W. A. MOZART

W. A. MOZART

HERMANN ABERT

Translated by Stewart Spencer
Edited by Cliff Eisen

YALE UNIVERSITY PRESS
NEW HAVEN AND LONDON

Published with assistance from the Annie Burr Lewis Fund

The Publisher acknowledges the vision and determination of John G. Ryden, former Director of Yale University Press, without whose initiative this project would not have been possible.

For information about this and other Yale University Press publications please contact:
U.S. Office: sales.press@yale.edu   yalebooks.com
Europe Office: sales@yaleup.co.uk   www.yalebooks.co.uk

Set in Minion by J&L Composition, Filey, North Yorkshire
Printed in Great Britain by St Edmundsbury Press Ltd, Bury St Edmunds

Library of Congress Cataloging-in-Publication Data

Abert, Hermann, 1871–1927.
  [W. A. Mozart. English]
  W. A. Mozart / Hermann Abert; translated by Stewart Spencer.
    p. cm.
  Includes bibliographical references and index.
  ISBN 978-0-300-07223-5 (alk. paper)
  1. Mozart, Wolfgang Amadeus, 1756–1791.
  2. Composers—Austria—Biography. I. Spencer, Stewart. II. Title.
  ML410.M9A6613 2006 2007
  780.92-dc22
[B]   2006023412

A catalogue record for this book is available from the British Library

10 9 8 7 6 5 4 3 2 1

Contents

Editorial note

Several years ago, when I read Abert for the second time – I had first read it as a graduate student – I was put in mind of a famous quote by Mark Twain: 'When I was a boy of fourteen, my father was so ignorant I could hardly stand to have the old man around. But when I got to be twenty-one, I was astonished at how much the old man had learned in seven years' ('Old Times on the Mississippi', *Atlantic Monthly*, 1874). In 1980 or so, Abert seemed to me to be a relic of the past, famous to be sure, but essentially a Romantic trawl through Mozart's life and works, impressionistic and overly metaphorical in its analyses, of little real value to 'modern' Mozart scholarship. Re-reading it, however, I couldn't put the book down: its 'impressionistic and overly metaphorical' analyses resonated strongly with how I've come to hear Mozart's music, the historical and generic overviews are still among the best ever written, and the discussion of Mozart's life – even if I fundamentally disagree with a central tenet of Abert's book (but more on that below) – is balanced and level-headed, free of the blinding prejudices against Mozart's father, or Archbishop Colloredo, or the Viennese public that have marred Mozart biography since the 1920s, giving Mozart credit where credit is due, but blame where blame is to be apportioned.

Abert's book is a revision of Otto Jahn's *W. A. Mozart*, published in four volumes between 1855 and 1859 and revised in 1867 (taking into account the discoveries of Ludwig Ritter von Köchel's 1862 *Chronologisch-thematisches Verzeichniss sämmtlicher Tonwerke Wolfgang Amadé Mozart's*). Up to that time, at least, Mozart biography was chiefly based on three important works: Friedrich Schlichtegroll's 'Joannes Chrysostomus Wolfgang Gottlieb Mozart', published in the *Nekrolog auf das Jahr 1791* (Gotha, 1793); Franz Xaver Niemetschek's *Leben des k. k. Kapellmeisters Wolfgang Gottlieb Mozart nach Originalquellen beschrieben* (Prague, 1798); and Georg von Nissen's *Biographie W. A. Mozarts nach Originalbriefen* (Leipzig, 1828). Nissen's biography, in particular, had an authority that few were willing to challenge: a Danish diplomat, he was Constanze Mozart's second husband and based his work (unfinished at the time of his death in 1826 but redacted and published soon afterwards) chiefly on letters and other documents still owned by Mozart's widow. Other early writings on Mozart were more aesthetic treatises than biographies. These included Ignaz Arnold's *Mozarts Geist: Seine kurze Biografie und ästhetische Darstellung seiner Werke* (Erfurt, 1803) and Alexandre Oulibicheff's *Nouvelle biographie de Mozart suivie d'un aperçu sur l'histoire générale de la musique et de l'analyse des principales Œuvres de Mozart* (Moscow, 1842–3; in German as *Mozart's Leben und Werke*, Stuttgart, 1859). Edward Holmes's *The Life of Mozart* (London, 1845) was chiefly based on Nissen.

Jahn (1813–69) was a philologist and archaeologist by training: his publications included studies of Greek mythology, editions of Persius and Juvenal, and important contributions to the history of Greek vase-painting; he was a professor at Greifswald from 1842 and at Bonn from 1855. According to the preface to his biography, the idea of writing a life of Mozart was suggested to him by the philosopher Gustav Hartenstein at Mendelssohn's funeral on 7 November 1847;

Jahn had originally intended to write a life of Beethoven but soon came to think that a life of Mozart was an essential preliminary. And the biography that he wrote was unprecedentedly large-scale, including an enormous mass of new material, all of it critically assessed. Jahn's biography was, in fact, the first full-scale, academically rigorous and independent biography of Mozart.

Jahn's biography was published twice more before World War I, in 1889–91 and 1905–7; both editions were overseen by the musicologist Hermann Deiters. The fifth edition – Abert's – appeared during the years 1919–21. But Abert's was no mere revision; rather, it was a thorough reworking of the text, with new, extended analyses, historical overviews of the genres in which Mozart worked and, above all, a rethinking of the relationship between Mozart's life and his works. Abert (1871–1927) was the ideal man for the job. The son of a Kapellmeister, he took his doctorate at Berlin in 1897 with a dissertation on Greek music and in 1902 he completed his *Habilitation* at Halle with a study of the aesthetics of medieval melody. He was appointed professor at Leipzig in 1920 and at Berlin in 1923; in 1925 he became the first musicologist ever elected as an ordinary member of the Prussian Academy of Sciences.

In revising Jahn, Abert believed not only that it was necessary to correct facts and report new discoveries, but also that Jahn's point of view was dated and – what was worse – bourgeois. As Abert saw it, Mozart had been 'idealized, constructed in true romantic yearning for a musical fairyland the prince of which was Mozart. . . . The enthusiasm [Jahn's] work aroused even among laymen had its reasons. It had, after all, been written for the same audience as that of Mendelssohn, Schumann and, to some extent, Brahms, the educated German middle-class with all of its advantages but also its limitations.'[1] I suppose the same criticisms – that his work is dated and written for *its* audience, an audience that increasingly came to see Mozart as the antithesis of a 'musical fairyland'[2] – could be levelled at Abert, but it has not been my brief to rewrite Abert's biography. Just the opposite, in fact: Abert's work is so monumental, so insightful (irrespective of the audience for which it was written), and so universal that it would be presumptuous to think it could be successfully revised and still remain Abert (just as Abert, though sometimes referred to as Jahn–Abert, is really no such thing). In any case, it is not our habit nowadays to feel that great works of the past need necessarily to be updated, that they have a limited lifespan beyond which they require 'modernization' (whether we ought to believe this or not is another question). For Abert, Jahn was an important foundation but not a monument to be preserved, either for its intrinsic value or for what it says about the culture within which it was created. For us, however, Abert is exactly that and more: a testament to its time and place but one that endures in the present.

My job, then, has been to preserve Abert's text but at the same time to correct some errors of fact, to revise the bibliographical references, and to note where recent Mozart research – especially with respect to sources, authenticity, chronology and contemporaneous documentary evidence – has helped refine or contradict Abert's arguments. To this end, I have thoroughly revised the footnotes and modernized their style: references are now given in abbreviated form with full details in

1. See Lenneberg, 'Hermann Abert's Biography of Mozart', 848.
2. Note, for example, Abert's admiration for Alfred Heuß's 'Das dämonische Element in Mozarts Werken', which he frequently cites.

the bibliography (in those cases where Abert left only sketchy or incomplete references, often to obscure literature, I have tracked down the citations and fleshed them out). I have also added more recent literature relevant to the topics he discusses. By the same token, I have tacitly corrected numerous inconsequential errors in the text, or augmented the information given there, including the spelling of names, birth and death dates, and some details of individuals' occupations or appointments or relationships. Where Abert's wrong facts have some bearing on his argument, however, I have retained his original text but added a discursive footnote with more recent information, at the same time pointing out the implications of this research for his conclusions; chiefly these concern sources, authenticity and chronology and, above all, Abert's view of Mozart's stylistic development. In these ways I hope to have preserved Abert's ideas – as well as a snapshot of Mozart scholarship *circa* 1920 – but at the same time to have rendered his book thoroughly up-to-date biographically and bibliographically. All editorial additions to the text (and they appear only in the footnotes) are indicated by the symbol ◆.

Other changes need to be noted here as well. Abert's citations from the Mozart family correspondence were derived from the then-standard edition by Ludwig Schiedermair (*Die Briefe W. A. Mozarts und seiner Familie*) which has now been superseded by the eight-volume edition by Wilhelm Bauer, Otto Erich Deutsch and Joseph Heinz Eibl (*Mozart: Briefe und Aufzeichnungen*). Accordingly, I have replaced all of Abert's original references with references to Bauer, Deutsch and Eibl. At the same time, I have given the dates of all letters so that they can also be located in any one of a number of English translations (there is, as yet, no complete edition of the letters in English; the most extensive selection is Emily Anderson's *The Letters of Mozart and his Family*). Similarly, all known documents relating to Mozart have been collected in Otto Erich Deutsch's *Mozart: Die Dokumente seines Lebens* (in English as *Mozart: A Documentary Biography*) and Cliff Eisen's *New Mozart Documents* (in German, with additions, as *Mozart. Die Dokumente seines Lebens: Addenda, Neue Folge*). Where Abert cites original documents, I have added references to these now-standard sources, where they can be consulted all at once. I have used a number of abbreviations throughout the footnotes for works that are cited many times. They are:

AmZ: *Allgemeine musikalische Zeitung* (the leading German music periodical of the time, first published at Leipzig in 1798)

Briefe: Wilhelm Bauer, Otto Erich Deutsch and Joseph Heinz Eibl, ed., *Mozart: Briefe und Aufzeichnungen* (Kassel, 1962–2006)

Documentary Biography: Otto Erich Deutsch, *Mozart: A Documentary Biography* (second edition: London, 1966)

Dokumente: Otto Erich Deutsch, *Mozart: Die Dokumente seines Lebens* (Kassel, 1961)

Dokumente: Addenda: Cliff Eisen, *Mozart: Die Dokumente seines Lebens. Addenda. Neue Folge* (Kassel, 1997)

New Mozart Documents: Cliff Eisen, *New Mozart Documents* (London, 1991)

Finally, Abert also included several lengthy appendices, some of which are now irrelevant or are incorporated, in various ways, in the text and footnotes and in works such as *Dokumente/ Documentary Biography*. I have retained five of these appendices but omitted the following: family documents and poems written about Mozart as well as other contemporaneous documents; church music texts; Mozart and Vogler; two letters from Mozart to Aloysia Weber; the texts of the choruses to *Thamos;* the controversy over the Requiem (much more recent and relevant material is footnoted in the main text); lists of Mozart's residences and portraits of the composer; a description of Leopold Mozart's list of Mozart's earliest compositions (see below, page 69 footnote 15); and a few music examples that do not add substantially to Abert's argument (at least not sufficiently for him to have included them in the main text).

Mozart's works are identified throughout by their numbers in Ludwig Ritter von Köchel's *Chronologisch-thematisches Verzeichniss sämmtlicher Tonwerke Wolfgang Amade Mozart's* (Leipzig, 1862, abbreviated throughout as K). A second edition of Köchel (K^3), edited by Alfred Einstein, was published in 1937 and a sixth edition (K^6), edited by Franz Giegling, Alexander Weinmann and Gerd Sievers, in 1964. Although changes in the chronology of Mozart's work have given rise to different numberings in these three versions of Köchel, most works continue to be known by their numbers in the first edition (for example, the 'Paris' symphony, K297, is listed as 300a in K^3 and K^6). For simplicity's sake, then, I have retained the original K numbers. In cases where a work is best identified by a number from a subsequent edition, however (such as some fragments or works not in the original edition), I have used the most common reference. In any case, all of Mozart's works, and all of the numbers assigned to them, are cross-referenced in K^3 and K^6, so any individual work can easily be found in any edition of the catalogue. Readers should be warned, though, that K numbers are used solely for the purpose of identification and that the information reported in even the most recent edition of Köchel is sometimes out of date: the catalogue should not be used, therefore, as the only reliable, factual guide to the date and authenticity of Mozart's works and their sources. Much of the information I have given here is based on research undertaken since 1964.

The heart of Abert's book is chapter 31, 'Mozart's Personality'. For all his discussion of biography, of social circumstance, of commerce and industry, patrons and the public, it is Abert's firm belief that, above all, Mozart's music expresses Mozart himself, his keen observation of, and boundless empathy for, his fellow man: '. . . it is impossible to separate his life from his music: in both, the same force is at work.' And it is here that I profoundly disagree with Abert: as I see it, Mozart *was* a keen observer of mankind, and boundlessly empathetic, but what he expressed in his music was *us*, not himself. Put another way, Mozart was the consummate artist, able to manipulate and cajole his listeners, to draw them in and draw them out, to *create* art, to *construct* art not for the sake of self-expression but to allow us to express ourselves. Yet this fundamental difference with Abert is exactly why I like the book so much: if I could, I would say exactly the same things about the music, I would describe it in exactly the same words and with the same images, for Abert's words and images correspond more or less exactly with how I hear the music. At the most basic level, then, Abert and I agree, not only that Mozart's music is profoundly expressive but also as to *what* it expresses. So it is really of little consequence, in the end, whether Mozart is expressing himself or expressing his listener. Either way, Mozart's is a compelling story: to whom, or to what, we attribute meaning in his music only determines the thrust and trajectory of the narrative, not its substance and not, ultimately, its effect. It is a story that can be read and told in a multiplicity of ways and Abert's, because his understanding of the music resonates so strongly within us, no matter what our view of Mozart's creative personality, remains perhaps the most compelling of all.

I am grateful to Yale University Press for asking me to revise Abert, and in particular to Robert Baldock, Malcolm Gerratt and Steve Kent for their editorial and production assistance, as well as their personal encouragement. The Arts and Humanities Research Council generously funded a semester's leave so I could complete my work, while Dominic McHugh kindly tracked down some bibliographical details and made other suggestions that have improved the book, as did Raphaël Taylor. Finally, I am particularly grateful to Stewart Spencer, who not only produced a magnificent translation, but also helped me correct some of my own mistakes and took a constructive interest in the book from start to finish.

Cliff Eisen
London, spring 2007

Preface

When the publishers of Otto Jahn's Mozart biography approached me a number of years ago and invited me to prepare a new edition, I was already acutely conscious of the insolubility of the problem with which I was faced. The two previous editions had been entrusted to Hermann Deiters, who saw it as his principal function to retain the character of Jahn's original with a rigour verging on the reverential. As a result, he limited himself in the main to additions and alterations of a biographical and antiquarian nature, leaving the rest – above all, the sections dealing with art history and aesthetics – untouched. This was an entirely legitimate approach as long as scholarship had made no significant advances since Jahn's day. But by the time of its fourth edition, it was increasingly impossible for his biography to maintain its former status as the leader in its field. The bases of our historical understanding have grown much broader since Jahn's day, the goals and methods of scholarship have changed, and, last but not least, we now hear and perceive Mozart's music in ways that differ fundamentally from those familiar to our grandparents. The dictum that the lives of great men must be rewritten at least once every fifty years demands its due in the present case, too. What is at stake is no longer Jahn, but Mozart. To work into the old biography all the new and far-reaching findings of recent years would have produced a hybrid text, destroying Jahn's unity and effectively preventing a new unity from emerging in its place. For better or worse, then, I was forced to accept that the work would have to be completely restructured.

The reproach that I have treated Jahn irreverently is one that I can repudiate with a good conscience. Anyone who thinks that the new work's principal purpose is to show how far we have progressed since Jahn's day has totally failed to understand my aim. To adopt a superior attitude to a sixty-year-old work requires no great skill, and the pitying tone with which many more recent writers already speak of Jahn says little for their sense of history. No one knows better than I that Jahn's Mozart represents an achievement whose historical importance cannot be equalled, let alone surpassed. Although his findings may now be out of date, his methodology and the whole way in which he treats his subject, superbly reconciling level-headedness and enthusiasm, constitute a legacy from which modern Mozart scholars may seek to escape only to their own detriment.

As a music scholar, Jahn was an out-and-out Romantic. The very fact that he chose biography as his main activity places him squarely in an age when our science was still in its infancy and the history of art was largely synonymous with the history of the artist. Although he had long since outgrown the naïve and anecdotal approach of the older period and had no time for its urge to rationalize everything, as a Romantic he acknowledged the artist's dependency on universal forces and was aware of the power of the unconscious and of history, but this awareness did not mislead him into denying the personality. Quite the opposite: one of his principal merits consisted in the fact that, not least on the strength of his analyses, he awakened and sharpened our understanding of artistic individuality in the history of music, too. With this, admittedly, came another genuinely Romantic feature: while observing and analysing Mozart's art from a historical point of view, he involuntarily came to idealize it. To him, it seemed like some distant fairyland on which he gazed with perpetually unrequited longing. This desire was intensified by the battle over Wagner that was currently raging in every quarter, a battle into which Jahn, too, was drawn as an outspoken opponent of Wagner. His Mozart bears clear signs of this struggle. If it is Mozart, rather than any other composer, who for a long time enjoyed the curious fate of being treated as the purest representative of an older and more 'authentic' art and of its 'hallowed' formal world and, as such, of being played off against the wicked innovators of the newer school, it is Jahn who was ultimately responsible for this. Yet this canonization of Mozart was not limited to Jahn's day alone, it also affected Mozart's relations with his predecessors. For Jahn, this whole process culminated in a single powerful high point, Mozart, in which all that was previously inchoate and imperfect came to glorious fruition. Italian music, in particular, suffered greatly from an approach clearly influenced by the heightened national awareness of the German Romantics and underpinned by the idiosyncratic treatment of sources adopted by Romantic historiographers, who were content to use them selectively in their attempts to gain universal insights. This is the point on which Jahn's work inevitably started to disintegrate: the historical bases of his view of Mozart proved to be too weak, with the result that the edifice that had been raised on them was sooner or later bound to begin to totter.

Jahn's idealized view of Mozart bore the stamp of Romanticism in every last detail. The audience at which it was aimed was the same as the one for which Mendelssohn, Schumann and Brahms wrote their music, namely, the German bourgeoisie of the day, with its intellectual curiosity and literary sophistication. This explains both the truthfulness and clarity of Jahn's account, two qualities that distinguish it from the vapidity and self-admiration of so many modern writers. Hence, too, the choice language and structure that scrupulously avoid all that is intrusive and inauthentic. Yet this, more than anything, betrays the limitations of Jahn's idealized view of his subject, which has something bourgeois and respectable about it, a picture of the composer intended for the drawing rooms of German middle-class homes, executed with taste and refinement but none the less geared to the taste and attitudes of its inhabitants. This is clear on a purely biographical level from Jahn's attempt to play down and euphemize those aspects of Mozart's personality and of his family to which the Mrs Grundys[2] of the world might conceivably take exception, while in his various conflicts with the outside world, especially with Archbishop Hieronymus Colloredo, he invariably took Mozart's part. But Jahn's analyses of the works suffer from the very same shortcoming. It is entirely typical of his whole approach that, in his view, one of the principal merits of Mozart's art was that the listener was spared the process of fermentation that it cost its creator. For him, Mozart was the master of an art that was fully finished and rounded off, the art of the most perfectly elegant proportions. For him, Mozart contained no surprises, no emotional depths, no passions that suddenly leapt to the surface. A composer who, in his own day, had been regarded as an unsettling Romantic, was now – in the 'Age of Romanticism' – treated as the embodiment of 'Classicism' as defined by the complacent bourgeoisie of the day, in other words, in the spirit of what Nietzsche termed an Apollonian beauty, pure and untroubled by any last vestiges of earthly passion. The land inhabited by Jahn's Mozart is like the Elysian Fields in Gluck's *Orfeo*, 'che puro ciel, che chiaro sol!' This was not only intended as a critique of Wagner but also as a perceptible reaction to the goings-on of the older Romantic

2. ◆ That is, a conventional or priggish person, based on a character from the play *Speed the Plough* (1798) by Thomas Morton (?1764–1838).

'Beethovenians', for whom Mozart and Haydn were already old hat. Here Jahn performed sterling service in restoring a sense of balance.

In short, Jahn's biography of Mozart is not only an example of historiography, it is also part of the history of its age, reflecting with peculiar accuracy its ideas and musical sensitivities. The present age is still struggling to break free from Romanticism and has abandoned idealistic, constructive thinking in favour of empiricism and realism, with the result that it has adopted a far stricter approach to its critique and use of sources. No longer content to proceed selectively, it now aspires to wholeness. But it also has a different attitude to the artist as such. Operating empirically, it strives to intellectualize the issues at stake, approaching the problem above all from a psychological standpoint and seeking to solve it by the subtlest possible dissection of the artist's style as the most intimate aspect of his personality. With his own analyses, Jahn was already in the best possible position to solve this problem, but he was repeatedly distracted from doing so by his preconceived ideal. Of course, it is granted to no age and to no biographer to deal with such a problem exhaustively, as it is in the nature of a creative genius that he reveals different aspects of that nature to each new generation. But it is our duty to account for our attitude towards him and to maintain our intellectual independence vis-à-vis our grandparents.

This is something that we have signally failed to do for far too long in the case of Jahn and Mozart. The most disastrous consequence of this is the universally held view that there is nothing more that can be said on the subject of Mozart in particular and of his age in general. For decades Jahn's findings have continued to be copied out and watered down – this has been a golden age for music journalism and one, moreover, that shows no sign of ending. In its day, Jahn's picture of Mozart was still a living force, but as it permeated the broader reaches of society, it began to grow increasingly pallid and fixed, until all that was left was a vague ideal of formal beauty behind which all that was best about Mozart – his personality – disappeared completely. The composer was now the 'eternally cheerful and youthful Amadeus' of our adolescent girls and old maids, a composer, moreover, whose great advantage was that it required little intellectual effort to appreciate his music. It is no wonder, then, that those observers who were dissatisfied with this philistine ideal now turned their backs on Mozart, thinking that in doing so they were being particularly progressive. For a long time, then, views of Mozart vacillated between a veneration which, for all its honesty, was backward-looking and toothless (here one thinks, for example, of Eduard Hanslick's rambling reviews[3]) and a high-handed rejection which, in one case at least, accused the enemy of conscious hypocrisy. And yet there are increasing signs among both musicians and scholars that in Mozart's case there is a genuine desire to go beyond the views of the Romantics. It is sufficient to compare Wagner's comments on Mozart with those of Robert Schumann to see what progress has been made in this respect. On a scholarly front, the first critical onslaught on Jahn's theory that Mozart was incomparably superior to all his predecessors and contemporaries was launched by Friedrich Chrysander in his well-known series of articles on *Mitridate*,[4] but another two decades were to pass before any further steps were taken along this road, at least as far as Mozart's operas were concerned. For the present, all full-length works on Mozart followed Hermann Deiters's example[5] and retained Jahn's basic approach. The most independent of these writers was Oskar

---

3. ◆ See, in particular, the ongoing Hanslick, *Sämtliche Schriften*.
4. ◆ Chrysander, 'Mitridate, italienische Oper von Mozart'.
5. ◆ In his edition – the third – of Jahn, *W. A. Mozart*.

Fleischer, whose *Mozart*, published in Berlin in 1900, has the additional merit of being the first to draw attention to such important points as Mozart's relations with Johann Christian Bach, while his appendix is notable for its extremely meticulous bibliography. Far less independent is Karl Storck, whose biography[6] follows Jahn closely, in some cases even taking over his phraseology. Where he attempts to go beyond Jahn, we find him on very shaky ground, and, in spite of individual insights, even his numerous and extensive divagations on the history of civilization – excursuses typical of a particular kind of modern writing on art – cannot blind us to the fact that Storck's study marks no advance on Jahn. Leopold Schmidt's life of Mozart[7] makes no pretentions to be anything other than a piece of popular music journalism.

All these writers merely followed in Jahn's footsteps. Rather better results have been achieved by some of the more detailed scholarly studies that have appeared since 1889. Bibliographically speaking, pride of place must go to Oskar Fleischer's aforementioned study and thereafter to Henri de Curzon's meticulously researched *Essai de bibliographie Mozartine*,[8] an attempt to collate all that has been written on Mozart from the earliest studies to 1905. Somewhat remarkably, it has so far proved impossible to found a scholarly journal devoted solely to Mozart similar to the yearbooks on Bach and Gluck and, for a time, on Beethoven and Wagner.[9] Its place continues to be filled by the *Jahresberichte des Salzburger Mozarteums*, edited and largely written by that indefatigable champion of Mozart, Johann Evangelist Engl. Since 1895, this journal has been joined by the *Mitteilungen für die Mozart-Gemeinde in Berlin*, founded by Rudolph Genée and essentially intended for a lay audience, hence the uneven quality of its contributions, those of its first editor being distinguished more for their enthusiasm than for their thorough knowledge of the subject. Alongside these articles, however, we find others by writers such as Albert Kopfermann, Max Friedlaender and Ernst Lewicki – the last-named a sensitive and knowledgeable writer of the younger generation – to whom Mozart scholars owe a lasting debt of gratitude. On 1 November 1918 the central committee of the Mozart-Gemeinde in Salzburg finally began publication of its *Mozarteums-Mitteilungen*, a journal that may well take on the role of the Mozart *Jahrbuch* that has been so badly lacking. Its editor is Rudolf von Lewicki of Vienna.

Biographically, too, decisive progress has been made. Jahn's biography alerted its readers to the vast importance of Mozart's letters,[10] yet, curiously enough, publishers long remained content to bring out mere selections, few of which added anything to Ludwig Nohl's long-overrated anthology. Between 1906 and 1912 no fewer than five such selections appeared, edited by Karl Storck, Max Weigel, Albert Leitzmann, Curt Sachs and Hugo Leichtentritt.[11] The long awaited critical edition finally appeared in 1914. Published by Georg Müller in Leipzig and Munich in 1914, it was edited by Ludwig Schiedermair and runs to five thick volumes, the fifth of which contains an iconography.[12] The first two are given over to Mozart's own letters, while the lion's share of the

---

6. ◆ Storck, *Mozart: Sein Leben und Schaffen*.

7. ◆ Leopold Schmidt, *W. A. Mozart*.

8. ◆ Curzon, *Essai de bibliographie Mozartine: Revue critique des ouvrages relatifs à W. A. Mozart et ses œuvres*.

9. ◆ Here Abert refers to the *Gluck-Jahrbuch*, edited by him and founded in 1913; the *Bach-Jahrbuch*, published by the Neue Bachgesellschaft from 1904; Theodor Frimmel's *Beethoven-Jahrbuch*, begun in 1908; and the *Richard-Wagner Jahrbuch*, edited by Ludwig Frankenstein from 1906.

10. ◆ The first work to include significant quotations from Mozart's letters was Nissen, *Biographie W. A. Mozarts: Nach Originalbriefen, Sammlungen alles über ihn Geschriebenen, mit vielen neuen Beylagen, Steindrücken, Musikblättern und einem Facsimile*.

11. ◆ Storck, *Mozarts Briefe in Auswahl*; Weigel, *Mozarts Briefe*; Leitzmann, *Mozarts Briefe*; Sachs, *Die Briefe Mozarts*; and Leichtentritt, *Mozarts Briefe*.

12. ◆ Schiedermair, *Die Briefe W. A. Mozarts und seiner Familie*.

third and fourth volumes falls to Leopold, with Mozart's mother represented by forty, his sister by sixteen, Constanze by four and Maria Anna Thekla Mozart by two. The letters are edited with exemplary care, with only a few unimportant passages omitted from Leopold's letters. The orthography and language of the originals have been meticulously preserved, and a brief – almost too brief – commentary provides information on individuals named in the letters, as well as on the background to them and the works mentioned. Here, then, we have a reference tool of the first order and one, moreover, that will provide Mozart biographers with the secure foundations that they have lacked for far too long. In particular, the characters of the two main correspondents, father and son, emerge for the first time in the full light of day, with the result that even non-experts will find reading these volumes a source of particular pleasure. In short, they deserve a place of honour in the history of letters as a literary genre: the stark contrast between these letters and the sentimental and belletristic letter-writing of Mozart's day shows clearly that a century reviled as mawkish none the less had a more robust, not to say coarse, side to it.[13] Schiedermair preferred to keep the individual members of the family separate, although I myself would have thought it better to have arranged the letters in the form of a series of dialogues. In assessing collections of letters, we rightly complain if only one of the correspondents is allowed to speak, as letters are never autonomous documents: each presupposes an interlocutor to whom the writer accords a certain influence over him by making contact with him in the first place. In the case of the Mozarts, we are fortunate that in the majority of cases – especially where the all-important relationship betweeen father and son is concerned – we are able to follow closely the cut and thrust of their correspondence. How subtly the letters of each party are distinguished from each other, with Wolfgang's impressionistic missives offset by Leopold's pedagogical divagations! And how clearly the often highly dramatic tensions between them emerge! Had this correspondence been presented in dialogue form, we should have had a biography in letters, a biography which, given the approach preferred by Schiedermair, the reader now has to piece together for himself from two volumes, a procedure that involves not a little effort.[14] The 'picture book' – as I am tempted to rename the iconographical fifth volume that is intended for more than just classical philologists – is a cause for gratitude, even if it has turned out to be something of a ragbag. Remarkably, it omits at least one person who was immensely important in Mozart's life: Süßmayr. Are there really no surviving pictures of him in Vienna?[15]

Mozart's biographer is also indebted to Albert Leitzmann for his study on Mozart's personality,[16] which is a virtually complete compilation of contemporary accounts of the composer's character and appearance. Not all these eyewitness accounts are equally valuable, but in their totality they vividly capture the impression that Mozart left on the world around him. Many, of

---

13. ◆ Among numerous interpretations of the family correspondence, see in particular Hoesli, *Wolfgang Amadeus Mozart: Briefstil eines Musikgenies*; Mančal, 'Briefe – nur "Briefe"? Vorüberlegungen zur Informationsbewertung einer Quellengattung der Mozart-Forschung'; Schroeder, *Mozart in Revolt: Strategies of Resistance, Mischief and Deception*; and Serwe, 'Komposition und Disposition: Über rhetorische Strukturen in Mozarts Briefen'.

14. ◆ Schiedermair has now been superseded by the seven-volume Bauer, Deutsch and Eibl, *Mozart: Briefe und Aufzeichnungen* [hereafter *Briefe*], which gives the letters in chronological order; a recently published eighth volume, edited by Ulrich Konrad, includes corrections, additions and further commentary. A complete edition in English has not been published although a significant selection, also given in chronological order, appears in Anderson, *The Letters of Mozart and his Family*; further, see Marshall, *Mozart Speaks*; Spaethling, *Mozart's Letters, Mozart's Life*; and Eisen, *Mozart: A Life in Letters*.

15. ◆ Schiedermair's 'picture book' has been superseded by Deutsch, *Mozart und seine Welt in zeitgenössischen Bildern*. Apparently pictures of Süßmayr do not survive.

16. ◆ Leitzmann, *Mozarts Persönlichkeit: Urteile der Zeitgenossen*.

course, say far more about the personality of the eyewitness in question than they do about Mozart himself.[17]

As for the dating of Mozart's works, a much expanded and revised edition of Köchel's old catalogue[18] – after Jahn, the most important of the older books on Mozart – was published in Leipzig in 1905. Edited by Paul von Waldersee, it is based on additional information entered in Köchel's own private copy of his catalogue, while also taking account of all the findings of Mozart scholarship since 1877, the year in which Köchel died. The volume's aims and layout remain the same, and the dating of Mozart's works is substantially unchanged. That a great deal remained to be done in this area, especially in terms of the works written before around 1780, was proved by later scholars, both Köchel and Waldersee having adopted Jahn's often outdated findings when dating the works on stylistic grounds. But this second edition is invaluable above all for Carl Victor Reusch's biography of Köchel, which is reproduced in the foreword.[19]

Of the aesthetic and historical writings on Mozart, only the most basic can be mentioned here. All specialized studies must be dealt with individually when the time comes. Some of these writings involve research that is not specifically concerned with Mozart but with his predecessors and contemporaries, but which for precisely this reason has provided us with an entirely new basis for an understanding of his style. The first area of Mozart's output to benefit from these researches was his instrumental music. In 1902 Hugo Riemann published the first of a series of volumes on the Mannheim symphonists,[20] and this was soon followed by a similar series on pre-classical composers in Vienna.[21] In this way, new light has been shed on the roots of the classical instrumental style and, hence, of Mozart's instrumental style – a light, be it added, of which Jahn had seen only the vaguest glimmer. All three classical composers now appeared within a completely new historical context, the three most important links in which were the symphonic schools in Mannheim, Vienna and north Germany. In Mozart's case, there proved to be a close link between him and the Mannheimers during his years of development, a link that became clearer as a result of Riemann's research on the music of Johann Schobert. Johann Christian Bach and Schobert have emerged with increasing clarity as the two composers who had the greatest influence on Mozart's

---

17. ◆ The now-standard documentary source is Deutsch, *Mozart: Die Dokumente seines Lebens* [hereafter *Dokumente*]; for an English translation, see Deutsch, *Mozart: A Documentary Biography* [hereafter *Documentary Biography*]. Supplements to Deutsch include Eibl, *Mozart: Die Dokumente seines Lebens. Addenda* and Eisen, *New Mozart Documents*.

18. ◆ Köchel, *Chronologisch-thematisches Verzeichniss sämmtlicher Tonwerke Wolfgang Amadé Mozart's*, first published in 1862.

19. ◆ Köchel has been substantially revised twice since Abert's time: by Alfred Einstein (1937), whose edition is heavily indebted to the work of Wyzewa and Saint-Foix (see below); and by Franz Giegling, Alexander Weinmann and Gerd Sievers (1964). This last benefited from early work on the *Neue Mozart-Ausgabe*, which started publication in 1955, but is in many respects now superseded by more recent research on Mozart sources, chiefly the work of Wolfgang Plath on the chronological development of Mozart's handwriting, and Alan Tyson's study of the types of paper found in Mozart's autographs. Plath's work is largely represented by his 'Beiträge zur Mozart-Autographie I: Die Handschrift Leopold Mozarts' and 'Beiträge zur Mozart-Autographie II: Schriftchronologie 1770–1780'; Tyson's most influential studies are collected in his *Mozart: Studies of the Autograph Scores*. For other important sources, including authentic and contemporaneous manuscript copies and first editions, see Haberkamp, *Die Erstdrucke der Werke von Wolfgang Amadeus Mozart: Bibliographie*; Eisen, 'The Mozarts' Salzburg Copyists: Aspects of Attribution, Chronology, Text, Style and Performance Practice'; and Edge, 'Mozart's Viennese Copyists'. For a general summary of Mozart sources and their evaluation, see Eisen, 'Sources for Mozart's life and works'. In what follows, I have relied on these studies and noted where present-day thinking on the chronology of Mozart's works differs from Abert's, and, where necessary, to sketch the implications of the revised chronology. Concerning Köchel, see Deutsch, 'Aus Köchels Jugendtagen'; Biba, 'Ludwig Ritter von Köchel (1800–1877): Zur Erinnerung an seinen vor 100 Jahren erfolgten Tod' and 'Ludwig Ritter von Köchels Verdienste um die Mozart-Gesamtausgabe'; Rehm, 'Nochmals: Ritter von Köchels Verdienste um die "Alte Mozart-Ausgabe"'; Engelbrecht, 'Ludwig Alois Friedrich Köchel (1842 Ritter von) (1800–1877)'; and Thomas Konrad, 'Ludwig Ritter von Köchel'.

20. ◆ Riemann, *Sinfonien der Pfalzbayerischen Schule: Mannheim Symphoniker*, including works by Johann Stamitz, Johann Anton Fils, Ignaz Holzbauer, Carl Joseph Toeschi, Christian Cannabich, Carl Stamitz, Franz Ignaz Beck and Ernst Eichner.

21. ◆ Horwitz and Riedel (Heft 1) and Wilhelm Fischer (Heft 2), *Wiener Instrumentalmusik vor und um 1750*, including works by Monn, Wagenseil, Schlöger and Starzer.

development, an influence of which Jahn was barely aware. Following on from this research, a number of recent scholars, notably Guido Adler and his pupils in Vienna, have examined the products of Viennese 'classicism' from a stylistic point of view: here one thinks above all of Wilhelm Fischer's article in Adler's *Studien zur Musikwissenschaft*.[22] These enquiries have proved especially fruitful in the case of Mozart in that Jahn had taken only the most general interest in his style and failed to examine it in any systematic way. The present writer offered a number of new insights into Mozart's earliest development in an article on Leopold Mozart's notebook of 1762 published in the *Gluck-Jahrbuch*.[23] Here particular attention was drawn to Leopold's relations with the older north German school associated with Sperontes.

It has taken longer for writers to follow up Chrysander's investigations into Mozart's operas and to progress beyond the standpoint held by Jahn. The first decisive move in this direction was taken by Hermann Kretzschmar in his essay 'Mozart in der Geschichte der Oper', first published in 1905 in the *Jahrbuch der Musikbibliothek Peters* and reprinted in his collected essays (ii.257–79). Here Kretzschmar, writing with exemplary lucidity and succinctness, points out the direction that research must take in tackling Mozart's operas. The whole historical background that was either missing in its entirety from Jahn or sketched in garbled form now emerges in clear outline, with Italian music in particular finally being given its historical due. Needless to say, Mozart's own works, too, can now be seen in a new light. Meanwhile, the importance of the music of his predecessors and contemporaries both for Mozart himself and on its own terms became clear from the reissue of works by Holzbauer, Graun, Jommelli, Traetta, Gassmann and Umlauf, while the recent revival of scholarly interest in Gluck has likewise helped to shed new light on Mozart.

But it was two French scholars, Théodore de Wyzewa and Georges de Saint-Foix, whose magnum opus – *Wolfgang Amédée Mozart: Sa vie musicale et son œuvre, de l'enfance à la pleine maturité (1756–1777)* – represents the greatest advance on Jahn.[24] Although it deals with only the first twenty-one years of Mozart's life, offering no more than a summary overview of the rest of it, it has succeeded in placing Mozart scholarship on completely new foundations. Its methodology may not have been entirely new, but never before in the history of music had it been applied on such a scale and with such consistency. It is a wholly modern work, inspired by the psychology of art and, as such, represents the clearest possible rejection of the Romantics' theory that there is a close link between an artist's work and the outward circumstances of his life. Mozart's life concerns the two authors only to the extent that it offered him new artistic experiences. Here alone, in their view, lay the source of Mozart's art, not in the various conflicts and crises of his outward existence. This way of observing the situation is inspired by the new and entirely valid insight that of all the great composers, Mozart was the one who was the most sensitive to artistic impressions, the one whose ability to adapt was matched only by his need to adapt and by a gift for spontaneous emotion that he retained to the very end. The authors then set to work with admirable consistency, dividing Mozart's output until 1777 into no fewer than twenty-four periods, each of which was influenced by one or more models. For the later years, they argue in favour of ten such periods.

22. ◆ 'Zur Entwicklungsgeschichte des Wiener klassischen Stils'; further, see Adler, *Der Stil in der Musik* and *Handbuch der Musikgeschichte* (including 'Periodisierung der abendländischen Musik' and 'Die Wiener klassische Schule'). Concerning Adler, see Heinz, 'Guido Adlers Musikhistorik als historisches Dokument' and Dömling, 'Musikgeschichte als Stilgeschichte: Bemerkungen zum musikhistorischen Konzept Guido Adlers'.

23. ◆ Abert, 'Leopold Mozarts Notenbuch von 1762'.

24. ◆ Here Abert refers to the first two volumes of Wyzewa and Saint-Foix, *Wolfgang Amédée Mozart: Sa vie musicale et son œuvre*, with the subtitle: *de l'enfance à la pleine maturité (1756–1773)*, published in 1912. Subsequent volumes – the complete work is published in five parts – appeared to 1946, the last three Saint-Foix's work exclusively; Wyzewa died in 1917.

Their findings are quite literally astonishing for what they have to tell us about the formal aspect of Mozart's works, especially his instrumental music. Above all, the authors have succeeded in establishing an entirely new chronology for Mozart's works, effectively undermining that of both Jahn and Köchel on many important points and leaving the reader in awe at the perceptiveness with which works previously thought to be undatable can now be dated, in some cases to the nearest month.[25] The majority of these datings are convincing or at least highly plausible. All that could be achieved by this method has been achieved here, and in view of the wealth of new results that are found in these two volumes, that hackneyed epithet 'epoch-making' is certainly justified here. Only in the case of the operas could the authors' methodology have paid greater dividends. Here, curiously enough, they are far less knowledgeable about the sources than they are in the case of the instrumental music. The various trends in Mozart's day are not clearly distinguished, still less is the uniqueness of individual composers properly grasped, so that in this area much still remains to be done, in spite of sensitive comments on the development of individual forms. Yet even here there is one important new finding: the influence of French *opéra comique* on Mozart's music turns out to be far greater than had previously been thought to be the case.

In spite of its outstanding advantages, the work of Wyzewa and Saint-Foix none the less invites criticism of its overall design and aims, above all in the context of the relationship between Mozart's life and art. Earlier writers believed that an artist's works were directly inspired by all that befell him in his life. According to this doctrine, the artist first had to experience something which he then turned into music on the strength of the gifts that had been granted him. This is the well-known theory of imitation in all its various guises. Wyzewa and Saint-Foix go to the opposite extreme and argue that there is absolutely no link between an artist's life and his creativity. But it seems to me that both views are based on a false assumption, namely, that the life of a genius such as Mozart is lived in the same world of activities and contingencies as that of the non-artist and of the man who is merely talented. It is sufficient in this context to compare Mozart's life with that of his father. Throughout his life, Leopold was immensely proud of the fact that he was self-taught and self-made, but, when looked at closely, his life turns out to have been no more than a series of random occurrences that he simply accepted or used to his own advantage, revealing a greater or lesser degree of cleverness in the process. But music was an arbitrary activity that he pursued only when professional obligation or inclination prompted him to do so, yet he could equally well ignore such promptings if he felt it right to do so. Music was not a primitive life force but acquired its rules from religion, morality, courtly and bourgeois convention and so on. For a genius like Mozart, by contrast, artistic creativity was the most basic expression of existence. He could not simply write music when he wanted to. For him, there was no causal connection between wanting to do something and being able to do it. Rather, music was an imperative. As a result, his works are not simply expressions of, or reflections on, his life, but the very meaning of that life. And so the 'outward' circumstances of his fate were neither 'essential' nor 'non-essential' to his music but from the very outset were inextricably bound up with it, influenced, as they were, by the same instincts and forces. All that was mere chance in Leopold's life was transformed into destiny in that of his son. This explains much of what strikes the self-assured philistine as 'naïve', 'unworldly' and even as 'incomprehensible' in Mozart's every thought and action. The same daemon that inspired his works guided him on his journey through life to its grim and sombre ending.

---

25. ◆ Many of Wyzewa and Saint-Foix's datings, based chiefly on musical style, have proved incorrect; see again note 18.

But there is another problem that our two French writers failed to solve: for them, Mozart's art is like a mosaic, made up of a series of influences to which he succumbed in the course of his life as a result of chance. This rationalistic desire to bring clarity and order to a varied picture is typically French, but, quite apart from the fact that it is a fatal error to see genius as the sum total of the influences that affect it, this approach provides us with no answer to two main questions: how did Mozart choose which of his many models to adopt? And which elements did he appropriate from each of them and make his own? Why did Johann Christian Bach and Schobert, for example, affect him more deeply than the incomparably greater Gluck? Not even ordinary mortals imitate things if they do not already contain within them the nucleus of what they are imitating. In the case of the genius, this selective process already bears within it the stamp of creativity: it is his first attempt to assert himself in the face of tradition, to cast aside what inhibits him and is alien to his nature and not just to imitate all that he feels drawn towards but, at the same time, to recast it and make it his own. This is a crucially important point, but it is one that does not receive its due at the hands of Wyzewa and Saint-Foix, with their piecemeal approach to creativity. Here Mozart the imitator of other composers' ideas overshadows Mozart the creative artist, with the result that we lose sight of the wood for the meticulously painted trees. But we should never forget that what was so great about Mozart was his own self and its creative ability, not the material on which he tried out those abilities. And so it is the biographer's principal duty to identify what was most unique about his subject, a uniqueness that finds expression in varying forms at varying stages of his development but that ultimately remains the same. Mozart's art is like a finely polished crystal that reveals different colours with the changing light, while never altering its basic substance.

Given the importance of Wyzewa's and Saint-Foix's work, it was a cause for celebration that it found a home for itself in Germany, too, very soon after its appearance. Paraphrased and abbreviated, its findings were incorporated into the first volume of Arthur Schurig's two-volume life of Mozart.[26] Schurig describes himself as the 'vassal' of his two French predecessors and sticks closely to their findings on an aesthetic and historical level. His admiration of them is as high as his estimation of Jahn is low, with the result that his study represents what is hitherto the most vehement rejection of Jahn's Romantically idealized view of Mozart and, as such, is not without importance in terms of the history of ideas. Schurig feels justified in throwing out all the old lumber and in his enthusiasm even goes so far as to dismiss the founder of modern scientific music biography as intellectually and morally backward. However much a breath of fresh air may have been necessary in the musty studies of Mozart scholarship, such extreme remarks not only insult the man at whom they are directed, they also harm the cause of academic progress. The situation is not as straightforward as Schurig thinks in the case of either Jahn himself or another figure for whom he conceives a remarkable dislike, Leopold Mozart, who, for Jahn and his successors, had been cast in the role of the ideal father of a great man, but who is depicted by Schurig as a narrow-minded and self-opinionated philistine. Here, too, an idea which in itself is sound is taken to extremes. Above all, there is a lamentable lack of any attempt to see Jahn and Leopold Mozart as the intellectual products of their age, an attempt that would have proved extremely helpful in the one case as in the other. At the same time, this would have led more deeply into the problems raised here and guarded the writer against excessive subjectivity. There is one point, at all events, that Schurig has in common with Leopold, the pronounced streak of rationalism that seeks to reduce everything

26. ◆ Schurig, *Wolfgang Amadeus Mozart: Sein Leben und sein Werk auf Grund der vornehmlich durch Nikolaus von Nissen gesammelten biographischen Quellen und der Ergebnisse der neuesten Forschung dargestellt*; the second edition appeared in 1923 under the title *Wolfgang Amade Mozart: Sein Leben, seine Persönlichkeit und sein Werk.*

and everyone to a particular, clear and simple formula and, wherever possible, to speak in the language of stereotypes. Hence, too, his fondness for Wyzewa and Saint-Foix. Inevitably, his view of Mozart is geared to this whole approach. It is highly instructive to compare the Romantic picture of Mozart with its modern counterpart: while the former attempts to idealize everything, including even the unimportant aspects, and to raise them to the level of something exceptional, the latter seeks, conversely, to reduce everything to the level where it can be grasped and understood and, by restoring it to the 'real' world, to counter the hero worship of earlier writers. The circumstances of Mozart's life and, to a large extent, his character, too, now seem positively ordinary, his education more than modest and his range of ideas as simple and primitive as possible. At a time when the cult of the personality has acquired an element of hysteria, this sober way of looking at Mozart seems initially more than welcome, clarifying the issue in a number of areas, notably in its powerful refutation of the apparently ineradicable and sentimental legend bound up with Mozart's visit to Berlin, and thereby providing us with something akin to a sense of liberation. But in other areas such as the unproven and sensationalist account of Mozart's seduction by Constanze, it again proves wide of the mark. In general, of course, what matters is whether this new picture of Mozart by a man who, as a modern thinker, prides himself on his freedom from prejudice does not, in fact, involve a narrowing of our intellectual perspective and whether we have not simply exchanged one set of prejudices for another. Are we really justified in attempting to rediscover our own 'reality' in a creative artist such as Mozart? After all, the life of a genius runs along completely different lines from that of a non-artist, inhabiting a different world and assuming different forms, and is by no means as simple as the non-artist, applying his own standards to it, assumes it to be. Even the reports by Mozart's own contemporaries needed to be treated with caution as most of them offer an idealized portrait of what their authors believed themselves or wanted to believe. Only where they offer raw facts can they be trusted, but these facts invariably prove tangential to Mozart's central activities. We shall be able to understand the artist in his entirety only to the extent that we can experience his works for ourselves: no critical skill on our part and no amount of expertise should mislead us into thinking otherwise. And herein lies the principal weakness of Schurig's biography: it is a product of the same aesthetic intellectualism that thrived in every kind of artistic journalism in the years leading up to the outbreak of the last war. This explains not only its basically rationalistic approach, but also its urbane, cool and self-assured tone, all qualities that are ultimately derived from the French. Schurig's vassal-like dependence on his French predecessors goes far beyond his adoption of their findings and affects his book's whole thrust and methodology, including the very way in which he depicts his subject. To the biography proper a few very useful chapters have been added, such as those on the Mozart family tree and, especially, the composer's relations and descendants.

A completely different aim was pursued by Josef Kreitmaier's *W. A. Mozart: Eine Charakterzeichnung des großen Meisters nach den literarischen Quellen*. Kreitmaier also rejects earlier attempts to idealize Mozart, not only as an artist but as a man, too, while still finding much that was 'noble and lovable' about him, even if this was not enough to immortalize his name independently of his music. The picture that he presents creates a very sympathetic impression through its thoughtfulness, warmth and popular tone. That Mozart's credentials as a good Catholic are particularly well stressed – sometimes excessively so – is clearly attributable to the fact that the author is a member of the Order of Jesuits. He, too, of course, makes no attempt to derive Mozart's personality from his works, even though these were the most basic expression of his nature and even though the early masses and, more especially, Mozart's idiosyncratic approach to the individual sections of the mass could have told us a great deal about his views on religion.

There has recently been an increase in studies of Mozart as an opera composer, an increase due, in part, to a renewed interest in the aesthetics of opera as such and one, moreover, that has come from the most varied quarters. In his *Musikästhetik des 18. Jahrhunderts*, Hugo Goldschmidt seeks to throw critical light on the eighteenth century's musico-aesthetic principles in general and to trace their development through their various manifestations, an attempt all the more welcome in that this is a field that had hitherto been barely explored, for all that it was a particularly serious gap in our understanding of the period: after all, the music aesthetics of the eighteenth century had one great advantage over its modern equivalent in that it was still confined to the world of practical music-making, achieving its results not by speculation but by drawing inferences from the music of the period. But Goldschmidt's book is also of value for Mozart because of its particularly detailed engagement with opera, allowing him to establish an aesthetics of opera on the basis of the teachings of the time and to throw new light on all the burning issues of the day, including the respective contributions of intellect and imagination to the musical drama, the relationship between Italian and French opera and, finally, the uniqueness of Gluck. Last but not least, Goldschmidt helps us to judge Mozart from an aesthetic point of view.

Hermann Cohen approaches Mozart from a completely different angle – that of philosophy – in his study *Die dramatische Idee in Mozarts Operntexten*. The contrast with eighteenth-century writers on the aesthetics of opera is clear not least from the fact that Cohen virtually ignores all questions of musical form, for which he evidently has no understanding. The openings of Italian arias that he adds to the German openings in the case of *Die Entführung aus dem Serail* and *Die Zauberflöte* prove beyond doubt that he has signally failed to grasp the stylistic distinction between *opera buffa* and singspiel. And his sideswipes at Wagner likewise invite dissent. Above all, it should nowadays be impossible to print statements such as his claims that opera developed out of oratorio or that the German art song emerged from Pamina's aria. Yet in spite of all these shortcomings and in spite of its curious mixture of aesthetics and ethics, Cohen's study includes a number of excellent and fruitful ideas. It offers the most intelligent account yet of the old parallel between Mozart and Shakespeare,[27] while the sections on the relationship between tragedy and humour, on Mozart's inspired way of creating contrastive characters and on the position of *Così fan tutte* in Mozart's output are stimulating in the extreme, drawing attention to a field that music scholars have all too often ignored. At the same time, this approach has produced a number of very odd results, including the author's defence of *Don Giovanni* against the charge of immorality and the Gretchen-like role allegedly played by Donna Elvira, both of them ideas that have as little to do with Mozart as they have to do with Shakespeare.

In the wake of the philosopher, the stage director has finally demanded a say in the form of Ernst Lert's study *Mozart auf dem Theater*. Lert was led to undertake his investigations by his productions of Mozart's operas in Leipzig, and the result is an edifying sign of the breath of fresh air that has begun to leave its mark on performances of Mozart's operas in recent times. After all, the ballast of a highly dubious and un-Mozartian tradition has been dragged around on our stages for far too long. Lert knows very well that the solution to this problem is not simply improvements in stage technology but that all such enquiries must necessarily go to the very heart of Mozart's dramatic art. Until now, Mozart has been virtually ignored as a stage director, and it is this aspect that Lert places at the very centre of his study, an aspect that emerges as far more important than has been assumed until now. Mozartians are additionally in Lert's debt for his investigations into

---

27. ◆ See Vom Hofe, 'Die Konstellation des Genies: Raffael und Shakespeare in Mozart. Mozarts Kunstgeist in parallelisierter Deutung des frühen 19. Jahrhunderts'.

the various forms of opera that existed in Mozart's day (investigations undertaken from the standpoint of the theatre historian) and of the links between their style and that of the spoken drama. Only the section on the history of music reveals serious gaps, as well as risky hypotheses and downright errors. Lert ends his study by suggesting ways of staging all the operas with the exception of *La finta semplice*, which, for reasons best known to the author, is wholly ignored. All these suggestions have the advantage of having been tried out in practice in Leipzig. Even where they invite criticism, they are stimulating and provide food for further thought. All these sections may be commended to the attention of singers, conductors and directors, whose sense of style, where Mozart is concerned, still leaves a lot to be desired. Similar aims, albeit with no account of the musico-historical background, are pursued by Emil Gerhäuser in his *Stuttgarter Bühnenkunst*, which includes a whole series of suggestions for staging Mozart's work and which is additionally important as it takes as its starting point Bernhard Pankok's new designs for all the operas, designs that are among the most artistically satisfying to have been produced by modern theatre design.

It goes without saying that the present work attempts to deal critically with all the findings of modern scholarship. I have tried to establish the historical facts of every genre in which Mozart took an interest, especially the long-neglected field of opera. But the reader should not expect a detailed account. After all, our principal concern is the genius of Mozart, not a history of opera or the symphony or whatever. As a result, we can deal only with the most essential – living – aspect of these older composers and their influence on Mozart's music. And even here I have been forced to be selective: in those cases where there is widespread evidence for the same influence, I have concentrated on those aspects in which that influence finds clearest expression. And these older composers can be seen as relevant to Mozart only if we can turn them into living forces, as they were for their contemporaries, including Mozart himself. Somehow, therefore, we must succeed in recreating and reliving Mozart's own response to them. A list of mere names is of no more use here than ready-made concepts and labels. I must leave the reader to decide to what extent my choice of material is valid.

I have already explained why I have not adopted the practice so popular with modern music biographies and dealt first with Mozart's life and only then with his works. Instead, the individual works are discussed within the context of the period of his life to which they belong. Only with *Il re pastore* have I made an exception and dealt with it alongside the other *opere serie*. As for the chronology of the individual works, I have carefully reexamined the dates proposed by Wyzewa and Saint-Foix and in the majority of cases adopted their findings. But I have retained the numbering of Köchel and Jahn, merely adding details of the relevant volume in the collected edition.[28]

Nor is it my wish to have to put the case yet again for the traditional division of the works into sacred, dramatic, vocal and instrumental. All these genres have their own stylistic rules that need to be respected, but they do not necessarily help the biographer who has to deal with the artist as an individual. For him, the universal conceals what is individual, unique and new, in short, the genius. In the case of *Le nozze di Figaro* and *Don Giovanni* we shall have to set out from the standpoint of *opera buffa*, in that of *Die Entführung* and *Die Zauberflöte* from the standpoint of the

---

28. ◆ Here Abert refers to the collected edition of Mozart's works published by Breitkopf & Härtel beginning in 1877 and commonly referred to as the AMA. As noted in the editor's preface, I have deleted Abert's AMA references except where they bear directly on his argument: Mozart's works are by now so well known as to make them unnecessary solely for the sake of identification. The AMA has, in any case, been superseded by the *Neue Mozart-Ausgabe* (hereafter NMA).

German singspiel, yet here, too, the genius proves to be an innovator who not merely recreates the genre but causes it to fragment. This is clear not least from the writings on *Don Giovanni*, with commentators evidently still unable to answer the question as to whether we are dealing here with a 'comic' or a 'tragic' opera. Moreover, this principle of dividing the works by genre means that ones that are linked on an internal level are forcibly wrenched apart. *Die Zauberflöte*, for example, is far closer to the *Requiem*, the *Ave, verum corpus* and even to the great instrumental works of the previous period than it is to its 'companion piece', *La clemenza di Tito*, for all that this last-named work is another example of 'dramatic' music. And what is the connection between *Der Schauspieldirektor* and *Die Entführung aus dem Serail*? For all its charm, the former constitutes one of Mozart's professional obligations, rather than a fully-fledged work of art in its own right.

We know that most of Mozart's works were in fact commissions and that, in keeping with the practice of the older, pre-Beethovenian period, they were the result of external circumstances. A living tradition still existed at this time, a summation of formal and stylistic rules acknowledged and felt by all, whether they were the patrons responsible for issuing the commissions or the artists responsible for carrying them out. No artist could afford to ignore them. The main question with all these older composers, including – as the last in the line – Mozart himself, concerns the way in which each individual artist sought and found a balance between this tradition and his own archetypal experience as an artist. When seen from this point of view, Mozart's works, too, can be divided into three groups, the first of which comprises those in which his genius conformed to tradition without further ado, in some cases even subordinating itself to that tradition. These are the works written *sub specie momenti*, experiments and compromises that may be compared to shavings lying around on his workshop floor. They include the dramatic and symphonic works written for various celebrations, the pieces intended for pupils and for individual singers, with their specific vocal demands, and so on. The second group consists of those works that are still part of the tradition described above, but here the tradition is permeated and hence transformed and enriched by the elemental force of the artist's own experience, its range of forms increased in consequence. Typical of this group are the great keyboard concertos of the 1780s, which still clearly embody the old ideal of music written to divert society, while at the same time adopting a personal approach to that ideal and reinterpreting it accordingly. In the works of the third group, finally, the artist's archetypal experience, his basic emotion comes to predominate, with the result that the tradition is completely overshadowed by it. Here the focus of the artist's interest passes from the receptive element – his audience in society – to the artist himself. In these works, tradition is annealed by the fires of Mozart's genius to the point where it finally falls away like ash, allowing entirely new shapes to emerge. Here it is a matter of total indifference whether the genius expresses himself directly, as in the great symphonies and string quintets, or whether he uses the medium of an essentially alien subject matter, as in his great operas. It is here, above all, that we can see most clearly the relationship just discussed: in *Idomeneo*, the archetypal artistic experience is far more powerful than in *La clemenza di Tito*, a work that belongs in the second group, while this experience is at its most powerful in *Le nozze di Figaro*, *Don Giovanni* and *Die Zauberflöte*. Needless to add, the dividing line between these three groups is not always clear-cut: there are hybrid and composite forms that it is a particular pleasure to explore.

What is particularly characteristic of Mozart and, indeed, allows us to speak of him in the same breath as Goethe (a popular but otherwise exaggerated parallel) is his urge to give shape and form to his experiences from his earliest youth. Unlike the young Haydn and, at a later date, the young Schubert and Schumann, he was never able to allow the raw material of his emotions simply to pour out unchecked. Initially, he preferred to eschew all obvious signs of originality and to seek out among his numerous models those features that were best suited to confirming and fostering this urge to create coherent forms. This urge expressed itself unconsciously at least until the end of his various visits to Italy, becoming conscious throughout the following period up to and including *Idomeneo*. From the time of *Die Entführung aus dem Serail* until the end of his life, it found its most mature expression. As a result, this tripartite division of Mozart's output strikes me as the most natural. A number of recent writers have seen in the second of these periods the influence of the *Sturm und Drang* movement in contemporary German literature and art, a movement that has recently come back into fashion. And there is no doubt that Mozart's music – especially *Idomeneo* – has a great deal of the *Sturm und Drang* about it, but it is not in itself *Sturm und Drang*, for even the most tempestuous outbursts of this period still reflect the urge to create formal structures and to transform naturalism into culture. It is sufficient to recall the way in which Mozart took up and developed the legacy of Johann Schobert – one of the most unequivocal representatives of the *Sturm und Drang* movement in music – in order to appreciate the gulf that divides him from that movement.

I was fortunate in being able to complete most of the preparatory work on this book before the outbreak of war: only French and English libraries remained inaccessible during that time, but their holdings are not so significant as to persuade me to delay publication until some unforeseeable date in the future. It was Italian libraries that I invariably found the most helpful and that naturally produced the most plentiful yield in terms of the historical foundations of Mozart's art. In particular, I am grateful to the late Rocco Pagliara of the Naples Conservatory Library, to Francesco Mantica of the Santa Cecilia Library in Rome, to Francesco Vatielli of the Library of the Liceo Musicale in Bologna and to the staff of the Casanatense in Rome. I am also indebted to the staff of the Biblioteca Estense in Modena, the Marciana in Venice and the Library of the Monastery at Monte Cassino. I do not need to add that the various public and private libraries in Germany and Austria, especially those in Vienna, Berlin, Munich and Dresden, have been unfailingly helpful in my own case, too. Here I have largely been able to make up for the loss of access to the libraries in Paris and London. I am likewise immensely grateful to the Mozart Archives in Salzburg and to their director, Johann Evangelist Engl, not least for his permission to transcribe and photocopy a large number of original documents. The task of proof-reading was made easier by my old friend Professor Bechtel of Halle, who was his usual helpful self, while my pupil Rudolf Gerber helped me to prepare the index.

Last but not least, I should like to thank my publishers, Breitkopf & Härtel, who have supported me in every way and pressed ahead with publication of this work in spite of the critical times in which we live.

Inasmuch as this study is intended to take up Jahn's legacy, its outward presentation has remained the same, especially in terms of the relationship between text and annotation. But I have tried to reduce the number of footnotes as far as possible and removed all references to older works that are no longer of value as primary sources. I have also followed Jahn in slightly modernizing the orthography of the letters from which I have quoted as it does not seem to me necessary to torment the reader with Mozart's often chaotic spelling merely for the sake of a little historical colour. Readers interested in the history of the Salzburg dialect will have to go back to the original orthography, as given by Schiedermair, and will find in Mozart's letters a first-rate source. But that is not the purpose of the present study. At the same time, a comparison between the passages cited by Jahn and Schiedermair's edition of these letters brought to light a number of misreadings on Jahn's part, most of them based on his lack of knowledge of the south German dialect. In general, all that has survived of Jahn's original are a mere handful of pages, including passages in which, for the sake of brevity, he paraphrased sections from Mozart's and Leopold's letters. Even in those passages where, in common with other Mozart biographers, I have accepted Jahn's findings, I have recast them in a different form for the sake of the work's overriding stylistic unity. (These findings invariably relate to the details of Mozart's life.) I have also taken over some of Hermann Deiters's additions, indicating them as such with the reference [Deiters's note].

This study is appearing at a very dark time for our German fatherland, perhaps the darkest that it has ever known. Its consequences are bound to be felt by the world of German scholarship, too. Although the country's inward and outward collapse has not affected its leading position in scholarship, it too will have to preserve its strength and guard against weariness and trivialization. Together, art and scholarship are destined to play a part in the intellectual renewal of German life. We shall not, of course, achieve this goal through nebulous dreams or by feebly marvelling at foreign achievements. Rather, we must bethink ourselves of the living intellectual and moral forces that lie locked away within our own people and, armed with these forces, begin the task of rebuilding. Mozart had a sure feeling for the German character. 'If only a single patriot had been in charge, things would look very different', he once wrote.[29] 'But that, of course, would be an everlasting blot on Germany if we Germans were seriously to begin to think as Germans – to act as Germans – to speak as Germans – and even – to sing as Germans!' Even today, these words still ring out like a bright-toned fanfare. In the course of a long reign marked by the happiest concord between himself and his people, the noble prince [Duke Wilhelm zu Württemberg] to whom this study is inscribed understood these words as few others have done, and as a result he is the only person who, as he lives out his days in retirement in the silent depths of the forest, may justifiably apply to himself the words of the poet who once wrote that he – the prince – may 'boldly lay his head in every subject's lap'.[30] May he accept this book as a modest token of ancient Swabian loyalty!

Halle an der Saale, October 1919   Hermann Abert

Preface to sixth edition

No research of any fundamental importance that would have required significant revisions to the text has appeared since this volume first appeared, and so the present second (sixth) edition is essentially unchanged, the main difference being that most of the corrections formerly included in the appendix to the second volume have now been incorporated in the text, at least to the extent that this was technically possible. A number of other minor errors and misprints have been corrected and individual findings, including Hermann Spieß's research on the *Adoramus*, have been taken into account.

Leipzig, Christmas 1922   Hermann Abert

29. ◆ *Briefe*, iii.393 (letter of 21 May 1785).
30. ◆ Justinus Kerner, 'Der reichste Fürst'.

Childhood

Wolfgang Amade Mozart was no more a child of Vienna than were the other two composers traditionally yoked together as Viennese 'classics': Joseph Haydn and Ludwig van Beethoven. He was born in Salzburg, but his father's family could trace back its roots to Swabia and to the old imperial city of Augsburg, where they had settled by the middle of the seventeenth century. The earliest recorded mention of the name, which is variously found as Mozert, Motzart, Motzhardt and Motard, dates back, in fact, to the early years of the century: among the pupils at the Augsburg Choir School – a training ground for the cathedral choristers and a first stage in the careers of a number of later choir masters and conductors – was one Johann Mozart, a pupil of Christian Erbach and, to all appearances, highly gifted as a musician. The oldest known representative of the name to take an interest in music, he completed his studies in 1613, but then entered the Monastery of the Holy Rood.[1] It is unclear, however, whether he was related to Wolfgang's oldest identifiable forebear, David Mozart, who came to Augsburg from the nearby village of Pfersee and was granted citizenship and the right to trade as a mason.[2] David Mozart was born around 1620, married Maria Negeler from Lechhausen on 25 January 1643 and died on 28 January 1685. His three sons, Daniel (1645–83?), Hans Georg (1647–1719) and Franz (1649–94), were master-masons like their father. The youngest of the three, Franz, married Anna Härrer (or Harrer) from Oberpüchrhain (?–1703) on 30 January 1678. He was Mozart's great-grandfather. *His* eldest son, Johann Georg Mozart (*b* 4 May 1679; *d* 19 February 1736),[3] became a master-bookbinder in Augsburg. His first wife, whom he married in 1708, was Anna Maria Peter, the widow of a bookbinder by the name of Banneger, while his second wife, whom he married on 16 May 1718, was Anna Maria Sulzer (1696–1766), the daughter of a master-weaver from Baden who later settled in Augsburg. She bore him eight children: six sons and two daughters. One of the sons died in infancy, while another two – Joseph Ignaz (1725–96) and Franz Alois (1727–91) – followed in

1. See Kroyer, *Gregor Aichinger: Ausgewählte Werke*, LXVII–LXVIII; and Ursprung, *Jacobus de Kerle*.
2. See Buff, 'Mozarts Augsburger Vorfahren'; see also Engl, *Festschrift zur Mozart-Centenarfeier in Salzburg am 15., 16. und 17. Juli 1891*. Mozart's family tree may be found prefaced to the opening chapter of Schurig, *Wolfgang Amade Mozart*; see also i.511–12. The oldest representative of the name to be recorded in Augsburg is Christoph Mozart (Stoffel) in 1551, although it has no more proved possible to establish a link between him and the composer than with the painter Anton Mozart, who was born around 1575. Nor has it been possible to establish a connection with the surgeon Leopold Mozart, who was born at Pfaffstädt near Mattighofen in around 1765, or with the latter's brother, the musician Philipp Mozart; see the *Jahresbericht des Mozarteums*, xxiii (Salzburg, 1903), 18. Caution is all the more advisable in that the name of Mozart and its manifold variants is relatively common in south Germany. ◆ Further, see Breitinger, 'Ältester väterlicher Abstammungsnachweis aus Augsburg'; Layer, 'Zur Tätigkeit des Augsburger Barockbaumeisters David Mozart und seiner Söhne im Donautal. Ein Beitrag zur Geschichte der Architektur Dillingens im 17. Jahrhundert'; Schöttl, 'Mozarts Ur-Urgroßvater'; and Kessler, 'Der Ur-Urgroßvater W. A. Mozarts als Erbauer des Achteckaufsatzes auf dem Dillinger Stadtpfarrkirchenturm'.
3. The oil painting in the Mozarteum depicts not him, but his son Leopold; see Engl, *Festschrift zur Mozart-Centenarfeier in Salzburg am 15., 16. und 17. Juli 1891*, 21. ◆ This picture is reproduced in Deutsch, *Mozart und seine Welt*, 33.

their father's footsteps and became master-bookbinders in Augsburg. But it was the oldest of them, Johann Georg Leopold (*b* 14 November 1719),[4] who was the first member of this family of honest craftsmen to show any musical talent. Unlike Johann Sebastian Bach, Wolfgang Amadè could look back on only a single generation of musicians.

Even as a child, Leopold was already distinguished by his astuteness of mind, and his father was determined that he should enter the Church, with the result that, on the recommendation of his godfather, the canon of St Peter's, Johann Georg Grabherr, he became a chorister in the monastery choirs of the Holy Rood and St Ulrich's.[5] In earlier centuries, most Catholic musicians began their formal training as choristers, a training that provided a sound practical and theoretical foundation for their careers, not least because their duties extended far beyond the framework of the liturgy. As late as 13 October 1777 we find Leopold writing to his son and recalling how, as a chorister at St Ulrich's, he had taken part in a performance of a cantata on the occasion of the wedding of a local privy counsellor, Andreas Felix Oefele.[6] And it seems likely that it was during this period at the monastery that he laid the foundations for an organ technique that was to excite attention during his years as a student. In 1777, Wolfgang was introduced to one Franziskus Erasmus Freysinger in Munich and wrote to tell his father that Freysinger 'still clearly remembers Messenbrunn, where Papa (this was news to me) played the organ amazingly well. "It was quite frightening," he said, "to see him working away with his hands and feet, but absolutely amazing – he was quite a fellow. My father thought the world of him. And how he fooled the clergy about becoming a priest!"'[7]

Later, Leopold Mozart rarely had a good word to say for the inhabitants of Augsburg, dismissing them in a letter to his son as 'Abderites'.[8] Equally strained were his relations with his siblings, whom he accused of having exploited their mother's weakness to his own disadvantage. They themselves, of course, had no scruples about petitioning him for his help.

Leopold matriculated at the University of Salzburg in 1737, intending to remain there for two years.[9] This did not mean that he abandoned his interest in music. Quite the opposite: for generations, the universities had been among the staunchest supporters of music in Germany, and legion were the famous musicians who had frequented the groves of academe. According to the university records, Leopold studied logic and probably also jurisprudence. Within a year of matriculating, he was publicly commended at an examination, but by 1739 his name had vanished

---

4. The house in which he was born in the Frauengasse [number 30] now bears a commemorative plaque. ◆ For a transcript of his baptism certificate, see *Dokumente*, 3, *Documentary Biography*, 4. ◆ Leopold Mozart's birthplace has now been restored as a museum, including not only exhibitions but also an important library housing early manuscripts and prints of Leopold Mozart's works. See Mančal, *Mozart-Schätze in Augsburg* and 'Die "Zengersammlung". Zu einem der wichtigsten Bestände des Augsburger Mozarthauses'; <http://www.deutsche-mozart-gesellschaft.de/mozart/service/mozarthaus.htm>. For other Mozart memorials in the Augsburg area, see Kluger, *Die Mozarts: Die deutsche Mozartstadt Augsburg und die Mozartstätten in der Region*. Documents relating to the marriage of Leopold Mozart's parents, as well as his birth and baptism, are reproduced in *Dokumente*, 3–4, *Documentary Biography*, 3–4.
5. St Ulrich's was one of the Benedictine monasteries that had helped to endow the University of Salzburg and that continued to offer it financial support; see Mayr, *Die ehemalige Universität Salzburg*, 4. It was presumably this connection that persuaded Leopold to study in Salzburg. ◆ Concerning Leopold's early years in Augsburg and musical life there, see Ernst Fritz Schmid, 'Leopold Mozart' and 'Neues zu Leopold Mozarts Bildungsgang'; Münster, 'Neues zu Leopold Mozarts Augsburger Gymnasialjahren'; Layer, *Eine Jugend in Augsburg: Leopold Mozart 1719–1737*; Mančal, 'Augsburg "Meine Vaterstadt" (L. Mozart 1756), "die vatterstadt meines Papa" (W. A. Mozart 1777), "meine eigentliche Stammstadt" (Fr. X. W. A. Mozart 1821)'; and Krautwurst and Zorn, *Bibliographie des Schrifttums zur Musikgeschichte der Stadt Augsburg*.
6. *Briefe*, ii.52 (letter of 12/13 October 1777).
7. *Briefe*, ii.47–8 (letter of 11 October 1777).
8. *Briefe*, ii.72 (letter of 18 October 1777). ◆ Leopold's reference is to the dimwitted denizens of the Thracian city of Abdera.
9. See Hammerle, *Mozart und einige Zeitgenossen*.

from the university rolls: clearly, music had triumphed over his more scholarly inclinations;[10] the attempts to lure him back to the Church that Mozart mentions in his letter of 1777 may merely have served to confirm him in this resolve. His definitive decision dates from 1740, when the president of the cathedral consistory, Count Johann Baptist Thurn-Valsassina and Taxis, took him into his service as valet and musician, a combination of duties by no means uncommon at this time. That same year, Leopold dedicated to his patron the first of his compositions to be engraved at his own expense, his *Sonate Sei per Chiesa e da Camera A T R E Due Violini e Basso*. The accompanying letter speaks gratefully of the manner in which the count had rescued him 'dalle dure tenebre d'ogni mio bisogno, e stradato ver l'orizzonte della mia fortunata'.[11] During the next three years, Count Thurn allowed his valet to pursue his musical interests to the full. In 1741 and again in 1743 Leopold wrote passion cantatas, both entitled *Christus begraben*, and in 1742 he composed a Latin school opera for the University, a companion piece to his son's *Apollo et Hyacinthus* that was performed in the smaller of the University's halls on 18 May 1742 under the title *Antiquitas personata*.[12] Only the scenario is extant, whereas in the case of the two passion cantatas – wrongly described by Mozart as oratorios – only the librettos have survived. In all likelihood, the librettist in each case was Jakob Anton Wimmer.[13]

Both cantatas were almost certainly performed during Lent at the archbishop's court,[14] which would mean that Mozart had already endeared himself to Archbishop Siegmund Count von Schrattenbach when the latter appointed him fourth violinist in his court orchestra in 1743. By 1758 Leopold had advanced to the position of second violinist, and in 1763 he was appointed deputy Kapellmeister at the same time that Lolli was appointed Kapellmeister.[15] In 1757 we also

10. The question depends on whether or not we regard Leopold as the author of the notes in Marpurg's *Historisch-kritische Beyträge zur Aufnahme der Musik*, iii.184–5. Relying on the University records, Hammerle (*Mozart und einige Zeitgenossen*) denies that he was, but Seiffert, in his introduction to *Leopold Mozart: Ausgewählte Werke*, IX, draws attention – rightly in my own view – to the correspondence between Marpurg and Mozart and to the unmistakably Mozartian tenor of the whole report. ◆ Compelling as it is to believe that Leopold's musical inclinations – genetically passed on to Wolfgang? – led him to abandon his academic career, in fact he was expelled from the University in 1739 for poor attendance and 'indifference'. On other occasions he had also shown he was a hot-head (see n. 15). The notes in Marpurg mentioned by Abert refer to the 'Nachricht von dem gegenwärtigen Zustande der Musik Sr. Hochfürstlichen Gnaden des Erzbischoffs zu Salzburg im Jahr 1757' (Report on the Present State of the Musical Establishment at the Court of His Serene Highness the Archbishop of Salzburg in the Year 1757). For the passage referring to Leopold Mozart, see *Dokumente*, 13, *Documentary Biography*, 11. For an English translation of the entire 'Report', see Zaslaw, *Mozart's Symphonies*, 550–7.

11. Max Seiffert, *Leopold Mozart: Ausgewählte Werke*, XII. ◆ Further, see Hochradner, '"Meistens nur um eine Uebung in der Radierkunst zu machen". Leopold Mozarts kompositorisches Erstlingswerk: Die Sonate Sei (1740)'.

12. Max Seiffert, *Leopold Mozart: Ausgewählte Werke*, XIII–XVII, reproduces the text of the first passion cantata.

13. Hammerle, *Mozart und einige Zeitgenossen*, 13ff., and Köchel, *Chronologisch-thematisches Verzeichniss*, 32, argue that the initials J. A. W. are those of the curate Johann Adam Wieland. ◆ In fact they are the initials of Ignaz Anton Weiser, a Salzburg businessman and mayor of the city from 1772 to 1775. Here Abert confuses two settings of *Christus begraben*, an original from 1741 and a thorough-going revision from not later than 1755. The music for both is lost although printed librettos survive in the library of the University of Salzburg (shelfmarks 4058.I and 4064.I); the text of the 1741 version is printed in Max Seiffert, *Leopold Mozart: Ausgewählte Werke*, XIII–XV. Leopold's 1743 cantata was *Christus verurtheilt*, the libretto of which also survives in the library of the University of Salzburg (shelfmark 4062.I). With the exception of the last three lines ('Reliquum apparatuum dabit Theatrum. / Ut in Omnibus Glorificetur / Deus'), the text of *Antiquitas personata* is given in Seiffert, *Leopold Mozart: Ausgewählte Werke*, XV–XVI. See Carlson, 'The Vocal Music of Leopold Mozart (1719–1787): Authenticity, Chronology and Thematic Catalog', 183–93.

14. In his petition of 1778 (reproduced in Pirckmayer, 'Zur Lebensgeschichte Mozarts', 145 [*Briefe*, ii.462]), Leopold reports that he has been in the service of the archiepiscopal see for thirty-eight years. In this position, too, he continued to bear the title of 'Hochfürstlicher Salzburgischer Kammerdiener'. See also the report on the wedding service in Engl, *Festschrift zur Mozart-Centenarfeier in Salzburg am 15., 16. und 17. Juli 1891*, 16, where further details of Leopold's career may be found. In 1753, for example, he was reproached for writing a letter of complaint about one of the counts of Thurn und Taxis and a local priest by the name of Egglstainer and required to make a formal apology. For Leopold's appointment as deputy Kapellmeister, see *Dokumente*, 21–2, *Documentary Biography*, 20.

15. See Hammerle, *Mozart und einige Zeitgenossen*, 26 and 28; and Max Seiffert, *Leopold Mozart: Ausgewählte Werke*, XXV. ◆ For Leopold's appointment as deputy Kapellmeister, see *Dokumente*, 21–2, *Documentary Biography*, 20.

find him described as court composer, a title bestowed as a sign of special distinction and one that conferred on its holders a status approaching that of the Kapellmeister himself.[16] According to Leopold's own account, the orchestra numbered thirty-three players at this date,[17] but to these should be added the tower warder and his colleagues, and a sizeable contingent of court and field trumpeters, who were pressed into service whenever the need arose.[18] Leopold worked under no fewer than seven different Kapellmeisters: Matthias Siegmund Biechteler (1706–43), Karl Heinrich Biber von Bibern (1743–9), Johann Ernst Eberlin (1749–62), Giuseppe Francesco Lolli (1763–78), Domenico Fischietti (1772–83), Jakob Rust (1777–8) and Luigi Gatti (from 1783).[19] In addition to these instrumentalists, there was also a vocal ensemble consisting of thirty soloists and choristers and fifteen boys, all of whom took part in performances of sacred music.[20] These boys were taught by Leopold Mozart – from 1744 on the violin and from 1777 on the keyboard, too.[21]

The orchestra was kept busy, performing both sacred and secular music,[22] and this circumstance, coupled with the lessons that Leopold gave both privately and as part of his official duties, meant that life was not at all easy for him, not least because, as a conscientious employee, he saw it as a point of honour to place music on a sound footing.[23] And, like his contemporaries, he was also required under the terms of his employment to write music. Even so, it is clear from his surviving correspondence with the Augsburg publisher Johann Jakob Lotter[24] that he still found time to write a number of pieces for the city's collegium musicum, including *The Musical Sleigh-Ride*, *Peasants' Wedding* and a sinfonia 'pastorale'. In 1756 Lotter published his violin tutor, and in 1759 he and Eberlin wrote a set of twelve pieces, *Morning and Evening*, for the mechanical organ at Hohensalzburg.[25]

16. ◆ It is by no means clear that the title 'court composer' conferred any official status: the term is known only from the 'Report' and does not otherwise occur in court records; quite possibly, if Leopold is the author of the 'Report', it represents little more than self-aggrandizing.

17. See Marpurg, *Historisch-kritische Beyträge zur Aufnahme der Musik*, iii.184–5. See n. 10, above.

18. Max Seiffert, *Leopold Mozart: Ausgewählte Werke*, lists the individual players.

19. ◆ For Biechteler, see Rosenthal, 'Zur Stilistik der Salzburger Kirchenmusik von 1600 bis 1730', and Hochradner, 'Matthias Siegmund Biechteler: Leben und Werk eines Salzburger Hofkapellmeisters'; for Biber, Chafe, *The Church Music of Heinrich Biber*, 71–7; for Eberlin, Pauly, 'Johann Ernst Eberlin's Concerted Liturgical Music'; Schneider-Cuvay, 'Die Instrumentalwerke Johann Ernst Eberlins'; Manfred Schmid, *Mozart und die Salzburger Tradition*; Haas, 'Eberlins Schuldramen und Oratorien'; Cuvay, 'Beiträge zur Lebensgeschichte des Salzburger Hofkapellmeisters Johann Ernst Eberlin'; and Layer, 'Johann Ernst Eberlin'; for Gatti, Gehmacher, 'Luigi Gatti: Sein Leben und seine Oratorien'. Concerning musical life in Salzburg generally, including Kapellmeisters mentioned by Abert for whom there is still no specialized literature, see Constantin Schneider, *Geschichte der Musik in Salzburg*; Hintermaier, 'Die Salzburger Hofkapelle von 1700 bis 1806: Organisation und Personal'; Eisen, 'Salzburg under Church Rule'; Schuler, *Mozarts Salzburger Freunde und Bekannte: Biographien und Kommentare*; and Schimek, *Musikpolitik in der Salzburger Aufklärung: Musik, Musikpolitik und deren Rezeption am Hof des Salzburger Fürsterzbischofs Hieronymus Graf Colloredo*.

20. Marpurg, *Historisch-kritische Beyträge zur Aufnahme der Musik*, iii.90ff., and Max Seiffert, *Leopold Mozart: Ausgewählte Werke*, XXVIII–XXIX. ◆ For an account of orchestras in Salzburg, see Eisen, 'Mozart's Salzburg Orchestras'.

21. See Leopold's own self-assured remarks in *Briefe*, ii.381 and 454 (letters of 29 June and 27 August 1778).

22. Max Seiffert, *Leopold Mozart: Ausgewählte Werke*, XVIIff., reproduces not only the Salzburg church and court calendar but also the announcements of all the court celebrations in 1757.

23. Schubart, *Ideen zu einer Ästhetik der Tonkunst*, 157.

24. The surviving letters are in the Grasnick collection in the Königliche Bibliothek, Berlin. Excerpts are reproduced by Max Seiffert, *Leopold Mozart: Ausgewählte Werke*, XXX. ◆ Leopold's correspondence with Lotter survives in the Augsburg Stadtarchiv, the Augsburg Leopold Mozart Museum, and the Staatsbibliothek zu Berlin. For a modern edition, see *Briefe*, i.3–48 and v.3–30.

25. The pieces for January, April, August, November and December are by Eberlin, the remainder by Leopold. Leopold took care to capture the mood of the individual months in his music, later transcribing these pieces for keyboard. His pieces for May ('Menuetto Pastorale') and September ('The Hunt') can still be heard on the instrument to this day. ◆ Despite numerous changes over the years – in 1820 the Salzburg gunsmith Gitzl set six new pieces on the drum and in 1853 the Austrian national anthem was added – the organ mechanism is now, for the most part, returned to its 1753 state. The drum and pins were restored in 1892 by the Salzburg organ builder Matthäus Mauracher and reset by the Viennese organ builder Franz Janisch to include the Austrian national anthem (after Haydn), the anonymous 'Alter Choral', Paul Hofhaimer's 'Lydia, dic', Mozart's 'Komm, lieber Mai', Michael Haydn's 'Sehnsucht nach dem Landleben', Eberlin's 'Menuetto' and 'Lullaby', and Leopold Mozart's 'The Hunt' and 'Menuetto

Nor was Leopold merely a local celebrity known only within the confines of Salzburg, as a number of writers would like us to think. In 1753 – three years before the publication of his violin tutor – Lorenz Mizler appointed him a member of his Society of Musical Sciences in Leipzig, an appointment about which Leopold informed his publisher on 24 November:

In the utmost confidence: I have received a letter from a distant place informing me that they are thinking of appointing me a member – do not be alarmed – – or – – do not laugh – – a member of the Corresponding Society of Musical Sciences. Heavens! What a fillip! But don't go telling tales out of school, as it may be no more than a rumour. I'd never have thought it; and I can say that on my word of honour.[26]

On 23 June 1759, Friedrich Wilhelm Marpurg, who had founded a similar society in Berlin, wrote to his colleague in Salzburg:

The Society is minded to publish its periodical articles in the form of letters, and it proposes to take the liberty of addressing these letters to persons of merit, insight and taste. Could the aforesaid Society, in this endeavour, Sir, make a more auspicious beginning than with you?[27]

These contacts between Leopold and north German musicians deserve far more attention than they have received hitherto, not least because of their importance for the young Mozart's artistic development. But Leopold also succeeded in making contact with the leading music publishers of his time, a contact which, given the fact that works of music at this date were closely bound up with the needs of the day and could expect to find only a very limited market, presupposes a solid artistic reputation on his part. The Nuremberg dealer Johann Ulrich Haffner published his three keyboard sonatas as part of his *Œuvres mêlées*, and from 1762 onwards Gottlob Immanuel Breitkopf's Leipzig catalogues announced no fewer than twenty of his works, although only seven of these have survived.[28]

It is not true to claim, as some writers have done, that, when he saw the first glimmerings of Wolfgang's genius, Leopold abandoned composition and lived only for his son's education: his official duties, if nothing else, would have prevented him from doing so; and he himself informs us that he wrote a number of sacred works during the brief period that he spent in Salzburg between his two longer visits to Italy.[29] In Rome in 1770, spurred on by Wolfgang's successes,

Pastorello'. Two National Socialist songs added to the drum in 1938 were removed after 1945. Although the *Musical Sleighride, Peasant's Wedding* and sinfonia 'pastorale' were performed by the Augsburg collegium musicum, it is uncertain if the works were written specifically for them. The *Musical Sleighride*, for example, was also given at the Salzburg court.

26. Max Seiffert, *Leopold Mozart: Ausgewählte Werke*, XXXV.

27. Marpurg, *Kritische Briefe über die Tonkunst* iii/3, 184–5 [*Dokumente*, 13, *Documentary Biography*, 11].

28. ◆ Several of these lost works, as well as numerous previously unknown compositions by Leopold Mozart, have been recovered or discovered since Abert's time. For a thematic catalogue of the church music, see Carlson, 'The Vocal Music of Leopold Mozart (1719–1787): Authenticity, Chronology and Thematic Catalog', and for the symphonies Eisen, *Leopold Mozart: Ausgewählte Werke I: Sinfonien*, XVI–XXVIII. For a complete, non-thematic list of all Leopold's works, see Eisen, 'Mozart, Johann Georg Leopold'.

29. *Briefe*, i.505 (letter of 14 December 1774). ◆ Here Abert misrepresents Leopold's letter, in which he asks his wife to send to Munich the scores of two litanies, one by Wolfgang (K125), and one of his own, which he describes as in D major, 'a recent one [by me] which begins staccato violin and double bass . . . ; in the Agnus Dei the second violin has triplets throughout'. Almost certainly this is the litany Carlson IB2, the autograph of which is dated 1762, not a work composed – as Abert implies – in Salzburg between the Italian journeys; for a modern edition, see NMA X/28/3–5/1. It is likely that his last work (unfinished) is the mass K116, formerly attributed to Wolfgang and composed in Vienna and Salzburg in 1768 and 1769.

he even roused himself sufficiently to write a symphony.[30] None the less, his output during this later period cannot be remotely compared with what he produced at an earlier date. Given his numerous journeys and the various other efforts bound up with his son's education, it comes as no surprise to find his Muse growing increasingly taciturn, until she finally fell silent altogether. During his final, embittered years, he even denied her existence completely and laid her to premature rest.

Leopold Mozart was a self-made man and, as such, an idiosyncratic, independently minded individual. In their desire to idealize everything to do with their hero, most older biographers, headed by Jahn, turned him into the ideal father of a youthful genius, painting a romantic portrait of his character that does not correspond to the facts. More recently, the pendulum was swung too far in the other direction, and the venerable patriarch has had to make way for a figure whose character is made up, in the main, of weaknesses such as pedantry, obstinacy, vanity, envy and petty-bourgeois complacency, with the result that Leopold now seems very much to have been his son's nemesis.[31] This curious volte-face merely proves how hard it is to remain objective towards the fathers of great men, especially when – as is the case here – they have a character of their own. The rationalistic attempt to reduce their characters to certain stereotypes constitutes the main obstacle in the way of our deeper understanding of their real personalities. Leopold Mozart is the best possible example of this.

Leopold's Swabian extraction had a decisive impact on his character. His typically phlegmatic, often ruminative approach to life, his tenacity in pursuit of his goals (a tenacity often verging on sheer stubbornness) and his idiosyncratic and dry sense of humour all reveal the Swabian, as does the remarkable shrewdness that he showed in his dealings with others. He was forever trying to gain a clearer understanding of people and their lives, the better to be able to use them for his own advantage, and as a result gradually came to despise and, finally, to hate his fellow human beings. 'People are all villains,' he wrote to his son in 1777, 'the older you get and the more contact you have with other people, the more you will realize this sad truth. Just think of all the idle and wheedling promises and of the hundred things that have already befallen us, and draw your own conclusion as to how much you can rely on people's help, since in the end everyone soon finds, or invents, a plausible excuse and blames some third party for the fact that all his good intentions came to nothing.'[32] In Leopold we see a true disciple of the Enlightenment, his pessimism only one aspect of a character entirely typical of the age: he was the product of the same dream of a more perfect world that gave rise in those of a less stoical disposition to the infatuated longing for a true communion of souls in the belief that such an exchange of ideas would in some way ennoble the mind.

It was not, of course, an unworldly, inactive pessimism that Leopold Mozart espoused. He was saved from this by his strength of will and especially by his immutable sense of duty towards himself and, later, towards his son. This is the aspect of his personality that first and most frequently strikes the observer and has resulted in the fact that some writers have turned him into

30. It is wrongly attributed to Wolfgang in the complete edition of his works: AMA XXIV, no. 4; see Max Seiffert, *Leopold Mozart: Ausgewählte Werke*, XXXVIIIff. ◆ The symphony is K81; see below, n. 62.
31. Schurig, *Wolfgang Amade Mozart*, i.38, goes further than anyone in this. ◆ For an even more extreme view, see Solomon, *Mozart: A Life*; a more balanced picture is presented in Halliwell, *The Mozart Family: Four Lives in a Social Context*.
32. *Briefe*, ii.75 (letter of 20 October 1777). Needless to say, it was his professional colleagues who were his chief target here; see *Briefe*, ii.257: 'I avoided all acquaintances and, mark you, particularly all familiarity with people of our own profession' (letter of 5 February 1778).

the heroic embodiment of the most total self-denial, while others see him as a pedant of limited imagination. Both views are wrong.

Leopold's sense of duty was largely grounded in his religious beliefs. He was a devout Catholic and regulated his dealings with the Church with the same painstaking care that he evinced within his own household. There was a certain bigotry about his actions: it was, for example, with almost pathological anxiety that he shielded his family from the dangerous influence of other creeds. On 15 December 1777, he wrote to his son: 'Perhaps I may ask whether Wolfgang has forgotten about confession? – – God must come first. It is from Him that we must expect our temporal happiness, and at the same time must think of our eternal salvation: young people don't like to hear such things, I know, I was once young myself; but, thank God, I always pulled myself together again, in spite of all the foolish pranks of my youth, avoiding all threats to my soul and never losing sight of God and my honour or of the consequences, the *dangerous* consequences.'[33] This final remark already points clearly to the powerful influence of Enlightenment ideas on Leopold's religious beliefs. He expressly rejected the reproach that he was holier-than-thou and a hypocrite.[34] Above all, however, he was attracted by that aspect of the Enlightenment that in north Germany found its classic exponent in Christian Fürchtegott Gellert. Indeed, Leopold's admiration for Gellert is a striking example of the high regard in which the Leipzig poet was held in both denominational camps, and we shall shortly find him introducing his son to the world of the Protestant anthem. It comes as no surprise, therefore, to discover that, in spite of his attachment to the Church, Leopold became a Freemason towards the end of his life.

In the case of the principles which, methodical as ever, he applied to his son's education, it was again religion that invariably had the last word. In its sincerity and grandeur, the manner in which Leopold struggled to reconcile this most pressing of all his concerns with the dictates of his conscience raises him high above any reproach of narrow-minded pedantry, and it alone would suffice to make him worthy of his great son. In the course of his turbulent life he learnt how important it is for a person to work at improving himself. And this was to be his son's guiding principle, too: 'The greatest art is to get to know oneself, and then, my dear son, do as I do, and make sure that you also get to know other people properly.'[35] Here, too, Wolfgang's best teacher was the living example of his father, who, in spite of his self-assurance, never forgot the import-ance of self-discipline. His aim was that of all fathers who have struggled to get on in the world: his son was to do better in life than he himself had done and to achieve a position in the world that was worthy of his talent. And from the very outset, it was sheer hard work that he held out to him as the way to achieve this end. The greater the genius, the greater the sense of responsibility in the eyes of God and the world and the greater, too, the obligation to follow the example of the parable of the talents and put his money to the exchangers in order that he might enter into the joy of his Lord. This was his motto in life and one that he never tired of holding out for his son to emulate until it became second nature to him.

Whatever he could do to smooth Wolfgang's way for him he did with his usual circumspection and lively tenacity. There was not infrequently a certain violence to his actions on such occasions, an autocratic element that did not always redound to his children's advantage. On their travels, for example, he placed demands on their health to which they were simply not equal, as is clear from

---

33. *Briefe*, ii.188 (letter of 15 December 1777).
34. *Briefe*, ii.79 (letter of 23 October 1777).
35. *Briefe*, ii.284 (letter of 16 February 1778).

their frequent illnesses. But a no less important role in Mozart's upbringing was played by the thought of mutual gain. Yet, given the pitiful conditions in which they lived in Salzburg, it is impossible to criticize Leopold for wanting to profit from his children. No more should we condemn him for the obsequious air which, his normal misanthropy notwithstanding, he was fond of adopting towards his superiors. After all, such an attitude was all too deeply rooted in the social status of the musicians of the time. Less attractive, by contrast, is the importunate, even strident, tone that he assumed when presenting his children to the world as 'prodigies of nature', a sales technique in which he had no hesitation in knocking a year off Wolfgang's age. In such cases he would stop at nothing in his burning ambition to enhance his children's reputation, an ambition that sometimes assumed the strangest forms. Artistically, too, his practical nature, when combined with all manner of personal dislikes, was often to his son's decisive disadvantage. There was something demagogic about his taste in art, with the result that he saw his son's salvation as closely bound up with the then fashionable love of what he termed 'popular' art. It was this, too, that defined his limitations in the artistic sphere as elsewhere, so that Wolfgang was forced in directions from which he was later able to escape only with great difficulty, if at all.

In short, Leopold Mozart was no saint. But nor was he an empty-headed philistine. He was a strong-willed individual who commanded respect, in every aspect of his character a product of the Enlightenment, and it is from this standpoint alone that his strengths and weaknesses should be judged. Only an oversensitive dilettante would regard these weaknesses as a source of martyrdom for Wolfgang. What Mozart inherited from his father was not only the living example of strength of character reinforced by self-discipline and sense of duty but also a serious and lofty attitude to art that remained with him all his life. We may be confident that the author of a treatise on violin playing would bring up his children to be more than mere artisans. His intellectual outlook went far beyond that of a mere musician, but took in politics, history, philosophy, literature and art. As a true rationalist, he was, of course, immensely proud of his knowledge, but it was also something that he regarded with the utmost seriousness, a seriousness clear from his dealings with Gellert. As a strict Catholic, he was keen to show his admiration for the poet of the Protestant Enlightenment. He received the following reply:

> I would have to be very insensitive not to be touched by the extraordinary kindness with which you honour me; and I would be the most ungrateful of men to have read you kind letter without feeling some sense of recognition. No, my very dear sir, I accept your love and friendship with the very same sincerity with which you offer them to me. And so, my dear sir, you enjoy reading my writings and encourage your friends to read them, too? Without wishing to boast, I may say quite sincerely that I scarcely hoped to receive this reward from the place from which it has come. Does 'The Christian' – one of my more recent poems – also meet with your approval? I am almost tempted to answer this question myself and say yes. Its contents, together with the nobility of character which, without realizing it, you revealed in your letter to me and my own honest intentions seem to permit me to say yes.[36]

36. Nissen, *Biographie W. A. Mozarts*, 10–11. ◆ Gellert's undated letter to Leopold almost certainly dates from the 1750s or 1760s; Leopold's original letter to him is lost. For the complete text, see *Briefe* i.236–7.

Leopold's letter may have been written in the wake of the gift of a volume of Gellert's poems that Baron von Bose gave the then seven-year-old Mozart in Paris with the request that he set them to music 'so that the unfeeling despiser of religion may read them and pause, or may hear them and fall to his knees and worship God'.[37] Later, in 1770, Mozart wrote to his sister from Milan to report the poet's death.[38] But Leopold's letters also contain countless passages in which he speaks of politics, military history, culture and economics, making it clear that there was much for Wolfgang to learn in other areas besides music, areas permanently closed to the children of other musicians. All in all, Leopold was really not unworthy of being the father of a great artist.

Towards the end of his life, Leopold virtually abandoned composition, thereby laying the foundations for the dismissive attitude to his own music that has dominated writings on the subject from Schubart[39] to the present day. Yet the high regard in which he was held by his contemporaries ought to give us pause for thought. More recently, attempts have been made – with some success – to do justice to his works both historically and artistically.[40] After all, this question is closely bound up with the no less important question of the father's influence on his son.

Leopold Mozart was a prolific composer,[41] with a work-list that includes not only various masses, litanies and other sacred compositions of greater or lesser length, but also an impressive series of symphonies (including the programmatical occasional works), concertos, divertimentos and keyboard pieces. His report also mentions 'theatrical pieces'.[42] Barely two-thirds of these works have survived, but enough of them have been reprinted in recent years to allow the lay listener to gain an idea of Leopold's abilities.

As far as the sacred works are concerned, we shall have to accept the existing view that they reveal a well-schooled and technically competent musician lacking in imagination. Indeed, we could go further and claim that whole movements strike entirely the wrong note, being lightweight and playful where the words demand gravity and dignity, while others – in keeping with the court's demand that church services should last no more than three-quarters of an hour[43] – were barely elaborated at all and incapable, therefore, of doing full justice to their words. Of course, it would be wrong to lay the blame for most of these weaknesses at Leopold's door, inasmuch as they are

37. ◆ *Briefe*, i.140 (letter from Leopold to Lorenz Hagenauer, 1 April 1764). Bose's dedication of Gellert's 1757 *Geistliche Oden und Lieder* to Mozart reads: 'Take, little Orpheus of seven years, this book from the hand of thy admirer and friend! Read it often, – and experience its divine songs, and lend them (in those blessed hours of perception), thy irresistible harmonies; so that the unfeeling despiser of religion may read, – and attend! – that he may hear them – and bow down, and pray to God.' See *Dokumente*, 29, *Documentary Biography*, 28.

38. *Briefe*, i.309 (letter of 26 January 1770). ◆ Yet Mozart's letter is hardly sympathetic to the poet or to his father: he puns on Gellert's name (as 'gelehrt', or 'learned') and notes that since his death he had composed no more poetry.

39. Schubart, *Ideen zu einer Ästhetik der Tonkunst*, 157: 'His style is somewhat old-fashioned, but thorough and full of contrapuntal understanding.' Schubart's assessment was echoed by Jahn, *W. A. Mozart*, fourth edition, i.7ff., and, even more, by Wyweza and Saint-Foix, *Wolfgang Amédée Mozart: Sa vie musicale et son œuvre*, i.4–9, who denied that Leopold had any creative gifts at all or that he exercised any influence on his son.

40. First by Renz, 'Leopold Mozart als Komponist', and especially by Max Seiffert, *Leopold Mozart: Ausgewählte Werke*. ◆ More recently, see Plath, 'Zur Echtheitsfrage'.

41. See Marpurg, *Historisch-kritische Beyträge zur Aufnahme der Musik*, iii.185 and, especially, the list drawn up by Max Seiffert, *Leopold Mozart: Ausgewählte Werke*, XLIff., together with the additions and corrections in Liebeskind, 'Leopold Mozart: Ausgewählte Werke', 361–2. ◆ See n. 28 above.

42. Gerber (*Altes Lexikon* i.977, *Neues Lexikon* iii.474) also mentions *Semiramis*, *La finta giardiniera* and *Bastien und Bastienne*, but these are plainly by Wolfgang. It is no longer possible to know what Gerber meant with his reference to the intermezzo, *La cantatrice ed il poeta*. ◆ In a letter of 3 December 1778, Wolfgang wrote to his father about his work on the first act of a melodrama based on Otto von Gemmingen's *Semiramis*, which he intended to bring home to Salzburg and finish there (*Briefe*, ii.516). No trace of the work survives and possibly it was never started. The source of Gerber's information – and the attribution of the work to Leopold – remains unknown.

43. *Briefe*, i.532–3 (letter to Giovanni Battista Martini, 4 September 1776).

endemic to all church music at this time, a state of affairs that may also help to explain Wolfgang's own attitude to his father's sacred music.[44] Even so, these works give us a valuable insight into the type of church music then favoured in Salzburg and into the tradition in which the young Wolfgang grew up.[45] Many of them, moreover, allow us to draw useful comparisons with Wolfgang's own settings of the same words.

The situation is totally different, however, in the case of most of Leopold's instrumental music.[46] Here he was not inhibited by any outward constraints and was able to allow his talent free rein, with his three surviving keyboard sonatas in particular affording conclusive evidence of his originality.[47]

Comparisons with Carl Philipp Emanuel Bach are not especially helpful, of course, not least because they ignore Mozart's development sections which, lacking Bach's thematic resourcefulness, sound positively old-fashioned in comparison, limited as they are to transpositions and the sort of sequencing of which Leopold was particularly fond.[48] By contrast, Leopold's tendency to strike a more serious, grandiloquent note recalls the north German Bach, as does his attempt to impose a sense of conceptual unity on his opening allegros: only the third sonata has a contrastive second subject, whereas in the case of the other two, the second subject is derived from the first.[49] Another progressive feature is the choice of three-movement form, although here, too, we find a remarkable vacillation between principles associated, on the one hand, with north Germany and, on the other, with Austria and, more especially, with Vienna. The final movements of the first two sonatas are cast in traditional sonata form, while the third follows the example set by Georg Christoph Wagenseil in his keyboard divertimentos, with a menuetto and trio in a minor tonality, the latter thematically integrated into the movement as a whole – a procedure frequently found elsewhere in Mozart's music.[50] Progressive, too, is the performing technique demanded by these sonatas: with their playful brilliance, crossing of hands, octaves in the bass and effective changes of register, they are on a technical par with Domenico Scarlatti's sonatas, while at the same time revealing the more recent influence of Carl Philipp Emanuel Bach. Under this heading comes the art of ornamentation in its broadest sense, including sighing motifs, turns, broken chords[51] and the like, all mannerisms that have encouraged writers to see in Leopold Mozart a member of the

---

44. *Briefe*, iii.262 (letter of 29 March 1783): 'What we should like to have as well, my dearest father, would be some of your finest church music, for we like to amuse ourselves with all manner of masters, ancient and modern.' On receipt of his father's letter declining to send any such items, Mozart wrote again, this time regretting that 'true church music is to be found only in attics and in a worm-eaten condition' (*Briefe*, iii.264, letter of 12 April 1783).

45. ◆ Abert's opinion reflects the predispositions of his time, favouring instrumental music over church music and a stricter separation between sacred and secular music. However, considering the importance of counterpoint for Mozart's musical development, it is important to note the extent to which Leopold and other Salzburg composers of the time may have represented a *stile antico* model for Wolfgang; see Manfred Schuler, 'Zum Stile antico in Leopold Mozarts kirchenmusikalischem Schaffen'. By the same token, instrumental and secular vocal styles, also frequently found in Leopold's church music, were similarly important for Wolfgang's early musical education; see, for example, Eisen, 'Mozart e l'Italia: Il ruolo di Salisburgo'. Further, see below.

46. This was recognized, with his customary perspicacity, by Chrysander, 'Mitridate, italienische Oper von Mozart', 104ff.

47. Max Seiffert, *Leopold Mozart: Ausgewählte Werke*, 3ff., dates these sonatas to 1762/3; see Faißt, 'Beiträge zur Geschichte der Claviersonate', 82, and Friedlaender, 'Leopold Mozarts Klaviersonaten', 38–40. ◆ Based on dates of publication discovered since Abert's time, the first sonata was composed not later than 1759, the second not later than 1760, and the third by 1762–3.

48. Only in the opening movement of the F major sonata do we find at least an incipient attempt at thematic development. Reminiscent of the opening bars of a number of symphonies by the Viennese composer Georg Matthias Monn, the three beats of the main theme ♩♩♩𝄽 recur in augmentation in the bass in the development section.

49. ◆ Further, see Manfred Hermann Schmid, 'Zu den Klaviersonaten von Leopold Mozart'.

50. The finale of the F major sonata likewise breathes the spirit of an Austrian suite, with the second subject appearing here as a minuet. The kinship between father and son emerges with particular clarity here.

51. Significantly, Leopold makes as little use of the then highly fashionable Alberti bass as Carl Philipp Emanuel.

'Mannheim school'.[52] But, quite apart from the fact that Bach, too, can be shown to have used these mannerisms, it is entirely possible that inspiration came from a totally different quarter – just as it did in the case of Johann Stamitz himself, namely, from Italian *opera buffa*. There is no doubt that individual reminiscences in these sonatas are proof positive of Leopold's familiarity with the Mannheim style.[53] But these reminiscences are of a superficial nature, and Leopold remained unaffected by its principal characteristic, which was its modern, revolutionary spirit. Although Leopold cannot be numbered among the most modern composers of his day in spite of all the progressive features in these sonatas, these works are none the less distinguished by their individual, characteristic tone that faithfully reflects his tenacity, a tenacity that refused to do things by halves and often bordered on sheer obstinacy. They are the most inspired of all Leopold's known instrumental works; and they are by no means lacking in impassioned, sombre traits, revealing their qualities with particular force in their sections in minor tonalities, each of which appears as though from nowhere. It was from Wagenseil and, hence, from Scarlatti that Leopold learnt this ability to allow sudden and surprising shadows to pass over a scene of relaxed enjoyment. But whereas, in the case of Wagenseil and Scarlatti, the scene generally brightens again very quickly, Leopold is fond of lingering over such pessimistic moods, a feature found not only in his own music but also in that of his great son. There is a sense of well-calculated contrast between the solemn and powerful opening allegros and the final movements, which are filled with the spirit of Austria, while the slow middle movements are, inevitably, their least individual sections.

This picture is nicely complemented by the six divertimentos for two violins and cello that appear to have been written as a group in 1760.[54] They, too, are in three movements. In spirit, they are true divertimentos, in other words, works written to entertain in the best sense of the word, formally clear-cut, popular in tone, filled with a lively grace and spiced with an idiosyncratic, even sometimes surly, sense of humour.[55] Here, too, there is no lack of sombreness, not to say, pessimism. With the exception of the first piece, all are in minor tonalities (although even here the final menuetto includes a pensive trio in G minor), while their outer movements, too, contain sudden flashes of passion when least expected.[56] But there are also examples of a dreamy inwardness that looks forward to Wolfgang's own music:[57]

52. See Riemann, *Sinfonien der Pfalzbayerischen Schule II*, XVI–XVII.
53. Compare, for example, the opening of the third sonata with that of Johann Stamitz's G major symphony: Riemann, *Sinfonien der Pfalzbayerischen Schule II*, XXXIX.
54. Nos 1, 2 and 4 are edited in Max Seiffert, *Leopold Mozart: Ausgewählte Werke*, 37ff. ◆ It is likely that these works were composed before 1760: at least one of them (the G major) survives in a copy from the Benedictine monastery at Lambach that can be dated to the 1750s. The earliest unequivocal dated reference to the divertimentos is their appearance in a thematic catalogue of the Leipzig publisher Breitkopf in 1762.
55. ◆ For a recent discussion of 'divertimento', and in particular the term's use in the mid-eighteenth century to denote all soloistic ensemble music, not just the entertaining, popular or even frivolous, see Webster, 'Towards a History of Viennese Chamber Music in the Early Classical Period'.
56. For a particularly revealing example, see the first ten bars of no. 1, in which the strains of an Austrian march are repeatedly and brusquely interrupted. The opening movement of no. 6 contains equally austere passages.
57. Second subject of the opening movement of no. 3.

The outer movements are structured along similar lines to those of the sonatas, although everything is more succinct here.[58] Thanks to the delightful interplay between the violins, whose frequent crossing of parts recalls a much older style, these are immensely gratifying works to perform and deserve to be revived. Leopold's other chamber works fail to achieve the same high level as these divertimentos. In their level of invention and thematic writing, his *Sonate a tre* are manifestly juvenilia, while in his actual trios with obbligato keyboard, the trio writing is still underdeveloped, although, formally speaking, they are far more progressive, with certain details clearly revealing their composer's distinctive hallmarks.[59]

Largely occasional in character, Leopold's concertos and symphonies are relatively uneven in quality. But it is in his programmatic works that this occasional character is most apparent. And it is these last-named works – *The Musical Sleigh-Ride*, the *Sinfonia burlesca*, the *Sinfonia pastorale*, the *Divertimento militare* and *The Peasants' Wedding* – to which Leopold owes his continuing reputation. We now know that he was by no means alone in composing such pieces, but that, thanks to the French educational ideal, programme music was particularly popular at this time with audiences and artists alike. It is unnecessary to go back as far as older composers such as Froberger, Kerll, Kuhnau and Georg Muffat: later composers, too, contributed to the genre – and not just with their endless hunts and tempests. Suffice it to mention Telemann's *Don Quichotte*, Dittersdorf's six Symphonies after Ovid's *Metamorphoses* and Mysliveček's symphonies on the various months of the year, the last-named a counterpart to Leopold Mozart's works for mechanical organ. Above all, however, the young Joseph Haydn began his career as a writer of symphonies with programme works of this kind. There is no denying their affinities with the sort of dramatic pantomimes then being written in southern Germany and Austria by composers such as Deller, Rudolph, Starzer, Toeschi and Gluck (in *Don Juan*)[60] and, indeed, the movement headings of Leopold's *Sinfonia burlesca* ('Signore Pantalone' and 'Harlequino') place the piece firmly within this tradition. Elsewhere, the main difference between Leopold and the other composers mentioned is that, as with the songs of his compatriot, Christian Friedrich Daniel Schubart, he avoids the more elevated themes drawn from Nature, legend and history, preferring instead to explore the everyday world of the common people. Rollicking peasants, carefree huntsmen, soldiers accompanied by the strains of fife and drum, coachmen, a lively sleigh party – these were the things that were dear to his heart. Nor did he attempt to draw a veil over their more coarsely comical aspects, as in 'The Girl Trembling with Cold' on the sleigh-ride and 'The Regrets of the Bridal Bouquet' in *The Peasants' Wedding*. The realism of the subject matter is reflected in the means deployed, with *The Peasants' Wedding* demanding not only a three-part rustic string orchestra with winds, but also musette and hurdy-gurdy, while the *Sinfonia pastorale* includes a part for a cow-horn, *The Musical Sleighride* five tuned bells. In the *Divertimento militare*, the string orchestra is contrasted with a second group of instruments made up of horns, trumpets, and pipe and tabor. Nor was Leopold afraid of introducing extra-musical effects, such as the sound of a whip in *The Musical Sleighride* and pistol shots in *The Peasants' Wedding*. It is this last-named

58. An exception is the opening movement of no. 6, the development section of which gives the impression after just a few bars that it is on the point of moving on to the recapitulation, only for it to settle into a lengthy section in C sharp minor before finally debouching into the actual recapitulation.

59. The opening movement of the A major trio is reproduced by Max Seiffert, *Leopold Mozart: Ausgewählte Werke*, 57ff., and comprises two contrastive themes, a relatively lengthy development section characterized by its persistent use of a minor tonality and a full-length recapitulation into which the composer slips unnoticed with his sequential second subject. This regressive feature, too, is reminiscent of Wolfgang's own style.

60. Abert, 'J. G. Noverre und sein Einfluß auf die dramatische Ballettkomposition', 29ff., and Abert, *Ausgewählte Ballette Stuttgarter Meister aus der 2. Hälfte des 18. Jahrhunderts*; see also Niedecken, *Jean-Georges Noverre*.

piece that reveals the greatest realism: teeming with cheeky popular melodies that are often like street songs in character, as well as with drone basses and cheers, it does not shy away from parodies of actual peasant music: here, too, Leopold anticipates Wolfgang's 'village musicians'. There is no denying the divertimento-like character of all these pieces, with only the huntsmen's and soldiers' music suggesting loftier artistic ambitions. The remaining symphonies likewise afford ample proof of the way in which the boundaries between the two genres were still only vaguely defined at this time. The number of their movements varies from two to six, while marches and dance movements of various kinds reveal their affinities with the serenade. It is clear that in writing his symphonies Leopold entertained no higher ambitions than he did with his divertimentos. In his final symphony in D major,[62] he admittedly comes strikingly close to the Italian style in his attempt to meet the expectations of his audiences in Rome, but his approach is broader and more cautious, while offering remarkable pre-echoes of Wolfgang.[63] Yet not even here does he transcend the bounds of Gesellschaftsmusik. Both in theory and practice, then, Leopold clearly favoured a 'popular' approach,[64] with the result that he is at his most immediately appealing in those of his movements that are dancelike in character, but even elsewhere he introduces popular themes in his attempt to ensure that audiences got their money's worth.[65] The most backward-looking feature of these symphonies is their development sections,[66] although even here we find, at least in some of them, an attempt to create a marked contrast between their first and second subjects,[67] while the recapitulation is generally complete (in the Viennese manner) and sometimes even extended.

61. The *Sinfonia pastorale* includes a similar feature in the false G sharp in the violins in the final movement:

This is an effect that Wolfgang recalled in his *Galimathias musicum* and in the introduction to scene 2 of *Bastien und Bastienne*. In the context of Beethoven's 'Pastoral' symphony, it is also worth drawing attention to the pastoral motif that recurs repeatedly in this symphony:

62. See above; also Max Seiffert, *Leopold Mozart: Ausgewählte Werke*, XXXIX–XL. ◆ It is not clear that the symphony referred to by Abert, K81, is by Leopold or even by Wolfgang, to whom it is also attributed. The work, published in NMA IV/11/2, survives in an early, non-authentic manuscript in the Gesellschaft der Musikfreunde, Vienna (shelfmark XIII 20026), attributed to Wolfgang. But it was also advertised by Breitkopf in 1775 as a symphony 'da L. Mozart'. Further, see Allroggen, 'Zur Frage der Echtheit der Sinfonie KV Anh. 216 = 74g'; and Eisen, 'Problems of Authenticity among Mozart's Early Symphonies: The Examples of K. Anh. 220 (16a) and 76 (42a)' and 'The Present State of Research on Leopold Mozart's Symphonies'. Leopold's last, approximately dateable symphony is G16, the so-called 'New Lambach', probably composed *c*1767. At one time, it, too, was claimed for Wolfgang. For an account of the debate concerning the symphony's authorship, see Zaslaw, *Mozart's Symphonies*, 127–38. Further, see Allroggen, 'Mozarts Lambacher Sinfonie: Gedanken zur musikalischen Stilkritik'.
63. Cf. the opening movement's cantabile second subject and various melodic features in the andante.
64. Under this heading come titles such as 'De gustibus non est disputandum' and 'Non è bello quello che è bello ma quello che piace'. ◆ These subtitles are each attached to two symphonies attributed to Leopold Mozart: for 'De gustibus non est disputandum', see the symphonies D1 and D2 (in Eisen, *Leopold Mozart: Ausgewählte Werke I: Sinfonien*; Seiffert 3/3 and 3/4); for 'Non è bello quello che è bello ma quello che piace', see the symphonies D3 and D13 (Seiffert 3/5 and 3/15).
65. Cf. the second subject of the final movement of the D major symphony ('Non è bello' etc.), a subject that recalls a well-known folksong and that also forms the basis of the menuetto from the *sinfonia da camera* in F major (Seiffert 3/18; Eisen, *Leopold Mozart: Ausgewählte Werke I: Sinfonien*, F1).
66. The development section of the opening movement of the D major symphony (Seiffert 3/15; Eisen, *Leopold Mozart: Ausgewählte Werke I: Sinfonien*, D13) consists of only eight bars.
67. The D major symphony (Seiffert 3/15; Eisen, *Leopold Mozart: Ausgewählte Werke I: Sinfonien*, D13) even uses a change of time-signature and tempo to point up this contrast.

On the whole, Leopold Mozart's symphonies are examples of an art in transition, but an art in which older stylistic elements are allowed more scope than newer ones. There is no doubt that the 'Mannheim school' left its mark here, too, but again it is only individual reminiscences and mannerisms[68] of a superficial nature that we find here. Of Stamitz's true spirit there is no more trace than in the sonatas. Their transitional nature is also clear from the forces for which they are scored: with their figured bass, the *sinfonie da camera* still indicate a harpsichord accompaniment and the use of soloists,[69] whereas the others are intended for more than one instrument to a part, but with no harpsichord.

In short, the main merit of these symphonies lies in their folklike features of a rustic or intimate nature. But here, too, we find the same tendency for the carefree picture suddenly to cloud over, albeit less frequently than in the divertimentos.[70] And here, above all, we find a wholly unmistakable affinity between father and son, inasmuch as this 'demonic' feature is as typical of the latter as it is of the former.[71] And Wolfgang's cantabile style is likewise already found in many of Leopold's allegro themes,[72] albeit far less pronounced and with Leopold's lightweight, salonesque tone invested from the outset with an animation and gallantry absent from his writing, which remains firmly wedded to solid bourgeois values. But there are clearly identifiable links between the two composers on points of detail, too. Leopold, for example, is fond of using syncopation to convey agitation,[73] while his melodic writing is notable for its tendency to include figurations spiced with chromatic *note cambiate* or with suspensions and the like, so that it assumes a remarkably tormented aspect.[74] The harmonic writing, finally, is distinguished not only by its characteristic use, already mentioned, of minor tonalities,[75] but also by repeated chords of a sixth to express silent reverie or thrusting urgency.[76] These are all features that recur in Wolfgang's works, infinitely intensified and spiritualized. Nor are such features limited to his early works, in which respect they differ from the direct reminiscences of Leopold's style that are confined to his early period. It is hard to see how writers could have denied the most obvious influence – that of his father – on a composer as receptive to foreign influences as was the young Mozart. Of course, Leopold was no genius, but an independent artist whose achievements, judged by the standards of their time, merit our respect. At all events, it would be a miracle if this influence were the only one not to have left its mark on Wolfgang's music.[77]

But all doubts as to Leopold's seriousness of purpose as an artist are dispelled by his *Versuch einer gründlichen Violinschule* of 1756.[78] Although this was not the first such work of its kind (in

---

68. The most striking reminiscence is the one between the opening of the D major symphony and the beginning of Stamitz's orchestral trio in E major. ◆ Concerning Mannheim symphonies generally, see Eugene K. Wolf, *The Symphonies of Johann Stamitz*.
69. The D major symphony (Seiffert 3/7; Eisen, *Leopold Mozart: Ausgewählte Werke I: Sinfonien*, D5) is even an offshoot of the old concerto grosso, except that here the concertante element is not carried through to its strict conclusion.
70. Cf. the C minor theme in the first movement of the F major symphony (Seiffert 3/18; Eisen, *Leopold Mozart: Ausgewählte Werke I: Sinfonien*, F1) and Leopold's fondness for minor-key trios in his menuettos: in the trio of the F major symphony, the main theme is simply transposed from F major to D minor.
71. Heuß, 'Das dämonische Element in Mozarts Werken'.
72. Cf. the opening bars of the third and sixth divertimentos.
73. Cf. Seiffert, *Leopold Mozart: Ausgewählte Werke*, 17 and 23.
74. Under this heading comes the variation of a musical idea when repeated; see Max Seiffert, *Leopold Mozart: Ausgewählte Werke*, 10.
75. Once he has reached a minor tonality, Leopold often clings to it tenaciously; see Max Seiffert, *Leopold Mozart: Ausgewählte Werke*, 12–13.
76. Max Seiffert, *Leopold Mozart: Ausgewählte Werke*, 7 and 23.
77. ◆ Further, see Eisen, 'The Present State of Research on Leopold Mozart's Symphonies'.
78. A long series of letters that Leopold wrote to his friend and publisher in Augsburg, Johann Jakob Lotter, while the volume was at press in 1755 and 1756, attests to the conscientious care that he lavished on matters of correct terminology and orthography and on ensuring that the volume was correctly printed. ◆ See p. 4 n. 24 above.

spite of his own and Jahn's assumption that it was[79]), it far surpassed its predecessors in its influence and longevity. Its success was well founded, for what Leopold strove to achieve here and what he offered his readers was far more than mere technical instruction. Once again, the inspiration came from north Germany, with not only its title but its whole spirit suggesting the influence of the *Versuch einer Anweisung die Flöte traversière zu spielen* by Frederick the Great's fellow flautist and composer in residence, Johann Joachim Quantz.[80] Mozart follows Quantz in his basic principle that technique should be a means to an end, that end being a performance that is both tasteful and soulful. As a result, Mozart's tutor became for violin playing what that other Quantz-inspired treatise – Carl Philipp Emanuel Bach's *Versuch über die wahre Art das Clavier zu spielen* of 1753 – was for keyboard players, a performance manual, and since eighteenth-century composers expected their interpreters to make their own contribution to the performance of their works, thereby placing completely different demands on them from those placed on today's performers, Mozart's treatise shares with the other two mentioned the distinction of being our principal source of information on the way that music was performed at this time.

In his basic belief that the performer's task lay in correctly realizing the music's underlying 'affections', Leopold reveals himself a willing pupil of Carl Philipp Emanuel Bach, their points of agreement even extending to individual sentences: 'In practising, every care must be taken to find and to render the effect which the composer wished to have brought out. . . . In a word, all must be so played that the player himself be moved thereby' (218).[81] For the violinist, this aim is achieved through the bow-stroke, which Leopold describes as 'the medium by the reasonable use of which we are able to rouse in the hearers the aforesaid emotions. I mean that this can be done if the composer makes a reasonable choice; if he selects melodies to match every emotion, and knows how to indicate the appropriate style of performance' (114). Elsewhere he notes that 'there exist, unfortunately, enough . . . would-be composers, who . . . put a patch by the side of the hole' (124), instead of placing it over the hole itself. Again: 'Many a would-be composer is thrilled with delight and plumes himself anew when he hears his musical Galimathias played by good performers who . . . know how to make the whole miserable scribble bearable to the ears of the listeners by means of good performance' (215). As for Bach,[82] so for Mozart, the ultimate aim was a simple, natural cantabile line, with the instrumentalist imitating the art of singing as far as possible (51). 'And who is not aware that singing is at all times the aim of every instrumentalist; because one must always approximate to nature as nearly as possible' (101–2). Here Leopold is particularly critical of those virtuosos who 'tremble when they have to sustain a long note or play

79. See the preface to Leopold's treatise and Jahn, *W. A. Mozart*, i.12. Other eighteenth-century treatises are Montéclair's *Méthode pour apprendre à jouer du violon* (1711–12) and Geminiani's *The Art of Playing on the Violin*, published in 1751. ◆ Further, see Corrette, *L'école d'Orphée, méthode pour apprendre facilement à jouer du violon dans le goût françois et italien* (1738), and Bremner, *The Compleat Tutor for the Violin* (c1750), both of which also appeared before Leopold's *Gründliche Violinschule*.

80. Three editions appeared in the eighteenth century, in 1752, 1780 and 1789. A new edition was supervised by Arnold Schering in 1906. ◆ Additionally, a Dutch translation was published at Amsterdam in 1754; for a modern English translation, see Reilly, *On Playing the Flute*.

81. [The references to Leopold's *Violinschule* here are taken from the translation by Editha Knocker; see the bibliography.] Cf. Bach III § 2: 'What comprises good performance? The ability through singing or playing to make the ear conscious of the true content and affect of a composition.' §13: 'A musician cannot move others unless he too is moved. He must of necessity feel all of the affects that he hopes to arouse in his audience.' [English translations from C. P. E. Bach's *Versuch* are from the edition by William Mitchell.]

82. Bach advises the keyboard player to listen to proficient singers as often as possible; see II §12: 'Above all, lose no opportunity to hear artistic singing. In doing so, the keyboard player will learn to think in terms of song. Indeed, it is a good practice to sing instrumental melodies in order to reach an understanding of their correct performance.'

only a few notes singingly, without inserting their usual preposterous and laughable frippery' (51). They are condemned all the more roundly in that they generally lack the necessary understanding to know where to ornament the music without introducing errors into the piece (170). Among other failings committed by virtuosos are the use of a tremolando on every note, making it sound as though the performers had the palsy (203); the 'perpetual intermingling of the so-called flageolet' (101); and the tendency on the part of would-be virtuosos either to press ahead or to drag the tempo, a tendency that destroys all sense of time:

> Many, who have no idea of taste, never retain the evenness of tempo in the accompanying of a concerto part, but endeavour always to follow the solo-part. These are accompanists for dilettanti and not for masters. When one is confronted by many an Italian songstress or other such would-be virtuosi, who are not able to execute in correct time even that which they learn by heart, even entire half-bars have indeed to be allowed to drop out in order to rescue them from public disgrace. But when a true virtuoso who is worthy of the title is to be accompanied, then one must not allow oneself to be beguiled by the postponing or anticipating of the notes, which he knows how to shape so adroitly and touchingly, into hesitating or hurrying, but must continue to play throughout in the same manner; else the effect which the performer desired to build up would be demolished by the accompaniment. A clever accompanist must therefore be able to judge a concert performer. To a sound performer he certainly must not yield, for he would then spoil his tempo rubato.[83] What this 'stolen tempo' is, is more easily shown than described. But on the other hand, if the accompanist has to deal with a *soi-disant* virtuoso, then he may often, in an adagio cantabile, have to hold out many a quaver the length of half a bar, until perchance the latter recovers from his paroxysms; and nothing goes according to time, for he plays after the style of a recitative (223–4).

Leopold's principal aim was to produce 'an honest and virile tone' (58). 'For what can be more insipid than the playing of one who has not confidence to attack the violin boldly, but scarce touches the strings with the bow (which is often held by two fingers only); and makes so artificial and whispering a sound right up against the bridge of the violin that only the hissing of a note here and there is heard and the listener knows not what is meant thereby; for everything is merely like unto a dream' (96).

The greatest emphasis is laid, of course, on a strictly methodical approach to teaching: 'Here lies really the greatest error committed by masters as well as pupils. The first often have not the patience to wait, or they allow themselves to be led astray by the disciple, who deems himself to have done all if he can but scratch out a few minuets. Indeed, many a time the parents or other guardians wish to hear that sort of untimely little dance at an early stage and then think miracles have happened, and how well the money for the lessons has been spent' (61; *cf.* 112–13). Above all, Leopold is anxious not to make things too easy for the pupil, for whom no effort must be too great. At the beginning of a set of bowing exercises, for example, he writes: 'The more distasteful they are the more am I pleased, for that is what I intended to make them' (88). In other words, he was keen to prevent the student from getting used to playing from memory.

---

83. Incomprehensibly, this important piece of evidence for the use of rubato in early music is denied by many of today's purists; see Kamieński, 'Zum "Tempo rubato"'. ◆ Further concerning rubato, see Hudson, 'Stolen Time: The History of Tempo Rubato'; and Rosenblum, 'The Uses of *Rubato* in Music, Eighteenth to Twentieth Centuries'.

Modelled on north German lines, this violin tutor became an exercise in musical thinking,[84] and while Leopold concedes that natural aptitude may sometimes 'make up for a lack of learning' and that 'a man with the greatest talent has, alas, never had the opportunity of studying science' (101–2), this does not mean that the rule itself is invalid or that the greatest demands are no longer placed on pupil and teacher alike.

These are also the principles according to which Leopold brought up his own son. We have every reason to be grateful to him for this, too, for it was to this upbringing that Wolfgang owed his lofty and pure conception of art.

The treatise was particularly well received in north Germany. Friedrich Wilhelm Marpurg, to whose judgement Leopold had appealed in his preface, duly praised the volume when announcing its publication: here was revealed 'the sound and skilled virtuoso, the rational and methodical teacher, the learned musician'; and he compared its author to Geminiani,[85] hoping in the process to induce Leopold to contribute to his periodical. Zelter wrote: 'His *Violinschule* is a work which will be worth using as long as the violin remains a violin; moreover it is well written.'[86] But even a south German writer and composer such as Schubart thought that 'By his *Violinschule*, written in very good German and with deep insight, he has earned great merit. The examples are excellently chosen and his "fingering" is by no means pedantic. Although he inclines towards the school of Tartini, he allows his pupil more freedom in his handling of the bow than the latter.'[87]

The volume is certainly well written and, as such, is a faithful reflection of the man himself, with its lucid intellect and dry, sometimes caustic wit.[88]

A man of such character and intellectual aspirations could not, of course, feel at ease in a position of subservience or even among equals, and the longer he remained in Salzburg, the more he suffered from the town's narrow-mindedness. The court looked askance at independent natures in its service, while his colleagues repelled him either by their intellectual poverty or their dissolute lifestyle. The townspeople eventually came to value him as a good music teacher, but otherwise felt no particular warmth or personal affection for him. He himself did not feel to be part of them. 'The Salzburgers', wrote Schubart, 'are much given to low comedy. Their folksongs are so amusing and burlesque that it is impossible to hear them without shaking with laughter. The spirit of Hanswurst[89] shines through each and every one of them, and their melodies are generally admirable and exceedingly beautiful.'[90] Though it found favour with Schubart, it was precisely this spirit of buffoonery that was so profoundly antipathetic to an individual as phlegmatic as Leopold

---

84. There are even references to the links between performance, on the one hand, and rhetoric and poetry on the other, links familiar to an earlier period from the very title of Johann Sebastian Bach's *Inventions*: 'Here we see also that a good violinist must have this knowledge. For a sound composer this is indispensable, for otherwise he is the "fifth wheel on the wagon"' (101).

85. Marpurg, *Historisch-kritische Beyträge*, iii.160–3. [*Dokumente*, 12, *Documentary Biography*, 10].

86. Riemer, *Briefwechsel zwischen Goethe und Zelter*, iii.125.

87. Schubart, *Ideen zu einer Ästhetik der Tonkunst*, 157. ◆ Mozart's *Violinschule* appeared in a second edition in 1769/70 and a third, posthumous edition in 1787; it was reprinted, updated and taken as a model for violin instruction until well into the nineteenth century.

88. ◆ Further concerning the *Violinschule*, see Petrobelli, 'Leopold Mozart e la "Ausbildung" di Wolfgang' and Angelucci, 'La forma della comunicazione nel sistema didattico della "Violinschule" di Leopold Mozart'. For an overview of the history of Leopold Mozart scholarship generally, see Mančal and Plath, *Leopold Mozart: Auf dem Weg zu einem Verständnis*; and for a discussion of Leopold as a rational, self-aware thinker, see Mančal, 'Der Mensch als Schöpfer seiner Wirklichkeit'.

89. When playing the part of Hanswurst, Josef Anton Stranitzky wore Salzburg peasant costume, with a slapstick and broad-rimmed pointed hat (see Flögel, *Geschichte des Grotesk-Komischen*, ii.315ff.), and spoke Salzburg dialect (see Sonnenfels, *Gesammelte Schriften*, vi.372). His typical qualities are coarseness, stupidity and clumsiness. According to a Salzburg proverb: 'He who comes to Salzburg will become stupid in his first year, a cretin in his second and a Salzburger in his third.' ◆ Further, see Asper, *Hanswurst*.

90. Schubart, *Ideen zu einer Ästhetik der Tonkunst*, 158.

Mozart. And there were other things, too, for which father and son reproached the people of Salzburg, although many of the things to which they objected – especially their fondness for gossip and slow-wittedness – were typical of the provinces in general, rather than of Salzburg in particular. In short, Leopold was exposed to all the less attractive sides of provincial life, with the inevitable result that some of it rubbed off on him.

Leopold married Anna Maria Pertl[91] on 21 November 1747. The daughter of the Pflegekommissar at Sankt Gilgen in the Salzkammergut, she had been born at Hüttenstein near Sankt Gilgen on 25 December 1720. 'Today is our wedding anniversary,' Leopold wrote to her on 21 November 1772. 'It was 25 years ago, I think, that we had the excellent idea of getting married, although we had had this idea many years previously. All good things take time!'[92] They were regarded at the time as the handsomest couple in Salzburg, and surviving portraits certainly confirm this assessment.

The dictum – based on Goethe's example – that great men essentially owe their talents and training to their mothers does not apply to Mozart: Maria Anna Pertl in no way rose above the average for her sex. The only marked feature of her character that she passed on to her son was her propensity for coarse humour, a propensity common to Salzburgers as a whole. In general, she adopted a far more relaxed and carefree view of life than her husband and took ample advantage of the female prerogative to prefer the personal to the universal. As a result, she was always well informed about personal and family relationships, not only in Salzburg but elsewhere. She was astute and had excellent powers of observation. Above all, she understood her husband's phlegmatic and painfully conscientious nature and did all she could to spare him the numerous troubles and worries that stemmed from it, a task that cannot have been easy, given his perpetual mistrust, and there is no doubt that she will have drawn a veil over many an unpleasant incident not merely out of prudence, but also from fear. Yet she was utterly devoted to him and willingly submitted to the strict regime to which he inevitably and unquestioningly subjected her. But she had little authority over their children, a problem that became particularly apparent during her visit to Paris when, against her better judgement, she was able neither to curb her son's high spirits nor to resist his charm. That she had an ear for music emerges from her assessment of Ignaz Holzbauer's *Günther von Schwarzburg* in Mannheim,[93] as well as from her delight in performances of operas and plays in general; no less striking is the interest that she took in the political events and wars of the day.

In short, husband and wife complemented each other to felicitous effect, and it was on this complementarity that the true and sincere love rested that bound them not only to each other but also to their children. It was a pure and healthy spirit that reigned in the Mozart household and ruled their moral lives, and Anna Maria must take much of the credit for this. Above all, she was a true mother to her children, who invariably sought refuge with her when their father's strict hand weighed unduly heavily upon them. Wolfgang loved and admired her to distraction, and what he lost in her is clear from the moving letter that he wrote to Joseph Bullinger following her death in Paris.

Of the seven children born to this marriage, only two survived infancy: a daughter, Maria Anna ('Nannerl'), who was born on 30 July 1751 (see Appendix I), and a son, Wolfgang, who was born

---

91. Also written Bertl.
92. *Briefe*, i.462 (letter of 21 November 1772). ◆ For Anna Maria Mozart's baptismal record, as well as the Mozarts' marriage registry, see *Dokumente*, 4, *Documentary Biography*, 4–5.
93. *Briefe*, ii.108–9 (letter of 8 November 1777).

on 27 January 1756.[94] His birth almost cost his mother her life, and it was only after some time that she recovered from a debility that gave rise to considerable concern.

Nannerl showed such a decisive aptitude for music that her father soon began to teach her the piano.[95] These lessons left a deep impression on her younger brother, who was around three years old at this time: he, too, sat at the keyboard and could amuse himself for long periods picking out thirds, which he would then proceed to play, while at the time expressing his delight at what he had discovered. He could also recall prominent passages from the pieces that he heard. Even before he had reached his fourth birthday, his father had already begun to teach him a number of minuets and other pieces on the keyboard, and it was not long before he was able to play them with total accuracy and in perfect time. Soon he was moved to write music of his own and was still only four when he wrote his first short pieces, which he played to his father and which the latter duly notated [K1].[96]

Most of the anecdotes that relate to Mozart's early years and tell of his awakening genius come from a letter written soon after the composer's death and addressed to the latter's sister. Its author, Johann Andreas Schachtner (1731–95), had attended the Jesuit school in Ingolstadt and acquired a thorough grounding in literature in addition to training as a musician.[97] His translation from the Latin of Franz Neumayer's sacred drama *The Conversion of Saint Augustine* was praised by no less an authority than Johann Christoph Gottsched, who claimed that one could almost say he wrote good German and, indeed, that he also wrote good German poetry.[98] We shall later encounter Schachtner as one of Mozart's German librettists. He became court trumpeter in Salzburg in 1754 and was a regular visitor to the Mozarts' home. The following affectionate letter bears eloquent witness to his devotion to the family:

Most gracious lady!

Your kind letter was forwarded to me from Salzburg to the Hammerau, where I was visiting my son, an official at the local prefecture; from my desire always to be of service to everyone, and particularly to the Mozart family, you can judge how painful it was for me to be prevented from complying with your request at once. But to the point, and to your first question: what your late brother's favourite pastimes were in his childhood, NB apart from his preoccupation with music.

This question can have no answer; for no sooner had he begun to busy himself with music than his interest in every other occupation was as dead,[99] and even children's games had to have

---

94. His full name appears in the parish register as Joannes Chrysostomus Wolfgangus Theophilus (Leopold wrote 'Gottlieb', the godfather was called Theophilus). In early letters he also added his sponsor's name Sigismundus. In many of his early works and in the Paris engraving of 1764 he is called J. G. Wolfgang, but later he regularly called himself Wolfgang Amadè. ◆ Baptismal records for Leopold and Anna Maria's seven children are reproduced in *Dokumente*, 5–11, *Documentary Biography*, 5–9.

95. ◆ Concerning the possibility that Nannerl also had composition lessons from Leopold, see Plath, 'Leopold Mozart und Nannerl: Lehrer und Schülerin. Fragmentarische Bemerkungen zu zwei Fragmenten'.

96. See Schlichtegroll, 'Joannes Chrysostomus Wolfgang Gottlieb Mozart', and Nottebohm, *Mozartiana*, 96.

97. See Hammerle, *Mozart und einige Zeitgenossen*, 46.

98. Gottsched, *Das Neueste aus der anmuthigen Gelehrsamkeit*, xi (1761), 60ff. ◆ Abert's text continues: 'It may have been this that persuaded Gottsched to write a preface for a volume of Schachtner's verse and to note here that both with these poems and with a later sacred drama, *Humanity's Wanderings*, he had shown that "neither then nor now should he have written poetry".' The apparent contradiction of this sentence with the previous one remains unresolved. *Die menschliche Wanderschaft* is the first part of the sacred singspiel *Der laue Christ*, performed about early March 1771; cast in three parts, the second, *Der büßende Sünder*, was composed by Michael Haydn and the third, *Der sterbende Fromme*, by the court musician Joseph Krinner. See de Catanzaro and Rainer, *Anton Cajetan Adlgasser (1729–1777): A Thematic Catalogue of His Works*, 188.

99. On 16 February 1778 Leopold wrote to his son: 'As a child and a boy you were serious rather than childish and when you sat at the keyboard or were otherwise intent on music, no one dared joke with you. Why, even the expression on your face was

a musical accompaniment if they were to interest him; if we, he and I, were carrying his play-things from one room to another, the one of us who went empty-handed always had to sing or fiddle a march the while. But before he had begun music, he was so ready for any prank spiced with a little humour that he could quite forget food, drink and all things else. He became so fond of me – for, as you know, we saw much of each other – that he would often ask me ten times in one day if I loved him, and when I sometimes said no, just for fun, bright tears welled up in his eyes, so tender and kind was his good heart.

2nd question, how he behaved as a child when the great admired his musical talent and art.

In truth, he showed no pride or awe whatsoever:[100] for he could in no wise better have satisfied these than by playing to people who had little or no understanding of music; but he did not want to play unless his audience were great lovers of music, or he had to be deluded into thinking them such.

3rd question. What branch of learning did he like best? Answer: in this respect he was easily led, it was of small matter to him what he was given to learn; he simply wanted to learn, and he left the choice to his dearly beloved father[101] as to what field he was to work in – it seemed as if he understood that nowhere in the world could he have found a tutor, much less a guide, to equal his unforgettable father.

Whatever he was given to learn occupied him so completely that he put all else, even music, on one side; e.g. when he was doing sums, the table, chair, walls, even the floor were covered with chalked figures.[102]

4th question. What characteristics, maxims, timetable, peculiarities and inclinations towards good and evil did he have?

Answer. He was of a fiery disposition, no object held his attention by more than a thread. I think that if he had not had the advantageously good education which he enjoyed, he might have become the most wicked villain, so susceptible was he to every attraction, the goodness or badness of which he was not yet able to examine.

Some particular points worth marvelling at, concerning the fourth and fifth year of his age, the veracity of which I could swear to.

I once went with your father to the house, after Thursday service; we found the 4-year-old Wolfgängerl busy with his pen:

Papa: What are you writing?

Wolfg.: A keyboard concerto, the first part is nearly finished.

Papa: Show me.

so serious that, when they saw your precocious gifts and the expression on your face, which was always so serious and thoughtful, many perceptive people from several different countries doubted whether you would live to reach a ripe old age'; *Briefe*, ii.283.

100. 'As a boy you were so bashful that you used to burst into tears when people praised you too much'; *Briefe*, ii.284 (letter of 16 February 1778).

101. 'He was so obedient, even in trivial matters, that he never received any physical punishment. He loved his father with exceptional tenderness.' In a letter of 12 February 1778, Leopold recalls how, each evening before going to bed, Wolfgang would stand on a chair and sing a duet with him, the tune of which was said to be Wolfgang's own, while the nonsensical words sounded vaguely Italian, 'Oragnia figa tafa'. Wolfgang would then kiss his father on the nose and promise that when he grew old, he would put him in a glass case and honour him. Only then would he go to bed; see *Briefe*, ii.273 and Berchtold zu Sonnenburg, 'Noch einige Anekdoten aus Mozarts Kinderjahren', 300. The tune of this 'Oragnia figa tafa' is reproduced by Leitzmann, *Mozarts Persönlichkeit*, 11, and turns out, on closer examination, to be a childlike variant of the old Dutch song *Wilhelmus van Nassouwe*, here combined with other folklike features. First printed in 1607, the tune is still sung in Germany to a whole series of songs, including Fouqué's *Frisch auf zum fröhlichen Jagen* and Eichendorff's *Nach Süden nun sich lenken*; see Friedlaender, *Das deutsche Lied im 18. Jahrhundert*, ii.11. We shall encounter this tune again in Mozart's music. One of the boy's favourite sayings was 'Papa comes right after God'.

102. This sentence was written on a separate sheet of paper.

Wolfg. It's not ready yet.

Papa: Show me, it's sure to be interesting.

His father took it from him and showed me a smudge of notes, most of which were written over ink-blots which he had rubbed out. (NB: Little Wolfgangerl, knowing no better, plunged the pen to the bottom of the inkwell each time, and so, when he put it to the paper, a drop of ink was bound to fall off each time, but he was equal to it, and drawing the palm of his hand across it, wiped it away, and wrote on.) At first we laughed at what seemed such a galimatias, but his father then began to examine the most important matter, the notes and music; he stared long at the sheet, and then tears, tears of joy and wonder, fell from his eyes. Look, Herr Schachtner, he said, see how correctly and properly it is all written, only it can't be used, for it is so very difficult that no one could play it. Wolfgangerl said: That's why it's a concerto, you must practise it till you get it right, look, that's how it goes. He played, and managed to get just enough out of it for us to see what he intended. At that time he had the notion that to play a concerto and work a miracle must be one and the same.

One further thing:

Madame, you will remember that I had a very good violin which Wolfgangerl used to call the 'butter violin' because of its soft and full tone. One day shortly after your return from Vienna [in early 1763] he played on it and could not find words to praise it highly enough; one or two days later I came to see him again and found him amusing himself with his own violin. He at once said: How's your butter violin? and went on fiddling away at his fantasia. Finally he thought a moment and said to me: 'Herr Schachtner, your violin is tuned half a quarter-tone lower than mine, if you left it tuned as it was last time I played it. I laughed at this, but Papa, knowing the child's extraordinary sense of pitch and memory, asked me to fetch my violin and see if he was right. I did so, and he was right.[103]

Shortly before this, in the days after your return from Vienna, Wolfgang having a little violin that he got as a present in Vienna,[104] our former very good violinist, the late Herr Wenzl,[105] came to us. He was a beginner in composition and brought 6 trios with him, which he had written while your father was away and asked your father for an opinion on them. We played the trios, Papa playing the bass with his viola, Wenzl the first violin, and I was to play the 2nd violin. Wolfgang had asked to be allowed to play the 2nd violin, but Papa refused him this foolish request, because he had not yet had the least instruction in the violin, and Papa thought that he could not possibly play anything. Wolfgang said: You don't need to have studied in order to play 2nd violin, and when Papa insisted that he should go away and not bother us any more, Wolfgang began to weep bitterly and stamped off with his little violin. I asked them to let him play with me; Papa eventually said: Play with Herr Schachtner, but so softly that we can't hear you, or you will have to go; and so it was. Wolfgang played with me; I soon noticed with astonishment that I was quite superfluous, I quietly put my violin down, and looked at your Papa; tears of wonder and comfort ran down his cheeks at this scene, and so he played all 6 trios. When he had finished, Wolfgang was emboldened by our applause to maintain that he could play the 1st violin too. For a joke we made the experiment, and we almost died for laughter

---

103.   As Abraham has shown, this passage says little about the sensitivity of Wolfgang's hearing, as such a subtle sense of absolute pitch is hardly exceptional; 'Das absolute Tonbewußtsein', 53.

104.   But see *Briefe*, i.51 (letter of 16 October 1762), according to which Wolfgang already had a violin in his possession on his visit to Vienna in 1762.

105.   ◆ Wenzel Hebelt (c1736–69), court violinist from 1757 to 1769.

when he played this part too, although with nothing but wrong and irregular positions, but in such a way that he never actually broke down.

In conclusion. About the delicacy and fineness of his ear.

Until he was almost 9 he was terribly afraid of the trumpet when it was played alone, without other music. Merely to hold a trumpet in front of him was like aiming a loaded pistol at his heart. Papa wanted to cure him of this childish fear and once told me to blow my trumpet at him despite his reluctance, but my God! I should not have been persuaded to do it; Wolfgangerl scarcely heard the blaring sound, when he grew pale and began to collapse, and if I had continued, he would surely have had a fit.

This is the best I can do with the questions you ask; forgive my dreadful scrawl, I am so worn out that I can do no better. With all esteem and due respect I am

	Madame
Salzburg	Your most humble servant
the 24th April	Andre Schachtner
1792	Trumpeter to the Prince-Bishop[106]

Another witness of the boy's astonishing early development was Placidus Scharl, a Benedictine who taught at the Salzburg Gymnasium between 1759 and 1770 and who took a lively interest in music and poetry. According to his biographer,[107] who was relying in turn on his diary jottings, Scharl had frequent occasion to admire Wolfgang's musical talents and to lavish little presents on him for the hours of enjoyment that he gave him. 'He was still unable to span an octave with his short little fingers,' Scharl recalled in his memoirs, 'but he leapt over it with extraordinary speed and amazing accuracy.' It was sufficient to give him the first theme that came to mind and ask him to improvise a fugue or an invention, and he would develop it through every tonality 'with remarkable variations and constantly changing progressions'. Extemporization was his greatest passion. Mozart even promised to write something specially for Scharl.

Mozart's first public appearance also dates from this time, although not as a keyboard player. On 1 and 3 September 1761 a play by one of the prefects at the Salzburg Gymnasium, Marian Wimmer, *Sigismundus Hungariae rex*, with incidental music by Johann Ernst Eberlin, was performed in the University Theatre to mark the archbishop's name-day. Of the 146 persons listed in the cast, one of the 'Salii' [dancers] was played by 'Wolfgangus Mozhart'. Also listed here is one Dr Antonius de Mölk, a name that we shall encounter again.[108]

Even more important for Mozart's artistic beginnings, however, are two sources of a musical nature that have survived only by chance. In keeping with an earlier custom whereby music teachers either wrote their own exercises or at least compiled them themselves, Leopold Mozart prepared a book of exercises for each of his children. These are not in fact studies, but are what were called *Handstücke* for the keyboard, pieces that pupils were encouraged to play as a way of recovering from the exertions of purely technical exercises. The exercise book for Nannerl was donated to the Salzburg Mozarteum in 1864 by the Grand Duchess Elena Pavlovna, unfortunately

106. The original of this letter [present location unknown] was owned by Aloys Fuchs, who communicated its contents to Jahn (*W. A. Mozart*, i.29ff.) Both Schlichtegroll and Nissen drew on it [*Dokumente*, 395–7, *Documentary Biography*, 451–3, translation amended].

107. Sattler, *Ein Mönchsleben aus der 2. Hälfte des 18. Jahrhunderts: Nach dem Tagebuche des P. Placidus Scharl O.S.B. von Andechs*, 157 [*Dokumente*, 440–1, *Documentary Biography*, 512, translation amended].

108. See *AmZ*, new series, ix (1874), 138, and Hammerle, *Mozart und einige Zeitgenossen*, 1–2 [*Dokumente*, 15–16, *Documentary Biography*, 13–14].

in a badly mutilated and incomplete state.[109] It contains minuets and similar short pieces, although later sections also include longer works such as a set of twelve variations written by Leopold and musical visitors. Each of these variations is the work of a different composer, some of whom – Agrell, Fischer and Wagenseil – are mentioned by name.[110] Wolfgang, too, used this volume in his lessons,[111] and his own first attempts at composition were transcribed here by his father, in two cases with headings: 'Di Wolfgango Mozart 11 May 1762' [K4] and '16 July 1762' [K6].

The second notebook, which was intended for Wolfgang's own use, has survived complete. It was generously made available to the present writer a number of years ago by its then owner, the well-known Strasbourg gynaecologist Wilhelm Freund. Attention had previously been drawn to its existence by Rudolph Genée, albeit only briefly and relatively superficially.[112]

On the verso of the first folio is the note: 'To my dear son Wolfgang Amadée on his sixth name-day from his father Leopold Mozart. Salzburg, 31 October 1762.' At the date in question, father and son were not in fact in Salzburg, but in Vienna, and Wolfgang had just recovered from a serious attack of scarlet fever (see below). None the less, I am not convinced by the claim advanced by Wyzewa and Saint-Foix that the book was started in Vienna.[113] Leopold's influence on Wolfgang's earliest compositions and the unlikelihood that he would have taken such a detailed task upon himself while travelling both speak decisively against this assumption. It is far more likely that he started it in the immediate wake of Nannerl's notebook, and there is little doubt that Wolfgang was introduced to at least some of its contents in the course of his lessons with his father.

The volume contains a total of 135 pieces divided into twenty-five 'suites'. Both the choice and the order of the keys are modelled on the order of Johann Sebastian Bach's inventions and sinfonias. All that survives of the older suite, of course, is the uniform tonality and (at least in the majority of cases) the dancelike character of the individual movements, but their number and sequence are entirely arbitrary,[114] with only the introductory pieces proving the exception to this rule: in the vast majority of cases, these are settings of sacred texts taken from what Leopold calls a 'New Anthology of Sacred Songs'. This has since been shown to be an anthology published in Wernigerode in 1752 by Count Heinrich Ernst zu Stolberg-Wernigerode. With a single

109. *Recensionen*, x (1864), 512. The oblong folio volume is titled 'Pour le Clavecin. Ce livre appartient à Marie Anne Mozart 1759'. It was complete when Fröhlich examined it (*AmZ*, xix [1817], 96), but now a number of folios are unfortunately missing. Excerpts are reproduced by Nissen and the volume as a whole is reprinted in AMA XXII, nos 1–4, 12. ◆ Some of the missing leaves have now been identified; they include K1a–f, 2, 3, 5 and 5b; see Tyson, 'A Reconstruction of Nannerl Mozart's Music Book (Notenbuch)'. For a complete modern edition of the notebook, see NMA IX/27/1.
110. ◆ Concerning the identification of the authors in the 'Nannerl Notebook', see NMA IX/27/1, XIII–XVIII.
111. By the eighth menuetto, Leopold has added a note: '*Wolfgangerl* learnt the preceding menuetto in his 4th year.' Similar remarks are entered later, too, such as: 'This menuetto and trio were learnt by Wolfgangerl on 26 January 1761, a day before his 5th birthday, at half past 9 at night in half an hour.' ◆ In fact, Leopold's notation after the eighth menuetto reads: '*Wolfgangerl* learnt the preceding 8 menuettos in his 4th year.' See NMA IX/27/1, 3–8 and 9–11.
112. Genée, 'Mozarts musikalische Erziehung und ein bisher unbekannt gebliebenes Notenbuch von Leopold Mozart'. The original is now owned by Dr L. König of Kiel. A complete copy is in the possession of the present writer. A detailed study of the volume may be found in Abert, 'Leopold Mozarts Notenbuch von 1762'. ◆ The following discussion needs to be read with caution: it has since been determined that the 1762 notebook probably dates from c1750 and is a falsification; see Plath, 'Leopold Mozarts Notenbuch für Wolfgang (1762) – eine Fälschung?'. While this in itself does not detract from the notebook's importance as evidence for how music was studied at mid-century (as several similar examples from Salzburg show; see Eder, *Salzburger Klaviermusik des 18. Jahrhunderts*), it undermines Abert's subsequent arguments concerning some important influences on the young Wolfgang as well as what he describes as 'Leopold's methodical mind and comprehensive knowledge of the literature'; it does not, as a result, show 'Wolfgang's development in an entirely new light'. Abert's argument is further complicated by his attribution to Mozart of the song *Geheime Liebe* K150, which is in fact by Leopold. Further, see Biener, 'Zu Leopold Mozarts Liedern'.
113. Wyzewa and Saint-Foix, *Wolfgang Amédée Mozart*, i.25.
114. Only the 23rd suite reflects the older German sequence of allemande – courante – sarabande – menuetto – gigue, with, in this case, a final polonaise. Indeed, no fewer than twelve of the suites end with a polonaise.

exception,[115] the texts selected by Mozart also come from this volume, whereas for their melodies he used the well-known north German collection by Johann Friedrich Gräfe (1711–87), *Sammlung verschiedener und auserlesener Oden,* or, to be more precise, its first three parts, which were published in Halle in 1737, 1739 and 1741.[116] In fact, Stolberg's texts are, for the most part, sacred parodies of secular poems from Gräfe's collection. For Leopold, the only two composers worth including were Gräfe himself and Conrad Friedrich Hurlebusch (1696–1765); the former is represented by eight pieces, the latter by eleven. In his use of parody – the underlaying of new words beneath originals which, in the case of Gräfe, were already instrumentally coloured – Leopold reveals himself as the true disciple of a tendency that had come to dominate the German song as a result of French influence as transmitted by the Leipzig-based poet and anthologist Sperontes and his *Singende Muse an der Pleiße* of 1736–45. Here, too, we have the source of its aesthetic aberrations and its harnessing together of serious sacred texts and comic secular tunes, often to the detriment of the language's natural stresses.

Only in nineteen cases does Mozart give the names of the composers whose works he has used. Of these, the most frequently named is Georg Philipp Telemann (1681–1767), who generally appears under his pen-name of 'Melante' as the composer of eleven minuets[117] and one fantasia.[118] Carl Philipp Emanuel Bach is represented by two minuets and a march,[119] the Halle-based composer Gottfried Kirchhoff by a four-movement 'sonatina',[120] Balthasar Schmid from Nuremberg by two minuets plus alternative versions,[121] the great Johann Adolf Hasse by a polonaise[122] and an otherwise unidentified 'Mons. Bosse' by a murky.[123] But it would be wrong to assume that Mozart himself was the composer of the other pieces, as their style is completely different from his own. For some, I have been able to identify their sources. The polonaise no. 3/5 and menuetto no. 7/7, for example, both come from Sperontes' *Singende Muse,*[124] while the polonaise no. 21/5 is by Johann Nikolaus Tischer (1707–74).[125] The menuetto no. 24/6 is a keyboard arrangement of the menuetto from the sinfonia to Hasse's opera *Cleofide* of 1731. And the 'Huntsmen's Song' no. 4/9, finally, turns out to be an ornamented version of an old German pseudo-folksong contained in Johann Friedrich Dreyßer's *Dantzbüchlein* of 1720, much as the burlesque no. 20/4 is based on a old German folksong. Other reminiscences of well-known pieces, often only a few bars in length, include the beginning of no. 4/3, which recalls Johann Sebastian Bach's 'Lied von der Tabakspfeife'; but such echoes are probably only the result of chance.

In general, the keyboard pieces can be divided into three groups, the first of which comprises movements inspired by the German folksongs and folk dances that were particularly popular in manuscript collections in south Germany during the eighteenth century.[126] A few include headings: here one thinks of the aforementioned 'Huntsmen's Song', the 'Swabian Dance' (no. 9/5), the 'Smith's Courante' (2/1), the 'Trumpet Piece' (4/11) and the 'Horn Piece' (12/5). The highlight of this group is the 'March du Bredau' (4/2). The second group is made up of examples of the most

115. No. 18/1, which is by Christoph Julius Mevius.
116. See Friedlaender, *Das deutsche Lied,* XLI and Kretzschmar, *Geschichte des neuen deutschen Liedes,* i.204ff.
117. All are taken from *Sept fois sept et un menuet* (Hamburg, 1728).
118. *Fantaisies pour le clavecin. 3 douzaines* (after 1737), part iii, no. 1.
119. All are missing from Wotquenne, *Thematisches Verzeichnis der Werke von Carl Philipp Emanuel Bach.*
120. No. 1/2–6.
121. No. 17/2–3.
122. No. 14/6.
123. No. 15/3.
124. Buhle, *Sperontes Singende Muse an der Pleiße,* 40 and 233.
125. *Sechs leichte und dabey angenehme Clavier-Parthien Jungen Anfängern zur Übung,* part iii, 13.
126. Kretzschmar, *Geschichte des neuen deutschen Liedes,* 166ff.

fashionable music of the time, a period when the latest works by Domenico Scarlatti were beginning to leave their mark on German keyboard composers. It includes fantasias, free allegros, 'arias' (at least to the extent that these are not pure dances) and the 'Kirchhoff' sonatina.[127] Cast in binary and ternary form,[128] they all place supreme demands on their performer's technique and interpretative skills. The third and largest group, finally, is given over to dance movements of French inspiration. Here Sperontes's modernizing influence no doubt accounts for the fact that older dances such as allemandes and courantes have largely been displaced by the newer and more fashionable dances such as the minuet and polonaise that he himself favoured.[129] Wolfgang could study all the different types of binary and ternary form by reference to these dances: here we find minuets with two sections of equal length alongside others in which the second section is often substantially longer than the first, while monothematic movements coexist beside others in which the second section is based on material that is either wholly or partially new. Nor is there any lack of minuets with an 'alternativo' (also described as a 'trio'). And these pieces are also extraordinarily varied in character, with some still revealing the strait-laced dignity of the older dance forms, while others revel in their grace and capriciousness, with a third group even suggesting an element of sombreness and pain. Only the popular rusticity and wit of a composer such as Haydn is missing, and there is no doubt that in this respect the notebook anticipates the later type of Mozartian minuet. No less pronounced is the distinction between songlike minuets and others purely concerned with playful figures.

Rondo form, finally, is represented by a number of pieces.

With few exceptions, the harmonic writing and use of modulation are both extremely simple. There is no trace, for example, of the sudden interplay between major and minor that had rapidly become popular in south Germany in the wake of Scarlatti. Only rarely do we find a figured bass, although the young composer naturally had to add the harmonies where they were missing. To acquaint him with this important aspect of the older way of performing music was no doubt one of the main aims of the volume. On the other hand, Leopold took very seriously the task of writing out the ornaments, and a comparison between his song movements and Gräfe's originals provides valuable information on the way such pieces were ornamented at this time.

Technically, the pieces are relatively undemanding – as one might expect, given the boy's abilities – and are limited to the chordal and scalic figures usual around 1750. The most advanced pieces reveal the influence of Domenico Scarlatti with their crossing of hands, octaves in the bass and changes of register. Leopold has also added the fingering in one piece (no. 3/5).

In short, this volume is an important source of domestic music around the middle of the eighteenth century. Its systematic arrangement sets it clearly apart from the other manuscripts of the period, which are invariably an arbitrary collection of pieces, and once again affords evidence of Leopold's methodical mind and comprehensive knowledge of the literature. It also shows Wolfgang's development in an entirely new light, for it is clear from this volume that this development was far more influenced by the north German school than has been suspected hitherto. In part this influence was decidedly beneficial, inasmuch as it taught him the importance of clarity of thought and of clear, incisive formal structures and showed him what can be achieved with simple, characterful writing and taut rhythms, even without complex harmonic writing.

---

127.   ◆ Abert's reference here is to a well-known violin sonata by the German composer Gottfried Kirchhoff (1685–1746).
128.   There is something study-like about the D major fantasia no. 6/3, with its broken chords. Harmonically, this is one of the most delightful of all these pieces. With its mixture of passage-work and recitative-like adagio episodes, the A minor fantasia no. 22/2 recalls the fantasias of Gottlieb Muffat. A number of the arias (nos 6/2 and 14/4) may be transcriptions of violin pieces.
129.   There are 48 minuets and 16 polonaises.

More problematical was the fact that he received his earliest impressions of the art song from the school of Sperontes, a school whose one-sided predilection for dance song and parody had already been superseded in north Germany by composers such as Telemann. Indeed, it took Mozart some considerable time to rid himself completely of this dubious inheritance. Even as late as 1772, his song *Geheime Liebe* K150[130] continues to recall Sperontes not only in its choice of words by Günther but also in its verbal reminiscence of the song *Liebste Freiheit, fahre hin*,[131] just as his first original song, *An die Freude* K53, belongs in this context by dint of its strict four-bar structure. With its pronounced love of the dance song, *Bastien und Bastienne*, too, continues to breathe this same spirit. Its final sign of life is found in the two French songs, K307 and 308, that Mozart wrote in Mannheim in 1778.

It was, however, on Mozart's earliest compositions that this volume left its most palpable traces, and it is significant that, with a single exception, they are all minuets.[132] Although all of them date from 1761 and 1762 (in other words, before the date of the volume's dedication[133]), their form and content make it clear that Wolfgang was already familiar with the style that is found here. Of the minuets, three (K2, 4, 5) have the same bass – presumably provided by Leopold with the aim of encouraging Wolfgang to use it as the starting point for minuets of differing character. The first is a starched, old-fashioned affair reminiscent of Telemann, while the second flows along and the third adopts a more capricious tone. Form, harmonic[134] and melodic writing are exactly the same as in the exercise book of 1762. The first two belong together to the extent that they are developed from a single motif that is also found in the trio of the first of them.[135] They also have the advantage over the other three in that they reveal a songlike tone and childlike manner that finds expression in the first of them not least in its tendency to revel in folklike thirds.[136] The allegro K3 likewise adopts a hearty south German folklike tone. It is also Mozart's first fully developed ternary song, with a repeat of its first section.

Common to all these works is their extraordinarily clear and lucid form. Even so, we must beware of drawing overhasty conclusions about the boy's progress at this time, for behind them all stands his father, ordering and improving and refusing to countenance any shortcomings or other inelegancies. We shall shortly find a remarkable example of the sort of music that Mozart produced when his father's guiding hand was lacking.

---

130. ◆ See n. 112 above.
131. Buhle, *Singende Muse an der Pleiße*, 23.
132. AMA XXII, nos. 1–4, 12; XVIII, no. 1 (2nd menuetto). See n. 133.
133. Wyzewa and Saint-Foix, *Wolfgang Amédée Mozart*, i.28, argue that the G major menuetto comes at the end of this series, even though it has hitherto been regarded as Mozart's first composition and even though Nannerl claims he wrote it when he was five. But their reasons for doing so are not compelling. First, it would have to be shown that Nannerl followed her father's example in making Wolfgang a year younger than he really was, and, secondly, there were already plenty of precedents for combining a menuetto and trio at this date. We could equally well regard our piece as coeval with the first F major menuetto on 'internal' grounds – in this case, on the grounds of motivic unity. ◆ Abert's assertions here are difficult to justify. Of Mozart's eight earliest works, all of them composed between early 1761 and July 1762, only four are menuettos (K1d, 2, 4 and 5), three are allegros (K1b, 1c and 3) and one is an andante (1a).
134. Only the regular modulation of the second part of each piece to the minor of the subdominant points not to the exercise book but to south German keyboard music inspired by Italian composers.
135. Here we can obviously see Leopold's influence at work; see above.
136. Cf. Schachtner's letter quoted above.

2

Travels of the child prodigy

It was in 1762 that Mozart's years of travel began and with longer or shorter interruptions they were to last a whole decade. As with so much else, it was his father who both instigated this period in his childhood and who planned its subsequent course. His aim was to introduce his son to the world of music, initially as a virtuoso, and, in that way, to smooth his path as a composer. This was to remain the custom from the sixteenth century right up to the end of the eighteenth century and to the time of the young Beethoven: anyone wanting to succeed as a composer first had to make a name for himself as a practising musician.

Of the first visit to Munich that Leopold and his two children undertook in January 1762 we know only that it lasted three weeks and that Wolfgang and Nannerl performed for the elector.[1] Far more important was the visit to Vienna on which the three of them set out on 18 September 1762.[2] They had to break their journey in Passau and spend five days there after the local bishop demanded to hear the child prodigy, whose performance he rewarded with a ducat. From there they moved on to Linz. Their travelling companion was Ernst Johann, Count Herberstein, who at that date was a canon at Passau Cathedral and who, as Bishop of Passau in 1785, recalled in conversation with Leopold how the young Wolfgang had reacted when he saw an old beggar fall into the water. In Linz they gave a concert under the patronage of the regional governor, Count Leopold Schlick. The young Count Karl Hieronymus Pálffy, who was paying a courtesy call on Countess Schlick, heard so much about the young prodigy that he was persuaded to stop the mail coach outside the town hall and attend the concert with the countess. He listened in utter astonishment. The Mozarts continued their journey from Linz by boat, putting in to shore at Ybbs, where their travelling companions, two Minorites and a Benedictine, said Mass, while the six-year-old Wolfgang amused himself on the organ, performing so well that the Franciscans who were lunching with some guests left the table and hurried across to the choir, where they were almost struck dumb with amazement at what they found there. On their arrival in Vienna,[3] Wolfgang was also instrumental in helping the family through customs: according to Leopold, he made friends with the customs officer, showing him his keyboard and playing him a minuet on his little violin,

---

1. ◆ The only evidence for this trip is a reminiscence of Nannerl Mozart from 1792. See *Dokumente*, 399, *Documentary Biography*, 455.
2. It is possible to reconstruct this journey in some detail thanks to Leopold's letters to the merchant Lorenz Hagenauer (*Briefe*, i.49–69). Leopold had been living in Hagenauer's house when Wolfgang was born, and was still living there. Hagenauer proved a loyal and dependable friend, ever willing to help him in word and deed and even advancing considerable sums of money. It is understandable, therefore, that Leopold kept him informed about the financial success of the journey. See also Nannerl's reports in Nottebohm, *Mozartiana*, 96–7. ◆ Johann Lorenz Hagenauer (1712–92) owned houses at 7 and 9 Getreidegasse. Leopold had rented the third floor of the house at number 9 in late 1747.
3. ◆ Although Abert does not give exact dates for the trip, they can be reconstructed on the basis of the family letters and other documents. The Mozarts were in Passau from 20 to 26 September and Linz from 26 September to 4 October, where their concert was on 1 October. They arrived at Ybbs on 5 October and at Vienna the next day.

with the result that they were simply waved through. Throughout the whole journey he was cheerful and quick-witted, confiding in everyone, especially the officers, as though he had known them all his life, endearing himself through his childlike, open character and astonishing his listeners by his gifts as a virtuoso.

Leopold had good reasons for attaching particular importance to Vienna, for in no other city in the German-speaking world had music prospered as it had in Vienna since the days of Maximilian I. Ultimately, it was the imperial house itself that was to thank for this state of affairs: from Ferdinand III to Charles VI it had produced an unbroken line of eminent composers who had taken the lead in the struggle to assert the rights of the art of *nuove musiche* that had crossed the Alps from Italy. Charles VI is known to have accompanied and conducted operas and other works from the harpsichord,[4] but it was under Ferdinand II that music really began to play an important role in the education of members of the imperial family. Charles VI's daughter, Maria Theresia, for example, was trained as a singer and was still only seven when, in 1725, she appeared in an opera by Fux to mark the churching of her mother, the Empress Elisabeth, later telling Faustina Hasse, 'in pleasantry', that she 'thought herself the first, meaning the oldest, *virtuosa* in Europe'.[5] In 1739 she performed a duet with Senesino in Florence, singing so well that the famous castrato is said to have wept tears of joy, and even in later years she retained an excellent singing voice.[6] Her husband, Franz I, was also musical, and music was certainly not neglected in the upbringing of the imperial family. In 1750 three of the empress's daughters performed the cantata *La rispettosa tenerezza* by Reutter and Metastasio to mark their mother's name-day,[7] and in 1762 four archduchesses sang and acted in the opera *Il trionfo di Clelia*, reappearing two years later in a performance of Metastasio's and Hasse's *Egeria* to mark Joseph's coronation as king of Rome, when Burney declared that they 'sung and acted very well, for princesses'.[8] In 1765 they performed Gluck's *Il Parnasso confuso* to celebrate Joseph II's second marriage.[9] Joseph was himself a good singer who also played the cello, but he was known above all for his skill as an accompanist, a skill that presupposed a thorough knowledge of the art.

The court's example soon encouraged the aristocracy to follow suit, and it was not long before virtually every aristocratic household had its own private orchestra of greater or lesser dimensions, a state of affairs that constitutes one of the most glorious chapters in the history of the Austrian nobility, for without it the whole of Viennese 'classicism' would be unthinkable. No one familiar with the lives of Gluck, Haydn and Beethoven can fail to appreciate the part played by the aristocracy, in the best sense of the term, in the work of these composers. Mozart, too, was to enjoy such beneficence on his very first visit to Vienna.

Counts Herberstein, Schlick and Pálffy had already alerted the Viennese court and aristocracy to the approaching prodigies, and it was not long after their arrival that Leopold was invited to present them at Schönbrunn on 13 October. Their appearance proved the first of a series of bril-

4. See Köchel, *Die Pflege der Musik am österreichischen Hofe vom Schlusse des XV. bis zur Mitte des XVIII. Jahrhunderts*; see also Adler, 'Ferdinand III., Leopold I., Joseph I. und Karl VI. als Förderer der Musik', 252–74, and Adler's two-volume edition of the *Kaiserwerke* published in Vienna in 1892/3. ◆ More recently, see Wollenberg, 'Vienna under Joseph I and Charles VI'.
5. Burney, *The Present State of Music in Germany*, i.252. The duchesses also appeared in an opera to mark the empress's birthday in 1735. Metastasio, who wrote the libretto and rehearsed the singers, could not find words enough to praise the princesses' skill and charm; see Metastasio, *Opere postume*, i.175ff. ◆ Fux's 'opera' was the *festa teatrale Giunone placata*, first given on 19 November 1725.
6. Burney, *The Present State of Music in Germany*, i.251.
7. Metastasio, *Opere postume*, i.401.
8. Burney, *The Present State of Music in Germany*, i.253. ◆ Hasse's *Il trionfo di Clelia*, on a text by Metastasio, was given at the Burgtheater on 27 April 1762.
9. Anton Schmid, *Christoph Willibald Ritter von Gluck*, 115.

liant successes in which their audiences' love of sensation played at least as important a part as any purely musical interest. On their very first visit, the children were required to perform from three until six, with the emperor treating Wolfgang as a 'little wizard', requesting him not only to play the keyboard in the normal way but also to perform all manner of tricks such as playing with one finger alone and with a cloth covering the keyboard. But even at this early date, the young Mozart already insisted on his rights as an artist. Not satisfied with his distinguished listeners alone, he demanded to see the famous keyboard player Georg Christoph Wagenseil (1715–77), who taught Maria Theresia and her children:[10] 'Let him come, he understands these things.' And when Wagenseil arrived, the boy announced: 'I'm playing one of your concertos, you'll have to turn the pages for me.' But an even more touching impression was made by his genuinely childlike, uninhibited behaviour. He took to the Archduchess Marie Antoinette (later queen of France) when she picked him up after he had fallen on the polished floor. 'That's good of you,' he said, 'I intend to marry you.' And he explained the reason why: 'Out of gratitude, she was kind to me, while her sister troubled herself about nothing.'[11] But he also jumped up into the empress's lap and kissed her, and when the emperor played the violin with Wagenseil, the boy made known his feelings from the antechamber in the form of lively exclamations: 'Ouch!' 'That was wrong!' and 'Bravo!'[12] Of course, the court not only paid the usual fee, but also showered the children with gifts of every kind. Nannerl received a court dress belonging to an archduchess, Wolfgang a lilac-coloured costume with wide double gold braiding that had been intended for the Archduke Maximilian and in which he was subsequently painted. And the children were also fêted by the local aristocracy. Prince Hildburghausen, the imperial vice-chancellor Count Colloredo and Bishop Esterházy invited them to their homes, and they were invariably fetched by carriage and handsomely rewarded. Needless to say, all the women soon fell in love with Wolfgang. But these days of wine and roses were brought to a sudden end by a violent attack of scarlet fever that confined the boy to his bed for two weeks at the end of October. Although his admirers generally sympathized with his plight, there is no doubt that they were also afraid of catching the illness themselves, a fear that persisted even after he had recovered. An invitation to Preßburg from a family of Hungarian aristocrats was, therefore, all the more welcome to Leopold, and although his leave of absence from Salzburg was already over, he duly set off on 11 December, in spite of the poor weather and travelling conditions that were so bad that he and his family were often in fear of their lives. On their return to Vienna, they attended a dinner given in honour of Field-Marshal Daun by Countess Kinsky, returning to Salzburg in early January 1763.[13]

Mozart's principal instrument at this time was still the harpsichord, which he already played with astonishing skill,[14] but he also turned increasingly to the violin and organ.[15] His knowledge

10. Metastasio, *Opere postume*, ii.31; Burney, *The Present State of Music in Germany*, i.326; and Marpurg, *Kritische Briefe über die Tonkunst*, ii.141–2.

11. Nissen, *Biographie W. A. Mozarts*, 9.

12. Rochlitz, 'Verbürgte Anekdoten aus Wolfgang Gottlieb Mozarts Leben', *AmZ*, i (1798/9), 856. ◆ Here Abert mixes fact – Mozart's jumping into the empress's lap – with unsubstantiated anecdote. Rochlitz's account of Mozart's reaction to the emperor's violin playing is probably fiction. And while it cannot be established that Mozart wanted Wagenseil to turn the pages for him, it is at least possible, considering that Wolfgang was by this time already acquainted with Wagenseil's keyboard concertos (see Eisen, 'Mozart and the Four-Hand Sonata K. 19d', 94–5). The original source of this anecdote is Niemetschek, *Leben des k. k. Kapellmeisters Wolfgang Gottlieb Mozart*, 6–7.

13. ◆ Mozart took to bed from 22 to 31 October, the family was in Pressburg from 11 to 24 December, and they left Vienna on 5 January 1763.

14. In the presence of musically literate audiences, Mozart would play concertos and other examples of high art, whereas others were fobbed off with dances and other trifles in the style of the pieces found in his exercise book.

15. *Briefe*, i.50–51 (letter of 16 October 1762).

of theory, by contrast, was still developing, and here there was much that his father still had to teach him. We already know the influences to which he was exposed by Leopold, but to these a new one was added in Vienna: that of Viennese keyboard music under its principal exponent, Georg Wagenseil.

The boy's education had reached the point where, after a brief rest in Salzburg, Leopold set out again with both children for a second, longer journey.[16] Their chief destination on this occasion was Paris, and the intention was to call at all the German courts on the way, for it was here that music was principally cultivated in Germany at this time. Indeed, it was with some pride that Leopold stressed that in the course of their journey they had dealings only with members of the aristocracy and persons of rank and that they were obliged to travel in style both on account of their health and 'for the sake of the court's reputation'. Because it was summer, they generally had to visit their princely admirers at their summer residences.

The journey began on an inauspicious note on 9 June:[17] at Wasserburg a wheel on their carriage broke and they were stranded in the town for twenty-four hours until it was repaired. 'The latest news', wrote Leopold on the 11th, 'is that in order to amuse ourselves we went to the organ and I explained to Wolferl the use of the pedal. He immediately tried it out, then shoved away the stool and preludized standing, operating the pedal as though he had been practising for months. Everyone was amazed, another example of God's grace that many people receive only after much effort.' Throughout the journey, Wolfgang gave frequent proof of his skills on the organ and, as his father repeatedly reports, was generally admired for his organ playing even more than for his performances on the harpsichord.

They arrived in Munich on 12 June 1763 and immediately went to Nymphenburg. Here they were introduced to the elector by Prince Karl August von Zweibrücken, who knew them from Vienna. They were well received and on several occasions played for both the elector himself and for Duke Clemens, with Wolfgang performing on both the harpsichord and the violin; according to his father, he played a concerto for the elector and 'extemporized between the cadenzas'. Here they met two visitors from Saxony, Baron Hopfgarten and Baron von Bose, whom they saw on several subsequent occasions and with whom they became good friends, a friendship renewed and consolidated during the Mozarts' visit to Paris. They arrived in Augsburg on 22 June and put up at the 'Three Moors',[18] remaining in the town for two weeks and giving three concerts on 28 and 30 June and 4 July,[19] when their audience was made up almost exclusively of Lutherans. In its edition of 19 July 1763, the Salzburg *Europaeische Zeitung* included a report dated 'Augsburg, 9 July':

The day before yesterday, in the morning, the deputy Kapellmeister to the court of Saltzburg, Herr Leopold Mozart, left here for Stuttgart with his two remarkable children, to continue his

---

16.   ◆ In the interim, Leopold had on 28 February 1763 been promoted to deputy Kapellmeister in Salzburg; that same evening Wolfgang and Nannerl played at court. See *Dokumente*, 21–2, *Documentary Biography*, 20.

17.   The main sources for this journey are Leopold's letters to Hagenauer, a number of family anecdotes in Nissen and information gleaned from Nannerl (Nottebohm, *Mozartiana*, 97–8). Also of interest are the brief notes that Leopold jotted down in the course of the journey containing the addresses of the people with whom they came into contact, a note of the hostelries where they stayed and remarks on the sights that they visited. It is clear from these notes how observant Leopold was. They were published by Schurig, *Leopold Mozarts Reise-Aufzeichnungen 1763–1771*. ◆ Leopold's travel notes are also given in *Briefe*, i.69, 73–4, 78, 81–2, 84–5, 96–101, 110–12, 117–20, 142–5, 192–8, 200, 214–17 and 227.

18.   See Buff, 'Mozarts Augsburger Vorfahren', 30.

19.   According to Nannerl, '2 academies'; see Nottebohm, *Mozartiana*, 97 [*Dokumente*, 399, *Documentary Biography*, 455].

journey to France and England by way of the greatest courts in Germany. He afforded the inhabitants of his native city the pleasure of hearing the effect of the quite extraordinary gifts that God has bestowed on these two dear little children in such abundant measure, gifts of which the Herr Kapellmeister has, as a true father, taken such indefatigable care that he is now able to present the musical world with a girl of 11 and, what is incredible, a boy of 7 on the harpsichord as a marvel of both past and present. All connoisseurs have found that what a friend in Vienna wrote some time ago about these celebrated children and what appeared in the local *Intelligenz-Zettel* is not only true (incredible though this seemed), but even more worthy of admiration.[20]

From Augsburg, the Mozarts made their way to Ludwigsburg and the summer residence of Duke Karl Eugen of Württemberg, but, although armed with letters of recommendation from the canon of Salzburg Cathedral, Count von Wolfegg, to both the Master of the Hounds, Baron von Pöllnitz, and the senior Kapellmeister, Niccolò Jommelli, they failed to gain an audience with the duke. Suspicious as ever, Leopold blamed Jommelli, whom he accused of being a sworn enemy of all foreign virtuosos and of having driven away virtually all the German artists from the court and replaced them with Italians. In fact, Leopold's remarks in this context are as exaggerated as his claims concerning Jommelli's salary. The Italian composer was extraordinarily kind and obliging by nature and it is clear that he had no intention whatsoever of 'weeding out' the German artists at the local court.[21] At all events, he had no hesitation in receiving Wolfgang and, by Leopold's own admission, conceded that 'it was amazing and hardly believable that a child of German birth could be such a musical genius and so intelligent and passionate'.[22] Although this remark no doubt reflects the Italian's sense of superiority, it also reveals his true appreciation of Wolfgang's gifts. If the Mozarts failed to gain an audience with the duke, the reason lay entirely with the volatile and despotic nature of a man whose passion for the theatre and female artists was currently plumbing new depths. None the less, it is clear from Leopold's account that their visit left a deep impression. Here was a court where theatrical and artistic interests were pursued with unprecedented luxury under an unprincipled but musically gifted and educated prince, a court that may subsequently have seemed to Leopold to have offered a foretaste of Versailles. Nor did his ever-watchful eye fail to notice the powerful military presence in the town. We shall later have more to say about Jommelli and Mozart's attitude towards him. Of the virtuoso performers in the Stuttgart orchestra, Leopold mentions only Pietro Nardini (1722–93), a pupil of Tartini: 'It would be impossible to hear a finer player for beauty, purity, evenness of tone and singing quality, but he has a very light touch.'[23]

From Ludwigsburg the Mozarts travelled to Schwetzingen, the summer residence of the Elector-Palatine Karl Theodor, who received them on 18 July on the recommendation of Prince Karl August von Zweibrücken and Duke Clemens of Bavaria. A concert was arranged for them at the court and lasted from five until nine; the children proved the talk of Schwetzingen, and even the electoral couple joined in the applause. Most important of all, however, Mozart got to know the famous Mannheim orchestra and its novel manner of performing. 'The orchestra is

20. ◆ *Dokumente*, 24, *Documentary Biography*, 23 (translation amended).
21. See Abert, *Niccolò Jommelli als Opernkomponist*, 65, 79 and 97ff.
22. *Briefe*, i.76 (letter of 11 July 1763).
23. ◆ *Briefe*, i.77 (letter of 11 July 1763).

undeniably the best in Germany,' Leopold wrote, 'and is made up entirely of young people of good character, not drunkards, gamblers or rakes [an unmistakable sideswipe at Salzburg], so that both their behaviour and their playing are altogether admirable.'[24] Leopold was also struck on this occasion by the playing of the flautist Johann Baptist Wendling. At the same time, however, he informed the God-fearing Frau Hagenauer that since leaving Wasserburg they had not had a holy-water stoup and only rarely a crucifix in their rooms. It was difficult to obtain Lenten fare in the Palatinate and when they did, it was badly prepared, 'for everyone eats meat; and who knows what they have given us – basta! It's not our fault!'[25]

They made a detour to Heidelberg, where Wolfgang played the organ at the Church of the Holy Ghost, so astonishing his listeners that on the orders of the local magistrate, his name and full particulars of his visit were inscribed on the instrument in memory of the occasion. Unfortunately, all trace of this inscription has been lost.

In Mainz, they were unable to perform at court on account of the illness of the elector, Emmerich Joseph von Breidbach, but instead gave two concerts at the 'Roman Emperor', netting a total of 200 florins in the process.[26] Here they met the soprano Anna Lucia de Amicis, who was on her way home from London with her father and other members of her family. By 12 August the Mozarts were in Frankfurt,[27] where they caused such a stir with their concert on the 18th that three more were hastily arranged. The advertisement of 30 August 1763 indicates what was on offer:

> The universal admiration aroused in the minds of all listeners by the skill of the 2 children of the Kapellmeister to the Salzburg court, Herr Leopold Mozart, a skill never previously seen or heard to this extent, has led to a threefold repetition of a concert originally intended to be given only once. Indeed, it is this universal admiration and the request on the part of various great connoisseurs and music lovers that has prompted the decision to give what will definitely be their last concert today, Tuesday 30 August, at 6 o'clock in the evening in Scharf's Hall on the Liebfrauenberg, when the girl, who is in her twelfth year, and the boy, who is in his seventh, will not only play on the harpsichord or fortepiano, the former performing the most difficult pieces by the greatest masters, but the boy will also play a concerto on the violin, accompany symphonies on the keyboard and completely cover the manual or keyboard with a cloth, on which he will play as though he had the keyboard before his eyes; he will also accurately name any notes that may be played to him from a distance, singly or in chords on the keyboard or on every imaginable instrument including bells, glasses and clocks. Finally he will improvise not only on the fortepiano but also on an organ (as long as one wishes to listen and in all the keys, even the most difficult, that may be named for him), in order to show that he also understands the art of playing the organ, an art completely different from that of playing the harpsichord.[28]

24. *Briefe*, i.79 (letter of 19 July 1763).

25. *Briefe*, i.80 (letter of 19 July 1763). 'In Mannheim they were invited to perform before the Elector-Palatine', recalled Nannerl; but since she says nothing about the performance in Schwetzingen, it seems likely that she was confusing the two places. That the travellers also stayed in Mannheim is clear from Leopold's letter in Nissen, *Biographie W. A. Mozarts*, 41. ◆ *Briefe*, i.78–81 (letter of 19 July 1763).

26. Information from Nannerl. ◆ *Dokumente*, 399, *Documentary Biography*, 455.

27. Woelcke, 'Mozart in Frankfurt', 103–21. We know that the family stayed at 3 Bendergasse on this date because Leopold scratched details of their visit on one of the window panes in his room. The concert on the 30th, and presumably the earlier ones too, were held at Scharff's Hall on the Liebfrauenberg.

28. Belli-Gontard, *Leben in Frankfurt am Main*, v.25. The announcement ends: 'Admission, a small thaler per person. Tickets to be had at the Golden Lion.' ◆ *Dokumente*, 25–6, *Documentary Biography*, 24–5.

It was on this occasion that Goethe heard Mozart play. 'I saw him when he was seven,' the poet later told Eckermann, 'when he gave a concert on his way through the town. I myself was around fourteen, and I still clearly remember the little man with his wig and sword.'[29]

In Koblenz, where Baron Walderdorf and the imperial ambassador, Count Pergen, introduced the two children to the elector of Trier, Johann Philipp von Walderdorf, they saw a great deal of the privy councillor Baron Kerpen, who was head of the local nobility and whose seven sons and two daughters almost all played the harpsichord, while some also played the violin and cello and sang. The Mozarts performed at court on 18 September, then moved on to Bonn, but the elector of Cologne, Maximilian Friedrich, Count of Königseck-Rothenfels, was not in residence, and so they remained only long enough to admire the palace's two exceptionally valuable beds and bath, together with its remarkable galleries and concert halls with their paintings, clocks, inlaid tables and porcelain. They also saw the most varied rarities in Poppelsdorf and Falkenlust, whereas in Cologne they noted only 'the dirty minster or cathedral'. In Aachen, where they gave a concert,[30] Princess Amalie, the sister of Frederick the Great and a woman well known for her love and knowledge of music, was currently taking the waters. She attempted to persuade Leopold to take his children to Berlin, but he refused to be sidetracked. 'She has no money,' he wrote, pragmatic as ever; 'if the kisses that she has given my children, and especially to Master Wolfgang, were all new louis d'or, we'd be happy enough; but neither the landlord nor postmasters allow themselves to be fobbed off with kisses.'[31] In Brussels, where Prince Karl of Lorraine, the brother of the Emperor Franz I, resided as governor and commander-in-chief of the Austrian Netherlands, they had to wait until they were able to organize a full-scale concert, but they used the unexpected delay to study the paintings of the old Dutch school. The young Mozart will have been attracted above all by the flute-playing figures and singing birds of the mechanical-instrument maker, Adam Lambman. The local musicians will have had less to offer him: although Leopold mentions composers such as Friedrich Schwindl (1737–86) and Pierre van Maldere (1729–68), whose comic opera *La bagarre* was performed in Paris in 1763, they were not especially distinguished, for all their advocacy of the modern Mannheim style.[32]

In Brussels we again encounter Mozart as a composer, this time with an allegro in C major for keyboard that was later to be reworked as his first Paris violin sonata K6 and that Leopold entered in Nannerl's exercise book on 14 October. This allegro has recently been seen as the opening movement of a keyboard sonata, its other movements appearing elsewhere in the volume in the form of an andante K8/2, menuetto (the second minuet of this same piece) and allegro K9a.[33] Given the nature and aim of this volume, such a hypothesis is doubtful at best, and it is far more likely that it was only when the allegro was reworked for the violin sonata that the three movements were combined and a new finale added.

29. Eckermann, *Gespräche mit Goethe*, ii.178–9.
30. According to Nannerl; Leopold's letter to Hagenauer is silent on this point.
31. *Briefe*, i.104 (letter of 17 October–4 November 1763).
32. ◆ The Mozarts were in Koblenz from 18 to 27 September, Cologne from 27 to 29 September and Aachen from 30 September to 2 October (the concert was probably on 1 October). They arrived in Brussels about 5 October and gave their 'full-scale concert' on 7 November; see Eisen, *New Mozart Documents*, 16.
33. See Wyzewa and Saint-Foix, *Wolfgang Amédée Mozart*, i.27. If one assumes that the first three movements belong together (although their keys of F and C major are no compelling reason for making this assumption), I would think it more likely that the sonata ended with the menuetto, as do so many well-known models. It is most improbable that it also included the aforementioned allegro, a piece whose authenticity even Köchel called into question (K5b). After all, the allegro K3 appears in the volume as an independent piece. ◆ K5b, a fragmentary andante in B flat major, is unquestionably by Mozart: the autograph, formerly part of the so-called 'Nannerl-Notenbuch', is now privately owned in Switzerland.

Leopold arrived in Paris with his children on 18 November. The impressions with which they were assailed from every quarter may have been difficult even for Leopold himself to assimilate, well versed in the ways of the world though he was. In the case of Mozart, they continued to resonate even as late as the period of *Le nozze di Figaro* and *Don Giovanni*. It was with some astonishment that they observed the tremendous contrasts that rent the French state from top to bottom and that had been made worse by the war with England and Prussia, a war that had ended barely twelve months earlier, with little glory for the French: on the one hand were the aristocracy and clergy, in sole possession of all the privileges of their day and representatives of a hedonistic approach to life that bordered on sheer folly, and, on the other, the exploited masses, virtually without any rights and barely assured of their livelihood and property, while over them all was a monarchy whose representative, Louis XV, had long neglected his duties as a ruler in his pursuit of a life of pleasure. The state was effectively run by the now elderly Madame de Pompadour. But already a struggle had begun to overturn this unnatural state of affairs, and the *ancien régime*, which counted on the victory of reason and existing mores to maintain the status quo, had been called into question by Rousseau throwing down his gauntlet and arguing that universal human happiness could be achieved only by the total abandonment of existing cultural values. His *Nouvelle Héloïse*, *Émile* and *Contrat social* had all appeared shortly before the Mozarts' arrival in Paris, and all had shown the two darkest aspects of contemporary society – marriage and children's education – in a disturbing new light, while ultimately declaring war on the present system of monarchical rule.

These contrasts were particularly striking in the aristocratic circles in which the Mozarts found themselves almost without exception in Paris as elsewhere. The most unbridled hedonism – summed up in the crass idea of the 'sacrament of adultery' – coexisted with an enthusiastic belief in the virtues of the 'beautiful soul', a belief entirely typical of the Age of Sensibility and one that owed much to Rousseau's writings. Sober Enlightenment values were found side by side with effusive sentimentality, unnatural sophistication with an immoderate love of Nature. For the first time in his life, the young Mozart was exposed to a world that he was to depict with such masterly astuteness in the works of his maturity. Nor was it hard to find living Don Juans, demonic sensualists who frequented these circles which, well read in Plutarch, were especially fond of the heroism of immorality.

But, for all its faults, this society also had its good points in the form of freedom of thought, formal elegance, the play of intellect, wit and tender emotion and, finally, that seductive dream of universal human happiness to which we ultimately owe *Die Zauberflöte*. Many of these traits, especially the curious mixture of hedonistic gallantry and brooding contemplation, were already subliminally present in Mozart's character, and they now assumed physical form in the midst of a bewildering whirl of novel experiences. There is no doubt that he learnt an infinite amount about the formal aspect of art in Paris, but at least as important was the part played by his visits to the French capital, both now and, more especially, later, in terms of the development of his own personality.

Of particular interest in this context is a letter that Leopold wrote to Maria Theresia Hagenauer, in which he describes his initial impressions of Paris:

Whether the women in Paris are beautiful, I cannot say, and for good reason, for they are painted so unnaturally – like the dolls of Berchtesgaden – that, as a result of this frightful make-up, even a naturally beautiful person is unbearable in the eyes of every honest German. As for religion, I can assure you that it will not be hard to fathom the miracles wrought by women saints in France; the greatest of them are performed by those who are neither virgins nor wives nor widows, but are all performed during their lifetime. . . . Enough! It is already hard enough to tell who is the lady of the house here. Everyone lives as he likes and, if God is not especially merciful, the French state will go the same way as the Persian Empire. . . . I can assure you that it does not require an eye-glass to see everywhere the devastating consequences of the recent war, for the French insist on continuing to lead lives of superficial splendour on the grandest scale, with the result that only the *fermiers* are rich, while the masters are deep in debt. The greatest wealth is divided among 100 persons, a few big bankers and *fermiers généraux*, and most money, ultimately, is spent on Lucretias who do not, however, stab themselves. . . . In winter the women wear not only fur-trimmed clothes, but even collars or scarves and instead of flowers in their hair, fur ornaments, and fur armlets on their arms &c. But the most ridiculous thing of all is a sword-band (which is the fashion here) wound round and round with fine fur – a good idea, as it prevents the sword from freezing. On top of their idiotic desire to be fashionable in all things, there is their great love of comfort, which means that this nation no longer hears the voice of Nature and also explains why everyone in Paris sends new-born children to be brought up in the country. So-called governesses, who are licensed for this very purpose, take these children to the country, and each of them has a large book, with 'father' and 'mother' &c in it; and then at the place where the child is taken, the name of the nurse or, rather, of the peasant and his wife, is entered by the local vicar. This is done by persons of high and low rank alike, and they pay a trifle for it. But you soon see the pitiful consequences of it, for you'll hardly find a place full of so many miserable, mutilated people.[34]

On their arrival in Paris, the Mozarts put up with the Bavarian ambassador, Maximilian Emanuel Franz Count von Eyck, at the Hôtel Beauvais in the Rue Saint-Antoine.[35] (The ambassador's wife was a daughter of Salzburg's high chancellor, Georg Anton Felix, Count Arco.) But the plentiful supply of recommendations from members of the aristocracy and diplomat corps that they had brought with them proved ineffectual, with the single exception of a letter to Friedrich Melchior Grimm that had been given them by the wife of a Frankfurt businessman. Grimm had been born in Regensburg in 1723 and studied in Leipzig, where he sat at the feet of Ernesti and Gottsched, whom he idolized to distraction.[36] He moved to Paris in 1748 and, as secretary to August Heinrich Count Friesen and later to the Duke of Orleans, gained entry to all the best circles. Of decisive influence on his subsequent development was his acquaintance with Rousseau, Diderot, d'Alembert and other figures involved in the *Encyclopédie*, in which he, too, had a hand. Against this background, it is little wonder that he became one of the staunchest champions of Italian opera in the *Querelle des Bouffons*. As early as 1752 he published an annihilating critique of Destouches's *Omphale* in the *Mercure de France*, following it up in 1753 with a satire in the same vein, *Le petit prophète de Boehmischbroda*, and, together with Guillaume Raynal and Jacques-Henri Meister, founded the *Correspondance littéraire, philosophique et critique*, a chronicle that has ensured that, as its principal contributor, Grimm remains inextricably linked with the cultural history of the *ancien régime*. Intended for a select readership at court and in society, this journal remains a source of the first importance for music of the years between 1747 and 1790.[37] That it

34. *Briefe*, i.121–5 (letter of 1 February 1764).
35. Now 68 rue François-Miron; see Wilder, *Mozart: L'homme et l'artiste*, 22.
36. See Danzel, *Gottsched und seine Zeit*, 343ff.
37. See Kretzschmar, 'Die Correspondance littéraire als musikgeschichtliche Quelle'.

none the less needs to be treated with caution is due to the personality of its principal contributor, for Grimm was not sufficiently well trained as a musician to do justice to the art that he was describing, nor was he the man to let slip the opportunity for a flash of wit or eloquent turn of phrase, even if it meant violating the truth in the process. Yet he was just the sort of journalist that Paris society deserved, invariably au fait with all that exercised its members from the world of high politics to the lowest gossip, no less familiar with their views and tastes and, finally, a raconteur of brilliant wit who was never at a loss for words. In keeping with the contemporary practice of mutual adulation, Sainte-Beuve described him as 'the classic critic'.

It was, then, the exceptional, unprecedented nature of the Mozarts' visit that persuaded Grimm to take the German prodigies under his wing. Even Leopold forgot his usual mistrust in the face of a man whom he described as this 'great friend' and as this 'man of learning and a great philanthropist. . . . He brought our business to court; he made all the arrangements for the first concert . . . and will do the same for the second. . . . So you see what a man can do who has good sense and a kind heart. . . . He has been in Paris for over 15 years and knows how to steer things in the right direction so that they inevitably turn out as he wishes'.[38] Indeed, even in his views on art the normally critical Leopold allowed himself to be completely led by Grimm. 'The whole of French music is not worth a sou,' he informed Maria Theresia Hagenauer, 'but the French are now starting to make drastic changes, and in 10 to 15 years French taste, I hope, will have disappeared altogether.'[39]

In Paris as elsewhere, their initial aim was to be heard at court. They arrived at Versailles on Christmas Eve and, according to Leopold's letter of 1 February 1764, remained there for two weeks. The detailed report of the visit that Leopold submitted to the archbishop has unfortunately not survived. The most important person present was, of course, Madame de Pompadour. 'She must have been very beautiful, for she is still good-looking,' Leopold informed Frau Hagenauer. 'She is tall and stately, stout and portly, but well-proportioned, blonde and very like the late Therese Freysauff,[40] while her eyes are rather like those of Her Majesty the Empress. She is extremely dignified and uncommonly intelligent.'[41] According to Nannerl's much later account, she had Wolfgang placed on the table in front of her but refused to allow him to kiss her when he bent forward to do so, prompting him to ask indignantly: 'Who's this woman who won't kiss me? Even the empress kissed me.'[42] A more friendly attitude was shown by the royal princesses, who flouted etiquette and spoke with the children not only in their rooms but also in public, kissing them and allowing their hands to be kissed in turn. On New Year's Day the Swiss Guard led the family into the banqueting hall and they remained present at the court dinner; Wolfgang had to stand next to the queen, who handed him morsels of food and spoke to him in German, before translating everything into French for the benefit of Louis XV, who did not understand German, of course. Leopold stood beside Wolfgang, while mother and daughter stood on the other side of the king, beside the dauphin and Madame Adélaïde. The boy also had a chance to play the organ in the chapel at Versailles in the presence of the court, who again applauded his performance.[43] Only when they had performed at Versailles were they admitted to, and admired by, aristocratic

38. *Briefe*, i.141 (letter of 1 April 1764).
39. *Briefe*, i.126 (letter of 1 February 1764).
40. Here is meant Therese Freysauff of Salzburg. ◆ Maria Theresia Freysauff von Neudegg (1712–57) was the daughter of the local tax collector Johann Sebastian Freysauff (1685–1767).
41. *Briefe*, i.125–6 (letter of 1 February 1764).
42. Wolfgang was particularly proud of his association with the empress. When he was about to perform for a member of the local aristocracy at one of the minor German courts, a courtier tried to encourage him, whereupon the lad retorted that he was not afraid as he had already played for the empress.
43. According to Nannerl; see Nottebohm, *Mozartiana*, 98 [*Dokumente*, 399, *Documentary Biography*, 455–6].

circles. A small oil painting, now in the Louvre, depicts the young Wolfgang seated at the keyboard in the salon of the Prince of Conti surrounded by a large gathering of members of the nobility.[44] And only after they had performed on frequent occasions at private gatherings did they give two full-scale concerts on 10 March and 9 April 1764. Both were held in the small private theatre of a local member of the aristocracy, Monsieur Félix, that was normally used for performances of plays mounted by the nobility. Permission to hold these concerts at all was a mark of special favour, as it ran counter to the *privilèges* enjoyed by the Concert Spirituel as well as by the French and Italian theatres, and was granted only at the request of a large number of distinguished patrons. Both concerts were brilliantly successful in every respect.

While Nannerl could stand comparison with the leading Paris virtuosos of the day, Wolfgang astonished his listeners not only with his abilities on the harpsichord, violin and organ but with other demonstrations of his gifts. Both at public concerts and private gatherings he not only sight-read the accompaniments of French and Italian arias but even transposed them at sight, an ability that presupposes total command of continuo playing. But he was also capable of improvising the accompaniment of an Italian cavatina whose bass line he did not know, and of improvising the accompaniment differently each time the piece was played. Most important of all, he now appeared in public for the first time in a series of free improvisations, an art still widely practised and, indeed, demanded at that time but one that has now unfortunately been almost completely lost. All of this we learn from Grimm, who could not conceal his pride and satisfaction that this latest 'sensation' had turned out so successfully.[45]

No less important, however, is the information that we glean from Leopold's letters concerning the people they met in Paris: they came into contact with virtually all the capital's most prominent artists. Of these, pride of place must go to the Silesian harpsichordist and composer Johann Schobert, a man about whom we know only that, according to Mozart,[46] he was briefly in Augsburg and that from around 1760 he was harpsichordist to the Prince of Conti in Paris, where he died on 28 August 1767 as a result of eating poisonous mushrooms. He was the most celebrated keyboard player in Paris at this time, but also enjoyed great acclaim as a composer[47] and was the first true representative of the Mannheim school to come Mozart's way. We shall later have occasion to discuss his influence on him. The initial impression, it must be said, was distinctly unfavourable, with Leopold referring to 'mean Schobert who cannot conceal his envy and jealousy and who is making himself a laughing stock in the eyes of Monsieur Eckard, who is an honest individual, and many others. . . . Monsieur Schobert is not at all the man he is said to be. He flatters you to your face, but is the falsest of men. But his religion is the religion in fashion. May God grant

44.   ◆ This painting, by Ollivier, is reproduced in Deutsch, *Mozart und seine Welt*, 6. Further, see Hanning, 'The Iconography of a Salon Concert: A Reappraisal'. For Mozart's performance at the Prince of Conti's, see Daniel Meyer, 'Deux vedettes chez le Prince de Conti'; and for Conti, see Turrentine, 'The Prince de Conti, a Royal Patron of Music'.
45.   Grimm, *Correspondance littéraire*, iii.367–8. See also the account by Jean-Baptiste-Antoine Suard, *Mélanges de littérature*, v.337: 'He was 6 to 7 years old. I heard him play the harpsichord at the Concert spirituel and in private houses. He astonished all music lovers with the facility and precision with which he executed the most difficult pieces. He could accompany from a full score at sight. He would improvise at his instrument, and in these extemporized capricci he revealed the happiest touches of melody and already showed a deep feeling for harmony.' [*Dokumente*, 54–5 and 428, *Documentary Biography*, 56–7 and 497; translation amended].
46.   *Briefe*, ii.70 (letter of 17 October 1777).
47.   For a summary of Schobert's life and works, see Riemann's introduction to *Johann Schobert: Ausgewählte Werke*, which also includes eyewitness accounts by Schubart, Burney, Grimm and others as well as by Goethe's sister, Cornelia. Also of importance are Wyzewa, 'Un maître inconnu de Mozart', 35ff.; Wyzewa and Saint-Foix, *Wolfgang Amédée Mozart*, i.65–80; Hiller, *Wöchentliche Nachrichten und Anmerkungen die Musik betreffend*, i.134–5; and Junker, *Zwanzig Komponisten*, 89ff. ◆ Further, see Saint-Foix, 'Les premiers pianistes parisiens, I: Jean Schobert, vers 1740–1767'.

that he sees the errors of his ways!'[48] Leopold reacted far more favourably to Schobert's principal rival in Paris, Johann Gottfried Eckard (1735–1809), who, like Leopold, hailed from Augsburg and who had been living in the French capital since 1758. We know from Wolfgang's letters, too,[49] that Eckard's art was highly regarded. We shall have more to say about both Eckard and another of the composers mentioned by Leopold, Leontzi Honauer, in the context of Wolfgang's own works. All these names attest to the important role played by German musicians in Paris at this time, an importance confirmed by advertisements of the publishers La Chevardière and Venier, who were currently publishing works not only by Johann Stamitz but also by Christian Bach and Joseph Haydn.[50]

Of the music that the Mozarts heard in France, Leopold spoke particularly appreciatively of the choruses in a number of the sacred works that they encountered at Versailles. But it is opera – the declared favourite of the Parisians and, as such, of greater interest to them than the whole instrumental repertory combined – that commands our attention here. The extent to which the pride of the French nation, the old *tragédies lyriques* of Lully and Rameau, had fallen into disfavour with audiences is clear from the fact that all the surviving accounts of the revival of Rameau's *Castor et Pollux* on 23 January 1764 describe it as the epitome of boredom, and later works by Mondonville and Bernard de Bury fared no better.[51] All the greater, then, was the acclaim accorded to productions at the Comédie-Italienne, whose leading representatives at the time of Mozart's visit were Duni (*Les deux chasseurs* and *Le milicien*), Philidor (*Le bûcheron*, *Blaise le savetier*, *Le maréchal ferrant* and *Le sorcier*) and Monsigny (*Rose et Colas*). And Mozart could also have heard *Bastien et Bastienne*, to a libretto by Marie Justine Favart, at the court theatre in Versailles.[52] Although he did not, of course, attend performances of all these works, he could have heard their principal numbers played on the streets of the capital. At all events, it is clear that these popular French songs will not have escaped his attention. Their witty and waspish verses, in which no aspect of state or society was sacrosanct, are a faithful reflection of the spirit of the times.

It is no wonder that, given this wealth of new impressions, Mozart, too, felt his own creative drive reassert itself. At the end of January 1764 his father had four of his sonatas for keyboard and violin engraved,[53] and then sat back to observe the furore that they produced when people read on their title-page that they were the work of a seven-year-old boy. He himself thought they were good – and not just because they had been written by a child. He was particularly pleased with an andante 'in a quite unusual style'. Later, when it emerged that in the final trio his correction to three consecutive fifths in the violin part had been ignored, he consoled himself by arguing that

48.   *Briefe*, i.126–7 (letter of 1 February 1764).

49.   *Briefe*, i.513 (letter of 30 December 1774).

50.   Wyzewa and Saint-Foix, *Wolfgang Amédée Mozart*, i.60. ◆ Further concerning Parisian musical life at this time, see Mongrédien, 'Paris: The End of the Ancien Régime'; Dufourcq, *La musique à la cour de Louis XIV et de Louis XV d'après les mémoires de Sources et Luynes, 1681–1758* and 'Concerts parisiens et associations de "Symphonistes"'; Burton, 'Les académies de musique en France au XVIIIe siècle'; and Pierre, *Histoire du Concert Spirituel, 1725–1790*.

51.   Bachaumont, *Mémoires secrets*, ii.13, even goes so far as to claim: 'C'est le système de Copernic mis en action, il est très bien exécuté: reste à savoir pourquoi le système de Copernic dans cet opéra?' ◆ Concerning the reception of *Castor et Pollux*, see Dill, 'The reception of Rameau's *Castor et Pollux* in 1737 and 1754' and *Monstrous Opera: Rameau and the Tragic Tradition*. Jean-Joseph de Mondonville's (1711–72) later works include the *tragédie Thésée* (1765) and the *opéra-ballet Les projets de l'Amour* (1771); Bernard de Bury's (1720–85) works include the *ballets héroïques Palmyre* (1765) and *Zénis et Almasie* (1765 but apparently lost; see also n. 135 below).

52.   Wyzewa and Saint-Foix, *Wolfgang Amédée Mozart*, i.55.

53.   Of these sonatas, several movements appear as keyboard pieces in the abovementioned exercise book, *viz.*: K6, movements 1–3; K7, 3rd movement; K8, movements 1–2. K8 is dated 21 November 1763 in Leopold's hand; and K9 almost certainly dates from December 1763 or January 1764. Both collections are titled *Sonates pour le clavecin, qui peuvent se jouer avec l'accompagnement de violon*, that is, they would be performed with or without violin. See *Briefe*, i.126 and 177 (letters of 1 February 1764 and 3 December 1764).

they might be seen as 'proof that Wolfgangerl wrote these sonatas himself, something which, naturally enough, people may not have been willing to believe, even though it is true'.[54] The two sonatas to be engraved first (K6 and K7) were dedicated to the king's second daughter, the good-natured Princess Victoire who, like her sisters, was musical. They were handed over personally at Versailles. The other two (K8 and K9) were inscribed to Madame la Dauphine's lady-in-waiting, the strait-laced *précieuse* Comtesse de Tessé.[55] Grimm wrote a dedication in Wolfgang's name describing both the boy and his dedicatee in lively terms, but to Leopold's regret she rejected it as she did not want to be praised, with the result that a simpler dedication had to be used instead.[56]

The two prodigies were showered with honours, gifts and poems in their honour. Louis Carrogis de Carmontelle, a well-regarded amateur portrait painter,[57] produced a group portrait of the family that was engraved by Delafosse at Grimm's instigation.

It was in the proud knowledge that his son was now firmly ensconced in the minds of Parisian audiences that Leopold left Paris with his two children on 10 April 1764. At Calais, Nannerl noted in her diary that she 'saw how the sea runs away and comes back again'. The packet was full, so they hired a boat of their own for the crossing to Dover, in the course of which they all suffered acutely from sea-sickness; a servant whom they had taken with them from Paris arranged the journey for them and helped them to find their bearings in London, where they arrived on 22 April.

The atmosphere in London was completely different from the one that reigned in France, where the country was drifting irresistibly towards revolution. At the same time, there is no doubt that in the years around 1765 England scarcely merited the enthusiastic praise lavished upon it by Voltaire in his *Letters concerning the English Nation*, although visitors must have been struck no less by its inhabitants' tireless industry, by their delight in hard work (a delight sustained by their great sense of nationalism) and by their astonishing successes in trade and commerce than by their self-conscious, often coarse high spirits. After all, the recent war[58] had brought the country an unforeseen increase in power and especially in its naval supremacy.

In other areas, of course, Britain's ascendancy had been bought at a price, and it is no accident that from the beginning of the eighteenth century – the date when trade first began to affect the country's policies – England ceased to be one of the leading musical nations and had to make do either with foreign imports or with a level of musical achievement that failed to rise above the parochial.[59] Its royal house's links with Germany lured many a leading German musician to England, none more so than Handel, who was then at the height of his powers. Mozart himself had the opportunity to become acquainted with a large number of Handel's works;[60] and Handel's pupil and confidant, Johann Christoph Schmidt (or John Christopher Smith, as he now styled himself), was still active at the English court. George III was himself very musical, even if he lacked

54. ◆ *Briefe*, i.177–8 (letter of 3 December 1764). As for the andante 'in a quite unusual style', *Briefe*, v.103, following Wyzewa and Saint-Foix (*Wolfgang Amédée Mozart*, i.82) identifies this as the second movement of K7. The tempo marking there, however, is 'adagio' and the movement is more likely to be the unusual andante of K9.

55. Goncourt, *La femme au XVIIIIème siècle*, i.71–2.

56. *Briefe*, i.141 (letter of 1 April 1764). ◆ The dedications of K6–7 and K8–9 are reproduced in *Dokumente*, 30 and 33, *Documentary Biography*, 29–30 and 31–2.

57. See Vichy, *Correspondance complète*, i.207. ◆ Carmontelle's group portrait is reproduced in Deutsch, *Mozart und seine Welt*, 5.

58. Here Abert refers to the Seven Years' War (1756–63).

59. ◆ For accounts of musical life in England at this time, including views contrary to Abert's characterization of it as in decline, see Burrows, 'London: Commercial Wealth and Cultural Expansion'; William Weber, 'London: A City of Unrivalled Riches'; Johnstone and Fiske, *Music in Britain: The Eighteenth Century*; McVeigh, *Concert Life in London from Mozart to Haydn*; and Ehrlich, 'Economic History and Music'. More generally, see Clark, *English Society, 1688–1832*, and McKendrick, Brewer and Plumb, *The Birth of a Consumer Society: The Commercialization of Eighteenth-Century England*.

60. ◆ For Handel performances in London at this time, see Stone, *The London Stage, 1660–1800: Part 4 (1747–76)*.

the detailed knowledge of music evinced by many of his Continental counterparts. In particular, he was influentially fond of Handel's music. Queen Charlotte was trained as a singer and also played the keyboard – 'very passably for a queen', to quote Haydn.[61]

In the field of opera, Gay's and Pepusch's *The Beggar's Opera* was still pulling in the crowds at Covent Garden with its folksongs,[62] but more important for Mozart were the Italian operas at the King's Theatre, which was currently being run by Colomba Mattei and, thereafter, by the violin virtuoso Felice Giardini and the singer Regina Mingotti. Here Mozart could have heard operas by Johann Christian Bach, Niccolò Piccinni, Mattia Vento and Giardini himself, as well as a number of pasticcios by a whole range of different composers.[63] But he also became better acquainted with singers from the company, notably the castrato Giovanni Manzuoli, who had been born at Florence in around 1725 and who was now one of the most acclaimed singers and actors of his day: after early successes in Italy, he had taken London, Madrid and Vienna (1760)[64] by storm, returning to London in 1764 where, engaged on the most advantageous terms, he was the cynosure of the operatic scene, exciting audiences to 'a universal thunder' of applause with his singing and acting.[65] Together with his fellow castrato, Ferdinando Tenducci (1736–90), he was the first great singer to impress Mozart and, out of his friendship for the composer's family, even deigned to give the boy singing lessons. Mozart made use of his new skill while still in London,[66] and the following year, during his visit to Paris, Grimm reported that he had clearly learnt from Manzuoli and, in spite of his weak voice, was none the less capable of singing with both feeling and good taste.

But the greatest influence on the young Mozart was that of two artists of German birth who were currently setting the tone on the London musical scene: Carl Friedrich Abel and Johann Christian Bach. Abel[67] had been born at Cöthen in 1723 and had been a pupil of Johann Sebastian Bach at the Thomasschule in Leipzig. Between 1746 and 1758 he was a member of the Dresden Hofkapelle and *c*1764 became chamber musician to Queen Charlotte. He remained in London more or less uninterruptedly until his death in 1787. Abel was not only an extremely prolific composer but also the last virtuoso of any importance on the gamba. Johann Christian Bach, for his part, was the first composer to leave a decisive and lasting mark on Mozart in the most disparate areas. The youngest son of Johann Sebastian, he was born on 5 September 1735[68] and was initially taught by his father, but on the latter's death in 1750 went to study with his brother,

61. Pohl, *Mozart und Haydn in London*, 99. ◆ Concerning George III, Queen Charlotte and musical life at court, see Scholes, 'George III as Music Lover'; Harley, 'Music at the English Court in the Eighteenth and Nineteenth Centuries'; and Broughton, *Court and Private Life in the Time of Queen Charlotte: Being the Journals of Mrs. Papendiek.*
62. Pohl, *Mozart und Haydn in London*, 82 and 89. ◆ Further, see Gilman, 'The beggar's opera and British opera'; Moss, 'Popular music and the ballad opera'; and Richardson, 'The beggar's opera, and forms of resistance'.
63. Pohl, *Mozart und Haydn in London*, 71ff. Three of Bach's works were in the repertory at this time: *Orione* (19 February 1763), *Zanaida* (7 May 1763) and *Adriano in Siria* (26 January 1765). ◆ For the King's Theatre, see McVeigh, *Concert Life in London from Mozart to Haydn*; Nalbach, *The King's Theatre, 1704–1867: London's first Italian opera house*; Petty, 'Italian opera in London, 1760–1800'; and Gibson, 'Italian Opera in London, 1750–1775: Management and Finances'.
64. Metastasio, *Opere postume*, ii.272.
65. Burney, *A General History of Music*, ii.868; see also Kelly, *Reminiscences*, i.7.
66. See Nottebohm, *Mozartiana*, 99: 'The son also sang arias with the greatest feeling.' ◆ Early on in his stay in London, Mozart apparently gave a concert with Manzuoli at the Berkeley Square residence of Lord and Lady Clive; see Woodfield, 'New light on the Mozarts' London Visit: A Private Concert with Manzuoli'.
67. See Pohl, *Mozart und Haydn in London*, 155ff., and Burney's biography in Cramer's 1820 edition of Abel's adagio. ◆ Further, see Knape, *Karl Friedrich Abel: Leben und Werk eines frühklassischen Komponisten*; Charters, 'Abel in London'; and Holman, '"A solo on the viola da gamba": Carl Friedrich Abel as a performer'.
68. See Max Schwarz, 'Johann Christian Bach', 401–54.

Carl Philipp Emanuel, in Berlin, continuing to perfect his keyboard playing and, at the same time, coming into contact with Italian opera. He went to Italy in 1754 – the only member of his family to do so – and entered the service of Count Agostino Litta in Milan, completing his studies with Padre Martini in Bologna and converting to Catholicism. In 1760 he became organist at Milan Cathedral. During these years he was increasingly drawn to opera, and his *Catone in Utica* was staged in Naples in 1761, to be followed in 1762 by *Alessandro nell'Indie*.[69] A whole series of sacred compositions also date from this period. It was soon after this that he received a commission from Colomba Mattei to write an opera for London, an invitation that is also a visible sign of Bach's new status as a fully-fledged representative of the now dominant trend of Italian opera. *Orione* and *Zanaida* proved spectacularly successful, and Bach was appointed music master to Queen Charlotte on a salary of £300. He founded the Bach–Abel Concerts with Abel in 1764, a venture that was to have a lasting impact on the capital's concert life. Among the composers whose works were performed at these concerts were not only Bach and Abel themselves, but also Joseph Haydn, while leading virtuosos from all over Europe added lustre to their programmes. *Adriano in Siria* (1765) was followed by *Carattaco* (1767) and a whole series of pasticcios: *L'Olimpiade* (with Piccinni) in 1769, *Orfeo* (with Gluck and Guglielmi – one of many attempts to make Gluck's opera more palatable to audiences by bringing it closer to the Italian style) in 1769/70 and the oratorio *Gioas, rè di Giuda* in 1770.[70] It is no wonder, therefore, that Bach also received commissions from abroad at this time: for Mannheim he wrote *Temistocle* in 1772 and *Lucio Silla* in 1774. Mozart is known to have studied *Lucio Silla* in some depth at this date.[71] The two composers met again in Paris in 1778. (*Amadis de Gaule* was performed in the French capital in 1779, albeit with scant success.) 'You can well imagine his delight and my own delight when we saw each other again', Mozart wrote to his father on this occasion. 'Perhaps his delight wasn't as genuine as mine, but you can't deny that he's a man of honour and that he deals justly with people; I love him (as you know) with all my heart – and respect him, and it is a fact that he has genuinely praised me, not only to my face but in the presence of others – and has done so, moreover, not in any exaggerated way, as some people affect, but in all seriousness.'[72]

Bach died on 1 January 1782.[73] His reputation and historical position rest not only on his operas but, more especially, on his symphonies and keyboard music,[74] to which we shall return in a moment in the context of Mozart's own music.

Fortune smiled on the Mozarts no less in London than it had done in Paris. By 27 April they had already been received at court, a reception that exceeded all expectations, as Leopold wrote to inform Lorenz Hagenauer:

---

69. *Demofoonte* dates from 1758 but it is not certain whether Bach wrote all this opera or only parts of it; see Max Schwarz, 'Johann Christian Bach', 442. ◆ The *Demofoonte* to which Bach contributed one aria was by Antonio Ferradini.

70. ◆ According to Warburton, *The Collected Works of Johann Christian Bach, 1735–1782: Thematic Catalogue*, Bach contributed six arias, one duet, ballet music and a chorus to the performance on 7 April (except for four arias, all of these are lost); for a performance on 17 April he contributed three arias. Further, see Warburton, *The Collected Works of Johann Christian Bach, 1735–1782*, volume 9.

71. *Briefe*, ii.120 and 304 (letters of 13 November 1777 and 28 February 1778).

72. *Briefe*, ii.458 (letter of 27 August 1778).

73. The only London opera that needs to be added to the foregoing list is *La clemenza di Scipione* (1778). ◆ Further concerning Bach, see Terry, *John Christian Bach*; Young, *The Bachs, 1500–1850*; Gärtner, *Johann Christian Bach, Mozarts Freund und Lehrmeister*; and Roe, 'J. C. Bach (1735–1782): Towards a New Biography'.

74. A detailed list of these works, together with a note of their present whereabouts, may be found in Max Schwarz, 'Johann Christian Bach', 442ff. ◆ For an up-to-date list of J. C. Bach's works, see Warburton, *The Collected Works of Johann Christian Bach: Thematic Catalogue*.

The kindness with which both His Majesty the King and the Queen received us is indescribable. . . . You wouldn't have thought from their friendly nature that they were the king and queen of England. It's true that at every court we've visited we've been met with the most extraordinary courtesy, but what we experienced here surpassed anything previously encountered. The following week we were out walking in St James's Park. The king came driving along with the queen, and although we were differently dressed, they still recognized us and not only waved to us, the king opened the window and leant out, smiling, nodding and waving to us, especially to our Master Wolfgang, as he drove past.[75]

By 19 May they were invited back to the court, where they performed to a select group of listeners from six until ten in the evening. The king presented the 'unbeatable' Wolfgang with pieces by Wagenseil, Bach, Abel and Handel, all of which he sight-read; on this occasion, he also performed on the king's organ, playing so impressively that his listeners were even inclined to think him a better organist than a harpsichord player. He then accompanied the queen in an aria and a flautist in a solo, ending up by improvising 'the most beautiful melody' to the bass line of a Handel aria. 'It is beyond your wildest dreams', wrote Leopold. 'What he knew when he left Salzburg is the merest shadow of what he knows now.'[76] Eleven days later we find Leopold writing to Hagenauer again: 'It's enough that my little girl is one of the most skilful players in Europe, even though she is only twelve, and that my boy, in a word, already knows in his eighth year what one would expect from a man of forty. In short, people who haven't seen and heard it for themselves simply don't believe it. You yourself and everyone else in Salzburg can have no idea, for the affair has taken such a completely different turn.'[77] The impression left by Bach, however, was to last the rest of Wolfgang's life: he felt powerfully drawn to a man whose personality was so closely akin to his own in so many important respects.[78] And Bach fully recognized the magnitude of Mozart's gifts. He enjoyed performing music with him, placing the boy on his knees and playing through sonatas with him with each of them taking a number of bars in turn, but with a precision that persuaded listeners than only one person was playing; or he would start a fugue that Wolfgang would then take over and complete.

Although the season was officially over, Leopold none the less thought it was worth taking a risk and presenting Wolfgang to a wider public, introducing him as 'the greatest Prodigy that Europe or that Human Nature has to boast of'.[79] It was decided to hold the concert on 5 June – a shrewd choice, as this was the day after the king's birthday, an event attended by impressive celebrations that drew a large and distinguished gathering to London. The gamble paid off and Leopold was able to report that he had 'had another shock, namely, the shock of earning 100 guineas in 3 hours', with the result that he was able to send a respectable sum back to Salzburg.[80] Anxious to commend himself further to English audiences, he arranged for a second concert to be held at Ranelagh House on 29 June 'for the Benefit of a Public useful Charity'. According to the *Public Advertiser* of 26 June, Mozart would 'perform several fine select Pieces of his own Composition on the Harpsichord and on the Organ, which has already given the highest Pleasure, Delight, and

75. *Briefe*, i.149 (letter of 28 May 1764).
76. *Briefe*, i.151–2 (letter of 28 May 1764).
77. *Briefe*, i.154 (letter of 8 June 1764).
78. See Fleischer, *Mozart*, 27. It is to Fleischer's credit that he was the first writer to draw attention to the links between Bach and Mozart, links that completely escaped Jahn's notice.
79. ◆ See, for example, the notice published in the *Public Advertiser* for 21 May 1764 (*Dokumente*, 35, *Documentary Biography*, 34).
80. Pohl, *Mozart und Haydn in London*, 101 [*Briefe*, i.153 (letter of 8 June 1764)].

Surprize to the greatest Judges of Music in England'.[81] It was at this juncture that Leopold Mozart fell seriously ill with a throat infection while returning from a concert at the home of the Earl of Thanet. On 5 August[82] he moved to Chelsea to recover, remaining there with his family for seven weeks. During this time, Mozart was not allowed to touch any musical instruments in order not to interfere with his father's recovery, and so he used the time to write symphonies, his sister later recalling that he once turned to her while working on them with the words: 'Remind me to give the horn something worthwhile to do.'[83] The horn was then a popular instrument in England, and for some time to come it received preferential treatment at Mozart's hands. From this period date the symphonies in B flat, E flat and D major (K17, K16, K19), Mozart's first attempts to write instrumental music in a more elevated style.[84]

After seven weeks the family returned to London and on 25 October were again received at court. This date marked the fourth anniversary of the king's accession, and the occasion was cele-brated both at court and in the city. In token of the royal favour, Leopold had six of Wolfgang's new sonatas for harpsichord and violin or flute engraved at his own expense. Inscribed to Queen Charlotte (the letter of dedication is dated 18 January 1765 and elicited a payment of fifty guineas from the queen), these six sonatas K10–15 went on sale on 20 March.[85]

On 21 February, and after repeated postponements, the two 'Prodigies of Nature' gave a further concert. To quote the *Public Advertiser* of that date, 'All the Overtures [that is, symphonies] will be from the Composition of these astonishing Composers [*sic*], only eight Years old'.[86] In the event, the political situation and the king's illness detracted from the success of the occasion, while 'other pleasures' discouraged members of the public from attending, with the result that the receipts were less than had been hoped. Only after repeated announcements and references to the children's imminent departure was another concert held on 13 May at a reduced price. 'It was quite enchanting', reported the *Europaeische Zeitung*, 'to hear the fourteen-year-old sister of this little virtuoso playing the most difficult sonatas on the keyboard with the most astonishing dexterity, while her brother accompanied her extempore on another keyboard.'[87] Mozart also played on a

81. Nannerl's claim (Nottebohm, *Mozartiana*, 99) that 'all the symphonies were composed by the son' must rest on a misun-derstanding. At all events, Leopold has nothing to say on this point. Nannerl also reports that they everywhere played 'a concerto on 2 keyboards' (see below). ◆ It is unclear whether the reference is to one or more concertos: Nannerl writes 'Concert auf zwey Clavier' although the context suggests several different works may have been played. See *Dokumente*, 400, *Documentary Biography*, 456.

82. This is the date given by Nannerl, whereas Pohl says it was the 6th: *Mozart und Haydn in London*, 106. ◆ According to Leopold's letter 9 August (*Briefe* i.161) the family arrived at Chelsea on the evening of 6 August.

83. Berchtold zu Sonnenburg, 'Noch einige Anekdoten', 301.

84. Here I adopt the dating of Wyzewa and Saint-Foix, *Wolfgang Amédée Mozart*, i.99–102, who assume that K17 was written during the summer of 1764, K16 in January 1765 and K19 in the spring of 1765. The manuscripts of the last two bear the word 'London', but there is nothing to help us date the first of them. The symphony in E flat major K18 is not by Mozart but by Abel; see Wyzewa and Saint-Foix, *Wolfgang Amédée Mozart*, i.97. There is also considerable doubt over the authenticity of the minuet in C major K25a, which Köchel dates to 1765. ◆ Concerning the dating of K16 and K19, see Zaslaw, *Mozart's Symphonies*, 32–5 and 45–7 (where K19 is dated to Holland, 1765–6). Concerning K17, which is probably by Leopold Mozart and may date from not later than 1756, see Eisen, 'Contributions to a New Mozart Documentary Biography', 620–3. K25a is by Kozeluch; see Deutsch, 'Kozeluch ritrovato'.

85. *Briefe*, i.170–85 (letters of 27 November, 3 December 1764, 8 February and 19 March 1765). They were advertised as going on sale on 20 March 1765. ◆ See *Dokumente*, 43, *Documentary Biography*, 43–4.

86. Pohl, *Mozart und Haydn in London*, 123; the works in question were presumably the ones listed above. [See *Dokumente*, 42, *Documentary Biography*, 42].

87. *Europaeische Zeitung*, lxiii (6 August 1765) [*Dokumente*, 47, *Documentary Biography*, 48]. There are other signs, too, that Mozart had not been forgotten in Salzburg during his absence. On 3 January 1765, 'there was a party at Court, in the course of which was performed a small *Cammer-Musique*, composed by the young son of Mozart, the resident Vice-Kapellmeister here, who is at present in London together with his son'; court diary quoted Pirckmayer, *Über Musik und Theater am f.e. Salzburger Hofe, 1762–1775* [*Dokumente*, 39, *Documentary Biography*, 38]. The piece in question may have been one of the sonatas written in Paris.

two-manual instrument with pedal-board made for the King of Prussia by Burkat Shudi,[88] who had 'conceived the good notion of having his extraordinary instrument played for the first time by the most extraordinary keyboard player in the world'. From now on, Leopold repeatedly invited audiences to hear the young prodigies perform in private and to set them whatever tests they liked. Initially the performances were held at their lodgings every day from twelve till two, later in a room that he hired for the purpose at a second-rate tavern. As a special feat, it was promised that 'the Two Children will play also together with four Hands upon the same Harpsichord, and put upon it a Handkerchief, without seeing the Keys'. It was in London that Wolfgang wrote his first piece for four hands, a piece that encouraged Leopold to claim, incorrectly, that it was the first sonata for four hands ever to have been composed.[89]

The child prodigy's abilities and achievements were put to the test in June 1764 by Daines Barrington, a man well respected in his day as a barrister and natural scientist. Barrington, who later wrote a detailed report on his observations, had obtained a copy of Mozart's birth certificate in order to ascertain his age and had taken care to ensure that all the information he received was fully reliable. Barrington set Mozart the usual tests, requiring him to sight-read difficult pieces and hearing him sing and accompany confidently and tastefully from an unfamiliar score, after which he invited him to extemporize a love song of the kind that Manzuoli might sing in an opera. Wolfgang immediately began to declaim words appropriate to an introductory recitative, followed by a piece inspired by the word *affetto* (love) about as long as a normal two-part aria. In exactly the same way, he then improvised a 'Song of Anger' on the word *perfido* (faithless man), working himself up to such a pitch of enthusiasm that he struck the keyboard like a man possessed, sometimes rising in his chair. Barrington remarked that although these improvisations were not especially remarkable, they still rose far above the ordinary and 'shewed most extraordinary readiness of invention'.[90] It is clear, therefore, not only that the boy was remarkably advanced on a purely technical level, allowing him to handle the rules and forms of composition with a certain freedom, but that his artist's imagination already inspired him to acts of genuine creativity. It is interesting to see here the first stirrings of the sense of drama that was later to become one of the constituent elements of Mozart's artistic personality and to discover how, even at this early date, he was already capable of giving fixed form to specific passions. Evidence of this comes from a tenor aria K21, *Va, dal furor portata*, written in London in 1765. Cast in regular *da capo* form, it admittedly shows few signs of originality but none the less reveals a sure sense of characteristic expression.

Towards the end of their stay, the Mozarts visited the British Museum, the natural historical and ethnographic curiosities of which were listed by Nannerl. In response to a request from the museum, Mozart handed over not only his engraved sonatas but also a manuscript work, K20.[91] It is a brief four-part madrigal, *God is our Refuge*, possibly based on a given melody, in which case

88. See Burney, *The Present State of Music in Germany*, ii.145–6. ◆ Concerning Shudi, see Dale, *Tschudi, the Harpsichord Maker*.
89. Nannerl once owned two pieces for four hands, which she described as Mozart's first such piece. Both are lost. See Nottebohm, *Mozartiana*, 139. ◆ The sonata for four hands K19d, discovered in 1921, was for many years thought to be the four-hand sonata composed by Mozart in London in 1765. It seems likely, however, that Mozart and his sister did not perform four-hand sonatas but four-hand concertos, and that K19a is not by Mozart at all. See Eisen, 'Mozart and the Four-Hand Sonata K. 19d'.
90. *Philosophical Transactions of the Royal Society*, lx (1771), 54–64, reprinted in Barrington, *Miscellanies*, 279–325. Meanwhile in Vienna, Mozart's name was mentioned in the context of the age at which Jews could be baptized: Mozart, it was argued, already had the necessary powers of discrimination by his seventh year of life; see Hanslick, *Geschichte des Concertwesens in Wien*, 121. ◆ Abert's assertion notwithstanding, the exact date of Barrington's tests is unknown. The report is reprinted in *Dokumente*, 86–92, *Documentary Biography*, 95–100.
91. Pohl, 'Über Originalhandschriften von Mozart, Haydn etc.'.

the way in which it has been adapted, if nothing else, affords remarkable proof not only of the boy's skill but also his ability to grasp and reproduce a particular form.[92]

A totally different aspect of the young Mozart emerges from a collection of forty-three pieces which, according to a note by his father, were written in London in 1764.[93] This collection of pieces cannot be regarded as a sketchbook in the Beethovenian sense as Mozart never returned to it. Rather, it should be seen as an exercise book in which the young composer experimented with the most varied forms and – most important of all – did so on his own, without his father's help. The volume presumably dates from the period of involuntary inactivity in Chelsea when Leopold was ill and Wolfgang was unable to play the harpsichord.

The view that Mozart had already scaled the highest peaks of achievement as a composer while still in London is completely contradicted by this notebook, and much of the praise lavished on the works of this period should no doubt be accorded to Leopold, who in a number of cases was presumably solely responsible for beating them into shape. Readers content merely with marvelling at Mozart's talent may be disappointed, but the more rational among us will be relieved to discover that, although Mozart developed sooner and quicker than ordinary mortals, he none the less evolved along sound lines, without any supernatural leaps and bounds. That he was not even able to rely entirely on his inner ear at this time we may infer from the numerous irregularities that he would undoubtedly have noticed and removed with the help of a keyboard. But there are also many compositional errors, generally in the case of the more complex contrapuntal and harmonic exercises.[94] In short, this was still his weakest side at this time. His melodic writing, too, is far from maintaining the same high level throughout. Above all, we find a weakness here with which he had to contend for many years to come and that was basically the negative side of his wealth of ideas: instead of sticking to the idea that he had chosen and developing it, he would simply replace it with new ideas whenever he felt like doing so. Sometimes this tendency to jump from one idea to another seems designed very much to provoke, as though the boy, freed from his father's tight rein, wanted to play the part of the angry young man (no. 28[95]), but generally this piecemeal approach to composition not only reveals considerable clumsiness but seriously detracts from any unified effect.

With few exceptions, these pieces are simple binary dances, rondos and sonata movements, with the dances clearly modelled on those contained in Leopold's sketchbook of 1762:[96] the large number of minuets – twelve – reinforces this suggestion. Also included is a whole series of contredanses evidently inspired by Mozart's impressions of Paris, although a number of them, such as nos 5 and 32, are shot through with Austrian and, specifically, Bohemian dance rhythms. On the whole, these dance movements are among the volume's most successful pieces, not least on

---

92. The Secretary of the British Museum wrote to thank Leopold on 19 July 1765: 'Sir. I am ordered by the *Standing Committee* of the Trustees of the British Museum, to signify to You, that they have received the *present of the musical performances of your very ingenious Son* which You were pleased lately to make Them, and to return You their Thanks for the same. *M. Maty.* Secretary' [*Dokumente*, 45, *Documentary Biography*, 46]. ◆ Concerning the Mozarts' gift, see King, 'The Mozarts at the British Museum'.

93. It was among the manuscripts that Ernst von Mendelssohn-Bartholdy presented to the German Kaiser in 1908. Kaiser Wilhelm II in turn entrusted them to the Königliche Bibliothek in Berlin. The incipits of individual pieces appear in KAnh. II 109b. The volume as a whole was edited by Georg Schünemann and published by Breitkopf & Härtel in Leipzig in 1909 under the title *Mozart als achtjähriger Komponist: Ein Notenbuch Wolfgangs*. ◆ Here Abert refers to the so-called 'London sketchbook', now in the Biblioteka Jagiellońska, Kraków. Works from the notebook are listed in Köchel as 15a–15ss and are published in NMA IX/27/1, 99–168.

94. It is surely no accident that the fugue no. 43 was left unfinished: even its chordal subject shows how remote the boy was at this time from the spirit of the fugue; see also nos 7, 10, 15, 19, 20, 21 and many more.

95. In no. 6 (bars 5ff.), a reminiscence of Handel's *Messiah* – correctly identified as such by Heuß, '[Review]', 181–2 – clearly threw Mozart off course. As such, it affords a good example of the boy's receptivity to artistic impressions.

96. ◆ But see again p. 28 n. 112 above; the 1762 sketchbook is a forgery.

account of their markedly childlike tone, which one seeks in vain in the published compositions of this period. In no. 31, the opening bars clearly recall *Das Veilchen* and are already remarkable for the rapt *cantabilità* typical of Mozart's later works. Nor is there any lack of contrast here. In the first part of each movement, the consequent phrase is generally totally different from the antecedent, and the second section, too, often begins with new ideas before reverting to the closing phrase of the first. Even so, everything fits effortlessly together, with the harmonic writing proceeding along regular lines, while the impression of unity is enhanced by the fact that in the minuets both sections are of equal length.[97] In the case of the rondos, it is striking that their episodes – like the trios in the minuets of Wagenseil and, in part, of Leopold Mozart – are invariably in a minor key. In four cases (nos 11, 18, 32 and the second episode of no. 33) we already find examples of Wolfgang's later tendency to stick tenaciously to the sombre minor mood.[98]

The sonata movements fall well short of the advances made by other German composers at this time, including even Leopold Mozart himself. This is clear from their second sections, most of which are of the same length as their first sections (in no. 26 the second section is shorter than the first). In particular, there is no full recapitulation, which is replaced, rather, by an abbreviated or much-compressed form of the subject-group.[99] As a rule, the development sections mostly begin with the first subject in the dominant,[100] but all too often this is followed by all manner of new ideas, which are treated with considerable freedom, after which Mozart simply reverts to the earlier group of ideas. There is also a certain amount of disorganization within the subject-groups. Although there are several examples of the tripartite division into first, second and third subject-group found at its simplest in Wagenseil's divertimentos opp. 1–4 (see nos 14, 15, 17), the subject-group of no. 19 finds the young composer attempting to cram as many themes as possible into the space available. It is clear that what motivated him was not pleasure in the detailed working out and marshalling of the ideas but in the changes of mood and especially in his wealth of ideas *per se*.[101] The influence of Johann Christian Bach is unmistakable in these movements, an influence evident not only on a formal level but in many revolutionary features in which the boy may be found striving – generally unsuccessfully – for a particularly incisive and 'modern' expression (no. 29). Nor is there any lack of direct reminiscences, with the opening bars of no. 37, for example, replicating one of Johann Christian's favourite turns of phrase (see also no. 2):[102]

Most of the pieces were evidently intended for the keyboard, as is clear both from their overall character (note, in particular, nos 4 and 27, two hunting pieces probably written as tributes to his father) and from their technique, a technique whose virtuosity is often considerably more

97.   Eccentricities such as those found in no. 6 and in the A minor menuetto no. 10, where the first section ends in F major, are rare. No. 32, too, is extremely awkwardly written, and the listener is bound to be struck by the sudden chromaticisms of the second section – a childishly clumsy precursor of the composer's later manner.

98.   It is worth mentioning here that 27 of these pieces are in flat keys, only 9 in sharp keys; five are in minor tonalities.

99.   Only no. 22 has a full recapitulation. ◆ Abert's expectation here is unreasonable and reflects later nineteenth- and earlier twentieth-century views of 'sonata' form: full recapitulations became the norm only later.

100.   At this point, no. 21 has the sort of surprising change of harmony that is typical of the later Mozart and that is achieved here by means of a simple unison shift.

101.   The only piece that is genuinely unified is no. 1, a position that it no doubt occupies precisely because of its uniformity.

102.   It is found on three occasions in *Catone* (act 1, scenes 2 and 5, and act 3, scene 6). The role that it plays in Gluck's *Orfeo* and in both his Iphigenia operas is well known. It also occurs in the Countess's first cavatina in *Le nozze di Figaro* ('Porgi amor').

advanced than that of the 1762 sketchbook.[103] Conversely, Alberti basses are as rare here as they were there.[104] Other pieces, however, go beyond the keyboard in their scope: no. 7 seems to have been written for the organ, while nos 29 and 35[105] appear to be sketches for symphonic andantes or, in the case of no. 28, for an orchestral minuet.

In short, this sketchbook, which has survived only by a stroke of good fortune, provides us with the most remarkable evidence of Mozart's first period. Here we see the boy feeling his way towards the most varied forms and styles and assimilating older and newer impressions; here and there we also find portents of the later composer, foremost among which is the tendency to allow himself to be carried along on the floodtide of his own ideas. In general, however, these pieces are far from revealing a 'prodigy of Nature': while the boy is occasionally successful, especially when he remains within the bounds of his childlike talent, he no less clearly remains an apprentice to his profession and, in some case, no more than a rank amateur.

The Mozarts left London on 24 July 1765 and, after spending a day at Canterbury, stayed for the rest of the month at Bourne Place, the country seat of Sir Horace Mann.[106] Princess Caroline of Nassau-Weilburg was particularly keen to hear the children and so, in response to repeated entreaties from the Dutch ambassador, Leopold decided to go to The Hague, even though he had not been planning to do so.[107] It was presumably to justify his long absence that he stressed the urgency of this invitation: his leave of absence had long since expired and he had already received repeated reminders to hurry back to Salzburg, whereas he himself was concerned only to carry through with God's help the enterprise that he had undertaken in God's name. 'I hope everything will turn out well, we're nearly there', he wrote. 'God won't abandon an honest German.'[108] On 1 August the Mozarts crossed to Calais, a journey which, with a favourable wind, took them three and a half hours, and from there they travelled to Dunkerque, where they visited the sights, before continuing their journey to Lille. Here father and son fell ill and were obliged to rest for four weeks. They had still not fully recovered when they left for Ghent, where Wolfgang played on the large new organ in the Church of the Bernardines. In Antwerp he played on the cathedral organ. From here they travelled via Rotterdam to The Hague, arriving on 11 September and taking rooms at the 'Ville de Paris', a third-rate tavern much frequented by artists. They were well received by the Prince of Orange and his sister, Princess Caroline.[109] By the 20th the *Leydse Courant* had already reported on the boy's presence in the town and his successful appearance at the governor's court. His first public concert was on 30 September. Here, too, it was announced in advance that 'all the overtures [that is, symphonies] will be from the hand of this young composer', and music lovers were invited to 'confront him with any music at will, and he will play everything at sight'.[110] The orchestra was made up of local musicians, many of whom figure

103. See, in particular, no. 14. ◆ See n. 96 above.
104. See the fragmentary no. 38 with its crossing of hands. Here Mozart probably had in mind the andante from his father's third sonata, which is in the same key. Wyzewa and Saint-Foix (*Wolfgang Amédée Mozart*, i.135) ascribe to Bach this custom of repeating the same phrase in both hands, but there are already several prototypes in the 1762 exercise book.
105. Heuß, '[Review]', believes that no. 35 is a transcription of a work by another composer, but his reasoning is unconvincing. ◆ NMA IX/27/1, XXV, similarly sees no reason to think no. 35 may be a transcription of a work by another composer.
106. ◆ At Canterbury, Mozart may have given a public concert. See Roscoe, 'Two 18th-century non-events', 18.
107. In his first letter from The Hague (*Briefe*, i.200 (letter of 19 Sept. 1765)), Leopold announces that he was intending to return home via Milan and Venice, an indication of the care with which he planned his journeys.
108. *Briefe*, i.190 (letter of 9 July 1765).
109. A detailed account of Mozart's stay in the Netherlands may be found in Scheurleer's excellent study, *Mozart's verblijf in Nederland*.
110. The announcement in the *'s-Gravenhaegse Vrijdagse Courant* reads: 'Met permissie zal de Heer *Mozart*, Musiek Meester van den Prins Bisschop van *Saltzburg*, de eer hebben op Maentag den 30 September 1765, in de Zael van den Ouden Doelen in's Hage een *Groot Concert* te geeven, in het welke zyn Zoon, oud maar 8 Jaeren en 3 Maenden, beneevens zyn Dogter, oud 14 Jaeren, Concerten op het Clavecimbael zullen executeeren. Alle de ouvertüres zullen zyn von de Compositie van dien jonge Componist

in Leopold's list of people they met. The conductor was Christian Ernst Graf or Graaf, who was born in Rudolstadt in 1723 and who wrote an aria for the governor's installation on which Mozart composed a set of variations K24.[111] On 12 September Nannerl had succumbed to a serious illness that confined her to her bed for several weeks, during which time she became delirious, with the result that on 21 October she was given extreme unction. 'Anyone listening to the conversation that the three of us – my wife, myself and my daughter – had on many an evening, when we convinced her of the vanity of this world and of the happy death of children, would not have done so with dry eyes, while Wolfgangl amused himself with his music in the other room.'[112] They also arranged for masses to be said for Nannerl in Salzburg. One Sunday, when her condition was giving especial cause for concern, Leopold read the Gospel '*Domine, descende.* Come, Lord! before my daughter dies.' Princess Caroline had sent her own private physician, Thomas Schwencke,[113] and on this particular Sunday he began a new course of treatment that proved so successful that Leopold had every reason to hope that Nannerl would soon be fully recovered, a recovery reinforced by that Sunday's Gospel reading: 'Thy daughter slept: thy faith hath helped thee.' No sooner had Leopold got over this fear, however, than Wolfgang developed a fever, subjecting Leopold to an even more severe trial. He, too, was ill for several weeks, during which time he was nursed by a certain Padre Vincenzo Castiglione, who had practised medicine in England and the Netherlands for thirty years and who, at Leopold's suggestion, now resolved to return to his native Italy as a cleric. In spite of his illness, Wolfgang remained mentally alert and a board had to be placed over his bed for him to write on. Even when he had virtually no strength in his tiny hands, it was only with difficulty that he could be prevented from writing and playing. From January 1766 dates the soprano aria *Conservati fedele* K23,[114] a setting of an aria from Metastasio's *Artaserse* that Mozart wrote for the princess. His second concert took place on 22 January and was advertised in the same way as the first one. It emerges from the announcement that the family had in the meantime moved to another address. By the end of January they were in Amsterdam, where they remained for four weeks and where Wolfgang gave two concerts made up entirely of instrumental music of his own composition. The first was on 29 January 1766 and was advertised in the *Amsterdamsche Dingsdagsche Courant* and the *Haerlemse Courant*,[115] while the second took place on 26 February.

die nooyt zien weerga gevonden hebbende, de goed-keuring van de Hoven van *Weenen, Versailles* en *London* heeft weggedraagen. Die Liefhebbers kunnen na hun plaisir hem Musiek vorleggen, hy zal het zelve voor de vuyst speelen. Jeder billet vor een Persoon is 3 Guldens, en voor een Heer en Dame f. 5. 5. 0. De Entree-Billetten worden uytgegeven by den Heer *Mozart*, Logeerende op den Hoek van de Burgwal, alwaar de *Stadt Parys* uithangt, als mede in den Ouden Doelen' [*Dokumente*, 49–50, *Documentary Biography*, 49–50].

111. ◆ The violinist and composer Christian Ernst Graf (or Graaf) (1723–1804) was composer to the Dutch court from 1757 or 1758.

112. *Briefe*, i.206 (letter of 5 November 1765).

113. Schwencke was director of the Anatomical Theatre and personal physician to the governor; see Scheuleer, *Mozart's verblijf in Nederland*, 76 (Deiters's note).

114. ◆ In fact, K23 was composed at The Hague in October 1765 (cf. the dated autograph in the Bibliothèque nationale, Paris). Abert's dating derives from a copy by Leopold Mozart, now in the Bayerische Staatsbibliothek, Munich. The Munich manuscript transmits a revised version of the aria.

115. The announcement in the *Amsterdamsche Dingsdagsche Courant* and the *Haerlemse Courant* ran as follows: 'Le Sr. *Mozart*, Maître de Chapelle du Prince Archevêque de Saltzbourg, aura l'honneur de donner Mercredi le 29. Janvier 1766 un grand Concert, à la Salle du Manege à Amsterdam, dans lequel son Fils, âgé de 8 ans et 11 mois, et sa Fille, âgée de 14 ans exécuteront des Concerts sur le Clavecin. Toutes les Ouvertures seront de la Composition de ce petit compositeur, qui, n'ayant jamais trouvé son égal, a fait l'Admiration des Cours de Vienne, Versailles et Londres. Les amateurs pourront à leur gré, présenter de la Musique; il exécutera tout à Livre ouvert. Le Prix par Personne est f. 2. On distribuera les Billets chez J. J. Hummel, Marchand de Musique sur le Vygendam. Les Mrs. auront la bonté de se pourvoir des billets, parce qu'on ne recevra point d'Argent à la Porte'. The announcement was repeated on 25 and 28 January; on the final occasion, it was announced that tickets were to be had from 'Sr. Mozart, qui loge au Lion d'Or dans la Warmoestraat' and that 'N.B. Ils joueront sur un clavecin à quatre mains'. The Mozarts must have arrived in Amsterdam between the two days mentioned [*Dokumente*, 50, *Documentary Biography*, 51].

According to the preliminary announcement for the second concert: 'Ces deux Enfants Exécuteront non Seulement des Concerts sur différents clavecins, mais aussi sur le même à 4 Mains, et le Fils jouera à la Fin sur l'Orgue de ses Propres Caprices, des Fugues et d'Autres Pièces de la Musique la plus profonde.'[116] As evidence of the claim that the concerts would include only instrumental music of Wolfgang's own composition we may cite the three-movement symphony in B flat major K22 that had been completed in The Hague. Although all public entertainments were banned during Lent, these concerts were allowed to go ahead as 'the dissemination of these children's miraculous gifts served to praise God', a justification that struck the strict Catholic in Leopold as devout and well-considered, for all that the decision emanated from members of the Reformed Church.[117]

At this juncture the Mozarts were summoned back to The Hague for the festivities marking the installation of the Prince of Orange, who had attained to his majority on 8 March 1766. Both Leopold and Nannerl state that the date was 11 March, but this was presumably the day on which they themselves were received at court.[118] Wolfgang had been asked to write six sonatas for harpsichord and violin for Princess Caroline, and these were duly engraved with a dedication (K26–31).[119] He also had to write several arias for the princess, together with other 'trifles' that were printed at this time and that include a set of keyboard variations on an aria written for the celebrations accompanying the prince's installation (K24) and another on a melody that was 'sung, played and whistled by everyone in Holland' (K25). This last-named piece was a set of variations on the old Dutch song (and the world's oldest known national anthem) *Wilhelmus van Nassouwe*, the words of which are ascribed to the Dutch writer and statesman Philip Marnix van St Aldegonde. The tune was first published in Melchior Franck's *Opusculum etlicher newer und alter Reuterliedlein* in 1603, thereafter in Adriaen Valerius's *Neder-landtsche gedenck-clanck* of 1626.[120] This song has been performed at every patriotic celebration in Holland since then,[121] and was also heard on the occasion of the present installation.[122] For a concert held at the same time Mozart wrote a quodlibet, a type of orchestral piece particularly popular in southern Germany at this date and a precursor of today's potpourri. A compilation of various well-known melodies, each wittily contrasted with its neighbours and appropriately orchestrated, it ended with a fugue on *Wilhelmus van Nassouwe*. Mozart described the result as a *Galimathias musicum*, and Leopold entered it in the catalogue of his son's compositions that he kept until 1768. It survives in two versions, the relationship between which has yet to be satisfactorily explained.[123] Nor have all the tunes been

116. The same advertisement announces that the sonatas for keyboard and violin opp. 1–3 could also be bought at Hummel's. ◆ *Dokumente*, 51, *Documentary Biography*, 52.
117. Scheurleer, *Mozart's verblijf en Nederland*, 94, found no evidence in the Amsterdam archives that Mozart had been granted a special favour. He also draws attention to the fact that two other artists had given concerts the previous day.
118. A detailed account of the festivities and of the 'unique illuminations' mentioned by Leopold may be found in Scheurleer, *Mozart's verblijf en Nederland*, 103–4.
119. ◆ Mozart's dedication is published in Eisen, *Dokumente: Addenda*, 7–8, Eisen, *New Mozart Documents*, 11–12.
120. See Erk and Böhme, *Deutscher Liederhort*, ii.106ff. and Bohn, *Die Nationalhymnen der europäischen Völker*, 16–17. Wolfgang was already familiar with German variants of this song.
121. See *Matthesons Mithridat wider den Gift einer welschen Satyre*, 162ff.
122. The six sonatas written at The Hague (K26–31) were advertised by the *'s-Gravenhaegse Vrijdagse Courant* on 16 March 1766. The variations K24 were titled: *Een Nederduitsch Air op de Installatie van Z. D. H. Willem den V Prinz von Oranje etc. etc. etc. door C. E. Graaf in musiek gebragt, en door den beroemden jongen Compositeur J. G. W. Mozart, oud 9 Jaaren, mit konstige Variatien vermeerdert, à 12 stuivers*. The variations K25 were advertised as follows: *Het bekende Airtje Wilhelmus von Nassau etc., gevarieért voor't Clavier door gemelden jongen Mozart, à 6 stuivers* [*Dokumente*, 51–2, *Documentary Biography*, 52–3].
123. The autograph score in the possession of Daniel François Scheurleer in The Hague contains only ten movements, which are reproduced in AMA XXIV/24, no. 12, together with Leopold's additions and corrections. Orchestral parts have survived in the collection of Charles Malherbe in Paris (formerly in the possession of Monsieur Cathelineau) that are in the hand of neither Leopold nor Wolfgang: here the movements are not only in a different order, but some are omitted and four new ones have been

identified. The opening is based on a well-known quotation from Handel, which Mozart develops at length in the manner of a festive French overture. But instead of the expected allegro, the harpsichordist now steps forward and regales his listeners with a delightful little piece in the style of the Hussar dances and related tunes that were extremely popular in German manuscript collections of this period. A brutal orchestral fermata is followed by a manneristic minuet reminiscent of the Gesellschaftsmusik of the time. The obligatory trio begins by striking a sullen note (it is cast as an adagio in D minor), followed by a tempestuous pounding and a few expectant chords, after which the German folksong *Ich wollt es wäre Nacht* suddenly enters on the horns, suggesting that we are dealing with some nocturnal amorous escapade;[124] in the following adagio the spurned lover duly disappears in the opposite direction, his tail between his legs. The following group of movements introduces us to a rustic celebration, with Wolfgang evidently recalling his father's *Peasants' Wedding*, just as there are clear reminiscences of the latter's *Sinfonia pastorale* in the movement in G major. With the allegretto, village musicians enter, to be followed in turn by another clodhopping dance with drone basses, raised fourth[125] and a Bavarian folk tune still popular to this day, after which the music grows more subdued, and the basses strike up the song *Wilhelmus van Nassouwe* as the subject of the final fugue. The whole piece was particularly dear to Leopold's heart and, in consequence, there is little doubt that he himself played no little part in its composition. It is important for showing that the impressions left by the family's recent travels were still not strong enough to sever the links that bound them to autochthonous German folk music.

Leopold, too, was both flattered and honoured at this time by a Dutch translation of his violin tutor, which was presented to him in the course of the celebrations marking the prince's installation.[126] The presentation was made by the publisher in the company of the Haarlem organist, who invited Wolfgang to play on his famous instrument, an invitation that he took up the following day.

The Mozarts remained in The Hague for a further five weeks after the celebrations were over, and the children performed at court on several occasions during this period. Following their

---

added (a molto allegro in D major, an andante in D minor, an allegro in D major and a presto in D major). Both Scheurleer and Deiters (i.53–4) believe that this is the version that Mozart himself regarded as definitive. But Wyzewa and Saint-Foix (*Wolfgang Amédée Mozart*, i.158) point out – quite rightly, in my view – that in this version the opening movement is in a different key from the final fugue. This runs counter to traditional practice in quodlibets: even large-scale multi-movement examples of the *Tafelkonfekt* ultimately return to the key of their opening movement. It seems to me that the key sequence is carefully calculated in Mozart's original version, inasmuch as it leads gradually from flat keys to sharp keys. It is of some interest in this context that the Malherbe Collection includes not only the orchestral parts already mentioned but also the autograph full score of a symphony in D major with the note 'Composed in Milan in 1770'. It comprises three of the movements contained in the parts, together with a new menuetto and bears the same burlesque stamp as the *Galimathias*, its similarities even extending to individual solo instruments. It is by no means out of the question, therefore, that the version that survives in full score was the original, intended for performance in the Netherlands, and that the extended version represented by the surviving orchestral parts was the basis of a later performance in Milan. Italian audiences were less familiar with German quodlibets and their jokes, and it is entirely possible that Mozart hoped to appeal to them with a parody of what was the more familiar form of the symphony; see Wyzewa and Saint-Foix, *Wolfgang Amédée Mozart*, i.158 and 291. ✦ The source situation for the *Galimathias musicum* is clearer now than it was in Abert's day. The Malherbe and Scheurleer sources are partly autograph sketches now in the Bibliothèque nationale, Paris (shelfmark Ms. 242), and the Koninklijke Bibliotheek, The Hague (shelfmark 4J41), respectively. A set of orchestral parts, used by the Mozarts to perform the work in Donaueschingen, survives in the Universitätsbibliothek Karlsruhe (shelfmark D-DO Mus. Ms. 1403). The 'symphony' described by Abert is now taken to be nos 1–4 of K32.

124. See Erk and Böhme, *Deutscher Liederhort*, ii.618–19. Joseph Haydn, too, used this tune as the basis of his capriccio for keyboard; see Carl Ferdinand Pohl, *Joseph Haydn*, ii.324.

125. In this, too, Leopold had anticipated Wolfgang.

126. Leopold Mozart, *Grondig Onderwys in het behandelen der Violin*, 4. The full announcement is reproduced in Scheurleer, *Mozart's verblijf in Nederland*, 120. Here we read 'der Viool' instead of 'der Violin'. The deluxe edition that was handed over to the governor is now in the Royal Library in The Hague. According to Scheurleer, it was in mid-March that Mozart played on the Haarlem organ. ✦ It is now thought Mozart's performance took place in early April; see Eibl, *Wolfgang Amadeus Mozart: Chronik eines Lebens*, 27.

departure, they gave further concerts in Amsterdam on 16 April and in Utrecht a few days after that. (This later concert is confirmed by the minutes of the local collegium musicum for the 18th.[127]) They then continued their journey to Paris, stopping off in Mechlin to call on their old friend Archbishop Johann Heinrich, Count of Frankenberg, and arriving in the French capital on 10 May.[128] Here they stayed at rooms provided by Grimm, who reports that both Nannerl and, more especially, Wolfgang had made remarkable progress in the intervening months, but that audiences more interested in the miracle of such precocious virtuosity than in the incomparably more important development of an exceptional genius now seemed less inclined to get excited than they had done on the earlier occasion. Even so, they had to perform at Versailles on several occasions, and the Princess of Orléans – later the Duchess of Condé – deemed it an honour to present Wolfgang with a brief rondo of her own composition for keyboard and violin.[129] Here, too, they received a visit from Crown Prince Karl Wilhelm Ferdinand of Brunswick – the Brunswick Achilles, as Winckelmann called him,[130] not least as a result of the laurels that he had garnered during the Seven Years' War. 'He is a very pleasant, handsome and friendly gentleman', wrote Leopold. 'On entering the room he asked me whether I was the author of the book on the violin.'[131] According to Burney, he was a man of 'taste and discernment' and could play the violin so well that a professional musician could make his fortune from it.[132] He is reported to have said that many Kapellmeisters would die before learning all that Wolfgang was already capable of achieving, and, indeed, the boy emerged triumphant, or at least with credit, from various contests with the most distinguished organists and harpsichordists, including tests of his powers of improvisation. On 12 June he wrote a brief Kyrie for four-part chorus and strings K33. Based on a French song tune, it shows the boy once again swimming with the tide of French music.

They left Paris on 9 July and, at the invitation of the Prince of Condé, made their way to Dijon, where the Burgundian Estates were currently in session,[133] and from where they travelled to Lyons. Here they stayed for four weeks and met a merchant by the name of Meuricoffre, who on several occasions had to entertain Mozart by singing an Italian song with his spectacles perched on the tip of his nose. In Geneva, where they found the town in a state of unrest, they remained for three weeks; and in Lausanne they were obliged to remain for five days at the insistence of the local nobility, especially Prince Ludwig of Württemberg (the brother of Duke Karl Eugen), who proved particularly welcoming.[134] From here they moved on to Berne, where they stayed for a week, and thence to Zurich, where they remained from 19 September to 3 October.[135] Here they spent an

127. 'Monsr. Mozart Virtuoso, het Collegie verzogt hebbende om't gebruik van het orchest en instrumenten, is zulks naa deliberatie hem op den ouden voet en conditien geaccordeert' [Dokumente, 52–3, Documentary Biography, 54]. The concert took place on 21 April.

128. According to Marianne, it was the end of April; see Nottebohm, Mozartiana, 101; but Leopold's travel diary gives 10 May as the date; see Schurig, Leopold Mozarts Reise-Aufzeichnungen, 47.

129. The piece is reproduced in Nissen, Biographie W. A. Mozarts, 114–16; see also Nottebohm, Mozartiana, 118.

130. Winckelmanns Briefe, iii.95, 98 and 104; see also Goethe, Briefe an Frau von Stein, ii.278–80. ◆ This visit took place on 26 May 1766; see Eisen, Dokumente: Addenda, 9, New Mozart Documents, 12–13.

131. Briefe, i.224 (letter of 7 June 1766).

132. Burney, Carl Burney's Tagebuch seiner Musikalischen Reisen, iii.258. ◆ The second half of this sentence is not by Burney but was added by his German translator; it is not found in The Present State of Music in Germany, ii.322.

133. Poisot, Lecture sur Mozart à propos du 116e anniversaire de la naissance de ce maître.

134. According to Nannerl, they remained for eight days; see Nottebohm, Mozartiana, 101.

135. ◆ Some of Abert's dates are questionable. As far as we know, the Mozarts were in Geneva from 20 August to about 10 September, Lausanne from 11 to 16 September, Berne from 18 to about 26 September and Zurich from about 28 September to 3 October; see Eisen, New Mozart Documents, 16. In addition to the concerts at Zurich and Donaueschingen mentioned by Abert, the Mozarts also performed at Dijon on 18 July, at Lyons on 13 August (at which an apparently lost work by Bernard de Bury, not mentioned in Grove, L'acte d'Hilas was also given; cf. Abert's reference to de Bury above), and at the Munich court on 22 November. His works from this time include lost solos for flute composed at Lausanne (K33a) and lost solos for violoncello composed at Donaueschingen (K33b). Documents concerning the return trip to Salzburg are reproduced in Dokumente, 56–65

enjoyable time with the Geßner family, so that it was with heavy hearts that they left. Among the various books that they were given as souvenirs of their stay were Salomon Geßner's collected works, which their author inscribed as follows:

> Take, most valued friends, this present with the same friendship with which I give it to you, and may it be worthy of keeping my memory ever alive with you! Continue long to enjoy, honourable parents, the fairest fruits of education in the happiness of your children: may they be as happy as their merits are extraordinary. At the tenderest age they are the pride of the nation and the admiration of the world. Fortunate parents! fortunate children! Do not, any of you, ever forget the friend whose high regard and love for you will remain as lively all his life as it is today.
>
> Zurich, 3 October 1766   Salomo Geßner[136]

They also appeared in public in Zurich at a concert organized by the local collegium musicum, at which orchestral works were performed.[137]

They continued their journey via Winterthur and Schaffhausen, where they spent a pleasant four days. In Donaueschingen, where they were already expected, they were received by Prince Joseph Wenzeslaus's director of music, Franz Anton Martelli. They remained in the town for twelve days, on nine of which they gave concerts between five and nine in the evening, on each occasion performing a different programme. On their departure, they were showered with gifts by the prince, who was moved to tears by the occasion. In Biberach, at the instigation of Count Fugger of Babenhausen, Mozart competed on the organ with Sixtus Bachmann, who, his senior by only two years, had already created a stir with his abilities as a musician. 'Each did his utmost to dispute the other's advantage, and the competition ended very honourably for both.'[138] They then made their way to Munich, travelling via Ulm, Günzburg, Dillingen (where they performed for the prince) and Augsburg, and arriving in the Bavarian capital on 8 November. The very next day they presented themselves at the prince elector's table. Wolfgang had to write out a piece in pencil on a theme several bars long that the prince elector sang to him and which he then played to general astonishment in the prince's private music room.[139] Mozart again fell ill in Munich, with the result that they had to turn down an invitation to visit Regensburg. The family finally arrived back in Salzburg towards the end of November 1766.[140]

---

and *Documentary Biography*, 58–67. Among others, a letter of 5 September 1766, from Voltaire's publisher Gabriel Cramer to the librarian Johann Rudolf Sinner, is worth quoting: 'We have here a young German who is strongly recommended to me from Paris, nine years of age; he plays the harpsichord as it has never been played, he reads everything at sight in a moment; he composes instantly on every possible theme; with all that he is gay, child-like, high-spirited, in short one dare not describe him for fear of not being believed' (*Dokumente*, 57, *Documentary Biography*, 59).

136.   ◆ *Dokumente*, 58, *Documentary Biography*, 60–1.

137.   ◆ See Fehr, 'Die Familie Mozart in Zürich': according to a note from its treasurer, the society was instructed 'to pay 28 pounds to a Salzburger for symphonies and serenades'; see also 'Nachrichten . . . Zürich' (*Dokument*, 65, *Documentary Biography*, 69).

138.   Bossler, *Musikalische Korrespondenz der Teutschen Filarmonischen Gesellschaft* (24 November 1790), 163–4 [*Dokumente*, 333, *Documentary Biography*, 379].

139.   ◆ On 10 November Leopold wrote to Hagenauer, 'yesterday – Sunday – we visited His Highness the Elector at table and were most graciously received. Even while we were still at table, Wolfgangl had to compose a piece while standing beside the elector, who sang the beginning or, rather, a few bars of the theme, and he then had to play it for His Highness after dinner in the music room' (*Briefe*, i.231–2). *Briefe*, v.168, identifies the work as the lost *Stabat mater* K33c. Given the circumstances, however, including the secular nature of the occasion and the court and the fact that Mozart then performed the work, it is improbable that he was asked to compose a smaller church work; more likely it was a short keyboard work.

140.   ◆ In fact, the family arrived home on 29 November, on which date Beda Hübner, librarian at St Peter's, Salzburg, noted in his diary, 'I cannot forbear to remark here also that today the world-famous Herr Leopold Mozart, deputy Kapellmeister here, with his wife and two children, a boy aged 10 and his little daughter of 13, have arrived to the solace and joy of the whole town' (*Dokumente*, 63, *Documentary Biography*, 67).

3

Works from the Grand Tour

The way in which a great artist confronts tradition in his earliest experiments in his chosen field is one of the most important pieces of evidence that we have in seeking to understand his personality – not because of the revelations that they may contain (in most cases, there are no such revelations or, if they exist at all, only on a very modest scale), but because of the critical approach that the artist consciously or unconsciously adopts to that tradition. What I mean by this is the element of selectivity: from the wealth of ambient phenomena, each artist decides from the outset to work within a specific, limited field that corresponds most closely to his character. No doubt external circumstances play an important role here, but their importance should not be overestimated, still less should they be regarded as uniquely determinative, for no artist imitates anything unless he already bears its seeds within himself: everything alien to his nature will sooner or later be discarded.

The nature and extent of such criticism varies enormously from one artist to the next. In some – and here one thinks of the young Haydn, Schubert and Schumann, for example – it is determined almost exclusively by their unchecked, youthful temperament and is the product of feeling and imagination, hence it always finds such radical expression. These are the angry young men who consciously reject tradition, appearing on the scene as innovators and, most significantly of all, proclaiming a message that is not only new but out-of-the-way, extreme and one that takes risks. The other group is represented in the main by Bach and Beethoven and knows nothing of such violence. Instead of rejecting tradition in a purely emotional way, these artists do everything in their power to assimilate it and in that way to come to terms with it. Significantly, it is the most strong-willed individuals in the history of music who have proceeded in this way, acting in accordance with a carefully worked-out plan and placing both imagination and their appreciation of art at the service of clearly articulated artistic ideals. They are not interested in saying something new at any price but, rather, in ensuring that what they have to say is expressed in the clearest and most convincing manner in terms of both form and content. The difference between these two groups emerges most clearly in their relationship to existing forms: the former group makes a conscious effort to break out of the stranglehold of these forms, while the latter attempts to refashion and adapt them from within, with the result that the break with existing traditions becomes visible only later.

The young Mozart cannot be accommodated in either of these two groups. In neither form nor expression does he appear as a conscious innovator, but nor do we find him criticizing tradition in the sense of setting himself a particular goal which he then pursues in furtherance of his own development. He was perhaps the most sensitive of all our great composers. His artistic surroundings had a far livelier influence on him, new impressions stirred him far more profoundly than is generally the case with musicians, and he never lost his basically childlike ability to treat even everyday occurrences as something new. As a result he was influenced by all the musical currents of his time and during his early years especially he resembled the young Goethe in abandoning himself to them unconditionally and without any particular plan, fluttering from flower to flower like a butterfly; only gradually did he begin to feel a desire to take conscious control over all this wealth. Intensely creative by nature, he not only assimilated new impressions but also imitated them. All the trends with which he came into contact in the course of his life, whether in the field of vocal or instrumental music, inspired him to mimic them, suggesting that his adaptability was no less astonishing than his *need* to adapt. He gave himself utterly to whichever composer happened to have made the most powerful impact on him at any given moment, sometimes getting under the skin of his model to such an extent that it is virtually impossible to distinguish the work of the pupil from that of the master. Not that this prevented him from subscribing to a new ideal only a few weeks later and giving his work an entirely new sense of direction. Very few composers were able to exert any lasting influence on the young Mozart. Of these, the most important were Schobert and Johann Christian Bach. It is difficult, therefore, to speak of a specific school in Mozart's case, as he was always the pupil of the master to whom his young soul had currently attached itself with limpet-like tenacity.

It would be dangerously misleading, however, to see in Mozart's development only the chaotic workings of chance. As with all great artists, he was able to make connections in an entirely personal way. The method adopted by philistines, whereby the nature of genius is calculated by totting up the number of identifiable 'influences', is even less appropriate here than elsewhere. Not even Mozart imitated anything if he was not already predisposed to do so, and if he felt particularly drawn to this or that composer, it was because he was unconsciously aware that the model in question reflected a particular aspect of his own character to an unusually pure extent. As a result, all the foregoing artists were of exceptional influence on him, but less because of what they gave him than because of what they roused from slumber in his soul and stirred into active life. His innermost nature demanded such confirmation of his own emotional and conceptual world, it sought to clarify its own needs in order not to be constantly at the mercy of new possibilities. Goethe once wrote, with reference to himself: 'How hard it is for a man to find himself and help himself in time, without tradition or teachings to fall back on.'[1] The young Mozart is living proof of the truth of this remark. He assimilated a vast number of different influences, but, like the young Goethe, he later instinctively rejected many of them as incompatible with his own nature. In many of his early works he was content to play the role of naïve imitator, without any claim to particular originality, with the result that he developed not in a straight line, but in fits and starts, in individual waves, just as the sea casts up a great deal of mud in producing a single pearl.

The young Mozart first entered the public arena with a set of sonatas. Twenty years earlier it would probably have been a suite, a form that was then enjoying its heyday in the hands of Johann Sebastian Bach and Handel, with the result that for a long time it overshadowed the keyboard sonata, as developed by Johann Kuhnau by analogy with the violin sonata.[2] It was, in part, the suite itself that was responsible for its change of fortune: while French composers proved to be zealous guardians of the individual types of dance and their distinctive rhythms, the Italians sought increasingly to remove these distinctive features in favour of more subjective type of expression and a more brilliant impact, so that the old allemandes, courantes, gigues and so on were finally replaced by character pieces of a more general kind, with little to recall the old dances apart from their binary

1. Letter to Charlotte von Stein (10 February 1787). See Goethe, *Goethes Briefe an Frau von Stein*, ii.278–80.
2. ◆ See Arbogast, *Stilkritische Untersuchungen zum Klavierwerk des Thomaskantors Johann Kuhnau;* for a very early account of Kuhnau and his historical importance, see Becker, 'Die Klaviersonate in Deutschland'.

form.[3] The decisive step in this direction was taken by Domenico Scarlatti (1685–1757) in his *Essercizi*. As such, he was the first significant representative of the modern spirit in eighteenth-century keyboard music.[4] Generally cast in a single movement, these pieces all reveal the hand of genius in terms of both form and content. They laid down the principles of first-movement sonata form for both the types that we find in Mozart: in the first type, the second section begins with the first subject in the dominant, before a purely melodic development section leads back to the second half of the first section, while in the second type the development section is followed by a repeat of the whole of the first section, albeit in condensed form. In Germany, too, the suite soon developed from its original dance form to one that was purely musical. In Johann Sebastian Bach's 'German Suites', for example, the old genre has been so extended and spiritualized as a result of the composer's profundity of approach that it is no longer possible to speak of dance movements; they simply show that the suite was no longer a force to be reckoned with.

It was the sonata that now came into its own, although it inevitably took a while for it to achieve a fixed and universally acknowledged form. One possible approach was pointed out by Scarlatti in his two-movement *Essercizi*, while the other, more important way ahead was suggested by the three-movement form of the Italian concerto. In turn, Bach's 'Italian Concerto' and related works opened up new prospects for the keyboard sonata.[5] Meanwhile, the old four-movement *sonata da chiesa* continued to flourish in Germany, albeit combined with all manner of suite-like features.[6] This, indeed, is the hallmark of all such transitional periods, namely, that lesser composers champion the new, while not wanting to alienate their audiences by abandoning the old. In consequence, keyboard music continued for a long time to draw its strength from curiously hybrid forms, with unadulterated suites not infrequently appearing under the title of sonatas.[7] In other cases, the piece may be cast in the three-movement form of a sonata, but, as a concession to public taste, an extra movement will be added at the end in the form of a minuet or polonaise, the two most popular dances at this time.[8] Indeed, the minuet managed to force its way into both symphonies and sonatas as the one surviving element of the older suite, appearing both as the middle movement and, even more frequently, in final position.[9] In the circumstances, it comes as no surprise to discover that the number of movements in these sonatas varies from two to half a dozen, and that they are cast not only in the forms already mentioned but in others that were still

3. ◆ Concerning the suite, see Riemann, 'Zur Geschichte der deutschen Suite'; Quittard, 'Les origines de la suite de clavecin'; Reimann, *Untersuchungen zur Formgeschichte der französischen Klaviersuite mit besonderer Berücksichtigung von Couperins Ordres*; Mollie Parker, 'Some Speculations on the French Keyboard Suites of the Seventeenth and Early Eighteenth Centuries'; and Mas, 'Influence française sur l'évolution de la suite instrumentale en Allemagne'.
4. Max Seiffert, *Geschichte der Klaviermusik*, 419ff. ◆ More recently, see Sutcliffe, *The Keyboard Sonatas of Domenico Scarlatti*.
5. See Spitta, *Johann Sebastian Bach*, ii.629–32.
6. Cf. the Kirchhoff sonata cited above.
7. This is certainly true of the sonatas of Amandus Roffeld and Christian Gottfried Krause, both of whom were content to write works with a fast or slow movement of a generalized character combined with a series of dances. But even Wagenseil's A major Sonata is no more than a complete four-movement suite harking back to the earlier style (see Sächsische Landesbibliothek, Dresden, shelfmark *Sammelband mus. c. Ch. 6 no. 6*). ◆ Christian Gottfried Krause (1719–70), a lawyer and composer of songs, is now best known for his *Von der musikalischen Poesie* (Berlin, 1752). See Marks, 'The Rhetorical Element in Musical *Sturm und Drang*: Christian Gottfried Krause's *Von der musikalischen Poesie*'.
8. This is the standpoint of the Dresden composer Christlieb Siegmund Binder, for example. In much the same way, Johan Joachim Agrell's op. 2 sonatas comprise three regular movements followed by an 'Aria', alongside minuets and polonaises. ◆ Christlieb Siegmund Binder (1723–89) was court organist at Dresden. The Swedish composer Johan Joachim Agrell (1701–65) was active at Kassel and Nuremberg; his sonatas op. 2, published in 1748, are available in a modern edition, ed. Laura Cerutti (Padua, 1994).
9. ◆ Recent research suggests that it is more probably the quick tempo finale that was a late addition to the symphony. Many early three-movement works in the genre end with a minuet.

current at this time.[10] The influence of the suite is often felt, too, in the fact that the movements are generally all in the same tonality.[11]

The first and most far-reaching attempt to bring order to this confusion was undertaken by Carl Philipp Emanuel Bach in his very first sets of printed sonatas, the 'Prussian' sonatas of 1742 and the 'Württemberg' sonatas of 1743. Not only did he establish three-movement form as the standard and, following Scarlatti's example, cast the first movement in what was to become the 'Classical' tripartite form of exposition, development and recapitulation, he also steered the sonata in a new direction in terms of its very nature and ideational content. To describe the music of this remarkable man as '*galant*', as writers are fond of doing, fails to do justice to an art in which features of the old-style Enlightenment are constantly cross-fertilized with the spirit of the *Sturm und Drang* and even of the later Romantic movement.[12] In many respects, he is, in fact, the very opposite of a *galant* composer, at least to the extent that this term is taken to imply a playful approach to ideas and feelings marked by grace on the one hand and *Empfindsamkeit* or sensibility on the other. In spite of all his modishness and the sometimes ill-defined exuberance that characterizes all such innovators, Bach in his sonatas demands far more than this from his listeners, often drawing them away over strange peaks and troughs and, through harmonic writing of often savage audacity, forcing them – true son of Bach that he is – into areas of their emotional lives that could hardly be further removed from those explored by *galant* composers such as his brother Johann Christian. In his hands, the sonata, and especially its opening movement, came to trace the course of an emotion along constant, well-ordered lines. It was not any sense of delight in a roving imagination or in the lively interplay of opposites that inspired him, but the north German appreciation of discipline and order and the quest for organic unity. As a true precursor of Haydn, he often develops his second subject from his first, but it is above all in his development sections that he establishes entirely new principles. Here earlier composers had been content to develop and juxtapose the main melodic ideas in a manner notable chiefly for its simplicity. Bach dissects these ideas, breaking them down into smaller sections, shedding new light on them and attempting to exhaust their expressive potential in every conceivable manner. In this way, and apparently taking his cue from his father, he raised thematic development to the basic principle of the modern sonata, with the result that the sonata inevitably acquired a completely different emotional content. Before, the development sections had often been no more than transitional passages leading back to the recapitulation, but now they became central to the movement as a whole, bearing the greatest emotional load within the musical argument and thereby investing the recapitulation with a completely different aspect. But, as further proof of his stylistic sensitivity, he also did everything he could to exclude all elements of the suite. The full implications of this step were not immediately recognized, with a whole number of his successors taking over the three sonata movements but continuing to append various dance movements to them, thereby demonstrating only that they had failed to grasp the true spirit of the Bach sonata. This was a spirit which, like

10. Giovanni Marco Rutini's F major sonata has an instrumental recitative as its middle movement, while Wagenseil launches his sonata no. 11 from the aforementioned collection with a French overture. ◆ Rutini (1723–97) was active at Prague, Dresden, Berlin and St Petersburg, as well as in Italy. See Torrefranca, 'Il primo maestro di W. A. Mozart (Giovanni Maria Rutini)'; Sanders, 'Early Italian prototypes of the classic sonata-rondo form'; and Pestelli, 'Mozart e Rutini'.
11. By contrast we often find a tendency to modulate to the minor and major of the same degree, a tendency also found in many suites of the period.
12. See the excellent article by Steglich, 'Karl Philipp Emanuel Bach und der Dresdner Kreuzkantor Gottfried August Homilius im Musikleben ihrer Zeit', esp. 60ff., and Jalowetz, 'Beethovens Jugendwerke in ihren melodischen Beziehungen zu Mozart, Haydn und Ph. E. Bach', esp. 419ff. For a completely different account of the genesis of the modern style, see Torrefranca, 'Le origini della sinfonia: Le sinfonie dell'imbrattacarte (G. B. Sammartini)'.

that of the operatic sinfonias of Alessandro Scarlatti, aspired to single-movement form: in some of Bach's two-movement sonatas, the slow movement has been reduced to a few transitional bars.[13] But with his new type of thematic development, which lent a firm backbone of support to Scarlatti's ternary allegros, Bach laid the foundations for the Classical sonata. In this respect, too, it was a long time before his ideas found general acceptance. Quite apart from the far higher demands placed on composers by this kind of approach, the older Italian form continued to assert its rights until well into the Classical period, triumphing above all in southern Germany and undergoing a transformation in the hands of Georg Christoph Wagenseil that brought it closer to the south German spirit. It is hardly surprising that in Vienna – the home of popular dance music – audiences were reluctant to forgo dance movements in sonatas, and, indeed, we have already seen the extent to which Wagenseil, too, sought to satisfy this demand in individual sonatas. Conversely, he achieved a more unified approach in his keyboard divertimentos opp. 1–4.[14] Two-thirds of these pieces are in three movements (fast–slow–fast), but what is so characteristic about them is the decisive role played by the minuet that has been taken over from the suite and that generally appears in final position, more rarely in central position.[15] But even the other works, which are all in four movements, acquire their four-movement form by no more than an additive process, with an andante *and* a menuetto interpolated between the two outer movements.[16]

This form clearly betrays the influence of Wagenseil's Italian contemporaries such as Baldassare Galuppi (1706–85), Giuseppe Antonio Paganelli (1710–c1763), Domenico Paradies (1707–91) and Giovanni Battista Pescetti (c1704–66), except that in their case we find much greater freedom in the order of the movements, with the minuet often replaced by movements in much freer forms, especially flowing gigues.[17]

The internal structure of the allegro movements also differs from that found in the sonatas of Carl Philipp Emanuel Bach. But Wyzewa and Saint-Foix go too far when they claim that they are all in two sections and that they merely repeat the second section of the first part.[18] Even Scarlatti had returned to the opening of his first section in individual movements in order to repeat it, albeit in condensed form; and his successors repeatedly fell back on this device,[19] with Wagenseil

13. Friedemann Bach adopted this principle in his keyboard sonatas in C and F major; see Falck, *Wilhelm Friedemann Bach*, 70ff.

14. There are four sets of six divertimentos each. The first is dated 1753 and includes a preface that is important in terms of the way in which these works should be performed. ◆ Wagenseil's divertimentos opp. 1–4 were published at Vienna in 1753, 1755, 1761 and 1763 respectively. Further, see Scholz-Michelitsch, *Georg Christoph Wagenseil* and 'Georg Christoph Wagenseil als Klavierkomponist: Eine Studie zu seinen zyklischen Soloklavierwerken'. For a thematic catalogue of his keyboard works, see Michelitsch, *Das Klavierwerk von Georg Christoph Wagenseil: Thematischer Katalog*. The divertimentos opp. 1 and 2, edited by Scholz-Michelitsch, are published in modern editions by Doblinger (Vienna, 1975 and 1996, respectively).

15. Twice we also find the form allegro – più allegro – menuetto, a form clearly influenced by Scarlatti's two-movement *Essercizi*, to which a further menuetto has been added here.

16. Only once (op. 2 no. 4) do we find a polonaise in addition to a minuet in central position; in op. 4 no. 5 the three movements are preceded by a ricercata.

17. ◆ For Baldassare Galuppi (1706–1785), see Raabe, *Galuppi als Instrumentalkomponist*; Pullman, 'A Catalog of the Keyboard Sonatas of Baldassare Galuppi (1706–1785)'; Sartori, 'Le sonate per cembalo di Baldassarre Galuppi'; and Di Mauro, 'A Stylistic Analysis of Selected Keyboard Sonatas by Baldassare Galuppi (1706–1785)'. For Giuseppe Antonio Paganelli (1710–c1763), see Schenk, *Giuseppe Antonio Paganelli*, and Eitner, 'Die Sonate. Vorstudien zur Entstehung der Form'. And for Giovanni Battista Pescetti (c1704–1766), see Degrada, 'Le sonate per cembalo e per organo di Giovanni Battista Pescetti'. More generally, see Hoffmann-Erbrecht, *Deutsche und italienische Klaviermusik zur Bachzeit* and Sanders, 'The Keyboard Sonatas of Giustini, Paradisi, and Rutini: Formal and Stylistic Innovation in Mid-Eighteenth-Century Italian Keyboard Music'. It is likely that Mozart was familiar with Paganelli's and Galuppi's sonatas, several of which were published at Nuremberg by Haffner; not only was Haffner the publisher of Leopold's keyboard sonatas, but Mozart's father also occasionally acted as his agent at the annual Salzburg book fairs.

18. Wyzewa and Saint-Foix, *Wolfgang Amédée Mozart*, i.38.

19. A readily accessible example is the second movement of Galuppi's A major sonata in Pauer's *Alte Meister*, iii.

in particular tending – like the Viennese symphonists – to include a complete recapitulation or to shorten it only slightly. The decisive difference between, on the one hand, the Italian and south German sonata and, on the other, the north German sonata, which is itself ultimately Italianate in spirit, lies in the fundamentally different way in which the ideas are developed. In contrast to Bach's logical method, the south German composers, with Wagenseil at their head, continued to subscribe to Scarlatti's principle of a free but purely melodic treatment of the ideas, while not entirely excluding the introduction of new motifs in their development sections. This more naïve south German art came to affect the sonata from a totally different quarter: what mattered now was not the depiction of a well-ordered thought process, but the imaginative interplay of changing ideas and moods. In consequence, the subject-group is now at least as important as the development section. Wagenseil was one of the first composers to experiment with three subjects, and although they are not yet as sharply distinguished from one another as was later to be the case, there is none the less a palpable difference between them: first subject, second subject (in the dominant) and concluding phrase.[20]

There is no trace in Wagenseil of Bach's harmonic musings: only the sudden shift from major to minor and back again is found here, often to a wearisome extent. It is Scarlatti's influence that we may detect both here and in the brilliance and elegance of the writing.[21] But there is another influence at work, an influence that was to prove extremely important for the sonata's subsequent development: Austrian folk music. Reminiscences of folksongs, lively march rhythms, brief expressions of delight and melodies in parallel thirds and sixths such as we have already encountered in the music of both Leopold and Wolfgang himself, all belong under this heading, as do secluded little scenes from Nature and other 'tales from the Vienna woods'.[22] In this way, the old spirit of the suite slipped back into the sonata, where it rejoined that of the minuet. The flower that was to spring from this combination of folk music and high art is clear from Joseph Haydn's example.

Needless to say, lesser talents often tried to combine north German sonata form with its Italian and south German counterpart, either using now one, now the other model in different works or even attempting to merge them together in one and the same piece. We have already seen an example of this in the case of Leopold Mozart, while Wolfgang was to encounter other examples among German composers whom he met on his visit to Paris. The first of these was Johann Gottfried Eckard,[23] a composer who took over three-movement form and thematic development from his teacher, Carl Philipp Emanuel Bach,[24] but who then proceeded to adapt the form to Parisian taste and, under Italian influence, to produce a style more pleasing and better suited to the salon. Both in its formal design and style and even in its un-Bachian use of an Alberti bass, Mozart's first sonata points to Eckard as its model. But Leopold, to whom we no doubt owe the definitive form of all these works, is clearly represented, too, with the sequencing in the develop-

20. These concluding themes are all very brief and frequently popular in tone. Harmonically speaking, they are usually based on the cadence IV–V–I.
21. Mozart also found plenty of examples of an Alberti bass in Wagenseil's works. Wyzewa and Saint-Foix (*Wolfgang Amédée Mozart*, i.37–45) are wrong to claim that it was only in Paris that Mozart encountered this device.
22. Generally this folklike tone emerges in the first subjects, while the second subjects are figurative in character.
23. See Wyzewa and Saint-Foix, *Wolfgang Amédée Mozart*, i.41–5. The most important work in this context is Eckard's *Six sonates pour le clavecin* of 1763. ◆ Concerning Johann Gottfried Eckard (1735–1809), see Reeser, *Ein Augsburger Musiker in Paris: Johann Gottfried Eckard (1735–1809)*, and Komlós, *Fortepianos and their music: Germany, Austria, and England, 1760–1800*. Eckard's complete works for keyboard are published in Reeser and Ligtelijn, *Johann Gottfried Eckard: Œuvres complètes pour le clavecin ou le piano forte*.
24. Wyzewa and Saint-Foix rightly draw attention to Bach's influence here. The note about the *Versuch* in Ernst Ludwig Gerber's *Neues historisch-biographisches Lexikon der Tonkünstler*, ii.16, is evidently an error, but none the less indicates that he had lessons with Bach.

ment section, individual figurative phrases and the way in which the andante is developed from a single motif along the lines of many symphonic movements.[25] In the final movement, by contrast, we find evidence of another composer who was soon to supplant Eckard in Mozart's estimation, Johann Schobert.

However antipathetic Schobert may have been to the Mozarts as a man, there is no doubt that, for a young artist like Wolfgang, he was the most fascinating figure that Paris had to offer at this time. He was a true child of the *Sturm und Drang*, irritable and restless, often burning with a demonic fire and, in particular, always open to new experiences. The very fact that he wrote violin sonatas, trios and quartets with obbligato keyboard and in that way laid the foundations for today's chamber music with piano is in itself sufficient to ensure him a prominent place in the history of music.[26] That Mozart added a violin part to his first sonatas, even if only *ad libitum*, is the first visible sign of Schobert's influence. Unfortunately, we still know virtually nothing about this remarkable man's education.[27] All that we can say for certain, on the basis of his works, is that he was clearly influenced by the Mannheim school. This emerges not only from their lively, revolutionary character and their delight in contrastive moods in general, but also from a whole host of specific reminiscences, with Schobert's minuets, for example, being virtually indistinguishable from Stamitz's.[28] Other features, by contrast, suggest Vienna and the influence of Wagenseil: the order of the movements, with the minuet in final or central position; the tripartite division of the subject-group; the surprising minor-key effects (especially the impassioned minor-key trios in the menuettos); and, finally, many of the allegro themes, some of which include brief, skipping motifs, while others are made up of scurrying semiquavers. There is no doubt that Schobert was introduced to his type of Viennese keyboard music in Vienna itself while on his way from Silesia to Paris. Conversely, there is no reason to assume that he made a detour to Italy.[29]

Unlike the younger members of the Mannheim school, Schobert was not the man to allow all these influences to become mere mannerisms. Instead, he developed them in such a way as to produce a living, highly personal style. Even his abilities as a pianist (indeed, as a modern piano player) enabled him to transfer the orchestral effects of the Mannheimers to the keyboard. In its rich-toned sonorities and especially the virtuosic autonomy of the writing for the left hand, his keyboard style goes far beyond anything that Mozart had previously known. But in terms of his music's expressive values, too, Schobert was the right man at this time for Paris audiences who, in the wake of Rousseau, regarded grand passions as the right of human nature. Schobert was one of the very few musicians before Mozart who can be described as 'sentimental' in the Schillerian sense of the term,[30] and this explains his immense appeal to a young composer like Mozart who was clearly a kindred spirit. In Schobert, Mozart rediscovered two basic aspects of his own character:

25. The final phrase of the opening movement, which Wyzewa and Saint-Foix argue derives from Eckard, occurs at the very same point in Leopold's A major trio (Max Seiffert, *Leopold Mozart: Ausgewählte Werke*, 58) and was no doubt common property at this period. By contrast, there is a surprising turn of phrase in bars 5–8 of the menuetto that clearly recalls Stamitz and that is the first such reminiscence in Mozart's works.
26. Among his most important predecessors are Johann Sebastian Bach's sonatas for violin, gamba and flute with keyboard obbligato and Rameau's *Pièces de clavecin*, but Schobert differs from all these works not only in terms of his more modern style, but also, and above all, through the dominant role of the keyboard, although one cannot, of course, go so far as to treat the string instruments merely as an *ad libitum* addition, as we can in the case of Mozart's Paris sonatas; see Riemann, *Johann Schobert: Ausgewählte Werke* VIII–IX.
27. ◆ Johann Schobert's early history remains largely unknown; born around 1735, he was active in Paris from 1760 or 1761. He died in 1767.
28. Riemann, *Johann Schobert: Ausgewählte Werke*, XV.
29. Wyzewa and Saint-Foix, *Wolfgang Amédée Mozart*, i.73.
30. I am thinking here only of the sudden shifts of mood within individual themes. The use of contrast was, of course, familiar to the older generation of composers, although such contrasts were differently treated here in fast and slow movements.

the pronounced emotionalism that inspired broad cantabile themes even in his allegros and the tendency to include sudden, unexpected outbursts of passion. Take, for example, the cantabile themes in Schobert's two piano quartets in E flat major.[31] For the demonic aspect, conversely, Schobert's development sections offered Mozart examples aplenty. When set beside Carl Philipp Emanuel Bach's art of thematic transformation, they still seem relatively old-fashioned and, indeed, often introduce completely new material. On the other hand, we frequently find here outbursts of savage passion that are in blatant contrast to the customary practices found in Gesellschaftsmusik of this order. A striking example of this is the D minor sonata,[32] in which the development section begins without any warning and consists solely of dark harmonies gliding into and out of each other, with razor-sharp *sforzato* accents and extraordinarily low bass notes, before being swept away, just as surprisingly, by a surly *unisono*. In this way, Schobert created a completely new type of development section that could be described as fantasia-like in contrast to the logical development of ideas found in Carl Philipp Emanuel Bach. Its principal characteristic is an imaginatively agitated harmonic style that glides from key to key through a series of often daring harmonic sequential curves, more improvised than actually worked out, but immediately gripping in its emotional expressivity and very often of great virtuosity and brilliance. It is no wonder that minor tonalities play a decisive role here and entirely logical – from a psychological point of view, too – that the recapitulation should likewise be affected by this. This Schobertian type of development section turned out to be tremendously important for Mozart and is repeatedly found even during his later period, when he had in general swung round to the type of approach represented by Bach and Haydn. And Schobert's chromatic writing, too, occasionally assumes the same curiously dour and impassioned tone as it later did with Mozart, a tone so different from the lachrymosity of the earlier period. Even his figural writing betrays Schobert's desire to make his language more expressive. Passages that would earlier have run as follows

now acquire the following form:[33]

In this and the following passage[34]

the affinity with Mozart is particularly clear.[35]

---

31. Riemann, *Johann Schobert: Ausgewählte Werke*, 83 and 94.

32. Riemann, *Johann Schobert: Ausgewählte Werke*, 36–7.

33. Sonata op. 20 no. 3, first movement; see Wyzewa and Saint-Foix, *Wolfgang Amédée Mozart*, i.114.

34. Riemann, *Johann Schobert: Ausgewählte Werke*, 48.

35. ◆ Further concerning Schobert and his influence on Mozart, see Irving, 'Johann Schobert and Mozart's early sonatas'; David, *Johann Schobert als Sonatenkomponist*; Turrentine, 'Johann Schobert and French Clavier Music from 1700 to the Revolution'; and Hunkemöller, *W. A. Mozarts frühe Sonaten für Violine und Klavier. Untersuchungen zur Gattungsgeschichte im 18. Jahrhundert*. For a comprehensive account of the eighteenth-century keyboard sonata, with detailed descriptions of works by the composers mentioned here as well as many others, see William S. Newman, *The Sonata in the Baroque Era* and *The Sonata in the Classic Era*.

Not all of Schobert's works are on the same high level, of course, and, for all his genius, he failed to achieve a true distillation of his talents. But what Mozart saw in him was enough to draw him completely under his spell. This is clear even from the nod of appreciation that we find in the first subject of the final movement of his first sonata.[36] But it is the sonatas in D major and G major K7 and K9 that are most powerfully affected by Schobert's spirit. The development sections in the first movements of both these works contain remarkable outbursts of Schobertian passion,[37] expressed with the means already described, with especially stark contrasts within the narrowest possible confines in the andante from the G major sonata.[38] The progressive technique, in which both hands are equally employed, is also Schobertian, as is the passionately dark tone of the trios from the menuettos,[39] all but one of which (K6) follow Wagenseil's example and are in minor keys. The menuettos themselves reveal a pronounced cantabile element that we noted in the 1764 exercise book and that is no doubt similarly derived from Schobert. With its popular melody embedded in a tendril-like growth of trills and triplets, the G major sonata is an especially fine example of this.[40]

In spite of all these borrowings from Eckard and Schobert, these sonatas clearly reveal Mozart's own hand. Yet not all the points that emerge in this way are to his credit: here one thinks of the tendency in the first two sonatas simply to juxtapose two- and four-bar periods, a tendency that betrays the beginner;[41] the cadences that destroy all sense of development; the chains of sequences that recall his father's example; and, once again, the sheer profligacy of the themes. The first movement of the D major sonata, for example, has no fewer than five subjects, instead of the usual three, even going so far as to add a sixth in the development section; indeed, even within the narrow confines of a minuet we sometimes find new and sharply contrastive ideas in its second section (K7 and K8). That this tendency was deeply rooted in Mozart's nature has already been emphasized. On the whole, however, the young Mozart already reveals himself as a perfect gentleman able to move with confidence in polite society, lively, gallant and full of youthful high spirits. Indeed, he is already in sufficiently fluent command of the language spoken in these social circles that one almost overlooks the absence of genuinely childlike features as found in his exercise book. But there are other aspects of his character that emerge clearly, notably the remarkably insistent emotions of an overflowing heart as found, for example, in the G major adagio from K7. With its mounting sense of yearning, its dreamily pulsating fifth in the tenor,[42] its anguished

36. See the thematic catalogue in Riemann, *Johann Schobert: Ausgewählte Werke*, XXI, no. 9.
37. In K9 Mozart even delights in beginning the recapitulation, like Schobert, in the minor, only for this to turn out to be a false alarm. Wyzewa and Saint-Foix (*Wolfgang Amédée Mozart*, i.84) are probably right to suspect Leopold's influence in this belated return to conformity.
38. With the unison writing and rumbling trill in the third bar of the consequent phrase, we find an outburst of pent-up emotion of a kind not encountered in Schobert but which already looks forward to the later Mozart. Also worth noting here is the way in which for the first time in his career Mozart has included precise dynamic markings. Mention should finally be made of the unexpected entry of the chromatic sobbing motif in bar 18ff. of the second section.
39. Like many of Schobert's pieces, the trio from K9 consists merely of a series of harmonies, without any underlying melodic idea.
40. Wyzewa and Saint-Foix (*Wolfgang Amédée Mozart*, i.85) suggest that this piece is inspired by a French *ariette*, but my own feeling is that it is based on a south German folksong whose traces can be still be found in the andante from symphony no. 45 (K95) and in the variations from the A major sonata K331. Rietsch, 'Ein Sonatenthema bei Mozart', 278–80, was the first writer to draw attention to this dependency, but, somewhat surprisingly, he failed to include the present menuetto in his survey, even though it is in the same key as the original song, G major. It has to be conceded, however, that the second half of the work moves completely away from the melody of the song in question. ◆ It is questionable whether the symphony K95 is in fact by Mozart; see Eisen, 'Problems of Authenticity among Mozart's Early Symphonies'.
41. The opening movement of the C major sonata [K6] is a particularly striking example of this.
42. The prototype of this triplet movement appears to lie in a number of symphonic and concerto adagios from this period; see also no. 35 from the 1764 exercise book. The bass was one of the favourite devices of Schobert's Muse: see Riemann, *Johann Schobert: Ausgewählte Werke*, 94 and 112.

chromaticisms and the muted agitation of its syncopations,[43] it could have been written by no other composer at this time.

Formally speaking, these sonatas still hark back to the world of Wagenseil, with their allegros, andantes and menuettos and trios. The opening allegros are all in three sections and begin the recapitulation with the first subject.[44] In comparison with the keyboard part, the violin part rarely progresses beyond a few hesitant imitations and, in stark contrast to Schobert, has no independent contribution to make.

A very different aspect is revealed by the sonatas written in London and The Hague, K10–15 and K26–31. It is not, however, as though Mozart had broken completely free from his former models. Indeed, Schobert's spirit continued to leave its mark on his style right up to the end of his life, simply because the two men were kindred spirits. But the older impressions were now joined by new ones whose principal mediator was Johann Christian Bach. It was not, however, a change that took place overnight: the sonatas K10, K11 and K13 are still in three movements, while K13 and K14 additionally include complete recapitulations as found in works of the earlier period. Parisian taste is discernible in points of detail, too.[45] In other respects, however, we find far greater freedom here in terms of both the number and order of the movements: K12 and K15 are in two movements, while K14 comprises two allegros followed by a minuet, a development that shows Mozart turning his back on Wagenseil and Schobert and moving towards the Italians. There is little doubt that Leopold – his weather-eye trained, as always, on the taste of local audiences – had a hand in this development. Thoroughly Italianate is the andante from K12, the expressive cantabile melody of which suffuses the movement from beginning to end. Italianate, too, are the recapitulations of the opening movement of K10 and the final movement of K15, both of which are limited to the second subject. It is clear, moreover, from the opening bars of K15 that Mozart was now writing for Handel's adopted homeland. But the most important aspect of all is the way in which these sonatas reveal Mozart drawing progressively closer in his style of writing to the language of Johann Christian Bach.

Bach's significance for our Classical instrumental style has become clear only relatively recently.[46] That he deserves to be numbered among the Mannheim progressives is beyond doubt; but whether he should simply be regarded as a pupil of Stamitz or whether he brought with him from Italy other distinctive features of his style apart from his 'singing allegro' is still very much open to question. The Italians have always hailed him as one of their own, and not without good reason, for the works that he wrote during his years in Italy, especially his operas, show clearly the extent to which he had become Italianized. Indeed, his own natural disposition encouraged this development. He was the most mawkish and effeminate of Bach's sons, but also the most volatile and adaptable. These basic aspects of his character remained unaffected even by the spirit of

43. The syncopation is already found here in the form that was to be typical of Mozart's later rhythmical language.
44. Only the C major sonata is an exception here: not only is it in four movements, but only the second subject is repeated in the recapitulation.
45. Cf. the menuetto en carillon from K14, a playful exercise in the keyboard's highest register. Wyzewa and Saint-Foix (*Wolfgang Amédée Mozart*, i.103) also argue that in the second movement of K13 Mozart was imitating French *complaintes*. Both here and in the following second menuetto, the listener will note the way in which Mozart clings tenaciously to the minor tonality.
46. See Max Schwarz, 'Johann Christian Bach'; Riemann, *Präludien und Studien*, iii.181ff., and *Handbuch der Musikgeschichte*, ii.3 and 131. ◆ More recently, see Freeman, 'Johann Christian Bach and the Early Classical Italian Masters'. Further, see Derr, 'Composition with Modules: Intersections of Musical Parlance in Works of Mozart and J. C. Bach'. More generally, see Gärtner, *Johann Christian Bach, Mozarts Freund und Lehrmeister*. For an edition of Bach's keyboard music, see Warburton, *The Collected Works of Johann Christian Bach 1735–1782*, volume 42. The trio by Pergolesi is possibly not authentic; it is not listed in the Pergolesi worklist in *New Grove*. Riemann's edition was published by Breitkopf & Härtel (Leipzig, n.d.).

Mannheim, and while he was uncompromising in adopting the new and subjective manner (a manner for whose change of mood his Italian operas already afforded important precedents), the antitheses in his character did not allow him to avoid the highs and lows that Stamitz did, but nor did they draw him into the morass of emotionalism inhabited by Schobert. With him, everything was more mannered and more elegant, the Italianizied German in him finding expression in the preponderance of grace and elegiac sentiment over passion and deep emotion. That this implies no reproach is clear, not least, from his Mannheim quartets, all of which are entirely worthy of a pupil not only of Johann Sebastian and Carl Philipp Emanuel Bach but also of Padre Martini.

In short, Bach taught the young Mozart a modernized Italian manner that had undergone the most recent stylistic developments and that the younger composer proceeded to adopt in his keyboard and violin sonatas. Among the features that he took over were the indeterminate number and order of the movements, a tendency to vacillate between the two types of recapitulation (although from K16 onwards Mozart invariably opts for the second, incomplete type) and, finally, the introduction of new forms such as the rondo, both in its French guise (with a single subsidiary section in the minor[47]) and in its German equivalent (with several episodes[48]).

Within the movements, too, a new spirit starts to stir under Bach's influence. Bach had already brought with him from Italy the tendency to write cantabile allegro themes,[49] and this tendency finds increasing expression in the young Mozart's compositions, too,[50] from now on becoming an ever more marked feature of his fast movements. Although Mozart did not invent these cantabile allegro themes, the inspiration for which came from every conceivable quarter,[51] there is no doubt that he created a new style by drawing on them and by combining them with antithetical elements,[52] a style, moreover, that transcended anything his predecessors had achieved in terms of self-contained unity and that was ultimately rooted in his own personality.

It was in London, too, that Mozart learnt to rethink the relationship between individual ideas. The older German sonata composers – notably Carl Philipp Emanuel Bach and Wagenseil – had set little store by stark contrasts between first and second subjects, tending, rather, to treat the second subject as no more than an offshoot of the first. With Johann Christian Bach, conversely, they are sharply contrasted from the outset in keeping with the Mannheim model and also clearly separated by means of emphatic cadences. This new spirit could hardly be further removed from the manner adopted by Carl Philipp Emanuel Bach and Joseph Haydn, for both of whom unity of ideas was paramount. But it is a spirit that also left its mark on Leopold Mozart in the opening movement of his third sonata, and it is no accident that Leopold's second subject reappears in slightly modified form in the first movement of Wolfgang's C major sonata K14.

In general, Mozart's style became more fluent and elegant under Bach's influence. His quick movements, especially his rondos, are now characterized by Bach's typically lively and effervescent rhythms, whereas the sort of melodic writing found in Bach's slow movements, with their blend of Italianate sweetness and German wistfulness, is still relatively sparsely represented in these sonatas, for all that it was to accompany Mozart throughout his career as an opera composer. But it is in his six Dutch sonatas (K26–31) that Mozart comes closest to Bach's style: indeed, it has even

47. Cf. the final movement of K11, in which the second subject – related thematically to the first – is a minuet.
48. Cf. the final movement of K12; see Wyzewa and Saint-Foix (*Wolfgang Amédée Mozart*, i.110) for an account of the difference between the two types.
49. Cf. Pergolesi's well-known trio in G major in Riemann's *Collegium musicum*, no. 29, first movement.
50. Cf. the opening movements of K10, K13, K14, K28, K29 and K31.
51. Cf. also Johann Stamitz and, of particular relevance in Mozart's case, Schobert. The third of Carl Philipp Emanuel Bach's 'Prussian' sonatas in E major also contains an allegro cantabile theme.
52. Cf. K14, where the cantabile motif is reached only with the lively semiquaver passage.

proved possible to identify a specific model for them in the form of Bach's *Six sonates de clavecin* op. 5.[53]

Bach's influence thus complemented Schobert's to particularly felicitous effect. Whereas Schobert had struck a dark-toned chord in Mozart's breast, Bach reflected the more rapt and optimistic side of his nature. Of course, one did not automatically replace the other, for it is clear that, in spite of all these influences, Mozart emerges from these sonatas as a fully unified personality. Even here, the moods suddenly darken, and the first four bars of K15 reveal an abrupt change of mood underscored by the dynamic markings (*f* and *p*)[54] that remained typical of Mozart's thematic writing until the time of the 'Great' C major symphony ['Jupiter']: a powerful opening followed unexpectedly by a quiet and contemplative passage – the spirit of Mannheim given a Mozartian twist. In the rondo's episodes, too, Mozart clings tenaciously to the minor mode.[55] Yet none of the three sets of variations from this period[56] contains a single passage in the minor, even though minor variations were already commonplace at this time in the works of composers such as Eckard and Honauer.[57] There is, however, one variation in each of these three sets that stands apart from the others by dint of its attempt to explore a new aspect of the theme: in K31 it is a curiously agitated syncopated variation, in K24 and K25 one of those richly ornamented, deeply felt adagios that are also found in Mozart's later variations and that are clearly his own invention. In general, however, these variations are purely melismatic in character and rarely depart very radically from the melodic line of the theme. Not until the variations on *Wilhelmus van Nassouwe* do we find a desire to invest each variation with its own individual character and thus to enhance the expressive potential of the theme by developing it in different directions.

Nor, finally, should we forget the links that Mozart forged in England and the Netherlands with the art of his south German homeland. The *Galimathias musicum* provides the clearest evidence of the extent to which these autochthonous strains continued to resonate within him. They also appear from time to time in his sonatas. It was in the course of this detour that Mozart first encountered Gluck.[58]

Since Bach and Abel have been shown to be the models for three of the four symphonies written in London and The Hague,[59] little purpose would be served by interrupting our narrative at this

53. See Wyzewa and Saint-Foix, *Wolfgang Amédée Mozart*, i.150–51. ◆ At the time Mozart wrote these sonatas it is likely that he was acquainted with not only J. C. Bach's op. 5 but also the sonata op. 17 no. 3, an autograph copy of which was given to the Mozarts during their visit to London in 1764–5. See Eisen, 'The Mozarts' Salzburg Music Library'.

54. The rondo of K12 is particularly important from the standpoint of dynamics: note, for example, the *forte* passages that erupt in the middle of the phrase in the allegro, bars 66–8.

55. The minor-key character is further intensified in K30 by the performance marking 'poco adagio' and by the authentically Mozartian syncopation on a sustained note.

56. K24, K25 and K31, final movement.

57. Wyzewa and Saint-Foix, *Wolfgang Amédée Mozart*, i.147; conversely, there are no examples of minor-key variations in Leopold Mozart's work: see Max Seiffert, *Leopold Mozart: Ausgewählte Werke*, 30ff. ◆ Most literature on eighteenth-century keyboard variations is concerned with works by Haydn, Mozart and Beethoven. For some account of variations by other composers, see Kurt Fischer, 'C. Ph. E. Bachs Variationenwerke' and 'Zur Theorie der Variation im 18. und beginnenden 19. Jahrhundert'; Helm, 'C. P. E. Bach and the Great Chain of Variation'; Reijen, *Vergleichende Studien zur Klaviervariationstechnik von Mozart und seinen Zeitgenossen*; and Marshall, *Eighteenth-Century Keyboard Music*.

58. The theme of the rondo from K12 is identical with the second subject of the sinfonia from Gluck's *Il re pastore* of 1756; their common source was probably Wagenseil's divertimentos op. 4, i.3. In the rondo from K30 we suddenly hear a minor-key variant of the opening of the song *Der hat vergeben* from the *Augsburger Tafelkonfekt*; see the examples in Lindner, *Geschichte des deutschen Liedes*, 26.

59. See Wyzewa and Saint-Foix, *Wolfgang Amédée Mozart*, i.98–102 and 126–31, where the writers draw attention to Bach's *Six Overtures* op. 3 and to Abel's symphonies op. 7. ◆ Further, see Gersthofer, 'Mozarts frühe Sinfonien und ihre Londoner Vorbilder: Überlegungen zum Verhältnis Mozart – Abel – J. C. Bach'; Zaslaw, *Mozart's Symphonies: Text, Context, Interpretation*, 16–43; and, more generally, Gersthofer, *Mozarts frühe Sinfonien (bis 1772): Aspekte frühklassischer Sinfonik*.

point and offering a survey of the genre as a whole.[60] All Bach's stylistic peculiarities have already been described, and all of them recur here, with even Mozart's handling of the orchestra closely following this model, especially in respect of the relative lack of independence of the winds. As with Bach, so with Mozart, it is not merely their three-movement form that reveals these pieces' affinity with the Neapolitan operatic sinfonia (which at this date had only recently broken free from the complete opera), but also their whole attitude, from the triadic themes and repeated bass notes of their opening movements to their frequent Italian aria cadenzas. To this, Bach brought a more subjectively coloured thematic writing inspired by German models, a sharp contrast between first and second subjects and the use of rondo form for the final movement. All of this is found in Mozart. And yet even when we concede that he must have been helped by his father, it is impossible not to admire the way in which he not only mastered this form with as much skill as speed, but also was able to fill it out in various ways with his own world of ideas and feelings. The very first subject of K16 affords eloquent evidence of this:

A lively and energetic attack in the antecedent phrase is followed by calm and devout self-communing in the cantabile consequent phrase, which is almost three times as long. Mozart, like Faust, harboured two souls within his breast, and here we find them nestling together in the closest possible association. The opening movement of K19 is also typically Mozartian in a number of ways: note the weary minor-key syncopations that insinuate themselves into the second subject and the almost literally terrifying unison A sharp (on the weak beat of the bar) that begins the development section and induces a sense of eerily frightening gloom lasting two whole bars – a passage which is also our first example of the lapidary harmonic shifts that Mozart was later fond of using to introduce his development sections. As in the sonatas, the development sections themselves proceed along purely melodic lines, but with repeated modulations to minor tonalities, and they invariably issue into the second subject. These short-winded second subjects have a trio-like character to them and, as such, recall the sort of sinfonias – especially the buffo sinfonias – that could be heard in theatres at this time. The final rondos are the least Mozartian sections of these works. Conversely, the G minor andante from K22 is a highly significant piece, authentically Mozartian in its mixture of calmly composed seriousness and insistent despair; with the B flat major entry in bar 16 the listener would be forgiven for thinking himself transported to the world of the andante from the 'Great' G minor symphony (K550).[61] The winds, too, speak a more eloquent language here: in the andante from K16, we hear a well-known phrase from the later period on the horns:

60. ◆ Although Abert mentions only Bach and Abel as influences on Mozart's first symphonies, Wolfgang's first acquaintance with works of this sort can probably be traced back to Salzburg and the relatively little-known repertory of symphonies by his father and his contemporaries; at least some of the gestures noted by Abert as common to both Wolfgang's and Leopold's sonatas can also be found in the orchestral works. See Eisen, 'The Present State of Research on Leopold Mozart's Symphonies' and, for editions of selected works, Eisen, *Orchestral Music in Salzburg*. An account of the surviving Salzburg repertory is given in Eisen, 'The Salzburg Symphonies: A Biographical Interpretation'.

61. See Kretzschmar, *Führer durch den Konzertsaal*, i.168ff., and Schultz, *Mozarts Jugendsinfonien*.

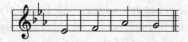

By contrast, the four-movement B flat major Symphony K17 stands completely apart from the others that make up this series. Its opening movement has no second subject and in essence is developed out of its main theme, but it makes up for this omission by having a complete recapitulation. Nor is its powerfully march-like character[62] in keeping with the theatrical note that is struck by the other works in this series. Together with the menuetto, it harks back, rather, to the Viennese serenade.[63] All in all, it seems highly unlikely that this work was written in London.[64] More probably, it dates from the later period in Vienna and was presumably finally abandoned, a suspicion that receives some support from the unfinished state of the autograph score. The menuetto is a remarkably backward-looking piece, its preoccupation with the basic motif and the thematic link between the menuetto and trio[65] both recalling Mozart's oldest works of this kind.[66]

62.   The bass line is again typical of Schobert; the theme comprises six bars, rather than four, a feature frequently found in the sonatas and derived from the Italian aria.

63.   See Schultz, *Mozarts Jugendsinfonien*, 15–16.

64.   This attribution was first called into question by Wilder, *Mozart*, 28; Wyzewa and Saint-Foix, by contrast, remain convinced that it was written in London.

65.   It is described here as Menuetto II, a description that recalls the older tradition. Such motivic links between both parts are also found in Haydn's C major symphony of *c*1764: see *Joseph Haydns Werke*, ed. Eusebius Mandyczewski, ii, no. 20. ◆ Haydn's symphony Hob. I:20 is now thought to date from before 1766, possibly as early as 1762; see Webster and Feder, *The New Grove Haydn*, 95.

66.   ◆ The stylistic anomalies of K17 are probably accounted for by the fact that it is almost certainly not by Mozart but by his father, Leopold, and dates from 1756 or earlier. Abert is also incorrect to identify an unfinished autograph score: no such document has ever existed. See Eisen, 'Contributions to a New Mozart Documentary Biography', 620–3.

4

Studies in Salzburg

Leopold Mozart had achieved all that he had set out to achieve: the tour had brought him and his children all the artistic and material rewards that he could possibly have wished for.[1] But the children now needed time to recover from the various illnesses from which they had suffered en route and that were a clear indication that there were limits to what they could do. Wolfgang in particular had proved to be of a delicate constitution and a sensitive disposition. There had been times on their travels when he burst into tears, so much did he want to return home. He had cried especially when he heard that his friend the young Cajetan Hagenauer had entered Salzburg's Benedictine monastery: he thought he would never see him again, but once he had recovered from the news, he resolved to visit him at St Peter's as soon as he returned home; they would then catch flies and play at bows and arrows together. At the same time, however, the journey had increased his youthful self-esteem. When a member of the local aristocracy confessed that he did not know how to address the boy and finally opted for the neutral 'we', Wolfgang is said to have retorted: 'I do not recall, Sir, ever having seen you anywhere else but here in Salzburg.' On the whole, however, his childlike ways remained unaffected. He continued to romp around in his room with his father's stick and to play with his favourite cat while ostensibly playing the piano. But he was also beginning to harbour grander plans: he wanted to write an opera that would be performed solely by people he knew in Salzburg. Evidence of the child's lively imagination comes from his 'Kingdom of Back', of which he himself was the ruler: his subjects consisted entirely of children on whom he lavished endless presents. He even prevailed on a servant to draw a map of the kingdom, while he himself dictated the names of its towns and cities.[2]

But his father was now more ambitious than ever and began to question whether a provincial town like Salzburg was a suitable place for his children's talents to unfold. Shortly before their return to Salzburg, he had written to Lorenz Hagenauer:

God (who has been far too good to a wicked person like me) has bestowed such talents on my children that, quite apart from my duty as a father, they alone would encourage me to sacrifice everything to their education. Every moment that I lose is lost for ever, and if ever I knew how precious time is for young people, I know it now. You know that my children are used to work: but if they were to get used to hours of idleness on the grounds that one thing gets in the way of another, my whole plan would come to grief. Habit is an iron shirt, and you yourself know

---

1. See *Historisch-Moralische Belustigungen des Geistes oder ermunternde Betrachtungen über die wunderbare Haushaltung Gottes in den neuesten Zeiten* (Hamburg, 1765), Part vii; 'XVIe discours', *Aristide ou le citoyen* (11 October 1766); and Hiller, *Wöchentliche Nachrichten und Anmerkungen die Musik betreffend*, i (25 November 1766), 174 [*Dokumente*, 46–7 and 58–63, *Documentary Biography*, 46–7, 61–5 and 67].
2. Marianne's reminiscences in Nottebohm, *Mozartiana* 137 [*Dokumente*, 426, *Documentary Biography*, 493].

how much my children and especially Wolfgangl still have to learn. But who knows what people are planning for us on our return to Salzburg? Perhaps we'll be met in such a way that we shall be only too happy to pack our bags and leave. But at least, God willing, I shall bring my children back to their native country. If they're not wanted, it won't be my fault. But people won't get them for nothing.[3]

Mozart's education is shrouded in mystery. We do not know whether he attended school on Salzburg and, if so, which school: indeed, it is by no means out of the question that the energetic Leopold, who set such store by his own erudition, taught his children himself.[4] None the less, we can gain at least a vague idea of the course that his education took. It included not only reading and writing (it is to be hoped that none of his contemporaries regarded his poor spelling as a matter for personal reproach) but also arithmetic, a discipline that seems to have given him particular pleasure.[5] That he may also have been taught history and geography is suggested by a manual found among his father's posthumous papers.[6] Languages played a preponderant role: Latin, Italian (a language indispensable for musicians of the period), French, and, if we may believe Schlosser, a little English.[7] The aim of these studies was essentially practical, and naturally the boy's various journeys were of immense benefit to him here. Conversely, there is very little evidence that Mozart read any German literature as a youth: we know only that he was in contact with Gellert, Geßner and Count Stolberg. On the other hand, it is inconceivable that he was totally cut off from literature in a university town like Salzburg and in a house as cultured as that of his father's.[8] Modern writers have a tendency to wrinkle their noses in distaste at his evident liking of Gellert and Wieland, but it must be asked what Austrian literature could have offered him by way of compensation at this time. It was presumably through Sperontes that he became acquainted in his youth with a writer such as Johann Christian Günther.[9] We shall later have more to say in a different context about other aspects of his early education, including, in particular, his knowledge of foreign literature.

That his father continued with his usual thoroughness to take responsibility for his musical education is clear, above all, from an exercise book now preserved in the Mozart Archives in Salzburg and almost certainly dating from this period.[10] The volume in question runs to

3. *Briefe*, i.232–3 (letter of 10 November 1766).
4. ◆ Almost certainly this was the case. Concerning Mozart's education generally, see Halliwell, *The Mozart Family*.
5. See Schachtner's reminiscences cited above and *Briefe*, i.339 and 349 (letters of 21 April and 19 May 1770), in which Mozart asks his sister to send him his arithmetic book.
6. *Kürtziste Universal Historie, Nach der Geographia Auf der Land-Karte zu erlernen, Von der studierenden Jugend des Bischöfflichen Lycei zu Freysing. Geschrieben von P. Anselmo Desing, Ord. S. Bened. Ensdorf Cum facultate Superiorum et Priv. Spec. Sac. Caes. Maj. Im Verlag Johann Gastl zu München und Stadt am Hof nächst Regensp. 1756.* A second volume that may come under this heading is the *Atlas des enfans* of 1760 found among Mozart's own papers at the time of his death. See Engl, 'Studien über W. A. Mozart', 36–7. ◆ Concerning Mozart's library, see *Dokumente*, 497–8 and 509–10, *Documentary Biography*, 587–9 and 601–2, as well as Konrad and Staehelin, *allzeit ein buch*.
7. Schlosser, *W. A. Mozarts Biographie*.
8. ◆ Concerning the Salzburg Benedictine University, see *Universität Salzburg 1662–1962–1972: Festschrift* and, more generally, Dopsch, *Geschichte Salzburgs: Stadt und Land*.
9. ◆ More likely it was Mozart's father who brought Günther's works to his attention; during the 1750s or 1760s Leopold composed at least three Günther settings, *Die großmüthige Gelassenheit, Bey dem Abschiede* and *Die Rangordnung. Die großmüthige Gelassenheit* and *Bey dem Abschiede* were incorrectly attributed to Wolfgang by Köchel (K149 and in connection with K150). *Die Rangordnung* is cited in connection with K150.
10. The present writer has in his possession a photographic reproduction of this volume; see also Tanejew, 'Der Inhalt des Arbeitsheftes von W. A. Mozarts eigenhändig geschriebenen Übungen', 29–39. ◆ The following needs to be read with caution. The exercise book referred to by Abert is now known to represent materials used by Mozart to teach his student Franz Jakob Freystädtler in Vienna in 1786 or 1787. As such it sheds light on neither Leopold's teaching of Mozart nor Wolfgang's deepening theoretical knowledge. It does, however, give insight into Wolfgang's teaching methods. For a facsimile, see NMA X/30/2.

eighty-two pages and is divided into four sections, each of which was separately numbered by Wolfgang.[11] In spite of claims to the contrary by Jahn and Deiters,[12] it does not contain exercises in thoroughbass, but in strict counterpoint. These exercises break off before the end of the final section on three-part counterpoint, no doubt because the Mozarts had set out on a further tour. It is clear from the volume as a whole that Leopold had now identified the main gap in his son's musical education. The individual exercises are based on the principal treatise of the time, Johann Joseph Fux's *Gradus ad Parnassum* of 1725, in Lorenz Mizler's translation (1742). (That Mizler's translation was used emerges from a reference to page 56 of the 'book' and to the intervals of augmented second and augmented and diminished third, which are not mentioned in the original.) The volume was written by father and son together, with Leopold generally beginning each new type by listing the rules and giving examples of the same, followed by a classic example that Wolfgang was then left to imitate. Wolfgang's exercises are heavily corrected and offer ample evidence of the extent to which he was still groping his way in this new field, an impression in no way diminished by the gallows humour of his marginal remark at one point: 'Sign. d'Alto, marchese Tenor, duca Basso.'

The volume contains examples of only two- and three-part counterpoint based on traditional cantus firmi taken in the main from Fux. The intervals between the contrapuntal voice and the cantus firmus are marked with figures, leading some writers to conclude, erroneously, that these are exercises in figured bass. The exercises in three-part counterpoint are written on three staves. Both types include examples of every genre up to and including the 'Contrapunctus cum ligaturis' and 'floridus'.[13]

In short, Mozart's knowledge of theory was deepened by these exercises, but was still far from complete. The results of these studies may be seen in the surviving works from this period.

The boy's services as a composer were commandeered soon after his return to Salzburg: to mark the anniversary of the archbishop's ordination on 21 December 1766 he wrote a *licenza* – a piece of music in homage of the archbishop that followed on from the actual celebrations.[14] It appears that Mozart wrote other works for the court but that these have been lost: Leopold's catalogue for this year mentions six four-part divertimentos for various instruments, six trios for two violins and cello, marches and minuets for orchestra, and fanfares for trumpets and timpani.[15]

---

11. The pages were later numbered consecutively in pencil by Nissen.

12. Jahn, *W. A. Mozart*, fourth edition, i.59.

13. Under this same heading comes a single sheet that Vincent Novello received from Mozart's widow in 1829 and that he later donated to the British Museum. It contains on four lines a figured bass set in four different ways. The accompanying melody is not included. According to Thomae ('Vier Mozart-Handschriften', 483), these lines are not in the *Gradus ad Parnassum*.

14. The description in the Salzburg court diary runs as follows: 'Lastly there was a *licenza* consisting of a recitative and aria, the music of which was composed to everyone's admiration by young Wolfgang Mozart, son of the Vice-Kapellmeister and a remarkable boy ten years of age, complete master of the harpsichord, only just arrived here from England' [*Dokumente*, 67, *Documentary Biography*, 71]. Of the two surviving pieces of this kind (K36 and K70), this will have been the first.

15. ◆ Abert's suggestion that these lost works were written for Salzburg is probably incorrect. Leopold's *Verzeichniß alles desjenigen was dieser 12jährige Knab seit seinem 7ten Jahre componiert, und in originali kann aufgezeiget werden* was presented by him to the Viennese court in late 1768 and gives no specific information concerning the divertimentos, trios and other works. Given the practice of music at the Salzburg court and the kinds of works composed by Mozart while on tour, it is more likely that they were written before the family's return to Salzburg on 29 November. In any case, Abert's description of the works is overdetermined. Leopold's list mentions '6 Divertimenti à 4. für verschiedene Instrumenten als Violin, clarino, Corno, flautotrav: fagotto, Trombone, Viola, Violoncello &c.' (K41a), which could refer to works (but only six) in a variety of scorings, not necessarily six trios for two violins and cello and six four-part divertimentos for various instruments. The fanfares for trumpets and timpani are listed together with 'Viele Stücke – für 2 Clarini – für 2 Corni – für 2 Corni di Baßetto' as K41b; the marches and minuets are K41c and 41d, respectively. For an edition of the *Verzeichniß*, see *Briefe*, i.287–9; for an attempt to sort out its references, see *Briefe*, v.207 and Zaslaw, 'Leopold Mozart's List'.

The archbishop was initially sceptical about the boy's miraculous gifts and, according to Daines Barrington, had him locked away in a room for a week, cut off from all visitors. During this time he had to write an oratorio to a given text. Wolfgang duly completed the piece, which was greeted with universal applause when it received its first public performance.

The oratorio (K35) was first performed at court on 12 March 1767 and was printed in Salzburg in 1767 with the following title-page:

The Obligation of the First and Foremost Commandment (Mark 12:30): 'And thou shalt love the Lord thy God with all thy heart, and with all thy soul, and with all thy mind, and with all thy strength.' In three Parts set forth for Consideration by J. A. W.[16]

Part I set to music by Herr Wolfgang Motzart, aged 10 years.

Part II by Herr Johann Michael Heiden, Concert Master to His Serene Highness.

Part III by Herr Anton Cajetan Adlgasser, Chamber Composer and Organist to His Serene Highness.

The action takes place in a pleasant landscape with a garden and a small wood. Singers:

A lukewarm and afterwards zealous Christian: Herr Joseph Meisner.

The Spirit of Christianity: Herr Anton Franz Spitzeder.

Worldliness: Jungfer Marie Anna Fesemayr.

Divine Mercy: Jungfer Maria Magdalena Lipp.

Divine Justice: Jungfer Marie Anna Braunhofer.

According to the introduction, it was the consideration 'that there is no more dangerous a state of mind than a lukewarm interest in the matter of salvation' that inspired the performance of a work aimed 'not only at delighting the senses but also at entertaining the mind in a profitable way'. 'In the first part, the memory and reason of the same [the lukewarm Christian] are exercised by the tireless and loving zeal of the Spirit of Christian Virtue with the assistance of Divine Mercy and Justice; in the second part reason is defeated, the will to submit is made ready and finally, in the third part, this latter is entirely freed from the fear and vacillation that still cling to it.'

The text is in verse and, in keeping with contemporary practice, is lavishly larded with Latin quotations from the Bible. As will be abundantly clear from the following examples, it is entirely at one with the prosaic and bombastic character of contemporary poetry.

Mozart's original score[17] is headed, in Leopold's hand, 'Oratorium di Wolfgango Mozart composto nel mese di Marzo 1766'. This date must be an error, as the Mozarts were then in the

---

16. According to Köchel, these initials refer to Johann Adam Wieland (1710–74), who became curate in Golling and Anthering in 1734, vicar in 1766 and rector of Friedorfing in 1767. But Hammerle (*Mozart und einige Zeitgenossen*, 6 and 18) is much more likely to be right in identifying the author as Jakob Anton Wimmer, who was born at Mühldorf in 1725 and who studied at Salzburg's Grammar School and University, before taking the name Marianus and entering the monastery of Seeon in 1744. Four years later he became a minor canon and shortly afterwards was appointed professor and prefect at the Salzburg Grammar School. From 1763 to 1769 he was prior at Seeon and, following his resignation, active at Maria Plain in Salzburg. From 1772 to 1780 he taught at Lauterbach, where he was also responsible for his young charges' spiritual welfare. He retired from this position in 1780 and returned to Seeon, where he died in 1793. He had considerable experience of music, was friendly with Leopold Mozart from an early date and, as we noted above, wrote various librettos for him. As early as 1742 he is described as 'Menander Aulicus' in a list of actors. He was the University's *comicus*. See Sattler, *Ein Mönchsleben aus der 2. Hälfte des 18. Jahrhunderts*, 135. ◆ Recent research suggests that the initials J. A. W. refer to Ignaz Anton Weiser (1701–85), mayor of Salzburg from 1772 to 1775. Many years earlier, Weiser had written the text of Leopold's cantatas *Christus verurtheilt* (by 1743) and *Christus begraben* (by 1755) as well as the oratorio *Der Mensch ein Gottesmörder* (by 1753).

17. The autograph was discovered by Ferdinand Pohl in the Royal Library at Windsor; see his article, 'Mozarts erstes dramatisches Werk', 225–33.

Netherlands. The piece was presumably begun at the end of 1766 and completed in March 1767. In the printed libretto, Wolfgang is described as '10 years old'. A second performance was given on 2 April.[18]

The score runs to 208 pages and bears the unmistakable signs of its author's age, not only in its tentative handwriting, with its numerous smudges and ink blots, but also in a number of errors in the notation and performance markings, to say nothing of the words of the arias, laboriously scrawled between the vocal line in the local orthography (Leopold himself wrote out the words of the lengthy recitatives). It was not an easy task: not only was this Mozart's first foray into the field of elevated vocal music, but he was also constrained by a demanding and longstanding tradition. It is hardly surprising, therefore, to find him occasionally casting round for existing models, which he found both in his father and in the Salzburg Kapellmeister Johann Ernst Eberlin, who had died in 1762. Of Leopold's 'oratorios', only two arias have survived,[19] but these resemble Wolfgang's not only in terms of their form, but also in their Italianate expressivity, in the care with which they attempt to capture the sense of the words and in their meaningful use of coloratura. By contrast, twelve of Eberlin's oratorios have survived in their entirety.[20] They show him to have been one of the genre's leading German representatives at this date and, at the same time, explode the myth that Salzburg was a musical backwater during these years. Eberlin was a progressive composer who sought to combine the prevailing Italian style with German elements, while simultaneously throwing his own by no means inconsiderable talent into the scales.[21] It was Eberlin who was Mozart's chief model, not only in spirit but on points of individual expressive detail and even in respect of thematic reminiscences.[22] It was Eberlin's idea to preface such a piece with a single-movement sinfonia (the elaboration of which recalls Johann Christian Bach), his, too, the careful handling of the accompanied and unaccompanied recitatives. This in itself is all the more remarkable in that, under Italian influence, Mozart later adopted an increasingly negligent approach to *secco* recitative. Here we still find that emphatically German spirit that had long been a regular feature of these movements. Mozart's declamatory style is not only outstanding in its own terms, but also reveals a genuine sympathy with the subject matter, while his harmonies generally reflect the course of the developing dialogue. Indeed, he even attempts from time to time to flesh out the individual characters. The frivolous character of Worldliness is particularly notable from this point of view. Note, for example, how dismissively he treats his enemy, Christianity:[23]

---

18. In the *Protocollum praefecturae Gymnasii Universitatis Salzburgensis* we read: '1767, 12 March, Thursday: holiday. (After dinner.) At half past six in the Hall there was sung an oratorio set to music by D. Wolfgang Mozart, aged 10 years, greatly skilled in composition.' And later: '1767, 2 April, Thursday: holiday. The music of the first oratorio repeated in Hall.' See Hammerle, *Mozart und einige Zeitgenossen*, 5–6 [*Dokumente*, 68 and 70, *Documentary Biography*, 72 and 74].

19. ◆ It is unclear to which arias Abert refers. Two oratorios by Leopold Mozart survive complete: *Der Mensch ein Gottesmörder* (1753) and the *Oratorium pro Quadragesima* (date uncertain). See Eisen, 'Mozart, Johann Georg Leopold'.

20. The autograph scores are in the Proske-Musikbibliothek at Regensburg. ◆ The source of this assertion is unclear. By present-day reckoning, ten oratorios by Eberlin survive in their entirety and one more is partially lost; see Pauly and Hintermaier, 'Eberlin'. The autographs are in the Bischöfliche Zentralbibliothek (Proske-Musikbibliothek), Regensburg.

21. See Schering, *Geschichte des Oratoriums*, 357–8. ◆ For a more recent account of the genre, see Smither, *A History of the Oratorio*, esp. volume 2: *The Oratorio in the Baroque Era*.

22. See Schering, *Geschichte des Oratoriums*, 359–60. Also worth mentioning here is the concertante trombone in the sixth aria: see Wyzewa and Saint-Foix, *Wolfgang Amédée Mozart*, i.184. In Leopold's *Litaniae Lauretanae* in E flat major, the Agnus Dei is likewise a solo with obbligato alto trombone. ◆ Leopold's litany is published in NMA X/28/3–5/1a.

23. Recitative before the aria 'Schildre einen Philosophen'.

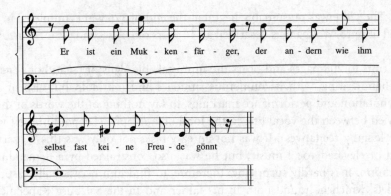

For particular high points in the text Mozart switches to accompanied recitative and here, in keeping with contemporary custom, he exaggerates to make his point, with Christianity, for example, conjuring up the following picture of the 'gaping maw of Hell', an image previously written off as *secco* recitative:

The accompanied recitative of the Christian stretching himself as he wakes from a deep sleep is realistic in the extreme:

The Christian then palpably feels all the terrors of death and the Last Judgement and even hears ghostly reminiscences of motifs from Divine Justice's previous aria (*pianissimo* violins *con sordini* and an additional fanfare on the alto trombone).[24]

The bulk of the score is made up, of course, of arias: three for tenor and four for soprano. All are cast in the older form, with a binary A-section, a B-section to different words, and a *da capo* of the A-section. The B-section tends to involve a different tempo and to have a different time-signature.[25] Only 'Schildre einen Philosophen' has no middle section, but has a change of tempo in its main section. A more modern feature is the tendency in the opening ritornellos to distinguish between the first and second subjects by means of abrupt cadences, a tendency that Mozart had picked up from Johann Christian Bach. The arias are unadulteratedly Italianate, even down to their carefully considered coloratura writing, which invariably reveals restraint and which Leopold generally retouched. It is, however, with astonishing assurance that Mozart operates within this framework, successfully creating a number of outstanding atmospheric images that make up for their lack of originality with the authenticity of their emotion. Listen, for example, to 'Manches Übel will zuweilen', with its warm and heartfelt appeal.[26] The first number, 'Mit Jammer muß ich schauen', also deserves to be mentioned here on account of the sustained note of anguish of its opening section, as does 'Hat der Schöpfer dieses Leben', which is notable for its Handelian subject. This last-named aria is sung by Worldliness, a figure remarkable for its inchoate characterization: for all his wicked worldly ways, there is almost a sense of chivalry and true style about him. Nor is he lacking in a sense of sarcasm.[27] The final trio is no more than an aria sung by each of the voices in turn, a pleasant enough piece with simple imitative writing. The orchestra, too, helps to characterize the dramatis personae: in his aria 'Jener Donnerworte', the Christian is accompanied by a

24. Later, at the mention of the 'voice', the entry of the muted strings is particularly effective.
25. In 'Erwache, erwache' it is even divided into an allegro and an adagio.
26. Mozart later reused this aria in *La finta semplice* ('Cosa ha mai la donna indosso').
27. Compare the eloquent melisma at the words 'mit betrübten Augenlichtern' in 'Schildre einen Philosophen', with the gentle humour of the brief andante section, 'Dann hast Du ein Bild getroffen', in the same aria.

concertante alto trombone as the voice of the Last Judgement, while his seducer, Worldliness, is joined by two flutes in 'Schildre einen Philosophen'. The second aria, 'Ein ergrimmter Löwe brüllet', is remarkable for its concertante winds and an independent onomatopoeic figure in the second violins, the recitative 'Wie, wer erwecket mich?' for the fact that the violas play in octaves with the violins in the Viennese tradition. Indeed, the violas are regularly divided throughout the work as a whole: in this repect, too, the boy was clearly keen to show that he was fully abreast of the times.

More or less the same picture emerges from a shorter cantata for two voices simply called *Grab-Musik* (K42). It, too, was evidently written for Lent in 1767. Cast in the form of a dialogue between the Soul (bass) and an Angel (soprano), it is an example of the older tradition of sacred dialogue. The words sound as though they may be the work of a local poet from Salzburg. The piece begins without further ado with a recitative for the Soul:

> Wo bin ich? bittrer Schmerz!
> ach jener Sitz der Liebe,
> mein Ruh, mein Trost, das Ziel all meiner Triebe,
> und meines Jesu göttlichs Herz,
> das reget sich nicht mehr,
> und ist vom Blut und Leben leer.
>
> Was für ein herbes Eisen
> konnt dieses süßeste und allerliebste Herz zerreißen?

[Where am I? Bitter pain! Ah! the seat of love, my peace, my consolation, the goal of all my instincts and my Jesu's godly heart: it stirs no more and is bereft of life and blood. . . . What kind of cruel sword could rend this sweetest and dearest of all hearts?]

There follows the aria:

> Felsen, spaltet euren Rachen,
> trauert durch ein kläglichs Krachen,
> Sterne, Mond und Sonne flieht,
> traur, Natur, ich traure mit.
> Brüllt, ihr Donner, Blitz und Flammen,
> schlaget über dem zusammen,
> der durch die verruchte Tat
> dieses Herz verwundet hat.

[Rocks, open wide your jaws, may your pitiful roar express your grief; stars, moon and sun, flee; mourn, Nature, I shall mourn too. Roar, you thunder, lightning and flames, together engulf the man who by his wicked deed has wounded this heart.]

The music to this aria shamelessly exploits all the most sensational effects associated with Neapolitan opera of the period, with the listener spared none of its excesses, from noisy fanfares with widely leaping intervals to elaborate and showy coloratura writing and garish tone-painting in the orchestra. The middle section modulates from D minor to E flat major and B major and finally to E minor, thereby constituting a classic example of the often completely unplanned harmonic schemes of these sections. Among notable features are the evident reminiscence of a theme from one of Leopold's arias,[28] a dynamic range that recalls Johann Christian Bach's love of extreme contrasts and the fact that, in keeping with the newer type of aria, Mozart shortens the *da capo* by half. The following soprano aria, 'Betracht dies Herz', has all the hallmarks of a German song, not only in its brief binary form but even in its melodic writing. The choice of the key of G minor – and this point may be made here once and for all – is not Mozart's but derives from Italian operas of the time, where it is invariably the key of grief and mourning. But even here Mozart already uses more characterful harmonies to strike the more anguished note of muted passion that distinguishes his own G minor laments from the mawkish sentimentality of their Italian counterparts. How authentically he feels the Phrygian phrase in the third and fourth bars of the ritornello and the insistent chord of a fifth that brings this opening passage to an end. And how beautifully he extends the final phrase to create an anguished *adagio* coda, a decision influenced by the words 'Ergib dich, hartes Herz, zerfließ in Reu und Schmerz!' (Yield, hard heart, melt in contrition and anguish). An expressive accompanied recitative built up from one and the same orchestral motif is followed by a duet for the two solo voices. It is binary in form, with the voices entering in succession in keeping with the Italian tradition, before coming together in thirds and sixths. As in *Die Schuldigkeit des Ersten Gebots*, imitative writing is found here on only a modest scale. The expressive language is tender and natural, with no trace of sentimentality, with the exception of a handful of modishly playful figures:

For a later performance, probably in the mid-1770s,[29] Mozart added a final chorus introduced by a brief recitative. The chorus is a homophonic ternary movement which, for all its melodiousness,

28. 'So straft Herodes die Verräter'; see Max Seiffert, *Leopold Mozart: Ausgewählte Werke*, 167ff.
29. Jahn speculates 'before 1775', whereas Wyzewa and Saint-Foix, *Wolfgang Amédée Mozart* (ii.288), assume that the revival took place during Lent 1775 or 1776. They are no doubt correct to point to affinities with Mozart's sacred music of 1776. ✦ Jahn was probably right. Paper and handwriting studies suggest a date of *c*1773.

strikes a particularly insistent note of imprecation. Mozart's final contribution to Passion music was the aria *Kommet her, ihr frechen Sünder* K146, a rather undistinguished piece that likewise dates from the 1770s.[30]

Another relatively insignificant piece – and certainly far inferior to the oratorio and *Grabmusik* – is the offertory *Scande coeli limina* K34 that Mozart wrote for the Feast of Saint Benedict (21 March) immediately after his return to Salzburg. The piece was intended for the monks of the monastery at Seeon, who were on friendly terms with his family.[31] Stylistically speaking, the soprano aria is all too reminiscent of a Parisian comic opera,[32] while the following four-part chorus with its stiff and dry part-writing once again reveals the gaps in Mozart's contrapuntal skills at this time. By contrast, the offertory *Inter natos mulierum* K72, which tradition likewise associates with the monastery at Seeon, must be dated on stylistic grounds to a later period.[33]

There was one further occasion during the spring of 1767 when Wolfgang's services as a composer were required by the authorities in Salzburg: in keeping with a Jesuit tradition, the students at the town's university regularly mounted performances of plays, both at the end of the academic year (that is, in late August or early September) and sometimes on other festive occasions, too. A small theatre was erected for the purpose in 1657, followed in 1661 by a larger theatre with twelve sets that were universally admired. As a rule, a Latin play written by the professor of poetry or another cleric (referred to as the *comicus*) was performed by 'the Benedictine muses', that is, the students from the various classes at the university. The subject matter was taken from the Bible, from ancient or more recent history and, more rarely, from pagan mythology and sought to propagate a particular moral doctrine.[34] In keeping with a long-standing tradition dating back to the days of the old Italian spoken theatre, a short Latin opera on a related subject was interpolated between the acts of the *tragoedia* or *comoedia*, with the first part being performed as a prologue before the actual play, while the following acts or scenes (termed *chori*) were staged between the acts of the drama, much as intermezzos or ballets were performed between the acts of an *opera seria*. The musical setting was entrusted to members of the court music: among composers mentioned by surviving librettos are Biechteler von Greiffenthal, Eberlin, Adlgasser, Meißner, Michael Haydn and Leopold Mozart. Singers from the court music would help out by taking on the more difficult roles.

On 13 May 1767 the tragedy *Clementia Croesi* was performed by pupils from the syntax class, in other words, students in the penultimate year of their course in the humanities. On this occasion the musical adjunct was *Apollo et Hyacinthus seu Hyacinthi Metamorphosis*, to a score by Mozart (K38). According to the printed libretto, 'the author of this piece of music is the noble D. Wolfgangus Mozart, aged eleven, son of the noble and strict Kapellmeister, D. Leopoldus Mozart'.

30.   Jahn and Köchel both assume that it was written during the early 1770s, whereas Wyzewa and Saint-Foix (ii.246) suggest a date of 1779/1780. A copy in Munich is headed, in Leopold's hand, 'Aria de Passione D. N. Jesu Christi di Wolfgango Amadeo Mozart'. ◆ There is no firm evidence for the dating of this work. The sole surviving authentic copy (Munich, Bayerische Staatsbibliothek, shelfmark Mus. Mss. 1280) is on a type of paper commonly used in Salzburg throughout the 1770s.
31.   According to Schafhäutl, Mozart wrote down the piece in pencil when the prelate complained that they had no offertories for the Feast of Saint Benedict. ◆ Karl Schafhäutl's account appears in the foreword to his 1851 Munich edition of the offertory. No authentic sources for the work survive: both its dating and attribution to Mozart are doubtful.
32.   See Wyzewa and Saint-Foix, *Wolfgang Amédée Mozart*, i.181–2.
33.   ◆ Bibliographical evidence supports a later dating as well. Although there is no autograph, a copy in the Salzburg cathedral archives (shelfmark A1123) also appears to date from the mid- to late-1770s.
34.   A list of the plays performed between 1621 and 1727 appears in Sedelmayr, *Historia almae et archi-episcopalis Universitatis Salisburgensis*, 112ff.; see also Hammerle, *Mozart und einige Zeitgenossen*, 2, 12, 17 and 59–60. ◆ For a more recent account of this repertory, see Boberski, *Das Theater der Benediktiner an der alten Universiät Salzburg (1617–1778)*.

Following the performance, Wolfgang played the keyboard, astonishing his listeners with his pianistic abilities until late into the night.[35]

The cast was as follows:

Oebalus, king of Lacedaemonia (tenor)	The Most Illustrious and Learned D. Matthias Stadler (Scholar in Theology, Morals and Law)
Melia, Oebalus's daughter (soprano)	Felix Fuchs, of the Kapelle (Grammar)
Hyacinthus, Oebalus's son (soprano)	Christianus Enzinger, of the Kapelle (Rudiments)
Apollo, received by Oebalus as a guest (alto)	Joannes Ernst, of the Kapelle
Zephyrus, friend of Hyacinthus (alto)	Josephus Vonterthon (Syntax)
First Priest of Apollo	Josef Bruendl (Poetry)
Second Priest of Apollo	Jacobus Moser (Syntax)

The old legend has been freely adapted by the librettist in the manner of an Italian opera: for the greater good and edification of the young students, Melia is here the beloved of Apollo and Zephyrus, while Hyacinthus is barely motivated as a character. And the piece ends with a marriage befitting the rank of the participants. It is difficult to speak of a dramatic plot in the usual sense of the term. Instead, individual situations arise that provide an excuse for long arias and duets of a thoroughly traditional kind. The Latin text, too, has had to be adapted to meet traditional requirements. The dialogue is in iambic *senarii*,[36] while the choruses and arias are in free rhymed verse. The result is not inappropriate, but extremely flat, with individual sections modelled on Italian opera librettos.

Following a brief two-part overture of simple but effective structure, the action begins with a recitative for Hyacinthus and Zephyrus. The latter reveals his love of Melia and his jealousy of Apollo. Oebalus and Melia enter in order to offer up a sacrifice to Apollo, who is invoked in a chorus:

> Numen o Latonium,
> audi vota supplicum,
> qui ter digno te honore
> certant sancte colere.
> Hos benigno tu favore
> subditos prosequere.

[O god born of Latona! Hear the prayers of thy supplicants, who strive to worship thee that art thrice worthy of that honour. Grant that they may be attended by thy favour.]

---

35. *Protocollum Praefecturae Gymnasii Universitatis Salisburgensis:* '13 May, Wednesday. In the morning short schools on account of phlebotomy. After dinner was given the Syntaxists' comedy written by the Very Reverend Professor [Rufinus Widl from Seeon Monastery], and by desire performed by his students, which gave me the greatest pleasure. I congratulate the Professor on the public applause. The music for it, composed by Wolfgang Mozart, a youngster of eleven, delighted everybody, and in the evening he gave us notable proofs of his musical art on the harpsichord' [*Dokumente*, 70, *Documentary Biography*, 75].
36. ◆ Lines of six iambic feet traditionally found in Classical Latin plays.

The sacrifice is not accepted, and a flash of lightning destroys everything. Hyacinthus attempts to calm the distraught Oebalus and assure him that the gods have not always been so vindictive:

> Saepe terrent numina
> surgunt et minantur,
> fingunt bella
> quae nos angunt,
> mittunt tela
> quae non tangunt;
> at post ficta nubila
> rident et iocantur.

[Often the gods cause terror, rise up and threaten, cause wars that harm us, shoot arrows that do not hit their mark; but after the mock storm clouds they laugh and jest.]

Apollo now appears and asks to stay with Oebalus as Jupiter has banished him. The two men exchange pleasantries, after which Apollo delivers himself of an aria in which he expresses his gratitude. There now follow the first two acts of *Clementia Croesi*. Oebalus then tells his daughter that Apollo wants to marry her. She is happy to fall in with his plans and expresses her delight in an aria notable for its elaborate passage-work:

> Laetari, iocari
> fruique divinis honoribus stat,
> dum Hymen optimus
> taedis et floribus
> grata, beata
> connubia iungit et gaudia dat!

[My lot is to rejoice, be merry, enjoy the honour done to me by the god, now that excellent Hymen, with torches and garlands, joins the happy, blessed marriage knot and brings me joy.]

But Zephyrus now enters with the news that Hyacinthus has been killed by Apollo. Melia thereupon declares that she cannot marry him, Oebalus plans to banish him, and Zephyrus sing an aria expressing the hopes aroused in him by this latest turn of events. Apollo now arrives, unmasks Zephyrus as Hyacinthus's murderer and calls on the winds to carry him away to Aeolus's cave. Incensed by this new act of violence, Melia showers him with reproaches, spurning him in a duet and bidding him be gone, while he protests his love and complains at her harshness. The third and fourth acts of *Clementia Croesi* now follow, after which Hyacinthus is borne in on a bier. Dying, he announces in an accompanied recitative that it was Zephyrus who murdered him, provoking Oebalus to vent his anger in an aria. When Melia tells him that Hyacinthus has been killed and that she herself has banished Apollo, he gives her a piece of his mind, fearing that the offended god will punish them in his anger. Their sentiments find expression in a duet. But Apollo now appears, transforms Hyacinthus into a flower and forgives Oebalus and Melia, assuring them of his favour. He accepts her hand in marriage and in a final trio all express their contentment.

Like the text, the music, too, is inspired by Italianate models. At every turn we encounter favourite phrases of Johann Christian Bach, and in Melia's aria ('Laetari, iocari') we even find a reminiscence of Handel. Nor is there any lack of south German features.[37] Style and structure are the same as in the oratorio. With two exceptions,[38] the arias are all cast in the ternary *da capo* form typical of Hasse's operas, and the same is true of the largely homophonic duets.[39] On the whole, the music leaves a decidedly weaker impression than was the case with the oratorio: most of the numbers have something conventional and forbidding about them, a state of affairs bound up not only with the stilted text but also with Mozart's evident weakness in Latin,[40] which prevented him from approaching the subject with ultimate self-assurance. Only in the duet between Melia and Oebalus ('Natus cadit') does he manage to imbue the music with any real warmth and life. Even the instrumentation here is worthy of note, with its horns, muted first violins, pizzicato second violins and divided violas, and while the saccharine wistfulness and little chromatic sighs of the melodic writing infallibly recall Johann Christian Bach, the expression is natural and genuine, with the father's melodic line delightfully ornamented by the daughter as she laments the loss of her lover. Hyacinthus's aria ('Saepe terrent numina') is important for other reasons: not only does it introduce three contrastive themes in its opening ritornello, but even after the singer's entry it lovingly explores all manner of details in the text (note, for example, the chromatically rising figure at the word 'surgunt'). The result is a disjointed series of tiny independent musical ideas that only rarely give the impression of a coherent melodic line. We shall often encounter this type of writing in Mozart's early Italian operas. Otherwise the piece is relatively lacking in features that might point to the later composer. One exception is the interrupted cadence on the chord of a sixth on the subdominant that Mozart continued to favour even as late as *Die Zauberflöte* and that we find here in the following passage from Zephyrus's aria ('En! duos conspicis'), where the character asks insistently:

Another exception is the sudden chromatic clouding over of the music on the word 'beata' in Melia's aria 'Laetari, iocari fruique' at bars 92–3, a chromaticism not justified by the text.

Nor are the recitatives on a par with those of the oratorio. Sketchy passages reminiscent of Mozart's later manner are found alongside others of considerable expressive force, notably between 'En! duos conspicis' and 'Discede crudelis' and at the start of the second chorus.[41] As in the oratorio, the orchestra is handled with a certain independence and with the flexibility vis-à-vis the text that we already find as a legacy of *opera buffa* in the works of Johann Christian Bach and his contemporaries. The brief single-movement overture – here called an Intrada – closely follows

37. Cf. the middle section of the duet 'Discede crudelis'.
38. Following the example of Johann Christian Bach, the aria 'Jam pastor Apollo' repeats only the foreshortened ritornello in the *da capo*, while 'En! duos conspicis' and 'Tandem post turbida fulmina' have no middle section in the older sense of the term.
39. In 'Natus cadit' Melia enters with the main theme on the dominant.
40. On this point, see *Briefe* i.290 (letter of [?1769]).
41. The recitative for Oebalus and Melia, 'Amare numquid filia', is also remarkable for its chromatically descending bass line. Significantly, Mozart dealt cursorily with the unfavourable signs from the gods (the *secco* recitative between the first two numbers), using *secco* recitative for a passage on which the Italian composers of the period would have lavished all manner of onomatopoeic effects.

the model of the overture to *Die Schuldigkeit des Ersten Gebots*: here, too, we find the divided violas so typical of both works. The final group contains an example of the widely-spaced intervals and rhythms which, entirely typical of Mozart, suddenly break the melodic thread:

Until recently it was usual to include among this already remarkable list of works the four keyboard concertos in F, B flat, D and G major (K37, 39–41) that were believed to have been written in part by Mozart and in part by his father in April, June and July 1767, although even earlier scholars were puzzled by the fact Leopold made no mention of them in his otherwise meticulous catalogue of 1768. We must be grateful to Wyzewa and Saint-Foix for demonstrating that these are not original works but transcriptions of pieces by other composers,[42] their aim being to provide the children with new and grateful works to perform on their forthcoming visit to Vienna. The four concertos are arrangements of the following pieces:

K37: the opening movement is the initial allegro from Raupach's op. 1 no. 5,[43] while the final movement is based on the opening movement of Leontzi Honauer's sonata op. 2 no. 3;[44] K39: the first and third movements are taken from the opening allegro and finale of Raupach's op. 1 no. 1, the andante from the first movement of Johann Schobert's op. 17 no. 2;[45]
K40: the opening movement is a transcription of the first movement of Honauer's op. 2 no. 1, while the andante is arranged from Eckard's sonata op. 1 no. 4;
K41: the first and third movements are based on the first movement and finale of Honauer's op. 1 no. 1, the andante on the andantino from Raupach's op. 1 no. 1.

With few exceptions, this selection shows that Mozart was more interested in superficial brilliance than inner meaning. The originals themselves are left untouched, but a relatively lengthy tutti is added to the beginning of each sonata movement, with a second, shorter tutti appended at the end. A third is inserted between the subject group and the development section. For the rest, the orchestra plays no more than a supportive, accompanying role; the free cadenza is generally introduced by the solo with support from the orchestra, less frequently by the tutti. In certain movements, however, we find a fourth tutti, generally immediately before the recapitulation. The extended opening tuttis of the opening movements and occasionally those of the final movements, too, derive their thematic material from the first subject of the sonata movement, but then generally contrast it with a second subject following the example of Johann Christian Bach. It is significant, however, that with a single exception (K37/1), Mozart does not take up the second subject from his source but, rather, concentrates on the final group or, as in K37/3, on a later episode from the rondo.

But far from adapting these works by Raupach, Honauer and others in a purely mechanical way, Mozart more often than not places the stamp of his own genius on them. Right at the beginning

---

42. Wyzewa and Saint-Foix, *Wolfgang Amédée Mozart*, i.187–92; see also Wyzewa's 'Un maître inconnu de Mozart', 35–41.
43. On Raupach, see Gerber, *Historisch-biographisches Lexicon der Tonkünstler*, ii.239.
44. According to Wyzewa and Saint-Foix, the andante is by Schobert, but no trace of this work can be found among his surviving compositions. ◆ No source has been identified for this movement; possibly it is the only one among the concertos that is entirely original to Mozart.
45. Edited by Wyzewa and Saint-Foix and published with Mozart's concerto movement by Breitkopf & Härtel in 1908. ◆ For a more recent publication, see the edition by Jean-Patrice Brosse (Courlay, 1995).

of K37, for example, he brings out the characteristic, agitated syncopations in Raupach's movement, and in the third tutti of K39/1 the orchestra takes over the soloist's playful figure and clothes it in a sombre minor tonality from which the soloist escapes only with difficulty. But it is Schobert's andante that he adapts most freely: the pounding bass motif that appears only in the second part of Schobert's movement is not only transferred to the first part of Mozart's movement, it is even placed at the very beginning in the powerful orchestral unison, its weighty emotionalism thereby acquiring a much darker hue. K41 offers further examples of Mozart's independent approach, especially in terms of the ideas of his own that he introduces into the opening tuttis of all three movements.[46] Although Johann Christian Bach's influence on these works is unmistakable, with their thematic bipolarity, their predilection for superficial brilliance and their neglect of a concertante element in favour of the soloist, it would none the less be absurd to compare them with the English Bach's own keyboard concertos.[47] The transcription of three sonatas from Johann Christian's op. 5 set of sonatas should clearly be regarded as an earlier exercise of the same kind (K107).[48]

Although no other datable works have survived from this period in Salzburg, a number of more recent scholars[49] are inclined to argue that several other pieces were written at this time. Chief among these pieces is the undated Symphony in F major K76. In terms of its style and, above all, its structure, it is clearly an early work, while the evident reminiscence of Rameau[50] in the theme of the final movement points to the period of the journey to Paris. On the other hand, the inclusion of a minuet points in the direction of southern Germany. We may assume, therefore, that it was written either in Salzburg or immediately afterwards in Vienna.[51]

---

46. Mozart's treatment of the orchestra reveals constant advances from one concerto to the next. K40 has trumpets, while K41 has flutes (instead of oboes).

47. On Bach's keyboard concertos, see Daffner, *Die Entwicklung des Klavierkonzertes bis Mozart*, 36ff. ◆ Further concerning K37 and 39–41, see Eybl, 'Mozarts erster Konzertsatz: Die Pasticcio-Konzerte KV 37, 39, 40, 41 im zeitgenössischen Wiener Kontext', and Escal, 'Les concertos-pastiches de Mozart, ou la citation comme procès d'appropriation du discours'.

48. Wyzewa and Saint-Foix, *Wolfgang Amédée Mozart* (i.160–61) date them to the period between April 1765 and April 1766. ◆ Paper and handwriting studies suggest a date of 1772 for Mozart's arrangements. Further, see Bieler, *Binärer Satz – Sonate – Konzert: Johann Christian Bachs Klaviersonaten op. V im Spiegel barocker Formprinzipien und ihrer Bearbeitung durch Mozart*, and Steinbeck, 'Zur Entstehung der Konzertform in den Pasticcio-Konzerten Mozarts'. More generally, see John A. Meyer, 'The keyboard concertos of Johann Christian Bach'.

49. Wyzewa and Saint-Foix, *Wolfgang Amédée Mozart*, i.178–81.

50. Gavotte (allegro gai) from *Le temple de la Gloire*. ◆ Rameau's *opéra-ballet Le temple de la Gloire*, to a text by Voltaire, was performed at Versailles on 27 November 1745.

51. Wyzewa and Saint-Foix draw attention to the similarity between the opening movement and the overture to *Die Schuldigkeit des Ersten Gebots*, but in doing so they overlook the completely different kind of development section. In the overture it is thematic, whereas in the symphony it departs from the main ideas and returns to the second subject only after an agitated modulation. A thematic link between menuetto and trio was something that Mozart had already encountered in his father's works; see above. ◆ The stylistic anomalies of K76 are probably accounted for by the fact that it was almost certainly not composed by Mozart, but by Leopold. See Eisen, 'Problems of Authenticity among Mozart's Early Symphonies'.

5

First operas in Vienna

It was no doubt the news that Archduchess Maria Josepha of Austria was to marry King Ferdinand IV of Naples at the end of 1767 that persuaded Leopold to set off for Vienna with his whole family on 11 September. Clearly he hoped to take advantage of so opportune an occasion and show the most brilliant of audiences what progress his son had made since their last visit to the city.

They did not linger over their journey but stopped only briefly at Lambach, where they had to dine with the prelate, and then at the monastery at Melk, where Wolfgang was recognized by the organist when he went to try out the instrument.[1]

In Vienna they made an unpromising start and were unable to attend the court as the beautiful and universally loved Princess Maria Josepha was suffering from smallpox, from which she died on 15 October, the empress's name-day. As a result, it was also impossible for the Mozarts to perform in the homes of the local aristocracy. They were on the point of leaving the city but were detained by the suggestion that the emperor might still want to hear them. While they were waiting, Leopold mentions that they attended performances of Hasse's *Partenope*, in which they particularly enjoyed the dancing of the famous Gaetano Apolline Baldassare Vestris, and of Florian Gassmann's *Amore e Psiche*. But the smallpox epidemic continued to rage in the city and so he and his children fled to Olmütz (Olomouc) at the end of October.[2] Not even here were they safe, however, and first Wolfgang, then Marianne fell ill with the disease. Count Leopold Anton von Podstatsky, the dean of Olmütz Cathedral and canon of Salzburg Cathedral (hence his acquaintance with the Mozarts), offered to provide accommodation for the whole family: exceptionally, he himself was not afraid of the illness. The family stayed at the deanery and, thanks to the care and medical attention that they received, the children recovered, although the symptoms were so severe that for nine days Mozart was unable to see at all. Even after he had recovered, he still had to look after his eyes for several weeks and so, in order to prevent him from becoming bored, the court chaplain, Johann Leopold Hay, who was a brother of Maria Theresia Josepha von Sonnenfels[3] and who later became bishop of Königgrätz, would visit him every day and keep him entertained with card tricks that the boy soon learnt for himself. Wolfgang also used this period of enforced leisure to learn fencing, throwing himself into it with his usual enthusiasm: both now and later he was always keen on physical exercise.[4] When he was fully recovered, he wrote an aria for the little daughter of the doctor who had treated him, Joseph Wolff, a piece that Leopold recalled in a much later letter of 28 May 1778.[5]

---

1. ◆ Along the way, the family also stopped at Vöcklabruck, Linz, Strengberg, St Pölten and Purkersdorf.
2. ◆ Concerning smallpox and vaccinations in the eighteenth century, see Halliwell, *The Mozart Family*, 70–2 and 122–6.
3. Georg Forster, *Sämtliche Schriften*, vii.270.
4. Berchtold zu Sonnenburg, 'Noch einige Anekdoten', 301.
5. ◆ *Briefe*, ii.363.

They set off back to Vienna on 23 December but broke the journey in Brünn (Brno), where they spent two weeks as guests of Count Franz Anton Schrattenbach, the brother of the archbishop of Salzburg, who had wanted them to give a concert on their way from Vienna to Olmütz. Here, according to Leopold, they were shown 'special consideration' by members of the local aristocracy.

They arrived back in Vienna on 10 January 1768 but now encountered one difficulty after another, although they were at least received at court somewhat sooner than they had expected. The Empress Maria Theresia had barely heard of the life-threatening illness from which the two children – both of whom she had earlier admired – had recovered when, on 19 January, she summoned them to court. The emperor himself came into the anteroom and ushered them into his mother's presence. The only other people in attendance were Duke Albert of Saxe-Teschen and the archduchesses. They remained with the imperial family for two hours.[6] The empress took Anna Maria Mozart into her confidence, speaking to her as one mother to another, asking about all the details of the children's illness and of their grand tour, taking her hands in sympathy and stroking her cheeks, while the emperor spoke about music and other matters with Mozart and his father, causing Marianne to blush to the roots of her hair. The Mozarts felt deeply honoured by such exceptional affability, and their patriotic hearts beat faster, but the visit proved less than rewarding in other ways. The empress gave them a beautiful, if worthless, medal, but she had given up going to the opera or theatre since her husband's death and no longer maintained any musicians at court, so that an invitation to perform there could come from the emperor alone. And Joseph gave little sign of the generosity towards artists that had earlier been regarded as an essential token of a prince's prestige and as a sign of royal favour. Leopold was not the only musician to be disenchanted by such thrift. Members of the nobility followed the court's example and avoided displays of extravagance, hoping in that way to endear themselves to the emperor. During the Shrovetide carnival, the only entertainment was dancing, with balls of every description following each other with dizzying speed. And whereas, at an earlier date, the members of the local nobility had vied with each other in holding the most brilliant soirées at which the leading virtuosos of their day were almost always invited to perform, the balls were now held in public halls, with the costs shared by all.[7] Leopold mentions that the court in fact benefited from this arrangement by taking out a lease on all the dances, balls and other spectacles and in that way sharing the profits with the other lessees. In the circumstances, it made little difference to Mozart that he was held in high regard in the most respected circles and by the most influential music lovers: among his admirers, Leopold singles out the chief equerry Count Dietrichstein, whom he describes as 'all-powerful with the emperor', Fräulein Josepha von Guttenberg, 'who is the left eye of the empress', and the much-travelled physician Alexandre-Louis Laugier, a man who, according to Burney, possessed 'a most active and cultivated mind', especially where music was concerned, and whose house was 'the rendezvous of the first people of Vienna'.[8] Among Mozart's patrons was Juan Carlos, Duke of Braganza, an outstanding individual whose courage and character had been tested by the Lisbon earthquake and by his time as a volunteer with the Austrian army.[9] In the course of his travels he had acquired a profound knowledge of the world and was noted for his sensitive

6. According to Marianne, the children also performed on this occasion, but Leopold makes no mention of this. ◆ *Dokumente*, 401, *Documentary Biography*, 458.

7. ◆ See Witzmann, '"Amici, al ballo, al gioco . . .": Wiener Ballkultur zur Mozartzeit'; for a brief contemporaneous description, see the passages from Johann Pezzl's *Skizze von Wien* (Vienna, 1786–90), translated in Landon, *Mozart and Vienna*, 149–50.

8. Burney, *The Present State of Music in Germany*, i.247; see also Dutens, *Mémoires d'un voyageur*, i.853–4.

9. Garat, *Mémoires sur la vie de M. Suard*, ii.218–20; see also Dutens, *Mémoires d'un voyageur*, i.347–8. ◆ Juan Carlos, Duke of Braganza (1719–1806) was living in exile in Vienna at the time.

understanding,[10] sociable nature and fine ear for music.[11] It was to him that Gluck dedicated his opera *Paride ed Elena* in 1770, declaring in his famous dedication that what he looked for in the duke was not so much a patron as a judge who, sufficiently knowledgeable about the great principles of art, would bring to bear on the subject a mind 'fortified against the prejudices of convention'. The Mozarts also found favour and support with Prince Kaunitz, a sophisticated connoisseur,[12] but a man so absurdly concerned for his own health that he refused to admit Wolfgang to his presence until there was no longer any trace on the boy's face of the red marks left by the smallpox. According to both Marianne and Leopold,[13] a 'major concert' was held for the children in March at the home of the Russian ambassador, Prince Dmitri Mikhailovich Galitzin.

Leopold had little to say in defence of Viennese audiences in general:

That the Viennese, generally speaking, have no desire to see serious and sensible things, have little or no idea of them and want to see only foolish stuff, dancing, devils, ghosts, magic, Hanswurst, Lipperl, Bernardon, witches and apparitions is well known, and their theatres offer daily proof of this. Even gentlemen wearing the sash of some order or other will clap their hands and laugh themselves sick over a ribald remark or simple joke, but during the most solemn scene, the most moving and beautiful action and the wittiest figures of speech, they will gossip so loudly with some lady or other that other honest people cannot understand a single word.[14]

Leopold had evidently suffered numerous disappointments of this kind, but his opinion of Viennese taste in matters of art is none the less very one-sided, based, as it is, on less elevated types of popular entertainment.[15] Among the things that musicians could hear and study at this time it emerges not only from Wolfgang's works from this period, but also from Gluck's remark that Vienna had 'always been the first to shake off the yoke of vulgar prejudice in order to clear a path for perfection'.[16] It was in Vienna, after all, that Gluck's second great reform opera, *Alceste*, had been staged for the first time in 1767. But by now, of course, Mozart had lost his appeal as a 'child prodigy' and audiences had far less time for his progress as an artist. And his fellow musicians acknowledged him as their equal only to the extent that they visited on him the old vices of their profession, envying him both his income and his skills. Leopold has the following to say on this point:

I was told that all the keyboard players and composers in Vienna were opposed to our advancement, with the sole exception of Wagenseil, but *he* is ill at home and so he cannot help us or contribute to our advantage. The chief maxim of these people has been to take the greatest

10. Zimmermann, *Briefe an einige seiner Freunde in der Schweiz*, 96.

11. Burney, *The Present State of Music in Germany*, i.255

12. ◆ Wenzel Anton Fürst Kaunitz-Rietberg (1711–94) was the Imperial ambassador to Turin, posted to the Austrian Netherlands, and from 1750 to 1753 Imperial ambassador to Paris. After his return from the French capital he was appointed *Staatskanzler*. The Mozarts had met Kaunitz during their first visit to Vienna in 1762.

13. *Briefe*, i.261 (letter of 30 March 1768); see also Nottebohm, *Mozartiana*, 103 [*Dokumente*, 401, *Documentary Biography*, 458].

14. *Briefe*, i.254 (letter of 30 Jan. 1768). ◆ 'Lipperl' is a diminutive of Philipp and refers to a comic character in the Hanswurst tradition; Bernardon was the stage name of the actor Johann Joseph Felix von Kurz (1717–84). The character of Hanswurst dates back to 1519 and first appears in a stage play in the middle of the sixteenth century. Further, see Asper, *Hanswurst*.

15. See Gervinus, *Geschichte der poetischen National-Literatur der Deutschen*, iv.384ff.; Devrient, *Geschichte der deutschen Schauspielkunst*, ii.191ff; and Sonnenfels, *Gesammelte Schriften*, v.157–8 and 191–2; see also Sonnenfels's letter to Christian Adolf Klotz in his *Briefe über die wienerische Schaubühne*, i.2ff.

16. Preface to *Alceste*.

possible care to avoid every occasion of seeing us and of acknowledging Wolfgangerl's abilities. And why? So that on the many occasions when they might be asked whether they had heard the boy and what they thought of him, they could always say that they had not heard him and that it could not possibly be true; that it was all jugglery and nothing but a joke; that it was pre-arranged; that he was given music he already knew; that it was ridiculous to think that he could compose, and so on. That, as you can see, is why they are avoiding us. For people who have seen and heard him cannot say such things without running the risk of losing their honour. But I managed to catch out one of these people. We had arranged with someone to let us know when he was going to be there. He was then to come and give this person an exceptionally difficult concerto that was to be put before Wolfgangerl. And so we turned up, and he had the opportunity of hearing his concerto played by Wolfgangerl as if he knew it by heart. The astonishment of this composer and keyboard player, his comments and the things he said in expressing his amazement made us realize the truth of what I said a moment ago, and finally he said: 'All I can say as an honest person is that this boy is the greatest man alive.' I couldn't believe it.[17]

But a single incident of this kind, however gratifying, could do little to offset the envy and mania for belittling Mozart's achievements that pursued its silent and destructive course. It was at this juncture that the emperor himself put forward an idea which, if realized, would have shown Mozart's exceptional abilities in the most brilliant light: he invited the boy to write an opera, adding that he would particularly like to see him conduct it from the keyboard. Father and son lost no time in agreeing to the suggestion, not least because a successful outcome would not only establish their reputation in Vienna, but would also prepare the ground for Mozart's conquest of Italy and its theatres. The emperor let his wishes be known to the impresario Giuseppe Affligio. Leopold himself was fully aware that the fate of any opera depended, for the most part, on the performers, and he was able to win over singers for an opera that could expect an exceptional degree of public interest on account of its composer's youth, with the result that they, too, urged Affligio to entrust the young composer with an opera. Affligio declared himself willing to do so and drew up a contract agreeing to stage the work and to pay Mozart a fee of one hundred ducats.

The singers currently engaged in Vienna for *opere serie* were not particularly distinguished. As early as 29 September 1767, Leopold had reported that Hasse's opera – *Partenope* – was a beautiful work, but that the singers were 'nothing out of the ordinary for such a festive occasion. Signor Tibaldi is the tenor and Signor Raucini from Munich, the leading castrato. The prima donna is Signora Deiber, the daughter of a violinist at the Viennese court.'[18] Therese Teyber had studied with Tesi and Hasse. But Gluck had been unwilling to entrust *Alceste* to these singers, and when the production opened in Vienna on 26 December 1767, it was with Bernasconi in the title role. Tibaldi sang Admetus. The Mozarts were in Olmütz by this time, but following their return to Vienna they had an opportunity to hear what Leopold called 'Gluck's sad *Alceste*'.[19] It is a remarkable coincidence that, at the very moment that he was on the point of writing his first opera,

17. *Briefe*, i.256–7 (letter of 30 January 1768).

18. ◆ *Briefe*, i.239 (letter of 29 September 1767). Giuseppe Tibaldi (1729–c1790) was later the original Aceste in Mozart's *Ascanio in Alba* and Venanzio Rauzzini (1746–1810) the original Cecilio in *Lucio Silla*; it was for Rauzzini that Mozart later composed the motet *Exsultate jubilate* K165. In fact 'Signora Deiber' is more likely to have been Elisabeth Teyber (1744–1816), the elder sister of Therese Teyber (1760–1836), who was the original Blonde in *Die Entführung aus dem Serail*.

19. As Nissen points out, it is conceivable that Leopold was using this term to draw a distinction between *opera seria* and *opera buffa*. The full context reads: 'There are no singers here for serious operas. Even Gluck's sad opera *Alceste* was performed entirely by *opera buffa* singers. He too is now writing an *opera buffa*' [*Briefe*, i.258 (letter of 30 January 1768)]; see Nissen, *Biographie W. A. Mozarts*, 134.

Mozart was in Vienna to see Gluck taking *his* first and decisive steps in the direction of his operatic reforms, and it may perhaps have been this youthful memory that later prompted him to study *Alceste* with such evident enthusiasm. In the case of Leopold, by contrast, it is understandable that his own education, based, as it was, on the traditions of Italian music, made him less responsive to Gluck's reforms. That there were many in the audience who thought as he did emerges from conversations that Sonnenfels heard at the first night of *Alceste*, conversations gleaned not in the gods but in the pit, where the nobility traditionally sat: 'This is uplifting! Nine days without plays and then, on the tenth, a *De profundis*! – What? Tears are envisaged? Maybe I'll shed some – out of boredom! – No, it's simply throwing one's money away! An admirable entertainment, watching a foolish woman dying for the sake of her husband!'[20]

The members of the *opera buffa*, by contrast, were outstandingly good,[21] and so the Mozarts chose an *opera buffa*. The libretto was provided by the Florentine poet Marco Coltellini, who had been living in Vienna since 1763 or 1764 and who in 1769 even became Metastasio's successor as *poeta cesareo*. In 1772 he went to St Petersburg as poet to the Russian imperial court. As a poet he initially adopted Metastasian models, earning the latter's praise for doing so,[22] but in Vienna he switched his allegiance to the reformist camp and, together with Frugoni and the celebrated Calzabigi, became a leading exponent of the new and more serious type of opera libretto. In his *Ifigenia in Tauride*, set by Traetta in 1763, he first achieves that simplicity in the basic dramatic idea that Calzabigi and Gluck were later to proclaim as the fundamental principle of their new music drama. In the field of *opera buffa*, however, he continued to plough a traditional furrow, and his libretto for Mozart's *La finta semplice* K51 is no exception.

Mozart lost no time in setting to work on the commission in order to ensure that the opera could be given at Easter: on completing the first act, he sent it off to the singers, who, according to Leopold, expressed their total satisfaction and admiration for it. But Coltellini now delayed things by taking so long with the alterations demanded by both the composer and the singers that it was not until after Easter that he had completed them. Mozart refused to be troubled by this, but continued to work on the opera, eagerly and enthusiastically, writing new arias whenever he was asked to do so and soon completing a respectable-sized score in three acts comprising twenty-five numbers and running to 558 manuscript pages.

Meanwhile various individuals had begun to intrigue against the opera. The idea of allowing a twelve-year-old boy to conduct from a keyboard where Gluck was regularly to be seen was thought by many to be undignified, and people knew how to make their feelings known. Leopold initially suspected Gluck of being party to these intrigues. On 30 January, it is true, we find him writing: 'I have even won Gluck over to our side, though, I admit, only to the extent that, even though he is less than whole-hearted in his support, he may not let it show, as our own patrons are also his.'[23] But six months later he was to write on this very point: 'All the composers, amongst whom Gluck is a leading figure, undermined everything in order to prevent the opera from being a success.'[24] This is undoubtedly an exaggeration. Why should Gluck have been afraid of a novice like Mozart?

20. Sonnenfels, *Gesammelte Schriften*, v.155–6.
21. For a more detailed assessment, see Sonnenfels, *Gesammelte Schriften*, v.290ff. ◆ Concerning *opera buffa* in Vienna at this time, see Heartz, 'Goldoni, opera buffa, and Mozart's advent in Vienna', and, more generally, Rice, 'Vienna under Joseph II and Leopold II'.
22. Metastasio, *Opere postume*, ii.278 and 290; see also Arteaga, *Le rivoluzioni del teatro musicale italiano dalla sua origine fino al presente*, ii.126 and, above all, Hugo Goldschmidt's introduction to *Tommaso Traetta: Ausgewählte Werke*.
23. ◆ *Briefe*, i.257 (letter of 30 January 1768).
24. ◆ *Briefe*, i.270 (letter of 30 July 1768).

Given his seriousness of purpose, he is far more likely to have regarded the whole affair, including the way in which Leopold made such a fuss of his twelve-year-old son, as no more than a mild distraction, and, outspoken as he was, he made no secret of his feelings.[25] But even at this early date Leopold seized the opportunity to align himself and his son with the old school, a school represented by Metastasio and Hasse – 'the father of music', as Leopold called him. In this he was no doubt helped by the fact that Wolfgang had been prepared for this battle over the merits and demerits of the new music drama by the impressions that he had gained in London. Leopold prevailed upon both Metastasio and Hasse to swear that thirty operas had been performed in Vienna 'which in no respect can touch this boy's opera that they both admired in the very highest degree'. But the Mozarts' enemies now turned the tables on them. Rumour had it that Leopold had helped his son on his earlier works, and so it was now said that the new opera was not by Wolfgang at all, but by his father. The boy himself was said to be incapable of writing such a work. Leopold was equal to such a calumny: at the homes of Prince Kaunitz, the Duke of Braganza, Metastasio, Hasse and the Kapellmeister to the Prince of Hildburghausen, Giuseppe Bonno,[26] he would throw open a random volume from Metastasio's works and invite Wolfgang to provide a musical setting, with orchestral accompaniment, of whichever aria he hit upon. It was a test that left no one in any doubt about the boy's technical skills and assurance. This is confirmed not only by Marianne but also by Niemetschek, who refers to the 'testimony of respectable persons who were present at such tests'.[27]

In spite of Leopold's efforts to counter them, the incessant attempts to undermine the new opera finally affected the artists intended to perform it. The orchestra was urged to refuse to allow itself to be conducted by a boy; and the singers, who had earlier declared themselves well satisfied with music that they described as grateful, now began to fear for the success of the production when they saw how much effort was being expended on preventing it from going ahead. They, too, now thought it would be to their advantage to scuttle the production, with the result that when-ever it seemed appropriate they spoke of the work with a dismissive shrug of the shoulders. Leopold complained at the singers' duplicity, claiming that some of them barely knew the music and that they had had to learn it by ear. He was particularly critical of Count Zeil, 'who believed that all the musicians were in favour of Wolfgang, as he too judged by appearances and knew nothing of the inner wickedness of these beasts'.[28] Now even Affligio began to have doubts about the venture and to think that it might harm his reputation: after all, he had agreed to put on the opera mainly because he hoped that the boy's youth would prove a particular draw. Affligio[29] was an adventurer and gambler who had obtained his officer's commission by fraud and duly risen to the ranks of lieutenant colonel. His complete lack of any understanding of art is clear from an occasion when he was present at a bull-baiting and two dogs were pitted against a Hungarian steer. He turned to a friend and commented: 'You see, I prefer these dogs to Aufresne and Neuville', two leading actors whose careers he had done much to promote.[30] He took over as impresario on 16 May 1767, gaining a dubious immortality by virtue of the unfortunate role that he played on more

25. Burney, *The Present State of Music in Germany*, i.255.
26. See Wellesz, 'Giuseppe Bonno'. ◆ More recently, see Meloncelli, 'Un operista italiano alla corte di Vienna' and Heartz, *Haydn, Mozart and the Viennese School*, 115–20.
27. ◆ *Dokumente*, 401, *Documentary Biography*, 459.
28. ◆ *Briefe*, i.278 (letter of 14 September 1768).
29. This is now the usual form of the name. Wlassak's *Chronik des Burgtheaters* (16) prefers the form Afflisio.
30. Johann H. F. Müller, *Abschied von der National-Schaubühne*, 72.

than one occasion in the struggle between the legitimate theatre and the local harlequinades.[31] He was finally sent to the galleys for forgery.[32] This was the sort of man that Mozart had to deal with. Making all manner of excuses and holding out the finest promises, he postponed the opera from Easter to Whitsuntide, then delayed it again until the emperor returned from Hungary, putting one opera after another into rehearsal and secretly countermanding his instructions each time Leopold wrung from him the promise to have *La finta semplice* copied and rehearsed. Although the emperor asked Wolfgang on several occasions what progress he was making on the piece, the court had no influence in the matter, as Affligio was wholly independent. He had taken out a lease on the theatre and had to bear all the costs, including granting free admission to the emperor and his family. Moreover, he had promised the aristocracy and especially Prince Kaunitz that he would reintroduce French plays, which had been dropped from the repertory in 1766, and this he duly did in 1768, but, according to Leopold, it was at a cost of 70,000 florins and at great personal loss to himself. Kaunitz had, in fact, imposed this condition on Affligio without the emperor's knowledge and although he now attempted to persuade Joseph to share the costs, the attempt failed. In the circumstances, no influence could be brought to bear on Affligio from this quarter, and Leopold had no alternative but to deal with the impresario's excuses one by one. Only when Affligio had run out of excuses did he agree to give the opera if Leopold insisted, but it would do him no good, he went on: he would ensure that it was a fiasco and that it was booed off the stage. There is no doubt that Affligio would have been as good as his word, with the result that Leopold was left with no alternative but to abandon the production. In order to salvage his reputation, he submitted a formal complaint to the emperor on 21 September,[33] and Count Johann Wenzel Spork, who was director of court and chamber music and a fanatical music lover, was asked to carry out an investigation. That it failed to produce any results was only to be expected.

The affair had dragged on for nine months, and Leopold and his family had had to survive throughout the whole of this period on little more than the meagre savings from their earlier tour. Leopold's income in Vienna was negligible, and the salary that he had received in Salzburg as first violinist in the prince-archbishop's orchestra and as violin teacher at the chapter house had been withdrawn in March with the comment that he could remain in Vienna as long as he liked, but that he would not be paid in his absence. He was too proud to appeal to his patron, Count Schrattenbach, the archbishop's brother, and beg him to use his influence to restore to him a salary which 'in the opinion of most of the courtiers' he did not deserve. None the less, he had to take steps to secure his position at least for the foreseeable future, as rumour had it that even this was in doubt: it was now being claimed that he had made a fortune in Vienna and that Wolfgang had received 2000 florins for his opera. Leopold attempted to justify himself to the archbishop, pointing out that he could not have anticipated Affligio's baseless actions, but that he was now obliged to have the opera performed in Vienna as it was an *opera buffa* and, as such, geared to local conditions and resources. Had it been an *opera seria*, Wolfgang would have placed it at the feet of his most gracious lord and master and given Vienna no further thought. The reputation of the archbishop himself was at stake: artists employed and recommended by him should not be treated as 'liars, charlatans and impostors who venture forth, with his gracious permission, to throw dust in people's eyes like common conjurors'. He must do everything in his power to justify his son and,

31.   Johann H. F. Müller, *Genaue Nachrichten*, i.13.
32.   Carpani, *Le Haydine*, 82 and Kelly, *Reminiscences*, i.103–4. ◆ Further concerning Affligio, see Croll and Wagner, *Vita di Giuseppe Afflisio: Lebensgeschichte des Giuseppe Afflisio. Aus dem Nachlaß von Bernhard Paumgartner*.
33.   ◆ *Briefe*, i.279–83.

hence, their prince in the eyes of people who, 'because they have breathed the air of a city that is home to the emperor and who serve foreign princes, look on with contempt and speak mockingly and dismissively of foreign princes'. As a Christian, he felt duty-bound to convince non-believers by means of a miracle, 'which God has allowed to see the light in Salzburg':

> If it is ever to be my duty to convince the world of this miracle, it is so now, when people are ridiculing whatever is called a miracle and denying all miracles. That is why they must be convinced. Was it not a great joy and a tremendous victory for me to hear a Voltairean [Grimm] say to me in amazement: 'For once in my life I have seen a miracle; it's the first one!' But because this miracle is so obvious and, therefore, not to be denied, they want to suppress it. They refuse to let God have the honour. They think that it is only a question of a few years and that it will then be perfectly natural and cease to be a divine miracle. So they want to withdraw it from the eyes of the world, for how could it be more visibly revealed than at a public spectacle in a large and populous city?[34]

These remarks were clearly directed at the archbishop's bigotry and sanctimoniousness.

None of these difficulties, however, was allowed to come between Leopold and his principal goal, a goal that was ultimately to be served by Wolfgang's opera. As before, he continued to regard this period in Vienna as no more than a staging post on the road to Italy. As early as May 1768 he had written to Hagenauer:

> This is what makes it easy for me to get permission to travel to Italy, a journey which, taking all the circumstances into consideration, can now be postponed no longer and for which I have received from the emperor himself all the necessary introductions to Florence, the Imperial States and Naples. Or should I perhaps stay in Salzburg in the empty hope of some improvement in my fortunes, watching Wolfgang grow up and allowing myself and my children to be made fools of until I reach an age that prevents me from travelling and Wolfgang is so old and long in the tooth that he no longer attracts admiration for his merits? Is my child to have taken his first step with this opera in Vienna for nothing, and is he not to hurry on with firm steps along the road to which he is now so whole-heartedly committed?[35]

And on 30 July we find him complaining:

> You see how one has to fight one's way through the world. If a man has no talent, he is unhappy enough; but if he has, envy pursues him in proportion to his ability. . . . All sensible people must to their shame agree that it is a disgrace to our nation that we Germans are trying to suppress a German, to whom foreign countries have done justice by their great admiration and even by public acknowledgements in writing. But by patience and perseverance one must convince people that our adversaries are wicked liars, slanderers and the most envious of creatures.[36]

---

34. ◆ The preceding account is based largely on Leopold's letter to Hagenauer of 30 July 1768 (*Briefe*, i.271–3). In fact, Leopold wrote twice to Archbishop Schrattenbach, as references in letters of 11 May and 24 September 1768 show.
35. *Briefe*, i.264 (letter of 11 May 1768).
36. *Briefe*, i.273 (letter of 30 July 1768).

A glance at *La finta semplice* K51 shows us, of course, that far too much praise has been lavished on the twelve-year-old Mozart's work by observers from Leopold tc Jahn and Deiters. Only writers with an inadequate insight into the history of the genre could conclude that the work is not merely as good as, but better than, most similar pieces. We shall later see that it was only with *La finta giardiniera* that Mozart emerges as a serious, if as yet unequal, competitor as a composer of *opere buffe*. The earlier work, by contrast, may be briefly dealt with here as the musical equivalent of a schoolboy's essay.

Coltellini's text is no more than an average example of a particular type of comic-opera libretto at this time. Action and characters remain within well-defined confines. A Hungarian officer, Fracasso, is billeted on two wealthy bachelors, the self-important and at least in theory extremely misogynistic Don Cassandro and his brother, the timid, simple-minded and amorous Don Polidoro. Fracasso is conducting an affair with their beautiful sister, Giacinta. In keeping with the old *buffa* tradition, Fracasso's servant Simone is currently carrying on with Giacinta's maid Ninetta. But the brothers refuse to accept Fracasso as their brother-in-law, and so, on Ninetta's advice, Fracasso's sister, the wily Rosina, tricks them into falling in love with her and thereby persuading them to agree to the two marriages. She arrives at their home disguised as the 'make-believe simpleton' of the title,[37] and soon ensnares the two bachelors. The resultant confusions are entirely burlesque in character and constitute the main action of the opera. Finally the two brothers are told that Giacinta and Ninetta have fled with all their valuables, persuading them to promise their sister's hand to whoever recovers them. Fracasso and Simone succeed in doing so, and, to the brothers' great amazement and to scenes of general merriment, Rosina, who had previously given her hand in marriage to Cassandro, admits to her deception.

It is clear from Coltellini's libretto that audiences were still extremely partial not only to the bourgeois *comédie larmoyante* pioneered by Piccinni in *La buona figliuola* but also to the older type of *opera buffa* that was aimed at pure comedy. The result is a situation comedy of burlesque proportions, with all the usual scenes of beatings, drunken excesses and duels alongside the fustian and erudite outpourings that were ultimately intended as a parody of *opera seria*. The characters, too, recall the masks of the older *commedia dell'arte* tradition, with even the lover Fracasso retaining some of the features of the braggart Capitano Spavento. One suspects that Coltellini deliberately gave this libretto to the young Mozart in the belief that he would best be able to deal with these crudely drawn characters. Of all the challenges that they presented, the most grateful was no doubt that of Cassandro, the opera's most consistent and fully rounded character. But even in his opening aria, 'Non c'è al mondo altro che donne', the composer comes to grief, as he was bound to do, simply because he lacked the necessary knowledge of life in general and of his fellow human beings in particular. What did the twelve-year-old boy know about the misogyny and hostility to marriage on the part of an old bachelor, especially when seen in the distorting mirror of the Italian *buffa* tradition? He saw in Cassandro only a good-natured old blusterer and wrote an aria light years away from the scintillatingly, even fiendishly witty philippics of a composer like Paisiello or Guglielmi. It is significant that whenever his imagination found solid support in opportunities for commonplace tone-painting, he reveals greater independence in his handling of the text. In Cassandro's second aria, 'Ella vuole ed io torrei', the image of boiling blood, with its typically Italian 'blo blo', and the simile of the poodle raising its paw for some meat, then barking and howling when beaten, raise the work to an altogether higher plane, lending it a verve for which

37. This was a popular motif at this time and is also found, for example, in Paisiello's *La frascatana* of 1774.

the aria's lively orchestral writing is, of course, largely responsible.[38] But the most successful of Cassandro's arias is, 'Ubriaco non son io': clearly, the figure of the drunkard was familiar to the composer from his days in Salzburg. Listen to the way in which the orchestra staggers in right at the beginning, then passes without a break into foolish-sounding staccato semiquavers that almost recall the Bacchus duet in *Die Entführung aus dem Serail*:[39]

The way in which the orchestra gives the lie to Don Cassandro's claim that he is not drunk is nicely observed. Equally delightful is the passage in the second part of the aria where the orchestra keeps reminding him of his intoxicated state. Indeed, the orchestra plays an important role throughout the opera as a whole, its careful part-writing recalling not only Mozart's own education to date but also – as emerges from Gassmann's works[40] – more general practices among Viennese *opera buffa* composers at this time. The same is true of Mozart's handling of the following *secco* recitative, with its tone-painterly progressions in the bass of a kind frequently found in Cassandro's part. Also under this heading comes the dialogue between Cassandro and Rosina in the Pantomima in act two, scene seven, in which the exchange is largely conducted in the orchestra.[41] But this scene was also tailor-made for the singers, whom Mozart had to keep happy. By this stage in his career, Francesco Caratoli, who was playing the part of Don Cassandro, was less of a singer than an actor, skilfully compensating for his lack of a voice by occasionally overacting in an effort to please the groundlings.[42]

By contrast, Mozart hardly knew where to begin with the doltish figure of the lovesick Don Polidoro, revealing a cluelessness already apparent from the fact that for Polidoro's first aria, 'Cosa ha mai la donna indosso', he fell back on Christianity's aria 'Manches Übel will zuweilen' from *Die Schuldigkeit des Ersten Gebots*. Here the physician speaks calmingly of the painful operations that are sometimes necessary to cure an illness, whereas in the later work we are dealing with the first stirrings of love in the heart of a foolish old bachelor.[43] Evidently Mozart had recourse to this aria because he thought that he had been particularly successful in capturing a sense of tender emotion and was sufficiently naïve as to believe that it was equally appropriate to the new situation, the

38. The original ending of this aria was discarded by Mozart and replaced by a new one. Part of the original survives and is reproduced in NMA II/5/2, 411. Here, Mozart underscored the word 'porco' with some appropriate tone-painting in the orchestra, but the abrupt ending is more awkward than original.

39. The bass line should be read an octave lower than written.

40. See the section on *opera buffa* below.

41. The instruments play a similarly pantomimic role in act two, scene sixteen of Gassmann's *La contessina*.

42. Sonnenfels, *Gesammelte Schriften*, v.297; Burney, *The Present State of Music in France and Italy*, 94; and Johann H. F. Müller, *Genaue Nachrichten*, i.73. According to Müller (ii.132), he died in Vienna in 1772 at the age of 67. ◆ Little is known of Francesco Caratoli (c1705–72), who had earlier served as chamber musician to the Duke of Modena and was active in Vienna from about 1763.

43. It is difficult to understand how Jahn and Deiters (i.89) could be so enthusiastic in their praise of this aria, even going so far as to claim that it reminds them of Cherubino: after all, we are dealing here not with a naïve youth but with an old bachelor of relatively advanced years.

psychological complexities of which were completely lost on him. Moreover, he intended the part for the tenor Gioacchino Garibaldi, whose beautiful voice was particularly affecting in slow passages but whose coloratura technique was sadly deficient, while as an actor he made ungainly attempts to model himself on Caratoli.[44]

Nor can Polidoro's second aria, 'Sposa cara', be regarded as a success. It is in two sections, but each section is further divided into three contrastive subsections, with Mozart setting each new idea in turn, without drawing them together to form a unified whole. The first section is addressed to Rosina and, in terms of its atmosphere, recalls the world of Johann Christian Bach, while its melodic line is not dissimilar to that of a Viennese song.[45] But the second section, directed at Don Cassandro, makes do with a not particularly skilful juxtaposition of hackneyed *buffo* phrases. The only original feature here is, once again, the writing for the violins, the surly figurations of which depict the violent gestures of the indignant Cassandro. In the third section, too, it is the instruments that have the lion's share of the action.

Of the two servants, Simone and Ninetta, it is Simone who comes off best, although not even here is there any trace of the manic high spirits of the Italian characters of this kind. None the less, his three arias ('Troppa briga', 'Con certe persone', and 'Vieni, vieni, o mia Ninetta') reveal a natural, stolid humour. It is significant, however, that in most of the passages where Mozart imitates the genuine Italian *buffo* style with its rapid patter and other realistic ingredients, the result is oddly unmusical and ineffectual: it is clear that he is familiar with the style but that he imitates only its superficial aspects, while remaining impervious to its inner nature, in other words, its close link between singing and acting. He is at his most successful in the aria 'Con certe persone vuol esser bastone', where we find a delightful, if not entirely original, feature in Simone's exclamation 'Madama, bastone!' which he interjects into the final ritornello, thereby summing up the aria's principal idea. The intended singer, Domenico Poggi, combined a pleasing and well-trained voice with a delightful style of acting free from exaggeration. He was popular with connoisseurs of the theatre.[46]

The part of the servant girl Ninetta can have been intended only for Antonia Bernasconi, who had already triumphed as Sandrina in both Piccinni's *La buona figliuola* and Sacchini's *La contadina in corte*.[47] Here, too, Mozart fell far short of the vivacity and liveliness of his Italian models. Her three arias – 'Un marito, donne care' and the two versions of 'Sono in amore', of which the older is the better of the two – are partially or wholly minuet-like in character and, as such, reflect the influence of Viennese songs and French *opéras comiques* typical of Viennese *opere buffe* of this period. Her most successful number is her lively and charming little song, 'Un marito, donne care', even if its lightly scored opening had been a regular feature of the Italian *buffa* tradition since the time of Pergolesi's *La serva padrona*.[48]

Giacinta is one of those semi-serious characters who, when judged by our own standards, is impossible to deal with and who seems to exist only to be shoved around like some pawn in a game of chess. In her first two arias ('Marito io vorrei' and 'Se a maritarmi arrivo') she paints a portrait of her future husband in the best *buffa* tradition. In the first, she announces:

44. Sonnenfels, *Gesammelte Schriften*, v.296. According to the *Teutscher Merkur*, iii (1789), 210, he appeared in Rome as late as 1780 as a toothless old man. ◆ Garibaldi died sometime after 1792; he was born in 1743.
45. Cf. the opening bars of the second-act finale in Haas, *Florian Gassmann: La contessina*, 254.
46. Sonnenfels, *Gesammelte Schriften*, v.293–4; Johann H. F. Müller, *Genaue Nachrichten*, i.79; Kelly, *Reminiscences of Michael Kelly*, i.66–8.
47. Sonnenfels, *Gesammelte Schriften*, v.299–300. ◆ In light of the importance Abert attaches to Gluck's *Alceste* of 1767, it is worth noting that Bernasconi's greatest success was in that opera.
48. The reminiscences of *La serva padrona* are so numerous that we must assume that Mozart was familiar with the work.

Marito io vorrei, ma senza fatica,
averlo, se comoda, lasciarlo, se intrica.

[I'd like to be married, but without the trouble. I'd like to have him if he does what I want and leave him if he's a nuisance.]

He should be 'a man of intelligence, but made of wood'. Here Coltellini contrasts Fracasso's impetuous courtship with the placidity of a character who dislikes any sudden excitement, but Mozart strikes a note that is roguish and sentimental by turns, and the situation scarcely improves with her somewhat livelier second aria: not even here is there any trace of a more sharply delineated characterization. Only with her third aria ('Che scompiglio'), in which she expresses her fears following her ostensible flight, does she enter a world of tragic emotion. Here Jahn and Deiters speak of an intentional caricature.[49] If this is so, Mozart has failed in what he was trying to achieve: in such cases contemporary audiences were accustomed to quite different images of horror from Italian *buffa* composers. It seems to me, rather, that the boy took a much more serious view of the situation. At all events, the words elicited from him an aria which, in certain important respects, already looks forward to the mature composer's distinctive style. The tonality of C minor, the eerily ascending opening motif:[50]

and the tenacity with which the minor tonality is maintained, with only brief modulations to a brighter major: these are all devices that Mozart was later to use in order to express the sinister and wildly impassioned. In its whole approach, the part of Giacinta was tailor-made for Teresa Eberardi, whose pleasing contralto voice was praised by Sonnenfels, although he added that her trill was by no means flawless and that her acting was not free from artificiality.[51]

No doubt as a result of pressure applied by the tenor Filippo Laschi, it was the part of Fracasso that caused Mozart the greatest difficulty, with the whole of his first aria ('Guarda la donna in viso') having to be rewritten, as was the middle section of his third ('Nelle guerre d'amore'). Laschi was essentially a *buffo* tenor, but he also played the part of lovers, and here listeners were disturbed by the fact that he could no longer reach certain notes, a fact that he managed to disguise only with difficulty by transposing the notes in question or by introducing coloratura passages. His tone quality, moreover, was now distinctly unpleasant.[52] In both form and character, all Fracasso's arias

49. *W. A. Mozart*, i.95.
50. This clearly looks forward to the C minor serenade K388 and related works; only the filled-out harmonies and Italianate *Trommelbässe* still reveal the beginner.
51. Sonnenfels, *Gesammelte Schriften*, v.301. ◆ Teresa Eberardi was active at Vienna from 1766.
52. Sonnenfels, *Gesammelte Schriften*, v.293. ◆ The tenor Filippo Laschi (*fl*1739–89) had been active at London, Brussels and Turin before appearing in Baldassare Galuppi's *Li tre amanti ridicoli* at the Burgtheater in January 1765; further, see Weiss, 'La diffusione del repertorio operistico nell'Italia del Settecento: Il caso dell'opera buffa'. The two versions of 'Guarda la donna in viso' are published in NMA II/5/2, 60–8 (revised version) and 403–10 (original version).

are *serioso* in style, although the earlier version of 'Guarda la donna in viso'[53] was originally in the *buffa* tradition. It was replaced by an extremely straitlaced number, so that in the end there was virtually no trace left in the music of the character's only prominent characteristic, his daredevilry as a soldier.

Mozart lavished particular care on the titular heroine, Rosina: here he clearly set out to give of his best, casting around for viable models in the rich repository of his operatic memories. The part was evidently intended for Clementina Baglioni, whose voice, according to Sonnenfels, had 'a silvery tone, was as flexible as one could wish, and carried admirably'. Her singing was 'not reckless, but correct; her gestures, when she chose, were easy and becoming'.[54]

With her very first, songlike aria ('Colla bocca e non col colore') she strikes a delightfully intimate Piccinnian note supported by flutes and strings, the divided violas frequently playing in octaves with the violins. By contrast, her characterful echo aria ('Senti l'eco') inevitably recalls the world of Johann Christian Bach not only in terms of its instrumentation (strings, english horns, *corni da caccia* and solo oboe) but, more especially, in the tenderness of its melodic line. The echo effects in the solo oboe part extend even as far as the coloratura writing and may possibly be a reminiscence of Gluck's *Orfeo*. The second part of the aria is an allegro grazioso that proves something of an anticlimax. But the highlight of the opera as a whole is Rosina's two-part aria in which she pleads with the 'amoretti' or Cupids not to torment her ('Amoretti'). Here, too, the instrumentation is exceptional (strings with corresponding violas and bassoons), but the vocal writing also reveals greater freedom and nobility of utterance, at times achieving the expressive intensity of the later Mozart. Once again, of course, we may see the boy's revered mentor, Johann Christian Bach, peering over his young charge's shoulder. With its charmingly erotic stamp, the piece explores territory familiar to Italian opera composers of the period, while its numerous sighs and ornaments both breath the spirit of the Rococo. Not only was it Mozart's first significant achievement in this field, it also reveals his ability to strike a more personal note. Chief among its features is the return to E major towards the end of the piece, with its mounting sense of longing: all in all, an aria like this would have been to the credit of many a mature composer. In Rosina's fourth aria ('Ho sentito a dir'), by contrast, Mozart fails almost completely in his attempt to depict the 'feigned simplicity' of the title: psychologically speaking, he was unequal to such a challenge.

Formally speaking, these arias are cast either in simple binary *Liedform* in the manner of a cavatina, or they adopt a two-part form that was particularly popular at this time, in which each part is further divided into individual sections distinguished in terms of their tempo and time-signature. Only Fracasso's arias are in the ternary form associated with *opera seria*, albeit with a more modern foreshortening of the *da capo*. Understandably, the young Mozart did not dare to experiment with novel forms in individual cases, as did the great exponents of Italian *opera buffa*. In the ternary duet for Cassandro and Fracasso ('Cospetton cospettonaccio'), with its delightful description of the duel so feared by the elder of the two characters, the focus of interest lies in the orchestra, which appears to side with Fracasso, repeatedly laying into Cassandro with its whistling cuts and thrusts.

The three multi-sectional finales follow the course of the action, each section distinguished in terms of tempo and time-signature. These, too, remain firmly within traditional confines: the

---

53. Its opening recalls the beginning of Leopold Mozart's third keyboard sonata; see Max Seiffert, *Leopold Mozart: Ausgewählte Werke*, 22.
54. Sonnenfels, *Gesammelte Schriften*, v.300. ◆ Clementina Baglioni (d. after 1783) was probably the daughter of the tenor Francesco Baglioni. She made her Viennese début in Hasse's *Il trionfo di Clelia* in 1762.

unity of the individual sections is achieved either by a main theme that keeps returning in the manner of a rondo or by some recurrent and memorable motif in the orchestra. In the first- and second-act finales, Mozart follows Piccinni's lead and takes up ideas from earlier sections. But there is, of course, virtually no trace of the drama and life found in Italian finales of the period. Even important turning points in the plot such as the flight of the two women in the second act and the denouement in the third are dismissively dealt with in a spirit of harmless merriment, without any sense of tension. The weakest element is again the vocal writing, with individual sections even recalling the genre's infancy, when the melodic line was simply divided up between the various parts without any regard for individual characterization. But even when Mozart follows the words closely and uses a whole series of motifs, he fails to grip his listener. Only in the case of the cowardly and tearful Polidoro do we find at least the first stirrings of a more sharply delineated characterization in all three finales. Like the Introduzione, the final sections of these three numbers are all carefree examples of the homophonic *Liedform* found in the Italian *opere buffe* of this period.

As a whole, Mozart's first opera must be accounted a failure as a drama, although it still deserves an occasional airing on account of the comparisons that may be drawn with his later works and that certainly do the boy credit. None the less, he was simply not mature enough at this stage in his career to rise to such a challenge, and yet, if he lagged far behind his fellow composers, this is simply a sign of his healthy and natural development. It is impossible, however, not to marvel at the boy's ability to assimilate the *buffa* style. Even here, he is already familiar with most of its characteristics, from the popular to the coarsely realistic. He is also familiar with its vocal and, above all, its instrumental style. Of course, he begins by merely reproducing its more superficial aspects, the true *buffa* spirit still remaining a closed book to him, hence his inability to make the sort of impression that the Italian composers of the period were capable of creating. Ultimately, what we find here are echoes of the various stimuli that any *buffa* composer could find in Vienna at this time, from local songs and singspiels to French *opéras comiques* and, most important of all, the independent treatment of the orchestra inspired by the sort of instrumental music that was currently flourishing in the city. This, indeed, was the area in which Mozart was most at home, whereas his handling of vocal lines is still largely lacking in freedom, unmusical and, hence, ineffectual.[55] The overture marks a considerable advance on the D major symphony of 16 January 1768 K45, with which it shares various themes and their treatment, but not its menuetto, which Mozart omitted. But the piece's instrumental garb has become much richer and, most important of all, the additional winds are used not merely to reinforce the other instruments but to speak an independent language of their own, producing sonorities that place the old ideas in an entirely new light. (Listen, for example, to the first movement's final subject group.)

In the autograph score, the changes that Mozart was required to make by his singers are clearly visible. But Leopold's hand, too, has left its mark here in the form of virtually all the tempo and performance markings, together with the names of the characters and instruments. And there is no doubt that Leopold's influence extended well beyond such superficial aspects of the work: after all, this was a field still largely unfamiliar to Wolfgang. It is, of course, no longer possible to prove this point.[56]

---

55. To defend Affligio and his contemporaries at Leopold's expense, as Wyzewa, Saint-Foix and Schurig have done, is simply not possible, so serious are these shortcomings. Even if Leopold exaggerated in order to make his point, it certainly did not need months of malicious delaying tactics to draw the boy's attention to the inadequacies of his work.
56. ◆ For details, see the critical report to NMA II/5/2.

To a certain extent, Leopold was compensated for the disappointments bound up with this opera by a commission from another quarter. He and his family had been introduced to Anton Mesmer,[57] who was later to become famous for his method of healing his patients by 'animal magnetism' and who, having married into money, kept a well-appointed house in the Landstraße district of Vienna that proved a popular meeting place for a whole host of well-educated people, including Franz Reinhard von Heufeld. Mesmer was a keen music lover and had a small theatre in his garden, where he now proceeded to stage Mozart's little German singspiel, *Bastien und Bastienne* K50.[58]

The work is ultimately based on Jean-Jacques Rousseau's intermezzo *Le devin du village*, the genesis of which Rousseau himself describes in the eighth book of his *Confessions*.[59] His aim in writing the piece had been to offer his compatriots an alternative to the Italian *buffo* intermezzos that had first been heard in Paris in 1752 during a visit by a touring Italian company and that had given rise to the famous dispute over the respective merits of French and Italian music. He decided to write it while staying at Passy and completed it within the space of only six weeks.[60] At a private rehearsal at the home of the famous French historiographer Charles Pinot Duclos, the work caused something of a sensation, and de Cury, the Intendant des Menus Plaisirs, finally obtained permission for it to be performed at court. The work was duly given at Fontainebleau in the king's presence on 18 and 24 October 1752, with Marie Fel as Colette and Pierre de Jélyotte as Colin. It left a deep impression. The first public performance took place at the Académie Royale de Musique in Paris on 1 March 1753, and once again proved brilliantly successful.[61] Rousseau's tunes were soon on everyone's lips, including even those of the king, who reputedly sang 'J'ai perdu mon serviteur' from morning to night 'with the worst voice in his entire kingdom'. As late as 1774 it was applauded with the same enthusiasm as Gluck's *Orphée*,[62] and, to the astonishment of German observers, was still being performed to immense acclaim in 1819 and 1821, before finally disappearing from the stage in 1864.[63] The action is simple in the extreme.

57. That the person in question was indeed the proponent of 'animal magnetism' was first propounded by Nissen, who speaks of 'the well-known friend of the Mozart family'. Jahn, by contrast, assumed that it was a doctor of medicine of the same name (see Helfert, *Die österreichische Volksschule*, i.132–3). More recently, Deiters (i.100) has drawn attention to the younger Mesmer's letter (Nohl, *Mozart nach den Schilderungen seiner Zeitgenossen*, 210) in which there is talk of Leopold's 'Swabian friends'. The inventor of 'animal magnetism' was also from Swabia – he was born at Iznang near Radolfzell – which means that Nissen was right. ◆ In Vienna the Mozarts were friendly with two members of the Mesmer family, Franz Anton Mesmer (1734–1815), the proponent of animal magnetism, and his cousin Joseph Conrad Mesmer (1735–1804). Franz Anton was later accused of medical deceitfulness and left Vienna in 1778, taking up residence in Paris. See Deutsch, 'Die Mesmers und die Mozarts'.
58. On the strength of *Briefe*, i.484–5 (letter of 21 July 1773), Lert (*Mozart auf dem Theater*, 330) assumes that it was an open-air theatre made from box hedges. ◆ There is no unequivocal evidence that *Bastien und Bastienne* was performed at Mesmer's; the first to assert this was Nissen, *Biographie W. A. Mozarts*, 127. As it happens, Mesmer's garden theatre was not completed in 1768, although this in itself does not rule out a performance at his house. It has been suggested, too, that Mozart may have started work on the opera in Salzburg as early as 1767 (see NMA II/5/3, X–XII), although it is worth noting that the autograph is written entirely on paper from Mozart's stay in Vienna.
59. Schelle, *Berliner Musik-Zeitung Echo*, xiv (1864), 384–5. ◆ Further, see Tyler, 'Bastien und Bastienne'; Blank, 'Jean-Jacques Rousseaus Devin du Village'; and Rousseau, *Le Devin du village*.
60. See Jansen, *Jean-Jacques Rousseau als Musiker*, 158ff.; Pougin, *Jean-Jacques Rousseau musicien*; and Tiersot, *Jean-Jacques Rousseau*, 99ff.
61. On 23 June 1753 Friedrich Melchior Grimm wrote to Johann Christoph Gottsched, '"Le devin du village" est un intermède charmant dont les paroles et la musique sont de M. Rousseau'; see Danzel, *Gottsched und seine Zeit*, 351. On 15 December 1753 Grimm went on to describe it in his *Correspondance littéraire* (i.92–3) as an 'intermède agréable, qui a eu un très-grand succès à Fontainebleau et à Paris' and, a short while after, as an 'intermède français très-joli et très-agréable' (i.112–13). Later he invariably omitted all reference to it whenever discussing Rousseau's musical accomplishments, mentioning only his failed opera *Les muses galantes*.
62. La Harpe, *Correspondance littéraire*, ii.59.
63. *AmZ*, xxi (1819/20), 841 and xxiii (1821), 141; see also Berlioz, *Voyage musical en Allemagne et en Italie*, i.389 and Jansen, *Jean-Jacques Rousseau*, 185. *Le devin du village* was revived as late as 1890: see Pougin, *Jean-Jacques Rousseau*, 91. ◆ Concerning

Colette, a shepherdess, is disconsolate because her lover Colin has left her. She visits the village soothsayer in search of help and advice. He tells her that the lady of the manor has ensnared Colin but that the latter continues to love her. He will visit her, but she must punish him by feigning indifference and in that way rekindle his love for her; she promises to do as the soothsayer suggests. Colin now enters in turn and tells the soothsayer that he is cured of his delusion and is returning to his Colette. When the soothsayer explains that she now loves another, he begs him to help; the soothsayer promises to conjure up Colette by means of a magic spell and Colin may then try his luck with her. Colette duly appears and with some difficulty plays the part of the aloof beauty, but when Colin rushes away in despair, she calls him back and a scene of tender reconciliation follows, accompanied by renewed protestations of love and fidelity. The soothsayer receives his thanks and reward, and the assembled countryfolk join in celebrating the lovers' new-found happiness, which finds expression in a series of couplets.

There was every reason why this piece should be so tremendously successful, for in it we may detect a breath of the revolutionary spirit that two years earlier had inspired the first of Rousseau's famous *Discourses*, even though there is no denying that the pastoral world depicted here was firmly bound up with the very society that Rousseau so despised. None the less, the piece contained enough that was new and kept its distance not only from the rhetoric and high emotion of the French *tragédie lyrique* but also from the tendency towards caricature manifest in the Italian *buffa* tradition: in Rousseau's view, both were at odds with his basic principle that a work should be natural. Thus his tale of a village soothsayer has become a pastoral idyll which, according to his own later explanation,[64] takes place among shepherds. The music, too, had to reflect their simple customs. But the songs that these shepherds sing are essentially French in origin (and hence emphatically anti-Italian), and Rousseau has been outstandingly successful in capturing the natural grace and peculiar rhythmic vitality of this folk art.[65] This is also true of the recitatives,[66] for the delivery of which Rousseau gives the singers the clearest possible instructions. Here, too, he avoids both the over-emphatic emotionalism of *opera seria* and the cursoriness of the Italian *secco* recitative: his own recitatives mirror the words, presupposing a style of declamation that is correct, emotionally charged and invariably natural.

For all its success, *Le devin du village* was, of course, the work of a talented amateur,[67] but its historical significance is for that very reason no less great than the acclaim with which it was greeted by contemporary audiences.[68] Above all, it became a powerful ally of the French comic operas that were now coming into fashion: even their titles – *Rose et Colas*, *Annette et Lubin* and so on – make this parentage plain. It is no surprise, therefore, to find the work soon being parodied – the surest

---

the reception of Rousseau's *Le devin du village*, see Waeber, 'Le Devin du village de Jean-Jacques Rousseau: Histoire, orientations esthétiques, reception, 1752–1829'; for its adaptation in English, see Voisine, 'Le *Devin du village* de Rousseau et son adaptation anglaise par le musicologue Charles Burney'. Further, see Thalker, 'Rousseaus *Devin du village*', and Verba, *Music and the French Enlightenment*.

64. Rousseau, *Dictionnaire de musique*, entry under 'Pastorale', 366.

65. For further details on this and the following points, see Arnheim, 'Le devin du village von J. J. Rousseau und die Parodie "Les Amours de Bastien et Bastienne"'.

66. See also Rousseau's article 'Récitatif' in his *Dictionnaire de musique*, 399–404.

67. On the alleged contribution of Philidor and Francœur, see Arnheim, 'Le devin du village', 692ff. It was even claimed that Rousseau had written only the words and that the music was the work of a composer in Lyons (see *AmZ*, xiv [1812/13], 469; see also Castil-Blaze, *Molière musicien*, ii.409ff.), an accusation contested by Grétry in his *Mémoires*, i.276 and iii.306. Rousseau hoped to refute this charge by writing a second work, but the result was not a success: see La Harpe, *Correspondance littéraire*, ii.370 and Adam, *Souvenirs d'un musicien*, 202.

68. An English version by Burney (1766) proved a failure; see Parke, *Musical Memoirs*, ii.93. German versions were published by Gottlieb Leon in *Der teutsche Merkur*, ii (1787), 193ff., and Carl Dielitz (Berlin, 1820).

sign in Paris at this time that a piece was a runaway success. Moreover, the parodies generally went beyond mere satire and, taking their cue from the original, included similar texts set to popular melodies, the whole spiced with genuine humour and occasionally even with allusions to events of the day. The true home of these pieces was the Comédie-Italienne, where over the years every major success at the Académie Royale found a parodistic echo. And so we find a parody of Rousseau's piece being staged at the Comédie-Italienne on 4 August 1753 under the title *Les amours de Bastien et Bastienne*.[69] Its authors were Harny de Guerville[70] and the popular Marie-Justine-Benoîte Favart, a singer and actress as charming as she was witty.[71] The parody went one step further than Rousseau and turned his rustic and sentimental Arcadians into real peasants who express corresponding sentiments in their local dialect. The result is completely natural in its coarse and homely way. Marie-Justine-Benoîte Favart herself established her reputation in the role of Bastienne,[72] appearing in a sleeveless linen smock and wooden clogs, the novelty of which outraged critics but delighted the general public. She was even painted wearing this costume and apostrophized in bombastic verses by her friend, Claude-Henri de Fuzée, the Abbé de Voisenon. The parody is in surprisingly good taste, revealing considerable skill and a very real sense of dramatic characterization. As always, the individual numbers were sung to popular melodies. In Rousseau's version, for example, Colette's first aria begins with a sentimental outburst, 'J'ai perdu tout mon bonheur' (I've lost all my happiness), whereas the more down-to-earth Bastienne sings 'J'ai perdu mon ami' (I've lost my lover) to the tune of a song that was popular at this time, 'J'ai perdu mon âne' (I've lost my donkey). This single example may suffice to indicate the nature and aim of the parody as a whole.

In 1764 *Les amours de Bastien et Bastienne* found a German translator in the person of Friedrich Wilhelm Weiskern,[73] and it was Weiskern's text, with a mere handful of alterations, that Mozart set.[74] Weiskern produced a continuous dialogue interrupted at appropriate points by individual arias and duets. These numbers – eleven arias, three duets and a trio – do not always correspond to the ones in Rousseau, and, indeed, it seems unlikely that he was familiar with *Le devin du village*. Some arias have several strophes, but Mozart set only the first. The French parody has been involuntarily travestied with an ineptitude that beggars belief, as may be seen from the various forms of the opening aria:

69.   Favart, *Théâtre de M. Favart*, i. A libretto printed in Amsterdam in 1758 bears the note: 'Représenté à Bruxelles Nov. 1753 par les Comédiens français sous les ordres de S. Alt. Roy.'
70.   Grimm, *Correspondance littéraire*, iv.400 and 417; on Harny de Guerville, see Cucuel, 'Notes sur Jean-Jacques Rousseau musicien', 289.
71.   ◆ Abert neglects to mention the third author of *Les amours de Bastien et Bastienne*, Favart's husband Charles-Simon Favart (1710–92). See Iacuzzi, *The European Vogue of Favart: The Diffusion of the Opéra-Comique*; Pougin, *Madame Favart: Étude théâtrale*; and Pendle, 'L'opéra-comique à Paris de 1762 à 1789'. Further concerning parodies of *Le devin du village*, see Darlow, 'Les parodies du Devin du village de Rousseau et la sensibilité dans l'opéra-comique français'.
72.   See *Dictionnaire du théâtre*, vi.228–9 and *Theaterkalender* (1776), 100.
73.   *Bastienne, eine französische Opéra comique. Auf Befehl in einer freyen Übersetzung nachgeahmt von Fr. W. Weiskern* (Vienna, 1764). For a number of the songs, the original French melodies were retained, but the remainder were newly written. The work was performed in Vienna, in Brünn in 1770, in Prague in 1772 and in Hildesheim in 1776 (Johann H. F. Müller, *Genaue Nachrichten*, i.31 and ii.213; *Abschied von der National-Schaubühne*, 137).
74.   Nissen names Schachtner as the librettist. Perhaps Schachtner was involved in versifying the prose dialogue, a number of scenes of which Mozart later set as recitative – a task that proved a waste of time, and one that he never completed. The recitatives for Colas are written in the alto clef, persuading Wüllner, who edited the work for the AMA, to argue that these were written for a later performance that did not in the event take place but at which the role of Colas would have been sung by a contralto. ◆ In fact, Schachtner contributed significantly to the version set by Mozart (for his now-lost autograph text, see Orel, 'Die Legende um Mozarts "Bastien und Bastienne"') and a comparison of Mozart's setting with other surviving texts shows that he included material from Weiskern's original, by Johann Müller (1738–1815), an actor involved in early performances of *Les amours de Bastien et Bastienne* in Vienna, and Schachtner. See Tyler, 'Bastien und Bastienne' and NMA II/5/3, VIII–IX.

Rousseau	Favart
	(Air: J'ai perdu mon âne)
J'ai perdu tout mon bonheur;	J'ons pardu mon ami!
J'ai perdu mon serviteur;	Depis c'tems-là j'nons point dormi,
Colin me délaisse.	Je n' vivons pû qu'à d'mi.
Hélas! il a pu changer!	J'ons pardu mon ami,
Je voudrois n'y plus songer:	J'en ons le cœur tout transi,
J'y songe sans cesse.	Je m' meurs de souci.

Weiskern

Mein liebster Freund hat mich verlassen,
Mit ihm ist Schlaf und Ruh dahin;
Ich weiß vor Leid mich nicht zu fassen,
Der Kummer schwächt mir Aug' und Sinn.
Vor Gram und Schmerz
Erstarrt das Herz,
Und diese Not
Bringt mir den Tod.

[My dearest friend has abandoned me. With him, sleep and peace of mind have fled. I am beside myself with grief, my eyes and mind grow weak with such wretchedness. My heart is numb with sorrow and pain, and this suffering will be the death of me.]

Although Weiskern uses Viennese dialect in places, the text remains wooden and flat:

Bastienne

Ganz allein
Voller Pein
Stets zu sein
Ist kein Spaß
Im grünen Gras![75]

[Always to be completely alone, full of grief, is no joke in the green grass!]

Bastien

Geh, du sagst mir eine Fabel,
Bastienne trüget nicht.
Nein, sie ist kein falscher Schnabel,
Welcher anders denkt als spricht.

[Get away with you, you're making it up. Bastienne wouldn't deceive me. No, she's no liar who says one thing and thinks another.]

Passages such as these already look forward to the poetic diction of the later Viennese singspiel.[76]

75. In the opera, the last two lines have been changed, probably by Mozart himself, to 'Bringt dem Herz / Nur Qual und Schmerz' (brings the heart only torment and pain). Other changes are noted in the critical commentaries to AMA V/3 and NMA II/5/3.
76. A comparison with passages from a translation of Metastasio that was published in Vienna in 1769 and that are cited by Hiller (Über Metastasio und seine Werke, 17ff.) reveals certain affinities.

In tackling *Bastien und Bastienne*, Mozart was required to switch from *opera buffa* to German singspiel and assimilate new stylistic principles, but it is a step that he takes with his characteristic assurance. Of course, the innocent world of the singspiel was much closer to the boy's imagination than the far more complex demands of the *buffa* tradition. But at the same time, it was far harder in Vienna at this time to find suitable models for such an approach. True, improvised comedy was particularly popular here and music was an important aspect of it, thereby laying the foundations for the later singspiel tradition, with Joseph Haydn, for example, beginning his operatic career with a work of this kind, a setting of Joseph Felix von Kurz's *Der neue krumme Teufel*. But all these works were more or less burlesque in character, whereas it is significant that Mozart conceived of his own piece rather in the pastoral tradition, thereby bypassing Favart and Harny and returning to Rousseau's original conception. And works of this kind were very thin on the ground in Vienna at this period.[77] Although writers are fond of appealing in this context to the founder of the north German singspiel, Johann Adam Hiller, comparisons between Hiller and Mozart's first contribution to the genre need to be drawn with considerable caution,[78] for Hiller, too, suffered much from the profound aversion of the Viennese to the art of north Germany, and isolated performances of his works before 1768 all ended in failure.[79] Moreover, a comparison between Mozart's *Bastien und Bastienne* and Hiller's three relevant singspiels – *Die verwandelten Weiber* (1766), *Lisuart und Dariolette* (1766) and *Lottchen am Hofe* (1767) – shows that the only points that the two composers had in common were their general aims and their predilection for the popular form of the song as a genre. On points of detail, by contrast, they went their separate ways. Above all, Mozart retained far more of the character of the German singspiel by ignoring such Italianate ingredients as coloratura arias and the three-movement sinfonia favoured by Hiller. The sources on which the boy drew in writing this work must be sought elsewhere, primarily in the Parisian *opéras comiques* of Duni, Philidor and Monsigny, whose tunes still echoed in his ear from the time of his visit to Paris.[80] In numbers such as 'Ich geh' jetzt auf die Weide', 'Würd' ich auch', 'Geh', du sagst mir eine Fabel', 'Dein Trotz vermehrt sich' and especially 'Befraget mich ein zartes Kind', with its curious cross-rhythms, he brilliantly captured the vital and witty rhythms of all three of these French composers.[81] But other influences, too, are identifiable, influences that can be traced not to Hiller but to the popular south German song tradition whose traces we have already encountered in Mozart's music on more than one occasion. This influence may be found not only in individual reminiscences and certain turns of phrase[82] but, more especially, in the heartfelt tone of many of the sustained melodies, where there is no trace of sentimentality: listen,

77. See Robert Haas's introduction to *Ignaz Umlauff: Die Bergknappen*, XXIII.

78. See, for example, Wyzewa and Saint-Foix, *Wolfgang Amédée Mozart*, i.239. Their remarks must be treated with extreme caution, given their description of Hiller's lieder as 'lieds viennois'.

79. See Haas, *Ignaz Umlauff: Die Bergknappen*, XXIII.

80. ◆ During Mozart's stay in Paris in 1763–4 and 1766, works by Egidio Duni (1708–75), the famous chess-player François-André Philidor (1726–95) and Pierre-Alexandre Monsigny (1729–1817) performed at the Comédie-Italienne included *Le milicien* (1 January 1763), *Les deux chasseurs et la laitière* (23 July 1763) and *Le rendez-vous* (16 November 1763) by Duni; *Les fêtes de la paix* (4 July 1763) and *Le sorcier* (2 January 1764) by Philidor; and *Rose et Colas* (8 March 1764) by Monsigny.

81. See Wyzewa and Saint-Foix, *Wolfgang Amédée Mozart*, i.239.

82. Cf. the beginning of the aria 'Ich geh' jetzt auf die Weide', which could be by Schubart; for an analogy with the middle section of this same aria, see Rattay, *Die Ostracher Liederhandschrift*, 57–8; for an analogy with bar 9ff. from 'Geh', du sagst mir eine Fabel', see the *Augsburger Tafelkonfekt* in Lindner, *Geschichte des deutschen Liedes*, 72, and for an analogy with the beginning of 'Großen Dank dir abzustatten', see Lindner, *Geschichte des deutschen Liedes*, 96. There are also affinities between Mozart's lieder and the Ostracher Liederhandschrift (Rattay, *Die Ostracher Liederhandschrift*, 91).

for example, to 'Mein liebster Freund', 'Wenn mein Bastien einst im Scherze', 'Meiner Liebsten schöne Wangen' and the second section of 'Kinder! Kinder!'. Such numbers reveal the born song composer, a composer capable of combining a popular tone with high art to consummate effect and, in terms of sheer invention, they already raise Mozart far above Hiller, whose singspiel songs often enough bear traces of the dust of a bygone, periwigged age. And for this very reason, *Bastien und Bastienne* is far superior to the superficially much more demanding *La finta semplice*. On that occasion, Mozart had struggled to rise to a challenge that was far beyond him, whereas now, albeit in a far more modest context, he was able to give of himself. Bastienne's delightful little song, 'Er war mir sonst treu und ergeben', would not be to the discredit of a volume of songs by the mature composer. Of course, the work as a whole is no mature masterpiece, especially in terms of its characterization, but this shortcoming is by no means as problematical within the context of its harmless action as it was in the case of *La finta semplice*, quite apart from which Mozart has succeeded in turning at least the magician Colas into an independent figure who functions as an effective foil to the lovers. And, as before, it is the orchestra that is used above all to achieve this aim, even though it is employed with far greater restraint than in the earlier work. Colas is introduced with an earthy entrance aria ('Befraget mich ein zartes Kind') complete with drone (with augmented fourth) that looks back to earlier works by Leopold Mozart and to the *Galimathias musicum* of 1766, while his hocus-pocus aria ('Diggi, daggi') – another piece emphatically in a minor tonality – again gives the orchestra an independent part to play.

All the vocal numbers are in simple binary *Liedform*. The occasional tendency to subdivide them into two parts, each with its own time-signature, suggests not so much Hiller (for whom such a division is by no means the general rule) as the influence of the almost contemporary *La finta semplice*. The four ensemble movements are likewise simple songs in which the voices occasionally merge in the simplest harmonies – generally in folksong-like thirds and sixths – while the closing trio is distinguished only by its fuller sonorities and richer instrumentation.

Mozart's assured grasp of style is also clear from the single-movement overture, the design of which is as simple and straightforward as possible. It has only a single theme, which recurs in the course of the piece first in the dominant and then in the tonic, finally modulating very quietly to the subdominant and thereafter setting the mood for the opening aria. This is the first time that Mozart uses the overture to announce the standpoint from which he expects the listener to observe the subsequent action. The theme begins by striking a pastoral note:

The melody and its accompaniment, and especially the tendency to hold on to the tonic or dominant or often both together, conjure up the sounds of a musette, and in the course of the rest of the aria the first violin often repeats the tonic on the open G string or D string. The similarity with the main theme of Beethoven's 'Eroica' symphony is no doubt purely fortuitous.[83]

All these features mean that a work that is now gratifyingly returning to the modern operatic repertory was very much an interloper in the world of the Austrian theatre of the 1760s.[84] Its historical importance is undisputed. The present-day scholar may derive a certain pleasure from observing the twelve-year-old Mozart contributing to the two genres in which he was later to garner his finest laurels: the Italian *opera buffa* and the German singspiel. In the first, he initially failed, while with the latter he created his first genuinely viable work for the theatre.[85]

One of Bastien's arias ('Geh', du sagst mir eine Fabel') was published with a piano accompaniment in a Viennese newspaper, where it appeared with different words ('Daphne deine Rosenwangen') alongside another song, *Freude, Königin der Weisen*, to words by Johann Peter Uz (K52 and 53).[86] With its uniform rhythms (all the lines begin with the same rhythmic figure), minimal modulations and melodic commonplaces, this song recalls the *Lieder der Teutschen* that had first appeared in Berlin in 1767. In its originality of expression, it is far less advanced than the songs that make up the singspiel. Both these songs, it may be added, had a precursor in the little soprano duet, *Ach was müssen wir erfahren?* K43a, for which no accompaniment has survived but which evidently postdates the death of the Archduchess Maria Josepha on 15 October 1767.[87] (Its second line runs: 'Alas, Josepha is no longer alive.')

The three symphonies from this period all find Mozart moving increasingly away from the formal Italian features of a composer like Johann Christian Bach and towards the Viennese school. They are K43 in F major, which dates from the end of 1767;[88] K45 in D major, the autograph of which is dated 16 January 1768; and K48 in D major, dated 13 December 1768.

Ultimately, the Viennese symphony, too,[89] is derived from the operatic sinfonias of Alessandro Scarlatti. But, as in opera, so in the field of the symphony, Viennese composers soon struck out in

83. The similarity becomes even greater when the theme is repeated in G major. This seems to have been a popular theme at this time. The Stuttgart court musician and composer Christian Ludwig Dieter (1757–1822) offers the following version in the overture to his singspiel *Das Freischießen* (1787):

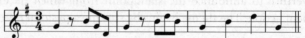

See Abert, *Herzog Karl Eugen von Württemberg und seine Zeit*, vii.597.
84. See Kretzschmar, 'Mozart in der Geschichte der Oper', ii.273.
85. The chronological relationship between the two works is indicated by Leopold Mozart in his worklist, which places *Bastien und Bastienne* before *La finta semplice*. It is possible that Mozart already had his eye on this subject while still in Paris, but there is no evidence to support the claim made by Wyzewa and Saint-Foix (*Wolfgang Amédée Mozart*, i.238–9) that he had already begun work on the score in Salzburg in 1767, a claim that they advance on the strength of the French character of individual numbers. ◆ The evidence of Mozart's autograph also suggests a later date: it is written entirely on a type of paper used by Mozart only in Vienna in 1767–8.
86. Rudolf Gräffer, *Neue Sammlung zum Vergnügen und Unterricht*, iv.80 and 140; cf. Chrysander, 'Mozarts Lieder', 17. The volume was published in August 1768, so that Bastien's aria, at least, must have been completed by that date ◆ In fact, the song was first published as a supplement to the December 1768 issue of the *Neue Sammlung zum Vergnügen und Unterricht*, so Bastien's aria was not necessarily completed by August.
87. Marianne attests to its authenticity but wrongly dates it to 1763; see Malherbe, 'Autographiana: Albums musicaux et feuilles d'albums', 23. ◆ The fragmentary autograph, now in the Bibliothèque nationale, Paris, seems to be entirely in Leopold Mozart's hand. It is possible, then, that the work is by him, not Wolfgang.
88. ◆ It is possible that K43 was started in Salzburg and finished in Vienna, or even that it predates the trip to Vienna in its entirety. The autograph is written on a type of paper that Mozart used in Salzburg during the first half of 1767.
89. Cf. the introductions to Horwitz and Riedel, *Wiener Instrumentalmusik vor und um 1750. Heft 1*, and Wilhelm Fischer, *Wiener Instrumentalmusik vor und um 1750. Heft 2*; see also Kretzschmar, *Führer durch den Konzertsaal*, i.86ff. ◆ Further concerning early Viennese symphonies, see Larsen, 'Zur Entstehung der österreichischen Symphonietradition (ca. 1750–1775)' and 'Zur

a direction of their own, largely under the influence of the same composer, Johann Joseph Fux (1660–1741). From him derives one of the principal characteristics of the Viennese symphony, the predilection for strict counterpoint that had already played a significant role in the symphonies of the first important representative of the Neapolitan symphony in Vienna, Antonio Caldara (1670–1736).[90] A second characteristic of the Viennese school may also be found here, namely, the Scarlattian delight in concertante writing, a characteristic whose influence may still be felt in Haydn's early symphonies. But the most important element was the gradual usurpation of the symphony by Austrian folk music. It is clear from the works of composers such as Corelli, Bach and Handel that in itself such an impregnation of high art by popular elements was by no means new, but what *was* new was the remarkable energy with which it was taken up in Vienna, which was, after all, the classical home of popular music and popular art in general. The emergence of the serenade[91] and the new spirit that entered the symphony with Joseph Haydn were the two most important historical consequences of this development. Needless to say, it was a development that did not happen overnight, nor one that followed a linear progress. Even in Haydn's early symphonies we may still hear clear echoes of the Italian overture, while there is no mistaking its tone in the works of Georg Reutter (1708–72). The main pre-Classical representatives of the Viennese school were Georg Matthias Monn (1717–50), Georg Christoph Wagenseil (1715–77) and Joseph Starzer (1728–87).[92] A symphony in D major by Monn dating from 1740 is the first known example of a piece that interpolates a minuet between the second and final movements, without, however, establishing four-movement form as the general rule in Vienna. Even Haydn continued to vacillate on this point in his early symphonies. More important than the question whether the minuet was first introduced into the symphony in Vienna or Mannheim, however,[93] is the tendency to include a complete recapitulation in the opening allegro, without any fore-shortening, thereby emphasising the movement's ternary structure. This was a tendency already clearly pronounced in the symphonies of Monn and one that was soon to be raised to the level of a general principle by Wagenseil. Even the contrast between first and second subject is already

Vorgeschichte der Symphonik der Wiener Klassik'; more generally, see Reese, *Grundsätze und Entwicklung der Instrumentation in der vorklassischen und klassischen Sinfonie*; Apfel, *Zur Vor- und Frühgeschichte der Symphonie*; Kunze, *Die Sinfonie im 18. Jahrhundert: Von der Opernsinfonie zur Konzertsinfonie*; and Heartz, *Haydn, Mozart and the Viennese School, 1740–1780*.

90. ◆ The most recent catalogue of Fux symphonies remains Köchel's. For Caldara's symphonies, see Toscani, 'Introduction'.

91. ◆ The notion of the serenade and its relationship to the symphony is problematic. Aside from the ambiguousness of the term's use in Vienna, in Salzburg it is fair to say that the serenade, a large multi-movement orchestral work often including concerto movements, *preceded* the symphony as a defined 'genre'. If that is the case, then some symphonic repertoires derive from the serenade (as is the case with several of Mozart's works of the 1770s) and are not, as Abert suggests, coincident with them. See Eisen, 'The Scoring of the Orchestral Bass Part in Mozart's Salzburg Concertos' and Kearns, 'The Orchestral Serenade in Eighteenth-Century Salzburg'.

92. ◆ For Reutter, six of whose symphonies survive in the library of the Gesellschaft der Musikfreunde, Vienna, see A. Peter Brown, 'The Trumpet Overture and Sinfonia in Vienna (1715–1882): Rise, Decline and Reformulation', and for Monn, Rudolf, 'The Symphonies of Georg Mathias Monn (1715–1750)'; a thematic index and editions of five symphonies are published in Rudolf, *Georg Mathias Monn: Five Symphonies*. For Wagenseil, see Kucaba, 'The Symphonies of G. C. Wagenseil', Scholz-Michelitsch, *Das Orchester- und Kammermusikwerk von Georg Christoph Wagenseil: Thematischer Katalog*, and Kucaba, *Georg Christoph Wagenseil: Fifteen Symphonies*. Further, see Wellesz and Sternfeld, 'The Early Symphony'.

93. This question remains unresolved. All that can be said with any certainty is that, in the face of this vacillation on the part of Viennese composers, Johann Stamitz adopted a much more strenuous approach in introducing the minuet into the symphony, so that, although the Viennese were chronologically the first to do so, it was Stamitz who established it as a general principle. It would appear that the idea for doing so came from the divertimento, which juxtaposed free movements and dances, privileging the minuet from an early date. The formal difference between these works and symphonies was often so slight that they are often described interchangeably as sinfonias, partitas and so on. The partita in B flat major by Matthäus Schlöger of 1722 is actually a symphony, with an extra minuet inserted before the finale – an instructive example of the direction in which things were moving; see Wilhelm Fischer, *Wiener Instrumentalmusik vor und um 1750. Heft 2*, and Kretzschmar, *Führer durch den Konzertsaal*. ◆ On the vexed terminological question of symphonies, partitas and similar titles, see Webster, 'Towards a History of Viennese Chamber Music in the Early Classical Period'; on Stamitz, see Eugene K. Wolf, *The Symphonies of Johann Stamitz*.

found here, although the second subjects are not yet cantabile in character, but are mostly short-winded imitative structures, their *piano* character and reduced scoring still clearly recalling the old concerto. In general, Monn is a remarkably inferior composer. His lively and intelligent fugal writing is conservative in the best sense of the term,[94] but the same cannot be said of the pronounced Italian manner of his allegro themes and of his outmoded and often schematic development sections. But a more progressive spirit may be found in the cheeky, folklike themes of his final movements and in the adagios that are intended to serve as introductions and that forge a link between the Grave sections of the old French overture and Joseph Haydn's contemplative introductions. The harmonic language of these last-named movements is often extraordinarily bold and marks out Monn as an early representative of the *Sturm und Drang*. Nor is there any lack of a sense of drama, with Monn occasionally even looking forward to the introduction of the instrumental recitative that was to be of such importance for Haydn and Beethoven.[95]

Wagenseil's contribution to the development of the symphony consists not only in his establishment of ternary form in the opening movement but in an increased emphasis on the folk element and especially a more careful, sometimes even thematic development section. Here, too, Italianisms have to contend for supremacy with more progressive features: Wagenseil is fond of surprises and all manner of contrasts in terms of dynamics, movement types, periodic structure and especially shifts between major and minor, in which regard he had a particular influence on both Haydn and Mozart. Joseph Starzer is unfortunately known to us only through his quartets (which he called divertimentos) and ballet scores. His symphonies are no longer extant.[96] His ballets, especially those with tragic scenarios in the Noverre tradition, are superior to those of his fellow composers in terms of their power and realism,[97] and writers on the early history of programme music will undoubtedly have to pay greater attention to his music in the future. His quartets, too, reveal a composer of above-average abilities whose treatment of form is inspired in its freedom and who has several points in common with Mozart in terms of their emotional worlds, especially where rapt passion and wistfulness are concerned.[98]

By 1769 Joseph Haydn had produced more than three dozen symphonies, which can be dealt with only very briefly here.[99] Unlike Mozart but like Gluck and Beethoven, Haydn was already a mature composer when he entered upon what was to become his principal field of activity,[100] but for that very reason he immediately towered head and shoulders above all his predecessors and contemporaries, drawing together the strands of all their various achievements, including formal mastery, especially of the opening movement; the tendency to use contrapuntal procedures and concertante textures in a way which, already imbued with the spirit of modernity, first comes to fruition here; and the penchant for a more popular tone and universal intelligibility. At the

---

94. It must be stressed that these are not fugues in the older sense of the term, but fugal movements in sonata form. The final movement of Mozart's 'Great' C major symphony [K551] is a further example of this.
95. Cf. the opening movement of the sinfonia a quattro in B flat major in Wilhelm Fischer, *Wiener Instrumentalmusik vor und um 1750. Heft 2*, 41, one of the most daringly experimental works in the entire volume.
96. ◆ Twelve symphonies by Starzer have since been discovered in the Národná Muzeum, Prague.
97. On his ballets, see Abert, 'J. G. Noverre und sein Einfluß auf die dramatische Ballettkomposition', 40ff.
98. Cf. the chromatic sections in the opening movement of the C major divertimento and the melodic writing in the third movement of the same work; also the first subject in the first movement of the A minor divertimento.
99. See Kretzschmar, 'Die Jugendsymphonien Joseph Haydns'. ◆ Further concerning Haydn's early symphonies, see in particular Landon, *The Symphonies of Joseph Haydn*; Gerlach, 'Joseph Haydns Sinfonien bis 1774: Studien zur Chronologie'; and Webster, *Haydn's 'Farewell' Symphony and the Idea of Classical Style: Through-Composition and Cyclic Integration in his Instrumental Music*.
100. His first symphony dates from 1759. ◆ Possibly this was composed as early as 1757; see Webster and Feder, *The New Grove Haydn*, 94. Abert's description of Haydn's symphonies as 'his principal field of activity' reflects the nineteenth-century bias privileging orchestral (or 'absolute') music. Haydn, of course, was equally active as a composer of vocal music.

same time, the thematic writing in his development sections and, indeed, the striving for thematic unity in general reveal the influence of Carl Philipp Emanuel Bach, whereas of all the Classical composers, Haydn was the least affected by the spirit of Mannheim. But what makes these works so great is the towering personality behind them. In these early symphonies there is still something youthful and untamed, an aspect that emerges on a purely superficial level in the programmatic character of individual works and in their boldly realistic elaboration. But even his typically south German delight in such a tremendous variety of forms attests to this very same feature. There is scarcely a single area untouched by his imagination: wildly fantastical effusions figure alongside a more coarsely common touch, silent rêverie beside sparkling wit, sombre soul-painting beside familiar images drawn from nature and everyday life. And yet a keen-eyed, lucid artistic understanding helps to marshal all this great variety, an understanding manifest on the one hand in his ability to draw together all four movements to create a coherent atmospheric whole and, on the other, in features such as the start of the recapitulation of the opening movement of symphony Hob. I:24, the minor tonality of which is wonderfully motivated by the impassioned character of the preceding development section. In much the same way, the lively tone of his final movements is sometimes muted by a second subject in the minor in the spirit of a French rondeau. Finally, the quintessentially Haydnesque wit of his false recapitulations, which we find even at this early date, is part and parcel of this superior play of intellect, with the listener suddenly surprised by the entry of the first subject in the middle of the development section, giving the impression that the recapitulation has already begun, only for the subsequent course of the musical argument to reveal that the composer has only been joking after all.

In short, the symphonic tradition that the young Mozart encountered in Vienna was on an incomparably higher level than that which he had studied and even essayed himself following the example of Johann Christian Bach, and there is a certain pleasure to be derived from observing the way in which he gradually approached this new symphonic style, while occasionally relapsing into the older Italian manner.[101] Initially, he was attracted to its formal characteristics, especially by the idea of including a minuet.[102] And it is significant that it is in these movements that his independence is most marked: Mozart's minuets retain far more of the stately, aristocratic character of the old dance movement than the much more uninhibited minuets of Haydn, while enhancing that character through their additional energy, an energy that has something challenging, even headstrong, about it (cf. K43). From K45 onwards, the trios, conversely, no longer serve merely to fill out the movement,[103] but are in sharp contrast to the main dance. This contrast reveals itself initially, of course, only in a generalized change of mood and in the fact that the trio is scored for strings alone: there is as yet no trace of Haydn's idyllic wind movements, just as Mozart's instrumentation in general still seems relatively old-fashioned beside the richly developed concertante style of the Viennese school. Viennese influence is further suggested not only by the complete recapitulations in the opening movements of K45 and K48 and the tendency to have the violas playing in unison with the violins,[104] but also by certain melodic features such as the lively themes of the finales and the marchlike Andante theme of K 48.[105] But it was only gradually

---

101. ◆ Like all previous (and most later) accounts of Mozart's early symphonies, Abert ignores the Salzburg tradition. See Eisen, *Orchestral Music in Salzburg.*
102. On account of its extremely dubious chronology, the symphony K17 is excluded from the present considerations. ◆ As already noted, K17 is almost certainly by Leopold Mozart.
103. It may be added that in one case (Hob. I:20), Haydn, too, develops the trio motivically from the main movement, just as Mozart had done at an earlier date.
104. Haydn first introduces this doubling in the andante of his A major symphony Hob. I:14.
105. The andante of K43 is identical with the duet 'Natus cadit' from *Apollo et Hyacinthus.*

that Mozart assimilated the specifically Austrian folk idiom as exemplified by Haydn: as we have seen, the folklike features embodied in his music until now were derived in the main from south-west Germany rather than from Austria.

On the whole, the new influences that are to be found in these three works are more or less counterbalanced by their Italianate features: not for some time was Mozart to rid himself of the noisy ostentation of his themes, to say nothing of their generalized character and festive rhetoric. Of Viennese contrapuntal procedures there is scarcely a trace. Formally, too, these works continue to vacillate between the two different traditions: structurally, the outer movements of K43 are still indistinguishable from similar movements by Johann Christian Bach. Above all, however, it is the relatively brief development sections, with their lack of any thematic development, that afford the clearest possible proof that Mozart had yet to enter properly into the spirit of the Viennese school.

None the less, there are a number of individual points at which Mozart's own personality still shines through this remarkable mixture of the old and the new. All of them are features that in many cases take us far beyond the framework of the symphony as a form of social entertainment. Among them are a theme which, like some curiously silent and thoughtful intruder, suddenly joins the noisy banquet in the final subject group of the opening movement of K45; the furtive envoi of the winds in the final movement of K48; and the whole of the first subject of this last-named symphony:

This is a veritable battle theme, plunging downwards in giant steps from the plagal G major and then forcing its way back up again in a genuinely Mozartian syncopation. And the movement goes on as it began, with a motif notable for its helplessly hesitant rhythm and tentative figure on the oboes, then a second subject made up of semiquaver figurations behind which one senses a discreetly imploring cantilena. This symphony is in general the most progressive of the three in terms not only of the foregoing features but also of its Viennese-influenced contrapuntal procedures and its more independent treatment of the winds.

By contrast, the B flat major quintet K46 for two violins, two violas and cello must be later than the date entered in an unidentified hand in the only surviving copy of the work: 25 January 1768. Stylistically, it must be later, and the fact that it is a transcription of the four main movements of the wind serenade K361 of 1780 clearly suggests a date later than 1780. The error is further under-lined by the fact that the same unidentified hand claims that it was written in Salzburg, whereas Mozart was in Vienna on the date in question. Indeed, the whole manuscript is almost certainly not by Mozart at all,[106] although this does not of course exclude the possibility that he was responsible for the transcription.[107]

In spite of all the disappointments bound up with the non-performance of Wolfgang's opera, Leopold must none the less have derived some satisfaction from the fact that one of his son's works

106. See Wyzewa and Saint-Foix, *Wolfgang Amédée Mozart*, ii.425; Jahn, *W. A. Mozart*, fourth edition, i.109 and K¹, 43.
107. ◆ Modern opinion dismisses K46 as an anonymous arrangement that has nothing to do with Mozart.

now received a public airing in Vienna. They had been introduced to the famous Jesuit priest Father Ignaz Parhamer, who, following the departure of the Protestants from Salzburg in 1733, had taken an active part in restoring the Catholic faith[108] and who later assumed an influential position in Vienna, not least as father confessor to the Emperor Franz I from 1758 onwards. In 1759 he took over the management of the city's orphanage, expanding its activities, reorganizing it and, during his long tenure as its director, transforming it into an institution whose fame extended far beyond the city itself.[109] In all such Jesuit establishments in Germany, music was taught along lines similar to those found in the conservatories in Venice, with the students being trained to perform at church services.[110] So thorough and successful was this training that the Emperor Joseph even thought of employing them for his opera.[111] Parhammer occasionally invited the Mozarts to dine with him, and when the foundation stone for the new Orphanage Church was laid in the Rennweg in the summer of 1768, they met the emperor and he spoke to Wolfgang about *La finta semplice*. The latter was now asked to provide music for the consecration of the church and to write not only a mass and offertory but also a trumpet concerto suitable for performance by a boy.

The performance, which Wolfgang himself conducted,[112] took place on 7 December 1768 in the presence of the court and, as Leopold wrote to tell Hagenauer at the time, helped to restore their reputation, which their enemies had hoped to destroy by preventing the performance of *La finta semplice* from going ahead, with Wolfgang demonstrating both to the court and to the large audience present that he could hold his own as a composer.

The local newspaper provides public testimony to this:

On Wednesday the 7th Her Imperial and Royal Majesty, together with the Archdukes Ferdinand and Maximilian and the Archduchesses Maria Elisabeth and Maria Amalia, was pleased to visit the orphanage on the Rennweg in order to attend the solemn consecration and first service in the newly built church. On either side of the entrance to the church were stationed all the assembled companies of bodyguards with their bands and three choirs of trumpets and timpani. The royal party was received at the main door of the said church by His Eminence the Cardinal Archbishop and the local Archbishop, together with their clergy, to the most joyful strains of trumpets and timpani, followed by a discharge of guns and cannons. The service of dedication was then conducted with the usual ceremonies by His Eminence the Cardinal Archbishop, after which Mass was said by the Suffragan Bishop Franz Anton von Marxer to the sound of the repeated discharge of firearms.

All the music for the High Mass was sung by the choir of orphans and was specially composed for the occasion by the 12-year-old son of the Kapellmeister to the Prince-Archbishop of Salzburg, Herr Leopold Mozart. Wolfgang Mozart is already well known for his very special

108. Friedrich Nicolai, *Beschreibung einer Reise durch Deutschland und die Schweiz im Jahre 1781*, iv.648–9.

109. Nicolai, *Beschreibung einer Reise*, iii.228–30.

110. Burney, *The Present State of Music in Germany*, i.221–2.

111. Müller, *Abschied von der National-Schaubühne*, 237.

112. It was customary at this period to beat time in church music, whereas operas and instrumental pieces were conducted from the keyboard; see Schünemann, *Geschichte des Dirigierens*, 154–5; see also *Briefe*, i.286 (letter of 14 December 1768). ◆ Concerning conducting in the eighteenth century, see Camesi, 'Eighteenth-Century Conducting Practices'; Koury, *Orchestral Performance Practices in the Nineteenth Century: Size, Proportions, and Seating*; Galkin, *A History of Orchestral Conducting in Theory and Practice*; and Siepmann, 'The history of direction and conducting'.

talents, and his music, which he himself performed and conducted with the utmost precision, met with universal acclaim and admiration. He also sang in the motets.[113]

The music for the mass and trumpet concerto is lost,[114] although a Missa brevis in G major K49 for four voices, strings and organ has survived. Leopold entered it in his catalogue after the mass, so that it presumably dates from December 1768.[115] Not long after the performance of the *Waisenhausmesse*, the Mozarts returned to Salzburg, arriving back in the town on 5 January 1769.[116]

113. *Wienerisches Diarium*, 99 (10 December 1768) [*Dokumente*, 78, *Documentary Biography*, 84–5 (partial translations)].
114. ◆ As is the music for the offertory K47b also performed on this occasion.
115. That it is not the same as the *Waisenhausmesse* was shown by Deiters (i.110). Conversely, Deiters believes that it was the C minor mass K139 that Mozart wrote for the celebrations in Vienna in 1768, a view adopted by Kurthen, 'Studien zu W. A. Mozarts kirchenmusikalischen Jugendwerken', 211ff. But this seems to be ruled out on stylistic grounds: the G major mass is the work of a beginner and cannot possibly date from the same year as the far more advanced K139. See Wyzewa and Saint-Foix, *Wolfgang Amédée Mozart*, i.422. ◆ Paper studies, however, suggest that K139 is indeed the so-called 'Waisenhausmesse', its proximity to K49 notwithstanding: all of the autograph is written on a type of paper used by Mozart in Vienna in 1768.
116. This is the date given by Hagenauer's diary. Marianne states that it was in December 1768 but this was presumably the date at which they set off. ◆ Although the date of the Mozarts' departure from Vienna remains unclear, documents show that they visited Melk on 28 December, that they left the next day for Linz and that on 4 January 1769 they were in Lambach. It is likely, then, that the family arrived home on 5 January; see *Dokumente*, 79, *Documentary Biography*, 86.

6

Gesellschaftsmusik and church music
in Salzburg, 1769

The archbishop evidently felt flattered by all that Mozart had achieved in Vienna and now attempted to make good what the young Salzburger had failed to complete there. Accordingly, he gave instructions for *La finta semplice* to be staged in Salzburg, even though it was an *opera buffa* and, as such, required special performers in the guise of *persone buffe*. The playbill read as follows:

La Finta Semplice Dramma Giocoso per Musica
Da rappresentarsi in corte per ordine di S. A. Reverendissima
Monsignor
Sigismondo Arcivescovo
e Prencipe
di Salisburgo
Prencipe del S. R. I.
Legato Nato della S. S. A.
Primate della Germania e dell antichissima famiglia
dei conti di SCHRATTENBACH. etc. etc.
Salisburgo Nella Stamperia di Corte 1769.

Personaggi.

Fracasso, Capitano Ungarese
Il Sig. Giuseppe Meisner.
Rosina Baronessa Sorella di Fracasso,
la quale si finge Semplice
La Sig. Maria Maddalena Haydn.
Giacinta, sorella di Don Cassandro e
Don Polidoro
La Sig. Maria Anna Braunhofer.

Ninetta Cameriera
La Sig. Maria Anna Fösömair.
Don Polidoro Gentiluomo sciocco
Fratello di Cassandro
Il Sig. Francesco Antonio Spizeder.
Don Cassandro Gentiluomo sciocco
ed Avaro Fratello di Polidoro
Il Sig. Giuseppe Hornung.
Simone Tenente del Capitano
Il Sig. Felice Winter.

Tutti in attual servizio di S. A. Reverendissima etc.
La Musica è del Signor Wolfgango Mozart in Età di Anni dodici.[1]

---

1. Transcribed from a copy in Nottebohm, *Mozartiana*, 103. The original playbill was subsequently rediscovered and published by Köchel in 'Nachträge und Berichtigungen zu von Köchels Verzeichnis der Werke Mozarts', 495 [*Dokumente*, 82, *Documentary Biography*, 89–90]. ◆ Although there is no firm evidence that this performance took place, surviving evidence makes it likely. In addition to the playbill mentioned by Abert (now lost), a libretto dated 1769 was published in Salzburg and according to Nannerl Mozart's letter to Breitkopf & Härtel of 23 March 1800 (*Briefe*, iv.343), a copy of the score was available in the court music

Performances of this nature were held either on the archbishop's name-day or on some other festive occasion, when a special theatre was erected in the archbishop's palace.[2] The works were performed either by members of the court – in 1748 *La clemenza di Tito* was given by the 'signori paggi di corte', who also took the female roles – or by members of the *Kapelle*. Surviving librettos show that generally, if not always, it was local musicians who were asked to write these works.[3] In ceremonial operas of this kind, the individual thus celebrated was usually addressed in person at the end of the work, mostly in the form of a recitative and aria that was normally followed by a chorus; this address, which was totally unconnected to the action of the opera, was known as a *licenza*.[4] Two such works by Wolfgang have survived and both were addressed to Archbishop Siegmund von Schrattenbach, who died in 1771. One is a tenor aria K36, the other a soprano aria K70. Both include lengthy recitatives and attest to the boy's growing accomplishment in his handling of musical form.[5]

Mozart spent most of 1769 in Salzburg, calmly continuing with his studies, even if we do not know exactly what these studies entailed.[6] Among the works from this period are seven minuets for two violins and bass – veritable dance movements that he wrote on 26 January (K65a) – and two instrumental pieces (presumably serenades) performed at the university on 6 and 8 August.[7] That these were not the only occasional works from this period is clear from Wolfgang's letter to Marianne of 4 August 1770, in which he lists the incipits of various cassations.[8] These are the cassations K63 in G major for two violins, two violas, bass, two oboes or flutes and two horns, K99 in B flat major for two violins, viola, bass, two oboes and two horns, and a lost work in D major.[9] Stylistically related is the serenade in D major K100 for two violins, two violas, bass, two oboes (or flutes), two horns and two trumpets. Whether these works include any of those intended as *Finalmusik* for the university is no longer certain. Equally unresolved is the question whether any of them had been written before the Mozarts went to Vienna in 1767.[10]

archives. Concerning the libretto, see Angermüller, 'Ein neuentdecktes Salzburger Libretto (1769) zu Mozarts "La Finta semplice"'. The singers mentioned on the playbill include Maria Magdalena Lipp (Rosina), Joseph von Arimathaea Hornung (Don Cassandro), Franz Anton Spitzeder (Don Polidoro), Maria Anna Braunhofer (Giacinta), Maria Anna Fesemayr (Ninetta), Joseph Nikolaus Meißner (Fracasso) and Felix Winter (Simone), all of them attached to the court music. Further, see NMA II/5/2, XIV–XIX and XXXV.

2. See Pirckmayer, *Über Musik und Theater am f. e. Salzburger Hofe 1762–1775*.

3. ◆ For an account of Italian opera in Salzburg from 1703 to 1768, including works by both local and non-Salzburg composers, see Eisen, 'Mozart e l'Italia'.

4. The various ways of presenting these works are described by Pietro Metastasio, *Opere postume*, i.300ff.

5. ◆ K70, composed for Sarti's *Vologeso*, may have been intended for a performance on 28 February 1767 or, later, for a performance in March 1769. K36, on the other hand, dates from 1766 when it was performed on 21 December to celebrate the anniversary of the consecration of Archbishop Schrattenbach.

6. A few dates are given by Keller, 'Wolfgang Amadeus Mozart in Salzburg im Jahre 1769'. Cajetan Hagenauer had entered them in his diary, which is still preserved at St Peter's in Salzburg and which attests to his continuing interest in Mozart's development [*Dokumente*, 83, 85–6 and 92, *Documentary Biography*, 91, 93–4 and 101].

7. See Hammerle, *Mozart und einige Zeitgenossen*, 8: '1769. 6 August. (Menstrual Sunday). At night, in honour of the Professor of Logic, music composed by the most excellent boy Wolfg. Mozart. – 1769. 8 August. Tuesday. Holiday. The Physicians' music, written by the same boy.' Hagenauer's diary for 6 August reads: 'Today was the Logicians' *Final-Musik*, composed by young Wolfgangus Mozart [*Dokumente*, 83, *Documentary Biography*, 91].' Keller assumes that this was a dramatic piece, but no such work is known from this period. As we shall see later, the term *Finalmusik* was used to describe an instrumental work.

8. *Briefe*, i.378 (letter of 4 August 1770).

9. ◆ This 'lost' work, K62, is in fact the march associated with the serenade K100.

10. See Wyzewa and Saint-Foix, *Wolfgang Amédée Mozart*, i.200–208. Here the authors argue on stylistic grounds that K99 and K100 must date from 1767, K63 from 1769. In the present writer's opinion, internal arguments alone are insufficient to date works whose composition was influenced in no small way by external circumstances, including the available forces and other random factors. ◆ Although the dates of K63, K99 and K62+100 remain uncertain, all three are now generally thought to have been composed in 1769.

In writing these works, Mozart entered a field that was extremely popular in Austria at this time. The old Austrian orchestral suite had never really died out here and now enjoyed something of a revival in the immediate run-up to Viennese Classicism. But its spirit had remained unchanged. This was not an art that sought to storm the gates of heaven but one that sought out the common folk in the streets and in their homes, regaling them in ways both great and small and bringing beauty and joy to their everyday lives with cheerful, familiar sounds that were well within their powers of comprehension. This national programme of musical education played no small part in the high regard in which the Austrian nation has always been held. As early as 1684 a visitor to Vienna reported that 'in the evening we seldom failed of Musick in the Streets',[11] and in 1794 observers were still able to write of all manner of serenades being sung and played in the streets of the city.[12] Only the name, structure and instrumental resources had changed, with the pieces now described as cassations,[13] serenades, divertimentos and notturnos. Indeed, even the term 'symphony' would sometimes mean a serenade, just as in keyboard music the title 'sonata' often meant a suite. Structurally, the newer works were no different from the older ones in continuing to hesitate over the number of their movements, but of the earlier dances only the minuet and popular polonaise survived. Even the old French overture, which had traditionally opened the piece, had given way to a lively march with which the performers took up their positions before launching into the serenade proper. It is clear not only from this but also from the lively final movements that this music largely depended for its effectiveness on being performed in the open air. Gradually, however, the symphony began to assert its influence, with the first and final movements of the serenade, as well as the andante, slowly growing closer in structure and character to the corresponding movements of the symphony. From the harnessing together of two slow movements, two minuets and two outer movements there emerged a six-movement piece which, formally speaking, was to play an important role in Mozart's later works, even though he never accepted it as binding.[14] But one of the most significant differences between the older and newer forms was the disappearance of the large string orchestra. These new divertimentos and so on are

11. Edward Brown, *A Brief Account of Some Travels in divers Parts of Europe*, 14.1.

12. For a detailed account, see Pohl, *Joseph Haydn*, i.107ff.

13. The origins of this term remain obscure, with Jahn's derivation from 'gassatim gehen' (Jahn, *W. A. Mozart*, third edition, i.847–8) no more satisfactory than that offered by Wyzewa and Saint-Foix (*Wolfgang Amédée Mozart*, i.201), whereby the word means 'fragmented' little symphonies, in other words, symphonies with pauses between the individual movements. Not even the derivation from *gran cassa* or bass drum proposed by Riemann with reference to the introductory march (see Riemann's *Musiklexikon*, eighth edition, 532) can be correct. The most likely explanation is that it means 'farewell piece'. Evidently it was an old technical term used by the musicians. The term *Finalmusik*, by contrast, refers to compositions that bring to an end a concerto or similar piece. ◆ *Finalmusik* does not refer to a concluding work but to a multi-movement orchestral work performed at the Salzburg University graduation ceremonies. As such it is used by the Mozarts to designate function and is not a genre. The normal title for such works is serenade. Concerning the meaning of titles such as divertimento, cassation, notturno and serenade, see also Unverricht, *Gesellschaftsgebundene instrumentale Unterhaltungsmusik des 18. Jahrhunderts*; further, see Webster, 'Towards a History of Viennese Chamber Music in the Early Classical Period'.

14. ◆ Abert is incorrect to claim that the six-movement form of the serenade was standard for Salzburg. Among Mozart's Salzburg works in the genre – in particular those composed for weddings, ennoblements and the university graduation ceremonies – none is in six movements: K63, 99, 204 and 320 ('Posthorn') have seven movements, K100 and 203 eight movements, and K250 ('Haffner') nine movements. Similarly, a serenade by the court violinist Joseph Hafeneder , possibly from 1776 or 1777, also has seven movements, while two serenades by Michael Haydn (MH86 of 1767 and MH407 of 1785) have eight and seven movements, respectively. Nor is it the case that the symphony encroached on the serenade – more likely it was the other way around. In Salzburg, serenades – characterized chiefly by their inclusion of both symphonic and concerto movements – probably predate independent symphonies. Accordingly, it may be that symphonies were in large part seen as deriving from the serenade tradition, rather than in competition with it. For Hafeneder's serenade, see Kearns, *Six Orchestral Serenades from South Germany and Austria. Part 2*; for Michael Haydn's serenades, see Sherman and Thomas, *Johann Michael Haydn (1737–1806): A Chronological Thematic Catalogue of His Works*, 33 and 141. For a brief account of the relationship among serenade, symphony and concerto in Salzburg, see Eisen, 'The Scoring of the Orchestral Bass Part in Mozart's Salzburg Keyboard Concertos: The Evidence of the Authentic Copies', 417–19.

all examples of chamber music and gave substantial impetus to its subsequent development in the form of the string quartet.[15] Here, too, we find signs of the occasional character of the medium as a whole: if the performers included outstanding soloists among their number, the composer would have no hesitation in including one or more movements in which they could display their abilities to the full. Conversely, inferior players might occasionally be teased by the inclusion of wrong notes. In short, this whole genre is a veritable treasure trove of the subtlest sonorities and tonal effects, while its themes often alluded to people and places bound up in some way with the outward circumstances of the serenade. In consequence, the young Mozart was by no means lacking in models either in Vienna or in Salzburg, where both his father and Michael Haydn[16] were particularly fond of the genre. And theirs was the type of serenade that Mozart now modelled himself upon in the three works already mentioned. K63 and K99 both open with a march, which is even repeated at the end of the second of these pieces, while both K63 and K100 provide for solo contributions, with a solo violin appearing in one of the seven movements of the first-named work, while no fewer than three of the movements in K100 involve solo writing for oboe and horn. In both cases, there is a clear distinction between soli and tutti in the manner of a concerto grosso.[17] The opening movements are cast in sonata form with a brief development section and a recapitulation that is either complete or omits the main theme, while the final movements are diaphanous rondos (as in K63 and K100) or (as in K99) further examples of sonata form, but with two themes that differ in terms of both tempo and time-signature. In his Andante movements, Mozart is especially fond of emphasizing the serenade-like character of the piece by means of mutes, pizzicato accompaniments and romance-like melodic writing. These movements, too, generally depart from the home key, usually modulating to the subdominant, while the minuets, of which there are invariably two, revert to the principal tonality. Particularly delightful are the cheekily folklike and humoristic features that are far less common in the symphonies. There is something irresistibly comical, for example, about the way in which the main theme, now heard in diminution, steals away *pianissimo* in the final subject group of the march from K63, while K99 is especially notable for its folklike tone.[18] No less remarkable, however, is the finale of K63, an out-and-out hunting piece whose folklike theme wanders good-humouredly from tonality to tonality. The most sophisticated of these pieces is K100, the opening movement of which is notable for its typically Mozartian wealth of musical ideas, from its noisy beginning (which resembles nothing so much as an Italian overture) to the remarkable tension of the pedal-point passage and the A minor theme that enters mysteriously and eerily, before finally coming to a rest, seemingly at a loss, on a solid fermata, and, finally, to the surly humour of the boisterous unison of the final subject group. Here, too, there are passages where the mood grows darker, especially in the trios of some of the minuets (notably K63/iv and K100/vii) and in the episodes of the rondos. Yet the prevailing serenade-like character of these works is not affected by all this, and the overriding atmosphere is one of contentment, charm and flirtatious good humour.

15. Sandberger, 'Zur Geschichte des Haydnschen Streichquartetts', 2–3. ◆ Sandberger's account is now considered out of date. See Webster, 'Towards a History of Viennese Chamber Music in the Early Classical Period'.
16. A selection is given by Perger, *Johann Michael Haydn: Ausgewählte Werke.* ◆ It is unlikely that Michael Haydn was 'fond' of the genre. In general it represented a commission, not a compositional choice, and of the two such works by Haydn that are known, only one dates from this time: MH86 of 1767. The other, MH407, was written in 1785. See Sherman and Thomas, *Johann Michael Haydn*, 33 and 141–2. On the serenade generally, see Kearns, 'The Orchestral Serenade in Eighteenth-Century Salzburg', and *Six Orchestral Serenades.*
17. In the third movement, we even find the typical six-four chord with fermata for the cadenza.
18. Under this heading we may also include the canon from the first menuetto of K63, the first example of its kind in Mozart's oeuvre. Haydn's first symphonic menuetto in his G major symphony (Hob. I:3) includes a canon in its main section, while the menuetto from the later G major symphony (Hob. I:23) even extends the canonic writing to the trio.

With his first mass in G major K49, Mozart entered a world to which he was repeatedly to be drawn between now and the onset of his maturity as a composer. Admittedly, these Masses are all youthful works lacking the ultimate in real-life experience: one has only to think of the *Requiem* to appreciate the vast gulf between them. Moreover, Mozart was born in an age whose ideal in terms of church music had lost much of its earlier purity and rigour. To criticize this trivialization or even, as Beethoven was later to do, to attempt to offset it with a new and purer ideal would no more have occurred to the young Mozart than it would have struck him to regard himself as a reformer in other areas. Here, as elsewhere, he initially allowed himself to be swept along by the most disparate artistic impressions (which is why it is such a great mistake to judge these masses by the same unvarying standards) and only gradually did he begin to find himself on firm ground that he could emphatically call his own. For this reason, if for no other, an examination of his masses is instructive in the extreme, as they provide us with a highly graphic picture of the various influences at work on the genre as a whole at this time. But their artistic merits, too, should not be undervalued, even if they cannot, of course, compare with his mature works in other areas. Students interested in the psychology of the artist will derive particular pleasure from observing the way in which Mozart gradually creates his own formal and expressive world and how individual types keep recurring (their minor differences notwithstanding), before reappearing more than ten years later in the *Requiem* in their most deeply spiritualized form.

The first two masses in G major and D minor (K49 and K65) form a self-contained group to the extent that they still belong to the older, more rigorous type of mass to which composers like Eberlin and, to a lesser degree, Leopold Mozart still subscribed.[19] Compared with the sort of mass that Mozart was later to get to know during his studies with Martini, this type is, of course, already demonstrably impure, but Hasse's tendency to give the music its head at the expense of the words, and his subordination of the poetic to the purely musical element, does not yet strike the listener with such blatant force. As a result, there is as yet no trace of elaborate images with their frequent textual repetitions or of an attempt to force the individual ideas within the text into the usual musical forms. The structure is brief and succinct, and Mozart is content to state the individual ideas only once. The second characteristic of the older style is the much reduced role of the orchestra: in the first of the two masses under discussion, it has virtually no independent part to play, although by the second we already find it being used in a more modern way.[20] And the fact that contrapuntal procedures are not limited to specific passages, as was later to be the case, but permeate the work as a whole still recalls the older tradition, as does the division of the chorus into two concertante groups, to say nothing of isolated echo effects and bass patterns, notably in the Benedictus from K65. Mozart's allegiance to the old school and, at the same time, his inexperience are further seen in the fact that he has no inhibitions about working with tried and tested thematic material. And so we find the following well-established theme with the diminished seventh

19. ◆ Concerning church music in Salzburg, see Rosenthal, 'The Salzburg Church Music of Mozart and his Predecessors' and 'Zur Stilistik der Salzburger Kirchenmusik von 1600 bis 1730', and Manfred Hermann Schmid, *Mozart und die Salzburger Tradition*. Abert's suggestion that Eberlin and Leopold Mozart continued to subscribe to an older tradition, however, is exaggerated; see n. 39 below.
20. ◆ It is worth noting here that the first mass, K49, was composed in Vienna in October or November 1768 while the second, K65, was completed in Salzburg on 14 January 1769. The differences between them may relate to local performing traditions.

recurring throughout these masses in a whole series of variant guises. Familiar from Bach[21] and Handel, it occurs in the bass in the 'Hosanna' from K65 and in the 'Crucifixus' and 'Qui cum Patre et Filio' from K49, before making a final appearance in the Kyrie from the *Requiem* K626. In the fugue subject of the 'Et vitam venturi saeculi' in K49, by contrast, we hear a much earlier model – a hexachord subject with intervals of a fourth – familiar from the first fugue of Bach's *Well-Tempered Clavier*:

et   vi - tam ven - tu - ri sae - cu - li   a - - - men

Further examples include the 'Dona nobis pacem' from K65, with its ascending and descending scalar themes and double counterpoint; the 'Miserere' from the Gloria of K49, with its diminished second;[22] the chromaticisms in the 'Crucifixus' from K49; and, above all, the Benedictus from K65, a setting which, with its old-fashioned bass part, strict part-writing and austere and solemn standpoint, was to find few successors. This was clearly a movement that was close to Mozart's heart, if we may judge from the fact that he revised it no fewer than four times.[23]

No less traditional is the division of the individual parts into tutti and solo, and especially the basic conception of the movements as a whole and of their subdivisions in particular, including individual images such as those associated with the words 'ascendit', 'descendit' and 'vivos et mortuos'. Among examples of this use of traditional topoi are the darker colouring for the 'Qui tollis', 'Et incarnatus est' and Agnus Dei; the fugal character of the 'Et vitam' and 'Cum Sancto Spiritu', which in these particular Masses is limited to a single exposition; and the conscious and stark contrast between the 'Crucifixus' and the 'Et resurrexit'. The message of the Resurrection is here proclaimed by the dense choral mass, declaiming it in the ecstatic tone that was typical of the older masses and that was to achieve so magnificent an apotheosis in Beethoven's great *Missa solemnis*. Finally, mention may be made of the division of the Agnus Dei into two contrasting sections, together with the attempt, common to both masses, to point up motivic links between the 'Et unam sanctam' and earlier movements. (In K49 such links are established with the 'Et resurrexit' and in K65 with the 'Patrem omnipotentem' and 'Et vivificantem'.) On the whole, writers have tended to overlook the extent to which these later works continue to reveal the age-old desire to impose a sense of motivic unity on the mass. K49, for example, is dominated by a melodic type whose principal feature is a stepwise ascent through a fourth followed by a descent to the third, harmonized as I–(IV)–V–I. In its simplest form, it is found at the very beginning of the Kyrie:

21. Cf. cantata 106, *Gottes Zeit ist die allerbeste Zeit*.
22. Cf. the second Kyrie from Bach's B minor mass. ◆ While it is true that there are occasional similarities with works by Bach, it is not the case that the examples cited by Abert served as specific models for Mozart: there is virtually no evidence that Mozart was familiar with any of these works before his move to Vienna in 1781. The case with Handel may be different and Mozart could have become acquainted with some of his church music during the family's stay in London in 1764–5.
23. These versions are reproduced in NMA I/1/1. Wyzewa and Saint-Foix (*Wolfgang Amédée Mozart*, i.254) even surmise that the final version was written for a later performance. It is very likely that the piece is based on an as yet unidentified model.

This is followed by the first variant of the motif, a variant that draws on an inverted form of the subsidiary motif (*b*):[24]

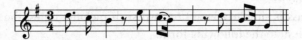

An expanded version appears at the beginning of the Gloria:

And, with the same beginning, starting on the tonic, it is also found in the fugue subjects of the 'Cum Sancto Spiritu'[25] and 'Et vitam venturi':

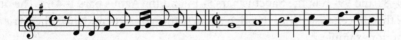

Expanded to a hexachord, it is also concealed in the theme of the 'Hosanna':

A more succinct form, with an energetically rising interval of a fourth,[26] occurs in the 'Et resurrexit':

And yet another variant, this time with an ascending fifth, is found in the 'Patrem omnipotentem':

A more expressively intensified version is heard in the 'Laudamus te' and 'Quoniam tu solus sanctus', where the intensification is achieved by raising its first half by a sixth and returning to the tonic via a descending sixth:

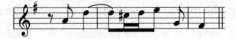

Other sections – especially those that breathe an atmosphere of sombre brooding or mystery – are linked together less by their shared themes than by a meaningful choice of tonality and part-writing:

---

24. In turn, this version also generates the melody of the 'Et in Spiritum Sanctum'.
25. The whole ending of this movement, from the antepenultimate 'Amen' onwards, is nothing more nor less than a powerful intensification of this idea, a circumstance that may help to explain the otherwise striking closure on the third.
26. It returns, meaningfully filled out, at the 'Et unam sanctam'. Also under this heading comes the 'Et iterum venturus est'.

in the case of the 'Qui tollis', 'Et incarnatus est' and Agnus Dei, for example, this is achieved by the use of chromaticisms and by the fact that the sequence of modulations assumes an exceptional character in consequence.

The D minor mass is similarly based on two such melodic types, the first of which may be reduced, at its simplest, to the following form:

In this way, it already contains within itself a chromatic nucleus (see the Kyrie bars 1–7, the Credo bars 1–8, 70–88 and 99–106, the Sanctus bars 8–14 and the Agnus bars 1–4).[27] The other type is a scalar figure that descends stepwise through a fourth, fifth or sixth and links the Kyrie to the 'Dona nobis pacem', for example:[28]

At the same time, an inversion of this theme[29] appears in long note-values in the bass of the 'Dona nobis pacem', followed immediately by the original motif of a fourth with a contrapuntal accompaniment derived from the other main motif. Meanwhile, in the middle movements, the most disparate versions of the scalar theme may be found at work: see the Gloria, bars 38–40 (the fugue subject of the 'Cum Sancto Spiritu'); the Credo, bars 55–63 and 125–133; and the Credo, bars 167–171 ('Et vitam venturi') – identify by movement and bar numbers; even the Benedictus is based on it. But what gives this Mass a particularly unified stamp is its minor tonality, to which Mozart clings with remarkable tenacity, abandoning it only briefly within individual movements. Not even the Sanctus and Benedictus are exceptions here, and only the Credo has a section ending in the major. It is more than likely that there was a particular reason for this – perhaps the work was written for some funeral service or other.[30]

In general, the second mass is already much more modern than the first, a modernity clear both from the more independent contribution of the orchestra and from its opening Kyrie. In K49, the Kyrie's faster main section is through-composed, with the Christe only slightly set apart by dint of its modulations,[31] but, far from forming a separate section, it remains inextricably linked to the Kyrie. In K65, by contrast, the movement is already a consummate example of cyclical ternary

27. The diminished fourth in the third bar of the allegro from the Kyrie returns in the second and third bars of the 'Et incarnatus est'.
28. The framework of the theme, which contains a striking reminiscence of the well-known Protestant hymn, is marked by crosses.
29. The inverted form is also found at the words 'genitum non factum' on p.39, 1st system.
30. See Wyzewa and Saint-Foix, *Wolfgang Amédée Mozart*, i.253. ◆ K65 was composed for the opening of the forty hours' devotion at the University (Collegiate) Church in Salzburg and performed there, in the presence of the archbishop, on 5 February 1769.
31. The reader may note, in particular, the endings of the individual sections in both masses: there is still no sign of the general move towards the dominant that was later to make itself felt under the influence of aria and sonata form. Indeed, the subdominant is as yet more common than the dominant.

form, with the Christe as its middle section, except that the words 'Kyrie eleison' do not coincide with the repeat of the opening but are already heard during the transitional passage leading back to the repeat. Otherwise, however, the musical argument follows the text to the letter, even in the solo sections, which differ from those in the later masses only in the far greater restraint of their coloratura writing. In the Credo in the D minor mass, we even find the words 'et in Spiritum Sanctum, Dominum', 'Et vivificantem', 'Qui ex Patre Filioque procedit' and 'Qui cum Patre et Filio' sung together, while divided among three different parts, as is also the case in related works by Leopold Mozart.[32]

No one will expect a boy of Mozart's age to reveal any great originality of conception. Even so, his genius still shines through in individual passages, notably in the beautiful modulation to the major in the Credo of K49 at the words 'homo factus est'. Using the simplest of means, Mozart movingly describes Christ's incarnation:

Even at this early date, the two settings of the 'Et incarnatus est' are among the finest movements within their respective works. And in each case, the Sanctus is particularly brief, its basic character being one of ethereal lightness: in K49, the rising chains of syncopations produce the effect of floating in space, while a similar impression is achieved in K65 through the brief and gently rocking orchestral motif. No less effective here is the concertante interplay between the two choral groups. The Benedictus from K49 is one of those movements whose melodic character comes closest to Mozart's later practice, without, of course, quite matching it. Here, above all, the most obvious solution would have been to create a self-contained, unified whole, but, instead, Mozart simply strings together independent melodies that have nothing in common but their general mood of naïve and charming warm-heartedness: one is reminded of Goethe's 'half in a childish pattern, half with a heart for God'.[33] We have already mentioned the Benedictus from K65, but the movement is also remarkable from an orchestral point of view, inasmuch as the motif from the Sanctus is heard on the first and second violins at the very beginning, as though in an echo, while at the final 'qui venit' the listener will fleetingly note a motif modelled on the one found at the appearance of the heavenly hosts in Handel's *Messiah*:[34]

32. In general, Leopold is clearly one of his son's principal models in terms of his structural succinctness: cf. his *Litaniae de venerabili*, in D major, cited above.
33. *Faust* I, ll.3781–2.
34. The recitative 'And suddenly there was with the angels' preceding the chorus 'Glory to God' (no. 15).

This same motif then recurs throughout the first section of the Agnus Dei, suggesting the radiant crown of the heavenly apparition of the Lamb.[35] The orchestra thus provides a quite remarkable link between the last three movements. The basic character of both these settings of the Agnus Dei is a vague sense of awe that shudders before God, the Eternal. The melodic writing is largely declamatory in style, whereas the harmonic writing glides along in a series of extraordinarily bold progressions which, especially in K49, already appear to ask questions of the afterlife – very much in the manner of Mozart's later works. The 'Dona nobis pacem' in this mass is on a much lower level than this, but with its natural, childlike tone, it successfully avoids the superficially brilliant but ultimately vacuous nature of a number of later settings of this section of the mass. The 'Dona nobis pacem' from K65 achieves this end by means of its stricter procedures. A curious halfway house between these two early masses and their successor is the offertory *Veni Sancte Spiritus* K47.[36] Not only does it use more elaborate orchestral forces (four-part strings, oboes, horns, trumpets and timpani), it also emerges as a far more self-confident work in terms of its prelude and interludes and its independent accompanying figures. Other 'modern' features may be found in its tendency to move closer to ternary form and its consciously contrasting themes. Conversely, the treatment of the text, the division of labour between soli and tutti, and the character of many of the motifs such as those at the words 'et tui amoris' and 'allelujah' look back to the earlier masses. The orchestral accompaniment, too, is awkward and contains too many vacuous commonplaces. All in all, we gain the picture of an artist trying to imitate a new style that he has just got to know but still equal to the task that he has set himself. Perhaps this work really is a preliminary study for Vienna.[37]

The so-called *Dominicus* mass K66, by contrast, pursues a totally different course. It dates from October 1769, when Mozart's friend Cajetan Hagenauer celebrated his first mass at St Peter's in Salzburg.[38] (As noted above, the young Mozart had wept openly at Hagenauer's decision to enter

35.   It is also found in the Italian version of Gluck's *Alceste* when the queen appeals to the god in act one, scene four.

36.   Leopold's catalogue lists two offertories, one – the present *Veni Sancte Spiritus* – entered before the two operas, the other – a 'grand offertory' – after the two masses. This means that the offertory performed in Vienna on 7 December 1768 was not the first, as previously assumed, but the second. Whether this last-named work is identical with the Benedictus K117, as Deiters assumes (Jahn, *W. A. Mozart*, fourth edition, i.112n.), is questionable on both internal and external grounds. It is more likely that the second offertory, like the *Missa solemnis*, has been lost. See Wyzewa and Saint-Foix, *Wolfgang Amédée Mozart*, i.243. ◆ Abert is probably correct that the second 'lost' offertory is K47b. Certainly it is not identical to the Benedictus K117, which on the basis of paper types in the autograph appears to date from Salzburg, 1769. The *Missa solemnis*, however, is not lost; as noted above, it is K139.

37.   Wyzewa and Saint-Foix, *Wolfgang Amédée Mozart*, i.243. ◆ The notion that K47 is a preliminary study for Vienna is complicated by the work's uncertain date. If, as is presumed, it is identical to the 'Veni Sancte Spiritus à 4 Voci 2 Violini 2 Hautb: 2 Corni, Clarini, Timpani, Viola e B 1768' in Leopold Mozart's list, then it was composed during Mozart's stay in the imperial capital, not earlier. On the other hand, no autograph survives and the earliest known copy, a manuscript now at the Diözesanarchiv, Graz (shelfmark Mariazell 333), may date from as late as 1771 or early 1772.

38.   *Briefe*, i.394–5 (letter of 6 October 1770). Dominicus Hagenauer became abbot at St Peter's in 1786. He also held the post of general tax gatherer for the abbacy. See Koch-Sternfeld, *Die letzten dreißig Jahre*, 78, 299 and 326. The entry in Hagenauer's diary reads as follows: '15 Oct. At 9 o'clock today P. Dominicus celebrated his first Mass. Music for the Mass composed by Dom. Wolfgangus Mozart, 14 years of age, which in every one's opinion was most elegant. . . . After dinner, Dom. Wolfgangus Mozart played on the great organ for half an hour to the astonishment of all.' The celebrations were followed the next day by a banquet at the home of Cajetan Hagenauer's father. It ended with music performed by Leopold and his children. Cajetan's diary entry for the 16th reads: 'The neophyte celebrated Mass at the Nunberg. Afterwards he was invited by his father to a dinner held at his house in the Nunthal. . . . Dinner . . . lasted until about a quarter past four. When it was over, Dom. Mozart, Second Master of the Court Chapel Music, with his two famous children, held a concert. The daughter first played the clavier, then Wolfgangus, a

the Benedictine abbey at Salzburg as Father Dominicus in 1764.) Liturgically and in terms of its instrumentation, it is a *missa solemnis*, while on a stylistic level it marks a transition from the older tradition still practised in Salzburg to the newer tradition as represented by Hasse, a tradition which, in Vienna too, had gradually taken over. Even now, of course, Mozart was still unable to break completely free from the older style, as is clear, for example, from his handling of the bass in both the Benedictus and the Agnus Dei and from the melodic writing in the fugal 'Cum Sancto Spiritu' (with its reminiscence of the fugue on 'Et vitam venturi' in K49) and 'Hosanna'.

The most notable feature of this new style is the way in which the masses of this period are flooded with expressive and formal elements from contemporary operatic and instrumental music, a development that brought with it a far greater emphasis on soloists and instruments and, above all, far more elaborate imagery than before. The focus of the whole now shifts to the music at the expense of the poetry. Whereas in the two older masses the form emerged quite naturally from the close correspondence between music and words, the words now have to be adapted to fit the existing forms of two- and three-part aria and sonata, and with these inevitably come all their rules of modulation, their melodic formulas, including the well-known cadenza with fermata and trill, and much more besides. Needless to say, the coloratura writing was no longer content merely to decorate individual ideas in a more or less cursorily picturesque manner, but, as in the operas of the period, acquired a rank luxuriance all of its own.[39]

Although there is still the same striving for motivic unity here, it assumes new forms. The older type is recalled only by the 'Laudamus', 'Domine Deus' and 'Et in Spiritum Sanctum', in other words, the three main solo movements, in which the affinities extend to the melodic writing, two-bar structure and operatic character of the writing. Conversely, Mozart now uses the orchestra to forge a link between the work's major subsections, even if he as yet stops short of imposing a sense of overriding unity upon the work as a whole. The entire Credo, for example, is notable for an ostinato bass that repeatedly points back to the beginning, a device that derives from Hasse[40] and that Mozart later developed in the most varied ways.

The influence of sonata form is already evident in the allegro of the Kyrie: note the two sharply contrasting subjects, the closure on the dominant with an orchestra interlude, then a return via the first subject to the home key and a recapitulation not of the first, but of the second, subject. The arias, by contrast, are largely cast in the binary form typical of Italian and especially French comic opera, making it abundantly clear that it was not only the form of opera, but its spirit, too, that entered the mass at this time. Mozart has yet to break free again from the charming but textually meaningless trifling and coloratura glitter of these movements. The worst example of this

youth aged thirteen, sang [and] played the violin and the clavier to everyone's amazement. Which things finishing at about 5.30, the Most Reverend Abbots departed' [*Dokumente*, 85–6, *Documentary Biography*, 93–4]. During the morning, Mozart had conducted the mass on the Nonnberg. Presumably it was a repeat of the mass performed the previous day.

39. ◆ As noted above, Abert misrepresents the 'modernity' of church music in Salzburg, which frequently included gestures and forms typical of secular vocal music, opera in particular. The Benedictus of Leopold Mozart's mass Seiffert 4/2, for instance, is a fully-fledged *da capo* aria; similarly, *da capo* arias can be found throughout the church music of Eberlin and Adlgasser. Church music in mid-century Salzburg included not only local works but also works by Italian composers, among them Diogenio Bigaglia (*c*1676–*c*1745), the Viennese-based Antonio Caldara (*c*1670–1736), Gioseffo Carcani (1703–79) and Gioseffo Maria Carretti (1690–1770), as well as Niccolò Jommelli's *Requiem* of 1756. Numerous Italian operas were performed at court as well, including several by Caldara, Hasse's *Cajo Fabricio* (1732, performed at Salzburg in 1737) and *Leucippo* (1747, performed at Salzburg in 1756), Bernasconi's *Temistocle* (1740 and apparently performed at Salzburg the same year), Gioacchino Cocchi's *La maestra* (1747, performed at Salzburg in 1756), Giuseppe Sarti's *Vologeso* (1754, performed at Salzburg in 1766–7) and Antonio Sacchini's *Olimpiade* (1763, performed at Salzburg in 1768). See Eisen, 'Mozart e l'Italia: Il ruolo di Salisburgo'.

40. See Walther Müller, *J. A. Hasse als Kirchenkomponist*, 60ff. ◆ Concerning Hasse and Viennese church music generally, see MacIntyre, *The Viennese Concerted Mass of the Early Classic Period*.

failing is the polonaise rhythm of the 'Quoniam', where the listener is inevitably reminded of Sperontes,[41] although the 'Et incarnatus', too, is too lightweight to be wholly successful. This, it may be added, is the first time in Mozart's works that we find a pointer to an intimate scene beside the Infant Jesus' manger. At the same time, contrapuntal procedures break free from their close historical link with homophonic, chordal textures and take refuge in specific passages, no longer seeming an essential element in terms of the style of the work but an extra seasoning that allows the composer to display his abilities in strict counterpoint. Their principal domain is the 'Cum Sancto Spiritu' and 'Et vitam venturi', in which fully worked-out fugues now replace the single exposition of the subject. Here, too, however, the poetic element is upstaged by the purely musical, academic aspect. These, moreover, are the only passages in which the orchestra, at least in the main, simply accompanies the singing; elsewhere it maintains a strict independence, which it achieves in two different ways. Either – as in the allegro from the Kyrie – it strikes the same note as contemporary instrumental Gesellschaftsmusik,[42] or it complements and deepens the mood of the section, conjuring up a picture of the situation or state of mind in a manner reminiscent of the dramatic music of the period. It was inevitable, of course, that the first of these two approaches should produce results which, superficially brilliant, were internally incoherent and incapable of exploring the text in an adequate fashion, but the second approach proved an asset to the mass, even if it simultaneously jolted it appreciably further down the road to full-blown drama. Take the 'Qui tollis': its profound impact rests, on the one hand, on its brooding harmonies and, on the other, on the two-part accompanying motif in the strings, first a semiquaver figure that trickles down incessantly in a typically Mozartian manner and, secondly, a darting quaver motif. Note also the constant echo-like interplay between *forte* and *piano*. The 'Crucifixus', too, is treated in a markedly dramatic way, with only the chromaticisms at the end (at the word 'passus') harking back to the older manner. In the Sanctus, by contrast, the orchestra weaves a glimmering halo of radiance around the movement as a whole. Particularly instructive in terms of what they tell us about the gradual development of the new style are the Benedictus and Agnus Dei: the former does not yet breathe the spirit of that transfigured delight in the appearance on earth of the Son of God that we find in its successors. Indeed, at one point it even gives the impression that it is about to return to the anguished dourness of its immediate predecessor, while its use of strict counterpoint similarly sets it apart from Mozart's later manner. On the other hand, the orchestra is handled here in an emphatically modern way, with glittering semiquavers spinning a halo around the heavenly apparition. The Agnus Dei adopts the newer approach not only in its melodic writing in the soli but also in the role of the orchestra in general, with its remarkable shift of atmosphere within the first few bars of the introduction. Conversely, the treatment of the bass and the austerity of the choral writing still reflect the older tradition.

By and large, the interplay between tutti and soli reflects older practices, except that the individual movements are now much longer, with only the Credo proving to be an exception: here only the 'Et incarnatus est' and the 'Et in Spiritum Sanctum' are solo movements. The Agnus Dei and 'Dona nobis pacem', by contrast, are divided between solo and chorus.

---

41.   A trace of Sperontes's spirit may also be found in the melody of the 'Dona nobis pacem'; see the comments above concerning the song *Geheime Liebe* K150. ◆ As already noted, K150 is by Leopold Mozart. The reference to Sperontes [Scholze, Johann Sigismund] is to the *Singende Muse an der Pleiße*, a popular and widely-disseminated collection of German strophic songs published in Leipzig in 1736, 1742, 1743 and 1745.

42.   A purely musical effect derived from sonata form is the cantabile theme of the soli with its primitive, dancelike accompaniment.

This was the first great stylistic change in Mozart's church music and it was to have lasting consequences. That he succeeded in taking this step is once again evidence of his peculiar and rapid ability to assimilate the views of others. He had not yet managed to write a perfect masterpiece (even when judged by the standards of his day), and his works still bear individual traces of the older tradition, but he had struck out purposefully in a new direction and adopted a course which, with few deviations, he was never again to leave.

7

First Italian Journey

As we have already seen, Leopold Mozart regarded all his family's travels, including their visit to Vienna, as no more than a prelude to his long-planned assault on Italy. This was no mere whim on his part but sprang from a still widely held view at this time, a view rooted in a tradition stretching back some two hundred years. Just as today's visual artist is expected to complete his studies in Italy, so in the eighteenth century the German musician needed to study in Italy if he was to find fame and fortune at home. There is no doubt that this demand also had serious drawbacks for German artists at the time: only those artists who had sufficient resources at their disposal could afford to study in Italy or – as was more usually the case – if they were supported by an aristocratic patron. The majority of artists remained cut off from such patronage, resulting in a yawning gulf between those on whom fortune smiled and those on whom she turned her back. Among the latter group, German cantors and organists were particularly disadvantaged. Not even Johann Sebastian Bach was able to study in Italy and had to pay for this lack of education by remaining no more than a local celebrity whose reputation during his own lifetime extended no further than the confines of Saxony and Thuringia. It says much for Leopold's perceptiveness and his capacity for self-denial, therefore, that in spite of his modest means he now set off on his own initiative on what was bound in the circumstances to be a fairly risky undertaking: Wolfgang, he was resolved, would study much-vaunted Italian music at source.[1]

Even at this late date, Italy could still pride itself on being the promised land of music, although its ancient and uncontested hegemony had already been undermined by national aspirations beyond the Alps, especially in France and, more recently, in Germany, where instrumental music had blossomed with sudden and surprising speed. But the foundations on which its authority was based were still as solid as ever, being grounded, as they were, in the Italian nation's natural predisposition and aptitude for music and, especially, in the comprehensive and organized way in which music was cultivated so that talent was constantly nurtured and pleasure for ever rekindled. With its characteristic melodies and rhythms so closely attuned to the southern temperament, folk music continued to flourish among both the high and the low. As in Vienna, so in Italian towns and cities, the streets re-echoed with serenades of every description on balmy summer evenings,[2] while the close links that had always existed in Italy between folk music and art music may be regarded as little short of ideal. Not only in *opera buffa* but in all the more serious types of music,

---

1. ◆ While it is true that the Italian journeys say much for Leopold's perceptiveness, he was not as disadvantaged as some other German musicians. Because of Salzburg's geographical proximity to Italy and successive archbishops' close ties to Rome (many of them had studied at the Collegium Germanicum), it was not uncommon for local composers and singers to spend periods touring Italy or studying there.

2. In an entry in his *Italian Journey* dated 30 July 1787, Goethe reports that 'until nearly morning, there are still groups in the street, singing and playing, one occasionally hears duets as beautiful as in any opera or concert': *Jubiläums-Ausgabe*, xxvii.80; see also the description of the cart full of musicians that 'made its pleasure rounds through the nocturnal city': xxvii.87.

including church music, the Italians believed as a matter of principle that even the most highly developed art forms should be linked to ideas that were universally intelligible. Even today the Italians have managed to avoid the deep chasm between high art and popular art that exists in present-day Germany.

Given so harmonious a working relationship between the folk and the nation's artists, it comes as no surprise to discover that an appreciation of, and enthusiasm for, music were shared by members of every social class and, indeed, that the Italians set greater store by their music than by their no less highly developed visual arts. Here the artist found an audience trained by constant practice, rewarding the good things on offer with genuine Mediterranean enthusiasm, while equally capable, of course, of judging all shortcomings with implacable rigour. One would have to go back to the time of the ancient orators to find an equally impassioned interest and, at the same time, an equally highly developed technical understanding of an artist's achievements.

It was the Church – the traditional upholder of musical culture since the early Middle Ages – that was largely responsible for teaching young people music. Monasteries and religious institutions of every description were keen to take advantage of the musical resources at their disposal and adapt them to their own ends. But, starting in the sixteenth century, it was the conservatories that were of the most vital importance. In keeping with their name, the earliest such institutions were intended only to look after destitute orphans and provide them with a musical education. The first to be established was the Conservatorio di Santa Maria di Loreto in Naples, which was founded by Giovanni di Tapia in 1537 and followed during the next sixty years by the Conservatorio della Pietà dei Turchini, the Conservatorio dei Poveri di Gesù Cristo and the Conservatorio di Sant'Onofrio, all of them in Naples. Venice, too, could boast four similar institutions: the Ospedali della Pietà, dei Mendicanti, degli Incurabili and dell'Ospedaletto ('delle Donzelle Povere'), the last-named exclusively for young girls. The products of a genuinely charitable concern, these institutions were the pillars on which Italian's hegemony in the world of music was to be built, more especially during the seventeenth century, when the new art of unaccompanied solo song came into being. This was an art that they adopted with an energy and an enthusiasm difficult to imagine today. The young pupils' studies lasted several years, setting store by a general education and ultimately producing some of the country's most accomplished singers, instrumentalists and composers. Even as late as the eighteenth century, virtually every Italian composer of any significance studied at one of these schools and even during his later career regarded it as a supreme honour to run such an institution, at least for a time. The astonishing wealth of Italian singers and especially opera composers whose often incredible productivity supplied not only the home market but foreign opera houses, too, is entirely due to these conservatories.[3]

Alongside these democratic institutions, however, Italy could also boast others, no less venerable, that served the hereditary and educated aristocracy as temples of music: the academies. These last-named organizations were made up of scholars, artists and art-loving amateurs and were a product of the Renaissance, acquiring a standing that was of immense importance not only for the history and theory of music but for its performing practices, too. It was to these organizations that opera owed its very existence and from them that the new genre of instrumental music received every possible encouragement. The Accademia degli Arcadi in Rome and the Accademie della Crusca and degli Elevati in Florence were well known, but no less important for the history of music were two institutions in Bologna, the Accademia dei Filomusi, which was established by

---

3. ◆ See, for example, Denis Arnold, 'Orphans and Ladies: The Venetian Conservatories (1680–1790)'.

Adriano Banchieri in 1615, and the Accademia dei Filarmonici, which Count Vincenzo Maria Carrati founded in 1666 and whose members continued to be held in the highest regard even in Mozart's day, numbering among their ranks some of the most famous composers and theorists of their age, while discouraging less qualified musicians from joining by means of a strict entrance examination. To be a member of such an institution was regarded as one of the highest honours available to any musician.[4]

Opera had become increasingly central to the country's musical concerns, being regarded, as before, as the culmination of Renaissance art and allowing the Italians to see themselves as the only true heirs of classical antiquity. By the date of Mozart's arrival in the country, *opera buffa* had come to enjoy a status equal to that of its elder sister, with the Italians quite rightly regarding it as the most fitting reflection of their national spirit. To receive a commission – a *scrittura* – was a composer's highest ambition, and musicians such as the two great teachers Francesco Durante and Padre Martini who acquired their reputations away from the world of opera were very much the exception in this regard. Like most of the older genres, operas, too, were written to commission, but they were also occasional compositions in the sense that the individual work ceased to exert any influence once the outward circumstances that had produced it no longer existed. Relatively few famous operas were staged in theatres other than the one where they first saw the light of day, with impresarios generally taking care to ensure that their audiences heard only new works. In consequence, not even famous opera composers ever had an opportunity to rest on their laurels but were forced to turn out one work after another with a frequency and fecundity that now seem to us inconceivable.

But the preponderant role played by opera also brought with it serious dangers. Admittedly, the situation in Mozart's time was not as grave as it was later to become, when the almost exclusive interest in opera virtually prevented instrumental music from developing any further and as a result undermined the international reputation of Italian music. On the other hand, the damage that this caused was already clearly evident in church music by the date of Mozart's first visit to the country. Most opera composers also wrote for the church and generally had to reckon on having their works performed by opera singers and instrumental virtuosos, so that it was hardly surprising that the spirit of opera gradually infiltrated church music and jeopardized its dignity and purity. In much the same way, the dramatic decline in the standard of the old church choirs drove more and more composers to take refuge in solo songs and instrumental works, helping to foment a crisis from which Italian church music has still not escaped even today. Attempts to counter this pernicious development, including the one undertaken by Padre Martini in Bologna, remained ineffectual in the longer term.

In spite of these danger signals, Italy's domination in the world of music remained essentially unshaken at this time, with Spain and England acknowledging its ascendancy virtually without reserve. But even in France – the only country to have a firmly established national school of music – there was an Italian faction that had been steadily growing since the middle of the seventeenth century. Germany, for its part, had long been able to boast of little more than its Protestant chorales and the organ music based upon them. In all other genres, Germany remained an Italian province, with only odd exceptions such as the short-lived efflorescence of German opera culminating in Reinhard Keiser's contribution to the genre serving to confirm the rule.[5] Above all, German opera houses were entirely in Italian hands from around 1720 onwards, presenting not

---

4. ◆ In general, see Maylender, *Storia delle Accademie d'Italia.*
5. Kretzschmar, 'Das erste Jahrhundert der deutschen Oper'. ◆ See also Klaus-Peter Koch, *Reinhard Keiser.*

only the works of Italian composers at German courts but also showcasing Italian poets, singers and, for the most part, instrumentalists.

The counterpart of these Italian emissaries to Germany was the respectable number of German musicians who visited Italy to study the native tradition at source. The first of these pilgrims was Hans Leo Haßler, who travelled to Venice in 1584 to study with Andrea Gabrieli. Haßler was followed by Heinrich Schütz in 1609 and, in the eighteenth century, by a whole series of opera composers from Handel, Hasse, Gluck and Johann Christian Bach to Mozart. Mozart was the last in the series, and it is largely to his credit and to that of Joseph Haydn, whose career was already independent of Italy, that the 'Roman campaigns' of German musicians now came to an end, a handful of exceptions such as Meyerbeer and Nicolai notwithstanding.

Leopold himself had been unable to visit Italy in his own youth and so, in order to pave the way for his son, he astutely addressed himself to the one person whose influence still dominated the world of music and who had already cleared a path for countless musicians from both Italy and Germany, including Haydn. Johann Adolf Hasse – the 'father of music' – had given Leopold a letter of recommendation in Vienna. Dated 30 September 1769, it was addressed to his friend the Abbate Giovanni Maria Ortes in Bologna and provides an extremely interesting account of both father and son:

I have made the acquaintance here of a certain Sig. Mozart, *maestro di cappella* to the Bishop of Salzburg, a refined man of spirit and of the world; and who, I believe, knows his business well, both in music and in other things. This man has a daughter and a son. The former plays the harpsichord very well, and the latter, who cannot be more than twelve or thirteen years of age, is already a composer and a master of music. I have seen the compositions that must be his own, which certainly are not bad and in which I have found no trace of a boy of twelve; and I dare not doubt that they are by him, seeing that I took him through various tests on the harpsichord, on which he let me hear things that are prodigious for his age and would be admirable even for a mature man. Now his father, wishing to take him to Italy to make him better known there, therefore wrote to me asking me to give him at this moment some letters of recommendation, and I shall take the liberty of sending him one for you.[6]

The said Sig. Mozart is a very polished and civil man, and the children are very well brought up. The boy is moreover handsome, lively, graceful and full of good manners; and knowing him, it is difficult not to love him. I am sure that if his development keeps due pace with his years, he will be a prodigy, provided that his father does not pamper him too much or spoil him by means of excessive praise; that is the only thing I fear. Here you have a long letter from me: please accept it in the spirit in which it is intended, etc.[7]

Leopold had no wish to delay a moment longer in setting out for Italy, so confident was he that Mozart would enjoy an even more rapid and brilliant success with impressionable Italian audiences. And in this he was not mistaken. On the other hand, he was soon forced to realize that no financial gain could be expected from the journey, as the concerts or *accademie* were generally organized by private societies or by public organizations that did not charge admission. At best,

6. It is clear from this letter that Leopold already planned to leave Salzburg on 24 October. ◆ Hasse then goes on to ask Ortes to advise Mozart and to introduce him to others.
7. First published with the Italian original by Kretzschmar, 'Hasse über Mozart'. On the letters to Ortes in general, see Kretzschmar, 'Aus Deutschlands italienischer Zeit', 149–50 [*Dokumente* 84–5, *Documentary Biography*, 92–3 (translation slightly amended)].

the artist could expect to receive some trifling remuneration from the organizer. Leopold wrote to inform his wife of this fact soon after his arrival in Italy, but repeatedly stressed that, even if he had not made his fortune, he 'always had a little more than necessary' and, because he never lost sight of his principal aim, was altogether satisfied.

Shortly before they set off, Wolfgang was formally appointed Konzertmeister to the archbishop, and he appears in this capacity in the Salzburg court calendar from 1770 onwards.[8]

Father and son left Salzburg on 13 December 1769.[9] Throughout their journey through the Tirol and Upper Italy, they were able to take advantage of the numerous personal links that bound these regions to Salzburg, either in the form of business contacts or through members of the cathedral chapter whose aristocratic dependants, many of whom had studied in Salzburg, had settled or held appointments here. As a result, there was no lack of letters of recommendation to introduce the travellers to the most varied circles wherever they went. Their first stop was at Innsbruck, where they arrived on 15 December and were well received by Count Johann Nepomuk Spaur, the brother of the Salzburg Cathedral canon. Shortly afterwards, at an academy organized by the local aristocracy and held – probably on the 15th – at Count Künigl's, Wolfgang sight-read a concerto, which he then received as a present, together with twelve ducats. He was supported by several local musicians, including the violinist Franz Sebastian Haindl, the organist Georg Paul Falck and the horn player Franz Joseph Schauer. In its edition of 18 December, the local paper mentioned the laurels garnered by Mozart on his earlier travels, adding that at the above-mentioned concert he gave 'the most splendid proofs of his quite peculiar skill' and thus 'lent new lustre to his fame'.[10]

They resumed their journey on the 19th and travelled via Steinach and Brixen to Bozen, where they alighted at The Sun. From there they moved on to Rovereto, where Leopold was agreeably surprised to meet an old friend of his in the person of the regional governor Nicolò Cristani, who had been brought up by one of his relations in Salzburg and received violin lessons from Leopold; Cristani thought that Wolfgang was like his mother, whom he could still remember very clearly. Meanwhile, the members of the aristocracy to whom the Mozarts had been recommended – Leopold mentions Counts Massimiliano Settimo and Domenico Antonio Lodron, Baron Gian Giulio Pizzini and Giovanni Battista de Cosmi – showered all manner of gifts on them and even organized a concert at the home of Baron Giovanni Battista Todeschi, who had been one of Wolfgang's admirers since the time of their visit to Vienna. 'I don't need to tell you what a credit Wolfgang has been to us all,' Leopold reported. By the time that he went to play on the organ in the main church the next day,[11] reports of his visit had spread through the town and the building

8. Hagenauer's diary for 27 November reads: 'Today Dom. Wolfgangus Mozart, a youth of fourteen years, received permission to travel to Italy and also an official letter granting him the title of *Concert-Maister* and promising him, upon his return from Italy, the remuneration due to that office' [*Dokumente*, 86, *Documentary Biography*, 94–5].

9. The sources for this journey are the letters of Leopold and Wolfgang, together with the information given by Marianne and reproduced by Nottebohm, *Mozartiana*, 104 [*Dokumente*, 402–3, *Documentary Biography*, 458–60]. Also of importance in the context of this first visit to Italy is a brief autograph list of all Mozart's acquaintances written in his own hand and now preserved in the Munich Staatsbibliothek; see Sandberger, 'Mozartiana'. Unfortunately, it contains only the names of the relevant individuals in Innsbruck, Bozen, Rovereto and Naples. As Hagenauer correctly states, the Mozarts left Salzburg on 13 December, not on the 12th as Leopold and Marianne jointly claim. As a result, the dates on which they left Innsbruck and Steinach were both a day later than those given by Leopold, who had taken an old diary with him. Only in the course of the journey did he replace it with a new one. According to his travel diary, the Mozarts stayed in the following towns in the course of their first visit to Italy: Innsbruck, Steinach, Brixen, Bozen, Egna, Rovereto, Verona, Mantua, Cremona, Milan, Parma, Bologna, Florence, Rome, Naples, Turin and Venice; see Schurig, *Leopold Mozarts Reise-Aufzeichnungen 1763–1771*, 16, 49ff., 62. ◆ The letters and travel diaries from the Italian journeys are reproduced in full in *Briefe*, i.292–483. They are written by both Mozart and his father.

10. ◆ This was the *Innsbrucker Montägige Ordinari Zeitung*, see *Dokumente*, 92, *Documentary Biography*, 101.

11. Leopold's diary also mentions a 'Capellmeister abbate Pasqui' (presumably an error for Pasquini), who was no doubt the church's *maestro di cappella*.

was so full that 'some very strong fellows had to go on ahead and clear a way for us to the choir, where we then had to wait for over five minutes before we could get to the organ'.[12]

Even greater was the enthusiasm that greeted them in Verona. Operas were currently being performed every evening, and so it was only on the seventh day that they were able to organize a concert. While they were waiting, they were assailed by invitations from a veritable army of admirers, including the Marchese Alessandro Carlotti, Count Giusti del Giardino and the violinist Locatelli.[13] In the presence of a gathering of hand-picked cognoscenti, Wolfgang performed a symphony of his own composition, sight-read the most difficult pieces and wrote not only an aria to a given text, which he then proceeded to sing himself, but also various other pieces on given themes. His announcement that he wanted to try out the organ in the Church of San Tommaso led to a repetition of the same sort of scenes as those that had taken place in Rovereto. There were so many people packed into the building that they had to enter it via the monastery, and even then they would never have reached the organ if the monks had not taken them into their midst and ushered them into the choir. When the performance was over, the throng was even greater, as everyone wanted to see the diminutive organist. The newspapers vied with each other in hailing his achievements, while poets sang his praises in verse. Foremost among Mozart's admirers was the Receiver General, Pietro Lugiati, who commissioned a life-size oil portrait of him at the keyboard and in a letter of 22 April wrote to the boy's mother to report on the honour accorded him, expressing his warm admiration for the 'raro e portentoso giovane'.[14]

They arrived in Mantua on 10 January and, in spite of the cold, were in good health, although, as Leopold wrote to tell his wife, the effect of the air and open fires on Wolfgang's complexion was such that he looked as though he had been through a campaign, as his face was reddish brown, especially about the nose and mouth, 'just like the face of His Majesty the Emperor'.[15] Here, too, they were well received by members of the music-loving nobility, with Marianna Bettinelli, in particular, looking after Mozart like a mother and weeping openly when he left. Margherita Sartoretti invited them to have lunch with her and the following day sent one of her servants with a bowl containing a magnificent bunch of flowers. The flowers were tied with ribbons, with four ducats woven into them, and, resting on top of them, was a poem written by Signora Sartoretti herself.[16] She also gave Wolfgang some skin cream to rub into his chapped hands. The concert organized by the Accademia Filarmonica took place on 16 January at their splendid *teatrino*, with Wolfgang providing the main attraction. The following programme gives an idea of the various concerts in which Mozart took part in Italy:

Series of Musical Compositions to be Performed at the Public
Philharmonic Academy of Mantua on the Evening of the 16th
of the present month of January 1770
on the Occasion of the Arrival of the Most Highly Skilled Youth
Signor Amadeo Mozart.

12. ◆ *Briefe*, i.298–9 (letter of 7 January 1770).
13. ◆ Here Abert seems to confuse the famous violinist Pietro Antonio Locatelli, who died in 1764, with a local Innsbruck businessman, Michelangelo Locatelli.
14. The portrait is reproduced by Schiedermair, *Die Briefe W. A. Mozarts und seiner Familie*, v.12. Schiedermair is no doubt right to argue that the artist is the 'pittore Cignaroli' mentioned by Leopold in his travel diary. ◆ See also Pietro Lugiati's letter to Anna Maria Mozart: 'I have conceived such a regard for him that I had him painted from life' (*Dokumente*, 108–9, *Documentary Biography*, 119–20). The artist, however, is now considered to be Saverio dalla Rosa; for a reproduction, see Deutsch, *Mozart und seine Welt*, 11.
15. ◆ *Briefe*, i.303 (letter of 11 January 1770).
16. ◆ Sartoretti's poem is given in *Dokumente*, 98–9, *Documentary Biography*, 108–9.

1. Symphony composed by Sig. Amadeo.
2. Harpsichord Concerto presented and performed by him at sight.
3. Aria by a Professor.
4. Harpsichord Sonata performed at sight by the youth and variations of his own invention extemporized and subsequently repeated in a key other than that in which it is written.
5. Violin Concerto by a Professor.
6. Aria simultaneously composed and sung extempore by Sig. Amadeo, with the proper accompaniment performed on the harpsichord, to words made for the purpose, but not previously seen by him.
7. Another Harpsichord Sonata, composed and performed by the same on a musical theme proposed to him extempore by the first violin.
8. Aria by a Professor.
9. Oboe Concerto by a Professor.
10. Fugue composed and performed by Sig. Amadeo on the harpsichord and brought to a proper conclusion according to the rules of counterpoint on a simple theme submitted to him extempore.
11. Symphony by the same, performed with all the parts on the harpsichord from a single violin part openly submitted to him extempore.
12. Duet by Professors.
13. Trio in which Sig. Amadeo will play an improvised violin part.
14. Final symphony by the said composer.[17]

The concert was a brilliant success, and the applause was tremendous, with one newspaper reporting that 'after various private trials to which our Masters and Professors of music have subjected him these last few days that he has stayed here, they cannot sufficiently assert that this youth appears to them to be born to vanquish all the experts in the art; and this view accords well with that of a noted literary man of Verona . . . that he is a miracle of music and one of those freaks of Nature, just as Ferracina was born to shame mathematicians, Corilla to humiliate all poets.'[18]

It is clear that what most impressed the reporter was the apparently miraculous nature of such precocious attainments. Whereas it was already astonishing to find a boy of Mozart's age performing so impressively on the harpsichord and violin, to say nothing of his singing, his performance as a virtuoso was all the same decidedly less impressive than his achievements as a composer. Here, too, the emphasis was placed on improvisation – the ability to rise spontaneously to various challenges, while obeying the rules of music, an ability that presupposed not only an extremely lively imagination but also total confidence in the handling of musical form. But Mozart also reports on his operatic impressions in Verona and Mantua: in Verona he heard an opera entitled *Ruggiero*,[19] and in Mantua, on 10 January 1770, he attended a performance of Hasse's *Demetrio*. His reaction[20] is entirely typical of his whole later outlook, being both assured and

---

17. ◆ *Dokumente*, 96–7, *Documentary Biography*, 106.
18. ◆ *Dokumente*, 97–8, *Documentary Biography*, 107–8. Concerning the poet Corilla Olimpica (Maria Maddalena Morelli), see nn. 49 and 50 below, and Dixon, 'Women in Arcadia'.
19. The composer's name is not given, although it cannot have been Hasse, as assumed by Wyzewa and Saint-Foix, *Wolfgang Amédée Mozart*, i.272, as Hasse's *Ruggiero* was not written until 1771. ◆ The most likely possibility appears to be Guglielmi's *Ruggiero* (Venice, 1769).
20. *Briefe*, i.6–7 (letter of 26 January 1770): 'The opera at Mantua was nice. They played Demetrio [Mozart wrote 'Denetrio'], the prima donna sings well, but quietly, and if you don't watch her acting, but only her singing, you'd think she wasn't singing at

honest, lacking in effusiveness, but acutely perceptive in a way that was typical of Salzburg's inhabitants in general and, finally, graphic in the extreme. Only about the music does he say nothing, as he still feels himself to be lacking in confidence in this area, but also because he does not want to praise at random. All the more critical is he, conversely, of the singers and especially the dancers, and it is remarkable that even at this early date the future dramatist already sets special store by acting. An echo of the performances that he attended was a setting – unfortunately lost – of the aria 'Misero tu non sei' from act one, scene four of Metastasio's *Demetrio*.

In Cremona the Mozarts heard a second opera by Hasse, *La clemenza di Tito*,[21] before continuing their journey to Milan, where they arrived in late January and found secure and comfortable accommodation at the Augustine monastery of San Marco. A lay brother waited on them, and when they were shown to their rooms, they found that their beds had been warmed, so that (to quote Leopold) 'when he goes to bed, Wolfgang is always very happy'. They were particularly helped by the governor general, Count Karl Joseph von Firmian (1716–82), who had been brought up for a time in Salzburg, where his elder brother, Leopold Anton Eleutherius, was archbishop until 1744. After studying in Salzburg and Leiden,[22] he had travelled widely in France and Italy, before becoming ambassador in Naples. Here Winckelmann met him and praised him as one of the worthiest representatives of his nation.[23] In 1759 he became governor general of Lombardy, generously making available to others his considerable collections and doing much to encourage artists and scholars. The Mozarts, too, were most warmly received by him, and it was thanks to his good offices that they were admitted to the most distinguished families and able to enjoy the pleasures of the carnival to the full.[24] At the opera, they got to know Niccolò Piccinni, who was currently producing his *Cesare in Egitto* there.[25] Mozart himself performed at a public concert and various private soirées, garnering the usual laurels. Among the musicians who tested his abilities, the most important was undoubtedly Giambattista Sammartini (1700/01–75), who numbered Gluck among his pupils and who was one of the leading exponents of Italian sacred and instrumental music at this time. He was organist at several churches in Milan and *maestro di cappella* at the monastery of Santa Maria Maddalena.[26]

all, she can't open her mouth, but whines all the time, but that's nothing new. The seconda donna looks like a grenadier and has a powerful voice, too, but her singing isn't at all bad, considering this is the first time she has acted. Il primo uomo il musico sings beautifully, but his voice is uneven, he's called Casselli. Il secondo uomo is already old and I don't like him, his name is [space left blank in autograph for addition of name]. Of the tenors, one is called Otini, he doesn't sing badly, but rather stolidly, like all Italian tenors, he's a great friend of ours; I don't know what the other one's called, he's still young, but nothing special. Primo ballerino: good. Prima ballerina: good, it's said she's not bad looking, but I've not seen her close to, the others are like all the rest: a grotesco was there who jumps well. . . . The orchestra wasn't bad.'

21. A description of it may be found in the same letter of 26 January 1770.

22. Mayr, *Die ehemalige Universität Salzburg*, 12–13. Here he had founded a literary society whose libertarian aspirations were strenuously opposed by the authorities.

23. Winckelmann, *Briefe*, i.271, 279, 324; ii.48. Schlözer ranks him alongside Münchhausen: Doering, *Leben A. L. V. Schlözer's*, i.96–7, 276, 313. See also Dutens, *Mémoires d'un voyageur qui se repose*, i.327, and *Der teutsche Merkur* (1789), iii.301.

24. In keeping with local custom, they had to have costumes specially made, consisting of cloaks and cowls reaching down to their shoulders (see *Der teutsche Merkur* (1775), iii.247–8). Leopold thought that the costume 'suits Wolfgang amazingly well', but shook his head at the idea that 'in my old age I too have had to take part in this tomfoolery' (*Briefe*, i.314–15, letter of 17 February 1770).

25. The title on the full score is *Cesare e Cleopatra*. The identity of the composer of the *Didone* mentioned by Mozart is uncertain, but it cannot have been Jommelli, as surmised by Wyzewa and Saint-Foix (i.272) as [the third version of] his *Didone abbandonata* was first staged in Stuttgart in 1763. ◆ *Briefe* v.228 also claims the *Didone* was Jommelli's, Abert's argument notwithstanding. Other possibilities include settings by Gian Francesco de Majo (1770), by Giacomo Insanguine (1770) and by Niccolò Piccinni (1770).

26. See Torrefranca, 'Le origini della sinfonia: Le sinfonie dell'imbrattacarte (G. B. Sammartini)', and Saint-Foix, 'La chronologie de l'œuvre instrumentale de Jean Baptiste Sammartini'. ◆ More recently, see Inzaghi and Prefumo, *Giambattista Sammartini*, and Churgin, 'The Italian Symphonic Background'. The claim that Sammartini was *maestro di cappella* at Santa Maria Maddalena derives from Burney; there is no evidence to support this assertion.

Mozart was also introduced to two young and accomplished castratos, one of them fifteen years old, the other sixteen, and it was for them that he wrote a handful of Latin motets and perhaps also the overtly operatic aria *Quaere superna* K143 and the offertory K117.[27]

Keen to help the ambitious young composer, Count Firmian organized a brilliant soirée at his *palazzo* that was attended, among others, by the Duke of Modena and his daughter and also by the Cardinal Archbishop. Here, in the presence of a hand-picked audience, Mozart was required to prove that he was capable of writing serious dramatic music and to set 'three arias and a recitative' by Metastasio.[28] The *pièce de résistance* was a large-scale aria with accompanied recitative from act three, scene five of *Demofoonte*, the famous and frequently set *Misero pargoletto* K77. With its lofty note of dramatic seriousness and freedom from all histrionic bombast, the piece sounds like Mozart's farewell to the school of Hasse, a school that had greeted him with open arms on his arrival in Italy. Nowhere in his later operas, all of which are influenced by more modern models, was he to achieve this same lofty tone. Particularly remarkable is the unity of the underlying mood, which even extends to the aria thanks to the use of individual reminiscences. Its principal vehicle is the syncopated rhythm on broken triads in the bass, which Mozart uses for the first time here in any consistent way in order to achieve a sense of supreme dramatic excitement. We have already seen how he had prepared for this move in his instrumental works, but he now received a new impetus in the form of Piccinni's *Cesare in Egitto*, which uses this device with striking frequency[29] and which is also the inspiration behind Mozart's divided violas.[30] Far less successful, by contrast, are the three arias from *Artaserse*, *Fra cento affanni* K88, *Per pietà, bell'idol mio* K78 and *Per quel paterno amplesso* K79. Particularly regrettable are the tawdry coloratura excesses that are found here but that are significantly missing from the aria from *Demofoonte*. Formally speaking, all four works find Mozart adopting a more progressive stance, with the old *da capo* – a staple of Hasse's operas – now replaced by more modern, freer and more volatile forms. Mozart passed the test that was set him and received from Firmian not only a snuffbox containing twenty *gigliati*,[31] but also – a most welcome gift – an edition of Metastasio's works. But the most important result of this evening and, indeed, of their stay in Milan as a whole was the *scrittura* that Wolfgang received for the forthcoming *stagione*. On condition that the prince-archbishop allowed him to do so (and the Mozarts lost no time in applying for and obtaining his permission), Wolfgang was to write the first opera of the new season, for which the leading singers of the time – Caterina Gabrielli, her sister Francesca and Guglielmo Ettore – would be engaged. The fee agreed was one hundred *gigliati*, with free accommodation for as long as Mozart was required to stay in

27. See Wyzewa and Saint-Foix, *Wolfgang Amédée Mozart*, i.284–7. On this question, see also Jahn, *W. A. Mozart*, i.318, and K⁶, 123–4 and 153. The suggestion that K143 was intended for insertion in K117 in rightly disputed by Nottebohm in his critical commentary to AMA III/2. ◆ It is unlikely that K143 was composed in Milan; both the type of paper on which the autograph is written and Mozart's handwriting suggest it was written in Salzburg towards the end of 1773. Similarly, K117 may have been written in Salzburg in early 1772.

28. Thus Leopold in *Briefe*, iii.24 (letter of 13 March 1770). Although Leopold does not mention the aria that goes with this recitative, there are in fact four arias, three of which are from *Artaserse*, namely, the two already mentioned and *Fra cento affanni* K88; see also Wyzewa and Saint-Foix, *Wolfgang Amédée Mozart*, i.287–91. ◆ The identity of the 'three arias and a recitative' remains uncertain. For a summary of earlier suggestions, a redating of *Fra cento affanni* to some time after the Firmian concert, and an argument for K71, K83 and two other texts from Metastasio's *Demofoonte*, see Pryer, 'Mozart's operatic audition: The Milan concert, 12 March 1770: A reappraisal and revision'.

29. In Caesar's arias in act one, scene one, and act two, scene three, and in Cornelia's aria in act three, scene six.

30. ◆ Abert seems to imply that in K77 Mozart for the first time writes for divided violas. However, this scoring was not uncommon in Salzburg and Mozart himself had used it in several earlier works; see, for example, *Die Schuldigkeit des Ersten Gebots* K35, the *Grabmusik* K42, the symphony K43, the mass K66 and the offertory K117.

31. A Florentine gold florin was worth about one ducat.

Milan. The libretto was to be sent on, so that he could familiarize himself with it in advance. The recitatives had to be submitted by October, and Mozart himself agreed to be back in Milan by the beginning of November in order to be able to complete the opera with the singers present and prepare it for performance over the Christmas period. These conditions were all the more acceptable in that they allowed the Mozarts to spend the intervening months travelling around Italy unhindered, while Wolfgang himself was still left with enough time to complete the opera at his convenience.

After leaving Milan, Mozart wrote his first quartet K80 at Lodi on 15 March, completing it – as he himself noted – at seven o'clock in the evening.[32] In Parma the famous soprano Lucrezia Aguiari ('la Bastardella') invited the Mozarts to supper and sang three arias for them, thereby confirming her reputation for extreme agility and fabulous top notes.[33] Here they were also received by Margrave Giovanni Luca Pallavicini with an affability that reminded them of their reception at Count Firmian's.[34] On 26 March Pallavicini organized a brilliant concert at his house attended by some one hundred and fifty members of the higher aristocracy, including the Cardinal Legate Antonio Colonna Branciforte and, at the head of the cognoscenti, Padre Martini, even though the latter had officially given up attending concerts. The guests started to assemble at half past seven, and it was not until towards midnight that they began to think of leaving.

Leopold wrote home to report that they were particularly popular in Bologna and that Wolfgang was admired even more than elsewhere, as Bologna was the home of so many scholars and artists. Here they met the famous La Spagnoletta (Clementina Spagnoli), the castrato Giuseppe Manfredini, the brother of the *maestra di cappella* Vincenzo Manfredini, who was also known as a writer and who had visited the Mozarts in Salzburg in 1769 on his return from St Petersburg,[35] and the famous soprano castrato Giuseppe Aprile.[36] Leopold reckoned that Wolfgang's fame would now spread like wildfire to the rest of Italy, as Padre Martini had set him the most challenging tests and Martini, who had spoken of Wolfgang with the greatest admiration, was 'the idol of the Italians'. Giovanni Battista Martini[37] (1706–84) was a Franciscan priest who enjoyed the highest reputation in Italy at this time, not only as a church composer, but even more as a theorist, historian and teacher. Although only one volume of his scholarly *Storia della musica* (1757) had been published by this date and his classic study of counterpoint[38] was still in preparation at the time of the Mozarts' visit to Bologna, he was regarded even at this date as a universally venerated oracle in all matters of music not only in Italy but elsewhere, too. The owner of a uniquely magnificent library,[39] he was invariably surrounded by students and in constant correspondence with musicians, scholars and princes. He was often asked to settle disputes, and his

32. ◆ See *Briefe*, ii.326 (letter of 24 March 1778). This information is noted on Mozart's autograph; originally in three movements, a fourth movement was added to the quartet in Vienna in 1773 or in Salzburg sometime between 1773 and 1775.
33. She could reach c''''. As Leopold reports in his letter of 24 March (*Briefe*, i.326), Wolfgang wrote down some examples of her passage-work. ◆ Further, see Giazotto, *La Musica a Genova nella vita pubblica e privata del XIII al XVIII secolo*, 201, 233–4.
34. See *Briefe*, i.327 (letter of 27 March 1770).
35. See *Briefe*, i.377 (letter of 4 Aug. 1770).
36. See Kelly, *Reminiscences*, i.74–6. ◆ Concerning Aprile, see Mamy, 'Tradizione pedagogica del canto a Napoli: Giuseppe Aprile'.
37. See Della Valle, *Memorie storiche del p. m. Giambattista Martini*; Federico Parisini, *Della vita e delle opere del Padre G. B. Martini*; Leonida Busi, *Il Padre G. B. Martini*; and Gandolfi, *Elogio di Giovanni Battista Martini*. ◆ More recently, see Zaccaria, *Padre Giambattista Martini*; Vecchi, *La musica come arte e come scienza*; and Callegari Hill, 'Padre Martini and the Accademia filarmonica of Bologna'.
38. *Esemplare ossia Saggio fondamentale pratico di contrappunto sopra il canto fermo* (Bologna, 1774–6).
39. Burney, *The Present State of Music in France and Italy*, 202–3. ◆ See also Schnoebelen, 'The Growth of Padre Martini's Library'.

advice was regularly sought whenever new appointments were made: a word from Padre Martini was the best possible recommendation. His authority was all the more willingly accepted in that his immense knowledge was combined with great modesty and a perpetual readiness to help others through his teachings, advice and recommendations. He remained affable and calm[40] and, at the same time, circumspect even in his learned disputations. Inevitably, Leopold was more than anxious to win over such a man to his son's cause. Each time they visited him, Mozart was given a fugue to elaborate, with Martini writing out only the 'duces and the guide with a few notes' for him. On each occasion, the result was to the complete satisfaction of the great contrapuntalist.

Mozart met Bologna's other leading musician at this time, a man who could hardly have been more unlike the learned Padre Martini: Carlo Broschi (1705–82), better known as Farinelli, was a pupil of Porpora and had made his public début as Metastasio's Angelica in 1722, a début that laid the foundations for a close friendship between the singer and the young poet, who invariably called him his 'caro gemello'. It was a relationship that was to influence the whole course of Italian opera. Farinelli went on to enjoy an unprecedentedly successful career not only throughout Italy, but also in Vienna and London.[41] From 1737 he was the declared favourite of King Philip V of Spain, before retiring to a luxurious villa in 1759 to devote himself to the arts and sciences. Here he received his fellow artists with the delightful refinement of the man of the world, continuing to astonish them with his singing even in old age.[42] Reports not only of the compass and beauty of his voice, but also of his technique and execution, are legendary.[43] Indeed, he seems very much to embody the greatness and power of the art of singing in the eighteenth century, an art of which not even the most extraordinary achievements of the nineteenth century can give us a proper idea but which ensured that the history of the music of this period is largely the history of singing and of singers. The age in which Mozart grew up still bore traces of Farinelli's influence, and even though singers no longer enjoyed the absolute hegemony of old, it is not without significance that, as a youth, Mozart was deeply and lastingly impressed by these great representatives of the art of fine singing.[44]

The travellers arrived in Florence on 30 March and found a warm reception thanks to the letters of recommendation that they had brought with them from Austria. The imperial ambassador Count Rosenberg lost no time in announcing their arrival at court, where Grand Duke Leopold was pleased to receive them, recalling their earlier visit to Vienna and enquiring after Marianne. Wolfgang performed at court on 2 April, an occasion that lasted five whole hours. He was accompanied by the famous violinist Pietro Nardini, and was given the most testing fugues to play and most complicated themes to elaborate by the director of music in Florence, the Marquis de Ligniville: he performed these various feats 'as easily as one eats a piece of bread'.

Ligniville – whose various titles included Prince of Conca and Chamberlain to the Court of Tuscany – was a cultured amateur musician and had written a *Salve regina*[45] and a *Stabat mater* for three voices, both of which he had had engraved. In a preface written by the academy, of which he himself was a member, the first of these works was held out as a fine example of contrapuntal

40. See Grétry, *Mémoires*, i.91; Meißner, *Bruchstücke zur Biographie J. G. Naumanns*, i.150ff.; and Burney, *The Present State of Music in France and Italy*, 200–1.
41. See Désastre, *Carlo Brioschi*, and Chrysander, *Georg Friedrich Händel*, ii.378ff. ◆ More recently, see Mamy, *Les grands castrats napolitains*, and Cappelletto, *La voce perduta: vita di Farinelli evirato cantore*.
42. See Burney, *The Present State of Music in France and Italy*, 210–12.
43. Mancini, *Pensieri, e riflessioni pratiche sopra il canto figurato*, 152ff.
44. See Dittersdorf, *Lebensbeschreibung*, 90–1.
45. See Burney, *The Present State of Music in France and Italy*, 261.

procedures and one, moreover, that followed the old Roman school as represented, among others, by Padre Martini. Wolfgang prepared a fair copy of nine of the thirty canons in the *Stabat mater*, and their style also finds an echo in the *Kyrie a cinque con diversi canoni* (with three five-part canons at the unison) K89. An autograph sketch also survives including not only the first canon of the Kyrie but also a four-part canon that begins as follows:[46]

Five elaborate puzzle canons follow, all of them explicitly marked 'di Mozart':[47]

---

46. In the complete edition of Mozart's works (AMA III/2), the canon is reproduced on the basis of a copy in the archives of the Gesellschaft der Musikfreunde in Vienna and is described as a 'canon for five voices'. In the autograph sketch in the Königliche Bibliothek in Berlin (bound into a volume entitled *Varia Instrumentalia*), the canon is in four parts, as reproduced by Jahn. It appears that the copyist was misled by the fact that Mozart wrote out the canon on a special line above the four voices, adding a sign after each three-bar group to the effect that the following voice had to enter at this point. As in the complete edition, the additional line is in A major; see Deiters in Jahn, *W. A. Mozart*, fourth edition, i.134n. ◆ For a facsimile and transcription of the autograph sketch, see NMA X/30/3.

47. These five puzzle canons are sketched on the same folio as the one in the Königliche Bibliothek in Berlin that also includes the previous canon. Deiters compared them with the autograph and made the necessary corrections. The fourth note from the end in no. 5 is unclear but, according to Deiters, it is probably a quaver.

4 Canon. Tertia pars si placet.

Con - fi - te — bor ti - bi Do ———— mi-ne.

in gen - ti - bus et no-mi - ni tu - o can - ta ———— bo.

5 Canon. Ter voce ciemus.

The - ba - na bel - la can - to, Tro - ja - na can - tat al - ter.

Tro - ja - na can - tat al - ter, The - ba - na bel - la can - to.

The first four of these are modelled on the vignettes with which Martini decorated his *Storia universale* (i.67 and ii/1.41).[48] He gave a copy of the volume to Leopold in Bologna and, with his well-known receptivity to new impressions, Wolfgang clearly lost no time in imitating the master's contrapuntal skills.

In Florence they met their old friend from London, the singer Giovanni Manzuoli, and Mozart was delighted to hear that he had been approached by the authorities in Milan to sing in the boy's new opera. In order to win him over, Wolfgang gave him his arias to sing, together with the ones written as test pieces in Milan. He also became very friendly with the thirteen-year-old Thomas Linley, the son of an English composer, who was studying with Nardini and who had already achieved such feats as a violinist that he was said to be almost as good as his teacher. The two boys met at the home of Maddalena Morelli, who, as 'Corilla',[49] was famous as an *improvisatrice* and who was crowned poetess on the Capitol in 1776.[50] During the few days that the Mozarts spent in Florence, the two boys became inseparable, tirelessly competing with each other 'not as boys, but as men'. Both of them cried copiously when they had to say goodbye, and Tommasino – as Linley was known in Italy – brought Mozart a poem written for him by Corilla.[51] According to Burney,[52] Linley and Mozart were talked of all over Italy as the two most promising geniuses of the age, and Kelly recalled[53] that in Vienna Mozart spoke warmly of Linley and of the great expectations dashed by his premature death.[54]

'I wish you could see Florence and the surrounding countryside and the situation of the town', Leopold wrote to his wife; 'you'd say that one should live and die here'.[55] Both he and Wolfgang

48. On the mottos, see Martini, *Esemplare*, ii.XXV.
49. See Barthold, *Die geschichtlichen Persönlichkeiten in Casanovas Memoiren*, ii.177.
50. See Schubart, *Deutsche Chronik*, iii (1776), 499, 554, 613.
51. ◆ This poem is reproduced in *Dokumente*, 105, *Documentary Biography*, 115–16.
52. Burney, *The Present State of Music in France and Italy*, 255.
53. Kelly, *Reminiscences*, i.225–6.
54. He was drowned in a boating accident in 1778; see Parke, *Musical Memoirs* (London, 1830), i.204. According to Edward Holmes, Linley's brother Ozias owned an Italian letter from Mozart to Thomas. ◆ Mozart's letter to Linley is published in *Briefe*, i.388–9 (letter of 10 September 1770). Further, see Beechey, 'Thomas Linley, Junior'.
55. ◆ *Briefe*, i.331 (letter of 3 April 1770).

were reluctant to leave, but they had little time to lose if they were to reach Rome in time for Holy Week. It was a difficult journey. The weather was so appalling that they were often tempted to retrace their steps and return to Salzburg, the countryside was largely unfarmed, and the inns were filthy and unwelcoming, with nothing to eat but a few eggs and broccoli. They finally reached Rome at midday on the Wednesday before Easter (11 April) to the sound of such cataclysmic claps of thunder that they were reminded of a twenty-one-gun salute. They were just in time to hear a performance of Allegri's *Miserere* in the Sistine Chapel. And here Mozart famously gave proof of his excellent ear and impeccable powers of recollection[56] by writing out from memory the famous setting of the Fiftieth Psalm by Gregorio Allegri, who had been a member of the papal choir from 1629 to 1644. The piece is scored for five- and four-part choir, with a final section in which the two choirs come together in nine-part counterpoint. Performed every Wednesday and Friday in Holy Week,[57] it was universally regarded as the *ne plus ultra* of its genre and as the high point of the Passion music performed in the papal chapel,[58] so that, as Leopold reports, it is hardly surprising to find that the choir was anxious to prevent it from falling into unqualified hands.[59]

Needless to say, Wolfgang's feat caused something of a sensation, especially when he declaimed the piece in the presence of one of the singers from the papal choir, a certain Cristofori, and the latter recognized it. His mother and sister in Salzburg both expressed the fear that, by writing out the *Miserere*, Wolfgang might have committed some offence and get into trouble, but Leopold assured them that this was not the case and even encouraged them to tell the archbishop what had happened.[60]

Father and son initially tried to attend all the Holy Week and Easter Week services. 'Our fine clothes, the German tongue, and my usual freedom of manner with which I instructed my servant to speak to the Swiss guards in German and order them to make way for us soon helped us through everywhere.'[61] Leopold was no doubt pleased when Wolfgang was taken for a German courtier or even a prince, while he himself was assumed to be his tutor. At the cardinals' table, Wolfgang stood next to Cardinal Pallavicini, attracting his attention, so that the cardinal asked him his name. When Mozart told him, Pallavicini expressed astonishment: 'So you're the famous boy about whom I've been told so much.'[62] They had an affable conversation, in the course of

---

56. Rochlitz embroiders his narrative as usual: Rochlitz, *Für Freunde der Tonkunst*, ii.180–1.
57. On the intervening Thursday, the *Misereres* of Anerio, Nanino and Scarlatti were performed by way of a change, at least until 1714 when they were replaced by the setting by Tommaso Baj. Since 1821 Allegri's *Miserere* has been performed only once, and the third work has been a setting by Baini; see Baini, *Memorie storico-critiche della vita e delle opere di Giovanni Pierluigi da Palestrina*, ii.195ff; also Kandler, *Über das Leben und die Werke des G. Pierluigi da Palestrina*, 96ff.
58. See Goethe's 'Italian Journey', *Jubiläums-Ausgabe*, xxvii.249; Burney, *The Present State of Music in France and Italy*, 284–91; Spohr, *Selbstbiographie*, ii.37ff.; and Mendelssohn, *Reisebriefe aus den Jahren 1830 bis 1832*, 124ff. and 177ff. The way in which the work was performed was also important in this respect: Metastasio (*Lettere*, i.99) reports that the *Miserere* that had inspired him in Rome made absolutely no impression on him in Vienna. Reichardt, too, speaks dismissively of the work: Reichardt, *Musikalischer Almanach*.
59. Leopold exaggerates somewhat (*Briefe*, i.334–5, letter of 14 April 1770), for, as Burney admits (*The Present State of Music in France and Italy*, 287–91), the pope had copies made for the Emperor Leopold, the king of Portugal and Padre Martini, and the pope's *maestra di cappella* Giuseppe Santarelli gave him a copy which he, Burney, had printed in London in 1771. It was also performed in Florence, and here, too, Burney was offered a copy (252). In the light of this, we must regard as an exaggeration Baini's claim that no full score or copy of the *Miserere* had ever existed: see Sievers, 'Das Miserere von Allegri', 69–71.
60. *Briefe*, i. 349 (letter of 19 May 1770).
61. ◆ *Briefe*, i.334 (letter of 14 April 1770).
62. ◆ *Briefe*, i.334 (letter of 14 April 1770).

which the cardinal complimented Mozart on his Italian and even spoke a few words in execrable German.

Once the church services were over, the Mozarts started to send out their twenty letters of recommendation and were duly received with the usual magnificence by various members of the local aristocracy, including the Chigi, Barberini, Bracciano and Altemps families. Soirée followed soirée with exhausting rapidity, and at each of them Mozart had to perform. As Leopold noted, the astonishment at his achievements grew greater the further south they travelled. Moreover, 'Wolfgang's knowledge does not stand still, but increases from day to day, so that the greatest connoisseurs and masters are at a loss for suitable words to express their admiration'.[63]

It goes without saying that, in spite of his operatic commission, Mozart had continued to compose throughout this period, although the only works to be dated are two arias from Metastasio's libretto for *Demofoonte* (act one, scene thirteen, and act two, scene six): *Se ardire, e speranza* K82 and *Se tutti i mali miei* K83 date from April and May.[64] Although flawless from a formal point of view, these two soprano arias are palpably inferior to their predecessors in terms of their musical content.

Throughout all this, Mozart never lost sight of his family and friends in Salzburg, corresponding with his sister on the subject of dance music and asking her to send him some new Haydn minuets. In return he sent her a newly written contredanse.[65] Leopold added a note to the effect that Wolfgang 'would like Herr Cyrillus Hofmann to make up the steps for it; when the two violins play as leaders, only two persons should lead the dance, but whenever the orchestra comes in with all the instruments, the whole company should dance together. It would be best if it were danced by five couples. The first couple should begin the first solo, the second couple should dance the second one, and so on, as there are five soli and five tuttis.'[66] Here, too, they met Joseph Meißner, who was on his way back from Naples to Salzburg: Wolfgang appeared with him at the German College of Jesuits, where they performed at the invitation of Albert von Mölk, who was currently studying there.

In Rome they stayed with the papal courier, Steffano Uslenghi, on the Piazza del Clementino. Here they were most hospitably entertained and did not have to pay on leaving, which they did on 8 May. Travelling in the company of four Augustinian monks, they took the usual road to Capua, where they attended a ceremony at which an aristocratic nun took the veil, and arrived in Naples on the 14th. Twelve days later Leopold wrote to his wife:

> The situation of this town pleases me more and more every day, and Naples itself is not bad on the whole. But I wish the populace here were not so godless and that certain people, who do not for a moment imagine that they are stupid, were not as stupid as they are. And how superstitious they are! Superstition is so deeply rooted here that I can say for certain that heresy now reigns supreme and is regarded with the utmost indifference.[67]

63. ◆ *Briefe*, i.338 (letter of 21 April 1770).
64. The symphony K81 of 25 April is by Leopold. ◆ In fact, the authorship of this work is uncertain. A catalogue from 1775 by the Leipzig publisher Breitkopf credits the work to Leopold; a manuscript, possibly from the 1770s and now in the library of the Gesellschaft der Musikfreunde, Vienna, however, is attributed to Wolfgang.
65. A contredanse from this period is listed by Köchel (123) and included in NMA IV/13/1/1. Whether it was the work sent to Salzburg remains open to question.
66. ◆ *Briefe*, i.335–6 (letter of 14 April 1770).
67. *Briefe*, i.352 (letter of 26 May 1770). The sideswipe at 'certain people' is clearly aimed at the king; see below.

At court, they were graciously received by Queen Caroline, whom Wolfgang knew from Vienna, but Ferdinand IV was his usual offhand self. 'I'll tell you the kind of person the king is when I see you', wrote Leopold. 'It's not the sort of thing one can put into writing.'[68] As a result, they did not perform at court. Conversely, the all-powerful prime minister, the Marchese Bernardo Tanucci, took them under his wing, and the aristocracy followed his example. In consequence they often drove in convoy down the Strada Nuova and along the Molo, with two footmen carrying torches on the foot-board of their princely carriage. They also frequented the homes of the nobility, including those of the Princess of Francavilla, Princess Belmonte (an old friend of Metastasio's[69]) and especially the English ambassador, Sir William Hamilton, who knew the Mozarts from London and who was also known to Goethe. His house was a meeting place for artists and scholars. He himself was a violinist of the school of Giardini, while his first wife was an excellent keyboard player whose art of ornamentation and affecting playing were universally admired.[70] It gave Leopold particular pleasure to report that she trembled at having to play for Wolfgang. Among the acquaintances with whom they renewed contact in Naples were Baron Fridolin Tschudi from Salzburg, Jean Georges Meuricoffre from Lyons and Simon Doncker from Amsterdam.[71] In this way the Mozarts were able to organize an extremely well-attended concert on 28 May.[72]

At the opera, too, they were able to hear a number of new works. The two main theatres associated with *opere buffe*, the Teatro dei Fiorentini and the Teatro Nuovo, were dominated in the main by Piccinni and Paisiello.[73] But the performances at the San Carlo began on 30 May – the king's name-day – with Jommelli's *Armida abbandonata*, to words by Francesco Saverio De Rogatis. Anna Lucia De Amicis sang Armida, while Giuseppe Aprile was Rinaldo.[74] This was the first opera that Jommelli had written following his return to Italy from Germany and, at the same time, the first major disappointment that he suffered in his life. Mozart merely repeated the general view when, in a letter of 5 June 1770, he described the work as beautiful but too serious and old-fashioned for the theatre.[75] Jommelli's next two operas, *Demofoonte* (4 November 1770) and *Ifigenia in Tauride* (30 May 1771),[76] proved even less successful. We shall shortly have occasion to look more closely at the reasons for these setbacks in the career of a composer who had once been so highly acclaimed. On a personal level, Jommelli welcomed the Mozarts with his usual affability, and, if he had not already been under contract to Milan, Wolfgang would even have been invited to write an opera for the San Carlo by the impresario Giovanni Amadori, to whom he was introduced by Jommelli. Among other leading lights of Neapolitan opera whom Mozart met at this time were Pasquale Cafaro, Gian Francesco de Majo and his father Giuseppe, Gennaro Manna, Pasquale Tarantini, Girolamo Abos and especially Giovanni Paisiello. Leopold's diary also mentions the castrato

68. *Briefe*, i.366 (letter of 30 June 1770).

69. Metastasio, *Opere postume*, iii.258.

70. Burney, *The Present State of Music in France and Italy*, 333; Cramer, *Magazin der Musik*, i (1783) 341; and Kelly, *Reminiscences*, i.29. ◆ See also Deutsch, 'The First Lady Hamilton'.

71. Scheurleer, *Mozart's verblijf in Nederland*, 98.

72. Marianne mentions a 'big concert at the home of the imperial ambassador Count Kaunitz': Nottebohm, *Mozartiana*, 106; see also Nissen, *Biographie W. A. Mozarts*, 205; and Wurzbach, *Mozart-Buch*, 21 [*Dokumente*, 403, *Documentary Biography*, 459].

73. Florimo, *La scuola musicale di Napoli e i suoi conservatori.*, iv.68 and 128. ◆ Further, see Croce, *I teatri di Napoli, Secolo XV–XVIII*; Cantone and Greco, *Il Teatro del Re. Il San Carlo da Napoli all' Europa*; and Michael Robinson, *Naples and Neapolitan Opera*.

74. Florimo, *La scuola musicale di Napoli*, iv.241.

75. *Briefe*, i.358; his earlier impression had been different: 'è una opera che è ben scritta e che mi piace veramente': *Briefe*, i.355 (letter of 29 May 1770).

76. Leopold reports on the failure of *Demofoonte* in his letter of 22 December 1770: *Briefe*, i.410. On this whole background, see Abert, *Niccolò Jommelli als Opernkomponist*, 89ff.

Caffarelli (Gaetano Majorano) – said to be as wealthy as he was avaricious – and the violinist Emanuele Barbella.[77] But they also visited the surrounding area and saw the local sights, including Pozzuoli, Baia and Cape Miseno, Vesuvius ('and the two buried cities where they are excavating rooms from antiquity'), Caserta, Capodimonte and so on. As before, Leopold was struck by the local population's 'terrible superstition and the amount of the most godless idolatry; but you mustn't think I mean only the *lazzaroni* from among the common people, no, even people of distinction are deeply superstitious'.[78]

On 25 June they set off for Rome, travelling post-haste and arriving in the city after a journey lasting twenty-seven hours that was not without its mishaps and that left Mozart so exhausted that no sooner had they arrived than he fell asleep in an armchair. In Rome they found new impressions waiting for them, and also new honours. On the Feast of St Peter and St Paul they attended a public festivity with illuminations and witnessed the handing over of the Neapolitan tribute, and on 8 July Mozart was presented with the Order of the Golden Spur by the pope.[79] It was the same order as the one awarded to Gluck, but it made a far deeper impression on Leopold than it did on Mozart himself. Although his compositions during the next few years were to include the note 'Del Sign. cavaliere Mozart', the title 'Ritter Mozart' subsequently disappeared, never to reappear, in marked contrast to 'Ritter Gluck', whose title became an inseparable part of his name both in his own day and later. Mozart again had his portrait painted in Rome, on this occasion by Pompeo Batoni.[80]

The Mozarts left Rome on 10 July and continued their journey via Città Castellana, Loreto and Senigallia, arriving back in Bologna on the 20th[81] and intending to remain here until Mozart had finished his opera for Milan. They found attractive accommodation outside the town on Count Pallavicini's estates, where Mozart soon struck up a close friendship with the count's son, who was the same age as himself: 'He plays the keyboard, speaks German, Italian and French and has five or six teachers a day for lessons in various sciences and other exercises', Leopold reported. 'He is already imperial chamberlain.'[82] Mozart was troubled only by the loss of his singing voice as a result of the onset of puberty: he no longer had any high or low notes, and could not sing even five notes in tune, so he was no longer able to perform his own songs. Here, too, they met the well-known opera composer Josef Mysliveček (1737–81), otherwise known as 'Il Boemo', who was completing an oratorio for Padua and due to write an opera for the 1772 carnival in Milan. 'He's an honest fellow,' wrote Leopold, 'and we've become close friends.'[83] But their main contact was with Padre Martini. They were now the best of friends, visiting him every day and holding long discussions with him on the history of music. These conversations, combined with the great contrapuntalist's teachings, were to leave their mark on Wolfgang's work, and a whole series of sketches in difficult contrapuntal forms that can be dated to this period on the strength of their handwriting are no doubt bound up with the studies that Mozart undertook at Martini's urging. Particularly important is a three-part *Miserere* K85 for alto, tenor and bass with a figured continuo part headed 'del Sigr. Caval. W. A. Mozart in Bologna 1770'. It was clearly written not only under

77. Sandberger, 'Mozartiana', 67–8; and Burney, *The Present State of Music in France and Italy*, 333–4.
78. *Briefe*, ii.360 (letter of 9 June 177).
79. On this order, see Dittersdorf, *Lebensbeschreibung*, 76.
80. The Batoni portrait, now considered inauthentic, is reproduced in Deutsch, *Mozart und seine Welt*, 289.
81. See Corrado Ricci, 'Mozart e Bologna (con documenti inediti)'.
82. *Briefe*, i.379 (letter of 11 August 1770).
83. ◆ See Nascimbene, 'Mysliveček e i Mozart a Bologna. Documenti, cronaca e critica'.

Allegri's influence but, more especially, under that of Martini, while towering above all Mozart's earlier sacred works in terms of its freer style and what, in part, is its deeper and more independent expressive language – the first important evidence of a more mature approach to contrapuntal procedures stemming from Martini's teachings and example. The last three movements – a 'Quoniam', 'Benigne' and 'Tunc acceptabis' – are written in another hand and are clearly not by Mozart, but perhaps by Martini himself in an attempt to express his approval by means of a formal example of his own.[84]

On 13 August the Mozarts, together with Burney,[85] attended a performance of a mass and vespers, the ten individual movements of which were written by members of the Accademia Filarmonica, each of whom conducted his own contribution. In response to an application submitted under the terms of its constitution, the society subsequently decided to elect Mozart himself a member of their body as a *compositore*, once he had completed the requisite test. It was an honorary title that the society was fond of awarding to outstanding composers and was of particular significance for church composers as Benedikt XIV, in a papal bull of 1749, had entrusted the society with the task of overseeing music in Bologna, with the result that only its own members could become *maestri di cappella* in the city, and even at other churches in the Papal States membership of the Accademia Filarmonica served as a substitute for any formal examination.[86] In the present case the distinction was all the greater in that, according to the society's rules,[87] members had to be twenty years of age or more and had to have spent a year in each of the lower classes of *cantori* and *suonatori* before being accepted into the highest class of *compositori*. Leopold's description largely coincides with that found in the society's minutes:

On 9 October he had to appear in the Hall of the Academy at four o'clock in the afternoon. There, in the presence of the members of the society, the Princeps Accademiae and the two Censores, all three of whom are old *maestri di cappella*, put before him an antiphon taken from an antiphonal, of which he then had to produce a four-part setting in an anteroom, to which he was taken by the Beadle, who locked the door behind him. When he had completed it, it was examined by the Censores and all the *maestri di cappella* and composers, after which a vote was taken by means of black and white balls. As all the balls were white, Wolfgang was called in and all the members applauded as he entered and congratulated him when the Princeps Accademiae

---

84. Among Mozart's surviving sketches are three four-part movements with figured bass: an *Adoramus* K327, a *Justum deduxit Dominus* (KAnh. A4) and an *O sancte fac nos captare* K 326. All appear to be written in Leopold's hand. The last two may very well date from the Bologna period. Jahn (*W. A. Mozart*, fourth edition, i.146) believes them to be the work of Padre Martini, while Wyzewa and Saint-Foix (i.389) date them to the spring of 1771. The *Adoramus*, by contrast, has recently turned out to be by Quirino Gasparini: see Spieß, 'Ist die Motette "Adoramus te" (K327, Krit. Ges. Ausg. Ser. III, Nr. 30) von W. A. Mozart?' ◆ Abert is correct to point to Gasparini as the composer of K327; the composer of K326 and KAnh. A4 is the Salzburg Kapellmeister Ernst Eberlin. But while it has been traditional to date these early contrapuntal exercises to Italy, Leopold Mozart's copies actually date from considerably later, probably Salzburg, c1783.
85. Burney, *The Present State of Music in France and Italy*, 236: 'I must acquaint my musical reader, that at the performance just mentioned, I met with M. Mozart and his son, the little German, whose premature and almost supernatural talents so much astonished us in London a few years ago, when he had scarce quitted his infant state. Since his arrival in Italy he has been much admired at Rome and Naples.'
86. Grétry, *Mémoires*, i.91; Kandler, *Cenni storico-critici intorno alla vita ed alle opere del celebre compositore di musica Giovanni Adolfo Hasse detto il Sassone*, 21. The edict is reproduced in Tognetti, *Discorso su i progressi della musica.* ◆ Further concerning the Accademia Filarmonica, see Vecchi, *L'Accademia Filarmonica di Bologna (1666–1966): Notizie storiche, manifestazioni* and 'L'Accademia Filarmonica e le sue fonti storiche: Padre G. B. Martini . . . ridimensionato'; Callegari Hill, *L'Accademia filarmonica di Bologna 1666–1800: Statuti, indici degli aggregati e catalogo degli esperimenti d'esame nell'archivio, con un'introduzione storica*; and Gambassi, *L'Accademia Filarmonica di Bologna: Fondazione, statuti e aggregazione.*
87. *Statuti ovvero costituzioni de' Signori accademici filarmonici di Bologna* (Bologna, 1721).

announced, in the name of the society, that he had been accepted as a member. He thanked them, and with that it was all over. . . . Throughout all this I had been locked in the Academy library on the other side of the hall. Everyone was amazed at the speed with which he had completed the task, as many people had spent three hours over a three-line antiphon. NB. I should add that this is no easy task, as in this kind of composition many things are not allowed, as had previously been explained to him. He completed it in a good half hour.[88]

Under the terms of the society's ancient constitution, candidates were given a cantus firmus from the Gregorian antiphon and required to produce an *a cappella* setting for four, five or eight voices that obeyed the rules of strict counterpoint and observed the laws of harmony peculiar to the old church modes.[89]

Wolfgang did not approach this task unprepared. A reworking of the cantus firmus *Cibavit eos* K44 survives, written in his childish hand, and is evidently a practice piece, probably produced under Padre Martini's supervision.[90] His actual test piece (K86) involved a freely imitative, contrapuntal treatment of the accompanying parts over a cantus firmus in the bass. Taken from the Roman Antiphonal, the melody of the cantus firmus had to remain intact, but its rhythmic divisions could, conversely, be changed. The original, in Mozart's hand, is preserved in the Accademia Filarmonica archives in a volume containing various other test pieces, mostly by pupils of Martini. It was discovered here and published as part of the complete edition of Mozart's work.[91]

The Mozarts arrived in Milan on 18 October. A planned detour via Florence, Pisa, Livorno and Genoa had to be cancelled on account of Leopold's continuing indisposition following his earlier accident. Wolfgang now threw himself with a will into the task of completing his opera, *Mitridate, rè di Ponto*, a setting of Vittorio Amedeo Cigna-Santi's adaptation of Giuseppe Parini's translation of Racine's tragedy of the same name. Cigna-Santi was a native of Turin, where the opera had already been performed in 1767 in a setting by the local *maestro di cappella*, Quirino Gasparini.[92]

88. *Briefe*, i.396 (letter of 20 October 1770).

89. The conditions were made more difficult in 1773. An Italian who passed the examination at the beginning of the nineteenth century reported that he was required to submit three different settings of a given melody. First, he had to produce a four-part setting of the cantus firmus in falsobordone, in other words, a simple harmonization. The second involved a 'disposizione di parte', with the cantus firmus in one part and the other parts either in canon or imitation. The motivic writing tended to be based on the cantus firmus itself, generally in rhythmic diminution. Strict imitation was not prescribed: it was sufficient to produce a pseudo-vocal setting with similar figures in the successive entries of the different voices. The third part of the test consisted in a *fuga reale*, a complete fugue following the rules of the church mode of the cantus firmus, in which one of its phrases had to serve as the fugue subject, while other sections served as episodes; see Gaspari, *La musica in Bologna*, 27–8.

90. ◆ This assertion has since been proven false. K44 is an incomplete copy by Mozart of a seventeenth-century antiphon by Johann Stadlmayr, from his *Musica super cantum gregorianum* (Regensburg, 1625); see Hintermaier, 'Zur Urheberschaft des Introitus Cibavit eos KV 44/73u'. Mozart's copy was not made in Italy but in Salzburg, probably in 1769.

91. Bound into the files was a second version, written by Padre Martini and copied out by Mozart. A second copy of this version survives in Mozart's own hand in the Mozarteum and includes a note in Leopold's handwriting: 'Dal. Sigr. Cavaliere Amadeo Wolfgango Mozart di Salisburgo. Scritto nella sala dell' accademia filarmonica in Bologna li 10 d'Ottobre 1770.' This version was published as Mozart's actual test piece K86. His submission was not without a number of errors and was described in the society's minutes as 'satisfactory in the circumstances'. Presumably Martini worked through the piece with Mozart and showed him how to solve the problem that he had been set. The boy then took the corrected version away with him (see music example). Wyzewa and Saint-Foix (i.327) erroneously reproduce the opening bars of Martini's piece. See also Gaspari, *Gazzetta musicale di Milano* (9 May 1858); Gaspari, *La musica in Bologna*, 28; Fétis, *Biographie universelle des musiciens et bibliographie générale de la musique*, vi.226ff.; Köchel, 'Nachträge und Berichtigungen zu von Köchels Verzeichnis der Werke Mozarts', 495, and Nissen, *Biographie W. A. Mozarts*, 226. In Nottebohm's note in his critical commentary in the complete edition of Mozart's works, the sentence 'the manuscript in the Mozarteum in Salzburg is a copy of Mozart's composition' should presumably read 'a copy of Martini's composition'.

92. The ultimate fate of this great adversary of the Roman empire was a popular operatic subject at this time, especially since Apostolo Zeno's *Mitridate* of 1728. But only Gasparini's and Mozart's versions are based on Racine. ◆ In fact, at least fifteen other settings of *Mitridate* are based on Racine, including versions by Scarlatti (1707, as *Il Mitridate Eupatore*); Bioni (1722); Capelli

Mozart had made a start on the *secco* recitatives in Bologna, and these were the first sections of the opera to be completed. Indeed, he worked at such a speed that, by his own account, his fingers ached. But the arias – in keeping with contemporary custom – were written only after detailed consultation with the singers, who had a considerable say in the matter. And Wolfgang tried to accommodate them as best he could. They made life difficult for him by arriving late and leaving him almost no time to write their arias. Leopold did what he could to help Wolfgang conserve his energies and in particular refused to allow him to compose after a meal, generally preferring to go walking with him instead. The mental effort involved in so important a commission made the boy moody and he repeatedly reminded his mother and sister to pray for a successful outcome, so that 'we may be happy together again'. At the same time, Leopold wrote to his friends in Salzburg, asking them, as a favour, to write cheerful and amusing letters in order to distract him. Needless to say, they had to contend with the usual vexations that every conductor, especially one who is foreign and young, has to put up with from what Leopold called this 'canaille of virtuosos'. But Leopold was not afraid of the difficulties involved and was resolved to face them with the necessary 'presence of mind and constant vigilance'. In this way, he wrote, they would win through 'like Hanswurst through a mountain of shit'.[93]

The first of the singers to arrive was not Caterina Gabrielli but Antonia Bernasconi, the daughter of a valet to the Duke of Württemberg. She had been taught singing by her stepfather Andrea Bernasconi, who worked as Kapellmeister in Munich from 1 August 1753.[94] With her, the Mozarts fought and won their first battle. The young composer's enemies had hoped to use her in their attempts to undermine his authority, with one of his opponents in particular trying to persuade her to reject the arias and duet that Mozart had written for her and to replace them with the corresponding numbers from Gasparini's opera, which the individual in question – his identity remains unknown – had thoughtfully provided for that purpose. But Bernasconi refused to be party to this shameful deal and, indeed, was said to be 'beside herself with pleasure' at the arias that Wolfgang had written with her voice specifically in mind. Even her old and experienced coach, Giovanni Battista Lampugnani, who worked through the part with her, had nothing but praise for her arias. Another storm on the theatrical horizon was caused by the tenor Guglielmo Ettore, who was a member of the Munich ensemble but who had recently appeared to great acclaim in Padua.[95] Fortunately, this storm, too, was averted, but the intrigues bound up with the production must have been tiresome in the extreme as Leopold later reminded his son of them when he needed to boost his spirits in Paris. The last of the singers to arrive was not Manzuoli but Santorini, who had recently sung in Turin and been introduced to the Mozarts in Bologna. He arrived in Milan on 1 December. The first performance was on the 26th.

The rehearsals got off to a good start, with even the copyist having done his job so well that only a single mistake was discovered at the rehearsal for the recitatives. The singers, moreover, were on their best behaviour. 'As far as I can judge without a father's partiality,' wrote Leopold on 8 December, 'I think Wolfgang has written the opera well and with great intelligence.'[96] The

(1723, as *Mitridate re di Ponto, vincitor de sè stesso*), Caldara (1728), Giai (1730), Porpora (1730), Aliprandi (1738), Terradellas (1746), Graun (1750), Sarti (1779), Sacchini (1781), Tarchi (1785), Nasolini (1796, as *La morte di Mitridate*), Zingarelli (1797, as *La morte di Mitridate*), and Tadolini (1827).

93. ◆ *Briefe*, i.401, 402 (letters of 3 and 10 November 1770).
94. See Rudhart, *Geschichte der Oper am Hofe zu München*, i.138–9.
95. Burney, *The Present State of Music in France and Italy*, 139–40. ◆ Further, see Wignall, 'Guglielmo Dettore – Mozart's 1st Mitridate'.
96. *Briefe*, i.407.

first rehearsal with the full – and much-reinforced – orchestra[97] took place in the Sala di Ridotto on 17 December, followed two days later by a second rehearsal in the theatre itself. By now, everyone had been won over by the new opera, as Leopold reported:

> Before the first rehearsal with the small orchestra, there were plenty of people who previously had cynically dismissed the music as worthless juvenilia and prophesied its failure because, so they claimed, it was impossible for such a young boy – and, what is more, a German[98] – to write an Italian opera or, great virtuoso though he might be, to grasp and apply the *chiaro ed oscuro* that is necessary in the theatre. Since the evening of that first brief rehearsal, these people have all gone very quiet and not uttered another syllable. The copyist is utterly delighted, which bodes well in Italy, where, if the music turns out to be a success, the copyist can sometimes make more money by marketing and selling the arias than the Kapellmeister can by composing them.[99] The singers are entirely satisfied and altogether delighted, especially the prima donna and primo uomo, who are utterly enchanted with their duet.[100]

The orchestra, too, was pleased with the demands placed on it, and its leading players – Fioroni, Sammartini, Lampugnani and Colombo – declared their support for the work. In short, it looked as though the company could count on victory even before the first night.

The production opened on 26 December under Mozart's own direction, its successful outcome even exceeding expectations. With the exception of those of a handful of the subsidiary characters, all the arias were followed by astonishingly enthusiastic applause, including cries of 'Evviva il Maestro! Evviva il Maestrino!' One of Bernasconi's arias was encored. At the second performance, the applause was even greater, and two of the arias and the duet were encored. But as it was a Thursday and the following day was a day of fasting and most people wanted to eat at home, it was necessary to keep the performance as short as possible. Even so, it lasted a good six hours, including the ballets that were included at the end of each act. On 5 January 1771 Leopold was able to write to his wife:

> Our son's opera is still running to universal applause and, as the Italians say, is *alle stelle*. Since the third performance the two of us have been listeners and spectators, sometimes in the stalls and sometimes in the boxes or *palchi*, where everyone is eager to speak to the Signore Maestro and see him at close quarters. . . . . The Maestro is obliged to conduct the opera from the orchestra only on the first three evenings, when Maestro Lampugnani accompanied at the second keyboard. Now that Wolfgang is no longer conducting, Lampugnani plays the first keyboard and Maestro Melchior Chiesa the second one.[101]

97. According to Leopold, it consisted of 14 first violins, 14 second violins, 2 harpsichords, 6 double basses, 2 cellos, 2 bassoons, 6 violas, 2 oboes and 2 flutes ('which, if there are no flutes, always play with 4 oboes'), 4 horns and 2 trumpets, making a total of sixty players in all: *Briefe*, i.408 (letter of 15 December 1770). Two weeks earlier, Leopold reported an incident that struck him as barely credible, above all in Italy: 'As we were leaving the house yesterday, we heard . . . two beggars, a man and a woman, singing together in the street and they sang the whole song together in fifths, without missing a note. I have never heard this in Germany. At a distance I thought that they were two persons, each of whom was singing a different song. But when we came up we found that they were singing together a beautiful duet in perfect fifths' (*Briefe*, i.406–7, letter of 1 December 1770).
98. Once, while Dittersdorf was playing the violin in Bologna, a member of the audience called out: 'Come è mai possibile, che una tartaruga tedesca possa arrivare a tale perfezione!': Dittersdorf, *Lebensbeschreibung*, 92.
99. When the Mozarts left Milan, the full score had to remain behind as the copyist had received orders for five complete copies, to say nothing of individual arias.
100. *Briefe*, i.408 (letter of 15 December 1770).
101. *Briefe*, i.414 (letter of 5 January 1771).

The opera was given some twenty times in all, always to full houses and with the same degree of applause. In its edition of 2 January 1771, the local newspaper assured its readers that the young composer 'studia il bello della natura e ce lo rappresenta adorno delle più rare grazie musicali'.[102] Members of the audience dubbed Mozart the 'Cavaliere filarmonico', a title more or less confirmed by the Accademia Filarmonica of Verona when it elected him the society's *maestro di cappella* on 5 January 1771.

Once the performances were over, there was no lack of opportunities to relax. The Mozarts were on friendly terms with the governor's secretary, Leopold Troger, and his daughter, Marianne D'Aste, was more than happy to feed them on liver dumplings and sauerkraut, which Wolfgang had specifically asked for. They were also frequent guests of Count Firmian, and on 4 January there was a concert at which Wolfgang was required to sight-read a new and attractive but difficult concerto. They also visited Turin, where they saw what Leopold describes as 'a magnificent opera'[103], returning to Milan on 31 January 'to see the second opera' and, after a brief stay in the city, travelling on to Venice, where they arrived on 11 February and found a most friendly welcome in the house of a local businessman by the name of Wider, a business friend of Lorenz Hagenauer, whose son Johannes had also stayed with the family. Even though Johannes had always spoken highly of them, Leopold assured his wife that he himself could never speak highly enough of them: never before had he met such honest, helpful and polite people. While in Venice, they enjoyed the delights of the local carnival. They were soon introduced to the homes of all the local nobility, with the result that magnificent gondolas were permanently at their disposal, and many was the time that they would bob up and down on the city's lagoons. One soirée gave way to another, and they were to spend every evening at the opera or some other place of entertainment. A concert that they gave proved brilliantly successful.[104]

They set off home on 12 March, spending a day in Padua, where they visited two of the city's leading musical lights: the Franciscan priest Francesco Antonio Vallotti (1697–1780), who was regarded at this time as Italy's leading organist and as Martini's equal as a theorist and contrapuntalist, and the composer Giovanni Ferrandini (*c*1710–91), who was director of chamber music in Munich (Tartini had died the previous year). Wolfgang also performed on the magnificent organ at the Church of Santa Giustina. Here, too, he was invited to write an oratorio – a setting of Metastasio's *Betulia liberata* that he could compose at his leisure on his return home. In Vicenza they were detained for a few days by the bishop, a member of the house of Cornaro, whom they had got to know in Venice. And they also spent a few days in Verona, where they stayed with their old friend Pietro Lugiati, who gave a magnificent party in Wolfgang's honour. But the most important item in Mozart's luggage when he arrived back in Salzburg on 28 March 1771 was a commission for a new opera for the 1773 carnival in Milan, the fee for which had even been raised to 130 *gigliati*.

We know very little about Mozart's activities during the six months between his first and second visits to Italy, but there seems little doubt that the period passed off peacefully and that he continued with his studies. Only four works from this period can be dated with any certainty: the oratorio *Il sogno di Scipione* K126, the *Litaniae Lauretanae BVM* in B flat major K109 of May 1771,

102. ◆ For the full report, see *Dokumente*, 117, *Documentary Biography*, 130–1.

103. ◆ The operas playing in Turin at this time included Paisiello's *Annibale in Torino*, Gaetano Pugnani's *Issea*, and Ignazio Platania's *Berenice*.

104. ◆ Mozart's concert in Venice took place on 5 March. For a review, published in the *Staats- und gelehrten Zeitung des hamburgischen unpartheyischen Correspondenten* on 27 March 1771, see Eisen, *Dokumente: Addenda*, 18, *New Mozart Documents*, 20.

the *Regina coeli* K108 also of May 1771, and the G major symphony K110, which dates from July. But we shall also have to date a whole series of other works to this period on stylistic grounds.

At the same time, various mysterious passages in the fifteen-year-old Mozart's letters to his sister from the coming months suggest that he was now becoming more sexually aware, and although we do not know the identity of the beauty who set his heart ablaze in the summer of 1771, it seems likely that it was one of Marianne's friends who was just on the point of marrying. None the less, it is clear from his letters – which, no doubt in deference to Leopold's strict upbringing, are extremely reserved in tone – that this turn of events did not plunge him into an abyss of Wertherian despair. Evidently it was no more than a schoolboy infatuation, though no less important for all that in that it marked the advent of manhood and, with it, a maturity that was soon to find expression in his music.

8

Second and third Italian journeys

On 18 March 1771 Leopold wrote to his wife from Verona:

> Yesterday I received a letter from Milan announcing one from Vienna that I shall receive in Salzburg and that will not only amaze you but bring our son undying fame.[1]

The letter in question was a commission inviting Mozart to write a serenata for the wedding of Archduke Ferdinand and Princess Maria Beatrice Ricciarda d'Este of Modena, the daughter of Prince Ercole Rainaldo. The celebrations were due to begin in Milan on 15 October 1771, and Mozart now found himself in the most illustrious artistic company: the principal work on the programme, *Ruggiero*, was entrusted to Metastasio and Hasse, while the words of the serenata were the work of one of Milan's most distinguished poets, Giuseppe Parini (1729–99), who currently held a chair in rhetoric at the city's university and who was particularly admired as a satirist.[2] The result – *Ascanio in Alba* K111 – was an allegorical pastoral of a kind that was then in fashion. The dances were by Jean Favier. As was usual at this time, Parini was first required to submit his poem to the Viennese court for their approval, so that it was not until the end of August that Mozart was able to see it for himself and not until the beginning of September that he could make a start on it, as a number of additional changes had proved to be necessary. But from that moment onwards he made extremely rapid progress on it. The choruses and recitatives were finished by 13 September, so that it was hardly surprising that his fingers ached from so much writing.[3]

He and his father had left Salzburg on 13 August and, after a brief rest in Verona, where they were again guests of Pietro Lugiati, they arrived in Milan on 21 August.[4]

According to his letter of 5 October 1771, it was on this occasion that Mozart made the acquaintance of the soprano Caterina Gabrielli, who had only just arrived in Milan and who was as famous for her whims and amorous escapades as for her vocal abilities.[5] The Mozarts also renewed

---

1. *Briefe*, i.426.
2. See Wiese and Percopo, *Geschichte der italienischen Litteratur*, 513ff. (with a portrait).
3. *Briefe*, i.439 (letter of 21 September 1771). On 24 August Mozart described their accommodation in Milan in a letter to his sister: 'Upstairs we have a violinist, downstairs another one, beside us a singing teacher who gives lessons and in the end room opposite ours an oboist. It's great fun composing! gives you lots of ideas': *Briefe*, i.432.
4. On all three journeys they took the same route to Milan, except that on their third visit they first broke their journey at St Johann, with another break in Brescia before they arrived in Milan.
5. The impression that she made on Mozart is clear from a letter that he wrote to his father from Mannheim on 19 February 1778: 'Those who have heard Gabrielli will say that she was good only at passage-work and roulades, but because she sang in such a unique way she won their admiration, except that by the time they had heard her four times they no longer admired her. She could not find favour in the longer term; people soon get tired of passage-work, and she had the misfortune of not being able to sing. She was incapable of sustaining a semibreve properly, she had no *messa di voce*, she did not know how to hold on to a note, in a word she sang with artistry but not with understanding': *Briefe*, ii.287.

acquaintance with Marianne Davies and her 'glass organ', as well as with Josef Mysliveček, who was in Milan to write an opera for the forthcoming carnival.

This time, thanks to his secure position and to the fact that he was in favour with the Viennese court, Mozart's dealings with his performers passed off smoothly. The tenor Giuseppe Tibaldi visited the Mozarts almost every day, arriving at eleven and remaining for lunch until one, while Wolfgang continued to compose.[6] Another frequent caller was Manzuoli, who on this occasion was contractually engaged to appear in the new work.

Mozart's dealings with Hasse[7] could likewise not have been more cordial. It was a curious quirk of fate that brought the two composers together at this juncture: whereas Hasse had done so much to reform Italian opera, Mozart was later to overcome the Italians' hegemony in Germany. Hasse was not only a great artist but also a great man, who had actively campaigned on Mozart's behalf in Vienna. It was on this occasion that he is said to have exclaimed: 'This boy will put us all in the shade.'[8]

The festivities[9] began on 15 October with the arrival of a large number of foreign visitors anxious to see the archduke's triumphant entry, followed by the wedding service in the cathedral and, later, by a concert and reception at court. On the 16th a public banquet was held for more than four hundred newly married couples, all of whom had received dowries from the empress, and in the evening Hasse's *Ruggiero* was performed in the Regio Ducal, which had been specially decorated for the occasion. Two magnificent ballets, Picq's *La corona della gloria* and Favier's *Pico e Canente*, were performed between the acts. And on the 17th, following a brilliant procession of carriages up and down the Corso, Wolfgang's serenata was performed. Even after the first rehearsals Leopold was already able to write to his wife and predict with some pleasure that the work would be a success.[10] In this he was not mistaken, and the applause was so great that

---

6. ◆ Concerning Tibaldi, see Petrobelli, 'Un cantante fischiato e le appoggiature di mezza battuta: cronaca teatrale e prassi esecutiva alla metà del '700'.

7. Hasse had written to Ortes on 23 March 1771: 'Young Mozard is certainly marvellous for his age, and I do love him infinitely. The father, as far as I can see, is equally discontented everywhere, since here too he uttered the same lamentations. He idolizes his son a little too much, and thus does all he can to spoil him; but I have such a high opinion of the boy's natural good sense that I hope he will not be spoilt in spite of the father's adulation, but will grow into an honest fellow': Kretzschmar, 'Hasse über Mozart' [*Dokumente*, 120–1, *Documentary Biography*, 134].

8. Carpani, *Le Haydine*, 83; and Kandler, *Cenni storico-critici intorno alla vita ed alle opere del celebre compositore di musica Giovanni Adolfo Hasse detto il Sassone*, 27. Mennicke (*Hasse und die Brüder Graun als Symphoniker*, 433–4) casts doubt on the authenticity of this remark by pointing out that Leopold is silent on the subject.

9. Parini's description of the festivities was published in Milan in 1825 under the title *Descrizione delle feste celebrate in Milano per le nozze delle L. L. A. A. R. R. l'arcid. Ferdinando e l'arcid. Maria Beatrice.* ◆ A captivating contemporaneous description of the festivities was published in the *Augspurgische Ordinari Post-Zeitung* for 28 September 1771: 'Everything is lively here on account of the grand and expensive preparations for the forthcoming wedding of his Royal Highness Archduke Ferdinand to the Princess of Modena. An opera by the famous Metastasio, *Il Ruggero*, or Heroic Gratitude, will be presented. The most famous singers in Italy are being called here to perform this opera, the music of which is composed by the famous Hasse, a Saxon, and Kapellmeister to the Elector of Saxony. All of the sets will be designed and arranged with the greatest magnificence. The ballets, choreographed by Messrs Pich and Favre, and Mesdames Binetti and Blasge, will be exceptionally fine and the performance will include 40 dancers. Similarly, other theatrical spectacles will be very elegant and various in their presentation. The Facchini company will be seen in a magnificent masquerade, with decorative emblems appropriate to the occasion. Each day three hundred persons will dine at court, where there will be masked balls, and at the theatres masked balls will also take place. Moreover, the theatres will be magnificently lighted, as will the whole city, three nights in a row, and for three evenings tickets to the theatrical performances will be distributed gratis. There will be races with horses and also races with light carriages. A part of the race course will be converted into a gallery, covered with the interlaced boughs of verdant trees, and beautifully lighted, and underneath 150 poor maidens, to be married the same day to 150 similar young men, and given dowries by the royal bridal couple, will dine and celebrate their weddings. Two fountains will flow with wine instead of water, various orchestras with musicians will perform and, finally, a serenade, entitled *Ascanio in Alba*, composed by Abbate Parini and set to music by Herr Mozzart, will be performed. Numerous other entertainments, impossible to describe, will also be given, and it is expected that an astonishing number of visitors will arrive here to see them' (Eisen, *Dokumente: Addenda*, 19, *New Mozart Documents*, 20–1).

10. *Briefe*, i.440 (letter of 28 September 1771).

the work had to be repeated the next day. By the end of the festivities it had been performed more often than *Ruggiero*. 'I'm sorry to say so,' wrote Leopold, 'but I simply can't tell you how much Wolfgang's serenata has overshadowed Hasse's opera.'[11] He also mentions that Franz Xaver Kerschbaumer, the young son of a Salzburg businessman, had attended the performance on the 24th and seen the archduke and archduchess demand encores of two of the arias and how they had shown Wolfgang every mark of their approval. And on this occasion the composer was suitably rewarded, receiving not only his fee but also a gold watch from the empress. Inlaid with diamonds, it had a excellent likeness of Maria Theresia herself painted in enamel on the back.[12]

Among the high points of the festivities, which lasted until the end of the month, were a spectacular procession of masked *facchini* wearing local costume on the 19th, a race for Barbary horses on the 22nd, another race for horse-drawn carriages – *calessetti* – on the 28th and, on the 24th, a *cuccagna* at which vast amounts of food were handed out to the local populace[13] and the fountains flowed with wine. On this last-named occasion, the Mozarts were lucky to escape serious injury when a large piece of scaffolding erected for the spectactors collapsed and more than fifty people were killed or injured. It was purely by chance that they had arrived late and not occupied the seats reserved for them but, instead, had started to look for alternative seating on the court balcony.

With the opera out of the way, Mozart wrote two more works in November, a symphony K112 and a divertimento K113. Both works may have been intended for a concert or, alternatively, they may have been written in response to some commission or other.

While he was staying in Milan, Mozart also signed a contract with the Teatro San Benedetto in Venice to write a second opera for the 1773 carnival.[14] It is difficult to see how this commitment could have been reconciled with the one he had entered into for Milan, but perhaps the impresario in Venice agreed to make concessions. In the event, the Venice commission fell through, and the opera was entrusted to Johann Gottlieb Naumann, whose setting of Giovanni Ambrogio Migliavacca's *Solimano* proved a great success.[15]

Not until mid-December[16] did the Mozarts return to Salzburg, where Mozart completed a new symphony K114 on the 30th and shortly afterwards fell seriously ill.[17] In the meantime, the Mozarts' circumstances had changed considerably in Salzburg. On 16 December 1771 Archbishop Siegmund Schrattenbach had died after a long illness, and on 14 March 1772, after protracted

---

11. *Briefe*, i.444 (letter of 19 October 1771). ◆ Leopold's appraisal is confirmed by contemporaneous newspaper accounts; see, for example, the *Notizie del Mondo*, published in Florence on 26 October 1771: 'The opera has not met with success, and was not performed except for a single ballet. The serenata, however, has met with great applause, both for the text and for the music' (Eisen, *Dokumente: Addenda*, 19, *New Mozart Documents*, 21).

12. The watch was later acquired by a Viennese businessman, Joseph Strebl, who used to go bowling with Mozart in Mödling: see *Süddeutsche Musikzeitung*, i (1856), 4. More recently, it was acquired by an art dealer in Pest by the name of Joseph Wagner: see Wurzbach, *Mozart-Buch*, 178. Unfortunately, this picture of imperial favour also has its negative side: it had occurred to Archduke Ferdinand to take the young composer into his service and so he wrote to his mother Maria Theresia on the subject. Her reply is dated 12 December 1771: 'You ask me to take the young Salzburger into your service. I do not know why, not believing you have need of a composer or of useless people. If, however, it would give you pleasure, I have no wish to hinder you. What I say is intended only to prevent your burdening yourself with useless people and giving titles to people of that sort. If they are in your service it degrades that service when these people go about the world like beggars. Besides, he has a large family': Arneth, *Briefe der Kaiserin Maria Theresia an ihre Kinder und Freunde*, i.92 [*Dokumente*, 124, *Documentary Biography*, 138].

13. *Der teutsche Merkur*, iii (1775), 240; *Briefe*, i.445–6 (letter of 26 October 1771).

14. ◆ *Dokumente*, 121, *Documentary Biography*, 135.

15. See Meißner, *Bruchstücke zur Biographie J. G. Naumann's*, i.279.

16. According to Marianne, it was on the 13th, whereas Leopold, in his letter to Breitkopf of 7 February 1772, states that it was the 15th [*Briefe*, i.456].

17. According to a remark made by Marianne in a letter to Joseph Sonnleithner, a watercolour shows Mozart after he had recovered from this illness. ◆ It is not clear to which picture Abert refers here.

deliberations, a successor was appointed in the person of Hieronymus Joseph Franz de Paula, Count Colloredo, who had previously been bishop of Gurk. It was not a popular choice in Salzburg, where the local population had enjoyed considerable freedoms under the lax regime of Colloredo's predecessor and now feared, with some justification, that they would be kept under a much tighter rein.[18] Mozart was invited to write an opera to celebrate his entry into the town and the traditional display of homage on 29 April 1772.[19] Another serenata or *azione teatrale*, *Il sogno di Scipione* K126 is a setting of words by Metastasio that had already been set by Luca Antonio Predieri for the birthday of the Emperor Charles VI on 1 October 1735. On that occasion, the work had referred to the unfortunate events in war-torn Italy, but now it was effortlessly reinterpreted to refer to the archiepiscopal celebrations – an example of the nonsense that audiences were prepared to put up with in occasional operas of this kind. Even the *licenza* was taken over whole-sale, the only concession to the changed circumstances being the substitution of the name 'Girolamo' for the earlier 'Carlo'.[20] It is believed that the work was performed in early May 1772.[21]

The other dated compositions from this period are the symphony K124 of 21 February and the *Litaniae de venerabili altaris sacramento* in B flat major K125 of March 1772. The month of May saw the composition not only of a *Regina coeli* K127 but also of three symphonies K128, 129 and 130. In June Mozart wrote a divertimento K131 and in July and August three more symphonies K132, 133 and 134. Three other works – all of them divertimentos for string quartet K136–138 – are dated 1772. It seems likely that all these works, together with various others which, although undated, can be ascribed to this period on stylistic grounds, were written for specific occasions in Salzburg. Mozart did not always meet with a favourable response: Burney, for example, was told by an acquaintance that the young Mozart was still regarded as 'a great master of his instrument', but that, to judge by his orchestral works, he was 'one further instance of early fruit being more extraordinary than excellent'.[22]

At least on one level, Colloredo's appointment brought the young composer a superficial advantage when he was confirmed in his position as Konzertmeister on 9 August, now on an annual salary of 150 florins.[23]

On 24 October father and son set out once again for Milan in order to give themselves plenty of time to prepare for the new opera. They spent a night in 'dreary' Bozen, where Mozart wrote a quartet 'to while away the time',[24] and on 31 October they celebrated Mozart's name-day with a party at the home of the Pizzini brothers at Ala. Then, following their usual visit to Verona to see Lugiati, they arrived in Milan on 4 November. Here Leopold was again affected by the dizziness and headaches from which he had already suffered in Salzburg as the result of an earlier accident,

18. See Koch-Sternfeld, *Die letzten dreißig Jahre*, 36ff.
19. Leopold had already written to Breitkopf to order oboes and bassoons from Karl Augustin Grenser in Dresden for the forthcoming election [*Briefe* i.455; letter of 7 February 1772].
20. Mozart initially took over the name Carlo and only later replaced it with Girolamo.
21. Mozart later rewrote the *licenza* aria, but it is impossible to conclude from this that the work as a whole was given a second performance. ◆ Contrary to Abert's assertion, *Il sogno di Scipione* was originally conceived by Mozart to celebrate the 50th anniversary, on 10 January 1772, of Schrattenbach's ordination. It was only after the archbishop's death on 16 December 1771 that the work was pressed into service to celebrate Colloredo's ordination: the name 'Carlo', representing Schrattenbach, was crossed out in the score and replaced by Girolamo, representing Colloredo. Concerning the performance on 29 April 1772, see Eisen, *Dokumente: Addenda*, 21, *New Mozart Documents*, 22.
22. Burney, *The Present State of Music in Germany*, ii.323. ◆ Burney's assessment is not his own but that of Louis De Visme, who had written to him from Munich on 30 November 1772; see Eisen, *Dokumente: Addenda*, 24, *New Mozart Documents*, 23.
23. Pirckmayer, *Über Musik und Theater am f. e. Salzburger Hofe 1762–1775* [*Dokumente*, 127, *Documentary Biography*, 142].
24. ◆ *Briefe*, i.457 (letter of 28 October 1772). ◆ Almost certainly the quartet was one of K155–160, the set composed by Mozart in Italy.

in addition to which he was tormented by all manner of 'thoughts of Salzburg' evidently caused by his change of employer: he was no doubt fearful for his son's future in the event of his failure to find a suitable position for him.

The opera that Mozart had to write was *Lucio Silla*, to a libretto by the Milanese poet Giovanni de Gamerra.[25] On this occasion, Wolfgang brought some of the completed recitatives with him, but he may as well not have bothered, as the librettist had in the meantime shown his text to Metastasio and the latter had changed a great deal and interpolated a new scene. Even so, Mozart had still left himself with enough time to rewrite the existing recitatives and to set the remaining ones, in addition to composing the choruses and overture. Only two of the singers had arrived so far: Felicità Suardi, who had sung in Parma in 1769 and who was now cast in the role of the *secondo uomo*, and the *ultimo tenore*. Milan was deserted, as most of the population was still in the country, and only the d'Aste family was there to welcome them as old friends. Mysliveček was also in residence. The next singer to arrive was Venanzio Rauzzini (1746–1810), an outstanding soprano castrato, as well as an accomplished keyboard player and by no means insignificant as a composer. Since 1766 he had been in Munich, where Burney met him after he had already agreed to perform in Mozart's opera.[26] His first aria was soon finished: Leopold thought that it was in a class of its own and that Rauzzini sang it like an angel.[27] After a difficult journey, the prima donna, Anna Lucia De Amicis, arrived from Venice on 4 December, but there was still time, as the first performance was not until the 26th. Between now and then, Mozart had to write another fourteen numbers, including a trio and a duet 'that might as well count as four', he told his sister in a letter of 5 December. 'It's impossible for me to write much,' he went on, 'as I don't know anything and, secondly, I don't know what I'm writing, as I can think of nothing but my opera and run the risk of sending you not words but an entire aria.'[28] Anna Lucia De Amicis (*c*1733–1816) studied with Vittoria Tesi and began her career singing comic operas before turning to *opere serie* under the influence of Johann Christian Bach in London in 1762. For the last four years she had been married to a physician from Venice by the name of Buonsolazzi and was accompanied to Milan by her young daugher Sepperl. Although the Mozarts knew her from the time of their visit to Paris, she was initially inclined to make life difficult for them, but familiarity soon bred understanding and they became the best of friends. She was extremely happy with all three of her arias, to the principal one of which Mozart had added some new and extraordinarily difficult passage-work.[29]

25. Gamerra was born at Livorno in 1743 and, after taking holy orders and becoming an abbot, subsequently became 'Tenente nelle Armi di Sua Maestà Imp.', in other words, a soldier, while at the same time turning out a large number of sentimental comedies. In 1786 he even conceived the idea of founding a tragi-comic national theatre in Naples. He died in 1803. See Croce, *I teatri di Napoli*, 628ff. ◆ Concerning de Gamerra, see de Gamerra, 'Osservazioni sullo spettacolo in generale, . . . per servire allo stabilimento del novo Teatro nazionale'; Masi, 'Gio. De Gamerra o il segreto d'un cuor sensibile' and 'Giovanni de Gamerra e i drammi lagrimosi'; and Candiani, *Libretti e librettisti italiani per Mozart*.

26. Burney, *The Present State of Music in Germany*, i.126 and 148–9.

27. Rauzzini also appeared in Naumann's *Armida* in Padua and on that occasion the composer was heard to say of him that 'he has all the best qualities, sings like an angel and is an admirable actor'. He settled in England in 1774, first as a singer and, until his death in 1810, as a singing teacher, in which capacity he was held in the highest regard; see Kelly, *Reminiscences*, i.10; Parke, *Musical Memoirs*, ii.51; and Rudhart, *Geschichte der Oper am Hofe zu München*, i.149–50. ◆ Concerning Rauzzini, see Sands, 'Venanzio Rauzzini: Singer, Composer, Traveller'; Hodges, 'Venanzio Rauzzini: "The First Master for Teaching in the Universe"'; and Michot, 'Le créateur de Cecilio: Venanzio Rauzzini'. For Suardi, see Bouquet, *Storia del Teatro Regio di Torino I: Il Teatro di Corte dalle origini al 1788*, and Angermüller, 'Die Sänger der Erstaufführung von Mozarts Dramma per musica "Lucio Silla" KV 135, Mailand, 26. Dezember 1772. Morgnoni – de Amicis – Rauzzini, Suardi – Mienci – Onofrio'.

28. ◆ *Briefe*, i.465 (letter of 5 December 1772). ◆ For an account of Mozart's composition of *Lucio Silla* and Leopold's correspondence concerning the opera, see NMA II/5/7/1, XVII–XVIII.

29. The Abbate Cardanelli, a contemporary of Mozart, reports that De Amicis asked Mozart to submit arias to her in draft form so that she could examine and pass comment on them. But he brought her a finished aria, which she declared to her liking, at which point Mozart allegedly produced two more complete settings of the same text; see Schizzi, *Elogio storico di W. A. Mozart*, 26ff.; and *AmZ*, xx (1818), 93. The story is scarcely credible.

Even after the rehearsals, Leopold continued to think that she sang and acted like an angel and that the whole of Salzburg would be amazed to hear her.

They were still waiting for the tenor Cordoni to arrive when the news reached them that he was too ill to appear. The theatre secretary was immediately despatched to Turin and, at the same time, a courier was sent post-haste to Bologna in search of a decent replacement who was not only a good singer but also, and in particular, 'a good actor with a handsome presence in order to play Lucio Silla creditably'.[30] But no such individual could be found and so they finally had to make do with a church singer by the name of Bassano Morgnoni who had appeared only a handful of times on stage in his native Lodi but had yet to sing in a major theatre. He arrived on 17 December, by which date the rehearsals were already in full swing, and on the 18th Mozart wrote two of his four arias. On 21, 22 and 23 December a series of large parties were held for the higher aristocracy at Count Firmian's house, with musicians on hand to perform vocal and instrumental music from five in the afternoon until eleven at night. Mozart performed on all three occasions, and on the 23rd he even had to play as soon as the guests arrived. The latter then graciously condescended to exchange a few words with him. The dress rehearsal passed off without incident and the first night, too, was a success, in spite of a number of mishaps.

Performances at the opera regularly began an hour after the Ave Maria,[31] but by half past five the theatre was already completely full. The archduke rose from table only shortly before the Ave Maria and still had to write five letters sending his New Year greetings to Their Majesties in Vienna; and, as Leopold added, he wrote very slowly. As a result, not only the singers, who were already suffering from first-night nerves, but the audience, too, were kept waiting, hot and impatient, until after eight o'clock. During the prima donna's first aria, the tenor from Lodi had to express his anger by gesticulating wildly, but in his efforts to surpass himself he unfortunately gave the impression that he was 'about to box her ears and strike her on the nose with his fist'.[32] This provoked laughter in the audience, confusing De Amicis, who did not immediately realize who they were laughing at, with the result that she did not sing well all evening. The situation was made worse when the archduchess applauded Rauzzini at his first entrance: he had sent word to her that he would be unable to sing from sheer terror, thereby assuring himself in advance of the court's indulgent applause. By way of consolation, De Amicis was invited to an audience at court the next day, and from then on the opera passed off smoothly. In spite of all this, the work itself found favour from the outset, and the applause increased from one performance to the next. Normally the first opera in the season was poorly attended unless it was particularly well received, but *Lucio Silla* was given more than twenty times to such packed houses 'that it was hardly possible to slip in'. At each performance several of the arias had to be repeated, although it was generally De Amicis who had it all her own way.[33] Or so Leopold reported.[34]

For Rauzzini, Mozart wrote a motet, *Exsultate, jubilate* K165, which received its first performance at the Theatine Church on 17 January 1773.[35] It is, in fact, a dramatic solo cantata: only the words are sacred, whereas the music, inevitably geared to the voice of the singer who commissioned it, is purely operatic and, as such, a further example of the spirit that informed church

30. ◆ *Briefe*, i.465 (letter of 5 December 1772).
31. ◆ This was about a half hour after sunset.
32. ◆ *Briefe*, i.472 (letter of 2 January 1773).
33. Contemporaries seem to have been very eager to know whether or not the opera was a success. Naumann, for example, noted in his diary on 2 January 1773: 'I went to Colloredo's and heard news of the opera in Milan' [*Dokumente*, 129, *Documentary Biography*, 144].
34. ◆ *Briefe*, i.471–2 (letter of 2 January 1773).
35. See Mozart's letter of 16 January 1773: *Briefe*, i.475–6.

music at this time. Particularly noteworthy is the independent role played by the oboes and, more especially in the section in A major, by the violas.[36] Later – on 6 February – Leopold reported that Mozart was working on a quartet.[37]

Leopold repeatedly postponed the date of their departure, initially on the pretext of wanting to see the second opera, then pleading a violent attack of rheumatism that he claimed had confined him to bed. But the real reason for his delay lay in the fact that, actively supported by Count Firmian, he was hoping to obtain a post for Mozart at the Florentine court of the Archduke Leopold, to whom he also sent a copy of the new opera. The archduke seemed initially disposed to look favourably on the idea, and Leopold evidently hoped to continue the negotiations from Milan. And even when these negotiations eventually came to nothing, he still expected the archduke to put in a good word for him and, in consequence, turned his thoughts to another grand tour. 'But do save some money,' he admonished his wife, 'for we must have money if we want to travel; I regret every farthing that we spend in Salzburg.'[38]

Towards the end of their stay in Milan, the Mozarts received a visitor from Salzburg in the person of one of their orchestral colleagues, the horn player Joseph Leutgeb. Although he was there on business, he also seems to have enjoyed himself in the city.

They finally left Milan in early March, as they had to be home by the first anniversary of the archbishop's election on the 14th. They duly arrived back in Salzburg on the 13th.

With this, Mozart's involvement with Italian theatres came to a definitive end. He received no further *scritture* and not even his successful Italian operas found their way north of the Alps. Admittedly, his new employer in Salzburg was not in favour of his artists going off on tour and rarely allowed them leave of absence. At the same time, however, *Lucio Silla* appears not to have been the overwhelming success that Leopold – laying it on particularly thick – claims it to have been in his letters home. A glance at the score explains the reason for this. Mozart's art was now in a state of transition and undergoing a transformation that was to take him well beyond the confines of traditional *opera seria*. We must now examine this change in greater detail.

According to the latest research, Mozart returned from his final visit to Italy as an out-and-out 'Romantic', profoundly affected by the very same spirit that was responsible for the *Sturm und Drang* movement in contemporary German literature.[39] Certainly, all his works from the end of this period are characterized by an underlying tone that is remarkably subjective and often deeply impassioned and sombre: there is something more confessional about them than what we find in any of their predecessors. But we must remember that the spirit of the *Sturm und Drang* movement, with all its contrastive moods, had always been second nature to Mozart and that the darker aspects of our inner lives were by no means unexplored in his earlier compositions, as is clear, more especially, from those that he wrote under Schobert's influence. Until now, however, his cheerful childlike nature had served as an effective counterbalance. If these darker aspects now emerge more prominently, the reasons must be sought neither in any literary influences (from which Mozart was in any case cut off in upper Italy at this time) nor in some searing personal experience (about which we know nothing) but simply in the sheer force of the impressions of the

---

36. ◆ In 1779 or 1780 Mozart revised the motet for performance in Salzburg by the castrato Francesco Ceccarelli; see Münster, 'Die beiden Fassungen der Motette *Exsultate, jubilate* KV 165'.
37. ◆ One of K155–160.
38. ◆ *Briefe*, i.475 (letter of 16 January 1773).
39. The term 'Romantic' is, of course, open to misunderstanding, but is taken from Wyzewa and Saint-Foix, *Wolfgang Amédée Mozart*, i.468–522. ◆ See also Landon, 'Crisis Years: *Sturm und Drang* and the Austrian Musical Crisis'.

last three years, impressions that assailed the mind of a young composer who, now on the brink of manhood, prepared to bid farewell to Italy. Until then, he had scarcely had time to draw breath at such a wealth of changing impressions but now, as he set off back home, they lay siege to his adolescent heart, forcing from him music of such passion that even he himself must sometimes have marvelled at it.

Nor is there any doubt that his visits to Italy were also of importance to him on a purely personal level, although it would be wrong to conjure up the shade of Goethe here: not only did Goethe come to Italy sixteen years later as a mature individual with completely different intellectual goals, but his whole way of observing people and things was exceptional, even at this date. To adopt an effusively modern and neo-Romantic approach and accuse Leopold of being an unimaginative philistine is a sign of the most crass dilettanism, and we can only be grateful to the Italians that this approach has lost much of its appeal following the events of 1915. Between Mozart's visits to Italy and Goethe's there lies a fundamental shift in our whole attitude to foreign lands and nations, and this shift is largely associated with the name of Jean-Jacques Rousseau.

Goethe's description of his Italian journey begins, like virtually every subsequent account, with a series of more or less colourful images of the Alps. Of this we find not a single word in the accounts of either Mozart or his father. At best, Leopold thought that 'the country near Innsbruck seemed to me a bit like the road to Hallein near Kaltenhausen', but otherwise he had 'nothing to report'.[40] Far more frequent are the references to the difficulties of crossing the Alps, to the snow and dirt and so on. Bozen struck Leopold as 'dreary', while Mozart even described it as a 'pigsty'.[41] There is not a single trace of the Romanticism usually associated with mountain scenery, and the Mozarts are still clearly in thrall to the essentially classical view of nature typical of the generation before Rousseau, in whom the wild beauty of the mountains inspired only terror and unease. This is also the view of their trusty literary companion, Johann Georg Keyssler, in his own account of his travels.[42] Only after the Mozarts had descended into the Valley of the Po do we find more frequent accounts of their impressions of nature. Leopold had earlier written that his favourite scenery was the Swabian countryside, with its delightful mixture of woods and fields and parks, and in Italy, too, it is clear from his praise of Naples that what attracted him most was the jocund charm of its park-like landscapes. As a true disciple of the Enlightenment he never forgot the element of fruitful fecundity.[43] Vesuvius, by contrast, left little impression on him, and when they visited the Phlegrean Fields near Naples, it was the legends and history bound up with them that interested Leopold more than their natural beauty.[44]

And it is this older view of nature that finds expression in Mozart's music. In comparison with Gluck, Haydn and Beethoven, his music contains far fewer images of nature, and where they do occur (and here one must discount the traditional storm scenes and the like), nature is seen not as

40. *Briefe*, i.293 (letter of 15 December 1769).
41. *Briefe*, i.457 (letter of 28 October 1772) and i.458 (letter of 28 October 1772).
42. Keyssler, *Neueste Reisen durch Teutschland, Böhmen, Ungarn, die Schweitz, Italien und Lothringen*. The journeys themselves were undertaken between 1729 and 1731.
43. *Briefe*, i.359–61 (letters of 9 and 16 June 1770). ◆ Although Leopold may not have written much about the impressions he gained in Italy, he was not unresponsive to what he saw there; an extensive collection of engravings purchased by him on the 'Grand Tour' and in Italy survives in the Salzburger Museum Carolino Augusteum; see Angermüller and Ramsauer, '"du wirst, wenn uns Gott gesund zurückkommen läst, schöne Sachen sehen". Veduten aus dem Nachlaß Leopold Mozarts in der Graphiksammlung des Salzburger Museums Carolino Augusteum'.

something sublime and awe-inspiring but as something idyllic and delightful and, as such, still clearly indebted to the spirit of the Italian Renaissance.

It was through engravings and books that Leopold sought to recapture specific impressions of nature both for his own and his family's benefit, and the same is true of his artistic impressions. Here, too, he took his cue from Keyssler and made a point of studying the monuments of classical antiquity. Yet, as before, there is no trace of any emotionalism or Romanticism: the predominant approach is historical and antiquarian, so much so that one is sometimes reminded of the delight in curiosities felt by the mirabiliaries of old. Of all the arts, it was architecture that most interested Leopold, while Italian painters seem – significantly – to have made far less impression on him than the old Dutch masters had done.

Essentially, Leopold was no different from other travellers at this time, for whom nature and art were of only peripheral interest, something that they were happy to admire along the way but which they never regarded as objects worth studying in their own right. What Enlightenment travellers looked for in their travels was, above all, an increase in understanding, a greater knowledge of the world at large and a more moral outlook on life: by getting to know the people, society and political systems of foreign countries, they hoped to hone their powers of judgement and improve their minds. And it was certainly these considerations that were uppermost in Leopold's thoughts. Conditions in Naples, Easter Week in Rome and the carnival in Milan were far more important to him and his son than any artistic impressions. But it is unfair to impute these universally held views to any alleged personal limitations on Leopold's part[45] or to assume, simply because his impressions differed from our own, that he was somehow unresponsive. The picture of the dimwitted philistine visiting the Eternal City with his half dreamy, half simple-minded son is one that we may happily leave to modern Goethe Societies: it is every bit as distorted as many of the more idealizing images of Mozart that date from the 'Age of Romanticism'.

In all this, Mozart was, of course, influenced by his father. No doubt, the exertions and commissions bound up with these journeys often took their toll, quite apart from the approach of puberty, so that his occasional tiredness is not hard to explain. Yet none of this affected his receptivity to new impressions. His letters to his sister are lively and astute, full of youthful high spirits and sometimes also of ribald banter, and if they have little to say about the people and countries they visited, except on a purely musical level, this certainly does not mean that Mozart was impervious to all impressions: even what he has to say about music reveals him as someone with no time for prolix and effusive enthusiasms. Praise is very rare, and even then it is extremely reserved. But the most striking aspect of all – and it is one that time and again transcends all the amusing and often caustic jokes – is his exceptionally observant eye. Every impression leaves its mark on the thirteen-year-old boy and does so, moreover, from the most disparate directions, while nothing could be further from his thoughts than to idealize or suppress any one of these impressions at the expense of another. His keen and penetrating gaze immediately recognized the living play of the most varied forces behind people and objects, revealing the born dramatist. It was a perspicuity that was bound to be increased by his contact with a nation like the Italian nation. On his earlier tours, Mozart had come into contact with only one particular social class, but now he got to know an entire nation, a nation with a naïve and realistic approach to life that was always ready to instil a little drama into its day-to-day activities. Above all, he came to realize the extent to which *opera*

---

45. See Schurig, *Wolfgang Amade Mozart: Sein Leben und sein Werk*, i.232. Schurig plays off Winckelmann, Goethe and Heinse against Leopold Mozart.

buffa, even in its now much more refined guise, was deeply rooted in the people. The world that in *La finta semplice* he had still had to depict on the basis of hearsay was now revealed to him in all its wealth of characters, with the result that it is not just on a musical level that *La finta giardiniera* towers above its predecessor.

In short, the Mozarts' visits to Italy were free from all Romantic associations and from the sort of lyrical effusions that are all too common today, yet in their way they were no less important in terms of Mozart's own later development. What is significant is the completely open way in which Mozart allowed impressions to work on him. There is no trace of self-deception, but a remarkable propensity for irony in his comments on acknowledged and acclaimed figures in the world of art and, indeed, in the world at large. The acclaim of the multitude impressed him as little as the papal order. Instead, his love of his country and of his family time and again finds expression in his letters. Those to his sister often give the impression that the two of them have been apart for only a few hours. He talks to her about Haydn minuets[46] and asks her to send him his arithmetic book as he does not want to forgo his favourite activity even in Italy.[47] Leopold, too, was keen to see Mozart continue to work to the best of his abilities, with a whole series of compositions attesting to the importance that he attached to an abiding sense of duty. Among the literary impressions that Mozart received in Italy, the most important were those left by the works of Metastasio, by an Italian translation of the *Arabian Nights* that he was given in Rome and that he read with immense pleasure,[48] and by Fénelon's *Télémaque*.[49]

To this point, Mozart's education had concentrated largely on instrumental music, but now he fell completely under the spell of Italian vocalism, an art already highly developed by this date. Of course, even his existing works reveal his innate propensity for a vocal style, but from now on the relationship between the vocal and instrumental elements in his music, far from achieving a state of balance, gradually favours the former. However important the instrumental works that he was later to write, in his heart he was more on the side of vocal music, with his innovations in the field of instrumental music consisting of his introducing cantabile elements into *Spielmusik*.[50] Italy made a decisive contribution to this fundamental feature of his music, and even though he later moved consciously away from the Italians in his general artistic principles, he remained true to their singing style.

A second gap in his existing knowledge was filled in Italy when the living essence of counter-point – familiar to him until now almost solely from its academic aspect – was revealed to him by Padre Martini.[51] And again it was singing that proved decisive here. Under Martini's guidance he learnt to see the individual voices in their independent melodic and rhythmic life and, in conse-quence, to grasp the poetic aspect of this style, and since Martini was a born teacher who set out

---

46. *Briefe*, i.323 and 349 (letters of 24 March and 19 May 1770).
47. *Briefe*, i.339 and 349 (letters of 21 April and 19 May 1770).
48. *Briefe*, i.372 (letter of 21 July 1770).
49. *Briefe*, i.388 (letter of 8 September 1770).
50. This term is generally applied to Baroque instrumental music that is within the grasp of amateur performers.
51. ◆ The traditional view, that Mozart's acquaintance with contrapuntal practice (as opposed to theory) can be traced first to his acquaintance with Martini and, later, to his exposure to Bach, is an exaggeration. It ignores the rich tradition of contrapuntal church music in Salzburg with which Mozart was not only familiar, but participated in. See, in particular, Manfred Hermann Schmid, *Mozart und die Salzburger Tradition*.

from the living works of an earlier generation of composers, Mozart had the opportunity to get to know Italian music of a bygone age. As such, it was an extremely effective counterweight to the modish influences of opera and one, moreover, whose blessings had already benefited many an Italian composer such as Jommelli.[52]

Mozart's visits to Italy marked the end of his childhood not only as a human being but also as an artist and in doing so laid the foundations for his subsequent development as a man.

52. See Abert, *Niccolò Jommelli als Opernkomponist*, 183. ◆ In addition to his instruction from Martini, Mozart's contrapuntal education also included studying works by local Salzburg composers; see Rosenthal, 'The Salzburg Church Music of Mozart and his Predecessors' and 'Zur Stilistik der Salzburger Kirchenmusik von 1600 bis 1730'; and Manfred Hermann Schmid, *Mozart und die Salzburger Tradition*.

9

Opera seria

Of all the products of the Renaissance, opera is undoubtedly the most remarkable. To all the other arts and sciences much-vaunted classical antiquity was revealed either through direct observation or on the basis of a fully authenticated tradition. But when, at the end of the sixteenth century, the members of the Florentine circle centred upon Count Giovanni de' Bardi and Jacopo Corsi, together with the poet Ottaviano Rinuccini and the two composers Jacopo Peri and Giulio Caccini, proposed a new classical ideal, the image that they had in mind was almost as impenetrable to today's observer as it was to them, revolving, as it did, around the music of classical antiquity, of the natural truth of which these enthusiastic Platonists were no less convinced than they were of the moribund and 'barbaric' nature of contemporary counterpoint. The first fruits of this struggle soon manifested themselves in a new form of accompanied solo song, but, under the influence of the powerful element of drama that had been an integral part of Italian music from the sixteenth century onwards, it was not long before it left its mark on drama, too, producing the very first music drama in the form of Peri's *Dafne*. Written to a libretto by Rinuccini, *Dafne* was performed in Corsi's Florentine home in 1597–8.[1] Its text still clearly encapsulates the spirit of contemporary Italian pastoral poetry, while at the same time reflecting a new and different ideal which, occasional distortions notwithstanding, was to remain in force until Mozart's day and beyond. This new ideal was classical tragedy. Even in Florence, there was a firm belief that with the new work of art not only had a new type of music been created, so, too, had a higher form of drama, and the solemn, almost religious strains of the first Venetian overtures breathe this same idealistic spirit.

To this lofty Renaissance ideal, opera owed not only its choice of subjects (a range that for more than two hundred years was to be limited to classical legend and history before receiving a modest boost from the storehouse of Italian Romanticism) but also, and more especially, the various dramatic reforms from Gluck to Wagner, all of which sought to rescue opera from its various wrong turnings and restore it to its ancient ideal.

The most pressing question for opera composers – the question of the relationship between words and music – was solved by the Florentines in favour of the words, a solution which, in keeping with their classical prototype, treated recitative as the basis of opera and did so, moreover, with a rigour never achieved by any of their successors. The poet enjoyed a unique privilege, and to this the musician yielded on every level. Only in the choruses, which were included in conformity with the classical model, did the composer's art have a chance to unfold with any greater freedom. That

1. On the early years of opera, see Solerti, *Gli albori del melodramma*, and Ambros and Leichtentritt, *Geschichte der Musik*, third edition, iv.283ff. ◆ The early history of opera has been widely investigated since Abert's time. For more recent accounts, see Nagler, *Theatre Festivals of the Medici, 1539–1637*; Palisca, 'The "Camerata Fiorentina": A Reappraisal'; Palisca, *The Florentine Camerata: Documentary Studies and Translations*; Sternfeld, *The Birth of Opera*; and Parker, *The Oxford Illustrated History of Opera*.

this approach cut both music and drama off from important forms of expression was soon recognized by artists, and we must thank Claudio Monteverdi (1567–1643) not only for devising a new relationship between the natural cadences of the words and the melodic line that answered the needs of the drama, but also for having been the first opera composer to have recognized and exploited the dramatic linguistic power of the instruments at his disposal.[2]

But this state of balance was not to last. As a reflection of Greek tragedy, opera had acquired a powerful didactic element. But once it emerged from the world of intellectuals, as it did with the opening of the Teatro San Cassiano – Venice's first public opera house – in 1637 and found a new audience in a broad cross-section of the population that had absolutely no time for classical tragedy, its whole nature was bound to change. High drama was replaced by ordinary theatre, with the material element favoured at the expense of the spiritual and the populace gratified rather than educated. As at every other turning point in the history of music, poets led the way, while composers fell into two camps: the first, under Francesco Cavalli (1602–76), sought – sometimes highly successfully – to rescue all that could be salvaged for the drama, while the second, under the leadership of Antonio Cesti (1623–69), consciously aligned itself with the new spirit in opera, not even shying away from the introduction of farcical elements and doing everything in its power to encourage that spirit with a plentiful supply of popular songs. Only now did 'closed' forms find their way into opera, first and foremost of which was the aria, while the dramatic recitative fell more and more into disrepute, allowing a third enemy of drama to usurp the world of opera in the guise of vocal virtuosity. These are the basic features of opera during the period when the Venetians held sway from 1637 to 1690.[3]

The Venetians were followed by the Neapolitans, whose reign lasted from 1690 until 1800.[4] It is to them that opera owed its unexpected revival, at least on a poetic level, after the decline of the earlier period. For the first time since the days of Rinuccini, opera again acquired a literary cachet, and once more the driving force was the idea of classical drama that now awoke to new life. Opera was increasingly affected by the spirit of the Italian Risorgimento, a development for which two highly gifted poets can legitimately claim the credit: Apostolo Zeno (1668–1750)[5] and Pietro Metastasio (1698–1782), the younger and more imaginative of the pair, who soon completely overshadowed his older rival.

Even in Mozart's day, Metastasio[6] was still the undisputed ruler of the Italian operatic stage and, quite apart from his poetic gifts in general, he brought specific qualities to his task that made his

2. See Vogel, 'Claudio Monteverdi'; Ambros and Leichtentritt, *Geschichte der Musik*, iv.533ff.; Heuß, 'Die Instrumental-Stücke des "Orfeo"'; Goldschmidt, 'Claudio Monteverdis Oper: Il ritorno d'Ulisse in patria'; Kretzschmar, 'Monteverdi's "Incoronazione di Poppea"'; and Goldschmidt, *Studien zur Geschichte der italienischen Oper im 17. Jahrhundert* (reprint of *L'incoronazione*). ◆ Also see Tomlinson, *Monteverdi and the End of the Renaissance*; and Rosand, *Opera in Seventeenth-Century Venice: The Creation of a Genre*.
3. Salvioli, *I teatri musicali di Venezia nel secolo XVII*; Kretzschmar, 'Die venetianische Oper und die Werke Cavallis und Cestis'; Ambros and Leichtentritt, *Geschichte der Musik*, iv.616ff.; Wellesz, 'Cavalli und der Stil der venetianischen Oper von 1640–1660'; and Riemann, *Handbuch der Musikgeschichte*, ii/2, 187ff.
4. See Florimo, *La scuola musicale di Napoli e i suoi conservatorii*. ◆ Further see Michael Robinson, *Naples and Neapolitan Opera*, and Degrada, 'L'opera napoletana nel Settecento'.
5. Fehr, *A. Zeno und seine Reform des Operntextes*. ◆ More recently, see Robert Freeman, 'Apostolo Zeno's Reform of the Libretto' and *Opera without Drama: Currents of Change in Italian Opera, 1675–1725*.
6. Calzabigi, 'Dissertazione su le poesie drammatiche del signor abate Pietro Metastasio', *Poesie del signor abate Pietro Metastasio*, i.xvii–cciv; Burney, *Memoirs of the Life and Writings of the Abate Metastasio*; Mussafia, *Pietro Metastasio*; Wiese and Percopo, *Geschichte der italienischen Litteratur*, 441ff.; Zito, *Studio su Pietro Metastasio*; Gubernatis, *Pietro Metastasio: corso di lezioni fatte nell'Università di Roma nell'anno scolastico 1909–1910*; and Wotquenne, *Alphabetisches Verzeichnis der Stücke in Versen aus den dramatischen Werken von Zeno, Metastasio, und Goldoni*. ◆ Concerning Metastasio, see Saccenti, 'Metastasio e altro settecento'; Knighton and Burden, 'Metastasio, 1698–1782'; and Hilscher and Sommer-Mathis, *Pietro Metastasio, uomo universale (1698–1782)*.

generation think of him as a born opera librettist. His poetry was essentially musical. In his dealings with singers and composers he had developed his musical gifts to the point at which he felt and knew exactly what was required of him to produce a text that lent itself to music. Not only could he sing ('come un serafino', as he joked in a letter to Farinelli[7]), he could also play the piano and could even compose a little,[8] finding that it helped him to find true poetic inspiration if he could improvise on the piano. He himself said that he never wrote the words of an aria without also setting it to music in his own head: in other words, he first had to be completely clear in his own mind what its musical character involved.[9] He made young composers such as Salieri[10] and Martinez[11] declaim the texts that they were setting and advised them on the correct musical expression.[12]

However much Metastasio may have acknowledged music's ability to breathe life into the drama and complement the text,[13] he still insisted on the poet's rights. The assumption that in Neapolitan opera the singers and composer said everything and that the poet had nothing to say is a grave error, and even the great Hasse was given a detailed lesson in the poet's intentions on the occasion of *Attilio Regolo*,[14] with Jommelli even receiving a stern rebuke, albeit one couched in the most courteous terms, on account of his allegedly overladen instrumentation.[15] Singers fared no better if they neglected the emotional truth of the words that they were singing at the expense of superficial virtuosity. And it was with total self-assurance that Metastasio insisted that, as tragedies, his librettos would hold his listeners in thrall even if they were performed without music.[16]

If Metastasio was the poetic idol of virtually the whole of the contemporary civilized world, then there were good reasons for this: few poets captured the whole spirit of that world as comprehensively as he did. In the field of opera, he lent the Enlightenment the most effective support imaginable and, like most of its other representatives, he also took up and developed French tragedy, as is clear from the conditions that he describes and the characters that he puts on stage, all of whom bear the heroic and courtly stamp of the French. He, too, was imbued with the Enlightenment's tremendous respect for rules and rational thinking: he began by devising a particular heroic quality and only then created the individual character to go with it. Far from attempting to reflect the whole range of human life in its constantly changing facets, the main aim of this poetry was didactic. As a result, his characters are not individuals in the modern sense of the term. Rather, they embody certain qualities that are often impressed upon the listener with a *naïveté* that recalls nothing so much as plays intended for children.

No less rationalistic are the plots of his dramas, with the one exception of *Attilio Regolo*. Even though the intrigue as such is bound to have far less appeal for us Germans than for the Italians and French, unless it is accompanied by a genuine art of characterization, we must none the less

7. Metastasio, *Opere postume*, i.324.
8. He mentions some of his works in *Opere postume* (i.386 and 402) and also in conversation with Burney: see Burney, *The Present State of Music in Germany*, i.296–7. Some of these works have appeared in print: thirty-six *canoni*, for example, were published by Artaria in Vienna in 1782.
9. Metastasio, *Opere postume*, i.384.
10. Mosel, *Ueber das Leben und die Werke des Anton Salieri*, 62.
11. Metastasio, *Opere postume*, iii.109.
12. Mancini, *Pensieri, e riflessioni pratiche sopra il canto figurato*, 247.
13. Metastasio, *Opere postume*, ii.47.
14. Metastasio, *Opere postume*, i.344ff.; see also ii.355.
15. Hermann Abert, *Niccolò Jommelli als Opernkomponist*, 352.
16. Metastasio, *Opere postume*, ii.329–30; see also Mancini, *Pensieri, e riflessioni pratiche*, 234–5, and Carlo Goldoni, *Mémoires* i/20, 110. Friedrich von Hagedorn thought that a number of Metastasio's operas were consummate tragedies in their own right (see his *Sämmtliche poetische Werke*, v.113).

concede that in matters of both intellect and taste he was far superior in his handling of intrigue not only to his Venetian predecessors but also to his successor Scribe. And the same is true of his treatment of that area of our emotional lives in which the plot is almost always played out, namely, love. Admittedly, love is depicted here, as with most rationalist dramatists, not as a passion but as a form of *galant* behaviour, in other words, as a social phenomenon. In every conflict, it is convention that has the last word, hence the fact that, although the characters' emotions may be in a state of turmoil, there is rarely the sense of any grand passion. Within these confines, however, Metastasio moves with undeniable taste and assurance. Above all, his poetry breathes the spirit of a sophisticated aristocratic society. It has style and, as such, towers far above that of all his earlier and later rivals. Form and content are a perfect match and, indeed, the form of Metastasio's verse is among its greatest strengths. It, too, is unambiguously aristocratic, with the poet determined to show off his wide reading, erudition and elegance and to hold out to the listener the pearls of his wisdom set in the choicest verse. The most obvious example of this is to be found in the general aphorisms that are couched in finely turned poetry and that may also have influenced the young Schiller, who grew up, after all, in a similar atmosphere. Equally important in this context is the delicacy with which he often controls the complex fates of his heroes and appears to flirt with disaster, but pride of place must go to the consummate technique that seems to leave no dull patches in the dialogue and knows exactly how to hold the listener's unceasing attention through the iridescent play of language.

In short, Metastasio's librettos are not poetry in the highest sense of the term but an art form intended for fashionable society, albeit one of a particularly sophisticated kind. A product of rules that were well thought through, it could easily be learnt and, as such, found many imitators, notably in the work of Verazi and Gamerra, even if the librettos of these last-named poets lack the spirit and formal elegance of the original.

In the outward form of his dramas, Metastasio took over the various forms that Neapolitan opera had adopted under its founder, Alessandro Scarlatti (1660–1725).[17] All that remained of the formal variety of old was the recitative and aria, while the aria in turn had essentially been reduced to a single type. The chorus had disappeared by 1650.

This impoverishment of the formal variety of opera, which had already been clearly foreshadowed during the latter part of the Venetian period,[18] is striking proof of the extent to which views on the relationship between music and drama in opera had changed. With the great Venetian composers, music and drama had been intimately interconnected, but now each began to go its own way, with the drama being assigned to the new type of *secco* recitative in which music had only the most modest part to play, while the music was represented by the aria, which in turn came to occupy a position more or less outside the drama. In this disjunction lay the Achilles' heel of the whole genre, a weakness which, in spite of the progress made in other areas, was soon to be recognized as such not only by its outspoken opponents but more especially by those composers who with increasing energy sought to pluck out the evil from their midst. The problem that had to be solved at all costs if *opera seria* was to have any future was how to reunite drama and music in opera and to do so, moreover, in such a way that the dramatic parts of the work received an injection of musical blood, while the musical parts were injected with greater drama. To its

17. See Dent, *Alessandro Scarlatti*. ◆ Also see Strohm, 'Alessandro Scarlatti and the Settecento'; Zanetti, 'Il teatro: Alessandro Scarlatti'; Grout, *Alessandro Scarlatti: An introduction to his Operas*; and Lindgren, 'Il dramma musicale a Roma durante la carriera di Alessandro Scarlatti (1660–1725)'.
18. This can be seen quite clearly from Carlo Pallavicino's *La Gierusalemme liberata* of 1687. (For a modern edition of this work, see Abert, *Carlo Pallavicino: La Gierusalemme liberata*.)

attempts to solve this problem Italian opera owed one of the most brilliant high points of its career, even though it remained bogged down for far too long in purely musical reforms. It was Gluck and his librettist Ranieri de' Calzabigi who finally realized that salvation could ultimately come only if they dispensed with the current type of libretto, which was now seen as the root of all evil.

Secco recitative was accompanied by the harpsichord alone,[19] its very name indicating that it did not set out to produce a full-toned musical effect.[20] Although the whole course of the drama unfolded in these sections, they are made up of no more than the most cursory form of *Sprechgesang*, with the dialogue raised only to the level of fixed musical notation. For many composers, *secco* recitative was not even a part of the opera that was actually 'composed', but was an improvised extra of which they would write only the bass and sometimes not even that, preferring to leave everything to the singers. Other composers entrusted these sections to younger assistants.[21] But even those composers who wrote them out in full showed by the cursory, uninvolved tone and mechanical repetition of fossilized formulas that as musicians they were simply capitulating to the demands of the performers. And it was the performers who were the primary object of attention on the part of the audience, assuming that the latter were listening at all,[22] and it was as actors that singers often enjoyed some of their greatest triumphs in these sections. But there was another kind of recitative in Neapolitan opera, the *recitativo accompagnato*, in which the singers were joined by the orchestra and the declamation, in particular, assumed a more expressive musical character. Accompanied recitatives occur in those sections of the libretto that deal with emotional crises before or after important decisions and generally lead into an aria. Invariably introduced with great skill by Metastasio, these passages gave the composer an opportunity to show off his abilities to the full and it is here that we find the most significant achievements of Neapolitan opera. None the less, it must be emphasized that not even these passages are dramatic, as the action does not move forward here. Rather, these sections are free, lyrical monologues[23] that reflect the dramatic tension of the preceding or following scene, fulfilling an aim that the aria was prevented from achieving by virtue of various shortcomings that we shall mention in a moment and allowing the hero to give direct expression to feelings stirred up by the present dramatic situation. Not until the period immediately before Gluck do we find the first attempts to draw the dramatic action into the *accompagnato*, a development that inevitably opened up extraordinarily important new horizons for the subsequent course of opera.

Textually speaking, the arias were based on the two lyrical quatrains that Metastasio almost always used to bring his scenes to an end. The idea was that they would encapsulate the entire emotional content of these scenes in a single lyrical outpouring and thereby maintain a connection with the drama. In fact, Metastasio achieved this aim in only a handful of cases, a failure due to the fact that, as a true rationalist, he regularly lapsed into speculation and in that way forgot to be natural and direct. These aria texts are the best possible proof that Metastasian poetry sprang not from real life but from the workings of a rational mind. Some of these arias are merely decor-

19. The harpsichord provided only the supporting harmonies; for an examination of the way in which these parts were realized, see Max Schneider, 'Die Begleitung des Secco-Rezitativs um 1750'. The bass notes of this instrument decay very quickly, and so they were sustained by an accompanying string bass. ◆ More recently, see Borgir, *The Performance of the Basso Continuo in Italian Baroque Music*; Howard Mayer Brown and Sadie, *Performance Practice: Music after 1600*; Christensen, *Die Grundlagen des Generalbassspiels*; and Ledbetter, *Continuo Playing According to Handel*.
20. See Kretzschmar, 'Aus Deutschlands italienischer Zeit', ii.140ff.
21. This is also said to have been the case with Mozart's *La clemenza di Tito*.
22. Abert, *Niccolò Jommelli als Opernkomponist*, 122.
23. Dialogue scenes of this kind are rare and, as before, of a purely lyrical nature.

ative: they are like rhetorical flourishes bringing the scene to an end, but, in spite of their formal brilliance, their content is so generalized and vague that they could easily be transferred from one opera to another without further ado – as frequently happened. So universal was their applicability that they suited every context because, at bottom, they suited none. Even when the poet explored the underlying situation in greater detail, the feelings and passions that he wanted to depict were often first passed through the winnowing-mill of reason. His heroes do not give direct expression to their feelings but launch into rational explanations of them, speaking in images and similes instead of revealing their own inner lives. These virtuoso simile arias tend to derive their imagery from the sea and are the products of a profoundly rationalistic spirit and in both poetry and music long prevented the creative imagination from taking flight.

It comes as no surprise to discover that these circumstances made it much easier for a further enemy of drama in opera – vocal virtuosity – to acquire its tyrannical stranglehold over the stage. Singers tended to regard their arias merely as an opportunity to display their abilities, forcing composers to heed their demands and even insisting on interpolating arias from other works and, in some cases, by other composers.[24]

In the circumstances, it is hardly surprising that composers had such a difficult time. There was a period immediately after Scarlatti when they simply severed the already weak links between music and drama and high-handedly allowed the sensual charms of their music to overwhelm the listener, and even during the later period we still find frequent lapses into music pure and simple. Yet we must not forget what was genuinely – and increasingly – significant about these arias. With the passage of time, composers succeeded more and more in drawing from Metastasio's verse all that lent itself to deeper emotional expression and in that way bypassed the jumble of rational reflections and comparisons in order to concentrate on the underlying emotion itself: where the poet, for example, had the desperate hero comparing his own situation with that of a shipwrecked sailor on the storm-tossed sea, the composer would no longer depict the wind and waves but the mood of despair itself. In this way, composers adopted a creative approach to the texts they were setting, reestablishing the dramatic connection that the poet, entrenched in his rationalist views, had failed to make. The individual situation that had inspired the poet to produce only intellectual imagery now became a genuine inner experience for the composer. Needless to say, composers were not always successful in this, and in simile arias in particular they often enough went no further than replicating the outward imagery. But the fact that they succeeded at all and became increasingly conscious of the creative challenge facing them raises their achievements far above the level of routine work and pseudo-art, a reproach far too readily levelled at them by writers of an earlier generation. Their operas – including their arias – reveal a real wealth of genuine art, in other words, art that is grounded in emotional experience and that continues to be valid today. But since it is genuinely dramatic, it can only be fully understood if the listener is aware of the overall context, and it is impossible to sound an urgent enough warning against the enforced divisions of number opera, divisions into which even Gluck's operas are broken down in so many modern editions.

Given the extra scope that the composer acquired in this way, it is only to be expected that the main difference between the Neapolitan aria and its Venetian counterpart lay in its greater length. Venetian composers said only what was necessary, contenting themselves often with only the sketchiest of hints, whereas Neapolitan composers were fond of going into elaborate detail and

---

24. Writers distinguished between a whole series of subtypes including the *aria cantabile*, the *aria di portamento*, the *aria di mezzo carattere*, the *aria parlante* (*agitata*) and the *aria di bravura* (*agilità*); see John Brown, *Letters upon the Poetry and Music of the Italian Opera*, 29ff.; see also Goldoni's advice to librettists in his *Mémoires*, i.102–3. ◆ See also Westrup and Hunter, 'Aria'.

lingering over their ideas. The themes of their arias are much more expansive by nature, with the composers in question seeking not merely to skate over the surface, but to explore their contents in full. The result is a detailed and in-depth portrait of the hero's soul, with the art of variation and development playing a not inconsiderable part in the musical argument. Coloratura writing, too, is one of its basic expressive devices.[25] Although it could, in theory, have served the drama admirably, it had in fact become little more than a parasitical growth on the tree of opera even by Caccini's day, and the demands of vocal virtuosity turned it into an end in itself, with instrumental music, too, now beginning to exert a noticeable influence on it to the extent that singers prided themselves on their ability to rival instrumental virtuosity. It was these coloratura excesses that did most to harm the reputation of the genre as a whole,[26] even though we should not forget that alongside excrescences such as Konstanze's 'Martern aller Arten' from *Die Entführung aus dem Serail* there are also examples of the genuinely dramatic use of coloratura techniques.

Not even Scarlatti severed the links between opera and the music of the common people. The only difference was that the popular music of Venice was now replaced by its Neapolitan counterpart with all its sicilianas, appoggiaturas, slides, interrupted cadences, triplets and so on. But with Scarlatti, this folk tone was successfully held in check by a serious and often impassioned underlying tone of a highly distinctive kind as well as by a fine sense of poetical form. In much the same way, Scarlatti's detailed exploration of the emotional content of the text shows that he took the drama seriously.

The ternary *da capo* aria – the *only* form acknowledged by the exponents of Neapolitan opera – was already in use by around 1650 and began to dominate opera in the hands of later Venetian composers such as Pallavicino and Steffani.[27] It is in three sections, the third of which is merely a repeat of the first, except that the singer now had to decorate the melodic line, just as Italian audiences always expected singers to regale them with renewed samples of their ability to improvise ornaments even in encores. The first section was based on the opening quatrain of the text, the second – which was invariably shorter – on the second quatrain. This middle section was either motivically dependent on the first or, more frequently, conceived in terms of a contrast in respect of both tempo and time-signature. And whereas the first section served largely as a vehicle for the art of singing, the second allowed the composer to have a greater say and to display his harmonic skills.[28] The *A*-section was divided in turn into two subsections separated by an abrupt cadence

25. Goldschmidt, *Die Lehre von der vokalen Ornamentik.*

26. ◆ On the other hand, Burney (*The Present State of Music in France and Italy*, 213–14) reports an entertaining anecdote that shows how virtuosity, even mindless virtuosity, was appreciated by contemporary audiences. It concerns a performance in Rome in 1722 by the famous soprano castrato Farinelli: 'There was a struggle every night between [Farinelli] and a famous trumpet player on the trumpet, in a song accompanied by that instrument: this, at first, seemed amicable and merely sportive, till the audience began to interest themselves in the contest, and to take different sides: after severally swelling out a note, in which each manifested the power of his lungs, and tried to rival the other in brilliancy and force, they had both a swell and a shake together, by thirds, which was continued so long, while the audience eagerly waited the event, that both seemed to be exhausted; and, in fact, the trumpeter, wholly spent gave it up, thinking, however, his antagonist as much tired as himself, and that it would be a drawn battle; when Farinelli, with a smile on his countenance, shewing he had only been sporting with him all this time, broke out all at once in the same breath, with fresh vigour, and not only swelled and shook the note, but ran the most rapid and difficult divisions and was at last silenced only by the acclamations of the audience.'

27. See Johann Georg Sulzer, *Allgemeine Theorie der schönen Künste*, i.104ff. ◆ Concerning Pallavicino, see Glixon, 'Recitative in Seventeenth-Century Venetian Opera: Its Dramatic Function and Musical Language', and Rosand, *Opera in Seventeenth-Century Venice: The Creation of a Genre.* Concerning Steffani, see Riemann, *Agostino Steffani: Ausgewählte Werke*, vii–xxiii.

28. It very often ended on the minor of the dominant. According to Arteaga, it was the singer Baldassare Ferri from Perugia (1610–80) who invented the aria with ornamented *da capo.* Whether or not there is any truth in this claim, it is clear that singers played a major role in the development of this form; see Arteaga, *Le rivoluzioni del teatro musicale italiano dalla sua origine fino al presente*, ii.262. ◆ Also see Conestabile, *Notizie biografiche di Baldassarre Ferri, musico celebratissimo*, and Baiocco, 'Su Baldassarre Ferri, cantante evirato del Seicento'.

on the dominant or in the parallel tonality and was followed by a ritornello. It was the second of these two subsections that was normally the principal focus of coloratura interest, while its development-section-like character and return to the first section (which may or may not have been foreshortened) recall the corresponding section of a sonata movement. It came to a rest on a fixed formula [see p.164] that functioned as the point of departure for the singer's freely improvised cadenza. As a rule, there were four ritornellos: at the beginning, at the end of each section of the first part, and at the end of the second. All of them derived their musical ideas from the themes of the aria itself. But in Neapolitan opera the instruments never fell silent in the way that they did – with the exception of the harpsichord – in Venetian opera. Sometimes they doubled the vocal line and at other times they provided harmonic support, generally in quavers or crotchets, but they might also occasionally strike out on their own. In this regard Scarlatti often went further than his successor Hasse, with concertante writing not only for virtuosic strings and winds but even for whole sections. Central to the Neapolitan orchestra was the three-part string family of two violins and bass, from which the violas and, thereafter, the cellos broke free as independent voices only at a later date. As before, it was the harmony instruments – lutes, theorbos and harps or, more usually, one or more harpsichords – that provided solid harmonic foundations. Traditionally, this part was not notated but had to be independently executed by the performers with or without the help of a figured bass. The conductor led the entire performance from the harpsichord. The wind department of the Neapolitan orchestra generally comprised oboes and horns, although we may assume as a matter of course that the bass was reinforced by bassoons. Flutes were used only to add a specific sense of colour in pastoral or idyll-like numbers. Except where they were used as solo instruments,[29] the winds either doubled the violins or served to reinforce the harmonies.[30] Moreover, they were not used in pairs, as in modern orchestras, but in choirs, in other words, there would be approximately half as many winds as there were strings. It is additionally worth pointing out here that the ancient practice of concertante playing in older music also affected the dynamics of the performance, with the *piano* passages – especially at the point where the voice enters – achieved not by having the entire orchestra play more quietly but by reducing the number of players.[31]

Trumpets and timpani generally appear only in scenes of a festive or martial stamp, while only very exceptionally do we find instruments such as the english horn and chalumeau, the latter the forerunner of the clarinet. The clarinet itself is found only after 1750, making its first appearance not in opera houses but in symphony orchestras.[32]

The seating plan of the Dresden orchestra may serve as an example of the sort of arrangement that was generally found at this period. It is the seating plan used by Hasse and was regarded as a model of its kind:[33]

29. Colouristic effects are not uncommon here, especially in *ombra* arias in which the shades of dead people are invoked and the winds are often used to represent them; see Abert, *Niccolò Jommelli als Opernkomponist*, appendix exx. I and III.

30. The question whether the wind parts were dependent on the resources available, allowing them to be included or omitted at will, is one that deserves closer examination than it has received hitherto. The fact that some works exist in two versions, with and without winds, appears to suggest that this was, indeed, the case.

31. For a general introduction to orchestral resources at this time, see Mennicke, *Hasse und die Brüder Graun als Symphoniker*, 266ff. ◆ A fuller account can be found in Spitzer and Zaslaw, *The Birth of the Orchestra*, 137–79.

32. See Riemann, *Sinfonien der Pfalzbayerischen Schule I*, XVI; Mennicke, *Hasse und die Brüder Graun*, 277ff.; and Georges Cucuel, 'La question des clarinettes dans l'instrumentation du XVIIIe siècle'. ◆ Abert is generally correct; although a few German court orchestras acquired clarinets by the 1730s (Spitzer and Zaslaw, *The Birth of the Orchestra*, 25), they did not become common until later.

33. Rousseau, 'Orchestre', *Dictionnaire de musique*; see also Kandler, *Cenni storico-critici intorno alla vita ed alle opere del celebre compositore di musica Giovanni Adolfo Hasse detto il Sassone*, pl. 1; and Fürstenau, *Zur Geschichte der Musik und des Theaters am Hofe zu Dresden*, ii.290–93. When he met Burney in Vienna in 1772, Hasse confirmed that the details given by Rousseau were correct in every way; see Burney, *The Present State of Music in Germany*, i.345. ◆ For additional seating plans of early orchestras, see Spitzer and Zaslaw, *The Birth of the Orchestra*, especially 350–3.

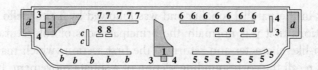

1. Harpsichord of the conductor
2. Harpsichord of the second accompanist
3. Cellos
4. Double basses

5. First violins
6. Second violins
7. Oboes
8. Flutes

a Violas
b Bassoons
c Horns
d Trumpets and timpani on a raised platform

Apart from the arias, the only other numbers worth mentioning under this heading are the relatively brief and songlike cavatinas that were frequently linked to accompanied recitatives. Largely made up of duets and, much less frequently, trios,[34] the ensemble movements, too, were cast in the form of arias. Neither the poet nor the composer attempted to present the individual characters here as antithetical types, and many of these movements are distinguished from the solo arias merely by dint of their fuller sonorities and the fact that they are set for more than one voice.[35] Only in the wake of Hasse and under the influence of *opera buffa* are more individualized numbers encountered here. As in Venice, the chorus was limited to very brief movements at the end of the piece, and even these were often performed by the soloists. None the less, composers from Hasse onwards sought to regain the ground that had been lost in this way by adopting the French model and, at the same time, by restoring to their former importance the ballets that had previously been interpolated between the acts and, more especially, the independent orchestral pieces that were now restricted to festive and martial marches. The Neapolitan sinfonia is distinguished from its Venetian counterpart by its fixed ternary form. It begins with a resolutely festive allegro followed by an andante intended as no more than a brief transition, and it ends with a second fast movement of an even more festive stamp than the first. We have already noted the way in which this three-movement form, including the tripartite division of the opening section, contains within it the seeds of the later classical symphony. Unlike the Venetian sinfonia, however, the Neapolitan sinfonia had absolutely no connection with the ensuing drama, but was simply a piece of festively sparkling, Mediterranean music, which explains why the sinfonia of one opera could so effortlessly be transferred to another. In short, these introductory numbers were yet further examples of pieces that stood apart from the drama.

The costumes and scenery of Neapolitan operas were possibly even more spectacular and costly than those of Venetian opera. The scenery painters, machinists and cutters were scarcely less important than the performers themselves, and, indeed, even the printed wordbooks contributed to the general luxuriousness of the occasion. But it was the singers, of course, who were the most expensive item on the budget, with the prima donna and *primo uomo* – in other words, the castrato – taking the lion's share. The institution of the castrato[36] can be traced back to the last two decades of the sixteenth century and began to leave its mark on opera in the years around 1650, both Monteverdi and the early Cavalli having preferred the four natural vocal

---

34. In all Metastasio's librettos there is only a single quartet. It occurs in act three, scene nine of *Catone in Utica.*

35. Following Scarlatti's example, the first singer normally begins these pieces by stating the theme, which is then repeated by the second singer, after which their voices combine in simple homophonic textures. Only later do we find more elaborate techniques, including canonic procedures and double coloratura.

36. See Ambros and Leichtentritt, *Geschichte der Musik,* 463ff. ◆ Also see Rosselli, 'The Castrati as a Professional Group and a Social Phenomenon, 1550–1850', and Bergeron, 'The Castrato as History'.

registers.[37] It was in Neapolitan opera, however, that castratos really came into their own, and it is highly significant that, with its cult of singing, this period in history was oblivious to the repellent, unnatural and undramatic nature of this practice.[38] Although castrato singers were pitilessly mocked in literature and especially in *opere buffe*,[39] such attacks were directed not at their singing but at their outward appearance, their effeminacy and their increasingly intolerable arrogance. But their singing, which was believed to combine the tone colour of a boy's voice with the lung power of a man's, was still felt to embody the highest of all vocal achievements.[40] Some distance behind these principals came the singers of the secondary roles in the shape of one or more tenors and the other female singers: the prima donna and castrato made sure that the roles given to these rivals were neither too substantial nor too grateful.[41] Bass voices had gradually disappeared from serious opera even under Venetian composers.

There is no doubt that as a result of the control exerted by these singers the composer, who generally received one hundred ducats for his contribution, was constrained in a way that now seems to us inconceivable. Yet the surviving works afford ample proof of the fact that time and again composers were able to triumph over these limitations and press vocal virtuosity into the service of their own artistic aims, aims that they achieved either through sheer energy, as in the case of Handel and Gluck, or through diplomacy. Today, the great singers of the time – the castratos Senesino (Francesco Bernardi), Caffarelli (Gaetano Majorano), Farinelli (Carlo Broschi) and Girolamo Crescentini and the sopranos Vittoria Tesi, Faustina Bordoni, Francesca Cuzzoni, Regina Mingotti, Lucrezia Aguiari, Caterina Gabrielli and others – are mere names, and neither the distinctly anecdotal accounts of their triumphs nor the arias intended for them can give us a clear picture of their living art.[42]

Initially, operas were performed only during carnival (26 December to 30 March), but later two more seasons or *stagioni* were added, the first from Easter Monday to 15 June, the second from 1 September to 30 November. At royal courts, it was, of course, princely birthdays, weddings, ceremonial visits and the like that were generally the occasion for operas. Here, under the direction of an intendant, the company was usually more settled than in towns and cities where the

---

37. Soprano and alto were sung by women, occasionally also by boys. The institution of the castrato found little favour among German singers. On 9 March 1775, the secretary to the Saxon legation, Johann Friedrich Unger, reported in his diary on the unsuccessful appearance of a German castrato from Rastatt: 'On jugera heureusement pour la postérité de notre nation que les allemands ne réussiroient jamais dans ce genre' (Hauptarchiv, Dresden, loc. 3292).

38. Not infrequently in love duets the part of the man was higher than that of the woman.

39. See Marcello, *Il teatro alla moda*; see also Goldoni's *L'impresario di Smyrna* and Jommelli's *La critica* in Abert, *Niccolò Jommelli als Opernkomponist*, 426ff.

40. See Heinse's comment on Pachierotti, 'o benedetto il coltello, che t'a tagliato li coglioni', in Heinse, *Schriften*, ii.103–4; see also the same writer's *Hildegard von Hohenthal*, iii.19.

41. There was even a recognized system of court etiquette among the singers, with the prima donna enjoying the right to have her train carried by a page boy – and by two page boys if she was playing the part of a princess. They followed her around the stage. She occupied the place of honour on the right of the performers as she was generally the most distinguished person in the piece. In 1748, Faustina Bordoni sang the role of Dircea in *Demofoonte*, a character who is acknowledged as a princess only later in the opera. None the less, she demanded that she be given precedence over the singer playing the part of Creusa, and Metastasio himself was obliged to intervene in order to settle the dispute and persuade her to defer to her rival; see Metastasio, *Opere postume*, i.282ff.

42. See Mancini, *Pensieri, e riflessioni pratiche*, 14ff. ◆ Concerning these singers, see Mazzeo, *I tre 'Senesini': musici ed altri cantanti evirati senesi*; Faustini-Fasini, 'Gli astri maggiori del bel canto napoletano: Gaetano Majorano detto "Caffarelli"'; Rosselli, 'The Castrati as a Professional Group and a Social Phenomenon, 1550–1850'; Barbier, *Farinelli: Le castrat des lumières*; Mamy, *Les grands castrats napolitains à Venise au XVIIIe siècle*; Cappelletto, *La voce perduta: Vita di Farinelli evirato cantore*; Vitali and Boris, *Carlo Broschi Farinelli: Senza sentimento oscuro*; Lucarelli, 'Girolamo Crescentini: La vita, la tecnica vocale analizzata attraverso alcune sue arie tipiche'; Ademollo, 'Le cantanti italiane celebri del secolo decimottavo: Vittoria Tesi'; Högg, *Die Gesangskunst der Faustina Hasse und das Sängerinnenwesen ihrer Zeit in Deutschland*; Buelow, 'A Lesson in Operatic Performance Practice by Madame Faustina Bordoni'; Müller von Asow, 'Regina Mingotti: Eine italienische Primadonna aus österreichischer Familie'; and Casavola, 'La più grande interprete di Traetta: Caterina Gabrielli'.

local impresario tended to engage his performers only for a particular run of performances. Smaller towns that could not afford a theatre of their own were visited by the large number of touring opera companies that existed at this time.[43]

It will be abundantly clear from all that has been said that, notwithstanding the lofty goals of its creators, opera was by no means immune from decay: there were simply too many temptations to lapse into superficiality and to lose all sense of drama, and it was to these temptations that Scarlatti's immediate heirs, notably Leonardo Vinci (*c*1696–1730) and Nicola Porpora (1686–1768), now proceeded to succumb. It was not that any of these composers – especially that ill-mannered favourite of the Graces, Leonardo Vinci – lacked talent or musical training (such a charge is emphatically refuted by Vinci's dazzling melodic gifts and masterly *accompagnato* scenes), but that they were wholly innocent of the self-denial of the genuine dramatist: they worked hurriedly, skating over the surface and all too often failing to find the right tone by dint of their desire either to gratify their audiences with pleasing melodies or to achieve purely virtuosic effects. The *opere serie* of the hugely gifted Giovanni Battista Pergolesi (1710–36)[44] and the great church composer Leonardo Leo (1694–1744)[45] deserve to be taken more seriously from a purely musical point of view, yet they lack any real dramatic substance. In Pergolesi's case, the predominant tone is one of tender-hearted lyricism and, as such, it occasionally reminds one of Mozart, whereas Leo's music is curiously reserved and even arid in character.[46] It was left to Johann Adolf Hasse (1699–1783)[47] to bring a true sense of drama to opera, and the immense reputation that he enjoyed soon helped to ensure that the principles that he represented acquired more widespread acceptance. He may be described as a member of the Neapolitan school to the extent that, for him, the focus of attention in opera was directed solely at the singing. In each and every one of his views on drama, he was Metastasio's natural ally, as is clear not only from his evident sense of form and, its bewitching sensual appeal notwithstanding, the aristocratic beauty of his musical language but also from his art of characterization, an art in perfect accord with Metastasio's poetic principles as expounded above. Indeed, there are times when he even succeeds in breathing real individual life into the librettist's characters, all of whom are imbued, in turn, with the spirit of the Enlightenment. His seriousness of dramatic purpose is evident even in his *secco* recitatives, their characterful declamation and harmonic writing providing an important pointer to the expressive possibilities contained in this neglected form. In the course of his long life, Hasse was inevitably affected by the increasingly powerful influence of the Risorgimento that sought to revivify opera by reintroducing choruses, dance and independent instrumental movements, a development that ultimately culminated in Gluck's music dramas. But it was Hasse's pupils who really saw this development through to its logical conclusion and who in doing so bring us close to Mozart himself. All of these composers, including Gluck in his pre-*Orfeo* Italian operas, managed to make as much dramatic capital as feasibly possible out of Metastasio's texts, not even shying away from shortening the *secco* sections and introducing ensembles and choral scenes whenever they felt that the drama demanded it. But even existing forms now took on a new life, with the *secco* recitatives

43.   The most famous were those of the brothers Pietro and Angelo Mingotti and the one run by Giovanni Battista Locatelli; see Müller von Asow, *Angelo und Pietro Mingotti*.

44.   See the excellent study by Radiciotti, *G. B. Pergolesi*. ◆ Also see Degrada, '"Lo frate 'nnamorato" e l'estetica della commedia musicale napoletana'.

45.   Leo, *Leonardo Leo, musicista del secolo XVIII e le sue opere musicali*; Dent, 'Leonardo Leo'; and Piovano, 'A propos d'une récente biographie de Léonard Leo'. ◆ Further, Degrada, 'L'opera napoletana' and Pastore, *Don Lionardo: vita e opere di Leonardo Leo*.

46.   ◆ Concerning Leo, see Strohm, 'Die italienische Oper im 18. Jahrhundert', and Markstrom, 'The Operas of Leonardo Vinci'.

47.   Kandler, *Cenni storico-critici intorno alla vita ed alle opere del celebre Giovanni Adolfo Hasse dello il Sassone*; Mennicke, *Hasse und die Brüder Graun*; and Kretzschmar, 'Aus Deutschlands italienischer Zeit', ii.148ff. Hasse's *La conversione di Sant'Agostino* of 1750 is edited by Schering. ◆ Also see Millner, *The Operas of Johann Adolf Hasse*, and Strohm, *Dramma per musica: Italian opera seria of the eighteenth century*, 271–93.

either making explicit the sense of drama already implicit in them[48] or, wherever possible, being replaced by accompanied recitatives to produce great dramatic scenes, while in the arias a purely melodic vocal line frequently had to make way for a more declamatory line. Harmonically and instrumentally, too, the arias acquired a new vitality. Of the composers who fall under this heading, neither Domènech Terradellas (1711–51) nor David Perez (1711–78) is of relevance in the context of Mozart: the former was long dead, and the latter was in faraway Lisbon. Conversely, Mozart was in touch – and often in personal contact – with Niccolò Jommelli (1714–74), Tommaso Traetta (1727–79) and Gian Francesco de Majo (1732–70). Both Jommelli and Traetta came into direct contact with the German and French spirit, the former through his years in the two cities that were most receptive to reform, namely, Vienna and Stuttgart, the latter through his work in Parma and Vienna. It was Jommelli who was the true pioneer of the new art, a master of the freely structured, large-scale *scena*, chorus, ensemble, and of dramatic orchestral music, an artist of an austere, often brooding seriousness that earned him the nickname 'the Italian Gluck'.[49] Yet, of all the composers under review, he was the one who influenced Mozart the least: the two men were simply too different from each other in terms of their character and views on art.[50] More marked was the influence left by Traetta, the most versatile and imaginative member of this school.[51] In his setting of Coltellini's *Ifigenia in Tauride* (1763), he even succeeded where Jommelli, over-faithful to Metastasio, had failed and came close to the Gluckian ideal on a textual level, too. Dramatically, of course, Mozart is as remote from Traetta as he is from Jommelli, although on a purely musical level there was a great deal in Traetta's music that attracted him, notably its elegiac tone[52] and grace.[53] At the same time, Traetta was a master of the subtly stylized folk

---

48.   This is something that Gluck, in particular, did in his pre-reform operas; see Abert, 'Glucks italienische Opern bis zum "Orfeo"', 9ff. This is a specifically German characteristic that is also found in the case of Hasse and Graun, although David Perez, in his *Solimano* of 1757, similarly includes a large number of performance markings in his *secco* recitatives.

49.   See Abert, *Niccolò Jommelli als Opernkomponist*. ◆ Also see Strohm, *Die italienische Oper im 18. Jahrhundert*.

50.   It is not enough merely to point out individual reminiscences here; see Abert, *Niccolò Jommelli als Opernkomponist*, 214. Even the Mozartian first subject of the aria from act two, scene three of *Caio Mario* (Abert, *Niccolò Jommelli*, 195) is a melodic commonplace found in many Italian operas at this time:

51.   A selection of Traetta's works is edited by Goldschmidt (*Tommaso Traëtta: Ausgewählte Werke*) with a valuable introduction to Traetta's life and works. ◆ See Bloch, 'Tommaso Traetta's Reform of Italian Opera'; Morea, *Tommaso Traetta: Riformatore del melodramma*; Strohm, 'Tradition und Fortschritt in der opera seria: Tommaso Traetta: *Ifigenia in Tauride* (Wien, 1763); Christoph Willibald Gluck: *Il Telemaco, o sia l'isola di Circe* (Wien, 1765)'; and Riedlbauer, *Die Opern von Tommaso Trajetta*.

52.   Whether anguish finds expression in childlike emotion, sovereign surrender or violent passion, we invariably find a foretaste of the spirit of the later Mozart. Particularly striking is the austere use of the key of G minor.

53.   Castor's aria from act one, scene six of *I Tindaridi* contains a remarkable pre-echo of Mozart's violin sonata K301:

The entry of the voice in this aria recalls *Die Entführung aus dem Serail*:

melody, as is clear, for example, from the mandolin canzonetta from his serenata *Le feste d'Imeneo* of 1760,[54] a piece of considerable interest in the specific context of Mozart. This leads us on to another characteristic feature of this period that was to emerge even more clearly in later years, namely, the growing influence of *opera buffa* on *opera seria*. It is a feature found not only in the aforementioned folklike songs but, above all, in a suppler handling of the vocal line and especially of the orchestra, where there is now a growing number of brief but vivid motifs, and, finally, in the more elaborate ensembles which in Jommelli's *opere serie* already aspire to more individual characterization.

The most profound influence, however, was that left by the youngest of the present group of composers, Francesco di Majo, even though here, too, the influence was musical rather than dramatic.[55] Majo never left Italy and so he never moved as far away from Italian taste as did Jommelli, for example. As a composer, he stood on the cusp between two different traditions: on the one hand, Jommelli's seriousness of dramatic purpose is still clearly evident in his works, while on the other we already find that more modern, hedonistic spirit for which Jommelli had had no time, and it is striking that it is very much this aspect of Majo's art that left the greatest impression on Mozart, with the two composers revealing marked affinities[56] in their expression of tender-hearted emotion in all its varied gradations. Indeed, the similarities even extend to points of detail such as the soft-edged melodic lines shot through with chromatic features, the slippery harmonies based on chords of a sixth and so on. A few examples from *Astrea placata*, *Ipermestra* and *Eumene*[57] may serve to illustrate this point:

54. Goldschmidt, *Tommaso Traëtta: Ausgewählte Werke*, 99ff. Pieces such as the middle section of the present canzonetta or the passage reproduced on 138ff. come very close to the corresponding numbers from Piccinni's *La buona figliuola*.
55. See Abert, 'Joh. Christian Bachs italienische Opern und ihr Einfluß auf Mozart'. ◆ Also see Carli Ballola, 'Mozart e l'opera seria di Jommelli, De Majo e Traetta', and DiChiera, 'The Life and Operas of Gian Francesco de Majo'.
56. Kretzschmar, 'Mozart in der Geschichte der Oper', ii.262. Another possible intermediary, of course, is Johann Christian Bach, who, like Mozart, was profoundly influenced by Majo, with all three composers revealing the same tendency to end individual phrases and periods with a dreamily ascending fifth; see the beginning and imperfect cadence of the main theme (a and b) from Linceo's aria from act one, scene nine of *Ipermestra*:

57. *Astrea placata* received its first performance in 1760. Among the participants listed in the score are Manzuoli and the tenor Anton Raaff, and it may have been one or both of these singers who introduced Mozart to the work. *Ipermestra* dates from 1768, *Eumene* from 1771. Only the opening act of *Eumene* is by Majo: the second is by Giacomo Insanguine, the third by Pasquale Errichelli. The fourth example is remarkably reminiscent of the middle section of Orpheus's 'Chiamo il mio ben così' from the first act of Gluck's opera. Also worth mentioning here is the theme of Eumene's aria from act one, scene nine of the same work, a theme of the sort often favoured by Johann Christian Bach and later destined to acquire classic status in the hands of Gluck and Mozart. It is also found sporadically, of course, in works by some of the older Neapolitan composers, notably in Arbace's aria from act two, scene one of Perez's *Artaserse*:

The same thematic type can then be traced through Majo, Bach and Gluck's *Orfeo ed Euridice* and both *Iphigénie en Aulide* and *Iphigénie en Tauride* to the Countess in *Le nozze di Figaro*.

Astrea, Overture, middle movement

Astrea I 7, Giove's Aria

Ipermestra I 6, Plistene's Aria

Non è   la mia spe - ran - za,   la mia spe-

ran - za   lu - ce del ciel se - re - no,

lu - ce del ciel se - re - no   im - pon - ga vi - ta o

mor - te,   im - pon - ga o vi - ta o mor - te, leg - ge per me sa - rà.

But Majo also did more than any other member of Hasse's school to break a lance for the more modern kind of orchestral writing associated with *opera buffa*. With him, there is a pronounced tendency for the instruments no longer to double the vocal line or to provide only homophonic or contrapuntal accompaniment but for them to take a brief yet vivid orchestral motif and subject it to various transformations in keeping with the changing mood of the piece. Examples from *Ricimero* (1759) and *Ipermestra* may serve to illustrate the affinity not only with *opera buffa* but also with Mozart:[58]

Example 47e is also instructive for the light that it sheds on the remarkably tortuous, subjective language of many of Majo's figures. On the level of rhythm, Majo also reveals a far more striking predilection for the use of syncopation at moments of agitation than we find in any of his contemporaries. Here, too, he comes close to Mozart.[59]

Formally, Majo's operas also herald the dawn of a new era. Although, as a rule, he still prefers the old *da capo* aria *à la* Hasse, he also experiments with two other, more modern forms, one of which foreshortens the *da capo* by as much as half, while the other dispenses altogether with the *B*-section of the older type, accommodating the second quatrain of the text within the second part of the *A*-section and investing it with the harmonic features of the former middle section; the *A*-section is then repeated, generally in modified form. The result was a far more compact ternary structure that is still found in works such as *Idomeneo*, for example.[60] But the internal structure of these arias is also affected by the new spirit: as early as *Ricimero* (1759) we already find opening ritornellos made up of two contrastive themes clearly separated by an imperfect cadence (act one, scenes eight and ten; and act three, scene five). Although Majo was not responsible for this innovation, he was still fond of using it, a point he shares with Johann Christian Bach, in whose sonatas

---

58. Example a) is taken from Ermelinda's accompanied recitative in act one, scene ten of *Ricimero*. The other four examples are from *Ipermestra*: b) comes from Ipermestra's aria in act one, scene three; c) comes from Plistene's aria in act two, scene seven; and Examples d) and e) are taken from the duet in act two, scene ten.

59. See also Artemisia's aria from act one, scene nine of *Eumene*:

cor fan — no i mo — — ti del mio_____ cor

60. The order is now as follows: main section (1st quatrain) ending on dominant, subsidiary section (2nd quatrain) designed either as development section or in contrast to the previous section, with return to home key, followed by repeat of main section in home key; see act two, scenes seven and eight of Majo's *Ipermestra*.

we have already observed a similar procedure – living proof of the vital interaction at this time between vocal and instrumental forms. (A further example of this interaction is the way in which the second subjects are sometimes entrusted to solo instruments, thereby recalling the world of the concerto.[61])

In his coloratura writing, Majo adopts an older, more measured approach than Bach, but in his instrumentation, in spite of some genuinely dramatic traits,[62] we find him making concessions to the newer, more undramatic spirit, especially in arias with concertante instruments in which the virtuosic writing for these latter virtually monopolizes the listener's attention.[63]

The *opere serie* of Baldassare Galuppi (1706–85)[64] provide a similar picture to those of Majo, except that their underlying tone is less redolent of the Age of Sensibility. He, too, follows older models in terms of both form and content, but, chronologically speaking, he is even more advanced than Majo in the bithematicism of his ritornellos, notably in *Demofoonte*, a work which, as we know, was familiar to Mozart.

Even in this dramatic period, the sinfonias are remarkably antiquated in tone. Ever since Vinci's day the old Scarlattian model had been dominated by tinkling harmonies of highbrow aspirations but in curious contrast to the dramatic aims of Hasse, Jommelli and others. The opening section begins mostly with triadic themes often built up over noisily repeated notes in the bass:

Hasse, *Senocrita*

Terradellas, *Merope*[65]

Jommelli, *Ricimero*

61. In act three, scene five of *Ricimero*, the second subject is entrusted to solo violas.
62. Under this heading come the viola parts, which were also to be of importance to Mozart. Other dramatic features include the combination of strings, mandolins and flutes in act one, scene one of *Astrea placata*, and in Ipermestra's cavatina ('Ah non mi dir') from act three, scene six of *Ipermestra*, the muted strings and oboes, together with *voci umane* notated in the bass clef – presumably another oboe-like instrument: see Sachs, *Real-Lexikon der Musikinstrumente*, 418a.
63. Typical of this development is the aria 'Sol di virtù verace' from act two, scene six of *Astrea placata*, in which even the ritornello is a virtuoso showpiece for bassoon. No less showy are the four concertante trumpets in act two, scene twelve of *Arianna* ('Per trionfar pugnando').
64. Alfred Wotquenne, *Baldassare Galuppi*; and Piovano, 'Baldassare Galuppi: note bio-bibliografiche'. ◆ Also see Wiesend, *Studien zur opera seria von Baldassare Galuppi: Werksituation und Überlieferung – Form und Satztechnik Inhaltsdarstellung, mit einer Biographie und einem Quellenverzeichnis der Opern*.
65. Identical with the sinfonia from *Artaserse*.

Majo, *Ipermestra*[66]

This is a musical idiom that we can continue to trace through to Mozart not only in operatic sinfonias, but also in the sinfonia concertante and sonata. The better composers, foremost among whom was Jommelli,[67] tried to offset it with more individual second subjects (often in the minor), but even here the development sections rarely progress beyond meaningless note-spinning. The best movements are the andantes, which are either cast in *Liedform* (often with wind solos) or are developed out of a brief but memorable motif, while the binary final movements, mostly in triple time, generally breathe a spirit of superficial, noisy revelry. Only gradually – and only after it had broken free from opera – did the sinfonia recover from its decline in Italy and, more especially, in Germany.

The works of Jommelli and Traetta failed to survive their creators. At almost the same time that Gluck completed the journey which they themselves had started and staged his *Orfeo* in Vienna, thereby creating a type of music drama that was new from both a musical and a poetic point of view, the Italian nation once again grew weary of drama in opera. It was at this time that Jommelli's final operas all proved to be failures in Naples. Composers, too, saw which way the wind was blowing, not least because there was, after all, space for the just and the unjust alike in the many mansions of Metastasio's house.

There is little point in asking what would have become of Mozart's Italian operatic style if it could have ripened in the sun of Jommelli and Traetta. The circumstances in which he found himself, to say nothing of his father's constant concern to appeal to the widest possible audiences, drove him from the outset into the modernist camp and the arms of the 'neo-Neapolitans',[68] in whose art the spirit of Vinci and his colleagues was currently enjoying a glorious revival. Its principal characteristic was still the preponderance of music over drama and of the sensual over the intellectual or spiritual. Yet even these composers were still capable of scoring the odd success in terms of tender-hearted, trifling charm thanks to their pronounced melodic gifts; but whenever the music was meant to draw blood in the Gluckian sense, the older seriousness of dramatic purpose was replaced by mere rhetoric, seeking to compensate for the lack of genuine emotion by means of all manner of high-flown phrases, wide-ranging intervals, interminable runs and so on. It goes without saying that the bane of coloratura that not even the school of Hasse had been able to root out now grew still more rankly than before. But even the *secco* recitative suffered a dramatic decline, becoming formulaic and lifeless and often completely losing touch with the course of the drama. In much the same way, the glorious choral writing of an earlier age survived only in isolated instances. Admittedly, not even this school was incapable of producing grandiose effects,

66. This type is often encountered in Mozart's works and may also be found at an earlier date in Hasse's sinfonia to *Il re pastore*.
67. See Abert, *Niccolò Jommelli als Opernkomponist*, 151. Second subjects in the minor are also found in Perez's *Il Siroe* of 1740 and in Terradellas's *Didone abbandonata* [of 1750].
68. Kretzschmar, 'Mozart in der Geschichte der Oper', ii.262.

especially in the arias, most of which now subscribe to the second of the forms described above. And these composers also succeeded in creating numbers of an inspired melodic vein, with the musical ideas worked out with consummate skill. The orchestra, especially, became not only more varied but also more adaptable than in the previous period, although here, too, there is a noticeable tendency to indulge in outward showiness, with arias with virtuosically handled obbligato instruments among the particular favourites of these composers.

The leading member of this school, and the one who was also to exert the greatest influence on Mozart's operatic writing, was Johann Christian Bach.[69] Bach's whole view of life and art predisposed him to join the neo-Neapolitan camp,[70] with the result that he also became one of its principal spokesmen. Formally speaking, he had in fact begun his career with *Catone in Utica*[71] as a loyal follower of Hasse, retaining the old form of the *da capo* aria in every last detail.[72] Only with *Alessandro nell'Indie* (1762) and its successors do the two more modern forms start to penetrate his works, initially in only isolated ways but later more comprehensively, yet at no point did Bach decide in favour of one of them to the exclusion of the other. In both *Temistocle* and *Lucio Silla*, he still uses the two forms interchangeably and in some cases has no hesitation in going back to the older type as exemplified by Hasse. But the arias with a foreshortened *da capo* incorporate a new feature inasmuch as the repeat he does not mechanically omit the first part of the *A*-section but begins with the main theme and only subsequently curtails the musical argument, so that the *da capo* now offers a concise overview of the aria's main ideas. In his early operas, Mozart, too, soon returned to this type of aria, a type of far greater psychological subtlety than any of its alternatives.

In terms of their internal structure, Bach clearly followed Majo's example, developing into a master of stark contrasts and thereby leaving the profoundest mark on his contemporaries and successors, most notably, of course, on Mozart himself. From *Alessandro* onwards, there is rarely an instance in his sinfonia allegros or in the great opening ritornellos of his arias where we do not find sharply contrasting second subjects[73] that are generally prepared by means of emphatic half-cadences. That they tend in the earlier works to recall the solo or concertino in character suggests the influence of the instrumental concerto.

Expressively, too, Bach is very much a neo-Neapolitan in his earliest operas: contrived and insistent in his high-flown emotion, self-indulgent in his use of coloratura but, conversely, generally sincere and felicitous in matters of sweetness and tenderness. He is far less reserved than the more austere Majo in terms of melodiousness and sensual beauty and there are times here when he achieves genuinely bewitching effects of a kind equalled by none of his contemporaries. Alongside such examples of Italianate euphony, however, we also find a remarkably rapt, sometimes even dreamy tone – perhaps the only aspect of these operas that points to their creator's German provenance. Here we already find ourselves at the very portals of Mozart's own art. Listen, for example, to the theme of the Andante from the sinfonia to *Catone in Utica*:

69. See Abert, 'Joh. Christian Bachs italienische Opern'. ◆ More recently, see Downes, 'The Operas of Johann Christian Bach as a Reflection of the Dominant Trends in Opera Seria, 1750–1780', and Warburton, 'A Study of Johann Christian Bach's Operas'.
70. This is stressed, quite rightly, by Johann Friedrich Reichardt in his *Musikalischer Almanach*.
71. Although Gerber claims that this work was written in 1758, Schwarz is almost certainly right to dispute this: Max Schwarz, 'Johann Christian Bach', 410–11. At all events, the work was first staged in Naples in 1761.
72. Burney, in his *General History of Music* (iv.483), must therefore stand corrected.
73. Actual 'cantabile' themes are not found until Bach moved to London.

Or take the middle section of the aria 'Non ti minaccio' from act one, scene two of the same opera:

Or here, finally, is the almost Romantic main melody from the duet 'Se mai turbo' from act one, scene nine of *Alessandro*:

Elsewhere, too, the listener is reminded at virtually every turn of Mozart's range of expression. Here, for instance, is an excerpt from the aria 'Digli che son fedele' from act two, scene nine of *Alessandro*. Note the scalar passages and the interval of a fourth in the melodic line, an interval found even more frequently in Bach than in Majo:

Much the same is true of the aria 'Va ritorna' from act two, scene two of *Catone*:

   Another of Bach's characteristic features to be found in these early operas is his predilection for pieces with obbligato instruments, generally virtuosic writing for winds, especially oboes and bassoons. As for his treatment of the *secco* recitatives, by contrast, it is significant that they are not even notated in his two Neapolitan operas.

   Bach's London operas take up and develop the features already found in Naples. Modern forms of the aria become more prevalent without ever entirely displacing the older type, while other new forms that were added later include the rondo, first found in *Carattaco* (1767), the large-scale ensemble inspired by the *buffa* finale and first found in *Temistocle* (1772), where it remains more of a purely musical number than a dramatic one, and, finally, choruses of an often Gluckian character.[74] But the orchestral contribution, too, is expanded, notably through the addition of clarinets

74.   The chorus 'Fuor di quest'urne dolenti' from act one, scene seven of *Lucio Silla* is motivically and instrumentally linked to the preceding *recitativo accompagnato*. Textually and musically it recalls the opening chorus from *Orfeo*, a work that Bach arranged for performances in London in 1770 and Naples in 1774, on both occasions adding new pieces of his own; see Engländer, 'Zu den Münchener Orfeo-Aufführungen 1773 und 1775'.

in *Orione* (1763), a use with which Mozart was evidently already familiar, therefore, before his first visit to Mannheim. Bach was presumably introduced to them while passing through Paris.[75] The exceptional nature of these instruments during the early years of their existence both in *opera seria* and *opera buffa* is clear from their use in creating particular moods, notably in the *ombra* aria in act one, scene four of *Lucio Silla*, although they are also found, of course, alongside the other wind instruments in the tuttis in fast movements, notably in the aria 'Ah si resta' from act three, scene five of *Temistocle* and in the first section of the overture to *Lucio Silla*. But all the concertante winds are handled with consummate virtuosity, rivalling the vocal line in its coloratura extravagances and occasionally even revelling in free cadenzas in the opening ritornellos, as in act one, scene ten, and act two, scene five of *Temistocle*.

In one respect, Bach stands head and shoulders above the other neo-Neapolitans, and that is in his orchestral writing, perhaps the only characteristic that he inherited from the school of his great father. He is not content simply to allow the instruments to double the vocal melody or to settle for primitive harmonic accompaniments but frequently allows the instruments to go their own way and even within the orchestral writing strives to provide independent parts for the inner voices, either through the use of imitation or in the tone-painterly way in which Jommelli, for example, had treated his second violins.[76]

The thematic contrasts within the aria ritornellos became more marked in London to the extent that the second subjects, previously more notable for their figural writing, now became genuinely cantabile in character. But they had also grown considerably longer, with the result that many of them now resemble the subject-groups of Bach's sonatas or even the opening tuttis of his concertos. Yet even here the impression that one gains is less of a music dramatist attempting to reduce the content of his arias to the lowest common denominator in terms of their antithetical moods than of a south German writer of symphonies concerned with a subject-group consisting of a first subject and a contrastive second subject. Here, too, the musician prevails over the dramatist. As an example of the way in which these cantabile themes are introduced and handled, the reader is referred to the following ritornello from the aforementioned aria from *Zanaida*:

75. In the aria 'Se spiego le prime vele' from *Zanaida* they appear together with taille, oboe and horn, while in both *Temistocle* and *Lucio Silla* we find instruments described as 'clarinetti d'amore' and invariably notated in F major, two in the violin clef and one in the bass clef.
76. Abert, *Niccolò Jommelli als Opernkomponist*, 143 and 159–60.

It was as a melodist that Bach really came into his own in London, and there is no doubt that a large number of his themes and melodic turns of phrase continued to exert a subliminal influence on Mozart even during the latter's years of maturity. A mere handful of examples must suffice:

Orione, aria 'Se volete eterni dei'

Mi - su - ra - te i gior - ni mie - i   cogl' af - fet - ti

Adriano, aria 'Son sventurato'

b) Clar.

Bn.

Carattaco, aria 'Sposa raffrena'

da   pa - ce al tuo do-

lo - re   l'af - - fan - no   del mio   co - re

Temistocle II ɪɪ, quartet

ah stel - le incle - men - ti,   se va - ghe non sie - te   a

me   di - vi - de - te_____   quest' al - ma,   quest'

Lucio Silla, aria III 5

al - ma   del   sen

But Bach developed a particular type of movement in London that was based on Italian models and that had already been foreshadowed in *Catone* and *Alessandro*. It is a type that can be traced through to Mozart and consists of a slow movement in E flat major generally described as a largo,[77] its beautifully sinuous, often bewitching melodies used to express dark and infatuated yearning or even muted fear. They are rêveries filled with a sense of sweet nostalgia and an emphatically German tone of a kind achieved by neither Majo nor Piccinni, the two composers closest to Bach in terms of affinity of outlook. One might even suspect the influence of Handel, except that there is no trace in the far more tender-hearted Bach of any sense of cruelty or misanthropy. This type of aria culminates in Ilia's 'Se il padre perdei' from act two, scene two of *Idomeneo* and in the Countess's cavatina from *Le nozze di Figaro*.

We have already had more than one occasion to note Johann Christian Bach's influence on Mozart. In fact, the younger composer remained committed to Bach's vocal style throughout his life, even after he had inwardly outgrown the fashionable ways of this most *galant* of all Bach's sons.

77. For the older Neapolitan composers, E flat major was the key of dark, solemn emotion and was used especially in invoking deities and in scenes involving ghosts; see Abert, *Niccòlo Jommelli als Opernkomponist*, 179.

In short, the spirit of neo-Neapolitan opera was already second nature to Mozart even before he came into direct contact with its Italian exponents.[78] Nor was it long before he met one of its oldest Milanese representatives, Giovanni Battista Lampugnani (1708–88). To the extent that his few surviving operas allow us to pass judgement at all, the picture is much the same as with Johann Christian Bach, except that Lampugnani's melodic writing is less inventive and his orchestration less brilliant than Bach's. And Bach is decidedly more modern in his use of contrastive themes. On the other hand, both composers share certain features with a third composer, Gaetano Latilla (1711–1788), whose operas reveal even greater imagination but, at the same time, a greater dramaturgical carelessness than those of Lampugnani, tending to bring out the demagogue on the operatic stage. In the works of all three composers, there is the same sense of exalted emotion in their serious arias and the same endless displays of coloratura roulades – frequently and indifferently on words such as 'la', 'siete' and so on. Latilla's finest opera was *Antigono* (1775) and is thoroughly modern in its lavish instrumentation and in the way in which its arias are structured. (It even includes a rondò.) As such, it is an ideal and particularly effective example of this whole trend. Of far greater importance for Mozart, however, was Niccolò Piccinni (1728–1800), who was later to be an opponent and, finally, a supporter of Gluck. Piccinni's forte lay in *opera buffa*, of course, but it was precisely this that made him such an important innovator in the field of *opera seria*, too. We have already seen how, in Majo's case, individual stylistic features found their way from *buffa* to *seria*, but Piccinni pursued this goal with far greater seriousness of purpose than any of his predecessors or rivals. This is especially true of his handling of the orchestra. From *Ciro riconosciuto* (1759) onwards, the accompaniments of whole arias tend to be based increasingly on brief but graphic orchestral motifs reminiscent of *opera buffa* that could be adapted in the most varied ways in keeping with the psychological vagaries of the drama. In turn, the relationship between voice and orchestra began to shift in the direction of the *buffa* model: in some cases the orchestra begins an interlude, in the course of which the voice enters completely unexpectedly, while in others the two forge poetically highly effective motivic links extending over entire scenes as in act two, scene nine of *Demetrio*, act three, scene seven of *Artaserse* and especially act two, scene twelve of *Alessandro*, where Piccinni reveals a subtle poetic intentionality in repeating a motif from act two, scene five). This is entirely typical of the thoughtful approach of a composer who, although no out-and-out dramatist, achieved his principal effects by means of subtle details of this kind.[79] But his extraordinarily flexible handling of his orchestra, with its background in the *buffa* tradition, also allowed him to make advances in other areas, too. From *Zenobia* (1756) onwards, we find all manner of features in his orchestra that modern writers have hitherto been inclined to ascribe to the influence of the Mannheim school[80] and that include the 'sigh', the *Vögelchen* and the *Walze* or 'roller'. The crescendo, too,[81] is found here with striking frequency and, as in works of the Mannheim school, is combined with sequentially rising motifs. Particularly memorable effects of this kind, including ones over sustained notes, could have been heard by Mozart in *Cesare e Cleopatra* in 1770. It is highly unlikely that Piccinni owed all these characteristics to Stamitz, as they are already found in his earliest works, while his entire oeuvre shows us that, of all the Italian composers, he was the one with the least time and understanding for purely instrumental music.

---

78. ◆ In addition to performances of Italian opera heard by Mozart on the Grand Tour and in Vienna in 1768, he was also acquainted with the *opera seria* style from church and theatrical music produced in Salzburg during the 1750s and 1760s; see Eisen, 'Mozart e l'Italia: Il ruolo di Salisburgo'.
79. ◆ See Strohm, *Die italienische Oper im 18. Jahrhundert*, and Michael Robinson, *Naples and Neapolitan Opera*.
80. See Riemann, *Sinfonien der Pfalzbayerischen Schule: Teil I*.
81. From *Zenobia* onwards, Piccinni always describes it as an 'accrescendo'.

In short, he must have drawn his inspiration from other sources. In the case of the crescendo, the source of inspiration was undoubtedly Jommelli,[82] whereas all the other features can be shown to derive from Italian opera, especially comic opera. What Stamitz owed to Italian opera deserves to be the object of a special study, which would at least serve to prove what is already likely on internal grounds, namely, that the great stylistic change between the older and newer members of the Classical school was due not to a single composer and his school but to far more wide-ranging developments. This does not, of course, affect the great and characteristic contribution that Stamitz made to all this and in no way belittles his importance for German instrumental music.[83]

The concertante style of which Piccinni, like all his contemporaries, was particularly fond now became lighter and more elastic in his hands. Solo winds are often accompanied by broken chords on the strings in an entirely modern manner but also occur with expressive and independent motifs, as in the aria 'Bell'alma se ancora' from act three, scene thirteen of *Ciro*:

82. Abert, *Niccolò Jommelli als Opernkomponist*, 446.
83. ◆ Concerning Stamitz, see Eugene K. Wolf, *The Symphonies of Johann Stamitz*.

But Piccinni also handles questions of musical form with the remarkable freedom of a born composer of *opere buffe*. He is particularly fond of the brief songlike cavatina, and from *Cesare e Cleopatra* onwards we also find the rondo in addition to the traditional three types of aria.[84] Fast arias are often preceded by slow introductions whose musical ideas occasionally recur in the following Allegro in long note-values. And Bach's influence is discernible in the way in which the themes of his ritornellos grow increasingly contrastive in the course of his development.

There is, of course, even less trace of heroic force in Piccinni's writing than in any of the other composers already discussed. As man and artist, he was placid, thoughtful and even dreamy by nature. His serious operas have none of the sensual charm of Bach's and are occasionally monotonous and over-indebted to the *empfindsam* tradition. At the same time, however, the essential tender-heartedness typical of the neo-Neapolitan composers not infrequently acquires a highly sympathetic, intimate and heartfelt aspect. Here, too, his skill as a *buffa* composer worked to the advantage of his *opere serie*, with the subtly stylized folk tone of a naïve or elegiac character typical of *opere buffe* recurring throughout the whole of Egle's part in *Zenobia*. But an equally instructive example is the aria 'Deh lasciami' from act two, scene four of *Caio Mario*, with the theme ending on a note of heartfelt yearning on the third:

This affecting, heartfelt tone is found in Piccinni's operas each time he wants to express yearning or urgent entreaty, as in the aria 'Mi scacci sdegnato' from act two, scene two of *Artaserse*, a theme later taken over by Mozart:[85]

Sometimes it even adds a touch of nobility to the coloratura writing, as in the aria 'Dovrei, ma no' from act one, scene two of *Didone*:

---

84.   The older form as exemplified by Hasse survived longest in the great bravura arias. Even as late as act three, scene eight of *Ciro* (cf. act three, scene one of *Zenobia*) we still find a number of individual pieces written in a remarkably strict style that recalls no one so much as Piccinni's teacher, Leonardo Leo.

85.   Later taken over into 'Care pupille' in act one, scene six of *Cesare e Cleopatra*.

The Romantic characteristics often displayed by artists of this kind are also found in the case of Piccinni, and none of his contemporaries was as adept as he at exploiting the sudden shifts between major and minor, a feature which the example of Domenico Scarlatti reveals to have been common to all Italian composers at this time. In scenes such as those in which dark clouds suddenly obscure a picture of radiant sunlight or, conversely, a ray of brilliant sunlight pierces the gloomy mists, we see what a sensitive tone-poet Piccinni could be and how, under the weight of the poetic idea, he sometimes even departs from the beaten track.[86] And in some of his arias in minor tonalities, he tends to wallow in the mood of gloom to such an extent that the major tonality is barely explored.[87]

These are all characteristics that were bound to find a lively echo in the young Mozart's mind, and we do indeed find palpable traces of Piccinni's style in a number of his arias.

Far more rough-hewn as a character was Cherubini's later teacher, Giuseppe Sarti (1729–1802), a composer whose oeuvre was, of course, less important for Mozart's early operas than for *Idomeneo* and *La clemenza di Tito*. None the less, his works show clearly that it was still possible to strike dramatic sparks from neo-Neapolitan opera, at least if the composer in question was capable not only of sentimentality and flirtatiousness but also of a more serious and virile tone. As a result, Sarti became the most important representative of this school, with Heinse not only numbering him among the older Neapolitans but placing his *Giulio Sabino* on an even higher plane than Gluck's *Iphigénie en Tauride*,[88] an assessment due, no doubt, to Sarti's great dramatic *accompagnato* scenes in which he towers head and shoulders above all the other neo-Neapolitan composers. But the form and style of his arias, and his virtuosic handling of the orchestra all point the way ahead, just as the manner in which many of his arias are more concerned with superficial effectiveness than with dramatic seriousness, together with his tendency to indulge in excessive coloratura, indicates that the self-denial of the older generation was now a thing of the past.[89] In spite of this, Sarti was unique among his contemporaries in being able to retain a vital understanding not only of the style of Metastasio's art but also of the greatness of the old Renaissance ideal, an ideal to which he sought to do justice with all the sophisticated means at his disposal in his finest opera, *Giulio Sabino* (1781). He was also successful in extending its outward form, privileging the multi-sectional aria and especially the rondo alongside what were then the most modern forms of aria and doing so, once again, on the model of *opera buffa*. Here, moreover, we regularly find a gavotte-like, often rather monotonous type of melody demonstrably influenced by the French composers of the period and later employed in the allegro section of Sesto's rondo

---

86. In the duet in act two, scene four from *Zenobia*, Tiridate answers – surprisingly – with a new theme in the minor, while in act two, scene ten of *Catone*, the trio that had begun in the major ends in the minor.

87. Cf. act two, scenes six and ten of *Demetrio* and act two, scene nine of *Antigono*.

88. Heinse, *Hildegard von Hohenthal*, v.251 and vi.11. ◆ Also see Wiesmann, 'Giuseppe Sartis *Giulio Sabio* als representative Opera seria der Haydn-Zeit'.

89. Entirely typical of this trend is the final scene of *Giulio Sabino*, from act three, scene four onwards, in which an extremely dramatic solo *scena* is followed by an extraordinarily banal duet. ◆ Further, see Lippmann, 'Tendenzen der italienischen Opera seria am Ende des 18. Jahrhunderts'.

'Deh, per questo istante solo' from act two of Mozart's *La clemenza di Tito*. Note also the rondo 'Bella dea' from Sarti's *Alessandro e Timoteo* of 1782:[90]

Sarti's operas contain few examples of ensembles and choruses, the principal exception being *Alessandro e Timoteo*, arguably the most formally varied work of the whole school[91] and one written, significantly, for the Francophile court at Parma. On the other hand, his orchestration is extremely flexible and superficially brilliant.[92] Symptomatic of this whole approach is the fact that in the aria 'Men bramosa' from act two, scene nine of *Ciro* – a thoroughly old-fashioned piece in every way – he includes a harpsichord solo of a kind extremely rare in opera at this time. The orchestra makes a positive contribution to the accompanied recitatives, sometimes even including brief independent movements. Here, too, of course, we find a peculiarity of Sarti's that recurs in many of his arias and again recalls the young Mozart, namely, a tendency to be profligate in his use of motifs: Sarti also reveals an unusual wealth of ideas, some of which are popular in tone, as in scenes five and eleven from act two of *Giulio Sabino* (on both occasions making a mockery of the words):

90. Although not described as a rondo, this particular type of aria is also found in other works by Sarti, notably in act one, scene thirteen of *Cleomene* (1788) and act one, scene four of *Ifigenia in Aulide* (1777).

91. In addition to large-scale *recitativi accompagnati*, it also includes numerous ballets, ensembles and choruses, with the ballets for the Furies clearly influenced by Gluck.

92. Here, too, *Alessandro* is especially remarkable, its orchestra – which Sarti handles with virtuosic skill – including not only clarinets (also found in *Ifigenia* in 1777) but also *corni piccoli*, english horn and *serpentone*. Occasionally Sarti even writes for two orchestras.

On other occasions, by contrast, the tone is more artful and often surprisingly modern, notably in scenes eleven and five from act two of *Cleomene* and act two, scene five of *Ifigenia*:

In all three examples, the affinities with Mozart are plain to see.

Another composer who belongs under this heading is Pietro Alessandro Guglielmi (1728–1804).[93] He, too, was particularly successful as a composer of *opere buffe* and he, too, introduced *buffa* elements into the world of *opera seria* in the form of an increased dependency on folk-like dance and march tunes, brief but animated orchestral motifs and a fondness for generating tension by introducing brief recitatives into his arias. Here he was much helped by his idiosyncratic and lively rhythms, with syncopated motifs such as the following, by no means an exception:

. And rondo form based on French melodies of a kind already found in the case of Sarti is a favourite of his not only in his arias but also – and this is a further sign of the influence of *opera buffa* – in ensembles which, like choruses, become increasingly common in Italian *opere serie* from the time of Piccinni's defection to the *Gluckiste* camp.[94] But Guglielmi also reveals his neo-Neapolitan allegiances in the undramatic and often monotonous tone of many of his serious arias,[95] in the showy insistence of his coloratura displays and in his dazzling orchestral textures with his many concertante arias and striving for novel tonal effects.[96] He shares with Sarti the tendency to introduce as many contrasting ideas as possible into his ritornellos and, indeed, into his arias in general, thereby taking one of Johann Christian Bach's characteristics to its logical extreme. Formally speaking, his arias alternate between the older and newer types;[97] from *opera buffa* comes the frequent habit of prefacing a fast section with a slow one. In spite of all his

93.   Bustico, *Pier Alessandro Guglielmi: Appunti biografici*, and, above all, Piovano, 'Elenco cronologico delle opere (1757–1802) di Pietro Guglielmi (1727–1804)'. ◆ More recently, see Mary Hunter, 'Some representations of *opera seria* in *opera buffa*' and Lipton, 'The opere buffe of Pietro Alessandro Guglielmi in Vienna and Eszterháza'.

94.   Cf. *Felicità d'Anfrisio* (1783) and *Enea e Lavinia* (1785). ◆ *Felicità d'Anfrisio* is not an opera, but an unstaged 'componimento dramatico' or cantata.

95.   The so-called *Bettelkadenz* is particularly common in Guglielmi's works.

96.   Under this heading come the cello solo and *voce umana* in *Enea e Lavinia*, the harp and four horns in *Felicità* and, in *Laocoonte* (1787), the division of the players into a *banda* comprising oboes, clarinets and horns and an orchestra. The clarinets are used to great effect from *La Semiramide riconosciuta* (1776) onwards.

97.   Especially in *La Semiramide riconosciuta*.

weaknesses, Guglielmi none the less succeeded in creating scenes of genuine dramatic weight, notably in the brilliant orchestral description of the burning of the temple in *Enea*, the freely structured oracle scene in *Laocoonte*[98] and the conjuration of Ajax's ghost in *Ifigenia in Tauride*.

Although the overtures of all these composers still largely recall the superficiality of the earlier period, they also show traces of the rejuvenating influence that the now more vigorous sinfonia concertante had begun to exert on the original form. As in *opera buffa*, we already find single-movement sinfonias such as the one that launches Guglielmi's *Laocoonte*. The French form becomes more common, and in Neapolitan opera there are attempts – inspired by French *opéras comiques* of the period – to forge closer links between the three separate movements in order to ensure that the third movement constitutes a thematic continuation of the first, with the Andante appearing as more of an episode in consequence. The most loosely structured and regressive episodes are still the development sections, where it is by no means uncommon to find new themes introduced.[99] In the subject-groups, by contrast, the second subjects are now in clear contrast to the first subjects, most notably in the case of Bach, while Piccinni and Lampugnani continue to vacillate between the older and newer types. But these second subjects are manifestly influenced by the *opera buffa* sinfonia, being remarkably short-winded and, in a way that is reminiscent of the old concertino, generally entrusted to only three instruments, often without a bass and not yet remotely cantabile in character:[100]

98. This is a large-scale, multi-sectional number in the style of a *buffa* finale with rondo-like repeats. The oracle itself speaks, of course, in the usual *accompagnato* manner with sustained chords on the strings, but makes up for this banality with a characteristic motif in the *banda* (horns and bassoons) that also dominates the following scene.

99. Bach, *Temistocle* (1772) and *Lucio Silla* (1775); Piccinni, *Caio Mario* (?1757) and *Il gran Cid* (1766); Latilla, *Antigona* (1753); and Guglielmi, *Ricimero* (1777) and *La Semiramide riconosciuta* [1776].

100. Cf. the second subjects in works by the Viennese symphonists discussed above.

The recapitulations, too, have yet to assume a fixed form, but continue to vacillate between the foreshortened and unforeshortened types, while here, too, there is an occasional tendency to include an entirely new theme as in Piccinni's *Caio Mario* and Bach's *Lucio Silla*. In Sarti's *Giulio Sabino*, finally, we find a stretta, albeit one that fades away at the end in an extended diminuendo.[101]

Whereas the slow movements scarcely changed in terms of their structure and character, the final movements of the sinfonias to Bach's *Lucio Silla* and Sarti's *Ciro*[102] are both cast in the form of a rondo. In *Caio Mario* and *Artaserse*, by contrast, Piccinni simply repeats the opening movement – a remarkable attempt to recall the fact that the sinfonia was originally a single-movement piece.

This, in outline, is the background against which Mozart wrote his *opere serie*. Although we shall still have to examine many more detailed influences, the general nature of these remarks will not be affected by this. Of course, the works that we have been examining do not bear close dramatic scrutiny: they are often ripe for decay, and yet they reveal an idiosyncratic, highly developed style that rendered them capable of grandiose, genuine effects. That it was no easy matter to compete with the Italians, still less to beat them at their own game of *opera seria*, was to be clearly demonstrated by Mozart's example.

---

101. The sinfonia to *Alessandro* is a single-movement piece that leads directly into the opening chorus.
102. In view of the early date of this work (1754), the modern form of this movement is bound to seem odd, and it is extremely likely that the sinfonia was in fact written for a later revival.

10

Early operas and the oratorio
La Betulia liberata

The series of stage works that begins with *Mitridate* and ends with *Il re pastore* again bears traces of Leopold's influence. It was he who showed Mozart the way ahead, his single aim being to help his son find fame and fortune through lasting success in Italy, and, given Leopold's well-known principles, such success could be achieved, he was convinced, only if Mozart aligned himself unconditionally with the camp that now had the whip hand, in other words, the neo-Neapolitans. Wolfgang agreed to this plan all the more willingly in that he had already acquired a thorough taste for this kind of music as a result of his contacts with Johann Christian Bach: from the outset he regarded it as his duty to strive to emulate the most up-to-date and successful opera composers of his day and, if possible, to surpass them. In short, it was neither idealism nor reforming zeal but purely practical considerations that led him to *opera seria*. But readers will understand Mozart's early operas only if they judge them by the standards of the neo-Neapolitans and determine the extent to which Mozart managed to match those standards. Only when this relationship is clear shall we be in a position to say how important these works were for Mozart's own development.[1]

The cast-list of *Mitridate, re di Ponto* K87 is as follows:[2]

Mitridate, re di Ponto e d'altri regni, amante d'Aspasia	Sign. Cav. Gugl. d'Ettore virtuoso di camera (Tenore).
Aspasia, promessa sposa di Mitridate, e già dichiarata regina	Sig. Antonia Bernasconi (Prima Donna. Soprano).
Sifare, figliuolo di Mitridate e di Stratonice, amante d'Aspasia	Sig. Pietro Benedetti, detto Sartorino (Soprano. Primo uomo).
Farnace, primo figliuolo di Mitridate, amante della medesima	Sign. Giuseppe Cicognani (Contralto).
Ismene, figlia del re de' Parti, amante di Farnace	Sign. Anna Francesca Varese (Seconda Donna. Soprano).
Marzio, tribuno Romano, amico di Sign. Farnace	Gasp. Bessano (Tenore).
Arbate, governatore di Ninfea	Sign. Pietro Muschietti (Soprano).[3]

---

1. Earlier writers, including Jahn, were inclined to regard Mozart as the Italians' superior in the field of *opera seria* as elsewhere, but such a view could no longer be sustained once Italian music, previously vilified only on the basis of hearsay, became better known. The way to a better understanding was paved by Friedrich Chrysander in a series of articles on *Mitridate*; see Chrysander, 'Mitridate, italienische Oper von Mozart'; see also Kretzschmar, 'Mozart in der Geschichte der Oper', ii.259–60.

2. See Chrysander, 'Mitridate', and Wyzewa and Saint-Foix, *Wolfgang Amédée Mozart*, i.341–9. Among older studies, see Sonnleithner, 'Über Mozarts Opern aus seiner frühen Jugend'. A copy of the wordbook is lodged in the Berliner Bibliothek [now the Staatsbibliothek zu Berlin].

3. ◆ Concerning the singers at the first performance, see Angermüller, 'Die Sänger der Erstaufführung von Mozarts "Mitridate, Re di Ponto" KV87'.

Before setting off on his campaign against the Romans, Mitridate (the historical King Mithridates of Pontus) has promised to marry Aspasia and has entrusted her to the care of his two sons, Sifare and Farnace. He is falsely reported dead, whereupon Farnace sues for Aspasia's hand, causing her to seek refuge with Sifare, who is already secretly in love with her. The ensuing rivalry between the two brothers is cut short by the return of the king, who brings with him a bride for Farnace in the person of Ismene. Mitridate soon learns of his sons' relations with Aspasia and of Farnace's treacherous dealings with the Romans and decides to kill both them and Aspasia. Aspasia prepares to drink from the poisoned goblet but Sifare dashes it to the ground. Meanwhile, Farnace has been thrown into prison by his father and subsequently released by the Romans. He sees the error of his ways and joins forces with his father and brother. Together they destroy the Roman fleet, but in the course of the battle, Mitridate is fatally wounded. With his dying breath, he entrusts Aspasia to Sifare, while Farnace now agrees to marry Ismene. The opera ends with a quintet in which the surviving characters swear vengeance on Rome's tyrannical rule.

Excluding its overture, the opera comprises twenty-four numbers made up of twenty-two arias, a duet ('Se viver non degg'io') and the final quintet.[4] The autograph score appears to be lost,[5] although several individual numbers have survived in variant versions, attesting to the fact that Mozart was obliged to rewrite several of them, no doubt to satisfy the singers rather than himself. No fewer than four drafts of Mitridate's opening aria, 'Se di lauri il crine adorno', are extant; Aspasia's aria, 'Nel grave tormento', begins in one version, only to break off again in its opening section; and five other numbers were completed before being rejected in favour of later versions.[6]

The libretto is an instructive example of the affinities between the Metastasian tradition and the French writers of the period, with the rhetorical heroism of the text, its complex intrigue and grand historical background all recalling Metastasio, and only the latter's glittering eloquence

---

4. A third-act aria for Aspasia included in the wordbook is missing in its entirety. ◆ Almost certainly this was not set by Mozart – as the family correspondence notes, it was common for the wordbook to include material that served to explain the action but was not composed. In the case of *Mitridate*, several lines of recitative not set by Mozart were included in the wordbook as well as second strophes for the arias 'Quel ribelle', 'Tu, che fedel mi sei' and 'Vado incontro'.

5. According to Waldersee, the autograph score was auctioned by Friedrich Stage of Berlin; it has not been possible to discover the identity of the buyer. In 1890 a Dr H. Watson discovered nine original numbers in Manchester at a bookseller's by the name of Cornish; see his letter to *The Musical Times*, 1 July 1890. These nine numbers included those listed by Jahn (see the next note). Also included among these manuscripts were the original autographs of the keyboard concertos in B flat and A major K238 and K488 that had been owned by Stage and Jean Baptiste André in Berlin. The items listed by André were included by Johann Anton André in his handwritten catalogue. In other words, these pieces formed a self-contained group, and it was presumably only those discovered by Watson that were auctioned. We have little choice but to conclude that the complete autograph manuscript of *Mitridate* is lost [Deiters's note]. ◆ The autograph score of *Mitridate* remains lost; the best surviving source is a manuscript copy, now in the Biblioteca do Palácio nacional da Ajuda, Lisbon (shelfmark 45/III/22–24), that was produced by the Teatro Regio Ducal, Milan, in 1771.

6. They are as follows: Aspasia's aria 'Al destin che la minaccia' in G major, worked out in detail, with a good deal of passage-work, fairly stilted; Ismene's aria 'In faccia all'oggetto' in B flat major, with an allegretto middle section in G minor, also in 3/4 time, extremely attractive, without being in any way distinguished; Sifare's aria 'Lungi da te, mio bene' in D major, with a long and sustained, if uninspired, cantilena; it breaks off in the triple-time middle section in G major; the duet in E flat major elaborated in much greater detail, adagio and allegro both repeated. Many passages in thirds but, on the whole, somewhat stilted; Mitridate's aria 'Vado incontro al fato estremo' in F major, proud and powerful in its expression, with harmonic writing that is unusually bold and striking. Perhaps this is why the singer rejected it: the aria that replaced it is in no way exceptional in this respect. The information given by Köchel on the basis of André's catalogue must relate to this same material, in spite of a discrepancy over the final number. It has not been possible to establish who was responsible for this error. Nothing is known about the present whereabouts of the autograph manuscripts of these numbers [Deiters's note]. ◆ Mozart's extant drafts for *Mitridate* are now housed in the Bibliothèque nationale, Paris (shelfmark MS 244). They include versions of the arias 'Al destin che la minaccia', 'In faccia all'oggetto', 'Lungi da te, mio bene', 'Nel grave tormento', 'Son reo', 'Vado incontro al fato estremo', 'Se di lauri il crine adorno', the duet 'Se viver non degg'io', the recitative 'Respira alfin' and the beginning of an orchestral ritornello to an aria for Sifare. The version of 'Vado incontro' found in most editions of the opera, including the NMA, is not by Mozart: apparently d'Ettore managed at the last minute to substitute the version from Gasparini's 1767 setting of the text; see Peiretti, '"Vado incontro al fato estremo": Eine bisher fälschlich Mozart zugeschriebene Arie'. Further, see Wignall, 'The Genesis of 'Se di lauri''.

missing. Even so, the libretto is one of the better examples of its kind: skilfully constructed, it would have provided opportunities for genuine dramatic effects, if only its composer had not been a fourteen-year-old German boy. Once again Mozart was confronted by a challenge to which he was not yet emotionally equal.

All that he could bring to his task was his rich musical vein, and it was entirely natural, therefore, that in writing this opera he wanted only to create an effective, large-scale piece. He was fortunate that his aim coincided with the demands of contemporary audiences. Had he written it during the heyday of Jommelli and Traetta, it is more than likely that not even his gifts as a child prodigy would have safeguarded him from failure.

In the circumstances – and this is true not only of *Mitridate*, but of all Mozart's Italian works up to and including *Il re pastore* – there can be no question, therefore, of any consistent dramatic characterization. The sombre majesty of the oriental potentate was as much of a closed book to the boy as the heroic suffering of the lovesick Aspasia and Sifare, and he had little choice but to fall back on the universal and frigid theatrical emotion of the neo-Neapolitans, the principal characteristics of which he had assimilated with his characteristic adaptability. But his naïve approach is clear from Aspasia's very first aria ('Al destin che la minaccia'), the main theme of which runs as follows:[7]

This outburst of fury accompanies words that are a simple prayer to God. In highly emotional arias such as these we seek in vain for signs of the later Mozartian spirit. He is more successful, by contrast, at expressing pain and yearning, and here Italian models and his own innate talent come together to felicitous effect. Aspasia's G minor aria, 'Nel sen mi palpita', for example, is entirely typical of the later composer in terms of its modulatory procedures – it rarely migrates to major tonalities – and dour chromaticisms, to say nothing of its mood of wistful nostalgia, a mood rendered all the more affecting by being so understated. Only the writing for the voice fails to achieve this same high level. In much the same way, Ismene's songlike aria, 'Tu sai per chi m'accese', is distinguished by its appealingly simple and heartfelt tone. And in other *empfindsam* numbers, Mozart takes up and successfully develops his Italian models. The two long numbers in E flat major – Aspasia's *ombra* scene in act three, scene four ('Ah ben ne fui presaga!–Pallid'ombre che scorgete') and Farnace's aria ('Già dagli occhi il velo è tolto') – reveal the influence of Johann

---

7. See Kretzschmar, 'Mozart in der Geschichte der Oper', ii.263.

Christian Bach, while the allegro melody of 'Parto, nel gran cimento' derives from Piccinni's *Cesare e Cleopatra*, a work whose traces may also be glimpsed in 'l'orgoglio d'un audace', bars 41–4.

But it is not only on a dramatic level that Mozart lags behind the Italians in these early operas: on a purely musical level, too, he still leaves much to be desired. Although he successfully and skilfully imitates not only their two most up-to-date types of aria – the foreshortened *da capo* and condensed ternary form – but also the binary cavatina, there is still a curious sense of unease about their internal structure: clearly he has yet to fathom the principal secret of Italian music, namely, the organic unity of its melodic writing, a unity that is preserved in spite of all its breadth and wealth of detail.[8] Instead of calmly developing his ideas, he all too often breaks off and catches his listeners off-guard by introducing new motifs that spring inexhaustibly from his ever-fertile imagination. Elsewhere, too, there is often too much of a good thing: in the example quoted above, for instance, the theme itself is weighed down with *fioriture*, something the Italians were right to avoid, not introducing any ornamentation until the second part of the A-section, by which time the melodic framework was already firmly established. To make matters worse, the coloratura writing here is set to wholly inappropriate words.

By the same token, the relationship between voice and orchestra still remains to be clarified. Clearly Leopold had impressed on Mozart the fact that in an Italian opera he should not allow his symphonic skills free rein, and so the first half of the opera, in particular, is notable for accompaniments which, in their simplicity, must have sounded distinctly old-fashioned at this time. But then his previous training reasserts itself and from around 'Nel grave tormento' [act two, scene eight] onwards the instruments become increasingly prominent in the German manner.[9] Yet there are very few signs of the flexible handling of the orchestra that Piccinni had shown and that exploited the expressive potential of the instruments without detracting from the prior claims of the vocal line.

The opening ritornellos are generally broadly structured and, as a rule, adopt the Bachian model in having two contrasting themes divided by a sharply delineated imperfect cadence. Only exceptionally, as in 'So quanto a te dispiace', does the second of these themes have a cantabile character. Far more frequently, it is designed as a solo in contradistinction to the preceding tutti. In the aria itself, these second subjects are generally reintroduced only when the words of the opening section are repeated for the first time, with the result that right from the outset the aria's principal poetic idea assumes two different forms which, musically speaking, could hardly reveal a greater sense of contrast. Bach and the Italian composers were likewise fond of such contrasts, but in their case their second subjects do not rival their first subjects in importance from the outset but are introduced through the back door, as it were, in the course of the musical argument and, as a result, do not threaten the hegemony of the principal musical ideas. There is no intimation here of Mozart's later and genuinely dramatic ability to harness together the most disparate moods within a single aria. Rather, it was simply a delight in his own wealth of ideas and in purely musical contrasts that inspired him here.

In short, *Mitridate* represents a considerable advance on its predecessors in purely technical terms, but it falls far short of its Italian models in respect of its command of the Italian vocal style.

A striking feature of the work is the *secco* recitatives, the declamatory style of which Mozart, clearly recalling the German approach, took far more seriously than the Italian composers of the

---

8. ◆ Also see Gandolfi and Mora, 'La forma dell'aria nelle opere milanesi di Mozart'.
9. See Wyzewa and Saint-Foix, *Wolfgang Amédée Mozart*, i.346–7.

period. The declamation here is generally flawless and there is a real attempt to reflect the underlying emotion, at least to the extent that Mozart was capable of feeling such emotions. Conversely, the relatively numerous accompanied recitatives are markedly inferior to the recitative from *Demofoonte*, 'Misero pargoletto' K77, discussed above, in spite of Mozart's profligacy in introducing new motifs.

Apart from the final quintet – the usual cursory, bonhomous *envoi* – the only ensemble is the duet ('Se viver non degg'io'), the expansive binary form of which recalls the world of *opera buffa*. Its raptly voluptuous first section is one of the finest episodes in the opera, with the usual pair of horns joined for the occasion by a second pair.

The brief overture reveals the influence of Piccinni in its outer sections, with their short-winded second subjects, their insistence on introducing new ideas into their development sections, in spite of the brevity of the latter, and the great crescendo in the final presto, while the intimate march theme of the middle section recalls Mozart's Austrian homeland.[10]

Lucio Silla K135 dates from 1772 and is a setting of a libretto by Giovanni da Gamerra that was revised, according to the preface to the printed wordbook, by Metastasio. The cast-list was as follows:[11]

Lucio Silla, dittatore	Sgr. Bassano Morgnoni (Tenore).
Giunia, figlia di Cajo Mario e promessa sposa di Cecilio	Sgra. Anna de Amicis-Buonsolazzi (Prima donna).
Cecilio, senatore proscritto	Sgr. Venanzio Rauzzini (Soprano. Primo uomo).
Lucio Cinna, amico di Cecilio e nemico occulto di Lucio Silla, patrizio Romano	Sgra. Felicità Suarti (Soprano).
Celia, sorella di Lucio Silla	Sgra. Daniella Mienci (Soprano).
Aufidio, tribuno, amico di L. Silla	Sgr. Giuseppe Onofrio (Tenore).

The senator Cecilio has been outlawed by Silla (Sulla) but returns in secret to Rome and is told by Cinna that Silla has had him declared dead in order to be able to claim his bride Giunia for himself. But Giunia spurns him, and so he resolves to kill her. The lovers celebrate their reunion in a sombre mausoleum. Silla asks his sister Celia to help him persuade Giunia to change her mind, but in vain. Meanwhile, Cecilio and Cinna decide to murder him. But the attempt on his life fails and the lovers resolve to die together. Silla now declares his willingness to forgive them all in order to restore peace to his heart. He permits the two couples – Cecilio and Giunia, on the one hand, and Cinna and Celia, on the other – to marry, then steps down as dictator and restores freedom to Rome.

One sympathizes with Metastasio's feeling that this libretto was in urgent need of improvement, but even with its alterations it remains one of the weakest products of the Metastasian school, contradictory in its characterization, cluelessly incompetent in its handling of the plot, and arid and stilted in expression.[12] From a dramatic standpoint, any attempt to set this libretto to music

10. ◆ Further concerning *Mitridate*, see Adlung, *Mozarts Opera seria 'Mitridate, re di Ponto'* and Gianturco, *Mozart's Early Operas*, 74–98.

11. ◆ Concerning the singers at the first performance, see Angermüller, 'Die Sänger der Erstaufführung von Mozarts Dramma per musica "Lucio Silla" KV 135'; also see Adrian, 'Rolle und Bedeutung der Kastraten in Leben und Werk Wolfgang Amadeus Mozarts'.

12. ◆ For a facsimile of the libretto distributed at the first performance, see Angermüller, *W. A. Mozart: Lucio Silla*.

was doomed from the outset. Yet such a standpoint was of no more interest to Mozart on this occasion than it had been with *Mitridate*: audiences at this time were prepared to put up with any amount of poetic nonsense as long as the music was effective and grateful from the singers' point of view. Like *Mitridate*, *Lucio Silla* is a genuine child of the neo-Neapolitan spirit, albeit markedly more progressive in style and part of the trend that allowed Sarti to enjoy his greatest triumphs during this same decade.[13] This is clear not only from the choruses but also from the accompanied recitatives, which are far more numerous than in *Mitridate*. The very first chorus ('Fuor di queste urne dolenti'), which is set in a gloomy mausoleum and dependent on the opening scene of Gluck's *Orfeo* for both its underlying idea and even its poetic diction, introduces us to a new feature that was missing from *Mitridate* and that is grounded in Mozart's own personal development. Between finishing the one opera and starting the next, the boy had entered his years of adolescence. The feeling for grand tragic passion that had been absent from *Mitridate* now entered his adolescent soul with elemental force, and it is entirely to be expected that the novel feelings that now stirred in his breast struck him initially as something exceptional, not to say extraordinary. The mausoleum scene was an old favourite among composers of *opere serie*, but now, when Giunia appeals to the shade of her dead father, Mozart responds by empathizing with the whole fantastical and demonic nature of the scene. Admittedly, he uses the same devices as those regularly found in *ombra* scenes in Italian operas, from the E flat major tonality, syncopations and tremolandos to the ghostlike strains of the wind instruments, but alongside these we also find at almost every turn evidence of an exceptionally lively imagination in the form of all manner of unusual melodic and especially harmonic touches, including bold transitions designed to heighten the sense of tension and novel instrumental turns of phrase. Nothing similar had been found on this scale in any of the Italian composers of the period nor, indeed, in Mozart himself until now. Contemporary listeners who recalled *Mitridate* may well have quailed at these early signs of his youthful genius: even the opening andante is exceptional in every way.

The following accompanied recitative for Cecilio ('Morte, morte fatal') is unusually richly scored for strings, oboes, bassoons, horns and trumpets. Here Mozart adopts his usual approach and keeps introducing new motifs into the orchestral writing, but in this case it serves to heighten the sense of nocturnal eeriness, conjuring up the sound of the wind rustling in the cypress trees and of a ghostly lament rising up from the vaults, and even the sudden switch from horror to effortfully suppressed jubilation in Cecilio's breast at Giunia's approach is of compelling dramatic life. It is with a brief but genuinely Mozartian crescendo that the orchestra leads into the chorus's dirge, a number that includes a solo section for Giunia inspired by French models. Its mood of solemnity notwithstanding, this chorus, too, suggests a sense of agitation with its pungent harmonic and dynamic accents and frequently shifting orchestral motifs, some of which, freely transformed, are taken over into the solo section. Judged by the standards of Italian melody, this solo is again somewhat lacking in unity and too restless, yet it has a characteristic charm of its own thanks to the contribution of the instruments: it is as though Giunia keeps finding new reasons to lament her situation as a result of the disjointed sighs that are heard in the winds but that seem to issue from the tomb on her dead father's lips. The section rises to a magnificent climax at the end with *sforzato* chords in the orchestra and lamenting violas. The succeeding chorus repeats the first in a slightly altered form[14] and in doing so strikes a more impassioned note. A comparison with Orpheus's great scene of lamentation in Gluck's opera would not, of course, be appropriate here

13. ◆ Also see Candiani, 'Giovanni De Gamerra e il libretto del "Lucio Silla"'.
14. The opening phrase of the solo section is identical, moreover, with the two choral entries.

as the two scenes could hardly be more different in terms of their form and expression.[15] But this scene in *Lucio Silla* is our first encounter with Mozart not only as a dramatist but also as a masterly exponent of the demonic, and it is all the more valuable in that it was to be some considerable time before Mozart explored this field again. The love duet that follows ('D'Eliso in sen m'attendi') takes us right back to the unadulterated Italian manner, although there is no denying the beauty of the almost Schumannesque writing for the winds at the beginning or of the sombre shadow cast by the word 'ombra' and, finally, of the bright A major, a tonality which, after all the preceding terrors, has an emphatically liberating effect. The whole piece – two-thirds of which consist of simple homophonic writing for the voices – is unambiguously Italian in its exclusively musical character.[16] It is hard to resist the conclusion that on this occasion it was the pupil who inspired the teacher. It is also worth drawing attention here to the affinities between the opening of Bach's duet and Blonde's aria 'Durch Zärtlichkeit und Schmeicheln' from *Die Entführung aus dem Serail*, the only exceptions being the greater contribution of the orchestra and a handful of individual features such as the typically Mozartian chromatic shift in the oboes (*a–a* sharp–*b*) in the allegro (bars 90–2), a shift that serves to ratchet up the tension.

That the opera contains two more choruses ('Se gloria il crin ti cinse' and 'Il gran Silla che a Roma in seno') is due to the progressive influence of Johann Christian Bach.[17] The second is a rondo with a choral refrain that reflects French influence. The trio ('Quell'orgoglioso sdegno') recalls a tendency on the part of many Italian composers of *opere buffe* to distinguish between the three different characters, namely, the overbearing Silla, the ardent Cecilio and the love-sick Giunia. It is in his depiction of Giunia's all-consuming love that Mozart is most successful. There is, of course, a greater sense of drama here, but this sort of approach was not invented by Mozart and there is no direct connection between it and his later skill at writing large-scale ensembles.

Four types of aria are found here – not only the two found in *Mitridate* (one with the *da capo* reduced by half, the other the condensed ternary aria), but also the type created by Johann Christian Bach, in which the *da capo* is shortened but without omitting the main musical idea,[18]

---

15. Both musically and dramatically, Bach's style is far closer to Gluck's than Mozart's, except that its severity is tempered by a note of tender-hearted wistfulness.
16. Bach structures his duet in exactly the same way as Mozart. Its allegro begins as follows:

17. ◆ For further comparisons of Mozart's and J. C. Bach's settings of the text, see Warburton, 'Lucio Silla – by Mozart and J. C. Bach' and Fauquet, 'Regards sur "Lucio Silla" de Jean-Chrétien Bach'.
18. See Cecilio's 'Il tenero momento' and 'Ah se a morir mi chiama' and Cinna's 'Nel fortunato istante'. Wyzewa and Saint-Foix, *Wolfgang Amédée Mozart* (i.487), also include Cinna's 'Vieni ov'amor t'invita' and Celia's 'Se lusinghiera speme' and 'Quando sugl'arsi campi', but these numbers are in fact cast in other forms: 'Vieni ov'amor t'invita' and 'Quando sugl'arsi campi' have a complete, albeit modified, *da capo*, whereas the *da capo* in 'Se lusinghiera speme' is reduced by half.

and, finally, a fourth type, which is found in the most important arias and consists of two sections of approximately similar length but starkly contrasting moods and involving no repeat of the first section.[19] The models for this fourth type are no doubt to be sought in *opera buffa* and in Sarti. Significantly, it is two of Giunia's arias ('Dalla sponda tenebrosa' and 'Fra i pensier più funesti di morte') that are cast in this unusual form. Here, and in the scene at the mausoleum, Mozart genuinely catches the mood of ardent and impassioned emotion, and one feels quite clearly how powerfully this heroic character fired his youthful imagination, in spite of the character's high-flown outpourings. It is with real adolescent infatuation that he interprets her as an austerely majestic figure devoid of all sense of mercy. Indeed, he is even naïve enough to treat her second aria ('Ah se il crudel periglio'), the words of which suggest only helpless fear, as a vow to be avenged on Silla, a vow couched in the highly emotional musical language of an Italian vengeance aria in which the coloratura is far in excess of anything found in *Mitridate*.[20] Her two most important arias ('Parto, m'affretto', 'Fra i pensier') are preceded by accompanied recitatives that are both notable, once again, for their wealth of musical motifs and for their strikingly sombre and agitated tone. The first of these arias acquires its curiously unstable character from its almost constantly interrupted vocal line and from an insistent figure in the violins that is repeated with stubborn obstinacy and that makes no attempt to disguise its origins in opera buffa:[21] Even the dynamics are the same.

Thematically speaking, the aria has little new to offer, as phrases such as this are part of the stock-in-trade of Neapolitan opera:

But the aria's fragmented modulatory character is certainly remarkable, with the E flat major chord that suddenly erupts after the section in G major, for example, creating the effect of a thunderbolt. Even finer is Giunia's fourth aria ('Fra i pensier'), an anxious andante already tinged with a presentiment of death, in the opening bars of which we can already hear her lover's final sighs in the flutes and violas, followed by a feverishly hurried allegro that hammers out the main idea in Giunia's heart with an almost Gluckian intensity:

19. Transitional forms are 'Il tenero momento', in which the second section includes reminiscences of the first section and repeats the introductory ritornello at the end, and, similarly, Silla's 'D'ogni pietà mi spoglio'.
20. ◆ For a discussion of this aria, see Mahling, '". . . new and altogether special and astonishingly difficult": Some Comments on Junia's Aria in "Lucio Silla"'.
21. The analogous motif in act one, scene four of Piccinni's *Ciro* is as follows:

Ma   per   mag - gior   mio   duo - lo

Here, too, the orchestra plays an important part in the musical argument, driving it towards its conclusion in an agitated final ritornello.

Mozart paid even greater heed to Venanzio Rauzzini, who was playing the part of Cecilio, than he did to Anna Lucia de Amicis, tailoring the role not only to suit his vocal range (from *a* to *a''*) but also to reflect his degree of education. Rauzzini had a solid grounding in theory and was himself a composer, with the result that Mozart wrote some particularly challenging arias for him. His third aria ('A se a morir mi chiama'), for example, includes intervals such as the following, each of which attests to the singer's secure sense of pitch:

om - bra, om - bra   om - bra, om - bra fe - del

Cecilio's first aria ('Il tenero momento') is introduced by an expressive recitative and begins with a sustained note popular with castrato singers at this time. But it adopts far too emotional an approach to the 'tenero affetto' described in the text,[22] while the final aria ('Pupille amate') with which Cecilio seeks to comfort Giunia immediately before his death has turned out far too light-weight and even frivolous in tone. In the third scene of act two, by contrast, Mozart again reveals a significant advance on his earlier style, an advance apparent even from the introductory *secco* recitative. The motivically unified accompanied recitative, 'Ah corri!', is thrillingly effective thanks to its realistic screams and bold harmonic writing. No less inspired is Mozart's decision to take over into the following aria the three-note motif first heard in augmentation in the recitative. It is to these three chords, repeatedly thundered out by the full orchestra, that the aria owes its overriding sense of unity, a unity that prevents it from falling apart as a result of its constant – and typical – alternation of contrasting moods and themes.

In both of Silla's arias ('Il desio di vendetta e di morte', 'D'ogni pietà mi spoglio'), Mozart was obliged to take account of Morgnoni's want of experience, with the result that they are lacking in all virtuosity. But even so, the character remains very much the traditional theatrical villain, with only the oboes and violas in the second part of his second aria adding a touch of typically Mozartian tension and investing the figure with a slightly more personal aura.

Of Celia's four arias, the two in *Liedform* ('Se lusinghiera speme', 'Quando sugl'arsi campi') are notable for the graceful, heartfelt tone that Mozart favoured for young women of this kind. Her two others ('Se il labbro timido', 'Strider sento la procella') fail to rise above the average, and the same is true of the single aria for the second tenor, Aufidio ('Guerrier, che d'un acciaro'), and Cinna's three arias ('Vieni ov'amor t'invita', 'Nel fortunato istante', 'De' più superbi il core').

As a result, the opera features all the characteristics of Neapolitan opera, in some cases intensi-fied, alongside traces of a totally alien spirit that embrace not only the opera's impassioned, revo-

22. This emotion is better expressed by Bach in his andante.

lutionary tone[23] but also the role of the orchestra. Mozart falls even further short of the purely vocal ideal of the Italians in *Lucio Silla* than he had done in *Mitridate*, a failure due, not least, to the fact that during the intervening period he had again been working chiefly on instrumental music in Salzburg.[24] His opera orchestra has become not only more expressive, but also more ambitious, sometimes accompanying and elucidating the action on stage in a highly poetical manner, but equally often exerting an oppressive influence on the vocal line, especially when the composer adopts his familiar tendency of continually introducing new episodes instead of developing the motifs he has already chosen. The vocal writing is also more instrumentally coloured than in *Mitridate*, and the inner life of the orchestra is more varied, with the first and second violins, for example, going their separate ways – further testimony to the influence of Johann Christian Bach. The violas, too, break free from the bass and are often divided, while the winds in particular constantly surprise the listener not only with their independent and expressive motifs but also through their idiosyncratic sonorities. Mozart's lively imagination is revealed most clearly in the interludes, but the majority of the large-scale preludes, with their contrastive themes,[25] are likewise superior to anything found in the Italian tradition at this time. We have already had occasion to comment on the peculiar importance of the accompanied recitatives, of which there are more in *Lucio Silla* than in any other opera by Mozart. The *secco* recitatives, by contrast, are uneven in quality, and it is not hard to identify the passages where Mozart's imagination caught fire and he suddenly rises above the more conventional, albeit invariably well-declaimed, sections to achieve real dramatic verve in which a by no means insignificant part is played by the harmonic writing (see especially the second and ninth scenes of act two and the fourth scene of act three).

The sinfonia's opening allegro resembles that of its predecessor even to the extent that in both cases a new theme is introduced into the development section. But the middle section of the ternary andante brings with it a pointer to what is to come in the form of that half eerie, half anguished passage in the minor, in which genuine passion suddenly finds untrammelled expression. (The pointer, it must be conceded, is not motivic, but operates on a less literal level.) No less characteristic here are the sharp dynamic accents. The final section is an effervescent rondo with a wittily varied theme.[26]

---

23. Here, too, one is struck by the dynamic markings, which are more careful than usual and which include a sudden interplay between *piano* and *forte*, frequent *sforzati* and crescendos.

24. ◆ Mozart, at least, was pleased with several of the arias from the opera. He had copies made of 'Se il labbro timido' in Salzburg in January 1777, of 'Ah se il crudel periglio', also in Salzburg but in 1773/4, and two copies of 'Pupille amate', one of which suggests he may have performed the aria in Vienna as late as 1786; see Eisen, 'The Mozarts' Salzburg copyists', 303.

25. It is striking that three arias ('Vieni ov'amor t'invita', 'Il tenero momento' and 'Il desio di vendetta e di morte') all include the same second subject in slightly altered guise. In each case, the model is Paisiello (see below):

This template is repeatedly – and famously – found in much of Mozart's music.

26. ◆ Concerning the possibility that Mozart redacted this overture into a symphony, see Hintermaier, 'Eine vermutlich authentische Sinfonie-Fassung der Ouvertüre zu Mozarts Lucio Silla KV 135'. For other settings of the same text, see Esch, *"Lucio Silla": Vier Opera-Seria Vertonungen aus der Zeit zwischen 1770 und 1780*. For Paisiello's setting in particular, see Lippmann, 'Mozart und Paisiello: Zur stilistischen Position des "Lucio Silla"'.

The two 'dramatic serenades' or *azioni teatrali* of 1771 and 1772 are congratulatory cantatas cast in dramatic form of a kind commissioned by the hundred for all manner of festive occasions by seventeenth- and eighteenth-century princes, aristocrats and even members of the middle classes (a notable example is Bach's *Der zufriedengestellte Aeolus*[27]). Central to each work was, of course, the distinguished individual whose life and achievements were being celebrated, and in each case the individual in question was more or less blatantly flattered in mythological, allegorical or Arcadian guise. Outward pomp was what mattered, with the drama coming a poor second. Moreover, these mythological masques were far shorter than the usual ceremonial operas, in only one act and with none of the scene divisions of *opera seria*. As a rule, they were performed only once and regarded as secondary to the *opera seria* proper.[28] This explains why the young Mozart was commissioned to write the serenata, while the opera itself was entrusted to Hasse.[29]

In the case of *Ascanio in Alba* K111, the librettist Giuseppe Parini[30] attempted to satisfy all the demands of a festive occasion such as the wedding of Archduke Ferdinand of Austria and Maria Beatrice Ricciarda d'Este.[31] The characters are gods, heroes and shepherds; there was no stinting on sets, choruses and ballets; and the work teemed with flattering references to the newly wedded couple. Several well-known artists were engaged for the performance,[32] as is clear from the surviving libretto:

Venere	Signora Falchini (Seconda donna, Soprano)
Ascanio	Signore Manzuoli (Primo uomo, Mezzo-soprano)
Silvia, ninfa del sangue d'Ercole	Signora Girelli (Prima donna, Soprano)

27. Bach's work is also a priceless parody on the whole tradition of *Zopfmusik*.

28. See Marpurg, *Historisch-kritische Beyträge zur Aufname der Musik*, iii.44–5.

29. ◆ And yet, Mozart's serenata was far more successful than Hasse's opera. In a letter to his wife on 19 October 1771 Leopold wrote that 'We are constantly addressed in the street by cavaliers and other people who wish to congratulate Wolfgang. In a word, *it grieves me*, but Wolfgang's serenata has so overshadowed Hasse's opera that I cannot describe it' (*Briefe*, i.444). Leopold's opinion is apparently confirmed by a notice in the Florentine *Notizie del Mondo* for 26 October 1771: 'The opera has not met with success. . . . The serenata, however, has met with great applause, both for the text and for the music.' Similarly, the *Wienerisches Diarium* for 6 November 1771 reported that 'the serenata received universal applause for its composition and very excellent music.' See Eisen, *Mozart Dokumente: Addenda*, 19–20, *New Mozart Documents*, 21.

30. Reina, *Opere di Giuseppe Parini*, iv.

31. ◆ A detailed description of the festivites was published in the *Augspurgische Ordinari Postzeitung* for 28 September 1771: 'Everything is lively here on account of the grand and expensive preparations for the forthcoming wedding of his Royal Highness Archduke Ferdinand to the Princess of Modena. An opera by the famous Metastasio, *Il Ruggero*, or Heroic Gratitude, will be presented. The most famous singers in Italy are being called here to perform the opera, the music of which is composed by the famous Hasse, a Saxon, and Kapellmeister to the Elector of Saxony. All of the sets will be designed and arranged with the greatest magnificence. The ballets, choreographed by Messrs Pich [*recte* Picq] and Favre, and Mesdames Binetti and Blasge, will be exceptionally fine, and the performance will include 40 dancers. Similarly, other theatrical spectacles will be very elegant and various in their presentation. The Facchini company will be seen in a magnificent masquerade, with decorative emblems appropriate to the occasion. Each day three hundred persons will dine at court, where there will be masked balls, and at the theatres masked balls will also take place. Moreover, the theatres will be magnificently lighted, as will the whole city, three nights in a row, and for three evenings tickets to the theatrical performances will be distributed gratis. There will be races with horses and also races with light carriages. A part of the race course will be converted into a gallery, covered with the interlaced boughs of verdant trees, and beautifully lighted, and underneath, 150 poor maidens, to be married the same day to 150 similar young men, and given dowries by the royal bridal couple, will dine and celebrate their weddings. Two fountains will flow with wine instead of water, various orchestras with musicians will perform and, finally, a serenade, entitled *Ascanio in Alba*, composed by Abbate Parini and set to music by Herr Mozzart, will be performed. Numerous other entertainments, impossible to describe, will also be given, and it is expected that an astonishing number of visitors will arrive here to see them.' See Eisen, *New Mozart Documents*, 20–1, *Mozart Dokumente. Addenda*, 19.

32. The three main singers also appeared in Bologna in 1763 in Gluck's *Il trionfo di Clelia*; see Dittersdorf, *Lebensbeschreibung*, 88–9.

Aceste, sacerdote   Signore Tibaldi (Tenore)
Fauno, uno dei principali pastori   Signore Solzi (Soprano)[33]

Venus descends to earth with a large retinue of spirits and with her grandson Ascanio. She informs him that she intends him to marry the beautiful nymph Silvia, who is sprung from Hercules and who lives in the country that she loves more than any other. But Silvia tells the priest Aceste that she is already in love with a youth who has appeared to her in a dream. On the advice of the goddess, Ascanio decides not to reveal his true identity but to observe Silvia and in that way to test her. Meanwhile, Silvia has been told by Aceste that Venus plans to marry her to Ascanio and with them found a new city. As its first building, the votaries of Venus conjure up a magnificent temple during the entr'acte ballet. In the second act, the lovers are finally united by Venus after a series of misunderstandings. She reminds her grandson of his duties as a ruler, and the work ends with her return to Mount Olympus.

Fauno's account of the country's tutelary goddess, together with Aceste's speech to the departing Venus and the goddess's own words, contain such clear allusions to Maria Theresia that it is inconceivable that the reference was not picked up by listeners. Nor would eyebrows have been raised at the fact that the empress was equated with Venus. By the same token, the nymph Silvia is said to be descended from Hercules, the Italian form of which – Ercole – was not uncommon in the d'Este household. A pupil of Minerva and the Muses and a paragon of virtue and modesty, she is clearly modelled on the Princess Maria Beatrice, whose intellect, literary gifts and kindness were universally praised.[34] There was less that could be said of Archduke Ferdinand, and the poet's portrait is little more than a thumbnail sketch of a fair-haired youth with rosy cheeks. It is significant that, however much Parini may stress the importance of mutual affection based on beauty and intellectual merits, he none the less singles out as the highest of all virtues the ability to subordinate affection to duty, a prioritization entirely appropriate to a princely wedding. The wedding had not, in fact, been without its difficulties,[35] and worries had been expressed about relations between the young couple.[36]

The two-volume, 480-page autograph score contains twenty-two numbers.[37] The ballet music, which ran to eight separate numbers, survives only in the form of a bass line in a copyist's hand.[38]

---

33. Antonia Maria Girelli-Aguilar had sung Eurydice in Gluck's *Orfeo* in Parma in 1769, while Giuseppe Tibaldi (1729–*c*1790), by now somewhat advanced in years, had created the role of Admetus in Gluck's *Alceste* in 1767. ◆ Further concerning the singers, see Angermüller, 'Die Sänger der Erstaufführung von Mozarts Festa teatrale "Ascanio in Alba" KV 111'.

34. Björnstahl, *Briefe*, ii.296; *Der teutsche Merkur*, iii (1789), 299–300.

35. *Erinnerungen an Meyer*, i.77.

36. 'The archduke and his wife are well and very happy', Leopold wrote on 26 October 1771. 'This will be a cause of particular pleasure for Her Majesty the Empress, as people were worried that he wouldn't like his bride, as she is unattractive; but she's uncommonly friendly, agreeable and virtuous, with the result that everyone likes her, and she has completely won over the archduke, for she has the best heart and the most pleasant manners in the world' (*Briefe*, i.446).

37. ◆ The important sources for *Ascanio in Alba* include not only the autograph score, now in the Staatsbibliothek zu Berlin, but also a manuscript copy in the Gesellschaft der Musikfreunde, Vienna (shelfmark MS Mantuani 17798A), with autograph entries by Mozart.

38. The ballets in particular were frequently conducted from the bass part at this time. Generally they were not by the composer of the opera but were the work of second-rate musicians, hence Leopold's insistence that Wolfgang should also compose the dance music (*Briefe*, i.435, letter of 7 September 1771). The Mozarteum in Salzburg contains the sketch of a setting of Noverre's ballet *Le gelosie del seraglio* (see Noverre, *Lettres sur la danse et sur les ballets*, 419ff.). Noverre's ballet was performed in Lyons in 1758 (see Niedecken, *Jean-Georges Noverre*, 21). The sketch runs to thirty-two numbers, the first two of which are notated on two systems, the rest on one. Apart from various indications as to the use of wind instruments, it also includes the names of the performers: Casacci (Cassani), Salomoni, Pick, La Binetti and La Morelli. At the beginning of the sketch are three words whose meaning is impossible to fathom: Revmatismo, Otiulla(?), Allcinao(?). It has always been assumed that this ballet was intended for the entr'acte of *Ascanio in Alba*. The handwriting certainly suggests the period around 1771 and Leopold mentions at least two of the same dancers – 'Mr. Pick' (= Le Picq) and 'Mad Binetti' – in his letter of 13 September 1771 (*Briefe*, i.437). But in his letter

Mozart's serenade is neither dramatic nor of particular importance for its composer's inner development. Even so, it has one great advantage over many similar works, including Gluck's *Le nozze d'Ercole e d'Ebe* of 1747,[39] in that it serves its purpose by dint of its sheer variety. Right from the outset, it offered its listeners something which, if not altogether new, was at least unusual, with the curtain rising immediately after the sinfonia's opening allegro, a movement which, in terms of its structure and spirit, is virtually indistinguishable from the two analogous movements of the operatic sinfonias discussed above.[40] As a result, the andante is not only played but danced – according to Leopold, the dancers at the first performance were 'eleven female persons, namely eight spirits and the Graces, or eight Graces and three goddesses'.[41] In the final allegro the sixteen dancers are joined by a chorus of thirty-two.

It was almost certainly this use of the chorus to which the work owed much of its success. In fact, the choruses were probably a concession to Viennese taste,[42] as it is clear from Gluck's example[43] that local audiences were not prepared to forgo the chorus in occasional pieces of this kind. Five of Mozart's choruses are combined with dancing, while two are independent. The majority of them allude to the course of the action, with the second of them referring to it no fewer than five times. This is a pastoral chorus for men's voices (tenor and bass) accompanied by flutes, oboes, horns, bassoons, cellos and basses, and, with its frequent repetitions, is instrumental in conveying the essentially Arcadian tone of the work as a whole. It has a counterpart in the two choruses for women's voices in the second part of the work, both of which are distinguished by their lively part-writing. The second is a three-part setting, the canonic entries of which reflect the young girls' bemusement at Silvia's behaviour with surprising vividness. The four-part choruses, too, are admirably effective, their homophonic character in no way affected by brief but pertinent passages of imitative writing. The chorus of jubilation that recurs on more than one occasion, framing the opening part of the work, stands out by dint of its middle section in which the men and women appear as separate groups. (When the chorus is repeated, this section is omitted.) But the most interesting number is the chorus 'Scendi celeste Venere', a remarkably high-flown piece that is introduced by a great crescendo and twice repeated after brief passages of *secco* recitative,

---

of 21 September 1771 (*Briefe*, i.438), he speaks of *two* great ballets after the first and second acts, each of which was to last three-quarters of an hour. We know the entr'acte ballet from the bass part in Berlin. It would seem, therefore, that *Le gelosie del seraglio* was originally intended to end the serenata but that it was later discarded for reasons that are unclear – perhaps on account of its excessive length. This was the first time that Mozart had tackled a Turkish subject of the kind that was so popular at this period, and it is clear that he made a serious attempt to capture the exotic local colour. In no. 7 we find a theme, initially in A major, that he was later to use in the final movement of his A major violin concerto K219 where it is again intended to create a sense of exotic colour. Transposed to A minor, it reappears as the main subject of the finale of the present ballet. In general, Mozart sticks close to the example of the dramatic ballets of Deller, Rudolph, Starzer and others (see Abert, *Ausgewählte Ballette Stuttgarter Meister*). The basis is French, but alongside this the listener will also hear strains of Austrian, Bohemian and Hungarian folk music. Only the large-scale, freely structured scenes of Deller and Rudolph are missing. See Niedecken, *Jean-Georges Noverre*, 54–5. ◆ Further, see Plath, 'Der Ballo des "Ascanio" und die Klavierstücke KV Anh. 207'; Dahms, 'Entlehnungspraktiken in der zweiten Hälfte des 18. Jahrhunderts und zur Ballettmusik aus Mozarts "Ascanio in Alba"'; and, more generally, Hansell, *Opera and Ballet at the Regio Ducal Teatro of Milan, 1771–1776: A Musical and Social History*.

39. See Abert, *Christoph Willibald Gluck: Le nozze d'Ercole e d'Ebe*.

40. Cf. the sinfonia to Jommelli's *Fetonte* in Abert, *Niccolò Jommelli: Fetonte*.

41. *Briefe*, i.436 (letter of 13 September 1771). André surmised, no doubt correctly, that a surviving symphonic movement K120, the paper and handwriting of which match those of the score of *Ascanio in Alba*, was intended to complete the sinfonia if the latter were to be performed on its own; see Wyzewa and Saint-Foix, *Wolfgang Amédée Mozart*, i.402–3.

42. ◆ Further, see Gallarani, 'La festa teatrale tra Vienna e Milano'.

43. Gluck's three Viennese operas *Le cinesi* (1754), *L'innocenza giustificata* (1755) and *Tetide* (1760) all have relatively large choruses. Hasse's two *feste teatrali*, *Egeria* (Vienna, 1764) and *Partenope* (Vienna, 1767), include not only choruses but also a large number of accompanied recitatives, while *Partenope* additionally abounds in dances. ◆ The generic designations of Gluck's works are *componimento dramatica* (*Le cinesi*), *festa teatrale* (*L'innocenza giustificata*) and *serenata* (*Tetide*).

its darkly coloured middle section successfully capturing the sense of awe-struck terror in the presence of divinity.

The trio ('Eccovi alfin') begins with a purely musical andante followed by an allegro in which we find the first signs of an attempt at individual characterization. As such, it may be regarded as a precursor of the trio from *Lucio Silla*. The allegro section is later repeated.

The arias are mostly in concentrated ternary form and are markedly more impersonal than in the operas. In Silvia's aria ('Spiega il desío le piume') Mozart recalls Mitridate's four horns, while Ascanio's aria ('Torna mio bene, ascolta') is scored not only for strings, flutes, bassoons and horns but also for two serpents – members of the cornett family.[44] Only rarely does the writing acquire a note of any real power, the main exceptions being the end of Silvia's aria ('Infelici affetti miei'), the note of yearning insistency of which recalls the later Mozart, and the beautiful, full-toned but calm final phrase, the impact of which is diminished only by the fashionable sighs tacked on to the very end.

The accompanied recitatives likewise fail to reach the same high standards as those found in the operas of this period. On two occasions – act one, scene two, and act two, scene two – there is a remarkable attempt not only to impose a greater sense of unity on the orchestral writing along the lines of the scene from *Demofoonte* but also to repeat certain sections of the text. In the *secco* recitatives, too, there are very few passages in which Mozart achieves any greater warmth of expression.

Each of the eight dances comprises a fast section followed by a slower one.[45] At least to the extent that it is possible to judge from the surviving bass line, they were dance movements in the style of Deller, Rudolph and Starzer and were evidently not based on any programme. Only the largo (no. 7) is cast in a somewhat freer form. Nos 1 and 2 are binary, nos 3 and 4 ternary (with no. 4 in *da capo* form). No. 5 is a French rondeau with a middle section in the minor, and the same is true of the finale, although here the bass part in the middle section is silent, suggesting that it was a trio. The finale as a whole was almost certainly a contredanse of the kind that composers were fond of writing by way of a conclusion to their ballets.[46]

The second serenata was *Il sogno di Scipione* K126. Dating from 1772, it, too, was a one-act allegory based on classical models.

The young Scipio falls asleep in the palace of Massinissa and is visited by visions of Costanza (Constancy) and Fortuna (Fortune). They demand that he choose one of them as his guide in life. Other characters who appear include his dead forebears Scipio Africanus and Aemilius Paulus, who tell him about the immortality of the soul and the vanity of all earthly things. Scipio expresses a wish to remain with them, but they remind him of his historical mission and send him on his way. The goddesses renew their battle over Scipio's soul and he finally chooses Costanza. His decision precipitates violent threats from her rival accompanied by thunder and lightning, at which point he wakes up and declares his intention of remaining true to Costanza.

The text contains repeated – and transparent – allusions to the background against which the work had first been performed on 1 October 1735 to celebrate the birthday of Charles VI, who had just suffered a series of disastrous defeats in Italy. Nowhere are these allusions more explicit than

44. ◆ See Bevan, 'The low brass'.
45. No. 4 has the rare tempo marking 'Allegrino'.
46. See Abert, *Ausgewählte Ballette Stuttgarter Meister*, 61, 122 and 151. The libretto is closely based on Cicero's *Somnium Scipionis*, albeit combined with a narrative by Silius Italicus, in the fifteenth book of whose *Punica* Virtus and Voluptas appear to Scipio in a dream, obliging him to choose between manly virtue and a life of sensual pleasure. In keeping with the new situation, Metastasio has replaced Virtus and Voluptas by Costanza and Fortuna. ◆ Further concerning *Ascanio in Alba*, see Dahms, 'Mozarts Festa teatrale "Ascanio in Alba"'; Hortschansky, 'Mozarts Ascanio in Alba und der Typus der Serenata'; and Gianturco, *Mozart's Early Operas*, 99–119.

in the speeches for Africanus and Costanza. None the less, the work ends with the usual *licenza* containing a specific reference to the dignitary being celebrated, followed by the traditional congratulations in the form of an aria and concluding chorus.

If the text was thought suitable for a revival in Salzburg, it was no doubt on account of its philosophical and moral trappings, an aspect singled out for particular praise as a model of its kind, even in purely dramatic terms. There can be no question, however, of any plot here. Audiences evidently did not take exception to the fact that Scipio joins in the action and sings while dreaming, while his awakening at the end was even praised by Metastasio himself and held out as exemplary.[47]

Mozart clearly had as much difficulty relating to this tale of supernatural beings as modern audiences do, and it is significant that he reserves his most characteristic writing for the moments when the hero falls asleep and wakes up again. The former is depicted by flutes in a *sommeil*, a scene-type popular with Italian composers of this period. It begins as the slow movement of the sinfonia, before leading directly into the first scene by means of a diminuendo that fades away to almost nothing.[48] Scipio's awakening, by contrast, takes place during the only accompanied recitative in the whole work. Noisy rather than substantial, it includes the first example in Mozart's works of a motif associated with tumult that he must have picked up from Italian composers of the time:

On this occasion, however, it still lacks the syncopated harmonies that were later to be generally associated with it. The remaining recitatives are all of the *secco* variety, even in Costanza's account of the Pythagorean harmony of the spheres, a passage which Italian composers would have seized with both hands as an opportunity for an accompanied recitative. But Mozart was evidently attracted by the idea of using *secco* to distinguish between the temperamental figure of Fortuna and the more thoughtful Costanza. In their arias, by contrast, there is little sign of any such distinction, and even the three Roman heroes – all cast as tenors – are virtually indistinguishable as characters, assuming that we may speak of any characterization at all in their arias. All ten arias are similar to those in *Ascanio in Alba*, except that they are even more brilliant and scored for richer orchestral resources. On a purely formal level, three of these arias ('Lieve sono al par del vento', 'Voi colaggiù ridete' and 'Quercia annosa su l'erte pendici') are important inasmuch as they repeat both main ideas within the foreshortened *da capo*, a form subsequently taken over into *Lucio Silla* (see above). A second version of the *licenza* ('Ah perchè cercar degg'io') survives, its handwriting and style both suggesting that it belongs to a later period.[49] Most of the arias from this period are notable for the brief and often cursory nature of their middle sections, in which the modulatory procedures of the earlier period, as represented by Hasse, survived longer than anywhere else.

Of the two choral movements, the final chorus ('Cento volte con lieto sembiante') is in no way exceptional, whereas the chorus of heroes ('Germe di cento eroi'), with its rushing upper strings, has a certain power and dignity, while still falling short of the choruses from *Ascanio in Alba* in terms of its vital impact. Its imitative writing, too, remains tentative.

---

47. Metastasio, *Opere postume*, i.301.
48. This sinfonia, too, could be performed as a self-contained symphony, K161, with the addition of a final movement, K163.
49. Wyzewa and Saint-Foix, *Wolfgang Amédée Mozart* (ii.340), date it to 1776. ◆ Both palaeographical and historical evidence make it more likely that the *licenza* was revised in March or April 1772 in anticipation of a performance in Salzburg on 29 April 1772 to celebrate the election of Archbishop Colloredo.

The final work in the present series is *Il re pastore* K208. It was written in Salzburg in 1775 in honour of Archduke Maximilian. The cast-list is as follows:

Alessandro, re di Macedonia.

Aminta, pastorello, amante d'Elissa, che, ignoto a se stesso, si scuopre poi l'unico legittimo erede del regno di Sidone.

Elisa, nobile ninfa di Fenicia, dell'antica stirpe di Cadmo, amante d'Aminta.

Tamiri, principessa fuggitiva, figiuola del tiranno Stratone; in abito di pastorella, amante di Agenore.

Agenore, nobile di Sidone, amico di Alessandro, amante di Tamiri.

The plot, in outline, is as follows.[50] Alexander the Great has captured Sidon, and the city's tyrannical ruler, Strato, has taken his own life. Alexander decides to replace him with the son of the last legitimate ruler, Abdalonimus,[51] who is now living incognito as a shepherd, Aminta. Aminta has fallen in love with a noble Phoenician girl by the name of Elisa, and she with him. First, however, Alexander tests Aminta in order to be sure of his sense of kingship, then offers him the throne at the very moment that he learns that he has the permission of Elisa's father to marry her. At the same time, Alexander announces his intention of allowing his friend Agenore to marry Strato's daughter, Tamiri, with whom Agenor is secretly in love. The usual confusions ensue, until finally Aminta, torn between virtue and love, renounces the throne out of his love for Elisa, and Tamiri declares her love for Agenore. Moved by such magnanimity, Alexander unites the two couples, confirming Amita as ruler of Sidon and promising to conquer another kingdom for Agenore.

Metastasio's libretto dates from 1751 and was originally set by Giuseppe Bonno for a performance at the Viennese court, when the performers were four ladies-in-waiting and a gentleman of the court.[52] It is, in fact, a dramatic pastoral and, as such, is part of the same tradition as *Ascanio in Alba*. For the Salzburg performance the second and third acts were telescoped together, the dialogue radically reduced and several arias cut, but without seriously affecting the text. Aminta's first aria was replaced by another with accompanied recitative, and a further accompanied recitative was added for Aminta immediately before the duet at the end of act one. The brief final chorus made way for a kind of finale for soli and tutti. The role of Agenore was recast as a tenor.[53] Aminta was sung by the soprano castrato Tommaso Consoli. But, apart from this, we know nothing about the cast or the performance itself.[54]

50. Metastasio names Justinian (xi.10) and Curtius (iv.3–4) as his sources. Both historians tell how Alexander the Great visited Sidon and discovered Abdalonimus, a distant descendant of the royal house, living in poverty as a gardener. Alexander then raised him to the throne, considering him worthy of it by virtue of his beauty and nobility of mind.
51. Characteristic of Metastasio's whole approach is the care he took to avoid this ill-sounding name ('un nome ipocondriaco'); see Metastasio, *Opere postume*, ii.12 and 35.
52. Metastasio, *Opere postume*, ii.31ff.; Grimm, *Correspondance littéraire*, vi.17–18. Metastasio himself suggested it to Farinelli as a suitable subject for a *festa teatrale*. It was set many times, notably by Sarti (Pesaro, 1752), Hasse (Hubertusburg, 1755), Gluck (Vienna, 1756), Giuseppe Zonca (Munich, 1760), Jommelli (Ludwigsburg, 1764), Piccinni (Florence, 1760), Pietro Alessandro Guglielmi (Venice, 1767) and Galuppi (Parma, 1762). ◆ Other settings include those by Giuseppe Bonno (Vienna, 1751), Felice Giardini (London, 1765), Anton Bachschmidt (Eichstätt, 1774), Antonio Ferradini (Madrid, 1756), Matteo Rauzzini (Dublin, 1784), Antonio Mazzoni (Bologna, 1757) and Giovanni Lampugnani (Milan, 1758).
53. Metastasio had already suggested this change to Farinelli; see Metastasio, *Opere postume*, ii.31.
54. The account of the general archiepiscopal receiver for 15 May 1775 contains a reference to the engagement of both Consoli and the flautist Johann Baptist Becke: 'To Leop. Mozart, Kapellmeister to His Highness the Prince, for food, drink, etc., served by the Sternbräu to the two virtuosi engaged from Munich. 98fl. 47xr.'; see Pirckmayer, 'Zur Lebensgeschichte Mozarts', 138 [*Dokumente*, 138, *Documentary Biography*, 154]. ◆ *Il re pastore* was performed at the Salzburg Residenz on 23 April 1775.

Mozart's surviving two-volume autograph score runs to 284 pages. On a purely musical level it represents a considerable advance on *Ascanio in Alba*, an advance explicable in terms of the works that Mozart had written in the interim, not least of which was *La finta giardiniera*. On a dramatic level, by contrast, it remains as unconvincing as before, with no sign of any characterization or of any real passion. What we have instead is the whole rhetorical language of the neo-Neapolitan composers, with their wide-ranging intervals, ill-judged coloratura and so on. Indeed, Mozart even goes a stage further by adopting a strikingly careless approach to the *secco* recitatives, falling back on hackneyed phrases for even the agitated and emotionally charged passages in exactly the same way that Italian composers did.[55] At the same time, he takes an evident delight in virtuosic orchestral effects, including the writing for solo violin and pairs of flutes, english horns, bassoons and horns in Aminta's rondo aria ('L'amerò, sarò costante'), the four horns in Agenore's aria ('Sol può dir come si trova') and especially the virtuoso flute part in Alessandro's aria ('Se vicendo vi rendo felici').[56]

The arias all adopt the modern, concentrated ternary form found in *Ascanio in Alba*, the only novel feature being the two rondo arias ('L'amerò, sarò costante' and 'Se tu di me fai dono') modelled on similar pieces by Bach and Piccinni. The E flat major rondo ('L'amerò, sarò costante') that has recently reentered the repertory is cast in the form *ABACA*, with a brief coda that repeats the first and last two bars of the main theme before dying away *pianissimo* in the orchestra. The *C*-section also includes material from *B*. Although this aria can trace back its origins to the music of Johann Christian Bach, it already reveals a genuinely Mozartian blend of fire and graceful dreaminess, while also containing a whole series of ideas that were later to be particular favourites of Mozart, such as:

None of these phrases, of course, can deny its origins in Piccinni, yet they create an incomparably more powerful and distinctive impression in the case of a far more universal composer like Mozart thanks to his ability to highlight them through the use of powerful contrasts. Elsewhere, too, we encounter authentically Mozartian ideas such as the impassioned syncopations (often accompanied by excessive *sforzato* markings) and the relentlessly minor-key *da capo* of Agenore's C minor aria ('Sol può dir come si trova'). This tendency in minor-key movements to exclude from the repeat all the more cheerful images that had been admitted the first time round in order to intensify the piece's sombre character is entirely typical of Mozart and one that continues to dominate his instrumental music even as late as the great G minor symphony of 1788.

Within the arias, the middle sections are no longer as concise and old-fashioned as before but come closer in character to development sections, a trend in which we are no doubt right to see the influence of instrumental music and, more especially, of the concerto.[57] This same trend is no

55. A novel feature for Mozart, if not for the Italians, is the brief four-part passage in act two, scene thirteen.
56. After spending some years as a student and then a soldier, Johann Baptist Becke (1743–1817) studied the flute with Wendling and became an outstanding practitioner on the instrument. He was invited from Munich for the performances.
57. ◆ The connection between aria and concerto, with specific reference to the aria 'Ah, se il crudel periglio' from *Lucio Silla*, the violin concerto K216, and the keyboard concerto K238, is discussed in Feldman, 'Staging the Virtuoso: Ritornello Procedure in Mozart, from Aria to Concerto'.

doubt also responsible for the extended initial ritornellos, some of which are strikingly similar to the opening tutti of a violin concerto. Indeed, the role of the orchestra in general is again extremely important, albeit far less demanding and overwhelming than in the earlier works. Here, too, Mozart has learnt his lesson: in spite of the riches that it contains, his orchestra remains flexible, its textures translucent, failing to delve as deeply into the innermost recesses of the characters' emotional lives as was the case with *Lucio Silla*, but making up for this shortcoming by proving far more economical with its musical ideas. At the same time, the vocal writing is freer and more songlike. By Italian standards, of course, Mozart has yet to achieve the right balance between the two.

The duet for Elisa and Aminta ('Vanne a regnar ben mil') comprises an andante and ternary allegro with a coda and, with its heartfelt and rapt expression and Rococo ornamentation, is one of the opera's finest numbers. It was clearly Piccinni who suggested the appealing and entirely appropriate idea of reintroducing the melody and accompanying figures from the andante into the allegro with only a change of rhythm. The finale ('Viva l'invitto duce') consists of three choral strophes divided by two brief homophonic duets.

The overture stands apart from all its predecessors not only by virtue of its key (C major) but also, and more especially, as a result of its one-movement form. It ends with an entirely new and wonderfully tuneful melody that leads directly into the opening scene. This is a French practice to which Gluck, too, had subscribed long before *Alceste*.[58] The overture, which is otherwise unrelated to the drama,[59] is in simple binary form without a proper development section, its unity guaranteed by its main theme, which migrates from part to part.[60] The second subject is suppressed in the second section in favour of the new idea just mentioned.

We may conclude this account of Mozart's early operas by examining his oratorio of 1771, *La Betulia liberata* K118. A setting of words by Metastasio, it is an example of a Neapolitan oratorio and, as such, is comparable to an *opera seria* in many, if not all, of its principal characteristics.

As in the field of opera, so in the oratorio,[61] the two poets Apostolo Zeno and Pietro Metastasio did much to bring about reforms. In both cases there was a need to turn the tide of poetic decline, as even oratorios, by turning increasingly away from the Bible and adopting subjects from hagiography, had been slowly sucked into the maelstrom of fantastical sensationalism that had turned Venetian opera into a caricature of the classical ideal. Both Zeno and Metastasio now returned to the Bible and especially the Old Testament as a quarry for their themes – librettists had always tended to avoid the New Testament on account of the hallowed figure of Christ – and strove to invest the oratorio with a purer moral and religious content. Of course, there is no question here

---

58. For the first time in *La contesa de' numi* of 1749, then in *Il re pastore* of 1756.

59. This overture, too, Mozart later turned into a fully-fledged symphony by adapting the first section of the opening aria and adding a final movement [K120]. ◆ Further concerning French and Italian overtures in the eighteenth century, see Prunières, 'Notes sur les origines de l'ouverture française'; Botstiber, *Geschichte der Ouvertüre*; Demuth, *French Opera: Its Development to the Revolution*; Hell, *Die neapolitanische Opernsinfonie in der ersten Hälfte des 18. Jahrhunderts*; and Kunze, *Die Sinfonie im 18. Jahrhundert*.

60. Wyzewa and Saint-Foix, *Wolfgang Amédée Mozart* (ii.228), point out its affinities with the theme of the allegro section from the overture to *Così fan tutte*.

61. Since oratorio plays only a modest role in Mozart's output, I shall dispense with a historical overview of the subject. (The account given by Jahn and taken over by Deiters has long been superseded.) Instead, I shall merely draw attention to the standard work by Schering, *Geschichte des Oratoriums*. See also Pasquetti, *L'oratorio musicale in Italia*; Alaleona, *Studi su la storia dell'oratorio musicale in Italia*; and Kretzschmar, *Führer durch den Konzertsaal*. ◆ All of these works are now superseded by Smither, *A History of the Oratorio*.

of Handel's impressive way of turning whole nations into the heroes of his oratorios: even as oratorio librettists, Zeno and Metastasio remained true rationalists, spinning the silken thread of their sonorous verses not on the basis of inner experience but in the light of the new rules that they first devised, then applied to their poetry. The poetic element was necessarily subordinated to moral instruction and edification, as is clear from what now strikes us as the curious theological, philosophical and moral debates in which the heroes engage with each other. None the less, both Zeno and the incomparably more imaginative Metastasio succeeded in creating works within these limitations that make it easy to understand how they were able to maintain their reputation until well into the nineteenth century. Indeed, Metastasio's oratorios are in many respects even finer than his operas,[62] inasmuch as his didactic aims are easier to square with the former than with the latter, with his heroes adopting a less importunately heroic tone and the love intrigue vanishing completely. In consequence, the heroes' inner conflicts, however limited in scope, come more into their own here, while the masterly dialogue and the brilliant poetry in which it is clothed are in no way inferior to those in his operas. Particularly praiseworthy, finally, is his ability to create three-dimensional characters in spite of the absence of any on-stage action.[63]

The didactic aim of these works emerges most clearly in those pieces that tell of the battle between worldly and spiritual forces and the inevitable victory of the latter. One such work is Mozart's *Davidde penitente* of 1785. A second group, including the present *La Betulia liberata*, reveals God's power and strength through the heroic actions of a woman and, as such, forms a counterpart to the operas about heroines that were popular at this period. The third group is represented by Zeno's *Tobia* and looks forward to the later bourgeois melodrama and plays about family life.

In contrast to the operas of the time, the Neapolitan oratorio was in only two acts and contained only six or seven arias. At the beginning or end of each act there would be a chorus, although this might also appear elsewhere in the piece. Another point that distinguished opera from oratorio was the importance attached not only to ensembles, but also to the accompanied recitatives and to more elaborate orchestral writing. In all other respects, however, the formal repertory of Neapolitan oratorios was the same as for *opere serie*, namely *secco* and accompanied recitative and the *da capo* aria.[64] Oratorio also responded to the various changes in taste, while avoiding its more egregious lapses. Like operas, oratorios were written to commission and often had to be completed within a very short space of time. Above all, however, they were no more successful than operas in avoiding the pitfalls of vocal virtuosity.

It was only after the death of Scarlatti that the Neapolitan oratorio enjoyed its finest hour in the works of Leonardo Leo, who set standards that were later occasionally equalled, but never surpassed, by other Italian composers. In Germany, the genre's principal representative was again Johann Adolf Hasse,[65] and it was on him, rather than on the elderly Eberlin, that the young Mozart

62. Metastasio himself called them not tragedies but, far more modestly, 'componimenti sacri'.
63. ◆ Specifically with respect to K118, see Thoma, '"Betulia liberata". Bemerkungen zum literatur- und geistesgeschichtlichen Hintergrund des Mozart-Oratoriums KV118'.
64. Scheibe, *Der critische Musikus*, i.216.
65. See Kamieński, *Die Oratorien von Johann Adolf Hasse*, reprinted in Schering, *Johann Adolph Hasse: La Conversione di Sant' Agostino*. ◆ More recently, see Koch, *Die Oratorien Johann Adolf Hasses: Überlieferung und Struktur* and Monterosso, 'L'oratorio in Bologna nel secolo XVIII' (including remarks on Leo).

modelled his own oratorio.[66] The merits of Hasse's style were no less suited to oratorio than to opera, including, as they did, an emphasis on *cantabilità*, on clarity and transparency of style, an aristocratic reserve in the expression of violent passion and, at the same time, a sureness in his dramatic vision that enabled him to concentrate on the essence of his subject and to ignore all that was peripheral and incidental.

The legend of Judith was treated as follows by Metastasio in a libretto that was set by numerous other composers.[67] The characters – or *interlocutori* – are:

> Ozia, principe di Betulia.
> Giuditta, vedova di Manasse
> Amital, nobile donna Israelita.
> Achior, principe degli Ammoniti.
> Cabri ⎫
>   ⎬ capi del popolo.
> Carmi ⎭
> Coro degl abitanti di Betulia.

The town of Betulia is currently besieged by Holofernes. Its inhabitants are in despair, but Judith now enters and accuses them of pusillanimity. Her simile aria ('Del pari infeconda') may be taken as an example of style of Metastasio's poetry:

> Del pari infeconda
> d'un fiume è la sponda,
> se torbido eccede,
> se manca d'umor.
> Si acquista baldanza
> per troppo speranza,
> si perde la fede
> per troppo rumor.

[The bank of a river is equally barren if there is too much turbulence or a lack of moistness. Rashness comes from too much hope, confidence is lost through too much noise.]

Judith announces that she has taken a great decision but that she is not yet able to reveal what it is. Meanwhile, she invites the townspeople to pray. There follows an episode revolving around the

---

66. ◆ Here Abert underestimates the importance of the Salzburg repertory for Mozart, a repertory transmitted in large part by Leopold's teaching and advice. Eberlin's oratorios and oratorio-like works, mostly composed in the 1740s and 1750s, included *Die Allmacht Gottes, Die beste Wahl der christlichen Seele, Der büssende hl. Siegmund, Christus-Petrus-Debora-Sara, Petrus und Magdalena, Pro sepulchro Domini, Sedecias* and *Der verlorene Sohn*; see Haas, 'Eberlins Schuldramen und Oratorien'. Similarly, Leopold's oratorios were also influential on Wolfgang, including *Der Mensch ein Gottesmörder* and the *Oratorium pro Quadragesima*; see Eisen, 'Leopold Mozart Discoveries'.

67. First set in Vienna by Georg Reutter the younger (1734), then by Jommelli (1743), Holzbauer (1760), Cafaro (1746), Gassmann (1772), Salieri (revised 1821), Sales (1783), Schuster (1796), Seydelmann (1774), Naumann (1805) and Jacob Schuback (1773). ◆ Other settings include those by Andrea Bernasconi (1754), Mysliveček (1771), Giuseppe Calegari (1771), Mattia Stabingher (1783), Francesco Pitichio (1786), Giuseppe Scolari (1768), Anfossi (?1781), Giuseppe Giordani (1796) and a German version, *Judith, oder der Entsatz Bethuliens*, by Johann Michael Demmler (1780).

heathen prince Achior, whom Holofernes has banished to Bethulia for lauding Jehovah's power and who he hopes will share the townspeople's fate. Festively attired, Judith now asks to leave Bethulia. The chorus (in the distance) expresses its amazement at this turn of events.

The second part of the work opens with a lengthy theological discussion between Ozias and Achior in which the former attempts to demonstrate that there is only one God. In its moment of supreme need, Judith now returns to the town with the severed head of Holofernes and describes what she has done. Achior declares his readiness to convert. Charmis announces that, following Holofernes' death, the Assyrians have been slaughtered while fleeing. The work ends with a hymn of thanksgiving for Judith and the chorus.

The surviving autograph score runs to 382 pages and comprises fifteen numbers.[68] In its whole approach to the subject, as well as in many modulatory and melodic details[69] and its use of a Gregorian melody in its final chorus, it reveals Mozart's debt to Hasse,[70] while other features, such as the shortened *da capo*, the use of thematic contrast, the elaborate coloratura writing and the handling of the orchestra, place the work in the immediate vicinity of the composer's early operas. The fact that Mozart set himself higher goals here than he did in his operas is clear, not least, from the overture. Although it is in three movements, its outer movements are thematically linked, with neither of them containing any other theme apart from the principal musical idea. Even more important, however, is the fateful, almost inconsolable tone of the overture, a tone sustained in the middle movement and discharged in the final section in a paroxysm of wild defiance. This is the first time in Mozart's music, moreover, that the key of D minor emerges in all its eerie solemnity, making one wonder whether it was modelled on the overture to Gluck's *Alceste*, a piece in the same key and further related to Mozart's by dint of its motif of a third.

The three choruses are no less exceptional in character. Although the first ('Pietà, se irato sei') consists only of three brief, homophonic, refrain-like interjections in Ozias's solo, these bitter strains encapsulate the nation's whole despair, a despair only with difficulty held back, while at the same time underscoring the soloist's sustained and hopeless lament. The chorus that ends part one ('Oh prodigio! Oh stupor!) is again homophonic, but is far more broadly structured, with the people's astonishment at Judith's undertaking finding expression in brief, generally declamatory phrases, their agitation in a series of impassioned orchestral figures. The whole scene is observed through the eyes of the dramatist. This whole approach emerges even more clearly from the final chorus ('Lodi al gran Dio'), the nucleus of which is a hymn of thanksgiving for the liberated Bethulians, with interjections from Judith in which she tells of her victory over their enemies. But whereas she vents her feelings in curiously agitated, subjective terms, the chorus avails itself of the old and hallowed language of the Church in the form of the following melody:

68.   André wrote to Jahn to report that, according to a copy of the wordbook that was unknown to Jahn, the work was performed during Lent 1786 – not in Vienna, as Sonnleithner had told him – and that Mozart appeared to have written two extra numbers, an introductory chorus 'Qual fiero caso' and a quintet 'Te solo adoro'. He suspected that they were in Berlin, but no trace of them has been found there. ◆ On 21 July 1784, Mozart wrote to his sister asking for the score of *La Betulia liberata*: he was to compose an oratorio for the Viennese Tonkünstler-Sozietät and thought he might mine the earlier work for a number or two (*Briefe*, iii.319). Additionally, a printed copy of the libretto, dated 1776 and used by Gassmann as the basis for his setting, may derive from Mozart's estate: the title page was altered to read '1786' and a later notation describes it as including corrections by Metastasio made specifically for a setting by Mozart. However, the corrections are not by Metastasio, there is no trace of two extra numbers, and no surviving evidence suggests the work was either revised or performed by Mozart. See NMA I/4/2, VII–VIII.
69.   These include a predilection for a striding bass or for a bass line that indicates the harmonies by means of *sforzato* quavers, a procedure found far more frequently here than in the operas.
70.   See Schering, *Geschichte des Oratoriums*, 238–9.

Andante

Lo — di al gran Di — o che op — pres — se gli em — pi ne — mi — ci

suo — i, che com — bat — tè per no — i

che tri — on — fò co — — sì.

This is the two-part trope of the ninth church mode (the *tonus peregrinus*) associated with the psalm *In exitu Israel de Aegypto*, the same melody that was to be used in the *Requiem* at the words 'Te decet hymnus'.[71] Here the melody is heard four times, on each occasion in a different, albeit invariably homophonic, setting, with the orchestral accompaniment, in particular, being noticeably different. On the fourth occasion its second section is slightly altered, even in the tenor. The inspiration behind this passage was almost certainly Hasse, who used the chorale melody *O Lamm Gottes* in the Pilgrims' Chorus from his oratorio *Sant'Elena al Calvario*. But the impact of this melody is substantially increased by being contrasted with Judith's solo interjections, in which subjective emotion is given free rein, with the melody tending towards a more declamatory style and finding expression in generally brief phrases. In short, it is the text that conditions the form here, which explains why the orchestra plays such a retiring role. Even in this early work, then, Mozart typically combines ecclesiastical objectivity with subjective emotion. Here we find the first traces of the spirit that was later to inform the *Requiem* and that could hardly be more different from the operatic style of similar choruses of jubilation in other oratorios of the period, although this style, too, finds expression in the *allegro* closing chorus.

Mozart also lavished greater care on the *secco* recitatives, again following Hasse's example, if not achieving the standards set by his predecessor, an achievement none the less impressive in view of the fact that Metastasio did not make life easy for him with passages such as Achior's outline history of the Jews. Characteristic of Mozart's approach is the great dispute about polytheism and monotheism at the beginning of part two, a lively and graphic argument conducted between Ozias

71. It is also the basis of the old chorale *Mein Seel erhebt den Herrn*. The melody appears at the same point in Michael Haydn's *Requiem* in B flat major and, more recently, in Friedrich Kiel's *Requiem* in A flat major. ◆ See also Croll, 'Im tonus peregrinus: Bemerkungen zur "Betulia liberata" von Mozart'.

and Achior in brief and pointed phrases behind which the listener can almost see the characters' gestures. The actual climax of the debate[72] is introduced by a lively progression in the bass; three more such progressions in the bass are heard later when Achior vacillates for the first time but as yet remains unconvinced. The use of sequencing in his declamatory line is also highly effective.[73] Indeed, the declamation reveals a number of intelligent details, notably at Achior's words 'Io ripugnanza alcuna nel numero non veggo', while Ozias' pontificating tone is also very well caught.[74]

Judith's two accompanied recitatives are motivically more unified than those in the operas, a state of affairs that is once again probably due to Hasse. At the same time, their often acute characterization reveals Judith as a forerunner of Giunia in *Lucio Silla*. Her long account of her actions – one of Metastasio's most exciting scenes – inspired Mozart to write a very special kind of piece, with sustained chords on the strings, generally in their higher register, replacing his usual plethora of disparate motifs and lending the character a somewhat rapt air. All the more striking, then, are the brief motifs that interrupt these chords, especially the one heard at the very beginning at Holofernes's overbearing question, then Judith's eerie, catlike gesture as she springs to her feet (just before the word 'sorgo') and, finally, the twitching of Holofernes's dead body ('balzar mi sento').

There is little that needs to be said about the arias. On a formal level, they are more carefully planned than those in the operas and, above all, more richly instrumented and more independent. With three exceptions ('Ma qual virtù non cede', 'Di tua vittoria' and 'Con troppa rea viltà), all require at least double wind.

The middle sections of the arias continue to be relatively old-fashioned in character, whereas the main sections at least reveal an occasional attempt to use for poetic ends the thematic contrasts[75] that in the operas had generally still been conceived in purely musical terms. Listen, for example, to the remarkable syncopated theme in the minor in Judith's aria ('Terribile d'aspetto'): this same theme had already been heard at the same point in her first aria ('Del pari infeconda'), albeit in the major – clearly an echo of the attempts to impose a sense of motivic unity on the works that we have already noted in the case of the masses. On the other hand, both these arias – both, significantly, are simile arias – are noticeably lacking in vital warmth, and much the same is true of Ozias's arias. But as soon as the characters cease to moralize and speak to the people ('Pietà, se irato sei' and 'Lodi al gran Dio'), Mozart's creative gifts rise to an appreciably higher level. How vivid and true to life, for example, are the choral entries in Ozias's scene with the people ('Pietà, se irato sei'), each entry successfully adding a far greater sense of urgency to the soloist's singing within only a handful of bars. Both here and in the final scene that we discussed earlier Mozart not only equalled his Italian models but far surpassed them. Even the homophonic and essentially declamatory chorus that brings part one to an end ('Oh prodigio! Oh stupor!) is full of character, with the austere and rhythmically taut writing for the orchestra playing a not inconsiderable role

72. At Ozias's question 'credi, Achior, che possa cosa alcuna prodursi senza la sua cagion?'

73. This device had been used by Gluck, with great success, in his pre-*Orfeo* operas. Inspired by Hasse, it was very infrequently used by Mozart. Gluck often used these sequences – mostly based on chromatic progressions in the bass – to sum up and intensify a whole group of ideas, whereas Mozart tends to stick to individual words and concepts in his *secco* recitatives. Nor is there any sign here of Gluck's subtle distinctions between different types of cadence (perfect, medial and phrygian); see Ralph Meyer, 'Die Behandlung des Rezitativs in Glucks italienischen Reformopern'.

74. All the more grating is the effeminate, fashionable and almost flirtatious tone of the aria, which contains no sense of religious conviction but merely demonstrates the superficial manner in which composers of the period set about solving problems of this kind.

75. See especially Amital's aria ('Quel nocchier che in gran procella'), in which the gracefully fluttering second subject has absolutely nothing to do with the image of a tempest at sea but serves merely to produce a sense of musical contrast.

in its effectiveness. It is not just astonishment at Judith's decision that finds expression here, one also has the feeling that her heroic feat has breathed new life and courage into the hearts of a despondent nation.

Among the arias of the secondary characters, Amital's ('Con troppa rea viltà) is particularly notable for the second subject of its adagio and its beautiful and contrite coda over a pedal point. Bass voices, too, were allowed in oratorios,[76] and the present representative is Achior, whose account of the monstrous Holofernes, in one of the rollicking bass arias so common in the eighteenth century ('Terribile d'aspetto'), occasionally verges on the comical. Mozart even includes parts for solo trumpets here.

These attempts at drama on Mozart's part during his Italian period present us with a colourful and motley picture. On a biographical level, they are of supreme interest, providing further startling evidence of the boy's astonishing ability to adapt immediately to new styles. Suffice it to compare *Mitridate* with *Ascanio in Alba* and *La Betulia liberata*: for all their similarities, Mozart had no difficulty in grasping the stylistic differences between the three genres of opera, serenade and oratorio. But he also changed decisively during these three years on both an artistic and personal level as he entered into early manhood, and nothing is more rewarding or more moving than to observe the passion coursing through his veins from the time of *La Betulia liberata* and *Lucio Silla* onwards. Yet these early works also show us the limits to his youthful genius, limits imposed in spite of and, in part, because of his precociousness. He was a child of a northern land, a barbarian country where even infant prodigies took longer to develop than in the south. As a boy he was not yet equal to writing dramatic works. As an artist he brought to his task only his musical genius, but even here he first had to assimilate qualities that were second nature to Italian composers. He was hindered, moreover, by his upbringing, which had been devoted, in the main, to instrumental music, with the result that the symphonist was forever looking over the shoulder of the opera composer. Even Mozart was forced to realize that a work of art as unified as an Italian opera required time and careful thought. No doubt his works from this period include individual blooms from the land of his genius that it was not even given to any of the Italian composers of the time to pluck, but these works remain markedly inferior to their Italian models in terms of their stylistic unity and, more especially, their vocal writing, while the worst excesses of the Italian school happily find a place here, sometimes even in exaggerated guise. Mozart's years of apprenticeship were not yet over, and we do both him and ourselves a disservice if we attempt to treat these products of his immaturity as the ineffable creations of an immortal genius.

---

76. See Mattheson, *Critica musica*, i.110–11: 'That the deep bass voices bring great majesty, harmony and force to a piece is undeniable; but whether the result is always agreeable or whether there is not also something uncivilized and terrifying about it, I leave the listener to decide.' In this context, the reader may recall figures such as Handel's Polyphemus and Bach's Zeolus.

11

Church and instrumental works, 1769–1773

Alongside the operas and other works discussed in the previous chapter, Mozart's visits to Italy also witnessed the composition of an impressive number of other pieces, only a few of which were commissioned by individuals and institutions in Italy: the majority were composed for his archiepiscopal employer in Salzburg during the breaks between his trips to Italy. Pride of place under this heading goes to a series of sacred works.

We have already discussed sacred music in Salzburg in the context of Leopold Mozart.[1] Austerely devout and opposed to all suspicion of worldliness, Archbishop Schrattenbach had taken a particular interest in church music, believing that his Kapelle's principal function lay in its contribution to church services.[2] His successor, Hieronymus Colloredo, extended his frugality to the Salzburg Kapelle, further alienating his musicians as a result of his severity of temperament. Contemporaries felt that under him music in Salzburg deteriorated rather than improved,[3] even though he was more concerned with the court's prestige than Schrattenbach had been and made a number of individual improvements.[4]

The composition of the archbishop's Kapelle during Wolfgang's time was the same as it had been during Leopold's, comprising, as it did, thirty men's voices alongside a boys' choir of fifteen. These last-named the archbishop not only maintained: he also provided for their education.[5] Schrattenbach allowed the few surviving castratos to die out, while at the same time sending the daughter of the cathedral organist, Maria Magdalena Lipp, to study singing in Italy, appointing her a court singer in 1765. She married Michael Haydn soon afterwards [on 17 August 1768]. Colloredo engaged another castrato in the person of Francesco Ceccarelli, but the latter proved a mediocre singer and, on a purely personal level, contemptible as an individual.[6]

---

1. See above and Hammerle, *Mozart und einige Zeitgenossen*.

2. ◆ Abert's portrait of Schrattenbach is overdrawn: the Archbishop was fond of worldly splendour, the church music composed for him was strongly influenced by the Italian style (and by Italians, such as Caldara, who were active both in Vienna and Salzburg) and Italian opera was given not infrequently at court; see Eisen, 'Mozart e l'Italia: Il ruolo di Salisburgo'.

3. Koch-Sternfeld, *Die letzten dreißig Jahre*, 255; Burney, *The Present State of Music in Germany*, ii.322; and Schubart, *Ideen zu einer Ästhetik der Tonkunst*, 157.

4. Believed to be by Leopold Mozart, this report was published by Marpurg in his *Historisch-kritische Beyträge zur Aufnahme der Musik*, iii.183ff. Much information may be gleaned from Mozart's correspondence. Pillwein's *Biographische Schilderungen oder Lexikon Salzburgischer, teils verstorbener, teils lebender Künstler* is as superficial in its treatment of musicians as the later *Biographien Salzburgischer Tonkünstler*. ◆ For an English translation of Leopold's report, see Zaslaw, *Mozart's Symphonies*, 550–7.

5. Particularly outstanding singers such as the tenor Felix Winter and the baritone Joseph Nikolaus Meißner were even sent to Italy to study and later engaged as soloists. For more details on Meißner, who was also active as a composer, see Marpurg, *Historisch-kritische Beyträge*, iii.190–91; Schubart, *Deutsche Chronik*, ii (1775), 408; Dreßler, *Theater-Schule für die Deutschen, das ernsthafte Singe-Schauspiel betreffend* (1777), 42; and Hammerle, *Mozart und einige Zeitgenossen*, 53. ◆ Also see Hintermaier, 'Die Salzburger Hofkapelle'.

6. ◆ Ceccarelli was nevertheless a close friend of the Mozarts, who seem not to have such had a low opinion of his singing; see, among others, Mozart's and Leopold's letters of 3 and 10 December 1778 (*Briefe*, ii. 517 and 519).

The orchestra was likewise kept up to strength thanks to reinforcements in the form of three trombone players made available by the tower watchman and the six trumpeters and timpanists who, as part of the Futtermeisteramt, took their place between the archbishop's equerry and his lackeys in the social hierarchy of the court.[7] Leopold's account of the way in which these forces were distributed is worth quoting here:

In the cathedral church, the main organ is at the back, by the entrance to the church, while at the front, near the choir, there are four side organs, with a small choir organ beneath them in the choir itself. It is here that the choristers are positioned. The main organ is used only for performing preludes in choral works, otherwise one of the side organs is used, namely, the one nearest the altar on the right-hand side, where the soloists and basses are positioned. Opposite them, by the left-hand side organ, are the violinists and so on, and on the other two side organs are the two choirs of trumpets and timpani. The lower choir organ and violone play with them in tuttis. The oboe and transverse flute are rarely heard in the cathedral church, the horn never. As a result, all these gentlemen play the violin in church.[8]

Since 1750 the cathedral's principal organist had been Anton Cajetan Adlgasser (1729–1777), a pupil – and later son-in-law – of Johann Ernst Eberlin. An outstanding organist and accompanist, in 1764 he was sent by the archbishop to Italy to further his studies. His sacred works continued to be performed in Salzburg even after his death.[9] Of less importance was the second organist, Franz Ignaz Lipp, who was Michael Haydn's father-in-law. They were joined in 1774 by Anton Paris, the son of the second organist, who had died in 1760.[10]

Eberlin was succeeded as Kapellmeister in 1763 by Giuseppe Francesco Lolli, a native of Bologna, whose surviving compostions include a handful of oratorios and sacred works.[11] Domenico Fischietti was appointed titular Kapellmeister in 1772. He hailed from Naples and had also made a name for himself as a writer of *opere buffe*. He moved to Dresden in 1765 as music director of Giuseppe Bustelli's opera company[12] and was engaged as church composer in the city in 1766, but in 1772 he was dismissed from his post for lack of achievement.[13] His opera *Il mercato di Malmantile* was performed at Maggerbill in 1763 in honour of Countess Pálffy, the sister of Archbishop Colloredo, and it may have been this performance to which he owed his appointment in Salzburg. Here, too, he seems to have promised more than he delivered, and Mozart's letters are full of contempt for his scant achievements.

7. Altenburg, *Versuch einer Anleitung zur heroisch-musikalischen Trompeter- und Pauker-Kunst*, i.26–7.

8. Marpurg, *Historisch-kritische Beyträge*, iii.195. A similar arrangement is demanded by Mattheson in *Das neu-eröffnete Orchestre*, i.158–9.

9. See Keller, 'Wolfgang Amadeus Mozart in Salzburg im Jahre 1769', 41–2, and Hammerle, *Mozart und einige Zeitgenossen*, 31. ◆ Concerning Adlgasser, see Constantin Schneider, 'Zur Lebensgeschichte des Salzburger Komponisten A. C. Adlgasser'. For a thematic catalogue of his works, see de Catanzaro and Rainer, *Anton Cajetan Adlgasser: A Thematic Catalogue of his Works*.

10. For a note on their duties, see Leopold Mozart's account in Marpurg, *Historisch-kritische Beyträge*, iii.187–8. ◆ Concerning Lipp, see Aigner, 'Der Eggenfeldener Lehrersohn Franz Ignaz Lipp (1718–1798)', and Hintermaier, 'Die Salzburger Hofkapelle', 223–6; for Paris, see Hintermaier, 'Die Salzburger Hofkapelle', 309–12.

11. ◆ See Haas, 'Beiträge zur Geschichte der Oper in Prag und Dresden' and Engländer, 'Domenico Fischietti als Buffokomponist in Dresden'.

12. Hiller, *Wöchentliche Nachrichten und Anmerkungen die Musik betreffend*, i.53.

13. Fürstenau, *Beiträge zur Geschichte der königlich sächsischen musikalischen Kapelle*, 161 and 164; see also Teuber, *Geschichte des Prager Theaters*, i.268. Fischietti was with Bustelli first in Prague, then in Dresden. His operas *Vologeso* and *Nitteti* were performed in Prague in 1764 and 1765 respectively. ◆ Further, see Hintermaier, 'Die Salzburger Hofkapelle'.

With Lolli as Kapellmeister and Leopold Mozart as his vice-Kapellmeister, Joseph Haydn's younger brother, Johann Michael (1737–1806),[14] was appointed Konzertmeister and orchestral director in Salzburg, an appointment made on the recommendation of a nephew, Archbishop Sigismund of Großwardein, whose Kapellmeister he had been since 1757. There was little contact between the Mozarts and the Haydns. Haydn was fond of whiling away his time over a glass of beer or wine, a tendency that was bound to strike the strict and sober Leopold as all the more reprehensible in that he neglected his official duties in the process. 'Who do you think has been made organist at Holy Trinity?' Leopold asked his son in a letter of 29 December 1777. 'Herr Haydn. It's a joke! He'll be an expensive organist; after every Litany he knocks back a quart of wine and then sends for Lipp, who is himself something of a tippler, to take the other services for him.'[15] On 29 June 1778, we find Leopold writing again: 'In the afternoon, with the archbishop present, Haydn played the organ during the Litany and the *Te Deum*, but so badly that we were all shocked [. . .]. He was only slightly drunk, but his head and hands weren't together. [. . .] Haydn will drink himself into a dropsy in a few years or, at any rate, he'll get lazier and lazier the older he becomes, as even now he's too lazy to do anything.'[16] Even the behaviour of Haydn's wife must have given cause for offence, as we find Mozart making fun of her in a letter to the Abbé Bullinger of 7 August 1778: 'Frau Haydn, it's true, is in poor health; she has a very ascetic lifestyle and has been overdoing things. But there are so few like her! – I'm surprised she hasn't lost her voice long ago, what with her constant scourgings and flagellations, her hair-shirts, unnatural fasts and night prayers.'[17] Leopold will have preferred his family to have no closer dealings with the Haydns, especially as he himself had so little time for Haydn's own behaviour: 'How I'd like to hear him talking to the Italians in Italy', he wrote on 8 December 1777. 'They'd certainly say: "Questo è un vero tedesco!"'[18] Although private tensions and petty jealousies of a kind that so easily arise in such parochial circumstances may perhaps have influenced Leopold's unfavourable opinion of Michael Haydn, he excepted the artist from his condemnation. Admittedly, he thought on hearing Haydn's opera *Andromeda e Perseo* in 1787 that his younger colleague had no aptitude for the theatre and that the arias for the main characters could have been written for a boy chorister, but he had nothing but praise for the incidental music to *Zaire* that Haydn wrote in 1777, describing it in detail in a letter to his son and adding that the archbishop had done Haydn the honour of saying at table that he had not thought him capable of writing such a work: he should drink not beer but only Burgundy and as a reward receive six kronthalers.[19] But when he says of him, in his letter of 24 September 1778, 'You would surely not deny Haydn his achievements in music',[20] it is his sacred works that he is referring to, and these Wolfgang duly copied out as part of his studies. From Vienna, Wolfgang wrote to his father on 4 January 1783, asking him to send him 'a few contrapuntal pieces by Eberlin

14. Schinn and Otter, *Biographische Skizze von Michael Haydn*; Engl, *Zum Gedächtnis Johann Michael Haydns*; and Otto Schmid, *Johann Michael Haydn*. A selection of his masses may be found in Klafsky, *Michael Haydn: Kirchenwerke*, and of his instrumental works in Perger, *Michael Haydn: Instrumentalwerke*. ◆ Further, see Heinz Schuler, 'Johann Michael Haydn und sein Salzburger Familienkreis'; MacIntyre, *The Viennese Concerted Mass of the Early Classic Period*; Croll and Vössing, *Johann Michael Haydn, sein Leben, sein Schaffen, seine Zeit: eine Bildbiographie*; and Sherman and Thomas, *Johann Michael Haydn (1737–1809): A Chronological Thematic Catalogue of his Works*.
15. *Briefe*, ii.212.
16. *Briefe*, ii.379–80. A similar point is made by Riesbeck in his *Briefe eines reisenden Franzosen*, i.357. Later, as we know, Haydn achieved a reputation for great industry.
17. *Briefe*, ii.440.
18. *Briefe*, ii.175. Wolfgang described Anton Schweitzer as being 'as dry and smooth as our Haydn, but better-spoken' (*Briefe*, ii.161; letter of 3 December 1777).
19. *Briefe*, ii.25 and 36 (letters of 30 September and 6 October 1777).
20. *Briefe*, ii.485.

copied out on small sheets of paper and bound in blue, and some things by Haydn'.[21] And on 12 March 1783 he wrote again: 'The "Tres sunt" copied out in my own handwriting must be somewhere at home.' He wanted these works in order to be able to perform them at the Sunday concerts at van Swieten's house, additionally requesting Haydn's latest fugues. 'I should very much like them to hear the *Lauda Sion*', he wrote in the same letter. 'The fugue *In te Domine speravi* has been much applauded, as have the *Ave Maria* and *Tenebrae*.'[22] Among the unpublished papers found on Mozart's death were two further fugues on *Pignus futurae gloriae* from litanies by Michael Haydn, both of them copied out in Mozart's own hand.[23]

In the history of Catholic church music and especially of one of its greatest glories, the mass, the rapid decline in musical standards must be laid firmly at the door of the Neapolitan school.[24] Stylistically, this period is characterized by the fact that solo singing increasingly displaced choral singing, while the instrumental contribution increased in size and scope. But, unlike polyphonic choral singing, all these devices are essentially unecclesiastical in character. Indeed, there was a time when solo singing was considered the born enemy of true church music inasmuch as it was regarded as the expression of an individual personality, while *a cappella* music, with its 'impersonal' stamp, was deemed uniquely suited to performance in church. This is, of course, an extremely one-sided view: composers such as Josquin, Palestrina and Lassus left the imprint of their own personality on the art of their time in exactly the same way that later composers did, and to regard the development of accompanied solo song as the birth of individuality in music would be to misunderstand the whole nature of artistic creativity. What we *can* say is that, in expressing their personal feelings, the composers of an earlier age never transgressed the limits of the church's universality of emotion, but regarded themselves as the legitimate spokesmen of that universality, firmly convinced, as they were, that this framework still left them with enough room to express more personal beliefs. As a result, they succeeded in solving the main problem of all church music – how to reconcile the demands of the Church with a more popular appeal – and did so, moreover, in a way that was perfectly suited to their age. In this they were sustained by the revival of a more general ecclesiastical spirit, a revival summed up in the Council of Trent.

None the less, it was inevitable that, following the rise of solo singing, composers should feel tempted to go beyond generalities and seek to express their own subjective emotions. After all, the main aim of the Florentine Hellenists had consisted in allowing the form of a movement to develop freely from the text and from its individual words and ideas. The following period showed clearly

---

21. *Briefe*, iii.248. This volume is mentioned in Gottfried Weber, 'Weitere Nachrichten', 290–1. According to a note by Aloys Fuchs, it contained the following works written out in full score in Mozart's hand: Michael Haydn, *In te Domine speravi*, fuga a 4 voci 2 Viol. Org.; Eberlin, *Missa canonica a 4 voci Organo* (three different settings); Eberlin, *Recessit pater noster a 4 voci*; Eberlin, *Tenebrae factae sunt a 4 voci Org.*; Eberlin, Graduale pro Dominica in Palmis *Tenuisti a 4 voci Org.*; Eberlin, Offertorium pro Dominica in Palmis Improperium a 4 voci Org.; Eberlin, Communio pro Dominica in Palmis *Pater si potest a 4 voci Org.*; Michael Haydn, *Tenebrae a 4 voci Org.*; Eberlin, 3 Motetti *In nomine Domini; Christus factus est; Domine Jesu a 4 voci*; Michael Haydn, *Ave Maria* pro Adventu Domini a Sopr. solo c. rip.; Eberlin, *Benedixisti a 4 voci Org.*; Eberlin, *Cum Sancto Spiritu*, fuga a 4 voci; Eberlin, *Kyrie*, fuga a 4 voci; and Eberlin, *Cum Sancto Spiritu*, fuga a 4 voci. ◆ This manuscript collection, now at the British Library (shelfmark Add. MS 41633), includes not only the works described above (and listed in K[6] as Anh. A71–88) but also Anh. A14, an Ave Maria by Michael Haydn. It is not the case, however, that the copies are by Wolfgang: with the exception of Anh. A14, they are by Leopold Mozart. Wolfgang's copy of Anh. A14 was probably made in Salzburg some time between 1773 and 1775; Leopold's copies date from various times during the 1770s.
22. *Briefe*, iii.259.
23. ◆ These are Anh. A11 and Anh. A12. The former (now at the Bibliothèque nationale, Paris), and based on a work of April 1764, was probably copied out by Mozart during his stay in Salzburg in 1783, while the latter (now at the Staatsbibliothek zu Berlin), based on a work of March 1776, may have been copied towards the end of 1783.
24. See Kretzschmar, *Führer durch den Konzertsaal*, ii/1.181ff. ◆ On the mass generally, see Schmidt-Görg, *Geschichte der Messe*; Ursprung, *Die katholische Kirchenmusik*; Blankenburg, *Die Messe*; and MacIntyre, *The Viennese Concerted Mass of the Early Classic Period*.

that, in itself, church music had nothing to fear from this development as long as it was practised by composers who were perfectly clear in their own minds about the seriousness of the challenge facing them. In the Protestant world, where the new style was particularly suited to the desire to give practical expression to religious convictions, it even produced a new and magnificent harvest – not, it is true, in the field of the mass, but in that of the new form of the cantata.

As the seventeenth century pursued its course, the mass acquired an orchestral component, but composers still shied away from introducing solo singing. When its time finally came, under the Neapolitan composers, it was not as the result of any consolidation of religious beliefs struggling to find expression in some new and subjective way, but, on the contrary, in consequence of a reduction in religious feeling and increasing confusion in the basic tenets of church music, hence the growing influence of operatic music at this time. It was not solo singing as such that caused this decline but the unecclesiastical use to which it was put, a use closely bound up with the decline in religious life in eighteenth-century Italy. Above all, the traditional guardian of church music – the clergy – failed in its appointed task for, in spite of all the decrees of the Council of Trent, they had become increasingly secularized and were no longer capable of providing any much-needed moral guidance. The schools of the period, however, were dominated by the Jesuits, whose religious teachings were shrewdly geared to their own claims to power, while the true representative of spiritual culture, the aristocracy, was itself increasingly concerned with questions of secular power and content to fulfil its religious duties on a purely superficial level, meeting its spiritual needs – always assuming that it had any – through philosophy, rather than through religion. It is no wonder, therefore, that church music was affected by this decline in religious life, the signs of which are still evident in Italy, even today.

The basic problem was that neither the Church nor its musical servants had the strength any longer to criticize the sort of music that was inspired by opera, but merely adopted it in an increasingly thoughtless way. Traces of this spirit may be found even in the works of more serious composers such as Durante and Leo, but it was Hasse's generation that was worst affected by it, depriving church music of two of its principal characteristics, without which it can never fulfil its true function: virility and mysticism. The effeminate sentimentality of the century as a whole now took possession of the mass, too, so that only rarely was it able to produce a more virile tone, and whenever composers attempted to strike such a note, the works in question all too often resembled the operas of the period in bearing all the hallmarks of blatant, empty and stilted emotionalism. At the same time, the tawdry *fioriture* of opera found their way into church music, where they naturally led to far worse distortions than they had ever done in opera. But even the sublime and transcendental rarely found a place in this music any longer, with composers no longer capable of summoning up any sense of inspiration or mystic interiority, but descending, rather, into workaday routine and communing with their God in a tone of petty and even jovial informality that could hardly have been less appropriate. From informality to thoughtlessness is but a single step, and composers now wrote down the first thing that entered their heads without worrying about the meaning of the words, turning the fundamental principle of the Renaissance style into its diametrical opposite.

Choral singing suffered especially badly during this period. It is clear from classic works of this kind that a meaningful combination of choral and solo singing could produce an impressive increase in expressive possibilities: suffice it to recall the profoundly thoughtful way in which Bach, for example, uses this combination in his B minor mass to bring out the historical and personal aspect of the Christian faith. The Neapolitan composers, by contrast, and especially the later ones, forfeited these advantages by failing to eliminate choral singing completely and by treating what remained in so careless a manner that it lost virtually all its ancient dignity. Even now, dim memories of the old importance of contrapuntal procedures lived on in the constant choral fugues, but such fugues are insipid in their subjects and arid in their elaboration, with richly varied organic life replaced by moribund craftsmanship and with many of these fugues no more than empty products of a mindless insistence on clinging, limpet-like, to a custom that was now barely understood.

This shortcoming, too, was largely bound up with the looser structures that now typified organized religion. The clergy stood idly by as church choirs went into free fall,[25] with their numbers and, with them, their standards much reduced, so much so that in some places the congregation fled the building before the figural singing began.[26] Choirs of the size of those found in Salzburg and Munich were very much the exception. In the circumstances, it was only natural for composers to place the main emphasis in their masses on solo singing, and here, as in opera, castratos played an increasingly important role. What is more, instruments now came to play a more independent part than they had done in the past.

Here, there was already a long-standing tradition on which to draw, inasmuch as the old *sonate da chiesa*, as well as a large number of church concertos including Corelli's concerti grossi, were intended to be performed during church services. But as the *sonata da chiesa* became increasingly indistinguishable from chamber works in terms of both form and character, it came to be replaced by the newer type of sonata and even by symphonies and solo concertos.[27] A worrying aspect of this practice was the fact that more often than not no attempt was made to ensure that the pieces chosen were suitable for performance in church, with the result that purely secular works such as Haydn's symphonies that were originally written as *Tafelmusik* or for academies were now taken over into the mass.[28]

All in all, it was the same spirit as that already familiar to us from the world of opera that increasingly proclaimed the absolute precedence of the sensual over the spiritual.[29] The ecclesiastical character of the works in question – especially masses – suffered considerably in consequence, but even qualities such as popular appeal and universal intelligibility were reduced to the level of shallowness, triviality and worse.

No doubt some of the better composers were conscious of this problem. A leading figure from Mozart's own day to whom we have already had occasion to refer is Padre Martini, who in his teachings and writings was tireless in recalling the classical age of Italian church music. But he and people like him could do little to stem the rising tide, not least when Hasse himself joined the enemy camp.[30] In Germany, too, the Neapolitan type quickly became established, albeit not without a good deal of opposition, the most significant of which came from Johann Joseph Fux in Vienna, a composer who in his own masses had done all that he could to bring about a revival of the art of Palestrina and the Dutch composers within a modern context. As such, he was a

25.   Burney, *The Present State of Music in France and Italy*, 14, 22, 117, 176, 182 and 229.
26.   Schubart, *Ideen zu einer Ästhetik der Tonkunst*, 128 and 347.
27.   Max Seiffert has published excerpts from some of the Mass sinfonias by the Bohemian composer Franz Habermann (1706–83) in the *Kirchenmusikalisches Jahrbuch*, xviii (1903). For more on this custom, see Dittersdorf, *Lebensbeschreibung*, 22 and 91–2, and Burney, *The Present State of Music in France and Italy*, 181 (Burney describes a Venetian performance of a mass by Galuppi, scored for six orchestras).
28.   ◆ See Zaslaw, 'Mozart, Haydn, and the *Sinfonia da chiesa*'.
29.   See Kretzschmar, *Führer durch den Konzertsaal*, ii/1, 199ff. Two writers who have attempted to rescue the reputation of this whole trend are Lorenz, *Haydns, Mozarts und Beethovens Kirchenmusik und ihre katholischen und protestantischen Gegner* and Schnerich, *Der Messentypus von Haydn bis Schubert* and *Messe und Requiem seit Haydn und Mozart*.
30.   ◆ Further, see Witzenmann, 'Stilphasen in Hasses Kirchenmusik'. And for some aspects of Neapolitan Mass settings, see Hochstein, 'Die Gestaltung des Gloria in konzertierenden Messvertonungen "neapolitanischer" Komponisten'.

remarkable witness to the practical and historical aspirations of a century generally dismissed as unhistorical. He, too, of course, was denied any lasting success, and the Viennese mass once again fell completely under Neapolitan influence in the hands of Georg Reutter the younger. In Salzburg as well, a worthier tradition was kept alive, with Orazio Benevoli (1605–1672) composing his famous fifty-three-part mass for the inauguration of the cathedral on 24 September 1628.[31] Scored, in reality, for two eight-part choirs and their respective orchestras, it is a work which, for all the originality of its tonal combinations, none the less preserves its sacred character.[32] Even at a later date, valuable artistic work went hand in hand with a more careful treatment of the chorus, as is clear from the masses of both Eberlin and Michael Haydn. And in both of Mozart's early masses this old and distinctive spirit continues to make itself felt.[33] Mozart himself reports on local conditions in Salzburg in a letter to Martini of 4 September 1776 that is also of value for what it tells us about his assessment of his own church music:

I live in a country where music enjoys scant success, and although a number of them have already left, we still have some excellent teachers here, in particular some composers of great wisdom, learning and taste. As for the theatre, we are in a bad way because of the lack of singers. We have no castratos and are unlikely to find any, because they want to be well paid: and generosity is not one of our failings. Meanwhile, I am amusing myself by writing for the chamber and the church, and here we have two excellent contrapuntalists, namely, Signor Haydn and Adlgaßer. My father is maestro di cappella at the cathedral, which gives me a chance to write as much as I like for the church. Also, my father has already served this court for 36 years and knows that the present archbishop is neither able nor willing to put up with people who are getting on in years, and so he no longer puts his whole heart into his work, but has taken up literature, which has always been a favourite study of his. Our church music is quite different from Italian church music, and is becoming more so all the time, so that even the most solemn Mass said by the archbishop himself, including the whole of the Kyrie, Gloria, Credo, Epistle sonata, Offertory or motet, Sanctus and Agnus Dei, must last no longer than 3 quarters of an hour. This type of composition requires special study, and even so a mass should have all the instruments – trumpets, timpani, etc. It's a pity that we're so far apart, my very dear Signor Padre Maestro, I have so much to tell you![34]

We have already mentioned the way in which Mozart took up and developed Hasse's particular brand of mass. It remains only to add a few remarks on its nature and history.

Even at this late date, the *missa solemnis* was still distinguished from the *missa brevis*. The former treated the individual subsections as independent, large-scale movements, whereas the latter admitted only the five best-known movements as a self-contained entity, with the subsections being merely alluded to rather than singled out as autonomous sections.[35]

---

31. ◆ This work is now thought possibly to be by Heinrich Biber; see Hintermaier, '"Missa salisburgensis": Neue Erkenntnisse über Entstehung, Autor und Zweckbestimmung'. Further concerning Viennese church music at this time, see Riedel, *Kirchenmusik am Hofe Karls VI. (1711–1740): Untersuchungen zum Verhältnis von Zeremoniell und musikalischem Stil im Barockzeitalter*.

32. See Adler, *Orazio Benevoli: Festmesse*.

33. For a recent study, see Kurthen, 'Studien zu W. A. Mozarts kirchenmusikalischen Jugendwerken (bis zur 1. italienischen Reise)'. ◆ Further, see Manfred Hermann Schmid, *Mozart und die Salzburger Tradition*.

34. *Briefe*, i.532–3. The original is in Italian. See also *Allgemeine Musik-Zeitung*, xxiii, 683ff. ◆ Although this letter is signed by Mozart, it is otherwise entirely in Leopold Mozart's hand, and may have been composed by him.

35. ◆ Concerning the *missa brevis* and *missa solemnis* traditions, see MacIntyre, *The Viennese Concerted Mass of the Early Classic Period*.

It did not occur to the Neapolitan composers to revise their basic attitude to the five mass movements. Indeed, they were prevented from doing so not only by a centuries-old tradition but by the words of the mass themselves, which trace in clear and graphic outline every stage in man's dealings with God: humble devotion in the Kyrie, praise and thanksgiving in the Gloria, a firm declaration of faith in the Credo, mystical contemplation and adoration in the Sanctus and guilt-laden entreaty and compassion in the Agnus Dei. Even when they singled out individual passages such as the 'Qui tollis' in the Gloria and the 'Et incarnatus est' and 'Crucifixus' in the Credo, the Neapolitan composers continued to respect the old and great tradition. But their basic error was to adopt far too superficial an approach to man's dealings with God. Even Bach himself, in the themes of his B minor mass, sets out from an approach that is universally human, popular and comprehensible, but then proceeds to use this as a bridge by which to lead his listener's imagination into the realms of the highest art. The Neapolitan composers, by contrast, did not merely remain on the level of this popular folklike tone, they watered it down and thus became so hopelessly outdated and trite that their music often seems like a caricature of the religious ideas contained in the text. There is barely a trace here of any attempt to explore the symbolism of the words of the mass. Quite the opposite: the text itself grows increasingly incidental, with many composers concerned only to write effective pieces of a powerful, festively brilliant, idyllic or elegiac stamp, pieces, in short, into which the words are then inserted with greater or lesser skill. It is impossible to speak any longer of any musical clarification of the words, still less of any attempt to illustrate the meaning of the text and explore every one of its subtlest ideas. This failing emerges with particular force from the great complexes of the Gloria and Credo, although here it has to be conceded that these movements had always proved a challenge to composers on account of the abstract and speculative concepts that they contain. The Neapolitan composers made light of this problem, recognizing only those passages that were musically grateful or ungrateful and turning the grateful sections into the structural pillars of the whole work and leaving the others to fend for themselves. It was left to Beethoven to sweep away this purely musical approach to the words of the mass, so that, for him, there were no longer any main sections and subsidiary sections, even in the Credo. But even elsewhere the prevalence of purely musical considerations was clearly felt, notably in the interplay between solo and choral writing and in the way in which whole movements were cast in aria or sonata form. Of course, composers cannot be criticized merely for taking over these forms as such, but only for not adapting them to their new surroundings with sufficient seriousness of purpose and for taking over not just the actual form but also its secular spirit.

Ternary form is also found in the case of Mozart's Kyries, often after a brief slow introduction. Here the form emerges naturally from the text to the extent that the 'Christe eleison' is a gentler-toned middle movement between the two Kyries and is often entrusted to the soloists.[36] In terms of its musical content, even this section already shows clear signs of decline: its *allegro* character is significant, and even in cases where composers adopt a rigorously contrapuntal approach, the appeal for mercy often rises to Heaven with no real sense of inner involvement or fervour.

In much the same way, the Gloria,[37] with its mood of jubilation and thanksgiving, frequently acquires an element of secular and festive brilliance that tends to be expressed in rushing string

36. Even here, as we shall see, there are fluctuations that can be explained only in purely musical terms.
37. The opening words, 'Gloria in excelsis Deo', are intoned by the priest before the altar in the prescribed manner, and the choir then enters with the words 'Et in terra pax'. The same applies to the beginning of the Credo, where the choir enters only with the words 'Patrem omnipotentem'. As a result, the opening words are frequently not set. On other occasions, by contrast, the choir repeats the words intoned by the priest.

figures and over-instrumentation, and even the soloist's entrance in the 'Laudamus te' all too often strikes a secular note through its use of tawdry coloratura to express a sense of joy. As for the interplay between soloist and chorus, Mozart generally follows tradition, which in this case meant striving for musically effective contrasts, although with the passage of time he sought increasingly to entrust the more semantically important sections of the text to the chorus. The most important of these sections is the threefold appeal to Christ at the words 'Qui tollis', the movement's ideational middle section that introduces the only darker note into an otherwise brightly lit picture. Here Mozart's imagination, too, invariably takes wing, above all with the help of harmonic writing that is as surprising as it is austere and full of character. Of course, not even in Mozart's case does the following section always manage to maintain this same high level, either in the soloist's 'Quoniam tu solus Sanctus' or in the usual final fugue on 'Cum Sancto Spiritu'. Here and at the words 'Et vitam venturi saeculi' in the Credo we find the two main areas where composers allowed their fugal imaginations to run riot and where Archbishop Colloredo rightly put his foot down. Mozart, too, only slowly broke free from the spell of tradition.[38] In general, however, his masses reveal that it was very much the Gloria that he strove to invest with increasingly individual and deeper life.

Based as it is on the Nicene Creed, the Credo is the wordiest and most conceptually dense of the movements that make up the mass. Rejoicing in the strength of their religious beliefs, composers of an earlier generation had sought to deal with this section by adoping a virile and even austere underlying tone which, when combined with characterful part-writing, invested this profession of faith with a genuinely religious, fixed expression. Here, too, the school of Hasse adopted a far more superficial approach to dogma, refusing to explore the individual metaphysical ideas contained in the text but remaining on the level of what can be grasped by the senses. This element was then singled out at the expense of the others.[39] In general, the spirit of contemporary church music finds particularly faithful expression in these movements, the overall mood being one of animation, vigour and briskness, with joviality and brilliance replacing composure and inward awe. Only rarely do composers appear conscious of the deeper significance of the words: this emerges most obviously at the section dealing with Christ's incarnation and Passion, the 'Et incarnatus est' and 'Crucifixus', although here, too, two fundamentally different approaches coexist alongside each other. One of them is spiritual and sees Christ's incarnation as a mystery, while the other is material and authentically Neapolitan, an approach that takes as its starting point the popular scene in the manger and accordingly has no inhibitions in drawing on pastoral siciliana melodies.[40] In the 'Crucifixus', too, it is usually the singers' and instruments' lower register that is exploited, with the resurgent 'Et resurrexit' designed to provide an effective contrast to it. In the distribution of the text between soloists and chorus, it is again purely musical considerations that tend to prevail here: the fact that at the words 'Et in Spiritum Sanctum', for example, the third person of the Trinity often has to make do with an extremely lightweight and trifling solo can be explained only in terms of the desire to create an exclusively musical contrast. As we have already observed, the ending, as before, is a fugue which, as Beethoven's great mass shows us, may well

38. ◆ Generally, see Rosenthal, 'The Salzburg Church Music of Mozart and his Predecessors' and Manfred Hermann Schmid, *Mozart und die Salzburger Tradition*.

39. Typical of this approach is the popular use of tone-painting to underscore individual words and ideas such as the reference to the dead at the words 'iudicare vivos et mortuos' and 'resurrectionem mortuorum', or the idea of descent and ascent at 'descendit de coelis' and 'ascendit in coelum', and so on. Mozart, too, follows this example. ◆ Further, see Walther Müller, *Johann Adolf Hasse als Kirchenkomponist* and Hansell, 'Sacred Music at the Incurabili in Venice at the Time of J. A. Hasse'.

40. This view underpins the 'Et incarnatus est' even as late as Mozart's great C minor mass K427.

suggest the idea of eternal life, even though his predecessors fall far short of this ideal in terms of the manner of their execution.

But the most difficult challenge that faced composers not only in the Gloria but, even more so, in the Credo was how to weld together such a wealth of ideas and produce a unified whole. The older method, adopted by Padre Martini and, uniquely, by Mozart in his K115, was to dispense with the idea of a formal link and stick as closely as possible to the text.[41] Now, however, we find attempts to round off the whole complex of ideas from a musical point of view and thus to produce a clearer structure either by repeating certain themes in the manner of cyclical forms or ensuring a sense of unity by means of recurrent orchestral motifs. As a final possibility, the main ideas contained in the text could be impressed on the listener by dint of frequent repetition: here one thinks especially of the word 'credo' itself. In this respect Mozart was to prove a true pioneer, and traces of his influence can still be seen even in Beethoven.

As for the Sanctus, the situation had changed with the passage of time, with the result that the Benedictus, which had originally been only a brief interlude, now tended increasingly to become the main section, thereby reducing the Sanctus to the role of a mere introduction. Invariably kept very brief, the Sanctus opens the movement on a note of awestruck sublimity and is followed by the 'Pleni sunt coeli', a longer, more animated and festively brilliant movement that ends with the fugal 'Hosanna'. All three sections are entrusted to the chorus. By contrast, the Benedictus,[42] with its tone of childlike trust, is a favourite among Viennese composers and, as such, is regularly set for solo voices – either one or, in Mozart's case, preferably four. The movement lies embedded between the surrounding movements like an intimate idyll, and Mozart left his mark on it so visibly that his whole approach to it was later to be regarded as authoritative. The 'Hosanna' is then normally repeated either complete or in part and sometimes also merged with the Benedictus. Alongside this type, however, we meet a second type, albeit much less commonly found, that strikes the sort of austere, even sombre note more usually associated with the Agnus Dei, giving the impression that the last-named movement is already casting its shadows in advance and that the sight of the Lamb of God has produced a feeling of profound contrition within the composer's breast. These movements are generally also characterized by far stricter part-writing.

The two-part structure of the Agnus Dei is already dictated by the text, with the first part a guilt-ridden prayer for mercy, the second a plea for peace. Musically, this contrast finds expression in a slow movement (the Agnus Dei) followed by a fast one ('Dona nobis pacem'). The Agnus Dei is often scored for a soloist alternating with the chorus. Here, moreover, is another of the passages where most composers strike a note of greater profundity, be it elegiac or emotionally charged. All the more crass, then, tends to be the contrast with the 'Dona nobis pacem', in which the secularization process plumbs depths unusual even by Neapolitan standards. One has the impression that by this stage in the proceedings the composers in question were already outside the church and on their way home, so smugly jovial and trifling does this final plea for peace appear. Not even Mozart himself always succeeded in avoiding this pitfall.

Mozart began, but failed to complete, a number of masses at this time. Their handwriting may be dated to the years between 1770 and 1772, suggesting that they were written under Martini's

41. ◆ Abert's observation that K115 is unique is in a way prescient since it happens that the mass is almost certainly by Leopold Mozart; his incomplete, autograph draft survives in the André archive at Offenbach. Later copies were the basis for editions attributed to Wolfgang, chiefly that in AMA XXIV no. 28 (a modern edition, correctly attributed to Leopold, ed. Reinhold Kubik, was published by Carus-Verlag [Neuhausen-Stuttgart, 1989]). It would seem, then, that by Abert's lights at least, it is Leopold who was the 'true pioneer'.
42. In Mannheim, the Benedictus was replaced by an organ voluntary: see *Briefe*, ii.102 (letter of 4 November 1777).

influence. The new world that was opening up to the young composer at this time is best reflected in the C major mass K115, the autograph score of which has been dated by more recent scholars – almost certainly correctly – to the late summer of 1770.[43] Here everything points to the older school of Italian church music as promulgated by Padre Martini – the accompaniment scored solely for organ, the strict counterpoint from start to finish and even the motifs, as is clear from the beginning of the Kyrie, which is introduced by a five-bar adagio:

Another tendency that resurfaces here is the attempt to create motivic links between the individual movements. The Kyrie theme just quoted, for example, is a condensed version of the previous Adagio, its principal characteristics being its descent into subdominant harmonies and reascent to dominant and tonic harmonies by means of a rhythmically intensified variant of the two short note-values. Both continue to be in evidence in the following movements, with the tendency to modulate to the subdominant not only in stark contrast to the Neapolitan predilection for dominant endings but characteristic of the mass as a whole, as may be seen from the eight bars of the Sanctus.

In no other mass did Mozart move as far away from the Neapolitan spirit as he did on this occasion, his independence evident not least in the extreme brevity of the individual movements: one almost feels that he is afraid of allowing his emotions free rein here but that, instead, he lavishes the greatest possible care on bringing out the meaning of the words. The whole spirit of the work is more earnest and dignified (listen, in particular, to the 'Et incarnatus est', the bold harmonic secrets of which already anticipate the *Requiem*), and only the rather uninspiring subject of the final fugue in the Credo (a section otherwise worked out with great skill) recalls the older Salzburg manner. One can only regret the fact that Mozart's return to Salzburg prevented him from becoming Martini's more permanent ally and promulgating a type of mass which, although

43. Wyzewa and Saint-Foix, *Wolfgang Amédée Mozart*, i.324–5, draw attention to the similarity between the paper and handwriting found here and those found in the works written in Bologna at this same period. ◆ But see again n. 41. It is unclear to which mass fragments Abert refers – traditionally, very few incomplete church works by Mozart have been attributed to this period and most of them are not authentic: the Kyrie K91 (K[6] Anh. A17) is by Georg Reutter and the Kyrie K221 (K[6] Anh. A1) by Eberlin. The mass K116 is by Leopold Mozart and the authenticity of K140 is uncertain. Only the D minor Kyrie K90 dates from this time (mid-1772).

condemned at the time as old-fashioned, was none the less full of character and genuinely religious in style.[44] The fragmentary F major mass K116 breaks off at the words 'sedes ad dexteram Patris', and although its contrapuntal procedures and close link between the Kyrie and 'Christe' clearly reveal Martini's influence, it already includes brief orchestral interludes in the Neapolitan manner. Stylistically speaking, the Kyrie in C major K221 may also date from this period, even though it has no slow introduction and its 'Christe' has a subject of its own. Possibly it was intended for a *Requiem* and may therefore belong together with two other movements in the same manuscript, a three-part vocal movement with missing text and a Lacrimosa KAnh.21.[45]

But of all the works from this period, the one that provides the greatest contrast with the Bolognese style is the great *Missa solemnis* in C minor or, rather, in C major[46] K139 that probably dates from early 1772. Not only does Mozart now return to his most up-to-date manner, he piles on its operatic features to an extent that is found nowhere else in his works. The mass revels in the most extreme dramatic contrasts and, in particular, contains nocturnal images – notably in the opening sections of the Kyrie and Agnus Dei and in the 'Qui tollis' and 'Crucifixus' – that are bolder than anything found in any of the other works from this period. There must have been some specific reason for this flight of fancy on the part of Mozart's genius; and the remaining movements, too, reveal his desire to produce something special.[47] The four sections just mentioned not only share a minor tonality, they are also exceptional by dint of their harmonic writing and instrumentation – with the exception of the 'Qui tollis', all are scored for three trombones in addition to strings and oboes. Mozart was evidently at pains to mitigate the bright underlying tone of the Neapolitan mass by underscoring the darker aspects of our emotional lives, and he does so as a veritable member of the *Sturm und Drang*, as, indeed, he is in this case. In consequence, he abandons his usual more lyrical standpoint and moves over into the field of drama, increasing the sense of human suffering until it encompasses the torments of eternal damnation. Even the opening Kyrie conjures up a scene from hell, with a thrice-repeated cry from the entire massed chorus followed by whole-bar rests during which we hear a typically Mozartian figure in the first and second violins,[48] a descending, fate-laden triadic motif answered by a dull sob in the trombones and violas, and followed at once by a tremolando shudder that passes through the full orchestra. To this may be added harmonic writing as bold as it is austere and, above all, the lapidary brevity of the whole – this opening section must certainly have given the Salzburgers pause for thought. In much the same spirit, the entirely declamatory and homophonic 'Qui tollis', with its trembling triplet accompaniment and restless, curiously agitated bass motif, points in the

---

44. ◆ This paragraph needs to be read with caution: none of the works described by Abert is by Mozart. The mass K116 (which also includes K⁶Anh. A18, 417B and Anh. 19) is a late but incomplete work by Leopold Mozart, probably from 1768; K221 is a copy by Leopold Mozart of a Kyrie by Eberlin from before mid-1772; and Anh. 21, listed in the most recent edition of Köchel as Anh. A2, is a copy from before mid-1772 of a Lacrimosa also by Eberlin.

45. With its almost Bachian ostinato bass, the beautiful Lacrimosa is strikingly different in style from the other works written under Bolognese influence. Whether this *Requiem* is the mass for Count Spaur mentioned by Leopold Mozart (*Briefe*, ii.362, letter of 28 May 1778) or the C major mass K259 is impossible to say; see Jahn, *W. A. Mozart*, fourth edition, i.187; and Wyzewa and Saint-Foix, *Wolfgang Amédée Mozart*, i.388. ◆ KAnh. 21 (K⁶ Anh. A2) is not a work by Mozart but a Lacrimosa by Eberlin copied by Leopold Mozart not later than mid-1772 and possibly considerably earlier.

46. Only the first sections of the Kyrie and Agnus Dei are in C minor. The 'Qui tollis' is in F minor. All the other movements are in the major. ◆ Present-day scholarship now assigns K139 to Vienna, 1768; almost certainly it is the so-called 'Waisenhausmesse' composed by November of that year and first performed in Vienna on 7 December 1768.

47. Wyzewa and Saint-Foix, *Wolfgang Amédée Mozart*, i.423, suggest the funeral ceremonies for Archbishop Schrattenbach at the end of 1771 or beginning of 1772, whereas Jahn argues that this was the mass for Count Spaur. ◆ It now seems more likely that the 'Spaur' mass is K258. If K139 is in fact the mass composed by Mozart in 1768 – as seems likely – then it could not have been written for Schrattenbach's funeral ceremonies. In any case, a Requiem was commissioned from Michael Haydn for that occasion (Klafsky I/8, MH155).

48. Cf. the opening movement of the keyboard fantasia in C minor K475 of 1785.

direction of those operatic scenes in which ghosts are conjured up. This sense of emotionally charged drama culminates in the 'Crucifixus', in which the strangely unnerving sound of the muted trumpets is answered by an agonized groan in the orchestra. Only then does the chorus enter, intoning its cry of disconsolate wretchedness in brief despairing phrases, before slowly sinking into a state of calm resignation, while the calls on the trumpets simultaneously fade into silence. Drama returns as the solo soprano rises, lark-like, into the air from this deathly silence with her scalar 'Et resurrexit'. Finally, even the Agnus Dei creates the impression of a graveside scene, with its trombone tune – heard three times in the course of the movement – initially striking a note of dull lament, before ascending triplet motifs produce a curious feeling of agitation. But even here we find a sense of stark dramatic contrast, as the chorus intones the 'Miserere' in long note-values, while the strings are suddenly seized by a violent triplet movement.

The dramatic, almost theatrical nature of these sombre images introduces a surprising new note to Mozart's masses, yet they remain introductory or episodic in character, and the main movements remain essentially unaffected by this development: if we except his formal changes, Mozart remains entirely on Neapolitan ground here. The solo contributions to the 'Quoniam' and 'Et in Spiritum Sanctum' (both of them cast in binary aria form), the siciliana duet of the 'Et incarnatus' (another scene in a manger) and the like are purely operatic, trifling in tone and decked out with tawdry *fioriture*. The 'Quoniam' in particular is strikingly dancelike, half minuet, half polonaise. Thoroughly modern, too, is the sonata form of the Kyrie's allegro section,[49] while the attempt to impose a sense of motivic unity on the orchestra emerges with even greater clarity here than it did in the last C major mass. The Kyrie and 'Christe' are not yet treated as separate entities in the allegro, but instead Mozart adds a separate section in the 'Christe' for the four soloists, a section which, although it has turned out far too lightweight for its contents, reveals great skill and effectiveness in its part-writing and especially in the interplay between the four vocal lines.[50] The allegro is then repeated – a further example of the excesses that point in the direction of the *Sturm und Drang*. By contrast, the Gloria is lacking in all sense of motivic cohesion, consisting, as it does, in a whole series of stark contrasts that again reveal the dramatist in Mozart. And it is to Mozart the dramatist that we owe the remarkable form of the 'Gratias', which adopts a form particularly prevalent in this mass, with a slow introduction followed by an allegro section. Although the text is extremely brief at this point and in itself scarcely suggests the use of contrast, Mozart has produced an antithetical structure that he has then proceeded to underscore with all the harmonic and compositional means at his disposal. Never again was he to draw such a sharp distinction between the words 'propter magnam gloriam tuam' and the 'gratias agimus tibi'. Only the fugue on the words 'Cum Sancto Spiritu' rolls along like a river in full flood. It, too, has a revolutionary element to it in the form of the tritone interval of its subject and its great length, while its technique, structure and expressivity all mark it out as a great advance on Mozart's earlier style.

The Credo picks up on the earlier attempt,[51] in K 66, to impose a sense of motivic unity on the whole complex of ideas, and on this occasion it achieves its aim with incomparably greater skill. In the earlier mass, the linking element had been an ostinato bass motif in keeping with the older tradition, whereas now it is an energetic scalar figure on the violins that returns in the full

49. The second subject for the soloists recalls an old folk tune that we have already encountered in an earlier piece by Mozart: see Rattay, *Die Ostracher Liederhandschrift*, 57–8.

50. As a rule, the Neapolitan composers treated the Kyrie and 'Christe' as three separate movements, with the third of them either a repeat of the opening Kyrie or a fully worked-out fugue.

51. ◆ Given that K66 is later than K139, the relationship between the two Credos is the reverse of that suggested by Abert and the following discussion should be read with a grain of salt.

orchestra at the 'Et resurrexit', 'Et unam sanctam' and, finally, at the beginning and end of the fugue on the words 'Et vitam venturi saeculi':

Here Mozart consciously addresses a problem that was to preoccupy him incessantly from now on. It is significant that he began by attempting to solve it by orchestral means, for, with the exception of a mere handful of passages, the instruments in this mass are totally independent when compared with the voices. In spite of this scalar motif, the Credo is again designed, above all, with effective dramatic contrasts in mind. The final fugue on 'Et unam sanctam' is cleverly prepared not only by the theme itself but also by the more independent treatment of the individual voices. The decision to include a new 'Hosanna' in the Benedictus is strikingly and emphatically inspired by the same concern for dramatic contrast, resulting in the entire movement becoming a dialogue between soloist and chorus. And, as in the Kyrie, Mozart again gilds the lily by repeating the 'Hosanna'.

One wonders what Padre Martini would have said about this work of his pupil, a work which, borne aloft on the wings of the dramatist and deploying the most up-to-date means, takes the listener from heaven to hell, passing through the world of human existence on its way. Whatever his reservations, he would surely have seen in it the fruits of his teachings and applauded the genuinely cantabile vocal writing that sets it apart from its Salzburg predecessors. But in terms of its form and content, too, it represents a tremendous advance on these earlier works, and we shall later have occasion to observe its traces in virtually every bar of its successors.

Mozart's earliest litanies date from this same period. The litany is a sung prayer which, like the mass, begins with the 'Kyrie eleison' and ends with the 'Agnus Dei, miserere nobis' (without the following 'Dona nobis pacem'). Between these sections comes a whole series of prayers that vary depending on the particular circumstances in which the litany is performed. In consequence, it is impossible to speak of a fixed form and, in general, the work does not build to a climax. Musically speaking, the piece as a whole is conceived as a dialogue between a prayer leader (soloist or chorus) and a chorus, with the former stating the object of the request and invoking the saints, after which the latter joins in with frequently repeated formulas such as 'Ora pro nobis' and 'Miserere nobis'. As a result, the refrain played a special role here from time immemorial. That the litany was not difficult to set to music but, rather, that it was particularly well suited to providing composers with a quite special field of expression is clear from older settings dating as far back as Heinrich Schütz.[52] As with the mass, it was the Neapolitan composers who ushered in the period of decline.

Mozart's first litany in B flat major K109[53] dates from May 1771 and is an example of a *Litaniae Lauretana*, an invocation to the Virgin Mary.[54] The musical images of the Mother of God that are depicted here have always reflected those found in the visual arts: for all their underlying majesty and purity, they have a great sense of charm and often of intimacy and rapt devotion, while more popular elements can also occasionally be discerned. Mozart's litany is no exception: in form, it is extremely concise and rarely avails itself of contrapuntal procedures. Instead, it explores the meaning of the text with some care, an aspect no doubt due to Padre Martini's influence. The

52. Examples may be found in Proske, *Musica divina*, iv.319ff.
53. On Mozart's first two litanies, see Chrysander, 'Mozarts Werke: Litaneien und Vespern'. ◆ Further, see Krutmann, 'Mozarts Litaneien'.
54. ◆ See Klaver, *The Litany of Loreto*.

instrumentation, too, harks back to the earlier period, with two violins (including crossing of parts) and bass, together with a trombone in the 'Salus infirmorum'.[55] A further distinctive feature of the work is its approach to the question of form, with the individual movements welded together to create a unified entity thanks to skilful reminiscences and variants of its principal ideas.[56]

Even in the opening Kyrie the listener is bound to be struck by the way in which the music reflects the text at the words 'Miserere nobis' and 'Sancta Trinitas' (marked *forte*). In the 'Sancta Maria' the voices of the four soloists constantly overlap with each other, while the chorus adds its invocatory interjections. The result is a piece of genuine Neapolitan tenderness, but without any of the excesses of that school, a piece that revels constantly, yet charmingly, in its adoration of the Mother of God. A far more austere tone is struck in the 'Salus infirmorum', a choral number built around the contrast between the distress felt by Christians and their powerful faith in the Virgin's assistance. The most lightweight movement is the 'Regina angelorum', which is entrusted to the four soloists. Far more substantial is the 'Agnus Dei', which begins with a moving entreaty, before striking a more impassioned note with the entry of the chorus, then finally – and surprisingly – dying away with a muted sob in a dark-hued B flat minor, a fine example of the unexpected way in which more sombre emotions may surface and which, as we have already repeatedly observed, is entirely typical of Mozart. Movements of this kind show that the 'Romantic crisis' of 1773 already had its antecedents less in the world of opera than in the composer's sacred music.

The *Litaniae de venerabili altaris sacramento* K125 is Mozart's second contribution to the genre and dates from March 1772. More serious in character than its predecessor, it consists of invocations of the Holy Sacrament, almost all of which are dogmatic and transcendental in nature, placing the same sort of demands on the composer as the Credo in the mass and, as a result, finding far better and less secular solutions in the older period than in the hands of the Neapolitans.

Stylistically speaking, Mozart's litany stands in the same relation to its predecessor as the C minor mass does to the Bolognese Mass: it adopts the most up-to-date Neapolitan manner, most strikingly in the opening Kyrie, which resembles a movement from a contemporary symphony with added chorus, and in the two solo arias, 'Panis vivus' and 'Panis omnipotentia', which are faithful to their operatic models even to the extent of replicating their coloratura flourishes and typical final cadenzas. The fact that the Salzburg litany also contains a specific sense of local colour in terms of its structure and character is clear from a comparison with Michael Haydn's litany in G minor[57] and, even more, from Leopold Mozart's litany in C major.[58] Mozart's readiness to follow in his father's footsteps is revealed by correspondences not only in terms of tempo and time-signature (only the Agnus Dei has a different time-signature), but especially by his choice of keys, except that in Wolfgang's case everything is a whole tone lower. Both agree, moreover, in their interpretation of the individual movements. What matters here is less the fugal form of the 'Pignus', since this form was dictated by tradition and in Mozart's case, in spite of its characterful theme, is far

55. ◆ Mozart had a precedent in this: Leopold's litany in E flat major, Seiffert 4/7–8, also included a trombone solo at 'Salus infirmorum' (later reworked by Mozart for oboe); see Eisen, 'The Mozarts' Salzburg Copyists', 287–9.

56. Jahn's dismissive reaction to the piece, which he describes as 'solid and assured, but earth-bound' (i.309), shows a fundamental inability to recognize the distance that Mozart had travelled in the meantime.

57. Published by Breitkopf & Härtel in Leipzig, this is a more mature and more serious piece than Mozart's and clearly dates from a much later period; see Wyzewa and Saint-Foix, *Wolfgang Amédée Mozart*, ii.434. ◆ Haydn's litany MH228 dates from 26 March 1776.

58. Max Seiffert, *Leopold Mozart: Ausgewählte Werke*, 188ff. ◆ Leopold's C major litany (Seiffert 4/1) was written in the 1750s or early 1760s at the latest.

too long[59] and certainly more studied than inspired. Far more interesting is a comparison between the three slow introductory movements in both works – the 'Verbum caro factum', the 'Tremendum' and the 'Viaticum'. Although both reveal the same basic approach, Leopold's work resembles nothing so much as a preliminary study for Mozart's consummate realization, with the latter astonishing his listeners with music that is among his most inspired at this time. In the 'Verbum caro factum' the mystery of the incarnation of the Word inspires one of those sombre minor-key canvases observed through the eyes of genius that we have already encountered on several occasions in these sacred works: through a constant flood of sequences, the bold, dark-toned harmonies finally glide down into a shadowy B flat minor accompanied by agitated triadic figures on the violins. A similar sense of awestruck terror affects the 'Tremendum', with Wolfgang taking over his father's tone-painterly tremolando on the strings, although the concluding allegro is, of course, as colourless in the one case as it is in the other. In the 'Viaticum', too, the borrowings extend even to the dynamic markings, including the *f* and *p* at the words 'in Domino morientium', and the closure on the dominant of B flat minor.[60] Even so, Mozart towers far above his father in the profoundly thoughtful, almost dramatically exaggerated way in which he depicts the deaths of those who have died believing in God and the contrite prayer of those who have been left behind on earth. The Agnus Dei, too, begins with a solo[61] in both composers' works and ends with a choral section in which Mozart uses a number of individual motifs from the solo section, which, with its wide-ranging melodic intervals, *fioriture* and cadenzas, is again authentically Neapolitan in spirit. In the chorus, too, the instruments are almost more important than the voices, and only the 'Miserere' brings us a little closer back to the sacred tradition with its anguished chromaticisms and a plagal cadence that dies gently away into nothingness.

Other works from this period that can be dated with relative certainty include two motets, both settings of the *Regina coeli* and dating from May 1771 (K108) and May 1772 (K127). Both are laid out and treated on exactly similar lines and demonstrate only that the spirit of Neapolitan music had infiltrated the motet, too, with its aria-like solos, highly developed orchestral style and light-weight choral writing that only rarely avails itself of imitative procedures. There is virtually nothing here to remind the listener of Padre Martini. Conversely, the outer movements resemble nothing so much as the corresponding movements of a symphony with their subject group, brief development section and complete recapitulation. As a result, it is the instruments that have the greatest contribution to make here. The slow middle movements, too, resemble symphonic andantes in their structure and character,[62] while adopting an operatic cantabile style. Only the second such movement of both works, the 'Ora pro nobis', contains more individual Mozartian features alongside the tender-hearted melodies that were common at this time.[63] Here, at the same time, is the only opportunity for darker, more serious emotions, with the whole of the rest of the work adopting a tone that is either operatically emotional or lively and carefree, a tone invariably

---

59. Mozart cut three passages and made corresponding changes. The original form of this movement, together with the 'Viaticum', may be found in the critical commentary to NMA I/2/1.

60. The movement originally closed in B flat major.

61. At the beginning, Leopold has added above it: 'The solo in the Agnus Dei will be transposed for Herr Meißner.' This and other remarks added by Leopold and relating to questions of tempo and performance markings for the organ part will no doubt have been made with a specific performance in mind.

62. At this point in K108 we find a favourite phrase of Mozart's, a phrase borrowed from the Italian composers of the period and later taken over into both Blonde's first aria from *Die Entführung aus dem Serail* and *Das Veilchen*.

63. Among such features in the first setting is Mozart's fondness for the flattened second degree of the minor scale, while the second setting is notable for the chromatic treatment of the vocal line in the first bar in E flat major, a treatment already reminiscent of the *Ave verum*.

associated in the minds of Neapolitan composers with a good deal of brilliance and noise. The division of labour between solo[64] and chorus is the same as in the second Litany.

In terms of its style and handwriting, the offertory *Benedictus sit Deus* in C major K117 must date from an earlier period and was almost certainly written during Mozart's first visit to Milan in February 1770.[65] The middle section is a soprano aria and was intended for one of the two castratos to whom Mozart had been introduced there. In the main, the two choruses hark back to the older Salzburg tradition, and only the use of the eighth psalm tone[66] in the second subject of the 'Jubilate' suggests something of the new impressions gleaned in Milan's churches:

Psalmum di - ci - te no - mi - ni   e - ius, da - te glo - ri - am lau - di   e - ius

The choral voices intone the melody in succession to a figural orchestral accompaniment, with the chorus responding on each occasion with a powerful 'Jubilate'.

According to one tradition,[67] the offertory *Inter natos mulierum* K72 for St John the Baptist's Day was written in June 1769 immediately after Mozart's visit to Paris, but undoubtedly belongs to the later period.[68] Mozart is said to have been very fond of Franz Xaver von Haasi – Father Johann Baptist – at the monastery at Seeon and whenever he visited the monastery he would jump up, stroke his cheeks and sing:

Mein Han - serl, liebs Han - serl, liebs Han - serl!

It is with this melody that the offertory begins: Mozart is said to have sent his friend a copy as a present on the occasion of his name-day in 1769. But this tradition is emphatically contradicted by the progressive style of the piece, the broadly structured orchestral prelude of which already suggests a later period, as do the free contrapuntal writing and the skilful way in which the theme is repeated in the manner of a refrain after various episodes of a jubilatory or contemplative character ('ecce agnus Dei'), all of which imply a greater degree of maturity on Mozart's part. This is one of the most unified of Mozart's sacred works from this period, a piece of uniquely distinctive character and of a consistently high level of achievement. As such, it almost certainly dates from the end of this period, rather than from its beginning.[69]

In the case of the *Tantum ergo* in B flat major K142, Mozart's authorship seems doubtful, not so much on account of its slight merit[70] but because none of his other works contains anything comparable to the present predictable responses of chorus and soloist in such short phrases. A second

---

64. The privileged role of the soprano in the second *Regina coeli* is due to the fact that it was written for Maria Magdalena Lipp. According to Leopold (*Briefe*, ii.337, letter of 12 April 1778), it was later sung by Ceccarelli. ◆ Further concerning K108 and 127, see Aringer-Grau, *Marianische Antiphonen von Wolfgang Amadeus Mozart, Johann Michael Haydn und ihren Salzburger Zeitgenossen*.

65. Wyzewa and Saint-Foix, *Wolfgang Amédée Mozart*, i.286. ◆ It now seems likely that the offertory dates from Salzburg, 1769.

66. On 4 October 1777, Lepold wrote to his son: 'I am enclosing the chorale tones, which you may occasionally find useful or even necessary; one has to know everything' (*Briefe*, ii.34).

67. Jahn, *W. A. Mozart*, i.66.

68. ◆ Abert's reference to Paris is confusing: presumably he means Vienna (the family had last been in Paris in 1766).

69. Wyzewa and Saint-Foix, *Wolfgang Amédée Mozart*, i.372–3, date it to June 1771. (St John the Baptist's Day falls on 24 June.) ◆ Modern scholarship generally dates K72 to 1771, although even this is not certain: the earliest surviving source for the work dates from the later 1770s. See Eisen, 'The Mozarts' Salzburg Copyists', 281–6.

70. Thus Wyzewa and Saint-Foix, *Wolfgang Amédée Mozart*, ii.426.

Tantum ergo K197, conversely, reveals all the stylistic characteristics of the motets of this period. It is scored for chorus and orchestra alone. There is no reason to deny its authenticity, as Jahn does,[71] not least because it includes some of Mozart's favourite phrases, such as the progression *c″* sharp–*d″*–*g″*–*f″* sharp at the words 'veneremur cernui'.

Scored for four-part chorus and organ, the *De profundis* in C minor K93 is utterly different in character.[72] As is clear from the autograph manuscript, it was originally to have included two violins, a scoring which, like its interdependence of words and music,[73] recalls Mozart's first Marian litany. In the present instance, however, there is no trace of any contrapuntal procedures, with the piece being largely declamatory in style. It is clearly modelled on church psalmody, with the melody of the old liturgical Gloria plain to hear in the doxology that is tacked on at the end. The harmonic writing is as straightforward as it is expressive, with the piece as a whole genuinely prayer-like in tone and imbued with a simplicity that speaks directly to the heart. Particularly beautiful is the sense of elation achieved in the Gloria and the gradual return to silent solemnity at the end. The motet *Iustum deduxit Dominus* K326 must also be dated to this period on stylistic grounds.

Mozart's sacred works also include a series of sonatas for two violins, bass and organ that he wrote between now and 1780. We know from his letter to Martini that in Salzburg a sonata was performed between the Epistle and Gospel, at least until 1783, when it was replaced by a gradual at Colloredo's behest. This was a custom that harked back to the old church sonata (the *sonata da chiesa* in contradistinction to the *sonata da camera*) and had already produced a number of classic examples, including works by Corelli and Dall'Abaco. Mozart's contributions to the genre inevitably show that the old note of religious solemnity had long since disappeared: they are neither solemn nor reverential in tone, and they afford no evidence of stricter procedures. The focus is on the string instruments, with the organ reduced to its historical role of supporting and filling out the harmonies. Wherever it is conceived in more independent terms, Mozart has merely expended a little more care on notating the part, but there is no question here of an obbligato role for the instrument.

Mozart's first dated sonata (K212) was written in 1775, but recent scholarship has shown, with some certainty, that all five pieces – K67–69 and K144–145 – date from this same period,[74] the first three from its beginning, the last two from its end.[75] This attribution is based partly on the character of the handwriting and the choice of paper (which plays an important, if not decisive, role in dating these works) and partly on stylistic arguments. All are single-movement works cast in first-movement sonata form with a subject-group comprising two antithetical themes plus a final group, a very short development section and a recapitulation that is initially entirely faithful but which later assumes more variety. In terms of their character, all five pieces fit easily into the

71. Jahn, *W. A. Mozart*, i.318. ◆ Abert is right to question the authorship of K142 which, with the exception of the 'Amen', is apparently by the Mainz Kapellmeister Johann Zach. But Jahn was probably correct in his assessment of K197, which is not by Mozart but also by Zach. Concerning the authenticity of these works, and of the 'Amen' to K142, see Eisen, 'The Mozarts' Salzburg Copyists', 271–2.

72. ◆ This paragraph also needs to be read with caution. K93 is not by Mozart but by Georg Reutter; Wolfgang's manuscript copy (now in the British Library, London) was written down some time between 1787 and 1791. By the same token, K326 is by Eberlin; the undated manuscript (now in the Biblioteka Jagiellońska, Kraków) is in Leopold Mozart's hand.

73. Wyzewa and Saint-Foix, *Wolfgang Amédée Mozart*, i.386–7, likewise date this piece to the summer of 1771. (They also include a facsimile of the first page of the autograph score.)

74. Wyzewa and Saint-Foix, *Wolfgang Amédée Mozart*, i.383–5 and 431–3.

75. Wyzewa and Saint-Foix date the former to May–July 1771, the latter to January–March 1772. ◆ Although K67–69 are likely to have been composed in Salzburg in 1771 or 1772, K144 and 145 probably dated from 1774. Further concerning Mozart's epistle sonatas, see Tangeman, 'Mozart's Seventeen Epistle Sonatas' and Harmon, 'The performance of Mozart's Church Sonatas'.

picture of the other church music of this period, with themes that are, in part, bombastically rhetorical in the manner of Neapolitan opera sinfonias and, in part, charming and graceful, but in every instance unchurchlike and, as such, entirely typical of the popular chamber music of this time. Specifically Mozartian features are relatively rare, but include the final group of K145 with its contrast between surly outburst and meek retreat:

In assessing the sacred music that Mozart wrote in Salzburg, we need to remember that, unlike most of his contemporaries, he had at his disposal a well-schooled choir that could look back on a long and venerable tradition already exploited by composers such as Eberlin. It is to this circumstance that we owe the fact that, whatever concessions he may have made to solo singing and instrumental music, Mozart left inviolate the chorus's traditionally dominant position in church music. If he had had to write for the average choir of his day, with its one or two soprano voices, soloists and instruments would undoubtedly have taken control in his masses and similar pieces. Here, however, he had before him a choir equal to the highest demands placed upon it. That fortune had smiled on him in this way was later brought home to him in Mannheim, for we find him writing to his father on 4 November 1777 to announce that he dare not have any of his masses performed here as the singers are so irredeemably awful that composers would have to write, in the main, for the instruments.[76] Jahn is wrong, of course, when he writes that, as a result of this, Mozart wrote cantabile choral movements from the outset.[77] This is true to only a limited extent and applies, above all, to the works written under Martini's influence. Mozart's vocal style in both his secular and sacred works is, in general, instrumentally coloured, a circumstance due to the fact that his main field of activity was always instrumental music. His vocal achievements must not be underestimated, but they were not sufficient to offset the instrumental influences of his early years. The view of Mozart as a natural genius in terms of vocal writing is one of those Romantic and idealistic fictions that do not bear close examination. Even at this date, of course, there are already signs of a greater degree of balance, but it was not until later that the two aspects were to be evenly matched.

As in his operas, the writing for the solo voices takes account of the forces available. Both Maria Magdalena Lipp and Maria Elisabeth Sabina Meißner were no mean virtuosos, and much the same may be said of Maria Anna Braunhofer and Franz Anton Spitzeder.[78] Yet none of them was so exceptional as to inspire the composer to write new and distinctive works. Their parts are written out in full, including the ornaments, with only the final cadenzas left for them to improvise. The dynamic markings, too, are more frequent here than in the earlier works.

Leopold's report cited above spells out the role of the organ in accompanying these works. Its chief representative was the side organ to the right of the altar, where the soloists and basses were positioned; if the chorus was involved, they would be joined by the lower choir organ supported by a violone (double bass). The main organ was used only for preludes on more festive occasions – in other words, as a solo instrument. In modern performances, where two organs are not

76. *Briefe*, ii.101.
77. Jahn, *W. A. Mozart*, i.323.
78. ◆ Concerning these singers, see Heinz Schuler, *Mozarts Salzburger Freunde und Bekannte: Biographien und Kommentare*, 135–8, 140, 145–9, 156–9, 223–4 and 267.

normally available, the organ will be reserved for the choruses and the accompaniment entrusted to a harmonium or harpsichord. The bass line is meticulously figured – sometimes in Leopold's hand – in all the sacred works with the exception of the sonatas. The choral writing was reinforced by three trombones played by tower watchmen: in the tutti sections they doubled the three lower choral parts. In the surviving scores, their parts are generally not notated, but only the passages where they are silent. The solemn sound of these instruments recalls an ancient practice dating back to the early days of instrumental music. Only rarely in Mozart's works, by contrast, are trombones used as solo instruments.

Trumpets and timpani tended to be deployed in the solemn mass. Like his father, Mozart used not only the old clarino register familiar from Bach but also the *vulgano* and *principale*, which could play only the notes *e*, *g* and *c*.[79] Leopold's statement that the oboe and flute were rarely played in the cathedral and that the horn was never heard here was no longer true even by Wolfgang's time. The more modern and operatic Mozart's religious style becomes, the more frequently these instruments appear,[80] even if they are initially handled with greater reserve than in his operas and never treated as soloists. Clarinets are still absent, whereas Leopold mentions four bassoonists who in keeping with the older tradition reinforced the bass line in movements scored for wind instruments. Their number recalls the old tendency to use the winds in choirs and implies a relationship between strings and winds that is noticeably different from the one that obtains today.[81] In his treatment of the strings, too, Mozart moves progressively closer to the modern operatic style: pseudo-archaic pieces such as the Marian litany are still limited to the old three-part writing, with frequent crossing of the violin parts and the violas doubling the basses, but the other pieces treat the viola with growing independence. The fondness for rushing violin figures[82] (a fondness also found in Leopold's case, albeit on a much reduced scale, and designed to create the impression of particularly full sonorities) may have been encouraged by the architecture of Salzburg Cathedral, but such writing is part and parcel of the theatrical religious style of the Neapolitan school. Leopold's letter of 1 November 1777 includes an extremely important account of a performance of one of Michael Haydn's masses:

I was extraordinarily taken by it, as there were 6 oboists, 3 double basses, two bassoons and the castrato. . . . Ferlendis and Sandmayr played the oboe solos. The ripieno oboists were the oboist at Lodron's, a student whose name I don't know, the chief watchman[83] and Obkirchner, while Caßl and the choirmaster Franz Knozenberger were the double-bass players beside the organ, alongside the trombones. Estlinger[84] played with the bassoons, Hofer and Perwein sat beside the oboists on the violinists' platform. What I particularly liked was that the oboes and bassoons are very similar to the human voice, so the tuttis seemed to be purely vocal music for a very large contingent of voices, while the sopranos and altos, reinforced by the 6 oboes and alto trombones, balanced out the tenors and basses, and the *piano* was so majestic that I could easily have done

79. See Altenburg, *Versuch einer Anleitung zur heroisch-musikalischen Trompeter- und Pauker-Kunst*; also Eichborn, *Die Trompete in alter und neuer Zeit* and *Das alte Clarinblasen auf Trompeten*; and Mahillon, *La trompette, son histoire, sa théorie, sa construction*. ◆ For a modern account of trumpets, see Herbert and Wallace, *The Cambridge Companion to Brass Instruments*.

80. The consciously archaic Marian litany does not include them, whereas they do appear in the *Litaniae de venerabili altaris sacramento*.

81. ◆ See Eisen, 'Mozart's Salzburg Orchestras'.

82. It was evidently this that Burney criticized in *The Present State of Music in Germany*, ii.322.

83. It would appear from this that the tower watchman could also turn his hand to the oboe.

84. Joseph Richard Estlinger was a double-bass player by training. ◆ Estlinger was also important as a court music copyist who also worked privately for the Mozarts; see Eisen, 'The Mozarts' Salzburg Copyists'.

without the oboe solos. . . . I should add that Brunetti stood behind Ferlendis, Wenzel Sadlo behind the bassoonists and Hafeneder[85] behind the other oboists, watching Haydn throughout the performance and beating time on their shoulders, otherwise it would have fallen apart in places, especially in the fugues and running-bass[86] accompaniments.[87]

But Mozart was not only kept busy writing sacred works during this period, he was no less active in the field of instrumental music, a type of music which – as we have already noted – was made up exclusively of occasional compositions. Within the social lives of the nobility and the well-to-do, the main role was played by music written by composers under contract and performed by private orchestras, with composers required to regale their employers not only on special occasions such as visits by social equals, family celebrations and so on, but also on a more mundane and workaday level: works would be performed at table and whenever the family came together in the evening. On each occasion, the main attraction of such works was their novelty: employers of this kind were not best served with older and discarded compositions, as they staked their honour on having new works written to order. Even Joseph Haydn, whose productivity in the field of the symphony is bound to seem astonishing today, was forcefully reminded by his employer in 1765 'to apply himself to composition more industriously than hitherto'.[88] Nor were the composer's employers content merely to listen to the pieces that they had commissioned, but frequently took part in performances themselves, revealing themselves in the process as virtuosos of no mean ability. Among the many princely performers on the flute – an instrument particularly popular in domestic music-making at this time – were Frederick the Great, Margrave Friedrich of Bayreuth, Duke Carl of Courland and Prince Joseph Friedrich of Hildburghausen.[89] The Prince Elector Maximilian III of Bavaria played the gamba, the Prince Elector Karl Theodor the cello, Prince Nikolaus Esterházy the baryton and Archduke Maximilian the viola.[90] Like Tsar Peter III and Prince Karl Wilhelm Ferdinand of Brunswick, Archbishop Colloredo had chosen the violin,[91] which he often played alone after lunch.[92] In the evening, he would perform with the other members of his orchestra. Mozart objected to playing the violin at court, prompting his father to remonstrate: 'As a music lover, you will not consider it beneath your dignity to play the violin in the first symphony any more than the archbishop himself does, to say nothing of the courtiers who now play with us.'[93] Needless to say, the involvement of amateurs did not always improve standards.[94] Neukomm reports that Brunetti used to sit beside the archbishop and, whenever there was a more difficult passage, would pick up his viola and surreptitiously retune it. Colloredo allowed Brunetti to do this and each time such a passage came up is said to have remarked: 'Brunetti will retune his instrument now.' Mozart himself had a low opinion of his employer's musical abilities, and on 26 September 1781 we find him writing to his father from Vienna about the singer Johann

85. Three violinists; Sadlo's main function was to play the horn.
86. 'bei laufenden Baß-Obligationen' = running basses (from 'basso obbligato').
87. *Briefe*, ii.96.
88. Pohl, *Joseph Haydn*, i.248.
89. Cramer, *Magazin der Musik*, i.776 and 783; Reichardt, *Briefe eines aufmerksamen Reisenden die Musik betreffend*, ii.121; and Dittersdorf, *Lebensbeschreibung*, 29.
90. Schubart, *Ideen zu einer Ästhetik der Tonkunst*, 123; Burney, *The Present State of Music in Germany*, i.95; Dies, *Biographische Nachrichten von Joseph Haydn*, 55–6; and Cramer, *Mazazin der Musik*, ii.959.
91. Hiller, *Wöchentliche Nachrichten*, v (1770), 178–9 and 207–8; and Burney, *The Present State of Music in Germany*, ii.322.
92. Koch-Sternfeld, *Die letzten dreißig Jahre*, 314.
93. *Briefe*, ii.485 (letter of 24 September 1778).
94. See Jahn, *W. A. Mozart*, i.330, for the joke told by Haydn.

Fischer 'who has an excellent bass voice (in spite of the fact that the archbishop told me he sang too low for a bass and that I assured him he'd sing higher next time)'.[95]

At these concerts, virtuosos played a pre-eminent role. Whenever the make-up of the *Kapelle* was discussed, due regard was paid to them, with foreign artists being employed where necessary. In the larger towns and cities, many virtuosos earned their living by appearing at the academies that were held on a daily basis.[96] Moreover, a great deal of orchestral music was performed, as concerts were both long and frequent.[97] Count Firmian's musical soirées, for example, lasted from five until eleven: the programme for a single concert is known to have included a number of symphonies by Johann Christian Bach and four by Sammartini,[98] while on another evening Dittersdorf had to perform twelve new violin concertos by Benda.[99] At a private concert at the home of the Prince Elector of Bavaria, Burney heard two symphonies by Schwindl, an aria by Panzacchi, a scene from an opera by the Dowager Electress of Saxony performed by the composer herself, a gamba trio by Schwindl played by the Prince Elector, two arias sung by Rauzzini and Guadagni and, finally, a gamba solo performed by the Prince Elector.[100] At a private concert in Dresden, each half of the concert included a symphony, a violin concerto, a flute concerto and an oboe concerto. As a rule, provisions were also made for other forms of entertainment such as card games and conversation. Colloredo in fact prescribed strict limits to the hours when music could be performed in the evening: on 17 September 1778 we find Leopold writing to his son to reassure him that performances generally lasted only from seven until a quarter past eight and tended to include only four pieces, a symphony followed by an aria, then either another symphony or an aria and, finally, a further aria – 'and with that addio'.[101]

Responsibility for these performances was divided on a weekly basis between the court composer and the Kapellmeister. Whichever of the two was on duty was free to choose which pieces might be performed and the order in which they were played,[102] at least to the extent that orders from on high did not ordain differently. As a result of his father's position, Mozart was always able to hear performances of his own attempts at instrumental composition. Particular emphasis was placed on new works, especially on festive occasions,[103] and it is to the same custom that produced Bach's Brandenburg Concertos and Joseph Haydn's symphonies that we owe the relatively large number of Mozart's symphonies. Only with Beethoven does a new spirit enter the world of music, with the artist no longer working to commission but enjoying complete freedom in the choice and execution of his material. Judged by the standards of his own time, Mozart's

95. *Briefe*, iii.162.
96. *Briefe*, iii.159 (letter of 19 September 1781).
97. Dittersdorf's account of the musical household of the Prince of Hildburghausen is entirely typical; see Dittersdorf, *Lebensbeschreibung*, 67–9.
98. Burney, *The Present State of Music in France and Italy*, 101.
99. Dittersdorf, *Lebensbeschreibung*, 45.
100. Burney, *The Present State of Music in Germany*, i.138–40.
101. *Briefe*, ii.482. Baron von Boecklin visited Salzburg in the 1780s and thought that church music in the town was good, with several fine wind players, but that 'the concert orchestra on the other hand is by no means particularly brilliant; although there are nevertheless a few excellent and well-known musicians to be found, who in sonatas and concert pieces mitigate these shadows by their charming playing; and indeed, shed a light over their weak accompanists which to a visitor often conveys a most favourable impression of the whole'; *Beyträge zur Geschichte der Musik, besonders in Deutschland*, 28–9 [*Dokumente*, 335–6, *Documentary Biography*, 382]. ◆ It is likely that Leopold's comment to Mozart is a complaint, not reassurance.
102. Marpurg, *Historisch-kritische Beyträge*, iii.186.
103. For the name-day of the Bishop of Großwardein, Dittersdorf wrote a solo cantata, a choral cantata, three symphonies and a violin concerto; see Dittersdorf, *Lebensbeschreibung*, 117.

output, in purely quantitative terms, was even more modest than Haydn's: at this date, a dozen symphonies a year was certainly not seen as a sign of particular industry.

In Salzburg, as elsewhere, the prince's example was followed by the well-to-do and respected middle classes, who likewise commissioned works of music to celebrate special occasions, as is clear from Mozart's 'Haffner' serenade [K250] and the 'Antretter' [K185, a serenade] and 'Lodron' divertimentos [K247, K287]. It was hardly surprising, therefore, that instrumental music continued to dominate Mozart's creative output.

It scarcely needs to be added that all these works were occasional pieces to the extent that they had to take account of the forces at Mozart's disposal.[104] Here, too, fate was kind to Mozart, for although the Salzburg orchestra was not among the front rank, it was none the less appreciably above average, and Colloredo seems to have lavished particular attention on it following the reproach – to quote Burney – that it was 'more remarkable for coarseness and noise, than delicacy and high-finishing'.[105] Schubart had particular praise for the wind instruments, especially the trumpets and horns. In 1770 the orchestra[106] normally comprised between ten and twelve violins and violas, two or three cellos and as many double basses, three horns, two or three oboes (of whom two also played the flute), three or four bassoon players and the choirs of trombones and of court and field trumpeters and timpanists already mentioned. On festive occasions the numbers were correspondingly increased, with many players doubling on strings and winds, depending on the demands of the piece in question. The trumpeters in particular were taken on only on condition that they could also play the violin or viola. It is more difficult to determine the extent to which a harpsichord was used in performances of these Salzburg symphonies.[107] This, after all, was a transitional period during which the old continuo instrument gradually disappeared from the orchestra, albeit at varying speeds, depending on the place in question. We have already noted how methodically Leopold Mozart proceeded in this respect. Wolfgang, like Haydn, no longer includes a figured bass, suggesting that, following his father's example, he no longer reckoned on a harpsichord. Yet this is highly unlikely, given the style of his works prior to his visits to Italy.[108] A few clues are contained in Leopold's oft-cited report listing Adlgasser and Lipp as organists *and* harpsichordists and expressly referring to their 'accompaniment in the chamber'.[109] A handful of references in his letters reinforce this view. That *Mitridate* reckoned on two keyboards is clear from his letter of 5 January 1771,[110] but only a single passage in a later letter of 30 September 1777 contains any reference to the way in which instrumental music was accompanied in Salzburg. Discussing Michael Haydn's incidental music to *Zaire*, Leopold writes: 'Although it was only instrumental music, the court harpsichord [*Hofflügl*] had to be brought over [i.e., to the theatre] for Haydn to play on.'[111] This seems to suggest that a harpsichord accompaniment in an instrumental piece was the exception at this time. But whether this was also the case in 1770 is open to question. As long as Mozart was well and truly under Italian influence, we may well assume the existence of a

---

104. Under this same heading comes the role of the trumpet in Bach's Brandenburg concertos.
105. Burney, *The Present State of Music in Germany*, ii.322. The reader will recall the earlier reference to rushing violin figures in Mozart's sacred works.
106. See Leopold Mozart's account quoted above and Seiffert's edition of his works, *Leopold Mozart: Ausgewählte Werke*, XXVff.
107. ◆ For a summary of performance practice issues in these works, see Zaslaw, *Mozart's Symphonies: Context, Performance Practice, Reception*, 445–509.
108. In the estimation of Adler, *Wiener Instrumentalmusik vor und um 1750*, XXVff., Viennese symphonies still reckoned on a harpsichord.
109. Marpurg, *Historisch-kritische Beyträge*, iii.186–7; here Adlgasser is praised as a particularly fine accompanist on the harpsichord.
110. *Briefe*, i.414.
111. *Briefe*, ii.25.

harpsichord accompaniment, as there are numerous passages here that demand to be filled out harmonically, either because the violas are playing in unison with the double basses or because there is a large gap between the upper and lower voices that needs to be filled. Only from 1773 onwards, with the growing influence of German and, specifically, Viennese music, does this support become increasingly dispensable, but it is impossible, of course, to say from exactly which work the harpsichord was first omitted.[112]

The symphony remained the chief of the instrumental forms espoused by Mozart. It is highly characteristic of him that, unlike Haydn, it was only at a relatively late date and then only with some hesitation that he took over one of the two main forms that played such an important role in the evolution of the modern symphony, namely, the French overture. Definitively established by Lully as an essentially two-movement piece,[113] it consisted of a slow movement (grave) with characteristically stately dotted rhythms and a far longer second section which, from Lully's time onwards, was a fugal allegro. The grave accompanied the solemn entrance of the king and his retinue into the theatre, but was increasingly treated as an introductory movement, while the quicker second section was regarded as the actual heart of the piece. Like the opera that followed it, the overture, too, faithfully reflected the spirit of the festivities that were held at the French court, with their rhetorically coloured ceremonial and an essential character which, however emotionally charged, none the less followed certain strict rules of etiquette. This basic character was long retained in the German orchestral suites that were inspired by Parisian practices and disappeared only with the emergence of the Viennese Classicists, and here the French overture's two-movement form proved particularly useful in assimilating the new intellectual content. Haydn was especially fond of it and revealed a masterly ability to prepare the ground psychologically for his later symphonic allegros with a profoundly thoughtful or dreamy introduction, while Beethoven tended to use it to allow the main ideas of his allegros to rise up, as it were, from the twilight world of the unconscious and assume a fully three-dimensional form.

Mozart, by contrast, long remained loyal to the Italian symphony, a type that assumed its definitive form in the hands of Alessandro Scarlatti. As is clear from its andante movements, a number of which are restricted to a mere handful of bars, this type tended to be a single-movement work and, after the varied and volatile world of the Venetian sinfonia that often borrowed its themes from the opera itself, it is the true representative of the Neapolitan spirit, a spirit which, in the overture, too, was keen to linger, growing expansive and reworking its themes at leisure. As such, it affords brilliant proof of the Italians' refined sense of form, being clear and readily comprehensible in outline and, thanks to the straightforward manner in which its antitheses are distributed, well suited to assimilating the most disparate ideas. As we have seen, Scarlatti's successors were not remotely capable of exploiting these advantages, and even with serious dramatists the sinfonia remained by far the weakest part of the opera.

Not until the 1740s do we find signs of any improvement, as the sinfonia started to break free from opera and to lead a life of its own. From the outset, higher intellectual demands were placed on these 'academy symphonies', and these demands, in turn, were bound up with the profound revolution in people's thinking that was currently affecting the whole of educated Europe and whose principal spokesman was Rousseau. In the case of composers, too, the new and idealistic

---

112. ◆ If Haydn's practice at Eszterháza is relevant – and it is not entirely clear that it is – the early symphonies may have reckoned without a keyboard continuo; see Webster, 'On the Absence of Keyboard Continuo in Haydn's Symphonies'.
113. See Prunières, 'Notes sur les origines de l'ouverture française'. ◆ Further, see Botstiber, *Geschichte der Ouvertüre und der freien Orchesterformen*.

approach to Nature initially found expression in a fundamental denial of all that had gone before. The Enlightenment lacked any sense of history and of that modern, salutary counterweight to all radical trends; for the Enlightenment, the old was simply old-fashioned or, rather, 'unnatural' and 'untrue', an attitude that sprang directly from what was then a universal belief in the absolute progress of art. As a result, the change in attitudes took place with astonishing speed, with one of the most enthusiastic supporters of the new, Johann Christian Bach, for example, not hesitating to dismiss his great father as 'an old big-wig'.[114]

And it was the symphony which, replacing the old suite as the main type of orchestral music, now became the chief arena in which this great stylistic change occurred. As a form, it was created neither by a single composer nor by a single school but was tackled equally in every country, with only the results turning out to be different. If Germany now finally took over as the leader in the more discriminating kinds of instrumental music, it undoubtedly owed this advantage to the excellent organization of its musical institutions, which encompassed the broadest sections of the population. Intellectually, too, the Germans were particularly well prepared for the new style. Essentially irrational by nature, they had accepted rationalism only reluctantly and only when imposed from outside. But in the middle of the eighteenth century, when the tyranny of reason was finally broken in the home of rationalism itself – in other words, in France – the Germans, too, began to have second thoughts. The principal feature of the new style – the sudden shifts of mood – is the best possible proof of this, for here the genuinely German urge for those natural emotional values in art that lie beyond mere cognition found altogether surprising, but apt expression. For Germans, this style was the natural and uninhibited expression of their own essential nature and was bound, therefore, to lead to a new and grandiose artistic ideal, while repeatedly finding a counterbalance in the innately logical temperament of the Romance nations.

None the less, we must not underestimate the independent role that Italy, in particular, played in this general development. Pergolesi's example shows that its roots go back to a relatively early date. Moreover, Italy had an art form in *opera buffa* which, with its pronounced emphasis on naturalness and its opposition to conventional rules, was clearly related to the new spirit, and we have already had frequent occasion to note the way in which many of its stylistic features coincided with those of the newer type of symphony.[115] The chief aim of the innovators – greater fluency and volatility of expression and freedom in the interplay of moods – is one that *buffa* composers had, for the most part, already achieved. Moreover, the sinfonias of *opere buffe* were treated more loosely, but also more naturally, than those of *opere serie*, and their influence on the concert symphony may be seen even in composers of the Viennese school.

Academies played a major part in the development of the Italian symphony, as did the private concerts of the aristocracy, which even in Mozart's day were still a flourishing institution. Both aspects are adequately attested in his letters. Conversely, we still have very little information about the detailed state of composition at this period. Fortunately, the work of at least one composer has recently been examined in greater depth, a composer who was not only one of Italy's leading instrumental composers but whose works are known to have been studied by Mozart:

114.   ◆ For more recent, more detailed and in some respects different accounts of the early history of the symphony, see Kunze, *Die Sinfonie im 18. Jahrhundert: Von der Opernsinfonie zur Konzertsinfonie*; Larsen, 'Zur Entstehung der österreichischen Symphonietradition (ca. 1750–1775)'; and Hell, *Die neapolitanische Opernsinfonie in der ersten Hälfte des 18. Jahrhunderts.*
115.   Johann Adam Hiller was not completely wrong, therefore, when he described 'current taste' as 'more comic than serious'; *Wöchentliche Nachrichten*, i (1766), no. 26.

the composer in question is Gluck's teacher, Giovanni Battista Sammartini.[116] Sammartini's symphonies were clearly written under the influence of opera, their themes often songlike in character and, with their notorious repeats and closures and absence of counterpoint, aria-like in style. The old operatic sinfonia continued to make itself felt in various boisterous themes, alongside which we also find more individual figures closer to the world of *opera buffa*. Even in progressive movements such as these, Sammartini's symphonic writing remains carefree and salonesque, with no darker or deeper resonances, but their musical language certainly has character and sometimes even an infectious verve, tending to exploit brief, uninhibited and sometimes even bold and challenging motifs and revelling in contrasts, not within the themes themselves, but in terms of their juxtaposition. It is easy to imagine the impression left on contemporary audiences by this lively, if frequently aphoristic, interplay of ideas, while even the development sections occasionally accommodate thematic interlopers. The second subjects are, in part, short-winded trio-like ideas in the *buffa* style and, in part, themes that are already genuinely cantabile in character. But Sammartini sets no store whatsoever by developing his themes, and it was no doubt this that prompted Joseph Haydn to dismiss him as a 'hack composer'. His development sections include few pointers in the direction of thematic transformation and are frequently no more than brief bridge passages. His recapitulations generally omit the first subjects, while his andantes and finales (there are no minuets) are distinguished from the older type only by their more individualized expression. Only in the later works are the final movements cast in rondo form.

Conversely, Sammartini was one of the most progressive composers in contemporary Italy in terms of his instrumentation, and here, too, the influence of the *buffa* style is unmistakable. His orchestral writing is remarkable for the extraordinary volatility of the individual voices, albeit with the exception of the winds, which continue to be used soloistically or to reinforce the other instruments and, as such, rarely go beyond existing practices. The strings, on the other hand, lead colourful and often eventful lives, with much traditional crossing of parts in the first and second violins and independent writing for the violas, and with angular, challenging, noisy and brilliant figures that clearly recall the world of *opera buffa* and that can still be found in the semiquaver quavers in the overture to *Iphigénie*[117] by Sammartini's pupil, Gluck. Indeed, all Gluck's early Italian operas contain frequent reminiscences of his mentor's music.[118]

But the most important Italian composer at this time was Giuseppe Tartini (1692–1770), a detailed study of whose life and works we still await from his fellow countrymen. His passionate and revolutionary nature made him the obvious ally of the forces of progress, and his symphonies could hardly be further removed from the older type of symphony, with their tendency to encapsulate impressions of life and Nature and to incorporate wildly impassioned ideas. Another composer who deserves to be mentioned here on account of the four-movement form of his *Sinfonia funebre* is Pietro Antonio Locatelli (1695–1764). Finally, as we have already seen, Johann Christian Bach grew up in this Italian environment.[119]

---

116. Torrefranca, 'Le origini della sinfonia: Le sinfonie dell'imbrattacarte (G. B. Sammartini)'; Saint-Foix, 'La chronologie de l'œuvre instrumentale de Jean Baptiste Sammartini' and 'Les débuts milanais de Gluck', 28ff.; and Wyzewa and Saint-Foix, *Wolfgang Amédée Mozart*, i.276–8. See Sammartini's E flat trio op. 1/3 and the Sammartinian overture in Abert, *Christoph Willibald Gluck: Le nozze d'Ercole e d'Ebe*.

117. ◆ It is not clear here whether Abert means *Iphigénie en Aulide* (1774) or *Iphigénie en Tauride* (1779).

118. See Abert, 'Glucks italienische Opern bis zum "Orfeo"'.

119. ◆ Concerning Locatelli, see Dunning, *Intorno a Locatelli: Studi in occasione del tricentenario della nascita di Pietro Antonio Locatelli* and Eynard, *Il musicista Pietro Antonio Locatelli: Un itinerario artistico da Bergamo a Amsterdam*. And for J. C. Bach, see Tutenberg, *Die Sinfonik Johann Christian Bachs*.

Among the younger generation of composers, Luigi Boccherini (1743–1805) is particularly important in the context of Mozart: he was the first of the Italians to reveal undeniable traces of German influence – first of the Mannheim school, later of Haydn. But his music remained, in essence, Italian in tone, as is clear from its recurrent note of sensibility. Yet, under German influence, his talent grew increasingly serious and, on a technical level, more painstaking. In the field of the symphony, he was particularly keen on rondo form in final position and in this respect, too, was an important influence on the young Mozart.

But, in spite of all these promising beginnings, Italian instrumental music failed to acquire the same rights as opera, whereas in Germany the symphony soon came to enjoy a period of unsuspected prosperity. Here, far more than in Italy, it was supported by the great mass of the general public – not just the princes and the nobility, but also by students and the middle classes through countless amateur associations or collegia musica. Huge numbers of symphonies were written at this time, but, even so, demand often outstripped supply. And whereas symphonies had previously circulated in manuscript form, they were now printed for the first time and sold like hot cakes. For composers, the main centres were Vienna, Mannheim and Berlin.

We have already dealt in some detail with the Viennese symphony and its school, a school that sought, in the main, to meet the new demand for natural truth by introducing large numbers of popular elements, while at the same time taking over from the older tradition its rigorous approach to orchestral writing. A substantially different role in the continuing development of the German symphony was played by the Mannheim school under the leadership of the brilliant Johann Stamitz[120] (1717–57). Like their Viennese counterparts, but unlike the north Germans, the members of the Mannheim school are notable for the naturalness of their ideas and their affinities with the folk, even though Stamitz himself came from Bohemia. This, however, was far from being the most important of their sensational innovations – innovations praised in extravagant terms by so many of their contemporaries, while condemned by others, especially in north Germany, on the grounds of stylistic impurity.

Compared with all his fellow composers, not only was Johann Stamitz uniquely talented, but it was he, more than any other, who most clearly identified the new problems that had to be solved and who managed to provide the most logically consistent solutions.

The stylistic change that distinguishes the two great peaks of 'classical' German music – the Saxon and Thuringian school on the one hand and the Austrian school on the other – is the result, at bottom, of two very different approaches to art. Its first representatives regarded it as the higher, 'more natural' form. Here, of course, there can be no question of ascent or decline but only of a fundamentally new art in which is reflected a whole new approach to life and the world. The older classicism of Corelli, Bach and Handel had been an art of perfect proportions, with each and every one of their works consisting of self-contained, fully finished sections, each theme and even each motif leading an independent existence complete unto itself and embodying a single mood that may undergo manifold minor changes but which essentially retains the same basic character.[121] When these composers wanted to introduce a change of mood, they would do so by means of a new theme which, like all the others, would be self-contained. The result, in short, was the most

---

120.   See Riemann, *Sinfonien der Pfalzbayerischen Schule I–II*; see also Riemann, *Handbuch der Musikgeschichte*, ii/3, 133–4; and Mennicke, *Hasse und die Brüder Graun als Symphoniker*. ◆ More recently, see Eugene K. Wolf, 'On the Origins of the Mannheim Symphonic Style'; Hosler, *Changing Aesthetic Views of Instrumental Music in 18th-Century Germany*; and, above all, Eugene K. Wolf, *The Symphonies of Johann Stamitz: A Study in the Formation of the Classic Style*.
121.   A good example of this is the aria 'Ich will bei meinem Jesu wachen' from Bach's *St Matthew Passion*.

perfect order, with one fully rounded picture following another and no new mood ever being introduced before the old one was completely exhausted. In spite of the far more modern resources at his disposal, Joseph Haydn is still part of this older tradition. The newer tradition, by contrast, had a totally different attitude: it was not concerned with perfection in each individual section and had no time for clear-cut boundaries and stasis, but only for the idea of movement, of becoming and of looking beyond itself, in short, of what Wagner was once to describe so aptly as 'the art of transition'. Its aim was not to replicate ready-made moods, but to show those moods developing, not some calmly radiating emotion, but feelings that fluctuate, with all their tensions, explosive outbursts and, above all, sudden changes of mood. Contrasts that were previously entrusted to two different themes now collide with each other unexpectedly within the same theme, with fixed forms now replaced by changing shapes, and with calm giving way to movement. It is this new type of *durchbrochene Arbeit* and its attendant disjointed moods that makes this music seem so much more 'modern'. As such, it is a faithful reflection of a world profoundly affected by Rousseau's teachings and, with its consciously revolutionary stance, a true counterpart of the contemporary *Sturm und Drang* movement in literature.[122] Here, too, it did not emerge overnight but traced back its roots to the earlier period and to a time when Handel, for example, already approximated to the new approach. Its first conscious and consistent advocate was Stamitz with his Mannheim colleagues, but its first classical representative was Mozart, a position he owes not merely to his musical genius, which towered far above all his predecessors, but, most of all, because it was an accurate reflection of his new view of the world, a view that sees in the human soul an overriding unity behind the most disparate forces that are in a constant state of flux and interaction. That this lay deep within him is something we saw in the case of the theme of his very first symphony. It was only natural, therefore, that time and again he felt drawn to the Mannheim composers.[123]

Ultimately, of course, the mature Mozart transcended these models, too, and finally came to look down on them from the Olympian heights of his own artistic personality. The Mannheim composers suffered the same fate as so many pioneers, becoming intoxicated with the new phenomena that they had produced and not infrequently confusing cause with effect. This is the reason why they lapsed into superficial mannerisms in such a relatively short space of time. But even in the case of the brilliant Johann Stamitz, it was clear that he was consciously fighting a revolution and that storm and stress was his natural element: he liked the sudden, motley interplay of phenomena *per se*, so that the main attraction of his music is its impulsiveness and disjointedness, its sense of surprise and its cult of genius. As a result, he not only introduced contrasting and, above all, sentimental features into his fast movements, thereby picking up and developing a feature already found in Italian composers at this time, he also extended and transformed thematic procedures. Even in the opening movements of his six orchestral trios op. 1, the listener is bound to be struck by the fact that, although the first subjects remain in the tonic, they are extraordinarily discursive and, at the same time, divided into contrastive sections. But Stamitz is not content for his second subjects to bring with them a complete change of mood for, far from coming straight to the point, he uses these sections to regale the listener with new surprises, his second subjects not

122.   ◆ In general, see Loewenthal, *Sturm und Drang: Kritische Schriften*; Kenneth Clark, *The Romantic Rebellion*; Michael Mann, *Sturm- und Drang-Drama: Studien und Vorstudien zu Schillers 'Räubern'*; and specifically with respect to music, Landon, *Haydn: Chronicle and Works*, ii.266–393.

123.   ◆ Abert's intensely pro-Germanic bias is perhaps overstated here; although Mozart was clearly drawn to the Mannheim style, there is no compelling reason to think that he was attracted to it above all others.

merely forming a contrast with the first subjects but incorporating a further contrast in the form of a third subject that is generally as far removed as possible from the field of emotions explored in the first two. It either serves as a concluding group, in which case it is more broadly developed before reverting to the original mood by means of a sudden shift of atmosphere,[124] or it is followed by yet another subject in fourth and final position.[125] As a result, his allegros contain not two subjects, plus appendages, as before, but three or four, and these in turn are made up of several subsections, each of which is more or less independent in terms of its range of expression. It is clear from this that this new type of emotional expression necessarily brought with it a new approach to form.

But these sudden shifts of emotion also found their way into the individual sections that make up the themes themselves, revealing themselves in the juxtaposition of completely different rhythmic patterns, in the introduction of fermatas and sudden silences in the whole orchestra and, in more general terms, in the original use of 'eloquent' rests and the like, but, above all, in a new type of dynamics that led, quite logically, to a mass of dynamic markings in works by the Mannheim composers that was in stark contrast to the thrift of the earlier generation. Their scores teem with endless sequences of *forte* and *piano* markings, of *sforzatos* and crescendos ending in a sudden *piano*, and so on.

The famous 'Mannheim crescendo' deserves a section all to itself. The source of considerable astonishment at the time,[126] it complements the features discussed hitherto to the extent that the effect that it sought to achieve was one of transition rather than contrast, increasing the sense of tension in a way not known until then, before allowing the pent-up emotion to erupt with the force of a veritable explosion.[127] Although we find increases and decreases in volume in works of the earlier period, the basic dynamic character of the melody in question – be it *forte* or *piano* – was not affected by these minor gradations but, on the contrary, merely confirmed. The dynamics of the earlier period relied, in the main, on echo effects involving the immediate juxtaposition of *forte* and *piano* and were achieved by dividing the orchestra into tutti and soli or, at all events, into individual groups, each with its own sonority. Even in Bach's scores, the performance marking *forte* indicates that the passage in question is to be performed by the tutti, whereas a *piano* presupposes the concertino. This practice excluded any consciously designed and developed crescendo, which became possible only when *piano* and *forte* were no longer achieved by dividing and reuniting the whole orchestra but by having them performed by the whole orchestra playing together. This new effect is first found in Italy in works by Jommelli and Piccinni, and in Germany in works by Stamitz. In Italy, where symphonic writing failed to develop, it culminated in the great crescendos of Rossini and his successors, with their hankering after sensation, while in Germany it found its supreme expression in Beethoven, who brought to the device an intensity and a depth that had been absent from it hitherto.[128]

These great crescendos – which, incidentally, had a prototype in the early Neapolitan opera sinfonia with its main themes striving upwards over a pedal point[129] – involved more than mere performance markings but affected the inner life of the work, inasmuch as they had to be prepared

---

124. See op. 1/1 in Riemann, *Sinfonien der Pfalzbayerischen Schule I*, 4.

125. See the D major symphony op. 3/1 in Riemann, *Sinfonien der Pfalzbayerischen Schule I*, 16–7.

126. See Burney, *The Present State of Music in Germany*, i.94; Schubart, *Ideen zu einer Ästhetik der Tonkunst*, 130, and *Leben und Gesinnungen*, i/14.153; and Reichardt, *Briefe eines aufmerksamen Reisenden*, i.11.

127. On this point, see Heuß, 'Über die Dynamik der Mannheimer Schule', 433ff. ◆ For a more recent study of crescendo, see Manfred Hermann Schmid, 'Typen des Orchestercrescendo im 18. Jahrhundert'.

128. See Heuß, 'Über die Dynamik der Mannheimer Schule', 448.

129. As a result of the superficiality of the composers that we have been discussing, the psychological aspect of this effect is barely explored.

and built up and, finally, discharged in a powerful *forte*. In turn, this meant that the individual sections within the movement were now extended and expanded. As a result, we find, alongside sudden, relatively brief outbursts of passion, large-scale outbursts that spring from tremendous psychological pressure and, like some unleashed natural force, drew contemporary listeners into their sway.[130]

This same spirit also dominates the development sections.[131] Although they are predominantly thematic and only rarely introduce new material, their main concern remains the composer's delight in the colourful and exciting interplay of ideas, rather than any attempt to describe the developing course of a particular emotion. It is this, more than anything else, that distinguishes the Mannheimers' approach from that of the north German and 'classical' composers, and it is striking that Stamitz, in stark contrast to the Viennese, begins his recapitulations with a shortened version of the main theme, rather than with its complete restatement, and that the contrastive ideas are then reintroduced in random order in the course of its subsequent development. A further important feature of Stamitz's style is his total eschewal of all fugal procedures and of the various other contrapuntal techniques of the earlier period, including running and ostinato basses, ostinato rhythms and the like. Conversely, his works contain plentiful examples of free imitation that are clearly and advantageously distinguished from the transparent homophony of the *galant* composers of the period. Finally, his orchestral writing was one of the most powerful incentives in finally evicting the harpsichord from the symphony orchestra.

These, then, are the principal features of Stamitz's style, compared with which the lesser ones are far less important.[132] Admittedly, these latter are found so often in the Mannheimers' symphonies that they are an integral part of the picture, but very few of them are original Mannheim features. The 'sigh', whose origins lie in Italian vocal ornamentation, is common to all of Stamitz's precursors and contemporaries,[133] while the remaining characteristics such as the *Vögelchen* and *Bebung* have already been mentioned in the context of *opera buffa*:

Symphonic themes such as the following are firmly rooted in the Neapolitan opera sinfonia:[134]

130. Riemann, *Sinfonien der Pfalzbayerischen Schule I*, 16 and *Sinfonien der Pfalzbayerischen Schule II*, 29.
131. It may also be noted here that Stamitz frequently dispenses with any repeat of the subject-group in his symphonies.
132. Riemann in his introduction to *Sinfonien der Pfalzbayerischen Schule II*.
133. See Heuß, 'Zum Thema: "Mannheimer Vorhalt"', 273ff.
134. It is far more interesting to follow the new spirit as it enters the old framework in Stamitz's hands; note, for example, the beginning of his op. 3/2:

Nor should we forget that the majority of these 'mannerisms' are ornamental in character. Whereas such ornaments had previously been left to the performer's discretion, the Mannheimers now followed Gluck's example and wrote them all out just as they wrote out their dynamic markings, with the result that even the physical appearance of the notes on the page looks different.

With greater or lesser variations, all these stylistic features recur in all the remaining movements. Formally speaking, the most regularly structured are the slow movements, sonata movements with predominantly melodic development sections and shortened recapitulations. In terms of their character, two types may be distinguished: an idyllic andante often made up of enchanting Rococo images produced by means of generally short themes, and an elegiac type with a much slower tempo marking. It was to this last-named type that Stamitz committed his most profound expressions of muted ardour.[135] Movements such as these occasionally look forward to Beethoven.

The last two movements strike a note of unadulterated joy. Although Stamitz was not the first composer to include a minuet in a symphony, it was almost certainly he who established its right of domicile. His minuets are spiritually related to Mozart's, for even where they are whimsical and trifling, their main sections still bear the imprint of powerful virility, but they are also notable for their concise and definite character, so that their initial section is often only eight bars in length. The trios are often more expansive and give vent to more contemplative[136] or, as with Viennese composers, to more popular and idyllic emotions. In the sonata-form finales, the sense of *joie de vivre* become positively infectious, and there is something challenging and provocative about the *prestissimo* movements in 2/4 time, with their staccato crotchet themes.[137]

The most independently minded of the Mannheim composers after Stamitz was Franz Xaver Richter (1709–89). Far more thoughtful and pensive than Stamitz, he is the only member of the Mannheim school who did not dispense entirely with the contrapuntal procedures of the older tradition, a tradition also recalled by his Italianate main subjects,[138] even though their treatment

Italianate features include the introductory chords and the *Trommelbass* pedal point, whereas Stamitz himself is clearly behind the idiosyncratic theme with its against-the-grain syncopation and the tremendous crescendo with its explosion of pent-up energy, both of which features recall Beethoven's *Leonore* overture. The introductory chords of the 'Eroica' symphony were a last ghostly echo of the opening bars of this old Italian sinfonia.

135. See Kretzschmar, *Führer durch den Konzertsaal*, i/1, p.98.
136. Among the orchestral trios, op.1/1 and 4 are good examples of the first type, while op. 1/2 and op. 5/3 are good examples of the second type.
137. Op. 1/1.
138. An exception is his symphony op. 4/5, with its Mozartian cantabile subject. ◆ Concerning Richter, see Lebermann, 'Zu Franz Xaver Richters Sinfonien'; Pečman, 'Franz Xaver Richter und seine "Harmonische Belehrungen"'; and Reutter, 'Franz Xaver Richters Bemerkungen über das Komponieren einer Sinfonie in Kompositionstheorie und Kompositionspraxis'.

reflects the entirely modern Mannheim spirit, with its predilection for striking contrasts and tremendous emotional tension. His thematic writing, however, reveals not just a well-trained technician but also an extremely versatile poet capable of reordering and reinterpreting his ideas in a highly intelligent manner. Also worth mentioning here is the fact that Richter occasionally prefers three-movement form and sometimes runs his first two movements together without a break.

Of the remaining members of the Mannheim school, we have already made the acquaintance of one of Mozart's earliest models, Johann Schobert. In general, however, the Mannheimers suffered the same fate as all new trends in art that are rooted in the personality of a single revolutionary artist, producing a backward-looking, epigonic art that becomes obsessed with superficial mannerisms and loses sight of its originator's aims. The 'Mannheim goût' acquired a distinctly unpleasant taste especially in the area of dynamics, with such contrasts now being introduced simply to make an effect and with crescendos, notwithstanding the effort expended on them, ending up vacuous and thin. These symptoms of decline may be found alongside a number of more successful features in the works of Anton Fils (1733–1760), Carl (1745–1801) and Anton Stamitz (1750–between 1796 and 1809), Franz Beck (1734–1809), Ernst Eichner (1740–77) and also of Christian Cannabich (1731–98), whom we shall meet again in the context of Mozart's visit to Mannheim.[139] In one respect, all these composers took up and developed the tradition along entirely logical lines, pointing the way from Haydn and Mozart to Beethoven, whose spiritual affinity with the Mannheimers in terms of his treatment of the orchestra has recently, and rightly, been stressed. In Mannheim, it now became customary for the full orchestra to play where it had formerly been the practice to alternate between one section of the orchestra and the full orchestra. As a result, the old relationship between strings and winds no longer obtained: the winds were no longer used merely to reinforce the strings, but nor were they given brief solos as they had been under the older dispensation. They now enjoyed equal rights with the strings and in this capacity sought to merge with them in a way that extended their colouristic and thematic contribution in a way that could not have been envisaged only a short time previously.[140]

Events in north Germany took a rather different turn from those in the south of the country.[141] Here composers set out, in the main, from the type of operatic sinfonia promulgated by Hasse, and, indeed, the latter's theatrical sinfonias were often performed in the concert hall. The principal feature of the north German symphony throughout the classical period and beyond was the particular care lavished upon it from a compositional point of view, with the difference between the north and south German temperament reflected in the symphony just as it was in the

139. Samples of their work may be found in Riemann, *Sinfonien der Pfalzbayerischen Schule I-III.* Cannabich's B flat major symphony (*Sinfonien der Pfalzbayerischen Schule III*, 3ff.) positively teems with Mozartian features. None the less, considerable care is needed in deciding who influenced whom, as Mozart could just as easily have influenced Cannabich as the other way round. ◆ Further, see Littger, *Johann Anton Fils (1733–1760): Ein Eichstätter Komponist der Mannheimer Klassik*; Vít, 'Kompositionsprinzipien der Sinfonien des Anton Fils'; Sondheimer, 'Die formale Entwicklung der vorklassischen Sinfonie' and 'Die Sinfonien Franz Becks'; Reissinger, *Die Sinfonien Ernst Eichners (1740–1777)*; Waldkirch, *Die konzertanten Sinfonien der Mannheimer im 18. Jahrhundert*; Eugene K. Wolf and Jean K. Wolf, *The Symphony at Mannheim: Johann Stamitz, Christian Cannabich*; and Henze-Döhring, 'Orchester und Orchestersatz in Christian Cannabichs Mannheimer Sinfonien'. More generally, see Sondheimer, *Die Theorie der Sinfonie und die Beurteilung einzelner Sinfoniekomponisten bei den Musikschriftstellern des 18. Jahrhunderts.*
140. See Heuß, 'Über die Dynamik der Mannheimer Schule', 452ff.
141. See Mennicke, *Hasse und die Brüder Graun*; Flueler, 'Die norddeutsche Sinfonie zur Zeit Friedrichs des Großen und besonders die Werke Ph. Em. Bachs'; and Kretzschmar, *Führer durch den Konzertsaal*, i/1, pp. 103ff.

keyboard sonata. Chronologically speaking, the first two composers to be dealt with here are the brothers Carl Heinrich (1702/3–1759) and Johann Gottlieb Graun (1703/4–1771). Of the two, Carl Heinrich was emphatically the more old-fashioned of the two, while Johann Gottlieb was distinguished by his more characterful invention and more careful handling of his themes.[142] He, too, was affected by the new spirit to the extent that he operates with palpably contrasting moods, albeit only within relatively large-scale structures: within one and the same theme he does not indulge in such sudden shifts. On the other hand, both he and, in part, his brother reveal the principal characteristics of the later north German symphony, namely, the restriction to three-movement form and the tendency to engage in imitative procedures and thematic development. Also worth mentioning under this heading is Johann Gottlieb's predilection for unusually lavish orchestral forces and concertante writing for the most disparate instruments. In general, of course, the Grauns' style is still in a state of flux, with the old frequently appearing alongside the new, Italianate features alongside what were later to be regarded as distinctively north German ones. It was in the hands of Carl Philipp Emanuel Bach that the north German school enjoyed its first great triumphs and, in consequence, first acquired its true significance.[143] Although Bach's very real historical importance rests far more on his keyboard sonatas, the stylistic principles that he established here were also of use in the field of the symphony. We have already examined the impact of Bach's thematic writing on instrumental music in the context of the contrast between north and south German principles, and it is sufficient to refer the reader to our earlier account. With its tendency towards logic and order, it was an ideal complement to the more imaginative approach of the south Germans.

Whereas Joseph Haydn inclined, in the main, towards the Viennese and north German schools and whereas Beethoven inclined towards the north German and Mannheim schools, the situation with a composer as receptive to, and as eager for, new impressions as Mozart is inevitably far more complex. Even in the field of the symphony, it is impossible to speak of any conscious approach at this time: sometimes he flirts with one school, sometimes with another, sometimes even with the Italians, while also allowing local influences to affect him. No doubt he felt closest to the Viennese and Mannheim schools – to the former as a result of his origins and the principal areas of his activity, to the latter by his psychological make-up, to which we have already had frequent occasion to refer. Of all the composers discussed, Carl Philipp Emanuel Bach was the last to influence him. In view of the constant interaction of all these disparate influences, it is not easy to identify in detail his relations with each school in turn, for at least as important as that which he took over from them is that which, consciously or unconsciously, he rejected. Here, especially, we find important insights into his nature as an artist.

One immediate consequence of his visits to Italy was that the gradual rapprochement with the Viennese symphony that had revealed itself in the works written immediately before his departure from Salzburg now came to a temporary end, as Italian influence made itself felt in its place. Only one symphony can be dated with any certainty to the time of his first visit and his subsequent brief sojourn in Salzburg: K114 of 30 December 1771. Conversely, the majority of the later symphonies – in other words, those written between late December 1771 and the end of the period under discussion – can be dated with some precision. On the other hand, we have a whole series of

---

142.   Examples may be found in Mennicke, *Hasse und die Brüder Graun*, 208ff. Three trio sonatas are reproduced in Riemann's *Collegium musicum*.
143.   ◆ See Günther Wagner, *Die Sinfonien Carl Philipp Emanuel Bachs: Werdende Gattung und Originalgenie*.

undated works – K74, 76, 84, 95, 97 and Anh. 216 [K[6] Anh. C11.03] – that are not on the same high level as the other pieces written in Salzburg in 1772 but which are clearly distinguished from the works of 1769 by virtue of their unambiguously Italianate manner. This circumstance, coupled with Mozart's own claim of 4 August 1770 that he had 'already written four Italian symphonies',[144] makes it relatively certain that these works date from 1770 and early 1771. Attempts to date them any more accurately within this period may produce more or less plausible findings but cannot lay claim to absolute certainty, not least because the circumstances in which individual pieces were written often played as great a part in their final form as any purely artistic factors.[145]

As a result, Mozart's development as a composer of symphonies follows the same erratic course as that of the composer of Masses: he picked up the tradition of German music in Salzburg in 1769, but then, as soon as he set foot on Italian soil, he became an Italian, only to attempt to find his way back to the world of the German symphony during the periods that he spent in Salzburg between his three visits to Italy. And even after the German symphonic style had won the day, his works continue to reveal traces of recurrent lapses into the Italian manner. Leopold, for ever concerned with superficial success, may well have played a significant part in this state of affairs, but, more generally, it was the logical outcome of Mozart's own artistic nature and of his peculiar receptivity to passing impressions. Such adaptability should not be seen, however, as uncritical imitation. Quite the opposite: at the very moment that the boy was developing into manhood, he was beginning to think for himself and to draw consciously on the whole wealth of ideas at his disposal; and by the end of this period he stood before the world as his own man, in spite of all his borrowings from other composers.

Italianate influence is most pronounced in the three symphonies in D major,[146] K84, 95 and 97, and the G major Symphony K74. Two of these four works (K74 and 84) have no minuet and two (K74 and 95) run the first two movements together. And none of their opening movements repeats the subject-group. Stylistically, too, all four are unadulteratedly Italianate, with the light-weight, even threadbare nature of their main subjects and their short-winded second subjects recalling Sammartini and his colleagues. (The striking similarity of their first subjects is in itself sufficient to suggest that all four works date from the same period, while their second subjects inevitably remind the listener of the sort of resources associated with the older trio.) Above all, however, these opening movements reveal an authentically Italian garrulousness that revels in the endless repetition of the same ideas and is more concerned with impressive brilliance and elegance than with the profundity of those ideas. As with Italian composers, the development sections are cursory in the extreme, regularly introducing new ideas but never extending beyond very brief transitions innocent of any thematic development.[147] The recapitulations are complete or foreshortened and restate the thematic material unaltered: neither here nor elsewhere is there any trace of contrapuntal procedures or variation technique or of any of the other thematic devices designed to display a composer's abilities.

144. *Briefe*, i.377.
145. With their usual astuteness, Wyzewa and Saint-Foix (*Wolfgang Amédée Mozart*, i.278–84) have sought to order the works of this period, although their precise datings have only approximate value, of course. ◆ Beyond problems of dating, many of the works cited by Abert are of uncertain authorship: only K74 survives in the composer's autograph and can be confidently attributed to Mozart; K76 is almost certainly by his father. The following discussion should be read in the light of Eisen, 'Problems of Authenticity among Mozart's Early Symphonies'.
146. The key of D major is by far the most common in symphonies of this period, as orchestras were dominated by the string section at this time and, as a result of the frequent use of open strings, it produced the fullest sonorities.
147. In K84 the development section is only ten bars long.

Yet not even here was Mozart able to deny his German training or his own innate personality. The former emerges from individual reminiscences of the German song tradition, notably in the theme of the andante from K95,[148] from the frequent octave doublings in the melody and in the retention of the minuet in K95 and 97, whereas Mozart's own personality is clear from odd and unexpected outbursts of an emotionalism unknown to the Italians (as at the beginning of the development section of K97 and in the G minor episode from the rondo of K74), as well as from a number of strikingly tender subsidiary ideas such as the second subject of K74. On the other hand, the handling of the orchestra still bears all the hallmarks of the Italian style, with the strings as the focus of interest and the winds serving only to reinforce them.[149]

In the following series of works – K73,[150] 75, 98, 110, 112 and Anh. 216[151] – it is fascinating to follow the way in which Mozart progressively divests himself of his Italian guise following his return from his first visit to the country. Even here, of course, we still find unrepeated subject-groups, unvaried recapitulations and brief, unthematic development sections, and there are still many reminiscences of the Italian manner in his choice of themes. Alongside all these features, however, we find traces of a new spirit. A theme such as the following from K73

brings with it a change of mood that could hardly be less Italian but that is like an intensified version of the Mannheim manner. Not since Mozart's very first symphony had any of his works boasted such a dramatic change of mood. The andante of K112 is audibly indebted to Johann Stamitz. But Viennese influence is even more pronounced, as is clear from the reappearance of contrapuntal procedures and the more sophisticated use of the orchestra – especially the winds – resulting from the influence of the concerto. In the menuetto of K110, for example, the contrapuntal writing achieves the density of a complete canon. And here a new composer enters Mozart's field of vision, a composer under whose spell he was increasingly to fall from now on: Joseph Haydn. In the opening movement of the same symphony, the first subject not only exerts a melodic influence on the second subject, it even returns after it, thereby acquiring a dominant position in the movement that has nothing to do with Italian models and everything to do with Haydn. Indeed, even the development section includes an as yet pale reflection of procedures associated with Haydn inasmuch as it reveals tentative attempts at thematic development. Further

148.   It is the same melody as the one that occurs in the menuetto from K9.
149.   In K84 we even find the Sammartinian violin figure that was also taken over by Gluck. The andante contains a modest attempt to produce a more distinctive colouristic effect.
150.   This symphony bears the date '1769', entered in an unidentified hand, but this date cannot be reconciled with the progressive style of the piece. ◆ Nevertheless, both paper studies and handwriting analysis confirm a date of 1769–70. The apparent anomalies in Mozart's stylistic development may therefore have more to do with Abert's inclusion of several uncertain symphonies in his study, and the conclusions he draws from them, than with the style of K73 itself.
151.   Only the beginning of this symphony was known to Köchel, but the complete score has since been located in the Royal Library in Berlin. ◆ This symphony, which lacks an autograph or any other unequivocal evidence of Mozart's authorship, is listed as Anh. C11.03 in the most recent edition of Köchel. Although the score mentioned by Abert has subsequently disappeared, the symphony was published in 1910 by Breitkopf & Härtel. Of the other symphonies mentioned by Abert, K75 and 98 are also problematic and possibly not by Mozart.

signs of Haydn's influence may be found in the tauter rhythms and in the minuets with their independent and often idiosyncratic basses.

The impact of the concerto style may also be seen in the way in which the wind instruments break free from their role of accompanying or reinforcing the rest of the orchestra: even in the second theme of the andante from K73, for example, we already find the flutes and first violins going completely separate ways, while in the allegro from K112 the second subject on the oboes and *divisi* violas is repeatedly interrupted by two bars of a string concertino. Although Mozart still has a long way to go before he achieves the total fluency of Haydn's orchestra, he is already successful in echoing his solo and tutti effects at the start of his fast movements.

Also new is the suppression of the carefree, nimble-footed Italian character of the final movements in favour of a different tone drawn, in part, from German folk dances (K75) and, in part, from French gavottes (K73 and 110). Of significance here is the fact that in his final rondos Mozart regards his episodes – here, too, they are generally distinguished by their particularly characterful expression – no longer simply as contrasts but as a way of complementing the main sections, thereby bringing rondo form closer to sonata form and in the process demonstrating yet another of his debts to Haydn.

This group of works is also notable for the way in which it shows Mozart's independence of spirit gradually breaking through. On a purely superficial level, this emerges from the increasingly frequent pre-echoes of the composer's later masterpieces, as in the menuetto from K110:[152]

Even more striking is the reminiscence in the broadly flowing soulful cantilena of the slow movements (notably in K110), a cantilena that avoids the usual periodic divisions and achieves its sense of contrast from within, by intensifying or suddenly changing the emotion that is being depicted.

These German influences survived Mozart's second visit to Italy, during which time he wrote little symphonic music. The symphony in F major K112 demonstrably belongs to this period – it is dated 2 November 1771 – and makes a handful of concessions to Italian taste in terms of its themes and orchestration, but none of this obscures its essentially German tone.[153] In the case of a second symphony in F major, K98, Mozart's authorship seems doubtful in the extreme.[154]

In the following series of works, Mozart advances purposefully along the road on which he has set out, and in works such as the two symphonies in A major K114 and 134 and the symphony in F major K130 scales heights only rarely achieved in the subsequent period. The typical tone of the Italian overture gives way to more individual themes, often of genuinely Mozartian *cantabilità*. But

---

152. The trio, too, contains a reminiscence of the trio from the clarinet trio K498.

153. Wyzewa and Saint-Foix (*Wolfgang Amédée Mozart*, i.403–6) argue that this work is an example of Italian recidivism, but against this must be set the frequent shifts of mood, the expressive final subject-group and the impassioned tone of the development section in the opening movement, to say nothing of the Stamitz-like andante and of the partly German, partly specifically Mozartian features of the menuetto (with its trio!) and of its rondo finale, with its two episodes.

154. Its authenticity is attested only by Fuchs and Gall and in consequence was accepted, with reservations, by Köchel. Wyzewa and Saint-Foix (*Wolfgang Amédée Mozart*, i.406–8) defend its authenticity but, in the present writer's view, on insufficient grounds. The work contains a number of features that cannot be squared with the type of symphony that we have been discussing: these features include the suppression of half the second subject and the new final subject-group in the recapitulation, the sentimental character of many of the themes even in the menuetto (the plethora of 'sighs' recalls the Mannheim school) and the often highly mannered approach to dynamics that is again reminiscent of the Mannheimers. The opening bars of the trio even include a favourite phrase of Stamitz's. ◆ See also Eisen, 'Problems of Authenticity among Mozart's Early Symphonies'. There is little reason to think K98 is by Mozart; a second copy of the work, now at Stift Weyarn in Germany, is attributed to 'Hayden'.

they are treated entirely in the spirit of Haydn, in other words, with preference being given to the main ideas. Haydn's increased influence is also apparent in the free handling of the soli.[155] Most important of all, however, is the fact that Mozart now attempts for the first time to merge the four movements together to create a tauter conceptual unity and in that way to broach the most important problem facing composers of symphonies at this time. In K130 it is the strict thematic and contrapuntal writing[156] and intelligent treatment of the soli[157] that link the four movements together, while in K134 it is the Romantic element, an element that finds expression in a mixture of inward rapture, bizarre whimsy and impassioned outbursts that storm the very portals of heaven. This particular creation of the young fireball, whose works of this period – with the exception of the 'Haffner' serenade – are largely unknown, deserves to be revived.

Given Mozart's close cooperation with, and admiration of, Michael Haydn (1737–1806), it is only to be expected that the latter's music, too, should have left its mark on Mozart's.[158] Like his brother, he was a product of the Viennese school and, like him, was essentially optimistic by nature. And like Mozart, he was receptive to Italian influences and – a subjective feature – was fond of exploring the ideas of the moment. The beautiful, regular flow of Mozart's andantes from this period may also be due to Michael Haydn's influence, even though the latter, as the less sensitive of the two, not infrequently falls back on fashionable ideas. Moreover, Haydn tends to append the main idea as a coda to his recapitulations, and Mozart does the same at this period. Unlike the two Haydns, however, Mozart is fond of treating the new element not, in the first instance, as thematic confirmation but merely as a brilliant climax in the style of an Italian stretta. Finally we may mention the concluding fugues of Michael Haydn's symphonies, as it was almost certainly these that were the inspiration behind the final movement of Mozart's last great C major symphony. In general, however, Haydn was incomparably more important in the field of chamber music than he was in that of the symphony.

Of Mozart's shorter orchestral works, suffice it to mention the contredanse K123, a work which, with its five soli and five tuttis, corresponds to Mozart's description as reported by Leopold in his letter of 14 April 1770.[159]

It was at seven o'clock in the evening of 15 March 1770, at Lodi, that Mozart completed his first string quartet K80, a circumstance that he was fond of recalling even in later years. Although the string quartet was already a flourishing genre in Germany at this time, cultivated, as it was, by composers in Mannheim and Vienna (especially by Joseph and Michael Haydn), it was in fact the Italians who first inspired Mozart to contribute to the medium. It was a medium that was the most idiosyncratic fruit of the great change in style that affected all the arts at this time, gradually finding acceptance in the years after 1750: in keeping with its orchestral style, every previous 'quartetto' (or 'sinfonia a quattro') proves on closer examination to be a string symphony with harpsichord accompaniment. Older types of chamber music, too, invariably reckoned on a basso continuo. Only with the gradual disappearance of the latter was the way open for an independent treatment of all four voices. Historically speaking, this first became discernible in the case of the

---

155. The handling of the triplet motif in the andante of K133 is entirely typical of Haydn, even down to the witty unison writing in the basses.
156. The second part of the trio suddenly harks back to the theme of the menuetto, an eccentric feature common to most of the trios in this group of works.
157. Like K132, it has four horns in addition to flutes.
158. A selection of his works, with an introduction, may be found in Perger, *Michael Haydn: Instrumentalwerke.* ◆ More generally concerning the symphonies discussed here, see Zaslaw, *Mozart's Symphonies*, 156–245.
159. *Briefe*, i.335–6.

divertimento, which was also the starting point for Haydn's string quartets.[160] At the same time, however, the new genre came increasingly close to the modern sonata and symphony in terms of both form and content. Needless to say, this was not a development that took place overnight. Of pre-classical composers of quartets,[161] some still reckoned on a continuo or at least evoked its memory through the noticeable stiffness of their bass parts, while others adopted an orchestral style that had little to do with chamber music and that made no secret of its indebtedness to the *sinfonia a quattro*. Yet others attempted to treat all four voices as equals, but failed to rise above the relatively lightweight form of the divertimento. Even in Haydn's early works there is still no clear-cut division between quartets and symphonies, and not until his 'Russian' quartets of 1781 can we speak of fully developed works on a par with the symphony.[162]

In Italy, composers such as Sammartini, Tartini and Boccherini were of no less importance for the string quartet than they were for the symphony. Chronologically speaking, precedence goes to Sammartini with his *Concertini a quattro istromenti soli* of 1766/7,[163] all of them three-movement works in the order allegro–andante–menuetto or andante–allegro–menuetto. They are all written in the same lively and accessible and, at the same time, loosely structured and aphoristic manner as his symphonies. The influence of the old trio sonata is still clearly audible in the self-effacement of the two lower parts vis-à-vis the violins, both of which are treated independently. Even the bass leads a more autonomous existence than before, while still frequently recalling the practices of the old continuo.[164]

This is precisely what we find in Mozart's first attempt to write a string quartet:[165] there is as yet no trace of a genuine quartet style; the main argument is disputed by the two violins; and even though the viola is handled more independently than was the case with Sammartini, the bass is still largely continuo-like in character. The most original movement is the allegro, with its solmization theme in the development section, although not even here is any deeper significance apparent.

The next three quartets in D major, B flat major and F major K136–138, are divertimentos in the manner of Joseph and Michael Haydn and were clearly written as a set in Salzburg in 1772.[166] They, too, are three-movement works. In terms of their style and form, they reflect Italian models,

160.   See Sandberger, 'Zur Geschichte des Haydnschen Streichquartetts', 41ff. Haydn's and Mozart's early quartets still tend to be called notturnos and divertimentos. ◆ The idea that the string quartet and divertimento represent two different genres, and that the former derives from the latter, is effectively debunked in Webster, 'Towards a History of Viennese Chamber Music in the Early Classical Period'.

161.   For examples of chamber works by composers of the Mannheim school, see Riemann, *Mannheimer Kammermusik des 18. Jahrhunderts*.

162.   ◆ For a contrary view, see Webster, 'The Bass Part in Haydn's Early String Quartets'.

163.   See Wyzewa and Saint-Foix, *Wolfgang Amédée Mozart*, i.301–4.

164.   ◆ Further concerning Italian quartets, see Churgin, 'Did Sammartini Influence Mozart's Earliest String Quartets?'; Cattoretti, '1771–1773: Gli ultimi quintetti per archi di Giovanni Battista Sammartini, i primi di Luigi Boccherini' and *Giovanni Battista Sammartini and his Musical Environment*; Churgin, 'Sammartini and Boccherini: Continuity and Change in the Italian Instrumental Tradition of the Classic Period'; Speck, 'Mozart und Boccherini: Zur Frage der Italianità in Mozarts frühen Streichquartetten' and *Boccherinis Streichquartette Studien zur Kompositionsweise und zur gattungsgeschichtlichen Stellung*; Lehmann-Gugolz, *Deutsches und italienisches Wesen in der Vorgeschichte des klassischen Streichquartetts*; and Finscher, *Studien zur Geschichte des Streichquartetts, i: Die Entstehung des klassischen Streichquartetts: Von den Vorformen zur Grundlegung durch Joseph Haydn*.

165.   The charming rondeau was added later, probably in 1772/3. ◆ More likely it was added in Vienna in late 1773 or in Salzburg in early 1774.

166.   Only K136 is known to date from this year, but the style of all three pieces clearly suggests a self-contained group. Quartets were often published in sets of six at this time, suggesting that Mozart wrote a further three works that are now lost – perhaps KAnh. 211–13; see Wyzewa and Saint-Foix, *Wolfgang Amédée Mozart*, i.440–41. ◆ These works, listed in K⁶ as Anh. C20.2–20.4, are now thought to be by Joseph Schuster.

especially in respect of the role of the two violins and bass, whereas a number of contrapuntal and thematic passages already reveal the Haydns' German influence. Common to all three pieces is a Romantic element which finds expression in impassioned minor-key outbursts that cloud the musical picture in the development sections and which, in the andante of K137, already dominates the first and third subjects.

At the end of October 1772, while on his way to Milan, Mozart wrote a further quartet 'to while away the time' and, according to Leopold's letter of 6 February 1773, a third was written in Milan itself.[167] There is no doubt that these are part of the set of six quartets in D, G, C, F, B flat and E flat major K155–160 that clearly belongs to this period on the strength of its script and style. As such, the set dates from the time of *Lucio Silla* and, for the reasons already adduced, is of particular importance for Mozart's development, an importance confirmed by the artistic qualities of all six works. Mozart's progress is evident less from their form than from their expression. Their basis is still Italianate, albeit with a greater number of German, and specifically Haydnesque, features, chief among which are their thematic, albeit as yet brief, development sections. And the historically predominant role of the two violins is undermined, partly by the pre-eminence of the first violin and partly by the way in which the two upper voices are pitted against, and contrasted with, the two lower parts. Other passages in which we can appreciate the advances made by Mozart in the direction of a true quartet style include various contrapuntal sections and whole movements such as the andante of K157, in which the themes are taken up by each of the instruments in turn. But the real value of these pieces is a more personal one.[168] While discussing *Lucio Silla*, we had occasion to draw attention to the wealth of new ideas that were opened up to the adolescent composer under the overwhelming impact of recent events. In *Lucio Silla*, they found expression in the field of high tragedy, whereas in the present string quartets they assume a far more direct and highly personal character, and it is significant that it was the quartet and violin sonata – the two new forms best suited to expressing subjective emotions – to which the young Mozart confided his new world of feelings. There was one aspect of his character in particular that now sought forceful expression, an aspect that we have observed only sporadically in his earlier works: a dark and brooding passion that often descends into pessimism and that finds clearest expression in his middle movements, of which four, significantly, are in minor tonalities. Although their second subjects are initially in the major, they reveal their true character only in the recapitulation, where they, too, are sucked into the minor-key framework. None of Mozart's earlier slow movements achieves the same intensity as the E minor lament in the first version of K156,[169] with its implacable tread, or the veiled anguish of the andante from K158, through whose billowing mists we repeatedly hear a yearning but plaintive cry of almost recitative-like freedom. Another movement that belongs under this same heading is the dark and defiant G minor andante from K159, in which we already find the wildness and vain striving for freedom typical of so many of the composer's later movements in G minor. His allegros, too, are imbued with the new spirit – in the case of the sonata movements it is in the development sections[170] that this spirit is most clearly heard, while in the final rondos it is in the minor-key episodes,[171] and in the minuets, the trios.

167.   *Briefe*, i.457 and 480 (letters of 28 October 1772 and 6 February 1773).
168.   It is to the credit of Wyzewa and Saint-Foix that they recognized the psychological importance not only of the present quartets but also of the contemporary violin sonatas, whereas Jahn (*W. A. Mozart*, i.355–6) passed over them with surprising indifference.
169.   The second adagio was apparently intended for the definitive version of the piece.
170.   Cf. the shadowy beginning of the development section of K158.
171.   In K157 the third subject-group harks back to the first, a merging of sonata form with rondo form that we have already observed in the case of the symphonies.

But, above all, it finds expression in themes such as the following from the beginning of K157, in which the instrumental melody seems on the point of bursting into song:

Writing such as this is as far removed from the Italian overture as it is from Joseph Haydn's effervescent allegros. Rather, it is the expression of a heart which, full to overflowing, seeks to put its feelings into song. Only now does Mozart's instrumental style acquire the songlike colouring that it is to retain from now on, albeit with many fluctuations, and this affects even the figurative passages.

The six violin sonatas in F major, C major, F major, E flat major, C minor and E minor K55–60 are clearly related to the quartets, but are more personal and impassioned in expression. Wyzewa and Saint-Foix date them, with some probability, to the winter of 1772/3,[172] citing as their evidence not only their affinities with the quartets but also their curious mixture of German and Italian features. Particularly remarkable is Mozart's reliance on what was already the outmoded form of the chamber sonata or suite, with a slow prelude and series of dancelike movements, in this case minuets and the rondos also favoured by Mozart in his quartets. In K57–60 we also find the same unity of key-signature that was a feature of the old suite. Sonata movements of a more modern stamp are very much the exception. The conscious attempt to create an archaic atmosphere emerges with particular clarity from the slow movements, where the bass line, rhythms and even the melodic writing attest to this same propensity. It is as though Mozart suddenly felt drawn to the older art of Corelli and his successors, an art to which Sammartini had also paid tribute in a number of his works.[173] Italianate, too, is the discursiveness of the minuets and the songlike nature of the melodic writing that recalls a broadly flowing operatic aria. Alongside these features, however, we also find ideas that could be by Haydn himself and that include the main themes of the rondos of K57, with its genuinely witty, Haydnesque coda, and of K59, the second episode of which boasts an idea *all'ongarese* entirely worthy of Haydn. Nor should we forget in this context

---

172. Jahn and, following him, Köchel date them to 1768, but this is simply impossible on both formal and stylistic grounds. As a result, these important sonatas have acquired the ill-deserved reputation of being insignificant juvenile pieces and, as such, have been excluded from all current editions of Mozart's violin sonatas. Wyzewa and Saint (*Wolfgang Amédée Mozart*, i.502–13) were the first to raise well-founded objections to this incomprehensible under-evaluation, and as a result these works have recently been published by Breitkopf & Härtel in an edition by Hermann Gärtner titled *Romantische Sonaten*. ◆ Abert's enthusiasm notwithstanding, K55–60 are now universally accepted as spurious; the question of their authorship is discussed in detail in the preface to NMA X/29/2. What follows needs to be read with caution.

173. Wyzewa and Saint-Foix (*Wolfgang Amédée Mozart*, i.507) draw attention to six sonatas by Sammartini dating from 1766 as Mozart's immediate model.

the unity of the menuettos in K57 and K58, a unity achieved, in part, by canonic procedures and, in part, by strict thematic writing.

But all these influences take second place to the often volcanic eruptions of genuinely Mozartian melancholy and passion. As in the quartets, the listener is bound to be struck by the important role of minor tonalities and the impressive number of performance markings. The development sections are particularly impassioned in tone, exploring all manner of sombre recesses of the composer's emotional life, often in great chains of melodic and harmonic sequences, and ranging from mere lightning flashes of passion to their full demonic discharge. The old Schobertian spirit is also found here, but invested with an intensity that is entirely Mozart's own. Even in the themes themselves passion often surfaces with sudden vehemence: K58, for example, begins on a note of heroic strength, but by the fourth bar there is a desperate attempt at a *fortissimo* outburst, an attempt that sinks back on a resigned *piano* to a fragmented form of the motif in diminution. It is no wonder, then, that in listening to these sonatas we are reminded for the first time of Beethoven: the similarity between the *dolce* theme of the allegro of K60 and an idea in the final movement of Beethoven's C minor sonata is surely not accidental.[174] In general, these works are typified by a constant ebb and flow of expression that goes far beyond anything found in the works of the Mannheim composers, while avoiding their great crescendos and eruptions of pent-up emotion.[175] Among other details, suffice it to mention the brief coda to the adagio of K56, which already anticipates the succinct and yet eloquent plagal epilogues to Mozart's later andantes. The composer's handling of rondo form in the final movements of these sonatas is inimitable in its freedom, with some of the episodes conceived as antitheses and, as in the E flat minor episode of K58, leading quite unexpectedly into areas of darker emotion, while others appear to emerge from the main theme as if of their own volition. The result is a sense of pulsating life teeming with fresh and enthralling ideas. As a set, these sonatas are finer even than the quartets, each individual piece having its own distinctive atmosphere that finds expression in each of its three movements in various shades of intensity.

No less striking, finally, is Mozart's developing understanding of the relationship between keyboard and violin and, more particularly, his progress in keyboard writing, progress that throws brilliant light on his unflagging studies in this area. The inspiration behind his keyboard style is still Domenico Scarlatti, but Scarlatti as transmuted by Schobert. Octave doublings, crossing of the hands and Alberti basses are by no means infrequent, and the figurative writing has become more individual, not least as the result of a powerful injection of chromatic elements. Free counterpoint, too, plays a by no means insignificant role. But what is especially striking is the highly effective use of all the instrument's registers, allowing Mozart to achieve colouristic effects that often sound very modern, as in the deep rolling basses in the allegro and the heartfelt E major cantilena that enters in the instrument's lower register in the final movement of K60, in the opening movement of which Mozart writes out the cadenzas in full for the first time.

Only exceptionally is the violin treated as the keyboard's thematic equal, but where it is so treated, the writing proves exceptionally effective, as in the second subject of the largo from K57

---

174.   There is also a striking similarity between the theme of the rondeau from this same sonata and the main theme from the final movement of Beethoven's violin sonata op.12/2. Nor, however, can we overlook the spiritual affinity between the present sonata and Mozart's own violin sonata in E minor K304: readers may care to compare not only the key, but also the character of the two allegro themes and the E major episodes in the menuettos.

175.   The second section of the tempo di menuetto from K55 includes a great crescendo build-up that one expects will culminate in a return of the main theme, instead of which it issues in a timid *piano* completely unlike anything found in the Mannheim composers – with an additional *calando* marking. Only then does the main theme reappear.

and in the F minor episode from the same sonata's final rondo. Otherwise the instrument is entrusted only with accompanying figures, skilful imitative writing and sustained notes which, although designed only to fill out the harmonies, often produce highly effective sonorities. (Note, for example, the *c'* at the beginning of the final movement of K57.)

In short, these violin sonatas are far from being merely youthful works that can be summarily dismissed before we proceed to the main business of the day. Rather, each movement bears within it the infallible hallmark of genius and of a sense of self-awareness which, fired by searing passion, was growing increasingly assured at this very time. As such, these sonatas are more important than many of Mozart's later works, for all that the latter may be more mature from a formal point of view. Goethe's *Götz von Berlichingen* appeared in 1773, his *Werther* in 1774. Just as Goethe's poetic genius caught the mood of the *Sturm und Drang*, so Mozart's musical genius reflects its spirit of aspiration in these six sonatas.

Other chamber works that demonstrably date from this period are the *Concerto ossia Divertimento* in E flat major K113 for string quartet, two clarinets and two horns written in Milan in November 1771; the divertimento in D major K131 for string quartet, flute, oboe, bassoon and four horns composed in Salzburg in June 1772; and the divertimento in E flat major K166 for two oboes, two clarinets, two english horns, two horns and two bassoons, the autograph of which is dated Salzburg, 24 March 1773. The divertimento in B flat major K186 is scored for identical forces and presumably dates from this same period. This was the first time that Mozart had used clarinets, a use which suggests that these pieces were intended to be performed at the home of some Milanese patron or other, as there were no clarinets in the Salzburg orchestra.[176] Conversely, the divertimento K131, with its four virtuoso horns, affords brilliant proof of the abilities of Salzburg's horn players. But all these works are true divertimentos in terms of both form and spirit. The number of movements varies from four to seven, with K131 as the most elaborate: not only does it have two finales (one in sonata form, the other in rondo form), but the first of them is preceded by a Haydnesque adagio introduction, the first example of such a practice in Mozart's works. Of the two menuettos, the second has two trios, the first three: in the first, the musical argument is entrusted to the horns, in the second to the woodwinds, while in the third both groups engage in dialogue with each other. Both menuettos include an unnecessary coda which, in the case of the first, repeats the whole of the main section, while in the case of the second, the repeat is limited to its first half in the full orchestra. Particularly remarkable is Mozart's grasp of sonority and the freedom with which, even here, he approaches questions of practical music-making. Popular instrumental jokes are also in evidence. In general, these works are examples of witty and stimulating light music, with few traces of the impassioned tone of the instrumental music of the period. Only in the soulful adagios of K131, 166 and 186 do we find the graceful and enraptured tone, with its delight in cantabile melodies, that is characteristic of these other instrumental works.

It remains only to mention a handful of relatively short vocal works from this period, namely, the as yet unpublished aria *Non curo l'affetto* from Metastasio's *Demofoonte* that Mozart wrote for

---

176. ◆ While Mozart's first use of clarinets in an original composition was probably the divertimento K113, earlier, in London in 1764 or 1765, he had added them to an arrangement of C. F. Abel's symphony op. 7 no. 6 (K18, K⁶ Anh. A51). And while it is true that clarinets were not part of the Salzburg court orchestra, they were used by military and civil bands; for a thoroughgoing discussion of wind instruments in Salzburg, see Birsak, *Das Große Salzburger Blasmusikbuch*. The *Concerto ossia Divertimento* K113 was originally composed by Mozart for two clarinets, two horns, two violins, viola and basso; sometime later, probably in Salzburg in early 1773, he revised the work to include two oboes, two bassoons and two english horns as well. See Blazin, 'The Two Versions of Mozart's Divertimento K. 113'; both versions are published in NMA IV/12/2.

the theatre at Pavia in 1771 and that is stylistically at one with the arias from *Mitridate*,[177] and two German songs to words by Johann Christian Günther, *Ich hab es längst gesagt* K149 and *Was ich in Gedanken küsse* K150.[178] Both are deeply undemanding works in the style of the north German school, a school recalled by the German subtitle of the second ('In the tempo of a certain secret pleasure'), while its opening is identical to that of a song by Sperontes.[179] The rigid structure of the dance song continues to dominate both these works. On an expressive level, the first is more successful than the second, with a certain good-natured roguishness imbuing the melisma on the word 'längst', the gruff turn of phrase at 'plagt' and the thundering bass at 'billt'.

177. Discussed by Wyzewa and Saint-Foix, *Wolfgang Amédée Mozart*, i.350–2.

178. ◆ All three of these works are problematic: the two songs are by Leopold Mozart, not Wolfgang, while the aria *Non curo l'affetto* K74b lacks authentic sources and cannot be claimed absolutely for Mozart.

179. Buhle, *Sperontes Singende Muse an der Pleiße*, 23. This opening phrase is found on several occasions in Leopold Mozart's notebook (see above).

12

On the way to La finta giardiniera

We know virtually nothing about Mozart's life during the period between his return from Italy in March 1773 and his departure for Vienna the following July. All that we can say for certain is that in May 1773 he wrote a symphony K181 and a concertone for two violins K190 and that in June he composed a mass K167. It is likely, however, that he also spent this period completing not only the two sets of quartets and violin sonatas discussed in the previous chapter but also various works such as the second clarinet divertimento that had been commissioned in Milan.[1] But the principal new impression of this period was undoubtedly bound up with the completely new situation resulting from the election of Schrattenbach's successor as archbishop.

The Mozarts' relations with Archbishop Schrattenbach had been tolerable, even though the latter had been unhappy with Leopold's repeated and lengthy absences and with his tendency to return only after his leave of absence had already expired. Wolfgang, it is true, had been given the post and title of Konzertmeister at the Salzburg court in 1769, but it was an unpaid appointment, and even after the performance of *Ascanio in Alba*, Leopold thought it highly unlikely that the archbishop would remember Mozart if the question of remuneration were to arise.[2] In the event, however, Colloredo granted him an annual salary of 150 florins in 1772, and Mozart continued to draw this salary until 1777, so that the archbishop's own sister, Countess Schönborn, 'absolutely refused to believe that (oh, blessed memory) my entire salary used to be 12 florins and 30 kreutzers a month'.[3]

For most earlier writers on Mozart, including even Jahn, Archbishop Colloredo played the same sort of role in their subject's life as Duke Karl Eugen did in Schiller's, being regarded as the unjust oppressor of innocent genius. Such writers were all the more convinced that they were in the right in that both Leopold and his son present a highly unfavourable picture of Colloredo and his character in their letters. In the process, these writers have overlooked the fact that the opinion of neither Mozart himself nor of his perpetually suspicious father was impartial but that it generally bore the stamp of personal ill will.[4] Admittedly, Colloredo was never a popular figure in Salzburg: he had been elected in the face of considerable local opposition, and the good people of Salzburg showed their disapproval in no uncertain terms at the time he took up his office.[5] But here, too, their feelings were not entirely pure, as it soon transpired that the new broom was keen to sweep

---

1. ◆ See Blazin, 'The Two Versions of Mozart's Divertimento K 113'.
2. *Briefe*, i.450 (letter of 16 November 1771).
3. *Briefe*, ii.13 (letter of 26 September 1777). ◆ The decree of 21 August is reproduced in *Dokumente*, 127, *Documentary Biography*, 163.
4. The following entry in Hagenauer's diary is clearly influenced by Leopold: Leopold 'had the misfortune of always being persecuted here and was far less popular than elsewhere, namely, in the largest cities in Europe'; see *Dokumente*, 258, *Documentary Biography*, 293. Pirckmayer, 'Zur Lebensgeschichte Mozarts', attempts to salvage the archbishop's reputation; see also Deiters in Jahn, *W. A. Mozart*, fourth edition, i.394, n.37. ◆ More recently, see Eibl, 'Die Mozarts und der Erzbischof'.
5. See the account in Koch-Sternfeld, *Die letzten dreißig Jahre*, 44–5.

clean and do away with many of the slovenly practices that had endeared his predecessor to them. Colloredo was a shrewd, clear-thinking individual powerfully drawn to Enlightenment ideas, well-read and, at the same time, sufficiently tenacious and energetic to put his convictions into practice. In the process he revealed an exceptional understanding of human nature and refused to be misled by flattery or hypocrisy. From the outset he dealt firmly with the easygoing local population and if he was sometimes cold and ruthless,[6] it was not to get his own back for the frosty welcome that he had received but because he was convinced that this was the quickest and surest way of putting his plans into practice. His officials and advisers and, indeed, all his subordinates were timidly respectful of the brusqueness of a man who had little time for praising others or for acknowledging their achievements. He deferred to members of the higher aristocracy, but everyone else was peremptorily treated as an inferior.[7] This was, of course, a bitter pill to swallow for those who had got to know the old and affable archbishop, but the new regime brought the province a whole series of important reforms, chief among them an overhaul of its ruinous finances. Of course, Colloredo shared the view of all enlightened despots at this time, that the lives of their subordinates must necessarily be governed by princely dictate and that the subject should invariably look up to his ruler as his benefactor. But this was a precept that was accepted by all artists in the pay of princes of the time, and the majority were happy to put up with it. If things turned out differently in Mozart's case, the blame must lie as much with Colloredo's employees as with the archbishop himself. After all, Leopold himself could be something of a tin-pot tyrant unwilling to accept another's authority, in addition to which he soon discovered that his usual diplomatic skills, which had proved so successful with other powerful rulers, made little impression on Colloredo. The old archbishop had tacitly allowed Leopold to pursue his life's goal of helping his son to find fame and fortune in the big wide world, whereas the new one demanded the strictest observance of his terms of service, a demand based on what, from his own point of view, was the eminently reasonable principle that his Kapelle existed in the first instance for the benefit of his own court and not for the courts of others. There is no doubt that from the outset he regarded Leopold as the sort of official who needed to be kept on a tight rein, thereby placing Leopold in a predicament and fomenting a conflict of loyalties that was bound to be particularly testing for as phlegmatic a person as his servant. The two men also seem to have developed a personal antipathy to each other: from the very beginning the prince with the unsmiling lips and the keen expression in his two grey eyes, of which the left one was rarely fully open,[8] inspired feelings of deep mistrust in his self-willed deputy Kapellmeister who, where Mozart was concerned, seemed capable of anything. Meanwhile, as we have seen and as we shall have further occasion to see, Leopold was tireless in his often devious attempts to free his son from Salzburg's trammelling constraints.

But not only did Leopold have to face Colloredo's endless criticisms, so, too, did Wolfgang. In this case, the reason appears less to do with the fact that Count Ferdinand von Zeil, who later became Bishop of Chiemsee and whose generous withdrawal from the list of archiepiscopal

---

6. See Riesbeck, *Briefe eines reisenden Franzosen*, i.158: 'As a thinker, the present prince cannot be praised sufficiently highly, but of his heart I cannot speak. He knows that he is not very popular with the Salzburgers, and so he despises them and shuts himself off from them.'

7. On 19 February 1778 we find Wolfgang writing to his father: 'I didn't dare contradict them, partly because I wanted to make some good friends, and partly because I'd come straight from Salzburg, where we're discouraged from contradicting anyone'; *Briefe*, ii.286.

8. A characteristic of the archbishop noted by Koch-Sternfeld, *Die letzten dreißig Jahre*, 312–13.

candidates resulted in Colloredo's appointment,[9] was particularly supportive of him, than with the boy's boisterous high spirits and quick wit, both of which seemed to need curbing. Even so, Colloredo was in no doubt about the boy's exceptional talent, and he expended some effort on retaining his services. In spite of his notorious thrift, it is hard to believe that he treated him in a particularly offhand manner in order to avoid having to increase his salary.[10] After all, it was he who offered the sixteen-year-old composer 150 florins, and even his later salary of 450 florins shows him being treated more, rather than less, favourably than the other musicians.[11] The Italians, it is true, received more, but this was standard practice at all the princely courts in Germany: Salzburg was in no way exceptional in this respect. And a glance at the list of musicians in the archbishop's Kapelle[12] makes it impossible to argue that foreigners were somehow favoured: the only Italians in the Salzburg Kapelle were Lolli's successor as Kapellmeister, Domenico Fischietti, the violinist Antonio Brunetti, the cellist Antonio Ferrari, the oboist Giuseppe Ferlendi and the castrato Francesco Ceccarelli. No doubt Colloredo, like most princely rulers of the time, preferred Italians, even though he sometimes treated even them harshly[13] and Salzburg was no different from elsewhere in terms of the improprieties committed by these foreigners and the tensions caused by their contacts with the Germans.[14] But we know from his visit to Stuttgart that Leopold invariably suspected Italian intrigues behind every real or imagined slight, even when he had no grounds for such suspicions. And he successfully inculcated this mistrust of Italians in his son. The archbishop ensured that Wolfgang received his fair share of official commissions, even though there was never any question of any extra payment. Indeed, he was under no obligation to offer any such payments, just as he rarely offered the other musicians any tokens of his special favour. Moreover, his whole approach to Mozart's music was coloured by his private views on the subject, and here we shall have to revise our existing prejudices, at least as far as church music is concerned. His enlightened attitude is attested not least by his ban on the usual dry fugal writing in masses and his replacement of organ sonatas by sung graduals. Also, it is clear from his pastoral letter of 1782 that he actively championed German hymns in church services. In the case of secular music, by contrast, his tastes seem to have been predominantly Italian, with the result that he found much to criticize in Mozart's music.[15] In this context Leopold reports his offensive remark that Mozart knew nothing about music and should betake himself to some conservatory or other in Naples in order to study the subject properly.[16] But this comment comes from the

9. Koch-Sternfeld, *Die letzten dreißig Jahre*, 43.
10. Jahn, *W. A. Mozart*, fourth edition, i.394.
11. Pirckmayer, 'Zur Lebensgeschichte Mozarts', rightly draws attention to this fact, citing in evidence a list of local salaries.
12. Max Seiffert, *Leopold Mozart: Ausgewählte Werke.* ◆ For a full account of the Salzburg court music during the eighteenth century, see Hintermaier, *Die Salzburger Hofkapelle*.
13. Meißner was one of his favourites, but, according to Leopold's letter of 6 October 1777 (*Briefe*, ii.36), even he received a warning from the chief steward to the effect that, having been prevented from singing because of a cold, 'he must sing and perform regularly in the church services or else he will be dismissed. Such is the great favourite's reward.'
14. Burney comments pertinently in this context: 'The musicians of almost every town, and every band in the service of a German prince, however small his dominions, erect themselves into a musical monarchy, mutually jealous of each other, and all unanimously jealous of the Italians, who come into their country: for my own part, as a bystander, who had no share in these quarrels, and was not in the least interested in the event, I thought I could see prejudice operating strongly on both sides. As to the Italians, however, it must be acknowledged that they are caressed, courted, and frequently rewarded with double the salary that is paid even to such natives as have the claim of superior merit'; see his *The Present State of Music in Germany*, ii.336–7.
15. Wolfgang writes ironically from Mannheim on 4 November 1777: 'I played this concerto to him [Ramm] today on the pianoforte at Cannabich's, and although people knew I'd written it, it was well received. No one said it wasn't well written, because the people here don't understand such things – they should ask the archbishop, he'll soon put them right'; *Briefe*, ii.101.
16. *Briefe*, ii.204 (letter of 22 December 1777 to Padre Martini).

time immediately after their breach with Colloredo and shows only the depths of irritation to which both parties had sunk. In the archbishop's case, his tetchiness was short-lived and he later acknowledged Mozart's mature artistry ungrudgingly and without resentment. In short, it was no act of capricious despotism on the prince's part that led to the final breach but the incompatibility of their characters and views.

For a convinced supporter of the Enlightenment like Colloredo, music was of only material benefit to mankind. Here, too, he had time only for neatness and correctness and hated the irrational element that could not be controlled by the intellect. But, as we have seen, the feelings that were stirring in the young composer's heart in the years around 1773 could never be reconciled with this well-regulated sense of order, as a voice demanded to be heard that was bound to strike the princely prelate not merely as unsettling but as positively dangerous. The definitive breach was repeatedly deferred, not least because Mozart kept his daemon in check and accommodated his employer's tastes. But the differences between them simmered on in secret. This was Mozart's first confrontation with the older dispensation in art, a dispensation represented by the aristocracy and one, moreover, in which his father, too, had been inextricably caught up. It was a confrontation that was to have profound implications and, given the uncompromising sincerity of both parties, was bound to end with Mozart resolving to honour God rather than Man and to go his own way as his own master, without any patronage or protection.

When Colloredo travelled to Vienna in the summer of 1773, Leopold decided to follow suit. Initially, he planned to remain there only briefly, but as the days turned into weeks, Leopold asked if he and Wolfgang might be allowed to stay on as well, a request that Colloredo granted. That the aim of the visit was to find a more permanent appointment for Mozart in Vienna is as good as certain: it was already being rumoured in Salzburg that Leopold was counting on the demise of the already ailing Florian Gassmann. Naturally, he indignantly rejected such suspicions,[17] but his letters contain various clues as to all manner of ulterior motives. In the event, none of these wishes came true. Although Gassmann died in 1774, his post as Hofkapellmeister passed to the former court composer Giuseppe Bonno,[18] and elsewhere, too, Mozart found that all doors were closed to him. Not even at court did he have any luck on this occasion. Although they were graciously received by the empress, the emperor did not return from Poland until September and appears not to have received the Mozarts.

In the circumstances, the Mozarts drew little comfort from their contacts with old friends and acquaintances such as Alexandre-Louis Laugier, Nicolò Martínez, Jean-Georges Noverre, Giuseppe Bonno, Joseph Leopold von Auenbrugger and his two musical daughters,[19] and Johann Gottlieb Stephanie and his wife. They received a particularly warm welcome at the Mesmers' home in the Landstraße district, where music was still regularly performed. Mesmer himself had been taught to play the musical glasses by Marianne Davies,[20] and Mozart too tried his hand at the instrument

17. *Briefe*, i.496 (letter of 4 September 1773).

18. See Wellesz, 'Giuseppe Bonno (1710–1788): Sein Leben und seine dramatischen Werke'. ◆ More recently, see Hadamowsky, 'Leitung, Verwaltung und ausübende Künstler'; Meloncelli, 'Un operista italiano alla corte di Vienna: Giuseppe Bonno (1710–1788)'; and Heartz, *Haydn, Mozart and the Viennese School 1740–1780*.

19. *Briefe*, i.486 (letter of 12 August 1773). Friedrich Nicolai, *Beschreibung einer Reise durch Deutschland und die Schweiz im Jahre 1781*, iv.554; Cramer, *Magazin der Musik*, i.928.

20. Marianne Davies – Leopold invariably writes Devis – made her public début on Franklin's glass harmonica in 1762; see Pohl, *Mozart und Haydn in London*, 61. ◆ Marianne Davies (1743/4–1819) travelled extensively throughout Europe in the 1760s and 1770s with her sister, the soprano Cecilia Davies; they were active in London during the 1780s but later faded into obscurity. See Matthews, 'The Davies Sisters, J. C. Bach and the Glass Harmonica'.

at this time, with Leopold even professing a keen interest in acquiring a set.[21] They also had to attend the eighth wedding anniversary of the younger Mesmer, who was now working as a school inspector.

Their visit to Vienna coincided with the suppression of the order of Jesuits. Leopold followed their expulsion with considerable interest, commenting that many good Christians were of the view that the pope should concern himself with questions of faith and leave the Jesuits in peace if they were really as poor as the Capuchins. In Rome their property had been appropriated 'ad pias causes' – for religious causes, which was easily done, or so Leopold argued, as all that the pope took was used for such causes. But the Viennese court had refused to accept the first papal Brief, preferring to retain for itself the right to use property of the Jesuits in whatever ways it wished. Leopold also thought that the millions received from the Jesuits would whet the court's appetite for a few more expropriations of a similar kind.[22]

Among the sadder experiences of their visit was the death of Franz Joseph Niderl von Aichegg, a doctor from Salzburg with whom they were on friendly terms and who had come to Vienna to be operated on for kidney stones, only to die as a result of the operation.

Wolfgang had brought some work with him. For a celebration planned by the Antretter family, he had agreed to write a *Finalmusik* in the form of a large-scale serenade K185 that he sent back to Salzburg and that was performed there in early August under Meißner's direction. He then set to work on six quartets K168–173, though it is uncertain whether these were commissioned works.[23] This same autumn also saw the first version of the first two choruses from *König Thamos*. The *Dominicus* mass K66 was performed under Leopold's direction 'in the octave of the Feast of St Ignatius', in other words, on 7 August, a week after the feast day on 31 July. Performed by the Jesuits at their church Am Hof, it met with exceptional acclaim. The Theatine Fathers invited the Mozarts to lunch and to their service on the Feast of St Cajetan, but the organ was not good enough for a concerto, and so Mozart borrowed a violin from his young friend Teyber, the brother of the soprano Therese Teyber,[24] and was brazen enough to perform the concerto on the violin, making such an impression that eight years later, as soon as he recalled performing a violin concerto in the choir in 1773, a lay brother immediately recognized him.[25]

There was no opportunity to make any money, causing Leopold to comment wryly that the fatter he was growing, the thinner his purse was becoming. He admitted to his wife that he had had to raise some funds, but reassured her that this meant only that he needed money, not that he required a doctor. Also, he had his reasons for remaining in Vienna – 'the situation will change, it's bound to. Cheer up and keep well, God will help us!'[26]

Meanwhile, all his attempts to free his son from his forced labour in Salzburg had proved unavailing, at least for the time being, and they returned to Salzburg in early October. But Mozart also took back with him some lasting artistic impressions, echoes of which we shall, as usual, discover in his later works. Above all, he had renewed contact with the world of opera. The battle lines between the *Gluckistes* and the party of Metastasio and Hasse had grown even more deeply

21. *Briefe*, i.484 (letter of 21 July 1773).
22. See *Karl Leonhard Reinhold's Leben*, 5ff. and Pichler, *Denkwürdigkeiten aus meinem Leben*, i.36.
23. Four are dated August, the remainder September.
24. ◆ Probably this was not Therese Teyber's brother Anton (1756–1822), who at the time was in Italy, but their father Matthäus (c1711–85), a violinist in the imperial Hofkapelle; see *Briefe*, v.334.
25. *Briefe*, iii.105 (letter of 11 April 1781). ◆ Abert seems to have conflated two performances here. Mozart's mass was given at the Jesuit church Am Hof on 8 August; the performance of the violin concerto at the Kajetaner-Kloster was on 7 August; see Eibl, *Chronik*, 50.
26. *Briefe*, i.491 (letter of 21 August 1773).

entrenched since his last visit to Vienna: Gluck's third reform opera, *Paride ed Elena*, had been staged in 1770 and the score published more or less simultaneously with a further sharply-worded preface. Meanwhile, Gluck was working on *Iphigénie en Aulide*.[27] But older composers such as Hasse and Traetta were still far from forgotten. *Opera buffa*, too, continued to flourish, not only in its original form in the works of composers such as Galuppi, Piccinni, Anfossi and others, but also in a form closer to the Viennese tradition, the foremost representative of which was Florian Gassmann. Among younger composers, Antonio Salieri had recently come to prominence. Instrumental music, too, was currently enjoying something of a revival, with Joseph Haydn increasingly taking over from the older generation of composers, including Wagenseil, Starzer, Vanhal and Gassmann. And from church music came the most varied impressions, with the older and 'truer' style still gaining a hearing alongside the most up-to-date works.[28]

On his return to Salzburg, Mozart is known to have written the following datable works: two masses in F and D major K192 and 194, a Marian litany K195, two psalms for a vespers K193, a symphony in D major K202, a keyboard concerto in D major K175 and a revised version of the string quintet K174 that he had probably begun before leaving for Vienna.[29] A whole series of other orchestral works dates from this period, but they can be dated only with difficulty because the original date on the autograph scores has been rendered more or less illegible by a later and careless hand. The works in question are three symphonies K199–201, two serenades or divertimentos K203 and 205 and the bassoon concerto in B flat major K191, if we may believe André's note 'a Salisburgo li 4 di Giugno 1774'.[30]

For the rest of 1773 and the whole of 1774, Mozart's life reverted to its old routine.[31] But for the 1775 carnival he received a commission to write a comic opera for Munich, an invitation that he almost certainly owed to the admirable prince-bishop of Chiemsee, Count Ferdinand von Zeil, a loyal supporter of Mozart who spent several years in Munich on archiepiscopal business. The Elector Maximilian III, too, had earlier proved one of Mozart's most active advocates, and Colloredo could not refuse him his request to allow Wolfgang leave of absence to write the opera. Having studied extensively, the elector was extremely talented as a musician and had written a number of sacred works, in addition to which he played the gamba 'divinely', according to Naumann. Burney assured his readers that, with the exception of the celebrated Carl Friedrich Abel, he had never heard so excellent a gamba player. His sister was the dowager Electress of Saxony, Maria Antonia Walpurgis, who was currently staying in Munich. As a poetess, she was known as 'Ernelinda Talea, pastorella Arcada', but her talents also extended to singing and to the composition of Italian operas

---

27. See Burney, *The Present State of Music in Germany*, i.262, and for a detailed account of conditions in Vienna in the autumn of 1772, i.202–367. ◆ *Iphigénie en Aulide* was premièred at Paris in 1774.

28. Burney, *The Present State of Music in Germany*, i.214.

29. ◆ K174 was revised in December 1773, the litany and symphony were written in May 1774, and the two masses in June and August 1774, respectively; the vespers K193 dates from July 1774.

30. ◆ Although Abert is correct in claiming that the dates on Mozart's autographs of these works have been tampered with, they are nevertheless mostly readable: K199 dates from April 1773, K201 from April 1774 and K203 from August 1774. Only the dates of K200 (November 1773 or 1774) and K205 (probably July 1773) are uncertain. The implication that all of these works postdate the trip to Vienna is therefore slightly inaccurate: the symphony K199 was composed before the Mozarts left for the imperial capital; this was also probably the case with K205.

31. In his petition of 1777 (*Dokumente*, 145–6, *Documentary Biography*, 162–3), Mozart mentions that *three* years earlier he had asked for permission to travel to Vienna and that on that occasion the archbishop had declared that he had nothing to hope for and would do better to seek his fortune elsewhere. Since he was in Vienna in 1773 and since he travelled to Munich at the end of 1774, albeit with Colloredo's permission, it is doubtful whether this petition was submitted in 1774. Perhaps Mozart is referring to his earlier stay in Vienna; he may well have made a mistake over the date [Deiters's note].

to her own librettos.[32] In short, orchestras and singers received considerable support in Munich's churches and opera houses, even though musical standards still fell short of those in Mannheim at this time.[33] The court held regular concerts, and, as for the theatre, *opera seria* shared the honours with German comedy and Italian *opera buffa*,[34] with performances regularly ending with a ballet, usually on a tragic subject, a trend set by Jean-Georges Noverre, who was already engaged in Vienna by this date.[35]

Mozart left for Munich with his father on 6 December.[36] They stayed in a small but comfortable apartment placed at their disposal by Johann Nepomuk Pernat, whom Leopold describes as 'chanoine e grand Custos de Notre Dame', i.e., canon of the city's Frauenkirche, and who showed them more courtesy and honour than they felt that they deserved, frequently putting himself out for them from a sense of genuine friendship. It was bitterly cold throughout the journey and, in spite of every precaution, Wolfgang again found himself suffering from a complaint that had plagued him repeatedly during his youth, toothache on one side of his mouth, with the result that his swollen cheek kept him in his room for a whole week. They then met the various people with whom they would be dealing and received a friendly welcome wherever they went.

Mozart had brought part of his opera with him from Salzburg, although we do not know which sections. Like so many others, this production, too, was dogged with difficulties: following the first rehearsal, the opening night was postponed from 29 December to 5 January, so that the singers could learn their parts. In the event, this proved an over-optimistic assessment of the situation on Leopold's part, and the first night was again put back, this time to 13 January. In other respects, too, the situation at the theatre seems to have been fairly tense, if we may believe Leopold's report of 30 December:

> You must know that Maestro Tozzi, who this year is writing the *opera seria*,[37] wrote an *opera buffa* this time last year, and contrived to write it so well that it killed the *opera seria* written by Maestro Sales.[38] Now it so happens that Wolfgang's opera is being performed before Tozzi's, and when people heard the first rehearsal, they all said that Tozzi was being paid back in his own coin, as Wolfgang's opera would certainly kill his. I do not like such things and am trying to silence such remarks as far as possible by raising endless protests, but the whole orchestra and everyone who heard the rehearsal say they have never heard finer music and that every aria is beautiful.[39]

32. Karl von Weber, *Maria Antonia Walpurgis, Churfürstin zu Sachsen*; Petzholdt, 'Biographisch-litterarische Mittheilungen über Maria Antonia Walpurgis von Sachsen'; Fürstenau, 'Maria Antonia Walpurgis, Kurfürstin von Sachsen: Eine biographische Skizze'; Schering, *Johann Adolph Hasse: La conversione di Sant'Agostino*, vi–vii.

33. Burney, *The Present State of Music in Germany*, i.142–76; Schubart, *Leben und Gesinnungen*, section xvi; and Rudhart, *Geschichte der Oper am Hofe zu München*, i.196ff. ◆ Concerning Mozart and Munich generally, see Münster, *'Ich bin hier sehr beliebt': Mozart und das kurfürstliche Bayern*.

34. One of our main sources is the journal kept by the secretary to the Saxon legation, Johann Friedrich Unger (Dresdener Hauptarchiv lo. 3292), a source inadequately used by Rudhart in his *Geschichte der Oper am Hofe zu München*. Among the *opere buffe* listed by Unger for the period 1774/5 (that is, up to the time of Mozart's departure) but ignored by Rudhart are *L'amante deluso, L'isola d'amore, La locanda, Il villano geloso, La contadina in corte, La serva astuta, Lo sposo burlato, La pupilla ed il ciarlone, L'amore artigiano, Il cavaliere per amore* and *La sposa fedele*. Rudhart also fails to mention a performance of *La Betulia liberata* on 23 May 1775, a performance described by Unger as 'oratoire ou operette'; see Engländer, 'Zu den Münchener Orfeo-Aufführungen 1773 und 1775', 34. During the carnival, the *opera buffa* was always performed with an 'académie en masque'.

35. A ballet called *Docteur Faust* turns up on 12 February 1775.

36. According to Nannerl, they left on 9 December; see Nottebohm, *Mozartiana*, 108. But a letter written by Leopold in Munich is already dated the 9th.

37. *Orfeo ed Euridice*; on this travesty of Gluck's work, see Engländer, 'Zu den Münchener Orfeo-Aufführungen 1773 und 1775', 26ff.

38. *Achille in Sciro*.

39. *Briefe*, i.513 (letter of 30 December 1774).

The performance on 13 January 1775 turned out to be a brilliant success, with Mozart's opera followed by a ballet, *La nymphe parjure protégée par l'Amour*. Mozart himself wrote to his mother the next day to report that the theatre had been 'packed to the rafters' and that 'after each aria there was a terrific noise, with people clapping and shouting "Viva Maestro"'. At the end he was graciously received by the elector and electress.[40]

On 15 January 1775 the secretary to the Saxon legation, Johann Friedrich von Unger, noted in his diary: 'On Friday Their Electoral Highnesses were present at the first performance of the *opera buffa: La finta giardiniera*; the music was universally applauded; it is by young Mozart of Salzburg, who is here at the moment. He is the same who went to England and elsewhere at the age of 8 to be heard on the harpsichord, which he plays supremely well.'[41] That the work was sensationally successful is clear from the fact that the composer is not only – exceptionally – mentioned by name but also described in detail, a privilege accorded to no other composer. Writing in his *Deutsche Chronik*, Christian Friedrich Daniel Schubart noted that he 'heard an *opera buffa* by that wonderful genius *Mozart*; it is called *La finta giardiniera*. Flashes of genius appear here and there; but there is not yet that still altar-fire that rises towards Heaven in clouds of incense – a scent beloved of the gods. If Mozart is not a plant forced in the hot-house, he is bound to grow into one of the greatest musical composers who ever lived.'[42] Of the performers themselves, it was said that Rossi and Rosa Manservini were made for *opera buffa*. Rossi was as good as his cousin in Stuttgart in comic roles, while Manservisi was said to have the voice, music, person and everything else necessary to raise her above the average singer.[43]

On this occasion, Mozart had the pleasure of having his sister with him to witness his triumph. Thanks to a good friend, they had managed to find suitable accommodation for her with a certain Frau von Durst, 'the widowed wife of a salt merchant from Reichenhall, whom Herr von Mölk often drove over to visit and whom we frequently heard him mention', Leopold explained in a letter of 16 December 1774: 'She is a young woman of about 26 or 28, a brunette, with dark eyes, very retiring, sensible and well-read. She does not care for the society of philanderers and is very courteous and pleasant.'[44] Marianne arrived in Munich on 4 January with Frau von Robinig and found a pleasant enough apartment waiting for her, with a harpsichord on which she could practise as much as she liked. Other visitors from Salzburg who came for the carnival include Maria Barbara Gertrudis ('Waberl') Eberlin, Maria Anna Aloisia ('Louise') von Schiedenhofen, Siegmund von Antretter and the young Franz von Mölk, who, according to Mozart's letter of 11 January 1775, 'was so astounded by the *opera seria* that he kept crossing himself, so we were thoroughly ashamed of him, as it was clear that he had never been anywhere except Salzburg and Innsbruck'.[45]

An involuntary witness of Mozart's successes was Archbishop Colloredo, who paid an official visit to the elector in January 1775.[46] In the event, he arrived only after the first night and left again before the second performance. Inevitably, he heard a great deal about Mozart's new opera during

---

40. *Briefe*, i.516 (letter of 14 January 1775).
41. ◆ *Dokumente*, 135, *Documentary Biography*, 150–1.
42. ◆ *Dokumente*, 138, *Documentary Biography*, 153.
43. Rudhart, *Geschichte der Oper am Hofe zu München*, i.161–2. In his letter of 12 November 1778 (*Briefe*, ii.506) Mozart expresses his indignation at the fact that Count Seeau was claiming that his *opera buffa* had been hissed off the boards in Munich: if people actually went to Munich, they would discover that the opposite was the case. Given the other reports, Seeau's claim need not detain us here. Even the fact that Mozart received no further *scrittura* from Munich cannot be taken as evidence that *La finta giardiniera* was a failure, whatever Wyzewa and Saint-Foix, *Wolfgang Amédée Mozart*, ii.178, may claim to the contrary.
44. ◆ *Briefe*, i.506 (letter of 16 December 1774).
45. ◆ *Briefe*, i.515 (letter of 11 January 1775).
46. Koch-Sternfeld, *Die letzten dreißig Jahre*, 348. Unger reports that the authorities in Munich organized a concert for him on 22 January 1775. The only operas he heard were *La pupilla ed il ciarlone* and *Il barone di Torreforte*. Unger reports that he left on 26 January.

his time in the city, even though Leopold's account of the congratulations showered upon them by the whole court, to which the archbishop is said to have responded only by nodding his head and shrugging his shoulders, seems an exaggeration on the part of a proud father.[47] None the less, it is unlikely that Colloredo was pleased to see Mozart appearing at a foreign court.

The second performance could be given only on the Friday, but it proved problematical as the *seconda donna*, whom Leopold in any case found wretched, was ill. As a result the opera was savagely cut in order for the performance to be able to go ahead at all. This second performance was scheduled to take place on Mozart's birthday, and he himself was determined to attend: 'Otherwise my work will be quite unrecognizable, for very strange things happen here.'[48] His remarks refer to the sordid affair between the [music] director Antonio Tozzi and Countess Törring-Seefeld, an affair that ended with Tozzi fleeing to Italy and the countess decamping 'with a great deal of money and jewellery'.[49] This untoward turn of events threw the company into disarray and meant that Mozart's presence was urgently required. In the event, *La finta giardiniera* was not given on 27 January but was replaced by *Il cavaliere per amore*.[50] A second performance took place on 3 February, the third and final one on 3 March, when the concluding ballet was *Le braconnier*.[51]

Mozart also had to perform some of his sacred music in addition to his opera: his B flat major litany (K125) was performed at the canonical hours on New Year's Day, together with Leopold's setting of the same text; and on two subsequent Sundays two short masses – evidently those in F and D major K192 and 194 – were performed at the Hofkapelle.[52] A few days before his departure, the elector invited him to write a contrapuntal motet for the Offertory at Mass the following Sunday. The result was the *Misericordias Domini* K222.[53] Mozart thought very highly of this piece and sent a copy of it to Martini the following year as a sample of his abilities. Martini, too, liked it.[54] Mozart also performed on the harpsichord during his time in Munich and to this end had brought with him his D major concerto K175. His sister had to bring not only some variations by Eckard, but also his own Fischer variations K179 and a number of sonatas.[55] Schubart writes in his *Deutsche Chronik*:

> Just imagine, brother, how enjoyable it was! Last winter in Munich I heard two of the greatest keyboard players, Herr Mozart and Herr Captain Beecke.[56] My landlord, Herr Albert, is much

47. *Briefe*, i.517 (letter of 18 January 1775).

48. ◆ *Briefe*, i.516–17 (letter of 14 January 1775).

49. Leopold reports on the incident in detail in *Briefe*, i.523 (letter of 21 February 1775); Schubart, *Deutsche Chronik*, 324, mentions it without naming names; see also Rudhart, *Geschichte der Oper am Hofe zu München*, i.162.

50. Unger, journal entry of 29 January 1775.

51. Unger, journal entry of 5 March 1775. Present at the second performance was the elector of the Palatinate, who returned to Mannheim that same evening. ◆ Abert's dates are off by one: the second and third performances of *La finta giardiniera* took place on 2 February and 2 March, respectively.

52. *Briefe*, i.522 (letter of 15 February 1775). There is nothing in Leopold's letter to indicate that these were new works. ◆ In fact, this letter makes no mention of a litany performance. According to *Briefe*, v.355, the mass K192 may have been performed on 12 February and the mass K194 on 19 February.

53. Nissen, *Biographie W. A. Mozarts*, mistakenly dates it 1781; see Leopold's letter of 11 December 1777 (*Briefe*, ii.183). ◆ See also Münster, 'Mozarts Kirchenmusik in München im 18. und beginnenden 19. Jahrhundert'.

54. *Briefe*, i.532–3 (letter of 4 September 1776).

55. *Briefe*, i.513 (letter of 30 December 1774) and *Briefe*, i.509 (letter of 21 December 1774). The sonatas by Wolfgang may be the three lost sonatas KAnh. 199–201. ◆ Knowledge of these three sonatas, listed in current editions of Köchel as 33d, 33e and 33f, derives from a letter of Nannerl Mozart to the Leipzig publisher Breitkopf, of 8 February 1800; see *Briefe*, iv.312–3. A fourth lost, early sonata, K33g, has no demonstrable connection to Mozart; it is known only from an incipit in Breitkopf & Härtel's in-house catalogue of Mozart's works.

56. On Ignaz von Beecke (1733–1803), see Schiedermair, 'Die Blütezeit der Öttingen-Wallerstein'schen Hofkapelle', 107ff. ◆ More recently, see Munter, 'Ignaz von Beecke (1733–1803) und seine Instrumentalkompositionen', and Ernst Fritz Schmid, 'Ignaz von Beecke'.

taken with the great and the beautiful and has an excellent fortepiano in his house. There I heard these two titans vying with each other at the keyboard. Mozart sight-read everything that was put before him, however difficult. But it was no good: Beecke far surpassed him. Winged speed, charm, melting sweetness and a thoroughly individual, self-cultivated taste are the cudgels that will almost certainly never be wrested from this Hercules's hands.[57]

This persuaded the amateur musician Baron Thaddäus von Dürnitz, whose principal instrument, apart from the keyboard, was the bassoon, to invite Mozart to write a set of six keyboard sonatas K279–284, the fee for which was never, in fact, paid. Stylistically, these six works were almost certainly completed during the Munich period,[58] rather than shortly before his visit to Paris, even though he often played them in the French capital.

In the light of all these successes, Leopold hoped that Mozart would be invited to write the *opera seria* for the 1776 carnival. We do not know why his hopes came to nothing. Even in Salzburg there were rumours that Mozart would enter the elector's service. That such rumours were profoundly unwelcome to Leopold is clear from the affected indifference with which he greeted what he called this 'gossip': there is no doubt that nothing would have suited him better, but he had no wish to be reproached in Salzburg for entering into secret negotiations with Munich. They returned to Salzburg on 7 March 1775, having enjoyed to the full the delights of the Munich carnival. Indeed, Leopold even thought that the celebrations had gone on a little too long.

Mozart's *Missa in honorem Sanctissimae Trinitatis* in C major K 167 dates from June 1773[59] and is the first of his masses to exclude the chorus. Like the D minor mass (K65), it also dispenses with violas, but makes up for this by including in most of its movements four trumpets and timpani, in addition to two oboes. In terms of its general style, it picks up where its predecessor, K139, had left off, albeit not without a number of often far-reaching differences. Above all, it eschews its forerunner's pronounced sense of drama, its tendency to revel in stark contrasts and its whole *Sturm und Drang* ethos. By contrast, there is now a far greater attempt to achieve a sense of formal and motivic unity between the individual movements, and the earlier development in the direction of first-movement sonata form, with its thematic and modulatory procedures, is now complete in both the Kyrie[60] and Gloria. The Credo, conversely, is cast in a form – a kind of free rondo – that Mozart was to use from now on with great frequency, developing it and making it his own. Initially, two sections – the 'Et incarnatus est' (including the 'Crucifixus') and the 'Et in Spiritum Sanctum' – stand out as independent episodes, while the remainder form a separate entity with a main theme and two second subjects that return after each of these episodes, generally in varied form and in a different order. The fugue on the words 'Et vitam venturi' follows as a large-scale coda, which also includes a return of the basic orchestral motif of the entire allegro:

---

57. ◆ *Dokumente*, 138, *Documentary Biography*, 153.
58. Wyzewa and Saint-Foix (*Wolfgang Amédée Mozart*, ii.166) date K279 to the Salzburg period, K280, 281 and 283 to the autumn of 1774, and K284 to February/March 1774. They consider K282 to be a reworking of an older piece. ◆ For a different view of the chronology of the sonatas, see Plath, 'Zur Datierung der Klaviersonaten KV279–284'.
59. See Waldersee, 'Neue Publikationen der Mozart-Ausgabe', 737.
60. The 'Christe' is again inserted in a most curious place, namely, towards the end of the middle section, with sharp dynamic accents and dark-toned harmonies, ending with a gentle half-cadence.

This is a structure that affords excellent evidence of Mozart's sense of form. With it, he created a musical form that not only was effective in itself but had the additional advantage of being easy to grasp and of making it significantly simpler for him to explore the individual ideas in the text. The principle of recurrent orchestral motifs is also more strictly carried through on this occasion, and the Kyrie motif

even recurs in the second part of the 'Dona nobis pacem' – Mozart's first attempt to provide a motivic link between the opening and closing movements of the mass. It has to be said, however, that all these motifs are of a positively secular tone and would be more at home in an *opera buffa* than in church, but this is a characteristic that they share, of course, with every Neapolitan mass of the period. The balance between voices and orchestra, especially in the homophonic sections, has shifted considerably towards the orchestra when compared with the earlier mass, with the result that the voices sometimes sound as though they are merely filling in the harmonies, notably at the beginning of the Gloria. In other sections such as the 'Et in Spiritum Sanctum' and 'Benedictus', there is virtually no difference between them in terms of their treatment of the motivic material. The only exception is the Agnus Dei, but its whole conception sets it apart from earlier settings of this section of the text, even though it retains the traditional two-part structure with contrasting tempos, with the heavy emotional pressure of the first section giving way to an inward, childlike plea. But the 'Dona nobis pacem' is a strictly contrapuntal setting for all four voices accompanied by a brief counter-motif in imitation and ending in an effusive homophonic coda, with the return of the contrapuntal subject bringing the work full circle.

This brings us to the final feature that distinguishes this Mass from earlier ones and at the same time looks forward to the following mass in F major (K192): the far greater role played by contrapuntal procedures. Of course, we are not dealing here with a return to much earlier practices, when counterpoint permeated the entire piece. Even now, it remains confined to traditional sections within an essentially homophonic work and is merely episodic in character. But where it does appear, we are not dealing merely with timid attempts at imitative writing but with broadly developed structures such as the whole of the middle section of the Kyrie.[61] Here we shall not go far wrong in suspecting Michael Haydn's influence. In terms of their range of expression, too, these sections mark a considerable advance on their predecessors, with the old dry scholasticism in particular replaced by a freer and, above all, a more cantabile spirit that points unmistakably in the direction of Padre Martini and of Mozart's lessons with him.

Little has changed in terms of Mozart's approach to textual detail, except that – as we have already observed – the contrasts are now less stark. The mystical strains of the 'Et incarnatus' raise this section far above the scene in the manger found in the previous mass, yet here, too, the 'Et in Spiritum Sanctum' is the most lightweight and operatic part of the whole work, even though it is sung by the entire ensemble. Conversely, the Benedictus – again in three sections – has turned out to be more anguished in tone than its predecessor, a tone that it owes above all to the imitative writing in the violins and the suspensions in the oboes. As in the majority of these early masses, the least individual sections are the Sanctus and the 'Hosanna'.

---

61. Fugato themes rising stepwise to the fifth are a particular feature of this mass: see the middle section of the Kyrie, the third theme of the Credo and, as a chromatic version, the 'Crucifixus'.

The F major mass K192 was completed on 24 June 1774 and is regarded by many as the finest of Mozart's early masses.[62] Certainly, it far transcends all its predecessors in terms of the motivic unity of its individual sections and the increased contribution of contrapuntal techniques, while at the same time striking out in directions that listeners familiar with Mozart's earlier works could hardly have foreseen. On a purely superficial level, one is inevitably struck by Mozart's recourse to the old orchestral forces of the D minor Mass: two violins, bass and organ. Not only does this signify a conscious decision to forgo the brilliant effects associated with the use of woodwinds and brass, it also suggests a reversal of the policy adopted in the previous Masses, although this does not, of course, mean that the orchestra is again reduced to the simple task of doubling the voices and filling out the harmonies.

The Kyrie is again a sonata movement with two subjects, development section (the 'Christe') and recapitulation. Even here, however, there is already a noticeable attempt at motivic unity: the second subject, which is introduced by the soprano soloist, is accompanied in the orchestra by the first subject that was originally heard in the chorus, while in the 'Christe' both chorus and orchestra derive their thematic material from the orchestral prelude to the whole movement – further proof that Mozart draws no distinction between vocal and instrumental themes or, rather, that he simply adapts the vocal line to suit the two instrumentally conceived themes, neither of which, it must be added, is particularly religious in tone:

The Gloria, by contrast, strikes a completely different note from the outset, with the choral sopranos entering like heavenly heralds to announce a theme of transfigured exuberance:

Here is a theme that is no less important on account of its expressive yet restrained accompaniment. And it is shortly answered by canonic entries for the soloists introducing a motif of genuinely Mozartian suavity – the first time in Mozart's works that such a contrast has been found:[63]

These are the two main ideas (*a* and *b*) which, alternating with various episodes, dominate the entire movement, recurring in varied guise and migrating through all four voices. As a result, the movement assumes the following form: A–B–C (the episode from the 'Laudamus te' to 'gratias', with an orchestral motif based on *a*)–A–B–D (the 'Domine fili' episode, with the same orchestral motif)–A–B–E (the 'Qui tollis' episode, as before)–F (the 'Quoniam' episode, with individual reminiscences of earlier orchestral motifs)–G (the independent[64] fugato on 'Cum Sancto Spiritu')–B–A. Here, too, then, we find the same free rondo form that allowed Mozart to maintain the basic mood of blissful rêverie, while allowing emotions such as wistfulness ('qui tollis') and strength to have their say. This all springs from the composer's imagination with astonishing ease and bears the unmistakable imprint of his genius.

The Credo is even more unified and, from a formal point of view, is unique among Mozart's masses. Its main motif is repeated twelve times, dominating not only the musical but also the poetical structure to the extent that it repeatedly interrupts the text in the manner of a parenthesis with its single or repeated cries of 'Credo'. It is also found in sections such as the 'Crucifixus', 'Confiteor' and 'Et vitam venturi' that had formerly been motivically independent. It is derived from the liturgy – specifically from the beginning of the intonation of the *Magnificat* in the third tone or of the Gloria:

This had been a familiar feature of sacred music since the time of the Dutch composers,[65] and in Mozart's day it found its way into secular music, too,[66] recurring throughout his entire corpus of works, including the great C major symphony.[67] It dominates the present movement so comprehensively that all other passages that had earlier generated independent images – the 'Et incarnatus est', the 'Et resurrexit' and the 'Et in Spiritum Sanctum' – are now cursorily episodic in character. At the end it once more places its seal on the movement as a whole. In general, the words are repeated less frequently in this movement than in the Gloria, which had always been more frugal

63. This motif is clearly the germ-cell of the famous melody of Schubert's *An den Mond* (1815) [Deutsch 311].

64. The rhythm of the final phrase ♪♪ ♩ ♩ | ♩ looks back to the 'Quoniam'.

65. It occurs in one of Alessandro Scarlatti's masses: see Reißmann, *Allgemeine Geschichte der Musik*, iii.39ff. It is also found in Michael Haydn's gradual *Qui sedes*. ◆ Haydn's gradual, listed as IIa/3 in Klafsky's catalogue and 444 in the catalogue of Sherman and Thomas, dates from 1 September 1787.

66. See, for example, the finale of Joseph Haydn's D major symphony Hob. I:13.

67. See also the Sanctus of the C major mass K257, the B flat major symphony K319, the first movement of the violin sonata in E flat major K481, and the final fugue of the C major symphony K551. It also appears at the words 'Credo in unum Dominum' in Schubert's first mass in F major, a work profoundly influenced by Mozart.

in its verbal repetitions, and in this it stands in stark contrast to its predecessors. Even the two inevitable fugal sections at the end of the Gloria and Credo have been reduced to a single statement of their subjects. Here, too, we find Mozart falling back on the older ideal in which the words were of paramount importance. The older tradition is also recalled by Mozart's almost fastidious avoidance of the modulation to the dominant characteristic of the various aria and symphony forms: the subsections of both the Gloria and the Credo end either on the tonic and its minor or – as in Mozart's earliest masses – in the region of the subdominant. The Credo even has a recurrent and expressive orchestral formula for this:

In addition to the main motif, however, individual subsidiary ideas are also freely repeated – here one thinks of the 'Deum de Deo' in the 'Et iterum venturus est', the 'Per quem omnia facta sunt' in the 'Qui locutus est', and the 'Descendit' in the 'Et unam Sanctam'. Orchestral motifs, too, are repeated in meaningful ways. Also worth noting, finally, is the almost regular alternation of homophonic and contrapuntal sections, with the main motif generally, but not always, containing within it the potential for contrapuntal exploitation. In short, this Credo is the most unified mass movement of Mozart's youth. The Sanctus, too, rises to significant heights in its freely polyphonic opening section, with the heavenly host hurrying in from every side to sing God's praises to the strains of a curiously agitated, genuinely Mozartian syncopated accompaniment. Unfortunately, the 'Hosanna' again relapses into convention. The succinctly ternary Benedictus, by contrast, maintains a note of dreamy charm without descending into the operatically saccharine. And the Agnus Dei, finally, introduces a note of drama that Mozart otherwise goes out of his way to avoid in this mass. The soloists alternate with the chorus, the latter uttering their cries of 'Miserere' in an enharmonic style that sometimes looks forward to the very end of Mozart's life:

A violin figure accompanied by bitter-sounding syncopations and positively revelling in its sense of anguish completes this picture of suffering, and only the final recidivist 'Dona nobis pacem' brings with it a surprising return to unadulterated Neapolitanisms.

It will be seen, therefore, that the most disparate aspirations cross-fertilize here. On the one hand, Mozart falls back on the older and more distinctive tradition of sacred music, seeking to curtail the purely musical excesses and restore the words to their rightful importance. (The far greater role of counterpoint falls under this heading too.) At the same time, however, he is keen to take advantage of the formal advances found in his previous mass and to merge them with these older features. There is no doubt that in producing these large-scale, unified atmospheric portraits in free rondo form Mozart made a significant contribution to the Mass, influencing other composers such as Michael Haydn[68] in the process. Alongside these movements, however,

68. See Klafsky, 'Michael Haydn als Kirchenkomponist', 22.

we also find a whole series of others, including the Kyrie, 'Hosanna' and 'Dona nobis pacem', that reveal recidivist leanings and fail to break free from their old dependency on opera and instrumental music. As a whole, the work is a fine example of Mozart's art, but a comparison with the *Requiem* is out of place here not only because of the greater mastery but also because of the greater experience of life that Mozart had acquired between 1774 and 1791.

Mozart made no further attempts to explore the territory mapped out in his F major mass, and by the date of its successor, the D major mass K194 of 8 August 1774, we already find the earlier principles much diluted.[69] It resembles its predecessor in its instrumentation and in its avoidance of textual repetitions, but while there is also an attempt at motivic unity, it finds expression in different ways. The Kyrie is again in three sections and is as unecclesiastical in tone as its predecessor, albeit far more unified thematically. Conversely, the Gloria and Credo are again far more loosely structured, with the familiar episodes now reclaiming their ancient right and with the Credo even revealing the old change of tempo. In the Gloria, the main idea returns only once, at the words 'Cum Sancto Spiritu', and although it recurs more frequently in the Credo, the manner of its return is idiosyncratic in the extreme, either slipping in suddenly, as though through the back door (as in the 'Et resurrexit'), or with its subdivisions rearranged ('Et exspecto resurrectionem' and its continuation). This second alternative is a new and intelligent way of forging internal links and was to prove fruitful in the longer term, too. Equally striking is the absence of the two final fugues, but, by way of compensation, the 'Et resurrexit' begins with a fugato that returns in the final 'Amen' in the Credo. Harmonically, too, this mass has its own distinctive personality, favouring minor tonalities even in sections such as the 'Quoniam' and 'Et in Spiritum Sanctum' that are normally in a bright major key. This tendency to prefer minor keys even affects the Agnus Dei, which is again divided between soloists and chorus: the soloists begin in the minor, while the chorus replies in the major before succumbing, too, to the minor-key mood. Apart from a handful of episodes such as the expressive and well-structured 'Qui tollis' and the 'Et incarnatus',[70] the importance of this Mass rests rather on its later movements, especially its Sanctus, in which Mozart – evidently following Joseph Haydn's example – links together the 'Pleni sunt coeli' and the 'Hosanna'. Like most of Mozart's settings of this section, the Benedictus is in the subdominant and, in spite of its basically Italian tone, reveals specifically Mozartian features in terms of its melodic writing and the rhythmic structuring of the text.[71] The interplay between soloists and chorus in the Agnus Dei continues into the 'Dona nobis pacem'. Cast in sonata form, this movement recalls nothing so much as a secular dance, for all its cantabile charm.

Important though the role of counterpoint undoubtedly is in this mass, it is appreciably less pronounced than it had been in the F major mass, a development clear, not least, from the suppression of the two final fugues. As if by way of compensation, the instruments acquire far greater prominence than before. The overall character is pleasing rather than profound, and the archbishop will certainly have preferred this piece to its predecessor.

Similar stylistic developments may be seen in Mozart's other sacred works from this period. The Marian litany in D major K195 dates from 1774 and, compared with K125, is thoroughly modern in character. In other words, it exudes a positive joy in life that has little to do with religion. And, like the C major mass, it is heavily influenced by the instrumental style of the time. The Kyrie, for

---

69. Wyzewa and Saint-Foix (*Wolfgang Amédée Mozart*, ii.157–9) draw attention to the affinities with Joseph Haydn's G major mass of 1772. ◆ Hob. XXII:6, the so-called 'Nicolaimesse'.

70. It is curious that Mozart gives the words 'et homo factus est' to a different soloist. We have already seen that he is particularly fond of emphasizing these words.

71. See Handke, 'Zur Lösung der Benedictus-Frage in Mozarts Requiem', 110–11.

example, is a fully worked-out sonata movement with a slow introduction which, its brevity notwithstanding, is expressive in the extreme. The instrumental floodtide rolls along with so broad a sweep that it often takes no account whatsoever of the words. At the same time, however, the contrapuntal writing is extremely skilful and effective – the piece as a whole is entirely in the spirit of the religious Enlightenment, intelligent and brilliant, but without placing excessive demands on the listener's mind and imagination. The 'Sancta Maria' is likewise cast in sonata form. It, too, fails to strike a deeper note but comes close to the world of opera in its solo sections, to which the chorus generally replies only with its 'Ora pro nobis'. As such, it could hardly be more different from the 'Salus infirmorum', an extremely important number built entirely around the contrast between the chorus's impassioned emotionalism and the gentler entreaties of the solo voices. Both groups, moreover, have their own distinctive accompanying motifs in the orchestra, with the dotted rhythm of the choral accompaniment recalling later movements written under the influence of Bach and Handel. A curiously questioning transition leads into the 'Regina angelorum', a further example of sonata form, on this occasion a highly operatic tenor solo with choral responses and elaborate coloratura that runs along traditional lines. No less virtuosic, albeit far more expressive, is the soprano solo with which the chorus alternates in the Agnus Dei, a movement that acquires its distinctive character through a series of chromatic features in the melodic line and surprising harmonic shifts, notably at the beautiful 'parce nobis'. Similarly remarkable are the dynamic contrasts towards the end.

A *Dixit Dominus* and *Magnificat* in C major both date from July 1774 and form the beginning and end of a vespers setting K193. The remaining psalms were presumably set by another of Salzburg's composers. Characteristic of both these movements is Mozart's careful exploration of the words, making these the best examples of his declamatory word-setting from this period. Equally impressive is the cantabile style of the two final fugues. The other sections reveal only a modest, but none the less impressive, use of counterpoint. That Mozart was keen to set the words as accurately as possible is clear from the very beginning, with its emphatic entry in all four voices peremptorily interrupted before trumpets and timpani introduce the word of the Lord. The trumpets are also prominent – significantly – at the words 'Iuravit Dominus'. Within this movement, Mozart's imagination was particularly fired by the idea of the word 'confregit'. Even more significant as an achievement is the *Magnificat*, the theme of which, introduced by the tenor soloist, belongs to the third canticle tone of the *Magnificat*. The bass immediately launches into a counter-subject:

Together, they provide the basic material for the movement as a whole, in the course of which individual ideas such as 'timentibus', 'fecit potentiam', 'dispersit' and 'humiles' are singled out in keeping with ancient custom. The desire for a unified structure is no less evident than in the Masses. Only the doxology is independently treated in both movements, being divided into two sections in each case: the Gloria is freely contrapuntal, while the 'Et in saecula' is treated as a strict fugato. On both occasions the main theme is rigidly preserved, constantly recurring with no intermediary ideas. On the second occasion it is followed by a magnificent plagal coda. Also worth mentioning, finally, is the remarkably veiled tone of the two Glorias.

With the exception of a handful of passages in the F major mass, all the sacred works of this period are overshadowed by the motet *Misericordias Domini* K222. The piece has, in fact, been variously assessed. When Mozart sent it to Padre Martini in September 1776, he was assured that it had 'all the qualities which modern music demands, good harmony, mature modulation, a moderate pace in the violins, a natural connection of the parts and good taste'.[72] Martini hoped that Mozart would continue to make such good progress. Of course, his reference to 'modern music' implies marked reservations, as he was a well-known champion of the older ideal and a critic of modern music. Later the work was as one-sidedly praised by Ulïbïshev as it was criticized by Thibaut for its unsatisfactorily contrasting moods, before Jahn again leapt to its defence.[73] Thibaut's crassly schoolmasterly view that Mozart should have made either the 'Misericordias Domini' or the 'Cantabo in aeternum' – but not both – the basic idea of the work fails to acknowledge the composer's right to use his art to forge a psychological link between separate ideas. The present piece is an inspired example of this right. The tersely homophonic setting of the words 'Misericordias Domini' to a constantly shifting accompaniment of dark and sombre harmonies suggests a composer held spellbound by the figure of the crucified Christ, while the 'Cantabo in aeternum' inspires him to free counterpoint and elaborate melismas. But however animated the expression of gratitude, Mozart never loses sight of the reasons for that gratitude, and time and again anxious harmonies, sharp dissonances and chromatic part-writing remind us that man's redemption was bought at the price of Christ's death on the Cross: suffice it to recall the two oppressive pedal points shortly before the end. A composer who had grown up in the Neapolitan tradition would have had at his disposal a quite different means of expressing boundless jubilation. Although this work bears all the hallmarks of a test piece in its conscious, but never insistent use of counterpoint,[74] it remains a characteristic example of Mozart's independent and increasingly profound approach to the text.

Of the symphonies dating from this period, those in C, D, B flat and E flat major K162, 181, 182 and 184 form a separate group on account of their three-movement form.[75] Other features that encourage us to treat them together include their main themes, all of which recall those of an Italian overture, a number of individual melodic similarities and, above all, the idiosyncratic structure of their opening movements. On a purely superficial level, these movements are remarkable for the absence of a repeat sign, while on an internal level, the listener will be struck by the lack of any development in the German sense of the term: instead, the main ideas are simply transposed to related tonalities in keeping with ancient Italian custom. We know that the D major symphony was written in May 1773, and so we shall not go far wrong in dating the others to the same period, namely, the months between the Mozarts' return from Italy and their departure for Vienna.[76]

72. ◆ *Dokumente*, 142, *Documentary Biography*, 158.
73. Oulibicheff, *Nouvelle biographie de Mozart*, ii.333; Thibaut, *Über Reinheit der Tonkunst*, 191–2; Jahn, *W. A. Mozart*, i.320–21. See also Kretzschmar, *Führer durch den Konzertsaal*, i.512–13. Wyzewa and Saint-Foix (*Wolfgang Amédée Mozart*, ii.210–13) see in it no more than an exercise, however inspired. For an analysis, see *AmZ*, x (14 October 1807), 43ff.; see also *AmZ*, xiii (1 May 1811), 315.
74. As Stadler (*Verteidigung der Echtheit des Mozart'schen Requiem*, 10) points out, the first subject of the 'Cantabo' is borrowed from Eberlin's offertory, *Benedixisti Domine*, but reworked by Mozart in a thoroughly idiosyncratic manner.
75. In K181 and 184 the three movements are additionally linked together by transitions in the manner of an Italian overture.
76. Wyzewa and Saint-Foix (*Wolfgang Amédée Mozart*, ii.7) even presuppose the existence of a set of six symphonies that Mozart is said to have written in response to a commission from Milan. ◆ In fact, all four works are dated on Mozart's autographs: K162 on 19 or 29 April 1773, K181 on 19 May 1773, K182 on 3 October 1773, and K184 on 30 March 1773. Accordingly, one work – K182 – dates from *after* Mozart's return to Salzburg from Vienna, where he stayed from 16 July to about 24 September 1773.

In spite of Mozart's renewed contacts with Italy, these works are not lacking in German features, including their more individual treatment of the orchestra (a treatment influenced by the concerto) and the hint of Viennese influence in the middle movements of the symphonies in D and C major. But their most delightful aspect is their personal, impassioned tone, a survival from the violin sonatas that affects the E flat major symphony most of all, the D major symphony somewhat less. The E flat major symphony introduces a more sombre note into its festive overture-like strains, with the E in the strings and bassoons in bar 4. It is a mood that assumes a terrifying aspect in the unison writing that follows, while the restless haste of the second subject fails to bring any respite. But the high point of the symphony is the C minor Andante, which is introduced by a transitional passage full of tremendous tension and built up, in the Italian manner, on a brief motif that Mozart subjects to imitative procedures. The anguished, even desperate, mood of this movement takes us far beyond the confines of Gesellschaftsmusik. The winds add their voices with heavy, oppressive off-beat chords or intrude independently upon the musical argument. The first violin already includes examples of the eloquent, almost recitative-like brief solo passages typical of the later Mozart. And the finale is introduced by a brusquely unexpected passage on the winds, and although it yields to more cheerful ideas, it fails to silence the fighting spirits. In terms of its mood, therefore, this symphony provides a link between the six violin sonatas and the following G minor symphony K183. This work, too, forms part of a group of which only a single piece – the D major symphony K202 – can be dated with any certainty (5 May 1774), but the other works in the group – the symphonies in G minor and G, C and A major, K183 and 199–201 – reveal so many formal and stylistic similarities with it that we shall not go far wrong in dating them all to the period between Mozart's visits to Vienna and Munich.[77] On a formal level, all these symphonies differ from their predecessors by reintroducing a minuet. Internally, they are notable for their markedly grander, more heroic stamp, a development behind which writers are no doubt correct in seeing the influence of the impressions left by Vienna. They are much more broadly structured than their predecessors, with their development sections no longer purely transitional in character. Although these sections are not yet strictly thematic as they are in the case of Joseph Haydn, still preferring to spin out their main themes by means of sequencing, the Italians' pleasantly conversational tone has now been abandoned, and there is a remarkable, often passionate energy that never loses sight of its goal and that ultimately achieves that goal in genuinely Mozartian ways with all manner of poetic surprises.[78] Moreover, all these movements have relatively lengthy codas inspired by Michael Haydn. Internally, too, we find a greater verve: the themes are more significant and, thanks to the increased role of counterpoint and of the thematically independent winds, they are developed in far deeper ways. The desire to impose a sense of conceptual unity on all four movements is particularly noticeable here, especially in the two most important symphonies in G minor and A major,[79] whereas the D major symphony falls markedly short of this ideal: indeed, this work

77. The subject of the allegro of K 200 is remarkably similar to the corresponding theme of K182. ◆ K199 belongs chronologically with the earlier group of symphonies composed before the journey to Vienna: the autograph of this work is dated ?10 April 1773. K201 is dated 6 April 1774; K200 may be from 12 or 17 November 1773 or, more likely, 1774 (the date on the autograph has been tampered with). Although Abert's dates are sometimes incorrect, this does not necessarily undermine the validity of his stylistic assertions. Rather, it suggests that Mozart's stylistic development and exploitation of a wide range of affective gestures is more multifaceted and non-linear than argued by nineteenth- and early twentieth-century scholars.
78. Generally they begin with a motif derived from the final group, here too anticipating the later Mozart.
79. Wyzewa and Saint-Foix (*Wolfgang Amédée Mozart*, ii.120–31) suggest Joseph Haydn's symphony Hob. I:44 ('Trauersinfonie') of around 1772 and Vanhal's contemporary G minor symphony as the models of K183 and Michael Haydn's A major symphony of 1774 as the model of K201.

generally finds Mozart re-entering the world of ordinary *galant* light music evidently designed to appeal to the archbishop. But the symphonies in G minor and A major afford splendid proof of Mozart's multifaceted imagination. The A major symphony K201 breathes a spirit of vigorous delight in life, with humour in the Andante and impressions of nature in the finale, while the G minor symphony K183 – Mozart's most significant contribution to the medium for some time to come – captures to perfection the mood of impassioned pessimism that has found repeated and forceful expression in Mozart's works from the time of *Lucio Silla*. It is additionally memorable on account of its striking similarities with the great G minor symphony K550 of 1788, similarities that extend not only to individual motifs[80] but to its entire outlook. Even its opening theme, launched by the oboes and accompanied by typically Mozartian rebellious syncopations in the strings

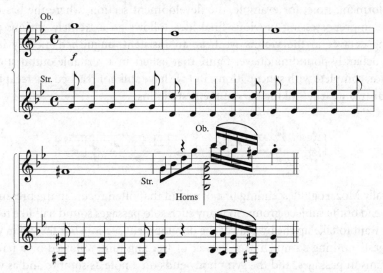

introduces us to a wildly seething state of mind which, with its mixture of defiance and hopelessness, is far from being dispelled by the two second subjects, although these latter are not, of course, on the same high level of musical invention. The first of these second subjects springs to life in B flat major after a helpless imperfect cadence on D, only to break off again with an Italian slide motif.[81] It is important – once again – for its syncopations and for a menacing rhythm in the four horns that recalls Gluck: ♩ ♫ ♩ 𝄾 With the actual second subject, too, the emphasis lies more on the restlessly pounding bass and syncopated accompaniment than on the melody which, in spite of its ornamentation, is not in fact very original. All the intermediary groups, by contrast, are full of the most personal and impassioned expression, in addition to which they are free of all routine. The development section begins by attempting to master the sense of emotional pressure in a thematically new passage[82] notable for its canonic writing, but here, too, the result is helpless abdication. And the movement's brief coda ends with a final outburst of anguish to the accompaniment of a new rhythm reminiscent of a funeral march. The andante is filled with the same sense of inner unrest, and although the manner in which that unrest finds expression is more subdued

80. Note the subdued return to the recapitulation in the opening movements of both works. Only in the earlier work do the strings finally abandon their hopeless enterprise, leaving the winds to force the return of the recapitulation through two crescendo chords of almost literally explosive power.

81. It is strikingly reminiscent of the opening movement of Johann Stamitz's orchestral trio in E major.

82. The new theme returns in the first subject of the finale, but continues along different lines.

and less defiant, the result is a greater sense of brooding, with more confident thoughts rarely in evidence.[83] As in the 1788 symphony, the menuetto openly takes up the struggle again. Characteristic of this movement, too, is the constant interplay between defiant attack and timid withdrawal. Entrusted to the winds alone in the manner of a serenade, the trio is the only section of the symphony to conjure up an affecting picture of happiness and peace, only to fade away again like a brief but beautiful dream. The old and grimly determined ill humour then asserts itself, tiger-like, in the final movement's first subject, only now it seems even more unsettling than it had been in the opening movement, with which this section shares both its massive unison passages and wild syncopations. Lacking the grim joviality of the 1788 finale, it presents a picture of passion constantly seething, finding expression now in a desperate indictment of fate, now in plaintive self-torment: note, for example, the development section, where the basses' cyclopean sport with the unprepossessing previous final idea follows an extremely curious passage: over shrill flickering octaves in the violins we hear an insistent, anguished melody in the basses, followed by a defiantly pounding quaver figure that ushers in a veritable outburst on the dominant of G minor, complete with syncopations. But we have still not reached the recapitulation, and instead we hear two wearily sinking bars in the first violins:

This is a typically Mozartian descending line of a kind that often recurs in the present movement, notably at the end of the subject-group. So many such solo passages sound half like recitatives. The coda seems to want to take up the by-play of the development section, but the violin writing in the third bar suggests nothing so much as a shower of freezing rain, followed by a few defiant and unrestrained unison passages, and the symphony ends on a note as sombre and as wildly impassioned as it began. As a whole, the work has as little in common with the Gesellschaftsmusik of the period as with the liberating atmosphere of a Haydn finale, still less of its Beethovenian equivalent. It is entirely possible that Mozart wrote this self-confessional piece in a cheerless hour when suddenly overcome by an awareness of his cramping conditions in Salzburg. No less likely is it that the archbishop, whose view of music was such that he would never have sanctioned such an infringement of the rules of decent behaviour, will have reproached the composer for writing it. Be that as it may, Mozart initially refrained from all further such outbursts and returned to more conventional channels. The conflict was temporarily resolved.

Of the divertimentos from this period, pride of place goes to the D major serenade K185 that was written for the wedding celebrations of the young Judas Thaddäus von Antretter, the son of one of the councillors in the War Department at the Salzburg court. It received its first performance in Salzburg in early August 1773.[84] In all likelihood it was performed with the march in D major K189, a dignified andante in sonata form entirely suited to the high social standing of the dignitary in question. If so, it will have been played, in keeping with ancient custom,[85] while the

83. Here, too, the tension-filled introduction of the recapitulation, with the expressive cadenza in the violins, is remarkable.
84. See *Briefe*, i.485 and 486 (letters of 21 July and 12 August 1773). ◆ Concerning the Antretter family, and music written for them by Mozart, see Heinz Schuler, *Mozarts Salzburger Freunde und Bekannte*, 202–10.
85. ◆ It is more likely that these two works were composed almost a year apart. While K203 dates from August 1774, recent paper studies and handwriting chronology suggest that the divertimento K205 was composed in 1773.

players took up their positions and again at the end of the serenade. The work is in seven move-ments, the main ones being scored for strings, oboes, horns and festive trumpets, with flutes replacing the oboes in the fourth and fifth movements, and with a concertante solo violin in the second and third. In terms of its structure and thematic material, the work is clearly indebted to Joseph Haydn, an influence evident, not least, from the dominant role of the first subjects in the subject-groups, but also from the extended development sections, most of which are thematic in inspiration. In the fifth and seventh movements, we even find examples of genuinely Haydnesque wit, with the sudden appearance of the first subject in the development sections fooling the listener into thinking that the recapitulation has already begun. Equally Haydnesque are the witty handling of the winds, the taut rhythms of the minuets, and the melodic writing in the second andante and finale. The two movements involving the solo violin bear all the hallmarks of a concerto. The second is a rondo in which the main idea is entrusted to the tutti, the subsidiary ideas to the soloist. As a whole, the work is a genuine serenade of a positively festive and *galant* stamp. A more profound note breaks through only in the slow introduction to the finale,[86] which ends with a powerful crescendo and a series of brilliant fanfares.

The divertimento in D major K205 for violin, viola, bassoon, bass and two horns and the sere-nade in D major K203 for string quartet, two oboes/flutes, bassoon, two horns and two trumpets probably also date from this period.[87] Whereas the former strikes the harmlessly carefree note of Viennese street music, bearing a striking resemblance to works by Joseph Haydn not only in its formal structure but also in certain motifs, the latter aspires to an altogether higher level, more especially in its slow movements. The G major andante is one of the most poetically inspired sere-nade movements ever written by Mozart, with a coda whose entirely new and tender oboe melody descending to the subdominant is in no way inferior to the magical epilogues of the composer's later Andantes.[88] The second, third and fourth movements are like a three-movement violin concerto and, as such, are among the most brilliant and virtuosic sections of the work. Although structurally related to the corresponding movements in the 'Antretter' Serenade, this episode is on an altogether larger scale, recalling the composer's actual concertos, nowhere more so than in the andante, where the solo instrument's broadly flowing melodic line, overflowing with expression, already points clearly ahead to the later violin concertos. The most loosely structured movement is the finale, the main theme and crescendo build-up of which recall a number of final movements by composers of the Mannheim school.

Both these pieces reveal an outstanding appreciation of the qualities of the violin. Mozart had favoured the violin, alongside the keyboard, from his earliest youth, performing on it as a soloist both during his first grand tour and on his first visit to Italy. But in Rome he gave up performing on the instrument in public, even though he still had regular lessons. In Salzburg his official duties required him to play the violin at court concerts; in 1773 his father thought it cheeky of him to borrow a violin and play a concerto on it at the Church of the Theatines.[89] From that date onwards he threw himself increasingly into playing the violin and here, too, developed into a virtuoso, albeit more at his father's instigation than out of any inner inclination of his own. Just as playing the violin

---

86. Its beginning recalls the opening of the C major symphony K338 of 1780.
87. The march K290 is scored for similar forces to K205 and was no doubt intended to be performed with it. In much the same way, the D major march K237 presumably goes with K203.
88. It is also worth noting that this movement is motivically linked to the slow prelude to the whole work.
89. *Briefe*, i.486 (letter of 12 August 1773).

at court was a burden to him, so he seems to have felt little inclination for the instrument and no real confidence in his abilities. 'You yourself do not know how well you play the violin,' Leopold wrote to him on 18 October 1777, 'if you will only do yourself credit and play with energy, with your whole heart and mind, yes, just as if you were the first violinist in Europe.'[90] Even so, Mozart practised regularly and diligently so that on 6 October 1777, following his departure for Munich, we find Leopold writing to him: 'Whenever I return home, I feel a slight sense of melancholy, for whenever I approach the house, I always imagine I can hear you playing the violin.'[91] And from 1773 onwards, Mozart's works for the violin include an increasing element of bravura, indicating the composer's technical progress. His main rival was Brunetti,[92] who was engaged as solo violinist but who was happy to give credit where credit was due. 'Brunetti now praises you to the skies', Leopold informed his son in a letter of 9 October 1777. 'And when I mentioned the other day that you played the violin *passabilmente*, he exclaimed: "Cosa? Caz[z]o! se suonava tutto! questo era del Principe un puntiglio mal inteso, col suo proprio danno"' (What? Shit! Why, he could play anything! That was a mistaken idea the prince persisted in, to his own loss).[93]

Following his departure from Salzburg in September 1777, Mozart performed in public on the violin in Munich and Augsburg, reporting ironically on his successes from Munich on 6 October: 'How they all stared! I played as though I were the greatest fiddler in all Europe!'[94] And from Augsburg, on 24 October: 'I performed a symphony and played Vanhall's B flat concerto on the violin to universal applause. . . . In the evening at supper I played my Strasbourg concerto, which went very smoothly. Everyone praised my beautiful pure tone.'[95] Later these reports cease, and we find Leopold asking, with some concern: 'I suppose you didn't practise the violin while you were in Munich? I'd be very sorry if that were true.'[96] And somewhat later: 'I imagine your violin is hanging up.'[97] No doubt it was. On his return to Salzburg Mozart again had to play the violin,[98] but following his move to Vienna he gave up performing on the instrument and, as we know, he later tended to prefer the viola whenever he played in quartets or was otherwise involved in performances. Not without interest, however, are his comments on other violinists such as the foolish Karl Michael von Esser,[99] whose soulful *adagio* playing Leopold singled out for special mention, while also commenting, of course, on his love of all manner of tricks more suited to a circus showman. It is significant that even as a six-year-old Mozart had little time for such showmanship: coming straight to the point, as usual, he informed him when they met in Mainz that he played well, but added too many notes and should play the music as it was written.[100] Much later, on 22 November 1777, we find Mozart himself writing about Ignaz Fränzl (1736–1811), who was then Konzertmeister in Mannheim:

90. *Briefe*, ii.72 (letter of 18 October 1777).
91. *Briefe*, ii.37 (letter of 6 October 1777).
92. ◆ Antonio Brunetti (*c*1744–1786) was Hofmusikdirektor and Hofkonzertmeister at Salzburg from 1 March 1776.
93. *Briefe*, ii.41–2 (letter of 9 October 1777). ◆ The word 'cazo' is a misspelling of the Italian expletive *cazzo*, which is of doubtful etymology but can loosely have the meaning as translated.
94. *Briefe*, ii.41 (letter of 6 October 1777).
95. *Briefe*, ii.82 (letter of 24 October 1777).
96. *Briefe*, ii.41 (letter of 9 October 1777).
97. *Briefe*, ii.150 (letter of 27 November 1777).
98. ◆ It is not clear that this was the case. Mozart's new appointment was as court and cathedral organist with accompanying duties at the keyboard; probably he did not play the violin at all. See *Dokumente*, 163, *Documentary Biography*, 183–4.
99. ◆ (?Karl) Michael von Esser (1737–*c*1795) was Konzertmeister of the court orchestra at Kassel from 1761, and from 1764 a freelance, travelling virtuoso.
100. Leopold reports this in his letter of 7 December 1780, *Briefe*, iii.50.

I had the pleasure of hearing Herr Fränzl . . . play a concerto on the violin. I like him very much. You know I'm no great lover of difficulties. He plays difficult things, but you're not aware that they're difficult, you think you could play them yourself. That's real playing. He also has a very beautiful, round tone. He never misses a note, you can hear everything; it's all clearly defined. He has a beautiful staccato, played with a single bow-stroke, up or down, and I've never heard anyone play a double trill as he does. In a word: he's no wizard, but a very sound fiddler.[101]

This assessment is important not only on account of its technical understanding and all-pervasive seriousness of artistic approach but also because of the typically Mozartian vividness of the description: we can actually see the man standing there with his violin.

Mozart's first concertante work of any importance for the violin was the concertone K190 for two solo violins and orchestra. Dated 31 May 1774, it is a late example of the old concerto grosso: the concertante instruments are not only the two solo violins but also the oboes and, to a lesser degree, the cello. The concerto form is not yet fully developed,[102] whereas the soli and tutti are already sharply distinguished in the Tartinian manner, except that Mozart, in keeping with the whole thrust of his inclinations following his return from Italy, places far more emphasis on contrapuntal procedures than the Italians. Scarcely an idea is introduced, especially in the first movement, that is not immediately taken up and subjected to imitative procedures. The invention is not particularly original but is profoundly influenced by the Italians, as is the violin technique and the final minuet in the 'long taste' of the Italians. Here the main section is entrusted to the tutti, the trio, by contrast, to the soloists. Clearly the most stimulating aspect of the challenge facing Mozart was the problem of the concertante writing, a problem that he solved with great skill and vitality and with a commendable feeling for sonority. The most successful movement is the andante, which, like individual sections of the menuetto, comes closest to the German style and which brings the concertante groups and their respective themes closer together, thereby producing a delightful, if well-mannered dialogue with no trace of dramatic excitement.

In December 1773 Mozart returned to a field that was to prove particularly attractive to him and wrote his piano concerto in D major K175.[103] He often played the work on his visits to Mannheim and Paris and in 1782 replaced the final allegro with a new rondo K382.[104]

The earliest keyboard concertos were essentially no more than piano reductions of violin concertos intended for use by amateurs. Johann Sebastian Bach, for example, is known to have

---

101. *Briefe*, ii.137–8 (letter of 22 November 1777).

102. ◆ Recent literature suggests that concerto 'form' was not fixed in the late eighteenth century and that the genre included a number of concerto 'styles', the most attractive and successful of which was Mozart's. For a summary, see Eisen, 'Concerto. §3. The Classical Period'.

103. On Mozart's keyboard concertos in general, see Schering, *Geschichte des Instrumentalkonzerts*, 160ff.; Daffner, *Die Entwicklung des Klavierkonzerts bis Mozart*; and Reinecke, *Zur Wiederbelebung der Mozartschen Clavier-Conzerte*. ◆ Further, see Girdlestone, *Mozart et ses concertos pour piano*; Hutchings, *A Companion to Mozart's Piano Concertos*; Landon, 'The Concertos: (2) Their Musical Origin and Development'; Edwin J. Simon, 'The Double Exposition in the Classic Concerto' and 'Sonata into Concerto: A Study of Mozart's First Seven Concertos'; Forman, *Mozart's Concerto Form: The First Movements of the Piano Concertos*; Charles Rosen, *The Classical Style* and *Sonata Forms*; Leeson and Levin, 'On the Authenticity of K.Anh. C 14.01 (297b), a Symphonia Concertante for Four Winds and Orchestra'; Küster, *Formale Aspekte des ersten Allegros in Mozarts Konzerten* and *Das Konzert: Form und Forum der Virtuosität*; Robert Forster, *Die Kopfsätze der Klavierkonzerte Mozarts und Beethovens: Gesamtaufbau, Solokadenz und Schlußbildung*; Roeder, 'Das Klassische Konzert. Kapitel: Wolfgang Amadeus Mozart' and *A History of the Concerto*; and Irving, *Mozart's Piano Concertos*.

104. ◆ In 1777 or 1778, Mozart also revised the oboe and first horn parts; see Hortschansky, 'Autographe Stimmen zu Mozarts Klavierkonzert KV 175'.

produced a whole series of such transcriptions of works by other composers,[105] while also writing the *Italian Concerto* in 1735, a work which, based on the selfsame models, is the first important original keyboard concerto, albeit without orchestra. But Bach also blazed a trail for the keyboard concerto with orchestral accompaniment, and it was this lead in particular that his pupils followed with especial enthusiasm. As with the older violin concerto, three-movement form, derived from the Neapolitan sinfonia, remained the norm, surviving into the modern age with none of the interpolated movements that came to characterize the symphony. In the hands of Viennese composers such as Wagenseil, the final movement acquired the elements of a suite in the form of a minuet, which was later replaced by a rondo – the favourite form of the *galant* age – under the influence of Johann Christian Bach. Thanks to the numerous collegia musica, the keyboard concerto proved a particularly popular form, acquiring the characteristics that were to distinguish it until Mozart's time and beyond. Even at this date, the concerto remained Gesellschaftsmusik, its tone set by amateur musicians, yet thanks to the refinement and wit of eighteenth-century society it maintained a far higher standard than what was later to be described as salon music. Its subsequent development reflects the basic problem of the whole genre, namely, the relationship between solo and tutti, not to mention the growing influence of the new symphonic style and the fundamental changes to keyboard technique and playing brought about when the old harpsichord was replaced by the new fortepiano.[106] The north Germans under Carl Philipp Emanuel Bach remained loyal to the old concept of the concerto, treating the solo and tutti as completely equal partners and concentrating both here and in the sonata on logic and objectivity. For Carl Philipp Emanuel in particular, the concerto remained an affair of the brain rather than of the senses, no matter how great the demands it placed on the performer, and his concertos, like his sonatas, have lost none of their musical value: after all, the trend that he represented was ultimately to culminate in the piano concertos of Beethoven.

In south Germany, matters took a rather different turn. As we noted in the case of the sonata, it was a development that was due in part to Italian influence and in part to local conditions. Of particular significance is the fact that the north Germans clung far more tenaciously to the old harpsichord concerto, whereas the south Germans very soon allowed themselves to be seduced by the novel sounds of the fortepiano. Even with Wagenseil, the keyboard is already the main character in the concerto, and since it speaks in an unadulterated Viennese dialect, his keyboard concertos not infrequently create the impression of divertimentos for keyboard with accompanying orchestra: it is scarcely possible to speak of a genuine dialogue between the two. Similar goals were pursued by Johann Christian Bach, whose keyboard concertos soon proved even more successful than those of his brother and, as such, were of supreme importance not only for Mozart but for other composers, too. He, too, largely obscured the dialogue-like nature of the concerto, transferring the focus of interest to the keyboard and investing it with all the delights not only of the new type of playing, with its figurations and passage-work, but, in particular, of the new

105. See Schering, 'Zur Bachforschung'.

106. It was invented by Bartolomeo Cristofori (1655–1732) in Florence in 1711 and introduced to Germany by Gottfried Silbermann (1683–1753) of Freiberg. Andreas Silbermann's pupil, Johann Andreas Stein (1728–92) of Augsburg, founded the 'German' ('Viennese') hammer action together with his son-in-law Andreas Streicher (1761–1833). Streicher was a childhood friend of Schiller, while Stein is a familiar figure from Mozart's biography. ◆ For more recent literature on the early history of the piano, see Colt and Miall, *The Early Piano*; Badura-Skoda, 'Zur Frühgeschichte des Hammerklaviers'; Komlós, *Fortepianos and their Music: Germany, Austria, and England, 1760–1800*; and Pollens, 'The Pianos of Bartolomeo Cristofori' and *The Early Pianoforte*.

cantabile tone. At the same time, he introduced to his concerto allegros the contrastive second subjects that we have already encountered in his aria ritornellos and sonatas.

This important incursion of sonata form into the field of the concerto radically altered the form of these opening movements,[107] resulting in Bach's case in the following typical form: (i) large-scale orchestral tutti with two independent subjects; (ii) solo based on the first subject with pianistic embellishments and generally also with the addition of brief subsidiary ideas; (iii) relatively brief tutti based on first-subject material and modulating to the dominant; (iv) solo based on the second subject in dominant, also with brief additions; (v) brief tutti based on the end of the second subject; (vi) development section based on existing or new ideas for the soloist with light accompaniment from the orchestra; (vii) recapitulation of the subject-group in the same order by the tutti and solo, but with shortening of individual sections; the second subject is followed by a full-scale cadenza, after which the movement ends with a tutti derived from the second subject.

Based on the principle of first-movement sonata form, this form very quickly conquered the German market with the exception of north Germany, and Mozart, too, took it over largely unchanged. Its character is the same as in all Bach's music: a carefree delight in life, with no awareness of any emotional tensions or crises, ingratiating and elegant part-writing, and a skilful exploitation of sensuous sonorities. In Germany, this basic tone was altered in keeping with local symphonic schools, but here, too, the concerto remained a form of light music designed to entertain amateurs even as late as the years of Mozart's maturity.

In spite of his debt to his famous model, Mozart none the less makes its clear to his audience that he has no intention of treading a well-worn path in his D major concerto. The novel features that he has to offer lie both in its energetic basic tone, which assumes a positively heroic dimension in the final movement, and in the idiosyncratic manner with which he adapts to the existing framework. Now even the soloist's brief link passages, which in Bach's works had largely involved passage-work, become independent, with expressive ideas that lend greater depth to the overall picture, just as the purely virtuosic element is far less self-regarding than in many a later concerto. But the orchestra, too, intervenes in the musical argument in a more significant manner, returning to the first subject in both the development section and the final tutti and thereby striking out in a different direction from the one adopted by Bach. Here the spirit of the Haydnesque symphony lives on, a spirit keen to see Bach's variety subjected to the law of uniformity. The second movement is a particularly poetical Andante. It, too, is cast in first-movement sonata form, albeit on a smaller scale, with the tension-filled dialogue between soloist and orchestra in its central section pointing the way ahead to entirely new expressive possibilities. The witty changes in the recapitulation and the individual nature of the orchestral accompaniment likewise betray a spirit of independence. But the final movement must have caused contemporary audiences to prick up their ears, with the usual carefree rondo replaced by a strict sonata movement, complete with elaborate counterpoint, that functions as the climax of the concerto as a whole. Here, it is not only the free handling of the form that is new but, more especially, the inspired ability to achieve a sense of unity in variety. In spite of the wealth of subsidiary ideas, the self-conscious power expressed by the main idea is never interrupted. Mozart was right to keep performing this concerto: it contains within it the most beautiful dreams of his youth and a boisterous discovery of life mixed with raptness verging on very real melancholy.

---

107. A parallel may be found in the works of Johann Schobert.

The bassoon concerto in B flat major K191 is constructed on similar lines, except that the finale is a rondo of minuet-like character. Characteristic of this movement is the fact that the episodes are no longer all of equal weight, but that the main section and the first subsidiary section return after the great minor-key intermezzo, thereby recalling the rondos of Johann Christian Bach. The virtuosic element emerges more forcefully than in the D major keyboard concerto, and the overall character is lighter and more elegant. In general, the work is clear evidence of the popularity enjoyed by wind concertos at this time, especially in Germany.

Among the chamber works of this period, the first – chronologically speaking – is the string quintet in B flat major K174. Both the trio from the menuetto and the finale survive in alternative versions, suggesting that Mozart revised the work for a later performance. The autograph score is dated December 1773, a date which, it is more than likely, refers to the revised version.[108] If so, the first version must be earlier and was probably written soon after Mozart's return from Italy, where the composer had got to know Sammartini's quintets. In Salzburg he found a model in the form of similar works by Michael Haydn, and it was this that he soon adopted.[109] The present piece bears all the hallmarks of a divertimento,[110] as, indeed, do the related works by Michael Haydn. Other Haydnesque features include the three codas and the frequent questions and answers between first violin and first viola. But the most important aspect of all is the progress apparent between the two versions. Here one thinks not so much of the Trio (although the new version, with its charming echo effects, is far superior to its predecessor) as of the inspired reworking of the finale on the basis of existing material. In its earlier version, the finale had brought the piece as a whole to a carefree end, but now, as in the contemporary symphonies and the keyboard concerto, it becomes the work's actual climax. Previously, it had begun with the semiquaver theme in simple three-part harmonies, but now Mozart prefaces this subject with a new theme of a Viennese stamp, with the result that the existing subject now appears as its very antithesis. No longer, moreover, is it accompanied by three-part harmonies but is contrapuntally intensified: the earlier harmless game now becomes a large-scale complex in which antithetical forces vie with each other with considerable energy. The second subject, too, has acquired additional power, and at the end of the subject-group the basses alone come swaggering along with a Haydnesque variant of the first subject that is answered in canon by the second violins. The development section, too, has been much expanded, turning this into one of the longest movements of its kind in Mozart's whole output. The first half is the same in both versions, but then the new subject suddenly appears – not, as one at first imagines, as the beginning of a Haydnesque recapitulation, but as the vehicle of a new development section, with the recapitulation only gradually being reached after what, in part, are some desperate efforts. Also new is the coda, in which the old first subject, marked *forte*, is contrasted with the new one, marked *piano*, thus producing a dramatic antithesis. Clearly, it was the upswing in Mozart's productivity inspired by his impressions of Vienna that

108. See Wyzewa and Saint-Foix, *Wolfgang Amédée Mozart*, ii.26–30 and 113–15.

109. Wyzewa and Saint-Foix (*Wolfgang Amédée Mozart*, ii.27) suggest Michael Haydn's C major quintet as Mozart's immediate model. That the quintet was far less popular in Germany than the quartet is clear from Joseph Haydn's response to Andreas Romberg to the effect that he had not written any quintets because he had never been invited to write one. ◆ Concerning K174, its revisions and its indebtedness to Michael Haydn, see Wolf-Dieter Seiffert, 'Mozarts "Salzburger" Streichquintett'.

110. ◆ Abert uses the term 'divertimento' in the sense understood by the nineteenth and early twentieth centuries: as light, entertainment music. For a more historically informed account, demonstrating that 'divertimento' was the most common eighteenth-century term for soloistic ensemble music generally, light or serious, see Webster, 'Towards a History of Viennese Chamber Music in the Early Classical Period'.

persuaded him to end this quintet, originally conceived as a divertimento,[111] in the grand symphonic style and to transfer its whole intellectual weight from the first movement to the last.

It was under the immediate impression of Viennese chamber music and, especially, Haydn's two sets of string quartets, the op. 17 set of 1771 and the 'Sun' Quartets op. 20 of 1773,[112] that Mozart wrote his six string quartets K168–173. Dating from August and September 1773, they may have been written to commission and are Mozart's first four-movement quartets (with minuet). A few minor formal variations such as the final fugues in K168 and 173, the set of variations in first position in K170, and the *adagio* introduction to K171[113] may likewise be laid at Haydn's door. The final movements are cast not only in sonata form but also in rondo form. Internally, too, Haydn's influence is unmistakable, notably in the strictly thematic development sections in the opening movements,[114] even though there are still evident traces here of the old sequential procedures, thereby proving that Mozart had not yet fully entered into the spirit of Haydn's art of exegesis. But more than once Mozart comes close to the older composer's conceptual and atmospheric world. Not only the minuets include examples of Haydn's occasionally bizarre sense of humour (a sense of humour essentially foreign to Mozart's nature), the slow movements, too, find him attempting to match the thoughtful seriousness of his Haydnesque models, with the sombre brooding of the F minor andante of K168 containing a direct reminiscence of Haydn's string quartet op. 20 no. 5, also in F minor:[115]

And both the theme and the variations of the opening movement of K170 are a faithful reflection of their Haydnesque model. In general, these works reveal a decisive advance on their predecessors in their handling of the quartet style, an impression due, not least, to their more careful contrapuntal writing and, at least in part, their greater range of expression. On the other hand, they occasionally lag behind their predecessors in terms of their emotional immediacy. One often has the impression that Mozart felt inhibited in the face of his great model and that he was attempting to make up for his lack of assurance by the meticulousness of his writing, an impression already suggested by the formally flawless but somewhat academic final fugue of the first quartet.[116] On the other hand, he is sometimes tongue-tied and taciturn where the substance of his themes might

111. In bars 7–9 of the second movement we also find an idea that was later to play an important role with Beethoven and the Romantics:

112. These quartets were published in 1774 but were written the previous year; see Wyzewa and Saint-Foix, *Wolfgang Amédée Mozart*, ii.57–61. ◆ Haydn's quartets op. 20 were composed in 1772, not 1773; see Webster and Feder, *The New Grove Haydn*, 108.
113. Completely untypical of Haydn, of course, is the repeat of this adagio after the allegro: Mozart's own idea, it follows naturally from the whole character of the movement.
114. With the exception of K172, which in other respects too is the least significant of the set. Here the development section follows the older tradition in introducing a new theme.
115. This theme is also found in Handel's *Messiah* [chorus 'And with his stripes', also in F minor] and in the Kyrie in Mozart's *Requiem*. It belongs to an old family of themes: see Max Seiffert, *Geschichte der Klaviermusik*, 205ff.
116. Only later did Mozart add the final unison passage.

have demanded a broader treatment, as in the middle movements of K171 and 172. At the same time, however, there are also passages where the authentic Mozart stands before us in all his greatness: here one thinks not only of the cantabile first subjects of most of the Allegros but of whole movements such as the opening movement of K171. Entirely worthy of Haydn is the profound introduction with Mozart's favourite phrase at the very beginning:

Note, too, the genuinely Mozartian semiquaver figure in the second violin that accompanies the entreating melody of the first violin:

But the mood of rêverie is not yet over, and the allegro, too, begins on a note of otherworldly wistfulness:

Only then, completely unexpectedly, does the music take wing. Highly poetic, this vision returns in the two lower voices in the brief development section and, again, at the end of the Allegro. Towering above this whole series of works, however, is the final quartet, K173, in which even the minor tonality is significant. Its opening movement has a portentous subject entirely reminiscent of Gluck[117] that is answered by a defiantly pounding motif, so that the whole painfully agitated movement is based on the clash between these two moods, before defiance wins the day in the coda. The andantino, admittedly, strikes far too trifling a note, and it is not until the menuetto that we return to the earlier atmosphere, a curiously fragmented movement in its shifting moods, with only the trio bringing a sense of calm. With its chromatic subject,[118] the final fugue reverts to the earlier tone of aggrievement:

117. In K169, too, the main theme of the andante recalls the famous oboe solo from 'Che puro ciel' in *Orfeo ed Euridice*, while the second subject (in F major) has the breadth and pace of many of the orchestral motifs from the recitatives in *Alceste*. The prominent role of the first violin in this movement recalls older Viennese composers, as well as Joseph Haydn.
118. 'Chromatic' fugues of this kind are also familiar to the earlier period, except that on this occasion the chromatic writing is limited to the framework of a tetrachord. The retrograde form of the theme

plays an important role here and involves a transitional motif familiar to Mozart from many other contexts.

On a purely technical level, it is far from perfect, but on an expressive level it is far more successful than that of the first quartet, with a far greater sense of life, while the calm resignation of the coda is positively moving.[119]

Mozart first entered the field of the keyboard sonata with his six sonatas K279–284.[120] Dedicated to Baron von Dürnitz, they frequently featured on his programmes in Mannheim and Paris. The often substantial differences between the individual pieces in terms of both structure and character suggest that on receipt of the commission Mozart turned to an older portfolio,[121] although it must be noted that at this date the sonata had not yet acquired the same fixed form as the symphony. Alongside the two Haydnesque sonatas K280 and 281, we find one in E flat major K282 that is formally indistinguishable from a Romantic violin sonata, while the D major sonata K284 points to French models with its rondeau en polonaise and final movement in the form of a set of variations. The fashionable, markedly Italianate style of the Viennese composers is followed most faithfully by the whole of the first sonata and by the allegro of the third, with its contentedly loose structure and a playful tone that revels in figurative themes, broken chords and Alberti basses. In the other sonatas, the development sections are now more worthy of the name and, as such, recall Haydn, whose influence may also be detected in a number of the transitional themes and final movements (cf. nos 2, 4 and 5). The rondo of the third sonata is already notable for its vitality and verve. But there is nothing confessional about these sonatas in the way that the quartets were, and only rarely are there fleeting traces of the Romanticism of those works.[122] In this regard, only the sixth sonata goes its own way. This is also the first work fully to exploit the expressive possibilities of the new fortepiano, whereas the others do not really go beyond the old clavichord technique. In the opening movement's development section the clear blue sky suddenly clouds over, and the listener is drawn into a seething maelstrom of passions on the basis of a motif derived from one of the subsidiary ideas.[123] Finally the melodic line disappears completely, and only after Mozart has hurriedly explored a whole circle of minor tonalities does he return to the main theme by way of a brief crescendo. This is the Schobertian side of Mozart's character, an aspect that suddenly breaks out here with elemental force. The final movement is a set of variations inspired by French models, and here, too, Mozart's genius seems to catch fire in the course of his work on the movement. The first few variations explore the theme melodically on the basis of certain playful figures, but from the mournful minor variation onwards the poetic element wins the upper hand, striving to discover new aspects of the theme in the eighth, ninth and tenth variations,[124] with the ninth and tenth in particular already powerfully reminiscent of Beethoven's

119. ◆ Recent scholarship tends to identify in K168–173 the influence of the Viennese milieu generally, rather than Haydn specifically (and exclusively); see A. Peter Brown, 'Haydn and Mozart's 1773 Stay in Vienna: Weeding a Musical Garden'.

120. ◆ Concerning the dates of these sonatas, and the possibility of an earlier set, now lost, see Plath, 'Zur Datierung der Klaviersonaten KV279–284'.

121. Thus Wyzewa and Saint-Foix, *Wolfgang Amédée Mozart*, ii.166–70 and 185–96. Only the last of the set is specifically said by Mozart to have been written for Dürnitz: *Briefe*, iii.319 (letter of 9 June 1784).

122. Only the dynamics reveal an almost bizarrely idiosyncratic approach to the contrast between *piano* and *forte* (cf. the adagio of no. 2), while crescendo effects are still rare; cf. the contrasts between the first and second appearance of the rondo theme in no. 6.

123. The opening motif is also found in Beethoven's 'Kreutzer' sonata [op. 47], also in A minor.

124. Note in particular the way in which the chromatic beginning of the second section of the theme is intensified in expression.

manner. Unfortunately the adagio variation follows fashionable taste and fails to maintain this same high level.

These variations have two precursors in the variations on a minuet theme by Johann Christian Fischer K179 and on 'Mio caro Adone' from Salieri's *La fiera di Venezia* of 1772 K180. Both date from more or less the same period.[125] But whereas the former are in essence purely ornamental in keeping with the custom of the time and never lose sight of the melodic line,[126] the Salieri variations adopt the older German model, a practice still followed by Joseph Haydn in his A major variations and, later and on a far larger scale, by Beethoven: instead of concentrating on the outward, melodic aspect of the theme, he varies its spiritual content and in that way produces entirely new shapes. Fischer's minuet remains permanently recognizable, whereas Salieri's aria has no choice but to be turned into a whole series of brief but independent character pieces, of which the last one abandons its basic rhythm and even resembles a little song from a French musical comedy, with the Italian *Bettelkadenz* that follows striking a half-humorous note. Of course, these pieces are of no great significance, but the underlying principle is remarkable. Only rarely in his later works did Mozart return to it.

This whole series of works culminates in the *opera buffa La finta giardiniera*. The libretto is the work of an unknown poet[127] that was first set by Pasquale Anfossi and staged at Rome's Teatro delle Dame during the 1774 carnival. In order to do it justice we must first take a closer look at the history of the whole genre, which was, of course, to be of such importance for Mozart. This is all the more necessary in that the genre has been shabbily treated by earlier writers. Here, too, lies one of the largest gaps in Mozart scholarship, with the proud structures of *Figaro* and *Don Giovanni* lacking a historical foundation. All the more remarkable, therefore, is the method adopted by men like Jahn, who, with their cursory treatment of a handful of precursors selected at random, simply declare Mozart to be the culmination of the whole genre. Here we need to examine the whole question all over again.

---

125. According to Wyzewa and Saint-Foix (*Wolfgang Amédée Mozart*, ii. 86–9 and 170–3), the Fischer variations are later than the Salieri set. ◆ This hypothesis is borne out by studies of Mozart's paper types and the chronological development of his handwriting: K180 dates from Vienna, 1773; K179 was composed in Salzburg during the summer of 1774.

126. The theme recalls that of Gluck's 'Che farò senz'Euridice'.

127. According to Wiel, *I teatri musicali veneziani nel Settecento*, 361, the text is a translation from the French, but no evidence has been found to support this claim. ◆ Concerning the possibility that the text may be by the papal chamber servant, secretary to Prince Giustiniani, and Arcadian academician Giuseppe Petrosellini (1727–after 1799), see Angermüller, 'Wer war der Librettist von *La finta giardiniera*?' and NMA II/5/8/1, IX.

13

Opera buffa

Opera seria was intended from the outset to educate its audiences, and it never forgot its origins even in the days of its greatest popularity. *Opera buffa*, by contrast,[1] was a child of the people from the very beginning, remaining so in essence in spite of all attempts at greater stylization. In it the spirit of the Italian nation produced one of its most quintessential and delightful expressions, and it owed this in the main to the fact not only that it remained in close contact with the Italian people but that it fell back on ancient material that had belonged to the Italians from time immemorial: characters and jokes that had delighted classical antiquity return in the works of Piccinni and Paisiello.

The old saw that the common people are more inventive in comedy than in tragedy is doubly true of the Italians. Their naïve sense of realism, their keen eye for human weaknesses and for the comedy of everyday life make them natural clowns. To this may be added their pronounced propensity for mimicry that has always encouraged them to triumph over the dreariness of the daily round by treating it as a matter for comedy, and it is significant that, far from remaining content with a faithful reflection of everyday life, they have always preferred to observe it through the concave mirror of caricature. Caricature is thus the principal characteristic of popular Italian comedy from the time of the old Roman Atellan farces to the *opere buffe* of more recent times. This explains their violent, coarsely sensual character and their tendency to single out one particular characteristic at the expense of all the others, treating it as something larger-than-life. In themselves, these characteristics – self-importance, good-naturedness, avarice and so on – do not need to be comical, but they become so through exaggeration. By preference, they are associated with particular social classes, an association felt to be especially amusing: thus we have the braggart soldier, the pedantic scholar, the sophistical lawyer and so on. Subtler features derived either from an ironical insight into the relative limitations of the material world or from a sense of idealism are essentially alien to this earthy, popular farce.

It was entirely natural for *opera buffa* to pick up the tradition of the improvised *commedia dell'arte* that was derived from popular farce and for it simply to take over its characters unchanged: Pantalone, the old Venetian merchant, Dr Graziano, the self-important pedant from Bologna, Captain Spavento from Naples (a throwback to the old *miles gloriosus*), the two wily servants Arlecchino and Brighella from Bergamo, the stuttering Tartaglia and – a particular favourite of the Neapolitans – the crafty Pulcinella. From an early date these characters were joined by others from abroad: the pugnacious German drunkard, the French rake and the excessively formal Spaniard. The plots of *opere buffe* were likewise markedly influenced by those of

---

1. See Scherillo, *L'opera buffa napoletana durante il Settecento: Storia letteraria*; and d'Arienzo, *Die Entstehung der komischen Oper*. ◆ Further, see Della Corte, *L'opera comica italiana nel '700: Studi ed appunti*; Strohm, *Die italienische Oper im 18. Jahrhundert*; Sadie, *History of Opera*; and Herbert Schneider and Wiesend, *Die Oper im 18. Jahrhundert*.

improvised comedy: their intrigues are generally unsubtle and not infrequently abound in conscious implausibilities. The main concern is situation comedy of the most grotesque kind possible that flies in the face of logic and reason. Of course, we also find various attempts in both literary and musical comedy to introduce a note of greater refinement to this unadulterated popular art form and to raise it to a higher level, and in its most important aspects, including the way in which it descended into sentimentality, sung comedy followed the same historical course as spoken comedy, with Goldoni's appearance on the scene representing an important turning point for both. In *opera buffa*, however, the popular spirit had a powerful ally in music which, even at times of supreme artistic ambition, retained a living memory of the origins of the whole form. Often enough we find composers insisting on the right to be popular and natural in the face of opposition on the part of their own librettists, whose attempts at stylization not infrequently lead to artifice and high-flown extravagance.

The element of mimicry played at least as important a part in the external form of *opera buffa* as the dramatic and musical components. Indeed, during the earlier period it was decisive. We all know the Italians' exceptional talent for mimicry and that even today the Italian actor can express at least as much through his acting as through his words. It is no wonder, therefore, that mime also played a leading role in popular musical comedy, even exerting an important influence on the way in which the dramatic and musical aspects developed. In its earliest form it may be found in the Florentine carnival processions, the Neapolitan *farse cavaiole* and the comedies of the *bagattellisti* and similar primitive folk plays that have rightly been seen as the breeding ground for *opera buffa*.[2] Of course, these knockabout mime shows, which often enough recalled the high-wire acts of the old *histriones*, were later refined, but even in its fully developed form, *opera buffa* still contains a goodly drop of the old *jongleur*'s blood. This is clear from the numerous songs that were actually danced and, even more, from the well-known types of scenes involving physical violence such as beatings,[3] as well as from the disguises that have been familiar to the Italians from time out of mind and, most of all, from the obvious pre-eminence enjoyed by the performer over the poet. The worst infringements of logic were forgiven the poet as long as his technical command of the stage was sufficient to allow him to create situations of great tension and roles that were grateful for the actors. *Opera buffa* also took over the old practice of improvised comedy whereby individual actors would step outside the action and dazzle the audience with the clash between illusion and reality. Figaro's 'Aprite un po' quegl'occhi', for example, still recalls the old *buffa* practice of allowing the individual actor suddenly to address the audience.

But it was not only the performer to whom the *buffa* poet had to submit: he also had to yield to the musician. During the early days of the genre it was no doubt the hit song that the librettist often enough had to take into account as best he could. The doctrine of the serious music drama, according to which the composer had to be the poet's faithful and even obsequious servant, never caused the composer of *opere buffe* a moment's concern. Quite the opposite: *buffa* composers demanded only that the poet should abide by musical considerations and give them the opportunity to show off their abilities to their greatest advantage. The poet's subordination to

---

2. See Sandberger, 'Roland Lassus' Beziehung zur italienischen Literatur'. The old southern Italian villanella reckoned not only on music but also on dance and mime: see Chrysander, 'Ludovico Zacconi als Lehrer des Kunstgesangs', 308–10. ◆ Villanella is a generic term describing popular songs originating in Naples during the period 1530–1650; see Cardamone, *The Canzone villanesca alla napolitana and Related Forms, 1537–1570*, and DeFord, 'Musical Relationships between the Italian Madrigal and Light Genres in the Sixteenth Century'.

3. When *opera buffa* became more respectable with the passage of time, the old *bastone da bastonare*, while not disappearing completely, was replaced by mere threats. Osmin's 'Erst geköpft, dann gehangen' from *Die Entführung aus dem Serail* is a survival of this old spirit of knockabout comedy.

the musician affects the work in every way, including even formal details: the numerous repeats of brief phrases in most *buffa* arias, for example, are not just comic exaggerations but instances of the musician's right to dictate the poet's actions. For the same reason, *opera buffa* differs from *opera seria* in originating not in dramatic recitative but in the musical form of the song in all its manifestations. Its close links with Italian folk music are immediately apparent, although no detailed proof has yet been adduced to support this claim, of course. But it is to this that *opera buffa* owes its chief advantage over *opera seria*, namely, its naturalness, a quality that it never lost even in times of degeneration. While the formal repertory of *opera seria* shrank to the point where only the *da capo* aria remained, *opera buffa* never forfeited its right to freer forms, acknowledging not only the simple strophic song but also the two-, three- and four-part aria, as well as longer composite forms, and thanks to the Italian's sophisticated sense of structure, composers were always able to press this wealth of forms into the service of the drama. On an internal level, too, we find the greatest variety and adaptability: although the melodic writing developed its own elaborate *buffa* style over the centuries, it never lost touch with popular music. Coloratura techniques are also found in *opere buffe*, but only to the extent that composers made fun of their unnaturalness and used them as a vehicle for parody. Only during the period of the genre's decline do we find composers introducing coloratura writing for serious effect.

This wealth of forms reflects an outer life that was not only richer but also better suited to the genre's natural disposition. To castratos *opera buffa* remained closed, acknowledging only the two natural male voices and, above all, according the bass voice, which had vanished from *opera seria* since the time of Monteverdi, hitherto unsuspected honours. But ensembles and choruses, too, found a permanent and well-appointed home here, regardless of the rejection from which they suffered at the hands of composers of *opere serie*. The old custom whereby the performers of a folk comedy would present themselves to the audience at the beginning and end of the piece led ultimately to two of the genre's most important forms, the *introduzione*, which was often an independent ensemble before the first act, and the finale. But even in mid-act, ensemble movements were by no means unusual. Recitatives, too, had a different function in *opera buffa* from the one they fulfilled in *opera seria*. Since we are not dealing here with any profound dramatic developments but only with dialogue based on real life, albeit with all manner of accents and highlights, *secco* recitative, with its fluent parlando, was entirely appropriate, capable, as it was, of expressing these lightning-quick battles of words with no sense of ponderousness, reflecting the volatility of the Mediterranean temperament, while at the same time giving the actors every opportunity to display their mimetic skills. It is no wonder, therefore, that *secco* recitative came into its own far sooner in *opera buffa* than it did in *opera seria*. Accompanied recitative, too, found a use here, albeit on a more modest scale, while achieving its greatest effects when parodying *opera seria*.

It might be thought that, such were its advantages, *opera buffa* would soon have challenged the hegemony of *opera seria*. But this did not in fact happen. Rationalism had little time for such earthy popular art, with the result that *opera buffa* long had to make do with second- or third-rate poets, with even Goldoni conceding that his own *buffa* librettos were inferior in quality.[4] Goethe, conversely, championed Italian *buffa* texts, astutely acknowledging that they should be judged not

---

4. Goldoni, *Mémoires*, ii.226–7. ◆ Also see Ortolani, *La riforma del teatro nel Settecento e altri scritti*; Weiss, 'Venetian Commedia dell'Arte "Operas" in the Age of Vivaldi'; Emery, *Goldoni as Librettist: Theatrical Reform and the drammi giocosi per musica*; Messina, *Carlo Goldoni: vita, opere, attualità*; Pieri, *Il teatro di Goldoni*; Pietropaolo, *Goldoni and the Musical Theatre*; and Padoan, *Problemi di critica goldoniana*.

only according to the poet but also according to the 'composer and actor'.[5] Even today, this remains the only legitimate standpoint: we have no right merely to repeat the condemnation of eighteenth-century adherents of *opera seria*[6] and to parrot criticisms based solely on the poetic aspect of *opera buffa*. Nor should we forget that, once it had been fully accepted, *opera buffa*, too, attracted gifted poets of the stature of Giambattista Lorenzi.

Of course, it took a long time for *opera buffa* to gain acceptance in this way. Generally, it was only the smaller theatres that were open to the *buffonisti*, and often enough they had to make do with barns and the like.[7] For a long time they were associated in the popular imagination with the old troupes of travelling actors, hence their carelessness over scores, a carelessness that has meant the loss of many a valuable work.

Two forms of *opera buffa* have come down to us: the intermezzo and the fully-fledged opera. The earlier assumption that the second type developed out of the first can no longer be sustained in the light of the most recent research. Rather, both types more or less coexisted, and not even in the heyday of the fully developed form did the intermezzo disappear altogether. Its earliest traces may be found in Venetian opera, with comic scenes interpolated into a serious plot and with servants as their protagonists. Often these comic scenes involved a parody of the preceding serious scene.[8] Certainly, there is no mistaking the affinities between these 'servi ridicoli' and the masks of the *commedia dell'arte* tradition.[9] About the same time, however, the fully-fledged comic opera was first summoned into life, a form for which the madrigal comedies of Striggio, Croce, Vecchi and Banchieri had already prepared the ground in the sixteenth century.[10] Its home was Rome and its founder – by a strange quirk of fate – was the later Pope Clement IX who, as Cardinal Giulio Rospigliosi, wrote two comic librettos: *Chi soffre speri*, set by Virgilio Mazzocchi and Marco Marazzoli in 1637, and *Dal male il bene*, which was set by Antonio Maria Abbatini and Marazzoli in 1654.[11] Both works are the first attempts to ennoble *opera buffa* by borrowing from literary models, with the former harking back to Tuscan peasant comedy, the latter to Calderón. And these earliest attempts at stylization suffered the same fate as most later attempts, with the comic, popular sections proving far superior, on an artistic level, to the more serious parts and, hence, incapable of merging with them to produce an organic work of art. The music, conversely, already contains within it important elements of the later *buffa* tradition, with *secco* recitative for the dialogue, popular types of dance song for the self-contained numbers, and ensembles – still, of course, purely musical rather than dramatic in character – for the ends of the acts. First heard in Florence in 1657, Jacopo Melani's *La Tancia* already combines Roman and Venetian influences: the grotesque conjuration of the devil in the third act is also the first example of an *opera seria* being parodied within a fully-fledged *opera buffa*,[12] thereby broaching a theme that was to be found

---

5. Goethe, 'Italienische Reise' (*Jubiläums-Ausgabe*), xxvii.157, 186–7 and 233; see also Riemer, *Briefwechsel zwischen Goethe und Zelter*, i.322.
6. Goldoni, *Mémoires*, ii.305; Arteaga, *Le rivoluzioni del teatro musicale italiano dalla sua origine fino al presente*, iii.140ff. Jahn, *W. A. Mozart*, fourth edition, i.235, adopts a similar standpoint.
7. Dittersdorf, *Lebensbeschreibung*, 36–7.
8. Kretzschmar, 'Die venetianische Oper und die Werke Cavallis und Cestis'. ◆ On the development of the intermezzo, see Michael Robinson, *Naples and Neapolitan Opera*; Strohm, *Die italienische Oper im 18. Jahrhundert*; and Troy, *The Comic Intermezzo: A Study in the History of Eighteenth-Century Opera*.
9. The stuttering figure of Tartaglia was extremely popular. ◆ See Pirrotta, 'Commedia dell'arte and Opera', and Pandolfi, *La commedia dell'arte: storia e testo*.
10. ◆ See Detenbeck, 'Dramatized Madrigals'.
11. Goldschmidt, *Studien zur Geschichte der italienischen Oper im 17. Jahrhundert*, i.87ff. and Ambros, *Geschichte der Musik*, third edition, iv.513ff. ◆ Further, see Canevazzi, *Papa Clemente IX poeta*.
12. Specifically a parody of the scene in Cavalli's *Giasone* (1649), in which Medea invokes the spirits of the underworld; see Goldschmidt, *Studien zur Geschichte der italienischen Oper*, 121 and 371ff.

again and again in *opere buffe* even as late as Mozart's time. This was also the first major confrontation between the two genres and, as such, proof of the growing hostility towards *opera buffa* on the part of the old Renaissance work of art even at this time. From now on, *opera seria* was to have no more implacable and, at the same time, no more obdurate critic than *opera buffa*.

In Naples at this time we find in Francesco Cirillo's *Orontea* (1654) an important contribution to *opera buffa*[13] that paved the way for the city's prominent role from the time of Alessandro Scarlatti. Scarlatti[14] began by adopting the Venetian model and larding his serious operas with comic scenes. Gradually, however, they came to occupy a specific place at the ends of the acts, while at the same time we begin to find the practice of transferring them from one opera to another. Shortly afterwards they broke completely free from *opera seria*, acquiring an independent action of their own and finding a new home as intermezzos between the acts of serious operas. It is not clear who first took the decisive step in this direction, although there is no doubt that Hasse, with his intermezzos of 1723–30, played an important role in this development.[15]

Scarlatti's comic scenes generally involve an old woman sung by a tenor and a young servant, and include more or less obvious pointers to all the characteristics that were to constitute the later style, namely, popular sicilianas (with the much-loved Neapolitan sixth) and the seeds of those natural melodies that were later to be developed with such supreme artistry. Here, too, music played its part in the vacillation between illusion and reality that is so typical of this whole kind of comedy. Here the singer steps out of his part, his melodic line suddenly degenerates into primitive scales or even *secco* recitative, or else he prattles on incessantly in brief little motifs that are often more like mere interjections than musical shapes.[16] From now until Mozart's day and beyond, rapid parlando was to be the principal characteristic of the Italian *buffa* style. It was Scarlatti, too, who must take the credit for the greater effectiveness with which instrumentation was now placed in the service of the comedy.[17]

Scarlatti's *Il trionfo dell'onore* of 1718[18] is a fully-fledged *opera buffa* of remarkable freshness, not least of whose progressive features is its eschewal of the Neapolitan dialect that was later to become traditional. In the event, *opera buffa* developed along other lines, taking as its starting point a more primitive type of work represented by Antonio Orefice's *Patrò Calienno de la Costa*, a setting of a libretto by 'Agasippo Mercotellis' first staged in 1709. In the case of both Orefice and his immediate successors, only their librettos, written in Neapolitan dialect, have survived.[19] This *cummedeja in museca* is a faithful reflection of the life of the people in Naples under its viceroys. Alongside local types, we also find Spanish soldiers, Armenian tradesmen and even Turkish arch-enemies rubbing shoulders with the old masks – Pulcinella with his Zeza, Captain Spavento in his guise as the bane of the Moors, Matamoros, and so on. The texts and almost certainly the music, too, were based virtually without exception on folksongs, while improvisation will have continued to play an important role in the acting.

13. D'Arienzo, *Die Entstehung der komischen Oper*, 25ff.
14. Dent, *Alessandro Scarlatti*, 127ff. and 48–9. ✦ Also see Grout, 'Alessandro Scarlatti: An Introduction to his Operas'; Hucke, 'Alessandro Scarlatti und die Musikkomödie'; and Lütolf, *Alessandro Scarlatti und seine Zeit*.
15. The intermezzos from Scarlatti's *Scipione nelle Spagne* of 1714 were performed as an independent piece in Bologna in 1730.
16. For examples, see Dent, *Alessandro Scarlatti*, 52 and 126.
17. Cf. the bassoon in Delbo's aria from act one, scene five of *Il prigioniero fortunato* (1698).
18. Dent, *Alessandro Scarlatti*, 127, draws attention to the similarity of the text with that of Mozart's *Don Giovanni*.
19. See Scherillo, *L'opera buffa napoletana*, 102ff. ✦ Seven arias survive from Orefice's *Le fente zingare* of 1717; see Pastore, 'Le "arielle co'wioline" di Antonicco Arefece'.

The first surviving scores date from the following generation – the generation of Vinci, Leo and Pergolesi.[20] By now the texts have changed, and alongside purely comic and popular scenes we also find more serious scenes of a more sentimental nature, no longer written in dialect and revealing the influence of Metastasio,[21] whose star was currently in the ascendant. Indeed, there is even the suspicion that he, too, tried his hand at writing the words for an *opera buffa* with the intermezzos inserted in *Didone* in 1724, a successful parody of vocal virtuosity. His authorship, however, remains contested.[22]

Meanwhile, Leonardo Vinci had proved himself a born *buffa* composer with *Li zite 'ngalera* of 1722, a model of its kind.[23] He, too, derived his inspiration from Neapolitan folk music, while permanently enriching the repertory with a whole series of melodic types expressive of comedy. He and his age loved brief, skipping motifs, often syncopated or with slides at the end of the phrase, as in the following examples from scenes five and twelve of act one of *Li zite 'ngalera*:

Sicilianas, frequently in minor tonalities and bearing all the hallmarks of southern Italian folk music, are surprisingly well represented here. In much the same way, rapid *presto* passages in triple time and made up of identical notes from now on form one of the principal features of the *buffa* style and are presumably derived from a particular type of folksong. One example among many is Ciccariello's song in act three, scene nine, in which he heaps abuse on a fellow character:

---

20. Somewhat apart stands Francesco Bartolomeo Conti (1681–1732), whose *tragicommedia Don Chisciotte in Sierra Morena* was written for Vienna in 1719; see Mattheson, *Critica musica*, i.98; for a note on Johann Abraham Peter Schulz, see Gerber, *Neues historisch-biographisches Lexikon der Tonkünstler*, i.772. ◆ Further, see Williams, *Francesco Bartolomeo Conti: His Life and Music*.
21. See Scherillo, *L'opera buffa napoletana*, 105ff.
22. It is striking that Metastasio himself never mentions these pieces.
23. For a detailed account, see d'Arienzo, *Die Entstehung der komischen Oper*, 73ff. The only other works by Vinci that can be considered here are the intermezzos from *L'Ernelinda* (1726). Nothing else has survived. ◆ Since Abert's time, sources have been discovered in the Naples Conservatory for Vinci's *Albino e Plautilla* (1723) and an aria from his *Il corteggiano affettato* (1728) and in the Conservatorio 'G. Verdi', Milan, for *Erighetta e Don Chilone* (1728). Further, see Markstrom, 'The operas of Leonardo Vinci'.

Two other survivals of the older tradition are cuckoo calls (act one, scene twelve) and echo effects (act two, scene eleven).

But Vinci also reveals himself from the outset as a master of slapstick comedy. He is additionally fond of interpolating passages of recitative into his arias, so that the lively marchlike duet in act three, scene nine,[24] for example, is suddenly interrupted by the following:

In the Captain's aria in act three, scene six, Vinci uses two trumpets and *fioriture* to paint a picture of a vainglorious braggart, while in the Doctor's aria, 'Questo è il mio recipe', from the second intermezzo in *L'Ernelinda*, the language of chromaticism is parodied:

On a formal level, Vinci's works are especially important for the appearance of arias alongside folksongs – mostly the ternary *da capo* aria, with all its traditional features except for coloratura.[25] Indeed, this may be taken as further proof of *opera buffa*'s increasing attempts to align itself with *opera seria*. As with Scarlatti, the ensemble sections are still purely musical, rather than dramatic: the trio in act two, scene thirteen is even cast in the form of a *da capo* aria. Of the finales, the third is headed 'cantano e suonano' in the manner of the old comedies and, as such, offers the company the opportunity to take its leave of the audience. The second comprises a quarrel and, in spite of Colangelo's repeated 'vecchia mascarone', is likewise purely musical.[26] The orchestral contribution is still very modest, with whole sections of the score performed by the singers alone.

Leonardo Leo's *opere buffe* are written in the same style as Vinci's, except that there is a more pronounced tendency here to include more serious songs. He is also more thorough in his work as a *buffa* composer, and more earthy in his humour, an aspect particularly apparent in his parodies.[27] His finales, too, are more varied and more serious,[28] with the finale of *Lo matrimonio annascuso* already divided into two sections, yet not even here is there any trace of any greater

24. D'Arienzo, *Die Entstehung der komischen Oper*, 87ff.
25. A remarkable hybrid form is Belluccia's aria in act one, scene two, with the dal segno markings in the first section.
26. The first has survived in only incomplete form, but is notable for its recurrent violin figure:

This is the first attempt at the richly developed motivic writing for the orchestra that was to typify later works. On the finales of these composers in general, see Dent, 'Ensembles and Finales in Eighteenth-Century Italian Opera'. ◆ Further, see Heartz, 'The Creation of the Buffo Finale in Italian Opera'.
27. In act one, scene five of *Lo matrimonio annascuso* there is a parody of simile arias about storms at sea, and in act two, scene six of the same work there is a delightful parody of the pastoral obsessions of *opera seria*.
28. The quartet in act one, scene fourteen of *L'Alidoro* (1740), for example, is a canon. ◆ Also see Pastore, *Leonardo Leo*; Hardie, 'Gennaro Antonio Federico's *Amor vuol sofferenza* (1739) and the Neapolitan Comic Opera'; and Degrada, 'L'opera napoletana'.

sense of drama. On the other hand, the orchestra is now conceived in more independent terms, and it comes as no surprise to find that Leo is the author of the first surviving comic opera overtures: like their serious counterparts, they are in three movements, but with a minuet in final position (*La semmeglianza de chi l'ha fatta*, 1726; *Lo matrimonio annascuso* [1727]; and *L'Alidoro* [1740]). The minuet from the sinfonia to *Lo matrimonio annascuso* even includes a balletto with two concertante orchestras.

The art of the Neapolitan *opera buffa* achieved its first high point in Pergolesi's intermezzo *La serva padrona* of 1733.[29] The composer's ambitions are clear from his decision not only to dispense with dialect but also to avoid the siciliana, whose appearances had become excessive. The fresh folk tone has been preserved but with an element of stylization designed to support the characterization. Such stylization is more apparent in the case of the cunning servant Serpina, who is a veritable child of the people, than with the sullen old Pantalone character, Uberto. The work's principal advance on its predecessors lies in its comic characterization and its inspired ability to draw every last drop of humour from the situation. Pergolesi also includes extremely subtle motivic reminiscences of other works. The characters themselves are by no means novel, but the individual freedom with which they are treated has ensured that the piece is a classic of its kind, as effective today as it ever was. Indeed, its influence may be noted in countless later works.[30] By contrast, Pergolesi's actual *opere buffe* follow traditional models with their use of dialect and popular types of movement. In terms of their subject matter, they are remarkable, in part, for their use of parody and, in part, for their sentimental features.[31] Formally, they are notable for their attempt to invest the ensembles, which are cast in aria form, with greater dramatic life.[32]

It was under the next generation of composers – the generation immediately before Mozart – that *opera buffa* witnessed its finest hour. At the same time, however, it assumed a quite different aspect, at least from a purely poetical standpoint. Essentially, it adopted the same course as contemporary spoken comedy, attempting to break free from the spirit of the old improvised farce and work its way towards a more subtle kind of musical comedy. It is no accident that it was Goldoni who played the principal role here. The old masks were now relegated to the subsidiary roles of the servants. These latter were also the only characters who still spoke in dialect. Instead, more serious characters – the *parti serie* – now assumed greater prominence in the form of lovers whose vicissitudinous fates now constitute the main action. The old comic characters did not allow themselves to be completely upstaged, of course, and, indeed, a few new ones were added, especially the character of the notary, who was introduced by Pietro Trinchera.[33] In general, musical comedy was far more resistant to stylization than spoken comedy, and there was never any question of a merger between the two antithetical worlds of tragedy and comedy of the kind found in Shakespeare. The delight in earthy situation comedy generally maintained the upper hand over

29. The Paris performances of 1752 notoriously led to the founding of the French genre of *opéra comique*. From this period date the various French interpolations that later found their way into German vocal scores. Abert, *Die Magd als Herrin*, goes back to the old Italian *buffa* version of the score.

30. The first such traces may be found in act one, scene eight ('Questa cosa') and scene eleven ('Chiano meo') of Leo's *L'Alidoro* (1740), then in Majo's intermezzos of 1752 (now in the Biblioteca Casanatense in Rome), as well as in the *licenza* of Gluck's *Le nozze d'Ercole* and in Mozart's *La finta semplice*.

31. Cf. his *Il maestro di capella*, the main operatic parody since the intermezzos of Metastasio's *Didone*. ◆ Presumably Abert refers here to *Il maestro di musica*, a pastiche performed at the Paris Opéra on 19 September 1752, based largely on Pietro Auletta's *Orazio* but including two arias and a duet by Pergolesi. Further, see Degrada, '"Lo frate 'nnamorato" e l'estetica della commedia musicale napoletana'.

32. Cf. the trio in act two of *Lo frate 'nnamorato* of 1732.

33. ◆ See Martorana, 'Trinchera, Pietro'.

finer emotions, and there remained no shortage of mad disguises, mistaken identities and stupid misunderstandings, to say nothing of scenes involving drunkenness, beatings and duels. Above all, however, librettists and composers poked greater fun than ever at *opera seria*, mocking its outward forms and musical style, including its love scenes, ghosts, simile arias and accompanied recitatives.

With the introduction of a pair of sentimental lovers, the plot or intrigue began to play a more important role in *opera buffa*, too. Generally, these plots involved marriages, with the lovers finally united only after various dangers, among which the motif of abduction played a major role. Another popular figure is the unfaithful lover who, after a series of infidelities in the style of Don Giovanni, finally and remorsefully returns to his patient bride. But with these sentimental characters, *opera seria* finally gained its revenge on its over-boisterous sister. And it is here, above all, that we can see the growing stylistic influence of Zeno and Metastasio. It was now that their *galant* pathos and ornate rhetoric found a home for themselves in *buffa* poetry, on more than one occasion driving composers to introduce coloratura techniques and thereby to come perilously close to the pitfalls of *opera seria*. Even a certain didacticism on the part of these librettists finds expression here either in their insistence on one particular aspect of their characters' lives (an aspect usually indicated by names such as Buonafede and Tagliaferro) or in their choice of a moralizing subtitle such as *Don Giovanni ossia Il dissoluto punito*. In this way, *opera buffa* drifted inexorably towards the bourgeois *comédie sentimentale*, a transformation already complete by the date of Piccinni's *La buona figliuola* (*La Cecchina*) to a libretto by Goldoni that was first performed in Rome in 1760. Piccinni's *dramma giocoso* tells the affecting tale of a female foundling who, after various ordeals, turns out to be of noble birth[34] and who is finally united, therefore, with the Marchese whom she loves. There is no longer any trace here of comedy in the older sense. The work's tremendous success is proof, if proof be needed, of the extent to which it reflected the sentimental tendencies of the day. Of importance in this context is its source, Samuel Richardson's novel *Pamela* (1740), whose apotheosis of virtue now conquered the operatic stage.[35] *La buona figliuola* inspired a whole series of imitations, most of which are poetically on a far lower level. With its saccharine sentimentality and smugly philistine morality, the whole genre descended to the level of theatrical fodder, and even the comic servants and so on who were now reintroduced in order to entertain audiences were affected by this egregiously homespun tone.

These sentimental heroes and heroines cannot, of course, compare with the fully-rounded characters of *opera seria*. Genuinely profound emotion is even rarer here than it is there, not least because audiences recoiled from it. The young men are distinguished by their social amiability and personal courage, but there is something curiously inexpressive about their feelings of love. The most successfully drawn characters are the seductive beaux who are the immediate precursors of Count Almaviva and Don Giovanni and who, apart from their generally highly implausible decisions to mend their ways, are powerfully influenced by the social norms of the period. Conversely, the young heroines are not lacking in authentic features, in spite of their often excessive sentimentality, while frequently surprising the spectator with their sometimes completely unexpected fickleness and with a level-headedness that never loses sight of marriage, however infatuated they

---

34. These recognition scenes were to become very frequent from now on and are mocked in act two, scene one of Piccinni's *Lo sposo burlato* of 1769: 'Un personaggio che si sia perduto, si riconosce a un neo, a un segno che ha sul braccio, a una medaglia antica, ad un monile, al tratto ed al portamento signorile.'

35. ◆ See Hunter, '"Pamela": The Offspring of Richardson's Heroine in Eighteenth-Century Opera'.

may be. It is significant that poets and composers generally treat them, with undisguised pleasure, as the cheated party: the old implacable and wholly unsentimental spirit of *opera buffa* was never completely exorcized. The reader should not imagine that the *comédie larmoyante* simply replaced the old *opera buffa*, for even now works were still being written in the style of the old comedies, a style that audiences refused to forgo, in spite of all the attempts to stylize the genre,[36] and a new hybrid art known as *opera semiseria* emerged, combining the old and the new – Rousseau and Neapolitan earthiness – with greater or lesser success.

It is significant that these works continue to lack a political dimension, and not even social differences emerge as clearly as in French operas and the German singspiel. Of course, even here the lower orders are generally favoured in terms of their character and – a far more important aspect in the eyes of Italian audiences – their wit and skill. But the aristocracy, too, comes into its own, and if individual classes and professions are mercilessly mocked, there is none the less a noticeable lack of social satire. Even literary satire is poorly represented. The squabbles between Goldoni and Gozzi occasionally surface, of course,[37] the bluestockings remain the butt of many a literary joke,[38] and in the depiction of the French characters who appear in these pieces we find something of the satirical wit of Maffei and Alfieri and of their hostility to the Gallomania of the time. On the whole, however, their mockery is directed less at universal types than at individual phenomena and current trends. The only exceptions are the parodies of *opera seria*, which now became even more outrageous than they had been previously, with even Gluck joining in.[39]

Venice had a special role to play here,[40] as its theatres retained more of the spirit of the early comic operas than they did in the case of tragedy. Venice, moreover, was a democracy, where a keener satirical wind blew than in Naples under its viceroys, and even during the seventeenth century travesties of classical legends were already hugely popular. During the second decade of the eighteenth century the most vicious of all satires of *opera seria* and its practices was written in Venice in the guise of Benedetto Marcello's *Il teatro alla moda* (1720), the spirit of which soon infected all *opera buffa* librettos. The principal representative of Venetian *opera buffa* was Giuseppe Maria Buini (1687–1739), who was active both as a librettist and as a composer, although only his librettos have survived.[41] While, as we have seen, satire was by no means unknown in the theatres of Naples, its occurrences are relatively rare, whereas in Venice it became very much of a subspecies of *opera buffa*, and both Goldoni and the composer Baldassare Galuppi were lastingly influenced by the *buffa* spirit of their native Venice, a spirit very much concerned with current events.[42]

---

36. It is significant that the version of Piccinni's work preserved at the Naples Conservatory under the title *La Cecchina zitella* reintroduces dialect for individual characters and also draws on comic episodes inspired by the older tradition. Mozart's own *Così fan tutte* is a setting of a *buffa* text of the older type.

37. In Goldoni's libretto for Piccinni's *La bella verità* (1762), for instance.

38. Under this heading comes Lorenzi's satire of the Greek scholar Saverio Mattei in *Socrate immaginario* (1775), one of the best *buffa* texts of the time.

39. See below. In act two, scene nine of Anfossi's *Il geloso in cimento* (1774), one of the characters, Fabio, reads an opera libretto and exclaims: 'Oh quanto che impazziscono i poveri poeti nel compor questi drammi!'

40. ◆ See Helmut Christoph Wolff, *Die venezianische Oper in der zweiten Hälfte des 17. Jahrhunderts* and Mancini, Muraro and Povoledo, *I teatri del Veneto*.

41. See Dent, 'Giuseppe Maria Buini'.

42. Particularly instructive in this context is Goldoni's libretto to Piccinni's *La bella verità* of 1762, which deals with the rehearsals for a serious opera. The first character to appear is the impresario, who bewails his bitter lot with the words: 'Il mestiere è malandrino, ma nol posso abbandonar.' In the first-act finale he is won over by his coquettish prima donnas, who demand the most impossible things of him, demands that lead to a series of outbursts of anger. But the theatre poet fares no better. In act one, scene eight, for example, his activity is belittled: 'Quando il libretto è fatto, forse si è fatto il men.' He cannot protest at the singers' wishes, and in the first-act finale they bark at the by now desperate man: 'Just write down what no one will understand.' Much the same treatment is meted out to the *maestro al cembalo*: he, too, is a necessary evil, and he remains the object of the

The Neapolitan playwright and librettist Francesco Cerlone (1722–c1812) opened up a completely different world of *opera buffa*, as did Gozzi for the genre as a whole: this was the world of the supernatural and of fairytales, even though Cerlone rarely rose above illusionistic tricks.[43] One notices that, as the genre gained in popularity, so librettists began to crave new themes, often resorting to the most fanciful and senseless inventions.

The artistic merit of these librettos, in which the starkest contrasts jostle for attention, remains relatively low and, with few exceptions, it follows fashionable taste, with the result that it very soon went out of fashion. Only a handful of poets rose above the mass of their colleagues with their higher dramatic ambitions: here one thinks not only of Goldoni himself but of Giambattista Lorenzi (1719–1805) and Giovanni Battista Casti (1724–1803). In their hands – and especially Casti's – *opera buffa* cast aside all final traces of its Neapolitan origins and came to represent Italian musical comedy in general.[44]

A far more edifying picture emerges when we turn to musical aspects, with composers taking full advantage of the *droit de seigneur* granted to them by *opera buffa* and allowing their imaginations to be far more actively stimulated by the freedoms that it permitted them than *opera seria* was ever able to do with its far stricter rules. It was they who first breathed genuine life into this curious mixture of comedy and sensibility, lending it a stylistic unity that librettists had all too often failed to achieve. Every opera composer of the time was keen to turn his hand not only to serious opera but also to comic opera, and the majority proved more successful in the latter than they did in the former. By Mozart's day, Italian *opera buffa* had reached such a pitch of perfection that it was almost impossible to beat it at its own game.

At least to the extent that it was rooted in folk music, the melodic element proved the least progressive, preferring titillation and amusement to originality: time and again we find the same little skipping motifs, the same little free appoggiaturas, the same melodic lines in short note-values, while the old rhythmic models – especially the siciliana – refused to lie down and die. The harmonic writing and part-writing remained equally straightforward, with the melodies generally designed to be accompanied in thirds or sixths and with harmonic surprises still limited to sudden shifts from major to minor and vice versa. At the same time, however, the naturalistic language of *opera buffa*, with its eschewal of ordered melodic structures, and the orchestra's contribution to the drama are both expanded in ways that an earlier generation could never have anticipated, with its tentative steps in this direction now developed into a system that opened up new horizons for the musical drama, taking it far beyond the traditional confines of *opera buffa*.

The influence of Metastasio and his school on librettos naturally affected the music, too, producing a whole series of arias that were now intended to be taken seriously, rather than treated as parodies, and that were placed in the mouths of the lovers, in particular. In terms of both form

female singers' amorous attentions only so long as no aristocrats present themselves. For him, love in the theatre is like the phoenix 'that no one has yet seen'. (Much the same is true of Don Alfonso's attitude to women's fidelity in Mozart's *Così fan tutte*.) The head of the costume department is also brought in to sort out the costumes of the nagging women. Also important is the praise lavished on Bologna as a particularly good theatrical centre (act one, scene four), as well as the comic argument over dancing (act three, scenes seven to ten). A similar cultural portrait reminiscent of Marcello's *Il teatro alla moda* may be found in Jommelli's *La critica* (1766), where the status of castratos and the difference between French and Italian opera is also examined from a comical standpoint. See also Chiari's *L'amore in musica* (1760), Joseph Haydn's *La canterina* (1766), Gassmann's *L'opera seria* (1769) and Guglielmi's *L'impresa d'opera* (1765). Later offshoots of this tradition include Mozart's *Der Schauspieldirektor*, Lortzing's *Die Opernprobe* and, most recently, Richard Strauss's *Ariadne auf Naxos*. ◆ Abert's reference to Chiari cannot be traced; generally the only known setting of *L'amore in musica* is Antonio Boroni's *dramma giocoso* of 1763.

43. Scherillo, *L'opera buffa napoletana*, 196ff.

44. ◆ See van den Bergh, *Giambattista Casti (1724–1803): L'homme et l'œuvre* and Muresu, *La parola cantata: Studi sul melodramma italiano del Settecento*.

and character, they are often indistinguishable from those found in *opere serie*, right up to the point of including elaborate *fioriture*. Even now, of course, the tendency to use the coloratura passages for parodistic ends still gains the upper hand, but we also find a handful of cases in which there is no longer any trace of parody. Here, too, it was consideration for the singers that persuaded composers, including Mozart himself, to attempt this mixture of styles.

The formal range of *opera buffa* was extended, with the threat posed by the *da capo* aria in Vinci's day soon being overcome. The actual *da capo* was now limited, in the main, to those arias that came closest to the ones found in *opere serie*, while the *buffa* aria enjoyed particular favour alongside popular song forms. Its most common form – often described as a cavatina – was in two sections, frequently followed by a climactic coda or stretta that was occasionally treated as an independent section. But we also find four-part arias and even composite forms, which in Mozart's day generally consisted of a combination of a slow section and a quick one. And last but not least there is rondo form.

But the greatest change to *opera buffa* came about through the increasing importance of the ensembles or *pezzi concertati*, which more and more broke down the usual sequence of recitative and aria, assuming increasingly free forms in the process. Only the opening number or *introduzione*, which now tended to be treated as a separate number between the sinfonia and opening act, was still generally cast in popular forms such as the refrain song and rondo. But the most momentous step involved the position and structure of the finales. Initially this change affected merely the endings of the first two acts: only later was the third-act finale – which until then had been a simple and cheerful closing song – turned into a fully-fledged ensemble.

This was a form that was to be immensely important not just for *opera buffa* but for other types of opera, too, yet its history, even today, remains confused if for no other reason than that, as so often where opera is concerned, writers have tended to consider only the musical side of things and to ignore the libretto. In terms of their words, all the finales discussed so far are no more than lyrical afterthoughts to a plot that is already finished. Either the dramatic tension that has preceded it is discharged in a more or less animated atmospheric portrait or, in the best *buffa* tradition, the opera ends with a general comic moral directed as much at the performers themselves as at the audience. However subtly nuanced these atmospheric portraits may be in detail, they are emphatically not dramatic in the true sense of that term: the action does not advance here any more than it does in the solo aria. This explains why, both musically and textually, these ensembles could be accommodated within the existing range of forms – in this case the ternary aria. They are almost exclusively arias for several voices,[45] distinguished from individual arias only by their fuller sonorities and notable chiefly for their total inability to draw any distinction between the individual characters. But this was bound to change as soon as musicians hit upon the idea of transferring the dramatic high point of the action, which in the past had often enough been relegated to a passage of recitative, to the finales, and to flesh them out musically. This confronted composers with a challenge that could not be solved by means of the cyclical aria. It was a challenge that could be met in various ways, depending on the weight that individual composers gave to musical form as such. The most consistent and, at the same time, most dramatic solution was that proposed by Nicola Logroscino, who stuck to the course of the action, writing music that followed that action as closely as possible. To use a modern expression, he wrote through-composed finales

---

45. Although the binary finales in Leo's *Lo matrimonio annascuso* and Jommelli's *Don Trascullo* are formally freer in design, they remain purely musical structures.

that paid no heed to existing forms.[46] This surprisingly progressive approach meant a total rejection of existing practices, while at the same time calling into question the sway that the composer had hitherto held over the librettist in *opere buffe*, and for that very reason – in spite of Logroscino's initial successes – it failed to find lasting favour with audiences. The second type of solution, which we may call the 'chain finale', consisted in breaking down the action into its individual phases, each of which was then depicted in music using an existing form. Such a complex might well comprise a dozen or more sections, but its unity was assured by means of a home key that was asserted at the beginning and end and sometimes also in the middle of the piece. With its immense variety, this form was particularly well suited to the comedy of many finales and to the sort of insane surprises on which they generally relied for their effect. They offered the listener a series of gripping images, of each of which he could gain a clear overview. But they caused problems for composers as soon as the latter attempted to interpret and treat these whole complexes as self-contained units. Initially, composers sought a way out of this problem simply by repeating individual sections within the finale, and there is no doubt that they achieved a greater sense of unity in this way, but the approach remained purely mechanical. At this juncture, a third form emerged as a far more adaptable alternative: it turned the repetition of certain main ideas into an immutable law and thereby produced an organic, elaborately structured whole in the form of a rondo. In essence, this was another purely musical form, but it was far more flexible than the others and, with its opposition between a main theme and various subsidiary themes, was far more able to adapt to the twists and turns of the plot, while maintaining a sense of unity and, above all, a sense of clarity as a result of the regular recurrence of its refrain. The earliest fully-fledged example of a rondo-form finale is the first-act finale of Piccinni's *La buona figliuola*, which is also a good example of the way in which the ends of the drama may be served by the principle of variation when combined with rondo form. The chain finale and rondo finale now dominated the entire development of the genre up to and including Mozart, with various hybrid forms that even occasionally comprised through-composed movements. These forms became more varied and multifarious as the desire for unity was increasingly joined by a further desire to build to a climax. Even the generation of composers before Mozart was no longer interested merely in sudden changes of scene, but was keen to explore events from a psychological point of view, interpreting the outward situation as the result of inner tensions and attempting with increasing skill to prepare the ground for these inner tensions, building them up to a climax and finally allowing them to find release with almost literally explosive force. It is significant that this subtler kind of comedy achieved its supreme expression in Germany.

There is another regrettable gap in our knowledge of the history of the genre at the beginning of the period under discussion, as only a single work – *La zingara* – has survived by its principal representative, Rinaldo di Capua (*c*1705–*c*1780).[47] We are rather better informed about Nicola Logroscino (1698–1764/5), who, according to the latest research, was one of the leading champions of the new *buffa* style.[48] With him, the more subtle kind of *buffa* drama, hitherto found only

---

46. Among Logroscino's surviving works, this is first found in *Il governatore* of 1747. Logroscino's role in the historical development of the finale was long misunderstood, a state of affairs finally remedied by Kretzschmar in his article 'Zwei Opern Nicolo Logroscinos'. ◆ Further, see Prota-Giurleo, *Nicola Logroscino, 'il dio dell'opera buffa' (la vita e le opere)*.

47. Spitta, 'Rinaldo di Capua'. ◆ A source has since been discovered in Stockholm for di Capua's *Il capitan Fracasso*, a 1768 revision of his 1745 intermezzo *Il bravo burlato*.

48. Kretzschmar, 'Zwei Opern Nicolo Logroscinos'. ◆ Also, see Pagano, 'L'inserimento di Nicolò Logroscino nella realtà musicale palermitana'.

in the intermezzo, was taken over into the fully-developed *opera buffa*. We have already spoken of his most important innovation while discussing the newer types of finale. But as a true dramatist he brought a number of other novel ideas to *opera buffa* by freeing it from the rank excesses of the siciliana and *da capo* aria. It is largely to Logroscino's credit that *opera buffa* was now distinguished from *opera seria* in the main by its far wider range of living forms. His whole *buffa* style is the result of a conscious dramatic decision: it was in this spirit that he took up and developed all his fore-runners' achievements – the contrast between folk art and high art, the tendency to interweave recitative-like[49] and realistic sections into his melodic lines, and the brief and vivid motifs that he often repeats – while at the same time substantially adding to them from his own repertory of original ideas.

Among Logroscino's contemporaries and successors, the school of Hasse initially gave little heed to *opera buffa*, bent, as it was, on reforming *opera seria*. In his *Don Trastullo* of 1749, Jommelli reveals himself as the master of grotesque parody that he was to remain even as a composer of *opere buffe*. While breathing real dramatic life into *opera seria*, he simultaneously mocked the genre in his *buffa* works, mercilessly pillorying every one of its participants, right down to the prompter and costumier. The principal merits of his style – his elaborate ensembles and dramatic orchestral writing – are also found to advantageous effect in his *opere buffe*. His ensembles, admittedly, are somewhat phlegmatic in tone, but they group the voices together in an extremely lively manner and are largely successful in their attempt to treat the characters as individuals. His last and most important *opera buffa*, *La schiava liberata* (1768), reveals the influence of Piccinni not only in its sentimental sections but also in its finales. We shall have occasion to return to this piece when discussing the poetic prototypes of Mozart's *Die Entführung aus dem Serail*.[50]

In Traetta's output, too, *opera buffa* occupies a relatively modest place alongside his *opere serie*, while showing signs of an impressive and independent talent already apparent in his first surviving opera buffa, *Buovo d'Antona* (Venice, 1758[51]), with its large number of pieces of particularly picturesque charm, including songs for the rustic miller's lad and the mendicant pilgrims, a great comic aria about the law, a lullaby, a hunting piece and so on. But Traetta also explored new aspects of parody, notably in his grotesque vision of the drunken Giannino in act two, scene nine of *Le serve rivali* of 1766 and in the bizarre scenes involving magic and madness in *Il cavaliere errante* of 1778. Not even Gluck is spared here.[52] Elsewhere, however, Traetta is far more restrained in his use of caricature than the other Neapolitan composers and in this respect is closer to Galuppi: to delineate a character is at least as important to him as to caricature it. One of the principal merits of his style, whether in *buffa* or *seria*, is the variety of his invention, to which he brings a warmth and nobility that were also to influence Mozart,[53] as the following examples reveal:[54]

---

49. The brief passages of recitative that serve to increase the tension in the arias of Mozart's *Le nozze di Figaro* derive ultimately from Logroscino.
50. See Abert, *Niccolò Jommelli als Opernkomponist*, 403ff.
51. Goldschmidt, *Tommaso Traetta: Ausgewählte Werke*, XIV.
52. In act two, scene two, the ensorcelled Guido thinks that he is Orpheus and launches into a bizarrely instrumented version of Gluck's 'Che farò senz'Euridice'. But Melissa's aria in act one, scene five, 'Agli amanti son pietosa', clearly alludes to the same piece.
53. A number of examples are given by Kretzschmar, 'Mozart in der Geschichte der Oper', ii.269. ◆ Further, see Riedlbauer, 'Tommaso Trajetta – Ein Wegbereiter Mozarts', *Die Opern von Tommaso Trajetta* and 'Zur stilistischen Wechselwirkung zwischen Niccolò Jommelli und Tommaso Trajetta'.
54. *Le serve rivali*, act one, scene eight and *Il cavaliere errante* act one, scenes one, seven and five.

The triadic motifs in the final example are particularly reminiscent of Mozart. Note also the following example from act two, scene seven of *Buovo d'Antona*:

Il cavaliere errante also reveals Viennese influence, especially in its songlike melodies and more careful writing for the inner voices (the frequent Alberti figures in the second violins come under this heading).[55] Traetta's orchestral language is extraordinarily volatile and varied and includes a

55. In the final section of the overture to *Il cavaliere errante* we even find a theme of markedly Hungarian coloration.

large number of onomatopoeic jokes such as twittering birds and motifs associated with smithery and work in general. But we also find less weighty figures of a positively Mozartian stamp. The following example is typical of *Buovo d'Antona*:[56]

In his finales, Traetta differs from Logroscino, remaining within the confines of musical form but treating that form with inspired freedom.[57] And from *Le serve rivali* onwards we also find significant repeats of earlier themes in later numbers. The finales of *Il cavaliere errante*, finally, are among the most progressive of their age, full of drama and climaxes and drawing effective contrasts between individual characters and whole groups before combining them as more or less elaborate ensembles often involving canonic procedures and, at the same time, allowing the orchestra to make an active contribution to the drama. Although Traetta was not primarily a *buffa* composer and was clearly influenced by the genre's true representatives in Naples and Venice, he none the less created a work which, in spite of its worthless libretto,[58] was to bequeath to posterity a number of important ideas.

But it was in the hands of the neo-Neapolitan composers that *opera buffa* enjoyed the most unexpected upturn in its fortunes. The principal credit for this development must go to Niccolò Piccinni,[59] whose tender-hearted and sentimental *La buona figliuola* (*La Cecchina*) of 1760 reveals him as a master of the *comédie larmoyante*.[60] If it were not for its fashionable text, this work would still be effective today. In its time, it proved unexpectedly innovative, offering subtly drawn characters in place of coarse popular comedy and ruthless caricature, with a note of tenderness and intimacy replacing the raucous comic laughter of its predecessors and instantly capturing the hearts of its listeners. Piccinni was the first Italian composer to demand his audience's sympathy, rather than merely their contempt, for his characters and in this was to be particularly important for Mozart. Admittedly, he fails to explore the territory of which he has taken possession and achieves neither the weight of Mozart's highly contrastive characters nor his blend of seriousness and humour. This is clear even from the isolated *buffa* elements found in *La Cecchina*, some of which – notably in the Marchese's aria in act one, scene six – are at odds with the situation and characterization and, as a result, create a highly disruptive impression. Piccinni's most successful character is the German soldier Tagliaferro, who, although heavily influenced by the older tradition of the fire-eating bully, reveals a good-natured, worthy streak that transcends caricature and turns him into a real-life figure. The other characters, too, are remarkable for their creator's attempts to explore them from various angles: in the case of the heroine, for example, there is a childlike *naïveté* in addition to her sensibility, while the coquettish character of her rival

56. In Guido's aria in act two, scene four, the heroic opening is followed by a section containing the words 'Senti tu adesso il resto, perchè l'istoria è bella, via fatemi un balletto ch'io fò da suonator', at which we suddenly hear the solo violin of the ballet violinist in the orchestra.

57. The second-act finale of *Buovo d'Antona* includes a graceful folklike round accompanied by a chitarrone.

58. It may also be noted that Guido's timorous servant Calotto, who is always bewailing his fate, has certain features in common with Leporello (act one, scene one) and that, like Papageno, he even contemplates suicide: in act two, scene ten, he asks the audience 'Non v'è alcuno che trattenga un disperato?'

59. Abert, 'Piccinni als Buffokomponist', 29–42. ◆ More recently, see Bellucci la Salandra, 'Opere teatrali serie e buffe di Nicolò Piccinni dal 1754 al 1794'; Hunter, 'The Fusion and Juxtaposition of Genres in Opera Buffa, 1770–1800: Anelli and Piccinni's "Griselda"'; Capone, *Piccinni e l'opera buffa: Modelli e varianti di un genere alla moda*; and Di Profio, *Niccolò Piccinni, musicista europeo*.

60. ◆ Also see Popovici, *La buona figliuola von Nicola Piccinni*.

Sandrina has a certain sinisterness to it. The Marchese, finally, is not merely conscious of his status as a member of the aristocracy but is almost neurotically sensitive. As a whole, the work breathes a gentler spirit of greater intimacy than the older tradition had done.

This tendency to explore the emotions of tenderness and intimacy is typical of all Piccinni's *opere buffe*. Of course, he is no less masterful in his handling of the coarser *buffa* style in all its manifold forms, as may be seen from the following passage from Bartolo's aria in act one, scene four of *La locandiera di spirito* (1768). Note, in particular, the similarities with Leporello's aria:[61]

In passages such as these, however, Piccinni is particularly dependent on precursors and contemporaries such as Paisiello. He is drawn more to the tender, intimate and elegiac than to the agitated and coarsely comical, as is additionally clear from his relations to folk music. As with all composers like him, these relations are particularly close, although here, too, he prefers to stick to the charming, cheerful and melancholy side of the folksong. Here we have an example in 3/8–metre from the first-act finale of *I viaggiatori* of 1775:

Other melodies bubble with effervescent high spirits, as in the following example from act one, scene three of *Enea in Cuma* (1775). The same sort of melodies recur in *Don Giovanni*:

Above all, however, we find wistful minor-key sicilianas, often conceived as serenades, a legacy from a much earlier period that Piccinni developed with particular skill.[62] A splendid example of

---

61. The characteristic interval of a seventh frequently found in Mozart's works, too, is also used by Piccinni in serious arias to express extreme emotion, as in the third-act finale of *Le gelosie* (1755) and act two, scene two of *Le donne vendicate* (1763).
62. In his earlier operas, including *La scaltra letterata* (1758), they are still particularly frequent, in keeping with the older tradition. Here, too, they are purely musical in character.

his ability to place such numbers in the service of the characterization is Sandrina's little song in act one, scene five of *La buona figliuola*, which begins as follows:

None of Piccinni's contemporaries could match his ability to write a wittily stylized folk melody in this way. And few of them were able to put the simple form of the strophic song to such poetic use. Here Mozart found the models not only for Osmin's first aria, with its art of variation, but for the exotic harmonies of Pedrillo's serenade. Piccinni invariably treated such numbers as atmospheric character pieces and mood paintings, harking back to them in the subsequent course of the opera in subtle and poetic ways. His *introduzioni* are independent numbers that precede the action itself and tend to be cast in popular forms such as the rondo or round with a refrain.

In other types of number, too, Mozart was particularly attracted to the above-mentioned aspects of Piccinni's muse.[63] Two excellent examples occur in *Il mondo della luna* of 1770, the first taken from the overture, the second from the *dolce sinfonia* that depicts the lunar landscape in act two, scene one:

63. For examples, see Abert, 'Piccinni als Buffokomponist', 37.

In Lesbina's aria from act one, scene three of *La molinarella* (1766) we hear Barbarina's voice (note also the key of F minor):

And at the beginning of the second-act finale of *La Corsara* (1771) we hear the seductive tones of Don Giovanni:

Other favourite phrases of Piccinni – especially at cadential points – recur in Mozart:

Significantly, all these examples are taken from the *galant* and sentimental aspect of Piccinni's art, few from his coarsely comical side. But Mozart learnt even more from his motivic writing, with which his treatment of the orchestra is closely bound up. Here we find one of his strongest points and one, moreover, that affords an excellent demonstration of Piccinni's lively imagination. The way in which Piccinni produces whole numbers with proudly arching melodic curves from entirely unprepossessing and even prosaic material can only be called masterly.[64] Indeed, he even ventures down avenues previously explored by Scarlatti and Logroscino but left untouched by Mozart, creating motivic links across whole scenes. It is by no means uncommon for the quick second section of his binary arias to repeat the main motifs from the first part either note-for-note or in varied guise. But it is the orchestra that enjoys the lion's share of the motivic writing. In the history of the *opera buffa* orchestra Piccinni blazed a distinctive trail, going far beyond anything achieved even by Logroscino. Many of his aria themes are devised in such a way that the orchestra begins and the voice continues or vice versa, while in other numbers we find the motivic material divided equally and constantly between the two. But it is chiefly in his *buffa* scenes that the instruments often have the biggest role to play. In the quartet from act one, scene three of *Il barone di Torreforte* (1765), the main role is taken by the following orchestral motif (a motif that recalls *Die Zauberflöte*):

64. In act two, scene four of *I furbi burlati* (1773 [originally produced as *La furba burlata*, 1760]) he even develops a full two-part song from Minicuccio's brief recitative-like interjections.

Generally, however, it is brief and lively motifs from which the number as a whole is developed, and it is these that are the main vehicles of all the devilish tricks that he plays in these *buffa* numbers. Here are a few examples:[65]

Other composers, notably Paisiello, may have created more graphically memorable motifs, but few can match him in the intelligence with which he develops them. In comparison to other Italian composers, he is relatively uninterested in novel orchestral effects,[66] the main exception being his frequent use of the crescendo. But no one could beat him in terms of the adaptability and quick-wittedness of his orchestral language, and here there is no doubt that he was of decisive influence on Mozart's *buffa* orchestra. Nor, finally, should we forget the many independent orchestral numbers that serve to depict a particular situation, or the witty way in which the vocal style of *opera buffa* is transferred to the instruments, with the result that, instead of regular melodies, we suddenly find a motley assortment of all manner of brief giggling and chattering motifs.

None of Logroscino's successors saw any reason to abandon the wealth of forms that he bequeathed to them. With Piccinni, too, the simple song is found alongside the various types of aria, all of which are handled with the greatest freedom. He is especially fond of a form consisting of a slow and fast section, both of which are generally repeated and often separated by a very brief recitative designed to increase the sense of tension. Piccinni is no less fond of this device than Logroscino.

Among his ensembles,[67] those conceived in purely lyrical terms adopt the form of solo songs, while the more dramatic ones are already closer to finales in their more varied structure. The finales of his earliest operas are still purely musical aria finales, and it looks as though he approached his new rondo finales via his rondo-like *introduzioni*, except that the form is now far more highly elaborated. The wealth of dramatic life that he was able to find in this form, especially by combining it with variation form and thematic development, is really quite astonishing. In the aforementioned finale from *La buona figliuola*, for example, the little duet for Sandrina and Paoluccia that is the main theme of the rondo recurs on no fewer than eight occasions after numerous interludes, sometimes note-for-note, sometimes in varied guise, but always recogniz-

---

65. Example (a) comes from act one, scene one of *La scaltra letterata*; (b) is from the first-act finale of *Vittorina* (1777); and (c) and (d) are from the *introduzione* and act two, scene four of *Gli sposi perseguitati* (1769).

66. In this respect, Piccinni's *opere buffe* are indistinguishable from his serious operas. *Vittorina*, which unfortunately cannot be dated [*Vittorina* dates from 1777] but which, as a sentimental comedy, must postdate *La buona figliuola*, includes clarinets, while *I furbi burlati* of 1773 has a 'voce umana' notated in the bass clef. Piccinni is also very fond of the sort of orchestral jokes that date back to an earlier tradition, whereby every instrument mentioned in the text immediately appears in the orchestra: examples include act one, scene one of *La scaltra letterata*, the second-act finale of *Il barone di Torreforte*, and act one, scene eight of *Il curioso di se stesso* (1767). ◆ No work by the title *Il curioso di se stesso* appears to be known. Possibly Abert refers to *Il curioso del suo proprio danno* of ?1755/6, revised by Antonio Sacchini as *Il curioso imprudente* at Naples in 1761.

67. The duets in which one of the character's contributions are limited to a mere handful of comic interjections are no more than pseudo-ensembles.

able as the principal idea symbolizing the hostile forces that refuse to release poor Cecchina from their clutches. But we also find frequent examples of the chain finale, both in its simplest form as a series of thematically independent sections held together only by their relationship to a home key,[68] and in a more subtle form whereby later links in the chain include repetitions or more or less clear reminiscences of earlier links[69] – what one might regard as a transfer of the rondo principle to the series as a whole. Within the individual sections, by contrast, we find the greatest freedom, with songs and arias alternating with accompanied recitatives (a relatively rare type in Piccinni's works) and rondos. Two devices are used, above all, to create climaxes: either a particular theme takes increasing control of the entire orchestra and cast so that it finally assumes the form of a veritable triumphal procession,[70] or the psychological forces that motivate the action find expression in a variety of contrasting themes supported by an orchestral motif that indicates the general mood. These contrasting themes produce a highly dramatic interplay of living forces from which one of the themes finally emerges victorious.[71] Although these finales are essentially concerned, above all, with a specifically Italian kind of larger-than-life situation comedy, Piccinni also attempts to use the music to depict his characters as real individuals. The separate groups are often contrasted with one another with a razor-edged sharpness reminiscent of Mozart. Piccinni's finest numbers are distinguished by their elaborate, free polyphony, including examples of the popular form of the canon.[72]

The three-movement sinfonias to Piccinni's *opere buffe* contain no special features to distinguish them from those of his serious operas, although we occasionally find a programmatical element.[73] *Sui generis* is the sinfonia to *La finta baronessa* of 1767, the slow movement of which is inserted between the two parts of its fast movement. This fast section then returns in the third-act finale. In *I viaggiatori*, the sung introduction replaces the final movement of the sinfonia.

The sentimental, effeminate figure of Niccolò Piccinni has a far more virile counterpart in Giovanni Paisiello (1740–1816).[74] Admittedly, he too made a modest contribution to the sensibility of the Neapolitan school and ultimately, if belatedly, threw in his lot with the Piccinnian *comédie larmoyante*.[75] But in his case the sentimental element is held in check by a goodly dose of sincere and natural boyishness that time and again brought him back to earthy, popular musical comedy. This is evident not least from his texts, in which we even encounter the old figures of Pulcinella and his Carmosina.[76] Folk instruments such as the *colascione, salterio, zampogna* and mandolin[77] (the last-named particularly important for Mozart) are by no means rare in his scores, which also contain Neapolitan street cries and improvised lute serenades.[78] The folk element also

---

68. Only in parodies of *ombra* scenes does Piccinni abandon the well-worn path of the most closely related tonalities. Here we regularly find the inevitable E flat major and even A flat major, regardless of what may have gone before.

69. Particularly good examples may be found in the second-act finale and in the quartet in act three, scene four of *I furbi burlati* and in the first-act finale of *La pescatrice* (1766).

70. As in the first-act finale of *Gli amanti mascherati* (1774).

71. Act one, scene eight, and act three, scenes one and two of *I viaggiatori*.

72. Cf. the second-act finale of *Enea in Cuma*; for an example of canonic procedures, see act two, scene three of the same work.

73. In *La molinarella, Il mondo della luna* [originally *Il regno della luna*, 1770] and *Enea in Cuma*.

74. See Abert, 'Paisiellos Buffokunst und ihre Beziehung zu Mozart'. ◆ Further, see Faravelli, *Mozart e Paisiello*; Lippmann, 'Paisiello und Mozart in der Opera Buffa'; and Strebel, '"Nun ist der Paesiello Hier (. . .)" – Mozart's Beziehungen zu Giovanni Paisiello'.

75. His principal contribution to this field is *Nina o sia La pazza per amore*, a hugely successful work in his own day first seen in Caserta in 1789. But Paisiello's first non-dialect opera, *La frascatana* of 1774, also belongs under this heading.

76. *L'osteria di Marechiaro* (1769) and *Gli amanti comici* (1772). There is nothing in the wordbooks to indicate the presence of these characters, only in the scores do they appear.

77. The mandolin first appears in act one, scene three of *L'osteria di Marechiaro*, after which it is found on frequent occasions. It sometimes also occurs in *opere serie*, notably in 'Se un core annodi' from act two, scene eight of Hasse's *Achille in Sciro*.

78. In act one, scene seven of *I scherzi di amore* (1771), Saverio and Marzia sing an 'improvisata a 2' to a lute accompaniment.

affected Paisiello's style in general, of course, but unlike Piccinni, he was fascinated by its coarse and realistic aspect. His stylized folk tunes are fresher, more earthy and often more brazen than Piccinni's. Paisiello is the creator of those provocatively ambling themes that not infrequently come close to street songs and that allowed the lower orders to make their superiors feel small. The present example is taken from act two, scene two of *Il re Teodoro* (1784):[79]

In much the same way, the young women who in Piccinni's works tend to lapse into sentimentality speak an earthier language in Paisiello, a language more sincerely natural, now practical, now pert, but always free from excessive sentimentality. Blonde, Zerlina and Despina clearly breathe this same spirit and so, to a lesser extent, does Susanna. This tendency towards coarse humour soon led Paisiello to explore the world of foreign folk music or, rather, what his generation believed to be foreign folk music. The buccaneering librettist Francesco Cerlone gave him ample opportunities with *La Dardané* (1772),[80] and Pasquale Mililotti rendered a similar service with his libretto for *L'arabo cortese* (1769). Both these works were to be important in the context of Mozart's *Die Entführung aus dem Serail*. Allusions to French chansons of a kind so popular at this period are also found here.[81]

But Paisiello took up and developed the actual language of *opera buffa* in a far more idiosyncratic way than Piccinni and in this he was to prove one of Mozart's most important models. He appears almost literally inexhaustible in inventing those primitive and realistic motifs that share a demonstrative avoidance of regular melodic structures. A whole series of examples may serve to illustrate this point:[82]

79. Mozart's 'Conoscete, signor Figaro' comes under this heading, except that on the lips of the Count the tone is now ironical.
80. In terms of its subject matter, this piece is strikingly similar to Gotter's German singspiel, *Das tartarische Gesetz*. ◆ Gotter's singspiel was set by Franz Seydelmann (c1779), Johann André (1779), Johann Rudolf Zumsteeg (1780) and Georg Benda (1787).
81. In scene two of *Il duello comico* (1774) and in act one, scene two of *Le astuzie amorose* (1775). Also worth mentioning here is the use of the minuet to indicate *galant* dignity. See also act one, scene eight of *I filosofi immaginari* (1779) and Leporello's 'catalogue aria'. ◆ Abert's dates and titles appeared to be slightly confused here: *Il duello comico* is the title of the 1776 Paris version of Paisiello's original *Il duello* produced at Naples in 1774.
82. Example (a) is taken from act one, scene seven of *Il re Teodoro*; (b) is from act one, scene twelve of *La vedova di bel genio* (1766); (c) is from the *introduzione* to *Gli amanti comici*; and (d) comes from act two, scene seventeen of *L'amor contrastato* (1788).

The grotesque intervals of a seventh are far more frequent here than in Piccinni. Above all, the octave intervals breathlessly hissed out in the style of Mozart's Osmin play an important role in scenes of comic rage in Paisiello's *opere buffe*:

Paisiello also favours scalar motifs involving sequencing that often explore the whole of the singer's vocal range. Or, again, there are triadic motifs rising gaily upwards:[83]

In the true *buffa* manner, Paisiello tends to harp at length on such motifs, just as his particular strength – unlike Piccinni's – lies in exaggeration.[84] It is a strength that is revealed especially in his numerous parodies of *opera seria*, the grotesque effectiveness of which is due to all manner of devices, including melody, harmony, rhythms, coloratura and instrumentation. Like Osmin, his *buffo* basses are fond of the sinister, diatonic or chromatic descent of a fourth to the dominant, as in Catuozzo's aria, 'La femmena chi è', from act one, scene six of *I scherzi di amore e di fortuna* (1771):

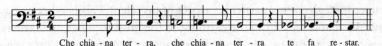

Che chia - na ter - ra,   che chia - na ter - ra   te   fa   re - star.

Osmin's interrupted cadence on the flattened submediant is also frequently found here.[85]

Paisiello's volatile but invariably memorable rhythms are likewise rooted in folk music. Particularly important here, as it is for Mozart, is his use of syncopation to express genuine or caricatured passion. One example among many is the following from act two, scene twelve of *L'idolo cinese* (1767), which is also important on account of its accompanying orchestral motif:

già   ti   co - no - sco   ap - pie - no

83. In act one, scene seven of *L'idolo cinese* (1767) and the *introduzione* to *La frascatana* (1774).
84. In the opening aria from *La finta maga* (1768), Giacomo repeats the same note no fewer than twenty-two times.
85. The prototype, of course, is Uberto's second aria in Pergolesi's *La serva padrona*.

In the orchestra, however, syncopations over broken triads in the basses are used by both Paisiello and Mozart to express a sense of eeriness or insidiousness, as in act two, scene six of *La finta maga per vendetta* (1768):

But the rhythm associated with a boundless love of life that recurs throughout Don Giovanni's 'champagne aria' also derives from Paisiello, as is clear from Don Peppe's aria in act one, scene one of *La vedova di bel genio* (1766), where it similarly permeates the whole number:[86]

It is no wonder that, given this particular aspect of his talent, Paisiello became such a master of contrasts, contrasts that extend from the earthiest to the most sophisticated, where only the most attentive listener is aware of the joke.[87] And they appear not only one after the other, but also simultaneously in his ensembles. In his finales the sustained melodies of the serious characters are often accompanied by the insane *buffa* patter of the others, allowing the individual characters to emerge with even greater clarity than with Piccinni.

In his treatment of the orchestra, too, Paisiello comes close to Mozart, albeit in a very different way from Piccinni. His orchestra is much more lavish and brilliant, containing, as it does, not only the folk instruments mentioned above but often trumpets and horns (both frequently 'con sordini'), too. Among concertante wind instruments, the clarinet is a particular favourite of Paisiello's.[88] But the strings, too, are not infrequently divided, and sometimes we even find two orchestras.[89]

---

86.   See also act two, scene fourteen of *Il credulo deluso* (1774) and the third-act finale of *Il re Teodoro*.
87.   Particularly popular is the milksop who vacillates endlessly between desperate courage and helpless fear, a state recalled by Pedrillo's aria, 'Frisch zum Kampfe'.
88.   It is instructive to see how Paisiello uses the clarinet: initially it appears only as an exceptional device in scenes depicting Elysium and the Underworld (scene eight of *Il duello comico* and the second-act finale of *I scherzi di amore*), a usage that survives in the natural idyll of the second-act finale of *I filosofi immaginari* and the dream narration in act two, scene seven of *Il re Teodoro*. Later it is used in the entirely modern manner to express burgeoning passion and desire.
89.   In act one, scene two of *Le astuzie amorose*. In Frasconio's aria in act one, scene nine of *La Dardané*, pizzicato and coll'arco occur in alternate bars in the violas and basses. Instrumental jokes may be found in the second-act finale of *L'osteria di Marechiaro* and in act one, scene ten of *La Dardané*.

No less varied than the make-up of Paisiello's orchestra is its use within the drama, and here, once again, he comes closest to Mozart. One example among many is the staccato motif in broken triads in the comic bassoon that accompanies Doctor Bartolo in act one, scene five of *Il barbiere di Siviglia*, just as it accompanies Leporello in his 'catalogue aria'. Or take the ghostly horn melody that represents the 'mostro' in the second-act finale of *L'arabo cortese* or the tender wind themes which, as with Mozart, appear as the second main subject in emotionally charged arias.[90] In the recitative preceding the duet for Lisetta and Taddeo in act three, scene one of *Il re Teodoro* we already hear a lively military march that later grows louder as Taddeo assumes the airs of a commander, his daughter those of a princess. As such, it forms a counterpart to Mozart's famous 'Non più andrai'. It is clear, then, that these ideas were already in the air and that it needed only a superior poetic mind to turn them into a new and meaningful system.

The role of recurring orchestral motifs is the same as in Piccinni, except that Paisiello's are earthier and more trenchant, and he is also fond of combining them in pairs. The popular slides and mordents appear in his works in all manner of different forms, as do pounding motifs based on the interval of a fourth. Particularly common are the twitching and trembling motifs that are also found in Mozart:[91]

90. We already find this at the phrase 'se penso a quel core' in act one, scene ten of *Il furbo malaccorto*.
91. Example (a) comes from the first-act finale of *L'idolo cinese*; (b) is from act one, scene nine of *La luna abitata* (1768); (c) is from the *introduzione* to *Gli amanti comici*; (d) is from the second-act finale of *Le astuzie amorose*; (e) is from the first-act finale of *Il credulo deluso*; (f) is from act two, scene one of *La finta maga*; (g) is from act one, scene eight of *La molinara*; and (h) comes from the second-act finale of *La frascatana*.

Especially frequent are the *Walzen* attached to the end of individual vocal phrases, as in act one, scene two of *La somiglianza de' nomi* (1771):

Paisiello's particular strength lies in his ability to transform these motifs harmonically, allowing him to achieve surprising effects that sometimes look forward to Schubert. In the orchestra, it is the winds that play a far greater role in this development than was the case with Piccinni.

In his approach to questions of form, by contrast, Paisiello followed in the footsteps of his predecessor, with the structure and inner design of his arias revealing an even greater freedom, if possible, especially in terms of the links between voice and orchestra.[92] Here, too, the predominant form is the binary aria consisting of a slow section followed by a quick one.[93] More serious numbers are cast, by preference, in the form of cavatinas and ternary arias with shortened *da capo*. Contrastive themes are very common, but unfortunately there is also an even greater tendency than with Piccinni to indulge in empty effects and tawdry coloratura, even where there is no hint of any parody. It is a pitfall that, as we know, Mozart himself did not always succeed in avoiding.

In general, however, Paisiello reveals himself as the most inspired and most versatile of melodists, and on this point in particular he exercised the greatest influence on Mozart. Indeed, there is a striking echo of Figaro's aria 'Aprite un po' quegl'occhi' in Sandrina's aria from act two, scene three of *Il re Teodoro*, an echo which, given the misogynistic thrust of the text, is scarcely coincidental. The motif that accompanies the words 'son rose spinose' is heard four times in each case:[94]

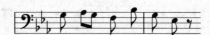

There is no doubt an intentional quotation here.[95] Elsewhere in Mozart's musical vocabulary, we find a remarkable number of features that he shares with Paisiello. Indeed, many of his favourite phrases such as the freely introduced chromatic suspensions and motifs that descend either triadically or stepwise from the fifth are by no means uncommon in Paisiello:

92. If a *buffa* aria begins with a large-scale and ambitious ritornello in the older tradition, one can be fairly certain that what follows will be a parody.
93. The reverse order is found in act one, scene four of *Il barbiere di Siviglia*, a reversal due – as with Leporello's 'catalogue aria' – to the words.
94. In Paisiello's case, the aria is in A major.
95. This is additionally clear from the fact that in Paisiello's case the motif is the main idea, whereas in Mozart's case it is merely an episode.

In Ottavio's 'vengeance aria' in act three, scene one of *Gli amanti comici*, we hear pre-echoes of Donna Elvira:

And in Zafira's aria from act one, scene three of *La Dardané*, it is Donna Anna's voice that we hear:

In act one, scene six of the same opera, the following passage occurs in the orchestra:

And in act two, scene seven of *I scherzi di amore*:

A whole series of motifs was to be important for Mozart on account of their rhythms which, peremptory or disjointed, serve to increase the tension. The following are all found frequently in Paisiello:

Paisiello's *introduzioni* and finales are structurally similar to Piccinni's, but on average they are more powerfully compelling from a dramatic point of view. Certainly, one looks in vain in Piccinni's *opere buffe* for a scene as lively and as exciting as the bandits' battle in the *introduzione* to *Il furbo malaccorto* (1767). Paisiello's finales, like Piccinni's (and clearly under his influence), developed from purely musical structures to dramatic ones, resulting in a varied sequence of song- and aria-like sections and, especially, free dramatic rondos. Characteristic of his operas is the important role of the accompanied recitative and of the independent orchestra, both of which are bound up with his predilection for extensive parodies of *opera seria* in his finales.[96] In general, every twist in the action brings with it a new section, although we also find Piccinni's motivic links here.[97] As a result, the main difference between the two composers has less to do with questions of form than with the far greater emphasis on the comic element in Paisiello's works. Here the insane and eccentric spirit of Italian comedy runs riot, with the unlikeliest contrasts brought into sharp conflict to produce a state of confusion whose unbridled comedy was later to be matched by Rossini but never by Mozart.[98] The love scenes and natural idylls that are scattered throughout

96 . In time, the name of Gluck was to be added to these parodies; on *Il credulo deluso*, see Abert, 'Glucks italienische Opern bis zum "Orfeo"'. Paisiello's *Socrate immaginario* belongs under this same heading.

97.   A paragon of symmetry is the first-act finale to *La vedova di bel genio*, the first three and last three of whose seven sections are motivically linked; the second and sixth are merely episodic in character, while the pivotal fourth section also has its own music.

98.   In the second-act finale of *L'osteria di Marechiaro*, the grieving Lesbina begins by summoning up the shade of her dead husband; her minor-key aria 'Placati sposo amato' is highly emotional, whereas the shade of her dead husband maintains a major tonality to the accompaniment of permanent chuckles in the orchestra. After a few brief bars of recitative, there is a sudden Mozartian shift from G to E flat major. An exaggeratedly emotional ensemble describes the effect of these events on those present. Pluto and Proserpina are then invoked (a 42-bar pedal point on E flat with tremolando). The Count, who is also involved in this scene, steps completely outside his role with his insane *buffa* patter, and from now on the whole action revolves around the characters' mockery of the hysterical Lesbina who, to general merriment, ends by apostrophizing the 'sfere armoniche' and by calling on each of the instruments in the orchestra in turn. Also worth mentioning in this context is the cackling of hens ('com'a gallina voi strillate cà cà cà') in the second-act finale of *Il furbo malaccorto*, with which the comic characters accompany the earnest Count and Ginevra. The second-act finale of *L'arabo cortese* deals with a foiled abduction, with Osmirone's triumphant cursing powerfully reminiscent of Mozart's Osmin.

Paisiello's works seem to exist only to stem the insane floodtide for a moment, so that it can then burst forth again with all the greater violence. The writing for the voices, too, is generally filled with tremendous dramatic life, with Paisiello bringing out the interplay of individuals and whole groups with assurance and great firmness of purpose.

Whereas the characterization in Piccinni's works all too easily descends to an undistinguished mean, the versatile Paisiello offers a far greater range of openly comic characters. In many cases there are clear links between them and Mozart's characters. The Oriental Osmirone in *L'arabo cortese*, for example, clearly influenced Mozart's Osmin in his mixture of self-importance, low cunning, brutality and a sense of humour that borders on the sinister, just as Pedrillo has acquired a number of features of the character of Miccio in the same opera. In much the same way, the aristocratic heroes of Paisiello's operas such as the Cavaliere Giocondo in *La frascatana* and Count Almaviva in *Il barbiere di Siviglia* remain lively and seductive in spite of their lack of scruples and, as such, are manifestly the precursors of Mozart's Count and Don Giovanni. Significantly, however, Paisiello long proved unequal to the depiction of deeper emotions and in the case of his female characters veered between Piccinnian sentimentality and po-faced over-emotionalism. Only in his later works does he finally manage to create genuine, heartfelt emotions, and there is no doubt that the Rosina of his *Barbiere di Siviglia* is far more successful in this respect than Rossini's heroine.

In terms of both form and content, Paisiello's sinfonias are more varied than Piccinni's. In his later works, we find single-movement sinfonias alongside the usual three-movement type. A remarkable transitional form is also found in which the andante – as in Mozart's overture to *Die Entführung aus dem Serail* – is merely episodic in character, with the opening allegro being further developed after the andante has ended.[99] The way in which the ideas are ordered and developed is as loose in Paisiello's case as it was in Piccinni's. Piccinni's important attempt to forge a thematic link between sinfonia and finale was repeatedly imitated by Paisiello, notably in *Le astuzie amorose* (1775).[100] Here, in the recapitulation, we find a completely new cantabile theme of a trio-like character that returns in the first-act finale at the words 'lire canore vogliamo sentir':

99. Cf. the sinfonias to *Gli amanti comici*, *Le astuzie amorose* and *La finta maga*. In *L'osteria di Marechiaro*, the andante also replaces the second subject and is twice repeated before the final allegro begins.
100. Cf. the sinfonia to *Il duello comico*, which is identical to the one used in *La frascatana*.

Even this brief list of examples will be sufficient to show what Mozart was most attracted to in Paisiello: it was far less the love of earthy *buffa* caricature, which, as an end in itself, he never seriously considered, than the sincerely naïve and, at the same time, lively and impassioned aspect of his art and, above all, his exploitation of highly effective contrasts. On a technical level, there was much that he could learn from Paisiello's handling of the orchestra in terms not only of its new expressive resources but also the dramatic and psychological use of the different instruments. Mozart failed to equal, let alone surpass, his predecessor's achievements in this regard, and it was left to Rossini to develop this particular *buffa* tradition. There is no point, after all, in praising Mozart for something he did not achieve and, indeed, that he made no attempt to achieve in the works of his maturity. His stage works are built on different foundations: he willingly, but not uncritically, took over the numerous building bricks that the Italians were able to offer him, but the edifice that he produced with them looked quite different from the bold and airy structures of Italian *opere buffe*.[101]

Another composer whose talents as a composer of *opere buffe* are firmly rooted in the popular tradition is Pietro Guglielmi (1728–1804). Yet there is something *galant*, almost reckless about his style that sets him apart from the earthier Paisiello. Typical of this style are his cheerful march tunes with their dotted rhythms, such as the following example from act one, scene three of *Le due gemelle* [1787]:

Sometimes we are even reminded of Weber, as in act one, scene nine of *Il matrimonio in contrasto* of 1776, which begins as follows:

101.   ◆ Further concerning Paisiello, see Hunt, *Giovanni Paisiello: His Life as an Opera Composer*; Della Corte, *L'opera comica italiana nel '700*; Blanchetti, 'Tipologia musicale dei concertati nell'opera buffa di Giovanni Paisiello'; and Lippmann, '"Il mio ben quando verrà": Paisiello creatore di una nuova semplicità'.

Rondo themes in the style of Sarti that ultimately derive from French influence and that we later find in Mozart's *La clemenza di Tito* likewise occur in these *opere buffe*, as in the allegro from the aforementioned aria from *Le due gemelle*:

Everything that Guglielmi wrote in this folk tone is instantly convincing as a result of its warmth and charm and manliness. In the following menuetto from the first-act finale of *I finti amori* (1784), where Lesbina introduces Pancrazio to society, we even hear the cavalier-like tone of the menuetto from Mozart's *Don Giovanni*:

Guglielmi also went his own way in expressing comedy. His *buffa* style has a distinct element of grotesqueness about it, operating far more than Paisiello's with those tiny, naturalistic motifs that create their comic effect by dint of obstinate repetition. Often enough he allows his characters to prattle on in very short note-values set to a single pitch, and there is something irresistibly comic about the scene in the *introduzione* to *L'azzardo* when Gebra suddenly loses her composure:

This sudden tendency for the well-ordered melodic line to be broken down by scales and patter motifs or by rests and fermatas had a profound influence on Mozart. Take the following example from act one, scene eight of *Il matrimonio in contrasto*:

And here is a passage from act one, scene three of *La bella pescatrice* [1789]:

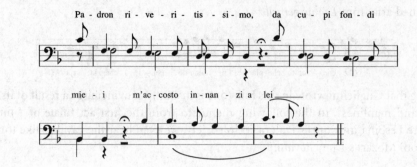

Even coloratura assumes a grotesque character in Guglielmi's hands, as in the duet from act two, scene three of *I finti amori*:

But Guglielmi also combines great skill in the art of variation with these cheekily insolent melodies. The main theme of the aria 'Io sò qualche costumano le donne' from *I viaggiatori ridicoli* [1768] is entirely typical of the composer:

Later, as the character's anger at the women reaches its climax, it assumes the following form:[102]

Guglielmi's handling of the orchestra likewise reflects this fondness for a folk element and for the grotesque and includes concertante lutes, guitars and postillion trumpets,[103] and even a death knell in a grotesque parody of a death scene.[104] Guglielmi is also fond of brief, angular orchestral motifs such as the following, which he develops over highly volatile harmonies:

102. Cf. numbers such as the quartet in Mozart's *Così fan tutte* ('La mano a me date').
103. In act one, scene two, and the first-act finale of *I finti amori*.
104. Three timpani tuned to E flat, G and B flat in *Il matrimonio in contrasto*.

Guglielmi's arias include large-scale codas with highly effective climaxes, while rondo form is particularly favoured in the solo songs. But Guglielmi emerges at his most brilliant and most characteristic in his ensembles – not just in his finales, but more especially in the broadly structured, multisectional numbers that occur in the course of his acts, often equalling the finales not only in their length but also their dramatic life and their capacity for surprise. Here one thinks, for example, of the great sextet in act two, scene six of *Le due gemelle*, which depicts a music lesson[105] and is also notable for the brilliance of its orchestration. Guglielmi's overtures, too, are particularly varied, with single-movement sinfonias appearing alongside French overtures in two movements and Italian ones in three.[106]

Pasquale Anfossi (1727–97) proves himself to be a true pupil of Piccinni in his preference for the *comédie larmoyante*, a genre represented by his most successful and, for Mozart, most important works: *L'incognita perseguitata* (1773), *La finta giardiniera* (1774) and *La pescatrice fedele* (*La vera costanza*, 1776). His skills were honed at the school of Piccinnian sentimentality and, as a result, he was most successful at expressing tender longing, infatuation and melancholy. Songs such as these delighted contemporary audiences with melodies which, no matter how tender-hearted, always retained their sense of nobility. And it was these that left the greatest mark on Mozart, as the following examples will show:[107]

105.   This number also contains important information about vocal techniques of the time. When the female pupil ornaments the word 'restò' with elaborate *fioriture*, she is told: 'Il maestro avrà sbagliato restò; sopra l'ò non si solfeggia, quel passaggio non ci và.' Later, too, he remains unhappy with the coloratura: 'Il maestro bastonate!'

106.   ◆ Further, see Piovano, 'Notizie storico-bibliografiche sulle opere di Pietro Carlo Guglielmi (Guglielmini) con appendice su Pietro Guglielmi'; Hunter, 'Some representations of opera seria in opera buffa'; Lipton, 'The opere buffe of Pietro Alessandro Guglielmi in Vienna and Eszterháza: Contributions to the Development of opera buffa between 1768 and 1793'; and DelDonna, 'The operas of Pietro Alessandro Guglielmi (1728–1804): The Relationship of His Dialect Operas to His Opere Serie'.

107.   Exx. (a) and (b) are from act two, scenes one and four, respectively, of *L'incognita perseguitata*; exx. (c) and (d) are from act one, scene six, and act two, scene twelve, respectively, of *La pescatrice fedele*; ex. (e) is from act one, scene thirteen of *Il geloso in cimento* (later taken over into the first act of the pasticcio *I tre gobbi*); and ex. (f) is from act two, scene two of *La finta giardiniera*; for further examples, see Kretzschmar, 'Mozart in der Geschichte der Oper', ii.268. ◆ Also see Tintori, *L'opera napoletana*; and Mattern, *Das Dramma giocoso: 'La finta giardiniera': Ein Vergleich der Vertonungen von Pasquale Anfossi und W. A. Mozart.*

e lo giu - ro ai vo - stri

d)

lu - mi che son fon - ti di bel - tà.

e) Con un

te - ne - ro so - spi - ro, ah Ro - si - na mi di-

ce - va e la ma - no mi strin - ge - va tut - to af-

fet - to e tut - to ar - dor

f)

To adopt a teasing, charming note suits him particularly well. Genuine, effervescent comic themes such as the following from the sinfonia to *La finta giardiniera*, with its scurrying quavers reminiscent of *Le nozze di Figaro*, are by no means uncommon:

And there is also an element of roguishness that reminds the listener of Mozart, as in Serpetta's aria from act one, scene nine of the same opera:

Anfossi, finally, is the source of the performance marking 'Andantino grazioso' that we often find in Mozart's works. But Anfossi has another aspect to him, an aspect that links him to Paisiello and Guglielmi, namely, his fondness for the grotesque and picturesque. The vivid and rapid *buffa* patter and incessant repetition of brief motifs to which we have already referred are found in all his operas,[108] with the result that his lovers' tender and wistful songs coexist alongside larger-than-life caricatures of the real *buffa* characters. Anfossi also explores new facets of the traditional types of scenes, notably the scene with the notary in the first-act finale of *Lo sposo di tre* (1763), the scene with the treasure-hunter in the first-act finale of *L'avaro* (1775) and the storm scenes in second-act finale of *La pescatrice fedele*, and in the first-act finale of *Il geloso in cimento* (1774). He is also especially fond of what one might term 'instrument arias',[109] while another speciality of his art is the comic scenes from military life in the spirit of Figaro's 'Non più andrai'.[110]

108. In the first-act finale of *L'incognita perseguitata*, the whole sentence 'Fermate, sentite! Che caso spietato! La bella Gianetta

così modestina così semplicetta adesso è fuggita!' is sung to the same three-note motif:

The following motif is regularly used by Italian composers to express the idea of toil (*faticar*):

It is repeatedly used by Anfossi, notably in the first-act finale of *L'avaro* and in the aria about war in act one, scene thirteen of *L'incognita perseguitata*. In act two, scene nine of *La pescatrice fedele* the milksop Villotto initially fails to produce a melodic line consisting of anything more than a single note, endlessly repeated.

109. Act one, scene two of *La finta giardiniera*; the tuning of the violins familiar from *Don Giovanni* is also found is act three, scene seven of *La pescatrice fedele* and in act one, scene one of *Il geloso in cimento*.

110. Act one, scene thirteen of *L'incognita perseguitata*, act one, scene three of *L'avaro*, and act one, scene twelve of *La pescatrice fedele*.

As for his aria types, Anfossi prefers strophic and binary form, with the two parts of the latter distinguished by time-signature and tempo,[111] but we also find multisectional numbers, as in act one, scene thirteen, and act two, scene ten of *Il geloso in cimento*. This is a form that is found especially in the third-act duets that were now becoming a regular feature of Italian operas. Generally they depict the coming together of the lovers and as such serve as a substitute for the third-act finale, which was often omitted in consequence. Finally, we also find large-scale, multisectional solo scenes with accompanied recitatives and relatively lengthy cavatina-like movements, as in act two, scene ten of *La pescatrice fedele*.[112] The finales themselves tend to be cast in rondo form, following Piccinni's example, revealing a desire for unity that finds expression, above all, in the references to earlier sections and in the way in which the individual sections are developed at length. The progress that Mozart reveals in his treatment of the finales in *La finta giardiniera* is due, in the main, to Anfossi. We shall have more to say about his setting of this libretto in the context of Mozart's opera.

The numerous other composers of *opere buffe* in Naples at this time added little new to the tradition described above, although some of them, such as Sarti and Martin, we shall encounter again when discussing Mozart's works. Antonio Sacchini (1734–86) was later to become one of the most important representatives of the Gluckian music drama. At the time in question he was noted, rather, for his charm and exceptional gift for melody. *La contadine in corte* of 1765 is heavily influenced by Piccinni in terms of its form and character,[113] captivating its listeners with its wealth of folklike ideas and eloquent orchestral motifs. If suitably revised, it would almost certainly prove successful even today. Also worth mentioning here on account of his personal dealings with Mozart is Domenico Fischietti (*c*1725–after *c*1810). His *dramma giocoso* of 1758, *Il signore dottore*, treads a well-worn path without achieving the level of its predecessors, although in a second work, *Il mercato di Malmantile* (1757), he at least produces a lively picture of a marketplace that the quack Rubbicone honours with a visit. The comedy, of course, is fairly coarse-grained.[114] The second-act finale contains a pre-echo of *Don Giovanni*:

The fact that Venice was able to remain independent of Naples in the field of *opera buffa* was due, above all, to Baldassare Galuppi (1706–85), who was often known simply as 'Il Buranello' from his birthplace at Burano.[115] Although he was, of course, familiar with the art of Naples and

111. This is not an innovation on Anfossi's part, as assumed by Wyzewa and Saint-Foix, *Wolfgang Amédée Mozart*, ii.198, but is already found in Paisiello and Galuppi.

112. Here, too, we find a textual allusion to Orpheus and his lyre, an allusion encountered with striking frequency in the wake of Gluck's opera. A similar complex of ideas occurs in act two, scene fifteen of Mozart's *La finta giardiniera*. Note also the great six-part duet in act three, scene five of this last-named opera.

113. Also worth mentioning in this context is his meaningful use of reminiscence motifs. ◆ Also see Prota-Giurleo, *Sacchini a Napoli*.

114. We even find double-bass solos in the instrumental jokes in the aria in act three, scene four. ◆ Further concerning Fischietti, see Engländer, 'Domenico Fischietti als Buffokomponist in Dresden', and Kipper, *Musikalische Aktion in der Opera buffa: Il mercato di Malmantile von Carlo Goldoni*.

115. See Wotquenne, *Baldassare Galuppi*; and Piovano, 'Baldassare Galuppi: note bio-bibliografiche'.

was no less generous than his Neapolitan colleagues in sprinkling his scores with sicilianas,[116] he was none the less able to go his own way, displaying an independence due in part to his native talent and in part to the particular Venetian tradition, although the lack of surviving scores makes it difficult for us to explore this tradition in detail.[117] Many of the characteristic features of Galuppi's *opere buffe* were already found in Venetian operas in the seventeenth century, notably the idiosyncratic combination of earthiness and brevity that sets them apart from Neapolitan loquaciousness. Where he does not obviously speak the language of Naples, his aria themes all have something curt and often provocative about them, but they are all the more powerfully effective in consequence. Most of them differ from Neapolitan themes in their specific, eloquent rhythms that are not content with traditional templates but successfully seek more individual forms. Here, too, the basis is folk music, but, unlike the Neapolitan composers, Galuppi is markedly fond of anapaestic and dactylic rhythms – the very ones that had literally swamped Venetian opera during its period of decline a century earlier.[118] His introductions and final ensembles contain most examples of this folklike feature. *L'inimico delle donne* (1771) even ends with a pre-echo of Papageno:

But Galuppi is particularly fond of all manner of rhythmic distorions to the basic four-in-a-bar metre when dealing with a particular characteristic. In act two, scene ten of *Il filosofo di campagna* (1754), for example, Lesbina attempts to lead Nardo up the garden path by playing the part of the *finta semplice*:

Act one, scene seven of the same opera includes a good example of Galuppi's dramatic way of breaking off the rhythm at the end of a phrase, generally from the third to the fifth:

116. In *Li tre amanti ridicoli* (1761) the serenades of all three lovers are sicilianas (act two, scenes five to seven).
117. Dent, 'Ensembles and Finales in Eighteenth-Century Italian Opera'.
118. See Abert, *Carlo Pallavicino: La Gierusalemme liberata*, ix.

Mozart made particular use of Galuppi's energetic march rhythms with their insurgent syncopations, as in the first-act finale of *L'inimico delle donne*:

And none of his Italian compatriots could beat Galuppi when it came to using rhythm for comic ends. He is familiar, of course, with tried-and-tested Neapolitan devices such as rapid patter to the accompaniment of realistic motifs, but he is far more sparing in his use of them and, more importantly, he introduces them at totally unexpected places, sometimes even in the theme itself, whereas the Neapolitan composers always wait until the piece is already under way. Take the following example from act two, scene twelve of *I bagni d'Abano* (1753):

This is Galuppi in a nutshell: a rhythmically interesting roguish tune, the vivid little marginal sketch in the bass, the unison and, finally, the completely unexpected way in which the vocal line breaks free – and all this is compressed into six bars of music. It is hardly surprising that his sense of humour is somewhat dry, even gruff but, for that very reason, particularly impressive.

Galuppi's melodic vein is equally uninhibited, preferring unusual intervals, freely introduced suspensions and so on, and it may have been Galuppi who encouraged Mozart to use his characteristic interval of a seventh, notably in *Don Giovanni*. In act one, scene three of *L'amante di tutte* (1760), Mingone looks down superciliously on his fellow humans and rejoices in what he thinks is his new-found wealth:

The following phrases are also common:[119]

And a reminiscence of Cherubino occurs in Agnesina's aria in act two, scene six of *L'inimico delle donne*, in which she laments the fate of women:

   With his peculiarly comic talent and his ability to draw not only on caricature but on other, more subtle means of expression, Galuppi could have posed a far greater threat to the Neapolitan composers if he had not been so careless in dashing off his works. In his evocation of local colour, he is at least their equal as a result of the overtly picturesque element in his music. Scenes such as the hunt in the first-act finale of *Il re alla caccia* (1763), with its clip-clop of horses' hooves and bray of horns, or the seascape in the first-act finale of *La partenza e il ritorno de' marinari* (1764), which recalls the rapt trio in *Così fan tutte*,[120] or the grotesque scene in the Chinese temple in the second-act finale of *L'inimico delle donne* are among the most successful examples of local colour at this time. Needless to add, the orchestra plays a leading role here, with Galuppi differing from

119.   See also act two, scene five, and the third-act finale of *Il filosofo di campagna*; act two, scene five *et passim* in *Il marchese villano* (1762); and act one, scene six of *La partenza e il ritorno de' marinari* (1764).
120.   The similarity extends to the murmuring accompaniment of the first and second violins playing in thirds.

his Neapolitan rivals in that his motifs are not merely comical in a generalized way but more substantial and individual, as in the following examples from the second-act finale and act three, scene five of *L'amante di tutte*:

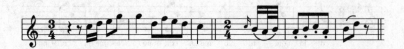

Above all, however, these motifs are intelligently introduced at significant points in the action, rather than dominating the stage from the outset, as they do with the Neapolitan composers. In terms of superficial orchestral colour, of course, Galuppi is content with traditional practices and, as such, is markedly inferior to the Neapolitans.[121]

Galuppi's handling of questions of form reveals great intelligence and adaptability. Especially noteworthy is his careful treatment of *secco* recitative, which finds expression more especially in his wittily animated bass lines. In the arias themselves, the popular strophic song plays a major role. No less astonishing is the variety with which he manages to treat the inevitable siciliana, from the consciously lyrical to the charming and melancholic and, finally, to an intentionally exotic tone. Although his operas include bravura *da capo* arias, these are largely overshadowed by freer forms of which the brief cavatina is particularly popular. Among the various types of aria, the most important is the binary type with a change of time-signature and tempo, with both sections being repeated. But the repetition is rarely literal, generally involving variation and expansion, often with a stretta-like coda that serves as a climax. These variations are Galuppi's particular strong point. The allegro section is often no more than a free variation of the andante.

Galuppi is strikingly sparing in his use of ensembles within the acts. The only regular feature is the folklike *introduzione* that is also found in the works of Neapolitan composers, although he is also fond of the multisectional duet that contains within it a miniature drama, with the alienation and reconciliation of the lovers building to an effective climax.[122] At the same time, Galuppi was particularly important for the development of the finale. Although he was familiar with the Piccinnian rondo-finale,[123] he soon reveals a desire to provide a thematic link between the individual sections, a desire already apparent in the second-act finale of *I bagni d'Abano*. From a poetic point of view, these thematic allusions are often even more subtly elaborated than was the case with Piccinni. But we also find a freer form of the finale in his works, with the main stages of the action depicted in a series of independent sections set as traditional closed forms or, in the manner of Logroscino, in freer forms, depending on the particular situation. This type of finale is already found in *I bagni d'Abano* and *Il filosofo di campagna*. But in each case the finale ends with a carefree, homophonic ensemble, no matter how conflictual the situation on stage. That the finale was still in a state of flux is clear from the many individual numbers to which the other members of the cast make only a fleeting contribution. But Galuppi soon learnt how to divide the ensemble into separate groups and play them off against each other with considerable dramatic skill. Indeed,

121. A double orchestra features in act two, scene two of *Il re alla caccia*; and the ottavino finds delightful use in act one, scene one of *L'amante di tutte*. Particularly common is the use of pizzicato in the violins in the many guitar serenades. A typical example of the 'instrumental aria' is Onofrio's aria in act one, scene nine of *Li tre amanti ridicoli*, which even includes some witty double-bass solos.

122. It is often found in the third act, effectively replacing the extended finale, which is generally missing here.

123. It is first found – evidently under Piccinni's influence – in *L'amante di tutte* (1760). The first two finales of *Il marchese villano* (1762) are both rondos in the freest sense of the term.

one of the main attractions of his finales lies in the living interplay between these different groups, an attraction increased by the fact that each part has its own motif of genuinely Galuppian power, which is developed in the course of the finale.[124] In general, the difference between the Neapolitans and the Venetians emerges with particular clarity here: the former are more animated and more high-spirited, while the latter are earthier and coarser but often also more characterful. Galuppi's ability to create highly effective scenes is especially apparent here: one thinks, for example, of the ball scene in the second-act finale of *I marinari* (a scene which, with its minuet, is particularly important for Mozart) and the supper scene in the first-act finale of *L'amante di tutte*. In both cases, it is the orchestra that is largely left to depict the festivities.

Only in his later works, and evidently under Neapolitan influence, do Galuppi's operatic sinfonias reveal a more individual aspect, especially in terms of the contrasts between their themes. Yet even here he occasionally falls back on folk music, as in the final section of the sinfonia to *L'amante di tutte*.[125]

From Venice we have a direct link with Vienna in the person of Florian Gassmann (1729–74), who spent part of his formative years in Venice. *Opera buffa* came to Vienna in 1757 with Giuseppe Scarlatti but soon acquired a different aspect as a result of its encounter with other genres, notably French comic opera, autochthonous Viennese folk music and Viennese instrumental music. Not even Mozart was able to resist this combination. Together with a number of lesser talents such as Florian Deller (1729–73),[126] Gassmann is the main representative of this Viennese *buffa* style,[127] which differs from the Italian tradition mainly in its melodic and orchestral writing. Alongside genuinely Italian aria themes we find others reminiscent, in part, of Viennese songs and, in part, of French *opéras comiques*.[128] These are songs of more individual life and more freely structured, with broader melodies, and here Gassmann clearly prepared the way for Mozart, especially in those cases where he is concerned to express innocence and yearning.[129] But he often – and successfully – attempts to deal consciously with the whole range of stylistic elements.[130] Another feature that he shares with Mozart is the far more subdued nature of his comedy, which rarely achieves the boisterous mirth of the Italians. Instead, we find signs of a more complex psychological characterization that is no longer content with mere caricature. *La contessina*, in particular, includes some fine examples of the mixture of contradictory features within one and the same character.[131] But Gassmann is particularly fond of using the orchestra to achieve this end. From its sinfonia onwards, this work contains numerous carefully elaborated inner parts that are markedly different from the more negligent Italian manner. Such care reflects the influence of Viennese

124. Cf. the beginning of the finale of *Li tre amanti ridicoli*.
125. ◆ Further concerning Galuppi, see Della Corte, *Baldassare Galuppi: profilo critico* and *L'opera comica italiana nel '700*, especially i.141–72 and ii.216–46 ; and Heartz, 'Vis comica: Goldoni, Galuppi, and L'Arcadia in Brenta'.
126. See Abert, 'Die dramatische Musik'.
127. Donath, 'Florian Leopold Gassmann als Opernkomponist'; see also Abert, 'Joh. Christian Bachs italienische Opern und ihr Einfluß auf Mozart'.
128. In Smorfiosa's aria in act one, scene eight of *L'opera seria* (1769) we even find an echo of Amor's first aria from Gluck's *Orfeo ed Euridice*.
129. For examples, see Donath, 'Florian Leopold Gassmann', 126 and 200–1; see also Haas's edition of *La contessina*, 51, 99, 106, 254 *et passim*.
130. In *La contessina* (no. 22), the disguised Marquis sings a French chanson, and in the second-act finale the disguised peasant sings a minor-key siciliana; but we also find French influence in the Contessina's cavatina (no. 4), with its coquettish syncopations, as well as in the third-act finale. (The opening of the cavatina also contains pre-echoes of the menuetto from *Don Giovanni*.)
131. A good example is Pancrazio's aria (no. 3), with its constant changes of mood, which also find expression in the dynamics. But perhaps the best example is the Contessina's aria (no. 9), which is a miniature masterpiece in terms of its conscious vacillation between conflicting emotions.

instrumental music, as does the tendency to write for concertante instruments. Not only the sinfonias afford evidence of this tendency (the sinfonia to the third act of his *L'opera seria* even includes a complete sonata-form fugue of a kind found in Michael Haydn's contemporary symphonies), so, too, does the orchestral writing in the arias and other vocal numbers. In this way, the witty motivic writing in the orchestra in Vienna acquired a new subtlety: many of Gassmann's numbers are simply orchestral pieces with a light declamatory coating.

This same tendency to adopt stricter procedures is also found in Gassmann's ensembles, with their frequent brief canons. Note, too, the effectiveness with which the different voices are grouped together to create a sense of contrast à la Galuppi and their ability to build to a climax, an ability that is often highly effective when combined with suitable words.[132] Formally, these ensembles are notable for their immense variety, extending from rondo form to freer, through-composed sections. The arias, too, reveal a remarkable variety, in spite of their usual preference for binary form. The individual handling of the *secco* recitative is a legacy of Galuppi.[133]

Admittedly, Gassmann was not one of the major composers of *opere buffe* and, in general, he never succeeded in breaking free from the Italian model. But we find in his works traces of an attempt to internalize the whole genre and, in particular, to individualize the various types. The way in which in *La contessina*, for example, he observes and contrasts the two characters of Pancrazio – trustingly innocent, yet self-possessed – and the proudly aristocratic and eccentric countess is in itself sufficient to explain the opera's success: the graphic contrast between these two social classes was based on real life and was to bulk large, of course, in *Le nozze di Figaro*. But there are other aspects of Gassmann's character, too, that remind us of Mozart. Just as he includes cantabile themes in his sinfonias, so in his *opere buffe* he sets store by a more subtle characterization, treating his characters as a combination of various living forces, rather than exaggerating a single characteristic. Nor, finally, should we forget his gift for parody, a gift which in *L'opera seria* (a setting of words by Calzabigi that is also one of our most graphic accounts of operatic conditions at this time) assumes an altogether grotesque dimension.[134]

132. Gassmann frequently achieves this degree of effectiveness either by shortening the note-values, as in the Contessina's vocal line in the first-act finale and in the trio (no. 19), or by bringing the individual vocal lines closer and closer together, as in the first- and second-act finales.
133. See Haas's edition of *La contessina*, XI.
134. ◆ Further, see Heartz, *Haydn, Mozart and the Viennese School 1740–1780* and Kleinertz, 'Musik als Parodie: Bemerkungen zu Florian Leopold Gassmanns Dramma giocoso La contessina'.

14

La finta giardiniera

The list of characters is as follows:

Don Anchise Podestà di Lagonero, amante di Sandrina (tenor)
La Marchesa Violante Onesti, amante del Contino Belfiore, creduta morta, sotto nome di
    Sandrina in abito di giardiniera (soprano)
Il Contino Belfiore, primo amante di Violante ed ora di Arminda (tenor)
Arminda, gentildonna Milanese, prima amante del Cav. Ramiro ed ora promessa sposa al
    Contino Belfiore (soprano)
Il Cavaliere Ramiro, amante di Arminda dalla stessa abbandonato (soprano)
Serpetta, Cameriera del Podestà innamorata del medesimo (soprano)
Roberto, Servo di Violante, che si finge suo cugino sotto nome di Nardo in abito da
    giardiniero, amante di Serpetta, da lei non corrisposto (bass)

    The Marchesa Violante Onesti has been injured by her lover, the Conte Belfiore, in a fit of jealousy. Believing he has killed her, he flees, whereupon she herself sets out in disguise in search of him. She is accompanied on her search by a faithful servant, Roberto. Both are taken on as gardeners by Don Anchise, the Podestà (mayor) of Lagonero, she as Sandrina, he as Nardo. Don Anchise falls in love with his beautiful gardener and as a result neglects his chambermaid Serpetta, whom he had previously been courting and for whose favours Nardo now sues in vain. Serpetta resents the intrusive presence of Sandrina and Nardo. Also staying with Don Anchise as his house guest is Count Ramiro, who was the lover of Don Anchise's niece, Arminda, before being dismissed in favour of Belfiore.

    The opera begins with the festive preparations for the reception of Arminda and Belfiore. Ramiro tells the Podestà that he is unhappy in love, then leaves. In turn, Don Anchise attempts to declare his love for Sandrina, but is repeatedly interrupted by Serpetta. Sandrina tells Nardo that she is thinking of leaving in order to escape from the Podestà's importunate attentions. She complains about men's faithlessness. Ramiro re-enters to complain about women's faithlessness, while Nardo complains about Serpetta's hard-heartedness. The proud and foppish Conte Belfiore arrives and welcomes the capricious Arminda as his bride. There follows a tiff between Nardo and Serpetta, after which Sandrina discovers that Arminda is Belfiore's bride, causing her to faint. Arminda calls on Belfiore to help and Ramiro, too, comes running in. To their utter consternation, the four lovers recognize each other. The Podestà arrives and demands an explanation, but in vain. Instead, Serpetta stokes the fires of his jealousy by telling him that she has just seen Belfiore flirting with Sandrina. He decides to keep an eye on them. Sandrina confesses that she is Violante, and Belfiore throws himself at her feet in contrition. The others characters arrive, heap obloquy on the pair, and the first act ends in general confusion.

The second act opens with Ramiro reproaching Arminda with being unfaithful, a charge repeated by Arminda to Belfiore, whereupon Serpetta adds her voice of condemnation by pouring scorn on Nardo. There follows a further scene between Sandrina and the repentant Belfiore in which she declares that she was merely expressing the sentiments of her acquaintance Violante. Belfiore apologizes and takes her hand in order to kiss it, only to find that he is holding the hand of the Podestà, who has slipped in unobserved. Belfiore rushes out in dismay. The Podestà declares his love for Sandrina, at which point Ramiro accuses Belfiore of murdering the Marchesa Onesti and demands that he launch an official enquiry in his capacity as mayor. The Podestà postpones the wedding and questions Belfiore, whose answers merely serve to increase his suspicions. At this point Sandrina reveals her true identity as Violante, only to encounter disbelief. Alone with the Count, she declares that she is not really Violante but that she had merely hoped to save him through their physical similarity. Serpetta now tells the Podestà and Ramiro that Sandrina has fled, but then tells Nardo that Arminda has hidden her in a nearby forest in order to prevent her from disturbing her wedding to Belfiore. All then meet in the darkness of the forest, an encounter that gives rise to all manner of mistaken identities. Only when Ramiro arrives with torches does their confusion turn to recriminations, which in turn give way to astonishment at the discovery of Sandrina and the Count, who have both been reduced to madness by this bewildering turn of events.

The third act begins with Serpetta pouring scorn on Nardo for his continuing infatuation, after which Sandrina and Belfiore, still insane, arrive and put him to flight. In turn, the Podestà is sent packing by Serpetta, Arminda and Ramiro, who is again spurned by Arminda. To the strains of a lullaby, Sandrina and Belfiore recover from their madness and in the following duet she finally yields to his entreaties. On hearing this news, Arminda is reconciled with Ramiro, Serpetta with Nardo. Only the Podestà is left on his own.

That the libretto is directly inspired by Goldoni's and Piccinni's *La buona figliuola* is immediately apparent. Both are examples of the genre of *comédie larmoyante* that had come into fashion following the success of Samuel Richardson's *Pamela*. In both, the main character is a virtuous young woman who, after surviving all manner of dangers and temptations, finally turns out to be a member of the aristocracy. In both works, moreover, she disguises herself as a gardener. The main difference between the two is that Piccinni's libretto is much more classical in tone than Mozart's: in the former work, the action develops along relatively simple and transparent lines, whereas in the latter it becomes obscure and often tasteless as a result of the various additional ingredients intended to inject a certain sensationalist piquancy into the proceedings. The poet[1] evidently wanted to be the servant of two masters: on the one hand, he wanted to write a modern sentimental comedy, while on the other he was unwilling to forgo the old traditional *buffo* characters and motifs. The result is a hybrid piece clumsily cobbled together from a mass of disparate elements that often fly in the face not only of good taste but even of basic common sense. We must bear such comparisons in mind if we want to do justice to *Così fan tutte*.

Of Mozart's original score (K196), only the second and third acts have survived in two separate volumes running to a total of 344 sides. The first act is missing and there is no known copy of the Italian score, so that the recitatives of act one are no longer extant.[2]

---

1. ◆ This is now thought to be Abbate Giuseppe Petrosellini; see NMA II/5/8/1, IX.
2. A copy of the first act with German words in the Munich Library appears to be based on Mozart's autograph score. In the AMA, the first act includes only the German words. ◆ The copy, which probably dates from around 1800, is now in Munich, Bayerische Staatsbibliothek (shelfmark Mus. mss. 5593). Other important, surviving sources for the opera include score copies from *c*1800 in the Mährisches Museum, Brünn (shelfmark A17.036), and the library of the Gesellschaft der Musikfreunde, Vienna (shelfmark Cod. Mus. 18.649).

Around 1780 Mozart revised the work and turned it into a German singspiel referred to as *Das verstellte Gärtner-Mädchen* in Heinrich August Ottokar Reichard's *Theater-Kalender* of 1781.[3] It was performed under this title in Frankfurt in 1789.[4] It is not known who prepared the German translation, but it may have been Johann Andreas Schachtner: if so, he revealed considerably greater skill than in his other poetic effusions. Copies of the full score have survived, and a number of arias were published by André under the title *Die Gärtnerin aus Liebe*. A complete vocal score was later published by Karl Ferdinand Heckel in Mannheim. Leopold Mozart entered the German words in the original full score and at the same time made a handful of insignificant changes to the vocal line for reasons of prosody.[5] For the Munich performances, by contrast, various cuts were made to the recitatives and to four of the arias ('Vorrei punirti indegno', 'Una damina, una nipote',

3. ✦ The impetus for this revision was probably the visit to Salzburg of Johann Heinrich Böhm's travelling theatrical troupe; Böhm played Salzburg from early April to early June 1779 and again from September 1779 to the beginning of Lent 1780. See Fellmann, *Die Böhmsche Theatertruppe und ihre Zeit*; Deininger, 'Die deutsche Schauspielergesellschaft unter der Direktion von Johann Heinrich Böhm, einem Freunde der Familie Mozart, in Augsburg in den Jahren 1779 und 1780'; and Rech, 'Böhm und Schikaneder: Zwei Salzburger Theaterimpresarios der Mozart-Zeit'.

4. The work was performed as *Sandrina oder die verstellte Gräfin* by Böhm's company in Frankfurt on 2 April 1782; see Carl Valentin, *Geschichte der Musik in Frankfurt am Main vom Anfange des XIV. bis zum Anfange des XVIII. Jahrhunderts*, 256.

5. There exists a further adaptation with a new German text, of which Jahn (*W. A. Mozart*, first edition, i.367ff.) knew only the Hauser fragment. The complete orchestral score and wordbook of this *Gärtnerin aus Liebe* are lodged in the Dresden Landesbibliothek (Sammlung Öls 65). In this version the characters have German names: the Podestà is the Governor of Lagonero, Arminda is Agnese, Belfiore is the Count of Aosta, Ramiro is the Marchese Grimaldi, Sandrina–Violante is Röschen–Juliane, and Serpetta and Roberto are Friederike and Philipp. 'Mio padrone, io dir voleo' is missing. The libretto includes a number of important stage directions: the andantino that begins the first-act finale, for example, is headed 'as though in a dream'; and at the adagio ma non molto we read: 'As soon as they stop singing, all remain motionless, as though thunderstruck.' Even more important, however, is the fact that the allegro section of 'Care pupille, pupille belle' is here sung by both the Count and the Governor (Podestà) alternating with each other, so that the section beginning 'Padrone stimatissimo' is now sung by the Podestà, while the second section, 'Destin maledettissimo' and so on, is given to the Count, a redistribution that naturally adds to the comic effect in no small way. The spoken dialogue is freely adapted from the *secco* recitatives and in act one, scene seven includes a highly topical reference to Lavater: here Agnes consults a book illustrating physiognomic types and containing pictures of faithless lovers, one of which resembles the Count. Even more far-reaching are the musical changes, which consist in often extensive cuts and much heavier orchestration. The ritornellos in particular are frequently reduced to only a few bars, but there are also cases, notably in 'Ah non partir . . . Già divento freddo' and 'Tu mi lasci', where whole sections have been cut. Elsewhere ('Si promette facilmente') individual passages have been transposed or ('Da Scirocco a Tramontana') actual changes have been made. The orchestral revisions consist, on a purely superficial level, of the addition of trumpets (clarini), timpani and especially clarinets. Incomparably more important, however, is the forward-looking use of the strings – especially the violas and cellos – and winds. These last-named instruments are used in a manner entirely reminiscent of the later Mozart, providing a bridge at the end of individual thematic sections by means of brief but expressive phrases, while also adding colour. Above all, they combine with the strings in the new manner established by the Mannheim composers, who no longer used them merely in individual passages but throughout each piece in general. Almost all the string episodes are permeated by the sound of the wind instruments, but the solo writing, too, is far more striking, as is clear from the orchestral jokes in 'Dentro il mio petto io sento' and 'Da Scirocco a Tramontana'. With the single exception of 'Un marito, oh Dio, vorrei', the instrumental colour is substantially altered in every number: in 'Welche Pracht! welche seltne Schönheit', for example, the original oboes have been replaced by flutes and clarinets. The original subject groups have been retained (as have the coloratura flourishes), but with occasional variants. 'Care pupille, pupille belle', for instance, now begins as follows:

Dynamic and tempo markings are both more carefully indicated than in the familiar version of the score. In short, this adaptation is entirely independent both musically and textually and in every respect represents a marked improvement on the original. The changes are by no means as insignificant as Jahn claims but clearly reveal a specific approach and an extremely skilful hand. The handwriting of both the words and the music belongs to the 1780s rather than the 1790s, and so it is entirely possible that Mozart took up the work again following his return from Paris and that the revisions date either from Salzburg or from his early years in Vienna. The instrumentation in particular reveals the same delight in new sonorities as is also found in *Idomeneo*, for example. The other evidence leaves us in the lurch, of course. If, conversely, we assume that this version is the work of another arranger, he must have had an excellent knowledge of Mozart's style and have been a composer of particularly refined and assured taste.

'Ah non partir . . . Già divento freddo', 'Mio padrone, io dir volevo'). (The passages in question are indicated either by being scored through in red or by being pasted over.) For one scene, an abbreviated version of the dialogue was newly set by Mozart. The shortened version of the arias was taken over into the German adaptation of the work, although this verson also includes one aria ('Chi vuol godere il mondo') marked in red with the words 'to be omitted'. That Mozart himself was involved in these revisions is clear from two accompanied recitatives that have survived in his own hand on separate sheets of paper and that were retained in the German version of the work. The *secco* recitatives of the Italian original were replaced by spoken dialogue, with the German cues entered in another hand. We do not know whether Mozart also took this opportunity to make changes to the music, although this was certainly his usual practice. At all events, these changes cannot have been far-reaching, as the whole style of the score essentially reflects the state of his artistic development around 1775.

That Mozart was familiar with Anfossi's score[6] emerges from fact that a number of pieces[7] are designed along similar lines. There are also individual echoes.[8] But this is the full extent of Mozart's dependency on his Italian colleague.[9] Far more important than these superficial similarities is his clear attempt to break free from Anfossi. A comparison between the two works is highly instructive for the light that it sheds on Mozart's growing independence vis-à-vis his models. Whereas Anfossi remains true to type and writes a quintessential Italian *opera buffa* with clearly delineated characters, Mozart attempts to create a more individualized work. Genre scenes of a kind that Anfossi conjures up in a single number are now spread over two or even three sections. Where Anfossi begins straightaway with a fully developed melodic line, Mozart starts with a passage of recitative. And features that Anfossi lovingly elaborates are conscientiously avoided, while others that Anfossi neglects are fully worked out. Above all, there is no mistaking Mozart's desire for greater psychological and dramatic depth. That he sometimes departs quite radically from the *buffa* style and, in spite of his superior gifts as a musician, falls short of Anfossi's stylistic mastery will become clear shortly. If this work is particularly important in terms of Mozart's development, it is because it is his first attempt at a practical critique of the Italian *buffa* manner, for all that the critique is not yet entirely successful.

La finta giardiniera clearly marks a distinct advance on *La finta semplice*, yet it would be wrong to speak of it in the same breath as *Le nozze di Figaro*: even in his choice of libretto, Mozart is far from scaling the peaks that he was later to achieve as a dramatist. Admittedly, his later mastery shines through at various points and most of the numbers are so manifestly Mozartian in style that it is impossible to imagine them as the work of another composer, yet this very fact demonstrates that it is possible to be a gifted and accomplished musician long before one becomes a musical dramatist. Mozart was still only nineteen and lacked the necessary maturity of character, outlook and experience, and instead of exploring the characters and their actions in depth, his approach remained superficial and unduly concerned with detail. It is enough to glance at the individual

6. Textually, the two works are identical, the only exception being the opening section of the mad scene in the second-act finale (from 'Mio Tirsi' to 'grato piacer'), which is missing from Anfossi's version. Conversely, Mozart did not set the second part ('Senti l'ussignuolo') of the duet 'Tu mi lasci' in act three, scene five.

7. In both operas, for example, a sung *introduzione* takes the place of the sinfonia's third section.

8. Notably in the arias of Ramiro ('Se l'augellin sen fugge'), Arminda ('Si promette facilmente'), Belfiore ('Da Scirocco a Tramontana'), Serpetta ('Un marito, oh Dio, vorrei', 'Chi vuol godere il mondo') and the Podestà ('Mio padrone, io dir volevo').

9. Wyzewa and Saint-Foix, *Wolfgang Amédée Mozart*, ii.198, place far too much emphasis on this dependency: the vast majority of the formal characteristics that they ascribe to Anfossi are also found in other contemporary Italian composers.

characters to see the truth of this remark. With most of them, it is simply impossible to gain a self-contained and unified picture on the strength of their various utterances. Instead, one has the impression that Mozart wrote not entire parts but only individual arias. Of course, the way in which he did so is entirely typical of him and throws significant light on his development as a dramatist (we shall return to this point in a moment), but to insist that his art of characterization is still in its infancy in this opera is by no means the same as denying its very existence.

The character of Sandrina is clear proof of this. Her first aria ('Sarei felice appieno') breathes the same spirit of mischievous dalliance as we find with all the young women in Italian opera who complain at the unfaithfulness of their wicked menfolk, yet it is mixed with an element of innocence in the melodic writing that derives from Viennese *opera buffa*. At the same time, however, we learn absolutely nothing about her heartfelt anguish. How differently Piccinni's long-suffering heroine expresses herself in her first number, to say nothing of Mozart's Countess. Only in her second aria ('Geme la tortorella') does Sandrina strike a more individual note. The text is that of a fashionable simile aria about a lovesick turtle-dove (a popular theme at this time[10]), whose cooing is depicted – in the Italian tradition – by the orchestra. Yet her grief finds expression in a moving and genuinely Mozartian mixture of charm and melancholy. By contrast, her third aria ('Un voce sento al core') clearly reveals the novice dramatist with its lack of inner unity. Here the text contains three different ideas: the coquettish flattery addressed to the infatuated Podestà, the reference to how unhappy she would be if he chided her, and the popular *buffa*-like appeal to the lovely ladies in the audience. Mozart adopted a different stylistic approach to each of these three ideas, treating them in highly contrastive ways and even striking a profoundly tragic note in the second section, where there is a palpable lack of the parodistic element that the Italians invariably added at such points. We shall encounter further examples of these sudden outbursts of heightened emotion and unmitigated tragedy, all of which were evidently meant to be taken seriously.

A completely different Sandrina emerges from her last two arias ('Crudeli, fermate, crudeli' and 'Ah dal pianto, dal singhiozzo'). Here the poetic situation, depicting the abandoned young woman prey to all the terrors of the dark forest, derives from the tried-and-tested stock-in-trade of *opera seria*, with its traditional *lamento* scenes, but Mozart is guilty of heaping Pelion upon Ossa by intensifying the tragic component and ignoring the way in which the character has previously been depicted.[11] The result is an emotionally charged scene that could easily come from an *opera seria*. Here Sandrina suddenly grows in stature and becomes a heroine in the grand tradition, expressing herself in highly idiosyncratic ways. The first of these two final arias is dominated by a wildly impassioned motif in the violins with a diminished fourth and *forte* final beat:

10. Cf. the opening chorus from Gluck's *Orfeo ed Euridice.*
11. No less remarkable is the fact that Mozart has combined this great scene not only with the following finale (a combination implied by the plot) but also with Serpetta's preceding aria, which has nothing in common with it and is even separated from it by a scene change.

It is constantly accompanied by typically Mozartian syncopated harmonies and a defiant motif in the bass that is repeated in the Gluckian manner:

In turn, this last-named motif is accompanied by *forte* chords in the woodwind on the final beat of the bar.

In the face of this agitated turmoil in the orchestra, the vocal line rarely succeeds in rising above a few desperate outbursts and, apart from a single brief attempt to launch a melodic line, is confined to declamatory phrases. This is no longer what Jahn terms the 'breathless anxiety of a tender-hearted and timid young woman'[12] but the indignant despair of a tragic heroine, a sentiment audibly combined with the desire for vengeance. But the whole aria breathes a curiously agitated, typically Mozartian spirit of impassioned utterance, with its resigned minor-key character and its characteristic dissonances and modulations familiar from the composer's Masses and symphonies. The orchestral motifs from the aria are then taken over into the following *accompagnato*, which ends quietly with a surprising enharmonic shift to A minor. Sandrina's cavatina ('Ah dal pianto, dal singhiozzi') shares with its predecessor the same sense of disquiet in the orchestra, the same declamatory writing in the vocal line and the same heightened emotion. Far from growing calmer, the character descends into a state of utter hopelessness, a state that acquires its ability to move the listener through its brief melismatic motifs in the vocal line and interplay between oboe and bassoon. It is followed by an *accompagnato* with onomatopoeic figures in the orchestra that gives way in turn to the finale, a transition effected in a typically Mozartian manner with broken chords in the strings that help to maintain the sense of tension. In itself, this tragic scene constitutes a significant achievement on the composer's part, but it falls completely outside the framework of a normal *opera buffa*. Of course, even the Italians occasionally included individual tragic arias in their *opere buffe*, but they would never have introduced such a sustained note of seriousness as this, unless they were writing a parody, which is out of the question here. In terms of its characterization of Sandrina, too, the scene stands entirely apart. The role was written for Rosa Manservisi, who was highly praised by contemporaries both as a singer and as an actress.[13]

No less inconsistent is the characterization of the role of Count Belfiore, assuming that we may speak of characterization at all in this context. The part was created by the *buffo* Felice Rossi,[14] although the character is no more comic by nature than Sandrina, being one of those popular and generous cavaliers who, consciously or unconsciously, are always in thrall to more than one woman at once. As a perfect gentleman, he begins by praising Arminda's beauty ('Che beltà, che leggiadria'), striking a note of manly ardour that occasionally anticipates Belmonte. All the more bewildering, then, is his *buffa* aria ('Da Scirocco a Tramontana'), in which he regales the hapless

---

12. Jahn, *W. A. Mozart*, fourth edition, i.243. Strangely enough, Jahn also stresses the 'charm of beauty and grace' in Sandrina's A minor cavatina.

13. Schubart, *Deutsche Chronik*, ii (1775), 267; and Burney, *The Present State of Music in Germany*, i.147. Mozart re-encountered her in Dresden in 1789, and it was here that she later died, having lived to a ripe old age.

14. ◆ Apparently the role was not taken by Rossi but by Johann Evangelist Walleshauser (1735–1816, known as Giovanni Valesi), who later sang the part of the High Priest of Neptune in *Idomeneo*. See Hans Schmid, 'Zur Biographie des bayerischen Hofsängers Giovanni Valesi (Walleshauser)'.

Podestà with a lengthy account of his aristocratic accomplishments told with pompous conceit.[15] Not only is the aria inappropriate in this context, it is also decidedly inferior to its models in terms of its comic effect. In Sandrina's presence, the vain fop quickly reverts to his former role as a lover, who in his next aria ('Care pupille, pupille belle') expresses his feelings with far greater sincerity than he had towards Arminda. Here is an aria full of real emotional depth of a kind typical of Mozart. That it ends on a comical note is the result of the situation on stage, with the Count taking hold of the Podestà's hand, thinking it to be Sandrina's. His part again descends into fatuousness when he goes mad on stage ('Ah non partir . . . Già divento freddo'). Mad characters are by no means unusual with the composers of Italian *opere buffe*,[16] but they are invariably comic figures that librettists, too, tended to use to parody *opera seria*, as is the case with the present scene, with its thunder and lightning, its various other natural phenomena and its reference to the Elysian Fields. Mozart, too, begins by striking an emphatically tragic note,[17] but the orchestral writing – its motifs constantly and importunately changing – betrays a sense of parody that comes clearly to the fore in the following aria in E flat major, and while its slow section is tragic in tone, the orchestra again teems with all manner of motifs familiar to Mozart's listeners from the *opere buffe* of the period. Initially, too, the vocal line incorporates *buffa* elements. The menuetto section gives somewhat homely expression to the joy felt at recovering from madness. It is framed by an independent orchestral idea which, as Sonnleithner was the first to point out, recalls both the trio from the menuetto of the D major symphony K385 ('Haffner') and a few bars from the opening allegro of the great E flat major symphony:[18]

Of the lovers' two duets, the first ('Da bravi seguitate') follows on from Nardo's comic aria and finds the lovers still in thrall to madness. Compared with similar pieces by Italian composers adept at using grotesque exaggeration to invest these absurd situations with an additional comic element, Mozart's duet has turned out to be far too serious, with the result that the listener experiences the painful embarrassment of the situation twice over. The lovers' great scene in act three ('Tu mi lasci') is on a far higher level, with its exploration of what is a standard theme in such scenes: the lovers' mutual recognition, followed by temporary discord and ultimate reconciliation. The *dolce sinfonia* to whose strains they wake from their slumbers and, hence, from their madness dominates the beautiful and expressive *accompagnato* with its manifold variations. Sandrina's rejection of the Count in the following adagio recalls the older style of Scarlatti, with the same musical ideas divided between the two parts, so that their plan to separate is belied by the music. The following andantino in 3/8-time brings with it a rapprochement. Here it is the orchestra that generally takes the lead, notably at the beginning, where the oboes proclaim the lovers' true feelings in a moving manner that already looks forward to the later Mozart. We see the characters

15. This is an old motif that is also found in Galuppi's *Il filosofo di campagna* (act two, scene four), *Il marchese villano* and *L'amante di tutte* (act one, scene seven) and Gassmann's *La contessina* (act two, scene six), not to mention Molière.
16. Cf. Traetta's *Il cavaliere errante* discussed above.
17. The pizzicato effect in the andante episode in B flat major derives from Neapolitan *ombra* scenes; see also 'Sì, aspetta' in act three, scene two of Gluck's *Orfeo ed Euridice*.
18. The beginning of the vocal line, by contrast, harks back to a motif from the finale of *Bastien und Bastienne*.

approach each other, step by step, until finally they are reconciled and their happiness finds expression in an Italianate allegro shot through with Mozartian features. With its ardent and typically Mozartian rhythms and melodic outline, one particular motif stands out as a heightened version of Sandrina's main motif from the first-act finale (see below):

dal pia - ce - re, dal con - ten - to già mi bal (za)

It ends with a jubilant coloratura passage that includes a *Bettelkadenz* of a kind very popular with Anfossi, too.

Alongside the work's two main characters, we find a second pair of lovers who are anything but comic in conception: Arminda and her faithful lover Ramiro, whom she constantly mistreats. Later in his career, Mozart was to draw a conscious contrast between the two couples in order that each might lend psychological support and depth to the other. But in the present case there is barely the glimmer of an attempt at such a contrast. As before, individual arias were composed with no regard for any overriding characterization, still less with any concern for the remaining characters. In her opening aria, Arminda appears as a young woman who is as agitated as she is cunning but who, in spite of her aristocratic lineage, lapses into the tone of an artful chambermaid. In her second aria, by contrast ('vorrei punirti indegno'), she is entirely the offended aristocrat thirsting for vengeance. *Pace* Jahn,[19] this aria is most emphatically not parodistic in intent: there is no evidence whatsoever for such a reading. Rather, it is a typically Mozartian G minor movement in all its bitter passion, seething with disquiet and thereby proving that Mozart took the situation entirely seriously, adding considerably to this sense of seriousness by dint of his own individual temperament. We do not know who sang this role in Munich. The role of Ramiro, conversely, was evidently written for a castrato, probably the outstanding soprano castrato Tommaso Consoli (*c*1753–after 1811), who joined the Munich *Kapelle* in 1773 and who was also invited to take part in the gala performance of *La finta giardiniera* in Salzburg. Here, too, we find further evidence of the work's affinities with *opera seria*: the role is entirely serious in character. Yet, for Italian audiences, such sentimental and unhappy lovers were invariably figures of fun. This is not the case with Mozart. Ramiro's entrance aria ('Se l'augellin sen fugge') is entirely serious in terms of its words, form and expression and there is even something moving about its note of calm composure, with only its middle section, in which he speaks of the anguish of love, striking a more agitated and genuinely Mozartian note. Equally arresting is the brevity and violence with which Mozart forces the music back to the *da capo*. The tenderness typical of all such lyrical youths in Italian operas of the period finds further expression in his later aria ('Dolce d'amor compagna'), in which he sings of his hopes and of his love, albeit with a coloratura flourish on the word 'te' that seems imposed on the piece from the outside. But Ramiro's part, too, brings with it a surprise in the form of his final aria ('Va pure ad altri in braccio'), with its outburst of oddly unbridled anger. Note especially the opening ritornello which, as so often in this opera, is entirely independent, not returning until the very end:

19. Jahn, *W. A. Mozart*, i.243.

The melody's chromatically descending line, the two intervals of a sixth and the urgency of the chromatically ascending line at the end are all unmistakably Mozartian. This aria is a counterpart to Arminda's ('Vorrei punirti indegno'), except that it is more vehement and demonic in expression. It is difficult to imagine a bolder or more powerful contemporary description of the despair of a fatally wounded heart than we find at the words 'già misero mi vuoi' and so on. Here, too, Mozart took a thoroughly tragic view of the situation.

The Podestà is a genuinely *buffo* role. As proud of his job as he is dimwitted, the permanently besotted village mayor is a favourite figure in *opera buffa*, and Mozart, too, respected this typology, except that – presumably for personal reasons – he entrusted the role to a tenor rather than to a bass.[20] As a result, the Podestà, at least, emerges as a unified character. Even so, his opening aria – an additional number composed for the German version of the work – does not really fit into this picture, but is an example of a popular type of aria in which the instruments mentioned in the text are heard to comic effect in the orchestra, with the violas in particular being introduced to extremely witty effect by means of a sudden interrupted cadence on B flat. At this point the Italian version includes an aria which, in keeping with the situation on stage, is addressed to Sandrina, 'Dentro il mio petto io sento'. That Mozart himself composed it is beyond doubt.[21] In the Podestà's second aria ('Un damina, una nipote'), it is the man's affected dignity that finds expression, while his third ('Mi padrone, io dir volevo') is a delightful, if overlong, account of the torments of a man assailed on every side. Especially remarkable here is the extremely flexible and independent writing for the orchestra, which already looks forward to the later composer.

The two comic servants Serpetta and Nardo are introduced together in a brief strophic song that could almost have been written by Anfossi ('Un marito, oh Dio, vorrei'). Like the rest of her kind, Serpetta is an out-and-out egoist, malicious and spiteful. As in the Italian operas of the period, she conceals her true character in both her arias ('Appena mi vedon' and 'Chi vuol godere il mondo') behind a charming, mischievous exterior. There is, of course, no trace of the sophistication of Mozart's later soubrettes.[22]

As Violante's faithful servant, Nardo reveals real spirit, but it is a spirit hardly suited to the role of the infatuated simpleton who pursues Serpetta in spite of all the rebuffs that he suffers. His arias feature all manner of tone-painterly effects, including a hammering motif in his first aria ('A forza di martelli') that in the following allegro gives way to a successful imitation of Anfossi's *buffa* style, with its rapid, angular motifs and its grotesque chromatic conclusion. His second aria reveals a skilful handling of rondo form. Here he tries to win Serpetta by complimenting her in various languages and styles, for all of which Italian operas provided plentiful models: at one point he assumes the role of a Frenchman with a rhythmically taut minuet richly ornamented with trills,

20. A tenor was not, of course, entirely unknown here; see Arteaga, *Le rivoluzioni del teatro musicale italiano dalla sua origine fino al presente*, iii.147 and ii.415.
21. *Briefe*, iii.43 (letter of 2 December 1780). Leopold had it copied for Schikaneder.
22. Her arias contain two unmistakable pre-echoes of *Le nozze di Figaro*: 'und schweige zu allem' ('So bald sie mich sehen', bars 11–23) and 'la voglio' ('Chi vuol godere il mondo', bars 106–123).

later becoming an Englishman with a ramrod-backed anglaise. In his third aria ('Da bravi segui-tate') he regales the lovers with a description of the general confusion in the heavens to an increas-ingly agitated orchestral accompaniment; his interjection, 'sono incantati già', already anticipates Leporello's eloquent impishness.

The 'Introduction' to the opera is also the third section of the sinfonia, the first two sections of which are geared to a note of Italian high spirits. It is a fresh-toned homophonic ensemble for Sandrina, Serpetta, Ramiro, Don Anchise and Nardo and is filled with a sense of nuptial celebra-tion. Its third section is a repeat of its opening section. Between them comes a middle section in which each of the soloists expresses his or her own thoughts and situation in appropriate terms, while all the motifs from the outer sections are repeated in suitably modified forms. In this way, Mozart skilfully introduces us to the opera's plot by means of this well-rounded and motivically unified introduction. Admittedly, it belongs far more to the older type of introduction in which the individual characters are introduced one by one, rather than to its later, genuinely dramatic successor, but within these limitations Mozart moves with great assurance and with an unmistak-able sense of dramatic purpose. An even better example is the first-act finale, which is cast in the form of a septet ('Numi! Che incanto è questo') and begins with an impassioned *accompagnato* for the Count interrupted by Sandrina's affecting lament. This is followed by an Allegro into which a motif expressive of whimpering fear is introduced between brief and hurried interjections, before being taken up by the whole ensemble and raised sequentially towards G minor. In an inspired application of the strophic principle, all the characters now have a chance to speak: each begins with the same melodic line that comes to a rest on a single note, the men in the major, the women in the minor, but the way in which the melody continues differs from person to person, depending on his or her character. This section ends with an ensemble passage based on a fragmented melodic line of a kind often found in Italian operas of the period, with even individual words broken up by rests. Above them, the oboes intone a sustained lament in typically Mozartian fashion. The hand of the master emerges still more clearly in the transition to the following adagio and in the adagio itself, with the music modulating from E minor to E flat major (the key associ-ated with otherworldly powers) within two bars by means of broken chords in the bass and synco-pated writing in the upper voices. To the emotionally charged sound of the horns, the Podestà now enters, initially deeply embarrassed, then displaying a mixture of dignity and appeasement due in part to the interval of a seventh that is characteristic of the later Mozart. Abashed, the remaining singers answer in chorus, the syncopations in the orchestra now dissolving into brief semiquavers with rests. And the music modulates from G minor to D major with the same degree of boldness as we found at the beginning of this number, with the result that the appearance of the village mayor assumes the aspect of a visitation from another world and thereby stands out from the finale as a whole. By now the Podestà has recovered his equanimity and vents his anger in no uncer-tain terms. Of all the sections that make up this multisectional finale, this D major episode is the most Italianate, with the melodic line encompassing all the characters, who are barely differentiated. The following G major allegro is the culmination of the entire finale, a rondo treated with both freedom and wit. Its main theme points backwards to Piccinni and forwards to the second-act finale of *Le nozze di Figaro*:[23]

---

23. We must not overlook the introductory quaver figure in *La finta giardiniera*, a figure generally entrusted to the oboes and calculated to invest the motif with a special degree of tension.

Initially, the theme remains the preserve of Sandrina and Belfiore, with the result that it is on them that the limelight falls, with the remaining characters confined to the more or less extended episodes, the most characteristic of which are the comic interludes for Serpetta and the Podestà and Arminda's ironical outburst in E minor, with its eloquent oboe solo. Only towards the end do the other characters take up this theme, but whereas it had previously been heard in the minor, it is now in a bright and penetrating major. And it is also treated canonically in a brilliant example of mordant irony, with the lovers still marooned in their minor tonality and barely able to make any headway in the face of a *force majeure*. This section is a masterpiece not only of characterization but also of gripping tension and of the way in which the language of the orchestra can be exploited to such lively effect. Only rarely did Italian composers produce anything as good as this. Unfortunately, the rest of this finale fails to maintain this same high level: the allegro in 3/4-time continues to play off the individual characters against one another and successfully maintains the same excitable tone, but, in spite of the use of orchestral motifs to portray the sense of confusion, the homophonic final ensemble relapses into the manner of so many Italian final choruses that seek only to bring the act to an effective and brilliant conclusion without serving any higher dramatic purpose.

The second-act finale ('Fra quest' ombre, o questo scuro') is likewise described as a septet. It, too, is multisectional, but with fewer – albeit longer – sections than before. From a purely musical point of view it is as superior to the first-act finale as it is inferior to it in terms of the subtlety of its characterization and its ability to build to an effective climax. It is, of course, the text that is largely to blame for these shortcomings, and even the mature Mozart would have been powerless in the face of so absurd a mad scene. In the first section the whole company meets in the forest and one case of mistaken identity follows another. Here Mozart was essentially left to depict the strangeness of the situation, which he did by adopting the tried-and-tested Italian model and shifting the centre of interest to the orchestra, with more or less declamatory writing for the voices. The result is a picturesque passage that captures both the frightening noises of the forest at night and the characters' timid whispering as they tiptoe to and fro; the skipping basses and chuckling woodwind repeatedly ensure that the situation does not become too serious. And the orchestra remains in control when Ramiro arrives and the tempo changes to allegretto. He is accompanied by servants with torches – delightfully represented by flutes and horns – that suddenly throw light on the situation and reveal all the cases of mistaken identity.[24] On the whole, however, this scene involves only situation comedy of the Italian kind, with no attempt to delineate the characters in any greater depth. In the following section in C major, the general sense of ill-humour finds forceful expression in an emotionally charged motif that returns in the course of the section in the manner of a rondo theme. The episodes are sharply contrasted and are intended to show how the two main characters gradually go mad under the pressure of the main theme, with the various groupings among the characters emerging entirely naturally. With its wind postludes (including a reference to Gluck and Orpheus's lyre), the brief pastorale for the two mad lovers is not without a certain piquant charm, but the end effect is of a slapstick humour of a particularly boorish kind. Here, too, Mozart attempts to build to a large-scale climax, and Sandrina's ecstatic 'Che giubilo è questo' even harks back unconsciously (and with cruel irony) to the main motif from the first-act finale. And while the present finale closes on a note of greater agitation than its predecessor, none of this alters the fact that, however much artistry may have been lavished on this section, it is all set at naught by the silliness of the libretto.

The third-act finale ('Viva pur la Giardiniera') is described simply as a 'Coro' and is a homophonic, if richly orchestrated, ensemble in which the characters issue their standard invitation to the audience to enjoy life.

The *secco* recitatives contribute to the unevenness of the score. The majority are very sketchy, but a number already reveal the quick-fire manner of the Italians, notably in Belfiore's interrogation by the Podestà with its rapid succession of question and answer and animated writing in the basses. Elsewhere – in act three, scene six, for example – Ramiro's emotionally charged aria already casts its shadows over his preceding recitative: here the word-setting is far more expressive than usual.

If *La finta giardiniera* cannot be hailed as a masterpiece, it is none the less of considerable importance for Mozart's development as a dramatist. It reveals, above all, that his dramatic gifts first found expression not in his arias but in his ensembles, where the characters are sharply contrasted. In the arias, conversely, the joins and contradictions are all too plain to hear. This is entirely natural: where the plot moves quickly, with a lively exchange between characters, the eye of the budding dramatist sees his characters in sharper outline than in the monologues of the arias, which placed greater demands on his artistic understanding. Technically, of course, the

---

24. The later Mozart would no doubt have conflated the change of tempo with this effect on the wind instruments, as he did at the well-known passage in the sextet 'Sola sola in buio loco' from *Don Giovanni*.

ensembles presuppose greater mastery, but Mozart was already so advanced in this regard that such passages were no longer likely to cause him any difficulties.

Even more important, however, is the unusual role of tragedy in this opera. By Italian standards, these sudden outbursts of authentic passion devoid of any suspicion of parody were inconceivable, all the more so in that – as we have seen – the characterization is all over the place. Anfossi's opera is innocent of the passions by which Mozart's characters are suddenly wracked, but remains firmly entrenched in the *buffa* tradition, ensuring that while its characters display no depth of emotion, they are not riddled with contradictions either. As a result, the overall impression is of a more harmonious opera that is aesthetically more pleasing than Mozart's, however inferior it may be to the latter in terms of its wealth of invention and sheer originality. But in writing this opera, Mozart took his first tentative step on a road that was to lead to *Le nozze di Figaro*. He was loath to treat deep-seated emotions as no more than a source of ridicule and wherever his librettist allowed him to do so, he emphasized these emotions with all the demonic ardour of his soul, breaking down the barriers of Italian *opera buffa* as effectively as he had done with drawing-room music in many of his instrumental works. For the first time in its history, *opera buffa* acquired a powerful injection of tragic elements, but the result, for the moment, was not the greater nobility and depth that we find later, but a fragmentation of the whole genre. Of course, this is Mozart's first attempt to tear the masks from the faces of his Italian characters and allow them to speak the language of the heart and, as such, it is of supreme importance for his inner development, but he was not yet mature enough to appreciate the common roots of tragedy and comedy and to be able to grasp the interplay of comic and tragic motives in all their depth and truth. Nor was it yet clear to him that he would need a completely new style in order to achieve this synthesis. For now, comedy and tragedy appear alongside each other, with no inner or outer connection, comedy in the motley of *opera buffa*, tragedy in the guise of *opera seria*. *La finta giardiniera* is the work of a young genius driven in a new direction by a dark and irresistibly powerful force. At the time, it was unclear to him where this road might lead. Only to the artist who had known life's harsh vicissitudes was the goal to be revealed in all its blinding clarity.

15

Mozart in Salzburg, 1775–1777

It will be clear from what has been said why, in spite of being a great initial success, *La finta giardiniera* disappeared from the Munich stage after only three performances, while all the other hopes that Mozart had secretly placed in Munich proved as empty as those that Leopold had pinned on Vienna only a short time earlier. It is no wonder, therefore, that it was with extremely mixed feelings that father and son returned to Salzburg, where their old and silent battle with the archbishop awaited them anew. Mozart's next works indicate that, perhaps at his father's suggestion, he was prepared to make an initial attempt to adopt the taste in music that currently prevailed at court. That he did so only with a sense of inner reluctance is clear from the vast majority of them. On a superficial level, his artistic activities were the same as before his visit to Munich: in addition to his duties in the *Kapelle*, he also had to write whatever works were required of him for the church and for court concerts,[1] quite apart from the considerable demands on his time by the aristocracy and respected members of the local middle classes. It is striking that not a single symphony dates from this two-year period,[2] and it is more than likely that Colloredo was so appalled at Mozart's earlier symphonies, with their personal and revolutionary stamp, that he refused to countenance any further experiments in this field. Significantly, Leopold, who was himself still wedded to the old ideal of music as a means of social entertainment, seems to have shared this view, as he wrote to Mozart on 24 September 1778: 'It is better if what does you no honour remains unknown, which is why I have not had any of your symphonies copied, because I knew in advance that, when you are older and have more insight, you will be glad that no one has a copy of them, even though you were pleased with them when you wrote them. One becomes more discriminating with time.'[3]

In April the archbishop received a visit from Maria Theresia's youngest son, the Archduke Maximilian (1756–1801), who had recently caused the French queen some embarrassment as a result of his tactlessness at the Paris carnival.[4] Later to become archbishop of Cologne, he arrived in Salzburg following a brief visit to Munich, and it was to mark this occasion that Mozart was invited to set Metastasio's *Il re pastore* as a *festa teatrale*. There was little time left, as the performance was fixed for 29 April, with a serenata by Fischietti arranged for the previous day.[5]

---

1. ◆ It is not strictly true that Mozart was 'required' to compose for the church and court concerts; according to the decree appointing him court organist in 1779, he was obligated only 'as far as possible [to] serve the court and the church with new compositions made by him' (*Dokumente*, 163, *Documentary Biography*, 183). For the possible implications of this formulation and Mozart's response to it, see Eisen, 'The Salzburg Symphonies: A Biographical Interpretation'.
2. ◆ While it is true that Mozart composed no new symphonies during this period, a manuscript now in Berlin (Staatsbibliothek zu Berlin, shelfmark Mus. ms. autogr. W. A. Mozart KV 250) shows that he did redact the serenade K250 as a five-movement symphony (movements 1, 5, 6, 7 and 8) in 1776 or 1777; apparently he performed the work again in Vienna *c*1785. Other serenades were also revised as symphonies, including K204 and K320.
3. *Briefe*, ii.485. ◆ A different reading of this letter may be that Leopold was not concerned with the idea of music as 'social entertainment' but, rather, with suppressing what he considered less successful juvenilia.
4. Campan, *Mémoires sur la vie privée de Marie Antoinette*, v.107–8.
5. ◆ See Schwindt-Gross, 'Zwei bisher unbekannte Salzburger "L'isola disabitata"-Vertonungen'.

For the performances, Colloredo invited the castrato Tommaso Consoli and the flautist Johann Baptist Becke to travel to Salzburg from Munich. On the 24th, according to the diary of one of the members of Maximilian's retinue, 'In the evening as on the preceding days, *musique* was chosen for the entertainment. . . . At the end of the *musique*, the famous young *Mozart* was heard on the keyboard and played various things by heart with as much art as pleasantness.'[6]

Of Mozart's sacred works, only one can be dated with any certainty to 1775, his epistle sonata K212. Conversely, the following year witnessed the composition of no fewer than four masses K257, 258, 259 and 262, three of which date from the end of the year.[7] In March 1776 he wrote the litany in E flat major K243 and the offertory *Venite populi* for double chorus K260,[8] and in April two more epistle sonatas K244 and 245. In 1777 there followed a further mass, K275,[9] a gradual *Sancta Maria*, K273, dated 9 September, and a further sonata, K274.

Of Mozart' secular works from this period, pride of place must go to the six divertimentos K213, 240, 252, 253, 270 and 289 that he wrote as *Tafelmusik* for Colloredo.[10] Scored for two oboes, two horns and two bassoons, they date from June 1775 to the end of the period under discussion.[11] Later known as the 'Haffner' serenade, the [march and] serenade K249 and 250 were written for the wedding of the Salzburg burgher Franz Xaver Späth and Elise Haffner, the daughter of the respected local businessman and current mayor Siegmund Haffner[12] and was performed on the day before the wedding ceremony, which took place on 22 July 1776. But Mozart was now in demand with the local aristocracy, too. For the name-day of the Countess Antonia Lodron (13 June) he wrote serenades in both 1776 and 1777. Both are mentioned on frequent occasions in his letters.[13] The rehearsal for the 1777 piece was attended by Joachim Ferdinand von Schiedenhofen,[14] who also reports that on 25 July 1777 a serenade was rehearsed at the home of the grocer Giovanni Battista Gussetti. The work, Schiedenhofen goes on, had been written for Nannerl's name-day, 26 July, and consisted of a symphony, a violin concerto played by Mozart himself and a flute concerto performed by Cassel.[15] Presumably the divertimento K251 of July 1776 was likewise intended for Nannerl's name-day. Nothing more is known about the circumstances surrounding the composition of two other works from this period, the serenade K204 of 5 August 1775 and the Serenata notturna K239 of January 1776.[16]

6. ◆ *Dokumente*, 137, *Documentary Biography*, 152–3.
7. ◆ The dates of these masses are uncertain: K258, 259 and 262 may date from 1775; see Tyson, 'The Dates of Mozart's *Missa brevis* K. 258 and *Missa longa* K. 262 (246a)'.
8. ◆ It is not clear that K260 was composed in March.
9. ◆ Although it is almost certain to have been composed in 1777, the earliest authentic source for the mass (Augsburg, Stadt-und Staatsbibliothek, shelfmark H⁺8) may have been copied as late as early 1780.
10. ◆ There is no evidence these works were composed for Colloredo.
11. ◆ Mozart's authorship of K289, although likely, is not certain. No authentic sources for the divertimento survive; the earliest extant copy is a nineteenth-century manuscript in the Bayerische Staatsbibliothek, Munich.
12. See Koch-Sternfeld, *Die letzten dreißig Jahre*, 30 and 187.
13. In his letter of 3 October 1777, Mozart mentions the 'two cassations for the countess' that Leopold describes as the Lodron serenades. The 'last cassation in B flat' that Wolfgang played in Munich (see his letter of 6 October 1777, *Briefe*, ii.41) is the divertimento K287 for string quartet and horns. The earlier piece – K247 – is in F major and dates from June 1776. ◆ The scoring of K287 is probably two horns, two violins, viola, violoncello and double bass.
14. The *Finalmusik* rehearsed in Schiedenhofen's presence on 9 August 1775 and performed on 23 August is the 'Antretter' serenade K185. ◆ Although the serenade K185 was apparently composed for Judas Thaddäus von Antretter's graduation from the Salzburg Benedictine University, this was in 1773. It is more likely that the work Schiedenhofen heard rehearsed on 9 August 1775 was the serenade K204, the autograph of which is dated 5 August 1775.
15. ◆ Joseph Thomas Cassel (?–1788) was court double bassist from 21 June 1777 to 28 December 1788.
16. ◆ Given its date of composition in August, it is likely that K204 was composed for the annual graduation ceremonies at the Salzburg Benedictine University; concerning this tradition, see Kearns, 'The Orchestral Serenade in Eighteenth-Century Salzburg'. The occasion for which K239 was composed remains unknown.

That Mozart now had a firm foothold within the ranks of the aristocracy is also clear from his keyboard compositions. The C major concerto K246 was written in April 1776 for one of his pupils, the Countess Antonia Lützow, who was the wife of the commandant of Hohensalzburg, Count Johann Nepomuk Gottfried von Lützow, while the concerto for three keyboards K242 was composed in February 1776 for the Countess Lodron and her two daughters, Aloisia and Josepha.[17] Mozart's dealings with the nobility and especially with their womenfolk, some of whose younger members received music lessons from the now twenty-year-old composer and who were no doubt worshipped with all the fervour of his young heart, not only increased his self-esteem but also brought out the whole gallant side of his character. The works of this period reveal the aristocratic ideal of music with particular élan, an élan that in turn reflects the composer's inner involvement. This period was also memorable for a visit from a representative of the great world of music outside Salzburg, the famous French pianist Mlle Jeunehomme,[18] whom Mozart later reencountered in Paris. In January 1777 he wrote for her his concerto in E flat major K271, while the concerto in B flat major K238 that he wrote that same month [but a year earlier, in 1776] appears to have been intended for his own use. Nothing further is known about the circumstances surrounding the composition of the five violin concertos of 1775, K207, 211, 216, 218 and 219,[19] which were followed by a sixth, K271a, in 1777,[20] but all demonstrate Mozart's lively interest in the instrument at this time. From August 1776 dates the B flat major trio K254 for keyboard, violin and cello, a work also known as the 'Divertimento à 3'.

Secular vocal works are in a distinct minority, being limited to a handful of arias that Mozart wrote, in keeping with the custom of the times, as insertion arias for individual singers. In May 1775 he wrote two *buffa* arias, 'Con ossequio, con rispetto' (K210) and 'Si mostra la sorte' (K209), which were followed in October by 'Voi avete un cor fedele' (K217) for a character called Dorina.[21] In September 1776 he wrote the *buffa* aria 'Clarice cara mia sposa' (K256) for the tenor Antonio Palmini[22] and the tragic *scena* and rondo 'Ombra felice' (K255) for the contralto castrato Francesco Fortini, the latter to words that had already been set by Michele Mortellari in *Didone abbandonata*.[23] And finally, in August 1777, he wrote an alternative setting of the great *scena* and aria 'Ah lo previdi' (K277) from Paisiello's *Andromeda* for Josepha Duschek. Josepha Duschek was the wife of the Prague pianist Franz Duschek and was herself an accomplished singer and pianist. She came to Salzburg on family business in the summer of 1777 and soon became friendly with Mozart, a friendship to which we shall often have occasion to refer in the course of our narrative. This setting of 'Ah lo previdi' – one of his last works before he left Salzburg and arguably one of his finest concert arias – affords eloquent proof of the profound effect that this kind and beautiful woman had on his highly susceptible heart.

17. ◆ The concerto K242 also survives in an authentic version for two keyboards.
18. In his letters, Mozart refers to her variously as Jenomé and Jenomy. ◆ 'Jeunehomme', a name invented by Wyzewa and Saint-Foix, has been identified as Victoire Jenamy (1749–1812), the daughter of Mozart's friend, the ballet master J. G. Noverre. See Lorenz, 'Konzert für Klavier und Orchester Es-Dur, KV 271 (1777) "Jenamy" (bisher "Jeunehomme")'.
19. In 1776 Mozart wrote an alternative adagio K261 for the A major concerto. It is believed to have been intended for Antonio Brunetti; see *Briefe*, ii.42 (letter of 9 October 1777). ◆ The first of the violin concertos, K207, is now thought on the basis of Mozart's handwriting to date from 1773.
20. Wyzewa and Saint-Foix, *Wolfgang Amédée Mozart*, ii.375–6, are entirely justified in doubting whether the surviving score represents the original version of 16 July 1777. ◆ Neither the authenticity nor the date of the concerto is certain. A dated autograph (Salzburg, 16 July 1777) is alleged to have been known in Paris by 1837 but all trace of this source has disappeared.
21. ◆ Almost certainly this aria was intended for a production of Baldassare Galuppi's *Le nozze di Dorina* (act one, scene four).
22. ◆ For Niccolò Piccinni's *L'astratto ovvero Il giocatore fortunato* (1772).
23. Wyzewa and Saint-Foix, *Wolfgang Amédée Mozart*, ii.339. The words of the aria come, in fact, from act two, scene thirteen of Metastasio's *Issipile*. In 1783 Mozart asked his father to send this aria to him in Vienna: *Briefe*, iii:264 (letter of 12 April 1783).

These were also the final years that Mozart spent in his family home in a state of unsullied harmony. By the time that he returned from Paris in 1779, his mother was dead and the rift that had opened between him and his father was never to heal. The harsh realities of life to which he was first exposed on this journey in any case ensured that the relationship was no longer as close as it had been. For the present, however, he could still enjoy all the blessings of family life, blessings based on a strict sense of religious duty, conscious morality and a heartfelt and trusting affection between its individual members. No doubt Mozart felt the importance of a father's support at a time when he was gradually having to learn to stand on his own two feet. His life as a child prodigy, when his laurels had been relatively easily won, was now behind him, and among his first bitter discoveries was the realization that those laurels had been heaped on the prodigy rather than on the artist. The world had willingly forgiven the child whenever his genius had led him away from the beaten track, but now that he was growing into manhood, it regarded such aberrations as dangerous and not to be tolerated. The genius's battle with the philistines was now beginning to assume palpable forms in Mozart's life, prompting him to criticize his own works, persuading him to sort out in his mind what his aims really were and, above all, increasing his self-awareness and self-assurance, a development which, in turn, increased his hatred of his petty-minded enemies. It was during this period in Salzburg that it gradually became clear to him that the world is willing to accept the gifts of genius as long as they reflect its own desires and opinions, while implacably opposing all his higher demands. Mozart had no difficulty dealing with his more petty-minded critics. More dangerous, by contrast, was the storm that was brewing in the archbishop's palace, for here his very livelihood was at stake. There is no doubt that he was increasingly aware of this danger and that he did all he could to arm himself against it. In this he naturally looked to his father for help. 'After God comes Papa.' His father had proved a pillar of strength in the past, and so Mozart clung to him again now.

Leopold was sensible enough to realize that, with his son's increasing maturity, it was time for him to redefine their relationship. In his most recent letters he had already attempted to change the earlier tone from that of a tutor to that of a fatherly adviser and friend whose concern was not so much to guide his son's genius along certain paths as to give him the strength of character needed to make the right use of his gifts. But Leopold would not have been Leopold if this concession had not had its own very specific limitations. Although gossip continued to leave him cold, especially in Salzburg, he had very particular views on life, views that his family had to accept unconditionally and which, as we have seen, were concerned in the main with questions of utility. Even in his plans for his children's future, superficial advantages were uppermost in his mind: only here did he see the indispensable precondition for the full development of their talent. This principle may be applicable to people of average ability, but as a rationalist at heart, he utterly failed to appreciate the true nature of genius, whose workings are influenced by no external aims. As a result, father and son came into the sharpest conceivable conflict, with Leopold wanting to bring order, rules and a sense of purpose to his son's artistic activities, while Mozart felt himself to be a creative artist in the sense understood by Herder, an artist who acknowledges no human, non-artistic rules. Needless to say, this difference of opinion led to conflicting views on the artist's relationship with his audience. For Leopold as for the whole of aristocratic society, which set the tone in music at this time, it was the audience that was paramount, whereas for Mozart the main emphasis was shifting slowly but surely to the creative artist, in which respect Beethoven was his logical successor.

As long as Mozart was still developing as man and artist, it goes without saying that he submitted to his father's principles. But as soon as he became aware of the wealth of his inner life, conflict was inevitable. Of course, this change took place only very gradually, and during the period in Salzburg with which we are now concerned a state of temporary equilibrium had been reached between the two parties. But it was a state that was bound to end as soon as one or the other of them was put to the test. Leopold's supreme demand – that his son should work in an orderly and efficient way – was beneficial even now. Here, after all, Leopold saw the basis of all bourgeois existence and progress. Apart from his official duties, he had abandoned all his other activities, including even teaching, which was one of his main sources of income, simply in order to keep a better eye on Wolfgang's work.[24] In addition to composing music of his own, Wolfgang also had to write out other composers' works, thereby following a well-established practice.[25] And he was often warmly praised by his father for his enthusiasm and hard work.

A whole series of these exercise books has survived, all of them enclosed in greyish blue covers and containing works in Mozart's hand, ordered and titled by his father, and it may be that Mozart's peculiar practice of sticking to a particular type of manuscript paper over a certain period of time (a practice that is not unimportant for dating his works) goes back to this suggestion of his father's.[26]

In addition, there were his advanced technical studies in the piano, violin and organ, his activities at court and private commissions and, finally, his teaching: Mozart's days were certainly well filled. Meanwhile, his general education was not neglected. Above all, his father ensured that he studied Latin and that his knowledge of French and Italian, gained during his visits to those countries, was not allowed to lie fallow. And Leopold, ever the rationalist, wrote to his son on 18 December 1777, exhorting him to miss no opportunity 'to dip into other useful branches of knowledge', to train his mind 'by reading good books in various languages' and, finally, 'to practise those languages'.[27] Unfortunately, we do not know what Mozart was given to read and what attracted him in particular.[28] It was entirely typical of Leopold, however, that he made both his children keep a joint diary,[29] which they wrote up every evening, making a note of all that they had learnt and discovered in the course of the day. In this way, he hoped to encourage them to pay attention to all that was going on in the world around them.

For all its patriarchal rigour, family life in the Mozart household was by no means lacking in warmth and affection. As before, a mother's hand smoothed away the rough edges of Leopold's strictness of character, while the relationship between brother and sister was marked by an unalloyed sincerity free from all petty jealousies. They were always the best of friends: Nannerl

24. ◆ The source for this incorrect assertion is Nannerl's reminiscences of 1792; see *Dokumente*, 398, *Documentary Biography*, 454. As the family correspondence shows, Leopold continued to perform his duties at court well into the late 1770s and early 1780s: he was on occasion director of the weekly court concerts and conducted at the Cathedral; he continued to teach at the chapel house; and he was frequently responsible for purchasing instruments for the court as well as finding and hiring personnel.
25. ◆ Concerning Mozart's (and Leopold's) copying of works by other composers, as well as other printed and manuscript music owned by them, see Eisen, 'The Mozarts' Salzburg Music Library'.
26. ◆ Presumably Abert refers to a manuscript in the British Library (shelfmark Add. ms. 41 633) with copies of works by Michael Haydn and Ernst Eberlin (K⁶ Anh. A14 and A71–88). Of these, however, only Anh. A14, an 'Ave Maria' by Michael Haydn, is copied by Mozart; the remainder are by Leopold Mozart. The copy of Anh. A14 probably dates from 1773–5; the others were written down at various times during the 1770s. For details, see Eisen, 'The Mozarts' Salzburg Music Library', 131–4.
27. *Briefe*, iii.190 (letter of 18 December 1777).
28. ◆ Some indication of Mozart's reading habits may be gained from the inventory of books made at the time of his death in 1791; see *Dokumente*, 497–8 and 509–10, *Documentary Biography*, 587–9 and 601–2. For a more detailed account, see Konrad and Staehelin, *allzeit ein buch*.
29. Unfortunately, only a brief fragment has survived; see Lewicki, 'Mozarts Jugendtagebuch'. ◆ For a modern edition of the diary, see *Briefe*, ii.541–6 and iii.3–12, 33–5, 39–41, 44 and 47. It is by no means clear, as Abert suggests, that Leopold 'made' Wolfgang and Nannerl keep this diary; the nature of the entries suggests that it was a private, if hardly secret, account of their daily life in Salzburg, a document that Mozart, as a mischievous brother, frequently intruded upon with irreverent entries of his own.

regarded her brother's successes with ungrudging pride and willingly put up with his endless teasing and the colourful language in which it was couched, because she knew that she could count on him through thick and thin. They were also on the best of terms with their domestic staff: the serving maids were no more overlooked in their letters[30] than their canary and their dog Pimperl, to whom mother and son regularly sent their 'love and kisses' from Paris. We shall encounter other examples of Mozart's love of animals.

Nor was there any lack of distractions and pleasures in Mozart's life. Leopold ensured that his son lost any inhibitions he may have had and learnt to comport himself with assurance in society, a comportment to which Mozart brought his own special gifts thanks to his amiable nature. In Salzburg at this time, as elsewhere, it was effectively only the higher nobility who combined a genuinely high level of education with a knowledge of music, and with few exceptions they were enthusiastic in their support of Mozart. Foremost among his champions were the Counts Virgilius Maria and Franz Lactanz Firmian, brothers of the governor-general of Lombardy; Virgilius Maria was the dean of Salzburg cathedral and well versed in world literature, while Franz Lactanz was Salzburg's chief steward and exceptionally knowledgeable about painting.[31] Also deserving of mention in this context are the local canon Count Anton Willibald Waldburg zu Wolfegg und Waldsee, who had made a thorough study of architecture; the chief equerry Count Leopold Joseph Kuenburg; the bishop of Chiemsee, Count Ferdinand Christoph von Waldburg-Zeil;[32] the grand chamberlain Count Georg Anton Felix von Arco; the lord-marshal Count Nikolaus Sebastian von Lodron; and the captain of the archbishop's bodyguard, Count Leopold von Lodron. Mozart was admitted to most of these households, he performed at their social gatherings and was allowed to give lessons to their daughters. It was not long before he had a whole series of female patrons among the ranks of the aristocracy. Writing from Milan on 17 February 1770, for example, Leopold informed his wife that 'Wolfgang kisses most humbly the hands of Her Excellency the Countess von Arco and thanks her for the kiss she sent, which is far more precious to him than many young ones'. Admittedly, a true understanding of art could not always be taken for granted in these aristocratic circles,[33] but we should not underestimate the extent of Mozart's dealings with the local nobility: the detailed knowledge of the customs and opinions of the aristocratic world of this period that we find in *Le nozze di Figaro* and *Don Giovanni* rests entirely on the composer's own observations.

The lower aristocracy – known locally as 'der wilde Adel' and represented by countless individuals all bearing the title 'Edler von' – generally had no money of their own but derived what income they could from the many minor offices at court. But their incomes had remained the same for years, preventing them from leading lives commensurate with their social standing. In consequence, they were all the more notable for their obsessive desire for titles and pride in their new-found nobility. Mozart did not have to look far to find living models for his Belfiore, although

---

30. Prior to Wolfgang's return from Paris, 'Tresel' repeatedly reports on how many capons she has bought for him.
31. Although Count Franz Lactanz Firmian held Mozart in high regard, he seems to have understood nothing about music, for on 9 July 1778 (*Briefe*, ii.395) we find Mozart writing to his father in the context of the need to improve the Salzburg orchestra: 'The chief steward should have nothing to say to me in musical matters, or on any point relating to music. For a courtier can't do the work of a Kapellmeister, but a Kapellmeister can well be a courtier.'
32. On these individuals, see Riesbeck, *Briefe eines reisenden Franzosen*, i.155ff., and Koch-Sternfeld, *Die letzten dreißig Jahre*, 40. ◆ Genealogical and biographical details of Mozart's Salzburg friends and contemporaries are extensively described in Heinz Schuler, *Mozarts Salzburger Freunde und Bekannte*.
33. In his letter of 2 October 1777, Mozart praises Count Salern of Munich as a true connoisseur: 'He really understands musique, for all the time he kept on shouting "bravo", where other noblemen would take a pinch of snuff, blow their noses, clear their throats or start a conversation' (*Briefe*, ii.29).

their number also included families of no mean culture.[34] He was in relatively close, albeit super-ficial, contact with some of these families, especially the younger ones, but these contacts gradu-ally grew more remote again during his years of maturity. Among the friends of his youth we find, for example, Marianne's hapless suitor, one Herr von Mölk, who is mentioned in Mozart's letter of 26 January 1770. The son of Salzburg's court chancellor, he visited the Mozarts in Munich and attended a performance of *La finta giardiniera*, expressing such 'astonishment' and 'crossing himself' so often that the Mozarts were downright ashamed of someone who had clearly never been further than Salzburg and Innsbruck.[35] At least in his youth, Mozart was much more taken by Anna Barbara (Waberl) von Mölk: according to his letter of 13 September 1771, he was looking forward to receiving another present from her similar to the one she had already given him for some recent minuets. That there was no lack of opportunity for such youthful infatuations is clear from mysterious hints in his letters to his sister, inviting her to visit so-and-so – she knows who he means – and greet her affectionately (letters of 24 and 31 August 1771, 28 October, 7 and 21 November 1772, and 28 and 30 December 1774[36]). At the time of his second visit to Italy, it appears from a reference in a letter from Leopold that it was one of the daughters of the archbishop's personal physician, Silvester Barisani, who was the object of his attentions. Among other friends from this period were Heinrich Wilhelm von Heffner,[37] the son of the local syndic Franz Friedrich von Heffner, and Basilius von Aman, although his friendship with the latter was of only brief dura-tion.[38] And finally there was Joachim von Schiedenhofen, whom we have already encountered on numerous occasions and who incurred Mozart's anger for marrying into money.[39] The diary that he kept and that was quoted by Jahn lists all the visits paid by the Mozarts, revealing that the latter were in fairly regular contact with the families of Johann Ernst von Antretter, who was a councillor in the Salzburg War Department; Joachim von Schiedenhofen auf Stumm, a counsellor to the Salzburg consistory and later privy councillor; the privy councillor Franz von Mölk and the consis-torial councillor Albert von Mölk; the archbishop's private physician and court doctor Silvester Barisani; the lord high steward Dominicus von Chiusole and the Gilowskys von Urazowa, who numbered a privy councillor, a chamber furrier[40] and a court surgeon among their ranks. Visits were paid in the afternoon or evening and lasted several hours, during which time the participants indulged their fondness for gaming or for making music. Regular entertainments are also mentioned, including sharp-shooting and a gambling club; the families also attended concerts and masked balls together.

We know little about the Mozarts' dealings with the middle class, of which they were after all still members. On one occasion – in a letter dated 8 January 1779 – we find Mozart tersely announcing that he cannot bear the Salzburgers, whose language and lifestyle he finds so intoler-able.[41] His reaction is no doubt exaggerated and reflects the views of his father, whose reserve and pride in his own education caused offence among Salzburg's middle classes on more than one occasion. Among their closer acquaintances was Lorenz Hagenauer, a man of no mean education,

---

34. See Riesbeck, *Briefe eines reisenden Franzosen*, i.156; and Koch-Sternfeld, *Die letzten dreißig Jahre*, 256–7.
35. *Briefe*, i.515 (letter of 11 January 1775).
36. ◆ *Briefe*, i.432, 434–5, 457–9, 462, 511 and 513–14.
37. See letters of 18 August 1771, 21 November 1772 and 15 September 1773. Heffner was already appearing in school plays in 1759, so he was evidently older than Mozart; see Hammerle, *Mozart und einige Zeitgenossen*, 8 [Deiters's note].
38. See letters of 3 and 24 March 1770 (*Briefe*, i. 317–19 and 323–4).
39. See letters of 3 March, 19 May and 4 August 1770 (*Briefe*, i. 317–19, 347–50 and 376–8).
40. According to Pirckmayer, *Über Musik und Theater am f. e. Salzburger Hofe 1762–1775*, 11 and 23–4, Franz Anton Gilowsky von Urazowa was the author of the court diaries that express admiration for the young Mozart.
41. *Briefe*, ii.536 and ii.438 (letters of 8 January 1779 and 7 August 1778).

who loyally supported the Mozarts in word and deed. For many years he was their landlord, and the numerous letters that Mozart wrote to him while away from home afford splendid proof of the position of trust that existed between them. His wife, by contrast, emerges as something of a bigot. We have already had frequent occasion to mention their son Cajetan, who was friendly with the young Mozart. Another friend of the family who enjoyed the trust of father and children alike was the cleric Joseph Bullinger, who had studied at the Jesuit Seminary in Munich and who now worked as a tutor in the Salzburg home of Count [Leopold Ferdinand] Arco. The 'loyal' Bullinger was 'always an important person' in the Mozart household. In the letters that Wolfgang wrote whenever he was away from home, he not only invariably asked to be remembered to his 'best friend Bullinger', he assumed that his best wishes would always be passed on, sometimes appealing to him directly and asking that important secrets be divulged to no one but Nannerl and Bullinger. When his mother died in Paris, it was to Bullinger that Mozart first wrote, asking him to break the news to his father as gently as possible, a task that Bullinger performed both skilfully and sympathetically. When Mozart was finally forced to return to Salzburg, it was to Bullinger that he poured out his troubled heart. Bullinger's feelings for Mozart were no less sincere. For some weeks during his return from Paris to Salzburg, there was no news of Mozart, but during this time the family continued to take communion and attend confession, with the 'excellent' Bullinger – to quote Leopold's letter of 19 October 1778 – 'praying daily for you at Holy Mass'.[42] Leopold, too, had every reason to regard Bullinger as his best and truest friend, as he ran into debt during Mozart's absence and the latter helped him out with a not inconsiderable loan. As a result, he confided in him in everything, telling him all there was to tell about Wolfgang and conferring with him on what should be done. Their relationship was well known in Salzburg, and when it was decided to lure Mozart back to the town, it is clear from Leopold's letter of 11 June 1778 that it was Bullinger who was asked to act as intermediary.[43] He also seems to have been musical as he was a member of a private orchestra that met every Sunday at eleven. On 11 October 1777, following his departure for Paris, Mozart wrote to ask him 'to make an authoritative pronouncement' in his name and present his 'compliments to all the members of the orchestra'.[44] Mozart's acquaintances were fond of visiting the home of the paymaster of St Peter's, Joachim Rupert Mayr von Mayrn, and Mozart later recalled the many happy hours that he himself had spent there. We have already mentioned the family's earlier contacts with Placidus Scharl, who taught at the Salzburg grammar school from 1759 to 1770.

As a town, Salzburg was addicted to pleasure, and under Archbishop Colloredo's more liberal and enlightened approach to public entertainments, there were ample opportunities for the locals to enjoy themselves.[45] A chronicler of conditions in Salzburg reports that 'the country's ruler goes hunting and attends church; those closest to him attend church and go hunting; those who come next to them in rank eat, drink and pray, and the whole of the lower orders pray, drink and eat. The two last-named classes make love in public, the two first-named in secret, they all live for pleasure.' In the town hall, a large room was set up in 1775 with a number of side-rooms, where during the carnival season masked balls were held on a regular basis under the eye of the local

42. ◆ *Briefe*, ii.497–500.
43. ◆ *Briefe*, ii.373.
44. ◆ *Briefe*, ii.49.
45. *Literarische Anekdoten auf einer Reise durch Deutschland*, 228–9; Riesbeck, *Briefe eines reisenden Franzosen*, i.159; and Koch-Sternfeld, *Die letzten dreißig Jahre*, 157. ◆ For a comprehensive survey of Salzburg's social, political and cultural history, see Dopsch, *Geschichte Salzburgs: Stadt und Land*.

magistracy. At other times of the year, concerts, society events and gambling took place here.[46] Mozart was fond of dancing and playing jokes and regularly distinguished himself at masquerades. Schiedenhofen reports that he once entertained all and sundry at a peasants' wedding and that on another occasion he dressed up as a barber's boy.[47]

The favourite pastime in Salzburg as elsewhere was the theatre. In 1775 Archbishop Colloredo had a new theatre built on the right bank of the Salzach, with a special committee in charge of its artistic and financial management under the chairmanship of Count Lodron. During the winter months, it provided a home for touring companies from Munich and even from France,[48] and there were also sledging parties and assemblies. In the summer months, too, the surrounding area was popular with visitors, as was the royal park at Hellbrunn about an hour's distance away.[49] Only rarely did Mozart join in the fun. Although we find his father writing to him on 12 February 1778, 'Have I not provided you with all manner of entertainment at all times and helped you to enjoy yourself in honourable, decent ways, often at great inconvenience to myself',[50] his straitened circumstances prevented him from enjoying these pleasures with any frequency. After all, the rise in prices that Leopold attributed, not without good reason, to the perverse system of government,[51] made it increasingly necessary for him to order his life along strict lines and to be prudently thrifty. He spelt out these conditions in a letter to his son of 5 February 1778:

> Since the time of your birth or even before, in other words, since the time of my marriage, it has been very difficult for me to support a wife, seven children, two maids and Mama's mother on my monthly income of around 20 florins and to meet the expense of childbirth, deaths and illnesses. If you think it over, you will realize that not only have I never spent a farthing on the smallest pleasure for myself but that without God's special mercy and in spite of all my efforts I would never have succeeded in keeping out of debt. . . . When you were children, I gave up all my time to you in the hope that not only would you be able to provide for yourselves later on, but that I, too, might live to enjoy a comfortable old age, justifying before God the education that I had given my children, living a life free from all further care, worrying only about my soul's salvation and calmly contemplating death.[52]

But he was thrifty within reason. 'Do not buy inferior materials,' he wrote to his wife on 26 October 1771, 'for to buy shoddy stuff is no economy.'[53] The Mozarts' simple lifestyle and the modest nature of their entertainments is well illustrated by the fact that within the Salzburg area one of the principal pastimes was sharp-shooting. A number of their more immediate friends had formed a kind of small guild of marksmen who met every Sunday at the homes of each of the families in turn. The family whose turn it was to host the meeting was responsible for providing the target, a task that gave rise to all manner of jokes. They always made a special effort to

46. A plan for this ballroom was drawn up by the architect Wolfgang Hagenauer; see Hammerle, *Mozart und einige Zeitgenossen*, 75.
47. ◆ This was on 18 February 1776; see *Dokumente*, 140, *Documentary Biography*, 155.
48. See Riesbeck, *Briefe eines reisenden Franzosen*, i.157; Koch-Sternfeld, *Die letzten dreißig Jahre*, 157; and Pirckmayer, *Über Musik und Theater*. ◆ Further, see Hintermaier, 'Mozart und das Theater am Salzburger fürsterzbischöflichen Hof' and 'Das Fürsterzbischöfliche Hoftheater zu Salzburg (1775–1803)'; Dahms, 'Das musikalische Repertoire des Salzburger Fürsterzbischöflichen Hoftheaters (1775–1803)'; and Kutscher, *Vom Salzburger Barocktheater zu den Salzburger Festspielen*.
49. Riesbeck, *Briefe eines reisenden Franzosen*, i.159. There was also a theatre here: see Hammerle, *Mozart und einige Zeitgenossen*, 65.
50. ◆ *Briefe*, ii.278.
51. For more details, see Koch-Sternfeld, *Die letzten dreißig Jahre*, 28ff.
52. *Briefe*, ii.256–7.
53. ◆ *Briefe*, i.446.

decorate the target with a picture that referred to local events and to the foibles of the participants. These pictures had to be accompanied by an explanation in verse, and the Salzburgers' propensity for jokes and ridicule found a ready outlet here, depending on the abilities of the versifier. Bolts were fired at this target from an air-gun and modest bets produced a source of income for the society that allowed them to pay for occasional entertainments. Its members had met so often that the meetings were relaxed and amusing, drawing them even closer together. In a letter of 11 November 1780, Leopold reports on an incident that illustrates the degree of ribaldry that members evidently felt was permissible on such occasions. One of the participants, Katherl Gilowsky, liked to be courted but did not take these things very seriously. On the day in question she had the misfortune to trip on the step of a shop she was entering and to fall most indecorously, in which position she was then portrayed on the target, with a suitable poem inscribed to her, and exposed to the jokes and ribaldry of the company.[54] These shooting competitions were always referred to in family letters, particularly entertaining paintings on the targets were invariably described and, since absent members were represented by substitutes, a careful account of the profits and losses at each meeting was kept. Even after he had moved to Vienna, we still find Mozart writing to his sister on 4 July 1781: 'I suppose it will soon be time for the marksmen's annual dinner. I beg you *solemniter* to drink the health of a loyal marksman; and when it's my turn to provide the target, let me know and I'll have one painted.'[55]

Conversely, the Mozarts' dealings with their fellow musicians in Salzburg were far less cordial, and it was really only to the loyal Schachtner that they were bound by ties of closer friendship. For a whole variety of reasons they had no real contact with the rest of them, even if, like Michael Haydn and Cajetan Adlgasser, they commanded their unquestioning respect. It was with reference to conditions in Salzburg that Leopold praised the Mannheim orchestra in a letter of 19 July 1763, describing the players as 'young and of good character, not drunkards, gamblers or dissolute black-guards, so that both their behaviour and their playing are admirable'.[56] Mozart later confirmed this view, writing to his father from Paris on 9 July 1778 to report that under Cannabich's direction 'everything is taken seriously', that there was total discipline and they all led respectable lives, in contrast to Salzburg: 'This is one of my main reasons for detesting Salzburg – those coarse, slovenly, dissolute court musicians – no honest man of good breeding could possibly live with them – far from wanting to associate with them, he would be bound to feel ashamed of them. This probably explains why music isn't popular with us and why it's not respected.'[57] We must not forget, of course, that these remarks conceal a good deal of personal bitterness. No doubt the general tone of the Salzburg Kapelle left something to be desired, and the envy shown by his colleagues must sometimes have sorely tried Mozart's patience. At the same time, Leopold's self-conscious reserve and Mozart's thoughtless and even spiteful remarks were scarcely calculated to make things easier. There is no doubt that both parties added unnecessarily to each other's difficulties.

These years witnessed the completion of a large number of works of unequal worth, with the pieces intended for the court in particular appearing to reveal a certain awkwardness and even disinterest and to suggest that Mozart was only reluctantly complying with the views of his paymasters in Salzburg.

---

54. *Briefe*, iii.15. ◆ Leopold actually writes 'she revealed her bare arse'.
55. ◆ *Briefe*, iii.138. Concerning target-shooting, see Günther G. Bauer, 'Bölzelschießen – das "Dartfieber" der Mozartzeit. Salzburg, 1770–1795' and 'Spielen in Salzburg im 18. Jahrhundert'.
56. ◆ *Briefe*, i.79.
57. *Briefe*, ii.395.

Of the Masses that date from this period, the first chronologically was probably the C major Mass K220. It may date from the beginning of 1775.[58] Its most immediately striking feature is its almost total eschewal of contrapuntal procedures, an eschewal that makes this work the very antithesis of the F major Mass. Even the two final fugues in the Gloria and Credo have disappeared,[59] with Mozart apparently concerned above all to write a particularly accessible, formally translucent and, in a word, popular work. The prevailing tone is one of sentimental intimacy, sometimes verging on the secular, and only in the 'Qui tollis' and 'Et incarnatus est' do we find the authentically Mozartian, profoundly emotional sounds and harmonies with which he regularly speaks of the divine mystery at these points in the Mass. Formally, too, this work is somewhat unusual. On the most superficial level, the listener is bound to be struck by the way in which the music of the Kyrie returns for the 'Dona nobis pacem' of the Agnus Dei, a procedure that is also found with both Joseph and Michael Haydn and that Süßmayr later adopted when completing the *Requiem*. Also new is the recourse to the orchestral accompaniment of the 'Pleni sunt coeli' at the repeat of the Hosanna. Whereas the more loosely structured Gloria acquires its sense of unity essentially from a recurrent motif in the orchestra, the Credo is again cast in free rondo form, with the main sections entrusted to the chorus and distinguished from the episodes for the soloists by dint of a particular ostinato rhythm in the bass; here, too, one particular orchestral motif recurs throughout the whole movement. As such, it is a remarkable attempt to explore a new aspect of rondo form. The four masses of 1776 – K257–259 and 262 – are likewise all in C major.[60] The first three date from November and December, while the fourth, according to the latest research,[61] was written in around May. Stylistically speaking, it is a particularly varied work, not only assigning a major role to contrapuntal procedures, but again revealing a profound commitment to the spirit of contemporary instrumental music. Even the opening Kyrie begins with two themes that are contrapuntally combined, and in the 'Dona nobis pacem', too, double counterpoint plays an important, if less well-defined, role.[62] The Gloria and Credo again include final fugues,[63] the second of which has an extremely eloquent subject.[64]

But instrumental features, too, are powerfully represented, not least by the practice – also found in the symphonies of this period – of delaying the return of the main themes until the end of the recapitulation. The 'Et in Spiritum Sanctum', moreover, begins with a long, aria-like ritornello. This is the most secular movement of all, its melodic writing, too, harking back to Mozart's very first masses.[65] A light and charming number, it strikes a folklike tone not least by dint of the fact that the choir repeats the soloist's words in the manner of a refrain, with the final repeats audibly reminiscent of Orpheus. Formally speaking, neither the Gloria nor the Credo has anything new to offer, the only exception being in the 'Et resurrexit', where the Credo is indicated by its tempo alone. In general, this is a work of considerable brilliance but no special warmth, the only

58. Thus Wyzewa and Saint-Foix, *Wolfgang Amédée Mozart*, ii.208; they are no doubt right to identify this work with the 'short mass' which, according to Leopold's letter of 15 February 1775 (*Briefe*, i.522), had been performed in the Munich court chapel only a short time previously. ◆ Although Abert may be right, K220 cannot be dated with certainty; the earliest surviving source, a manuscript copy now in the Salzburg Cathedral archives, dates from 1775 or 1776.

59. This is, of course, the result of the archbishop's recent ban on fugues at this point in the mass.

60. ◆ Concerning the dating of these works, see above, n. 7.

61. Wyzewa and Saint-Foix draw attention to its stylistic affinities with the litanies and to the fact that surprisingly few dated works have survived from the month of May.

62. Both themes appear at the end in augmentation.

63. This indicates that K262 was written not for the court but for some private occasion.

64. According to Wyzewa and Saint-Foix, *Wolfgang Amédée Mozart*, ii.299, the contrapuntal writing here contains a reminiscence of the C minor fugato from the sixth keyboard sonata in Johann Christian Bach's first set of such pieces.

65. Cf. the corresponding passages in K66 and 139.

exceptions being the episodes in the Gloria and Credo already mentioned. The 'Qui tollis' is one of the most inspired and, at the same time, most dramatic passages in any of these Masses: it begins on a note of ponderous sacred seriousness accompanied by a sharply rhythmical motif in the orchestra, but with the third bar a shudder runs through the chorus (marked *piano*) and in the sixth and seventh bars there follows an altogether unexpected outburst of despair ending on a fermata. What remains is the hopeless sobbing of the 'miserere nobis'. At the same time, the bass line descends chromatically from G to B over chords that keep changing enharmonically. This procedure is thrice repeated, with increasingly intensified harmonic expression, producing a dramatic effect that is as shattering as it is genuinely Mozartian. Equally heightened is the expressive language in the 'Crucifixus' and, finally, in the Agnus Dei. Here, too, the chorus enters on a note of great confidence but is drawn into the mood of subjective agitation through the soloist's turbulent 'miserere' with its interval of a diminished seventh. Its second entry in the Agnus Dei proceeds along identical lines to its entry in the 'Qui tollis', producing a wonderful effect by means of an interrupted cadence in E flat major: a confident *forte*, a timid *piano* and – again on the words 'peccata mundi' – a sudden outburst of passion that simultaneously brings with it the most abrupt enharmonic shift. The same psychological process is at work in both cases.

The second mass in C major K257 takes this populism a stage further but does so in the best sense of the term. Although the work is not especially profound, it remains one of Mozart's most successful sacred works in terms of the beauty and nobility of its melodic writing and its sonorities. Here it is not so much the influence of opera that makes itself felt as the spirit of German song, lending the work as a whole its calm and intimate character and avoiding all sense of excess. As such, the work leads on naturally to Schubert's earliest masses. Formally, too, it is exceptionally clear and translucent. The Gloria consists of one main movement that is repeated at the end – at the 'Quoniam' – in extended form. Between them lie two episodes: first, the 'Domine Deus' in the dominant, involving the popular interplay between solo and choral refrain with one particular motif in the orchestra and, second, the choral 'Qui tollis' in the subdominant, again with a particular motif in the orchestra that is heard in the bass in its original version and in the violins in a trilled version; this motif is later recalled in the final section at the words 'Jesu Christe' which, sung in a whisper, create a profoundly poetical impression. In the Credo, by contrast, Mozart recalls the procedure adopted in his F major mass, constantly repeating the Credo motif. But whereas in the earlier work it had generated the music for every section of the Mass, it now remains unchanged as a special liturgical motto theme exerting no influence on the subsequent musical argument. The free rondo form is retained without this quotation.[66] Here, too, the 'Et incarnatus est' is a pastorale[67] freely, but palpably, linked to the 'Crucifixus', a link between Christ's birth and death that is found in all these masses. In the Sanctus the listener is struck by Mozart's recourse to the theme of the Credo from the F major mass. The Benedictus is one of the sweetest and raptest movements of its kind, creating the impression that Mozart was unwilling to abandon so lovely an idyll. And the Agnus Dei, too, stresses the idea of childish trust far more than that of contrition, which casts only isolated shadows over the picture. Only right at the end of the movement do we find a repeat of the psychological process that we encountered in the previous mass. The orchestra, too, plays a significant role in what is again an extremely beautifully and clearly structured movement, but – a novel feature – it is motivically linked to the following 'Dona nobis

---

66. *Pace* Wyzewa and Saint-Foix, *Wolfgang Amédée Mozart*, ii.347, the 'Et resurrexit' is identical with the beginning.
67. Particularly remarkable here, as before, is the emphasis given to the 'et homo factus est' by means of the dynamics and by the chromatic coloratura that later returns in the minor at the words 'et sepultus est'.

pacem'. The second subject of the Agnus Dei provides, as it were, a framework for the whole of the 'Dona nobis pacem'. In itself, the 'Dona nobis pacem' is relatively secular and primitive, but a genuinely Mozartian feature may be found in the entry of the two female soloists, whose chromatic figure appears to beckon first to the other soloists and then to the chorus to join them. Of the two masses that date from December 1776, K258 and 259, the second is by far the more insignificant, taking simplicity to the point of aridity. A novelty is the organ solo in the Benedictus,[68] at the end of which an inspired image of the transfigured son of God floating down from Heaven is conjured up over a powerful pedal point. Far more important, however, is the other C major mass, K258, in which even the far more careful contrapuntal writing is indicative of Mozart's greater involvement in the work. His progress from the purely musical to the poetic is also clear from the relationship between words and music. Essentially, it marks a return to the style of Padre Martini, a return also clear from the striking restraint of the orchestral writing, although here, of course, Mozart avails himself of entirely modern resources. The Gloria, for example, is through-composed in respect of the vocal writing, but in the violins we find an accompanying figuration that runs through the entire section in the most varied versions and variants, thereby demonstrating that not even here was Mozart willing to forgo a sense of motivic unity. The Credo, by contrast, includes rondo-like allusions to the main theme in both the vocal and orchestral writing.[69] The old tradition of word-painting at 'descendit' is given particular emphasis here through the unison writing in all four voices, with a curious inner link established with the rising unison lines at 'Et resurrexit'. Particularly beautiful, once again, is the episode of the 'Et incarnatus est', with the redemptive 'Et homo factus est' breaking free from the tenor soloist's anguished line with a surprising modulation to the major, only for the choral cries of 'Crucifixus' and the insistently rising line in the bass to cast a sombre veil over the radiant image, which finally sinks back into night and death – through its sheer brevity, this passage creates a moving link between Christ's birth and Passion. In the present mass, too, the pendant to this section is the 'Qui tollis', which is again repeated three times, each time a whole tone lower (A, G and F minor). But in the Benedictus, Mozart once more establishes the first word of the text as a motto theme that the chorus subjects to the most disparate variations and interjects into the soloists' vocal textures. A glittering triplet accompaniment in the violins seems to suggest a vision of God. The Agnus Dei is again linked to the 'Dona nobis pacem', this time without the usual change of tempo. This prayer for peace unexpectedly insinuates itself into the freely developing musical argument, and only at the end does a brief and independent fugato appear in the form of a plagal coda. In spite of its unity, the movement is none the less notable for its remarkable sense of disquiet, a mood due in the main to the unison figure in the first and second violins that pursues its restless course before finally taking over the vocal line, too.

The final mass from this Salzburg period, the mass in B flat major K275,[70] generally adopts the same stylistic model as its predecessor, but without exploring the same depth of religious feeling. The opening bars of the Kyrie are in themselves symptomatic of its tender and pleasing underlying tone:[71]

---

68. See *Briefe*, ii.362 (letter of 28 May 1778).
69. Bars 3ff. in the 'Et resurrexit' and in the 'Et unam sanctam'.
70. It was performed on 22 December 1777, in other words, after Mozart had already left Salzburg. The parts, which are at Stift Lambach, give 1777 as the year of composition.
71. This was a favourite theme among eighteenth-century composers and one that Mozart learnt from Johann Christian Bach. It also appears in the 'Qui tollis'.

Ky - ri - e   e - lei - son

The soloists have a greater role to play than the chorus, homophony a greater role than counterpoint. At the same time, however, the older tradition reasserts itself in the combination of various texts in the Gloria and Credo. In the Gloria it is impossible not to be struck by the veiled tone of the opening. This movement is completely through-composed and held together only by recurrent motifs in the orchestra. Even more extreme in this regard is the Credo, which is dominated by the following theme[72] and its various subdivisions that occur with a persistence not found in any previous work:

Indeed, the motif (a) even returns in the accompanying figure in the Sanctus and Benedictus. The theme is both a motto theme and an accompanying figure designed to impose a sense of unity on the work, recurring in the most disparate forms and disappearing from sight only in the 'Et incarnatus est' before reappearing again at the word 'passus'. Whereas the earlier masses had all used different music to describe Christ's birth and Passion, here the music is the same, except that the chorus enters on the word 'Crucifixus'. And as in all these other masses with the exception of K262, the two traditional fugues are missing, an absence that suggests that they were intended for the court. Conversely, the present Sanctus begins – exceptionally – with a fugato later joined by an ostinato accompanying figure, whereas the Hosanna – normally set as a fugue – is now homophonic. No movement explores greater depths than the Agnus Dei: the declamation, part-writing and doubling of voices and instruments are all masterly. Listen, for example, to the tension-laden unison bar in the orchestra leading into the chorus's outburst and often repeated in the course of the movement:

This is one of the most moving of all Mozart's settings of the Agnus Dei. At the end he appears about to launch straight into the 'Dona nobis pacem', then suddenly remembers the old bipartite division and turns the 'Dona nobis pacem' into an independent movement. Its main theme returns with curious obstinacy in all the voices, allowing no other ideas to emerge:

72. According to Lorenz, it is based on the folksong *Bauer häng den Pummerl an*, but cf. the final movement of Bach's violin sonata in A major (BWV1015). Perhaps both composers had the same folktune in mind.

do - na no - bis pa - - cem

Here, too, we find Mozart avoiding all routine and keeping a constant look-out for new formal possibilities, especially those that might allow him to enhance the piece's formal and atmospheric unity.

The *Litaniae de venerabili altaris sacramento* in E flat major K243 of March 1776 is a striking work not least as a result of the unevenness of its individual sections. Whole movements such as the 'Panis vivus' and 'Dulcissimum convivium' hark back to the bravura style of opera, and it speaks volumes for contemporary attitudes to church music that the second of these arias leads directly into as liturgically strict a movement as the 'Viaticum', in which the choral sopranos are entrusted with the Gregorian Corpus Christi hymn, *Pange lingua gloriosa*, treated here as a cantus firmus. The accompaniment is not contrapuntal but harmonic and colouristic, with oboes, bassoons, horns, trombones and two muted violas providing the harmony, while the violins add their pizzicato voices, generally in broken chords, recalling the manner already familiar from death scenes in operas and from other scenes involving ghosts. The overall impression is as solemn as it is picturesque. The preferential treatment accorded to the instruments is typically Neapolitan and is found not only here but also in the Agnus Dei which, cast in the form of a rondo for soprano soloist and concertante flute, oboe and cello, is a charming but – given the nature of the text – unduly playful piece. A totally different picture emerges from the previous 'Pignus', which is a large-scale, fully developed fugue. No mere contrapuntal study, it speaks directly to the listener's heart with its mood of wistful melancholy. It is not a vocal fugue, however, but could equally well be written for instruments. Of the other movements, the boldly conceived and sombrely majestic 'Tremendum' stands out not least by virtue of the fact that, contrary to earlier practice, it includes a setting of the words 'panis omnipotentia, verbi caro factus, incruentum sacrificium, cibus et conviva'. Of the remaining movements, the music of the Kyrie returns in abbreviated form at the end of the Agnus Dei. All these movements strike the same note of amiable sincerity with no particular depth, a tone familiar from the other masses that date from this period in Mozart's life.

Another work that may date from the same period as K243 is the offertory *Venite populi* K260 for four-part double chorus, two violins ad libitum, bass and organ, a piece that is a counterpart to the polychoral instrumental works of this period. Its main feature once again is not its contrapuntal writing but the echo effects that Mozart had encountered in the works of Michael Haydn and others and that he now deployed with his unique and considerable gift for mimicry. Two fast sections involving contrapuntal procedures based on the same subjects frame a homophonic section that forms the literal and psychological centre of the work with its heavy, mysterious harmonies. The contrapuntal sections, conversely, are imbued with a spirit of animation and vitality but are otherwise undemanding. By contrast, the gradual *Sancta Maria, mater Dei* for the Feast of the Blessed Virgin Mary K273 and the offertory *Alma Dei creatoris* K277 are among Mozart's finest sacred compositions from this period. The first one has been interpreted – possibly with some justification – as a votive offering to the Virgin Mary prior to Mozart's departure for Mannheim.[73] Both works reveal not only a ternary structure related to sonata form but a genuinely

---

73. Wyzewa and Saint-Foix, *Wolfgang Amédée Mozart*, ii.396.

moving inwardness of emotion.[74] And in both, the simple and heartfelt language recalls the world of the German song.[75] Whereas the gradual is a purely choral work, the offertory is an *alternatim* piece for soloist and chorus. But the style of writing is the same in both, in other words, it is basic- ally homophonic, with very few attempts at counterpoint, while the orchestral writing, too, largely follows the voices. There is much here, especially in the gradual, that looks forward to the *Ave verum corpus* of 1791, but these earlier works still lack the element of tender suffering that is so typical of the later Mozart.

The church sonatas of this period[76] likewise reveal considerable progress. Of course, there is no more sign here of a spirit of religious orthodoxy than we find in any of their predecessors and, apart from the fact that they are all single-movement works, they remain indistinguishable from the composer's secular instrumental compositions. But Mozart now experiments with new combi- nations of sounds: in two cases (K244 and 245) he treats the organ as an independent concertante instrument, and in a third (K278) he adds oboes, trumpets, timpani and cellos to the traditional trio, while the bass line, too, acquires a new and more animated life. Style and structure are the same as in the instrumental works of this period. The development sections are generally thematic and on occasion rise to impressive heights. Indeed, their verve and, less often, their sheer passion place them on a par with Mozart's finest achievements of these years.

The sacred works that Mozart wrote before 1777 do not always reveal any real purity of religious feeling, a state of affairs attributable in part to the composer's youth and in part to the depths to which the genre had sunk at this time. But to pass quickly over them by appealing to Bach and Beethoven, as many writers do, is to do them a grave injustice. It is, after all, a boy expressing his ideas and feelings about life and death, and in the circumstances we can scarcely expect any basic new revelations of the kind that we might find with an older man tempered by life's struggles. More than any other compositions, Mozart's sacred works reveal how much more rapidly he had developed as an artist than as a man. His faith was firmly rooted in traditional dogma, in which respect he was totally unlike Beethoven, who struggled to achieve that faith within the work of art. But he also knew that within the ecclesiastical framework there was sufficient scope for individual feelings. And it is on this basis that the outlines of his personality emerge in his sacred works with surprising clarity. Here, too, a comparison with Joseph Haydn is extremely instructive. Haydn's church music is firmly grounded in the here-and-now and is at its finest where it seeks to express a positive attitude to life in all its different aspects. It is far less successful in expressing powerful and dark emotions, and it generally stops short of setting foot inside the portals of the mysteries alluded to by the words of the Mass. With Mozart, too, a tone of childlike confidence also plays an important role, and the expression of joy often goes beyond what was permitted by the Church. At the same time, however, we also find a more sombre, even otherworldly note. It is no accident that it is those sections of the text which, in terms of dogma, are the most profound and most moving and which include the 'Qui tollis', the 'Et incarnatus est' and the Agnus Dei that are the

74. The ornamentation of the fifth degree of the scale at the 'Amen' in K273 is a very popular melodic type from now on in Mozart's works and is found as late as *Die Zauberflöte* at the words 'Wir wandeln durch des Tones Macht' in the second-act finale.
75. A more effeminate tone is struck by the undated offertory *Sub tuum praesidium* K198, a duet which, according to the Göttweig parts, is scored for soprano and tenor; in the Bludenz parts, it is scored for two sopranos. Wyzewa and Saint-Foix, *Wolfgang Amédée Mozart*, ii.427, argue that it was originally a setting of different words, but offer no evidence for this claim. ◆ There is no unequivocal evidence that K198 (K⁶ Anh. C3.08) is by Mozart; the earliest surviving source, a manuscript copy in the Gesellschaft der Musikfreunde, Vienna, is of uncertain date and provenance.
76. On plausible grounds, Wyzewa and Saint-Foix, *Wolfgang Amédée Mozart*, ii.293–5, also ascribe the undated sonatas in F and A major K224 and 225 to this same period. ◆ Paper and handwriting studies suggest that K224 and 225 date from later, probably early 1780.

high points in most of Mozart's masses. Here we find the same outbursts of darkly glowing passion that we recognized as indicative of Mozart's individuality in all his other works. Here, too, are the unexpected changes of mood within a short space of time that we noted earlier. The allegro movements speak the common language of the age in far clearer terms than the adagios, with the settings of the 'Dona nobis pacem' turning out to be too lightweight in the majority of these masses: it is as though, in begging for peace, we are already standing outside the church in the thronging bustle of the street. In general, the fast sections are less popular in their appeal than with Haydn but reveal greater power and energy, with an element of grandeur that is missing from Haydn's masses. A contributory factor here is the formal structure of the majority of these movements, a structure that is eloquent in its brevity and, as such, far superior to the garrulousness of so many of the Italianate masses of the period. Whether it be the dramatist who wields the pen, as in K139, or the lyric poet, as in the later works, the majority of these images attest to a manly taciturnity that is in itself sufficient to create an impression. This formal assurance is one of the greatest merits of these works and is aimed above all at ensuring that the individual movements are as fully rounded and as unified as possible. At the same time it helped the young and increasingly successful composer in his exploration of the different stylistic trends to which his genius, in need of models as ever, was no less exposed here than it had been before. Nothing could be further from the truth than to assume that Mozart subscribed to one particular type to the exclusion of all others. Barely two of these works are stylistically identical: in each, there is a different balance between words and music, voice and instruments, homophony and counterpoint. In the process, Mozart criticized – albeit unconsciously – the various stylistic trends of his time. In turn, this explains why these sacred works are so important in terms of his own artistic development – quite apart from the numerous passages which, casting aside all earthly trammels, speak the language of genius.

Of the serenades, pride of place goes to the two divertimentos for string quartet and two horns K247 and 287. Both were written for the name-day of Countess Antonia Lodron, the first in 1776,[77] the second in 1777. Like their predecesors, they too afford clear evidence of Mozart's debt to Michael Haydn in this field: the latter's influence is evident not only in their overall character but also on points of formal detail, including, for example, the variations and instrumental recitative in the B flat major divertimento.[78] But there is no longer any trace of the schoolboy awkwardly imitating his mentor's model. Once Haydn's ideas have passed through the fire of Mozart's imagination, they seem no more than a shadowy image alongside all that is new. The stimuli that the younger composer received from his older colleague are important for the historian and psychologist alike, but the artistic result is entirely independent and towers as far above its model as genius towers above mere talent, however powerful it may be. There is no doubt that with these two works Mozart created two models of their kind, so outstanding, indeed, that it was to be a long time before even Mozart himself could match his own achievement. He does not yet move outside the divertimento's traditional world of emotion, so that pessimism and tragedy appear only very rarely, as in the recitative already mentioned, a passage that no doubt reflects some personal experience. In general, however, these are examples of music written for polite society, albeit of

---

77. The march in F major K248 no doubt goes with this piece.
78. In the case of K247, Wyzewa and Saint-Foix, *Wolfgang Amédée Mozart*, ii.300–1, draw attention to a notturno of 1772 and the B flat major divertimento of 1774. A comparable model in the case of K287 is said to be a string quintet in B flat major from 1776. ◆ Presumably the references here are to Michael Haydn's F major notturno Perger 106 (MH185) and B flat divertimento Perger 92 (MH199). No 1776 string quintet by Haydn is known; possibly Abert means the divertimento Perger 234 (MH 209), the earliest surviving source for which is dated 1777 although it may have been composed earlier.

the noblest and wittiest kind that gives the greatest scope to his poetical imagination. They are also filled with all the youthful fire of a chivalrous and visionary soul. Moreover, each of the movements that make up these works is on the same high level, revealing an astonishing wealth of succinctly captured moods. In the F major divertimento, for example, the powerful love of life of the opening allegro is followed by a vaguely French andante – one of the most graceful pieces ever penned by Mozart – and by the soulful rêverie of the adagio, while the solemn introduction to the finale even foreshadows the world of the priests in *Die Zauberflöte*. The finale, too, reveals French influence and, in spite of its loose structure, draws the listener into its sway with its effervescent high spirits. The B flat major divertimento scales even higher peaks in terms of both its musical ideas and the way in which all six instruments merge together to create a genuine chamber-music style: note the powerful sense of enjoyment evoked by its opening movement, with its rustic ländler; the fine brushwork in its second movement, which is cast in the form of a set of variations; the witty and manly minuets; the broadly flowing, genuinely Mozartian cantilena of the adagio that already looks forward to movements such as the adagio from the famous G minor quintet of 1787; and the finale, one of the most ebullient final movements that Mozart ever wrote. Sonata form is treated even more freely in the first of these works than it is in the second, with even the subject-group bringing with it a remarkable range of ideas. Here, however, the themes are no longer carelessly juxtaposed in the aphoristic manner found in the earlier pieces: what is so special about these two later works is the astonishing naturalness with which one idea is developed from another, so that the listener is never aware of the transition. The same art of motivic development is also revealed by Mozart's handling of ternary form: take the two menuettos from K287, the second sections of which both strike the listener as recapitulations, and yet when the opening section returns, it has been transformed with inspired freedom, coaxing entirely new possibilities from the melodic material. As befits a serenade, the development sections are not symphonic in their rigour, but, thematically speaking, they stick to the point and play wittily with the main subject. The allegro of K247 gives greater scope to contrapuntal procedures, while that of K287 gives the first violin a chance to show off. All the outer movements are surprisingly broadly struc- tured and elaborated, and in this respect the finale of K287 provides a pointer to the later symphonies. Among more detailed points, it is worth mentioning that throughout these two works Mozart is fond of omitting the beginnings of his main subjects in the recapitulations but of introducing them into his codas to produce a more emphatic ending. It is again Michael Haydn's influence that can be detected here, yet the eloquent brevity of these codas is quintessentially Mozartian, as is clear more especially from K287. As far as his treatment of the instruments is concerned, both works reveal a slight preference for the first violin, a preference entirely typical of serenades in general. The writing for the two horns is far less independent in the second of the two works than it is in the first, just as the chamber-music style is more subtly and rigorously applied in the later work than in the earlier one.

It is clear that Mozart was at pains to impose a specific and distinctive character on each of these pieces. Scored for strings, two oboes (doubling flutes), two horns, two trumpets and bassoon, the D major serenade K204 of 1775[79] is a work of outward, sometimes even superficial, brilliance, in which the tendency towards concertante effects plays a major role. With its constant interplay between Viennese andantino and allegro, the final movement represents a remarkable attempt to

---

79. Köchel's date of 1772 must be rejected on stylistic grounds; see Wyzewa and Saint-Foix, *Wolfgang Amédée Mozart*, ii.241–2. Mozart describes the work as a 'symphony' in a letter of 4 January 1783 (*Briefe*, iii.248). ◆ In fact, K204 is dated 5 August 1775 on the autograph manuscript.

combine sonata form and rondo form. Even finer is the divertimento in D major K251 of 1776.[80] Scored for string quartet, oboe and two horns, it is notable not least for its blend of French stylistic elements (its march and menuetto with variations and the theme and structure of its rondeau) with reminiscences of popular German songs. The thematic unity of its opening Molto allegro recalls Joseph Haydn, making it one of the most unified of all Mozart's suite movements from this period, while none the less creating the impression of a piece dashed off with inspired ease. But it is with the 'Haffner' serenade in D major K250 that we find Mozart pursuing the most elevated aims.[81] The work is scored for strings, two oboes (flutes), two bassoons, two horns and two trumpets, a lavishness of resources that indicates Mozart's desire to ensure that the wedding in the mayor's house was celebrated in style. This desire on Mozart's part finds further expression in the unusual number of movements and the breadth with which they are elaborated, a breadth which, in the case of the rondeau, becomes positively distended. This is a real musical epithalamium, now emotionally highly charged, now delightfully confiding, now wittily garrulous, but always showing the respect due to the couple in question. Only once – and this is indicative of Mozart's particular empathy with this piece – does the mood cloud over and even become sombre, namely, in the inspired G minor menuetto, which suddenly reveals the whole dark, pessimistic side of Mozart's emotional life. Here the composer consciously strikes out in a direction that was to lead straight to the sombre world of the C minor serenade K388, a world that could hardly be further removed from that of the suite. An especially noteworthy aspect of the opening movement is the forward-looking and highly intelligent motivic link between the introductory allegro maestoso and the following allegro, a link maintained until its very last bars. Elsewhere, too, Mozart continues to explore new aspects of older forms, notably in the virtuosic rondeau and in the second andante, where rondo form is combined with variation form.

Somewhat apart stand the six divertimentos for two oboes, two bassoons and two horns K213, 240, 252, 253, 270 and 289 that date from 1775–7. All were written to be performed at the archbishop's table, hence the modest length of their individual movements, their loose structure and carefree, lightweight character. In the earlier ones, Mozart still retains 'classical' four-movement form, but later adopts a freer approach to it, beginning with a slow movement and following it up with sets of variations and pure dance movements such as polonaises, simple rondos and so on. In one particular case – the final movement of K252 – he even recalled an old folksong, probably familiar to him from the *Augsburgisches Tafelkonfekt*.[82] These undemanding movements seem to have given him particular pleasure, if we may judge by their ebullient wit and high spirits and by their ability to treat even the simplest ideas in new and fascinating ways. Of incomparable charm are the dancelike idylls of many of the trios in the menuettos that already look forward to Schubert's German dances. A no less significant feature of these divertimentos is the striking number of pre-echoes that they contain of Mozart's later masterpieces:[83] listen, for example, to the syncopated theme of the variations in K253. As for their instrumentation, the earlier works suggest

---

80. Probably written for Nannerl's birthday. The 'Marcia alla francese' that appears at the end of the autograph manuscript (see Nottebohm's critical commentary on this passage) evidently replaces the marches that generally introduce and conclude such works.

81. The march K249 goes with this serenade. This work has nothing to do with the later 'Haffner' symphony K385, which is likewise based on a serenade.

82. *Andere Tracht*, no. 7. The same tune is found in one of Joseph Haydn's G major symphonies and in the rondo from Beethoven's piano concerto op. 15. It also recurs in the first-act finale to *Die Zauberflöte*; see Friedlaender, *Das deutsche Lied im 18. Jahrhundert*, i.72ff.

83. Cf. the beginning of the second section of the andante in K213; the final subject-group in the opening movement of K252; and the subject-group of the opening movement and main subject of the finale of K270.

writing for violins, while the later ones exploit the wind sonorities to masterly effect. The two undated divertimentos for two flutes, four trumpets and four timpani K187 and 188 no doubt served similar aims.[84] The first is in ten short dancelike movements, the second in six. Both were presumably written for the 'processions with trumpets and timpani' listed by Leopold in his catalogue. Individual movements do indeed sound like fanfares of a kind intended to accompany the arrival of distinguished dinner guests, while others may have been performed as individual dishes were carried to table. In the main, the flutes are entrusted with the melodic line, with the trumpets serving to accompany them and, more especially, to add a certain colour. Neither of these pieces lays claim to any greater depth.

A final group comprises the serenades for multiple ensembles, which were no doubt positioned apart in order to enhance the effect. In the serenata notturna K239, a solo string quartet[85] is contrasted with a ripieno string quartet plus timpani. To judge by the piece's humorous quality, it was probably written as New Year music in 1776, with the larger of the two orchestras intervening hesitantly but, as a result, all the more wittily and sometimes even impertinently in the soloists' *galant* musical discourse. In the rondeau it even provides a wholly unexpected flourish. On this occasion, the entrance march replaces the opening allegro, but the departure of the players, too, is suggested in the rondeau by the lively Viennese march tune of one of its episodes. This tune is introduced by the soloists in a remarkably high-spirited adagio and, at its later return, is heralded by a ghostlike pizzicato, before being accompanied and poetically transfigured by a glittering figure. As the whole, the work reveals a whimsical sense of humour.

A second notturno K286 features no fewer than four ensembles, each consisting of two horns and a string quartet. With the exception of the trio in the menuetto, which is scored either for only one ensemble or for all four together,[86] the work as a whole relies on a threefold echo effect, with the first ensemble stating the melody, the second entering with its second half in the manner of an echo and the third repeating half the echo. As a result, all that is left for the fourth ensemble is the final bars. The overall effect is of the initial melody gradually appearing to fade away in different directions. Here we find a humorous use of a principle that had been universally valid in an earlier age and one that Joseph Haydn had already used in his double string trio of 1767. But what for Haydn had been mere playfulness is raised by Mozart to the level of genuine art, for the echo effects that we find in this work have nothing superficial about them but emerge from its design and structure. Even without them, the piece has an importance all of its own. Indeed, some of the themes are designed in such a way that the echo section is an inalienable part of them. Alongside them we find passages of irresistible humour, notably in the menuetto, with its interlocking fanfare motif on the eight horns producing a sudden and mysterious flood of sound that assails the listener from every direction.

Although the term 'divertimento' was already somewhat old-fashioned by this date,[87] Mozart also used it for his first piano trio in B flat major K254 of August 1776. The menuetto-like character of

---

84. In keeping with its more mature style, the second must belong to a later period, perhaps 1775/6; see Nottebohm's critical commentary in AMA IX/4. ◆ K187 is not an original composition by Mozart but an arrangement of the gavotte from Gluck's *Paride ed Elena*, first given in Vienna on 3 November 1770. The arrangement dates from 1773–5. K188 was probably written in mid-1773.
85. ◆ In fact, the solo string quartet in K239 consists of two violins, a viola and a double bass.
86. The trio was added later and the manner of its execution is not indicated. ◆ The idea that the trio of K286 is a later addition to the work was first mooted by Nottebohm in his critical commentary to the AMA edition of the notturno. There is, however, no evidence to support this assertion: Mozart's autograph is lost and the earliest surviving source is a manuscript made for Otto Jahn *c*1850 (Staatsbibliothek zu Berlin, shelfmark Mus. ms. 15345).
87. ◆ It was not as old-fashioned as Abert surmises; see James Webster, 'Towards a History of Viennese Chamber Music in the Early Classical Period'.

the final movement certainly recalls the older practice. Conversely, the independent writing for the violin alongside the keyboard in the second and, in part, the third movement reveals the modern influence of Johann Schobert, while the opening movement – like Haydn's six trios of 1766[88] – is rather an example of a 'keyboard sonata with accompanying instruments'. As with Haydn, the cello is almost slavish in following the keyboard bass. In terms of its artistic merits, K254 falls far short of the great divertimentos of 1776, with only the adagio and its soulful cantilena scaling the same peaks as Mozart's finest works of this period.[89] Another work that creates an unfinished impression is the remarkable trio in B flat major for two violins and cello K266. In the forces on which it draws, including the merely accompanying role of the bass and the frequent crossing of parts in the violins, it harks back to older models, but stylistically speaking it is abreast of its age. The second section of the opening movement is unique among Mozart's works to the extent that it is thematically unrelated to the first section.

In a letter of 8 December 1777, Leopold mentions two keyboard sonatas for four hands that Mozart presumably wrote for himself and his sister. We have already encountered this genre in the context of the Mozarts' visit to London, where Leopold even declared that his son had invented the keyboard duet.[90] All that this proves, of course, is that the Mozarts themselves were unfamiliar with the genre at this time. Equally questionable is whether Johann Christian Bach, whose earliest sonatas for four hands were published in 1770 as his opp. 15 and 18, was inspired by Mozart or whether he was following an older Italian tradition. After all, such a work does indeed exist, albeit undated, in the form of a piece by the Neapolitan composer Niccolò Jommelli. This repertory cannot have been extensive, of course, and it was thanks to Mozart that it gained acceptance, at least in Germany. But, with the exception of the last two sonatas of 1786 and 1787 (K497 and 521), we are completely in the dark about the dating of these works. Stylistically speaking, the earliest seems to be the one in D major K381, as its ideas and thematic writing both point clearly to Italy. The distribution of these ideas between the two performers is still comparatively primitive and generally goes no further than echo effects or simple accompaniment of the melodic line by one or the other player. It almost certainly dates from the time of Mozart's visits to Italy.[91] Far more mature as a piece is the B flat major sonata K358, which is probably one of those mentioned by Leopold in his letter and, to judge by its style, dates from around 1774.[92] The second would appear to be lost.[93] K358 is distinguished from its predecessor above all by its more skilful exploitation of the nature of four-handed playing, with a number of sections already dialogue-like in character.

88.   ◆ The identity of these works is unclear.
89.   Wolfgang performed it in Munich in 1777 (see *Briefe*, ii.40, letter of 6 October 1777). In 1778 Nannerl performed it in Salzburg with Anton Janitsch and Josef Reicha (see *Briefe*, ii.242, letter of 26 January 1778).
90.   ◆ But see Eisen, 'Mozart and the Four-Hand Sonata K. 19d' and Sühring, 'Eine vierhändige Sonate – "bis dahin noch nirgends gemacht"?'. Further, see again p. 44 n. 89 above.
91.   Relying on a passage in a letter of 24 November 1781 (*Briefe*, iii.176) Köchel dates the work to 1781, but the passage in question refers to the sonata for two keyboards K448. Wyzewa and Saint-Foix, *Wolfgang Amédée Mozart*, i.428–31, assume that the piece – of which they write in remarkably dismissive terms – dates from the period between December 1771 and March 1772. We shall never know the exact date. On a more general point, see Niecks, 'Pianoforte four-hand compositions'. According to Niecks, Leopold was right and Burney's duets for two performers of 1777/8 are the first surviving works for four hands that can be dated with any degree of certainty.
92.   Wyzewa and Saint-Foix, *Wolfgang Amédée Mozart*, ii.145–6. Köchel has been misled by a passage in Mozart's letter of 27 June 1781 (*Briefe*, iii.135) to assign it to 1780.
93.   To harness this work together with an unfinished sonata K357 is ruled out on stylistic grounds. Wyzewa and Saint-Foix, *Wolfgang Amédée Mozart*, ii.417, even argue that this fragment dates from 1786. ◆ Almost certainly the two sonatas described by Leopold are K358 and 381, not K358 and a lost work. K381 is probably the earlier of the two: both the paper of the autograph and Mozart's handwriting date it to the summer or autumn of 1772; K358 was probably composed in late 1773 or early 1774.

The fact that Mozart conquered the field of the violin concerto by writing no fewer than five such works within the space of a single year – K207, 211, 216, 218 and 219 – is not unimportant and at the very least shows the attraction that the medium enjoyed at this time.[94] By 1775 little remained of the older Vivaldian model that Mozart had undoubtedly got to know in Italy and that emphasized the recurrent tutti ideas. Although Vivaldi's three-movement form had survived, the concerto's structure and inner design had perceptibly changed under the influence of both the aria and first-movement sonata form. Other influences at work were those of the French violin concerto of Viotti that gave greater scope to the purely technical, virtuosic element[95] and, finally, local influences that were particularly strong in Germany, which, in Mozart's case, meant Vienna.[96] As a result, the concerto had gradually acquired what might be termed an international character that helps to explain the widespread popularity of these works.

Mozart brought all his sympathies to the new genre, as is clear not only from the sheer number that he wrote but also from his attempt, here as elsewhere, to explore new aspects of the form and to test its load-bearing capacity. He retained the genre's three-movement form and also the sonata form of the opening movement, including the latter's traditional division into four tuttis framing three solos. This framework is clear in the first two concertos and remains discernible in the following ones, too, in spite of manifold modifications to it. The broadly structured opening tuttis all represent fully developed symphonic subject-groups that are then worked out in the following solo either thematically or by means of new episodes. Mozart reveals quite exceptional mastery in his treatment of the themes as stated by the orchestra, a mastery especially evident in the development sections. Haydn's thematic writing is more alien to him than ever, and yet the unity of mood is carefully retained. The impression is of a free and imaginative approach to the given ideas, with a glorious harvest of melody suddenly coaxed from apparently infertile soil, while on other occasions a veil of melancholy or even passion is abruptly drawn over an image of cheerfulness and charm, only for the earlier mood to be reasserted by means of witty reminiscences of the main themes. Here Mozart reveals impressive artistry, the intellectual content of which grows from concerto to concerto, leaving little scope for any purely technical, virtuosic element: it is clear that the composer had no time for pyrotechnics. His passage-work is based in the main on scales and broken chords and is effective without being obtrusive. Above all, an extremely emotional and imaginative *cantabilità* keeps pure virtuosity in constant check. The recapitulations omit the opening tutti, but otherwise proceed along regular lines until they reach the soloist's free cadenza, followed by the final tutti. Within these opening movements, there are minor modifications to sonata form, most significantly in the A major concerto (K219), where, following the initial tutti, the soloist interpolates a strangely agitated, almost recitative-like adagio over a mysteriously whispered accompaniment – one of those subjective features that emerges even more clearly from the andantes and final movements.

94. In the form in which it has come down to us, the E flat major concerto K268 cannot be by Mozart, but it contains so much that is clearly authentic that it seems reasonable to assume that Mozart's sketches were worked up by an otherwise unidentified arranger (perhaps Süßmayr or the publisher of the orchestral parts, Johann Anton André); see Rudorff's critical commentary and Wyzewa and Saint-Foix, *Wolfgang Amédée Mozart*, ii.428–9. ◆ Studies of Mozart's handwriting show that K207 probably predates his other violin concertos and was composed in 1773. The concerto K268 (Anh. C14.04 in K⁶) is possibly not by Mozart; the earliest source for this work is an edition by André from 1799. See Landon, 'Controversial Köchels: On the authenticity of Mozart's sixth and seventh violin concertos', and Lebermann, 'Mozart–Eck–André. Ein Beitrag zu KV 268'.
95. See Schering, *Geschichte des Instrumentalkonzerts*, 166ff.
96. ◆ This account is probably incorrect. Vivaldi's concertos had little or no currency by the 1770s and Viotti, so far as is known, had yet to compose a violin concerto (his earliest surviving work in the genre appears to date from c1781). It is likely that the chief influences on Mozart's concerto thinking were the Salzburg serenade tradition and the Viennese concerto, in particular those of Wagenseil; see Eisen, 'Concerto'.

The slow middle movements – especially those of the last three concertos – are splendid examples of the noblest *cantabilità*, professions of an adolescent's infatuated soul that go straight to the heart in their chaste purity. Here one thinks above all of the sweet rêverie of the G major concerto (K216), the romance-like brevity of which recalls the French tradition; particularly poetical is the ending, with the soloist opening his eyes once again and calling out a final farewell to the wonderful vision before him. Scarcely inferior is the andante of the penultimate concerto (K218), a single uninterrupted cantilena for the solo violin expressive of burgeoning yearning. And finally there is the adagio of the fifth concerto, with its mood of suppressed agitation and anguish. It is easy to understand why Brunetti, having studied this movement,[97] asked Mozart to write another one. K261 is on the same high level from an artistic point of view but lacks its predecessor's profoundly personal stamp.

The final movements, too, are products of a youthful spirit that here becomes positively boisterous. Even on a formal level, they reveal an outspoken delight in all manner of innovations. Apart from the first, which is cast in sonata form,[98] and the last, which is described as a 'Tempo di Menuetto', all are headed 'Rondeau', a heading that leaves us in no doubt as to their French models. Yet the form itself is handled in the most varied ways. In the first concerto in D major (K211), the tutti is treated as a recurrent refrain, whereas in the finale of the A major concerto the older dance form of the minuet and trio is combined with rondo form to remarkable effect. In much the same way, rondo and sonata form interact in the second D major concerto (K218). But the most surprising aspect of the last three finales is the unmistakable strain of folk music that they contain. In essence, such surprises are French, but the manner in which they are introduced suggests something of the spirit of the old Austrian suite, while Mozart's predilection for changes of tempo recalls the old quodlibets with their paratactical juxtaposition of the tunes of different folksongs. Even in the allegretto episode in the finale of K216 we can already hear quite clearly an old German folksong,[99] while the musette theme of K218

seems to conceal behind it the 'Straßburger' mentioned in Leopold's letters.[100] In the finale of the A major concerto the strains of a graceful minuet are even interrupted by gypsy music that creates a most eerie impression. It is an effect borrowed from Joseph Haydn, who deploys it relatively frequently in comparison with Mozart's own very sparing use of the practice.

In short, these violin concertos occupy a very special place in Mozart's output. They are the products of a self-assured, even exuberant youthful ardour that revels now in tender infatuation, now in boisterous high spirits, while light-heartedly playing with the parameters of the form. Of course, we shall search in vain for the revolutionary advocate of the *Sturm und Drang* in these

97. See *Briefe*, ii.42 (letter of 9 October 1777).
98. This movement, too, was later replaced by the rondo K269 for Brunetti; see *Briefe*, ii.10 (letter of 25 September 1777).
99. This is a type that can be traced to *Wilhelmus van Nassouwe*; see Erk and Böhme, *Deutscher Liederhort*, iii.52, 58, 214, 310, 494.
100. *Briefe*, ii.36 (letter of 6 October 1777). Liebeskind ('Mozarts Konzert mit dem Straßburger', 8) draws attention to the similarity with the musette in Dittersdorf's 'Carnival' symphony, where it is described as a 'ballo Strasburghese'. Jahn believes that the work in question is K216 or 219, while Lewicki argues that it is the recently rediscovered violin concerto in D major (see below).

works: the hedonistic, brilliantly witty tone of an art designed to entertain aristocratic society is rarely troubled here, with the first D major concerto in particular a veritable model of elegant French-style salon music. Not even in the great keyboard concertos of the first half of the 1780s did Mozart stray beyond these confines. The violin concertos stand in the same relation to these keyboard concertos as the creations of a young gentleman to those of a mature man no longer concerned with wit and whimsy but with matters of substance. For that reason if for no other, these works breathe far more of the spirit of France than the keyboard concertos, a spirit that finds expression not only in individual formal details but, above all, in their preferential treatment of the soloist and in their fluent, elegant style, a style which, in contrast to that of the keyboard concerto of 1773, eschews all virtuosity. Not even in the later violin concertos can we speak of any real rivalry between solo and tutti, so much is Mozart at pains here to replace their schematic interplay by more individual writing and to give the orchestra a more symphonic function. Rarely does the orchestra's role extend beyond that of providing transitions and an accompaniment. The difference between Mozart and his French counterparts consists merely in the fact that he subordinates the technical to the musical and never treats it as an end in itself. Moreover, in discussing the French features in these works,[101] we risk overlooking their non-French aspects, which are no less prominent, namely, the German influence on the melodic writing and Italian influence in terms of both violin technique (Tartini and Nardini are the principal figures in this respect[102]) and, to a lesser extent, the melodic writing. The opening theme of the A major concerto, for example, contains a clear echo of one of Vivaldi's ideas.[103]

An unexpected pendant to this series of concertos was rediscovered only recently in the form of a further concerto in D major. Formerly in the possession of François-Antoine Habeneck, the autograph manuscript is now lost, but it is known to have been dated 'Salisburgo le 16 di Luglio 1777'.[104] There are no grounds for doubting its authenticity: it reveals so many Mozartian features that any other composer is simply out of the question. The only argument is whether the present version is the original one of 1777.[105] The technical demands, including the use of the instrument's highest register and the intervals of a tenth, are considerably greater than those in the earlier concertos and suggest a later adapter, perhaps Baillot or Eugène Sauzay. The surviving cadenzas are deeply unimpressive and certainly not by Mozart. But the revisions have not gone beyond the purely technical: the formal differences between this and the earlier concertos are paralleled within the earlier group, and we already know that Mozart's love of experimentation found particularly fertile ground in his violin concertos. Even so, the concerto's traditional form is still clearly recognizable in both the overall design and the structure of the individual movements, with the usual

---

101. These influences are particularly stressed by Wyzewa and Saint-Foix, *Wolfgang Amédée Mozart*, ii.231–5, in their analyses of these works: they see Gaviniés and Guénin as Mozart's principal models.
102. See Schering, *Geschichte des Instrumentalkonzerts*, 174.
103. Schering, *Geschichte des Instrumentalkonzerts*, 91.
104. It has survived in two old copies, one of which was prepared by Eugène Sauzay for the French violinist Pierre Baillot and is now in the private ownership of Julien Sauzay in Paris, while the other formed part of the collection of Aloys Fuchs and is now lodged in the Staatsbibliothek in Berlin. It was this second copy that was used by Albert Kopfermann for the edition published by Breitkopf & Härtel in Leipzig. See in particular Ernst Lewicki's reviews in 'Musikalien' and the *Dresdener Anzeiger* (16 June 1907); for a detailed analysis, see Heuß, 'Mozarts siebentes Violinkonzert'. ◆ K271a is almost certainly not authentic. Neither the Berlin copy, which dates from *c*1824–5, nor the privately owned copy, dated 1837, provides compelling evidence of Mozart's authorship. See Mahling, 'Bemerkungen zum Violinkonzert D-dur KV 271ⁱ'.
105. Wyzewa and Saint-Foix, *Wolfgang Amédée Mozart*, ii.375–6, assume that the 1777 version was revised in around 1779/80, a revision that was far-reaching on both a formal and instrumentational level, as the surviving score cannot be reconciled with Mozart's style in 1777. But their reasons are not compelling, and both writers run the risk of curtailing the genius's creative right in their methodological determination to channel Mozart's stylistic development along firmly prescribed lines.

four tuttis and three solos effortlessly identifiable in the opening movement, for example. But everything is now on a larger scale, with the relationship between solo and tutti both more idiosyncratic and psychologically more interesting. The themes are now not only more numerous, they remain in neither the same place nor the same hands, but migrate with total freedom from tutti to solo and back again, sometimes even appearing in places where we would least expect to find them. In the recapitulation of the opening movement, for example, the soloist begins with the first subject, which the orchestra immediately arrogates to itself, a procedure that already looks forward to Beethoven's use of dialogue. Entirely new, however, is the way in which a basic idea first stated by the tutti is poetically varied and explored: the andante affords a particularly fine example of this. Here the orchestra launches into a melody born from the spirit of German song, but even before it has finished, the soloist enters on a sustained *d'''* and plays the melody through to the end. But instead of repeating it from start to finish, as it did in the earlier concertos, it entrusts this task to the orchestra, ornamenting the melodic line with trills, broken chords and floating sighs that create an impression that is charming and yearning by turns. French ideas that were aimed in essence at virtuosic brilliance are now suddenly raised to a new and higher level, entering a world of poetry similar to the one that we later find in the middle movement of Beethoven's violin concerto. The final rondo, too, is markedly different from its predecessors in its breadth of structure and the number of its themes, to say nothing of the manner of their distribution between tutti and solo. Conversely, it shares with them a decidedly popular theme that is repeated several times before bringing the movement to a close.[106]

The important role played by the orchestra is reflected in its extremely careful and intelligent treatment, notably in the freedom with which the winds and violas are used. In this regard, the present piece provides a link between the earlier works and those written in Mannheim and Paris. In general, the listener is conscious of the fact that Mozart wrote this piece with the Paris public in mind: brilliance and charm are its basic characteristics, and superficial effects, especially of a purely technical order, play a far greater role than in the earlier concertos. Even so, there is also a contemplative element to the work, notably in the second subject of the opening movement and the final movement's theme in B minor, which is introduced with typically Mozartian abruptness.

As companion pieces to the violin concertos, three keyboard concertos invite our attention: K238 in B flat major dates from January 1776; K246 in C major was written for Countess Antonia Lützow in April 1776; and K 271 in E flat major was written for the French pianist Mlle Jeunehomme and dates from January 1777.[107] Here, too, the most striking feature is the fact that, their formal similarities notwithstanding, each has its own distinctive character in keeping with the circumstances of its composition. It is hard to imagine a greater contrast than that between the C major and E flat major concertos: the former is an example of the wittiest drawing-room music, while the latter is the work of an artist who feels sufficiently mature to impel listeners in the outside world to pay heed to his own world of ideas. Common to all three works is the avoidance of virtuosity as an end in itself, although all three were written with the keyboard clearly in mind, with the last two in particular demanding an outstanding performer. The three-movement form

---

106. It later reappears as the gavotte no. 6 in the ballet *Les petits riens* of 1778; Lewicki even sees in it the 'Straßburger' mentioned above.
107. That Mozart's reputation as a composer had already spread far beyond Salzburg is confirmed by Ernst Christoph Dreßler who in his *Theater-Schule für die Deutschen*, 46, writes: 'I cannot possibly refrain from drawing the attention of Germans to Messrs Mozart and Schröder [that is, Johann Samuel Schröter], two extraordinary geniuses, musicians, clavier players and composers; not we alone, but foreigners too know their merits' [*Dokumente*, 151, *Documentary Biography*, 169]. ◆ Concerning 'Jeunehomme', see p.342 n.18 above.

with final rondo is the same as in the violin concertos, a form also recalled by the menuetto episode in the final movement of the third. But all these works also share a number of individual features, such as the sequential writing in the development sections, which are still the most virtuosic passages in these works. This is a feature to which Mozart returns again and again, in spite of Haydn's example. Among features that bear Mozart's personal imprint is the alternately fanciful and passionate harmonic writing that glides along through minor tonalities by preference – a further echo of Schobert's manner. For the rest, however, these three works are significantly more advanced than the six violin concertos. Progress is discernible not only on the level of thematic development but also on that of the relationship between solo and tutti, producing a work in the E flat major concerto that is entirely worthy of standing alongside the later great keyboard concertos. Admittedly, we still find the surfeit of themes characteristic of the young Mozart, but the way in which he treats them is little short of inspired. Here one thinks first and foremost of the remarkable links between individual themes, with the beginning of one often hooking into the end of another, giving the impression that each idea keeps generating the next one. But the way in which they are developed is equally individual. In essence at least, it does not yet correspond to Haydn's art of logical exposition but aims at giving freer rein to the imagination. Precisely for this reason, however, it is no longer the disjointed manner of the early works that we find here, but a conscious handling of the wealth of ideas at his disposal. Nothing is forgotten, but the individual ideas often occur at the most surprising and least expected points, now in the solo, now in the tutti. Often it is no more than an echo of a theme that is added to another one – as a way of rounding it off, for example. Consider, for instance, the role played by the *espressivo* recitative-like ending of the first subject of the andantino before it brings the movement to an end on a note of broken-hearted hopelessness in the deeply affecting coda.[108] Hand in hand with this approach goes a relationship between solo and tutti that is markedly different from anything found before and that can best be described as dialogue-like. In the earlier works, the two had been strictly divided, with the tutti reduced to a merely accompanying role during the soli, but here we find a more flexible interplay between them, one that goes far beyond questions of pure sonority and affects the work's inner life. Take the very beginning of the concerto: the orchestra enters with a powerful herald-like call, and at once the keyboard answers in manly agreement. And so it goes on: although the old division into four tuttis and three soli is clearly discernible, the links between orchestra and keyboard are none the less closer, with both participants striving for greater variety within the existing framework. Indeed, it is clear from the opening that the themes are now devised with this interplay in mind. Sometimes one of the participants will not allow the other to finish but picks up the thread before the end: listen, for example, to the way in which the soloist enters with a trill at the very end of the opening tutti.[109] Essentially, Mozart is here returning to the older concept of the concerto as represented at this date by Carl Philipp Emanuel Bach, who regarded the medium as a veritable contest between two equal partners. The result is a whole series of completely new and varied psychological contrasts that naturally also affects the way in which the themes are developed. The middle movement, in particular, offers some splendid examples of this. Needless to say, the keyboard remains the feminine partner in this dialogue, a role in keeping with its relative lack of power at this time, its function being to sing, to calm and occasionally also to entreat

108. This is very much the way in which Beethoven used the instrumental recitative, the first such example being in the adagio from his C major concerto.
109. ◆ Further, see Keefe, *Mozart's Piano Concertos: Dramatic Dialogue in the Age of Enlightenment*.

and to grieve; energy and defiance remain the preserve of the orchestra. As we have already noted, virtuosity is always subordinate to the musical idea and never self-satisfied. Also worth mentioning here is the soloist's extremely poetical art of variation. In the second and third of these concertos Mozart wrote out several of the cadenzas in full, but they serve only as bridge passages and, as a result, are figurative rather than thematic. In the final movement of the E flat major concerto they are remarkably agitated and fanciful in character.[110] The orchestral writing in this last-named work, by contrast, is remarkably free in character and already looks forward to the last of the violin concertos, especially in terms of the independent writing for the winds, which occasionally assume sole responsibility for accompanying the soloist.

Between these three solo concertos came the concerto in F major for three keyboards K242 that dates from February 1776 and that was dedicated to Countess Antonia Lodron and her daughters Aloisia and Josepha. It is a contribution to the genre of the old concerto grosso, with the interaction and interplay between the three keyboards aimed more at timbral effects than at any thematic development. The third keyboard is noticeably less prominent than the other two and in the second and third movements in particular is largely content to reinforce the harmonies and to add brief echoes to phrases in the other two instruments, somewhat in the style of the fourth ensemble in the Notturno described above. Evidently Josepha had yet to reach the standard of her mother and elder sister. No doubt it was for this reason that Mozart transcribed the work for two keyboards, a transcription probably made soon afterwards and involving no great loss to the musical argument.[111] In the original, Mozart exploits the tonal effect of the three keyboards with great skill and not without humour, while the orchestra has a far less prominent role to play than in the solo concertos. Of some importance are the cadenzas that Mozart wrote out in full and which, with the exception of the final movement, involve all three players: they are no longer purely figurative, as in the works discussed so far, but constitute free fantasias on all the different themes that have been heard in the rest of the movement. As a result, we have our first pointer here to the way in which Mozart himself used to treat the free cadenzas when performing his own concertos. As with the concerto for Countess Lützow, the work's underlying tone is that of sophisticated music for aristocratic society. Only briefly, as in the first development section, do darker shadows flit past, but the adagio is a rêverie of a sweetness in no way inferior to the other middle movements of this period.

Secular vocal music is represented only by the occasional arias already mentioned. Formally speaking, the comic ones among them – K209, 210, 217 and 256 – are more or less on a level with *La finta giardiniera*. The first two tenor arias from May 1775, 'Si mostra la sorte' and 'Con ossequio, con rispetto', are notable for their independent writing for the orchestra. Far more valuable from an artistic point of view is Dorina's aria 'Voi avete un cor fedele' K217, which consists of a constant interplay between an andantino grazioso and an allegro. Particularly striking is its heart-

---

110. ◆ In general, Mozart's piano concerto cadenzas are confusingly described in the literature. For K238, cadenzas survive for all three movements (K626a/I/5–7); for K246 cadenzas from the late 1770s survive for all three movements (K626a/I/9, 12 and *deest*), from the late 1770s for the first two movements (K626a/I/9 and 12), and from c1779 for the first two movements (K626a/I/10 and 14); for K271, cadenzas and lead-ins from c1777 for all three movements are known (K626a/I/16, 18 and *deest*) as well as cadenzas from 1784 or 1785 for the first two movements (K626a/I, 15, 17, 19 and 20) and lead-ins for the third movement (K626a/I/21 and 22) sent by Mozart to his sister in a letter of 15 February 1783 (*Briefe*, iii.256). All of the cadenzas and lead-ins are edited in NMA X/31/3.

111. ◆ The arrangement for two pianos of K242 probably dates from 1779 or 1780. Cadenzas for the three-piano version are written directly in the autograph score; cadenzas for the two-piano version are known from the surviving authentic parts.

felt and impassioned tone, which in its slow section comes very close to that of a German song. This willingness to explore the emotional depths of the text goes beyond Italian practice and, like the lively writing for the orchestra, looks forward to the later Mozart. By contrast, the tenor aria 'Clarice cara mia sposa' K256 of September 1776 is a typically Italian *buffa* aria describing a vain-glorious captain who 'in tempo commodo d'un gran ciarlone' prattles on about how he will get his way, while a certain Don Timoteo keeps trying to interrupt him with the brief recitative-like interjections typical of *opera buffa*. This torrent of words is poured out in the usual Italian manner in a veritable orgy of triplets and the swiftest possible parlando. It is virtually impossible to trace any real melodic line here. All the more important, therefore, is the authentically Italian, merrily chuckling motif in the orchestra that accompanies this floodtide of words with its witty harmonic volatility:

A tragic note, by contrast, is struck by the recitative and aria 'Ombra felice' K255 for contralto written in September 1776 for Francesco Fortini for insertion in Michele Mortellari's *Didone*.[112] The brief but highly expressive recitative ends with a sudden and genuinely Mozartian modulation which, as an expression of profound and authentic emotion, anticipates the opening words of the aria, 'Io ti lascio'. Mozart again treats the two basic moods of the text – the sorrow of parting and the pain of abandonment – as two separate sections, each of which is repeated, one slow section and one fast, but linked together by a common refrain, 'Vengo, oh ciel, deh lascia, oh pena', a notable attempt to express the conceptional unity of mood on a formal level also. The ending, too, repeats the opening bars of the andante before the allegro brings the aria to a rapid conclusion, effectively reflecting the vacillating mood of the whole. These emotions are expressed with real truth and nobility, without recourse to coloratura, with the allegro in particular filled with seething passion of a genuinely Mozartian kind.[113]

The finest of these pieces is the great solo *scena* for Andromeda that Mozart wrote for Josepha Duschek[114] in the summer of 1777. 'Ah, lo previdi' K272 is one of the last works that he wrote before leaving Salzburg and one of his most magnificent contributions to the genre, unusual not least for the fact that, unlike most arias of this kind, it does not build to a passionate climax but traces the course of an emotion that gradually dies away, ending in a rapt rêverie and, finally, a resigned and broken-hearted return to reality, this concluding section again very finely observed from a psychological point of view. The opening recitative leads via a brief and violent outburst to the agitated conflict of emotions that typifies the work as a whole, with the two main antitheses – suppressed anguish and wild passion – finding masterfully succinct expression within the first few bars. The harmonies modulate constantly and abruptly, passing without any clear break into the first cavatina, one of those genuinely Mozartian numbers woven from passion and despair and

---

112. ◆ The text is from Mortellari's *Arsace*, first produced at Padua in 1775.
113. As late as 12 April 1783 we find Mozart asking his father to send him this aria; see *Briefe*, iii.264.
114. See above; see also Leopold's letter of 15 December 1780 (*Briefe*, iii.57), in which the latter reports that Josepha Duschek was wanting Mozart to write her another aria but that he, Leopold, had declared this to be impossible at present.

achieving no real resolution. Here the sense of agitation reaches its highest pitch, with the vocal line reduced now to brief and breathless phrases, now to urgent outbursts of explosive violence. The orchestra, too, is in a state of turmoil with its syncopations, off-beat rhythms and unison writing, but it enters a plea for the ungrateful but still loved Perseus in the form of a beautiful motif that follows straight on from Andromeda's initial outburst of anger:

But in an extraordinarily poetical stroke, this motif is then used at the end of the cavatina to restore the earlier calm, and in the following recitative the only emotion left is pain at the feeling of loss. This passage breathes a far greater sense of calm than the opening recitative, although Mozart's predilection for chromaticisms and harsh modulations is entirely true to Andromeda's character. The orchestral motifs are more tender, more entreating, more songlike, with some of them – notably at the word 'infelice' – striking the same natural tone that Gluck, too, adopted in such cases. In the following cavatina, however, nothing remains of the earlier mood of wild passion but tender, feminine self-sacrifice. As always with arias that deal with the River Lethe, the tone is rapt and visionary. And Mozart also includes the wind solos favoured by Italian composers in these circumstances, while the sense of mystery is further underscored by the use of muted first violins and violas and by pizzicati in the second violins and basses. But it is the vocal line that is all-important here, almost literally overflowing with tender infatuation, as though a sense of gentle ease were slowly stealing over the hapless Andromeda's limbs after the painful tensions of the past, and only right at the very end, as the final phrase of the cavatina returns fitfully in the allegro, does the old feeling of agitation flare up once more, but only, of course, to sink back down again. The scene dies away in a shadowy *piano*, as though some dreamlike vision were fading from sight. The whole scene reveals a master of musical psychologizing and makes it clear what Mozart could have achieved in *opera seria* at this time if only he had received a commission.[115]

All these arias are scored for the sort of orchestra usually found in Neapolitan operas of this period. The recitatives are accompanied by strings alone.[116]

115. When Mozart sent this *scena* to Aloysia Weber in July 1778, he added a note (in Italian): 'Most of all, I advise you to heed the expression marks, to think carefully about the meaning and the force of the words, to make a serious attempt to put yourself in Andromeda's situation and position and, in short, to imagine that you really are this character' (*Briefe*, ii.420, letter of 30 July 1778).

116. The aria with German words, *Der Liebe himmlisches Gefühl* K119, which has survived only in the form of a vocal score, was almost certainly originally in Italian. Jahn's suggestion (*W. A. Mozart*, fourth edition, i.265, n. 3) that it dates from the period of Mozart's early Italian operas is highly unlikely, given its advanced style, but it is equally doubtful whether, as Wyzewa and Saint-Foix claim (*Wolfgang Amédée Mozart*, ii.426), it can be dated to 1782 on the strength of a handful of reminiscences of *Die Entführung aus dem Serail*. Perhaps it is a further insertion aria for an opera by another composer and dates from the same period as the other works discussed in this chapter. ◆ Mozart's authorship of *Der Liebe himmlisches Gefühl* is uncertain; the earliest surviving source is a piano score published by Breitkopf & Härtel in 1814.

Mozart wrote no songs during this period.[117] In Salzburg they would no doubt not have been appreciated, not least because even in Vienna lieder composition was still in its earliest infancy. And the few foreign virtuosos who passed through Salzburg were naturally disinclined to familiarize audiences with the unprepossessing genre of the German song. And so it was not until he moved to Vienna that Mozart himself embarked on his period of song – if we can speak of such a thing in this context.

Mozart was twenty-one when he left behind him the confines of Salzburg and set out into the big wide world of music. He was a virtuoso on one instrument, the harpsichord, on which he was one of the foremost exponents of his day, and he was well above average on two others, the violin and the organ. And thanks to his early maturity and prolificity, he could stand comparison as a composer with any of his elders. By now he had written almost three hundred works embracing every musical genre with the exception of independent organ music and a cappella works, a genre which in any case was everywhere in decline at this time.[118] The only exceptional aspect of Mozart's output at this time was his youth, not his prolificity as such, which was the hallmark of every composer in the age before Beethoven and a natural consequence of the contemporary practice whereby works were written to commission. Of course, Mozart's standing in the world of music was still modest in the extreme. The noisy successes of his childhood had long since faded from memory, and even the laurels that he had garnered in Italy had not been sufficiently long-lasting to help him acquire any real reputation in his homeland: there were very few people in Germany who had even heard of the operas he had written for Italy. And the situation had been much the same with La finta giardiniera in Munich. Meanwhile, as a result of the decentralization of musical life in Germany at this time, the sacred works and instrumental pieces that he had written in Salzburg remained confined to a very limited area, with few of them finding their way beyond the immediate vicinity. The situation was somewhat better in the case of his standing as a virtuoso, for here he had already caused something of a stir, at least in south Germany and Austria, although he could not for a moment compete, of course, with the international virtuosos of his day.

None the less, Mozart's development was both healthy and, in keeping with his character, harmonious. There was nothing forced or unwholesome about it, and if it was volatile, then this merely reflected his own artistic nature. But above all as a human being he developed along natural and healthy lines. With his return from his final visit to Italy, the youth matured into manhood, albeit not without suffering the physical and psychological crises necessarily bound up with this change. His view of the world grew clearer and broader, and he gradually began to evolve a philosophy of his own. Such a view was entirely typical of someone of his age, basically optimistic, but permeated with that unconscious wistfulness and yearning that characterize adolescence. And the cares of life also began to make themselves known all too clearly in his employer's hard school. As we have seen, these cares even affected his productivity, although ultimately they could do little serious harm. Above all, however, these years of adolescence found Mozart's development as a

---

117. *Pace* Jahn and Deiters (*W. A. Mozart*, first edition, iii.349, and fourth edition, i.265), the canzonetta *Ridente la calma* seems to me not to date from this early period, not least because the keyboard part is written out in full, something that we find only much later in Mozart's lieder. A more accurate dating of this delightful if not especially significant piece is not possible. ◆ *Ridente la calma* is also uncertain as a work by Mozart; no source for the work is known before Breitkopf & Härtel's edition of 1799. Possibly the work is by Mysliveček; see Flothuis, 'Ridente la calma – Mozart oder Mysliveček'.
118. ◆ Mozart had written four a cappella works by this time: the motet 'God is our Refuge' K20, composed at London in 1765; the lost *Stabat mater* and fugue K33a and 41f, listed in Leopold Mozart's 1768 catalogue of his son's work; and the antiphon 'Quaerite primum' K86, Wolfgang's exercise for the Bolognese Accademia filarmonica, composed in October 1770.

person catching up with that as an artist: during his childhood, the artist had far outstripped the man. Thanks to his astonishing adaptability and formal skills, he had succeeded in solving problems here to which he was not yet psychologically equal. But now he began to gain an inner understanding of the spirit and problems of contemporary art and to pass from mere imitation to independent composition, even though he continued to commit the errors of his youth, albeit on a smaller scale. As before, the most serious of these mistakes was closely bound up with his principal strength, his teeming imagination, the result of a restless and dissipated nature that preferred to introduce two new ideas rather than exhaust one of them from a thematic point of view. Here, too, the fermenting wine was beginning to be fined at least to the extent that the young genius no longer allowed himself simply to be driven along by his own wealth of ideas but sought to introduce some discipline and order to the whole of this varied world. Indeed, we even see the first promising signs of an attempt at strictly thematic development, an attempt inspired by Joseph Haydn. Yet the works of this 'young Mozart' have a very special charm to them, such is their *galant* ardour, their often sudden outbursts of emotional anguish and their profligate flood of ideas. Writers who restrict themselves to the works of the final decade of his life, as they all too often do, know only half the artist.

We have already seen how, at least from the time of their most recent visit to Vienna, Leopold Mozart had made all manner of attempts to find his son a post away from Salzburg, and it seems likely that he resumed contact with Padre Martini chiefly with a view to his obtaining a new position for Mozart, even if only in Italy. His attempts were unavailing. Meanwhile, the atmosphere in the archiepiscopal palace was growing perceptibly cooler. The real reason for this growing tension must be sought in the fact that, as the works of 1777 make clear, the now mature composer could no longer bring himself to subscribe to an ideal from which he had grown increasingly remote. And, not having set foot outside Salzburg since 1775, he felt an urgent need to reacquaint the world with his gifts as a virtuoso and remind people of his skills as a composer. It will have been with silent envy that he observed Mlle Jeunehomme and the few other visitors from the outside world whom fate had brought to Salzburg. And so he began, very quietly, to plan a new grand tour, a decision clear from the numerous new concertos that he composed during these last two years.

Much as Leopold aided and abetted him in this resolve, he remained concerned at the thought of its execution, not least because of what he knew of Mozart's character. For some time, Mozart had harboured the notion – typical of an adolescent – that the whole family should set out on this grand tour and live off its proceeds until such time as they found a permanent appointment. But, as Leopold later wrote to his son in a letter of 18 December 1777,[119] he was sufficiently experienced to know that circumstances had changed since Mozart's childhood and he was entirely against the idea of exposing his family to so uncertain and arduous a future. But to allow his son to set off on his own was equally unacceptable to him. He knew how helpless Mozart was in all practical matters, especially when travelling, as he 'knew little about the different sorts of money and had no idea about packing and suchlike necessities'. And all his old mistrust of the honesty and reliability of his colleagues came flooding back, so convinced was he that they would feel only envy and resentment towards his son. It was his greatest worry that Mozart was so different from him in this respect, and, keen-eyed as ever, he had already realized that, with his honest and good-natured character, his youthful impetuosity and sharp tongue, he was by no means the man to win through

119. *Briefe*, ii.190–4.

and assert himself in the face of the world's hurly-burly. His words of 16 February 1778 are highly significant in this regard:

> My son! You are hot-headed and impulsive in everything. Your whole character has changed since your childhood and boyhood. As a child and boy you were serious rather than childish, and whenever you sat at the harpsichord or were otherwise occupied with music, no one dared play even the slightest joke on you. Why, even your expression was so solemn that, observing the premature burgeoning of your talent and the invariably grave and thoughtful expression on your face, many discerning people in different countries doubted whether you would live to a ripe old age. But it seems to me that you are now far too ready to retort in a bantering tone to the very first challenge that confronts you – and that, of course, is the first step towards undue familiarity etc., which anyone who wants to preserve his self-respect will try to avoid in this world. . . . It is just your good heart that prevents you from detecting any shortcomings in a person who roundly praises you or who speaks highly of you and flatters you to the skies, so you give him all your trust and love; and yet, as a boy, you were exceptionally modest and used to cry when people praised you too much. The greatest art of all is to know oneself and then, my dear son, do as I do and try to get to know other people properly.[120]

Nor had Leopold failed to notice how rapidly his son has developed as an artist during the last few years, even though he can only have suspected his true greatnesss, being no longer in a position fully to understand it. At all events, he was afraid – and with good reason – that worldly wisdom would not keep pace with the sacred fire that was burning within him. And finally he feared the moral dangers that awaited his inexperienced son as the latter left behind him his parental home, forsaking Salzburg's middle-class way of life and setting off into the big wide world. And so he kept advising him to be patient and, both as man and artist, to prepare as conscientiously as possible for this great journey.

But force of circumstances proved more powerful than Mozart's vacillating father. By 1777 the arguments between Mozart and the archbishop must have become particularly violent as the letters that father and son exchanged shortly before Mozart set out for Mannheim[121] speak of all manner of annoyances and even of 'baseness'. In June they petitioned the archbishop for permission to leave on a grand tour lasting several months, a request that the archbishop flatly dismissed on the grounds that he needed his players for the forthcoming visit of the Emperor Joseph II. Later, of course, he declared that he could not tolerate the thought of members of his orchestra 'going round begging'. Wolfgang, however, was allowed to go on his own as he was on only part-time service. Leopold was about to agree to this compromise, albeit with a heavy heart, when Colloredo raised new objections. Mozart's petition, to which we owe our knowledge of all these events, continues:

> Parents take pains to enable their children to earn their own bread, and they owe this both to their own interest and to that of the State. The more of talent that children have received from God, the greater is the obligation to make use thereof, in order to ameliorate their own and their parents' circumstances, to assist their parents, and to take care of their own advancement and

---

120. *Briefe*, ii.283–4.
121. *Briefe*, ii.111 (letter of 8 November 1777); and *Briefe*, ii.129 (letter of 17 November 1777).

future. To profit from our talents is taught us by the Gospel. I therefore owe it before God and in my conscience to my father, who indefatigably employs all his time in my upbringing, to be grateful to him with all my strength, to lighten his burden, and to take care not only of myself, but of my sister also, with whom I should be bound to commiserate for spending so many hours at the harpsichord without being able to make profitable use of it.

May Your Serene Highness graciously permit me, therefore, to beg most submissively to be released from service, as I am obliged to make the best use of the coming September, so as not to be exposed to the bad weather of the ensuing cold months. Your Serene Highness will not take this most submissive request amiss, since already three years ago, when I begged for permission to travel to Vienna, Your Highness was graciously pleased to declare that I had nothing to hope for and would do better to seek my fortune elsewhere.[122]

On 28 August His Serene Highness added a note in his own hand to this petition: 'To the Exchequer with the observation that father and son have permission to seek their fortune elsewhere, according to the Gospel.' Leopold's dismissal was rescinded in a later decree on the grounds that Colloredo wanted peace and quiet in his Kapelle and had therefore left him in his old position.

Wolfgang's dismissal caused something of a stir in Salzburg and, according to Leopold's letter of 9 October 1777, even Brunetti thought 'Questo era del Principe un puntiglio mal inteso, col suo proprio danno': 'This was a mistaken idea the prince persisted in, to his own loss.'[123] The archbishop's immediate entourage shared the general sense of regret. In his letter of 4 October 1777, Leopold reports that the lord high steward Count Franz Lactanz Firmian had bought four horses and was looking forward to the pleasure that they would give Mozart, of whom he was very fond. But on his return to Salzburg he had learnt to his dismay of the latest turn of events. Shortly afterwards he was paying his respects to Colloredo, when the latter exclaimed: 'Now we have one man less in the orchestra.' Firmian replied: 'Your Grace has lost a great virtuoso.' 'Why?' 'He is the greatest keyboard player I have ever heard in my life; on the violin he rendered very good service to Your Grace and he is a first-rate composer.' At this the archbishop went very quiet.[124] On 29 June 1778, the local canon, Count Franz Joseph Starhemberg, admitted that Mozart's complaints were fully justified and that all the foreigners at the Salzburg court had admired only the young Mozart. He included himself among these admirers.[125]

Leopold, too, was a worried man, as the journey was now to take place under particularly unfavourable circumstances and he himself was unable to accompany his son. But the die was cast and it was now a question of preparing for the undertaking in such a way that Mozart got the most out of it and, above all, found a permanent appointment elsewhere. The cost of the journey was to be covered by means of concerts and commissions. And, as before, it was only princely residences that were considered as suitable ports of call. In drawing up his plan of action, Leopold could rely on his own numerous connections and his topographical knowledge, and there is something almost touching about the zeal with which he thought of even the smallest detail in his attempt to smooth his son's way for him. In particular, he was tireless in impressing upon him that the main aim of his journey was to acquire a reputation, money and a fixed appointment. This practical advice was only too opportune as Mozart set off into the world with the *naïveté* of a

122. The petition is reproduced by Pirckmayer, 'Zur Lebensgeschichte Mozarts', 140 [*Dokumente*, 145–6, *Documentary Biography*, 162–3].
123. ◆ *Briefe*, ii.41–2.
124. *Briefe*, ii.34–5 (letter of 4 October 1777).
125. *Briefe*, ii.380.

young and impetuous artist, firmly believing that his art would help him to overcome every obstacle. The happy prospect of leaving Salzburg added further to his carefree attitude and encouraged him to believe that his worried father was seeing things in far too black a light. So concerned was Leopold that he decided to send his wife on the journey with Mozart.

He knew, of course, that Anna Maria was no substitute for himself and that, however great her love for her son, she had neither the energy nor the ability to keep the young hothead on what he regarded as the straight and narrow. But at least she was a seasoned traveller and could keep an eye on the outward aspects of the journey, especially the financial side, in which regard Leopold had particular doubts about his son's competence. Here he demanded that mother and son should keep him fully informed, so that he would always be ready to come to their aid in word and deed. Yet even in this respect Anna Maria was not always entirely reliable, revealing a negligence that was due in part to her indulgence towards her son and in part to her congenital idleness, even though she sometimes claimed to be so tired from packing that she 'could shove her feet in her face'.[126] On the other hand, Leopold had complete trust in her when it came to Mozart's health. 'But I beg you, my dear Wolfgang', he wrote to his son on 28 September 1777,

> not to indulge in any excesses, for from your youth up you have been used to a regular life. You must avoid hot drinks, as you know that you soon get hot and that you prefer the cold to warmth, clear proof that your blood has a tendency to over-heat and immediately starts to boil. And so strong wines and drinking too much wine are bad for you. Just think how unhappy and depressed you would make your mother in a far distant land, not to mention myself.[127]

In particular, however, Leopold regarded the presence of Mozart's mother, whom the composer loved with childlike trust, as a moral safeguard. As a result, he believed, Mozart would behave himself. And he held out his own example in his attempt to encourage his son to show the greatest circumspection in his dealings with the world:

> I made the acquaintance and sought only the friendship of people of position – and, what is more, among these I associated only with older people, never with young fellows, not even if they were of the highest rank. I never invited anyone to visit me in my rooms with any frequency, as I wanted to remain completely free, and I always thought it more sensible to visit others when it suited *me*. For if I do not like the man or if I have work or business to do, I can stay away, whereas if people come to see me and behave badly, I know not how to get rid of them; and even a person who is not unwelcome to me will often prevent me from getting on with some urgent task. You are a young man of 22, so you do not have that seriousness of purpose that comes with age and that might discourage any young fellow, of whatever rank – be he an adventurer, joker or trickster, young or old – from seeking your acquaintance and friendship in order to draw you into his company and then by degrees bend you to his will. One drifts imperceptibly into these traps and then cannot get out again. I shan't even mention women, as the greatest reserve and prudence are necessary here, Nature herself being our enemy, and he who does not act with all prudence and show the greatest reserve will exert himself in vain later on in his attempts to escape from the labyrinth: this is a misfortune that

---

126. ◆ Letter of 11 October 1777 (*Briefe*, ii.48).
127. *Briefe*, ii.17. Mozart attempted to allay his father's fears in his reply of 2 October 1777: 'I eat very little, drink water, finally with dessert a small glass of wine'; *Briefe*, ii.29.

generally ends only in death. How blindly we may often be led on by what seem initially to be meaningless jokes, flatteries and jests etc. but at which Reason, when she awakens, is ashamed – this you yourself may perhaps already have discovered; I do not want to reproach you for this. I know that you love me not merely as your father but also as your truest and surest friend.[128]

But Leopold went even further. He must have known what this journey would cost and that he needed to provide the travellers with money not only for the journey itself but for all eventualities. He had no resources of his own and so, for better or worse, he ran up debts. As before, Hagenauer and Bullinger proved willing to help. Together with Nannerl, he reduced his household to the barest essentials, even deciding to return to teaching, which he had given up some time previously.

My dear Wolfgang, not only do I not distrust you, even in the slightest, but I place all my trust and confidence in your childlike love. Our future depends on your common sense, which you certainly possess, if only you will listen to it, and on favourable circumstances. These latter we cannot command, but you will always act according to common sense. I hope so, and I beg you.

These words are taken from Leopold's letter of 5 February 1778[129] and afford the clearest evidence of the cares and wishes that preoccupied him at this time. But his self-regard was also stirred. His son was not to go round begging but travel as an artist who commanded respect not least through his outward appearance. After all, he himself had always set store by travelling in a manner befitting his rank. And so the best clothes were singled out, compositions were chosen with which Mozart could introduce himself to the world, and everything packed into a 'chaise', a particularly comfortable form of transport.

128.   *Briefe*, ii.257–8 (letter of 5 February 1778).
129.   *Briefe*, ii.257.

16

Munich and Augsburg

Mother and son left Salzburg early on the morning of 23 September 1777. Until the very end, Leopold had struggled manfully to conceal his emotions, with the result that he forgot to give Mozart his father's blessing, but, as soon as they had left, he collapsed in a chair, utterly disconsolate. Nannerl, too, could not stop crying and did not recover until evening, when the two of them attempted to take their mind off things by playing a game of piquet.[1]

Meanwhile, Wolfgang set off through the autumnal morning mists beside himself with happiness. The nightmare of Salzburg was finally over and he felt that a weight had been lifted from his shoulders, helping to reconcile him to saying goodbye to his father and sister and causing his father's admonitions to fade even further from his mind. Entirely characteristic of the light-hearted, childlike frame of mind with which he set out into the world is the first letter that he wrote to his father from Wasserburg 'undecima hora noctis' – at eleven o'clock in the evening of the day of his departure.[2] For him, the most remarkable incident on their journey was the sight of a 'lop-sided cow, a thing we'd never seen before'. They also met two acquaintances from Memmingen, one of whom, Jakob von Unold, asked that his best wishes be conveyed to Leopold and 'to my brute of a sister'. Only right at the end of his letter does Mozart remember that he has left his 'diplomas' at home, in other words, the diplomas attesting to his membership of the Academies of Bologna and Verona – the very documents on which Leopold had laid such special emphasis. This alone will have given him pause for thought, in spite of Mozart's earlier attempts to allay his fears:

> Viviamo come i principi [We are living like princes], all that we lack is Papa; but it is God's will, all will yet be well. I hope that Papa is well and as happy as I am; I'm being very good. I'm like another Papa and taking care of everything. I've just asked if I can pay the postilions as I can deal with these fellows better than Mama. . . . Both of us beg Papa to look after himself . . . and remember that our Mufti H. C.[3] is an idiot, but that God is compassionate, merciful and loving.[4]

Their first port of call was Munich. Given the present situation and his earlier failure to gain a foothold there, Leopold expected little in the way of success, but there was no avoiding a further such attempt. Armed with the diplomas in question, Mozart could show the Elector Maximilian that he was thoroughly accomplished as a composer. All that he needed to do was to find some influential patrons and demonstrate his abilities by means of some new commissions.

---

1. ◆ This account derives from Leopold Mozart's letter of 25 September 1777 (*Briefe*, ii.84).
2. *Briefe*, ii.6–7 (letter of 23 September 1777).
3. Hieronymus Colloredo.
4. ◆ *Briefe*, ii.7 (letter of 23 September 1777).

Mother and son lodged with Franz Joseph Albert, the 'learned landlord' [of the Black Eagle] with whom they had become friendly on their previous visits to the city.[5] Wolfgang's first audience was with the intendant of Munich's court theatres, Count Joseph Anton Seeau.[6] Already apprised of the composer's dismissal, he gave Mozart a friendly reception and advised him to appeal without delay to the elector either in person or in writing. No one knew better than he that Munich currently lacked a decent composer.

Mozart also called on the prince-bishop of Chiemsee, Ferdinand Christoph Count Waldburg-Zeil, who was detained in Munich on diplomatic business. He, too, put in a good word with the elector on Mozart's behalf, but, like the prince-bishop, was told that it was 'still too soon'. Even the electress herself had promised to help, but in the event was forced to 'shrug her shoulders' and to doubt that anything would come of the plan.[7]

Mozart received confirmation of this when he was introduced to the elector by the influential cellist Franz Xaver Woschitka (1728–96) just as the elector was on the point of going hunting. Mozart reported on their conversation in a letter to his father of 30 September 1777:

When the elector came up to me, I said: 'Your Highness will allow me to throw myself most humbly at your feet and offer you my services.' 'So you've left Salzburg for good.' 'Yes, Your Highness, for good.' 'Why's that? Have the two of you fallen out?' 'Certainly not, Your Highness, I just asked him for his permission to travel and he refused, so I was forced to take this step, though I'd long been thinking of leaving, as Salzburg is no place for me, that's for sure.' 'Good Heavens, there's a young man for you! But your father's still in Salzburg?' 'Yes, Your Highness, he too throws himself &c. I've already been to Italy three times, I've written three operas, I'm a member of the Bologna Academy, where I had to pass a test at which many maestri have toiled and sweated for 4 or 5 hours, but which I completed in an hour: this may serve to show that I'm capable of serving at any court. But my only wish is to serve Your Highness, who is himself a great . . . .' 'Yes, my dear child, but I have no vacancy. I'm sorry, if only there were a vacancy.' 'I assure Your Highness that I'd be a credit to Munich.' 'I know, but it's no good, there's no vacancy.' He said this as he was walking away. I commended myself to his good graces.[8]

Although there was no longer any hope of an appointment at court, Seeau none the less attempted to find some other way of keeping Mozart in Munich. He was not only intendant at the theatre but also, in part, entrepreneur: the elector paid for the orchestra and ballet, contributing an annual subsidy of 9000 florins towards the income, which was Seeau's to keep. With this sum he had to run the theatre and ballet and engage members of both companies, most of whom were local and whom he could pay as little as eight to twelve florins a month.[9] Italian operas were presented only during the carnival and at major court festivities – and then generally free of charge. In addition to plays, there were also tentative steps to stage German operas, which meant adaptations of Italian and French operas, as there were still no original German operas here: Munich had no more time than Vienna for Hiller's north German singspiels. (It was not until the following year that the Viennese singspiel was to blossom into life.) With Mozart at its head,

5. Johann Heinrich Friedrich Müller, *Abschied von der National-Schaubühne*, 215.
6. Rudhart, *Geschichte der Oper am Hofe zu München*, i.134–5.
7. ◆ See Mozart's letters of 26 and 29 September 1777 (*Briefe*, ii.11–14 and 21–4).
8. ◆ *Briefe*, ii.23–4 (letter of 30 September 1777).
9. Müller, *Abschied von der National-Schaubühne*, 219.

Munich would have had the opportunity to take the lead in this new development, for although Mozart had proclaimed himself an enthusiastic champion of Italian opera only a short time earlier in a letter to Padre Martini, he was now completely sold on German opera. For the first time an aspect of his character emerges that is frequently overlooked, his sense of German nationalism. It is an aspect which, after a few further flirtations with Italian art, was increasingly to dominate his music from now on.[10]

Seeau asked the bishop of Chiemsee whether, with a little financial support, Mozart might be persuaded to remain in Munich, but the bishop naturally doubted this. Seeau also hoped that Mozart might himself make some proposal along these lines. The composer's letter to his father of 2 October 1777 includes an extremely vivid account of his impressions of German opera and, in particular, of the singer Margarethe Kaiser:

The leading soprano is called Keiser and is the daughter of a cook by a local count, a very attractive girl, pretty on stage. I haven't yet seen her from close quarters. She was born here. When I heard her, it was only the third time she'd appeared in public. She has a beautiful voice, not large, but not weak either, very pure, good intonation. Her teacher is Valesi [Johann Baptist Walleshauser (1735–1816)], and it's clear from her singing that he understands both the art of singing and how to teach it. Whenever she holds a note for a few bars, I've been surprised at the beauty of her crescendo and diminuendo. She takes her trills very slowly, which I like, as they'll be all the cleaner and clearer when she wants to take them more quickly later on: quick trills are in any case easier than slow ones. People really like her here – and I number myself among them. Mama sat in the stalls; she went in at half past four as she wanted to be sure of a seat, but I didn't go in until half past six, as I have free access to all the boxes, enough people know me here. I was in the Brancas' box. I kept my opera-glasses trained on Mlle Keiser, and she often drew a tear from me; I often shouted brava, bravissima, as I kept thinking that this was only the third time she'd appeared on stage. The piece was called the Fishermaiden [*La pescatrice*], a very good translation based on the music of Piccinni. They still don't have any original works. They'd also like to have a German *opera seria* – – and they want me to write it.[11]

This wish was shared by Klemens Huber, who had already seen and heard Mozart at Mesmer's during his most recent visit to Vienna in 1773 and who now renewed his acquaintance at Albert's in the course of one of his regular evening visits to the latter's hostelry. Huber was Seeau's assistant at the theatre and, to quote Mozart, his job was 'to read through the plays that they are intending to perform and to improve, spoil, add to or make cuts to them'.[12] This editing process may well have been necessary as the directors performed everything sent in to them and were even contractually obliged to rehearse everything written by local authors. And since 'virtually every student and lower-ranking official fancied himself as a writer' at this time, the theatre was 'inundated with rubbish'.[13] It could hardly be a matter of indifference to a man like Huber that a composer as talented as Mozart might be lost to the Munich theatre.

10. In his letter to Leopold cited below, he writes: 'I am *very popular* here, and how much more popular I'd be if, through my music, I could help to advance the cause of the German national theatre? And there's no doubt this would happen, for as soon as I heard the German singspiel, I was already very keen to write something' (*Briefe*, ii.29, letter of 2 October 1777).
11. *Briefe*, ii.29–30.
12. ◆ *Briefe*, ii.12 (letter of 26 September 1777).
13. Müller, *Abschied von der National-Schaubühne*, 219.

Others shared this view, with Baron Rumling, for example, complimenting Mozart: 'I love the theatre, good actors and actresses, good singers of both sexes and a fine composer like yourself!' In reporting this remark in his letter to his father of 2 October 1777, Mozart added: 'Only words, it is true, and it's easy to talk, but he's never spoken like this to me before.' Count Joseph von Salern (1718–1805)[14] was in overall charge of music and opera in Munich. Mozart visited him on successive days, performing 'several things from memory, including the two cassations for the countess [Lodron] and, by way of a conclusion, the *Finalmusik* with the rondo, all of them by heart'.[15] Salern applauded most warmly, prompting Mozart to comment that he only wished the elector had been present to hear his remarks. He felt that he was a match for any living composer.

Mozart also renewed contact with earlier acquaintances and friends, including the soprano castrato Tommaso Consoli, the flautist Johann Baptist Becke and, notwithstanding his father's ban, the composer Josef Mysliveček, who was then in hospital suffering from venereal disease. At a private concert at Albert's, he met a pupil of Tartini's, whose name he gives as Dubreill,[16] and whom he thought of as a fine orchestral player with excellent intonation. As it turned out, his high opinion was misplaced:

We began with 2 Haydn quintets, but to my dismay I found I could hardly hear him; he was incapable of playing 4 bars in a row without losing his way; he couldn't work out the fingering and had only a nodding acquaintance with short rests. The best one can say about him is that he was very polite and praised the quintets, but apart from that – . . . I then played the concertos in C, B flat and E flat and then my trio. And a fine accompaniment I received: in the adagio I had to play his part for 6 bars. Last but not least, I played my latest cassation in B flat and they all opened their eyes in amazement! I played as though I were the finest fiddler in all Europe.[17]

One of Mozart's most loyal friends proved to be his landlord, Franz Joseph Albert, who was also a great music lover.[18] In an attempt to persuade Mozart to remain in Munich, he offered to find ten good friends, each of whom would contribute a ducat a month, producing 600 florins a year. It would be easy, he went on, to persuade Seeau to commission new works from him, so that he could reckon on an annual income of 800 florins. Mozart was enthusiastic about the plan and set about devising ways of surviving until it could be put into practice. The concerts would be held every Saturday in Albert's hall, starting in November and lasting until May, by which date foreign visitors, too, could be counted on coming. Maria Anna was in agreement with his plan, but Leopold, not without reason, had reservations, doubting whether these 'ten charming friends' would be found and, even if they were, whether they would keep their word. Unless the matter

14. Rudhart, *Geschichte der Oper am Hofe zu München*, i.130.

15. *Briefe*, ii.28–9 (letter of 2 October 1777). The cassations were K247 and 287, the *Finalmusik* probably K250. ◆ While it is likely that K247 and 287 were performed by Mozart on this occasion, the identity of K250, a grand serenade, is less certain; probably it was the divertimento K251 that was given. Further, see Bär, 'Die Lodronischen Nachtmusiken', and Münster, 'Mozarts Münchener Aufenthalt von 1777, der "H: von Hamm" und "die Finalmusik mit dem Rondeau auf die letzt"'.

16. Jahn, *W. A. Mozart*, fourth edition, i.408, turns him into a cleric, but Schiedermair (*Die Briefe W. A. Mozarts und seiner Familie*, i.72n) is more likely to be correct in identifying him with the electoral court musician Charles-Albert Dupreille. ◆ Dupreille (1728–96) was a violinist in the Munich court orchestra.

17. *Briefe*, ii.40–1 (letter of 6 October 1777). ◆ The two quintets were probably by Michael Haydn, while the three keyboard concertos were K238, 246 and 271. The trio was K254 and the cassation K287. Michael Haydn's quintets are Perger 106 (MH 185, dated 21 December 1772) and Perger 109 (MH 189, dated 1 December 1773).

18. On one occasion he organized a wind serenade for Mozart and on another hosted 'a religious wedding or *altum tempus ecclesasticum*, at which there was dancing, but I danced only 4 minuets – among all the women present, there was only one who could keep in time'; *Briefe*, ii.39 (letter of 6 October 1777).

were resolved at once, Mozart should on no account waste time and money awaiting an outcome that was by no means certain.

Mozart, of course, believed that he could survive in Munich even without such a subsidy. Albert and his other friends would provide him with food, and he reckoned on at least 300 florins from Seeau for four German operas a year, part serious, part comic, in addition to a benefit perform-ance of each, which he calculated at a further 500 florins. But this plan, too, struck Leopold as flawed, quite apart from the question of honour: 'I agree that if you were alone,' he wrote to Mozart on 6 October 1777, 'you could live in Munich. But it would do you no honour, and how the archbishop would scoff at you. You can live like that anywhere, not just in Munich. You mustn't belittle yourself and throw yourself away like this. There's absolutely no need for that yet.'[19] He insisted on their leaving Munich as soon as possible. 'Fine words, praise and cries of bravissimo pay neither postmasters nor landlords', he reminded Mozart on 15 October. 'As soon as you find that you can earn no more, you must try to get away at once.'[20] His 'good friends' could continue to work on his behalf in his absence. And so Mozart took his leave of Count Seeau, as he explained in his letter of 3 October:

> I was with Count Seeau at 8 this morning, was very brief and said only: 'Your Excellency, I've come simply to explain myself and my business here. I've been criticized for not going to Italy. I've spent 16 months in Italy and, as everyone knows, written 3 operas. The rest Your Excellency will see from these papers.' I showed him my diplomas. 'Your Excellency, I am showing these to you and telling you this only so that, if ever my name is mentioned and any injustice is done me, Your Excellency may be justified in taking my part.' He asked me if I was now going to France. I said I was staying on in Germany. But he thought I meant Munich and said, laughing delightedly, 'So you're staying on here?' 'No,' I said. 'I'd like to have done; and to tell the truth, my only reason for wanting anything from the elector was so that I could have kept Your Excellency supplied with compositions without asking for anything in return. It would have been a pleasure.' At these words he even shoved back his night-cap.[21]

And that was the end of the matter. In spite of the honour that he had accorded Mozart and in spite of his amiability, Seeau was a man of caution who mistrusted Mozart's great youth and clearly did not have a sufficiently high opinion of his Italian successes to entrust him with a post. As luck would have it, it was at precisely this moment that Mozart was offered an opportunity to add to his Italian laurels – or so, at least, it seemed. Josef Mysliveček was currently in Munich, where his opera *Ezio* had been performed during the carnival, followed during Lent by his oratorio *Abramo ed Isacco*, both to great acclaim.[22] He had now been invited to write a work for the forth-coming carnival in Naples and gave Mozart to understand that he, too, might be asked to write an opera for Naples, even drafting a letter for him to send to the impresario Don Gaetano Santoro. Mozart was particularly keen to compose another opera and, almost beside himself with happiness, wrote to his father on 11 October 1777:

---

19. *Briefe*, ii.35. Nannerl, too, wrote to Mozart on 5 October 1777: 'It would do you no credit to stay on in Munich without an appointment. It would do us far more honour if you could succeed in obtaining a post under some other great lord. You're bound to find one.'
20. *Briefe*, ii.57.
21. *Briefe*, ii.31–2 (letter of 3 October 1777).
22. Müller, *Abschied von der National-Schaubühne*, 222–3.

I'm still certain of my 100 ducats from the carnival, and once I've written something for Naples, I'll be in demand everywhere. And, as Papa is well aware, you'll find the occasional *opera buffa* performed there in spring, summer and autumn and you can write to keep your hand in and pass the time. It's true that you don't make very much, but it's still something and brings you more honour and credit than 100 concerts in Germany, and I'm happier when I've got something to compose, as this, after all, is my one delight and passion. And if I secure an appointment or if I have hopes of settling down somewhere, the *scrittura* will be an excellent recommendation, give me prestige and add to my value. But this is only talk – I speak as I feel – – if Papa were to prove me wrong, I'd accept his arguments, however reluctantly; for I have only to hear an opera discussed, have only to sit in a theatre and hear the players tuning their instruments – and I'm completely beside myself.[23]

Leopold was by no means opposed to this plan but thought that it could – and should – be pursued without losing sight of Mozart's main objective. Accordingly he made contact with Mysliveček, but by 25 January 1778 we find him expressing the conviction that Mysliveček was merely using him and holding out the promise of a commission only in the hope that Leopold would do something for him in return. Be that as it may, nothing came of the commission. And Leopold was no more successful in obtaining a commission for Mozart to write an opera for Ascension Day in Venice: the impresario Michele dall'Agata did not even reply to his two letters.

The artistic impressions that Mozart gained in Munich at this time will not have been very different from those gleaned on his earlier visit in 1775. And his creative energies, too, seem to have lain fairly fallow. He himself mentions hearing only six 'duets' for violin and keyboard by the Dresden court Kapellmeister Joseph Schuster (1748–1812), describing them as 'not bad' and indicating that, were he to remain in Munich for any length of time, he would write something similar himself.[24] Needless to add, this plan remained unfulfilled.

The travellers left Munich at midday on 11 October, arriving in Augsburg later that same evening. In response to detailed instructions from Leopold in his letter of 25 September 1777, they put up at The Lamb in the Kreuzgasse 'where the tariff is 30 kreutzers for lunch, the rooms are comfortable and only the best people stay there – Englishmen and Frenchmen'.[25] They received a warm and friendly welcome at the home of Mozart's uncle, Franz Alois, where Mozart struck up a friendship with the latter's lively daughter, Maria Anna Thekla, that more than made up for the coolness shown them elsewhere in the town.

Leopold further insisted that a meeting be arranged without delay with one of his oldest acquaintances, the local magistrate Jakob Wilhelm Benedikt Langenmantel. Mozart has left a particularly vivid account of his visit to the home of the puritanical local tyrant, whose family included his 'overdressed son, the latter's long-necked young wife and simple-minded old lady',[26] so that Leopold was reminded of Wieland's Abderites. Even so, he introduced himself to the family by performing at the keyboard, improvising, sight-reading and playing 'some very pretty pieces by a certain Edelmann'.[27] This passage is important as one of the few references in Mozart's letters to the fact that even before he arrived in Paris he was already developing an interest in French keyboard music.

23. *Briefe*, ii.45–6 (letter of 11 October 1777).
24. *Briefe*, ii.41 (letter of 6 October 1777).
25. ◆ *Briefe*, ii.9.
26. ◆ Here Abert misreads Mozart's letter which describes Langenmantel's wife as 'long-legged' [*langhachsigten*], not 'long-necked'.
27. *Briefe*, ii.54 (letter of 14 October 1777). ◆ Jean-Frédéric Edelmann (1749–94) lived in Paris from 1774 to 1789. He enjoyed a European reputation as a keyboard composer.

Of all the people that Mozart visited in Augsburg, the most important was the famous keyboard instrument maker Johann Andreas Stein (1728–92), who had studied with Gottfried Silbermann and gone on to develop 'German action'. Acting on his father's advice, Mozart introduced himself to Stein as 'an unworthy student of Herr Sigl in Munich', but his playing very soon gave him away. Stein was delighted: '"Oh," he cried and embraced me, crossing himself and making faces, so pleased was he to see me.'[28] Mozart was no less fascinated by Stein's instruments and immediately sent his father a lengthy report that is indicative not only of his interest but, more especially, of his powers of observation and expertise:

Before I'd seen any of Stein's work, I'd always preferred Späth's keyboard instruments, but I now have to revise my opinion and award the palm to Stein's as they damp much better than the Regensburg ones. When I strike hard, the sound ceases as soon as I produce it, whether I keep my finger on the note or raise it. No matter how I touch the keys, the sound is always even, it never jars, never grows stronger or weaker, never fails to sound; in a word, it's always even. It's true that he won't sell a pianoforte of this kind for less than 300 florins, but the effort and labour that he expends on it can't be paid for. Unique to his instruments is their escape action. Not one maker in a hundred bothers about this; but without escapement it's impossible to avoid jangling and vibration after the note's been struck. When you touch the keys, his hammers fall back again the moment they strike the strings, whether you hold down the keys or release them. When he's finished a keyboard like this (as he himself says), he first sits down and tries all kinds of passages, runs and jumps, shaving and working away until it can do everything; for he works only for the benefit of music, not for his own benefit, otherwise he'd be finished much sooner. He often says: 'If I weren't such a passionate music lover and didn't have some slight skill at the keyboard, I'd long since have lost all patience with my work; but I love instruments that don't let the player down and that last.' His instruments certainly last. He guarantees that the sound-board[29] won't break or split. When he has finished making a soundboard for an instrument, he puts it outside, exposing it to rain, snow, the heat of the sun and all the devils to make it crack, then he inserts wedges, gluing them in, to make it strong and firm. He is perfectly happy for it to split, as you're then assured that nothing else can happen to it. He often even cuts into it himself, then glues it together again and strengthens it in this way. He's finished three forte-pianos of this kind, it wasn't until today that I played on them again. . . . The device that you work with your knee is also better than on other instruments. I barely need touch it and it works; and as soon as you remove your knee, you don't hear the least reverberation.[30]

Mozart not only used these new instruments for his own performances, from now on his keyboard compositions bear clear signs of these impressions. But Stein also took advantage of Mozart's visit to consult him on his daughter's education: Maria Anna Stein (1769–1833) was regarded as the 'child prodigy of Augsburg', having given her first keyboard recital in April 1776 at the local Patrizierstube, eliciting universal admiration and receiving a medallion from the local nobility.[31] She later married the harpsichord maker Andreas Streicher, who was an early friend of

28. *Briefe*, ii.55 (letter of 14 October 1777).
29. Curiously, Mozart spells the word 'Raisonance-Boden'.
30. *Briefe*, ii.68–9 (letter of 17 October 1777).
31. See Schubart, *Deutsche Chronik*, iii (1776), 239, and Friedrich Nicolai, *Beschreibung einer Reise durch Deutschland und die Schweiz im Jahre 1781*, vii.156–7.

Schiller, and, as Frau Nannette Streicher, later played a notable role in Beethoven's life. Mozart's comments on her – like those on artists in general – are of razor-sharp perceptiveness, but objective and, above all, relevant to the object in hand and instructive for his own views on the matter:

As for his daughter, anyone who sees and hears her without laughing must, like her father, be made of stone. Far from sitting in the middle, she sits right up at the treble end as it gives her more room to move and more opportunity to pull faces. She rolls her eyes and smirks; whenever a passage is repeated, she plays it more slowly the 2nd time round; and if it comes round again, even more slowly the 3rd time. Whenever a passage is played, the arm must be raised as high as possible, and it has to be the arm, not the fingers, that indicate how the passage is stressed – and she goes out of her way to do this in as ponderous and ungainly a way as possible. But the best thing of all is when she comes to a passage that should flow perfectly smoothly but where the fingers have to be changed, here she pays virtually no attention but, when the moment arrives, simply omits the notes, raises her hand and starts again as though nothing has happened, a method by which she's much more likely to strike a wrong note, which often produces a curious effect. I'm writing this simply to give Papa an idea of keyboard playing and teaching, so that he may derive some benefit from it when the time comes. Herr Stein is quite mad about his daughter. She's 8 and a half and still learns everything by heart. Something may come of her as she's genuinely gifted; but in this way she'll get nowhere, as she'll never achieve any real velocity as she does everything possible to make her hands heavy. She'll never acquire the most essential, most difficult and most important thing in music, which is a sense of tempo because from her earliest years she has done all she can not to play in time. Herr Stein and I discussed this point for a good 2 hours and I've almost converted him. He now asks my advice on everything. He was quite foolishly fond of Beecke. Now he sees and hears that I play better than Beecke,[32] that I don't pull faces and yet play so expressively that, as he himself confesses, no one has been able to get such good results from his pianofortes. Everyone is amazed that I can always keep in time. What they simply can't understand is that in tempo rubato in an Adagio, the left hand should ignore the right; with them, the left hand always follows suit.[33]

To the amazement of the composer Friedrich Hartmann Graf and the organist Johann Adam Schmidbaur, Mozart sight-read a relatively difficult sonata by Beecke, a piece he described as 'miserabile al solito' – 'wretched as usual'.[34]

It was not only as a pianist, however, that Mozart elicited general astonishment, but also as an organist and violinist:

When I told Herr Stein that I'd like to play on his organ [in the Barfüßerkirche] as the organ is my passion, he was very surprised and said: 'What, a man like you, such a fine harpsichordist, wants to play on an instrument that has no sweetness, no expression, no *piano* or *forte* but is always the same?' 'That doesn't mean anything. In my eyes and ears the organ is the king of

---

32. Even Colloredo acknowledged that Mozart was better than Beecke, although only his intimates were apprized of this; see Leopold's letter of 29 June 1778 (*Briefe*, ii.381).
33. Here we see his father's pupil; *Briefe*, ii.83 (letter of 24 October 1777).
34. ◆ Friedrich Hartmann Graf (1727–95) was music director of the Protestant church and St Anna's Gymnasium in Augsburg. Johann Adam Joseph Schmidbaur (?–1786) had been cathedral organist at St Ulrich's since 1742.

instruments.' 'Well, as you like.' And so we set off together. It was clear from what he said that he didn't think I'd achieve much on his organ but would play it just like a harpsichord. He told me that Chobert[35] had already asked to see the organ. 'I was rather nervous,' he said, 'as Chobert had told everyone and the church was fairly full. And I thought, of course, that he'd be all spirit and fire and speed, which isn't suited to the organ, but as soon as he started I changed my opinion.' All I said was: 'But, Herr Stein, surely you don't think I'm going to run around on your organ?' – – 'Ah, with you, it's quite another matter.' We reached the choir, I started to improvise, whereupon he began to smile; then a fugue. 'I can well believe you like playing the organ,' he said, 'as you play so well.' At first the pedal seemed a bit strange as it wasn't divided. It started with C, then D and E followed in the same row. With us, D and E are above, as E flat and F sharp are here. But I soon got used to it.[36]

Mozart also played on the organ at St Ulrich's Monastery (the instrument was reached by a staircase that was 'perfectly horrible') and frequently went to the Monastery of the Holy Cross, where he was invited to dine on 19 October. According to his letter of the 24th, he performed there during the meal:

In spite of their poor fiddling, I prefer the monastery players to the Augsburg orchestra. I performed a symphony and played Vanhall's Violin Concerto in B flat to general applause. The dean is a fine and amusing fellow; he's a cousin of Eberlin, is called Zöschinger, he knows Papa quite well. At supper that evening I played the Strasbourg concerto [K216]. It went very smoothly. Everyone praised the beautiful pure tone. Afterwards they brought in a small clavichord. I improvised and played a sonata and the Fischer variations. Then the others whispered in the dean's ear that he should hear me play something in the organ style. I said he should give me a theme, but he didn't want to, so one of the monks gave me one. I put it through its paces and in the middle (the fugue was in G minor) started off in the major, playing something quite comical, but at the same tempo, then the theme again, but this time backwards; finally I wondered whether the comical theme could also be used as a fugue subject. – – I didn't waste much time in asking but used it immediately, and it went as accurately as if Daser [a tailor in Salzburg] had fitted it. The dean was absolutely amazed. 'Why, it's simply phenomenal, that's all I can say,' he said, 'I'd never have believed it, you're quite a fellow. My abbot told me, of course, that never in his life had he heard anyone play the organ as convincingly and with such seriousness of purpose.' He'd heard me a few days previously, when the dean was away. Finally someone produced a sonata in the fugal style, and I was asked to play it. But I said: 'Gentlemen, this is too much; I have to admit that I shan't be able to play this sonata straightaway.' 'Yes, I can well believe that,' said the dean, with some alacrity, as he was entirely on my side, 'it's too much to expect, there's no one who could play it.' 'Even so,' I said, 'I'd like to try.' I kept hearing the dean calling out behind me: 'Oh, you rogue! You rascal, you, you –!' I played till 11 o'clock. I was bombarded and besieged with nothing but fugue subjects.[37]

35. ◆ Here Mozart means the poet, journalist, writer on music and composer Christian Friedrich Daniel Schubart (1739–91), who had moved to Augsburg in 1774 and established the *Deutsche* (or *Teutsche*) *Chronik*, a periodical devoted to politics, literature and music. The next year Schubart moved to Ulm but his criticisms of policies pursued by the Catholic Church and various courts angered the nobility and he was imprisoned at the fortress Hohenasperg for ten years. See DuBois, 'Christian Friedrich Daniel Schubart's Ideen zu einer Ästhetik der Tonkunst: An Annotated Translation'; Wertheim and Böhm, *C. F. D. Schubart: Briefe*; and Honolka, *Schubart, Dichter und Musiker, Journalist und Rebell: Sein Leben, sein Werk*.
36. *Briefe*, ii.69–70 (letter of 17 October 1777).
37. *Briefe*, ii.82 (letter of 24 October 1777).

This passage is instructive not only for what it tell us about Mozart's abilities on the organ and his contrapuntal skills – skills largely overshadowed in his works of the last two years by a more lightweight, *galant* tone – but also, and more particularly, for the way in which he used to improvise at this time. He did not launch blindly into a piece, but from the outset had the broad outlines of ternary form in his mind's ear. Within this form, however, he liked to surprise his listeners. Whereas the opening section was in G minor, the middle section was in a major key and 'comical' in tone. In the recapitulation the subject was heard in inversion, with Mozart trumping his own ingenuity by combining it contrapuntally with the theme of the middle section. This is the old practice of improvisation, whereby the performer sets out from another composer's ideas or from common property, using it as a way of firing the listener's imagination, while preserving a clear sense of fully-rounded form – and it is this last-named feature that is quintessentially Mozartian.

In order to thank the abbot, Bartholomäus Christa, for his hospitality, Mozart gave him his masses in F major (K192) and C major (K220) and his *Misericordias* (K222). As for a *Litaniae de venerabili altaris sacramento* he referred the monks to his father and in his letter to Leopold of 20 November 1777 suggests his most recent litany in E flat major (K243) as a suitable piece to send them.[38]

Generally, of course, Mozart was unimpressed by the standard of music in Augsburg, which he found 'heartily bad' and enough 'to give one a fit', hence his constant anxiety when being accompanied. There had also been some difficulty in organizing a concert in the town. The young Jakob Alois von Langenmantel had promised to arrange a concert at the Stube simply for the local patricians, but, having fully exploited Mozart's abilities at a private gathering under his own roof, he withdrew his offer, arguing that 'the patricians were out of funds'. And the Abderites, with Langenmantel at their head, tactlessly teased Mozart at table over the value of his papal order, an incident that he brought to an end with a few well-chosen words. None the less, he appears not to have worn the cross again. He was also drawn into the bitter arguments between the two confessions.[39] He had promised to attend one of the weekly concerts organized by a patrician society at the Geschlechterstube[40] and possibly also to perform for them. But since it was Catholics who had treated him so shabbily, he preferred to give a concert for only a few friends and connoisseurs. Stein now mobilized the Evangelical party, who persuaded Mozart to attend their concert at the Bauernstube[41] and perform one of his symphonies, for which he sat with the violins, together with a concerto and a sonata. Leopold disapproved of his son's behaviour and in his letter of 20 October 1777 commented pointedly that 'they would have had great difficulty in dragging *me* to their beggarly concert'.[42] The proceeds confirmed his prejudices, with Mozart receiving only two ducats from Augsburg's fanatical music lovers.

Somewhat more successful was the concert arranged on 22 October by Mozart's friends in Augsburg, foremost among whom was Count Wolfegg:

---

38. A mass in C minor that he is said to have written at this time and that Gathy ('Un manuscrit inédit de Mozart', 90–1) considered genuine is plainly inauthentic; see Jahn, *W. A. Mozart*, i.418. Quite apart from the non-Mozartian nature of the work, it would be unusual for Mozart not to have told his father about the commission. ◆ The mass is listed in the sixth edition of Köchel as Anh. C1.10. A copy in the Bayerische Staatsbibliothek, Munich (shelfmark Mus. mss. 4754), derives from the Holy Cross monastery, but the work is not by Mozart.

39. See Schubart, *Leben und Gesinnungen*, ii/17.15; and Riesbeck, *Briefe eines Franzosen über Deutschland*, ii.55.

40. Cramer, *Magazin der Musik*, ii.126.

41. In Mozart's crudely comical list of the participants (*Briefe*, ii.66–7), Jahn (*W. A. Mozart*, i.419) sees a counterpart to Goethe's list of guests at Hanswurst's wedding.

42. ◆ *Briefe*, ii.73–4.

The count kept running round the hall, saying: 'I've never heard anything like it in all my life.' He said to me: 'I must say I've never heard you play as you did today; I'll tell your father as soon as I get back to Salzburg.' What does Papa think we played immediately after the symphony? – The concerto for three keyboards [K242]. Herr Demmler[43] played the first, I the second and Herr Stein the third. On my own, I then played my most recent sonata in D, the one for Dürnitz [K284], then my concerto in B flat [K238], then another solo – a fugue in C minor in the style of the organ – and then all of a sudden a magnificent sonata in C major, out of my head, with a rondeau to finish with. There was a regular din of applause. Herr Stein kept making faces and grimacing in his amazement; Herr Demmler couldn't stop laughing. He's a strange fellow, whenever something takes his fancy, he laughs terribly. In my case he even started to curse.[44]

An 'incomparable article in the Maschenbauerische Zeitung no. 213' that gave Leopold a good deal of pleasure may perhaps have been written by Christoph von Zabuesnig, whose fine poem Leopold had already commended to Wolfgang's attention. Conversely, the income from this concert, at which Mozart 'displayed the whole of his powers',[45] was by no means brilliant: the receipts amounted to ninety gulden, with expenses of sixteen gulden and thirty kreutzers. Wolfgang had no reason to revise his views on the local nobility as expressed in his letter of 16 October 1777:

I may say that if it were not for my good uncle and aunt and my delightful cousin, I should have as many regrets at coming to Augsburg as I have hairs on my head. I should say something about my dear little cousin, but I'll save it up till tomorrow, as you have to be very clear-headed to praise her as much as she deserves. – It is now early on the 17th and I hereby declare that our little cousin is beautiful, intelligent, charming, clever and amusing; this is because she has mixed with people a good deal and has also spent some time in Munich. It's true, we're well suited to each other, as she too is a bit naughty;[46] we both like teasing people for the fun of it.[47]

A charming and innocent flirtation developed between the two of them,[48] and when Leopold commented on it, Wolfgang leapt to his cousin's defence, claiming in his letter of 25 October 1777 that not for a moment was she 'infatuated with priests. Yesterday, to please me, she dressed up as a Frenchwoman, which makes her 5 per cent prettier.'[49] He gave her his portrait in a small medallion and she had to promise to have her own portrait painted showing her wearing French costume. Not content with this, he asked his father to send her a souvenir from among the various presents they had received on their earlier travels: a double fichu from his mother and a box or toothpick case or the like from himself. After the delightful times they had spent together, their

43. The organist Johann Michael Demmler (1748–85).

44. *Briefe*, ii.83–4 (letter of 24 October 1777).

45. Stetten, *Kunst-, Gewerb- und Handwerks-Geschichte der Reichs-Stadt Augsburg*, 554 ◆ *Dokumente*, 165–6, *Documentary Biography*, 186.

46. The word 'schlimm' that Mozart uses here is still used in Austria as a popular expression for someone who is fond of teasing others in a rather lewd manner.

47. *Briefe*, ii.66 (letter of 16/17 October 1777).

48. ◆ Maria Anna Thekla Mozart (1758–1841) was the daughter of Leopold's brother Franz Alois. It is unusual that Abert says little about Wolfgang's scatological correspondence with her, a correspondence that has traditionally provided considerable fodder for discussions of Mozart's personality and burgeoning sexuality – perhaps Abert was intent here on showing Mozart in the best possible light, overwhelmed instead by his 'morally upright' love for Aloysia Weber. He does, however, give an extended selection from the Bäsle letters in Appendix III below. See Eibl, 'Zur Überlieferungsgeschichte der Bäsle-Briefe', and Kühn, 'Komik, Humor und Musikalität in Mozarts Bäslebriefen'. For conflicting interpretations of their scatological content, see Solomon, *Mozart: A Life*, and Schroeder, *Mozart in Revolt: Strategies of Resistance, Mischief and Deception*.

49. *Briefe*, ii.85 (letter of 25 October 1777).

parting was commensurately painful, as Stein himself wrote to inform Leopold, while expressing his astonishment and praise at Mozart's musical accomplishments.[50]

Immediately after Mozart left Augsburg[51], Leopold seized the opportunity of his son's name-day – 31 October – to appeal to the latter's conscience:

> I am to congratulate you on your name-day. But what can I wish you that I don't always wish you? – – I wish you the grace of God, that it may follow you everywhere and never forsake you, and it will never forsake you if you are diligent in fulfilling the duties of a true Catholic Christian. You know me. – I'm no pedant, no bigot, still less a hypocrite, but you'll surely not refuse a father's request? It is that you take thought for your soul's welfare, so that in the hour of his death you may cause your father no anxiety and that in that dread moment he may have no reason to reproach himself for having neglected your soul's salvation. Farewell! Be happy! Be sensible! Honour and respect your mother, who now has to shoulder a great burden of responsibility in her old age. Love me as I love you. Your truly solicitous father.[52]

Mozart's reply is couched in the sort of respectful tone that children regularly adopt when discussing such serious matters with their parents:

> I kiss Papa's hands and thank him most humbly for his congratulations on my name-day. Papa must not worry; God is always before my eyes, I acknowledge His omnipotence, I fear His anger; but I also recognize His love, His compassion and tenderness towards His creatures; He will never forsake His servants. If it is according to His will, so let it be according to mine. So all will be well – I must be happy and contented. And I'll certainly do all I can to follow to the letter the instructions and advice that you were kind enough to give me.[53]

On 26 October, mother and son travelled to Hohen-Altheim via Donauwörth and Nördlingen. Hohen-Altheim was the country seat of Prince Kraft Ernst von Oettingen-Wallerstein and he was currently in residence there. Music played a particularly important role in the cultural life of this tiny court,[54] with an orchestra numbering among its players such famous virtuosos as the violinist

50. This provided Leopold with an opportunity to depict 'the sad parting of two tearful people, Wolfgang and his cousin' on the target for their next shooting competition: 'A girl from Augsburg stood on the right and handed a parting bouquet to a young man in riding boots who was about to leave, while in the other hand she held an enormous linen sheet which trailed along the ground and with which she dried her tearful eyes. The young dandy had a similar linen sheet with which he was doing the same, while in his other hand he held his hat containing the bull's eye, where it could be seen more easily than on the bouquet. Above it were the words:

> Adieu, Mistress Cousin! Adieu, my dear Cousin!
> Good luck on your journey, good health and fine weather!
> We've spent a whole fortnight in pleasure together.
> It's this that makes parting so sad for us twain.
> Hateful fate! Hardly met and yet sundered again!
> Who wouldn't weep at such undeserved pain?'

Wolfgang remained in correspondence with his cousin.
51. ◆ In fact this was three days before he left.
52. *Briefe*, ii.79 (letter of 23 October 1777).
53. *Briefe*, ii.84–5 (letter of 25 October 1777).
54. See Lang, *Memoiren*, i.56ff., and especially Schiedermair, 'Die Blütezeit der Öttingen-Wallerstein'schen Hofkapelle'. ◆ Further, see Sterling Murray, 'Bohemian Musicians in South German Hofkapellen during the Late Eighteenth Century' and *Seven Symphonies from the Court of Oettingen-Wallerstein, 1773–1795*.

Anton Janitsch, the cellist Josef Reicha and the oboist Markus Berwein. The conductor was the much-travelled Antonio Rosetti, who was also a distinguished instrumental composer in his own right[55] and who, according to Schubart, was able to bring out 'the subtlest and often most imperceptible gradations of sound'.[56] Mozart also made contact with Ignaz von Beecke, an outstanding pianist and prolific composer, who was stationed in Wallerstein with a regiment of dragoons and in charge of music at court. Leopold, of course, suspected that Beecke was jealous of his son: he had been told that Wolfgang had pranced around while playing the violin and generally behaved very foolishly, giving Beecke an excuse to denigrate his abilities as an artist. Wolfgang remonstrated with some warmth, assuring his father that he had behaved 'perfectly seriously'. And he spoke of Beecke in only the most amicable terms: the latter had received him well, had given him all manner of good advice in the event of his deciding to go to Paris and had invited him to play for him. They had also discussed Vienna, including the emperor, who, according to Beecke, knew something about counterpoint but 'was no great lover of music'. As a result, Beecke had played him only 'fugues and suchlike childish nonsense'. The music that was performed in the imperial apartments would drive a dog away, he concluded. They also discovered that music gave them both headaches: in Beecke's case, it was good music that did so, in Mozart's case, bad music.

Mozart's main reason for breaking his journey at Hohen-Altheim was to give a concert for the prince, who had once invited him to visit him in Naples. But nothing came of the plan as Kraft Ernst was suffering from depression and unable to listen to music. None the less, the travellers were delayed in Hohen-Altheim for several days because Maria Anna was suffering from catarrh.

---

55. See Kaul's introduction to *Anton Rosetti: Ausgewählte Sinfonien*.
56. Schubart, *Ideen zu einer Ästhetik der Tonkunst*, 169.

17

Mannheim

The travellers arrived in Mannheim on 30 October 1777. Although Mozart's stay in the town was to bring no marked improvement to, or clarification of, his outward situation, in spite of all the hopes that he pinned on it and the length of time that he delayed here, it was to prove all the more significant in terms of his development as both man and artist.

Jesuit-trained, the ruling elector, Karl Theodor,[1] had studied at the universities of Leiden and Louvain and even while still a student developed a clear predilection for French culture, a predilection fostered by his personal friendship with Voltaire. The court at Versailles was his model as it was Karl Eugen's in Württemberg, except that, in keeping with the Palatinate's geographical position, French ideas infiltrated the country far more effectively than was the case with Swabia. In 1773, Christian Friedrich Daniel Schubart even thought that the Palatinate could 'be regarded far more readily as a colony of Frenchmen than of German provincials'.[2] Although the region had subsequently embraced German nationalism, this French undercurrent had not been lost and was to leave its mark on Mozart. In this regard, Mannheim was a natural stepping stone on the composer's road to Paris.

In terms of its life and customs, too, Mannheim was a miniature Paris, a scene of brilliant bustle with a rank array of priests, court favourites and mistresses battening upon the body politic, while men of dubious honour found ample opportunity to fish in troubled waters. Karl Theodor was partial to science and art and not ungifted, but he was also weak-willed and lacking in character, setting the tone for both better and worse, with the result that his ambitious cultural plans were in the crassest contrast to the superficial and boundless hedonism of life at court. Yet even if the brilliance of Mannheim's world of music was the product of its prince's love of ostentation rather than of any true artistic appreciation, science and art were encouraged to lasting effect. To Karl Theodor, Mannheim owed its library and natural history museum, an academy of drawing and sculpture, collections of painters and engravings and a classical gallery with plaster casts of well-known sculptures – the first of its kind in Germany.[3] Meanwhile, the spirit of German nationalism was increasingly making itself felt alongside French influence thanks to Frederick the Great and his various feats. One of its early champions was the publisher Christian Friedrich Schwan, a familiar figure from Schiller's life who laid the foundations for German opera by translating French comic operas. In 1775 Karl Theodor placed himself at the head of this movement when he founded the *Kurpfälzische Deutsche Gesellschaft* whose aim was to mobilize all the available intellectual forces and purge the German language of foreign elements, rationalize orthography and

1. Karl Theodor was born in 1724 and came to power in 1743. He became elector of Bavaria in 1778 and died in Munich in 1799.
2. Schubart, *Leben und Gesinnungen*, i/14.136.
3. Schubart, *Leben und Gesinnungen*, i/14.145; Goethe, *Dichtung und Wahrheit*, part iii, book 11; Schiller, *Die Rheinische Thalia*, i (1785), 176ff.; Herder, *Aus dem Nachlaß*, iii.371–2 and 374; and La Roche, *Briefe aus Mannheim*, 233.

promulgate good taste.[4] It was a programme that bears clear traces of the spirit of Johann Christoph Gottsched. Klopstock's presence in the town in 1775 was not without influence on this development. Its members included local worthies such as Otto Heinrich von Gemmingen, Anton von Klein, Wolfgang Heribert von Dalberg and the artist Friedrich Müller. But attempts to persuade such established writers as Lessing[5] and Wieland[6] to join were inevitably unsuccessful.

It was not long, of course, before these nationalist aspirations embraced the theatre,[7] the first step in this direction being the disbandment of the French troupe of actors in 1770;[8] court and society began to derive greater pleasure from German plays, with the Marchand troupe performing original German singspiels alongside translations of French comic operas. The Mannheim National Theatre was built between 1775 and 1777, and no less a figure than Lessing was invited to run it,[9] but negotiations with him very soon foundered.[10]

In the event, the nationalist movement had a far greater impact on opera than on spoken drama, a state of affairs due not least to the fact that Mannheim already enjoyed a reputation as what one writer called 'a paradise for musicians'.[11] As fate would have it, the new German national opera was roused from its slumbers in the very same corner of south-west Germany that had seen its last sign of life some fifty-five years earlier, before Italian opera had asserted its all-powerful sway.[12]

The impetus came from Wieland. Performances of singspiels by the Seyler troupe had encouraged him to think in terms of fully-fledged serious operas alongside the existing singspiels which, with their songlike character and spoken dialogue, were only an imperfect substitute for opera. But such operas – and here we find an echo of the old Renaissance ideal – should reflect 'the taste of the ancients, albeit with a handful of modifications appropriate to the age'.[13] Wieland found a suitable collaborator in Anton Schweitzer (1735–87), who was then Kapellmeister of the Seyler company and who likewise came from the world of the singspiel. Schweitzer's works had filled the susceptible poet with a 'frenzy of enthusiasm for the lyric theatre'.[14] The result was the opera *Alceste*, which received its first performance in Weimar on 28 May 1773. Wieland himself placed its music not only above that of the leading Italians but even above that of Gluck's *Alceste*.[15] Here he found the realization of his musico-dramatic ideal, with the composer subordinated to the poet

4. Schubart, *Deutsche Chronik*, ii (1775), 729–30; Häusser, *Die Geschichte der rheinischen Pfalz*, ii.943ff.; Ernst Schmidt, *Lessing: Geschichte seines Lebens und seiner Schriften*, ii.330–31.

5. Schmidt, *Lessing*, ii.330–31.

6. Wieland, *Briefe an J. H. Merck*, i.105ff. and ii.105.

7. See Walter's authoritative study, *Geschichte des Theaters und der Musik am kurpfälzischen Hofe* and the same author's *Archiv und Bibliothek des Großherzoglichen Hof- und Nationaltheaters zu Mannheim*.

8. Walter, *Geschichte des Theaters*, 246.

9. Ernst Schmidt, *Lessing*, ii.330–31; Johann Friedrich Müller was in Mannheim in December 1776 and in his *Abschied von der National-Schaubühne* (207ff.) reports remarks by both the elector himself and his minister Hompesch to the effect that there was a general sense of enthusiasm in the town at the prospect of Lessing's appointment.

10. Walter, *Geschichte des Theaters*, 267ff.

11. Jacobi, *Aus F. H. Jacobi's Nachlass*, i.273. Wieland wrote to Merck, 'I have to go to Mannheim: for once in my life I really want to – and have to – sate myself on music, and when or where shall I ever find a better opportunity?' (*Briefe an Merck*, ii.116). Klopstock, too, travelled to Mannheim specifically for the music (*Briefe an Merck*, ii.51). According to Schubart (*Deutsche Chronik*, ii [1775], 183), the Mannheimers 'delighted in gratifying his great taste'.

12. Kretzschmar, 'Das erste Jahrhundert der deutschen Oper', 292. ◆ Also see Ott, 'Von der frühdeutschen Oper zum deutschen Singspiel'.

13. *Euphorion*, i.529.

14. Maurer, *Anton Schweitzer als dramatischer Komponist*. ◆ Further, see Würtz, 'Anton Schweitzer and Christoph Martin Wieland: The Theory of the Eighteenth Century Singspiel'; Bauman, *North German Opera in the Age of Goethe*; and Hortschansky, 'Musiktheater in Mannheim als gestelltes Bild'.

15. Letter to Klein, *Morgenblatt* (1820), no. 160; on *Alceste* in general, see Seuffert, *Prolegomena zu einer Wieland-Ausgabe*, v.26.

and with words and music mutually complementary, and his 'Letters on the German Singspiel Alceste'[16] attest to his pride and satisfaction at the progress that he had achieved. Of course, such an innovation was bound to elicit not only great enthusiasm but also violent censure and even satire,[17] with writers berating Wieland for his dependence on Metastasio, objecting to the lack of proper characterization and drama, describing the orchestration as overloaded and dismissing the whole as effeminate and monotonous.[18] A number of these reproaches, such as that of monotony and the excessively thick orchestration, are undoubtedly justified, but the comparison with Metastasio does little more than scrape the surface: after all, the Italian librettist's chief character-istic – his complex intrigues – has been completely removed. Conversely, Schweitzer's attempt to follow his poet in exploring the subtlest recesses of his characters' emotional lives is eminently laudable, and if he failed to create an entirely satisfactory music drama, the fault lay in part with the excessively lyrical nature of the libretto and in part with his own inability to handle large-scale form: here we see the consequences of his schooling in the small-scale forms of the singspiel. However successful individual details and however significant some of those details may be, the work as a whole lacks a sense of gripping dramatic momentum. For all its importance, it remains no more than a tentative attempt to create a fully-fledged German opera.

Even so, the work created a sensation and proved a lasting success in Weimar, soon finding its way to other theatres.[19] Karl Theodor mounted a brilliant performance in Schwetzingen on 13 August 1775.[20] The exceptional nature of the occasion was not lost on contemporaries: here was a German opera to a libretto by a German poet, set to music by a German composer, sung by Germans and applauded by a German prince. The following summer Wieland was commissioned to write a new opera for Mannheim and to supervise Schweitzer's setting of it.

Mozart, too, got to know *Alceste* in Mannheim. He ascribed its success first and foremost to the fact that it was the first German opera,[21] later writing to his father on 18 December 1778: 'The best thing about melancholic Alcestis (apart from some of the beginnings, middles and ends of a handful of arias) is the beginning of the recitative "O Jugendzeit" – and it was Raaff who ensured that this was so; he phrased it for Hartig [the Admetus] and in that way introduced true expres-sion into it; the worst part about it all (though most of it is bad) is undoubtedly the overture.'[22]

Encouraged by success, the authorities in Mannheim ventured a further step down this particu-lar road by drawing on local resources. The result was the opera *Günther von Schwarzburg*[23] to a libretto by the former Jesuit Anton Klein who taught philosophy and belles lettres at Mannheim University and who was one of the most enthusiastic members of the circle of writers around Christian Friedrich Schwan, while at the same time evincing less commendable qualities as an opportunist and lick-spittle. The music was by the local Kapellmeister Ignaz Holzbauer

16. Wieland, 'Briefe an einen Freund über das deutsche Singspiel, *Alceste*'.

17. Apart from Goethe's farce, which was provoked by Wieland's comparison of *Alceste* with Euripides, there was also a parody by Einsiedel and Seckendorff, *Orpheus und Euridice* (1779); see Maurer, *Anton Schweitzer als dramatischer Komponist*, 24.

18. See Maurer, *Anton Schweitzer als dramatischer Komponist*, 23–4; Zelter (*Der Briefwechsel zwischen Goethe und Zelter*, iii.38) was put off by Wieland's panegyric, but conceded that Schweitzer was talented, even if he was inferior to Georg Benda.

19. For the statistics, see Maurer, *Anton Schweitzer als dramatischer Komponist*, 22–3.

20. *Der teutsche Merkur*, iii (1775), 268ff., and Schubart, *Deutsche Chronik*, ii (1775), 535, 575, 716 and 720.

21. *Briefe*, ii.161 (letter of 3 December 1777).

22. *Briefe*, ii.523 (letter of 18 December 1778). ◆ For contemporaneous writings on *Alceste*, see Wieland, 'Briefe an einen Freund [F. H. Jacobi] über das deutsche Singspiel, *Alceste*', and Dreßler, *Gedanken, die Vorstellung der Alceste, ein deutsches ernsthaftes Singspiel betreffend*. Further, see Maurer, *Anton Schweitzer als dramatischer Komponist*, and Würtz, 'Anton Schweitzer and Christoph Martin Wieland: The Theory of the Eighteenth Century Singspiel'.

23. *Günther von Schwarzburg: Ein Singspiel in drei Aufzügen für die Kurpfälzische Hofsingbühne*, published by Schwan in Mannheim in 1777.

(1711–83)[24] and the work received its first performance on 5 January 1777 in a lavish production[25] in the large and magnificent opera house. In advance of the performance, Schubart had already welcomed the 'salutary revolution in taste',[26] and the piece was well received not only in Mannheim itself but elsewhere, too. As before, the critics[27] objected to many aspects of the libretto, and even Wieland spoke of a 'so-called opera', shying away from reviewing it in the pages of the *Teutscher Merkur*.[28] From his own point of view, there is no doubt that he was right for, unlike his own libretto to *Alceste*, that of *Günther von Schwarzburg* was a watered-down version of Metastasio, displaying all the latter's gallantries, intrigues and elegant saws but with far less of his wit and poetical powers. Even so, its patriotic subject matter was preferable in many eyes to the theme of *Alceste*, which still had half an eye on the Renaissance ideal, while the music merely served to underline this superiority. Minister Hompesch opined that the work was neither French nor Italian in style but that it contained original German ideas,[29] while Schubart found in it an expression of all that was German, coloured by Latin charm.[30] Others again spoke of its mixture of grandeur and gentle grace.[31] Far more important, however, is the reaction of the hypercritical Mozart, who saw the opera on the day of his arrival in Mannheim and who, by his own standards, was relatively enthusiastic: 'Holzbauer's music is very beautiful', he wrote to his father on 14 November 1777. 'The poetry is unworthy of such music. What surprises me most of all is that someone as old as Holzbauer[32] still possesses so much spirit; you wouldn't believe what fire there is in the music.'[33] And there is no doubt that this music continued to reverberate in Mozart's soul even as late as *Die Zauberflöte*.[34] Compare, for example, the opening of this last-named work with Rudolf's aria 'Wenn das Silber deiner Haare' in act two, scene five of *Günther von Schwarzburg*:

24. Kretzschmar, *Ignaz Holzbauer: Günther von Schwarzburg*. The beautifully engraved score was published by Götz in Mannheim and dedicated to Karl Theodor, 'the most illustrious patron of music, under whose august protection the Palatinate theatre has first hymned the praises of a German hero'.
25. The sets were painted by Lorenzo Quaglio; and the ballet was based on a scenario by Lauchéry and composed by Cannabich. According to Burney in *The Present State of Music in Germany*, i.92, it cost 'near four thousand pounds' to stage an opera in Mannheim during the carnival.
26. Schubart, *Deutsche Chronik*, iii (1776), 630–1. The opera was successfully revived in Mannheim in 1785; see Schiller, *Die Rheinische Thalia*, i (1785), 185–6.
27. A detailed review appeared in the *Rheinische Beiträge*, i (1777), 377ff.; see also Vogler, *Betrachtungen der Mannheimer Tonschule*, i/1.116ff.; Kraus, *Etwas von und über Musik*, 34–5; and Düntzer, *Frauenbilder aus Goethes Jugendzeit*, 258–9.
28. See Wieland, *Briefe an Merck*, i.100.
29. Müller, *Abschied von der National-Schaubühne*, 208–9. ◆ For a modern edition, see Pelker, *Günther von Schwarzburg: Singspiel in drei Aufzügen*.
30. Schubart, *Ideen zu einer Ästhetik der Tonkunst*, 131.
31. *Musikalicher Almanach*, i (1782), 23–4.
32. Holzbauer was now sixty-seven. He had been to Italy in 1747 [probably from 1744 to 1747], then spent three years in Vienna and worked in Stuttgart from 1751 to 1753.
33. *Briefe*, ii.125 (letter of 14 November 1777).
34. See Kretzschmar, *Ignaz Holzbauer: Günther von Schwarzburg*. He, too, singles out the opening bars of the overture.

Or take Asberta's aria in act one, scene five:[35]

Dein Haupt wird heut die Kai - ser - kro-ne schmücken

In terms of both form and character, the opera clearly betrays Holzbauer's Italian training and is not free of the shortcomings of the Italian school, namely, sentimentality, frivolity and superficial emotion, so that on the whole it is no more possible to speak of a new German operatic style in the case of *Günther von Schwarzburg* than we could in the case of *Alceste*. None the less, Holzbauer's contemporaries were right to detect traces of a German spirit in it. These traces may be found in the work's seriousness of dramatic purpose and in Holzbauer's independent attitude towards his material. A clear commitment to the task in hand informs every bar of the music, and since he was fully at home in the large-scale forms of Italian opera, he was more successful in achieving his aims than Schweitzer had been. The sense of dramatic structure that was absent from Schweitzer's work is emphatically present here, as is clear not only from the large number and importance of the accompanied recitatives, but also from the free and idiosyncratic treatment of the arias and the poetical exploitation of the instruments, a feature of the Mannheim instrumental school. Of course, a true German opera still lay some distance away in the future, but *Günther von Schwarzburg* was among its principal forerunners and there is no doubt that it fully deserved Mozart's praise.

Wieland and Schweitzer followed up this opera with a new work, for which Wieland had already received a commission from Hompesch during the summer of 1776.[36] Schweitzer's choice fell on *Rosemunde*, a choice in which he was no doubt encouraged by the publication that year[37] of the poem of that name by Klamer Eberhard Karl Schmidt. Little can Wieland have suspected that the subject would go down so badly with the many mistresses of an elector whose own marriage was currently under severe strain. Wieland's initial enthusiasm suffered a serious setback when both Goethe and Jacobi declared the libretto a failure and Hompesch demanded that the last two acts be rewritten. Indeed, Wieland was on the point of withdrawing his services completely, even though Schweitzer had already set three acts ('enchantingly beautifully'), but he finally agreed to

35. This same opening is also found in Gluck's *Die frühen Gräber* and Neefe's *Da schlägt die Abschiedsstunde*; see Kretzschmar, *Geschichte des neuen deutschen Liedes*, i.272. I can confirm Kretzschmar's hypothesis that both derive ultimately from an Italian melodic type.
36. Wieland, *Briefe an Merck*, ii.76
37. See Maurer, *Anton Schweitzer als dramatischer Komponist*, 28.

Hompesch's insistent demands and revised the ending of the work.[38] Although he was dissatisfied with the result, he thought that people would come from twenty or thirty miles around to hear Schweitzer's music and that, on hearing it, they would forget all the libretto's shortcomings.[39]

Wieland was also invited to attend the performance in person, and although he was dissatisfied with his contribution and had reservations for family and financial reasons, he could ultimately not resist the desire 'to sate himself on music', quite apart from the fact that his friends Friedrich Heinrich Jacobi, Sophie La Roche and her daughter Maximiliane Brentano had promised to come to Mannheim, too.

As a result of the revisions, the first performance was delayed from the elector's name-day, 4 November 1777, to the following January. Schweitzer himself arrived in Mannheim in early December to superintend the rehearsals, although by this date all the preparations, including work on the lavish sets and costumes, were already complete. Mozart immediately made contact with him. 'He is a good, worthy, honest fellow,' he told his father in his letter of 3 December 1777, 'dry and smooth like our [Michael] Haydn, but better-spoken':

> There are some very beautiful things in the new opera and I've no doubt that it will be a great success. *Alceste* was very popular but isn't half as fine as *Rosamunde*. Of course, the fact that *Alceste* was the first German singspiel had a lot to do with this. It no longer makes such a deep impression on people who are carried away only by novelty.[40]

On one occasion Schweitzer was ill and so Mozart himself had to replace him and 'conduct a rehearsal at Wendling's with a few violins'.[41] But the more often Mozart heard the new piece, the more unfavourable his opinion became and on 18 December we find his mother writing: 'Schweitzer's new opera is being rehearsed every day. Wolfgang does not like it at all; he says there's nothing natural about it, everything is exaggerated and not well written from the singers' point of view; we must wait and see how the production turns out.'[42] On 10 January we find Mozart himself writing on the subject of *Rosamunde*: 'It is – good, but nothing more, for if it were bad, they couldn't stage it, could they?'[43] And on 11 September 1778 he even complained about Aloysia Weber's 'miserable' role:

> She has one aria where, to judge by the ritornello, something good might be expected, but the voice part is alla Schweitzer, like dogs barking; she has a single type of rondeau, in act 2, where she has an opportunity for sustained singing and can show off her voice; yes, unhappy the singer, male or female, who falls into Schweitzer's hands, as he'll never learn how to write for the voice, however long he lives.[44]

38. See Jacobi, *Auserlesener Briefwechsel*, i.262ff.; and Wieland, *Briefe an Merck*, ii.93, i.102 and i.118–19.
39. Wieland, *Briefe an Sophie von La Roche*, 184 and 187–8.
40. *Briefe*, ii.161–2.
41. *Briefe*, ii.197 (letter of 18 December 1777).
42. *Briefe*, ii.196.
43. *Briefe*, ii.222.
44. *Briefe*, ii.477. Holzbauer was said to have suffered untold agonies when *Rosamunde* was put into rehearsal in 1780, with Minna Brandes in the title role and Federico Toscani as the King. Of Schweitzer, Holzbauer told Heinse: 'He's a genius; when he gets it right, he's divine; but there are other times when he sounds to be in a brandy-induced stupor'; see Koerte, *Briefe zwischen Gleim, W. Heinse, and J. von Müller*, i.424. A detailed review appeared in the *Rheinische Beiträge*, i (1780), 330ff. and 497ff.; see also Klein, *Über Wielands Rosamund, Schweizers Musik und die Vorstellung dieses Singspiels in Mannheim*.

The audience was particularly keen to meet Wieland, whom the Mannheimers regarded as the most popular German poet of his day.[45] Mozart, too, was anxious to make his acquaintance. Wieland arrived on 21 December and was as pleased with his reception by the elector as with the attention paid by the general public. He wrote to Johann Heinrich Merck on 27 December: 'For the present I can say only that I am well in body and soul as I am playing no other role than my own and, I think – or at least it seems to me, I'm doing very well. – May God grant that things do not go *too well* for me among these people! But I have ensured that this will not be so!'[46] Mozart's opinion of him, by contrast, is entirely typical of his own independence of mind in the face of even acknowledged and acclaimed figures:

I've also got to know Herr Wieland, though he doesn't know as much about me as I know about him, as he's heard none of my works. I'd imagined him quite differently. He strikes me as slightly affected in his speech; a rather childish voice, always quizzing you over his glasses, a certain scholarly uncouthness and even at times a stupid condescension. But I'm not surprised that he deigns to behave in this way here (though it may be different in Weimar and elsewhere), as people stare at him as though he's dropped from Heaven. Everyone is embarrassed in his presence, they say nothing and stand stock-still, listening carefully to every word he utters; – it's just a shame they have to wait so long, as he has a speech impediment that makes him speak very slowly and means that he can't say 6 words without stopping. Apart from that, he has an excellent mind, as, indeed, we all know him to have. But he has a frightfully ugly face, covered with pock-marks, and a rather long nose; as for his height, I'd say he's a little taller than Papa.[47]

After Wieland had got to know him, Mozart wrote to his father again:

Now that he has heard me twice, Herr Wieland is utterly enchanted with me. The last time, after showering all manner of compliments on me, he said: 'I'm really happy I've met you here!' And with that he pressed my hand.[48]

The performance of *Rosamunde* was set for 11 January 1778, but on 30 December the Elector Maximilian of Bavaria died, and Karl Theodor decided to leave for Munich without delay,[49] with the result that the performance was cancelled. A further rehearsal was held at the theatre for Wieland's sake, after which the poet returned to Weimar.[50]

An examination of the opera confirms Mozart's reaction on all its essential points, a reaction that was shared by Holzbauer, too.[51] It fails to match its predecessor in terms of melodic invention and *cantabilità*, while attempting to surpass it in its orchestral effects.[52] Particularly notable are the clear French influences not only in the overture, but also in the independent orchestral numbers

---

45. Schubart, *Leben und Gesinnungen*, xiv/1.157.
46. Wieland, *Briefe an Merck*, i.121.
47. *Briefe*, ii.207 (letter of 27 December 1777).
48. *Briefe*, ii.222 (letter of 10 January 1778).
49. Häusser, *Geschichte der rheinischen Pfalz*, ii.957–8.
50. Wieland, *Briefe an Merck*, ii.122 and 124. *Rosamunde* was not performed in Mannheim until 20 January 1780; see Maurer, *Anton Schweitzer als dramatischer Komponist*, 29. ◆ For a contemporaneous reaction to *Rosamunde*, see [Vogler], 'Ueber die Musik der Oper *Rosamunde*'.
51. Maurer, *Anton Schweitzer als dramatischer Komponist*, 29–30.
52. Especially striking is the use of the French-inspired reminiscence motif; see Maurer, *Anton Schweitzer als dramatischer Komponist*, 61.

and, above all, in the extended choral scenes. The arias, by contrast, reveal the familiar hallmarks of Neapolitan rhetoric. Of the German spirit that had left its mark on Holzbauer's *Günther von Schwarzburg*, there is thus very little evidence, and it comes as no surprise, therefore, to discover that the work's success was limited in the main to Mannheim.

In this way Mozart witnessed the historically important initial attempts to create a national German opera.[53] We shall shortly have occasion to see the response that they elicited in a mind already responsive to German opera following his recent experiences in Munich.

Thanks to the excellent training that they had received at Holzbauer's hands, most of the leading singers at the Mannheim opera were Germans.[54] Among them was Dorothea Wendling née Spurni (1736–1811), who was described by one commentator as 'the German Melpomene of Mannheim's Golden Age'[55] and who was universally admired for her technically consummate and heartfelt singing. According to Wieland, she even surpassed Mara: for him, she was the embodiment of true singing, a singer who spoke the language of the heart and soul, each note being the living expression of the purest, most intimate emotion and her whole singing the continuous unfolding of a beautiful line.[56] Her physical beauty – Heinse saw in her features the affectionate, dewy-eyed, ardour-dampening essence of a woman's love and at the same time the volatility and mercuriality of passion[57] – and her outstanding gifts as an actress[58] raised her performances to an altogether exceptional level. Less important, although still highly commendable as a singer, was her sister-in-law Elisabeth Augusta Wendling née Sarselli (1746–86), whose career was repeatedly interrupted by illness. Another singer of the first rank was Franziska Danzi (1756–91),[59] who later married the oboist Ludwig August Lebrun and who was on leave in London at the time of Mozart's visit to Mannheim.[60] She impressed not only through her beauty but also by the range of her voice, which was equal to all the demands placed on it.

The most famous singer in Mannheim at this time was the tenor Anton Raaff, who was already nearing the end of his career. He had been born at Holzem[61] near Bonn in 1714 and studied at the Jesuit grammar school in Bonn. The elector Clemens Augustus had then paid for his training as a singer, engaging him in 1736 on a salary of 200 thalers and finally taking him with him to Munich. From there he went to Bologna to study with Bernacchi. In 1738 he sang at Maria Theresia's wedding and in 1742 returned to Bonn from where he toured various German courts.[62] There

---

53. Further see Lühning, 'Das Theater Carl Theodors und die Idee der Nationaloper'; and for a more general account of music at Mannheim, Finscher, *Die Mannheimer Hofkapelle im Zeitalter Carl Theodors*.

54. See Walter, *Geschichte des Theaters*, 227ff.

55. Heinse, *Sämtliche Schriften*, iii.221.

56. Wieland, *Briefe an Sophie von La Roche*, 191. A more critical note was struck by Schubart in his *Ideen zu einer Ästhetik der Tonkunst* (144): 'She distinguished herself as one of our finest opera singers, appearing in French, Italian and German pieces, but in far more comic works than tragic ones. She soon developed a wobble – which creates the most unfortunate impression in serious declamation.'

57. Koerte, *Briefe zwischen Gleim, W. Heinse, und J. von Müller*, i.424.

58. Jacobi, *Auserlesener Briefwechsel*, i.279. ◆ Further, see Corneilson, 'An Intimate Vocal Portrait of Dorothea Wendling. Mozart's "Basta, vincesti" – "Ah non lasciarmi, no" K. 295a'.

59. See Burney, *The Present State of Music in Germany*, i.90; *A General History of Music from the Earliest Ages to the Present Period*, iv.481 and 508–9; Schubart, *Ideen zu einer Ästhetik der Tonkunst*, 142; and Busby, *A General History of Music, from the Earliest Times to the Present*, ii.361. ◆ Also see Höft, 'Komponisten, Komponistinnen und Virtuosen'.

60. Wieland, *Briefe an Merck*, i.108.

61. Gerber, *Neues historisch-biographisches Lexikon der Tonkünstler*, iii.789, claims that Raaff was born at Gelsdorf in the duchy of Jülich, on which point he is followed by Walter, *Geschichte des Theaters*. For more general information on Raaff, see *AMZ*, xii (1810), 857–77, and Walter, *Geschichte des Theaters*, 231ff. ◆ Also see Freiberger, 'Anton Raaff (1714–1797): Sein Leben und Wirken'; Petrobelli, 'The Italian Years of Anton Raaff'; Angermüller, '"ein Gottförchtiger, erlicher Mann": Anton Raaff, Mozarts erster Idomeneo'; and Schwarte, '"in des Fedi Parnass . . .". Bildnisse des Sängers Anton Raaff (1714–1797)'.

62. In 1749 he appeared in Vienna in Jommelli's *Didone abbandonata*; see Metastasio, *Opere postume*, i.359.

followed a lengthy period of foreign travel, during which time he added to his reputation: from 1752 to 1755 he was in Lisbon, from 1755 to 1759 in Madrid, where he worked under Farinelli,[63] and from 1759 to 1769 in Naples.[64] It was not until 1770 that he returned to Germany. When Karl Theodor invited him to enter his service, the modest Raaff declared that he would deem himself happy indeed if the elector were to be satisfied with his scant remains. In Schubart's opinion, Raaff's was the most beautiful tenor voice he had ever heard, equally full and pure from bass to alto.[65] He demonstrated perfect mastery in the art of singing combined with admirable skills not only in sight-reading but also in ornamenting the vocal line and improvising cadenzas. His delivery, moreover, was so filled with emotion that 'his beautiful heart seemed to echo in his singing'. He was also unusually perceptive in his judgements and capable of calm contemplation. To these assets were added the purest and clearest enunciation so that not a single syllable was lost in even the largest halls. Of course, Schubart was not deaf to the fact that Raaff's voice was already beginning to develop a marked vibrato.[66] The most critical voice within these universal plaudits was again that of Mozart, who first heard Raaff in *Günther von Schwarzburg* and reported his impressions in his letter to Leopold of 14–16 November 1777:

Herr Raaff sang 4 arias – about 450 bars in all – in such a fashion as to make you realize that his voice is the principal reason why he sings so badly. Anyone who hears him begin an aria without simultaneously recalling that it is Raaff, the once famous tenor, who is singing is bound to burst out laughing. It's a fact; I thought so myself: if I didn't know that this was Raaff, I'd double up laughing, but as it is, I just take out my handkerchief and hide a smile. And he's never been much of an actor, or so people tell me here; you need to have heard him, without seeing him: and he doesn't have a good presence.[67] In the opera he had to die and while dying sing a very very very long and slow aria, and he died with a smile on his lips, and towards the end of the aria his voice gave out so badly that people could stand it no longer. I was sitting next to Wendling the flautist in the orchestra. Earlier, he'd complained that it was unnatural for a man to keep singing until he died, as it was too long to wait. So I said to him: 'Just be patient, he'll soon be gone, I can hear it.' 'I, too,' he said and laughed.[68]

Only when Mozart had heard Raaff more often did he do the singer greater justice. Yet even now he found Raaff's style of singing insufficiently simple. In a letter written in Paris on 12 June 1778 he explains his reaction in greater detail, making it clear that, fond as he was of Raaff, he was unable to bring himself to offend the singer, while standing by his convictions:

For his début here at the Concert Spirituel he sang Bach's *scena* 'Non sò d'onde viene' – which is in any case a favourite of mine. It was the first time I'd really heard him sing. I liked what I heard – in other words, within this particular style of singing, even though the style itself – the

63. On his successes there, see Reichardt, *Berlinische musikalische Zeitung*, i (1805), 278. Raaff left Lisbon shortly before the earthquake and, in gratitude for his salvation, paid for a chapel to be built at Holzem.
64. Here he met Naumann in 1767 and his singing is even said to have cured the Princess Belmonte-Pignatelli of the melancholy caused by the death of her husband; see Gerber, *Neues historisch-biographisches Lexikon*, iii.789, and Haug, 'Raff'.
65. Schubart, *Leben und Gesinnungen*, i/14.154.
66. Schubart, *Ideen zu einer Ästhetik der Tonkunst*, 136–7.
67. Local tradition remembered Raaff as a fairly tall thin man with dark brown hair and attractive features; see Thayer, *Ludwig van Beethovens Leben*, eighth edition, 407ff. [Deiters's note].
68. *Briefe*, ii.125.

Bernacchi school[69] – isn't to my taste. For my own taste, he's too inclined to adopt a cantabile style. I admit that when he was younger and in his prime this must have been very effective and taken people by surprise – I like it myself, but he overdoes it, it often strikes me as laughable. What I do like is when he sings short pieces such as certain andantinos, but also certain arias, which he sings in his own particular style. Each in his own way. I can well imagine that his great strength was bravura singing and to the extent that his age allows it, you can still tell that this was the case, a good chest and long breath and then – these andantinos. His voice is beautiful and very agreeable. If I close my eyes when listening to him, he reminds me very much of [Joseph Nikolaus] Meißner, except that Raaff's voice strikes me as more agreeable. . . . Meißner, as you know, has the bad habit of making his voice tremble at times, . . . but Raaff doesn't do this, which is something he, too, can't abide. As far as a real cantabile is concerned, I prefer Meißner to Raaff (although I don't like everything about him, as, in my view, he too overdoes it). But in terms of bravura, passage-work and roulades, Raaff is his superior, and then there's his excellent, clear enunciation, which is beautiful, and then, as I've already said, his andantinos or little canzonettas. He's written four German songs that are really quite charming.[70]

That Raaff was a good singer but no actor was universally acknowledged. As for his private life, it was morally blameless. Religious by nature, he held ethical views that were no less rigorous than his artistic convictions. Occasionally he would let out a torrent of abuse, but basically he was good-natured and well-disposed towards others, a true friend and generous to the point of self-sacrifice. It is typical of Mozart's candid nature that he was as attached to Raaff as a fellow human being and friend as he was critical of his work as an artist.[71]

Another distinguished tenor at Mannheim was Raaff's pupil Franz Hartig (1750–1819).[72]

Church music in Mannheim, by contrast, was not to Schubart's liking: he found it too mawkish and operatic, arguing that 'nothing is more profane than a Lamb of God in the cooing neo-Italian tradition, babbled out with no feeling for Heaven, and a Kyrie that drivels on like a beautiful young actress to a fast and frivolous metre with music to match'.[73] Accordingly, he ranked Holzbauer's sacred works below his operas, finding them lacking in contrapuntal rigour.[74] In doing so, he failed, of course, to appreciate the independent poetical mind at work in these Masses, failed to appreciate the 'charming piety that is by no means devoid of depth and which, on a formal level, expresses itself succinctly in various ways, achieving a splendid impact that is calculated with a sure hand'.[75] Mozart was rather more appreciative here: 'He writes very well,' he told his father

---

69.   ◆ The Italian alto castrato Antonio Maria Bernacchi (1685–1756), considered by some to be the finest singer in Europe, had founded a singing school in Florence; his pupils included Raaff, Guarducci and Amadori. See Frati, 'Antonio Bernacchi e la sua scuola di canto'; and Dean and Knapp, *Handel's Operas 1704–1726*.

70.   *Briefe*, ii.377–8.

71.   After appearing as Idomeneo in 1781, Raaff retired from the operatic stage, seeing few friends and dividing his time between devotional exercises and reading. He died in Munich in 1797.

72.   'We recently had the virtuoso Hartig here', Jacobi wrote to Wieland on 8 June 1777. 'You should hear this man sing! We performed the recitative from Alceste, "O Jugendzeit, o goldne Wonnetage", four times. I wish you could have had the pleasure of hearing him sing even this one recitative'; Jacobi, *Auserlesener Briefwechsel*, i.272. See also Mozart's letter quoted above. ◆ The tenor Franz Christian Hartig (1750–1819) was active at Mannheim from 1777 at both the Nationaltheater and the court theatre; among his chief roles was that of Karl in Ignaz Holzbauer's *Günther von Schwarzburg*.

73.   Schubart, *Leben und Gesinnungen*, i/14.155; see also Walter, *Geschichte des Theaters*, 180ff.

74.   Schubart, *Ideen zu einer Ästhetik der Tonkunst*, 132.

75.   Kretzschmar, *Ignaz Holzbauer: Günther von Schwarzburg*, xii.

on 4 November 1777, 'with a good sacred style. He also knows how to write for voices and instruments, and he writes good fugues.'[76]

But there is no doubt that he was appalled at the decline in musical standards in the Mannheim church choir and thought it would be impossible to perform any of his own masses there:

> Why? – On account of their shortness? – No, everything has to be short here, too. – Because of the sacred style? – Not at all, but because, given the present circumstances, you have to write chiefly for the instruments as you can't imagine anything worse than the voices here. 6 sopranos, 6 altos, 6 tenors and 6 basses against 20 violins and 12 basses is just like 0 to 1; isn't that so, Herr Bullinger? The reason for this is that the Italians are now in very bad odour here. They've only 2 castratos, who are already old. They'll simply be left to die off. The soprano would in fact prefer to sing alto as he can't get the high notes any longer. The few boys[77] they have are pitiful, while the tenors and basses are like our funeral singers.[78]

But the situation with the organ was even worse, and here Mozart's contempt for the two court organists knew no bounds:

> They have 2 organists who alone would be worth a special visit to Mannheim. I've had a chance to hear them properly, as it's not the custom here to sing a Benedictus, instead the organist has to play the whole time. The first time I heard the second organist, the second time the first one. But I value the 2nd one even more highly than the first, for when I heard him I asked who it was who was playing the organ. 'Our second organist.' He plays abominably. When I heard the other one, I asked who it was. 'Our first one.' He played even more abominably. I think if they were thrown together, something even worse would come out of it. You'd die laughing watching these gentlemen. The second is like a mudlark, you can see from his face what he's up to. But the first wears spectacles. I went and stood by the organ in the hope of learning something from him. At every note he lifts his hands high in the air. But his great strength is his 6-part playing, which he mostly plays in fifths and octaves. As a joke, he often omits the right hand altogether and plays with his left hand alone. In a word, he can do as he likes, he is complete master of his instrument.[79]

But Mannheim was famous chiefly for its instrumental music, with the local orchestra universally regarded as the finest in Europe. It numbered more players than was usual, especially in the winds,[80] and from 1759 included clarinets, which were still extremely rare in Germany at this

76. *Briefe*, ii.102 (letter of 4 November 1777). ◆ Further, see Eduard Schmitt, *Kirchenmusik der Mannheimer Schule*.
77. Cf. Wieland's comment on 'dressed-up schoolboys' in these choirs; *Die Abderiten*, book 1, part 3, chapter 5.
78. *Briefe*, ii.101 (letter of 4 November 1777).
79. *Briefe*, ii.102 (letter of 4 November 1777).
80. An account of the orchestra in 1756 may be found in Marpurg, *Historisch-kritische Beyträge zur Aufnahme der Musik*, ii.567; see also Riemann, *Sinfonien der Pfalzbayerischen Schule*. For a report from 1767, see Hiller, *Wöchentliche Nachrichten und Anmerkungen die Musik betreffend*, ii.167ff. See also Walter, *Geschichte des Theaters*, 207ff. On 4 November 1777, Mozart wrote to his father: 'The orchestra is very good and strong; on either side 10 or 11 violins, 4 violas, 2 oboes, 2 flutes and 2 clarinets, 2 horns, 4 cellos, 4 bassoons, 4 double basses and trumpets and timpani' (*Briefe*, ii.101). Here, as elsewhere, two platforms were built in the opera house to accommodate the extra trumpets (see above). ◆ Also see Spitzer and Zaslaw, *The Birth of the Orchestra: History of an Institution*, 256–62.

time.[81] 'Ah, if only we too had clarinets,' Mozart wrote to his father on 3 December 1778. 'You can't imagine what a splendid effect a symphony makes with flutes, oboes and clarinets.'[82]

Even more than the number of its players, the Mannheim orchestra was praised for its novel performing style.[83] Here *piano* and *forte* were reproduced in all their gradations, and the crescendo and diminuendo were executed in a completely new way that only the Stuttgart orchestra under Jommelli came close to imitating.[84] And the strings and winds were combined in a wholly new way.[85] In short, the Mannheim orchestra was the object of universal astonishment.[86] The elector was fully aware of its merits and invited its members to perform at his regular concerts, taking part himself and contributing in no small way to the history of the German symphony.

Even the composition of this orchestra was new. In 1756 we find an unusually large complement of twenty violins against four violas, four cellos and two double basses, but only two oboes, two flutes, two bassoons and four horns. This balance between winds and strings is entirely modern: under the older dispensation,[87] such a body of strings would have been offset by ten oboes and ten bassoons. As a direct result of this, a new performing style evolved, replacing the older system of dynamics with a newer one, whereby dynamic levels underwent a graduated change rather than being based on register.[88] It also brought with it a totally different relationship between strings and winds. We have already seen how this new performing style was not limited to questions of technique but affected the very life of the work itself. Nor was it a question any longer of leaving the execution to the conductor's discretion: here, too, the Mannheim symphonists paved the way for a new age by indicating dynamic markings on a far greater scale than their predecessors had done, with the result that the conductor now ceded one of his most important functions to the composer. Meanwhile, another of the main supports of the older type of music, the continuo, was dealt its death blow in Mannheim,[89] and although it continued to survive for a little longer, pieces with more elaborate inner parts now began to proliferate.

The progenitor of all these innovations was Johann Stamitz. Although he had died many years previously [in 1757], his numerous pupils and successors had successfully kept his tradition

81. See above. Jahn's claim, in *W. A. Mozart*, fourth edition, i.434–5, that it was in Mannheim that Mozart first got to know the clarinet as an orchestral instrument needs correcting in the light of this. Burney, *The Present State of Music in Germany* (i.94–5), complained only at the impure intonation of the winds, but this was a problem endemic to all the orchestras with which he was familiar.
82. *Briefe*, ii.517 (letter of 3 December 1778). ◆ Presumably Mozart refers here to the use of clarinets as an orchestral instrument; in Salzburg they had for some time been a part of civil and military bands. See Birsak and König, *Das große Salzburger Blasmusikbuch*.
83. Burney, *The Present State of Music in Germany*, i.92–5; Schubart, *Leben und Gesinnungen*, i/14.152–3; and *AmZ*, i (1798/9), 882.
84. Reichardt, *Briefe eines aufmerksamen Reisenden die Musik betreffend*, i.11, wrote of the Berlin orchestra: 'Of the swelling and disappearance of a long note or even of several successive notes which, if I may express myself in this way, passes through every shade of light and dark and is so masterfully executed in Mannheim, I shall not even speak here, as Hasse and Graun never availed themselves of it.' Reichardt adds that Jommelli was the first to use this device, causing listeners gradually to rise from their seats during the crescendo, not drawing breath until the diminuendo, when they finally noticed that they had been holding their breath; he had experienced this effect for himself in Mannheim.
85. Schubart, *Ideen zu einer Ästhetik der Tonkunst*, 130.
86. Schubart, *Ideen zu einer Ästhetik der Tonkunst*, 130: 'No orchestra in the world has ever beaten the Mannheim orchestra in its manner of execution. Its *forte* is a thunderclap, its crescendo a cataract, its diminuendo a crystal stream babbling away into the distance, its *piano* a breath of spring.'
87. See the list in Mennicke, *Hasse und die Brüder Graun als Symphoniker*, 270ff.
88. See Heuß, 'Über die Dynamik der Mannheimer Schule', 433.
89. Riemann, *Sinfonien der Pfalzbayerischen Schule*, XVII–XVIII. Significantly, Marpurg's list does not mention a harpsichordist. ◆ Abert's assertion here is something of an exaggeration: continuo continued to be performed at least until the end of the eighteenth century (whether orchestral lists name keyboardists or not). Its decline and eventual dissolution was gradual, depending on changes in local tastes and performing practices, and often tied to specific genres.

alive. The Mannheim orchestra continued to unite within its ranks some of the finest musicians of their day: among the violinists were Christian Cannabich, Carl Joseph (1731–88) and Johann Baptist Toeschi (1735–1800), Ignaz Fränzl (1736–1811) and Wilhelm Cramer (1746–99); the viola players included Carl Stamitz (1745–1801) and the flautists Johann Baptist Wendling (1723–97). The oboists were Ludwig August Lebrun (1752–90) and Friedrich Ramm (*c*1741–1813), while the bassoonists included Georg Wenzel Ritter (1748–1808) and the horn player Franz Lang.[90] All were among the foremost virtuosos of the age. On Stamitz's death the difficult task of maintaining a sense of orchestral discipline among players of this calibre passed to his pupil Christian Cannabich (1731–98). Cannabich had studied in Italy with Jommelli,[91] and by 1775 he was working alongside Holzbauer in Mannheim, a function that points to the importance of the post of first violinist in the town. Cannabich was also a talented composer,[92] but, thanks to the training he had received at Stamitz's hands, his main strength lay in his activities as leader, soloist and teacher. Most of the violinists in the Mannheim orchestra were his pupils, which naturally contributed greatly to the uniformity of their playing. He examined all the means and conditions necessary to create orchestral effects, perfecting violin technique in particular in order to train competent ripieno players. He combined insight and an innate talent for conducting[93] with 'the best of German hearts'[94] and the reputation of leading a moral, sober lifestyle, ensuring that he enjoyed the respect and affection of his players and in this way guaranteeing the highest performance standards.

In short, the European reputation of music in Mannheim was well-grounded. In opera, the Italian foundations of the genre had not yet been undermined, of course,[95] although an important step had been taken in choosing German subjects and engaging German singers who challenged the hegemony of their Italian colleagues. But French influence, too, was particularly forcefully felt in Mannheim, a state of affairs encouraged not only by the Palatinate's geographical location and by the elector's personal predilections but also by the conscious decision of the school of Hasse to embrace such influences. Mannheim's artists received the most varied stimuli and advantages from Karl Theodor's links with Paris. If Mannheim failed to become one of the leading centres of

---

90. ◆ See Fuhrmann, *Mannheimer Klavier-Kammermusik*; Lebermann, 'Biographische Notizen über Johann Anton Fils, Johann Anton Stamitz, Carl Joseph und Johann Baptist Toeschi' and 'Zur Genealogie der Toeschi'; Eugene K. Wolf, 'Mannheimer Symphonik um 1777/1778 und ihr Einfluß auf Mozarts symphonischen Stil'; Würtz, *Ignaz Fränzl: Ein Beitrag zur Musikgeschichte der Stadt Mannheim*; McVeigh, *The Violinist in London's Concert Life, 1750–1784: Felice Giardini and his Contemporaries*; Höft, 'Komponisten, Komponistinnen und Virtuosen'; and Griswold, 'Mozart's "Good Wood-Biter": Georg Wenzel Ritter (1748–1808)'.
91. His lessons with Jommelli are attested by Hiller (*Wöchentliche Nachrichten*, 21 September 1767). But they cannot have lasted from 1760 to 1763 as Walter (*Geschichte des Theaters*, 212) assumes, as Jommelli was working in Stuttgart at this time. They took place in 1753/4: see Adolf Sandberger's article in the *Festschrift Hermann Kretzschmar*, 130. Cannabich is also important in terms of the historical parallels between Jommelli and the Mannheimers on the question of the crescendo. ◆ Cannabich studied with Jommelli in Rome from about 1752 to July 1753, then followed him to Stuttgart, where he remained until February 1754.
92. In addition to operas and symphonies, he also wrote ballets; see *AmZ*, new series, viii (1870), 310, and Niedecken, *Jean-Georges Noverre*, 56. ◆ Concerning Cannabich, see Beck, 'Geschichte und Genealogie der Hofmusikerfamilie Cannabich, 1707–1806'; Groman, 'The Mannheim Orchestra under the Leadership of Christian Cannabich'; and Eugene K. Wolf, *The Symphony at Mannheim: Johann Stamitz, Christian Cannabich* and 'Mannheimer Symphonik um 1777/1778 und ihr Einfluß auf Mozarts symphonischen Stil'. Cannabich's Mannheim ballets included *Ceyx et Alcyone* (1762–3), *Renaud et Armide* (1768), *Roland furieux, ou Angélique et Médor* (1768), *Le rendez-vous* (1769 or earlier), *Les mariages samni(s)tes* (1772), *Médée et Jason* (1772), *Admette et Alceste* (1775), *L'embarquement pour Cythère, ou Le triomphe de Vénus* (1775) and *Orphée dans l'isle de Sirènes* (1775–6); at least eleven others composed between 1758 and 1778 are lost. See Kloiber, *Die dramatischen Ballette von Christian Cannabich*.
93. Schubart, *Ideen zu einer Ästhetik der Tonkunst*, 137; *Musikalischer Almanach für 1782*, 6–7.
94. Schubart, *Leben und Gesinnungen*, i/14.152; *AmZ*, v (1802/3), 276.
95. A list of all the operas, oratorios, ballets and so on that were performed in Mannheim may be found in Walter, *Geschichte des Theaters*, 362ff. On the musical life of Mannheim in 1765, see also Closson, 'Pascal Taskin', 239–40. ◆ Further, see Eugene K. Wolf, 'The Mannheim Court'; and Corneilson, 'Opera at Mannheim, 1770–1778' and 'Reconstructing the Mannheim court theatre'.

German opera, it none the less achieved this distinction in the field of instrumental music, an achievement that it owed to the genius of Johann Stamitz.

By a stroke of good fortune, Mozart was able to experience Mannheim's literary and musical heyday at first hand and soak up its atmosphere before it came to a sudden end with the court's removal to Munich [in 1778]. But, as we have seen, he differed from Schubart, who felt only enthusiasm at what he found, and maintained his usual independent, critical outlook. In spite of his natural receptivity to new artistic impressions, he never for a moment felt constricted or oppressed by this wealth of new ideas but consorted with Mannheim's luminaries as though they were his equals, charming and winning them over, but candid and self-confident. From the very outset he was surprised that, although his name was already familiar to them, they treated him with so little respect. On the day after his arrival he met the violinist Christian Franz Danner (1757–1813) at Cannabich's and went with him to a rehearsal, where some of the musicians treated him unsympathetically and even with ill-concealed contempt, making fun of his unprepossessing appearance – a point on which Mozart remained very sensitive throughout the whole of his life. More important, however, is the fact that he narrowly avoided attending a rehearsal of Handel's *Messiah*. Mannheim was only the third German town after Berlin and Hamburg to perform Handel's oratorio.[96] The conductor in Mannheim was Georg Joseph Vogler (1749–1814), a man whom Mozart found profoundly unattractive and who contented himself with performing only the first part of the work, omitting the whole of the second part 'as no listener will want to sit through such arid music'.[97] And even the first part was performed in an almost incredible paraphrase in the style of an Italian opera libretto.[98] It was preceded by a *Magnificat* by Vogler himself, the rehearsal for which so wearied Mozart that he left before the start of the Handel. Evidently he also avoided the performance on 1 November, preferring to attend 'a high mass in the *Kapelle*'.[99] As a result, he missed Vogler's performance of *Messiah*, a performance which, whatever its deficiencies, was still of considerable historical importance.

Conversely, it was not long before he won the hearts of Mannheim's musicians through the sheer force of his personality and his achievements as an artist. Following his experience of Salzburg, he was agreeably surprised by their far higher level of culture. And he also found that relations between the prince and his artists were of an informality that was the exact opposite of the situation in Salzburg. Like Schubart before him,[100] he was soon accepted into their social circle, even though, like Schubart,[101] he very quickly discovered that the easygoing manners of the court had already affected a number of artists.

He soon struck up a cordial friendship with Cannabich, and the two men visited each other on a daily basis, when they were joined by Mozart's mother. Mozart often dined with Cannabich at lunchtime, and it was not long before he was invited to dine with him in the evenings as well. These evenings were spent in animated conversation and music-making, after which Mozart generally produced a book from his pocket and read. His humorous confession of 14 November 1777 reflects the light-hearted mood of these meetings:

---

96. See Max Seiffert, 'Die Mannheimer "Messias"-Aufführung 1777'.
97. Vogler, *Betrachtungen der Mannheimer Tonschule*, ii.280.
98. Max Seiffert, 'Die Mannheimer "Messias"-Aufführung 1777', 65.
99. *Briefe*, ii.101 (letter of 4 November 1777).
100. Schubart, *Leben und Gesinnungen*, i/14.152.
101. Schubart, *Leben und Gesinnungen*, i/14.162; see also Riesbeck, *Briefe eines reisenden Franzosen*, i.341.

I, Johannes Chrysostomus Amadeus Wolfgangus Sigismundus Mozart, hereby plead guilty and confess that yesterday and the day before (not to mention several other occasions) I didn't get home till midnight; and that from 10 o'clock until the said hour I was at Cannabich's in the presence and company of Cannabich, his wife and daughter, the Treasurer, Ramm and Lang, with whom I did frequently and without any difficulty, but quite easily, perpetrate rhymes, the same being, moreover, sheer nonsense, . . . and that I did so in thought and word, but not in deed. But I wouldn't have behaved so godlessly if our ringleader, known as Lisel,[102] hadn't egged me on and incited me; and I must admit that I thoroughly enjoyed myself. I confess all these sins and transgressions from the bottom of my heart, and in the hope of having to confess them very often, I firmly resolve to go on with the sinful life that I've begun. And so I beg for the holy dispensation, if it can be easily obtained; if not, it's all the same to me, as the game will go on all the same, lusus enim suum habet ambitum, as the late Meißner says, Chap. 9, p. 24, as does Saint Ascenditor, patron of burnt soup coffee, musty lemonade, almondless milk of almonds and especially strawberry ice full of lumps of ice, as he himself is a great connoisseur and artist in ices.[103]

That they also made music goes without saying, and within days of his arrival Mozart had already performed all six of his sonatas (K279–284), one after the other. Cannabich was fully alive to, and appreciative of, his exceptional talent, even taking advantage of his presence to ask him to prepare playable keyboard reductions of his ballets. But self-interest was certainly not the reason for his actions: both he and his wife loved Mozart as if he were their own son, taking a lively interest in his well-being and repeatedly proving to be loyal friends. The magnet that drew Mozart to their house and held him there for some time was Cannabich's eldest daughter Rosa. She was then thirteen and, as Mozart wrote to tell his father on 6 December 1777, was 'a very pretty and charming girl, very intelligent and mature for her age; she's serious, doesn't say much, but what she does say is said in a delightful and friendly tone'.[104] On the day after his arrival on 31 October 1777, she performed for him and, discovering that she played very well, he started to work on a sonata for her as a favour to her father. The opening allegro was completed that very same day. 'Young Danner asked me how I intended to write the andante', Mozart went on in his letter of 6 December. 'I said I intended to make it fit Mlle Rosa's character. – When I played it, she liked it a lot. Young Danner told me so afterwards; it's true: the andante is just like her.' On 8 November he wrote the rondo at Cannabich's – 'as a result they wouldn't let me leave'. While working on this sonata with Rosa, Mozart was all the more struck by her talent in that he found her playing careless: 'Her right hand is very good, but her left, unfortunately, is completely ruined. . . . If I were her regular teacher, I'd lock up all her music, cover the keys with a handkerchief and make her practise, first with her right hand and then with her left, nothing but passage-work, trills, mordants etc., very slowly at first, until each hand was properly trained. I'd then undertake to turn her into a first-rate keyboard player.'[105]

102. Cannabich's daughter Elisabetha (1776–?).
103. *Briefe*, ii.123–4.
104. *Briefe*, ii.170. That she was very attractive at this time emerges from a remark in an unpublished letter from the painter Ferdinand von Kobell to Wolfgang Heribert von Dalberg: 'How many such sweet and priceless moments Heaven granted me through my delightful dealings with the beautiful Rose Cannabich. My memory of her is of a Garden of Eden to my heart!' An equally enthusiastic description appears in the *Musik- und Künstleralmanach für 1783*, 27–8. By 1786 she was known as Madame Schulz.
105. *Briefe*, ii.124 (letter of 14–16 November 1777).

It was not long before Mozart was giving Rosa Cannabich regular lessons – an hour a day – and he was more than happy with the results. 'Yesterday', he wrote to his father on 6 December 1777, 'she gave me the indescribable pleasure of playing the whole of my sonata most admirably. The andante (which must *not be taken too quickly*) she plays with the utmost feeling; and she likes playing it.' Leopold cast his expert eye over the piece and on 11 December 1777 pronounced it a curious work, having 'something in it of the rather mannered Mannheim *goût*', but not enough to detract from Mozart's own style.[106]

Mozart also came into closer contact with the outstanding flautist Johann Baptist Wendling, who had been a member of the Mannheim orchestra since 1752 and who kept open house. He was introduced to Wendling by Cannabich and describes the extreme courteousness of his hosts:

> The daughter [Augusta], who was once the elector's mistress, plays the harpsichord most prettily.[107] I then played myself. I was in such excellent spirits today that I can't describe it – I improvised everything and then played three duets with violin that I'd never seen by a composer I've never heard of. They were all so delighted that I had to kiss the ladies. In the daughter's case, this was no hardship as she's not at all bad-looking.[108]

He also wrote a French song for Augusta Wendling, who Wieland thought looked so much like a Madonna by Raphael or Dolci[109] that it was impossible not to address a 'Salve Regina' to her.[110] She herself provided the words and performed it so well that it was then sung every day at the Wendlings, who were said to be 'positively mad about it'. Mozart promised to write more songs for her, and at least one was later begun.[111] He also sketched a recitative and aria for Augusta's mother, Dorothea. She herself chose the text from act two, scene four of Metastasio's *Didone abbandonata*, 'Ah! non lasciarmi, no, bell'idol mio'. Mother and daughter were said to be 'completely mad' about this aria, too. Since we know from his sketches that Mozart always tended to write out the vocal line and bass in full and generally also gave indications as to the accompaniment, it was possible to sing and accompany the aria from such a draft.[112] Wendling, too, did not go away empty-handed, as we learn from a letter of 22 November 1777 that a concerto of his, scored by Mozart, was rehearsed at Cannabich's the previous day (K284e). Although he disliked the flute as an instrument and distrusted flautists, Mozart evidently made an exception in Wendling's case. 'You know,' he told Wendling's brother, who had teased him on the subject, 'it's not the same with your brother. First, he's by no means a bad player and, secondly, you don't live in constant fear that the

---

106. As Nottebohm, Köchel, Deiters and, most recently, Heuß ('Zum Thema: Mannheimer Vorhalt') assume, this work was presumably the C major sonata K309. On the other hand, Scheibler ('Mozarts Mannheimer Klaviersonate') argues that it was K311. It seems to me that the critical passage in this context is Mozart's comment in his letter of 14–16 November 1777: 'The andante . . . is full of expression and must be played accurately and with the exact shades of *forte* and *piano*, as marked'; *Briefe*, ii.124. The andante of K309 has more performance markings than any other movement in these works: only 12 of its 79 bars are without a dynamic marking of one sort or another, and many attest to the 'mannered goût' of which Leopold speaks. ◆ Further, see Patier, 'Vers une meilleure compréhension de l'expression de Léopold Mozart: le "vermanierierte Mannheimer Goût"'.

107. Schubart, *Ideen zu einer Ästhetik der Tonkunst*, 144. According to *Briefe*, ii.165 (letter of 3 December 1777), she was always ill.

108. *Briefe*, ii.110 (letter of 8 November 1777).

109. ◆ Presumably Abert's reference here is to the Florentine Carlo Dolci (1616–86), who specialized in devotional paintings.

110. Wieland, *Briefe an Sophie von La Roche*, 192; see also Koerte, *Briefe zwischen Gleim, W. Heinse, and J. von Müller*, i.424.

111. The two songs written in Mannheim will have been the French songs *Oiseaux, si tous les ans* K307 and *Dans un bois solitaire* K308.

112. The sketch was later elaborated as K486a; see *NMA* II/7/2. ◆ Apparently Mozart's aria was inspired by a setting of the same text by Galuppi; see Plath, 'Mozart und Galuppi'.

next note will be either too low or too high – you see, it's always right, he has his heart and ears and the tip of his tongue in the right place and doesn't think that all he has to do is blow and splay his fingers, and he also knows what "adagio" means.'[113]

Mozart also got to know the oboist Friedrich Ramm (1744–c1811) at Cannabich's, valuing him for his artistry and refined, attractive tone and immediately presenting him with a copy of his oboe concerto. According to his letter of 4 November 1777, Ramm was 'beside himself with delight'.[114] The work became his war-horse and he played it five times that winter (see Mozart's letter of 13 February 1778). Audiences liked it 'even though people knew it was by me'. But Mozart also introduced himself to Mannheim audiences as an organist and harpsichordist. Of his violin playing, by contrast, we hear no more. In his letter of 13 November 1777 he offers his father the following whimsical account of his organ playing:

Last Sunday – for fun – I tried out the organ in the chapel. I came in during the Kyrie and played through to the end, and after the priest had finished intoning the Gloria, I played a cadenza. It was so different from what they're used to here that everyone turned round to stare, especially Holzbauer. He said to me: 'If I'd known you were going to do that, I'd have put on a different mass.' 'Yes,' I said, 'so that you could have caught me out!' Old Toeschi and Wendling were standing next to me throughout this. People were helpless with laughter; now and then the music was marked pizzicato, and each time I just touched the keys very lightly. I was in the best of spirits. Instead of just playing the Benedictus, the organist has to play all the time here, so I took the theme of the Sanctus and developed it as a fugue. They all stood there gaping. Finally, after the 'Ite, missa est', I played a fugue. The pedal is different from ours, which confused me a bit to begin with, but I soon got used to it.[115]

On 18 December the new organ in the Lutheran Church was put through its paces and all the local conductors were invited to attend. According to Mozart's mother, a 'distinguished Lutheran' called on them and 'most courteously' invited Mozart to attend. He reported that it was 'very good, both the pleno and the individual stops' but had no time for Vogler, who was playing it, and so he played only a prelude and fugue, but promised himself that he would return there shortly with the various families with whom he was on friendly terms and 'amuse himself spendidly on the organ'.[116] On another occasion, he played for an hour and a half on the organ in the Reformed Church, an instrument praised as outstanding by contemporaries.[117]

The admiration that he inspired as a keyboard player is clear from his mother's report of 28 December 1777:

Everyone thinks the world of Wolfgang, but he plays very differently from the way he did in Salzburg – there are pianofortes here that he plays so extraordinarily well that people say they've never heard anything like it. In a word, everyone who hears him says he has no equal. Even though Beecke was here and Schubart, too, they all say that Wolfgang far surpasses them in

113. Wolzogen, 'Zur Mozart-Biographie', 82; see also Schubart, *Ideen zu einer Ästhetik der Tonkunst*, 143.
114. *Briefe*, ii.101 (letter of 4 November 1777). The concerto has unfortunately not survived. ◆ In fact, the oboe concerto is K314, which in Abert's time was thought to be a flute concerto; see the discussion of Mozart's commission from Dejean below.
115. *Briefe*, ii.120.
116. ◆ *Briefe*, ii.206–7 (letter of 27 December 1777).
117. Schubart, *Leben und Gesinnungen*, i/14.147.

beauty, taste and refinement, and they're all absolutely amazed at the way he improvises and sightreads whatever is placed in front of him.[118]

In Mannheim, keyboard skills lost ground to virtuosity on orchestral instruments, so that Peter Winter, as a true product of the Mannheim school, could not play the harpsichord at all and never derived any pleasure from what he described to his friends as mere tinkling.[119] Even so, there was no lack of opportunity for Mozart to pit himself against other keyboard virtuosos. The Abbé Johann Franz Xaver Sterkel (1750–1817) was one of the most famous keyboard players of his day and during Mozart's visit to Mannheim he travelled to the town from Mainz, where he was pianist and chaplain to the elector.[120] 'The day before yesterday,' Mozart wrote to his father on 26 November 1777, 'I spent the evening at Cannabich's as usual, and Sterkel joined us. He played five duets, but so fast that it was hard to make out what he was playing, it wasn't at all clear, and not in time; everyone said the same. Mlle Cannabich played the sixth and, to tell the truth, better than Sterkel.'[121] Mozart particularly disliked Sterkel's attempt to impress his listeners by playing everything quickly and by sight-reading, an attempt to cover up his artistic shortcomings. A similar criticism was levelled at Vogler, except that in this case Mozart was even more outspoken. In his letter to his father of 17 January 1778 he reports on his meeting with Mannheim's only keyboard virtuoso at a large gathering in the town:

> After dinner he sent to his house for two harpsichords tuned to the same pitch and also for his boring engraved sonatas. I had to play them while he accompanied me on the second keyboard. He then insisted that I should send for my own sonatas. NB: I should add that before dinner he had sight-read my concerto after a fashion (the one that the daughter of the house plays and that was written for Countess Lützow [K246]).[122] The first movement went *prestissimo*, the andante *allegro* and the Rondo, believe it or not, *prestississimo*. The bass he generally played differently from the way it was written and sometimes he even rewrote the harmonies and the melodic line. Nothing else is possible at such a speed; your eyes can't see the music and your hands can't grasp it. Well, what do you call this sort of thing? This kind of sight-reading – is all one to me. Listeners (I mean those who deserve the name) can say only that they've *seen* the music and seen someone playing. They hear, think and feel as little as he does. You can well imagine that it was unbearable as I couldn't bring myself to say to him: '*Far too quick.*' Besides, it's much easier to play something quickly than slowly: in passage-work you can leave out odd notes without anyone noticing; but is that a good thing? – When playing at speed you can change the right and left hands without anyone seeing or hearing; but is that a good thing? – And in what does the art of sight-reading consist? In this: in playing the piece at the right speed, as it ought to be played, playing all the notes, appoggiaturas etc. with the necessary expression and taste, so that you think that the performer actually composed it himself. His fingering, too,

118.   *Briefe*, ii.208.

119.   Obituary in *AmZ*, xxviii (1826), 466.

120.   Max Maria von Weber, *Carl Maria von Weber: Ein Lebensbild*, i.248. ✦ Further concerning Sterkel, see Scharnagl, *Johann Franz Xaver Sterkel*; Gottron, *Mainzer Musikgeschichte von 1500 bis 1800*; Fuhrmann, *Mannheimer Klavier-Kammermusik*; and Komlós, 'The Viennese Keyboard Trio in the 1780s: Sociological Background and Contemporary Reception'.

121.   *Briefe*, ii.146–7.

122.   'In terms of his ability to sight-read, Vogler may well be unbeatable and, indeed, unique': *Musikalische Realzeitung*, i (1788), 61; see also *Musikalische Korrespondenz der Teutschen Filarmonischen Gesellschaft*, i (1790), 119 and iii (1792), 379; see also Schubart, *Ideen zu einer Ästhetik der Tonkunst*, 133ff. Many writers expressly preferred Beecke and Mozart to Vogler; see *Musikalische Realzeitung*, ii (1789), 262 [*Dokumente*, 307–8, *Documentary Biography*, 350].

is miserable: his left thumb is like that of the late Adlgasser, and all descending runs in his right hand he does with his first finger and thumb.[123]

The profound dislike of his famous colleague that finds expression here is something of which Mozart never made any secret.[124] On a personal level, he had no complaints: 'Herr Vogler was most insistent on making my closer acquaintance', he told his father on 17 January 1778. 'He kept pestering me to go and see him but finally overcame his pride and paid me the first visit.'[125] Envy cannot have been the reason for Mozart's aversion, as this was a vice of which he remained innocent all his life, however common it may be among other musicians. Nor does his attitude seem, at least in the first instance, to have been inspired by the orchestra's antipathy to Vogler, although the players certainly regarded Vogler as an intruder who had gained his comfortable position in Mannheim by stealth, violating the rights of others and intriguing against men of outstanding merit like Holzbauer. The purple stockings that he was entitled to wear as papal protonotary struck them as bizarre;[126] and the fact that he always included a prayerbook when sending his music to societies and often kept his visitors waiting until he had finished praying was seen as an example of putting on airs.[127] There were complaints about his arrogance and intolerance. And his own achievements were felt to fall far short of his own extravagant claims for them. This was the verdict on Vogler among the people with whom Mozart was on friendly terms in Mannheim. On a personal level, however, he is more likely to have been put off by the streak of vanity and theatricality in Vogler's character.[128] Vogler had seen a great deal of the world and in the process had acquired a not inconsiderable degree of general education. But he never came to terms with the feelings seething within him and remained at odds with himself throughout his entire life. This, too, may explain Mozart's antipathy, just as it may help to explain the young Schumann's enthusiasm. In Vogler's art, the charlatan is hard to distinguish from the true artist: elements lacking in balance and even in good taste figure alongside others of great significance, backward-looking elements alongside ones that only a later age was to appreciate and develop. It comes as no surprise to discover that Vogler felt he could turn his hand to anything. Thus we find him writing not only fashionable pieces such as *The Shepherds' Joy Interrupted by a Thunderstorm* for organ (a companion piece to Beethoven's 'Pastoral' symphony) and a choral ode *Lob der Harmonie* but also a C major symphony of 1815 that is full of character in spite of its academic mannerisms, and especially church music which, a few lapses into demagoguery notwithstanding, far surpasses all his other works, including those written for the stage.[129] He is particularly important as a theorist and teacher: among his pupils were Justin Heinrich Knecht, Franz Danzi, Peter Winter, Johann Gänsbacher, Carl Maria von Weber and Giacomo Meyerbeer, a role of honour that at the very least

123. *Briefe*, ii.227–8.
124. On 4 November 1777 he wrote: 'Deputy Kapellmeister Vogler, who wrote the mass that they performed recently, is a vacuous musical joker, a man who imagines he can do a lot but who in fact can do very little'; *Briefe*, ii.101–2.
125. *Briefe*, ii.227.
126. *Musikalische Realzeitung*, i (1788), 70.
127. *Musikalische Realzeitung*, i (1788), 77; and Forkel, *Musikalischer Almanach*, iv (1789), 135.
128. See Fröhlich, *Biographie des großen Tonkünstlers Abt G. J. Vogler*; Schafhäutl, *Abt Georg Joseph Vogler*; James Simon, *Abt Voglers kompositorisches Wirken*; Max Maria von Weber, *Carl Maria von Weber*, i.177–8; Gottfried Weber, *Caecilia*, xv (1833), 40–1; and Walter, *Geschichte des Theaters*, 188ff. ◆ Vogler (1749–1814), active at Mannheim from 1775 to 1780, was best known as a keyboard player and theorist; see Kreitz, 'Abbé Georg Joseph Vogler als Musiktheoretiker'; Grave and Grave, 'In Praise of Harmony: The Teachings of Abbé Georg Joseph Vogler'; Betzwieser, 'Singspiel in Mannheim: *Der Kaufmann von Smyrna* von Abbé Vogler'; Georg-Helmut Fischer, 'Abbé Georg Joseph Vogler: A "Baroque" Musical Genius'; and Corneilson, 'Vogler's Method of Singing'.
129. ◆ Presumably Abert means Vogler's 'Satisfactions Sinfonie' of 1799, revised in 1806 as the 'Baierische national Sinfonie' and published by André of Offenbach *c*1815.

presupposes a man of some importance. As a result Vogler played a significant and undeniable role in the history of early Romanticism, being one of the few composers at this time to draw attention to the importance of the folk music of other countries, notably Scandinavian and Slav.

As we have seen, Mozart was by no means the sort of man to allow his artistic judgement to be dictated by others, even by good friends, and, being honest and well-balanced by nature, he was put off from the outset by Vogler's contradictory character. That his friends shared this view was no doubt gratifying, but only to the extent that it confirmed his own impression. We must be satisfied with his judgement even if on this occasion, too, it overshoots the mark with typically Mozartian asperity. That he did not keep his views to himself but showed by his behaviour how he felt is understandable in light of what we know about his character. Equally certain, of course, Vogler felt deeply hurt by this. The naturally distrustful Leopold immediately assumed that Vogler was secretly conspiring against his son, but Mozart's letters do not support this assumption.[130] Among Vogler's followers at this time was Peter Winter (1754–1825), who played the violin in the Mannheim orchestra from 1754 and who was described by a contemporary as 'virtually Vogler's only friend and companion, at least his only close friend'. The same writer regretted that Winter made daily sacrifices to Vogler's vanity,[131] even though he later refused to be described as Vogler's pupil.[132] He seems to have conceived a dislike of Mozart at this time that later became a sore point for the latter.

As a result of his attitude to Vogler, Mozart became all the more intimate with the other members of the Mannheim orchestra. Both Wendling and Ramm were thinking of travelling to Paris during Lent and joining the bassoonist Georg Wenzel Ritter, who had gone on ahead of them. There they would give concerts together. A composer and keyboard player such as Mozart was the best possible companion in the circumstances, and Wendling suggested that he should accompany them. Here, then, we find the first mention of a plan to go to Paris. Mozart fell in with it at once and wrote to his father on 3 December 1777:

> If I stay here, I shall go to Paris during Lent in the company of Herr Wendling, the oboist Herr Ramm, who is an excellent player, and the ballet master Herr Lauchéry.[133] Herr Wendling assures me that I shan't regret it. He has twice been to Paris and only just got back. He says it's the only place to earn money and a proper reputation. 'You're a man who can do anything. I'll show you the way to go about it. You must write serious operas, comic operas, oratorios – anything. Once you've written a couple of operas for Paris, you'll be assured of an annual income. Then there's the Concert Spirituel and the Académie des Amateurs, where you get 5 louis d'or for a symphony. If you give lessons, the usual fee is 3 louis d'or for 12 lessons. Then you can get sonatas, trios and quartets engraved *par souscription*. Cannabich and Toeschi send lots of their music to Paris.' Wendling is a man who knows the value of travel. Write and tell me what you think. It seems to me useful and sensible to travel with a man who knows Paris (as it is now) like the back of his hand, as it has changed a great deal. I'll not be spending any more, indeed I don't think I'll spend half as much, as I'll only have myself to pay for, since Mama

130. The vague comment in his letter of 10 December 1777 ('I know well enough who was the cause') is not enough to support this claim; *Briefe*, ii.179. Later, too, Vogler acknowledged Mozart's greatness; see Schafhäutl, 'Moll und Dur in der Natur', 40 [Deiters's note].

131. *Musikalische Realzeitung*, i (1788), 70.

132. Winter's obituary in *AmZ*, xxviii (1826), 354.

133. Étienne Lauchéry had been ballet master in Mannheim since 1774. ◆ Concerning Lauchéry (1732–1820), see Dahms, 'Etienne Lauchéry, der Zeitgenosse Noverres' and 'Das Repertoire des "Ballet en action": Noverre-Angiolini-Lauchéry'.

would stay here, probably with the Wendlings. Herr Ritter, who's an excellent bassoon player, is off to Paris on the 12th. If I'd been on my own, I'd have had the best possible opportunity; he told me so himself. The oboist, Ramm, is a most excellent, amusing and honest fellow, around 35, who has already travelled a great deal and as a result has plenty of experience. The chief and best musicians here are very fond of me and genuinely respect me, they never call me anything but 'Herr Kapellmeister'.[134]

Mozart's mother was not averse to the idea and on 11 December 1777 we find her writing to her husband:

As for Wolfgang's visit to Paris, you must think it over and let us know if you approve; at this time of the year Paris is the only place to achieve anything. Monsieur Wendling is an honest fellow whom everyone knows, he's travelled widely and has already been to Paris more than 15 times, he knows it like the back of his hand, and our friend Herr von Grimm is also his best friend and has done a lot for him. So make up your mind, whatever you decide is fine by me. Herr Wendling has assured me that he'll be a father to him, he loves him as if he were his own son, and he'll be as well looked after as if he were with me. As you can well imagine, I don't like to let him go, nor do I like the idea of having to travel home on my own, it's such a long way; but what's the alternative? I'm too old to undertake such a long journey to Paris, quite apart from the expense. To travel with a party of four is cheaper than travelling alone.[135]

A necessary precondition of this plan was Mozart's continuing presence in Mannheim until such time as they left for Paris in the spring. His primary objective, therefore, was to obtain a post in the elector's *Kapelle*, and in this his friends did what they could to help him. As he reports in his letter of 4 November 1777, Holzbauer had lost no time in introducing him to the intendant Count Savioli, when Cannabich also happened to be present:

Herr Holzbauer spoke to the count in Italian, suggesting that His Excellency might grant me the favour of hearing me; I'd been here 15 years ago, when I was 7; now I was older and bigger, in music, too. 'Ah,' said the count, 'that is – –', goodness knows who he thought I was. Cannabich immediately broke in, but I pretended not to hear and started talking to some other people, but I noticed that he was speaking to him about me with a serious expression on his face. The count then said to me: 'I hear you are a passable keyboardist.' I bowed.[136]

The elector was holding court at this time and on the first of his court-days Savioli introduced Mozart to the electress, who received him most graciously, recalling his visit of fifteen years earlier, even though she did not recognize him at once. On 6 November a grand concert was held at court and Mozart played a concerto, later – before the final symphony – improvising a piece and playing a sonata:

---

134. *Briefe*, ii.162.
135. *Briefe*, ii.180.
136. *Briefe*, ii.101.

The elector, electress and whole court are very pleased with me. On the two occasions that I played at the concert, the elector and she came right over to the harpsichord. After the concert Cannabich arranged for me to speak to the court. I kissed the elector's hand. He said: 'I think it must be about 15 years since you were last here.' 'Yes, Your Excellency, 15 years since I had the honour –' 'You play incomparably well.' When I kissed the princess's hand, she said: 'Monsieur, je vous assure, on ne peut pas jouer mieux.'[137]

The electress, too, held out the prospect of an invitation to play for her, but no date was agreed, and it was not until a few days later that he received a present from the elector, a gold watch worth twenty carolins that he viewed with very mixed feelings.[138]

Meanwhile, Leopold had followed this whole turn of events with the greatest interest. As early as 1 November 1777 he had insisted categorically:

I want you to get something to do in Mannheim. They're always performing German operas, perhaps they'll ask you to write one? If so, you know that I don't need to urge you to adopt a natural, popular approach of a kind that everyone easily understands; the grand and sublime is suited to grand subjects. Everything in its place.[139]

Leopold was evidently thinking of singspiels and had as yet no idea of what Schweitzer and Holzbauer were doing. Soon after this he started to make further enquiries about Mozart's plans for Paris. He, too, had given some thought to the idea of his son's appearing in Paris, but for the time being he saw it only as a last resort, given the cost and difficulties bound up with such a journey. For the present, he repeated his former advice not to remain longer than necessary in Mannheim without the firm prospect of an appointment. Mozart's friends could continue to be of assistance to him even in his absence, but he himself should be performing elsewhere, both to earn some money and to introduce his name to wider audiences. He had made enquiries in various quarters. As a result, he thought that Frankfurt and Bonn were not worth considering, but pinned his hopes, rather, on Mainz, where, with the help of the local Konzertmeister Georg Anton Kreußer, he believed it was possible to organize a series of concerts both at the court of the art-loving elector[140] and in the town itself. Another possibility was Koblenz, where Mozart had already commended himself to the Elector Clemens through a work written down at table in 1763. After these excursions, they could always return to Mannheim, as long as there remained the prospect of their being able to survive the winter there. In general, of course, Leopold was not happy with their dependency on Mannheim, whereas Mozart himself was only too pleased to be talked into staying in the town, so stimulating was the company. The elation he felt made him see his prospects in an unduly favourable light. But his mother allowed herself to be persuaded by both Mozart himself and by his friends and was happy to be reassured that Mozart's best course of action was to remain in Mannheim.

---

137. *Briefe*, ii.109–10 (letter of 8 November 1777).
138. In his letter of 13 November 1777, he writes: 'Forgive me, but I've now got 5 watches. I'm seriously thinking of having an additional pocket on each leg of my trousers and whenever I visit some great lord I'll wear both watches (which is in any case now the fashion), so that they won't take it into their heads to present me with another one'; *Briefe*, ii.119.
139. *Briefe*, ii.99.
140. See Schubart, *Ideen zu einer Ästhetik der Tonkunst*, 182.

Initially, everything seemed to go well. The elector even commended Mozart to his natural children[141] in order to have his opinion concerning their musical education. Mozart's report on the meeting is contained in his letter of 8 November 1777:

> I talked to the elector as to an old friend. He's a most gracious and kindly person. He said to me: 'I hear you wrote an opera for Munich.' 'Yes, Your Highness, I commend myself to Your Highness's good graces, my greatest wish is to write an opera here; please don't forget me completely. Thanks and praise be to God, I know German too', and I smiled. 'That can easily be arranged.' He has a son and three daughters. The eldest daughter and the young count both play the harpsichord. The elector asked me in all confidence about his children. I answered quite frankly, but without disparaging their teacher. Cannabich agreed with me. On leaving, the elector thanked me most politely.[142]

A few days later he played for the elector again, improvising a fugue on a given subject. Then, on Cannabich's advice, he called on Count Savioli to ask whether the elector might be prepared to take him on during the winter as his children's music teacher. Savioli told him to wait until the present round of celebrations at court was over and Mozart, trusting as ever, agreed. He drew 150 florins from his banker and begged his father not to indulge in 'idle speculation', a request that inevitably earned him a sharp rebuke. It is easy to understand why Leopold was so vigorously opposed to this propensity for making plans without any solid foundation and that he complained with particular bitterness at the fact that he had been told about them only after the event. He was also angry that Mozart had not asked his permission to withdraw money that he, Leopold, had scraped together with so much difficulty and only by running up debts. His wife, too, was taken to task for her careless bookkeeping. 'Such a journey is no joke,' he told her on 24 November 1777:

> You've no experience of it. You should have more important things on your mind than practical jokes; you should be attempting to arrange a hundred different things in advance, otherwise you'll suddenly find yourself in a mess and with no money – and where there's no money, you'll have no friends either, even if you give a hundred lessons for nothing, write sonatas and, instead of devoting yourself to more serious matters, play the fool every evening from 10 till 12. Then ask for credit! All jokes will suddenly cease – and the most ridiculous face will all at once become very serious.[143]

Maria Anna responded on 11 December with a summary account of their outgoings:

> My dear husband,
> You demand to know how much we've spent on our journey. We sent you Albert's bill, which was 300 florins. Wolfgang told you we were 24 florins out of pocket, but he didn't include the concert expenses, which were 16 florins, or the landlord's account. And so, by the time we reached Mannheim, we'd no more than 60 florins left, so we'd not have had much left if we'd

141. They were his children by the actress Josepha Seyffert (Countess Heydeck). The son, Carl August, 1769–1823, later became Prince of Bretzenheim, while the daughters married into money; see Häusser, *Geschichte der rheinischen Pfalz*, ii.934.
142. *Briefe*, ii.110.
143. *Briefe*, ii.144.

set off again after a fortnight. The cost of travel has gone up a lot as everything has become so much more expensive; it's not what it used to be, you'd be amazed.[144]

The tetchy and somewhat sheepish tone of Mozart's letter of 29 November, in which he rejects his father's charges, shows that he felt the truth of the latter's remarks and the extent to which this reminder of his filial obligations roused him from the comfortable life that he was leading in Mannheim:

If you attribute my behaviour to negligence, thoughtlessness and laziness, I can only thank you for your opinion and sincerely regret that you do not know your own son. I am not careless, but merely prepared for anything and am able, in consequence, to wait patiently for whatever may come and endure it – provided that my honour and the good name of Mozart are not affected. Well, if it must be so, so let it be. But I must ask you right away not to rejoice or grieve prematurely; for come what may, all is well as long as one remains healthy; for happiness exists only in the imagination.[145]

But Leopold did not even agree with his son's moral philosophy and with great composure offered him a detailed critique of his claim that happiness is merely a product of the imagination. His argumentation is worthy of a thinker like Christian Garve.[146] In particular, he reminds Mozart of the situation that arises when one has to pay for something and has no money. 'My dear Wolfgang, this is a moral saw only for people who are forever discontented.'[147]

We now learn in greater detail about Mozart's efforts to win over the elector. He begins by attempting to reassure his father about Cannabich's attitude and conduct:

I spent the afternoon [following his first meeting with Savioli] at Cannabich's, and as it was on his advice that I'd been to see the count, he asked me at once whether I'd done so. – I told him everything. He said to me: 'I'd very much like you to stay with us for the winter; but I'd like it still more if you could get a permanent post.' I said: 'There's nothing I'd like more than to stay here with you, but I really don't know how it could be arranged on a permanent basis. You've already got two Kapellmeisters, so I don't know what I could be, as I wouldn't want to be Vogler's subordinate!' 'Nor would you be,' he said. 'None of the musicians here is under the Kapellmeister or even under the intendant. The elector could make you his chamber composer. Wait, I'll discuss it with the count.' – The following Thursday there was a big concert; when the count saw me, he apologized for not having mentioned the matter, but the elector was still holding court, and as soon as it was over, namely on Monday, he'd certainly put in a word. I let 3 days go by and when I'd still not heard anything, I went to make enquiries of him. He said: 'My dear Monsieur Mozart' (that was Friday, in other words, yesterday), 'they were out hunting today, so I wasn't able to speak to the elector; but by this time tomorrow I'll certainly be able to give you an answer.' I asked him not to forget. To tell the truth, I was a little annoyed when I left him and decided to take my 6 easiest variations on Fischer's minuet to the young count. I'd

---

144. *Briefe*, ii.180.
145. *Briefe*, ii.153.
146. ◆ Concerning the philosopher Christian Garve (1742–98), see Wölfel, *Christian Garve: Gesammelte Werke*.
147. ◆ *Briefe*, ii.175 (letter of 8 December 1777).

already copied them out here expressly for this purpose, hoping that this would give me a chance to speak to the elector in person. When I arrived, you can't imagine how delighted the governess was to see me. I was received most politely; when I took out the variations and told her that they were for the count, she said: 'Oh, that's good of you, but do you also have something for the countess?' – 'Not yet,' I said, 'but if I stay here long enough to have time to write something, I shall –' 'By the way,' she said, 'I'm glad that you'll be staying here for the winter.' 'What? That's the first I've heard of it!' – 'How strange! Most curious! The elector recently told me so himself. "By the way," he said, "Mozart is staying here all winter."' – 'Well, if he said so himself, he should know; for it goes without saying that I can't stay here without the elector.' I then told her the whole story. We agreed that the next day, namely today, I should return after 4 o'clock and bring something with me for the countess. 'You'll speak to the elector before I get here, and he'll still be here when I arrive.' I went there today, but he didn't come. So I'll go again tomorrow. I've written a rondeau for the countess. Haven't I now got reason enough to remain here and await the result? – Should I leave now that the most important step has been taken? – I now have a chance to speak to the elector in person. In all probability I think I'll stay here for the winter; the elector likes me, thinks highly of me and knows what I can do. I hope to be able to give you some good news in my next letter. But once again I beg you not to rejoice too soon or to worry and, above all, not to confide in a soul apart from Herr Bullinger and my sister.[148]

But progress was very slow, and in his next letter of 3 December 1777 Mozart could still only report on various incidents that seemed to indicate a successful outcome to the matter:

Last Monday, after attending his natural children morning and afternoon for 3 days in a row, I finally had the good fortune to meet the elector. We all thought that our efforts were once more to be in vain as it was already late, but finally we saw him coming. The governess immediately invited the countess to sit at the harpsichord, and I sat beside her and gave her a lesson, and that was how the elector found us when he came in. We got up; but he told us to continue. When she'd finished playing, the governess was the first to speak and said I'd written such a beautiful rondeau. I played it; he liked it very much. At length he asked: 'But will she be able to learn it?' – 'Oh yes,' I said, 'I just wish I might have the good fortune to teach it to her myself.' He smiled and said: 'I'd like that too; but wouldn't her playing suffer if she had two different teachers?' – 'Oh no, Your Highness,' I said, 'all that matters is whether she has a good teacher or a bad one. I hope Your Highness will not doubt me – and will have confidence in me.' – – 'Oh, most certainly,' he said. The governess then said: 'Monsieur Mozart has also written some variations on Fischer's minuet for the young count.' I played them, he liked them very much. He now joked with the countess, whereupon I thanked him for the present. He said: 'Well, I'll think it over; how long do you intend to stay here?' – 'As long as Your Highness commands, I've no other commitments, I can stay as long as Your Highness commands.' And with that it was over. I was back there again this morning, when I was told that the elector had again said yesterday: 'Mozart is staying here for the winter.' Well, we're now in the thick of it and I'll have to wait. I lunched with Wendling today for the 4th time. Before we sat down, Count Savioli came in with Kapellmeister Schweitzer, who had arrived yesterday evening. Savioli said to me: 'I spoke to the elector again yesterday, but he still hasn't made up his mind.' I told him I'd like to have a word

148. *Briefe*, ii.153–4.

with him. We went over to the window. I told him about the elector's doubts and complained that it was taking so long and that I'd already spent so much money here, and I begged him to persuade the elector to take me on permanently as I feared he'd give me so little during the winter that I wouldn't be able to stay; he should give me work, I like work. He told me he'd certainly suggest it to the elector, but it couldn't be this evening as he wasn't going to court today; but he promises to give me a definite answer tomorrow. Well, I leave it to fate. If he doesn't keep me on, I'll insist on my travelling expenses as I've no intention of giving him the rondeau and variations for nothing. I assure you that I'm completely calm as I'm certain that, whatever happens, all will turn out for the best, I've placed myself entirely in God's hands.[149]

But on the following days, too, the elector's answer remained the same: a shrug of his shoulders indicating his continuing refusal to come to a decision. Not until 10 December 1777 was Mozart able to report on the outcome of all these negotiations. It was as his father had always assumed it would be:

There's nothing to be hoped for at present from the elector. The day before yesterday I attended the concert at court in order to get a reply. Count Savioli carefully avoided me, so I sought him out and when he saw me, he shrugged his shoulders. 'What,' I said, 'still no answer?' – 'I'm sorry,' he said, 'unfortunately nothing.' – 'Eh bien,' I said, 'the elector could have told me so himself.' – 'Yes,' he said, 'but he still wouldn't have made up his mind even now if I'd not urged him to do so and made it clear to him that you'd been hanging on for so long and were using up all your money at the inn.' – 'It's that that annoys me most of all,' I retorted, 'it's not very nice. But I'm most obliged to you, Count (he's not addressed as Excellency), for having taken such an interest in me and I'd be grateful if you would thank the elector on my behalf for his gracious if belated reply.' And I assured him that he would never have regretted it if he had taken me on. 'Oh,' he said, 'of that I am more certain than you think.'[150]

This unexpected turn of events left as disagreeable an impression on Mozart's friends as it did on the composer himself. He went to see Cannabich, only to discover that the latter was out hunting. And so he reported the matter to Cannabich's wife:

Mlle Rosa was 3 rooms away and busy with the laundry, but when she had finished she came in and said to me: 'Are you ready?' For it was time for her lesson. – 'I'm at your command,' I said. – 'But,' she said, 'we must have a really serious lesson today.' – 'We certainly must,' I retorted, 'as we shan't have the chance much longer.' – 'Why's that? Why's that? What is it?' – She went to her mother, who told her. 'What?' she said, 'Is it true? I can't believe it.' – 'Yes, yes, quite true,' I said. She then played my sonata very seriously; believe me, I couldn't stop myself from crying; by the end, mother, daughter and treasurer were all crying as she had been playing the very sonata that's the favourite of the whole house. 'Listen,' said the treasurer, 'if Herr Kapellmeister leaves (that's all they ever call me here), he'll make us all cry.' – I must say that I have some very good friends here, it's in circumstances like these that you get to know them.

---

149. *Briefe*, ii.160–61.
150. *Briefe*, ii.177.

For Wendling, in particular, this outcome was most unwelcome. When Mozart told him, he 'went very red in the face and said very heatedly: "We must find means of keeping you here, at least for 2 months, until we can go to Paris together."' When Mozart arrived for lunch the next day, he had already devised a plan that seemed eminently satisfactory. Among Mozart's friends and admirers was a Dutchman (Dejean or Dechamps[151]) with a private income. Known as 'the Indian', he was willing to pay 200 florins for three short and simple flute concertos and a couple of flute quartets. Cannabich, for his part, would find Mozart at least two pupils who would pay well. And he could have some duets for violin and keyboard engraved by subscription. He could have lunch and supper at Wendling's and Councillor Serrarius was prepared to offer him accommodation. Mozart was happy at the prospect of being able to remain in Mannheim and thought he would have enough to keep him busy for the next two months with three concertos, two quartets and between four and six duets 'for the keyboard'. He was also thinking of writing a new large-scale Mass and of presenting it to the elector. The very next day he set off to find a small and cheap apartment for his mother.

Leopold found it entirely natural that Wendling should try to keep Mozart in Mannheim as they needed a fourth person for their journey to Paris and they could not have found a better companion than Mozart. He was reassured that the situation was now clearer. And he was pleased that his son did not have to continue his journey in the depths of winter. But he also thought that the plan could be realized only if they could count on their Dutchman. If this were not the case, they would have to leave for Mainz forthwith. On no account, however, should mother and son be separated: 'As long as Mama remains there, you and she must live together', he wrote on 18 December 1777. 'You should not and must not leave Mama alone and at the mercy of others as long as she is with you and you with her.' The few florins that a larger apartment would cost were not worth worrying about, and Maria Anna could not return home at present. 'In the meantime be sure to stay with her and take care of her, so that she lacks nothing, just as she cares for you.' In this, Leopold was thinking not only of his son's health but also of his moral and religious well-being. He had already expressed his concern on his point in his letter of 15 December:

> May I ask whether Wolfgang is not getting a little lax about confession? God must come first! It is to Him that we must look for our temporal happiness, while at the same time thinking of our eternal salvation; young people do not like to hear such things, I know, I was young myself; but, thank God, I always pulled myself together, in spite of all my foolish pranks, avoiding all the dangers to my soul and never losing sight of God and my honour and the consequences – the very dangerous consequences.[152]

Maria Anna reassured her husband that Mozart had attended confession on the Feast of the Immaculate Conception [8 December], and although they rarely heard Mass during the week, they always did so on Sundays, when Mozart himself went to the Hofkirche. Mozart, too, wrote to his father to justify himself, not without a certain touchiness:

> As I have already told you, your last letter gave me a great deal of pleasure, it's true! Only one thing annoyed me somewhat – the question as to whether I wasn't perhaps getting a bit lax

---

151.   ◆ Ferdinand Dejean (1731–1797) was a surgeon with the Dutch East India Company from 1758 to 1767; see Lequin, 'Mozarts ". . . rarer Mann"'; and Moolenijzer and Bunge, *Mozart en de Hollanders: een winter in Mannheim*.
152.   *Briefe*, ii.188.

about confession! – I've nothing to say to this; but just let me ask you one thing, and that is not to have such a low opinion of me! I like to enjoy myself, but rest assured that I can be as serious as the next man. Since I left Salzburg (and even in Salzburg itself) I've met people who, although 10, 20 and 30 years older than me, have talked and behaved in ways that I'd be ashamed to imitate! So I most humbly beg you once more to think better of me.[153]

In these circumstances, the Mozarts were particularly grateful for an offer of accommodation, including heating and lighting, from Privy Court Councillor Serrarius, in return for which Mozart was to give lessons to his host's daughter. Although Maria Anna was left on her own a great deal, while Mozart went about his business, she felt perfectly happy at the inn: they had excellent beds, the service was good, and in the evening she dined with Serrarius's wife and daughter, gossiping with them till half past ten and also being invited to spend most of the afternoon there. Serrarius's fifteen-year-old daughter, Therese Pierron, had already been playing the harpsichord for eight years, but Mozart seems not to have been drawn to her by any exceptional talent as there is rarely any mention of 'the young lady of the house'. None the less, she learnt one of his concertos [K246] under his supervision and performed it at a large party at her parents' home. On a subsequent occasion she played the third and easiest of the solo parts in his concerto for three keyboards. And on 11 March 1778, just before leaving Mannheim, he wrote a keyboard sonata with violin accompaniment for her, K296. He also gave composition lessons to young Christian Franz Danner, in return for which his mother had lunch at the Danners.[154] He himself ate at the Wendlings. 'Wolfgang', wrote his mother, 'is so busy composing and giving lessons that he hasn't time to call on anyone. So you can see that we can remain here quite comfortably for the winter, and all of this has been made possible by Monsieur Wendling, who loves Wolfgang as though he were his own son'.[155] Mozart gave his own account of his day-to-day activities in his letter of 20 December 1777:

We can't get up before 8 o'clock, as it doesn't get light in our room (which is on the ground floor) until half past eight. I throw my clothes on and at around 10 I settle down to compose until 12 or half past; I then go to Wendling's, where I can write a little more until half past one, when we have lunch. By the time we've finished it's already 3, and I then have go to the Mainzischer Hof to give a Dutch officer [Ferdinand Guillaume Duval de la Pottrie] a lesson in gallantry and thoroughbass, for which – if I'm not mistaken – I'm receiving 4 ducats for 12 lessons. I have to be home by 4 in order to teach the daughter of the house; we never start before half past four as we have to wait for the lights. At 6 I go to Cannabich's and give Mlle Rosa her lesson; I remain there for supper, after which we talk or sometimes gamble, in which case I always take a book from my pocket and read – as I used to do in Salzburg.[156]

In short, there was some truth to Maria Anna's remark, in her letter of 14 December 1777, that Mozart was so busy that he no longer knew whether he was coming or going. And it was with justified contentment that she was able to add that Leopold could not possibly imagine in what high esteem Mozart was held by the local orchestra and other people in the town: they all said that there was no one to touch him, and his music was lauded to the skies. At around the same time, there

153. *Briefe*, ii.199.
154. ◆ Christian Franz Danner (1757–1813), active at Munich and Zweibrücken, was Cannabich's godson; his only known work is a violin concerto composed at Munich in 1785. See Pisarowitz, 'Allerhand Neues vom vergessenen Mozart-Schüler Danner'.
155. ◆ *Briefe*, ii.195 (letter of 18 December 1777).
156. *Briefe*, ii.198–9.

are various references in the correspondence that passed to and fro between Salzburg and Mannheim to Mozart's beard, which was now so noticeable that it had to be removed. In reply to Leopold's question whether it was to be cut off, singed or shaved, Maria Anna duly noted that 'We have not yet called in the barber to deal with Wolfgang's beard, we've just been cutting it with scissors; but this won't do for much longer, and the barber will soon have to tackle it'.[157]

Mozart had first expressed a wish to write a German opera in Munich, but neither there nor in Mannheim had he been able to achieve this increasingly consuming ambition. At this juncture, it suddenly looked as though Mozart might be able to do so in Vienna, and on 11 January 1778 we find him writing to his father:

> I know for a fact that the emperor is planning to establish a German opera in Vienna and is making a serious attempt to find a young Kapellmeister who understands German and who is talented and capable of creating something new; Benda of Gotha is applying, but Schweitzer hopes to get it. I think it would be good for me, but only – of course – if it's well paid. If the emperor gives me 1000 florins, I'll write a German opera for him; if he won't keep me, it'll be all the same to me. Please write to all our friends in Vienna and tell them that I'd be a credit to the emperor. If he's not prepared to accept me on any other terms, let him take me on a trial basis – what he does then is all the same to me. Adieu. But please set things in train straightaway, otherwise someone may beat me to it.[158]

Leopold was not the man to remain idle in such circumstances and he immediately appealed to Franz von Heufeld,[159] whom he knew from his earlier visits to Vienna and whom he regarded as both knowledgeable and influential. Heufeld was now asked to use that influence to obtain an appointment for Mozart. As chance would have it, Leopold had just received a series of letters from Joseph Mesmer in Vienna, asking why Mozart did not come to the city, where there was 'plenty of room for a great talent'. He could have free board and lodging and everything else as long as he liked, and his friends would ensure that he received an income. But Mesmer's letters held out little prospect of an operatic commission, and in his letter of 29 January 1778 we find Leopold commenting that the emperor seemed no different from the archbishop in this respect: both men wanted something good, as long as it cost very little. Heufeld's letter of 23 January 1778 finally threw some light on the matter. Leopold communicated its contents to his son:

> What has happened is that His Majesty the Emperor, to whose hands his mother has entirely entrusted the theatre, intends to start a German comic opera. All commands proceed from His Majesty to the company through the Chief Chamberlain, Count von Rosenberg, and a kind of council consisting of the leading actors and actresses has been established for the sharing and distribution of the pieces and parts. For the opera, which is to be united to the national company,[160] those engaged as extra singers are Dlle Cavalieri and Schindler's daughter, whose

157. ◆ *Briefe*, ii.198 (letter of 20 December 1777).
158. *Briefe*, ii.222. In early December the emperor had invited Johann Heinrich Friedrich Müller to engage the tenor Franz Christian Hartig for Vienna; see Müller, *Abschied von der National-Schaubühne*, 254ff. Although the plan came to nothing, Mozart must have heard about it and known exactly what was going on in Vienna.
159. Franz Reinhard von Heufeld (1731–95) wrote for the Viennese theatre and was repeatedly involved in running it; see above [Deiters's note].
160. In 1776 the then lessor, Count Kohary, went bankrupt, whereupon the emperor himself took over the administration of the theatre, which now became known as the National Theatre rather than the Court Theatre.

married name is Lange, as well as a bass whose name escapes me. They recently had the first rehearsal for the first opera [*Die Bergknappen*], for which Herr Weidmann has furnished the text and the violist of the theatre orchestra, Herr Umlauf, has composed the music; the performance is to take place soon. All this is for the moment only a trial, to see whether anything is to be done with the Germans in this department. What is certain, however, is that for the present no musical composer will be specially taken on, particularly as *Gluck* and *Salieri* are in the Emperor's service. To recommend anyone to the sovereign would be a sure means of not finding a place for the person recommended. Nor is there any middleman through whom he could be approached, since, being himself a connoisseur, he arranges and chooses everything according to his own idea and fancy. Everybody knows this, and no one dares to come forward with suggestions and recommendations. In this way His Majesty has made his own choice of *Gluck*, *Salieri*, and for some time now, of most of the people in his service. I might give you some examples, too, of people who appealed straight to the sovereign and failed to succeed. I cannot approve of the way in which you intend to go about it, and that is the reason why I refrained from taking any steps by means of a petition, because I am convinced in advance that it would be useless and indeed disadvantageous. At the same time, another, more laudable and surer way remains open whereby good talents may find their fortune with the sovereign, namely by their works, for in this respect all men are considered eligible. If your son will take the trouble of setting some good German comic opera or other to music, to submit it, to leave his work to the imperial judgment and then to await a decision, he may succeed in being admitted, if the work pleases. In that case, however, it would probably be necessary to be here in person. About Benda and Schweitzer your son need not worry. I am ready to guarantee that they will not be admitted. They have not the reputation here that is theirs elsewhere. Perhaps even Wieland has since his visit to Mannheim relinquished some of the high opinion he had had of these people.[161] I read a letter from him of the 5th inst., in which he admits that he had come to see music in a very different light at Mannheim than he had ever done before.[162]

This letter found Mozart in high spirits – we shall discover the reason for this in a moment – and so he was all the more dismayed to have his hopes dashed. Moreover, his self-esteem had been raised by the lively interest taken in him and in his works by his friends in Mannheim, so that he felt insulted by the suggestion that he should write a comic opera 'on chance' and at his own risk. He refused to be treated as a beginner and was particularly offended by the familiarity with which Heufeld referred to him as his 'dear Wolfgang'.

As chance would have it, a further prospect opened up in Salzburg at this time. The town had been shocked by the news that Adlgasser had suffered a stroke while playing the organ in church on 21 December 1777 and had died that same evening. It soon emerged that the authorities were not averse to the idea of reappointing Mozart, and in his letter of 12 January 1778 Leopold reported on the hints that he had been given in this regard and the steps that they were suggesting he might take:

His Excellency the Chief Steward has just told me that His Grace commanded him to ask Haydn and me whether we knew of a very good organist who must, however, be a first-rate harpsi-chordist and, at the same time, of good appearance and presence, to teach the ladies. – 'What?'

---

161. Wieland had recommended Schweitzer for the post in Vienna; see Müller, *Abschied von der National-Schaubühne*, 188.
162. ◆ For Heufeld's letter, see *Briefe*, ii.235–7.

I said, 'did His Grace mention me too?' 'Yes, you in particular,' he replied with a smile. – I answered: 'I know nobody who has all these qualities.' – 'If there is such a person in Mannheim, then he can make his fortune.'[163]

But even if Leopold had wanted to follow up these suggestions, Mozart would certainly have remained impervious to them.

At the same time, however, Leopold launched a further assault on Mannheim: in December 1777 he sent Padre Martini a portrait of Mozart that Martini had requested and simultaneously seized the opportunity to ask him to use his influence with the elector.[164] Obliging as ever, Martini promised to write to Raaff and put in a good word for Mozart. Although the political situation was at present unfavourable, he went on, he was sure that his recommendation would later bear fruit. Although no letter reached Raaff, Mozart appears to have used the occasion to commend himself to the tenor and become better acquainted with him, as he informed his father on 28 February 1778:

I went to see Raaff yesterday and took him an aria that I've recently written for him. The words are 'Se al labro mio non credi, bella nemica mia' etc. I don't think the text is by Metastasio.[165] He liked the aria a lot. You have to be very careful when dealing with a man like Raaff. I specifically chose this text as I knew that he already has a setting of these words, but he'll prefer mine as it will be easier to sing. I told him he should say quite candidly whether it suited him or if he didn't like it, I'm prepared to alter the aria or even to write another one. 'God forbid,' he said, 'the aria must remain as it is, it's very beautiful, only I'd be grateful if you could shorten it a little, as I'm no longer able to sustain such a piece.' – 'Most gladly, as much as you want,' I replied. 'I made it a little longer on purpose, as you can always cut it, whereas it's not so easy to add to it.' After he'd sung the second part, he removed his glasses and, looking at me with eyes wide open, said: 'Beautiful! Beautiful! That's a beautiful *seconda parte*.' And he sang it three times. As I was leaving, he thanked me most politely, and I assured him in return that I would arrange the aria in such a way that he would undoubtedly enjoy singing it. For I like an aria to be tailored to a singer like a well-made suit of clothes.[166]

Meanwhile the date of Mozart's departure for Paris was drawing closer. His father's letters are full of sound practical advice and, as usual, no detail was too trivial for his consideration. Not even the price of cabs was overlooked. Above all, however, Mozart was instructed to prepare for a long stay in Paris: it was not enough to remain there for only a few weeks or months if he wanted to make a name for himself in the French capital. As for Maria Anna, he should ensure that she returned to Augsburg, safely and in comfort, at the beginning of March. And Leopold reminded his son with some force to look after his health and keep to the straight and narrow: it would be the death of him if he discovered that Mozart had been ensnared by a woman. He appended a long

---

163. *Briefe*, ii.224.
164. Martini had dedicated the second part of his *Storia della musica* to the elector in 1770 and was in regular correspondence with him.
165. Mozart was right: the words are by an unidentified librettist. ◆ The text is now thought possibly to be by the Florentine poet Antonio Salvi (1664–1724). Further, see Giuntini, *I drammi per musica di Antonio Salvi: Aspetti della 'riforma' del libretto nel primo Settecento.*
166. *Briefe*, ii.304. The autograph is headed 'Aria per il Sigre Raff di Amadeo Wolfgango Mozart. Mannheim li 27 di Febr. 1778' and reveals the corrections and not inconsiderable cuts that Mozart made at Raaff's request.

list of earlier patrons and friends in Paris, all of whom were worth looking up. At the same time he was urged to consort only with persons of quality,[167] not to lead a life of dissipation and, in particular, to keep a safe distance from his colleagues, avoiding Gluck, Piccinni and Grétry if at all possible: 'De la politesse, et pas d'autre chose!' In consequence, he should depend on Friedrich Melchior Grimm above all, as the latter had proved a friend in the past. And he should never forget what he owed to God, who had bestowed such exceptional gifts on him.

All the greater, then, was Leopold's astonishment when Mozart wrote to him on 4 February 1778 and announced that he was abandoning his planned trip to Paris with Wendling and the others:

Mama and I have talked the matter over and are agreed that we do not like the sort of life that the Wendlings lead. Wendling is a basically honest and most excellent person, but unfortunately he has no religion, and his whole family is the same; it is enough to say that his daughter has been someone's mistress.[168] Ramm is a decent fellow, but a libertine. I know myself, I know that I have enough religion never to do anything that I wouldn't do openly before the whole world; but the mere thought of being with people whose way of thinking is so different from mine (and from that of all honourable people), even if only on a journey, horrifies me. But of course they can do as they like; I don't have the heart to travel with them; I'd not have a moment's pleasure and wouldn't know what to say; for, in a word, I don't entirely trust them. Friends who have no religion don't last. I've already given them a hint of what's coming. I've said that during my absence [in Kirchheim-Bolanden, from 23–29 January 1778, and Worms, from 29 January–2 February 1778] 3 letters arrived and that I can say only that it's unlikely I'll be able to travel with them to Paris; perhaps I'll join them later, but perhaps I'll go elsewhere, they mustn't count on me.[169]

Maria Anna added a note to the effect that she had never liked the idea of Mozart's going off with Wendling and Ramm but had raised no objections as she would not have been listened to. In her next letters, too, she insisted that this was the truth: Wendling and Ramm were bad company and could easily have led Mozart astray. 'It is perfectly true', she assured Leopold, 'that Herr Wendling is the best fellow in the world, but his whole household knows nothing about religion and has no time for it; mother and daughter never go to church from one end of the year to the next, never go to confession and never hear mass, but are always going off to the theatre; they say the church is unhealthy.'[170]

Leopold was not a little surprised to discover that mother and son had suddenly noticed their hosts' irreligious ways only after so lengthy an acquaintanceship. 'It is a good thing that you did not travel with these people,' he wrote on 16 February 1778, 'but you long since noticed the evil streak in them and yet, throughout the whole of the period during which you associated with them, you didn't trust your father – who is so concerned about you – to write to him about it and

---

167. 'You can always be perfectly natural with people of high rank; but with everybody else please behave like an Englishman'; *Briefe*, ii.272 (letter of 9 February).
168. Wolzogen, 'Zur Mozart-Biographie', 81, reports that, according to a family tradition, this report was untrue but that, during Wendling's absence in Paris, the elector lured Augusta Wendling to his palace under the pretext of making music with his natural children, and raped her. She was said to have died in a madhouse in 1778. But Karl Theodor went to Munich in January 1778, before Wendling left for Paris, and as late as the summer of 1780 Heinse saw Augusta and her mother at the theatre in Munich, describing the former as looking like 'a perfect hundred-petalled rose'; Koerte, *Briefe zwischen Gleim, W. Heinse, und J. von Müller*, i.224.
169. *Briefe*, ii.252.
170. *Briefe*, ii.291 (letter of 22 February 1778).

ask him for his advice, and it shocks me to think that your mother did not do so either.'[171] To this there was little that Mozart and his mother could say, except that they had been blinded to Wendling's lack of religious principles by the high esteem in which he was otherwise held and by his genuinely excellent qualities.

Meanwhile, Mozart had found other reasons for not going to Paris, as he explained in his letter of 7 February 1778:

I have already told you in my previous letter of my main reason for not going to Paris with these people. My second reason is that I've now given careful thought to what I'd have to do there. I couldn't manage without pupils, but I'm not made for that sort of work. I've living proof of this here. I could have had 2 pupils; I went to each of them 3 times but, finding one of them out, haven't been back. I'll gladly give lessons as a favour, especially if I can see that a pupil is talented and is pleased and keen to learn. But to have to go to a house at a certain hour – or to have to wait at home for someone – that's something I can't do, however much money it may bring in for me. This is something I find impossible, something I leave to others who can do nothing but play the harpsichord. I'm a composer and was born to be a Kapellmeister; I've neither the right nor the ability to bury my talent for composition, a talent with which God in His goodness has so richly endowed me (I may say this without conceit as I feel it now more than ever), and yet that is what I'd be doing if I took on lots of pupils, as it's a highly unsettling profession. I'd rather neglect the keyboard than composition, as keyboard playing is only a sideline with me, though, thank God, a very important one.[172]

He had, he went on, already told Wendling this, adding that if Wendling could achieve anything definite for him, he would happily follow him to Paris – 'especially if it were to write an opera. I'm very keen to write an opera, French rather than German, but Italian rather than French or German. The Wendlings are all of the opinion that such a piece would be exceptionally successful in Paris. I've no fears on that point for, as you know, I can adopt and imitate virtually every kind and style of composition.'

This passage is important for two reasons: first, it reveals that, after his previous preference for German opera, Mozart was vacillating and veering back to the Italian tradition. Secondly, the self-assurance expressed at the end shows clearly that Mozart himself was in no doubt about his own ability to adapt.

Leopold's reply is dated 23 February. His remonstrations are fully justified:

You would rather give lessons as a favour, yes, of course you would! And you'd rather leave your old father in need; the effort is too great for a young man like you, however good the pay, and no doubt it's better for your 58-year-old father to run around for a pitiful payment in order to earn the necessary means to support himself and his daughter by the sweat of his brow and, *instead of paying off his debts*, support you with what little is left, while you in the meantime can amuse yourself by giving a girl lessons for nothing. My son, think about it and listen to common sense. Are you not behaving more cruelly towards me than our prince? . . . God has given you excellent powers of judgement, but it seems to me that there are 2 things that occasionally

171. *Briefe*, ii.283.
172. *Briefe*, ii.264.

prevent you from using those powers properly, . . . a little too much *pride* and *self-love* and also the fact that you immediately become too *familiar* and pour out your heart to all and sundry.[173]

In his letter of 16 February 1778 Leopold had already reassured his son on the question of giving lessons in Paris:

In the first place, no one is going to dismiss his teacher at once and engage you; secondly, no one would dare to ask you, and you yourself would take on only the occasional lady who is already a good player and who wants to learn something about interpretation, and such work would be well paid. . . . Such ladies would also make every effort to collect subscribers for your music. Everything is done by such ladies in Paris, they're great keyboard lovers and there are many who play very well. These are the people for you. As for composition, you can make money and gain a reputation for yourself by publishing keyboard works, string quartets etc., symphonies, perhaps a collection of good French arias with keyboard accompaniment like the one you sent me and, finally, operas. – What objection do you have to this? – – With you, everything has to be done at once, even before people have seen you or heard any of your music.[174]

For the first time we find Mozart being less than honest with his father in his letters to him. His proud declaration concerning his true profession as a composer is genuinely Mozartian and, like his reluctance to teach, was sincerely meant, but, in spite of his essential piety, the doubts that he raises on religious grounds simply do not ring true. It did not need Leopold's ever-watchful eye to see that this unexpected turn of events had other, deeper causes that had clouded his son's clear vision. Wendling was disconsolate that Mozart was not accompanying him. Mozart attempted to persuade himself that the reason for his dismay was not friendship but self-interest. And so he allowed Wendling and Ramm to set off for Paris on 15 February, albeit not without a certain feeling of apprehension. 'If I thought that my not going with them to Paris would annoy them very much,' Mozart wrote to his father on 14 February 1778, 'I should regret having stayed here; but I hope that this isn't the case, at all events the road to Paris is still open to me.'[175]

Leopold was not unhappy with this arrangement, but he was dismayed at Mozart's comments in his letter of 4 February 1778: 'I propose to remain here and finish off Dejean's music at my convenience, I'll then get my 200 florins; I can stay here as long as I like, as neither board nor lodging costs me anything.' 'If you examine your conscience,' Leopold had written to him on 11 December 1777, 'you will find that you have put off doing many things.' On 12 February 1778 he wrote again:

I was amazed when you wrote that you propose finishing off the music for Monsieur Dejean's at your convenience. – So you still haven't delivered it? And you were thinking of leaving on 15 February? and even went trailing off to Kirchheim? . . . Well, that doesn't matter, but, good God! Suppose that Herr Wendling were to play a trick on you and Monsieur Dejean were not to keep his promise! After all, the plan was simply for you to wait and travel with them. Send me word by return of post so that I know how things stand.[176]

173. *Briefe*, ii.293–6.
174. *Briefe*, ii.284.
175. ◆ *Briefe*, ii.280.
176. *Briefe*, ii.278.

The news that Mozart had sent in the meantime was by no means reassuring:

Herr Dejean is also leaving for Paris tomorrow and, because I've finished only 2 concertos and 3 quartets for him, he has given me only 96 florins (4 florins too little, assuming half the original fee). But he'll have to pay me in full, for that's what I agreed with the Wendlings, I'll send on the rest. It's entirely to be expected that I've not been able to finish it. I never have an hour's peace here; I can write only at night, so I can't get up early as well. Also, one's not always in the mood for work. Of course, I could scribble things down all day long: but a work of this kind goes out into the world, and I really don't want to feel ashamed at seeing my name on it. And, as you know, I always lose interest whenever I have to write for an instrument I can't stand; by way of a diversion I've also been writing some duets for keyboard and violin and done some work on the Mass. I'm now hard at work on the keyboard duets as I want to have them engraved.[177]

In a letter written from Paris on 20 July 1778, Mozart mentions only 'two flute quartets', while his later letter of 3 October 1778 speaks of 'the flute concerto'. Two quartets for flute, violin, viola and cello have survived. The first, K285, is in D major and dated 25 December 1777, while the second, K298, is in A major. According to a note added to the manuscript in a different hand, it was written in Paris in 1778.[178] The flute concertos K314 in D major and K313 in G major, together with the andante in C major for flute and orchestra K315, were evidently likewise undertaken for Dejean.[179] The keyboard duets were the violin sonatas K301–306 that were later published in Paris; on 28 February 1778 we find Mozart writing that he still had to compose two of them: 'There's no hurry as I can't have them engraved here. Nothing can be done here by subscription, it's a miserly place, and the engraver won't do them at his own expense but wants half the proceeds. So I'd rather have them engraved in Paris, where the engravers are happy to get something new and pay handsomely and where it's easier to get things done by subscription.'[180]

That Mozart was so behindhand with his work came as a particularly bitter blow to Leopold, who had clearly reckoned on income from this quarter to cover the costs of his son's stay in Mannheim and the journey to Paris. Again he saw himself obliged to intervene and write, with some concern, on 5 February 1778:

---

177. *Briefe*, ii.281. ◆ The fragmentary Kyrie K322, which apparently dates from this time, may represent the only surviving work on the mass mentioned by Mozart, which is otherwise unknown.

178. ◆ It now seems that the two surviving quartets for Dejean are K285 and – if it is genuine – K285a, which is known only from an edition published in 1792. Another flute quartet, K285b, probably dates from c1781 (like K285a its authenticity has also been questioned) while K298, Abert's choice for the second quartet, almost certainly dates from late 1786 or early 1787: aside from the apparently late paper of the autograph, the first movement is based on an early 1780s song by Franz Anton Hoffmeister, 'An die Natur', and the third movement cites the cavatina 'Chi mi mostra chi m'addita' from Paisiello's opera *Le gare generose*, first given in Vienna on 1 September 1786. The note on the manuscript of K298 is clearly incorrect.

179. ◆ In fact, K314 is not an original flute concerto but, rather, the oboe concerto composed by Mozart for Ferlendis in Salzburg in early 1777 (see *Briefe*, ii.278). It is possible that a flute version – which in Abert's time was considered authentic (and the oboe concerto lost) – is by Mozart and was arranged by him to fulfil Dejean's commission. It is unlikely, however, that the arrangement used today, based on a faulty, late eighteenth-century manuscript now in the library of the Mozarteum, is identical to Mozart's version. Further, see Heinrich Wiese, 'Zur Entstehungsgeschichte der Flötenkonzerte'.

180. *Briefe*, ii.305 (letter of 28 February 1778). According to its heading, one of these sonatas, K304, was not completed until Mozart was already living in Paris. The whole set was published by Sieber in Paris in 1778 and dedicated to the electress. The autograph scores are owned by Baron Ernouf, who acquired them from Sieber's widow [Deiters's note]. ◆ As Abert notes, Mozart wrote that two sonatas remained to be composed. The second, after K304, was K306: although the autograph to this work is undated, it is written on paper used by Mozart in Paris in 1778. For Mozart's dedication of the set, see Haberkamp, 'Eine bisher unbekannte Widmung Mozarts an die Kurfürstin Maria Elisabeth von Bayern zur Erstausgabe der Sonaten für Klavier und Violine KV 301–306'; Eisen, *Dokumente: Addenda*, 28, *New Mozart Documents*, 27–8.

We've done everything in our power to make you happier and, through you, to bring happiness to ourselves and to set your future at least on a firmer footing, only fate has willed it that we should not achieve our aim. As you're aware, I am in very deep waters as a result of the latest step that we've taken and you know that I'm now in debt to the tune of 700 florins and I simply do not know how I am going to support myself, Mama and your sister on my monthly salary, for as long as I live I can't expect to receive another farthing from the prince. So it must be as clear to you as the noonday sun that the future of your old parents and your good sister, who loves you with all her heart, is entirely in your hands.[181]

Not a day passed without Nannerl noticing her father's worries and difficulties. He did not know how he was going to pay the bills that had arrived in January, still less how he could afford the new clothes that he needed. Fully alive to the seriousness of the situation, she redoubled her efforts at the keyboard and with great difficulty learnt the arts of improvisation and continuo playing: it was clear to her that on her father's death she would have to see to the needs of herself and her mother. She was deeply upset by the bad news from Mannheim and spent much of the day in tears, precipitating Mozart's ill-tempered remark – in his letter of 19 February 1778 – that she 'should not cry over every minor mishap'. His father's reply of 26 February 1778 was clearly calculated to shame him:

Your sister was not crying over a minor mishap when she wept over your letter: and yet when you wrote that you had not received the 200 florins, she said 'Thank God it's no worse than that'. Until now we've always thought of her as very self-interested, but she knows that to help you her own savings must be sacrificed.[182]

The reason for this total failure on Mozart's part was an experience that was to be of supreme importance for his development as both man and artist. Even in the past he had not been indifferent to feminine charms, but his previous affairs of the heart had taken the form either of gallant infatuation, as with the young female members of the Salzburg aristocracy, or, in the case of his cousin in Augsburg, light-hearted teasing. But in Mannheim love first assailed his young soul with all the force of a springtime storm, seizing hold of his entire being to an extent that he was never again to feel and initially extinguishing all thoughts of his family and future. As was only to be expected, it was art that had laid the foundations for love, with admiration at exceptional musical gifts quickly developing into a consuming passion for the singer of his heart, a passion that was fuelled not least by the fact that under the influence of this love the young woman in question had achieved her true potential as an artist and become conscious and appreciative of her own talents as a singer. Pity too played a part, with Mozart feeling sorry for the straitened circumstances in which the young woman and her family lived. Aloysia Weber was the second daughter of Fridolin Weber, who had been born in 1733 and who had worked as a senior civil servant for the Schönaus. Although his life remains shrouded in some mystery,[183] it appears to have known its fair share of adventure. He is said to have studied law in Freiburg and to have taken his doctorate in theology,

181. *Briefe*, ii.256.
182. *Briefe*, ii.301.
183. See Max Maria von Weber, *Carl Maria von Weber*, i.6–7, although Weber's information is by no means reliable, of course; see also Walter, *Geschichte des Theaters*, 308–9.

a claim that is already hard to credit.[184] He was appointed his father's successor in 1754. But he must also have been a good singer as it was in this capacity that Karl Theodor invited him to Mannheim, where he appears in local records as a bass singer from 1765 to 1778, initially on a salary of 200 florins a year, later rising to 400.[185] It was no doubt this paltry pay that persuaded him to look for other sources of income as a copyist and prompter. Even so, his circumstances remained modest in the extreme, not least because he had a large family to support, his wife Maria Cäcilia Stamm, whom he married in 1756, having born him five daughters and one son.[186] Of these only the four daughters Josepha, Aloysia, Constanze and Sophie were still alive in 1777. Aloysia, who was also known as Luise, was then seventeen and already relatively experienced as a singer. Mozart first mentions her in the context of a visit to Kirchheim-Bolanden and Worms that he undertook with the Webers, but without his mother, at the end of January 1778:

As from next Wednesday [23 January] I'll be spending a few days with the Princess of Orange at Kirchheim-Bolanden; I've heard so many good things about her here that I've finally decided to go. A Dutch officer who's a good friend of mine[187] got a terrible dressing-down from her for not taking me with him when he went to wish her a happy New Year. I'll get at least eight louis d'or as she's extraordinarily fond of singing and so I've had four arias copied out for her, and I'll also give her a symphony as she has a nice little orchestra and gives concerts every day.[188] Having the arias copied won't cost much, as this has been done by a certain Herr Weber, who'll be going with me. He has a daughter who's an excellent singer with a beautiful pure voice, and who's only 15. All she lacks is the ability to act, otherwise she could be the prima donna on any stage. Her father is a thoroughly honest German who is bringing up his children very well, which explains why the girl is pursued here. He has 6 children, 5 girls and a boy. For the last 14 years he and his wife have been obliged to survive on 200 florins, but because he has always carried out his duties conscientiously and provided the elector with an extremely talented soprano, he now gets a grand total of 400 florins. She sings my aria for de Amicis with the horribly difficult passage-work [*Lucio Silla*, 'Ah se il crudel'], and sings it admirably; she'll also sing it at Kirchheim-Bolanden.[189]

Mozart reported on this 'holiday trip' in his letter of 4 February 1778:

As soon as we got there, we had to send a list of our names to the castle; early the next morning the Konzertmeister, Herr Rothfischer, came to see us. . . . In the evening – it was Saturday – we went to court, where Mlle Weber sang 3 arias. I'll pass over her singing – in a word, it was excellent! I told you about her merits in my recent letter, but I can't end without telling you something more about her, as it's only now that I've really got to know her and as a result discovered her true strengths. We had to dine afterwards at the officers' table. The next day we walked quite a distance to church, as the Catholic church is some way off. That was Sunday. We were again

184. Mozart generally did all he could to exaggerate Weber's merits, but signally fails to mention this degree, in spite of the fact that he could clearly have impressed his father with it.
185. Walter, *Geschichte des Theaters*, 302 and 308. Weber's younger brother, Franz Anton, was the father of Carl Maria von Weber, so that Constanze Mozart was an actual cousin of the composer of *Der Freischütz*.
186. ◆ Abert's source for the assertion that Weber had five daughters is uncertain. Only four are known: these include, in addition to Aloysia and Constanze, Josepha (*c*1759–1819) and Sophie (1763–1846). The son was Johann Nepomuk (1760–?80).
187. Ferdinand Guillaume Duval de la Pottrie.
188. This is confirmed by Schubart, *Ideen zu einer Ästhetik der Tonkunst*, 192.
189. *Briefe*, ii.226–7.

invited for lunch, but there was no music in the evening as it was Sunday – so they have only 300 concerts a year. We could also have dined at court in the evening but we chose not to, preferring to remain at home by ourselves. We would gladly and unanimously have done without the meals at court, as we never enjoyed ourselves better than when we were on our own together; but we had to give some thought to saving some money – we had quite enough to pay for as it was. The next day, Monday, there was another concert, another on Tuesday and another on Wednesday. Mlle Weber sang 13 times in all and played at the keyboard twice – her playing isn't bad at all. What surprises me most is how well she sight-reads. Would you believe it, she sight-read my difficult sonatas – *slowly*, but without a single wrong note! On my honour I'd rather hear my sonatas played by her than by Vogler. I played 12 times in all, and once by request on the organ in the Lutheran Church, and presented the princess with 4 symphonies but received only 7 louis d'or, in silver, mind you, and my poor dear Mlle Weber only 5. . . . Basta! We've lost nothing by it and still made a profit of 42 florins and had the immense pleasure of making the acquaintance of a thoroughly honest, good Catholic Christian family; I'm only sorry that I didn't get to know them long ago. . . . By the way, you mustn't be too surprised when I tell you that I've only 42 florins left out of 77. This is merely the result of my delight at finding myself in the company of honest, like-minded people again. I could hardly do other than pay half the expenses; but I shan't do so on our other journeys, I've already told them that I'll pay only for *myself*. – We then stayed 5 days at Worms, where Weber has a brother-in-law, who is dean at the monastery; I should add that he's terrified of Herr Weber's barbed pen. We had a great time and lunched and dined every day with the dean. I may say that this little journey really forced me to practise the keyboard. The dean is a most excellent and intelligent man. – Well, it's now time for me to stop; if I were to write down all that I'm thinking, I'd run out of paper.[190]

The mood of jollity that typified this journey is also clear from the comic poem that Mozart sent to his mother from Worms on 31 January.[191] Here he mentions four quartets that he was planning to write and a concerto that he was saving for Paris. Evidently he was still trying to conceal from his mother his deeper feelings and aims, at least to the extent that he had any identifiable aims at this time.

190. *Briefe*, ii.251–4.
191. Nottebohm, *Mozartiana*, 47 [*Briefe*, ii.245–7]. ◆ Mozart's poem reads:
Dearest Madam, darling Mummy,
Spread the word round: butter's yummy. / Lift your hearts and praise the Lord / For giving us our just reward! / Still, our travels aren't so funny / 'Cos we've got so little money. / But we're well: no sound of mucus / Or of head colds to rebuke us / For our lifestyle; though catarrh / Affects some other folk, so far / We both have managed to avoid it. / Gas builds up and others void it / Both before and after meals when they / Let rip with farts whose noise, I'd say, / Would wake the dead. But yesterday / The queen of farts was here to stay, / With farts as sweet as honey but / A voice as hoarse as any chestnut. / We've been away for seven nights / And in that time shat many shites. / Herr Wendling will be cross, his 4 / Quartets are not yet in full score. / But once I'm back across the Rhine / I'll knuckle down, step into line / And write his works, for I don't fancy / Being called an idle nancy. / As for the concerto, this must wait till we / Reach Paris, where I'll toss it off as ea- / Sily as shitting. And yet, if I'm to tell / The truth, I'd rather roam the world than dwell / Upon the past with men I so condemn / That it now makes me sick to think of them. / And yet I have no choice, we've got to stick / Together, even though I'd rather lick / Herr Weber's arse than Herr Ramm's head. I'd say / A slice of it beats Wendling's any day. / Our shitting won't offend the Lord a bit, / Still less if we tuck in and eat our shit. / We're honest folk. Who tries to part us dies! / Between the 4 of us we've got 8 eyes, / Not counting those on which we sit. This verse / Must stop. I hope I shan't make matters worse / By saying that on Monday next I trust / I'll have the honour to embrace you. Just / Let me tell you, though, that by the time / I see you, I'll have shat my breeches. I'm /
Worms, the 1778th January
in the year 31.

Your loving child
Both scurvy and wild
Trazom.

On his return to Mannheim, Mozart spent virtually all his time with the Webers, attempting to train Aloysia's voice and working with her on all the arias that he had brought with him; [in his letter of 14 February 1778] he even asked his father to forward an 'aria cantabile with coloratura indications', some cadenzas and whatever else might be suitable. He then set about creating an opportunity for her to perform, as he explained to his father in his letter of 14 February 1778:

Yesterday there was a concert at Cannabich's, when all the music was by me, except for the first symphony, which was by Cannabich. Rosl [Rosa Cannabich] played my concerto in B flat [K238], then, by way of a change, Herr Ramm played my oboe concerto for the 5th time – the one I wrote for Ferlendis, which is proving quite a sensation here; it's now Herr Ramm's *cheval de bataille*. After that Mlle Weber gave a splendid performance of de Amicis' aria di bravura. I then played by old concerto in D major [K175] as it's such a favourite here, and then I improvised for half an hour, and after that Mlle Weber sang de Amicis' aria 'Parto, m'affretto' [from *Lucio Silla*] and was loudly applauded. And finally there was my sinfonia to *Il re pastore*.[192]

Finally Mozart wrote an aria for Aloysia, *Non sò d'onde viene*, to words from act three, scene six of Metastasio's *L'Olimpiade*, together with an introductory recitative 'Alcandro, lo confesso' (K294). The words are placed in the mouth of King Cleisthenes who, it later turns out, has condemned his own son to death for attempted murder. Here the character expresses his astonishment at the tender feelings that overcome him on pronouncing his verdict: compassion alone cannot possibly be the reason. Mozart reinterpreted this situation in the light of his own experience: he, too, felt overpowered by a previously unknown emotion in which compassion may originally have played a part but which he was unable to explain. Almost uniquely in Mozart's oeuvre, the result is an aria divorced from its dramatic context, with words that provide no more than the starting point for a profoundly personal confession. It is no wonder, therefore, that the setting was particularly close to his heart, not least because, when writing it, he could not get Aloysia's voice and singing out of his mind, as he explained in his letter of 28 February 1778:

For practice I've also set the aria *Non sò d'onde viene*, which was set so beautifully by Bach; because I know Bach's setting so well, because I like it and because it's always running through my head, I wanted to see whether, in spite of all this, I could write an aria completely unlike his. – It's not at all like his, not at all like it. At first I intended it for Raaff, but even the beginning seemed to me too high for Raaff, and I liked it too much to alter it, and because of the writing for the instruments, it seemed to me better suited to a soprano. And so I decided to write this aria for Mlle Weber. I put it to one side and took out the words of 'Se al labbro' for Raaff. But in vain. I simply couldn't work on it as the first aria kept coming back to mind. And so I wrote it, firmly resolved to tailor it to Mlle Weber's voice. It's an andante sostenuto (preceded by a short recitative), then the middle section, 'Nel seno a destarmi', then the sostenuto again. When it was finished, I said to Mlle Weber: 'Learn the aria yourself, sing it as you like; then let me hear you and I'll then tell you in all honesty what I like about it and what I don't like.' After two days I went to see her and she sang it for me, accompanying herself. I was forced to admit that she sang it as accurately as I could have hoped and just as I'd have taught her myself. It's now the best aria she has; and it's bound to do her credit whenever she goes.[193]

---

192. *Briefe*, ii.282. ✦ Concerning the oboe concerto, see note 179 above.
193. *Briefe*, ii.304–5.

That this confidence was amply justified became clear at a concert held at Cannabich's on 12 March, shortly before Mozart's departure. Also on the programme was Mozart's concerto for three keyboards, extremely well performed after only three rehearsals by Rosa Cannabich, Aloysia Weber and Pierron Serrarius:

> Mlle Weber sang 2 arias of mine, 'Aer tranquillo' from *Il re pastore* and my new one, *Non sò d'onde viene*. With the latter my dear Mlle Weber did herself and me indescribable honour. Everyone said that they'd never been as moved by an aria as by this one; but then she sang it as it should be sung. As soon as the aria was over, Cannabich called out loudly 'Bravo, bravissimo maestro! Veramente scritta da maestro!' This was the first time I'd heard it with instruments. I wish you could have heard it too, just as it was played and sung on this occasion, with this accuracy of interpretation, *piano* and *forte*. Who knows, perhaps you'll still hear it – I hope so. The players wouldn't stop praising the aria and talking about it.[194]

Mozart also sent the new aria to his father, but with the request that no one else be allowed to sing it as it was written specifically for Aloysia Weber and fit her like a glove.

Mozart's reluctance to go to Paris is easily explained by his feelings for Aloysia Weber, unwilling though he was to admit this to himself. He wrote to his father on 4 February 1778, 'I cannot possibly travel with people, with a man, who leads a life of which a mere stripling would be ashamed, whereas the idea of helping a poor family, without harming myself, delights my very soul.' And there is no doubt that he meant it: he was literally consumed by his desire to free this family from its straitened circumstances. Yet it was his love of Aloysia Weber that was the tacit, but overwhelming, reason for his actions. The direction in which his thoughts were leading may be inferred from a remark of his when he discovered that an old friend, Johann Ferdinand von Schiedenhofen, had married into money:

> His, I daresay, is another of those money matches, nothing more. I'd not like to marry in that way; I want to make my wife happy, not make my fortune through her. So I'll let things be and enjoy my golden freedom until I'm well enough off to be able to support a wife and children. If Herr von Schiedenhofen was obliged to choose a rich wife, that's because he's a member of the nobility. People of noble birth must never marry from inclination or love but only from self-interest and all manner of secondary considerations; it simply wouldn't suit such high-born persons to love their wives after the latter have done their duty and brought into the world a bouncing son and heir. But we poor commoners not only have to marry a woman we love and who loves us in return, but we may, can and, indeed, want to marry such a woman because we're neither noble, nor highly born, nor aristocratic, nor rich, but lowly born, humble and poor, so we don't need a rich wife, as our riches – being in our heads – die with us, and these no one can take from us unless they chop off our heads, in which case we no longer need them.[195]

Leopold will no doubt have shaken his head in bewilderment at this outpouring, but he was persuaded to interfere in what he perceived as his son's muddled situation by a hare-brained plan

---

194. *Briefe*, ii.326–7 (letter of 24 March 1778).
195. *Briefe*, ii.263–4.

that the Webers, bent as ever on their own advantage, had already been talked into accepting and that promised to kill two birds with one stone: first, Mozart would be able to remain close to Aloysia until such time as he could call her his own and, secondly, he would be able to write operas. And so we find him writing to his father on 4 February 1778 and announcing his wish to remain in Mannheim for the time being and complete the works he has started:

In the meantime Herr Weber will endeavour to obtain concert engagements for me and we'll travel to them together. When I travel with him, it's just as if I were travelling with you. The reason I like him so much is that, quite apart from his personal appearance, he is just like you and has exactly the same character and way of thinking. If my mother were not, as you know, too lazy to write, she'd say the same. I must admit that I really enjoyed travelling with them. We were happy and relaxed; I was hearing a man talk like you. I had nothing to worry about; if my clothes got torn, I found them mended; in a word, I was waited on like a prince. I've become so fond of this unfortunate family that I want only to make them happy, and perhaps I can do so. My advice is that they should go to Italy. So I wanted to ask you if you'd be kind enough to write to our good friend Luggiati, the sooner the better, and enquire how much and what is the most paid to a prima donna in Verona – the more the better, one can always climb down, – perhaps it would also be possible to get the Ascensa in Venice. As for her singing, I'll wager my life that she'll be a credit to me. Even in the short time that she's known me, she has greatly profited from my instruction, and how much greater will be the improvement by then! I'm not worried about her acting. If our plan succeeds, we – Monsieur Weber, his 2 daughters and I – will have the honour of visiting my dear Papa and my dear sister for a fortnight on our way through Salzburg, my sister will find a friend and a companion in Mlle Weber, for, like my sister in Salzburg, she has the reputation here for good behaviour, her father is like mine, and the whole family is like the Mozart family. Of course, there are envious people, as there are at home, but when it comes to the point, they have to speak the truth: honesty is the best policy. I must say that I'm looking forward enormously to coming with them to Salzburg, if only so that you can hear her sing. She sings superbly the arias I wrote for de Amicis, both the bravura aria and 'Parto, m'affretto', as well as 'Dalla sponda tenebrosa'. I beg you to do all you can to get us to Italy; you know my greatest concern is to write operas.

I'll gladly write an opera for Verona for 50 zecchini, if only so that she can make her name; if I don't write it, I fear she'll be wasted. By that time I'll have made so much money on the other journeys that we propose making together that it won't matter to me. I think we'll go to Switzerland, perhaps also to Holland, do write to me soon. – If we stay anywhere for long, the eldest daughter will be very useful to us: we'll be able to manage our own household, as she knows how to cook. . . .

Send me an answer soon, I beg you. Don't forget how much I want to write operas! I envy everyone who writes one; I could weep from sheer vexation whenever I hear or see an aria. But Italian, not German; *seria*, not *buffa*. . . . Well, I've told you everything that's been weighing on my heart, my mother is entirely of one mind with me. . . . I kiss your hands 1000 times and remain until death your most obedient son.[196]

196. *Briefe*, ii.252–4.

In a later letter of 14 February 1778 Mozart repeats his request:

I beg you to take an interest in Mlle Weber; I can't tell you how happy I'd be if she could make her fortune; husband, wife and 5 children on an income of 450 florins! On my account, too, don't forget about Italy; you know my desire and passion. I hope all will go well; I place my trust in God, who will not forsake us. Now farewell, and don't forget my requests and recommendations.[197]

That Mozart's mother was not, of course, quite as happy to fall in with his plans as he assumed emerges from a postscript to his letter of 4 February 1778. The same postscript also makes it clear that she had absolutely no influence over her son:

My dear husband,
    You will have seen from this letter that whenever Wolfgang makes new acquaintances, he immediately wants to sacrifice his life and property to them. It's true, she sings wonderfully well, but we mustn't ignore our own interests. I never liked the company of Wendling and Ramm but didn't venture to raise any objections and wouldn't have been believed in any case. But as soon as he got to know the Webers, he immediately changed his mind. In a word, he prefers other people's company to mine, for if I remonstrate with him about things I don't like, he objects. So you yourself will have to consider what's to be done. . . . I'm writing this in the utmost secrecy, while he's eating, as I don't want to be caught.[198]

Mozart could hardly have dealt his father a harsher blow had he tried. It was a revelation, moreover, that Leopold felt had been lifted straight out of the pages of a novel. He was so distraught that he could not sleep. His worst fears had been realized with his discovery that in his goodness of heart and familiarity his son could play such a mean trick on him. But he was not the man to brood for long. Action was required, and without delay. His reply of 12 February 1778 deserves to be quoted here *in extenso*:

My dear son,
    I've read your letter of the 4th with amazement and horror. I'm beginning to answer it today, the 11th, having been unable to sleep all night and am so exhausted that I can write only slowly, one word at a time, but I have to finish it by tomorrow. Until now, thank God, I have been in good health, but this letter, in which I recognize my son only by that failing of his that makes him not only believe everyone as soon as they open their mouth, but lay bare his kind heart to all who flatter him with their fine words and allow himself to be swayed by others, so that he is led by fanciful ideas and ill-considered, impractical projects to sacrifice his own name and interests and even the interests and claims of his old and honourable parents to those of strangers – this letter dismayed me all the more in that I had hoped, not unreasonably, that recent events, together with the various reminders I'd given you both here in person and in writing, might have convinced you that not only for the sake of your own happiness but in order for you to gain even a basic livelihood and finally attain your desired goal in a world of men who are in varying degrees good and bad, fortunate and unfortunate, it was imperative for you to guard your kind heart by the strictest reserve, to undertake nothing without the most careful consideration and never let

197. *Briefe*, ii.282. ◆ See note 184 above.
198. *Briefe*, ii.255.

yourself be carried away by enthusiastic ideas and dangerously blind fancies. My dear son, I beg you to read this letter carefully – take time to reflect on it – merciful God, those moments of happiness for me are gone when, as child and boy, you never went to bed without standing on a chair and singing to me 'Oragnia figatafa' and ending by kissing me again and again on the tip of my nose and telling me that when I grew old you'd put me in a glass case and protect me from every breath of air, so that you could always have me with you and honour me.[199] Listen to me patiently, then.

You're fully aware of our difficulties in Salzburg, you know how hard it is for me to get by and why I kept my promise to let you leave, and you know all my troubles. There were 2 reasons for your journey – either to find a decent and permanent appointment or, if this should fail, to go off to some large city where large sums of money can be earned. Both plans were designed to assist your parents and help your dear sister, but above all to bring you fame and honour in the world, something partly achieved in your childhood and partly in your youth, but it now depends on you alone to raise yourself by degrees to a position of eminence such as no musician has achieved before you. You owe this to the exceptional talent that you've received from a most beneficent God, and it depends only on your good sense and way of life whether you die an ordinary musician forgotten by the whole world or a famous Kapellmeister about whom posterity will read in books, – whether, waylaid by a woman, you die bedded on straw in an attic full of starving children, or whether, after a life of Christian contentment, honour and renown, you leave this world with your family well provided for and your name respected by all.

Your journey took you to Munich – you know the reason why – but there was nothing that could be done there. Well-meaning friends wanted to keep you there – your wish was to remain there. It was decided to form a company – I don't need to go over it all again. At the time you thought the scheme was workable, – I did not – read what I wrote in my reply. You have a sense of honour. Would it have done you honour – assuming the plan had come to anything – to have depended on 10 people and their monthly charity? – On that occasion you were quite amazingly taken with that little singer at the theatre and wanted nothing better than to come to the assistance of the German stage: now you declare that you don't even want to write a comic opera. No sooner were the gates of Munich behind you than (just as I prophesied) your whole company of subscribers had forgotten you – what would have become of you in Munich then? – Ultimately it is all God's will. – In Augsburg too you had your little romance and amused yourself with my brother's daughter, who has now had to send you her portrait. The rest I wrote to you in my first letters to Mannheim. When you were at Wallerstein you caused the company great amusement, taking up a violin, dancing around and playing, so that people described you to absent friends as a merry, high-spirited and foolish fellow, giving Herr Beecke an opportunity to disparage your achievements, although your compositions and your sister's playing (as she has always said 'I'm only my brother's pupil') have since persuaded these two gentlemen to see you in a different light, so that they now have the very highest opinion of your music and are in fact more inclinded to run down Herr Beecke's inferior compositions.

In Mannheim you did very well to ingratiate yourself with Herr Cannabich. But your efforts would not have borne fruit if he himself had not been seeking a twofold advantage. I've already written to you about the rest. Then Herr Cannabich's daughter was showered with praise, her

199.   In his reply of 19 February 1778, Mozart returned to this point: 'The days when, standing on a chair, I used to sing to you "Oragna fiagata fà" and finish by kissing you on the tip of your nose are gone indeed, but does this mean that I honour, love and obey you any the less on that account? I'll say no more' [*Briefe*, ii.286].

character depicted in the Adagio of a sonata, in short, *she* was now your favourite. – Then you got to know Herr Wendling. Now *he* was your truest friend – I don't need to tell you what happened next. Suddenly you got to know Herr Weber and everything that had happened before is now forgotten, *this* family is now the most honourable, most Christian family and the daughter is to have the leading role in the tragedy to be played out between your own family and hers, and in the frenzy into which your kind and too open heart has thrown you, you think all your ill-considered fancies as reasonable and as unfailingly practicable as if they were the most natural thing in the world.

You are thinking of taking her to Italy as a prima donna. Tell me if you know a prima donna who, without first having performed many times in Germany, has walked out on to the stage in Italy as a prima donna. How many operas did Signora Bernasconi sing in Vienna, operas, moreover, of the most emotional kind produced under the most critical eye and instructions of Gluck and Calzabigi! And how many operas did Mlle Deiber [that is, Teyber] appear in in Vienna under Hasse's direction – first having been taught by the elderly soprano and very famous actress, Signora Tesi, whom you saw at Prince Hildburghausen's and whose blackamoor you kissed as a child! How many times did Mlle Schindler[200] appear on the Viennese stage after making her début in a private production at Baron Fries's country seat under the direction of Haase and Tesi and Metastasio? – Did any of these people dare to appear before the Italian public? And how much patronage and what powerful recommendations they needed in order to achieve their aim! – Princes and counts recommended them, and famous composers and poets vouched for their ability. And you want me to write to Luggiati to say that you'll write an opera for 50 ducats, even though you know that the Veronese have no money and never commission new operas? I'm now to be mindful of the Ascensa, even though Michelagata [that is, Michele Dall'Agata] hasn't so much as replied to my last 2 letters. I'm quite willing to believe that Mlle Weber sings like a Gabrielli, that she has a powerful enough voice for the Italian stage and so on, that she is built like a prima donna and so on, but it's absurd of you to vouch for her ability to act. There's more to it than that, and old Hasse's childish efforts on behalf of Miss Davies, however kindly and well-meant, merely succeeded in banishing her for ever from the Italian stage, where she was hissed off on the very first night and her part given to de Amicis.[201] Even an experienced male singer, let alone a woman, is bound to tremble at his first appearance in a foreign country. And do you think this is all? – By no means. – Ci vuole il possesso del teatro [One must have a stage presence]. This is particularly true of a woman and her dress, hairstyle, finery and so on. But you know all this yourself, if only you'd think it over; I know that a close examination of all this will convince you that your plan, though well meant, needs *time* and *a lot of preparation*, and a totally different approach is required if it is ever to be carried out. What impresario wouldn't laugh if one were to recommend him a girl of 16 or 17 who has yet to set foot on a stage!

---

200. Katharina Leidner was born in 1753 and brought up by the husband of her stepsister, Philipp Ernst Schindler, appearing under this name in Vienna before making a name for herself in Italy and London. In 1777 she married Johann Baptist Bergopzoomer. Further engagements followed in Braunschweig in 1780 and, three years later, in Prague, where she died in 1788.
201. Cecilia Davies (?1756–1836) was the younger sister of the famous harmonica player, whom she accompanied on her travels. During her stay in Vienna, she stayed in the same house as Hasse and studied with him; see Burney, *The Present State of Music in Germany*, i.275–6. She appeared in Naples in 1771 and it must have been here that the incident mentioned by Leopold took place. On her return to London, she was acclaimed as a rival of Gabrielli; see Busby, *A General History of Music*, ii.359, and Burney, *A General History of Music*, iv.499–50. Later she also appeared in Florence, where she was known as 'L'Inglesina'. She returned to London in 1785 and retired (after 1791). ◆ Further, see Matthews, 'The Davies Sisters, J. C. Bach and the Glass Harmonica'.

As for your proposal (I can hardly write when I think about it), your proposal to travel with Herr Weber and, be it noted, his 2 daughters – it almost robbed me of my reason. My dearest son! How can you have allowed yourself to be taken in even for an hour by such a horrible idea, which must surely have come from someone else? Your letter reads like a novel. Could you really have decided to set off into the world with strangers? – To ignore your reputation – your old parents, your dear sister? – To expose me to the mockery and ridicule of the prince and of the *whole town that loves you*? – Yes, to expose me to mockery and yourself to contempt, for I've told everyone who asked me that you were going to Paris, whereas now you're intending to wander around at random with strangers. No, it surely requires only a moment's thought for you to abandon the whole idea. – So that you can see just how rash you're being, let me tell you that the time is fast approaching when no sensible person could think of such a thing. Conditions are now such that it's quite impossible to guess where war may break out next, as regiments are everywhere either on the march or under marching orders. – To Switzerland? – To Holland? – There's not a soul there all summer, and in winter you can just about earn enough in Berne and Zurich not to die of starvation, otherwise there's nothing. And Holland now has other things to think about apart from music, quite apart from which half one's takings are eaten up by Herr Hummel[202] and concert expenses, and in any case what would become of your reputation? This is something only for lesser lights, for second-rate composers, for scribblers, for a Schwindl,[203] a Zappa,[204] a Ricci[205] and so on. Name one great composer who would deign to take such an unworthy step! – – *Off with you to Paris*! and soon! Find your place among great people – aut Caesar aut nihil! The mere thought of seeing Paris should have preserved you from all these flighty ideas. *From Paris the name and fame of a man of great talent resounds throughout the whole world, there the aristocracy treats men of genius with the greatest deference, respect and courtesy, there you'll see an attractive way of life in astonishing contrast to the coarseness of our German courtiers and their ladies, and you'll become proficient in French.*

As for the company of Wendling and the rest, you simply have no need of it. You've known them long enough – and did your Mama not realize? Were you both blind? – No, I know what it was. Your mind was made up and she didn't dare to oppose you. It angers me that neither of you had the confidence and honesty to give me a proper report; you behaved in exactly the same way with the elector, but in the end it was bound to come out. You wanted to spare me any annoyance, but you end up emptying a whole slops' bucket of annoyances on my head and almost killing me. You know, and have 1000 proofs of it, that God in His goodness has given me sound judgement, that I still have my head screwed on and that in even the most complicated situation I have often found a way out and foreseen and guessed aright: so what has prevented you from asking me for my advice and from always acting as I desired? My son, you should

202.   Johann Julius Hummel was a music publisher in Amsterdam. In return for a handsome fee, he also acted as an agent for visiting artists, a role that seems to have been necessary to ensure decent box-office receipts; see Scheurleer, *Mozart's verblijf in Nederland*, 35.

203.   According to Gerber, 'Friedrich Schwindel is a most agreeable and popular composer, who is still alive, but he is inconstant and restless and stays in a place only long enough to gratify his propensity for pleasure'. He was in The Hague in around 1770, then went to Geneva and from there to Mühlhausen and Lausanne. He died in Karlsruhe in 1786. ◆ Schwindl (1737–86) was active in Germany, the Netherlands and Switzerland.

204.   Francesco Zappa (*fl*1763–88) was a cellist who toured widely. ◆ Further, see Tajetti, 'Francesco Zappa: Violoncellista e compositore milanese'.

205.   [Francesco] Pasquale Ricci was born in Como in 1732. He toured widely and may have met Leopold Mozart in the course of his travels. He then lived in Paris before returning to Como, where he died in 1817. ◆ Also see Staral, 'Zwei Klavierschulen des späteren 18. Jahrhunderts von Francesco Pasquale Ricci'.

regard me not so much as a stern father but as your best friend – haven't I always treated you as a friend, served you as a servant and even provided you with all possible entertainments and enabled you to enjoy all honourable and seemly pleasures, often at great inconvenience to myself? – –[206]

This letter is a worthy memorial to Leopold. In it he carefully but firmly opens his son's eyes. Particularly noteworthy is the skill with which he avoids all mention of the main bone of contention, Mozart's love of Aloysia Weber. Indeed, the whole of the Weber family, whose ulterior motives the distrustful Leopold undoubtedly saw straight through, comes off remarkably lightly, with Leopold even suggesting that Mozart entrust Aloysia's future training to Anton Raaff, who was said to have considerable influence over Italian impresarios. But first she should attempt to gain some stage experience in Mannheim, even if the work was unpaid. 'That you take pleasure in helping the afflicted is something you've inherited from your father; but above all you must think of your parents' welfare, or else your own soul will suffer eternal damnation.'

In this way Leopold forgot all the misgivings that he had had with regard to the visit to Paris, except that, instead of Wendling and Ramm, it would now be Maria Anna who accompanied Mozart and saw that everything went smoothly: they, after all, needed him more than he needed them. Leopold himself would take care of the money and credit notes. Above all, Paris offered the greatest protection from the threatening danger of war.

Leopold's appeal to Mozart's finer feelings – his sense of duty, his ambition and his filial love – was not in vain. With a heavy heart but a sense of childlike submission he yielded to his father's wishes and replied on 19 February 1778:

I'd always assumed that you'd disapprove of my journey with the Webers, but I never had any such intention – *in our present circumstances*, of course; but I gave them my word that I'd write to you about it. Herr Weber doesn't know how things stand with us, and I'll certainly not tell anyone. It was merely that I'd wished I were in the position of not having to consider anyone else and that we were all well off, with the result that in the heat of the moment I forgot how impossible it is to carry out this plan at present and also forgot to tell you about it, something which I'm doing now. . . . What you say about Mlle Weber is all true; and even while I was writing you, I knew as well as you that she's still too young and needs to learn how to act and that she must first gain experience on stage; but with some people one often has to proceed by degrees. These good people are as tired of being here as – you know who I mean and where; and they think that every scheme is practicable. I promised them that I'd tell you everything; but when the letter was on its way to Salzburg, I kept telling them that she must be patient a little longer and was still a little too young and so on. They accept everything I say as they think very highly of me. On my advice her father has engaged Madame Toscani (the actress) to give his daughter acting lessons. Everything you say about Mlle Weber is true, except that she doesn't sing like a Gabrielli; I wouldn't like it at all if she sang like that. Those who have heard Gabrielli say she can sing only passage-work and roulades; . . . in a word, she sings with skill but with no understanding. But Mlle Weber's singing goes straight to the heart and she prefers singing cantabile. I only recently introduced her to passage-work in my great aria, because she'll have to sing bravura arias if she goes to Italy; of course, she'll never forget how to sing cantabile as that is her natural bent.[207] . . . So now you know everything, I still commend her to you with all my heart.[208]

Mozart had finally found true happiness in love, and suddenly to see that happiness destroyed affected him deeply, so that for several days he was confined to his bed. Once again he repeated his old motto, this time with tears in his eyes: 'After God comes Papa.' But he did not accept his father's advice without question, and the inner estrangement between father and son that began during his journey to Paris and finally became insurmountable was powerfully fuelled by the present incident. Mozart felt offended not only in his love but also in his honour:

You can think of me what you like, but please think nothing ill of me. There are people who think that no one can love a poor girl without having evil designs, and that beautiful word maîtresse – wh.re to the rest of us – is really much too beautiful! – I'm no Brunetti or Mysliveček! I'm a Mozart, but a young and right-thinking Mozart, and so I hope you'll forgive me if in my eagerness I sometimes get over-excited.[209]

At the same time he refused to regard his relationship with Aloysia as over. Quite the opposite: the more lonely and unhappy he felt in Paris, the more attractive was the thought of the happiness of sharing his life with hers, and he was forced to drink this particular cup to its last bitter dregs before he was finally cured of his feelings for her. It was with the firm resolve of finally getting his way and in the equally firm belief that Aloysia would be true to him that he faced up to his new and uncertain future. Of course, he said nothing about these secret plans to his father, but the latter knew his son too well not to sense what was happening, precipitating an insidious conflict between them that affected first Aloysia, then the Webers in general and culminating in Mozart's marriage and the ultimate cooling off of what had once been so close a relationship.

For the present, Leopold again offered his son his paternal advice as the latter prepared to set off for Paris with his mother:

My heart is heavy indeed now that I know you'll be further away from me than ever. While you can no doubt imagine something of what I feel, you cannot know all that weighs on my heart. If you take the trouble to recall what I did for you two children in your tender youth, you'll not accuse me of cowardice but, like everyone else, grant that I am, and always have been, the sort of man who has the courage to risk everything. But I always acted with the greatest caution and consideration that were humanly possible – there's nothing anyone can do about accidents, as only God can see into the future. . . . You'll be entering a completely different world; and you mustn't think that it's mere prejudice that makes me see Paris as such a dangerous place, *au*

207. In his *Ideen zu einer Ästhetik der Tonkunst*, 135–6, Schubart writes of Vogler that 'His singing teaching is also highly praised. The outstanding soprano Aloysia Lange in Vienna is an example of his teaching. She has high notes and low notes and sings them all with the greatest accuracy. She is equally adept at singing at full voice as at half voice. Her portamento, her vibrato and her ability to sustain a note, her exceptional accuracy when sight-reading, the subtleties in her performance, her *mezzotinto*, the lightness with which the notes pour forth as though taking wing, her incomparable fermatas and cadenzas, to say nothing of her majestic and dignified bearing – all these she owes in the main to this great teacher.' Some of these merits must also have been to Mozart's credit, for if she was taught by Vogler at all, it must have been later, in Munich. Moreover, Johann Christian Brandes reports that Kirnberger and others specifically warned his daughter Minna against having lessons with Vogler; see Brandes, *Meine Lebensgeschichte*, ii.260. ◆ Further concerning Vogler, see p.406 n.128 above.
208. *Briefe*, ii.285–7.
209. *Briefe*, ii.290 (letter of 22 February 1778).

contraire, I have absolutely no reason to believe, on the basis of my own experience, that Paris is so very dangerous. But my situation then and your present one could hardly be more different.[210]

After explaining this in detail and offering advice appropriate to the situation, Leopold ends with the words:

I know that you love me not merely as your father but also as your truest and surest friend; and that you know and realize that our happiness and unhappiness are, so to speak, in *your* hands as much as in God's: it depends on you whether I live to a ripe old age or die sooner rather than later. If I know you as well as I think I do, I have nothing but happiness to look forward to, and this alone must console me for being robbed by your absence of a father's delight at hearing you, seeing you and holding you in my arms. Live like a good Catholic, love and fear God, pray most ardently to Him in true devotion and trust and lead so Christian a life that, even if I never see you again, the hour of my death may be free from anxiety. From all my heart I give you a father's blessing and remain until death your faithful father and surest friend.

The thought of their separation brought home to both parties a sense of what they were losing. The concerts that Mozart organized prior to his departure in order to introduce himself, his works and his pupils to a wider audience finally revealed his exceptional achievements and in every quarter he heard how unhappy the Mannheimers were to see him go: not only the local musicians but many other cultured individuals who had the town's cultural well-being at heart valued him. Among the latter was the author of *Der deutsche Hausvater*, as Mozart explained in his letter of 24 March 1778:

Before leaving Mannheim I had copies of the quartet [K80] that I wrote one evening at the inn at Lodi, the quintet [K174] and the Fischer variations [K179] made for Herr von Gemmingen. He sent me an extremely polite note, expressing his pleasure at the souvenir that I'd left for him and enclosing a letter for his good friend Herr von Sickingen, adding 'I'm certain that you will be a greater recommendation for the letter than it can possibly be for you'. He sent me 3 louis d'or to cover the costs of the copying. He assured me of his friendship and asked for mine in return. I must say that all the courtiers whom I met, together with the court councillors, chamberlains and other worthies, as well as all the court musicians, were very reluctant and sorry to see me go. There is no doubt about it.[211]

As he explained in his letter of 28 February 1778, he had derived a certain consolation from the prospect of finding opportunities to write music in Paris:

There's nothing I'm looking forward to more than the Concert Spirituel in Paris, as I'll presumably have to write for them. The orchestra is said to be so good and large, and my favourite type of composition, the chorus, can be performed to a high standard there; and I'm very pleased that the French set such store by choruses. The only fault found with Piccinni's new opera

---

210. *Briefe*, ii.255–7 (letter of 5 February 1778).
211. *Briefe*, ii.326.

Roland[212] is that the choruses are too spare and weak and the music as a whole is a bit too monotonous; but otherwise it was well received. Of course, they're used to Gluck's choruses in Paris. But rely on me; I'll do everything in my power to bring honour to the name of Mozart; I'm not at all worried on that score.[213]

Mozart still had to say goodbye to his beloved Aloysia. This, too, he reported on quite openly in his letter of 24 March 1778:

Out of the goodness of her heart Mlle Weber has knitted me 2 pairs of mittens in filet, which she has given me as a souvenir and as a small token of her gratitude. And Herr Weber copied out all I need without asking for a fee, making me a present of the paper and also giving me a copy of Molière's comedies (as he knew I'd not yet read them), with the inscription: 'Recevi, amico, le opere del Moliere in segno di gratitudine e qualche volta ricordati di me' [Accept, my friend, the works of Molière in token of my gratitude and think of me sometimes]. And when he was alone with Mama, he said: 'Our best friend and benefactor is leaving us. Your son has done a lot for my daughter and taken an interest in her, she can never be grateful enough to him.' – They wanted me to have supper with them on the eve of my departure, but I had to decline as I had to be at home. Even so, I had to spend two hours at their house before supper; they never stopped thanking me and wishing they were in a position to show me their gratitude. When I left, they all broke down and cried. I'm sorry, but it brings tears to my eyes just to think about it. He came downstairs with me and remained standing by the door until I'd turned the corner, calling out after me 'Adieu'.[214]

The three arias that Mozart wrote in Mannheim are closely related not only chronologically but also in terms of their style. Even if the name of Johann Christian Bach did not figure so frequently in Mozart's letters of this period, we would still be able to tell from these three works that Mozart felt particularly attracted by his old ideal at this time. All three are examples of the sentimental type of aria which, partly inward, partly wistful, reveals the sort of ravishingly beautiful melodic writing that was especially popular with Johann Christian.[215] On a formal level, the tenor aria *Se al labbro* adopts the older model of Johann Adolf Hasse, except that the *da capo* is limited to the repeat of the main section, with the influence of the earlier middle movements still evident in the form of their modulatory restlessness. The second aria, *Non sò d'onde viene*, adopts the more modern practice of incorporating its middle section – an allegro agitato – into its main section, with the repeat being treated with inspired freedom: not only do its motifs appear here in a different order, with the main theme – first heard in the orchestra in the middle of the piece – creating a particularly beautiful impression, they are also subjected to imitative procedures and their expressive content intensified. The beginning of the recapitulation, for example, is of a remarkable psychological truth, using a motif from the allegro and only gradually re-establishing the earlier mood. The third aria, *Ah, non lasciarmi*, is another example of modern ternary form.

212. Piccinni's first opera for Paris, *Roland*, had been staged on 27 January 1778.
213. *Briefe*, ii.305.
214. *Briefe*, ii.327–8.
215. See above. Even the tonalities of these arias are significant in this respect: two are in E flat major, the third in B flat major. All, moreover, are slow, with their allegros forming mere episodes. ✦ Further, see Kunze, 'Die Vertonungen der Arie "Non sò d'onde viene" von J. C. Bach und Mozart'.

Here two bars of recitative are interpolated before the recapitulation and, as before, the earlier ideas are varied and expanded, before building to a wholly unexpected climax in a new coda.

Common to all three arias, moreover, is their rich orchestral apparel, with flutes, bassoons and horns in addition to the usual strings. *Se al labbro* additionally calls on oboes, *Non sò d'onde viene* on clarinets. Here and in the independence and freedom with which these wind instruments are used, we see the influence of the Mannheim *goût*, an influence also revealed by the detailed dynamic markings. What is particularly striking here is the fact that Mozart was clearly fascinated in the first instance not by the famous crescendo and diminuendo effects but by the tendency to luxuriate in all manner of sudden contrasts and by more intimate subtleties in performance such as *smorzandos* and *mezza voce* effects.

In *Se al labbro*, Mozart's wish not to tax Raaff unduly is clear both from the absence of *fioriture* and the limited compass of *f* to *g'*. Yet these very limitations reveal the extent of Mozart's mastery. Its note of tenderness notwithstanding, the adagio contains a powerful if suppressed passion already evident from the main theme's syncopations, bursting forth with typically Mozartian suddenness at the words 'aprimi il petto', before yielding once more to a mood of placid wistfulness. The result is a portrait of a deeply wounded nature making its final and already half-resigned attempts to gain a hearing. And how poetically the wind instruments are used here, with oppressive writing for the bassoons followed by a curiously agitated motif in the flutes over string tremolandos and sustained wind chords. In general, the accompaniment is as discreet as it is eloquent and free from all clichés. But what chiefly distinguishes this piece is its masterly unity of mood: here there is no longer any tendency to digress and introduce new ideas. Instead, the emotional mood remains the same, flowing along with no awkward breaks to disrupt the continuous flood of music, with each idea emerging from its predecessor as though as a matter of course. Only the middle movement brings with it a different picture, creating a mood of self-torment with its restless harmonies and imitative procedures involving voice and orchestra.

The two soprano arias are both introduced by brief accompanied recitatives. As with earlier arias, the strings alone are heard here and the writing is motivically unified. Of the three arias, the most atmospherically unified is *Ah, non lasciarmi*. There is no ritornello, but, instead, the main theme is reached via a typically Mozartian passage that is as brief as it is surprising from a modulatory point of view. With all the fervour of a loving woman, Dido – who has nothing of the operatic heroine about her here – clings to her lovelorn anguish, repeatedly returning to the main idea, 'Ah, non lasciarmi!' In the brief but eloquent recitative she stammers the phrase as though half crazed, whereas in the coda the same words are introduced by three tense new bars of writing for the winds and followed by an unexpected outburst of passion. Characteristic of the whole aria are the brief, sobbing phrases in the vocal line that often resemble mere interjections and the eloquent fermatas at the end of each section, as though the melodic thread had suddenly snapped. There is a prominent role for two solo bassoons, but in general the orchestra is even more subdued than in the foregoing aria, which is remarkably free of *fioriture* and of all the other hallmarks of the sort of emotional rhetoric associated with Neapolitan opera.

But the jewel of this group of pieces is Aloysia's aria *Non sò d'onde viene*. We have already seen how Mozart abandoned Metastasio's dramatic framework and turned the aria into an expression of private emotion, so that only the opening bars of the recitative still recall King Cleisthenes. Even on the most superficial level, the aria is remarkable for the fact that Mozart here writes for clarinets in addition to bassoons. And even in the ritornello, the winds no longer appear as a self-contained mass but enter in succession, leading up to the powerful outburst in the fourth bar, followed by a sudden dying away of the emotion in the mysteriously shuddering figure in the second violins that accompanies the rapt cantilena in the first. The ritornello ends with a brief and harshly accented syncopated motif. As a whole, it is entirely typical of the later Mozart's preludes. Like Johann Christian Bach, the Italian composers of the period were fond of incorporating into their ritornellos the contrastive moods of the following aria, but these moods were invariably neatly separated, generally by a cadence. Mozart by contrast set out with the aim of combining the emotions depicted and, unlike Gluck, whose art of characterization was concerned with the constant and the typical, sought to depict what was volatile and individual. As a result, he does not single out only one of the character's features and treat it as the dominant one but sees in every human being a combination of the most disparate psychological forces that are in a state of constant interaction and succession. It is in the depiction of his characters' richly animated emotional lives that we find the greatest difference between Mozart and Gluck as dramatists. As such, this art of characterization is closely related to the new spirit that informs Mozart's instrumental music.

As a result, even the introduction to this aria already contains within it all the emotions that dominate what follows: dreamy infatuation, sweet torment, anxious foreboding and utter shock all come together here in a state of flux. With the entry of the human voice comes a sense of sweet-toned rêverie, yet it acquires a more individual character through the motifs that flare up in the violins in their lowest register. The first of the fermatas that is so characteristic of this aria is followed by a passage expressive of anxious foreboding, its mood evoked by suspended harmonies and a mysterious rustling in the second violins and including at its heart a repeat of the words 'Non sò d'onde viene'. With their note of helpless entreaty, they reveal a high degree of psychological subtlety. This section ends with an extraordinarily eloquent coloratura flourish on the word 'scorrendo', involving a curiously wayward vocal line that plunges erratically downwards. The following allegro agitato is characterized by a sense of breathless, anguished haste, with heavy chords in the winds and shrill interjections from the flutes struggling in vain to break free. Finally this section forces itself back to the *prima parte* (see above) by means of tied harmonies so often found in Mozart's works in similar situations:

Here the mood is intensified by means of dissonant *note cambiate*.[216] Although based on a Bachian prototype, everything about this aria is new and idiosyncratic, including the instrumentation, accompanying figures and coloratura writing. Not surprisingly, Jahn was reminded of Donna Elvira.[217] This wonderful aria ends with an orchestral postlude that dies away on a note of virginal tenderness. As a whole it throws a brilliant light on Aloysia's technique and interpretative skills, which were clearly quite exceptional for a girl of only fifteen.[218]

216. The figure in the second violins is the same as the one in the first violins in augmentation.
217. Jahn, *W. A. Mozart*, i.480.
218. In 1837 Mozart's widow gave Anselm Hüttenbrenner a folio [now in the Bibliothèque nationale, Paris] in Mozart's hand containing a coloratura version of the final section of this aria, from the repeat of the 3/4 time-signature. The folio later passed into the hands of the autograph collector Johann Nepomuk Kafka in Vienna. It bore the following entry in Constanze's hand: 'Genuine manuscript by Wolfgang Mozart, received from his wife Constanze von Nissen, widow of the late Mozart of Salzburg, 30 March 1837'; see *Neue Wiener Musikzeitung* for 1 November 1889. Evidence for the date of the manuscript may be found in

On 19 March 1787 Mozart set the same words again, this time for the bass singer Ludwig Fischer: K512. On this occasion, however, he took as his starting point the dramatic situation in Metastasio's original libretto. As a result, the aria goes its own way. (The recitative, by contrast, still clearly recalls the initial version in its overall design and tremolando motif.) There is no longer any sense of burgeoning passion, urgency or exquisite foreboding: here is a man and king who is seized by tender feelings that he does not understand and who half reluctantly attempts to suppress them. Everything is more forceful and dignified, with the opening 'quel gel che scorrendo', for example, revealing a wonderfully dark and majestic brilliance. This aria, too, was written for a singer of the first order and, like the aria for Aloysia Weber, appears to have been composed with Fischer's voice especially in mind.

The two songs for Augusta Wendling – *Oiseaux, si tous les ans* K307 and *Dans un bois solitaire* K308 – reflect the contemporary custom among composers of this period of setting French song texts. Mozart's models were the *ariettes* of French *opéra comique*, a genre in part lyrical, in part narrative in character. They are Mozart's first through-composed songs, with the second of them already looking forward to *Das Veilchen* in the way that it depicts a complete dramatic scene with its frequent changes of tempo and a keyboard part which, written out in full, provides an independent illustration of the events depicted in the text. The first song, too, begins by striking the rhythmically taut note of the French *ariette*, the brief, charming and occasionally even semi-humorous marginal illustrations in the keyboard clearly recalling the works of Philidor, Monsigny and Grétry. German, by contrast, are the elements of gravity and inwardness which, in the second song in particular, come close to overburdening the Rococo pastoral idyll depicted in the text.

The two flute concertos [*recte* flute and oboe concertos, respectively] K313 and K314 are clearly related to the violin concertos and, as a result, must date from this same period.[219] They are very similar works in terms of their structure and character and, although inferior to the violin concertos in respect of their depth and the originality of their ideas, they none the less contain a number of surprising details of a highly poetic and individual stamp: the main theme of K314, for example, returns virtually unchanged in Blonde's aria, 'Welche Wonne, welche Lust'. But these works also contain clear echoes of French comic opera, notably in the final rondo of K313 and in the slow movements of both concertos. Equally French is the tendency to accompany the soloist only with the first and second violins, as in the older type of trio. Formally speaking, both works recall the violin concertos in almost every detail. Particularly witty, as before, is the way in which the individual ideas are linked together: in the opening movement of the D major concerto, for example, the actual solo theme is developed from what initially appears to be a wholly unprepossessing motif in the final subject-group of the tutti. And the rondeau of this same work contains a delightful moment just before the penultimate return of the main theme when the soloist is evidently undecided whether to opt for the main theme itself or the subsidiary theme. These concertos are less influenced by the specific 'Mannheim *goût*' than the contemporary keyboard sonatas, with Mozart far more sparing in his use of dynamic markings. On the other hand, the

Mozart's letters of 12 March 1783 ('My sister-in-law sang the aria *Non sò d'onde viene*'); 12 April 1783 ('I'll also take the opportunity to send you the varied vocal line of the aria *Non sò d'onde viene*'); and 21 May 1783 ('I'm sending you herewith the varied vocal line of *Non sò d'onde viene*, and only hope that you may be able to read it') (*Briefe*, iii.259, 264, 269 and 273). The vocal line found in this coloratura version is not entirely the same as that found in the full score and must therefore have been transcribed from a version that is no longer extant; see NMA X/30/3 and the critical report to NMA II/7/2 [Deiters's note]. ◆ A further leaf in Mozart's hand, now at the Stadtarchiv, Braunschweig, gives a varied version of the first part of the aria. See NMA II/7/2.
219.   Given the freedom with which Mozart handles the solo and tutti here, it is impossible to follow Jahn and date them to an earlier period; see Jahn, *W. A. Mozart*, i.362. In both slow movements, as well as in the separate andante K315, the influence of the violin concerto in G major K216 is plain to hear, even down to the beautiful farewell for the soloist.

Mannheim spirit is evident in his treatment of the orchestra, most notably in the independent writing for the second violins and, above all, the violas. As for the writing for the solo instrument, no less an authority than Moritz Fürstenau observed that it reveals total understanding of the flute's qualities and technique and of the individual effects that can easily be obtained on it,[220] even if it is clearly indebted to violin technique.

The flute quartet in D major K285 of 25 December 1777 is not dissimilar in character, with even the opening bars reflecting the Mannheim spirit with their numerous sighing figures. The most original of its three movements is the central adagio with its pizzicato strings and romance-like melody on the flute abruptly curtailed by a whole bar's rest. The most substantial movement, by contrast, is the opening allegro with its meticulous part-writing and a development section which, by Mozart's standards, is longer than usual but impassioned in tone and thematically unified. Its coda likewise has recourse to earlier motifs.[221] The A major quartet (K298) was similarly written for Dejean.[222] According to a note added to the autograph score in another hand, it was written in Paris, a provenance confirmed by its suite-like form, with its theme and variations, menuetto and rondeau.[223] The whole of this brief work is the product of a mood of carefree high spirits that assumes a positively playful guise in the witty final rondeau, in which the main theme recurs in all four parts.

The two keyboard sonatas of the Mannheim period, K309 in C major and K311 in D major, bring us back to German territory after Mozart's flirtation with French ideas in their immediate predecessor, K284, with which the second is related not only in terms of its tonality but also its main theme. Yet they assume a totally different place within the German tradition. First, it is impossible not to be struck by their greater dimensions: in both the opening movements and the final rondos we are no longer dealing with individual themes and their final and transitional groups but with entire thematic complexes characterized, as before, by sudden and surprising changes of mood. The very beginning of the C major sonata is an excellent example of this, with its surgingly heroic ascending line followed, by way of an answer, by a gentle sighing motif reminiscent of Johann Stamitz:

The rondo of K311 likewise contains whole sections – notably at the beginning – where the listener is constantly torn back and forth between the most disparate moods. It was the Mannheimers' more expansive form and their revolutionary changes of mood that initially attracted Mozart to this style, in keeping with his own individual nature. For the present, however, we find no trace of

220. See Jahn, *W. A. Mozart*, i.473–4.
221. The first of them already recalls the main theme of the opening movement of the string quintet in G minor K516.
222. ◆ This is incorrect; see n.178 above.
223. The final rondeau bears the whimsical title: 'Rondieaoux. Allegretto grazioso, ma non troppo presto, però non troppo adagio, così – così – con molto garbo ed espressione.' The theme of the rondeau is almost identical to that of the aria 'Chi mi mostra, chi m'addita' from Paisiello's *Gli schiavi per amore* [originally staged in Naples in 1786 as *Le gare generose*, but revived in London in 1787 as *Gli schiavi per amore*]. It is not entirely clear when this opera was written, but in all probability it was during the early 1780s. If so, we have evidence of the Italian composer borrowing from Mozart's work, a borrowing that is by no means implausible, given the close contacts between the two men; after all, Paisiello occasionally played quartets with Mozart; see Kelly, *Reminiscences*, i.238; see also Stratton, 'Coincidence or Design', 450. ◆ Because K298 is now known to date from late 1786 or early 1787, Abert's hypothesis that it represents evidence of Paisiello borrowing from Mozart is incorrect.

their other distinguishing feature, their great dynamic extremes. Although crescendo and diminuendo markings appear more frequently than before, they are used only in the older sense of providing expressive nuances within individual phrases, rather than to convey the large-scale emotional tensions characteristic of the Mannheim style.

These sonatas teem with *forte* and *piano* markings, and nowhere more so than in the andante of K309. Indeed, there are times when the mannerism becomes almost anti-musical, persuading writers to see in K309 the sonata criticized by Leopold as an example of the 'mannered Mannheim *goût*'.[224] To judge from this musical portrait, Rosa Cannabich must have been quite a scamp. Mannheim influence may also be found in the orchestral character of the keyboard writing. Even K284 had been designed for the new pianoforte, but now we find Mozart eagerly attempting to transfer to the keyboard the magic of the Mannheim orchestra, an attempt apparent not only from the more careful handling of the inner parts and the denser textures in general, but also from the broadly arching violinistic melodies, the rapid broken octaves, sevenths and sixths that replace the tremolando, and, finally, the discreet wind sounds, staccato basses and so on. Even the level of purely pianistic virtuosity is considerably greater, with the influence of the concerto perceptible not only in the free cadenza in the rondo of K311 but elsewhere, too. In particular, the art of ornamental variation plays an important role here: scarcely a theme is repeated that is not more or less broken down into arabesques.

Haydn's keyboard style, by contrast, is recalled by the length and thematic character of the opening movements and by the importance of their development sections. The improvisatory spirit of K284 has disappeared, although the sense of Mozartian passion remains. The development section of K309 is based on the movement's only main theme, dying away on a double echo after outbursts of melancholy and defiance. Although the development section of K311 begins by striking a similar note and remains, in the main, in the minor, it then introduces an unexpectedly virtuosic element that in the recapitulation even leads to the main theme's initial suppression. This passage in K311 is additionally notable for the fact that it is based on secondary material in a manner typical of the later Mozart. A similar freedom of approach dominates the final rondos, where there is no sense whatsoever of any schematicism, as Mozart handles his main themes and episodes with sovereign freedom, on each occasion singling out one of them for preferential treatment, shortening, altering and combining it with other themes and, as in the opening movements, adding a coda. The result is a further stage on the journey that was to lead to the later rondos in the style of Carl Philipp Emanuel Bach. Never before had Mozart written as witty a movement as the rondo of K311.

A totally different picture, at least on a superficial level, emerges from the five Mannheim 'keyboard duets', in other words, the violin sonatas K296, 301–303 and 305 in C, G, E flat, C and A major.[225] Of these, only the first is structurally reminiscent of the two keyboard sonatas just discussed. The remainder are all two-movement works and resemble each other not least in the dance form of their second movements. Only in K305 do we find a set of variations in this position. Whereas the earlier series of works had been based on Italian models, the predominant influence is now French, inasmuch as even at this late period French composers still took the suite as

224. See Heuß, 'Zum Thema: Mannheimer Vorhalt', 277–80. Mannered, by the standards of the time, is the penultimate theme of the opening movement's subject-group in K311, which is first played *piano*, then *forte*, producing a sort of inverse echo effect.
225. The first was written for Therese Pierron on 11 March and was published by Artaria in Vienna in 1781 together with K376–380. The remainder were engraved and appeared with K304 and K306 in Paris in 1778 and dedicated to Karl Theodor's wife, the electress Elisabeth Maria of the Palatinate.

their starting point.[226] German, by contrast, are the opening movements[227] with their strictly thematic development sections in the Haydnesque manner[228] and the way in which their final subject-groups often have recourse to the principal themes. The Mannheim style is recalled by the large number of themes and their broadly structured design, as well as by the detailed and highly contrastive dynamics. Only rarely do we find crescendos, although where they do occur, they add a special piquancy. Significantly, only one – in K301 – builds to a broad climax and a release of tension in the sense intended by the Mannheim composers.[229] Finally, we may note the influence of the 'duets' of Joseph Schuster (1748–1812), works that Mozart held in high regard and that he took with him on his journey.[230] Although it is no longer possible to be certain, Schuster seems to have been one of the few composers in Germany who took up Schobert's ideas and developed them with any enthusiasm. Schuster's divertimentos are predominantly three-movement works, the first being cast in sonata form, the last often adopting the primitive outlines of a suite (rondo with mineur, polacca, anglaise and so on). But we also find freer forms of a kind illustrated by the opening movement of K303. In one of Schuster's divertimentos in D major,[231] development section and recapitulation are even interrupted by a lengthy recitative for the violin that leads directly into the andante. The subjective, imaginatively impassioned character of his development sections is another feature that links him to Schobert and Mozart,[232] while other features such as the slow and vaguely Mediterranean sicilianas and the lively German folktunes give his sonatas their picturesque quality. But Mozart's most obvious debt to Schuster is in his melodic writing and his technique of combining the two instruments. After a slow introduction, the allegro of Schuster's G minor sonata, for example, begins as follows:

---

226. In the rondo of K301, Mozart even reverted to the much older French form of rondeau with an episode in the minor that he had abandoned some time previously. In their general character, the dance movements, like the variations, indicate French influence.

227. With the exception of K303, in which an introductory adagio alternates with an allegro in the manner of a *buffa* aria, all are cast in sonata form.

228. In K301 and K305, the themes are inverted. Otherwise, however, we already find Mozart's later tendency to construct his development sections from subsidiary ideas.

229. By contrast, the release of tension in the great crescendo in the opening movement of K302 lasts only two bars. It is followed by a sudden *piano* wholly atypical of the Mannheim style.

230. The chronology of Schuster's violin sonatas remains to be resolved, of course, but there is no doubt that on stylistic grounds the five 'Divertimenti da camera a cembalo e violino' that are lodged in Dresden must predate Mozart's works.

231. In the Öffentliche Landesbibliothek in Dresden. ✦ Schuster's sonatas have been published in an edition edited by Wolfgang Plath (Kassel: Bärenreiter, 1971).

232. Note, for example, the mysterious return from the allegro to the adagio in the G minor sonata with the sustained chords in the violin and broken chords in the keyboard.

And in the andante of his G major sonata we find the following:

But it is above all in his handling of the two instruments that Schuster appears most obviously to be an intermediary between Schobert and Mozart. The whole essence of the 'Classical' violin sonata lies, of course, in the increasingly powerful emphasis on concertante writing for the keyboard and violin, thereby granting greater scope to the virtuoso. With Schobert, this type of approach is still in its infancy and the keyboard remains in the ascendant. With Schuster, by contrast, the concertante principle is already clearly present: not only do both instruments have their own individual themes derived from the characteristics of each instrument in turn, but they also enter into dialogue on the same theme and even on individual sections of it. New effects are essayed,[233] notably a tendency shared by both Schuster and Mozart for the violin to hold on to the fifth, while the keyboard theme is developed above or below it. Often the two instruments will start together but then go their separate ways in order to achieve this precise effect:

233. Among these effects is the pizzicato that Schuster was particularly fond of using.

Thanks to Schuster, then, Mozart's earliest violin sonatas are stylistically up-to-date in their concertante approach. To Schuster he owes his abilty to progress beyond the technique of the 'Romantic sonatas'; and it is to Schuster and to French influence, of course, that we owe his avoidance of their wider circle of moods. The Mannheim sonatas have none of the sense of a struggle with emotional chaos that we find in the earlier works. Instead, the spirit is that of the suite, the prevailing mood one of joviality and pleasure in existence. Only in the slow movements is the idyllic tone usually found here transfigured by the magic of Mozart's poetry, with the andante of K296, for example, emerging as one of the loveliest and dreamiest movements that he ever wrote, while in K302 the youthful high spirits of the opening movement give way to a sense of noble, manly melancholy that raises the main theme at the end to the level of utter sublimity. Here rondo form is invested with a psychological depth previously unknown in Mozart's works. But both andantes finally end in those wonderfully poetical codas that are now found with increasing frequency in Mozart's adagios and that bear all the hallmarks of his genius.[234]

The last work to be mentioned here is an isolated four-part Kyrie in E flat major K322 for soloists, chorus and orchestra. It presumably forms part of the mass on which Mozart is known from his letters to have worked in Mannheim. In accordance with conditions in Mannheim, the vocal writing is extremely simple. All the richer, by contrast, is the orchestral contribution, in which even the dynamics point to this period in Mozart's life. The expressive language of this ternary movement is as simple as it is dignified.

---

234. ◆ Further concerning Schuster, see Engländer, 'Les sonates de violon de Mozart et les "Duetti" de Joseph Schuster', 'Problem kring Mozarts violinsonat i e-moll K. 304', 'Die Echtheitsfrage in Mozarts Violinsonaten KV 55–60', 'Die Dresdner Instrumentalmusik in der Zeit der Wiener Klassik' and 'Nochmals Mozart und der Dresdner Joseph Schuster'. It is worth noting, further, that four quartets by Schuster were at one time attributed to Mozart (KAnh. C20.01–04).

18

Arrival in Paris: *Tragédie lyrique*

Mother and son left Mannheim on 14 March 1778, travelling in their own chaise, which they sold to their hired coachman at the end of a journey lasting nine and a half days: 'We thought we'd not be able to hold out to the end', Mozart wrote to his father from the French capital on 24 March.[1]

Now that the die had been cast, all the hopes that Leopold had placed in Paris were revived with redoubled force. Conscious though he was of the vast difference between the present situation and their previous visit of 1764, when Mozart had had a much easier ride as a child prodigy, he none the less hoped that their former patrons would still remember them and that audiences would be favourably impressed by Mozart's much greater mastery. But it was on Friedrich Melchior Grimm that he pinned his greatest hopes: Grimm, after all, had proved a staunch friend in the past, and the two men had remained in contact in the interim. Grimm had even visited Salzburg in the company of two Russians by the name of Rumyantsev[2] and was said to be looking forward to hearing Mozart. He duly attended Mozart's concert in Augsburg on 22 October 1777, but did not make himself known as he was in a hurry to continue his journey. Now he discovered that Mozart was on his way to Paris. Trusting as ever, Leopold had confided in him his difficult situation and commended his son to him. On 6 April 1778 he wrote to the latter, suggesting that he should approach Grimm himself:

I now urge you most emphatically to earn or, rather, to preserve by a *complete and childlike trust* the favour, love and friendship of Baron Grimm, to consult him on all matters, not to do anything on your own initiative or on the basis of any preconceived ideas and always to take account of your own interest and, in this way, of *our common interest*. People lead very different lives in Paris from those familiar to you in Germany, and the French have a most peculiar way of expressing themselves politely, of commending themselves to others, seeking patrons, introducing themselves and so on, so that on the last occasion Baron Grimm instructed me on the subject, and I asked him what I should say and how I should express myself. Tell him that I am his most obedient servant and that I have reminded you of this, and he will confirm the truth of what I say.[3]

Once again, however, the normally astute and distrustful Leopold failed to see through Grimm, only on this occasion his failure was all the more glaring. Although he did not underestimate Grimm's influence, which was even greater now than it had been in 1764, he assumed that Grimm

---

1. See Fournier, 'Mozart à Paris 1778' [*Briefe*, ii.326].
2. ◆ Probably Counts Nikolay Petrovich and Sergey Petrovich Rumyantsev, Russian diplomats.
3. *Briefe*, ii.333–4.

was far more interested in his son than was in fact the case. For all that Grimm found Mozart sympathetic as a person, he had less time for him as an artist, seeing in him merely another of the countless German musicians who were seeking fame and fortune in Paris at this time. The appeal of the child prodigy for whom all doors had once opened had now faded, and Paris knew little about his more recent achievements as a virtuoso and even less about his abilities as a composer. It was now necessary for Mozart to find a position for himself in Paris, a need that both he and his father signally failed to appreciate, the former through his new-found sense of self-confidence following his successes in Mannheim, the latter through his boundless faith in Mozart's inherent talent. Their failure to recognize this was to prove their mutual undoing. Grimm, it is true, offered to smooth Mozart's way for him, but then demanded that Mozart should assert himself in the face of all his rivals, and when Mozart failed to do so, partly as a result of his lack of experience of business and of the world in general, partly because he was confused by the mass of new impressions, Grimm's interest in him began to cool.

Paris was a particularly difficult place for musicians at this time. In Mannheim Mozart had seen the first signs of reawakening life on the part of German opera, but now he found himself pitched into the thick of the controversy surrounding Gluck and Piccinni. This was the *affaire* that currently exercised the whole of Paris, creating an extremely tense situation whose historical course may be recalled in outline here.

France had achieved political unity long before Germany and, thanks both to this and to the country's deep-rooted national consciousness, the French already had a national opera, having had the good fortune to find in Jean-Baptiste Lully (1632–87) a composer who, although Florentine by birth, was sensitive to the needs and taste of the French court. By picking up an old autochthonous tradition, he was able to give the French a national music drama whose spirit far outlasted Lully's own individual art.[4] Lully's starting point was the dramatic ballet, a form which, as the *ballet de cour*, had already been at the centre of court festivities under Louis XIII.[5] The whole court took part in these celebrations, with the king himself playing the leading role. These ballets consisted of a series of dances only loosely linked together by a dramatic idea and accompanied partly by singing and partly by instruments.[6] Here, indeed, we find one of the principal sources of French music in general and, more especially, the source of two of its strongest points, its painterly, programmatical aspect and its ability to depict situations in realistic ways. In 1672 Louis XIV created the Académie Royale de Musique as the chief focus of French opera and here Lully, acting with the king's blessing, transformed the *ballet de cour* into opera,[7] while leaving untouched its essential kernel, with the result that French opera retains its balletic character to this day. In

4. See de Noinville, *Histoire du Théâtre de l'Opéra en France depuis l'établissement de l'Académie royale de musique, jusqu'à présent*; Castil-Blaze, *Théâtres lyriques de Paris: L'Académie impériale de musique de 1645 à 1855*; and Nuitter and Thoinan, *Les origines de l'opéra français* (see also Hermann Kretzschmar's review article in *Vierteljahrsschrift für Musikwissenschaft*, iii [1887], 477). For biographies of Lully, see Lajarte, *Bibliothèque musicale du Théâtre de l'Opéra*; Radet, *Lully, homme d'affaires, propriétaire et musicien*; Prunières, *Lully: Biographie critique*; and La Laurencie, *Lully*; see also Rolland, *Musiciens d'autrefois*, 107ff. ◆ Further, see Prunières, 'Lully and the Académie de musique et de danse'; Borrel, *Jean-Baptiste Lully: Le cadre, la vie, la personnalité, le rayonnement, les oeuvres, bibliographie*; Scott, *Jean-Baptiste Lully*; Couvreur, *Jean-Baptiste Lully: Musique et dramaturgie au service du prince*; Wood, *Music and Drama in the Tragédie en musique, 1673–1715: Jean-Baptiste Lully and his Successors*; and Gallois, *Jean-Baptiste Lully, ou La naissance de la tragédie lyrique*.
5. See Prunières, *Le ballet de cour en France avant Benserade et Lully*. ◆ Also see Silin, *Benserade and his Ballets de cour*; McGowan, *L'art du ballet de cour en France, 1581–1643*; Isherwood, *Music in the Service of the King: France in the Seventeenth Century*; Christout, *Le ballet de cour au XVIIe siècle*; and Canova-Green, 'Le ballet de cour en France'.
6. Wasielewski, 'Die Collection Philidor'.
7. A similar *privilège* had already been granted to Lully's two principal predecessors, the poet Pierre Perrin and the composer Robert Cambert, in 1669, but it was then withdrawn in Lully's favour. ◆ Further, see Auld, *The lyric art of Pierre Perrin, founder of French opera*; and Borowitz, 'Lully and the Death of Cambert'.

France, as in Italy, the ultimate impetus behind the growth of opera came from the Renaissance,[8] with both Lully himself and especially his librettist Philippe Quinault adopting classical tragedy as their elevated model.[9] But this model assumed a totally different aspect in the minds of French artists from the one that prevailed in Italy. In France, after all, the classical ideal had already been realized in what was seen as an exemplary manner in French classical tragedy. The Italians, by contrast, lacked such a precursor. It was only natural, therefore, that the *tragédie lyrique*, as the French – significantly – called it, should have followed a similar course, not least because the tragedies of Corneille and Racine reflected the national temperament with paradigmatic accuracy. As a result, French opera was far more closely bound up with national art and culture than Italian opera had ever been, a circumstance that saved it from the rapid decline that typified Italian opera librettos. Behind French opera lies the whole of the self-contained, ramified culture of the court and society of the age of Louis XIV, with its typically French rationalistic basis, its striving for logic, order and clarity, and a sense of courtly manners that dominated every form of thought and feeling and regarded the natural and the *bienséant* as wholly synonymous. As in spoken tragedy, so in the *tragédie lyrique*, everything was lit by the bright light of reason. Its heroes were not characters in the sense of an individual mixture of manifold psychological forces but the embodiment of certain rationally conceived characteristics designed to appeal to human reason, with even passion appearing not as a primal experience but as a rational thought process. Equally rationalistic is its outward form of expression, with rhetoric taking precedence over poetry (in this we may detect the influence of late Gallo-Roman antiquity) and with writers favouring the grand heroic gesture and a form as transparent as it was finely polished. German audiences may well be left cold by this world of French tragedy and may even be put off by it, but for French audiences both then and, to a lesser extent, even now, it has always been the uninhibited and natural expression of their underlying nature.

Needless to say, the role of music was strictly circumscribed in these works, with the most Romantic of all the arts forced to suffer the most from the iron rule of rationalism, which simply denied the existence of its principal area of concern, namely, the world of the unconscious and the secrets of the psyche. The creative imagination was subordinated to the intellect and nothing was admitted that refused to submit to the dictates of utilitarianism. As a result, music, too, was invested with a twofold purpose: on the one hand, it had to clarify the concepts contained in the text and, on the other, it had to make those abstract ideas more accessible to the senses and, hence, more enjoyable by clothing them in the concrete garb of sounds.[10] Lully achieved the first of these aims through his use of a type of recitative that closely followed the text and that was modelled on the sort of declamation found in classical tragedy.[11] The second he achieved by means of *airs* and other dancelike movements borrowed from the old *ballet de cour*. Here, too, the supreme law was

8. As early as the end of the sixteenth century, a society had been formed in Paris similar to that of the Florentine academies. Its most important member was the poet Pierre de Ronsard. See Tiersot, 'Ronsard et la musique de son temps'. ◆ Also see Lebègue, 'Ronsard et la musique'; Jeffery, 'The Idea of Music in Ronsard's Poetry'; and Howard Mayer Brown, 'Ut musica poesis: Music and Poetry in France in the Late Sixteenth Century'. For histories of early French opera, see McGowan, 'The Origins of French Opera'; and Kennedy, 'The First French Opera'.
9. See Lindemann, 'Die Operntexte Ph. Quinaults vom literarischen Standpunkte aus betrachtet'. ◆ Further concerning Quinault, see Gros, *Philippe Quinault: Sa vie et son œuvre*; Brooks, *Bibliographie critique du théâtre de Quinault*; and Norman, 'The *tragédie-lyrique* of Lully and Quinault: Representation and Recognition of Emotion' and *Touched by the graces: The libretti of Philippe Quinault in the context of French classicism*.
10. See Goldschmidt, *Die Musikästhetik des 18. Jahrhunderts*, 267–8.
11. See Rolland, *Musiciens d'autrefois*, 143ff. ◆ Further concerning Lully's recitative, see Palisca, 'The Recitative of Lully's Alceste: French Declamation or Italian Melody?'; Beaussant, 'Le récitatif lulliste'; Leslie E. Brown, 'The *récit* in the Eighteenth-Century *Tragédie en musique*'; and Couvreur, 'Le récitatif lulliste et le modèle de la Comédie-Française'.

intelligibility, with most of these numbers being based on 'programmes', that is to say, on sets of ideas that were clearly prescribed from a conceptual point of view and that the composer merely had to illustrate with his music. Elsewhere, too, his course was clearly marked out for him, and there could never be any question of his reinterpreting the text in the spirit of music. In consequence, the decorative, picturesque element plays a decisive role in French opera from the very outset. Lully had led the way in this, presenting a whole series of scenic types of a heroic or idyllic stamp, with obsequies, sacrifices, priestly ceremonies, storms at sea, *tempêtes* and other natural phenomena gradually becoming a fixed part of later operas not only in France but in the rest of Europe, too. It would be wrong, of course, to suggest that these scenes bear any resemblance to those of later German Romanticism, for which Nature was filled with a sense of foreboding: these *tragédies lyriques* dealt only in illusionistic tricks designed to titillate the intellect.

But in the longer term music could not be denied its due, and even Lully – an Italian by birth – was too independent a musician to submit to this restrictive rule without putting up some resistance. Not only in his recitatives (especially in the later works), but in his choruses, too, there are plentiful examples of music's creative potential. On the whole, however, he remained bound by prevailing tastes, and it is no accident that the most sensual and profound elements of music – rhythm and harmony respectively – were the least developed in his music. As with the poets of the period, it is here that we invariably find the same easily comprehensible patterns. Even the strictly syllabic nature of his melodic writing belongs under this heading,[12] as does the often unbalanced nature of his recitatives, which are frequently interrupted by brief sections reminiscent of dance songs and, finally, the short-windedness of his self-contained numbers, in which he anxiously avoids any temptation to linger over more elaborate images. All this merely shows that, in spite of Lully's great talent, opera, too, was intellectualized under Louis XIV and incorporated into the rationalistic system that prevailed in all the arts at this time. But the reader should not imagine that such strict rules were regarded as restrictive or even as unnatural. Quite the opposite. For educated men and women at this time, the world of the court was the world *tout court*: all that the court contained within its confines was natural, whereas everything outside it, especially the lower orders, was of no interest whatsoever, with the result that when this world came under attack,[13] the attack was directed both at its unnaturalness and its narrowness of outlook. The old neoclassical spirit still informs the works not only of Gluck but of Meyerbeer, too.

The question was merely how long music could sustain this subjugation of artistic creativity to intellect, a situation that music was the least willing of all the arts to accept. In this, it acquired a powerful ally in French audiences' growing awareness of Italian opera. As early as 1645, Sacrati's *La finta pazza* and Rossi's *L'Orfeo* were both heard in Paris, followed in 1660 and 1662 by two of Cavalli's operas, *Serse* and *Ercole amante*.[14] Even at this early date, a small group of like-minded individuals with an interest in Italian culture had been formed and was quietly promoting its ideal,

---

12. Of course, singers began to ornament these melodic lines even during his lifetime; see Goldschmidt, *Die Lehre von der vokalen Ornamentik*, 76ff. ◆ More recently, see Howard Mayer Brown and Sadie, *Performance Practice: Music after 1600*; and Frederick Neumann, *Ornamentation in Baroque and Post-Baroque Music. With special emphasis on J. S. Bach* and *Performance Practices of the Seventeenth and Eighteenth Centuries*.

13. In his first real opera, *Cadmus*, Lully had included a number of comic features, but it is significant that these features disappear completely from his later works; see Rolland, *Musiciens d'autrefois*, 171ff. ◆ Also see Prunières, 'La première tragédie en musique de Lully: Cadmus et Hermione' and Wood, *Music and Drama in the Tragédie en musique, 1673–1715: Jean-Baptiste Lully and his Successors*.

14. ◆ Rossi's *L'Orfeo* was first heard at the Palais Royal in Paris on 2 March 1647. According to Loewenberg, *Annals of Opera*, 20, an unidentified Italian opera was performed at the Palais Royal in February/March 1645, followed by *La finta pazza* on 14 December 1645.

resting its case on a view that had already been expressed with some force in the sixteenth century – in other words, long before Rousseau – that the French language was wholly unsuited to music.[15]

Initially, at least, Lully's *tragédie lyrique* found no immediate successor worthy of that name, with most of the composers who followed in his wake content to imitate his style and with only André Cardinal Destouches (1672–1749) and the rather more important André Campra (1660–1744) going beyond it, the former by transferring Lully's tone-painterly writing for the orchestra to the vocal soloists, the latter by introducing to the Académie Royale the scenes of Italian peasant life that had previously been seen only in Paris's suburban theatres. By now the Italian party had grown noticeably stronger and felt sufficiently emboldened to launch a powerful attack on the Lulliste *tragédie lyrique*. In 1702 the Abbé Raguenet published his *Parallèle des italiens et des françois* in which he encouraged composers to break free from the world of French opera and join the Italian camp,[16] thereby unleashing a literary feud that lasted almost a century and ended only with Gluck's historic victory. Meanwhile an unexpected saviour had emerged in the person of Jean-Philippe Rameau (1683–1764),[17] who came to the defence of a genre threatened both by these Raguenet-inspired attacks and by his Italian rivals. Rameau had already acquired a name for himself as a keyboard composer and, even more, as a theorist (his *Traité de l'harmonie* appeared in 1722), and he was fifty by the time that he conquered the operatic stage with *Hippolyte et Aricie* in 1733, astonishing both factions with the unusual nature of the piece, with even Lully's supporters initially believing that their ideal was under threat and only gradually accepting that Rameau was not their enemy but their hero's outstanding successor. The Italian camp had a clearer perception of what was happening, and Rousseau, who increasingly assumed the role of their spiritual leader, made no secret of his hatred of Rameau, dismissing him as a 'destillateur d'accords baroques'. The feud continued to be waged in the columns of the press with an intensity second only to that fought by the followers of Gluck and Piccinni. Above all, it confused public opinion, so that it was not until 1748, when the Académie Royale finally threw its whole weight behind him, that Rameau found general acceptance.

Rameau is one of the rare exceptions to the rule that practice goes before theory in the evolution of art. As a theorist and aesthetician, he had demanded that music be freed from the bonds of the doctrine of rationalism, yet as a composer he never once departed from the Lulliste tradition in his own operas, the chief of which are *Hippolyte et Aricie* (1733), *Castor et Pollux* (1737),

15. Although it was Lully who was largely responsible for helping French national opera to achieve its ultimate victory, one of his works none the less contains a passage that is important as an example of this opposite tendency: in the famous dialogue between French and Italian music in *La raillerie* (1659), the two allegorical figures point out each other's shortcomings, with French music criticizing its Italian counterpart for its 'chants tout languissants' and its 'fredons [trills] ennuyeux', before going on, 'La manière dont je chante, exprime mieux ma langueur; quand ce mal touche le cœur, la voix est moins éclatante.' French music also protests explicitly: 'Je n'ordonne point du tien, mais je veux chanter au mien.' On this whole development, see Kretzschmar, 'Die Correspondance littéraire als musikgeschichtliche Quelle', ii.210–25. ◆ More recently, see Thomas, *Aesthetics of opera in the Ancien Régime, 1647–1785*.

16. Raguenet, *Paralèle des italiens et des françois, en ce qui regarde la musique et les opéra*; an annotated German translation appeared in Mattheson, *Critica musica*, i.91ff., and in Marpurg, *Kritische Briefe über die Tonkunst*, i.65ff., 89ff., 113ff. and 398ff. [An English translation from 1709 is reprinted in *Musical Quarterly*, xxxii (1946), 411–36.] Both Mattheson and Marpurg also included the riposte by Jean Laurent Le Cerf de la Viéville, *Comparaison de la musique italienne et de la musique françoise*, that was reprinted as volumes ii–iv of later editions of Bourdelot's *Histoire de la musique et de ses effets depuis son origine jusqu'à présent*. See also Raguenet, *Défense du Parallèle des italiens et des françois*. ◆ Further, see Storer, 'Abbé François Raguenet: Deist, Historian, Music and Art Critic', and Cowart, *The Origins of Modern Musical Criticism: French and Italian Music 1600–1750*.

17. See Pougin, *Rameau: Essai sur sa vie et ses œuvres*; Laloy, *Jean-Philippe Rameau*; and Lionel de La Laurencie, *Rameau*. ◆ Further concerning Rameau, see Gardien, *Jean-Philippe Rameau*; Kintzler, *Jean-Philippe Rameau: Splendeur et naufrage de l'esthétique du plaisir à l'âge classique*; Paquette, *Jean-Philippe Rameau: Musicien bourguignon*; Dauphin, *La musique au temps des encyclopédistes*; and Thomas, *Aesthetics of opera in the Ancien Régime, 1647–1785*.

Dardanus (1739) and *Zoroastre* (1749).[18] Even their librettos mark them out as products of the same spirit. Formally, too, they follow similar lines, with their recitatives in particular adopting Lully's model with their razor-sharp rhetorical declamation and frequent changes of time-signature. The vocal numbers are still cast in the older forms and, as such, are brief and easy to follow. None the less, these works also include features that represent a marked extension of Lully's system, allowing an element of musical subjectivity to enter into them, while leaving its rationalistic character untouched. With their large- and small-scale contrasts and climaxes, Rameau's operas are living organisms in a way that Lully's are not, and although his characters continue to represent certain typical qualities and remain fundamentally impervious to irrational, elemental feelings, not developing, but presenting the same immutable and clearly intelligible picture from start to finish, the musician in him allows his creative abilities far greater scope within these particular limits. While the music is not allowed to complicate the characterization as laid down by the librettist, it enjoys total freedom in the way in which it is realized and in the interplay of light and shade. It is no wonder, therefore, that Rameau was able to coax new and unexpected blossoms from the two areas that his predecessor had found to be especially infertile and to invest rhythm with the virtually inexhaustible vitality that remains the principal strength of French music today and which, as with Gluck, was pressed into the service of a dramatic characterization; and his harmonic language was raised to a height that confused and even stunned the adherents of the old school. Above all, however, Rameau's art of orchestration achieves a level of excellence which, technically and expressively, places him on a par with the greatest practitioners of his century. He, too, sets out from a programmatical idea in his overtures and other instrumental movements, but he reveals an astonishing ability to discover all the musical possibilities hidden in a template designed to appeal primarily to the intellect. Thanks to Rameau, the old art of French ballet acquired a new and firm support, and if this type of music – like its offshoot, programme music in general – continues to dominate French and sometimes even German music to this day, the decisive impulse behind this development came from none other than Rameau.

There is no doubt, however, that the spirit of Italy left its trace on Rameau's operas no less than that of France, although details such as the introduction of *fioriture* and even of the *da capo* aria are less important in this respect than the greater dramatic exploitation of vocal solos and the emancipation of the music in general from Lully's narrow confines. Rameau's genius was far too independent to allow itself to be tied to a single model. Receptive to the currents of his time, while remaining true to himself, he created works aimed not at overthrowing existing traditions but at renewing those traditions from within. He accepted the old rationalistic operatic norm as an immutable rule and never for a moment thought of questioning it, but within this framework he attempted, wherever possible, to allow the emotions to find their rightful expression, as they had in fact been straining to do long before Rousseau arrived on the scene. In this respect, Rameau's operas go as far as was then conceivably possible. At the same time, of course, they showed that even in opera rationalism could not be overthrown by emotion alone but that it first needed to be transformed, with its fixed and lifeless rules once again felt to be living forces and with thinking itself becoming an inner experience again. It was left to Gluck to achieve this aim and to complete the journey already started by his inspired predecessors in French no less than in Italian opera. But one can understand how Gluck felt increasingly drawn to Rameau, whose art was the indispensable precursor of his own operatic reforms.

---

18. See Goldschmidt, *Die Musikästhetik des 18. Jahrhunderts*, 107ff.

Scarcely had Rameau persuaded Lully's supporters to recognize his merits and united behind him the advocates of French opera when the Italians regrouped their forces and launched a further attack. In August 1752 an Italian *opera buffa* company appeared in Paris under the direction of Eustachio Bambini [1697–1770] and obtained permission to perform comic intermezzos at the Académie Royale. They began with Pergolesi's *La serva padrona*, which, after some initial hesitation on the part of the capital's audiences, eventually took Paris by storm. Other works followed.[19] Everything about these performances was praised, from the music to the leading performers, although neither Pietro Manelli nor Anna Tonelli was among Italy's leading singers. There was even praise for the way in which the harpsichordist conducted the work from the keyboard, a method much preferred to the audible beat of Lully's staff striking the ground. But the new type of opera found the supporters of the older type still at their posts, provoking the famous battle between the nationalist *coin du roi* and the opposing *coin de la reine*, which was sympathetic to Italian ideas.[20] Among the Italian faction was Friedrich Melchior Grimm, who won his first literary spurs at this time with his *Lettre sur Omphale* of 1752, in which he attacked Destouches's opera with more enthusiasm than understanding.[21] He followed this up in 1753 with his *Vision du petit prophète de Boehmischbroda*, a lampoon couched in Biblical terms, in which he poured scorn on the older type of opera, dismissing its characters as mere marionettes and prophesying that, if its advocates persisted in supporting it, a decline in good taste would inevitably follow.[22] Like the rest of the *encyclopédistes*, Diderot sided with Grimm, their antagonism towards Rameau already fuelled by the latter's attack on the *Encyclopédie*.[23] But the most vocal of Rameau's critics was Jean-Jacques Rousseau. In his battle against the old order, the old national opera – which was, indeed, an accurate reflection of the older type of society – struck him as the *ne plus ultra* of unnaturalness. He repeated the old adage that the French language was unsuited to music and set out to prove that French vocal music was an absurdity.[24] For the opposing faction this was tantamount to insulting the French nation, with the result that he received death threats and even risked a period of incarceration in the Bastille.[25] Fortunately, the threat was not realized. Instead, Paris found itself awash in a veritable flood of satirical pamphlets penned by the supporters of the Bouffons and their enemies. With the exception of the writings of the leading figures on both

19. See Hiller, *Wöchentliche Nachrichten*, v.331ff.; Jansen, *Jean-Jacques Rousseau als Musiker*, 159ff.; Spitta, 'Rinaldo da Capua'; and Hirschberg, *Die Enzyklopädisten und die französische Oper im 18. Jahrhundert*, 12ff. The operas performed by the Bouffons were Pergolesi's *La serva padrona* and *Il maestro di musica* [a pasticcio based largely on Auletta]; Orlandini's *Il giocatore*; Latilla's *La finta cameriera* and *Gli artigiani arricchiti*; Rinaldo di Capua's *La donna superba* and *La zingara*; Cocchi's *La scaltra governatrice*; Sellitto's *Il cinese rimpatriato*; Jommelli's *Il parataio*; Ciampi's *Bertoldo in corte*; and Leo's *I viaggiatori*.
20. The leaders of both parties regularly sat beneath the boxes of the king and queen. ◆ The King's side was stage left, the Queen's side stage right.
21. Kretzschmar, 'Die Correspondance littéraire als musikgeschichtliche Quelle', ii.212–13. ◆ Concerning Grimm, see Oliver, *The Encyclopedists as Critics of Music*; and Doussot, *Grimm et la musique d'après 'La correspondance'*.
22. Reprinted in Grimm, *Correspondance littéraire, philosophique et critique*, xv.315ff. Grimm wrote to Gottsched to report on its extraordinary success, prompting the latter's wife to write a similar piece directed at Christian Felix Weiße's operetta *Der Teufel ist los*; see Danzel, *Gottsched und seine Zeit*, 350–1, and Jansen, *Rousseau als Musiker*, 192. As Jansen points out (193), even in France Rousseau was long regarded as the author [Deiters's note]. See also Tiersot, *Jean-Jacques Rousseau*, 111ff.
23. Cf. his satirical novel, *Le neveu de Rameau*, which Goethe translated into German. ◆ For an English translation, see Barzun and Bowen, *Rameau's Nephew*.
24. Rousseau propounded this view in his well-known *Lettre sur la musique française* of 1753, an essay whose views were already adumbrated in his anonymously published *Lettre d'un symphoniste de l'Académie royale de musique à ses camarades de l'orchestre*, also of 1753. See Jansen, *Rousseau als Musiker*, 199ff., and Tiersot, *Rousseau*, 125–6. On the aesthetic views of Rousseau and the *encyclopédistes*, see especially Goldschmidt, *Die Musikästhetik des 18. Jahrhunderts*, 85ff.
25. Grétry, *Mémoires*, i.279. ◆ Further, see Sacaluga, 'Diderot, Rousseau et la querelle musicale de 1752: Nouvelle mise au point'; Kiernan, 'Rousseau and Music in the French Enlightenment'; Dauphin, *Rousseau musicien des Lumières*; Verba, 'Jean-Jacques Rousseau: Radical and Traditional Views in his Dictionnaire de musique'; Eigeldinger, *Jean-Jacques Rousseau et la musique*; Kumbier, 'Rousseau's *Lettre sur la musique française*'; and Gülke, *Rousseau und die Musik*.

sides, the debate involved a good deal of mud-slinging and was more notable for the intellectual agitation of its contributors than for their factual accuracy.[26] By March 1754 the Italian company had been driven from Paris at the instigation of the nationalist party, which naturally included the members of the Académie Française,[27] although their supporters remained as voluble as before, demanding again and again that French opera receive an injection of new blood from its Italian counterpart.

This was not just a life-and-death struggle among musicians: music was merely the excuse to launch a preliminary assault on the older form of French culture in general. At the very time when that culture found its supreme artistic expression in Rameau's operas, Rousseau was preparing to declare war on it and deliver its *coup de grâce*. His new doctrine of Nature, after all, consisted in the first instance in an outright denial of all that existed and an attack on its intellectual basis in rationalism: feeling, not intellect, was what mattered, and the inalienable rights of the individual mattered more than those of all-powerful society. Unsurprisingly, it was opera – the most prominent outpost of the old order – that bore the brunt of Rousseau's attack. In this way, the *Querelle des Bouffons* became the first noisy echo of the new spirit of radicalism. The Italian works in Bambini's repertory were merely an excuse, albeit a particularly suitable and effective one, inasmuch as Italy was the only nation at this time that had a counterweight to Renaissance opera in the form of its *opere buffe*. But the basic question over which partisans and opponents fought – in most cases unwittingly – was not concerned with the relative merits of French or Italian opera but with ways in which the new ideal of an emotionally charged naturalism could be realized on the operatic stage in place of existing social norms and stylization. Rousseau himself was clearly aware of this when he wrote *Le devin du village*, thereby disproving his own theory that French was unsingable as a language.

It was entirely natural that the new spirit initially spurned the old *tragédie lyrique*, which it regarded as hopelessly reactionary, and turned instead to the new and more popular musical comedy that promised greater freedom of artistic expression. Yet the question remained open as to whether the older form of opera could not, after all, be reconciled with this new spirit and whether, in consequence, it could still be rescued. It was to be left to Gluck to provide the answer to this question and to do so, moreover, in a gloriously affirmative manner.[28]

---

26. For a general account, see Pougin's article, 'La querelle des bouffons'; see also Jullien, *La musique et les philosophes au dix-huitième siècle*; Jansen, *Rousseau als Musiker*, 188ff.; Hirschberg, *Die Enzyklopädisten und die französische Oper*; and Tiersot, *Rousseau*, 111ff. ◆ Further, see Boyer, *La Guerre des Bouffons et la musique française*; Launay, *La Querelle des Bouffons*; Wokler, 'La Querelle des Bouffons and the Italian Liberation of France: A Study of Revolutionary Foreplay'; and Isherwood, 'Nationalism and the *Querelle des Bouffons*'.

27. Grimm, *Correspondance littéraire*, i.114.

28. ◆ Further concerning late seventeenth- and early eighteenth-century French opera, see Lagrave, *Le théâtre et le public à Paris de 1715 à 1750*; Rice, *The Performing Arts at Fontainebleau from Louis XIV to Louis XVI*; Cowart, *The Origins of Modern Musical Criticism: French and Italian Music 1600–1750*; La Gorce, *L'opéra à Paris au temps de Louis XIV: Histoire d'un théâtre*; Kintzler, *Poétique de l'opéra français de Corneille à Rousseau*; and Charlton, *French Opera 1730–1830: Meaning and Media*.

19

Opéra comique

The precursors of French *opéra comique*[1] were the Italian actors who were engaged by Louis XIV and who specialized in improvised comedy. In their performances we find two of the principal features that were later to typify the new genre: the pronounced tendency to adopt a satirical approach to current affairs, whether of a political, social or artistic nature, and their delight in parodying *opere serie*. Italian was soon replaced by French as the language in which these works were performed, and improvisation gave way to written texts. Nor was it long before street songs began to be interpolated into these works in the form of the vaudevilles[2] that were extremely popular at this time as a comment on contemporary events. In 1697 these Italian actors were expelled from France for insulting Mme de Maintenon,[3] but their spiritual heirs were the comedians who appeared at Paris's annual fairs, notably the Foire St Germain and the Foire St Laurent, accompanying their performances with music. In 1715 these players found an outstanding poet in the person of Alain-René Lesage (1668–1747), who had already made a name for himself as the author of *Le diable boiteux*. Lesage's works, too, are mainly comedies with interpolated songs in the style of the city's vaudevilles and functional middle-class music, yet these songs are already used for the purposes of characterization and to depict particular situations,[4] generally with parodistic intent. In 1716 the 'Italiens' were readmitted to the court and they immediately helped themselves to the innovations made by Lesage in his vaudeville comedies.[5] Both the Opéra and the Comédie-Française saw the fair theatres as a threat to their livelihood, and for a time – in 1744, for example[6] – the latter were suppressed, until finally in 1762 they reached an agreement with the Comédie-Italienne.[7]

---

1. See Contant d'Orville, *Histoire de l'opéra bouffon*; Desboulmiers, *Histoire du Théâtre de l'Opéra Comique*; Desarbres, *Deux siècles de l'opéra*; Bernardin, *La Comédie italienne en France et les Théâtres de la foire et du boulevard (1570–1791)*; Font, *Favart, l'opéra-comique et la comédie-vaudeville aux XVIIe et XVIIIe siècles*; and Calmus, *Zwei Opernburlesken aus der Rokokozeit*. ◆ Further, see Cucuel, *Les créateurs de l'opéra-comique français*; Carmody, *Le répertoire de l'Opéra-Comique en vaudevilles de 1708 à 1764*; Gourret, *Histoire de l'Opéra-Comique*; Vendrix, *L'opéra-comique en France au XVIIIe siècle*; Charlton, *French Opera 1730–1830: Meaning and Media*; and Herbert Schneider and Wiesend, *Die Oper im 18. Jahrhundert*.
2. The word 'vaudeville' is said to derive from 'voix de ville'. The earlier term was 'pontneuf' (a reference to one of Paris's chief arterial routes at this time). Later the 'pontneuf' became the ordinary street song in contrast to the more elevated vaudeville; cf. the opening scene of Charles Collé's *L'isle sonnante*. The term 'opéra-comique' essentially meant a serious opera that was comically distorted, in other words, a parody. These works were collected by Evaristo Gherardi and published as *Le théâtre italien*. ◆ On the vaudeville and 'voix de ville', see Lesure, 'Eléments populaires dans la chanson française au début du XVIe siècle'; Levy, 'Vaudeville, vers mesurés et airs de cour'; Barnes, 'Vocal Music at the "Théâtres de la Foire" 1697–1762, i: Vaudeville'; Heartz: '*Voix de ville*'; Bill Smith, *The Vaudevillians*; Gidel, *Le vaudeville*; Herbert Schneider, *Das Vaudeville: Funktionen eines multimedialen Phänomens*; and Philip Robinson, 'Vaudevilles et genre comique à Paris au milieu du XVIIIe siecle'.
3. ◆ Françoise d'Aubigné, marquise de Maintenon (1635–1719), was the mistress of Louis XIV.
4. Lesage published his plays in his *Théâtre de la Foire*. His *Télémaque* of 1715 is reprinted in Calmus, *Zwei Opernburlesken*. See also Campardon, *Les spectacles des foires*, and Soubies and Malherbe, *Précis de l'histoire de l'Opéra-Comique*. ◆ Further, see Robinson, 'Vaudevilles et genre comique à Paris au milieu du XVIIIe siècle'.
5. Their works are published in the anthology *Les parodies du nouveau théâtre italien*.
6. See Favart, *Mémoires et correspondances littéraires, dramatiques et anecdotiques de C. S. Favart*, i.17–18.
7. *Mémoires de Favart*, i.203–4, 214–15 and 228–9.

The principal step in the development of comedy with vaudeville interpolations to fully-fledged comic opera was taken by the poet Charles Favart [1710–92], the husband of Marie-Justine-Benoîte Favart [1727–72], who was famous in her own right as an actress, singer and dramatist.[8] For a long time, these home-grown products survived alongside translations of Italian works that were adapted to suit local tastes.[9] The most successful of these indigenous works was *Les troqueurs* (1753), an adaptation by Jean-Joseph Vadé of a tale by La Fontaine set to music by Antoine Dauvergne.[10] None the less, it was several years before Favart managed to win over any musicians to the new genre. In fact, the most important of the collaborators to ally himself to the cause of French *opéra comique* before Philidor and Monsigny was based not in Paris but in Vienna: between 1758 and 1764, Christoph Willibald Gluck set a whole series of texts by Favart, either wholly or in part, thereby ensuring a place for himself in the history of comic opera.[11]

Although French composers and their librettists were initially influenced by their Italian counterparts, they very soon tired of the underlying qualities of *opera buffa*, with its reliance on the old character masks and, especially, on caricature and slapstick comedy, and struck out in a direction of their own. From the outset, their comic operas were firmly grounded in everyday life, drawing their principal material from their mockery of public and private figures and the situations in which those figures found themselves. *Opera buffa* took as its starting point the stereotypes of human nature, while *opéra comique* was timely and topical, with the result that the librettos of these last-named works could easily provide us with an outline of French cultural history up to the time of the Revolution, so faithfully do they reflect the life of the social classes to which the old order was ultimately to fall victim. It was these works – not Mozart's *Le nozze di Figaro* – that were the true harbingers of the Revolution. They also have the advantage of being much more varied than the Italian works of the period. Comedy as such was not their exclusive aim but was increasingly counterbalanced by sentimental and, later, by serious elements that occasionally bordered on tragedy, until in the end even works such as Beethoven's *Fidelio* and Cherubini's *Médée* were described as *opéras comiques*, a term that by this date referred only to the piece's purely external form.

In these works, the everyday world replaces classical legend and history, while the bourgeoisie supplants the aristocratic world of the court. The real hero is now the bourgeois in all his manifold manifestations, including the *fermier*, landowner and artisan. Moreover, poets and composers alike were interested not only in individual representatives of the middle classes but also in their activities and took particular pleasure in depicting the homely atmosphere in middle-class households, including their daily chores,[12] to say nothing of military marches, harvest festivals, grape-picking festivals, scenes in courts of law, tavern scenes and scenes set in the antechambers of the nobility, or else the characters were depicted gambling or playing blind man's buff and so on. In addition, we find a whole series of descriptions of nature, foremost among which were the storm scenes taken over from *opera seria*. The authentically French art of depicting the outward situation

8. See *Théâtre de M. et Mme Favart, ou Recueil des comédies, parodies et opéra-comiques*; Font, *Favart*; and Pougin, *Madame Favart: Étude théâtrale.* ◆ Also see Iacuzzi, *The European Vogue of Favart: The Diffusion of the Opéra-Comique*; Herbert Schneider, 'Zur Gattungsgeschichte der frühen Opéra-Comique'; Bruce Alan Brown, *Gluck and the French Theatre in Vienna*; and Vendrix, *L'opéra-comique en France au XVIIIe siècle.*

9. *La serva padrona*, for example, appeared in 1754 in an adaptation by Pierre Baurans entitled *La servante maîtresse*, while Rinaldo di Capua's *La zinzara* was reworked the following year by Favart as *La bohémienne*.

10. ◆ Concerning Dauvergne, see Paulin, *La vie et les œuvres d'Antoine d'Auvergne.*

11. See Tiersot, *Gluck*, 34ff.

12. Loveplay while ironing the washing was a popular theme that is familiar to us from *Fidelio*. No less popular were the expectant spinning scenes with their attendant songs, a type of scene that was later taken over by German Romantic opera.

that had already been essayed in the *tragédie lyrique* proved immensely successful here and left a decisive mark on German opera, too, until well into the nineteenth century.

The nobility is also well represented, and respect for the refined manners of gentlemen of the old school is still a frequent feature of these works. None the less, there is an increasing tendency to take the aristocracy to task, either by depicting its representatives as frivolous and violent or by portraying them in such idealized terms that the gap between ideal and reality is instantly apparent. Much the same is true of the clergy and the educated classes, with doctors coming in for particular criticism.[13] Mayors, bailiffs and so on come off relatively lightly, being closer in rank to the bourgeoisie. There are even occasional sideswipes at the king himself.[14]

There are obvious links here with Diderot's plays about contemporary middle-class life, in which the characters are no longer depicted merely as representatives of certain typical qualities but are seen, instead, in the context of their obligations to society, with the plot drawing its lifeblood from an accurate reflection of the circumstances in which those lives were led. Didacticism and especially sentimentality also play a role here, with the former – an offshoot of the older rationalism – revealing itself with particular clarity in the fondness for petit-bourgeois morality proclaimed in the final number. Indeed, the whole plot is regularly geared to such epigrammatical morals as 'On ne s'avise jamais de tout'; and in individual cases such as Favart's *La belle Arsène* (1773), with its disputation about love and its allegorical goddess 'Indifference', the influence of the older rationalistic didacticism is still unmistakably present.[15]

In general, however, it is the new ideas of the age that predominate here, with Rousseau's 'Gospel of Nature' rehearsed in all manner of variants,[16] from praise of Nature at her earthiest to the sweetly scented descriptions that have nothing whatever to do with actual Nature.[17] Unlike the degenerate, teeming towns and cities, the countryside was seen as the true home of Nature, with all the intimacy of family life now opened up to opera.[18] Of course, sentimentality also caught on under Diderot's influence,[19] bringing with it gossipy virtue, persecuted innocence, 'hearts of gold' and floods of tears. Just as Piccinni's *La buona figliuola* had introduced the sentimental comedy to Italy, so in France the *comédie larmoyante* proved tremendously successful with works such as *Le déserteur* (1769) by Sedaine and Monsigny. But, thanks to the talents of its poets and the wide-ranging nature of its subject matter, *opéra comique* soon strove to distance itself from these aberrations and to achieve a higher synthesis that sought to embrace both tragedy and comedy.

This early period of *opéra comique* also witnessed the first stirrings of Romanticism. Under composers like Duni, Philidor and Monsigny, fairy-tale motifs appeared here for the first time, with marvels proving especially popular. There was, however, nothing fantastical about the spirit

---

13. In Sedaine's *Félix* of 1777, the three intriguing sons of good old Morin are an officer, a cleric and a senior civil servant, but all three are outright egoists.

14. In Sedaine's *Le roi et le fermier* of 1762, the king is well disposed but ill advised. None the less, Grétry's *Richard Cœur-de-lion* constitutes an enthusiastic glorification of royalist sentiments.

15. In other cases such as Duni's *L'isle des foux* of 1760, a kind of musical ship of fools that is in fact a parody of Goldoni's *Arcifanfano*, such didacticism is ridiculed.

16. The closing moral of Sedaine's *Rose et Colas* (1764) is, 'Il faut seconder la nature puisqu'elle vous fait la loi'.

17. The most repugnant example of this may be found in pieces such as Philidor's *Zémire et Mélide*, a dramatization by Fenouillet de Falbaire of Salomon Geßner's *Der erste Schiffer*.

18. 'Où peut-on être mieux qu'au sein de sa famille?' asks a character in Marmontel's *Lucile* (1769).

19. ◆ On Diderot, see Oliver, *The Encyclopedists as Critics of Music*; Doolittle, *Rameau's Nephew: A Study of Diderot's 'Second Satire'*; Farmer, 'Diderot and Rameau'; Heartz, 'From Garrick to Gluck: The Reform of Theatre and Opera in the Mid-Eighteenth Century' and 'Diderot et le Théâtre lyrique'; Paul Henry Lang, 'Diderot as Musician'; Fubini, *Les philosophes et la musique*; Didier, *La musique des lumières*; Coulet, *Diderot: Les beaux-arts et la musique*; Durand-Sendrail, *Denis Diderot: Écrits sur la musique*; Verba, *Music and the French Enlightenment*; and Dauphin, 'La musique au temps des encyclopédistes'.

world of the *comédie-féerie*, which remained solidly grounded in petit-bourgeois reality and invested with a certain irony. Not until the age of Marmontel and Grétry was a link to be forged with Romanticism.

That the librettists of these *opéras comiques* were well versed in literature is clear from the wealth of literary motifs that are found in their works, with their own inventions skilfully mingled with all manner of borrowings from popular and high-brow literature from both home and abroad. Alongside features from Italian *opere buffe* we find others not only from spoken comedy but also from tragedy and fairy tales. Much rarer, by contrast, is the tendency to ridicule *opera seria*, as this was the function of actual parodies.[20] As in Italy, there was much play with disguises and long-lost kinsfolk, while the major role of confidants, squires and servants, together with the presence of certain caricatures, likewise reminds us of the Italian composers of the period: one such figure is the old lover who is led by the nose and who, as with the Italians, is often the young heroine's guardian. Yet even these characters are invariably solidly grounded in French surroundings and, as it were, have taken French nationality. But we also find a large number of new ideas, including the love of a mere portrait, letter duets, the tendency of village orators to lose their way while speaking and to grind to a halt, dungeon scenes, old governesses and, finally, politicizing women, all of which left their mark on later operas.

There is no doubt that it was this variety which, drawing its strength from everyday life, gave popular French operas a decisive advantage over their Italian counterpart,[21] an advantage due not least to the talent and skill of their librettists, foremost among whom were Favart, Michel-Jean Sedaine (1719–97) and Jean-François Marmontel (1723–99).[22] All were as inexhaustible in devising new situations as they were adept at producing gripping plots. Above all, they were more successful than the Italians at merging serious and comic elements. To this may be added a living, forceful language, be it in prose or verse, that rarely sounds unnatural, no matter how rhetorically exaggerated it may be. As a result, the view of a composer like Beethoven, that only in Paris could decent librettos be found, was not without justification. It was a state of affairs that was due, above all, to the fact that the librettists in question still followed the example of Quinault and Lully, working together in the closest possible contact with their respective composers. Composer and librettist took account of the other's idiosyncrasies and for this reason, if for no other, could generally count on a successful collaboration.

On a formal level, the main difference between French and Italian comic operas consisted in the fact that in the former most of the sections that served to advance the plot were entrusted not to singing but to the spoken dialogue. It is this feature – inherited from the age of the vaudeville comedy – that turns French comic opera into something of a cross between spoken and sung drama, giving rise to an aesthetic problem that composers did not always succeed in solving. (For Italian composers, with their subtle sense of style, this was never a problem.[23]) German composers initially adopted the French solution in their singspiels, not opting for through-composed operas until much later. Although we find examples of accompanied recitatives (indeed, these recitatives

---

20. Ghosts are conjured up in Louis Anseaume's *Le soldat magicien* (1760) and Antoine-Alexandre-Henri Poinsinet's *Le sorcier* (1764), for example. Original musical parodies may be found in Charles Collé's *L'isle sonnante* (1767) and Grenier's *La mélomanie* (1781).

21. Even Goldoni concedes this point in his *Mémoires*, ii.227ff.

22. ◆ On Sedaine, see Gisi, *Sedaine: Sein Leben und sein Werk*; Günther, *L'œuvre dramatique de Sedaine*; Arnoldson, *Sedaine et les musiciens de son temps*; Charlton and Ledbury, *Michel Sedaine, 1719–1797: Theatre, Opera and Art*. Concerning Marmontel, see n.72 below.

23. Grimm declares this mixture of dialogue and singing to be barbaric in the extreme; *Correspondance littéraire, philosophique et critique*, iv.166, vi.120, 209.

take up more and more room under Italian influence), they appear only at critical junctures and, as with the Italians, are tragically measured in tone, a tone that French composers continued to maintain even after they had arrogated the Italians' greater freedom of expression. A further survival of the age of the vaudeville, at least during the first decade of the new genre's existence, is the inclusion of numerous songs whose tunes could be assumed to be familiar to the audience, with the result that they were not printed in the published scores: instead, only their opening line or some other marker was given such as 'Air: Tous vos apprêts', 'Air des échos italiens' or 'Menuet de Dardanus'.[24] Only with Grétry do these songs disappear. Also included under this heading are the regular final ensembles described as 'vaudevilles', popular rounds in which the individual characters each sing a strophe illustrating the moral of the piece alternating with a refrain sung by all and generally containing the actual moral.[25] But the other vocal numbers, too, breathe a popular, folklike spirit. They are generally described as *ariettes*.[26] Subdivisions include the romance, a tender, elegiac love song; the chanson, which with its barbed and epigrammatical jibes still clearly recalls the old satirical street songs; and especially the songs that are narrative in character, either captivating little numbers in the style of folk ballads (Pedrillo's serenade from *Die Entführung aus dem Serail*, for example, belongs under this heading) or graphic accounts of real events, a speciality of French comic operas that survived until relatively recently.

The form of these songs extends from simple strophic settings to the large-scale *da capo* aria modelled on that of the Italians. Particularly popular was a type of song derived from the old *ballet de cour*, with a main section in the major combined with a subsidiary section in the minor, followed by a repeat of the main section, in short, the form of the old French rondeau that we have already encountered in instrumental music.

Songs for two, three or more voices are particularly well represented. Here, too, clarity of musical form was especially close to the hearts of French composers, with the result that they generally avoid the multisectional finales of Italian *opere buffe* with their numerous subdivisions. And it is clear from many of these numbers that they are conceived and designed along musical, rather than dramatic, lines. Alongside such numbers, however, we also find as many movements that handle their form with real dramatic freedom and acquire a degree of animation superior to that of the average Italian work. Among traditional devices is one whereby a father begins by striking a note of dignified calm, only for his high-spirited daughter to interrupt him with her rhythmically lively chatter after a few bars. In the ensemble passages, too, the individual characters and groups are distinguished in the liveliest manner imaginable thanks to the use of extraordinarily varied rhythms. The highly effective combination of solo, ensemble and chorus that was typical of tragic opera from the time of Rameau was also exploited to the full by the composers of comic operas. The chorus, too, was represented here, for all that its role was initially not dramatic but intended only to provide a superficial background in the form of peasants', huntsmen's and soldiers' choruses. Not even ballets were entirely excluded.[27]

The roots of this vocal style may be found in the dance song and in the closely related popular songs cultivated by the French middle classes. It drew its peculiar strength from its use of rhythm, and here *opéra comique* achieved a far greater range of expression than may be found in the works

24. These examples are taken from Philidor's setting of Anseaume's *Le soldat magicien* of 1760.
25. This was also a favourite place for all manner of satirical allusions.
26. Hence the older terminology according to which the work as a whole was described as a 'comédie mêlée d'ariettes', while a duet was an 'ariette dialoguée'. ◆ See Bouissou, 'Ariette'; and Couvreur and Vendrix, 'Les enjeux théoriques de l'opéra-comique'.
27. A large-scale ballet is found in act three, scene five of Duni's *La fée Urgèle* of 1765.

of any other nation. Often enough it is still possible to hear in these numbers the older dance types such as the gavotte and menuet. That this posed the danger of imbalance was recognized by composers themselves, who sought to breathe more individual life into their vocal numbers by dint of meaningful and pointed declamation in the finest French tradition. But it was only under the growing influence of the Italians that French composers began to write melodic lines of noticeably greater breadth. Traditionally, their melodies were strictly syllabic, admitting of only very brief melismas at best, and while passages of coloratura may be found in the subsequent course of the number, their aim is invariably to add a touch of tone-painterly colour and generally also to instil a note of humour into the proceedings. They are never used in the wildly extravagant manner of the Italians. By contrast, the comic operas of the French followed the lead of tragic opera and found a particularly effective ally in the orchestra, developing the techniques of the *tragédie lyrique* to felicitous effect. Even in the works of composers such as Philidor and Monsigny, we not only find more independent writing for the violas, but the winds, too, speak a more individual language. Indeed, compared to the vocal line, the whole orchestra has far more to say than its Italian counterpart: above all, the listener is aware that music's chief function is 'to paint', to quote the then current view as espoused by writers such as Charles Batteux [1713–80].[28] Individual details in the text are lovingly coloured in by one or other of the instruments, but even large-scale orchestral canvases are found here, with the voice merely providing an explanatory programme. In short, the typically French love of picturesque detail characterizes this genre, too, and there is no lack of exotic, lively, elegiac and idyllic genre scenes of exceptional charm. The old trio episodes are invested with novel aspects, and we also find numbers that make use of pizzicato and *con sordino* effects and so on: in a word, the influence of Rameau's art of instrumentation is plain to hear. And *opéra comique*, especially from the time of Grétry, was also to prove of great historical importance in terms of its reintroduction of the old leitmotivic principle. Conversely, it was only later that an overture became a regular feature of these works. Most are single-movement pieces in first-movement sonata form, usually with a thematic development section (only rarely is it based on new material), clearly influenced by the Italian *buffa* model.[29] But we also find ternary movements in the Italian manner, with a minuet reminiscent of the *sonata da camera* in final position. The actual French overture, with its grave and allegro sections à la Lully and Rameau, is studiously avoided. On the other hand, the overture based on a free programme, drawing its ideas wholly or in part from the following opera or pursuing other poetical goals, now began to enjoy increasing popularity. With Grétry it was even incorporated into the opera, either by including singing while the curtain was still lowered or by being performed as incidental music with the curtain already raised. Here, then, we find the roots of the nineteenth-century programme overture. Finally, we also encounter the practice of entr'acte music, which consists either in the repetition of an earlier number or in new music of a programmatical kind designed to cover a scene change.[30] In short, the whole argument over entr'acte music, to which Lessing had already added his own contribution, was ultimately French in origin.

The composer essentially responsible for establishing *opéra comique* as a higher art form was, like Lully, an Italian by birth: Egidio Romualdo Duni (1708–75). After a string of operatic

28. ◆ See Becq, *Genèse de l'esthétique française moderne: De la raison classique à l'imagination créatrice, 1680–1815*; Modica, *Il sistema delle arti: Batteux e Diderot*; and Kintzler, *Poétique de l'opéra français de Corneille à Rousseau*.
29. An early example of a ternary-form overture (presto–andante–prestissimo) is that to Monsigny's *Les aveux discrets* (1759), a work described as an 'intermède'.
30. The first entr'acte of Philidor's *Tom Jones* (1765) is a repeat of the overture, the second his 'symphonie de nuit'. The first entr'acte of Monsigny's *Le roi et le fermier* (1762) is an *orage* that passes straight into the following act.

successes in his native Italy, he spent some time at the Francophile court in Parma before moving to Paris in 1757. Here his deep understanding of the French style enabled him to change the course of comic opera.[31] He abandoned its flightier aspects, including its tendency to court ephemeral success, and raised it to the level of a fully-fledged work of dramatic art by concentrating on a unified plot that proceeds along logical lines, with consistent characterization. Above all, the music was now placed entirely in the service of the drama. Duni's Italian background stood him in particularly good stead when it came to melodic invention,[32] although the brief but vivid motifs of Pergolesi's generation still continue to be found here.[33] Equally, he made use of the realistic *buffa* language of his fellow countrymen, but in deference to French taste he remained relatively sparing in its application, preferring dancelike melodies animated by lively declamation. A good example of the meaningful merger between the French and Italian styles is Follette's aria in act two, scene four of *L'isle des foux* [1760]:

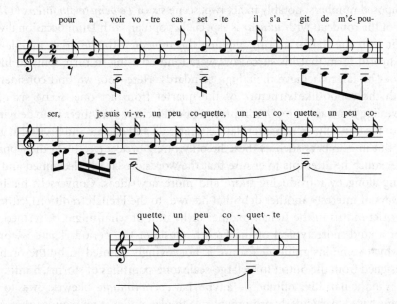

Duni was a master of musical characterization, and it is easy to see why he was so attracted by the rogues' gallery of *L'isle des foux*. But the more serious character of the squire Lahire in *La fée Urgèle* (1765) is no less impressive as a fully-rounded character, a comic combination of grim loathing of his profession and secret pride at the adventures that he has known in the course of it. As such, he is an important precursor of Leporello.[34] Candor in *Les moissonneurs* (1768) is a typical example of one of the landed gentry of the day and is far more convincingly portrayed and

31. In his foreword to *Le peintre amoureux* (1757) Duni rails against Rousseau's thesis that the French language is unsingable, adding that he himself honours it as 'la langue qui m'a fourni de la mélodie, du sentiment et des images'. He also draws Rousseau's attention to the fact that *Le devin du village* contradicts the composer's own doctrine. ◆ See Kent Maynard Smith, 'Egidio Duni and the Development of the Opéra-Comique from 1753 to 1770'; Isherwood, *Farce and Fantasy: Popular Entertainment in Eighteenth-Century Paris*; and Artuso, *Monsieur Egidio Romualdo Duni tra scuola napoletana e opéra-comique*.
32. Coloratura writing, too, is more common in Duni's works than in those of his successors.
33. There are still many reminiscences of *La serva padrona* not only in Duni's works but also in those of Philidor and Monsigny and even of the young Grétry.
34. See Kretzschmar, 'Mozart in der Geschichte der Oper', ii.267. Even the words of his first aria recall Lorenzo Da Ponte: 'Trouver un objet friand, / N'y toucher qu'avec un gand, / Sans pain, sans vin vivre de gloire, / Passer chaque nuit et tout le jour sans boire, / Trouver son bien pris et sa douce amie, / Voilà les profits de la chevalerie.'

invested with far greater dignity than in Favart's stilted libretto.[35] Only exceptionally does Duni's sense of humour extend to caricature: there is something restrained and often morose about him, with the result that the two boastful milksops in *Les deux chasseurs* (1763) are among his most successful characters. But he is also adept at expressing a sense of heartfelt lament: here he was helped by the elegiac and vaguely exotic *sicilianas* of his native Italy.

To a large extent, Duni's works owe their effectiveness to their astonishing formal variety and flexibility. Here, too, we see the influence of the Italian school. Not only is he conversant with all its different forms, from the simple binary chanson to the *da capo* aria and larger, composite forms, but he uses them in meaningful ways in the service of the drama.[36] How wittily, for example, rondo form is used in Sordide's aria in act one, scene four of *L'isle des foux* to suggest the fool's recurrent *idée fixe*. Much the same is true of strophic and aria form, with both displaying a freedom and flexibility that Duni's successors did not always manage to achieve. We even find through-composed numbers, notably in act two, scene six of *Le peintre amoureux* (1757). The old French form of the rondeau with *mineur* is especially popular, with Duni occasionally attempting to combine it with the Italian aria by aligning the *mineur* with the aria's middle section and producing a hybrid form that his successors were fond of using in turn. Only in his numerous ensembles does he fail to achieve their high standards. Here, too, we find considerable formal freedom, with the rondo-like structure of the quartet from act one, scene six of *Le peintre amoureux* revealing Duni as an important precursor of Piccinni. And there is no denying his adroit exploitation of the typically French interplay between solo and chorus and his skill at grouping the participants. But in numbers such as these he only rarely breaks free from their purely musical basis, however much he attempts to ensure that the words are clearly declaimed and to keep the drama flowing along by introducing more and more new ideas. Conversely, his instrumental writing is always of interest (another debt that he owes to the French tradition), either as a result of recurrent brief motifs in the Italian manner or by dint of what might be termed picturesque marginalia of a kind more typical of the French music of the period. There is barely a single number in which some insignificant feature is not lovingly painted in by the orchestra, while others are designed from the outset to be large-scale tone-paintings of storms, hunting scenes and so on. But it is in the narrative numbers – a type that *opéra comique* likewise owes to Duni – that the instruments have a particularly prominent role to play, and it is no wonder, therefore, that his orchestral writing, too, is highly progressive in character. Whole arias of an idyllic stamp are accompanied only by a trio of instruments, generally oboes or flutes with violins providing the bass line.[37] Elsewhere, too, we find wind solos aplenty, string writing with *con sordino* and pizzicato effects, crescendos and *demi jeu*, in which the orchestra is divided. In short, Duni showed the way ahead for composers of comic opera in almost every single respect.[38]

One of the leading chess players of his day, François-André Danican Philidor (1726–95)[39] was far more Italian than the Italian Duni. This is clear not so much from many of the formal and

---

35. As an idyllic *comédie larmoyante*, this work is a direct precursor of Monsigny's *Le déserteur*.
36. Even the *airs* that are not included in the printed libretto but whose words and music are assumed to be familiar to the audience are adapted to suit the course of the drama in question.
37. In act one, scene four of *Les deux chasseurs* (1763) there is even a bass aria.
38. The overture to *Le peintre amoureux* is still reminiscent in character of the opening allegro of an Italian overture, while that of *Les deux chasseurs* is already an example of programme music, providing a link with the opening scene of the opera. For all its wealth of detail, Grimm's opinion of Duni is relatively superficial: *Correspondance littéraire*, iv.164–5, 414, v.140, 369, vi.63, vii.126. ◆ Further, see Charles E. Koch, 'The Dramatic Ensemble Finale in the Opéra Comique of the Eighteenth Century'.
39. ◆ See Brian Harley, 'Music and Chess'; and Rollin, *Philidor: Il musicista che giocava a scacchi*.

especially melodic features that his works contain, nor even from the important role played by accompanied recitatives and by his fastidiously noisy ritornellos with their two contrasting themes, but especially from what, by French standards, was his pronounced predilection for caricature and for the Italianate means used to express it. Philidor possessed a particularly well-developed streak of realism and was fond of depicting situations and characters in relatively earthy terms, not shying away from even fairly coarse burlesque effects. There is an impish humour to the way in which he introduces such lifelike figures as a coachman constantly cracking his whip,[40] a braggart soldier whose warlike actions are recalled in a martial coda to his aria,[41] much as in Mozart's *Le nozze di Figaro*, a working smith with bellows and hammer motifs,[42] and so on. Even falsetto singing[43] and the inarticulate stammer of a woman unable to speak à la Papageno[44] are depicted with comic realism. It is hardly surprising, therefore, to find that his parodies of serious operas – especially those of Rameau – are particularly grotesque in character.[45] Needless to say, it is the orchestra that is used to create these portraits, its painterly function employed to novel and telling effect.[46]

This desire to depict the individual characters in a mere handful of brush strokes (for all that those strokes are generally exaggerated) prompted Philidor to undertake an important step and extend his ensembles and at the same time to invest them with greater depth. That there are far more such ensembles in Philidor's works than in Duni's is immediately apparent, but their most progressive feature lies, rather, in the fact that Philidor's keen dramatic eye detected a whole series of potential ensembles in his texts that his predecessors had failed to notice. Even in his duets[47] we already find him striving to distinguish between his characters as sharply as possible (in this respect his duets could hardly be more different from Scarlatti's), and the contrastive motifs that are used in this way are generally retained until the end of the number in question. But Philidor avoids the multisectional ensembles of the Italian composers of the period: ensembles with three independent sections are already the exception, and as a rule he prefers ternary aria form or rondo form, both of which are handled with considerable freedom. At the same time, however, his attempts to ensure that the dramatic situation and *dramatis personae* are sharply characterized have resulted in a highly advanced and effective dramatic polyphony that finds expression in all manner of quick-witted imitations and affords brilliant proof of his technical skills as a composer. Particularly popular is the canon, the older form of the *geselliges Lied*, and in act three, scene one of *Tom Jones* – a picturesque tavern scene involving four drunkards – we even find an unprecedented *a cappella* canon for four tenors.[48] In this way, Philidor succeeds in creating extraordinarily gripping ensembles while remaining within the framework of lucid musical form.[49] He is no less

---

40. In act two, scene two of *Le maréchal ferrant* (1761).
41. In scene one of *Le soldat magicien* (1760).
42. In act one, scene one of *Le maréchal ferrant*.
43. The voice of the frightened Blaise is heard to tremble in the grotesque conjuration scene in act two, scene seven of *Le sorcier* (1764), while Julien imitates the voices of the imagined ghosts in every vocal register – voix de fausset, de basse, de hautecontre and du nez.
44. In the septet in scene eighteen of *Le bûcheron* (1763).
45. In scene fourteen of *Le soldat magicien* and act two, scene seven of *Le sorcier*.
46. Under this heading come all manner of bird calls and other voices of nature such as a braying ass (act one, scene ten of *Le maréchal ferrant*), the sound of skittles (scene ten of *Sancho Pança*, 1762), large-scale hunting scenes (act one, scene three of *Tom Jones*), the sound of pealing bells (act one, scene three of *Le maréchal ferrant*) and so on.
47. The very first number of his first opera, *Blaise le savetier* (1759), is proof of this.
48. Equally witty is the canon scene for the creditors in scene eight of *Le bûcheron*.
49. A good example is the quintet in scene seventeen of *Le jardinier et son seigneur* (1761).

successful, finally, in exploiting the comic potential inherent in the interplay between solo and ensemble or chorus.[50]

Philidor's melodic writing is heartfelt, lively and full of surprising features, chief of which is his fondness for Phrygian scales, even though his real strength lies not so much in the tender and serious as in the comic and coarse. Here he is much influenced by the Italians and, in his later tendency to go to the very limits of what is permissible, by Gluck.[51] Italianate, too, are his sudden shifts between major and minor, which he exploits with remarkable wit.[52] But even in his own particular field, he succeeds in creating a number of original ideas that were later to leave their mark on Mozart. Take, for example, the sullen unison melodic writing of the trio in scene six of *Sancho Pança*:

Or consider his predilection for motifs that begin broadly, only to break off abruptly, as in act one, scene three of *Le maréchal ferrant*:[53]

Note, finally, the use of chromaticisms in act two, scene one of *Zémire et Mélide*, which are far more prominent than they had been with Duni. Typically French are the dance songs,[54] among which chansons and romances are now increasingly common. Especially noteworthy is his fondness for gavotte rhythms. In his arias, Philidor also favours ternary form with a change of tempo and varied *da capo*, although the French rondeau is also a popular form with him.[55] His works almost always end with a vaudeville in the form of a simple, dancelike solo song with a refrain for the whole company. The individual participants sing either the same tune or new *mineur* episodes. In certain cases, the final verse is followed by a complete choral refrain motivically related to what

50. As in scene four of *Sancho Pança*, where various artisans, delivery men and so on wait upon the man they assume to be the governor, with the portrayal of the pompous tailor adding a particularly delightful touch.

51. Reminiscences of *Orfeo* occur in act one, scene six of *Le sorcier* and in Clitandre's scene (no. 3) in *L'amant déguisé* (1769). Equally Gluckian is the aria in act one, scene one of *Zémire et Mélide* (1773). In his serious opera *Ernelinde* (1767) he is even guilty of plagiarism.

52. There are good examples in scenes five and eight of *L'amant déguisé*.

53. Cf. the opening allegro of Mozart's wind serenade in B flat major K361.

54. In Clitandre's song in scene eight of *L'amant déguisé*, Philidor dispenses with any accompaniment.

55. In act one, scene one of *Le sorcier*, even the ritornello is divided into major and minor sections.

has gone before. But it is in his accompanied recitatives and their generally elaborate orchestral passages that Philidor reveals his greatest advances over his predecessors.[56]

In contrast to Philidor's coarse-grained virility we find in Pierre-Alexandre Monsigny (1729–1817) a composer of a far more sensitive and feminine nature.[57] It was with Monsigny that the playwright Michel-Jean Sedaine (1719–97) chose to collaborate. His reputation has suffered badly at the hands of a writer like Grimm, who accused him of dilettantism,[58] but whose dismissive opinion was as wide of the mark as it was with Philidor and Duni. Monsigny's first opera, *Les aveux indiscrets* (1759), is historically important as an admittedly unique attempt to adapt the style of the *tragédie lyrique* to that of comic opera. The dialogue is through-composed as 'récitatif obligé'; ballet plays a significant role; and the arias have something austere and archaic about them.[59] Later, too, contrapuntal procedures are prominent, although they are not used as a dramatic device in the way that Philidor had used them, but as a purely musical way of adding spice to the musical textures. Indeed, Monsigny sometimes even writes regular fugues, including one – in act two, scene ten of *Le déserteur* (1769) – based on a much older theme that is also familiar from Mozart:

O ciel quoi? tu vas mou - rir!   O ciel, quoi? tu vas mou - rir!

But Philidor's cheeky dramatic contrasts are only rarely found in Monsigny's ensembles, where the purely musical underpinning remains more or less visible throughout, and if these numbers are dramatic in character, they generally owe this quality not to their part-writing, but to their highly effective design, to the interplay between solo and chorus, their exciting rhythms and melodic writing and, above all, to Monsigny's original and independent treatment of the orchestra. Thanks to Monsigny, the formal range of *opéra comique* was considerably increased at this time. Although he, too, sets out from the chanson, rondeau and aria and is often clearly concerned to achieve maximal brevity and concision, there are other occasions where he attempts to breathe life into the form and expand it from within, an aim in which he is particularly helped by the art of variation. Elsewhere he strives to combine individual numbers by means of accompanied recitatives, independent orchestral movements and so on, creating larger complexes and in that way achieving a sense of large-scale form.[60] It was Monsigny who played the most decisive role

56. In scene fifteen of *Sancho Pança*, there is a constant interplay between battle music and pastoral music. Grimm was unable to make up his mind about Philidor: see his *Correspondance littéraire*, ii.346, iii.401, vi.14, 145 and xii.468. He was particularly critical of Philidor's relations with Gluck: *Correspondance littéraire*, ix.378. ◆ Further concerning Philidor, see Bonnet, *Philidor et l'évolution de la musique française au XVIIIe siècle*; Rushton, 'Philidor and the Tragédie Lyrique'; Vendrix, *L'opéra-comique en France au XVIIIe siècle*; and *Recherches sur la musique française classique* (Philidor issue).

57. ◆ See Druilhe, *Monsigny*; Heartz, 'The Beginnings of Operatic Romance: Rousseau, Sedaine, and Monsigny'; Charlton, *Grétry and the Growth of Opéra-Comique*; and Pendle, 'L'opéra-comique à Paris de 1762 à 1789'.

58. Grimm, *Correspondance littéraire*, iii.136, vi.208, ix.463. He ascribes all Monsigny's good points to his librettist Sedaine. The composer's cause was championed, conversely, by Genlis in her *Mémoires inédits pour servir à l'histoire des dix-huitième et dix-neuvième siècles*, ii.21–2.

59. Under this heading come the carefully figured bass, the archaizing bass line and the reminiscences of Handel in act one, scenes one and four.

60. In act one, scene ten of *Le roi et le fermier* [1762], the three strophes of the duet are repeatedly interrupted by the lowering storm, which reaches its climax during the entr'acte after the curtain has fallen and which does not abate until the duet in act two, scene one. Also relevant in this context are not only the great final scene in act three of *Le déserteur*, in the second half of which rondo form is cleverly used, but also the rondo-like ending of *La belle Arsène* of 1773. The interplay between soli and tutti is especially effective in act three, scene twelve of *Félix* (1777).

in bringing *opéra comique* closer to the *comédie larmoyante*, while at the same time attempting to mitigate its sentimentality by investing it with greater depth and emotion. In this he was helped, above all, by his rich and original melodic vein. Although this vein also included a certain number of *buffa* elements, Monsigny none the less managed to create an independent melodic style whose great strength lies in its ability to express gracefulness, dreaminess and wistfulness. Here we find a clearly recognizable link between Monsigny and Mozart, especially the Mozart of *Die Entführung aus dem Serail*, a link that finds expression less in individual reminiscences such as the following[61]

61. The Cadi's *ariette* in act one, scene six of *Le cadi dupé* (1761) and Eleonore's *ariette* from scene ten of *Le faucon* (1771). Monsigny was particularly fond of the performance marking 'amoroso'.

ce qu'il a dans l'â - me

than in more general characteristics such as roguish warm-heartedness and heartful infatuation. In this context, Belmonte and Blonde are clearly prefigured by Durbin in *L'isle sonnante* (1767), another opera about an abduction, and by Eleonore in *Le faucon* (1771).[62]

This light-hearted aspect of Monsigny's music finds expression in powerfully arresting rhythms and occasionally achieves a momentum reminiscent of Beethoven. All the more remarkable, then, is the fact that it is coupled with a note of contemplation and even of pensive brooding. And it is here that, of all the French opera composers, Monsigny comes closest to Mozart. Even the means of expression employed by both composers are related, namely, the characteristic and often completely unexpected use of a minor tonality, harsh chromaticisms and solid syncopations. An example from Célénie's scene in *L'isle sonnante* may serve to make this clear:

---

62. ◆ Concerning Mozart and Monsigny in particular, see Ernst Fritz Schmid, 'Mozart und Monsigny'.

The tendency for the mood to shift within the narrowest possible confines signifies a great advance on Duni and Philidor and was another feature that was bound to attract Mozart to this music. That the origin of this development is probably to be sought in instrumental music, and almost certainly in Stamitz himself,[63] is suggested by the fact that in Monsigny's case it is above all the independent orchestral part that reveals this innovation. With the exception of the symphonies of the Mannheim school, there are no other scores at this time in which the dynamics are so carefully and so consistently marked as they are in Monsigny's. These scores literally teem with large- and small-scale crescendos and diminuendos (including ones affecting only single notes), sforzatos and sudden entries marked *fortissimo* or *pianissimo*, and so on. Even the overture of *Les aveux indiscrets* (1759) includes a large-scale crescendo culminating in a fermata at the end of the development section. And as in all similar overtures, the main theme returns at the end of the recapitulation 'en diminuant'. In the later works we occasionally find crescendos covering an entire strophe (scene nine of *Rose et Colas* [1764]), diminuendos that bring a large-scale, agitated scene to a *pianissimo* close (act one, scene sixteen of *Félix*) and, finally, the brief crescendos which, half violent, half nervous, occur before the return to the main theme and that are also found in a number of Mozart's works. In the main, all these devices are used to depict the outward situation, but many also have a psychological function. The following example of Monsigny's treatment of his orchestra from act two, scene eight of *L'isle sonnante* inevitably recalls the eerie scales of *Don Giovanni*:

Or take the following canon between vocal line and bass in act three, scene five of *La belle Arsène*:

O dieux, est - il pos - si - ble   que

---

63. Remarkably, this principal ally of the Mannheimers in Paris is only fleetingly mentioned by Riemann, *Präludien und Studien: Gesammelte Aufsätze zur Ästhetik, Theorie und Geschichte der Musik.* If this hypothesis is true, Gossec would not be alone in borrowing from Stamitz.

Monsigny's scores demand to be performed with extreme care. They contain a large number of picturesque orchestral scenes of every description and, in consequence, an impressive array of novel colouristic devices.[64] It is not only that the writing for the violas is almost always independent of the basses and that for the cellos frequently so, but that pizzicato effects are used in entirely new and picturesque ways.[65] Equally novel is the concertante writing for winds and strings. Following Duni's example, whole arias are accompanied only by a trio comprising a wind instrument and both violins. Monsigny is particularly fond of the bassoon as a solo instrument, but he also uses the piccolo in a highly characteristic manner.[66]

In short, Monsigny's operas are varied in the extreme, not least because he also makes extensive use of accompanied recitatives,[67] while the traditional range of forms is treated in the freest possible way, often including brief recitatives. In all these areas, Philidor was the more vivid and, in terms of musical characterization, the more significant of the two, but Monsigny was the more intimate and, above all, the more modern with his love of more complex psychological problems. In keeping with the older French tradition, the instruments of the orchestra had already played a relatively important role in the works of Duni and Philidor, but in Monsigny's operas they speak a far more progressive language that reflects the stylistic changes that were taking place at this time. This also emerges from the great care that he lavishes on his entr'actes and overtures. As we have already noted, a number of these entr'actes are already drawn into the action. In most cases, however, they draw their material from a particularly significant vocal number and repeat it in a different, ear-catching instrumentation. Monsigny attaches far more weight to his overtures than

64.   Even so, the continuo is prescribed in virtually all Monsigny's operas.
65.   Notably in the night scene in act two, scene six of *Le maître en droit* (1760) and in Lise's account of the monk's song in scene eight of *On ne s'avise jamais de tout* (1761).
66.   In act three, scene one of *Le roi et le fermier* and in scene six of *Le faucon* (1771).
67.   Mostly, they are extremely intelligently combined with the following aria, as in act two, scene two of *Le roi et le fermier*. An example of a recitative becoming increasingly melodic may be found in act three, scene five of *La belle Arsène* (1773).

Philidor had done. Some are single-movement numbers, others are in three sections, some are independent, others programmatical and linked to the opera.[68] With its mass of colourful ideas and anticipation of the opera's finale, the overture to *Le déserteur*, for example, already looks forward to the programmatical potpourri overtures of the nineteenth century.

A new chapter in the history of the *opéra comique* begins with André-Ernest Modeste Grétry (1741–1813), who was born in Liège and who studied in Rome, before settling in Paris and, from 1768 until well into the Napoleonic era, writing a whole series of brilliant *opéras comiques* that proved lastingly successful not only in France but in Germany, too.[69] Jahn's claim[70] that it was only under Grétry that *opéra comique* became the true representative of the French national character in music for the stage fails to do justice to the achievements of Philidor and Monsigny, but there is no doubt that it was Grétry who substantially extended the genre's range of subjects, while consolidating its internal structure and clarifying its goals. Grétry was far more conscious of what he was trying to achieve than his predecessors had been.[71] Although his thinking often lacked the ultimate in clarity, he was an exceptionally multifaceted and thoughtful individual whose mind teemed with ideas that were not to be realized until a much later date: here one thinks, for example, of the covered orchestra, the symphonic poem and the reform of singing in schools. If his music had been as profound as it was broadly based, he would have been an artist of the first order. But his talent did not extend to the darker sides of human existence, while as a person he lacked clarity and decisiveness, in spite of all his new ideas. Yet of all the musicians in Paris at this time, Grétry had the keenest ear for the numerous new demands made of the operatic stage by Rousseau and the *encyclopédistes*. In Jean-François Marmontel (1723–99) he found a gifted and like-minded poet.[72] Both were genuinely convinced of the truth of the new gospel and proved honest advocates of the new faith in humanity that currently captivated the whole of civilized society. But they were no longer satisfied with operatic subjects drawn from the workaday bourgeois world and instead had recourse to literary themes and, to a lesser extent, to ideas already adumbrated in operas of the earlier period. The most important of these new subjects were Romantic in the sense that they introduced an element of magic:[73] a work whose tremendous success has ensured it a place in the annals of opera and whose influence was to be felt most lastingly in the world of the German singspiel was *Zémire et Azor* of 1771, one of the principal forebears of later 'Romantic' opera, even though the differences between the two should not be underestimated. After all, even this fairy-tale opera is an unmistakable offshoot of the spirit of

68. In *Le roi et le fermier*, the opening aria, with its varied motifs, forms the third section of the overture.
69. See Brenet, *Grétry*; and Curzon, *Grétry*. ◆ Also see Clercx, *Grétry, 1741–1813*; Froidcourt, *La correspondance générale de Grétry*; Lenoir, *Documents Grétry dans les collections de la Bibliothèque Royale Albert 1er* and *Grétry: Lettres autographes conservées à la Bibliothèque Royale Albert 1er*; Hasquin and Mortier, *Fêtes et musiques révolutionnaires: Grétry et Gossec*; and Vendrix, *Grétry et l'Europe de l'opéra-comique*.
70. Jahn, *W. A. Mozart*, fourth edition, i.507.
71. His reminiscences and views on art may be found in his *Mémoires, ou Essais sur la musique*, the first volume of which was published in Paris in 1789. All three volumes appeared in 1797 and were reprinted in Brussels in 1829. Karl Spazier published excerpts, with some additions of his own, in Leipzig in 1800 under the title *Grétrys Versuche über die Musik*. Although the work is not free of vanity and superficiality, it leaves a powerful impression thanks to the wealth of its ideas and the vividness of its descriptions. ◆ For a modern edition, see Grétry, *Memoiren: oder, Essays über die Musik*.
72. ◆ See Ehrard, *De l'Encyclopédie à la contre-révolution: Jean-François Marmontel (1723–1799): études réunies*; Pendle, 'The Opéras Comiques of Grétry and Marmontel'; Cardy, *The Literary Doctrines of Marmontel*; Kaplan, 'Marmontel et "Polymnie"'; and Niderst, 'Marmontel et la musique'.
73. 'Romantic' is used here in the traditional sense of the opposite of 'Classical'. Essentially, even the older type of opera, with its fondness for the miraculous, was Romantic in character, especially when it avoided subjects drawn from classical antiquity. But works such as Gluck's *Orfeo* and *Armide* were particularly close to Romanticism in their overall outlook.

Rousseau, a spirit whose ideal was no longer sought in the uncultured world of ordinary people but in a purely imaginary universe.[74] Even the element of magic is often no more than an extra ingredient grafted on from the outside, and there is certainly no sense of foreboding or subjectivity here, while even the scenes of nature remain firmly within the existing framework of picturesque local colour. There is still no question of nature as a living force. Of considerable importance, by contrast, is the principal motif, whereby a curse-laden individual on whom a magic spell has been cast is released from that spell by the true love of a young woman, a motif especially popular with the German singspiel and central to the librettos of many later operas. Grétry took a further important step with *Richard Cœur-de-lion* (1784), to a libretto by Jean-Michel Sedaine, which tells of King Richard's adventurous rescue after many years of captivity. As such, it is a prototype of the *Schreckensopern*[75] that enjoyed particular popularity during the Revolution as a reflection of the bloody events that were taking place in the world at this time. An echo of it may still be found in Beethoven's *Fidelio*.

It was not only to these innovations that Grétry owed his immense and lasting success, but also to his own musical gifts. He was far more multifaceted than his two predecessors and, above all, was able to invest the emotional language of his time with a natural and (in the best sense of the term) popular form of expression. The seething passion of the Revolutionary period was no less integral to his work than its sentimental effusions, an aspect which, in Grétry's case, occasionally degenerates into mawkish sentimentality. These were features which, in the minds of contemporary audiences, more than made up for his lack of talent and of true greatness and depth. After all, they were joined by a further advantage that was particularly important to French audiences, an extraordinarily lively dramatic imagination that rarely let him down. Grétry was able to invest his subjects with original and gripping situations; his characters are drawn from life; and thanks to his careful setting of the text, he brings to the popular style a genuinely dramatic spirit. In the case of his melodies, too, we can concur with Johann Abraham Peter Schulz[76] when he writes of the 'semblance of familiarity': thanks to the way in which music and poetry are merged, these melodies spring effortlessly and naturally from the singers' lips, while at the same time revealing all the iridescent melodic and rhythmic delights of the French chanson.

This produces a wonderful flexibility in Grétry's handling of musical form. Although he added little to existing forms, remaining content to explore song forms, aria forms and, in his own particular case, the binary Italian *buffa* aria, he handles them with a degree of dramatic freedom, especially in his later works, that sometimes makes it hard to recognize the old outlines. In particular, he is fond of combining the ternary Italian aria with the French rondeau (with *mineur*): many of the middle sections of his arias are in the minor and are also of considerable length, whereas the *da capo* is frequently much curtailed. But even where this is not the case, the *da capo* is varied either vocally or instrumentally, generally building to an extremely effective climax; in addition, the order of the themes is sometimes changed, or else the existing ones are extended, brief new episodes introduced and so on. In a word, Mozart could learn a great deal from Grétry in terms of

---

74. Under this heading come the remote nations such as the Hurons in *Le Huron* (1768) and the Middle Ages in *Aucassin et Nicolette* (1779), a work significantly subtitled 'Les mœurs du bon vieux tems'. Both these works are precursors of the exoticism and courtly Romanticism found in operas of the later period.

75. See Kretzschmar, 'Über die Bedeutung Cherubinis für die Gegenwart', ii.340.

76. ◆ Schulz (1747–1800) was largely responsible for the music articles from S to Z in Sulzer, *Allgemeine Theorie der schönen Künste*.

the flexibility of his musical language. In his later works in particular we often find that the middle movement of an aria is an accompanied recitative or even an orchestral number involving mime. And whereas the older types of song such as the romance had always seemed more or less like interpolations, however great the attempt to take account of the outward situation, they now emerge naturally from the dramatic context.[77] Indeed, Blondel's song in *Richard Cœur-de-lion* is repeated so often and at so many salient points that it becomes the main idea of the opera, with Grétry using the technique of the reminiscence motif far more logically and dramatically than Italian composers such as Piccinni had done. Here, too, then, Grétry was to prove particularly important for nineteenth-century music in general.[78] In the course of the genre's development, finally, we find an increasing number of large-scale scenes freely made up of recitative, solo songs, ensembles, choruses and independent orchestral movements, all of which largely anticipate the standpoint of composers such as Boieldieu, Adam and Auber. It is not to belittle the merits of his predecessors to claim that it was Grétry who ultimately raised *opéra comique* from the world of the petit-bourgeois singspiel and invested it with higher aims. For a time, at least, he even attempted to set the dialogue in a way that was through-composed, but soon abandoned this idea.[79] Conversely, he was never interested in interpolating well-known songs.

That Grétry's five years of apprenticeship in Italy left a profound mark on his art is clear not only from the formal design of many of his arias but also from their melodic writing. It is not difficult to single out certain turns of phrase and cadential forms popular with southern composers.[80] Indeed, there are even times when the Italian style is parodied to delightful effect.[81] Far more important, however, are the greater verve and breadth of Grétry's melodies, which break down the fixed framework of French dance rhythms and point to Italy. Conversely, he is relatively sparing in his use of the realistic language of Italian *opera buffa*. By the same token, caricature and parody are found even less frequently in his own works than in those of his predecessors.[82] Yet these Italian features cannot disguise the underlying Frenchness of his works. Here, too, this consists in his use of much earlier types of song, except that, as we have already noted, they are imbued with the spirit of drama. Mozart frequently comes close to Grétry in his unadulterated folklike tone, as in the two following examples:[83]

---

77. Note Bredau's curiously sultry soldier's song in act two, scene two of *Aucassin et Nicolette* (1779).

78. Cf. the call of the cockerel and vulture in *La fausse magie* of 1775. ◆ Further, see Vendrix, *L'opéra-comique en France au XVIIIe siècle*; Koch, 'The Dramatic Ensemble Finale in the Opéra Comique of the Eighteenth Century'; and Charlton, *Grétry and the Growth of Opéra-Comique*.

79. *Colinette à la cour* (1782), *L'embarras des richesses* (1782) and *La caravane du Caire* (1783) are through-composed, but spoken dialogue returns in *Richard Cœur-de-lion* (1784) and *Panurge* (1785).

80. In Linval's aria in scene thirteen of *La fausse magie*, we even find a reminiscence of Paisiello (see above):

81. Notably in Juliette's aria in act one, scene six of *L'amitié à l'épreuve* (1770) and in the Italian Woman's aria in act two, scene five of *La caravane du Caire*.

82. In *Le jugement de Midas* (1778), Marsyas imitates the style of *tragédie lyrique* in the 'goût de nos aïeux', while Pan sings in the style of a popular song and Apollo votes in favour of natural singing as found in *opéra comique*.

83. The first is from act three, scene four of *L'amitié à l'épreuve*, the second from act three, scene three of *L'amant jaloux*.

The typically French melodic line with rapid repeated notes has left its mark on his writing. The first-act finale of *L'amant jaloux* [*Les fausses apparences*] of 1778, for example, includes a situation closely related to the one found in *Le nozze di Figaro*, where one of the characters, jealous by nature, demands that a closet be opened in which he suspects a rival to be hidden. When the door is opened, the general surprise finds expression as follows:

Neither these nor similar reminiscences should be regarded as conscious borrowings, of course, but merely as evidence of Mozart's growing affinity with *opéra comique*. Even so, he was profoundly indebted to Grétry in terms of his melodic writing, a debt evident not only from his vocal works but from his instrumental compositions as well. His gift for striking a folklike and, at the same time, dramatic note, to say nothing of the melodic and, more especially, rhythmic flexibility of his musical language, both found active encouragement here. It is significant that Mozart was particularly impressed, on the one hand, by the fresh-toned, charming aspect of Grétry's music and, on the other, by its heartfelt, melancholic strain. It was unlikely, by contrast, that he would find much genuine large-scale emotion and passion in a composer who was relatively feeble and lacking in independence in this regard.[84] Nor did he follow Grétry in watering down the folk-like element and turning it into something insipid and philistine.[85] But neither did he adopt another of Grétry's characteristics: the curiously highly charged and urgent melodies, generally in equal note-values and simply but powerfully harmonized, that left such a profound mark on

---

84. The only number that could be included under this heading is Eumene's solemn bass aria in act three, scene six of the second version of *Les mariages samnites* (1776), with its exploitation of the singer's lowest register.
85. Grétry helped to popularize a sentimental melodic type that was later to be widely used, the eleven-syllable line with a three-quaver anacrusis and feminine ending (as in the line 'Denkst Du daran, mein tapfrer Lagienka'); cf. the duet in scene four of *Silvain* (known in Germany as *Erast und Lucinde*) of 1770.

Beethoven.[86] In the final chorus of *Raoul Barbe-bleue* (1789) we can even feel the hot breath of the *Marseillaise* on our necks.

At the same time, Grétry uses realistic devices to create a sense of tension: note, for example, the rests that he introduces at particularly critical junctures[87] (in this, too, he looks forward to Beethoven); the tendency to declaim on a single note;[88] and especially the expressively declaimed but very brief adagio passages that generally precede the recapitulation in his allegros and that are frequently found in Mozart's works, too. Grétry introduces coloratura procedures more frequently than his predecessors, but they are used to excess only in numbers that are either clearly Italianate or parodistic in character. His melodic writing is at its most felicitous when he seeks to render simple, natural feelings, but, like Duni, he is also adept at expressing a sullen, slightly sinister type of humour[89] and at depicting female *préciosité*.[90] Only in the case of the two areas to which his wider range of subjects led him, the Romantic and the exotic, did he not infrequently fail to find the right tone.[91]

But it was for his extended ensembles that the younger generation of composers and especially Mozart had particular reason to be grateful to Grétry. Although many of these numbers are still purely musical even in Grétry's case, they are none the less well adapted to suit the dramatic situation: here one thinks, for example, of the delightful trio for the three daughters awaiting their father's return in act two, scene one of *Zémire et Azor*. In the genuinely dramatic numbers, by contrast, especially those in which the action moves forward, Grétry achieves a flexibility and freedom of form far superior to anything found in any of his predecessors' works. The individual characters are sharply distinguished from each other, and Grétry reveals a typically French sensitivity in choosing apposite moments at which to contrast soloists and ensemble and create groups. Song form, aria form and rondo form (with one or more episodes) are all treated with mounting freedom; old motifs are replaced by new ones when it is right for them to be replaced, but are then repeated at significant points; and song and declamation are sensibly kept apart, resulting in

86. One example is the ensemble in act three, scene four of *L'amitié à l'épreuve*:

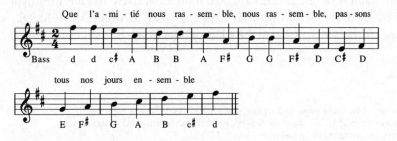

In Beethoven's case, this melodic type can still be found even in works such as the *Choral Fantasy* and the final movement of the ninth symphony.

87. In act three, scene five of *L'embarras des richesses* (1782).

88. As in the Gypsy's prophecy in scene fourteen of *La fausse magie* and the reading out of the letter in the first-act finale of *Les événemens imprévus* (1779).

89. Cf. the two heroes in *Les deux avares* (1770).

90. In act one, scene one of *L'ami de la maison* (1771) and act three, scene five of *Le magnifique* (1773).

91. There is little that is specifically exotic about the Arabs in act one of *La caravane du Caire*, for example. Conversely, the Romantic atmosphere is well caught in act two, scene five of *Richard Cœur-de-lion*.

extended ensemble scenes in which the earlier single-movement structure increasingly yields to a multisectional design. Here, of course, there is no mistaking the influence of the Italian *opera buffa* finale, an influence that is also apparent in the tendency to repeat earlier passages in varied form.[92] Grétry reveals particular skill at gradually building up these large-scale movements, initially beginning with an aria or duet, after which further voices enter at random, until we suddenly find ourselves dealing with a large-scale dramatic ensemble,[93] to which the chorus then adds its voices in a considerable number of cases.[94] In this frequent inclusion of the chorus, especially to depict the outward situation, French comic opera was markedly and undeniably superior to its Italian counterpart: far from using the chorus merely to produce fuller sonorities, it generally drew on it for genuinely dramatic effects.[95] Choruses become more numerous, especially in works such as *Colinette à la cour* (1782), which resembles a serious opera in other ways, too, notably in its inclusion of dances and recitative in place of spoken dialogue.[96] Initially Grétry simply took over the vaudeville as the final number, but from 1773 he dispenses with it in favour of freer ensembles. But in *La fausse magie* and *L'amant jaloux*, for example, he again adds a vaudeville as an individual element within a longer finale.[97]

In his accompanied recitatives, too, Grétry largely follows earlier French models, although his later works, in particular, include Italian turns of phrase, notably at cadential points. The declamation is razor-sharp and vivid, and even performance markings are found here from time to time.[98] But, in order not to weary his listeners, Grétry, too, is fond of including brief dance numbers in his recitatives, another French practice that can still be found in Meyerbeer's works. We have already mentioned the frequent brief passages of recitative interpolated into the vocal numbers, passages that were to become the melodramas in the *Schreckensopern* of the later period.[99] These recitatives draw their particular strength from the composer's thoughtful use of the orchestra, which brings us on to a further original aspect of Grétry's operas. Even on a superficial level, his orchestra is far more colourful than that of any of his predecessors, with *Le Huron* (1768) the first of his works to demand clarinets,[100] while *Colinette* includes a 'flûte' and 'hautbois de tambourin' (act three, scenes six and nine). A mandolin – an instrument also of importance for Mozart – appears in act one, scene one of *Les deux avares* (1770) and in act two, scene fourteen of *L'amant jaloux*; a harp features in act one, scene six of *L'amitié à l'épreuve* (1770); and there is a triangle in several of his oriental operas, notably in act two, scene two of *La caravane du Caire* (1783). But even more traditional instruments are used more extensively and more idiosyncratically: here one thinks above all of the piccolo, which is sometimes used to conjure up the sultrily sensuous and exotic atmosphere that we later find in the Bacchus duet from *Die Entführung aus dem Serail* and in

92. See scene twenty of *La fausse magie* and act one, scene five of *Les événemens imprévus*.
93. In act two, scene three of *Les mariages samnites* and act three, scene three of *L'amant jaloux*.
94. Notably in act one, scene ten of *La rosière de Salency* (1773).
95. Note, for example, the chorus of Janissaries that is linked to the previous duet in act three, scene three of *Les deux avares*.
96. In act three, scene eight of *Colinette à la cour* we even find two choruses elaborately contrasted.
97. Within an individual act, it is also found in act two, scene three of *Les mariages samnites*.
98. For the first time in act two, scene thirteen of *Le Huron*.
99. In act three, scene seven of *Les mariages samnites*, the exciting climax of the duet, in which the character is named, is treated, without warning, as recitative.
100. In scene four, which includes the significant note: 'Si l'on n'a point de clarinettes, les hautbois peuvent jouer leurs parties en jouant un ton plus haut.' The piece in question is a pastoral siciliana.

Monostatos's aria in *Die Zauberflöte* – in both cases clearly under Grétry's influence.[101] Even the strings are used in special ways,[102] while the orchestra as a whole is occasionally pressed into the service of a painterly dynamic, either through being positioned off-stage[103] or through the use of marches that gradually die away, an effect that Mozart inverted and used almost immediately in *Idomeneo* and, later, in *Le nozze in Figaro*.[104]

There are countless independent orchestral scenes of greater or lesser extent that illustrate the text and situation and often continue along entirely independent lines.[105] In terms of his ability to depict the surroundings and the milieu in which the action takes place, none of Grétry's rivals could compete with him, and in his finest works his orchestral language clearly looks forward to the later period and especially to Romanticism. *Zémire et Azor* offers some instructive examples of this: whereas the depiction of the magic cloud is still influenced by the older tradition, the Genies of the Arts appear in act three, scene four to the sound of sustained and solemn chords that are later transformed into a fiery tremolando.[106] Azor's aria in act four, scene three resembles Florestan's in the way in which it builds to an urgent and optimistic climax only to sink back again, as though broken, in its orchestral postlude. And in act four, scene four, Zémire performs her act of redemption to the sound of horns (in part off-stage), echoing flutes and glittering triplets in the violins. Finally in this context we may mention the solo violin that accompanies Blondel in *Richard Cœur-de-lion* and serves as his musical trademark. Most of these motifs reveal a degree of inventiveness that is as powerful as it is felicitous, and a number clearly anticipate Mozart. One such motif, which is particularly common with Grétry, is a tutti entry followed by a descending staccato scale (often in thirds) in the violins, as in act three, scene two of *La rosière de Salency* (1773):

Or take the brusque and peremptory figures in scene twenty of *La fausse magie*:

There is even a direct pre-echo of *Le nozze di Figaro* in act three, scene eight of *Le magnifique* (1773):

---

101. Cf. the aria of the Negro Amilcar in act one, scene eight of *L'amitié à l'épreuve*. (Here the character is held out as an ideal example of natural man.) Also worth mentioning in this context is Pan's flute in act one, scene two of *Le jugement de Midas*.

102. In act three, scene one of *L'ami de la maison*, we find the performance markings 'sur la touche' (on or over the fingerboard) and 'au chevalet' (*sul ponticello*).

103. In act three, scene six of *Zémire et Azor*.

104. Cf. the fourth part of the overture to *Le magnifique*. It is impossible not to be reminded of Beethoven by the sustained note on the trumpet, gradually growing louder, that is heard in the second entr'acte of *Raoul Barbe-bleue* to signal the approaching rescuers and that is repeated in act three, scene two, where it interrupts events.

105. The first act of *Zémire et Azor*, for example, ends with a complete 'symphonie qui exprime le vol du nuage'.

106. A similar effect may be found in act three, scene three of *Panurge* in the recitative that introduces the Dance of the Goblins.

In the vocal numbers, too, the orchestra is exceptionally liberal in adding picturesque comments: where it is not independently employed, it often seeks to embellish the vocal line and invest it with a sharper outline by means of rhythmic variation.

Although Mozart largely ignores Grétry in his letters, the new world that was opened up to him in this way must have exercised his imagination. Nor is it any wonder that Grétry was the man of the moment in Paris. It was he, after all, who had fully opened up an area to *opéra comique* that had been dear to French hearts from the very beginnings of French opera: the art of ballet in the wider sense of intelligent programme music in general. Less important in this context are his ballet scenes as such, although even they for the most part are organically integrated into the plot,[107] than the large-scale, picturesque and dramatic genre pictures that Grétry succeeded in investing with as much realism as poetry. Here we find not only the usual storm scenes,[108] hunting scenes, battle scenes and scenes from military life, but also novel images such as a woman adorning herself with jewellery, a music lesson and rustic celebrations of every kind, alongside aristocratic balls, convoys of captives, Turkish watchmen, prophetic gypsies with all manner of jiggery-pokery, singing contests and so on. Above all, however, there are whole bands of Romantic goblins of every description. Although Grétry did not always manage to strike the right note in these scenes and many of these intruders speak an emphatically petit-bourgeois language, there are other scenes in which he did indeed succeed in introducing a genuinely novel note that was to find an audible echo during the later period.

It is hardly surprising to find that these programmatical tendencies on Grétry's part influenced his overtures, too, with only a tiny minority of them remaining free of this influence. The majority are in one or three movements. The single-movement overtures and the opening allegros of the three-movement overtures are cast in a loosely structured sonata form tending towards binary form, with the recapitulation generally reduced to one of the two main themes and with the main theme tending to return only at the very end in keeping with Parisian practice.[109] Thematically speaking, the development sections are generally very free. Only in the rarest cases are the three-movement overtures modelled on the Italian sinfonia. Instead, their movements are freely arranged according to the individual programme.[110] Especially frequent is a form that Mozart imitated even

---

107. Notably in act two, scene fourteen of *Colinette à la cour*, a ball scene in which the dancing is directly linked to the finale.
108. Pierrot's account of his maritime adventures in scene seven of *Le tableau parlant* (1769) was particularly famous in this regard.
109. The overture to *La rosière de Salency* is very loosely structured, in which respect it recalls Mozart's overture to *Les petits riens*.
110. The overture to *L'ami de la maison* – allegretto–menuetto–rondo – is suite-like in character.

as late as *Die Entführung aus dem Serail,* where a slow movement is interpolated between the two main sections of an allegro.[111] In his later works Mozart prefers the form of the French overture, with a slow section followed by a fast one, a preference presumably due to Gluck's influence, yet even here the programme continues to be determinative.

Virtually all these programmes are scenic in nature, with the result that many of them positively demand to be played with the curtain raised. The overture to *Zémire et Azor* depicts the way in which a blissful idyll is disrupted by a storm that continues to rage throughout much of the opening act. The overture to *Le jugement de Midas,* by contrast, begins by conjuring up Midas's ass's ears, followed by a detailed description of Apollo's fall from the heavens. That to *Aucassin et Nicolette* includes old Garin's call 'Aucassin! Mon fils!' Particularly picturesque is the overture to *Le magnifique* which describes in its four sections a convoy of prisoners that takes place behind the scenes and that is described by two young women.[112] The overture to *Richard Cœur-de-lion,* finally, opens with a brief, fanfare-like passage, then immediately calls on the chorus. In the circumstances it comes as no surprise to find that the majority of these overtures pass straight into the opening scene without a break.

Grétry lavished just as much care on his entr'acte music. Generally he takes up a particularly remarkable number from the previous act, which he then proceeds to repeat, giving extra piquancy to the instrumentation and often adding a set of brilliant variations.[113] In other cases he uses the overture or one of its sections.[114] But there are others, finally, that continue to spin out the dramatic thread along independent lines.[115]

To this point, Mozart had been dependent upon Italian models in the field of comic opera, but now he was introduced to a composer who, essentially different from his Italian colleagues, was bound to open up his field of vision in no uncertain ways. Although Grétry's works had no depth to them, they none the less had two great merits, those of naturalness and of liveliness and variety. It would have been little short of a miracle had Mozart remained impervious to these impressions. In contrast to his earlier *opere buffe,* he did not merely imitate them, of course, but assimilated their spirit. As a result, there are far fewer direct reminiscences of Grétry than there are of the Italian composers of the period, and in general it is only the freer approach and more flexible style that remind us of the French manner. Yet these aspects are often so pronounced that one wonders how a writer such as Jahn could have ignored this relationship completely.

Alongside these three main practitioners of comic opera, such lesser composers as Nicolas-Médard Audinot (1732–1801), Stanislaus Champein (1753–1830), Nicolas Dezède (1740/5–1792) and others are of far less importance for Mozart. None of them added substantially to the picture already described.[116] But there is little doubt that the older *tragédie lyrique* had increasing difficulty in asserting itself in the face of this rudely flourishing genre. Virtually no new and viable *tragédies*

---

111. This form is first found in *L'amitié à l'épreuve.*
112. Botstiber, *Geschichte der Ouvertüre und der freien Orchesterformen,* 151–2. The first movement is headed 'Fuga', the second includes an 'air d'Henri IV', while the third is remarkable for its cantus firmus in the bass.
113. In the second entr'acte of *La rosière de Salency* he takes up a melody from act three, scene six of the opera.
114. In the first entr'acte of *L'amitié à l'épreuve,* the slow middle section is repeated.
115. One example is the second entr'acte in *Raoul Barbe-bleue.*
116. The oldest of them was Nicolas-Médard Audinot, whose *opéra comique Le tonnelier* (1761) enjoyed great popularity for a time in Germany under the title *Der Faßbinder.* A canon quartet deserves mention in the context of Beethoven's *Fidelio.*
◆ Further, see Isherwood, *Farce and Fantasy: Popular Entertainment in Eighteenth-Century Paris*; Wild, *Dictionnaire des théâtres parisiens au XIXe siècle*; and Pendle, 'L'opéra-comique à Paris de 1762 à 1789'.

lyriques were being written any longer, and audiences were increasingly turning their backs on those of older composers such as Rameau. The earlier type of opera found itself in an even more parlous state than it had been before Rameau's intervention. Once more, however, there was help at hand in the form of a powerful ally, a foreign composer who adopted a far deeper and far more logical approach to the problem of reforming serious music drama than even Rameau had done and who breathed new life into the old Renaissance ideal, investing it with a hitherto unknown purity. His name was Christoph Willibald Gluck. Gluck's arrival in Paris changed everything, unleashing a new and embittered struggle from which the German composer finally emerged victorious.

20

The music dramas of Gluck

Christoph Willibald Gluck (1714–87)[1] studied first with Bohuslav Černohorský in Prague and then with Giovanni Battista Sammartini in Milan.[2] Between 1741, the year in which his first opera *Artaserse* was first performed,[3] and 1750, the year in which he married, he led an eventful and unsettled life, travelling around Europe as a composer of Italian operas, initially in the service of Italian and English theatres, then in that of the touring companies run by the brothers Pietro and Antonio Mingotti, with whom he is known to have visited Prague, Dresden, Leipzig, Hamburg, Copenhagen and possibly Graz, as well as Holland and Belgium.[4] During the course of these years of travel he was assailed by the most disparate artistic impressions, although the greatest of them – his acquaintance with Handel and with the music of Rameau – were not to bear fruit until the period of his operatic reforms. In general, Gluck's Italian operas coincide in their aims with those of Hasse and his school, a school among whose members Jommelli was temperamentally the closest to Gluck. Gluckian is the fondness for strict motivic procedures, especially in the orchestra, the writing for which was still heavily influenced by Sammartini. Gluckian, too, is the careful word-setting in the *secco* recitatives, which even now are already strikingly dramatic in tone and supported by expressive harmonies. And Gluckian, finally, is the orchestral colour, which in places is already surprising for its later 'Romantic' manner and which is found in particular in scenes of a darker or more impassioned character. As a matter of principle, the Metastasian type is still strictly preserved. Indeed, Gluck remains far behind Jommelli and Traetta in the freedom of his aria forms, to say nothing of his handling of the accompanied recitatives and his introduction of ensembles and choruses.[5] In 1758 he began to explore the world of French comic opera, in the history of whose development he was to play an important role. Although this may appear to have been a step in the opposite direction, his later reform operas are inconceivable without this

1. See Anton Schmid, *Christoph Willibald Ritter von Gluck*; Marx, *Gluck und die Oper*; de Desnoiresterres, *Gluck et Piccinni*; Ernest Newman, *Gluck and the Opera*; Wotquenne, *Thematisches Verzeichnis der Werke von Chr. W. v. Gluck*; and Tiersot, *Gluck*; see also Kretzschmar, 'Zum Verständnis Glucks', ii.193–209, and Wortsmann, 'Die deutsche Gluck-Literatur'. ◆ Generally, see Einstein, *Gluck*; Prod'homme, *Gluck*; Tenschert, *Christoph Willibald Gluck, der große Reformator der Oper*; and Anna Amalie Abert, *Christoph Willibald Gluck*. Further, see Mueller von Asow, *The Collected Correspondence and Papers of Christoph Willibald Gluck*; and Howard, *Gluck: An Eighteenth-Century Portrait in Letters and Documents*.
2. ◆ Abert's assertion that Gluck studied with Bohuslav Černohorský in Prague cannot be documented; he enrolled at the Prague university in 1731 but did not graduate. Gluck was in Milan from 1737; the claim that he studied with Sammartini derives from Carpani, *Le Haydine*, second edition, 64.
3. See Saint-Foix, 'Les débuts milanais de Gluck', 28–46.
4. Müller von Asow, 'Gluck und die Brüder Mingotti'. ◆ Also see Müller von Asow, *Die Mingottischen Opernunternehmungen: 1732 bis 1756* and *Angelo und Pietro Mingotti*; and Strohm, 'The crisis of Baroque opera in Germany'.
5. On these operas, see Kurth, 'Die Jugendopern Glucks bis Orfeo'; see also Hermann Abert, *Christoph Willibald Gluck: Le nozze d'Ercole e d'Ebe* and 'Glucks italienische Opern bis zum "Orfeo"'. ◆ Concerning Jommelli and Traetta, see McClymonds, 'The Evolution of Jommelli's Operatic Style' and *Niccolò Jommelli: The Last Years, 1769–1774*; Casavola, *Tommaso Traetta di Bitonto (1727–1779): La vita e le opere*; Morea, *Tommaso Traetta: Riformatore del melodramma*; Riedlbauer, *Die Opern von Tommaso Trajetta*; and Martinotti, 'Italiani e italianisti a Vienna da Bonno a Salieri'.

groundwork, for it was here that he first became aware of the entirely new concepts of naturalness and dramatic characterization and, above all, of the need for a totally different relationship between words and music and a far greater formal variety than he had been used to in *opera seria*. For the first time in his career he had the chance to collaborate on a type of art that breathed the spirit of Rousseau's new ideal of nature and that was free from all convention, seeing its ultimate goal in a revival of the spirit of the folksong. This was an art that Gluck found far more attractive than is generally believed: nor was it only the tone of French songs that he successfully attempted to imitate, the youthful memory of Austrian and even Bohemian folksongs was suddenly rekindled. From the standpoint of the loftier kind of drama, these were only modest works, of course, but they enabled him to learn how to handle musical characterization within the succinct and small-scale forms of the song and to draw closer to a goal that was to strike the later reformer as of paramount importance in drama, namely, to express each musical idea in its most appropriate form, using as few and as simple means as possible. Even *Orfeo ed Euridice* already demonstrates the truth of this remark: the famous 'Cerco il mio ben così' in the opening act could never have been written in this form without the experience of these *airs nouveaux*.

At the same time – 1761 – Gluck took a further important step with his dramatic ballet *Don Juan*, to the plot of which we shall have occasion to return in the context of *Don Giovanni*. It is clear from remarks by the poet Gasparo Angiolini that in terms of its aims this was already a reform work, albeit limited to the world of dance.[6] Angiolini's demand for significant characters and simple plots, together with the markedly philological nature of his remarks, suggest affinities with Calzabigi[7] and indicate the same intellectual background, namely, the circle surrounding the Viennese intendant Count Giacomo Durazzo.

The members of this circle could count on Viennese opera's traditional resistance to fashionable trends from Italy.[8] Their aims, which had found increasingly clear expression in the sung and spoken drama for almost a century, finally assumed the form of a specific programme. As in the years around 1600, so it was the ideal of classical tragedy that was now revived, an ideal to which the spoken drama aspired through its introduction of choruses, while opera aimed for similar results by means of a completely new approach to its texts. It was a movement that was to lead ultimately to Schiller's *Die Braut von Messina* and Goethe's *Pandora* and, in parallel, to the music dramas of Gluck.[9] Metastasio's librettos, too, had purported to imitate classical drama, though they contained little of the classical spirit, unless we count the late Roman antiquity that is also found in Metastasio's unacknowledged French models. With the passage of time, the absence of one of the principal features of classical tragedy – the chorus – was increasingly keenly felt, and as librettists and composers became more familiar with French opera, so there were ever more vocal demands for a reinvigoration of Italian opera by means of a revival not only of the chorus, but of the dancing and instrumental music found in French works of this period. One of the most enthu-

---

6. The principal reformer was Jean-Georges Noverre. ◆ See Lynham, *The Chevalier Noverre: Father of Modern Ballet*, and Tugal, *Jean-Georges Noverre, der große Reformator des Balletts*.
7. Angiolini adopted an even more rigorous approach than Noverre in this regard, with the result that in his introduction to *Les Horaces et les Curiaces* the latter attacked him for his 'pantomime sans danse'. ◆ Concerning Angiolini, see Tozzi, *Il balletto pantomimo del Settecento: Gaspare Angiolini*; Dahms, 'Anmerkungen zu den "Tanzdramen" Angiolinis und Noverres und zu deren Gattungsspezifik' and 'Wiener Ballett zur Zeit Metastasios'; Brown, 'Elementi di classicismo nei balli viennesi di Gasparo Angiolini' and 'Metastasio und das Ballett'.
8. See Kretzschmar, 'Zum Verständnis Glucks', ii.199–201. ◆ In general, see Bruce Alan Brown, *Gluck and the French Theatre in Vienna*; further, Puncuh, 'Giacomo Durazzo: Famiglia, ambiente, personalità'; and Gallarati, 'La poetica di Giacomo Durazzo e la *Lettre sur le méchanisme de l'opéra italien*'.
9. See Burdach, 'Schillers Chordrama und die Geburt des tragischen Stils aus der Musik'.

siastic advocates of reform, Count Francesco Algarotti, openly voiced this demand in his *Saggio sopra l'opera in musica* of 1755.[10] Within Germany, Vienna was certainly the most fertile ground for such a suggestion, as it was necessary only to revive the aspirations of composers such as Johann Joseph Fux and Carlo Agostino Badia, aspirations that had been realized barely a generation earlier on the Viennese stage.[11] Of course, this purely formal expansion still left a great deal of work to be done. Composers could add as many choruses and dances to Metastasian texts as they liked (and as members of the Hasse school did with increasing frequency), but the end product was still the same, an expression of that rationalistic current in intellectual thought in which convention and fixed rules triumphed over nature and humanity, and the imagination was used, by preference, for purely decorative ends. Even before Gluck appeared on the scene, it was clear to the members of this group that if reforms were to be made, they must start with the texts. The pillars on which rationalism was built in Germany had already been undermined by a new wave of ideas that had come first from England and then from France: freedom from convention and the liberation of emotion from the tyranny of reason – this basic principle of the new doctrine was already an integral part of the thinking of the advocates of reform in Vienna. But it is Ranieri de' Calzabigi (1714–95)[12] who deserves the credit for applying the new spirit to Italian opera. Calzabigi began his career as an ardent champion of Metastasio and as the editor of his compatriot's works, and now Count Durazzo recommended Gluck to him as a composer well suited to implementing his new ideas. The three operas *Orfeo ed Euridice* (1762), *Alceste* (1767) and *Paride ed Elena* (1770) were the fruits of their collaboration. As Gluck's Italian reform operas, they belong together as a self-contained group. The series of French operas that followed begins with *Iphigénie en Aulide*.

Like Metastasio, Calzabigi was not a true poet but a man of letters endowed with skill and good taste and, above all, an acute observer of the various trends in contemporary opera. He himself admitted that he merely gave the clearest expression to his predecessors' ideas, yet he will always be remembered as the man who progressed from mere speculation to artistic achievement and who, above all, helped Gluck to see precisely what his new goals were. In radical upheavals such as these, the last word is invariably spoken not by the speculative theorist but by the creative genius. However highly we rate Calzabigi's contribution, Gluck will always remain the true soul of the reform movement, for whereas Calzabigi may have been clever enough to devise these new ideas, it was Gluck who felt them on their deepest level.

Of decisive importance was the fact that Calzabigi had the courage to grasp the nettle and break free from the stranglehold of the Metastasian tradition. As a result, Gluck's reforms – like Wagner's a century later – began not with music but with the words, and musical reform ultimately proved to be only a natural consequence of poetic reform. Calzabigi's aim was to reassert the legitimate claims of individual emotion in the face of rationalistic convention. As a poet, he himself was prevented from achieving this end since he lacked the divine spark needed to do so, but he was intelligent enough to know how to ignite that spark in the soul of his musician and produce a white-hot flame. He set out from the belief that the plot should be as simple as possible, with

10. ◆ For a partial translation, see Fubini, *Music and Culture in Eighteenth-Century Europe: A Source Book*, 435–7 and 443–51. Further, see Cerami, 'Il Saggio sopra l'opera in musica di Francesco Algarotti: Analisi e critica nel contesto culturale del XVIII secolo'.
11. See Kretzschmar, 'Zum Verständnis Glucks'.
12. See Welti, 'Gluck und Calsabigi', 26–42; Lazzeri, *La vita e l'opera letteraria di Ranieri Calzabigi*; and Michel, 'Ranieri Calzabigi als Dichter von Musikdramen und als Kritiker'. For a German translation of Calzabigi's 1790 *Risposta*, see Einstein, 'Calzabigis "Erwiderung" von 1790'. As a member of the Arcadian Academy in Rome Calzabigi adopted the name of Liburno Drepanio. ◆ Further, see Piscitelli, 'I libretti napoletani di Ranieri de' Calzabigi'; Bellina, *Ranieri Calzabigi: Scritti teatrali e letterari*; and Del Monte and Segreto, *Christoph Willibald Gluck nel 200° anniversario della morte*.

Horace's 'denique sit quidvis simplex dumtaxat et unum'[13] as the model for all that he wrote. Metastasio's whole system of complex intrigues thus collapsed. But Calzabigi was sufficiently clever to realize that he also needed to block off the source of such unnaturalism, namely, Metastasio's *galant* view of love as a social phenomenon. It is here, perhaps, that his greatest achievement lies. Orpheus and Alcestis are no longer social beings whose actions and feelings are consciously or unconsciously adapted to conform to the moral code of an invisible aristocratic public. There is no longer any trace of love in the *galant* sense of the term: in both works, love exists only in its supreme ethical form as the love between husband and wife. And such fidelity proves itself not in some petty intrigue created by human hand but in a struggle with death itself. The sublime notion of love triumphing over death is one that Metastasio had often toyed with in a purely superficial way, but it now became the driving force of two entire dramas. But the idea is so overpowering, especially in *Orfeo*, that it robs the characters of their individuality, draining every last ounce of marrow from their bones. It is impossible to speak of Orpheus and Alcestis as characters in the sense in which we can speak of Agamemnon or Thoas as characters. They draw what life they have purely and simply from the underlying idea and are thus closer to allegory than to the concept of dramatic character. It is for this reason that the character of Cupid in *Orfeo ed Euridice* does not fall as far outside the action as is generally argued to be the case. Calzabigi was wrong to think that he was returning in this way to classical antiquity as the characters in classical drama are individuals, not universal symbols, in spite of all their simplicity.

None the less, he could be proud of his innovation. The fact that he placed great and simple ideas at the heart of his dramas was in itself sufficient to mark a tremendous advance on Metastasio, for whom such ideas had merely been a pretext for parading his modish gifts. Now music dramas finally had plots that developed through an emotionally charged, internally consistent series of antitheses. The call of 'back to nature' that coincided at this time with the demand for an end to convention thus won a decisive victory in the art of Italian libretto writing.

Even so, Calzabigi was unable to sever all his links with Metastasio: he was far too much of a rationalist for that, as is clear, not least, from his extensive speculations on the rules governing the new drama, speculations that preceded his work on the drama and continued even while he was engaged on it. As a result, his stage works are not elemental poetic experiences but considered and ordered illustrations of a preconceived theory of drama. Although he went beyond Metastasio's conventional handling of his subject matter, he remained bound by his predecessor's general method. Calzabigi's heroes, like Metastasio's, are not unique, individual characters but the embodiment of certain characteristics based on his own observations: he, too, began with particular qualities and created his characters on the strength of them. That he failed to attain the same high level as his classical models even in his interpretation of his subjects is clear from his uninspired, euhemeristic account of the legend of Alcestis.[14] But Calzabigi was a rationalist even on points of detail, including his curiously stylized bombast, his fondness for alluding to all manner of recondite legends, his tendency to produce subjective effects by means of objective portrayals and formal clarity, and, finally, various aspects of his poetic diction. Admittedly, he makes a genuine effort to avoid Metastasio's self-conscious eloquence, notably his predecessor's similes, but there is still the same delight in finely polished form, the same attempt to display his erudition and to show

---

13. This quotation from Horace's *Epistles* iii.23 appears as a motto at the head of the score of *Alceste*.
14. For Calzabigi, Alcestis is a tender-hearted wife whose husband is suffering from an infectious disease. She tends him and saves him but in the process is herself infected by his illness, with the result that she can ultimately be saved only by an experienced and sympathetic physician; see Einstein, 'Calzabigis "Erwiderung" von 1790', 72.

off his elegance and the breadth of his reading, and his audiences were no more spared his sententious moralizing than had been the case with Metastasio.

On the other hand, he succeeded in an area in which Metastasio had known only failure, conceiving his scenes from the outset in such a way that the composer no longer needed to side-step the drama, while the dramatist no longer needed to be afraid of trespassing on the composer's preserves. This was a natural consequence of his simplified approach to the drama and it is one that was to prove immensely important: instead of the intricate ratiocinations that had been necessary to advance the plot in Metastasio's librettos, Calzabigi was able to invest the dialogue with a far greater degree of emotion, meeting the musician halfway and enabling him to restore the aria to its dramatic context. Even for Calzabigi, the aria was still the 'perorazione del discorso e conclusione della scena', just as it had been for Metastasio, but it no longer served merely as a sensual or conceptual embellishment but as a genuine climactic conclusion to the individual emotion aroused in the earlier part of the scene. In this way, one of the basic shortcomings of Neapolitan opera – the dislocation of drama and music – was avoided, and it was now only a question of how the musician would follow up these suggestions.

Gluck, too, began his career as a rationalist of the old school. Not only his personality, in which thinking of something was tantamount to wanting it,[15] but also his whole background, especially his upbringing by the Jesuits at Komotau (Chomutov), predisposed him to adopt this outlook. But unlike so many of his contemporaries, including Calzabigi, he was not content to fall into line with the others. For Calzabigi, the whole rationalistic system of thinking and of writing poetry was an immutable fact of life. Gluck, by contrast, was a man of tremendous intellectual resolve, the sheer force of which caused this ossified system to melt and achieve new life. All the traditional princi-ples became living forces again thanks to his ability to assimilate every last one of them and make them uniquely his own. Rationalist thinking had always lacked inner experience, but with Gluck that lack was at last made good to the extent that thought and experience now became one. In this way he succeeded in salvaging the highest and purest achievements of rationalism in opera, marking both the culmination and end of that movement.

As a result Gluck quickly outgrew his librettist. Although Calzabigi's characters had cast aside their old conventional masks, they did not acquire a life of their own until they had drunk the warm blood of Gluck's personality as an artist. In this they may be said to resemble the Homeric shades. Common to both the composer and his librettist was the fact that they gave precedence to the thinker over the artist and to the forces of order over those of creative disorder. Order, clarity and logic – rationalism's old ideals – were also Gluck's ideals, as is clear in particular from his char-acterization of his heroes. For Gluck, too, they are not characters in the modern sense of the term, they are not unique figures combining within them the most disparate emotional and psycho-logical forces, but representatives of specific, clear and intelligible ideas reduced to their simplest formulas, with the result that all other characteristics are bound to seem secondary or to disappear altogether. As a result he is unfamiliar with the modern concept of dramatic psychological devel-opment, and herein lies the decisive difference between his own approach to drama and that of the later period, including Mozart. For Calzabigi, the classical image of Orpheus as the embodiment of the bard's ideal beauty is fixed for all time and it remains so even in situations such as his very first strophe and his famous 'Che farò', where one would expect very different emotions, namely, grief and despair. Of course, these emotions still come into their own, but in the recitatives: this,

---

15. See Heuß, 'Gluck als Musikdramatiker'.

then, is an art that is well ordered and carefully considered. For Calzabigi, the most important consideration is always his depiction of the underlying idea, for the sake of which he reduces everything to the most basic antitheses within which there is no longer any room for psychological complications of a modern kind. Yet in the wonderful plasticity of these scenes and their inspired emotional consistency it is impossible not to see the way in which thinking and hypothesizing are transformed into an emotional experience for Gluck. This takes us far beyond Calzabigi, revealing a relationship between poet and composer that allows us to see their differing attitudes to rationalism in the clearest possible light: Calzabigi remained entrenched in it, whereas Gluck triumphed over it by turning its rules into living forces.

But this basic principle of Gluck's art also conditioned his attitude to music.[16]

The earlier view that Gluck found composition relatively difficult and that he therefore made a virtue of a necessity by subordinating the musician to the poet[17] is one that becomes impossible to sustain when we recall his prolific years in Italy. Nor does one have the impression that the specifically musical element gave Gluck any difficulty as an artist. And, given his way of working, there was certainly no question of this to begin with. As we have seen, the thinker invariably took precedence, and it was only when the building was complete that the composer was allowed to set foot inside it,[18] and even then his task was limited to not altering or concealing the basic outlines of the finished structure but simply to reinforcing them and making them clearer. In this way the composer became the servant not of the poet Calzabigi (as is so often claimed) but of the thinker in Gluck, a thinker who had annealed the libretto in the refining fires of his intellect. Never were the creative forces as strenuously subjected to the forces of order as they were here. Indeed, Gluck even thought that he could banish the ambiguity and irrationality of music from the language of the music drama. He openly admitted that music, especially its melodic aspect, was limited in its means,[19] a claim that places him at the very opposite end of the spectrum to Mozart. But it also explains the whole nature of his music, which aimed for simplicity and clarity (and hence, in Gluck's mind, for all that was natural), even if a number of 'absolute' musicians today regard it as merely primitive. And it further explains his elemental rhythmic effects and his antipathy to coloratura and to every kind of dramatic polyphony, which he inevitably found confusing and unnatural; and, finally, it explains one of the principal characteristics of his music, its declamatory style, with each individual thought and concept chiselled out with the hardness of steel. In the area of recitative, this had the momentous consequence of replacing the old *secco* recitative with *accompagnato*, but with the passage of time it also, and increasingly, affected the melodic lines of his arias. As a result, the two sections of the older type of opera, the 'unmusical' *secco* and the 'purely musical' aria, which had been drifting further and further apart, were brought together again in a new-found unity based on a totally different conception of the relationship between words and music, a concept that reflected the underlying principle that only the libretto could be allowed to determine the way in which the music itself was expressed. Essentially, the whole new structure of the music drama was the natural consequence of these underlying principles. This is especially true of the displacement of the *da capo* aria and its replacement by more varied forms ranging from the

16. See Heuß, 'Gluck als Musikdramatiker', 282.

17. See, for example, Jahn, *W. A. Mozart*, fourth edition, i.518ff.

18. Gluck's well-known remarks on this subject may be found in Anton Schmid, *Gluck*, 425: 'Before I set to work, I attempt above all to forget that I am a musician. I forget myself in order to see only my characters.' See also Schmid, *Gluck*, 433–4: 'Once I have sorted out the composition of the whole [that is, the overall design] and the characterization of the main characters, I consider the opera finished, even though I have not yet written down a single note. This groundwork normally takes about a year and not infrequently makes me very ill, in spite of which many people regard it as tantamount to writing light songs.'

19. Anton Schmid, *Gluck*, 427.

simple song, the natural expressive force of which Gluck had already explored in his comic operas, to the freest through-composed numbers.[20] Of course, he had a number of Italian forerunners in this regard, foremost among whom were Jommelli and Traetta, but they had abandoned the struggle while it was still half finished, leaving Gluck to stay the course and fight on with implacable resolve, achieving a monumental uniformity of style of which his predecessors had never even dreamt. Gluck no longer admitted to any distinction between the dramatically important and the less important: with him, the unimportant had already been removed even before the first musical sketches were made.

Where the Italian composers had taken only the most tentative steps, Gluck was far more consistent in introducing choruses, dances and autonomous instrumental music – a further formal innovation. Here we may detect the influence not only of the old Viennese school, but also of the Italian composers of the period, to say nothing of Rameau and Handel. But, of all his predecessors, only Handel had revealed such resolve in turning the chorus into one of his *dramatis personae*. There is no longer any trace here of the search for outward splendour or simply for a fuller-toned musical effect: either the chorus functions as the hero's dramatic antagonist, as in the scene with the Furies in *Orfeo*, or it etches in the atmospheric background, as it does with compelling force in *Alceste*. Entirely worthy of Handel is the way in which Gluck, in *Paride ed Elena* and later works, uses the chorus to extend the scope of the opera until it assumes a universal dimension. And he treats dance in the same way, even if he is sometimes too keen to imitate the French style, especially in his Parisian operas. Moreover, as we have seen, attempts had already been made by Noverre and his school to reform the world of dance. But solo singing, choruses and dance are no longer placed alongside each other in a non-organic way, but are treated as links in a living, dramatic organism in the form of dramatic scenes which, although anticipated in various details by his predecessors, are systematically raised by Gluck to the point where they support the whole structure of his dramas.[21]

Gluck's music dramas, finally, are inextricably bound up with an important development in terms of the orchestra. It is significant that he treats the two most elemental aspects of music – rhythm and orchestral tone colour – in particularly characterful ways. Following up French ideas, he was able to exploit the expressive force inherent in the timbre of each individual instrument, especially the winds, often investing it with such dramatic power that one can legitimately describe him as the forefather of the later 'Romantic' art of orchestration.[22] But even here he is never concerned with the purely sensuous side of his newly expressive language but only with its dramatic aspect. Such passages are intended to seem exceptional, and modern 'adaptors' are guilty, therefore, of traducing Gluck when they turn these passages into the general rule in their attempts to curry favour with their audiences.

It is extremely dangerous to judge Gluck's dramatic language by the standards of later composers such as Mozart and Wagner. It follows its own rules, and we ourselves must respect them, come what may. It is innocent of the later delight in psychological problems, but in its basic

20. In the light of what we have said, Calzabigi's declaration that it was only in *Orfeo ed Euridice* that he finally showed Gluck the correct form of declamation in his recitatives and drew his attention to the themes of his arias and choruses requires no further comment. In 1794 he even thought that he had discovered in Paisiello the true 'philosophical' composer.

21. As a result there is nothing more foolish than the division of scenes like that with the Furies into individual numbers. Although found in many of today's vocal scores, this sort of compartmentalization amounts to a massacre of the score. The same is true of Mozart's operas, as it is of those of any dramatist who deserves to be taken seriously.

22. It is no accident that it was precisely this aspect of Gluck's works that Berlioz particularly admired; see Kretzschmar, 'Zum Verständnis Glucks', ii.203.

ideas and their development it follows only the goal of supreme simplicity and clarity, qualities that only a judge who swears blind by psychology could ever regard as primitive. Listeners who really understand Gluck will feel his art to be no less genuine than that of his successors. Indeed, they will even regret that, disregarding all later progress, an appreciation of such elemental opposites has been lost as a result of the subsequent interest in individual characterization. Take *Orfeo*: the scene of lamentation (a scene doubly moving on account of its suppressed sadness) is followed by the tremendous climax of the scene with the Furies, the high point of the work as a whole, with its sense of a life-and-death struggle and its wistful echo in the bright yet faraway world of Elysium. With the final act comes the gradual dying away of emotion. This tendency to create a three-part structure with the greatest tension in the middle is found in *Alceste* and the majority of the later works. In it we may again detect an echo of 'classical' French tragedy, and it certainly introduces us to a further merit of the Gluckian music drama, that of total organic unity, in which each section has a particular function to fulfil.

The individual characters in *Orfeo* are as typical of Gluck as its structure: the hero is the bard who sings of the purest beauty, a beauty which in keeping with Winckelmann's ideas is Apollonian rather than Dionysian; and Eurydice is typically ruled by female desires. Between them is the allegorical figure of Cupid, whose Rococo wings are clearly visible in his first-act aria. It is no accident that there is more Italian blood in this work than in any other by Gluck. Individual reminiscences of particular models no doubt mark it out as Gluck's first attempt at a reform opera,[23] but they cannot detract from its importance as a reform work. That it was regarded as such is evident not least from its lukewarm reception and from the various attempts to revise it and thus to align it with current tastes.[24]

From *Alceste* onwards, Gluck no longer made any secret of his reformist aspirations. The basic problem is the same: the victorious struggle of a mortal raised above him- or herself by the force of a moral idea and locked in conflict with the divine representative of dull and ineluctable fate in the form of death. But the two main characters have not only exchanged roles when compared with *Orfeo*, they have also risen above the innocent, fairy-tale world of that work and entered the realm of high tragedy. The semi-unconscious desire that leads Orpheus to the shades of the underworld becomes the blinding light of conscious morality in the case of Alcestis. Unlike Orpheus, she follows no youthful impulse, but as a wife and mother she forces herself to reach the ultimate decision, while remaining every inch a queen and revealing that inner and outer regality from start to finish. In exactly the same way, Admetus is forced to suffer all the torments of his destiny in a state of total awareness. In this way the antitheses found in *Orfeo* are made incomparably deeper, even if they are not more complicated. The three-part structure is again in evidence: first there is the overwhelming increase in tension such as few other operas can boast in the whole history of the genre, a tension that mounts throughout the whole of the opening act and culminates in act two, scene five, when Admetus finally forces his wife to utter her terrible confession. As with *Orfeo*, it has to be conceded that the release of tension is less successfully achieved. The succession of opposites, too, reveals undeniable progress: they are now more numerous and their effects more subtly calculated.

23. The opening scene recalls the famous *tombeau* in Rameau's *Castor et Pollux*, while the scene with the Furies bears a strong resemblance to a similar scene in Traetta's *Ifigenia in Tauride*. And the beginning of the scene in Elysium is reminiscent, finally, of the scene in which Rinaldo falls asleep in Traetta's *Armida*; see Abert, *Christoph Willibald Gluck: Orfeo ed Euridice*. We have already noted the influence of *opéra comique* on the brief, songlike numbers. Among such numbers is the final one of all, which, formally speaking, is a complete vaudeville.
24. See Engländer, 'Zu den Münchener Orfeo-Aufführungen 1773 und 1775', 26ff.

Not only has the drama gained in depth, so too has the expressive range of the music, revealing a breadth and profundity that are particularly clear from the instrumental sections of the recitatives as well as from the choruses and their combination of solo singing and dancing. Although this signifies a marked increase in French influence, Gluck's achievement here, as elsewhere, far exceeds all his models, with the ancient device of repeating individual choral numbers now producing whole blocks of scenes of unprecedented monumentality.

In spite of all these merits and notwithstanding its aggressively worded preface, *Alceste* was by no means an outright success. Although there were a few enthusiastic voices raised in its defence,[25] these were offset by the eloquent silence of such authorities as Hasse. There were only two productions in Italy, one in Bologna in 1778, the other in Naples in 1785,[26] but neither led to anything further. Nor did the opera fare any better at its first foreign staging in Christiansborg in Denmark,[27] while in northern Germany it was rejected almost completely not only by King Frederick himself[28] but also by his musicians.[29]

Gluck came out fighting, expressing himself in no uncertain terms in his preface to *Paride ed Elena*, complaining at the public's tepid response and at the stupidity of the musicians and declaring his intention of remaining true to his new ideal. Unfortunately Calzabigi proved unequal to the new challenge, and in both its five-act structure and its treatment of its subject matter, *Paride ed Elena* is a failure, albeit one that is not without interest in terms of its transitional nature and its anticipation of the French operas that were to follow. Here the dramatic conflict does not stem from a basic idea that determines everything in advance, be it plot or *dramatis personae*, but from the antagonism between two characters. For this to work, the characterization would have had to be in the style of *Iphigénie en Aulide*, but it was Calzabigi's misfortune to imagine that he could get by here with his earlier approach. As before, he tried to achieve his effects by means of elemental antitheses, and it is typical of his whole manner that he highlighted the contrast between his two main characters by giving it a universal dimension and seeing in it a clash between Europe and Asia and, hence, between culture and barbarism. But this contrast remains no more than a detail when compared with the matter in hand, the manner in which the fatal affair develops. And it is precisely here that Calzabigi came to grief. The idea that love is a source of ruin as soon as it assumes the form of a primeval force and boundless passion is entirely typical of the 'Age of Reason'; but the rationalist in Calzabigi lacked the power of inner experience to carry this through into the drama. As a result, Love remains a pale child of reason, for all that she is the main character whose presence permeates the piece, and matters are only made worse by the fact that the action is spread over five whole acts. Not even Gluck was able to overcome this problem, even though the work reveals an undeniable advance in terms of its musical characterization. His Paris is an inspired and genuinely Gluckian creation: he is the Asiatic hero who, in Gluck's eyes, has not enjoyed the principal blessings of a civilized education, blessings that include clarity of mind and firmness of will. As such, he represents those chaotic instincts which, for Gluck, were the root of all evil. Helen is his antithesis, no Circe-like figure but a majestic princess who, as Gluck says, is still 'respected by Hector' even after committing so heinous a crime and whom he therefore subtly

25. Sonnenfels, *Briefe über die wienerische Schaubühne*; Hiller, *Wöchentliche Nachrichten*, iii (1768), 127ff.; and Riedel, *Ueber die Musik des Ritters Christoph von Gluck*, IXff.

26. Ricci, *I teatri di Bologna nei secoli XVII e XVIII*, 625ff., and Florimo, *La scuola musicale di Napoli e i suoi conservatorii*, iv.350. ◆ Loewenberg, *Annals of Opera*, 295–8, also lists performances in Padua in 1777 and Florence in 1786.

27. See Wotquenne, *Thematisches Verzeichnis der Werke von Chr. W. v. Gluck*, 208.

28. *Allgemeine deutsche Bibliothek* x/2.31; Nicolai, *Beschreibung einer Reise durch Deutschland und die Schweiz im Jahre 1781*, iv.529; and Reichardt, *AmZ*, iii (1800/1), 187 and xv (1813), 612.

29. Agricola, *Allgemeine deutsche Bibliothek* xiv/1.3ff. and especially Forkel, *Allgemeine deutsche Bibliothek* x/2.29ff.

portrays in her cruel reserve even towards her own retinue of earthy athletes. But it is for precisely this reason that there is something unsatisfactory about her final change of heart. The conflict between nature and religion so masterfully embodied by Agamemnon (see below) is still barely sketched out here. Gluck himself appears to have been aware of these shortcomings and never returned to the piece but merely helped himself to individual numbers when writing his later works.

Paride ed Elena proved no more of a breakthrough for Gluck than his earlier operas had done. Viennese audiences could make nothing of Gluck's art of ethnographical characterization, an art which for today's listeners is the most accessible aspect of the work. It is no wonder, therefore, that he accepted an offer from the then attaché to the French embassy in Vienna, François Louis Gand Leblanc du Roullet, to write his next opera for Paris. Du Roullet himself was keen to prepare a libretto based on Racine's *Iphigénie en Aulide*. It was thus Du Roullet who took the decisive step and gave a new direction to Gluck's operatic reforms, exchanging an Italian basis for a French one. Du Roullet was entirely right to predict that success would come more easily to Gluck if he pursued this new course. The German temperament, in which the chaotic and elemental element has always been particularly pronounced, had offered dull and instinctive resistance to this implacable dramatic logic, and only the upper echelons of Viennese society, who had in any case been favourably disposed to the French educational ideal, had been won over to Gluck's cause. Paris, by contrast, was the home of the rationalist 'classical' drama, the city of Racine and Corneille: here Gluck's art was very soon felt to reflect the national spirit, a spirit that saw in logic, clarity and order the supreme goals of human endeavour. Rationalism had started life in Paris in the form of 'classical' tragedy. After a lengthy period of paralysis it had now been restored to life and returned to its old home with the Gluckian music drama, and it was no accident that Gluck's first French work was based on a piece by Racine.

In spite of everything, it must none the less have seemed a risk to appear just now before Paris audiences with a new opera that harked back to the old *tragédie lyrique*. As we have seen, the old type of opera à la Rameau had sunk considerably in general esteem since the time of the *Querelle des Bouffons*, and for Rousseau and the whole of the younger generation it had become the epitome of unnaturalness and backwardness. Even so, it was Gluck who very soon emerged as the almost total victor, with even Rousseau finally proving to be one of his most ardent supporters. The reason for this apparently surprising turn of events lay in the fact that, unlike the radical *Bouffon* faction that had dismissed the older type of opera out of hand, Gluck had been able to distinguish between its outward manifestation and its universal intellectual aims.[30] He abandoned the former but retained the latter as something to which he himself could relate. Yet even in *Iphigénie en Aulide* he found himself confronted by a whole series of new problems that forced him to pursue a rather different course from the one he had taken so far. The heroes of his three most recent operas had all embodied certain elevated ideas and these alone, with the result that all purely human features had effectively disappeared. Now he was dealing for the first time with characters which, while not individuals in the modern sense, were none the less firmly rooted in a particular area of human culture. But this meant a different concept of dramatic action inasmuch as the plot was no longer derived from a particular moral idea but from the interplay between the characters. With *Iphigénie en Aulide* Gluck immediately found himself confronted by his most

---

30.   ◆ See Herbert Schneider, 'Gluck and Lully'.

difficult challenge: the character of Agamemnon, torn between his love as a father and his duty as a king or, as Gluck himself put it, between nature and religion.

Yet even when faced by these new challenges, Gluck did not waver from his principles. In the first place, he adopted exactly the same attitude to French verse as he had done towards Metastasio's: everything had to go that was still bound up with the old conventions and with the views and moral concepts of the age of Louis XIV. At the same time, however, he retained the old rationalistic creative principle that was aimed at clarity and order, except that in this case too he based it on inner experience. As a result he gave back to the French a purified image of their own temperament and it was not long before he was able to unite both enemy camps under his banner. The adherents of the older type of opera were suborned by the force of his thinking, while the champions of the new were won over by his weight of experience.

In this way Gluck developed a new and distinctive art of characterization. The characters' conventional masks were removed, and although these masks were not replaced with individual features in the sense understood by modern psychology, still less did he attempt to portray them as capable of development in the sense in which we understand this term today, even so he strove to reduce them to the simplest possible stereotypical formulas. Although Achilles and Iphigenia were no longer 'prince Achille' and 'princesse Iphigénie', as Jahn believed,[31] he was not interested, either, in depicting the psychological development of their relationship. For him, Achilles remains the murderous son of Peleus of the *Iliad*, Iphigenia the tender, maidenly young woman who suffers patiently till the end. Likewise in depicting the character of Agamemnon, Gluck's main concern remained his two basic motifs, nature and religion, with other characteristics such as anger and the desire for vengeance receiving his attention only to the extent that they served to deepen the underlying conflict. Everything that might be construed as unique or fortuitous was strenuously removed, and only what was typical remained. This explains why the action proceeds in a series of broad and simple sweeps. The characters never change, and so there are no unexpected complications in terms of the plot. Everything is reduced to the simplest concepts with implacable acuteness of vision, yet there is none of the sense of cold calculation that one often finds with the older rationalist dramaturgy: the whole of this splendid system is not merely the product of deep thought but is genuinely lived. Gluck's characters are as far removed from Mozart's as is humanly possible, yet the impression that they create is no less profound, thereby offering clear proof that there are different ways of experiencing the life of the soul and, hence, of creating dramatic characters. Only the philistine succeeds in forcing these different possibilities into the straitjacket of a particular system.

That Gluck aligned himself with French opera on a formal level, too, was only natural, not least as a result of the French language, whose peculiarities he studied with wonted resolve. But what finally emerged, in spite of all his readily identifiable models, was none the less something new, something specifically Gluckian, as is clear, not least, from his recitatives. Gluck brought with him from Vienna his ideally steely and dramatic declamatory style, which needed only to be slightly modified to suit the spirit of the French language. At the same time, however, he welded together all his existing achievements to create a new style that ranges from the *secco* and *accompagnato* recitatives of the Italians[32] and the *récitatif mesuré* of the French to fully developed arioso akin to the melodic line of an aria. Conversely, the declamatory nature of his melodic writing is perceptibly increased in the arias, with the words gaining an increasing influence on Gluck's vocal style – hence,

---

31. Jahn, *W. A. Mozart*, i.523.
32. Highly significant in this context is the gradual disappearance of the typical Italian cadence with descending fourth.

too, his emphatic rejection of the old coloratura principle whose 'unnaturalness' he had already attacked, of course, in *Orfeo ed Euridice*. The choruses, by contrast, are the least progressive aspect of the new work, although here, of course, it was difficult to improve on *Alceste* and *Paride ed Elena*. Likewise, the ballet increased in size rather than in kind: in spite of Gluck's attempt to incorporate this element into an organic whole, he was obliged to make certain concessions to French taste. Significantly, the number of such movements reverts to more modest proportions in *Iphigénie en Tauride*.

The ground was prepared for the new piece by two open letters in the *Mercure de France*, the first, in October 1772, from Du Roullet to the director of the Académie Royale, Antoine Dauvergne, and the second, in February 1773, from Gluck himself. Thanks to his connections with the Viennese court, Gluck finally managed to win over the dauphine, Marie Antoinette, to his side. The first performance took place on 19 April 1774 at the end of a six-month rehearsal period during which Gluck's strength of purpose had been tested to its limits by the obstinate resistance on the part of the singers and orchestra.[33] Although this first performance was less than wholly successful, the second found greater favour. There was, of course, resistance to the work from the outset, and it was not long before arguments were raging on both sides.

This is not the place to trace the various stages in this dispute. The initial reaction in both the French and Italian camps was one of bemusement, but they soon roused themselves and offered concerted resistance. Gluck, too, found a number of enthusiastic admirers, foremost among whom were the Abbé Arnaud, the editor of the *Gazette littéraire de l'Europe*, and Rousseau himself. They were later joined by Jean-Baptiste Suard, who styled himself 'L'Anonyme de Vaugirard'.[34] Gluck himself consolidated his position with a French reworking of *Orfeo*, which was unveiled on 2 August 1774 but which was, of course, no more successful from a dramatic point of view than its predecessor had been.[35] This in turn was followed by adaptations of two older and less important works, *L'arbre enchantée* (27 February 1775) and *Cythère assiégée* (1 August 1775), both of which proved deeply disappointing to Gluck. *Alceste* followed on 23 April 1776 in a reworking by Du Roullet, a version which, while making a number of decisive improvements to Calzabigi's libretto, introduced the character of Hercules, a change of distinctly doubtful dramatic value.[36] This version, too, was initially unsuccessful, and it was not until later that audiences began to take an interest it. But Gluck now decided to offer Parisian audiences two new works, rather than recycling his older ones, and with his customary resolve chose two texts by old Quinault himself: *Roland* and *Armide*.

While he was still working on these two operas in Vienna, the supporters of Italian opera were inspired by his example to implement a plan which, although long cherished, had invariably come to nothing in the past: they invited one of the most respected Neapolitan composers, Niccolò Piccinni, to Paris. His invitation was the work of Madame Du Barry; Jean-François de La Harpe; the influential Neapolitan ambassador to Paris, the Marchese Domenico Caracciolo; and ultimately

33.   Cramer, *Magazin der Musik*, i (1783), 561; Genlis, *Mémoires inédits pour servir à l'histoire des dix-huitième et dix-neuvième siècles*, ii.248–9; Desnoiresterres, *Gluck et Piccinni*, 85ff.

34.   ◆ See Vendrix, *Aux origines d'une discipline historique: La musique et son histoire en France aux XVIIe et XVIIIe siècles*; and Alfred C. Hunter, *J.-B.-A. Suard, un introducteur de la littérature anglaise en France*.

35.   The aria 'L'espoir renaît' is not by Bertoni, as was formerly assumed, but by Gluck himself; see Julien Tiersot's introduction to the Pelletan edition of *Orphée et Eurydice*, LIXff. ◆ The current view is that although the arias have some resemblances, both composers were writing for the same singer, who demanded that they customize their writing to his preferences; hence their similarities. The original accusation stems from Coquéau's 1776 *Entretiens sur l'état de l'Opéra de Paris* (see Lesure, *Querelle des Gluckistes et des Piccinnistes*, for a facsimile of Coquéau; and Howard, *Gluck: An Eighteenth-Century Portrait in Letters and Documents*, 202).

36.   Hercules's first-act aria is not by Gossec, but comes from Gluck's own *Ezio* of 1750.

Queen Marie Antoinette herself, whose Italian sympathies were now newly revived. Marmontel declared his willingness to revise Quinault's *Roland* for Piccinni, resulting in a strongly worded letter from Gluck to Du Roullet that the latter proceeded to publish.[37] This was the letter that sparked the famous quarrel between the Gluckistes and the Piccinnistes that soon inflamed the whole of Paris but that was effectively no more than a latter-day version of the old antagonism between the French and Italian operatic ideals, except that thanks to Gluck's towering personality the French ideal had now acquired a purity that ensured its spiritual and intellectual ascendancy from the outset.[38]

Gluck was not the man to allow himself to be intimidated by this turn of events and he never saw any serious danger for his music drama in the sort of Italian opera that he himself had long since routed. The attacks of the Italian faction were a cause of considerable annoyance, of course, but like all determined individuals he drew renewed strength from the struggle. He even enjoyed entering the arena from time to time and joining in the general feud with his usual reckless causticity. Piccinni, by contrast, was not in the least belligerent by nature. He arrived in Paris on the last day of 1776, his hopes of a brilliant future fired by the city's patrons of the arts. But it did not take him long to realize that he had entered a lions' den, and the longer he was exposed to these squabbles, the less this kind, inoffensive and, above all, peace-loving man felt equal to the struggle. He had neither the inclination nor the talent to be a party leader. Added to this was his ignorance of the French language, which seriously impaired his abilities to deal with the outside world and also caused him great difficulties in composing *Roland*.[39] It was with mounting anxiety, therefore, that he watched events unfold, especially when Gluck angrily abandoned his own plans to set Quinault's libretto and started rehearsing *Armide* in July 1777. The first night followed on 23 September. Although Gluck had proudly predicted that the work would be a success, informing even the queen herself of this fact,[40] it was again slow to make an impression, drawing full houses only after La Harpe had lambasted it and Gluck had called for help on L'Anonyme de Vaugirard. Its initially cool reception was no surprise, of course, as its Romantic character and pronounced sensuality seemed to set it apart from the 'classical' Gluck of the earlier works. Not every listener noticed right away that, with his customary resolve, Gluck had sought and found the most suitable forms of expression for these completely different characters. Meanwhile, the rehearsals for *Roland* were proceeding apace. The controversy raged with particular fury at this time, but Gluck, who was well aware of the need to draw a distinction between the man and the work,[41] insisted on strict discipline from singers and musicians alike. Piccinni, meanwhile, grew more and more pessimistic and was already resolved to return to Naples on the day after the first performance on 27 January 1778. Contrary to his expectations, however, it proved a total triumph.[42] Its success was certainly

37. *Année littéraire* 1776, viii.322. The letter dates from the end of the year; see Tiersot, *Gluck*, 178. ◆ It is not clear which letter Abert refers to here; Gluck wrote to Du Roullett twice, on 2 and 13 December 1775; see Mueller von Asow, *The Collected Correspondence and Papers of Christoph Willibald Gluck*, 75–9.

38. See Desnoiresterres, *Gluck et Piccinni*, and Thoinan, *Notes bibliographiques sur la guerre musicale des Gluckistes et Piccinnistes*. A collection of the most important essays and pamphlets was published by Le Blond, *Mémoires pour servir à l'histoire de la révolution opérée dans la musique par M. le Chevalier Gluck*. ◆ Concerning the quarrel of the *Gluckistes* and *Piccinnistes* and its importance, see Lesure, 'Querelle des Gluckistes et des Piccinnistes' (facsimiles of original documents); Rushton, 'Music and Drama at the Académie Royale de Musique (Paris), 1774–1789' and 'Iphigénie en Tauride: The operas of Gluck and Piccinni'; and Schmierer, 'Die deutsche Rezeption der Querelle des Gluckistes et Piccinnistes'.

39. Marmontel, who also taught him French, each day had to translate the libretto for him, section by section; see Marmontel, *Œuvres complètes*, ii.15; see also Ginguené, *Notice sur la vie et les ouvrages de Nicolas Piccinni*, 25ff.

40. Campan, *Mémoires sur la vie privée de Marie Antoinette*, 7 and 131.

41. See Genlis, *Mémoires inédits*, ii.248 and Ginguené, *Notice*, 45–6.

42. Grimm, *Correspondance littéraire*, ix.500 and x.23.

merited, as the work teems with beauties all of its own and attests to the surprising ease with which Piccinni was able to adapt and assimilate the new style. Yet this very fact spelt the defeat of the Italian faction in Paris, for the work that the composer of their choice had offered them was anything but the Neapolitan opera that they had expected him to write: with its choruses and dances, its orchestral recitatives and earnest sense of drama, it resembled nothing so much as a work by the hated Gluck, except that the Italian delight in making music and, above all, Piccinni's tender-hearted and dreamy inwardness found greater expression here. Although the arguments continued to rage for some time, the dispute effectively ended in 1778, when the elderly, world-famous Italian composer showed exceptional magnanimity and resolve in bowing before Gluck's greatness and becoming his pupil instead of his enemy. His response was imitated not only by other Italians in Paris, including Sacchini, for example, but it also brought new blood to the old Italian opera by offering powerful support to the minority of composers who had already been won over to the idea of reintroducing the chorus into their works.

21

Mozart in Paris

Thanks to the unprecedented success of *Roland*, Piccinni was still the hero of the hour when Mozart and his mother arrived in Paris on 23 March.[1] But the Gluckistes had not been idle and were busily giving their adversary a piece of their mind in a whole series of different forms ranging from serious polemic to light-hearted parody.[2] On 27 April 1778, a month after his arrival in the city, Mozart could have attended a performance of *Les trois âges de l'opéra*, an opera by Grétry to words by Alphonse de Vismes,[3] in which the characters of Lully, Rameau and Gluck appeared in a succession of scenes depicting the whole history of the genre, including Italian *opera buffa*.[4] In this way Mozart would have been able to see this most topical of operatic controversies treated in theatrical guise. But wherever he turned, there was no escaping it, whether in the theatre or the concert hall, in newspapers or the salons of the aristocracy and even in the street. And his whole future depended on his own particular reaction to it.[5]

That it was exceptionally difficult for a newcomer to make any impression in these circumstances must have been clear to him from the outset, and even if it was not, advisers such as Grimm made no secret of the difficulties. To remain neutral in the general debate was tantamount to renouncing success from the outset. But to assert himself alongside Gluck and Piccinni, as Leopold hoped,[6] would have required far greater artistic prestige than Mozart currently enjoyed in the world and especially in Paris. Only by acting clear-headedly and energetically could he achieve his ends; anyone who in the present mayhem did not know exactly what he or she wanted and who did not join one or other of the two parties ran the risk of falling beneath the bandwagon's wheels.

There were various ways in which a young artist could catch the public eye. Mozart himself was temperamentally disinclined to take part in the literary feud. After all, he simply could not understand why men of letters should cudgel their brains over matters which, in his view, were of concern only to musicians. But nor could he understand why composers argued over rules before writing a note of music. The second possibility, to which Leopold had directed his son with some insistence, was to find influential patrons at court and among the nobility. Although his contacts in Vienna had been unable to provide him with a letter of recommendation to Queen Marie Antoinette, Leopold had already sent his son a long list of members of the aristocracy whom

---

1. The opera's takings totalled 60,000 livres for twelve performances. By 19 March it was being parodied in the form of Dorvigny's *La rage d'amour*; see Bachaumont, *Mémoires secrets*, xi.185.
2. Marmontel was mockingly said to live in the 'rue des mauvais paroles', Piccinni in the 'rue des petits-champs', whereupon Gluck was banished to the 'rue du grand hurleur'; see Bachaumont, *Mémoires secrets*, xi.108 and 115.
3. The brother of the director of the Académie Royale de Musique.
4. In his preface, the poet apologizes to Piccinni for not including him, too; see Bachaumont, *Mémoires secrets*, xi.250.
5. ◆ Concerning musical life in Paris at this time, see Salinger, *Mozart à Paris*, and Mongrédien, 'Paris: The End of the Ancien Régime'.
6. *Briefe*, ii.442 (letter of 13 August 1778).

Mozart was enjoined to call on.[7] In the event, barely a single one of these names appears in Mozart's letters, and it was not long before he abandoned such visits altogether:

You say that I ought to call on lots of people in order to make new acquaintances and revive the old ones. But this is impossible. It's too far to go on foot – or too muddy, for it's indescribably dirty in Paris. To take a carriage means that you have the honour of paying 4 or 5 livres a day, and all for nothing. People pay their respects, and that's it. They arrange for me to come on such and such a day; I then play for them and they say: 'Oh, c'est un prodige, c'est inconceivable, c'est étonnant.' And, with that, adieu. At first I spent a lot of money driving around – often to no purpose, as the people weren't at home. If you're not here, you can't imagine how tiresome this is.[8]

The same letter mentions a particularly humiliating experience that must have been the last straw for a self-respecting artist like Mozart:

Monsieur Grimm gave me a letter to Madame la Duchesse de Chabot,[9] and so I drove there. The main object of the letter was to recommend me to the Duchesse de Bourbon[10] (who was in a convent the last time I was here[11]), to reintroduce me to her and remind her of my existence. A week went by without any news. But she had asked me to call on her after a week had gone by, and so I kept my word and returned. I had to wait ½ an hour in a large, freezing, unheated room that didn't even have a fireplace. At last the D. de Chabot appeared, politeness itself, and asked me to make the best of the keyboard in the room as none of her others was in good condition. She suggested I should have a go. I said I'd be only too pleased to play something but that it was impossible at present as my fingers were numb with cold, and I asked to be taken to a room where there was at least a fire. 'Oh oui, Monsieur, vous avez raison,' was her only reply. She then sat down and began to draw for the next hour in the company of some gentlemen who all sat in a circle round a big table, while I had the honour to wait. Windows and doors were open, not only my hands were cold, so were my whole body and feet, and my head was starting to ache as well. So there was a deep silence, and I didn't know what to do for cold, headache and boredom. I kept thinking that if it weren't for Monsieur Grimm, I'd leave at once. Finally, to cut a long story short, I played on that miserable, wretched pianoforte. But what annoyed me most of all was that Madame and all her gentlemen didn't stop drawing for a moment, but went on as before, so I had to play to the chairs, table and walls. In these unfavourable circumstances, I lost my patience and, having begun the Fischer variations [K179], played only half of them, then got up. I was showered with praise. I said the only thing I could say, namely, that I couldn't do myself justice on this instrument and that I'd like to come on another day when a better one would be available. But she wouldn't hear of my going and so I had to wait another ½ hour for

7. *Briefe*, ii.258–60 (letter of 5 February 1778).

8. *Briefe*, ii.344–5 (letter of 1 May 1778). Grimm confirmed these difficulties: 'C'est une chose très fatigante de courir les quatre coins de Paris et de s'épuiser à parler pour montrer' (*Briefe*, ii.446; letter of 13 August 1778).

9. The Duchesse de Chabot was a daughter of Jean-Baptiste, Marquis de Roucy (1707–46), and is mentioned by Galiani as an acquaintance of Grimm and Madame d'Épinay; see Galiani, *Correspondance inédite*, ii.305.

10. The Duchesse de Bourbon was a daughter of the Duc d'Orléans and sister of the then Duc de Chartres, later Philippe Égalité. Only a short time previously she had been the cause of a sensational duel between the Duc de Bourbon and the Conte d'Artois; Grimm, *Correspondance littéraire, philosophique et critique*, x.1ff.

11. That is, during Mozart's first visit to Paris in 1763/4. The duchess had entered a convent at the age of fifteen and remained there for some years; see Genlis, *Mémoires inédits sur le XVIIIe siècle et la révolution française*, iii.84.

her husband to come. But he then sat down beside me and listened with great attention and I – I forgot the cold and my headache, and in spite of the wretched instrument I played as I always do when I'm in a good mood. Give me the best instrument in Europe but with listeners who understand nothing or who don't want to understand and feel nothing for what I'm playing, and I get no pleasure from it. I told Monsieur Grimm about it afterwards.

As a result of his aversion to paying calls, Mozart acquired very few pupils and in this way lost what would have been one of his principal sources of income. And, of course, all his old dislike of teaching came flooding back:

You mustn't think it's laziness – no! – it's just that it goes against my genius and against the way I live my life – you know that I live only for music – that I'm immersed in it all day – that I like thinking about it, studying it and pondering on it; but I'm prevented from doing this by the life I'm leading here.[12]

None the less, Mozart was grateful to Grimm for at least one promising contact. Following a sensational court case involving his secretary Tort de la Soude,[13] the Comte de Guines had been recalled from his post as French ambassador in London in 1776 and had settled to Paris, where he enjoyed the special favour of the queen.[14] Leopold, too, set the greatest store by this contact and hoped that his son would be commissioned to write something for the festivities that were expected to follow the queen's forthcoming *accouchement*.[15] De Guines was a great music lover and, according to Mozart, played the flute extremely well. His daughter was an equally fine harpist.[16] Mozart duly received an invitation to wirte a concerto for these two instruments (K299).[17] He also taught the daughter composition for two hours a day, in return for which he was promised a handsome fee. It is to these lessons that we owe Mozart's own lively account of his teaching methods in his letter of 14 May 1778:

She has lots of talent and genius and, in particular, an incredible memory, as she plays all her pieces, around 200 in all, by heart. But she has doubts about her abilities as a composer, especially with regard to ideas; but her father (who, between ourselves, is somewhat too much in love with her) says she has plenty of ideas and that it's mere diffidence – she simply has too little confidence in herself. Well, we'll see. If she gets no ideas (for at present she genuinely doesn't have any), it's a waste of time – God knows, I can't give her any. Her father's intention isn't to make a great composer of her. She's not, he said, to write operas, arias, concertos or symphonies, but only grand sonatas for her instrument and my own. I gave her her fourth lesson today, and

12. *Briefe*, ii.427 (letter of 31 July 1778).
13. See Louis de Loménie, *Beaumarchais et son temps*, ii.89–90; Dutens, *Mémoires d'un voyageur qui se repose*, ii.59ff.; and Deffand, *Lettres*, iii.172ff. and 297.
14. Deffand, *Lettres*, iv.107.
15. *Briefe*, ii.364 (letter of 28 May 1778). The dauphine, Marie Thérèse Charlotte, afterwards Duchesse d'Angoulême, was born on 19 December 1778.
16. *Briefe*, ii.356 (letter of 14 May 1778); see also Genlis, *Mémoires inédits*, i.288–9. The daughter, who was endowed by the king himself, married the Comte de Charlus (afterwards the Duc de Castries) during the summer of 1778 and died in childbirth in 1780; see Deffand, *Lettres*, iv.52.
17. According to Joseph Frank, these were Mozart's least favourite instruments; see Frank, 'Aus den ungedruckten Denkwürdigkeiten der Aerzte Peter und Joseph Frank'. In her letter of 5 April 1778 (*Briefe*, ii.329), Maria Anna erroneously states that Mozart had written two concertos, one for the flute and one for the harp, an error perpetuated by Nannerl in Nottebohm, *Mozartiana*, 109.

as far as the rules of composition and harmony go, I'm fairly pleased with her – she filled in quite a good bass for the first minuet that I set her. She has already started to write in three parts. We're getting on well, but she soon becomes bored and there's nothing I can do to help her – I can't go on to the next stage, it's still too soon, even if she were a genius, which unfortunately she isn't – everything will have to be done by the book. She has no ideas – nothing comes. I've tried everything possible; among other things, I hit on the idea of writing out a very simple minuet and seeing whether she could write a variation on it. – But it was a waste of time. – Well, I thought, she simply doesn't know where to begin – and so I started to write a variation on the first bar and told her to go on in the same vein and stick to the idea – in the end it went quite well. When it was finished, I told her to begin something of her own – only the treble part, the melody – well, she thought about it for a whole quarter of an hour, but nothing came. So I wrote down 4 bars of a minuet and said to her: 'You see what an idiot I am, I've started a minuet but can't even finish the first part. Would you mind finishing it for me?' She thought that she couldn't. Finally, after a lot of effort, something emerged. I was happy to see anything at all. She then had to finish the minuet, I mean just the treble. For her homework I asked her only to vary my four bars and make something of them – to devise a new beginning, using the same harmonies if necessary, as long as the melody was different. I'll see tomorrow what she has done.[18]

The experienced Leopold responded to this naïve account on 28 May:

You write that you have today given the duke's daughter her fourth lesson and you already want her to write down ideas of her own – do you think everyone has your genius? – It will come with time. She has a good memory. Eh bien! Let her steal or, to put it more politely, let her apply what she has learnt. There's nothing you can do until she gains self-confidence. You've started her off on the right path with variations, so carry on! – If Monsieur le Duc hears a short piece by his daughter, he'll be beside himself with delight; this is a lucky contact.[19]

But Mozart remained convinced that his pupil was 'not the sort of person who is made for composition'. She was 'heartily stupid and heartily lazy'.[20] When she became engaged, her lessons finally came to an end, although not before de Guines had attempted to buy off Mozart by offering him three louis d'or, an offer that Mozart indignantly rejected.

With few exceptions, he was no more successful with his colleagues in Paris than he was with the local aristocracy. Here he took all too seriously his father's advice to maintain the lowest possible profile. Gluck himself was in Vienna at this time, but Mozart was introduced to Piccinni, without, of course, having sought him out:

I spoke to Piccinni at the Concert Spirituel – whenever we bump into each other, he is very polite to me and I to him, but I have made no attempt to become better acquainted with him or with any other composers – I know what I'm doing – and they do too – and that's enough.[21]

18. *Briefe*, ii.356–7 (letter of 14 May 1778).
19. *Briefe*, ii.364–5 (letter of 28 May 1778).
20. *Briefe*, ii.397 (letter of 9 July 1778).
21. *Briefe*, ii.397 (letter of 9 July 1778).

Among the other musicians who set the tone in Paris at this time, Mozart mentions only the Walloon composer François-Joseph Gossec (1734–1829), describing him as 'a very good friend and a very dry man'.[22] But he has absolutely nothing to say about the representatives of *opéra comique*, especially Grétry.[23] The other musicians whom he mentions were either relative nonentities such as the horn player in the Chapelle Royale, Jean Joseph Rodolphe (1730–1812),[24] the Bohemian horn virtuoso Giovanni Punto (Johann Wenzel Stich, 1746–1803) and the Italian Giuseppe Cambini (1746–1825), who had studied with Martini and who was a favourite of Gossec's, or else they were old friends from Mannheim such as Wendling, Ritter, Ramm and especially Raaff. Wendling had already done much of the groundwork necessary for Mozart's visit. There was no longer any reference to the dangers that he posed as a freethinker. Instead, we find Mozart's mother declaring on 5 April 1778: 'He really is a true philanthropist, and Monsieur von Grimm has urged him to do his best to make Wolfgang known, as he has more influence as a musician.'[25] It was only now, however, that Mozart became more closely acquainted with Raaff, not least when he realized that he, too, had the Webers' interests at heart: not only did Raaff promise to give Aloysia lessons, he also approved of Mozart's love of her. Mozart also had the unexpected pleasure of renewing contact with his old teacher from London, Johann Christian Bach, who came over in August 1778 to write a French opera for Paris. Bach brought with him his friend, the castrato Giusto Ferdinando Tenducci, whom Mozart likewise knew from London. All three men were delighted to see each other again, as is clear from the unusually heartfelt expressions of love and respect found in Mozart's letter of 27 August. Bach introduced his young friend to the Duc de Noailles,[26] and the latter invited all three men to stay with him at St-Germain, where they spent several enjoyable days together. For Tenducci, Mozart wrote a *scena* for voice, keyboard, oboe, horn and bassoon that was performed by German members of de Noailles's private orchestra (K315b). Unfortunately, it is no longer extant.[27]

If we stand back for a moment and consider Mozart's modest contribution to the musical life of Paris during these six months, it will be clear that, superficially at least, this was a time of failure for him. The first person to realize this fully was his adviser Friedrich Melchior Grimm. Although he had initially given Mozart one letter of recommendation after another, he soon noticed what little use Mozart was making of them and so he allowed him increasingly to go his own way. By 31 July Mozart was already telling his father that Grimm had complained that he was 'not sufficiently active' and 'not running around enough'.[28] And it was not long before Leopold received similar

22.   *Briefe*, ii.332 (letter of 5 April 1778). ◆ Further concerning Gossec, see Prod'homme, *François-Joseph Gossec*, and Mongrédien, *La musique en France, des Lumières au Romantisme: de 1789 à 1830.*

23.   ◆ See Vendrix, *L'opéra-comique en France au XVIIIe siècle*. In his *Mémoires*, i.84, Grétry described a less than convincing meeting in Geneva with a child prodigy: 'Once in Geneva I met a child who could play everything at sight. His father said to me before the assembled company: so that no doubt shall remain as to my son's talent, write for him, for tomorrow, a very difficult sonata movement. I wrote him an allegro in E flat; difficult, but unpretentious. He played it and everyone except myself believed that it was a miracle. The boy had not stopped; but following the modulations, he had substituted a quantity of passages for those which I had written' (*Dokumente*, 415–6, *Documentary Biography*, 477). The child prodigy is presumed to be Mozart: Grétry had moved to Geneva in 1766 and the Mozarts visited there between 22 August and about 10 September that year.

24.   A selection of his dramatic ballets may be found in Abert, *Ausgewählte Ballette Stuttgarter Meister aus der 2. Hälfte des 18. Jahrhunderts.*

25.   *Briefe*, ii.330 (letter of 5 April 1778).

26.   There were two marshals called de Noailles in Paris at this time, one a duke, the other a count. The duke was the father of one of Mozart's former patrons, the Comtesse Tessé, and like her was a great lover of art and literature; see Loménie, *Beaumarchais*, i.206–7.

27.   Tenducci must have taken it back with him to London, as Burney mentions it admiringly in Barrington's *Miscellanies*, 289 [*Dokumente*, 166, *Documentary Biography*, 187]; see Pohl, *Mozart und Haydn in London*, 121–2.

28.   *Briefe*, ii.426 (letter of 31 July 1778).

complaints from Grimm himself.[29] Grimm, moreover, was not entirely confident about Mozart's artistic achievements, and it was this that annoyed Mozart more than anything else. Grimm doubted Mozart's ability to write a French opera and repeatedly drew his attention to the Italian school. There is no question that Grimm's advice was honestly meant. He was, after all, a staunch supporter of the Italian party. But Mozart was naturally distrustful (a characteristic inherited from his father), and these feelings now increased, not least because he was so put off by Grimm's inability 'to do you a kindness without constantly rubbing your nose in it'.[30] By the end he was describing Grimm as stupid, clumsy, base and false[31] and even convinced that his old patron was his personal enemy. Of course, Grimm was not entirely irreproachable or honourable as a person,[32] otherwise he would scarcely have risen to such a position of influence in Paris, but his contemporaries also praised his willingness to help others and his kindly disposition.[33] Moreover, Mozart seriously overestimated the importance of his own position in Paris if he thought that a man like Grimm was attempting to undermine it. Given the modest role that Mozart was playing in Paris at this time, he really had no need to make any such attempt. He remained Mozart's patron until the end, well-meaning if invariably maintaining the distance required by his reputation, and although there is no doubt that he will have regretted the fact that Mozart did not follow his advice, there is no evidence that he allowed himself to get worked up as a result. At all events, there is absolutely no reason to question his sincerity, a sincerity based at least in part on his high regard for Leopold Mozart.

As a result of all this, the Mozarts' dealings with a man in whom they had placed their greatest hopes ended on a note of the deepest disharmony. Grimm himself was bound to find Mozart increasingly baffling as a person: with his curious mixture of self-confidence and dreaminess, the latter explored the whole of Paris's motley musical scene, listening silently but attentively to all that was going on around him and finally coming to the depressing conclusion that Paris was not the right place for him. Mozart never felt comfortable in Paris, and the longer he remained there, the less he liked the French. 'They are not nearly so polite as they were 15 years ago', he wrote to his father on 1 May 1778. 'Their manner now borders on rudeness and they are frightfully arrogant.'[34] He was appalled by their general immorality[35] and complained to Ritter that he could find 'no pleasant, honest point of contact with people'. More and more, he told his father on 18 July 1778, he longed to escape from his present surroundings, finding Paris 'totally at odds' with

29. Grimm's letter to Leopold, the contents of which Leopold passed on to his son on 13 August 1778, runs as follows: 'He is too trusting, too inactive, too easy to catch, too little intent on the means that may lead to fortune. To make an impression here one has to be artful, enterprising, daring. To make his fortune I wish he had but half his talent and twice as much shrewdness, and then I should not worry about him. For the rest, he can try but two ways here to make a living. The first is to give harpsichord lessons; but, not to mention that one cannot get pupils without a great deal of activity and even mountebankery, I am not sure that his health would be good enough for him to sustain that profession, for it is a very tiring thing to run to the four corners of Paris and to exhaust oneself in explanations. And then this profession will not please him, because it will keep him from writing, which is what he likes above all things. He might therefore give all his time to that; but in this country the great public knows nothing about music. Consequently everything depends on names, and the merit of a work can be judged by only a very small number. The public is at the moment ridiculously divided between Piccinni and Gluck, and all the argument one hears about music is pitiable. It is thus very difficult for your son to succeed between these two parties. – You see, my dear *maître*, that in a country where so many mediocre and even detestable musicians have made immense fortunes, I very much fear that your son will not so much as make ends meet.' *Briefe*, ii.442 (letter of 13 August 1778).
30. *Briefe*, ii.474 (letter of 11 September 1778).
31. *Briefe*, ii.474–5 (letter of 11 September 1778).
32. Sainte-Beuve, *Causeries du lundi*, ii.158ff. and vii.226ff.; Genlis, *Mémoires inédits*, iv.3–4; and Merck, *Briefe*, ii.282–3.
33. Jacobs in Samuel Hoffmann, *Lebensbilder berühmter Humanisten*, 15.
34. *Briefe*, ii.345 (letter of 1 May 1778).
35. *Briefe*, ii.406 and 410 (letters of 18 and 20 July 1778).

his 'genius, inclinations, knowledge and sympathies'.[36] There is something touching about the way in which this German artist, far from home, was assailed by an increasingly ardent longing for that homeland and its way of life. 'I pray to God every day to give me grace to hold out here with fortitude and to be an honour to myself and the whole of the German nation.'[37] It is with angry pride that he compares himself with Piccinni 'even though I am only a German'[38] and repeatedly takes heart from the thought that he is an 'honest German'.[39] This pronounced sense of patriotism had found occasional expression in the past and is an essential element in Mozart's make-up, setting him apart not only from Haydn but from Beethoven, too.

Mozart was no less outspokenly critical of French music than he was of the French character, and on 1 May we find him writing to his father:

> If this were a place where people had ears to hear, hearts to feel and some measure of understanding or taste for music, I'd laugh heartily at all that has happened, but (as far as music is concerned) I'm surrounded by nothing but beasts and animals. But how can it be otherwise, for they're just the same in all their actions, emotions and passions – there's no place in the world like Paris. You mustn't think I'm exaggerating when I talk about the music here in these terms. Ask anyone you like, provided he's not a native Frenchman, and (if he knows what he's talking about) he'll say exactly the same.[40]

Here, of course, Mozart found himself on common ground with Grimm. As early as 5 April we find him writing to his father: 'Baron Grimm and I often vent our musical rage on the music here, just between ourselves, of course. In public we shout "Bravo bravissimo" and clap till our hands hurt.'[41] Rousseau himself would not have disowned Mozart's comments on the unmusical nature of the French language, which both men regarded as the root of all evil. And French singers, Mozart went on, were no better than the French language. 'The devil himself must have invented the language of these people', he wrote on 31 July.[42] On the 9th he had complained even more bitterly:

> If only the confounded French language weren't so damned impossible where music's concerned. It's hopeless. German is divine in comparison. And then there are the singers! In fact, they shouldn't be called singers at all, as they don't sing but scream and howl at the tops of their voices.[43]

In the light of all this, Mozart could hardly be expected to play a significant role in the arguments currently raging in Paris. Ultimately, he remained on the sidelines, even though – as we shall see – he had the opportunity and, in spite of Grimm, the intention – initially at least – to take Gluck's part. The reason for his failure to act was certainly not due solely to the unfavourable circumstances in which he found himself at this time nor yet to the congenital indolence inherited

36. *Briefe*, ii.409 (letter of 18 July 1778).
37. *Briefe*, ii.346 (letter of 1 May 1778).
38. *Briefe*, ii.474 (letter of 11 September 1778).
39. *Briefe*, ii.368 (letter of 29 May 1778).
40. *Briefe*, ii.346 (letter of 1 May 1778).
41. *Briefe*, ii.332 (letter of 5 April 1778).
42. *Briefe*, ii.427 (letter of 31 July 1778).
43. *Briefe*, ii.387 (letter of 9 July 1778).

from his mother, even though a more purposeful and energetic response would have spared him many a disappointment. No, it lay rather in the fact that in art as in life he held completely different views from those that were being so hotly debated in Paris. The times were past when, as boy and youth, he had impulsively aligned himself with each new trend that awoke a response in his young heart. He was now conscious of his own wealth of experience and began to question all new impressions and to wonder where his present direction was taking him. In his earlier quarrel with Colloredo he had, for the sake of his genius, sacrificed the sort of position that every ordinary musician had to endure at this time. The son of a self-respecting middle-class household, he had stood up to a representative of the old traditional order, urged on, as he was, by an artistic conscience whose voice had already led him far from the established idea of aristocratic art. In coming to Paris he had entered the citadel of that art, an art whose foundations had been severely undermined by Rousseau and his followers, only to be spiritually renewed by Gluck, quite apart from which the old spirit of rationalism of the age of Louis XIV that had first summoned this art into existence was still far from dead, as was clear from the way in which the arguments over opera were currently being conducted. For what, after all, was all this insistent theorizing and argumentation if not the old methodology of rationalism according to which rules first had to be devised before artists could set about implementing them?

As the son of a much later age, Mozart had virtually no interest in this older form of rationalism. Thought processes, it is true, played an important role with him, as is clear from his letters as much as from his works themselves, and nothing could be further from the truth than the widely held view of him as a 'naïve' artist who composed only when inspired to do so. But the dominant and decisive aspect of his artistic nature had nothing to do with thinking. He had an instinctive feeling for art, but he was not ruled by it. Just as important was the emotional element, an equally powerful and primary inner force. And it is on the unique combination of these two forces that the secret of his music's harmonious impact rests. As a result, the feud that was being conducted in the Paris press was bound to remain essentially unintelligible to him, at least to the extent that it related to French opera. Here he was confronted by a type of music in which order, fixed rules and convention were far more important than creativity, a system of priorities that was bound to have an inhibiting effect on someone like himself, who held completely different views. Although he conceded that the best thing about French opera was its librettos, even though, to his mind, they were already starting to deteriorate in quality,[44] he was unable to summon up any lasting enthusiasm for this heroic and courtly world in which poetry was overshadowed by rhetoric.

But he still had difficulty coming to terms with Gluck's works, all of which, with the exception of *Iphigénie en Aulide* and *Armide*, he already knew. Many writers have rightly lamented this fact,[45] but it lies deep in the essentially differing natures of the two composers. To consider those natures in purely musical terms is to address the problem from the wrong angle. What they have in common is merely their ruthless honesty towards themselves, but in their attitude towards their art they could hardly have been more different. Unlike Gluck, Mozart refused to allow the thinker precedence over the artist, and it would never have occurred to him to forget, even for a moment, that he was a musician. His art was the expression of order and creativity at one and the same time. Indeed, in his youth the musician had taken precedence over the thinker. For the same reason, he

---

44. *Briefe*, ii.389 (letter of 3 July 1778).
45. See Kretzschmar, 'Mozart in der Geschichte der Oper', ii.266.

was bound to feel totally alienated by Gluck's keen-eyed, conceptual way of creating his characters. Although Mozart's characters, too, are nicely observed, he was attracted by diversity as much as by simplicity, by the individual as much as the typical and by the sum total of ideas, feelings and passions that make characters what they are. As a result, his works attest – in a way that Gluck's do not – to the appeal of the fortuitous (to use an expression of Heinrich Wölfflin's[46]). There is a breath of freshness and surprise that is very much due to the musician. But it would be rank dilettantism to argue that these differing attitudes to art reflect an absolute difference in quality, as each composer gave uniquely pure and consummate expression to his basic creative principles. There is one thing alone that this contrast adequately explains, namely, the fact that they could never find any common ground on which to meet. Mozart's interest was inevitably directed, first and foremost, at Gluck's music, in other words, at what was secondary. He never succeeded in fathoming his older colleague's magnificent system of thought. Only in this way can we understand the otherwise perplexing fact that, whereas Mozart was normally so receptive to other artistic impressions, even those left by far less significant thinkers, he had so few points in common with the most important of his contemporaries. Shortly before he left for Paris, Mozart told his father that what fascinated him most about Gluck's works was their choruses.[47] And his attitude remained essentially the same even later. Admittedly, reminiscences of Gluck now become more frequent in Mozart's works up to and including *Die Zauberflöte*. Indeed, he sometimes even constructs entire choral scenes along Gluckian lines. But none of this extends beyond the music. Neither here nor elsewhere is there any sign of a genuine intellectual engagement with the Gluckian music drama and its underlying aesthetic.

In these circumstances Piccinni's Gluck-influenced *Roland* made little impression on Mozart. The Italian *opere buffe* that he got to know in Paris likewise had little that was new to offer him and in part were already familiar to him.[48] Striking, by contrast, is his total silence with regard to *opéras comiques*, more especially since the works in question were by no means only the latest examples of the genre. French scores had long enjoyed a considerable advantage over their Italian equivalents in that they were engraved and, as a result, generally available. There is no doubt that Mozart also got to know older works in this way.[49] All of Duni's works were in print at this time, as were many of Philidor's, up to and including his *Femmes vengées* of 1775. Everything of Monsigny's was available, while the list of Grétry's published operas included *Isabelle et Gertrude*, *Le Huron*, *Lucile*, *Le tableau parlant*, *Silvain*, *Les deux avares*, *L'amitié à l'épreuve*, *L'ami de la maison*, *Zémire et Azor*, *Le magnifique*, *La rosière de Salency*, *La fausse magie*, *Matroco*, *Le jugement de Midas* and *Les trois âges de l'opéra*. To these may be added contributions by Gossec, especially *Les pêcheurs* (1766), *Toinon et Toinette* (1767) and *Le double déguisement* (1767), Dezède (*Julie*, 1772; *Les trois fermiers*, 1777; and *Zulima*, 1778) and Desormery (*La fête de village*, 1775, and *Myrtil et Lycoris*, 1777).[50]

46. Wölfflin, *Kunstgeschichtliche Grundbegriffe*, 158.

47. *Briefe*, ii.305 (letter of 28 February 1778).

48. The works in question were Pergolesi's *La serva padrona*, Piccinni's *Le finte gemelle*, Anfossi's *Il curioso indiscreto*, and Paisiello's *Le due contesse* and *La frascatana*.

49. In his letter of 29 May 1778, Mozart reports that Count Sickingen had 'nearly 30 operatic scores' in his collection (*Briefe*, ii.368). The music-publishing business was positively thriving at this time thanks to the numerous *privilèges* that had been granted to local dealers; see Brenet, 'La librairie musicale en France de 1653 à 1780', and Cucuel, 'Quelques documents sur la librairie musicale du XVIIIe siècle'. ◆ Further concerning Mozart and Sickingen's library, see Corneilson and Wolf, 'Newly identified manuscripts of operas and related works from Mannheim'.

50. ◆ Further, see Angermüller, 'Theateraufführungen während Mozarts Paris-Aufenthalt 1778 (23. März-26. September 1778)'. More generally, see Noël and Stoullig, *Les annales du théâtre et de la musique*; Pitou, *The Paris Opera: An Encyclopedia of Operas, Ballets, Composers and Performers*; and for Italian opera, Brenner, *The Théâtre Italien: Its Repertory 1716–1793*.

Whether it was his dislike of the French character (a character that finds particularly clear expression in these works) or his fear of local competition that discouraged Mozart from making his own contribution to the genre, he was none the less unable to resist its influence, an influence still plainly evident in a work such as *Die Entführung aus dem Serail*.

With few exceptions, Mozart concentrated on instrumental music during his months in Paris. Indeed, this in itself is enough to show that he was forced to play second fiddle at this time, for whatever successes French instrumental music might have chalked up, it was music for the stage, in all its different manifestations, that enjoyed the favour of both audiences and composers. This brings us back to Mozart's fate in Paris.

His initial impression was anything but favourable. His mother discovered to her horror that everything was now half as expensive again. As a result, they had to make do with a small, dark apartment, where there was not even room for a keyboard instrument and Maria Anna Mozart felt that she was 'under arrest'. Understandably, they initially clung to their fellow Germans, and here Mozart was fortunate to find a good friend in Count von Sickingen, the Palatine ambassador to Paris, to whom both Gemmingen and Cannabich had written letters of recommendation and to whom he was introduced by Raaff:

> He's a charming man and a true connoisseur of music, of which he's passionately fond. I spent 8 hours all alone with him. We spent the whole morning, afternoon and evening until 10 o'clock at the keyboard, going through all kinds of music – praising it, admiring it, analyzing it, discussing it and criticizing it.[51]

'He loves Wolfgang more than anyone', his mother confirmed. Above all, Sickingen took a lively interest in Mozart's compositions.

Thanks to his friends from Mannheim, Mozart was able to gain a hearing at the Concert Spirituel, the oldest organization of its kind in Europe. Anne Danican Philidor, the elder half-brother of the opera composer, had been granted a *privilège* by the king in 1725, allowing him to give concerts in the Salle des Suisses at the Château des Tuileries on religious holidays when the theatres were closed. There were twenty-four such concerts a year.[52] Instrumental music and sacred vocal works were performed. The director at this time was Joseph Legros (1739–93), to whom Mozart was introduced by his friends from Mannheim and who placed his own harpsichord at Mozart's disposal. Legros was happy that at a time when everyone was preoccupied with opera, he was able to obtain Mozart's services for an organization in whose programmes foreigners had been particularly preponderant of late. It was not long before he invited Mozart to write a new work for him, as Mozart informed his father in his letter of 5 April:

> Kapellmeister Holzbauer has sent a *Miserere* here, but as the choirs in Mannheim are weak and poor, whereas here they are strong and good, his choruses would be ineffectual; and so Monsieur Le Gros has asked me to write some others. – The opening chorus remains Holzbauer's. 'Quoniam iniquitatem meam' etc. is my first one, an allegro. The second, an adagio, 'Ecce enim in iniquitatibus'; then an allegro: 'Ecce enim veritatem dilexisti' as far as the 'Ossa

---

51.   *Briefe*, ii.368 (letter of 29 May 1778).
52.   Noinville, *Histoire du Théâtre de l'Opéra de l'Académie de Musique en France*, i.164ff.; and Fétis, *Curiosités historiques de la musique*, 325ff. An account of musical life in 1770 may be found in Burney, *The Present State of Music in France and Italy*, 14–51.
◆ For a complete account of the Concert Spirituel, see Pierre, *Histoire du Concert Spirituel 1725–1790*.

humiliata'. Then an andante for soprano, tenor and bass soloists: 'Cor mundum crea' and 'Redde mihi laetitiam', but *allegro* as far as 'ad te convertentur'. I've then written a bass recitative, 'Libera me de sanguinibus', and a bass aria by Holzbauer follows, 'Dominus labra mea'. The 'Sacrificium Deo spiritus' is an *andante* aria for Raaff with oboe and bassoon solo, and so I've added a short recitative, 'Quoniam si voluisses', with obbligato oboe and bassoon, as recitatives are now very popular here. 'Benigne fac' as far as 'Muri Jerusalem', an andante moderato for chorus. Then 'Tunc acceptatis' to 'Super altare tuo vitulos', an allegro with tenor solo (Le Gros) and chorus. Finis. – I can honestly say that I'm heartily glad to have finished this hack work, it's a curse when you can't write at home and you're pressed for time. Thank God I've finished it and I hope it'll be effective. When he saw my first chorus, Monsieur Gossec, whom you must know, said to Monsieur Le Gros (I wasn't there at the time) that it's charming and will certainly make an impression: the words, he said, are well arranged and, without exception, admirably set.[53]

In the event, the fates were to prove unkind to Mozart's first composition for Paris, no trace of which has survived (K297a). On 1 May we find him writing to his father:

I should add in passing that my work on the choruses was in fact a waste of time, as Holzbauer's *Miserere* is in any case too long and found little favour, so that they gave only 2 of my choruses instead of 4 and, as a result, left out the best bits. But this didn't matter very much, as few people knew I'd written any of the music and many of them didn't know anything about me. But there was considerable applause at the rehearsal. I myself am very pleased with my choruses (as I attach no importance to Parisian praise).[54]

But Mozart fared no better with his second composition, a sinfonia concertante in E flat major (K297B), written at the instigation of Giovanni Punto and his friends from Mannheim and scored for flute (Wendling), oboe (Ramm), horn (Punto) and bassoon (Ritter). He describes it to his father in his letter of 1 May:

There's been another hitch with the sinfonia concertante. I think something's going on behind my back. No doubt I have my enemies here, too. Where haven't I had them! But it's a good sign. I had to write the sinfonia at great speed and it cost me a lot of hard work, but the 4 performers were – and still are – completely infatuated with it. Le Gros kept it for 4 days, saying he was going to have it copied, but I kept finding it lying in the same place. Finally, the day before yesterday, I couldn't find it but, after searching carefully among the music, I found it hidden away. I pretended not to notice, but asked Le Gros: 'A propos, have you given the sinf. concertante to be copied?' 'No, I'd forgotten.' Of course, I can't order him to have it copied and performed, so I said nothing, but on the 2 days when it should have been performed, I went to the concert. Ramm and Punto came up to me, incandescent with rage, and asked why my sinfonia concert. wasn't being performed. – 'I don't know. It's the first I've heard of it. I know nothing about it.' – Ramm flew off the handle and in the green room cursed Le Gros in French, saying it wasn't very nice of him and so on. What annoys me most about the whole affair is that Le Gros never said a word to me about it – I was the only person to be kept in the dark. If only he'd made an excuse and said that there wasn't enough time or something of the kind – but to

53. *Briefe*, ii.331–2 (letter of 5 April 1778).
54. *Briefe*, ii.345 (letter of 1 May 1778).

say nothing at all – but I think that it's Cambini, an Italian maestro here, who's behind it all, as in all innocence I offended him at our first meeting at Le Gros' house. He has written some quartets, one of which I heard at Mannheim, they're really quite attractive, and so I praised them to him and played him the beginning. But Ritter, Ramm and Punto were there and wouldn't leave me in peace but insisted that I go on, telling me that what I didn't know I could make up. So I made it up after a fashion, and Cambini was completely beside himself and couldn't help saying: 'Questa è una gran testa!' I don't think he can have liked what he heard.[55]

Leopold replied that Mozart was no doubt right to be suspicious, but none the less tried to placate him.[56] In the light of experiences such as these, he was ultimately unable, of course, to dispel his son's mounting dismay. It was soon after this that Jean Joseph Rodolphe offered to secure Mozart a post as organist at Versailles, as Mozart reported to his father on 14 May:

It pays 2000 livres a year, but I'd have to spend 6 months a year in Versailles, the other 6 in Paris, or wherever I like: but I don't think I'll accept it. I'll have to consult my friends; 2000 livres isn't all that much money. In German money, it would be, of course, but not here; it works out at 83 louis d'or and 8 livres a year, which in our own money is 915 florins and 45 kreutzers (which would, of course, be a lot), but here it's only 333 thalers and 2 livres – that's not very much. It's frightening how quickly a thaler disappears here! It doesn't surprise me that people hold the louis d'or in such low regard here, as it's worth very little; 4 of these thalers – the same as a louis d'or – are spent in no time.[57]

Leopold urged Mozart to give the offer careful consideration, always assuming that Rodolphe had any real influence:

Don't reject it out of hand. Remember that you'll earn 83 louis d'or in 6 months – and that you've still got the other 6 months to earn some money in other ways; – also, it's presumably a life appointment, whether you're ill or well; – you can resign it at any time; – you'd be at court and, therefore, in the daily presence of the king and queen and, as a result, closer to achieving true happiness; – if there were to be a vacancy you could obtain one of the two posts of Kapellmeister; – if the marriage produces an issue, you'd become keyboard teacher to the young princes, which would be very well paid; – no one could stop you from writing for the theatre and Concert Spirituel etc. or from having your music engraved and dedicating it to the influential acquaintances that you'll have made, as many ministers stay at Versailles, at least during the summer; – Versailles is a small town in itself or at least it has lots of distinguished inhabitants, among whom you'd surely find the odd pupil; – and, finally, this is the surest way of

---

55. *Briefe*, ii.345–6 (letter of 1 May 1778).
56. Mozart sold the work to Legros without keeping a copy of his own. Although he planned to reconstruct it from memory (*Briefe*, ii.492; letter of 3 October 1778), he evidently found no occasion to do so. None the less, a copy exists in the Staatsbibliothek in Berlin. ◆ Here Abert treats as identical Mozart's lost sinfonia concertante and a similar work attributed to him and believed possibly to transmit some of the original. K297B is the lost sinfonia concertante for flute, oboe, horn and bassoon; KAnh. C14.01 is a sometimes Mozartian-sounding work for oboe, clarinet, horn and bassoon that is preserved in a nineteenth-century manuscript. Concerning the history of this manuscript, and a consideration of the style of the work, see Levin, *Who Wrote the Mozart Four-Wind Concertante?* Also see NMA X/29/1, which includes an edition of KAnh. C14.01 and a further discussion of its authenticity.
57. *Briefe*, ii.358 (letter of 14 May 1778).

obtaining the queen's patronage and making yourself popular. Read this to Baron von Grimm and hear what he has to say on the subject.[58]

But Grimm and his other friends shared Mozart's belief that little would come of such a post. And while he was keen to find an appointment, it would have to be as a Kapellmeister and well paid.

In Paris as elsewhere, Mozart was anxious to write an opera, and here too his prospects initially seemed propitious. He had renewed contact with Noverre, who had come to Paris at the queen's invitation in 1776 and been appointed *maître de ballet* at the Académie Royale de Musique.[59] Mozart was invited to dine with him as often as he liked, and Noverre used the occasion to attempt to persuade him to write a music drama in the style of Gluck. Noverre himself chose the subject – the lives of Alexander and Roxana – and even found a poet willing to work it up into a libretto. The text of the opening act was finished by early April, and on 14 May we find Mozart expressing the hope that he would soon have in his hands the entire two-act opera.[60]

The state of excitement induced in Leopold by this plan is entirely typical of him. It was the pragmatist in him, the man obsessed with outward success, who now emerged, acknowledging his son's talent for 'imitating everything' and advising him to study French taste in depth, to accustom himself to the intonational patterns of the French language and not to be overhasty, but to discuss the text and compositional drafts in detail with Grimm and Noverre. Even Voltaire made a habit of listening to his friends' advice. 'It is a question of making a name for yourself and earning some money, and then, when we can afford to do so, we'll go to Italy again'[61] – as he was perfectly well aware, this prospect was bound to make a deep impression on Mozart. The latter made no secret of the difficulties that would be caused by both the 'confounded French language' and by French singers, but in his letter of 31 July he expressed his conviction that he would master them.

By 3 July little progress had been made in the matter of an opera on the subject of Alexander, but a second idea had now been suggested, as Mozart reported to his father:

> As for the opera, the situation is now as follows. It is very difficult to find a good poem; the old ones, which are the best, are not suited to the modern style, and the new ones are all useless; poetry – the only thing the French can be proud of – is getting worse by the day, and yet the poetry is the one thing that must be good here as they understand nothing about music. – There are now two operas in aria that I could write, one en deux actes, the other en trois. The one en deux is 'Alexandre et Roxane' – but the poet who is writing it is still in the country. The one en trois is a translation of 'Demofoonte' (by Metastasio) interspersed with choruses and dances and adapted for the French stage,[62] but I've not seen anything of this one either.[63]

Mozart remained convinced that this plan would be realized and on 31 July we find him writing: 'Whenever I imagine that all is going well with my opera, as I often do, I feel my whole body is on

58. *Briefe*, ii.365 (letter of 28 May 1778).
59. See Grimm, *Correspondance littéraire*, ix.174ff.; Wlassak, *Chronik des k.k. Hof-Burgtheaters*, 26; Pohl, *Joseph Haydn*, ii.121 and Niedecken, *Jean-Georges Noverre*, 30ff. ◆ Further, see Lynham, *The Chevalier Noverre: Father of Modern Ballet*; Tugal, *Jean-Georges Noverre, der große Reformator des Balletts*; and Dahms, 'Mozart und Noverres "Ballet en action"'.
60. *Briefe*, ii.332 and 357–8 (letters of 5 April and 14 May 1778).
61. *Briefe*, ii.341 and 354 (letters of 20 April and 11 May 1778).
62. Cherubini (1788) and Johann Christoph Vogel (1789) both produced French versions of *Démophon*.
63. *Briefe*, ii.389 (letter of 3 July 1778).

fire and tremble from head to foot with my desire to teach the French once and for all to know, value and fear the Germans.'[64]

Even now Leopold continued to counsel patience: Mozart cannot possibly expect theatre directors and audiences to hail him as a great composer when they knew him only as a keyboard player, and so he should persevere in his attempts to maintain his patrons' interest in him.[65] In spite of all this, the project remained dormant. Shortly before he left Paris, Mozart told Noverre once again that he would write the opera if Noverre could guarantee that it would be performed.[66] Noverre was unable to offer any such undertaking, and so, after months of negotiations, the whole plan came to nothing. The only trace that it left on Mozart's music was his contribution to the ballet *Les petits riens*, which was performed on 11 June 1778 at the end of Piccinni's *Le finte gemelle*. As was usual with these ballets, only Noverre was named as the author. The work disappeared after a handful of performances and was not rediscovered until 1872, when Victor Wilder found a score in the Paris Opéra library. It is published as K299b, with the omission of the first six numbers, which are not by Mozart.[67]

The first indication that Mozart was planning to write a ballet for Noverre occurs in his letter of 14 May.[68] But when Leopold enquired after it some time later and asked about the proceeds, he received a somewhat embarrassed reply:

As for Noverre's ballet, all that I ever said was that he might possibly do a new one. He needed only half a ballet and so I wrote the music for him – in other words, 6 numbers are the work of other composers and consist of nothing but wretched old French airs; the overture and contredanses, 12 pieces in all, are by me. – This ballet has already been given 4 times to the greatest acclaim. – But I'm now absolutely determined not to write anything unless I know in advance what I'll get for it, as this was just a favour for Noverre.[69]

Jahn[70] argues that Noverre used this ballet to fob Mozart off with mere promises about an opera, but there are no grounds whatsoever for assuming such an act of treachery on Noverre's part. Rather, Mozart seems to have seriously overestimated the extent of Noverre's influence: ever since he had been appointed *maître de ballet*, the latter had found his position repeatedly undermined by his enemies and there had been times when he was completely stymied.[71] And the same was true of the then general administrator of the Académie Royale, Anne-Pierre-Jacques de Vismes, who was on friendly terms with Noverre and who was ultimately responsible for deciding which new works were accepted for performance. He, too, was heavily criticized for various changes that he had made to the way in which the theatre was being run (among other innovations he allowed the Italian opera company to alternate with the French one). Above all, however, he had had no success with French works, with the exception of Gluck's, and it is hardly surprising,

64. *Briefe*, ii.427 (letter of 31 July 1778).
65. *Briefe*, ii.457 (letter of 27 August 1778).
66. *Briefe*, ii.473 (letter of 11 September 1778).
67. See Wilder, 'Mozart à Paris en 1778: Une partition inédite ("Les petits riens")', 418–19. A piano score by Renaud de Vilback was published in Paris by Heugel et Cie. More recently, Breitkopf & Härtel published a vocal score by Otto Taubmann as well as two orchestral editions of the score. ◆ The score, not an autograph but a contemporary copy, is now in the library of the Bibliothèque nationale, Paris. The complete work is published in NMA II/6/2.
68. *Briefe*, ii.357–8 (letter of 14 May 1778).
69. *Briefe*, ii.397 (letter of 9 July 1778).
70. Jahn, *W. A. Mozart*, fourth edition, i.551ff.
71. Niedecken, *Noverre*, 31–2.

therefore, that he was so lukewarm about a plan for an opera by a newcomer like Mozart. And what of Mozart himself? In spite of his enthusiastic remarks in his letters, he clearly did not pursue the matter with sufficient resolve, no doubt because, for the reasons given earlier, he felt increasingly insecure in a field that was so alien to him. If matters had proceeded smoothly, he would presumably have done all he could to sort things out, but evidently he could summon up no real interest in this kind of work. As a result, he failed to take advantage of the one and only opportunity that he had to make closer contact with the Gluckian music drama.

He was, however, to enjoy *one* success as a composer in Paris. Although he had broken off all dealings with Legros following the affair with the sinfonia concertante, he bumped into him again in early June when visiting Raaff, who had taken rooms in the same building. Legros apologized profusely and again invited Mozart to write a symphony for the Concert Spirituel, an invitation that Mozart found irresistible. By 12 June he was already in a position to play through the new work – K297 – to Count Sickingen and Raaff:

> They both liked it very much. I too am very pleased with it. But whether other people will like it I do not know – and, to tell the truth, I really don't care; for who won't like it? I can vouch for the *few* intelligent French people who may be there; as for the stupid ones – I see no great harm if they don't like it. – But I hope that even these idiots will find something in it to like; and I've taken care not to overlook the *premier coup d'archet* – and that's enough! What a fuss these boors make of this! What the devil! – I can't see any difference – they all begin together – just as they do elsewhere. It's a joke.[72]

In the event, the symphony proved a huge success with its listeners, as Mozart reported in his letter of 3 July 1778:

> It was performed on the Feast of Corpus Christi [18 June] to unanimous acclaim. I hear that there was even a report on it in the *Courier de l'Europe*. So it has been exceptionally successful. I was very worried at the rehearsal, as I've never heard worse playing in my life, you can't imagine how they scraped and scratched their way through it twice in succession. I was really very worried and would like to have rehearsed it again, but there was so much else to rehearse and so there was no time. So I had to go to bed in a state of some anxiety and feeling angry and discontented. The next day I'd made up my mind not to go to the concert at all, but in the evening the weather was fine, and so I finally decided to go, determined that if it went as badly as it did at the rehearsal, I'd go up to the orchestra, take the violin from the hands of the first violin, Herr La Houssaye, and conduct it myself. I prayed to God in His mercy that it would go well, for it is all to His greater honour and glory, and behold! the symphony began. Raaff was standing beside me. In the middle of the opening Allegro there was a passage that I knew people would like; the whole audience was carried away by it, and there was tremendous applause. – But I knew when I wrote it what sort of an effect it would make, and so I introduced it again at the end, with the result that it was encored. They liked the Andante, too, but most of all the final

---

72. *Briefe*, ii.378–9 (letter of 12 June 1778). It was the imposing impression made by the loud tutti passage played by a large orchestra, usually at the start of a work, that gave rise to this expression (*coup d'archet*). Raaff also told Mozart about a well-known witticism by Evaristo Felice Dall'Abaco in this context: 'He was asked by a Frenchman at Munich or somewhere – "Monsieur, vous avez été à Paris?" "Oui." "Est-ce que vous étiez au Concert Spirituel?" "Oui." "Que dites-vous du premier coup d'archet? Avez-vous entendu le premier coup d'archet?" "Oui, j'ai entendu le premier et le dernier." "Comment, le dernier? Que veut dire cela?" "Mai oui, le premier et le dernier – et le dernier même m'a donné plus de plaisir."'

Allegro. I'd heard that all final Allegros, like all opening Allegros, begin here with all the instruments playing together, generally in unison, and so I began mine with just the 2 violins, *piano* for the first eight bars – immediately followed by a *forte*; the audience (as I expected) said 'Shh!' at the *piano* – then came the *forte*. – The moment they heard the *forte*, they started to clap. I was so happy that as soon as the symphony was over I went off to the Palais Royal and had a large ice, said the rosary, as I'd vowed to do, and then went home.[73]

With Legros, too, the ice now melted, and, according to his letter to his father of 11 September, Mozart not only wrote a symphony for the Concert Spirituel (the work in question was probably K311A[74]) but was even invited to compose a French oratorio for the coming Lenten season. In the event, Legros was not entirely happy with the andante of the D major symphony, which he thought was too long and too prone to explore remote keys. Mozart, of course, thought differently, but to please Legros replaced the movement with a new one that even he himself soon came to prefer.[75] In its revised version, the new work was repeated on 15 August.

More violin sonatas were written to add to the series started in Mannheim. Of the final tally of six, the E minor sonata K304 was definitely composed in Paris (the manuscript includes the note 'à Paris') and the same is almost certainly true of the piece in D major K306.[76] Mozart now attempted to find a publisher who would pay him handsomely for all six works.[77] The keyboard sonata in A minor K310 must likewise date from Mozart's time in Paris.[78] Moreover, in a letter of 20 July to his sister the composer himself speaks of 'a number of sonatas for keyboard alone' that he planned to send to her.[79] In other words, he must have written other sonatas in Paris besides the one in A minor. In a later letter of 9 June 1784 he mentions three keyboard sonatas 'that I once sent to my sister, the first in C, the second in A and the third in F' (K330–332).[80] It is possible,

73. *Briefe*, ii.388–9 (letter of 3 July 1778). ◆ According to the *Courrier de l'Europe* for 26 June 1778, 'The Concert Spirituel on Corpus Christi Day began with a symphony by M. Mozart. This artist, who from the tenderest age made a name for himself among keyboard players, may today be ranked among the most able composers' (*Dokumente*, 158, *Documentary Biography*, 176). For an account of the Concert Spirituel orchestra, see Angermüller, 'Wer spielte die Uraufführung von Mozarts "Pariser Symphonie" KV 297?'.

74. *Briefe*, ii.473 (letter of 11 September 1778). The second was performed on 8 September, a performance confirmed by the announcement of the concert in the *Journal de Paris*; see Wilder, *Mozart: L'homme et l'artiste*, 115. On 3 October, moreover, Mozart wrote to tell his father that he had sold the two overtures (that is, symphonies) and a sinfonia concertante to Legros. The parts for the B flat major overture were discovered by Julien Tiersot in the library of the Paris Conservatoire, marked 'à l'imprimerie du Conservatoire Faubourg Poissonnière'; see Köchel, *Chronologisch-thematisches Verzeichnis sämtlicher Tonwerke Wolfgang Amade Mozarts*, second edition, 599. ◆ It is now generally thought that Mozart was untruthful in his letter to Leopold and that he did not write a second symphony for Paris but played an older work instead; see Tyson, 'Mozart's Truthfulness'. Nevertheless, there is an entry in the most recent edition of Köchel for this supposedly lost work, K311A. The overture discovered by Tiersot, KAnh. C11.05, survives in an edition published during the first years of the nineteenth century; it transmits a work that is considered stylistically distant from Mozart and almost certainly spurious. Further, see Zaslaw, *Mozart's Symphonies*, 331–4.

75. *Briefe*, ii.398 (letter of 9 July 1778). ◆ The two movements are an andante in 6/8 and an andante in 3/4. Although it is generally thought that the 3/4 andante transmitted by the first edition of the 'Paris' symphony represents Mozart's replacement, Tyson, 'The Two Slow Movements of Mozart's Paris Symphony K. 297', argues that the reverse may be the case.

76. The final movement was started as an andante grazioso e con moto on 16-stave upright paper, but Mozart then crossed this out and began the movement again, this time as an allegretto, which he wrote out in its entirety on oblong paper. ◆ The paper type of the autograph confirms the dating of K306 to the time of Mozart's stay in Paris.

77. See Leopold's letter to Breitkopf of 10 August 1781: 'The six sonatas dedicated to Her Highness the Electress of the Bavarian Palatinate have been published by Herr Sieber in Paris. . . . He took them from my son in Paris for 15 louis d'or, 30 copies and complete freedom to dedicate them to whoever he wished' (*Briefe*, iii.149).

78. According to Nottebohm's critical commentary to K310, the heading of the autograph manuscript reads 'di Wolfgango Amadeo Mozart. Paris 1778'. ◆ Nottebohm's report is correct; the autograph is now housed at the Pierpont Morgan Library, New York.

79. *Briefe*, ii.410 (letter of 20 July 1778).

80. *Briefe*, ii.318–19 (letter of 9 June 1784).

therefore, that these three sonatas, too, were written in Paris, rather than during the later period,[81] a conclusion confirmed by the style of all three pieces, especially the one in A major. In his letter of 20 July, Mozart additionally speaks of a Praeambulum said to have been written for his sister's name-day – 'not the kind of prelude that passes from one key to another, but only a sort of capriccio with which to try out a keyboard'.[82] Whether this piece is K 395 seems highly doubtful on stylistic grounds.[83] Conversely, there seems little doubt that the three sets of variations on three French *ariettes*, *Lison dormait*, *Ah vous dirai-je Maman* and *La belle Françoise* (K264, 265 and 353) were all written in Paris,[84] where *thèmes variés* were immensely popular at this time. Finally, at least the first part of the recitative and aria *Popoli di Tessaglia* for soprano – a setting of a *scena* from Calzabigi's *Alceste* – dates from July 1778.[85]

In the midst of all these activities, Mozart was struck by a particularly heavy blow of a personal nature. His mother had begun to feel unwell soon after arriving in Paris, a condition largely due to their unhealthy accommodation and inadequate food at the Hôtel des Quatre Fils Aymon in the Rue du Gros Chenêt. She was ill for three weeks in May and, once she was better, thought of moving to alternative accommodation with its own kitchen. But in June she fell ill again; she was duly bled and on 12 June wrote to her husband to say that in spite of pains in her arm and eyes, she was feeling well. Soon after that, however, her condition deteriorated markedly. The doctor sent by Grimm was unable to do anything, and after two anxious weeks, during which Mozart remained at her bedside, she died peacefully on the evening of 3 July. His only support during the whole of this difficult time was a musician by the name Franz Joseph Heina, an old acquaintance of his father's, who together with his wife often visited Maria Anna in her loneliness.[86] Mozart's first thought on recovering from his initial grief was his father, who had no idea that his wife was even unwell. In order to prepare him, he wrote to announce that his mother was seriously ill and, at the same time, wrote to his friend Bullinger, revealing the whole truth of the matter and asking him to break the news to his father as gently as possible. A few days later he wrote again, this time sending a detailed report, comforting his father and attempting to reassure him by giving him a full account of his own situation. These letters[87] are further proof of the genuine affection that existed between parents and children in the Mozart household, while also attesting to Mozart's sensitivity and tact. The reasons that he adduces in order to comfort his father and the manner in which he expresses those reasons are, admittedly, inspired more by his father's teachings than by his own experience of life, but precisely because of that they were justified when

81. This view is shared by Wyzewa and Saint-Foix, *Wolfgang Amédée Mozart*, ii.406, whereas Jahn and Köchel argue that all these works (which, it may be added, were published together) date from 1779. ◆ Recent research on Mozart's autograph manuscripts suggests that neither Abert, Wyzewa and Saint-Foix, Jahn nor Köchel is correct: almost certainly K330 and 331 were composed in Vienna some time between 1781 and 1783; K332 may date from the same period or possibly slightly earlier, Salzburg or Munich, 1780–1.

82. *Briefe*, ii.409 (letter of 20 July 1778).

83. Wyzewa and Saint-Foix, *Wolfgang Amédée Mozart*, ii.406. Deiters (Jahn, *W. A. Mozart*, fourth edition, ii.165) argues that this must be one of the '4 Préludes' mentioned by Mozart in his letter of 10 October 1777, but this is ruled out by the explanation concerning K395 that Mozart himself gives in his letter of 20 July 1778 (*Briefe*, ii.410–11). ◆ It now seems likely that K395 is in fact the work sent by Mozart to his sister; see Christoph Wolff, 'Mozarts Präludien für Nannerl: Zwei Rätsel und ihre Lösung'.

84. Wyzewa and Saint-Foix, *Wolfgang Amédée Mozart*, ii.405–6. ◆ These works, too, were probably composed in Vienna between 1781 and 1783. Abert falls prey here to the biographically-based assumption, common in earlier Mozart research, that French-titled or related works must have been composed in Paris in 1778. Further, see the introduction concerning biography and assumptions about chronology and style generally.

85. See Friedlaender, 'Briefe aus Goethes Autographensammlung: Zwei Schreiben W. A. Mozarts', 108.

86. ◆ Franz Joseph (François) Heina, a horn player in the service of Baron Bagge, was married to the Paris publisher Gertrude Heina.

87. For the letter to Bullinger, see *Briefe*, ii.390–91 (letter of 3 July 1778). Mozart's letters to his father of 3 and 9 July may be found in *Briefe*, ii.387–90 and 393–9, while Leopold's letter of 13 July appears in *Briefe*, ii.400–4.

addressing his father and, as such, bound to ring true. Moreover, so serious a sense of personal loss helped to transform the youth into a man: for all his genuine grief, he none the less looks towards the future with manly gaze and thinks above all of how to support and comfort his father and sister. And so we find him writing on 31 July:

> Sad as your letter made me, I was none the less beside myself with joy when I heard that you had taken it all as it should be taken – and that as a result I need have no fears for my most beloved father and my dearest sister. As soon as I read your letter, I fell to my knees and thanked the dear Lord from the bottom of my heart for this blessing. . . . Now, thank God, I am perfectly well and healthy, only occasionally do I have attacks of melancholy – but I find that the best way to get rid of them is to write or receive letters; this cheers me up again.[88]

Mozart no doubt knew that Leopold must now have been doubly anxious on his son's behalf, and it is touching to see how, in the course of his next few letters, he attempts to come to terms with his grief by means of detailed accounts of his various activities; all the minor irritations of the past are now forgotten, and even Mozart's handwriting, which his father had criticized for being so careless, is now visibly neater.

Mozart's friends had already returned to Mannheim when his mother died, and so he was left entirely on his own. Grimm and his mistress, Madame d'Épinay,[89] took pity on Mozart and provided him with board and lodging, an offer he was all the more willing to accept in that it involved him in no appreciable expense or any other inconvenience. He even found himself obliged to borrow money from Grimm, a debt which gradually crept up to as much as fifteen louis d'or. But, as Mozart wrote to reassure his father, Grimm was in no hurry to be paid back.

But this close personal contact with Grimm merely served to increase Mozart's criticisms of his benefactor and deepen his distrust from one day to the next. The two men understood each other less and less. Grimm resumed his former attempts to put Mozart on what he thought was the right path as man and artist, but Mozart felt insulted by this and the longer he remained in the Grimm household, the less edified he was by the tone that prevailed there. The full extent of the yawning void between them became clear in the aftermath of Voltaire's death on 30 May. For Grimm, this was an event of the utmost importance, whereas Mozart's reaction is summed up in his letter to his father of 3 July: 'That godless, archvillain Voltaire has pegged out like a dog, like an animal – that's his reward!' Here too we can see the lingering effects of Mozart's religious education.[90]

---

88. *Briefe*, ii.422 (letter of 31 July 1778).

89. It was by a curious quirk of fate that Mozart was brought into contact in this way with the most typical representative of the world of the courtesans who left their mark on the whole of French society at this time. Louise-Florence-Pétronille Tardieu d'Esclavelles, Marquise d'Épinay (1726–83) made up in wit what she lacked in beauty. A friend of both Rousseau and Voltaire, she had been married to a dissolute husband, after which she passed through various hands before finally attaching herself to Grimm, who had ingratiated himself with her by his immoderate praise of her musical compositions. Writing of her memoirs, Sainte-Beuve declared: 'Ils ne sont pas un ouvrage, ils sont une époque' (Sainte-Beuve, *Causeries du lundi*, ii.190). They were published by Paul Boiteau in Paris in 1863. See also Perey and Maugras, *Une femme du monde au XVIIIe siècle: La jeunesse de Madame d'Épinay, d'après des lettres et des documents inédits*; and Toth, *Französisches Salonleben um Charles Pinot Duclos 1704–1772*. On 9 July 1778, we find Mozart writing to his father: 'I am writing this in the house of Madame d'Épinay and M. Grimm, with whom I am now living, I've a pretty little room with a very pleasant view and, so far as my condition allows it, I'm happy' (*Briefe*, ii.394).

90. *Briefe*, ii.389 (letter of 3 July 1778). In spite of Arthur Schurig's claims to the contrary, there is no evidence that this passage refers to the fact that Voltaire died without receiving the blessing of the Church; see Schurig, *Wolfgang Amade Mozart*, i.480. ◆ For a different interpretation, see Schroeder, *Mozart in Revolt*, 104–5.

In the circumstances, it is hardly surprising to find Mozart growing increasingly anxious to leave Paris. And since his wife's death, Leopold, too, shared this desire, albeit for totally different reasons, as he was afraid that, robbed of his mother's support, Mozart would fall into bad company. Although Leopold's fears were unfounded, Mozart's failures and worries in Paris rekindled memories of Aloysia Weber, a prospect that he now found all the more attractive in that he had discovered in Raaff a sympathetic listener in whom to confide his troubles. By the end of June we find Mozart engaged in lively correspondence with her father Fridolin Weber in Mannheim. His excuse for renewing contact was the court's planned transfer to Munich. It was left to the discretion of the individual members of the court orchestra whether they followed the court to Munich or remained in Mannheim on their existing salaries. Weber poured out his heart to Mozart, bewailing the fact that, given his ruinous finances, he would find it difficult to move to Munich. In this way, Mozart also heard about all the insults that Aloysia had suffered at the hands of her enemies, with the result that his old and heartfelt interest in the family's fate was reawoken. More level-headed than before, he now restricted himself, of course, to the role of the considerate adviser anxious to warn the family against ill-considered actions, discouraging Aloysia not only from contemplating the uncertainties of Paris but also from accepting an engagement in Mainz, where the Seyler company was currently appearing but had no opening for a singer of her gifts. The extraordinarily warm tone of his letter leaves us in no doubt that Mozart's old hopes had most certainly not been abandoned: 'If I had no father and sister to whom I must sacrifice everything and whom I must try to support,' he concludes his letter to Fridolin Weber, 'I would renounce my own interests with the greatest of pleasure and concern myself with your own interests alone, for, if I may think only of myself, my entire happiness consists in your welfare, pleasure and happiness.'[91]

Conversely, Mozart hoped that he might come closer to his goal of marrying Aloysia by becoming Kapellmeister to the elector of Bavaria. His predicament is clear from his letter to her of 30 July: 'I shall have no peace of mind until I am certain that your merits have been justly rewarded – but I shall know supreme happiness only on that day when I have the infinite pleasure of seeing you again and embracing you with all my heart – this is all that I long for, all that I desire – only in this desire and wish shall I find comfort and peace.'[92]

When writing to his father, of course, Mozart said nothing about his secret desires but concentrated instead on his application for the post of Kapellmeister.[93] With this, Leopold was in complete agreement and again activated Padre Martini. The prospects seemed promising, not least because the electoral orchestra was well disposed towards Mozart. Count Sickingen promised his support, while in Munich itself, Holzbauer's advanced age made the appointment of a younger Kapellmeister and opera composer a matter of urgent necessity. But the threat of war now intervened and threw everything into uncertainty, prompting Mozart to reveal his hand and reveal his worries about the Weber family, whom he commended to Leopold most insistently. Leopold's reply was dated 27 August 1778 and made it abundantly plain that such thoughts were out of place until Mozart had taken steps to ensure his own well-being and that of his family. All his high-flown

91. Only two letters have survived, one to Fridolin Weber dated 29 July 1778, the other to Aloysia of 30 July 1778 (*Briefe*, ii.414–21). See Friedlaender, 'Briefe aus Goethes Autographensammlung'.

92. *Briefe*, ii.421 (letter of 30 July 1778); the original is in Italian.

93. Only Mozart's letter of 3 July (*Briefe*, ii.389) contains a number of vague hints in this direction: 'I've something in mind for which I pray daily to God. If it's His divine will, it will succeed, and if not, then I'll also be content – at least I'll have done what I can. When all this has been organized and has turned out as I want, you too will have to do what you can, otherwise the whole affair will remain unfinished, so I hope you'll be kind enough to do so.'

plans were merely castles in the air, he went on, with the result that Mozart must remain in Paris until such time as a decision had been taken.

In the event, the decision came sooner than Mozart had expected, and, contrary to all his expectations, it was in favour of Salzburg. Following Adlgasser's sudden death on 21 December 1777, Bullinger had discovered that the court was not ill-disposed to the idea of reappointing Mozart as organist and Konzertmeister on a monthly salary of fifty florins. He could later be appointed Kapellmeister. But the prince could not make the first move. Perceptive as ever, Leopold saw the embarrassment in which the parties found themselves and decided to do all he could to exploit the situation for his son's advantage. He informed the latter about a conversation that he had had with the canon of Salzburg Cathedral, Count Franz Joseph Starhemberg, in the course of which he acted 'in as masterly a manner as Ulysses', to quote Mozart himself.[94] The count had beaten about the bush in an extraordinarily incompetent way for some considerable time, before finally exclaiming:

'Your son ought to be here!' – 'Bravo!' I thought, 'I've caught you out! What a pity this man isn't a great statesman or an ambassador!' – I then told him we should talk quite frankly and asked whether people hadn't done everything in their power to drive him [Mozart] from Salzburg. I started at the beginning and omitted nothing of all that had happened, so that his brother was utterly amazed and he himself could only say that it was the plain truth. We then got on to the orchestra – I spared no detail – and he agreed that it was all perfectly true and finally told his brother that all the foreigners who had come to the Salzburg court had admired the young Mozart and him alone. He kept trying to talk me into writing to my son on the subject, but I told him I couldn't do so, it would be a waste of effort and my son would only laugh at such an offer; it would only be possible if I could give some indication of the salary that he would receive, as I couldn't even hope for an answer if it was the same salary as someone like Adlgasser got. Indeed, even if His Grace decided to give him 50 florins a month, it was extremely doubtful that he'd accept. The three of us left the house together as they were off to the riding school, I accompanied them and we continued to talk the matter over, I stuck to what I had said earlier, while he stuck to his assertion that he was interested only in my son. . . .

Well, I must tell you that the prince is not going to get a good organist who is also a good harpsichordist; he's now saying (but only to his favourites) that Beecke is a charlatan and a joker and that Mozart far surpasses them all; as a result, he'd prefer to have someone he knows, rather than pay a lot of money for someone he doesn't yet know. If he were to offer less money, he couldn't promise any income from pupils as there are very few of them, I've got most of them already, quite apart from the fact that I have a reputation for being the best teacher. – That's the crux of the matter! My dear Wolfgang, I'm not writing all this with the aim of persuading you to return to Salzburg – I set absolutely no store by what the archbishop says, nor have I said a word to the countess[95] but have been avoiding meeting her as she could interpret my least remark as submissiveness and importunacy. They must come to me – and in order for me to agree to anything, the terms they offer must be extremely favourable and advantageous, and that's most unlikely. Let's wait and see what happens – but don't speak too soon.[96]

94. ◆ *Briefe*, ii.396 (letter of 9 July 1778).
95. Maria Franziska, Countess von Wallis (1746–95), was Colloredo's sister. She maintained her own court in a side wing of the archiepiscopal residence, facing the cathedral.
96. *Briefe*, ii.380–81 (letter of 29 June 1778).

Mozart hated Salzburg even more than he hated Paris and replied with a crude attack on the town's 'coarse, slovenly, dissolute court musicians'.[97] But when the elderly Kapellmeister Giuseppe Lolli died about 11 August, the same time as Mozart's mother died, the question of a successor became critical, forcing Leopold to abandon his earlier caution. Following his wife's death, he felt all his old desire rekindled to see his son close beside him in a secure position, and so the ever-helpful Abbé Bullinger had to accept the difficult task of overcoming Mozart's fundamental objections to the idea. Bullinger duly wrote to Mozart, explaining that the conditions under which he would be appointed in Salzburg were so favourable that he owed it to his family to accept them. And Salzburg, although small, was not a disagreeable place to be. Moreover, the archbishop was planning to appoint a second soprano in addition to Maria Magdalena Haydn, so that Aloysia Weber's appointment was by no means out of the question. Mozart replied quite candidly in his letter to Bullinger of 7 August 1778:

> My dear friend, you know how I detest Salzburg – not only because of all the injustices that my dear father and I have endured there and which, in themselves, would be sufficient to make me want to forget such a place and wipe it from my thoughts for ever. But let's forget all that and try to arrange things so that we can live there respectably; to live respectably and to live happily are two very different things, and the latter I could never do (without witchcraft) – there would inevitably be something unnatural about it! . . . It will always be the greatest pleasure for me to embrace my dearest father and sister, and the sooner the better; but I can't deny that my joy and delight would be twice as great if I could do so elsewhere, as I have *more* hope of being able to live pleasantly and happily anywhere but there.[98]

It was not because Salzburg was a small town that he was reluctant to return, he continued, but because it was no place for a man of his talents: the local musicians were not respected and there was no theatre or opera house. He concluded with a bitterly satirical account of conditions in Salzburg.

Meanwhile, Leopold had reminded the archbishop of his existence by petitioning him on the subject of Lolli's appointment.[99] And in his letter of 27 August he informed Mozart of a conversation that he had had with the countess:

> Finally she asked me whether you wouldn't come if the archbishop offered me Lolli's salary and if he offered you Adlgasser's, which would come to 1000 florins a year – I'd already worked this out; and so all I could say was that, if the offer was genuine, I had no doubt that you would accept it for my sake, while she herself added that there was absolutely no doubt that the archbishop would allow you to go to Italy every 2 years, as he himself always maintains that from time to time one needs to hear something different, and that he would provide you with letters of recommendation. If this were to happen, I could certainly reckon on our having a guaranteed income of at least 115 florins a month and, as things stand at present, more than 120. . . . In this way we'd be better off than elsewhere, where things are twice as expensive, and if you don't need to be so careful about money, you can easily find ways of entertaining yourself. But

97. ◆ *Briefe*, ii.395; letter of 9 July 1778.
98. *Briefe*, ii.438 (letter of 7 August 1778).
99. ◆ For Leopold's unsuccessful petition to Colloredo, see *Briefe*, ii.462.

the main thing is that I'm not banking on all this, as I know how hard it is for the prince to take this decision. That the countess is entirely serious and could wish for nothing better is beyond doubt, and it's only right that old Arco, Count Starhemberg and the bishop of Königgrätz should want to see this come to pass. But, as is always the case, they have their own reasons for this, as I've told you a thousand times: the countess is afraid, no less than old Arco, that I too shall leave and they'll have no one to teach the harpsichord; I have a reputation for being a good teacher and can prove it. They don't know who else they could get or when, and if they were to get someone from Vienna, would he give 12 lessons for 4 florins or 1 ducat, when he could get 2 or 3 ducats elsewhere? – It has put them all in a quandary. But, as I've already said, I'm not counting on it as I know the archbishop: although it's certain that in his heart he wants to have you, he can't make up his mind – which is curious when he has to *give*.[100]

Once again, Mozart refused to discuss this letter in detail, but at this point specific offers suddenly arrived from Salzburg, as we learn from Leopold's letter of 31 August:

You don't like Paris and on the whole I don't blame you. Until now I have been worried about you in both heart and mind, and in spite of a minister, I had to play a very difficult role, since, my anxieties notwithstanding, I had to pretend to be happy in order to make everyone believe that all was well with you and that you had money in abundance, even though I knew the opposite to be the case. I very much doubted that I would get my way because, as you know, we could expect little from so proud a prince following the step that we'd taken, and I knew that your sudden defection had annoyed him considerably. But, thanks to my valiant perseverance, not only have I got my way, with the archbishop agreeing to everything both for me and for you (you'll have 500 florins), but he even apologized for not being able to appoint you Kapellmeister at present, but you're to take my place if ever it's too much trouble for me or I'm unable to do the job myself; he said that he had already meant you to have a better salary, etc. – in a word, and to my astonishment, the most courteous apology. Even more! He has raised Paris's[101] salary by 5 florins so that he'll now take charge of most of the services, and you'll be appointed Konzertmeister as before. So together we'll receive an official salary of 1000 florins a year, as I've already told you. Everything now depends on whether you think I've still got a sound head on my shoulders and you think I've acted in your best interests – and whether you want me dead or alive. I've thought it all through. The archbishop has declared that, if you want to write an opera, he'll allow you to travel wherever you like; he excused his refusal to allow us leave last year by saying that he couldn't bear to see people travelling around begging. In Salzburg you'll be midway between Munich, Vienna and Italy. It'll be easier to write an opera for Munich than to get an appointment there, for where are German opera composers to be found? And how many? – Following the elector's death, they're all unemployed, and there's another war in the offing. The Duke of Zweibrücken is no great lover of music. But I don't want you to leave Paris until I have the decree, duly signed, in my hands, as the prince is at Laufen this morning. – Mlle Weber has really whetted the appetites of the prince and everyone else; they positively demand to hear her, they can stay with us. It seems to me that her father has no brains; I'll arrange things better for them if they are prepared to do as I say. You must put the case for her here, as he wants a

---

100. *Briefe*, ii.454–5 (letter of 27 August 1778).
101. Anton Ferdinand Paris (1744–1809) was the third court organist in Salzburg.

second soprano alongside the castrato to perform an opera. . . . My next letter will tell you that you are to leave Paris.[102]

Mozart now complied with his father's wishes, albeit with a heavy heart. 'When I read through your letter,' he wrote on 11 September, 'I trembled with pleasure, as I could already see myself in your arms. It is true, as you yourself will admit, that no great fortune awaits me in Salzburg, but when I think of embracing you, my dearest father, and my dear sister with all my heart I know of no other happiness.'[103] Of course, he continued to be deeply concerned about musical standards in Salzburg, and only the prospect of being able to escape from the town every other year persuaded him to accept the position. 'A man of mediocre talent will remain a mediocrity, whether he travels or not, but one of superior talent (which, without being godless, I cannot deny is true in my own case) will go to seed if he always remains in the same place.' The prospect of seeing Aloysia Weber again filled him with inordinate pleasure. Indeed, he was already afraid that audiences might not like her in Schweitzer's *Rosamunde* because the role lay awkwardly for her voice, and he urged his father to do all he could to help her until such time as he himself returned home. In the shorter term, he asked to be allowed to visit the Webers in Mannheim on his way back to Salzburg.

Leopold lost no time in declaring Mozart's decision to be the right one.[104] His hopes of being invited to write a German opera for Munich would in no way be affected by this, he went on, as his new post would allow him ample opportunity 'for study and speculation'. Moreover, he would no longer play the violin in the court orchestra, as he had done previously, but the harpsichord, from which he would direct the performances, a point on which Mozart had laid particular emphasis. Only occasionally would he have to play the violin at court concerts, and it was hoped that he would do so gladly, as a music lover, so to speak. These concerts would last only from seven until a quarter past eight, as in general only four pieces would be performed, a symphony followed by an aria, then either another symphony or a concerto and, finally, a second aria.[105] They could also enjoy good company and afford entertainments as they would no longer have to look to every kreutzer that they spent. Of course, as Leopold knew very well, it was Aloysia, rather than the prospect of balls, plays and target-practice, that was the principal lure for Mozart. And here, too, Leopold was to prove remarkably accommodating, promising to do all he could to promote her appearances in Salzburg. In his letter of 3 September, he writes on this subject: 'As for Mlle Weber, you really mustn't think that I'm opposed to this acquaintance. All young people must be left to make fools of themselves. You can continue to write letters to each other as before, I shan't ask you about them, still less shall I demand to read them. Moreover, I'll give you some advice – there are enough people here whom you know very well and can have your Weber letters addressed to someone else and kept secret if you think you're not safe from my curiosity.'[106] Mozart was understandably mortified by such mordant irony and on 15 October we find him writing to Leopold to

102. *Briefe*, ii.460–61 (letter of 31 August 1778).
103. *Briefe*, ii.472 (letter of 11 September 1778).
104. *Briefe*, ii.463–5 (letter of 3 September 1778).
105. *Briefe*, ii.482 (letter of 17 September 1778). ◆ Abert misrepresents Leopold's correspondence with Wolfgang on this point: he did not promise his son that concerts at court would be curtailed; rather the passage is a description of the sorry state of music in the archdiocese and reads more like a complaint on Leopold's part, an indictment of the Archbishop's seeming lack of interest in his music establishment.
106. *Briefe*, ii.465 (letter of 3 September 1778).

say that the 'poor girl' had been very worried about him because a letter to her in Mannheim had gone missing. 'You'll laugh? – I'm not laughing. I'm touched by it, I can't help it.'[107] But Mozart had also heard at around this time that Aloysia had been taken on as an opera singer in Munich on a handsome salary.[108] He made no secret of his mixed feelings at this news:

That Mlle Weber, or rather my dear Mlle Weber, is now receiving a salary and in this way has finally been given her due delights me as much as might be expected from someone who has taken such an interest in her. I continue to commend her to you most warmly; unfortunately, I must now give up all hope of what I had so much wanted, namely, that she should be given an appointment in Salzburg, for the archbishop would never give her the salary she's now drawing. The only possibility now would be for her to come to Salzburg for a time for sing in an opera.[109]

At the same time, this news rekindled in Mozart his old desire for a permanent post at the Bavarian court and revived his old hatred of Salzburg. Indeed, he even attempted to exert pressure on Colloredo by demanding an increase in his salary:

My dearest father, please use this opportunity to make the archbishop think that I may not return to Salzburg after all, so that he may decide to increase my salary, for, listen, it upsets me even to think about it. The archbishop can't pay me enough for such slavery in Salzburg! As I say, I feel only pleasure at the thought of seeing you, but only annoyance and anxiety when I see myself back at this beggarly court. The archbishop had better not give himself airs with me as he used to before – if he does, it's quite likely that I'll pull a long nose at him![110]

Indeed, the prospect of returning to Salzburg even made Mozart see his fate in Paris in a more favourable light. Once it had been decided that he would leave, Grimm insisted that he should be ready to depart in a week's time, but this in itself was enough to incur Mozart's displeasure. He had fees to claim from Legros and de Guines and also maintained that not only did he still have to write six trios for which he would receive a handsome fee, but he also had to read the proofs of the sonatas that were already being engraved[111] and, finally, to sell the works that he had brought with him to Paris. Indeed, when Grimm offered to pay for his journey to Strasbourg – an offer that Leopold rightly saw as proof of Grimm's friendship – Mozart, in a fit of ill temper, interpreted it as an act of base treachery. Even as late as 15 October, we find him writing from Strasbourg to tell his father that he considers his journey to Salzburg the greatest folly in the world; the weighty counterarguments of his friends, he goes on, were offset only by the love that he felt for his father:

107. *Briefe*, ii.495 (letter of 15 October 1778).
108. Mozart later discovered in Mannheim that her salary was 1000 florins, while that of her father was 400 florins, with a further 200 florins as prompter; see also Leopold's letter of 24 September 1778 (*Briefe*, ii.485).
109. *Briefe*, ii.494 (letter of 15 October 1778).
110. *Briefe*, ii.507 (letter of 12 November 1778).
111. He hoped to sell his three keyboard concertos (K238, 246 and 271) and possibly also his six difficult keyboard sonatas (K279–284) to the engraver for cash. It is unclear whether he succeeded in this, although the works in question do not appear to have been engraved. Leopold also advised Mozart to remain in touch with publishers in Paris, so as to be able to exploit his contacts in future. In a letter to Breitkopf of 10 August 1781, Leopold mentions 'Trois airs variés pour le clavecin ou Fortepiano' that were engraved by Heina in Paris. These were the variations on Fischer's minuet, the variations on 'Mio caro Adone' from Salieri's *La fiera di Venezia*, which Leopold mentions in his letter of 28 December 1778, and the variations on 'Je suis Lindor' from Baudron's incidental music to Beaumarchais's *Le barbier de Séville* (K179, 180 and 354).

And I thought to myself that if I had not had to put up with such annoyance in the house where I was lodging and if the whole affair had not degenerated into one row after another, in other words, if I'd had time to think the matter over coolly, I'd certainly have asked you to remain patient a little longer and allow me to remain in Paris; I assure you that I'd have gained honour, reputation and wealth there and would certainly have got you out of debt. But the deed has now been done; – you mustn't for a moment suppose that I regret it, for you alone, my dearest father, you alone can sweeten for me the bitterness of Salzburg, and you will do so, I'm sure of that; but I must confess that I'd arrive in Salzburg with a lighter heart if I knew that I wasn't in the service of the court – this thought alone is intolerable![112]

In the meantime, Mozart had sorted things out in Paris and sent his mother's effects and other heavy items of luggage straight to Salzburg.[113] He himself left the city of 26 September, as ill-tempered and disgruntled as when he had arrived there.

In spite of the lack of outward success, Mozart's trip to Mannheim and Paris was none the less one of the most important events in his life. Until then he had been shielded from life by his anxious father, but now he was forced to come to terms with the world on his own. In the process he discovered much that was good, but also suffered many disappointments, and on a purely human level fate treated him particularly cruelly during these months. But the experience gained from adversity brought with it a new sense of maturity, proving far more valuable to Mozart as an artist than all his recent years in Salzburg had done. In Mannheim he was introduced to the new instrumental style at its source, a style to which he had already long been drawn in many ways. And, whereas he had previously been influenced in the main by Italian opera, Paris introduced him to a completely new type of drama in both comedy and tragedy, while initiating him into the aesthetics of opera in a way of which he had previously had no inkling. Even though he failed to achieve any lasting empathy with all the new impressions to which he was exposed here, more of those impressions stuck than he himself was willing to admit. The actual number of works that he was commissioned to write in Paris was few, of course, but their repercussions were still being felt at the time of *Idomeneo* and *Die Entführung*, and even as late as *Le nozze di Figaro* and *Die Zauberflöte*.[114]

The original scenario of the ballet *Les petits riens* K299b has not survived and we know its contents only from a brief review of the first performance in the *Journal de Paris*.[115] From this it

112. *Briefe*, ii.495–6 (letter of 15 October 1778).
113. The trunk arrived back in Salzburg before Mozart. Leopold noted that his wife's gold watch was missing and asked whether Mozart had pawned it. 'As for the watch,' Mozart replied on 18 December 1778, 'you guessed rightly, I pawned it but got only 5 louis d'or for it' (*Briefe*, ii.523). He also reported that he had exchanged a jewelled watch and the watch given him by the elector for a French watch worth 20 louis d'or.
114. This emerges from a later remark of Mozart's to Joseph Frank, who found him studying French scores and asked whether it was not better to study Italian works: 'In respect of melody yes, but in respect of dramatic effectiveness no. Moreover, the scores which you see here are, apart from those of Grétry, by Gluck, Piccinni, Salieri, and there is nothing French about them but the words', see Frank, 'Aus den ungedruckten Denkwürdigkeiten', 28 [*Dokumente*, 476, *Documentary Biography*, 561].
115. *Journal de Paris*, 12 June 1778, quoted from Wilder, *Mozart*, 105: 'It consists of three episodic scenes almost detached from each other. The first is purely Anacreontic: Cupid taken in the net and caged; it is very agreeably composed. Mlle Guimard and the younger M. Vestris display all the grace contained in the subject. The second is the game of blind-man's buff; M. d'Auberval, whose talent the public finds so agreeable, plays the principal part. The third is one of the rogueries of Cupid, where he shows two shepherdesses another shepherdess disguised as a shepherd. Mlle Asselin plays the shepherd and Mlles Guimard and Allard the two shepherdesses. The two shepherdesses fall in love with the supposed shepherd, who, to undeceive them, eventually bares her breast. This scene is made very piquant by the intelligence and the grace of these three famous dancers. We must add that at the moment where Mlle Asselin enlightens the two shepherdesses several voices cried *bis*. The varied figures with which this ballet ends were much applauded' [*Dokumente*, 158, *Documentary Biography*, 175–6]. According to Grimm, the dubious nature of the denouement was criticized by certain sections of the audience.

appears that the work was divided into three scenes, the first of which was Anacreontic, the second comic and the third pastoral. Their principal purpose was to provide popular dancers of both sexes with a chance to display their abilities. There is little trace of Noverre as a reforming spirit of the drama, and as such the work is one of those that he dismissed in his theoretical writings as a *divertissement de danse* rather than as a ballet.[116] This also emerges from the music, in which there is no sign of the large-scale programmatical orchestral scenes that go beyond the scope of the older type of dances and that we find in the works of Deller and Rodolphe, for example: everything takes place within the usual orchestral confines, with only the occasional abrupt change of tempo (as in nos 7 and 9) or a fermata (in no. 18) suggesting a specific action on stage. In general, however, the shorter numbers are typically Parisian dances in binary or, more frequently, ternary form, while the longer ones are closer in form to that of the French rondeau with minor episode.

The score is written in a neat hand[117] and runs to twenty-one numbers including the overture, which more or less tallies with Mozart's claim that six of the numbers were by other composers and that he himself was responsible for a dozen. (He is no more specific than this.) Wilder is no doubt right to dismiss the first six numbers as the 'wretched French airs' mentioned by Mozart himself and to acknowledge thirteen as Mozart's own.[118] These thirteen were duly taken over into the complete edition of Mozart's works. The composer's ability to capture the style of French dance music is really quite remarkable, with the rhythmical stamp of the individual types of dance admirably reproduced.[119] On similar occasions in the past he had often made use of folk tunes pure and simple, but this time he remained entirely within the framework of aristocratic society, even in the case of the pastoral drones in no. 14, where they evidently accompany an 'entrée des bergers'. No less in evidence are the piquant instrumental effects of the French composers of the period: no. 9, for example, is cast in the form of a old-style trio with two violins and a flute, except that the flute is constantly answered by a second flute in the manner of an echo.[120] Particularly attractive in terms of its sonorities is the semiquaver accompaniment in the gavotte no. 12 with clarinets and bassoons in octaves, an accompaniment that is transferred to the second violins and violas in the second subject.[121] No one, of course, will expect any greater depth of inspiration from such 'petits riens', yet most of these numbers – especially nos 12, 14 and 15–18 – reveal the whole magic of Mozart's charm and roguishness, while the mineur of no. 18 in G minor could only be by Mozart, such is its tone of gentle lamentation, its bitter accents and its anguished chromaticisms. Other numbers, too, contain pre-echoes of much later works.[122] The most substantial number is the overture, a single-movement piece in keeping with standard practice in the ballets of this period, the lavish instrumentation of which contains audible echoes of the Mannheim style, notably in the way in which the winds are thematically exploited. The movement's relatively loose structure likewise reflects balletic practice, lacking the usual modulation to the dominant and with only the contrastive second subject – a sustained theme of genuinely Mozartian stamp – recalling

116. Noverre, *Lettres sur la danse et sur les ballets*, 26.
117. Wilder, *Mozart*, 108. ◆ As noted above, the score is a contemporaneous copy, not Mozart's autograph.
118. The second number is the song 'Charmante Gabrielle' from the time of Henri IV; see Wilder, 'Mozart à Paris en 1778: Une partition inédite', 815.
119. No. 15 is described in the score as a 'Gavotte gracieuse', but is in fact a gigue.
120. According to Wilder, the following number (NMA no. 10), which is scored for strings alone, depicts the capture of one of the characters in the game of blind man's buff.
121. The main melody is taken from Mozart's most recent violin concerto, a borrowing paralleled by the thematic affinity between the A major violin concerto and the ballet *Le gelosie del seraglio*.
122. The flute melody of no. 9 looks forward to *Die Zauberflöte*, while the main melody of no. 11 looks forward to the final movement of the piano quartet in E flat major K493 of 1786.

the old sonata form. There is no question, of course, of any thematic development, yet there is no denying the intelligent way in which the numerous musical ideas are reordered, varied and combined with new ideas in the manner of French comic opera overtures. Among such ideas is one which, typical of Paisiello, occurs towards the end of the overture and already looks forward to *Le nozze di Figaro*:

Characteristic of the entire piece is an energetic life-enhancing sense of rhythm that finds expression not least in the high-spirited syncopation of the second bar and, more especially, in various rapid anapaestic figures in the accompaniment.[123] Typically Mozartian is the thoughtful, quiet ending to this bustling, festive piece.

In terms of both form and character, the 'Paris' or 'French' symphony in D major K297 is largely a concession to French audiences, whose intellectual abilities Mozart notoriously held in low regard. On 11 September 1778, for example, we find him writing to his father to the effect that his older symphonies would find little favour in Paris: 'In Germany we prefer length, but in fact it is better to be brief and to the point.'[124] Here Mozart is referring first and foremost to the absence of repeats. He was pandering to the taste of Paris's music lovers not only with the 'premier coup d'archet' and the *piano* opening of the final movement (the latter, be it added, clearly modelled on similar works by Haydn) but also with all manner of other dynamic and orchestral delights which, as before, reveal the influence of the Mannheim school. Above all, however, there is the superficially brilliant, demagogic aspect of the work, an aspect that includes the conscious avoidance of depth and originality in the basic ideas and their development and, the desire for brevity notwithstanding, a certain volubility that insists on repeating familiar material as though afraid that the listener might not yet have understood it properly. As a result, all the themes of the opening movement are more or less connected, but with no attempt being made to exploit their affinities and make psychological capital out of them and with the development section proving one of the most threadbare ever produced by Mozart. It is difficult, therefore, to find anything specifically Mozartian in the symphony's first two movements, still less to discern any progress between it and its immediate predecessors. Even the andantino[125] is a quintessential expression of the age of Rococo, carefree and dainty, with not even the sudden *forte* unison passages implying any real

123. Something similar may be found in the second subject of the opening movement of the C major violin sonata K296. ◆ Further, see Dahms, 'Mozart und Noverres "Ballet en action"'.

124. *Briefe*, ii.476 (letter of 11 September 1778).

125. Two versions of this movement have survived in Mozart's hand, the first one longer, the second one shorter. The sketch of this movement includes the complete melodic line and most of the bass line. Other instruments are included at individual points in order to indicate a particular motif. After drawing up his guidelines in this way, Mozart then worked out the individual detail, rarely changing anything and only occasionally making necessary cuts. If, in the process of elaborating the sketch, he came across a passage that struck him as too distended or even as dispensable, he struck out the passage and went on to the next section. Apart from a handful of relatively brief passages, the main sections affected by this process are a lengthy return to the main theme effected by means of an imitative figure and, shortly afterwards, a lengthy passage with flute and oboe solo. After the entire movement had been revised in this way, Mozart then prepared a rough copy of the whole that corresponds to the printed version of the score. In the first movement, too, Mozart made a number of often considerable cuts. The earlier andante that was performed first in Paris is printed in a Paris edition of the symphony; it is less significant as a composition and Mozart was right to replace it. It is notable, for example that the cello is used here as a melody instrument. See Köchel, *Chronologisch-thematisches Verzeichnis* K297 (with additional note). ◆ Here Abert apparently refers to the shorter 3/4 andante. For an account of Mozart's sketches, see Ulrich Konrad, *Mozarts Schaffensweise*, 140–1 and 291–2.

sense of threat. If the final movement is the most captivating of the three, it owes this fact above all to its second subject, which is introduced in canon in the winds – a procedure adopted by the Mannheim composers.[126] Its continuation in a sudden minor tonality is no less typically Mozartian. Indeed, this idea already bears within it the demonic features of the C minor concerto K 491:

But this second subject also raises the development section to a new and greater height, with an extraordinarily effective release of tension at the passage in D minor where the rhythm of the first subject-group suddenly appears in the winds. The section ends with a series of chords alternating, beat by beat, between winds and strings. The recapitulation adopts the model of the French comic operas of the period, with the themes regrouped and varied, but in such a way that the main theme always has the last word.

The symphony's outer garb is particularly striking. After all, the forces available to Mozart in Paris allowed him to produce 'the glorious effect of a symphony with flutes, oboes and clarinets' and at the same time to write for horns, bassoons, trumpets and timpani. His writing for the clarinets is in fact remarkably restrained. Not only are they absent from the middle movement (so, too, are the trumpets and timpani), but they play an extremely limited role in the working out of the thematic material, at least when compared with that of the other winds. It is clear that Mozart was more interested in giving a particular shade to the symphony's overall tone colour than in giving them prominence as soloists.

Incomparably more important is the sinfonia concertante in E flat major K297B, an offshoot of the old German concerto grosso for winds.[127] The influence of the Mannheim school is clear above all from its broadly structured opening movement, with its greater number of contrasting themes and the symphonic character of its very first tutti. As in the earlier concertos, tutti and soli are strictly separated, but the orchestra is limited to the role of a mere accompanist during most of the solo sections, the main exceptions being passages such as the soloists' very first entry. Generally, however, Mozart appears to be pandering to French taste. The development section is largely entrusted to the soloists, their musical material made up in part of new ideas and, in part, earlier secondary motifs. Only once does the tutti assert itself with the second subject in the minor, introducing one of those sombrely thoughtful, typically Mozartian passages from which the main theme suddenly emerges in the recapitulation as though the mists have abruptly lifted. In general, the movement is dominated by a sense of energy and lively animation, while the themes[128] are far

126.   ◆ Concerning possible Mannheim influences on the 'Paris' symphony, see Eugene K. Wolf, 'Mannheimer Symphonik um 1777/1778 und ihr Einfluß auf Mozarts symphonischen Stil'.
127.   ◆ But see n.56 above. In fact, Abert here describes not K297B but KAnh. C14.01. For the concerto grosso, see Hans Engel, *Das Concerto grosso*, and Walther Krüger, *Das Concerto grosso*; for the sinfonia concertante, see Brook, 'The Symphonie Concertante: Its Musical and Sociological Bases', and McCredie, 'Symphonie Concertante and Multiple Concerto in Germany, 1780–1850: Some Problems and Perspectives for a Source-Repertory Study'. Specifically with respect to Mannheim, see Waldkirch, *Die konzertanten Sinfonien der Mannheimer im 18. Jahrhundert*.
128.   The opening features a favourite theme of Mozart's, which is already found in an earlier symphony (K132) and which later returns in a well-known keyboard concerto (K482).

fresher and more individual than in the symphony. At the end of the typically foreshortened reca-pitulation is a cadenza for all four soloists that is carefully constructed from motifs heard in the rest of the movement. The ternary-form adagio, which is also in E flat major,[129] is a rêverie of authentically Mozartian sweetness in which the soloists engage in dialogue not only with the orchestra but also among each other. This deeply felt movement draws to a close on a note of muted bliss with the beautiful entry of the final tutti theme. The final movement is a set of varia-tions and is another concession to Parisian audiences, with the theme entrusted to the soloists and with a pizzicato accompaniment by the tutti that recalls nothing so much as a guitar. The influ-ence of the Parisian *opéra comique* could hardly be more evident. And, as in the operatic vaude-villes of the period, the tutti adds a refrain to the theme that is itself varied after every alternate variation. In keeping with the local fashion at this time, the variations themselves are purely melodic and largely designed to allow the instruments to engage in the most varied forms of dialogue, with only the penultimate one culminating not in the refrain but in a recitative-like adagio that leads in turn into the final variation, which is in a different time-signature and tempo. The sustained melodic line that suddenly enters at this point, immediately before the end and in place of the expected refrain, is almost religious in character, with a magnificence that already looks forward to Beethoven.

The concerto in C major K 299 for flute and harp is an example of the elegant, carefree music associated with the salons of the era, with even its opening movement being looser in structure than the work just discussed and with a rather more liberal approach to new ideas, especially in the solo writing. The most delightful passage in this movement is its development section, with the harp initially attempting to stick to the thematic material, while the flute insists on introducing new ideas, some of which even gain acceptance. The result is one of those harmonically fasci-nating, fantasy-like development sections involving sequencing that Mozart ultimately owed to Schobert. As we shall see, it was at precisely this moment that memories of Schobert came flooding back to Mozart with peculiarly vivid intensity. The heartfelt idyll of the middle movement is followed by one of Mozart's freest rondos, the essentially Italianate theme of which, now harnessed to the rhythms of a French gavotte, will later be found again in transmuted form in the romance from *Eine kleine Nachtmusik* K525. The principal appeal of this movement lies in its great variety and in the constant reordering, variation and instrumentation of the various musical ideas.

Far more important, on average, than these large-scale compositions are the chamber works and keyboard pieces that Mozart wrote in Paris. Not for a long time have we heard Mozart strike so profoundly tragic a note as he does in the violin sonata in E minor K304. Was it his memory of the emotional upheavals of Mannheim that overwhelmed him here, or was it the feeling of lone-liness in a foreign, hostile city? Like its predecessors, it is in two movements and at least superfi-cially recalls the Parisian practice of the time with its minuet in second position, yet there is not a single bar in the whole of this work that is not deeply, nay, passionately felt. The opening move-ment is a constant battle between weary resignation and uncontrollable defiance; rarely did Mozart write wilder unison passages or more searing syncopations. On this occasion, the devel-opment section is strictly thematic and non-episodic. Here the mood of resignation sinks to the level of a quiet sobbing until an eerie unison demon whips up the mood again to the terrible scream with which the recapitulation begins. And there is no let-up: after the giant strides of the

129. ◆ In fact this is a strike against the work: none of Mozart's concertos includes a middle movement in the tonic.

canon, the movement collapses in the expressive coda on a note of renunciation. The second movement is pointedly headed 'Tempo di Menuetto', rather than 'Menuetto'. Here the mood grows milder, producing a sense of wistful melancholy, yet towards the end it becomes clear that the fighting spirit of old is still far from dead: with its curiously penetrating, impassioned motif and a brief, convulsive outburst, the coda brings to an end a work that expresses an important, deeply pessimistic and genuinely Mozartian trait in consummate form unsullied by any digressions. Only once does a brighter ray of light fall on the sombre picture, in the magical E major trio, yet its role within the work as a whole is no more than that of a fleeting vision of happiness. The D major violin sonata K306 is completely different in character. Here is a work that exudes great strength and reveals an outward brilliance that recalls the concerto not least in formal details such as the final-movement cadenza. The development section of the opening movement is again modelled on similar passages in Schobert, a fantasia on a subsidiary motif from the first subject-group that races along in a series of broad sequences through all manner of remote harmonies.[130] Darker shadows pass briefly over the scene, notably in the middle movement's development section with its final syncopations reminiscent of *Don Giovanni*, while the final movement alternates between a capricious French allegretto and an effervescent Italian allegro, a form that Mozart had used by preference in his violin concertos.

Among the keyboard sonatas of this period, the one in A minor K310 takes pride of place. It is Mozart's first tragic sonata and recalls the E minor violin sonata in its strict adherence to its poetic model, its perfect formal proportions and, finally, in the very nature of that model, the only difference being that on this occasion the contrasts are more broadly based and more implacable. The first subject strides along in Mozart's heroic rhythm to quaver chords that are conceived along orchestral lines, but with the sighlike motif in the second bar it acquires an element of anguish, as a result of which the overall mood of the movement is that of manly resolve resisting dull and painful pressure. The second subject allows scope for virtuosity in a way unsuspected in any of Mozart's previous works; that the emotions depicted here avoid the merely playful is clear not least from Mozart's favourite rhythm ♪♪♪♪♩ 𝄾 | which always signifies extreme excitement in his works. The development section is again based on a sequential idea à la Schobert, except that here we find especially strident dissonances and sudden shifts from *fortissimo* to *pianissimo* as though we are passing through a stormy nocturnal landscape lit time and again by flashes of lightning. The recapitulation, too, acquires an extra degree of excitement not only from the transfer of the main theme to the bass with the tremolando in the right hand, but also from the interpolation of two impassioned bars before the final subject-group and, above all, from the use of a minor tonality that is maintained throughout the whole of this section. The andante, admittedly, is initially successful in striking a calmer note, but here, too, the development section brings with it a surprisingly abrupt descent into the darkest recesses of passion, a descent achieved, as before, by Schobertian sequencing techniques. Rarely in his later works did Mozart write harsher dissonances. In the final movement the spirits conjured up only with difficulty in the andante join hands in a demonic and peculiarly Mozartian dance, resulting in one of the composer's most remarkable sonata movements that races along, restless and inconstant, with only a brief ray of light in the form of the A major interlude. And it ends on a note of wild defiance, with none of the

---

130. There is real psychological subtlety to the way in which, following this outburst, the recapitulation begins not with the main theme – which is reserved for the very end – but with the second subject.

liberating resolution in the Beethovenian sense of that term.[131] Movements of this kind are in themselves sufficient to refute the view of a composer who endlessly revelled in beauty.

Of the three other keyboard sonatas that were probably written in Paris (K330–332),[132] the one in A major – K331 – departs most markedly from the formal structure observed in the earlier works, with the characteristic opening allegro replaced by a set of variations on a slow theme, while the slow middle movement is now a minuet and the finale a French rondeau with the picturesque addition 'alla Turca'. All three movements, moreover, are in the same key. All this suggests a suite rather than a sonata, and the present piece is certainly a suite in spirit.[133] This surprising step can be explained, however, by reference to the influence of French keyboard music: here, too, the sonata retained its links with the suite far longer than any other genre. We have already discussed the folklike melody of the theme, which is here cast in a unique light by the dreamily repeated fifths in the middle voice and by various dynamic surprises. With the exception of the third and fourth, the variations are all in fact double variations, with the theme newly varied at its return in the first section and followed each time by a sudden shift to *forte* that is nowhere anticipated by the theme. As a result, each stem puts forth two flowers, as it were, one of them in pastel shades, the other in far brighter colours. In the first variation, the theme is broken down into Rococo figurations expressive of both charm and yearning, whereas the second acquires a touch of humour, not least as a result of the obstinate D sharp in the accompaniment and the following grotesque faunlike leaps with appoggiatura in the bass. There follows the starkest of contrasts in the form of the impassioned third variation, its implacably restless passion becoming positively eerie at the passage in octaves in the right hand; the fourth rocks gently along as though blissfully dreaming; and the fifth variation is a yearning adagio, in which not only the melodic line but the figurations, too, begin to sing. The sixth and final variation is an allegro, energetic and whimsical by turns, with a change of tempo and a brief coda by way of a half-roguish *envoi*. In this way, each variation is a character-piece unto itself, while never straying too far from the melodic line of the theme. Common to all six is a uniquely enchanting melodiousness producing a veritable magic garden through which we wander as though guests of Armida herself. With its remarkable but constant shifts of mood, the main section of the menuetto[134] makes way for more serious, even sombre thoughts, while the trio harks back to the mood of the fourth variation, not least with its crossing of hands. Only in the second section do intruders[135] disrupt the proceedings in the form of barbaric unison octaves – are these the janissaries of the finale already beating at the gates of Paradise? This final movement is Mozart's first contribution to the Turkish local colour that was then popular, especially in *opéras comiques*, and as such was particularly influenced by Gluck's *La rencontre imprévue*. Characteristic of this local colour is the sharply dotted, rattling rhythm that seems to suggest the clash of cymbals.[136] The movement comprises two sections, one in the minor, the other in the major, the former capturing the essential nature of these characters, creeping along with catlike stealth, but at the same time revealing a certain ungainliness, while the latter expresses all their lurid savagery and sinister lechery. In the section in F sharp minor one can almost hear

---

131. Heuß, 'Das dämonische Element in Mozarts Werken', 184, rightly points out the affinity between the main subject of this movement and that of the final movement of Beethoven's op. 23, which is also in A minor.

132. ◆ But see n.81 above.

133. A similar course was later adopted by Beethoven in his A flat major sonata op.26.

134. The main theme is taken from the C major sonata K309.

135. Compare the Calender's aria in act one, scene two of Gluck's *La rencontre imprévue*.

136. A whole series of related motifs may be found in the overture to Gluck's opera, a piece that also left a profound mark on the Turkish colour of *Die Entführung aus dem Serail*.

the piccolos that Mozart always uses to conjure up these sensuous moods. And in the coda, finally, this sense of oriental fanaticism finds release in all its naturalistic madness.

The two other sonatas, K330 in C major and K332 in F major, not only revert to the old form, they also share the same wealth and lively interplay of ideas. With the exception of its heartfelt and, in its minor section, deeply impassioned slow movement, the C major Sonata remains within the framework of tasteful salon music and was probably written for a pupil. The F major Sonata, by contrast, is a far more ambitious piece. Its opening movement positively bursts with contrasting themes, some of which recall songs and comic operas, while others, such as the D minor idea, suddenly erupt from the darkness like ghosts with typically Mozartian unpredictability and cast a pall over the scene for some considerable time. The recalcitrantly Schobertian development section also comes under this heading. The Adagio revels in rapt figurations and ornaments and, as such, is pure Rococo, yet here, too, the idiosyncratic interplay of major and minor introduces a new and highly personal element. The almost unbearable tension produced by this wealth of ideas then finds release in the Presto, a virtuosic movement of a brilliance that Mozart rarely achieved in any of his later sonatas. It is cast in sonata form, but its most interesting feature is less its superficial brilliance than its kaleidoscopic interplay between the most disparate ideas. This movement, too, could hardly be further removed from the thematic thrift and compactness of a composer like Carl Philipp Emanuel Bach or Joseph Haydn. The whimsical ending brings with it a further surprise, dying away *pianissimo* and *calando*.

Of the three sets of variations on French songs that almost certainly date from this period (K264, 265 and 353),[137] none achieves the poetic intensity of the opening movement of K331, but they all surpass it in terms of superficial virtuosity. In keeping with French custom, Mozart uses the genre in order to open up the floodgates of his pianistic technique, and generally each variation allows him to treat a different technical problem – he is not interested in writing character-pieces in the spirit of the A major sonata. Instead, we find, in no particular order, exercises in scales, broken chords and various other figures, studies in octaves, thirds and staccato effects, crossing of hands, chains of trills and so on, generally divided between both hands. Even the adagio variations, which appear on a regular basis, seem to exist only to demonstrate the virtuoso art of ornamentation. The eighth variation on *Lison dormait* is a classic example of this. In the final variations, tempo and time-signature change on a regular basis. Here Mozart surpasses himself in creating the most brilliant impression. The variations on *Lison dormait* even include a brilliant cadenza, followed both here and in the variations on *La belle Françoise* by a calm coda which, in the best French tradition, picks up the theme itself. Although these works contain much that is charming and lively and, as a group, far surpass the fashionable variations of the period, there are few traces in them of the true, great Mozart, the only honourable exceptions being the minor-key variations, especially in *Lison dormait* and *Ah vous dirai-je Maman*, their profoundly thoughtful chromaticisms making them seem like intruders at a brilliant ball.

With the *scena Popoli di Tessaglia* K316 that he wrote for Aloysia, Mozart entered into direct competition with Gluck's *Alceste*;[138] and on account of his friends Ramm and Ritter he also added

---

137. ◆ See n.84 above.

138. According to Köchel, the autograph score was headed 'Scena per la Sgra. Weber, di Wolfgango Amadeo Mozart mpr. Monaco li 8 di gennajo 1779'. This was presumably the date on which it was handed over to Aloysia. The published version was based on a copy owned by Otto Jahn. ◆ The location of Mozart's autograph for K316 was unknown during Abert's time; it has since resurfaced at the Biblioteca do Palácio nacional de Ajuda, Lisbon. The work is published in NMA II/7/2.

parts for oboe and bassoon obbligato. Of course, there is virtually nothing about the piece that could really be said to be Gluckian, unless it be the way in which the recitative is carefully divided up along syntactic lines, something that the younger composer clearly picked up from his elder colleague. Otherwise, the approach could hardly be more different. In Gluck's case, Alcestis is an unapproachable princess even in the *secco* recitative, a queen who is fully able to control her grief:

Po - po - li di Tes - sa -glia, ah mai più giu -sto fu il vostro pian - to

With Mozart, by contrast, she enters after a wildly impassioned orchestral prelude with a stunned outburst:

Po - po- li di Tes - sa - glia, ah   mai   più giu -sto fu il vo-stro pianto

This sense of sudden uncontrolled anguish dominates the whole recitative, the accompaniment to which is built up from only a few expressive themes, with harmony used with surprising boldness to enhance the underlying expression. Gluck's Alcestis is both a wife and a queen who is able to maintain her dignity in the presence of her people even while suffering the bitterest anguish; Mozart's, by contrast, carries her grief out into the street, her feelings as a woman making her forget herself as a ruler. Again, it is not poverty of invention[139] that prompts Gluck to use such extreme economy of means on a purely musical level, but the desire to depict this aspect of his heroine's character with the least possible display of extravagance, and in this he is admirably successful. Mozart, on the other hand, is unstinting in his use of musical means to depict Alcestis's emotion, and although he produces an excellent picture of a soul at war with itself, there is no trace of the chaste and majestic figure bearing her lot with fortitude in the way in which Gluck imagined her. And the way in which Mozart's heroine pours out his feelings in her aria is deeply untypical of Gluck – it is here, after all, that Gluck's Alcestis rises to the full height of her being. The second half of Mozart's *scena* reverts to the style of Neapolitan opera, with lengthy *fioriture* on unimportant words ('ha') and virtuoso writing for the two obbligato instruments, indulging in the insistently self-regarding displays of coloratura excess with which Italian prima donnas traditionally expressed their burning desire for revenge – and this in spite of the fact that Alcestis says that only the woman in whose breast there beats a mother's heart can understand her suffering. On the other hand, this section is laid out along clear lines: both the sense of violent inner agitation and the silent anguish of the mother's heart find expression here, the former, admittedly, in a fairly conventional manner, while the latter, by contrast, is an extremely beautiful and truthful section in C minor, whose sudden descent to A flat major already looks forward to Schubert. More

---

139. Jahn, *W. A. Mozart*, fourth edition, i.592.

successful is the andantino. Here, too, there is no trace of Gluck's austere chastity, of course, and there is excessive coloratura: what has become of Gluck's brief and veristic coloratura flourish on the word 'raggio', for example! Yet a calm and tender sadness finds noble expression here, not least as a result of the syncopated and chromatic melodic line. The aim of providing Aloysia with a grateful showpiece is all too apparent, of course: it was designed to give her an opportunity to demonstrate her mastery not only in the tasteful execution of the elevated Italian manner but also in legato singing and coloratura. The vocal writing has a range of two octaves, from g' to g'''.

22

Homecoming

Leopold was keen for Mozart to return home by the quickest possible route, which would take him via Strasbourg. But as the days turned into weeks and he had still received no news that Mozart had in fact arrived in Strasbourg, he began to grow concerned. 'I have confessed and received Communion together with your sister', he wrote on 19 October, 'and I have prayed God most earnestly to preserve you. Our excellent Bullinger prays daily for you at Holy Mass.'[1] The blame for the delay lay with Grimm who, in spite of his promise to provide Mozart with a diligence, which would have covered the journey from Paris to Strasbourg in five days, had forced him to travel by stagecoach, a journey of twelve days that inevitably caused both father and son considerable annoyance. Mozart endured the strain for a week before breaking his journey at Nancy, where he stopped off with a German merchant from Paris who had travelled widely and with whom Mozart had grown very friendly. The next day – 4 October – the two men hoped to find an inexpensive way of continuing their journey but were again delayed and it was not until around the middle of the month that Mozart finally reached Strasbourg, from where he wrote to his father on the 15th:

This is a miserable dump, but the day after tomorrow, Saturday the 17th, I shall be giving a subscription concert *all by myself* (so that I don't have any expenses) to please a few good friends, including both amateurs and connoisseurs; – if I had an orchestra, it would cost over 3 louis d'or, including lighting, and who knows whether we'd bring in as much as that?[2]

This was a wise precaution, inasmuch as we learn from Mozart's next letter of 26 October 1778 that the proceeds of this 'concert of sorts' were just three louis d'or:

The main takings consisted in the shouts of 'Bravo' and 'Bravissimo' that rang out on every side – Prince Max von Zweibrücken also honoured us with his presence. I don't need to tell you that everyone was pleased. I wanted to set off back home immediately afterwards, but I was advised to stay on until next Saturday and give a big concert at the theatre; – but to the astonishment, indignation and shame of all the inhabitants of Strasbourg, the receipts were exactly the same. . . . But I must say that the applause and clapping made my ears ache as much as if the theatre had been full. Everyone who was there loudly and publicly criticized their fellow citizens; and I told them all that, if I could reasonably have imagined that so few people would come, I'd gladly have given the concert for free, simply for the pleasure of seeing the theatre full. Certainly, I'd have preferred it that way, as, upon my word, there's nothing more depressing than a large

1. *Briefe*, ii.500 (letter of 19 October 1778).
2. *Briefe*, ii.496 (letter of 15 October 1778).

T-shaped table laid for 80 with only 3 at dinner, – and then it was so cold! But I soon got warm, and – in order to show these gentlemen of Strasbourg how little I cared – I played lots of pieces for my own amusement, including one more concerto than I'd promised, – and in the end I extemporized for a while. – Well, that's all over – at least I've covered myself in honour and glory.[3]

Mozart also gave two public concerts on the town's two fine Silbermann organs in the Neukirche and Thomaskirche and since the roads were impassable as a result of flooding and he was unable to continue his journey, he decided to 'amuse' himself and others on his name-day – 31 October – by giving a further concert at the suggestion of various friends, including the Frank brothers and a Herr de Beyer. The proceeds amounted to a grand total of one louis d'or. It is hardly surprising, therefore, that he had to borrow some money for the rest of his journey, a loan that was to cause him considerable annoyance several years later.

The dilatory nature of Mozart's return hardly gives the impression that he was in any particular hurry to get back to Salzburg, and he was easily talked into making a detour to Mannheim, rather than travelling via Stuttgart, the extra distance being compensated by the better roads and the availability of a post coach. This news again induced a state of extreme alarm in Leopold, and the irritable, tetchy and impatient tone of his letters of 19 and 23 November[4] can be explained only by reference to his secret fear that all his plans for Salzburg might yet be undermined at the very last moment by Mozart's visit to Mannheim. That the latter's journey there was a matter especially close to his heart was something that the rationalist in Leopold was constitutionally incapable of understanding.

Mozart left Strasbourg on 3 November and arrived in Mannheim three days later. Here he reminisced with friends and caught up with all the latest news from Marie Elisabeth Cannabich, who had remained behind in the town. Although many of his acquaintances, including the Webers, had already moved to Munich, he was still warmly welcomed wherever he went. 'There is a regular scramble to have me', he reported on 12 November. 'In a word, Mannheim loves me as much as I love Mannheim.'[5] Inevitably, all his old hopes were rekindled, encouraged by all manner of rumours, including one to the effect that the elector would soon be returning to Mannheim as he would be unable to endure the allegedly coarse Bavarians for long. As always, theatrical gossip was rife. It was at this point that Mozart wrote to tell his father that Colloredo would have to raise his salary. And the prospect of remaining in Mannheim now became even more seductive when he was offered an opportunity to write for the theatre there.

By the time that Mozart arrived back in Mannheim, the local theatre had recovered from the disruption caused by the sudden departure of the court, and although Baron Wolfgang Heribert von Dalberg had failed in his attempt to get the University of Heidelberg transferred to Mannheim, the elector had none the less followed up his suggestion and, by a decree dated 1 September 1778, had set up a national theatre in the town with an annual grant from the court of 5000 florins. Dalberg was its first intendant. A man of limited creative abilities, he took his duties very seriously and regarded it as a matter of personal honour to restore the Mannheim theatre to

---

3. *Briefe*, ii.501–2 (letter of 26 October 1778).
4. *Briefe*, ii.508–15 (letters of 19 and 23 November 1778).
5. *Briefe*, ii.505 (letter of 12 November 1778).

its former reputation.[6] It was not until 1779, of course, that the theatre's golden age began with the appointment of the leading members of the Gotha Court Theatre, foremost among whom was August Wilhelm Iffland. But this is a period in its history that belongs in a life of Schiller,[7] rather than in that of Mozart. In the shorter term, Dalberg had to seek help elsewhere. At the time of Mozart's visit in November 1778, he had engaged Seyler and his troupe of actors,[8] who performed once a week, giving both spoken plays and singspiels and in that way generating a mass of works by local men of letters and composers that Wieland ridiculed in his *Abderiten*.[9] It is no wonder, then, that Mozart hoped for a last-minute reprieve from the 'slavery' that awaited him in Salzburg, and so we find him writing enthusiastically to his father on 12 November:

I may be able to earn 40 louis d'or here, though I'd have to remain here for 6 weeks, or 2 months at the most. The Seyler company is here – I expect you already know them by reputation; Herr von Dalberg is their manager and won't let me go until I've written a duodrama for him; in fact, it didn't take me long to make up my mind, as I've always wanted to write this kind of drama. I don't know whether I told you anything about this type of piece the first time I was here. – On that occasion I saw a piece of this kind performed twice and was utterly captivated by it! Indeed, I've never been so agreeably surprised by anything, as I'd always imagined that such a piece would fail to leave any impression. – I expect you know that there's no singing in it, only dialogue, with the music as a sort of obbligato recitative; sometimes there's also dialogue during the music, which then produces the most wonderful impression. – The work I saw was Benda's *Medea*; – he's written another one, *Ariadne auf Naxos*, both of them really excellent. You know that of all the Lutheran Kapellmeisters, Benda has always been my favourite; I like these two works so much that I carry them around with me. Well, you can imagine my delight at having to write exactly what I want. – Do you know what I think? – I think that most recitatives should be treated in this way in opera – and only occasionally sung, when the words can be well expressed by the music.[10]

The duodrama that Mozart was supposed to write was a setting of *Semiramis* by his old patron, Otto Heinrich von Gemmingen, and the present passage from his correspondence is particularly important in that it reveals the extent to which the melodrama, as popularized in Germany by Georg Benda, could interest even as critical an observer as Mozart. In practical terms, too, it must have been well suited to the dubious vocal resources of the Seyler company. Alongside this project, however, we also find a plan for an opera: Dalberg had written the libretto for an opera *Cora*[11] and had already entered into negotiations on the subject with both Gluck and Schweitzer,[12] but as

6. See Walter, *Geschichte des Theaters und der Musik am kurpfälzischen Hofe*, 314ff. ◆ Further concerning the Mannheim theatre, see Eugene K. Wolf, 'The Mannheim court'; Finscher, *Die Mannheimer Hofkapelle im Zeitalter Carl Theodors*; Welck and Homering, *176 Tage W. A. Mozart in Mannheim*; and Corneilson, 'Reconstructing the Mannheim court theatre'.

7. See Karl Berger, *Schiller*, i.331ff.

8. ◆ Abel Seyler (1730–1800) was the director of a travelling troupe that was particularly successful during the period 1769–79, when it held extended appointments at Weimar (1771–4) and Gotha (1774–5). Further, see Schlösser, *Vom Hamburger Nationaltheater zur Gothaer Hofbühne*; Pies, *Prinzipale: Zur Genealogie des deutschsprachigen Berufstheaters vom 17. bis 19. Jahrhundert*; and Bauman, *North German Opera in the Age of Goethe*.

9. See Walter, *Geschichte des Theaters*, 274ff.

10. *Briefe*, ii.505–6 (letter of 12 November 1778).

11. According to the *Beitrag zur pfälzischen Schaubühne*, *Cora* – 'a musical drama' – appeared incapable of being set to music or staged.

12. Gluck's correspondence on the subject was published in the *Süddeutsche Musikzeitung* (1854), 174; Schweitzer's involvement in the project is attested by Dalberg's correspondence of 1778. ◆ See Mueller von Asow, *The Collected Correspondence and Papers of Christoph Willibald Gluck*, 163–4.

neither of them seemed sufficiently reliable, he now tried to win over Mozart to the idea. The latter wrote to him on 24 November:

Herr Baron! You know me; I'm not motivated by self-interest, especially when I know that I'm in a position to render a service to as great a lover and as true a connoisseur of music as you are. Quite the opposite. I know, too, that you will certainly not want me to suffer any losses here; – and so I take the liberty of stating my final conditions in this matter, as it's impossible for me to remain here any longer in a state of uncertainty. I undertake to write a monodrama for 25 louis d'or, to remain here for 2 more months, to make all the necessary arrangements and to attend all the rehearsals etc.; but on condition that, whatever happens, I'm paid by the end of January. That I expect free admission to the performance goes without saying.[13] You see, my dear Baron, that this is all I can do; if you consider the matter carefully, you'll see that I'm acting with considerable discretion. As for your opera, I assure you that I'd very much like to set it to music. But, as you yourself will admit, I could not do so for 25 louis d'or, because (even at a low estimate) it would involve at least twice as much work as a monodrama; – and what would deter me most is the fact that, as you told me yourself, Gluck and Schweitzer are already working on it. But let's assume that you were willing to give me 50 louis d'or for it, as a man of honour I'd still discourage you from such an undertaking. An opera without male and female singers – what an idea! Still, if in the meantime there's any prospect of its being performed, I wouldn't refuse to accept this commission as a favour to you; – but it would be no mean task, I can swear to that on my word of honour. – I've told you clearly and candidly what I think and ask only that you let me know your decision as soon as possible. If I could have it today, I should be all the more grateful, as I've heard that someone is travelling alone to Munich next Thursday and I'd very much like to take advantage of this opportunity.[14]

There were other ways, too, in which Mozart felt encouraged to turn his hand to composition at this time: 'An Académie des Amateurs, like the one in Paris, is about to be started here', he reported on 12 November. 'Herr Fränzl is to lead the violins, and I'm just writing a concerto for keyboard and violin.'[15]

But Leopold lost no time in nipping these plans in the bud:

You're hoping for an appointment in Mannheim? An appointment? What does that mean? You're not to take up an appointment in Mannheim or anywhere else at present, I refuse to hear the word 'appointment'. If the elector were to die today, a whole battalion of musicians in Munich and Mannheim would be forced to set off into the big wide world and beg for a living, as the Duke of Zweibrücken already has a 36-strong orchestra and the present orchestra of the Bavarian Electorate and Mannheim costs 80,000 florins a year. The people in Mannheim are fools if they imagine that the elector will leave Munich. . . . The main thing is that you now

---

13. Brandes reports that actors had to pay for tickets for opera performances in which they were not actively involved; see Brandes, *Meine Lebensgeschichte*, ii.277–8.

14. *Briefe*, ii.515–16 (letter of 24 November 1778).

15. *Briefe*, ii.506 (letter of 12 November 1778). The concerto remained unfinished. A 120-bar fragment appears in AMA XXIV, no. 21a (see also K315f). ◆ At the head of the fragmentary concerto for violin and keyboard, Mozart wrote, 'Concerto per il Cembalo e Violino / di Wolfgango Amadeo Mozart. – Mannheim li . . . di . . . 1778'; it is published in NMA V/14/2. Among the handful of known programmes for the academy's concerts from the 1780s, three included works by Mozart: on 15 May 1785 Dalberg performed a Mozart keyboard concerto; an 'overture' (that is, a symphony) was given on 9 December 1785; and on 20 January 1786 a quartet was performed. See Eisen, *Dokumente: Addenda*, 103–5, *New Mozart Documents*, 98–102.

return to Salzburg. I don't wish to hear anything more about the 40 louis d'or that you might earn there. Your whole aim seems to be to ruin me financially simply in order for you to go on building your castles in the air.[16]

And Leopold ended his letter by insisting that Mozart resume his journey forthwith. A few days later, however, he returned to the offensive, evidently still unsure that he could count on his son's compliance. On this occasion he even declared himself in agreement with Mozart's love of Aloysia, adding that the oboist in Salzburg, Joseph Fiala, had told Colloredo so much about her that she could easily come to Salzburg; his other friends in Munich would also find an open house whenever they called on him. He even tried to win his son over by holding out the prospect of another visit to Italy, but for this too, he went on, Mozart would first have to take up his post in Salzburg:

It is absolutely vital that you take up this post, unless – that is – you are motivated by the most confounded and malicious idea of exposing your father to shame and ridicule, your father who is so concerned for you and who has sacrificed every hour of his life to his children in order to bring them credit and honour, as I am not in a position to pay off a debt that amounts in total to 1000 florins, unless you make it easier for me to do so by drawing your salary here, in which case I would then undoubtedly be able to pay off more than 400 florins a year and still lead a splendid life with the two of you. . . . If it is God's will, I plan to live a few more years, pay off my debts – and then, if you want to, you can have your own obstinate way; – but no! You have too good a heart! You're not malicious, just thoughtless, – all will be well in the end.[17]

In response to this latest appeal, Mozart promised to leave Mannheim on 9 December, but not without first springing a further surprise on his father: 'I'm leaving next Wednesday, and do you know how I'm travelling? With the Imperial Abbot of Kaisheim. When a good friend of mine mentioned me to him, he immediately recognized my name and said how pleased he'd be to have me as a travelling companion; he's a most amiable man (in spite of the fact that he's a priest and a prelate), so I'll be travelling via Kaisheim and not via Stuttgart.'[18] Again it was inordinately difficult for him to tear himself away from Mannheim, not least because he had found in Marie Elisabeth Cannabich a sympathetic and well-disposed friend, whom he found it particularly painful to leave.

But he did not want to abandon his monodrama either and, because of his claimed 'fondness' for this type of work, he decided to complete the first act with no thought of any fee. The rest he would write when he got back home, he announced, although in the event he evidently did not do so.[19]

16. *Briefe*, ii.509 (letter of 19 November 1778).
17. *Briefe*, ii.512–15 (letter of 23 November 1778).
18. *Briefe*, ii.517 (letter of 3 December 1778).
19. On 9 August 1799 Mozart's widow wrote to Breitkopf & Härtel: 'There's a work here that I myself did not know. Stadler found the whole thing so admirable that he advised me against publishing it piecemeal. It is an opera and melodrama, both at the same time. Even the text is beautiful' (*Briefe*, iv.82). Nottebohm (*Mozartiana*, 126) assumed that this was the music to *Semiramis*, a work which, with the exception of a handful of parts for the overture, is no longer extent. But the expression 'opera and melodrama' could also refer to *Zaide*, of course. In Heinrich August Ottokar Reichard's *Theaterkalender* for 1779, 137, we read 'Mozard . . . Kapellmeister at Salzburg; begins *Semiramis*, a musical drama by Baron Gemmingen' [*Dokumente*, 162, *Documentary Biography*, 180], a piece of information presumably gleaned from a private source. Subsequent issues of the *Theaterkalender* regularly claim that the work was finished, but no record of a performance has ever been found. The only other mention of it is Gerber's inclusion of it in a list of Leopold Mozart's compositions alongside *Bastien und Bastienne* and *Die verstellte Gärtnerin*. As we pointed out earlier, this can be explained only by reference to the fact that after Leopold's death the early works by Mozart that he had had in his safekeeping were believed to be by Leopold himself. For this reason, if for no other, we must therefore assume that Mozart completed *Semiramis*, either wholly or in part. It remains unclear why it did not find its

In Kaisheim, too, Mozart broke his journey for the sake of the amiable prelate, after which the two men travelled on to Munich, where they arrived on 25 December. As Leopold rightly foresaw, Munich, too, was a dangerous distraction, as Mozart had the prospect of renewing contact here with his old friends from Mannheim and especially with Aloysia Weber. Indeed, he had even summoned his cousin from Augsburg with the mysterious promise of an important role that she might perhaps be able to perform in Munich.

Once again Leopold had to spell out the fact that only by taking up his appointment in Salzburg would Mozart be able to relieve the whole family of its crippling burden of debt. In short, he should not attempt to persuade Cannabich or anyone else to detain him any longer but set off with the first mail coach of the new year. His warning was all too apposite as Cannabich and Raaff were both 'working relentlessly' for Mozart and, on their advice, he had already decided to write a Mass for the elector and would be able to hand over to the electress herself the six sonatas (K301–306) that he had just received from Paris.[20] Leopold now put his spoke in all these projects, with the result that Mozart was now doubly depressed – not only was it now certain that he could no longer escape his fate in Salzburg, but he was also afraid that he would receive an unfavourable welcome on his return home. In his predicament he turned to his old friend, the flautist Johann Baptist Becke, who attempted to console him by reminding him of his father's kindness, but in doing so merely added to his depression. 'Never in my entire life have I written anything worse than this letter,' he told his father on 29 December, 'I really can't write at all, I feel so tearful. I hope you'll write soon and console me.'[21] Becke, too, wrote to Leopold:

He burns with desire to embrace his dearest and most cherished father, which will ensue as soon as his circumstances here will permit; but he almost made me dispirited too, since for a whole hour I hardly succeeded in staying his tears: he has so good a heart. Never have I seen a child who carried more feeling and love for his father in his bosom than does your son. He is assailed by some fear lest your reception of him may not be as tender as he wishes. I, however, hope for something very different of your paternal heart. . . . His heart is so pure, so childlike, so frank towards me, how much more must it be towards his father. Only to hear him speak is to accord him justice as the best of characters, the most honest and upright of men.[22]

Leopold duly wrote and promised his son a 'tender and pleasant' welcome, adding that even the party that was due to be paid for out of the autumn surplus from the target-practice club had been postponed because of his tardiness in returning home and that a further delay was now impossible,

---

way back into his own hands, as the rest of his operas did, and why, following his death, it was not acquired by André. Rössig's *Versuche im musikalischen Drama* includes an entry similar to that found in Reichard's *Theaterkalender*: '*Semiramis*, a musical drama by Baron Gemmingen, is now occupying Herr Mozard, Kapellmeister at Salzburg' [*Dokumente*, 162, *Documentary Biography*, 180]. See Jahn, *W. A. Mozart*, fourth edition, i.585. Gemmingen's text does not appear to have been published either. ◆ *Pace* Abert, it is likely that Gerber – who cast his net widely in his search for information about contemporaneous composers – took his listing of *Semiramis* from Reichard's *Theaterkalender*, which is ambiguous in its identification of the work's author (at the time, the Mozart generally known as 'Kapellmeister at Salzburg' was Leopold). As such, there is no argument to be made concerning the derivation of the attribution based on the survival or non-survival of the work in Leopold's estate. The most compelling argument against Wolfgang's composition of even part of *Semiramis* is that he did not remain in Mannheim either to compose or direct it, having promised Dalberg that, if he had the commission, he would.

20. ◆ *Briefe*, ii. 535; letter of 31 December 1778.
21. *Briefe*, ii.529 (letter of 29 December 1778).
22. ◆ *Dokumente*, 161–2, *Documentary Biography*, 179–80.

otherwise Colloredo might rescind his order appointing Mozart, an order signed four months previously.[23] Mozart answered this charge on 8 January 1779:

I assure you, my dearest father, that I am looking forward with all my heart to returning to *you* (but not to Salzburg), as your last letter convinces me that you now know me better than before! There was never any other reason than this doubt for my long delay in returning home and for the sadness which in the end I could no longer conceal, so that I opened my heart completely to my friend Becke. What other reason could I have had? I've no cause to fear your reproaches; I've done nothing wrong (by which I mean nothing that would not become a Christian and a man of honour). In a word, I am looking forward to seeing you and to spending the happiest and pleasantest of times, but only in your own company and that of my dearest sister. I swear to you on my honour that I cannot bear Salzburg or its inhabitants (I mean those who were born there); their language and lifestyle are completely intolerable to me.[24]

Mozart's depression had, in fact, another cause, namely, the end of his relationship with Aloysia Weber, which had left a bitter aftertaste. He had stayed with the Webers and been able to hear for himself the progress that she had made. This was the occasion on which he handed over the aria *Popoli di Tessaglia* (K316), work on which had revived his feelings for her while he was still in Paris. It was his final offering to her as a lover. In spite of Leopold's fears that Fridolin Weber would cease to acknowledge Mozart now that he no longer needed him, her father behaved towards Mozart as of old, and it was Aloysia herself who was heartless enough to make it clear to him that, now that better prospects beckoned to her as a singer, she had no further need of her old friend. Mozart was devastated, but did not reveal how he felt. Instead, he adopted an even more frivolous attitude, sat down at the piano and sang in a loud voice: 'I gladly give up the girl who doesn't like me.'[25] Deep down, of course, he was profoundly hurt, and it was only later that he became fully conscious of the extent of the danger from which he had just escaped. On 16 May 1781, we find him writing to his father: 'I was a fool, I admit, about Aloysia Lange, but what man isn't when he's in love! But I really did love her and even now feel that she's not a matter of total indifference to me – it's a good thing, then, that her husband is a jealous fool who won't let her out of his sight, so that I rarely have a chance to see her.'[26]

In this way a journey that had already witnessed so many disappointments ended on a note of the most painful disharmony for Mozart. Not a single one of his proud dreams had come true, and

23. The decree appointing Mozart court organist on a salary of 450 florins a year is dated 17 January 1779, while the letter to the archbishop's exchequer is dated 26 February 1779. Both documents were published for the first time by Pirckmayer, 'Zur Lebensgeschichte Mozarts' [*Dokumente*, 163–4, *Documentary Biography*, 182–4]. If Leopold writes on 31 December 1778 that the decree 'is now four months old', he must be relying on the provisional assurances that he had been given, unless he is thinking of another decree, agreeing to an increase in salary of 100 florins a year for Leopold himself, an agreement that was now exactly four months old.
24. *Briefe*, ii.536 (letter of 8 January 1779).
25. This is the version of events given by Nissen, *Biographie W. A. Mozarts*, 415–16. Nissen also reports that, as a sign of mourning and in keeping with French custom, Mozart arrived in Munich with black buttons on his red coat (a coat that he may be seen wearing in the portraits from this period), a dress code that Aloysia appears not to have liked. On the other hand, it is difficult to believe Nissen's later claim that Aloysia's younger sister Constanze felt so sorry for Mozart that she made her first overtures to him at this time.
26. *Briefe*, iii.116–17 (letter of 16 May 1781). In later years, Aloysia, too, seems to have felt a certain wistful sadness when recalling this period in Munich: the vocal line of her aria K538 that Mozart wrote out for her in 1788 includes a quotation, in her own hand, from the love duet from Metastasio's *L'Olimpiade*: 'Nei tuoi giorni felici pensa qualche volta al "Popoli di Tessaglia".'
◆ Paper studies show that the written-out vocal part (or particella) to K538 probably dates from the time of Mozart's visit to Mannheim in 1778; the full score of the work was completed only ten years later, in 1788.

the most beautiful of all had now burst like a bubble, leaving only the hated prospect of Salzburg as his ineluctable fate.

The profound sense of grief that he took home with him is the best possible proof of the important role that his love for Aloysia Weber played in his whole development. It had swept through his young heart like a spring storm, allowing him to feel its whole force and bringing him not only supreme happiness but utter desolation, too. He was heavily in debt both to his father and to others and was not spared the painful conflict between the voice of emotion and his artistic conscience. But, unlike his father, he still believed that he could serve both masters when Aloysia's fickleness suddenly brought him back to earth. There is undoubtedly something tragic about the fact that he suffered such profound disillusionment at a time when his young heart had barely begun to blossom, but the joys and sorrows of his love also drove the artist in Mozart to strike out in a wholly new direction, opening up areas of his emotional life that he had previously avoided with only the vaguest idea of what they contained. If the onset of Mozart's maturity is normally dated to the time of *Idomeneo*, we should not forget that one of the reasons for this was Aloysia, whose flirtatious fickleness helped a great artist finally to achieve a real sense of inner maturity.

On 7 January 1779 Cannabich introduced Mozart to the Electress Elisabeth Maria, who gave both him and his sonatas a cordial reception. He also saw Schweitzer's *Alceste* – this was the 1779 carnival opera – and, after further reminders from his father, he finally left Munich in the company of a Salzburg businessman, Joseph Franz Xaver Gschwendtner, who was travelling in comfort. He arrived back in Salzburg with his cousin on 15 January 1779.[27]

27. ◆ It is unclear whether the 'Bäsle' actually travelled with Mozart on this occasion, or whether she joined him in Salzburg only on 20 January.

23

Service at the Salzburg court

After all the cares of recent months, Leopold had finally got his way and gave the prodigal a suitably warm reception. A new chest for Mozart's clothes was waiting for him in his bedroom, as was his old clavichord, and the cook – Tresel – produced copious quantities of his favourite dish, capon. The chief steward, Franz Lactanz von Firmian, had already offered him the use of his horses, to which Johann Nepomuk Prex added his 'fine little bay'. And numerous other friends also let him know how pleased they were to see him again. He was especially happy, finally, to have his cousin for company. The difficult weeks in Munich had transformed his old foul-mouthed flirtation into a relationship of the closest trust. The mere fact that she had accompanied him back to Salzburg was in itself sufficient to raise his spirits. Of course, even in Munich, Maria Thekla had already been forced to realize that the only role left for her was that of the submissive provider of comfort and protection and that any other hopes that she might have placed in her cousin could now be abandoned for good. But she put a brave face on things, mastered her emotions and proved a loyal support to Mozart during his first dreary weeks back in Salzburg.

And Mozart certainly needed her support, as his relationship with his father had changed markedly in light of all that had passed between them in the course of the last twelve months. It was not that his old and sincere respect for his father had in any way diminished, but his struggles in Paris had brought him a sense of greater emotional maturity and, as a result, made him more critical, quite apart from the fact that he had found in Leopold his most implacable adversary on the two points that meant most to him, his love for Aloysia Weber and his loathing of Salzburg. The irritable and tetchy tone of the letters that passed between them was a new and disturbing sign of this latest turn of events, and neither Leopold nor his son had been entirely honest with the other during this period, Leopold's lack of openness being due to calculation, Mozart's to the moral dilemma in which he found himself. His affair with Aloysia had ended, of course, in the way that Leopold had hoped, but Mozart's aversion to his post in Salzburg – a post foisted on him by Leopold against his will – remained as powerful as ever, leaving a thorn in his side that not even his most heartfelt filial affection and the sense of obedience inculcated since birth were capable of removing. His battle with the outside world and with Colloredo was now to be fought alongside a more insidious conflict with his father, and since, with the passing years, Leopold became increasingly inflexible and obstinate in his conviction that his son's salvation lay in his complete and utter subjection to his own wishes, the outcome was all too predictable: inwardly isolated, the young composer went his own way, a journey that was to lead him to the highest peaks of artistic achievement and to the blackest depths of human despair.

Mozart knew exactly what awaited him in Salzburg. His low opinion of his fellow Salzburgers' level of education and artistic understanding may have been exaggerated,[1] but it was clear that

---

1. As late as 26 May 1781, we find him writing to his father: 'Whenever I play [in Salzburg] or any of my works is performed there, it's as if the audience was made up of tables and chairs'; *Briefe*, iii.121.

Colloredo would hardly be overjoyed to welcome back a former employee who had previously resigned his position and agreed to accept it back only by force of circumstances. Still less was he likely to change his views on music for Mozart's sake, and he was an astute enough judge of men to know that the latter's dilatory return was a true indication of his lack of interest in the post.

It was against this unfavourable background, then, that Mozart took up his new appointment. No letters have survived from this period, with the result that we know very little about the outward circumstances of his life, with the exception of the dates of individual works.[2] In general, however, his life returned to its old familiar routine, the only difference being his new and irrepressible sense of bitter discontentment. Even his desire for work, he confessed to his father in his letter of 26 May 1781, periodically deserted him: 'Why? Because I was never happy.'[3] A few weeks earlier, on 8 April 1781, he had made a similar point: 'To waste one's youth in inactivity in such a hole is really very sad – and such a loss.'[4] In fact, this last remark tends, rather, to reflect Mozart's anger at recent events in Vienna. On the whole, these years had been remarkably productive, certainly far more so than the period spent in Paris. He was never short of commissions, and his post as court and cathedral organist (for as such he now appears in the Salzburg court almanac) gave him ample opportunity to write instrumental and sacred music, even though he remained bound, as before, by prevailing tastes and by the resources that were available to him.

It is noteworthy that Mozart now reverted to writing symphonies. A symphony in G major (K318)[5] is dated 26 April 1779, another in B flat major (K319) bears the date 9 July 1779; and a third in C major (K338) is dated 29 August 1780. It seems, therefore, that Colloredo was no longer as dismissive of Mozart as a symphonist, although the fact that only three such works survive from this period suggests that he still harboured certain reservations.[6] Scored for four-part strings, two flutes, two oboes, two horns (posthorn), two bassoons, two trumpets and timpani, and centred upon a two-movement 'concertante', the D major serenade K320 appears to have been written with a particularly festive – possibly middle-class – occasion in mind.[7] The divertimento in D major K334 almost certainly dates from 1779 as well.[8]

2.   ◆ Some details are known from a diary kept by Nannerl Mozart between 26 March 1779 and 4 December 1780. And several of the entries are by Mozart, reporting on his daily activities. On 24 March 1780, for example, he recorded his attendance at church, his visits with Lodron and Schachtner, and his card playing; on 25 March he went to Hagenauer's 'to see the horses shit (zum Hagenauer die Pferde scheissen zu sehen)', he played cards, and visited the Mannheim musician Eck and his son. Nannerl Mozart reported on her attendance at church on 26 March and her visit with the Lodrons; on 28 March the Mozarts played quartets at home, then put in an appearance at court to hear Eck play. The diary is reproduced in *Briefe*, ii.541–6, 549–55 and iii.3–12, 33–7, 39, 41, 44 and 47. Further, see Geffray and Angermüller, *"meine tag Ordnungen": Nannerl Mozarts Tagebuchblätter 1775–1783 mit Eintragungen ihres Bruders Wolfgang und ihres Vaters Leopold*.

3.   *Briefe*, iii.121 (letter of 26 May 1781).

4.   *Briefe*, iii.104 (letter of 8 April 1781).

5.   Otto Jahn's argument (*W. A. Mozart*, fourth edition, i.597) that the work in question is a theatre overture is unconvincing.

6.   ◆ For a different interpretation, that Mozart's symphonies were not primarily intended for performance at court and were a provocation to the Archbishop, see Eisen, 'The Salzburg Symphonies: A Biographical Interpretation'.

7.   André additionally owned a separate copy of these two movements that was headed 'Sinfonia concertante' by Mozart. In other words, they were intended for a specific performance such as the one that took place in Vienna on 23 March 1783. Of the two marches K335, one was presumably intended for this serenade. ◆ Niemetschek suggested that K320 was composed for Archbishop Colloredo's nameday on 30 September. However, the date on the autograph, 3 August, suggests that it was composed as a *Finalmusik* for the university graduation ceremonies that summer. The copy of the sinfonia concertante derived from the serenade and owned by André (now in the Stadt- und Universitätsbibliothek, Frankfurt) is almost certainly the copy used by Mozart to perform the work in Vienna on 23 March 1783. It is possible that both marches of K335 are associated with K320, the first as a processional, the second as a recessional.

8.   ◆ An autograph does not survive for K334 and no documentary evidence confirms its composition in 1779. The style of the work, however, makes a date of 1779 or 1780 credible.

Two important concertos also date from this period, the E flat major concerto K365 for two keyboards that was believed by André to date from 1780,[9] and the sinfonia concertante in E flat major K364 for violin and viola[10] that was probably written during the autumn of 1779.

Mozart's duties in church produced a no less substantial crop of works. As organist he had to perform on feast days, and although this was normally limited to accompanying the singing and playing the usual interludes at certain points in the service, it none the less gave him a chance to extemporize, something he had always enjoyed doing. But a number of epistle sonatas also date from this period (K328, 329 and 336), as do two masses in C major, the first of which – the 'Coronation' mass K317 – is dated 23 March 1779,[11] while the second, K337, dates from March 1780.[12] Related to these works in terms of their style and handwriting are various fragmentary masses including the Kyrie in C major K323, the ending of which – from bar 38 onwards – was lost and later completed by Stadler.[13] Also worth mentioning here are two other incomplete Kyries K258a and 196a, the first with organ obbligato, the second in strict counterpoint.[14]

Alongside these masses we find not the earlier litanies but two vespers settings, one from 1779, the other from 1780 (K321 and 339). Vespers traditionally consisted of a series of five psalms ending with a setting of the *Magnificat*, with each psalm forming a self-contained whole that culminated in the *Gloria Patri*. The six individual movements were generally unrelated, with even the tonality being very freely handled. (For Mozart, as for other composers, only the two outer movements, the *Dixit Dominus* and *Magnificat*, were regularly in the same key.) Far from providing a unifying element, the *Gloria Patri* was treated differently in every psalm. As a result, the individual psalms were often interchanged and even harnessed to settings by other composers. As the two main movements, only the *Dixit Dominus* and *Magnificat* were regularly reset, with other existing settings then interpolated between them.

Among individual sacred works, a *Regina coeli* in C major K276 probably belongs to this period on stylistic grounds.[15] Finally, Mozart also contributed to the field of the German hymn with his

9. Wyzewa and Saint-Foix, *Wolfgang Amédée Mozart*, ii.407, assume that it was written in 1779. Mozart played it in Vienna on 23 November 1781, when the second pianist was Josepha Auernhammer. For this occasion, Mozart wrote out additional parts for two clarinets on a separate sheet. ◆ Paper studies suggest that Wyzewa and Saint-Foix are correct, that K365 is likely to have been written in 1779, not 1780. Whether Mozart composed clarinet parts for his performance with Josepha Auernhammer in 1781, however, or for a possible later performance, is uncertain: although the existence of such parts is not in question, Mozart's autographs are lost. 1781 would, in any event, represent an early use of the instruments in a Mozart concerto; the first of his keyboard concertos to include clarinets is K482 of December 1785. Trumpet and timpani parts to K365, published by Breitkopf & Härtel in 1881 as part of their complete works of Mozart, are almost certainly spurious.
10. The viola part is written in D major, so that the instrument has to be tuned up a semitone, the aim being to give it a more penetrating tone and make it easier to play.
11. According to research undertaken by Johann Evangelist Engl and based on Father Placidus Bernhardski's chronicle of St Peter's of 1782, this mass was written to commemorate the anniversary of the coronation of the miracle-working statue of the Virgin at the pilgrimage church of Maria am Plain in the wake of the deprivations of war in 1744. The precious crown was consecrated by the pope on 4 June 1751; see Engl, 'Mozarts Krönungsmesse'. ◆ This hypothesis is now considered doubtful; more likely the nickname derives from a performance of the mass in connection with the festivities marking the coronation of Emperor Leopold II in Prague in 1791.
12. Bound into Mozart's autograph score of this mass, which is currently lodged in the Österreichische Nationalbibliothek in Vienna, is a fragmentary version of the Credo (as far as the 'Et in Spiritum Sanctum'), with the tempo marking 'Tempo di Ciaccona'. Orchestral parts [from 1825] also survive at St Peter's in Salzburg [shelfmark Moz 130.1]; these are the work of Mozart's contemporary, the Seekirchen organist Mathias Kracher, and show, for example, that, with the exception of the obbligato passages, the bassoons double the basses; see Nottebohm's critical commentary.
13. The work was originally published with this ending under the heading *Regina coeli*. ◆ Paper studies suggest that K323 is more likely to date from 1790 or 1791.
14. ◆ Paper studies suggest that K258a and 196a do not date from this period but from considerably later, K258a some time between 1787 and 1791, and K196a between 1787 and 1789.
15. Wyzewa and Saint-Foix, *Wolfgang Amédée Mozart*, ii.408. ◆ Mozart's autograph is lost.

two settings K343.[16] Indeed, he seems to have taken a renewed interest in lieder in general at this time, as his three settings of songs from Johann Timotheus Hermes's novel *Sophiens Reise* (K390–392) also appear to date from this period or from his early years in Vienna.

But the most striking aspect of Mozart's works from this period is his increasing interest in the theatre, a predilection that was to culminate in *Idomeneo*. In the shorter term, of course, he was obliged to make do with productions in Salzburg. At the time of his return in January 1779, it was Johannes Böhm's company that was performing in the town. Böhm was followed in 1780 by Emanuel Schikaneder, who was currently making a name for himself with performances of both operas and plays.[17] Schikaneder soon became very friendly with the Mozarts and was even invited to join their target-practice sessions. As a result, it was not difficult for him to persuade Mozart to write an aria for one of his productions, although in the event it was not completed until midway through preparations for *Idomeneo*. The piece is no longer extant.[18]

More important than these individual pieces is the incidental music to *Thamos, König in Egypten* K345, which also dates from this period and is likewise bound up with Schikaneder's Salzburg performances. The libretto is the work of Baron Tobias Philipp von Gebler who, in spite of his elevated position as vice-chancellor of the Imperial and Royal Bohemian Court Chancellery, was one of a whole group of men keen to raise theatrical standards in Vienna.[19]

It appears from Gebler's correspondence that Mozart had already set the two choruses 'Schon weichet dir, Sonne' and 'Gottheit, über alle mächtig' in 1773, immediately after the play had been written.[20] Encouraged by one or the other of the aforementioned companies, he now took up the

---

16. It remains unclear whether the Passion aria *Kommet her, ihr frechen Sünder* K146 also dates from 1780, as argued by Wyzewa and Saint-Foix, *Wolfgang Amédée Mozart*, ii.408. On stylistic grounds, it must be later than Köchel's date of 1772 and, to judge by Leopold's heading 'Aria de passione D. N. Jesu Christi', was evidently intended for a Lenten performance in Salzburg. ◆ K343 is more likely to have been composed in Vienna or Prague about early 1787. Although no autograph survives, both were published in Prague in 1788 and in a letter of May 1787 Mozart wrote (ambiguously) to his friend Gottfried von Jacquin: 'Here is . . . the church song' (*Briefe*, iv.48). K146 cannot be dated with certainty although there is no question that it dates from the 1770s.

17. Schikaneder's repertory included not only works by Shakespeare (*Hamlet, Macbeth* and *King Lear*) but also some of the latest works by dramatists such as Lessing and Leisewitz; see Komorzynski, *Emanuel Schikaneder: Ein Beitrag zur Geschichte des deutschen Theaters*, 6–7. ◆ Concerning Salzburg's theatrical life at this time, see Saint-Foix, 'Le Théâtre à Salzbourg en 1779–1780'; Prossnitz, 'Vom fürsterzbischöflichen Hoftheater zum Stadttheater (1775–1893)'; Hintermaier, 'Mozart und das Theater am Salzburger fürsterzbischöflichen Hof' and 'Das Furstbischöfliche Hoftheater zu Salzburg (1775–1803)'; and Dahms, 'Das musikalische Repertoire des Salzburger Fürstbischöflichen Hoftheaters (1775–1803)'. Specifically with respect to Böhm and Schikaneder, see Rech, 'Böhm und Schikaneder. Zwei Salzburger Theaterimpresarios der Mozart-Zeit'; Deininger, 'Die deutsche Schauspielergesellschaft unter der Direktion von Johann Heinrich Böhm, einem Freunde der Familie Mozart, in Augsburg in den Jahren 1779 und 1780'; and Friedrich Johann Fischer, 'Emanuel Schikaneder und Salzburg'.

18. See Mozart's letter of 22 November 1780 (*Briefe*, iii.27). Mozart also appears to have promised an aria to Böhm; see his letter to his cousin, 24 April 1780 (*Briefe*, iii.4). ◆ Although Mozart's aria for Böhm appears never to have been written, his aria for Schikaneder, 'Die neugeborne Ros' entzückt', K365a, has been partly recovered since Abert's day: thirty bars survive in a fragment now owned by the Mozarteum, Salzburg. The aria, for soprano, two violins, two horns and double bass, takes as its text a portion of act four, scene six of *Wie man sich die Sache denkt! oder Zwey schlaflosen Nächte* by J. G. Dyk after F. A. C. Werthes and Carlo Gozzi; see Edge, 'A Newly Discovered Autograph Source for Mozart's Aria, K. 365a (Anh. 11a)'.

19. See his obituary in the *Wiener Zeitung*, xxxi (1786); see also Gervinus, *Geschichte der poetischen National-Literatur der Deutschen*, iv.590; and Goedeke, *Grundriß zur Geschichte der deutschen Literatur*, iv.75. Gebler's works for the stage were published in Prague and Dresden in 1772/3. *Thamos* appears in iii.305ff. A copy of the Prague edition with a note in Leopold's hand – in other words, perhaps the very copy that Mozart himself used – was available to Wüllner. The work was performed at the Kärntnertor-Theater in Vienna in 1774 [Deiters's note]. The correspondence between Gebler and Christoph Friedrich Nicolai for the years between 1771 and 1786 was published by Werner in Berlin in 1888 under the title *Aus dem Josephinischen Wien*. ◆ Leopold Mozart's copy of the Prague edition of *Thamos* is now housed at the Mozarteum.

20. On 13 December 1773 Gebler wrote to Nicolai: 'I enclose the music for *Thamos*, in any case, as set not long ago by a certain Sgr. Mozart. It is his own original score, and the first chorus very fine'; Werner, *Aus dem Josephinischen Wien*, 51 [*Dokumente*, 131, *Documentary Biography*, 146]. On 14 Feburary 1775 Gebler wrote again, this time expressing the hope that Koch's company might perform *Thamos* in Berlin, adding: 'The good *Magister* Sattler, who had written the first music for it (I believe, however, that I sent the better music by Mozart to your Excellency) has died in the meantime from consumption'; Werner, *Aus dem Josephinischen Wien*, 65 [*Dokumente*, 136, *Documentary Biography*, 151]. Deiters (Jahn, *W. A. Mozart*, fourth edition, ii.811ff.) is

old idea, completely revised the second chorus, reinstrumented the first, while leaving the basic musical ideas untouched, and added the entr'acte music.[21] Also added for the Salzburg performances – possibly by Schachtner – was a third chorus missing from Gebler's stage play. Fate looked no more kindly on this second version than it had on the first one, and on 15 February 1783 we find Mozart writing to his father: 'I'm really sorry that I shan't be able to use the music of "Thamos", but the piece proved a failure here and is now among the discarded works that are no longer performed. It deserves to be given, if only because of the music, but this is unlikely, which is certainly a pity!'[22] Later – probably for Mozart's Lenten concerts in Vienna – the words of the first and third choruses were replaced by sacred Latin texts ('Splendente te, Deus' and 'Ne pulvis et cinis superbe te geras').[23]

As with *Thamos*, Mozart's work on a German singspiel to words by Schachtner appears to be bound up with these same productions in Salzburg. The piece was still incomplete[24] when Mozart left for Munich in November 1780, but he none the less asked his father to forward it so that he could play it to Cannabich.[25] Later Leopold wondered whether it was possible to arrange a performance in Vienna, but Mozart replied on 18 April 1781: 'As for Schachtner's operetta, there's nothing that can be done – for the reason I've told you so often. . . . I didn't want to contradict Stephanie; I merely said that, with the exception of the lengthy passages of dialogue, which could easily be altered, the piece is very good, but not for Vienna, where they prefer comic works.'[26]

There is no doubt that the work in question[27] is K344, which André published under the by no means inappropriate title of *Zaïde*[28] and which Mozart completed with the exception of the overture and final number. His original score, which includes no title, is carefully marked up for performance. To judge by its overall character, the text is almost certainly based on an as yet

no doubt right to argue that Mozart's music dates from the period of his visit to Vienna between July and October 1773, when he must have got to know the poet personally. This assumption is supported by Leopold's remark of 18 September 1773: 'Wolfgang is busy working away at something' [*Briefe*, i.503]. It is unclear why the work was not performed at this time. Like Sattler, Mozart set only the first two choruses – the third one does not appear in the play. According to the critical commentary in AMA, the autograph score of this first version is lost, but is in fact in the Staatsbibliothek in Berlin [now the Staatsbibliothek zu Berlin]. ◆ The dating of Mozart's music for *Thamos* remains uncertain. According to Tyson, *Mozart: Studies of the Autograph Scores*, 24–5, the different papers of the autograph suggest dates of 1776 or early 1777 for both the choruses and entr'actes. An analysis of the handwriting, however, puts the choruses in 1779 or 1780; see Plath, 'Beiträge zur Mozart-Autographie II: Schriftchronologie 1770–1780', 173. In this instance, Tyson is inclined to accept Plath's dating.

21. On stylistic grounds, Wyzewa and Saint-Foix, *Wolfgang Amédée Mozart*, ii.117, argue that, with the exception of the melodrama, the entr'actes, too, date from this earlier period, and that only instrumental changes were made at the later date. ◆ See the previous note.

22. *Briefe*, iii.256.

23. Copies of both choruses with Latin words were found among Mozart's unpublished papers. ◆ This assertion cannot be confirmed. It is likely, however, that neither contrafactum has much, if anything, to do with Mozart; both were published well after his death. See KAnh. B zu 336a (345). Further with respect to *Thamos*, see Küster, 'Mozarts "Thamos" und der Kontext'; Landon, 'Mozart's incidental music to Thamos, König in Ägypten (K.345)'; and Lütteken, '"Es müsste nur blos der Musick wegen aufgeführt werden": Text und Kontext in Mozarts Thamos-Melodrama'.

24. On 11 December 1780 Leopold writes that, because of the period of national mourning, nothing can be done with Schachtner's drama: 'It's better that this is so, as the music isn't quite finished' (*Briefe*, iii.53).

25. *Briefe*, iii.90–91 (letter of 18 January 1781).

26. *Briefe*, iii.107–8 (letter of 18 April 1781).

27. As early as 1799, we find the *Intelligenzblatt* of the *AmZ* (ii.21) asking the question: 'Among Mozart's unpublished papers is a German singspiel, probably written in 1778 or 1779, untitled, in which the following characters appear: Gomaz, Zaide, Sultan, Zaram, Soliman, Osmin, etc. If anyone knows the title of this singspiel or, if it has been published, knows where it appeared, he is earnestly entreated to inform the publishers of this journal.' No response appears to have been received.

28. *Zaïde, Opera in two acts by W. A. Mozart*. Full score [and vocal score], Offenbach, Joh. André. André added an overture and final chorus for performance purposes, an addition to which it is impossible to take exception. The music was reproduced unaltered, but changes were made to the words by Carl Gollmick. Schachtner's text is, admittedly, insufferable, but indispensable to our understanding of Mozart's music. Wüllner argues that the lost libretto was in three acts, the third of which was not set at all. ◆ For a modern, critical edition, see NMA II/5/10.

unidentified French original. Several of its themes resemble those of *Die Entführung aus dem Serail*, and it was no doubt because of this that Mozart did not return to the work at a later date.[29]

But all these works were ultimately placed in the shade by a commission that was finally to represent the fulfilment of Mozart's most ardent ambitions after so many disappointments, when the Munich court asked him to write the *opera seria* for the 1781 carnival. Acting on the advice of his various friends among the singers and instrumentalists in Munich, the electoral couple had recalled his existence, and Colloredo was obliged to keep his word and allow Mozart to travel to Munich to fulfil the terms of his contract, a visit to which he was no doubt all the more ready to agree out of a sense of obligation to a neighbouring court. The chosen librettist was Giambattista Varesco, who had been court chaplain in Salzburg since 1766. The choice had the great advantage that Mozart, who was fully conversant with conditions in Munich, could remain in constant personal touch with his librettist. When a German translation was later found to be necessary, Mozart recommended his old friend Schachtner, so that it was with some pride that Leopold was able to inform Breitkopf that the opera was an exclusively homegrown product.[30]

As the basis of the text, the Munich court chose an old French libretto by Antoine Danchet which, previously set by Campra, had first been performed in Paris on 12 January 1712 and revived there in 1731.[31] The result was *Idomeneo, re di Creta*, which transformed the old five-act *tragédie lyrique* into a Metastasian Italian *opera seria* with French additions, foremost among which were its choruses. The cast list ran as follows:

Idomeneo, re di Creta	Il Sign. *Raaff*, virtuoso di camera.
Idamante, suo figlio	Il Sign. *Dal Prato*.
Ilia, prencipessa Trojana, figlia di Priamo	La Sign. *Dorothea Wendling*, virtuosa di camera.
Elettra, prencipessa, figlia d'Agamennone re d'Argo	La Sign. *Elisabeth Wendling*, virtuosa di camera.
Arbace, confidente del re	Il Sign. *Domenico de' Panzacchi*, virtuoso di camera.
Gran Sacerdote di Nettuno	Il Sign. *Giovanni Valesi*, virtuoso di camera

Once the libretto was finished in October 1780, Mozart started work on the score. Only then did he set off for Munich in order to complete it, which he did in accordance with contemporary practice in consultation with the singers. Following a journey by mailcoach that 'jolted the very souls' from their bodies and allowed them not a minute's sleep, he wrote to his father on 8 November 1780: 'My arrival here was happy and enjoyable!'[32] He was now fully occupied, as the opera had to be rehearsed, staged and, in part, written. It is impossible to say how much of it was finished by

29. The work received its first performance in Frankfurt am Main on 27 January 1866. It was revived in Vienna in 1902 in a version by Robert Hirschfeld (see his 'Mozart's "Zaide" in der Wiener Hofoper') and again in Karlsruhe in 1917, this time in an adaptation by Anton Rudolph. A vocal score of this version was published by Breitkopf & Härtel.

30. *Briefe*, iii.149 (letter of 10 August 1781); see Jahn, *W. A. Mozart*, fourth edition, i.613.

31. *Dictionnaire des théâtres* iii.126ff. ◆ Abert's reference here is not clear. It could be to any number of works, but possibly de Leris, *Dictionnaire portatif historique et littéraire des théâtres*. The complete text appears in Jean-Nicolas Francine, *Recueil général des opéra*, xii/1.

32. Nannerl's claim that her brother left on 8 November must, therefore, be incorrect; see Nottebohm, *Mozartiana*, 109. Nissen, *Biographie W. A. Mozarts*, 416, gives the date as 6 November; see also Mozart's letter of Saturday 16 December (*Briefe*, iii.60). ◆ In his letter of 16 December, Mozart writes, 'Next Monday it will be six weeks that I've been away from Salzburg.'

the time he arrived in Munich – probably the bulk of the recitatives and possibly the whole of the first and perhaps a section of the second act. This, at least, would seem to be the conclusion from references to completed numbers in his early letters from Munich.

He encountered only goodwill in every quarter and was able, therefore, to set to work in the best of spirits. Count Seeau, whom he described as 'moulded like wax by the Mannheimers',[33] complied with his every wish, and if they occasionally came to blows, causing Mozart to swear at him, the count always gave way in the end. The elector, too, gave him a warm welcome. 'I almost forgot my best news', he wrote to his father on 15 November 1780: 'Last Sunday after the service Count Seeau presented me en passant to His Highness the Elector, who was very kind to me and said: "I'm glad to see you here again." When I said that I'd do my best to retain His Highness's approval, he clapped me on the shoulder and said, "Oh, I've no doubt that all will go well" – a piano piano, si va lontano! [slow and steady wins the race!]'.[34] The aristocracy, too, was well disposed to Mozart. Cannabich introduced him to Countess Paumgarten née Lerchenfeld, who was the elector's current favourite. 'My friend is everything in this house,' he reported on 13 November 1780, 'and now I am too; it's the best and most useful house for me here, because of them all has gone well for me and, God willing, will continue to do so.'[35] As a result, Mozart was able to reassure his father that his opera would be a tremendous success. 'Don't worry about my opera', he wrote on 24 November 1780. 'I'm sure that it will all go well. – No doubt it will be attacked by a small cabal, but they'll presumably be made to look very foolish, for the most distinguished and influential families of the nobility are on my side, and the leading musicians are all for me.'[36] He singled out Cannabich for particular praise in this respect.[37]

The singers and orchestra could be relied on not to engage in intrigues. Mozart was as anxious to please them as they in turn were delighted with the result. In the course of their work together, it proved necessary to make certain changes to the libretto in order to adapt it for the stage, and Varesco was repeatedly asked either to undertake these changes himself or to agree to the suggestions that were put to him.

Of the singers, it was the soprano castrato Vincenzo dal Prato who caused Mozart the most problems. The latter had barely arrived in Munich when we already find him reporting on this whole 'sorry story. I've not, it's true, had the honour of meeting the hero dal Prato, but from the description I've been given, I'd almost say that Ceccarelli is better, as his breath often gives out in the middle of an aria and, note well, he has never appeared on stage and Raaff is like a statue. Well, you can imagine the scene in Act I [the meeting between Idomeneo and Idamante].'[38] Personal acquaintance with dal Prato did nothing to allay his misgivings: 'As for my molto amato castrato dal Prato,' he wrote on 15 November, 'I'll have to teach him the whole opera.'[39] And, a week later: 'He has to learn his entire role like a child, he doesn't have a farthing's worth of a method.'[40] Dal Prato was also the stumbling block in the quartet, which had to be rehearsed six times before it worked. 'He's completely useless', Mozart complained on 30 December 1780. 'His voice wouldn't

33. ◆ *Briefe*, iii.13 (letter of 8 November 1780).
34. *Briefe*, iii.20 (letter of 15 November 1780).
35. *Briefe*, iii.16 (letter of 13 November 1780).
36. Thanks to the mediation of the imperial ambassador Count Hartig, Aloysia Weber had already been appointed leading soprano in Vienna, and her whole family had followed her there. It is wrong, therefore, to claim that Mozart's visit to Munich was bound up with his affair with her.
37. *Briefe*, iii.29–30 (letter of 24 November 1780).
38. *Briefe*, iii.13–14 (letter of 8 November 1780).
39. *Briefe*, iii.20 (letter of 15 November 1780).
40. *Briefe*, iii.28 (letter of 22 November 1780).

be so bad if he didn't produce it in his throat and larynx. But he has no intonation – no method – no feeling, he just sings like the best of the boys who come to audition for a place in the chapel choir.'[41]

His good friend Raaff also caused him problems, but of a totally different kind. The tenor was extraordinarily touchy, and in deference to his age Mozart changed whatever he could:

Raaff is the best and most honest man in the world, but – so set in his ways as to make you sweat blood – as a result, it's very difficult to write for him, but also very easy if you choose to write commonplace arias such as his first one, 'Vedrommi intorno' etc. When you hear it – it's good, it's beautiful; but if I'd written it for Zonca, it would have been better suited to the words; he's too fond of everything that's cut and dried and pays no attention to expression. – I've just had problems with him over the quartet. – The more I think about this quartet in the theatre, the more effective I think it will be, and everyone who has heard it played on the harpsichord has liked it; only Raaff thinks it'll be ineffectual; he told me when we were alone together – non c'è da spianar la voce – it's too restricting. As if the words in a quartet should not be spoken rather than sung! He simply doesn't understand this kind of thing. All I said was: 'My dearest friend, if I knew of a single note in this quartet that needs altering, I'd do so at once; but – there's nothing in this opera that I'm as pleased with as I am with this quartet, and when you've heard it sung together, you're bound to change your mind. With your 2 arias, I've made every effort to help you, and shall also do so with the third one and I hope that I'll be successful; – but where trios and quartets are concerned, the composer must have his way.' With that he said he was satisfied.[42]

Following the rehearsal, Mozart wrote again on 30 December 1780, announcing that Raaff was 'delighted to find that he was wrong about the quartet and no longer has any doubts about its effectiveness'.[43] He ran through Raaff's first aria with him on 14 November and the next day reported that the singer was pleased with it. Two weeks later the tenor's second-act aria produced a similar response:

The man's as infatuated with his aria as any young and ardent lover with his beauty, he sings it at night before going to bed and in the morning when he wakes up. . . . He told Herr von Viereck . . . and Herr von Castel: 'In the past I've always altered my parts to suit me, both in recitatives and arias; but this time nothing's been changed, there isn't a note that doesn't suit me etc.' In a word, he's as happy as a king.[44]

Even so, malicious gossip was rife, as Mozart reported to his father on 27 December 1780:

A propos, Becke told me the other day that he had written to you again after the last rehearsal but one and among other things had said that Raaff's second-act aria goes against the words. 'So I am told,' he said, 'but I know too little Italian – is it true?' 'If only you'd asked me about it first and written about it afterwards! I must say that whoever said that knows very little Italian.'

41. *Briefe*, iii.77 (letter of 30 December 1780). ◆ Further, see Heriot, *The Castrati in Opera*, 121–2.
42. *Briefe*, iii.72–3 (letter of 27 December 1780).
43. *Briefe*, iii.77 (letter of 30 December 1780).
44. *Briefe*, iii.40 (letter of 1 December 1780).

The aria is very well suited to the words. You hear the "mare" and the "mare funesto", and the passage-work suits "minacciar", fully expressing the sense of threat in "minacciar". And it's the most brilliant aria in the opera and always universally applauded.[45]

The two other male singers were both members of the old Munich Opera. The 'old and honest' Panzacchi had been an outstanding singer and a fine actor in his day, but he was past his prime, and the tenor Valesi too, although fully deserving of his reputation, was now more in demand as a singing teacher than on stage. One sympathizes with Leopold, therefore, when he writes on 11 November 1780: 'What you say about the singers is depressing; in the circumstances, the best thing will be for you to get on with writing the music.'[46]

With the two sopranos, by contrast, Mozart had no problems at all. The Wendlings were friends of his and devoted to him; they agreed to all his suggestions and were happy with whatever he did. 'Mme Dorothea Wendling is arcicontentissima with her scene and insisted on hearing it played three times in succession', Mozart wrote home on 8 November 1780,[47] and they later agreed on her second-act aria, too. 'Lisel Wendling', he reported on 15 November, 'has also gone through her two arias half a dozen times and is very pleased with them: I have it from a third party that both the Wendlings were full of praise for their arias.'[48]

Mozart was kept busy rehearsing and composing – in the meantime he also found time to complete the aria for Schikaneder – even though he was suffering from a heavy cold. The household remedies recommended by his father brought a certain relief, but his work on the score did not help his catarrh, with the result that he was improving only slowly.

In Munich he met Gertrud Elisabeth Mara (1749–1833), who had recently left Berlin. 'I'm sorry to say that I don't like her', he told his father on 13 November 1780. 'She doesn't do enough to match up to a singer like Bastardina (this, after all, is her repertory) and does too much to touch the heart like Weber or any intelligent singer.'[49] He was no more edified by her singing than by her own and her husband's behaviour: according to his later letter of 24 November 1780, 'conceit, arrogance and unblushing effronterie' were 'written all over their faces'.[50]

The first act was rehearsed at the end of November and proved outstandingly successful, as Mozart informed his father on 1 December:

The rehearsal went off extremely well. There were only 6 violins in all, but the requisite number of winds. No one was admitted apart from Seeau's sister and young Count Seinsheim. . . . I can't tell you how pleased and amazed they all were. But I never expected anything else, and I can assure you that I went to the rehearsal in as relaxed a frame of mind as if I'd been going to a lunch party. Count Seinsheim said: 'I assure you that I was expecting a great deal from you, but I certainly didn't expect *that*.' The Cannabichs and all who frequent their house are real friends

45. *Briefe*, iii.72 (letter of 27 December 1780).
46. *Briefe*, iii.15 (letter of 11 November 1780).
47. *Briefe*, iii.14 (letter of 8 November 1780).
48. *Briefe*, iii.20 (letter of 15 November 1780). ◆ Further, see Everist, '"Madame Dorothea Wendling is arcicontentissima": The performers of *Idomeneo*'.
49. *Briefe*, iii.18 (letter of 13 November 1780).
50. *Briefe*, iii.29–31 (letter of 24 November 1780). Similar stories are reported by Forkel, *Musikalischer Almanach für Deutschland*, ii (1783), 122; by Riemer, *Briefwechsel zwischen Goethe und Zelter*, ii.264–5 and iii.378ff.; and by Niggli, 'Gertrud Elisabeth Mara'. ◆ Further concerning Mara, see Riesemann, 'Eine Selbstbiographie der Sängerin Gertrud Elisabeth Mara'; Kaulitz-Niedeck, *Die Mara: Das Leben einer berühmten Sängerin*; and Anwand, *Die Primadonna Friedrichs des Großen*.

of mine. As I was walking back to Cannabich's house after the rehearsal (we still had a lot to discuss with the count), Mme Cannabich came out to meet us and embraced me, delighted that the rehearsal had gone so well – Ramm and Lang had already been there, delirious with happiness. The good lady – a true friend of mine – had been alone in the house with her sick daughter Rosa, worried sick on my account. Ramm told me (when you get to know him, you'll say that he's a true German as he tells you to your face exactly what he's thinking): 'I really must say – he said – that no music has ever made such an impression on me, and I can assure you that I must have thought of your father a good 50 times and of how pleased he'll be when he hears your opera.' But enough of this! – My catarrh got worse during the rehearsal. You naturally get over-heated when honour and reputation are at stake, however calm and collected you may be at first.[51]

The success of the rehearsal was confirmed from another quarter, as Leopold reported in his letter of 15 December 1780:

Fiala has just been to see me and has shown me a letter from Herr Becke, full of praise for your music to act I; he writes that he wept tears of joy and delight when he heard the music and that everyone maintains it's the most beautiful music they've ever heard, that it's all new and strange etc.; that they're now about to rehearse act II – and that he'll write to me again in person. . . . Well, thank God, everything's going well.[52]

None the less, Leopold continued to remonstrate with Mozart, not only on the subject of his persistent cold but also on the nature of the opera itself. As in earlier years, so we find him writing on 11 December 1780: 'I advise you when composing to consider not only the musical, but also the non-musical public: – you know that for every ten real connoisseurs there are a hundred ignoramuses; – so don't neglect the "popular" style, which also tickles long ears.'[53] Mozart refused to be persuaded by this argument. 'As for the "popular" style,' he replied on 16 December 1780, 'don't worry, there's music in my opera for all kinds of people – except for those with long ears.'[54] It is clear from this that Mozart refused to be bullied by his father any longer and had achieved his independence as man and artist.

Meanwhile, rehearsals were proceeding apace. During the afternoon of 16 December the first two acts were rehearsed at Count Seeau's. The parts had now been copied, and so there were twelve violinists. This rehearsal, too, went well, as Mozart wrote to inform his father on 19 December 1780:

The orchestra and the whole audience discovered to their delight that the second act is actually more expressive and original than the first. Both acts will be rehearsed again next Saturday, but in a large hall at court, something I've long been wanting as there simply isn't enough room at Count Seeau's. The elector will listen (incognito) from an adjoining room. As Cannabich says, we'll have to rehearse as if our very lives depend on it. At the last rehearsal he was dripping with perspiration. . . . You'll have gathered from my letters that I'm well and – happy. After all, anyone

---

51. *Briefe*, iii.39–40 (letter of 1 December 1780).
52. *Briefe*, iii.56 (letter of 15 December 1780).
53. *Briefe*, iii.53 (letter of 13 December 1780).
54. *Briefe*, iii.60 (letter of 16 December 1780).

would be glad to be finally rid of such a great and laborious task – and with honour and glory: I've almost finished, – all that's missing are three arias and the final chorus from Act III, the overture and the ballet – et adieu partie![55]

The feeling of satisfaction was even greater after the following rehearsal, as we learn from Mozart's letter of 27 December 1780:

The last rehearsal went splendidly, it was held in a large room at court, the elector was there, too. This time we rehearsed with the full orchestra (in other words, with as many players as there's room for in the opera house). After the first act the elector called out 'Bravo' in a particularly loud voice, and when I went over to kiss his hand, he said 'This opera will be charming, it's bound to do you credit.' As he wasn't sure whether he could stay much longer, we then had to perform the concertante aria and storm from the beginning of act II. Afterwards he again expressed his approval in the friendliest way and said with a laugh: 'Who'd have thought that such great things would be hidden in such a small head?' He also praised my opera very highly at the levée the next day.[56]

The elector also spoke favourably about the music that evening at court and Mozart was reliably informed that after the rehearsal he had said: 'I was very surprised – no music has ever made such an impression on me – it's magnificent music'.[57]

These latest successes, too, were duly reported in Salzburg: 'The whole town is saying how good your opera is', Leopold wrote to his son on 25 December 1780. 'The first report was from Baron Lehrbach; the court chancellor's wife told me that he'd said your opera was everywhere being praised to the skies. The second was Herr Becke's letter to Fiala, which Fiala made everyone read.'[58] And Becke wrote to Leopold, too, reporting that 'the chorus during the storm in the second act is so powerful that even in the heat of midsummer everyone's spine is bound to run cold'. He was particularly fulsome in his praise of Dorothea Wendling's concertante aria ['Padre, germani']. The Mainz violinist, Karl Michael von Esser, had given a concert in Salzburg and later wrote from Augsburg to report on the first two acts of the opera, which he had heard 'che abbia sentito una musica ottima e particolare, universalmente applaudita'. 'In a word,' Leopold added, 'it would take me far too long to repeat all the praise. I hope act III produces the same impression, and am all the more certain that it will in that the greatest passions are expressed here and the subterranean voice is bound to astonish and terrify.[59] Basta, I trust people will say: finis coronat opus.' Mozart, who was anxiously trying to complete the score, replied on 30 December 1780: 'The third act will be *at least* as good as the first two, but I think it will be infinitely better and that people will be right to say: finis coronat opus.'[60] But he had his work cut out for him: 'My head and hands are so full of the third act', he wrote on 3 January 1781, 'that I wouldn't be surprised if I turned into a third act myself. This alone has cost me more trouble than an entire opera, as there's hardly a scene

55. *Briefe*, iii.64–5 (letter of 19 December 1780).
56. *Briefe*, iii.71–2 (letter of 27 December 1780).
57. ◆ *Briefe*, iii.77 (letter of 30 December 1780).
58. *Briefe*, iii.69–70 (letter of 25 December 1780).
59. 'The accompaniment to the subterranean voice', Mozart wrote on 3 January 1781, 'consists of only 5 instruments, namely, 3 trombones and 2 hand horns that are positioned in the same place as the voice comes from. The whole orchestra is silent at this point' (*Briefe* iii.79). Mozart had had a further argument with Count Seeau over this arrangement.
60. *Briefe*, iii.76–7 (letter of 30 December 1780).

in it that's not extremely interesting.'[61] He was gratified to discover at the rehearsal that it was indeed felt to be far superior to the first two acts.

Leopold urged Mozart to ensure that he was in the orchestra's good books as so much depended on the players:

> Do your best to keep the whole orchestra in a good mood, flatter them and, by praising them, keep them well-disposed towards you; I know your style of writing – it requires constant and unusually close attention from the players of every instrument, and to keep the orchestra at such a pitch of hard work and alertness for at least three hours is no joke. Everyone – even the worst viola player – is deeply touched if you praise him to his face and, as a result, works even harder and pays even more attention, and such politeness costs you no more than a word or two. But – you know all this yourself – I mention it only because it's not always possible to say anything at the rehearsal, and so you then forget about it, and because it's only when the opera is staged that you really need the whole orchestra's friendship and enthusiasm. The whole orchestra's position is then quite different, and all the performers must be even more attentive than ever. You know that you can't make friends of them all. There always has to be an undercurrent of doubt and 'yes, but . . .'. People doubted whether the second act would be as new and as good as the first act. Now that this doubt has been overcome, few will have any doubts about the third act. But I'll wager my head that some people will doubt whether your music will be as effective on stage in the theatre as it is in a room. And here you really need the greatest enthusiasm and good will on the part of the whole of the orchestra.[62]

On its own, the opera was not long enough to fill a whole evening and, as there was to be no special ballet, but only a divertissement related to the plot of the opera, Mozart had the 'honour' (to use his own expression in his letter of 30 December 1780) of writing the music for it. 'But I'm very glad, because all the music will now be by one composer.'[63] He was kept busy with these 'confounded dances' (K367) until mid-January, unable to think of anything else, including his health. Finally, on the 18th, he was able to write to his father: 'Laus Deo, I've survived!'[64]

Throughout these hectic preparations, the day of the performance drew ever closer. Leopold was worried that the death of the Empress Maria Theresia on 29 November 1780 would lead to the cancellation of the production, but Mozart was able to reassure him at once that no theatres would be closed as a result. Shortly afterwards Leopold was alarmed by a rumour that the electress was incurably ill but discovered to his relief that the rumour was 'a whopping lie'. Initially the first night was fixed for 20 January 1781, but this was then put back to the 22nd and finally to the 29th. The final dress rehearsal was now scheduled for the 27th, Mozart's birthday, a delay with which the composer was more than happy: 'In this way we'll be able to rehearse more frequently and with greater care.'[65]

That the opera was held in high regard had become clear in Salzburg even before the opening night and was a matter of great satisfaction not only for Mozart's friends, with Johann Nepomuk Prex, for example, speaking of the 'inexpressible delight' with which he had heard of the 'great

61. *Briefe*, iii.79 (letter of 3 January 1781).
62. *Briefe*, iii.70 (letter of 25 December 1780).
63. *Briefe*, iii.76 (letter of 30 December 1780).
64. *Briefe*, iii.90 (letter of 18 January 1781).
65. ◆ *Briefe*, iii.85 (letter of 11 January 1781).

credit that Mozart had brought to the people of Salzburg'.[66] Among those who travelled to Munich for the first performance were Maria Viktoria von Robinig and her family, two of Silvester Barisani's daughters and, from the orchestra, Joseph Fiala.[67] Leopold himself was 'looking forward to the excellent orchestra like a child' and was determined to travel to Munich with his daughter as soon as he could get away. For the time being, however, he bided his time, as he feared that Colloredo would refuse to allow him to go but had heard the latter would himself be leaving for Vienna. In the circumstances it suited his plans very well that the first performance was postponed until after the archbishop had already set off for Vienna. Leopold left Salzburg on 25 January in order to be able to attend the final dress rehearsal and first night. Mozart had made arrangements for both his father and sister to stay with him at his rooms at the 'Sonneck' in the Burggasse, even though conditions were so cramped that they were obliged to 'live like gypsies and soldiers' for the duration of their stay.[68]

The presence of Leopold and Nannerl in Munich has almost certainly deprived us of a detailed account of the first night of *Idomeneo* and its successful outcome. The *Münchner Staats-, Gelehrte und Vermischte Nachrichten* of 1 February 1781 limited its coverage to the following article:

> On the 29th day of last month the first performance of the opera *Idomeneo* took place at the new opera house here. The text, music and translation – all are by natives of Salzburg. The decorations, among which the views of the sea port and the temple of Neptune are especially effective, were masterpieces of our famous local theatre architect, the court councillor Herr Lorenz Quaglio, and were universally admired.[69]

But it is clear from all that we know about the opera's reception during the rehearsals that it must have been a brilliant first night.

We do not know how much Mozart was paid for *Idomeneo*. That it was not very much emerges from Leopold's letter of 11 December 1780: 'What about the score? Aren't you going to have it copied? You must consider what you are going to do and make some sensible arrangement. For a payment like this you can't leave your score behind.'[70] Mozart replied to this point on the 16th: 'As for having my score copied, there was no need for me to beat about the bush, I told the count quite frankly. It was always the custom in Mannheim (where the Kapellmeister was certainly well paid) for the original score to be handed back to him.'[71] The three-volume autograph score is now in the Staatsbibliothek in Berlin.[72] Although hastily written, it is an extremely neat fair copy in which virtually nothing has been altered, with the exception of an occasional passage of recitative. As usual, the individual numbers were written separately and then inserted into the score. As in other scores, the double-bass part is written in a larger size to facilitate the task of the keyboard continuo

66. ◆ *Briefe*, iii.83 (letter of 8 January 1781)
67. *Briefe*, iii.83 (letter of 8 January 1781).
68. ◆ *Briefe*, iii.88 (letter of 11 January 1781).
69. Reprinted in the *Augspurgische Ordinari-Postzeitung* of 5 February 1781 [*Dokumente*, 170, *Documentary Biography*, 191–2, translation emended]; see also Rudhart, *Geschichte der Oper am Hofe zu München*, 168.
70. *Briefe*, iii.53 (letter of 11 December 1780).
71. *Briefe*, iii.60 (letter of 16 December 1780).
72. ◆ The autograph is now split between the Staatsbibliothek zu Berlin (act 3) and the Biblioteka Jagiellońska, Kraków (acts 1 and 2). Further, a score produced in Munich in 1781 in connection with the production, and including autograph changes by Mozart, survives in the Bayerische Staatsbibliothek (shelfmark St.th. 265 (1)); the score includes numerous authentic readings not included in the NMA edition of *Idomeneo*. For details, see Sadie, 'Genesis of an operone', 38–44.

player. It transpires from Leopold's letter to Breitkopf of 10 August 1781 that there were plans to have the full score printed: 'People tried hard to persuade us to have the opera printed or engraved, either the full score or a keyboard arrangement. There were already subscribers for some 20 copies, including His Highness Prince Max von Zweibrücken etc., but my son's departure for Vienna and subsequent events obliged us to postpone everything.'[73] The original score of the ballet music is also lodged in the Staatsbibliothek in Berlin [now the Staatsbibliothek zu Berlin].

In later years, too, Mozart continued to think particularly highly of *Idomeneo*.[74] Soon after establishing himself in Vienna, he thought of revising it and of mounting a production in the city, but in the event the plan came to nothing. In 1786 a group of aristocratic amateurs performed the work at the home of Prince Karl Auersperg, prompting Mozart to undertake a number of changes to the score, but these stopped short of a thorough revision.[75] Since then[76] *Idomeneo* has enjoyed the occasional revival but without finding a permanent place for itself in the repertory. Most of the blame for this state of affairs must be borne by the antiquated libretto, whereas Mozart's music has always been praised by connoisseurs.[77]

Mozart had been granted six weeks' leave of absence by Colloredo, and even this had been obtained only with great difficulty. At the end of this period Mozart was afraid that he would be peremptorily summoned back to Salzburg, a thought that was all the more unbearable, given his successes in Munich. And so we find him writing to his father on 16 December 1780:

A propos, what about the archbishop? By next Monday I shall have been away from Salzburg for 6 weeks. You know, my dearest father, that I'm in Salzburg only for your sake, for, by God, if it had been left to me, I'd have wiped my behind with my last contract before leaving this time; for I swear to you on my honour that it's not Salzburg itself but the prince and his proud nobility who are growing more unbearable by the day. I'd be only too pleased if he'd write to me and say that he no longer needs me: given the great patronage that I now enjoy here, both my present and future position would be sufficiently assured – save for deaths, which no one can guard against but which are of no consequence to a man of talent who is single. – But I'd do anything in the world to please you, – and I'd find it easier to bear it if I could occasionally get away for a short time, just to draw breath. You know how difficult it was to get away this time, unless there were some compelling reason it wouldn't even be worth thinking about – it's enough to make you weep just to think about it, so away with the thought – – adieu! . . . Come

73. *Briefe*, iii.149 (letter of 10 August 1781).

74. See Rochlitz, 'Verbürgte Anekdoten aus Wolfgang Gottlieb Mozarts Leben', 51. Of course, the reason that Rochlitz gives is, in the main, incorrect. ◆ Also see Solomon, 'The Rochlitz Anecdotes: Issues of Authenticity in Early Mozart Biography', 16–17.

75. ◆ The Viennese performance took place on 13 March 1786. On this occasion Mozart composed the duet 'Spiegarti non poss'io' K489 to replace the duet 'S'io non moro a questi accenti' (act two, number 20) and the scena 'Non più, tutto ascoltai – Non temer, amato bene' K490 to replace the beginning of act two; he simplified Idomeneo's act two aria 'Fuor del mar'; and he made changes to two of the ensembles including Idamante, the terzet at the end of act two, and the quartet in act three. In the production itself, Idamante was taken by a tenor.

76. In Vienna, *Idomeneo* was performed five times in Treitschke's translation in 1805 (according to Wlassak, *Chronik des k. k. Hof-Burgtheaters*, 101, it was also given in the city on 14 May 1806); a further four performances were given in 1819: written communication from Köchel based on information received from Ferdinand Pohl [Deiters's note]. The most recent version of the opera is the one by Ernst Lewicki; see his 'Zur Wiederbelebung des Mozartschen Musikdramas "Idomeneus": Ein Wort der Anregung und praktische Vorschläge'. ◆ Times change: *Idomeneo* is now considered one of Mozart's early masterpieces, a view that has given rise not only to an extensive literature (see especially Rushton, *W. A. Mozart: Idomeneo* and the references there) but also to regular performances at major opera houses. For a short account of the opera's reception in the nineteenth and early twentieth centuries, see Rushton, *W. A. Mozart: Idomeneo*, 83–94.

77. Even Reichardt, who otherwise rarely had a good word to say about Mozart, described the opera as the purest work of art ever written by the composer; see his highly favourable review in his own *Berliner musikalische Zeitung*, ii (1806), 11–12.

to Munich soon and hear my opera – and then tell me whether it's wrong of me to be depressed when I think of Salzburg. Adieu![78]

Leopold replied on 25 December 1780 and attempted to reassure Mozart on the question of his leave of absence:

In regard to your six weeks' leave of absence, I'm resolved not to make any move or to say anything: but if I'm questioned, I'm resolved to say that we'd understood that you'd be allowed to stay on in Munich for six weeks after writing the opera in order to attend the rehearsals and the performance, as I could hardly think that His Grace the Prince could expect an opera of this kind to be composed, copied and performed etc. in the space of only six weeks.[79]

For understandable reasons Mozart again hoped to find employment in Munich and even to invite his father to join him there, a plan to which Leopold raised no objections. Above all, Mozart sought to remind the authorities in Munich of his work as a church composer, in which context we find him writing to his father as follows on 13 November 1780:

Would you be good enough to send me the scores of the 2 masses that I brought with me and also the mass in B flat [K275]. Count Seeau will be talking about them shortly to the elector. I'd like people to get to know some of my compositions in this style, too. I've heard only one mass by Grua [Franz Paul Grua, 1753–1833, Kapellmeister from 1779]; you can easily write half a dozen such works a day.[80]

This period evidently saw the composition of a new sacred work, the great Kyrie in D minor K341, both its character and the untypical resources for which it is scored (four-part strings, two flutes, two oboes, two clarinets, two bassoons, four horns in D and F, and two trumpets and timpani) recalling Munich and *Idomeneo*. It is no longer possible to say whether it is an independent work or a fragment of an unfinished mass.[81]

Another work which, in terms of its instrumentation, falls outside the framework of Mozart's Salzburg compositions and which may likewise have been written in Munich is the serenade in B flat major K361. Dated 1780, it is scored for two oboes, two clarinets, two basset-horns, two bassoons, four horns, cello and bass.[82] Mozart may have written the work for the outstanding

---

78. *Briefe*, iii.60–61 (letter of 16 December 1780).
79. *Briefe*, iii.70 (letter of 25 December 1780).
80. *Briefe*, iii.19 (letter of 13 November 1780).
81. ◆ In the absence of an autograph or other unequivocal evidence, the dating of K341 to Munich is conjectural. Tyson, *Mozart: Studies of the Autograph Scores*, 27, suggests that it may be contemporaneous with other fragmentary church works composed in the late 1780s.
82. On its possible links to the string quintet K46, see above. Wyzewa and Saint-Foix, *Wolfgang Amédée Mozart*, ii.409 and 421, date the romance and theme and variations to the end of Mozart's life, a dating which on stylistic grounds has much to commend it. The work was repeatedly transcribed and may be identical with the serenade 'for 13 instruments' mentioned by Schink at a concert of Stadler's in Vienna in 1784; see Schink, *Litterarische Fragmente*, ii.286. The third trio of the second menuetto survives only in the printed parts and was not taken over into AMA, although it is included in the critical commentary to this edition. ◆ K361 is now generally thought to date from 1784 and to be the work described by Schink in his *Litterarische Fragmente*: 'I heard music for wind instruments today, too, by Herr Mozart, in four movements, glorious and sublime. It consisted of thirteen instruments . . . and at each instrument sat a master (*Dokumente*, 206, *Documentary Biography*, 232–3). Although the number of movements mentioned by Schink does not tally with the number of movements in K361, it is possible that the work was not performed in its entirety. Stadler's concert was advertised in the *Wienerblättchen* on 23 March 1784: 'Herr Stadler . . . will hold a musical concert for his benefit at the I. & R. National Court Theatre, at which will be given, among other well-chosen pieces, a great wind piece of a very special kind composed by Herr Mozart' (*Dokumente*, 198, *Documentary Biography*, 223).

resources of the Munich orchestra, with whose members he is known to have been on friendly terms.

Two other works written in the immediate aftermath of *Idomeneo* are the concert arias *Ma che vi fece . . . Sperai vicino* K368 from act one, scene four of Metastasio's *Demofoonte* and *Misera! dove son . . . Ah! non son io* K369 from the same librettist's *Ezio*.[83] The second of these pieces are written for the Countess Josepha Paumgarten. The two songs with mandolin accompaniment (K349 and 351) may likewise have been written for friends in Munich,[84] while the loyal Ramm was rewarded with the quartet in F major K370 for oboe, violin, viola and cello.[85]

While working on *Idomeneo*, Mozart saw virtually no one except the Cannabichs, but following the arrival of his father and sister in the city he started to socialize and to enjoy himself, deriving particular pleasure from the carnival. Even as late as 26 May 1781 he still recalled this period:

> It is true that in Munich I involuntarily placed myself in a false light by enjoying myself too much – but I swear to you on my honour that, until my opera had been staged, I never set foot in a theatre or went anywhere except to the Cannabichs. . . . That I then enjoyed myself too much was due to the folly of youth. I thought to myself: 'Where are you going? To Salzburg! So you should have a good time.'[86]

It was essentially Colloredo whom Mozart had to thank for this life of reckless pleasure, for, following the death of the Empress Maria Theresia, the archbishop was detained in Vienna. In keeping with aristocratic practice, he had taken a sizeable retinue with him, including a number of his finest musicians. Now Mozart, too, was summoned to join him in Vienna, and he duly set off on 12 March. He had been away for so much longer than the six weeks originally agreed that the archbishop's patience had evidently finally snapped, and it appears that Colloredo was determined from the outset to remind his recalcitrant Konzertmeister in no uncertain terms of his contractual duties and stamp out any further desire for independence on his part. Mozart presumably had no inkling of what was in store and was no doubt looking forward to revisiting Vienna, where, following the end of the period of national mourning caused by the death of the Empress Maria Theresia, the musical life of the capital was again in full swing and he was eager to be heard in aristocratic circles. Colloredo lost no time in putting a spoke in his wheel. He no doubt had ulterior motives in offering Mozart accommodation in his own lodgings and from the very beginning treated him as a servant. Mozart's letters from this period contain a graphic account of the social status of musicians at this time, for the treatment that he received was not based on any particular malice of Colloredo's part but on a long-established custom that Mozart must have found especially irksome following his liberated life in Munich. When he arrived in Vienna on

---

83.   ◆ The autograph of K369 is dated Munich, 8 March 1781; K368, however, is undated and on the basis of its paper type is more likely to have been written in Salzburg in 1779 or 1780, before Mozart left for Munich.

84.   The second bears the note '1780 for Herr Lang', a horn player in the Munich orchestra. ◆ This note, however, is not by Mozart and the dating of K351, though plausible, is not certain.

85.   ◆ This date, too, is uncertain. The notation on the autograph, 'Munic 1781', is possibly not by Mozart.

86.   *Briefe*, iii.121 (letter of 26 May 1781). Leopold was meanwhile negotiating with Breitkopf: 'I have long been hoping that you would print something of my son's, surely you won't judge him by the keyboard sonatas that he wrote as a child? You will not, of course, have seen a note of what he has written in recent years, except perhaps the 6 sonatas for keyboard and violin that he had engraved in Paris: for we allow very little to be published. You might see what you can do with a couple of symphonies or keyboard sonatas, or with quartets, trios etc. You need give us only a few copies, only so that you see something of my son's style of writing. I have no wish to persuade you against your will, but the idea has often occurred to me because I see works engraved and printed that arouse only my pity' (*Briefe* iii.93; letter of 12 February 1781).

16 March, he found two of his old colleagues – the castrato Ceccarelli and the violinist Brunetti – already there:

I arrived here yesterday, the 16th, thank God, all on my own in a post chaise – at 9 in the morning. . . . Now for the archibishop. I have a charming room in the very same house where the archbishop is staying [the House of the Teutonic Order in the Singerstraße]. Brunetti and Ceccarelli are staying elsewhere. Che distinzione! – My neighbour is Herr von Kleinmayr [chairman of the Court Council], who showered all manner of courtesies on me on my arrival; he is a most charming man. We lunch at midday, unfortunately a bit too early for me. Our party consists of the two valets – the two who attend to His Grace's bodily and spiritual needs –, the contrôleur [Ernst Maximilian Köllenberger], Herr Zetti [the *Kammerfourier* or private messenger], the confectioner, 2 cooks, Ceccarelli, Brunetti and *mea parvitas*. The two valets sit at the top of the table, but at least I have the honour of being placed above the cooks. – I can almost see myself back in Salzburg. – The others crack stupid, coarse jokes at table; but no one does so with me, as I never say a word, or if I have to speak, I always do so with the utmost gravity; as soon as I've eaten, I leave. There's no meal in the evening, instead each of us is given 3 ducats – which goes a long way. His Grace is kind enough to bask in the glory of his house-hold, while robbing us of any means of earning a living and not paying us into the bargain. – We gave a concert yesterday at 4 o'clock, and at least twenty people of the highest rank were there. Ceccarelli has already had to sing at Palffy's [the archbishop's brother-in-law]. Today we're off to Prince Galitzin [the Russian ambassador], who was here yesterday. – I'm just waiting to see if I get anything; if I don't, I'll go to the archbishop and tell him straight to his face that if he won't let me earn anything, then he must pay for me, as I can't live off my own money.[87]

Leopold, who had already returned to Salzburg with his daughter, was inevitably alarmed by the tone of this letter and, seeing the stormclouds brewing, did what he could to placate his son, only to provoke the following reply:

What you say about the archbishop – about the way I gratify his ambition – is partially true; – but what good is all this to me? I can't live off it. Believe me when I say that he's like a screen. – What distinction does he confer on me? – Herr von Kleinmayr and Bönike [private secretary to the archbishop and a member of the Ecclesiastical Council] have a separate table with His Lordship Count Arco [Karl Joseph Felix Arco, the chief steward]; – it would be a distinction for me if I sat at their table, rather than with the cooks and the valets, who, when they're not sitting in the best seats, have to light the chandeliers, open the doors and wait in the anteroom when I'm within. And then, when we're summoned to a house where there's a concert, Herr Angelbauer [*recte* Johann Ulrich Angerbauer, one of the archbishop's private valets] has to wait outside until the gentlemen from Salzburg arrive, when he sends a lackey to show them in. When I heard Brunetti recount this in conversation, I thought: 'Just wait till I come along!'

So, the other day, when we had to go to Prince Galitzin's, Brunetti said to me in his usual polite way: 'Tu, bisogna che sei qui sta sera alle sette, per andare insieme dal Prencipe Gallizin, l'Angelbauer ci condurrà.' – Hò risposto: 'Và bene – ma se in caso mai non fossi qui alle sette in punto, ci andate pure, non serve aspettarmi, sò ben dove stà e ci verrò sicuro' ['You must be here

87. *Briefe*, iii.93–4 (letter of 17 March 1781).

at seven this evening, so we can go together to Prince Galitzin's. Angerbauer will take us.' I replied: 'All right. But if I'm not here at seven o'clock sharp, just go ahead. You needn't wait for me. I know where he lives and will be sure to be there.'] I went on my own on purpose, as I'm ashamed to go anywhere with them; – when I got upstairs, Herr Angelbauer was already standing there, waiting to tell the lackey to show me in. But I took no notice, either of the valet or the lackey, but walked straight on through the rooms to the music room, as the doors were all open, – and went straight up to the prince, paid him my respects and stood there talking to him. I'd completely forgotten about Ceccarelli and Brunetti, who were nowhere to be seen but were hidden away behind the orchestra, not daring to come forward.[88]

It emerges from this that the archbishop, in keeping with the custom associated with his rank, used to take his servants and the members of his orchestra with him when he visited other households in order to parade them there, and he was no doubt particularly proud to be able to show off an artist like Mozart. But he went no further than this. Just as the works commissioned from resident composers were anxiously prevented from falling into the hands of third parties, so it was traditionally believed that the composers in question existed only to serve their employers' needs, and Colloredo was merely acting in accordance with the practices associated with his own social class when he rigorously prevented Mozart from engaging in any independent artistic activities while in Vienna. Only in the low rates of pay that he offered did he differ from most of his fellow employers.

On one occasion Colloredo had his musicians perform for his father, old Prince Rudolph Colloredo, who gave each of them five ducats. The demands that he placed on Mozart himself at his concerts emerge from the latter's letter to his father of 8 April 1781:

Today – I'm writing this at 11 o'clock at night – we had a concert at which 3 of my pieces were given, all of them new, of course: a rondeau for a concerto for Brunetti, a sonata with violin accompaniment for me, which I wrote last night between 11 and 12, but in order to be able to finish it in time, I wrote out only the accompaniment for Brunetti and retained my own part in my head, and then a rondeau for Ceccarelli that he had to repeat.[89]

Colloredo had given him four ducats for the first concert but offered him no further payment on the present occasion. 'What really angers me', he wrote on 11 April, 'is that the very same evening that we gave this shitty concert, I was invited to the Countess Thun's but of course I couldn't go, and who should be there but the emperor! Adamberger and Frau Weigl were there, and each of them got 50 ducats! What an opportunity!'[90]

88. *Briefe*, iii.97–8 (letter of 24 March 1781).
89. *Briefe*, iii.103 (letter of 8 April 1781). The three pieces were K373, dated 2 April 1781; K372, of which only the opening allegro survives complete (see Jahn, *W. A. Mozart*, fourth edition, i.695); and K374. A variant of the ending of this aria, with simpler *fioriture*, is included by Waldersee with his critical commentary. ◆ It is more likely that the sonata is K379, the autograph of which was written down in two stages, consistent with the description in Mozart's letter; see Riggs, 'Mozart's Sonata for Piano and Violin, K. 379: Perspectives on the "One-hour" Sonata'. Mozart completed only 65 bars of K372; the remainder of the movement is by Maximilian Stadler; see the facsimile in NMA X/30/4, 70–4.
90. *Briefe*, iii.105 (letter of 11 April 1781). Valentin Adamberger (1740 or 1743–1804) was the well-known tenor; Anna Maria Weigl was the mother of the composer and currently engaged as a soprano at the German National Theatre in Vienna. ◆ Further concerning Adamberger, see Angermüller, 'Ein Mozart-Tenor aus Niederbayern: Johann Valentin Adamberger zu seinem 260. Geburtstag'; Barak, 'Valentin Adamberger – Mozarts Belmonte und Freund' and Münster, 'Mozart ". . . beym Herzoge Clemens . . .": Ein Beitrag zum Thema Mozart in München'.

In spite of the archiepiscopal ban, Mozart none the less managed to score some successes of his own. He renewed contact with the Meßmers, with Johann Michael von Auernhammer and his 'fat daughter' and with the elderly Kapellmeister Giuseppe Bonno. At Bonno's home, one of his symphonies was rehearsed to great acclaim: 'There were 40 violins, double winds, 10 violas, 10 basses, 8 cellos and 6 bassoons.'[91] But it was his new contacts that filled Mozart with the greatest hope and encouraged him to turn his attention to the Emperor Joseph II himself:

This evening [24 March] I'm going with Herr von Kleinmayr to meet one of his good friends, Court Councillor Braun, who – everyone tells me – is one of the greatest lovers of keyboard music.[92] I've twice dined with Countess Thun and go there almost every day, she's the most charming and amiable lady I've ever met, and she thinks very highly of me. . . . I've also lunched with Count Cobenzl [Court and State Chancellor in Vienna]. . . . My chief object here is to introduce myself to the emperor in some suitable way, as I'm absolutely determined that he should *get to know me*. I'd like to whip through my opera with him and then play him some fugues, as that's the sort of thing he likes. – If only I'd known that I'd be in Vienna for Lent, I'd have written a short oratorio and performed it in the theatre for my benefit, just as everyone does here. I could easily have written it in advance, as I know all the voices here. How I'd like to give a public concert, as is the custom here; but – I wouldn't be allowed to, I'm quite certain of that: just imagine – as you know, there's a society in Vienna that gives concerts for the benefit of musicians' widows at which everyone donates their services – the orchestra is 180 strong[93] – no virtuoso with even a modicum of love for his neighbour refuses to play if the society asks him to do so, as in this way you can ingratiate yourself with both the emperor and the general public. – Starzer was asked to invite me and I agreed at once, while adding that I'd first have to obtain the consent of my prince – and I had no doubt that he'd let me as it's a charitable organization and unpaid as it involves only doing a good turn; *he wouldn't let me*. All the local nobility took it amiss, – I'm sorry if only because I wouldn't have played a concerto but – because the emperor sits in the proscenium box – would simply have extemporized (Countess Thun would have lent me her beautiful Stein pianoforte) and played a fugue and then the variations on 'Je suis Lindor'.[94] Whenever I've played this programme in public before, I've always had the greatest applause as the pieces set each other off so well and because everyone has something to his or her taste; but pazienza![95]

On this occasion, Colloredo was finally obliged to give in. The Pension Fund for the Widows and Orphans of Viennese Musicians that Florian Gassmann had set up in 1771 had patrons in high

91.   *Briefe*, iii.106 (letter of 11 April 1781). The symphony in question may have been K338. It was presumably the same work as the one performed at the Tonkünstler-Sozietät on 3 April 1781; see below.
92.   'One of the greatest experts on music among amateurs is Imperial Court Councillor von Braun. He is particularly appreciative of the works of the great Philipp Emanuel Bach; in this he has, of course, the vast majority of the public in Vienna against him'; see Nicolai, *Beschreibung einer Reise durch Deutschland und die Schweiz im Jahre 1781*, iv.556.
93.   On this society, see Carl Ferdinand Pohl, *Joseph Haydn*, ii.134; Pohl, *Denkschrift aus Anlaß des hundertjährigen Bestehens der Tonkünstler-Sozietät in Wien*; Hanslick, *Geschichte des Concertwesens in Wien*, 6ff. Mozart wanted to become a member of the Society in 1785, but, although he had often donated his services both as a pianist and as a composer, he was refused admission as he was unable to produce his birth certificate; see Pohl, *Denkschrift*, 17 and 18; and Hanslick, *Geschichte des Concertwesens*, 17. Dittersdorf claims that the orchestra was 200-strong for the first performance of his oratorio *L'Esther* in 1773; see Dittersdorf, *Lebensbeschreibung*, 156. Johann Caspar Riesbeck speaks of 400 performers in his *Briefe eines reisenden Franzosen über Deutschland an seinen Bruder zu Paris*, i.276. ◆ Further, see Edge, 'Mozart's Viennese Orchestras'.
94.   In Leipzig, too, in 1789 Mozart played the variations on 'Je suis Lindor' K354 after a free fantasy.
95.   *Briefe*, iii.99 (letter of 24 March 1781).

places and the four concerts that it gave annually – two during Advent and two during Holy Week – were immensely popular with artists and public alike. With the help of the aristocracy, Starzer finally cornered Colloredo at the concert at Prince Galitzin's and managed to obtain his permission for Mozart to appear at the concert on 3 April 1781.[96] The occasion proved a triumphant success for Mozart, who not only performed his symphony but also played a concerto, as he reported on 4 April: 'I can truthfully say that I was very pleased with the Viennese public yesterday. I played at the concert for the widows at the Kärntnertor-Theater. I had to begin all over again, as there was no end to the applause.'[97] Against this background, a concert devoted exclusively to Mozart's own music promised to be a brilliant success: 'The ladies even offered to distribute the tickets. . . . How much do you suppose I'd make if I were to give a concert of my own? But this arch-oaf won't let me – he refuses to allow his people to make a profit, but only a loss.' That Mozart's irritation had already reached an alarming level is clear from other remarks, too. Above all, Mozart again made it clear in his letters to his father that it was only as a favour to the latter that he was showing Colloredo any consideration at all. In short, the situation was already inflammatory when the archbishop announced his intention of sending his musicians back to Salzburg. The explosion that followed was inevitable, as Mozart clearly felt that if he was forced to leave Vienna just as he was beginning to make an impression in the city, he might as well abandon all hope for the future. On 4 April Brunetti told him that he had heard from Count Arco that Colloredo would give them their fares and that they were to leave by Sunday at the latest. Anyone who wished to remain longer could do so, but only at his own expense. Mozart decided to feign ignorance until such time as Count Arco spoke to him in person, at which point he would make his intentions known. Clearly he had already made up his mind to remain in Vienna, where he was confident of earning vast sums of money. And he ended his letter by blurting out the truth: 'I can't tell you what pleasure it will give me to thumb my nose at the archbishop – but I'll do so with the greatest politeness, and he won't be able to do a thing about it.'[98]

On 8 April it was announced that the musicians had to return home in two weeks' time. Leopold was deeply alarmed at Mozart's plans and the risk that they involved. Once again, his son's independent actions filled him with the gravest misgivings, not least because Mozart was on the point of relinquishing a post that he had only recently obtained for him after endless worries and exertions. Once again he tried to hold Mozart on a tighter rein and to entreat him to be circumspect and not risk his job in this frivolous way, but the traces were already beginning to slip from his grasp. Mozart's reply is dated 8 April 1781:

> My dearest father, I love you dearly, you can see this from the fact that for your sake I renounce all my wishes and desires; if it weren't for you I swear on my honour that I wouldn't hesitate for a moment to leave the archbishop's service – I'd give a grand concert, take on four pupils and

96. The poster for this 34th concert read as follows: 'Herr Mozart, Knight, will then be heard on the pianoforte all by himself. He was already here himself as a boy aged seven, and even then earned the general applause of the public, partly in the matter of composition and partly in that of art altogether, as well as for his especial skill and delicacy of touch'; *Neue Wiener Musikzeitung*, xxxv (1852) [*Dokumente*, 173, *Documentary Biography*, 195]. The concert also included a performance of Albrechtsberger's *Die Pilgrime auf Golgotha*. According to Pohl, *Joseph Haydn*, ii.145, this was the first time that a piano concerto had been performed in public in Vienna.

97. *Briefe*, iii.101 (letter of 4 April 1781). Four days later we find him writing: 'What delighted and surprised me most of all was the amazing silence – and also the cries of "Bravo!" while I was playing. This is certainly an honour in Vienna, where there are so many – and so many good – pianists'; *Briefe*, iii.103 (letter of 8 April 1781).

98. *Briefe*, iii.102 (letter of 4 April 1781).

within twelve months I'd have got on so well in Vienna that I'd be earning at least a thousand thalers a year. I assure you that I often find it difficult to throw away my good fortune like this.[99]

On 11 April Mozart again complained:

When I think that I'll have to leave Vienna without bringing home *at least* 1000 florins, I can't tell you how unhappy it makes me. For the sake of an evil-minded prince, who plagues me every day and pays me only a lousy 400 florins, you expect me to throw away a thousand florins? I'm sure I'd earn that amount of money if I gave a concert.[100]

More than anything else, Mozart wanted to be presented to the emperor, and, if he left Vienna, he would have to abandon this plan, too:

I can't tell the emperor that if he wants to hear me, he'll have to hurry up as I'm leaving in however many days it is – you simply have to wait for things like this. Besides, I can't stay here – and don't want to either – unless I give a concert; – still, even if I have only two pupils here, I'd still be better off than at home; but – when you have 1000 or 1200 florins in your pocket, you can ask for a bit more and also be better paid. But this misanthrope won't allow this – I'm bound to call him this, as that's what he is, and the whole of the nobility calls him that, too.[101]

Moreover, there was a good chance of a post falling vacant in Vienna in the not too distant future: Bonno was getting on in years and when he died, Salieri was bound to replace him, while Starzer would move up into Salieri's post. But no one knew who might succeed Starzer. Could a better successor be found than Mozart himself?

Leopold continued to counsel prudence and with a heavy heart Mozart duly promised to comply with his wishes. But by 28 April the situation had degenerated to the point where Mozart had no hesitation in writing to his father:

You are looking forward to seeing me again, my dearest father! – That alone can persuade me to leave Vienna – I am writing all this in plain German[102] *as the whole world must know that the archbishop of Salzburg has only you to thank, my dear father, for the fact that he did not lose me yesterday for good (I mean, as far as he himself is concerned).* We had a grand concert here yesterday – probably the last. It was a great success, and in spite of all the obstacles put in my way by His Grace, I still had a better orchestra than Brunetti, as Ceccarelli will tell you; I had so much trouble arranging all this, but it's easier if I tell you about it in person, rather than writing about it. But if anything like it were to happen again (which I hope it won't), I can assure you that I'd lose all patience, and you'd certainly forgive me for doing so. And I beg you, my dearest father, to allow me to return to Vienna next Lent, towards the end of the carnival – this depends on you alone, not on the archbishop, for, if he won't let me, I'll go all the same – it certainly won't be a disaster for me, most certainly not! – Oh, I'd be more than happy for him to read this. But you must promise me in your next letter – for only on this condition shall I return to

99. *Briefe*, iii.104 (letter of 8 April 1781).
100. *Briefe*, iii.105 (letter of 11 April 1781).
101. *Briefe*, iii.105 (letter of 11 April 1781).
102. Here Mozart purposefully refrains from using the coded language that he and his father generally preferred when discussing matters of relative importance.

Salzburg – but it must be a definite promise, so that I can give my word to the ladies here. Stephanie is going to give me a German opera to write. And so I await your answer. . . . I still can't say when or how I shall leave. It's unfortunate that nothing can be got out of these people – then suddenly they'll announce: 'Allons, be off with you!' One moment we're told that a carriage is being got ready for the contrôleur, Ceccarelli and me to travel home in, then the next moment we're told that we're to return by the diligence, then again that we'll be given our diligence fares and can travel as we like – which would certainly be my preferred option; now in a week, now in 2 weeks, now in 3 weeks, then again even sooner – God! We don't know where we are and can't make any plans. . . . Yesterday, after the concert, the ladies kept me at the harpsichord for a whole hour, I think that if I'd not slipped away, I'd still be sitting there; I thought I'd already played quite enough for nothing.[103]

Later – on 13 June 1781 – we find Mozart recalling these same events in a further letter to his father:

Even after the last concert was over, I went on playing variations – on a theme given to me by the archbishop – for a whole hour, and the applause was so universal that if the archbishop has any human feelings at all, he must have felt some pleasure; but, instead of showing me – or, for all I care, not showing me – his pleasure and satisfaction, he treats me like a street urchin and tells me to my face to clear off, saying that he can get hundreds of people who'd serve him better than I do.[104]

The outcome was inevitable. Mozart himself has left the following account of the events of 9 May 1781:

I'm still seething with anger! and you, my dearest and kindest father, are bound to feel as I do. My patience has been tried to the point where it has finally snapped. – I am no longer so unfortunate as to be employed by the Salzburg court – today was a happy day for me; listen. Twice that – I really don't know what to call him – has said to my face the greatest *sottises* and impertinences that I refuse to repeat in order to spare your feelings, and if I didn't immediately get my own back for them, it was only because you, my dearest father, were constantly in my thoughts. He called me a knave and a scapegrace and told me to be off – and I – I put up with it all, – even though I felt that not only my own honour was being impugned, so, too, was yours, but – as you would have it so – I said nothing. Now listen. A week ago the footman came up and told me to move out at once – the others had all been told the day of their departure, but not me; so I hurriedly stuffed everything into my trunk, and old Mme Weber was kind enough to offer me her house. Here I have an attractive room, and the people are willing to help and supply me with all the things that you often need in a hurry but can't have (when you're alone). I planned to travel home by the ordinaire on Wednesday (in other words, today, the 9th), but I was unable to collect the money due to me, so I postponed my departure till Saturday. – When I presented myself today, the valets told me that the archbishop wanted to give me a parcel to take back with me; when I asked whether it was urgent, they said, yes, it was extremely important. 'Well, I'm sorry that I shan't have the pleasure of serving His Grace but (for the reason already given) I

103. *Briefe*, iii.108–9 (letter of 28 April 1781).
104. *Briefe*, iii.128 (letter of 13 June 1781).

can't leave before Saturday; I'm no longer staying here but have to pay for my own expenses, so it's clear that I can't leave until I'm in a position to do so, as no one will want to see me ruined.' Kleinmayr, Moll, Bönike and the two valets agreed with me. – When I then went to see him – that reminds me, I must first tell you that Schlauka [one of the archbishop's valets] had advised me to say that the ordinaire was full, which would be a more compelling excuse for him than the real one – so, when I went to see him, the first thing he said was: *Archb.*: 'Well, when are you leaving, young fellow?' – *I*: 'I intended to leave this evening, but all the seats were taken.' – It then all came pouring out – I was the most dissolute boy he knew; no one served him as badly as I did; and he advised me to leave today, otherwise he'd write home and have my salary stopped, – it was impossible to get a word in, he just went on and on. I listened to it all quite calmly; he lied to my face when he said my salary was 500 florins;[105] and he called me a wretch, a scoundrel and a cretin – oh, I really can't tell you everything he said. Finally my blood began to boil and I said: 'So Your Grace isn't satisfied with me?' – 'What? how dare you threaten me? You cretin, O you cretin! There's the door! I want nothing more to do with such a miserable knave.' – Finally I said: 'And I don't want anything more to do with you either.' – 'Well, go then.' – *And I* – as I was leaving – 'I mean it, you'll have it in writing tomorrow.' Tell me, my dearest father, shouldn't I have said this sooner rather than later? – Listen. My honour means more to me than anything, and I know that you feel the same. Don't worry about me, my future is so assured here that I'd have left even if I'd had absolutely no reason to do so; but now that I *have* good reason – *three* good reasons, in fact – I'd gain nothing by staying on, au contraire, I twice acted like a coward and simply couldn't do so a third time. As long as the archbishop remains here, I'll not give a concert. It's simply not true that I'll get a bad name with the nobility and the emperor himself – the archbishop is hated here, most of all by the emperor; he's furious that the emperor didn't invite him to Laxenburg. I'll send you some money by the next post to show you that I'm not starving. But please cheer up as my good luck is only now beginning, and I hope that my own good luck will be yours, too; send me a coded message that you're pleased – as you ought to be – but in public you can rail at me as much as you like, so that none of the blame falls on you. If, in spite of this, the archbishop is in the slightest bit impertinent towards you, you should come to Vienna at once with my sister. I assure you on my honour that all three of us can live here, though I'd prefer it if you could hold out for another year. Don't send any more letters to the House of the Teutonic Order or enclose them in their parcels – I don't want to hear another word about Salzburg – I hate the archbishop to distraction. . . . Just write on your letters: To be delivered Auf dem Peter im Auge Gottes, 2nd Floor. Write soon and tell me that you're pleased with me, as this is the only thing still missing to make my happiness complete.[106]

Mozart immediately carried out his resolve and wrote to inform his father of it on 12 May:

You know from my last letter that I've asked the prince for my dismissal – as he himself asked me to leave; even at the two previous audiences he'd said to me: 'Clear off if you're not prepared to serve me properly.' He'll deny it, of course, but, as God is my witness, it's true. Is it any wonder then that (after being driven to distraction by remarks such as 'knave', 'scoundrel', 'youngster', 'rake' and all the other expressions that graced his lips) I finally took his 'Clear off' in its literal sense?

---

105. This was in fact the amount promised him, but Mozart later insisted that he had been paid only 400 florins a year.
106. *Briefe*, iii.110–12 (letter of 9 May 1781).

The next day I gave Count Arco a petition to present to His Grace and at the same time returned my travelling expenses, which consisted of 15 florins 40 kreutzer for the diligence and 2 ducats for subsistence. He refused to accept either and told me that I couldn't resign without your consent, father. 'That's your duty,' he said. – I assured him that I knew my duty towards my father as well as he did and possibly better and that I'd be very sorry if I first had to learn it from him. 'Very well,' he said, 'if he's satisfied, you can ask for your dismissal; if not, you can ask for it all the same.' A nice distinction. – All the edifying things that the archbishop said to me during my three audiences, especially the last one, and all the subsequent things that this fine servant of God said to me had such an admirable effect on my health that in the evening I had to leave the opera in the middle of the first act and return home and lie down; I was very feverish – I was trembling all over – and staggered along the street like a drunkard, I also stayed at home the following day (yesterday) and spent the whole morning in bed, as I'd taken tamarind water.

The count has also been kind enough to write some very flattering things about me to his father [the chief chamberlain, Count Georg Anton Felix Arco], all of which you'll probably have had to swallow by now. Of course, there'll be a number of passages in them that are based on pure invention, – but if you write a comedy and want applause for it, you have to exaggerate and not stick too closely to the truth, – and you mustn't hold it against these gentlemen that they're so anxious to serve their master. Without getting too worked up (my health and life are very dear to me and I'm only sorry that I'm forced to do so), I just want to deal with the main charge against me concerning my terms of service. I didn't know I was a valet, and it was this that proved the last straw. I ought to have idled away a couple of hours each morning in the antechamber; of course, I was often told that I should allow myself to be seen, – but I could never remember that this was part of my duties, and it was only when the archbishop summoned me that I always turned up on time.

I only want to tell you of my inflexible determination, but so that the whole world may hear. If I were offered a salary of 2000 florins by the archbishop of Salzburg and only 1000 elsewhere, I'd still go elsewhere, – for instead of the extra 1000 florins I'd enjoy good health and peace of mind. – And so I hope that, by all the fatherly love that you have lavished on me since childhood and for which I can never thank you enough (least of all in Salzburg), if you wish to see your son well and happy, you'll say nothing to me about this whole affair but simply forget it – a single word would be enough to enrage me and – if only you will admit it – yourself as well. Now farewell, and be glad that your son isn't a coward.[107]

That same day Mozart wrote to his father again, but on this occasion he adopted a more intimate tone, confident that his remarks were safe from prying eyes:

In the letter that you've received by post I spoke to you as though we were in the presence of the archbishop. Now, my dearest father, I am speaking to you completely alone. Let us pass over in silence the injustice with which the archbishop has treated me from the very beginning of his reign, the incessant insults, all the impertinences and *sottises* that he has uttered to my face and the undeniable right that I have to leave him, for none of this is in doubt. I shall speak only of what would have led me to leave him in any case – even if I'd not been insulted.

---

107. *Briefe*, iii.112–14 (letter of 12 May 1781).

Here I have the finest and most useful contacts in the world, I'm liked and respected by the greatest families, I'm shown all possible honour, and, what's more, I'm paid for it – so why should I languish in Salzburg for the sake of 400 florins, pining away without remuneration or encouragement and of no use to you, when I can certainly be of use to you here? – Where would it all have ended? – always the same: I'd have had to put up with mortal insults or else I'd have had to leave. – I need say no more, as you know this is true. But let me say only this: the whole of Vienna knows my story, – the whole of the nobility is urging me not to allow myself to be led by the nose any longer.

My dearest father, people will come to you with fine words, but they are snakes and vipers, – all worthless souls are like this, disgustingly proud and haughty, but always ready to crawl – horrible! The two valets have seen through the whole scandalous affair. Schlauka, in particular, said to someone: 'I – I really can't say that Mozart is in the wrong, – in fact, he's entirely in the right, – I'd like to have seen him treat me in that way! He treated him like a beggar, I heard him – infamous!' The archbishop knows he's done wrong, hasn't he had ample opportunity to realize this? has he mended his ways as a result? No! so let's have done with him! – If I'd not been worried that you might have suffered in consequence, things would long since have been very different. – But, in the main, what can he do to you? – Nothing. – Once you know that all is going well with me, you can easily manage without the archbishop's grace and favour, – he can't take away your salary, and besides you always do your duty; and I can guarantee that I'll succeed, otherwise I'd not have taken this step, – though I admit that after this insult, I'd have left in any case – even if I'd had to beg; for who will let himself be bullied, particularly when he can do better elsewhere? So – if you're afraid, pretend to be angry with me, call me whatever names you like in your letters, as long as we two know how things stand, – but don't allow yourself to be led astray by flattery – be on your guard.[108]

Leopold, of course, thought differently. His son's step upset all his plans and, by exposing Mozart to an uncertain future, struck him as an act of youthful folly. He could never get used to the idea that his son could ever take charge of his own destiny, and his letters of this period betray the same degree of bitterness as we encountered in his letters to Paris. He tried every means in his power to make his son 'see reason', even at this late stage, but Mozart remained implacable: to return to Salzburg would redound not only to his disadvantage but also to his discredit, and so he rejected all his father's warnings and reproaches, adopting a tone which, without concealing his feeling of mortification, none the less reveals the clear and purposeful gaze of the now fully mature composer and, as such, is gratifyingly different from the irritable and even petty tone of his father's letters. Leopold seized the opportunity to confront his son with a whole catalogue of sins, including his old complaint that Mozart had an irresponsible attitude to money. Mozart duly replied to this charge on 26 May 1781:

Believe me when I say that I have changed completely – apart from my health, there is nothing I consider more necessary than money. I am certainly no miser – and it would be very difficult for me to become one – and yet people here think that I'm more disposed to be mean than to squander my money – and that surely is enough to begin with. – As for pupils, I can have as many as I like; but I don't want too many, – I intend to be better paid than the others, and so I prefer to have fewer. It's a good idea to get on your high horse a bit at first, otherwise you're at a permanent disadvantage and must then follow the common herd.[109]

Leopold also brought up the subject of the debts that he had incurred on Mozart's behalf and the latter was bound to be particularly offended by the remark that he would forget them in Vienna as quickly as he had been forgotten by Aloysia Weber.[110] He replied to this point on 9 June 1781:

That you compare me with Mme Weber amazes me and left me feeling depressed for the rest of the day. – This girl was a burden to her parents until such time as she was able to earn her own keep; – but as soon as the time came when she could show them her gratitude (remember that her father died before she had earned a brass farthing here), she abandoned her poor mother, attached herself to an actor and married him – and her mother has never had *that much* from her.[111] Good God! – my sole aim, God knows, is to help you and the rest of us; do I have to repeat it a hundred times that I can be of more use to you here than in Salzburg? I beg you, my dearest, kindest father, don't write any more letters like that, I entreat you; they serve only to provoke me and to disturb my peace of mind. – And I – I now have to compose and need a cheerful mind and a calm disposition.[111]

He even sent his father twenty ducats, apologizing for the fact that he could not spare any more at present. In the course of the years that followed several more such sums were sent to Salzburg. But Leopold also disapproved of the fact that his son had resumed contact with the Webers, fearing a resumption of his earlier affair, a fear that Mozart emphatically rejected while freely admitting to his former feelings and praising Frau Weber's willingness to help him.

Finally, various good friends managed to retail all manner of rumours concerning Mozart's allegedly immoral lifestyle in Vienna, with Ludwig Gottfried von Moll, especially, claiming that he was in the city 'only on account of the women' and even mentioning one woman in particular. Once again, Mozart was quick to defend himself: 'I am as liable to err as any young man,' he wrote on 13 June 1781, 'but for my own consolation I might wish that all were as free from sin as I am. You may perhaps believe things about me that are not true; my chief fault is that, *judging by appearances*, I don't always act as I should.' Nor, he went on, did he have any cause to reproach himself on religious grounds: he heard Mass every Sunday and every Holy day, even though he

109. *Briefe*, iii.120 (letter of 26 May 1781).
110. Aloysia had moved to Vienna in 1779 (see Blümml, *Aus Mozarts Freundes- und Familienkreis*); she sang at the Tonkünstler-Sozietät on 12 and 14 March 1781 (see Pohl, *Denkschrift*, 56) and married the actor Joseph Lange on 31 October 1780 (see Werner, *Aus dem Josephinischen Wien*, 105). Lange's own account of his wife's career is far more flattering: 'Unfortunately, her father was killed by a stroke, robbing both her and her family of his support. She was inconsolable and this, together with her deep mourning and my wish to help the family in both word and deed, made me all the more attractive to her. Her heart found a sympathetic response in mine, allowing her cares to be lifted, and so she decided to marry me, hoping to find in her husband the friend that she had lost in her father. By dint of her fine talent she was able to contribute to the upkeep of her family, and so I settled an annuity of 700 florins on her mother for the duration of her life and paid her an advance of 900 florins that the family had received from the court authorities'; Lange, *Biographie des Joseph Lange, k. k. Hofschauspieler*, 116ff. Mozart's harsh judgement was evidently influenced by her mother, whom he himself later saw in a far less favourable light. ◆ Further concerning Aloysia Lange, see Barak, 'Buff, Herz und Vogelsang – Die Theaterfamilien Stephanie, Lange und Adamberger im Wien Mozarts'; Breitinger, 'Aloisia Lange, die erste große Liebe Mozarts'; and Gidwitz, '"Ich bin die erste Sangerin": Vocal profiles of two Mozart sopranos'.
111. *Briefe*, iii.127 (letter of 9 June 1781).

interpreted fasting to mean 'abstaining, that is, eating less than usual. . . . Rest assured that I do have religious feelings, and should I ever have the misfortune (which God forbid!) to fall into evil ways, I shall absolve you, my dearest father, from all responsibility.'[112]

But Leopold continued with implacable insistence to demand that Mozart withdraw his resignation, claiming that he owed it to his sense of honour to do so. In his letter of 19 May, Mozart spelt out his feelings more clearly than ever:

> My dearest father, I too don't know how to begin this letter, as I can't get over my astonishment and shall never be able to do so as long as you continue to think and write as you do. I must confess that there isn't a single line in your letter by which I recognize my own father! – a father, no doubt, but not the finest and most loving father who cares for his own honour and for that of his children – in a word, not *my* father. But it must have been a dream, you've now woken up and don't need me to reply to any of your points in order to be more than convinced that – *now more than ever* – I can never abandon my resolve. . . . You say that the only way to save my honour is to abandon my resolve. – How can you be guilty of such a contradiction? Did it not occur to you when you wrote this that, by withdrawing my resignation, I'd be the basest person in the world. The whole of Vienna knows that I've left the archbishop – and knows why – knows that it's because my honour was insulted – and insulted, moreover, three times, and you expect me publicly to prove the opposite? – to make myself out to be a coward and the archbishop a worthy prince? – No one can do the former, I least of all, and the latter God alone can achieve, if He chooses to enlighten him. . . . For your sake, my dearest father, I was prepared to sacrifice my good fortune, my health and my life, – but my honour I hold more dearly than anything else, as you should, too. . . . My dearest, kindest father, ask anything of me that you like, but not that – anything but that – the very thought of it makes me tremble with rage.[113]

Mozart's first letter of resignation was dated 9 May and was either not accepted or put to one side. Presumably it was assumed at court that he would yield to pressure from his father. According to Mozart's letter of late May 1781, the archbishop was regarded in Vienna as an 'arrogant, conceited ecclesiastic who despises everyone here'[114] and who evidently saw no reason to temper his attitude. Count Arco, by contrast, took it upon himself to act as intermediary and invited Mozart to attend what he hoped would be an amiable meeting, but in the event it passed off coolly and produced no results, not least because Mozart was convinced that his father had no reason to fear any repercussions of his actions in Salzburg.[115] Instead, he gave the count a second letter of resignation but the latter failed to pass this on to his employer 'from lack of courage and from his love of fawning'. At the same time Mozart discovered that Colloredo was about to leave Vienna and had no thought for anything else. Beside himself with anger, Mozart drafted a third petition in which he explained the whole situation, adding that it was now necessary for him to present the

112. *Briefe*, iii.129–30 (letter of 13 June 1781).
113. *Briefe*, iii.117–20 (letter of 19 May 1781).
114. *Briefe*, iii.123 (letter of between 26 May and 2 June 1781).
115. On the prevailing tone in Salzburg, see Mozart's letter of 2 June 1781, in which he reports his conversation with Count Arco: 'That this incident took place in Vienna is the archbishop's fault, not mine; if he knew how to treat people with any talent, it would never have happened. My dear count, I'm the most equable person in the world, as long as they are the same with me.' 'Well,' he said, 'the archbishop considers you an extremely conceited person.' 'I can well believe it,' I said, 'as I am towards him; I treat people as they treat me; if I see that someone despises me and has a low opinion of me, I can be as proud as any peacock'; *Briefe*, iii.124 (letter of 2 June 1781).

petition in person.[116] He duly appeared in Colloredo's antechamber on 8 June, shortly before the archbishop's departure, and asked for an audience, at which point Arco finally lost his temper. After a heated exchange, in the course of which the count called Mozart a 'clown' and a 'knave' and much else besides, the latter was kicked out through the door. Mozart was left with no alternative but to 'decamp and take to my heels as I had no wish to show the same disrespect to the prince's apartments as Arco had already done'. That Colloredo had consented to this violent resolution to the affair – as Mozart, in the heat of the moment, assumed – is out of the question, as he had clearly no idea of the course that events had taken. He concealed his anger, said nothing and passed over the affair by pretending to remain calm. To allow himself to be visibly upset by the behaviour of one of his servants ran counter to his most fundamental principles.

Mozart's anger was understandably directed at Count Arco, and in his letter of 13 June we find him swearing to seek out an opportunity to return Arco's kick, even if it should be in the open street:

I'm not demanding any satisfaction from the archbishop, as he's not in a position to grant me the sort of satisfaction that I'm after; but one of these days I'll write to the count and tell him what he may confidently expect from me as soon as good fortune allows me to meet him, no matter where it may be, provided only that it's not a place where I'm bound to show him respect.[117]

Leopold was frankly alarmed at the idea of his son attacking a member of the aristocracy, but Mozart wrote to reassure him on 20 June 1781:

It is the heart that ennobles a man, and though I'm no count, I may still have more honour in me than many a count; but whether he be a count or a valet, the moment a man insults me, he's a scoundrel. I first intend to tell him quite reasonably how badly and wickedly he's behaved – but ultimately I'll have to assure him in writing that he can expect a kick up the arse from me and a couple of thick ears into the bargain.[118]

Mozart declined all his father's attempts at mediation, although in deference to the latter he finally agreed not to send his threatening letter to Count Arco.

Mozart was once again a free man, and on this occasion he was additionally free from his father's yoke. The older and newer attitudes to art had been thrown into even sharper relief than ever: a secure appointment at a princely court meant more to Leopold than anything else, and for this he was even prepared to pay the price of personal humiliation. Mozart, by contrast, upheld the right of artistic conscience not to sacrifice the artist's innate calling to the taste of an individual prince. As a result he had now broken free from his father's tutelage once and for all.

Of course, Mozart had to pay a high price for his freedom. With the success of *Idomeneo*, his pride as an artist had increased immeasurably, persuading him to see everything unconnected

116. The 'three memoranda' that Mozart mentions in his letter of 9 June 1781 (*Briefe* iii.126) could be the three petitions of 9 May, late May and 8 June, so that we do not need to assume a greater number.
117. *Briefe*, iii.129 (letter of 13 June 1781).
118. *Briefe*, iii.133 (letter of 20 June 1781).

with Salzburg in a particularly rosy light. In Vienna, too, he unthinkingly assumed that his music, which more than ever sprang from his heart, would speak to the hearts of his audiences and that the aristocracy would consider it only natural to do all that they could to support him. For all the frequency of his father's reproaches, he still tended to take empty remarks at face value. It was only with his departure from Salzburg, therefore, that he began to learn life's lessons at first hand and to gain a much deeper understanding of human nature.

24

Sacred and instrumental works, 1779–1781

The two masses in C major K317 and 337 (they are the ninth and tenth that Mozart wrote in this key[1]) add little new to the type of setting described in an earlier chapter, while at the same time constituting often highly idiosyncratic variants on that type. The first, for example, reuses music from its Kyrie in its 'Dona nobis pacem', but the quotation, far from being literal, adds to the sense of climax: what had merely been hinted at in the Kyrie is now fully realized at the end of the mass. For its part, the Kyrie departs from existing practices by adopting a slow tempo, its first, sharply dotted section being repeated in varied guise after a somewhat faster middle section. The Kyrie of the second mass, by contrast, is a continuous binary movement that clearly establishes the more intimate, tender tone of the work as a whole. In K317, the Gloria is a large-scale two-part complex, with the 'Qui tollis' as its middle section. The way in which the main theme is reached in the 'Qui sedes' is extremely impressive: in the 'Miserere'[2] it retreats to the inner parts, only to reassert itself again in the 'Quoniam'. This ternary structure is also vaguely discernible in the Gloria of the second mass but is obscured by the fact that the second subject of the main section with its distinctive orchestral motif[3] extends from the 'Domine Deus' to the 'Quoniam', soon taking charge again at the repeat and in this way effectively becoming the movement's principal idea. The Credo of K317 is cast in rondo form and is again particularly unified in structure; typically Mozartian are the rhythm of the bass part, the remarkably veiled tone that steals in with the 'Et in unum Dominum' and the inspired expansiveness at 'mortuorum', a feature also found in the other mass, whose Credo is more or less similarly structured. In both, the main episode is the 'Et incarnatus est'. With its declamatory choral writing, mysterious harmonies and incessantly downward sweeping figure in the violins,[4] the F minor movement of K317 is altogether exceptional. But the Sanctus, too, strikes an entirely new note thanks to a recurrent motif in the orchestra heard in the unison strings, its trilled motif later taken over into the 'Hosanna', which on this occasion is not fugal in texture. The main theme of the 'Benedictus' is somewhat superficial and lively in a manner all too reminiscent of an *opéra comique*, but even here we find Mozart introducing novel ideas by incorporating the theme as an episode in the following 'Hosanna'. In K337 the reverse is the case, with a more modern-sounding 'Sanctus' followed by a 'Benedictus' of a contrapuntal rigour

1. ◆ This assumes that the mass K115 is by Wolfgang when in fact it is by Leopold; and although K115 (Seiffert 4/2) was known to Abert only as a fragment, a complete copy survives in the library of St Peter's, Salzburg (shelfmark *Moz 15.1*). Accordingly, K317 and 337 are Mozart's eighth and ninth masses in C major, respectively.
2. As Hugo Riemann has pointed out, this theme recalls the menuetto from a keyboard trio by Johann Christian Bach; see Riemann, *J. C. Bach: Trio in D Dur*.
3. This characteristic scalar motif with its introductory interval of an octave is a precursor of the analogous motif in the first trio from *Don Giovanni*.
4. It recalls the analogous figure in Bach's B minor mass: on both occasions the poetic idea is the same.

unique in Mozart's masses, even though we have already encountered examples of more austere settings of this section alongside the usual type in which charm and tenderness are the prevailing emotions. Even the theme has something agitated, almost wild to it as a result of the curtailment of the motif in the second bar, and its tortured development takes it through keen dissonances and sombre minor-key harmonies before the main theme is finally reached in the bass via chromatically descending basses involving constant changes of tonality and it eventually dies away with one of Mozart's favourite half-cadences. No less typically Mozartian is the sudden insurgence of C major with the 'Hosanna'. This is certainly a highly unusual interpretation of a movement in which the sight of the Lamb of God inspires a sense of the deepest and most hopeless contrition rather than jubilation. In the two 'Agnus Dei' settings, where such ideas might more traditionally be expected, the tone is far more relaxed. Both are solo numbers, and both look forward in striking ways to the Countess's two arias in *Le nozze di Figaro*, with the main theme of 'Dove sono' anticipated by K317 (only the 3/4 time-signature and a number of minor melodic details are different), while K337 includes at the very least a clear pre-echo of 'Porgi amor'. Also of note are the two tonalities, with the first 'Agnus Dei' in F major, the second in E flat major, a tonality that Mozart would never have risked until now. Of the two settings of the 'Dona nobis pacem', the first is more sombre and dignified than the second, whose only relatively individual features are its surprising modulation to A flat major, its augmentation of the theme at its later appearance and its *morendo* ending.[5]

In terms of their instrumentation, both masses recall long-established practices in Salzburg, with no violas and with the trombones doubling the chorus. None the less, there are also clear signs of the influence of both Mannheim and Paris, with chorus and orchestra (and, within the latter, strings and winds) organically merged in a quite different way from before. Among the work's more novel features are its concertante effects within individual bars, including the highly poetical ending of the first 'Kyrie' and the middle section of the second, with its brusque dynamic contrasts,[6] while the thematic role of the winds is now considerably enhanced (note the beautiful 'bonae voluntatis' in the 'Gloria' from K317).[7] But it is in the 'Agnus Dei' of K337 that Mozart's delight in concertante writing emerges more prominently, with solos for oboe, bassoon and organ. With few exceptions, the choral writing is homophonic but eminently vocal in style.

The incomplete masses from this period likewise reveal an extraordinary diversity in terms of both form and content. Cast in sonata form and with carefully elaborated orchestral writing, the Kyrie in C major K323 seems like a spiritualized throwback to an earlier age.[8] Of the two unfinished Kyries (both of which are similarly in C major), one – K258a – is notable for its concertante organ part, the other for its exceptionally strict contrapuntal writing.[9]

That Mozart was able to achieve far more original results when not hampered by the prevailing taste in Salzburg is clear from his Munich Kyrie K341, the very tonality of which – D minor – is

---

5. There is the same sense of muted valediction as in the menuetto from the F major violin sonata K377 of 1781.

6. In the Gloria of K337 (bars 62–3), the words 'Jesu Christe' are sung *a cappella*, the unexpectedness of the device creating a particularly poetical impression.

7. Also new are the slides in the violins at the beginning of the Gloria of K317.

8. ◆ It now appears that the mass fragment K323 dates from considerably later, some time after 1787. Its apparent 'throwback to an earlier age' is possibly explained by Mozart's renewed interest in church music at the end of the 1780s and early 1790s, when he applied to succeed Leopold Hofmann as Kapellmeister at St Stephen's in Vienna.

9. ◆ K258a is now thought to date from 1787 or later, about the same time as the Kyrie K422a (previously thought to date from 1783).

remarkable: not since his early missa brevis of 1769 had Mozart written a mass in this key.[10] Its sheer verve and, at the same time, its seriousness of purpose recall that this was the period of *Idomeneo*: in a word, this setting towers over all previous Kyries not only in its external dimensions but in its ideas and uniformity of mood. A ternary work, it eschews a strictly thematic treatment of its musical material but flows along in a free and broad river of emotion. Its basic mood is one of profound seriousness of purpose mingled with a feeling of sadness which, with its numerous chromatic features, often comes close to resignation. Equally typical of Mozart is the frequent and unexpected clash between impassioned *forte* outbursts and quietly imploring *piano* passages (especially beautiful in the middle section at the contrast between the Kyrie and the Christe eleison). In general, the sense of passion increases gradually throughout the first half of the piece, culminating in the wildly agitated, dotted unison figures in the strings, before slowly subsiding and finally dying away at the end as though in the remote distance. A particularly fine feature here is the way in which the *da capo* section appeals directly to Christ. The choral writing is essentially homophonic, the orchestral accompaniment as elaborate as it is independent, enhancing the mood in a curious way and immersing the work as a whole in authentically Mozartian melodiousness.

The two vespers settings K321 and 339, by contrast, bring us back to Salzburg, where, as in settings of the mass, concision and brevity were the order of the day. That Mozart was consciously following a long-standing tradition here is clear, not least, from his recourse to the old three-part string orchestra and generally limited instrumental resources.[11] In terms of their overall character, too, these vespers are emphatically more earnest and churchlike in tone than the Masses and, with their stricter contrapuntal procedures, aspire to higher goals, with the result that the operatic features are now far less pronounced. Even here, however, the character of the individual movements was firmly circumscribed by tradition, notably in the case of the contrapuntal treatment of the *Laudate pueri*, the relaxed worldliness of the *Laudate Dominum* and the adagio introduction to the *Magnificat*. This is also the only slow episode in the whole work, every other section being marked 'allegro' – another indication that this type of church music was more concerned with power and brilliance than with inwardness and reverence. As with the Gloria and Credo movements in the masses, the individual movements are cast in the form of free rondos, with certain main ideas alternating with several episodes. Indeed, it is in the varied ways in which this material is combined (a treatment that extends to brief individual motifs, especially in the accompaniment) that one of the principal attractions of these works lies. Conversely, there is virtually no thematic development here. The lesser doxology – the 'Gloria Patri' – that ends each psalm is not set to the same music each time but invariably draws on the motivic material provided by the foregoing psalm, rounding it off in an atmospheric and highly effective manner. It is not hard to imagine the extent to which Mozart was evidently attracted by the challenge of providing a different musical setting of these words on each occasion that they appear.

10. ◆ The dating of this work is similarly uncertain – no autograph or authentic copy survives. Although it is traditionally dated Munich, 1780, possibly it was written later.
11. Apart from the organ (which is used only once as an obbligato instrument), the accompaniment comprises two violins and bass, trumpets and timpani (these only in the *Dixit Dominus* and *Magnificat*) and trombones doubling the chorus. The violas regularly double the bass, whereas the writing for the cello is often independent of the double bass, a feature only very rarely found in earlier works. At one point, Mozart also writes for an ad libitum solo bassoon.

Both settings open with the *Dixit Dominus*, in which the words 'Dixit Dominus Domino meo' are traditionally stressed. In both cases, this is followed by an animated section which, in the first setting, is rather more at pains to explore the meaning of the individual words and involves a livelier interplay between soloists and chorus than the second setting, which, more generalized in tone, introduces the soloists only at the 'Gloria Patri'. In both cases, the choral writing is largely homophonic.

The second psalm, *Confitebor tibi Domine*, is on a particularly elevated spiritual plane in the case of K321, a choral setting in E minor with solo interjections. The sinner's admission of guilt and the idea of divine majesty are interlinked here in an individual and highly poetical manner. While the soprano soloist confesses her guilt in a spirit of noble melancholy, the entry of the chorus brings with it a journey of exploration through a series of dark-toned dissonances, notably at the mysteriously awestruck 'memoriam fecit mirabilium suorum'. The sharply dotted orchestral motif returns almost in the manner of a refrain and on each occasion injects an extra dose of manly dourness into the proceedings. But this time the 'Gloria Patri' steals into the repeat of the opening as though from nowhere, creating a particularly beautiful effect. The second setting achieves nothing like this elevated note at this point, contenting itself, rather, with an expression of solemn strength. At the end the 'Gloria Patri' is cleverly linked to the preceding orchestral interlude.

With the exception of a handful of painterly features and its thoughtful orchestral accompaniment, the third psalm – the *Beatus vir* – has few individual qualities in either setting, but exudes the usual sense of confident joviality in the traditionally colourless and bustling manner. Here, too, the chorus constantly alternates with the soloists,[12] without interrupting the overall sense of forward momentum. The second setting allows rather more scope to contrapuntal procedures than the first.

Just as the 'Pignus' was traditionally the composer's chief opportunity to indulge in strict counterpoint in the litany, so this role was taken in vespers settings by the *Laudate pueri*, and Mozart's setting is no exception, with both movements acquiring a consciously old-fashioned colour. Neither movement, however, is a strict fugue. Instead, Mozart prefers to adopt freer contrapuntal procedures that clearly take account of the text. In K321[13] he begins with a perpetual canon on the expressive theme first stated by the soprano:

The effect is of all the singers converging from every side to join together in praising God. But after a perfect cadence, this image soon changes and a picturesque theme now enters:

---

12. The second setting even includes a long passage of coloratura triplets on the word 'exaltabitur'. On the alternative continuation of this movement from bar 12 onwards (a continuation that Mozart then discarded), see the critical report to NMA I/2/2.
13. This Laudate was first published by Diabelli in Vienna (*c*1830) as an offertory, *Amavit eum Dominus et iusti*.

a so - lis or - tu us - que ad oc - ca - sum

The voices finally combine in a homophonic outcry of joy at the words 'excelsus super omnes gentes', although a feeling of humility also finds expression in the course of the following section, before a further cry, liturgical in character, floats down from the soprano, who is cast in the role of a herald:

quis si - cut Do - mi - nus De - us nos - ter

The view before us broadens to take in God on high:

qui in al - - - tis ha - bi - tat

And the question posed by this movement now fades away on a phrygian cadence to tremendous effect. The following section is accompanied by a trilled motif in the violins inspired by the idea of 'suscitans' in the text. Here the psalmist's 'inopes' and 'pauperes' receive their due reward. The herald's call now strikes up anew, this time in the contralto, and the whole development is repeated, partly expanded and cleverly varied, now homophonic, now imitative in texture, before finally affecting the 'Gloria Patri', too. In turn this section reworks earlier themes in free counterpoint, culminating in a broad coda and ending with a pedal point on the dominant that swells to a mighty *fortissimo*. The result is a movement that would have delighted Mozart's old teacher, Padre Martini, not only on account of the liturgical tenor of its principal ideas but also because of the genuinely vocal part-writing, which is skilfully adapted to the words.

The corresponding movement in K339[14] is even stricter and more elaborate in its procedures but, precisely because of this, it is less eloquent in its motivic writing and less poetical in its expressiveness, a lack for which it compensates with its rather more unified structure. Its principal theme is the traditional fugue subject with an interval of a diminished seventh:

Lau - da - te pu - e - ri Do - mi - num

This subject is first developed along regular lines on its own, before being combined with a simple scalar motif. In the third section, the main theme is heard in counterpoint with its inversion. And in the 'Gloria Patri', finally, theme and inversion appear simultaneously over a tonic pedal:

14. First published by Diabelli in Vienna (*c*1851) as an offertory, *Sancti et iusti*.

Meanwhile a new and shimmering motif enters in the violins. At the end the first two motifs are divided between the vocal lines and accompaniment, where they build to a typically Mozartian climax. A disjointed, chromatically descending 'Amen' follows, and the movement ends on a note of ponderous, almost sombre earnestness. It is planned and executed with the greatest artistic understanding, with homophonic procedures playing only a brief and episodic role, yet the overall impression is one of musical intelligence and hard work rather than of any genuinely poetical exploration of the material.

The fifth movement is a homophonic solo setting of the psalm *Laudate Dominum* and, overtly secular in character, could hardly be in starker contrast to the preceding movements. Indeed, K321 is openly operatic in its melodic writing and coloratura excesses, with an organ obbligato thrown in for good measure. In the case of the second of these vespers settings, by contrast, the movement is a pastoral idyll of the most cloying raptness,[15] simple to a fault and supported by a solo bassoon. At the end the chorus creates a particularly beautiful effect by repeating the whole movement as the 'Gloria Patri'.

The two concluding settings of the *Magnificat* both hark back to their respective opening movements in terms of their tonality, instrumentation and overall mood. They cannot, of course, be compared with the far more elaborate, independent settings of this text, as the greatest brevity was demanded here. And in the second setting, Mozart creates only a generalized genre painting in music. But in the first he manages to invest the *Magnificat*'s traditionally favourite ideas such as the 'humiles, dispersit, fecit potentiam' with the appropriate expression. Indeed, he even goes a stage further before the mention of the 'sanctum nomen eius', ending the previous section on the dissonance *e* flat–*f* sharp–*a*–*c'* with a fermata and then suddenly plunging down into a dark E flat major (*piano* with trombones), as though overcome by the awestruck shudder of religious devotion – one of the most individual passages in this vespers.

Although both these vespers are similar in terms of their overall design and their basic approach to their individual movements, Mozart's attitude to his material is none the less markedly different in each case. It is not, as Jahn assumes,[16] simply the difference between harmony and counterpoint that distinguishes these two works, but rather the fact that, at least in its main movements, the first setting places the music in the service of the poetry, whereas the second uses the poetry only as the starting point for broadly characterized atmospheric portraits of a purely musical kind. But it is precisely this preponderance of the purely musical element that prevents us from placing K339 on the same high level as K321, at least as a sacred work.

Stylistically speaking, the *Regina coeli* in C major K276 may also belong to this period, with both the treatment of the motifs and the interplay between chorus and soloists tending to confirm this

15. Earlier published by Diabelli as a gradual (*c*1851); Rheinberger's vocal score was published in Berlin in 1873; see *AmZ*, new series (1873), 718 and 766.
16. Jahn, *W. A. Mozart*, fourth edition, i.611ff.

dating. It is a single-movement work of a powerful and carefree brilliance only briefly interrupted by the calm and ardent 'Ora pro nobis'. It must remain an open question whether the soprano aria *Kommet her, ihr frechen Sünder* K146, which was evidently intended for insertion in a German sacred oratorio, also dates from 1780.[17] Although not a substantial piece, it is stylistically so advanced that it is impossible to date it as early as 1772.[18] Conversely, the two hymns *O Lamm Gottes* and *Als aus Ägypten* K343 appear to belong to the end of Mozart's Salzburg period, at least if we may judge by their autograph score.[19] Both breathe a sense of great warmth and natural emotion. The three epistle sonatas K328, 329 and 336 resemble their predecessors in being single-movement works, loose in texture and light in character. All three treat the organ as an obbligato instrument, while K329 is additionally scored for two violins, oboes, horns, trumpets, timpani and bass. A novel feature of K336 is the influence of the concerto, with the opening movement resembling the opening allegro of a concerto scored for modest forces and with the solo organ the beneficiary of the composer's particularly lavish attention. Even a free cadenza is demanded of the soloist. But as in K329, the development section is reduced to no more than a few transitional bars.

Common to the three symphonies in G, B flat and C major K318, 319 and 338 is the absence of a minuet, an omission that represents a concession to the prevailing taste in Salzburg.[20] Not until Mozart moved to Vienna did the B flat major symphony acquire its menuetto.[21] Also missing from all three works are repeat signs in their opening allegros. The G major symphony additionally stands apart from the other two inasmuch as it interpolates its slow movement between the development section and foreshortened recapitulation of its fast movement, a procedure that Mozart had got to know in French comic opera overtures, especially those of Grétry. In general, these works are characterized by their marked progress in the direction of the composer's later, grandly symphonic style.[22] Even those passages such as the opening movements of the G and D major symphonies that are still dominated by the festive tone of the Italian overture soon find that tone undermined by more individual features: in the case of the G major work, for example, this is immediately achieved by the intimate consequent of bars 3–5 (a passage reminiscent of similar moments in Cherubini), while in the case of the D major symphony it is replaced by an energetic march tune that finally – and suddenly – modulates to the minor in a surprisingly Romantic way. The second subjects, too, reveal far greater depth. The tendency to write cantabile themes that distinguishes Mozart from Haydn had been evident, of course, from an early date, but now these songlike melodies acquire a more personal character, often breaking through the traditional periodic structures and exploring every last recess of the underlying emotion and, as a result,

---

17. See Wyzewa and Saint-Foix, *Wolfgang Amédée Mozart*, ii.408. ◆ The dating of *Kommet her* is uncertain; the earliest surviving source (Mozart's autograph does not survive) was copied in the mid- or late 1770s.
18. Thus Jahn's dating, *W. A. Mozart*, fourth edition, i.68.
19. ◆ It is more likely that the two hymns K343 date from the late 1780s: they were first published in Prague in 1788, and earlier, in May 1787, Mozart wrote to Gottfried von Jacquin that he was sending him a 'church song' (*Briefe*, iv.48).
20. ◆ It is not true that symphonies in Salzburg generally had three movements. On the contrary, four-movement symphonies are slightly more common: of Michael Haydn's sixteen symphonies composed there during the 1760s and 1770s, nine are in four movements; and of Mozart's twenty-three Salzburg symphonies of the 1770s, thirteen are in four movements. It was normal practice, too, for three-movement symphonies to conclude with a minuet and trio rather than an allegro, as later became the norm.
21. This is clear not only from the handwriting but also from the fact that it is written on a separate sheet of paper inserted into the autograph. Mozart also began a menuetto for the C major symphony but on this occasion failed to complete it. ◆ Paper studies suggest the menuetto of K319 was added some time between 1783 and 1785.
22. See Schultz, *Mozarts Jugendsinfonien*, 77ff., and Kretzschmar, *Führer durch den Konzertsaal*, fourth edition, i.173ff.

becoming the central idea of the whole movement, as in the opening allegro of K338, where the second subject-group is more than twice as long as the first. Indeed, the move towards greater *cantabilità* is so powerful in this series of works that even the new ideas that – as in the earlier pieces appear in the development sections – are largely songlike in character. Likewise, the transitional groups are generally more individual and better integrated into the underlying mood, and even the development sections, however free and untypical of Haydn they may be, are no longer content to grant untrammelled sway to the composer's freely ranging imagination but attempt to bring a sense of order to a world that is admittedly only loosely related to the rest of the work, an aim achieved more especially by means of stricter procedures, with double counterpoint playing an increasing role here. In terms of the structure, design and especially the instrumentation of these works, the impressions left by Mannheim are still clearly fresh in Mozart's mind: note, in particular, the more frequent use of crescendo transitions in place of the earlier sudden alternation between tutti and concertino. The winds, meanwhile, not only enjoy complete thematic freedom but – in keeping with the Mannheim model – they also enter into an entirely new relationship with the strings.

The B flat major symphony, which follows its heroic and emotionally charged predecessor by a matter of only a few months, reveals that, in spite of the slavery of his Salzburg years, Mozart none the less knew serenity and contentment. It is one of the composer's most amiable compositions, its first movement an idyllic miniature genre painting, now roguish, now raptly effusive, now lit by little Romantic half-lights, and not even the unexpected spirit of the liturgy that slips into the development section from the Credo of the F major mass succeeds in disturbing the sense of contented activity. The andante, too, finds it hard to break free from this idyll,[23] and it is not until the menuetto, the remarkably intelligent instrumentation of which is in itself sufficient to mark it out as a product of the later period, that Mozart strikes a more vigorous and, occasionally, even darker note. Its trio is based on an oboe melody from the second section of the first subject-group.[24] The final movement gives unbridled expression to a very real sense of delight in existence, the main vehicle of this delight being an effervescent and fiery triplet motif that darts through the whole of the orchestra, appearing now as the main idea, now as a mere accompaniment. The movement as a whole resembles nothing so much as a delightfully animated funfair attended by the most varied types, from nobility to commoners. Finally even a band of village musicians turns up with the old *Bettlertrio* of oboes and bassoons:

The principal charm of this movement lies in the large number and lively interplay of its individual images and in the intelligent way in which they are introduced. Take the first subsidiary idea, for example: although it follows on from what has gone before, it none the less introduces an element of surprise by modulating to G minor. But here, too, Mozart feels the need for an injection of *cantabilità*, which takes the form of a new motif in the development section:

23. Its second subject is an example of one of Mozart's favourite melodic ideas, an idea borrowed from Paisiello and later used in the clarinet trio K498.
24. The same melody returns, rhythmically altered, in Schubert's Impromptu in A flat major op. 90/4.

This then becomes what is effectively the second main theme of the movement as a whole. It is developed sequentially in the old Schobertian manner but avoids the earlier capriciousness by dint of its stricter contrapuntal treatment.

As we have already noted when discussing its first subject, the C major symphony contains an especially large number of Romantic features that repeatedly impede the powerful sense of forward momentum inherent in its main theme. Among these features in the opening movement are the broadly flowing cantabile theme; the final subject-group, which again vacillates between minor and major and interpolates three calmly contemplative bars for the strings in the midst of a noisy tutti; and, finally, the development section which, after an imperious opening, is suddenly – as though by magic – forced in the direction of the mysteriously whispering section in A flat major. There follows a deeply eloquent dialogue between strings and winds that ends on a note of whispered bemusement, at which point the recapitulation enters with typically Mozartian abruptness. Not even this development section is thematic, of course, but introduces a particularly large number of new ideas, while still holding the listener's attention by dint of its careful structure. All three allegros end with a coda derived from the main idea, a tendency already found in Mozart's earlier works but now reinforced by his exposure to the overtures of French comic operas. The andante of the C major symphony is the first to add more manly features to the Arcadian idyll that is usually found here and is strikingly modern in other ways, too, not least in its treatment of the strings, which resemble nothing so much as a string quartet, and in the remarkable way in which the most varied moods are interwoven, allowing the work's underlying Romanticism to find particularly clear expression. This wonderful movement ends with a coda which, for all its simplicity, is eloquent in the extreme. The final movement, too, includes Romantic features, above all in its development section which on this occasion is at least loosely connected to the main theme and which leads the listener through all manner of different moods, some of them idyllic, others strangely agitated. Generally, however, the movement is dominated by a vigorous sense of richly animated life, the effect of which is considerably enhanced by the meaningful interplay between concertante winds and strings. The subsidiary themes, too, are particularly felicitous and fiery in tone, clearly owing much to Grétry's influence, so that the movement as a whole creates a delightful impression in spite of elements of the older Italian style which, even here, still dare to put in an occasional appearance.

The concerto in E flat major for two keyboards K365 places considerably greater technical demands on its performers than the earlier triple concerto, suggesting that Mozart wrote it not for his pupils but for himself and his sister. At all events, the two soloists go their own way, harmoniously and contentedly, as did Mozart and his sister: they engage in lively debate on the subject of the same themes, repeating each other's ideas, varying them, interrupting each other and occasionally indulging in a certain disputatious teasing, but without their basic amity being disturbed by any serious differences of opinion. In spite of an occasionally free approach to matters of musical form, including the opening movement's wittily varied recapitulation, the work as a whole proceeds along clear and well-structured lines. Its basic character is one of impetuous joviality rising to mischievous good humour in the final rondo, not least as a result of Mozart's use of a folksong already heard in his earlier divertimento K252. In its treatment and dynamics the orchestra reveals the influence of the Mannheim school and, in keeping with its French model,[25] it is overshadowed by the soloists, even though the sustained chords in the winds introduce a new and highly effective element into the work.[26]

Even more inspired is the sinfonia concertante in E flat major for violin and viola K364, with the broadly structured, symphonic tutti of its opening movement already revealing that proud but dark-toned splendour so often found in Mozart's emotionally charged allegros in E flat major. As in the opening tutti of the final movement, the monumental solidity of this block of orchestral sound is reinforced by the curious insistence on sticking so rigidly to the home key: even the second subject is introduced by the winds in E flat major. To the accompaniment of an imperious trilled motif, the musical argument moves via a powerful crescendo based on a pedal point typical of the Mannheim school towards an outburst of defiant passion, but after four bars it sinks back on a typically Mozartian note of resignation involving syncopations and chromaticisms, thereby preparing the way for the more friendly approach of the two soloists, who now break into this final subject-group. But the orchestra's defiant attitude is in no way broken by this. There is no real sense of concertante writing anywhere in this work, at least in the sense that Carl Philipp Emanuel Bach would have understood that term (the soloists are far too dominant for this), but each of the orchestra's independent interventions invariably adopts the old impassioned tone. With their note of entreaty and challenge, the solo themes, too, are under considerable emotional pressure. (Their large number and the broad manner in which they are developed both recall the symphonies of this period.) In the development section the orchestra responds to a new imprecatory theme from the soloists with its old trilled motif and in the end evidently feels in a sufficiently mellow mood to add its old second subject to their virtuosic goings-on, resulting in a genuine dialogue of a concertante kind. Conversely, of course, the orchestral tutti is considerably curtailed at the reca-pitulation, and it is only with difficulty that the orchestra manages to reintroduce at least its second subject into the proceedings, only to make up for lost ground following the figurative cadenza (which is written out in full) and ending the movement with a gruff and imperious outburst. The same relationship between soli and tutti dominates the andante, the only difference being that the sense of inner ardour now finds more muted and subdued expression. Some of the tutti themes such as the portentous third theme with its syncopations in the first violins clearly hark back to corresponding ideas in the opening movement. And in both movements the recapit-ulation is used to build to an impressive climax. The result is a middle movement that is one of the most substantial of its kind among Mozart's works to date. The spell is broken by the final movement and by its commonplace theme, a theme familiar to all listeners at this time. The spirits of darkness have vanished, but the earlier strength remains, allowing this movement to scurry along in a mood of self-conscious joviality. The two solo instruments are treated in more or less the same way as the two keyboards were treated in K365. In a word, they engage in peaceful rivalry, with one and the selfsame melody sometimes divided between the two different instruments. Yet, when set alongside Mozart's other concertos from this period, the work as a whole remains one of his most significant achievements.

25. This suggests that the work was written soon after his return; see Wyzewa and Saint-Foix, *Wolfgang Amédée Mozart*, ii.407. In his letter of 27 June 1781, we find Mozart writing from Vienna and asking his father to send him 'the sonata in B flat for 4 hands and the 2 concertos for 2 keyboards' (*Briefe*, iii.135). In his letter of 24 November 1781 he reports that he has performed the concerto 'à Due' at a concert with Josepha Auernhammer (*Briefe*, iii.176). This accords with the fact that parts for two clarinets were added on a separate sheet of paper for the performance in Vienna. The second concerto mentioned here is undoubtedly the one originally scored for three instruments and later transcribed for two [K242].
26. The final movement also contains a number of striking pre-echoes of *Die Zauberflöte*.

The two brief rondos for horn (K371) and violin (K373) are clear and straightforward and require no special comment.

A number of the serenades of this period are also outright successes, with even the first of them – K320 in D major – proving a worthy and witty addition to the genre.[27] Its two outer movements are thoroughly symphonic in stamp. The first – in which the slow introduction is repeated during the recapitulation in the allegro – is notable for an obstinate dotted rhythm that time and again brutally interrupts the second subject's burgeoning cantilena, while the latter is remarkable for a lengthy development section that is as witty as it is lively and which, on this occasion, sticks to the given themes in a manner reminiscent of Haydn. The andante of the 'Concertante' (the concertante instruments are pairs of flutes, oboes and bassoons) is an entrancing slow dance to the festive rhythm familiar from *Don Giovanni*: ♩ ♫♫ ♩ | ♩ ♩ 𝄽 Meanwhile, the six solo voices whisper, enthuse and languish. A far more serious note is struck by the andantino in D minor, which puts a peremptory stop to the delightful goings-on of the concertante. Here the mood is clearly reminiscent of the middle movement of K364, except that here there is a greater feeling of intimacy. The extent to which Mozart refined traditional figurations by introducing chromatic elements may be illustrated by means of the following passage from this same movement:

A sense of valediction hangs over this movement, a mood also indicated by the post horn in the second trio from the following menuetto: perhaps the work as a whole was intended for someone who, in Mozart's eyes, was lucky enough to be leaving Salzburg.

Even more colourful is the great wind serenade in B flat major K361.[28] It, too, begins with a substantial largo introduction that generates a real sense of tension, adopting the Haydnesque model that Mozart was to take up only hesitatingly in his symphonies. Both within the subject-group itself and, later, in the development section and, finally, in the coda, the vigorous, if abruptly curtailed, allegro theme gives rise to the most varied combinations, all of which throw the brightest possible light on Mozart's fertile imagination and his feeling for sonority. But the high point of the whole is the third movement, the adagio. Even its very first bar, in which the following bass figure seems to be conjured up out of the depths, points far into the future. This mysterious motif stalks through the bass line in quavers, almost uninterruptedly, accompanied in the inner voices by a rhythm that Mozart also used in later slow movements to represent dull, yet excited

27. In the autograph score, the flautino part has been left blank in the first trio: perhaps the player was intended to improvise it. One of the two marches in D major K335 presumably also belongs with this serenade. ◆ It is likely, in fact, that both belong to K320: traditionally marches were attached to serenades as both processionals and recessionals.
28. ◆ The dating of this work, traditionally assigned to 1781, is problematic. Although the bulk of the autograph is written on paper used by Mozart in that year, at least part is on paper from 1783 or 1784. The only documented performance of the work, by Anton Stadler at his Burgtheater concert on 23 March 1784, apparently confirms the serenade's later date.

agitation: ♩♪ ♪.♩♪ ♪.♪ Above it there soars – divided among various soloists – a cantabile line of indescribable depth of feeling and of magically beautiful sonority, woven together from yearning, rapt infatuation and tender melancholy, a melody of a kind heard in no previous serenade. That more serious and loftier thoughts may be found behind the work's cheerful innocence is clear not only from the introduction and from a number of gloomy passages in the opening movement but also from the first trio of the menuetto, with its dark and brooding gestures.[29] Romantic features are also found in the two movements that were added later: in the fifth, they may be heard in the combination of a slow and tender, half-whispered romance with a whimsical allegretto in the minor, in which the bassoons in particular develop a comical semiquaver figuration, while in the sixth they occur in the anguished fourth variation and in the whispered fairy tale of the fifth. (The sixth variation resembles nothing so much as an attempt to make good the lack of a menuetto.) By contrast, the final rondo is a carefree envoi of the older Mozartian type. The interplay between the various instruments could hardly be freer, and the part-writing is so independent that it is often no longer possible to speak of any distinction between leading instruments and accompanying ones. With wonderful assurance Mozart coaxes from each the best and most characterful sonorities, and it is precisely because of this that pieces such as this have again found such a sympathetic response in an age that is especially alive to the subtleties of instrumental colour. For Mozart, however, sensually beautiful sound was less important *per se* than the self-evident form in which he chose to depict the underlying artistic idea and the way in which it is developed.

The divertimento in D major K334 follows on naturally from K287 in B flat major in terms of both the forces for which it is scored and its overall design.[30] Indeed, it may even have been intended for the same performers, as the first violin part is markedly virtuosic in both works. Mozart's aforementioned tendency to maintain the character of a serenade in the two outer movements,[31] but to give expression to all manner of private emotions between them, is particularly evident here. The D minor variations on a sombre, semi-exotic theme,[32] with typically Mozartian syncopated outburst in the fourth bar, could hardly be further removed from the world of the serenade. Here, rather, is an example of funeral music that breathes a spirit of almost literally hopeless resignation, its D minor implacably fixed from the very first statement of its theme. Not even the variation in the major can break the spell but merely makes it seem more oppressive than ever, while the sixth variation brings with it a further nuance in the form of the wildly fantastical. In terms of their stolid earnestness, these variations surpass all their predecessors and may well reflect some of the sense of bitter renunciation that typified this period in Mozart's life. Once conjured into existence, this sense of renunciation affects the other middle movements, too, with even the menuetto including a sudden such outburst in the second section of its first subject-group – and this in spite of the fact that it is filled with a sense of French grace, its gently rocking melody stated by the first violin and viola in octaves and accompanied by guitar-like chords in the second violin in the manner of a genuine serenade. But the second menuetto not only has two trios in the minor

---

29. Its principal idea is an inversion of the theme of the Credo from the F major mass.
30. ◆ In the absence of an autograph, authentic copy or any documentary evidence concerning K334, its dating, and even its authorship, is uncertain (although on stylistic grounds it is likely to date from Mozart's last years in Salzburg, 1779 or 1780).
31. One of the subsidiary ideas in the final rondo is the same as the new idea that occurs in the development section of the opening movement of the B flat major symphony.
32. The counterpart to this is the set of variations in D minor in the violin sonata in F major K377, the second variation of which is even motivically related to the first variation from the present divertimento.

(with its intervals of a seventh, the first is particularly eerie in tone), its first subject-group also includes a number of darker elements, notably in the utterly inspired augmentation of the main theme at its second appearance; and it is significant that in most of these passages it is the key of D minor – the key most often associated with fate in Mozart's works – that repeatedly demands its due from the bright D major.[33]

The oboe quartet K370 is also serenade-like in character, a character only briefly abandoned by the serious tone of its middle movement, which is again in D minor. In the opening movement, the listener will be struck by the richly varied recapitulation, while the final rondo, with its markedly Gallic theme, is notable above all for the surprising and humorous way in which the main theme is repeatedly reintroduced.

There are passages in the keyboard sonata in B flat major K333 that reveal a quite remarkable interiority which, in the development sections of the first two movements, assumes a particularly impassioned tone, before pulling itself together for the final movement and strolling along in a spirit of carefree joviality (note the seventh-based exclamation of delight).[34] But this finale is also important as a further stage on the road to Mozart's later rondos in the manner of Carl Philipp Emanuel Bach: here Mozart is no longer satisfied with a loosely structured interplay between a main theme and several episodes, but examines the theme itself from different aspects, shedding new light on it and also varying the secondary motifs, while at the same time singling out what had originally been subsidiary or transitional elements and suddenly turning them into the heroes of the hour. In a word, the form as a whole is unified and spiritualized. Indeed, we even find a cadenza that invests one of these subsidiary motifs with positively heroic stature. In earlier works, of course, we already find signs of this new approach, with the final movements of the contemporary divertimentos, in particular, affording analogous examples.

The relatively virtuosic violin sonata in B flat major K378 still follows older models, with its opening movement's development section containing entirely new ideas and including a passionate outpouring of Schobertian sequencing. This movement is also notable for its large number of themes (including what might be described as two second subjects), all of which are developed at leisurely length.[35] The high point of the piece is its thoughtful E flat major andantino, in the third section of which the first part of the main theme is brilliantly juxtaposed with the second part of its second subject, before the movement's two main moods fade away, as though in a rose-pink twilight, in a wonderful coda of authentically Mozartian poetry.[36]

It is clear from the three solo scenes for soprano K368, 369 and 374, and especially from the freedom with which Mozart approaches the problem of their musical form, that all three were written in the shadow of *Idomeneo*. The first two combine a slow section with a fast one. (In the case of the first aria, these sections are then repeated.) Typical of both, moreover, is the way in which the words of the slow section are repeated in the allegros, but to different music. The first is an outright bravura aria, whereas the second proves more ambitious from the very outset. The third is a simple but charming rondo placed in the mouth of a character called Zeïra, with leisurely

33. It must remain an open question whether the march K445 belongs with this divertimento; see Wyzewa and Saint-Foix, *Wolfgang Amédée Mozart*, ii.407.

34. ◆ Although K333 is traditionally thought to pre-date Mozart's time in Vienna – and possibly to have been written as early as Paris, 1778 – recent studies show it was probably composed in Linz or Vienna in late 1783 (perhaps during Mozart and Constanze's return trip to Vienna from their visit to Salzburg).

35. Arnold Schering was the first to point out the similarity between the continuation of the second subject of the present piece and one of the ideas in a violin concerto by Johann Christian Bach; see Schering, *Geschichte des Instrumentalkonzerts*, 161.

36. The unfinished allegro K372 that was later completed by Stadler in a sophisticated but barely Mozartian manner has nothing special to offer us.

ritornellos[37] and a concluding refrain that returns again and again. In general, the work clearly recalls the French *opéras comiques* of the period.[38]

Mozart's lieder also reveal considerable progress. Although he retains the strophic principle throughout and although the addition of a mandolin in both *Komm, liebe Zither* K351 and *Die Zufriedenheit* K349[39] puts one in mind of purely popular songs of a social kind, these two songs,[40] for all that they are superficially extremely modest, none the less reveal Mozart's mastery in terms not only of their structure but also of their freedom from all convention. Each, moreover, has its own distinctive physiognomy. Although both seem fairly similar at first sight, *Die Zufriedenheit* breathes the same spirit of a heartfelt love of nature as the famous *Komm, lieber Mai* K596, while *Komm, liebe Zither* already reveals the seductive sensuality of Don Giovanni's mandolin-accompanied serenade. A completely different spirit informs the three songs *Ich würd' auf meinem Pfad* K390, *Sei du mein Trost* K391 and *Verdankt sei es dem Glanz* K392 from Johann Timotheus Hermes's novel *Sophiens Reise*. The most substantial of the three is the first, which, significantly, is again in D minor; for all its succinctness, it goes far beyond its excessively self-satisfied text to produce a picture of the deepest emotional conflict ranging from mute anguish to a wild railing at fate. How much space would a later composer have required, instead of the thirteen bars of Mozart's setting? Mozart achieves his aim simply by means of a melodic line[41] that faithfully reflects each change in the underlying mood and by dint of harmonic writing that remains firmly and characteristically wedded to its minor tonality, revealing a boldness unique in the lieder of this period. The second song, too, is full of personal touches, not least of which is its opening, which slips gently into the key of B flat major and in this way already looks forward to Schubert. The third song is characterized by the note of self-assurance with which the composer here treats the relationship between high and low; this, too, is quintessentially Mozartian.

37. The first of them already includes a brief canonic passage that is later heard in the first-act finale of *Die Zauberflöte* at the words 'und er lebte ohne sie in der besten Harmonie'.

38. The main theme is ultimately derived from the oboe melody of 'Che puro ciel' in Gluck's *Orfeo ed Euridice* and later reappears in the andante of the 'Jupiter' symphony.

39. According to Nottebohm, *Mozartiana*, 130, the keyboard arrangement of this song is not fully authenticated, but Deiters in his revised edition of Jahn (ii.72) is almost certainly right to attribute it to Mozart on the strength of the changes to the vocal line. ◆ The dating of both these works is speculative although they are likely to have been written in Munich in 1780. The intended accompaniment, however, is not clear; there are no autograph or early, authentic sources for these works.

40. The lullaby *Schlafe, mein Prinzchen* K350 (K[6] Anh. C8.48) was first published by Nissen in the appendix to his *Biographie W. A. Mozarts*, facing p. 20. In 1826 Nissen told André that, in the view of experts, the song was worthy of Mozart, even though the composer's sister could not recall her brother having written such a piece. Significantly, Nissen did not appeal to Constanze's testimony. In his critical commentary, Nottebohm draws attention to a number of flagrant violations in terms of word-setting and part-writing in Nissen's version of the work, violations that Mozart would never have allowed himself. Since then, doubts about its authenticity have repeatedly been voiced, notably by Jahn, Köchel, Deiters and Friedlaender, who first drew attention to the fact that it is a setting of a poem by Friedrich Wilhelm Gotter; see 'Mozarts Wiegenlied'. Conversely, Engl, 'Über die Lieder W. A. Mozarts und die Echtheit des Wiegenliedes: Schlafe mein Prinzchen, schlaf ein', insisted on Mozart's authorship. Shortly afterwards, Friedlaender was able to show that the song was written by Bernhard Flies and published under his name in 1795/6; see Friedlaender, 'Mozarts Wiegenlied'. The situation has now been complicated by the recent discovery of Constanze's diary (currently in the present writer's possession), which includes the following entry dated 27 September 1828: 'to Dr. F[euerstein], enclosing another work by my Mozart instead of the Lullaby'; see Bücken, 'Tagebuch der Gattin Mozarts'. In response to this revelation, Engl again came out in support of the song's authenticity: 'W. A. Mozarts Wiegenlied und Konstanzes Tagebuch'. Even so, the attribution remains doubtful, as Constanze is a far from reliable source on questions of authenticity. And if she intended to replace the song by another work by Mozart, does this in itself not suggest that she harboured doubts about its authenticity? Ultimately, however, it is the style of the song that causes the greatest misgivings: such a schematic division into exactly equal two-bar periods is found in no other song by the composer – even his simplest songs are more concerned with variety and personal features than this (see K349 and 351, for example). The present lullaby is the work of a talented musician, but not of a composer of genius, and if Mozart really is its composer, it must be one of his occasional compositions dashed off in a hurry. The melisma in the penultimate bar is not Mozartian but belongs to what was common currency in the lieder of this period.

41. If one examines the four strophes from the standpoint of their word-setting and mood, it appears that it was probably the last that inspired the melody of the work as a whole.

25

König Thamos *and* Zaide

Mozart's music for Gebler's *Thamos, König in Egypten* is his first and only contribution to the genre of incidental music, a genre whose origins can be traced back to the Middle Ages but which was later largely displaced by opera, before enjoying a revival in the second half of the eighteenth century, at the very time when the melodrama was beginning to find acceptance. It is significant that it was in France that this type of music was most widely cultivated.[1] In Germany, Johann Adolph Scheibe was the first to recall its existence – in practical terms in his incidental music to Corneille's *Polyeucte* and Racine's *Mithridate* (written for the Theater der Neuberin in 1738) and as a theorist in the sixty-seventh issue of his *Critischer Musikus*. Here we learn that the opening sinfonia should pave the way not only for the drama as a whole but also for the first scene; by the same token the entr'actes should not only round off the previous act but should also provide a transition to the mood of the following act; the concluding symphony, finally, should reinforce the impression left by the ending of the drama. Scheibe even offers special hints on the choice of instruments. His example was followed by Christian Gotthelf Scheinpflug with his incidental music to Racine's *Mithridate* (1754), by Johann Christian Hertel with his music to Cronegk's *Olint, Olint und Sophronia* and other plays and, finally, by Johann Friedrich Agricola, whose incidental music to Voltaire's *Sémiramis* inspired Lessing's theory of entr'acte music.[2] Here Lessing appeals explicitly to Scheibe, but whereas Scheibe had argued that the entr'acte should look both backwards and forwards, Lessing felt that its function should be limited to rounding off the previous act. In south Germany, Michael Haydn wrote incidental music for a production of Voltaire's *Zaïre* in Salzburg in 1777, and according to Leopold Mozart's extremely favourable account,[3] it was more in the spirit of Scheibe than of Lessing. Two years later the Abbé Vogler's incidental music to *Hamlet* was heard in Mannheim.[4] These endeavours were evidently encouraged by the entr'actes that were regularly found in French comic operas and which, as we saw above, attempted to solve this whole question in a whole variety of different ways.

Mozart's decision to set the two choruses from *Thamos* in 1773[5] was not merely his first timid attempt to conquer a new field of compositional endeavour, it was also his first artistic encounter with the Masonic ideas that were later to be so important for his whole future development as a

---

1. ◆ See Howard Mayer Brown, *Music in the French Secular Theatre, 1400–1550*; for incidental music in England, see Price, *Music in the Restoration Theatre*.
2. See Lessing, *Hamburgische Dramaturgie* i, nos 26–7. On the whole question, see Hanslick, *Suite: Aufsätze über Musik und Musiker*, 100–123. ◆ Christian Gotthelf Scheinpflug (1722–70) was Kapellmeister at Rudolstadt, in Thuringia. Johann Christian Hertel (1697–1754) was Konzertmeister at Eisenach from 1733 to 1741 and thereafter at the Mecklenburg-Strelitz court; in 1767 he also composed incidental music for German adaptations, by C. F. Weiße, of Shakespeare's *Richard III* and *Romeo and Juliet*. Johann Friedrich Agricola (1720–74) was a pupil of J. S. Bach; his music to *Semiramis* is lost.
3. *Briefe*, ii.25 and 36 (letters of 30 September and 6 October 1777).
4. Vogler, *Betrachtungen der Mannheimer Tonschule*, i.253ff. and 313ff.
5. ◆ The dating of the complex of manuscripts by Mozart relating to *Thamos* is uncertain, although it is likely the choruses were set in 1773; see Tyson, *Mozart: Studies of the Autograph Scores*, 241–51.

composer, for Gebler's drama – like Wieland's fairy tale, *Dschinnistan* – is heavily influenced by Jean Terrasson's Masonic novel *Séthos* that was first published in Paris in 1731.[6] (We shall return to both Gebler and Wieland in the context of *Die Zauberflöte*.) The plot of *Thamos* may be summarized as follows:

Menes, the king of Egypt, has been overthrown by Rameses in an insurrection in which he is universally believed to have been killed. But in fact he has taken the name of Sethos and is now working as high priest in the Temple of the Sun at Heliopolis. Here he rules wisely, retaining the love both of his daughter Tharsis who, ignorant of her father's identity, has likewise grown up under an assumed name, and of Rameses's son, Thamos. Following Rameses' death, Sethos–Menes voluntarily declines to accept the throne, preferring to let Thamos rule in his place. But Thamos's confidant, Prince Pheron, who loves Tharsis and who hopes that by marrying her he will be able to ascend the Egyptian throne, instigates a conspiracy against Thamos in which he is supported by the guardian of the Virgins of the Sun, the wild-eyed Mirza. Mirza manages to persuade Tharsis to renounce her love of Thamos, while the latter, ignoring every warning, continues to place his trust in Pheron. After numerous intrigues, Sethos enlightens the lovers. Pheron attempts to get his way by force of arms, whereupon Menes intervenes and reveals his true identity. Pheron is disarmed, and Thamos and Tharsis are reunited and restored to the throne. Mirza stabs herself, while Pheron is struck down by lightning for blaspheming God.

The absence of an overture is evidently attributable to the fact that the piece begins with a large-scale choral movement.[7] Of the entr'acte music, some of the pieces reflect Lessing's demand that they should merely pick up the ending of the previous act, while others are inspired by Scheibe's belief that they should provide a link between the two acts. Brief headings explain the contents of each of the individual numbers,[8] with the first of them, for example, introduced with the words: 'The first act ends with Pheron's and Mirza's decision to place Pheron on the throne.' Mirza ends with the words 'Mirza is a woman and does not tremble. You are a man: rule or die!' At this point the orchestra enters with three solemn chords, the solemnity of which is enhanced by rests, after which there begins a regular one-movement sinfonia, an allegro in C minor. In terms of the characterization of this and most of the following numbers, it has to be said at the outset that eighteenth-century programme music had far more modest aims than its nineteenth-century equivalent, which was concerned, rather, with lovingly detailed descriptions. Above all, it was far less inclined to depart from traditional forms in order to provide a faithful depiction of the underlying programme. Mozart's first entr'acte, accordingly, is in sonata form, with subject-group, development section, recapitulation and coda and, without being in any way exceptional, none the less manages to conjure up an appropriately atmospheric portrait by typically Mozartian means.

The programme of the second entr'acte is even more general in tone: 'Thamos's good character is revealed at the end of the second act. The third act begins with Thamos and the traitor Pheron.' Here, too, Mozart responds with a ternary symphonic movement, the only difference being that, following acknowledged practice, the first subject does not return until the very end, in the coda. But on this occasion, the themes are adapted to suit the two characters and are headed accordingly:

6. See Junk, *Goethes Fortsetzung der Mozartschen Zauberflöte*, and Komorzynski, *Emanuel Schikaneder: Ein Beitrag zur Geschichte des deutschen Theaters*, 118ff. In 1784 Gebler was Grand Master of the District Grand Lodge of the New Brotherhood; see Lewis, *Geschichte der Freimaurerei in Österreich*, 162, and Werner, *Aus dem Josephinischen Wien*, 119 and 157.
7. Whether the G major symphony K318 was intended as the overture to *Thamos*, as Jahn suggests, is highly questionable; see Jahn, *W. A. Mozart*, fourth edition, i.618. ◆ Zaslaw, *Mozart's Symphonies*, 344, also finds the association questionable.
8. Although some of the headings in the autograph score were added by Leopold, they undoubtedly reflect Mozart's own intentions, as Jahn has shown; see Jahn, 'Mozart-Paralipomenon', 173.

Here, too, we are dealing with very general contrasts depicted by means of traditional symphonic form, albeit contrasts expressed with sufficient clarity to satisfy contemporary listeners.[9]

The third entr'acte is far more specific. Here the heading begins with the words 'The third act ends with the conspiratorial exchange between Mirza and Pheron'. A wildly agitated G minor movement based on a typically Mozartian rhythm expressive of defiance races past at uncanny speed, after which the curtain rises on the fourth act with a melodrama for Tharsis (Sais). Even though Mozart gives only individual cues, there can be no doubt that the whole piece was performed as a melodrama. As such, it constitutes the first fruits of Mozart's encounter with the work of Georg Benda, inasmuch as it, too, is a large-scale monologue. The only unusual feature here is that there are none of the usual breaks in the music to allow the text to be declaimed. Instead, the piece flows along uninterruptedly from start to finish, with only the uniform tonality and the modulation to the dominant in the middle recalling the older procedure. Right at the end, the music of the opening is repeated – another feature modelled on Benda.[10] As a result, the music is particularly self-serving in this first of Mozart's attempts to write a melodrama; in *Zaide* he follows Benda more closely and adopts a much more measured approach, with the music not only accompanying the declamation of the text but also being interrupted by it.

The fourth entr'acte is a violent description of the 'general confusion' that reigns at the end of the previous act. Suddenly a solemn, dignified second subject enters. Constantly repeated, it dominates the development section, too, before finally propelling the D minor section of the recapitulation towards a radiant D major. It is Thamos himself who confronts the conspirators here and

9. Note the way in which Pheron is characterized here by harmonic and dynamic means (cf. the *sforzato* syncopations in the bassoons), while Thamos is characterized by melodic means, including a guitar-like accompaniment in the violins.
10. In place of the opening allegretto, Mozart originally wrote an andantino that is markedly French in influence, but which he later discarded – and with good reason – as too frivolous in tone.

in that way becomes the real hero of this number. A listener familiar with the drama would not have been in any doubt on this point either, so that in this way the number served its purpose.[11]

The final number is said to depict 'Pheron's despair, blasphemy and death', with an accompanying thunderstorm that begins only once the number has already started. Compared with its French models, this *orage* is a distinctly low-key affair, but, even while depicting the storm itself, Mozart takes care not to overlook the blasphemous figure of Pheron, whose diabolical nature is clearly laid bare in a remarkable unison motif:

At the end he falls to the ground to an imposing scalar figure,[12] with the result that Mozart makes no attempt to depict the gradual abatement of the storm, a description otherwise very popular at this period.[13]

If we step back for a moment and take a more general view of Mozart's first attempt to write programme music under the joint influence of the melodrama and the impressions gleaned in Paris, we note a tendency on his part to vacillate: in the first, second and fourth entr'actes he attempts to grapple with the programme by means of existing musical forms, whereas in the third entr'acte and in the final number it is to his credit that he prefers a much freer approach. On the whole, this was also the approach adopted by the composers of dramatic ballets at this time, composers who, in turn, had a profound influence on the melodrama. It is striking that Mozart was most successful in the two freer movements, in which the dramatic situation was such that his imagination was fired and all formal considerations were thrown to the four winds. The subject matter of the remaining numbers was far less suited to such personal involvement, and Jahn was quite right to observe that the drama was largely to blame for this.[14] Gebler's play dates from a period when the Viennese theatre was still under French influence, and its only novel element – its Masonic garb – was only too well suited to favouring the didactic at the expense of the dramatic. The fact that the play none the less proved a notable success[15] merely shows that, Lessing's pioneering work notwithstanding, French taste continued to dominate German literature at this time.

It was no doubt his Masonic aspirations, coupled with French influence and in particular that of Racine, that persuaded Gebler to add choruses to his play. Significantly, the scenes in question are two involving sacrifices and attended by large-scale hymns, the first of which occurs at the very

11. Jahn, too, recognizes this, of course, but not without adding a number of not entirely intelligible remarks inspired by his antipathy to programme music; see Jahn, *W. A. Mozart*, i.623.

12. Jommelli uses an identical figure to describe the deaths of both Phaethon and Clymene in *Fetonte*; see Abert, *Niccolò Jommelli: Fetonte*, 289 and 301.

13. All these numbers are scored for the usual Salzburg forces: four-part strings, oboes, horns and bassoons, with trumpets and timpani in the first, fourth and fifth interludes.

14. Jahn, *W. A. Mozart*, fourth edition, i.624.

15. When Gebler sent him a copy of the first act, Wieland had nothing but praise for it; see Wieland, *Auswahl denkwürdiger Briefe*, ii.14ff. Likewise he expressed his lively approval for the finished drama; *Auswahl denkwürdiger Briefe*, ii.26–7. Soon afterwards, however, we find him wanting to change the ending and complaining that the virtuous characters are idealized and the depraved ones demonized; see *Auswahl denkwürdiger Briefe*, ii.27–8. Ramler, Sulzer and Thümmel, too, spoke appreciatively of *König Thamos*; see Schlegel, *Deutsches Museum* iv.139–40, 153 and 159. It was immediately translated into French: see Wieland, *Auswahl denkwürdiger Briefe*, ii.30, and Werner, *Aus dem Josephinischen Wien*, 136. In 1780 an Italian translation was prepared by Colloredo's private secretary, Johann Ludwig von Berghoff. A copy of this translation in a de luxe binding that presumably reached Colloredo is included with Mozart's score. Evidently the composer thought of underlaying the music of his choruses with this Italian translation.

beginning and, sung by Priests and Virgins of the Sun, is addressed to the deity in the Temple of the Sun. The second is heard at the beginning of the fifth act and accompanies the coronation of the king. It, too, is performed by Priests and Virgins. These were the two choruses that Mozart had been inspired to set in 1773.[16] Structurally and thematically, the first of them was later taken over unchanged, with only the duets for male and female soloists between the choral sections being simplified. The imaginatively imitative accompaniment was not added until later. The original choral writing, by contrast, acquired a completely different, far richer instrumental guise. Not only did the addition of flutes mean changes to the oboe parts, but Mozart's whole approach to the instrumentation changed. In the first version, the orchestra operates along the lines found in the contemporary masses, whereas the later version reflects all the experience of the Mannheim symphonic school and French opera. This naturally had repercussions for the role of the chorus, which was no longer merely supported by the orchestra and complemented by the occasional tone-painterly treatment of individual details. Instead, the chorus now found in the orchestra an independent partner to add to and deepen the underlying mood. Mozart evidently felt that the first chorus could sustain this new competition from the orchestra without further ado, but in the case of the second he retained only the beginning and a few individual motifs. For the rest, he produced a new piece that was far more substantial not only in terms of its length but also in respect of its musical ideas, a worthy testimony to all that Mozart owed to Paris in spite of his apparent failure to make any immediate impression there.

Later the first and third choruses were underlaid with Latin words of a sacred nature that were subsequently translated, in turn, into German. The second was also given new words, and in this transmogrified form these choruses found their way into church and were long regarded as prime examples of Mozart's sacred music. Admittedly, they are bolder and more imaginative than most of the sacred works that Mozart wrote in his youth, but, in terms of the peculiar nature of their pathos and the subjective character of their emotions, they are far closer to the grand and religiously coloured scenes of sacrifice in French operas of this period than they are to church music. However obvious Mozart's delight in the fact that he could disregard Salzburg conventions, he was none the less sufficiently sensitive to stylistic nuance to draw a sharp dividing line between sacred and secular drama. These choruses reveal a remarkable and genuinely Mozartian mixture of dignity and energy, but they are laid out along such broad lines that they threaten to overwhelm the drama with their weight. Formally speaking, the first of them, which is addressed to the sun, is a cross between sonata form and rondo form. The large-scale choral section at the beginning is repeated in full at the end, while between them come three solo episodes in G, F and C major which in turn are rounded off by choral sections in the manner of a refrain. In this way Mozart created an effective contrast, with the chorus stressing the seriousness and dignity of the ceremony, while the soloists express its confident, cheerfully animated aspect. In the process, he explores the meaning of the words in meticulous detail. This he does not only through the declamation but also, and more especially, through the instrumentation: listen, for example, to the syncopations in

16.   Schweitzer thought that the composer of the two choruses intended for performance that Gebler sent to both Ramler and Wieland was a beginner, albeit one of considerable ability. These were the first two choruses set by Mozart: see Werner, *Aus dem Josephinischen Wien*, 141. Conversely, the 'Two Choruses for the Play Thamos by Mozart in a Vocal Score by C. Zulehner' published by Simrock in Bonn in 1829 are most emphatically not by Mozart; Wieland, *Auswahl denkwürdiger Briefe*, ii.30. ◆ Wieland's letter reporting Schweitzer's opinion — 'Our Schweizer . . . has found much that is fine in this music, and in general a great *ability* in its author, although he *guessed* immediately that he must still be a beginner' – is dated 19 May 1774; see *Dokumente*, 134, *Documentary Biography*, 149. It further points up chronological problems concerning Mozart's composition of the choruses and their assignment to 1773; according to the *Historisch-Kritische Theaterchronik von Wien* for 24 March 1774 (*Dokumente*, 133, *Documentary Biography*, 148), *Thamos* opened there only on Easter Monday of that year.

the violins right at the beginning, where they symbolize the rising sun;[17] or take the phrase accompanying the words 'des Lichtes Feindin, die Nacht' (light's enemy, night), sung to a darkly descending line that finally fades away, *piano*, like a shadow. No less memorable is the festive bustle that strikes up at the words 'schon wird von Egypten Dir neues Opfer gebracht' (already a new sacrifice is offered to you from Egypt).[18] And finally there is the emphatic setting of the word 'erhöre' (hear our prayer), which is later treated canonically at the description of the sun's eternal course. The two episodes for the men and girls are more intimate in tone, with the coloratura in the second chorus suggesting that these passages were intended for soloists. The first is filled with a sense of joyful strength, the second with intimate charm, not least as a result of a delightful motif that scurries past in the winds. In the third, the two parties initially alternate, before ending on a note of calm transfiguration similar to that found later in *Die Zauberflöte*. The second chorus opens with a festive adagio involving exceptionally busy orchestral writing. It, too, is cyclical in structure, with an extended middle section in A major (an allegretto in 3/4-time). It is on an even grander scale than the first chorus, which it none the less resembles in terms of its declamation, part-writing and orchestral treatment, while striking a darker and, at the same time, a more ecstatic note. The intimate idyll of the middle section lies embedded between the two outer sections (the third is a repeat of the first) and is accompanied by magical wind sonorities. It is the sort of movement that Mozart had come across in Grétry's works but which he now invests with his own particular brand of rapt infatuation. In the dotted writing at 'nie verstummet unser Chor' ('our chorus never falls silent') the listener can almost hear the gently transfigured, solemn tread of the Three Boys in *Die Zauberflöte*. The procession slowly disappears in the distance to the strains of a sustained and independent orchestral coda.

Such was the effectiveness of these two choruses that Mozart evidently felt encouraged to write a third which replaces the earlier orchestral description of Pheron's death and rounds off the drama as a whole. Following the Gluckian model, a High Priest enters and enjoins the populace to take note of Pheron's fall and hold their deity in awe. The chorus joins in and prays for protection for Egypt's new king. The text appears to have been written in Salzburg and may be the work of Schachtner.[19] Gluck's influence is plain not only from the implacable rhythm of the opening section but also from the terse yet expressive manner of the first two choral sections, while the Priest's vocal line already clearly adumbrates that of the Commendatore. Like two other numbers in the score (the orchestral allegro vivace assai and the concluding music to act 5), this final chorus is in Mozart's tragic key of D minor, a key which, as we have already seen, played a particularly important role in his works at this time. The chorus begins by taking up the orchestral melody, adding stark dynamic accents, after which a brief but tension-laden section in D major provides a transition to the jubilation of the final chorus, which, for all its unbridled joy, does not overlook the virtue of humility and also recalls its new ruler in a spirit of confidence and strength of purpose.[20]

It is entirely understandable that, prior to his departure for Paris, Mozart was self-avowedly looking forward to the fact that choruses – his 'favourite type of composition' – were so well performed in the French capital. Yet his choruses for *Thamos* would scarcely have turned out

---

17. The same device is used with a similar aim in the Queen of Night's first aria in *Die Zauberflöte*. Already found in the 1773 version, this predates Mozart's encounter with Benda's *Ariadne auf Naxos*.
18. The section beginning 'Erhöre die Wünsche' reappears in the first-act finale of *Die Zauberflöte* at the words 'Es lebe Sarastro'.
19. It is absent from both Gebler and the Italian translation.
20. There is a further pre-echo of *Don Giovanni* – this time it is Elivra's 'l'ultima prova dell'amor mio' from the second-act finale – at the words 'Schütze des Königs neue Krone'.

as magnificently as they did if it had not been for his stay in Paris, where the best possible models were to be found for this novel combination of chorus, soloists and orchestra. Even in his masses one or other of these elements had all too often been privileged at the expense of the others, but now all three merge to form a living organism. Above all, Mozart had learnt to appreciate the new principle's structural potential. The individual movements are flawless in their design, with their form appearing to reflect the composer's intentions as though of its own accord. Above all, there are no longer any of those stopgap passages that served only to pad out the preexisting formal framework. Not only is the choral writing free of all instrumental colouring, but it explores the meaning of the text as far as is humanly possible within the realm of vocal music. Everything else is left to the orchestra. This, too, reflects the experiences gathered in Mannheim and Paris, but does so in an entirely idiosyncratic way. All that is missing is clarinets. And whereas the trombones had always doubled the vocal lines in the sacred works written for Salzburg, instruments and voices now go their separate ways, the only exception being in the case of sustained chords. Instead, they occasionally form a group with either the horns or the trumpets. For their part, the horns also join forces with the woodwinds. In general, a glance at the score reveals that, except for a very short time, woodwinds and horns are in constant demand: in short, there is virtually no trace any longer of the earlier procedure whereby they were unharnessed from the strings in precisely determinable and recurrent sections of the score; winds and strings are used alongside each other as totally equal partners. But this is the instrumentational principle associated with the Mannheim school,[21] a principle to which Mozart comes far closer during this period than at any later time, when he returned increasingly to the Haydnesque principle of treating the woodwinds more subtly as a self-contained group. Inevitably this approach also had repercussions for the role of the strings, which are no longer simply the basis and principal register of the piece as a whole but fit in with it as *primus inter pares*, while additionally acquiring an entirely new function by dint of their merger with the winds. The result is the same relationship between winds and strings as there is, on a larger scale, between orchestra and chorus: there is no longer any concertante writing in the older sense but, instead, a working together of two equal bodies of sound that enter into the most varied and novel combinations with each other. A comparison with Mozart's older choral works leaves us in no doubt about the tremendous difference between them.

We may now turn to the German singspiel which, following André, has come to be known as *Zaide*. Only the text of the vocal numbers has survived, but on this basis it is possible to reconstruct the following plot:

Gomatz is a Christian who has fallen into the hands of the Sultan Soliman and won the love of Zaide, a member of Soliman's harem. Soliman has sued for Zaide's love, but in vain. She and Gomatz declare their love for each other after Gomatz has fallen asleep in the garden and she has left him her portrait. With the help of Soliman's favourite, Allazim, they attempt to flee but are betrayed and caught by the Captain of the Guard, Zaram, who escorts them into the presence of the terribly agitated Soliman. The sultan remains impervious to all pleas for mercy. Needless to say, the piece ends happily, but in what way can no longer be inferred from the text. An episodic figure only loosely connected with the plot is Osmin, a name frequently found in the Turkish operas of this time.

We shall have more to say on the nature and development of the German singspiel when we come to *Die Entführung aus dem Serail*. Here it is sufficient to note that we are dealing with a

21. See Heuß, 'Über die Dynamik der Mannheimer Schule'.

serious – in other words, tragic – piece,[22] the only comic number being Osmin's laughing song, which is just loosely grafted on to the rest of the work. On the whole, the librettist, Johann Andreas Schachtner, failed to rise to the occasion: not only did he adopt a thoroughly naïve approach to the old, tried-and-tested models, as in the lion, nightingale and tiger arias ('Der stolze Löw' läßt sich zwar zähmen', 'Trostlos schluchzet Philomele' and 'Tiger! wetze nur die Klauen'), but he remains firmly entrenched within existing parameters when it comes to the more generalized expression of emotion, with Soliman's outbursts of anger, for example, appearing for all the world like unintentional parodies of Metastasio's arias on the themes of anger and revenge. Even where the action develops along more individual lines and demands more colourful expression, as in Gomatz's simile aria ('Rase, Schicksal, wüte immer') or Allazim's enlightened effusions ('Ihr Mächtigen seht ungerührt'), he remains inept and insipid. The language, too, is symptomatic of the sort of demands (or lack of them) that a company like Schikaneder's placed on its audiences. Soliman's aria ('Ich bin so bös' als gut'), for example, includes the words:

Soliman	Zaide
Ich bin so bös' als gut,	Tiger! wetze nur die Klauen,
Ich lohne die Verdienste	Freu Dich der erschlichnen Beut',
Mit reichlichem Gewinnste;	Straf ein törichtes Vertrauen
Doch reizt man meine Wut,	Auf verstellte Zärtlichkeit.
So hab ich auch wohl Waffen,	Komm nur schnell und töt' uns Beide,
Das Laster zu bestrafen,	Saug der Unschuld warmes Blut,
Und diese fordern Blut.	Reiß das Herz vom Eingeweide
	Und ersätt'ge Deine Wut!
[I am as evil as I am good,	[Tiger! Just sharpen your claws,
I reward merit	enjoy the captured prey,
with ample profit,	punish foolish trust
but if people provoke my anger,	in false tenderness,
I also have weapons	just come quickly and kill us both,
to punish vice,	drink innocence's warm blood,
and these demand blood.]	tear our hearts from our insides
	and sate your anger!]

That Mozart was able to set such words at all is attributable not only to his alleged lack of critical acumen when confronted by such texts, but also to his irresistible urge to write for the stage again. His description of the libretto as 'very good' can only be understood in the context of the generally low standard of the librettos of southern German singspiels at this time. It is unlikely that he had acquired any deeper knowledge of the genre in Salzburg at this period,[23] and it seems probable that Schachtner, too, essentially adopted Schikaneder's style. That Mozart made no attempt to revive the work when he later got to know the singspiel at first hand in Vienna was certainly not

---

22. Hence Mozart's comment, cited above, that the piece was unsuited to Vienna, where audiences preferred comic works.
23. ◆ Theatrical life in Salzburg is now known to have been considerably more varied and active than was thought in Abert's day; consequently Mozart may well have acquired a 'deeper understanding' of the genre about this time, and in the years immediately after. See, in particular, Hintermaier, 'Das Fürsterzbischöfliche Hoftheater zu Salzburg (1775–1803)'; Dahms, 'Das musikalische Repertoire des Salzburger Fürsterzbischöflichen Hoftheaters (1775–1803)'; and Boberski, *Das Theater der Benediktiner an der alten Universität Salzburg (1617–1778)*.

due simply to its lack of comic features. That he was thinking only of a production in Salzburg is clear not only from the orchestral forces for which it is scored but also from the vocal writing, which is tailored throughout to singers of modest abilities.

There is scarcely a trace here of any conscious exploration of the characters' emotional lives of the kind that we later find in *Die Entführung aus dem Serail*. The music, too,[24] remains within traditional confines in terms of its characterization, with the long-suffering lovers far better drawn than their furious tormentor. The first act is devoted to Gomatz and Zaide alone and not only reveals a typically Mozartian charm and tenderness of emotion but already contains pre-echoes of the more richly varied emotional world of Belmonte and Konstanze. The Sultan Soliman, by contrast, fails to rise musically or dramatically above the level of a traditional theatrical villain, and his dark fury remains considerably less convincing than that found, for example, in *La finta giardiniera*.

But *Zaide* is stylistically important as Mozart's first attempt to combine elements of different genres,[25] an endeavour entirely typical of the Viennese singspiel in general. Mozart, however, has undertaken it on the basis of his own most recent impressions and in doing so produced something different. Completely *sui generis* is Osmin's aria ('Wer hungrig bei der Tafel sitzt'), which breathes the spirit of Italian *opera buffa* with its sparkling rhythms and carefree laughter. Its consequent phrase, moreover, keeps on returning in the manner of a refrain and, as such, is a good example of Mozart's free approach to questions of musical form. Likewise, the work contains only a single instance of a simple German folksong ('Brüder, laßt uns lustig sein'), a type of number ultimately inspired by the hugely popular 'Ohne Lieb und ohne Wein' from Johann Adam Hiller's *Die verwandelten Weiber* of 1766. With its note of heartfelt cheerfulness, it is a fine example of Mozart's talents as a lieder composer. Only rarely in his later career did he return to this natural folklike tone. In other numbers the songlike tone is more stylized and closer to that of an aria. Here the influence of French opera and especially Grétry is clearly audible, notably in Zaide's delightful first aria ('Ruhe sanft'), with its floating dance step, brief adagio episode, change of tempo and piquant orchestral accompaniment. The same is true of her second aria ('Trostlos schluchzet Philomele'), its rondo form and brief painterly features, especially in the orchestra, again recalling Paris. Its final ritornello even includes a new programmatical feature. But the jewel of this group of arias is Gomatz's ('Herr und Freund, wie dank' ich dir'), the only aria in the work that encompasses a conflict of emotions, for although Gomatz wants to thank his illustrious patron, Allazim, he cannot wait to rush into Zaide's arms. Mozart expresses his dilemma with a priceless sense of humour, but without allowing the youth's genuine gratitude to appear in any way perfunctory. That he is in a tearing hurry is made clear not only by his gabbled 'Doch ich muß dich schnell verlassen' ('But I really must leave you now'), with its Grétry-like scalar motif in the violins, but also, and more particularly, by the agitated 'Laß dich küssen, laß dich drücken' ('Let me kiss you and embrace you') at the beginning of the middle section of the aria, with its repeated quaver g'' in the first violins and pizzicato writing for the second violins and violas. Right at the end Gomatz returns, after having already hurried away, and with obvious sincerity sings the words 'Herr und Freund, wie dank' ich dir' ('Lord and friend, how grateful I am to you') to the same accompaniment, a fine example of Mozart's meaningful handling of his orchestra. A transition to the third group – the large-scale Italianate arias – is provided by Allazim's two arias ('Nur mutig, mein

24. For a detailed discussion, see Chrysander, 'Mozarts Werke: Zaide'. ◆ Further, see Betzwieser, 'Auf der Suche nach der verlorenen "Zaide": Die Probleme mit Mozarts Opernfragment'.
25. ◆ Also see Tyler, '"Zaide" in the development of Mozart's operatic language'.

Herze' and 'Ihr Mächtigen seht ungerührt'). Neither of them succeeds in breathing any real life into the uninspired text, although the second is at least notable for its sombre introduction, with its taut Gluckian rhythms, and for its harmonically fascinating middle section.

The true Italian aria is represented in the main by Soliman's two arias ('Der stolze Löw' and 'Ich bin so bös' als gut'). So serious and emotionally charged are these numbers that it is hard to avoid the impression that in depicting this character Mozart was pursuing a parodistic aim, in which respect he was certainly not alone in Turkish operas of the period: after all, the wholly unromantic eighteenth century was all too ready to see the funny side of these sinister figures. In the second aria, in particular, Mozart resorts to the stock-in-trade of *opera seria*, with its large-scale ritornellos and extended cadenzas, both features that he had otherwise long since abandoned. Formally, too, this aria harks back to an older type, even though there is no middle section à la Hasse and the main theme does not return until the end – a feature also found in the allegros of the composer's contemporary symphonies. There is no denying the humour not only in the exaggerated expression in general but also in a passage such as 'so hab ich auch wohl Waffen, das Laster zu bestrafen' ('I also have weapons to punish vice'), with its excited babble and typically Mozartian interval of a seventh to express a sense of malice. Allazim's earlier aria adopts a similar stance, with the roar of the 'proud lion' depicted with evident delight.[26] But what is good enough for Allazim's lion also turns out to be good enough for the tiger in Zaide's G minor aria ('Tiger! wetze nur die Klauen'). Here, too, it is hard to recognize the Zaide of her earlier arias, so highly charged is its pathos, although she admittedly strikes a more individual note than the raging sultan. Chief among these more individual features is the deeply felt middle section, which opens with a clear reminiscence of Gluck and in which Zaide appeals to her lover alone in a tone far removed from hatred and anger; freely and yet closely mirroring the words, the vocal line pours forth from the girl's anxious heart.

Among the work's most successful numbers are the ensembles. The simple binary duet for Zaide and Gomatz ('Meine Seele hüpft vor Freuden') describes the couple's bliss in tender heartfelt terms that far surpass those found in most of the other love duets in the singspiels of this period, in which high-flown sentiment alternates with homespun expression. There is a childlike grace to the way in which the delightful melody (note the five-bar periodic structure) passes from character to character before turning into simple homophony interrupted only by a brief canon at the moment of supreme happiness. The trio that ends the first act ('O selige Wonne') is another purely atmospheric portrait with no dramatic accents. The way in which the piece is structured as three independent sections, the key of E major, the brief *tempête* in the middle section and the character of the themes in the first and third sections all point to Grétry. The gently rocking first section harks back to the mood of the duet, while the middle section clouds over only briefly,[27] after which a feeling of confidence finds redoubled expression in the folklike tone of the broadly structured Allegro. A far more dramatic note is struck by the quartet ('Freundin, stille deine Tränen'), for here we are dealing not with a basic emotion that animates all four participants, but with often stark contrasts between them. The Sultan remains implacably angry, Zaide attempts to save her lover by sacrificing her own life instead, Gomatz tries to console her and Allazim feels a sense of the profoundest anguish at the fact that he cannot avert the disaster that he himself has caused. Mozart

---

26. The vocal line includes an old idea found in Piccinni that had already appeared in *La finta giardiniera* and that was later repeated in *Le nozze di Figaro*.
27. Mozart was satisfied with neither the words nor the music here and so he twice revised this passage: see the critical commentary in NMA II/5/10.

expresses all these sentiments with an assured hand, although the underlying tone is determined by the emotional world of the character who suffers the most, with the result that the Sultan's anger is kept within reasonable bounds. This is clear from the very outset, with the movingly imploring wind passage serving as a motto for the whole number and recurring three times in the rest of the quartet, where it accompanies not only the lovers' words 'Ach das Leben hat für mich keine Reize mehr in sich' ('Ah, life no longer has any attraction for me') but also Allazim's plea for mercy. It will later be heard at the words 'Selbst der Luft darf ich nicht sagen meiner Seele bittern Schmerz' (I may not even tell the air my soul's bitter anguish) in Konstanze's aria ('Traurigkeit ward mir zum Lose') from *Die Entführung aus dem Serail*. Mozart has compressed the whole action into a single ternary structure, with the individual emotions etched in either in the form of separate solo or group episodes or in that of elaborate dramatic polyphony. Although Zaide, Gomatz and Allazim all suffer in one way or another, they are subtly differentiated, Allazim as painfully resigned, Gomatz as a consoling figure who, in spite of his anguish, never forgets his manly enthusiasm, and the touchingly entreating Zaide. The brief and simple passage for the duetting lovers, 'Himmel, höre doch mein Flehen' ('Heaven, hear my prayer'), sounds like a final, heartfelt confession of their love, the passage 'Ach das Leben' ('Ah, life') like a calm and nostalgic farewell to life. The instruments, too, have an eloquent role to play here, as is clear not only from the wind passage just mentioned but also from Soliman's peremptory scales and the trembling triplets that accompany the resigned dialogue for the winds at Allazim's words. At each of the climaxes the four characters come together in a full ensemble, and it is significant that on each of these occasions it is Soliman who is invariably given precedence ('Alle Tränen nützen nichts' ['All tears are unavailing']), his peremptorily dotted rhythm initially forcing the others to do his will. But then they all break free from him (bar 42ff), an inspired dramatic stroke that occurs at the moment when his agitation is still rising and the lovers independently pour out their hearts in impassioned motifs that almost seem to acquire the clarity of physical gestures and Allazim, completely broken, succumbs to his anguish. At the same time an ominous murmuring rises in the unison instruments, as though everything is now out of joint – it is already Mozart the fully-rounded, great dramatist who is speaking here. The exceptionally clear and symmetrical structure of this number – its freedom notwithstanding – likewise reveals the master's hand. Nor should we forget the quiet ending, which seems to die away on the same note of helpless perplexity that Mozart was to use in similar situations in later works. If there is any aspect of this quartet that still recalls the earlier period, it is its great breadth, a breadth that attests to a youthful delight in composition. The later Mozart was always more succinct in such instances.

But the most remarkable stylistic element of this opera is its two melodramas ('Unerforschliche Fügung!' and 'Der stolze Löw'), which combine declamation with orchestral music to elucidate the action.[28] Significantly, the impetus behind this new type of descriptive music came from France, where Rousseau's *scène lyrique Pygmalion* – except for two of its numbers, the music is by Horace Coignet – was first performed in Lyons in 1770 and in Paris in 1775.[29] Rousseau's aim, in fact, was not to write a melodrama in the sense in which this term was later to be understood, but to

---

28. For a history of the melodrama, see Schletterer, *Das deutsche Singspiel von seinen Anfängen bis auf die neueste Zeit*, 225; Schmidt, 'Goethes Proserpina', 27ff. (together with Werner's appendix on pp.523ff.); and Istel, 'Die Entstehung des deutschen Melodramas', 9ff. ◆ Specifically with respect to *Zaide*, see Gersthofer, 'Zur Melodramtechnik in "Zaide"'.
29. Istel, *Studien zur Geschichte des Melodramas*; Jansen, *Jean-Jacques Rousseau als Musiker*, 293ff. Both writers also examine the question of Rousseau's contribution to the score.

improve the accompanied recitative in French opera, especially in terms of the acting. Only his well-known doctrine that the French language was unsingable persuaded him to exclude singing entirely. As such, the idea was not particularly new for anyone familiar with French music, as programmatical contributions from the orchestra were already a feature of both serious and comic operas, so much so that the orchestra seemed equal to every demand that was placed on it. In particular, the dramatic ballets of Noverre and his school, with their detailed orchestral tone paintings, already came close to melodrama. At the same time, Rousseau no doubt also recalled the great free solo scenes of Italian opera, and if, among his German successors, female protagonists are far more numerous than their male equivalent, this feature is already adumbrated in *opera seria*. Rousseau's experiment was widely applauded, a handful of critical voices notwithstanding.[30] By early 1772 *Pygmalion* had also been seen in Vienna, this time with music by Franz Asplmayr (best known as a composer of dramatic ballets), and on 13 May a performance followed in Weimar, on this occasion with music by Anton Schweitzer. Both settings are lost. But this same year also saw the composition of one of the most famous of eighteenth-century works, *Ariadne auf Naxos*, to a libretto by the actor Johann Christian Brandes based on the cantata of the same name by Heinrich Wilhelm von Gerstenberg. Brandes's aim was essentially practical, namely, to create a virtuoso role for his wife Charlotte, whose principal rival was Friederike Seyler. He, too, seems to have been thinking of the great monologues of Italian opera, but his wife had no musical training and so the new combination of instrumental music and spoken word struck him as something of a godsend. The first composer whom he approached was again Schweitzer, but the latter was prevented by his work on *Alceste* from completing the commission. When he was transferred to Gotha with the Seyler company in 1774, Brandes entrusted the text to the local Court Kapellmeister Georg Benda (1722–95), with whose music the work was first staged in Gotha on 27 January 1775.[31] So successful was it – thanks, not least, to Charlotte Brandes in the title role – that the poet Friedrich Wilhelm Gotter was encouraged to write a melodrama for her pathologically jealous rival, Friederike Seyler. The result was *Medea*. It, too, was set by Benda and received a no less triumphant first performance in Leipzig on 1 May.[32] It was not long before the reputation of these two works had spread to the whole of the civilized world.[33] The critical voices that even then had been raised against the whole new genre went entirely unheard,[34] such was the public's enthusiasm. Eminent poets provided contributions of their own, foremost among which was Goethe's *Proserpina*, and for a considerable time the majority of composers, including Neefe and Mozart himself, regarded the melodrama as the artwork of the future.[35]

So successful was Benda that Rousseau's star soon set, and for good reason. For irrespective of whether Benda knew *Pygmalion* or not, he succeeded in transforming the genre and turning it into something completely different. In the first place, he drew the ultimate consequences from its rela-

30. See de La Harpe, *Correspondance littéraire*, i.280ff.
31. See Brandes, *Meine Lebensgeschichte*, ii.140 and 157; and Istel, 'Die Entstehung des deutschen Melodramas', 150ff.
32. See Brandes, *Meine Lebensgeschichte*, ii.193; *Der teutsche Merkur*, iii (1775), 276ff.; and Istel, 'Die Entstehung des deutschen Melodramas', 231ff.
33. *Ariadne auf Naxos* was also performed to great acclaim in Paris in 1781; see Grimm, *Correspondance littéraire*, x.450.
34. Eberhard, 'Abhandlung über das Melodrama'; *Neue Bibliothek der schönen Wissenschaften*, xxxvii (1778), 177ff.; Forkel, *Musikalisch-kritische Bibliothek*, iii.250ff.; *Tagebuch der Mannheimer Schaubühne*, i.327ff.; Johann Georg Sulzer, *Allgemeine Theorie der schönen Künste*, iii.318ff.; *Rheinische Beiträge*, i (1780), 64ff., 261ff. and vi (1784), 459ff.; Herder, *Adrastea*, 484; and Zelter, *Eine Lebensbeschreibung nach autobiographischen Manuscripten*, 100–1.
35. See Reichardt, *Musikalisches Kunstmagazin*, i (1782), 86; and Neefe, *Gothaer Theaterjournal*, i (1777), 74.

tionship with the accompanied recitative and used the instruments not simply to underpin the gestural language of the actor or actress on stage but to depict both inner and outer action. As a result, he no longer distinguished between declamation and orchestral music (a distinction still fastidiously maintained by Rousseau). Not infrequently, the two proceed in tandem with each other, as in the recitative, but even where they go their separate ways, they do so over far shorter sections. The orchestral writing, too, proceeds entirely according to the principles of the accompanied recitative, with short and succinct motifs developed over a freely modulating bass and with the inclusion even of brief cavatina-like passages. In general, Benda's melodramas reveal a composer fully abreast of current developments in drama: the influence of both the Italian operas of composers such as Carl Heinrich Graun and Schweitzer's German *Alceste* are clearly audible,[36] but so, too, is that of the French music of the period, with its typical depictions of nature. Here one thinks in particular of the skilful leitmotivic use of individual ideas in the manner of Grétry.

In short, the tremendous success of these pieces is attributable not only to the rhetorical language of their texts (a language essentially French in origin and cleverly adapted to suit contemporary taste), but also, and above all, to their music, which attests to the talents of their creator and to his profound understanding of art. As such, they no doubt justified the praise of a composer as critical as Mozart.

It was Beethoven's mentor, Christian Gottlob Neefe (1748–98),[37] who introduced the melodrama into the German singspiel. As with the introduction of the accompanied recitative, it was an attempt to raise the genre as a whole to a new and higher dramatic level. Mozart, too, pursued this aim in *Zaide* by using melodramas to introduce his two main characters, Gomatz and Soliman. In the case of the latter, the melodrama is immediately followed by an aria, in much the same way that an accompanied recitative is followed by an aria. But the manner in which Mozart takes up Benda's lead reveals his independent mastery vis-à-vis his predecessor. There are no direct reminiscences: all that Mozart has taken over is the underlying principle. Unmistakable here is his attempt to make the two scenes contrast as much as possible: Soliman's melodrama is highly dramatic and impassioned, whereas that of Gomatz is rather more intimate and ultimately more idyllic. As before, the first is more successful than the second. It is noteworthy that Mozart is even more concerned than Benda to ensure that the orchestral contribution forms a continuous whole; there is scarcely a single passage that does not follow on logically and harmonically from what has gone before, with the result that the entire number could be performed without the words as a freely programmatical piece with no interruptions. Most of its elements are additionally linked together rhythmically and melodically, with Mozart also taking up Benda's practice of repeating certain principal ideas. The genre's main weakness – its harnessing together of unmusical recitation with an instrumental language that has been invested with additional musical depth – emerges all the more flagrantly here, within a singspiel, than it does with Benda, where there are no purely musical arias by way of invidious comparison. As an alternative structural vehicle to the accompanied recitative, the melodrama will always be open to criticism. But it was later used at critical junctures in the action by composers writing in the wake of French *Schreckensopern*, where, thanks to the impression created by its material sonorities and its meaningful use of motifs of

36. Sandberger, '[Review: Edgar Istel, Die Entstehung des deutschen Melodramas]'. ◆ Further, see Bauman, *North German Opera in the Age of Goethe*, 111–28.
37. See Lewy, 'Christian Gottlob Neefe'.

reminiscence, it creates a fine and even moving impression, most notably in Beethoven's *Fidelio*, Weber's *Der Freischütz* and Marschner's *Hans Heiling*. In the case of epic poems, too, its aesthetic shortcomings are less apparent, as is evident from the more recent contributions of Robert Schumann, Richard Strauss and Max von Schillings.

Mozart himself never returned to the melodrama, but his preoccupation with it was none the less to be of considerable, if indirect, benefit in terms of his approach to the accompanied recitative, whose affinities with the melodrama he had clearly divined from the outset. The best proof of this is *Idomeneo*.

26

Idomeneo

The plot of *Idomeneo* may be briefly summarized as follows:

Idomeneo, the king of Crete, returns home following the Fall of Troy. During his lengthy absence and subsequent wanderings his son Idamante has grown up. Idamante loves King Priam's daughter, Ilia, whom Idomeneo has sent back to Crete ahead of him as a prisoner of war. In turn, Idamante is loved by Agamemnon's daughter Electra, who has fled to the island following Orestes's murder of their mother. At the start of the opera, Ilia is violently torn between her feelings for Idamante and her honour as a Trojan woman. Idamante has heard that his father is returning and, in his delight, frees the Trojan prisoners and declares his love of Ilia. Reluctantly, she rejects him, whereupon he gives vent to his sorrow in an aria. The Trojans celebrate their release in a chorus, thereby arousing Electra's displeasure, whereupon the king's confidant Arbace brings news – false, as it turns out – that Idomeneo has perished in a shipwreck. Overcome by his grief, Idamante leaves, while Electra gives free rein to her jealousy and despair. The scene changes to the seashore, where Idomeneo's fleet can be seen foundering, with their crew in extreme distress. Idomeneo appeases the furious Neptune by vowing to sacrifice the first person he encounters. Once on dry land, he looks round in fear and horror to see who the victim will be. At this point Idamante enters and, after a lengthy conversation, father and son recognize each other. Deeply shaken, Idomeneo hurries away, forbidding his son to follow him. Idamante remains behind, alone, disconsolate at his father's incomprehensible severity. The entr'acte comprises a march, dance and chorus for the returning warriors.

In the second act, Idomeneo decides to evade his terrible obligation by sending Idamante and Electra to Argos, where she will ascend the throne. Arbace receives instructions to pass on these orders and promises to do so. Ilia welcomes Idomeneo and praises Idamante's kindness, assuring the king of her devotion. The latter realizes that she and Idamante are in love and feels more dismayed than ever. Electra, too, thanks him for showing mercy; left alone,[1] she expresses her delight that what she desire most has come true. A march and chorus for the warriors and sailors introduce the final scene in which preparations are made for Idamante and Electra to set sail for Argos. Electra, Idomeneo and Idamante, the last as perplexed as ever, express their varied feelings in a trio. To general dismay a terrible tempest breaks out and a sea-monster rises from the waves. Conscious of his guilt, Idomeneo offers to sacrifice his own life instead of that of his innocent son. The Cretans flee as the storm continues to rage.

The third act opens with Ilia telling the breezes of her love for Idamante. Idamante enters and declares that, since his father hates him and she rejects him, he will seek death in battle with the sea-monster. She now admits to loving him and the two are united in a duet. They are discovered

---

1. For Mozart's changes to this passage, see the critical commentary to NMA II/5/11.

by Idomeneo and Electra. In order to save his son's life, the king again orders Idamante to leave Crete. A quartet follows. Arbace announces the approach of the populace with the High Priest: they are demanding that the king free them from the depredations of the sea-monster. He expresses his hope that Crete's rulers may be saved. The High Priest demands that the king carry out his vow and name the victim. When Idomeneo names his own son, the Cretans express their grief. A march and prayer introduce the sacrifice, at which point a jubilant cry is heard in the distance and Arbace announces that Idamante has killed the sea-monster. Idamante enters, robed for sacrifice: he knows everything and is prepared to die. As Idomeneo raises his arm to deal the fatal blow, Ilia rushes in and, bidding him stay his hand, offers her own life instead. A lengthy argument ensues, interrupted only when Neptune's oracle bids Idomeneo abdicate in favour of his son, who is to marry Ilia. Consumed with anger, Electra rushes away. Idomeneo acknowledges the god's will and expresses his delight, and Idamante is crowned to dancing and singing.[2]

Varesco set out to turn his French source into an Italian *opera seria* of the most up-to-date kind, with French-style choruses, dances and orchestral extras.[3] In this he was following a trend that had started with the school of Hasse and that was currently represented by Johann Christian Bach and Giuseppe Sarti. He followed Danchet's original plot fairly closely, while omitting what seemed to him – with good reason – to be old-fashioned: chief among these omissions were the prologue, the various gods and other allegorical figures and two of the three confidants. He also dispensed with the motif whereby Idomeneo, too, sues for Ilia's hand and remodelled the ending: in Danchet's version, Idomeneo goes mad after renouncing the throne and Ilia's hand and kills Idamante with the sacrificial axe. Ilia dies by her own hand.

The influence of Metastasio is clearly discernible here, but it becomes even more apparent from the work's overall design, from the way in which the individual figures are characterized, from the various types of scenes and, finally, from the poetic diction: suffice it to mention the three-act structure, the division into *secco* and accompanied recitatives and arias (among which the simile arias, *ombra* arias and others concerned with nature imagery, to say nothing of Electra's invocations of the Furies, are all entirely typical of the period) and such specific motifs as Idomeneo's refusal to explain himself to his son, thereby abandoning the latter to the profoundest anguish through his apparent cruelty, and Ilia's willingness to die for her lover's sake, a willingness that gives rise to the 'ultimo amplesso' and the magnanimous rivalry so popular with audiences at this time. No less Metastasian are the colourless Arbace as confidant, the tender, wistful Idamante and the impassioned Electra as Ilia's rival. The borrowings extend even to the level of language, as may be judged from the use of antitheses (notably in Idamante's aria 'Il padre adorato') and the juxtaposition of similar or related concepts with no conjunction in order to increase the sense of tension ('Oh sdegno! oh smanie! oh duol!) in act one, scene six and 'amor, mercè, pietà' in Electra's aria 'Tutte nel cor vi sento'). Indeed, we even find direct borrowings from Metastasio's vocabulary, including some of his favourite expressions such as the very first words of the opera, 'Quando avran fine omai l'aspre sventure mie?' Conversely, all the choruses and processions are French in origin, with famous prototypes for the tempest and shipwreck to be found in Gluck's *Iphigénie en*

2. The legend of Idomeneus being caught unawares by a storm while returning home and vowing, like Jephtha, to sacrifice the first living creature he meets was known to classical antiquity. In these versions Idomeneus refuses to sacrifice his son, whereupon a plague breaks out and he is driven into exile by his people. The remaining details have been added by modern writers.
3. The wordbook, which was published by Franz Joseph Thuille in Munich, is headed 'Idomeneo, dramma per musica, da rappresentarsi nel teatro nuovo di corte per comando di S. A. S. E. Carlo Teodoro etc. nel carnovale 1781' (Idomeneo, a musical drama to be performed in the new court theatre during the 1781 Carnival at the behest of His Excellency the Elector Karl Theodor). It reproduces the complete dialogue, including those sections cut while Mozart was working on the score. ◆ For a facsimile of the libretto, see Warburton, *The Librettos of Mozart's Operas. II: The Works for Munich and Vienna.*

Tauride and for the scenes of sacrifice and the oracle in both *Iphigénie en Aulide* and *Alceste*. Various other features suggest that Varesco was familiar with Calzabigi and especially with *Alceste*: here one thinks above all of the contrast between peace in nature and disquiet within the character's heart in act one, scene seven, and the charge of injustice directed at Neptune and the following chorus that depicts the resultant sense of fear ('Corriamo, fuggiamo'). Even the occasionally ostentatious display of mythological lore ('Nettuno s'onori' and 'Oh ciel pietoso') has been taken over by Varesco from French librettos of the period as mediated by Calzabigi. The oracle – one of Rameau's operatic innovations – undoubtedly derives from Gluck's *Alceste*, where, thanks to its greater brevity, it creates a far more vivid impression than in Varesco's libretto, where it tends rather to speak the language that Calzabigi's *dei ex machina* use at the end of an opera.

These French ingredients, on which the composer laid special emphasis in keeping with his whole attitude towards the chorus, should not, of course, delude us into thinking that the work is not, after all, a regular *opera seria*, rather than a Mozartian contribution to the Gluckian music drama, as a number of commentators have claimed. Although a handful of scenes – especially the choruses – bear all the hallmarks of Gluck, the action as a whole, with its specific kind of intrigue and its systematic use of tension, could hardly be less Gluckian. How much more subtly is the conflict between divine injunction and paternal love depicted in the case of Gluck's Agamemnon than it is in that of Idomeneo, who seeks to trick the god out of his sacrifice by all manner of petty ruses, quite apart from the fact that this principal strand in the action is repeatedly entangled with the various affairs of the heart. Indeed, it is the Gluckian features that help to highlight the fundamental difference between the two genres, and the basic failing of the whole opera stems from the fact that neither the librettist nor the composer realized that any attempt to graft individual Gluckian shoots on to the ancient bole of *opera seria* could never be anything but an ineffectual half-measure.

As a dramatist, moreover, Varesco cannot be remotely compared with Metastasio: the scenes already mentioned are far more superficial and far less effective, his aria texts are of often chilling artificiality, and the dialogue in the recitatives is stiff and inept. On every point, the composer was left with a great deal to put right.[4]

Mozart, too, was chiefly concerned to write an *opera seria*, albeit one to which he planned to give extra depth and breadth by dint of his treatment of the orchestra and chorus: the work, after all, was to be performed by singers trained in the Italian tradition. Here, too, the basis was the interplay between *secco* recitative and aria, and even though this basis is obscured by the larger number of orchestral recitatives, it was certainly not abandoned altogether. Not for a moment did Mozart consider following Gluck's example, as Piccinni, for instance, had done in *Roland*, and replacing the *secco* recitative by its accompanied alternative. The arias, too, are Italianate in terms of their structure and character. There is no trace of either Gluck's songlike forms or of the rondo form that we find so frequently in the works of Bach and Sarti, for example. Even numbers made up of two independent sections of constrasting character are rare ('Non ho colpa', 'Vedrommi intorno' and 'S'io non moro a questi accenti'). More frequent are the ternary arias constructed along the lines already found in Mozart's early operas: an A-section ending on the dominant or in the relative key; a B-section that resembles a development section with frequent modulations and occasionally also with a change of key-signature and tempo ('No, la morte, la morte io non pavento'

---

4. ◆ Abert's harsh condemnation of Varesco appeals to the grand sweep of music theatre history and its heroes, without necessarily considering local theatrical cultures or librettists' immediate influences. Beyond the Metastasian and the Gluckian, Varesco may have had other specific dramatic goals in mind; see, for example, Kramer, 'Antike und christliches Mittelalter in Varescos Idomeneo, dem Libretto zu Mozarts gleichnamiger Oper'.

and 'Torna la pace al core'); and a more or less varied repeat of the A-section ('Non ho colpa', 'Se il tuo duol', 'Fuor del mar', 'Zeffiretti lusinghieri' and 'Se colà ne' fati è scritto'). But Mozart's favourite type of aria in this opera is the binary aria which, derived from *opera buffa*, had made increasing inroads into the serious operas of the period. The old B-section has here been reduced to a few transitional bars, with even the ritornello at the end of the A-section cut back to an absolute minimum. The thematically related second section, by contrast, is now invested with far greater intensity and depth thanks to the way in which the ideas are refashioned, varied and expanded. It is here, above all, that Mozart's artistry proves most successful ('Padre, germani, addio!', 'Tutte nel cor vi sento', 'Il padre adorato', 'Se il padre perdei', 'Idol mio, se ritroso' and 'D'Oreste, d'Ajace'). It is entirely typical of Mozart that even here, in *Idomeneo*, he is not concerned, as Gluck was, with self-contained portraits of his characters' emotional lives but with exploring their gradual development. There is no trace here of Gluck's lapidary and unambiguous musical language, no trace of his implacable rhythmic tread. From the outset, Mozart's arias examine the basic mood in far more varied detail, touching on peripheral areas of their characters' emotional lives and even introducing antitheses whose connection with the underlying emotion emerges only in the course of the aria's development. In a word, they build up the whole picture of the character on the basis of his or her individual features and do so, moreover, in the presence of the listener. In particular, Mozart introduces two themes into his A-sections that are clearly contrasted, with the second generally conceived as an intensified version of the first. Even here, the introduction of this second theme already affords many a splendid example of the inspired way in which Mozart was later to exploit the winds for psychological dramatic ends. Needless to say, this more thoughtful approach to form also affects the ritornellos, with the result that there is virtually no trace any longer of the old Neapolitan schematism, while the large-scale, concerto-like preludes typical of Johann Christian Bach and frequently found in Mozart's early operas, with their two themes separated by noisy half-cadences, have likewise almost completely disappeared. Instead, Mozart now reveals a fondness for approaching the aria's theme from the dominant and for launching into it from the accompanied recitative with almost explosive force ('D'Oreste, d'Ajace'). As a result of all these devices, *Idomeneo* achieves a formal unity that sets it clearly apart from the earlier operas, with their looser and often discursive structures. Only in a handful of arias, especially those of the subsidiary characters and in particular at cadential points, do we still find any trace of the older Italian distendedness.

That the melodic writing in the arias is entirely based on Italian models is a natural result of the whole spirit and language of the work. Coloratura, too, still plays a considerable part, even though it is used more sparingly than before and, according to Mozart's own admission, adapted to individual painterly words in the text. His earlier habit of introducing elaborate *fioriture* even into the theme itself is limited to a single aria ('Zeffiretti lusinghieri'), and here we find it on the word 'volate', in other words, at a point where even those composers of French *opéras comiques* who generally eschewed such devices would sometimes have allowed themselves a brief coloratura flourish. The free final cadenza is also still found in a number of cases ('Non ho colpa', 'Se il tuo duol' and 'Fuor del mar').

In short, Mozart was following in the footsteps of composers such as Sarti and other Italian contemporaries who saw the salvation of *opera seria* in a greater or lesser infusion of French blood, but without altering its basic Italian outlines. For this was the accepted form in Germany. The reader should not imagine that the hegemony of the Italians in the large-scale musical drama had already been broken by this date, whether by Gluck or by Schweitzer's and Holzbauer's attempts to write a national opera. Quite the opposite: the success of Gluck's reform operas had been limited, in the main, to Vienna, and, after a brilliant start, the attempts by Schweitzer and Holzbauer to create a German opera were threatening to grind to a halt. It is sufficient to recall the appalling bowdlerization of *Orfeo* in Munich – the city of *Idomeneo* – to realize the extent to which Germany was still governed by Italian taste.[5] It was only to be expected, then, that Mozart, who had grown up entirely within the tradition of *opera seria*, should align himself with what was then its latest tendency. That it was still capable, even now, of justifying its outstanding reputation is clear not least from the operas of Giuseppe Sarti. Historically, *Idomeneo*, too, takes its place in this tradition. From a dramatic point of view, this is Mozart's supreme achievement in the field of *opera seria*, far surpassing the later *La clemenza di Tito* in terms of its fire and dramatic power. That it marked a new era in the history of the genre or even that it represents the genre's crowning achievement will be claimed only by those who are insufficiently familiar with the contemporary or immediately preceding generation of Italian opera composers.[6]

Idomeneo is all the more important for Mozart's own development inasmuch as it constitutes the dividing line between the 'early' and the 'mature' Mozart. Here all the powerful impressions that had assailed him in the course of his last great tour of Europe find elementally explosive expression. Gone, however, is the earlier half-unconscious assimilation of foreign influences. Instead, Mozart is now fully aware of the immense richness of his own personality and is so successful in merging it harmoniously with traditional stylistic elements that the result, while clearly betraying its Italian and French basis, none the less bears the unmistakable imprint of his genius. Especially astonishing is the stylistic assurance with which he assimilates the achievements of the different schools, and if he is not entirely successful at maintaining the same high level dramatically, the blame must be laid, for the most part, not at his own door but at that of *opera seria* in general. He had no choice, of course, but to take over the genre as he found it: never for a moment did it occur to him to call it into question.

This is clear not least from the two arias of the *confidente* Arbace ('Se il tuo duol' and 'Se colà ne' fati è scritto'), which are only loosely connected to the plot and which therefore express only the most generalized sentiments in often highly pretentious verse. In turn, Mozart set them in the usual way for subsidiary characters, without any more individual features, the first a bombastically agitated Allegro, the second a sentimental Andante. Significantly, the Italianate style emerges with particular clarity here in terms of both form and character: note the numerous repetitions, extended cadential passages, wide-ranging intervals, lengthy ritornellos[7] and so on. Even the restless modulations of the older type of B-section have left their audible mark here. Evidently Mozart was also taking account of 'honest old' Panzacchi[8] when writing these arias, a singer who had grown up entirely within the old tradition. But Panzacchi was also a 'good actor', and it is to this circumstance that we owe the extended accompanied recitative that precedes his second aria. The main reason for this, according to Mozart, was the 'chiaro e scuro' of this scene, in other words, Arbace's vacillation between fear and hope,[9] but it is clearly no accident that in doing so he also drew on the performer's particular skills, with the whole structure of this recitative clearly recalling

5. See Engländer, 'Zu den Münchener Orfeo-Aufführungen 1773 und 1775'. ◆ Concerning Italian opera generally in Munich at this time, see Böhmer, *Karnevalsopern in München*.
6. Both Jahn and Deiters were still of this opinion, of course; see Jahn, *W. A. Mozart*, fourth edition, i.664.
7. Two whole pages were later cut from the first aria's unduly distended ritornello. ◆ See NMA II/5/11, 539–40.
8. ◆ The Italian tenor Domenico Panzacchi (1733–after 1805) was the first Arbace; concerning the singers at the premiere of *Idomeneo*, see Angermüller, 'Die Sänger der Erstaufführung des "Idomeneo" KV366'.
9. Curiously enough, Jahn, *W. A. Mozart*, i.664, has misunderstood this expression of Mozart (*Briefe*, iii.48, letter of 5 December 1780) and drawn from it some strange conclusions about Italian arias in general.

the melodrama and its constant interplay between the language of the text and the language of the orchestra. As if to confirm this, a principal motif from Benda's *Ariadne auf Naxos* is heard towards the end of the recitative (following the words 'ah, sordo è il cielo'), a motif that had been taken over in turn from act two, scene one of Graun's *Montezuma*.[10]

Mozart was no less limited by the singer in the case of the three solo scenes for Idamante ('Non ho colpa', 'Il padre adorato' and 'No, la morte, la morte io non pavento'): Vincenzo Dal Prato was far from equal to the demands placed on him, with the result that his arias are much less virtuosic in tone than was usual with castrato roles at this time.[11] In terms of his general characterization, Idamante is one of those long-suffering, wistful youths who had enjoyed increasing popularity in Italian operas since the days of Venetian hegemony. But Mozart was able to invest him with individual features, with the adagio of his very first aria already capturing the confusion of the disappointed lover by its chromatic inner voices and authentically Mozartian syncopations in the first violins. It is immediately followed by a brief and affecting confession of his love. No less authentic is his indictment of the gods that breaks out in the ensuing allego with its sinister trill-like figure in the winds. And the way in which the aria develops is likewise by no means as straightforward as would have been the case with the Italian composers of the period: despair, dull pain and love constantly overlap, with Mozart not only introducing the sudden minor-key harmonies so characteristic of this opera (notably in the eleventh bar with its insidiously creeping figure in the winds) but also calling on unexpected climaxes and abrupt changes of mood. How moving, for example, is the turn of phrase at the second 'che mio non è' and the brief larghetto episode at 'e non chiedo altra mercè'. Idamante's second aria is introduced by a particularly expressive accompanied recitative, in the course of which the bass line descends chromatically through an entire fifth in a series of powerful *sforzatos* beneath a hissing motif in the woodwinds: it is as though Idamante's soul were sinking into the depths of bottomless despair over this chain of dissonances. The aria, too, adopts the Italian practice and reflects the antithesis in the text ('il padre ritrovo e lo perdo'), and here, too, there is the same vacillation between resolve and sensibility and the same chiaroscuro of major and minor as in his first aria. It ends with a brief coda whose total sense of devastation could hardly be in starker contrast to the agitation of the recitative. As with his first aria, the orchestral ending fades away in a spirit of quiet wistfulness. The third aria, too, is preceded by a lengthy recitative. Its allegro section is the most markedly Italianate in style, while its slow middle section sings of approaching death with the mixture of sadness and rapt inwardness that the Italians have always been fond of adopting when expressing these ideas.

Mozart also had problems with his Idomeneo, Anton Raaff, who had become seriously set in his ways but who to a certain extent was able to overcome these shortcomings through sheer intelligence and good taste. As a result, the slow section of his first aria ('Vedrommi intorno') finds the composer clearly taking account of the tenor's old-fashioned style and of the fact that the singer preferred everything 'cut and dried'.[12] But it is difficult to square this tender-hearted, delicate aria with the terrible despair that Idomeneo feels as he comes ashore, and it is impossible not to hear in this number the typical *ombra* aria long familiar to the Italian composers of the time: even the

---

10. See Adolf Sandberger, *ZIMG*, vii (1905/6), 477.
11. ◆ In a letter of 22 November 1780 to his father, Mozart mentions a concert, on 20 November, at which the Italian castrato Vincenzo Dal Prato (1756–1828), the first Idamante, sang 'most disgracefully. I bet you he will never get through the rehearsals, still less the opera. Why, the rascal is rotten to the core' (*Briefe*, iii.28).
12. ◆ Idomeneo was the last operatic role sung by the German tenor Anton Raaff (1714–97). See Heartz, 'Raaff's last aria: A Mozartian idyll in the spirit of Hasse'.

winds that are cast in the role of otherworldly voices answering this sweet-toned lament derive from this tradition. Only with the great crescendo of the allegro section does this vision come to an end and the king's true state of mind is revealed. It is significant that this section, too, is in C minor with individual episodes, including the ending, in the major. In much the same way, Idomeneo's second aria ('Fuor del mar'), which Mozart described as 'the most splendid in the whole opera', is likewise based on an older Italian model, the simile aria on the subject of a storm at sea. But precisely because of this, its connection with the preceding recitative, in which the orchestra recalls all manner of motifs from Ilia's earlier aria, impressing them on the brooding king in a highly poetical manner, creates a somewhat frosty and conventional effect, and the same is true of the virtuosic features that could not of course be omitted from this genuinely heroic aria, even though Mozart prided himself particularly immodestly on his apt use of coloratura. Apart from a number of orchestral details, the importance of this piece lies rather in its bold harmonies more especially in its middle section, where, in keeping with the older tradition, they emerge with particular clarity. This desperate appeal to the 'fiero nume' modulates from A to F major with typically Mozartian abruptness in a series of brief and savage strokes, conjuring up a picture of a man who is wrecked both physically and emotionally. He is shaken to his very foundations, hounded from idea to idea, with no clearer form emerging, as in the following passage:

Idomeneo's third aria is prefaced by an expressive *accompagnato* which, motivically highly unified, describes in deeply felt and dignified terms the way in which the king breaks free from the psychological pressure upon him: the overall design strongly recalls that of a melodrama. The piece is in fact closely related to an earlier aria that Mozart had written for Raaff (K295) and which, it is clear from a complete surviving sketch,[13] was submitted to the singer for his approval. It begins with strains more appropriate to Sarastro, but then adopts a far more tender and sentimental tone, with its middle section in particular standing out as a Rococo idyll of the older type, while the recapitulation, conversely, offers a fine example of Mozart's skill at building to a sense of climax in passages such as this. Of course, when we consider the characterization of the king and his son in general, we shall find a lack of focus of a kind that recurs in *La clemenza di Tito*. This lack is less evident with Idamante, who coincides with the Italian stereotype of the long-suffering, wistful youth. But Idomeneo has acquired an excessive dose of sentimentality, no doubt out of consideration for Raaff. There is nothing in his arias to suggest the royal dignity that Hasse or even Gluck during his Italian period would have included here, while the terrible curse that weighs upon him produces a sense of secret pain and dark despair in his soul, but no feeling of manly resistance. Here we find ourselves at the very limits of Mozart's gift for *opera seria*: although he is capable of offering us individually moving and even harrowing emotional portraits, he cannot combine them in the way that Gluck and some of the leading Italian composers could do to create unified characters of a kind that he was so uniquely able to achieve in his *opere buffe* and German singspiels. These characters lack the spark that will bring them to life and make them instantly convincing. From a historical point of view, they are also far less autonomous than the later *buffa* characters, at least when compared with the Italians.

The female characters in *Idomeneo* share this same quality but each is far more unified than her male counterpart. They are also effectively differentiated from each other, with the gentle Ilia contrasted with the passionate Electra. Of course, even Electra has countless Italian predecessors as the spurned and ambitious lover, and with her appeal to the Furies in her very first aria ('Tutte nel cor vi sento') we again find ourselves in the presence of an extremely common Italian stereotype, yet it is one that Mozart is able to adapt to his own independent ends. The whole piece is a single outpouring of seething passion – there is no contrastive second subject – in which high-flown emotion finds no less powerful expression than regal dignity. Again there is a tense introduction over a dominant pedal point, with darting figures in the flutes suggestive of the Furies' snake-like heads and demonic trills in the violins. The voice then enters, but the vocal writing recalls nothing so much as a series of interjected outbursts rather than a genuine melodic line, the whole section underpinned by strident chords in the full orchestra and brief but realistically onomatopoeic motifs in individual instruments (especially the winds), isolated horn calls and so forth. But the torments of unrequited love also receive their due. Minor tonalities predominate, with even the second subject beginning in F minor rather than F major, and if the major suddenly breaks through, as at the words 'vendetta e crudeltà' in the second section, the effect is not one of liberation but of searing anguish. Much the same is true of the unison of voice and bass at the end. No less typical is the ending of the A-section, where, instead of the old ritornello, the orchestra

---

13. The middle section was not originally intended to form a contrast with the main section; four deleted bars from this initial version have survived in the sketch. ◆ The preliminary version of 'Se al labbro mio non credi – Il cor dolente' referred to by Abert is published in NMA II/7/2, 167–81.

wanders aimlessly through a series of violent *sforzatos* before finally coming to a rest on a terrible chord of a diminished seventh on B (with fermata), at which point the opening returns, but this time a whole tone lower, in C minor. The bravura element normally found in these arias is limited here to a handful of wide-ranging intervals and there is no coloratura at all. Electra's third aria ('D'Oreste, d'Ajace') is likewise a portrait of the Furies, with even its recitative painting a hellish picture of grief and despair. Electra's madness no longer finds expression here in individual outbursts but in broader melodic lines that make particular demands on the singer's upper register. In the orchestra, too, the same agitated trill-like figure is hounded to death virtually throughout the whole number, disappearing only during the second subject-group, where it is replaced by an intensely vivid depiction of the 'squarciatemi' and 'dolore' of the text: here, too, Electra's fury cannot entirely displace her feelings of love. The orchestra likewise goes its own way in terms of its motifs and tone colours, with both arias sharing not only the same lavish additional resources of trumpets, timpani and four horns but also the same characteristic viola sonorities. But Electra has a third aria ('Idol mio, se ritroso') that falls outside the framework of her character, her feeling of happiness finding so delightfully light, even playful expression here that it is impossible to recognize in her the proud and impassioned daughter of Agamemnon. Stylistically, too, it stands apart from her other two arias, tending to suggest the spirit of French comic opera rather than that of its Italian equivalent. Its second subject is heard in the orchestra in the course of its foregoing recitative, thereby forging a link between recitative and aria.

Only the character of Ilia remains consistent throughout her three arias ('Padre, germani, addio!', 'Se il padre perdei' and 'Zeffiretti lusinghieri'), a captive filled with calm nostalgia, heart-felt and tender in her affection for Idamante, radiating the whole charm of youthful grace and, above all, entirely truthful and natural in the expression of her feelings. As such, she is the most successfully characterized figure in the whole work. It is no wonder, then, that this is the one role in which the underlying Italian prototype has been developed along the most independent lines and the stylistic characteristics of the later Mozart emerge with particular clarity. Among these features are several that appear in the very first of these arias: the ritornello reduced to a few anxious sighs, the role of syncopation in the vocal line and accompaniment, the meaningful alternation between minor and major in the A-section, the emotionally charged cry of 'Grecia!' with its fate-laden pre-echo in the winds and, above all, the inspired climax achieved in the B-section on the strength of the simplest of variants. But the aria's Italianate foundations lie first and fore-most in its minor-key tonality, which is now maintained with very real obstinacy: only now, for example, does the second subject, which had earlier appeared in the major, find its full and exhaustive expression, and the brief and chromatically convoluted coloratura flourish at the end on the word 'odiare' now raises the sense of anguish to its highest possible pitch by the simplest and most truthful means.

But it is Ilia's second aria that reveals the truly mature composer. Notable on a purely superficial level for its four concertante instruments (flute, oboe, horn and bassoon), this aria reveals so many stylistic characteristics of Mozart's mature artistry that it is worth lingering over it in some detail. It is cast in the form of a simple two-part cavatina, with the second section merely a slight variant on the first. This first section is divided in turn into two parts of unequal length (we shall omit the introduction for the moment). The first covers the first two lines of the text ('Se il padre perdei, tu padre mi sei') and is twelve bars long, while the second section covers the remainder of the text and is twenty-seven bars long. There then follows a four-bar return to the A-section. The opening of the new section is marked by the entry of the new (wind) theme and the tonality of B flat major.[14] It is significant that Mozart treats the words 'soggiorno amoroso è Creta per me' as a separate unit, even though his librettist combined them metrically with the previous line. He had his own psychological reasons for doing this, as we shall soon have an opportunity to observe in greater detail. The subsections, too, are subdivided into two starkly contrastive parts, their division underscored both melodically and instrumentally. In the first section (bars 14–26) this is immediately clear. The second, conversely, is itself in three sections (bars 28–33, 33–39, 40–53), of which the second and third are more closely linked, as is clear from the half-cadence between them. But what is decisive here is the fact that each of these various parts introduces completely new and generally highly contrastive material: the existing material is not developed by means of repetition, sequencing or variation. From a psychological point of view, therefore, we have a great variety of different moods held together only by the uniformity of the underlying mood. But this characteristic extends even as far as the briefest elements that make up the melodic line: even within the first six bars of the vocal melody, the second phrase ('la patria, il riposo') brings with it a new idea already familiar from Paisiello, while the third (on 'tu padre') involves a completely unexpected outburst, with a *forte* accent, an interval of a seventh and rhythmically heavily accented, full-toned harmonies in the strings – a typically Mozartian feature. In short, this head-motif already contains within it three remarkably contrasted moods, namely, calm respect, profound sadness at the fate of the exiled Trojan (note the octave doubling of this affecting melody in the ritornello) and a sudden outburst of passion that equally rapidly subsides again – how subtly Mozart expresses the ambiguity of the words 'tu padre mi sei'. It is all held together by a constant syncopated rhythm that is only partially obscured by the little sighs on the main words and that always indicates inner agitation in Mozart's works. But the overriding sense of unity is achieved, above all, by the way in which this section builds perceptibly to a climax, with the outburst in the fifth bar prepared for by the previous semiquavers in the second violins. With the second section (bars 46–53) the winds take control in typically Mozartian fashion. The feeling of happiness that they express has something naïvely innocent about it: it is the heartfelt gratitude of a young woman who suppresses all other, secret thoughts. Only in the vocal line is there any sense of the old nostalgia.[15] The wind writing at the start of the second section is completely different, by contrast, bringing with it, as it does, the new idea of a 'soggiorno amoroso', whereby 'amoroso' is clearly associated with the notion of 'amore', in this case, Ilia's love of Idamante. There is a sense of burgeoning and yearning to the theme (note, in particular, the dynamics and phrasing). On both occasions the answer in the vocal line sounds like a cry of jubilation. Here Mozart uses the winds in a highly poetical way to proclaim the heart's secret desires. This time, too, he never abandons the single motif, which is even echoed in Idomeneo's heart at the start of the following scene. A further change of mood

14. It is tempting to place the entry of the second subject eight bars later (at 'or più non rammento'), which would make both sections the same length. Certainly, bars 20–39 form a self-contained whole divided only by the half-cadence on 'affanni'. But the cadence in bar 12 is so incisive and the ideas so emphatically separated that it is difficult to relate what follows to what has gone before. The formal ambiguity of these seven bars is part and parcel of the freer approach to form that will be characteristic of Mozart from now on. We shall encounter more such cases.

15. The repeat of the final 'tu padre mi sei' is authentically Italian, except that an Italian composer would have written:

It is above all the modulation to C minor in the second bar that is quintessentially Mozartian.

comes with bar 33. The winds disappear and the harmony, which until now has not extended beyond the tonic, dominant and supertonic, explores the keys of C, E flat and B flat minor. After an initial energetically ascending sixth, the melodic line settles down to a genuinely Mozartian chromatic line, with the words 'angoscie' and 'affanni' expressed as sighlike sequences in keeping with their meaning. Likewise the orchestral writing, which until now has been purely homophonic, assumes a sterner aspect and the feeling of anguish finally erupts in a sudden *forte* on the f sharp of 'affanni' with its following, highly effective melisma. The bassoon gloomily repeats the earlier semiquaver motif in the violins, this time in augmentation. And now, with bar 40, there follows a typically Mozartian contrast as Ilia rises above her torment, a contrast ushered in by the sustained fifth on the horn – an exceptionally poetical device that Mozart used countless times. He then appears to repeat the previous bassoon motif, but it is in fact the augmented form of the semiquaver motif from the next bar but one. Ilia's love of Idamante now breaks into the music, with no further attempt to conceal itself, while the text speaks only of 'gioia' and 'contento' in the most general terms. But Mozart's vocal writing at this point reveals the agitated line interrupted by rests that we often find at the end of his arias at such outpourings of intense emotion.[16] Here Mozart dispenses with the basses and solo horn, a sure sign that the emotional language has acquired an element of weightlessness and transfiguration. It is no wonder, then, that this motif, too, will later betray Ilia, when it returns in the following accompanied recitative. For the present, however, the instruments in their exuberance take over the motif from the singer and develop it with the scalar motif that Ilia then adopts as a coloratura flourish on the word 'contento'. The musical argument seems to push forward with a crescendo towards a full *forte* ending, but following the word 'contento' it moves off in a different direction, which, wholly untypical of Mannheim, is none the less genuinely Mozartian: the words 'il cielo mi diè' enter *piano* with a painfully tortuous syncopated coloratura, as Ilia's feelings of happiness of only a few moments earlier are suddenly overshadowed by this anxious thought of heaven – a fine example of Mozart's ability to depict the subtly complex emotional life of the soul. The brief orchestral postlude is again based on completely new material and consists of little more than a timid trembling answered by a few deep sighs in the basses and leading back, with eloquent Mozartian brevity, to the recapitulation. The result is the last remaining vestige of the prolix ritornellos that were found at this point in Italian operas. The recapitulation itself is motivically relatively literal, albeit with variants, all of which are aimed at increasing the expressive tension. One thinks especially of the interjection 'tu padre' that interrupts the first wind passage: even here Ilia already expresses her feelings more clearly than before. The second section indicates this increase in agitation by repeating the wind motif in different tonalities (A flat major, F minor and E flat major), and its consequent phrase, too, intensifies the expression by means of a further modulation and the searing intervals of a seventh in the vocal line. The coloratura on 'affanno' is now more extensive and appears twice in augmentation in the winds. With its note of jubilation, the following melody, too, is altered and intensified, not least by being taken up by the winds, with the concertante coloratura passage that follows even being repeated, significantly without the final chromatic coloratura heard earlier. The ending, too, draws on new motivic material and is four bars longer than before. One of these motifs (bars 103 and 105) is identical with the one from Belmonte's aria 'O wie ängstlich' from *Die Entführung aus dem Serail*, where according to Mozart himself it evokes

---

16. Other examples include the words 'Porgi amor, qualche ristoro' in the Countess's first aria in *Le nozze di Figaro* and at 'meinem Herzen mehr zurück' in Pamina's G minor aria, 'Ach, ich fühl's' in *Die Zauberflöte*.

the character's 'beating loving heart'.[17] The vocal line itself picks up the ending of the opening section ('tu padre mi sei'). The orchestral postlude is identical to that of the first part, dying away *pianissimo*. The introduction, by contrast, expresses the principal emotions that Ilia can convey to Idomeneo without further ado but as yet gives no indication whatsoever of her most private thoughts.

In short, this aria is particularly important for Mozart's operatic aesthetic. The most disparate feelings and ideas struggle for supremacy in Ilia's breast – her inborn maidenly modesty, her respect for the king, grief at her fate and, bound up with this, the memory of her happy life in Troy and, finally, her love of Idamante. Gluck would have produced a stereotypical portrait here, reducing everything to its simplest formula, whereas Mozart individualizes the character, allowing her emotions free rein and, unlike the economical Gluck, using a whole range of motifs that often displace one another within the narrowest confines. The result is a constant overlapping and combining of the most varied emotions, yet we never feel any sense of dissipation: instead, the most varied sentiments unconsciously merge to form a unified whole. This is a sign of supreme mastery. But the aria is also a perfect example of the way in which vocal and instrumental expression work together as the 'outer' and 'inner' action, an aspect of Mozart's artistry that many observers, unaware of the true facts of the matter, regard as an innovation of the modern music drama. The gradual emergence of Ilia's love – a feeling that she is obliged to conceal from the king – and, more generally, the whole impenetrable conflict between her outward situation and all that is going on in her mind are depicted here in incomparable fashion by the orchestra, and especially by the winds, which are used in a far more poetic way than we find with the Italian composers of the period. Hence the sense of compelling truth to Idomeneo's following words: 'Qual mi conturba i sensi equivoca favella!' ('How her ambiguous words disturb my mind!')

What has become of Johann Christian Bach's beautiful E flat major largos in Mozart's hands! Ilia's third aria ('Zeffiretti lusinghieri') emerges naturally from the exquisitely anquished mood of its recitative in A major. These gentle appeals to the 'zeffiretti, piante e fiori' were familiar from Italian opera, and Ilia's aria certainly has far fewer individual features than her other two. None the less, the charmingly wistful tone of the present idyllic aria is not hard to reconcile with her characterization elsewhere in the opera; the orchestral reminiscences of the A-section in the middle section are particularly appealing.

The duet for the two lovers ('S'io non moro a questi accenti') likewise remains within the traditional world of sensibility and grace, a handful of minor details excepted, and much the same can be said of the trio ('Pria di partir, o Dio!'), which fails to do justice to the dramatic situation with the resolve that the later Mozart was to show. Clearly, it was intended to do little more than provide a bridge between the delightful chorus that precedes it and the storm scene that follows.[18] Its andante section begins by striking a note that is positively Scarlattian. Here the characterization is only lightly sketched in – the anguished Idamante, the impassioned Electra and Idomeneo torn between feigned brusqueness and inner torment. But there is no real sense of confrontation here. With its upbeat syncopation, the following allego begins by recalling the andante's generalized mood of impassioned valediction, before appealing to the mercy of the gods in that half-transfigured tone later found in 'Wir wandeln durch des Tones Macht' in the second-act finale

---

17. *Briefe*, iii.162 (letter of 26 September 1781).
18. This is also the case with the second version, which was written after the rest of the work was finished. Motivically linked to the preceding recitative, it consists of a single continuous movement.

of *Die Zauberflöte*, the only difference being that the mood in *Idomeneo* is more agitated and less consistent. The quartet ('Andrò ramingo e solo') is on an incomparably higher level, a number that the composer continued to find affecting even much later in life.[19] Here Mozart insisted on having his own way in the face of his singers' demands. The result is a great two-part structure, the second section of which brings with it considerable changes, interpolations and additions. Two groups are contrasted with each other, in keeping with the situation on stage: on the one hand there are the lovers, on the other Electra and Idomeneo. Yet even within these two groups each individual is carefully characterized, so that even right at the outset Idamante's dark resolve is already contrasted with Ilia's affecting inwardness. Even more striking, however, is the sinister mood that imbues the number as a whole, adding an element of foreboding that is only fleetingly dispelled by isolated phrases from the lovers. Orchestral motifs portending disaster, insidious bass lines, syncopations and exceptionally bold and dark-toned harmonies all help to sustain this mood. Sometimes the dark storm clouds suddenly mass together, notably at the gloomily muted passage in B flat minor ('Ah il cor mi si divide') with its snakelike figure in the orchestra. Most impressive of all, however, is the polyphonic intensity of the part-writing in the second section of the quartet. At the end, Idamante repeats his resolve, 'Andrò ramingo e solo', and leaves, while isolated fragments of what had originally been the remainder of this motif echo after him in the orchestra.

But the real strength of *Idomeneo* lies in its choruses, an aspect that constitutes the most immediate reflection of Mozart's impressions of Paris. As with the French composers of this period, these choruses may be divided into staffage choruses (those normally linked to a ballet) and dramatic choruses. The first chorus ('Godiam la pace, trionfi Amore') is a good example of the first kind, its generalized dance character and inclusion of solo episodes both reflecting the French tradition, while its brilliant and noisy verve suggests Italian models. There are even closer links between the final chorus ('Scenda Amor') and French opera and – in terms of its melodic writing – comic opera in particular. The very heading of the final chorus of the opening act – 'Ciaconna' – recalls a dance form especially popular in ballet and opera at this time, a type of festive rondo with solo episodes that was, of course, completely different from the variations of the older period.[20] The second of these solo episodes is especially close to Grétry in terms of its rhythms and melody and even includes a change of tempo and time-signature. The number ends in the French manner with a brilliant crescendo that raises the pitch of festive celebration to a level of utmost splendour. The orchestral writing is completely independent of the voices, so that the chorus could be omitted and there would be no obvious lacuna. A transition to the dramatic choruses is provided by the Sailors' chorus ('Placido è il mar, andiamo'), one of the most delightful maritime numbers of the older genre. Not only is the form of the siciliana Italian, but it is impossible to hear this piece without thinking of the blue waters of the Mediterranean. The instrumentation is limited to the gentle sounds of flutes, clarinets and horns. The choral strophes are separated by a more animated solo strophe for Electra.

The dramatic choruses are on a far more inspired level, with Mozart's contemporary predilection for choral composition resulting in monumental examples of the tragic style. The external

---

19. According to Constanze's account in Hogarth, *Memoirs of the Opera*, ii.198. ◆ For an extended analysis of this number, see Heartz, 'The Great Quartet in Mozart's *Idomeneo*'.

20. Well-known examples occur in Gluck's *Iphigénie en Aulide* and his French version of *Alceste*.

impetus again came from Paris, although it should not be forgotten that both Jommelli and Traetta had already written great choral scenes, as, indeed, had Mozart himself in *Ascanio in Alba* and *Lucio Silla*. Gluck's influence is evident not only from their sublime and tragic seriousness of purpose but also from a number of formal and melodic features, although it is not so pronounced that the opera as a whole can thereby be regarded as a product of the Gluckian school. Even the first of these choruses ('Pietà! Numi, pietà!'), which depicts Idomeneo's shipwreck, reveals exceptional dramatic imagination that goes far beyond Varesco, who provides for only a single chorus of shipwrecked mariners, whereas Mozart distinguishes between a 'coro lontano' out at sea and a 'coro vicino' on stage. The former is in four parts and is largely accompanied by winds, while the two-part writing in the latter is supported by strings. Motivically, too, the two choruses are differentiated from each other. Common to both is merely their realistically disjointed mode of expression, a form that captures the characters' mortal fear. In the case of the mariners out at sea, this fear takes the form of a stammering and wailing intermingled with isolated cries of anguish, whereas what we hear in the case of those on shore are terrified, agitated calls for help. Only at the beginning does the off-stage chorus repeat the motif of the on-stage chorus like some demented echo. The same device recurs towards the end, where Mozart's imitative writing for the two choruses makes their cries of terror appear to reverberate confusedly on all sides. The orchestra, meanwhile, is left not only to evoke the tempest but – as its division indicates – to mirror the events in the minds and souls of the sailors. As before, the writing for the more distant chorus is notable for its far more anxious and timid motifs than those given to the on-stage chorus. The harmonic writing, too, is extremely dissonant and bold, including, as it does, conscious asperities such as the following, which is accompanied by the Gluckian nature motif of the *coro lontano*:

The choral scene at the end of act two ('Qual nuovo terrore!') is even more powerful. It, too, begins with a storm which on this occasion accompanies the appearance of the sea-monster. After a brief orchestral introduction based on subdominant harmonies, the whole chorus enters as a dense mass with its broad, realistic cries, whose recurrent heroic rhythm – a Gluckian mode of expression – is bound to strike Idomeneo as the deity's punitive voice even before the question 'Il reo, qual'è' ('Who is the guilty one?') is repeated four times. But the orchestra assumes responsibility for depicting the raging sea and roaring monster. As the number progresses, so its tonality increasingly vanishes, so that ultimately it is impossible to speak any longer of a basic key. It culminates in the fourfold question. And it ends three times on a heavily dissonant chord with a fermata that is answered by a brief and piercing interjection in the winds, a shattering climax entirely worthy of Gluck. As though gasping for air, Idomeneo then announces his decision to die in a strident D major. At the end, his plea for innocence and his indictment of Neptune are filled with anguish and dismay. Now the chorus intervenes for a second time ('Corriamo, fuggiamo quel mostro spietato'), this time as a frightened crowd scattering in every direction to the sounds of cries of horror and, as such, reminiscent of the crowd in act one, scene four of Gluck's *Alceste*. Hence Mozart's use of a 12/8 time-signature otherwise rarely found in his works, and hence, too, the largely imitative writing for the voices that answer each other now in anxiously stumbling motifs, now in long-drawn cries, coming together only occasionally to produce homophonic textures. The final disjointed phrases reach us from the remote distance. Also French in origin, finally, is the scene with priests in act two. For all its brevity, the orchestral introduction mirrors the events on stage: first, the king and his retinue appear, the former majestic yet visibly agitated, then come the priests in a sombre A flat major and, finally, the excitable, heaving crowd. The following recitative for the High Priest is closely based on the scene with the High Priest in act one, scene four of Gluck's *Alceste*. Even the recurrent motif

corresponds to Gluck's in every way apart from the typically Mozartian trill:[21]

But with its depiction of the approaching deity, Gluck's scene is even more solemn and mysterious, building to an irresistible climax lacking in Mozart's case. The third-act chorus ('O, o voto tremendo!') likewise begins on a Gluckian note, especially in terms of the mixture of horror and grief on the part of the populace, which continues to strike a note of disgruntled agitation. The sound of muted trumpets and muffled timpani adds to the feeling of oppressiveness until it becomes positively tormenting, and there is something deeply affecting about the unison passage for the chorus at the word 'Già regna la morte' ('Death now reigns'), with its note of dull lamentation from which the chromatically rising triplet figure in the winds seeks in vain to break free. Note how poetically it is taken up by the orchestra in the solo episode for the High Priest. No less emotionally charged, finally, is the chorus's threefold cry of 'O!', which leads back to the sombre mood of the opening after the brighter middle section. A touching postlude reintroduces a lighter note and leads into the beautiful march that introduces the sacrifice. It, too, is markedly influenced by the march from Gluck's *Alceste*, but the underlying note of solemnity is now joined by an elegiac tone that will later be heard to far greater effect in the March of the Priests in *Die Zauberflöte*. There follows Idomeneo's solemn prayer with choral accompaniment, a number that is one of the finest expressions of Mozart's genius ('Accogli, o rè del mar'). The solo melody is a supremely transfigured outpouring of *italianità*, heartfelt to the point of ecstasy, yet imbued with subdued and affecting sadness. But the priests sing their brief prayer to the single note c sharp with almost liturgical severity, descending at the end to f with a plagal cadence familiar from sacred music. The instrumentation, too, is particularly unusual, with wind sonorities seeming to hover over harplike pizzicato chords in the strings and etching in gently rocking imitative motifs and miniature marginal images. Only with the plagal cadence does the sense of movement come to an end on a devoutly sustained chord. The result is an atmospheric portrait of a kind that we shall look for in vain in either Gluck or contemporary Italian composers: for all its clarity, it reveals an unfathomable multiplicity of moods. The brief passage for off-stage chorus that follows is in stark and well-calculated contrast, its accompaniment for trumpets and timpani helping to turn it into nothing more nor less than a victory fanfare for voices and instruments.

Here, too, the bulk of the dialogue is entrusted to *secco* recitative, but there is very little sign here of the profound indifference to declamation that characterizes the *secco* passages in *La clemenza di Tito*. Indeed, the mere fact that Mozart originally set all the *secco* passages in the libretto but shortened them in the course of the rehearsals[22] shows that he kept a careful eye of this aspect of the

21. It reappears in the quintet (5) and the scene with the priests in the first-act finale of *Die Zauberflöte* and also as the main theme of the opening movement of Carl Maria von Weber's piano quartet in B flat major.
22. See the critical commentary to NMA II/5/11/1–2.

work, even though it was not the singing that was of paramount importance for him, of course, but the on-stage action. The execution is not consistent. Electra, for example, has a number of passages of recitative that are indifferently written and even feeble (act one, scene four, and act two, scene four), and there are still a number of important scenes such as Neptune's baleful command and the first encounter between Idomeneo and his victim Idamante that are treated as *secco*. But these passages are offset by others that explore the situation and characters with greater care. Yet here, too, there remains a wide gulf between Mozart and Gluck. The former comes closest to his older colleague in the elevated, solemn tone in which princes customarily address their people over sustained notes in the bass, as in act one, scene three. But even on those occasions where Mozart's *secco* recitatives are well handled, they are far less rigorously matched to the words than is the case with Gluck. With Gluck the recitatives grow out of the spoken language and its underlying emotion with wonderful naturalness. The sharpest possible distinction is drawn between individual sentences and, within these sentences, between parts of the sentence and even between individual concepts and words, with their emotional significance explored in depth, while the melodic line follows the subtlest inflections of the spoken melos and the harmonic writing has the task of etching in the emotional bases of the dialogue. With Gluck a single chord is often retained with iron resolve throughout an entire complex of ideas; if the emotion that he is depicting grows more intense while the underlying ideas remain the same, he tends to use melodic sequences over chromatically rising basses, achieving his finest results with this device in his recitatives.[23] It is significant that *Idomeneo* does not contain a single parallel to this. The declamation here is certainly not poor and on occasions it is even impressive: Mozart is generally capable, for example, of drawing an apt distinction between the individual characters in a particular passage of dialogue (here one thinks of father and son in act one, scene nine, and of Ilia and Idamante in act three, scene two – an especially well-declaimed number). It also includes some finely observed atmospheric portraits, notably the breathless Arbace in act three, scene eight, and the raptly wistful Ilia in act three, scene one. But Mozart does not proceed with anything like the same steadfastness of purpose as Gluck, and the results are far more variable. There are occasions when the beginning of a *secco* passage reveals an almost total lack of interest on his part, only for his enthusiasm to be gradually fired in the course of the number: act two, scene one affords a good example of this. But the most typical aspect of these recitatives is to be found not in their declamation but in their harmonic writing – in other words, on a musical level, rather than that of linguistic melody. Here Mozart adopts a far freer and bolder approach to modulation than Gluck, opening up completely new and surprising areas by means of an interrupted cadence or enharmonic change. Bound up with this is his particular predilection for animated bass lines in his *secco* recitatives, a device found relatively infrequently in Gluck and his Italian contemporaries. One example among many may be found in act one, scene eight.[24]

But it is the accompanied recitatives that have most increased in number and importance in comparison with the earlier operas. With a sure instinct Mozart has divided them up among the emotional high points of the work, and their treatment reveals great progress that is again due to the impressions gleaned in Paris and Mannheim. The principal role is played by the orchestra:

---

23. See Ralph Meyer, 'Die Behandlung des Rezitativs in Glucks italienischen Reformopern'.
24. ◆ For a different view of Mozart's recitatives, see Rushton, '"... hier wird es besser seyn – ein blosses Recitativ zu machen...": Observations on recitative organization in *Idomeneo*'.

there are far fewer passages in which the voice is supported only harmonically. Generally the orchestral writing proceeds independently of the voice, while at the same time serving to clarify it. We have already discussed the powerful impact of the melodrama, an influence especially apparent in the numerous passages in which orchestra and voice are so sharply differentiated that for long sections the vocal line is unaccompanied as mere musical declamation. Even the very first scene of the opera includes various examples of this. In general, these accompanied recitatives are distinguished from Gluck's not by virtue of their dramatic rigour but – as before – by their greater variety of mood and their more lavish musical execution. Only rarely does Mozart match Gluck's ability to work towards his goal in a straight line while building to a powerful climax. And unlike Gluck, but like his Italian colleagues, he produces finer and more individual results in contemplative and sentimental scenes, rather than in those of a darker, more impassioned character. Yet most of these scenes exhibit an astonishing range of emotions, with a remarkable variety of motifs liberally scattered among them. At the same time, there is no longer any trace of the careless, loosely structured design of the early operas but a determination, rather, to introduce a sense of poetic meaning and order to the overall structure. The motifs are generally developed, albeit very freely, returning at significant junctures as in the melodrama. (The most unified section in this respect is act three, scene eleven.) The majority of them are exceptionally eloquent and expressive, and some are even introduced canonically. As in the *secco* recitatives, the harmonic writing is particularly delightful here. Especially bold are the harmonies that develop over chromatically descending basses, a device of which Mozart was to remain very fond at a later date, too. They create an emotion that vacillates remarkably between agitation and resignation, notably at Ilia's 'tiranni i Dei non son' in act three, scene ten, with its tremolando in the second violins and eloquent little motif in the first. We have already commented on the way in which Mozart occasionally forges a highly poetical motivic link between a recitative and the following – and even the preceding – aria (act two, scene five, and act two, scenes two and three). The principle itself is, of course, older and is found, for example, in act one, scene seven of Jommelli's *Fetonte*. A case unto itself is the Voice of the Oracle ('Ha vinto amore . . . a Idomeneo perdona'), which Mozart set three times, on each occasion shortening it, as the first version struck him as far too long.[25] All three versions are accompanied by three trombones and two horns. Here, too, the Oracle in Gluck's *Alceste* was the model, except that Gluck's scene is not only shorter than Mozart's, it also has the advantage of stressing the otherworldly aspect of the apparition, an aspect derived from Rameau's idea of setting the vocal line to the same unvarying pitch. Gluck's Oracle has an awesome otherworldliness to it, whereas Mozart's – in spite of (or, rather, because of) the far greater musical resources lavished upon it and in spite of its strange majesty – remains rather more earthbound in all three versions. Of these, the second – shorter than the first – is the most effective.

A further aspect of the opera's advance over its predecessors, and one that should not be underestimated, is the fact that, at least at its most significant points, it prefers the great dramatic scene to the old interplay of recitative and aria. That it still falls short of Gluck's complex structures is the result of the Italian design of the libretto. None the less, Mozart created scenes of enthralling dramatic weight that approach their model in intensity, notably in the final scene of act two (from the trio onwards) and in the scene with the priests in act three (even though this scene ends, of course, in a passage of *secco* recitative). Elsewhere he not only runs individual numbers together

---

25.   The different versions of this scene are published in NMA II/5/11, 472–3 and 566–9. The crescendo and diminuendo on the wind chords in the first two versions rest on a suggestion of Leopold. ◆ Mozart described the reasons for his revision in a letter to his father of 29 November 1780 (*Briefe*, iii.34–5); further, see Manfred Hermann Schmid, 'Das Orakel in Mozarts *Idomeneo*'.

('Tutte nel cor vi sento' and 'Pietà! Numi, pietà!) but also, and above all, seeks to forge a closer link between recitative and aria. Most of the recitatives grow increasingly varied and expressive towards the end and, as in the *secco* recitatives, the bass lines grow more animated, while the introductions to many of the arias reveal the tonally curiously vacillating, tension-inducing character already mentioned, an aspect that allows the lyrical outburst of the aria to seem the natural and ultimate expression of pent-up emotion. This is especially true of Electra's first aria, and as this leads directly into the chorus of shipwrecked sailors at the end, the character's state of emotional upheaval is meaningfully linked to the turmoil affecting the elements.

But for contemporary listeners the most novel aspect of the work was Mozart's handling of his orchestra.[26] Certainly, no other opera by the composer reveals so rich and resplendent an orchestral garb, and time and again one can sense his delight in writing for the Munich orchestra and not being hoppled by the sort of restrictions that he was familiar with from Salzburg. All that he had learnt in Mannheim and Paris in terms of the art of instrumentation he now sought to apply to opera. The forces are those that he was also to use later, including the clarinets that he had particularly wanted to write for. Conversely he was never again to write for four horns, which he had occasionally used previously and which are employed several times in *Idomeneo*. In every case his aim was clearly to press this greater range of instruments into the service of the drama. Certain instruments are employed only once in the course of the work: here one thinks of the piccolo during the tempest ('Qual nuovo terrore!')[27] and of the trombones during the oracle – as is evident from the *Thamos* choruses and later from *Die Zauberflöte*, Mozart reserved trombones for moments of supreme religious solemnity. But there are no trumpets or timpani in the two storm scenes, and it is not until the chorus of fleeing Cretans – a number totally different in style – that Mozart first chooses to employ them. But, mindful of their festive associations in older Italian works, he also uses them in the dance choruses ('Nettuno s'onori!' and 'Scenda Amor'), in the chorus of mourning ('O, o voto tremendo!'), where their muted and muffled tone creates a remarkably subtle effect, and finally – and again in keeping with tradition – in two emotionally charged arias ('Fuor del mar' and 'D'Oreste, d'Ajace').

As for Mozart's treatment of the orchestra in general, our earlier comments on the choruses from *Thamos* remain valid, only more so. A number of fine examples of Mozart's poetical handling of the winds have already been mentioned in the case of individual arias. The old register-based concertante writing for strings and winds has now been replaced by total freedom. Often it is no more than a few notes that suddenly introduce a different colour into the music: take, for example, the brief but heavy sigh in the bassoons in the third and fourth bars of the very first aria or the perplexedly sobbing wind motif that precedes the allegro section of Idomeneo's entrance aria ('Vedrommi intorno'). Elsewhere the full winds combine in weighty rhythms and in sustained and howling chords as at the beginning of the second storm scene. The characteristic tone colours of the various instruments are admirably exploited not only on a superficial tone-painterly level but also to depict the characters' state of mind, with all three of Electra's arias, for example, typified by the same viola sonorities. No less typical of the work is a certain predilection for figures that steal through the winds in thirds and sixths to evoke a sense of the sinister ('Non ho colpa'); in Idomeneo's entrance aria (and later) they appear staccato; and in the prayer ('Accogli, o re del mar') they gradually work their way up through the orchestra from the bassoons to the flutes. Within the strings, too, new life stirs, not only in the independent and often *divisi*

---

26. See Komorzynski, *Mozarts Kunst der Instrumentation*, 13ff.
27. Here it once doubles the double basses at the upper octave.

violas that we have already encountered in Mozart's earlier works but more especially in the way in which the cellos now break free from the basses. In the march they create a curious effect by doubling the basses, but two octaves higher.

For all his delight in sensuous tonal effects, Mozart never loses sight of the underlying drama, with his treatment of the winds in particular revealing numerous passages entirely worthy of the later composer. And in spite of all this instrumental splendour, the rights of the human voice are never curtailed: as before, the voice remains the soul of the work as a whole.

Notwithstanding these merits, Jahn is emphatically wrong when he claims that in this opera Mozart laid the foundations for modern instrumentation.[28] This had long been achieved by Italian and French composers, to say nothing of Gluck and the Mannheim school. Indeed, *Idomeneo* still falls far short of Gluck in the invention and exploitation of certain 'Romantic', colouristic orchestral effects. In this respect, too, *Idomeneo* represents an important stage on a road that was clearly marked out in advance, but it was not yet the gateway to a new art.

Within the opera, the orchestra achieves full independence only in the ballets and three marches, the first of which is a powerfully festive march with brief French trio episodes. The second follows immediately on from the final note of Electra's aria and begins with its second section, thus plunging the listener *in medias res*.[29] Its principal effect is borrowed from *opéra comique* and consists in the gradual approach of the march, which begins *pianissimo* and *con sordini*,[30] rising to *fortissimo* through the gradual entry of more and more instruments. Electra interjects her reaction as though at random. With its constant rhythm ♩ ♪♪♩ ♪│♩, this march is authentically Mozartian, on more than one occasion recalling Figaro's wedding march. We have already mentioned the third and most attractive of these three marches.

The first of the dances that are linked to the opera is a chaconne, the beginning of which is identical to that of the chaconne from Gluck's *Iphigénie en Aulide*. The headings read 'Pas de deux de Mad. Hartig et Mr. Antoine', then 'Pas seul de Mad. Falgera'. The repeat of the main section is invariably headed 'Pour le Ballet'. One particular episode is the beautiful, genuinely Mozartian larghetto in B flat major ('Pas seul de Mad. Hartig'), after which a new section of the chaconne begins in D minor, before the whole company ends the movement with the main theme. But the orchestra leads directly into no. 2, 'Pas seul de Mr. Le Grand', in which an emotionally charged slow introduction is followed by a dainty allegretto that was, however, cut at the first performances. It ends with a sparkling più allegro and then ('Pour le Ballet') a further più allegro, a veritable riot of triplets with a large-scale Mannheim crescendo seasoned with suspensions. No. 3 is a charming Passepied with Mineur 'pour Mad[selle] Redwen'. The following gavotte (no. 4) has no performance instructions. It has a certain old-fashioned air to it, especially in its middle section, from which a delightful passage involving imitative interplay with the main theme leads back to the beginning. No. 5 is a passacaglia ('Pas seul de Mr. Antoine – Pas de deux de Mad. Falgera et Mr. Le Grand'). It, too, is a rondo-like movement with several episodes that only gradually assumed its definitive form on account of its excessive length.[31]

28. Jahn, *W. A. Mozart*, i.681.
29. Mozart does something similar with the march in *Le nozze di Figaro* and the menuetto in *Don Giovanni*. The same device is also employed by Spohr in the case of the menuetto at the beginning of *Faust*.
30. Mozart had to have the mutes for the trumpets and horns sent to him from Salzburg. ◆ See his letter of 5 December 1780 (*Briefe*, iii.48).
31. Two longer sections were drafted by Mozart but not taken over into the finished work. The whole pas de deux was then cut before the first performance. One of the folios on which this number was written is missing from the autograph score. According to the critical commentary, there were additional sketches on pp.39 and 42 of the present score, but these were later discarded. For a discussion of the ballet music, see Chrysander, 'Mozarts Ballettmusik zur Oper "Idomeneo"'. ◆ Further see NMA II/5/11/2, 623–6.

In general, these dances are less distinctive than the older types, with the chaconne and passacaglia in particular already very close to the rondo. Gluck's dances are more dour and more unequivocal in character, whereas Mozart's are more varied, with a greater delight in sheer music-making. Clear and simple, with no claims to any great profundity, they none the less reveal the whole charm of Mozart's graceful and apt approach.

The overture, by contrast, is magnificent in terms of both its design and its execution, a piece aglow from first to last with supremely tragic emotion. Instead of the three-movement Italian type, Mozart has opted for a single-movement form, evidently under Gluck's influence,[32] the only difference being that Gluck's brief slow introduction has been replaced by a seven-bar festive opening. The end of the overture likewise follows Gluck's example and leads straight into the opening scene. The last seven bars even include a clear reminiscence of the introduction to the overture to *Iphigénie en Aulide*. The opening, too, recalls this work,[33] although both composers were, of course, drawing on the festive tone of the Italian sinfonia in general. But with his darkly insidious crotchet motif, Mozart moves straight into the emotional world of the drama, the sombre basic tone of which is expressed above all in the numerous passing modulations to minor tonalities and the harshly piercing dissonances. Although the overture is in three sections, subject-group and development section pass imperceptibly into each other, such is the floodtide of passion that bears it along. The overture's notional second subject is in A minor: note its gentle sighs and its wonderfully comforting ascent to C major, the only passage in the piece that grants space to any greater sense of hope. In the recapitulation it is replaced by a rock-solid, twice repeated pedal point which the violins attempt to resist by means of an agitated melisma expressive of fearful pressure and dissonantly accompanied by what had originally been a subsidiary motif. The ending suggests nothing so much as meek capitulation, although not before the earlier sense of agitation has twice broken through in the form of two violent *sforzatos*.

Although *Idomeneo* does not mark a milestone in the history of opera – even if this has long been assumed to be the case by Jahn and others – it may none the less be seen as one in Mozart's own development. It is the first proof of the now fully mature composer's new dramatic powers following his visit to Paris, but at the same time it also shows beyond doubt that *opera seria* and tragic music drama were not the field in which his natural talent could prosper. Writers have long been misled by the admittedly undeniable fact that Mozart far outshines all his Italian rivals in terms of the strength and variety of his talents as a musician, but this in itself was not sufficient to give a new sense of direction to an entire genre such as *opera seria*. For this to have happened, it would have needed a far more critical engagement with the spirit of the whole genre than Mozart was capable of achieving on the strength of his existing outlook. It is enough to recall what he made of the singspiel in *Die Entführung aus dem Serail* and what he made of the *opera buffa* in *Le nozze di Figaro* to realize the truth of this remark. In these freer and more natural fields his dramatic creativity blazed a trail with elemental force, calling into existence something entirely new. In *Idomeneo*, by contrast, he failed to break free from his Italian models in spite of the work's teeming world of musical ideas. Above all, he failed to solve the problems inherent in the whole genre. As a result, his progress vis-à-vis his Italian contemporaries lies in the field of music, not of drama. Not even the tremendous choral scenes, which even today have lost none of their grandeur, alter this state of affairs, but merely point up the contrast with the Italian foundations of the work. It is no accident that *Idomeneo* was Mozart's last conscious attempt to conquer the field of *opera*

---

32. Single-movement overtures were also familiar to Mozart, of course, from French *opéras comiques*.
33. It later returns, barely changed, in the overture to *La clemenza di Tito*.

seria – La clemenza di Tito was no more than a guest appearance, as it were, an engagement that he accepted for wholly impersonal reasons, evincing a fine sense of style but carrying out the commission with no aim of reforming the genre.

It is also significant that the opera's success was limited to the few performances that he himself conducted in Munich. Apart from the amateur production in Vienna in 1786, the work never resurfaced, at least in the shorter term. Only when Mozart's later operas were firmly established in the repertory was it revived, partly out of curiosity, but without ever gaining a permanent place for itself in opera-house schedules. As with *La clemenza di Tito*, there were only isolated performances,[34] generally within the framework of complete cycles of Mozart's operas, from which it could not, of course, be excluded. More recently, there have been a number of notable attempts to revise the work in an attempt to bring it closer to modern taste.[35] These attempts are all the most commendable in that we owe it to an artist like Mozart to keep on reminding ourselves of those of his works that have never been popular with the broad masses. Of course, it is virtually out of the question that *Idomeneo* will ever be regularly staged, as the whole genre of *opera seria* is one that our present dramatic sensitivities are no longer able to accommodate.[36] We have enough difficulty, after all, in keeping Gluck's incomparably more powerful works alive in our opera houses.

---

34. An exception was Dresden, where, thanks to the advocacy of Joseph Tichatschek, the work remained in the repertory for several years following its first performance on 15 January 1854. ◆ Vocal scores of *Idomeneo* had appeared as early as 1797–8; the first full score was published in Bonn, by Simrock, in 1805. The opera had been given in German in Kassel as early as 1802 and in Vienna, also in German, in 1806. As Abert notes, however, there was no sustained performance tradition in the early decades of the nineteenth century.

35. The most recent version is by Ernst Lewicki; see his 'Auf Mozartschen Vorlagen fußende Bühnen-Neubearbeitung der ernsten Oper "Idomeneus"', and 'Zur Wiederbelebung des Mozartschen Musikdramas "Idomeneus." Ein Wort der Anregung und praktische Vorschläge'; see also Lert, *Mozart auf dem Theater*, 328ff. ◆ A notable modernization, slightly postdating Abert and undertaken by Richard Strauss in 1930/1, is described in Holden, 'Richard Strauss' performing version of *Idomeneo*'; also see Walton, 'The performing version by Richard Strauss and Lothar Wallerstein'.

36. ◆ History has to some extent proved Abert wrong: *Idomeneo* has enjoyed a revival both in the opera house and among writers on music – the work no longer represents 'dramatic sensitivities' we are unable to 'to accommodate'. Among recent, important works on *Idomeneo*, including historiographically-aware accounts of influence as well as analytical, source and documentary studies, see Platoff, 'Writing about influences: *Idomeneo*, a case study'; Rushton, 'Mozart and opera seria'; *Mozarts 'Idomeneo' und die Musik in München zur Zeit Karl Theodors*; Münster, 'Ich bin hier sehr beliebt': *Mozart und das kurfürstliche Bayern*. Among general resources, Rushton, *W. A. Mozart: Idomeneo*, is comprehensive. As his text for the opera, Abert used the Breitkopf & Härtel AMA edition of 1881, which was based on Mozart's autograph score (now split between the Staatsbibliothek zu Berlin and the Biblioteka Jagiellońska, Kraków). The discovery in 1981 of the original performing parts shows that Mozart made some last-minute revisions to the work, revisions not recorded in the autograph. Chiefly these include the re-insertion of Idamante's deleted aria 'No, la morte' and the fact that Raaff sang the first version of 'Fuor del mar'. These changes also affect the version of the work published in the 1972 NMA edition (II/5/11), although they are described in the later critical report; see Münster, 'Neues zum Münchner *Idomeneo* 1781'.

27

First steps in Vienna

While Colloredo was attempting unsuccessfully to persuade Leopold Kozeluch to succeed Mozart in Salzburg,[1] the latter was busily trying to find a permanent post for himself in Vienna. As early as 4 April 1781 he had written to his father: 'I assure you that this is a splendid place – and for my métier the best place in the world.'[2] His enthusiasm was fully justified, as Vienna was now more than ever the capital of German music, not only offering young artists a wealth of novel stimuli but also providing the best possible prospects for their material survival. The court, aristocracy and clergy continued to maintain their glorious musical traditions,[3] with the middle classes increasingly following their example. In no other German town or city was such a range of music as admirably organized as here, with the theatre in particular enjoying a new and promising revival.

As we have already seen, Mozart himself was exceptionally pleased with his reception in Vienna, where he hoped to make a name for himself as a keyboard player ('This is undoubtedly the land of the keyboard',[4] he told his father on 2 June 1781) and as a teacher, in that way preparing the ground for his début as a composer. It soon turned out, of course, that the moment of his arrival on the Viennese musical scene was singularly ill-timed as the aristocracy invariably repaired to their country seats with the onset of summer. For the time being, therefore, he could achieve nothing by putting on concerts, and for the present he found himself with only a single pupil, the Countess Rumbeke née Cobenzl, who went on to enjoy considerable acclaim as a performer.[5] No doubt Mozart could have had more pupils, but for understandable reasons he was unwilling to lower his price of six ducats for twelve lessons. Needless to say, these experiences were all grist to his father's mill, but Mozart refused to be daunted by them. The feeling of being rid of an intolerable burden kept all thoughts of depression at bay, and his letters from this period all breathe a spirit of confidence and contentment. He eagerly set about preparing for the coming winter, beginning by opening a subscription for six violin sonatas K296 and K376–380,[6] but in spite of the support of the Countess Thun and other female members of the nobility, only seventeen subscribers could be found. He also thought of organizing a concert during the coming Advent

---

1. Colloredo held out the offer of a salary of 1000 florins, but Kozeluch declined on the grounds that he was better off in Vienna. According to Mozart's letter of 4 July 1781 (*Briefe*, iii.136), Kozeluch told his friends that what most deterred him from accepting the offer was Mozart's own fate in Salzburg: if Colloredo treated a man such as Mozart in this way, how would he himself fare at the archbishop's hands?
2. *Briefe*, iii.102 (letter of 4 April 1781).
3. On 10 August 1781, Leopold Mozart wrote to Breitkopf: 'As His Grace the Prince treated my son extremely badly there [in Vienna], whereas all the higher nobility showed him every honour, they had no difficulty in persuading him to resign a post to which such a miserable salary was attached and to remain in Vienna' (*Briefe*, iii.148). ◆ Also see Rice, 'Vienna under Joseph II and Leopold II'.
4. *Briefe*, iii.125 (letter of 2 June 1781).
5. Schönfeld, *Jahrbuch der Tonkunst von Wien und Prag*, i (1796), 51.
6. They were published by Artaria in November 1781 as the composer's op. 2 and dedicated to Josepha von Auernhammer.

and of performing a new Italian cantata to words by Felice Rossi. Above all, however, he was keen to obtain another commission to write for the theatre. Indeed, his desire to do so was hardly surprising, given the current state of the Viennese theatre and its popularity with the audiences of the day. His letter to his sister of 4 July 1781 is the best possible proof that he now felt a profound need to renew his links not just with opera but with the theatre in general: 'My sole entertainment is the theatre; I wish you could see a tragedy here! I really don't know of any other theatre where all the different kinds of plays are *so well* performed; but here every role – even the smallest and least significant – is well taken and double-cast.'[7]

It should be clear from this passage that there is absolutely no justification for the curious attempts that have been made in recent years to cast doubt on Mozart's literary leanings. Indeed, no life of the composer can ignore the Viennese theatre of his day,[8] not least in view of the fact that it had such a decisive impact on the development of the singspiel in general.

As a result of the Counter Reformation, Austria had long been cut off from the literary life of the rest of Germany, but by the time of the Seven Years War the country was beginning to renew its contacts with the outside world. Gottsched's ideas slowly gained acceptance in Vienna as elsewhere, finding a lively response with the cultured aristocracy above all. Yet even in Mozart's day dramatists such as Cornelius Ayrenhoff and Tobias Philipp Gebler still subscribed to the French ideal. All the more dangerous was the threat posed to that ideal by the autochthonous popular theatre. Italian improvised comedy had found a natural ally in the inclinations of the Viennese national character and produced a unique local art form that was not only successful in resisting the influence of serious French drama but also gave a largely new direction to comic opera. From Italy came the art of improvisation and the character of Arlecchino, who was very soon completely nationalized as Hanswurst, while the Viennese themselves contributed a type of humour which, partly homespun, partly slapstick, but always good-natured, appealed chiefly to its listeners' emotions, rather than to their intellect, as Italian comedy did. It was Josef Anton Stranitzky (1676–1726) who created the Viennese Hanswurst.[9] Stranitzky was followed by Gottfried Prehauser (1699–1769), whose merits were acknowledged even by one of the character's most outspoken opponents, Joseph von Sonnenfels (1733–1817), and by Johann Joseph Felix von Kurz (1717–84), whose Bernardon was a modern variant of Hanswurst. The spoken – non-improvised – theatre found it hard to match such successes. In 1748 members of Friederike Neuber's disbanded company arrived in Vienna, sparking off violent opposition to the character of Hanswurst, who had even found his way into serious plays at this time.[10] Not until around 1770 was the victory of the spoken theatre assured, not least as a result of the intervention of the 'Austrian Lessing', Joseph von Sonnenfels.[11] His sobriquet notwithstanding, Sonnenfels was in fact distinguished from Lessing by virtue of his predilection for all things French and his profound contempt for popular art. There was, however, something genuinely rationalistic about his attempt to make 'true' culture – in other words, moral culture – and its nobler forms the theatre's principal aim. In this, he found active support not only from dramatists such as Ayrenhoff, Gebler, Klemm and Heufeld but also from the Emperor Joseph II himself. And it was his spirit that informed the

---

7. *Briefe*, iii.138 (letter of 4 July 1781).
8. See Devrient, *Geschichte der deutschen Schauspielkunst*, iii.117ff.; Pohl, *Joseph Haydn*, i.83ff., and ii.117ff.; and Weilen, *Geschichte des Wiener Theaterwesens* and *Geschichte des Burgtheaters*.
9. He was represented as a Salzburg peasant with a fool's wand and a green pointed hat.
10. In 1763, for example, the servant Norton in Lessing's *Miß Sara Sampson* was played as Hanswurst. ◆ See Asper, *Hanswurst*.
11. His most important work is his *Briefe über die wienerische Schaubühne*.

foundation of the Court and National Theatre in 1776.[12] Joseph himself proved even more far-sighted, of course, in sending the actor Johann Heinrich Friedrich Müller to Germany to engage other actors and seek out new ideas from such authorities as Lessing himself. Like his two colleagues, the Stephanie brothers, Müller also turned his hand to writing plays,[13] and during the heyday of the actor Friedrich Ludwig Schröder in the 1780s,[14] their works were performed alongside those of Shakespeare, Lessing, Goethe and Schiller. Even by this early date, however, the infamous theatre censor had already raised his head above the parapet. All the same, there was enough to fascinate a man such as Mozart, in addition to which the old Hanswurst was still far from dead, in spite of all attempts to silence him. When Karl von Marinelli founded his theatre in the Leopoldstadt in 1780,[15] for example, he resurfaced in regular farces as 'Kasperl', generally – as before – as the servant of the actual hero but now invested with a greater degree of cheekiness and coarseness. At the same time, a supernatural, fairy-tale element played a prominent role, albeit more with the aim of creating a sense of superficial, if undeniably effective, tension than in the sense understood by the later Romantics, hence the by no means inappropriate term 'comedy of machines' to describe this type of theatre. Its principal exponent was Philipp Hafner (1731–64),[16] while the character of Kasperl himself was created by the comic actor Johann Laroche (1745–1806). The genre as a whole was soon to produce its first great representative in Ferdinand Raimund (1790–1836), but even before that it had already made a deep impression on opera. Joseph II himself took an active interest in the development of his own Court and National Theatre,[17] and although he did not encourage German literature in the way that Klopstock had hoped he would, he saw in the theatre in general an essential tool for educating the nation and regarded it as a point of honour to ensure that his theatre in Vienna was the finest in the German-speaking world, hence his decision to reduce ticket prices[18] and make sure that it was not only the court and the aristocracy that could attend the theatre, but the whole of the educated bourgeoisie, too. This also had repercussions, of course, for the social status of actors, poets and musicians: previously regarded as socially disadvantaged, they were now welcomed into the salons of the aristocracy.[19] Even the emperor himself followed his artists' activities with warm and lively interest[20] and by relaxing press censorship summoned into existence a form of literary criticism that underpinned his educational aims in the most effective manner possible. In this way an audience came into being that brought together the educated members of all the social classes and responded to what was on offer with as much attention and understanding as genuine gratitude.[21] Shortly before Mozart arrived in Vienna, Friedrich Schröder and his wife became members of the National Theatre, where they worked alongside actors and actresses of the stature of Johann Heinrich Friedrich Müller, Joseph Lange, Josef Weidmann, Johann Brockmann, Karl Jaquet,

12. ◆ See Michtner, *Das alte Burgtheater als Opernbühne: Von der Einführung des deutschen Singspiels (1778) bis zum Tod Kaiser Leopolds II. (1792)* and Link, *The National Court Theatre in Mozart's Vienna.*

13. Sonnenfels's programme for 1770 is reproduced in Müller's *Abschied von der k. k. Hof- und National-Schaubühne,* 73ff.; see also Gebler's letters in Werner, *Aus dem Josephinischen Wien.*

14. ◆ See Friedrich Meyer, *Friedrich Ludwig Schröder.*

15. ◆ In fact, Marinelli's theatre was not founded until 1788.

16. His *Megära, die fürchterliche Hexe* (Berlin, 1764) is generally regarded as the first German *Zauberoper.*

17. ◆ See Payer von Thurn, *Joseph II. als Theaterdirektor: Ungedruckte Briefe und Aktenstücke aus den Kinderjahren des Burgtheaters.*

18. See Müller, *Abschied von der National-Schaubühne,* 95, and *AmZ,* xxiv (1822) 253.

19. Müller, *Abschied von der National-Schaubühne,* 79; and Lange, *Biographie des Joseph Lange,* 25.

20. Lange, *Biographie,* 65ff., and Meyer, *Friedrich Ludwig Schröder,* i.361; Gebler's letters are reproduced in Werner, *Aus dem Josephinischen Wien,* 76ff.

21. Pichler, *Denkwürdigkeiten aus meinem Leben,* i.78ff., and Meyer, *Friedrich Ludwig Schröder,* i.361–2 and 375.

Johann Baptist Bergopzoomer, Christian Gottlob and Johann Gottlieb Stephanie, Mlle Weidner, Maria Anna Adamberger,[22] Johanna Sacco, Maria Henriette Stierle and Maria Rosalia Nouseul – Mozart's enthusiasm was manifestly entirely justified.[23]

In Vienna, no less than elsewhere, the spoken theatre was closely associated with the German singspiel.[24] Here, too, of course, the singspiel had to overcome concerted resistance, but the emperor spoke out forcefully in favour of his 'National Singspiel' and disbanded the Italian opera and ballet in its favour. On 17 December 1777 Johann Heinrich Friedrich Müller received instructions to organize the new venture. As his inaugural production he chose *Die Bergknappen*, a setting of Paul Weidmann's libretto by Ignaz Umlauf (1746–96) that opened on 17 February 1778 to immense acclaim. Umlauf had previously played the viola in the court opera orchestra but now became Kapellmeister to the new venture.[25] The singers who took part in *Die Bergknappen* – the sopranos Catarina Cavalieri and Maria Henriette Stierle, the tenor Martin Ruprecht and the bass Franz Fuchs – had all been chosen by the emperor himself, while the chorus was taken from local churches. Müller took charge of the production. Its success encouraged Joseph to experiment further, while continuing to maintain a firm grasp on the repertory. *Die Bergknappen* was followed by fourteen other pieces in the course of 1778, including Benda's *Medea*.[26] But only five of these works were written in German (they were by Umlauf, Ordonez, Asplmayr, Bárta, Ulbrich and Benda), the majority being German translations of operas by Monsigny, Grétry, Martini and Gossec performed under the titles *Röschen und Colas*, *Der Hausfreund*, *Lucille*, *Die abgeredete Zauberey*, *Sylvain*, *Der Liebhaber von fünfzehn Jahren* and *Anton und Antonette* – a clear sign that *opéra comique* was firmly entrenched in Germany, too, at this date. The final work was Guglielmi's *La sposa fedele*, performed in German under the title *Robert und Kalliste*. A similar picture emerges from the repertory during the years that followed,[27] until the enterprise began to stagnate in 1783 as a result of internal arguments and a cooling off of interest on the part of the court, finally coming to an end in 1787, when the Italians were reinstated.[28] As we have already observed, the north Germans remained largely impervious to the Viennese singspiel. Individual attempts on the part of touring companies to stage works by Hiller, Wolf, Schweitzer and others failed to make any impression,[29] with Benda's *Der Jahrmarkt* proving a fiasco when staged at the Nationaltheater in 1779.[30] The contrast between north and south Germany (especially Austria) became increasingly pronounced.[31] Nicolai reports that in Vienna a number of otherwise intelligent and committed music lovers spoke to him about Carl Philipp Emanuel Bach not just with indifference but with positive loathing; for them, Kozeluch and Steffan were unsurpassed as keyboard composers.[32] Although this may appear exaggerated when we recall Joseph Haydn and the two Mozarts, it is certainly true of the mood in the public at large. Mozart, too, mentions 'Lutheran' composers, and

22. ◆ Here Abert also lists a 'Mlle Jacquet' who is, in fact, identical to Maria Anna Adamberger.

23. An overview of the situation and a characterization of the artists who were active at this time may be found in Riesbeck, *Briefe eines reisenden Franzosen über Deutschland an seinen Bruder zu Paris*, i.258ff.; Friedrich Nicolai, *Beschreibung einer Reise durch Deutschland und die Schweiz im Jahre 1781*, iv.587ff.; and Friedrich Meyer, *Friedrich Ludwig Schröder*, i.355ff.

24. See below; for further details, see also Müller, *Abschied von der National-Schaubühne*, 253ff.; Pohl, *Joseph Haydn*, ii.122; and especially Robert Haas's exemplary introduction to *Ignaz Umlauff: Die Bergknappen*, which also includes a detailed bibliography.

25. From 1789 he deputized for Salieri as conductor of the Imperial Court Orchestra.

26. For a complete list, see Haas's introduction to *Ignaz Umlauff: Die Bergknappen*, XII–XIII.

27. See Haas, *Ignaz Umlauff: Die Bergknappen*, XIVff.

28. ◆ The Italian opera was reinstated in 1783, not 1787.

29. Haas, *Ignaz Umlauff: Die Bergknappen*, XXIII.

30. Haas, *Ignaz Umlauff: Die Bergknappen*, XIV.

31. See the instructive remarks by Forkel, *Musikalischer Almanach für Deutschland*, ii.189ff.

32. Friedrich Nicolai, *Beschreibung einer Reise*, iv.556.

on one occasion we even find Adamberger speaking of a 'Lutheran way' of singing, which he defines as 'when one hears a beautiful voice in a singer such as he has received from nature and, further, when one perceives good musical training of a kind that is frequently found in north Germany, but also when there is no perceptible trace of the Italian school of singing that is uniquely able to produce a true singer'.[33]

In this way the Viennese National Singspiel lost its most talented performers[34] and had to make do with second-rate artists who had neither the inclination nor the skill to carry the whole genre forward. Nothing could be expected of Gluck in this regard, and as if to confirm this, the now elderly composer contented himself with a revival of *La recontre imprévue* in 1780, now staged in German as *Die unvermutete Zusammenkunft oder Die Pilgrime von Mekka*. In 1781 another of Vienna's leading lights, Gluck's pupil Salieri, added his own contribution with his Lustspiel *Der Rauchfangkehrer* to a mediocre text by Joseph Leopold Auenbrugger (1722–1809),[35] but for Salieri, too, the singspiel was no more than a sideline to his main activity. In the circumstances one can well imagine the extent to which Mozart arrived in Vienna buoyed up by hope. After all, at least some of the city's performing artists were of an excellence that placed no restrictions on a composer's imagination.

Foremost among these singers was the soprano Catarina Cavalieri (1755–1801), who had already appeared in *Die Bergknappen*. She was the daughter of a schoolmaster by the name of Cavalier from the suburb of Währing, had been taught singing by Salieri and created a sensation at her first public appearance for the Italian company in 1775, going on to enjoy a reputation as a virtuoso of the first order.[36] Maria Henriette Stierle (1762–99) came to opera from the spoken theatre and had made her Viennese début in 1777 in Lessing's *Minna von Barnhelm*, before turning increasingly to soubrette roles in singspiels. These outstanding performers soon attracted others, including the first wife of the actor Joseph Lange, Anna Maria née Schindler, although her brilliant career was cut short by her premature death in 1779.[37] Her successor, both on stage and in the marriage bed, was Aloysia Weber, who owed her appointment to the Viennese ambassador in Munich, Count Adam Franz Hartig, and who proved triumphantly successful in her very first role in Vienna, Hännchen in a German adaptation of Grétry's *La rosière de Salency*.[38] Prior to Aloysia's arrival in the city, Therese Teyber (later Mme Arnold) had been engaged for smaller roles, winning praise for her fresh-toned, youthful voice, whereas that of Barbara Fischer née Straßer from Mannheim, a technically proficient singer and fine actress, was already showing signs of wear by this time. They were joined in the summer of 1781 by Antonia Bernasconi (1741–1803), apparently at the insistence of Gluck himself, who was keen to foist his first Alcestis on an unwilling emperor. By now she was long past her best, as Mozart made clear in his letter of 27 June 1781: 'She's paid 500 ducats for singing all her arias a good comma higher; this is really an achievement, as she always stays in tune. She has now promised to sing a ¼ tone higher but she wants to be paid twice as much.'[39]

33. *Allgemeine Wiener Musikzeitung* (1821), 56.

34. In spite of Wieland's intercession, Schweitzer was not appointed; nor was Benda, even though he had declared himself not unwilling to accept the post; see Müller, *Abschied von der National-Schaubühne*, 185, and Forkel, *Musikalisch-kritische Bibliothek*, iii.340.

35. See Cramer, *Magazin der Musik*, i.353.

36. See Leopold von Sonnleithner, *Recensionen und Mittheilungen über Theater und Musik*, viii/2 (1862), 18ff. According to Gebler, 'She had a powerful and attractive voice, with low and high notes that one rarely finds in the same singer, and can sing the most difficult passage-work'; Werner, *Aus dem Josephinischen Wien*, 105. In spite of her unprepossessing appearance, she was also a good actress; see Friedrich Meyer, *Friedrich Ludwig Schröder*. ◆ Also see Gidwitz, '"Ich bin die erste Sängerin"'.

37. Lange, *Biographie*, 104ff., and Müller, *Abschied von der National-Schaubühne*, 259 and 261.

38. See Friedrich Meyer, *Friedrich Ludwig Schröder*, and Werner, *Aus dem Josephinischen Wien*.

39. *Briefe*, iii.135 (letter of 27 June 1781).

On 29 August 1781 we find him writing again:

It's true that in great roles in tragedy she'll always remain Bernasconi, but in lightweight operettas she's hopeless, as they no longer suit her; and – as she herself admits – she is more Italian than German, and on stage she speaks the same Viennese dialect as in ordinary conversation – just imagine! – and whenever she tries to correct her accent, it's like hearing a princess declaim in a puppet show. And her singing is now so bad that no one wants to write for her.[40]

Among the first male singers to be signed up were the gifted tenor Martin Ruprecht (1758–1800) and the bass Franz Fuchs (?–1785).[41] They were soon followed by three more tenors, Herr Souter (1743–83), Johann Ernst Dauer (1746–1812), an actor by profession but gifted with an attractive voice,[42] and, above all, Josef Valentin Adamberger (1740 or 1743–1804), who was summoned to Munich from Italy and who proved to be a well-trained, cultivated singer and a 'most respectable' actor. He specialized in playing young lovers.[43] Outstanding among the bass singers was Karl Ludwig Fischer (1745–1825), who was widely regarded as the leading bass in Germany at this time on account of the range, power and melodiousness of his voice and his thorough training both as a singer and as an actor. Two of the company's other basses were Johann Baptist Hoffmann and Friedrich Günther, while its baritones included Gottfried Heinrich Schmidt and Ignaz Saal. The orchestra numbered thirty-seven players.[44]

Mozart did not arrive in Vienna empty-handed but brought with him his score of *Zaide*, only to realize that the work was unsuited to the city. None the less, it found sufficient favour with the theatre's inspector, Gottlieb Stephanie the Younger, for the latter to promise to provide the composer with a new libretto for the Viennese stage.[45] Stephanie was well respected by the emperor, though the Viennese themselves thought him 'rude, false and slanderous'.[46] Mozart was too wary to agree to a commission without a binding agreement with the theatre's current manager, Count Rosenberg, who had offered him a cordial reception on each of his visits and warmly applauded the excerpts from *Idomeneo* performed at the home of the Countess Thun, an occasion at which both Sonnenfels and Mozart's later patron, Baron Gottfried van Swieten, had also been present. Moreover, Stephanie gave no reason to doubt his word, with the result that by

40. *Briefe*, iii.153 (letter of 29 August 1781).
41. Haas, *Ignaz Umlauff: Die Bergknappen*, X.
42. Müller, *Abschied von der National-Schaubühne*, 181, 189 and 194.
43. See Friedrich Meyer, *Friedrich Ludwig Schröder*, and Werner, *Aus dem Josephinischen Wien*.
44. The entire company for the period 1781–3, together with their salaries, is listed as follows by Meyer, *Friedrich Ludwig Schröder*, i.356–7 (see also Haas, *Ignaz Umlauff: Die Bergknappen*, XVII). For Adamberger, see Barak, 'Valentin Adamberger: Mozarts Belmonte und Freund'; Angermüller, 'Ein Mozart-Tenor aus Niederbayern: Johann Valentin Adamberger zu seinem 260. Geburtstag'; and Bauman, 'Mozart's Belmonte'. For Fischer, see Gottron, 'Kleine Beiträge zur Mainzer Musikgeschichte, I: Die Selbstbiographie des Bassisten Ludwig Fischer aus Mainz'.
Male singers: Adamberger (2133 florins 20 kreutzers); Souter (1200 florins); Dauer (?); Fischer (1200 florins); Günther (1200 florins); Schmidt (1200 florins); Ruprecht (700 florins); Hoffmann (600 florins); Frankenberg (400 florins); Saal (800 florins).
Female singers: Catarina Cavalieri (1200 florins); Aloysia Lange (1706 florins 20 kreutzers); Barbara Fischer (1200 florins); Therese Teyber (800 florins); Haselbeck (600 florins); Genovefa Brenner (400 florins); Anna Maria Saal (800 florins); Antonia Bernasconi (500 ducats).
The orchestra under Umlauf (850 florins) comprised 6 first violins, 6 second violins, 4 violas, 3 cellos, 3 double basses, 2 flutes, 2 oboes, 2 clarinets, 2 bassoons, 4 horns, 2 trumpets and timpani. Their combined salaries amounted to 16,124 florins. In his letter of 31 October 1780, Gebler makes no mention of Saal and his wife or of Bernasconi and Haselbeck but lists Joseph Ignaz Walter, Anna Maria Weiß, Katharina Schindler and, as expected, Celeste Coltellini; see Werner, *Aus dem Josephinischen Wien*, 103ff. ◆ See Edge, 'Mozart's Viennese Orchestras'.
45. As early as 18 April 1781 we find Mozart writing to his father: 'Young Stephanie will give me a new piece and, as he says, a good one, and if I'm no longer here, he'll send it to me'; *Briefe*, iii.107–8.
46. *Briefe*, iii.132 (letter of 16 June 1781).

9 June 1781 Mozart was able to inform his father that Rosenberg had invited 'the distinguished actor' Friedrich Ludwig Schröder to cast round for a decent libretto for him.[47] A week later the text was in Stephanie's hands. His initial reaction was that the first act was excellent but that the other three were less good. But if Schröder agreed to a reworking, something could be made of it. Mozart thought that the revisions should be left to Schröder and Stephanie.[48] In the event the text was rejected in its entirety, but a collaboration remained a possibility: evidently the emperor had decided to give Mozart a chance to prove himself as an opera composer. The latter had every confidence in Stephanie's abilities, arguing that he understood the theatre and rejecting his father's reservations in his letter of 16 June 1781. The following passage on opera composition is of particular importance for our understanding of the composer:

> Do you really think that I'd write an *opéra comique* in the same way as an *opera seria*? There shouldn't be anything playful in an *opera seria*, which should rather be learned and sensible, just as an *opera buffa* should be *less* learned and *more* playful and amusing. I can't help it if people want comic music in an *opera seria*; but here they draw a fine distinction between the two. I simply find that Hanswurst has not yet been fully rooted out from music, and in this the French are right.[49]

This passage shows clearly that Mozart was familiar with literary currents in Vienna at this time and that he had given serious thought to the attempts on the part of Italian and French composers and their librettists to combine comedy and tragedy in their operas. This is the first time that he expresses his views on a problem to which he himself was to provide so matchless a solution in all his masterpieces from now on following his initial failure with *La finta giardiniera*.

By the end of July the libretto that he had been hoping for had been found, as he informed his father on 1 August:

> The day before yesterday Stephanie Junior gave me a libretto for me to set. . . . The book is really quite good; the subject is Turkish and it's called *Belmont and Constanze or The Seduction from the Seraglio*. I'll use Turkish music in the overture, first-act chorus and final chorus. Mlle Cavalieri, Mlle Teyber, Monsieur Fischer, Monsieur Adamberger, Monsieur Dauer and Monsieur Walter will sing in it. I'm so pleased to be working on the libretto that I've already finished the entrance arias for Cavalieri and Adamberger and the trio that ends act one. Time's short, it's true, as it's meant to be performed in the middle of September, but the circumstances bound up with the date of the performance and, in general, all my other prospects have so raised my spirits that I can't wait to get back to my desk and get on with my work.[50]

The favourable circumstances to which Mozart is referring here consisted in the prospect of a visit to Vienna by Grand Duke Paul of Russia and his wife. The new opera was to be performed in the course of the attendant celebrations, and Mozart hoped, with good reason, that the emperor and Count Rosenberg would think all the more highly of him if he were to finish it in time for

47. *Briefe*, iii.127 (letter of 9 June 1781).
48. *Briefe*, iii.131 (letter of 16 June 1781).
49. *Briefe*, iii.132 (letter of 16 June 1781).
50. *Briefe*, iii.143 (letter of 1 August 1781).

them. For the present, however, he and Stephanie agreed to keep the plan to themselves. He was very happy, he went on, to be able to stay with friends where he could work undisturbed and his meals were provided both at midday and in the evening: 'They know that I'm generally hungry when I'm working.' He continued to work at fever pitch, writing to his father on 8 August 1781 to report:

I'll have to be brief, as I've just finished the Janissary chorus. . . . Adamberger, Cavalieri and Fischer are exceptionally pleased with their arias. . . . I played what I've finished for Countess Thun; she said at the end that she'd wager her life that people will like what I've written so far. – But on this point I don't give a rap about people's praise or criticism – not until they've heard or seen it in its entirety, right now I'm simply following my own feelings – but you can tell from this how pleased she must have been to say something like that.[51]

On 22 August he wrote to report that the first act was finished.[52] Shortly afterwards, however, he was relieved to discover that the grand duke would not be coming to Vienna until November, so that he could 'give more thought' to the opera (29 August 1781). On 26 September 1781 he wrote again to his father:

I now find myself in something of a predicament. The first act has been finished for over three weeks, as has an aria from the second act and the drinking duet (per li sig^{ri} vieneri), which consists entirely of my Turkish tattoo; but I can't do anything else at present as the whole story has been changed – and at my own insistence. The third act starts with a charming quintet or, rather, a finale, but I'd rather have this at the end of the second act. In order to achieve this, a lot has to be changed, in fact a whole new plot has to be added, and Stephanie is up to his eyes in work.[53]

But there was another reason why Mozart had to break off work on the opera: two of Gluck's operas had been chosen to mark the Russian visit – a German reworking of *Iphigénie en Tauride* and an Italian version of *Alceste*. The aim was to show their visitors 'what we Germans are capable of achieving,'[54] even though the emperor had little time for Gluck or his favourite soprano, Antonia Bernasconi.[55] This naturally put a spoke in Mozart's wheel, as he had been hoping at the very least to mount *Idomeneo*, which he was planning to revise 'in the French manner'. But he failed to get his way[56] and was forced to postpone his singspiel until the two Gluck operas had

51. *Briefe*, iii.145 (letter of 8 August 1781).
52. *Briefe*, iii.152 (letter of 22 August 1781).
53. *Briefe*, iii.163–4 (letter of 26 September 1781).
54. Cramer, *Magazin der Musik*, i.353, where it is claimed in error that Gluck's *Alceste*, *Iphigénie en Tauride* and *Orfeo* were given in Italian; see Müller, *Abschied von der National-Schaubühne*, 270 and Haas, *Ignaz Umlauff: Die Bergknappen*, XVII. The German translation of *Iphigénie en Tauride* was the work of Johann Baptist Alxinger; see Forkel, *Musikalischer Almanach für Deutschland*, ii.153, and Werner, *Aus dem Josephinischen Wien*, 103. It is significant that *Alceste* was given not in its new French adaptation but in its original Italian version.
55. *Briefe*, iii.152–3 (letter of 29 August 1781). Johann Friedrich Reichardt reports a conversation with Joseph II during the summer of 1783: 'Archduke Maximilian brought the discussion round to Gluck, whom both men appeared to honour as a great tragedian of the stage, but there were certain aspects about Gluck's operas that the emperor thought could be improved'; Reichardt, 'Bruchstücke aus Reichardt's Autobiographie', 667, and Schletterer, *Johann Friedrich Reichardt*, 326.
56. Although Mozart thought that a third large-scale opera would be too much, Gluck's *Orfeo* was none the less put into rehearsal alongside the other two works. It seems, therefore, that voices were raised in protest at the idea of reviving *Idomeneo*.

been put into rehearsal – 'and they still have a lot to rehearse'.[57] By mid-November, he had made a little more progress on his singspiel, but it was now far too late to stage it in honour of the 'bigwig', as Mozart described the grand duke.[58] The latter, travelling under the name of the Count von Norden, finally arrived with his wife on 21 November and on the 25th a gala performance of *Alceste* was given at Schönbrunn.[59] 'I've been casting around for some popular Russian songs', Mozart told his father on 24 November, 'in order to be able to play some variations on them.'[60]

The grand duke's visit had been preceded by another state visit on 11 November, this time from Duke Karl Eugen of Württemberg and his wife, Princess Elisabeth, together with Archduke Franz's intended bride and her brother, Prince Ferdinand. Mozart's description of the party is entirely typical: 'The duke of Württemberg is a charming person, as are the duchess and princess. But the prince is an 18-year-old stick and a real booby.'[61] Mozart hoped to be appointed the princess's music teacher, an appointment in which he counted on the help of his old patron from Salzburg, the Archduke Maximilian, who was the emperor's youngest brother and currently coadjutor to the elector of Cologne. In the same letter, we read:

The Archduke Maximilian sent for me at 3 o'clock yesterday afternoon. As I entered, he was standing by the stove in the first room, waiting for me, he came straight over to me and asked whether I was doing anything today. – 'Nothing at all, Your Royal Highness, and even if I was, it would always be an honour to wait on Your Royal Highness.' – 'No, I don't want to be a nuisance to anyone.' – He then told me that he was thinking of giving a concert that evening for his visitors from Württemberg. Perhaps I'd like to play something and accompany the arias, I was to return at 6 o'clock, when all the others would be there. So I played there yesterday.

Mozart made no secret of the fact that he thought that the archduke had changed for the worse:

When God gives a man a professional office, He also gives him understanding. And so it is with the archduke. But before he became a priest he was far wittier and far more intelligent and talked less, but more sensibly. You should see him now! Stupidity starts from his eyes, and he can't stop talking, always in a falsetto, he has a swelling on his neck, – in a word, he's a changed person!

But the archduke remained as friendly as ever with Mozart, persuading the latter to believe that as soon as he became elector of Cologne, the composer could count on becoming his Kapellmeister. The archduke also recommended Mozart as the princess's music teacher and had already received her consent when the emperor suddenly decided to appoint Salieri as her singing teacher instead.

---

57. *Briefe*, iii.165 (letter of 6 October 1781).
58. ◆ *Briefe*, iii.177 (letter of 24 November 1781).
59. *Wiener Zeitung* (1781), no. 95, appendix. *Alceste* was repeated on 13 [or possibly 3] and 27 December, while *Iphigenia* was staged on 9 December (see *Wiener Zeitung*, no. 99). *Orfeo* was performed in Italian on 31 December 1781; see Haas, *Ignaz Umlauff: Die Bergknappen*, XVII.
60. *Briefe*, iii.177 (letter of 24 November 1781). Mozart adds a highly colourful account of the social mix that occurred on this occasion and that the emperor ultimately found tiresome in the extreme: 'All I can say is that it serves him right; it never works, the mob always remains the mob'; *Briefe*, iii.178 (letter of 5 December 1781).
61. *Briefe*, iii.175 (letter of 17 November 1781).

Antonio Salieri (1750–1825)[62] had studied briefly in Venice before moving to Vienna with Florian Gassmann in 1766 and becoming the latter's pupil. Gassmann was held in high regard by the emperor and was able to persuade him to extend his patronage to Salieri, who was allowed to play in the emperor's private orchestra and win Joseph's favour as both man and artist. 'He cares for no one but Salieri', Mozart wrote resignedly on 15 December 1781.[63] It was entirely natural that Joseph preferred to appoint Salieri the princess's singing teacher: after all, he valued Salieri as a vocal composer, whereas, like most other people in Vienna, he knew Mozart only as a keyboard player, albeit one whom he held in high regard, so that on 22 December 1781 we find Mozart writing to his father to report that at table the emperor had recently given him 'the highest praise, adding: "C'est un talent decidè."'[64] On 24 December Joseph invited him to court to compete with Muzio Clementi, who had arrived in Vienna preceded by a reputation as an outstanding virtuoso on the keyboard.[65] Clementi later gave a report of the encounter – a trial of strength of a long-established kind – to his pupil Ludwig Berger:

> Having been in Vienna but a few days I received an invitation from the Emperor to perform on the fortepiano in his presence. On entering his music-room I found there someone whom, because of his elegant appearance, I took for one of the Emperor's chamberlains; but scarcely had we begun a conversation when it turned at once towards musical matters; and we soon recognized each other as Mozart and Clementi, brother artists, and greeted each other in the most friendly manner.[66]

Mozart reported on the subsequent course of the encounter in his letter to his father of 16 January 1782:

> The emperor (after we had paid each other enough compliments) declared that Clementi should begin. 'La santa chiesa cattolica!' he said, as Clementi is from Rome. – He improvised and played a sonata.[67]

'Also worthy of note here', Berger reports, 'is Clementi's original practice of extemporising quite long, very interesting and thematically developed interludes and cadenzas during the fermatas in his sonatas; this is what led him at that contest to choose a sonata which, though certainly suited to his purpose, yet in other respects was inferior to several of his earlier compositions in this genre. It was the following [op. 24 no. 2]:

62. Mosel, *Ueber das Leben und die Werke des Anton Salieri*; Hermann, *Antonio Salieri: Eine Studie zur Geschichte seines künstlerischen Wirkens*. ◆ Further, see Angermüller, *Antonio Salieri: fatti e documenti*; Rice, *Antonio Salieri and Viennese Opera*; and Heartz, *Haydn, Mozart and the Viennese School*.

63. *Briefe*, iii.179 (letter of 15 December 1781).

64. *Briefe*, iii.188 (letter of 22 December 1781).

65. Unger, 'Muzio Clementis Leben'. ◆ See Plantinga, 'Clementi, Virtuosity, and the "German Manner"' and *Clementi: His Life and Music*.

66. Clementi's account is virtually identical to Mozart's. Ludwig Berger heard it from him in 1806 and repeated it in his 'Erläuterungen eines Mozartschen Urtheils über Muzio Clementi' and *AmZ*, xxxi (1829), 467–8. A slightly different account based on Clementi's English obituary appeared in *AmZ*, xxxiv (1832), 657–8. The version given by Giuseppe Bridi in his *Breve notizie intorno ad alcuni più celebri compositori di musica e cenni sullo stato presente del canto italiano*, 51–2, again varies on points of detail in a way often found in such matters.

67. *Briefe*, iii.193 (letter of 16 January 1782).

and it is to this theme that we perhaps owe the genial and in its way unsurpassed allegro of the overture to *Die Zauberflöte*.[68]

Mozart again:

The emperor then said to me: 'Allons, off you go.' – I improvised in turn and played some variations, – then the grand duchess[69] produced some sonatas by Paisiello (wretchedly written out in his own hand),[70] and I had to play the allegros from them, after which he [Clementi] played the andantes and rondos. – We then took a theme from them and developed it on two pianofortes. The odd thing is that although I'd borrowed Countess Thun's pianoforte, I played it only when I played on my own, as that's what the emperor wanted, – and, by the way, the other instrument was out of tune and three of the keys stuck. – 'It doesn't matter,' said the emperor. Looking at it in a positive light, I assume that, because the emperor knows my skill and knowledge of music, he merely wanted to show consideration to our visitor. But I have it from a very good source that he was very pleased with me.

This is confirmed by Dittersdorf, who reports the following conversation with Joseph II:

Emperor: Did you hear Mozart play? – *I*: Three times. – *Emperor*: How did you like him? – *I*: As every connoisseur is bound to like him. – *Emperor*: Did you also hear Clementi? – *I*: I heard him, too. – *Emperor*: A few people, headed by Greybig, prefer him to Mozart. What's your own view? Out with it! – *I*: Clementi's playing is dominated purely by skill, Mozart's by skill and good taste. – *Emperor*: That's exactly what I said myself.[71]

The emperor afterwards sent Mozart fifty ducats 'which I can certainly do with'. Clementi was entranced by Mozart's playing:

Until then I had never heard anyone play with so much spirit and grace. Especially did an Adagio and several of his extemporized variations surprise me, for which the Emperor chose the theme on which we, accompanying each other by turns, had to play variations.[72]

Mozart's opinion of Clementi, by contrast, was as harsh as it was acerbically worded: 'Clementi is an excellent harpsichordist, but that is all', he wrote on 16 January 1782. Four days earlier he had written: 'Clementi plays well, so far as execution with his right hand goes; his greatest strength lies

68. When reissuing this sonata, Clementi felt it advisable to insist that it predated the overture: 'Cette sonate, avec la Toccata qui la suit, a été jouée par l'auteur devant Sa M. J. Joseph II en 1781; Mozart était présent.' The two works are certainly strikingly similar, but we should not forget that we are dealing here with a melodic type frequently found from the time of Hasse onwards.
69. According to Bridi, *Breve notizie intorno ad alcuni più celebri compositori di musica e cenni sullo stato presente del canto italiano*, the emperor had wagered with the grand duchess that Mozart would beat Clementi and won the bet.
70. Paisiello had written some keyboard sonatas and capriccios for the grand duchess.
71. Dittersdorf, *Lebensbeschreibung*, 175–6.
72. ◆ *Dokumente*, 464, *Documentary Biography*, 542. In addition to the sonata, Clementi also played the toccata op. 11.

in passages in thirds. But beyond that he doesn't have a kreutzer's worth of taste or feeling, – in a word, a mere mechanicus.'[73]

Later, when his sister got to know some of Clementi's sonatas in Salzburg, Mozart wrote to their father on 7 June 1783:

I have a few words to say to my sister about Clementi's sonatas. Everyone who plays or hears them will feel that they're worthless as compositions. They contain no remarkable or striking passages except for those in sixths and octaves, and I would ask my sister *not to waste too much time* on them, otherwise she'll ruin her controlled and even touch, and her hand will lose its natural lightness, flexibility and fluency. For what's the point of it all? Even if she manages to play the sixths and octaves at the greatest speed (which no one, not even Clementi, can do), she'll produce the most frightful chopping, nothing else. Clementi is a ciarlattano, like all Italians! He writes presto and even prestissimo and alla breve in his sonatas, but plays them *allegro* in 4/4 time. I know, I've heard him! What he does well are his passages in thirds; but he sweated over them day and night in London. Apart from this, he has nothing – absolutely nothing – not the slightest expression or good taste, still less any feeling.[74]

In order to explain the harshness of Mozart's judgement, Berger reports Clementi as saying that at this stage in his career he had chiefly cultivated brilliance and digital dexterity, delighting in 'those double-chorded passages and extemporized ornaments that were not in common use before his time'. Only later did he come to favour a cantabile, 'nobler' style of performance that he owed not only to listening to famous singers of the day but also to gradual improvements in English fortepianos whose earlier faulty construction had almost entirely ruled out the possibility of a cantabile legato style. This, Berger concluded, helped to explain Mozart's opinion of Clementi, as there could be no question of any ulterior motives, given the former's 'well-known honesty and straightforwardness'.[75]

One of the more influential figures at court, both politically and musically, was the emperor's valet, Johann Kilian Strack (1724–93), and Mozart duly set his sights on winning him over to his cause. And so, on 3 November 1781, we find Mozart writing to his father to report on a perform-ance of one of his own serenades at the home of Baroness Waldstätten, with whom he spent his name-day on 31 October. The work in question – K375 – had been written for St Theresa's Day (15 October) for the sister-in-law of the court portraitist Joseph Hickel. 'But the main reason for writing it', he continued, 'was to let Herr von Strack hear something of mine (he goes there every day), and so I put a little extra care into it: as a result it was much applauded.'[76] Mozart duly managed to strike up a friendship with Strack, although, as he told his father on 23 January 1782, 'these court flunkeys are never to be trusted'. When reports reached Salzburg that the emperor was planning to engage Mozart, the latter wrote to his father on 10 April 1782:

The reason I haven't written to you about this before is because I myself know nothing about it. It's true that the whole town is awash with rumours and that a whole crowd of people have

---

73. *Briefe*, iii.191–2 (letters of 12 and 16 January 1782).
74. *Briefe*, iii.272 (letter of 7 June 1783). Mozart's comments refer not only to the sonata but also to the toccata, which is headed 'Prestissimo'.
75. ◆ Further, see Komlós, 'Mozart and Clementi: A Piano Competition and its Interpretation'.
76. *Briefe*, iii.171 (letter of 3 November 1781).

already congratulated me on the subject – and I'm also ready to believe that there has been talk of it with the emperor and that he may even be considering it – but as of now I know nothing. Things are so advanced that the emperor is considering it, even though I've done nothing to encourage him. I've seen Herr von Strack on a handful of occasions (he's certainly a very good friend of mine) in order to let myself be seen and because I enjoy his company, but not so often as to make a nuisance of myself or to make him think I have some ulterior motive; and if he's a man of honour, he's bound to say that he's never heard me utter a single word that would have given him cause to think I'd like to remain here, let alone enter the emperor's service. We spoke only about music. – It is entirely on his own initiative, not out of self-interest, that he has spoken so favourably of me to the emperor. – If things have come so far without any help from me, there's no reason why the matter shouldn't be concluded in the same way. – If you make the first move yourself, you immediately receive less pay – the emperor is enough of a miser as it is. – If the emperor wants me, he must pay for me, as the honour of serving him is not in itself enough.[77]

Like all his predecessors on the Habsburg throne, Joseph II was highly educated as a musician with a particular fondness for strict counterpoint. He also had a decent bass voice that was trained in the Italian school,[78] and he could play the viola, cello and keyboard, in which last-named capacity he not only performed as an accompanist but could also score-read. As a rule, meals in the imperial household were followed by an hour's music-making. Three times a week there was a more substantial concert to which Gassmann and, later, Salieri and occasionally also Umlauf were invited. There was no audience, but the emperor himself always took part in the proceedings. Particularly popular were excerpts from operas and oratorios, and in this way both Joseph himself and the Archduke Maximilian familiarized themselves with operas that were due to be performed in public.[79] Performers were generally expected to sight-read, and the emperor is said to have derived particular pleasure from seeing them tested in this way.[80]

Joseph's fellow performers consisted mostly of a quartet of thoroughly mediocre players. The first violinist was Franz Kreibich (or Greibich),[81] whose curious mixture of timorousness and pomposity made him the butt of all the group's jokes.[82] Other members were Thomas Woborzill, Johann Baptist Hoffmann, Heinrich Bonnheimer, Joseph Krottendorfer and, as the life and soul of the group, Johann Kilian Strack, who played the cello, took charge of the scores and was not allowed to miss a single concert. His exceptional standing with the emperor naturally enhanced his status within the group and gave him considerable influence over the choice of pieces played. That the choice did not fall on the 'most modern' composers, Haydn and Mozart, goes without saying. Joseph, too, had little time for Haydn, or at least for earlier Haydn, a disliking attributable to his 'jokes', although he later adopted a more balanced approach.[83] Even so, it would be wrong to blame only Strack for the fact that works by Mozart and Haydn were not performed within the imperial household: Joseph was certainly no puppet in the hands of his valet. But he had grown

---

77. *Briefe*, iii.201 (letter of 10 April 1782).
78. See *AmZ*, xxiv (1822), 285.
79. See *AmZ*, xv (1813), 66; and Reichardt, *Musikalische Monatsschrift 1792*, 57. *AmZ*, xv (1813), 512, reports Mozart commenting on an aria by the emperor: 'The aria is no doubt good, but whoever wrote it is better.' There is no truth in this anecdote.
80. For an example, see Mosel, *Salieri*, 130–1.
81. ◆ Franz Kreibich (1728–97, not Greibich) was imperial director of chamber music.
82. Dittersdorf, *Lebensbeschreibung*, 177, reports a story of this kind.
83. See Pohl, *Joseph Haydn*, ii.112.

up essentially within the Italian tradition and, like the rest of the civilized world at this time, regarded every work of music from the standpoint of courtly and aristocratic Gesellschaftsmusik, in which regard both Haydn and – more especially – Mozart left something to be desired, as is clear, not least, from Joseph's comment on *Die Entführung*. In short, Mozart was faced with the same degree of incomprehension in Vienna as he had encountered in Salzburg, the only difference being that Joseph II proved far more tolerant and considerate than Colloredo had ever been. Indeed, he deserves our wholehearted respect inasmuch as, unlike so many tyrannical arbiters of taste in every period of history, he did not simply dismiss the latest trends in music and all the other arts but allowed them all to have their say, albeit with reservations. Although his idea of a German National Singspiel may have owed more to reason than to genuine desire, it none the less reveals a genuine far-sightedness and a tolerant attitude towards art. In the circumstances it was only natural for him to choose Salieri – another of the Italian composers of the period who have suffered much at the hands of earlier biographers, especially Mozartians, who, fired by a false sense of nationalism, have treated him as a spiteful intriguer and, worse, an incompetent musician. In fact, Salieri was a good-natured, benevolent individual of a markedly charitable disposition. By the time that he returned to Vienna in 1780 following an extended visit to his native Italy, he was widely regarded as one of the foremost Italian artists of his day. It is particularly to his credit that soon afterwards Gluck drew him into his circle and, by ceding to him Calzabigi's libretto to *Les Danaïdes*, effectively presented him to the world as his heir apparent. *Les Danaïdes* was premièred in Paris in 1784 under both composers' names. With it Salieri followed in Piccinni's footsteps and entered the world of the high-flown music drama, a move that inevitably led him away from Mozart in a way that was bound to have an adverse effect on personal relations between the two composers. Salieri was not envious by nature – this much is clear from his later dealings with Beethoven. Rather, he resembled the majority of the great Italian composers and adopted a tolerant attitude to his German colleagues. But the case of Mozart tested his impartiality to its limits. There is no doubt that he soon became conscious of Mozart's towering stature and it is clear from the many anecdotes that have come down to us that he remained exercised by it for the whole of the rest of his life, without ever being able to come to terms in his own mind with what to him was so unsettling a phenomenon. It was not merely their differing attitudes to Gluck that prevented any real rapprochement, Salieri was also suspicious of Mozart's brilliant virtuosity (a virtuosity denied to Salieri himself) and of the undeniable superiority of *Die Entführung aus dem Serail* over *Der Rauchfangkehrer*. Even so, there was no sense of personal animus.[84] Mozart was openly friendly towards all his artistic colleagues, 'even towards Salieri, who could not bear him', to quote Mozart's sister-in-law, Sophie Haibel, and Salieri was too astute to reveal his mistrust in public. Of course, Mozart's supporters in Vienna were convinced that Salieri was ill-disposed towards him, and it is no wonder, after all, that Salieri's views veered constantly between appreciation and passionate rejection[85] and that there were times when he made it clear which of them held the whip hand. When Salieri was unable to give Princess Elisabeth the keyboard lessons that

84. Anselm Hüttenbrenner was a pupil of Salieri's and reports his teacher saying that Mozart often visited him with the words: 'Dear Papa, give me some old scores from the court library. I'd like to look through them at your place.' So engrossed did Mozart become in these scores that he often missed his lunch; see Hüttenbrenner, 'Kleiner Beytrag zu Salieri's Biographie', 797.
85. Appreciative opinions may be found in *AmZ*, xxvii (1825), 412, and Hüttenbrenner, 'Kleiner Beytrag', 797; also Rochlitz, *Für Freunde der Tonkunst*, iv.345–6. Conversely, Otto Jahn, *W. A. Mozart*, fourth edition, i.732n., reports 'trustworthy witnesses' from a later period who claimed that, within his close circle of friends, Salieri spoke extremely dismissively and unjustly about Mozart's music; for a defence of Salieri, see Thayer, 'Mozart und Salieri'.

he had been hoping for, Mozart thought that he might be offered the post instead: 'All he can do is try to harm me in this matter by recommending someone else, which he's entirely capable of doing! But the emperor knows me; and the last time the princess was in Vienna she would gladly have had lessons with me'.[86] In the event, however, Salieri ensured that the post went to an insignificant musician by the name of Georg Summer, who went on to become court organist in 1791, leaving Mozart to console himself with the thought that Summer's paltry salary of 400 florins would be spent entirely on keeping up the appearances required by teaching so august a pupil.[87]

As a result, Mozart's position at court remained as uncertain as before. Although the emperor was not short of words of encouragement, he repeatedly succumbed to other influences that were more in tune with his own view of music. Above all, he was too parsimonious to appoint another Kapellmeister in addition to the ones already on his payroll.

For a time there seemed a prospect that Mozart might find employment with the son of the prince regent, Prince Alois Liechtenstein, whose income was reckoned to be 900,000 imperial florins.[88] Liechtenstein wanted to have his own wind band, for which Mozart would have arranged the pieces. It would have been only a modest appointment, of course, but at least it would have been a secure one, and Mozart was resolved to accept it only if he was appointed for life. But nothing came of this plan either.[89] Conversely, the winter months brought a few more pupils, including Josepha Barbara Auernhammer, Countess Josepha Gabriele Pálffy[90] and especially Maria Theresia von Trattner, the wife of the bookseller Johann Thomas von Trattner and, of the three, the one of whom Mozart was clearly the fondest.[91] They were later joined by Countess Zichy, so that Mozart's basic necessities were now taken care of. His six violin sonatas were published in November 1781,[92] and the following Lent, on 3 March, he gave a concert at which – on the advice of Countess Thun, Adamberger and others – he performed highlights from *Idomeneo* and played his old concerto in D major K175, with a new rondo in final position (K382;) that made a 'great impact'. When he sent it to Salzburg on 23 March 1782 he added: 'I wrote it specially for myself, and no one else but my dear sister must play it'.[93] He ended the concert with a free fantasia, a choice largely dictated by Clementi, who was planning a concert of his own at this time and who prided himself on his improvisatory skills.[94] Mozart also performed at other composers' concerts and at private gatherings. On 24 November 1781, for example, we find him writing to his father to report on a concert at the Auernhammers at which he played 'the concerto a due [K365] and a sonata for two keyboards [K448] that I wrote expressly for the occasion and that was a great

86. ◆ *Briefe*, iii.225 (letter of 31 August 1782).
87. *Briefe*, ii.194 (letter of 12 October 1782).
88. Riesbeck, *Briefe eines reisenden Franzosen über Deutschland an seinen Bruder zu Paris*, i.272.
89. The 'Cantata composed for Prince Alois von Liechtenstein by W. A. Mozart' KAnh. 242 [K⁶ Anh. C14.01] is undoubtedly spurious. ◆ Köchel notes that according to Wurzbach, *Mozartbuch*, 238, the work may be by W. A. Mozart jr.
90. She was one of Colloredo's nieces, prompting Mozart to ask his father to keep this news to himself, as he did not know how it would be received in Salzburg; *Briefe*, iii.248 (letter of 4 January 1783).
91. Citing Constanze as his source, Nottebohm, *Mozartiana*, 131, mentions two 'interesting letters on music' to her, while Niemetschek, *Leben des k. k. Kapellmeisters Wolfgang Gottlieb Mozart nach Originalquellen beschrieben*, 59, mentions a single letter. Unfortunately, none has survived. Conversely, Mozart paid Maria Theresia von Trattner a special tribute by dedicating to her his sonata in C minor K457 and his fantasia in C minor K475. ◆ Concerning the Trattners, see Rüdiger Wolf, 'Wiener Wirtschaftsadel um Mozart, 1781–1791', and Cloeter, *Johann Thomas Trattner*.
92. In the *Wiener Zeitung* of (8 December) 1781, no. 98, they were advertised as '6 Sonatas for the clavier with accompaniment for a violin by the sufficiently well-known and celebrated Herr Wolfgang Amadee Mozart, op. 2, 5 fl.' [*Dokumente*, 175, *Documentary Biography*, 198].
93. *Briefe*, iii.199 (letter of 23 March 1782).
94. Clementi left Vienna again at the beginning of 1782.

success'.[95] Following up an earlier tradition familiar from Johann Sebastian Bach, he also wrote pieces for his pupils, most of which were intended as exercises. On 20 June 1781 he completed a set of variations for Countess Rumbeke[96] and two weeks later he mentions in a letter to his sister[97] three 'new arias with variations'. (Of these, two were presumably K359 and K360. The third piece is unidentifed.)

Mozart clearly had his hands full and had every reason, therefore, to reject his sister's charge that he was a poor correspondent:

> When our father has finished his duties in church and you yourself have got rid of your few pupils, you can both spend the whole day doing what you like, writing letters that contain whole litanies, – but I can't do that. – I recently gave my father an account of my life and I'll repeat it for you now. My hair is always done by 6 in the morning and by 7 I'm fully dressed. I then compose till 9. From 9 till 1 I teach, then I eat, unless I'm invited out where they eat at 2 or even 3, like today and tomorrow at Countess Zichy's and Countess Thun's. I can't work before 5 or 6 in the evening and I'm often prevented from doing so by a concert; if not, I write till 9. . . . Because of these concerts and the uncertainty as to whether I may be called out, I can't count on being able to compose in the evening and so I make a habit – especially if I arrive home early – of writing a little before going to bed; I often go on writing till 1 – and then I'm up again at 6. – My dearest sister! if you imagine that I could ever forget my dearest and kindest father and you, then – but enough of this! God knows the truth, and that's enough to console me, – may He punish me if I ever forget you.[98]

Mozart also sent a few small gifts to his sister and father in Salzburg: the latter received a snuffbox and a pair of watch chains that he had been given by Count Szapary, while his sister received two bonnets made by Constanze Weber 'according to the latest Viennese fashion'. He regularly asked after his old friends in the town and above all still wanted to be regarded as an active member of the local crossbow club.

Meanwhile Mozart had also been working away at his opera. Although it had been delayed by Gluck's festival offerings and by changes to the libretto, it was now scheduled for immediately after Easter.[99] But the next we hear about it is on 8 May – well after Easter – when Mozart reports that he has just 'cantered through' the second act for Countess Thun.[100] The third was to follow on 30

---

95.   *Briefe*, iii.176 (letter of 24 November 1781). Mozart mentions this work – K448 – again in his letter of 15 December 1781 (*Briefe*, iii.179), where he describes it as a 'Sonate auf 2 Klavier'. As Deiters rightly points out (Jahn, *W. A. Mozart*, fourth edition, ii.180), this effectively disproves Jahn's assumption that the work in question was the sonata in D major K381 for four hands. According to Deiters, moreover, the date 1784 on the autograph manuscript of the sonata K448 is in Mozart's own hand. It would appear, therefore, that this sonata was written in 1781; see Schiedermair's commentary in *Die Briefe W. A. Mozarts*, ii.370. Wyzewa and Saint-Foix, *Wolfgang Amédée Mozart*, ii.409, likewise date it to 1781, though the month that they give – December – is clearly wrong. The same work is mentioned again in Mozart's letter of 9 June 1784 (*Briefe*, iii.318); there is no reason to adopt Schiedermair's assumption (*Die Briefe W. A. Mozarts*, ii.374) that this is the concerto K365. ◆ Abert's remarks here do not quite make sense: an autograph date of 1784 on the manuscript of K448 hardly proves the sonata is the work in question. In any case, the date '1784' does not stem from the composer, but from Johann Anton André, who purchased the manuscript from Constanze; accordingly it is irrelevant to the argument and it is possible that the date reported by Abert is a misprint. The dating of K448 to 1781 is based primarily on the conjunction of references in the family correspondence and the type of paper on which the autograph is written.

96.   *Briefe*, iii.134 (letter of 20 June 1781).
97.   *Briefe*, iii.138 (letter of 4 July 1781).
98.   *Briefe*, iii.197–8 (letter of 13 February 1782).
99.   *Briefe*, iii.196 (letter of 30 January 1782).
100.   *Briefe*, iii.208 (letter of 8 May 1782).

May, when we also find Mozart writing that 'We are to have our first rehearsal next Monday. I have to say that I'm really looking forward to this opera.'[101]

In the event, his pleasure was considerably reduced by the various intrigues that beset the production and that finally induced the emperor himself to intervene and order the production to open on 16 July.[102] It proved a brilliant success, with the packed house repeatedly calling for individual numbers to be encored and with more performances than of any other opera during the 1782 season.[103] Mozart himself sent his father a detailed account of the second performance:

> My opera was given yesterday for the second time. Can you believe that there was an even more powerful cabal yesterday than on the first evening? The whole of the first act was hissed, but they couldn't stop people from shouting 'bravo' during the arias. – I was relying on the closing trio; – but, as ill luck would have it, Fischer went wrong, with the result that Dauer (Pedrillo) went wrong too and Adamberger on his own couldn't make up for it, so that the whole effect was lost and for once it *wasn't repeated*. I was beside myself with anger, as was Adamberger, and said straightaway that I wouldn't allow the opera to be given again without a short rehearsal for the singers. In the 2nd act both duets were repeated, as on the opening night, and so was Belmonte's rondeau 'Wenn der Freude Thränen fließen etc.'. The theatre was almost fuller than on the first night; the previous day it had been impossible to get any reserved seats, either in the stalls or in the 3rd circle, and no boxes either. In 2 days the opera has brought in 1200 florins.[104]

Mozart's next report is dated 27 July 1782:

> My opera was given for the third time yesterday in honour of all Nannerls[105] and was universally applauded; as before the theatre was packed, in spite of the terrible heat. It's supposed to be given again next Friday, but I've protested as I don't want it to become hackneyed. I can truthfully say that people are absolutely mad about this opera. It's good to get so much applause.[106]

In spite of Mozart's protests, the work was given again on 30 July, with a fifth performance following on 6 August, when the theatre was packed as usual. While Mozart was busy transcribing the work for wind band,[107] he received a commission from Salzburg to write a new serenade for the Haffner family. He accepted out of his fondness for the family and in order to please his father,

101.   *Briefe*, iii.211 (letter of 29 May 1782).
102.   Pohl, *Joseph Haydn*, ii.123, and Haas, *Ignaz Umlauff: Die Bergknappen*, XVIII.
103.   According to a report from Vienna in Cramer's *Magazin der Musik*, i.352, the music was 'full of beauties. . . . It surpassed the public's expectation, and the author's taste and new ideas, which were entrancing, received the loudest and most general applause' [*Dokumente*, 189, *Documentary Biography*, 214; the report is dated 27 March 1783].
104.   *Briefe*, iii.212 (letter of 20 July 1782).
105.   ◆ The 26th was St Anne's Day.
106.   *Briefe*, iii.215 (letter of 27 July 1782).
107.   'You really can't imagine how hard it is to arrange something like this for wind band, so that it suits the instruments and loses none of its effectiveness', Mozart wrote to his father on 20 July 1782; *Briefe*, iii.213. ◆ Mozart's arrangement is either lost or was never finished. Blomhert, 'Mozart's own 1782 Harmoniemusik based on "Die Entführung aus dem Serail"', suggests that it survives in a manuscript copy formerly part of the princely music collection at Donaueschingen (now at the Universitätsbibliothek, Karlsruhe). Further, see Blomhert, *The Harmoniemusik of Die Entführung aus dem Serail by Wolfgang Amadeus Mozart: A Study of its Authority and a Critical Edition*.

even though he had to work late into the night and forward the individual movements piecemeal to Salzburg. On 27 July we find him writing home again:

> You'll be surprised to find only the 1st allegro, but there was no alternative, I've had to write a serenade in a hurry,[108] only for wind band though, otherwise I could have used it for you too. On Wednesday the 31st I'll send the 2 minuets, the andante and the final movement; if I can, I'll also send a march – if not, you'll just have to use the one from the Hafner music [K249] which hardly anyone knows). I've written it in D as you prefer that key.[109]

That Mozart's facility as a composer had its limits emerges from his cry for help of 31 July:

> You can see that I have the best of intentions, but what can't be done can't be done! I don't like to produce botched work, so I can't send you the whole symphony till next post-day.[110]

The final piece to go off was a short march,[111] which he sent off on 7 August, with the general instruction: 'The first allegro must be played with great fire, the last as quickly as possible.' Later he asked for the whole serenade to be sent back to him in Vienna so that he could perform it at his concert as a symphony, in other words, without the march and without one of the minuets.[112] On 15 February 1783 he wrote again to his father: 'The new Hafner symphony really surprised me, as I'd forgotten all about it; it's bound to leave a good impression.'[113] So preoccupied was Mozart with his opera and with his latest affair of the heart that he had completely forgotten a work that had once been such a torment to him.

Die Entführung aus dem Serail was staged no fewer than fifteen times in the course of 1782,[114] including a performance on 8 October in honour of the grand duke and his wife, whose return journey took them back through Vienna. Mozart had 'thought it advisable' to resume his place 'at the keyboard and conduct it, partly to rouse the orchestra that was beginning to nod off, partly (since I happen to be here) to appear before the attendant dignitaries as the father of my child'.[115]

The emperor's reaction to *Die Entführung* – 'Too beautiful for our ears and far too many notes, dear Mozart!'[116] – is entirely typical of the musical tastes of a man whose Italian education blinded him to Mozart's novel treatment of the orchestra.[117] Mozart replied quite frankly: 'Just as many notes, Your Majesty, as are necessary.'[118] Other members of the nobility, by contrast, were more

---

108. K388.

109. *Briefe*, iii.214–15 (letter of 27 July 1782).

110. *Briefe*, iii.216 (letter of 31 July 1782).

111. *Briefe*, iii.219 (letter of 7 August 1782). It is unclear whether this march was K408 or K445; see Jahn, *W. A. Mozart*, fourth edition, i.738, and Wyzewa and Saint-Foix, *Wolfgang Amédée Mozart*, ii.410. ◆ Recent studies of Mozart's handwriting and the paper types in his autographs suggest that K445 was composed earlier and probably belongs with the divertimento K334. It is likely that K408 is to be associated with the serenade composed for the Haffners.

112. The second menuetto was presumably written on separate pages and not kept as it was not needed in Vienna. For Vienna, flutes and clarinets were added to the two outer movements.

113. *Briefe*, iii.257 (letter of 15 February 1783).

114. See Haas, *Ignaz Umlauff: Die Bergknappen*.

115. *Briefe*, iii.239 (letter of 19 October 1782).

116. Niemetschek, *Mozart*, 34.

117. See also his remark to Dittersdorf, 'In his theatre pieces, he committed the sole mistake – as his singers often complained – of drowning them with his full accompaniment'; Dittersdorf, *Lebensbeschreibung*, 176.

118. Cherubini made a similar comment to Napoleon; see *AmZ*, xxxvi (1834), 21, and Hohenemser, *Cherubini: Sein Leben und seine Werke*, 205. ◆ It is not certain that Dittersdorf's report, or Joseph II's alleged reaction, is authentic.

enthusiastic. The highly cultured Prince Kaunitz[119] introduced himself to the composer and became one of his warmest admirers. And Mozart was especially surprised when Gluck requested an additional performance, made a number of pertinent remarks on the subject and the following day invited him to lunch.[120] The work remained in the repertory even after the National Singspiel had gone into terminal decline and was the last work performed by the German company on 4 February 1788.[121]

The opera also commanded attention outside Vienna. The widely travelled Prussian ambassador Johann Hermann von Riedesel, who was a close friend of Winckelmann, asked Mozart to send him a copy of the score so that he could arrange a performance in Berlin, even though André's setting of the text had already been given there to great acclaim. He even held out the prospect of a suitable fee. Mozart had sent the autograph score to Salzburg in order to acquaint his father with the work until such time as he could hear it for himself.[122] Now he wrote to ask him to have it copied in Salzburg, and when Leopold expressed doubts about the viability of the whole affair hastened to reassure him in his letter of 5 October 1782:

> I went in person to see Baron von Riedesel, who is a charming man, and, confident that the opera is already being copied, promised to let him have it by the end of this month or the beginning of November at the latest. Could I ask you, then, to make sure that I have it by then? But in order to relieve you of all worry and anxiety on the subject, which I most gratefully regard as proof of your love as a father, I can say only that I am most indebted to the baron for ordering the copy from me and not from the copyist [as was the custom in Italy], from whom he could have got it at any time by paying cash; – also I should be very sorry if my talent could be paid for once and for all – especially for one hundred ducats![123] – For the present I shall say nothing to anyone (simply because I don't need to); if it is performed – as seems likely (and as would suit me best of all) – people will obviously hear about it, but my enemies will not ridicule me as a result, nor will they treat me as a worthless churl, but will be only too pleased to give me an opera to write whenever I want to – though it's highly unlikely that I'd want to do so. I mean, I'll write an opera, but not stand idly by with 100 ducats in my pocket while the theatre makes four times as much in a fortnight; – no, I'd produce my opera at my own expense and make at least 1200 florins from three performances, – and then the management can have it for 50 ducats; if they don't want it, I'll have been paid and can produce it wherever I like. Anyway, I hope that you have never detected any sign of a tendency on my part to act basely. No one should act basely, – but neither should they be so stupid as to let other people profit from their work, which has cost them so much study and effort, and to renounce all further claims on it.[124]

But Leopold, mistrustful as ever, delayed preparing the copy and it was not until much later that one was made in Salzburg, by which time Mozart had been obliged to tell the ambassador the real reasons for the delay.

119. On Kaunitz, see *Biographie des Joseph Lange*, 98–9; Müller, *Abschied von der National-Schaubühne*, 100ff.; and Friedrich Meyer, *Friedrich Ludwig Schröder*, i.341, 343 and 346. ◆ Further, see Szabo, *Kaunitz and enlightened absolutism 1753–1780*.
120. *Briefe*, iii.219 (letter of 7 August 1782). ◆ In fact it was two days later.
121. Haas, *Ignaz Umlauff: Die Bergknappen*. It was not revived in Vienna until 23 September 1801.
122. The work was not performed in Salzburg until 1784.
123. Mozart seems to be exaggerating here. At all events, we find Schröder writing to Wolfgang Heribert von Dalberg on 22 May 1784: 'Mozart has got 50 ducats for *Die Entführung aus dem Serail*; I don't think he'll write one for less than that.' The usual fee for an opera was 100 ducats; see Dittersdorf, *Lebensbeschreibung*, 178.
124. *Briefe*, iii.235–6 (letter of 5 October 1782).

Die Entführung was performed in Prague in 1783 to immense acclaim.[125] Niemetschek reports:

I cannot speak from my own experience of the applause and the sensation which it aroused in Vienna – but I was witness of the enthusiasm which it caused among cognoscenti and amateurs alike when it was performed in Prague! It was as if all that we had previously heard and known had not been music! All were captivated – all wondered at the new harmonies, the original, never before heard passages for the wind instruments.[126]

Other towns and cities that heard *Die Entführung* in 1783 were Mannheim,[127] Frankfurt am Main (with Aloysia Lange),[128] Bonn[129] and Leipzig.[130] By 1784 it had reached Salzburg and Schwedt,[131] and by 1785 it had been performed in Kassel.[132] Breslau[133] and Koblenz first heard the work in 1787 (in the case of Koblenz, the work was chosen to inaugurate the new opera house).[134] Not until 1788 was it staged in Berlin,[135] while Stuttgart had to wait until 1795, a delay attributable to competition in the form of rival settings by Christian Ludwig Dieter in 1784 and by Justin Heinrich Knecht in 1790.[136] The opera also proved successful in northern Germany, although it failed to achieve the popularity enjoyed by Hiller's singspiels. Even smaller theatres snapped up the sensational work: the actor Anton Hasenhuth, for example, tells of a remarkable performance in Baden by Georg Wilhelm's troupe in 1783 or 1784, when Hasenhuth had to play the viola part, even though he barely knew how to handle the instrument.[137] Suddenly a diminutive figure emerged from the audience, sat down beside him and started to play. By the end of the overture the newcomer had had more than he could take of Hasenhuth's bungling and, angrily throwing down his viola, rushed away with the words 'You, Sir, are an absolute bumpkin!' But the opera proved a success, prompting Wilhelm to lay on a banquet for his company and, as he had been told that Mozart was in town, the composer, too, was invited. Hasenhuth was aghast to recognize in the guest of honour his fellow viola player, but the composer good-humouredly reassured him: 'I expect I was a bit impolite earlier today, but I didn't recognize you and the devil himself wouldn't have put up with such scraping and scratching!'[138]

---

125. *Briefe*, iii.295 (letter of 6 December 1783); see also Cramer, *Magazin der Musik*, i.999 [*Dokumente*, 194, *Documentary Biography*, 219], and Procházka, *Mozart in Prag*, 18–19.
126. Niemetschek, *Mozart*, 23 [*Dokumente*, 434, *Documentary Biography*, 404].
127. Koffka, *Iffland und Dalberg*, 136.
128. Carl Valentin, *Geschichte der Musik in Frankfurt am Main vom Anfange des XIV. bis zum Anfange des XVIII. Jahrhunderts*, 257.
129. Thayer, *Ludwig van Beethovens Leben*, i.76.
130. *Raisonnierendes Theaterjournal von der Leipziger Michaelismesse 1783*, 32–3; see also *Briefe*, iii.295 (letter of 6 December 1783).
131. *Litteratur- und Theater-Zeitung* (Berlin, 1784), part 3, no. 36, 160 [*Dokumente*, 205–6, *Documentary Biography*, 231–2].
132. Lynker, *Geschichte des Theaters und der Musik in Kassel*, 316.
133. Schlesinger, *Geschichte des Breslauer Theaters*, i.72.
134. Dominicus, *Coblenz unter dem letzten Kurfürsten von Trier*, 73.
135. Louis Schneider, *Geschichte der Oper und des Königlichen Opernhauses in Berlin*, 223.
136. Krauß, *Das Stuttgarter Hoftheater*, 100; see also Preibisch, 'Quellenstudien zu Mozarts "Entführung aus dem Serail"', 457.
137. Hadatsch, *Die Launen des Schicksals*, 94–5.
138. ◆ Anecdotes such as these are not uncommon for Mozart and probably represent a type of story, rather than actual fact. The most familiar describes Mozart's visit to the opera in Berlin, to hear a performance of *Die Entführung*: 'He stood at the entrance to the parterre, meaning to listen without being seen. But at one moment he too much enjoyed the execution of certain passages, at another he was unhappy with the tempos or found that the singers were adding too many ornaments . . . unconsciously he moved ever closer and closer to the orchestra, now humming and murmuring this tune, now that, now soft, now loud. Seeing the small homely man in the worn overcoat, people began to laugh, of which he was unaware, of course. Finally they came to Pedrillo's aria – "Frisch zum Kampfe, frisch zum Streite" etc. The management either had a defective score or wanted to improve it by substituting a D sharp for a D for the second violins at the frequently-repeated words "Nur ein feiger Tropf verzagt". Here Mozart could contain himself no longer: he called out in a loud voice in his usual forceful language: "Confound it! – It must be a D!" Everyone looked around, including several members of the orchestra. Several of the musicians recognized him and the word spread like wildfire through the orchestra and the theatre: Mozart is here!' See *AmZ*, i (10 October 1798), 20–2 and Solomon, 'The Rochlitz Anecdotes', 7–9.

Even professional critics were almost unanimous in their praise of the piece.[139] Of course, Mozart made virtually no money out of any of these productions outside Vienna, and even the profits that might have accrued to him if a vocal score had been published in time were lost as a result of his financial incompetence. And so we find Leopold complaining to his daughter on 16 December 1785:

> Well, what I warned you about my son has now come true. A vocal score of 'Die Entführung' has been published by the bookseller Stage in Augsburg for 7 florins and I forget how many kreutzers. It has been arranged by Canon Starck – and engraved in Mainz and trumpeted forth in the Augsburg papers with many praiseworthy remarks about the famous Herr von Mozart. If Torricella has already engraved a large portion of the score, he will lose out considerably and your brother will have wasted his time writing out 2 acts[140] which, with the exception of the 3rd, were already finished.[141]

Mozart's letters and compositions from this early period in Vienna, up to and including *Die Entführung aus dem Serail*, all reflect his feelings of happiness at being released from years of pressure. At no time in the past, with the possible exception of the months spent working on *Idomeneo* in Munich, had he allowed his genius such free rein and done so, moreover, with such a sense of pride, self-assurance and uninhibited verve. But it is not just his basically life-affirming nature that finds such forceful expression here,[142] works such as the great C minor wind serenade – one of the most important pieces that Mozart ever wrote – reveal that the other aspect of his character, its dark and wildly impassioned side, was also struggling to acquire far greater profundity. Stylistically speaking, French influence continues to make itself felt, but there are increasing signs of the impressions gleaned in Vienna, culminating in a further series of works which, thanks to his contacts with Gottfried van Swieten, reflect a third and particularly important model, that of the north German school of Carl Philipp Emanuel Bach and, hence, the music of Johann Sebastian Bach and Handel.

In this context, the two most important works are the serenades in E flat major K375 and C minor K388, both scored for winds and, as such, examples of a type of work that was particularly popular at open-air serenades. Generally, there were six such instruments, namely, pairs of clarinets, horns and bassoons, but composers often wrote for two additional oboes.[143] In the case of the E flat major serenade the oboes were added later, evidently in July 1782, an addition clearly apparent from the prominent clarinet sonorities in the later version, too. The C minor Serenade was scored from the outset for eight instruments. Common to both works is their subversion of the serenade's traditional character, a transformation which in the case of the second work amounts to a radical revision. Even the E flat major piece, for all that it begins by striking an almost

---

139. Detailed and positive reviews appeared in Cramer's *Magazin für Musik*, ii.1056ff. and in Knigge's *Dramaturgische Blätter* (Hanover, 1788), ii.21ff. The author of the last-named piece was Bernhard Anselm Weber. Copies of both these journals were among Mozart's modest collection of books. ◆ For the review in the *Dramaturgische Blätter*, see *Dokumente*, 287–8, *Documentary Biography*, 327–8.

140. Of Mozart's vocal score, only a few fragmentary excerpts from the arias of Konstanze ('Martern aller Arten') and Blonde ('Welche Wonne, welche Lust') have survived in the composer's own hand. The engraved vocal score of act one was advertised in the *Wiener Zeitung* no. 98 (1785), appendix.

141. *Briefe*, iii.471 (letter of 16 December 1785).

142. Thus the characterization of Wyzewa and Saint-Foix, *Wolfgang Amédée Mozart*, ii.409.

143. Eight instruments provided the *Tafelmusik* for the Emperor Joseph II and the Elector of Cologne, for example, and are also recorded at a celebration at the Berlin court in 1791; see *Musikalische Correspondenz*, ii (1791), 366. The *Tafelmusik* in the second-act finale of *Don Giovanni* and the serenade in *Così fan tutte* are both a true reflection of current practice. ◆ See Whitwell, 'The Incredible Vienna Octet School'.

importunately old-fashioned note, soon launches out in a highly personal direction, with the consequent phrase significantly repeated and expanded: here is a work that is no longer content to pay noisy and jocular tribute to the object of the serenade, but one that now casts ardent and yearning glances up at the windows and even utters heartfelt sighs that appear to wait in vain for an answer as the players fall momentarily silent. The whole of the first movement consists in a constant interplay between the strains of the older type of serenade and a more individual, Romantic manner whose chief representative is the wittily introduced second subject in B flat minor. Particularly idiosyncratic is the way in which this subject is replaced in the otherwise regular recapitulation by an entirely new and serenade-like theme, as though Mozart has had enough of the mood of rapt infatuation. But the sighs that had ended the earlier second subject unexpectedly attach themselves to the new one, too. The development section is very brief but based on existing material, maintaining the two basic moods, but on both occasions coming to a standstill on a fermata after only a few bars' development. In much the same way the coda opens with great ceremony with the first of the serenade's themes, only to fade away with an eloquent sigh in the oboes like some final, furtive parting kiss. Writers who number Mozart among the principal forerunners of Romanticism may justifiably appeal to the slow movement in support of their thesis, a movement which, like all the other movements, adopts the practice of the older suite and is in the home key of E flat major. The result is a love scene overflowing with emotion, a discreet and delightful whispering, and there is no denying the natural note that it strikes. This slow movement is framed by two minuets, both of which (and especially the second) are Haydnesque in manner. The main sections of both, together with the trio of the first, are ternary in structure. With its popular Haydnesque theme, the final rondo reverts to the world of the older serenade. The two thematically related episodes are full of good humour,[144] and the way in which Mozart then returns to his main theme is particularly witty and intelligent.

Not the least of the remarkable features of the second serenade is its key. A serenade in a minor tonality is effectively a contradiction in terms, at least by the standards of the time, when such a piece was expected to be a celebration of an exuberant delight in existence. Not even Mozart himself was ever to write another minor-key work of this kind. Rarely has a less similar set of twins been brought into the world than the 'Haffner' serenade[145] and the present remarkable piece, which could hardly be further removed from the traditional idea of a serenade. It is as though the Haffner commission, which forced Mozart to work so precipitately in the service of traditional art, automatically exposed the other aspect of his character, an aspect that declines to accept man-made rules of creativity but acknowledges its own laws alone. The main theme of the opening movement is already exceptional in character by dint of its unusual length – twenty-two bars: a darkly ascending unison phrase with an eerie interval of a seventh in the fourth bar that keeps returning as a veritable mark of Cain; a weary and fearful groping upwards through a series of syncopations; a new and wild outburst of passion; and, finally, a spirit of hopeless renunciation – contemporary listeners must have felt a curious tightening round their hearts on hearing this theme. A despondent calando seems to herald the entry of the second subject, only for it to be suddenly curtailed by an interrupted cadence that seizes hold of the musical line as though with the talons of a

---

144. The theme of the second, which is later contrapuntally reworked, provides a kind of explanation of the beginning of the first with its apparently unmotivated horn signal.

145. ◆ Here, of course, Abert refers to the serenade described in this chapter, which was eventually reworked as the 'Haffner' symphony K385. The serenade K250, composed for a Haffner family wedding in 1775, is the work usually referred to as the 'Haffner' serenade.

vulture. All the evil spirits are again unleashed and, ignoring the helpless pleading of the oboe, vent their fury in a demonically anapaestic unison motif. Only after calmness has again been established does the oboe slowly and effortfully grope its way towards the second subject. Admittedly, this broadly flowing cantilena allows brighter emotions to enter the piece, but it is clear not only from the melodic writing but also from its six-bar rhythmic structure that there can be no question of the sort of innocent merriment found in the older type of serenade. Almost at once the old spirit of defiance stirs in the following motif, which breathes a typically Mozartian power:

The only consequence of this ray of light is the absence of the earlier mood of dark despair, yet the anabatic final subject-group none the less has something convulsive and benumbing about it. The development section begins with an abrupt change of mood and a new and pensive idea, although the sforzatos that suddenly flash forth from it could hardly be more ill-omened, and this remarkable section duly breaks off in bewilderment after twelve bars with an ominous one-beat rest. There follows the movement's climax, with a frightening relapse into the old sense of despair and an inability to escape from the first subject's descending seventh that is now developed in *stretto*. Based on an earlier subsidiary motif, the development section ends on a note of the wildest emotional upheaval with a strident chord of a diminished seventh on C minor followed by a whole bar's rest. This, then, is the shattering result of this emotional struggle, a struggle that already anticipates the later Mozart: renunciation and resistance to the very last gasp. In this way new light is shed on the recapitulation too. It is typical of the composer that the second subject, like most other second subjects in his minor-key movements, now enters in the minor, thus finally revealing its true colours. Even the main theme of the andante bears within it a sense of silent suffering that acquires a positively touching aspect especially in the development section. The dialogue between the individual groups of instruments is particularly entrancing in this movement. Like many of Beethoven's scherzos, the menuetto harks back to the mood of the opening allegro. Its trio follows Haydn's example and includes a double canon by inversion, in which the four (*mezza voce*) voices, constantly pursuing each other, create a curiously restless, volatile impression.[146] The final movement is an allegro cast in the form of a set of variations on a theme of emphatically minor-key character.[147] The first four variations explore the theme in their separate ways, adding to the note of intensity. In the case of the first and fourth, it is its defiant and passionate aspect that they exploit, while in the second and third (with its authentically Mozartian syncopations and dissonant clash of suspensions and main notes) it is its demonic side. The fifth variation in E flat major begins with a horn motif that later returns in the trumpets in the famous passage from the sextet in *Don Giovanni* and is one of the few rays of light to pervade the work's underlying gloom. The horns attempt to cling to this moment of beauty, but the clarinets abruptly modulate to the minor and equally suddenly we find ourselves back with the theme, which has again been slightly altered in a passage whose simplicity reveals the hand of a master and, specifically, of Mozart. No less inspired is the seventh variation in which the theme's purely melodic outlines are obscured in a thoroughly Beethovenian manner, turning it into a kind of shadow of itself, before it finally sinks

---

146.   The two-part canon is entrusted to the oboes and bassoons, with the answering voice repeating the melody with the intervals inverted.

147.   For an excellent analysis, see Heuß, 'Das dämonische Element in Mozarts Werken', 179ff.

away over a pedal point. An oppressive silence follows, then suddenly the theme rings out once again, this time in a radiant C major.[148] It is as though Mozart had remembered at the very last moment that this work is actually a serenade and that it should leave its listeners with a cheerful impression. But the result is that this upbeat ending seems grafted on from the outside rather than internally motivated: after the sombre emotions that have been explored hitherto, the smile at the end seems somewhat conventional.

Mozart himself evidently felt that this work was far too serious to be a serenade, hence, presumably, his decision to rewrite it as a string quintet K406. His revisions probably date from before 1784[149] and involve minor alterations to the inner voices and accompanying figures and so on: the musical substance in general remained untouched. That a great deal was lost in terms of the work's sonorities will not, of course, have escaped the composer's notice.

Far more typical of the genre is the 'Haffner' serenade, which was later turned into a symphony K385 through the omission of its march and one of its minuets. Its opening movement in particular demonstrates the extent of Mozart's respect for the Haffner family. Its strikingly wide-ranging subject

dominates the entire movement in a manner more typical of Haydn, leaving no room whatsoever for a second subject. The theme passes from voice to voice, now in festive radiance, now in a secret whisper, providing ample opportunity for displays of contrapuntal mastery. A number of these counterpoints such as

add an element of wistfulness to the underlying joviality. A spirited allegro, the movement ends with a brief coda based on a motif familiar from the final fugue of the C major symphony. If this opening movement recalls Haydn in respect of its thematic unity, the andante points in more general terms to Vienna: a marchlike theme that ambles past in leisurely fashion gives way to all manner of subsidiary motifs that whisper and chuckle in turn: in all of these motifs, including the brief little trills and sudden *forte* outbursts, we are evidently dealing with impressions of nature and everyday life. No less a product of Vienna is the brevity and freshness of the menuetto, together with the songlike tone of its trio, the second section of which begins on an authentically Mozartian note of interiority. With the start of the final movement, it is none other than the Osmin of *Die Entführung aus dem Serail* who steps out on to the stage:

---

148. To interpret the major tonality as 'sinister', as Heuß does ('Das dämonische Element', 180), is frequently fully justified in Mozart's minor-key pieces, but I do not feel it is appropriate in the case of the present movement.
149. ◆ These are now thought to date from 1787 or 1788, about the time Mozart offered three string quintets on subscription, the C major K515, the G minor K516 and the arrangement of the C minor wind serenade.

A serenade-like section of somewhat fussy and festive pomp leads into the second subject that bears clear traces of Haydn's indirect influence. Equally Haydnesque is the return of the first subject in the home key only a few bars into the development section, leading the listener into thinking, mistakenly, that the development section has been omitted, an impression that Mozart increases on this occasion by following the first subject with the second one.[150] No less typical of Haydn, finally, is the long and, with its Romantic opening, extremely eloquent coda.

All these works mark a clear return to the style of Viennese instrumental music, a return apparent on the one hand from the choice of themes and on the other from the use of thematic development in place of fantasia-like development sections à la Schobert. The same is true of more or less all the other instrumental works of this period, most notably the four violin sonatas (K376 in F major, K377 in F major, K379 in G major and K380 in E flat major). Of these, the one exception is K380, its development section introducing new ideas in the older manner and indulging in impassioned harmonic sequencing. As such, it may date from an earlier period.[151] This powerfully emotional and virtuosic movement is followed by an Andante that likewise introduces a new and oddly gripping idea into its development section, finally culminating in a surprising outburst of dark and dour emotion – the climax of the pain-masked mood that makes this G minor movement one of the most moving of all these threnodies. The spell is broken by the final Rondeau, in terms of its musical substance the most lightweight of the work's three movements and a typical example of Mozart's approach to form at this time: broad, multisectional themes, the first episode in the dominant as in sonata form, and the second – now in the minor – equally wide-ranging, its impassioned defiance recalling the middle movement. Particularly attractive is the hesitant manner in which Mozart finds his way back to the main theme. K376 in F major is closely related to K380, except that it is more intimate and relaxed in tone. Here, too, the development section of its opening allegro begins with a new theme of childlike affectingness which, as before, sounds almost like the movement's notional second subject. Cleverly developing a subsidiary motif, this idyll builds in intensity before leading back to the recapitulation. The middle movement tells of the yearning that accompanies burgeoning love and is a consummate example of Mozart's now fully developed ability to create a balanced dialogue between the two instruments; there is something entirely self-evident about the way in which each of them takes up and develops the other's cantilena, and even where one merely accompanies the other, it does so independently in a manner appropriate to the instrument in question.[152] With its lively Viennese march theme ending in a surprising exclamation of delight, the final rondo is similar in design to that of the E flat major sonata, the only difference being that it is more elaborately and variedly structured.

150. Cf. the serenade K185.

151. ◆ Interesting as this speculation is, paper studies show that K380 almost certainly dates from the summer of 1781 and is exactly contemporary with K376, K377 and K379. It is worth noting, however, that these four sonatas were published by Artaria in December 1781 with two earlier ones: K296, composed at Mannheim on 11 March 1778, and K378, composed at Salzburg in 1779 or 1780. This fact may be in part behind Abert's speculation, since the autograph of K380 is not dated.

152. Note, for example, the whispering accompanying figure in the violin right at the beginning and the figure in the piano immediately afterwards.

Common to the two remaining sonatas, K377 in F major and K379 in G major, is the freedom with which the movements are ordered, a feature inspired by French models. Both works include sets of variations (a form frequently found in Mozart's works at this time), and the first additionally ends with a tempo di menuetto. The second further resembles a suite in its absence of a change of key and its interpolation of a movement in G minor between two in G major. In terms of their musical substance, these two works form the high point of the whole series. The opening movement of the F major Sonata is captivating in its fiery energy and, with its taut unity, is an admirable example of the new stylistic ideal that Mozart espoused in Vienna: the urgent triplet motion does not relent for a moment, thereby precluding any contrast between first and second subject. The strictly thematic development section likewise looks forward to the later Mozart in the way in which it suddenly foregrounds a rhythmic subsidiary motif:  But the recapitulation does not emerge unexpectedly from the mists, as it had done so often before, but forms the climax of a tremendous development that also involves a transformation of the first subject: there is no room any longer for what had originally been its second section (with the sigh) and instead it is replaced by a restless passage from the development section. The set of variations[153] forms a counterpart to the finale of the C minor serenade in more than one respect but above all through the way in which the minor-key character of its theme – the agitated tenor of which is further enhanced by the authentically Mozartian syncopation – is strenuously maintained throughout the entire movement. And, as in the serenade, this basic character is gradually intensified in the course of the first four variations, with the fourth variation and its wildly pounding accompanying motif forming the climax of the whole (note also the searing chromatic part-writing in the second section). That the childlike innocence of the following variation in the major is not conceived as a way of breaking the spell is clear from the final variation, a siciliana,[154] in which the mood becomes positively eerie. It is sufficient to consider the dynamics with their abrupt juxtaposition of *piano* and explosive *forte*, a clash unfortunately obscured by the crescendo markings in Ferdinand David's edition.[155] The deeply felt coda is one of the most beautiful epilogues that Mozart ever wrote, allowing the sense of anguish to die away at the end on a note of utter hopelessness. In spite of its charm, the finale too – a rondo with two consecutive episodes – has a wistful streak to it: following the nocturne of the set of variations, Mozart preferred not to return to the active vigorous mood of the opening movement, a mood recalled only fleetingly by the first middle movement. This movement is wisely headed 'Tempo di Menuetto' and is far removed from an actual dance. The coda is again particularly poetical in its impact as a result of its constantly delayed conclusion and a main theme that gently floats away at the end.

In the case of the second sonata, the listener might be left in some doubt as to its basic tonality. Is it G minor and are the two movements in the major intended merely to prepare the way for it and thereafter to break loose from it? Or is the minor-key movement no more than a sombre episode within a bright-toned framework? Listeners already familiar with this G minor movement in particular and with the composer's works in general will have no difficulty deciding that this is the nub of the sonata as a whole. There are few pieces in which Mozart has captured such a sense of explosive passion in so brief and concise a form. Where is the Italian loquacity found in the

153.   See Heuß, 'Das dämonische Element', 181.
154.   The theme returns in the finale of the D minor string quartet K421.
155.   ◆ Ferdinand David (1810–73) was a professor of violin at the Leipzig conservatory. His edition of the violin sonatas, published by Breitkopf & Härtel in 1866, circulated widely at the time.

earlier works? Even its development section has been reduced to a handful of bars, with the result that the modest, but eloquent, additions to the recapitulation create a correspondingly powerful effect. With its glorious cantilena, the G major adagio recalls the old Italian sonata, while the set of variations at the end is more redolent of the French school. Based on a folklike theme, these variations are a serenely cheerful and relaxed counterpart to the corresponding movement from the F major sonata. Both are founded on the same underlying principle in which the basic character of the theme is progressively intensified.[156] On this occasion, Mozart has also added a slow variation: as in the A major keyboard sonata, it is a richly ornamented cantilena that tests to the limits the performer's ability to produce a cantabile line. Pizzicato broken chords in the violin provide a guitar-like accompaniment. In keeping with the older tradition, the theme then returns *allegretto* and this delightful movement ends with a coda.

Over and above the interest afforded by their musical ideas, these sonatas are characterized above all by their perfect balance between poetry and concertante virtuosity. The older period is recalled only by their title 'Sonatas for keyboard with accompaniment for a violin', although there is in fact no longer any trace of an accompaniment in the sense that the violin is subordinated to the keyboard. The same technical demands are made of both performers, and both have an equal part to play in developing the musical argument. Alongside the older, simpler concertante style in which the whole theme is taken over by the other instrument, we also find one and the same melody divided between the two instruments in the form of a brief interplay (see above), with a witty dialogue involving fleeting imitations that is found especially in the two sets of variations. Although stricter contrapuntal procedures are not found, a few brief individual pointers in this direction are none the less included and, as such, are immensely poetic: note, for example, the suspensions in the violin in the second subject of the opening movement of K376 and in the minor-key variation of K379. In addition, there are many examples of piquant sonorities, including the expounding of the same melody in octaves in both instruments, sustained notes (especially beautiful at the very beginning of K376), the exploitation of every register and so on. Although Mozart's delight in virtuoso brilliance is more pronounced here than in the earlier works, it still falls short of the demands that are made in the later pieces. Virtuoso outbursts of temperament such as we find in the final movement of the A major sonata K526 and, later, in Beethoven's works will be sought here in vain. The advertisement for these six sonatas described them aptly in the following terms:

> These sonatas are the only ones of their kind: abounding in new ideas and bearing clear traces of their author's great genius as a musician, extremely brilliant and well suited to the instrument. At the same time, the violin accompaniment is so skilfully combined with the keyboard part that both instruments are constantly kept in equal prominence, so that these sonatas demand as accomplished a violinist as a keyboard player. But it is not possible to give a full description of this original work. Amateurs and connoisseurs must first play them through for themselves, only then will they discover that we have not been exaggerating.[157]

---

156. It is remarkable that the clouded minor-key harmonies at the beginning of the second section do not return until the variations. Here, however, they are found in the very first variation (for keyboard alone), a variation which, with its expressive figurations and independent middle voice, is an instructive example of what can be achieved with the old 'melodic' variation in the hands of a master.

157. See Pichler, *Denkwürdigkeiten*, i.90–91. ◆ This was not an advertisement but a review, first published in Cramer's *Magazin der Musik* for 4 April 1783; see *Dokumente*, 190, *Documentary Biography*, 214.

Openly virtuosic, by contrast, is the sonata in D major for two keyboards K448, a piece whose technical demands are in no way inferior to those found in the composer's keyboard concertos. From the outset it strikes a note of festive brilliance, evincing a breadth and looseness of structure unique in the works of this period. The development sections of the first two movements again introduce new themes, of which the one in the first movement briefly assumes an air of wild-eyed pathos before returning in triumph at the end. The final movement is cast in the form of a large-scale rondo, its theme resembling an inversion of the 'alla turca' of K 331, while its festive bustle occasionally recalls the figure of Blonde in *Die Entführung*.[158]

It is no accident that Mozart wrote a number of sets of variations during these early months in Vienna, when he was attempting to find some pupils and make a name for himself as a pianist. Variations were a particularly popular genre at this time. Two of them were based on French themes, *La bergère Célimène* K359 and *Hélas! j'ai perdu mon amant* K360, and are even scored for keyboard and violin.[159] With its wistful siciliana theme, the second is typical of all Mozart's works in G minor, a piece heavy with muted passion that swells perceptibly throughout the work and bursts forth all the more restlessly after the major-key variation. The two sets of keyboard variations on the March from Grétry's *Les mariages samnites* K352 and on 'Salve tu, Domine' from Paisiello's *Socrate immaginario*[160] K398 are so closely related that they must have been written at around the same time.[161] The Grétry variations are also very similar to the K331 set; the adagio variations are all of the ornamental cantabile type. Virtuosity plays an especially distinguished role in the case of the Paisiello set; typical of this showiness are the cadenzas in the three last variations, a mannerism to which Mozart was evidently introduced by Clementi. Although described as a 'rondo', the replacement finale (K382) for the D major concerto K175 is also cast in the form of a set of variations.

With the exception of *Die Entführung aus dem Serail*, Mozart found little time for vocal compositions at this time. On 10 April 1782 he wrote an occasional aria for Aloysia Lange, *Nehmt meinen Dank, Ihr holden Gönner* K383,[162] a simple piece comprising two strophes, the principal musical idea of which is identical to Pedrillo's A major melody from the allegretto of the quartet from *Die Entführung*. The accompaniment consists of broken chords in the pizzicato strings and brief and expressive solos for flute, oboe and bassoon. It is unclear whether any other occasional pieces date from this period, and it must remain an open question whether the aria *Der Liebe himmlisches Gefühl* K119, of which only the vocal score survives, was written at this time.[163]

---

158. The heartfelt and solemn second element of the first episode seems to have left its mark on the first episode in the rondo finale of Beethoven's first violin sonata, which is also in A major.

159. Remarkably, these two works are missing from all more recent editions of Mozart's violin sonatas with the exception of Litolff's, even though neither of them – and especially the second – deserves this neglect.

160. ◆ 'Salve tu, Domine' is not from *Socrate immaginario* (first given at the Naples Teatro Nuovo in October 1775) but from *I filosofi immaginari*, which had its premiere at the Hermitage in St Petersburg on 3/14 February 1779.

161. Mozart played variations on 'an aria from an opera called the Philosophers' at his concert on 22 March 1783; see *Briefe*, iii.262 (letter of 29 March 1783). It is possible that this work was K398. Paisiello's opera was first given in German in Vienna on 22 May 1781 [as *Die eingebildeten Philosophen*]. Grétry's march was not included in the opera until it received a new production in 1782, suggesting that both works date from the summer of 1782; see Wyzewa and Saint-Foix, *Wolfgang Amédée Mozart*, ii.410.

162. It was written for a benefit performance, but it has not been possible to establish which one.

163. Jahn, *W. A. Mozart*, fourth edition, i.265, dates it to a much earlier period (around 1771), whereas Wyzewa and Saint-Foix, *Wolfgang Amédée Mozart*, ii.410, propose a date of 1782, a dating no doubt suggested by the piece's striking echoes of *Die Entführung aus dem Serail*. ◆ The authenticity of *Der Liebe himmlisches Gefühl* is uncertain: an autograph or authentic copy is unknown, no documentary evidence unequivocally ties the work to Mozart, and the earliest known source is a vocal score published by Breitkopf & Härtel in 1814. The presumed dating '1782' is entirely speculative.

28

German singspiel

German opera had been established by Heinrich Schütz in the second quarter of the seventeenth century, but after a period of efflorescence as brief as it was promising, it was finally forced to abandon the field to Italian opera in the years around 1720.[1] All memory of it was so thoroughly wiped out that the new attempts to found a national German opera that started up in the middle of the eighteenth century had to begin again at the beginning and to do so, moreover, on a completely different basis. The new singspiel slipped in through the back door, as it were, on the coat-tails of the spoken drama with musical interludes, a genre that had never completely died out in Germany. Unlike the older form of German opera, this was intended from the outset to be in stark contrast with that quintessential product of the Italian Renaissance, *opera seria*. The same trend that produced *opera buffa* in Italy and *opéra comique* in France now seized hold of Germany, too, where there had likewise been a marked reaction to serious opera during the period of Italian domination.[2]

On this occasion the impulse came from England.[3] It was here that Gay's and Pepusch's famous *Beggar's Opera* had first been performed in 1728, itself a reaction against Italian opera and, at the same time, an incendiary satire on conditions at the English court at this period. Formally speaking, it was a mixture of spoken dialogue and popular folksongs[4] and, as such, resembled the early French vaudeville comedies by which it was manifestly influenced. The work was much imitated, and one of these pieces, *The Devil to Pay, or The Wives Metamorphos'd* (1731) by the Irish playwright Charles Coffey, a crude marital comedy involving elements of sheer fantasy, finally found its way to mainland Europe, where the well-known Shakespearian translator, Caspar Wilhelm von Bork, translated it into German.[5] It was first performed in Berlin by Johann Friedrich Schönemann's company in 1743 under the title *Der Teufel ist los, oder Die verwandelten Weiber*, presumably with the original English tunes.[6] It proved hugely successful, and as Schönemann was anxious to keep such a crowd-puller for himself, his colleague in Leipzig, Heinrich Gottfried Koch, who had eked out a living until then by staging Italian intermezzos,[7] decided to join forces with

---

1. In his *Nöthiger Vorrath zur Geschichte der deutschen dramatischen Dichtkunst* (Leipzig, 1757–65), 314, Johann Christoph Gottsched describes *Atalante*, first staged in Danzig in 1742, as the last German opera; see Kretzschmar, 'Das erste Jahrhundert der deutschen Oper', 270–93.
2. ◆ On the early history of German opera, see A. R. Neumann, 'The Changing Concept of the *Singspiel* in the Eighteenth Century'; Krämer, *Deutschsprachiges Musiktheater im späten 18. Jahrhundert*; and *Das deutsche Singspiel im 18. Jahrhundert*.
3. See Schletterer, *Das deutsche Singspiel von seinen Anfängen bis auf die neueste Zeit* (now largely outdated), and Calmus, *Die ersten deutschen Singspiele von Standfuß und Hiller*.
4. See Calmus, 'Die Beggar's Opera von Gay und Pepusch', 286ff., and *Zwei Opernburlesken aus der Rokokozeit*. ◆ For a modern edition, see Barlow, *The Music of John Gay's The Beggar's Opera*.
5. ◆ See van Boer, 'Coffey's *The Devil to Pay*, the Comic War, and the Emergence of the German *Singspiel*'. 'Bork' is properly Borck or Borcke.
6. Christian Heinrich Schmid, *Chronologie des deutschen Theaters*, 109–10; Plümicke, *Entwurf einer Theatergeschichte von Berlin*, 193–4.
7. Schmid, *Chronologie*, 159–60 and *Caecilia*, viii (1828), 277ff.

one of his friends, the poet Christian Felix Weiße, and to rework the piece for himself. Koch's répétiteur, Johann Standfuß, revised the musical numbers. This adaptation was staged in Leipzig on 6 October 1752 and again proved hugely popular. From the outset it was regarded as the first work of the new genre, prompting Gottsched to renew his old attacks on opera and to suffer a humiliating defeat in consequence.[8] In 1759 Koch staged a sequel in Lübeck under the title *Der lustige Schuster*, based on Coffey's *The Merry Cobbler*.

For the present, this was no more than a modest beginning, of course: these were plays with interpolated songs, and this dependency on the spoken theatre continued to plague the singspiel for some time to come. In particular, it meant that the performers were not trained singers but actors with an aptitude for singing, and as soon as any greater musical demands were placed on them, the results must have been woefully inadequate.[9] During the early period, however, when all that mattered was a lively and spirited performance and the vocal numbers were technically undemanding, the existing actors, including those of Koch's company, will have managed as best they could.[10] The formal repertory of the German singspiel was largely established by Weiße and Standfuß, with spoken dialogue for the unfolding action and simple, popular song forms for the musical numbers. The latter were chosen with due regard for the individual characterization and the situation on stage.

The Seven Years' War brought a temporary halt to this development, and when the singspiel reappeared on the scene in 1766, it presented a somewhat different aspect to the world. Weiße had spent some time in Paris in 1759–60 and had got to know early examples of *opéras comiques*, with their mixture of vaudevilles and well-known *airs*, prompting his decision to introduce this kind of music into Germany[11] and resulting in the supersession of English by French influence. In this way, the singspiel became caught up in the same trend as contemporary lieder which, under the influence of the Berlin school, espoused a folklike ideal modelled on the French *chansons* of the period. Weiße resurrected his old libretto for *Die verwandelten Weiber* and reworked it in the spirit of Sedaine's *Le diable à quatre*, retaining the spoken dialogue but adding considerably to the number of interpolated songs. Standfuß having died in the interim, Weiße turned to Johann Adam Hiller (1728–1804), and in this new guise[12] the work was performed by Koch's company in Leipzig on 28 May 1766. So successful was it that Hiller followed it up later that same year with a second piece, *Lisuart und Dariolette*. First performed on 25 November 1766, this new piece was a setting of a text by Daniel Schiebeler that the young poet himself described as 'romantic'.[13] It too was based ultimately on an English original,[14] albeit transmitted by Favart's *La fée Urgèle*. On this occasion, Hiller had set himself the task of writing a national German opera, and there is no doubt that he extended the formal range of the singspiel by dint of his borrowings from Italian *opera seria* and *opera buffa*, but without abandoning spoken dialogue. In the event, his high-flown plans found little favour with either the cautious Koch or with Weiße, who was biased in favour of French ideas. And the work itself must have opened their eyes to the fact that Hiller's talent fell far short of his intentions. The result was a return to French models, and with *Lottchen am Hofe*, an

8. Blümner, *Geschichte des Theaters in Leipzig*, 98ff.; Danzel, *Gottsched und seine Zeit*, 172ff.; and Minor, *Christian Felix Weiße und seine Beziehungen zur deutschen Literatur des achtzehnten Jahrhunderts*, 144ff.

9. See Reichardt, *Ueber die deutsche comische Oper*, 14 and *Briefe eines aufmerksamen Reisenden die Musik betreffend*, i.147.

10. Calmus, *Die ersten deutschen Singspiele*, 12ff.

11. Weiße, *Selbstbiographie*, 102ff.

12. A number of Standfuß's songs were taken over. ◆ These were published in Leipzig in 1770 by the firm of Junius.

13. See Schiebeler, 'Anmerkung zu Lisuart und Dariolette'; by 'romantic' Schiebeler understood the adventures of a knight errant that the Italians termed 'romantico'.

14. Calmus, *Die ersten deutschen Singspiele*, 27.

adaptation of Favart's *Ninette à la cour* first performed on 24 April 1767, Weiße and Hiller established a prototype[15] that was to remain immensely popular until Mozart's day. Although poets such as Johann Joachim Eschenburg and August Gottlieb Meißner drew their subjects from Italian *opera buffa*, they failed to displace French models, not least because the latter found increasing support in the growing tendency for French operas to be adopted in Germany.

In this way the singspiel became one of the principal vehicles of French cultural ideas on German soil, faithfully reflecting the changes witnessed by *opéra comique*, from the older period's pieces about peasants and artisans to the 'Romantic' works of the later period, with their magic spells, their tales of adventurous rescues and their idea of redemption. Their intellectual aims, too, were largely the same, revolving, as they did, around Rousseau's antithesis between town and country and between rustic innocence and the corruption of the upper classes. No less in evidence are allusions to the social conditions of the day, with a work such as *Lottchen am Hofe* already containing within it a palpable foretaste of the storm-laden atmosphere of *Le nozze di Figaro*. As in the French works of the period, burlesque comedy – which had still played a major role in Standfuß's pieces – is now replaced by the principal evil of the age, sentimentality, receiving active encouragement from that typical German quality of soulfulness that has so often been the bane of our nation. Above all, however, we encounter in Germany a greater tendency to moralize – a tendency already observed among the French writers of the period and one that naturally found a particularly fertile soil in Gottsched's city of Leipzig. Such a tendency, moreover, was bound to seem all the more unwelcome when stripped of the formal elegance of the French.

Weiße did not regard himself as a mere slave of the French, of course, but sought to nationalize French art: his nation was to acquire an art of its own, an art based in the most general terms on the French model but adapted to suit conditions in Germany. He knew exactly how the mass of his fellow Germans felt in the wake of the Seven Years' War: although they were now far more receptive to national ideas, their main concern was to enjoy their new-found peace and the resultant sense of order, whose blessings they hoped to enjoy in peace and quiet. In this way Weiße and Hiller succeeded in creating an art that sailed under the German flag and appealed to the nation as a whole, while making no claims to educate them. The success of their venture proved them right, and the new singspiel found favour with the broadest possible cross-section of the population, enjoying a degree of popularity that no dramatic genre had previously known. Such popularity proved extraordinarily beneficial not only to the singspiel itself but to the songs that were associated with it and, indeed, to German music in general: the Germans, too, now had their own national opera, as did the Italians, English and French. Here, too, of course, we find all the weaknesses that traditionally beset such 'bourgeois' art forms, chief of which is the tendency to regard everyday life as the only true reality, thereby leading inexorably to homeliness, philistinism and tedium. French comic operas had not been free of this failing, of course, but for the Paris of this time the 'mundane' had completely different connotations from those that obtained in the sleepy provincial German states, quite apart from which French poets had sufficient talent, imagination and formal adroitness to make up for this shortcoming or at least to disguise it. In Germany, by contrast, petty bourgeois values found far coarser and far more uninhibited expression, with the result that this world of provincial middle-class types, with their narrow, humdrum concerns and recurrent motifs, was unlikely to be satisfied by the refined tastes of the French. Indeed, it was far more likely to be repelled by it, especially when its *naïveté* degenerated into affectation and its

---

15. Hiller, *Lebensbeschreibung berühmter Musikgelehrten und Tonkünstler neuerer Zeit*, 311–12.

expressions of emotion turned into conventionalities and tearful sentimentality or when librettists, in an attempt to please their audiences, doled out their smugly philistine morality in shovelfuls. The situation did not improve when the range of subjects increased under the influence of works such as Grétry's *Zémire et Azor*, adding elements from the world of the supernatural and the fairy tale, as such additions were generally purely superficial and mechanical, while the essentially petty bourgeois nature of these works, with their roughly drawn characters, their frivolousness and their sentimentality, remained much the same as before. For a long time, therefore, the singspiel was the most stalwart ally of the bourgeois sentimental comedy in Germany. As a result it encountered a very mixed response among educated audiences, especially the literary public. Thanks to the tour undertaken by the Austrian actor Johann Heinrich Friedrich Müller, we know the reactions of a number of leading literary figures to the German singspiel. Lessing, for example, considered the combination of poetry and music so perfect 'that Nature herself seems to have intended it not so much as a combination as one and the selfsame art'. He also had much of relevance to say on the subject of the aesthetics of opera.[16] Yet he was outspoken in his dismissal of the singspiel, deriding it as 'the bane of our theatres; such a work is easily written, every comedy gives the author material for it, he adds some songs, and the piece is finished; our newly emergent theatre poets find that this requires little effort and that it is easier, therefore, than writing a good character piece'.[17] Johann Wilhelm Ludwig Gleim was even more acerbic in his judgement, describing the singspiel in an epigram as a witch

> die schlau wie Schlang' und Krokodil
> sich schleicht in aller Menschen Herzen,
> und drinnen sitzt, als wie ein Huhn
> auf seinem Nest und lehrt: nur *kleine* Taten tun
> und über *große* Taten scherzen![18]

[who slyly slips into all men's hearts like a snake and crocodile and sits there, just like a hen on its nest, and teaches us to perform only petty actions and pour fun on great ones.]

In short, both Gleim and, especially, Lessing doubted whether the genre as a whole could be raised to new artistic heights in this way and, indeed, its very character inevitably encouraged all manner of unqualified amateur poets to try their hand at it, thereby justifying fears of artistic stagnation. Weiße himself naturally resisted this pessimistic assessment:[19] operettas, he argued, were not works of high dramatic art, and he had no great hopes of helping his fellow Germans to come to a better understanding of art, but nor was he afraid that he would corrupt them. Rather, he wanted to instruct them in the delights of communal singing and in that way promote a sense of general conviviality.[20] In this, we may hear a clear echo of the impressions that he had gleaned in France and Berlin. Among other writers whose opinions were canvassed by Müller, Friedrich Wilhelm Gotter wrote singspiels of his own and, like Johann Benjamin Michaelis, was keen to consider more serious subjects. Understandably, he preferred not to express his opinion,

16. Lessing, *Werke*, xi.152ff.
17. Müller, *Abschied von der k. k. Hof- und National-Schaubühne*, 140.
18. Müller, *Abschied von der National-Schaubühne*, 146 and 157.
19. Müller, *Abschied von der National-Schaubühne*, 163.
20. Weiße, *Selbstbiographie*, 103–4; a similar point of view is put forward in the preface to *Die Apotheke*, p. VIII; see also Christian Heinrich Schmid, *Das Parterr*, 155–6.

commenting only that variety was the spice of life.[21] Wieland, by contrast, naturally gave his approval. After all, he had written the libretto for *Alceste* and, basing his views on Schweitzer's works, had already given a detailed account of the way in which he saw the singspiel developing. German singing, he opined, must first restore prestige to the German stage; although there was still a lack of comic and serious singspiels, poets would be found to overcome this shortcoming.[22] Even a musician such as Johann Friedrich Reichardt declared his opposition to the singspiel, while conceding that, since it existed, attempts should be made to improve it and exploit it as much as possible.[23]

Among the poets who took practical steps to address this problem were Goethe who, while still in Leipzig, had 'derived much pleasure from Weiße's operas that were undemandingly brought to life by Hiller'.[24] His singspiels differed from the usual sort by virtue of the fact that they were largely intended for social gatherings at the Weimar court, in other words, for a far more cultured audience than was generally the case. And, unlike Weiße, he pursued a secondary aim of attempting to come to terms in his own mind with the basic questions raised by music drama as a whole. His contributions confirmed Wieland's prognosis, improving the poetic aspect of the singspiel but leaving its basic nature untouched. None the less, they pointed out a possible way ahead, a way which, if it had been followed more rigorously, could have saved the genre from a good deal of inartistic mediocrity. What a wealth of ideas we find in these few singspiels by Goethe compared with the usual products. Instead of borrowing solely from *opéras comiques*, which his contemporaries felt were uniquely capable of answering all their prayers, Goethe had recourse to Spanish and English models in *Claudine von Villa Bella* and *Erwin und Elmire* respectively. Elsewhere, Swiss and German impressions of the countryside and its people were brought to life in *Jery und Bätely* and *Die Fischerin*, while in other works he drew on folksongs, legends and fairy tales, and in *Scherz, List und Rache* he even ventured into the world of Italian *opera buffa*. No less varied than their content was their formal range. The works of his *Sturm und Drang* period – especially *Claudine von Villa Bella* and *Erwin und Elmire*[25] – are closest to the Franco-German model, with prose dialogue and vocal numbers in verse. These were followed by *Lila, Jery und Bätely* and *Die Fischerin*, the last named a more improvisatory piece. That Goethe's singspiels are the source of a whole series of the most beautiful lyric poems, including *Das Veilchen, Erlkönig, Feiger Gedanken bängliches Schwanken, Ihr verblühet süße Rosen* and so on, is well known, but Goethe also devoted more and more care to the spoken dialogue, which in its cliché-ridden awkwardness had always been the singspiel's Achilles' heel.[26] This aim also coincided with his attempt to replace the French type of comic opera with the through-composed Italian type, his sure grasp of style having opened his eyes to the self-contradictory nature of the former. He now reworked *Claudine von Villa Bella* and *Erwin und Elmire* in this spirit, bringing them formally much closer to current attempts to create a through-composed German opera. Here, too, however, his basic aim was to raise the whole genre to a higher poetic level.[27] We shall have occasion to consider his comments

21. Müller, *Abschied von der National-Schaubühne*, 183–4.
22. Müller, *Abschied von der National-Schaubühne*, 188.
23. Reichardt, *Briefe eines aufmerksamen Reisenden*, i.141ff., *Ueber die deutsche comische Oper*, 6 and *Musikalisches Kunstmagazin*, i.161ff. ◆ Further, see Flaherty, *Opera in the Development of German Critical Thought*.
24. Goethe, *Dichtung und Wahrheit*, book 2, chapter 8.
25. Naturally only in their first versions. In her whole attitude – which reveals the influence of the *Sturm und Drang* – Claudine recalls the French school most of all. Her words, 'The closer we are to nature, the closer we feel to the deity', could equally well be found in many of the *opéras comiques* of the period; Goethe, *Werke* (*Jubiläums-Ausgabe*), xi.42.
26. Thus we find him writing from Italy on 14 September 1787: '*Erwin und Elmire* has already been half rewritten. I have tried to breathe more interest and life into the little piece and have thrown away the whole of the extremely flat dialogue. It's the work of a schoolboy or, rather, mere scribbling'; *Werke*, xxvii.109.
27. If, in the case of *Jery und Bätely*, he occasionally adopted the opposite approach, this was for superficial reasons.

on Mozart's *Die Entführung aus dem Serail* when we examine this last-named work in detail. On the whole, however, his singspiels – quite apart from their intrinsic poetic merits – are of considerable significance for the development of the genre as a whole inasmuch as they were the first and, for a time, the only attempt by a poet to develop the genre and prevent it from grinding to a halt.

Musically, too, there was initially a marked difference between Standfuß and Hiller. Standfuß was far more of a man of the people than Hiller: the few of his works that have survived express the same cheeky, even ribald spirit which, delighting in the here and now, is equally typical of the secular cantatas of the period, with their quodlibets and other jokes. This may help to explain certain peculiarities of his style such as the inclusion of brief passages of recitative within his songs and especially the sudden changes of time-signature and tempo that are used for comic effect. But it also explains the brief yet painterly *fioriture* that are often extremely witty and sometimes have the force of a physical gesture.[28] Admittedly, the amount of high art involved in these songs is modest in the extreme, but all the more sincere is their delight in natural simplicity. They are as far removed from affectation as they are from narrow-mindedness, two charges from which Hiller cannot always be exonerated, and at the same time they reveal a far greater gift for knockabout humour. Technically, too, they are less demanding and can no doubt be mastered by vocally gifted actors. Their melodic writing is entirely popular, with a preference for triadic intervals, while their rhythms, for all their simplicity, are striking and lively. On a formal level, most of the numbers are the briefest possible binary structures. The orchestra occasionally adds brief marginal comments of a picturesque kind.

In Hiller's hands, the singspiel continued its process of stylization, while consciously clinging to its popular basis. Hiller came to the genre from the rarefied Italian world of Hasse and Graun and, in terms of sentimentality, he never moved away from these two favourites of his. As a result, popular German and French influences were now joined by Italian influence in the form of *opera seria* and *opera buffa*. The former reveals itself in his handling of form and in the melodic writing in his serious numbers, the latter especially in his fondness for two-part comic arias with a change of tempo and in his borrowings from realistic *opera buffa* melodies.[29] On a formal level, however, it must be said straightaway that even in these artistically more ambitious numbers Hiller still strove for the greatest concision: fully developed arias of the Italian type are very rare.[30] In spite of this limitation, however, the way in which he condenses and varies his ideas when repeating them reveals one of the finest aspects of his artistry, an aspect that also had an influence on lieder composition. The French models to which Hiller had taken such exception in theory continued to leave their mark on his music not only in its general songlike character but even in terms of individual forms such as the rondeau,[31] vaudeville and similar combinations of solo sections and ensembles. Indeed, we even find entire scenes such as the *tempêtes* that were typical of the French

28. A good example is Jobsen's very first aria in *Die verwandelten Weiber*, which, with its change of tempo and dogged humour (note, in particular, the chromatic ascent through a fourth that inevitably recalls Mozart), is entirely typical of Standfuß's whole approach.

29. The widely held view that Hiller gave his high-ranking characters arias, while his peasants were entrusted with simple songs, is not true. Rather, he always used arias at moments of heightened passion, no matter who the character may be; see Calmus, *Die ersten deutschen Singspiele*, 43–4.

30. One such aria is Wilhelmine's 'Lebe wohl Du Land der Knechtschaft' in act two, scene ten of *Das Grab des Mufti*, with its lengthy ritornello and extended *fioriture*.

31. His rondeaux are remarkable not least because the theme is sometimes independently varied and repeated in other keys, an approach that also plays an important role in the instrumental rondos of Carl Philipp Emanuel Bach; note, for example, the quartet in act three, scene thirteen of *Der Aerndtekranz*.

works of the period.[32] Hiller's use of rhythm, finally, although never his strongest side, acquires a heightened existence as a result of this French input. If we also include his frequent and unwarranted use of elaborate *fioriture*, it becomes clear how extensive was foreign influence on the nominally German singspiel. But in spite of his greater culture, Hiller falls short of his predecessor in his failure to achieve the same degree of spontaneity as Standfuß in terms of either his humour or his ability to strike a high-spirited folklike note. Indeed, it is impossible to speak of any special talent for comedy at all. Instead, he attempts to make up for this deficiency by borrowing, in part, from Standfuß himself (especially the latter's older works) and, in part, from Italian and French comic operas, but without coming anywhere near his models. Although he is well aware of their tone-painterly jokes in both the vocal line and the accompaniment, to say nothing of the rest of their standard repertory of laughing and sobbing motifs, falsetto outbursts and whistling, his use of them generally lacks all sense of piquancy and originality. All too often, moreover, Hiller's folk tunes degenerate into petty bourgeois complacency and uniformity, just as those of his contemporaries in Berlin tend towards the arid and doctrinaire. Not even famous numbers such as Hannchen's 'Als ich auf meiner Bleiche' from *Die Jagd* are an exception to this rule: here, after all, is an example of a narrative song or romance taken over into the singspiel on the basis of French models, a hit of the kind that Mozart, too, contributed towards in Pedrillo's serenade in *Die Entführung aus dem Serail*.[33] Hiller is at his most successful in reproducing non-extreme moods such as harmless self-sufficient joviality and tender wistfulness; and it is with these, together with the homely element to his music, that he proved consistently popular with German audiences of the time. Nor can it be denied that in the majority of his songs he succeeded in conveying a succinct impression of the relevant characters and situations on stage. He also followed his French models in extending the formal repertory of the singspiel and introducing ensembles and even brief choruses, although the result is of a primitiveness long since outgrown by the Italian and French composers of the period. His trios and so on effortlessly divide the same tune among the different characters, often every two bars, and only occasionally – albeit more frequently in his later works – do we find a modest attempt to characterize the individual singers or at least to essay more independent part-writing. Here his successors still had a great deal to do. In the three-movement sinfonias to his operas Hiller sides unequivocally with the Italians, with only the absence of a complete cadence pointing in the direction of the French.[34]

As a result there was relatively little that Mozart could exploit in Hiller's works and use for his own ends. Essentially, his borrowings are limited to shared sources, as is the case with the second subject of Hiller's overture to *Der Aerndtekranz*:[35]

32. Especially in the highly successful storm sinfonia in D minor (!) in *Die Jagd*, which is motivically linked to the previous duet in exactly the same way as in the work's French source, Monsigny's *Le roi et le fermier*.
33. See Spitta, *Musikgeschichtliche Aufsätze*, 408, 410 and 413.
34. ◆ Further, see Kawada, *Studien zu den Singspielen von Johann Adam Hiller*.
35. The main theme is also worth mentioning on account of its pronounced *cantabilità*, a feature otherwise very rarely found in such surroundings.

and the theme of Lindfort's aria in act three of the same opera:

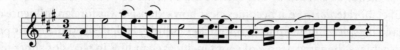

Both are typical examples of Hiller's way of adding old-fashioned ornaments to his basically Italian material.

The tremendous success of Hiller's singspiels was by no means limited to the theatre but also came to the aid of the popular songs that composers in Berlin were attempting to write at this time, bringing to the genre the very qualities that the Berliners themselves had been unable to provide: popular texts. In this way, Hiller helped, in Hermann Kretzschmar's words, to 'win over the so-called third estate to songs and, hence, to music'.[36] Long after Mozart's death, the singspiel remained one of the principal sources of domestic music-making in Germany.

Even during Hiller's day, however, the singspiel had already begun to grow both poetically and musically more ambitious. Its range of subjects and formal repertory were both expanded and its musical language in general was deepened. In this way, increasing demands were placed on the singers, of course. As performances of singspiels continued to be left to private impresarios who did not always have sufficient means to pay properly trained singers, the result was often mediocre and inadequate performances,[37] although we should be wary of generalizing on the strength of these reports as they are contradicted not only by other accounts but above all by the numerous scores with their often highly demanding vocal parts that were intended by their composers for very specific singers.

In spite of all the attacks that were launched against it by musicians and men of letters, the genre enjoyed increasing popularity, especially in north Germany.[38] In Berlin, for example, where Karl Theophilus Doebbelin first established regular performances in 1769, no fewer than 409 operas were staged between 1781 and 1783,[39] a number achieved not least as a result of the immense productivity of composers at this time. But since, for the reasons already given, north and central German composers had little influence on the Viennese, it will be sufficient to include only a brief survey of the most eminent of these figures. For the most part, they are the same as those who, as representatives of the Berlin school, were also of importance for the German lied.

It was Georg Benda[40] to whom the singspiel owed its greatest debt in the years between Hiller and Mozart. As we have already seen, Benda was one of the 'Lutheran composers' whom Mozart valued particularly highly. His most popular singspiels were *Der Dorfjahrmarkt* (1775),[41] *Walder* (1776), *Romeo und Julie* (1776) and *Der Holzhauer* (1778), all of them settings of texts by Friedrich Wilhelm Gotter and all revealing a surprising improvement on Hiller in terms of both form and

36. Kretzschmar, *Geschichte des neuen deutschen Liedes*, i.262.
37. See Reichardt's reports from Berlin and Leipzig in his *Briefe eines aufmerksamen Reisenden*, i.147 and ii.94; also Burney, *The Present State of Music in Germany*, ii.71–83; for Müller's report on Dresden, see *Abschied von der National-Schaubühne*, 173.
38. See *Deutsches Museum*, ii (1779), 268, and Plümicke, *Entwurf einer Theatergeschichte von Berlin*, 205ff. ◆ On north German opera generally, see Bauman, *North German Opera in the Age of Goethe*.
39. Louis Schneider, *Geschichte der Oper und des Königlichen Opernhauses in Berlin*, 209.
40. Brückner, 'Georg Benda und das deutsche Singspiel'.
41. ◆ *Der Dorfjahrmarkt* was a revision of Benda's two-act *Der Jahrmarkt*, also 1775.

content. From *Walder* onwards, we also find accompanied recitatives, a form which in the hands of the composer of *Ariadne* and *Medea* proved particularly effective in a work such as *Julie und Romeo*.[42] But even the forms drawn from popular music and art music that had already been taken over by Hiller are now used with a freedom that places Benda on a far higher level as a dramatist. Of particular importance for Mozart was Bärbchen's folklike strophic song, with its witty variations, in act one, scene five of *Der Dorfjahrmarkt*, while in other cases Benda breathed new life into the folklike tone of his songs by interpolating passages of recitative, as in scene seven of *Der Holzhauer*. Where the text requires it, he unhesitatingly breaks down existing forms and writes – for example – four-movement arias that combine a folklike tone with the strains of art music, as in act one, scene two of the same work, just as he frequently writes songs involving stark contrasts, with abrupt changes of time-signature and tempo. In *Julie und Romeo* he even creates large-scale formal structures made up of more than one scene (act three, scenes three and four), on one occasion achieving this end with the cyclical repetition of a choral number (act three, scenes one and two), a scene whose musical design, too, is reminiscent of Gluck. But it is his ensembles that reveal the greatest progress. Here Benda clearly learnt much not only from the French composers of the period but also from Italian *opera buffa*, as emerges not least from the recurrent orchestral motifs that are also familiar from Mozart and that are found, for example, in act one, scene eight of *Der Dorfjahrmarkt*:

Although Benda, too, still tends to be influenced by purely musical considerations in planning his formal structures, he none the less succeeds within this framework in portraying his characters and situations in far more clear-cut and vivid terms than Hiller had done, and in ensembles such as the quartet from *Walder* and the trio (no. 7) from *Der Holzhauer*, which also contains an ingenious echo of the aria no. 4, we already find ourselves on the same high level as Mozart's *Zaide* in terms of the effective grouping of voices and the art of characterization. In his overtures, too, we find a new spirit stirring under French influence. Indeed, the overture to *Der Holzhauer* seems to have been the immediate structural model for that of *Die Entführung aus dem Serail*, with the melody of the following slow aria for Wilhelmine interpolated between the two sections of its Allegro.

Although Benda's musical language prefers to strike a more popular note and does so, moreover, with masterly freshness, it none the less strives for emphatically higher goals than Hiller had done. This sometimes led him – as it led all Hiller's successors – to occasional excesses of high-flown Italian rhetoric and tawdry coloratura, but at the same time it helped him to refine his expressive language, which is far removed from Hiller's often homely tone. In his expression of warm and noble emotions, he often – and by no means fortuitously – resembles Mozart, and even the latter's sudden outbursts of passion within an otherwise calmly flowing melodic line are already found here, as in the Colonel's aria in act one, scene two of *Der Dorfjahrmarkt*:

---

42. Hiller had given the impetus to this development in act three, scene seven of *Lisuart und Dariolette*, in which Derwin keeps interpolating bars of recitative into an extended orchestral number. But this can hardly be called an accompanied recitative in the later sense of the term, and Hiller himself did not return to this point in any of his subsequent works.

No less frequently the music's inherently popular note is stylized to the point where it acquires an additional grace and emotional charge, as in Sophie's little rondo from *Walder*, with its delightful coloratura:

Valentin, too, expresses his joy at his impending happiness in a thoroughly modern manner in scene five of *Der Holzhauer*:

Both passages, moreover, reveal a further aspect of Benda's talent of which Hiller was largely innocent: a lively sense of humour that finds expression more especially in his orchestral writing,[43] which he develops not only on a technical level by means of his pronounced predilection for concertante effects, but also in a poetical manner: the instrumental mastery that he had acquired in the melodrama is clear at every turn. Among such features are the many poetic allusions in the ritornellos[44] and the orchestral writing in the martial aria in act two, scene one of *Der Dorfjahrmarkt* which, like so many of the older Italian pieces of this kind, is closely related in terms of its situation and execution to Figaro's 'Non più andrai'.

The singspiels by Benda's contemporary Johann André (1741–99) – *Der Töpfer* (1773), *Die Bezauberten* (1777), *Das tartarische Gesetz* (1779), *Das wütende Heer* (1780)[45] and *Die Entführung aus dem Serail* (1781) – are not on the same high level artistically as Benda's but they complement them in terms of their cheekily popular tone and slapstick humour: the spirit of Standfuß seems to be reborn here in a more modern guise. André's humour shimmers with the iridescence of shot silk, ranging from harmless tomfoolery to the surly and smug, while there are orchestral jokes aplenty.[46] The spirit of France is more in evidence here than it is in Benda's works, as is clear from his rhythmic and melodic writing,[47] his fondness for the rondo and, above all, the picturesque element that characterizes his works and that is found chiefly in his more or less fully developed orchestral tone-paintings, including his *tempêtes*.[48] In general, his orchestra is no less varied and brilliant than Benda's.[49] In his ensembles, too, he adopts the Parisian model and strives for loftier aims,[50] and from *Das tartarische Gesetz* onwards his accompanied recitatives find him successfully following in his contemporary's footsteps.[51] We shall have further occasion to consider his version of *Die Entführung aus dem Serail* when examining Mozart's setting.

The third composer who deserves to be mentioned here is Christian Gottlob Neefe (1748–98). In his earliest works – *Die Apotheke* (1771) and *Amors Guckkasten* (1772) – he remained very close to Hiller, whose whole spirit and formal world are still clearly recognizable in spite of his freedom of approach and more modern attitude in general. Here the affinities between the singspiel and the lieder of the Berlin school are particularly evident. Soon, however, Neefe felt a need to experiment and to strike out in a new direction, and although *Amors Guckkasten* represents a not entirely successful attempt to introduce classical mythology into the world of the German singspiel, *Zemire und Azor* (1776) finds him exploring 'Romantic' themes, while *Die Zigeuner* (1777)

43. Under this heading comes the witty instrumental flourish in the first drinking chorus in *Der Dorfjahrmarkt*.
44. Cf. scene three of *Walder*.
45. This work is textually important as a precursor of *Der Freischütz*, the wild hunt of which is prefigured in the 'wütendes Heer' of the present title.
46. In Robert's aria in act two, scene eight of *Das wütende Heer*, the voice suddenly breaks off on the words 'my little wife is turning me into a –', whereupon the oboes and bassoon imitate a cockerel's crowing, completing the image of the cuckold and, as such, providing a counterpart to a sort of joke about horns that was popular at this time: a further example may be found in *Le nozze di Figaro*.
47. The spoken interjections in the vocal numbers belong under this heading.
48. Cf. the depiction of the wild hunt in act two, scenes three and four of *Das wütende Heer*, the choral numbers of which reflect Gluck's continuing influence. This scene is also used in the overture in keeping with its Parisian model.
49. Clarinets are demanded even in *Der Töpfer*.
50. Note especially the quintet in scene seven of *Der Töpfer* and the two large-scale duets in act two, scene two of *Das tartarische Gesetz* and act one, scene twelve of *Das wütende Heer*.
51. ◆ See also Stauder, *Johann André: Ein Beitrag zur Geschichte des deutschen Singspiels*.

and *Adelheid von Veltheim* (1780) both introduce an exotic element. The last of these is also an Oriental abduction opera and, as such, one of the immediate precursors of Mozart's *Die Entführung aus dem Serail*. His most striking formal innovation was his introduction of a melodrama à la Benda into act two, scene one of *Adelheid von Veltheim*. Whether Neefe was familiar with Mozart's slightly earlier *Zaide* is doubtful.[52] Rather it appears that both composers independently hit upon the same idea, an idea that at the time was very much in the air. But the ensembles at the end of his acts also reveal a new aspect of Neefe's works. Even in the final divertissement of *Amors Guckkasten* – a number which, textually speaking, is a remarkable example of the depths of lascivity to which the otherwise prim and proper singspiel was capable of sinking – the principle of strophic variation is handled with the greatest freedom and a fine sense of dramatic effectiveness, while the two central acts of *Adelheid von Veltheim* both end in large-scale, multi-movement finales, the first of which is a chain finale, consisting of a series of movements in song form and aria form, while the second attempts to impose a unified, rondo-like structure on its individual elements by freely repeating a number of separate themes in evident imitation of Piccinni.[53] In terms of their dramatic vitality, of course, both fall short of Benda's far briefer ensembles. Indeed, there is on average more such life in Neefe's lieder and dramatic cantatas than in his singspiels, where it generally finds expression only in his more original numbers. There is also a pittoresque element here, notably in the duet for the two hypocritical women in act two, scene one of *Die Apotheke* and the *buffa* aria for the hypochondriac Trist in act two, scene four of the same work. On the other hand, the Turkish local colour in *Adelheid von Veltheim* finds expression only in the overture, a number which, with its constant interplay between normal orchestra and Janissary band, clearly prefigures Mozart's overture to *Die Entführung aus dem Serail*. But in *Amors Guckkasten*, Komus begins and ends his opening aria on a surprisingly witty fairground note:[54]

Neefe's dramatic strength lies in keenly observed individual scenes such as these. Conversely, there are few signs of any consistent characterization: although Enoch in *Die Apotheke* may be the exception that confirms this rule, Mehmet in *Adelheid von Veltheim* – the Osmin-like character of the piece – only rarely rises above the level of a good-natured blusterer in the singspiel tradition. In his singspiels, as elsewhere, Neefe generally proves outstanding and progressive as a melodist: his folklike songs, as well as his arias, all reveal an intelligent use of melodic development and of poetic allusions and repetitions. More than once they anticipate Mozart. In *Amors Guckkasten*, for example, Psyche sings the following in scene fifteen:

52.   ◆ It is virtually impossible that Neefe knew *Zaide*, which was neither performed nor published during Mozart's lifetime.
53.   The fourth is a curiously high-flown, strictly contrapuntal chorus.
54.   This recalls the serenatas of 1777; see Kretzschmar, *Geschichte des neuen deutschen Liedes*, i.275–6.

And in act one, scene eight of *Adelheid von Veltheim* we find:

In both cases, however, we are probably dealing with common Italian sources.

The north German singspiel was enthusiastically taken up and developed in the south-west of the country by the Stuttgart school, foremost among whose members were J. F. Gauß, Christian Ludwig Dieter and Johann Rudolf Zumsteeg, all of them former pupils of the Carlsschule in Stuttgart.[55] In Vienna, by contrast, it encountered concerted resistance that stemmed not only

---

55. In Swabia, a coarsely popular tradition had survived in both songs and drama. In contrast to the theorizing north Germans, Swabian composers saw the world's salvation in a return to the music of the folk. Proof of this assertion may be found in anthologies such as the Ostrach Liederhandschrift and Johann Valentin Rathgeber's *Tafel-Confect*, with its songs, quodlibets, comic cantatas and, above all, its singspiels, including *Die Schöpfung* by the well-known Swabian cleric and dialect poet Sebastian Sailer. Written in 1743, this last-named work predates Standfuß by several years. See Lach, 'Sebastian Sailers "Schöpfung" in der Musik'. The songs of Christian Daniel Friedrich Schubart also sprang from this same soil. On the singspiel composers of the Carlsschule, see Abert, 'Die dramatische Musik', 588ff. ◆ Concerning Dieter, see Haering, 'Christian Ludwig Dieter'; for Zumsteeg, see Völckers, *Johann Rudolph Zumsteeg als Opernkomponist*.

from political and denominational differences, but more especially from the independent musical culture of the Viennese, who were in no mind to sacrifice their own autochthonous art on the altar of foreign rivals.[56] Above all, established folk music resisted the introduction of Hiller's style. Although local audiences were generally well disposed to the singspiel as such, they preferred to rely on their own resources in capturing its folklike tone. Moreover, the singspiel found a related genre in the improvised comedy, a popular form of entertainment in Vienna, in which music had always played an extensive role, not just in the form of individual songs, but also in that of ensembles and choruses.[57] There was also the marionette theatre that was especially popular in Austria and that numbered Haydn among its composers,[58] drawing in Vienna as in Paris on parody.[59] Finally, there were the earliest attempts on the part of the Viennese to create a singspiel of their own, attempts first undertaken in the years around 1760.[60]

As a result, the ground was already well prepared for Joseph II's National Singspiel. Once a composer had been found who possessed talent, artistic understanding and a serious desire to aspire to higher ideals, Vienna could write a new chapter in the history of German opera. As always, a precondition for this development was the existence of suitable poets, and in Vienna there was an even greater lack of such librettists than in northern Germany. A glance at the repertory of the National Singspiel reveals a relatively varied picture, but it is one that, without adding any original features of its own, merely reworked existing motifs from French and Italian comic operas and from German comedies before and after Lessing, revealing more or less skill in the process. Gothic romances and ghost stories also left their mark on the genre, especially when combined with French *féeries* and magic operas, in which guise they contributed much to the popularity of the *Zaubersingspiel* in Vienna. Characterization is as derivative and as crude as the dialogue, which in terms of its flatness is markedly worse than that of *Die Zauberflöte*.[61]

Umlauf's *Die Bergknappen* is an instructive example of the musical style of these works.[62] Here numbers in the lowest Viennese popular taste coexist alongside more stylized pieces reminiscent of the contemporary art song, fully-fledged Italian coloratura arias (10) alongside *buffa* numbers, and we even find reminders of Fuxian counterpoint. To these may be added two musically highly effective choruses, a number of ensembles, among which a trio stands out for its excellent characterization of its individual participants, and finally a French round, with which the work ends. French, too, is the two-movement overture, which dispenses with a formal ending. In terms of its stylistic variety, *Die Bergknappen* is decidedly superior not only to Hiller and his school but even to Mozart's *Die Entführung aus dem Serail*.[63] All that the composer lacks is a dramaturgical conscience: not once did it occur to him to use these different styles for dramatic ends. Instead, he merely employs them to create a sense of musical variety, allowing his characters to sing now in this style, now in that, and in that way offending not only against the rules of dramatic character-

56. See Haas, *Ignaz Umlauff: Die Bergknappen*.

57. Joseph Haydn had begun his dramatic career in the winter of 1751/2 by setting Joseph Felix von Kurz's *Der neue krumme Teufel*; see Pohl, *Joseph Haydn*, i.153.

58. Pohl, *Joseph Haydn*, ii.356.

59. Haas, *Ignaz Umlauff: Die Bergknappen*, XXIV; see also, more generally, the *Theaterkalender von Wien für 1772*, 5ff.

60. Haas, *Ignaz Umlauff: Die Bergknappen*, XXIII, lists a number of these pieces, a list that also includes Mozart's *Bastien und Bastienne*.

61. Haas, *Ignaz Umlauff: Die Bergknappen*, XXV.

62. Reprinted in Haas, *Ignaz Umlauff: Die Bergknappen*; see also Alfred Heuß, 'Zu Umlauf's Singspiel "Die Bergknappen"'.

63. ◆ Further, see Reuter and Wächtler, 'Die künstlerische und historische Bedeutung des Singspiels "Die Bergknappen" von Ignaz Umlauf am Beginn der Geschichte der deutschen Nationaloper'.

ization but often against those of sound common sense. The possibilities inherent in the genre were to be revealed only by Mozart in *Die Zauberflöte*.

Mozart's own dismissive attitude to Umlauf in his letter of 6 October 1781 is cast in a new light by all this, as it refers specifically to the composer's unsystematic versatility:

> Umlauf, too, has to take his place in the queue, even though his opera is finished – it took him a whole year to write it, but (between ourselves) you mustn't think it's any good simply because it took him so long. I'd have thought that this opera (again between ourselves) had taken him 14 or 15 days, especially as he must have learnt so many operas by heart! – and all he had to do was sit down, which is no doubt what he did – you can hear it for yourself![64]

Into this tranquil world of Umlauf, Ordonez, Asplmayr, Ulbrich and their colleagues, Mozart's *Die Entführung* entered like some apparition from a fairy tale.

---

64. *Briefe*, iii.165–6 (letter of 6 October 1781).

29

Die Entführung aus dem Serail

That the dislike felt by the good people of Vienna for the north German singspiel was directed in essence at its music, rather than at its words, is clear from the popularity enjoyed among the city's composers[1] by the singspiel texts of the Leipzig businessman Christoph Friedrich Bretzner (1748–1807).[2] Bretzner owed his reputation not to any outstanding gifts as a poet – his librettos are little better than average – but to a keen nose for what the public at large expected of singspiels. He was able to turn his hand to anything, but as a poet who believed himself fully abreast of the age, he preferred Romantic, fairy-tale subjects. In spite of their limited value as works of art and their dependence on foreign models, his most popular texts – *Der Irrwisch* and *Das wütende Heer* – none the less have a certain historical importance: the former is a tale of 'Romantic' redemption, the latter a notable precursor of *Der Freischütz* and its wild hunt. With its Turkish local colour, his *Belmont und Constanze, oder Die Entführung aus dem Serail*[3] is one of a number of attempts to introduce new blood into the singspiel by means of all manner of exceptional stimulants. The plot is as follows: Belmont's lover Constanze has fallen into the hands of the Pasha Selim, who woos her in vain. Another prisoner in the pasha's seraglio is Belmont's former servant Pedrillo: his job is to oversee the pasha's gardens, and in the course of doing so he has caught the eye of Constanze's maid Blondchen. Pedrillo has managed to get word to Belmont of Constanze's whereabouts, prompting Belmont to set sail without delay, but, together with Pedrillo, he is initially rebuffed by the overseer Osmin. Then, to Osmin's intense annoyance, Pedrillo succeeds in introducing his old master to the pasha's service as an accomplished architect. The second act opens with a comic scene in which Blondchen sees off the violent and lascivious Osmin, followed by a more serious scene in which the pasha's advances are again spurned by Constanze. Pedrillo now forces some wine on Osmin and puts him out of harm's way, leaving the lovers to arrange their flight together the following night. In the third act, Belmont succeeds in escaping with Constanze at a sign from Pedrillo, but as Pedrillo himself is on the point of fleeing, he is captured by the semi-inebriated Osmin. Although they manage to break free, Osmin gives orders for them to be pursued, and both couples are taken prisoner and led into the pasha's presence. The latter initially orders them to be put to death but then recognizes his own son in Belmont and, in an act of clemency and forgiveness, allows the lovers to return home.

1. See Haas, *Ignaz Umlauff: Die Bergknappen*, XXV.
2. Kneschke, *Das deutsche Lustspiel in Vergangenheit und Gegenwart*. Bretzner's collected librettos were published in two volumes, the first (Leipzig, 1779) devoted to his operettas, the second (Leipzig, 1796) to his singspiels.
3. Published in Leipzig in 1781. The work was adapted into French by Charles Destrais in 1857 and by Prosper-Pascal in 1859; see Wilder, *Mozart: L'homme et l'artiste*, 168. For details of a modern Greek translation for a production in Alexandria on 6 February 1889, see the *Hamburgische Musikzeitung*, no. xxiv (1889).

It has so far proved impossible to find a specific Italian or French source for this libretto, and almost certainly none exists.[4] Rather, Bretzner's poem affords striking proof of his undeniable skill at picking up tried-and-tested ideas from the most disparate genres and periods and combining them together to create new crowd-pullers.[5] Neither the characters nor the situations are any more original than the individual motifs or the Turkish setting. The basic motif whereby two lovers are separated and then reunited is a basic ingredient of singspiels from every country, at least from the time when the genre developed into the *comédie larmoyante*, and not even the more unusual form of a forceful abduction was new. Indeed, these rescue stories were coming into vogue again at this very time. A no less ancient motif that Bretzner pressed into service for his own dramatic ends was the discovery that Belmont is the pasha's own son, a discovery that brings about the work's denouement. The lovers are indistinguishable from similar couples in the older singspiels;[6] like all their predecessors, they are concerned only with love and loyalty in the true spirit of rationalism, while their willingness to die for each other at the end is an idea derived from Metastasio. Pedrillo and Blondchen are throwbacks to the old *confidenti* of *opera buffa*, the former – craven by nature – being more typical of the genre than Blondchen, who has rather more French blood in her veins.[7] The two Turkish characters, finally, the pasha and Osmin, were also familiar to audiences from time immemorial: the Italian stage had known Turks since the days of Venetian opera, when they had impinged on the Venetian consciousness through their numerous predatory raids and wars; by the age of Neapolitan opera they were already appearing in both serious and comic operas. In every country, the composers of comic operas saw Turks as cruel pashas, sly merchants, insolent cadis, lascivious seraglio guards and so on, but soon the image of them changed under Rousseau's influence, and the savage Turk was replaced by his noble counterpart, a development encouraged by contemporaries' fondness for holding up remote nations as examples of how to behave and, as such, as the antithesis of corrupt European culture.[8] The status of Turkish operas was further enhanced by the growing popularity of the world of oriental fairy tales as found in Gozzi and elsewhere, a world that provided other features, including Pedrillo's outwitting of Osmin by offering him wine in spite of Muhammad's proscription.

Bretzner's Pasha Selim combines both these views, the cruel despot, as represented by Sultan Soliman in *Zaide*, and the noble foreigner. Osmin, by contrast, had long since been at home in *opere buffe* as the puffed-up, violent and lascivious oriental. Indeed, it is clear from his very name (and also from its augmentative form Osmirone) that we are dealing here with a stock type who is regularly found in Turkish operas in the guise of either a harem guard or palace overseer or the like.

A poet like Bretzner who knew how to write a well-made singspiel merely needed to help himself from this range of existing ideas to create a new and highly effective piece. None the less, a certain number of earlier works seems to have been singled out for preferential treatment, the oldest of them being Dancourt's and Gluck's *La rencontre imprévue* (*Die Pilgrimme von Mekka*) of

---

4. ◆ For a general account of French traditions in Vienna at this time, see Karro-Pélisson, 'Livrets et librettistes parisiens à la cour de Vienne au temps de Marie-Thérèse'.

5. See Preibisch, 'Quellenstudien zu Mozarts "Entführung aus dem Serail"'.

6. That they are Spaniards is also an ancient motif. As early as 1682 *Kara Mustapha* had contrasted Turks with two Spanish prisoners, Don Gasparo and Donna Manuela.

7. On their English nationality, see n.12 below.

8. Preibisch, 'Quellenstudien', lists a whole series of Turkish operas, although his list of *opere buffe* is in fact incomplete: suffice it to add Paisiello's *L'arabo cortese* and *La Dardané*, Grétry's *La caravane du Caire* (which also features a character called Osmin and a deaf mute) and Monsigny's fantastical *L'isle sonnante*. ◆ More recently, see Würtz, 'Das Türkische im Singspiel des 18. Jahrhunderts bis zu Mozarts Entführung aus dem Serail' and Head, *Orientalism, Masquerade and Mozart's Turkish Music*.

1764.[9] Here the basic idea of the plot is the same as in Bretzner, the main differences being that the abduction is nipped in the bud by the sultan, and the lover Ali and his servant Osmin are likewise orientals. Moreover, the main plot is repeatedly prevented from unfolding by a whole series of distracting episodes. Also worth mentioning here is Gaetano Martinelli's libretto for *La schiava liberata*, an *opera semiseria* that was set by Jommelli for Ludwigsburg in 1768 and by Joseph Schuster for Dresden in 1777.[10] Here the two European women are freed not through cunning and force but as the result of an amicable agreement, yet in terms of its characterization and the grouping of the individual figures, it is strikingly similar to Bretzner's piece. Each of Bretzner's characters has his or her counterpart in Martinelli, the only difference being that Martinelli's father and son – Soliman and Selim – have been replaced by a single figure in Bretzner, who combines the dignity and nobility of Martinelli's Soliman with the unrequited love and magnanimity of his Selim. The similarity in the way in which the various figures are characterized has even led to similar types of scenes, such as the jealous outburst between the doltish Pedrillo and the superior Blonde, Pedrillo's serenade and Osmin's *buffa*-like jealous fury in 'Erst geköpft, dann gehangen' (a scene that was, of course, written by Stephanie).[11] Bretzner will presumably have heard Martinelli's work in Dresden. But whether he also knew two related English works, Isaac Bickerstaff's *The Sultan: or, a Peep into the Seraglio* (1775) and *The Captive* (1769), is more doubtful.[12] All that these works demonstrate is that the subject of abductions in Turkish guise was internationally popular even before Mozart's day. On the other hand, Bretzner was undoubtedly familiar with Großmann's *Adelheit von Veltheim*, which likewise deals with an oriental abduction,[13] except that here the couple is German. Once again the seraglio guard Mehmed has a major role to play. And it may well be Adelheit who is responsible for the air of tragedy that invests the character of Konstanze in the version of Bretzner and Mozart. In general, however, Großmann's piece is on a far lower level poetically than Bretzner's.

Although Bretzner's text fails to take flight and has its fair share of the narrow-mindedness of the genre as a whole, it none the less towers far above its models in terms of its clarity and simplicity. Unlike Dancourt and Großmann, Bretzner did not encumber his plot with all manner of subsidiary figures and episodes, but ensured that it ran along straightforward lines from beginning to end. It is hardly surprising, therefore, that within twelve months of its publication in 1781 it had already been set by two composers, André and Mozart, who were followed in turn by the Stuttgart-based composer Christian Ludwig Dieter in 1784 and by Justin Heinrich Knecht of Biberach in 1790.[14]

Mozart himself was familiar with this kind of subject from *Zaide*, but the changes that he persuaded Stephanie to make to Bretzner's text are extremely important for our understanding of his whole approach to drama in general. Fortunately, he had no need on this occasion to take account of inadequate singers. Although the bravura technique of Catarina Cavalieri forced him

9. See Marx, *Gluck und die Oper*, i.271ff., and Preibisch, 'Quellenstudien', 443–4.

10. Abert, *Niccolò Jommelli als Opernkomponist*, 435ff., and Preibisch, 'Quellenstudien', 439ff.

11. In Martinelli's version, Albumazar threatens Giulietta's abductor: 'per li cappelli lo prenderei, con le mie mane lo graffierei, ne mai contento di strapazzarlo, di maltrattarlo, di bastonarlo, di fracassarlo farei che in polvere volasse ancor'; see Abert, *Jommelli als Opernkomponist*, 437.

12. Preibisch, 'Quellenstudien', 446ff. None the less, there is a remarkable affinity between Blonde, who is likewise described as an Englishwoman, and Bickerstaff's Roxelana, who in the presence of the harem guard – here, too, called Osmin – stresses her mistress's self-assurance and, also like Blonde, makes it clear to him that in the West women are used to being treated completely differently by their menfolk.

13. A résumé of the plot may be found in Lewy, 'Christian Gottlob Neefe', 58–9.

14. Nothing more is known about a setting by Anton Joseph Kuzzi mentioned by Gerber in his *Neues Lexikon der Tonkünstler*, iii.154. The remaining four settings are compared by Preibisch, 'Quellenstudien', 457ff.

to make a number of concessions,[15] he had a completely free hand in the case of Adamberger[16] and, especially, Fischer. The fact that in his hands Osmin outgrew all his models and became merely the first in a whole series of incomparable classic characters we owe, of course, not only to Mozart's genius, but also to the artistry of this exceptional singer and actor.[17] In Bretzner's version, Osmin had played only a minor role, but he now became one of the leading characters, as Mozart reported to his father in his letter of 26 September 1781:

> The opera began with a monologue, so I asked Herr Stephanie to turn it into a little arietta, and then, instead of having the two of them chattering away after Osmin's little song, I asked him to treat it as a duet. – We've given the part of Osmin to Herr Fischer, who certainly has an excellent bass voice – and this in spite of the fact that the archbishop told me he sang too low for a bass, but I assured him that he'd sing higher next time – and so we have to take advantage of a man like this, especially as he has the whole of the local public on his side. – But in the original libretto this Osmin has only one short song to sing and nothing else except the trio and the finale. So he's been given an aria in the first act and will also have one in the second. I've told Herr Stephanie exactly what I want in this aria – most of the music for it was already finished before Stephanie knew anything about it. – Here's only the beginning and the end, which is bound to be highly effective.[18]

In this way, the opera's protagonist and antagonist, Belmonte and Osmin, are sharply contrasted right from the outset, each with an exceptionally characterful number and without the need for any distended dialogue. And when we recall the highly poetical way in which Belmonte's 'arietta' is already prefigured in the overture, we shall see straightaway that Mozart approached his task from a completely different standpoint from Bretzner. In the second act, too, what had originally been spoken dialogue has been turned into a duet ('Ich gehe, doch rate ich dir') for Osmin's sake, this time with Blonde. Conversely, the vapid duet for Constanze and Blonde, 'Hoffnung, Trösterin im Leiden', was dropped in favour of a second aria for Blonde ('Welche Wonne, welche Lust'): joy at their impending rescue was initially to be expressed by Blonde alone. But Constanze, too, was given a new aria, so that what had originally been a duet was broken down, as it were, into two arias. This is the bravura aria 'Martern aller Arten', a number which, dramatically speaking, is undoubtedly a mistake, inasmuch as it merely repeats the existing situation.

Mozart's approach to the actual abduction is likewise highly revealing. In Bretzner's version, it takes the form of a large-scale ensemble at the beginning of the third act, starting with a duet for Belmont and Pedrillo, both of whom are lying in wait. The well-known romance ('Im Mohrenland

---

15. ◆ See Kretschmer, 'Mozarts "geläufige Gurgel": Die Sängerin Caterina Cavalieri'.

16. Adamberger was widely praised for his beautiful, genuine tenor voice and excellent training. Only at the top of his range was his emission felt to be somewhat nasal. See Friedrich Meyer, *Friedrich Ludwig Schröder*, i.368; also Werner, *Aus dem Josephinischen Wien*, 104. ◆ Further, see Bauman, 'Mozart's Belmonte'.

17. Writing in the *Musikalische Monatsschrift* for 1792 (67), Johann Friedrich Reichardt describes Fischer as 'an admirable bass singer whose voice has almost the depth of a cello and the natural height of a tenor [its range was C–a'], yet his low notes never grate and his high notes are never thin; his voice is flexible, secure and agreeable. In praise of his style of singing, it is sufficient to note that he is an excellent pupil of the great tenor Raaff, who was regarded – and is still regarded – as the leading tenor in the whole of the European singing world. He has more skill and ease in his throat than perhaps any other bass singer, and in terms of his acting he can hold his own on both the serious and the comic stage'. Gebler, for his part, called him 'an excellent bass who sings the lowest notes with a fullness, ease and pleasantness that one normally encounters only in the case of good tenors'; Werner, *Aus dem Josephinischen Wien*, 105.

18. *Briefe*, iii.162 (letter of 26 September 1781). Of the three other composers, only Knecht used Mozart's version.

gefangen war ein Mädel hübsch und fein') was incorporated into this duet.[19] Belmont then abducts Constanze, but when Pedrillo attempts to follow suit with Blondchen, Osmin appears and, although still half asleep, realizes what is afoot and has all four lovers hauled in by his guards. All their entreaties and attempts to bribe him prove unavailing but merely increase his anger and his thirst for vengeance, so that the number ends on a note of extreme agitation. Mozart immediately saw that he had the makings of a superb finale here, hence his desire to have 'this charming quintet or, rather, finale at the end of the second act'.[20] Bretzner's second act had in fact ended with a quartet in which the four lovers had expressed their confidence in relatively insipid terms. This abduction scene was to become the climax of the whole work only after Mozart had already started to compose the ensemble at the beginning of the third act.[21] This led to the need for 'a great change, indeed, for a whole new intrigue', as all that was left for the third act was the denouement following the pasha's act of forgiveness. The only alternative was for this act of forgiveness to be appended to the second-act finale, but this would inevitably have made the ending seem over-abrupt and resulted in an underlength opera. This reworking appears to have been frustrated by Stephanie's inability to devise a new intrigue for the third act. The abduction scene remained where it had previously been, at the start of the third act, but instead of being set as an ensemble, it was now treated as pure dialogue with the exception of Pedrillo's romance. And, as in the opening act, Belmonte and Osmin were again given a new aria apiece ('Ich baue ganz auf deine Stärke' and 'O, wie will ich triumphieren'); new words were written for the duet for Belmonte and Konstanze ('Meinetwegen sollst du sterben!'), although the situation remained unchanged; and one of Bretzner's arias for Konstanze, 'Ach mit freudigem Entzücken', was cut. The denouement, finally, was altered to take account of Viennese taste: now the pasha no longer forgives the lovers on recognizing his own son in Belmonte but pardons him out of sheer magnanimity in keeping with what, according to one report,[22] was a fashion in the city at this time. Bretzner had ended his text with a concluding moral to the effect that, although the sky often clouds over, a sunbeam invariably sweeps the clouds away. Stephanie replaced this with a vaudeville in which each of the characters in turn thanks the pasha for his magnanimity, after which the chorus sings his praises.

The end of the second act, too, was altered. Here Belmonte was given a further aria ('Wenn der Freude Tränen fließen') but, more importantly, Bretzner's insipid quartet was replaced by a new and more dramatic number that is a miniature drama all of its own, with the lovers reunited, then temporarily driven apart by jealousy, before finally being reconciled once again.

These changes give the lie to the claim advanced by many writers, including Wagner,[23] that Mozart indiscriminately set whatever texts came his way. Quite the opposite, he found much to object to in Bretzner's libretto and, more importantly, his suggested changes are all improvements, with the single exception of Konstanze's 'Martern aller Arten'. By investing the individual characters with sharper outlines, he was able to raise the whole action to a higher level and by turning Osmin into the lovers' principal adversary, he brought to its basic idea a far greater depth that went far beyond the confines of a traditional singspiel. All Mozart's additions constitute keenly observed musical portraits noted down by the musician with a keen eye for dramatic effectiveness and

---

19. For an account of the way in which André and Dieter handle this passage, see Preibisch, 'Quellenstudien', 471–2.
20. *Briefe*, iii.163 (letter of 26 September 1781).
21. The greater part of the duet for Belmonte and Pedrillo preceding the romance survives in the form of a sketch: see K389. ◆ This is published in NMA II/5/12, 436–41.
22. Cramer, *Magazin der Musik*, ii.1057. ◆ This report, published in the *Magazin der Musik* for 17 December 1786, is largely based on a passage from Johann Friedrich Schink's *Dramaturgische Fragmente* of late 1782; see *Dokumente*, 185–7 and 246–7, *Documentary Biography*, 209–11 and 281.
23. Richard Wagner, 'Oper und Drama', iii.246.

executed by Stephanie as far as the latter was able. Mozart had his librettist where he wanted him and was able, therefore, to defend him in his letter to his father of 13 October 1781:

Now to the text of the opera. – As far as Stephanie's work is concerned, you're right, of course – but the poetry is entirely appropriate for the character of the stupid, surly and malicious Osmin, and I know very well that the verses are not of the best, but they fit my musical ideas so well (they were already buzzing round in my head) that I was bound to like them; and I'll wager that when it's performed, nothing will be found wanting. As for the poetry in the rest of the piece, I really can't despise it. – Belmont's aria 'O wie ängstlich etc.' could hardly be better written for music. – Except for the 'Hui' and the 'Kummer ruht in meinem Schooß' [Grief reposes in my breast] (grief can't 'repose'),[24] the aria, too, isn't bad, especially the first part; and I don't know, but I'd say that in an opera the poetry must definitely be the obedient daughter of the music. – Why is it that Italian comic operas are everywhere so popular? in spite of the awfulness of their librettos? even in Paris, as I myself can attest? – It's because there the music reigns supreme and so you forget everything else. An opera is all the more likely to succeed when the plot is well worked out in advance and the words are written solely for the music, rather than added here and there for the sake of some awful rhyme (which, God knows, never contributes anything to the value of a theatrical performance, no matter what it may be, but tends rather to detract from it) – I mean words or even whole strophes that ruin the composer's whole idea.[25] – Verses are undoubtedly the most indispensable thing about music, but rhyme – solely for the sake of the rhyme – is the most detrimental; the people who set to work in this pedantic manner will always come to grief, together with their music. – Best of all is when a good composer who understands the theatre and is himself in a position to offer his advice encounters that true phoenix, an able poet – there's no reason then to be afraid of the applause of the ignorant. – Poets remind me of trumpeters and their professional jokes; if we composers were always to stick so closely to our rules (which were all well and good when no one knew any better), we'd produce music as worthless as their librettos.[26]

The letter ends on a typically self-ironical note: 'Well, I think I've wittered on for long enough and spouted quite enough nonsense.' Apart from his remarks on *Idomeneo*, this is one of the few passages in which we find Mozart expressing his opinion on what was then the highly contentious issue of the relationship between the words and the music in opera.

These remarks have been much misunderstood, especially after Mozart was unfortunate enough to be drawn into the arguments over Wagner's music dramas. As a result, they require a brief examination, not least because we are dealing here with the intellectual basis of his operas in general. We may begin by warning against the pernicious belief that there is a single immutable dramatic ideal to which some composers come closer than others. Our three greatest music

24. Konstanze was originally to have sung: 'Doch im Hui schwand meine Freude, / Trennung war mein banges Los; / Und nun schwimmt mein Aug' in Tränen, / Kummer ruht in meinem Schoß' ('But in a trice my joy vanished, separation was my anxious fate; and now my eyes are bathed in tears, grief reposes in my breast'). Note Mozart's criticism of the illogical 'reposing grief'. He had already written to his father on 26 September 1781 on the question of the word 'Hui': 'I've changed the "Hui" to "schnell" [quickly], in other words, "Doch wie schnell schwand meine Freude" etc. I really don't know what our German poets are thinking of; even if they don't understand the theatre, or at all events operas, they shouldn't make people talk as if they were addressing a herd of swine. Get a move on, porker!'; *Briefe*, iii.163.
25. Reichardt likewise rejects rhyme in his letter on musical poetry published as an appendix to his essay *Ueber die deutsche comische Oper*, 115.
26. *Briefe* iii.167–8 (letter of 13 October 1781).

dramatists of modern times – Gluck, Mozart and Wagner – prove that this is not so. Thanks not only to their differing personalities but also to the differing attitudes to drama shown by their respective ages, each of them adopted such an idiosyncratic and independent approach to the basic problem of music drama, namely, the relationship between poetry and music, as well as to the more general problem of drama, that we would do far better to investigate the rules that apply to each of them in turn than subordinate all three to some hypothetical universal rule that on closer inspection proves to be utterly hollow.

When a composer sets to work on a music drama or, indeed, on any vocal composition, he begins consciously or unconsciously by subjecting the text that he is setting to his critical scrutiny. There is certainly some truth to the dictum that a composer's dramatic gifts may be judged by his choice of text: as is clear from the works of the Neapolitan school and from Weber's *Euryanthe*, librettos whose poetic content fails to rise above the conventions of a particular age or whose basic design is anti-musical cannot be salvaged in the longer term by even the cleverest music. Yet the seam of gold that a libretto has to contain if it is to create a lasting impression does not need to be worked by the librettist himself: it is enough for it to be present and for the composer to be sufficiently inspired to discover it among the dross. But this immediately brings us to the basic question as to the different ways in which the musician may be inspired by the poet. The ideal case, whereby poet and musician are one and the same person, as they were with Wagner, is so rarely found that it can be dismissed without further ado. But even poets who are capable of couching their texts in genuinely poetic language and yet of creating them from the spirit of music are all too rare in the history of opera. Calzabigi came close to this ideal but because of his lack of innate creativity he still fell short of it, and it was left to Gluck to create works of lasting greatness. Yet, as we have already seen, he achieved this initially not as a musician but as a dramatic thinker. Gluck was the most extreme advocate of the view that the most important element in opera is its dramatic and poetic conception.

Mozart adopted a totally different approach. That there is no truth to the claim that he lacked all sense of critical acumen towards the texts that he set is clear not only from his remark that he studied 'a hundred little books' before setting to work on *Le nozze di Figaro* but also, and above all, from his remarks, quoted above, on the incompetence of contemporary librettists. With his keen eye for such matters, he could hardly have failed to see the depths to which the singspiel librettos of his time had sunk, and it is also clear from his wonderful and typically Mozartian comparison with the 'professional jokes of trumpeters' that he realized that the root of all evil lay in the dim-witted insistence on routine and the absence of any breath of fresh air. That he was au fait with the technical skills of these poets emerges from the vehemence of his remarks on their wretchedly jangling rhymes. Of course, this sorry state of affairs had already come to the notice of the more important of his predecessors, such as Benda, and there had been no lack of more or less successful attempts to breathe a greater degree of individuality into these marionette-like characters. But little progress had been made, as composers were repeatedly driven back to their old routines by their respect for poets and public alike. Mozart no longer felt this respect. Had he been of Gluckian stock, he would initially have looked round for a poet who could have cleansed the Augean stables for him and presented him with the model for a new and purified form of singspiel. But it was not in his nature to act in this way, and his immense creativity pointed him in a different direction. The nub of his whole aesthetic approach to opera lies in a single short sentence in the letter quoted above: 'Best of all is when a good composer who understands the theatre and who is himself in a position to offer his advice encounters that true phoenix, an able poet.' Shortly before this he draws a comparison between Italian comic operas 'in which the music reigns supreme' and a more ideal kind of opera 'in which the plot is well worked out in advance'. These two passages help to explain his other oft-cited and much-misunderstood comment that in opera 'the poetry must definitely be the obedient daughter of the music'. In Mozart's eyes, the best musician is not the one to whom the poet subordinates himself unquestioningly, but the one who, on the strength of a thorough understanding of 'the theatre' – in other words, an understanding of drama in its most general terms – is in a position to 'offer his advice', that is, to take the necessary initiative whenever the two collaborate. What we are dealing with here is certainly not a licence to the absolute musician to allow his artistry free rein with no heed for the libretto, but merely an appeal from the dramatically less qualified poet to the more qualified musician. Mozart was therefore entirely in the right in this, as he towered far above all the librettists of his day in terms of dramatic understanding, to say nothing of his inspired psychological insights. It was merely his ancestral right that allowed him to treat them in the way he did. After all, they rarely satisfied even his basic demand for a 'plan that was well worked out in advance'. The revisions that he asked Stephanie to make to Bretzner's text afford the best possible evidence of his views, for here we can see how parts of the scenario were completely revised in keeping with his conviction that the librettist's principal task was to divide up the individual solos, ensembles and choruses in what for the composer was the most dramatically effective way.

In short, Mozart began by allowing his librettos to work on his imagination in the most general terms, while guiding it in one particular direction.[27] Only then did the actual act of creation take place, but whereas in the case of Gluck this had been purely intellectual and rational, it was of an artistically creative and musical nature in the case of Mozart, who refused to accept the basic plot as fixed. For him, it was not an outline that the musician had only to colour in, but something that he at once recast in the fires of his musical and dramatic imagination. Not infrequently, the librettist's poetry was of no interest to him at all: the music of Osmin's first aria, for example, was already 'buzzing round' in his head even before he received the text. If, in such cases, the words more or less matched the image that he had in mind, he would allow them to stand, trusting in the power of his musical language to make whatever amends were necessary. Otherwise, they had to be changed. Writers have always admired Mozart's ability to extract gold from his often banal texts. The original lines are like helpless stammering beside the monumental language of his genius. As though by magic, his musical intuition raises all these homely figures high above the muddy waters of convention and places them firmly in the richly varied world of true humanity. He certainly never intended, as Schweitzer claims, 'to distract our minds from the inadequate texts by means of music that is beautiful in itself'.[28] Of course, beauty and elegant proportions are two of the principal characteristics of his music, but these merely reflected a universal requirement at this time, a demand to which even Gluck invariably submitted, in spite of his growing tendency to stress the declamatory nature of his texts. As with Mozart, his main concern was for dramatic expression, but whereas Gluck was led to declare war on the world of existing forms, Mozart – as we learn from the letter quoted above – stopped short of this, for all that he refused to regard the traditional 'rules' as inviolate and sacrosanct. The forms themselves, after all, were well suited to his dramatic ideal, especially when freely refashioned. Here, too, he recognized the importance of insisting on the rights of the musician over and above those of the poet.

---

27. ◆ Further, see Ulrich Konrad, '". . . mithin ließ ich meinen gedanken freyen lauf": Erste Überlegungen und Thesen zu den "Fassungen" von W. A. Mozarts Die Entführung aus dem Serail KV 384'.
28. Schweitzer, J. S. Bach, 432–3.

Of course, this ideal was quite different from Gluck's, inasmuch as it neither subordinated the whole to a monumental underlying idea,[29] as it did in Gluck's Italian operas, nor did it reduce the characters to the simplest formulas, as we find in his French reform operas. But for Mozart, even more than for Gluck, the characters were the main thing: for him, their depiction, development and interaction formed the actual substance of the drama, far more so, indeed, than the dramatic action as such. This explains why, even at the end of his life, he was still content to use spoken dialogue and *secco* recitative.[30] His imagination refused to use music at every single stage in the action, preferring to limit it to salient moments, where it depicts the development of the individual characters in large-scale, yet detailed psychological portraits, relying on the fact that the power of its language will continue to hold the listener in thrall even during these intermediary sections, until a new twist of the plot necessitates a change in these character portraits. If he thinks it appropriate to use music for a larger complex of events on stage, he opts not for the form of an orchestral recitative but that of a dramatic ensemble or finale. Even here, he is basically concerned not with dramatic developments as such but with the impressions left by them on the individual characters and with the changes brought about by this clash of personalities. It is no accident that even today Mozart remains the undisputed master of the dramatic ensemble. The unique alliance between poetic intuition and musical creativity within his personality allowed him to exploit a particular privilege of music and to do so, moreover, in consummate fashion: this privilege is music's ability to express the thoughts and feelings that animate different characters at one and the selfsame moment, while at the same time using the orchestra to indicate the outward situation.

Mozart's dramaturgy, in short, is first and foremost the dramaturgy of character. But even his concept of dramatic character differs from that of Gluck, whose characters are like personified concepts, acquiring their whole *raison d'être* from the ideas that they embody. All other emotions that are unrelated to this one idea are strenuously avoided. Here, too, conversely, Mozart reveals himself as a modern thinker, regarding the individual character not as the representative of a specific idea, but as an indivisible whole, combining living emotions, something unique and individual that bears within it the potential for development. Of course, Mozart's characters, too, are stereotypes, pointing beyond themselves to universals, but in spite of this they retain their individuality and never become lost in concepts or, worse, in allegory. This approach was dependent from the outset on the musician's creative powers, and his task consisted in shedding light on all his characters' complex emotions and on the psychological depths hidden from the poet. Each of Gluck's characters is made up of very few basic features and is fully developed from the outset, with the various stages in the action serving only to reinforce and intensify his or her underlying nature. Their basic unity notwithstanding, Mozart's characters, by contrast, are constantly developing, revealing more and more new facets and subsidiary characteristics that emerge and disappear again and which, far from destroying that unity, merely confirm it. This also explains why the characters that people Mozart's singspiels and *opere buffe* are far more true to life than Gluck's idealized figures. None the less, Mozart's understanding of reality was not the same as that of the contemporary representatives of the *Sturm und Drang* movement in literature, who were concerned only with the immediate present and with being 'of their time'. No, Mozart's concern – as emerges most clearly from his treatment of the *Figaro* material – was with what is true for all

---

29. The only exception to this rule is *Die Zauberflöte*.
30. The relatively insignificant role played by the orchestral recitative in Mozart's operas is entirely typical of this whole approach.

time. This is realism in the truest sense of the term, and it is to this that we owe the fact that his characters, even today, have lost none of their impact. They belong not to one age, but to every age.

Bretzner, it has to be said, was deeply unimpressed by the revisions undertaken by Mozart and Stephanie and in 1782 he wrote to one of the Leipzig newspapers:

A certain individual in Vienna by the name of Mozart has had the audacity to misuse my drama *Belmonte und Constanze* for an opera text. I herewith protest most solemnly against this infringement of my rights, and reserve the right to take the matter further.

Christoph Friedrich Bretzner, Author of *Das Räuschgen*.[31]

A second protest followed in 1783, this time against an 'unnamed person' who had 'interpolated a mass of songs in which occur truly heartbreaking and edifying verselets'.[32] It is not known whether Bretzner, who evidently took himself very seriously, took the matter any further.

The oft-heard claim that Mozart 'created German opera' with *Die Entführung aus dem Serail* betrays more enthusiasm than a true understanding of the historical facts of the matter. Both Schweitzer and Holzbauer had already attempted this very thing in Mannheim, albeit with only limited success. By contrast, *Die Entführung aus dem Serail* is a singspiel in both spirit and form, with its typical mixture of German, French and Italian features. Indeed, the character of Osmin has more Italian blood in him than was usual in German singspiels. Stylistically, therefore, the work has nothing new to offer: all that it contains already existed in embryo in the older singspiel, especially the Viennese variety. But listeners may well see something typically German in the determination with which Mozart went far beyond the confines of a piece intended merely to entertain and took the drama seriously as a reflection of human life. In this regard, there is no doubt that *Die Entführung aus dem Serail* was indeed of incalculable benefit in preparing the way for later German operas. But it was also the first of Mozart's works in which his dramatic muse fully revealed her own characteristic features. It is for this reason that it is *Die Entführung*, not *Idomeneo*, that forms the proud portal to the temple of his dramatic art.[33]

The profundity of Mozart's approach to his subject is clear even from the overture. The majority of the older singspiel overtures were more or less solidly wrought pieces lacking in any more individual features, with only a minority adopting the French model and seeking to forge an internal link with the opera as a whole or at least with its opening scene. Mozart adopts this French model, but does so in his own idiosyncratic and highly poetical way. Formally speaking, the piece is in extended sonata form, but, taking its cue from the Italian sinfonia, it has a brief slow movement in place of the development section. Yet this andante is really far too brief to be regarded as an

---

31. Wurzbach, *Mozart-Buch*, 261 [*Dokumente*, 187, *Documentary Biography*, 211]. ◆ The date '1782' is uncertain and reported only by Wurzbach; the original has not been found. Further, see Wolfgang Sulzer, 'Christoph Friedrich Bretzner: Sein Anteil an Mozarts Entführung aus dem Serail'.

32. *Litteratur- und Theater-Zeitung*, Berlin (21 June 1783), ii.398–40; see also Jahn, *W. A. Mozart*, fourth edition, i.759 [*Dokumente*, 191–2, *Documentary Biography*, 215–16].

33. Mozart gave the original score of the opera (K384) to his sister-in-law, Josepha Hofer, after she had given him particular pleasure by singing for him one evening. Later the score came into the possession of Paul von Mendelssohn-Bartholdy in Berlin and is now lodged in the Staatsbibliothek in the city. Not all the additional folios survive in André's collection. On 20 July 1782 Mozart wrote to his father: 'You'll find a lot of cuts in it, that's because I knew that the score is always copied out here at once; I gave my ideas free rein and only subsequently made occasional changes and cuts' (*Briefe*, iii.212). These changes and cuts are in fact more extensive and more substantial than in the majority of Mozart's scores. ◆ Surviving sources for *Die Entführung* include Mozart's autograph score (acts 1 and 3 at the Biblioteka Jagiellońska, Kraków; act 2 at the Staatsbibliothek zu Berlin) and a manuscript copy from 1782 with the composer's corrections, presumably the score used by him to direct the opera (Österreichische Nationalbibliothek, Vienna).

independent movement, with the result that the whole overture does indeed consist of a single movement, with an episode at its centre. This sense of unity is intensified by the fact that the second subject adopts Haydn's practice and, far from involving any sense of contrast, is derived from the first subject. Mozart himself set great store by the impression of concision: 'It is very short,' he wrote to his father on 26 September 1781, 'and keeps alternating between *forte* and *piano*, the Turkish music always entering with the *forte*, and it modulates through different keys, and I don't think anyone will fall asleep during it, even if they've not slept the whole of the previous night.'[34]

As for the character of the music, the listener is struck first and foremost by the oriental local colour, which is achieved by means of Janissary music. This is an idea that Mozart may have picked up from Gluck's *La rencontre imprévue*.[35] But there is a new feature here that not only keeps the Turkish element in check but determines the basic character of the overture as a whole. This is the secretive, fantastical whispering with which the theme – built up on simple triadic intervals – begins. A fairy-tale atmosphere envelops us, as it will later do in the allegro section of the overture to *Die Zauberflöte*, casting its spell on us and holding us in thrall till the very end with its secretive whispering and brightly darting flames. No less important in creating this inspired mood is the frequent and sudden alternation between *forte* and *piano* passages and the constant modulations, which underscore the sense of strangeness that right from the outset takes us far away from the conventional world of the older type of singspiel. Not until the ninth bar does the Turkish music enter, transporting us to the Orient, of whose fairy-tale world Mozart was especially fond. For him, the Orient was the land not only of brilliantly bright, intoxicating colours but also of a mysterious, sultry sensuality of a kind revealed in the opera even by Osmin. Within the overture, it is the passages in the minor which, suddenly stealing in, point to this other world. All at once the fantas-tical bustle breaks off and an outsider sets foot on the stage in a C minor heavy with grief and yearning. The concertante interplay between strings and winds is particularly effective here, as is the outburst on the fermata, where the whole sense of yearning finds particularly concentrated expression. But we barely have time to immerse ourselves in the plaintive strains of this image and to realize what is happening before we are again caught up in the earlier whirl of events, the piquancy of which is now increased by all manner of additional elements such as the clarinets and triangle at the beginning. The minor-key section at the end is also extended and intensified. This brilliant image then disappears on a questioning half-cadence as though behind a fine gauze, with the answer provided by Belmonte's aria, which follows without a break: 'Hier soll ich dich denn sehen, Konstanze!' The melody is that of the middle section of the overture, but now in C major, rather than C minor, a use of contrast as simple as it is poetic. The tension created by the minor key is thus released. The cry of yearning lamentation that had previously reached our ears from afar as though muted and repressed is now revealed as Belmonte's voice, the voice of the true lover who after 'all too many sufferings' has reached the shores of his longing and who now steps towards us as though out of the mists. In this way the overture reflects the outward mood of the opera, while at the same time indicating its basic theme, that of the true and innocent love that triumphs over all hostile forces.[36] Equally, it reveals what a true poet could make of the French link between overture and opera. This is not the more or less mechanical link forged by many of the

34. *Briefe*, iii.163 (letter of 26 September 1781).
35. The musical ideas themselves are on average far less exotic in stamp than in Gluck's overture or in the Janissary chorus ('Singt dem großen Bassa Lieder') or Mozart's well-known rondo alla turca from his A major sonata K331.
36. Wagner, too, stresses this particular character of the overture; see his essay 'Über die Ouvertüre', 195.

older singspiel composers, nor is it Grétry's pittoresque approach,[37] but is one that goes straight to the heart of the piece. Belmonte's aria is not only part of the overture, realizing the potential contained in its central section, it is also – as we shall see in a moment – very closely bound up with what follows. The result is a continuous complex of musical numbers whose individual members are linked to each other in a vital way. Only now do we understand the deeper meaning behind Mozart's laconic remark that, at his request, Stephanie had turned the original monologue into an 'arietta'. Few contemporary composers would have resisted the temptation to capture this mood in a large-scale Italianate aria. Mozart's composition is a simple song, like the following number for his adversary Osmin, and is barely longer than the overture's middle section. Here, too, the fairy-tale atmosphere is maintained, with the chivalric Belmonte expressing his deep love with pure and innocent sincerity and no trace of any emotional complications. His feeling of total happiness is dulled only by a sense of noble yearning that reaches its climax in the brief but emotionally charged coda, with its swelling wind accompaniment. No less succinct than the expression of ideal, morally unimpeachable love in Belmonte's opening aria is the expression of its antithesis in Osmin's following song ('Wer ein Liebchen hat gefunden'), in which unadulterated sensuality is coupled with lust and all manner of darker emotions, including jealousy, brutality and malice. Osmin is thus the first of the characters that Mozart introduces into his dramas by way of contrast, their aim being not to provide entertaining episodes but to allow the composer to throw his heroes into sharper outline. With Osmin as well, love is the force that motivates him, from his ungainly attempts to inveigle himself into Blonde's affections to his outbursts of savage cruelty. It is no accident that his opening number, like Belmonte's, is a love song. But the love that he feels remains brutally sensual and instinctive, diametrically at odds with the moral impulses that motivate Belmonte. What we find here is the same type of relationship as that between Don Giovanni and Leporello. Only by turning Osmin into the hero's principal antagonist was Mozart able to invest the work as a whole with a sense of drama: without his monstrous shadow the exemplary characters of the lovers would create no dramatic impact. And he owes his comic aspects, too, to more than merely an attempt on Mozart's part to remain within traditional confines: he is neither an unadventurous joker in the tradition of the German singspiel nor a caricature in that of *opera buffa*. Indeed, Mozart refuses to acknowledge the older type of comedy, and it was arguably his supreme intellectual feat to liberate opera from the artificial antithesis of high-flown heroism on the one hand and no less implausible comic distortions on the other and, in the case of both tragedy and comedy, to go back to their ultimate source in actual life. He is the greatest realist in the whole history of music drama, a composer whose characters are firmly and exclusively grounded in reality. In this way Mozart vastly extended our understanding of our fellow human beings, at least to the extent that this understanding affects music drama, merging tragedy and comedy in a highly idiosyncratic way and combining the highest with the lowest. Even in *La finta giardiniera* he had unconsciously worked towards this goal, but without success; and the ideal that he had vaguely glimpsed slipped between his fingers. By the time that he came to write *Die Entführung aus dem Serail*, his view of life had matured to such an extent that he was now able to grasp that ideal with both hands. Only now was he able to fathom his characters' lives and see in them individual, indivisible entities made up of powerful and weak forces that strive upwards and cling to the earth. In this way Mozart created a whole new picture of the world in his operas. His

---

37. Concerning Benda's *Holzhauer*, see above. The outward form of both numbers is identical, yet Benda's lacks the compelling poetic power inherent in the way in which the voice repeats the middle section of the overture. Also missing is the contrast between minor and major.

characters were bound to feel and act in ways completely different from those familiar from the past. They seek neither to embody specific ideas nor to amuse their listeners nor to appeal to them intellectually. Nor even was it their aim to 'imitate Nature', to quote an expression much favoured by rationalist aesthetics. Rather, they were themselves Nature, in other words, living creatures of arresting immediacy. This also explains why they are neither good nor evil in the sense of a common morality. They are not constantly judged by a moral code that has nothing to do with real life, rather is the yardstick real life itself. Mozart never felt called upon to pass judgement on his characters and does not, for example, interpret Don Giovanni's fall as a form of moral condemnation. Nor was it his intention to make his comic figures look ridiculous: his sense of humour is far less pointed and aggressive than that of his Italian contemporaries, but he also lacks their coldness and self-righteousness. These poor rogues are no pallid constructs but are drawn from life: suffice it to compare Leporello with the Latin members of his impressive ancestral line, and it will be clear at once that it was Mozart who tore the mask from this character's features. The claim that Mozart's opera is essentially no more than a witty piece for masks could hardly be more superficial.

But Mozart is also a dramatist in the far more modern sense in that his characters are closely interrelated. None of them stands on his or her own but emerges from the light and shade of the others, hence the richly teeming, endlessly animated life of these dramas and their pronounced realism, a realism that allows them to appear as fresh and true today as when they were first created. But let us return to *Die Entführung aus dem Serail*.

In the first part of his exposition, Mozart develops the characters of his protagonist and antagonist, Belmonte and Osmin, gradually bringing them into the sharpest possible focus. One number leads naturally to the other, with Osmin's elemental nature the first to be revealed ('Solche hergelauf'ne Laffen'), followed immediately by a more detailed exposition of Belmonte's character ('Konstanze! – O wie ängstlich').

Osmin's song consists of three strophes, each slightly varied and each throwing light on a new and different aspect of his character. The words are those of a harmless folksong sung while he is picking figs. Dieter's setting[38] shows how run-of-the-mill composers interpreted such numbers: it is a somewhat smug setting, striking a folklike tone and without any more individual features, the sort of song, in short, that any peasant girl might sing while out harvesting. What we find in the case of Mozart's Osmin, by contrast, is a song clearly expressive of his innermost character. For the first time in the history of the German singspiel, an entirely simple song is adapted to suit the character of the singer. Even the choice of a minor tonality – specifically G minor, which always has something special to say with Mozart – is significant. There is something murky and eerie about this song as it proceeds on its ponderous way with its eloquent thirds and fifths in the melodic line, its self-satisfied repeat of the final phrase at the lower octave and, finally, its tremendous ascent to the concluding 'Trallalera', with which the character's fanatical malice suddenly erupts with elemental force.[39] The following variations affect the instrumentation first and foremost, although there are also changes to the harmonic writing, including the sinister A flat in the second violins at the second 'Trallalera'. In the second strophe a brief motif is added in the winds, sounding half like a gesture, half like the noise of a wild animal; and in the third, the colouring becomes markedly

38. The opening is quoted by Preibisch, 'Quellenstudien', 459; the complete setting is reproduced in the appendix to Abert, *Herzog Karl Eugen von Württemberg und seine Zeit.* ◆ Further, see Mahling, 'Die Gestalt des Osmin in Mozarts Entführung' and Nägele, 'Belmont und Constanze in den Vertonungen von Dieter und Mozart'.
39. Mozart departs from traditional practice in stressing the word *trallaléra*: Dieter and his contemporaries all preferred *trállalerá*. The opening scene of Piccinni's *La notte critica* evokes a similarly sultry mood and even contains a direct melodic reminiscence of Mozart.

more sensuous as a result of the remarkably agitated octaves in the winds (now joined by a flute): at this very moment, moreover, the supremely jealous Osmin breaks out of the earlier tempo and launches into the Allegro. In this way, we first meet Osmin as a darkly wild-eyed figure, a character as inscrutable as he is ungainly and furtively lustful. The duet ('Verwünscht seist du samt deinem Liede!') follows without a break, with the enraged Belmonte bawling out Osmin's 'Trallalera' in a contemptuous echo, a remarkable, authentically Mozartian number that is formally completely free (only a handful of motifs are repeated) and of strikingly vacillating tonality. The result is a highly effective sense of contrast that is further increased by the lively characterization of the two adversaries and by a number of additional features, including Belmonte's repeated question.[40] The beast already begins to show his claws at the passage in A minor ('Seht selber zu'), with its unison writing for Osmin and the orchestra. Like many similar scenes, Mozart treats the following quarrel along French lines,[41] scoring it as a canon, with the very first attack already creating a deeply disturbing impression on account of its wailing motif and close intervals. Note, too, the vivid way in which Belmonte's praise of Pedrillo is turned on its head as a result of the imitative writing for Osmin in the minor. From the G minor passage onwards ('Es ist fürwahr ein guter Tropf'), the battle lines are irrevocably drawn up, with Osmin venting his rage in a *buffo*-like manner, while Belmonte's chromatically descending line suggests that, half ironically, he feels sorry for good Pedrillo – even the fairy-tale prince has his moments of good humour. The atmosphere continues to worsen, and the storm finally breaks in a D major presto. By now, both men are motivated by the same desire to see the back of the other and hurl the coarsest insults at each other in the form of the same boorish motif, with the bass line banging on after them in canon. The scene ends with a typically Italian quarrel involving brief, angular, repeated motifs, extended cries of rage and incoherent threats. The two characters are now joined by the scapegoat Pedrillo, and Mozart uses the opportunity to paint a portrait of Osmin whose roots, as we have seen, lie not in the text but in the composer's own dramatic perception of the character. The old man's rage produces a veritable bedlam of the most disparate emotions, their insane turmoil even flouting our formal expectations. His basic emotion is that of apparently total mastery over the situation, a complete sense of superiority – the sort of feeling which, in the case of individuals like Osmin, reduces all other feelings to silence and revels only in related forms of this one emotion. He refuses to countenance a ritornello but, following an eloquent and emotionally charged *forte* chord, launches into his sinister theme, with its grotesque coloratura, a theme which, expressive of his effortfully suppressed fury, proceeds via a powerful crescendo involving snarling trills and spiteful chromaticisms, before exploding in a descending octave. This is the naturalistic language of an Italian *opera buffa*, more especially one by Paisiello, and Osmin remains faithful to it throughout the whole of his aria. His outburst evidently does him some good, as it is with a certain smug superiority that he now insults his adversaries, describing them as 'fops' whose stealthy ways are vividly depicted by canonic entries in the violins. He bombastically boasts of his understanding of his fellow human beings, only to allow his self-assurance free rein in all its blatant brutality ('Eure Tücken, eure Ränke': 'Your malice, your intrigues'). Time and time again his bilious anger erupts, of course, and there is something sinisterly malevolent about his final 'sind mir ganz bekannt' ('are entirely familiar to me'), with its grotesque trill. Again his fury abates, and in his priceless 'ich hab auch

---

40. The orchestral motif that is heard at this juncture, the upper voice of which consists of quavers repeated at the same pitch as though between clenched teeth, recalls Johann Christian Bach, especially act one, scene six of *Catone* and the aria 'Solcar pensa un mar sicuro' from *Orione*.

41. Other examples include act three, scene five of Monsigny's *La belle Arsène* and the overture to Grétry's *Silvain*.

Verstand' ('I too possess understanding'), with its cunningly smirking oboe (in the second section of the aria, this motif is extended downwards into the lowest reaches of the bass register), the vain and self-righteous philistine has his say, adding to the note of savagery and demonism already associated with the character. It is entirely typical of the composer that in the course of this aria the different aspects of the same underlying emotion – anger, vainglory, violence and common vanity – are explored in rapid succession, generally with unexpected, elemental abruptness, creating a vivid picture of a mind dominated by only the basest instincts. For this, the flexible language of the Italian *opera buffa* stood the composer in the best possible stead. With the end of its second section, the aria draws to a regular close. But Osmin has not yet finished. On 26 September 1781, Mozart wrote to his father:

> The words 'Drum beim Barte des Propheten' etc. are taken at the same speed, but with quick notes, and as his rage continues to increase, the Allegro assai that follows in a totally different metre and a different key – just when you think it's all over – is bound to create the best possible effect. Just as someone in such a towering rage oversteps all the bounds of order and moderation and completely forgets himself, so the music must forget itself. But passions, whether violent or not, must never be expressed to the point where they excite disgust, and music, in even the most terrible situations, must never offend the ear but always remain a source of pleasure, so I haven't chosen a key foreign to F (the key of the aria), but one related to it – not the most closely related, D minor, but the more remote A minor.[42]

This passage, too, reveals the extent to which Mozart approached his task in full consciousness of what he was doing. But, *pace* Jahn,[43] it is simply not possible to regard this statement of intent as an aesthetic precept of timeless validity, as its demands can be understood only by reference to the date at which it was formulated. Rococo music does not, of course, exclude all possibility of depicting the passions, even if it tends towards the theatrical or the sentimental, but it takes great care to ensure that the beauty of the melodic line is preserved. Not even the most furious Medeas and Armidas forget this point in their arias, and in this respect, too, Mozart is entirely a product of his time. Indeed, it is already extremely daring of him to claim that the music should 'forget itself' here. After all, a writer such as Christian Gottfried Krause had argued that 'anger, madness and despair' should not be depicted in music at all.[44]

The first of the additional sections ('Drum beim Barte') retains the existing key-signature and, as a result, merely perpetuates the existing mood, while at the same time adding to its note of intensity. But a further aspect of Osmin's character finds forceful expression here: his cruelty. Even here the music already 'forgets itself', failing, as it does, to achieve a well-ordered melodic line, with Osmin merely hissing out his fifths and octaves between clenched teeth,[45] and doing so, moreover, on a different beat of the bar from the one that is actually indicated by the orchestra, with the result that everything seems to be out of joint. This manic tendency to stick to the same brief motifs

---

42. *Briefe*, iii.162 (letter of 26 September 1781).
43. Here, too, Jahn equates Mozart's art with 'all true art'; *W. A. Mozart*, i.769. ◆ Further, see Melamed, 'Evidence on the Genesis of *Die Entführung aus dem Serail* from Mozart's Autograph Score'.
44. Krause, *Von der musikalischen Poesie*.
45. A similar device is found in the aria 'Se mi scaldo, m'infurio, m'impesto' in act one, scene five of Paisiello's *La somiglianza de' nomi*. The aria in act one, scene one of this same opera also contains instructive parallels to Osmin's 'Eure Tücken, eure Ränke' and 'Mich zu hintergehen'. Needless to say, these are not conscious borrowings but merely proof of the extent to which Mozart fell back on the *opera buffa* tradition when creating the figure of Osmin.

– a further feature of *opera buffa* – is found to an even greater extent in the allegro assai, where the picture is rounded out with the addition of one final feature: Osmin's demonic fanaticism. Significantly, it is only now that Mozart presents his character in oriental guise by means of an instrumental race to the finish, the sinister nature of which is increased by its single-mindedness. A handful of naturalistic motifs enhances this impression, most notably the pungent and incisive mordant in the winds at the very beginning of this section.[46] Much the same impression is later created by the mindlessly provocative rhythm that accompanies the wildly scurrying strings[47] and piccolo: ♪♫ | ♩ ⅞ ♪♫ | ♩ . Here the contrast between the person that Osmin would like to be and the person he actually is is thrown into the sharpest relief, which is why the impression of comedy is most pronounced at this point. 'Osmin's rage', writes Mozart, 'is made to seem comical by the use of Turkish music.'

This aria is in a completely different league from even the finest achievements of earlier composers of singspiels and is followed by an aria for Belmonte in which the latter, too, reveals his innermost nature in clearer outlines than hitherto. Its A major is in conscious contrast to the foregoing A minor, with the result that the two enemies are brought into the sharpest focus. Indeed, this aria struck Mozart as so important that he set it to music immediately after receiving the libretto, as he wrote to tell his father:

> Now for Belmonte's aria in A major, 'O wie ängstlich, o wie feurig'. Do you know how it's expressed – and how the beating of his loving heart is indicated, too? – By 2 violins in octaves.[48] This is the favourite aria of all who've heard it, including myself, and it's tailor-made for Adamberger's voice. You can see the trembling and the faltering,[49] you can see his throbbing breast beginning to swell, which is expressed by means of a crescendo,[50] you can hear his whispering and sighing,[51] which is expressed by the first violins *con sordino* and a flute in unison with them.[52]

This aria is an outstanding example of Mozart's superb ability to portray his characters on the strength of a specific situation. Although Belmonte knows that he will see his lover again, he is so surprised to learn that their reunion is imminent that his delight at the prospect of seeing her again is mingled in a typically Mozartian manner with a painful recollection of the past and anxiety about the future, with this whole overwhelming torrent of emotions affecting him outwardly, too. Hence the important role of tone-painting here, and although it barely extends beyond the standard Italian devices of 'palpitare', 'vacillare', 'sospirare' and so on, it is so true to life and so well grounded in the whole situation that there is no sense that it has been grafted on from the outside, as one so often feels with the Italians. Even more importantly, Mozart adopts such a clearly focused approach to the whole scene that there are times when one almost has the

---

46. Something similar may be found in the wedding march from *Le nozze di Figaro*, where the aim is again to add an element of exotic colour.

47. The same incessantly repeated unison motif that ends the present number is also found at the words 'che brutto fracasso ve faccio vedè' in act two, scene three of Paisiello's *Le astuzie amorose*. The accumulation of threats recurs in act two, scene seven of the same composer's *La frascatana*.

48. See bars 9ff.

49. See bars 29ff.

50. See bars 35ff.

51. See bars 40ff. The main theme of the aria is strongly reminiscent of the second subject of the aria 'Pupille amate' from act three, scene five of Johann Christian Bach's *Lucio Silla*.

52. *Briefe*, iii.162–3 (letter of 26 September 1781).

impression of a dialogue. We hear, for example, the young woman's sighs and whispers, and immediately afterwards two phrases spring to Belmonte's lips in the exuberance of his emotions: 'Es wird mir so bange!' ('I feel so afraid') and 'Es glüht mir die Wange!' ('My cheek begins to glow'). In this way everything germane to the situation, no matter how small,[53] assumes physical form here, whereas André's and Dieter's heroes fail to emerge from behind the mask of an Italian castrato aria. In short, Belmonte's aria is a perfect example of Mozart's new-found art of handling the orchestra in a dramatically and psychologically appropriate manner. But its two sections – Mozart tends by preference to use binary form in this opera, too – also reveal a subtle increase in emotional intensity. In the second section there is no longer any sense of what Belmonte calls 'separation's anxious pain', which is replaced, rather, by a growing fear of the future, before a mixture of joy and ardent longing resurfaces at the end. In the orchestra, his lover's whispered words finally die away *pianissimo*.

As Mozart himself explained, the chorus of Janissaries that accompanies the Pasha's entrance comprises 'everything that you could demand of a chorus of Janissaries, short and lively and written entirely for the Viennese'.[54] It is in three sections, with a French solo episode in the middle, and is strikingly oriental in character, a character due not only to the Janissary instruments but also to the rattling rhythm, to a number of melodic features such as the brutally juxtaposed f″ and f″ sharp in the fifteenth bar and, especially, to the sudden modulation that recalls the overture.[55] In this way, the key of C major is reached via the foreign key of A minor.[56] The affinities with Gluck's overture to *La rencontre imprévue* are unmistakable.

Mozart originally intended the role of the Pasha Selim to be sung,[57] but in the end it remained a spoken part. The later Mozart would scarcely have left it at that, as it would have been easy for him to persuade Stephanie to introduce a number of arias. But at this stage in his career he saw no reason to depart from Bretzner's version. Given his own particular view of the subject, it was enough for Mozart to have a pair of lovers and their retainers, together with Osmin by way of contrast. The pasha, on the other hand, did not coalesce into a musical character for him. His position as Turkish pasha was sufficiently defined by his followers and by his hostility towards the lovers, while his unrequited love for Konstanze was made clear by his servant Osmin and by her arias. To have developed this character musically would not only have drawn the composer dangerously close to the world of *opera seria* (think of the character of Soliman in *Zaide*), it would also have made the simple affair of the heart between the two lovers unduly encumbered. Musically speaking, therefore, Mozart kept the character in the background, a course of action which, given the tendency of the singspiel to vacillate between spoken drama and opera at this time, was certainly not felt by contemporaries to be problematical. Even as late as Weber's *Oberon* we find a pendant to this practice.

Selim's first onslaught on Konstanze's heart is answered by an aria ('Ach ich liebte, war so glücklich') whose adagio section, with its disjointed, sighlike melodic writing and sustained notes in the winds, expresses in simple, heartfelt terms not only her anguish but also her fidelity to her lover.

---

53. Under this heading come not only the brief recitative, the very brevity of which creates an impression of elemental strength, but also the brief crescendo ending in a *piano* in the first two bars of the aria.

54. *Briefe*, iii.163 (letter of 26 September 1781).

55. Oulibicheff, *Nouvelle biographie de Mozart*, ii.375ff., recalls certain Russian folksongs that Mozart may perhaps have got to know while visiting Prince Galitzin.

56. Mozart was fond of using A minor for exotic scenes of this kind: other examples include the end of Osmin's aria and the rondo alla turca from the A major sonata K331, the rhythmic writing of which likewise recalls the present chorus.

57. This is indicated by Mozart's reference to the singer Joseph Walter in his letter of 1 August 1781 (*Briefe*, iii.143).

It is a worthy lover of Belmonte who stands before us here. Unfortunately the allegro section fails to sustain this high standard, and Mozart himself admitted that he had 'sacrificed Constanze's aria a little to Mlle Cavalieri's flexible throat. "Trennung war mein banges Los und nun schwimmt mein Aug' in Tränen" ['Separation was my anxious fate and now my eyes are bathed in tears'] – I've tried to express this as far as an Italian bravura aria will allow me to do so.'[58] This approach was by no means unknown in singspiels, of course, but it led to an irremediable disjunction in Konstanze's characterization, the two extremes of which are thrown into even sharper contrast in her two subsequent arias ('Traurigkeit ward mir zum Lose' and 'Martern aller Arten'). On the one hand we find a true match for Belmonte, a woman who expresses her feelings in a language that is simple, true and noble, while on the other we have a caricature of that image, an Italian prima donna who avails herself of the emotionally charged rhetoric of Medea and Armida, a short-coming that prevents us from placing *Die Entführung aus dem Serail* on the same high level as Mozart's later works, its undeniable merits notwithstanding. The Queen of Night's arias do not have such a disruptive effect as they are sung by a vengeful sorceress and queen, not by a simple young woman in love. And as always when Mozart ventures into the relatively uncongenial world of *opera seria*, his language loses much of its urgency and originality. Only a few individual features reveal the hand of the master – here one thinks not only of the treatment of the winds and the melodic writing, especially its chromaticisms, but above all the incorporation of the Adagio into the middle section of the aria. All the other elements, while capturing the mood in general, lack any sense of individual characterization, and the listener is particularly repelled by the senseless coloratura on the unstressed word 'my' in the phrase 'Grief reposes in my breast'. How differently Belmonte's 'loving heart' revels in its coloratura writing in his earlier aria.

In the trio ('Marsch, marsch, marsch!'), Belmonte and Pedrillo force their way past the furious Osmin into the pasha's house. Mozart reports on this number in his letter to his father:

> Now for the trio at the end of the first act. Pedrillo has passed off his master as an architect, in order to give him a chance to meet his Constanze in the garden. The pasha has taken him into his service; the overseer Osmin knows nothing of this and, being an ill-mannered lout and the arch-enemy of all strangers, is insolent and refuses to admit them to the garden. The beginning is extremely abrupt, and because the words lend themselves to it, I've produced a fairly decent three-part setting; but then the major enters *pianissimo* – it must go very quickly – and the ending will be very noisy, which is all you need at the end of an act: the more noise the better, and the shorter the better, so that people are not left too cold to applaud.[59]

Although this passage ends on a somewhat ironical note, it none the less shows that Mozart was more concerned with a lively depiction of the situation on stage than with any more subtle attempt at characterization. In this respect, as well as in terms of its brief and powerful motifs and stirring rhythms, the piece – and above all its section in the minor – is clearly influenced by the ensembles of certain *opéras comiques*. There are also individual examples of tone-painting, with Osmin's cudgelling motif ('or else I'll knock your brains out') closely related to a similar motif in *Die Meistersinger*. Following the fermata, the threatening bass figure and wind suspensions are used to depict a sense of bitter struggle. There is even an embryonic attempt at characterization: above all, it is Osmin who, again in a sombre C minor, sets the tone here, generally ignoring the others and

58. *Briefe*, iii.163 (letter of 26 September 1781).
59. *Briefe*, iii.163 (letter of 26 September 1781).

going his own way until the very end when, outwitted by them, he screams his furious 'March!' on the weak beat of the bar.

The second act introduces us to Blonde, whose aria ('Durch Zärtlichkeit und Schmeicheln') opens the proceedings. She is currently having to deal with Osmin who, as usual, is trying to get his way by force. Cast in the briefest possible rondo form, there is therefore something consciously mannered about her aria: she plans to show the doltish Oriental that Westerners woo with grace and good manners. Of course, Blonde has many predecessors in Italian and especially French comic operas, but she lacks the note of heartless coquetry that all too often is their one distinguishing feature. Her delightful mischievousness is in no way calculated but comes straight from the heart, from natural, warm emotion. This is a German feature, and Jahn is right to discover here the earliest traces of the naïve young women who are later found in so many German operas.[60] We have already noted that the aria's main theme is an old Italian idea. Its principal charm lies in the fact that, in spite of its mannered tone, it still manages to take a number of sideswipes at old Osmin, notably by means of its eloquent ascending octave on 'Tagen' and its comical coloratura on 'entweicht', which twice dies away with a hiss like escaping steam, on the second occasion rising to a high e''' – impressive proof of Therese Teyber's vocal accomplishments. Bound up with this are the surly demisemiquavers in the strings in the first episode,[61] a device that serves a similar purpose in works by both Guglielmi and Grétry[62] and that Mozart himself was later to use on frequent occasions.

Osmin pulls himself together for the following duet ('Ich gehe, doch rate ich dir'). Although he begins by thundering on as before, the tone he adopts is now markedly more good-humoured. Blonde starts by letting fly and overwhelming him with a torrent of abuse, initially preventing him from getting a word in edgeways. When he thinks that he has trumped her with his portentous descent into the lowest reaches of the bass register, she humiliates him with her merciless mimicry. Then, in the slow middle section in C minor, he launches into a melancholic melody, half lament, half love song. Although there is something touching about his shameless manner here, he remains as surly and uncouth as ever. Note, for example, the grotesqueness of his strained 'geplagt und geschoren' ('tormented and clipped'). But here, too, Blonde gives as good as she gets, decorating his melodic line in a way that is both delightful and mocking at one and the same time. By the second Allegro – a completely free repeat of the first – she has succeeded in taming him completely and it is now Blonde who sets the tone, rather than Osmin. All that remains for him to do is to turn tail and flee, frightened and submissive, availing himself in the process of her own melodic ideas. The orchestra offers a parting shot in the form of a veritable victory fanfare celebrating Blonde's triumph over the infatuated booby.

Konstanze's next aria ('Traurigkeit ward mir zum Lose') is introduced by a lengthy recitative, a form that Mozart uses relatively rarely when compared to his predecessors and contemporaries. Following a tension-laden opening in which the bass line suggests the full extent of the emotional pressures upon her, a sighlike motif floats in, followed by an agitated, sharply syncopated motif. The underlying emotion finally reaches a climax towards the end of the recitative, and immediately afterwards the aria itself begins with the strained and plaintive cry of 'Traurigkeit' ('sadness'), heard first in the winds and then in the voice, a superb example of Mozart's inspired way of introducing his listener to the mood of the piece not by some garrulous ritornello but by a brief and

60. Jahn, *W. A. Mozart*, i.775.
61. In the first version of this aria, they were heard twice; for more on these cuts, see the critical report to NMA II/5/2.
62. In act one, scene four of Guglielmi's *Il matrimonio in contrasto* and scene seven of Grétry's *Le tableau parlant*.

graphic motif. This aria is one of the high points of the opera, a status it owes not least to its note of affecting lament, the resigned colour of which already looks forward to the much later composer. The character that we see before us here is the Konstanze whom Mozart actually envisaged, simple, natural and without any false pathos. In terms not only of its key of G minor but of its whole expression, it takes its place in the line of development leading from Ilia in *Idomeneo* to Pamina in *Die Zauberflöte*. As before, it is a binary number, as the four introductory bars cannot be considered as an independent section, however intelligently and idiosyncratically they may lead us back to the beginning by means of the main idea. The second section, too, bears Mozart's unmistakable imprint, not only avoiding all the major-key modulations of the first section but sticking obsessively to the single key of G minor, which now infiltrates all the aria's other ideas, as though there were no longer any advice or help to be found elsewhere. Moreover, all the earlier ideas are now placed under increased emotional pressure and rendered gloomier or more intense, notably in the case of the appeal to the breezes (a topos familiar from *Zaide*), which in the first section had still allowed a modest shaft of light to enter the sombre picture. All the melodic and harmonic ideas that are typically found in Mozart's other G minor pieces are repeated here, including the important role of the sixth and flattened second degree, together with the typically Mozartian use of syncopation as the principal vehicle for inner agitation, the inspired elaboration of a phrase by dividing it between voice and instruments ('weil ich dir entrissen bin') and the mysterious introduction of a new idea by means of a brief and often merely rhythmical motif in the winds, especially the horns (as we find, for example, just before the words 'Gleich der wurmzernagten Rose'). This last feature is another of those that is part and parcel of the general view of Mozart as a 'Romantic' composer.

This beautiful image is, of course, immediately and disastrously ruined by Konstanze's next aria ('Martern aller Arten'). As we have already seen, it is dramatic to a fault and, by being treated as an Italian bravura aria, it makes a mockery of Konstanze's entire character. The instrumental writing is deeply impressive, with the usual large-scale forces of trumpets and timpani joined by a concertino of flute, oboe, violin and cello. Even the opening ritornello assumes the air of a concerto tutti with its various themes and cadenza and, as such, is in crass contrast to the sigh of the foregoing aria. Throughout the piece, the aim is to produce a concertante number of the most effective kind. The voice, too, begins by striking a note of Italianate pathos, even relapsing into the manner of Mozart's earlier operas by embellishing the theme with a lengthy coloratura flourish. Equally reminiscent of the composer's older style is the practice of failing to exploit all the themes in the ritornello and of introducing new ones instead. In spite of its ambitious garb, the aria is not a credit to Mozart as a dramatist but, at best, to his capabilities as a musician. Even as a musician, of course, he often enough falls back on commonplace phrases, raising himself to a significantly higher level only in those passages that are particularly grateful to the voice and in his intelligent exploitation of the sort of effects traditionally associated with a concerto. Even so, the tendency of the vocal line to mirror the concertino generally gives the impression of virtuoso ensemble writing for five solo instruments.[63]

Blonde now expresses her delight at the forthcoming abduction, on this occasion revealing herself as she is, full of life, cheerful and at the same time warm-hearted and sincere. There is

---

63. The older and longer version is reproduced in AMA, p.294ff. Writing in the *AmZ*, i (1798/9), 145, Friedrich Rochlitz reports that Mozart later undertook a thoroughgoing revision of the score, changing a great deal and cutting even more: 'I heard him play one of Constanze's main arias in both versions and regretted a number of discarded passages. – I expect it works at the keyboard, he said, but not in the theatre. When I wrote this, I was still too enamoured of the sound of my own voice and couldn't always work out how the piece should end.' It is impossible to say what Rochlitz is referring to here, as it was unlike Mozart to revise his works in this way.

something particularly high-spirited about the high *g″* that she hurls forth at the end. The orchestra, too, is in a notably good mood, from the cheerfully chuckling flutes and skittish second violins at the beginning to the scurrying string motifs at 'Ohne Aufschub will ich springen' that almost recall the elves of Romantic composers and, finally, to the light-hearted laughter in the instruments that send Blonde on her way.[64]

A totally different picture of Blonde's partner Pedrillo emerges from his aria 'Frisch zum Kampfe'. The Italian composers of the period treated such characters either as boobies or as the hero's cunning associate, admirably versed in all the ways of the world and representing an ideal that has always been held in particularly high regard by the Italian nation. Mozart's Pedrillo, by contrast, has his feet far more firmly planted on the ground, a lad whose heart is in the right place and who has every intention of seeing the plan through to the end. But there is one point on which he is vulnerable: he is a regular milksop. And the humour of his aria rests on the interplay between these two antitheses. He begins with what can only be described as war music with its trumpets and timpani, but by the time we reach the words 'Nur ein feiger Tropf verzagt' ('Only a cowardly rascal is afraid') he has already started to cower – evidently he is not exactly unfamiliar with the term 'cowardly rascal' – and immediately afterwards the hairs on the back of his neck start ever so slightly to stir. By the end he has cracked completely. As a result, even his belligerent outbursts acquire a forceful, forced expression, as though not entirely truthful. Particularly noteworthy in this context are the frequent fermatas at the end of each contrastive section. The ending itself is priceless, with Pedrillo's pugnacious trill followed by a coda in which the instruments of the orchestra independently return to the theme of the 'cowardly rascal'. At the end of this authentically Mozartian thumbnail sketch, we are still unclear as to how Pedrillo will act when the going gets rough. He lays into his arch-enemy Osmin with a bottle of wine in the famous drinking duet ('Vivat Bacchus! Bacchus lebe!'), which, in Mozart's own words, was intended 'per li sig^ri Vieneri' and 'consists entirely of my Turkish tattoo'.[65] Even the accompaniment, in which the Turkish orchestra is joined by a sensuously tingling flute, makes it clear that Osmin is the main hero, but it is also Osmin who sings the full version of the theme – significantly only after he has had a good swig of wine. The sober Pedrillo, meanwhile, gives only the outlines of the theme. In general, this number is cast in a form that Mozart was often to use from now on, a flexible form that hesitates between binary aria and rondo. Osmin's misgivings soon disappear, with the result that Pedrillo's courage visibly returns, and the sigh of relief behind Osmin's 'Nun wär's geschehen' ('Now the deed is done') is as earthy as all that he says and does. Supported by the bassoon, he launches into a jubilant song in praise of young women, and soon the whole 'tattoo' is going at it hammer and tongs under his direction, now with the full orchestra. Now it is the young ladies' turn once again, but this time with a new and curiously floating melody with no bass instruments, as though all manner of alluring creatures were beckoning to the old man through the mists of the tinkling triangle. The element of sensuality is significantly increased. And from now on Osmin's contribution to the main theme is limited to brief and disjointed phrases, chief of which is the rolling conclusion, which seems to give him particular pleasure – the only sign of his imminent state of complete inebriation. Mozart preferred not to describe the subsequent turn of events, including his falling asleep.

---

64. This aria, too, was shortened.
65. This passage (*Briefe*, iii.163, letter of 26 September 1781) suggests that Mozart was using an older piece here, but nothing is known of such a work. The familiar rattling rhythm in equal quavers is all part and parcel of the Turkish local colour.

This outburst of instinctive sensuality is followed by a further aria for Belmonte ('Wenn der Freude Tränen fließen') praising the happiness of true love. The infatuatedly pensive adagio is typified by the following idea, with its mixture of sentimentality and *naïveté*:

The allegretto, with its wind sonorities and Schubertian second subject, is filled with a sense of tender bliss at the prospect of possessing his beloved.[66]

The quartet that ends this act and that Mozart himself insisted on including here ('Ach Belmonte! Ach mein Leben!') differs fundamentally from Bretzner's, in which the characters express their hope that the plan will turn out well and which is therefore of only thematic interest. Instead, it reverts to the main idea of the whole work, that of true love between the two couples. The imminent abduction, with all its dangers, remains more or less in the background as the four characters are completely obsessed with the happiness of their love, a happiness now temporarily disturbed not from without but from within, as a result of their feelings of jealousy. Like an *opera buffa* finale, the quartet consists of a series of more or less extended sections, but it differs substantially from such finales by dint of the fact that it is not part of some more complicated situation comedy building to a dramatic climax. Instead, it is an inner development that is traced here, a miniature emotional drama based on the simple idea of happiness in love, rupture and reconciliation, hence the fact that the underlying tone of the quartet is lyrical rather than dramatic and, as such, admirably suited to the calm and innocent tenor of the whole work. On the basis of a commonplace Italian motif later heard in Leporello's 'catalogue aria',[67] Belmonte and Konstanze celebrate their first reunion on a note of sincere and innocent delight, from which all sense of past and future terror has been lost. The middle section in A major brings Blonde and Pedrillo into the foreground. Long familiar with each other, they turn their attention to more practical matters in the form of the forthcoming abduction, a discussion accompanied by a tense, whispering violin motif over an energetically ascending middle voice and a series of sustained notes in the bass.[68] Blonde has scarcely whispered the words 'if only the moment were already here' when the orchestra bursts in with the same phrase in a jubilant D major, thereby leading back to the beginning with typically Mozartian concision. This foreshortened repeat of the opening section brings all four lovers together in their delight at their imminent release. The new motif that accompanies them at the words 'voll Entzücken' ('full of rapture'), together with its division between voices and orchestra, points in the direction of Grétry. But following this outburst of happiness, the mood very quickly darkens as the two men begin to have doubts about their lovers' fidelity, doubts which, however slight, are far from unjustified, given the practices that were known to prevail in harems at this time. In the andante in G minor, a deeply oppressive atmosphere settles over the scene as a result of an insistently gnawing motif in the second violins and violas with its painful dissonances and syncopated accompaniment. The thought that the menfolk cannot bring

66. Both sections were subjected to extensive cuts in the final version of the aria, with an entire theme being omitted from the opening section and a lengthy coloratura passage from the second; see the critical report to NMA II/5/12.
67. See also Abert, *Jommelli als Opernkomponist*, 195 and 416.
68. A very similar motif appears at Figaro's words 'Mente il ceffo, io già non mento' in the second-act finale of *Le nozze di Figaro*.

themselves to express is twice uttered by the oboe with its half-humorous motif. No less appealing are the little variants in the negotiations between Pedrillo and Blonde. The gnawing motif is now missing and everything has become more terse and quick-witted.[69] The men express their misgivings in greater detail, both of them striking a note of deep embarrassment, Belmonte showing good manners, tact and reserve, while Pedrillo proves insolent, angry and hasty – yet there is a good deal of humour in this admission, not least because the main emphasis lies on the declamatory vocal lines. It provokes the same reaction in both women, only they express themselves differently, with Konstanze bursting into tears and Blonde boxing Pedrillo's ear. By the time that we reach the allegro assai in B flat minor the mood has turned quite nasty, as a surly motif,[70] endlessly repeated, seizes hold of the voices and orchestra before breaking off helplessly on a fermata. At this juncture the resolute Blonde rescues the situation, although, to judge by the Italian slide motif in the orchestra, she continues to harbour suspicions. In their embarrassment, the others simply repeat this motif in turn, culminating in a fermata rest followed by a sudden and totally unexpected outburst of feeling marked adagio. Here is one of those passages where Mozart rises far above the wretched doggerel of his librettist, maintaining the same high level throughout the whole of the A major andantino in 6/8 time. It is as though the lovers were finally shaking themselves free from all the trivial, all-too-human emotions that have occupied their thoughts until now. All four launch into this glorious yet gentle siciliana that hymns the central idea of the work as a whole: the power of an innocent fairy-tale love that is grounded in fidelity. Peace and silent bliss have stolen into their hearts to the strains of a lullaby mingled with those of Christmas,[71] while above it all there floats a note of piety pointing to heaven and to eternity and sublimity. Here the tone associated with the popular singspiel is supremely transfigured in a way that we shall not find again until *Die Zauberflöte*. This brief episode also casts its warming rays over the following allegretto that brings us back to earth again. The bright and conciliatory A major is maintained,[72] and the spirit of peace that had earlier seized hold of all four characters simultaneously now finds expression in each of them in turn. Here Mozart reveals his subtle understanding of human psychology by briefly recalling the earlier quarrel, but this time without any bitterness, with Blonde's ready tongue in particular refusing to be curbed: in a passage in 12/8 time, where she steadfastly maintains the same metre in spite of the 4/4 time of the others, she once again gives Pedrillo a piece of her mind, even though, in begging for her forgiveness, he has already shown the whole honest, good-natured side of his character. Following the celebratory mood of the Andantino, comic elements resurface, but far from cancelling out the earlier mood, they complement it to produce a picture of living humanity. It is entirely characteristic that just as it was the men who were the first to voice their suspicions, now it is the two women who ultimately restore a sense of peace and understanding. Particularly beautiful is the men's heartfelt yet painful plea for forgiveness towards the end, a plea that brings with it the finale's final modulation to the minor and entreating figures in the winds. The request is granted with firmness and assurance, and peace is sealed on a note of calm intimacy. The mood of happiness now finds expression in a final

69. Note also the way in which Blonde's staccato strings are offset against Konstanze's legato.

70. The same motif is found in Perichetto's aria in act three, scene four of Anfossi's *Il geloso in cimento*.

71. Note in particular the *e'* which, in spite of the changing harmonies, is maintained in the upper voice of the first two bars, making it sound like a pealing bell.

72. The A major tonality is strikingly effective after the earlier passages in B flat minor. Indeed, the whole choice of keys in this quartet is extremely instructive for what it tells us about Mozart's approach to tonality in general: in keeping with the changing moods, it modulates from D major to the darker flattened tonalities, including B flat minor, and thence to A major and finally back to D major.

section which, in keeping with the custom of the time, is brilliantly effective rather than profound, its whole spirit, rhythms and hint of canonic procedures recalling French models. Mozart even includes a large-scale Mannheim crescendo, combining it to splendid effect with unison writing in the strings.

As such, this finale could hardly be less Italianate: far from concentrating the action in a sudden and insanely confusing ensemble, it is – by Italian standards – extraordinarily lacking in drama. Even so, it is entirely at one with our overall view of Mozart: the principal danger that threatens the lovers comes not from without – not from the Pasha Selim and Osmin – but from within, from the stirrings of a narrow-minded jealousy that dares to assert itself here. These doubts must first be overcome before the lovers are equal to all the outward dangers and to the threats posed by their enemies. It is no accident that it is the transfigured world of A major that opens up at the very heart of this quartet.

Formally speaking, too, this ensemble goes its own way, admittedly reminding us now of the Italians, now of the French and even, as is clear from the A major section, of the German singspiel. But these traces of foreign influence affect only the surface of the piece: the underlying idea and its execution are and remain Mozartian. The former was essentially the work of the musician for which the librettist needed only to provide the poetical framework: after all, the whole number is based not on any external event, as was invariably the case with French and Italian composers, but on an inner occurrence whose individual phases seem to be born from the spirit of the music. And in the way in which the individual sections are fashioned, too, it is the musician who has the last word. It does not occur to Mozart to follow Logroscino's example, but, instead, to ensure that the form remains clear and intelligible, an approach that has nothing to do with thoughtlessness or respect for the ostensible sanctity of the world of existing forms. Rather, Mozart adopts an entirely creative and proactive approach to form, refashioning it until it produces everything he demands of it, varying, extending and curtailing its various sections and occasionally adding new ones, but without obscuring its basic outlines. For Mozart, form was not fixed and dead like the *da capo* aria of the Neapolitan composers, but something living and in a state of constant flux, reborn with each new creative act. In consequence, it is impossible to speak of the typical form of a Mozartian ensemble or finale in the way that one can speak of a finale by Logroscino, Piccinni or Galuppi, as no two movements are the same with him. All that they have in common is their matchless harmony of form and content.

Now that the lovers have undergone this process of inner transformation, their third-act numbers have a remarkably high-flown, transfigured quality to them. To judge by the preceding dialogue, Belmonte's aria ('Ich baue ganz auf deine Stärke') is intended to be interpreted as a love song sung beneath the seraglio windows and, as such, is similar to the songs sung there every evening by Pedrillo. The important role of the winds may well reflect this serenade tradition. The aria's tone of tender infatuation recalls the E flat major largos of Johann Christian Bach, with the resemblance extending in the present case to the melodic writing, too.[73] Yet there is no sense of mawkishness, and the melodic line, based in the main on triadic intervals, moves in a broad and manly sweep. Of all Belmonte's arias, this is the closest to the Italian style: a ternary structure with an independent middle section, it makes more lavish use of coloratura procedures, a lavishness clearly inspired by Adamberger.

---

73. See, in particular, the aria 'Non m'alletta' from act one, scene ten of *Temistocle*.

Textually speaking, Pedrillo's romance ('Im Mohrenland gefangen war ein Mädel hübsch und fein') is typical of a favourite type of number found in singspiels from Hiller's day onwards and treated by André, Dieter and Knecht in the usual ballad tone, ambling amiably along with no distinctive physiognomy. In his attempt to depict the exoticism of the 'land of the Moors', Mozart, by contrast, has created one of his most original compositions, remarkable not only for its ending, in which the guitar-like chords die away in the night-time darkness, but above all for its tonality, which vacillates incessantly between B minor, D major and F sharp minor. Even the harmonies supporting the vocal line are in a permanent state of flux.[74] The whole number has something incorporeal and ghostlike about it, a quality that also serves to give palpable expression to the uncertainty of the characters' situation, as the vocal melody, too, runs through all five lines without a break before coming to its curious end on the mediant. Its initial sense of valiant momentum grows markedly more subdued towards the close as the intervals shrink and acquire a sharper outline. The piece is unique in the singspiel tradition, combining, as it does, exotic charm with a close reflection of the situation on stage and the character of the singer.[75]

The aborted abduction is exactly what Osmin wanted, and his sense of triumph allows the cruel streak in his character to resurface. With his usual unbridled sensuality he allows it free rein in what Schumann would have termed the outrageous theme of his aria ('O, wie will ich triumphieren'), an aria that reveals Mozart's extremely subtle handling of rondo form:[76] time and again the idea of strangulation flares up without warning, generally following a fermata and with an enormous leap upwards. Only here is the piccolo used in the orchestra, its two non-harmonic notes vividly depicting Osmin garrotting his enemies. The two episodes add further features to this picture, partly complementing it, partly contradicting it: in the first, there is a sense of satisfaction at the fact that he will finally find peace and quiet again. For all his savagery, it is the indolent, anything-for-a-quiet-life philistine that re-emerges here. But first he permits himself a clod-hopping victory dance, then, following Paisiello's example,[77] he once again descends into the

---

74. It is built up of three sequences that descend stepwise through the scale (D major – A major, C major – G major, B minor – F sharp minor), except that the third is only half as long as the others in terms of the number of its bars, with this one half then being repeated.

75. Parisian *opéra comique* was fond of these atmospheric portraits full of local colour, as is clear from the Moroccan song 'Objet divin, femme féconde' in scene seven of Monsigny's *On ne s'avise jamais de tout* and from the Provençal song 'Toute fille en Provence' in Philidor's *L'amant déguisé*. On the harmonic writing, see act two, scene four of Galuppi's *I bagni d'Abano*:

Chi u - na don - na vuol pre - ten - de - re, il de-nar bi - so - gna spen - de - re, e ser - vi - re e sop - por - tar

The flattened second is frequently found in the sicilianas of the Italian *buffa* composers of the period: see, for example, act three, scenes one and seven of Paisiello's *L'osteria di Marechiaro*. ◆ Further, see Manfred Hermann Schmid, 'Die Romanze des Pedrillo aus Mozarts *Entführung*'.

76. Combined with aria form, a form recalled by the sequence of modulations and by the repeat of the first episode.

77. See Pillottola's part in the first-act finale of *L'idolo cinese*, where we also find Paisiello sidestepping into the minor of the subdominant; see also Catuozzo's aria in act one, scene six of *I scherzi d'amore e di fortuna*.

lowest depths of the bass register in his search for peace and quiet,[78] settling first on an A, then on a low D, while a handful of sinister natural sounds are heard in the orchestra, together with a dull rumbling sound. The image is that of a badly domesticated animal that may suddenly wake up and spring at your throat. Far more dangerous and even demonic is the second episode ('Schleicht nur säuberlich und leise'), with its grotesque intervals of an octave and ninth and dissonant suspensions in the accompaniment: behind them lies not only Osmin's whole fanatical savagery but also a good dose of his quintessential complacency. The third episode is remarkable for its use of coloratura to depict Osmin's 'little song of joy', lumbering, blustering its way down to a low E, then skipping back up again through a staccato scale to a trill – the perfect picture of a brutal sensualist who remains uncultured even when enjoying himself.[79] By the end Osmin is no longer capable of forming an orderly melodic line but simply avails himself of odd phrases and fragments of his main theme, flogging them to death in his delight at the thought of imminently strangling his enemies. Finally all that is left are two notes, the tonic and the dominant. Here the enemy of the two lovers and the slave of base instincts is revealed once again in all his grotesque grandeur, albeit already overshadowed by the superior wit of the lovers whose path he darkens one last time. It is the old conflict between sensuality and morality that is fought out here, and just as the former finds its most unrestrained expression in Osmin's aria, so the latter achieves its ultimate transfiguration in the following duet ('Meinetwegen sollst du sterben!'), where it faces its severest test. Only the introductory recitative recalls the threat hanging over the lovers, with its tension-laden *sforzato* motif and, more especially, its restless modulations. The two lovers are sharply distinguished, Belmonte inwardly agitated, Konstanze calm and composed. In the opening section of the duet, by contrast, Konstanze's anguish at her lover's unhappiness and the certainty that the power of her love will triumph over death find markedly clearer expression on her lips. Her resolute outburst

has a rapt, otherworldly quality unique in the operas of this period. Her own and Belmonte's emotions grow more ardent and insistent, finally erupting in all their intensity in an allegro unfairly described by Jahn as less successful:[80] rather, it is a wonderful, if slightly too discursive, hymn to the power of love that once again leaves the librettist's words far behind it. The melodic line is largely made up of what might best be compared to floating arches and contains both individual Italian and French elements, while audibly capturing the German folk tone. Especially noteworthy is the fact that, a number of individual *sforzato* accents notwithstanding, the entire allegro is marked *piano*, maintaining a note of calm and intimate rapture, so that it is wrong to perform it as a heroic duet of the Italian kind.[81]

78. Highly idiosyncratic and, indeed, unparalleled in the operas of this period is the *colla parte* writing for the clarinet at this point

79. The orchestra, too, joins in here with its primitive unison writing.

80. Jahn, *W. A. Mozart*, i.767.

81. For enthusiastic assessments of this duet, see Tieck, *Dramaturgische Blätter* (1825–6), ii.315, and Berlioz, *A travers chants*, 243.

The final number begins with a vaudeville in the good old French tradition ('Nie werd' ich deine Huld verkennen'),[82] the beginning of which is based on a type of melody extremely well known at this time.[83] The tune does the rounds of the various characters,[84] with the whole company joining in the final moral at the end of each strophe and with only Osmin stepping out of line. Annoyed by Blonde, he refuses to allow the others to join in after her own strophe, chiming in with the old tune but soon being overcome by bile and, a weak-willed slave of his instincts, relapsing into the wild onslaught from the ending of his first aria. This, too, is answered by the self-contained ensemble, but on this occasion it is initially not the original vaudeville melody but a remarkably high-flown tune, the tone of which recalls certain sections of the quartet. The number ends with a general chorus, the colour and execution of which are related to those of the earlier chorus ('Bassa Selim lebe lange!').

Mozart himself admitted that he was anxious to appeal to Viennese tastes when writing this opera. But it is instructive to follow the way in which he regarded some features of the highly disparate Viennese singspiel as worth taking over, while rejecting others. Missing, above all, is the low popular local tone that we find in Umlauf and, in a more sophisticated guise, in the songs of Papageno. Missing, too, is the opposite of this tone, the strict contrapuntal writing found, once again, in Umlauf and, in its supremely transcendent form, in *Die Zauberflöte*. Of the other stylistic elements, the emotionally charged tone of the Italian aria is the only one that Mozart has not yet succeeded in integrating organically into the overall context. Conversely, the roles of Osmin and Pedrillo find him borrowing consciously and successfully from the Italian *buffa* style, not by slavishly imitating it but by exploiting and developing it in the service of a far deeper characterization that is much truer to life. The influence of the French *opéra comique* likewise proves to be more pronounced than has been assumed to be the case hitherto: it is most visible in those scenes in which Mozart was at pains to portray the outward surroundings and to depict a particular situation in an especially vivid manner. And it is also found in Blonde's part. But the actual love story, at least to the extent that it revolves around Belmonte, Konstanze's G minor aria and the nub of the finale, is told in the refined tone of the German song, except that in the case of Belmonte's arias in particular it is combined with a good measure of warm Italianate melody. Of course, the German and Italian elements are not yet as perfectly merged as they will later be with Tamino and Pamina, but the few unresolved leftovers are unimportant beside the tremendous overall progress, a state of affairs due first and foremost to Mozart's artistic intuition and to the triumph of his own unique personality and his new attitude to art and to the world. It was this that allowed him to take the countless building blocks assembled by greater and lesser talents before him and on their basis to erect a structure capable of resisting all the vicissitudes of time. Where his librettists had failed in spite of their best endeavours, the musical genius succeeded. Goethe was right when he wrote: 'All our efforts to confine ourselves to the simple and the restricted went for naught when Mozart arrived on the scene. *Die Entführung aus dem Serail* knocked everything into a cocked hat, and there has never been any question of staging our own piece, which was so carefully worked out.'[85] Carl Maria von Weber, too, hit the nail on the head with his wonderful remarks: 'I would even go so far as to say that in *Die Entführung* Mozart's experience of art reached its full maturity and that what came later was his experience of the world. Operas like *Figaro* and *Don Giovanni*

---

82. A famous example from the field of serious music drama is the final number from Gluck's *Orfeo ed Euridice*.
83. See, for example, act one, scene seven of Traetta's *Il cavaliere errante* and act two, scene four of Grétry's *Zémire et Azor*.
84. The instrumentation changes from strophe to strophe: Belmonte has only strings to accompany him, but Konstanze is then joined by a bassoon, Pedrillo by an oboe and Blonde by a flute.
85. Johann Wolfgang von Goethe, *Italienische Reise* (report for November 1787).

justified his contemporaries' expectations of further such works from him; but with the best will in the world he could never have repeated *Die Entführung*. It is as though Mozart had here expressed the very essence of every human being's youthful happiness, something that can never be recaptured and whose charms are inextricably connected with its weaknesses.'[86] The peculiar charm of the work does indeed lie in the youthful innocence and freshness with which Mozart treats his subject, qualities reminiscent of a fairy tale. There is as yet no sign of any deeper emotional complications, with the lovers' joy and anguish finding expression in ways as straightforward as they are immediate. Not even Osmin could be deemed problematical, his savagery notwithstanding. The whole story moves towards its denouement with the self-evident optimism of a fairy tale, which does not need to explain or justify any of its individual details, and Osmin finally disappears like some evil spectre. The musical expression, too, is of strikingly youthful freshness, whether in the form of exuberant heartfelt confessions or outbursts of morbid humour. The opera dates from a happy period in Mozart's life, as his personal circumstances changed, raising him to the very apogee of human existence.[87]

86. Weber, *Carl Maria von Weber*, iii.191.
87. ◆ For a recent, general account of the opera, see Bauman, *W. A. Mozart: Die Entführung aus dem Serail*. Further, see Csampi and Holland, *Wolfgang Amadeus Mozart: Die Entführung aus dem Serail*; Dent, *Mozart's Operas: A Critical Study*; Hocquard, *L'Enlèvement au Sérail (Die Entführung aus dem Serail) précédé de Zaïde*; Kunze, *Mozarts Opern*; Mann, *The Operas of Mozart*; and Osborne, *The Complete Operas of Mozart: A Critical Guide*.

30

Engagement and marriage

Aloysia Weber's father, Fridolin, whom Mozart had known since Mannheim, died in Munich in 1779. The following year Aloysia married the actor Joseph Lange and at the same time was engaged by the National Singspiel in Vienna, an engagement that persuaded her mother, Cäcilie Weber, to move to Vienna, too, where she was accompanied by Aloysia's three unmarried sisters, Josepha, Constanze and Sophie. Their straitened circumstances forced them to sublet their rooms, and Mozart was delighted to be able to move in with his old friends and forget life's daily cares. As early as 2 May 1781 – while he still had unfinished business to sort out with the archbishop – he was already living with Frau Weber 'auf dem Peter im Auge Gottes im 2. Stock', that is, on the second floor of the house known as 'Zum Auge Gottes' at no. 11 Am Peter.[1] Leopold immediately began to suspect that his son would be ensnared by the Weber family all over again, not least because Mozart had again expressed sympathy with their plight.[2] Indeed, Leopold had even heard rumours that Mozart was planning to marry one of the daughters. Accordingly, he insisted that his son should move to another address, a demand that provoked the following reply, dated 25 July 1781:

I repeat that I have long been thinking of finding lodgings elsewhere, simply because people are gossiping; and I'm only sorry that I'm obliged to do so on account of a stupid rumour, not one word of which is true. I just wish I knew what pleasure certain people take in spreading reports that are wholly without foundation. Simply because I'm living with them, I'm marrying the daughter! There was no talk of our being in love; they skipped over that bit, no, I just take rooms in the house and get *married*. If there was ever a time when I've thought *less* of getting married, it is now. For (although the last thing I want is a wealthy wife) if I could now make my fortune by marrying, I couldn't possibly pay court to anyone as I have other things on my mind, God hasn't given me my talent simply for me to hitch myself to a wife and waste my youth in inactivity. I'm only just starting to live, why should I make my own life a misery? I've nothing against marriage, of course, but at present it would be a disaster for me. – Well, there's no alternative; even though it's untrue, I must at least avoid the appearance of such a thing, even though the appearance rests on nothing more than the fact that I'm living here. Unless people come into the house, they can't even say whether I have as much contact with her as with God's other creatures, for the children rarely go out, and when they do, it's only to the theatre and I never go with them, as I'm generally not at home when the play begins. We went to the Prater on a couple of occasions and her mother came, too, and as I was in the house at the time, I couldn't refuse to go with them, but at that stage I still hadn't heard any of these foolish rumours. I must also

---

1. *Briefe*, iii.112 (letter of 9 May 1781).
2. *Briefe*, iii.127 (letter of 9 June 1781).

point out that I was allowed to pay only for myself,[3] and now that her mother has heard this talk for herself and has also heard it from me, I have to say that she herself no longer wants us to go about together and has advised me to move in order to avoid any further unpleasantness; she says she wouldn't like to be the cause, however innocent, of my misfortune. – So this is the only reason why I've had it in mind to move for some time (since people have started to talk), although, as for the truth of the matter, I've no reason to do so; but as for these chattering tongues, I've every reason; – if it weren't for these rumours, I'd hardly think of leaving, for although I'd easily find a nicer room, I could hardly find anything more convenient or meet such friendly and obliging people. Nor do I mean to say that I am ill-mannered towards the mademoiselle to whom people imagine I'm already married and that I never speak to her, but I'm not in love with her; I fool around and have fun with her when time permits (which is only in the evening, when I dine at home, as in the morning I remain in my room, writing, and I'm rarely at home during the afternoon) and – that's all. If I had to marry all the women with whom I've ever shared a joke, I'd have at least 200 wives. . . . Now farewell, dearest and best of fathers, believe your son and trust him, as he cherishes only the most kindly feelings towards all honest people and why should he not do the same in the case of his dear father and sister? Believe him and trust him more than certain people who have nothing better to do than to slander honest folk.[4]

Even so, Mozart found it extremely difficult to tear himself away from Frau Weber's rooms. The Mesmer family offered to put him up at their apartment on the Landstraße, but conditions there were not to his liking. 'Meßmer', he wrote on 13 July 1781, 'has Righini (formerly an *opera buffa* singer and now a composer) staying with him and is his great friend and protector, but Frau Meßmer is even more so.'[5] He was much happier with the Webers. Johann Michael von Auernhammer and his 'fat daughter' Josepha, who enjoyed no mean reputation as a pianist, tried to persuade him to live near them. 'I see Herr von Auernhammer virtually every afternoon,' he wrote on 27 June 1781, 'the young lady is a fright, but her playing is delightful, except that in cantabile playing she lacks the true, delicate singing style and clips everything.'[6] But, according to Mozart himself, the rooms that they wanted to foist on him were 'fit only for rats and mice, but not for human beings. At noon you can find the stairs only with a lantern. The room could be described as a small closet. . . . Even the owner's wife called the house a rats' nest; in a word, it was a dreadful sight.'[7] Mozart also suspected that the family had ulterior – non-artistic – motives, and when

3. According to Riesbeck, *Briefe eines reisenden Franzosen über Deutschland*, i.193, it was the custom in Vienna for women to be paid for by their male companion on these outings, even if he was not at all close to them. Mozart will also have been thinking of his father's earlier reproaches about this open-handedness towards the Webers.

4. *Briefe*, iii.140–2 (letter of 25 July 1781). Leopold's letters have not survived, but were presumably destroyed by Constanze for all too obvious reasons.

5. *Briefe*, iii.139 (letter of 13 July 1781). Mozart subsequently had harsh words to say about Vincenzo Righini (1756–1812), whose later works were much influenced by his own: 'He writes very prettily. He isn't lacking in depth, but he's a great thief, selling his stolen goods in public in such abundance and such vast quantities that people can scarcely digest them'; *Briefe*, iii.153 (letter of 29 August 1781). On 14 September 1812 Zelter wrote to Goethe, 'For us, he was what Salieri, for example, was for the Viennese, perhaps somewhat livelier in character than Salieri, but much the same in terms of breadth and height'; Riemer, *Briefwechsel zwischen Goethe und Zelter*, i.328–9. See also *AmZ*, xvi (1814), 875.

6. *Briefe*, iii.135 (letter of 27 June 1781). Other critics praised her only for her capacity for hard work: see *AmZ*, vi (1804), 471 and vii (1805), 469; also Reichardt, *Berliner musikalische Zeitung*, i (1805), 128. She last appeared in 1813, when the critic of the *AmZ*, noting that she had 'once excelled as a keyboard player in Vienna', described her playing as 'finished and pedantic, but cold and old-fashioned'; *AmZ*, xv (1813), 300 and 372. See also Hanslick, *Geschichte des Concertwesens in Wien*, 125.

7. *Briefe*, iii.150 (letter of 22 August 1781).

Leopold warmly recommended the house, he responded with the following highly characteristic letter, dated 22 August:

He is the finest man in the world – indeed, too much so, as it is his wife, the stupidest and most foolish gossip in the world, who wears the trousers, so that when she opens her mouth, he daren't utter so much as a single word. We've often been out walking together and he has begged me not to tell his wife that we've taken a cab or drunk a beer. Well, I simply can't trust a man like that. . . . He's a decent type and has been a good friend to me and I've often been able to have lunch at his house, but I never make a habit of letting people pay me for *my favours* – which couldn't in any case be bought with a plate of soup at midday. But people like that think they can. If I visit them, it's not for my own advantage, but *for theirs*. . . . I won't describe the mother, suffice it to say that at table it's all you can do not to burst out laughing – basta! You know Frau Adlgasser? Well, this *meuble* is even worse, as she's médisante into the bargain – in other words, stupid and malicious. Now for the daughter. If a painter wanted to paint the devil to the life, it would be her face that he'd have to choose. She's as fat as a farm wench, sweats so much that it makes you sick and goes about so scantily clad that you can read it as plain as anything: 'Please look here.' True, there's enough to see, quite enough, in fact, to strike you blind – but you're punished for the rest of the day if you're unfortunate enough to let your eyes wander in that direction. . . . Ugh! – I've already told you about her keyboard playing and I've also told you why she asked me to help her.[8] It gives me great pleasure to do favours for people, as long as they don't plague me. She's not satisfied if I spend two hours a day with her, but expects me to sit there all day, during which time she then tries to make herself attractive! – but, even worse, she's sérieusement in love with me. I thought at first that it was a joke, but now I know it for a fact; when I noticed it – she took various liberties with me, making tender reproaches, for example, if I arrived somewhat later than usual or couldn't stay for long and so on – I was obliged, in order not to make a fool of the girl, to tell her the truth as politely as I could. But it made no difference, she simply became more infatuated; in the end I was always very polite with her, except when she started fooling around, and then I was rude; – she then took me by the hand and said: '*Dear Mozart, don't be so cross – you may say what you like, but I really am very fond of you.*' Throughout the city people are saying that we're to be married and they're only surprised that I can choose such an apparition. She told me that when people say anything of this kind to her, she always laughs at it; but I know from a certain person that she says it's true, adding that we'll then go off on tour together. That annoyed me. So I recently gave her a piece of my mind and told her not to abuse my kindness. Now I no longer go there every day, but only every other day, and in this way I'll gradually stop seeing her altogether. – She's nothing but an infatuated fool; before she got to know me, she heard me in the theatre and said: 'He'll come to see me

8. She wanted to study the piano for a number of years before going to Paris and 'making a career'. In Cramer's *Magazin der Musik*, ii (1787), 1274, we read: 'Mme Auernhammer is an excellent mistress of the clavier, on which she also gives lessons. I have not heard her for a long time. She it was who supervised and corrected the engraving of many sonatas and ariettas with variations by Mozart at Messrs Artaria's.' She also turned her hand to variations of her own, performing them at her concerts and also having them published; see *Musikalische Korrespondenz*, ii (1791), 362, and iii (1792), 195. By 1799 she had published 63 opus numbers; see *AmZ*, ii (1799), 90. ◆ For the article in Cramer's *Magazin der Musik*, see *Dokumente*, 256, *Documentary Biography*, 290. Auernhammer's publications included variations on numbers from Paisiello's *La molinara*, Mozart's *Die Zauberflöte*, Viganò's *La figlia mal custodita*, Salieri's *La stessa, la stessissima* and Cherubini's *Les deux journées*, among others, as well as six German songs, two keyboard sonatas, a sonata for violin and keyboard and six minuets, also for keyboard. In general, see Deutsch, 'Das Fräulein von Auernhammer' and Hirasawa, 'Josepha Barbara von Auernhammer: Schülerin Mozarts, Pianistin, Komponistin'.

tomorrow and I'll play him his variations in the same style.' Because of this, I didn't go, as it was such a conceited thing to say and also because it was a lie, as I had never said a word about calling on her the next day.[9]

This did not, of course, prevent Mozart from joining forces with Josepha von Auernhammer and performing his double concerto K365 and sonata for two keyboards K448 at a concert at her home on 24 November 1781. The following year he played keyboard duets with her at one of his concerts[10] and in the autumn of that year even postponed a visit to Salzburg in order to be able to keep his promise to perform at her concert at the Kärntnertor-Theater.[11] Finally, it was to her that he dedicated the violin sonatas K296 and K376–380 that he published in 1781.

In early September Mozart moved to new rooms on the third floor at no. 1175 Am Graben,[12] a move accompanied by a further bitter argument with his father, whose mistrust of his son had now reached unprecedented proportions. Mozart's letter of 5 September strikes a particularly irritated note with its bitter complaint about 'all the nonsense that God knows who puts into your head' and its insistence that, in spite of all the gossip that has reached Leopold's ears, he will 'remain the same honest fellow as before'.[13] There is no longer any attempt to deny his relationship with Constanze and the reader has the impression, rather, that Mozart had left far more behind at Zum Auge Gottes than good friends and creature comforts. That Cäcilie Weber had observed her lodger's behaviour towards her daughters with no further thoughts in her head, as Mozart claims, is out of the question, given what we know of her character. With his commission to write *Die Entführung*, his future could hardly have looked rosier and it would have taken a woman far less unscrupulous than Frau Weber to have resisted the temptation to seize the opportunity with both hands, especially when she knew that she was dealing with an artist as guileless as Mozart. Three months later, Mozart saw himself obliged to tell his father everything in his letter of 15 December 1781:

I'm trying to secure a small but secure income here, one which, with the help of whatever chance may provide, will allow me to live here quite well – and then – to marry! – Are you appalled at this thought? I beg you, my dearest and kindest father, to listen to me. I have been obliged to reveal my hand to you, so you must also allow me to reveal my reasons, reasons, I may add, that are eminently justified. The voice of nature speaks as loudly in me as in others, louder, perhaps, than in many a big strong lout. I cannot live as most young people do nowadays. – In the first place, I am too God-fearing, secondly, I love my neighbour too much and am too honourable to seduce an innocent girl and thirdly . . . I care too much for my health to fool around with w . . . . s;[14] and so I can swear that I've never had any relations of that sort with a woman. And if I had had, I wouldn't have kept it hidden from you; after all, it's natural enough for people to err, and to err *once* would be mere weakness – although I wouldn't trust myself to promise that, having erred once, I'd not commit exactly the same error again. – I can stake my life on this. I know very well that, however powerful it may be, this reason is in itself not

9. *Briefe*, iii.150–2 (letter of 22 August 1781).
10. *Briefe*, iii.209 (letter of 25 May 1782).
11. *Briefe*, iii.240 (letter of 26 October 1782).
12. *Briefe*, iii.154 (letter of 5 September 1781).
13. *Briefe*, iii.154; letter of 5 September 1781).
14. ◆ Mozart wrote 'hurren' = 'whores', but Abert evidently couldn't bring himself to use this word.

sufficiently compelling, – but my temperament, which is more inclined to lead a life of peaceful domesticity than to make a great noise, – I, who from my youth onwards have never been accustomed to seeing to my own affairs, be it linen, clothing or the like, can think of nothing more necessary than a wife. – I assure you that I'm often obliged to spend money unnecessarily because I pay so little attention to such matters. – I'm convinced that I'd manage better with a wife (on the same income as I have now) than I do by myself, – and how many useless expenses would be avoided? – True, there would be other expenses instead, but you know what they are and can prepare for them, in a word you can lead a well-ordered existence. – In my eyes, a single person is only half alive – such are my views, I can't help it – I've thought about it enough and I shan't change my mind. – But who, then, is the object of my love? – Don't be appalled, I beg you. – Surely not one of the Webers? – Yes, one of the Webers! – but not Josepha – not Sophie – but Costanza [*sic*], the middle one. – In no other family have I come across such differences in character. – The eldest [Josepha, later Hofer] is a lazy, coarse and deceitful woman who's as cunning as a fox. – Frau Lange [Aloysia] is a false, malicious woman and a coquette. – The youngest [Sophie, later Haibel] – is still too young to be anything, – she's no more than a good-natured, if unduly frivolous, creature – may God keep her from being seduced! But the middle daughter, my good, dear Konstanze, is the martyr of the family, and, probably for that very reason, is the kindest, cleverest and, in a word, the best of them all; – she takes charge of everything in the house – and yet she can do no right. O best of fathers, I could fill whole sheets of paper with descriptions of all the scenes that we've endured in this house; if you wish, I'll do so in my next letter. – I'll stop prattling on in a moment, but first I must tell you more about my dearest Konstanze's character. – She's not ugly, but at the same time not exactly beautiful, – her whole beauty consists in two little dark eyes and a beautiful figure. She isn't witty but has enough basic common sense to be able to carry out her duties as wife and mother. It simply isn't true to claim that she's inclined to be extravagant – quite the opposite, she's used to being poorly dressed, for the little that her mother has been able to do for her children, she has done for the two others, but not for her. – It's true that she'd like to be neatly and cleanly – but not smartly – dressed; – and most of the things that a woman needs she can make for herself, and she does her own hair every day – she knows all about good housekeeping, has the kindest heart in the world – I love her and she loves me with all her heart – tell me, could I wish for a better wife? – I should add that when I gave up my post we were not in love but that this sprang from the tender care and attentions that I received (when I was living in their house). – And so I want nothing more than a small and secure income (of which, thank God, I have high hopes), in which case I shall never stop asking you to allow me to rescue this poor girl – and to make myself and her – and, if I may say so, all of us – happy. – Won't you yourself be happy if I am?[15]

In short, Leopold's suspicions had proved all too well founded, and, given his views on marriage and on the need for a secure income that he had already expressed in the case of Aloysia, it is not difficult to imagine his mood in the present instance. But he knew something that Mozart had failed to mention in the letter under discussion, namely, that Mozart had already had to give a written undertaking that he would marry Constanze, a piece of information that confirmed him in his view that mother and daughter had been intriguing against him. Once again he left no stone unturned in his attempts to avert the inevitable, but as before was soon forced to admit that he

---

15. *Briefe*, iii.180–2 (letter of 15 December 1781).

had lost control of his son. According to Mozart's later letter of 22 December 1781,[16] it had been the daughters' guardian, Johann Thorwart, who had insisted on the written promise of marriage. Thorwart was auditor to the court theatres and inspector of its wardrobe department. An influential figure in the theatre, he was highly regarded by Count Rosenberg and Baron Kienmayr and, at the same time, a sworn enemy of the Italians.[17] Mozart had somehow antagonized him, with the result that Thorwart had incited Cäcilie Weber against him, arguing that Mozart had no secure income and that he would ultimately abandon Constanze. In the end Cäcilie asked Mozart to speak to Thorwart in person:

> He came, I spoke with him, the result (because I hadn't explained myself as clearly as he wanted) was that he told the mother to forbid all contact with her daughter until I had come to a written agreement with him. . . . What else could I do? I had either to give a written undertaking or abandon the girl. Where is the man who, if he loves sincerely and honestly, can forsake the woman he loves? Would not the mother and the woman he loves not place the most terrible interpretation on such an action? That was my predicament. And so I drew up a document to the effect that *I bound myself to marry Mad^elle Constance Weber within the space of 3 years and that if I should change my mind and, as a result, be unable to marry her, she should be entitled to claim from me 300 florins a year.* Nothing in the world could have been easier for me to write. . . . But what did the angelic girl do when her guardian had gone? She asked her mother for the document and said to me: '*Dear Mozart! I need no written assurance from you, I believe what you say*', and tore up the document. This action made my dear Konstanze even dearer to me.[18]

The problem was that, thanks to Thorwart's indiscretion, the whole of Vienna already knew about the affair. Even so, Mozart thought, neither he himself nor Frau Weber was guilty of corrupting the young as it was completely untrue that the Webers had opened their house to him and offered him every opportunity to do what he wanted, only then to entrap him: he would never have set foot in such a house.[19] Peter von Winter, Mozart's old acquaintance from Mannheim,[20] had retailed to Leopold all manner of malicious tales about the couple, prompting Wolfgang to write an indignant letter of complaint: Winter, he averred, was unworthy of the name of a human being; his lifestyle was that of a beast, while his behaviour in general was that of a child, the purveyor of 'infamous lies' that Mozart would not refute by means of 'infamous truths', not least because Winter had once said to him: 'You're a fool to get married. You're earning enough money. You can afford to do so. Keep a mistress. What's stopping you? Some d . . . . . religious scruple?'[21]

Needless to say, Leopold was not satisfied with this answer, and we owe it to his persistent objections that Mozart has granted us so many involuntary insights into the goings-on within the

16. *Briefe*, iii.184–8 (letter of 22 December 1781).
17. Da Ponte, *Memorie di Lorenzo da Ponte da Ceneda scritte da esso*, ii.104; for a recent study of Thorwart, see Blümml, 'Johann von Thorwart'. ◆ Also see Blümml, *Aus Mozarts Freundes- und Familienkreis*.
18. *Briefe*, iii.186 (letter of 22 December 1781).
19. *Briefe*, iii.192 (letter of 16 January 1782).
20. Later, too, Winter was notoriously hostile to Mozart (see Biedenfeld, *Die komische Oper der Italiener, der Franzosen und der Deutschen*, 86), complaining that he had stolen from Handel (see Winter's obituary in *AmZ*, xxviii [1826], 468) and that he was responsible for driving soprano voices higher and higher (Biedenfeld, *Die komische Oper*, 212). His anger at opera composers who played the piano (*AmZ*, xxviii [1826], 467) was no doubt directed at Mozart in particular. That Winter was not as straightforward or as rude as he appeared has been well recognized (see Biedenfeld, *Die komische Oper*, 212), but there is no doubt that he was capable of spiteful intrigue; see also Jahn, *W. A. Mozart*, fourth edition, i.790.
21. *Briefe*, iii.187–8 (letter of 22 December 1781).

Weber household, thereby vouchsafing information that he would otherwise have kept from the outside world. On 10 April 1782, for example, we find him writing as follows:

Your postscript about her mother is justified only insofar as she likes drinking – – and more than a woman should. But – I've never seen her drunk, I'd be lying if I said I had. The children drink only water, and although their mother almost forces them to drink wine, she can't get them to touch it. This often leads to the most violent arguments – can you imagine a mother arguing in this way?[22]

Leopold's suspicion that Constanze's mother would exploit Mozart financially after his marriage was likewise only too well founded, as emerges from Mozart's letter of 30 January 1782:

Both she [Constanze] and I have long been aware of her mother's designs; but she will be proved wrong – as she wanted us (when we're married) to live with her (as she has rooms to let) – but nothing will come of this, as I would never agree to it, and my Konstanze still less, – au contraire – she intends to see very little of her mother, and I'll do all I can to ensure that she doesn't see her at all – we know her for what she is.[23]

But the same letter includes a heartfelt request in relation to Constanze herself:

Just one thing more – for without this I'd not be able to sleep in peace – don't suspect my dear Konstanze of harbouring such evil thoughts, – believe me, I couldn't possibly love her if she really thought such things. . . . Dearest, most beloved father – my only wish is that we may soon meet, so that you may see her and – love her – for – you love kind hearts – I know that!

A similar point emerges from his letter of 9 January 1782:

I can never be happy and contented without my dearest Konstanze, – and unless you, too, are satisfied, I should be only half content; so make me completely happy, my dearest, most beloved father.[24]

Mozart also appealed to his sister, trusting in the fact that they had been very close in times of emotional upheaval in the past and writing to her on 13 February 1782:

I compose till 9. I then go to my dear Konstanz, – though the pleasure of seeing each other is nearly always spoilt by her mother's embittered remarks – as I shall explain in my next letter to my father – hence my desire to set her free and rescue her as soon as possible. – I return home at half 10 or 11; – that depends on her mother's barbed remarks and my ability to endure them.[25]

22. *Briefe*, iii.200 (letter of 10 April 1782).
23. *Briefe*, iii.196 (letter of 30 January 1782).
24. *Briefe*, iii.190 (letter of 9 January 1782).
25. *Briefe*, iii.197–8 (letter of 13 February 1782).

At Mozart's bidding, Constanze also sent his sister all manner of little gifts, including handmade bonnets in the latest Viennese fashion, a small crucifix and a heart with an arrow through it that Mozart thought matched his sister's heart, which also had an arrow through it.[26] According to a letter of 20 April 1782, Constanze had that very day 'finally summoned up the courage to follow the impulse of her kind heart and write to you, my dear sister'.[27]

Nannerl was delighted with these little gifts, but her father continued to oppose the idea of his son's marriage: above all, he regarded marriage without any real prospect of being able to provide for Constanze as completely out of the question. But as Mozart himself admitted in his letter of 23 January 1782, these prospects remained dubious in the extreme:

Dearest, most beloved father! If I could have it in writing from our dear Lord that I would remain healthy and not fall ill, I'd marry my dear faithful girl this very day. I now have 3 pupils and so I'm earning 18 ducats a month. . . . I really need only one more, four would be enough, that makes 24 ducats, i.e., 102 florins and 24 kreutzers – with this sum you can manage here with a wife (living very quietly, as we desire). But if I were to fall ill, we'd have no money coming in. Of course, I can write at least one opera a year, give a concert every year and have some things engraved and published by subscription, and there are also paid concerts, especially when you've been living in a place for some time and are held in high esteem. But I'd prefer to regard these things as extras, rather than as something necessary. But if the bow won't bend, it must break, and I'd rather take this risk than wait any longer. Things can only get better, and the reason why I can't wait much longer is not only because of me, but mainly because of her. I must rescue her as soon as possible.[28]

Not even this letter persuaded Leopold to change his mind. Meanwhile, Mozart was being tormented not so much by his father's attitude but, at least for a time, by that of Constanze herself. A letter that he was forced to write to her on 29 April 1782 is extremely revealing in this regard:

Dearest and best of friends,

Surely you'll still allow me to address you by this name? You can't hate me so much that I'm no longer allowed to be your friend and you – no longer mine? – And – even if you don't want to be my friend any longer, you can't stop me from wishing you well, now that I've become so used to doing so. Do think over what you said to me today. Three times (in spite of all my entreaties) you gave me my marching orders and told me to my face that you want nothing more to do with me. It means more to me than it does to you to lose the object of my love, and I'm not so angry, thoughtless and stupid as to accept your rejection of me. I love you too much to take this step. And so I would ask you once again to reflect and think about the cause of all this unpleasantness, which came about because I was annoyed that you were so shameless and inconsiderate as to tell your sisters – in my presence, be it added – that you had let a young beau measure your calves.[29] No woman who cares for her honour does such a thing. It is a good maxim to do as your companions do. But there are many other factors to be considered here:

---

26. *Briefe*, iii.199 (letter of 23 March 1782).
27. *Briefe*, iii.202 (letter of 20 April 1782). Constanze's postscript may be found in *Briefe*, iii.203–4.
28. *Briefe*, iii.195 (letter of 23 January 1782).
29. This was a fairly widespread practice in games of forfeits and, given the looser morals of the time, was not in itself felt to be risqué. Mozart, by contrast, justifiably took offence as he was already engaged to Constanze at this time.

for example, are only good friends and acquaintances present? am I a child or a girl of marriageable age? in particular, am I already engaged? but, above all, are people of my own social standing present, or are my social inferiors or, even more important, my social superiors present? – Even if it's true that the baroness [Martha Elisabeth von Waldstätten] allowed it to be done to her, that's beside the point, as she's already past her prime (and can't possibly attract men any longer) – and in any case she likes that sort of thing. My dearest friend, I hope that, even if you don't want to become my wife, you'll never want to lead a life like hers. If it was impossible for you to resist the urge to take part – although it's not always good for a man to take part, still less for a woman – why in heaven's name didn't you take the ribbon and measure your own calves yourself (as all women of honour have done in such cases in my presence), rather than allow a young beau to do so (I – I – would never have done so in the presence of others but would have handed you the ribbon myself), still less a stranger about whom I know nothing. – But this is all behind us now, and a brief admission of your somewhat thoughtless behaviour on that occasion would have put everything to rights again and – unless you continue to take it amiss, my dearest friend – can still put everything to rights. You can see from this how much I love you. *I don't get as worked up as you do* – I think – I reflect – and I feel. *If you, too, can feel, if you have any feelings,* I know for certain that I shall be able to say quite calmly today that Konstanze is still the virtuous, honourable, sensible and loyal sweetheart of her honest and well-meaning Mozart.[30]

This tiff was soon forgotten, but it shows the extent to which Constanze, too, had inherited her fair share of her family's impetuous temperament. Meanwhile, however, rumours were continuing to circulate and becoming increasingly unbearable. The emperor, it is true, had spoken favourably of Mozart's marriage on the occasion of a meeting with Clementi and, in the process, had awoken all manner of empty hopes in him, but this had merely encouraged the Viennese to take a greater interest in his fate, not least as a result of the fame that followed on from the success of *Die Entführung aus dem Serail.* On 27 July 1782 we find him writing to his father on a note of utter despair, complaining that most people thought he was already married: Constanze's mother was angered by these rumours and both he and Constanze herself were tormented to death.[31] In their distress – we learn from Mozart's letter of 17 August 1782[32] – the lovers sought comfort in religion. But help was also forthcoming from a secular quarter. Baroness von Waldstätten née Schäffer had been praised for her keyboard skills as long ago as 1766 and had championed Mozart from the time of his first appearance.[33] She now took an interest in his engagement with Constanze. For her part, Constanze was evidently tired of being tormented by her mother and, as a result, accepted the baroness's offer of accommodation at her home at 360 Leopoldstadt. Admittedly, the baroness had a somewhat dubious reputation: she was separated from her husband and, like many female members of the aristocracy at this time, led a fairly dissolute existence, a state of affairs as familiar to Mozart as to the rest of Vienna, with the result that he regarded Constanze's dealings with the baroness with distinctly mixed feelings. Paramount, however, was his sense of gratitude towards her for encouraging his relationship.[34] Frau Weber, by contrast, was beside herself with fury and

---

30. *Briefe,* iii.205–7 (letter of 29 April 1782).
31. *Briefe,* iii.215 (letter of 27 July 1782).
32. *Briefe,* iii.220–1 (letter of 17 August 1782).
33. See Hiller, *Wöchentliche Nachrichten,* i (1766), 100.
34. On 4 January 1783 he warned his father: 'I've heard it from a third party that she'd like to have someone for herself, as she is planning to leave. Well, I just wanted to warn you that, if this is the case, you should be on your guard as she's as changeable

finally sought to bring her daughter back home by force. An undated letter that Mozart wrote to the baroness in the depths of his despair throws particularly revealing light on this whole sorry affair:

Most highly esteemed Baroness,

Mme Weber's maidservant has brought me my music, for which I had to give her a written receipt. – The maid told me something in confidence which, although I do not believe it could happen as it would bring disgrace on the whole family, is none the less possible when one knows how stupid Mme Weber can be; and as a result it causes me some concern. – Sophie arrived in tears, and when the maidservant asked her the reason, she said: 'Tell Mozart in secret to ensure that Konstanze returns home, as my mother is absolutely determined to have her fetched by the police.' – Are the police allowed to enter each and every house here? – Perhaps it's just a trap intended to lure her back home. – But if it can be arranged, the best plan would be for me to marry Konstanze tomorrow morning – or even today, if that were still possible. I don't want to expose my sweetheart to this shameful treatment – and they couldn't do so if she were my wife. – Something else; – Thorwath [sic] has been summoned to appear before them today. – My dear Baroness, could I ask you to let me have your friendly advice and to give us poor creatures a helping hand. – I'll be at home all day. . . . In the greatest haste. Konstanze knows nothing of this as yet. Has Herr von Thorwath been to see you? do the 2 of us need to visit him after lunch?[35]

Against this background, Mozart had to do everything in his power to marry Constanze, and so we find him writing to his father on 27 July 1782 and begging for his permission to marry:

Dearest, best of fathers, I must ask you, must ask you by all you hold dear in the world, to give me your permission to marry my dear Konstanze. – Do not suppose it's just for the sake of getting married, if that were all, I'd gladly wait. – But I can see that it is absolutely necessary for the sake of my honour and that of my girl, as well as for the sake of my health and state of mind. My heart is restless and my head confused – how can anyone think or produce any sensible work in these circumstances?[36]

A few days later, on 31 July 1782, he repeated his request:

In the meantime you will have received my last letter, and I do not doubt that with your next letter I'll receive your consent to my marriage; – you can't possibly object to it, and, indeed, it is clear from your letters that you have no such objections; for she is an honourable, decent girl of good parents, – I'm in a position to support her, – we love each other and want each other; . . . so there's no point in delaying. – It's better to put one's affairs in order – and act like an honest fellow! – God will always reward this; – I'll have nothing for which to reproach myself. –[37]

as the wind – but, however much she may imagine it, she's unlikely to leave Vienna, as she's been planning to do so for as long as I've had the honour of knowing her'; *Briefe*, iii.249. On making further enquiries, Mozart wrote to his father again on 8 January 1783 to say that the baroness was looking for a husband for *herself*, which could mean many things: rumours about her were rife and she was certainly weak-willed, but Mozart refused to speak ill of her as she had been very kind to him and he was obliged, therefore, to defend her as far as possible and, where this was impossible, to say nothing.
35. *Briefe*, iii.217–18 [where it is dated 'shortly before 4 August 1782'].
36. *Briefe* iii.215 (letter of 27 July 1782).
37. *Briefe* iii.216–17 (letter of 31 July 1782).

But Leopold continued to withhold his agreement, so disgruntled was he by the whole affair that not even the success of *Die Entführung aus dem Serail* afforded him any pleasure. Initially he seems not even to have looked at the copy of the score that Mozart sent him and merely complained that the latter had made himself unpopular in Vienna as a result of his presumptuous behaviour. Mozart was indignant at his father's acerbic humour:

So the whole world declares that by boasting about myself and by criticizing others I've made enemies of the professors of music and of others? – what world? – Presumably the world of Salzburg, for everyone here can see and hear enough to be convinced of the contrary; – and this may serve as my answer.[38]

Once again Mozart waited two more days for his father's blessing to arrive, a blessing of paramount importance to him. In the meantime, the Baroness von Waldstätten had not been idle and had swept aside all difficulties, even attempting to persuade Leopold to change his mind,[39] with the result that the wedding finally took place in the Stephanskirche on 4 August 1782. The wedding reception was arranged by the baroness herself.[40] The following day Leopold's consent arrived, together with a letter from Nannerl. Even so, Leopold could not resist the temptation to add that just as he himself could no longer rely on his son's support, so Mozart could expect nothing more from him. Mozart remained supremely indifferent to such a spiteful reaction and, sublimely happy, replied on 7 August:

My dear Konstanze – now (thank God) my actual wife – knew my circumstances and I had long since told her all that I could expect from you. But her friendship and love for me was so great that she willingly and joyfully sacrificed her whole future to my fate. I kiss your hands and thank you with all the tenderness that a son has ever felt for his father for your kind consent and father's blessing. . . . Next post-day my dear wife will ask her dearest, most beloved father-in-law for his paternal blessing and her beloved sister-in-law for her continuing friendship. – The only people present at the wedding were her mother and her youngest sister. – Herr von Thorwarth as guardian and witness for both of us, Herr von Zetto (district councillor), who gave away the bride, and Gilowsky [Katherl Gilowsky's brother, 'the gasbag'] as my best man. When we had been joined together, both my wife and I started to cry; all the others, even the priest, were moved by this and all of them wept to see how much our hearts were moved. – Our wedding reception consisted of a supper given for us by the Baroness von Waldstätten, which was actually more princely than baronial. My dear Konstanze is now looking forward a hundred times more to travelling to Salzburg! – and I wager – I wager that you'll delight in my happiness when you've got to know her, as I'm sure you'll agree that a right-minded, honest, virtuous and amiable wife is a blessing to her husband.[41]

---

38. *Briefe*, iii.216 (letter of 31 July 1782).
39. Leopold wrote to the baroness on 13 September 1782: 'I am delighted to hear that his wife does not take after the Webers, otherwise he would be unhappy; Your Ladyship assures me that she is a good person, and that is enough for me'; *Briefe*, iii.230.
40. According to Nissen, the music played on this occasion was a 'sixteen-part piece for wind instruments' of Mozart's own composition. The piece was presumably the serenade for thirteen wind instruments K361.
41. *Briefe*, iii.218–19 (letter of 7 August 1782). ◆ The wedding contract was signed one day earlier, on 3 August; the witnesses were Dr Franz Wenzel Gilowsky von Urazowa and Johann Carl Cetto.

This, then, was the outcome of the 'Entführung aus dem Auge Gottes', as Mozart jokingly called his marriage to Constanze. It was not a lucky star that looked down on their union. If Mozart had felt impelled to compare his wife's family with his parental home in Salzburg, the differences between them must have filled him with misgivings. Leopold's verdict on the Webers was only too well founded: they were decidedly lacking not only in moral fibre, but in self-discipline and all true nobility of emotion, preferring instead to give free rein to all their basest impulses. In this, their mother was their worthy leader, and in her daughters' guardian she found a like-minded accomplice. Entirely typical of the curious mixture of low cunning and callousness with which the pair of them sought to trap the young composer is the written promise of marriage that they made him sign. But, in spite of recent claims to the contrary,[42] there is no evidence that Mozart was seduced by Constanze and in that way forced to marry her. Such heavy artillery was most certainly not necessary with a man of Mozart's sensitivity: his well-developed sense of honour was sufficient to persuade him to keep his word once it had been given. Of course, one has the distinct impression that he was initially far more deeply involved with Aloysia than was now the case with Constanze. On that earlier occasion, love had assailed his young heart with all its tempestuous force and swept him along with total abandon. His love for Constanze, by contrast, did not possess the same elemental force but had begun as harmless teasing, with Mozart, true to character, no doubt letting himself go rather more than others would have done, and when his passions were then gradually inflamed, it was not hard for the cunning Frau Weber, working in collusion with Thorwart, to tighten the noose around him. Public gossip, in which the two of them played their part, and the resistance on the part of his father merely served to drive Mozart increasingly over to Constanze's side and to cast her in the role of a martyr misunderstood by the whole world and, as such, someone whom he had to rescue at all costs. There is no doubt that his love was honourable and profound and that it grew warmer the more he had to fight for it. But his declarations of love lack the passion and spontaneity that we found in the case of Aloysia, sometimes appearing almost forced in his letters to his father. Yet no praise is too high for the sincerity and moral probity with which he saw the matter through to its end, once he had committed himself to it. It was this that allowed him to emerge as the ultimate victor in the whole sordid affair, however much Frau Weber and Thorwart may have exulted in their successful ruse.

And what of Constanze? It is extremely difficult to gain a clear impression of her character at the time of her engagement and marriage. The majority of surviving reports date from the period of her widowhood and second marriage, by which time her character had changed appreciably under the influence of Mozart and, more especially, Nissen.[43] Yet the mere fact that she did change in this way may offer us the best possible insight into a character that is still inadequately explained, not least as a result of the unfortunate tendency on the part of many biographers to portray the wives of great men as either angels or she-devils.[44] It is not the task of the historian to pass judgement on his subjects' morals. Instead, he must simply stick to the facts of the matter and note that in Constanze's case, too, they are far too complex to allow us to dismiss her whole character more or less out of hand.

There is no doubt, of course, that her family's general moral turpitude had left its mark on her, too. This consisted, above all, in a total lack of self-discipline and of any finer feelings. Instead,

42. Schurig, *Wolfgang Amade Mozart*, ii.5.
43. See Jahn, *W. A. Mozart*, i.800–1.
44. Whereas the typically conscientious Jahn and Deiters content themselves with a cautious, if less than remarkable, character sketch, Schurig holds up Constanze as a veritable monster, encompassing within her all the basest qualities.

the members of the Weber family were ruled by their instincts, acknowledging only a single goal in life, namely, the gratification of whatever redounded to their immediate advantage. When they were not consumed by boundless passion, they wallowed in sentimentality, invariably following the impulse of the moment. Here one thinks in particular of Constanze's thoughtless attitude in her row with Mozart at the time of their engagement and perhaps also of her sudden decision to move out from under her mother's roof. And she was acting in exactly the same spirit when she tore up the infamous contract, an act motivated not by sensitivity but by a momentary fit of sentimentality. Even after Mozart's death the sentimental effusions that she wrote in his family album are all of a piece with her striking indifference towards his place of burial.

It simply will not do to dismiss such vacillations as the sign of a bad character, as such people lack the resolve to be evil, just as they lack the resolve to be good. Instead, they develop by adapting to their present environment, a process particularly well illustrated by Constanze. There is no doubt that, at the time of her engagement to Mozart, she was influenced by her mother and, as such, was entirely typical of the Weber family, as defined by Leopold. Nor is there any doubt that she loved him, albeit in her own instinctively sensual way, without any inkling of the moral foundations on which her future marriage should be based. But during her nine-year marriage to Mozart, her character began to change perceptibly under the influence of his personality. It was not that she now started to brood on moral matters or that she consciously sought to mend her ways. Rather, she gradually adopted his manner, naïvely and unconsciously and, needless to say, only to the extent that she was able to make any sense of it. A number of family features were unfortunately reinforced in this way: Mozart's fiery artistic temperament, his zest for life and his somewhat negligent manner were scarcely calculated to temper her volatile yet indolent nature, and Mozart was the last person capable of setting a good example and instilling in her a sense of domestic virtue. His praise of her good housekeeping skills may perhaps have been true when she was a young girl and still under her mother's strict discipline, but there is ample evidence to indicate that quite the opposite was true of her marriage with Mozart. He himself was incapable of running an efficient household, and since Constanze was far too unsure of herself to step into the breach, she found it easier to do as he did and to let things slide. Never for a moment did it occur to her that she had any particular obligations towards a man like Mozart. In short, his influence on the development of her character was in many respects far from beneficial and, indeed, was positively disastrous for them both in the longer term. Yet he was none the less able to bring out a number of other, more attractive aspects of her character. Anyone reading the diary that she kept towards the end of her life[45] will be agreeably struck by an element of genuine philanthropy and helpfulness that she revealed within her more immediate family. Here we find a note of true emotion alien to the Weber household but presumably acquired from the morally sensitive Mozart. In this respect, the latter was genuinely able to instil in her heart a ray of heartfelt kindness and humanitarian idealism and thus to temper her own instinctual nature. She was also a true and loving mother to her sons, even though it is significant that here, too, she was decidedly biased, preferring the younger Wolfgang to the older Karl. A further curious change of character occurred during her second marriage to Nissen, this decent, pedantic, run-of-the-mill husband, who brought her something she had lacked in her life hitherto: the security that is alone capable of giving vacillating natures of this kind the sense of solid discipline and order that they need. Whereas everything had been at sixes and sevens in the Mozart household, Constanze appears to

---

45. It was published in 1920 in the Salzburg *Mozarteum-Mitteilungen*. ◆ For a modern edition, see Angermüller, *TageBuch meines Brief Wechsels in Betref der Mozartischen Biographie (1828–1837)*.

have been a model housewife in her second marriage, meticulously conscientious and fully in control of the Nissen household. If Constanze Mozart had been even half as efficient and careful as Constanze Nissen appears to have been from her diary, Mozart would have been spared many worries and much hardship. In general, the picture of her that emerges from its pages is that of a not especially distinguished old woman obsessed with the minutiae of everyday life, naïvely devout and devoted to her family. It is certainly not the impression of a woman who had lived the best years of her life at the side of an artist of genius. Great events tend to be remembered by elderly people in particularly bright colours, yet her diary contains barely a trace of any clearer impressions of her life with Mozart that would indicate any deeper inner experiences. All that we find here are generalized expressions of love and devotion, with artistic impressions being strikingly few in number.

This is all the more puzzling in that Constanze, like her sisters, was by no means untalented musically. She 'played the harpsichord and sang most admirably',[46] and during this period Mozart dedicated various works to her. Strangely enough, the majority of these pieces remained unfinished. They include a sonata movement for two keyboards (K375c) headed 'Per la Signora Costanza Weber – ah' and the violin sonata in C major K403 of 1782 headed 'Sonate Première. Par moi W. A. Mozart pour ma très chère épouse'[47] and missing the last few bars of its final movement. Constanze also mentions a keyboard march.[48] But her forte was her singing. Although less gifted than her sisters Aloysia and Josepha, she was still a proficient singer and especially good at sight-reading, with the result that Mozart tried out a number of his works with her. He also wrote some solfeggio exercises 'per la mia cara Costanza' and 'per la mia cara consorte' (K393), as well as shorter 'esercizi' – technical exercises only a few bars in length.[49] The fragmentary aria *In te spero, o sposo amato* (K440)[50], which, according to her letter to Härtel of 25 February 1799, Mozart wrote specially for her, places demands on the voice in terms of its upper range and flexibility that recall Aloysia.[51] She sang not only at family gatherings but also in public, appearing as a soloist in both the C minor mass K427 in Salzburg in October 1783 and in a concert that she herself organized in Berlin in 1796.[52]

She was appreciative of serious music in general and often organized performances of sacred works by Michael and Joseph Haydn[53] at family celebrations at home. But she was particularly attracted to the fugues of Bach and Handel and, as we shall shortly see, she deserves at least some of the credit for the great change than overcame Mozart's whole style in 1782. It was no doubt this

46. Schönfeld, *Jahrbuch der Tonkunst von Wien und Prag*, i.43.
47. ◆ The paper on which the autograph of K403 is written suggests it dates from late 1784 or early 1785, not 1782.
48. This is presumably the opening march from K408 arranged for keyboard, a piece which, as Constanze notes in her letter to Härtel of 25 February 1799, begins in a way strikingly reminiscent of the D major march from *Idomeneo*; see Nottebohm, *Mozartiana*, 122, and Jahn, *W. A. Mozart*, i.801 [Deiters's note].
49. The second of the solfeggio exercises is based on the melody of the Christe from the C minor mass K427, but a whole tone higher and with a different ending. Constanze sang the soprano aria in this mass, so that these exercises were presumably written shortly before it. ◆ K393 is not a coherent 'work', but a diverse collection of five exercises written between 1781 and 1785.
50. From act one, scene two of Metastasio's *Demofoonte*; the opening bars of the draft are reproduced by Nissen, *Biographie W. A. Mozarts*, appendix, 28. ◆ For a modern edition of K440, see NMA II/7/4 and X/30–4.
51. For his wife, Mozart added a brief cadenza to the aria 'Al desio' that he wrote for Adriana Ferrarese del Bene for insertion in *Le nozze di Figaro*; see Thomae, 'Vier Mozart-Handschriften in der Bibliothek des British Museum in London', 485. ◆ It is not certain that the cadenza – which survives in a copy by the Viennese music dealer Lausch (British Library, London, shelfmark Add. Ms. 4316) – was written for Constanze.
52. ◆ For Constanze's performance in Salzburg, see *Dokumente*, 194, *Documentary Biography*, 219. Abert is apparently mistaken, however, in claiming that Constanze performed the work in Berlin in 1796. Her concert there, on 28 February, included selections from *La clemenza di Tito*, two unidentified arias and the overture to *Die Zauberflöte*; see *Dokumente*, 417, *Documentary Biography*, 479.
53. Niemetschek, *Leben des k. k. Kapellmeisters Wolfgang Gottlieb Mozart*, 64.

that brought husband and wife together so quickly. Of course, she never suspected what a great artist Mozart was, and it would be foolish to reproach her for this. But she undoubtedly realized that he was talented and, indeed, Nissen indicates that she 'felt more for his talent than for his person'.[54] Even so, this musical influence of hers had its limits, a state of affairs generally attributed to the fact that Mozart's creativity needed no such stimulus.[55] We hear that she was happy to tolerate his absent-mindedness whenever he was pursuing his own independent musical ideas and that she read him fairy tales and children's stories while he was working, stories that gave him all the greater pleasure the more farcical they were. He invariably asked her to read to him and was never disturbed when she did so.[56] Mozart evidently never missed the stimulus that so many nineteenth-century artists received from their highly educated wives, yet the fact that he did not allow Constanze to share in the wealth of his inner visions may be due to the fact that, her musical talents notwithstanding, she was not the person capable of understanding his view of the world in general and of art in particular. This was simply denied to her. For all her gifts, she lacked the talent to become his muse, and it was only long after his death, when his fame first started to fill the world and she received visits from enthusiastic admirers of his music from all over the world, that she gained a vague insight into the true greatness of the man who for nine years had led an undemanding and pitiful existence at her side.

Mozart, by contrast, was devoted to her with all the uncomplicated affection and gallantry that were his. With great sensitivity he soon discovered ways of maintaining and safeguarding her love, showing unfailing kindness in accepting her as she was and finally managing to overlook all the less attractive aspects of her character and bring to the surface all the positive emotions that she was capable of feeling. Above all, he got to know her love of life, which struck a chord in him, and he did all that he could to keep her in a good mood. The outward impression left on others by the Mozarts' marriage is recorded by the loyal Niemetschek:

> Mozart led a life of contentment in his marriage with Constanze Weber. He found in her a kind and loving wife admirably adept at adopting his own disposition and thus winning his whole trust and a power over him that she used only to prevent him from acting overhastily. He loved her and confided everything in her, even his petty indiscretions – and she repaid him with tenderness and loyal care. Vienna bore witness to this treatment and it is not without emotion that the widow recalls this period of her marriage.[57]

The carefree couple were soon a familiar sight in Vienna. While out walking in the Augarten one day, they were playing with Constanze's pet dog and she asked him to beat her by way of a joke, saying that the dog would then attack him in its fury. Just as he was doing so, the emperor came out of his summer house and saw them: 'Oh dear, married for only three weeks and he's already beating you!', whereupon Mozart laughed and explained the situation. When, in 1785, there was widespread gossip about Lange's unhappy marriage,[58] the emperor told Constanze in the course of one of their meetings: 'What a difference to have a decent husband!'[59] The tenor Michael Kelly likewise reports that Mozart was 'passionately fond' of his wife.[60] The letters that he wrote to her

54. Nissen, *Biographie W. A. Mozarts*, 415.
55. Jahn, *W. A. Mozart*, i.803.
56. Nissen, *Biographie W. A. Mozarts*, 689.
57. Niemetschek, *Leben des k. k. Kapellmeisters Wolfgang Gottlieb Mozart*, 63–4.
58. See also Friedel, *Briefe aus Wien verschiedenen Inhalts an einen Freund in Berlin*, 409.
59. *Briefe*, iii.412–13 (letter from Leopold to Nannerl of 17 September 1785).
60. Kelly, *Reminiscences*, i.225.

in later years, while travelling, offer eloquent proof of his tender feelings for her, and she herself later set great store by their becoming adequately known 'in his honour'.[61] She was often ill following the birth of their children – in 1789 her condition was even critical for several months – and during these periods his self-sacrificial attentions show him in the best possible light. He left no stone unturned in his attempts to ease her burden of suffering, however much his budget was stretched by her repeatedly taking the waters at Baden.[62] He frequently went out riding at five in the morning, but always left a note by his wife's bedside with instructions such as the following:

> Good morning, dear little wife, I hope you slept well, that nothing disturbed you, that you don't get up too suddenly, that you don't catch cold, don't bend, don't stretch, don't lose your temper with your servants and don't fall over the step in the next room. Avoid all domestic chores until I get home. As long as nothing happens to you. I'll be back at – o'clock.[63]

Another touching feature is mentioned by Sophie Haibel:

> Oh, how attentive M — t was when something was wrong with his dear wife. Thus it was once when she was seriously ill and I nursed her for 8 long months. I was just sitting by her bed, Mozart too. He was composing at her side; I was observing her sweet slumber, which had been so long in coming. We kept as quiet as the grave so as not to disturb her. Suddenly, an unmannerly servant came into the room. Moz. was terrified that his dear wife might be disturbed from her gentle sleep, tried to beckon the man to keep quiet, pushed the chair back behind him, but happened to have his pen-knife open in his hand. This impaled itself between the chair and his thigh in such a way that it dug in up to the handle in the thick flesh. Moz., who usually made such a fuss, did not stir but, biting back his pain, he only signalled to me to follow him. We went to the room in which our mother was living secretly, for we did not want the good Mozart to realize how ill she was, and that her mother was there in case of need. She bound him up and put oil of cubebs into his very deep wound; with this St John's oil she succeeded in healing him, and although he had to limp somewhat from the pain, he managed to conceal it and keep it from his dear wife.[64]

The care that Mozart lavished on his wife did not, of course, mean that he was entirely faithful to her. He himself admits that he was susceptible to feminine charms and fond of joking and fooling with every young woman whom he fancied. But things went further than these harmless flirtations, and although his hot blood and artistic temperament were not such that he went out of his way in search of extra-marital erotic experiences, there is no doubt that he made no attempt to avoid them either. We may believe him when he states that he was not interested in prostitutes, yet he was not exactly fastidious in his choice of his lovers' social standing. None the less, he was open enough to admit to these 'goings-on with chambermaids', as Constanze termed his affairs

61. Constanze Mozart, 'Noch einige Kleinigkeiten aus Mozarts Leben', 855.
62. Only on one occasion did an enthusiastic admirer of Mozart's music defray the costs of such a visit. A tripe-boiler by the name of Rindum, who did not know Mozart personally, arranged for Constanze to take the necessary baths in his own house and provided her with board and lodging, while steadfastly refusing to accept any payment; see Niemetschek, *Leben des k. k. Kapellmeisters Wolfgang Gottlieb Mozart*, 62 and Nissen, *Biographie W. A. Mozarts*, 686–7.
63. Mozart, 'Einige Anekdoten aus Mozarts Leben', 291; see also Nissen, *Biographie W. A. Mozarts*, 687.
64. Jahn, *W. A. Mozart*, i.804. During his wife's illness, he became so used to receiving visitors by placing a finger to his lips and whispering 'sh' that even after she had recovered, he continued to whisper 'sh' to his acquaintances whenever he met them in the street [*Dokumente*, 451, *Documentary Biography*, 526].

with these Zerlina-like figures, and she forgave him because, as she herself explained, he was 'so affectionate that it was impossible to be cross with him, you simply had to be friends with him again'. In fact, it is clear from her sister's remarks that this was not always the case and that there were sometimes violent arguments between the two of them, especially when Mozart's roving eye alighted not on chambermaids but on singers, whom Constanze rightly saw as more serious rivals for his affections.[65] It is no longer possible to say who these women were, although literary gossip, with its predilection for such things, has inevitably drawn up an entire catalogue of Leporello-like length from which barely a single one of Mozart's pupils and performers is missing. Indeed, Mozart has even been proposed as the real-life model for Don Giovanni, with commentators – especially today – regarding a particularly active love life as the principal sign of true artistry. Mozart was in fact never like Don Giovanni, and it is extremely unlikely that the great female figures in his operatic masterpieces are based on particular individuals. More probably they resemble his male characters in being products of his imagination. At all events, it is striking that not one of these alleged models has ever been identified. Mozart's gallant adventures must in any case be measured by the standards of morality that obtained in Vienna at this time.[66] Against this background, it is no more possible to dismiss the composer as a rakish Bohemian than it is to absolve him of all such 'sins', as the moralizing Jahn does.[67] We have no right to judge as exceptional an artist as Mozart by the standards of bourgeois morality but do well to accept him as he is.

Notwithstanding all this, the marriage suffered no lasting damage. Constanze, too, often gave her husband cause to reproach her for her excessively liberal ways. 'Of course I'm glad when you are happy,' we read in a letter of August 1789, 'I just wish you didn't sometimes make yourself so cheap. . . . A woman must always take care that she is respected, or else people start talking.'[68]

In spite of his occasional tendency to fly into a rage, Mozart sought constancy in his life, as is clear from a letter that he wrote from Prague on 4 November 1787 to one of his closest friends, Gottfried von Jacquin:

Well, dearest friend, how are you? I hope you're *all* as fit and as well as we are; you can't fail to be happy, dearest friend, as you possess everything that you can wish for at *your age* and *in your position*! especially now that you seem to have given up your earlier, somewhat restless lifestyle. So you've gradually become convinced of the truth of the little sermons that I used to inflict on you? You must have discovered by now that the pleasure of a fickle, changeable love could hardly be further removed from the bliss that comes from true and rational love. I expect you often thank me in your heart of hearts for my lectures! You'll end up making me quite conceited! – But, joking apart, – you should be grateful to me if you've become worthy of Fräulein N., as I played a not insignificant role in reforming or converting you.[69]

It was during the summer of 1791 that gossip about Mozart's ostensibly immoral lifestyle reached its greatest heights. Constanze was again taking the waters at Baden and he was staying with Emanuel Schikaneder, whose rakish behaviour was the talk of the town. The resultant sense

65. Schurig sees in Donna Elvira a reflection of Constanze, but in this case, in contrast to his normally deeply dismissive attitude towards her, he does her far too much honour; *Wolfgang Amade Mozart*, ii.308.
66. See Georg Forster, *Sämtliche Schriften*, vii.268.
67. Jahn, *W. A. Mozart*, i.805ff.
68. *Briefe*, iv.96–7 (letter of mid-August 1789).
69. *Briefe*, iv.58–9 (letter of 4 November 1787).

of freedom, coupled with Schikaneder's bad example, encouraged him to indulge in wild excesses, and as this was the final summer of his life, it was these goings-on that stuck in people's minds.[70]

Mozart's outward situation during the last ten years of his life affords a particularly depressing picture, made up, as it was, of an unbroken series of cares, privations and illnesses of every description which, when combined with his tremendous and occasionally feverish desire to work, slowly but surely undermined his already delicate health. He himself was largely to blame for this, of course. He lacked the ability to see things in their true light and, worse, lacked the resolve to turn them to his own advantage. Leopold was quite right to regard his marriage as ill-considered on practical grounds alone, as his prospects of earning a regular living had never been less good. But once the step had been taken, husband and wife should have seized firm control of their foundering vessel and all their possessions and, by their decisive actions, steered it away from the reef on which it threatened to be wrecked, while conserving their energies for the battle for survival. That Mozart himself was completely inexperienced in all financial matters is something we discovered long ago. He remained so in marriage. Good-natured to the last, he strove tirelessly, of course, to see to all his most immediate concerns and in particular to lighten his wife's crippling burden of care. But all his attempts in this direction remained isolated and aimless, undertaken, as they were, on the spur of the moment. Not once did the Mozart household feel the firm hand of a leader. But it is Constanze who must bear the lion's share of the blame for this, for it was her duty to step into the breach. As we know from her marriage to Nissen, she had considerable gifts as a housekeeper, but these gifts first had to be discovered and guided along the right lines by her husband, and Mozart was simply not the right person to do this. As a result, she remained a typical Weber, making demands on life, while not taking its obligations sufficiently seriously. The result was a disorderly and irregular lifestyle that merely undermined Mozart's health yet further.

In spite of the success of *Die Entführung aus dem Serail*, Mozart's reputation in Vienna still fell short of that of the musicians who, long established in the city, set the local tone. The Viennese knew virtually nothing about his early Italian operas, the success of *Idomeneo* had remained confined to Munich, and even *Die Entführung* had encountered reservations, not least on the part of the Emperor Joseph II. Finally, the sacred works that Mozart had written for Salzburg were largely unknown to the wider public.[71] In the eyes of the Viennese, composers such as Salieri, Bonno, Starzer and their like had achieved far more, to say nothing of Gluck. All these composers, moreover, held tenured posts, whereas one would have to be created specially for their newly-arrived rival. But the prospects of such an appointment at the thrift-conscious imperial court were very slight. And his failure to gain a position with Princess Elisabeth had drawn Mozart's attention to a number of other enemies of a different order, with the result that when, in spite of the acclaim, *Die Entführung* failed to produce the appointment that he had been hoping for, he decided to turn

---

70. Even Mozart's pupil, who normally defended him against the charge of 'debauchery', admits that this was true: see Jahn, *W. A. Mozart*, i.807. The depths to which this gossip could sink emerges from a report by Suard in his *Mélanges de littérature*, v.339: 'I have heard it said that he wrote *la Flûte Enchantée* only to please a woman of the theatre with whom he had fallen in love, and who had offered him her favours at this price. It is added that his triumph had very cruel consequences, and that he contracted from it an incurable disease of which he died shortly after. This fact seems to me to be very unlikely; *la Flûte Enchantée* is not the last of his operas, and when he composed it, his health was already seriously impaired' [*Dokumente*, 429, *Documentary Biography*, 498].

71. ◆ It is curious that the usually scrupulous Abert should make these claims: *Die Entführung* was effectively an unqualified success and there is no compelling evidence that Joseph II had reservations about the opera, at least not of the sort suggested here. Nor was it Mozart's fault that his church music was not widely known in Vienna: Joseph II's church reforms put a virtual halt to the composition and performance of church music in the city; in neither composing new works nor disseminating his earlier masses, Mozart was no different from other local composers.

his back on Vienna, flaring up, as he always did when a plan unexpectedly miscarried. The whole pride of the German artist in him finds expression in his letter to his father of 17 August 1782:

> The Viennese gentry (by which I mean the emperor in particular) shouldn't think that I'm on this earth solely for the sake of Vienna. – There is no monarch in the world whom I'd rather serve than the emperor – but I have no intention of begging for a post. I believe I'm capable of being a credit to any court. If Germany, my beloved fatherland, of which (as you know) I am proud, will not accept me, then in God's name France or England shall become the richer by another talented German – and to the shame of the German nation. You know very well that it is the Germans who have always excelled in virtually all the arts. – But where did they find their fortune? and make their reputation? – certainly not in Germany! – Even Gluck – was it Germany that made him the great man he is? – unfortunately not! Countess Thun, Count Zichy, Baron van Swieten, even Prince Kaunitz are all very annoyed with the emperor for not valuing men of talent more and for allowing them to leave the country. – Recently, when my name came up in conversation, the last-named told Archduke Maximilian that '*such people come into the world only once every 100 years and shouldn't be driven from Germany – especially when we're fortunate enough to have them in the capital*'. – You can't imagine how kind and courteous Prince Kaunitz was when I visited him; – at the end he said: '*I am much obliged to you, my dear Mozart, for having taken the trouble to visit me* etc.' And you wouldn't believe the trouble that Countess Thun, Baron van Swieten and other luminaries are taking to keep me here; – but – I can't go on waiting like this – and I won't be dependent on their mercy – I find that (even if he is the emperor) I really don't need his favours.[72]

Mozart was seriously thinking of going to Paris the following Lent and had already written to Legros in the hope that commissions from the Concert Spirituel and Concert des Amateurs would help him to find pupils; but it was really the Opéra on which he had set his sights.[73] He had already started using his French again and had even had three English lessons with a view to visiting England.[74] These plans were already being formulated within two weeks of his marriage, so that it is no wonder that Leopold raised express objections to them, even writing to Baroness von Waldstätten on 23 August 1782:

> I should be entirely reassured [about his marriage], were it not that I have detected in my son an outstanding fault, which is that he is far too patient or indolent, too easy-going, perhaps even too proud, in short, that he has the sum total of all those traits that render a man inactive: or he is too impatient, too hasty and will not wait. Two opposing precepts rule him – too much or too little, never the golden mean. If he is not actually in want, then he is immediately satisfied and becomes indolent and inactive. If he has to bestir himself, he feels equal to it and immediately wants to make his fortune. Nothing must stand in his way, but unfortunately it is the cleverest people and those who possess outstanding genius who have the most obstacles to contend with. Who is there in Vienna who would prevent him from pursuing his present career if only he had

72. *Briefe*, iii.220–1 (letter of 17 August 1782).
73. As we know, Gluck had recommended Salieri to the Paris Opéra in 1784 as a suitable composer for *Les Danaïdes*; see Mosel, *Ueber das Leben und die Werke des Anton Salieri*, 77ff.
74. A book containing essays and letters that Mozart used as English exercises was used as an accounts book in 1784; see Johann Anton André, *Thematisches Verzeichnis W. A. Mozartscher Manuskripte, chronologisch geordnet von 1764 bis 1784*, 3. ◆ Further, see *Briefe* iv.312 and 317.

a little patience? – Kapellmeister Bonno is ancient – when he dies, Salieri will be promoted and make room for someone else, and isn't Gluck an old man, too!? – My dear Baroness, tell him to be patient and kindly inform me of your opinion in this matter.[75]

On this occasion Leopold got his way and Mozart decided to delay his departure from Vienna, arguing that France and England would always be open to him.[76] Initially, moreover, he was pleased with the progress that he had made in Vienna. As a result of the collapse of the National Singspiel, it was impossible, of course, for him to continue along the road on which he had set out with *Die Entführung*. And he was overlooked when an Italian opera company was established. But in 1786 the emperor invited him to write *Der Schauspieldirektor* and *Le nozze di Figaro*.[77] On the other hand, the appointment that he most hoped for continued to elude him, and now he began to have serious thoughts about returning to England, an idea encouraged by a number of English-speaking visitors who frequented his house in Vienna at this time. These were Thomas Attwood (1765–1838), who had returned to Vienna from Italy in 1785 and become Mozart's pupil; and two members of the Italian Opera, the Irish tenor Michael Kelly and the soprano Nancy Storace, whose brother, the composer Stephen Storace, was also in Vienna for a time. Early in November 1786 Mozart wrote to his father to inform him of his decision to leave Vienna with Constanze during the second half of the coming carnival and to travel via Germany to England. But he could do so only if Leopold agreed to look after their two children and their maids during this period. 'I wrote him a proper letter,' Leopold informed his daughter on 17 November 1786, 'and promised that I would continue my letter with the next post. – [. . .] Not at all a bad arrangement, – they could travel at their convenience – might even die – might stay in England – – I'd have to run after them with the children and so forth, and as for the payment he offers me for the children and for the maids to look after them – basta! If he cares to do so, he'll find my excuse very clear and instructive.'[78] Clearly, Leopold's refusal to help was inspired by his old anger towards his son and daughter-in-law, a supposition confirmed by the fact that Nannerl had married in August 1784 and was currently lying in at his house. He later took in her newborn son Leopold, but omitted to mention this fact to Mozart. For the time being the latter abandoned his plans to go to England, only to revive them at the beginning of 1787, when his friends set off back to London. On this occasion Mozart agreed to follow them once Attwood had organized a subscription for a series of concerts or obtained a commission for him to write an opera for London. Again he hoped that his father would take charge of his children until he had decided whether to remain in England permanently or to return to Germany. Attwood, Kelly and the Storaces broke their journey in Salzburg to call on Leopold, a visit that delighted both parties[79] but failed to allay Leopold's

75. *Briefe*, iii.222–3 (letter of 23 August 1782).
76. *Briefe*, iii.224 (letter of 24 August 1782); see also Leopold's reassured letter to Baroness von Waldstätten, *Briefe*, iii.228–30 (letter of 13 September 1782).
77. ◆ Although Joseph II commissioned Mozart to compose *Der Schauspieldirektor*, he had to have his arm twisted – as Abert later argues – to agree to put *Le nozze di Figaro* into production (and then only after at least part of the work had been composed). It is not exactly the case, then, that Joseph 'invited' Mozart to compose the opera.
78. *Briefe*, iii.606 (letter of 17 November 1786).
79. Kelly, *Reminiscences*, i.277–9. Leopold, too, gave his daughter a full report of the meeting. The visitors were also invited to perform at the court and were very well received by Colloredo. ◆ Leopold's report appears in his letter of 1–2 May 1787: 'At half past 6 on Monday evening I received a note from *Mme Storaci*, the Viennese theatre singer, announcing that she'd arrived at the Trinkstube. I found her with her mother, who's English (the daughter was born in England), and also the Viennese theatre tenor Ochelly [O'Kelly], who's also English [*recte* Irish], another Englishman whom I didn't know but who's probably the cicisbeo of mother or daughter, her brother Maestro Storacci and a little Englishman called *Attwood*, who was sent to Vienna 2 years ago specially to have lessons with your brother. Madame Storaci had a letter of introduction from Countess Gundacker Colloredo,

reservations about his son's trip to England. On 2 March 1787 he told Nannerl that his visitors had insisted that Mozart 'would gain nothing by going to England in the summer and would arrive at the wrong time, that he should have *at least* 2000 florins in his pocket before undertaking this journey and finally that, unless he had already procured some definite engagement in London, he would have to be prepared, no matter how clever he was, to be hard up at first, with the result that he will have lost courage, particularly because the soprano's brother will of course write the opera for the next season'.[80]

Once again Mozart abandoned his plans, but on this occasion rumours were already circulating in Vienna,[81] prompting the emperor to offer him a permanent appointment and in that way to bind him to Vienna. Unfortunately Leopold did not live long enough to enjoy his son's change of fortune as he died on 28 May 1787. No post as Kapellmeister was currently available, and so Joseph appointed Mozart his chamber musician on an annual salary of 800 florins.[82] That it was not more was attributed to the influence of Johann Kilian Strack, yet there is no reason to regard this sum as derisory: it was a typical starting salary, and none of the musicians belonging to the imperial chamber received more. Still less can it be compared with the salary of a man like Gluck,[83] whom Maria Theresia had appointed imperial and royal chamber composer on 18 October 1754 on 2000 florins a year. Gluck was already an internationally celebrated composer at this time and had commended himself to the Viennese court by writing a large number of works for the imperial family. He died on 15 November 1787, mourned as a veritable prince of the world of music. It is impossible in the circumstances to reproach Joseph for paying less to a composer who, however promising, was still a relative newcomer.[84] For his part, Mozart was initially quite content with this salary. If he later felt offended, it was simply because he was given insufficient opportunity to earn it. He received far too few commissions from the court and felt paralysed as a creative artist. When he was required to write down how much he was worth on a sealed document, he added the embittered words 'Too much for what I am doing, too little for what I could do'.[85] He had been told, of course, that his salary would be increased as and when the opportunity arose, but the emperor never returned to this point. The final years of Joseph's life were filled with all manner of cares and, as a result, his interest in art and artists inevitably cooled, while his concern for the young Mozart soon faded into the background, not least in consequence of the latter's inability to remind the emperor of his existence.

Only on one occasion, if we may believe a widely reported tradition, did Mozart have a chance to extricate himself from all his artistic and financial problems, namely, when he was in Berlin in

and so she had to be *heard* and *well treated*, as she's returning to the theatre in Vienna after a year-long stay in London. From 10 till 2 on Tuesday morning I galloped round the town to show them this and that. We didn't get our midday meal till 2. In the evening she sang 3 arias and they left for Munich at *12 o'clock at night*' (*Briefe*, iv.28–9).

80. *Briefe*, iv.29 (letter of 2 March 1787).

81. In a report dated 23 April 1787 and published in Cramer's *Magazin der Musik*, ii (1787), 1273, we read: 'Some weeks ago, Mozart set off on a musical tour to Prague, Berlin and, it is said, even to London. I hope it redounds to his advantage and pleasure' [*Dokumente*, 255, *Documentary Biography*, 290]. And on 12 January 1787 we find Leopold writing to his daughter: 'I am still receiving reports from Vienna, Prague, and Munich that confirm the rumour that your brother is going to England' (*Briefe*, iv.7).

82. Niemetschek, *Leben des k. k. Kapellmeisters Wolfgang Gottlieb Mozart*, 30. A number of the details found in Rochlitz's account, which is itself based on information given to him by Constanze ('Verbürgte Anekdoten aus Wolfgang Gottlieb Mozarts Leben', 22–4), were corrected by Nissen, *Biographie W. A. Mozarts*, 535–8. According to Deiters's revisions to Jahn, *W. A. Mozart*, i.812, the emperor made the appointment in person, bypassing the usual report that would normally have been submitted by his Lord Chamberlain, Count Rosenberg. In the court and state records, Mozart appears under the heading of the 'Imperial and Royal Court Chamber Musicians' or 'Chamber Musicians', with the additional qualification of 'composer'. In other words, he was 'Imperial and Royal Chamber Composer', but not 'Kapellmeister in the actual service of his Imperial and Royal Majesty'.

83. Jahn, *W. A. Mozart*, i.812.

84. ◆ Further, see Link, 'Mozart's appointment to the Viennese court'.

85. Constanze Mozart, 'Einige Anekdoten', 291.

May 1789 and King Friedrich Wilhelm II offered him the post of Kapellmeister on a salary of 3000 thalers. Mozart is said to have answered, with tears in his eyes: 'Do you expect me to abandon my dear emperor?' The king is then reported to have promised to think the matter over and promised to keep his offer open, regardless of when Mozart might return. It is said that on his return to Vienna Mozart kept the matter to himself and that only at the insistence of his friends did he mention it to the emperor and ask for his dismissal. Joseph was apparently dismayed: 'What? You want to leave me, Mozart?' The latter, moved, had then replied: 'Your Majesty, I am at your service, I'll stay.' When a friend asked him whether he had taken the opportunity to ask for an increase in his Viennese salary, he replied indignantly: 'May the devil alone think of such things at a time like that!'[86]

A number of writers[87] have questioned the authenticity of this touching tale, and their reasons for doubting it are certainly compelling. At no point in his letters does Mozart himself mention an offer that would have had such a decisive impact on his future, and Niemetschek – normally so sensitive to such matters – is likewise unaware of it. The Berlin archives likewise contain no evidence to support such a claim.[88] Moreover, Mozart had undertaken the whole journey in the secret hope of obtaining an appointment in Berlin, so it is hardly likely that, having achieved his ambition, he would suddenly have abandoned the idea in a moment of mere sentimentality. He was never as foolishly feeble-minded as that. He would have had no reservations about accepting if such an offer had been made. Moreover, all his letters indicate that his devotion to Joseph II was not so great that he would have turned down an advantageous position elsewhere, while, for his part, King Friedrich Wilhelm II was not the sort of person who would unhesitatingly have created such a well-paid job for a complete outsider above the heads of his local musicians. At best, the two men may have discussed the possibility of an appointment, with no commitment on either side, discussions which, in the minds of imaginative and sensitive souls such as Rochlitz, were then transformed into the legend before us. It is a legend, moreover, that does Mozart a grave disservice, and it is high time that we ceased to regard such adolescent sentimentality as an integral part of his character. Once this has been done, we may also dispose of the claim that the commission to write the opera *Così fan tutte* was a reflection of the 'gratitude of the house of Austria'. This was the last commission that Mozart received from Joseph II, who died on 20 February 1790. Following the succession of Leopold II, Mozart hoped to be appointed second Kapellmeister alongside Salieri, who had taken over Bonno's post in 1788.[89] But again he was unsuccessful. In the light of these latest experiences with the Viennese court, he addressed an appeal to the city's magistracy, asking to be appointed Leopold Hofmann's assistant at St Stephen's. His request was granted, and Mozart was even told that he would be offered Hofmann's post in the event of the latter's death, but the elderly organist survived him, with the result that this prospect, too, came to nothing.[90]

86. The chief source of this tale, Friedrich Rochlitz, reports that the king divulged the contents of this conversation to various individuals and also to Constanze herself, during her stay in Berlin in February 1796. ◆ In fact, the story is a conflation of two anecdotes reported separately by Rochlitz; see Solomon, 'The Rochlitz Anecdotes', 9–11.

87. Schurig, *Wolfgang Amade Mozart*, ii.185–6, quite rightly raises objections to the authenticity of this account, whereas Jahn, *W. A. Mozart*, i.813, continues to believe it to be true.

88. All the material relating to Mozart's stay in Berlin has been collated and published by Friedländer in 'Mozarts Beziehungen zu Berlin'. ◆ Further, see *Dokumente*, 298 and 303–4, *Documentary Biography*, 340 and 346.

89. Mosel, *Salieri*, 132.

90. The claim that Mozart was offered Hofmann's post on his return from Prague in September 1791 (see Niemetschek, *Leben des k. k. Kapellmeisters Wolfgang Gottlieb Mozart*, 36) or even on his deathbed is disproved by Jahn, who produces documentary evidence in support of his claim: *W. A. Mozart*, i.814. Hofmann died in 1793 and was succeeded by Johann Georg Albrechtsberger.

Mozart was thus left to support himself by means of teaching and concerts, a fate that he shared with all musicians who, based in large towns and cities, could not survive on their fixed appointments. We already know that he felt no particular desire to teach and that he was not especially talented in this regard. In Vienna, as elsewhere, he regarded teaching as a necessary evil and, as a result, was never sought after by pupils. Only in the depths of financial misery did he make desperate attempts to find more pupils.[91] Above all, it was the commercial aspect of teaching that discouraged him: he really felt happy only when there was a personal bond between him and his pupil, as was the case with Maria Theresia von Trattner and Franziska von Jacquin, the sister of his friend Gottfried von Jacquin and later the wife of Leopold von Lagusius. He describes her in a letter written to her brother from Prague on 15 January 1787:

I kiss the hands of your sister (Signora Dinimininimi) 100,000 times, with the request that she practises hard on her new pianoforte – but this reminder is unnecessary as I can truly say that I've never had a pupil who was as hard-working and who showed so much enthusiasm as she does – indeed, I'm already looking forward to teaching her again with what little ability I have.[92]

It was for this admirable pianist that Mozart is believed to have written his trio for keyboard, clarinet and viola K498, a work dated 5 August 1786.[93] He also sent her his great C major sonata K521 for four hands on its completion on 29 May 1787, with the request that she 'tackle it at once, as it is rather difficult'.[94] Another of Mozart's more significant keyboard pupils was Babette Ployer, whose father's cousin was the Vienna agent of the Salzburg court. It was for her that he wrote the concertos in E flat major K449 of 9 February 1784[95] and G major K453 of 12 April 1784. He told his father about her in his letter of 9 June 1784:

Tomorrow there'll be a concert at Agent Ployer's house out in the country at Döbling, when Fräulein Babette will play her new concerto in G, I'll be playing the quintet [K452] and together we'll play the grand sonata for two keyboards. I'll fetch Paisiello in my carriage as I want him to hear my compositions and my pupil.[96]

We have already mentioned Mozart's aristocratic pupils, together with Josepha Auernhammer, whom he taught with good humour. That his pupils were mostly women is due to the fact that in aristocratic circles in Vienna at this time it was women who, thanks to their musical enthusiasms and taste, invariably set the tone.[97] But Mozart did have the occasional male pupil, including the

---

91. See his letter to Puchberg of 17 May 1790: 'I now have 2 pupils, but I'd like to have as many as 8 – try to put it about that I'm willing to give lessons' (*Briefe*, iv.108).
92. *Briefe*, iv.11 (letter of 15 January 1787). ◆ See Kraus, 'Mozart und die Familie Jacquin'.
93. Pichler, *Denkwürdigkeiten aus meinem Leben*, i.180. The work is known as the 'Kegelstatt' trio, ostensibly because it was written while Mozart was playing skittles (= *kegeln*), but this anecdote needs to be treated with great caution.
94. *Briefe*, iv.48 (letter of late May 1787).
95. See Mozart's letter of 26 May 1784: 'It's a concerto of a very special kind, written more for a small orchestra than for a large one' (*Briefe*, iii.315). ◆ See Keefe, '"An Entirely Special Manner": Mozart's Piano Concerto No. 14 in E Flat, K. 449, and the Stylistic Implications of Confrontation'.
96. *Briefe*, iii.318 (letter of 9 June 1784). ◆ Further, see Deutsch, 'Das Fräulein von Auernhammer', and Michael Lorenz, 'Gottfried Ignaz von Ployers Haus in Döbling – eine vergessene Mozartstätte. Nebst biographischen Bemerkungen zu Babette Ployer'.
97. See Riesbeck, *Briefe eines reisenden Franzosen*, i.292; Georg Forster, *Sämtliche Schriften*, vii.268–9; Friedrich Meyer, *Friedrich Ludwig Schröder: Beitrag zur Kunde des Menschen und des Künstlers*, i.360; and Schink, *Dramaturgische Monate*, ii.542–3.

well-known physician and great music lover Joseph Frank,[98] who had twelve lessons with Mozart in 1790 and who left the following graphic account:

> I found Mozart to be a little man with a broad head and fleshy hands; he received me rather coldly. 'Now,' he said, 'play me something!' I played him a fantasia of his own composition. 'Not bad,' he said, to my great astonishment, 'now I'll play it for you.' What a marvel! The piano became a completely different instrument under his fingers. He had had it amplified by means of a second keyboard, which he used as a pedal.[99] Mozart then made a few observations about the way in which I should play his fantasia. I was fortunate enough to understand him. – 'Do you play other pieces of my composition?' – 'Yes, sir,' I replied, 'your variations on the theme "Unser dummer Pöbel meint", and a sonata with violin and violoncello accompaniment.' – 'Good, I will play the piece to you; you will derive more benefit from hearing me than from playing it yourself.'[100]

As we know, the young Beethoven was similarly exposed to this initial and wholly characteristic reserve on Mozart's part. But Frank's report is also important for revealing the great emphasis that Mozart placed on the teacher's living example. It was this that persuaded him to revive the old relationship between master craftsman and apprentice and to take in individual pupils, including the most important of them all, the young Johann Nepomuk Hummel. Hummel was born on 14 November 1778 and arrived in Vienna in 1785 with his father, who became music director of Schikaneder's Theater auf der Wieden the following year. He caused a sensation when playing the keyboard for the first time in public at the age of only seven. It was another of Mozart's pupils, Freystädtler, who introduced Hummel to Mozart in 1787. The boy began by playing a number of his easier sonatas, in which the composer complained only that he took them too quickly, and then followed these up with a performance, from memory, of one of his most recent concertos.[101] Mozart thereupon accepted him as one of the family. We do not know to what extent Hummel had regular and, as it were, official lessons, but it is significant that he remained with Mozart for two years, living in the closest personal and artistic proximity with his great teacher and soon assuming responsibility for performing all the new keyboard pieces that found their way into the house.[102] In general, Mozart adopted a markedly relaxed approach to teaching, with Freystädtler, for example, being taught at an adjacent table during a game of skittles, while Attwood was sometimes invited to play billiards instead of having a lesson.[103] Hummel, for his part, was allowed to accompany his teacher to parties and even went with him to court, where he played both on his own and in duets with Mozart, who declared that the boy would soon outstrip him as a keyboard

98. See *Briefwechsel des Herzogs Carl August mit Goethe*, i.302–3.
99. On 12 March 1785, Leopold wrote to his daughter from Vienna: 'He has had a large fortepiano pedal made, which stands under the instrument and is about two feet longer and extremely heavy. It is taken to the Mehlgrube every Friday and has also been taken to Count Zichy's and to Prince Kaunitz's' (*Briefe*, iii.379). ◆ Concerning Mozart's pedal piano, see Maunder and Rowland, 'Mozart's pedal piano'.
100. *Deutsches Museum*, ii/1 (1852), 27–8 [*Dokumente*, 476, *Documentary Biography*, 561].
101. *Allgemeine Wiener Musik-Zeitung* (1842), 489; and Maximilian Johann Seidel, handwritten note.
102. Under this heading comes Edward Holmes's tale, repeated by Jahn, to the effect that, returning home from a party late one evening, Mozart found Hummel asleep in a chair, but woke him and made him play through a new piece for him; see Holmes, *The Life of Mozart*, 258–9; and Jahn, *W. A. Mozart*, i.817.
103. Holmes, *Life of Mozart*, 259; and Fétis, *Curiosités historiques de la musique*, 212–13.

performer. It is no wonder, therefore, that Hummel retained a lifelong affection for his teacher. He finally left him in November 1788 in order to embark on a concert tour with his father.[104]

In addition to keyboard playing, Mozart also taught theory, and it is to his lessons with a cousin of the Abbé Stadler[105] that we owe an exercise book from 1784, in the Vienna Court Library [now the Österreichische Nationalbibliothek], that gives us an insight into his teaching methods. According to this volume, the pupil was given a bass or melody to work up polyphonically. Mozart would then correct the exercise, briefly commenting on the errors in Italian or German and occasionally giving vent to his reactions in witty turns of phrase.[106] These exercises are, of course, of a purely technical nature. On the basis of exercise books such as these, including one – perhaps the one just mentioned[107] – that Zelter saw in Vienna, a 'brief thoroughbass method' was published under Mozart's name and frequently reissued.[108] With more advanced pupils, Mozart naturally adopted a different approach. Attwood, for example, gave him a volume of his own compositions to examine, and Mozart duly worked his way through them all, rewriting entire passages with the note 'I rather show at once how it ought to be done'.[109] For his part, Michael Kelly was sufficiently talented as a composer of 'little airs' to toy with the idea of studying counterpoint in greater depth, but Mozart sought to discourage him:

'Had you studied composition when you were at Naples, and when your mind was not devoted to other pursuits, you would perhaps have done wisely; but now that your profession of the stage must, and ought, to occupy all your attention, it would be an unwise measure to enter into a dry study. You may take my word for it, Nature has made you a melodist, and you would only disturb and perplex yourself. Reflect, "*a little knowledge* is a dangerous thing;" – should there be errors in what you write, you will find hundreds of musicians, in all parts of the world, capable of correcting them; therefore do not disturb your natural gift.'

'Melody is the essence of music,' continued he; '*I* compare a good melodist to a fine racer, and counterpointists to hack post-horses; therefore be advised, let *well alone*, and remember the old Italian proverb – "Chi sa più, meno sa – Who knows most, knows least." '[110]

More satisfying and far more successful were Mozart's appearances as a virtuoso at concerts in Vienna, and here his initial verdict on the city as 'the land of the keyboard' was amply borne out.

Concerts were traditionally held during Lent, when the theatres were closed, and took place either at the Burgtheater or in private houses belonging to the aristocracy. Invitations were usually

---

104. ◆ In London, Hummel met Charles Burney, who wrote to his daughter on 13 December 1790: 'It is odd that 30 years after his Master Mozart had been recommended to me, & played on my knee, on subjects I gave him, that this little Man shd also claim and merit my kindness' (Eisen, *Dokumente: Addenda*, 67, *New Mozart Documents*, 5). Further, see Grochotow, 'Mozart und Hummel'.

105. ◆ This was Barbara Ployer.

106. For example, 'Ho l'honore di dirla, che lei ha fatta la scioccagine (da par Suo) di far due ottave tra il 2 do Violino ed il Basso' and 'This E is very contrived. It's clear that it's been included here only to stop you from moving straight from one consonance to another – just as bad poets often write something stupid for the sake of the rhyme. From C to D you could have proceeded very prettily stepwise through nothing but filled-in thirds'; see Lach, *W. A. Mozart als Theoretiker*. ◆ Ployer's exercise book is also edited in NMA X/30/2.

107. Riemer, *Briefwechsel zwischen Goethe und Zelter*, iii.57. Stadler writes: 'Each time I look through these pages, I recall the great composer and take pleasure in seeing the way he approached his teaching'; Stadler, *Verteidigung der Echtheit des Mozart'schen Requiem*, 13–14.

108. ◆ Concerning Mozart's thoroughbass method, see p.828 n.52.

109. Holmes, *Life of Mozart*, 316.

110. Kelly, *Reminiscences*, i.228–9.

issued by subscription only.[111] Mozart, too, generally gave a concert during Lent. His first was early in 1782. Immediately afterwards he joined forces with Philipp Jakob Martin, a native of Regensburg who had studied with Bullinger at the Jesuit Seminary in Munich and who, according to Mozart's letter of 29 May 1782, was 'a very worthy young man who is trying to make his way in the world through his music, through his elegant writing and generally through his ability, intelligence and sound judgement'.[112] Martin had founded a society of amateur musicians of a kind that was extremely popular at this time and that met every Friday at the Mehlgrube.[113] Mozart describes the organization in his letter to his father of 8 May 1782:

> I'm sure you know that there are lots of amateurs here, and some very good ones, too, both men and women; but so far things haven't really worked out. This Martin has now received a charter from the emperor, together with the promise of his most gracious patronage, allowing him to give 12 concerts in the Augarten and 4 grand serenades in the finest squares in the city.[114] The subscription for the whole summer is 2 ducats. Well, you can easily imagine that we'll have enough subscribers, the more so in that I, too, am taking an interest in it and am associated with it. Assuming we get only 100 subscribers, each of us will make a profit of 300 florins (even if the expenses amount to 200 florins, which is most unlikely). Baron van Swieten and Countess Thun are also taking an interest. The orchestra is made up entirely of amateurs, the only exceptions being the bassoon players and the trumpeters and timpanists.[115]

The Augarten was laid out on the site of the old 'Favorite' in the Leopoldstadt and, having been restored by Joseph II, was thrown open to the general public by imperial decree in 1775. Over its gate ran the famous inscription: 'Place of public entertainment dedicated to all mankind by one who values it'.[116] The main building was entrusted to a landlord. For himself, the emperor built a small, simple house surrounded by a wooden fence. Here he would spend several days at a time, freely mingling with the crowds who came here to take their constitutionals. Many members of the local aristocracy would gather here, especially on Sunday afternoons,[117] with the result that Martin's scheme promised to be a success. The concerts were promenade concerts of a kind familiar from Handel's day in London. Mozart threw his whole weight behind them, as we learn from his letter of 25 May 1782:

111. See Friedrich Nicolai, *Beschreibung einer Reise durch Deutschland und die Schweiz im Jahre 1781*, iv.552; and Pichler, *Denkwürdigkeiten aus meinem Leben*, i.127–8.
112. *Briefe*, iii.210–11 (letter of 29 May 1782).
113. Friedrich Nicolai, *Beschreibung einer Reise durch Deutschland*, iv.552–3, reports on the announcement of a grand concert organized by amateurs, lingering in particular over its sixth paragraph: 'In adjacent rooms gambling tables will be kept available for all manner of drinking bouts, for each of which bets may be placed à discretion. The company will also be provided with all manner of refreshments on demand.' Nicolai insists that this kind of thing did not go on at the private concerts held by true amateurs that he attended in Vienna. See also Pohl, *Joseph Haydn*, ii.148ff. and Hanslick, *Geschichte des Concertwesens in Wien*, 69–70.
114. See the *Wiener Zeitung* for 1 June 1782 and Riesbeck, *Beschreibung einer Reise durch Deutschland*, i.276–7: 'For me, one of the most beautiful settings on recent summer nights was the so-called lemonade huts. Large tents are erected in some of the city's larger squares, where lemonade is dispensed at night. Often several hundred chairs may be found standing around, occupied by ladies and gentlemen. A short distance away is a large band of musicians, and the immense silence traditionally observed by even the largest crowd creates an indescribably wonderful effect. The excellent music, the solemn silence, the confidences inspired by the night, everything lends the scene a special appeal.' See also Schönfeld, *Jahrbuch der Tonkunst von Wien und Prag*, i.78.
◆ For the *Wiener Zeitung* notice by Martin, see *Dokumente*, 178, *Documentary Biography*, 201.
115. *Briefe*, iii.208–9 (letter of 8 May 1782).
116. Hormayr, *Wien: Seine Geschichte und Denkwürdigkeiten*, v/1.41 and 50.
117. Friedrich Nicolai, *Beschreibung einer Reise durch Deutschland*, iii.12ff.

Our first concert takes place at the Augarten tomorrow. Martin will be arriving at half past 8 with a carriage, we still have 6 visits to pay. I have to be finished by 11 as I'm then seeing Countess Rumbeke; I'm then lunching with Countess Thun – in her garden. The concert will then be rehearsed in the evening. There'll be a symphony by van Swieten and one by me, and an amateur singer, Mlle Berger, will sing; a boy by the name of Türk[118] will play a violin concerto and Fräulein von Aurnhammer and I will play the concerto in E flat for two pianos [K365].[119]

This first concert was well attended, with an audience that included the Archduke Maximilian, Countess Thun, Wallenstein [probably Countess Marie Elisabeth Waldstein], Baron van Swieten and many other music lovers. But we know nothing more about this venture, which presumably turned out less well than was initially hoped.[120]

For the following year's Lenten season, Mozart began by appearing at a concert on 11 March with his sister-in-law Aloysia Lange, performing his 'Paris' symphony (K297) from the Concert Spirituel, after which she sang his aria *Non sò d'onde viene* (K294), with new variations in the vocal line – what memories this must have stirred in Mozart! 'Gluck had a box beside the Langes, in which my wife was sitting', he told his father the next day. 'He couldn't find words enough to praise the symphony and aria and has invited all four of us to lunch with him next Sunday.' Mozart also played a concerto of his own composition: 'The theatre was very full and I was again so well received by the local public that I'm bound to feel pleased by their reaction. – I'd already left, but they wouldn't stop clapping and so I had to repeat the Rondeau – there was a regular torrent of applause.'[121] As a result, all the boxes were taken for his own concert on 22 March. The theatre, he told his father, 'couldn't have been fuller'. The programme was as follows:

1. The 'Haffner' symphony (K385) of the previous summer.
2. Ilia's aria, 'Se il padre perdei', from *Idomeneo* (K366), sung by Aloysia Lange.
3. The third subscription concerto K415 in C major, which had just appeared in print.
4. The *scena* for Countess Paumgarten (K369, *Misera! dove son - - Ah! Non so io che parlo!*), sung by Adamberger.
5. The brief sinfonia concertante from Mozart's last *Finalmusik* (K320).
6. The concerto in D major ('which is so popular here'), that is, K175 and its replacement finale, the rondo K382.
7. The scena 'Parto, m'affretto' from *Lucio Silla* (K135) sung by Therese Teyber.
8. A free improvisation by Mozart, which he began with a short fugue ('because the emperor was present'), followed by improvised variations on the aria 'Salve tu, Domine' from Paisiello's *I filosofi immaginari* and, in response to the tumultuous applause, a set of variations on the aria 'Unser dummer Pöbel meint' from Gluck's *La rencontre imprévue*.

---

118. On Franz Türke, see Schönfeld, *Jahrbuch der Tonkunst von Wien und Prag*, i.63.
119. *Briefe*, iii.209 (letter of 25 May 1782).
120. As late as 1791, Martin – now styling himself 'Directeur des Concerts d'amateurs' – was advertising his concerts in the Augarten, the Prater and at court; the advertisement, in the appendix of the *Wiener Zeitung* no. 45, strikes a somewhat pitiful note. These concerts were later continued under their vice-president Franz Georg von Keeß (but with little success): see Schönfeld, *Jahrbuch der Tonkunst von Wien und Prag*, i.74, *AmZ*, iii (1801/2), 46, and Hanslick, *Geschichte des Concertwesens in Wien*, 71.
◆ Concerning Viennese concert life generally at this time, see Morrow, *Concert Life in Haydn's Vienna*.
121. *Briefe*, iii.259 (letter of 12 March 1783).

9. A new rondò (K416 *Mia speranza adorata! — Ah non sai qual pena sia*), written for and performed by Aloisia Lange.

10. The final movement of the 'Haffner' symphony.

This programme is typical of the concerts given by artists at this time. The virtuoso had to prepare the ground for the composer, with the inevitable free improvisation as the *pièce de résistance*. Both in the eighteenth century and for a long time afterwards, it was by no means unusual, moreover, to break up a symphony and perform it piecemeal. 'The best thing about it', Mozart told his father in his letter of 29 March 1783, 'was that his Majesty the Emperor was there – how pleased he was and how he applauded me! He normally sends the money to the box office before going to the theatre, otherwise I'd have been fully justified in expecting more [than twenty-five ducats], as his delight knew no bounds.'[122] Even so, Mozart must have been pleased with the receipts, which, according to a contemporary report, amounted to some 1600 florins.[123] Shortly afterwards, Mozart repeated the C major concerto at a concert organized by Therese Teyber. When the audience demanded the final rondo by way of an encore, he surprised everyone by offering them a free improvisation that was loudly applauded. The emperor, too, remained to the end, not leaving his box until Mozart had left the platform.[124]

In 1784 Mozart planned not only two concerts at the Burgtheater during Lent but also six subscription concerts that would have included a performance of *Idomeneo*. In the event, the keyboard virtuoso Georg Friedrich Richter announced a series of Saturday concerts to which the aristocracy refused to subscribe unless Mozart himself performed at them, and so the latter promised to appear at three of Richter's concerts, while organizing a subscription of his own for three concerts at six florins. These took place on the last three Wednesdays in Lent, 17, 24 and 31 March, in the beautiful hall of the bookseller Johann Thomas von Trattner on the Graben.[125] Mozart sent his father a list of the subscribers, which ran to 174 names,[126] thirty more than his rivals Richter and Nancy Storace's husband, John Abraham Fisher,[127] had managed to collect. These concerts, too, proved outstandingly successful from both an artistic and a commercial point of view.[128] (It

122. *Briefe*, iii.261 (letter of 29 March 1783).

123. See Cramer's *Magazin der Musik*, i (1783), 578: 'Today the famous Chevalier Mozart gave a concert for his own benefit at the National Theatre, at which pieces of his already much admired composition were played. The concert was honoured with an exceptionally large concourse, and the two new concertos and other fantasias which Herr M. played on the fortepiano were received with the loudest applause. Our Monarch, who, against his habit, attended the whole of the concert, as well as the entire audience, accorded him such unanimous applause as has never been heard of here. The receipts of the concert are estimated to amount to 1600 gulden in all' [*Dokumente*, 190–1, *Documentary Biography*, 215].

124. *Briefe*, iii.265 (letter of 12 April 1783).

125. Friedrich Nicolai, *Beschreibung einer Reise durch Deutschland*, ii.636–7.

126. This impressive list includes not only the names of Mozart's well-known patrons such as Countess Thun, Baroness von Waldstätten, Count Zichy and Baron van Swieten, but also the Duke of Württemberg, the Prince of Mecklenburg and Princes Alois Liechtenstein, Auersperg, Kaunitz, Lichnowsky, Lobkowitz, Paar, Palm and Schwarzenberg. Other illustrious families included Batthyány, Dietrichstein, Erdödy, Esterházy, Harrach, Herberstein, Keglevich, Nostitz, Pálffy, Schaffgotsch, Starhemberg and Waldstein, together with the ambassadors of Russia, Spain, Sardinia, the Netherlands and Denmark, leading members of the city's financial community, including Johann Fries, Adam Adalbert Hönig von Henikstein, Ignaz or Joseph Ehrenfeld, Johann Adam Binnenfeld, Gottfried Ignaz von Ployer and Karl Abraham Wetzlar, and high-ranking civil servants and academics such as Joseph Izdenczy-Monostor, Anton Bedekovich von Komor, Alexius Leopoldus von Nevery, Johann Gottlieb von Braun, Franz Sales von Greiner, Franz Bernhard von Keeß, Anna von Pufendorf, Ignaz von Born, Karl Anton von Martini and Joseph von Sonnenfels – a veritable who's who of the cream of Viennese high society. ◆ Further, see Heinz Schuler, 'Mozarts Akademien im Trattnersaal 1784: Ein Kommentar zum Mozart-Brief – Wien, 20. März 1784'.

127. Kelly, *Reminiscences*, i.231–2 and Pohl, *Mozart und Haydn in London*, 169–70. ◆ According to *Briefe* (vi.177), Fischer may be the bass singer Johann Ignaz Ludwig Fischer.

128. See *Briefe*, iii.303–7 (letters of 3 and 20 March 1784).

was for them that Mozart wrote his concertos in B flat and D major K 450 and K451, which he completed on 15 and 22 March 1784 respectively.) And the same is true of the concerts given at the theatre, the first of which had to be postponed from 21 March to 1 April because of an opera performance at the home of Prince Alois Joseph Liechtenstein.[129] It was on this occasion that the piano quintet in E flat major K452 was first performed to tremendous acclaim:[130]

> I myself consider it the best work I've ever written. . . . How I wish you could have heard it; – and how well it was performed! To tell the truth, I'm completely worn out from so much playing – and it's greatly to my credit that my listeners *never* felt tired.[131]

On 22 January 1785 Leopold wrote to his daughter: 'I've just received ten lines from your brother, in which he reports that his first subscription concert will begin on 11 February and continue every Friday.'[132] On this occasion, Leopold was able to attend the first concert of the series in person. It took place at the Mehlgrube and was supported by more than 150 subscribers, each of whom had paid three ducats. On 16 February Leopold wrote again to Nannerl: 'The concert was magnificent, the orchestra splendid. In addition to the symphonies, a soprano from the Italian theatre sang two arias, then came a new and splendid keyboard concerto by Wolfgang that the copyist was still writing out when we arrived and your brother didn't even have time to play through the Rondo as he had to supervise the copying.'[133] This was the D minor concerto K466, one of Mozart's most important contributions to the medium. The second of the Mehlgrube concerts was no less 'magnificent',[134] and when Mozart gave a third concert at the Burgtheater, this time for his own benefit and featuring the first performance of his C major concerto K467, which he completed on 9 March 1785, the receipts of 559 florins were a matter of no little pride and satisfaction on Leopold's part, not least in view of the frequency of his son's appearances at this time.[135] On 13 February he had performed at a concert given by the soprano Luisa Laschi, playing the concerto K456 that he had probably written in 1784 for the Paris début of the blind pianist Maria Theresia Paradis. 'When your brother left the platform,' Leopold wrote to Nannerl, 'the emperor waved his hat and called out "Bravo, Mozart!" And when he came on to play, he was again applauded.'[136]

In 1786 Mozart organized three more concerts, this time with 120 subscribers.[137] To these, we owe three more concertos, those in E flat major K482 of 16 December 1785, A major K488 of 2 March 1786 and C minor K491 of 24 March 1786. The andante of the C minor concerto was encored at his concert on 7 April, the last of his concerts to be held at the Burgtheater.[138] Later that year he gave four concerts at the Casino during Advent, completing another new concerto – K503 in C major – on 4 December. In January 1787 he travelled to Prague and, in response to public demand, gave a major concert at the opera house, winning unprecedented acclaim from the

129. *Briefe*, iii.307 (letter of 20 March 1784).
130. The programme is reproduced by Pohl, *Joseph Haydn*, ii.145 [*Dokumente*, 198, *Documentary Biography*, 223].
131. *Briefe*, iii.309 (letter of 10 April 1784).
132. *Briefe*, iii.368 (letter of 22 Jan. 1785).
133. *Briefe*, iii.373 (letter of 16 Feb. 1785).
134. *Briefe*, iv.373 (letter of 21 February 1785).
135. *Briefe*, iii.378 (letter of 12 March 1785).
136. *Briefe*, iii.373 (letter of 16 February 1785). ◆ Although it is traditionally thought that Mozart composed K456 for Paradis, no unequivocal evidence confirms this. See Ullrich, 'Maria Theresia Paradis' große Kunstreise', 'Das Stammbuch der Maria Theresia Paradis' and 'Maria Theresia Paradis in London'.
137. *Briefe*, iii.484 (letter of 13 January 1786).
138. Supplement to the *Wiener Zeitung* (8 April 1786), no. 28 [*Dokumente*, 237, *Documentary Biography*, 271].

packed house for his improvisations at the end. He was three times called back to the platform. A second concert proved no less successful. Nancy Storace told Leopold that Mozart earned 1000 florins in Prague.[139]

Mozart could certainly not complain about the artistic and material proceeds of his activities as a virtuoso. A comparison with the sort of fees that singers could command would be out of place, however, as such fees had always been greater than those paid to instrumentalists.[140] None the less, there is no denying the great pleasure and satisfaction that these concerts gave him. Even if we did not have his letters, the concertos that he wrote for these occasions would attest to his sense of satisfaction, as all of them reflect his high spirits and unadulterated delight in music making, while at the same time revealing him at his most artistically mature. Even so, we can understand them fully only if we know the audience for which they were intended. Unlike today's audiences, Mozart's audience did not extend to every social class but included only the nobility and those members of the bourgeoisie who in the Vienna of Joseph II were currently striving to ape the aristocracy. In short, Mozart was appealing to only a limited cross-section of the broad mass of listeners who were receptive to music, a select band whose taste in music had been refined by the old aristocratic culture but which was now confined within certain limits, thereby leaving its mark on these concertos, too: they are among the most sophisticated and brilliant examples of Gesellschaftsmusik that we possess. In addition to these public concerts, Mozart also appeared at a large number of private concerts organized by the nobility. They, too, were held during Lent. We have already had frequent occasion to refer to domestic music making among members of the Austrian aristocracy. Their activities embraced not only instrumental music, but dramatic music, too. Mozart himself mentions an opera at the home of Prince Liechtenstein, and his *Idomeneo* was performed in 1786 at Prince Auersperg's private theatre near the Burgtor, where in 1782 an Italian opera had been performed in honour of Grand Duke Paul, followed by Gluck's *Alceste*,[141] with Countess Hatzfeld in the title role.[142] Much more common were the private ensembles of the nobility that ranged from fully equipped orchestras such as those maintained by Prince Esterházy and Prince von Hildburghausen[143] to wind bands for *Tafelmusik* and serenades and, finally, to simple string quartets. All these institutions left their mark on composers in no uncertain terms, generating a tremendous need for new pieces that composers sought to meet by writing sets of six or a dozen works at once, with the men and women who commissioned these pieces taking special pride in owning them and in being able to boast that none of the other members of their social class could lay claim to them. As a result, composers were forced to turn out works with a frequency which, by today's standards, verges on the unreal. Of course, a great deal of lightweight, pedestrian music was produced in this way, but Mozart's keyboard concertos demonstrate how these circumstances could also fire composers' imaginations. Virtuoso and composer went hand in hand at these private concerts, as elsewhere, with the organizers priding themselves on having

139. *Briefe*, iv.28 (letter of 2 March 1787).
140. Singers such as Nancy Storace and Celeste Coltellini not only received free accommodation and transport to and from the theatre, but a fee of 1000 ducats that they could augment by means of benefit performances, concerts and not insignificant extras, while Luigi Marchesi received 600 ducats and a valuable ring for six performances; see Müller, *Abschied von der k. k. Hof- und National-Schaubühne*, 8.
141. Schönfeld, *Jahrbuch der Tonkunst in Wien und Prag*, i.25.
142. Kelly, *Reminiscences*, i.201. A performance of *Axur* is mentioned by Schönfeld, *Jahrbuch der Tonkunst in Wien und Prag*, i.38. Mozart's final chorus for Sarti's *Le gelosie villane* K 615, which he completed on 20 April 1791, was likewise intended for amateurs.
143. Dittersdorf, *Lebensbeschreibung*, 23. The Bohemian aristocracy frequently used household servants in their orchestras; see Einstein, *Lebensläufe deutscher Musiker, iii: Adalbert Gyrowetz*, 9.

the most famous virtuosos of the day performing under their roofs. It is no wonder, then, that music was such a drain on the resources of the aristocracy, driving many of them to the verge of financial ruin.[144]

During the winter of 1782/3 Mozart was invited to appear at all the concerts organized by the Russian ambassador, Prince Dmitri Mikhailovich Galitzin. According to his letter of 21 December 1782, he was 'always fetched in his coach and brought home again and generally treated in the most generous way in the world'.[145] The following winter he appeared at the concerts held at the homes of Counts Johann Esterházy, Zichy and others. Between 26 February and 3 April 1784 he played not only at five concerts of his own and Richter's three academies, but also at Galitzin's and Esterházy's, appearing five times at the former's residence and no fewer than nine times at the latter's. 'I don't think I can possibly get out of practice in this way', he commented wryly.[146] He often took his own keyboard with him,[147] an instrument which, according to Leopold,[148] was transported to the theatre or elsewhere on at least twelve separate occasions between 11 February and 12 March. We do not know what fees Mozart commanded for these appearances, but the aristocracy traditionally rewarded outstanding artists in outstandingly generous ways, demonstrating an extreme warmth and informality which, their elevated status notwithstanding, was typical of the tone in such circles. Hosts such as Colloredo were very much the exception, and artists were unqualified in their recognition of such generosity and understanding. Mozart, too, felt entirely at his ease in these aristocratic salons, revealing not only an innate and true sensitivity and gallant amiability but also a profound self-assurance as an artist. But, unlike Beethoven, he did not allow his distinguished hosts to sense his superiority. In the circumstances, it is hardly surprising that, like a number of his fellow musicians, he became very friendly with individual members of the aristocracy such as Prince Karl Lichnowsky and Count August Hatzfeld, the latter an outstanding violinist whose performances of his quartets were very much to his liking.[149] It was for Hatzfeld that Mozart wrote the additional aria for Idomeneo with violin obbligato. His exceptional qualities were widely praised following his death in Düsseldorf in 1787, with Mozart adding his voice to their number in his letter to his father of 4 April 1787:

> I expressed my views to you on this point [death and dying] in connection with the sad death of my dearest and best friend, the Count von Hatzfeld. He was just 31, like me; I do not feel sorry for *him*, but pity both myself and all who knew him as well as I did.[150]

144. ◆ Concerning Viennese musical patronage at this time, see in particular DeNora, *Beethoven and the Construction of Genius: Musical Politics in Vienna, 1792–1803*.
145. *Briefe*, iii.244 (letter of 21 December 1782).
146. *Briefe*, iii.304 (letter of 3 March 1784).
147. Mozart's concert piano is now in the Mozarteum in Salzburg. A small, five-octave instrument by Anton Walter, it has a walnut case and a light touch, but a relatively powerful tone. The natural keys are black, the sharp keys white.
148. *Briefe*, iii.379 (letter of 12 March 1785). ◆ Mozart's Walter is now housed at the Geburtshaus Museum, Salzburg (Getreidegasse 9). For recent discussions concerning its mechanics and authenticity, see Latcham and Huber, 'Instrumentenkundliche Daten des Mozart-Flügels', and Latcham, 'Zur Frage der Authentizität und Datierung der Klaviere von Anton Walter zwischen 1780 und 1800', 'Historische Belege zum Mozart-Flügel', 'and 'Mozart and the pianos of Gabriel Anton Walter'.
149. See Cramer's *Magazin der Musik*, ii (26 July 1787), 1380ff. ◆ *Dokumente*, 260–1, *Documentary Biography*, 295: 'In Vienna he became acquainted and friendly with *Mozart*. He studied there and played his famous *quadros* under the author's guidance, and became so intimate with their composer's spirit that the latter became almost disinclined to hear his masterpiece from anyone else. Some two months before his death I heard him deliver them with an accuracy and fervour which excited the admiration of every connoisseur and enchanted the hearts of all.'
150. *Briefe*, iv.41 (letter of 4 April 1787).

Finally, Mozart also performed at his own rooms on Sunday mornings, regaling not only his friends with his playing, but also admitting paying audiences. Among regular visitors was Michael Kelly.[151] These concerts continued until the very end of his life, as did his involvement in private concerts at the homes of the local aristocracy.[152] Conversely, there is no record that he organized any public concerts of his own after 1787, and only two more works were added to the series of brilliant keyboard concertos written for these concerts: K537 in D major, which was completed on 24 February 1788,[153] and K595 in B flat major, completed on 5 January 1791 and introduced to Vienna on 4 March 1791 at a concert organized by the clarinettist Joseph Beer, the last occasion on which Mozart performed in public in the city.[154] His composition of his three great symphonies in the summer of 1788 indicates his intention of giving further concerts, an aim confirmed by his letters of the period,[155] but there is no evidence that this plan was ever realized. With the single exception of the concerto already mentioned, no further symphonies or concertos survive from the period after 1788, clear proof that Mozart organized no further concerts.[156] But what was the reason for this sudden drop in productivity, which robbed Mozart of his principal source of income and was thus one of the main causes of his financial hardship during the final years of his life? It is unlikely that the Viennese public had become tired of him overnight: after all, he had been brilliantly successful, both as a virtuoso and as a composer, in writing concertos for the aristocracy, while retaining his artistic independence. But from the time of *Le nozze di Figaro* onwards, he had started to outgrow the sort of music that served merely to amuse high society. The tremendous outburst of creativity that led to *Le nozze di Figaro*, *Don Giovanni* and the three great symphonies left him feeling more and more alienated towards that older ideal, while at the same time reducing his interest in public appearances. He had already said all that he had to say within that framework and had said it to the best of his abilities; now, as his life drew towards its close, his soaring genius guided him towards a new land no longer dominated by the taste of a single social grouping – however well educated that class may have been – but ruled by the artist's conscience alone, a land on whose horizon the dawn of Beethoven's art had already started to glimmer. It is hardly surprising that so few of his existing listeners could follow him in this, and even the concerts that he gave at home now began to sink in the general estimation.[157]

Today's composers derive the bulk of their income from the publication and sale of their works, but for Mozart, this was still an uncertain source of revenue. Although sales of sheet music were buoyant, the market was only a fraction of what it was later to become. Within his own lifetime, only his works up to his op. 18 (K451) were published,[158] and even this list did not include his

151. Kelly, *Reminiscences*, i.226.
152. On 10 February 1788, for example, he performed at the home of the Venetian ambassador; see Pohl, *Joseph Haydn*, ii.146 [*Dokumente*, 273, *Documentary Biography*, 310].
153. We know only that Mozart performed this concerto in Dresden on 14 April 1789; see *Briefe*, iv.83 (letter of 16 April 1789).
154. Pohl, *Joseph Haydn*, ii.147. ◆ Edge, 'Mozart's Reception in Vienna, 1787–1791', 89–90, speculates that K595 may have been performed by Barbara Ployer on 9 January 1791 at Adam Auersperg's.
155. *Briefe*, iv.65 and 66 (letters of early June and before 17 June 1788).
156. See Pohl, *Joseph Haydn*, ii.147, and Hanslick, *Geschichte des Concertwesens in Wien*, 124. ◆ Here Abert refers exclusively to keyboard concertos, excluding the clarinet concerto K622 of November 1791.
157. In the distressing letter that he wrote to Michael Puchberg on 12 July 1789, we read: 'I must mention that in spite of my wretched condition I none the less decided to give some subscription concerts at home . . . but even this plan has miscarried; – Fate is unfortunately so much against me, *though only in Vienna*, that even when I want to, I can't earn any money; a fortnight ago I sent round a list for subscribers, and so far the only name on it is *Swieten!*' (*Briefe*, iv.92). Mozart expressed the same wish in his letter to Puchberg of May 1790 (*Briefe*, iv.106, letter of early May 1790).
158. ◆ By this Abert does not mean that only works up to K451 were published in Mozart's lifetime; rather, he means that the opus numbers assigned to his publications only reached eighteen. Numerous works later than K451 were published in Vienna and elsewhere by the end of 1791, often without opus numbers. For a comprehensive summary of Mozart first editions, see Haberkamp, *Die Erstdrucke der Werke von Wolfgang Amadeus Mozart: Bibliographie*.

songs and variations. In the main, he was dependent on the old practice of copying and, like his colleagues, had to be on his guard against unqualified copyists. And because he was so negligent in this regard, his works were often copied and sold behind his back by third parties. But it was not only behind his back that such deals went on: he even had to look on helplessly while dealers such as Traeg, Lausch and Torricella advertised copies of his works in the press.[159] Only in the case of his keyboard concertos did he retain strict control of his right of ownership, refusing to allow them to be played by all and sundry. Only with the first three was he prepared to consider publication, initially planning to publish them himself for six ducats apiece,[160] but later offering them to the public on subscription for four ducats, 'beautifully copied and superintended by himself'.[161] He stuck to this price even when his father suggested that it was too much.[162] But he withheld the later concertos. The ones written in 1784 he sent to his father on 26 May 1784, together with a covering note: 'I'm perfectly willing to wait for their return, as long as no one else lays his hands on them. Only today I could have got 24 ducats for one of them, but I think it will be better for me to hang on to them for a few years and only then to have them engraved and introduced to a wider public.'[163] As a result he took only the orchestral parts with him whenever he went off on tour, performing his own part from a piano score which, according to Rochlitz,[164] consisted of only the figured bass and the principal musical ideas, with the figurations merely hinted at. The rest he added from memory. In 1788 he advertised copies of three quintets (K406, 515 and 516) for four ducats for the set.[165]

Although he frequently received no fee for the countless works which, in keeping with a long-held practice, he wrote for his pupils as well as for friends and acquaintances, other pieces that were commissioned from him were well paid. Here one thinks of the three quartets K575, 589 and 590 that he wrote for Friedrich Wilhelm II in 1789 and 1790 and for which he is said to have received a valuable gold snuffbox and one hundred friedrichs d'or.[166] For the *Requiem*, he was offered an advance of one hundred ducats, and he will no doubt have received other amounts for various dedications and for other pieces commissioned from him, including the adaptations of a number of Handel's oratorios that he prepared at van Swieten's request in 1788 and 1789. But these were random earnings and were offset by a larger number of unpaid commissions. The indignities to which Mozart was sometimes exposed in this way emerge with striking clarity from an incident reported by his widow:

159.   ◆ While it is true that music copyists were frequently unscrupulous, it is not clear that Viennese music dealers such as Traeg, Lausch and Torricella regularly cheated Mozart. In fact, this seems unlikely since for the most part they published (either engraved or in manuscript) the first editions of Mozart's works (this may be less true of the operas, over which Mozart had little control); the composer was, accordingly, their only source and he almost certainly was paid by them for his music. With the exception of Artaria (see Hilmar, *Der Musikverlag Artaria & Comp.: Geschichte und Probleme der Druckproduktion*), there are at present no detailed accounts of Viennese publishing practices during the 1780s.

160.   *Briefe*, iii.246 (letter of 28 December 1782).

161.   Supplement to *Wiener Zeitung* (15 January 1783), no. 5 [*Dokumente*, 187–8, *Documentary Biography*, 212]. The three concertos K413–415 were eventually published in Vienna as his op. 4.

162.   *Briefe*, iii.251 (letter of 22 January 1783).

163.   *Briefe*, iii.315 (letter of 26 May 1784).

164.   Rochlitz, 'Verbürgte Anekdoten aus Wolfgang Gottlieb Mozarts Leben', 113.

165.   Supplement to *Wiener Zeitung* (2 April 1788), no. 27 [*Dokumente*, 274 and 280–1, *Documentary Biography*, 312 and 319–20].

166.   *Neue Berliner Musikzeitung*, x/5 (30 January 1856), 35. ◆ In the end, the quartets were not sent to Berlin but sold to the Viennese publisher Artaria; see Mozart's letter of about 12 June 1790 to Puchberg: 'I've now been forced to give away my quartets . . . for a song, simply in order to have cash in hand' (*Briefe*, iv.110).

One of the Sunday concerts that Mozart gave in his rooms was attended by a Polish count, who was enchanted by what was then the new piano quintet with wind instruments [K452] that Mozart had written on 30 March 1784. He asked Mozart if he could find the time to write him a trio with flute obbligato, and Mozart promised to do so. The count had scarcely returned home when he sent Mozart one hundred and fifty gold sovereigns, with a most obliging note repeating his lively thanks for the pleasure that Mozart had just given him. In the light of the letter's contents, Mozart regarded the money that he had been sent as a generous gift and, expressing his most sincere thanks, sent the count the original score of the quintet that he had so much enjoyed – something he normally never did –, while at the same time taking great pleasure in telling everyone about the count's generosity. A year later the count came to see Mozart again and enquired after the trio; Mozart apologized and said that he did not yet feel in the right mood to write anything worthy of the count. 'In that case I don't suppose you'll feel in the right mood to return the one hundred and fifty gold sovereigns that I paid you in advance for it,' retorted the count. Mozart paid him back the sum, but the count kept the score of the quintet which, shortly afterwards and without Mozart's agreement, was engraved in Vienna as a quartet for keyboard and strings. Mozart was defenceless against such people and such conduct. All he could do was shrug his shoulders and say 'The blackguard'.[167]

Given Mozart's good nature, this was undoubtedly not a unique incident. And more than once he will have been the victim of pirated editions of shorter fashionable pieces such as variations. Longer works he published by subscription, which was the usual method adopted at this time, or else he sold them to publishers such as Torricella, Artaria and Hoffmeister. For his 'Haydn' quartets, Artaria paid him one hundred ducats, a fee normally offered only in the case of operas and doubly impressive inasmuch as these works were unlikely to become bestsellers.[168] Nissen's claim that the two piano quartets in G minor and E flat major K478 and K493 were only the first in a longer series agreed with Hoffmeister sounds entirely plausible.[169] According to Nissen, these two works sold badly and so Hoffmeister wrote off the advance and abandoned his plans to continue the series. These works, too, demanded a public that was only now coming into existence. Rochlitz's account of Hoffmeister's admonition ('Write in a more popular vein, otherwise I shan't be able to publish and pay for any more of your works') and Mozart's reply ('In that case I shan't earn any more and shall starve, but I don't care') undoubtedly trivializes the affair by couching it in such petty terms,[170] but there is no doubt that it reflects the facts of the matter, as is clear from Mozart's letter to Hoffmeister of 20 November 1785:

Dearest Hoffmeister,

I turn to you in my distress and beg you to help me out with some money, which I need very badly at the moment; I would also ask you to try to procure for me as soon as possible the thing you already know about. – Forgive me for continuing to trouble you; but as you know me and

---

167. See Jahn, *W. A. Mozart*, i.833–4. First published by Constanze Mozart in 'Einige Anekdoten aus Mozarts Leben', 289, then transferred to Prague and, translated from the French, repeated in *AmZ* vi (1803/4), 196. ◆ Further, see Eisen, *New Mozart Documents*, 77–82.

168. ◆ Further, see Ridgewell, 'Mozart's Publishing Plans with Artaria in 1787: New Archival Evidence'.

169. Nissen, *Biographie W. A. Mozarts*, 633. ◆ This anecdote is apparently confirmed by bibliographical evidence as well; see Haberkamp, *Die Erstdrucke der Werke von Wolfgang Amadeus Mozart*, 240 and 262.

170. Rochlitz, *Für Freunde der Tonkunst*, third edition, i.90.

know how anxious I am that your business should succeed, I am convinced that you will not take my importunity amiss but will help me as readily as I shall help you.[171]

An enterprising publisher in Berlin, Johann Julius Hummel, claimed that, although unmusical, he could cast a critical eye over the works that were submitted to him and see whether they were worth publishing. He did not have a good word to say about Mozart and even boasted that he had returned several of his works as unpublishable.[172]

As for the returns on Mozart's operas, Rochlitz's claim that Schikaneder not only paid him no fee for *Die Zauberflöte* but sold the score behind his back, in spite of his promise not to do so, is undoubtedly much exaggerated.[173] According to Seyfried,[174] Schikaneder paid the composer one hundred ducats and made over to Constanze the net proceeds on the sale of the score. But it is entirely possible that, following Mozart's death, he felt absolved of all further obligations towards his widow.[175] In Vienna, as elsewhere, the regular fee for an opera – in keeping with Italian practice – was one hundred ducats, and this is the sum that Mozart received for *Die Entführung aus dem Serail* and *Le nozze di Figaro*. *Don Giovanni* brought him 225 florins, *Così fan tutte* 200 ducats.[176] Bondini paid him one hundred ducats for *Don Giovanni* in Prague, and the city's Bohemian Estates are unlikely to have offered him less for *La clemenza di Tito*. In 1789 Guardasoni in Prague even promised Mozart two hundred ducats for an opera, together with fifty ducats for travelling expenses,[177] but the plan came to nothing.[178] As a rule, both composer and librettist could also count on the proceeds of benefit performances. Although Mozart does not explicitly mention such a performance in the case of *Die Entführung aus dem Serail*, there undoubtedly was one, and, as with *Le nozze di Figaro*, it will have brought a welcome boost to his income.[179]

In this respect, too, Mozart was no worse off, then, than his colleagues. We do not know what he received from foreign theatres for performances of his works. Although he expected a handsome fee for *Die Entführung* from the Prussian ambassador, it is unclear whether he ever received it. In general, income from these sources remained the exception at a time when authors' rights were acknowledged in neither theory nor practice. Here, too, the older Italian attitude prevailed, whereby an opera became the property of the theatre that had commissioned it. The score remained the possession of the impresario, who, with luck, might allow his copyist to make and sell copies, but the composer, too, might retain a copy and make further use of it if a suitable occasion arose. German court theatres tended to be run along more efficient lines than their Italian equivalents, where scores were often thrown away and lost. According to Mozart, composers in Mannheim and Munich kept their scores in order to dispose of them as they thought fit, and, as we have seen, Mozart was pleased that Riedesel approached him personally, rather than turning to his copyist, for the score of *Die Entführung*. But this was very much the exception. In general,

---

171. *Briefe*, iii.454 (letter of 20 November 1785). On the back of the letter, Hoffmeister added a note: '20 November 1785 with 2 ducats'; see *Neue Zeitschrift für Musik*, ix (1842), 164.
172. *AmZ*, i (1798/9), 547.
173. Rochlitz, 'Verbürgte Anekdoten', 83; and Nissen, *Biographie W. A. Mozarts*, 548–9.
174. *Neue Zeitschrift für Musik*, xii (1845), 180.
175. Komorzynski, *Emanuel Schikaneder: Ein Beitrag zur Geschichte des deutschen Theaters*, 31. ◆ Probably this is an exaggeration. It is almost certain that Mozart sold copies of the score during his lifetime (see Eisen, *Dokumente: Addenda*, 75, *New Mozart Documents*, 73); so did Constanze, immediately following his death (*Dokumente*, 377, *Documentary Biography*, 428–9).
176. ◆ Further, see Edge, 'Mozart's Fee for "Così fan tutte"'.
177. *Briefe*, iv.80 (letter of 10 April 1789).
178. Rochlitz is wrong to claim otherwise in *Für Freunde der Tonkunst*, ii.163.
179. For a benefit performance of his *Doktor und Apotheker*, Dittersdorf earned 200 ducats; see Dittersdorf, *Lebensbeschreibung*, 243.

theatre directors were under no obligation towards composers and they acquired works wherever they could. Mozart himself accepted this situation and, in his letter to his father of 6 December 1783, we find him expressing his delight that *Die Entführung* had been performed in Prague and Leipzig to great acclaim.[180] And he was content that *Le nozze di Figaro* was staged in Prague and *Don Giovanni* in Vienna. Whether he received any special payment for these performances we do not know.

It is, of course, pointless to apply modern standards to Mozart's music and to the conditions under which it was commissioned and performed, as it was the product, after all, of completely different social circumstances. In general, he was no worse off than many of his colleagues and, as a virtuoso, was for a time better off than they were, while his income continued to increase between the time of his marriage and 1786. In 1785 Leopold had occasion to observe his son at close quarters and on 19 March 1785 wrote to his daughter: 'I think that, *as long as he has no debts to pay off*, my son can now bank 2000 florins; the money is undoubtedly there and, as far as food and drink are concerned, their household is run along extremely economical lines.'[181] It is odd that Leopold, who knew very well how little Mozart was to be trusted with money, could have been so wrong on this point. In fact, Mozart was in constant financial difficulties from the time of his wedding onwards, and the worries and humiliations bound up with them contributed substantially to his early death. Within six months of his wedding we hear of a creditor refusing to extend the date of a bill of exchange and threatening to take Mozart to court, with the result that the latter was obliged to turn to Baroness von Waldstätten.[182] And in July 1783, just as he was on the point of leaving for Salzburg, another creditor stood in the path of his carriage and demanded repayment of the sum of thirty florins, a sum that Mozart had great difficulty in raising.[183] He had scarcely returned from Salzburg when he was caught unawares by a further demand for twelve louis d'or that he had borrowed from a certain Johann Georg Scherz in Strasbourg in 1778. While in Munich, Mozart had assumed that his father would settle this debt for him, but on 6 December 1783 he had to write to Leopold, begging him to stand surety for him for a month.[184] We have already described how, when short of funds in 1785, he was now obliged to turn to Hoffmeister.

None the less, all these were debts that he was able to pay off, if necessary, from the income from concerts and similar sources. This changed in 1786. From now on his situation grew progressively worse as these sources, too, dried up. The letters that he wrote to his friend Michael Puchberg from 1788 onwards are harrowing evidence of this. Puchberg was a member of a mainly Protestant guild of merchants who enjoyed certain privileges that were granted by the emperor and that included the right to maintain warehouses in Vienna and carry on a wholesale business in the city.[185] His first wife, who had died in 1784, was a member of the Salliet family, with whom Mozart's own family had been friendly since 1773.[186] Accordingly, it was probably not membership of the same Masonic Lodge that brought the two men together, although this no doubt served to strengthen the bond between them. Mozart's first surviving letter to Puchberg dates from June 1788[187] and

---

180. *Briefe*, iii.295 (letter of 6 December 1783).
181. *Briefe*, iii.380 (letter of 19 March 1785).
182. *Briefe*, iii.257–8 (letter of 15 February 1783).
183. Nissen, *Biographie W. A. Mozarts*, 475.
184. *Briefe*, iii.293 (letter of 6 December 1783).
185. Friedrich Nicolai, *Beschreibung einer Reise durch Deutschland*, iv.447–8.
186. *Briefe*, i.490 (letter of 21 August 1773). For more on Puchberg, see Pohl, *Joseph Haydn*, ii.238–9. He had a son and daughter, both of whom were musical.
187. *Briefe*, iv.65 (letter of early June 1788). For the dating of Mozart's letters to Puchberg, see Spitta, 'Zur Herausgabe der Briefe Mozarts'.

indicates that the latter had already helped his friend in various financial ways, but the second contains a request for a relatively large loan,[188] a request that Puchberg was unable, of course, to meet. Conversely, he willingly supported Mozart from now on with greater or lesser sums, whenever the latter was unable to raise the money necessary to pay his rent or for Constanze to take the waters and so on. By the date of Mozart's death these debts totalled 1000 florins, but Puchberg, who, as trustee, helped Constanze to sort out Mozart's estate, did not insist on immediate repayment, preferring to wait a number of years until Constanze's circumstances had improved.[189] But Mozart had to ask other friends, too, for loans, including Franz Hofdemel, who held a post in the law courts in Vienna and who made Mozart a loan of one hundred florins.[190] Needless to say, none of this led to any real improvement in his situation, and before setting off for Frankfurt in 1790 he had to pawn some silverware and jewellery merely in order to raise the money for the journey.[191] On another occasion during the winter of 1790/91, an acquaintance, Joseph Deiner, who was the landlord of the Golden Snake Tavern, came across Mozart and his wife dancing around in their study and asked whether the composer was giving his wife a dancing lesson, to which Mozart answered with a laugh: 'We're only trying to keep warm, it's freezing in here and we can't afford to buy any wood.' Deiner immediately offered them some of his own supply, and Mozart promised to pay for it as soon as he had some money.[192] In the end, there were no depths to which he was not obliged to sink. 'I can find no true friends,' he wrote to Puchberg on 17 May 1790, 'and so I'm obliged to resort to moneylenders.'[193] Certainly, the letters dating from the end of September 1790 tell of very shady dealings, with an unnamed individual prepared to advance 1000 florins in cash, together with a quantity of cloth, in return for a bill of exchange for 2000 florins signed by Mozart and Hoffmeister.[194] Although we hear no more about this usury, the mere fact that Mozart was prepared to countenance it is sufficient to indicate the problems that he was facing at this time.

That Mozart's self-esteem as man and artist suffered in these circumstances is clear from the letters that he wrote at this time, and as always his problems were made worse by malicious gossip on the part of his delightful contemporaries. After his death, it was said that he had left debts of 30,000 florins, and Constanze even had to write to the Emperor Leopold in order to deny such appalling calumnies and assure him that 3000 florins would be sufficient to cover all her late husband's debts. Leopold generously helped her in this,[195] and his successor, Franz II, even granted her a pension.[196]

Needless to say, observers knew exactly how Mozart had managed to run up such a burden of debt, and self-righteously drew attention to his dissolute, dissipated lifestyle.[197] Many of these

---

188. *Briefe*, iv.69 (letter of 27 June 1788).
189. Nissen, *Biographie W. A. Mozarts*, 686.
190. *Briefe*, iv.77–8 (letter of late March 1789). The bill of exchange is reproduced by Jahn, *Gesammelte Aufsätze über Musik*, 234 [*Dokumente*, 296, *Documentary Biography*, 338].
191. Nissen, *Biographie W. A. Mozarts*, 683.
192. *Morgen-Post* (Vienna, 28 January 1856), no. 28 [*Dokumente*, 478, *Documentary Biography*, 564].
193. *Briefe*, iv.108 (letter of 17 May 1790 or before).
194. *Briefe*, iv.112–14 (letters of 28 and 30 September 1790).
195. Niemetschek, *Leben des k. k. Kapellmeisters Wolfgang Gottlieb Mozart*, 40–1, and Nissen, *Biographie W. A. Mozarts*, 580–1.
196. ◆ Concerning Mozart's finances, see Moore, 'Mozart in the Market Place', and Steptoe, 'Mozart and Poverty'.
197. Contemporary attitudes are clear from a remark such as the following in Schlichtegroll's obituary: 'In Vienna he married Constanze Weber and found in her a good mother of the two children of their union, and a worthy wife who, moreover, sought to restrain him from many foolishnesses and excesses. Despite a considerable income, he yet, in consequence of his exceptional sensuality and domestic disorder, left his family nothing beyond the glory of his name, and the attention of a large public fixed upon them' [*Dokumente*, 410, *Documentary Biography*, 469]. One can understand why Constanze bought up the whole print-run of a reprint of this obituary when it was published in Graz in 1794 and expressed herself with some warmth when discussing

good friends even went so far as to complain about his appearance, in which he admittedly took great pride. He liked to be well dressed and was fond of lace, watch chains and so on,[198] hence Clementi's initial impression that he was one of the emperor's chamberlains. It may even be the case that he was not especially economical in his dress, but only a philistine would use this as a stick with which to beat him. As for food and drink, we may accept his father's verdict without further ado, a verdict in any case confirmed by his sister-in-law Sophie Haibel, who insisted that he ate only the simplest fare.

Much has been written about his fondness for spirits: even today, there are many people incapable of conceiving of an artist and especially a musician who does not consume vast amounts of alcohol. There is no doubt that Mozart was particularly fond of punch,[199] but Sophie Haibel insists that his love of 'a drop of punch' was never taken to excess.[200] According to one well-known account, he asked his wife to prepare some punch for him while he was writing out the overture to *Don Giovanni*, and we know that, whenever he was working particularly intensely, he liked to fortify himself with a glass of wine or punch. The music-loving Johann Martin Loibl, a member of the same Masonic Lodge and a councillor with the Hungarian-Transylvanian Exchequer, was Mozart's neighbour in the Schulerstraße and used to send the composer wine from his cellar whenever he heard Mozart playing the harpsichord and then stopping to knock on the wall.[201] But none of this is enough to brand Mozart a heavy drinker. The basically lower middle-class composer lacked the talent to be an alcoholic, just as he lacked the talent to be a rake like Don Giovanni. Convivial by nature, he no doubt joined in when others were celebrating, allowing his boisterous high spirits free rein. Indeed, he may even have got carried away, as sometimes happened in his binges with Schikaneder.[202] But he himself proved again and again that he needed no stimulants in order to compose, and the very appearance of his scores suggests quite the opposite of a composer destroyed by drink.

Yet he was certainly fond of good company. At home, parties were limited to small musical gatherings that Constanze occasionally organized for a few friends, when he particularly enjoyed listening to Haydn's music.[203] All the more eagerly did he attend the lively social gatherings that Vienna had to offer at this time not only to fellow artists but also to educated amateurs. Music played a significant role on these occasions, and so it is easy to understand that Mozart enjoyed a particularly privileged status as a virtuoso and, especially, as an improviser. But he was no less

with Rochlitz this attempt to blacken her late husband's memory; see Rochlitz, 'Verbürgte Anekdoten', 17–24. Even more disparaging is the account of Ignaz Arnold in *Mozarts Geist*, 65ff., in which he attempts to identify the causes of Mozart's early death: in addition to over-work, 'he was a loving husband, fathered four children and, outside marriage too, had a number of affairs of the heart with compliant actresses and other refined girls and women, something his good wife was happy to overlook. Together with his wife and children, he was often forced to starve while working assiduously and was exposed to the impertinence of creditors who demanded repayment of his debts. As soon as he came into possession of a handful of louis d'or, the situation quickly changed. Now pleasure was the order of the day. He got drunk on champagne and tokay, lived it up, and within days was back where he started. We know how often he undermined his own health, spending the whole morning drinking champagne with Schikaneder and the whole night drinking punch, before returning to work after midnight without allowing his body the least opportunity to recover.'

198. Nissen, *Biographie W. A. Mozarts*, 692.
199. Kelly, *Reminiscences*, i.226.
200. Nissen, *Biographie W. A. Mozarts*, 672.
201. Information given to Jahn's friend Theodor von Karajan by Loibl's daughter, Frau Klein, in Vienna; see Jahn, *W. A. Mozart*, i.847.
202. Rochlitz is alone in claiming that Mozart drank to fend off depression; 'Verbürgte Anekdoten', 495–6.
203. Niemetschek, *Leben des k. k. Kapellmeisters Wolfgang Gottlieb Mozart*, 64.

popular as a kind, gallant and, above all, entirely natural individual, whose fondness for jokes endeared him to everyone, with comic doggerel proving his greatest love.[204]

But he was also a passionate dancer, a passion that he had ample opportunity to indulge in a city as fond of dancing as Vienna was at this time.[205] Indeed, he sometimes even claimed that he had made more progress as a dancer than as a musician. Observers noted that he danced the minuet with particular elegance.[206] On 22 January 1783 he reports with particular pleasure on a private ball that he had held in his own rooms:

Last week I gave a ball in my own rooms; – but it goes without saying that the young beaux paid 2 florins each; we began at 6 in the evening and stopped at 7 – what? only an hour? – no, no – at 7 in the morning. You're wondering where I found the space?[207] Here I have a room 1000 feet long and one foot wide, a bedroom, an anteroom and a beautiful big kitchen; – there are another two beautiful big rooms next to ours, which are still empty – and so I used these for our ball – Baron Wetzlar and his wife were there, as was Baroness Waldstätten, Herr von Edlenbach, that gasbag Gilowsky, the young Stephanie et uxor, Adamberger and his wife, the Langes and so on.[208]

He was also fond of attending public masked balls, at which his old talent for character masks again came into its own. In the letter from which we have just quoted, he asks his father to send him his old Harlequin costume, as he hopes to go to the masked ball as Harlequin – 'but not a soul must know about it, as there are so many asses at the masked balls here, indeed, nothing but asses'. On the Monday before Shrove Tuesday – 3 March – he got together with several friends and performed a 'company masque' during a break in the dancing:

It consisted of a pantomime. . . . My sister-in-law was Columbine, I was Harlequin, my brother-in-law Pier[r]o[t], an old dancing master (Merk) Pantaloon, a painter (Grassi) the Doctor. Both the plot and the music for the pantomime were by me. The dancing master, Merk, was kind enough to coach us, and I must say we performed very well. . . . The verses, although only doggerel, could have been better, they weren't by me but had been cobbled together by the actor [Johann Heinrich Friedrich] Müller.[209]

All that has survived of this undemanding little piece – K446 – is a fragment of the violin part that includes brief references to the plot, such as: 'Pantaloon and Columbine quarrel – the Doctor arrives – Pantaloon acts as master of ceremonies – introduces him as a husband for Columbine –

204. Niemetschek, *Leben des k. k. Kapellmeisters Wolfgang Gottlieb Mozart*, 93: 'Mozart was also open to the joys of conviviality and friendship. Among good friends, he was as trusting as any child, full of high spirits that found expression in the funniest jokes. It is with sheer pleasure that his friends in Prague recall the wonderful times that they spent in his company; they can never find words enough to praise his kind and innocent heart; in his company, people forgot that they were in the presence of Mozart, the much-admired artist.' A similar point is made by Rochlitz, 'Verbürgte Anekdoten', 494–5. His brother-in-law, Joseph Lange, observed that Mozart invariably made the most outrageous jokes when occupied with large-scale projects; Lange, *Biographie des Joseph Lange*, 171–2.

205. Kelly, *Reminiscences*, i.204–5.

206. Kelly, *Reminiscences*, i.226, and Nissen, *Biographie W. A. Mozarts*, 692–3.

207. Mozart had recently moved to new rooms belonging to a wealthy Jew, Baron Raimund Wetzlar. ◆ Probably this was the previous December. Mozart's new lodgings were at what is today Wipplingerstraße 14.

208. *Briefe*, iii.252 (letter of 22 January 1783).

209. *Briefe*, iii.259 (letter of 12 March 1783).

Columbine is sad – Pantaloon flatters her – she is cross – they becomes friends again' and so on. Mozart was especially fond of skittles and billiards, which he played to a very high standard.[210] He had his own billiard table at home, where, if necessary, he played either with Constanze or on his own.[211] This was, of course, a luxury, albeit one fairly widespread in Vienna at this time.[212] His doctors attempted to turn this pastime to his advantage. In the spring of 1783 he was struck down by the influenza epidemic that gripped the whole of Vienna,[213] and in the summer of 1784 he again fell seriously ill, as Leopold reported to his daughter:

My son has been very ill in Vienna, – he sweated so profusely at Paisiello's new opera [*Il re Teodoro in Venezia*] that his clothes were all soaked and he had to go out into the cold air in search of his servant, who had his overcoat, as orders had been given not to admit servants to the theatre through the ordinary entrance. As a result, he and others caught rheumatic fever, which became septic when not taken in hand at once. He writes: '14 [*recte* 4] days running at the very same hour I had a fearful attack of colic, that invariably began with violent vomiting; I now have to be terribly careful. My doctor is Herr Siegmund Barisani who has been to see me almost every day since getting here; he's very highly thought of here; he's also very clever and you'll see that he soon gets on here.[214]

Barisani was the son of Silvester von Barisani, an old friend of the Mozarts in Salzburg, where he was private physician to the archbishop. An outstanding doctor in his own right, Siegmund later became 'Physikus Primarius' at the Vienna General Hospital. The lines that he wrote in Mozart's *Stammbuch* (now in the Mozarteum in Salzburg) on 14 April 1787 attest to the warm friendship and respect that existed between the two men:

> Though Britons, great in spirit as they are,
> Know how to pay their tribute to thy art,
> And rapt in admiration hear thee play
> With mastery thy keyboard instrument;
> Though Latins envy thy composer's skill
> And try to follow it as best they may;
> Though long thy art has won thee fame and bliss,
> By Bach and Joseph Hayden [*sic*] only match'd;
> Do not forget thy friend, whose happiness
> And pride it is to know he served thee twice
> To save thee for the world's delight. This boast
> Is yet surpassed by joy and pride to know
> Thou art his friend, as he is ever thine.

210. Kelly reports that he often played with Mozart but never won a game; *Reminiscences*, i.226.
211. Niemetschek, *Leben des k. k. Kapellmeisters Wolfgang Gottlieb Mozart*, 64.
212. Friedrich Nicolai, *Beschreibung einer Reise durch Deutschland*, v.219.
213. See Mozart's letter of 7 June 1783: 'Praise and thanks be to God, I'm completely recovered! But my illness has left me with catarrh by way of a keepsake, which was very kind of it' (*Briefe*, iii.271).
214. *Briefe*, iii.331 (letter of 14 September 1784); see also Jahn, *W. A. Mozart*, i.845–6.

Beneath this, Mozart wrote the following lines:

Today, 3 September, I was very upset to learn that this noble man, this dearest and best of friends, who saved my life, has died quite unexpectedly. – He is at rest! – but I, we, all that knew him well – we shall *never* be at rest again – until we have the good fortune to see him again in a better world – *and never again to part.*

As a physician, too, Barisani proved no less solicitous than as a friend. He knew Mozart's habit of often working until late into the night and of resuming his work the following morning while still in bed. Unable to wean him of this habit and conscious of the fact that he spent so much time sitting at the keyboard, he urged him at least to remain standing while writing and to keep moving as much as possible. For a time, Mozart went riding in the morning, but appears to have abandoned this practice after only a short time: although he seems to have enjoyed the exercise, he always retained a vestigial sense of fear.[215] All the more, then, did Barisani encourage him to play skittles and billiards as a way of keeping in trim, not least because neither of these activities prevented him from working.[216] In Prague it was noted that he kept humming a particular motif to himself while playing billiards and occasionally glancing at a book that he was carrying around with him. It was the first quintet from *Die Zauberflöte* that was going round and round in his head.[217] And in Duschek's wine garden in Prague, he worked on the score of *Don Giovanni* while playing skittles, rising from his seat when it was his turn to play and returning to it afterwards.[218]

Readers fond of lecturing great men on their middle-class lifestyles may take Mozart to task on these matters. But none of these convivial pleasures and pastimes went beyond what was generally acceptable in Vienna at this time, and they are certainly not sufficient to explain the financial meltdown from which his family fortunes suffered from 1786 onwards. Far worse damage was caused by his ingrained good nature. In Leipzig, for example, he not only granted the choir free admission to his concert, he secretly gave an expensive present to a bass singer who had particularly impressed him. And on another occasion he gave several ducats to an elderly and impoverished piano tuner who, stammering with embarrassment, had asked him for a thaler.[219] Whenever he had any money on him, he was incapable of turning aside those who were in need, even if it meant inflicting hardship on his own family. Visitors were welcome at mealtimes, especially if they brought with them a sense of humour, and Mozart was particularly pleased if his other guests enjoyed it, too. Inevitably his good nature soon attracted all manner of disreputable individuals – in Sophie Haibel's words, 'false friends, parasites who, unnoticed, sucked his life's blood, worthless men and women who served as court jesters and whose contact with him harmed his reputation'.[220] One such person was Anton Stadler, an outstanding clarinettist and, at the same time, an amusing and adaptable individual and, what is more, a fellow Freemason, who for that very reason was readily admitted to Mozart's table. On one occasion Stadler discovered that Mozart had received fifty ducats from the emperor and immediately pretended to be in desperate straits himself, declaring that he would be lost unless Mozart lent him this precise sum. Mozart needed

215. Griesinger, *Biographische Notizen über Joseph Haydn*, 30.
216. ◆ This anecdote is unconvincing, not least in its suggestion that Mozart, at the time of his visit to Prague (28 August to mid-September 1791), had not yet composed the first-act quintet from *Die Zauberflöte*. According to his letter of 2 July 1791 (*Briefe*, iv.143), Mozart had composed the whole of the first act, from the introduction to the finale, not later than June.
217. Nissen, *Biographie W. A. Mozarts*, 559–60.
218. *Bohemia* (1856), 118 and 122.
219. Rochlitz, 'Verbürgte Anekdoten', 81–2.
220. Nissen, *Biographie W. A. Mozarts*, 673.

the money himself but gave him two solid repeating watches to pawn, asking him to bring him the receipt and to redeem them in good time. The date in question came and went, and, rather than lose the watches, Mozart give Stadler fifty ducats, plus interest. Stadler kept the money and left the watches at the pawnbroker's. But Mozart failed to learn his lesson. Following his visit to Frankfurt in 1790, he asked Stadler to redeem some of the silver that he had placed in pawn and to convert the rest into cash. Stadler was suspected of having removed the receipt from Mozart's strong box, which was always open to the world, but in spite of this, Mozart provided him with the money to undertake a concert tour in 1791, not only giving him his travelling expenses but also letters of recommendation and a new concerto (K622), which he wrote for him only a few months before his death.[221]

Undoubtedly Mozart's good nature proved a liability here, resulting in flagrant injustices towards his own family, whose burden of care was increased by his frequent illnesses. But one wonders where Constanze was in all this. Why did she not intervene and prevent her naïve yet easily misled husband from committing such mistakes? Why did she not run his household along more orderly lines? Her own frequent illnesses are not sufficient of an excuse here,[222] as they certainly did not prevent her from behaving in her typically overbearing, impassioned manner. In spite of all attempts to justify her actions, there is no doubt that she failed to act on those very occasions where purposeful, selfless intervention was required and that in this way she incurred much of the blame for Mozart's increasingly serious financial problems, problems which in turn undermined his health.

It is entirely typical of Mozart that from time to time he made a sincere effort to put his affairs in order. The most notable occasion on which he did so was in 1784, when his reputation and income both began to rise as a result of his frequent appearances as a virtuoso. In February 1784 he not only started to draw up a detailed list of his works,[223] he also began to keep a note of his income and expenditure. According to André, his income from concerts, lessons, compositions and so on was noted down on a long, thin strip of paper, while his expenditure was entered in a quarto notebook that he had previously used for his English exercises. Not even the least item was overlooked:

| 1 May 1784 | two mayflowers 1 kreutzer |
| 27 May 1784 | starling 34 kreutzers |

Beside this last entry is a tune, with the note 'That was nice!'

221. Nissen, *Biographie W. A. Mozarts*, 683–4. In the inventory and valuation of Mozart's estate we find the following entry: 'By Herr Anton Stadler, I & R Court Musician without liability, owing 500 fl.' [*Dokumente*, 494, *Documentary Biography*, 585]. ◆ For a complete documentary record of Mozart's estate, see *Dokumente*, 493–511, *Documentary Biography*, 583–604.
222. See Jahn, *W. A. Mozart*, i.850.
223. Published by André under the title *W. A. Mozarts thematischer Catalog* (Offenbach, 1805 and 1828), this is our most important source for the dating of Mozart's works from 1784 onwards, placing their chronology virtually beyond doubt. ◆ For a description and facsimile, see Mozart, *Eigenhändiges Werkverzeichnis*.

This is the theme of the rondo of the G major concerto K453, which Mozart completed on 12 April 1784:

The fact that the starling was able to whistle this theme, while adding a comic variant of its own, was sufficient to persuade Mozart to buy the bird there and then. He continued to hold it in high regard and, indeed, was fond of all animals and especially birds. When it died, he buried it in his garden with a gravestone inscribed with sentimental verses of his own composition.[224]

It is significant that, whereas Mozart continued to make entries in his thematic catalogue until the time of his death, he kept a record of his income and expenditure for only a year, from March 1784 to February 1785. He then abandoned the task to his wife, who very soon lost all interest in the exercise.

This was typical of the Mozart household, which was built on nothing and afterwards, when it was already too late, was only inadequately supported by a modest salary, with random receipts tending rather to endanger its stability than to bolster it up. And it was run by a couple incapable of imposing any order on it, Constanze as a result of naïve egoism and indifference, Mozart thanks to a disposition grounded in his artistic nature. Shortages and worries, disappointments and humiliations of every description were the inevitable consequence. All in all, the final decade of Mozart's life was shrouded in a dark mist from which death alone was to release him. The brighter the star of his artistry shone, the more sombre his surroundings became. No doubt it was certain aspects of his own character that drove him down this slippery slope – his carelessness and, in particular, his lack of resolve and knowledge of human nature – but they sprang for the most part from the wellspring of his whole character, his teeming imagination, which time and again allowed him to rise above the confusion that reigned all around him. The more powerfully this inner world transfigured his whole being, the more indifferent he became to the outside world, whose troubles he bore as if they were unavoidable. As long as his imagination moved in the same direction as the expectations of the world at large and his art was the transfigured expression of a universal culture, it seemed as though his contemporaries could sustain his ship of state as it ploughed on its faltering course. But as soon as his genius severed this bond, it was bound to founder, even if he had been better able to steer it than was in fact the case. Herein lies the tragedy of his destiny.

224. Schurig, *Wolfgang Amade Mozart*, ii.311.

31

Mozart's personality

'He who would the poet understand must needs seek out the poet's land.' This dictum of Goethe's[1] is true of every creative genius, and Mozart is no exception. Only his own remarks can tell us anything about the innermost core of his being. Admittedly, we have a whole series of contemporary accounts of his personality at our disposal, providing a colourful mixture of the good and the bad,[2] and much is of value to the biographer, at least when subjected to the appropriate degree of critical scrutiny. Here the biographer will learn more about the impressions that this out-of-the-ordinary figure left upon ordinary humanity and he will also discover some of the problems to which Mozart was exposed in his confrontation with common reality. But these are not primary sources and, in general, they say far more about the personality of the individual writer than they do about Mozart himself, inasmuch as such writers invariably tend to introduce into their picture all the various features that they themselves thought they possessed – or at least which they wanted to possess. In this way, the picture of Mozart is more or less badly distorted. In much the same way, we need to be extremely careful when dealing with Mozart's allegedly 'authentic' remarks that occasionally appear in print. Recent experience has taught us only too well what over-imaginative and enthusiastic disciples can achieve in this respect.

Yet not even the primary sources – Mozart's letters and works – are all of equal value. The former are evidence of the first importance, not least in view of the impressionistic nature of most of them, and even those dashed off at the greatest speed contain at least an element of Mozart's character. But they were written *sub specie momenti* and were always influenced to a greater or lesser extent by the personality of the recipient: only very rarely did Mozart reveal his innermost nature here.[3] As a result, they, too, need to be approached with caution and to be complemented by the composer's works, for it is these alone that reveal who Mozart really was, they alone that show us his innermost, autonomous nature unaffected by external, random circumstances and influences. It is not that the Mozart who emerges from these contemporary reports and from his letters is a completely different person from the one who is found in his works: quite the opposite, it is the same forces that affect his outer life and his work as a composer. But we should be careful not to apply the standards of ordinary mortals to so exceptional an individual as Mozart. The true wellspring of his life was always his work as an artist: it affected the whole of his outward, bourgeois existence and, indeed, sometimes overwhelmed it to such an extent that he was no longer understood by the people around him. Even his own sister discovered this when she tried to reduce his character to a simple formula and described him as a child, a description that struck a chord

---

1. ◆ From his 'Noten und Abhandlungen zu besserem Verständnis des Westöstlichen Divans' (1819).
2. Collected by Leitzmann, *Mozarts Persönlichkeit: Urteile der Zeitgenossen.* ◆ In general, also see *Dokumente* and *Documentary Biography.*
3. ◆ For a more sceptical approach to Mozart's letters, and what they say concerning his personality and relationships, see Schroeder, *Mozart in Revolt.*

with contemporaries,[4] based, as it was, on the conviction – whether born of admiration or mild censure – that Mozart's world was essentially different from that of ordinary mortals. The underlying feeling was correct; yet, with the possible exception of Joseph Haydn, none of Mozart's contemporaries suspected that this world was in fact loftier and purer than their own, however much they may have been moved by his music. Theirs was an ordinary middle-class world conditioned by the state, religion, morality, social conventions and related forms of life; even those individuals who were naturally endowed with artistic talent regarded it as a special gift to capture in music the experiences gained in those areas. This is certainly an attitude shared by Leopold Mozart, but not by his great son. We would be guilty of comprehensively misunderstanding the latter's personality if we were to seek its motivating force anywhere other than in the urge to create. It was this that was the most basic form of his existence: it needed no external stimulus, while at the same time refusing to tolerate any arbitrary interruption. Artistic creativity constituted the true meaning of Mozart's life and, as a result, was also his destiny. We know that other great musicians such as Handel, Haydn and Beethoven regarded themselves as vessels of some higher power: their creative powers, they felt, went beyond them. Although Mozart is not on record as having said anything similar, this does not preclude the possibility that he, too, felt what Goethe termed the 'demonic'. Leopold could compose by summoning and dismissing his artistic muse at will, whereas Mozart's creativity brooked no external laws but forced his outward life to conform to *her* laws. In consequence, it is impossible to separate his life from his music: in both, the same force is at work.

Even so, the people around him sensed from his attitude to his environment that he experienced things in ways completely different from their own. The first thing to which the ordinary bourgeois objects in the lives and activities of men of genius tends to be their 'impractical' nature. Mozart, too, was impractical, although not in the original sense of the word, which would imply that he was averse to all forms of action and in favour of only thinking and feeling. Quite the opposite: he was capable of acting vigorously and purposefully, but only when it was a question of asserting this basic instinct in the face of all obstacles and other inhibiting factors, as he did in his struggle with Colloredo and later with his own father. On the other hand, he was thoroughly 'impractical' in the normal sense of the word, being incapable of exploiting the situation in which he found himself and failing to adapt to a whole series of random incidents that the vast majority of people confuse with taking control of their lives. But nothing could have been further from Mozart's mind: random events barely existed in his world, hence his carelessness and even indifference towards all those aspects of 'real' life that played such a part in his ultimate ruin. Even though he suffered as a result of this indifference, as he did at the end of his life, it was more like an agonizing dream from which he was repeatedly released by his creative urge, an urge that burst forth with all the greater force on these very occasions. It is significant that his involvement in the outside world increased at the very times when his art – however freely – operated within the confines of the sort of music traditionally written for society at large, as was the case between 1783 and 1786, whereas his interest began to flag immediately afterwards, when he was engaged on his

4. Nissen, *Biographie W. A. Mozarts*, 259, and Schlichtegroll, 'Joannes Chrysostomus Wolfgang Gottlieb Mozart', 82ff. Marianne's own words may be found in Nottebohm, *Mozartiana*, 111. It is the same concept as the one that Herder and others applied to Goethe, albeit in a censorious vein, and that Schopenhauer later used to define genius. ◆ For Nannerl's 'Data for a biography of the late composer Wolfgang Mozart', written for Schlichtegroll, see *Dokumente*, 398–405 (here 405), *Documentary Biography*, 454–63 (here 462). In fact, the comment attributed to Nannerl, that Mozart was an 'eternal child', comes from a passage added to the end of her memoir in another hand.

greatest works, a lack of interest that had such disastrous consequences for him on a material level. Indeed, even events that tend to leave a particularly deep impression on us soon lost their keenness under the pressure of his urge to work: here one thinks especially of the death of his mother in Paris, but it is also clear from the philosophically tinged letter that he wrote to his father immediately prior to the latter's death, that this death, too, had already lost its terrors for him.[5]

But what exactly was the reality which, hidden from his contemporaries, lay within the heart of this genius? Our own age is fond of examining the lives of great artists and, if possible, of saddling them with one or other of the philosophical systems that existed in their own day, an approach familiar from the example of Wagner and Schopenhauer. But Mozart was utterly lacking in any desire to develop an outlook on life along philosophical lines. Of course, he had a keen intellect and even in his creative work had no time for aimless daydreaming, but nothing could have been further from his mind than to build up his view of the world on conceptual processes as such, still less to posit a complete philosophical system. In this respect, too, he remained an artist, in other words, a sentient being whose world was one of opinions and feelings, not of concepts. He did not judge life by a particular set of epistemological principles but, quite the contrary, tended to judge these principles by the yardstick of life itself, thereby following Goethe's dictum to the effect that we are dependent on life, not on contemplation. Whenever he engaged in theoretical speculation, it was not for the sake of theorizing as such but because of some link with his own material existence.

When examining Mozart's personality, it makes no sense, therefore, to set out from the abstract world of ideas contained in his works and letters. Not even his attitude to religion brings us any closer to the actual nature of his view of the world, and the same is true of his relations with nature. Central to his view of the world was something altogether different: humankind. For Mozart, it was the individual human being who was the yardstick by which all else was judged. It was not through idle speculation in the Gluckian sense but through the instinct germane to genius that he gradually came to realize that nowhere is the conflict between the general and the specific more clearly and comprehensively depicted than in the individual human being.

In the circumstances, it is no wonder that his art drew its greatest strength from his wonderful ability to observe his fellow human beings.[6] This was an innate gift, occurring, albeit in a childlike form, even during his boyhood and finding expression in the remarkably keen-eyed and specific manner in which he characterized the artists he met. Initially, of course, these were performing artists, but the same was later true of creative artists and their works. The very first example, dating from 7 January 1770, is already typical of his whole approach:

[Giuseppe Afferi] un bravo cantante, un baritono, mà [is a fine singer, a baritone, but] sounds forced when he sings falsetto, but not as much as Tibaldi in Vienna. Bradamante . . . recita under an assumed name, I don't know which, ha una voce passabile, e la statura non sarebbe male, ma distona come il diavolo [her voice is tolerably good and she hasn't a bad presence, but she sings devilishly out of tune]. Ruggiero . . . un musico, canta un poco Manzolisch ed à una bellissima voce forte ed è già vecchio, ha cinquanta cinque anni ed à una [a castrato who sings rather like Manzuoli and has a very fine powerful voice and is already old, he's fifty-five and has a] flexible

---

5. ◆ Abert's hypothesis, that family tragedies had only a limited effect on Mozart's capacity for work, is open to question. The two most fallow periods in his compositional output followed the death of his mother in 1778 and (albeit at a distance of some months) the death of his father in 1787: at both these times his output tailed off dramatically.
6. See Heuß, 'Mozart als Kritiker'.

throat. Leone [Afferi's wife] . . . à una bellissima voce, ma è tanto susurro nel teatro che non si sente niente [has a most beautiful voice, but there's so much whispering in the theatre that you can't hear anything]. Irene . . . à una schnoffelte voce e canta sempre um ein Viertel zu tardi, ò troppo a buon ora [has a muffled voice and always comes in a beat too late or too soon].[7]

Among other examples that have survived are character sketches of Bernasconi, the two delightful Mannheim organists and especially Wieland. Typical of all of them is the implacable search for the truth, a search which, even in the case of good friends such as Raaff, never led to well-meaning idealizations but which, with their keen eye for detail and reluctance to praise, invariably remain objective. Virtually all these judgements could stand today. But nor is there any trace of moralizing bombast, merely a delight in observation as such and, above all, an attempt to distil the quintessence of the people in question.

This gift for observing his fellow humans was the source of Mozart's dramatic art and it is one, moreover, that he inherited from his father, the only difference being that the two of them made different uses of it. For the rationalistic Leopold, a man's character could be clearly divined by reason and intellect. In consequence, individuals were treated as fixed points in a cleverly devised system of coordinates that he used in his attempt to keep control of his life. In other words, his observations of his fellow men and women served a rational purpose for him, contributing to his own practical advantage. For Mozart, conversely, human character could not be reduced to a rational formula. Rather, it was a unique interplay of various psychological forces, never recurring in the same combination, with the result that he saw the whole of human existence as no more and no less than the development and interaction of these eternally changing creations of nature. To observe this inexhaustible wealth of figures and capture them in his works was the main aim of his life. In this, he always set out from their natural state, refusing to apply preconceived moral or utilitarian standards: for him, people were as they were, not as they ought to be or as he wanted them to be. Above all, he made no attempt to analyse them in terms of good or evil: after all, how could he be expected to apply his way of observing people to the struggle for material existence, a struggle which, to someone of his own disposition, was bound to seem remote, restrictive and random? This explains much that seemed puzzling and even inexplicable to normal people of his own time and that continues to seem so today: here one thinks especially of his innocence, credulousness and even his helplessness in his dealings with others, all aspects of his character that caused his father so many sleepless nights. Mozart is a striking example of the way in which it is possible to be brilliantly observant, yet still not be a judge of character in the traditional sense of that term.

On the other hand, Mozart's character protected him from his father's growing bitterness and misanthropy, encouraging an ever greater purity in his dealings with his fellow human beings and safeguarding him from the two main vices of musicians, envy and vanity.[8] The often highly unedifying spectacle that the average artist presents in his desperate pursuit of praise was alien to his

---

7. *Briefe*, i.301 (letter of 7 January 1770). The performance in question took place in Verona. The opera is believed to have been Guglielmi's *Il Ruggiero*. ◆ Mozart's letter is written in a wilful combination of Italian and German.

8. Readers wishing to describe Mozart as vain on the strength of certain superficial predilections such as the care he lavished on his clothing are welcome to do so, as the nub of his personality remains unaffected thereby, significant though such features may be for this character as a whole. After all, he himself always set out in his observations from the outward impression left on him by others. It is sufficient in this context to recall his reactions to performing artists: for him, their external appearance and above all their 'action', in other words, the manner of their performance and their ability to perform, were at least as important as their musical achievements. Under this same heading comes the great attention that he paid throughout his life to dance and to mime in general.

way of thinking and feeling. Not that this means he was unaware of his own merits. But he was well able to distinguish between pride and arrogance among artists. His breast swelled with a powerful sense of self-awareness as he grew increasingly conscious of the whole wealth of his inner life. His prize possession was his 'honour', to which he repeatedly returns in his letters, and whenever his artistic freedom was called into question, he was fearless in expressing his feelings. Yet even here he interfered only to the extent that it was necessary to ensure that nothing stood in the way of his genius. Never for a moment did it occur to him to derive personal advantage from this, still less to envy others their advantages and thus to defraud them. For fellow composers who acted in this way he had only an ironic smile, but he was incapable of feeling hatred or moral indignation, revealing merely the interest that he took in each new type of person that he encountered. Occasional outbursts of anger are the exception that confirms this rule.

His natural disposition also meant that he lacked any desire to contribute to people's moral improvement or to persuade them to mend their ways. Here, too, he went no further than what he saw all around him and what his artist's hand could fashion. Only towards the end of his life, when, under the influence of Freemasonry, he became more interested in ethical questions, do we encounter an ethical tendency in his works, although even in *Die Zauberflöte* the dewy-eyed nostalgia that we find here shows clearly that the ideal posited in this work remained no more than an ideal to the great realist in Mozart: in other words, it was something eternally unattainable.

Ultimately, however, Mozart's observations of others invariably threw him back on himself. Through them, rather than through introspection, he came to a better understanding of himself. It would be wrong to assume that, by studying others, Mozart lost sight of himself. Although his basic principle in all his dealings with others was to live and let live, this did not imply an impersonal approach, still less a refusal to engage in moral actions of his own. To understand and to forgive everything was certainly not his style. Quite the opposite: Mozart was a man with a genuine, conscious belief in morality, as far removed from the anti-morality of so many of the adherents of the *Sturm and Drang* movement as from the supra-morality of some of today's bohemian artists. In this, he owed much to the healthy atmosphere in his parents' house, but the remarkably sure sense of moral sensitivity that characterized him was ultimately uniquely his. Kindness and a willingness to help were other innate qualities, yet the moral code that he gradually worked out for himself was not a categorical imperative, as it was for Beethoven as the spiritual brother of Kant and Schiller, but simply emerged from the cultivation of his own basic nature. He was moral out of an inner need and, as a result, free from all narrow-mindedness. Leopold's morality was rooted in rationalism, Mozart's in his humanity. Extremely finely developed, his conscience reflects the whole of the eighteenth century's delicacy of sentiment and, just as it led him to victory in his fight with the archbishop and in his far more difficult struggle with his father, so it also helped him to survive the morass of the Webers' machinations at the time of his engagement. But, even though Mozart remained silent on the subject, it finds its most moving expression in his later behaviour towards Constanze when, following the initial onrush of passion, he was forced to realize that, instead of committing himself to a woman who was his equal and to whom he could reveal his innermost thoughts, he had married someone with whom he could merely share his bed and board. Here, too, we see the truth of the old adage: 'Marry in haste, repent at leisure.' In the case of lesser people, such a conflict tends ultimately to lead to total emotional insensitivity, but Mozart fought his way through and, although it was a painful experience, he suffered no long-term psychological harm. Not even here did he feel called upon to educate, but nor did it occur to him to repudiate a woman whose life was inextricably bound to his own by habit and inclination. With his innate good-heartedness, he invited her to share in every aspect of his being that she was capable of understanding and experiencing with him. That this did not include the finest and deepest things that he had to give he accepted as his inescapable fate, a fate that he was unable to change but that he had to bear with fortitude. The price of having to approach his highest goals alone he squared with his own conscience, demonstrating true nobility of mind in fulfilling to the very end the obligation placed on him by the dislocation between his own private world and the bond of matrimony that he had elected to take upon himself.

The principal source of Mozart's view of the world – his keen eye for the world around him – was also the starting point of two other important aspects of his character, his humour and his sense of irony. The primitive form that these two aspects assumed in his letters, not just during his adolescence but later, too, generally had precious little to do with wit. What we find here are old chestnuts of the worst kind, jokes normally bandied by orchestral musicians involving wordplay and rhymes verging on mere silliness. In short, we note that Mozart was born in the town that gave the character of Hanswurst his familiar guise.[9] Occasionally, we are even reminded of the coarse jokes of the popular poetry from south-west Germany.[10] But it is entirely characteristic of Mozart that these jokes always sound entirely natural: never once did it occur to him to play the conscious wit. And behind most of them we find the sense of unbridled delight at boldly transgressing the norms and conventions that the majority of his contemporaries took so terribly seriously. We already find this in the case of his penchant for punning. Fate had given him the name Mozart: why could he not equally well have been called Trazom or Romatz?[11] Even his grotesque rhymes appear in a different light when we recall his views on rhyme as such – at least in his later years. On a somewhat higher level is the Klopstockian ode contained in a letter to his cousin and signed 'The Honourable Pig's Tail'.[12] It was to Maria Thekla that he confided that side of his character that was content to enjoy the base pleasures of the moment: here he uses the ode to ridicule all thoughts of eternity that could mar that enjoyment. Many of his comic accounts of individual incidents that create their effect with the slapstick humour of a scene from an *opera buffa* already reveal that loftier sense of humour that we also encounter in his works, a humour involving the ability to empathize with his characters and, at the same time, to observe their actions and inactions as a disengaged spectator. He is capable of portraying the limited, conditional, transient aspect of a character as something that is true for all time and, at the same time, of measuring it by the absolute. He fully understands, for example, how a character like Papageno thinks and feels and, as a result, fashions the part entirely on the basis of the character's world of ideas. But he also knows how narrow this world is, a narrowness hidden from Papageno: he knows that Papageno can never share in the ideal, never be blessed by supreme happiness. On this contrast rests the comedy associated with the character, comedy that explores far deeper recesses of Papageno's emotional life than the jokes of the old Hanswurst, for all that Papageno is superficially Hanswurst's descendant. Only in this way was Mozart able to ensure that this popular favourite, who was generally only loosely associated with the plot and who served only to make audiences laugh, was organically integrated into the drama.[13]

9. ◆ In general, see Asper, *Hanswurst*.

10. Sources include anthologies such as the *Augsburger Tafelkonfekt* and the *Ostracher Liederhandschrift*.

11. On another occasion he invented funny names not just for himself but for everyone around him: *Briefe*, iv.11 (letter of 15 January 1787). In providing details for his marriage certificate he even called himself Wolfgang Adam instead of Amad.; see Hajdecki, 'Mozarts Taufnamen'. ◆ For a psychoanalytical interpretation of Mozart's marriage certificate, see Solomon, *Mozart: A Life*, 277–83.

12. *Briefe*, ii.548 (letter of 10 May 1779).

13. ◆ Further, see Winternitz, 'Gnagflow Trazom: An Essay on Mozart's Script, Pastimes, and Nonsense Letters', and Mieder, '"Nun sitz ich wie der Haass im Pfeffer": Sprichwörtliches in Mozarts Briefen'.

There is particular pleasure to be had from observing the way in which Mozart's sense of humour moved from satire to irony, the more he distanced himself inwardly from the Italians. The Osmin of *Die Entführung aus dem Serail* is still essentially a satirical character: keenly observed though he is and however much he emerges as a figure of flesh and blood, we do not have the impression that he is in any way related to Mozart himself and that these features caused him any problems of his own. This is the standpoint of Italian *opera buffa*, albeit one refined to the highest degree, a refinement due above all to the fact that there is no longer any trace here of the Italians' cold self-righteousness. But from *Le nozze di Figaro* onwards we have the sense that Mozart felt his characters' weaknesses and inhibitions for himself and that he was merely reproducing them from a superior standpoint. In this way, satire becomes that remarkably heart-warming irony that in *Le nozze di Figaro* completely replaces the traditional form of comedy and that even today remains unintelligible to the Italians. One often has the feeling that the composer, smiling serenely, is looking down on his own creations with a very real sense of pleasure. More than any other music dramatist he was capable of both living for the moment and living with the idealists and thus constantly playing off the one against the other. Until now, audiences at both serious and comic operas had never known an element of surprise in terms of either atmosphere or characterization, but in the case of Mozart's operas, they were never quite certain whether the comedy might suddenly turn serious or vice versa. Yet there was never the impression of anything arbitrary or random, only of real life at its most immediate. This marked a tremendous step forward on the road from theatre to real drama, and it was Mozart that opera had to thank for this.

Mozart's attitude to his fellow human beings also affected his attitude to society and the state. For individuals in Mozart's day, society was incomparably more important than what we understand by the term today, and certainly more important than the state. In the case of artists, it not only determined their material existence, it also affected their art. Unlike today's artists, artists in Mozart's day created their works not for the nation as a whole but for a particular group of privileged individuals, namely, high society. It is no wonder, then, that the vast majority of merely talented, non-creative artists believed that the main object of their art was to depict man as a social being and that in no circumstances could the clearly delineated boundaries of this field of impressions be transgressed. It would be wrong to dismiss this art out of hand as impersonal, as it offered individuals more than enough scope to express themselves, but feeling and expression were none the less limited to areas that society regarded as natural and permissible. When the rise of comic opera undermined high society's prior claims to the operatic stage, convention was not replaced by purely human values, it was merely that the old aristocracy now had to coexist alongside the middle classes and peasantry. Class, not mankind, remained the decisive factor. It is no accident that in both *opéra comique* and the German singspiel such great emphasis was laid on the depiction of the characters' environment or that a large number of the songs that they included consisted of ones associated with particular social classes. The various social classes and the clash between them also play a part in Mozart's operas, of course, but it is clear that he was not interested in these classes as such but only in the people who represented them, with all their desires, merits and foibles. Social structures, society and so on were only the forms within which the characters interacted. In the case of a character such as Count Almaviva, the older type of opera had focused first on his social status and only then on his attributes as a human being, regarding his affairs as a gentlemanly pastime. Mozart's count, by contrast, is motivated first and foremost by sexual desire in constant conflict with his self-importance, with his aristocratic status playing a part only to the extent that it is the outward expression of that self-importance and of his determination to insist on his ancient *droit de seigneur*. In short, what matters here is not so much the social as the human.

As a direct consequence of this, Mozart attaches little importance to his characters' environment and so on. Men and women attract him only as autonomous individuals, not as the product of material circumstances and conditions. Where we find examples of local colour, as we do in *Die Entführung aus dem Serail*, these are not merely an external addition. Beneath their oriental mask, the Osmins of the older type of opera were thoroughly western, often deeply boorish blusterers and curmudgeons, whereas in Mozart's case the Turkish element is part and parcel of the character.[14]

This also explains why Mozart was not a political animal: the state was of even less interest to him than society, with political theories belonging in the realm of abstraction, a world that could not be grasped through the senses and for which he therefore had no time. Here, as elsewhere, there was a vast gulf between him and his father, who was unusually interested in both the theory and practice of politics. For Mozart, conversely, political principles were a matter of almost total indifference and he had time only for the people who represented them, hence the fact that in his choice of friends he never allowed himself to be influenced by political considerations. Very rarely do we find sudden outbursts of the kind that occurred in 1782, following the British successes at Gibraltar, when he proudly called himself an 'out-and-out-Englishman'.[15] But these were no more than passing moods and they fade into total insignificance beside the fact that the most important political event that he lived to witness, the French Revolution, receives not a single word of mention in his letters. Never once do we hear him speak of freedom, equality, human rights and so on as universal demands. Whenever he came into contact with individuals who championed these principles, as occasionally happened in Masonic lodges, it was again the people who fascinated him, not the principles. As a result, readers will search his letters in vain for a political creed.[16] Admittedly, we encounter the occasional democratic effusion of a kind regularly found on the lips of the bourgeoisie at this time: on one occasion we read, for example, that it is the heart that ennobles the individual, not his social standing.[17] Elsewhere he writes that the well-to-do are incapable of friendship,[18] that the German princes are all niggards[19] and that he thinks little of the honour of serving the emperor.[20] Nor did his inborn sense of self-awareness desert him in aristocratic houses. Indeed, he always felt at his ease in these circles, finding friends and warm admirers here. Above all, he was completely lacking in Beethoven's demonstrative manner, a manner calculated to ensure that the aristocracy felt his superiority. Socially, too, he stuck to individuals, not to principles. He no more had it in him than Goethe to belong to a political party in the bourgeois sense of the term: here, too, the views that he held were emphatically his own. Striking, by contrast, are the frequent professions of Germanness that we have already encountered and that we shall encounter on many further occasions in the course of the following pages.[21] In this, Mozart was markedly different from both Haydn and Beethoven. That these were not

---

14. ◆ For a different view, see Head, *Orientalism, Masquerade and Mozart's Turkish Music*.

15. *Briefe*, iii.238 (letter of 19 October 1782).

16. ◆ In fairness, it should be noted that relatively few letters survive from the period after the death of his father in 1787 and that, for the most part, they are highly personal. As such they are unlikely to reflect on important current events, including the revolution in France.

17. *Briefe*, iii.133 (letter of 20 June 1781).

18. *Briefe*, ii.437 (letter of 7 August 1778).

19. *Briefe*, ii.318 (letter of 7 March 1778).

20. *Briefe*, iii.201 (letter of 10 April 1782).

21. The relevant passages may be found in *Briefe*, ii.21 (letter of 29/30 September 1777); ii.110 (letter of 8 November1777); ii.346 (letter of 1 May 1778); iii.220 (letter of 17 August1782); iii.254 (letter of 5 February 1783); and iii.393 (letter of 21 May 1785). See also Ernst Lewicki, 'Mozarts Deutschtum nach seinen Briefen'.

merely occasional outbursts is clear from their sheer number. Nor was this the egoistical patriotism of his father, a sentiment born of hatred and envy of the Italians, but the increasingly clear awareness that, thanks to the actions of Frederick the Great, intellectual forces were beginning to stir in Germany that he recognized as more closely related to his own view of the world than the spirit that blew in from abroad. As a result, he was not a patriot in the modern, middle-class sense of the term but was probably something more than this: he was pleased to have discovered new wellsprings of artistic strength on German soil and insisted on their exploitation in order to increase Germany's might and prestige. Even today, we may reckon this to his credit.

In the light of all that has been said so far, we shall have no difficulty in imagining that Mozart was particularly responsive to friendship. Just as he shut himself off from the world with no feelings of hatred, so he spent his whole life searching for a friend with whom he could share his innermost thoughts. It was not merely the delight in innocent amusement that repeatedly drove him to seek the company of others, but the urge to interact with them, to leave his mark on them and, in turn, to be enriched and have his burden of care lightened by them. The more the humanitarian ideal flared up in him, the more lively was his desire to give practical expression to his belief that we are all brothers. In this he was encouraged by his innate goodness of heart and his perpetual willingness to help his fellow human beings in times of inner and outer need. Yet he never forced himself on other people. On the contrary, he had the gift – again it was the result of his powers of observation – of instinctively examining every person who tried to approach him, of determining what he himself could offer that person and of treating them accordingly. In this respect he behaved towards his acquaintances in exactly the same way in which he behaved towards his wife, allowing them to share in his inner life only to the extent that they were able to understand it. With spontaneous jokers such as Leutgeb he played the part of the prankster, with aristocrats he was the gentleman. Only to a select few, including Bullinger, Count Hatzfeld and the Jacquin family, was he prepared to reveal more of himself. To no one did he reveal himself entirely. These were close, even intimate friends who gave him their love, respect and good will in abundance but who were unable to support him on his chosen course. A different situation arose with Joseph Haydn, at least from the time when they first became personally acquainted. Haydn was the only man of genius among Mozart's circle of friends who could give him what no one else could: not merely a woman's infatuated devotion, but manly criticism and, above all, a true understanding of his innermost needs as an artist. But even Haydn, as the child of another generation, was denied access to whole areas of Mozart's character. And, as a child of the people, Haydn had in any case neither the gift nor the desire to ponder such contrasts. But it is entirely characteristic of the relationship between the two men that Haydn's artistic influence on Mozart, which had never been less than considerable but which had varied in its intensity, not only became stronger as a result of personal contact, it also became more regular. Individuals had a far livelier influence on Mozart than abstract trends and systems.

Important though the role of friendship undoubtedly was in Mozart's world of experience, an even more significant role was played by love. Yet, although love accompanied him throughout the whole of his mature life, it must be noted at the outset that the way in which gossip-mongering philistines – whether of the moralizing or anti-moralizing kind – regularly treat this favourite topic of theirs in their lives of great men is not the right approach to the problem. Here, as elsewhere, the creative genius undoubtedly experiences love in a completely different way from the non-artist, irrespective of whether the latter holds typically petit-bourgeois views or whether he claims to be free of such prejudices. Passion is part of the genius's essential nature and does not need to be kindled by any particular incident. This is the meaning behind the remark attributed to Beethoven, that he had 'never been without a love'.[22] In Mozart, too, the desire for love was permanently present. This instinct is of paramount importance for the creative individual, but whether or not it is activated in individual cases is a matter of pure chance, with the result that it often fails to bring the person in question complete satisfaction. Of all artists, Mozart was particularly unfortunate in never being able to see his dream fulfilled. In this he differed from Schumann, for example, who found fulfilment with Clara Wieck. In the case of Aloysia Weber, he came close to it for a time; and there is some evidence that he did so again with Maria Theresia von Trattner. In the case of his wife Constanze, by contrast, he very soon saw himself further than ever from that goal and was forced as both man and artist to make do as best he could.[23]

This act of renunciation did not affect the desire for love that lay dormant within him. Rather, this desire appeared increasingly as the motivating force behind his stage works, and at least one recent writer has pointed out, quite correctly, that love is the basic theme of all Mozart's operas.[24] Yet we need to remember that this has been the case throughout the whole history of opera and presumably it will always remain so, as the emotional nature of music forces it in this direction as though of its own accord. Entirely new, however, was the way in which Mozart treated this age-old theme. Only in his early operas did he interpret love in its older sense as a form of gallantry, in other words, as a social phenomenon: here he was thrown back on earlier models as a result of his lack of personal experience. But for the mature Mozart, love was an elemental, natural force that elevates or debases the individual, liberating or crushing him, depending on the way in which it affects other aspects of his personality. As such it invariably became his destiny, no matter what the circumstances were in which he found himself. Faced with such an elemental phenomenon, we cannot, of course, apply moral standards or seek to draw a distinction between good and evil: for Mozart, love was neither a sin nor a means of redemption. Certainly, he did not exclude the possibility of love based on morality, as morality, too, was one of the realities of life, but it was not an ideal by which all else was to be judged. Indeed, he was fond of contrasting these various forms of love in one and the selfsame drama, notably in *Don Giovanni*, but also in *Die Zauberflöte*, a work that draws on other ethical ideas in this regard. As a result, we encounter this natural force in Mozart's works in the most disparate guises: as a demonic life force, as passion in its most varied gradations, as a moral force and as a dull natural instinct. As a distorted form of the last of these, we also find lasciviousness. No other composer in the whole history of opera came close to Mozart in his ability to experience love in all its facets and to depict them through his art. In his life, too, the different forms of the same feeling were in a state of constant turmoil, depending on which of his various women coaxed it from his soul. In this he genuinely resembles his own Don Giovanni, who likewise adapts the expressions of his sex drive to suit whichever female character he happens

22.   Wegeler and Ries, *Biographische Notizen über Ludwig van Beethoven*, 54.

23.   His changing view of marriage is highly significant in this context. From Mannheim he wrote to his father on 7 February 1778: 'I want to make my wife happy, not to make my fortune through her'; *Briefe*, ii.263. Shortly after settling in Vienna, he denied that he was thinking of marriage as he had 'other things' on his mind; *Briefe*, iii.140 (letter of 25 July 1781). But less than six months later we find him writing again to his father, expressing a far from idealistic view of marriage: 'The voice of nature speaks as loud in me as in others, louder, perhaps, than in many a big strong lout of a fellow' (*Briefe*, iii.180, letter of 15 December 1781). Bed, board and a roof over his head are now the reasons that Mozart adduces for marrying. Although a great deal of this letter is written with his father's views in mind, we already find an indication of his realization, gradually gained through his dealings with Constanze, that he will be forced into marriage with a woman who is not his intellectual and moral equal. ◆ Here Abert takes a harder line on Constanze than elsewhere in the text – again, it seems, to preserve his 'moral' view of the composer. Among a wealth of writings about Mozart and Constanze, see in particular Lauer, *Mozart und die Frauen*; Weißensteiner, *Die Frauen der Genies*; Allihn, 'Die Darstellung der Konstanze Mozart in der neueren Mozart-Literatur'; and Gärtner, *Constanze Mozart: After the Requiem*.

24.   Cohen, *Die dramatische Idee in Mozarts Operntexten*, 39.

to be dealing with at the moment in question. Mozart's love for Aloysia was fired by the purest and most ideal passion, whereas his relationship with his cousin, for all its warmth and sincerity, was ruled by a quite striking predilection for the most primitive, one could almost say the most animalistic, aspect of his character – and not only in terms of eroticism. In this context, one recalls the juicy language in which his letters to her are couched – but these examples are really all in a class of their own. Embarrassed prudishness is even less appropriate here than elsewhere,[25] but it would be equally wrong to take such remarks out of context and regard them as prime examples of Mozart's character. They can be understood only on the strength of his whole personality, as expressions of a sensuous individual who was not blind to the most basic aspects of human existence. The difference between Mozart and his contemporaries is merely that these latter considered such matters sufficiently important to include in works of art; with Mozart, conversely, only the character of Papageno shows the aspect that they assumed in his own artistic reality.

Here we already find ourselves confronted by great and apparently irreconcilable opposites in Mozart's personality. And yet they are not the only contrasts that made up his world of inner experience. The realization that this is so may well be one of the most important findings of recent Mozart scholarship, superseding the older view that believed it could see in Mozart's personality and art a self-contained unity of specific forces striving towards the same goal and thus affording an insight into the very basis of his character. Writers thought that they had successfully reduced the composer to one particular formula, a formula on the strength of which it was possible to make sense of all that he said and did as man and artist. A detailed study of his works has finally led to the realization that this was a fatal misunderstanding. It is simply impossible to find such a formula unless we think of the creative, formative instinct that finds expression in all his works and, for the most part, in his letters, too. But the forces that set this instinct in motion remain as obscure as ever. Recently a number of writers have drawn on Schiller's well-known theory of naïve and sentimental poetry, with some commentators declaring him a naïve artist,[26] while others regard him as an example of the sentimental artist[27] – eloquent proof that the case is still far from resolved. Schiller himself was especially wary of applying his theory to specific individuals, as he knew very well that nature, which creates men of genius, may well generate life but certainly does not produce clearly distinguishable types. Mozart's personality cannot be assigned to one or other of these categories without further ado. There was much about his character that was naïve, but he was also aware of the dilemma that faces the individual robbed of his essential unity, a conflict from which Schiller derived his concept of the sentimental. It is sufficient to compare him with the far more naïve figure of Haydn to be conscious of the full extent of the difference. Scarcely once in his letters does Mozart lay bare his most private thoughts and feelings. But we have already seen from the remarkable changes of mood that typify his music from his very first symphony onwards that one of his most basic characteristics was his ability to experience things in contradictory ways. It was this which, in the course of his subsequent career, was to make him the great dramatist that he became, a greatness simply inconceivable without such contradictions. All that he then needed

---

25. This point is rightly stressed by Schurig, 'Die Briefe Mozarts und seiner Familie', 8–9, who also draws attention to Rudolph Genée's incredible idea of burning the Bäsle letters on account of their 'appallingly unaesthetic' character. ◆ Abert is right, I think, to argue that the Bäsle letters cannot be taken out of context. But it is clear, too, that by banishing them to an appendix he hopes to subvert their potential to undermine Mozart's 'pure' and 'most ideal' passion for Aloysia. See also p.560 n.110.
26. See in particular Rutz in his well-known monograph *Musik, Wort und Körper als Gemütsausdruck*; similar views were later expressed by Hermann Nohl, *Typische Kunststile in Dichtung und Musik* and Lert, *Mozart auf dem Theater*.
27. Kretzschmar, *Führer durch den Konzertsaal*, i.169–70.

to do was to draw on the contradictory moods that existed within him and to embody them in the various characters in a particular drama, dividing himself among the individual figures and in that way laying the piece's foundations. Here, too, lay the ultimate source of his art of observation: precisely because his soul was capable of such varied forms of experience, it sought and invariably found the objects that allowed this gift to be tested. For Mozart, every individual had something new to offer, an unpredictable, unique mixture of psychological forces, the very uniqueness of which fascinated him more than anything else. In this way he succeeded in creating characters which, for all their simplicity, are often unfathomable in their variety. Above all, he differed from Gluck in not seeing his characters as endlessly unchanging but in a state of constant flux like some natural spectacle, and the experiences that he reproduced as an 'absolute' musician operated within these selfsame antitheses. We can also see this 'demonic' feature in his instrumental works, where its passions dart forth and disappear again with the speed of lightning. Hans Georg Nägeli found all this far from edifying and duly described the composer as a 'shepherd and a warrior, a sycophant and a blusterer' in whose music 'tender melodies often alternate with shrill and piercing sounds, graceful motion with violent impetuosity'.[28] Of course, Mozart had an undeniable zest for life, especially when he was young, but it is these sudden outbursts of pain and passion and even escapism that invest this zest for life with its underlying note of realism. With his growing maturity and depth of experience, these outbursts gain in frequency, with the result that in some of his later works the relationship is reversed. As a result of this, our understanding of Mozart's personality suffered an almost fatal setback in the days of Romanticism, when the angry young men of the time, foremost among whom was the young Schumann, were no longer able to grasp the emotional depths of Mozart's art, such was the pressure exerted by Beethoven's 'Titanism' – another composer only half understood. Yet Mozart was never a titanic figure either in life or in his music, however many ancient gods he may have overthrown: and he toppled them without a struggle and without complaint, merely by expressing and developing his own essential nature. He also had to leave behind him the followers of the *Sturm und Drang* movement of his own day, composers such as Stamitz and Schobert, for all that they were spiritually related to him in other ways: his aim, after all, was not to foment revolution for the sake of revolution, but to fashion and form that seething world in his own inimitable spirit. He took over neither its dull and untrammelled passion nor that other evil of the age, mawkish sentimentality. Of course, even Mozart was affected by the sentimentalism of the age of Rousseau: he wept when hearing Rosa Cannabich play[29] and, following the breakdown of his relationship with Aloysia, he wrote to his father: 'Today I can only cry – I've far too sensitive a heart'.[30] But he was far from indulging in the floods of tears shed by the 'beautiful souls' of the period, and in his music, too, his creative instinct kept him from wallowing unduly in emotion. Here, too, he strove to reproduce real life in as vivid a way as he could, avoiding sentimental effusions that existed for their own sake alone. It is sufficient to compare one of Johann Christian Bach's arias in the *empfindsam* style with an aria by Mozart to see the difference straightaway. We should be guilty, therefore, of fundamentally falsifying his character if we were to ascribe to him sentimental outbursts of the kind imputed to him at the time of his apocryphal summons to Berlin. As a true son of the Rococo, he was able either to conceal his inner anguish or to hide it behind insane jokes. According to Lange, he would regale the people around him with 'frivolous remarks' and platitudes whenever he was deeply involved in a large-

28. Nägeli, *Vorlesungen über Musik*, 158ff.
29. *Briefe*, ii.178 (letter of 10 December 1777).
30. *Briefe*, ii.529 (letter of 29 December 1778).

scale piece. His works provide more than adequate proof of his ability to transmute the sentimentality of the age through his art: suffice it to mention his long-suffering heroines Konstanze, the Countess, Donna Anna and Pamina, all of whom inhabit the same sweet and tender world and yet refuse to yield up even the tiniest part of their humanity to modish sentimentality.

In short, Mozart was not a 'problematical' figure in the modern sense of the term. He did not seek his ideals beyond his own character. Rather, his only ideal was to allow his innate qualities to reach their full maturity, and not even this was an ideal in the sense that freedom in its various manifestations was an ideal for a Kantian like Beethoven, namely, a belief that affected his whole conceptual and emotional life. Mozart never gave a thought to man's right of self-determination in the Kantian sense, a right that exercised Beethoven throughout the whole of his life. In consequence, he was involved in no heroic struggle with some suprapersonal fate – a struggle from which the later composer drew his greatest strength. Indeed, there will have been few great thinkers in contemporary Germany who were as remote from Kant's conceptual world as was Mozart. His work is far more like an extraordinary natural spectacle whose only aim was the fullest deployment of all its available forces. It was the fact that these forces were as powerful and elemental as they were varied and that, thanks to his tremendous creative gifts, they merged to form a harmonic whole that constitutes the true greatness of this unique man. Only in this way was he able to lend all his characters a symbolic value while retaining their individual stamp and elevate them to the level of universal types.

But this untrammelled development of his own underlying nature that was the true aim of Mozart's life was beset by difficulties and, as a result, was fraught with crises. These crises always occurred when a particular area of emotional experience had been exhausted and it was necessary, therefore, for him to redistribute his inner strengths. This happened on two separate occasions towards the end of his life, once between *Le nozze di Figaro* and *Don Giovanni* and, later, during the final year of his life, just before *Die Zauberflöte*. These transitional periods were accompanied by emotional upheavals that found explosive expression in one or more monumental works in a fundamentally different style. It was as though a new river had suddenly burst forth from unknown chasms and, following the old riverbed, forced its floodwaters into a completely new and unsuspected direction. But it is no accident that it was during these critical periods that these dark, impassioned and even pessimistic feelings were particularly clearly noticeable. The sense of shuddering upheaval that we find in Mozart's music at these periods is an expression of emotional crisis, a reflection of an inner turmoil that sometimes bordered on total nervous collapse. But it is also highly likely that these inner crises, following upon each other in rapid succession, also left their mark on Mozart's delicate constitution, too. Certainly, his health began to give way from the time of *Don Giovanni* onwards, and he was never again to make a full recovery.[31]

As we have already indicated, nature plays a relatively minor role in Mozart's works,[32] when compared with his principal object of interest, the individual human being. That he was a child of his totally unromantic age in his impressions of his visits to Italy is undeniable. Later, too, there is no evidence that he ever really appreciated nature at her wildest and most disturbing.[33] The few reports that we have tell of 'pleasant' countryside, in other words, charming, park-like landscapes. In his letter of 13 July 1781, for example, he describes the area around Reisenberg very much in the spirit of the eighteenth century: 'The little house is nothing much, but the country – the forest

31. ◆ For a biographical interpretation that develops Abert's ideas of 'crises', see Hocquard, *La pensée de Mozart*.
32. See Ernst Lewicki, 'Über Mozarts Naturliebe'. ◆ Further, see Heartz, 'Mozart's sense for nature'.
33. This was not the case with Beethoven: see Bekker, *Beethoven*, 192.

– in which he [Count Cobenzl] has built a grotto that looks just as if nature herself had made it. It's wonderful and very pleasant.'[34] And in 1788 he was pleased that his house outside Vienna had a garden.[35] It was here that the great E flat major symphony (K543) was composed. Likewise, both *Don Giovanni* and *Die Zauberflöte* were written, for the most part, in summer houses, in other words, in close contact with nature. Rochlitz, finally, reports that, while travelling through beautiful countryside, Mozart was often inspired by nature and complained that he had to think up his works indoors.[36] But it never occurred to him to travel in order to enjoy nature or to find inspiration for his art in impressions of nature, and there is no trace in his works of natural events in the style of Beethoven, for example. Rather, these works contain universally well-known topoi from Italian opera, including maritime set-pieces, Rococo idylls with rustling west winds and so on and night-time scenes of an agreeable or fantastical kind, in short, all those charming individual portraits of nature and of the countryside in which contemporary attitudes to nature found their most poetical expression. What we do not encounter are the moods and atmospheres associated with nature of a kind that we find today. Instead, the ideas and images are conceptually grasped, with the music moving in the same direction and attempting to increase the objective tangibility of these images with the means available to it, in other words, through obvious examples of tone-painting. The young Mozart knew no alternative. But from *Idomeneo* onwards we find traces of a new response to nature that later acquires artistic form in numbers such as Susanna's aria ('Deh vieni non tardar') from act four of *Le nozze di Figaro*. Natural events and the countryside are now no longer something fixed and unchanging, but are related to the emotional lives of the characters and in that way individually inspired. The minutely detailed natural event is replaced by an atmospheric and emotionally charged portrait in which nature and feeling become one. Suffice it to compare Susanna's aria with similar eventide idylls of an earlier age: to borrow a phrase from Beethoven, this aria contains far less 'painting than feeling' and, as such, is an atmospheric portrait breathing an indefinable spirit of a kind that we miss in even the finest depictions of nature from the older period. Even here, of course, we need to bear in mind that in his maturity, too, Mozart was fascinated less by nature as such than by people and by purely psychological concerns. But it is entirely typical of his character that on those occasions where he explores nature in greater detail he has already left far behind him the rationalistic view of nature that was content with mere descriptions. And his impressions of nature are more powerfully represented in his instrumental works than has generally been assumed to be the case until now: indeed, anyone who listens carefully enough to these works will recognize this at once. Here, too, Mozart reverted to older models, inasmuch as one of the principal characteristics of popular Austrian instrumental music was the fact that it attached particular importance not just to the Austrian people but also to the Austrian countryside. Scenes by the brook or in the forest and birdsong of every description are by no means unusual, with serenades – works meant to be performed out of doors – lending themselves in particular to these discreet evocations of nature. Mozart, too, was familiar with this tradition, his descriptions of nature ranging from purely superficial, often half-joking imitations of individual sounds from the world of nature to scenes – especially in some of his slow movements – in which nature seems to acquire a living presence. Yet even here we are invariably dealing with the charming or idyllic side of nature: there is no trace whatsoever of its sublimity, still less of its wildly fantastical aspect.

34. *Briefe*, iii.139 (letter of 13 July 1781).
35. *Briefe*, iv.66 (letter of 17 June 1788).
36. Leitzmann, *Mozarts Persönlichkeit*, 134–5.

That Mozart was a great animal lover is clear from every surviving source: his pets in the form of dogs and birds play a leading role in his letters. And, for a time at least, horses figured prominently in his life, as we hear of daily rides that he took in Vienna on medical advice. But he never became a keen horseman, as he could never overcome a certain fear of riding.

Mozart's attitude to religion was largely determined by his environment, but more especially by his upbringing, yet it developed along lines entirely consistent with his overall character. That he was brought up to believe in the strictest tenets of the Catholic faith goes without saying, given his father's nature. As a result, he shared Leopold's standpoint with regard to other confessions, albeit in a less virulent form. And so we find him drawing a clear distinction between 'Lutheran' composers and their non-Lutheran colleagues and expressing the wish in 1778 to be appointed to a Catholic court.[37] He remained a loyal member of the Catholic church until the very end of his life, even after he had already begun to criticize its dogmas. This is entirely understandable. His whole nature demanded that he should first perceive an object through his senses, for only in this way could he grasp it conceptually and creatively. Of all the various faiths, Catholicism was the one that struck the clearest chord in this regard. It, too, set out from the sensory and tangible, in that way pointing to the symbolic. Throughout the whole of his period of development, Mozart's entire attitude to religion was clearly influenced by his father, and even as late as 25 October 1777, the very form in which he couched his comments sounds like an echo of Leopold's own profession of faith: 'God is ever before my eyes, I acknowledge His omnipotence, I fear His anger, but I also acknowledge His love, His compassion and His tenderness towards His creatures. He will never forsake His servants – – if it is according to His will, so let it be according to mine, then nothing can go awry.'[38] Later, religious remarks become less frequent in Mozart's letters and we see his views growing more liberal, without, however, abandoning their Catholic basis. His occasional outbursts against 'priests' admittedly increase in number after he joined the Freemasons, but they do not deserve to be taken unduly seriously, not least when we recall that one of his best friends – Bullinger – was a priest. As always, Mozart's criticism was directed not at the priesthood in general but only at individual representatives. More important in this context are Leopold's frequent questions about the regularity with which Mozart went to confession and attended Mass, questions which at the very least suggest that he was not entirely certain of the answer. Mozart, as we know, had already begun to reinterpret some of the Church's directives, including its rules on fasting, and to place his own private gloss on them.[39] Far more important, however, is the fact that from a very early age, the mystic in him was as active as the dogmatist, a development clear from the sacred works of his youth, the sheer number and manner of elaboration of which are the best possible proof of his powerful need for religion. Here it is the sections of a mystical character such as the 'Qui tollis' and 'Et incarnatus est' which, as we have seen, afford the most striking evidence of their creator's depth of experience. Here we first find the desire to transcend all the barriers of dogma and reason and to approach the divine directly and in that way to experience inwardly what established religion sought to define conceptually. At the same time, we find here an expression of the

---

37. *Briefe*, ii.396 (letter of 9 July 1778).
38. *Briefe*, ii.85 (letter of 25 October 1777).
39. *Briefe*, iii.130 (letter of 13 June 1781). ◆ 'Don't worry about the good of my soul, most beloved father! – I'm just as likely to err as any other young man and by way of consolation wish only that others were as little likely to err as I am. – You may perhaps believe things about me that aren't true; – my main failing is that I don't always *appear* to act as I should. – It's not true that I boasted that I eat meat on all fast days; but I did say that I set little store by it and don't consider it a sin; for me, fasting means abstaining and eating less than usual. – I attend Mass every Sunday and feast day and, if I can make it, on weekdays too, but you already know that, father.'

authentically mystical yearning for the otherworldly that we should never forget when examining Mozart's personality, however much we may stress his zest for life in the here and now.

It was only natural that death and resurrection were of far less concern to the young Mozart than they were to the mature composer. That he believed implicitly in individual immortality, in eternal bliss and in reunion with all those who were dear to him and who had died before him is self-evident, given the nature of his religious convictions. It is clear, of course, from the relevant sections of his early Masses, especially his setting of the words 'et vitam venturi saeculi', that he had as yet no desire to escape from the world of dogma, as these passages remain entirely impersonal and traditional in tone. As always, he needed to experience the matter for himself in order to adopt a clearer approach to it. This experience came with the death of his mother in Paris, an event that he described to his father as follows:

In those distressing circumstances, there were three things that consoled me, namely, my complete and confident acceptance of God's will and the presence of so easy and beautiful a death, which made me think that in an instant she had become so happy – how much happier she is now than we are, so that at that instant I wanted to make the journey with her. – This wish and this desire provided me with my third source of comfort, namely, that she isn't lost to us for ever – that we shall see her again – that we shall live together more happily and more contentedly than in this world of ours.[40]

He expressed similar thoughts following Siegmund Barisani's death in 1787:

He is at rest! – but I, we, all that knew him well – we shall *never* be at rest again – until we are fortunate enough to see him again – in a better world – and *never more to part*.[41]

From now on Mozart was to be increasingly preoccupied by the thought of death and immortality and was particularly grateful to Freemasonry for giving him so many new ideas in this regard. Here one thinks first and foremost of the famous passage in his last letter to his father of 4 April 1787. Leopold was already very ill at this time, and it is remarkable to see how Mozart, now positively clairvoyant, had come to terms with his approaching loss, while dispensing philosophical words of comfort as though to someone on the point of setting out on his final journey in life:

Inasmuch as death (when looked at closely) is the true goal of our lives, I have become so familiar with this true friend of ours in recent years that his image is not only no longer frightening for me, but is really very calming and comforting! and I give thanks to my God that He has granted me the good fortune and given me the opportunity (you know what I mean) of seeing in it the *key* to our true happiness. – I never go to bed at night without reflecting that (young as I am) I may not live to see another day – yet none of those who know me could say that I am sullen or sad in their company – and for this blessing I daily thank my Creator and with all my heart pray that each of my fellow creatures may share it.[42]

40. *Briefe*, ii.394 (letter of 9 July 1778).
41. Schiedermair, *Die Briefe W. A. Mozarts*, ii.361 [*Dokumente*, 261, *Documentary Biography*, 29]. Note also Mozart's response to the death of Count Hatzfeld: 'I don't feel sorry for him, only for myself and all those who knew him as well as I did'; *Briefe*, iv.41 (letter of 4 April 1787).
42. *Briefe*, iv.41 (letter of 4 April 1787).

This is a completely different attitude to death from the one that we find with Goethe, for example. And it is also, of course, worlds apart from Johann Sebastian Bach's tremendously impressive motto in life: 'I am delighted to be departing this life and to be with Christ.' Here is the demonic longing for death felt by a Protestant believer for whom the Saviour robs death of all its terrors and turns it into the gateway to heavenly bliss. One can clearly feel the extent to which this problem exercised Mozart: it was now no longer a question of naïvely accepting Church dogma, but an inner experience involving the realization that death is entirely natural and therefore not something to be feared. Death comes not to judge or destroy us but to fulfil a natural law that lies within us all; as a result, it can be only our friend, not our enemy. Bound up with this realization is the belief in immortality that as before refuses to avail itself of the dogmatic ideas of the Church but acquires a mystical aura of a kind almost certainly fashionable in Masonic circles at this time.[43] Mozart does not speak here of eternal life – the Church's 'vita venturi saeculi' – but of our 'true happiness'. It is also highly significant that there is no notion here of divine judgement: for Mozart, the world to come meant freeing the individual from the clinker of earthly existence and in the final resort was, therefore, the ultimate fulfilment of his desire for a higher form of contemplation and experience than was granted to him on earth.

It would be wrong to ignore this mystical aspect, not least because it introduces a further antithesis into our picture of this great realist. It, too, expresses itself with varying degrees of intensity and frequently assumes different forms and objects. But it was the main reason for Mozart's ultimate decision to join the Freemasons in the hope of silencing the dull desire that lives in all of us, especially in creative types, namely, the desire to pursue the wondrous within our lives.

Mozart's literary, philosophical and historical education – what we nowadays call our 'general culture' – has been much discussed in recent years. Niemetschek was one of the first to regret that 'someone so exceptional as an artist was not also a great man in other walks of life',[44] and among Mozart's later biographers, this same view has been peddled by those many enthusiastic souls who can imagine a great man only as a kind of repository of the most disparate and exceptional characteristics and abilities. To this must be added the increasing tendency, first found among Romantic writers, to use great poets and statesmen as the yardstick by which to measure the educational ideal of others. That the shade of Goethe is regularly invoked in such circumstances is only natural among us Germans.

But writers forget that a poet's and politician's literary and historical education is on a completely different level from that of a musician. Of course, the talented musician cannot – and may not – dispense with a non-musical education, which he needs in order to find his way in the world, quite apart from the inspiration that it may offer him. Older musicians knew very well why they attended universities in their youth, while more recent generations could look to the Romantics as living examples of the value of a universal education. The composer who knows nothing beyond his own discipline has always cut a sorry figure. But if, as is only fair, we regard education not as the sum total of acquired knowledge but as the artist's hard-won ability to fathom the whole range of phenomena and to create his own view of the world, then other sources will be open to him that will be all the more varied, the greater his genius. We must not judge the genius – the natural individual – by the standards of the philistine, but nor should we judge him by those of the merely talented artist, whose inner life is insufficiently varied to be able to manage without

43. It is also entirely possible that Mozart was influenced here by Moses Mendelssohn's *Phädon*, a work that was part of his own private library [*Dokumente*, 498, *Documentary Biography*, 589].
44. Niemetschek, *Leben des k. k. Kapellmeisters Wolfgang Gottlieb Mozart*, 57.

external stimuli. Mozart's genius was possessed of this strength of inner experience. No one will deny that in his mature works he reflects – and thereby legitimizes – all the vital forces of his age with a purity achieved by no other contemporary save Goethe. But this understanding, the sheer breadth of which is a source of perpetual wonderment, came not from the study of literature, cultural history and politics but from his ability to observe his fellow humans and to fathom the forces that ultimately motivated them. At no point does he consciously hold up a mirror to his age or offer a cultural conspectus, and he is wholly innocent of all artistic pretentiousness. Yet his works contain such a wealth of culture that we would do well not to get unduly worked up at their 'unliterary' creator.

In any case, Mozart was by no means as badly educated as recent writers would have us believe. The situation with regard to other musicians of his day, especially Austrian musicians, was no doubt deeply deplorable (not even Joseph Haydn was an exception in this respect), with only their north German colleagues being far better placed as a result of their contacts with the classical poets. Mozart, by contrast, had the advantage not only of having been born in the university town of Salzburg but of being the son of a man of considerable learning who was anxious to know more. None the less, Leopold's attempt to give his son a systematic intellectual education failed to produce the desired result, as Mozart's education was ruled by chance rather than by any specific plan.[45] This is especially clear from the motley assembly of titles in his surviving library, the principal items in which were works by Geßner, Ewald von Kleist, Wieland, Metastasio, Molière, Frederick the Great and Moses Mendelssohn.[46] Here we need to be wary of leaping to overhasty conclusions. Mozart's earliest literary impressions probably came from Gellert and Count Stolberg, two poets of the Protestant Enlightenment, who were favourites of his father but who seem not to have been to his own liking.[47] The situation was different, however, with Wieland, another writer whom Leopold much admired. Here Mozart instinctively recognized a number of aspects of his own personality, foremost among which were his sensitivity and adaptability, including the ability to assimilate new impressions and use them for his own creative ends. Above all, however, there was his relaxed approach to people and objects. Later he came across Klopstock, but the latter's emotional rhetoric found little favour with him. This helps to explain why in 1782 he failed to complete a setting of a Klopstockian 'Ode to Calpe' by the Viennese Jesuit Michael Denis, a failure that he explained as follows in a letter to his father:

> The ode is sublime, beautiful, everything you could ask for – but – it is too exaggerated and bombastic for my sensitive ears. What's to be done? – The golden mean, namely, truth in all things, is no longer recognized or valued – in order to win applause, you have to write things that a coachman can sing or that are so unintelligible that people like them precisely because no one of intelligence can understand them.[48]

This is again Mozart the realist talking, a man incapable of being satisfied by the second best or by an artificially constructed reality. Yet throughout his life he felt a remoteness from Klopstock's effusiveness that he did not feel for its opposite extreme, popular poetry. That this was the result

45. ◆ For a contrary view, see the extensive discussions of Mozart's education throughout Halliwell, *The Mozart Family: Four Lives in a Social Context*.
46. Schurig, *Wolfgang Amade Mozart*, ii.318ff. ◆ For Mozart's estate inventory, listing his library, see *Dokumente*, 497–8 and 509–10, *Documentary Biography*, 587–9 and 601–2; further, see Konrad and Staehelin, *allzeit ein buch*.
47. *Briefe*, i.309 (letter of 26 January 1770).
48. *Briefe*, iii.246 (letter of 28 December 1782).

of his Swabian ancestry is beyond doubt.[49] A similar spirit informs Mozart's brief and innocent occasional poems,[50] to say nothing of the coarsely folklike aspect of his wit and sense of humour.

With the exception of his setting of *Das Veilchen* (K476) we have no evidence that Mozart was familiar with the works of Lessing, Herder, Goethe or Schiller, although this does not, of course, preclude the possibility that he knew at least some of them: he may not have been a great reader, but he was certainly an avid theatregoer. Even while he was still in Salzburg, there were all manner of plays that he could see, and not just school plays like *Apollo et Hyacinthus*.[51] Amateurs were particularly keen to stage all kinds of fashionable pieces, especially sentimental comedies, and the archiepiscopal theatre, too, performed not only operas but also spoken dramas, including Corneille's *Polyeucte*.[52] A new municipal theatre opened in 1775, bringing with it performances by touring companies, including those of Böhm and Schikaneder. Böhm had included Shakespeare's *Romeo and Juliet* and Lessing's *Minna von Barnhelm* in his repertory during the early seventies,[53] and we know that Schikaneder's Salzburg productions included *Hamlet*, *Macbeth* and *King Lear*, as well as *Julius von Tarent* by Johann Anton Leisewitz and Lessing's *Emilia Galotti*.[54] That Mozart saw at least *Hamlet* in the theatre we know from his own testimony,[55] and it is clear that he also took a great interest in Schikaneder's Salzburg productions.[56] The next stage in his literary education was Mannheim, with its German national aspirations, which also extended to opera and which left a deep impression on him. Once again, Shakespeare was represented by *Hamlet* and *Macbeth*, but there was also more work by amateur writers, whose literary endeavours elicited Wieland's ridicule.[57] In Paris, finally, Mozart found himself at the very centre of the literary world, and with the salon of Madame d'Épinay he entered one of the circles that set the intellectual tone at this time. His letters contain barely a trace of all this, and we know only that even if he did not read Voltaire's writings, he was at least familiar with their contents. The same will have been true of Rousseau. The Munich stage told a similar story to Mannheim's, with its markedly nationalistic tenor and strong dose of dilettantism and local patriotism. During the period of *La finta giardiniera*, Mozart was a frequent visitor to the theatre, where he could have seen not only Lessing's *Miß Sara Sampson* and *Minna von Barnhelm* but also German translations of French works by Molière, Marivaux, Regnard and Diderot.[58] Even his later librettist, Stephanie the Younger, was represented by a number of comedies. At the time of *Idomeneo*, by contrast, Mozart was too busy to attend the theatre with the same degree of regularity, and the only play he is known to have seen is Johann Gottfried Dyk's *Essex*. Yet these experiences, too, left little mark on his letters of the period. More enlightening in this respect are the letters that he wrote in Vienna. Here we learn of Mozart's active involvement in what was then the most burning issue of the day, the clash between the regular theatre and the popular figure of Hanswurst. Here, too, Mozart's delight in the theatre

49. See Abert, 'Schwäbisches bei Mozart', *Der Schwäbische Bund*. ◆ Also see Ernst Fritz Schmid, *Ein schwäbisches Mozartbuch*.
50. Collected by Batka, *W. A. Mozarts gesammelte Poesien*. ◆ In addition to the poems written by Mozart in his letters, *Briefe* (iv.164–7) also includes the lengthy, undated 'Der kunstreiche Hund' and Mozart's poem on the death of his pet starling (iv.49–50).
51. ◆ See Boberski, *Das Theater der Benediktiner an der alten Universität Salzburg (1617–1778)*.
52. A complete list is included in Pirckmayer's *Über Musik und Theater am f. e. Salzburger Hofe 1762–1775*.
53. Lert, *Mozart auf dem Theater*, 69. ◆ These portraits are reproduced in Deutsch, *Mozart und seine Welt*, 11 (Saverio dalla Rosa), 19–21 (Posch), 21 (Stock) and 287 (Bosio, now not considered authentic).
54. Komorzynski, *Emanuel Schikaneder: Ein Beitrag zur Geschichte des deutschen Theaters*, 6.
55. *Briefe*, iii.35 (letter of 29 November 1780).
56. *Briefe*, iii.28 (letter of 22 November 1780); see also Nannerl's answer, with the list of performances in *Briefe*, iii.35–7. ◆ Further, see Dahms, 'Das musikalische Repertoire des Salzburger Fürsterzbischöflichen Hoftheaters (1775–1803)'.
57. Walter, *Geschichte des Theaters und der Musik am kurpfälzischen Hofe*, 275–6.
58. Legband, 'Münchener Bühne und Literatur im 18. Jahrhundert', 422–3.

reached its high point. 'I wish you could see a tragedy here', he wrote to his sister in 1781. 'In general, I don't know any theatre where every kind of play is properly performed; but here every role, even the smallest and least significant, is well taken and double-cast.'[59] Evidently Mozart was as fascinated by high tragedies in the style of Sonnenfels and Ayrenhoff that he already knew from Gebler's *Thamos* as he was by popular pieces whose stereotypical characters he was soon to transfigure in his own works. And recent writers have justifiably emphasized the influence on Mozart's art of serious Viennese drama at this time in the form of the Burgtheater's burgeoning style.[60] Here, too, of course, our only evidence is the odd disjointed passage in his letters. His song texts likewise reveal no sense of any conscious literary choice, extending, as they do, from poems by Johann Christian Günther to Goethe's *Das Veilchen*, a poem that fell into his hands by mere chance. But we need to remember that songs at this time were not regarded as high art but were written for domestic consumption and convivial ends. There was still no question at this date of recreating the text in the spirit of music. It was left to Goethe to loosen the tongue of lyric poetry and music, with Mozart's setting of *Das Veilchen* affording a particularly fine example of the new sources of inspiration opened up to lieder by the poet's magic wand. In general, however, the song was an area of only peripheral interest to Mozart, a field that he tilled only occasionally, when invited to do so by others. His lyrical vein he poured into his instrumental works, not into songs. As for the poetic aspect of his operas, we have already seen not only that he had thought deeply about all the important questions of the day but that he stood head and shoulders above the majority of contemporary librettists in terms of both insight and judgement.

He took little interest, by contrast, in the visual arts and in history, even though, as a child, he had been taken to the most varied galleries and collections. Both in Italy and later his father attempted to instil in him a sense of history, but in vain. None the less, he seems to have possessed a fair talent for drawing. As early as 1770, while in Rome, he drew 'St Peter with his keys and with him St Paul with his sword and St Luke with my sister and so on and so forth'.[61] And in Linz in 1783 he drew an 'Ecce homo' that he particularly liked, presenting it to Constanze, who kept it as an example of his talent in this direction. His letters, too, contain a handful of further examples, albeit of a primitive kind.[62]

But how knowledgeable was Mozart about the history of music? The collection of scores that he left on his death is modest in scope[63] and no less random than his collection of books, having owed its existence for the most part to gifts and other eventualities. Yet, given the state of the music-publishing business at this time, it was not easy, even for musicians with a disposable income, to build up a systematic library. Modern preconceptions are completely out of place here. In any case, Mozart's private library was far from being the only source of his knowledge of the history of music and gives virtually no idea of the breadth of that knowledge, which extended from early Italian vocal music to his contemporaries Gluck and Haydn, while also including vocal music and *Spielmusik* of every kind. During his earliest youth, Mozart had been introduced not only to the local traditions of Salzburg and Vienna but also to the aesthetic theories of the north Germans in Berlin and Leipzig, writers whom Leopold held in particularly high regard. Their travels had taken

59. *Briefe*, iii.138 (letter of 4 July 1781).
60. Lert, *Mozart auf dem Theater*, 38ff. ◆ For a more recent listing, see Link, *The National Court Theatre in Mozart's Vienna*.
61. *Briefe*, i.336 (letter of 14 April 1770).
62. 'In drawing and arithmetic he showed considerable skill', noted his sister; see Nottebohm, *Mozartiana*, 110.
63. They are listed by Schurig, *Wolfgang Amade Mozart*, ii.326–7. It is also worth mentioning at this point Mozart's visit to the Mannheim observatory on 16 November 1778, a visit attested by his entry in the visitors' book; see *Mannheimer Geschichtsblätter*, xvi/11–12, 137–8 [*Dokumente*, 161, *Documentary Biography*, 179].

them to the main centres of contemporary music: in Italy, Mannheim and Paris he learnt all about the arguments that were then raging with peculiar ferocity and whose local forms he now got to know at first hand.[64] Martini, meanwhile, introduced him to some of the finest examples of early Italian music, and we have already seen how the young Mozart was particularly fired by these. Moreover, there were few contemporaries better qualified than Martini to draw Mozart's attention to the history of music as such. As a mature composer, Mozart later proved receptive to the art of Handel and Bach, at least to the extent that their works were available at this time. It will be clear from all this that few contemporary composers could rival him when it came to universality of education.

Even so, there was no sense of any real interest in history: Mozart had absolutely no time for the history of music in the modern sense of the term. The historical tradition, with all its ramifications, was of no more concern to him than the ideas and their various manifestations that today's historian sees behind the whole range of artistic phenomena. What fascinated him was only the individual artist and the art that he represented, and even these were of interest only to the extent that they were able to give him something personally. He wanted to fashion and create things, not simply to understand them, wanted to make the art of others part of his own art and in that way to enrich it. It was left to the Romantics to value and develop the ability to transport themselves back into the past and empathize with the artistic sensibilities of an earlier generation, and if, in spite of this, Mozart's music contains elements drawn from the past, this was simply the result of his receptivity, on which we have often had occasion to dwell, not of any conscious historical speculations.

In spite of the relatively large number of surviving portraits, it is not exactly easy to form any real idea of Mozart's physical appearance.[65] Quite apart from the portraits that are inauthentic and those that consciously idealize him, even those that attempt to be true to life fail in often significant ways to agree on what he looked like, suggesting that it was not easy to capture his likeness, for, whenever he was not sitting at the keyboard, he was in a state of permanent physical unrest, his facial expression for ever changing.[66] This betrays a high degree of nervous tension, but there seems little doubt that this was not innate: the portrait of him painted in Vienna in 1763, showing him wearing court dress, reveals a healthy, chubby-cheeked, childishly impudent boy. In all likelihood, it was the result of the stresses of so many journeys undertaken during his youth. From birth, Mozart was a delicate, but healthy, child, and the sickliness that found expression in his strikingly large number of illnesses was the gradual but inevitable result, in part, of over-exertion and, in part, of the restless and irregular working habits that his genius forced upon him. Some of the blame for this should no doubt be laid at Leopold's door, yet it has to be admitted that the care that is nowadays lavished on bringing up children in healthy ways simply did not exist in Mozart's day. The principle of 'mens sana in corpore sano' had yet to find general acceptance, especially among the children of musicians, with the result that Mozart's physical development not only lagged far behind his intellectual development, it remained positively stunted. In his sister's words, he was always 'small, thin, pale of complexion and completely devoid of all pretensions in terms of physiognomy and physique'.[67] The fact that his head was slightly too large for his body is further

64. ◆ In general, see Eisen, 'The Mozarts' Salzburg Music Library'.
65. ◆ Almost all of the known portraits of Mozart are collected in Deutsch, *Mozart und seine Welt*. Further, see Dieckmann, 'Mozart im Bilde: Die Porträts der Wiener Jahre'; Michaelis and Seiller, 'Ein unbekanntes Bildnis Wolfgang Amadeus Mozarts in der Berliner Gemäldegalerie'; and Sørensen, 'Ein Mozart-Porträt in Dänemark'.
66. Schlichtegroll, 'Mozart'.
67. Nottebohm, *Mozartiana*, 111 [*Dokumente*, 405, *Documentary Biography*, 462]. ◆ This comment, too, is written in a hand different from Nannerl's; see n.3 above.

proof that body and mind developed at different rates. The best description of his physical appearance is the one given by Niemetschek:

> Physically, this extraordinary man had no distinguishing features; he was small, and his face, with the exception of his large fiery eyes, said nothing about the greatness of his genius. His gaze seemed inconstant and absent-minded, except when he was seated at the keyboard; then his whole countenance was transformed! – – The unprepossessing nature of his appearance, his slightness of stature stemmed from his early mental exertions and from all lack of free exercise during his childhood. Although he was brought up by handsome parents and is said to have been an attractive child, he was committed to a sedentary way of life from his sixth year onwards, at which age he had already begun to write! And how much did he not write in his lifetime, especially during his final years! We know for a fact that Mozart particularly liked to play and compose at night, and as the work was often urgent, it is all too easy to imagine how so delicate a constitution was bound to suffer! His early death . . . must be ascribed to these circumstances above all others.[68]

It is clear from all this that in the course of time Mozart's characteristic sensitivity often enough developed into nervous tension, becoming morbid irritability during the final years of his life, when his physical strength was gradually undermined. He himself suffered from his unprepossessing appearance and, in an evident attempt to overcome this perceived shortcoming, laid special emphasis on his clothing. He was also particularly proud of his small and beautiful hands; even to see him playing the harpsichord must have afforded considerable aesthetic pleasure.[69] Indeed, his sister-in-law Sophie Haibel even reports that he used all manner of other objects such as hats, bags, watch chains, tables and chairs as substitute keyboards.[70]

Except for its size, there was nothing exceptional about his head. Only his ears were strikingly formed: he had no lobes, while the shape of the auricle was likewise abnormal. Yet such ears are not rare and, needless to say, their shape has nothing to do with the individual's hearing.[71] His hair was fair and seems to have been fairly thick. He was pale of complexion as a result of his many illnesses and unhealthy lifestyle, which also affected the inconstant and often dull expression in his blue eyes, which stared out on an alien world and suddenly flared up with a curious fire only when he was seated at the keyboard. At moments like these it was as though a completely different person had awoken within him: all sense of randomness, ordinariness and dejection fell away 'and his eye then acquired a restful expression, serious and concentrated; every twist and turn of the music reflected the emotion that he summoned forth through his playing and that he was able to arouse so powerfully within the listener'.[72]

Normally his other features, too, gave no indication that he was in any way exceptional as a person. The lines on his face were neither soft-edged nor of especially characterful harshness. His brow was broad, but not especially high, sloping backwards and continuing the line begun by the nose, which was divided from it by only a slight indentation. As a result, the line from the top of his brow to the tip of his nose formed an obtuse angle, with the bridge of the nose as its vertex.

68. Niemetschek, *Leben des k. k. Kapellmeisters Wolfgang Gottlieb Mozart*, 44.
69. Niemetschek, *Leben des k. k. Kapellmeisters Wolfgang Gottlieb Mozart*, 44.
70. Nissen, *Biographie W. A. Mozarts*, 267–8.
71. Holl, 'Mozarts Ohr: Eine anatomische Studie'.
72. Niemetschek, *Leben des k. k. Kapellmeisters Wolfgang Gottlieb Mozart*, 44.

The nose itself was relatively large, an aspect remarked by contemporaries. To judge by the surviving portraits of her, it seems to have been inherited from his mother. His mouth was normal, but expressive, the upper lip fairly large, the corners of the mouth turned slightly upwards. The chin was weakly developed and certainly gave no sign of any appreciative amount of resolve.[73]

In short, Mozart was neither attractive nor impressive in his appearance, although in his youth he was not without charm. The face that looks back at us from these portraits is fresh, intelligent and as yet unspoilt, revealing a healthy self-confidence. By the end of his life, of course, the gradual decline in his health was also reflected in portraits of him.

73. This description is based in the main on the portraits by Saverio dalla Rosa, Bosio, Posch and Dora Stock.

32

Relations with Constanze, friends and colleagues, 1782–1786

Although Mozart's wedding had taken place against so unfavourable a background, it still seemed as though fortune was going to smile on him again during his early years of marriage. The court, society and even his colleagues showered accolade upon accolade on him at each of his frequent public appearances, and even his financial situation improved to such an extent that, had he made even a modest attempt to put his affairs in order, he could have looked forward to a rosy future.

But there was one dark shadow that fell over these final years of happiness in Mozart's life: his father's anger at his marriage, an anger which, however much it may appear to have abated on a superficial level, continued to fester and, given all that we know about his character, inevitably assumed an element of obdurate bitterness. As early as 23 August 1782 we find him writing to the Baroness von Waldstätten to thank her for arranging the wedding:

> When I was a young lad, I always thought that philosophers were people who said little, rarely laughed and viewed the whole world with a permanently sullen expression on their faces. But my own experiences have utterly persuaded me that, without knowing it, I too must be a philosopher: for now that I have done my duty as a true father – now that I've made the clearest and most understandable representations in so many letters – now that I am convinced that he knows my trying circumstances, which are extremely difficult for a man of my age, and is aware of my humiliations in Salzburg – since he must realize that both morally and materially I am being punished for his conduct, – there is nothing left for me to do but to leave him to his own devices (for this is what he wanted) and to pray to God to bestow on him His paternal blessing and not withdraw His divine grace. But I shan't abandon the cheerfulness that is natural to me and which, in spite of my advancing years, I still possess, and I shall continue to hope for the best.[1]

Leopold had been forced to accept that he was gradually losing control of his son's upbringing even during the latter's visit to Paris. Mozart's marriage was merely the final staging post on this voyage of self-discovery. If Constanze had been a woman after his own heart, rather than a Weber, he might have relented and been content with the role of a fatherly friend. But the situation was now beyond repair, and the worst thing about it all was that events had proved Leopold right. How he felt we can only guess, as his letters to Mozart from this period have not survived – they were presumably destroyed by Constanze. All that we have are a few letters to his daughter, and it is clear from the passages relating to Mozart that he still felt his old admiration for his son's artistic achievements, whereas his private relations are either passed over in silence or described with open disapproval.

---

1. *Briefe*, iii.222 (letter of 23 August 1782).

Given his innate goodness, Mozart was incapable of feeling angry with his father for any length of time. He had acted as his conscience had dictated; now he was concerned only to reestablish his former close relationship with his father, to whom he continued to feel indebted on the very deepest level. He was, of course, completely clear in his own mind that there was no longer any question of his earlier dependency on Leopold and that the latter no longer had anything to offer him, especially on an artistic level. Yet he continued to feel a son's love for him and patiently bore his father's occasional unpleasantnesses. Even in these difficult circumstances, he retained all his old sensitivity, and although his letters to his father now become fewer in number and, above all, more factual in tone, he continued to respect him until the very end.[2]

Initially, of course, Mozart still hoped that his father would change his mind when he met Constanze, and so we find him suggesting the idea of a visit to Salzburg very soon after their wedding. They originally planned to make the journey at the beginning of October 1782, later postponing the visit to Leopold's nameday, 15 November. The first of these plans was thwarted by the state visit of the Russian Grand Duke Paul and his consort,[3] the second by the various concerts and lessons that Mozart had to give. These latter continued to be a problem throughout the whole of the winter, and by the spring of 1783 Constanze's advanced pregnancy proved the principal obstacle. Instead, Mozart now wrote to Leopold, asking him to be godfather to the child: 'Whether it be generis masculini or faeminini, it will be called Leopold or Leopoldine.'[4] The child turned out to be a boy and was born on 17 June, although in the event its godfather was not Leopold, but the Jewish Baron Raimund von Wetzlar, who had insisted on performing this role immediately after the child's birth.[5] Only now did plans for a visit to Salzburg assume a more definite form, not least as a result of the fact that Leopold had begun to doubt whether his son seriously intended to make the journey at all. But Mozart was in fact worried that Colloredo might seize the opportunity to have him arrested as he had left the archbishop's service without being formally released,[6] and so he suggested that they might meet in Munich. Only when Leopold had reassured them on this point, did the couple set out for Salzburg at the end of July.

Mozart did not arrive empty-handed but brought with him a number of movements of a large-scale mass, on which he had worked during the critical days of his engagement, at a time when Constanze had been ill.[7] The movements in question were the Kyrie, Gloria, Sanctus and Benedictus of his great mass in C minor K427. The Credo survives only as a fragment, while the

2. Between the letter of 9 June 1784 and the very last one that he wrote to his father on 4 April 1787, there is a hiatus of three years, a gap attributed by Mozart's sister to the fact that their father destroyed all the letters from this period because of their references to Freemasonry. This is highly probable. At all events, we know of no other reason why Mozart might have stopped writing to his father; see Nissen, *Biographie W. A. Mozarts*, XVI.

3. ◆ Grand Duke Paul arrived in Vienna on 4 October 1782. On 8 October Mozart conducted *Die Entführung aus dem Serail* at the Burgtheater in his presence.

4. *Briefe*, iii.272 (letter of 7 June 1783).

5. This first son, Raimund Leopold, died the following August; see Mozart's letter of 10 December 1783 (*Briefe*, iii.296), in which he speaks of the 'poor, bonny, fat, darling little boy'.

6. See *Briefe*, iii.270 and 279 (letters of 21 May and 12 July 1783).

7. Nissen, *Biographie W. A. Mozarts*, 476, reports that Mozart vowed to write this mass for his wife if her confinement passed off successfully, but this version of events is contradicted by Mozart's own letter of 4 January 1783: 'What you say about my moral obligation is quite correct; – there was good reason why it flowed from my pen – I made the promise in my heart of hearts and still hope to be able to keep it. When I made it, my wife was still unmarried – but as I was firmly resolved to marry her as soon as she was better, it was an easy promise to make. As you yourself know, however, time and other circumstances made our journey impossible; – as proof that I did indeed make this promise, I have the score of half a mass lying here waiting to be finished'; *Briefe*, iii.247–8 (letter of 4 January 1783). Perhaps Mozart vowed to complete the piece as the time of Constanze's confinement drew nearer but failed to find the time. None the less, this passage is extremely important, not only because of its reference to the mass, but more particularly because of the change of style that occurs in this work. The first sentence relates to a letter from Leopold that is no longer extant.

Agnus Dei is missing in its entirety.[8] The mass was rehearsed at the Kapellhaus on 23 October and performed at St Peter's on 26 October. Whether Mozart used movements from earlier masses to complete it we do not know: no evidence survives to support this assumption, and the work could in any case have been performed incomplete. Constanze was one of the two soprano soloists.

In Salzburg, too, Mozart remained active as a composer. Even as early as May 1783, the reintroduction of *opera buffa* to Vienna had reminded him of his old Salzburg librettist, Giambattista Varesco:

He might write me a new libretto for seven characters, . . . really comic on the whole. – And if possible, he ought to include two equally good female parts. One should be *seria*, the other *mezzo carattere*, but both should be equally good. – The third female character can be *entirely* buffa, as can the male ones, if necessary.[9]

Varesco had in the meantime proved to be a somewhat difficult customer. In June he had drafted a scenario for *L'oca del Cairo* that Mozart 'liked a lot', but had then questioned whether the piece would be a success, prompting Mozart to write to his father with the following important credo:

That Herr Varesco has doubts about the opera's success I consider deeply offensive – I can assure him that his libretto won't go down well if the music is no good. The music is the main thing in an opera, so if it is to find favour (and if, in consequence, he hopes to be rewarded), he'll have to alter and recast the libretto as much and as often as I wish and not follow his own inclinations as he hasn't the least experience or knowledge of the theatre.[10]

Mozart had expressed identical views to these at the time of *Die Entführung aus dem Serail*: what was important to him was the basic outline, which another poet could elaborate in his own words just as well as he could himself. Moreover, he was currently examining four other librettos by another poet. But in the meantime Varesco had given him the whole of the first act while he was in Salzburg, and by the time that he returned to Vienna, he had already completed a first draft of it. We shall have more to say about the opera's subsequent fate.

Also in Salzburg Mozart wrote two duets for violin and viola for Michael Haydn, K423 and K424. Haydn had been asked to write them by the archbishop but had been prevented from doing so by recurrent illness, with the result that Mozart, prompted by his old feelings of attachment for his former colleague, leapt into the breach on his behalf, rapidly completing the pieces in Haydn's rooms and handing them to Colloredo in his colleague's name.[11] Mozart may have been much amused by the idea of renewing contact with his old tormentor without the latter realizing it, but above all these pieces reveal how pleased he evidently was to be able to do his old friend a favour. Haydn continued to hold them in high regard, and Mozart, too, is believed to have thought particularly highly of them. Mozart also renewed contact at this time with the blind pianist Maria

8. Considerably more than half the mass was completed, suggesting that Mozart worked on it again after 4 January 1783. ◆ Paper studies show that the wind parts for the 'Gloria in excelsis Deo', 'Qui tollis', 'Jesu Christe' and 'Cum Sancto Spiritu', as well as the wind and timpani parts for the 'Sanctus', were composed in Salzburg in the summer or fall of 1783.
9. *Briefe*, iii.268 (letter of 7 May 1783).
10. *Briefe*, iii.275 (letter of 21 June 1783).
11. ◆ This story was first reported in Schinn and Otter, *Biographische Skizze von Michael Haydn*, 38–9. Further, see Eisen, *Dokumente: Addenda*, 82–4, *New Mozart Documents*, 30–1.

Theresia Paradis, who was currently staying in Salzburg and who was on friendly terms with Leopold.[12] He later wrote a concerto for her (K456).

Leopold's house, too, was a beehive of activity at this time. He had taken in the two children of the well-known theatre manager Theobald Marchand, who was then working in Munich: the fourteen-year-old Margarethe Marchand was taught singing and keyboard playing, her twelve-year-old brother Heinrich violin and keyboard.[13] Also living under his roof was the nine-year-old Johanna Brochard, the daughter of the famous actress, whom Leopold taught in 1783/4.[14] Mozart took a lively interest in all these pupils. In the case of Margarethe Marchand, whom Constanze knew from Munich,[15] he warned her that when singing she should 'not be so arch and coy, for cajolings and kissings are not always acceptable'.[16] He later met her again as Franz Danzi's wife in Munich. Heinrich Marchand, for his part, was instructed to 'concentrate hard on staccato playing, the only point on which the Viennese cannot forget La Motte'.[17]

The main purpose of the journey was of course to persuade Leopold to adopt a less hostile attitude to Constanze, but in this respect the visit proved unsuccessful. Although Leopold retained a sense of outward propriety, he remained inwardly unreconciled to the new situation, and it was especially unfortunate that Constanze and Nannerl failed to hit it off, a failure that cast a dark shadow over what had once been such a close relationship between Mozart and his sister. Mozart had hoped that his wife would be given some of the trinkets he had received in his youth,[18] but Leopold remained true to his word that his son's family could no longer expect anything from him and kept his cupboards firmly locked. Constanze was deeply angered by the reception that she received, and although she did not show it, she never forgave her father- and sister-in-law. Mozart, too, returned to Vienna disappointed and disgruntled.

The couple left Salzburg at the end of October, returning to Vienna via Vöcklabruck and Lambach, where, to the delight of his old friend the Abbé Schickmayr, Mozart accompanied an Agnus Dei on the organ and improvised other pieces on both the organ and clavichord. From there they travelled to Ebelsberg near Linz, where they found the whole of Linz's high society assembled for an opera performance at the home of the local prefect Hugo Franz Steurer. In Linz itself, where they arrived on 30 October, they were warmly welcomed at the home of old Count Thun. A concert was due to be held on Tuesday 4 November, and Mozart had to write a new symphony 'at breakneck speed'.[19] This was the symphony in C major K425, which according to Niemetschek was dedicated to Count Thun.[20] The G major symphony K444 that was previously[21] thought to have been the work in question has since turned out to be a piece by Michael Haydn for which Mozart provided only the adagio introduction.[22] We have already mentioned the *Ecce homo* that Mozart drew during this visit to Linz.

12. See *Wiener Musik-Zeitung* (1817), 289.
13. *Briefe*, iii.205 (letter of 29 April 1782).
14. See Lipowsky, *Baierisches Musik-Lexicon*, 36ff., and *Briefe*, iv.121 (letter of 4 November 1790).
15. See Constanze's letter of 19 July 1783; *Briefe*, iii.281.
16. *Briefe*, iii.292 (letter of 31 October 1783).
17. *Briefe*, iii.295 (letter of 6 December 1783). ◆ Franz Lamotte (c1751–80) was from 1772 a violinist in the Hofkapelle of Maria Theresia. Concerning Marchand, see Heinz Schuler, *Mozarts Salzburger Freunde und Bekannte*, 98–100 and 191–2.
18. Nissen, *Biographie W. A. Mozarts*, XVIII.
19. *Briefe*, iii.291 (letter of 31 October 1783).
20. See *Briefe*, iii.313 (letter of 15 May 1784).
21. See Jahn, *W. A. Mozart*, fourth edition, ii.8–9.
22. Saint-Foix, 'Zwei Berichtigungen zum Köchelschen Verzeichnis der Werke Mozarts'. ◆ Haydn's symphony (Sherman and Thomas, *Johann Michael Haydn (1737–1806): A Chronological Thematic Catalogue of His Works*, MH 334) dates from 23 May 1783.

Fifteen months later Leopold repaid his son's visit, staying with him in Vienna between 10 February and 25 April 1785. The critical tone of the letters that he wrote to his daughter during this period makes it all too plain that relations between him and his son had not improved in the interim. In the circumstances, Mozart's suggestion that his father should move to Vienna must have been made in the knowledge that it would be turned down. Even so, Leopold was sufficiently fair-minded to acknowledge that he thought his son's household was being run along orderly lines. He was also delighted to get to know his second grandson, Carl, whom he thought the spitting image of Wolfgang,[23] and he was very much his old self in praising his son's artistic achievements, which he had ample opportunity to admire during the current spate of concerts. On the day after his father's arrival in the capital, Mozart invited Joseph Haydn to perform quartets with them, and there seems little doubt that he played the viola, as he always did on such occasions.[24] Leopold reported on the event in his letter to Nannerl of 16 February:

> The new quartets were played or, rather, only the 3 new ones that he's added to the 3 we already have, – they're a bit easier but still admirably composed. Herr Haydn said to me: *'I say to you before God and as an honest man that your son is the greatest composer known to me either in person or by name; he has taste and, what's more, the greatest knowledge of composition'.*[25]

It is easy to imagine how proud Leopold must have felt on hearing these words, which will have seemed the finest possible reward for all his toil and labour. In Jahn's words, they 'added a silvery lustre to his life'.[26]

Leopold also had every reason to be satisfied with the successes enjoyed by his pupil Heinrich Marchand, who had accompanied him to Vienna and who appeared at the Burgtheater on 2 March and at the Tonkünstler-Sozietät on the 15th. He was also able to hear his old enemy Aloysia Lange on a number of occasions and evidently enjoyed her singing. Her husband, the actor Joseph Lange, painted Leopold's portrait at this time.[27] Leopold also called on the Fischers, surprising them and delighting them in equal measure with his visit.[28] And he also travelled to Klosterneuburg, where the Baroness von Waldstätten was currently in residence.

While in Vienna, Leopold allowed his son to talk him into becoming a Freemason, an event of some importance for our understanding of the two men. At least in part, Leopold's reasons seem to have been personal, as he already knew a whole series of individuals whom he admired and who were members of the order. Above all, however, it seems to have been his increasing interest in philosophy that persuaded him to join. The narrow-mindedness of Salzburg had served merely to increase his secret urge to aspire to higher things, and in becoming a Mason he believed that he could satisfy that desire. How far he succeeded in doing so, we do not know. Nor is it clear whether

23. *Briefe*, iii.374 (letter of 16 February 1785).
24. Michael Kelly reports on a performance at Storace's at which Haydn played the first violin, Dittersdorf the second, Mozart the viola and Vanhal the cello; see Kelly, *Reminiscences*, i.240–1. In his *Life of Mozart*, 266, Edward Holmes wonders whether Kelly's memory deceived him and whether he was confusing Haydn and Mozart, inasmuch as Haydn 'played the tenor very well, but it is doubtful whether he was sufficiently master of the violin to lead a quartet', whereas Mozart enjoyed a considerable reputation as a soloist at this time.
25. *Briefe*, iii.373 (letter of 16 February 1785).
26. Jahn, *W. A. Mozart*, ii.11.
27. The letter mentioning this portrait is reproduced by Nohl, *Mozart nach den Schilderungen seiner Zeitgenossen*, 296, but is missing from Schiedermair's edition. ◆ It is given in *Briefe*, iii.382 (letter of 25 March 1785).
28. *Briefe*, iii.379 (letter of 12 March 1785).

he joined the Lodge that was founded in Salzburg in 1783.[29] At all events, he seems to have discussed these questions in correspondence with his son.

On his return to Salzburg on around 11 May 1785 he was greeted by a decree from the Salzburg exchequer [dated 2 May 1785] informing him that, as he had been away for longer than the six weeks allowed under the terms of his leave of absence, he was 'to receive no pay until further notice', unless he were to return to Salzburg by the middle of May. He did not see his son again. In 1787 he paid a further visit to Munich with Heinrich Marchand, but never returned to Vienna. It is clear, however, from his letters to Marianne that he followed progress on *Le nozze di Figaro* and news of the work's success in Prague with all his old warmth of interest. And although he observed his son's material circumstances with mounting concern, he continued to refuse him any support, while freely dispensing advice that was generally accompanied by expressions of bitterness and harshness. Early in 1787 he began to feel ill but on 13 February wrote to his daughter from Munich:

I'm not feeling any worse on this journey and hope that the change of air and the activity will do me good; the end of the 67th year of my life and the start of the 68th have brought a great change to my old body: which is entirely natural! old people don't get any younger![30]

Soon afterwards he received a visit from Michael Kelly and the Storaces, who had lots of news of Vienna and his son. But his health then took a turn for the worse, prompting Mozart to write the letter of 4 April from which we have already quoted and to ask to be kept informed of subsequent developments.

Leopold again recovered and on 26 May 1787 even wrote to Nannerl to invite her and her family to spend Whitsun with him. He died two days later, on 28 May. Mozart was deeply shaken by the news, which was completely unexpected, even though he had been preparing for it for some time. 'You can imagine the state I'm in', he wrote to Gottfried von Jacquin in late May.[31] But he had no more time to brood on this occasion than he had done following the death of his mother. *Don Giovanni* was demanding his attention.

Mozart's relations with his mother-in-law, Cäcilie Weber, were initially no more satisfactory than they had been with his father. Although the couple did not live in the same house as she did,[32] an argument broke out during only their second visit, with the result that it was then decided to restrict their visits to the family's name-days. The situation later improved. 'Mozart grew increasingly fond of our late mother, and she of him', recalled Sophie Haibel. Mozart's goodness of heart eventually disarmed even this stubborn and mean-spirited woman. According to Sophie Haibel, he won her over chiefly by all manner of gifts of food that he took with him on each of his visits. Sophie was the youngest and clearly the most good-natured of the four daughters and was also the most frequent visitor to the Mozarts' home, performing sterling service in looking after not only Constanze during her frequent confinements and illnesses but also Mozart himself on the occasion of his final illness.

---

29. Kreitmaier, *W. A. Mozart: Eine Charakterzeichnung des großen Meisters nach literarischen Quellen*, 114–15.
30. *Briefe*, iv.24 (letter of 13 February 1787).
31. *Briefe*, iv.48 (letter of late May 1787).
32. See *Briefe*, iii.196, 223 and 226 (letters of 30 January, 23 August and 31 August 1782).

Mozart also became very friendly with the Langes,[33] whose marriage was proving unhappy, largely as a result of mutual jealousy.[34] Aloysia was sufficiently generous to admit that she initially did not understand Mozart's music and that only with time did she come to appreciate it, resulting in a genuine sense of comradeship that found expression in a number of arias that he wrote for her. We have already mentioned one of them, *Nehmt meinen Dank* (K383). A second, *Mia speranza adorata* K416, was written on 8 January 1783 and first sung by Aloysia at a concert at the Mehlgrube on 11 January 1783.

Further opportunities arose when the Italian opera company was reestablished and both Aloysia and Adamberger – who, as German singers, were much criticized at the Italian opera – invited Mozart to write two additional arias for them for Pasquale Anfossi's opera *Il curioso indiscreto*, which had been written in 1777 and which was first performed in Vienna on 30 June 1783. As always, Mozart was willing to help, but got into all manner of difficulties, as he explained to his father in his letter of 2 July:

The opera . . . was performed for the first time the day before yesterday, Monday; nobody liked it, except for my 2 arias, – and the 2nd, a bravura aria, had to be repeated. – I should add at this point that my enemies were so spiteful as to put it about in advance that 'Mozart wants to improve on Anfossi's opera'. I heard about this. And so I sent word to Count Rosenberg that I wouldn't hand over the arias unless the following statement was printed in the wordbooks in both German and Italian:

Avertimento

Le due Arie a carta 36 e a carta 102 sono state messe in musica dal Sigr. maestro Mozart, per compiacere alla Sigra. Lange, non essendo quelle state scritta dal Sig. maestro Anfossi secondo la di lei abilità, mà per altro soggetto. Questo si vuole far noto perchè ne vada l'onore a chi conviene, senza che rimanga in alcuna parte pregiudicata la riputazione e la fama del già molto cognito Napolitano.

This was duly included, and I handed over the arias, which were an indescribable credit both to me and to my sister-in-law: – and my enemies were completely confounded! – But then Herr Salieri played a trick that has harmed poor Adamberger more than me. I think I told you that I'd also written a rondeau for Adamberger. During a short rehearsal (before the rondeau had been written out), Salieri took Adamberger aside and told him that Count Rosenberg wouldn't like it if he added an aria and, as a good friend, he advised him against it. – Adamberger, annoyed at Rosenberg, didn't know how to get his own back, and was stupid enough to say, *with ill-timed pride*: 'All right, just to show that Adamberger is already well known in Vienna and doesn't need to make a name for himself by singing music specially written for him, he'll sing what's in the opera and will never again insert an aria as long as he lives.' What was the result? That he was a complete failure, as was only to be expected! – He now regrets it, but it's too late; if he were now to ask me to give him the rondeau, I'd refuse to do so. – I can easily use it in one of my own operas. – The worst thing about it all is that his wife's prophecy and mine has come

---

33. A medallion showing the two of them was published in the *Ephemeriden der Litteratur und des Theaters* (Berlin, 1785); see also Freisauff, *Mozarts Don Juan 1787 bis 1887: Ein Beitrag zur Geschichte dieser Oper*, 48.

34. See Lange, *Biographie des Joseph Lange*, 118, and Friedel, *Briefe aus Wien verschiedenen Inhalts an einen Freund in Berlin*, 409.

true and neither Count Rosenberg nor the management knows anything about it and it was therefore only a trick on Herr Salieri's part.[35]

The arias in question were *Vorrei spiegarvi, oh Dio* K418, written on 20 June 1783,[36] and *No, che non sei capace* K419, both of which were intended for Aloysia, and Adamberger's aria *Per pietà, non ricercate* K420, which dates from 21 June.[37] Aloysia probably sang her second aria on a subsequent occasion at a Tonkünstler-Sozietät concert in April 1791, when she also performed scenes from Paisiello's *Fedra*; on that occasion the name 'Clorinda' was changed to 'Aricia', one of the characters in *Fedra*.[38] One of her best roles was as Konstanze in Mozart's *Die Entführung aus dem Serail*,[39] a role that showed 'what a compass of voice she had'.[40] Stephen Storace likened her to La Bastardina in terms of both range and technique. As a result she chose *Die Entführung* for her benefit performance,[41] returning to the role on 25 November 1785 after recovering from a serious illness. In foreign centres of music, too, she triumphed as Konstanze, especially with the aria 'Martern aller Arten'.[42] The last aria that Mozart wrote for her was *Ah se in ciel, benigne stelle* K538, a setting of an aria from Metastasio's *L'eroe cinese* that he completed on 4 March 1788. To judge from all these arias, she was a singer in the Rococo tradition, adept at evoking a sense of charm, tenderness and sentimentality, tasteful in expression and with exceptional technical skills, but far less able to convey a sense of thrilling passion. According to Hufeland, writing in 1783, hers was the most beautiful voice he had ever heard, uncommonly attractive and ingratiating, but a little too small for the theatre.[43]

Far less gifted, albeit the possessor of a high and flexible soprano voice, was the eldest of the Weber sisters, Josepha,[44] who joined Schikaneder's company only after her marriage to the violinist Franz de Paula Hofer. Mozart is said to have had great difficulty in getting her to learn her parts. For her, too, he wrote an aria, *Schon lacht der holde Frühling* K580, which he completed on 17 September 1789 for insertion in a German adaptation of Paisiello's *Il barbiere di Siviglia*. It survives in draft score only.

In spite of his unfortunate experiences with Anfossi's opera, Mozart allowed himself to be talked into writing two extra numbers for Francesco Bianchi's comic opera *La villanella rapita*, which was

---

35. *Briefe*, iii.276 (letter of 2 July 1783). Aloysia's success is confirmed by a report in the Berlin *Litteratur- und Theater-Zeitung*, i/35 (1783), 599, and by Lange, *Biographie des Joseph Lange*, 119. The Italian text reads: 'The two arias on p. 36 and on p. 102 have been set to music by Signor maestro Mozart to oblige Signora Lange, those written by Signor maestro Anfossi not being commensurate with her ability, but meant for someone else. This must be notified, so that honour should be accorded where it is due, and this without prejudice to the reputation and fame of the already well-known Neapolitan.'
36. Whether the aria *Ah spiegarti, oh Dio* K178 represents the first and subsequently discarded version of this piece, as Jahn claims (*W. A. Mozart*, ii.19), is doubtful. Stylistically, at least, it must date from Mozart's early years in Vienna. A sketched version of K420 likewise exists. ◆ A complete version of K178 does not survive in Mozart's hand, only a sketch of the melody and text; other sketches on the same leaf are for K419 and K420, hence the dating of K178 to early 1783. For the sketchleaf, now in the library of Stanford University, see NMA X/30/3.
37. The autograph manuscript bears the note: 'Il Curioso indiscreto. Atto 2do per il Sig^re Adamberger, di Wolfgango Amadeo Mozart a Vienna li 21 di giunio 1783 – Rondò.'
38. See Nottebohm's critical commentary to AMA VI, no. 26. ◆ The programme for this concert is given in *Dokumente*, 344, *Documentary Biography*, 392–3.
39. She sang the role at the first performance of *Die Entführung* at the Kärntnertor-Theater on 25 November 1785, thereby misleading a number of writers into claiming that she was the first Konstanze; see Jahn, *W. A. Mozart*, ii.20, n.36. ◆ The first Konstanze was Catarina Cavalieri.
40. Kelly, *Reminiscences*, i.253.
41. *Briefe*, iii.296 (letter of 10 December 1783).
42. See reports in the *AmZ*, iii (1800/1), 659 (from Amsterdam) and iv (1801/2), 322 (from Paris).
43. 'Briefe an Salzmann von Gottlieb Hufeland', 92–3; see also Cramer's *Magazin der Musik*, ii (1784), 185.
44. For a recent study of Josepha, see Blümml, 'Josefa Weber-Hofer: Die erste "Königin der Nacht"', 7–8. ◆ Also see Gidwitz, 'Vocal Profiles of Four Mozart Sopranos'.

performed for the first time in Vienna on 25 November 1785. The two numbers were the quartet 'Dite almeno, in che mancai' K479 and the trio 'Mandina amabile' K480, written on 5 and 21 November respectively. At the end of 1783, the second daughter of the librettist Marco Coltellini, Celeste (1760–1829), had been engaged by the Emperor Joseph himself in Naples, where she had been singing successfully since 1779.[45] She appeared for the first time in Vienna in Paisiello's *La contadina di spirito*[46] and later took over from Nancy Storace, who temporarily lost her voice[47] at the first performance of her brother's opera *Gli sposi malcontenti* on 1 June 1785.[48] Although her vocal resources were modest, she made up for this deficiency by dint of her great musical education, her powers of expression and her excellent acting abilities, all qualities to which Mozart's two ensembles are demonstrably geared.[49] Outstanding among the male characters was the Pippo, Stefano Mandini, for whom Mozart later wrote the part of Count Almaviva. The tenor Vincenzo Calvesi as the Count and the second bass Francesco Bussani as Biaggio had less prominent roles.

It was not only singers, however, for whom Mozart wrote works at this time: he also provided pieces for instrumental virtuosos. In April 1784 the Viennese were regaled by a visit from the violinist Regina Strinasacchi (1764–1839), a lively and delightful girl from Ostiglia. Mozart thought her playing very tasteful and full of feeling,[50] an assessment confirmed by Leopold, who heard her in Salzburg in December 1785:

> She plays no note without feeling, even in the symphonies she plays everything with expression, and no one can play an adagio with more feeling than she does. Her whole heart and soul are in the melody that she is playing, and her tone is as beautiful as it is powerful. In general I find that a woman with talent plays more expressively than a man.[51]

It was for Regina Strinasacchi that Mozart wrote his violin sonata in B flat major K454. The piece was due to be performed at a concert at the Kärntnertor-Theater on 29 April 1784, but, as so often, he failed to write out the piece in time and it was only with difficulty that the violinist was able to extort her part from the composer on the eve of the concert. She had to rehearse it on her own the next morning. Mozart himself turned up at the concert with a sketch containing only the violin line and a few accompanying figures and modulations,[52] playing the work virtually entirely from memory and without any rehearsal, a feat observed by the emperor from his box by means of his lorgnette. In spite of this, the performers achieved an excellent rapport and were much applauded.[53]

45. See Kelly, *Reminiscences*, i.84, and Werner, *Aus dem Josephinischen Wien*, 106. On the other hand, it is not until 1781 that she appears as a buffa singer in the lists of performances given by Wiel in *I teatri musicali veneziani nel Settecento*, 356, and by Florimo in *La scuola musicale di Napoli e i suoi conservatorii*, iv.74 and 90. In 1789 she was hugely successful in the title role of Paisiello's *Nina* in Naples; see Florimo, *La scuola musicale*, ii.268.
46. See *Wiener Zeitung*, xxix (1785), appendix.
47. Kelly, *Reminiscences*, i.234.
48. See *Wiener Zeitung*, xlvi (1785), appendix.
49. See Cramer's *Magazin der Musik*, ii (1784), 62–3 and Reichardt's *Musikalische Monatsschrift*, 38.
50. *Briefe*, iii.311 (letter of 24 April 1784).
51. *Briefe*, iii.467 (letter of 7 December 1785).
52. In the autograph manuscript, which is in England [now Stockholm, Stiftelsen Musikkulturens Främjande], the keyboard part is, with few exceptions, written in a different ink from the violin part. Constanze's later claim that the sheet of paper was completely blank is, therefore, an exaggeration; see Constanze Mozart, 'Einige Anekdoten aus Mozarts Leben', 290; and George Grove in the *Athenæum* (27 July 1872).
53. In the *Wiener Zeitung*, liv (1784), 1560, Torricella announced: 'From the pen of the famous Herr Kapellmeister Mozart, will be published by subscription . . . 3 new *clavier Sonatas*, of which . . . the third is accompanied by a *violin*, as recently played at the theatre with general applause by the celebrated *Mlle Strinasachy* and Herr Mozart, and thus needs no further recommendation' [*Dokumente*, 200, *Documentary Biography*, 225–6]. The three works were K 284, 333 and 454.

Also in Vienna, Mozart renewed contact with an old acquaintance from Salzburg, the horn player Joseph Leutgeb, who had set up a cheese dairy in a 'little snail's house' in one of he city's suburbs in 1777, for which purpose he had borrowed some money from Leopold.[54] By the time that Mozart settled in Vienna, he was still living in pitiful circumstances and in no position to pay off the loan.[55] He was a decent horn player, albeit with no real education.[56] In addition to cheese making, he still made frequent appearances in the concert hall and it is to these that we owe a whole series of horn concertos by Mozart, all of which date from this period: K412 (cf. 514), 417, 447 and 495.[57] Of course, Leutgeb had to contend with the whole force of Mozart's exuberant high spirits. On one occasion, Mozart made him earn the piece by crawling around on the floor and collecting up the parts of his symphonies and concertos that he tossed around the room, while continuing to work at his desk. On another occasion he had to kneel behind the stove.[58] The autograph manuscripts of these concertos bear signs of these high spirits. K417, for example, is headed 'Wolfgang Amadé Mozart has taken pity on Leutgeb, ass, ox and fool, in Vienna on 27 May 1783', while K 495 is notated in four different colours of ink: black, red, blue and green. The autograph of the rondo of K412 and 514 even includes a little scene showing Leutgeb playing, with his mistakes all held up to public ridicule.[59]

Mozart continued to see Leutgeb until the time of his death, their contacts being especially frequent during Constanze's absence in 1791, when Mozart occasionally spent the night at his friend's house, maintaining the high-spirited tone of their friendship until the very end. A fifth work written for Leutgeb was the quintet for horn, violin, two violas and bass K407. The autograph manuscript of the piece, which dates from between 1782 and 1784, was owned by Leutgeb.[60]

Mozart's thematic catalogue contains an entry dated 1 April 1785 for an andante in A major for violin and orchestra, K470, the present whereabouts of which are unknown. We do not know whether this movement was intended for one of his violin concertos, although it was probably written for a virtuoso.[61] On one occasion, Mozart is said to have repaired to a coffee-house and written down a menuetto and trio for a beggar who had accosted him in the street, claiming to be a relation of his and later demanding the fee from his publisher.[62]

54. *Briefe*, ii.159 (letter of 1 December 1777).
55. *Briefe*, iii.209 (letter of 8 May 1782). ◆ Further, see Pisarowitz: 'Mozarts Schnorrer Leutgeb'.
56. Dittersdorf, *Lebensbeschreibung*, 45.
57. The heading on the Rondo K 514 – 'Vienna Venerdì santo li 6 Aprile 1797' – is clearly a joke, postdating the piece by a full ten years. ◆ Recent paper studies show that the two movements K412 and the incomplete K514 belong together and that both were composed in 1791. A completion by Süßmayr that was traditionally thought to be by Mozart (and represents the generally disseminated version of the concerto) is the source of the misinformation 'Vienna Venerdì santo li 6 Aprile 1797' which is, in any case, a misreading for '6 Aprile 1792' (presumably the date on which Süßmayr completed his text); Süßmayr introduced into the work a quote from the Lamentations of Jeremiah normally sung as part of the Good Friday service.
58. Jahn, *W. A. Mozart*, ii.31, n.67. Leutgeb died on 27 February 1811, relatively well off.
59. The tempo of the horn part, for example, is marked 'Adagio', while that of the orchestra is 'Allegro'. The rest of the autograph is interspersed with exclamations: 'A lei Signor Asino – Animo – presto – sù via – da bravo – Coraggio – e finisci già – bestia – oh che stonatura – Ahi! – oimè – bravo poveretto! – oh, seccatura di Coglioni! – ah che mi fai ridere! – ajuto! – respira un poco! – avanti, avanti! – questo poi va al meglio – e non finisci nemmeno? – Ah Porco infame! oh come sei grazioso! – Carino! asinino! – hahaha – respira! – Ma intoni almeno una, Cazzo – bravo evviva! – e vieni à seccarmi per la quarta, e Dio sia benedetto per l'ultima volta – ah termina, ti prego! – oh maledetto – anche bravura? bravo – ah! – trillo di beccore! – finisci? grazie al ciel! – basta, basta!'
60. Gottfried Weber, 'Weitere Nachrichten', 306, and Zawrzel and Krüchten, 'Anzeige', 203.
61. Jahn, *W. A. Mozart*, ii.35, considers two virtuosos as possible contenders: the violinist Felix Janiewicz, who was currently performing in Vienna, and Heinrich Marchand. ◆ The Polish virtuoso Felix Janiewicz (1762–1848) gave a concert at the Burgtheater on 26 February 1785, more than a month before the composition of K470; it is unlikely that the work was written for him. Further, see Berwaldt, 'Życie Feliksa Janiewicza' and 'Twórczość Feliksa Janiewicza'. K470 was also composed too late for Marchand's Viennese concerts on 2 and 14 March and his performance of a violin concerto at the Tonkünstler-Sozietät academy on 15 March. But he remained in Vienna until 25 April and the work could have been composed for him before he left.
62. See Parke, *Musical Memoirs*, ii.179–80.

Far too often Mozart allowed others to take advantage of his good nature, but it was an aspect of his character that also had its darker side in the form of his implacable and often highly personal criticisms of his fellow artists and their art. The sharp end of his tongue was felt especially by Italian singers, whose mannerisms he found more objectionable, the longer he had to put up with them. Certain composers, too, were not spared his censure, censure which, when the mood took him, he dressed in the garb of improvised keyboard parodies.[63] In Niemetschek's words, 'dissimulation and flattery were equally alien to his guileless heart and to do anything under duress was intolerable',[64] with the result that he inevitably won many enemies through his outspokenness, a hostility that his Italian adversaries made plain at performances of his works. Soon after his arrival in the city, he acquired a reputation among some of the Viennese as a braggart and a malicious critic[65] and for a time it even looked as though he might become a writer on music: on 28 December 1782 we find him writing to his father, 'I'd like to write a book – a short critique of music with examples – but, I need hardly add, not under my own name'.[66] This passage not only gives the lie to the idea of Mozart as a thoroughly naïve and uncritical composer, it also affords striking proof of the clarity with which he saw his own goals, especially since the time of *Idomeneo* and *Die Entführung aus dem Serail*. That the book was never written is beside the point: what matters is that his own work and that of his contemporaries forced him to reflect on his art at this time. By now he had long since outgrown his earlier practice of basing himself on a single model and, instead, he took the view that an artist must consciously examine all the trends of his time. In his own case this meant studying in depth the scores of French and Italian operas. In Vienna he became more critical than ever of the Italians, as is clear from his entirely apposite views on both Righini and Vicente Martín y Soler, the latter a composer who was then especially popular. He found much of Martín's music 'really very pretty, but in ten years' time no one will take any more notice of it'.[67] There were plenty of opportunities to make personal contact with the Italian composers based in Vienna now that an Italian company had been reestablished in the city, and a lesser person than Mozart would undoubtedly have avenged himself on them and their art for the many setbacks that he suffered. But here, too, he was able to distinguish between man and artist and maintained a good working relationship not only with a decent enough individual such as Stephen Storace but also with Paisiello, who was a far more dangerous rival. Paisiello arrived in Vienna from St Petersburg in 1784 and was immediately showered with the highest honours. His *Barbiere di Siviglia* was performed soon after his arrival in the city[68] and immediately afterwards he was invited to write a new opera, the libretto for which was entrusted to the distinguished court poet Giovanni Battista Casti. The result, based on Voltaire's *Candide*, was *Il re Teodoro in Venezia*, one of the most original and action-packed librettos of the period.[69] We already know what Mozart owed Paisiello on an artistic level, and he also thought very highly of his work.[70] It is no

63. Rochlitz, 'Verbürgte Anekdoten aus Wolfgang Gottlieb Mozarts Leben', 591–2.
64. Niemetschek, *Leben des k. k. Kapellmeisters Wolfgang Gottlieb Mozart*, 62.
65. *Briefe*, iii.216 (letter of 31 July 1782).
66. *Briefe*, iii.246 (letter of 28 December 1782).
67. Rochlitz, 'Verbürgte Anekdoten', 116; see also Sievers, *Mozart und Süßmayer: Ein neues Plagiat, ersterm zur Last gelegt, und eine neue Vermutung, die Entstehung des Requiems betreffend*, XXII–XXIII.
68. ◆ Paisiello arrived in Vienna in the summer of 1784 and his *Barbiere di Siviglia* was given on 9, 18 and 28 June, 5 July, and 11 August; the work was first performed there on 13 August 1783. See Link, *The National Court Theatre in Mozart's Vienna*, 27 and 42–6.
69. According to Joseph Frank, writing in Robert Prutz's *Deutsches Museum*, ii (1852), 24, the idea was suggested by Joseph II himself and was intended as a satire on Gustavus III of Sweden and his stay in Venice in 1783; see also Kelly, *Reminiscences*, i.238–9.
70. Rochlitz, 'Verbürgte Anekdoten', 115.

wonder, therefore, that he now sought him out in person. Of all the great opera *buffa* composers, Paisiello was the only one with whom Mozart came into relatively close contact. He insisted that one of his female pupils should play some of his works for his colleague's edification, and Paisiello asked to see a copy of the score of *Idomeneo* so that he might study it.[71] That same year, 1784, another great Italian composer passed through Vienna on his way to St Petersburg, Giuseppe Sarti, whom Mozart likewise got to know personally. 'Sarti is a good honest fellow,' he told his father on 12 June 1784, 'and I've played a great deal for him, finally also writing some variations on one of his arias, which gave him a lot of pleasure.'[72] Sarti later wrote a particularly supercilious and dismissive critique of individual passages in Mozart's quartets, complaining that only barbarians with no sense of hearing could take it into their heads to write like this. He listed errors 'of a kind that could be made only by a keyboard player incapable of distinguishing between D sharp and E flat' and he ended with the Rousseauesque words: 'De la musique pour faire boucher les oreilles.'[73] In fact, Sarti's critique is merely proof of the extent to which Italian musicians had lost touch not only with German music but with instrumental music in general at this time.

Mozart was no less uninhibited in his comments on composers of instrumental music. If he liked their work, he did everything in his power to champion it. Adalbert Gyrowetz, for example, later recalled the generous way in which Mozart introduced him to Vienna:

> He gazed at Gyrowetz, who was then still very young, with a very sympathetic expression, as if to say, 'Poor young man, you are entering the ways of the great world for the first time and are anxiously awaiting from your Destiny what the future will bring!' – . . . Cheered by his affability and kindness, he asked him to cast a glance at his youthful works, which consisted of six symphonies, and to give him his opinion on them. Mozart agreed to this request like the kind-hearted man he was, looked the pieces through, praised them, and promised the young artist that he would have one of these symphonies performed at his concert in the music room in the Mehlgrube, where Mozart was giving six subscription concerts [in 1785]; and thus it actually came to pass one Thursday. The symphony was performed in the music room in the Mehlgrube by the full theatre orchestra, and received general applause. Mozart with his innate goodness of heart took the young artist by the hand and presented him to the audience as the author of the symphony.[74]

Given his sharp-tongued independence of manner, Mozart naturally had his critics, but he remained indifferent to that fact: he was far too objective not to take seriously all the objections raised against him and his music, but his very objectivity persuaded him to reject out of hand the one reproach that struck at the very heart of his music, namely, that it was 'all too fiery in spirit and all too wide-ranging in its imagination'.[75] It was merely the prerogative of the genius that he exercised when faced with such philistinism. Among those who not only failed

71. Bridi, *Breve notizie intorno ad alcuni più celebri compositori di musica e cenni sullo stato presente del canto italiano*, 47.

72. *Briefe*, iii.318 (letter of 12 June 1784). These are the variations on 'Come un agnello' from Sarti's *Fra i due litiganti il terzo gode* K460. The work was hugely popular in Vienna at this time. The theme returns in the second-act finale in *Don Giovanni*. ◆ Sarti's opera was first given at Vienna on 28 May 1783 but the date of Mozart's variations is uncertain. K460 was published by Artaria in 1787 in a version with the theme and six variations; authentic sources for variations 3–6 do not survive. Later editions include two additional variations for which authentic sources are also lacking.

73. Anon, 'Auszug aus dem Sarti'schen Manuscripte, worin Mozart bitter getadelt wird'. ◆ Further, see Vertrees, 'Mozart's String Quartet K. 465: The History of a Controversy'.

74. Einstein, *Lebensläufe deutscher Musiker von ihnen selbst erzählt*, iii.12–13. ◆ There is no documentary record of this concert.

75. Rochlitz, 'Verbürgte Anekdoten', 145.

to understand him, but who additionally felt envy and jealousy, the most obdurate was Leopold Kozeluch (1747–1818). Kozeluch enjoyed a certain reputation in Vienna at this time as a keyboard player and teacher and also taught at court, one of several musicians who sought to attract attention by their smugness and constant complaints.[76] It was Haydn whom he initially had in his line of fire, and he even tried to rally Mozart to his cause.[77] When this attempt failed, he chose Mozart as the butt of his spiteful attacks, opining that the overture to *Don Giovanni* was deficient,[78] that of *Die Zauberflöte* too learned.[79] And at the Prague performances of *La clemenza di Tito*, he vented his spleen with such vehemence that he permanently forfeited the sympathies of his Bohemian countrymen.[80] Later he tried to compete with Beethoven in arranging Scottish folksongs, but Beethoven vigorously rejected all comparisons out of hand and dismissed his rival as 'miserabilis'.[81] In the lives of Vienna's three great classical composers, Kozeluch was cast in the role of Thersites. Beside him, Franz Kreibich was far less dangerous in his hostility to Mozart.[82]

Mozart's dealings with Gluck went no further than a few occasional meetings, all of which were instigated by the older composer. Mozart never succeeded in ridding himself of a vague sense of mistrust towards him, a mistrust assiduously kept alive by Leopold, who had always disliked Gluck.[83] But such was the great difference in their personalities and artistic aims, a closer relationship between Mozart and Gluck was in any case out of the question. Gluck's friendship with Salieri must likewise have aroused Mozart's suspicions. But it appears from all the surviving evidence that Gluck behaved not only correctly towards his younger colleague but generously and amicably. In much the same way, there appear to have been no closer contacts between Mozart and Dittersdorf, even though the latter admitted to holding Mozart in high regard. But Dittersdorf was in fact an irregular visitor to Vienna during this period.[84]

By contrast, Mozart's friendly relations with Joseph Haydn continued to deepen. We do not know when the bond between them was first forged. Haydn was still at Eszterháza when Mozart moved to Vienna, but often came to the capital either on his own or with his employer and was regularly acclaimed there as a composer. As a result, there were ample opportunities for the two men to meet. Even so, it is not until 24 April 1784 that Mozart first mentions Haydn's name in a letter to his father:

> Some quartets have just appeared by a certain Pleyel, who's a pupil of Joseph Haydn. If you don't know them, try to get hold of them, you'll find them worth the trouble. They're very well

76. ◆ In general, see Flamm, 'Leopold Koželuch: Biographie und stilkritische Untersuchung der Sonaten für Klavier, Violine und Violoncello', and Komlós, 'The Viennese Keyboard Trio in the 1780s: Sociological Background and Contemporary Reception'.
77. At a performance of a new Haydn quartet, he raised all manner of objections within Mozart's hearing, exclaiming at one particularly bold transition: 'I'd have done that differently!' 'So would I', retorted Mozart, 'and do you know why? Because neither you nor I would have hit on that idea!' See Niemetschek, *Leben des k. k. Kapellmeisters Wolfgang Gottlieb Mozart*, 61; Rochlitz, 'Verbürgte Anekdoten', 53; Griesinger, *Biographische Notizen über Joseph Haydn*, 105; and Nissen, *Biographie W. A. Mozarts*, 681. (Nissen refers specifically to Kozeluch.)
78. *Bohemia* (1856), 127.
79. Jahn, *W. A. Mozart*, ii.42.
80. *AmZ*, ii (1798/9), 596.
81. Thayer, *Ludwig van Beethovens Leben*, iii.271–2.
82. ◆ Thersites was the only rank-and-file soldier described in graphic detail by Homer: he was bow-legged, lame, his shoulders caved inward and his head, which came to a point, was shaped like a sugar loaf. Homer describes him as vulgar, obscene and 'teeming with rant'.
83. *Briefe*, ii.272 (letter of 9 February 1778). Mozart's comment in his own letter of 17 August 1782 – 'With regard to Gluck, I think exactly as you do, my dearest father' (*Briefe*, iii.220) – seems to imply a similar need for caution to the one advised by Leopold.
84. ◆ On Dittersdorf, see Heartz, *Haydn, Mozart and the Viennese School 1740–1780*, 433–52.

written and very pleasant, and you'll also see at once who his teacher was. Well – it will be a great day for music if Pleyel is one day in a position to replace Haydn.[85]

Although this letter indicates the depth of Mozart's respect for Haydn, it does not as yet suggest that they were in any closer contact. By the following year, however, we find Mozart addressing Haydn as 'mio caro amico' in the dedication of his six new quartets.[86] In February 1785, Leopold had reported that they were on very friendly terms at the time of his own visit to Vienna, and from now on we find Mozart using the familiar 'Du' form to address Haydn, who was his senior by twenty-four years. It is by no means out of the question that it was again Freemasonry that brought the two men closer together, as it was in early February 1785 that Haydn joined the order, albeit a different lodge from Mozart's.[87] The dedication to which we have just referred is a fine example of the way that Mozart's mind worked, revealing, as it does, not only sincere affection but also respect for his friend's seniority and genius: like a father with his children, so he entrusts his latest works to the goodwill of his trusted friend. Artistically, too, he felt profoundly indebted to Haydn: he owed it to himself to dedicate these quartets to the older composer 'for it was Haydn who taught me how to write quartets'.[88] According to Niemetschek, 'it was certainly touching to hear him speak of the two Haydns and other great composers: you no longer thought it was the all-powerful Mozart who was speaking, but one of their enthusiastic pupils'.[89]

Mozart's unqualified praise is all the more impressive when we recall that, although Haydn had a considerable following in Vienna at this time, he also had a number of powerful enemies, foremost among whom was the Emperor Joseph II himself. These people were no great lovers of Haydn's 'jokes',[90] and it is clear from their opposition that Haydn's idea of opening up the symphony to ideas drawn from the world of folk music was felt to be unstylistic by many members of the Italian faction. Moreover, many of Haydn's colleagues in Vienna will have regarded Prince Esterházy's Kapellmeister as an unwelcome intruder. In a word, Haydn had every reason to complain about the large number of people who envied and criticized him.[91] He was all the more delighted, therefore, to be acknowledged by a man like Mozart, whose greatness he himself admired without reserve – it is sufficient to recall his remarks to Leopold Mozart. He never tired of expressing this view both privately and publicly. When Franz Roth asked if he could stage one of his operas in Prague alongside *Le nozze di Figaro* and *Don Giovanni*, he replied:

> You ask me for an *opera buffa*. Most willingly, if you want to have one of my vocal compositions for yourself alone. But if you intend to stage it in Prague, I cannot comply with your wish, as all my operas are far too closely bound up with our company and, moreover, they would not

85. *Briefe*, iii.311 (letter of 24 April 1784). Ignace Pleyel (1757–1831) later became Kapellmeister of Strasbourg Cathedral and between 1792 and 1795 [*recte* between December 1791 and May 1792] was active in London, subsequently settling in Paris, where he worked as a composer and music publisher and ran a piano-making business.

86. *Briefe*, iii.404 (letter of 1 September 1785). ◆ For a slightly sinister interpretation of Mozart's dedication to Haydn, see Schroeder, *Mozart in Revolt*, 189–91.

87. Pohl, *Joseph Haydn*, ii.207–8. ◆ Further, see Chailley, 'Joseph Haydn and the Freemasons', and Hurwitz, 'Haydn and the Freemasons'.

88. Rochlitz, 'Verbürgte Anekdoten', 53 and 116.

89. Niemetschek, *Leben des k. k. Kapellmeisters Wolfgang Gottlieb Mozart*, 60.

90. Reichardt, 'Autobiographie', 667, and *Vertraute Briefe geschrieben auf einer Reise nach Wien und den österreichischen Staaten zu Ende 1808 und zu Anfang 1809*, ii.91; see also Dittersdorf, *Lebensbeschreibung*, 176–7. ◆ Concerning Haydn's 'wit', generally, see in particular Wheelock, *Haydn's Ingenious Jesting with Art*.

91. When sending a sonata to Artaria on 8 February 1780, he added a covering note: 'I hope to gain some honour by this work, at least with the judicious public; criticisms of the work will be levelled only by those who are jealous (and there are many such people).' Haydn's letters include many similar remarks.

produce the effect that I reckoned upon their producing when staged locally. It would be quite a different matter if I were to have the great good fortune of setting a completely new libretto for your theatre. But even then I should be risking a great deal, as very few people can brook comparison with the great Mozart. If I could only impress on the soul of every lover of music, and on the great and good of the land in particular, how inimitable are Mozart's works, how profound, how musically intelligent, how extraordinarily full of feeling (for this is how I understand and feel them), all nations would vie with each other to possess such a jewel within their frontiers. Prague should hold on to him – but should also reward him; for without this the history of great geniuses is sad indeed and gives posterity little encouragement to continue its exertions, which is why, unfortunately, so many promising intellects fall by the wayside. It angers me to think that this unique Mozart is not yet engaged by some imperial or royal court. Forgive me for getting carried away: I love the man too dearly.[92]

These lines were written in 1787, at a time when Haydn was unaware of Mozart's appointment in Vienna and was concerned about his material situation. When *Don Giovanni* gave rise to violent arguments in Vienna in 1788, Haydn was asked his opinion and is said to have replied: 'I cannot settle the argument, but I do know that Mozart is the greatest composer in the world at present.'[93] Yet Haydn was extremely proud of his own operas: in 1781 he assured Artaria that nothing like *L'isola disabitata* and *La fedeltà premiata* had been heard in Paris and perhaps not even in Vienna, while in March 1784 he announced that *Armida* had been performed to great acclaim and was said to be his greatest work.[94] Remarks like these help us to see his modesty vis-à-vis Mozart in its proper light. But the situation was no different in the field of instrumental and sacred music, with Haydn on record as having said that, even if Mozart had written only his string quartets and *Requiem*, he would still have achieved immortality.[95] With tears in his eyes, he insisted that he could never forget Mozart's keyboard playing: 'It went straight to the heart!'[96] Later, too, he never missed an opportunity to listen to Mozart's music and often claimed that he had never heard any of his works without having learnt something from it.[97] When he returned to the wilds of Eszterháza in 1790, he was woken by the 'accursed north wind' when 'dreaming of listening to *Le nozze di Figaro*'.[98] And he later urged the music publisher Francis Fane Broderip to buy Mozart's autograph manuscripts, adding: 'He was in truth a great musician. My friends often flatter me by saying that I have a certain genius, but he towered far above me.'[99]

On a personal level, dealings between the two men were sincere and straightforward. Mozart used to call Haydn 'Papa' in order to show his older friend his love and respect, involuntarily contributing to the mindless image of 'Papa Haydn' as a good-natured but hopelessly outmoded philistine, a misconception that many of today's involuntary comics have used in a misguided attempt to show that they themselves are not philistines. Contact between the two men was limited to a short period each year, as Haydn's employer felt no great love of Vienna and spent only a few

---

92. Niemetschek, *Leben des k. k. Kapellmeisters Wolfgang Gottlieb Mozart*, 51–2; and Nissen, *Biographie W. A. Mozarts*, 643. The remark that Haydn is said to have made at the coronation in Prague in 1791 – 'Wherever Mozart is, Haydn cannot show himself' (see Griesinger, *Biographische Notizen*, 104) – is apocryphal: Haydn was in London at this date.
93. Rochlitz, 'Verbürgte Anekdoten', 52.
94. Ludwig Nohl, *Musiker-Briefe*, 84 and 93; and Griesinger, *Biographische Notizen*, 25.
95. Stadler, *Verteidigung der Echtheit des Mozart'schen Requiem*, 27.
96. Griesinger, *Biographische Notizen*, 104.
97. Carpani, *Le Haydine ovvero Lettere sulla vita e le opere del celebre maestro Giuseppe Haydn*, 201–2.
98. Ludwig Nohl, *Musiker-Briefe*, 114.
99. Pohl, *Joseph Haydn*, ii.213.

months each winter in the city, rarely granting his Kapellmeister leave of absence to go there at other times of the year.[100] Although Prince Nikolaus died in 1790 and the Esterházy orchestra was disbanded shortly afterwards, allowing Haydn to move to Vienna, the latter was almost immediately called away to London by Johann Peter Salomon. Mozart advised him against going on account of his advanced age and ignorance of English, but Haydn replied that, although old, he was still sprightly and in full command of his faculties. And the language that he spoke was understood throughout the whole world.[101] The two friends met for the last time on the day of Haydn's departure, 15 December. As so often during these years, Mozart was assailed by thoughts of death and felt that he would never see Haydn again, with the result that the latter, deeply affected, ended up consoling him.[102] The two men never saw each other again, but it seems that during Haydn's absence all manner of good friends attempted to drive a wedge between the two of them.[103] Haydn was left utterly distraught at Mozart's premature death and never recovered from his sense of loss. In 1792 he wrote to Michael Puchberg from London: 'For quite some time I was completely beside myself at his death and couldn't believe that Providence would so quickly claim the life of so indispensable a man.'[104]

In short, Haydn was the only one of Mozart's colleagues who, worthy of being compared to him, came into closer personal contact and was able to understand him in his innermost essence as an artist. Here Mozart found true understanding. His other friends simply admired him, however well-meaning they may have been, expressing their enthusiasm, at best, for the effect that his music had on them, but without understanding his true nature. From Haydn, however, he was entitled to expect more. Yet we should not forget that Haydn's influence was limited, in essence, to questions of form. Mozart had a completely different relationship to this new 'model' from the one he had had with earlier influences such as Johann Christian Bach and Schobert, both of whom had had an emotional impact on him that also found expression in his music, thereby enriching his view of the world in one way or another. But this was far less the case with Haydn. The reason for this was not only that Mozart himself was far more independent at this time, but, more especially, because such a wide gulf separated him from Haydn's whole view of the world and his art. Haydn was the last musical prophet of an old, hermetically sealed culture, that of the *ancien régime*, with all its wit and delight in existence, whereas Mozart was the son of a younger, middle-class generation that had already undermined the foundations of that earlier culture.[105] All that was unified, clear and coherent for Haydn was already becoming a problem for Mozart. The self-contained nature of Haydn's view of the world, which ensured that he remained a part of that aristocratic culture, was one that Mozart first had to struggle to acquire through the sheer force of his own personality. In this way, Haydn, who combined the imaginative nature of the Austrians with the north German sense of the need for highly concentrated ideas, may well have given Mozart new forms and possibilities of expressing his innermost world of experience, but he did not add any new ideas to that world. The independent and harmonious development of Mozart's art was not

100. Griesinger, *Biographische Notizen*, 23.
101. Pohl, *Joseph Haydn*, ii.251.
102. *Ibid.*
103. On 13 October 1791 Haydn wrote to Maria Anna von Genzinger, 'My wife has written to tell me – although I don't believe her – that Mozart speaks very ill of me. I forgive him'; Ludwig Nohl, *Musiker-Briefe*, 135. But the source is unreliable: Haydn's wife, whom he himself described as a 'hellish brute', was 'malicious by nature and went out of her way in her attempts to annoy her husband'; Pohl, *Joseph Haydn*, i.197.
104. Nottebohm, *Mozartiana*, 10; see also Nohl, *Musiker-Briefe*, 140. As late as 1807, Haydn is reported to have said with tears in his eyes: 'Forgive me, I can't help crying when I hear the name of my Mozart'; *Zeitung für Theater, Musik und Poesie*, iii (1808), 207. ◆ Further concerning the relationship between the two composers, see Vignal, *Haydn et Mozart*.
105. Kretzschmar, *Führer durch den Konzertsaal*, i.169ff.

disrupted by Haydn's increased influence, but there is no doubt that Mozart's influence occasionally caused the elderly Haydn to depart from his wonted path, when he took over purely musical elements, without, however, empathizing with their intellectual basis.

In spite of all this, we should not underestimate the friendship between the two men. Although much about Mozart's view of the world and his art may have remained a closed book to Haydn, there was one thing which, as an artist who was Mozart's equal, he was uniquely qualified to understand: the inner need that fuelled Mozart's urge to work. After all, he himself was convinced that he was merely the vehicle of some higher power. Accordingly, he regarded it as his supreme duty as a friend to help Mozart in times of need and to fend off all the misunderstandings and hostility of the world around him, even if he himself was unclear about the direction in which Mozart's genius was taking him. This is clear from his verdict on *Don Giovanni* and his reluctance to 'settle the argument': he knew only that the object in question was far above all disparagement and mindless praise. This is the friendship of a truly great artist. A kindly fate provided Mozart with this friend at a time when he was beginning to feel increasingly isolated as man and artist. The help that he gained from Haydn's approval allowed him to forget the lack of comprehension and hostility on the part of others.

None of the other friends whom Mozart met during these years could compare with Haydn. Although they were loyal and supportive and he was able to engage in a lively exchange of ideas on ethical questions with many of them, especially with his fellow Freemasons, they had little understanding of his inner life and, hence, of his art, in spite of the many examples of *Gesellschaftsmusik* that we owe to these acquaintanceships. Of all these friendships, the most genuine seems to have been the one with the family of the famous botanist Nikolaus Joseph von Jacquin (1727–1817), the best account of which has been left by Karoline Pichler:

> Even some sixty or seventy years ago the family was already a shining beacon for the scientific world inside and outside Vienna and was also sought out by many on account of their agreeable conviviality. While scholars or those who wished to become so visited the famous father and his ambitious son and successor, Joseph Franz von Jacquin,[106] the younger generation gathered around the younger son, Gottfried, whom a well-developed mind and outstanding talent for music, combined with a pleasing voice, made the cynosure of a good-natured circle that also included his sister, Franziska, who is still with us in the person of Frau von Lagusius. For as long as I can remember, parties were held at their home on Wednesday evenings. In winter, too, when the Jacquin family lived at the Botanical Garden,[107] erudite conversations were conducted in the father's rooms, while we young people talked, joked, made music, played little games and in general were admirably entertained.[108]

Mozart was particularly close to the younger son, Gottfried, a fiery, troubled individual with a considerable talent for music. His album contains an entry in Gottfried's hand, dated 11 April 1787:

106. On 24 April 1787 Joseph Franz von Jacquin wrote in Mozart's album: 'Tibi qui possis / Blandus auritas fidibus canoris / ducere quercus / in amicitiae tesseram' (To thee who canst 'gently move the attentive oaks with thy melodious strings'. In token of friendship) [*Dokumente*, 256, *Documentary Biography*, 290]. ◆ The quotation is adapted from Horace's *Carmina*.
107. The Botanical Garden was created by Maria Theresia in the Landstraße suburb; see Friedrich Nicolai, *Beschreibung einer Reise durch Deutschland und die Schweiz im Jahre 1781*, iii.34–5. Mozart's contacts with the Jacquin family were inevitably particularly close when he, too, was living nearby. ◆ For another contemporaneous description of the Botanical Garden, see Johann Pezzl, *Skizze von Wien*, vi.159.
108. Pichler, *Denkwürdigkeiten aus meinem Leben*, i.179–80.

True genius without a heart is a thing of naught – for not great understanding alone, not imagination alone, nor both together, make genius – Love! Love! Love! that is the soul of genius.[109] [translation from Deutsch 289, where there are three 'Loves'].

It was Gottfried von Jacquin whom Mozart occasionally lectured on the subject of his affairs, stressing the 'bliss' that comes from 'deep and true affection'.[110]

The happiness felt by Mozart whenever he was with the Jacquins is clear from the letter that he wrote to Gottfried on 15 January 1787, describing his brilliant reception in Prague and, as such, typical of Mozart's high spirits at this time:

Today is the first opportunity I've had to ask after the health of your dear parents and the rest of the Jacquin household. I hope and trust with all my heart that you are all as well as we two. I have to say in all honesty that (although I enjoy all possible courtesies and honours here and although Prague is undoubtedly a very beautiful and agreeable place to be), I long to be back in Vienna, and, believe me, the main reason for this is unquestionably *your* house. When I think that, following my return, I shall enjoy the pleasure of your valued company for only a short time and shall then have to forgo this pleasure for a long time – perhaps for ever –, only then am I fully conscious of the whole extent of the friendship and respect that I feel for your entire family. Now farewell, dearest friend, dearest HinkitiHonky! That's your name, just so as you know, we've devised names for everyone on our journey, here they are. *I* am Pùnkitititi. My wife Schabla Pumfa. *Hofer* Rozka Pumpa. *Stadler* Nàtschibinìtschibi. *Joseph my servant* Sagadaratà. *My dog gauckerl,* Schamanuzky – Mme *Quallenberg* Runzifunzi. Mlle *Crux.* PS: *Ramlo* is Schurimuri. *Freystädtler* Gaulimauli. Be so kind as to inform him of his name. Now adieu. . . . Please give my kind regards to your worthy parents and embrace your brother (who could be called blatterizzi) 1000 times for me. I kiss your sister's hands (her name is Sigra. Dinimininimi 100,000 times. . . . Write soon. . . . I'll then see whether you are as truly my friend as I am yours and ever shall be.[111]

Mozart also wrote to Gottfried von Jacquin to report on the later preparations for *Don Giovanni* and on its success, regretting only that he and Giuseppe Antonio Bridi had not been present to share in his happiness.[112] The importance to him of the Jacquin household is clear from the postscript to his second letter:

Neither your dear parents nor your sister nor your brother asked to be remembered to me? – I find that incredible. – I put it down, my friend, entirely to *your* forgetfulness and flatter myself that I am not mistaken.

Giuseppe Bridi was a young businessman from Rovereto who was popular not only on account of his beautiful, well-trained tenor voice, but also because of his character and education.[113] He

---

109. ◆ *Dokumente,* 254, *Documentary Biography,* 289.
110. *Briefe,* iv.59 (letter of 4 November 1787).
111. *Briefe,* iv.11 (letter of 15 January 1787).
112. *Briefe,* iv.54–6 and 58–9 (letters of 15 October and 4 November 1787).
113. Reichardt, *Vertraute Briefe geschrieben auf einer Reise nach Wien,* i.466 and Kelly, *Reminiscences,* i.221.

took part in the performance of *Idomeneo* at Prince Auersperg's private theatre, probably taking the title role.[114] Later, too, he gratefully recalled Mozart's friendship for him.[115]

To this friendship we owe a whole series of works, the most important of which is the trio in E flat major K498 for pianoforte, clarinet and viola. Written for Franziska von Jacquin, it was completed on 5 August 1786. The other works are examples, rather, of intimate, often humorous domestic music making, the most famous of these pieces being the 'Bandl' terzet K441 ('Liebes Mandel, wo ist's Bandel?') that may date from 1783 and that owes its existence to mere chance: Mozart had given his wife a new ribbon that she wanted to wear while out driving with Jacquin but which she was unable to find. 'Dear little husband, where's the ribbon?' she exclaimed, whereupon husband and wife joined forces with Jacquin in their search for the missing item. Jacquin eventually found it but, instead of handing it over, waved it in the air, while the diminutive Mozarts struggled to wrest it from him. Pleas, vituperation and laughter all proved fruitless, until the Mozarts' dog ran barking between Jacquin's legs, prompting him to hand it over and to suggest that the scene might be the subject for a comic trio.[116] Mozart agreed, wrote the words himself in Viennese dialect, describing events in general outline and, after setting it to music, sent it off to Jacquin.[117]

Among other works for the Jacquin family, pride of place goes to three songs: *Am Geburtstag des kleinen Fritz* K529 and *Das Traumbild* K530, both of which were completed on 6 November 1787, and *Als Luise die Briefe ihres ungetreuen Liebhabers verbrannte* K520, which bears the note '26 May 1787, in Herr Gottfried von Jacquin's room, Landstraße'. It seems likely that six other works belong under this same heading, namely the six canzonettas for two sopranos and bass to Italian words, some of which circulated in Vienna under Gottfried von Jacquin's name.[118] Three of these are settings of poems by Metastasio, *Ecco quel fiero istante* K436, *Mi lagnerò tacendo* K437 and *Più non si trovano* K549.[119] The other three are *Luci care, luci belle* K 346, *Due pupille amabili* K439 and *Se lontan, ben mio, tu sei* K438. An accompaniment for two clarinets and basset-horn (or three basset-horns) survives in Mozart's hand. That these pieces were originally intended to be performed without any accompaniment, as Jahn believes,[120] seems to me extremely doubtful, given all that we know about contemporary performing practice. We must assume that there was at least a chordal keyboard accompaniment. That all these pieces gain enormously by the addition of the wind accompaniment is beyond question.[121]

114. *AmZ*, xxvi (1824), 92.

115. Bridi, *Breve notizie*, 51. His name is often mentioned in Constanze's diary: see Abert, 'Konstanze Nissens Tagebuch'. ◆ Concerning Bridi, see Bisesti and Muzi, 'Giuseppe Antonio Bridi. Un amico Roveretano di W. A. Mozart' and *Un'architettura iniziatica: Il Giardino Bridi a Rovereto dall'abbandono al recupero. Relazione storica*.

116. Thus Constanze's later account, in which she confused Jacquin with Gottfried van Swieten. A fragment of the original full score (with four-part accompaniment) includes the names Constanze, Mozart and Jacquin. The quintet *O come lieto in seno* KAnh. C17.04 that was published under Mozart's name in 1856 comes from Antonio Cartellieri's opera *Il segreto*. ◆ Further, see NMA X/30/4.

117. See Mozart's letter to Jacquin of 14 [recte 15] January 1787: 'As a matter of course we performed among ourselves a little "quatuor in caritatis camera" ("und das schöne Bandel Hammera")'; *Briefe*, iv.10. ◆ Paper studies show that K441 probably dates from 1786 or 1787, not 1783.

118. Conversely, Jacquin's bass aria *Io ti lascio, o cara* was long believed to be by Mozart; see K621a. ◆ The authorship of this work is unclear. What appears to be the second leaf of the otherwise-lost autograph survives in the library of the Mozarteum, Salzburg. On the other hand, in a letter of 25 May 1799 Constanze wrote that neither she nor other knowledgeable *Kenner* believed the work to be by Mozart (*Briefe*, iv.239). Further concerning the generic tradition of these works, see Wignall, 'Mozart and the "Duetto Notturno" tradition'.

119. K549 is the only one of these pieces that Mozart specifically mentions in his thematic catalogue under 16 July 1788, but the other five are all extant in autograph manuscripts [and apparently date from this time as well].

120. Jahn, *W. A. Mozart*, ii.57.

121. The autograph score of the accompanying parts to K437 is owned by Julius André of Frankfurt am Main, who also owns the autograph of the vocal parts of K437 [now privately owned in the United States]. The vocal parts of K436 and the first seven bars of K438 are owned by the abbey church of Kremsmünster. K346 and 439 could not be included in the AMA as their vocal

A pendant to the 'Bandl' trio is the comic quartet *Caro mio Druck und Schluck* K571a, a marital scene between Mozart, Constanze and two friends H. and F. The words are by Mozart himself and comprise a crude mixture of German and Italian. The piece survives in incomplete form. Also missing is the keyboard accompaniment, which Mozart probably did not write out.[122] He refers to the piece in his letter to Constanze of 13 April 1789,[123] suggesting that it may have been written shortly before he left for Dresden.

The final works that fall under the heading of Gesellschaftsmusik are the various canons that Mozart probably wrote throughout the whole of his time in Vienna. Here we find him cultivating an age-old type of folk music whose origins date back to the early centuries of polyphony. Among composers of his own acquaintance who took an interest in it were Padre Martini and both Michael and Joseph Haydn.[124] A number circulated under Mozart's name, although not all of them are genuine, of course.[125] It is of some importance for his interest in the genre, moreover, that he also copied out a number of older canons.[126] His thematic catalogue lists ten such pieces as his own work: *Alleluia* K553, *Ave Maria* K 554, *Lacrimoso son io* K555, *Grechtelt's enk* K556, *Nascoso* K557, *Gehn wir im Prater* K558, *Difficile lectu* K559, *O du eselhafter Peierl* K560a, *Bona nox* K561 and *Caro bell'idol mio* K562. With the exception of the three-part *Difficile lectu* and *Caro bell'idol mio*, they are all four-part settings. To these may be added the six-part *Laßt froh uns sein* K231 and three-part *Nichts labt mich mehr* K233, both with new words to replace the original text, which is better not repeated here, and the four-part *Lieber Freistädtler* K232.[127] Also extant in the form of autograph manuscripts are the six-part *Wo der perlende Wein* K347, the three-part *Heiterkeit und leichtes Blut* K507 and the canon for three four-part choirs *V'amo di core* K348.[128] None of these

parts appear to be missing. The accompanying parts were written out by Mozart on a separate sheet, with a note in his own hand on the first side: 'Of these four pieces each voice must be copied out – a further piece will follow' [Deiters's note]. ◆ K436 and K439 are included in NMA III/9, based on contemporaneous Viennese manuscripts; see the critical report. On 31 May 1800 Constanze wrote that the vocal parts to all of these works were written by Jacquin (*Briefe*, iv.356).

122. Constanze later asked Beethoven to add a bass part, only to notice that it did not need one. That an accompaniment is necessary emerges only from Mozart's copy. ◆ The dating and authenticity of K571a are uncertain: no autograph is known and an early copy owned by Breitkopf & Härtel is also lost; modern editions in AMA (XXIV/50) and NMA (III/9) are based on this lost copy.

123. *Briefe*, iv.81 (letter of 13 April 1789).

124. According to Carpani (*Le Haydine*, 113), Martini's *canoni berneschi* were in general circulation at this time. According to Neukomm (Jahn, *W. A. Mozart*, ii.61, n.47), a canon by Michael Haydn that circulated under Mozart's name, *Sch . . . nieder, armer Sünder*, was aimed at a particular person in Salzburg, while another of Michael Haydn's canons was published in *Caecilia*, xvi (1834), 212. Joseph Haydn had 42 canons of his own composition hanging framed in his bedroom. ◆ 'Scheiß nieder, armer Sünder', KAnh. C10.13, composed by Michael Haydn (MH 700) *c*1795–9.

125. In his collected edition, Nottebohm includes 21 canons in AMA VII, nos 41–61, and a further 3 in XXIV, 51–3. Of this last group, the first is textless and the second is identical to AMA VII, no. 45, albeit set to the original text. On the third, see Jahn, *W. A. Mozart*, i.134. ◆ For a more recent account of Mozart's canons, see NMA III/10, which includes twenty-nine works.

126. K227 is by William Byrd (1543–1623), published in Johann Mattheson's *Der vollkommene Capellmeister* (Hamburg, 1739), 409; K226 comes from Athanasius Kircher's *Musurgia universalis* (Rome, 1650), i.386; and K235 is by Carl Philipp Emanuel Bach as published in Johann Philipp Kirnberger's *Die Kunst des reinen Satzes* (Berlin, 1774), ii.325. According to Nottebohm (*Mozartiana*, 132), Constanze drew up a list in 1799, itemizing 13 canons said to exist in the original, but failing to include K557, which is unquestionably by Mozart.

127. ◆ Mozart's authorship of K231 is uncertain: the earliest source is Breitkopf's complete works edition of 1804, where it appears with the text 'Laßt froh uns sein'; the original text is 'Leck mich im Arsch'. K233, on the other hand, is by Wenzel Trnka; like K231, it is first known from Breitkopf's 1804 edition (original text: 'Leck mir den Arsch fein recht schön sauber'). K232 is also uncertain as a composition by Mozart. Concerning the original texts of these works, see Ochs, '"L.m.i.a": Mozart's suppressed canon texts'.

128. See Nottebohm's critical commentary. K348 was also published in Breitkopf's catalogue (133, no. 13) and in Nissen's *Biographie W. A. Mozarts* (appendix, 19), where it is described as an unfinished arietta. In the list already mentioned, Constanze distinguishes it from the other canons. Another canon, *Laß immer*, also appears to be authentically Mozartian and survives in the form of an adagio for two basset-horns and bassoon (K410). It is unclear, however, whether the vocal or instrumental version should be given priority. ◆ Almost certainly it is the instrumental version that should be given priority. The texted version is not known before Breitkopf's 1804 edition. The dates of these works are various: K347 and 507, both originally untexted, were probably composed in 1785 and 1786, respectively, while K348 dates from between 1782 and 1785.

three works appears to be the work of other composers and so we may assume that all are by Mozart. All the remaining pieces are either inauthentic or doubtful.[129] Most, moreover, are impossible to date. If Mozart entered eight four-part canons and two three-part canons in his thematic catalogue on 2 September 1788, these were presumably not pieces that he had just written, but older works that he was copying out for reasons that can no longer be ascertained. These also include the four-part canon K560 with the words: 'O you asinine Peierl! O you Peierline ass! You're as idle as a nag with neither head nor legs; there's nothing to be done with you, I'll see you hanged yet; you stupid nag, you're so idle! You stupid Peierl, you're as idle as a nag; O dear friend, I beg you, forgive me! Nepomuk! Peierl! Forgive me!'

These lines were addressed to the tenor Johann Nepomuk Peierl, who passed through Vienna in 1785 and met Mozart on that occasion. He and his wife had previously spent several years at the theatre in Salzburg and subsequently settled in Munich, where he died in 1800. He was often teased about his idiosyncratic accent, and so Mozart set a three-part canon to a text that achieves its comic effect precisely through its parody of Peierl's accent.[130] But when the singers turned the page at the end of the song, their eyes alighted on the other canon *O Du eselhafter Peierl*.[131] It was much applauded and performed on many subsequent occasions, with the words very slightly altered.[132] The canon on Freystädtler's name K232 [if it is by Mozart] must also have been written in Vienna, since it was here that Freystädtler became Mozart's pupil. The speed with which Mozart was able to write these canons emerges from a piece that he composed for the Thomaskantor Johann Friedrich Doles in Leipzig on the eve of his departure for Berlin, when Doles and his son asked Mozart for a line as a parting gift.[133] Within five or six minutes both father and son had a three-part canon apiece, initially without words. One was in long note-values and struck a mournful note, while the other was all in quavers and sounded jolly. Only when they realized that the two could also be sung together did Mozart write in the words, adding 'Lebet wohl, wir sehn uns wieder!' ('Farewell, we'll meet again') to one of them and 'Heult noch gar wie alte Weiber!' ('Just go on howling like old women') to the other. Unfortunately this double canon (K572a) has not survived. In the circumstances, it is no wonder that various other comic compositions in a similar vein were later attributed to Mozart, including the comic 'Schoolmaster' mass.[134]

As before, Mozart continued to write songs as favours for friends. The works that can be dated to the present period are *Die ihr einem neuen Grade* K468, a Masonic song to words by Joseph Franz von Ratschky that Mozart completed on 26 March 1785; three settings of poems by Christian Felix Weiße dating from 7 May 1785, *Der Zauberer* K472, *Die Zufriedenheit* K473 and

---

129. A well-known canon, *Im Grab ists finster* (to give it its less offensive title [the original text is 'Beym Arsch ists finster']), is of very doubtful authenticity, even though Leopold von Sonnleithner recalled having sung a three- or four-part strophic song to these words that was ascribed to Mozart (KAnh. C9.03). The canon *Hätts nicht gedacht, daß Fischgräten so stechen täten* that Zelter attributed to Mozart (*Briefwechsel zwischen Goethe und Zelter*, i.388) is by Wenzel Müller.

130. On Peierl, see Lipowsky, *Baierisches Musik-Lexicon*, 239–40. He was in Vienna between 1785 and 1787. The canon in question is *Difficile lectu mihi Mars et jonicu*, the last word of which became 'cujoni' when the canon was sung. ◆ Further, see Küster, *Mozart: A Musical Biography*, 305–11.

131. For more details, see *Cäcilia*, i (1824), 179–80, which includes a facsimile of the folio containing the two canons. ◆ A facsimile is also published in *Mozart: Bilder und Klänge*, 353.

132. In Mozart's thematic catalogue, the canon is listed as *O du eselhafter Martin*. André and, later, Siegfried Dehn in Berlin owned copies in Mozart's hand in which the name Martin was replaced by Jakob. ◆ The autograph is now in the library of the Mozarteum, Salzburg.

133. Rochlitz, 'Verbürgte Anekdoten', 450–1.

134. According to Carpani (*Le Haydine*, 112–13), it is by the canon of St Florian's, Franz Joseph Aumann, and was wrongly attributed to Michael Haydn. A copy in the Salzburg Mozarteum names Haydn as the composer and notes that Mozart added the two violins *ad libitum* (KAnh. C1.15). According to Köchel (KAnh. C9.02), the *Motet burlesque* ('Nocte dieque bibamus') is probably French in origin.

Die betrogene Welt K474 ; Goethe's *Das Veilchen* K476, completed on 8 June 1785; and a setting of Aloys Blumauer's *Lied der Freiheit* K506 that appeared in print the following year.[135] On stylistic grounds we may also date the following two songs to this period: *Wie unglücklich bin ich nit* K 147 and *O heiliges Band* K148. In neither case has it been possible to identify the poet. The former appears to be dedicated to Constanze,[136] while the words of the latter have Masonic associations.[137]

All these works reflect Mozart's underlying character, sometimes good-naturedly coarse, sometimes charming, but invariably revealing a very real love of life. At the same time, however, the urge to aspire to a higher, transcendental plane was increasingly demanding its due. Neither his domestic situation nor his dealings with his uneducated colleagues allowed him to satisfy this need, hence, no doubt, his decision to pin his hopes on an institution that was currently drawing virtually the whole of educated Vienna into its thrall: Freemasonry.

135. In the *Wiener Musenalmanach* for 1786.

136. According to contemporary accounts, it was aimed, as a joke, at the daughter of a bass player in Salzburg, the beautiful Therese Horeischy, but this seems highly unlikely in view of the whole tenor of the work. ◆ Abert's 'contemporary accounts' cannot be traced; the first reference to this anecdote is Köchel's original annotation to 147. K148 is based on a text by the poet Ludwig Friedrich Lenz.

137. These two songs were previously dated to a much earlier period. It is to Johann Evangelist Engl's credit that they have now been redated to the period after 1784. Engl's redating has been adopted by Wyzewa and Saint-Foix, *Wolfgang Amédée Mozart*, ii.426. ◆ Recent paper studies show that the earlier dating is probably correct: it is likely that both K147 and K148 were composed in Salzburg between 1774 and 1776.

33

Mozart and Freemasonry

Mozart's membership of the Masonic Order has left such a profound mark on our picture of him as both man and artist that it requires a chapter to itself. Indeed, an understanding of it is indispensable if we are to make any sense whatsoever of the whole of the rest of his intellectual and spiritual development.[1]

The second half of the eighteenth century bears an oddly schizophrenic stamp. Rousseau had freed feeling from the tyranny of rationalism and taught individuals to appreciate their value vis-à-vis society, but the old-style Enlightenment, far from having given up the ghost, continued to exert an influence in all manner of ways, either surviving in unadulterated form or adapting to the new ideals in an attempt to impregnate with its spirit the new ideas that it was unable to stamp out. For a time, the most disparate currents interacted: at the one extreme there was a mystical enthusiasm that not infrequently degenerated into extravagant sentimentality, while at the other there was the most sober rationalism and an idealized attempt to bring happiness to humanity and to enjoy life to the full in the here and now. One result of this state of turmoil was a new humanitarian ideal that is found in various guises in Lessing's *Nathan der Weise*, Schiller's *Don Carlos*, Goethe's *Iphigenie auf Tauris* – and Mozart's *Die Zauberflöte*. The proper study of mankind was now felt to be 'man', as contemporaries began to relate 'man' to himself and to free civilization from the trammels of convention and rebuild it from within. This self-reflection, which was often taken to the point of self-torment, was intended to acknowledge and regulate the individual's relationship with God and with his neighbour and thus open the way to the ideal of the 'virtuous' individual. But the term 'virtue' was used in an active sense, signifying the highest spiritual good that seemed attainable to civilized man at this time. All that helped religious individuals to understand their relationship with God was now to serve those of a secular bent in their attempts to develop and deepen their own personalities. But this propensity for self-observation was far

1. See Jahn, *W. A. Mozart*, fourth edition, ii.105ff.; Schubert, *Mozart und die Freimaurerei*; Fellner, 'Mozart als Freimaurer in der Wiener Loge "Zur gekrönten Hoffnung"'; Richard Koch, *Mozart: Freimaurer und Illuminaten*; Kreitmaier, *W. A. Mozart: Eine Charakterzeichnung des großen Meisters nach literarischen Quellen*. For a general introduction, see Lewis, *Geschichte der Freimaurerei in Österreich im allgemeinen und der Wiener Loge zu St. Joseph insbesondere*. ◆ The history of modern Freemasonry is generally traced to the Grand Lodge of England, founded in 1717; French and German Lodges, modelled on the British Grand Lodge, were established shortly thereafter and gained popularity in particular among the aristocracy, the professional classes, military officers and intellectuals generally. In part, the rise of Freemasonry can be seen as a reaction against political absolutism and religious intolerance, emphasizing brotherly love, charity and the absence, by and large, of normal social barriers. None the less, Freemasonry's beliefs and practices, together with its symbolic rituals, frequently aroused political and religious suspicion. For general information on Freemasonry, see Lennhoff and Posner, *Internationales Freimaurerlexikon*. For Mozart and Masonry in particular, see Landon, *Mozart and the Masons*; Autexier, *La Lyre maçonne: Mozart–Haydn–Spohr–Liszt*; Irmen, *Mozart: Mitglied geheimer Gesellschaften*; Rosenstrauch-Königsberg, 'Zur Philosophie der österreichischen Freimaurer und Illuminaten mit Blick auf Mozart'; Beales, 'Court, Government and Society in Mozart's Vienna'; and Thomson, *The Masonic Thread in Mozart*. A useful, factual account of Mozart and his Masonic connections and brothers is Heinz Schuler, *Mozart und die Freimaurerei: Daten, Fakten, Biographien*.

from cutting off individuals from each other. Quite the opposite: the feeling that all men were brothers – a feeling that grew immeasurably more powerful following the extirpation of the quasi-religious faith in social convention – gave rise to the conviction that this ethical ideal could be achieved only through mutual support and that only in this way could the eighteenth century's beautiful dream of universal human happiness be realized. In turn, this led to the enthusiastic cult of friendship of a kind never seen again, and the excesses produced by unbounded emotion do not need repeating here. Countless overt and covert societies were founded with the aim of promoting self-improvement, and although they did much positive ethical work, they were also responsible for a great deal of muddy and morbid mysticism. But the Church was driven into a highly defensive position, especially in the Vienna of Joseph II, a position that it found all the more problematic as it fell increasingly under the influence of 'freeethinkers'.[2] And it had particular difficulty at this time in holding the attention of the educated classes, while its most effect weapon – the Order of the Jesuits – had been wrested from its control in 1773. In radical circles such as the Illuminati, which was founded on 1 May 1776, there was no doubt a good deal of anti-ecclesiastical feeling, but on the whole the general attitude was one of tolerance, with the result that Freemasonry came to include a large number of Catholic believers among its ranks.[3]

It is no wonder, in the circumstances, that the Brotherhood flourished at this period as never before. Not only did its own ranks grow considerably in size, its numbers were also swelled by the affiliation of a whole series of other secret societies that had originally been independent, with its rites proving hugely attractive to contemporaries fired by a mystical urge for the miraculous and mysterious, and many educated individuals regarded it as a place in which they could aspire to the ethical ideal of the age while communing with each other as brothers. And, in spite of its mysterious ceremonial, the rationalistic aspect of contemporary thinking also received its due here. True, this alluring outer garment also concealed all kinds of uncertainties, superstitions and even downright lies. But the reason for this lay less with the Craft itself than with the general trends of the time: whenever men have dreamt of making the world a better place, miracle workers and swindlers have flourished. Nor were such people lacking in genius, as is clear from the examples of Casanova, Cagliostro and Schikaneder.[4] At the same time, however, some of the country's leading figures were also associated with the Fraternity in one way or another: here one thinks, above all, of Frederick the Great, Lessing, Herder, Wieland and Goethe, who, according to his correspondence with Ludwig Ysenburg von Buri, had joined a Masonic circle as early as 1764/5. In 1813 he recalled the Order again in his tribute to Wieland, whom he described as a 'noble poet, brother and friend'.[5] Wieland himself declared that the 'spiritual temple' of the Craft symbolized 'the earnest, active and continuous striving on the part of all genuine and honest Masons to come closer through tireless application, both individually and, as far as possible, with all their brothers, to the ideal of humanity, namely, to that which man, as a living rock in God's eternal city, is destined to be and to which he is already predisposed to become in his rough natural state'.[6]

---

2. See Kreitmaier, *W. A. Mozart*, 104–5.
3. ◆ Illuminati – a term sometimes used to refer to a shadowy, conspiratorial group that controls world affairs behind the scenes – is more commonly understood to refer to the Bavarian *Illuminati*, a group of freethinkers founded in Munich by the Jesuit-taught Adam Weishaupt, possibly in response to the conservative, Catholic policies of Elector Karl Theodor; in 1784, the Bavarian government banned all secret societies, including not only the Illuminati but also the Freemasons, who were thought to support them.
4. See Leopold Engel, *Geschichte des Illuminatenordens*.
5. Goethe, *Werke (Jubiläums-Ausgabe)*, xxxvii.11ff.
6. Wieland, *Werke*, liii.435. See Keßler von Sprengseysen, *Anti-Saint-Nicaise*, 62.

Thanks to Joseph's well-known tolerance, Freemasonry entered upon a golden age soon after his accession. The heart and soul of the movement was Privy Councillor Ignaz von Born (1742–91), who founded the Lodge 'Zur wahren Eintracht' in Vienna in 1781.[7] Its aim was to safeguard and advance the newly won freedom of thought and to combat monasticism, which was regarded as a breeding ground of superstition and zealotry. It was not long before Born rallied under his flag the most respected figures in Vienna's intellectual life at this time: Ignaz Aurelius Feßler,[8] Karl Leonhard Reinhold, Johann Baptist von Alxinger, Aloys Blumauer, Lorenz Leopold Haschka, Gottlieb Leon, Joseph Franz von Ratschky, Michael Denis, Otto von Gemmingen, Tobias Philipp von Gebler[9] and Joseph von Sonnenfels.[10] With the emperor's tacit approval, they embarked on an extensive literary campaign whose most effective weapons were Born's and Blumauer's satires on monasticism. The circle's scholarly organ was Blumauer's *Realzeitung*, which waged a dogged war on superstition and prejudice of every kind. More general Masonic interests were served by the *Journal für Freymaurer* (1784–6), which was also edited by Blumauer.[11]

Born soon had many imitators, and by 1785 there were no fewer than eight Lodges in Vienna, although quantity did not necessarily mean quality or greater depth. Indeed, Freemasonry became something of a fashion with the easy-going Viennese, with many joining the Brotherhood out of curiosity, from an outright belief in miracles or even to advance their careers.

The Craft carried on its activities with an almost absurd openness and ostentation. Masonic songs were printed, composed and universally sung. People wore Masonic badges as bibelots on their watches, ladies received white gloves from apprentices and journeymen, and many a fashionable article was described as being *à la franc-maçon*. Many men joined out of curiosity, entering the Order and at least enjoying the pleasures of the table. Others had other aims. At this date it was not unuseful to belong to the Brotherhood, which had members in all the colleges and which had succeeded in drawing to its bosom every director, president and governor. One Brother helped another; the Brotherhood provided mutual support, and those who were not members often found obstacles in their way: this attracted many new members. Others again, who were either more honest or more limited in their views, credulously sought to be initiated into higher mysteries and believed that in the Order they would receive information about secret sciences or the Philosophers' Stone and how to converse with spirits. There is no doubt, too, that the Masons did a great deal of good work: at their meetings, collections were often made for the poor and for the victims of accidents.[12]

It was at this juncture that Joseph II intervened.[13] In a handwritten note of 11 December 1785 he recognized the order on condition that it undertook certain reforms and placed it under state

---

7. *Karl Leonhard Reinhold's Leben*, 18–19; Schubert, *Mozart und die Freimaurerei*, 14–15. ◆ For Born, see Lindner, *Ignaz von Born. Meister der Wahren Eintracht. Wiener Freimaurerei im 18. Jahrhundert*; and for the Lodge 'Zur wahren Eintracht', see Heinz Schuler, 'Die St. Johannis-Freimaurerloge "Zur wahren Eintracht". Die Mitglieder der Wiener Elite-Loge 1781 bis 1785'.
8. On Feßler, see Schubert, *Mozart und die Freimaurerei*, 43–4.
9. Gebler was admitted to the Lodge in 1784; see Werner, *Aus dem Josephinischen Wien*, 157.
10. ◆ Mozart set poems or texts by several prominent Viennese Freemasons, including Blumauer's *Lied der Freiheit* ('Wer unter eines Mädchens Hand') K506, Ratschky's *Gesellenreise* ('Die ihr einem neuen Grade') K468 (see below), and the incomplete *Bardengesang auf Gibraltar* ('O Calpe! dir donnerts am Fuße') K386d by Denis.
11. ◆ Additionally, Born edited the *Physikalische Arbeiten der Einträchtigen Freunde in Wien*, which published articles on botany, ornithology, astronomy and geography.
12. Pichler, *Denkwürdigkeiten aus meinem Leben*, i.105–6; see also Werner, *Aus dem Josephinischen Wien*, 124 and 126.
13. It is reported that for a time Joseph toyed with the idea of becoming a Mason himself, not least when the Russian Grand Duke was admitted to the Order. In the event, nothing came of the idea; see Leopold Engel, *Geschichte des Illuminatenordens*, 193.

protection, but demanded that the eight existing Lodges be reduced to three. In doing so, he stressed that he knew nothing about its mysteries and had no wish to learn anything about them either. His aim seems, rather, to have been to ensure stricter control of the Brotherhood and in that way to protect it against the increasing number of attacks to which it was being subjected: in Bavaria, attempts to combat the Illuminati had led to the persecution of Freemasons.[14] It is no wonder, then, that Joseph's decree was interpreted by some as a sign of special favour, but by others as a near fatal blow to Freemasonry in general. Among the latter was Born himself, who was now repeatedly attacked,[15] prompting him to resign from his Lodge in 1786[16] and encouraging others, including Gebler,[17] to do the same. In spite of this and in spite of the growing number of attacks on the Brotherhood, he retained numerous supporters, including not only Johann Martin Loibl,[18] in whose rooms the Lodge now held its meetings, but also Mozart himself.[19]

It is impossible to say with certainty when Mozart joined the Brotherhood, but it must have been before March 1785, as Leopold was admitted at this time and Mozart was already a member.[20] It has recently been suggested that he was encouraged to join by Otto von Gemmingen, his old acquaintance from Mannheim, who had moved to Vienna in the summer of 1782[21] and soon afterwards become Grand Master of the Lodge 'Zur Wohlthätigkeit'.[22] Mozart himself was admitted to the Lodge 'Zur gekrönten Hoffnung im Orient in Wien', a Lodge that included many members of the aristocracy and men of means, with the result that it was reproached for indulging in a predilection for particularly lavish banquets.[23] On 11 December 1785 Mozart's Lodge was merged with two other Lodges, 'Zur Wohlthätigkeit' and 'Zu den drei Feuern', to form a new Lodge, 'Zur neugekrönten Hoffnung', whose Grand Master was Count Franz von Esterházy.[24]

14. ◆ It is now generally thought that Joseph's restrictions were largely intended to counteract what was seen as a threat posed by powerful, secret societies, although he himself, as well as many of his senior government officials, were not opposed to the Masons; his edict also permitted 'this Brotherhood, which consists of so many honest men who are known to me, truly to show itself useful to its fellow men and to learning'.

15. One such attack was his clash with Josef Kratter, the so-called 'Masonic auto-da-fé', that produced a whole series of pamphlets.

16. Voigt to Hufeland in Diezmann, *Aus Weimars Glanzzeit: Ungedruckte Briefe von und über Göthe und Schiller*, 46–7; and Baggesen, *Briefwechsel*, i.304.

17. Letter to Christoph Friedrich Nicolai of 17 April 1786; see Werner, *Aus dem Josephinischen Wien*, 126.

18. His daughter could still remember him preparing for these meetings, sitting in his official robes before a crucifix and reading the Bible by candlelight. At the meetings themselves the children were amazed to see the men sitting round the table and delivering themselves of earnest discourses.

19. ◆ Further concerning Viennese Freemasonry and various Lodges, see Guy Wagner, *Bruder Mozart: Freimaurer im Wien des 18. Jahrhunderts*; Zörrer, 'La franc-maçonnerie à Vienne et à Prague'; and Irmen and Schuler, *Die Wiener Freimaurerlogen 1786–1793. Die Protokolle der Loge 'Zur Wahrheit' (1785–1787) und die Mitgliederverzeichnisse der übrigen Wiener Logen (1786–1793)*.

20. Nissen, *Biographie W. A. Mozarts*, 642. Koch, *Mozart: Freimaurer und Illuminaten*, assumes that Mozart had joined by the autumn of 1784 as he wrote the *Lied zur Gesellenreise* (see above) in March 1785 and would have become a journeyman between six and twelve months after his initial admittance. But it is by no means certain that he wrote the song for his own candidature. See Kreitmaier, *W. A. Mozart*, 117. All that we can say for certain is that Mozart was a member of the Lodge by March 1785. See Engl, *Mozart*, 7, and Fellner, 'Mozart als Freimaurer'. ◆ In fact, Mozart's name was circulated as a candidate for admission to the 'Beneficence' Lodge on 5 December 1784 and he was promoted to the second grade by 7 January 1785 (*Dokumente*, 204 and 207, *Documentary Biography*, 230 and 233). The *Gesellenreise* K468, dated 26 March 1785 by Mozart, is now thought to have been composed to honour his father's joining of the Craft during his visit to Vienna that winter. Leopold was proposed at the 'Beneficence' Lodge on 28 March 1785 and admitted on 1 April. He and Wolfgang attended the 'True Concord' on 16 April, at which time Leopold was promoted to second grade and, on 22 April, to third grade (*Dokumente*, 213 and 214–16, *Documentary Biography*, 233 and 242–4).

21. See Friedrich Meyer, *Friedrich Ludwig Schröder: Beitrag zur Kunde des Menschen und des Künstlers*, i.380.

22. ◆ See Heinz Schuler, 'Die Mozart-Loge "Zur Wohltätigkeit" im Orient von Wien 1783 bis 1785. Entwicklung und Mitgliederbestand'.

23. *Briefe eines Biedermanns über die Freimaurer in Wien*, xl–xli.

24. ◆ The intellectual force behind the 'New Crowned Hope' Lodge was the dramatist and civil servant Tobias Philipp Gebler, the author of *Thamos*, for which Mozart had earlier written incidental music and choruses (K345).

Mozart's reasons for joining may be sought in his own character and in his development until now. Anyone disposed to see mere opportunism in his decision to join simply does not understand him.[25] We have already seen how his need for friendship and his humanitarian idealism had increasingly become the foundation on which his whole moral outlook was based. Setting out from Salzburg's petit-bourgeois backwater, he had visited virtually the whole of the civilized world and had with difficulty assimilated the various impressions that these journeys had left on him. By now he was leading a more settled existence and at the same time had become conscious of his own inner wealth. And so it was only natural that, like any other great man, he should feel an instinctive urge to come to terms with the world, especially with a world like his own, which was so full of unresolved contradictions. The Church alone could no longer satisfy him, even though he remained its loyal son. We already know that, like his father, he was often highly critical of its servants, the clergy,[26] and these criticisms naturally became more vocal once they had both joined the Brotherhood. But this in itself would certainly not have persuaded Mozart to become a Mason. Rather, he was seized by a general desire at this time to separate faith from the superficialities of the church service and to realize the demand for a close personal relationship with God through religious experience. Second only in importance to his relationship with God was his relationship with his neighbour as his brother and fellow human being. This relationship, too, was freed from its traditional shackles and placed entirely on the level of personal feeling. And all these goals were represented first and foremost by Freemasonry in contemporary Vienna. Within their ranks Mozart reencountered most of the educated men whom he regularly met in society. It now struck him as particularly worthwhile to join forces with them in order to solve life's ultimate questions,[27] to find opportunities to demonstrate his willingness to help others and to gratify his need for friendship. Between now and his death, therefore, he regarded the Brotherhood with total seriousness, as is clear, not least, from his final letter to his father.[28] To what extent the Order's mysterious ceremonial fired his artistic imagination is no longer possible to say. But it is significant that he planned to form a secret society of his own, 'The Grotto', and to draw up a set of

25. This is the view adopted by Goschler, *Mozart, d'après de nouveaux documents*, quoted by Wilder, *Mozart: L'homme et l'artiste*, 209. Kreitmaier, *W. A. Mozart*, 117, tends to the same view. But Mozart's attempts to obtain loans from Puchberg are insufficient evidence to support this claim.

26. Leopold's letter of 14 October 1785 (*Briefe*, iii.426), with its attack on bigotry and convents, is already clearly influenced by his Masonic beliefs.

27. According to Richard Koch, *Mozart: Freimaurer und Illuminaten*, the Lodge had a library comprising 1900 volumes, together with a Masonic archive, a reading room and a physics laboratory. It also supported the poor with considerable sums of money. A planned literary undertaking came to nothing as a result of Joseph II's reforms. None the less, the Lodge's membership also included a whole series of visionaries, including alchemists, Rosicrucians, Illuminati and 'Asiatic Brethren'. In 1788 Koch numbered among the Lodge's members a ruling prince (Anton von Hohenzollern-Sigmaringen), 36 counts, 1 marquis, 14 barons, 42 aristocrats, army officers, ambassadors, chamberlains, canons, civil servants and so on.

28. ◆ Letter of 4 April 1787 (*Briefe*, iv.41): 'I've just this minute received news that has come as a great blow – not least because I'd assumed from your last letter that, praise be to God, you were feeling well; – but now I hear that you're very ill! I don't need to tell you how much I long to receive some reassuring news from you; and I'm sure that I shall – even though I've made a habit of always imagining the worst in all things – when looked at closely, death is the true goal of our lives, and so for a number of years I've familiarized myself with this true friend of man to such an extent that his image is not only no longer a source of terror to me but is comforting and consoling! And I give thanks to my God that He has given me the good fortune of finding an opportunity – you understand what I mean – of realizing that death is the *key* to our true happiness. – I never go to bed without thinking that – young as I am – I may no longer be alive the next morning – and yet no one who knows me can say that I'm sullen or sad in my dealings with them – and for this blessing I give daily thanks to my creator and with all my heart wish that all my fellow creatures may feel the same.'

rules.[29] It is conceivable that he was dissatisfied with certain aspects of his own Lodge and that he therefore toyed with the idea of reforming it.

That he was well respected by his Lodge brothers is clear from the funeral oration that was delivered after his death:

> It has pleased the Eternal Architect of the world, to tear one of our most beloved, one of our most meritorious members from our brotherly chain. Who did not know him? who did not esteem him? – our worthy Brother Mozart. Scarcely a few weeks have passed since he was standing here in our midst, glorifying the inauguration of our Masonic Temple with his magical harmonies. – Which of us, my brethren, would then have suspected the thread of his life to be so short? Which of us would have thought that we would be mourning him three weeks later? – It is true – it is the sad lot of mankind to have to leave behind an often already distinguished career just as it is coming to fruition; kings die in the midst of their plans, which they bequeath to posterity unrealized . . . ; artists die after they have used the lease of life allotted to them to perfect their art to the highest degree – universal admiration follows them to the grave, entire nations mourn them, and the common destiny of these men is – to be forgotten by their admirers. But it is not true of us, my brethren! Mozart's premature death remains an irreplaceable loss for Art – his talents, already expressed in earliest boyhood, made him even then the rarest phenomenon of his generation; half Europe revered him, the great called him their darling, and we – we called him our Brother. However much propriety demands that we recall to mind his artistic talents, by so much the less should we forget to offer a fitting sacrifice to his excellent heart. He was a diligent member of our Order: brotherly love, a peaceable disposition, advocacy of a good cause, beneficence, a true, sincere sense of pleasure whenever he could help one of his Brethren with his talents: these were the chief characteristics of his nature. He was a husband, a father, a friend to his friends, a brother to his brethren; he lacked only the riches which would have enabled him to make hundreds as happy as he would have wished.

The poem appended to this oration contains the following lines:

> With gentleness and patience,
> A Mason heart and soul,
> He lifts our aspirations
> Towards a higher goal.
>
> The bond is snapped! We give him
> Our blessings and our love,
> Our brother-love shall guide him
> To harmony above.

---

29. See Constanze's letters to Härtel in Leipzig on 27 November 1799 and 21 July 1800 [*Briefe* iv.299–300 and 360–2]; see Nottebohm, *Mozartiana*, 131 and 133, naming Stadler as his confidant in this matter. But Stadler, she went on, was afraid of admitting to his involvement, given contemporary attitudes to Freemasonry. Stadler was an extremely dubious Freemason (see above), but his membership of the Order may help to explain, at least in part, Mozart's otherwise curious willingness to confide in him.

Oft in his footsteps treading
We sought out the bereaved,
The widow in her steading
His rarest gifts received;

He heard the orphans' blessing,
Clothes to the naked gave,
God's recompense confessing,
He takes it to the grave.

Midst flattery's siren voices
He shared his Brothers' lot,
In poor men's smiles rejoices,
His manhood not forgot.[30]

From time immemorial music had played an important role at Masonic gatherings, inspiring Mozart to contribute to them and compose a whole series of works intended for specific Masonic occasions. Needless to say, all are limited to men's voices and, with few exceptions, make few great technical demands.

The first of these works, the *Lied zur Gesellenreise* K 468, we have already encountered.[31] Two further songs appear to have been written that same year, 1785, to open and close a Lodge. The words suggest that the Lodge was 'Zur neugekrönten Hoffnung', which was established following Joseph II's orders to merge several existing Lodges. Both these songs, K483 and K484,[32] are scored for soloist and three-part chorus. As in the *Lied zur Gesellenreise* there is an organ accompaniment. In addition to these songs, we also have a series of cantatas, including the unfinished *Dir, Seele des Weltalls* K429, which may date from as early as 1783.[33] It survives in two versions, one for two tenors and bass, with piano accompaniment, the other – almost certainly a later reworking – for four-part chorus, strings, two oboes, two horns and bassoon.[34] In both this and

30. H[ensler], *Masonic Oration on Mozart's Death. Delivered on the Occasion of the Admission of a Master to the Most Worthy Lodge of St John called the Crowned Hope of the Orient in Vienna*, 8 [*Dokumente*, 392–5, *Documentary Biography*, 447–51].

31. The first three of the text's strophes may be found in the revised edition of Ratschky, *Gedichte*, 151; see Vaupél, 'Mozarts Freimaurer-Gesellenlied', 135. Constanze's version of the title, *Gesellenweise*, as given by Nottebohm (*Mozartiana*, 123) is incorrect, as is Kreitmaier's *Gesellenweihe* (*W. A. Mozart*, 117).

32. According to Lewis, *Geschichte der Freimaurerei*, 162, the participants were the two Sch–g [Schittlersberg] brothers and Mozart. The 'threefold fire' mentioned in the words of the first song may refer to the Lodge 'Zu den drei Feuern'.

33. Köchel and Wyzewa and Saint-Foix (*Wolfgang Amédée Mozart*, ii.413) assume that the work dates from 1783. ◆ Paper studies show that the fragment probably dates from 1786.

34. According to Nissen (*Biographie W. A. Mozart*, appendix p. 18, no. 10) and André, who owned the autograph score, the first chorus was scored for 2 tenors and bass with orchestra (1 flute, 1 clarinet, 2 oboes, 2 horns and strings). The vocal parts were written out in full, with a figured bass, while the accompaniment was sketched out in Mozart's usual manner, as was the following tenor aria. This aria was to have been followed in turn by a duet, of which only 17 bars have survived. In other words, the version with piano accompaniment seems to represent no more than a makeshift solution. ◆ It now appears that the version with piano accompaniment postdates the instrumentally accompanied version and that Mozart is unlikely to have had a hand in it. Also see the facsimile in NMA X/30/4, 136.

the following cantatas the elaborate writing for the tenor soloist suggests a trained singer, namely, Adamberger.

A further Masonic cantata by Mozart, *Die Maurerfreude* K471, was performed on 24 April 1785.[35] Leopold was present at this first performance. The Lodge members had assembled to honour Born, whom the emperor had recently rewarded for devising a new method of extracting metals by amalgamation.[36] The words were by Franz Petran, and the score was later published with a title-page engraved by Sebastian Mansfeld, with the proceeds going to the poor.[37] The work is scored for tenor soloist, male-voice chorus, two oboes, clarinet (suggesting the involvement of Anton Stadler), two horns and four-part strings.[38] A second Masonic cantata, K623, to words by Schikaneder,[39] was completed on 15 November 1791 and performed a few days later [on the 18th] to inaugurate a new Masonic temple. This is the last work that Mozart completed.

Vaguely related to these works is the cantata *Die ihr des unermeßlichen Weltalls Schöpfer ehrt* K619 of July 1791.[40] The poet was the Hamburg businessman Franz Heinrich Ziegenhagen, who evidently felt called upon to provide his own solution to the questions about education that had been fashionable since Rousseau's time and who, outdoing even Rousseau himself, sought to bring about a practical return to pure culture in his colonies at Strasbourg. As he points out in his monograph,[41] existing religions could not satisfy a truly enlightened generation. To illustrate his book – which affords all too palpable proof of the havoc wrought in many minds by the new ideas in education – Daniel Chodowiecki provided eight copperplate engravings, while Mozart was invited to write a song for Ziegenhagen's colony. Almost certainly he never saw Ziegenhagen's book and presumably agreed to his request only because the text contained Masonic ideas, a circumstance that clearly helped him to come to terms with this poem and its curious expression of wild-eyed rationalism.

35. ◆ *Die Maurerfreude* was given again on 15 December at the 'Crowned Hope'. On that occasion, Mozart also played a piano concerto and improvised while two visiting basset-horn virtuosos, Anton David and Vinzent Springer, also performed. See *Dokumente*, 225–6, *Documentary Biography*, 256–7. David and Springer had already been heard at the united 'Three Eagles' and 'Palmtree' Lodge on 20 October; on this occasion Mozart and Anton Stadler also performed (*Dokumente*, 223–4, *Documentary Biography*, 254).
36. *Wiener Zeitung* (1785), 32.
37. Lewis, *Geschichte der Freimaurerei*, 119–20.
38. A copy in the Munich Conservatory Library includes a revised text suitable for use in church. The final chorus has been rescored for four voices (soprano, alto, tenor and bass), and trumpets and timpani have been added to the orchestra. ◆ Further, see Brauneis, '"Wir weihen diesen Ort zum Heiligtum . . .". Marginalien zur Uraufführung von Mozarts "Kleiner Freimaurer-Kantate" und des ihm zugeschriebenen Kettenliedes "Zum Schluß der Loge"'. There is no reference to the Munich copy in the critical report to NMA I/4/4.
39. Lewis, *Geschichte der Freimaurerei*, 39. ◆ It now appears that the text is by Karl Ludwig Gieseke, who was at one time credited with the libretto to *Die Zauberflöte*. Gieseke, who played the role of the first slave in Mozart's opera, later became a professor of mineralogy at Dublin; see below.
40. On the background to this work, see Weber, 'Geschichte der Mozart'schen Hymne: "Die Ihr des unermeßlichen"', 210–11. An expanded version of the interpolated allegro that Mozart later discarded is reproduced in the critical commentary to AMA VII/40; see also Chrysander, 'Mozarts Lieder', 163.
41. *Lehre vom richtigen Verhältnisse zu den Schöpfungswerken und die durch öffentliche Einführung derselben allein zu bewürkende allgemeine Menschenbeglückung* (Hamburg, 1792). A second edition followed in 1794, this time under the title *Physidicaeologia* and without the author's name. Mozart's song appears in a four-page appendix. Ziegenhagen was born in 1753. After a brilliant start in life, he fell upon hard times and ended his life in 1806 at Steintal near Strasbourg.

But the most important of Mozart's Masonic compositions was the *Maurerische Trauermusik* K477 of July 1785. Written to mark the deaths of Count Franz Esterházy von Galántha and Duke Georg August von Mecklenburg-Strelitz,[42] it is scored for two oboes, clarinet, three basset-horns, double bassoon, two horns and strings.[43] From this extremely important work there is a direct link to the piece in which Freemasonry, albeit still shackled to the earth in all manner of ways, finds its supreme artistic expression in Mozart's hands. We shall have more to say about the Masonic associations of *Die Zauberflöte* in due course.[44]

42. Duke Georg August von Mecklenburg-Strelitz was a major general in the Imperial and Royal Armies, while Franz Esterházy von Galántha was Court Chancellor to Hungarian Transylvania and Grand Master of Mozart's Lodge, hence the exceptional nature of the composition. ◆ The circumstances surrounding the composition and performance of the *Masonic Mourning Music* have never been clear. If the date of the work, given as July 1785 in Mozart's own thematic catalogue, is correct, then it cannot have been written to mark the deaths of his two Masonic brothers (Georg August von Mecklenburg-Strelitz died only on 6 November and Franz Esterházy on 7 November), although it was performed at a funeral celebration for them held at the 'Crowned Hope' Lodge on 17 November. Autexier, 'Wann wurde die Maurerische Trauermusik uraufgeführt', speculates that the work existed in an earlier, texted version. It may be, however, that the date in Mozart's *Verzeichnüß* is wrong: the next item in it, the G minor piano quartet K478, is dated 'July' in the catalogue but 16 October on the autograph, which is more likely to be correct. It is possible, then, that both K477 and 478 were entered retrospectively by Mozart in his work-list and that he misremembered their dates of composition. Further, see Heinz Schuler, 'Mozarts "Maurerische Trauermusik" KV 477/479a: Eine Dokumentation'.

43. The two higher basset-horns and the double bassoon were added later. The claim made in the note to the complete edition that these two basset-horns were added to replace the two horns makes little sense to me as it would result in gaps in the musical argument. As appears from his catalogue, Mozart may initially have thought of something similar but after completing the task decided in favour of the expanded orchestra.

44. ◆ Two additional Masonic songs by Mozart, to texts by Gottlieb Leon, are known only from their texts: *Zur Eröffnung der Meisterloge* ('Des Todes Werk') and *Zum Schluß der Meisterarbeit* ('Vollbracht ist die Arbeit der Meister'); see NMA III/8, 78. Both are mentioned in the remarks to K483, although neither has a separate listing in the Köchel catalogue; their music appears to be lost. Autexier, 'Cinq lieder inconnus de Mozart', identifies three other, previously unknown Masonic songs by Mozart to Leon texts: *Bey Eröffnung der Tafelloge* ('Legt für heut das Werkzeug nieder!'), *Kettenlied* ('Wir singen, und schlingen zur Wette') and *Lied im Namen der Armen* ('Brüder! Hört das Flehn der Armen'). Robbins Landon, *Mozart and the Masons*, ingeniously identifies a previously unknown picture of Mozart in an anonymous late eighteenth-century oil painting of an Austrian Lodge ritual now housed at the Historisches Museum der Stadt Wien. It is reproduced in Landon's book and in Deutsch, 'Innenansicht einer Wiener Freimaurer-Loge'. Further concerning Masonic music generally and Mozart's relationship to it, see Strebel, 'Freimaurerische Musik und Loge' and 'La musique maçonnique dans la vie de la Loge' and Henri, *Mozart Frère Maçon: La Symbolique Maçonnique dans l'Œuvre de Mozart*.

34

In the service of the aristocracy and society

Alongside the Mozart who joked with his colleagues, sharing their light-hearted banter and colourful jokes, there was a second Mozart who, as a Freemason, sought to address life's ultimate questions, and a third Mozart, a musical gentleman, who was the hero of countless concerts and cynosure of distinguished private gatherings, a role that he played more than ever during the period under discussion. As in his childhood, Fortune again decked his brow with the laurel of the virtuoso and composer, before abandoning him to a lonely fate at the end of his life. All that a celebrated virtuoso could wish for at this time was his for the asking: court and high society – the two groups that set the tone – flocked to his concerts and applauded the works that he wrote for them. For some time he was as popular and as outwardly successful as any fashionable artist. He basked in this reputation to his heart's content, at least as long as his artistic conscience was able to reconcile the demands of his art with those of his audience's taste. This taste was by no means as limited and narrow-minded as is often assumed to be the case, but allowed individual artists to go their independent ways and to explore the very limits of what society considered admissible. Mozart's own works from this period, especially his keyboard concertos, afford striking proof of the extent to which it was possible to produce genuine works of art within the framework of the old social ideal. Indeed, they appear as the supreme transfiguration of that earlier type, while at the same time representing Mozart's ultimate achievement in this field. His genius and the power and authenticity of his world of inner experience protected him from the danger of superficiality. Once he had said all that he had to say in this area, he was honest enough, as always, to refuse to engage in mere routine work and, when his genius drew him in a different direction, he preferred to accept the martyrdom of his final years, rather than become entrenched in an emotional world that he had already outgrown, whatever the material advantages that might have accrued from his continuing to plough what was now a barren furrow. From 1786 onwards, audiences did not simply turn their backs on their erstwhile 'darling' in a moment of fickle whimsy, as is so often claimed to be the case. Rather, Mozart himself, urged on by artistic necessity, abandoned the paths along which his audiences were still capable of following him, with the result that the darling of all became, instead, an artist variously described as 'unsettling', 'Romantic' and even as 'lacking in style'.

We have already examined the superficial aspect of these activities, with their numerous concerts and other events, when discussing Mozart's finances, which, at least for a time, seemed destined to improve his lot. All that remains is to get to know the individual members of the aristocracy with whom Mozart came into contact at this time, without, however, ever becoming as friendly as he did with the members of the Jacquin family.

One of the earliest and most sympathetic of Mozart's acquaintances was the Countess Wilhelmine Thun née Ulfeld (1744–1800), whose husband Franz Joseph was the son of Mozart's patron in Linz. She was one of the leading lights in contemporary Vienna in terms of not only her rank and possessions but also her education and character and was one of the few women whom the emperor considered worthy of numbering among his more intimate circle of friends in the final years of his life: he would visit her in the evening, uninvited and informally, and while on his deathbed he wrote a heartfelt letter to her, bidding her a final farewell.[1] Burney wrote admiringly of her, claiming that she had 'nothing about her that reminds one of the pride or heaviness attributed by travellers to the Germans' and taking particular delight in her 'sallies of wit' and 'pleasant irony'.[2] She was an extremely generous woman, and her house was a meeting place for Vienna's most cultured circles. One of her admirers was Georg Forster who, in a letter to Therese Heyne,[3] lists a whole series of her friends and acquaintances, including Ignaz von Born, Otto von Gemmingen, the Austrian State Chancellor Wenzel Anton Prince Kaunitz-Rietberg, the erudite Privy Councillor Anton von Spielmann,[4] the 'kind and gentle' Count Cobenzl and old field marshal Count Hadik:

You won't believe how accommodating and friendly they are. You scarcely notice that you're with people of quality – at every moment you're tempted to forget it and treat them on a familiar footing as friends of equal rank – there's real physical contact when I'm with Countess Thun, the finest woman in the world, and her three daughters – three veritable Graces, each an angel in her own way. Their mother is one of the most admirable mothers I know; the children are innocence itself, as merry as the morning sun and full of the natural understanding and wit that I silently admire, just as I admire the understanding and wit of a certain dear girl whom I have in my control. The subtlest conversation, the greatest sensitivity, and at the same time complete openness, wide reading – and what they have read, they have properly digested and thought about – and a pure religion free from all superstition, the religion of a genuine and innocent heart that is familiar with Nature and Creation. These people gather at Countess Thun's almost every evening between nine and ten, and all manner of witty conversations are conducted, they play the piano, sing in German and Italian and even, when their enthusiasm gains the upper hand, dance.[5]

These were the same 'enlightened' circles as those that flirted with Freemasonry and that Mozart, too, frequented in Vienna. Music featured prominently, with the countess herself a first-rate harpsichordist. 'She plays the harpsichord with that grace, ease, and delicacy, which nothing but female fingers can arrive at', wrote Burney. 'Her taste is admirable, and her execution light, neat, and feminine.'[6] Her favourite keyboard composer at this time – 1772 – was Ignaz von Beecke, who, as he told Dalberg, wrote a sonata for three keyboards for her and her daughters in 1785.[7] Reichardt, too, enjoyed her patronage in 1783 and reports that both the emperor and the Archduke

1. Only the Princesses Liechtenstein, Schwarzenberg and Lobkowitz enjoyed a similar privilege; see Kelly, *Reminiscences*, i.209; Pichler, *Denkwürdigkeiten aus meinem Leben*, i.141; and Vehse, *Geschichte des östreichischen Hofes und Adels und der östreichischen Diplomatie*, viii.304–5. Her portrait is reproduced by Freisauff, *Mozarts Don Juan 1787 bis 1887: Ein Beitrag zur Geschichte dieser Oper*, plate 1. On the genealogy of the Thun family, see Leupold, *Allgemeines Adels-Archiv der österreichischen Monarchie*. ◆ Further, see Angermüller, 'Die Familie des "alten" Graf Thun'.
2. Burney, *The Present State of Music in Germany*, i.254–5
3. Georg Forster, *Sämtliche Werke*, vii.272.
4. Spielmann had a house in the Landstraße district. His wife and daughter were both excellent keyboard players. See Friedrich Nicolai, *Beschreibung einer Reise durch Deutschland und die Schweiz im Jahre 1781*, iv.554 and iii.37 and 291.
5. Georg Forster, *Sämtliche Werke*, vii.275.
6. Burney, *The Present State of Music in Germany*, i.216 and 292. She told Burney by way of a joke that she had previously played much better, but that 'she had had six children, and that "every one of them had taken something from her"' (i.292).
7. ◆ Beecke's sonata survives in a manuscript copy at the Oettingen-Wallerstein library, Regensburg.

Maximilian frequently attended her musical soirées.[8] Mozart was warmly received by her soon after his arrival in Vienna. She took a close interest in the genesis of *Die Entführung aus dem Serail*, and actively supported his attempts to gain a position at court.[9] Her son-in-law, Prince Karl Lichnowsky, was Mozart's friend and pupil.

Another house at which artists and scholars from Vienna and elsewhere met on a regular basis was that of the Court Councillor Franz Sales von Greiner (1730–98), the father of Karoline Pichler. Pichler, who was herself an excellent keyboard player,[10] has left the following account of these gatherings:

> Apart from poets such as Denis, Leon, Haschka, Alxinger and Blumauer, all of whom were famous names at that time, frequent visitors to our house also included men of strict science. And few foreign scholars and artists came to Vienna without bringing with them letters of recommendation to Haschka or directly to my parents. In this way we received visits from the famous traveller Georg Forster, Professors Meiners and Spittler, Becker and von Goeckingk, the actor Friedrich Ludwig Schröder and many musicians and composers, including Paesiello and Cimarosa; that we also entertained local artists such as Mozart, Haydn, Salieri, the Hickel brothers, Füger and others goes without saying.[11]

Another active patron of music and musicians was Privy Court Councillor Franz Bernhard von Keeß (1720–95), who also owned a valuable collection of scores and sheet music.[12] The amateur concerts in the Augarten were held under his auspices, while the society concerts that took place twice a week under his own roof were described by Adalbert Gyrowetz as follows:

> The leading virtuosi at that time in Vienna, and the leading composers, viz: Joseph Haydn, Mozart, Dittersdorf, Hoffmeister, Albrechtsberger, Giornovichi etc., etc. were gathered together; Haydn's symphonies were performed there. – Mozart was most usually to be heard performing on the fortepiano, and Giarnovichi, at that time the most famous virtuoso on the violin,[13] generally played a concerto; the lady of the house sang. One evening it so happened that Mozart did not appear right at the beginning of the concert, and everyone had been waiting for him for some time, for he had promised to bring a new song for the lady of the house. Several servants were sent to look for him; at last one of them found him in a tavern and asked him to come at once, because everyone was waiting for him and looking forward to the new song. Mozart then remembered that he had not yet composed the song; he at once asked the servant to bring him a sheet of music paper – when this had been done, Mozart began to compose the song in the inn itself, and when he had it ready, he took it to the concert, where everyone was waiting with the keenest expectancy. He was received in the most joyful manner, after a few gentle reproaches for his considerable lateness, and when he at last sat down at the pianoforte, the lady of the

8. Reichardt, 'Autobiographie', 668–9.
9. She died in 1800. Two years earlier Beethoven had dedicated his clarinet trio op. 11 to her.
10. Schönfeld, *Jahrbuch der Tonkunst von Wien und Prag*, i.19 and 70.
11. Pichler, *Denkwürdigkeiten aus meinem Leben*, i.92. On Nicolai's attacks on the Greiner household, see Werner, *Aus dem Josephinischen Wien*, 153.
12. *Wiener Zeitung* (1796), no. 29. ◆ Also see Eybl, 'Franz Bernhard Ritter von Keeß – Sammler, Mäzen und Organisator'.
13. See Dittersdorf, *Lebensbeschreibung*, 173.

house sang the new song with a voice that admittedly trembled a little, but it was none the less received enthusiastically and applauded.[14]

Mozart was also a welcome visitor at the home of Joseph and Marianne Martínez, the children of Nicolò Martínez, the Master of Ceremonies to the Apostolic Nuncio, in whose house Metastasio lived during the whole of his time in the city from 1730 until his death in 1782. It was Metastasio who had assumed responsibility for Marianne Martínez's education.[15] Her keyboard teacher was none other than Joseph Haydn, who, after leaving the choir school at St Stephen's in Vienna, eked out a pitiful existence in an attic in the same house.[16] Nicola Porpora, for whom Haydn played the piano, was also involved in her musical education. Later she was taught by Giuseppe Bonno, and made such good progress that she attracted attention as a singer, pianist and composer,[17] with even Hasse acknowledging her gifts.[18] In 1773 she was made an honorary member of the Accademia Filarmonica in Bologna,[19] which later awarded her a doctorate, as did the Accademia in Pavia. In 1782 her oratorio *Isacco* was performed at a Sozietätskonzert in Vienna.[20] Metastasio called her his 'Santa Cecilia'[21] and left his entire fortune to her and to her brother, who worked as a librarian at the Imperial and Royal Court Library.[22] As a result, she was able to maintain a large household in which music naturally played a prominent role. Kelly found her a lively and agreeable woman, in spite of her advanced age, adding that she was very friendly with Mozart and regularly invited him to her gatherings, when the two of them played his own sonatas for four hands.[23]

We have already had frequent occasion to mention the informal tone of these gatherings. Although the subjects discussed were no longer the same, these salons still exuded something of the wit and charm that had characterized royalist France before gradually spreading to the whole of the rest of the civilized world. Music enjoyed a privileged place at these gatherings. Without them, the symphony, string quartet and all the other types of chamber music would not have blossomed with the speed that they did. But vocal chamber music for one or more voices had not disappeared, and alongside the simple song, we also find the domestic cantata and polyphonic songs for soloists and chorus. There were good reasons why Mozart long felt at his ease in these circles, and it is no accident that the work that he wrote at the end of this period in his life – *Le nozze di Figaro* – is the most inspired musical portrait of the aristocratic circles in which he moved at this time.

Mozart was profligate with his musical gifts on these occasions, performing pieces of his own and by others as often as they would have him, and was especially tireless at improvisation,

14. Einstein, *Lebensläufe deutscher Musiker von ihnen selbst erzählt*, iii.11–12; see also Ludwig Nohl, *Musiker-Briefe*, 116, 136 and 145; and Pohl, *Joseph Haydn*, ii.150 [*Dokumente*, 474, *Documentary Biography*, 558–9]. ◆ It is unclear whether the song composed by Mozart is lost or whether the anecdote refers to one of his surviving lieder.
15. Cristini, 'Vita dell'abate Pietro Metastasio', i.ccvi; and Gubernatis, *Pietro Metastasio*, 194–5.
16. Pohl, *Joseph Haydn*, i.126–7 and 165–6.
17. Burney, *The Present State of Music in Germany*, i.306–10, 341–2 and 348, and Schönfeld, *Jahrbuch der Tonkunst von Wien und Prag*, i. 41–2.
18. Burney, *The Present State of Music in Germany*, i.348.
19. Mancini, *Pensieri, e riflessioni pratiche sopra il canto figurato*, 229–30.
20. *Wiener Musikzeitung* (1842), 70, and Schering, *Geschichte des Oratoriums*, 253.
21. Gerber, *Historisch-biographisches Lexicon der Tonkünstler*, i.888.
22. Gubernatis, *Pietro Metastasio*, 195.
23. Kelly, *Reminiscences*, i.252, and *AmZ*, new series, xv (1880), 406n. For an account of her life (1744–1812), see Gerber, *Historisch-biographisches Lexicon*, i.888 and Anton Schmid, 'Zwei musikalische Berühmtheiten Wien's aus dem Schönen Geschlecht in der zweiten Hälfte des verflossenen Jahrhunderts', 513 and 517. ◆ Further, see Stevenson, 'Marianna Martines = Martínez (1744–1812): Pupil of Haydn and Friend of Mozart'; and Godt, 'Marianna in Italy: The International Reputation of Marianna Martines (1744–1812)' and 'Marianna in Vienna: A Martines Chronology'.

provoking a number of his well-heeled hosts into complaining that he played for all and sundry. One thing alone he was implacable in demanding: an attentive audience. This self-evident right on the part of every artist – a right that even today is ignored by many a lay listener – is one that Mozart was no less keen to champion than Beethoven and every other great musician. 'Nothing', wrote Niemetschek, 'annoyed him as much as disturbance, noise or gossip during the music. Then this mild and cheerful man would become indignant in the extreme and express himself in the liveliest manner. It is well known that on one occasion he angrily rose from the keyboard while playing and quit his inattentive listeners. This was held against him in many quarters, but unjustly so.'[24] When the mood took him, he adopted a satirical approach to listeners he did not care for[25] and either refused to play at all or performed only trifles,[26] whereas with real connoisseurs, no matter what their social background, he almost had to be stopped. After his concert in Leipzig, for example, he returned to his rooms with an old violinist by the name of Berger in order to play for him 'as befits people who really appreciate music'. At around midnight he suddenly leapt to his feet, announcing that his visitor had heard him as he really was – 'anyone can play as I played earlier'.[27]

There is another member of the nobility who deserves to be mentioned here and who played an extremely important, if not always laudable, role in Mozart's life in Vienna: Baron Gottfried van Swieten (1733–1803) was the son of Gerhard van Swieten, the famous and influential personal physician to the Empress Maria Theresia. He was born at Leiden in the Netherlands in 1733 and moved to Vienna with his father in 1745. He was a lawyer by profession but was drawn specifically to diplomacy, in which capacity he accompanied the Duke of Braganza on his travels in 1768.[28] He was also passionately interested in music, at least to the extent that he was temperamentally capable of such passions, and additionally dabbled in composition: as early as 1769 he wrote some arias for Favart's *La rosière de Salency*, albeit with scant success.[29] He is also reputed to be the author of at least eight – and as many as twelve – symphonies, which, in Haydn's words, were 'as stiff as the man himself'.[30] After holding diplomatic posts in Brussels, Paris and Warsaw, he was appointed ambassador to Berlin in 1770, where he was given the thankless task of persuading Frederick the Great to accept Austria's terms in the second partition of Poland, whereby Austria demanded the secession of Silesia and Galicia in return for certain concessions. He also pressed Austria's claims to Serbia and a part of Bosnia.[31] At the same time he continued to pursue his musical interests. Friedrich Nicolai found in him an 'enthusiastic amateur and connoisseur of music and even a composer in his own right',[32] and there is no doubt that van Swieten thought that his own musical ideal had been realized in Berlin, with the result that his stay in the city affected the whole of his musical thinking from now on. Henceforth he threw all his weight behind an attempt to apply to Vienna the impressions that he had gained in Berlin.

24. Niemetschek, *Leben des k. k Kapellmeisters Wolfgang Gottlieb Mozart*, 57.
25. Rochlitz, 'Verbürgte Anekdoten', 49.
26. Niemetschek, *Leben des k. k. Kapellmeisters Wolfgang Gottlieb Mozart*, 61.
27. *AmZ*, xiv (1812), 106. ◆ Rochlitz's frequently unreliable anecdotes must be taken with a pinch of salt. Concerning this particular story, see Eisen, *Dokumente: Addenda*, 85–6, *New Mozart Documents*, 60–1. More generally, see Solomon, 'The Rochlitz Anecdotes: Issues of Authenticity in Early Mozart Biography'.
28. Rengger, *Zimmermann's Briefe an einige seiner Freunde in der Schweiz*, 96.
29. Grimm, *Correspondance littéraire, philosophique et critique*, 263 and 314.
30. Griesinger, *Biographische Notizen über Joseph Haydn*, 66–7. Mozart performed one of them at the Augarten in 1782.
31. Frederick replied: 'That's the sort of suggestion you could make if I had gout in the brain, but I've got it only in my legs'; see Oncken, *Das Zeitalter Friedrichs des Großen*, 508.
32. Friedrich Nicolai, *Beschreibung einer Reise durch Deutschland*, iv.556.

This was a somewhat foolhardy venture at this time. After all, we have already seen how great were the differences between north Germany and Austria in music. In the field of serious opera, the Berlin of Frederick the Great was still one of the safest strongholds of Italian taste à la Graun and Hasse; the king himself was no great friend of Gluck's reforms, and it was not until after his death that Reichardt was able to introduce them to Berlin. The singspiel naturally followed Hiller's lead. One new genre that van Swieten did encounter in Berlin and that came to artistic fruition in Vienna only much later was the German song. We have already mentioned the principal characteristics of the north German symphony and sonata. Here the Viennese tendency to strike a more popular note was almost entirely overshadowed by a propensity for artificiality that was to typify the north German symphony even as late as the Romantic period. The fondness for conceptualization that is found in the works of all north German composers and that invests them with a sense of strict logic and unity could easily degenerate into arid scholasticism in the hands of lesser composers, and this is clearly the case both here and in their attempts to write songs. But it finds its most striking expression in the extensive literary activities of these composers, with Friedrich Wilhelm Marpurg's *Die Kunst das Clavier zu spielen* of 1750 followed by Johann Joachim Quantz's *Versuch einer Anweisung die Flöte traversiere zu spielen* of 1752 and by Carl Philipp Emanuel Bach's *Versuch über die wahre Art das Clavier zu spielen* of 1753 and 1762. Marpurg's most important work, his *Abhandlung von der Fuge*, appeared in 1753/4, with a further edition in 1806, and was followed in 1755 by his *Anleitung zum Clavierspielen* and in 1755–8 by his *Handbuch bey dem Generalbasse und der Composition*.[33] Aesthetics and singing were also widely discussed: Christian Gottfried Krause's *Von der musikalischen Poesie* appeared in 1752, Christoph Nichelmann's study of melody, *Die Melodie, nach ihrem Wesen sowohl, als nach ihren Eigenschaften* in 1755, Johann Friedrich Agricola's *Anleitung zur Singkunst* (a translation of Tosi's Italian original) in 1757 and Marpurg's *Anleitung zur Singcomposition* in 1758. Meanwhile, between 1751 and 1767, Johann Georg Sulzer was publishing one theoretical treatise after another.[34] Only Johann Philipp Kirnberger's writings fall, in the main, outside this period, the chief of them being his *Grundsätze des Generalbasses* of 1781.[35] An intellectual by nature, van Swieten was particularly attracted by this theoretical approach to music, although it is highly unlikely that he ever understood precisely where this particular road was leading. Nor is this the place to consider in detail the aesthetic outlook of the Berlin school.[36] Suffice it to say that it, too, was transitional in character, with rationalistic elements appearing alongside others that were purely emotive in tone, while mathematics, ethics, rhetoric and even, in part, the mystic symbolism of the Middle Ages were all combined with aesthetic questions. Central to all these discussions was the doctrine of the 'affections', in other words, the passions and moods that were produced by music and that were believed at the time to be real, not merely apparent.[37] As a number of recent writers have shown, this is a doctrine that can ultimately be traced back to Descartes and Spinoza.[38] That it survived for a whole century and

---

33. ◆ Abert's account of Marpurg's writings is confused. The *Abhandlung von der Fuge* of 1753/4 was not reprinted in German in 1806 but only in 1858. The earlier date is presumably a mistake for the 1816 reprinting of a French translation that had first appeared in 1756.

34. ◆ In fact, Sulzer's chief theoretical work, the *Allgemeine Theorie der schönen Künste*, was published between 1771 and 1774; a second edition appeared in 1778–9 and an enlarged third edition, by F. von Blankenburg, in 1786–7.

35. The *Wahre Grundsätze zum Gebrauche der Harmonie* (1773) that circulated under his name is in fact by Johann Abraham Peter Schulz; see Schulz's testimonial in Gerber, *Neues historisch-biographisches Lexikon der Tonkünstler*, iv.146.

36. See Schering, 'Die Musikästhetik der deutschen Aufklärung'; and Goldschmidt, *Die Musikästhetik des 18. Jahrhunderts*, 131ff. ◆ Further, see Morrow, *German Music Criticism in the Late Eighteenth Century: Aesthetic Issues in Instrumental Music*.

37. Marpurg, *Kritische Briefe über die Tonkunst*, ii.273, even includes a list of 27 'affects' and their musical realization.

38. Schering, 'Die Musikästhetik der deutschen Aufklärung', 271.

was lovingly developed by composers such as Carl Philipp Emanuel Bach goes without saying, given the state of profound emotional turmoil that followed in the wake of Rousseau's unleashing of feeling. The doctrine of the affections was the inevitable musical concomitant of the age of Werther and the 'beautiful soul'. In spite of its lack of clarity on a number of aesthetic points, its great advantage was that it set out not from any preconceived theories but from living art, forcing musicians to stick to practical considerations, while at the same time taking account of practical issues by developing a complex science of performing practice that for the most part remains valid to this day. That it was melody that finally triumphed in the battle waged in Paris between Rameau and Rousseau on the relative merits of harmony and melody is well known. Indeed, this was one of the reasons why the music of Johann Sebastian Bach faded so quickly from the purview of the younger generation, including even that of his own sons. The older tradition, with its emphasis on polyphony and counterpoint, was forced to give ground to the newer emphasis on melody, which seemed to come closer to the ideal of an art that was 'natural'. Yet even here the break was not complete, as is clear from the example of the north German symphony and its predilection for strict counterpoint.

There was, however, a further reason for this predilection and it is one that was to prove important for van Swieten's taste in music and, through him, for Mozart, too. The Berlin school included among its number various composers who had studied either with Johann Sebastian Bach himself or with his pupils and who, untimely though their intervention may have been, spoke out in word and deed in favour of their mentor and in that way ensured that at least his keyboard works were still used for teaching purposes. Bach's manuscripts were collected, and even during van Swieten's years in the city, there was already a flourishing Bach community under the leadership of Marpurg[39] and Kirnberger, whose influence was later to be felt especially at the Singakademie.[40] It was thanks to individuals such as these that van Swieten was finally won over to Bach's cause. That his help was much appreciated emerges, not least, from the fact that it was to van Swieten that Forkel dedicated his biography of Bach, a work that was to be of such great importance in the history of the Bach movement.[41]

All these aims were actively championed in a whole series of music societies that were drawn from the ranks of the middle classes and that culminated in the foundation of Fasch's Singakademie in 1791.[42] A choral society had been founded by Frederick the Great's keyboard teacher, Gottlieb Hayne, as long ago as 1724, establishing a tradition continued in 1749, when Johann Philipp Sack formed a Musikausübende Gesellschaft that included orchestral musicians.[43] Even more important were the Amateur Concerts established by Friedrich Ernst Benda and Carl Ludwig Bachmann in 1770. Originally devoted to orchestral music, they soon drew on the services of vocal and instrumental virtuosos and every three or four weeks performed operas or large-scale choral works.[44] Needless to say, their repertory showcased such local favourites as Hasse, Graun and Carl Philipp Emanuel Bach, but Handel's oratorios, too, soon found a place in their programmes. Reichardt mentions a performance of *Judas Maccabaeus* in 1774,[45] and Nicolai,

39. See Marpurg's preface to the second edition of *Die Kunst der Fuge* (1752), reproduced in the Bach-Gesellschaft edition, xxv/1, XIVff.
40. Kretzschmar, *J. S. Bach: Werke* (Bach-Gesellschaft), xlvi, XIX.
41. Forkel, *Ueber Johann Sebastian Bachs Leben, Kunst und Kunstwerke*.
42. ◆ See Wade, 'Carl Friedrich Christian Fasch, Geburtshelfer des Musiklebens in Berlin'.
43. Sachs, *Musik und Oper am kurbrandenburgischen Hof*, 177–8 and 191.
44. Blumner, *Geschichte der Sing-Akademie zu Berlin*, 2–3.
45. Reichardt, *Briefe eines aufmerksamen Reisenden die Musik betreffend*, i.82.

writing in 1781, reports that *Alexander's Feast* and *Messiah* were also often heard there.[46] *Messiah* had already been performed in Hamburg on 15 April 1772.[47] Berlin was thus a centre of the German cult of Handel even before the famous massed performance of *Messiah* took place there in 1786.

At the time of van Swieten's residence in Berlin, the leading light of the Amateur Concerts was Friedrich Nicolai, a man of many parts who was greatly interested in music, to which he also turned his hand in a semi-professional way.[48] As a result of his leading position in Berlin's intellectual life and thanks to his friendship with Agricola, Marpurg and Reichardt, he soon acquired great influence over the musical life of Berlin,[49] an influence that extended to the whole of north Germany as a result of his *Allgemeine deutsche Bibliothek* that was published periodically between 1765 and 1806. It is no wonder, therefore, that the Berliners regarded themselves as a force to be reckoned with in the world of German music and that they were especially keen for the south Germans to feel their superiority. The Mannheimers had long suffered from this dismissive attitude, while Leopold Mozart could see it as a sign of great distinction that he was praised and acknowledged by the Berliners.[50] Other Viennese composers such as Wagenseil and Steffan were simply given a good dressing down by Marpurg,[51] while Nicolai even went so far as to claim that Vienna may have had the odd decent composer since Fux's day, but they had no one of the distinction of Telemann, Graun and Hasse or either Johann Sebastian or Carl Philipp Emanuel Bach, at least until Haydn arrived on the scene.[52] It is easy to imagine that justified pride not infrequently turned to arrogance, bias and argumentativeness, thereby causing the gulf between north and south to grow even wider than ever.

Gottfried van Swieten felt extraordinarily at home in this company. His earliest literary endeavours date from 1773, when his *Dissertatio sistens musicae in medicinam influxum et utilitatem* earned him a doctorate from Leiden University for its contribution to what at the time was a much-debated question. But he also played an active role in the musical life of his time, commissioning the six symphonies for strings from Carl Philipp Emanuel Bach that appeared in Hamburg in 1773, specifically asking that Bach should simply follow his genius and give no heed to the difficulties of performing them.[53] Above all, this period was notable for his boundless admiration of the strict contrapuntal style of the age of Johann Sebastian Bach and Handel, an admiration that turned him into an important mediator between this older tradition and the younger generation of Viennese composers. Given his markedly intellectual nature, it must remain an open question whether he ever achieved a true understanding of art beyond the limitations of his time or whether his commitment to this earlier tradition did not, rather, have a deeply reactionary element to it. A man like van Swieten could understand neither the emotional greatness of Handel nor the inwardness and profundity of Johann Sebastian Bach, and it was clearly only the scholastic aspect

46. Friedrich Nicolai, *Beschreibung einer Reise durch Deutschland*, iv.525–6.
47. Voß, *Briefe*, i.295–6.
48. Goeckingk, *Friedrich Nicolai's Leben und literarischer Nachlaß*, 95 and 29; and Schletterer, *Johann Friedrich Reichardt*, i.97–8.
49. Burney, *The Present State of Music in Germany*, ii.89–93 and 107.
50. ◆ Here Abert refers to the positive review of Leopold's *Versuch einer gründlichen Violinschule* published in 1757 in the *Historisch-kritische Beyträge zur Aufnahme der Musik* and Marpurg's 1759 invitation to contribute to the *Kritische Briefe über die Tonkunst*; see *Dokumente*, 10–11, *Documentary Biography*, 12–13.
51. Marpurg, *Kritische Briefe über die Tonkunst*, ii.141–2.
52. Nicolai, *Beschreibung einer Reise durch Deutschland*, iv.525–6.
53. Friedrich Reichardt, 'Autobiographie', 28–9; and Wotquenne, *Thematisches Verzeichnis der Werke von Carl Philipp Emanuel Bach*, 62. ◆ The symphonies are Wq. 182; in Helm's *Thematic Catalogue of the Works of Carl Philipp Emanuel Bach* they are numbered 657–62.

of their art – its astonishing contrapuntal mastery – that attracted him. Even so, he managed to acquire for himself an important position in the history of music, a position that he owed, in part, to his dogged propaganda on behalf of his own views and, in part, to his keen nose for aspiring and talented musicians: Haydn, Mozart and Beethoven all enjoyed the often dubious honour of his patronage. In December 1798 he himself admitted:

> As far as music is concerned, I go back to those times when it was still considered necessary to acquire a proper and thorough grounding in art before one started to practise it. Here I find sustenance for mind and soul, here I find a tonic whenever I have been demoralized by some fresh proof of declining standards in art. The men who console me are, above all, Handel and the two Bachs and, together with them, the few composers of our own day who, with firm tread, have followed in the footsteps of these paragons of truth and greatness and who have either promised to reach the goal or have already reached it. Undoubtedly it would have been reached by Mozart, had he not been snatched from us prematurely. Joseph Haydn, conversely, truly stands there.[54]

These are the old complaints of an amateur who swears by only one trend in art. It is significant that Mozart never fully reflected that ideal, and there may well have been times when he made old Gottfried van Swieten feel not a little uncomfortable.

It was around 1778 that van Swieten returned to Vienna, where he replaced his father as Prefect of the Imperial Library, before becoming President of the Court Commission on Education and Censorship in 1781. Here he was invited to draw up a timetable that was implemented throughout the whole country in 1783, when it elicited mixed reactions: while there were some who acknowledged van Swieten's understanding, there were many who found him lacking in the resolve necessary to carry through his plans.[55] In music, conversely, he showed no such lack. As a high-ranking civil servant, a former ambassador, the son of his father and, not least, as a man of means, he soon acquired a position of considerable influence in the musical life of Vienna. He became a veritable high priest of music (a type of individual still familiar to us today), proud of his understanding and invariably ready to dispense his views on art, all of which he regarded as the very last word on the subject. It is no wonder, therefore, that Viennese society went in quasi-religious awe of this patriarchal figure. 'When he attends a concert,' reported Johann Ferdinand von Schönfeld, 'our semi-connoisseurs never take their eyes off him, seeking to read in his features, not always intelligible to every one, what ought to be their opinion of the music.'[56] If anyone was heard talking during a concert, His Excellency would rise solemnly from his seat and, drawing himself to his full height, fix the guilty party with a long and withering gaze. Unfortunately, van Swieten differed from the majority of Viennese aristocrats in that he was extremely miserly by nature. Although he managed to raise considerable sums for artistic purposes and even contributed himself, his purse remained closed to the musicians themselves. Haydn experienced this for himself,[57] and as for Mozart, van Swieten exploited him to the hilt as a composer, but left him to

54. Anon, 'Aus einem Briefe des Herrn Geheimen Raths, Freyherrn van Swieten'.
55. Werner, *Aus dem Josephinischen Wien*, 6 and 153–4; Georg Forster, *Sämtliche Werke*, vii.273; and Kink, *Geschichte der Universität zu Wien*, i.539–40.
56. Thayer, *Ludwig van Beethovens Leben*, i.355.
57. Dies, *Biographische Nachrichten von Joseph Haydn*, 210; and Griesinger, *Biographische Notizen*, 66.

rot in want and destitution. It is ultimately van Swieten's fault that Mozart found his final resting place in a pauper's grave.[58]

In general, van Swieten lacked too many of the qualities needed to be a true patron of the arts: self-denial was unknown to him, and he had too little respect for the inner independence of the artists with whom he came into personal contact. Tyrannical in imposing his own tastes on others, he could be extremely tactless and demanding when his protégés proved unwilling to live up to his ideal. Even Haydn, who found more favour in his eyes than any other living artist, experienced this for himself, and how much more so will this have been the case with Mozart, who, in van Swieten's view, still had so much to learn. It was certainly not respect for his patron that induced Mozart to take a greater interest in the earlier types of music that van Swieten recommended to him, but, rather, the conviction that his own music would benefit as a result. And so he accepted the stiffly formal old man's quirks as part of the bargain.[59]

Van Swieten's name is first mentioned in Mozart's letters in May 1781.[60] Less than a year later, we find him writing: 'I go to Baron van Swieten's every Sunday at 12, and nothing is played there but Handel and Bach. I'm currently collecting Bach fugues, not only by Sebastian but also by Emanuel and Friedemann Bach.'[61] Ten days later he wrote to his sister: 'Baron van Swieten, whom I see every Sunday, has given me all the works of Handel and Sebastian Bach to take home (after I've played them through for him).'[62] In the same letter he speaks of van Swieten's collection of music,[63] which he describes as 'small in quantity, but great in quality'. And he goes on to ask his father to send him various works for this same purpose, including not only his own sacred compositions, but also pieces by Michael Haydn and Eberlin. Performances were given within a very small group, with no audience. Swieten himself sang discant, Mozart (who also accompanied) alto, Starzer[64] tenor and Anton Teyber[65] bass. Keyboard music in the same style was also played. Mozart originally intended to introduce his patron to Eberlin's fugues, but later decided against including them because they were 'far too trivial to deserve a place beside Handel and Bach. With all due respect for his four-part writing, his keyboard fugues are no more than long-drawn-out voluntaries.'[66] Mozart's change of attitude emerges with particular forcefulness from his letter of 12 April 1783:

---

58. All claims to the contrary, including those found in *Musikalische Korrespondenz der teutschen filarmonischen Gesellschaft*, iii (1792), 4, are incorrect. Even Niemetschek deleted from his second edition the claim that, following Mozart's death, van Swieten had assumed responsibility for the composer's children; Niemetschek, *Leben des k. k. Kapellmeisters Wolfgang Gottlieb Mozart*, 31. ◆ The article in the *Musikalische Korrespondenz der teutschen filarmonischen Gesellschaft* for 4 January 1792 – the first lengthy obituary of Mozart – claimed that 'immediately after the death of his friend Mozart, and in recognition of his services, [Baron van Swieten] declared himself ready to embrace as his own Mozart's children, who through the lack of an estate would be destitute, without shelter and education, and to replace their father and care for their future lives!' See Eisen, *Dokumente: Addenda*, 80, *New Mozart Documents*, 75.

59. ◆ For a general account of van Swieten, see Olleson, 'Gottfried van Swieten: Patron of Haydn and Mozart'.

60. *Briefe*, iii.121 (letter of 26 May 1781).

61. *Briefe*, iii.201 (letter of 10 April 1782).

62. *Briefe*, iii.202 (letter of 20 April 1782).

63. ◆ See Holschneider, 'Die musikalische Bibliothek Gottfried van Swietens'.

64. Starzer often performed at van Swieten's, appearing with the famous lutenist Karl Kohaut; see Griesinger, *Biographische Notizen*, 66.

65. Teyber was born in Vienna in 1756 and died there in 1822 as Imperial and Royal chamber composer. He was probably a brother of the singer Therese Teyber. Mozart met him in Dresden in 1789; see *Briefe*, iv.83 (letter of 16 April 1789). ◆ Almost certainly Mozart had known Teyber (who was in fact Therese's brother) from his early Vienna years: in November 1784, when Schikaneder mounted at production of *Die Entführung* at the Kärntnertor-Theater, Teyber composed an aria to substitute for 'Martern aller Arten' which could not be performed in the absence from the band of several virtuosos normally attached to the court theatre. See Eisen, *Dokumente: Addenda*, 33, *New Mozart Documents*, 33.

66. *Briefe*, iii.203 (letter of 20 April 1782).

Baron van Swieten and Starzer know as well as you and I that taste is continually changing – and, what is more, that this change of taste unfortunately extends even to church music, which it shouldn't do, but as a result true church music is found only in attics and in a worm-eaten condition.[67]

Mozart had never struck this note before, and it reflects the powerful impression produced on him by his new-found interest in early music. No one was more delighted by this development than Constanze, who soon encouraged her husband to undertake his own experiments in this field:

When Constanze heard the fugues, she fell hopelessly in love with them: she now wants to hear nothing but fugues, especially (in this type of composition) by Handel and Bach. As she has often heard me play fugues off the top of my head, she asked me if I'd ever written any down, and when I said no, she told me off in no uncertain terms for not noting down this most beautiful and artistic of all musical forms, and didn't stop begging me until I'd written down a fugue for her and that's how it came about. I deliberately wrote 'Andante maestoso' above it, so that it's not played too fast – if a fugue isn't played slowly, you can't make out the subject when it enters and as a result it fails to make any impression. If time and opportunity allow me, I intend to write 5 more and shall then present them to Baron van Swieten.[68]

Constanze did not have to beg for long, and Mozart was soon so deeply immersed in early music that from 1782 onwards we can justifiably speak of a new stylistic period that we shall shortly have occasion to examine in greater detail. He began by arranging five fugues from part two of Bach's *Well-Tempered Clavier* for two violins, viola and bass (K405 = nos 2, 7, 9, 8 and 5 of part two of *The Well-Tempered Clavier*, with no. 8 transposed to D minor[69]). A second set of such works (K404a) is made up of six more three-part fugues, five of which are by Bach (from *The Well-Tempered Clavier*, the six organ sonatas and *The Art of Fugue*), the sixth being by Wilhelm Friedemann. These last-named works are preceded by six adagio movements, only two of which are by Johann Sebastian, the remaining four probably being by Mozart himself.[70] Conversely, Mozart twice attempted to prepare a keyboard arrangement of Froberger's 'hexachord fantasia' that he found in Kircher's *Musurgia*,[71] but broke off after fifty bars on his first attempt and after only thirty-two on his second. Among his own works in the older style, pride of place must go

---

67. *Briefe*, iii.264 (letter of 12 April 1783). ◆ Mozart's metaphor of 'true church music . . . found only in attics and in a worm-eaten condition' is explained by the beginning of this passage: 'When the weather gets warmer, please search in the attic, under the roof, and send us some of your own church music.' Apparently this was where Leopold stored his earlier works.

68. *Briefe*, iii.202–3 (letter of 20 April 1782).

69. ◆ Additionally, a thirty-nine bar fragment of the B minor fugue, transposed to C minor, survives at the Státná Zámek a Zahrady, Kroměříž, Czech Republic; see NMA X/30/4, Fr 1782r.

70. See the important article by Ernst Lewicki, 'Mozarts Verhältnis zu Sebastian Bach', 163–79, and Wilhelm Rust's Preface to volume 9 of the Bach-Gesellschaft edition, XXVI. Wyzewa and Saint-Foix, *Wolfgang Amédée Mozart*, ii.412, likewise regard these four adagios as being by Mozart himself. All these transcriptions and new works survive only in manuscript form and were not included in the complete edition of Mozart's works. ◆ The attribution to Mozart of K404a is now thought to be unlikely. The source, which is unattributed, dates from 1785 or 1786 at the earliest and possibly as late as *c*1800. The notion that the adagios are by Mozart was invented by Rust, presumably on the model of K405. In general, see Kirkendale, 'More Slow Introductions by Mozart to Fugues of J. S. Bach?' and Tomita, 'Bach reception in pre-Classical Vienna'.

71. We have already seen that Mozart was familiar with Kircher's work; see above. On Froberger's fantasia, see Max Seiffert, *Geschichte der Klaviermusik*, 172, and Adler, *Johann Froberger: Orgel- und Clavierwerke*.

to his three-part prelude and fugue K394, which he sent to his sister on 20 April 1782 with instructions that she should memorize it. Evidently one of his earliest experiments of this kind, it was followed by the C minor fugue for two keyboards K426, which he completed on 29 December 1783 and arranged for string quartet in June 1788, when he added an introduction (K546). A whole series of other pieces which, although undated, clearly belong to this period on stylistic grounds, remained unfinished. The longest of these fragments is the four-part fugue in G minor, the last eight bars of which were completed by Maximilian Stadler (K401). The fugue in G major K375g breaks off after only twenty-seven bars, a second fugue in G major for two keyboards K375d after twenty-three. Of two others, only the opening bars survive. Both point clearly to Johann Sebastian Bach as their models. Two other fragments likewise recall Bach's gigues. Of these, the fugue in C minor K383d begins as follows:

Here is the opening of the F major fugue K383b:[72]

Surviving sketches in an exercise book currently lodged in Vienna[73] afford extremely valuable insights in Mozart's study of Handel and especially Bach. The first of these folios includes the theme of Handel's famous chorus 'See the conquering hero comes', while the fugue subject in G minor on the following side also bears a Handelian stamp.[74] But these are then followed by a series of sketches of fugues that are quite clearly inspired by Bach, their spiritual roots lying in *The Well-Tempered Clavier*. Take, for example, the theme of a fugue in E minor that Mozart twice developed:

72.   ◆ Although Mozart was occupied with fugues in 1782, many of the fragments traditionally thought to date from this time are either earlier or later: K401 is from *c*1772, K375g probably from 1776, K375d from 1785 or 1786, and K383b from 1787–9. Among fragments not described by Abert but listed in K[6] as dating to this period, K375e is possibly from 1772, K385k from 1781–2, K375f from 1782–3, K375h from late 1783 and 383d from 1783 or later. The clear implication is that Mozart was concerned with fugal writing throughout his life, not just around the time of his performances at van Swieten's.
73.   Headed by Stadler, 'Mozart's teaching in composition 1784'. The sketches are described in detail in Lach, *W. A. Mozart als Theoretiker*. ◆ The so-called *Freystädtler-Studien* are published in NMA X/30/2.
74.   Between them comes a sketch for bass voice of an evidently buffo character.

But Mozart also made a contribution to the older form of the keyboard suite: K399. Laid out along the lines of the old four-movement sequence of allemande, courante, sarabande and gigue with a French overture by way of an introduction, it breaks off after only six bars of the sarabande. The gigue is missing in its entirety. Only in its change of key signature does it depart from the older tradition.

Two final works to be mentioned here are the keyboard fantasias in C minor K396 and D minor K397,[75] both of which reveal the influence of the fantasias of Carl Philipp Emanuel Bach. In addition to these direct imitations of older formal models, however, the earlier tradition will be found to permeate Mozart's works in general, especially those written between 1782 and 1784: although unfinished (it, too, was completed by Stadler), the A minor sonata K402 for keyboard and violin is nothing more nor less than a fugue with an introduction in A major. We shall have to return to this great stylistic change in due course and discuss it in greater detail in a section of its own. It was clearly not an easy change for Mozart to make, and many of these pieces reveal the effort that they cost him. Equally characteristic is the large number of pieces that were left unfinished. Evidently Mozart was fascinated in the first instance by the technical problems involved, receiving more than he gave and writing these pieces for himself rather than for others. Even here, there are individual instances in which he succeeded in asserting his genius in the face of the overwhelming influence of these older composers, but in general he remained their pupil. Although this was undoubtedly an excellent training ground for him, the lack of freedom invariably bound up with such an exercise may also be palpably heard here. There is no period in Mozart's creative output in which old and new coexisted in such an unbalanced relationship as they did between 1782 and 1784. Here, too, we find the same temporary lack of stylistic assurance that regularly occurs at such times of change, with the result that during the next two years – the time of the great keyboard concertos – it even seemed as though the spirit of modern Gesellschaftsmusik threatened to drive these older influences away again. Yet they continued to work away secretly within him, and once the 'modern' tendency had peaked in his works, they gradually came to life again, so that during his final years he was able to merge old and new and create a personal style of his own. The most perfect products of Mozart's art – the great C major symphony, *Die Zauberflöte* and the *Requiem* – all reflect the influence of these older composers, while retaining their independence.

---

75. ◆ It is likely that K397 was left unfinished by Mozart. No autograph survives and the first edition, published in Vienna by the Bureau d'Arts et d'Industrie in 1804, lacks the concluding ten bars. These appear for the first time in the Breitkopf & Härtel *Œuvres complètes* edition of 1806. Possibly they were composed by Breitkopf's in-house editor, August Eberhard Müller. See Paul Hirsch, 'A Mozart Problem'. K396, a fragment for keyboard and violin, was arranged for keyboard and completed by Maximilian Stadler; Mozart's autograph is in the Goethe-Schiller-Archiv, Weimar.

35

Plans for new operas

Throughout this period Mozart continued to feel his old irrepressible urge to write an opera, a desire that naturally grew more powerful following the success of *Die Entführung aus dem Serail*. Towards the end of 1782 Rosenberg advised him to write another *opera buffa*, but although he made the most varied attempts to find a new libretto, nothing suitable came to light. Given the general situation at this time, the German singspiel represented his best hope, and he even received an offer of a text with the title 'Which Is the Best Nation?', but it proved to be a 'wretched affair' and he rejected it, adding that 'anyone who set it without having it completely altered runs the risk of having it hooted off the stage'.[1] Umlauf had no such qualms and his setting was duly hissed. Mozart wondered whether 'the poet or the composer will carry off the prize for general ghastliness'.

Six weeks later, on 5 February 1783, we find him writing to his father again:

A new opera is to be given next Friday, the day after tomorrow, the music (a gallimaufry) by a young local composer, a pupil of Wagenseil, who's called gallus cantans, in arbore sedens, gigirigi faciens; I don't suppose it'll be much of a draw, though it's bound to be better than its predecessor, an old opera by Gassmann ('La notte critica'), in German 'Die unruhige Nacht', that had difficulty surviving for 3 performances. This in turn had been preceded by the execrable opera by Umlauf that I told you about and that didn't even make it to a third performance; – it looks as though they want to kill off the German opera before its time, though it's coming to an end in any case after Easter; – and Germans themselves are doing this – shame on them![2]

The crisis currently affecting the German singspiel in Vienna had been caused in part by the poor quality of the words and music and in part by all manner of machinations instigated by Stephanie the Younger in his attempts to unseat the then director, Johann Heinrich Friedrich Müller. Stephanie had begun by sidelining Müller and then, on the committee that met to replace him, had caused so much dissension that he finally achieved his aim of being placed in charge of the whole enterprise. But the situation had by now deteriorated to the point at which the existing directors, Rosenberg and Kienmayr, and ultimately the emperor, too, lost all pleasure in the venture. In his heart of hearts, Joseph II had always been on the Italians' side, and now those of his friends who likewise supported the Italians and for whom the National Singspiel had always been

---

1. *Briefe*, iii.244–4 (letter of 21 December 1782).
2. *Briefe*, iii.254 (letter of 5 February 1783). Gallus's real name was Johann Mederitsch (1752–1835), who for a time taught the piano to Franz Grillparzer. His *Rose, oder Pflicht und Liebe im Streit* was premièred on 9 February 1783. Gassmann's *La notte critica* had been revived on 10 January.

a thorn in the flesh seized the opportunity to demand the reintroduction of the Italian opera. Foremost among these agitators was Salieri.

Mozart himself intended to be ready for every eventuality and continued to keep an eye open for Italian librettos, while secretly preferring the idea of writing a German opera. Of particular importance in this context is the following passage in his letter of 5 February 1783:

> In my last letter I asked you to keep reminding Gatti[3] about the Italian librettos and I do so again now; – – now I must tell you what I have in mind. I don't believe that the Italian opera will survive for long – and *I* – I too stick with the Germans. Even if it means more trouble, I prefer to do so. Every nation has its own opera – why shouldn't we Germans have one? Is German not as singable as French and English? – not more singable than Russian? – Well – I'm now writing a German opera *for myself*. I've chosen Goldoni's comedy 'Il servitore di due padroni', and the whole of the first act has already been translated; the translator is Baron Binder. But it's all still a secret until it's finished; – well, what do you think? Do you not believe that I'll make a success of it?[4]

This operatic plan is important, not only because the libretto derives from Goldoni, but more particularly because Mozart chose to embark on it without a commission, simply on his own initiative. This, of course, also explains why, given the situation at this time, the plan was never realized.

The decision to invite back the Italians was taken in the wake of a visit to the Kärntnertor-Theater by a French troupe of singers and actors, a visit that had enjoyed the emperor's special favour.[5] In the summer of 1782 they were invited to perform at Schönbrunn and given board and lodging at the palace. But in the event they were dissatisfied with their accommodation, and one of the actors even had the temerity to complain to the emperor in person at the wine that had been provided for them and that was said to be a burgundy. Joseph replied that the wine was good enough for him but he had no doubt that they could find a better one in France.[6] The company was dismissed and Rosenberg was given the task of finding an *opera buffa* troupe in Italy to which the Viennese could limit themselves in future. Even during 1782 Sacchini's *La contadina in corte* and Salieri's *La locandiera* had already been given in Italian. The German company was disbanded at the end of the current season on 4 March 1783, its more talented members joining the new Italian company, while those that had not already been given their notice were left to fend for themselves.[7] Between March 1783 and the spring of 1785 only a handful of performances were given in German, and most of these were benefit performances such as the one for Aloysia Lange on 25 January 1784, when Mozart himself conducted *Die Entführung aus dem Serail*.[8] Her benefit performance the following year was *Zemire* on 20 January 1785. Meanwhile, Adamberger had chosen Gluck's *Die*

3. Luigi Gatti was Kapellmeister in Salzburg at this time; see above.
4. *Briefe*, iii.255 (letter of 5 February 1783).
5. Friedrich Meyer, *Friedrich Ludwig Schröder: Beitrag zur Kunde des Menschen und des Künstlers*, i.358–9; and *AmZ*, xxiv (1822), 265. Gluck's *Orfeo* was given here in 1781; see Friedrich Nicolai, *Beschreibung einer Reise durch Deutschland und die Schweiz im Jahre 1781*, iv.537–8.
6. Kelly, *Reminiscences of Michael Kelly*, i.194; on the following, see especially Robert Haas's introduction to *Ignaz Umlauff: Die Bergknappen*, XIXff.
7. *AmZ*, xxiv (1822), 269. Schröder wrote to Dalberg on 21 October 1782: 'The German Opera has abdicated here, and the comedy [i.e., the spoken theatre] is being strengthened by Reineke and Opitz.'
8. See *Wiener Zeitung* (1784), no. 7 [*Dokumente*, 196, *Documentary Biography*, 221]. A repeat performance was advertised on 1 February.

Pilgrime von Mekka for his benefit performance on 15 February 1784. *Le déserteur* was given in German on 25 January 1785. By 1785 there were increasingly vocal demands for a return of German opera. The court assumed responsibility for running the Kärntnertor-Theater later that year, and although it opened with an Italian opera, Giuseppe Sarti's *Giulio Sabino*, on 4 August – a choice dictated by the fact that the castrato Luigi Marchei was then passing through the city – it was here that German opera was to find a new home for itself alongside Italian operas.

It was with decidedly mixed feelings that Mozart watched these events unfold. The struggle between the two types of opera had driven him increasingly into the German camp, and early in 1785 he even had an opportunity to write a German opera in memory of Mannheim, when Anton Klein sent him a libretto, with the request that he set it to music. The text was almost certainly *Rudolf von Habsburg* and, as such, an attempt to repeat the success of Holzbauer's *Günther von Schwarzburg*.[9] Mozart replied on 21 March 1785:

> As for the opera, I can say little more now than I could before. My dear Privy Councillor! My hands are so full that I can scarcely find a moment to call my own. As a man of great insight and experience, you yourself will know even better than I that something like this has to be read through with all possible attention and deliberation – and not just once, but many times. So far I have not had time to read through it even once without interruption. All that I can say at present is that I should not like to part with it yet; and so I would ask you to allow me to hang on to the piece for a little while longer. If I decide that I want to set it to music, I'd like to know in advance whether a production has already been fixed and, if so, where. – In terms of both poetry and music, a work like this doesn't deserve to have been written in vain. I look forward to receiving your clarification on this point.[10]

Had this plan been realized, the result would have been more than capable of standing comparison with the works of Schweitzer and Holzbauer, a fully-fledged German opera of a kind that was, however, already in decline. In the event, the plan seems to have foundered on the fact that Mozart had no firm guarantee that the work would be performed at all. In the same letter he goes on to vent his displeasure at the state of opera in Vienna at this time, at the same time revealing his lofty opinion of the calling of German art and doing so, moreover, with typically Mozartian candour:

> I've no information at present concerning the new German opera company, where (with the exception of the building operations at the Kärntnertor-Theater, which has been chosen for this very purpose) things are progressing only very slowly. – It's supposed to open in early October. For my own part, I don't hold out much hope for it. – To judge by what has been done so far, I think they have been trying to undermine the German opera, which may only temporarily have fallen by the wayside, rather than to help it to its feet and keep it going. My sister-in-law Mme Lange is the only singer allowed to join the German singspiel. – Mme Cavalieri, Adamberger, Mme Teyber, all Germans of whom Germany may be proud, have to stay at the Italian theatre – and compete with their own countrymen! – – – The number of German singers at present, both male and female, can almost be counted on the fingers of one hand! – and even if there are

---

9. Thus Jahn, *W. A. Mozart*, fourth edition, ii.253. On 20 January 1781 Klein submitted this text to the electoral Deutsche Gesellschaft in Mannheim and was much applauded for the piece; see *Rheinische Beiträge zur Gelehrsamkeit*, i (1781), 383–4. He later worked it up into a stage play that appeared in print in 1781.
10. *Briefe*, iii.392–3 (letter of 21 March 1785, incorrectly dated by Bauer/Deutsch/Eibl).

singers as good as, or better than, the ones I've mentioned, which I very much doubt, it seems to me that the directors of the theatre here are too anxious to make economies and too unpatriotic to offer large sums of money to strangers, when they have better singers, or at least equally good ones, whom they can get for nothing. – For the Italian company doesn't need them – as far as numbers go; it can cast every role from within the company. – The idea at present is to make do at the German opera with actors and actresses who sing only when they absolutely have to; – the most unfortunate part of the whole affair is that the directors of both the theatre and the orchestra have been kept on, as it's they who, as a result of their ignorance and idleness, have done most to ruin their own work. If only a single patriot had been in charge – things would look very different! – But then the National Theater, which was just beginning to blossom, would really flourish, and that, of course, would be an everlasting blot on Germany if we Germans were seriously to begin to think as Germans – to act as Germans – to speak as Germans – and even – to sing as Germans!!! My dear Privy Councillor, please don't hold it against me that I've got so carried away in my enthusiasm. Utterly convinced, as I am, that I am speaking to a true German, I have given rein to my tongue, something that is unfortunately so seldom possible nowadays that after such an outpouring a man might get rolling drunk, but without thereby running the risk of endangering his health.

The German opera opened on 16 October with Monsigny's *Félix* [*oder der Findling*] in André's translation. The company comprised the following singers: Martin Ruprecht and Ignaz Saal (both of whom were also members of the Italian troupe), Johann Ernst Dauer, Ferdinand Arnold, Emanuel Schikaneder (from 1785) and Messrs Grünberg and Rothe. The female singers were Therese Teyber, Aloysia Lange, Anna Maria Saal (who, like her husband, also sang for the Italian Opera), Maria Henriette Stierle, Frau Rothe and Fräulein Delop.[11] But the German company had far less to offer than its Italian rivals: in 1785 only two original German works were staged, Martin Ruprecht's *Die Dorfhandel, oder Bunt über Eck* and Franz Teyber's *Die Dorfdeputirten*, although the following year there were six German works,[12] and a further four in 1787.[13] The rest of the repertory was made up of translations of French and Italian pieces.[14] With this, the German opera in Vienna once again came to an end. The company was disbanded during the 1788 carnival and it was not until 1794 that a new attempt was made to stage German operas under Müller and Süßmayr.

In spite of the continuing success of *Die Entführung aus dem Serail*, Mozart was reemployed only once, and even this was not for a proper opera but for an occasional piece, albeit one of an exceptional character. On 7 February 1786 festivities were held at the Orangery at Schönbrunn in honour of the joint rulers of the Austrian Netherlands involving leading members not only of the Burgtheater but also of the German and Italian opera companies. Indeed, the event even seems to have been designed to highlight the differences between the two types of opera, as both of them – in keeping with a popular custom at this time – revolved around the same theme:

11. See Haas, *Ignaz Umlauff: Die Bergknappen*, XIX.
12. Umlauf's *Die glücklichen Jäger*, Schuster's *Der Alchymist*, Dittersdorf's *Der Apotheker und der Doktor*, Hanke's *Robert und Hannchen*, Dittersdorf's *Betrug durch Aberglauben* and Umlauf's *Der Ring der Liebe, oder Zemirens und Azors Ehestand*.
13. Dittersdorf's *Die Liebe im Narrenhause*, Ruprecht's *Das wütende Heer*, Schenk's *Im Finstern ist nicht gut tappen* and Kürzinger's *Die Illumination*. Becker's *Die drei Pächter*, mentioned by Pohl, *Joseph Haydn*, ii.380, was a translation; see Haas, Introduction to *Die Bergknappen*, XIX.
14. ◆ These included *Der lächerliche Zweykampf* (after Paisiello's *Il duello*) and *Die schöne Arsene* (after Monsigny's *La belle Arsène*) in 1786 and *Die Trofonius-Höhle* (after Paisiello's *La grotta di Trofonio*) and *Im Trüben ist gut fischen* (after Sarti's *Fra i due litiganti*) in 1787. See Link, *The National Court Theatre in Mozart's Vienna*, 81, 89, 108 and 111.

mockery of opera itself and its apparatus. The Italian piece was *Prima la musica e poi le parole*, a setting by Salieri of a text by Giovanni Battista Casti,[15] while the German work was Mozart's *Der Schauspieldirektor*[16] to words by Stephanie the Younger. A comparison between the two texts reveals the yawning void between the two genres in terms of their poetic taste and aesthetic culture. The cast was as follows:

Frank, a theatre manager		Gottlieb Stephanie the Younger
Eiler, a banker		Johann Franz Brockmann
Buff		Josef Weidmann
Herz	actors	Joseph Lange
Mme Pfeil		Maria Anna Stephanie
Mme Krone	actresses	Johanna Sacco
Mme Vogelsang		Maria Anna Adamberger
Vogelsang, a singer		Valentin Adamberger
Mme Herz		Aloysia Lange
Mlle Silberklang	singers	Catarina Cavalieri

The entire performance was intended to be repeated at the Kärntnertor-Theater on 11 February, but had to be cancelled as a result of Dauer's indisposition.[17] In consequence, *Der Schauspieldirektor* received only two more performances, on 18 and 25 February.[18] All the more egregiously, then, were the words and music tinkered with after Mozart's death in an attempt to keep the piece in the repertory.[19] In Weimar, Goethe rewrote Cimarosa's *L'impresario in angustie* – a setting of a related text that he had enjoyed in Rome in 1787[20] – and staged it in 1791 under the title *Die theatralischen Abenteuer*,[21] initially with Cimarosa's music, but later combining it with the entire score of Mozart's *Der Schauspieldirektor* and performing the result, to great acclaim, on 14 October 1797.[22] It was later repeated with additional changes[23] and also staged elsewhere.

In Vienna *Der Schauspieldirektor* was not revived until 1797, when it was given three performances. A revised version by Matthäus Stegmayer was seen in 1814.[24] In 1845 Louis Schneider hit on the idea of rewriting the entire text for a production in Berlin, with a cast that included Mozart himself: the plot now revolved around the composition of *Die Zauberflöte* and examined Schikaneder's influence on the work and Mozart's relationship with Aloysia Lange.[25] Since the

15. Mosel, *Ueber das Leben und die Werke des Anton Salieri*, 90.
16. Mozart called it a 'comedy with music'. In both the autograph score and the old wordbook, Buff is called Puf; see Rudolf Hirsch, *Mozarts Schauspieldirektor: Musikalische Reminiscenzen*.
17. ◆ Dauer was indisposed on 10, not 11, February; as a result, it was a performance of Umlauf's *Das Irrlicht* that was cancelled, not Mozart's *Der Schauspieldirektor*. Further performances were given on 18 and 25 February; see *Dokumente*, 231–2, *Documentary Biography*, 264. The cast list given here corresponds with that given in NMA II/5/15, not the list originally proposed by Jahn and taken over by Abert.
18. Haas, *Ignaz Umlauff: Die Bergknappen*, XX.
19. Genée, 'Zur Geschichte des Mozartschen Schauspieldirektor und der verschiedenen Bearbeitungen', 60–2.
20. Goethe, 'Italienische Reise', *Werke*, xxvii.81.
21. Goethe, 'Tag- und Jahreshefte 1791', *Werke*, xxx.14; and Burckhardt, *Vierteljahresschrift für Literaturgeschichte*, iii (1890), 478–9.
22. Morris, 'Goethe als Bearbeiter von italienischen Operntexten', 4–5.
23. Goethe, *Werke*, xiv.80. Goethe himself provided the songs 'An dem reinsten Frühlingsmorgen' and 'Bei dem Glanz der Abendröte', but in general Mozart's text underwent few changes; see Diezmann, *Goethe-Schiller-Museum*, 15–16.
24. Hirsch, *Mozarts Schauspieldirektor*, 18–19.
25. *Deutscher Bühnenalmanach* for 1861.

existing numbers were insufficient to go round, Schneider prevailed upon Wilhelm Taubert to score up a few more.[26] The result was one of those dramatic changelings all too familiar from our own day, ostensible portraits of the lives of famous men that never fail to impress our theatre audiences, providing them with a *bonne bouche* of no artistic merit. Inevitably Schneider's scissors-and-paste job was hugely successful and in 1856 even reached the *Bouffes Parisiens*.[27] A related piece is Rudolf Genée's *Der Kapellmeister*, which was first performed at a Mozart concert in Berlin on 13 March 1896, before being revived at the Krolloper. Here, too, Mozart appeared in person, with other numbers by the composer being interpolated into the original score.[28]

Two German arias survive in the form of a draft score and, to judge by their handwriting, belong to this same period.[29] Both were presumably intended as insertion arias in singspiels by other composers. The first is a bass aria, *Männer suchen stets zu naschen* K433, for a character known only as Wahrmund, while the second is a tenor aria for a character called Carl, *Müßt ich auch durch tausend Drachen* K435.

Meanwhile, much to Mozart's surprise, the Italian opera received a tremendous boost when the emperor, acting partly on his own initiative and partly in response to a suggestion of Salieri's, assembled a company that was acclaimed by audiences and connoisseurs alike.[30] It concentrated in the main on *opere buffe* but occasionally performed serious works, too, usually in honour of famous singers: in 1783 Gluck's *Iphigénie en Tauride* was staged in Italian as a vehicle for the elderly Bernasconi[31] and in 1785 Sarti's *Giulio Sabino* was performed with the castrato Luigi Marchesi.[32] Of the older generation of German singers, Ruprecht, Adamberger and Saal and, among the women, Cavalieri, Lange, Teyber and Saal all switched their allegiance to the Italian company.[33] The distinguished buffo Francesco Benucci[34] was invited to join the company in 1783, and although he returned to Italy later that same year, his replacement, Marchesini [the stage name of Luigi Marchesi], proved so inadequate that he was invited back to Vienna in 1784.[35] Other members included the excellent baritone Stefano Mandini,[36] the bass Francesco Bussani,[37] Pugnetti and Mozart's friend, the tenor Michael Kelly. Other singers who came from Italy in 1783 included Nancy Storace, who that same year had also appeared in Italy ('detta l'Inglesina'),[38] and Maria Mandini. They were joined in 1785 by Celeste Coltellini, Teresa Calvesi,[39] Mmes Molinelli and Nani, and the German soprano Elisabeth Distler.

26. The 'Bandel' trio K441 ('Liebes Mandel, wo ist's Bandel?'), the aria *Männer suchen stets zu naschen* K433, and the songs *An Chloe* K524 and *Die betrogene Welt* K474.

27. Wilder, *Mozart: L'homme et l'artiste*, 255–6.

28. The text is reproduced in *Mitteilungen für die Mozart-Gemeinde in Berlin*, ii (April 1896), 35ff.

29. The date in the autograph – 1783 – has been added by an unknown hand.

30. Reichardt, 'Autobiographie', 665–6; and Pichler, *Denkwürdigkeiten aus meinem Leben*, i.78.

31. *Litteratur- und Theater-Zeitung*, Berlin, i (1784), 14.

32. Müller, *Abschied von der National-Schaubühne*, 7–8. ◆ Also see Rice, 'Benedetto Frizzi on Singers, Composers and Opera in Late Eighteenth-Century Italy'.

33. On the other hand, Mozart's first Osmin, the outstanding bass Ludwig Fischer, was dismissed, much to Mozart's dismay.

34. He appeared in Venice during the 1778/9 season; see Taddeo Wiel, *I teatri musicali veneziani nel Settecento*. ◆ Also see Rushton, 'Buffo Roles in Mozart's Vienna: Tessitura and Tonality as Signs of Characterization'.

35. *Litteratur- und Theater-Zeitung*, Berlin, i (1784), 14 and 19. ◆ Marchesini was the stage name of Luigi Marchesi.

36. He, too, came from Venice: see Wiel, *I teatri musicali veneziani*, 309ff. In 1776 he had appeared in Parma: see Ferrari, *Spettacoli drammatico-musicali e coreografici in Parma dall' anno 1628 all' anno 1883*, 38. ◆ Further, see Paissa, '"Questo è il conte, alla voce il conosco": Stefano Mandini prima di Mozart (1774–1783)'.

37. Wiel, *I teatri musicali veneziani*, 247ff. According to Ferrari, *Spettacoli drammatico-musicali in Parma*, 40, he appeared in Parma in 1782. ◆ See also Rushton, 'Buffo Roles in Mozart's Vienna'.

38. Wiel, *I teatri musicali veneziani*, 372–3.

39. According to Ferrari, *Spettacoli drammatico-musicali in Parma*, Calvesi appeared in Parma in 1784.

The Italian opera opened on 22 April 1783 with a revised version of Salieri's *La scuola de' gelosi*, which proved so successful that it had to be repeated no fewer than twenty-five times.[40] Although Salieri's [*recte* Cimarosa's] second opera of the season, *L'italiana in Londra*, which opened on 5 May, was less of a draw, Sarti's *Fra i due litiganti il terzo gode* turned out to be the hit of the season.[41] On 26 July 1783 Schröder wrote that 'The Italian opera is proving a great draw, while the German theatre is playing to empty houses.'[42]

When composers were commissioned to write new works for the Italian opera, Mozart was initially as studiously passed over as he had been by the German company, his only contributions being extra numbers for Anfossi's *Il curioso indiscreto* in 1783 and Bianchi's *La villanella rapita* in 1785. Although his hopes of writing a German opera had now begun to fade, he still wanted to compose an opera and so he turned his attention to the Italian troupe, whose achievements had clearly impressed him. Even by the end of 1782 he had, on Count Rosenberg's advice, set out in search of an Italian text, and now the successes of the Italian company reinforced him in this quest. On 7 May 1783 we find him writing to his father:

> The Italian *opera buffa* has started up again here and is proving very popular. The *buffo* is particularly good, he's called Benucci. I've looked through at least 100 librettos – probably more – but I've hardly found a single one with which I'd be satisfied, all of them would at least need changing here and there, and even if the poet were prepared to agree to this, it would probably be easier for him to write a completely new text; – and in any case a new text is always better. We have a certain Abbate da Ponte here as poet. He currently has an enormous amount to do in revising pieces for the theatre – he also has to write an entirely new libretto for Salieri *per obligo*, which he won't finish for another 2 months,[43] after which he's promised to write a new one for me. But who knows whether he'll be able – or willing – to keep his word! – You know these Italians are very civil to your face! – enough, we know them! If he's struck a deal with Salieri, I'll never get anything out of him as long as I live – and I'd so much like to prove myself in an Italian opera.[44]

As we have seen, Mozart's eye initially fell on Varesco, with whom he made personal contact while he was in Salzburg. The result of their collaboration was Varesco's libretto to *L'oca del Cairo*.[45] At the outset, Mozart was genuinely enthusiastic about the project, but the deeper he became involved in it, the more his reservations increased. Varesco had to make endless changes and finally seems not only to have derived little pleasure from the undertaking but to have lost patience with Mozart, with the result that after 10 February 1784 there is no further mention of the work in Mozart's letters and *L'oca del Cairo* – K422 – remained a torso. By the time that he abandoned it, Mozart had completed one of the recitatives and sketched out an aria for Biondello.

---

40. The critic of the Berlin-based *Litteratur- und Theater-Zeitung*, i (1784), 313, was less enthusiastic: 'The leading soprano sings well, but her acting is unbearable, whereas that of the *buffo* is so natural that he is regarded as the best ever seen here. The others are not worth mentioning.'

41. Cramer, *Magazin der Musik*, ii (1784), 185.

42. Friedrich Meyer, *Friedrich Ludwig Schröder*, i.345. A list of the operas performed between 1783 and 1790 may be found in Pohl, *Joseph Haydn*, ii.379ff. ◆ For a recent, exhaustive account, see Link, *The National Court Theatre in Mozart's Vienna*.

43. *Il ricco d'un giorno*, which was premièred on 6 December 1784.

44. *Briefe*, iii.268 (letter of 7 May 1783).

45. Mozart held out the promise of a profit of 400–500 florins for the poet, arguing that 'it's the custom here for the poet to receive the takings of the third performance' (*Briefe*, iii.268, letter of 7 May 1783).

Six additional numbers survive in draft score, with the vocal lines and bass written out in full, as usual, and the orchestral part merely hinted at.[46]

Various attempts have been made to complete these fragments, too. Victor Wilder created a two-act *L'oie du Caire* by adding the overture and introduction from *Lo sposo deluso*, the trio from *La villanella rapita* and an additional arietta of dubious authenticity. The instrumentation was entrusted to Titus Charles Constantin,[47] and in this form the work was performed to great acclaim at the Fantaisies Parisiennes on 6 June 1867. Other productions opened at the Friedrich-Wilhelmstädtisches Theater in Berlin on 4 October 1867 and at Vienna's Theater in der Leopoldstadt on 15 April 1868, but neither was particularly successful.[48]

In spite of this setback, Mozart continued to toy with the idea of writing an Italian opera and although he did not return to the Goldoni text, he became interested in 1783 or 1784 in another, older[49] libretto, *Lo sposo deluso* (The Deluded Bridegroom), with the subtitle *La rivalità di tre donne per un solo amante* (The Rivalry of Three Women for the Same Lover, K430). The date of composition emerges from the fact that Nancy Storace is described as Signora Fischer: she had married the English violin virtuoso John Abraham Fisher, but it proved an ill-considered step, as he treated her badly and in 1784 he was banished from Vienna by imperial decree.[50] As Nancy Storace did not use her husband's name after this, Mozart could have employed it only for a short time after her marriage.

Mozart's own list of characters runs as follows:

Primo Buffo caricato: *Bocconio* [Sempronio] Papparelli, uomo sciocco e facoltoso, promesso in marito ad Eugenia.	Sigre. *Benucci.*
Prima Buffa: *Eugenia* [Emilia], giovane Romana di nobili natali, alquanto capricciosa e promessa in consorte a Bocconio, ma fida amante di Don Asdrubale.	Sgra. *Fischer.*
Primo mezzo carattere: *Don Asdrubale* [Annibale], uffiziale Toscano, molto coraggioso ed amante di Eugenia.	Sigre. *Mandini.*
Seconda Buffa: *Bettina* [Laurina], nipote di Bocconio, ragazza vana ed inamorata di Don Asdrubale.	Sgra. *Cavalieri.*
Secondo Buffo caricato: *Pulcherio* [Fernando], sprezzator delle donne ed amico di Bocconio.	Sgre. *Bussani.*

46. Varesco's handwritten libretto and the full score are in the Berlin Library [now the Staatsbibliothek zu Berlin]. A vocal score by Julius André was published in 1855. See Waldersee, 'Varesco's L'Oca del Cairo, nach dem Originalhandschrift herausgegeben', 693–4; Gollmick, 'Eine nachgelassene Oper Mozarts'; and Genée, 'Mozarts Partitur-Entwurf seiner Oper "L'Oca del Cairo"'. ◆ Further on *L'oca del Cairo*, see Everson, 'Of Beaks and Geese: Mozart, Varesco and Francesco Cieco' and Czucha, 'Mozart's "Die Gans von Kairo": Zum Verhältnis von Satire und Lustspiel am Beispiel eines Opernfragments'.
47. Wilder, *Mozart*, 203.
48. Wurzbach, *Mozart-Buch*, 39–40 and 162–3; and Hanslick, *Die moderne Oper*, i: *Kritiken und Studien*, 49–50.
49. This emerges from the fact that Mozart altered the names of the characters that the copyist had given incorrectly. During the winter of 1787 an opera entitled *Lo sposo deluso*, with music by a Cavaliere Pado, was staged in Padua; see *Musikalische Real-Zeitung*, (1788), 85.
50. Kelly, *Reminiscences*, i.231–2; and Pohl, *Mozart und Haydn in London*, 169–70.

Secondo Buffo mezzo carattere: *Gervasio*, tu-
tore di Eugenia, che poi inamorasi di Me-
tilde.   Sgre. *Pugnetti.*

Terza Buffa: *Metilde*, virtuosa di canto e ballo,
anch' essa inamorata di Don Asdrubale e
finta amica di Bettina.   Sgra. *Teiber.*

The work was to have been in two acts. The only numbers that survive complete are the overture and introduction (the one follows the other without a break) and the trio for Eugenia,
Asdrubale and Bocconio in act one, scene nine. Eugenia's aria in act one, scene three, and
Pulcherio's aria in act one, scene four, both survive in draft form. This opera, too, was ultimately
abandoned. Another incomplete draft that has survived is of a comic trio for three male voices,
'Del gran regno dell'Amazoni' (K434), which, as Jahn rightly surmises,[51] comes from the opera *Il
regno delle Amazzoni*, which was first performed in Parma in 1783, before turning up in Florence
the following year.[52] This was no doubt another of the many librettos that Mozart studied at this
time.

But all these plans fell victim to the fact that none of them was an official commission – an
indispensable prerequisite at this time. Even Salieri had difficulty for a while in asserting himself
in the face of the triumphs of Sarti and Paisiello, but he could at least point to a number of major
successes away from Vienna, notably *Semiramide* in Munich in 1782[53] and especially *Les Danaïdes*
in Paris on 26 April 1784, a production that he owed to Gluck's patronage. As a result, his influence
in Vienna was steadily growing.

It was at this juncture that a curious concatenation of circumstances brought Mozart into
contact with a poet who at a stroke relieved him of all his difficulties and, as a result of his
collaboration, ensured his undying fame. Emmanuele Conegliano was born at Ceneda in
Venetia on 10 March 1749 but adopted the name of the Bishop of Ceneda, Lorenzo da Ponte,
when he and his family converted from Judaism to Christianity on 29 August 1763.[54] He
entered a seminary with a view to training for the priesthood and was ordained in 1773, with
the result that from now on he invariably referred to himself as the Abbate da Ponte. This
marked the beginning of a career notable not least for its amorous intrigues and battles with
the authorities that meant that he never remained in the same place for long. In 1774 he joined
the staff of the seminary at Treviso, but here, too, his stay proved shortlived and in 1776 he
was banished from Venetia after he had written a poem satirizing political events in the region.
With the help of a forged letter from the librettist Caterino Mazzolà, he sought refuge north of
the Alps, arriving in Dresden in 1780 and then, armed with a letter of recommendation from

51. Jahn, *W. A. Mozart*, ii.275. ◆ K434 was probably written down later, about 1786.

52. Not 1782, as stated by Jahn (who relied on Fétis; see Ferrari, *Spettacoli drammatico-musicali in Parma*, 40). The librettist was
Giuseppe Petrosellini (also known under his Arcadian name of Ensildo Prosindio) and the composer Agostino Accorimboni; see
Cramer, *Magazin der Musik*, ii (1784), 556.

53. Rudhart, *Geschichte der Oper am Hofe zu München*, 170–1.

54. See *Schweizerische Musik-Zeitung*, lxii/12; and Marchesan, *Della vita e delle opere di Lorenzo da Ponte* (Treviso, 1900). Da
Ponte's *Memorie* were published in four volumes in New York between 1823 and 1827, with a second edition following in
1829–30. A German translation appeared in volumes 814–16 of Spindler's *Belletristisches Ausland* (Stuttgart, 1847); a revised
edition of Burckhardt's translation was published in Gotha in 1861; see *AmZ*, xl (1838), 676–7, xli (1839), 788–9 and xliv (1842),
769–70. ◆ The standard English translation, by Elisabeth Abbott, edited by Arthur Livingston, was published in Philadelphia
in 1929. Further concerning Da Ponte, see Bolt, *Lorenzo Da Ponte: The Adventures of Mozart's Librettist in the Old and New
Worlds*; Hodges, *Lorenzo da Ponte: The Life and Times of Mozart's Librettist*; and Hunter, *The Culture of Opera Buffa in Mozart's
Vienna.*

Mazzolà to Salieri, moving to Vienna in 1781. Mozart first mentions Da Ponte's name in his letter of 7 May 1783 as the librettist of Salieri's *Il ricco d'un giorno*:[55] by this date Salieri had already recommended him to Joseph II and obtained a post for him as poet to the court theatre alongside Giovanni Battista Casti. But Salieri's opera proved a failure, and composer and librettist fell out, with Salieri swearing that he would sooner chop off his own fingers than set another line of Da Ponte's to music. Instead, Salieri renewed his links with Casti and enjoyed considerable success with his setting of the latter's *La grotta di Trofonio*, which opened on 12 October 1785. This led in turn to a bitter clandestine struggle between Da Ponte and Casti, who was not only his superior as a poet but also already well known, with a number of powerful patrons, including Count Rosenberg himself. Casti at once set about attacking his rival in a number of different ways, now with ironic praise, now with open criticism, and in his libretto to *Prima la musica e poi le parole* he alluded unmistakably to Da Ponte as a theatre librettist. By now Da Ponte had forfeited the sympathies of a good many people with his arrogant manner, and it was not difficult for the tenor Michael Kelly to mimic him in one of the librettist's own operas, *Il Demogorgone*, which was set by Vincenzo Righini in 1786, the accuracy of Kelly's portrayal eliciting 'a universal roar of laughter and applause' from the first-night audience.[56] Da Ponte's main aim, of course, was to find decent composers for his texts, and the first such composer to come his way was Vicente Martín y Soler (1754–1806), who owed his sobriquet of 'Lo Spagnuolo' to his Valencian extraction. Following early operatic successes in Spain, Soler had turned his attentions to Italy, where he is first recorded in Caserta in 1779, superintending a production of his *Ifigenia in Aulide*.[57] Between 1779 and 1785 there followed an impressive series of other works – mainly *opere buffe* – for Turin, Lucca, Parma and Venice.[58] His final successes in Italy were in Venice and Parma during the 1784/5 season, after which he moved on to Vienna, where he enjoyed the patronage of the influential wife of the Spanish ambassador. Here Da Ponte, acting on the instructions of Joseph II, who was always well disposed to him, worked up Goldoni's *Le bourru bienfaisant* into a libretto for Martín y Soler, which proved a brilliant success when staged as *Il burbero di buon core* on 4 January 1786. Da Ponte was less fortunate with his librettos for Gazzaniga's *Il finto cieco* (20 February 1786) and Righini's *Il Demogorgone* (12 July 1786), with the result that he renewed contact with Mozart, to whom he had already held out the prospect of a libretto in 1783.[59] The outcome of their collaboration was *Le nozze di Figaro*.

Mozart's last two librettists, Da Ponte and Schikaneder, were typical representatives of a remarkable period in which cheats and adventurers lived alongside true men of genius. Da Ponte was by no means lacking in intelligence, but his rational, critical faculties were far more developed than any creative vein, with the result that he was much more adept at reworking other writers' ideas than at creating an original work such as *Così fan tutte*. He lacked the most important quality necessary to become a true poet, pursuing his literary activities partly as a business venture, partly

55. *Briefe*, iii.268 (letter of 7 May 1783). On Da Ponte's activities, see also Boas, 'Lorenzo da Ponte als Wiener Theaterdichter'.
56. Kelly, *Reminiscences*, i.235–7.
57. Florimo, *La scuola musicale di Napoli e i suoi conservatorii*, iv.246.
58. Wiel, *I teatri musicali veneziani*, 366–7; and Ferrari, *Spettacoli drammatico-musicali in Parma*, 42. Kelly's claim (i.189–90) that one of his operas was hugely successful when performed with Nancy Storace in Venice appears to rest on a confusion with another work, perhaps Salieri's *La scuola de' gelosi*, which was revived in the city in 1783; see Wiel, *I teatri musicali veneziani*, 373.
59. ◆ Abert's argument here makes little sense. As he notes later, Leopold Mozart already knew of Mozart's work on *Figaro* in November 1785 and Wolfgang himself dated the opera 27 April 1786 in his thematic catalogue. So it is unlikely that the failures of *Il finto cieco* and *Il Demogorgone* in February and July 1786, respectively, led Da Ponte to renew contact with Mozart.

out of vanity and ambition. His character, too, was dubious in the extreme, with women, gambling, political rabble-rousing and the desire to create one literary sensation after another occupying much of his time. His burning ambition found expression in an often grotesque desire to push himself forward, and, as his memoirs make clear, he was never a stickler for the truth, with the result that these volumes of reminiscences need to be treated with extreme caution. He may have been the most gifted librettist that Mozart found, but he was also the most unscrupulous.

According to his memoirs, he was introduced to Mozart at the home of Baron Wetzlar, who, like Da Ponte, was Jewish. Wetzlar offered to pay the poet a 'decent' fee and to ensure that Mozart's opera was performed in Paris or London if it was not accepted in Vienna. Da Ponte is said to have turned down this offer and to have suggested instead that they should complete the work in secret and surprise the emperor with it. When the choice of a subject was raised, Mozart proposed an adaptation of Beaumarchais' comedy *Le mariage de Figaro*, a work that had held the world in a state of breathless suspense since its first performance in Paris on 27 April 1784.[60] It was a bold choice, as Joseph II had banned performances of the stage play at Vienna's National Theatre. But Da Ponte none the less hoped to overcome these difficulties and secretly set to work on his adaptation, with Mozart keeping pace with him in setting it to music, so that the whole opera was finished within the space of six weeks. By a stroke of luck, their labours coincided with a general dearth of new operas, with the result that Da Ponte went straight to the emperor and apprised him of the new piece. Joseph II expressed reservations on two counts: first, he had banned the play and, secondly, Mozart may have been a fine composer of instrumental music, but the opera he had recently written – presumably *Der Schauspieldirektor* – was only so-so ('non era gran cosa'). Da Ponte sought to reassure him, insisting that he had made a large number of cuts to the play and removed those passages that might offend against common decency and concluding by expressing the hope that he had created a work worthy of a theatre under His Majesty's immediate patronage. And he also spoke up in support of Mozart, with the result that Joseph relented, sent a lackey in search of the composer and, having listened to a playthrough of a handful of numbers, gave instructions for the work to be put into rehearsal. Casti was incensed at this, as was his puppet Count Rosenberg, and as Rosenberg was unable to prevent the rehearsals from going ahead, he at least put as many spokes in the production's wheel as he possibly could.[61]

Thus runs Da Ponte's account of the genesis of *Le nozze di Figaro*. In general it no doubt corresponds to the actual course of events, even if individual aspects owe more to the poet's love of sensationalist detail than they do to the sober truth. Although Mozart himself left no account of his own, a surviving letter from Leopold to his daughter, dated 11 November 1785, may serve as independent testimony:

---

60. This is the version of events given by Da Ponte in his *Memorie*. According to this version, the idea was entirely Mozart's, and this is indeed likely to have been the case, as Da Ponte was the last person to hide his light under a bushel. Even so, Arthur Schurig, pursuing to its logical conclusion his remarkable hostility to Jahn (*Wolfgang Amade Mozart*, ii.69), argues that the suggestion was Da Ponte's simply because Nissen states that the initial idea came from the emperor: Nissen, *Biographie W. A. Mozarts*, 492. This cannot be true, but even if it is, it does not prove that Da Ponte chose to play second fiddle to Mozart out of sheer magnanimity. According to Kelly, Mozart was invited by the emperor to write an opera and chose *Figaro*; Kelly, *Reminiscences*, i.257–8.
61. Da Ponte reports a highly significant incident in this regard: Rosenberg simply cut the third-act ballet (during the wedding celebrations), claiming that he had the emperor's backing. Mozart was beside himself with anger and almost resorted to violence. When this scene was rehearsed in the emperor's presence, the ballet was omitted, with the result that the scene between Susanna and the Count made no sense at all. Joseph noticed and, following representations from Da Ponte, finally gave instructions for the ballet to be reinstated.

I've finally received a letter from your brother, it's dated 2 November and is all of 12 lines long. He apologizes for not writing more, but he's up to his eyes in work on his opera *Le nozze di Figaro*. He thanks me and the two of you for your good wishes and asks me to apologize to you in particular and say that he hasn't time to answer your letter just now and that, in order to keep the morning free for composing, he has now shifted all his pupils to the afternoon and so on and so forth. – I know the piece, it's a very tiresome play and the translation from the French will certainly have to be changed if it's to be effective as an opera. God grant that the plot turns out well, I've no doubts about the music. But there'll be a lot of running about and a great deal of discussion before he gets the libretto exactly right – and, such is his delightful habit, he has no doubt kept putting things off and let them slide, but now he'll have to set to work in earnest, as Count Rosenberg is prodding him.[62]

Leopold's account is clearly at odds with Da Ponte's claim that work on the score was kept a strict secret. In his thematic catalogue, Mozart entered the opera under the date of 29 April 1786, the day on which – in keeping with his usual practice – he wrote the overture.[63] Equally implausible is Da Ponte's claim that the work was completed within the space of six weeks. On the other hand, there seems to be some truth in his remark that the opera encountered considerable resistance even during rehearsals, as Leopold, too, speaks of 'astonishingly powerful cabals', behind which he suspected Salieri and his hangers-on.[64] Certainly, Mozart was overwhelmed with work at the time that he was completing *Le nozze di Figaro*. Even by the standards of his unusually busy life, this period was particularly fraught with commissions: between 5 November 1785 and 29 April 1786, his thematic catalogue lists not only a number of shorter vocal works but also two large-scale keyboard concertos in E flat major K482 and C minor K491, the violin sonata in E flat major K481 and *Der Schauspieldirektor*.

As the day of the first performance drew closer, so Mozart's situation became more difficult, as Kelly reports:

62. *Briefe*, iii.443–4 (letter of 11 November 1785).

63. The score is now lodged in the Berlin Library. Mozart continued to make changes to it even after copies had already been made; see the critical report to NMA II/5/16, and Genée, 'Mozarts Partitur der "Hochzeit des Figaro"' and 'Die ersten Entwürfe Mozarts zu "Figaros Hochzeit"'. ◆ Since the upheavals of World War II, Mozart's autograph to *Figaro* is now split between the Staatsbibliothek zu Berlin (acts I and II) and the Biblioteka Jagiellońska, Kraków, Poland (acts III and IV).

64. *Briefe*, iii.536 (letter of 28 April 1786). Leopold's source was Franz Xaver Duschek, who, together with his wife, had passed through Vienna in early April on his way to Salzburg in order to sort out a legacy. ◆ Cabals against *Figaro* were similarly reported in the Viennese press: on 11 July 1786 the *Wiener Realzeitung* reported that 'Herr Mozart's music was generally admired by connoisseurs already at the first performance, if I except only those whose self-love and conceit will not allow them to find merit in anything not written by themselves. The *public*, however (and this often happens with the public), did not really know on the first day where it stood. It heard many a *bravo* from unbiased connoisseurs, but obstreperous louts in the uppermost gallery exerted their hired lungs with all their might to deafen singers and audience alike with their St! and Pst!' (*Dokumente*, 243–4, *Documentary Biography*, 278). Similarly, an anonymous pamphlet (*Uiber das deutsche Singspiel den Apotheker des Hrn. v. Dittersdorf* [Vienna, 1786]) noted a 'conspiracy by the aristocracy and some influential musical scholars' that found nothing good 'that has not been wafted to us by a foreign breeze. And these scholars have gone to so much trouble to decry every honourable man as an idiot.... For this reason it came to the point that – the poor German muse, hunted from the stage in order to tyrannize our taste with foreign nations ... it was unlikely ever again to find a German opera at the National Theatre ... [or] to hear good music for an Italian singspiel by a German master. [But] they have completely lost their bet, for Mozart's *Nozze di Figaro* ... [has] put to shame the ridiculous pride of this fashionable sect' (Eisen, *Dokumente: Addenda*, 111–12, *New Mozart Documents*, 45).

There were three operas now on the tapis, one by Regini [*Il Demogorgone*], another by Salieri (the Grotto of Trophonius[65]), and one by Mozart, by special command of the Emperor. Mozart chose to have Beaumarchais' French comedy, "Le Mariage de Figaro," made into an Italian opera, which was done with great ability, by Da Ponte. These three pieces were nearly ready for representation at the same time, and each composer claimed the right of producing his opera for the first. The contest raised much discord, and parties were formed. The characters of the three men were all very different. Mozart was as touchy as gunpowder, and swore he would put the score of his opera into the fire, if it was not produced first; his claim was backed by a strong party: on the contrary, Regini was working like a mole in the dark to get precedence.

The third candidate was maestro di cappella to the court, a clever shrewd man, possessed of what Bacon called, crooked wisdom; and his claims were backed by three of the principal performers, who formed a cabal not easily put down. Every one of the opera company took part in the contest. I alone was a stickler for Mozart, and naturally enough, for he had a claim on my warmest wishes, from my adoration of his powerful genius, and the debt of gratitude I owed him, for many personal favours.

The mighty contest was put an end to by His Majesty issuing a mandate for Mozart's "Nozze di Figaro," to be instantly put into rehearsal.[66]

Events of this kind were by no means exceptional at this time, of course.[67] Here, too, the main troublemakers seem to have been the singers, at least if we may believe Niemetschek, who, adducing 'reliable witnesses', even claims that the singers tried to undermine the opera by introducing deliberate mistakes, with the result that, at Mozart's insistence, they were personally rebuked by the emperor at the end of the opening act.[68] This appears to be an exaggeration, as Kelly states emphatically that the opening performances in Vienna were especially good:

All the original performers had the advantage of the instruction of the composer, who transfused into their minds his inspired meaning. I never shall forget his little animated countenance, when lighted up with the glowing rays of genius; – it is as impossible to describe it, as it would be to paint sunbeams. . . . I remember that at the first rehearsal of the full band, Mozart was on the stage with his crimson pelisse and gold-laced cocked hat, giving the time of the music to the orchestra. Figaro's song, 'Non più andrai, farfallone amoroso', Bennuci gave, with the greatest animation and power of voice.

I was standing close to Mozart, who, *sotto voce*, was repeating, Bravo! Bravo! Bennuci; and when Bennuci came to the fine passage, "Cherubino, alla vittoria, alla gloria militar," which he gave out with Stentorian lungs, the effect was electricity itself, for the whole of the performers on the stage, and those in the orchestra, as if actuated by one feeling of delight, vociferated Bravo! Bravo! Maestro. Viva, viva, grande Mozart. Those in the orchestra I thought would never have ceased applauding, by beating the bows of their violins against the music desks. The little man acknowledged, by repeated obeisances, his thanks for the distinguished mark of enthusiastic applause bestowed upon him.[69]

65. This is incorrect: Salieri's opera had already been given on 12 October 1785.
66. ◆ Kelly, *Reminiscences*, i.253–5.
67. They were to be repeated almost immediately afterwards at the first performance of Martín's *La cosa rara* on 17 November; see Da Ponte, *Memorie*.
68. Niemetschek, *Leben des k. k. Kapellmeisters Wolfgang Gottlieb Mozart*, 25.
69. ◆ Kelly, *Reminiscences*, i.255–6.

According to Mozart's thematic catalogue – the wordbook has unfortunately not survived[70] – the cast for the first performance was as follows:[71]

Il conte Almaviva	Sgre. Mandini.
La contessa	Sgra. Laschi.
Susanna	Sgra. Storace.
Figaro	Sgre. Benucci.
Cherubino	Sgra. Bussani.
Marcellina	Sgra. Mandini.
Basilio } Don Curzio }	Sgre. Ochelly.[72]
Bartolo } Antonio }	Sgre. Bussani.
Barbarina	Nannina Gottlieb.[73]

The first performance took place on 1 May 1786, and its reception lived up to expectations.[74] 'Never', wrote Kelly, 'was any thing more complete than the triumph of Mozart, and his "Nozze di Figaro."' The house was packed to the rafters, and many numbers had to be repeated, with the result that the opera lasted almost twice as long as planned, but even by the end of the performance the audience continued to applaud and to call Mozart back on stage. On 18 May we find Leopold writing to his daughter: 'At the second performance of *Figaro's Wedding* in Vienna [on 3 May] five numbers were repeated and at the third [on 8 May] seven, including a short duet that had to be sung three times.'[75]

So brilliantly successful was the work that Joseph was obliged to ban encores,[76] a decree that provoked somewhat mixed feelings in the singers.[77] During its first year the opera notched up nine performances (1, 3, 8, 24 May, 4 July, 28 August, 23 [*recte* 22] September, 15 November and 18 December), making it one of the most popular Italian works of the period, although it found a

---

70. ◆ In fact, three copies are known, all of them in the Stadtbibliothek, Vienna. For a facsimile, see Warburton, *The Librettos of Mozart's Operas*.

71. It is striking that the cast includes none of the German sopranos whom Mozart had reckoned on using in *Lo sposo deluso* – Aloysia Lange, Catarina Cavalieri and Therese Teyber, but their absence is no doubt due to the various factions described by Kelly, who notes that Cavalieri was Salieri's pupil and, therefore, specially favoured by him; see Kelly, *Reminiscences of Michael Kelly*, i.109, 110 and 135–6.

72. Thus Mozart's own orthography; Kelly himself reports that he was called 'Okelly' in Italy; see Kelly, *Reminiscences*, i.139.

73. She later sang Pamina in *Die Zauberflöte*.

74. The *Wiener Zeitung* of 3 May 1786 (no. 35) included only a brief notice: 'Monday, 1 May, a new Italian Singspiel in 4 acts, entitled "Le nozze di Figaro", after the French comedy by Herr von Beaumarchais, adaped by Herr Abb. da Ponte, the theatre poet; the music for it is by Herr Kapellmeister Mozart. La Sign. Laschi, who returned hither not long ago, and la Sign. Bussani, a new singer, made their first appearances on this occasion, as the Countess and the Page' [*Dokumente*, 240, *Documentary Biography*, 274].

75. *Briefe*, iii.546 (letter of 18–20 May 1786). After the second performance, Joseph Weigl took over from Mozart, directing from the keyboard; see *Jahresbericht des Wiener Konservatoriums für Musik*, new series, vii (1866/7), 5 [Deiters's note].

76. Following the third performance of *Le nozze di Figaro*, the poster advertising the performance of *L'italiana in Londra* on 12 May 1786 included a note: 'It is hereby publicly intimated that from now on, in order not to exceed the duration fixed for singspiels, no piece for more than a single voice will be repeated' [adapted from *Documentary Biography*, 275]. By the autumn, the ban had already been forgotten again: see Pohl, *Joseph Haydn*, ii.125.

77. Kelly reports that, after issuing this decree, Joseph II approached Nancy Storace, Mandini and Benucci at a rehearsal and announced that he believed he had done them a favour as such constant repetitions '"must be a great fatigue, and very distressing to you". Storace replied, "It is indeed, Sire, very distressing, very much so;" the other two bowed, as if they were of the same opinion. I was close to His Majesty, and said boldly to him, "Do not believe them, Sire, they all like to be encored, at least I am sure I always do." His Majesty laughed.' ◆ Kelly, *Reminiscences*, i.259.

dangerous rival in Martín's *Una cosa rara*, which received its first performance on 17 November and found favour with both the audience and the emperor, who used the occasion to repeat his earlier view, voiced at the time of *Die Entführung aus dem Serail,* that 'it was the singers' constant complaint that he drowned them with his full accompaniment'.[78] As a result of the success of *La cosa rara, Le nozze di Figaro* disappeared from the Viennese stage during the whole of 1787 and 1788, not reappearing until 29 August 1789.[79]

78. Dittersdorf, *Lebensbeschreibung,* 176.
79. In June 1787 Balzer & Co. announced in the *Wiener Zeitung* (appendix to no. 49) that the great success of *Le nozze di Figaro* in Prague had persuaded them to publish Johann Baptist Kucharz's vocal score. They also advertised arrangements for wind instruments and the Abbé Cajetan Vogel's arrangement for string quintet. ◆ Manuscript, as opposed to printed, vocal scores of *Figaro* were available considerably earlier: Lorenz Lausch had advertised copies in the *Wiener Zeitung* on 1 July 1786; see *Dokumente,* 242–3, *Documentary Biography,* 276–7.

36

Mozart's artistic creativity

The nature of artistic creativity has always had a powerful attraction for the non-artistic section of humanity who, depending on their own disposition, tend to think of it in either mystical or rational terms. But there are also many who seek a middle way and regard the actual creative act as something not amenable to rational interpretation, whereas the subsequent elaboration of what has been created in this way belongs more or less in the realm of artistic appreciation, a distinction which, although generally only tentatively drawn, still smacks very much of rationalism. According to this view, the artist begins by drawing on his imagination, then on his intellect, with everything neatly ordered. If only clarity and order could be brought so readily to all such irrational matters.[1]

That the actual act of creation remains impervious to rational analysis is entirely natural, for it is an elemental expression of life, a psychological experience and, moreover, one that is alien to most people's world of experience. The only question is whether this creative act extends to the entire work and not just to its basic musical ideas, as these people imagine, and whether, in consequence, the intellect has no role whatsoever to play here. After all, we speak of intellectual art, in other words, art that makes no psychological sense because it is not based on inner experience, and we draw a very precise distinction between the textbook fugue of a beginner and the fugue of a composer such as Bach. At the same time, however, we speak of music which, because of its composer's unbridled imagination, fails to convey a sense of ordered, logical structure and, as a result, loses its effectiveness. In short, we assume a certain degree of theoretical insight on the part of every artist. But how does this 'artistic understanding' operate? What are its aims? And how is it distinguished from the freely creative imagination?

Artistic understanding is generally taken to mean an insight into a particular set of formal rules derived from existing works of art that have already proved their worth. Consciously or unconsciously, they impress themselves on the artist and give him a sense of direction. The average artist – the one who is merely talented – will allow himself to be guided by this insight in his work and will use it to test the products of his imagination, assuming that these do not already move in this direction at the moment of their conception. This is not the case with the artist of genius. It is not his calling to repeat old, familiar ideas in a new guise but to create something new: he is not bound by historical or aesthetic laws from the past. But it is not a question – as it was for the members of the *Sturm und Drang* movement – of simply ignoring the laws of art in general: our great German classics are the work of men and women fully aware of what is permissible and expedient in art. But artistic understanding may not always help them to adapt their work to conform to some preexistent theory. Rather, it helps them to devise a new rule for their new creation, a rule that must be obeyed if the work of art is to emerge in all its purity and in a fully convincing manner.

---

1. Abert, 'Über Aufgaben und Ziele der musikalischen Biographie', 427.

Here artistic understanding derives its standards not from outside but from the work of art itself, coming into operation not before the creative act but during it and thus assuming a creative aspect of its own.

This is not to be taken in the popular sense, of course: it is not as if artistic understanding creates the work of art by acting in prudent conjunction with the imagination. The intellect is no doubt capable of generating new ideas and of suggesting certain guidelines, whether in a positive sense or with critical intent, but it can never produce the musical ideas themselves. These remain the exclusive preserve of the creative imagination. The intellect is incapable of providing a musical organism with even the least transitional link without the psychological experience turning all of a sudden into a mere mathematical exercise: there is no point in deluding ourselves on this score. But the intellect can no doubt motivate the creative individual by keeping pace with his imagination, not as a strict critic for ever reminding him of a particular set of rules, but as his ally, an ally that shares the same new goals and lends its products the inner structure that may in certain cases be necessary. It may sometimes draw its attention to the error of its ways and persuade it to change direction, but a new creative act on the part of the imagination will always be needed before these changes become effective within the work itself. In most cases we are emphatically not dealing with a purely mechanical change or with the insertion of new links. With Mozart especially, we shall later have occasion to see how imagination and a creative understanding of art often go over the same old ground all over again merely for the sake of an apparently minor change, thereby allowing the new shoot to emerge as though organically from the old stem.

Needless to say, the whole of the creative process takes place in the artist's head. It is a process that culminates in the notes on the page, but these notes are no more than the end-product, communicating the work of art to the outside world. By contrast, the sketch, whether of brief and fleeting ideas or of relatively long pieces, serves to fix the work in the artist's memory at a particular stage of its genesis or, rather, to provide him with clues that enable him to call back to mind at any given moment the relevant artistic experience. These sketches are naturally of a primitive, abbreviated kind, using keywords, as it were, and no one should think that the artist himself heard the work in his inner ear in this cursory form. Of course, his sketches are of immense value for the genesis of the work, but what they reflect is not the mental work that went into them but only the superficial result of that work at one or more specific stages, and they do so, moreover, in a heavily abridged form intelligible only to the composer. Neither with Mozart nor with Beethoven[2] does the order of the sketches represent a steadily ascending line culminating in the definitive fair copy. In short, they do not afford an 'insight into the master's workshop', desirable though this insight may be. Beethoven left more sketches than average, Mozart fewer, but both composers created their works not on the page but in their heads, with the result that the greatest care is needed when interpreting their sketches, as we can never know how much the artist's imagination added here.

That Mozart himself never expressed any views on the creative process[3] is hardly surprising, given the fact that one tends not to waste words on a process as natural as breathing or the beating of a heart, and even if he had ever thought of doing so, he would almost certainly have lost interest again in the first flush of creativity. Moreover, the creative urge never really left him, even when he was preoccupied with other, non-artistic matters. He himself told his father that he was 'soaked in

---

2. See Nottebohm, *Beethoveniana, Zweite Beethoveniana*, and *Ein Skizzenbuch von Beethoven aus dem Jahre 1803*; see also Riemann, 'Spontane Phantasietätigkeit und verstandesmäßige Arbeit in der tonkünstlerischen Produktion'. ◆ For the best modern guide to Beethoven's sketches, see Johnson, Tyson and Winter, *The Beethoven Sketchbooks: History, Reconstruction, Inventory*.
3. The letter to the 'dear baron' mentioned below includes an extremely stupid passage on this subject.

music, immersed in it all day long'. He loved 'to plan works and to study and think about music'.[4] And Sophie Haibel recalled that

> he was always in a good mood, but even in the best of moods, he remained very pensive, always looking you keenly in the eye, replying in a considered way to everything, whether it be happy or sad, and yet he always seemed deep in thought and appeared to be working on something quite different. Even when he washed his hands in the morning, he would pace up and down the room and never stood still, but kept kicking his heels together and was always thoughtful. At table he often took a corner of the napkin, screwed it up tightly and wiped it back and forth beneath his nose, apparently unaware of what he was doing and often contorting his mouth as he did so.[5]

We have already had occasion to mention this inner agitation. Even his barber often had to chase after him with the ribbon for his pigtail whenever he suddenly got up and ran over to the harpsichord while his hair was being done.[6] And he continued to work on the piece in hand even while he was playing billiards or bowls or out riding, and the same was true when he was in company: his close circle of friends may well have suspected that, behind his witty conversation, his mind was still teeming with ideas, but the rest of the world was unaware of this. And if he was listening to music by other composers and it failed to hold his attention, he continued to work away at ideas of his own.

This explains his instinctive dislike of writing down his works. 'Everything has been composed – but it's not yet written down.'[7] This idea returns again and again in his letters in all manner of variants. It was a dislike that caused Leopold endless headaches. A model of bourgeois practicality, he tended to judge his son's achievements by their visible results, knowing all too well that even the finest works are of no use if they are not written down. As a result he was for ever nagging his son about 'not always putting things off', and he even accused him of a lack of application, a charge against which Mozart, from his superior standpoint, was fully justified in defending himself.[8] For him, writing out the piece was a purely mechanical process that took up time he would rather have spent on new works and that prevented him from giving his imagination free rein. The mental anguish caused by this outward constraint is palpable. His dislike of writing things down was reinforced by his phenomenal memory: once ideas had taken shape in his head, they were so firmly fixed that a long time could elapse before he wrote them down, and the circumstances in which he did so could be unpropitious in the extreme. Here one thinks of Constanze's account of the genesis of the third of the string quartets dedicated to Haydn – the one in D minor [K421] – which he wrote down during the birth of their first child in the summer of 1783.[9] Each time she cried out in pain, Mozart got up from his desk in order to reassure her, then returned to his work. He was working on the menuetto and trio when she gave birth. She specifically speaks of Mozart writing down the music, and so she cannot have been referring to the actual composition of the piece, even though this cannot be entirely ruled out, given what we know about his method of composition. An even more striking example of Mozart's lack of interest in the mechanical process of writing

---

4. *Briefe*, ii.427 (letter of 31 July 1778).
5. Nissen, *Biographie W. A. Mozarts*, 627–8.
6. Jahn, *W. A. Mozart*, fourth edition, ii.131.
7. *Briefe*, iii.78 (letter of 30 December 1780). ◆ Further, see Ulrich Konrad, *Mozarts Schaffensweise: Studien zu den Werkautographen, Skizzen und Entwürfen* and 'Neuentdecktes und wiedergefundenes Werkstattmaterial Wolfgang Amadeus Mozarts: Erster Nachtrag zum Katalog der Skizzen und Entwürfe'; for a specific example, Konrad, '"In seinem Kopfe lag das Werk immer schon vollendet": Bemerkungen zu Mozarts Schaffensweise am Beispiel des Klaviertrios B-Dur KV 502'.
8. *Briefe*, iii.121 (letter of 26 May 1780).
9. Constanze Mozart, 'Noch einige Kleinigkeiten aus Mozarts Leben', 854–5.

out the music is his own report of the genesis of the prelude and fugue that he sent to his sister in 1782.[10] In this case he worked out the prelude in his head while simultaneously committing the fugue to paper, apologizing to Marianne for the fact that, as a result, the prelude comes after the fugue in the autograph score.

In consequence, it is hardly surprising that Mozart sometimes delayed work on a score until it was almost literally wrung from him by force of circumstances. The most famous example of this is the well-known tale of the genesis of the overture to *Don Giovanni*, reported by Niemetschek as follows:

Mozart wrote this opera in Prague in 1787; it was already finished and had been rehearsed and was due to be performed in two days' time, but the overture-sinfonia was still missing. The anxiety and worries on the part of his friends, which grew with each passing hour, seemed merely to be a source of amusement to him; the more concerned they became, the more nonchalant Mozart pretended to be. Finally, on the eve of the first performance, having joked to his heart's content, he went to his room at around midnight, started to write and completed *this extraordinary masterpiece within a matter of hours.*[11]

Constanze adds a few details of her own to this entirely plausible account:

On the eve of the first performance of *Don Giovanni* in Prague, after the final dress rehearsal had already taken place, he told his wife that he intended to write the overture that night and asked her to make some punch for him and to remain by his side in order to keep him awake. She did so, telling him tales of Aladdin's lamp, Cinderella and so on, while tears of laughter rolled down his cheeks. But the punch made him so sleepy that he nodded off whenever she stopped and worked only when she told him these stories. But the effort involved, together with his drowsiness and frequent tendency to nod off and then suddenly start up again, made the work so difficult that his wife finally encouraged him to lie down on the couch and sleep, promising to wake him after an hour. But he slept so soundly that she did not have the heart to wake him and it was not until two hours later that she did so. It was now 5 o'clock. The copyist had been told to come at 7; by 7 the overture was finished.[12]

We owe another version to Anton Genast, who was a young actor in Prague at this time. According to this account, Mozart had drunk so much tokay at a party at the home of a local cleric that Genast and another friend had to take him home and put him to bed in an unconscious state; they themselves fell alseep on the couch. In the middle of the night they were woken by a noise: 'Mozart was sitting at his desk and working. Just after seven o'clock he entrusted the finished score to his friends with the request that they take it to the four copyists at the theatre so that it could be copied. The ink on some of the parts was still wet when they were placed on the music stands that evening.'[13] Other stories circulated, according to which Mozart had three overtures in his head, with Duschek and Bassi choosing the one in D minor. The other two were simply never written down.[14]

10. *Briefe*, iii.202 (letter of 20 April 1782).
11. Niemetschek, *Leben des k. k. Kapellmeisters Wolfgang Gottlieb Mozart*, 55–6.
12. Nissen, *Biographie W. A. Mozarts*, 520 and 651.
13. Genast, *Aus dem Tagebuch eines alten Schauspielers*, i.3–4.
14. See Lyser, 'Mozartiana: Mozart's Leben', 27; all the different versions are summarized by Freisauff, *Mozarts Don Juan 1787 bis 1887: Ein Beitrag zur Geschichte dieser Oper*, 31.

With their curious mixture of amazement and sensationalism, these tales are typical of the way in which ordinary people attempt to explain the otherwise inexplicable workings of genius. According to Constanze, there were even resourceful exegetes who claimed to hear in the music the composer's nodding off and starting up from his sleep. The tenacity with which philistines continue to believe in the image of the 'miracle of Mozart' that they have constructed for themselves is clear from an inauthentic letter from the composer to a 'dear, kind baron' that was already in circulation in Rochlitz's day[15] and that still resurfaces from time to time, when it is invariably described as 'previously unpublished'. Meanwhile, it continues to circulate in private ownership in countless copies. With the qualities ascribed to him here, Mozart could effortlessly appear at any second-rate nightclub as a 'musical phenomenon'.

If there is any truth to the story about the overture to *Don Giovanni* (and Mozart himself has nothing to say on the subject), it is that he had long since worked out the piece in his head and merely wanted to put off to the last minute the tiresome task of writing it down. In the popular imagination, this final, purely mechanical stage in the compositional process is assumed to be the only stage in that process, resulting in the highly unfortunate and, indeed, totally inaccurate picture of a composer who wrote with uncanny speed and facility, a picture that many people continue to accept even now.

Given Mozart's dislike of writing anything down (and we moderns should not try to emulate Leopold and equate this dislike with indolence),[16] it is entirely natural that a large number of his works were simply never written down. Strange though it may sound, only a part of his oeuvre has survived: the rest he himself kept from us. During his early years there were more such works than there were towards the end of his life, when he was driven by material necessity to write more of them down in order to turn his creativity to greater financial advantage.[17]

There is a widespread belief that Mozart wrote music more effortlessly than virtually any other composer in the whole history of music and that, as such, he was the exact opposite of Beethoven, for whom the act of creation became what he himself called 'a real effort'. This is a somewhat bold claim, of course, when we recall Beethoven's phenomenal gift for improvisation. If Beethoven wrote fewer works, the reasons for this certainly do not lie in a less fertile imagination but in the change that affected all musicians and the conditions under which they created works that had quite different spiritual and intellectual aims from those of the earlier period. But not even in Mozart's case did his large-scale works issue from his soul with the ease that many observers believe to have been the case. The works themselves are the best possible proof of this, for, however immediate our emotional response to them, they invariably create the impression of a conscious design, never of a flight of unbridled fantasy. Moreover, Mozart was completely clear in his own mind about the meaning and nature of his art from both a historical and an aesthetic standpoint. And, last but not least, the creative understanding of art of which we spoke earlier was something that he had in abundance. He himself described his 'Haydn' quartets as the fruits of a long and strenuous effort[18] and, prior to the first performance of *Don Giovanni* in Prague, he told the local conductor Johann Baptist Kucharz, 'No effort has been spared in producing something outstanding for Prague. I assure you, my dear friend, no one has taken as much trouble as I have

15. First published by Rochlitz, *AmZ*, xvii (1815), 561–2; reprinted in Jahn, *W. A. Mozart*, iii.496ff., and Schurig, *Wolfgang Amade Mozart*, ii.295ff.
16. See Schurig, *Wolfgang Amade Mozart*, ii.315.
17. See Nissen, *Biographie W. A. Mozarts*, 694: 'The great industriousness of the final years of his life consisted in the fact that he wrote more down.'
18. *Briefe*, iii.404 (dedication of 1 September 1785) [*Dokumente*, 220, *Documentary Biography*, 250].

in studying composition. I doubt whether there is a single famous composer whose works I have not studied diligently and in many cases more than once.' Even during the years of his maturity, the works of other great composers were still to be seen lying on his desk.[19]

The actual nature of the act of artistic creation will no doubt always remain hidden from us, yet it is clear from all that we know about Mozart's way of working that we should see in it not a voluntary act determined by external factors, but a vital expression of the most elemental kind. The musical 'idea' is not the result of some non-artistic experience but is the experience itself. Only in a handful of works forced upon him by professional necessity does Mozart's genius descend into the world of mere talent, treating art as an end in itself and deigning to imitate a reality that is not in fact his; here he allows himself to be inspired by something outside himself. Yet even here genius often demands its due and suddenly fires the alien reality with the glow of his own experience so that this alien reality finally falls away like ash. Think, for example, of the wind serenade in C minor [K388]. Moreover, Mozart's ability to experience the world expressed itself in different ways at different stages of his development. It is already at work, fully active, in his youth, but at this stage it still lacks all sense of clarity and independence, not yet drawing on its own resources but on its surroundings. The only genuinely Mozartian element here is the incredible openness to new ideas, the unbridled urge to imitate and the astonishing ability – in spite of the lack of elemental experiences – to achieve complete mastery of the most varied forms and styles within so short a time. Only later, following his return from Italy, did Mozart gradually acquire the strength to swim against the current, a current that he had hitherto allowed to carry him along, and become conscious of his own reality. At the same time, the elemental experience increasingly replaces the derivative experience in his works. The derivative experience is something he shared with other composers whose art he first had to transcend, while the elemental experience belonged to him and him alone. Only now did his way of working acquire its extraordinary originality.

It has often been noted that Mozart's ideas sprang from his brain not in a state of molten malleability but as fixed shapes harnessed and structured by a powerful sense of form. From the very outset, they are products of culture, not of nature. What is at work here, then, is that creative understanding of art that at the moment of the work's conception discovers the formal law inherent in it. But this suggests that when Mozart conceived the thematic material of a piece – in other words, its individual ideas – he was also conscious of its potential for organic development, a potential that in most cases was more or less realized. In short, the initial act of creation produced a tightly structured, clearly fashioned work at a single stroke. Particularly in the case of shorter occasional works, this initial conception may also have constituted the piece's definitive form: this was certainly true of the song written for Karoline von Keeß that he wrote in a coffee-house or the contredanses that he promised Count Johann Pachta in Prague in the early months of 1787. His failure to produce these pieces prompted the count to summon him to his home an hour before the meal and to give him writing materials with the instructions that he write the dances there and then as they were to be performed that very day. By the time that the meal had started, nine dances for full orchestra had been completed in full score.[20] In the case of longer pieces, the actual 'labour', as Mozart tended to call it, continued after the initial conception had

19. Niemetschek, *Leben des k. k. Kapellmeisters Wolfgang Gottlieb Mozart*, 85.

20. Nissen, *Biographie W. A. Mozarts*, 561. In his critical commentary to the AMA edition (40), Nottebohm doubts whether these nine works are the four quadrilles and five contredanses K510, some of which include titles such as 'La favorite', 'La fenite' (fuite? fenice?) and 'La pyramide', as neither the autograph nor the works themselves are of undisputed authenticity. In the sixth of these pieces a theme appears in the piccolos and bass drum that Carl Maria von Weber later used in his cantata *Kampf und Sieg*, describing it as an 'Austrian Grenadiers' March'; see Max Maria von Weber, *Carl Maria von Weber*, iii.97. Perhaps it was a traditional Austrian theme. ◆ K510 is now considered uncertain, and possibly not by Mozart. The idea that they were composed for Johann Pachta in Prague in 1787 derives from Jahn, *W. A. Mozart*, iii.457.

taken place, with the tonal image that he had first heard in his mind's ear forming the nucleus from which everything else was later organically developed, while being constantly refashioned and shaped. If we may extend the organic imagery, his imagination may often have produced rank or stunted offshoots that threatened to destroy the organism, in which case it was entirely typical of Mozart that, as we shall shortly discover from his sketches, he did not introduce the new shoot at the relevant point of fracture but retraced his steps and approached the critical passage again with the broadest of run-ups. Here, too, then, Mozart operated along entirely organic lines, never proceeding in a purely mechanical way but making changes within the context of the overall picture, rather than on the basis of an individual passage.

Mozart's surviving sketches give us occasional insights into this process but they are far from representing it in its entirety. Still less are they connected to it on a deeper level in the sense that the process would be incomplete or even impossible without them. Many are very brief and rapid jottings down of spontaneous ideas of a kind that Mozart's restless imagination was perpetually producing, even though he may have had no plans to elaborate them any further at this stage. In other cases, other circumstances may have prevented him from elaborating them. Mozart always used to carry around with him a portfolio containing blank sheets of manuscript paper in which he wrote down these ideas and that he jokingly called a portfolio for his stocks and shares.[21] Unfortunately, very few of these folios have survived. Mozart himself evidently set little store by them and by the need to keep them, suggesting that a considerable number of them were used and elaborated. One example of such a use is the first three lines of the first sketch: these are three brief attempts to start three different pieces, evidently keyboard works, none of which proceeded beyond this initial stage. The fugue subjects mentioned above likewise come under this heading.

During the years when Mozart was particularly responsive to new artistic impressions we can see how, even in conceiving his ideas, he stuck closely to these models, before attempting to reshape and develop them. Here, then, we are dealing not with original ideas, but with ones that are plainly derivative – with the creative imitation of foreign trends in music. In the sketches appended to Stadler's exercise book, for example, we suddenly come across Handel's chorus 'See, the conquering hero comes', followed by a number of sketches whose nucleus is clearly Handelian in inspiration, whether it be in terms of their melody and rhythm, as in the brief

or more generally, as in the following sketches:

The same is true of the fugue subjects modelled on Bach.[22]

21. Rochlitz, *Für Freunde der Tonkunst*, third edition, ii.179ff.
22. Lach, *W. A. Mozart als Theoretiker*, 33–4 and 77–8.

The sketches of works that Mozart started with the firm resolve of completing them are considerably more developed. The keyboard sketches on the folio just described are immediately followed by the first draft of the *buffa* trio for two basses and tenor K434, presumably from the summer of 1783,[23] a sketch that also survives in the form of a draft score. This latter is no longer a sketch in the usual sense of the term but a fair copy of a piece already fully worked out in Mozart's head but, for reasons that remain unclear, one that he failed to complete. The sketch itself contains only the initial germ cells.[24]

This last-named sketch represents the version in which Mozart heard the work in his mind's ear at the time that he wrote it down, a version fairly close to the form it finally assumed. Most of Mozart's sketches are of this nature, revealing, as they do, the artistic organism at an already fairly advanced stage of its development. The earlier sketches were either played out entirely within his head or have been lost as they were replaced by the later ones. But we must never lose sight of the fact that, whenever Mozart returned to such a sketch and whatever non-specialists may think, he did not simply turn it into a complete score in his head, but already heard the work in its entirety. In short, he was primarily occupied not with questions of notation but with musical images.[25] Prior to the final stage of composition, Mozart seems to have liked to make one final abbreviated draft, perhaps in order to mark it off from other works currently on the stocks, perhaps also simply because he wanted to document the importance that it had for him shortly before its completion. It is entirely conceivable that this modus operandi reflects Leopold's continuing influence. For such was Mozart's extraordinary musical memory that he did not need such an aide-mémoire. The tonal image that he had created in his mind's ear was so firmly lodged in his brain that it could be recalled to mind at any given moment. On his concert tours, for example, he generally played his keyboard concertos more or less from memory without first having had to learn them in the way that virtuosos generally do. Nor did he have any difficulty in occasionally going back to earlier works that he had not performed for some time.[26] In Prague – to take another example – he wrote out the trumpet and timpani parts for the second-act finale of *Don Giovanni* without having the full score in front of him. When he took the parts down to orchestra in person, he drew the players' attention to a passage where they would find a mistake, but he could not say whether there were four bars too many or four bars too few. It later turned out that there was indeed a mistake here.[27]

23. ◆ Paper studies suggest that this sketch dates from 1786.
24. The long ritornello was the first passage to be added to the score. This was no doubt the general rule with Mozart's vocal works: he set out from the dramatic characters and from their musical expression in the relevant situation on stage, allowing himself to be inspired by these to produce his instrumental introductions. The sketch begins with the melody for Polipodio on a single system with no indication of the harmonies. The first seven bars are the same as those found in the definitive version, but the sketch then includes a violin figure of which the full score retains only the final crotchet on *g″*, with the interlude based on it made a whole bar shorter. From this point onwards sketch and full score are identical, with the exception of a handful of minor changes such as the shortening of individual phrase endings from crotchets to quavers. But the sketch of Villotto's 'Dunque il grano etc.' continues with a completely different and uncharacteristic eight-bar passage that Mozart almost immediately discarded, deleting it and replacing it with the far livelier version found in the full score. The two staves that became available as a result of this deletion were then used to notate the imitative two-bar interlude which, in the full score, is allotted to the winds; motivically, it is the same as in the full score, but the manner of its elaboration is different. The phrase 'Per amor di Livia cara' is already present in the sketch, where it is followed by a whole bar's rest indicating that Mozart had the wind interlude in his head when sketching this passage. In the following passage, the elaborate coloratura on 'vagheggiar' is missing from the sketch. Three staves are used in the sketch for the passage where all three voices come together, but, conversely, there are no indications as to the accompaniment here, with not even the bass being notated. The last ten bars in the full score are missing from the sketch.
25. ◆ For an instance where Mozart was concerned with both notation and 'musical image', see Wolf-Dieter Seiffert, 'Mozart's "Haydn" Quartets: An Evaluation of the Autographs and First Edition, with Particular Attention to mm. 125–42 of the Finale of K. 387'.
26. Niemetschek, *Leben des k. k. Kapellmeisters Wolfgang Gottlieb Mozart*, 56, mentions an older concerto that Mozart played entirely from memory as he had forgotten to bring with him the soloist's part.
27. Nissen, *Biographie W. A. Mozarts*, 560.

That this ability to retain a whole piece extended to works by other composers was already mentioned in the context of Allegri's *Miserere*. Later, too, he revealed other instances of this same ability.[28]

This explains why, whenever he played new works of his own, Mozart performed his own part either almost entirely from memory or from a part that included only the most basic information – mere prompts for his memory. Here one thinks not only of his keyboard concertos but of the sonata that he performed with Regina Strinasacchi. But a large proportion of his sketches bear a similar imprint, including the one for his setting of Michael Denis's ode *O Calpe, Dir donnerts am Fuße*. The vocal line and bass are written out in full, with the accompaniment indicated in sufficient detail to allow even those with no immediate connection with the work to gain an idea of its definitive form. The same is true of the sketch of an aria intended for *L'oca del Cairo*, except that in this case the use of a clarinet is indicated at one point.[29] How much work preceded these sketches is no longer possible to say, still less whether these would have been the final versions, had these works been completed. The draft of the trio from *Lo sposo deluso* ('Che accidenti'), for example, has only its opening motif in common with the later version,[30] whereas the development section is totally different. Conversely, the vocal lines in the sketches of an aria for *Idomeneo* and of the tenor aria *Per pietà, non ricercate* K420 are virtually identical to those found in the finished score: the divergencies between them are few in number and insignificant in kind. This may also help us to evaluate the sketches for the incomplete movements of the mass in C minor, the *Requiem* and *L'oca del Cairo*: here, too, the vocal lines and bass are written out in full, while the accompaniment is limited to a handful of characteristic elements.[31] Indeed, even the complete full scores occasionally still reveal traces of this working method in the form of their different types of ink and handwriting, a hand that is more hurried in the later entries than in the earlier ones.[32]

Occasionally – and this is especially true of the major works – we can see how Mozart's imagination remains active up to the very last moment, affecting even apparently minor details. In his arias, for example, he sometimes adds little highlights and makes alterations, only a small number of which were undertaken to please his singers: by far the majority of these changes go to the very heart of the piece and its underlying characterization. One example of this is the Count's aria in *Le nozze di Figaro*, which originally ended as follows:

The second bar was then expanded to include the familiar four-bar coloratura passage that is so well observed from a psychological point of view, with the Count, in his wounded pride, once again

---

28. *Briefe*, iii.165 (letter of 6 Octopber 1781). ◆ '. . . I am beginning to become impatient at not being able to go on writing my opera [*Die Entführung*] . . . all my enthusiasm is for my opera and what would at other times require fourteen days to write I can now do in four. In one day I composed Adamberger's aria in A ['O wie ängstlich'], Cavalieri's in B flat ['Ach ich liebte, war so glücklich']and the trio ['Marsch, marsch, marsch! trollt euch fort!'], and copied them out in a day and a half.'
29. NMA II/5/13, 89.
30. NMA II/5/14, 112.
31. In the *Requiem*, this is the case from the 'Dies irae' to the 'Quam olim'; on *L'oca del Cairo*, see Genée, 'Mozarts Partitur-Entwurf seiner Oper "L'Oca del Cairo"', 274–5.
32. In his edition of the full score of the overture to *Die Zauberflöte*, André distinguished the first version from the later one by means of a different colour of ink. ◆ For a comprehensive account of Mozart's sketches, including transcriptions, see NMA X/30/3 and Ulrich Konrad, *Mozarts Schaffensweise*.

enjoying a foretaste of triumph in an unbridled outburst of instinctive pleasure. And how delightful is Figaro's inward smile as he declares his love for the disguised Susanna in the fourth-act finale of the same work:

un ri - sto - ro al mio cor con - ce - de - te

Compare this with the far weaker first version:

un ri - sto - ro al mio cor con - ce - de - te

In her duet with Fiordiligi ('Ah guarda, sorella') in *Così fan tutte*, Dorabella originally sang:

se fiam - ma, se dar - di non sem - bran scoc - car

The final version runs as follows:

se fiam - ma, se dar - di non sem - bran scoc - car

Here the earlier resolve has been transformed into roguish grace, a quality far better suited to Dorabella's character.

　The characteristic motif in Donna Anna's 'vengeance aria' ('Or sai chi l'onore') in *Don Giovanni*

Or sai chi l'o - no - re ra - pir a me vol - se chi fu il tra - di - to - re

was originally as follows:

Or sai chi l'o - no - re ra - pir a me vol - se chi fu il tra - di - to - re

Here the improvement affects not only the declamation (how well the main ideas of 'sai', 'rapir' and 'fu' are now brought out!), but also the ethos of the melody, which is no longer as emotionally overwrought in the style of an *opera seria* but more appropriate to the emotional world of a profoundly agitated young woman whose true characteristics emerge in the course of her aria.

Perhaps the most brilliant example of one of these last-minute changes is the Countess's aria ('Dove sono') in *Le nozze di Figaro*, the first section of the allegro of which (from bar 8) originally ended as follows:

The bars familiar to us now are written beneath the above and the original bass has been erased. Later in the Allegro, the three bars

were originally simply repeated after the orchestral interlude and were followed by

At this juncture Mozart interpolated an extra seven bars that are vitally important for the characterization of the Countess:

Here we suddenly catch a glimpse of the character's deeply wounded heart through all her hopes and longings,[33] and how subtly Mozart lays the foundations for the return of the main theme by repeating the opening motif ('mi portasse' and so on). Only now is the final, almost rapt 'mi portasse', with its interjected echo in the winds, fully motivated from a psychological point of view. No one listening to this passage will imagine for a moment that it is a later addition, so organically does it develop not only from the aria itself but from the very character of the Countess. A further

---

33. The C minor that suddenly enters here forges a conceptual link with bars 4–5 of the allegro.

example of the difference between a draft and its final elaboration may be found in Vitellia's aria from *La clemenza di Tito* ('Non più di fiori').

Much the same is true of Mozart's instrumental works. The andante from the C major symphony K551, for example, originally ended as follows:

In the final version, Mozart now reintroduces the whole of the main theme, and in that way achieves not only a more perfect formal ending but also a deeper emotional impact. Note also the eloquent little variant in the penultimate bar. In the trio from *La clemenza di Tito* ('Se al volto mai ti senti') the simple chordal accompaniment at the end of the andantino

was replaced by a far more individual figure

that again emerges directly from the situation on stage. As we shall see later, Mozart had particular difficulty with Susanna's aria ('Deh vieni non tardar') from act four of *Le nozze di Figaro* and especially with its ending. Here, too, the definitive version appears as the ultimate realization of the living organism, with the development on this occasion leading from elaborate detail to brevity. In much the same way, the overture to *Die Zauberflöte* originally included a transition to the second theme that was allotted to the clarinet:

But this insertion was later eradicated as inorganic.

Sometimes we find Mozart hesitating, when writing down his ideas, over the division into bars. The duet from *Die Zauberflöte* ('Bei Männern, welche Liebe fühlen'), for example, was initially notated as follows:

Only at the end did Mozart realize his mistake and carefully cross out all the barlines, before correctly notating it as follows:

In much the same way the initial barline in the quartet from *Così fan tutte* ('La mano a me date') was originally entered after the first quaver and in Sesto's aria from *La clemenza di Tito* ('Deh per questo istante solo') after the second crotchet.

Changes were occasionally made to the instrumentation, too. That the two wind chords in the second and third bars of the duet from *Die Zauberflöte* were originally missing is no doubt merely an oversight, but all the other alterations – and they are significantly few in number – were made for internal reasons. The introduction to *Die Zauberflöte* ('Zu Hilfe! zu Hilfe! sonst bin ich verloren') originally had trumpets and timpani in C from the very first bars, but Mozart then deleted them and added trumpets and timpani in E flat on a separate sheet for the entry of the Three Ladies. They are used only to accompany the words 'Stirb, Ungeheu'r, durch unsre Macht! Triumph!' ('Die, monster, by our power! Victory!') and then disappear again completely, an excellent example of Mozart's economical use of orchestral colour.[34] In much the same way the trumpets and timpani were removed from Leporello's first aria ('Madamina, il catalogo è questo'), and the same is true of the horns in the great *buffa* aria intended for *Così fan tutte* (K584). In Dorabella's aria ('È amore un ladroncello') the double bass was removed in those passages where the winds are used on their own. The three chords that originally followed Pamina's words 'Ich möcht' ihn sehen' in the second-act finale of *Die Zauberflöte* were originally entrusted to the strings, not to the winds. And in the trio from the same opera ('Soll ich dich Teurer nicht mehr sehn?') the accompanying figure in the lower instruments was initially allotted to the violins:

---

34. In his critical commentary to the *AMA* edition of *Die Zauberflöte*, Rietz suggests that they were deleted because of the difficulty of retuning the instruments, a perpetual problem at this time.

This was then erased and transferred to the violas, cellos and bassoons, while the violins etch in the off-beat crotchets. And in the G minor symphony there were originally four horns, but these were reduced to two after only a few bars.

In short, Mozart's imagination continued to invent new tone colours, and yet it is precisely here that the subsequent changes are fewest in number. In general, each musical idea was already associated with a particular sonority at the very moment of its creation. And these sonorities remained confined to the resources available at this time: unlike Johann Sebastian Bach and his successors, Mozart did not invent any new instruments. But within these limitations, his imagination constantly thought up new mixtures and combinations, often placing considerable demands on his performers.[35]

The final group of sketches does not deserve this name at all as we are dealing here with draft scores – effectively fair copies of finished works that Mozart failed to complete for one reason or another. Among such works are several unfinished masses from the composer's years in Salzburg and, from his Viennese period, six fragmentary string quintets, two quintets for clarinet and string quartet, a quartet for english horn and strings, nine string quartets, nine keyboard concertos, a keyboard quartet, two keyboard trios, two violin sonatas, a cello sonata, four movements for two keyboards and nine keyboard pieces.[36] It is significant that not one of these was reused by Mozart at a later date.[37]

As we have seen, Mozart regarded the task of preparing the final fair copy as the least agreeable of all his activities. But it would be wrong to assume from this that it was a purely mechanical process for him, as essentially he had to recreate the work in his mind before he could commit it to paper. And it was by no means unusual for him to make further last-minute changes. With other works, conversely, this ultimate dictate of the imagination seems to have caused him so little trouble that it even generated new ideas while he was writing out the piece, as is clear from the prelude and fugue for his sister.

In the light of all this, it goes without saying that Mozart did not need to have an instrument to hand when he was working on a piece. 'He never went over to the keyboard when he was composing', says Niemetschek. 'At the very moment of its conception, the whole work was revealed to him, clearly and as a living entity, by his imagination.'[38] Constanze, too, reports with striking *naïveté*: 'He never composed at the keyboard but wrote music as if it were a letter, trying out a movement only when it was finished.'[39] If this was the case, he then liked to play the piece at

---

35. When Stadler once asked Mozart to alter a passage that he found awkward to play, Mozart retorted by asking, 'Do you have these notes on your instrument?' When Stadler affirmed that he did indeed have them, Mozart went on, 'Then it's up to you to bring them out.' Jahn was told this by Sigismund Neukomm; see Jahn, *W. A. Mozart*, ii.146.

36. The work-list drawn up by Stadler was reproduced by Nissen and, carefully revised, by Köchel; see Stadler, *Verteidigung der Echtheit des Mozart'schen Requiem*, 9–10; Nissen, *Biographie W. A. Mozarts*, appendix, 18–19; and Köchel, *Chronologisch-thematisches Verzeichnis sämtlicher Tonwerke Wolfgang Amade Mozarts*, second edition, Anh. II 12–109 F.

37. ◆ Contrary to Abert's assertion, Mozart frequently started pieces, put them aside, and only completed them later; hence many finished works began life as 'fragments'. Examples from the piano concertos include K449 (started 1782–3, completed February 1784), K488 (started 1784–5, completed March 1786) and K595 (started 1788, completed January 1791). In general, see Tyson, 'The Mozart Fragments in the Mozarteum, Salzburg: A Preliminary Study of Their Chronology and Their Significance'; further, see Konrad, 'Fragment bei Mozart'. For facsimiles and transcriptions of all Mozart's fragments, see NMA X/30/4.

38. Niemetschek, *Leben des k. k. Kapellmeisters Wolfgang Gottlieb Mozart*, 54.

39. Nissen, *Biographie W. A. Mozarts*, 473. Beethoven, too, warned the young Cipriani Potter against composing with a keyboard to hand, but according to Czerny he himself often tried out passages on the piano during his earlier years; see Thayer, *Ludwig van Beethovens Leben*, iv.56. ◆ Nevertheless, the evidence of Mozart's letters suggests that he did compose at the keyboard. On 5 April 1778 Mozart's mother wrote to Leopold from Paris: 'we have to pay 30 livres a month, the entrance and the stairs are so narrow that it would be impossible to bring up a clavier. And so Wolfgang has to compose away from home, at Monsieur Legros', as there's a keyboard there' (*Briefe*, ii.330); and on 1 August 1781 Mozart wrote to his father: 'Now I'm going off to hire a keyboard because until there is one in my room I cannot live in it as I have so much to compose and not a minute to lose' (*Briefe*, iii.144).

once, either to his wife, who frequently had to sing along with him, or to friends. One evening, for example, shortly after finishing the duet 'Crudel, perchè finora' from *Le nozze di Figaro*, he performed the piece with Michael Kelly, who later recalled the event with a mixture of pleasure and pride.[40]

Observers were unanimous in praising Mozart's art of free improvisation at the keyboard, a skill we have already mentioned on several occasions. For Mozart, this was not a means of helping him to compose but an independent creative activity, the results of which were committed not to paper but to the instrument in question. And, needless to add, the absence of any of the final stages of composition outlined above ensured that this approach had an immediate, highly personal appeal to it. It is one, moreover, that represents the organism of the work of art more in a state of becoming than in one of completion. Yet here, too, we are dealing with a living organism, one that comes into being in exactly the same way as a work that is written down, involving, as it does, invention and an instinctive urge to create architectural forms. The art of free improvisation, almost completely lost today, was still actively cultivated in Mozart's time. Indeed, the whole art of continuo playing rested on it, and the pianist's improvisation of one or more pieces formed a fixed part of every concert programme. As in the earlier period, the performers set out from a given theme that might be familiar or even commonplace and, on the strength of their imagination, they sought to raise it to a higher artistic level. It is no accident that these improvisations were generally cast in the form of variations or, less frequently, fugues and rondos, whereas we far less frequently hear of sonatas being improvised. We have already encountered such feats on the part of the young Mozart. Later, however, free improvisation increasingly assumed a completely different role in his output, functioning as the principal field of activity for his restless imagination. Here, in his writing for the keyboard, he poured out the whole wealth of his inner life, expressing a very real physical energy that paid no heed to external aims and often presupposed no listener, existing for its own sake alone. Niemetschek reports that

> Even during his manhood he would spend half the night at the keyboard, these were in fact the hours when he created his heavenly melodies! During the silent calm of the night, when no object holds the senses in thrall, his imagination was at its most active, opening up the whole world of sound that Nature had implanted in his mind. Here Mozart was all emotion and harmoniousness – here the most wonderful harmonies flowed from his fingers! Only those who heard Mozart at such times knew the depth and whole range of his genius as a musician: freely and independently of all other considerations, his spirit was able to soar aloft and boldly explore the highest regions of art. At such times of poetic fancy Mozart created an inexhaustible storehouse of ideas, and from these he then effortlessly ordered and fashioned his immortal works.[41]

With the exception of the final sentence, which once again reflects the layman's view of improvisation as a transitional stage on the way to the 'finished' work, this is correct. No doubt while he was improvising, Mozart will have recalled individual ideas from works on which he was currently engaged and, conversely, while creating new works, he will have remembered ideas from particularly inspired moments of improvisation, but at best it was the musical material that provided a link between improvisation and finished work: as artistic achievements they coexisted alongside

40. Kelly, *Reminiscences*, i.258–9.
41. Niemetschek, *Leben des k. k. Kapellmeisters Wolfgang Gottlieb Mozart*, 54–5.

each other in total independence. Moreover, the particular qualities of the keyboard undoubtedly had an important role to play in his treatment of the material.

So abundant was the storehouse of Mozart's ideas that he was even successful in an area that has proved the undoing of many lesser composers: he divided his time between writing and improvisation. Between six and seven in the morning, he would compose – during his later years he generally did so in bed. And at ten he began his lessons. As a rule he did no more composing that day, unless there were exceptional circumstances that forced him to do so, as there were at the time of *Le nozze di Figaro*. Unsurprisingly this one hour generally proved too little and so he often had to give up the evening and even the night and devote himself to this unwelcome activity.[42]

Mozart's inspired art of improvisation inevitably caused a great stir, with listeners clamouring to hear him extemporize. As we know, he had no inhibitions about showing off in this way, as long as he found a willing audience: he tended to draw a distinction between different types of audience, allowing his imagination far less free rein in the presence of ignorant or unsympathetic listeners (always assuming that he deigned to play for them in the first place) than with true connoisseurs. If there were only a few such people among his audience, he gave the impression that he was playing for them alone.[43] Now he would raise himself to the full height of his improvisatory powers, revealing not only his whole depth and seriousness of character but also the wit that was so typical of him.[44] Legion are the enthusiastic accounts of his playing that have survived. One such eyewitness was Ambros Rieder, the choirmaster at Perchtoldsdorf, who died in 1855 at the age of eighty-four:

> As a young man I admired many an excellent virtuoso on both the violin and the piano; but who can imagine my astonishment when I was fortunate enough to hear the immortal W. A. Mozart not only perform variations on the instrument, but also improvise before a numerous and eminent gathering. For me, here was a phenomenon completely different from anything I had been used to hearing and seeing until then. The bold flight of his imagination that soared aloft to the highest regions, then plunged back down into the bottomless pit, is something that not even the most experienced musician could properly admire or marvel at. Even now, as an old man, I can still hear those heavenly, unfathomable harmonies in my mind's ear and I shall go to my grave utterly convinced that there has only ever been one Mozart.[45]

As an old man, Niemetschek told Aloys Fuchs: 'If I could ask God for one more pleasure on earth, it would be to hear Mozart improvise again on the keyboard; no one who has not heard him has the faintest idea of what he was capable of achieving.'[46]

In Leipzig the audience demanded an improvisation at the end of a long concert in the course of which Mozart had already played two concertos and accompanied other works for almost two hours:

---

42. ◆ Abert's account of Mozart's daily schedule is a misrepresentation of a letter to his father of 22 December 1781; conveniently enough it emphasizes the distance between Wolfgang's daily life and his composing. What Mozart writes, however, is that his hairdresser wakes him at six o'clock, he finishes dressing by seven, and that he writes until ten before giving lessons to Maria Theresia Trattner and Countess Rumbeke. It is significant that he does not write about 'composing' but about 'writing' (*Briefe*, iii.187).

43. *Allgemeine musikalische Zeitung*, Vienna, ii (1818), 62.

44. Rochlitz, 'Verbürgte Anekdoten aus Wolfgang Gottlieb Mozarts Leben', 590–1.

45. *Neue Wiener Musik-Zeitung*, xxv (29 May 1856), 97–8. See also Schink, *Litterarische Fragmente*, ii.288. In a report on Beethoven dated April 1799, we read: 'He reveals himself at his most advantageous in the art of free improvisation. Not since the death of Mozart, who remains for me the *ne plus ultra* in this respect, have I enjoyed this art as much as I have with Beethoven'; *AmZ*, i (1798/9), 525 [*Dokumente*, 480, *Documentary Biography*, 566]. ◆ Where Abert has 'unermeßlich', 'unfathomable', Deutsch has 'unvergeßlich', 'unforgettable'.

46. *Deutsche Musik-Zeitung*, (1861), 322.

He resumed his seat at the keyboard and played, becoming all things to all men. He began simply, freely and solemnly in C minor – but it is absurd to try to describe such a thing. Having paid more attention to the connoisseur here, he gradually allowed his imagination to return to earth and ended with the printed variations in E flat major.[47]

Johann Nepomuk Stiepanek reports on the concert that Mozart gave in Prague in 1787:

At the end of the academy, Mozart improvised on the pianoforte for a good half hour, raising the mood of the enraptured Bohemians to the highest pitch of enthusiasm, to such an extent, indeed, that he saw himself obliged by the tumultuous applause to return to the keyboard. On this occasion, the floodtide of his imagination created an even more powerful effect than before, with the result that his listeners were inspired to demand yet another piece. Mozart reappeared, inner contentment at the universal enthusiasm and recognition of his artistic achievements suffusing his features. More inspired than ever, he began for a third time, achieving unheard-of results, when suddenly a loud voice rang out in the pit, shattering the silence that reigned in the hall: 'From Figaro!' At that, Mozart introduced the motif from the popular aria 'Non più andrai, farfallone etc.', improvised a dozen of the most interesting and elaborate variations and ended this remarkable performance to scenes of the noisiest jubilation.[48]

Niemetschek, too, reports on this concert:

Mozart improvised alone on the keyboard for more than half an hour, raising our rapt delight to the highest pitch, after which the state of sweet enchantment found relief in a loud and over-whelming expression of acclaim. And, indeed, his extemporizations surpassed everything that a keyboard player could conceivably produce, combining, as they did, a supreme example of the art of composition with the most consummate performance skills.[49]

Improvisation also played a regular part in concert programmes at this time in the form of the cadenzas in concertos. According to Dittersdorf, it was at precisely this period that they began to assume the character of improvisations on a simple theme, a development which, as Dittersdorf surmises, took place because previously 'as a result of the performer's lack of skill, all that he had achieved in the concerto itself was ruined in the cadenza'.[50] We shall later have occasion to look in closer detail at the independent standpoint adopted by Mozart in his keyboard concertos.

We have already noted how Mozart's whole appearance changed dramatically while he was improvising, suddenly and unexpectedly allowing the leading artist to appear from behind the unprepossessing man as his imagination set to work. But, according to Rochlitz's account, there were also frequent occasions when he was engrossed in a silent, inner world of composition and 'without realizing it, he would hum and even sing out loud, becoming flushed with heat and brooking no interruption'.[51] But such behaviour, far from being unique to Mozart, is typical of most musicians: in the case of Beethoven, for example, it notoriously found expression in lively gestures and sometimes even in wild outbursts of intemperate anger.

47. Rochlitz, 'Verbürgte Anekdoten', 113. ◆ These are the variations on 'Je suis Lindor' K354.
48. Nissen, *Biographie W. A. Mozarts*, 517.
49. Niemetschek, *Leben des k. k. Kapellmeisters Wolfgang Gottlieb Mozart*, 40.
50. Dittersdorf, *Lebensbeschreibung*, 41–2.
51. Rochlitz, *Für Freunde der Tonkunst*, ii.180.

Mozart's activities as a teacher afford a completely different picture of him. The materials that he used for his teaching contain virtually no trace of the extraordinary changes that he himself had brought to music in terms of both expression and technique.[52] In general, he followed the same basic principles as those in which he had once been instructed by his father. In other words, the pupil had to devise a bass for a given melody or provide the outer parts for a given set of inner parts. And, like his father, he taught the rudiments of counterpoint by reference to Fux's *Gradus ad Parnassum*. It is almost a truism that creative artists only very rarely reveal any inclination to reflect on the principles of their style, still less to systematize them for the purposes of their teaching, and Mozart was by no means the only innovator in the history of art who, as a teacher, continued to subscribe to particularly reactionary principles. A certain progressiveness may be detected, at best, in his insistence that his pupils should always reduce the bass to the simplest line and on that basis make it increasingly smooth and animated. This simplest figured bass line, which Mozart called 'the foundation of the continuo', even had to be written out by his pupils on a third system beneath the actual bass. Here we may no doubt see the influence of the thoroughbass theory which in the wake of Rameau's teachings found many followers in Germany, too, from the middle of the eighteenth century. Mozart devised his own examples, and even the first of these is remarkable for its similarity to the theme of the Benedictus from the *Requiem*. As an illustration of Mozart's method we may quote its opening bars, together with its 'fundamental bass':[53]

Fundamental bass

52. See Lach, *W. A. Mozart als Theoretiker*. It is also to Lach's credit that he has established beyond doubt that the *Kleine Generalbaßlehre* said to have been published in 1847 and cited by various more recent writers does not in fact exist. ◆ Presumably Abert refers here to the thoroughbass treatise (*Kurzgefaßte Generalbaß-Schule*) first published under Mozart's name at Vienna in 1818, reprinted at Berlin in 1822 (*Fundament des General-basses*) and, in English translation, at London in 1823 (*Mozart's Practical Elements of Thorough Bass, with many Observations & Examples on Harmony & Counterpoint*). As early as 1796, the Viennese music dealer Joseph Heidenreich offered 'a hitherto unknown manuscript tutor for the learning of thorough-bass, by Mozart' (*Dokumente*, 418, *Documentary Biography*, 480), which may have been the basis for the later publications. On Mozart's teaching, see Alfred Mann, *Theory and Practice: The Great Composer as Student and Teacher*, 41–62, and the foreword to NMA X/30/1 (Attwood studies).
53. The upper voice is notated in the soprano clef. The example exists in two versions; see Lach, *W. A. Mozart als Theoretiker*, 51–2.

The second example includes an embryonic version of the melodic type found in the March of the Priests from *Die Zauberflöte*:

Bass F   C♯   D   A   B♭   A   F   E   C   F

D G F   E C   A G   F D   G   G   C   —

Mozart repeatedly returned to this and other melodies in his exercises, sometimes also varying them. This is the same tune as the one we found him using when teaching the young daughter of the Comte de Guines in Paris.[54]

54.   ◆ Further concerning Mozart's compositional process, see Ulrich Konrad, *Mozarts Schaffensweise* and 'Compositional Method'.

37

Profound changes in style: the influence of J. S. Bach, G. F. Handel and C. P. E. Bach

Mozart's introduction to the music of older and contemporary north German composers in 1782 inspired the last of the deep-seated changes in his style that resulted from alien influences, especially during his early years, and that led him to develop in new directions. That this music signified a more powerful inner experience than anything he had previously known is entirely understandable: in terms of both form and content, a completely new world was opened up to him here, as emotional areas were revealed to his all-encompassing mind that were bound to cast a powerful spell on him, strange though their outward expression must initially have seemed to him; and, significantly, it was not Handel – a far more accessible composer at this time – who drew Mozart into his thrall, but Johann Sebastian Bach, a composer who by this date was far more remote from popular taste and, indeed, almost completely forgotten, with even Johann Friedrich Reichardt rating Bach far below Handel in north Germany.[1] The reason for this lay not only with Mozart's far greater capacity for artistic experience but above all in the fact that, unlike his father, he had a far more open and uninhibited attitude to rationalism, which was the main stumbling block to a revival of Bach's music.[2] No doubt his own music was based on foundations for which 'nature' and 'truth' meant something completely different from what they had meant in Bach's day, but he was already beginning to realize that behind Bach's music – and in spite of the fact that it was now felt to be out of date – there was a world of elemental emotion. There is something remarkable about the spectacle of Mozart's interest in Bach, an interest unencumbered by all theoretical considerations and concerned with artistic impressions alone. What is involved here is not, of course, the sort of dully instinctive assimilation of foreign models that we found in the case of the young Mozart, but a clear and conscious attempt to penetrate to the heart of this music, an incessant endeavour to imitate its style and merge it with his own. Ultimately, this was always Mozart's aim. Conversely, it would never for a moment have occurred to anyone of his wholly unhistorical frame of mind to write consciously archaic works or to produce fugues and suites in the style of early music. That he achieved this aim in only insolated cases is understandable as the distance between early music and his own was too great even for *his* powers of assimilation to bridge and it was unlikely, therefore, that he would have succeeded in doing so at the very first

---

1. Johann Friedrich Reichardt, *Musikalisches Kunstmagazin*, i (1782), 196.
2. ◆ Abert is more inclined to a grand, spiritual narrative here than is fashionable at present. While it is undoubtedly true that there were stumbling blocks to a Bach 'revival' in the later eighteenth-century – even the choice of word, 'revival', is loaded – these are now thought to relate more to cultural differences between the Protestant north and the Catholic south, which relates in particular to specific genres, and to changes in taste and the social conditions under which music was performed and disseminated. By and large, Abert treats history as a continuous, self-aware sweep of ideas and intentions whereas Mozart, as he later notes, had little sense, or at least little self-awareness, of musical history. 'Revival' was not an eighteenth-century phenomenon, but a nineteenth-century one. By the same token, Abert's claim that Mozart's interest in Bach was 'unencumbered by all theoretical considerations' must be understood not as a dismissal of theory altogether, but as an attempt to secure the ultimate importance of theoretical study as a means to an expressive end, rather than an end in itself.

attempt. Indeed, Mozart himself seems to have realized this, and so it comes as no surprise to find that the number of his unfinished works rose markedly during this period. Many of them point clearly to the fact that he wrote them only for himself, for the purposes of private study.

On a superficial level, this change finds expression in a striking interest in the formal world of the earlier period. Fugues, preludes and suites now acquire greater prominence, as do two of Carl Philipp Emanuel Bach's favourite forms, the fantasia and the rondo. No less important is the fact that strict counterpoint now permeates Mozart's music to a hitherto unknown degree. Its influence is not always uniform, and there are very few signs of it in the concertos, for example, but it is a recurrent feature of the works written between the summer of 1782 and the end of 1783. Even after that date it does not disappear completely but is merely overshadowed by other influences, reappearing only after *Le nozze di Figaro*, when it assumes a different, more spiritualized aspect. In the present chapter we shall examine only those works that reflect Mozart's impressions of earlier classics in their freshest and most immediate form.

The first and greatest of these works is the C minor mass K427, the genesis of which has already been recounted. Only the Kyrie, Gloria, Sanctus and Benedictus were finished. Of the Credo, only the opening section was completed in draft score, including the choral voices and bass. Only the most essential elements of the accompaniment are indicated here. In the 'Et incarnatus', too, the vocal line is written out in full, together with the obbligato wind instruments and bass, with the rest of the accompaniment merely hinted at.[3]

What distinguishes this torso from all Mozart's other masses is its tendency towards monumentality, a feature it really shares with only the Munich D minor Kyrie K341. The individual sections are developed on a scale previously unknown in Mozart's works: the Gloria, for example, is in seven completely independent movements, a structure that reveals that in these large-scale complexes Mozart has abandoned his earlier attempts to use rondo form to impose a formal unity on these movements. Their sheer length, moreover, finds a counterpart in the resources that Mozart employs: whereas all his earlier choruses had been in four parts, there are now frequent examples of five-part writing and even an eight-part double chorus. In keeping with local practice in Salzburg, the orchestral forces include neither clarinets nor flutes but make up for this lack by drawing not only on oboes, bassoons and horns but also trumpets and timpani and even four trombones, although, as was usual in Salzburg at this time, these last-named instruments generally support the voices and only occasionally acquire an independent function.

But the most remarkable aspect of this work is the striking unevenness of its individual sections. Passages of an inspired magnificence that far surpasses anything found in the earlier Masses occur alongside others that bear the dusty imprint of a style that had long been out of fashion. Yet it is

3. The mass was completed by Alois Schmitt of Dresden in 1901, and both the full score and vocal score of this completion were published by Breitkopf & Härtel in Leipzig. For the missing sections, Schmitt drew, in part, on other masses and, in part, on individual surviving sacred works by the composer. Individual endings were newly composed and various changes were made to the accompaniment, too. The arrangement has the great merit of having reintroduced the mass to the sacred repertory, yet the manner of its completion raises considerable doubts. To replace the 'Crucifixus' by a 'Lacrymosa' from KAnh. A2 [in fact a composition by Eberlin, copied out by Leopold Mozart some time before mid-1772] may be permissible, but Schmitt was then obliged to write a new 'passus et sepultus' of his own. Less happy was the idea of using two Kyries (from K139 [1768] and [the fragmentary] K322 [1779]) for the 'Et resurrexit' and 'Et in unam sanctam'. And however skilfully they may have been undertaken, Schmitt's additions and retouchings are certainly not free from reproach. The only sections that can be welcomed unconditionally are the replacement of the 'Et vitam venturi' by the corresponding movement from K262 and of the 'Agnus Dei' by a repeat of the Kyrie, this last-named change inspired by the example of the *Requiem*. See Alois Schmitt, 'W. A. Mozarts große Messe in c-Moll, ihre Entstehung und ihr Schicksal'; Ernst Lewicki, 'Die Vervollständigung von Mozarts Großer c-Moll-Messe durch Alois Schmitt in ihrem Werdegang nach authentischen Quellen dargestellt'; and Thouret, 'Das Mozartfest der Königlichen Oper in Berlin', 141ff. ◆ Modern completions of K427 have been published by Richard Maunder (Oxford, 1990) and Robert Levin (Stuttgart, 2005).

the more inspired passages – and it is significant that they are nearly all choral movements – that afford the clearest evidence of the influence of Bach and Handel, with even the opening Kyrie falling under this heading: it is a large-scale ternary structure, the third part of which is a slightly abbreviated and modified repeat of the first, with the 'Christe eleison' as its middle section, clearly set apart from the others in terms of its tonality and other features, thereby constituting an oasis of welcome relief within a more sombre picture. Unlike most of the earlier Kyrie allegros, this is a movement characterized by austerity and dourness and, as such, an audible echo of the impressions left by Bach.

The introduction is only brief, with a wistful sighlike theme over a heavy and powerful rhythm in the bass and a perceptible increase in emotional tension (note, in particular, the entry of the winds) that finally finds release in the lapidary first entry of the tutti that resembles nothing so much as a fanfare. These four bars provide a monumental introduction to the Kyrie proper, whose main theme, with its chromatic descent through a fourth, has numerous forebears in the earlier period:

But this main idea, which expresses a sense of lamentation in archaically austere sonorities, is combined with two other ideas, first, the theme of the introduction, which is more tender, more modern and more subjective in expression, and, beneath it, as though a warning against the excesses of such sentimentality, an impassioned motif in the bass that again recalls an earlier generation. Initially, the first theme is developed along regular lines, while the second is treated contrapuntally, with only the lower pair of voices entering at the same time as the two themes. From this point onwards the mood grows increasingly agitated, as the bass line forces its way upwards over a three-quaver motif (on 'eleison') derived from the main theme. By the final 'Kyrie', the sopranos, accompanied by wildly leaping syncopations in the strings, are already reduced, as though in despair, to a single savage outburst:

At this point there is a sudden shift of mood with the entry of G minor: the first and third themes disappear and the orchestra repeats the introduction, while the choral sopranos take up its theme, which is now accompanied by the other voices with essentially homophonic textures but with chromatic part-writing of extreme expressivity. The sense of pain turns to a feeling of gentle wistfulness, which in turn provides a bridge to the genuinely Mozartian sweet infatuation with which God the Son is invoked in the 'Christe'. No less typical of Mozart is the brief two-bar transition that ushers in this section in E flat major: eloquent, swelling wind chords and a figure in the violins that trickles gently down. Mozart consciously eschewed all older stylistic elements in this 'Christe eleison', which is essentially cast in the form of a soprano solo to which the chorus occasionally adds a few refrainlike passages as though in a dream. The winds, too, contribute no more than a handful of highlights which, however scattered they may be, none the less create a profoundly poetic effect. But the soprano soloist begs for Christ's mercy with a fervour that almost literally overflows with rapt infatuation, remaining in the same tonality, but introducing more and more new ideas, of which the most prominent is this tenderly wistful phrase:

e - lei - son, e - lei - son, e - lei - - - son

Others, of course, reveal the dangerous proximity of Italian opera with their wide-ranging intervals, elaborate coloratura and, last but not least, the stereotypical cadenza. At the repeat of the first section, which begins in E flat major, the voices enter in quicker succession and in a different order, but the range of moods is the same. It ends with a brief coda in which the opening bar of the second theme is heard over a *pianissimo* timpani roll. The movement as a whole is an outstanding example of Mozart's ability to combine the austerity of the earlier style with his own predilection for depicting gentle and elegiac emotions.

The first movement of the Gloria – a common-time movement in C major – consists of two equal sections, with the second shorn only of its introduction. This section, too, is antithetical in structure, with the ecstatic jubilation of the actual 'Gloria' contrasted with the irenic 'Et in terra pax'. This in fact reflects an earlier practice, but what is new – and it is unique to Mozart – is the tone of anguished resignation that breaks through unexpectedly at the words 'bonae voluntatis', whereas the 'Gloria' itself, with its fanfare-like themes and clear echo of the 'Hallelujah' chorus from *Messiah*, creates a more superficial impression. This is even truer of the following 'Laudamus te', a veritable operatic aria in the older Italian manner with noisy drum-bass ritornellos, bombastic emotions and plentiful coloratura. Here we find Mozart relapsing into the most vapid operatic style, a style found only very rarely in the earlier masses, leaving the listener with the impression that, at van Swieten's bidding, he was consciously evoking the spirit of a composer such as Graun. If so, this section would be curious proof of the way in which Johann Sebastian Bach and Graun summed up 'the good old days' in the minds of people such as van Swieten.

By contrast, the shortest of the mass's movements, the five-part 'Gratias', achieves new heights of expressivity. The orchestral writing is dominated by a peremptory, broadly striding motif repeatedly answered by violins and basses – a clear echo of the old ostinato principle. The tonality is initially highly unstable, with essentially homophonic harmonies gliding along in heavy dissonances. Only gradually does A minor emerge as the basic key. The choral writing is declamatory in style, entering at once on a forceful *forte*, with only a single *piano* shudder passing through the ranks of the singers at the entry of the horns. Like the first two sections of the Gloria, this movement, too, dies away *piano* in the orchestra, yet the overriding impression is not that of the charming, inward tone with which Mozart and representatives of the older Neapolitan mass generally give thanks to the Lord at this point in the work: rather, it reflects the austere earnestness of purpose with which Bach, for example, approached this movement in his B minor mass.

The 'Domine Deus' is a duet in D minor. Accompanied only by strings, it begins in a manner reminiscent of a freer variant of Scarlatti, with a foreshortened and varied da capo. But it is innocent of the excesses of the 'Laudamus te'. Here the curiously muted tone of the 'Gratias' continues to make itself felt: suffice it to compare this passage with the introduction, where the ideas are paratactically juxtaposed in a typically Mozartian manner, with the third of them already bearing an anguished and impassioned imprint. The whole style is more austere, with imitative and especially canonic passages abounding in the vocal lines and the instruments.

In Mozart's earlier masses, the 'Qui tollis' had stood out for its individual treatment, and the present movement in G minor is no exception. Although only a torso, it remains the climax of the work as a whole, with even the resources expended upon it proving exceptional: two four-part choirs and full orchestra recall the old polychoral tradition. The movement is divided into two sections separated by a closure on the dominant. In keeping with its words, each section incorporates two different themes, one of which reflects the weight of the world's sins with unsettling gravity, while the 'Miserere' theme is almost like a half-sob. Initially Mozart seems to have thought of casting this movement in a form often found in Bach, that of a chaconne (or passacaglia) with ostinato bass, but the chromatically descending bass line – itself an echo from the past – returns only at the repeat of the main idea. All the more persistently, by contrast, does Mozart retain the sharply dotted rhythm in the string accompaniment – it, too, a legacy from an earlier period and an eloquent symbol of the ineluctable idea of the world's burden of guilt. No less symptomatic are the extraordinarily harsh harmonic sequences and the idiosyncratic avoidance of all perfect cadences: the listener is inevitably reminded of the Bachian image of an immense procession of penitents crowding towards the cross in dull despair and disappearing into the distance at the end, when the second choir sings its unison 'miserere'. It is an image that is also reflected in the strict interplay between the two choirs, resulting in a magnificence of imagination and unity of approach wholly unlike anything found in any of Mozart's earlier masses.

The 'Quoniam' in E minor is a trio for two sopranos and tenor cast in the form of a ternary aria. With its predilection for imitative procedures, it is related to the 'Domine Deus', but it acquires its special character from its fondness for syncopated rhythms and from the festive brilliance brought to the movement as a whole by the coloratura flourishes on the word 'Sanctus'. The 'Cum Sancto Spiritu' is again strictly fugal in the older tradition, but for the first time in his career Mozart introduces it with a six-bar adagio invocation of Christ's name, a resolute and, at the same time, highly charged profession of faith in the Redeemer. The fugue itself reveals great technical mastery, being clear and free of all artifice, while even the subsidiary ideas ('in gloria Dei Patris' and 'Amen') fully reflect the text. And yet it is impossible to avoid the impression of something cool and academic, an impression due not least to the archaic theme with its intervals of a fourth and compass of a hexachord. More individual features, especially ones involving chromatic part-writing, are found only in isolation. Among such features is the highly effective ending, in the course of which the unison voices assert the theme in the face of a figural accompaniment.

The surviving parts of the Credo find Mozart reverting to the style of his earlier masses, the only exception being that the choral writing is now in five parts: the festive, superficially brilliant overall character, the homophonic, declamatory choral writing with its contrapuntal elaborations at the end of the various sections, the free repetition of individual parts and, finally, the recurrent, pounding orchestral motif – all these aspects are familiar to us from earlier. The movement marks no real advance in the direction of greater interiority, and even the 'Et incarnatus est' – a soprano aria scored for strings and solo winds and based on a siciliana rhythm – marks a return to the earlier manger scenes. It begins with elements of typically Mozartian grace and suavity, but then, as a result of its coloratura trappings and a cadenza that also draws on concertante winds, it proceeds to reveal all the worst excesses of Neapolitan opera. One wonders whether Mozart would have retained this movement if he had ever completed the work.

Far more elevated in its inspiration is the Sanctus, which is again scored for five-part chorus and which is one of the most festive and, at the same time, exciting movements of its kind that Mozart ever wrote. It is linked to the 'Pleni sunt coeli', with the orchestra in particular revealing Heaven's increasingly overwhelming majesty in a series of powerful brush strokes. Above it there rises the idiosyncratically ecstatic jubilation of the 'Hosanna' fugue, which on this occasion is developed along strikingly broad lines, emphatically surpassing its predecessor in terms of its distinctively Mozartian inner life and erring only on the side of excessive length. Equally striking is the

Benedictus for four vocal soloists, another long movement remarkable for its bitter seriousness of purpose, although this last-named feature has a handful of predecessors among the older masses. Only once in the first section does a brighter emotion break through, when the theme is launched by the bass and broadly developed in a C major triad, but from the end of this section onwards minor tonalities prevail, and it is entirely typical of Mozart that, at its return, this theme raises the whole movement's note of resignation to a particularly elevated pitch. Here, too, the bass writing, harmony and counterpoint all recall earlier models.[4]

Perhaps it was the personal disappointments that Mozart endured in Salzburg that robbed him of any desire to complete this remarkable work. Not until 1785 was it to enjoy a curious resurrection in Vienna when Mozart was invited to provide an oratorio for the Tonkünstler-Sozietät concert on 13 and 17 March. In spite of the shortage of time, he accepted the commission as he saw it as a welcome opportunity to introduce the music of his mass, which he held in particularly high regard, to a larger audience. The chosen text was an adaptation of the popular oratorio subject of *Davidde penitente*,[5] the author of which, hithero unidentified, was no doubt one of the Viennese court poets. As we know from Johann Sebastian Bach, this retexting of existing music had never been regarded askance by composers of the older period, and the fact that these adapters often revealed a high degree of musical appreciation is clear from the present piece, the text of which is not only poetically impeccable but subtly adapted to suit the expressive content of the individual movements of the mass. All the existing movements were used with minimal changes, the only exception being the Credo, which once again remained unfinished (K469).[6] Conversely, Mozart added two new arias ('A te, fra tanti affanni' and 'Tra l'oscure ombre funeste') for Catarina Cavalieri and Adamberger, which he completed on 6 and 11 March respectively. In both cases their orchestral postludes lead directly into the following number. Both, moreover, are concertante arias, thus revealing the extent to which Mozart had already moved away from Bach and Handel by 1785.[7] And both adopt the popular practice of dividing the aria into a slow and fast section. Nor, finally, is there any trace of the *Zopfmusik* of the 'Laudamus te'. The andante of the first of these arias is notable for its tone of tender, veiled nostalgia, while that of the second seethes with suppressed passion. The fast sections, by contrast, have the lively, somewhat superficial verve of a number of Mozart's secular concert arias. The result is a work – half oratorio, half cantata – that is bound to create an ambivalent impression on present-day listeners but which was not without importance for the Viennese audiences of Mozart's day. The special status enjoyed by the Viennese oratorio under Fux had already been undermined by the modern Neapolitan style,[8] but the very fact that Mozart was able to risk offering the public a work of such austerity and to call it an oratorio suggests that the old tradition was still very much alive. It was probably only in Vienna at this time that the independent handling of the orchestra and the elaborate artistry of many of the

---

4. ◆ For a psychological reading of the C minor mass, see Cadieux, 'Linzer Schmerzensmann: de *la Grande Messe en Ut Mineur* K.427 au fantasme "Ein Kind Wird Geschlagen"'.
5. See, for example, Ferdinando Bertoni's *David poenitens* of 1775; see also Schering, *Geschichte des Oratoriums*, 235. ◆ Other examples include *Il pentimento di Davidde* (1722) by the Portuguese composer Francisco António de Almeida and Francesco Zannetti's *Il pianto di penitenza espresso dal Santo Re Davidde nel Salmo L* (1773).
6. It must have been particularly tempting to complete the 'Et incarnatus' as the Italian oratorios of the period favoured such solo movements. If Mozart failed to do so on this occasion, the conclusion would seem to be that he had already outgrown the movement.
7. In the tenor aria, the concertante instruments are flute, oboe, clarinet and bassoon.
8. Schering, *Geschichte des Oratoriums*, 195ff. ◆ Further concerning Fux, see White, 'The Oratorios of Johann Joseph Fux and the Imperial Court in Vienna'; Kanduth, 'The Literary and Dramaturgical Aspects of the Viennese *Sepolcro* Oratorio, with Particular Reference to Fux'; and White: 'The *Sepolcro* Oratorios of Fux: An Assessment'.

numbers could count on unanimous approval. Even so, the monumental grandeur of the choruses was a risk since, in the wake of Zeno and Metastasio, choruses had largely been suppressed in the Viennese oratorio as elsewhere, yet Mozart was still able to trust in the abiding appeal of the Fuxian tradition, and on this point he was not mistaken as *Davidde penitente* proved hugely successful not only in Vienna but elsewhere at German and foreign music festivals until well into the nineteenth century.

With his fantasia and fugue in C major K394 for keyboard, Mozart returned to a form that had already been perfected by Johann Sebastian Bach. Like the prelude and fugue, it is an example of a two-movement form that combines freedom and constraint in the most felicitous manner. But Bach's fantasias should not be regarded as the products of boundless improvisation, as the term was used by him to encompass the most varied formal structures.[9] It was only the freest of them – the *Chromatic Fantasia* and the fantasia of the fantasia and fugue in G minor for organ – that served as the starting point for the fantasias of the main representative of the later keyboard fantasia, Bach's son and pupil Carl Philipp Emanuel. This helps to explain the strongly subjective nature of these pieces, their concert-like character, their fondness for discursive passage-work and broken chords and, finally, their recitative-like sections and harmonic audacities. Many of these features found their way into Mozart's works. Even Carl Philipp Emanuel's first fantasia – included in his *Essay* as a final example – defines the prototype that he himself created and reveals all its essential elements:[10] a chordal opening with passage-work, a free and broadly structured recitative that gradually assumes the form of a kind of songlike cavatina (and, as such, represents the notional heart of the piece) and a final section that brings the work to an end by drawing freely on earlier ideas involving passage-work and recitative. The songlike middle section has a similar function to that of the fugal section in the older toccata-like fantasias. Occasionally we find several such middle sections, so that the piece as a whole acquires a rondo-like structure. Moreover, these songlike sections have a remarkably subjective, often Romantic stamp to them, looking forward to Beethoven and sometimes even to Mendelssohn.[11]

An essential feature of these fantasias is their abandonment of the orchestic rhythms that are expressed by means of the division into bars and which, as Bach rightly realized, are replaced by the natural speech rhythms of the recitatives.[12] There is no trace any longer of the stiff and regular rhythms of the earlier period. Instead, the music teems with motifs that are rhythmically lengthened and shortened, with ritardandos and accelerandos that may or may not be written out in full, with fermatas, brief adagio episodes embedded in fast movements and allegro episodes in slow movements, and with pauses in particular acquiring a hitherto unsuspected psychological significance.[13] In addition, there is the extraordinary harmonic writing for which the *Versuch* similarly provides specific instructions: 'When the performer is allowed adequate time to have attention directed to his work, he may modulate to remoter keys.'[14] There is no doubt that the boldness and breadth of these modulatory arcs is one of the principal features of these fantasias, and the

9. Spitta, *Johann Sebastian Bach*, i.432–5 and 661–4. Even the well-known three-part keyboard inventions were originally described as fantasias.
10. Bach himself stressed this didactic, programmatical aim in the *Versuch*: 'As stated earlier, it is especially in fantasias, those expressive not of memorized or plagiarized passages, but rather of true, musical creativeness, that the keyboardist more than any other executant can practice the declamatory style, and move audaciously from one affect to another. A short example is sketched in the final Lesson'; Bach, *Versuch über die wahre Art das Clavier zu spielen*, 86.
11. See, for example, the largo sostenuto from the C major fantasia of 1787.
12. *Loc. cit.* The main section of the C minor fantasia dispenses with barlines altogether.
13. See Steglich, 'K. Ph. E. Bach und der Dresdner Kreuzkantor G. A. Homilius im Musikleben ihrer Zeit', 70–2.
14. Bach, *Versuch über die Art*, 12.

changing harmonies often seem to adopt the later Romantic manner and to be the sole vehicle for the changing moods and their individual transitions and nuances. Third-based relationships, chromaticisms and enharmonic change are exploited to surprising effect, with the interrupted cadence and other 'rational deceptions' likewise playing an important role here.[15] Slipping from one dissonance to another, instead of resolving that dissonance, is not uncommon, while harmonies involving suspensions and passing notes become more idiosyncratic and varied. Chromaticisms, in particular, do not exist – as they do with the average *galant* composer – simply to tone down the asperities and irregularities in the diatonic line: rather, they are often used with the specific aim of creating such rough edges. Needless to say, these developments are paralleled by a freer approach to melody, as it, too, reflects the slightest changes in the underlying emotion, allowing the tension to build up and find release in unexpected ways, breaking down the normal periodic structure and so on. And yet even these fantasias reveal a firm desire to maintain a uniform mood in spite of their superficial freedoms and to allow each motif to develop organically from within itself,[16] even if this process attests to a greater degree of freedom than we find in any of the sonatas. Above all, Bach's importance lies in his redefinition of the whole nature of ornamentation. On the whole, the ornaments are no longer decorative *agrémens* in the older sense of the term, but organic components of the melodic line itself, an aspect that looks far beyond Mozart to Beethoven and even to the Romantics.[17] Other elements of Bach's style that anticipate Romanticism include his embedding of a covert melody within a chordal figuration and his use of arabesques to embellish and bridge over the different thematic sections. Nor, finally, should we overlook the purely tonal, genuinely pianistic nature of these fantasias, which are keyboard poems of the choicest kind. Alongside the emotional world of the *Sturm und Drang* movement – a world that interpreted 'Nature' in the main as a justification for grand passions – we already find pointers to the tender infatuation of the coming 'Age of Romanticism'.

Only two of Mozart's fantasias are dated: the C major fantasia (with accompanying fugue) K394 dates from the early months of 1782[18] and the C minor fantasia K475 is dated 20 May 1785. But the others, too, can be ascribed to this same period on stylistic grounds. Here, too, formal differences make it clear that it was only with some difficulty that Mozart finally mastered the genre. To judge by its style, the fantasia in C major K395 is almost certainly one of the composer's earliest contributions to the medium and has been dated by some authorities to 1778 or even 1777.[19] It is in three movements, beginning with an allegretto that alternates between a relatively sustained theme and free passage-work with no obvious division into bars (Mozart writes 'caprice' over it at one point). There follows a middle movement that is a curious mixture of adagio ideas and confused allegro sections, before a very fast capriccio brings the work to an end. The aphoristic character is especially noticeable here: none of the movements acquires a clearly contoured structure, but all reveal the hand of the improviser. The style is a remarkable mixture of Johann Sebastian and Carl Philipp Emanuel Bach, with the former recalled by the imitative writing in the opening movement and by a number of figures which, especially in the capriccio, will remind the listener of certain preludes from *The Well-Tempered Clavier*, while Carl Philipp Emanuel is recalled by the

15. Bach, *Versuch über die Art*, 123.
16. Steglich, 'K. Ph. E. Bach', 112–14. ◆ Further concerning Bach's fantasias, see Schleuning, *Die Freie Fantasie: Ein Beitrag zur Erforschung der klassischen Klaviermusik* and Schulenberg, 'Carl Philipp Emanuel Bach'.
17. In *Der critische Musikus*, Johann Adolph Scheibe sees one of the principal merits of the Berlin school in the fact 'that composers there are extremely sparing in their use of embellishments and ornaments, but those that are included are all the more choice and are brought out all the more subtly and nicely'.
18. ◆ See *Briefe*, iii.202 (letter of 20 April 1782).
19. ◆ The chronology of Mozart's handwriting confirms a date of 1777 for K395.

revolutionary features, the sudden shifts of mood, the numerous diminished chords, the chromaticisms and, above all, the ternary structure with the slow episode in the middle. The only difference here is that Mozart introduces a note of disquiet even at this point of lyrical repose. At this stage, then, Mozart had not yet fully come to terms with the aesthetic foundations of the form as a whole, with the result that the piece remains inadequately developed. In short, we should date it to the beginning of the period of his engagement with the music of Bach and Handel.

The fantasia prefaced to the C major fugue continues to reveal a remarkable vacillation in Mozart's approach to the form. It begins on a thoroughly un-Bachian note with a brief adagio in the style of the slow introductions to the symphonies of Joseph Haydn.[20] This section ends on the dominant of C major, thereby generating a sense of tension that Mozart could easily have resolved by introducing the fugue at this point. Instead, we have a free fantasia that begins, surprisingly, on the dominant-seventh chord and that recalls Bach in a number of essential details, not least in its extraordinarily bold sequence of broken chords. That it was these that first fired Mozart's imagination is not altogether unsurprising in a composer who knew his Schobert. Conversely, the cantabile middle section is conspicuous by its absence: evidently Mozart had no wish to give undue emphasis to any overtly pictorial ideas before introducing the Fugue. Instead, we find an effect clearly borrowed from Carl Philipp Emanuel Bach in the form of the note *b'* flat hammered out in quaver octaves over a triplet scale in the bass.[21] Equally typical of Bach is the repeat of this passage and the fondness for fermatas to add to the sense of tension. On the other hand, there is an almost total lack of recitative-like melodic lines, with only a handful of timid attempts to move in this direction proving little more than the exception to the rule. On the whole, the musical argument unfolds along figurative lines, stressing particular technical problems such as the crossing of hands and so on. In this it comes close to the older, prelude-like fantasias.[22] It is clear that, in spite of its tensions and general effectiveness, the overall impression left by this stylistically oddly vacillating piece is not yet wholly satisfactory. And this is even more true when we turn to the Fugue – actually a double fugue – in which the main subject, the vigorous fourths of which recall Johann Sebastian Bach,[23] is regularly joined by a second main idea in rolling semiquavers, the auxiliary notes of which lend the piece as a whole a curious note of asperity:

20. The reminiscence of the C minor fantasia K475 and the C minor sonata K457 is not without significance.

21. The prototype may be found in the adagio of [C. P. E.] Bach's sixth 'Württemberg' sonata [Wq. 49, Helm 36]. This, too, is the source of the twofold upward shift by a whole tone. It is clear from this that effects such as these – effects that were completely new at this time – left a powerful mark on Mozart's sense of sonority.

22. The descending sequence of diminished chords (bar 46) likewise seems to contain an echo of Johann Sebastian Bach: here one thinks, above all, of the gigue from the first partita, where the degrees are exactly the same, and of the toccata from the final partita for keyboard.

23. It is modelled on the opening fugue from *The Well-Tempered Clavier*; see also the subject of the unfinished fugue in G major K443 for string trio. The prototype, it must be added, was familiar to Mozart from his youth: see Max Seiffert, *Geschichte der Klaviermusik*, 413–14.

In this countersubject the spirit of the fantasia lives on, putting up all manner of resistance that forces the powerful main subject to have to keep on asserting itself. Although the fugue reveals all the arts of stretto, diminution and augmentation,[24] it none the less recalls Handel rather than Bach, with its freer and – from a pianistic point of view – more effective style.[25] As such, it is an admirable example of Mozart's independent ability to assimilate this older style, too, when the circumstances were right. The relatively unpianistic G minor fugue K401 is not on the same high level, for all that it, too, seems to have been inspired by a particular Bachian model of an austere and brooding kind.[26] On a formal level, it is not unworthy of its prototype, but as a character piece it falls far short of it. Mozart's supreme contemporary achievement in the field of the fugue is the four-part fugue in C minor with the following subject:

Its change of mood is entirely typical of Mozart, even if its opening bars, with their descent of a diminished seventh, hark back to a much older type.[27] Mozart originally wrote this piece for two keyboards (K426), a version which, even at that stage in the work's history, was something of a makeshift solution, as the fugue avoids all pianistic effects, being conceived in purely abstract terms and pursuing a similar goal – albeit on a far less grandiose scale – to Bach's *The Art of Fugue*. It was only logical, therefore, that Mozart should rearrange it for strings in 1788,[28] when he added a slow introduction (K546). The fugue is developed with both rigour and boldness and explores to the full the emotional antithesis of its subject, with its contrast between heroism and weary resignation. The prelude that Mozart added when undertaking this revision is particularly profound,[29] with the same opposition as in the fugue itself, except that here it gives the impression of appearing behind a veil. It is a genuinely Romantic twilight mood that enfolds us here (note, in particular, the bold enharmonic writing), with the battlefield brightening only at the entry of the fugue.

24. Augmentation occurs only once in the bass, just as it does in the C minor fugue from part two of *The Well-Tempered Clavier*.
25. Note the many passages in thirds and the octave doublings.
26. ◆ K401 appears to be considerably earlier than other works discussed here: the paper on which it is written suggests it was composed in the early 1770s.
27. See Max Seiffert, *Geschichte der Klaviermusik*, 206ff. It also forms the basis of the fugue subject of K402 and of the sketch K417c [for string quartet, written down some time between 1785 and 1789]. There is also a striking analogy between the present theme and the second number from Noverre's and Starzer's ballet *Les Horaces et les Curiaces* from 1774:

See Niedecken, *Jean-Georges Noverre 1727–1810: Sein Leben und seine Beziehungen zur Musik*, 45. Starzer was a member of van Swieten's inner circle of friends.
28. Beethoven, too, instrumented the fugue.
29. Although the changes appear slight, they are important for the underlying emotion, with Mozart removing the sighlike character of the second section by omitting the staccato dottings and extending the slurs: see the above example.

The two fantasias in C minor K396 and D minor K397 bring us even closer to the world of Carl Philipp Emanuel Bach.[30] The latter begins on a thoroughly Bachian note with its broken chords and continues to reveal its parentage at a number of later points, including the off-beat semi-quavers in the upper voice and the extensive use of passage-work. But this is also the first occasion on which Mozart introduces genuinely developed melodic ideas, which he handles in a totally un-Bachian manner, not as episodes, but as the main idea, whereas the free and rhapsodical motifs have only an introductory and transitional character. In short, Mozart felt that in this particular fantasia the actual nub of the work lay far more in the free elaboration of the melodic element and, more specifically, in all manner of sudden changes of mood that repeatedly transport the listener to a new emotional world. There is a genuinely Mozartian sense of entreaty and searching here, a mood repeatedly and violently disturbed, but the language of expression is far more aphoristic than with Bach, who prefers to subordinate all the different ideas to a single specific will. With the D major allegretto comes a sudden release from the sense of inner pressure. 'Then an image – a godlike image – appears before us,' to quote Goethe: the lovely songlike melody is likewise interrupted, but on this occasion it is not by a brusque and surly passage but by a festive cadenza, after which it disappears with the same sharp dynamic contrasts as were typical of the earlier section.

The C minor fantasia is cast in sonata form, as though Mozart had set out with the firm intention of creating a conscious contrast with the looser form of its companion piece. As such, it finds him striking out in a different direction again from that taken by Carl Philipp Emanuel Bach, with the older composer recalled only by the pianistic style, the free approach to melody and harmony and, above all, by the intelligent thematic treatment of the development section which, its freedom notwithstanding, sticks closely to the first subject, developing it in a way that is markedly different from Mozart's earlier development sections, with their rather looser structures. Fantasia-like, by contrast, is the melodic and harmonic writing, which, more recitative-like in style and literally teeming with chromaticisms, flows along with unbridled boldness. Here we find harsh dissonances such as the following:

This is one of Mozart's most impassioned and pensive keyboard pieces, and this underlying tone is maintained throughout: not even the third-based, self-assured second subject allows more than a glimmer of light to enter the musical argument, even at the end, where it returns in C major –

---

30. It will be noted that all the following fantasias are in minor tonalities.

one of the rare instances in one of Mozart's minor-key sonata movements in which the second subject is twice heard in the major.[31]

But all these works are no more than preliminary studies for the well-known fantasia in C minor K475 of May 1785, a work that astonished Joseph Frank when he heard it performed by Mozart. Here Bach's formal world is completely permeated by Mozart's fiery spirit, and the result is a work that is the finest example of its kind in the whole of the Classical period. It is again a true fantasia, with no sonata-like features, and comprises five completely independent movements. The final section repeats the opening in a slightly different guise, thereby producing a cyclical conclusion.

The adagio opens with a deeply resigned unison motif bowed down by the weight of destiny and answered at once by two anguished sighs – one is tempted to say 'in the winds', inasmuch as so many passages in the piece are orchestral in character. A dreamy rêverie of wonderful profundity is now developed on the basis of the main idea, migrating to the remotest keys with extraordinary boldness by means of chromatic passing notes, with a wild sforzato used to stress the main stations in its migrations.[32] The mood now grows more peaceful. Highly poetic is the gently pounding *d'* that is heard in the right hand alone following the arrival in the dominant. A sudden gust of wind erupts in the bass – it is the main motif reduced to demisemiquavers – before rushing through all the different registers and ending on the dominant of B minor, where it produces a state of extreme tension.[33] But instead of a section in B minor, what we find – wholly unexpectedly – is a songlike passage in D major of genuinely Mozartian, touching sadness, like a dream of carefree youth.[34] Yet all dreams must end, and the songlike melody breaks off in the second bar and the brief sighlike motif flutters helplessly upwards as though some unknown enemy were approaching. And the enemy does indeed appear, seizing upon the preceding seventh-chord harmony and bursting in from the darkness with violent force, ushering in a section that can only be described as dramatic inasmuch as we are dealing here with a contrast between two sections of which the first rushes in with the wildest passion, while the second attempts to prevent it, first with timid defiance, then with increasingly urgent entreaties. But with the entry of the first dotted bass motif, this second section is drawn into a veritable whirlpool of passion[35] that grows slightly calmer only on the dominant of B flat major but fails to achieve total peace. This time it is a virtuosic scalar passage that acts as mediator between the sections. In the following andantino the

31. The brief final section is clearly inspired by Joseph Haydn. An old copy of the C minor fantasia K396 from the collection of Alexander Posonyi includes a note to the effect that only the part up to the development section is by Mozart, whereas the rest was added by Stadler. I am grateful to Ludwig Scheibler of Godesberg am Rhein for drawing this to my attention. Given the striking use of C major for the second subject, this seems more than plausible. Similar reservations could be levelled at the development section, the strict thematic treatment of which is particularly odd in a fantasia, not least when we recall how long it took Mozart to adopt this kind of approach in his actual sonata movements. It is tempting to assume that Mozart originally planned a completely different continuation, more in keeping with the character of the fantasia, and that, as the result of a misunderstanding, Stadler turned the whole thing into a sonata movement. This would also help to explain the markedly virtuosic nature of this development section (a point emphasized by Scheibler), as well as its modulatory procedures, which depart in many respects from Mozart's usual practice. None the less, the development section is so full of ideas and character that Stadler must have been particularly inspired when writing it. The absence of an autograph makes a definitive decision impossible, but I tend to agree with Herr Scheibler that the information contained in the old copy is correct. ◆ The recovered autograph (now at the Goethe-Schiller-Archiv, Weimar) shows that Mozart composed only bars 1–27 of K396, that is, the material up to the double bar; the development and recapitulation are by Stadler. Posonyi's copy, now lost, was therefore correct.
32. Typical of the first sixteen bars is the uninterrupted chromatic writing in the bass.
33. The enharmonic respelling of the dominant-seventh chords as augmented six-five chords occurs on a small scale in bars 10–15, before being repeated on a larger scale with the transition from G major to B minor.
34. Note in particular the absence of any modulation here, in contrast to what went before.
35. Here we find chromatic modulations similar to those that occur in the first adagio; note also the constant instability of the tonality in both these movements, in contrast to the earlier D major movement.

mood is once again intensified to produce a melodic songlike movement, but it is no longer as purely contemplative as before, for the melody includes various signs of agitation:

These features include the rests between its individual members; the *forte* that suddenly erupts in the second bar, only to die away again as abruptly in the third (its impact must not be destroyed by an arbitrary crescendo and decrescendo); and, above all, the shift of the rhythmic ictus of the main motif (a) as a result of its being combined with the rising melodic line: twice it falls on the strong beat of the bar, but at its third appearance it falls on the weak beat, thereby generating the greatest possible tension. With all the greater resignation, then, does the music sink back on the following rhythm which, although related, is far calmer in tone:

With its scarcely controlled agitation, this section, too, is in ternary form, with repeats,[36] and, as before, the musical line starts to falter as it approaches the final repeat, clinging to the briefest of phrases as its final refuge. Although the following più allegro brings with it a new and powerful change of mood, it is none the less more closely associated with the previous section than was the case with the earlier pair of movements. It is in the same time-signature, is introduced along tonally regular lines, and its dominant rhythm ♩♪♪♪ | ♩ ♪ is anticipated by the andantino.

(This rhythm is later abbreviated to ♩♪♪♪ ♪.)

In addition, we find here a classic example of a cantabile figuration, with the following sequential melody developed in demisemiquavers in the uppermost of the inner parts:[37]

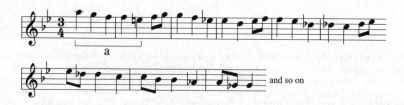

Finally it appears in two parts in the upper voice and in the lowest of the inner voices. Its basic motif (a) is likewise related to the andantino, except that on this occasion the melodic line invariably moves in a downward direction. This whole più allegro is designed to release the tension that has been building up until now. In the keyboard's lowest register, in A flat major, the forward

---

36. The repeat of the first subject with its magnificent cello melody again exploits the instrument's various registers to wholly admirable effect; the middle section begins like a wind trio transposed to the keyboard. ◆ Concerning a significant editorial problem in the andantino section of the fantasy, see Eisen and Wintle, 'Mozart's C minor Fantasy, K475: An Editorial "Problem" and its Analytical and Critical Consequences'.
37. The first beat is notionally tied to the *a″* of the previous bar.

momentum moderates, becoming half as slow again, and in its place there appears a type of passage familiar from the works of Carl Philipp Emanuel Bach and involving broken chords. Deeply expressive in character, it requires a highly poetical style of performance, not least because of the fact that it maintains a constant dialogue with a weighty chordal motif built up from the basic rhythm already mentioned. Finally a feeling of weariness takes over, as the sense of heaviness gains the upper hand and, to the sound of anxious and audible groans, leads back to the opening of the whole piece, an opening which, like some implacable fate, sweeps away all attempts to escape from it. But the repeat of the opening is on only a superficial level: it lacks all the earlier features of brooding and rêverie and from now on the key of C minor is firmly and unwaveringly established, with only the occasional descent into the region of the subdominant, while the dynamic contrasts are intensified. But how profoundly and truthfully Mozart has captured this fantasia's underlying emotional tone. By the end all attempts to find a means of escape have proved futile, and the feeling of resignation, which at the beginning had entered unconsciously, now seizes hold of the soul with pitiless clarity. Yet even these attempts to escape reveal the most marvellous psychological logic, operating according to the principle that the brighter the moments of hope, the crueller is the descent into despair. In this way, the D major episode and the first allegro go together, as do the andantino and più allegro, in which the sense of hope has already been dashed and turned to deep nostalgia (note also the contrastive use of keys in both pairs of movements). As a result, the musical argument moves towards its inconsolable ending as though of its own accord. But for precisely this same reason this fantasia is also a self-contained whole lacking in any prefatory character. Admittedly, Mozart later published it with the C minor sonata K457, showing that he set particular store by the fact that both inhabit the same world in terms of their atmospheric content. But he clearly did not think of the fantasia as a preparatory introduction in the older sense of the term. Conversely, the dedication to Maria Theresia von Trattner and the letters that he wrote to her about the piece suggest that it was composed in a state of heightened emotional excitement. Unfortunately, the letters in question have not survived.[38]

Mozart modelled himself particularly closely on the older style in his keyboard suite in C major K399, a piece that he regrettably failed to complete. The sequence of movements (French overture – allemande – courante – sarabande) shows that he was attempting to write four dances in keeping with the German norm at this time, as there seems little doubt that he was planning a gigue in final position. Whether this would have been preceded by any additional interpolations is open to question. On the other hand, the changing key-signatures owe more to sonata form than they do to the suite and reflect Mozart's own idiosyncratic approach to the medium, as does the unmediated transition from the fugue to the allemande. Stylistically speaking, the work is indebted more to Handel than to Bach, and, indeed, there are even individual reminiscences of the former. The allemande and especially the courante have a fluidity to them that has already outgrown their original dance character and that was favoured less by the French than by the Italians and, hence, by Handel. Yet this work, too, contains much that is typical of Mozart: and here, too, one notes above all that it was the characteristic harshness of the older style that attracted him. The most successful movements are the introductory dotted grave and the courante, in which double counterpoint is cleverly handled.

We may end this chapter by mentioning the two unfinished violin sonatas in A major K402 and C major K403. The former is a sonata in name alone and should really be described as a prelude

---

38.   ◆ See Nottebohm, *Mozartiana*, where Constanze is given as the source of the claim that Mozart wrote two letters to Maria Theresia von Trattner. Niemetschek (*Leben des k. k. Kapellmeisters Wolfgang Gottlieb Mozart*) mentions only one letter.

and fugue, although only the fugue recalls the earlier period.[39] Its second half was completed by Stadler in textbook fashion. Conversely, the two-part A major prelude, with its magnificent festive step recalling the minuet from *Don Giovanni*, is entirely worthy of the mature, *galant* Mozart and contains no archaizing features. The older period is more powerfully represented by the C major sonata, above all by its opening movement's somewhat inflexible main theme and development section. The most profound of its movements is its andante, the extraordinarily free thematic and harmonic writing of which clearly recall the fantasias. For whole stretches the writing is in three parts, yet the overall impression is not that of a study inspired by the older school but of an immediate outpouring of heartfelt melancholy.[40]

39. The chromatic descent of the lower melodic line through a fourth is another feature that recalls the older period. ◆ K402 probably dates from 1781, slightly earlier than Mozart's acquaintance with van Swieten and his sustained engagement with Bach's music. And possibly it was originally intended to be part of the set of accompanied sonatas published by him in December 1781 (K296, K376–380); the heading 'Sonata II^da' on the manuscript was subsequently struck through.

40. To judge by its first twenty bars, the final movement was intended to release the sense of tension and bring the work to an end on a note of serene joviality, but it is doubtful whether Mozart envisaged the playful note struck by Stadler in his attempt to complete the piece. Following the profundity of the andante, the *galant* ending – *galant* in the best sense of the term – seems emphatically too lightweight, quite apart from the fact that it shows not the least inkling of this whole change of style.

38

Chamber and orchestral works between Die Entführung *and* Figaro

We should be guilty of seriously underestimating the universality of Mozart's genius and his fine sense of style if we thought that north German composers monopolized his work to the exclusion of all other influences. By now he was no longer in any danger of being overwhelmed by any one particular model, as had occasionally been the case in his youth, not least because this influence was limited, in essence, to the genres to which he owed his knowledge of strict counterpoint, namely, church music and keyboard music. But he continued to develop organically throughout this period: the influence of Haydn, with whom he now entered into close personal contact, acquired a hitherto unsuspected intensity, and in the years leading up to *Le nozze di Figaro* his own imagination in particular acquired a breadth and depth that simply precluded any possibility of his limiting himself to a single model. Of course, the concertos required of him by his professional obligations now acquired a disproportionate predominance and for a time allowed the north German influence to be overshadowed. But they still left time for other concerns, and other aspects of his character demanded their due with peremptory force, aspects which neither the purveyor of musical trifles for high society nor the *galant* composer was able to satisfy: this much is clear from the contemporary string quartets, which are all the more significant in that they are among the few compositions that Mozart wrote on his own initiative, rather than in response to some external stimulus. For it is here, above all, that the influence of Mozart's study of Bach and Handel continued to make itself felt on the most obvious level. Here, too, of course, we see the dangers of attempting to impose any sense of 'order' on the work of a great artist.[1]

The six quartets dedicated to Haydn – K387 in G major, K421 in D minor, K428 in E flat major, K458 in B flat major, K464 in A major and K465 in C major – were written between 1782 and 1785.[2] Nine years had elapsed since Mozart's last quartets, which were similarly written under Haydn's evident influence. Now that the two men had become friends, Mozart could vie on equal terms with a composer whose own 'Russian' quartets [op. 33] had been published in 1781.[3]

Established in all its essentials by Joseph Haydn, the classic string quartet was the last and finest product of the great stylistic change that overtook German music in the course of the eighteenth century.[4] The cultivation of music was the preserve of the aristocracy throughout the whole of this

---

1. For one such attempt, see Wyzewa and Saint-Foix, *Wolfgang Amédée Mozart*, ii.410–13.
2. The individual dates are: 31 December 1782 (K387), June 1783 (K421 and probably also K428), 9 November 1784 (K458), 10 January 1785 (K464) and 14 January 1785 (K465). ◆ Mozart continued to revise the quartets after their composition, partly in response to his private performances of the works and partly in anticipation of their publication in September 1785. See Wolf-Dieter Seiffert, 'Mozart's "Haydn" Quartets: An Evaluation of the Autographs and First Edition, with Particular Attention to mm. 125–42 of the Finale of K. 387', 188–95.
3. Pohl, *Joseph Haydn*, ii.189 and 293ff.
4. ◆ Abert's teleological, 'great man' view of the history of the string quartet has been considerably revised since the early years of the twentieth century. Precursors of the genre may include the presumably orchestral *sonata a quattro* or *concerto a quattro*, the Italian *sinfonia* and the French *sonate en quatuor* and *ouverture à quatre*; closer in spirit and style are south German and

period, with the result that its orchestral style tended more towards chamber music than orchestral music in the later sense of the term, whereas the seventeenth century, by heaping a choral Pelion upon a choral Ossa,[5] was more concerned with mass effects.[6] Here, too, the Viennese classicists brought about a radical change, but at the same time opened up a rift: on the one hand, the increased use of tone colour and exploitation of the individual instruments, together with their complete freedom of movement within the work as a whole and, finally, the fullness and plasticity of sound achieved from Beethoven's day onwards led to the reemergence of an orchestral style of the grandest ambitions, while, on the other, the fondness for chamber music achieved its most internalized form in the string quartet. In both these areas it was Haydn who proved to be the true trailblazer.

In their formal design – a four-movement cyclical structure – these two increasingly disparate genres continued to remain closely linked. Only in their execution and style did they often go their own completely separate ways. The string quartet was domestic music to the extent that, unlike the orchestra, it did not invite other instruments from the most varied families to join in but remained limited to a single family of strings. As a result, it was excluded from the timbral effects available to the orchestra: *al fresco* paintings were impossible here, and external tonal effects could be achieved only to the extent that they were realizable within the body of solo strings. In turn, this meant that the sensual and physically expressive element was naturally overshadowed by its intellectual and spiritual aspect, an aspect which the quartet seemed tailor-made to express on the strength of its inherent and ideal combination of unity and diversity, for, although the four instruments are similar in terms of their origins and nature, they are very different in respect of their individual qualities, resembling the members of a highly developed family of whom each independently expresses common traits in his own individual manner. The fundamental principle of the string quartet is the strictest equality of all four voices.[7] It is this that distinguishes it from chamber music with piano, in which the domineering keyboard instrument forces the other players – always assuming that they refuse to be satisfied with their role as accompanists – to form themselves into groups, with the result that the true essence of this type of chamber music is a concertante style. This is also occasionally found in the string quartet, of course, except that here concertante playing is used not as a stylistic principle or for the sake of tonal effects but as a natural consequence of the way in which the ideas are developed based on the voluntary understanding of

Austrian symphonies in four parts, many of which are stylistically indistinguishable from one-to-a-part solo ensemble music. Quartets were first cultivated in south Germany, Austria and Bohemia, by Asplmayr, Ordonez, Dittersdorf, Vanhal, Starzer, Gassmann, F. X. Richter, Holzbauer, Camerloher, Christian Cannabich and Haydn; the usual title for such works was 'divertimento', which at the time designated solo instrumental music in general and was compatible with a variety of scorings, styles and character. It was not until about 1780 that modern titles such as quartet and quintet became common for 'serious' chamber music in the now standard scorings; this change in terminology does not, however, imply that earlier divertimentos were an independent genre of 'light', occasional music or that their scoring was variable. In general, see Geiringer, 'The Rise of Chamber Music'; Ludwig Finscher, *Studien zur Geschichte des Streichquartetts, i: Die Entstehung des klassischen Streichquartetts: Von den Vorformen zur Grundlegung durch Joseph Haydn*; Webster, 'Towards a History of Viennese Chamber Music in the Early Classical Period', and Jones, 'The origins of the quartet'. Further, see Hickman, 'The Nascent Viennese String Quartet' and 'The Flowering of the Viennese String Quartet in the Late Eighteenth Century'; Speck, *Boccherinis Streichquartette: Studien zur Kompositionsweise und zur gattungsgeschichtlichen Stellung*; and Oboussier, 'The French String Quartet, 1770–1800'.

5. ◆ In Greek mythology, the giants Otus and Ephialtes tried to overthrow the gods by piling Mount Ossa on Mount Olympus and then Mount Pelion on Mount Ossa.

6. See Schneider, 'Die Besetzung der vielstimmigen Musik des 16. und 17. Jahrhunderts' and Mersmann, 'Beiträge zur Aufführungspraxis der vorklassischen Kammermusik in Deutschland'.

7. ◆ The idea that the string quartet is fundamentally based on equality of the voices is a nineteenth-century, post-Beethoven view of the genre; at the end of the eighteenth century, writers distinguished between the *quatuor concertant*, in which the main thematic material is successively distributed throughout the ensemble; the *quatuor brilliant*, in which the first violin dominates and the other parts accompany; and the 'classical' quartet (typified by Haydn and Mozart), in which the four voices are treated as equals.

all four participants. Even if one of the voices temporarily assumes control, the others are always happy to agree to this: there is no sense in which they are mere orchestral padding (a concept increasingly abandoned by the string quartet). Rather, this 'accompaniment' leads a melodic life of its own in each voice, not merely supporting the upper voice but commenting on it and, as it were, allowing the other players to reflect on the main idea. The result is an art which, freed from all material charms, is concerned purely with ideas and with inwardness. Rather than ranging far and wide, it explores the depths, laying bare the most sensitive regions of the soul that cannot be reached by other instrumental combinations.

This is reflected in the style of these works. It is no accident that both Haydn and, later, Mozart devoted some considerable time to counterpoint on their way to perfecting the genre, a procedure which necessarily requires all the voices to be independent.[8] But, after studying counterpoint, they moved on: their ultimate goal was neither the strict polyphony of the older period nor the homophony of the *galant* age but a free combination of the two. What we find here is no longer the development of a theme in the sense of its changing relationship with various independent countermelodies but the drawing out of all the resources that it contains. These latter may occasionally find expression as independent countermelodies, but in the main they are created by dissecting the theme. As a result, thematic development plays a predominant role in this type of writing, too, with all four voices contributing equally to the musical argument. If there is one feature that sets this new type of chamber music more clearly apart from the older sort, it is the fact that the bass has lost its old character as a continuo instrument and is now treated on equal terms with the other lines. The symphony, too, is based on thematic procedures, of course, but it places them in the service of monumental effects, whereas the quartet style explores the world of the emotions in all its ramifications. As the whole genre grew increasingly spiritualized, so this was bound to affect the very nature of the themes, with the difference between those found in quartets and those used in symphonies becoming more and more noticeable: quartet themes are more delicate, intimate and complex, a development that culminates in Beethoven's last quartets.

The first composer to master this intimate style was Joseph Haydn, who found here a congenial field for his lively, fertile mind and profoundly logical imagination. But it should not be assumed that the later quartet style fell into his lap ready-made. Like Gluck, Haydn was one of those composers who developed very slowly, and however attractive his early works, it was not until he had turned fifty that he appears before us as the true 'great' Haydn,[9] a point that emerges with particular clarity from his quartets. The first set was advertised in 1763 but was written before this.[10] He himself called them cassations, a term reflected in their serenade-like tone and five-movement form.[11] Even the term 'sinfonia' refers to a period when sinfonia and quartet were not yet strictly segregated.[12] Indeed, some of these pieces even include figured basses. All this harks back to the earlier period, with the result that there is little sign in these works of the later thematic writing and independence of the four voices. Above all, the bass still bears clear traces of the old continuo. Strict counterpoint, too, is still largely avoided. Even so, these works are already superior

8. Sandberger, 'Zur Geschichte des Haydnschen Streichquartetts'.

9. ◆ For a contrary view, arguing on both historiographical and stylistic grounds that his earlier works also represent 'the true, great Haydn', see Webster, *Haydn's 'Farewell' Symphony and the Idea of Classical Style*.

10. Pohl, *Joseph Haydn* i.334ff. ◆ Haydn probably composed ten quartets (Hob. III:1–4, 6–8, 10, 12 and Hob. II:6) between about 1757 and about 1765.

11. ◆ For a corrective account of terminology in Haydn's early quartets, see Webster, 'Towards a History of Viennese Chamber Music in the Early Classical Period'.

12. See the op. 1 trios of Johann Stamitz and the op. 1 quartets of Carl Stamitz, all of which were intended to be performed by both solo and orchestral forces.

to all their rivals in terms of their variety of mood, their wealth of imagination, their folklike healthiness and effervescent good humour. The next set of quartets dates from 1773 [*recte* by 1771, op. 9] and by now four-movement form is the rule. Yet, although they mark an advance on their predecessors, the advance is one of degree, rather than of kind, unless we choose to see it in the markedly concerto-like writing for the first violin. Not until the 'Sun' quartets [op. 20] of 1773 do we find Haydn taking a significant step forward under the obvious influence of the north German school – most probably Carl Philipp Emanuel Bach's six great string quartets of that same year.[13] It is entirely typical of Haydn that the four voices acquire their independence here with the help of strict contrapuntal procedures and that Mozart, as Haydn's pupil, was immediately swept along by this development. The other main feature of the later Haydn's style – thematic development – likewise makes its first tentative appearance here. Movements such as the finale of the C major quartet (no. 34) show clearly how the later thematic writing developed as something new from the earlier contrapuntal procedures. Yet even this preference for counterpoint was only a single stage on a journey that was to lead to a new and even more important stage with the 'Russian' quartets of 1781. Haydn himself declared that they had been written 'in an entirely new and special way', a way that consists precisely in the fact that thematic development has passed through the refining fire of counterpoint. Variety is now replaced by uniformity, and the wealth of disparate phenomena is kept in check by a resolute insistence on unified formal structures. And it is the thematic writing that establishes this unity: by dissecting an idea, by breaking it down into its constituent parts and by allowing new ideas to emerge in this way, it invariably returns to itself, always remaining the centre of the musical argument to which – to quote a popular comparison of the day – 'four intelligent persons' make an equal contribution. But what is new about this approach is not simply that the individual idea is developed by the individual player as soon as he takes it up but that this act of developing the idea leaves an impression on the minds of the other players in the form of new ideas which, never expressed in so many words, accompany the debate in the hearts of all four of them. This inner process is not limited, however, to the development section but is already found during the exposition of the themes. We shall shortly encounter a fine example of this when we examine Mozart's first string quartet. The development section merely adds an element of drama to this whole process. On a superficial level it becomes more extensive and also combines counterpoint and free composition in an extremely varied and ingenious manner that was to have a profound effect on the whole later history of music. Only now did the string quartet become what it has remained to this day. No doubt Haydn later outgrew these 'Russian' quartets, touching on areas of our emotional lives that were still concealed from him in these works, so that the four players are no longer concerned with mere 'entertainment' but with grand intellectual ideas à la Beethoven, a development that more than justifies his comment on the 'moral character' of his symphonies and quartets. But the road to this goal had now been opened up and, as with the 'Sun' quartets, we now see Mozart taking his place beside the older composer and accompanying him on his journey to this important station, too. Yet it follows from this that, regardless of the artistic value of his own contributions to the medium, Mozart was cast in the role of a pupil – admittedly of a superior kind – in this particular field of instrumental music, while Haydn played the part of the teacher. 'From Haydn I learnt how to write string quartets', Mozart admitted with typical candour.[14]

---

13. ◆ The quartets Wq. 92 (Helm 516–521) were probably composed by 1768.
14. ◆ This comment is probably apocryphal.

That Mozart was none the less able to say something new within this Haydnesque world is clear from the debate that was sparked by these quartets in musical circles, with even Joseph II asking Dittersdorf for his opinion of them and concurring with the latter's comparison of Mozart with Klopstock and of Haydn with Gellert.[15] Mozart was less fortunate, by contrast, in the case of a Viennese review dated January 1787:

> The pity is only that he aims too high in his artful and truly beautiful compositions, in order to become a new creator, whereby it must be said that feeling and heart profit little; his new quartets for 2 violins, viola and bass, which he has dedicated to Haydn, may well be called too highly seasoned – and whose palate can endure this for long?[16]

In Vienna, Prince Kražalkovicz arranged for a private runthrough of these quartets and afterwards complained that the performance was full of wrong notes. When the players protested, he flew into such a rage that he tore up the parts. Conversely, he was very fond of Gyrowetz.[17] According to another report, the parts were returned to the publisher from Italy on the grounds that they were full of mistakes. It was these same works, of course, that formed the basis of Sarti's critique of Mozart.

In short, the initial impression left on contemporaries was of works that were confused, unclear and artificial.[18] Instead of smiling at this reaction, we would do better to try to understand it, not least because it contains a kernel of truth. Every teacher–pupil relationship involves a certain lack of freedom, at least on a technical level, and, as Mozart himself admitted, it was very hard for him to adapt Haydn's new technique to fit his own way of experiencing art. As we shall see, he was not always entirely successful in his attempts to solve this problem. Essentially, he was faced with a challenge similar to the one that had confronted him when he was studying Bach and Handel, except that on that occasion the gulf between his own style and that of his models was not so great. But his world of artistic experience was completely different from Haydn's, being far more irrational in character, with a tendency to allow his imagination to range freely and to court sudden psychological disasters that were avoided by a composer like Haydn, who had grown up in the north German tradition. The latter's style ultimately emerged as the natural consequence of his entire artistic growth, but Mozart first had to assimilate this style, a task that was all the more problematical for him, the greater his ambitions for these works and the deeper his world of inner experience. We may well believe him when he writes that these six quartets were the fruit of a long and laborious study. He may well have been able to master Haydn's technique relatively quickly as a result of his tremendous ability to assimilate new impressions, but it was much more difficult for him to apply it to his own world of emotions: after all, one of the most difficult things for even a great composer is to take over another's style while retaining his intellectual independence and to assimilate that style to such an extent that it appears as the natural expression of his very own

---

15. Dittersdorf, *Lebensbeschreibung*, 176–7. Leopold Mozart, too, approved of the comparison between his son and Klopstock: see Nissen, *Biographie W. A. Mozarts*, appendix, 62.

16. Cramer, *Magazin der Musik*, ii (1787), 1273–4 [*Dokumente*, 254–5, *Documentary Biography*, 290].

17. See Einstein, *Lebensläufe deutscher Musiker von ihnen selbst erzählt*, iii: *Adalbert Gyrowetz*, 14; see also Schönfeld, *Jahrbuch der Tonkunst von Wien und Prag*, i.77–8; and Constanze Mozart, 'Noch einige Kleinigkeiten aus Mozarts Leben', 855.

18. ◆ Some negative reactions notwithstanding, it is likely that Mozart's quartets were – on the contrary – popular and highly thought of. Not only were they quickly disseminated across Europe, but Artaria, the publisher, reprinted them at least 3 times before 1790, a sure sign that they were in demand. For a summary of the printing history of the 'Haydn' quartets, see Haberkamp, *Die Erstdrucke der Werke von Wolfgang Amadeus Mozart*, 182–4.

character and, therefore, as something new. Each time that Mozart achieves this and his own personality emerges clearly from behind Haydn's compositional style, we find ourselves in the presence of pieces that are not only entirely worthy of Haydn but that gave Haydn important ideas for his own later works. This is clear not least from the menuettos, half of which are in second position, the other half in third position.[19] With a single exception, they all include tempo markings. All, moreover, reveal an obvious attempt on Mozart's part to contrast the wit and popular humour of Haydn's minuets with a particular type of his own, a type more closely related to the subjective character-piece. The predominant tone is idiosyncratic and at times pugnacious, and in movements such as the menuetto of K421 we are no longer far removed from the menuetto of the great G minor symphony. Mozart achieves this effect by means of curious cross-rhythms that avoid regular eight-bar periods and that are found far less frequently with the more popular Haydn. The menuettos of K387 and K421 both begin with a ten-bar phrase, which in the earlier work is created by the 'curtain'[20] of the first two bars and in the later work by the sequential repetition of a two-bar motif. In much the same way the six-bar period of K428 results from lengthening the quaver motif in the second and third bars. Indeed, even in cases such as K458, where eight-bar periodic structure is to all appearances maintained, we none the less have the impression that each such period is made up of one section of three bars and another of five. Then there are all the dynamic and harmonic accents that appear to impede the regular progress of the movement, while even the part-writing serves not infrequently to obscure the natural divisions. The trios, finally, reveal this same tendency to develop in the direction of character-pieces. They are also fond of exploiting the old contrast between minor and major. Only in odd cases do we find one of the older types of dancelike idyll in which the tone alternates between roguishness and sheer verve.[21]

Yet even in those cases where the Haydnesque model seems all-pervasive, as in the final movements of K428, 458 and 465, we should never for a moment think in terms of slavish imitation, still less that Mozart felt under any compulsion to surrender his own personality, as these movements express a natural, effervescent joy in life that was common to both Mozart and Haydn, with the result that Mozart did not need to force himself to adopt a Haydnesque tone here: it was enough for him to add a few characteristic highlights of his own in order to assert his author's rights.

Nor should we imagine that Mozart's only model was Haydn's 'Russian' quartets, as his mind was always on the look-out for other models. Here one thinks above all of what, in the context of these quartets, is the disproportionately great role played by strict counterpoint. Here the influence may have been the older fugal finales of both Joseph and Michael Haydn, in addition to the 'Sun' quartets and, above all, the older classical composers whom Mozart had just been studying. It is almost possible to share the sense of pleasure that he himself must have felt at being able to apply his newly won knowledge to the field of the string quartet.

Finally, it must be acknowledged that these quartets also contain many examples of Mozart's earlier working method, with the fantastical and flighty spirit of Johann Schobert inhabiting the development sections of a number of their opening allegros. Indeed, the development sections of the opening movement of K458 and of the finale of K464 even include new themes, albeit in the

---

19. In Haydn's 'Russian' quartets, the proportion is 4:2.
20. The expression is Hugo Riemann's.
21. Even in terms of its outward sonorities, the trio of K421 belongs to the same type as the main section of the first menuetto of the divertimento K334.

spirit of a notional second subject (neither of these movements has a real second subject), and the new ideas are cantabile in nature. The development sections of the opening movement of K428 and, to a lesser extent, of K387 stress the aspect of virtuosity and include sequential modulations familiar to us from Schobert.

In short, the problem raised by these quartets is not such a simple one to solve. It is not sufficient to posit a single model – Haydn – or even to see that there were other intellectual forces at work. Here, too, the main question is what use Mozart made of all these elements and whether he succeeded in turning these *disjecta membra* into a new, living, Mozartian organism. He had long since outgrown the years when he had been content merely to imitate others and so we may assume as a matter of course that there was a specific artistic aim behind his use of these various stylistic components. Indeed, we have already established this in the case of the new themes that he introduced into his development sections. How beautifully, moreover, the strict counterpoint of the finale of K 387, with its raptly infatuated theme, seems to emerge as a natural, fully ripe fruit from the springlike buds and shoots of all that has gone before it!

Above all, however, Mozart was attracted to Haydn's use of thematic development in the widest sense of the term, with each of the lines treated as an independent voice, so that scarcely anything happens in one of the voices without the others being affected by it and adding their own autonomous comments, whether in agreement or contradiction. Here Mozart found a new form to express his world of artistic experience. As we have already seen, no essentially new ideas were added here: all that is best about these quartets is specifically Mozartian, in other words, independent of Haydn. But he was – and felt – deeply indebted to his friend for the fact that he had now learnt to express his own experience of life in a form that was all about spiritualization. It would be futile to ask whether he would have achieved this goal without Haydn's model. All that we can say for certain is that he would not have done so as quickly, as living people always left a more rapid and definite impression on him than abstract trends. On the other hand, he did not merely imitate anything that was not already dormant within him in embryonic form: his whole way of reacting to phenomena and of depicting various psychological forces in their constant interaction with each other inevitably drew him to a style in which all is teeming, restless activity. Here it is worth tracing the development of a single cadential motif from the first movement of K387 which, almost imperceptible on its first appearance, is introduced at the repeat of the main theme:

First it is treated to imitative procedures, then reshaped as follows:

After that, it reappears in an abbreviated, chromatic form:

And almost immediately after this, it recurs in contrary motion:

In much the same way, completely insignificant, formulaic motifs suddenly become the heroes of entire sections. Here one thinks of the following motif in the development section of the same movement:

The same is true of the following motif in the andante of the same work:

In the strictly contrapuntal movements, Mozart's imagination is literally inexhaustible in its invention of new counterpoints to the main subjects, with the A major quartet (K464) providing some particularly fine examples. Sometimes it is only a brief, rhythmically terse motif that invests an

entire movement with its overriding unity, as in the andante of K421:

Even at its first appearance in the main theme, it captured the composer's imagination to such an extent that, because of it, he extended the theme to five bars. With the exception of the dreamily beautiful episode in A flat major, it then dominates the whole movement right up to the very last bar, assuming the most varied guises as it does so. Related to this is a further feature of these works, namely, the occasional replacement of fully developed themes by brief, short-breathed motifs that are themselves developed by means of repetition, variation and the like on the basis of often extremely bold harmonies. Some of these motifs follow the older tradition and are derived from elements of the main themes (here one thinks of the beginning of the development section of the opening movement of K421), but others are independent ideas, as in the andante of K465:

   Sections such as these may well have reinforced contemporaries' secret

misgivings about Mozart the 'Romantic', and it is certainly the case that we come close here to the later Romantics' concern for detail, a concern that plays a major role in the opening movement of K458, where all manner of ethereal shapes pursue their sinuous and playful course throughout all four voices between the two solid pillars of the Haydnesque first subject and the notional, authentically Mozartian second subject, with which the development section begins:

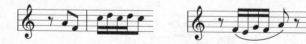

With its 'Tristanesque' sonorities, the whole of the slow movement of K428, finally, is an extended rêverie with no clear melodic structures, achieving a remarkable interiority missing from Mozart's earlier works.

In the circumstances, it is only natural that harmony should play a particularly important role here. In this, these quartets are markedly different from the contemporary concertos, which, as genuine products of the moment, are innocent of all such tendency to brood. In the quartets, by contrast, there is a sense in which Franz Schubert is already waiting at the door, so subtle and genuinely Romantic are the mood pictures that Mozart succeeds in conjuring up merely by means of exceptionally bold harmonies that are in a constant state of flux: listen, for example, to the remarkable twilit passages just after the return of the first subject in the andante of the G major quartet and at the start of the development section of the opening movement of the D minor quartet. At the same point in the C major quartet (K465) there is even a remarkable pre-echo of a passage in the development section of the opening movement of Schubert's B minor symphony. That Mozart did not shy away from dissonances here is clear from the fact that *c* and *c* sharp twice clash in different voices. The most famous passage in this context is the introductory adagio of the C major quartet:

This passage came in for much criticism until well into the nineteenth century, with writers such as Fétis and Oulibicheff even attempting to improve it.[22] An age that saw in Mozart only an out-and-out optimist simply did not know where to begin with this adagio. But the Mozart with whom we are dealing here was anything but an optimist. Like almost all other similar introductions, this adagio strives towards the dominant, which it finally reaches only after plunging deep down into the subdominant. As so often in the older period, the bass descends chromatically through a fourth, producing a regular sequence extending over the first nine bars – this, too, reflects an older practice. But Mozart was not content with the interval of a fourth in the bass and so he interpolated a further passage that reaches the dominant only by the roundabout means of E flat major and C minor, in other words, via its subdominant. On this harmonic basis there unfolds a psychological process of matchless concision. Initially, the key remains unclear: weary and resigned, the

22. For a full treatment of this subject, see Jahn, *W. A. Mozart*, ii.205–6. ◆ Further, see Vertrees, 'Mozart's String Quartet K. 465: The History of a Controversy'; Keefe, 'An Integrated "Dissonance": Mozart's "Haydn" Quartets and the Slow Introduction of K. 465'; and Irving, *Mozart: The 'Haydn' Quartets*, 76–8.

two middle voices begin to circle the fifth of the tonic and dominant, when the first violin suddenly intervenes like a flashing sword with its dissonant *a″*. This keenly cutting entry would create a much weaker impression if it were altered to *a″♭* on the grounds of 'correctness' and, at the same time, shortened by a whole beat. As it stands, it introduces a note of defiant resolve into the chaotic gloom. Twice this violent shift occurs, its crescendo suggesting an immense inner tension. For the time being, however, there is no sense of liberation, as the bass continues its implacable descent, drawing the first violin's melodic line with it, no matter how hard the latter may try to resist it. A new attempt to get under way by means of the same chromatic motif likewise comes to nothing, even though on this occasion it is finally taken up by the bass. The musical discourse ultimately comes to rest on the dominant, still unresolved, with a series of sharp dynamic accents. In other words, the idea that finds expression here is not merely that of a storm that blows over and clears the air. Rather, it is the basic mood of the work as a whole, the image of a mind weighed down by gloomy forebodings and attempting to come to terms with the emotional pressure that it feels. Once again, then, it is an expression of a purely personal kind that has little to do with the world of Gesellschaftsmusik, the difference being merely that on this occasion the process remains unconscious. Only in the allegro does the composer open his eyes, as it were, and continue the conflict on a conscious level. If the scales tip increasingly in the direction of confidence and hope here, there are still many passages in the later movements – notably in the trio in the menuetto and even in the final movement, where the light-heartedness at times acquires a particular stridency – that prove that the darker emotions have not been silenced altogether.

The C major quartet is the only one to include a slow introduction of Haydnesque provenance. And the theme and variations of the finale of K421 may likewise derive their inspiration from Haydn.[23] In their outward design, all six of these quartets stick to traditional form, with only the extended codas of the majority of the allegros proving in any way remarkable. The contrapuntal movements tend generally to put forth new shoots here, and in this respect the road to the final fugue of the C major symphony (K551) may be said to pass via these six quartets. But even the opening movement of the B flat major quartet (K458) includes a coda which, like many of Beethoven's codas, makes as if to strike out in the direction of a second thematic development section. These are no longer extended cadences but genuine epilogues that allow listeners to revisit the whole of the piece in their imagination, while occasionally also opening up new and unsuspected prospects at the end of their journey.

The range of different moods contained within these six quartets is little short of astounding. Each is a self-contained whole, with not a trace of routine about it. Even the first pair of works is a matchless example of the two principal aspects of Mozart's character: a life-affirming sense of strength and freedom speaks from the first of them, now charming, now teasing, but also showing manly resolve; in the finale, which on this occasion is not simply a cheerful *envoi* but the psychological high point of the work as a whole, it is combined with a mood of thoughtful tranquillity. The D minor quartet (K421), by contrast, is tragic in tone throughout. Free from all over-insistent bombast, it reveals the moving image of a mind that has been deeply hurt. In the development section of the opening movement (a section which, as we noted above, is masterful from a technical point of view), the sense of melancholy assumes a demonic expression of such novelty and inspired brilliance that we feel ourselves transported far beyond Mozart's day and into the age of Schubert. Later the tension-laden return to the recapitulation over an oppressive pedal point is

---

23. The fifth of the 'Russian' quartets also includes a set of variations on a siciliana theme.

wonderfully poetic, as, too, is the hopelessly resigned coda with its creeping progressions in the bass. Not even the andante brings with it a sense of release, in spite of its more welcoming opening, for it, too, contains an element of suffering that finds expression in powerful dynamic accents and which, in its 'Romantically' introduced middle section in A flat major, acquires a tender, elegiac tone. The menuetto harks back perceptibly to the mood of the opening movement, even intensifying its tone of pessimism to the point where it becomes one of harsh defiance. But Mozart now introduces the starkest conceivable contrast in the form of the trio's lovely, folklike idyll, the contrast creating an incomparable psychological effect as we, as listeners, seem to look down from wild mountain ravines on a distant flower-strewn landscape. But this is not, of course, the way that our journey is to take us, as the final movement draws its own conclusions from all that has gone before it and brings the work to an end on a note of resignation. It is significant that it is cast in the form of a set of variations, with Mozart declining to take up the struggle but preferring to stick to a single mood, the underlying character of which he typically tries to intensify in various ways, but without any attempt to invest it with any new aspects. With its persistently pounding rhythm, this siciliana theme has something obstinate and defiant about it,[24] while in the refrain-like passage for the first violin it acquires a note that is both piercing and sinister, so little is it concerned for the harmonic change in the other voices:

The result is a wild and ghostly dance that is almost literally numbing in its curious restlessness: there is not the least sense of liberation in the Beethovenian meaning of that term, with even the major-key variation maintaining a mood of inconstancy and volatility. The whole demonic nature of the movement breaks free in the final variation, a più allegro, not least as the result of the earlier motif which, increasing the tension by turning its semiquavers into triplets, flits through all four voices, finally and peremptorily claiming the last word. The whole quartet is moving testimony to the pessimist in Mozart, an aspect far too little known, for, in total contrast to Beethoven, he never succeeded in escaping from the dark forces that dwell within us.

The first subject of the E flat major quartet (K428) initially gives the impression that it intends to continue this pensive mood, but the consequent phrase brings with it a lighter tone, with the Romantic element confined to the opening bars and to the end of the development section, while the movement as a whole maintains the admittedly somewhat impersonal mood of innocent joviality. Only in the remarkably dreamy andante referred to above and in the exotically coloured trio of the menuetto does the spirit of Romanticism come into its own again, only to bow out in the finale, where it abandons the field to an outburst of positively Haydnesque high spirits. In turn, the following B flat major quartet (K458) appears to pick up this mood, with its opening movement coming closest of any to that of Haydn's equivalent movements, not only in terms of the character of its first subject,[25] but also in its absence of a second subject and its whimsical play with brief thematic particles. Only in the rapt and soulful musical idea which, as we noted above, is introduced into the development section do we see Mozart's eye gazing back at us. Here, too, the

---

24. It is related to the final variation of the F major violin sonata K377.
25. It recalls the then popular hunting themes or *chasses*.

middle movements are more intimate in character: note the sustained melody of the menuetto and, more especially, the adagio with its equally broadly flowing melodies, the dark-toned splendour of its opening and the glowing raptness of its second subject, which glides along on mysterious, almost Schumannesque harmonies. As before, the finale restores the mood of the opening movement. On this occasion it is a felicitous combination of Mozartian mischievousness and folklike humour à la Haydn, a humour already explicit in the movement's main idea.[26]

The A major quartet (K464) begins by striking a note of rapt infatuation, but it is not long before contrapuntal procedures take over, from now on lending the work as a whole its idiosyncratic stamp and revealing that behind this cheerful exterior are loftier and more serious thoughts. Even in this opening movement Mozart's mastery of variation technique is already fully developed, with new aspects being derived from each idea each time that it is repeated. The principle is Haydn's, but the use to which it is put is entirely Mozart's. The menuetto, too, catches the antithetical mood of the work as a whole within its first eight bars, while the trio forms an episode inspired by a feeling of the most cheerful serenity. Of particular significance is the final movement, a set of variations based on a theme that is woven together from thoughtful introspection and rapt fervour. Mozart begins in his usual manner with a melodic variation, but in a way that goes far beyond the usual figurations: note not only its general cantabile character but, more especially, its swelling syncopations and brief floating demisemiquaver motifs that begin with a rest. The following four variations are likewise largely confined to an intensification of the theme's basic character,[27] but the second section of the fifth variation, which once again takes up the free contrapuntal style of the work as a whole, then sets out with the firm intention of exploring new aspects of the theme, a voyage of discovery continued in the whole of the sixth variation. This is built up entirely on the dominant pedal point, which the bass maintains by means of the following capricious motif:

Above it there unfolds a new and deeply pensive melody that succeeds with difficulty in remaining cheerful. The movement as a whole is permeated by a particularly appealing good humour, making it hard for Mozart to take his leave of it. He follows it up with a kind of coda in which the above-cited bass motif moves up through each of the higher voices, maintaining its pedal-point character and unexpectedly becoming the principal protagonist, while its countermelodies increasingly lose their significance. But finally the first violin ushers back the main theme, as though the bass motif has been left in charge for too long. This final variation provides a highly original, condensed overview of all that has gone before it, beginning with the main theme as far as half way through the fifth bar and continuing with the second half of the thirteenth bar and thence to the end, thereby avoiding the modulation to the dominant. There then follows the beginning of the final third of the fifth variation, which is continued in a condensed form by the three upper voices, with the whimsical pedal-point motif recurring in the bass and finally being given the last word.

26. It is a condensed version of an old folksong to which Mozart had already alluded in the finale of his divertimento K252. The lengthening of the first two notes from crotchets to minims creates a particularly witty impression in the development section.
27. Note in particular the treatment of the theme's upbeat, which appears now in its original form, now in a simplified version comprising two quavers. The original rhythm generates some entirely new variants in the fifth variation.

The main theme of the finale begins chromatically:

It is in fact a sequence with a varied second element, with both elements developed contrapuntally in the course of the movement that follows,[28] a movement that sees the culmination of the work's contrapuntal tendencies. The serious, thoughtful basic mood now gains total control, displacing the rapt infatuation that finds episodic expression only in the first violin's Beethovenian line:

Even the lively final subject-group sounds challenging, rather than harmless. But Mozart does not forget the other aspect of his image, which finds clear expression in the rapt piety of the development section's new theme, which is the notional second subject of the movement as a whole:[29]

We have already mentioned the character of the opening movement of the C major quartet (K465). On this occasion the struggle to resist an undefined sense of psychological pressure leads not to hopeless resignation, as it did with the D minor quartet, but to liberation. Even the allegro's first subject breathes a spirit of tender yearning as it finally breaks free from the dark chaos of the introduction:

After all manner of 'Romantic' peregrinations, it brings the movement to a tranquil conclusion as though with a look of dreamy infatuation:[30]

28. Beethoven wrote out this movement in full score. ◆ Further, see Yudkin, 'Beethoven's "Mozart" Quartet'.
29. Its chromatic element – first in the bass, then in the upper voice – provides a notional link with the main theme.
30. Note the chromatic degree and the curtailment of the second bar.

But the work's crowning glory is its andante, of which Jahn[31] rightly says that it raises us up into a realm of blissful peace in which all memory of pain and passion is transfigured. Its emotional world embraces the heartfelt yearning of its gloriously sweeping main melody and the dreamily wistful transfiguration of its subsidiary sections, which float along on brief motifs. The second subject recalls a passage from the andante of the great E flat major symphony (K543) with its repeated notes, its dissonant entry and its imitative procedures. While the menuetto returns to the mood of the opening movement, with a trio of dark-toned passion, the sky brightens completely for the final movement. This is not the boisterous high spirits of Haydn but a more restrained joviality which in the episode in A flat major even strikes a note of noble infatuation, as a result of which Mozart succeeds here, too, in maintaining to the very end of the piece the antithetical mood established in the opening movement.[32]

Dating from the beginning of the present period, the two duos in G major K423 and B flat major K424 for violin and viola occupy a central position between the six 'Haydn' quartets and the following group. They were written as a favour for Michael Haydn but also as a tribute to him. It was as such that Haydn accepted these works and as such that Mozart laid such special emphasis on them. Inevitably, then, Haydn's stylistic influence is particularly marked, as is clear from the slow introduction of the B flat major piece, the predilection for extended codas and a number of other details. In general, both these works – and especially the first one – are still stylistically closely related to the string quartets, notably in terms of the independence of the voices, yet they are also related to the concertante chamber music of the period (note, in particular, the virtuosic predominance of the violin in the second of the pair). The six-eight time-signature of the middle movement of K424 and the gavotte-like themes of both finales come under this same heading. The G major piece is in general the more contrapuntal of the two, with numerous passages of imitative writing and even of canonic procedures, but it also repeats most of its themes by simply exchanging the two lines, resulting in the frequent crossing of parts. Haydn will have been particularly pleased by this work, the first movement of which is an especially fine example of the solidity of his style. Its development section is based on a free variant of the second subject[33] and a chordal subsidiary passage and again recalls the chamber music with keyboard. The adagio, too, is a fine example of Mozart's ability to mitigate the austerity of two-part writing, which admits of no full-toned harmonies, and to use broken chords in highly expressive ways. Take, for instance, the variant of the first simple viola figure in the fifth bar, which already looks forward to the magnificent tied chords in the adagio of the string trio in E flat major K563. In general, this movement is a fine illustration of Mozart's art of ornamental variation. Behind the dreamy character of this and the next middle movement we may well suspect the influence of Michael Haydn. The

31. Jahn, *W. A. Mozart*, fourth edition, ii.214.
32. ◆ Among the extensive literature on Mozart's 'Haydn' quartets, see in particular Allanbrook, '"Ear-tickling Nonsense": A New Context for Musical Expression in Mozart's Haydn-Quartets' and '"To Serve the Private Pleasure": Expression and Form in the String Quartets'; Bonds, 'The sincerest form of flattery? Mozart's "Haydn" quartets and the question of influence'; Irving, *Mozart: The 'Haydn' Quartets*; and Bockholdt, 'Liebe zu einer unterschätzten Komposition Joseph Haydns: Die Finalsätze von Haydns "Russischem" Quartett in G-Dur und Mozarts "Haydn"-Quartett in d-Moll'.
33. In its original form it reveals a marked affinity with the andante of Joseph Haydn's D major symphony Hob I:2, a work that in any case contains many reminiscences of Mozart.

rondo is based on a theme that is an old favourite of Mozart's[34] and, with its two episodes (the second and more important of which is in the minor), is structurally similar to the finales of the keyboard quartets. The minor-key episode stands out not only by dint of its strict canonic procedures but also because of its unusual modulation from E minor to G minor. No less beautiful is the way in which Mozart takes his leave of the main theme at the upper octave. In the case of the B flat major duo, even the slow introduction recalls Michael Haydn not only on a formal level but also in terms of its Romantic spirit. In contrast to its predecessor, the allegro exudes a feeling of contented high spirits, though the two movements are formally identical. It, too, has its whimsical moments in the form not only of brief motifs that break off unexpectedly, but also a perverse canon in the development section and a capricious conclusion to the coda. The middle movement comprises a richly ornamented siciliana for the violin, while the final movement is cast in the form of a set of variations on an extremely skittish theme, the humour of which is increased in the second and penultimate variations in particular, taking its leave in the brief coda in the form of a contented smile on the viola. One wonders whether the archbishop appreciated his former Konzertmeister's good humour. Inevitably, these variations fail to achieve the depth of expression found in the other variations of this period. Of some importance on a formal level is the fact that *both* the last variations are marked by a change of tempo and, in the case of the final variation, also by a change of time-signature, although the theme itself fails to reveal any new facets in the process.[35]

Stylistically speaking, the chamber works with keyboard form a self-contained group. Quite unlike the string quartets, they are in fact more like the concertos, and it is no accident that the vast majority of the works that involve a keyboard and more than two other instruments date from the period under discussion, when Mozart appeared with particular frequency as a concert pianist. As a result he approached them very much from the standpoint of the concerto, as is clear on a purely superficial level from the fact that, unlike the four-movement string quartets, they are all three-movement works, with a rondo finale. No less distinctive is the virtuosic writing for the keyboard, even though the last-named instrument never overshadows the others: there is scarcely a trace of any orchestral effects in the sense that the keyboard is the centre of attention and that the other instruments exist only to reinforce it and fill out the harmonies or that they are used, at best, for odd solo passages. Still less is the keyboard preponderant in a Schumannesque manner. Rather, the dominant stylistic principle is polychorality, with the keyboard and the self-contained mass of the other instruments contrasted with each other as two completely equal groups, frequently alternating with each other within the narrowest possible confines of one and the self-same theme, so that one party takes the antecedent, the other the consequent phrase. There are also occasions, especially in the slow middle movements, where the winds or strings are divided and their individual members are treated as concertante instruments. Then the keyboard accompanies them in a way which, although often virtuosic, is always translucent: the textures are mostly

---

34. Cf. the middle movement of the F major violin sonata K376. Behind the melodic line lies the old Swabian folksong idea from the theme of the set of variations of the keyboard sonata K331. On this Swabian element in Mozart, see Abert, 'Schwäbisches bei Mozart'.

35. ◆ Although Abert claims the duos are indebted to Michael Haydn's style, at least one contemporaneous writer thought that Haydn's duos sounded Mozartian. A review of six duos attributed to Haydn, published by Gombart of Augsburg about 1795, reads in part: 'Every movement of the third sonata is entirely filled with Mozart's spirit. Ah, the beautiful melodies, the rich harmony, the succession of the most exquisite ideas, the naïve simplicity, and their rich nobility, how they delight the calmly hovering heart with Elysian bliss!' It is uncertain which work this review describes: no copy of Gombart's print survives. It is not out of the question that it is K423, which has the same number and order of movements, and the same tempo indications, as Haydn's duo P127 (MH 335). See Eisen, *Dokumente: Addenda*, 82–4, *New Mozart Documents*, 30–1.

chordal and never insistent. This concertante approach is reflected in the compositional technique: the relatively strict counterpoint of the string quartets is absent and, indeed, we sometimes even find new ideas in the development sections. But even when the writing remains thematic, it is far looser in structure and tends to resemble a witty conversation rather than a detailed discussion of the themes in question. With the exception of the opening movement of the G minor quartet (K478), the overall mood of these works reflects a far greater zest for life than that of the string quartets, with the final movements in particular leaving the listener with an impression of real contentment. None the less, Mozart was sensitive enough to draw a fine stylistic line between his concertos and these chamber works. That he saw in them a genre with its own stylistic rules is clear from the fact that all three works are very closely related in terms of both form and content, especially in respect of their last two movements. All their middle movements, for example, are in 3/8-time and are larghetto-like in character, a character that remains unaffected by the fact that the middle movement of K478 is described as an andante. All, moreover, are representative of the same type of tender and often 'Romantically' thoughtful rêverie that avails itself of a musical language of magically beautiful sonorities. The finales, by contrast, are all *alla breve* allegrettos and virtually indistinguishable from one another in terms of their moods and their particular type of rondo form, with a main thematic group and two extended episodes, the second of which is in the minor, the individual elements of the group being interchangeable. All set out from themes reminiscent of French gavottes, with a tendency towards a more popular Viennese tone, with the movements as a whole resembling loosely structured dances that are now mischievous, now festively brilliant in character. There is barely a single dark cloud in the sky.

Only the first of these works – the quintet in E flat major K452 for keyboard, oboe, clarinet, horn and bassoon that Mozart held in particularly high regard – begins with a slow introduction, but it is one of such dimensions that it is easy to forget that it is an introduction. Even this particular section reveals all the characteristic features of this kind of chamber music: a strictly concertante style, often within the narrowest confines, and a highly ingenious handling of brief motifs. It is to this interplay between these motifs that we owe the remarkable tension that typifies this beautiful movement. In contrast to the string quartets, the harmonic writing both here and in the other works in this group is extremely simple and translucent, being limited here to the tonic and dominant. The allegro theme brings with it a change of mood: the keyboard begins on its own, softly and capriciously rapt in tone, but a *forte* tutti suddenly interrupts it, raising the tone to the point where we enter a world of manly strength. As usual, the roles are then reversed, after which there comes a transitional section in which Mozart, as so often in these works, allows the keyboard to indulge in a display of elaborate virtuosity, while the other instruments merely accompany it. The dialogue then continues, with question and answer alternating within as little as two bars in the second subject. And here, too, the roles are reversed at the repeat, but it is noteworthy that Mozart alters the way in which the same ideas are expressed in keeping with the expressivity of the instruments in question. With the motif that begins with a demisemiquaver scale, we find ourselves confronted by one of those rare passages that includes a brief attempt at a purely obbligato treatment of the voices: significantly, it resembles most of the passages similar to it in being cadenza-like in character.[36] The development section is very brief, but all the more ingenious for that. A modulatory echo effect in the winds based on the last two notes of the first section of the theme that was launched by the keyboard produces an increase in tension, after which the winds

---

36. These imitative cadenzas are offshoots of the earlier practice of improvisation; see Mersmann, 'Beiträge zur Aufführungspraxis', 118. We have already seen something similar in the sinfonia concertante K364.

make a stab at the main theme itself, but get no further than the first motif from the second bar, which they mischievously keep on calling to one another until we suddenly and unexpectedly find ourselves slipping into the recapitulation. But the winds have evidently enjoyed their thematic sport to such an extent that they now give the impression of wanting to continue it at the start of the recapitulation, resulting in a highly attractive variant of this last-named section. We have already mentioned the general character of the larghetto: its main emphasis lies less on its main theme[37] than on its various subsidiary ideas. The second subject introduces a wonderfully broad and flowing melody that is spun out phrase by phrase by the individual winds, while the keyboard accompanies them in broken chords. Its notional climax is the new theme in the development section, which the winds very soon take over and introduce to a harmonically extremely bold and strangely agitated passage with a half-cadence on the dominant of E minor, from which the keyboard attempts almost desperately to break free by means of contrasting dynamics. When the main theme enters again unexpectedly, it has the effect of bringing release. Similar lapses into 'Romanticism' are also found at corresponding points in the other works in this group. Here, too, the recapitulation is varied in order to add to the sense of climax. The rondo form of the finale could hardly be more different from the rondos of Carl Philipp Emanuel Bach, who, both here and in his sonatas, gradually drew the movement's whole expressive content from a single theme. In Mozart's case, unlike Bach's, this theme always appear in the same key, namely, the primary key. Here, too, we are concerned not with the development of the theme but with the juxtaposition of multisectional subject-groups, the individual elements of which are freely interchangeable, so that, for example, the second element of the first group is appended to the second or third and so on. In this way the minor-key episode culminates not in the expected main theme but in the first episode, which in turn is not continued along regular lines but passes into the second element of the main group. The virtuosity of the keyboard increases in the bridge passages, and shortly before the end we even find a regular concerto cadenza that is executed by all the instruments. The winds expound a motif familiar from the older period but new to this movement. Based around a suspension, it is treated to strict imitative procedures, while the keyboard is effectively left to play the role of an accompanist. It is one of the most delightful cadenzas that Mozart ever wrote out in full and, as such, may give us an idea of the intelligence and logic that he brought to bear on all his improvised cadenzas. The following section, too, brings with it something of a surprise, with Mozart offering us only the first eight bars of his main theme, even though he has already whetted our appetite for it with his cadenza, after which it seems to disappear again behind a veil. Off-beat octaves on the keyboard, first in quavers, then in quaver triplets and extended over three octaves, coupled with a melody in the winds that only slowly gathers momentum and that finally sounds almost like a good-humoured *buffa* ensemble, bring the movement to an end on a series of striking but genuinely Mozartian dynamic markings that should not be obscured by transitional crescendos.

The work's popularity is attested by numerous transcriptions, none of which, however, is by Mozart himself. Many are technically incompetent, and even the best of them fail to capture the sonorities of the original, which are its main attraction.[38] Beethoven, too, was inspired by the piece

---

37. Its underlying type is Italianate in provenance.

38. Even during Mozart's own lifetime, it was already published behind his back as a quartet for keyboard and strings. In Augsburg it was published by Gombart & C. as a 'Concertante pour Violon principale, Hautbois, Clarinette, Cor, Basson, Violoncelle, Alte et Basse par W. A. Mozart'. The wind writing was left unaltered, but the keyboard part was divided up among the strings in such a clumsy and amateurish manner as to preclude all possibility of Mozart's involvement. ◆ Other early arrangements include versions for keyboard, violin, viola and violoncello (published at Mannheim by Götz, at Vienna by Artaria, and at Mainz by Schott), and for keyboard four-hands (Bonn, Simrock). Concerning the publication of K452 as a keyboard quartet, see Eisen, *New Mozart Documents*, 77–8 and 80–1.

to write his own piano quintet op. 16 of 1797. The tonality and even the number and form of the individual movements (especially the slow introduction to the opening movement and the rondo form of the finale) are the same, while the concertante style in general was likewise taken by Beethoven as a model. Yet a comparison between the two works would be futile, as both are an accurate reflection of their creators' individual characteristics and, artistically speaking, are both on exactly the same high level.[39]

We may now consider the two piano quartets in G minor K478 and in E flat major K493 of July 1785[40] and 3 June 1786 respectively. Of these, the first, with its impassioned tone, comes closest to the world of the string quartets, with even its very first subject proving to be genuinely Mozartian in its unmediated contrast between heroic defiance and pensive brooding. It is also notable for its unusual length, with Mozart finding it hard to abandon the dotted rhythm of the opening: the same rhythm is heard now as an anguished lament, now in wild revolt, with the two parties even going thematically separate ways. The opposites are never reconciled. Not until the second subject does a calmer tone enter, only to bring this whole section to an end on a distinctly timid note. As with so many works of this period, the development section begins with the backward-leading motif from the previous closing bars, but it soon takes up the second subject in a free, augmented and, in the main, cantabile variant, and on the basis of this idea there unfolds a stretto for the two upper strings, a section which, twice interrupted by the keyboard's violent modulatory shifts, assumes an increasingly agitated and sombre character, especially when the semiquaver scales suddenly dart upwards. The main theme now reenters and by means of a defiant dialogue with this semiquaver motif finally leads back to the recapitulation. It, too, is initially changed to accommodate the movement's fighting spirits. Above all, however, Mozart follows his usual manner and remains within the tonality of G minor, the sombre mood of which also infects the second subject, producing a dark-toned picture that grows wild and demonic in the coda. The movement's contemplative aspect barely manages to assert itself in the affecting concertante interplay between keyboard and violin involving the following motif:

But immediately afterwards the main theme bursts forth in the strings in all its wildness, accompanied by a keyboard figuration in broken chords that is clearly not meant to be playful but that

39. Thayer, *Ludwig van Beethovens Leben*, ii.21 and 46ff. In the middle movement especially, there are clear reminiscences of Mozart – not, in fact, of the quintet, but of *Don Giovanni* and *Die Zauberflöte* – but these are almost certainly not intentional, as we also find them in many of Beethoven's other works from this period. Just as Mozart wrote two piano quartets, so he also seems to have intended to write a second wind quintet for keyboard, oboe, clarinet, basset-horn and bassoon: see K452a and Nissen, *Biographie W. A. Mozarts*, Appendix p.12, no. 10. ◆ K452a probably does not represent a 'second' quintet but an aborted attempt at a first quintet; the autograph, now in the library of the Mozarteum, Salzburg, is written on paper used by Mozart in 1783. Further, see Plath, 'Überliefert die dubiose Klavierromanze in As KV Anh.205 das verschollene Quintett-Fragment KV Anh.54 (452a)?'

40. Its exact dating is problematic: the opening bars are included in Mozart's letter to Sebastian Winter of 8 August 1786 (*Briefe*, iii.565–7), but this list of his 'latest births' naturally includes much older pieces. In his thematic catalogue, it appears alongside the Masonic funeral music under 'July'. On the other hand, the autograph score is dated 16 October in Mozart's own hand, and a passage in one of Leopold's letters (*Briefe*, iii.461; letter of 2 December 1785) confirms this later date. In other words, the work must at least have been started in July. Perhaps the present version is a revision undertaken with a view to publication. ◆ This is not the only instance where dates in Mozart's catalogue contradict the dates on his autographs: a flagrant example is the Masonic funeral music K477; see above, p. 782 n. 42. Apparently Mozart sometimes entered works in his catalogue retrospectively, without reference to his finished scores; see Leeson and Whitwell, 'Mozart's Thematic Catalogue'.

is designed to add to the general agitation.[41] At the end all the instruments join in a unison of almost spine-chilling force.

Like the opening allegros of the minor-key keyboard concertos, the present movement, too, departs from the world of emotion traditionally found here and stands completely alone as a profession of faith on the part of the demonic, impassioned Mozart. But, as if the composer had suddenly realized that he had revealed too much of this aspect of his character here, he reverts to his former, more sociable self in the movements that follow. Only in the mute wistfulness that hangs over the andante and in the curious restlessness of the almost incessant demisemiquaver scalar motifs do we seem to hear an echo of the earlier emotional turmoil. The movement is as clearly structured as it is unified in mood and repeatedly returns to the same motifs. And, for all its cheerful high spirits, the final movement, too, avoids any sense of frivolousness, its main theme's syncopations and upward thrust through a series of narrow intervals containing within them an element of agitation and tension. The range of themes in the first episode is significant, with motifs expressive of warm-hearted effusiveness, thoughtful grace[42] and folklike joviality succeeding each other in quick succession. The last of these themes – in D major – is Haydnesque in spirit, although its phrasing invests it with a whimsical, almost tomboyish element. The E minor episode, conversely, reintroduces the mood of battle that we found in the opening movement, with a brusquely noisy opening and a timid reply in the other instruments, which seem to be craving help. The rest of the movement, too, leads us into very dark, even sinister regions, until finally the strings attempt to break free with the main theme's opening motif. The sense of liberation duly comes, not, however, in the form of the expected main theme but – highly originally – with the first second subject on the keyboard, allowing the mood to brighten at last. Only once more, at the surprising interrupted cadence on E flat, do the work's 'Romantic' spirits assert themselves one last time.

The companion piece in E flat major is structured along identical lines, an identity that extends even to points of detail such as the rondo form of the finale. More intimate in character, it also reveals a greater love of life. Its opening movement begins with a genuinely Mozartian, dreamily cantabile theme[43] that is shortly joined by the rapt gaze of the second subject:

This is the movement's true hero, and it dominates the whole of the development section, which is again built up on sequences in the bass. Introduced in its simplest form in the concertante strings, it is later heard in stretto, revelling insatiably in the world of this single, virilely beautiful idea. In the coda, too, it once again places its seal on the piece as a whole. But the work's crowning glory is its larghetto in A flat major, a movement of an indescribable interiority of emotion. It, too, includes an element of rêverie that finds expression especially in the utterly inspired return to the opening, with its yearningly gliding harmonies, and in the no less magical coda, in which the main theme dies gently away surrounded by the tenderest of figurations. The basic character of the finale is innocent high spirits, coupled with a sense of tranquillity. The subsidiary idea

---

41. Note also in this context the melody concealed in the upper voice, where there is the clear sense of an effortful struggle.
42. This theme was also used by Mozart the following year as the basis of his D major rondo for keyboard K485.
43. The prototype of this theme may be found in Schobert's keyboard quartets; see Riemann, *Johann Schobert: Ausgewählte Werke*, 94ff. and 83ff.

keeps on interfering in the musical argument, even during the episodes, adopting all manner of delightful contrapuntal guises and even generating the theme of both the first episode and, indirectly, the minor-key episode on the basis of its last three notes. On this occasion, it produces no serious disruption, in spite of its length, but resembles, rather, a virtuoso keyboard fantasia. And various elements from other subject-groups ensure that the affair does not become too serious. As in the G minor quartet, the ultimate result is a return not to the beginning but to the first episode.

That these quartets bewildered their early audiences is clear from a report 'on the latest favourite music at grand concerts' that was published in Weimar in 1788:

On the keyboard it is Kozeluch, above all, who retains the ladies' affections, although Pleyel is beginning to get the better of him. At all events, there is a great deal of humour in Pleyel's music and more new and original invention than in Kozeluch's, even though it is impossible, of course, to deny even the latter a regular compositional style, elegance and a certain stream of natural ideas. – Mozart has now gone to Vienna as Imperial Kapellmeister. To every music lover of a philosophical bent he is certainly a remarkable man. He was an extremely precocious genius and, like a true virtuoso, was already playing and composing by his ninth year (and, indeed, even earlier), much to everyone's astonishment. But what is very unusual is not only that he was a skilled musician at an unusually early age, but that he matured in the happiest manner and, on reaching man's estate, continued to show steady development. We know the flashes of ephemeral genius from bitter experience! Where is its fruit when the right time comes? Where its solid durability? Not so in Mozart's case! A few words now on an odd phenomenon occasioned by him (or his fame). Some time ago a single quadro (for keyboard, violin, viola and cello) was engraved and published. Very ingeniously set, it requires the utmost precision in all four parts, but, even when it is well played, it seems that only connoisseurs of music are able and intended to enjoy it in the form of *musica di camera*. The report soon spread: 'Mozart has written a very special new quadro, and such and such a princess owns it and plays it!', exciting curiosity and leading to the rash resolve to perform this original composition at large and noisy concerts and to flaunt it *invita Minerva*. Many other pieces survive even mediocre performances, but this work of Mozart's is impossible to listen to when it falls into mediocre amateur hands and is badly played. This happened innumerable times last winter; nearly everywhere I visited and was taken to a concert, some young lady or pretentious middle-class demoiselle or some other impudent dilettante came up to me with this engraved quadro and fancied that it would be *enjoyed* at a noisy gathering. But it could *never* do so: everyone yawned with boredom at the incomprehensible racket of four instruments that did not keep together for four bars on end and whose senseless *concentus* ruled out any unity of feeling; but it *had to* please, it *had to* be praised. I can barely describe the obstinacy with which people attempted to enforce this view virtually everywhere I went. It is not enough to rail at this folly as an ephemeral *manie du jour*, as it lasted almost the whole winter and (to judge by all that I have additionally learnt from hearsay) showed itself far too frequently. [...] What a difference when this oft-mentioned work is performed with the greatest accuracy by four skilled musicians who have studied it carefully, in a quiet room where the suspension of every note cannot escape the listening ear, and in the presence of only two or three attentive persons! But, of course, it is impossible in those circumstances to imagine any éclat, any brilliant and modish acclaim or to obtain any conventional praise![44]

The trio in G major K496 for keyboard, violin and cello is something of a parergon to the quartets. Completed on 8 July 1786, it reveals the same three-movement form, the same concertante style and even similar details such as the gavotte-like *allegretto* theme of the finale. Frequently, however, the concertante writing is different in kind: although the proximity of the quartets emerges clearly from the more independent treatment of the cello, the older thoroughbass style has still not been completely forgotten. A number of passages recall the concertante writing of the violin sonata, with only the violin and keyboard engaging in discourse in this way, while the cello merely accompanies the keyboard's bass line. In other cases, the alternation between keyboard and strings is not fully carried through, so that in the development section of the first movement, for example, the keyboard bass and cello engage in dialogue together, followed by the violin and the keyboard's upper part. Finally – and especially in the andante – we find purely obbligato three- and four-part textures instead of concertante writing. In a word, the range of different techniques is considerably greater than in keyboard quartets and violin sonatas. Of course, this is less the result of a conscious endeavour than of a certain insecurity: the style of the modern keyboard trio has yet to be established. All the more unified, by contrast, is the work's conceptual design, with the trio, in particular, revealing a succinctness and a unity found nowhere else in Mozart's works. In the middle movement, there is no other musical idea to contest the main theme's hegemony. This movement is also a good example of another of the stylistic differences that distinguishes this piece from the keyboard quartets: the far more frequent appearance of contrapuntal procedures. In this respect, the trio is far more reminiscent of the string quartets. And, like the string quartets, it is fond of coaxing the most delightful contrapuntal textures from what in themselves are utterly insignificant subsidiary and transitional motifs (note, for example, the ending of the andante). The basic tone of the whole piece – energy and resolve – is unmistakably clear from the very first theme and assumes the character of a light-hearted feeling of power in the final movement, a set of variations on a genuine 'Rococo' theme. Only once does the feeling of happiness acquire a more hesitant note, in the fourth variation in G minor, one of the most touching atmospheric portraits ever created by Mozart. Here the violin becomes obsessed with a brief motif as though with an *idée fixe*:

This motif then descends to *g*, with a series of resigned fourths beneath it in the cello, as the keyboard winds its way above it in aimless desperation, its upper voice equally unable to tear itself away from the following motif of entreaty:

44. *Journal des Luxus und der Moden* (1788), 230–1 [*Dokumente*, 279–80, *Documentary Biography*, 317–18]. Rochlitz, too, thought that 'the spirit of the artist proceeds in a curious, alien manner, grand and sublime, like a manifestation from another world'; *AmZ*, iii (1800/01), 27.

The sound of anxious, heavy sighing and questioning rings forth from the middle section, after which we sink back into the old state of hopelessness. Movements such as these are particularly well suited to give the lie to the childish prattle of a number of recent commentators who have spoken of the 'undeveloped emotional lives' of the older composers. And how beautiful and moving is the sense of liberation in the rapturous adagio variation. Yet the idea of hopelessness was so deeply engraved on Mozart's soul that he conjures it up once again following the festive brilliance of the final variation. Now, in spite of all efforts to resist it, we are drawn back down into the sombre G minor, and the attempts to break free from it in the convulsively disjointed ending prove almost wholly unsuccessful.

The final work to be considered under this heading of concertante chamber music is the quintet in E flat major K407 for horn, violin, two violas and bass that was written for Joseph Leutgeb between 1782 and 1784.[45] It is not a quintet in the strict sense of that term but might better be described – by analogy with the violin sonatas – as a horn sonata, with the keyboard part taken by strings. It is really only the horn and first violin that are treated as concertante instruments, while the lower voices are largely limited to accompanying them. A three-movement work, it seems designed to complement the character of the good-natured Leutgeb – not very deep or significant, but full of natural healthy musicianship, with an earthy good humour also breaking through at various points, especially in the finale, thus allowing the piece to appear superior to the superficially far more demanding horn concertos.

The two violin sonatas in B flat major K454 and E flat major K481 betray their affinities with the concertos not only in their outward dimensions but also in the nature of their concertante writing, their virtuosity and the melismatic character of their middle movements, as well as on points of detail. A typical feature is the great wealth of ideas, largely cantabile in nature, even at points where Mozart otherwise prefers figurative themes, as in the final subject-groups. Equally noteworthy is his delight in formal experimentation. In K454, for instance, a development section in the spirit of a free fantasia[46] is followed by the actual development section at the start of the recapitulation, with the first subject completely transformed, while the second subject is impressively prepared by means of an entirely new transitional group. In K481 Mozart's favourite theme from the F major mass is introduced into the development section and developed in a series of harmonic arcs à la Schobert. It then reappears in the coda, where it is combined with the real final theme and with the second section of the first subject that was suppressed in the recapitulation. Elements such as these, to say nothing of the sheer variety and interplay of the ideas, lend these works an improvisational air that becomes all the more marked when we compare them with the C minor sonata K457 for keyboard alone. In K454 Mozart even had recourse to a slow introduction, which is also a perfect example of a type of concertante writing in which a phrase stated on one instrument is immediately repeated by another with a genuinely Mozartian melisma.[47] The

---

45.   ◆ Although K407 is likely to have been composed for Leutgeb, no contemporaneous evidence confirms this. Similarly, in the absence of Mozart's autograph, the dating is uncertain. According to Constanze's letter of 31 May 1800 to André (*Briefe*, iv.358), Leutgeb owned a copy of a quintet for horn, violin, two violas and violoncello, almost certainly K407.

46.   Mozart was particularly fond of including at this point a tension-laden cadence to the parallel minor tonality of G minor, a device familiar to him from older models. No less characteristic is the abrupt modulation to B flat major.

47.   The tension-laden keyboard motif that is based on three semiquavers is also found in the serenade K361.

allegro, conversely, adopts a different method of either dividing the same theme between the two instruments or of giving the violin independent or imitative countermelodies. The focus of both works is their slow movement, for rarely did Mozart write such nobly and profoundly felt elegies. Passages such as the subdued ardour at the start of the second section of the andante of K454 or the repeat of the main theme, with its intricate transitional melody divided between the two voices, are not easily forgotten. At the same time, we also find passages of unprecedented harmonic boldness, especially before the return to the first subject: rêveries of genuinely Mozartian 'Romanticism', they exploit enharmonic equivalents in the most original ways. The crowning glory is the adagio in A flat major of K481, a movement cast in rondo form, with each new version of the theme varied at its repeat in a typically Mozartian manner. Entrusted to the violin, the two sudsidiary themes in F minor[48] and D flat major are veritable pearls of noble *cantabilità*, with the second of them – a melody of the most rapt intensity – modulating far from the main key and finally conjuring up the image of the first subject in A major, very much in the spirit of the rondos of Carl Philipp Emanuel Bach – the only time that the violin is entrusted with this task. But almost immediately it returns in A flat major. The same thing happens in the coda, except that on this occasion it is interrupted by the enharmonic change from E major to F flat major and by the following aria-like cadenza that undoubtedly creates a somewhat frosty impression here. Of the final movements, that of K454 is a rondo with strikingly songlike subsidiary sections and very elaborate and ingenious returns to the main theme.[49] As with Mozart's violin sonatas in general, the finale of K481 is a set of variations on a Franco-Viennese theme, with the second and fourth variations standing out in particular, the former for its subtle chromatic melismas in the keyboard, the latter – a finely wrought character-piece in its own right – by dint of its independence vis-à-vis the theme. The last two are both double variations. A delightful motivic coda brings the work to an end.

On a superficial level, the most brilliant of the instrumental works of this period is the C major symphony K425, which Mozart completed in Linz on 3 November 1783. Even more than its predecessor in D major, it bears the imprint of Joseph Haydn.[50] This is clear, not least, from the slow introduction, with its transition from tension-laden pathos to dreamy contemplation, and the brilliant *forte* repeat of the allegro's main theme – another typically Mozartian idea. The writing for the basses, beneath the brisk march theme that follows, is likewise Haydnesque. But all these often demonstrative expressions of energy regularly culminate in passages of a remarkably pensive stamp, a character further intensified by the idiosyncratic writing for the winds. Note, for example, the latters' gentle echo of the *forte* idea in E minor that replaces the second subject. In the same way Mozart appends to the final subject-group (a subject-group which on this occasion is broadly developed) a further theme in the first violins alone which, as so often in the works of this period, is basically intended to lead back to the recapitulation but which very soon becomes the main character in the development section, only now revealing its true colours in the form of a yearning insistency. And Mozart returns to it in the coda, too, which is likewise developed at length, thereby demonstrating the importance that he attached to the contrast between the different moods in this work. The andante, too, involves acute dynamic accents and striking effects

---

48. The opening returns in the major in the first-act finale of *Die Zauberflöte* at the words 'Mir klingt der Mutter Namen süße' (bars 431–3).
49. Note in particular the return following the second episode, where the dominant of G minor again plays an important role.
50. It already reveals in embryonic form the structure of the later introductions that interpolate a cantabile section between the tension-laden pathos of the opening and the modulation, on the basis of a brief motif, to the dominant; cf. the 'Prague' symphony K504.

in the winds: think only of the surly *g* in the second subject with which the winds repeatedly oppose the strings. And think also of the beginning of the development section: here, too, what had originally been a transitional motif gradually turns into the actual hero of the hour. The Haydnesque features can no more be ignored in this movement than they can in the menuetto: indeed, they are found from the very outset in the form of the doubling of the first subject at the lower octave. Although the trio resembles a number of the trios in the string quartets in having no change of key-signature, it is none the less in welcome contrast to the main part of the movement. With its dynamic contrasts, the finale begins by striking a Haydnesque note, while even its second subject picks up a well-known idea of Haydn's, only to introduce a syncopation and place it under increased psychological pressure. By the time that we come to its continuation with its three-quaver motif migrating through all the voices by means of suspensions and causing the mood to grow increasingly anguished and oppressive, the writing bears Mozart's own unmistakable stamp. Only gradually does the old sense of festive joviality return. The development section is again based on what had earlier been a subsidiary idea and is entirely Haydnesque in spirit, subjecting the motif in question to an astonishing range of emotions, from tranquil rêverie and graceful tomfoolery to defiant strength, with a clearly perceptible ebb and flow of the underlying emotion.[51] The recapitulation is finally reached in an extremely thought-provoking way by means of one of Mozart's favourite chromatic motifs. As a whole, the symphony cannot, of course, compare with its great successors, yet it none the less introduces specifically Mozartian features to the emotional world of the salonesque symphony in the form of manly ardour in characteristic interplay with pensive brooding.[52]

One of Mozart's most individual orchestral works is the Masonic funeral music (*Trauermusik*) K477, with even its outward sonorities proving exceptional in character. Even more exceptional, however, is its musical form, which reveals the strictest unity, with the opening returning at the end. At its heart is a liturgical cantus firmus heard first on the oboes and clarinets, and then on all the wind instruments:[53]

In other words, we find Mozart returning to the world of the chorale setting, and in this regard the piece is a clear precursor of the corresponding movements from *Die Zauberflöte* and the *Requiem*. But there is something inspired about the almost dramatic way in which the melody is introduced and elaborated. It begins with four heavy sighs in the winds. While the last of them is

---

51. The winds have a significant part to play in this section, too.

52. ◆ Mozart apparently revised the 'Linz' symphony in 1784 or 1785; see Eisen, 'New Light on Mozart's "Linz" Symphony, K425'.

53. Mozart wrote out the melody on a separate sheet of paper in order not to make any mistakes when elaborating it. Evidently it had a particular significance for him. According to Jahn (*W. A. Mozart*, ii.118), the first five bars reproduce the first Psalm tone with the first difference (based on the Cologne Antiphonal), whereas what follows appears to be a local compilation of several Psalm tones for the penitential Psalm *Miserere mei Deus* that was traditionally sung at burials. The melody of the first section is found among the Roman differences of the beginning of the sixth Psalm tone, while that of the second occurs in the seventh tone. ◆ Autexier, 'Wann wurde die Maurerische Trauermusik uraufgeführt?', speculates that K477 may originally have been composed in a texted, vocal version (now lost), which might also account for the discrepancy in the dates assigned the work; see again, p. 782 n. 42.

still dying away in the oboes, a restlessly questing quaver figure is conjured up in the violins, culminating within three bars in a violent *forte*. From now on, winds and strings go their separate ways, the former with sustained expressions of mourning repeatedly shaken by *forte* outbursts, the latter with disjointed and rhapsodic interjections that seem to battle with the sombre mood in a spirit of impassioned anguish. Marchlike motifs interpose themselves, and two blasts on the winds announce the approach of the funeral procession itself as it enters upon the scene with the cantus firmus. In its first line, the melody does not yet express the dark and implacable majesty of death but has a mild and cheerful transfiguration to it that is more reminiscent of classical antiquity. Even the impression that is left by the violins is one of agitation rather than of an outburst of searing anguish – an extremely subtle psychological trait. Only when the full wind choir enters and the procession is close at hand does unbridled grief break forth. To the sound of thunderous march rhythms that now enter in the bass, we hear the rhapsodic motif familiar from before, but now with its melodic line uninterrupted yet strangely fissured like a series of violent tremors that shake the anxious heart to its very core. All that is left at the end is a syncopated figure in the violins that wanders aimlessly to and fro and a few incoherent sighs in the winds. Once again the sense of searing lament erupts, after which the motifs from the beginning reappear, returning to C minor in a more intensified form that is as brief as it is insistent. But the dynamic level drops back to *piano* with the entry of the six-four chord. The coda that is still to follow is unadulterated Mozart, with profound sadness in the chromatic line in the winds, accompanied by a muted sob in the violins. *Pianissimo* chords bring the work to an end with an unexpected, transfigured chord of C major. This is Mozart's musical acknowledgement of death: here there is no titanic struggle with an inescapable foe, for death as such has no terrors for him. What he feels is only the pain of parting, and to this he abandons himself without reservation, yet also without allowing himself to be bowed down by it.

The dances that date from 1784 – K461–463 – constitute a marked advance on their predecessors. Although the minuets are formally very brief (in each case the main movement and trio are only eight bars long) and although many of them never forsake their principal key, they are none the less full of witty and whimsical ideas, without ever going beyond the strict limitations of the dance. The trio generally forms an emotional contrast to the main section, and here we often find special instrumental effects, such as the popular octave doubling of first violin and bassoon. The contredanses – a genre that was hugely popular wherever French influence predominated – are far more ambitious. They consist of two or more lively movements in 2/4-time, sometimes also with a *mineur* and with a repeat of the beginning. In K463 Mozart combined a contredanse with a minuet, so that eight songlike bars of a slow minuet (no. 2 is specifically headed 'Adagio') frame a complete contredanse. Evidently this was a very popular combination in Vienna at this time. As with all such dances, the string writing is typically in three parts, with two violins and a bass.

39

The great keyboard concertos

For reasons already familiar to us, the keyboard concerto takes pride of place in Mozart's output between 1782 and 1786. During this period he wrote fifteen such works, most of whose dates of composition and origins we have already mentioned.[1] Of the remainder, the concertos K413 in F major, K414 in A major and K415 in C major must date from the second half of 1782, as Mozart published them by subscription in January 1783, writing to his father as follows on 28 December 1782:

> These concertos steer a mid-course between being too hard and too easy, they're very brilliant, pleasing to the ear and natural, without seeming empty; there are also passages here and there from which *connoisseurs alone* can derive any satisfaction – but in such a way that non-connoisseurs, too, are bound to be content, even if they don't know why.[2]

The concerto in F major K459 is dated 11 December 1784 and, like K451 in D major and K 488 in A major, is one of the pieces that Mozart kept back for himself or for a small circle of music lovers and connoisseurs.[3] The final work in this series is the concerto in C major K503, which was completed in Vienna on 4 December 1786.

Writing to his father on 26 May 1784, Mozart himself had the following to say about the concertos K449 in E flat major, K450 in B flat major, K451 in D major and K453 in G major:

1. There are also many surviving sketches from this period (K315f, 537a, 488a, 459a, 502a, 537b). A rondo in A major of 19 October 1782 is complete apart from a few gaps in the instrumentation (K386). A second one in D major (K382) was written in [February or] March as a replacement finale for the D major concerto K175. ◆ Recent studies of Mozart's autographs have suggested revised dates for the fragments mentioned by Abert. K459a was written down about April 1784, K502a in 1784 or 1785, K537a and 488a in 1785 or 1786 (K537a is traditionally dated February 1788), and K537b (traditionally dated February 1788) in 1785. K315f is an early fragment, dated Mannheim 1778, for a double concerto (keyboard and violin). Further, see Tyson, 'Mozart's Piano Concerto Fragments'. The source situation is particularly complicated for K386, the autograph of which was cut up and dispersed; at present, the following fragments are known: bars 1–22 (privately owned in the United States); bars 23–62 (privately owned in Germany); bars 63–78 (Royal College of Surgeons of England, London); bars 101–4 and 110–15 (University of Western Ontario, London, Canada); bars 118–32 (privately owned in Great Britain); bars 136–54 (University of Rochester, New York); bars 155–71 (privately owned in Japan); and bars 225–69 (British Library, London). Further, see NMA X/31/3.
2. *Briefe*, iii.245–6 (letter of 28 December 1782). ◆ It is not certain that the concertos were finished by January, as Abert suggests. Although Mozart offered them in the *Wiener Zeitung* on 15 January 1782, the advertisement clearly states that they 'will not appear until the beginning of April' (*Dokumente*, 187–8, *Documentary Biography*, 212). Apparently the subscription was not successful: on 26 April Mozart wrote to the Paris publisher Sieber offering him the works (*Briefe*, iii.266).
3. *Briefe*, iii.589–90 (letter of 30 September 1786). Mozart also played it, together with K537, at Leopold II's coronation in Frankfurt, with the result that it, too, is occasionally known as the 'Coronation Concerto'; see Köchel, *Chronologisch-thematisches Verzeichnis sämtlicher Tonwerke Wolfgang Amade Mozarts*, second edition, 431–2. ◆ Here Abert refers to K459. It is not certain, however, that Mozart performed this particular concerto at Leopold II's coronation; the only evidence for this assertion is the title page to André's 1794 first edition: 'Ce Concerto a été exécuté par l'Auteur à Francfort sur le Mein à l'occasion du Couronnement de l'Empéreur Léopold II'.

I really can't chose between these two concertos [K450 and 451] – they're both concertos that will make the performer sweat. But in terms of difficulty, the one in B flat beats the one in D. I'm curious to know which of the three you and my sister prefer – the one in B flat, D or G. The one in E flat doesn't belong under this heading. This is a concerto of a very special kind and is written for a small orchestra, rather than a large one – in other words, it's really only a question of the three great concertos. – I'm curious to know whether your opinion coincides with that of the *general* public here and with my *own*; of course, you have to hear all 3 works well performed and with all their parts.[4]

In terms of their outward form, these concertos are virtually indistinguishable from their predecessors, especially K271 in E flat major of 1777. Only in their internal design is there any appreciable difference. All of them are three-movement works, with the usual rondo finale replaced in only two cases (K453 and 491) by sets of variations on allegro themes: as so often elsewhere, we may see French influence in this. But there are other movements in which Mozart retains the old framework that had been established in essence by Johann Christian Bach, merely seeking to adapt it to his own individual ends. This conservatism is bound up with the style and thrust of this whole group of works, a group that still pays lip-service to the old ideal of art as a form of aristocratic entertainment in which the audience was at least as deeply implicated as the creative artist, for all that the latter was already attempting to conceive of it in a much more personal way and to reinterpret it as such.[5] The only exceptions to this are the two minor-key concertos K466 and 491, both of which abandon traditional territory in favour of the artist's archetypal experience, as a result of which they treat formal questions, too, in the freest and most independent manner.

The principal problem raised by the opening movements of these works – all of which are in sonata form – was the relationship between the first and second subject and, hence, the question of these subjects' distribution between tutti and solo.[6] There were various ways of solving this problem, with Johann Christian Bach one of the earliest composers to confront it.[7] Mozart himself was by no means disposed to accept the first solution that came his way and, indeed, one of the major attractions of these concertos is their freedom from all routine. But Mozart approached the problem from a far broader basis than Bach had done: after all, his works reflect the influence not

4. *Briefe*, iii.315 (letter of 26 May 1784). In an earlier letter (*Briefe*, iii.314; letter of 15 May 1784), Mozart notes that the concerto in E flat major could also be performed '*a quattro* without wind instruments', whereas the other three 'all have obbligato winds, and you rarely perform such music'. ◆ The same claim – that the concertos could be performed without winds – was made for K413–415 in Mozart's advertisement of 15 January 1783; see n. 2. Concerning K449, see Keefe, '"An Entirely Special Manner": Mozart's Piano Concerto No. 14 in E Flat, K. 449, and the Stylistic Implications of Confrontation'.
5. For general studies, see Franz Lorenz, *W. A. Mozart als Klavierkomponist*; Reinecke, *Zur Wiederbelebung der Mozartschen Clavier-Concerte*; and Schering, *Geschichte des Instrumentalkonzerts*, 160ff.
6. ◆ The 'origins' of concerto form have been hotly debated and it is by no means clear that 'sonata form' is the only model. See, among others, Blume, 'Die formgeschichtliche Stellung der Klavierkonzerte Mozarts'; Tovey, 'The Classical Concerto'; Landon, 'The Concertos: (2) Their Musical Origin and Development'; Edwin Simon, 'Sonata into Concerto: A Study of Mozart's First Seven Concertos'; Charles Rosen, *The Classical Style*, 185–263; Forman, *Mozart's Concerto Form: The First Movements of the Piano Concertos*; Charles Rosen, *Sonata Forms*, 69–95; Dubowy, *Arie und Konzert: Zur Entwicklung der Ritornellanlage im 17. und frühen 18. Jahrhundert*; Küster, *Formale Aspekte des ersten Allegros in Mozarts Konzerten*; Karol Berger, 'The First-Movement Punctuation Form in Mozart's Piano Concertos'; Webster, 'Are Mozart's Concertos "Dramatic"? Concerto Ritornellos versus Aria Introductions in the 1780s'; Feldman, 'Staging the Virtuoso: Ritornello Procedure in Mozart, from Aria to Concerto'; and Irving, *Mozart's Piano Concertos*. For contemporaneous theoretical descriptions, see Stevens, 'An 18th-Century Description of Concerto First-Movement Form' and 'Theme, Harmony, and Texture in Classic-Romantic Descriptions of Concerto First-Movement Form'; and Davis, 'H. C. Koch, the Classic Concerto, and the Sonata-Form Retransition'.
7. See Schering, *Geschichte des Instrumentalkonzerts*, 149. ◆ In addition to the literature cited in n. 6, see Daffner, *Die Entwicklung des Klavierkonzertes bis Mozart*; Hans Engel, *Die Entwicklung des deutschen Klavierkonzertes von Mozart bis Liszt*; and Sternfeld, 'The Concerto'. For J. C. Bach in particular, see John A. Meyer, 'The Keyboard Concertos of Johann Christian Bach and their Influence on Mozart'.

only of the different types of concerto that existed at this time but also of virtually every school of German instrumental music, most notably those associated with Mannheim and Vienna. The large-scale opening tuttis are entirely symphonic in character, recalling Mannheim not only in their broad sweep and the multisectional nature of their themes but also in their brilliant writing for winds, especially in the early works, whereas the later works recall the Viennese school in their more subtle treatment of the winds and their stricter thematic unity.[8] The result is a series of great symphonic subject-groups, except that they end not in the dominant, as they would in a symphony, but in the tonic. Yet their most striking feature is their division between first and second subject, the only question being whether the second subjects that appear here are later recognized as such by the soloist and applied to the movement as a whole. It is important to note from the outset, first, that all the tutti second subjects are conceived as being in contrast to the first subjects and are generally cantabile in character and, secondly, that Mozart, following a particular Bachian prototype, tends to introduce these subjects in the tonic.[9] The only exception here is K 449, with its sharply underlined dominant ending. Mozart was no doubt striving to create a sense of contrast here, but for the present did not exploit it to its full potential. In general he is fond of emphasizing the tonic in these tuttis and of modulating only fleetingly. In this context it is particularly worth listening to K459 and 491, whereas the other minor-key concerto – K466 – begins the second subject in the relative major, only to allow it to slip back very quickly into the tonic. A small minority of these works (K413 and 459) dispenses with any such contrast in their tuttis, delaying it until the solo, where it is introduced not at the soloist's first entry but only after the soloist has treated the main theme at length. But a far larger group replaces the solo with the second subject in the dominant, allowing its antithetical nature to emerge to its fullest effect (cf. K453). There is, finally, a third group in which the soloist takes absolutely no heed of the second subject in the orchestra, but introduces a new theme at the point where this second subject would normally enter: this is the case with the concerto in B flat major K450, which already contains a plethora of themes, as well as in K467 and K482, where the second subjects are even found in the minor of the dominant, and, finally, in the last two works in this series. This contrast between the two subsidiary themes sometimes even extends to the recapitulation: in K450, for example, the soloist briefly makes good the tutti's second subject, which had earlier been passed over. There is an almost palpable sense of delight to Mozart's attempts to explore more and more new aspects of this problem.

Thematically speaking, the orchestra's contribution generally comes to an end with these great symphonic opening tuttis. Although it still has a self-contained part to play at traditional points, namely, the end of the subject-group and at the beginning and end of the recapitulation, where it frames the soloist's free cadenza, it introduces no new ideas, limiting itself in the main to consolidating and rounding off all that has gone before. Only exceptionally, as in K459, is it left to introduce the second subject after the soloist has dealt with the main theme, but it is generally the soloist himself who is responsible for this task, with the orchestra left, at best, to make a belated contribution to the new idea.

8. The only exception is K449, in which the writing for the winds is singularly lacking in independence, confirming Mozart's own remark (see n. 4) that these instruments could be omitted if necessary. The main theme and final subject-group of K413 include direct reminiscences of Johann Stamitz. Later the final subject-groups tend to follow the north German and Haydnesque model and rework the main ideas. ◆ Recent paper studies suggest that K449 may have been started in the winter of 1782/3, coincident with Mozart's composition of K413–415, the three earlier concertos that he also noted could be performed without winds.
9. Even in his first three concertos, Beethoven struck out in a completely different direction here. In the C major concerto the tutti second subject is in G minor; in the B flat major concerto it is in D flat major; and in the C minor concerto it is in E flat major. In all three works, moreover, it is acknowledged by the soloist, too.

The first solo is likewise introduced in extremely varied and ingenious ways, especially in the later concertos. Although there is always an attempt on the soloist's part to pick up the tutti's opening idea, the idea itself may be varied, as in K413, while in other cases the link is made in an indirect way by means of an independent interpolation, as though the soloist needs time to get underway (K450) or as though he is tempted to go his own way and has to be brought to order by the orchestra (K467). There is definitely something improvisatory about these sections: just as the soloist takes his leave as an improviser in the great cadenzas at the end, so he is introduced as such here. The two minor-key concertos introduce their soli in particularly beautiful ways, thus underlining their special position within this series as a whole. In the D minor concerto the soloist begins with a new and extraordinarily expressive idea that already looks forward to Beethoven and that seeks to escape from its great psychological burden by means of a heartfelt entreaty. But as soon as the orchestra enters, he succumbs to a curious, nervous disquiet that immediately leads to the return of the sombre first subject: the soloist has no choice but to accompany its sinister tread with a half-defiant, half-desperate figuration. Much the same is true of the C minor concerto: here, too, the keyboard begins by striking an independent note, but is then drawn forcibly into the orchestra's world of emotion by the main theme's violent eruption in the orchestra; we can see quite clearly that the relationship between tutti and solo is based on a mental or psychological process that rests on the notion of contrast. In K503 the return of the main theme is even preceded by a long intermediary passage that begins as a dialogue, before the soloist breaks away in a spirit of free virtuosity. As a rule, however, the soloist takes up the main theme, either alone or accompanied by the orchestra. Sometimes he develops it figuratively, more rarely – as in K415 – he maintains his thematic independence vis-à-vis the orchestra. The main theme soon develops along independent lines, and the closer we get to the second subject, the more virtuosic the keyboard writing becomes – as is indeed the case in all bridge passages. This is even truer at the end of the 'second' subject group, before the entry of the tutti. These are always particularly playful passages that repeatedly delay the ending with the trilled cadence in favour of a display of brilliant virtuosity. The development sections are far more varied than in the other types of work from this period: some – K414, 415, 453 and 488 – adopt the older practice of introducing entirely new themes, while others – K413 and 459 – are strictly thematic. But what is decisive about all these passages is not so much this particular aspect as the surprising and ingenious revival of the old Schobertian principle of the fantasia development section. The main emphasis lies in the harmonic writing, which is in a constant state of flux, generally driving the same idea unaltered through the most varied keys. No attempt is made to gravitate towards a particular goal: instead, movement as such is all-important here, with the motifs that are carried along by it – initially primitive and chordal, in the later works thematic in character – serving only to strengthen the work's harmonic backbone. There is no question of any development section in the strict sense of that term. This harmonic framework is generally built up on bass sequences and is accompanied by particularly elaborate figurations and passage-work on the part of the soloist, whose virtuosity reaches its high point here. Some of these are highly 'Romantic' forays, which take the form of boldly arching paragraphs moving towards an unknown goal that is repeatedly hidden from view. Only at the beginning and end do we find relatively brief phrases of greater melodic and harmonic plasticity which, as with Schobert, are not unlike bridgeheads in terms of the function that they perform. In both minor-key concertos the same development-section principle is brilliantly subordinated to the train of thought of the work as a whole.

In these works as elsewhere, the entry of the recapitulation is rarely the result of large-scale tensions resulting from the underlying affects – a device favoured by Beethoven in particular.[10]

10. Among exceptions is the C minor concerto.

Rather, it tends either to follow on directly from the development section, entering as though through the mists, or to proceed via a series of brief false starts that may be defiant or dreamily wistful in character. Among memorable examples are the two quintessentially Mozartian bars in K466:

Indeed, Mozart occasionally goes out of his way to break off the build-up of tension shortly before it is due to find release. In K449, for example, he has already reached the dominant pedal point when he interpolates four pensive bars immediately before the entry of the recapitulation:

As before, the recapitulation begins by combining the first tutti and solo in a radically fore-shortened repeat. Here is a point at which Mozart's imagination proves particularly inspired: no two concertos are the same in this respect, their only point in common being their evident desire to treat both soloist and orchestra as concertante instruments within a relatively confined space. The foreshortened form does not prevent Mozart from occasionally developing individual ideas, as in K453, or even from reintroducing the new theme that had first been heard in the development section, as in K488. And the themes often reappear in a different order. But in general the recapitulations run along regular lines and the introduction of the free cadenza reflects the earlier tradition. Rarely does the soloist make any further contribution to the opening movement, the most notable exception being the highly poetical ending of the allegro of K491, which appears to fade away in the darkness of night.[11]

Most of the middle movements are in binary or ternary *Liedform*, generally with a highly poet-ical coda tacked on to the end. In two cases (K450 and 456) the movement is a set of variations, while in the case of K451, 466, 482 and 491 it is cast in rondo form, with Mozart preferring the French variant of main section plus *mineur* or *majeur*. In K466, the very heading – 'Romance' – indicates French influence. The themes are generally shared between both parties: either the soloist begins with the complete theme and the orchestra repeats it, or vice versa. Frequently the same theme is also divided between the two of them. Yet the main emphasis lies with the soloist, whose principal task is not to engage in a display of brilliant virtuosity (it is significant that the impro-vised cadenza so often found in the earlier concertos now disappears completely) but to unfold a cantabile line and to embellish it tastefully. Nowhere do we find such perfect examples of Mozart's subtle and yet expressive art of ornamentation[12] as we do in the soloist's variants on the tutti's

---

11. ◆ For a general, schematic outline of Mozart's concerto first movements, see Leeson and Levin, 'On the Authenticity of K. Anh. C 14.01 (297b), a Symphonia Concertant for Four Winds and Orchestra'.
12. We encountered earlier examples of this whole approach in a number of the adagio variations.

main themes in these concertos: listen, in particular, to K 415 in this respect. Except in the movements with a *mineur* episode, Mozart is less concerned here with a sharp contrast between the themes than with establishing a unified mood, with the result that most of the subsidiary subjects take up and extend the emotional world of the main themes, instead of ushering in a change in the underlying affect, hence the wonderful unity of all these movements, which afford brilliant proof of Mozart's lyrical gifts. But they also attest to his ability to refine the traditional middle movement in the fires of his genius and to free it from all trace of the transitory and merely fashionable. All vestige of the *galant* style as found in the works of Johann Christian Bach and, to a lesser extent, Carl Philipp Emanuel Bach has been expunged from these movements. In some of them, it is true, Mozart still clings to the older view that demanded an idyll or an elegy here, but everything is reinterpreted in personal terms and all trace of convention has vanished. Instead, most of them contain an element of contemplation and dreaminess that is also found in the related middle movements of the chamber works with keyboard[13] and which, when combined with the bewitching spell of the sonorities and melodic writing, produces a very special type of movement even within Mozart's output in general. Although other movements may be more profound, he never wrote anything as lovely or as sweet-toned as this. Their closeness to the composer's vocal music is undeniable: in some cases they approach the French *ariette*, in others a song from a serious German singspiel and in others again a sentimental Italian aria. And yet we always feel that the cantabile line is sustained by the instrumental soloist. Even today there are no pieces that are a better test of a pianist's ability to sustain a cantabile line. Listen above all to the andante of K 467, one of the most beautiful movements of its kind, effectively consisting of no more than a continuous melody accompanied by the tenderest tone colours in the orchestra. Yet even these rêveries have their Romantic, even terrifying stretches. In K 414, for example, we find the orchestra's final phrase spun out as though in a dream, while in K 453 there is an eloquent five-bar lead-in that precedes the actual theme. Note also the extremely bold modulation in K 449 and much else besides.[14]

With the exception of the two sets of variations in K 453 and 491, the final movements are all cast in rondo form, although only in the case of K466 is the movement in fact described as such.[15] The French influence that was sometimes also a feature of the middle movements is even clearer here, revealing itself not only in the choice of rondo form but in the very way in which that form is developed and even on points of thematic detail. Its principal characteristic is the interpolation of a great minor-key episode as a *mineur*, an episode absent from only a handful of these movements. The simplest form is the one in which this *mineur* remains the only episode, as in K449, while the most striking variant involves a change of tempo, as in K415. Generally, however, there are several episodes, rather than just the one, resulting in a fusion of the French and Italian types. The usual form includes three subsidiary themes, of which the one in the minor generally, but by no means exclusively, plays the principal role, producing the form ABACADA. In K415, 488 and 503 there are four or five episodes. The first may be in either the dominant or the tonic, but in the latter case it is so clearly set apart from the main theme and, as the musical argument unfolds, it goes its own way to such an extent that it deserves to be treated as an independent idea. But this form is handled with an astonishing wealth of wit and imagination, with the desire for uniformity

---

13. The affinity emerges most clearly from K450, 459 and 482.
14. ◆ Concerning Mozart's concerto slow movements, see Brück, *Die langsamen Sätze in Mozarts Klavierkonzerten: Untersuchungen zur Form und zum musikalischen Satz.*
15. The tempo di menuetto from K413 also falls under this heading.

emerging here, too, with ever greater clarity. In K449, for example, the main theme is so predominant that even the minor-key section has some difficulty in asserting itself. Sometimes the themes are in the same order, with the same sequence of modulations, as in first-movement sonata form, the only difference being that there is no development section (cf. K466), while in other cases, such as K459, the main theme is unexpectedly found in a completely free form within the episodes, demanding its due in defiant or mischievous fashion. Particularly ingenious, however, is the way in which the individual themes are rearranged and recombined with each other in the course of the movement. After a large-scale return based on motifs from the main theme, the listener naturally expects to hear the main theme itself, but this is suddenly displaced by a subsidiary subject – only one of many such surprises of which Mozart is capable here. This aspect is further reflected in the fact that there is no longer any rule governing the order of the tutti and soli. Only the main themes are generally stated by both, either one after the other or alternating with each other, but otherwise there is total freedom. Now one partner may take the lead, now the other. On some occasions the orchestra develops a theme sequentially to the accompaniment of virtuoso passage-work on the keyboard, producing effects similar to those found in the development sections of their opening movements, while on other occasions one of the partners – generally the soloist – clings obsessively to his theme, refusing to hand it over to the other partner or doing so only with great reluctance. The orchestra, too, occasionally begins to indulge in concertante practices, so that instead of two partners, we now find three. Generally the result is a witty and good-natured game, often inspired by sheer pleasure in sensuously beautiful sonorities, but in the more important concertos we also find deeper emotional conflicts.

Mozart is especially fond of turning the final return of his main themes into elaborate codas, and it is these sections, more than any other, that bear all the hallmarks of his genius. They are generally developed from the final tutti following the soloist's cadenza[16] and in most cases are highly specific in character, either reemphasizing one particular aspect of the earlier mood or taking stock of all that has gone before it. In K415, for example, Mozart picks up a brief motif from the first subject-group:

This motif gradually descends from the violins to the basses, where it brings the movement to an end with a mysterious purring sound. In K449 and 453 the main idea reappears, freely varied, with a change of tempo, while in K450 we find real hunting music in the form of a *chasse*.[17] And in the coda of K466, finally, the sombre minor-key mood is resolved – exceptionally – in a bright D major, with Mozart revelling in happiness and contentment, a feeling that is due, not least, to the half-humorous horn calls:

16. Neither K413 nor K488 has a cadenza.
17. Its nucleus is the fanfare in bars 16–18.

Mozart's rondos are only very loosely connected with the equivalent keyboard movements of Carl Philipp Emanuel Bach that are not only among the latter's most important works but also some of the most idiosyncratic keyboard pieces of the age.[18] Certainly, these links are far looser than they are in the case of the brief rondo in D major K 485. In terms of both their form and content, Bach's rondos are far freer and more subjective than his sonatas, even though their intellectual goal – the transformation of a theme by means of constantly changing shapes and colours – remains the same. It is not, however, strict logic that has the last word here, but the artist's free imagination, which reveals an almost literally inexhaustible volatility in the way in which the themes are repeatedly reexamined and cast in a new light. Sometimes they are varied, sometimes abruptly broken off and developed in completely new ways, but above all they are repeatedly given a new harmonic basis, migrating to the remotest keys at each of their subsequent appearances. Indeed, the harmonic language of these rondos is astonishingly bold, deliberately avoiding traditional, fixed modulatory patterns. Nor are their innovations confined to transitional passages but affect the whole structure's most basic elements, so that it is hardly surprising to discover here features that point far beyond the Classical period and look forward to the 'Age of Romanticism'. On the level of invention, too, these works are more idiosyncratic than the average sonata. Their themes are all highly distinctive, and there is no mistaking their links with the rondos of the young Beethoven, especially in terms of their rapt interiority.[19] In a word, these rondos – like the fantasias – reveal an alternative aspect of Bach's character, an aspect receptive to new and fashionable ideas. With their numerous interjections, questions, eloquent pauses and fermatas and sudden changes of mood, their whole musical language is clearly reminiscent of the *Sturm und Drang* movement, except that Bach has enough good taste and sense of logic to avoid the overwrought nature of the poets of this period.

Scarcely any of these basic features is found in Mozart's rondo finales, which draw far more closely on the Franco-Italian tradition than on that of Bach. This is already clear from their themes, where we find the same rhythmically piquant, effervescent spirit, except that here it glows with the fire of Mozart's genius. In particular, the themes with an *alla breve* time-signature and equal crotchets, as in K449 and 453, are obviously of French descent. But temperament comes before originality, and the same is true of the way in which these themes are developed, their aim being the most brilliant and colourful interplay of ideas, albeit under the hegemony of a single main idea, rather than changes to that idea. But it is in his harmonic writing that Mozart moves furthest away from Bach. In general, the basic ideas modulate according to a fixed pattern that usually admits of only the most closely related – fifth-related or relative – keys. It is not that these movements lack the inclination to explore more original harmonies, merely that this inclination finds expression only in bridge passages and in those places where the themes are developed, rather than while the themes are being presented. Without diminishing the artistic value of these final movements, we could almost claim that they are more genuine examples of Gesellschaftsmusik than their predecessors.[20] At all events, they are the fitting coping stones of the whole edifice, and Mozart was merely demonstrating his immense stylistic sensitivity when he eschewed the Bachian formal model here, a model which, although more up-to-date, belonged to a completely different emotional world.

---

18. 'The music that will be played in the New Jerusalem will undoubtedly include Bach's rondos': see Cramer, *Magazin der Musik*, i (1783), 35.
19. Compare, for example, the D major rondo from the *Zweyte Sammlung der Claviersonaten* [the second set of *Clavier-Sonaten nebst einigen Rondos für Kenner und Liebhaber*, Wq. 57] of 1780 with the final rondo from Beethoven's piano sonata op. 7.
20. Here, too, the exceptions are the minor-key concertos.

With the exception of the finale of K491, the movements that are cast in the form of sets of variations fail to achieve the profundity of the equivalent movements from the string quartets, even though they afford further examples of the composer's combinatory gifts and sense of sonority. The theme is always expounded by the tutti, with the soloist providing a figural variant of it in the first variation, where it is lightly supported by orchestral harmonies. The following variations, conversely, are generally double variations, in other words, each repeat of the two parts of the theme is newly varied, either in a related or a contrasting way. The relationship between tutti and soli plays a decisive role here, either with Mozart entrusting the theme to the orchestra, while the soloist accompanies it with rapid and often highly impassioned figurations, or both parties are strictly segregated, so that each of them emphasizes and intensifies a different aspect of the theme. The third variation of the middle movement of K456 and the fifth variation of the finale of K453 are both typical examples of this. Mozart is particularly fond of giving the tutti sections to the winds alone, with the result that these variations contain some particularly attractive timbral effects. The strings provide the soloist with light harmonic support. There are invariably minor (or major) variations, but none of the usual adagio variations. With the single exception of the coda variations, Mozart remains true to his general principle of merely intensifying the theme's basic character, rather than of exploring new aspects of it, as Beethoven did. In the presto finale of K453, the listener catches only a glimpse of the theme at the beginning but is regaled instead by a scintillating, tension-laden dialogue between, on the one hand, festive Italian bustle and the chuckling strains of an *opera buffa* and, on the other, strangely thoughtful ostinato basses with a sigh motif above them, until the theme itself finally rises up jubilantly in the keyboard and the winds good-naturedly take up and continue its final phrase. The coda of K491 is less extensive, but it too adopts an entirely free approach to the theme, throwing into even sharper focus than before the whole of this impassioned atmospheric portrait.[21]

One almost has the impression that in writing these concertos Mozart was conducting an experiment in order to see how far it was possible to reconcile the spirit of Gesellschaftsmusik with his subjective emotions as an artist. After all, he was still attached, at least in part, to the old order with its *galant* zest for life and intellectual curiosity. As a result, these concertos became classic examples of an art in which audience and artist both had an equal part to play, with social impressions and his own experiences as an artist in constant interaction. On some occasions, it is the social impressions that assert themselves, on others Mozart's own experiences, yet it is clear that here, too, the focus of his activity shifted from the audience and increasingly towards the composer, with the two minor-key concertos going furthest in this direction. With these two works, Mozart at least notionally picked up the tradition of Carl Philipp Emanuel Bach, who had struck an equally subjective and impassioned note in his own minor-key concertos. In the rest of the repertory, concertos in a minor key are very much the exception. The concerto in D minor – the key of *Don Giovanni*[22] – is especially Romantic in character, combining, as it does, sombre and even desperate brooding with an exuberant, transfigured inwardness.[23] The C minor concerto, by contrast, is

21. For Beethoven's enthusiastic verdict on it, see Thayer, *Ludwig van Beethovens Leben*, ii.78. ◆ For Mozart's concerto finales generally, see Brink, *Die Finalsätze in Mozarts Konzerten: Aspekte ihrer formalen Gestaltung und ihrer Funktion als Abschluß des Konzerts*; and specifically for movements in variation form, Sisman, 'Form, Character, and Genre in Mozart's Piano Concerto Variations'.

22. The only concerto that Johann Christian Bach is known to have written in a minor key is also in D minor; see Max Schwarz, 'Johann Christian Bach'. ◆ Recent research has uncovered two more minor key concertos by J. C. Bach, W69 and W73, both in F minor. The earlier of the two, W69, appears in the same set as the D minor concerto (W70) cited by Abert; see Warburton, *The Collected Works of Johann Christian Bach 1735–1782. Thematic Catalogue*, 122–4.

23. It contains various melodic types familiar from other great works. The Italian overture theme from the 'Jupiter' symphony is heard in the bass at the start of the very first movement, while the main theme from the same symphony's andante is concealed

entirely tragic in tone, combining, as it does, the titanic defiance of its opening allegro (an extraordinarily unified movement) with the genuinely Mozartian humour of its final allegretto, in which gruffness occasionally verges on malice. The middle movement introduces a brighter note only with its affecting, romance-like melody, while the subsidiary themes try to come to terms with the sense of emotional pressure, not, it is true, by defiance, but by heartfelt entreaty. These two works inevitably felt out of place in Vienna's concert halls, and it is no accident that the concept of the concerto is most radically developed in them. Yet the others, too, all reveal unique and self-contained atmospheric portraits. And they are also admirable examples of Mozart's approach to tonality, with the bright and sunny grace of the A major concertos K414 and 488 clearly distinguished from the festive brilliance of the D major concerto K451 and the more measured manly serenity of the G major concerto K453. Common to all three works in C major – K415, 467 and 503 – is a powerful, occasionally somewhat starchy dignity, which in the last of the group has to contend with all manner of dark undercurrents as a result of the constant and characteristic interplay between major and minor. The concertos in flat keys predominante in terms of both number and significance, with pride of place going to the two concertos in E flat major (K 449 and 482), both of which embody the whole dark splendour and majesty of the works that Mozart wrote in this key. By contrast, the two concertos in B flat major, K450 and 456, reveal an intimacy that frequently borders on anguish as a result of their proximity to the key of G minor, while the ones in F major – K413 and 459 – strike a more resolute, sometimes even harsh, note. Stylistically, too, these works reveal marked differences, their affinities notwithstanding: whereas some of them adopt the almost nonchalantly relaxed manner of music intended as popular entertainment, others, such as K453, bespeak a greater degree of artistry and others again even indulge in contrapuntal procedures: here one thinks of K415 and 459. But the later concertos lay special emphasis on thematic unity.[24] It is by no means only the main ideas that serve as Mozart's starting point, but often enough subsidiary motifs that initially seem extremely unprepossessing. The listener is reminded of a debate in which one of the participants suddenly takes up a particular idea from the previous speaker's remarks, an idea that the latter may not even have thought important but which he now proceeds to discuss as though it were a matter of life and death. In the development section of the opening movement of K456, for example, the orchestra initially becomes obsessed with the following high-spirited motif from the final subject-group:

A somewhat mannered form of this motif is then taken over by the soloist.

We have already had frequent occasion to mention the powerful French influence on these concertos. Among these influences are the relatively frequent march themes of the opening tuttis (K415, 453 and 459), which are typically found in French concertos of this period.[25]

There is a certain pleasure to be derived from comparing the themes of these concertos with those of the contemporary serenades and symphonies. The popular Viennese tradition finds

in the syncopations in the first violins above it. With its broken chords, the theme of the final movement resembles that of the finale from the G minor symphony, while the principal theme of the romance is of the *Veilchen* type. The sketch of an alternative opening of the finale is included in the Offenbach score of K450. ◆ For a modern facsimile and transcription of Mozart's sketch, see NMA V/15/4, 267. Also sketch volume.

24. In K456 the theme of the finale is even related to that of the andante.

25. See Schering, *Geschichte des Instrumentalkonzerts*, 163.

expression in only a handful of closing movements, and the noisy over-emotionalism of the Italian sinfonia is as good as banished altogether. Here, too, the listener is clearly aware of the ideal of this aristocratic art, which demanded of the artist as much intelligence and scintillating wit as he could muster, but frowned upon popular elements, which tended to be regarded as an expression of plebeian vulgarity.

Among the most fascinating aspects of these concertos are the tonal effects that stem not only from the concertante writing for orchestra and keyboard but also from within the orchestra itself.[26] Never before had Mozart used the winds and strings in such a varied and intelligent way in his orchestral writing. In the great opening symphonic tuttis, in particular, the two groups are closely and characteristically merged in the Mannheim manner, but more frequently the groups are subtly differentiated in the Viennese tradition, an approach that Mozart continued to prefer in his later symphonies, too. Above all, he uses them to bring out concertante effects within the tutti itself, so that there are occasions when three separate groups are involved: strings, winds and keyboard.[27] A particularly fine example of this may be found in the development section of the opening movement of K451. On some occasions, as in the middle movement of K413, the winds are content merely to echo the melody in the strings, while on other occasions – notably right at the beginning of K450 – the whole theme is divided between the two groups.

Mozart achieves his most idiosyncratic effects by allowing the soloist either to engage in a concertante dialogue, now with the strings, now with the winds, or to be accompanied now by the one group, now by the other. These were novel and surprising effects for audiences in Vienna at this time: never before had they heard such classic examples of the new and more spiritualized instrumental style. But there is no doubt that in this respect Mozart learnt a great deal that he was able to apply to his later masterpieces, the motivic language of which is already clearly audible here.[28] Compared with the violin concertos, the keyboard concertos represent a significant extension of the concept of the concerto, with its dialogue-like character increasingly emphasized, especially in the second half of this series of works, resulting in almost Beethovenian effects in the two minor-key concertos. Yet, such is the nature of this music and its choice of musical ideas that it must be admitted that this dialogue-like structure rarely results in extreme contrasts. Thesis and antithesis, effect and counter-effect generally move in only one direction, complementing each other and extending each other's range of expression, even amending each other on points of detail, but never leading to irreconcilable dramatic tensions in which one or the other partner is gradually forced to lay down his arms. Not even in the two minor-key concertos do these tensions extend to an entire movement, as they do, for example, in the middle movement of Beethoven's G major concerto. The contest is directed at the same goal, a goal to which both parties aspire in keeping with their respective strengths.

The keyboard style, too, is entirely at one with the general aims of this art. Counterpoint has a say only very rarely,[29] and then for only brief periods. It is significant that the listener often barely

---

26. The orchestral resources vary from concerto to concerto. Almost half of them demand trumpets and timpani. The old Neapolitan scoring for oboes and horns is limited to the earlier concertos (K413, 414 and 449). Later, flutes and bassoons are added, together with clarinets in K482. The most lavishly scored of these works is K491.

27. ◆ Further, see Keefe, *Mozart's Piano Concertos: Dramatic Dialogue in the Age of Enlightenment*.

28. In the finale of K449, for example, a motif familiar from the trio ('Soll ich dich Teurer nicht mehr sehn?') from *Die Zauberflöte* plays a preponderant role, and in the final group of the opening movement of K453 there is a palpable echo of the allegro theme from the overture to *Don Giovanni*, including its chromatic step, its pedal point and its diminished chord harmonies.

29. ◆ One significant exception is the double fugue at the heart of the finale to K459.

notices the double counterpoint in both hands, so effortlessly does the musical argument unfold. Only on a handful of occasions – notably at the start of the development section of K415 – do we sense the lingering influence of Mozart's studies with van Swieten. In general, however, the writing is entirely homophonic. Bound up with this (as we have seen) is the harmonic writing, which remains extremely simple in its basic textures. The emphasis here lies entirely on the melodic writing, with the soloist confronted by two main tasks: a cantabile style of playing and tasteful ornamentation in the broadest sense of the term. For Mozart's figurative style rests, for the most part, on the age-old art of breaking down longer note-values into shorter ones (embellishing the note by means of its neighbouring notes), filling out wider melodic intervals, broken chords and so on. Many figures are essentially no more than trills written out in full, producing the narrow chromatic progressions so typical of Mozart:[30]

We also find genuine chains of trills. They, too, rest by preference on a chromatic basis (*cf.* the middle movements of K450 and 482) and often prepare for the cadenzas.[31]

An even greater role is played by the turn. Highly instructive in this respect is the way in which, in the finale of K451, the soloist breaks down the outlines of the theme into a whole series of turns:

Another form of the turn that was a particular favourite of Mozart's also deserves to be mentioned here:

It is one of countless ways in which contemporary composers sought to animate the melodic line. Neither the turn nor other ornaments like it should be interpreted as integral elements of the melody itself. It would be wrong, therefore, to ascribe their frequent appearance to a lack of invention on Mozart's part. Rather, they are purely figurative in character and, as such, analogous to the ornaments familiar from the visual arts of the period, their aim being not to alter the work's basic outline but merely to breathe into it a sense of life.

30. End of the opening movement of K466; the phrasing is not in the original.
31. Opening movement of K414 and second movement of K415.

A combination of trill and turn occurs in a form that is often found in both hands and that was already familiar to the older period:  But Mozart develops these figures in highly appealing ways. Behind them lies a potential for polyphonic textures to the extent that one voice, with its trills or turns, sustains one note (generally the fifth), while the other sketches in an independent melody either above or below it. The following is only one of many such examples:

Related to this is another example that recalls the older tradition:

The result is a cantabile figuration with two or more melodies embedded within it of a kind that we have already observed with the great C minor fantasia. Note also the following passage from the opening movement of the C minor concerto:

Often this leads to striking dissonances, notably at the ostinato harmonies in the left hand beneath the trill on *d'''* in the right:

This brings us to the question of chordal textures, an aspect inextricably bound up with ornamentation in the broadest sense of the term. On closer examination, most of the simple scales prove to be designed to increase the impact of a particular chord. This is especially true of the sort of cadenza which, typical of arias of the period, is found at the end of the subject-groups:

Here the formal type is fixed, with its scales shooting upwards like rockets on arching triads, allowing the staccato quavers to sink back to earth again like flares, followed by the crackle of the trill and, inextricably bound up with it, the Alberti bass.

Mozart's chordal passage-work is handled with extraordinary freedom, from the simplest forms of broken chords to more complex variants involving altered notes. Generally he sticks to a four-note motif of which three are part of the chord, while the third generally forms an altered suspension from below:

Sometimes these motifs are extended by being combined with the ornaments mentioned above, as in the following example:

But sometimes two notes are alone sufficient to achieve the effect of a broken chord, as in the following example, taken from just before the recapitulation of the opening movement of the D minor concerto:

Here the two hands, setting out far apart, come together in the middle of the keyboard. Often the broken chords are divided between both hands and combined with scalar or decorative figures. Mozart is fond of underlining the first note by means of a heavily weighted crotchet in the bass:

Whenever Mozart writes passages for both hands involving a mixture of chords and ornamental figures, the listener can count on effects of a particularly dissonant and distinctive nature, as in the following excerpt from the opening movement of K467:

All non-chordal passage-work is generally limited to simple scales or to sections of such scales, with, at most, a handful of passing notes interpolated, as in the following popular figure, the main notes of which Mozart is fond of doubling at the lower octave:

Passages in thirds and sixths are often found, but they are divided between the two hands. As before, Mozart evidently had no time for Clementi's tricks involving thirds, even though they were familiar to him. When he writes passages in thirds and sixths, it is with a conscious eschewal of all virtuosity. Conversely, he is particularly fond of passages that involve the crossing of hands[32] and of playing in octaves, whether simple or broken.[33] The coda to the finale of K491 includes a passage that creates a thoroughly modern impression:[34]

We shall shortly have more to say about the idiosyncratic mixture of diatonic and chromatic writing in Mozart's keyboard style. Here it is sufficient to note that, their sprinkling of chromatic elements notwithstanding, the basic textures of his melodies are diatonic, with his harmonic language rarely affected by these chromaticisms. Here, too, these chromaticisms are used far less to tone down the melodic outlines than to enhance them, with Mozart employing them by preference to bridge the end of individual periods. Highly instructive in this regard is the solo writing at the beginning of the development section of K413:

32. A particularly distinctive example occurs in the final movement of K450.
33. The finale of K449 contains some particularly attractive instances of this.
34. ◆ Further, see Libin, 'The Emergence of an Idiomatic Fortepiano Style in the Keyboard Concertos of Mozart'.

Mozart is especially fond of including relatively brief chromatic elements in his figurative writing, thereby making it more varied and more lively, but only very rarely, as in the opening movement of K467, do we find a real sense of dissonant and tormented anguish:

Even the most primitive form of 'diminution' – the repetition of a single note – is found here, albeit used in very different ways. The first period of the beautiful larghetto from K491 ends as follows:

yet the most important element here is the rhythm, inasmuch as a sense of symmetry has to be established with the second bar. Compare the following passage from the finale of K453:

This – with the exception of the upbeat – is merely an extended diminution of the note *a''*, including the final turn, while the quaver rhythm is of only secondary importance. Instances of this are very common, generally involving the fifth degree, with its twofold potential for harmonization. It is invariably repeated staccato, while the musical argument continues above or below it. A third type of repeated note seems to represent an attempt to make up for the instrument's inability to swell the note. The example from K413 quoted above continues as follows:

Here the repeated notes[35] contain a palpable crescendo, an effect which, thanks to the use of syncopation, emerges even more powerfully during the following passage from the Larghetto in the same concerto:[36]

Occasionally, the repeated notes are replaced by octaves which, no matter where they appear in these concertos, are always used in a genuinely pianistic manner, rather than as an attempt to imitate a string tremolo, as is the case in a number of the keyboard sonatas. Above all, the reader will search in vain in these concertos for specifically orchestral effects on the keyboard. At most we find occasionally horn-like fifths with Handelian postilion motifs, as in the finale of K413:

Indeed, not even changes of register are used to create such bold effects as they are in many of the sonatas and fantasias.[37] In short, Mozart was not concerned in this type of keyboard writing to introduce any coloristic elements. Likewise, it is only within the course of this series that the two

---

35. With Mozart, the performance marking ⁀⁀ invariably indicates a heightened degree of expression.
36. Note also the way in which it is prepared by means of the turn and note, too, its resolution by means of the chromatic scale.
37. A good example of the way in which the various registers are exploited may be found in the minor-key variation in the finale of K453.

hands achieve total equality. (The left hand has, of course, long since lost the stiffness inherited from the age of the continuo.) In the later concertos, Mozart in fact sets particular store by introducing a figure in the right hand and then immediately transferring it to the left. But the main emphasis in this style lies in the field of melody, and so it is the right hand that receives the lion's share, no matter how active the left hand may be. Above all, it is to the right hand that Mozart entrusts the whole important area of cantabile playing, with the left hand essentially reduced to the role of accompanist, a role which, in the case of the true vocal melodies, generally involves the stereotypical form of an Alberti bass, a form far more frequently found in the concertos than in the sonatas.

Mozart's passage-work is distinguished less by its novelty and its wealth of figures (although contemporary audiences were bound to be struck by the extent to which he combined chromatic and altered notes here) than by its increased emotional expressiveness and by the composer's keen awareness of the affect that he was able to achieve by choosing individual figures. It is by no means a matter of indifference, for example, whether a succession of chords is broken once or several times, whether it introduces non-harmonic notes into the chord or even combines it with scalar motifs, and so on. Behind each of these figurations, however, we very often glimpse a vocal melody like a silver band behind pearls, now faint and almost incorporeal, now more clearly audible, while sometimes there may even be several melodies that perform their often sensuous dance behind the glinting play of notes. To give them special emphasis on the level of their material sonorities would be to destroy the aura of this poetry. Here neither digital dexterity nor routine can help, but only an unspoilt poetic sensitivity. And this is even truer of the genuine cantabile movements. Mozart's *adagio* cantilenas – a legacy of his Italian, French and German predecessors and contemporaries refashioned and reformed by a tremendous creative force – have always been the object of particular admiration but also of impassioned and, unfortunately, not always successful efforts on the part of keyboard performers. The best of these players have invariably realized that behind their apparent straightforwardness lies an extremely varied and highly complex emotional life. Other performers – quite wrongly – fail to detect any sense of passion here and replace it with elegance, beauty and melodiousness. In doing so, they commit the grave error of equating the free flow of passion with passion itself and in this way prevent themselves from the very outset from gaining access to an art such as Mozart's. For Mozart was no 'Rococo' composer of the older tradition, no longer a musician who could sing of his anguish in only charming strains, but nor was he a member of the *Sturm und Drang* movement. For members of this last-named movement, unbounded emotion was paramount, but for Mozart this was only of interest to the extent that it could be reduced to an artistic form. His concern was not nature, but culture. But this did not mean that he declined to reproduce passion in all its forms and that he favoured instead a weak and insipid ideal of beauty. Even if this had been his aim, he would have been utterly incapable of achieving it, as we are already sufficiently aware of the demonic, even volcanic aspect of his character, and we should be guilty of seriously underestimating the elemental nature of his artistry if we assumed that he was capable of simply excluding this essential kernel of his being from his music. Of course, the *Sturm und Drang* that raged and seethed within him was never enough for him either. Rather, he felt a constant urge to control this emotional raw material by imposing upon it a sense of artistic order. In the process he rejected much on which a later age perhaps laid greater emphasis, while at the same time adding other elements, but always aiming in the direction of greater purity and refinement. The noblest fruits of this development are the adagios under discussion. Their main emphasis lies not in their perfect formal structure and their sensuous beauty, glorious though these attributes may be, but in the weight of feeling that lies behind them and that embraces the whole vast range of our emotional lives, by no means concealing its inner glow but expressing it without any sense of hothouse emotion or overweening inwardness. It is sufficient in this context to recall the works of the later Romantics such as those of the young Schumann. Here everything is movement, agitation, boundless passion of a kind that any young composer may well imagine as the supreme goal of his art. With Mozart, by contrast, what matters is not the movement itself but the culmination of that movement in the form of the well-structured work of art.

Mozart remains rooted in the world of Rococo art to the extent that he willingly yields to contemporary society's delight in playful gestures and its need for ornamentation, qualities which, as before, we find in his concertos more than in his other instrumental pieces. This is clear from his elaborate use of ornamentation, without which his style would be inconceivable and which allows us to see in it the last and finest product of Rococo music. The fact that Beethoven soon struck out in an entirely new direction in this respect shows more clearly than anything else the radical revolution that began to affect music, too, in the 1790s. For what we find here is no purely mechanical curtailment of a type of figurative writing now regarded as old-fashioned but an entirely new way of forming melodies – the best possible proof that these ornaments were not merely a superficial extra but an essential element of Mozart's style.[38]

The term 'ornaments' should not be taken to refer only to the embellishments represented by the familiar shorthand symbols, as these are only the most superficial elements of this whole system of ornamentation. Indeed, it is highly significant that Mozart uses far fewer such signs than his predecessors and contemporaries, including even Carl Philipp Emanuel Bach and Joseph Haydn. He often writes out his ornaments in full, rather than using a contracted form, thereby announcing his wish to have them interpreted not as mere extras but as essential elements in the melodic line. At least from the time of his journey to Paris, he was also fairly meticulous in using the abbreviated forms of these ornaments, thereby relieving his performers of most of the difficulties that were so much feared during the older period. The earlier works contain more such symbols, no doubt as a result of his father's influence. The mature Mozart limited himself to the following:[39]

the trill ⁘⁘⁘, generally beginning on the main note and terminating on the lower note with a turn;[40]

the turn ∾, beginning on the upper auxiliary;

the arpeggio ⸴, often written out in small notes;

the appoggiatura, always written out using small notes of the value in which they are to be performed: ♩♩♪♪ ♪. Here it should be added that the semiquaver form is frequently notated as a quaver, in other words, as the symbol that was used for the short appoggiatura during the post-Mozartian period. Inevitably this caused a good deal of confusion in later editions and even today continues to give rise to serious distortions in the way in which Mozart's works are performed. In

38. Hans Gál, 'Die Stileigentümlichkeiten des jungen Beethoven', iv (1916), 60ff.

39. See the sections devoted to Mozart in the studies by Beyschlag, *Die Ornamentik der Musik* and Lach, *Studien zur Entwicklungsgeschichte der ornamentalen Melopöie*. ◆ Performance practice studies, including the size and make-up of ensembles, tempo, articulation and ornamentation, are more central to musicological research now than they were in Abert's day. Among the wealth of material relevant to the performance of Mozart's piano concertos generally (including the topics mentioned below, as well as some that are not), see in particular Howard Mayer Brown and Sadie, *Performance Practice*; Rosenblum, *Performance Practices in Classic Piano Music*; Clive Brown, *Classical and Romantic Performing Practice 1750–1900*; and Levin, 'Performance practice in the music of Mozart'.

40. The *Pralltriller* signs (⁘⁘⁘) that have passed into the printed edition prove on closer examination to be cursorily written trills: see Beyschlag, *Die Ornamentik der Musik*, 195.

general, Mozart sticks closely to these rules, one of his rare exceptions being the opening of the keyboard sonata K310:

Here the same sign represents a short appoggiatura on its first appearance, whereas on its second appearance – and this becomes clear in bar 10 – it represents a quaver, the value of which is deducted from the following crotchet.[41]

Far more important than these ornaments in the narrower sense of the term are the actual melismas, for what we are dealing with here are organic links in the melodic line, whereas the ornaments are purely superficial additions that could be omitted without destroying the melodic design: these are either melismas that have died out in the course of time and, as it were, turned to stone or – especially in the instrumental music – they serve to breathe life into the sonorities.[42] In the example cited above, the first appoggiatura is an ornament intended to accentuate the sound of the main note, whereas the second is a melisma that affects the very life of the melody itself by adding a feminine feature to its basically heroic character.[43]

This individual coloration is one of the most distinctive aspects of eighteenth-century style and, like so many other features of contemporary performing practice, it initially had an air of improvisation to it, with the result that it was the preserve not of the creative artist but of the performer. Theoreticians dealt with it in detail, listing the variation as its basic principle. Yet it is now clear that practical music making went far beyond what was demanded by these writers or even what was permitted by them.[44] But the more intellectualized these ornaments became and the more the performing artist introduced elements of his own personality into the work, the more the composer's attention was drawn to what he was doing. Some time before Mozart, composers had already begun to write out these passages in full, with the result that, instead of being improvised, they were now composed and became a fixed part of the works in question.

One can say that Mozart's slow movements are the culmination of all that could be achieved in this second, more advanced stage of the art of coloration. The old, purely melodic basic character is still clearly visible, as is the principle of variation that coaxes new embellishments from the self-same thought at each of its new appearances,[45] and yet we also find harmonic changes, just as we occasionally did earlier. Even so, these embellishments are no mere superficial trappings. For that, they are far too powerfully imbued with individual expression. Free from all formulas and clichés, they breathe an entirely personal spirit, with the tendency towards cantabile writing making the greatest contribution. As elsewhere, Mozart loosened the tongues of these favourites of the *galant*

---

41. This is also found elsewhere at the broken rhythm ♪♩♩; cf. the opening movement of K301. Other deviant forms are found, for example, at the start of *Das Veilchen* (♪ instead of ♪), no doubt in order to emphasize the strong melodic ictus, as well as in cases where Mozart, having notated the correct form at its first appearance (e.g., ♪), uses the simpler form at its later appearances: (♪). Space prevents me from examining this question in any greater detail.

42. Adler, *Der Stil in der Musik*, 110; and Lach, *Studien zur Entwicklungsgeschichte*, 85ff.

43. Mozart felt this himself, inasmuch as he generally wrote out this ornament in the subsequent course of the movement.

44. See, in particular, Mersmann, 'Beiträge zur Aufführungspraxis der vorklassischen Kammermusik in Deutschland', 141–2.

45. Mozart was also familiar, of course, with the other, older type of variation that was later taken up again by Beethoven on the most spectacular scale. Among later examples from Mozart's own works is the sixth variation from the finale of the serenade K388.

age, teaching them to exult and dream, to lament and to show defiance. Only a few of them still give the impression of being superficial stereotypes.

If I said earlier that the chief exponent of this ornamental style, in the wider sense of the term, was the soloist, I did not of course mean that the themes stated and varied by the orchestra are entirely free of such ornaments. Here we are dealing with a difference in degree, rather than a difference in kind. And the whole art of music at this time played a part in this, revealing itself in the works of those composers such as Johann Christian Bach and Mozart who were influenced by the sentimental Neapolitans and, to a lesser extent, in the works of a child of the Austrian people such as Joseph Haydn. But, however weak or powerful the influence may be, it is present in every case. One of its chief characteristics is its tendency to sidestep the long note that the listener naturally expects to hear on the strongest beat of the bar and to divide it into two notes, the first of which is split in turn into several notes which are either harmonic or, more frequently, non-harmonic (as in suspensions and the like[46]). A good example of this is once again the second bar of the A minor sonata (see above). This also explains the origins of the 'Mannheim sigh' that is derived from Italian vocal music and of other motivic endings such as the following:

Of these, the first is often found in the works of Johann Christian Bach and also of Stamitz and the young Mozart, but rarely in the works of the later Mozart. Closely related to these feminine cadences are the cadences involving a suspension that are so typical of this whole style and already treated with formulaic fixity by many composers of the period:

These replace the half-closure on the dominant and the authentic cadence:

But even without the afore-mentioned Lombardic rhythm, forms involving suspensions, whether prepared or free, play a decisive role in Mozart's works. Take, for example, the opening melody of the middle movement of K453:

---

46. See Wilhelm Fischer, 'Zur Entwicklungsgeschichte des Wiener klassichen Stils', 24–84.

And here is the beginning of the romance from K466:

In particular Mozart is fond of the altered suspension from below, as in the middle movement of K467:[47]

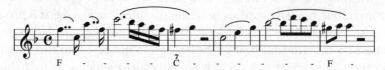

Closely related to this is his pronounced predilection for chromaticisms in general, in which respect he goes much further than any of his contemporaries not only in terms of his use of ornaments but in the very way in which he structures his themes. Here is an example from the middle movement of K451, with its final thirds:

As a result, this type of cantilena – unlike Beethoven's – bears a markedly feminine stamp. In the breaking down and relocation of heavy rhythmic accents, in the predilection for non-harmonic notes on the strong beat of the bar and in the impregnation of the whole melodic language with chromaticisms, there is undoubtedly a very real fear of simple, powerful effects. This is an art that proceeds along extremely cautious and contemplative lines. Although it affords hidden pleasures in its expression of happiness and grief, it is innocent of all active, strong emotions. What we find, instead, is a passive world in which the composer delights in tender emotions, thereby running the obvious risk of becoming monotonous. Not even Mozart, for all his versatility, was entirely successful in avoiding this danger, but it is clear from his mature works that he became increasingly aware of the problem and found inspired ways of avoiding it. No doubt he realized that this *gusto* was the result of a culture that was already moribund, having lost touch with the sort of natural conditions that were reflected in folksongs, for example.[48] But it still seemed particularly well suited to his concertos, and none of the themes of his middle movements is entirely free from it, least of all the larghetto of K491, which in consequence leaves a surprisingly modern impression.[49] The middle movements of K450 and 482 likewise attempt to intensify the range of expression by harmonizing various suspensions,[50] while others such as K467 restrict this mannerism to the phrase endings or, as in K456, to the second section of the theme.[51]

47. This also includes forms such as the one familiar from Paisiello: see above.
48. See Gál, 'Die Stileigentümlichkeiten des jungen Beethoven', 62. The songs of Papageno and other children of nature are likewise virtually free of it.
49. Only the six-four chord suspension in the second bar still recalls this, but its impact is immediately counteracted by the resolute interval of a falling fifth in the upper voice.
50. *Die Zauberflöte* contains a number of good examples of this particular type of harmonization: see especially 'O Isis und Osiris' and the end of 'In diesen heil'gen Hallen'.
51. A typical example of this is the theme of the andante from the 'Jupiter' symphony K551.

But it is in the solo passages that this type of melismatic writing achieves its full potential, as is clear, above all, from the very appearance of the notes on the page, with the numerous very short note-values. Even the larghetto of K413 affords a good example of this. Here the soloist begins by sticking very closely to the orchestra's theme, his only original contribution being the brief ornaments in the second and fourth bars. But from the moment that he begins to launch out independently in the fifth bar

we have before us an example of this style in its purest form, with all its characteristics: not a single rhythmic stress falls on a harmonic note, but all fall on suspensions. Of great significance here is the syncopation in the second bar, which Mozart particularly favours in place of the usual

sigh 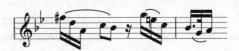 in order to underscore the fact that he has broken free from the natural rhythmic

accent. The result is always a particular sense of urgency in the melodic line. But Mozart goes even further: within the very first bar he balances out the wide interval between the *d″* of the third beat and the first *c‴* of the second bar by means of a scale in small note-values – on this occasion, it is diatonic, although on other occasions it is often chromatic – and he creates a new rhythmic motif by combining it with the afore-mentioned syncopations:

This is then varied twice – melodically and harmonically – in order to achieve a yet greater sense of urgency. This varied repetition of a melismatic motif is another of the hallmarks of Mozart's melismatic writing. A few bars later we find a second example:

But, far from being satisfied with such brief variants, Mozart is fond of creating an increase in tension, especially during harmonic sequences, an aim that he often achieves by his choice of motifs involving shorter note-values. The basic line of the motif in K453 (bars 74–6) runs as follows:

An ornamented variant of this motif migrates from A minor to F sharp major via E minor and B minor:

The motif is essentially still the same, with only its note-values adding to the sense of greater intensity. In general, Mozart made it a virtual rule to ensure that whenever the same idea was repeated by the soloist, it should be varied and intensified, often within the narrowest of confines, as in the andante of K414:

The effectiveness of these slow movements rests in the main on the clash between the simple form of the theme in the orchestra and the melismatic nature of the solo writing. Almost every concerto affords excellent examples of this, the sole exception being K467, in which the main theme is broken down into melismatic particles only in the episode in A flat major, while beneath it we find Mozart's characteristic habit of replacing the strong beat of the bar by a rest and continuing the melodic line on the weak beat with a series of individual, disjointed notes.[52]

In these circumstances, it comes as no surprise to find that intervals of more than an octave are rare. Where we do encounter them, the underlying style is that of an Italian aria with its enormous intervals – here one thinks of the siciliana of K488. Or else Mozart pursues emphatically virtuosic ends, as in the andante of K503. But in general he prefers smaller intervals and is particularly fond of allowing the soloist to reach the theme not directly but by means of a frequently chromatic scale.[53]

52. Very often Mozart embellishes the note in question by including the notes immediately above and below it, so that the basic line is decorated as follows:

53. This is the most primitive form of the lead-ins that we shall consider in a moment.

So far we have dealt only with the ornaments that Mozart himself wrote out and that he therefore regarded as essential. But there is also a whole series of other ornaments that are not included in the autograph scores or in most of the later editions yet which are indispensable if the work is to be correctly performed. The older tradition drew a far less clear-cut dividing line than the modern period between the creative artist and the performing artist but demanded that the latter should make a substantial creative contribution to the work of art at the moment of its performance. The further back in time we go, the fewer performance markings we find in manuscript sources relating to tempo, dynamics and the whole manner of the work's execution: this was always left to the executant. But this was only the beginning, for often enough the manuscripts include only a sketch of the melodic line, a skeleton outline that the performer had to clothe with flesh and blood. In other words, the latter was given the task of playing a creative role in the work's definitive form and of deepening and adding to its expressive content on the strength of his own intellectual and spiritual gifts.[54] Mozart's age, too, still reckoned in general on the performing artist's freely embellishing and varying the music before him, even though composers now adopted a more serious approach to the whole question of writing out the music in full. Carl Philipp Emanuel Bach notes: 'Altering while repeating is nowadays indispensable. One expects as much from every performer.'[55] And Mozart's keyboard concertos include striking examples of these 'random changes' that the player, of his own accord, has to make to the notes on the printed page. These changes are required whenever the composer repeats an idea and does not prescribe the varied form himself. Another important point concerns the fermatas preceding the reentry of the main theme, such as we find following the trill in the andante of K414. Here Mozart demands of his performer a cadenza-like interpolation of his own. He himself wrote a whole series of such 'lead-ins', as he called them, for his pupils in order to introduce them to this skill.[56] These passages are distinguished from the cadenzas that we shall discuss in a moment only by the fact that they are not as long, even though some of them are still quite substantial. In essence they resemble cadenzas, except that they are far less frequently thematic, tending rather to be purely figurative. Yet even here Mozart is occasionally able to play around in highly ingenious ways with individual elements of the preceding themes, as in the final movement of K415:[57]

In essence, these lead-ins also include all the solo passages that frequently precede the soloist's adoption of the main theme in the opening movement, except that on this occasion Mozart has

54. Kretzschmar, 'Einige Bemerkungen über den Vortrag alter Musik'. ◆ More recently, see Mishkin, 'Incomplete notation in Mozart's piano concertos'.

55. Preface to the *Sechs Sonaten fürs Clavier mit veränderten Reprisen* of 1760 [Wq. 50].

56. See the highly informative monograph by Reinecke, *Zur Wiederbelebung der Mozartschen Clavier-Concerte*, and Reinecke's edition of the concertos [published in the AMA]; a number of these lead-ins are included in AMA XXII. ◆ For a complete edition of Mozart's lead-ins and cadenzas, see NMA X/31/3.

57. AMA XXII, no. 17.

written out these passages in full and in some cases also lent them orchestral support, as in K450, for example, where the soloist is required to expand the first of the two closing fermatas and turn it into a special lead-in. In all these passages, the listener has the impression that the performer is keen to test his abilities before confronting his principal challenge. But that is not all: the soloist is required not merely to vary the musical line and provide independent transitions but also to fill in blank and spare passages and bring them to life, as in the following excerpt from the finale of K482:

These vast intervals are meant to be filled in by the soloist with virtuoso passage-work. But the thin two-part harmonies also have to be removed. Here we find the continuing influence of practices familiar from the age of the continuo.[58] Although there are fewer passages in Mozart's piano works involving thin, two-part harmonies that have to be harmonized by the performer, such passages none the less exist. They are particularly obvious in those places where there is a strikingly large gap between the two hands, as in the opening movement of K413 (bars 89–99).[59] Here the necessary additions are shown in smaller type:

58. Mersmann, 'Beiträge zur Aufführungspraxis', 107–8. ◆ Despite his nod in the direction of performance practice – uncommon for the time – Abert does not consider in detail the important practice of continuo. For recent discussion on this controversial topic, see Ferguson, 'The Classical keyboard concerto: some thoughts on authentic performance' and 'Mozart's Keyboard Concertos: Tutti Notations and Performance Models'; Manfred Hermann Schmid, 'Zur Mitwirkung des Solisten am Orchester-Tutti bei Mozarts Konzerten'; and Eisen, 'The primacy of performance: text, act and continuo in Mozart's keyboard concertos'.
59. ◆ A further example comes from the slow movement of the concerto K451. In response to a request from his sister, Mozart included in his letter of 9 June 1784 an elaborated version of what in the autograph is a bare-bones melodic outline to bars 56–63. See Eisen, 'Notation and Interpretation', 29.

Only rarely does Mozart write full-toned harmonies – notably in passages expressive of particularly highly charged emotion, as in the andante from K450. But this does mean, of course, that he would not have used them elsewhere. Here, too, the performer is left with considerable latitude. Nor is it possible to object if the performer, in his search for fuller sonorities, occasionally replaces Mozart's simpler accompanying formulas with fuller ones better suited to modern pianos or if he prefers open to closed harmony and exploits the compass of the modern concert grand and so on. For all that he is doing is applying the virtuoso's age-old right to present-day conditions. The only precondition is that he has enough artistic tact and sense of style to preserve the kernel of Mozart's artistry: no matter what he adds, the virtuoso remains the artist's servant and, ideally, his loyal confederate, consolidating and reinforcing his ideas, rather than confusing or suppressing them. The example of Carl Reinecke, one of the greatest Mozartians, may show everyone who is serious about Mozart's music, how this task should be approached.[60]

The great free cadenzas at the end of the two outer movements and, less often, of the middle movements too are now the last surviving trace of the art of free improvisation. Mozart wrote out a whole series of these cadenzas for his pupils (K624). All are believed to have been tailored to his pupils' individual needs and abilities, with the result that they do not give a full picture of his own practice. Even so, they may be regarded as a true reflection of that practice in terms of their length and the general nature of their execution. They could be described as extended 'lead-ins'. Demonstrating the freedom of the improviser, the composer draws on his repository of existing themes, selecting whatever seems to occur to him on the spur of the moment and playing with it in ways that are dreamily wistful and capricious by turn. First and second subjects, as well as all manner of unprepossessing secondary ideas, follow each other in no particular order. For a long time Mozart tended only rarely to linger over the same idea, generally preferring to lose himself very quickly in a whirl of passage-work which, much to the listener's surprise, would then throw up a new idea. The figurative writing, too, is extremely varied: now we find brilliant scales and chordal passages chasing each other across the keyboard's whole compass, now brief fragmentary figures interrupted by rests, now expressive melismas performed at a slower tempo. Especially

60. See his remarks on the 'Coronation' concerto in *Zur Wiederbelebung der Mozartschen Clavier-Concerte*, 25ff. ◆ For a table listing gaps in Mozart's scores where ornamentation may be required, see Flothuis, *Mozart's Piano Concertos*, 106–7.

towards the end of the cadenza – which consists exclusively of passage-work – this latter gains in intensity, whereas in the slow-movement cadenzas Mozart lays special emphasis on *cantabilità*. Apart from the figurations, no new ideas are introduced here, but the old ones are treated with an often astonishing originality, so that one sometimes has the impression that right at the end of the piece Mozart is making a joke of the matter and hinting at the still untapped expressive possibilities inherent in his themes.

Mozart's own cadenzas were presumably improvised anew at each performance and are therefore lost to us for ever, but the ones that he wrote out for his pupils may at least give us a vague idea of the spirit of these extemporizations and of their deeply subjective, imaginative and personal nature. The notated cadenzas contain passages that rarely occur in finished pieces, such as the accelerando that is written out in full in K626a/I/54 (K456):

But, above all, they teach us one thing that is generally overlooked nowadays, namely, that these cadenzas were relatively brief, a brevity that reflects their stylistic status as additions, rather than as the *res ipsa*.[61] One of the many aberrations of the age of the virtuoso in the early nineteenth century was the way in which performers became used to turning the cadenzas into vast virtuosic structures that adopted an increasingly high-handed approach to the work itself. In the light of all that has been said, it will be clear that this constitutes a grievous sin against the spirit of Mozart's art, an art which in the products of his maturity is strenuous in its avoidance of extreme garrulousness, to say nothing of virtuosic trivialization.

The same form, albeit on a far more modest scale, is found in the four horn concertos K412, 417, 447 and 495, except that the first of them has no slow middle movement, and its finale was not completed until 1787.[62] All of them have a so-called *chasse* – a rondo in 6/8-time – as their final movement, while the last two have a romance as their middle movement. The most striking feature of their opening movements is the cantabile character of their main themes, a character which, in the case of K495, it is left to the soloist to bring out after joining in the tutti as an orchestral instrument. (This feature is also found in K447.) As usual, these very brief tuttis introduce both subjects in the tonic,[63] in addition to which there is often a brief final group. The way in which Mozart allows the soloist to break into this in K495,[64] before he picks up the main theme, reveals a succinctness entirely typical of his concertos in general. None of the outer movements

61. Beethoven's equally brief cadenzas to K466 may be found in the complete edition of his works, IX/7, nos 11–12. Among later composers, Hummel, Moscheles, Reinecke, Linder and others have all published cadenzas to Mozart's concertos. ◆ Further, see Christoph Wolff, 'Cadenzas and Styles of Improvisation in Mozart's Piano Concertos', and Badura-Skoda, 'On Improvised Embellishments and Cadenzas in Mozart's Piano Concertos'.
62. ◆ As noted above, K412+514 is now thought to be an incomplete concerto from 1791.
63. The second subject of K 417 is the well-known favourite theme of both Paisiello and Mozart.
64. A figure that looks forward to the overture to *Le nozze di Figaro* appears in the strings at this point.

includes any appreciable deviations from the usual form. The range of ideas, too, is far more modest than in the keyboard concertos, even though there is no lack of surprising features, such as the bold and 'Romantic' harmonic language of the development section of K447. In general, however, the works are evidently tailored to Leutgeb's abilities as a horn player.

Of the works for keyboard alone, the most important is the sonata in C minor K457, which was completed on 14 October 1784 and which was Mozart's first contribution to the heroic type of sonata since the A minor piece that he had written in Paris in 1778. And yet what a difference between the two works even in terms of their keyboard writing! In the earlier piece, the impressions left by Mannheim were still fresh in Mozart's mind, with the result that K310 has a clearly perceptible orchestral character, whereas in K457 the style is purely pianistic and – as is easy to imagine – profoundly influenced by the contemporary concertos. Among these influences are the composer's delight in brilliant, virtuosic passage-work in the outer movements, the deeply expressive melismas in the adagio, in which the theme is varied at every repeat,[65] the exploitation of each register and much else besides. The final allegro requires the performer to intervene creatively on more than one occasion, notably at the fermata chord in bar 45, which he has to colour in the manner of a figurative lead-in (see above). A second intervention occurs at the point where the main theme is lengthened (*a piacere*) and each of the fermatas is likewise intended to be differently embellished.

Yet this brilliant outer garment is only the means by which Mozart creates a psychological portrait of a sombreness and passion found in no other sonata from his pen. It also bears all his characteristic hallmarks, as is clear, not least, from the opening movement's first subject, a defiantly rebellious triadic motif that recalls the Italianate Mannheim style,[66] followed by a complete change of mood in the form of an imploring phrase as its consequent, the climax of which is its interval of a seventh. This contrast finds extreme expression in the thematic writing, dynamics and register, affecting the whole character not only of this opening movement but of the sonata in its entirety. The result is a constant feeling of rebellion and of sinking back, of struggle and renunciation and, as so often in such cases, the movement ends on a note of sombre resignation. With its oppressive pedal point and, above it, chromatic and syncopated motifs, even the continuation of the theme captures the sense of sinister weight in highly dramatic terms, a weight that oppresses the soul at every such conflict. The opening is then repeated, but on this occasion – and, with a single exception, this will be the general rule from now on – without the contrasting consequent phrase. The change of mood that occurs in the theme within the narrowest possible confines later takes place over a longer period. First we hear a more cheerful idea which, in terms of its character and tonality, the listener would be tempted to regard as the second subject, were it not so remarkably short-winded and were it not, above all, to introduce a strident motif that very soon insists on striking out in a new direction:[67]

---

65. ◆ The rediscovery of Mozart's autograph in 1990 brought to light further ornamentations of the adagio theme; see Eugene K. Wolf, 'The Rediscovered Autograph of Mozart's Fantasy and Sonata in C minor, K. 475/457' and Plath and Rehm, *Wolfgang Amadeus Mozart: Fantasie und Sonate c-Moll für Klavier KV 475 + 457. Faksimile Ausgabe.*
66. On the Mannheim 'rocket', see Riemann, *Sinfonien der Pfalzbayerischen Schule. Teil 1*, XVI. Among the themes by Mozart that are relevant in this context are the first subject of the opening movement of K388 (also in C minor) and of K394. Examples from later works include the themes of the finales of the keyboard concerto in D minor (K466) and the symphony in G minor (K550). The same type of theme is also found in Beethoven's works, notably in the opening movements of the piano trio op.1/1 and the piano sonata op.2/1.
67. Significantly, it is suppressed in the recapitulation.

Only now do we hear the actual second subject, a yearning dialogue between high and low voice that explores to the full the mood that has been caught by this transitional idea. But we are abruptly roused from this dream, too:

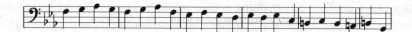

Again there is a wild outburst of passion followed by a sense of weary collapse. At the repeat, a concerto-like passage that explores the keyboard's whole compass is introduced, but it fails to affect the outcome. The final subject-group has to begin the build-up all over again, and, by drawing on a triplet motif earlier associated with the first subject and again reminiscent of the concertos, it eventually succeeds in bringing the movement to an end on a note of surly and somewhat desperate resolve. The main theme, now treated in canon for the first time, places its seal of approval upon it. This theme also dominates the whole of the development section, which is powerfully reminiscent of the development sections of the concertos. The theme slips through various harmonies, its melodic structure unchanged, accompanied in both hands in turn by the triplet figure that had joined it in the twenty-first bar. Only once does the transitional theme in F minor infiltrate itself. Yet, for all its strength, even this climax has something dogged about it. With the exception of its first bar, it remains entrenched in minor tonalities, and from its fifteenth bar onwards it is joined by a stubborn idea in the bass that constantly draws the musical argument downwards:

The proud theme sinks back in tatters, coming to rest on a heavy suspension with a fermata. The world of fate inhabited by this sonata yields neither to entreaty nor to defiance, with the result that the recapitulation sounds even more resigned than before. In its nineteenth bar and the following ones the contradictory moods burst apart even more irreconcilably than ever. This is the passage where the pseudo-second subject should enter, but instead the main theme, in triple canonic imitation, culminates in a new section as a result of enharmonic change – an effect identical to the one found in the opening movement of the G minor symphony K550. The D flat major that appears to enter so abruptly here and conjures up such an ineffably moving figure in the melody finally turns out to be the triad on the flattened second degree of C minor (in its second inversion) and, as such, leads along regular lines to the dominant via the six-five chord of the diminished seventh chord on the raised seventh degree of G minor, a passage that acquires a particularly 'Romantic' colour as a result of the sudden deep descent into the subdominant. (This is a procedure that occurs with increasing frequency in the works after *Le nozze di Figaro*.) This is the last brief glimpse of a major tonality that is granted to us: from now on, Mozart reverts to type and the musical argument proceeds entirely in C minor. To a certain extent, the coda takes stock of all that has gone before it: the main theme enters canonically, exerting the whole of its considerable force, followed by an abrupt descent into a cadenza that recalls nothing so much as an Italian aria. There follows one of the strangest endings that Mozart ever gave to a work: a dull unison in broken octaves in equal crotchets,[68] of which the fourth is invariably brutally accented, gradually descends into the depths of the keyboard's lowest register, where it finally dies away *pianissimo* as a gentle murmur, as though the curtain is slowly falling on a tragedy.[69] It is a tragedy that increasingly occupied Mozart's thoughts, the older he became: a tale of struggle and fatalistic renunciation.

The adagio is like an elegy woven together from yearning desire and silent grief, encapsulating the impression left on a deeply wounded mind by all that has gone before it. A ternary structure, it has an expansive middle section and an extended coda. As before, the musical language is that of the slow movements from the concertos, notably in terms of the expressive art of melismatic variation. But we also find the other characteristic features of Mozart's adagios, some of them intensified: note, for example, the *b'♭* in the sixth bar that turns out only after lengthy hesitation to be the altered suspension, a highly typical way of expressing helpless anguish. In terms of its *cantabilità*, the movement has no peers among Mozart's other sonatas, and more than once it almost literally seems to express human singing, so overwhelming is the emotion that it exudes. Even the structure of the themes suggests an extraordinary emotional intensity. The first of these themes is made up of three bars, a regular two-bar antecedent and a one-bar consequent which, melodically speaking, is completely new and which, as the variations reveal, is particularly emotionally charged. The middle section in A flat major likewise begins with a three-bar antecedent that also contains a hidden canon between the upper voice and the second of the middle voices. This subsidiary group begins on a note of deep and wishless rêverie, but it is soon drawn into the sense of remarkable urgency that is typical of the movement as a whole and that forges an emotional link with its neighbours. The virtuoso scalar passages disrupt the feeling of calm in no uncertain terms, with only the well-prepared return of the main theme appearing to hold out the promise of a means of escape. But Mozart suddenly reinterprets its dominant *b-flat'* as the mediant of G flat major and moves into this last-named tonality – in other words, further into the world of the subdominant and its associations of rêverie. The old routine reasserts itself, but this time with a significant increase in expressivity, resulting in an arioso that literally teems with emotion. All the more unexpected is the transition to a passage of mysterious whispering that moves irresistibly towards C minor, the relative of the tonic, E flat major. But as so often at this point in Mozart's works, what we find instead is a return to the main theme via a modulation, as brief as it is surprising, to E flat major. Its repeat is followed by a coda that brings the whole movement to an end on a note of calm and tranquillity, so that the rude awakening of the final movement – a formally curious structure – is all the more terrible and terrifying. Its opening, as far as its cadence in E flat major, is cast in sonata form, but no development section follows and instead we hear the first subject in the tonic, now combined with what appears to be a new theme in F minor. This, in turn, is followed by the first of the subsidiary subjects which, together with its continuation, is now treated in the manner of a recapitulation. But shortly before its final subject-group, another long section involving the first subject and the F minor theme is introduced, followed by an entirely new coda. The result is a remarkable combination of sonata and rondo

---

68. There may be an inner connection with the bass motif cited above.
69. Related to this, albeit far less tragic in tone, is the end of the finale of K452. ◆ Although these passages are related as regards their figuration, modern critics are hard-pressed to find the closing pages of K452 tragic in any respect.

form. In terms of its mood, the movement harks back to the opening molto allegro, with which it is even related thematically.[70] The mood, in short, is one of gnawing self-torment, with the syncopated suspensions succeeding one another without a break.[71] The pounding *forte* consequent again whips up the old sense of defiance, but there is now something sinister and fatalistic about it – there is no longer any possibility of escaping from the torment. Suddenly the theme flutters away over an abrupt dissonance followed by a whole bar's rest. As before, the answer sounds bereft of all hope, a five-bar phrase with a malevolent interval of a seventh that laconically cuts off all further argument. The pounding motif keeps on returning like a refrain, with or without its consequent phrases, determining the character of the movement in a quite exceptional way. There are virtually no transitional passages here to act as intermediaries between the extremes, with even the very first second subject entering abruptly, beginning by striking a note of relatively calm entreaty, but soon being caught up in the work's underlying mood of surly gruffness. At the point where this subject should be introduced for a second time, Mozart makes two attempts to move the musical argument forward, each attempt being interrupted by a whole bar's rest, before he interpolates the F minor theme, a touching lament within an implacable struggle:

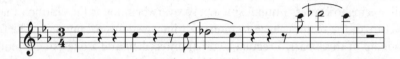

Time and again this is interrupted by wild *forte* blows – a highly significant variant of the earlier pounding motif. But at its next appearance the main theme is broken down into a whole series of expressive phrases with fermatas, where the performer can demonstrate his ability to decorate the line in a poetical manner. In this way, the emotional content is infinitely increased. Here, again, we find ourselves in the immediate proximity of human singing. The movement ends with a defiant coda that fails to bring any sense of catharsis, still less of liberation.[72]

Of the two keyboard rondos in D major K485 and in F major K494, the first is really a sonata movement that even includes a repeat sign. It is built up, however, on a single theme. But, following in the tradition of Carl Philipp Emanuel Bach, this theme modulates – surprisingly – to different keys in the development section and recapitulation and in general is treated with considerable freedom. Indeed, it is this that seems to have persuaded Mozart to use the term 'rondo'. Of course, the present piece, for all its charm, fails to rise to the heights of Bach's rondos. The F major rondo, by contrast, is a genuine rondo in the style of the keyboard concertos with several episodes, including a contrapuntal *mineur*. The main theme always appears in the tonic, each time in a different guise. The cadenza that appears towards the end is written out in full.[73] At the very end the main theme good-humouredly takes its leave in the keyboard's lower register over a running bass.

The sets of variations that date from this period – the eight variations on 'Come un agnello' from Sarti's *Fra i due litiganti* K460 and the ten variations on 'Unser dummer Pöbel meint' ('Les hommes pieusement') from Gluck's *La rencontre imprévue* K455 – likewise owe their expressive

---

70. Note in particular the second sections of the second subjects and the first ideas of the final subject-groups that follow.
71. Note also the change of register in the eighth bar.
72. The correspondence between motifs in the keyboard's highest and lowest registers that is found here is typical of this sonata.
73. ◆ Here Abert conflates the first version of K494 (composed 10 June 1786) with the later version published as the finale to the sonata K533 (3 January 1788). The twenty-seven-bar cadenza is found only in the sonata publication of 1788; it is lacking in the original rondo.

intensity to the influence of the concertos, an influence clear more especially from the increased virtuosity that exploits every register of the instrument and from the free, often cadenza-like transitions from one variation to the next. Mozart refuses to explore the dramatic situation, regarding the numbers in question merely as a musical substratum for his variations, hence his decision to abbreviate them to the usual, brief, binary themes.[74] In general, both works are constructed along similar lines, beginning with a purely figurative variation, including the theme in the bass in a later variation, incorporating a minor-key variation and an adagio variation and, in the later ones, tending towards large-scale, free, cadenza-like transitions and, in more general terms, to a more arbitrary and imaginative treatment of the themes, with regular changes of time-signature. The eighth variation of K460 even includes three variations, two motivically linked adagio variations in the major and the minor, and an allegro variation. The final variation of K455 runs along regular lines until shortly before the end, when the music suddenly modulates in a totally different direction and, following a cadenza, Mozart plays freely with the theme on the basis of its rhythm, until it finally appears in its original form following a tension-laden cadence. This is followed in turn by a brief thematic coda. Of the two, this is the more substantial work: from the fourth variation onwards, the second part of the theme is almost always subjected to a double variation, and the character of the individual variations is more clearly contoured. Suffice it to note the finely detailed writing in the fifth, sixth and seventh variations, all of which are more or less built up on the principle of double counterpoint: the first[75] with its weary chromaticisms, the second with the theme in the middle voice, while trills appear to ring out on all sides, and the third with its choice harmonies and counterpoint. The adagio variation is a model of ornamentation and notable, too, for its change of register in its second section. The Sarti variations are much more straightforward, with only the seventh variation being on a larger scale. This variation also begins with an extremely successful imitation of the somewhat lyrical tone of an Italian canzonetta.

---

74. In K455, bars 5–10 of the original have been omitted.
75. The third and fifth variations contain striking reminiscences of two variations from the violin sonata K379.

40

Choral works, lieder and arias

The choral movements included in the two Masonic cantatas K429 and 471 as well as in the Masonic songs with choral refrain (K483 and 484) are all characterized by a remarkably elevated tone that looks forward to *Die Zauberflöte*.[1] Indeed, there are often direct allusions to this work. In the chorus from the first cantata, the interplay of solemn splendour and tranquil humility creates a particularly powerful effect. *Die Maurerfreude* (K471), by contrast, begins with a great tenor aria of the binary Italianate type that strikes a simple, good-humoured tone with no sense of emotional bombast. There follows a brief recitative in which the Arioso stands out above all for its eloquent orchestral language. In turn this passes into a cheerfully animated movement reminiscent of Grétry, the second section of which is taken up by the chorus in the manner of a refrain. Both K483 and 484 fall under the heading of lieder.[2]

We have already traced Mozart's haphazard course through the field of the German lied and seen how he began with the older north German song, whose origins go back to Sperontes and how, under French influence, he then broke free from these narrow confines in Mannheim and succeeded in writing works that were not only more richly textured but sometimes positively dramatic in character. With the Hermes settings of 1780 (K390–392) Mozart took a step backwards, striving to achieve the greatest expression within the smallest space, hence the preponderant role of the declamatory writing here. The principle itself is north German, but the resources that Mozart uses, especially in terms of his harmonic writing, go far beyond this model. There then followed another gap of five years, at the end of which Mozart's lieder assumed a rather different aspect as a result of his falling under the decisive influence of the Viennese lied, which was then in its first flush of youth.

It would be a grave error to regard the Viennese song as a direct descendant of the north German lied, which by this date could already look back on a history lasting several decades – a time of hard work and notable successes, but also of many failures. After all, the whole genre had already witnessed a golden age in the seventeenth century, only to disappear from sight by the end of the century. It now had to be restored to life, a task that meant starting all over again from the beginning. And, given the general trend in German culture at that time, this could be done only under the aegis of the French. Yet, for all its initial successes, the very first such attempt – Sperontes's instrumental dance songs – proved misguided in the longer term.[3] The problem was a

---

1. ◆ The fragmentary K429 was probably written down in 1786; K471 was composed on 20 April 1785. Both K483 and 484 were composed for performance at the Lodge 'Zur neugekrönten Hoffnung' on 13 January 1786; see *Dokumente*, 229, *Documentary Biography*, 260.

2. ◆ Five additional Masonic songs have been discovered since Abert's day, including two from this period: *Zur Eröffnung der Meisterloge* ('Des Todes Werk') and *Zum Schluß der Meisterarbeit* ('Vollbracht ist die Arbeit der Meister'); both were probably written for performance on 12 August 1785. See Autexier, 'Cinq lieder inconnus de W. A. Mozart'. For three additional Masonic songs from 1790, see above, p.782, n.44.

3. See Kretzschmar, *Geschichte des neuen deutschen Liedes*, i.185ff.

difficult one to address and could not be solved simply by choosing instrumental pieces at random and making the words fit them as best they could, but it is entirely typical of the 'Age of Reason' that contemporaries sought an answer to this problem by speculating on a new principle of song composition: here, too, they struggled to formulate new rules to which composers would then have to conform. It was against this background that the 'Berlin' school assumed control in 1753, and it was to members of this school that the German lied owed the fact that, stylistically speaking, it was no longer dependent on keyboard music and arias but acquired a distinctive profile of its own, emphasizing the two points that even today remain central to lieder composition: a poetic text as the wellspring of the work and the ability to maintain the genre's intimate, lyrical character. The importance of the Berliners' contribution is in no way diminished by the one-sidedness with which they attempted to assert their theory and which had such an inhibiting effect on the development of the new genre. Its ultimate aim, after all, was pedagogical, rather than purely artistic, with the music intended to help the poetry to achieve greater urgency and in that way to make it more popular, thereby educating the widest circles and making them more socially adept.[4] This, too, is entirely typical of the spirit of rationalism, with individuality and creativity taking second place, sidelined by the rigorous demand that the songs should be so simple that members of the middle classes and peasantry could understand them even without piano accompaniment. The one aspect that now seems to us the most obvious and most important – the renaissance of the lied through the wellspring of the folksong – was of no interest to these people, who saw music as an aristocratic art form and regarded the folksong with deep suspicion. The French chanson was now held out as the unique ideal, which had the advantage that the hegemony of the Italian aria was now broken in domestic German music making, while bringing with it the concomitant disadvantage of encouraging the lied to develop within far too narrow confines. The palsied hand of rationalism soon lay hold of this new area, too, seeking as far as possible to prevent all irrational, creative forces – especially those bound up with music – from developing along natural lines. In this, it was helped by the sort of poetry that flourished at this period, inasmuch as it, too, sprang not from the depths of the heart but in essence from the mind, seeking to cheer and regale the spirit, while at the same time offering instruction and edification. In consequence, the musician had no choice but to follow this basic principle. It is no accident that the birth of 'classical' poetry was accompanied by an unexpected revival of lyricism in music. The battle to overcome Berlin's constraining rules had already begun with the earliest composers, but their first effective ally was Johann Adam Hiller and his singspiel songs. He, too, was still in thrall to the age of rationalism, yet the wave that now began to wash away the base of this whole system carried him far closer to a genuinely popular style than the Berliners had ever managed to achieve. Such was Hiller's mentality, however, that the results all too often turned to pedantry, yet the stilted shepherds and shepherdesses of the earlier period had at least been replaced by popular figures and, even more important, the theatre and, with it, the broad mass of the population had been won over to lieder. But salvation was at hand, and it came from within the ranks of the Berliners themselves, who now saw that musical reform was far less important than poetic reform, with composers such as Schulz, Reichardt and Zelter gaining access to classical poetry, with the result that the musical picture was utterly transformed.[5] While remaining true to the old Berlin principle of the poet's predominance

4. See Kretzschmar, *Geschichte des neuen deutschen Liedes*, i.234.
5. ◆ See Fischer-Dieskau, '*Weil nicht alle Blütenträume reiften*': *Johann Friedrich Reichardt, Hofkapellmeister dreier Preußenkönige: Porträt und Selbstporträt*; Barr, 'Carl Friedrich Zelter: A Study of the Lied in Berlin during the Late Eighteenth and Early Nineteenth Centuries'; and Fischer-Dieskau, *Carl Friedrich Zelter und das Berliner Musikleben seiner Zeit: Eine Biographie*.

over the musician (a right that Goethe invariably sought to uphold), they none the less freed the composer from his all too confining chains and came to the belated realization that in the longer term the French chanson could not satisfy German aspirations for the lied. This marked the end of primitive attempts to retrace the poet's words in music: from now on the composer was able to use all the resources at his disposal to elucidate and even to expand on the poet's ideas, while clearly remaining within the parameters of those ideas. As before, the poem remained something fixed, a given, and it was left to a later age to explore its subtlest psychological ramifications, to trace it back to its origins and on that basis to recreate it in the spirit of music.

This was the point that north German composers had reached when Mozart appeared on the scene with his lieder of 1780, yet, as with the singspiel, a vast gulf existed between their respective ideas: here, too, the south went its own way, obstinately insisting on its rights in the face of northern demands. While the Berliners eagerly debated the very nature of the song and enlisted their composers' support, the south German song initially gave only weak signs of life. But from Johann Valentin Rathgeber's *Tafel-Confect* onwards,[6] these signs were sufficient to show that if composers tackled the lied at all, it was with totally different preconceptions. We have already had repeated occasion to refer to the spirit of the south-west German – specifically Swabian – song and its importance for Mozart. Here there is no trace of any rationalist speculation, but, rather, a conscious debt to the genuine folksong, for the sake of which composers not infrequently eschewed any loftier ambitions. Schubart is a typical representative of this spirit. He emphatically rejected the Berliners' theoretical approach and was proud of the fact that his songs all came from the people. With Johann André, the Berlin school established its furthest outpost in southern Germany, but André remained an isolated phenomenon and was in any case much influenced by the south German character.[7]

The German song was silent for even longer in Vienna. After all, Gluck's Klopstock settings fall entirely outside this tradition, forming a pendant to his music dramas both in terms of his choice of poetry and in their musical setting, which is clearly related to the Berliners in respect of their simplicity and close dependence on the text. But Gluck reinterpreted the rules that had become ossified for the Berliners and treated them as living organisms, thereby returning to the wellspring of art – the aesthetic experience – that they themselves had lost sight of. It is the same attempt to overcome rationalism that we have already encountered in the field of opera.

The same richly varied musical culture that long prevented the singspiel from taking root in Vienna and that lent *opera buffa* so curious an aspect there was also responsible for the late development of the lied. The educated classes preferred high art, while the common people were content with the lower forms of popular poetry whose traces we have already observed in the singspiel. With the emergence of the National Singspiel, the spell was finally broken and a local lieder school gradually came into existence. Although its achievements were modest in the extreme and although in its choice of texts it compared badly with the now reformed taste of the north Germans, it was at least already distinctively Viennese in style.[8] This is not the place to examine its chief representatives, Steffan, Hoffmeister, Stadler, Kozeluch, Grünwald, Holzer and their

6. ◆ Rathgeber's two-part *Ohren-vergnügendes und Gemüth-ergötzendes Tafel-Confect*, a collection of popular songs that he edited and arranged, was published by Lotter in Augsburg between 1733 and 1737. Further, see Kleiner and Nowak, 'Nur wer die Musik liebt . . .': Valentin Rathgeber (1682–1750); and Krautwurst, 'Valentin Rathgeber OSB (1682–1750)'.
7. ◆ See Honolka, *Schubart, Dichter und Musiker, Journalist und Rebell: Sein Leben, sein Werk*; and Pretzsch, 'Johann André und seine Stellung in der Berliner Liederschule'. Further, see Schwab, *Sangbarkeit, Popularität und Kunstlied: Studien zu Lied und Liedästhetik der mittleren Goethezeit*.
8. See Kretzschmar, *Geschichte des neuen deutschen Liedes*, i.340ff., and, above all, Pollak-Schlaffenberg, 'Die Wiener Liedmusik von 1778 bis 1789'.

colleagues (towering above the rest of them was their only truly important member, Joseph Haydn), but a brief summary of their achievements is none the less necessary with specific reference to Mozart.

Like the Swabians, the Viennese did not come to the German song by theorizing about it, but unlike the former, they did not cling in the main to the art of the people. Rather, the popular element remains only one aspect of their lieder style, which they took over in the form already found in the singspiel. Alongside it – and at least as important – we also find the Italian aria (both *seria* and *buffa*), in addition to a well-developed style of instrumental music. As is generally the case with all new forms, these various elements initially featured alongside one another in a relatively inorganic state but gradually merged to form a new style far removed from that of the north German school, opening up the most disparate opportunities for novel expression. Alongside popular songs of the kind that we have already encountered in Umlauf's *Die Bergknappen*, we also find examples of a more lyrical type, in which the folklike form is imbued with the warm-toned, even sentimental melodies typical of the semi-serious songs of Italian *opere buffe*. Indeed, the coloratura writing even suggests the influence of *opera seria*, an influence that north German lieder composers did everything in their power to resist. Of course, various elements entered the Viennese lied at this time that were later found to be uncongenial and that it was obliged, therefore, to reject. But on one point it remained in advance of its north German equivalent, a status that it enjoyed as a result of its Italian qualities – a freer and more florid melodic writing that sometimes descended into sentimentality and monotony but never into aridity. Likewise the influences of instrumental music did more good than harm to the Viennese song. Not only did the role of the keyboard become freer and more independent in consequence, but the melodic and, more especially, rhythmic and harmonic writing benefited considerably, becoming more varied and more distinctive and thereby providing an effective counterweight to the effeminacy of the Italian vocal music of the period. French *opéra comique* and its *ariettes* also exerted a palpable, if weaker, influence.

In the circumstances, it is hardly surprising that the Viennese song took far less time to complete the distance that its north German equivalent had taken several decades to cover. From a very early date we find examples – admittedly still imperfect – of all the different types of lieder that were later developed by the composers of the Classical period. This state of affairs is all the more remarkable in that for some time to come the Viennese song was to remain markedly inferior to the north German lied on one essential point: its choice of poems. While composers in Berlin were already setting Klopstock and Goethe, their colleagues in Vienna were floundering around in areas of scarcely conceivable shallowness.[9] Generally it was local poets of the most modest abilities whose works were set to music, and it was only by accident that classic poems found their way into this company. This was bound up with the state of Austrian literature in general at this time, for only now was it stirring from a long period of paralysis. The men of letters had scarcely begun to feel the breath of the new spirit of poetry, so that we can hardly expect composers to have done so. Whereas men like Reichardt and Zelter were among the most literarily cultured figures of their age and in a position to get to know the new spirit of poetry through their personal dealings with the great poets of the period, their Viennese colleagues remained wedded to their lives of literary contemplation, with few opportunities to reveal any sense of taste or criticism. Not even Joseph

9. Reichardt regretted that, because of their words, he was unable to include among his *Lieder geselliger Freude* of 1796, i.VIII–IX, any of the works by 'such justifiably well-respected men as Haydn, Mozart and Dittersdorf'.

Haydn was an exception in this respect. Quite the opposite: even more than Mozart, Haydn was typical of Vienna's unliterary musicians.[10]

It was into this musically rich and promising but, in terms of its intellectual aims, still vague and unfocused world of the Viennese song that Mozart set foot with his contributions in 1785. On a superficial level, the song occupied the same place in his output now as it had done previously and as it did with other Viennese composers at this time: it was one of the parerga that he occasionally took in hand for friends or for other social ends, but without devoting any systematic attention to the medium as such. Even so, it appears from a letter that Constanze wrote to Härtel that he kept a special volume in which he entered poems that attracted him or that inspired him to set them. But the poems that came his way in Vienna were of the same low literary standards as those that we have already described. Although we know from his verdict on Michael Denis's ode that he was perfectly capable of maintaining his own independent standpoint here as elsewhere, he did not feel sufficiently qualified to explore the world of lyric poetry, great though his interest may have been in the dramatic poetry of the period. And he himself paid little heed to the fate of his songs, which for the most part remained in the possession of those for whom they were written. It never occurred to him to prepare copies of them, with the result that they frequently shared the same fate as his sets of variations. Often enough songs were ascribed to him for which he was not responsible, while, conversely, a number of his lieder circulated under the names of other composers.[11] He himself published only a very small handful of them.[12]

Although not a particularly significant piece, the Masonic *Lied zur Gesellenreise* of 26 March 1785 is none the less highly instructive for the light that it sheds on Mozart's change of attitude since the three Hermes's settings of five years earlier, with even the performance marking 'Larghetto' strikingly different in this regard: previously he had adopted the widespread practice found especially in north Germany and used German performance markings. But the song is also

---

10. ◆ The suggestion that Haydn was unliterary – perhaps a legacy of nineteenth-century teleological thinking and its tendency to downplay a broad cultural (that is, 'modern') awareness among composers before Beethoven – is no longer acceptable. For a reconstruction of his library and acquaintance with contemporary literature and poetry, see Hörwarthner, 'Joseph Haydns Bibliothek: Versuch einer literaturhistorischen Rekonstruktion'. Specifically with respect to Haydn's songs, see Brown, 'Song'; more generally, concerning Viennese songs, see Alberti-Radanowicz, 'Das Wiener Lied von 1789–1815'.

11. This confusion started soon after Mozart's death. An ostensibly complete collection of 33 songs was published by Rellstab in Berlin under the title *Sämtliche Lieder und Gesänge beim Fortepiano vom Kapellm. W. A. Mozart*, but contained only five authentic songs; see *AmZ*, i (1798/9), 744–5. The collection of songs included in volume 5 of the Breitkopf & Härtel edition of Mozart's works was based on information given by Constanze and the songs themselves are therefore authentic, but in many cases the words were adapted by Daniel Jäger. This edition contained 30 numbers, of which 21 are actual lieder. For the AMA (volume 7), Gustav Nottebohm reconstructed the original versions of 34 authentic songs. The song about Mozart's nose, *Schlaf, süßer Knabe*, mentioned by Wurzbach in his *Mozart-Buch*, 176, and said to be by Mozart himself, is a setting of a poem by Matthias Claudius. It is not known whether Mozart set it. The song included in *Caecilia*, xxv (1846) that is said to be by Mozart is a forgery. ◆ No doubt Abert refers here to the first (KAnh. C8.01) of the two known settings of *Schlaf, süßer Knabe* attributed to Mozart; probably the work is by Joseph Martin Kraus. Furthermore, no two accounts of Mozart's song output are identical: Breitkopf & Härtel identified twenty-one songs, the AMA thirty-four, the NMA (III/8) twenty-nine, and *New Grove* thirty-one (not including works such as the five lost Masonic songs referred to above or the fragmentary *O Calpe!* K386d). Among the songs considered by Abert to be by Mozart, at least three are spurious: K149, 150 and 151 are by Leopold Mozart. Additionally, at least fifty more songs, none of them by Mozart, were published under his name during the late eighteenth century and early years of the nineteenth century; see K⁶, 836–48 (Anh. C8.01–8.50).

12. Only five songs were published during Mozart's lifetime: the *Lied der Freiheit* appeared in the *Wienerischer Musenalmanach* for 1786. In 1789 *Abendempfindung* and *An Chloe* appeared under the title *Zwey Deutsche Arien zum Singen beym Clavier (1. Teil)*, followed by *Das Veilchen* and *Lied der Trennung* under the title *Zwey Deutsche Arien zum Singen beym Claiver (2. Teil)*. It has not been possible to substantiate the claim that *Des kleinen Friedrichs Geburtstag* appeared in May's *Wochenblatt zur angenehmen und lehrreichen Beschäftigung für Kinder in ihren Freistunden* in Vienna in 1787. For an excellent assessment of Mozart's lieder, see Chrysander, 'Mozarts Lieder'. ◆ Further concerning Mozart's songs, see Ballin, *Das Wort-Ton-Verhältnis in den klavierbegleiteten Liedern Mozarts*; and Rushton, 'Mozart's Lieder: A Survey'. In fact, *Des kleinen Friedrichs Geburtstag* was published by the Viennese Taubstummen-Institut (Institute for the Deaf and Dumb) in 1788 together with K474, 517, 518 and 529.

the first by Mozart to have a relatively lengthy prelude and postlude. Formally speaking, it is a binary work with the usual sequence of primitive modulations. But this simple form is imbued with the melodic lines of a sentimental Italian aria: with its chromatic suspensions and caressing melodic line, it could just as well appear in an emotionally charged scene in an opera such as *Così fan tutte*. Such warm southern melodies are rarely found in the north German song, which would not in any case give such importance to the melodic line at the expense of the declamation as is the case here. The *Lied zur Gesellenreise* was followed on 7 May by three settings of poems by Christian Felix Weiße, *Der Zauberer*, *Die Zufriedenheit* and *Die betrogene Welt*. Weiße's name is often found in the context of other Viennese lieder composers, suggesting that, however tenuous the links between the Viennese and the great German poets, more circumspect and mediocre writers such as Bretzner and Weiße – writers mocked by Goethe and Schiller in their *Xenien* as inhabitants of 'Leipzig's refuge of parochial taste' – were none the less popular in Vienna. These three poems are all good examples of this particular type of poetry, the first a stilted and lascivious pastoral episode, the second a painfully unnatural hymn to naturalness, and the third an expression of high-flown didacticism. But Mozart has transformed the first of these in a really quite remarkable way, abandoning the traditional Arcadian garb and offering an exciting dramatic snapshot of a young girl who has just experienced the first joys of love and whose cheeks are still flushed when she rejoins her friends, entering in breathless haste in the brief yet eloquent prelude. Note, too, the melodic writing: the more agitated she becomes, the more the lyrical and cantabile writing becomes dramatic and declamatory, a development reflected in the accompaniment, which follows no particular pattern but for the most part lightly traces the vocal line, only occasionally going its own way (notably in the third line at 'da fühlt ich': 'then I felt')[13] and finally plunging wildly and unexpectedly downwards during the interlude. As so often in his operas, therefore, Mozart composed this song over his poet's periwigged head and, as a born dramatist, introduces us to an emotional state between consciousness and presentiment that he was particularly good at depicting. He describes this state with total clarity in all its different stages, while never straying into the field of the cantata, as he did at an earlier date in his setting of the French song *Dans un bois* K308, but remaining strictly within the framework of the song. *Die betrogene Welt* shares this dramatic element, with all the characters that people this didactic text lovingly depicted in the music: the wealthy fool, the empty-headed fop and the frivolous Selimene. But no less vivid is the evocation of the magnificent celebrations in the piano and the sense of remorse that 'lags behind'. Particularly delightful is the consciously tedious tone of the moral of the tale: the world wants to be deceived, so let it be deceived! Of these two songs, the second makes more concessions to the Italian tradition than the first. Between them comes *Die Zufriedenheit*, a genuine Rococo song whose melodic writing is Italianate from start to finish.

It must have been pure chance that allowed Goethe's poem *Das Veilchen* to fall into Mozart's hands this very same year. He presumably got to know it from the Viennese collections of either Joseph Anton Steffan or Karl Friberth.[14] Mozart's setting dates from 8 June 1785, and among the points that it has in common with Steffan's is not only its tonality, but also its general metrical

---

13. This ingratiating and yet so agitated octave motif was often used by Mozart to depict such states of emotional presentiment; a further example may be found in Cherubino's aria 'Non so più cosa son' in *Le nozze di Figaro*.

14. Joseph Anton Steffan, *Sammlung Deutscher Lieder* (Vienna, 1778), i, no. 14; Karl Friberth, *Sammlung Deutscher Lieder* (1780), iii., no. 14. In Steffan's anthology, the poet is said to be Gleim, not Goethe. See also Friedlaender, *Das deutsche Lied im 18. Jahrhundert*, ii.164. ◆ Similarities between Mozart's and Steffan's settings of *Das Veilchen* notwithstanding, it is likely that Mozart was acquainted with the poem from Friberth's collection, a copy of which was part of Wolfgang's library; see *Dokumente*, 500, *Documentary Biography*, 591.

structure and even individual details such as the harmonic writing in the third and fourth bars.[15] The inspiration was no doubt indirect, nothing more, for neither Steffan nor any other lieder composer can match Mozart in terms of his independence of treatment and interpretation.[16] Above all, he abandoned the strophic structure of the original and, following the procedure adopted in the two earlier songs, treated it with total dramatic freedom. Indeed, he even went a stage further and introduced the recitative and appreciably increased the keyboard's independent contribution. The result is a genuine dramatic scene that draws the listener into the heart of the action with a vividness that is palpable. Right from the outside the two self-contained images of the violet and the young shepherdess are clearly distinguished, the former a picture of heartfelt tenderness, the latter one of almost provocatively youthful high spirits.[17] Unlike the violet, the shepherdess has a tripping, mercurial accompaniment and an independent painterly postlude that appears to be related less to her vocal line than to the pastoral strains of the shawm that are bound up with it. The girl's stepping on the little flower creates a deeply moving impression, its elegiac G minor lament striking the tone of an Italian aria, followed by a sudden ray of hope with the modulation to B flat major, and then the sense of catastrophe ushered in by the completely unexpected and harsh entry of the sombre E flat major. The disaster itself is described in recitative, not, of course, the coolly narrative tone of a *secco* recitative, but with extreme emotion, as though the narrator is struck dumb by the scene that he is obliged to witness. Hence, too, the appalled ascent of the voice to f'', followed by a rest. No less realistic are the falling sighs with which the sense of tension is released. And the way in which we suddenly slip into the dying violet's ecstatic outburst is little short of inspired. But Mozart also reveals a true sense of drama when he allows the narrator to have the final word and to express his feelings: 'das arme Veilchen!' ('the poor little violet'). This second brief recitative is a dramatic and psychological sequel to the first. Only now can the composer end the song on a genuinely lyrical note with an allusion to the popular refrain 'es war ein herzigs Veilchen' ('it was a delightful little violet'). For all his sympathy with Mozart, Goethe is unlikely to have approved of this setting of his poem, so untypical was it of the Berlin school. After all, Mozart had done something here that he, Goethe, was always keen to avoid: far from having been satisfied simply to set the poem to music and in that way to 'clarify' its meaning, he had recreated it in the light of his own imagination as a musician and thus brought to an end the poet's control over his own work. As such, *Das Veilchen* constitutes a glimpse into the promised land of the later Schubertian lied.[18] Who can say how the German song would have developed if this

15. Reprinted by Max Friedlaender in *Schriften der Goethegesellschaft*, xi (1896), 16–17.
16. A list of these similarities may be found in Friedlaender, *Das deutsche Lied*, ii.163–4. ◆ Eighteenth-century writers agreed with Abert; in January 1790 a reviewer for the *Musikalische Real-Zeitung* wrote that, 'From among the mass of settings with which the former song [*Das Veilchen*] has already been honoured and dishonoured, the reviewer is unacquainted with any but that by the late Kapellmeister *Schweizer* which could be set side by side with the present one [by Mozart]. Very surprising and uncommonly fine is the treatment of the text at the end, where Herr *M*. at the close of the third verse once more repeats the words 'Poor violet! It was a darling violet' and then ends with them. Would that such songs were studied by many a rising song composer as models for good vocal writing and pure harmony' (*Dokumente*, 317, *Documentary Biography*, 360–1). The earliest known setting of Goethe's poem appears to be by Karl Siegmund Freiherr von Seckendorff (1744–85) from 1777 or 1778.
17. A comparison between Steffan and Mozart is highly instructive for the light that it sheds on the difference between talent and genius. Steffan first modulates at the words 'es war ein herzigs Veilchen', obeying purely musical considerations, and for the same reason then interpolates an interlude. With the entry of the shepherdess he then reverts to G major. Mozart, by contrast, waits for the new character to enter before modulating to a different key, but then clings to that key as tenaciously as he had done to the old one. He does not allow the violet to expatiate at length but introduces the girl with dramatic suddenness, delaying the postlude until later, when it serves not just a musical purpose, but a highly poetic one, too. Note also the harmonic writing in this piece.
18. ◆ For a detailed analysis of *Das Veilchen*, see Schachter, 'The violet: An analysis of the music'.

isolated ray of our Classical poetry had not fallen on Mozart's oeuvre. Here was the 'true phoenix' that Mozart had so longed to find in opera.

The two Masonic songs K483 and 484 that Mozart wrote to open and close a lodge meeting already represent a significant decline.[19] With their division between solo and chorus, both are examples of the *geselliges Lied*. The keyboard, too, reverts to its old role as an accompanist. Only at the end do we find two brief postludes, the second of which bears a striking resemblance to one of the orchestral interludes from the opening act of Gluck's *Alceste*.

The origins of the 'Bandel' terzet K441 were described above. A typical example of this popular and comical kind of domestic music making, it is loosely structured round a main section and two episodes and involves a mixture of earthy Viennese humour and bubbling *buffa* jokes, a piece full of a harmless delight in music making that becomes comically eloquent towards the end. From first to last, it contains a whole series of delightful jokes behind which lies a carefully observed dramatic situation: when their high-spirited Viennese compatriot asks his question right at the beginning, he is recognized by the couple with a flourish and subjected to such a torrent of words that he no longer knows whether he is coming or going.

Most of the arias that date from this period were written for Aloysia Lange and Valentin Adamberger and include not only bravura pieces such as *No, che non sei capace* K419 but also a number of important works such as the *scena Mia speranza adorata* K416 of 8 January 1783. Although described as a rondo, it is not an example of the type of form that we have already encountered in Mozart's keyboard concertos, but is a binary aria comprising a slow and a quick section, each of which is developed at length and repeated. In other words, it is at least as much a binary aria as it is a rondo. The tenor aria *Per pietà, non ricercate* K420 is also described as a rondo and is made up of a slow ternary section followed by a binary allegro, but in this case the slow section is not repeated. Worked out in meticulous detail, both arias are highly individual works of great nobility of invention, with the second of them especially notable for the way in which the atmosphere of the piece is divided between strings and winds to great poetic effect. In general, these arias are excellent examples of Mozart's art of dramatic instrumentation, an art that was to find such brilliant expression only a short time later in *Le nozze di Figaro*. In the adagio from the soprano aria *Vorrei spiegarvi* K418, for example, the soloist's tender, yearning vocal line floats effortlessly over pizzicato strings evocative of a guitar and over sustained chords in the horns and bassoons, while the solo oboe adds its voice, alternating between lengthy and profoundly expressive phrases and brief and wistful sighlike motifs, creating a picture of repressed but exquisite anguish that is psychologically complemented in the most felicitous manner by the sense of convulsive haste with which the secret lover is urged to rush into his mistress's arms in the aria's allegro section. But the most important aria in this series of works is the tenor aria *Misero, o sogno o desto* K431 that was written for Adamberger. A dungeon scene, it includes the usual tormenting images that are here entrusted to the winds. Even the recitative introduces a note of Gluckian austerity into the harmonic writing, followed by the hero's appeal to the breezes to bear his greetings to his lover, a passage which, in stark contrast to the recitative, is a superb example of a cantilena as broadly beautiful as it is deeply felt. Here, too, the winds later make their own independent contribution, laying bare the lover's heartfelt wishes. Especially moving is the passage at

---

19. ◆ It is uncharitable of Abert – though in keeping with his sometimes misplaced absolutism – to dismiss Mozart's Masonic songs. Almost certainly they were composed both musically and expressively to suit the social situation in which they were performed and as representatives of a specifically Masonic song tradition different from the tradition of 'art' songs. As such they can hardly be described as 'a significant decline'.

the end where the whole orchestra comes together for the fervent entreaty, 'dì che per essa moro, che più non mi vedrà!' No less remarkable and authentically Mozartian is the allegro, with its blend of despair, anguish and indignation, while the tone colours provided by the winds repeatedly conjure up the demonic nature of the scene. The bass aria *Così dunque tradisci* K432 is likewise exceptional in character, in this case as a result of its tonality of F minor. Rarely was Mozart so successful in capturing a mood of dark, self-tormenting despair, and again it is the strings, with their incessant triplet tremolando, that are entrusted with the task of evoking the basic mood, while the winds etch in their wildly darting motifs and figures alternating with weighty columns of chords. The vocal line ranges widely over the singer's entire compass, with a particular predilection for wide and unusual intervals, such as we find at the following sinister passage:

ch'or mi sgri - da - - te ap - pres - so

It remains to mention the rondo for Idamante K490, with violin obbligato, that Mozart wrote on 10 March 1786 for Baron Pulini and Count Hatzfeld. It, too, comprises two sections, of which only the second can really be described as a rondo. Its theme is related to a type that we have already encountered with Sarti and that was particularly popular at this time, a gavotte-like theme with a two-crotchet upbeat that is pleasing rather than full of character. Indeed, the piece as a whole is clearly intended for the concert hall and notably lacking in drama. The vocal line explores a modest range of emotions, with only the virtuoso solo violin seeking to give any more personal expression to the emotions suggested by the words.

41

Operatic fragments between
Die Entführung *and* Figaro

While Mozart's fame as a virtuoso continued to grow, he was still largely ignored in the one area in which he longed to shine, that of the music drama. At this date the usual way to gain access to the theatre was by means of an operatic commission, but this route remained stubbornly closed to him, and so we find him casting round in the most disparate directions and even writing insertion arias for other composers' works merely in order to have an opportunity to work for the theatre. When the longed-for commission finally arrived and he was asked to write *Der Schauspieldirektor*, the piece succeeded only in engaging his professional interest but not in firing his imagination. And in the case of his own attempts to unearth a suitable text, fortune regularly left him in the lurch. Although he repeatedly tried to work himself up into a state of genuine enthusiasm, the fire soon died down again through lack of any real inner experience, as the conditions that his genius associated with an opera libretto were never met. He was incapable of summoning up his dramatic muse whenever he received orders from on high to do so, with the result that none of these attempts made any real progress.

This was the case with the earliest of these projects, Varesco's *L'oca del Cairo* (K422). Among the manuscripts found in Mozart's papers at the time of his death was the whole of the opening act written out in Varesco's hand, together with complete prose drafts of the second and third acts.[1]

The list of characters is as follows:

Don Pippo Marchese di Ripasecca, innamorato di Lavina, e credutosi Vedovo di
Donna Pantea sotto nome di Sandra sua Moglie.
Celidora loro unica Figlia destinata sposa al Conte Lionetto di Casavuota, Amante di
Biondello Gentiluomo ricco di Ripasecca.
Calandrino Nipote di Pantea, Amico di Biondello, ed Amante corrisposto di
Lavina Compagna di Celidora.
Chichibio Ma[e]stro di Casa di Don Pippo, Amante di
Auretta Cameriera di Donna Pantea.

The plot may be summarized as follows:

The vain and violent Don Pippo has repudiated his wife Donna Pantea and now believes her to be dead, but she is in fact living in hiding across the bay. Biondello, whom Pippo hates, is in love with the latter's daughter Celidora, but she is promised to Count Lionetto di Casavuota. Pippo

---

1. Varesco's autograph wordbook is in the Staatsbibliothek in Berlin. Only the opening act was worked up into a libretto that survives in two different versions, the second of them made at Mozart's suggestion. These were followed by a prose summary of the opera. All this material is reproduced by Waldersee in 'Varesco's L'Oca del Cairo, nach der Originalhandschrift herausgegeben'.
◆ Further, see the critical report to NMA II/5/13. For Mozart's sketches, see NMA X/30/4.

himself has designs on the latter's companion Lavina, who for her part has already agreed to marry Pantea's nephew Calandrino, who is also Biondello's friend. Pippo has imprisoned both women in a closely guarded tower. So assured is he of victory that he has promised him his daughter's hand in marriage if he can enter the tower within a year. Calandrino has therefore made an artificial goose operated by a man hidden inside it. Pantea will disguise herself as a Mooress and present the miraculous object to an astonished world. They hope that Pippo will let them show the goose to the girls, thereby allowing Biondello to gain access to the tower. In return, Calandrino will receive Lavina's hand in marriage.

The opera opens exactly a year after the wager took place and begins with preparations to welcome Count Lionetto, who is to attend the wedding of Pippo and Lavina. Calandrino discovers to his dismay that Pantea has been prevented from coming by a storm, and so they decide to enter the tower by a bridge. The chambermaid Auretta and her lover, the majordomo Chichibio, are bribed into removing Don Pippo's clothes and preventing him from going out. Biondello and Calandrino superintend the operations to build the bridge, while engaging the girls in the tower in a tender-hearted quartet. But Auretta and Chichibio have failed to keep a proper look-out and Pippo suddenly appears, violently disrupting the proceedings.

In act two, Pantea manages to land with her goose in spite of the storm, causing quite a stir at the annual fair. Chichibio informs his master, who summons Pantea into his presence. She claims that the goose has lost its voice during the storm but that it will regain it if it is allowed to eat a particular herb in a secret garden. Pippo escorts Pantea and her goose into the fortress garden, where they may also be seen by the two young women, who have been watching the fair in the market place from their tower window. An argument ensues involving Biondello, and Pippo, as the lord of the manor, has to settle it. The whole absurd business ends in general disorder.

Pantea conceals Biondello inside the goose and enters the tower, while Calandrino informs Pippo that in his despair Biondello has set sail in the teeth of the storm, an account that Auretta tearfully corroborates. Delighted, Pippo dresses for his wedding and sets off for the tower. The young women can be seen at the window, joking with the goose, much to the crowd's amusement. Pippo plans to marry Lavina as soon as Lionetto arrives, but the latter sends his excuses. He is about to proceed with the wedding without him when Pantea enters *in propria persona*. The goose begins to speak, as Biondello emerges from it and reminds Pippo of his promise, leaving the latter with no alternative but to put a brave face on things. Ruefully he returns to Pantea and all three couples live happily ever after.

Bizarrely adventurous plots of this kind were common currency in *opere buffe* at this time, although Varesco may well have been particularly proud of his wonderful goose, which reflected the contemporary love of such mechanical miracles.[2] Far worse, however, is the plot's lack of wit: the action plods along, with no sense of dramatic tension, while the characterization is either conspicuous by its absence or sketched out along the crudest lines. Mozart realized this at once, but initially thought that he could overcome the problem by undertaking various changes, and so he set to work without delay, as he informed his father in his letter of 6 December 1783:

Just three more arias to go, and then the first act of my opera will be finished. I can truthfully say that I'm completely happy with the *buffa* aria, the quartet and the finale and that I'm actually looking forward to the performance. And so I'd be sorry if I'd written this music in

---

2. ◆ For a broad-ranging discussion of *opere buffe* in Vienna at this time, see Hunter, *The Culture of Opera Buffa in Mozart's Vienna: A Poetics of Entertainment*.

vain, in other words, if what is absolutely necessary doesn't happen. Neither you nor Abbate Varesco nor I has given any thought to the fact that it will look bad and, indeed, may even wreck the whole opera if neither of the two principal women sets foot on stage until the very last minute but has to keep on walking around on the bastions or ramparts of the fortress. I may be able to rely on the audience remaining patient for one act, but they certainly won't be able to hold out for a second act, it's out of the question. This thought first occurred to me at Linz, – and so there's no alternative but to play some of the second-act scenes in the fortress. – Camera della fortezza. – The scene could be so arranged that Don Pippo gives orders for the goose to be taken into the fortress and we should then be introduced to the room in the fortress where Celidora and Lavina are. Pantea comes in with the goose – Biondello slips out – they hear Don Pippo coming, and Biondello becomes a goose again. One could introduce a good quintet here, which would be all the funnier in that the goose would join in. – I should add that my only reason for not objecting to this whole story about the goose is that two men of greater insight and judgement than I have not raised any objections to it, and those two people are you and Varesco. But there's still time to think of some alternative. Biondello once vowed that he would enter the tower; how he goes about it, whether in the form of a goose or by some other ruse is all the same. I think it should be possible to achieve a far more comical and natural effect if Biondello were to remain in human form. For example, the news that in his despair at not being able to enter the fortress Biondello has thrown himself into the sea could be brought in right at the start of the 2nd act, he could then disguise himself as a Turk or whatever and introduce Pantea as a slave girl (a blackamoor, of course). Don Pippo is willing to buy the slave girl as his bride, and so the slave dealer and the blackamoor are allowed into the fortress in order to be inspected. In this way Pantea has an opportunity to bully her husband and to be as rude to him as she likes, and so she'd have a better part, for the more comic an Italian opera the better. – Could I ask you to make my views known to Abbate Varesco and tell him to get on with it – I've worked hard enough as it is in this short time. Indeed, I'd have finished the whole of the first act if I hadn't needed to change the words in some of the arias, but please don't tell him this yet.[3]

But Mozart had by no means finished. By 10 December we find him writing again and expressing the hope that 'the 2 women could come down from the bastion even in the first act when they have to sing their arias, in which case I'd gladly agree to their singing the whole finale from on high'.[4] This could easily be arranged by a change of scene. But it was not long before Mozart presented a further set of demands, again revealing the extent to which he was involved in drafting these texts:

As for the opera – which is my most pressing concern – Abbate Varesco has written next to Lavina's cavatina 'a cui servirà la musica della cavatina antecedente' ['for which the music of the preceding aria will do'], that is, Celidora's cavatina. – But this won't work, as the words of Celidora's cavatina are all about hopelessness and despair, whereas those of Lavina's cavatina are about comfort and hope. – Besides, it's completely hackneyed and it has never been usual for one singer to echo the song of another. – At best, this can work for a soubrette and her lover, in other words, for the ultime parti [secondary characters]. I think the scene should start with a

3. *Briefe*, iii.294–5 (letter of 6 December 1783).
4. *Briefe*, iii.296 (letter of 10 December 1783).

beautiful duet, which could begin with the same words, with a short aggiunta for the coda. – The duet would be followed by the same dialogue as before. – e quando s'ode il Campanello della Custode [and when the duenna's bell is heard], Mlle Lavina, not Celidora, will be kind enough to remove herself, so that, as the prima donna, Celidora can sing a fine bravura aria. – I think this would be better for the composer, singer, spectators and audience, and the whole scene would undoubtedly be more interesting. – Moreover, they're hardly likely to tolerate the same aria from the 2nd singer after it has already been sung by the first. – I don't know what you both have in mind with the following suggestion: at the end of the newly interpolated scene with the two women in the opening act, Herr Abbate writes 'siegue la scena VIII. che prima era la VII. e così cangiansi di mano in mano i numeri' ['Scene VIII, formerly Scene VII, then follows, and thus the numbers are correspondingly altered']. – According to this description, I am to assume that, contrary to my wishes, the scene after the quartet, when both women sing their little songs in turn at the window, is to remain. – This is out of the question. – Not only would this make the act much longer, and to no purpose, but it would be very tedious. – It has always seemed to me ridiculous to read: – Celidora: 'Tu qui m' attendi, amica. Alla Custode farmi veder vogl' io; ci andrai tu puoi.' Lavina: 'Si dolce amica, addio.' (Celidora parte.) [Celidora: 'Wait for me here, my friend. I wish to show myself to the duenna. You may go later.' Lavina: 'Yes, sweet friend, goodbye.' (Exit Celidora.)] Lavina sings her aria. (Celidora comes back and says): 'Eccomi, or vanne' etc. ['Here I am, now go'] and now Lavina leaves, and Celidora sings her aria, – they relieve each other like soldiers on guard duty. – Also, it's much more natural that, having agreed as much in the quartet, the men should immediately set off to find the people needed to launch the attack and that the 2 women should quietly return to their apartments. The most they could still be allowed is a few lines of recitative. But I'm convinced that the scene was never meant to be retained and that Varesco simply forgot to indicate that it was to be omitted. – I'm most curious to know how you intend to get Biondello into the tower; – as long as it is amusing, I'm prepared to allow a certain unnaturalness here. I'm not worried about a few fireworks, the arrangements of the Viennese fire brigade are so good that there's nothing to fear from fireworks on stage. – After all, Medea is often given here, at the end of which half the palace collapses, while the other half goes up in flames.[5]

The final reference to the project occurs in Mozart's letter of 10 February 1784:

Every line of Herr Varesco's verse shows signs of haste! I hope that in time he'll see this for himself; that's why I'd like to see the opera *as a whole* (just let him jot it down), then one can raise fundamental objections to it; after all, we're in no hurry. If you were to hear what I've already finished, you wouldn't want it to be ruined either! and that can so easily happen! and it so often does. I've set aside what I've already written, and it's sleeping soundly. I'll wager that not one of the operas that may be performed before mine is finished will contain a single idea that resembles any of my own![6]

But Varesco lacked either the will or, more probably, the strength of purpose to satisfy Mozart's demands, and the opera remained a torso.

5. *Briefe*, iii.297–8 (letter of 24 December 1783).
6. *Briefe*, iii.300 (letter of 10 February 1784).

Apart from a recitative and tenor aria for Biondello, six numbers have survived in short score, all from act one. As usual, the vocal lines and bass are complete, while the ritornellos and accompaniment are merely hinted at.[7] Yet even the duet for Auretta and Chichibio ('Così si fa') is a significant achievement, fully worthy of the mature composer. It takes as its starting point a favourite theme of *opera buffa*, in which the superior young woman teases her jealous lover, before being reconciled with him at the end. But how subtly Mozart differentiates between the two characters right from the very beginning, with, on the one hand, the mischievous Auretta entirely confident of success and, on the other, the majordomo who, such is his jealousy, has great difficulty in maintaining the dignity by which he sets such great store.[8] He is already caught in her net during the first C major melody, which is clearly parodistic in tone. Here and in the following tearful episode we are still firmly in the world of an Italian *opera buffa*, but at the words 'siamo amici',[9] the lovers are reconciled in an authentically Mozartian manner expressive of unconditional sincerity and truth:

It is also significant that this theme is entrusted not to the voices but to the orchestra.

Auretta's aria ('Se fosse qui nascoso') is no less delightfully mischievous in tone. As a joke she allows herself to be kissed by Calandrino and then, having first made certain that Chichibio is watching them, describes the situation that would arise if her jealous 'Argus' were to see them. The whole number is full of dramatic life. She depicts the presence of her jealous lover with tragicomical pathos: we share her sense of horror and see him bickering and quarrelling, but then she insists that she is innocent and, with a delightful sense of humour reminiscent of Susanna, she describes his feeling of relief when he becomes aware of this. At the words 'o qui non c'è pericolo' her eyes light up with a smile of superior roguery. At the same time, this interplay of contrasting emotions fits with astonishing ease and self-evidence into the simple binary form associated with *opere buffe*. Chichibio's aria ('Ogni momento'), by contrast, is entirely Italianate in character, a typical philippic against the fickleness of women with brief and rapid parlando motifs. Mozart's ability to place this stereotypical form in the service of dramatic characterization was soon to be demonstrated again in *Le nozze di Figaro*. Here there is a generalized sense of comedy which, to judge by the proposed instrumentation (trumpets), would have been underscored by the composer's use of orchestral colour. In much the same way, the following duet for Auretta and Chichibio ('Ho un pensiero') is painted in the broadest brushstrokes that prelude any detailed characterization. As before, the orchestra is given a special role to play, with 'Astolf's horn' predominant at the end. Yet even here the individual ideas in the text are all given their due, while the orchestra, with its martial motif and little trill, is left to maintain a sense of unity. The next surviving fragment is a recitative of a lightweight *buffa* nature notable especially for the animated bass figures allotted to Don Pippo. In spite of the fact that it remains no more than a sketch and that the accompaniment, for all its importance, is as good as missing, his aria ('Siano pronte') makes it clear that Mozart

---

7. The full score is in the Staatsbibliothek in Berlin and was the basis of Julius André's edition of the vocal score in 1855; see Genée, 'Mozarts Partitur-Entwurf seiner Oper "L'Oca del Cairo"'. The beginning of Pippo's aria ('Siano pronte') is not in Mozart's hand. NMA II/5/13 also includes Mozart's surviving sketches.
8. There is a striking pre-echo of the duet (no. 16) from *Le nozze di Figaro*.
9. Initially only the bass is notated; the melody becomes clear only later at the words 'Sia ricetto l'alma mia'.

intended to treat the old man as a buffo character on the grandest scale.[10] The two final pieces are ensembles. The quartet ('S'oggi, oh Dei') is given over to the lovers' long-distance conversation and is the most intimate of the surviving numbers. It begins by striking a serious note with its expression of longing, but at the mention of Pippo's name, a mischievous smile plays round Biondello's lips. Although their situation is the same, the two couples are sharply contrasted. With the middle section comes a change of grouping, and the young women's anxious question is answered reassuringly and in canon by their menfolk. At this point the idea of the bridge is mooted, parodistically presented as an alternative between 'Charon's boat' and the 'bridge of Horatio Cocles'. The way in which all four participants immediately chip in with the words 'meglio il ponte piace a me' is genuinely amusing. They decide to set to work without further ado in a typically Mozartian allegro that clearly reveals their secret fears alongside their resolve. Typical of this is the timid *pianissimo* phrase on 'più non chiedasi perchè'. The ending, too, has something desperate about it. The finale ('Su via, putti, presto, presto!') is laid out along the grandest lines and is on the same high level as Mozart's later finales, with the individual phases of the action singled out with exceptional perceptiveness and transformed into highly effective scenes that succeed each other with a constant increase in tension. He begins with a lively account of the building of the bridge, with the thought of Lionetto being led by the nose expressing itself with typically Mozartian humour. In the section in 6/8-time, with its merry chatter and fanfare motifs, the sense of happiness turns to boisterous high spirits. Yet all at once the feeling of anxiety returns in the recitative and following adagio, with its strange orchestral accompaniment; and in the D minor section with its pounding anapaestic rhythm, Auretta comes rushing in to announce Don Pippo's arrival. She and Chichibio breathlessly report on the imminent danger, creating a particularly comic effect with their inability to break free from the line 'il marchese non c' è più'. Calandrino's attempt to calm them down proves futile, as does the decision by Auretta and Chichibio – heralded by the horns – to keep the old man under observation. The mood remains permanently blighted as fearsome chromaticisms that already anticipate the sextet from *Don Giovanni* seize hold of the melody and remain in control throughout most of the following section. A sudden shift to C major brings with it the much-feared figure of Don Pippo, his imperious singing driving the whole company before him like a flock of frightened birds. The threat becomes a reality within a matter of seconds, the guards arrive[11] and the felons, caught in the act, create an irresistibly comic impression with their cry of 'ah! siam traditi!' Pippo now lets fly with a rolling triplet motif familiar from *Le nozze di Figaro*, a solitary figure pitted against the solid mass of his enemies and one who, following an eloquent whole bar's rest, emerges in the brief andante maestoso as a splendid example of a pompously overwrought buffo bass. But his adversaries take heart, with the young women attempting to talk their way out of danger by adopting a delightfully light-hearted tone, while the men prepare for open resistance. The situation starts to get critical for Pippo and he calls on the guards to help him. Mozart kept the chorus in reserve for this presto, and they now enter independently, first calmly, adopting an attitude of official subservience, but then becoming increasingly agitated in turn. This final section creates a brilliant impression, with brief and excitable shrieks and lengthy cries on both sides and with the situation remaining unresolved until

---

10. ◆ At the time Abert wrote this chapter, only a 48-bar melody and bass version of Don Pippo's aria was known. In the meantime, a copy of the complete aria, almost certainly based on the lost original score, was discovered among the papers of Simon Mayr, Kapellmeister at Santa Maria Maggiore in Bergamo (now at the Biblioteca Civica, Bergamo, shelfmark Sala 32 D 8. 29/1). The complete aria is published in NMA II/5/13 Nachtrag.

11. Chichibio announces Pippo's arrival in highly graphic terms, the announcement then being taken up by the other characters in diminution.

the lovers lose heart at the *pianissimo* passage in G minor and finally turn tail. As a whole, the finale is all about atmosphere, and although there is little trace of any finer points of characterization, it can certainly stand comparison with Mozart's later finales in terms of its dramatic volatility and mounting tension, to say nothing of the clarity and succinctness of its design and the plasticity of the ideas chosen.

In 1784 Mozart turned his attentions to a further operatic project, but in the event *Lo sposo deluso* K430 was destined to suffer the same fate as *L'oca del Cairo*.

The plot of this opera is less recherché and, indeed, less silly than that of *L'oca del Cairo*, even though it, too, fails to rise above the average and remains on a far lower level than *Le nozze di Figaro* and *Don Giovanni*.[12] Central to the action is the wealthy but elderly Bocconio (Sempronio[13]), whose betrothal to the proud Roman patrician Eugenia is thwarted by all manner of *buffa* intrigues. His fortunate rival is the officer Don Asdrubale, in whom the other two female characters – Bocconio's empty-headed niece Bettina and the wily singer and dancer Metilde – have likewise fallen in love. The cast includes two other minor characters, the misogynistic Pulcherio (Fernando) and Eugenia's tutor, Gervasio (Geronzio). The action revolves around both the perpetually duped figure of Bocconio and Asdrubale, who is wooed on every side, and it seems to have been this that attracted Mozart to the libretto. Certainly, Bocconio is a buffo role in the best tradition, a character who, in the hands of a dramatist like Mozart, was bound to rise far above the world of caricature. And the gentleman officer who is courted by three different women already touches on a problem that was to occupy Mozart again in *Le nozze di Figaro* and, above all, in *Don Giovanni*. Most of all, the present piece bore within it the makings of a viable drama in a way that *L'oca del Cairo* did not. But fate threatened its survival from another quarter, as the work was not a commission but had been chosen by Mozart himself, with the result that, as things stood, it had little chance of being accepted for performance. It seems to have been Mozart's growing awareness of this that robbed him of any desire to continue working on it.[14]

The overture and sung introduction (here described as a 'quartetto') form a single number,[15] with the vocal section constituting a repeat of the opening symphonic allegro, now extended along the lines of a rondo. With its fanfares, slides and chuckling motifs, this is real Italian festive music of a kind that Mozart had not written for some considerable time: even the concertino-like character of the second subject can still be discerned here. Equally Italianate is the eloquent breadth, with Mozart modulating only to the dominant and back. A tender, particularly finely instrumented andante strikes a note of remarkable inwardness: one has the impression that Mozart was already gazing down on this world of love affairs with completely different eyes from his Italian colleagues. In the introduction the voices provide a kind of commentary on the opening allegro. Bocconio appears in all his finery in order to receive his bride, answering Pulcherio's malicious laughter with the following memorable passage:

---

12. The libretto – now in the Staatsbibliothek in Berlin – is reproduced in NMA II/5/14. 113–32. ◆ Mozart's autograph, now at the Biblioteka Jagiellońska, Kraków, is not complete, even for the few numbers he composed: the wind parts for the overture and opening quartet are entered in the score in another hand. Surviving sketches for K430 are reproduced in NMA II/5/14, 108–12.

13. Some of the original names were changed by Mozart in the copy prepared by a copyist ignorant of the Italian language.

14. ◆ Mozart's libretto is apparently based on *Le donne rivali*, by an unknown poet and set to music by Cimarosa; the opera was performed at Rome, Venice and Florence in 1780, and at Siena in 1782 (NMA II/5/14, XVI). Further, see Sannipoli, 'Dalle "Donne rivali" di Cimarosa allo "Sposo deluso" di Mozart: Alcune ipotesi sull'autore del libretto'; and Degrada, 'Lo Sposo deluso da Cimarosa a Mozart'.

15. For a similar example, see Piccinni's *I viaggiatori* discussed above.

The listener is bound to laugh at this, but at the same time inevitably feels pity for the deluded old man, for it is he who, with his mixture of infatuation and nervous excitement, is the true hero of this quartet. Pulcherio's supercilious irony becomes less important here, and, for the present, neither Asdrubale nor Bettina emerges as a fully rounded character. Rather, they strike a generally light-hearted note, with only occasional prominence given to Bettina's sharp tongue. The spirit of the old *introduzioni* can still be clearly felt here. Eugenia's aria ('Nacqui all'aura trionfale') survives only in the form of a sketch, but it is evidently a remarkable number. She is proud as only a Roman can be, so that she is all the more indignant when she is not received in the way she believes she deserves, as Bocconio has unfortunately not finished dressing. And so Eugenia begins by adopting the overwrought tone of an *opera seria* aria with its wide-ranging intervals, a tone to which she repeatedly returns.[16] At the beginning of the allegro she even works herself up in the manner of a 'furia delirante'. Time and again, however, she abandons the heroic air of the Capitol and, as an ordinary human being, expresses a sense of true feminine indignation, with no hint of any caricature. It is clear that Mozart was not aiming at caricaturing his heroine in the way that most Italians would have done but wanted to portray a woman who feels genuine pride but who, as a result of external circumstances, allows herself to be misled into adopting a note of comical exaggeration. If her only characteristic were her ridiculous pride as a Roman, she would be no better than Bocconio and, as such, a worthy bride for him, whereas she in fact feels a profound affection for the gallant Don Asdrubale. It is in this sense that we should interpret the coloratura writing at the end, with its distant allusion to the horn call of the postilion who will take her back to Rome.

A far less complete picture emerges from the sketch for Pulcherio's aria ('Dove mai trovar quel ciglio'). Here Pulcherio attempts to heal the rift between Bocconio and Eugenia following their disastrous first encounter. While drawing each partner's attention to the merits of the other, he naturally keeps to himself his grave misgivings about their future and ends up rejoicing in his own freedom. It is clear from the aria's general outlines that Mozart would have risen to this challenge in the most intelligent and ingenious way: when addressing Bocconio, Pulcherio speaks firmly, man to man, while his remarks to Eugenia are flattering and even comically infatuated. And the picture that he conjures up of the couple's demeanour in public is delightfully vivid. His own feelings, too, find lively expression. But there is no doubt that the orchestra would have made an important contribution here, and in this respect the sketch provides us with few indications.

Conversely, the trio ('Che accidenti! Che tragedia!') for Eugenia, Asdrubale and Bocconio in act one, scene nine is worked out in full. It occurs after Asdrubale and Eugenia have recognized each other: Eugenia had thought that Asdrubale was dead and faints, causing Bocconio to rush away in search of some means of bringing her round. For his part, Asdrubale was on his way to Rome in order to marry Eugenia and now heaps her with reproaches in the belief that she has been unfaithful

16. Note also the key of E flat major.

to him. Before she can explain herself, Bocconio returns and finds that the situation has changed completely. It is at this point that the trio begins, with Mozart treating it as a highly idiosyncratic atmospheric portrait. The plot does not advance here, and so he is content to rely on ternary form, which he invests with a remarkable degree of unity by constantly repeating the same motifs. The focus of interest is initially the orchestra, which, like so many of Mozart's later ensembles, begins with a brief introduction. Scored for winds and strings, it generates a real sense of tension not least as a result of its crescendo marking, before culminating in the *piano* main idea – another of Mozart's typical surprises. This whole section is authentically 'Romantic' in tone, completely eschewing any melodic writing but plunging the listener into the very heart of the action by exerting emotional pressure of a suddenness that creates a markedly sinister impression. The following theme, too, has an oddly agitated character with its insecurely groping unison and sudden sforzato. The listener simply does not know where it is all leading. The restlessly pounding motif that follows likewise adds to the tension, and here, too, the melodic writing reveals a remarkably disjointed, questing character that initially refuses to go away, with all three characters dumbfounded and forced to keep their feelings to themselves. Only at the syncopated passage[17] in B flat minor does the sense of pain suddenly erupt, bit it ebbs away again just as quickly. Here the three voices come together for the first time, finding common ground in the same basic emotion, however different its individual causes may be. From now on, they remain together, while the orchestra continues to go its own way. But not even now does the build-up of tension find any real release, remaining confined to the briefest of outbursts that flare up with the speed of lightning and die away again just as quickly. *Buffa* elements in the true sense of the term are found only infrequently here, the main exceptions being the appeal to the 'stelle irate' and at the first repeat of the words 'questa pena è troppo barbara'. Not even Bocconio emerges as a distinctive character. Nor will the listener expect to find any real sense of tragedy here. Rather, the various ideas and the design of the trio as a whole are notable for their superior sense of knavery that enables the listener to see things in the right light: he senses that the three characters are in a critical situation but he observes them from a superior vantage point and is aware, therefore, of the tragicomical nature of their plight.[18]

Alongside these two unfinished Italian operas, we find a completed German singspiel in the form of *Der Schauspieldirektor* K486 (see above). On a purely poetic level, it is far inferior to the Italian works, having neither a plot nor dramatic characters to offer its listeners. It is an occasional piece, and not even a particularly entertaining one at that. The same is true of the music, which sprang not from any inner necessity but merely from the composer's professional obligations. As a result, the work is innocent of genuine humour and limited to parody and to a generalized sense of comedy. Even the overture strikes this note, with its main motif

combining high-flown emotion and playfulness and, as a result of its strikingly broad and bombastic development, hinting at parody. And the concertino-like cantabile theme that is prepared

17. The fact that Bocconio sings 'una sincope m'afferra' at this point is undoubtedly an intentional joke.
18. ◆ Further concerning *L'oca del Cairo* and *Lo sposo deluso*, see Everson, 'Of Beaks and Geese: Mozart, Varesco and Francesco Cieco'; Czucha, 'Mozarts "Die Gans von Kairo": Zum Verhältnis von Satire und Lustspiel am Beispiel eines Opernfragments'; dell'Antonio, '"Il compositore deluso": The fragments of *Lo sposo deluso*'; and Zaslaw, 'Waiting for *Figaro*'.

for by an ambitious half-cadence wears a stereotypical mask that it removes only later, at the entry of the winds, when it assumes a note of good humour. The way in which the winds enter with the development section during the last two bars is remarkably ingenious. This section combines thematic development with the modulatory principle associated with Schobert. Not even here, of course, should we look for genuine passion. Quite the opposite: its high-flown emotion notwithstanding, the mood is merely well-mannered, once again suggesting the idea of parody. Only with the entry of the A flat in the basses does the true Mozart appear and usher in the recapitulation in the manner of his great symphonies by means of delightful imitations of the slide motif in the winds. With its high-flown emotional unison, the thematic coda takes the parody to hitherto unsuspected lengths. Indeed, the very fact that a large-scale symphonic allegro is used as an overture for this pitiful comedy suggests parodistic intent, a characteristic which, in its elaboration, throws a curious sidelight on Mozart's art, rather than revealing its innermost essence.

The arias for the two sopranos (Madame Herz's 'Da schlägt die Abschiedsstunde' and Mademoiselle Silberklang's 'Jüngling! Mit Entzücken') are both trial pieces that they have brought along with them and are laid out along similar lines, each consisting of a slow and a fast section. Both, moreover, are scored for four concertante winds.[19] Textually, too, they are related. Yet the manner of their elaboration could hardly be more different. The second is described as a 'rondo', although this relates more to the character of its first theme – a typical slow gavotte of a kind that we have already encountered on frequent occasions – than to its simple ternary form. Whereas the second soprano aligns herself with the French in this way, the first soprano throws in her lot with the Italians – and with Mozart. Her G minor larghetto bears all the hallmarks of his style in terms of its melodic writing, part-writing and instrumentation, although here too, of course, there is the faintest suspicion of parody.[20] In general, the first aria is more sentimental, the second more charming, a distinction entirely appropriate to the characters of Madame Herz and Mlle Silberklang. Both women oblige with a display of coloratura singing, although in neither case do we find any of the excesses associated with Italian opera. Both singers are more concerned to show off their top notes than to display their vocal flexibility.

Of all the numbers in the opera, it was evidently the trio 'Ich bin die erste Sängerin' that attracted Mozart the most, as this was the first number that he set, on 18 January 1786, whereas the rest of the work was not completed until 3 February. And it is, indeed, the high point of the work, with the sopranos squabbling because the director cannot decide between them, while the tenor tries vainly to placate them. Scenes such as this may well have been familiar to Mozart on the strength of his own experience. Cast in large-scale ternary form, with several shorter episodes, it creates a particularly comical impression as a result of the fact that the two women repeatedly seek to reassert the characters established in their two arias, only to be overcome by anger, causing them to relapse into exactly the same bickering tone. Here Mozart is fond of using imitative procedures, with the two singers scarcely allowing each other to finish what they are saying before the other breaks in and ends her sentence for her. Neither is willing to give her rival the last word, with

---

19. The ritornellos are missing from the autograph score but appear in copies of the full score and also in the vocal scores. They are entirely Mozartian in character, and so they have been taken over into the complete edition; see the critical commentary thereto. ◆ The earliest source for the ritornellos is a manuscript copy, now in the Pierpont Morgan Library, New York (shelfmark Cary 595), from c1800; they are also taken over in NMA II/5/15. Mozart's autograph is similarly in the Morgan Library (shelfmark Cary 206). Further, see Tyler, 'Aria as drama: A sketch from Mozart's *Der Schauspieldirektor*'.

20. Notably at the very beginning, in the sforzato accent in the horns that proclaim the hour of departure, then in the vocal line at the agitated words 'Wie fällt mir so was ein?' Authentically Mozartian is the melodic writing not only at the words 'Ich will dich begleiten' (cf. the C minor mass, 'Et incarnatus', bars 142–52) but also at the beginning of the allegro (cf. Zerlina's vocal writing in the duet 'Là ci darem la mano' from *Don Giovanni*).

the result that, with the entry of the triplet accompaniment, it is no time at all before they have forced each other up to a high *c‴*. The tenor, attempting to pour oil on troubled waters, provides a highly effective contrast, submitting to his difficult task in a spirit of resignation, his tedious homily in the andante episode scarcely sounding as though he means it, in spite of the enthusiastic contribution of the winds. Yet it is effective enough at the outset, producing some extremely well-mannered and strict polyphony ('nichts kann die Kunst mehr adeln': 'nothing can ennoble art more'). The women, too, know what they must do to preserve the dignity of their art, but their insight is short-lived. Shortly afterwards we hear a suspicious muttering in the lower clarinets, while scalar figures in the voices shoot up like rockets to *f‴*. The tenor continues with his unctuous address, as the two women continue secretly to hiss at each other 'I'm the leading singer', with the result that the argument soon breaks out again as violently as ever. They lay into each other with shrieks of 'adagio' and allegrissimo', so that the tenor is barely able to assert himself with his cries of 'piano! calando! pianissimo!' and so on. Even so, he succeeds in bringing the trio to an end on a genuinely Mozartian *pianissimo*. The piece as a whole bubbles with life, never coming to rest for a moment and yet remaining free of caricature. The closing number is a French-style vaudeville, as in *Die Entführung aus dem Serail*, and it is no accident that it is Mlle Silberklang who introduces the graceful *opéra comique*-like theme. Each of the characters contributes a strophe of his or her own in keeping with his or her character, after which all join together in a refrain reminiscent of Grétry. Finally they are joined by the actor Buff as the leading buffo in a grotesque C minor. Needless to say, he is incapable of singing properly, an inability that the actor Joseph Lange described with self-deprecating irony.[21] As a result, he is naturally excluded from the ensemble.[22]

---

21. Lange, *Biographie des Joseph Lange*, 126. ◆ Also see Barak, 'Buff, Herz und Vogelsang – Die Theaterfamilien Stephanie, Lange und Adamberger im Wien Mozarts'.
22. ◆ Further concerning *Der Schauspieldirektor*, see Penninger, 'Der historische Opernwettstreit von 1786: Untersuchungen zur Problematik der Gattungsbegriffe "Deutsches Singspiel" und "Opera buffa" in der Auseinandersetzung um Mozarts "Der Schauspieldirektor" und Salieris "Prima la musica, poi le parole" und Darstellung der vermeintlich konkurrierenden Position beider Komponisten anhand historischer Dokumente'; and Dittrich, 'Dichterlied und Damenzank: Zu Salieris "Prima la musica e poi le parole" und Mozarts "Schauspieldirektor"'.

42

Le nozze di Figaro

Beaumarchais's comedy *Le mariage de Figaro, ou La folle journée* was first performed at the Comédie-Française in Paris on 27 April 1784 and proved so spectacularly successful that within a very short space of time it had been repeated no fewer than sixty-eight times. Rarely had the Comédie-Française witnessed such a success, which Beaumarchais owed less to the poetic merits of the piece than to the circumstances leading up to its first performance, circumstances so remarkable that public interest in it was raised to the highest pitch and the production turned into a veritable *affaire*. Beaumarchais had begun the piece in 1778 and submitted it to the Comédie-Française in 1781, but, after reading the play in manuscript, Louis XVI had declared categorically: 'C'est détestable, cela ne sera jamais joué.' His ban inevitably stirred up public opinion in favour of the piece, which its wily author was able to build on by dint of astute publicity, until even highly placed individuals such as Grand Duke Paul, the Comtesse Lamballe and various ecclesiastical dignitaries regarded it as an honour to have Beaumarchais read them the play. At the same time, Beaumarchais continued to fight a bitter battle with the royal censor. A performance was due to be given before an invited audience of aristocrats in the theatre at the Hôtel des Menus Plaisirs on 13 June 1783, but at the last moment it was banned on royal instructions, resulting in a degree of displeasure at Louis's tyrannical actions that threatened his very authority. Three months later, on 27 September, the piece was finally performed at a private function given by the Comte de Vaudreuil on his estates at Gennevilliers for the Comte d'Artois and the Duchesse de Polignac. Beaumarchais had been overwhelmed with requests for the piece to be performed and had demanded a second censor's report, with the result that Louis finally gave his permission for this private performance to go ahead. Astute as ever, Beaumarchais had achieved what he wanted: a public performance was now inevitable, as the general public demanded the same right as the aristocracy. Beaumarchais now insisted on a further series of censor's reports and even on a tribunal drawn from the highest ranks of the aristocracy and educated classes, and in each case he encountered wholehearted approval, with the result that the king was finally forced to give in. The affair says as much about Beaumarchais's cunning and resolve as it does about the king's weakness and the seething tensions among the public at large. Even before the production had opened, Figaro had already won a complete and utter victory over his aristocratic enemy in the eyes and hearts of the broadest cross-section of the population.[1]

Le mariage de Figaro is the second of three loosely linked plays. The first, *Le barbier de Séville*, was premièred in 1775, while the last, *La mère coupable*, was not given until 1792. The links

---

1. For a full account of the whole background and a literary critique of the piece, see de Loménie, *Beaumarchais et son temps*; Lintilhac, *Beaumarchais et ses œuvres*; Toldo, *Figaro et ses origines*; Hallays, *Beaumarchais*; Genée, 'Caron de Beaumarchais und seine Lustspiele als Opernstoffe'; and Bettelheim, *Beaumarchais: Eine Biographie*. ◆ More recently, see Philip Robinson, *Beaumarchais: Homme de lettres, homme de société* and Conesa, *Trilogie de Beaumarchais: Écriture et dramaturgie*.

between the first two plays are in fact closer than between the last two, with the third marking a notable decline in Beaumarchais's artistic gifts.[2] Originally – and oddly – described by its author as an 'opuscule comique', *Le mariage de Figaro* revolves around a plot that may be summarized as follows:

Count Almaviva has married Rosine after having abducted her from her guardian Doctor Bartholo with Figaro's help in *Le barbier de Séville*. He has taken Figaro into his service, together with Rosine's duenna Marceline, and has also found room in his castle for Rosine's music master Bazile. It is not long before the fickle count tires of his wife and casts his eye on the Countess's maid, Suzanne, who is engaged to Figaro. Bazile is initially expected to help him. The play begins on the day fixed for Figaro's and Suzanne's wedding. Suzanne tells Figaro about the Count's designs on her and so he decides to thwart his master by bringing forward his wedding, while the Count does everything in his power to delay it in order to have Suzanne for himself. In this, he turns for help to Marceline, who is herself in love with Figaro and who has given him money in return for his written promise that he will either pay her back or marry her. She has no difficulty in gaining Bartholo's support, as this gives *him* the chance he has been looking for to wreak vengeance on Figaro and at the same time to escape from Marceline's claims on him: years ago she bore him a son who was stolen from them in infancy. These plans are now thrown into disarray by the impudent yet attractive page Chérubin, whom the Count has caught red-handed with his gardener's daughter, Fanchette, on whom he also has his eye. Chérubin is dismissed from the Count's services, and so he seeks out Suzanne in order to ask her to intercede with the Countess and ensure that he may remain. The Count interrupts their meeting, forcing Chérubin to hide behind a large armchair. The Count promises Suzanne a generous dowry if she agrees to meet him that evening, but she emphatically rejects his offer. Bazile now arrives, and the Count in turn is forced to hide behind the armchair while Chérubin slips out from behind it and hides in the chair itself, beneath one of Suzanne's dresses. Bazile attempts to win over Suzanne to the Count and, when she rejects him, too, he makes all manner of suggestive remarks about Chérubin, claiming that he not only enjoys Suzanne's favours but that he has also made advances to the Countess. The furious Count emerges from his hiding place and gives orders for the page to be sent packing without delay. He recalls how he found the latter hiding in Antonio's house and duly discovers him again, this time hiding in the chair. But Chérubin has heard everything that has passed between the Count and Suzanne, and so, in order to get rid of him while preserving his honour, he makes him an officer in his regiment with orders to take up his new post at once in Seville. Figaro now arrives with a group of peasants. His wedding will be the first to be celebrated since the Count abandoned the custom of the *ius primae noctis* at the time of his own wedding, and in their gratitude the peasants from his estate ask him to honour the ceremony with his presence and place the toque on Suzanne's head. In this way Figaro hopes to curtail the Count's activities. The latter promises to attend but asks for a few hours' delay in order to ensure that the celebrations are all the more magnificent.

Figaro has hatched a further plot against the Count, and the Countess, apprised by Suzanne of all that has been going on, is resolved to play her part in it. In order to win back her husband, she

---

2. On the differences between the male characters in *Le barbier de Séville* and *Le mariage de Figaro*, see Wilder, *Mozart: L'homme et l'artiste*, 214–15. ◆ Further, see Angermüller and Parodi, *Da Beaumarchais a Da Ponte*; and Miller, 'Die Komödie "Le mariage de Figaro" von Beaumarchais' and 'Die Schule der Intrige oder der Bürger als Parvenu: Zur Figaro-Trilogie von Pierre Augustin Caron de Beaumarchais'.

is not even afraid of subterfuge: the Rosine of *Le barbier de Séville* begins to stir within her once again. Figaro has arranged for Bazile to receive an anonymous letter warning him and the Count that his wife's reputation is at stake: he hopes that jealousy will prevent his master from interfering in his own wedding arrangements. At the same time, however, he plans to lull him into a false sense of security by having Suzanne keep their arranged tryst that evening, except that it will not be Suzanne who turns up in the garden but Chérubin, dressed as a girl. Chérubin, whom Figaro has instructed to remain behind at the castle, now arrives to change into his disguise. Depressed, he shows the others his commission, but it transpires that it has not been sealed. He takes the opportunity to reveal his feelings for the Countess, who momentarily seems not averse to responding to them, when suddenly there is a knock at the door. The Count has received the anonymous letter and in his jealousy has returned from hunting without a moment's delay. Chérubin hurries into the next room and the Countess locks the door behind him, but while the Count is interrogating his wife, he knocks over a chair. The Countess explains that it is Suzanne who is in the room but orders her to stay there and say nothing, while refusing to hand over the key to the Count. Beside himself with fury, the Count locks all the doors, then leaves to find an axe with which to break down the door to the closet, taking the Countess with him. Suzanne, who had been hiding in the alcove, frees the page, who escapes by jumping through the window into the garden. The Count and Countess return, and the Countess, faced with no alternative, admits that it is Chérubin in the closet, an admission that serves only to increase the Count's anger. To the couple's astonishment, Suzanne emerges from the room. The Countess regains her composure and both women declare that they were merely wanting to punish the Count as a joke and that this was why Figaro had written the letter. With some difficulty, the Count persuades them to forgive him. Figaro now arrives to announce that everything is ready for his wedding, but when the Count asks him about the letter, he becomes confused and it requires considerable persuasion on the part of the Countess and Suzanne to get him to confess. To add to their problems, Antonio now arrives, half drunk, to report that someone has just jumped out of the window and landed on his flowers. Figaro, who has spoken to the page, admits to the deed: he had been talking to Suzanne and jumped out of the window, such was his fear of the Count's anger. Antonio, of course, believes that it was Chérubin, but offers to return a piece of paper that he assumes that Figaro has lost. The Count's suspicions are aroused and, taking the paper, he asks Figaro what it is. The Countess recognizes the page's commission and whispers this piece of information to Suzanne, who in turn passes it on to Figaro. But at this very moment Marceline appears with Bazile in order to remind Figaro of his promise to marry her. Their arrival could hardly be more opportune for the Count, who promises to have the case properly investigated. At the same time, it provides him with a way of getting rid of Basile, who wants to marry Marceline himself, and of avenging himself on him for the anonymous letter.

Before the tribunal is convened, the Countess decides that instead of Chérubin she herself will dress in Suzanne's clothes and wait for the Count in the garden. Suzanne must tell the Count of her willingness to attend the tryst. The court decides that Figaro must pay Marceline and, since he is unable to do so, that he must marry her. But Figaro objects that he first has to obtain permission from his unknown parents, a remark that leads to the discovery that he is the son of Bartholo and Marceline and was stolen from them in infancy. They decide to have a double wedding. In this way Figaro has escaped from danger, but Suzanne now returns with money given her by the Countess in order to buy Figaro's freedom and is appalled to find him in Marceline's arms, but it does not take long to apprise her of the true facts of the matter.

During the wedding celebrations, Chérubin, with Fanchette's help, disguises himself as one of the peasant girls, but is recognized. Meanwhile, Suzanne gives the Count a billet-doux dictated by the Countess, stating where they should meet. It is sealed with a pin, which he is supposed to return to her as a sign that he agrees. Figaro notices the Count reading the letter and pricking himself with the pin and then learns from Fanchette that she is meant to return it to Suzanne. Beside himself with jealousy, he instructs his parents and friends to turn up for the assignation, when he himself plans to surprise and punish the guilty couple.

At dead of night, the Countess and Suzanne arrive in the garden, each dressed in the other's clothes, in order to put their menfolk to the test, as Suzanne, too, has been told by Marceline of all that has happened. Scarcely has the Countess been left alone when, to her horror, Chérubin arrives and, thinking that she is Suzanne, tries to steal a kiss from her. But at that very moment the Count steps between them, and it is him whom Chérubin kisses instead. The Count prepares to box the page's ears, but Figaro gets in the way and is sent reeling. The Count now turns his attentions to his wife and, thinking that she is Suzanne, heaps compliments upon her, giving her money and a valuable ring, before attempting to lead her away. But she escapes from him in the dark and he tries in vain to find her again. The next encounter is between the furious Figaro and Suzanne, still disguised as the Countess. She momentarily forgets to disguise her voice, allowing him to recognize her but, in order to tease her in turn, he suggests that they repay infidelity with infidelity, at which she reveals her true identity and gives him a box on the ears. It is not long, however, before they are reconciled, and when the Count returns in search of Suzanne, they resume their earlier love scene. Incensed, the Count calls on his servants to bring torches. Figaro's friends arrive, accompanied by the Countess, forcing the Count into the shameful confession that he has just been wooing his own wife with vows of love and gifts. The general confusion is brought to an end only by her act of forgiveness.

This brief résumé may serve to indicate only one aspect of the play's strengths: its art of intrigue or imbroglio.[3] As many writers have pointed out, this art has long been popular with Romance nations as a result of their rationalist character, but never before had there been a poet capable of handling its technique with such mastery as Beaumarchais. In *Le barbier de Séville* he had been largely content with a single intrigue, but in *Le mariage de Figaro* such intrigues proliferate on every side, with each character following his or her own secret course only to come into inevitable conflict with the others. In particular, Chérubin's insolent and impulsive behaviour places all the other characters in novel situations that have a disruptive effect on their lives. But the poet ravels and unravels all these strands to the plot with admirable ease and grace, avoiding obvious farce but revealing a superior wit that is genuinely suited to a comedy. Only at the end, when he needs to increase the tension, does he fall back on the stock-in-trade of the older type of comedy with its scenes of disguise and slapstick blows. Yet it is not only to the overall design of his plays that Beaumarchais owes his mastery in the field of intrigue but also to his own adventurous life which, far more than any *folle journée*, demanded his whole skill and cunning.

Of course, the situations, motives and characters of *Le mariage de Figaro* can all look back on a venerable tradition. Although the play is a unique blend of a comedy of intrigue with a comedy of characters, each of those characters has more or less obvious links not only with literary comedies but with the musical comedies of the French and Italians. Yet the treatment is thoroughly individual. In particular, Figaro differs from his countless literary predecessors in no longer being his aristocratic master's cunning accomplice but his most dangerous and ultimately successful enemy. It is easy to forget that he is a valet, so accurately is he depicted as a representative of the *tiers état*,

---

3. It appears from the first draft of the play that this intrigue was in fact the nub of the entire piece; see Lintilhac, *Beaumarchais et ses œuvres*, 259–60. There is no trace in this draft of the play's social or political aspect.

to which France already owed so many of its leading thinkers, skilful, cunning, a jack of all trades, intimately familiar with the aristocracy's manners and inclinations, including their artistic and philosophical leanings, and always ready to flatter them and use them for his own advantage, but above all waiting for the day when, to quote Count Münster, 'the antechamber will be brought into the salon'. It was to this Aristophanic feature that the piece owed much of its success. As we have already seen in the case of *opéras comiques*, this feature was by no means new, but it now found a particularly favourable soil in which to flourish, and in Beaumarchais it discovered a poet who had himself explored every aspect of this divided society, suffering personal injury in the process. Nor was he content with the traditional sentimental opposition between town and country but gave theatrical – and keenly satirical – expression to the contrasts as they actually existed, with the result that for us moderns his work is the most important literary harbinger of the Revolution. Needless to say, he himself had no such thought in mind: he simply wanted to write a comedy of intrigue drawn from fiction and real life, and inasmuch as social conditions in Paris at this time furnished him with the best possible basis for his intrigue, he needed only to seize the opportunity fearlessly and with both hands, and victory was assured. The Third Estate applauded its own hero in Figaro, yet – as is so often the case – the general enthusiasm also affected the aristocracy, in spite of the fact that they were the butt of Beaumarchais's attack: few spectators saw the writing on the wall, the king being one of the few who did so. The play quickly found a home for itself in German-speaking theatres in various translations.[4]

The relationship between Da Ponte's libretto and Beaumarchais's original has frequently been discussed.[5] Among the former's fiercest critics are the latter's staunchest supporters, who see in his libretto a total travesty of the original, an act of desecration mitigated only in part by Mozart's music.[6] But we must ask ourselves how librettist and composer viewed the original and whether it was ever their intention to compete with Beaumarchais in his own field or whether they merely used his work as the material basis for a new piece with entirely different intellectual aims. The question is closely bound up with the related issue of Mozart's contribution to the text. We have already addressed this point on a purely superficial level and answered it in the affirmative on the strength of Da Ponte's and Kelly's accounts. But internal arguments, too, speak in favour of Mozart's involvement. His letters demonstrate that he made an often important contribution to the librettos of *Idomeneo*, *Die Entführung aus dem Serail* and *L'oca del Cairo*. Is it likely that, having achieved total mastery as a music dramatist, he would suddenly have capitulated to his librettist? Of course, the far more talented Da Ponte caused him fewer problems than Stephanie and Varesco, but he will most emphatically not have abandoned his dramatic principles merely in order to please Da Ponte, who was a highly adaptable man of letters and astute enough to realize that it was entirely to his own advantage to meet the composer halfway. He could still bask in the reflected glory of the 'sensation' that *Figaro* was. (It is sufficient for the reader to imagine one of today's composers setting a witty social comedy – unfortunately no such examples exist – and turning it into an opera.)

4. One of the earliest was published in Berlin in 1785 by Johann Friedrich Unger. Of later translations, the most widely performed was that of August Lewald, which dates from 1839. ◆ A second translation, by Ludwig Ferdinand Huber and published at Dessau and Leipzig, similarly dates from 1785. That same year the work was also published in Vienna; according to the title page, the translation is by 'R . . . ch'.
5. Hanslick, 'Mozart'; Marchesan, *Della vita e delle opere di Lorenzo da Ponte*, 218ff.; Bulthaupt, *Dramaturgie der Oper*, 111ff.; Istel, *Das Libretto*, 169ff.; and the usual Mozart biographies. ◆ For a concise modern account, see Carter, *W. A. Mozart: Le nozze di Figaro*, 33–48.
6. This is the view taken by Schurig, *Wolfgang Amade Mozart*, ii.89ff.

The choice of genre was dictated by the prevailing circumstances: it had to be an *opera buffa*, a field in which Da Ponte had already proved his worth. It is in this sense that we should interpret his comment in his preface[7] that his intention was not to translate Beaumarchais, but to imitate him. The adaptation could not have entailed any particular difficulties as the original already contained many of the situations, characters and motives that had been traditional elements of *opere buffe* from time immemorial: here one thinks above all of the disguises and nocturnal confusions, but also of the situation surrounding the two duets ('Cinque . . . dieci' and 'Via resti servita, madama brillante') and Figaro's second aria ('Non più andrai farfallone amoroso') and so on. These passages needed only to be thrown into sharper relief in order to create a genuinely *buffa* impression. But Da Ponte added a whole series of typical *buffa* features not found in Beaumarchais's original. In particular, the three secondary characters of Bartolo, Marcellina and Basilio adopt an authentic *buffa* tone in their respective arias ('La vendetta', 'Presto avvertiam Susanna' and 'In quegl'anni, in cui val poco'), but so, too, do the main characters, including Figaro himself with the 'chitarrino' of his cavatina ('Se vuol ballare signor Contino'), the 'suonatori' of the second-act finale and, above all, his philippic against women ('Aprite un po' quegl'ochhi'), which Da Ponte wrote to replace the hero's infamous and highly political monologue in the fifth act of Beaumarchais's original.[8]

Even more important, of course, is the passage in Da Ponte's preface in which he apologizes for the length of his libretto, ascribing it to the 'multiplicity of the musical numbers that had to be made in order not to leave the actors too long unemployed, to diminish the vexation and monotony of long recitatives, and to express with varied colours the various emotions that occur, but above all our desire to offer as it were a new kind of spectacle to a public of so refined a taste and such just understanding'. This sounds very much like the principles that Mozart himself had enunciated at the time of *Die Entführung aus dem Serail*[9] and suggests very much that he operated along similar lines in the case of *Le nozze di Figaro*. In other words, he did not adopt an uncritical attitude to all that Da Ponte submitted to him but first agreed an overall plan with him which he then proceeded to elaborate on the basis of his own imagination as a musician, and it may well be the case here, too, that the music of one or other of the numbers was already in his head before he received the words. The role that Da Ponte played will have differed in degree, but not in kind, from that played by Stephanie.[10]

It has always been argued that the main difference between the play and the libretto is that Da Ponte removed the whole of the political satire. No doubt considerations for the Emperor Joseph played a part here, but the argument that political subjects do not lend themselves to a musical setting is untenable.[11] Admittedly, politics as such cannot be depicted in music, but it is clear from the whole history of French opera – both serious operas and comic operas – that the same is not

---

7. In Teuber, *Die Theater Wiens*, ii/2, part i, 78–9 [*Dokumente*, 239, *Documentary Biography*, 273–4].
8. The parodistic mention of the legend of Mars, Venus and Vulcan in the larghetto of the fourth-act finale also comes under this heading.
9. Lert, *Mozart auf dem Theater*, 372, rightly draws attention to this connection.
10. The most obvious departure from the French original and from the normal practice of *opera buffa* concerns the role of the Countess in Da Ponte's libretto, and here we may well be correct in recognizing Mozart's hand. Even the way in which she is introduced into the opera is significant: in Beaumarchais's original, we first meet her in act one, together with a whole group of other characters, whereas in the opera she is introduced at a far more visible point, at the start of act two, where she stands apart from the action, appearing in a lyrical solo scene that is later followed by a second such scene ('Dove sono i bei momenti'). Here we find ourselves dealing with one of the changes to the original that go beyond questions of dramaturgy and all other technical considerations, altering the innermost core of the work and inevitably producing a totally different piece.
11. See Jahn, *W. A. Mozart*, fourth edition, ii.292.

true of its effect on the emotional lives of those who practise politics and of those who are affected by it. In consequence, it would not have been necessary to remove all the political ideas contained in Beaumarchais's play, and it seems likely, therefore, that the real reason for their removal lay in Mozart's complete lack of interest in such ideas. All the siren calls of the approaching Revolution, including the notions of freedom, equality and social change, were mere abstract theories to him, lacking in tangibility and vitality. He simply did not know where to begin with them. As always, he was fascinated by people, not theories. Of course, the contemporary political picture, with its social conflicts, still plays an important role in the opera, certainly a more important role than in any of his other works, but it is not his main concern, being merely the outer form within which the individual characters act out their lives. What he wanted to write was not a moralizing play set in the 'Rococo Age' but a purely human comedy with no political or social aims. Not even the subject's oft-cited 'frivolity' was of any real concern to him: he was not interested in reducing it to some commonplace moral nor in deriving any particular pleasure from it. As long as they did not degenerate to the level of a sentimental comedy, the *opere buffe* of the time made no attempt to set any moral standards, but adopted a naïve and impartial stance, with no sense of moral outrage. In any case, eighteenth-century morality differed considerably from present-day views. Decay had begun to filter down from the top and was already affecting the other classes, finding eloquent expression, for example, in the light fiction of the day. Never for a moment did it occur to these writers to criticize society in the way in which Molière had done and as Ibsen was later to do. Rather, they subscribed to the principle of 'live and let live', attempting to see everything in the rosiest possible light and glossing over all shortcomings through their charming and witty accounts. From Wieland downwards, they were able to make silk purses out of sows' ears, and *opera buffa* adopted a similar line, albeit with incomparably less wit and good taste. But Vienna was arguably the one German-speaking city whose intellectual life most clearly reflected the strengths and weaknesses of this moribund culture. In the words of one observer, the whole place was dominated by 'a cheerful openness to every pleasure and a receptivity to all that was beautiful',[12] yet it was also aware of this moral laxity and knew that the conditions depicted in *Le nozze di Figaro* were entirely true to life. Not even Mozart was an exception here, but he felt neither particularly attracted nor repelled by these circumstances, not least because in pursuing his artistic goals he was not at all interested in presenting a moral picture of the age.

His keen eye no doubt recognized from the outset that here was a subject uniquely suited to his own particular approach to drama inasmuch as it offered him a wealth of living, yet contrasting characters who revealed unsuspected opportunities for psychological development thanks to the uncommonly gripping plot. A lesser composer would no doubt have dealt with it by drawing on the stock characters of *opera buffa*, but an astute observer like Mozart must have been attracted by the idea of breaking out of the old framework and allowing his unbridled creativity free rein. After all, we should be guilty of totally misunderstanding the nature of genius if we thought he would be content to imitate an existing model, even if that model were Beaumarchais. His aim was to create something new, his work was unique unto itself, no doubt dependent upon tradition in superficial ways, but independent of it in terms of its innermost essence. This is also the case with his attitude to Da Ponte's libretto and its affinities with *opera buffa*. This source, too, was melted down in his imagination, producing a new work that was essentially neither French nor Italian, nor even German (notwithstanding the claims of many a patriotic writer), but something specif-

---

12. Pichler, *Denkwürdigkeiten aus meinem Leben*, i.103–4.

ically Mozartian. And once again this transformation took place because he brought to the piece his own view of the world, which was that of the man of genius.

Few works are as well suited as *Le nozze di Figaro* to demonstrating the gulf that exists between what the man of genius feels about 'real life' and how the merely talented individual perceives it. For Beaumarchais, real life consisted in the national and social order of late eighteenth-century France with all its mounting problems, in other words, all that he could see around him. The same was true of *opera buffa*: it, too, invariably stuck closely to those aspects of real life that were of particular concern to contemporary society. For Mozart, by contrast, reality knew no such limitations, but embraced life in its totality. As such, it was completely independent of all that his own age regarded as real life: for him, it was no replica of a pre-existent entity but an archetypal image, with the result that here, too, he proved to be a true creator rather than a talented imitator. Of course, the symbols of the view of the world that he presented in *Le nozze di Figaro* were taken from a particular age – his own age – in a far more direct way than was the case with any of his other great operas. But the fact remains that they are symbols: all these characters point beyond the immediate present to a higher sphere of existence. Like all great works of art, *Le nozze di Figaro* is not topical but timeless, whereas Beaumarchais's play, for all its ebullient wit, remains inextricably bound up with its age, hence the disparate fates suffered by these two works.

In short, Mozart was concerned neither with politics nor with morality, neither with cultural and moral history nor with tickling his audience's intellect and wit. Rather, his aim was that of the creator who naively delights in his own ability to fashion characters who, freed from all moral bombast as well as from the contingencies of a particular reality, reflect an aspect of the eternal wealth of human existence viewed from the standpoint of an outstanding sense of irony. We may well be justified in complaining that Da Ponte's libretto has robbed the original of much of its glamour, with the result that – to state only the most obvious point – the character of Figaro has been reduced to the role of a valet, the very role from which Beaumarchais had raised him with so much wit and grace. In Mozart's hands, conversely, he is neither a political windbag nor a mischievous *buffo* servant, but a living person who wears no mask but has a richly complex emotional life, made up, as it is, from a curious mixture of *joie de vivre*, melancholy and a very real sense of moroseness. And the same is true of the other characters. They do not embody any specific qualities and ideas that lead by a process of logical necessity to this or that type of action but represent individual combinations of living emotional forces that express themselves either as qualities or as actions, hence their variety and originality and the fact that they are so true to life. They serve no purpose in any utilitarian sense, they prove nothing, but create their impact simply through their immediacy and through the plenitude of the life that they exude. This also explains Mozart's totally different interpretation of 'dramatic action', the purely objective aspect of which – the intrigue – was of no real interest to him, with the result that, with the exception of the plot's climaxes, he was perfectly happy to use *secco* recitative to depict its external development. The question that preoccupied him was simply the new forces unleashed in this or that character by the individual phases of the action. The sort of operatic comedy that was current at this time was either satisfied with a plot that was crudely cobbled together or else it tried to show that certain actions proceed from certain qualities and that these actions in turn have certain consequences. Mozart's characters are free of all didacticism, their actions merely the outward manifestation of these inner forces. This was why the subject of *Figaro* fascinated him so much, as he was able to stretch these characters to their limits and draw on every last reserve of their inner strength. They are constantly on the move and, unlike the stock characters from the older type of opera, are always developing new aspects to them. The piece reveals an almost inexhaustible vitality – not, however, in the way that we traditionally find in *opere buffe*, where violence is all too often done to the characters in an attempt to raise a laugh and real life is distorted by being limited to what is effective in the theatre.[13]

Yet in spite of its wealth of characters and its rich sense of life, there is a wonderful feeling of unity to the work, a feeling due to the fact that Mozart maintains a single basic mood and, above all, that it is refracted in a thousand different ways. *Le nozze di Figaro* has a basic theme, albeit not in the Gluckian sense of a monumental ethical idea that becomes clear in the course of the work as a whole. In Mozart's case we are not in fact dealing with an idea at all, but with a basic human instinct, the most powerful, indeed, of all: love. It is love that is the motivating force of the piece as a whole. Yet we must ignore all parallels with modern eroticism and its problems, to say nothing of the hothouse sensuality of so many literary philistines with an interest in sexuality. Nor is there any question of any moralizing tendency. In *Le nozze di Figaro* love figures as a purely natural force that reveals more and more new aspects of its nature depending on the way in which it combines with other instincts in individual characters. From an ethical standpoint, the result is now less, now more pure: in the case of the Countess it attains to true greatness thanks to the admixture – unique to her – of love and resignation, whereas with Cherubino it never rises above the stage of the unconscious and of wish fulfilment, leaving all ethical possibilities open. For Mozart, morality, too, is one of the realities that we have to face up to in life, a reality that exists alongside countless others, rather than transcending them, and if the Countess forgives her errant husband at the end and in that way releases the dramatic tension, this should not be interpreted as the triumph of virtue in the sense of a sentimental comedy, but as the natural outcome of the interaction of two living characters.

That the comedy in *Le nozze di Figaro* is totally different from anything that audiences had been used to until then was noted at an early date and, indeed, a number of critics with a particular sensitivity to questions of style even saw this as a cause for mild censure.[14] And yet this was merely the natural consequence of Mozart's whole approach to his subject. It could never have been his intention to beat the Italians at their own game in terms of madcap humour and sheer high spirits. All comedy rests on contrast. *Opera buffa* saw it in the contrast between reality and the distorted forms of reality that arose from singling out and grotesquely exaggerating individual qualities. The more rationalistic *opéra comique* adopted a less extreme approach to caricature but none the less judged its characters' behaviour by certain fundamental principles that it proclaimed either within the piece itself or, more commonly, in the closing moral. Not for a moment, however, did it occur to any of these authors to identify with their characters. Instead, they adopted a satirical stance towards them, merely depicting the limitations of others, limitations from which they themselves were free – or from which they thought that they were free. But Mozart added a far more subtle streak to this type of humour. In the case of the secondary characters of Bartolo, Marcellina and Basilio, he, too, comes close to the standpoint of *opera buffa*, yet without lessening his freedom of choice by any confining caricatures. He depicts them as a keen-eyed but essentially impartial observer whose weaknesses are alien to his nature. But he adopts a totally different approach to his

13. Hanslick speaks of the 'pronounced use of slow and moderate tempi' in this opera. But the marking for slow tempi, adagio, is not found at all in the opera (except in very brief transitional passages), and the term larghetto occurs only rarely, certainly less frequently than in many other *opere buffe*. The more frequent andante is not, however, a slow tempo, but a moderate one. Hanslick is right to note that duple time is more common than triple time, but it is unclear why duple time should lend itself more to the expression of carefree emotions than triple time; Hanslick, 'Mozart', 42.
14. See Stendhal, *Vies de Haydn, de Mozart et de Métastase*, 359; and Hanslick, 'Mozart', 42–3.

main characters, striking a note of irony rather than satire. He shares their joys and sorrows, treating these emotions as though they were his own, while depicting them from a standpoint far removed from theirs. It is this ability that sets him apart from the world of *opera buffa*, a world that generally moves its characters implacably to and fro like chess pieces merely in order to create a superficial effect, resulting in a completely different relationship between the spectator and the work in question. Mozart's subtle use of irony creates a psychological and emotional impact on his audience that is completely different from a mere appeal to their powers of deduction and their propensity for laughter.

Mozart saw no reason to alter the outward structure of *opera buffa*. Basing his libretto closely on Beaumarchais's stage play but shortening it as much as possible, Da Ponte used *secco* recitative for the action proper, while distributing the musical numbers throughout the piece, in which respect he acted in the spirit of – and probably also in accordance with the wishes of – the composer or, rather, the music dramatist. Some of these numbers allude to the outward situation only in the most general terms, while exploring their characters' emotional lives and resulting in clearly contoured character studies ('Porgi amor'). Others in turn depict a momentary mood that stems from the pressure of the present situation ('Aprite, presto'). The majority, however, allow the characters to develop before the audience's eyes in the light of the changing situation. But Mozart's principal means of advancing the musico-dramatic action lies in his ensembles, which are reserved for the climaxes, where the intrigue becomes a veritable imbroglio and brings the characters into such close proximity that the behaviour of one of them strikes sparks from another. In this respect, the second-act finale is a model of its kind, although Da Ponte, too, deserves some of the credit for this. After all, he was already familiar with the technique involved in writing finales. Although he initially conceived of such a number in a purely *buffa* spirit, he once described it, not inappropriately, as 'a little comedy all by itself'.[15]

In spite of a handful of uneven patches that are as nothing compared with the poetic capers tolerated in *opera buffa* generally, the text that Da Ponte submitted to the emperor was on the whole skilfully executed and certainly well above average. On no account should it be judged by the standard of the German translations that represent the darkest chapter in the whole history of the work.[16] The identity of the author of the first of these translations, which was performed, *inter alia*, in Berlin in 1790, remains unknown.[17] This was followed in 1791 by a version by Adolf von

---

15. In his memoirs, Da Ponte has the following to say about *Il ricco d'un giorno*: 'This *finale*, which must remain intimately connected with the opera as a whole, is nevertheless a sort of little comedy or operette all by itself, and requires a new plot and an unsually high pitch of interest. The *finale*, chiefly, must glow with the genius of the conductor, the power of the voices, the grandest dramatic effects. Recitative is banned from the *finale*: everyone sings; and every form of singing must be available – the *adagio*, the *allegro*, the *andante*, the intimate, the harmonious and then – noise, noise, noise; for the *finale* almost always closes in an uproar: which, in musical jargon, is called the *chiusa*, or rather the *stretta*, I know not whether because, in it, the whole power of the drama is drawn or "pinched" together, or because it gives generally not one pinch but a hundred to the poor brain of the poet who must supply the words. The *finale* must, through a dogma of the theatre, produce on the stage every singer of the cast, be there three hundred of them, and whether by ones, by twos, by threes or by sixes, tens or sixties; and they must have solos, duets, terzets, sextets, thirteenets, sixtyets; and if the plot of the drama does not permit, the poet must find a way to make it permit, in the face of reason, good sense, Aristotle, and all the powers of heaven or earth; and if then the *finale* happens to go badly, so much the worse for him!' It is the authentic spirit of *opera buffa* that we find speaking here. Da Ponte himself showed how it was possible to circumvent all these difficulties, and to do so, moreover, with skill and good taste, in the second-act finale in *Le nozze di Figaro*.

16. ◆ Early translations of *Figaro* include one by Christian August Vulpius and another – see note 18 below – by Baron Adolf Knigge, which included spoken dialogue instead of recitative and restored some passages from the original play; see Carter, *W. A. Mozart: Le nozze di Figaro*, 129.

17. Louis Schneider, *Geschichte der Oper und des Königlichen Opernhauses in Berlin*, 59.

Knigge prepared for Friedrich Ludwig Schröder.[18] Karl Ludwig Gieseke's translation was first heard in Vienna in 1792, followed two years later by a version by Christian August Vulpius, whose baleful spirit continues to haunt our theatres even today. For the complete edition of Mozart's works, Carl Niese[19] managed to root out the worst errors and excesses, but unfortunately added new ones of his own and left the task half finished. After all, many of the phrases used by Knigge and Vulpius have acquired proverbial status, with the result that there has been powerful resistance to their removal on the part of very many philistines. Yet our nation's debt of honour to one of our greatest masterpieces must one day be paid in full. That this will not be easy has been shown by recent attempts to translate *Don Giovanni*. What is needed is more than a thorough knowledge of Italian and of current operatic practices: the translator must be a poet in his own right, with a creative bent, someone who is familiar with the whole culture of that time and who does not merely 'know' Mozart but has inwardly digested him.[20]

Like all Mozart's overtures, that of *Le nozze di Figaro* was the last piece to be written. Jahn[21] thought that it was inspired by the subtitle of Beaumarchais's play, 'La folle journée', but it is hardly necessary to think in terms of the numerous intrigues and surprises of this 'crazy day', for, as we have already remarked, these were no more than a means to an end for Mozart. Moreover, he made an important change to the overture while working on it: in the original score the forward momentum suddenly falters on the dominant harmonies just before the return to the first subject, giving way to an andante con moto in 6/8-time, the main melody of which is entrusted to the solo oboe, with a pizzicato accompaniment in the strings:

18.   Knigge, *Aus einer alten Kiste: Originalbriefe, Handschriften und Dokumente aus dem Nachlasse eines bekannten Mannes*, 177; Friedrich Meyer, *Friedrich Ludwig Schröder: Beitrag zur Kunde des Menschen und des Künstlers*, ii.55. This translation was first heard in Hamburg. ◆ Further, see Whittaker, 'Karl Ludwig Gieseke: His life, performance and achievements'.
19.   ◆ AMA V/17, published in 1879.
20.   In 1793 Mozart's music was performed in Paris with the whole of Beaumarchais's dialogue; see Castil-Blaze, *L'Académie impériale de musique de 1645 à 1855*, ii.19. Beaumarchais approved of the idea in practice but criticized the actual performance; see Loménie, *Beaumarchais et son temps*, 595ff. A report in the *Berlinische musikalische Zeitung historischen und kritischen Inhalts* in 1793, 77, reads as follows: 'The music seemed to us beautiful, rich in harmony and very skilfully written. The melodic writing is agreeable, without being titillating. A number of the ensembles are of the highest beauty.' The French translation normally used today is by Barbier and Carré, even though it omits five of the original numbers; see Wilder, *Mozart*, 223. In Vienna, Mahler tried to incorporate the whole of Beaumarchais's trial scene into the opera and even wrote his own unaccompanied recitatives for the purpose – yet another example of the same hopeless attempt to reconcile two heterogeneous objects in the form of opera and spoken comedy. ◆ For an account of early French versions of *Figaro*, see Dudley, 'Les premières versions françaises du *Mariage de Figaro* de Mozart'; concerning Mahler's *Figaro* arrangement, which included newly-composed recitatives in act three, scene five, see Kende, 'Gustav Mahlers Wiener "Figaro"'.
21.   Jahn, *W. A. Mozart*, ii.332.

The folio on which this andante and the return to the presto appear has been torn out and the passage marked 'vi–de' struck out.[22] In other words, Mozart first attempted the sort of form that he had already used in the overture to *Die Entführung aus dem Serail*: a calmer picture was evidently meant to emerge from the animated background, with in this case a typical mixture of elegiac and piquant elements.[23] But even while he was working on the final stage of the fair copy of the overture, Mozart – exceptionally – was borne along so irresistibly by the bubbling floodtide of his Presto that this middle section was simply swept away.

If there were ever a time when the predilection of our modern intellectualizing age for foisting programmes on works of music were out of place, it is in the case of the present overture. It is not even possible to speak of a free association of any particular musical ideas here. Neither before nor since has the natural, unrestrained and instinctual urge to explore life's carefree, hedonistic aspect found such immediate expression as here. The piece – which is all about movement raised to its highest potential – steals in as though from a distance in its famous seven-bar opening phrase, needing two attempts to get under way. But now it stirs in every quarter, laughing, chuckling and triumphing, with new watercourses opening up as the floodtide rushes past, before the piece as a whole races towards its jubilant end in a bacchantic torrent entirely in keeping with Mozart's basic conception of his subject, an apotheosis of an untrammelled life force that could hardly be more infectious.

The overture's overall character also affects its form, which is that of a sonata without a development section: given the constant interplay between the various elements, there was simply no space for any thematic development of the material. But Mozart appends a large-scale coda that once again raises the pitch of excitement to hitherto unsuspected heights. Indeed, this constant movement may be felt even within the individual elements that make up the overture, including the grouping of the individual themes, its floodtide generating intensified shapes. The main theme is made up of three different elements: a unison motif to which the bassoon adds an ironical undertone,[24] then five bars in which a new motif is constantly tossed to and fro between the two

---

22. Whether this middle movement is the lost orchestral piece in D minor, as claimed by the *Deutsche Musik-Zeitung*, iii (1862), 253–4, is doubtful. ◆ For a facsimile of the transition to D minor and the first bars of the siciliana Mozart originally intended here, see NMA II/5/16/1, XXIII; further concerning K¹ Anh. 101 and its possible relationship to this passage, see Plath, 'Miscellanea Mozartiana I'.
23. The serenade-like character and orchestral colour recall Susanna's fourth-act aria ('Giunse alfin il momento – Deh vieni, non tardar').
24. On the rhythm of this theme, see the excerpt from Anfossi on p.319 above, and on its melody, see the beginning of Grétry's overture to *Les deux avares* and, above all, Salieri's overture to *Der Rauchfangkehrer* of 1781, which also features a violin unison. Even so, we should not see in these parallels anything more than fleeting, unconscious influences.

groups of wind instruments (and, as such, is a fine example of *durchbrochene Arbeit*) and, finally, the full tutti outburst which, with its *galant* wind sonorities, clearly recalls the analogous passage in the overture to *Don Giovanni*. In short, we already find the most disparate moods within these first few bars. And yet they are also closely related on an internal level, involving, as they do, the ideas of preparation, climax and the release of the tension that has been built up in this way. With what subtle psychological effectiveness Mozart uses the age-old Italian device of the pedal point[25] and dynamics, which avoid the usual crescendo but advance by fits and starts! At its repeat it is joined as though by chance by a cantabile counterpoint in the flutes that is entirely typical of the later Mozart. There follows a transitional group, again with two contrasting ideas, one consisting of rushing scales, the other built up on an exuberantly powerful rhythm ♩ | ♩ ♩ 𝄽 At the same time comes the first radical modulation to the dominant, all that has gone before having emphatically stressed the bright tonality of D major. The second subject in A major is prepared for by a clear-cut half-cadence in the manner of Johann Christian Bach, except that on this occasion it brings with it a slight sense of irony, as this second subject – ushered in with such great pomp – is one of Mozart's most original ideas. Although it is introduced in the Italian *buffa* manner by the three upper string voices, the note of eccentricity that it strikes is wholly without precedent. While the two lower voices lead the musical argument downwards through a series of regular sequences, the upper voice attempts to expound a cantabile theme. Even the fact that it twice comes to a rest on a sforzato *d″* sharp is disturbing, and the whole theme then bursts like a bubble in the Italian slide motif that comes as a total surprise. Although the oboes agree to accept it, it is only in order to bring it to an end in the way that they themselves desire, with an entirely new cadential motif. This second main section of the subject-group likewise introduces more and more new ideas. Initially, its capricious nature produces an extremely agitated, surly echo in the orchestra in which the powerful three-crotchet motif quoted above again plays a part. This also marks the first appearance of a minor tonality, resulting in a remarkable increase in emotional tension. A new and imperious motif now asserts itself in the basses beneath a flickering tremolando in the violins:

Yet it, too, soon acquires a sullen streak in the chromatic writing. Note the masterly way in which this motif is then recast by the violins to become timid and even supplicatory. But it is the chromatic element that is now intensified in the most inspired manner imaginable. Here, too, Mozart's unbridled life force has its critical moments, but the crisis is prevented from becoming too serious not only by the bassoon with its deeply untragic rapscallion-like caperings but also by the following passage in which the mood brightens without any sense of a struggle. Here in this final subject-group – the real cantabile theme of the overture as a whole – the sun emerges at last from behind the clouds, more radiant and earth-warming than ever, and it is with a heartfelt feeling of happiness that the beautiful melody ripples along on its A major harmonies. Immediately afterwards the earlier sense of wild turmoil re-enters, racing along to strident dominant-seventh

25. Note the role of the pedal point within the overture as a whole, where it takes up no fewer than 119 out of a total of 294 bars.

chords, before suddenly leading back to the recapitulation in a genuinely Mozartian manner with mysterious whisperings in thirds in the violins that already recall the main theme. This recapitulation begins by running along regular lines through a series of ingenious variants, before culminating in a coda which, typical of Mozart's handling of dynamics, includes the only example of a Mannheim crescendo, its uniqueness making it all the more effective in consequence. The tremendous build-up of tension is matched by a powerful release in which the three-crotchet motif now reveals its full force. Here Mozart is more generous in repeating individual sections, as though he finds it difficult to break free from this picture of an exuberant love of life. A brilliant fanfare brings the overture to an end.

The first act begins by taking a dramaturgical risk with two allegro duets ('Cinque . . . dieci' and 'Se a caso madama la notte ti chiama')[26] for the same two characters, but Mozart very skilfully differentiates between them by making the first a simple, carefree genre painting in the style of an Italian *introduzione*, while the second already contains a goodly drop of dramatic blood. The former presents the two characters in a state of total calm, with as yet no sign of the strain that is shortly to be placed on their relationship, but in the second the ripples have already started to spread across the drama's pondlike surface. This explains why the first of them has the broadest and most contented of all the opera's ritornellos. It introduces us to the number's two main ideas, one of which depicts Figaro measuring out the room, with the syncopated motif in the basses (supported by the bassoons) speaking volumes, while the music additionally reveals the remarkably tenacious resolve that characterizes all Figaro's actions. The second idea is launched by the winds and belongs to Susanna, who is admiring her wedding outfit with all the charm, sincerity and passion that are hers by nature.[27] But whereas Figaro's theme finally disappears, Susanna's gradually emerges as the duet's principal idea, repeatedly returning in the manner of a rondo's refrain. This is entirely typical: after all, Susanna has taken control of this relationship from the very outset, and it is only gradually that her more phlegmatic bridegroom gains a purchase on her melody and grows perceptibly more warm-hearted. Finally they both sing the same theme which, as such, becomes a symbol of their heartfelt premarital happiness. In terms of its melodic line, it is clearly derived from Piccinni,[28] but only Mozart himself could have invested it with such a naïvely heartfelt tone and, hence, with its actual soul. Reminiscent of Paisiello, the consequent phrase – which later returns on frequent occasions, notably in Susanna's fourth-act aria – adds an unmistakable note of resolve to the relaxed, yet mischievous, tone, revealing at a stroke the sort of characters that Figaro and Susanna are. This becomes even clearer in the second duet, in which the work's dramatic complications first make themselves felt, with even the key – B flat major instead of G major – being markedly darker. The form, too, is different: in this case the number consists of two independent sections divided by a brief recitative. The second section is followed by a coda based on motifs from the first, which itself is in ternary form, with full closure in the tonic. Initially

26. Mozart calls them duettinos, a term he uses for all the other duets in the opera, with the single exception of 'Crudel! Perchè finora', which is headed 'duetto'. The term clearly derives from the brevity of these numbers.
27. Note, in particular, the sudden eruption of the semiquaver motif in the violins at the word 'contenta' and the staccato triplets at 'sembra fatto inver', at which point we can almost imagine the colourful ribbons fluttering.
28. See act three, scene eight of his *Antigono* of 1771:

it seems like a continuation of the first duet, with Figaro – again supported by his bassoon – striking a note of harmless joviality: the tinkling bell is one of the most popular jokes from *opere buffe* of the period.[29] But Susanna destroys this future idyll once and for all: although she seems to strike the same note as Figaro, she suddenly slips into G minor. The surrounding landscape remains the same, but it is now lit by a threatening storm, with an eloquent outburst of anguish clearly audible in the oboes. Yet Susanna herself does not adopt an unduly tragic approach to what she says, as she is entirely sure of herself in her dealings with the Count. But Figaro's phlegmatic guilelessness provokes her into giving him a warning which, in view of his tendency towards jealousy, she knows will hit home. And she herself derives a thrill of pleasure from playing not only with the critical situation but also with Figaro. The music bubbles along, half jokingly, half sinisterly, as far as the sudden crescendo at the words 'ed ecco in tre salti'. Susanna gets no further than this, as the penny finally drops for Figaro, who, almost numb with horror, utters the words 'Susanna, pian pian', clinging – like his bassoon – to the final phrase of the theme, which he continues to repeat as though incapable of grasping the full horror of the idea. The final syllable is then extended, acquiring the force of a physical gesture and suggesting his refusal to hear any more. Susanna finds this particularly funny and in sheer exuberance goads him on. At this point a provocative, tingling, humming sound arises in the orchestra, always around the B flat in the bass: Figaro has come up against a brick wall, and Susanna can do nothing but leave him to let off steam on his fermata. But then she continues in the recitative,[30] revealing an excellent grasp of psychology, and it is not long before she draws him after her, increasingly taking control of him in this second section of the duet. She loves him dearly, but she cannot tolerate the least doubts in her loyalty. The brief lecture that she gives him could not be clearer in this regard. With her crystal-clear declamation underscored by the orchestra, she quickly whispers to him her 'Se udir brami il resto' ('if you want to hear the rest'), before allowing her emotions free rein: 'Discaccia i sospetti che torto mi fan' ('Banish those suspicions that do me wrong'). It will be noted that this whole section is framed by two fermatas. But Figaro has now lost all control, and there is something touching about the way in which he simply echoes Susanna's melody,[31] before ending a broken man. At this point the characters are thrown into sharper contrast than ever, Susanna with her pointed syncopations, Figaro still torn between anguish and suppressed rage. Their final bars reveal the full extent to which the harmless joviality of the opening has already been undermined: Figaro is reduced to a single phrase in which he has already sought refuge before, while Susanna again tells him to calm down. But there is something strange about the quiet, almost malicious purring sound with which the orchestra takes its leave, a clear sign of the unresolved tensions left by the duet as a whole.

In short, the two characters emerge from these two duets with unequivocal clarity: on the one hand, the lively, vivacious Susanna who loves resistance because it increases her feeling of being alive and who can therefore come to terms with difficult situations on the strength of her superior wit and, on the other, the phlegmatic Figaro, whose path through life – much to his own discomfort – is strewn with thorns and who is spurred into action only by outside pressure and only after he has brooded at length on his problems and put behind him all feelings of pessimism.

---

29. Note the comic contrast: the Countess rings her bell softly and gently, the Count loudly and forcefully, on the second occasion even appearing to tug violently at the bell pull.
30. These brief passages of recitative could already look back on a long history by this date: see above.
31. Note his descending melodic line in contrast to Susanna's and, indeed, the low register in general.

Initially he feels his courage return, a reaction helped by Susanna's warning. This is clear not least from the belligerent basses[32] in the recitative preceding his famous cavatina ('Se vuol ballare'). But in the cavatina itself he takes a furious delight in anticipating the time when he will make the Count dance to the strains of his 'chitarrino'. The dance that he plans for his master is not one appropriate to the latter's social standing, and it is hard not to smile at the thought of so elegant an aristocrat capering around to the sounds of this boorish folk tune with its earthy horn calls. But soon his malice becomes even clearer, revealing itself in the two cries of 'sì' that are hurled forth like so many challenges.[33] But in the second section, the outward description of the dance and the expression of Figaro's emotions repeatedly intersect, with a sense of furtiveness settling over the aria at the trilled motif in the violins and with the two *forte* outbursts at 'se vuol venire' and 'la capriola' breaking in like thunderclaps. The dance rhythms now cease completely, as Figaro's plans for revenge grow increasingly far-fetched, so much so, in the end, that he can no longer find words to express them.[34] At this point he suddenly changes tack and reminds himself of the need to stay calm. Again the sense of mysterious tension returns, this time in an intensified form in D minor: cunning and dissimulation will ensure his victory, an idea elaborated in the presto section of the aria, in which rhythm,[35] melody and orchestral accompaniment are all Italian. It is the Figaro of *Le barbier de Séville* whom we see here. In the light of all that has gone before, we cannot help wondering, of course, whether Mozart means his excitement to be taken ironically, in other words, whether, if things were to become serious, Figaro would in fact be too inhibited to act, however lively his initial response to the situation. And there does, indeed, appear to be a spirit of mischief abroad in the orchestra in the form of the limping syncopations in the second violins and violas in the postlude. Right at the very end this passage is even taken over by oboes and bassoons, as though the triumphant Figaro were suddenly to stumble as he is leaving.

And just as, in his thoughts, Figaro triumphs over the Count in this cavatina, so in the following aria ('La vendetta') Bartolo triumphs over Figaro – his old adversary from *Le barbier de Séville*. But the feeling of revenge brings out a completely different aspect of his character. In Figaro's case it finds an entirely naïve expression, adding to his own burden of care, but in Bartolo's it serves to increase his self-esteem, its effect being all the more comical in that it is lacking in any real justification. The humour of the piece lies in the contrast between the exaggeratedly bombastic manner in which, true philistine that he is, he proclaims his wisdom at the beginning of his aria and the pitiful conclusions that he draws from it. The opening is wholly Italianate with its empty bombast, fanfare-like melodies and additional timpani and trumpets, with Bartolo carrying on almost like the hero of an *opera seria*. His language strikes a far more individual note when he starts to talk about 'bassezza' and 'viltà', two concepts which, in spite of the contempt that he affects for them, are in fact far more familiar to him. This is an especially delightful passage not least on account of the ambiguity of the dismissive orchestral motif, with its imitative writing:

32. There is also something attractive about the lovesick glance that he shoots at Susanna during the andante.
33. For an analogous example from Galuppi, see above.
34. It is typical of Mozart that he forgoes the use of a crescendo here but prefers sforzato accents instead.
35. See above. In this regard the present section has affinities with Don Giovanni's 'champagne aria', 'Finch' han del vino'.

Shortly after this, the same motif is heard in diminution:

And it returns again and again in the course of the aria, each time that Bartolo works himself up into a frenzy at his own plans. 'Only fools are bashful, brave men delight in deeds',[36] we seem to hear the orchestra saying, although it remains an open question whether the instruments support Bartolo in this or whether, with their mockery, they are turning against him the reproach of 'bassezza' and 'viltà'. For the present, the thought of the difficulty of his task suddenly brings him down to earth: 'Il fatto è serio' ('The case is serious'), he sings, the remark underscored by a surprising modulation. But great minds do not lose their composure for long, and Bartolo continues with a complacent smile: 'Ma credete, si farà' ('But, believe me, I'll bring it off'). And, drawing on the sort of patter found in Italian *opere buffe*, he smugly rattles off a long line of sophistries, after which the orchestra mysteriously repeats back to him his 'è bassezza, è ognor viltà'. We then return to the beginning, as the hero draws himself up to his whole impressive height, except that at the mere mention of Figaro's name he is overcome by a feeling of common rage. He then appears to make a dash for the end of the aria with an Italian *Bettelkadenz*, the hollow bombast of which is clearly meant as a parody, but he is evidently left feeling dissatisfied, as he appends a further six bars of noisy but essentially vapid exultation.

Although Mozart includes more *buffa* features here, we still do not have the impression that the result is a caricature in the Italian style. This Bartolo is an angry, fastidious philistine almost beside himself with glee at his chance of wreaking vengeance on his enemy. As a result, there are good reasons why the aria is so full of sudden contrasts: often the musical argument breaks off without warning, only to continue in a completely different direction – the image of a mind lacking in all sense of conceptual and emotional discipline and, above all, ignorant of its own strengths. Mozart reveals great psychological insight in showing how this philistine initially works himself up into a frenzy over a triviality and then, as a result of the feeling of uncontrollable elation inspired by his agitation, how he is naturally forced to reveal the whole inadequacy of his character. Herein lies the comedy of the aria.

We now meet two women who, under the cloak of extreme politeness, feel only venomous hatred for each other. As such, they, too, recall the *buffa* tradition, allowing Mozart to treat their duettino ('Via resti servita') as a piquant situation comedy. The orchestra graphically describes their constant curtseying:[37]

The virtually uninterrupted triplet motion ensures that the feeling of tingling excitement is maintained from start to finish. Marcellina takes the lead in the vocal writing, with Susanna following

---

36. ◆ The quotation is from Goethe's *Rechenschaft*.
37. It is introduced from the dominant, thereby adding to the tension.

on with her superior wit: she clearly derives particular pleasure from this whole conversation, which turns increasingly into a cackling match, something that the two participants can hardly keep up in the longer term, of course, and here for the first time the triplet figuration ends. Note in particular the comical way in which Marcellina is struck dumb with anger in bars 33–35, while Susanna feels especially contented at the entry of the winds. At the corresponding passage in the second half of the duet, the contrast becomes even greater, with Marcellina breathlessly venting her anger, and Susanna, delightfully malicious, playing with her feelings in a coloratura flourish. In the orchestra (bars 66–67) we finally hear her Paisiello motif from the first duet.

Never in the whole history of the music drama has a boy's first half-conscious feelings of love, with all their ferverish excitement, exquisite anguish and total lack of direction, been depicted in a way that is so true to life as in Cherubino's famous opening aria ('Non so più cosa son, cosa faccio').[38] Time and again this unfocused sense of burning desire seems as though it will erupt in an outburst of passion, before sinking back into a blissful dream of happiness and joy, only for the boy to be carried away again on the floodtide of his emotions in pursuit of new goals which, as before, prove to have no firm foundations. Mozart is very much in his element in depicting a state of mind in which everything is flux and movement. As with Don Giovanni's well-known aria and Tamino's 'portrait aria' ('Dies Bildnis ist bezaubernd schön'), he is not concerned with a musical portrait or an 'imitation' of a particular natural state. Rather, the aria is itself an expression of the most elemental nature that sings about itself directly in all its iridescent movement. It begins with an orchestral introduction that features clarinets for the first time within the opera proper and that seethes with ill-defined emotion,[39] while the vocal line, expressive of feverish haste, is limited to an anapaestic metre. Entirely symptomatic of the boy's state of mind are the unexpected *forte* markings at the end of the first two lines, with their strained sighs in the winds above them, thereby giving the sense of breathlessness a deeply realistic aspect. But there then follows the first explosive outburst – significantly on the words 'ogni donna' ('every woman'), again with winds, while the word 'palpitare' ('to beat'), which no Italian composer would have ignored, remains in the shade. With the first second subject, the chromatic writing brings a new feature into the picture. There is something particularly touching about the way in which the sense of sweet torment forces the melodic line upwards, before allowing it to sink back again immediately after-wards in a bitterly anguished syncopated motif, while above it the clarinet expresses the whole sense of emotion with its sustained f' like some elemental sound from the world of nature. At 'un desio', the contrast between happiness and anguish becomes even clearer, especially when, at its repeat, the two wind instruments double the vocal line. Not even here is there any feeling of liber-ation, but, instead, we slip back to the beginning. Only with the second subsidiary section of the aria do we find any relatively lengthy rests in the vocal line. Here we sink even deeper into the mood of tender sensuality as a result of the rich-toned wind sonorities and the double motif in the strings.[40] The words are entirely typical of Rococo poetry with their natural imagery that even includes an echo, but it is the music that frees all these images from their state of ossification, eschewing the marginalia habitually found in such cases but which are really no more than a

---

38. Similar situations are familiar, of course, from Italian *opere buffe*. Here one thinks of Eugenio's tenor aria in act one, scene twelve of Galuppi's *L'amante di tutte*: 'Quando sono vicino a una femina, non v'è caso, non posso più star; sento un foco, una smania, un furore che pian piano crescendomi al core mi fa tutto di dentro avvampar.' But the tone is entirely gallant and there is no mention of any real anguish.

39. The accompanying figure is far from original but is intended merely to depict movement in general.

40. The motif in the first violins is an augmented form of the one found in the second violins.

backdrop, and depicting the entire situation on the strength of individual, heartfelt emotion. Nature and emotion become one: the traditional array of natural images created by the forces of reason has now been relegated to the junk room of history. In this regard, the present aria is important for the breakthrough of a new feeling for nature in music. In general, this section of the piece brings with it a powerful increase in emotional intensity, albeit not without a series of realistic interruptions, as is clear, not least, from the first fermata. And how strangely confused is the following attempt to get underway, an attempt that reaches the very height of passion at the second fermata on g'', only to sink back again as though broken! The same process is now repeated, except on a different basis.[41] And in bars 76–77 we find a new and affecting figure in the orchestra, too, a figure that seems to stroke the boy's fair locks as he dreams his fond dreams. Right at the end, at the words 'e se non ho chi m'oda, parlo d'amor con me' ('and if there is no one to listen to me, I'll talk about love with myself'), the lonely youth appears to start sobbing quietly, but he soon pulls himself together again and his feelings again take flight, with their mixture of self-pity and defiance so typical of youth. As a result, the aria ends on a note of increased desperation, an ending that takes the listener completely by surprise, as even the orchestra forgoes the usual postlude. The aria rushes past our ears like a spring storm that keeps changing its strength and direction. Its character also affects its form: as far as bar 51 it is cast in the form of a regular rondo. A surviving sketch[42] reveals that at this point a second episode in A flat major and a third repeat of the main theme were to have been included, but Mozart then deleted these passages and continued with the section (bars 51ff.) that he had originally intended as the coda, thereby producing a curious hybrid form which, by departing from the norm, provides a wonderful reflection of the character's vacillating state of mind.

The following trio ('Cosa sento! Tosto andate') is the first of the opera's dramatic ensembles and, as such, is particularly successful. Most of the Italian composers of the period would no doubt have entrusted this scene to *secco* recitative interrupted at best by an entrance aria for Basilio or by an aria for the Count expressive of his anger. But Mozart avoids all entrance arias here and instead points up the full dramatic contrast between the figures of the Count and Basilio. The Count's passion bursts forth like a white-hot flame within the first three bars, but almost immediately he recovers his composure, giving away nothing to a social inferior such as Basilio. He issues his orders condescendingly and with an emphatic and peremptory motif:

Only the motif's hesitant tread suggests a certain inner unease, and it is only at the *forte* outburst – when we literally hear him stamp his feet – that he finally regains control of the situation. This becomes clear straightaway from the incomparable character sketch of Basilio that follows:

41. The pedal point is particularly attractively used here to describe the state of dreaminess.
42. See the critical commentary in AMA. A vocal score of this aria with violin accompaniment in Mozart's hand was formerly in the possession of Julius André. ◆ For an edition of the vocal score, see NMA II/5/16/2, 618–24; the autograph is now owned by the Pierpont Morgan Library, New York (shelfmark MS 157). The sketch, now housed at the British Library (shelfmark Zweig 57) is reproduced in NMA X/30/3.

In mal pun-to   son quì giun-to,   per - do - na - te,   o mio   si - gnor!

This is the sort of melody typically found in Italian *opere buffe* to express submissive anxiety.[43] But there is also something furtive about it,[44] and, indeed, Basilio turns out in the course of this trio to be a villain of the worst sort, capable of stooping to the lowest depths. Initially, no one takes any notice of him, and although he repeats himself, our attention, for the present, is taken up by Susanna and her own anxieties. Throughout this number her role is typical of Mozart's desire to prevent the actors, as far as possible, from becoming inactive, as she vacillates constantly between genuine, sincere dismay and the attempt to regain control of the situation by pretending to be afraid and thus to get the two men out of the room at all costs. Initially, her fear is decidedly genuine, but at the words 'me meschina' they acquire a note of desperate exaggeration that leads directly to her pretending to faint. And so it goes on: genuine and feigned emotions keep overlapping, invariably finding expression in ways typical of Susanna's temperament, until finally, under the pressure of events, she is forced to abandon her pretence. But her faint in fact has an extremely unwelcome outcome for her, for, although the Count and Basilio are otherwise from totally different worlds, they find themselves occupying common ground when it comes to gentlemanly behaviour towards a woman, and there is something comical about the way in which Basilio takes the initiative and initially sets the tone. Splendidly amusing is the unexpected F major in which both set about their mission of mercy following Susanna's emotional F minor, and there is something genuinely *buffa*-like about the tone-painting used to describe the beating of her 'dear little heart'. Everything seems to be going according to plan for them, and even Susanna's earlier F minor sigh now appears in the major: Basilio can play the gentleman and escort Susanna to the chair, at which point she recovers with astonishing alacrity and seeks salvation in a show of righteous indignation. It is no accident that at her moment of greatest need she attempts to break out into the tragic key of G minor, but the other two refuse to follow her and, with another unexpected modulation, this time to E flat major, they insist all the more solemnly on their willingness to help. At this point Basilio, wanting to escape as quickly as possible from the whole unpleasant situation, retracts all that he has said about the page, ascribing it to mere suspicion, but the Count insists that Cherubino leave the castle, prompting both Susanna and Basilio to express their regret. The piece now appears to move back towards its beginning,[45] but their appeal provokes the Count, who

---

43. Cf. the sextet in act two, scene eight of Piccinni's *I viaggiatori*.
44. Note also the diminished intervals in the bass.
45. Here the music is strikingly reminiscent of Paisiello, notably the second subject of the overture to *La frascatana*:

justifies his decision by recalling the events at Antonio's house, first in a recitative in whose semi-quaver motif his fury clearly breaks through again, then by taking up Basilio's motif, as though to give the lie to the music master's last words: 'ed alzando pian pianino' ('and very very gently lifting the tablecloth'), he sings, descending through one and a half octaves in his furious pleasure and so discovering Cherubino in the armchair. This crisis is depicted in the music in an extremely original way. Virtually every contemporary and later composer would have responded with a *fortissimo* outburst on a dissonance in the orchestra, whereas Mozart, with no less truth and greater realism, describes a situation in which all the participants are simply struck dumb with amazement. There is no audible trace of spontaneous surprise, no reaction on the part of their minds or wills. All are dumbfounded, with the result that for a moment the music continues automatically like some well-oiled mechanism, before finally coming to a halt, having lost its driving force. The strings simply cling for support to Basilio's theme, turning it aimlessly to and fro, while far beneath them in the bassoons and, later, in the clarinets, too, the same motif begins to stir, but by now it has become sluggish, shapeless, as though bloated. Right from the outset one of the oboes and the two horns remain on the dominant, at octave intervals, as though reduced to a mysterious paralysis. For a while the dominant harmony continues to assert its hold, before the tension slackens and finally the whole mechanism comes to a halt on a fermata in the full orchestra. In much the same way the disjointed calls in the vocal lines sound like an unconscious, mindless stammering. Only Basilio's facial expression reveals a fleeting sense of malicious delight. Needless to say, the situation has now changed completely for all three characters, and while the Count has the satisfaction of having exposed Susanna's hypocrisy,[46] he is not exactly pleased as he himself has designs on her and cannot, therefore, be too critical of her. As a result his outburst of triumph is repressed and mixed with the bitterest irony, with the words 'onestissima signora' ('you paragon of virtue') set to the motif earlier associated with his peremptory behaviour, but on this occasion heard *pianissimo*, as though sung through clenched teeth. Susanna, meanwhile, has exhausted her whole art of dissimulation: far from having taken control of the situation, she now finds herself thrown back on the defensive, facing a situation as hopeless as it is desperate. It is Basilio, however, who feels the greatest sense of delight now that all his secret fears have been dispelled, and although he expresses himself, as always, in a thoroughly commonplace manner, there is no doubt about the genuineness of his reaction. To add to the humour, the orchestra joins in as he smirks and skips round the room. Indeed, he can even adopt the tone of the ironist with the words 'Ah del paggio quel ch'ho detto' ('What I said about the page was only a suspicion'). But immediately after all three voices have achieved their greatest degree of independence in the ensemble, they come together again in a homophonic passage that ironically uses the same melody as the one with which the two men had earlier described Susanna's beating heart. But now she herself joins in and does so, moreover, with bitter seriousness ('Accader non può di peggio; giusti Dei! che mai sarà': 'Nothing worse could come about! Heavens above, what's to happen?'), and so, as in so many of Mozart's ensembles, the same disquiet overwhelms all the participants. Of course, this does not mean that the tension is released or that the underlying emotion is somehow clarified, rather that the tension continues to mount inexorably, with no sign of any escape: it is as though some demon were driving these spirits before it, towards an unknown goal. The orchestra, too, suddenly acquires a curious sense of tingling movement as the figurations grow more intense, with all manner of brief crescendos that add to the sense of tension, only to burst again like bubbles.

---

46. Note the way in which he later decorates the words 'onestissima signora' with an eloquently syncopated melisma.

Finally an eerie string unison with offbeat wind harmonies rushes past *pianissimo*, with the three characters on stage briefly joining in one last time, after which the figure of Cherubino – the 'poverino' – flits through the orchestra once again like an imp, and the piece fades softly away in the dark like some half-crazed ghost.

This trio thus constitutes the first confrontation between the opera's two most spirited participants, the Count and Susanna, presenting them in the liveliest manner. This is our first meeting with the Count, who is immediately shown as a fully rounded character: with the sudden flaring up of his anger in the opening bars, he stands before us in all his elemental passion. Here he is no longer a gentleman pursuing his love affairs merely as a form of gallant sporting pastime. He has to fight for what he wants and suffer setbacks in ways unsuspected by the traditional Italian *contini* precisely because he is no longer a social being like them but a creature driven by natural instincts. He, too, of course, is an aristocrat to the very core of his being, a nobleman with all the demands and, at the same time, all the social obligations of his class. He insists on his rights in the case of Susanna, but in striving to achieve this aim, he is overcome by elemental sexual desire, a feeling intensified by her resistance. Here love is shown as a naked human instinct that breaks down the barriers of gallantry and blinds the Count to all other considerations, so great is his desire to possess Susanna. From now on he is torn to and fro between two equally powerful urges: on the one hand, his awareness of his own social standing and, on the other, passion or, to put it another way, culture and nature. Neither of these forces allows the other to develop to its full extent. Instead, they get in each other's way, inhibiting each other or forcing each other in different directions, and it is by this dichotomy that Almaviva's character and fate are circumscribed, raising his involvement in the drama far above a mere dalliance to the point where it acquires a universal human import. It is no wonder, therefore, that there are times when his characterization acquires a tragic element, especially at those moments when he himself suddenly becomes aware of that dichotomy ('Vedrò, mentr'io sospiro'). From the outset, therefore, he lacks what it takes to be a traditional *buffo* figure like all those crude and oppressive types who are intended only to make their audiences laugh. All his actions are sustained by the conviction that they are justified and a part of his nature. That this nature, with all its contradictions and inhibitions, invariably leads to feelings of inadequacy and lack of freedom is something that he himself fails to notice. But it is noticed by the spectator, and herein lies the humour of the character. This humour is far removed from the slapstick comedy of the sort of jokes normally found in *opere buffe*, but is rooted, rather, in the sense of irony mentioned above, something which, in spite of the Count's foolish behaviour, never allows us to forget the serious nature of the human fate that lies behind it.

But the trio also reveals another aspect of Mozart's dramatic bent: his highly effective use of contrast. While the two strong characters of the Count and Susanna get into increasing difficulties as a result of their hot-blooded temperament and lose control of the situation, Basilio – a crass opportunist of average abilities, who has never had to contend with emotional turmoil – strides increasingly confidently through the whole mess, finally regarding himself as the true hero of the piece. After all, he is able to enjoy the purest pleasure known to base individuals, which is to watch nobler natures suffer and at the same time to deliver himself of his philistine's platitudes. *Basilio triumphans* – an aspect worthy of Shakespeare.

Ultimately the present trio is one of the most magisterial achievements of its kind because it combines music and drama in a well-nigh ideal manner. This is something that could be achieved only by a composer in whose imagination the interplay between the dramatic characters was instantly transformed into sounds. He gives the music all the freedom that it needs to make its due effect, but, unlike the Italians with their tendency towards garrulousness, he never grants it too much freedom, investing the piece with a clear and obvious structure and ensuring by means of an economical repeat of individual ideas that the listener gains a convincing impression of a self-contained whole. Unlike Gluck and Wagner, Mozart was not interested in revolutionizing the architectural structure of the musical drama from without. Indeed, there was no need for any such changes, given the varied and vital formal repertory of *opera buffa*. Rather, he transformed it from within and did so, moreover, in a fundamental manner, coaxing from individual forms their ultimate potential. When touched by his breath, even forms that were already threatening to turn into mere routine suddenly took on a new lease of life and acquired a new meaning. In this way he not only regenerated existing forms, he also created new ones by transplanting elements from one to another, notably in the case of the ternary aria and rondo. The end result was no less new than had been the case with Gluck, as the musician who created this new formal world was also a dramatic genius: unlike Gluck, he was not the servant of the dramatist but his alter ego, whose directives he did not need to wait to receive, as he bore them within himself from the outset.

The present trio is an eloquent example of Mozart's new approach to dramatic form.[47] Following the brief and weightily gestural introduction that forcibly draws the listener into the

47. The first section (A) consists of a four-bar introduction, followed by the Count's theme (a) (bars 5–15), Basilio's theme (b) (bars 16–23), and Susanna's theme (c) (bars 23–27), together with a free repetition of the latter involving all three singers (bars 27–43). This section ends on the dominant. There follows the first great episode (B) (bars 43–100), which deals with the attempts of the two men, under Basilio's guidance, to help the unconscious Susanna, and her own attempts to keep them away from the armchair. It, too, is made up of a complex of several themes, an idea in F major (d) (bars 44–46), the tone-painterly continuation of which (d1) (bars 47–57) later plays an important role, and a transitional theme (c1) that belongs to Susanna and that is related to the theme (c). This brings with it a decisive modulation to A minor. In turn this is followed by a repeat of (d) in the unexpected and solemn key of E flat major (bars 70–84). Basilio hobbles afterwards with his theme (b) (bars 85–92), followed by a theme of Susanna's (c2) that is likewise related to (c). The accompaniment, with its groaning quavers, likewise proves to be important in the subsequent course of the trio (bars 92–100). Next comes the freely varied repeat of part (A) (bars 101–121), with the Count's theme (a) and the motif that accompanies (c2). This includes a shorter episode that begins with the recitative and ends with a lengthy development of (b) (bars 121–146) The Count's theme is now repeated (bars 147–155). There then follows the third great episode (C) (bars 155–201), which is also the climax of the dramatic polyphony and which begins by introducing a whole complex of new ideas that are divided among the different voices (e), but from bar 168 onwards the old theme (d1) is reintroduced, and finally Basilio cannot resist the temptation to resort to mockery and add his theme (b), which increasingly becomes the main idea of the whole section. Groups (d1) and (e) are then repeated, followed by the great coda, but, in spite of appearances, this does not introduce any new ideas, merely continuing the previous bass harmonies

in a simplified form:

Even the quaver figure has already been anticipated in the earlier part of the trio. The final bars, at least in the orchestra, are also entirely motivic. In short, the trio is structured along the following lines (superscript numbers refer to variants of the relevant ideas):

Introduction: 4 bars
Main section (A): themes (a), (b), (c): 39 bars
Section (B) (first episode): themes (d), (c1), (d), (b), (c2): 58 bars
Section (A1): themes (a1), (c2), recitative (b), (a1): 55 bars
Section (C) (second episode): themes (e), (d1), (b), (e), (d1): 46 bars
Section (D) (coda): motifs from d1 and c2: 21 bars.

The harmonic design is as simple as possible, with only sections (A) and (B) modulating, the former to the dominant, the latter returning via the relative minor and subdominant to the tonic: from (A1) onwards there are only fleeting modulations. All the more powerful, therefore, are the sudden harmonic shifts that are invariably motivated by Susanna, such as the F minor in (A) and the highly effective imperfect cadence in (B).

world of B flat major, we encounter a movement which, in view of its series of modulations and the repeat of its opening, we may initially take to be an extremely free example of cyclical form, were it not for the fact that it then develops along completely independent lines. The wealth of themes – the most important of which return in the course of the piece – suggests a rondo, but here too the rules are broken, as the main theme that is heard at the beginning fails to assert itself as such, its primacy disputed in particular by Basilio's theme, the hypocritical nature of which forces itself on most of the other themes in the manner of a refrain. This is also the only theme that retains exactly the same form each time that it is heard on the character's lips. In the case of all the other themes, Mozart avails himself of a device that he uses in astonishing combinations in many of his ensembles from now on, namely, variation technique. Yet this is far from being the same as the purely musical type of variation found in his instrumental works. Rather, it could be described as a form of dramatic variation that reveals total freedom in invariably following the changing situation on stage. Just as was the case at the return of the initial idea, only its main motif is taken up on the first occasion and then developed along completely free lines, while on other occasions all that remains is a certain characteristic element such as its rhythm, with everything else developing freely. As an example, consider Susanna's three episodes right at the outset ('Che ruina', 'Dove sono?' and 'È un' insidia'). All are sprung from the same musical stem, but take the form of new and different shoots. In other cases, a new idea may suddenly incorporate a continuation of an earlier one, but this always happens with total naturalness, never giving the impression of anything recherché or purely mechanical, precisely because it develops organically out of the situation. But a further factor is involved here. Mozart frequently repeats his themes to different words and in that way reinterprets them. That is to say, he uses a device associated above all with the nineteenth century and its use of the leitmotif. Ultimately, it rests on the poetic exploitation of the ideas and feelings evoked in the hearts and minds of his listeners. When the Count apostrophizes Susanna as 'onestissima signora' to the same tune that had earlier accompanied his indignant reply to her entreaty, 'Parta parta il damerino', the tune immediately recalls the earlier situation in the listener's mind, while merging it with the new idea produced by the different words and in that way generating a new emotional response. With the speed of lightning the music forges a link between the two situations even though there is no such link in the text. But there are also occasions where the music – still within the same number – suddenly grants completely unexpected insights into the characters' inner lives as a result of these associations,[48] while at other times the orchestra is temporarily cast in the role of the ideal spectator. Passages such as these audibly recall the principles later advanced by Wagner, but we should never forget that in Mozart's case all such phenomena spring from musico-dramatic considerations, whereas for Wagner and his predecessors they are based on poetic foundations, being only one dramatic means among many. It would never have occurred to Mozart to base a system on this: in his case the creative musician in him was far too powerful a force to be ignored.

The following chorus for the local peasants ('Giovani lieti, fiori spargete') is as straightforward as it is charming and combines festive Italian sonorities with the more intimate strains of the German song. The winds that are used throughout the piece – flutes, bassoons and horns – likewise recall the festive music associated with these people, producing a number that sounds like one of the wind serenades so popular in Vienna at this time. But it also includes more pastoral sounds, notably in the drone bass in the opening bars and in the interplay between the winds towards the

---

48. Cf. Bartolo's aria discussed above.

end, with the genuinely Mozartian gently rocking motif of the third bar. Here, too, finally, the dynamic markings are remarkable for their constant alternation between loud and soft: it is as though these worthy peasants keep having to remind themselves to calm down and show good manners in the presence of their lord.

Even during Mozart's lifetime, Figaro's aria 'Non più andrai' was the most popular number in the entire opera. Formally speaking, it is a simple rondo with two episodes, its memorable, vivid musical language presenting no difficulties of understanding, at least as long as the listener is not led astray by the German translators who have been so attracted by the thunder of battle that echoes throughout the second half of the aria that they fantasize about blood and corpses in the first half, too, where the original follows a completely different train of thought.[49] Here there is absolutely no mention of military matters. Instead, Figaro paints an ironical portrait of a young and elegant aristocrat, foppish, perfumed and fond of chasing the ladies. In short, he holds up to Cherubino a mirror of his life till now. The dashing march rhythms of the opening are admirably suited to this image: for real war music, this tune is far too elegant, while there is absolutely nothing martial about the second strophe, which presents us, rather, with an arresting picture of an aristocratic layabout with his ribbons flying in the wind, his feather-adorned cap on his well-groomed hair and his rustling silk clothes. Especially delightful here is the secret whispering and rustling in the orchestra. Only with the second episode ('Tra guerrieri, poffar Bacco') does an element of sharp contrast enter the aria, a contrast risibly obscured by the German translation. This second episode depicts the page's future fate in the army, and only now does the music acquire a martial air. Until now the orchestra has followed the vocal line with tender compliance, but from this point onwards it breaks free and noisily interrupts after virtually every phrase, with an active contribution not least from the trumpets and timpani and with both participants vying with each other in their description of military life. Only once does this wild torrent falter, at the delightfully subdued passage in E minor, where Figaro recalls the soldier's notoriously empty purse and we even find an eloquent fermata. But this mood quickly passes and now, in keeping with the text, a real *banda* appears, consisting only of winds (initially without trumpets and timpani) and playing a march that enters softly. Here the voice, with its blaring fanfare motifs, seems keen to assume the role of the missing trumpet. Once again the image of the aristocratic fop slips by, then the march reappears to Figaro's battle cry, 'Cherubino, alla vittoria, alla gloria militar!', this time with timpani and trumpets joining in with a dazzling fanfare, and as soon as Figaro finishes, the whole orchestra breaks in completely unexpectedly with this march tune. From every quarter the battle cries ring out, assailing the ears of the poor boy, whose thoughts are anywhere but with 'victory' and 'military glory'. Herein lies the humour of the piece, with Figaro, beside himself with happiness at being able to get rid of the dangerous youth, using the opportunity to deliver himself of an ironical homily. And he is delighted at being able to take out his anger on a member of the higher aristocracy. But this scene should not be allowed to descend to the level of a vulgar theatrical comedy, something to which the performer is all too easily misled by the German translation.

49. The original reads: 'Non più andrai, farfallone amoroso, / Notte e giorno d'intorno girando, / Delle belle turbando il riposo, / Narcissetto, Adoncino d'amor' ('No more, you amorous butterfly, will you go round fluttering by night and day, disturbing the peace of mind of all beautiful women, you little Narcissus, you little Adonis of love'). Compare this with the first strophe of the German translation that still disfigures the Peters score: 'Dort vergiß leises Flehn, süßes Wimmern, / Da wo Lanzen und Schwerter dir schimmern, / Sei dein Herz unter Leichen und Trümmern / Nur voll Wärme für Ehre und Mut! ('You can forget gentle entreaties and sweet whimperings when lances and swords flash around you. May your heart warm only to honour and courage when surrounded by corpses and ruins!')

We have repeatedly drawn attention to the affinities between the present scene and similar situations in Italian and French comic operas[50] and have even pointed to the existence of a particular type of 'military aria'. Yet the prototype is transformed in Mozart's hands into something new and individual as a result of the setting in which it is embedded: here the aria is no self-contained tour de force designed to titillate the senses, but an integral expression of Figaro's character and, at the same time, an extension of Cherubino's character inasmuch as it adds a further feature to our picture of his immaturity by revealing him as a young count. The first section of the aria is thus a counterpart to the second part of Leporello's 'catalogue aria'. On both occasions, an outsider presents a picture of the outward appearance of a gentleman, in the case of *Don Giovanni* a mature figure, in that of *Le nozze di Figaro* a young blade. Finally, Mozart used the aria to bring the opening act to an end in a highly effective manner, something on which he always laid great emphasis. Here the reader will recall the end of the opening act of *Die Entführung aus dem Serail* and the composer's remarks to his father on act endings in general. A comparison with the present aria reveals the tremendous dramatic progress that Mozart had made in the meantime. The first-act trio from *Die Entführung* had certainly generated considerable noise, but not much else besides, whereas the present aria is not only suitably noisy, it is also dramatic from beginning to end.

With the second act we are introduced to the exalted and noble portrait of the Countess ('Porgi amor'), who enters as though from another world. Her opening aria is a simple binary cavatina that creates a sense of tension and solemnity within its first two bars, with even the key of E flat major remarkable for its dark-hued ardour. The text is an appeal to the god of love of a kind that was popular at this time.[51] In relation to its overall length, the introduction is disproportionately long, yet is extremely succinct and Mozartian in character, eschewing the traditional structure of imperfect cadences and modulations to the dominant but preferring to juxtapose what are later to be the main ideas, bringing them together within the principal tonality in a way that is as free as it is concise and thereby granting us an insight into the turmoil within the Countess's breast. For the present, however, none of these feelings emerges with any greater clarity. Rather, the opposite is the case, with the emotions of longing, confidence, fearful presentiment and tender hope constantly overlapping. Yet the ritornello is no more than preparatory in character and gives no hint of the magnificent way in which the second half of the aria takes wing. The main theme begins in a typically Neapolitan manner that Mozart may have picked up from Johann Christian Bach or Gluck.[52] Among its Mozartian features are not only the syncopation in the third bar (which leads in turn to the lengthening of the sigh motif in the fourth bar) and its accompaniment with the anguished yearning of its chromatic *note cambiate*, but above all the completely free melodic structure of the consequent phrase.[53] The love of this woman for her faithless husband is no flickering will-o'-the-wisp, but nor is it an all-consuming flame. Rather, it is a pure and tranquil fire that suffuses her entire being. It, too, rests on a physical basis, of course, as becomes clear

50. See above; see also act one, scene eleven of Anfossi's *La vera costanza*; act one, scene two of Grétry's *L'ami de la maison*; and act two, scene eight of the same composer's *L'amant jaloux*.

51. See Abert, *Niccolò Jommelli als Opernkompnist*,179.

52. See above; see also act one, scene three of Bach's *Temistocle* and act one, scene seven of his *Lucio Silla*; also Ariene's aria in act three, scene nine of Sacchini's *Il Creso* of 1765. The most recent example was probably the largo of Carl Philipp Emanuel Bach's B flat major sonata from his fifth volume of keyboard sonatas of 1785. Many similar examples may also be found in Mozart's works from an early date, notably in the 'Agnus Dei' of the C major mass K337 (see above), where the writing is still entirely Italianate in character.

53. Most other composers develop the consequent phrase from the antecedent: notable examples include the Chorus of Priestesses at the end of the second act of Gluck's *Iphigénie en Tauride* ('Contemplez ces tristes apprêts').

as soon as we compare her to Gluck's embodiments of marital love. His heroes and heroines always have a lofty ethical mission in life, whereas in Mozart's case the emotion exists for its own sake alone as an elemental urge that floods and warms the Countess's whole being, drawing her to her lover in spite of all the obstacles that lie in her way and filling her with a trust that triumphs over all her grief and anguish. This love, too, transcends all sense of morality and is unconcerned with any attempt to convert her faithless husband but strives solely and instinctively for their reunion. The swelling clarinet theme in B flat major sounds like a memory of happier days that then forces from her the words 'O mi rendi il mio tesoro – o mi lascia almen morir' ('O give me back my loved one, or at least let me die'). That the Countess is far from being ascetic by nature is clear from the whole of the second half of her aria, from the fermata onwards. Melodically, this section strikes out in a wholly new direction, while repeating on a grand scale all that we have already observed on a smaller scale in terms of the structure of the individual periods. Here the full emotional force of the love that she feels for the Count breaks through with elemental intensity, a unique and powerful outpouring of temperament, an expression in song of a yearning desire that is bathed in the sweetest of sensual harmonies.[54] There is no place in her soul for gallant flirtatiousness, and if the Countess later intrigues against her husband, she does so only in the hope that in this way she will achieve her ends more quickly. But she is not inwardly divided in the way in which her husband is torn, and so she emerges as the stronger of the two of them, manifesting a strength to which he will ultimately succumb – 'strength', of course, in a dynamic, not in a moral, sense.

A totally different sort of love is revealed by Cherubino in his well-known canzona ('Voi, che sapete'). At this point in Beaumarchais's original we find an authentically French, semi-balladesque romance to the tune of *Marlbrough s'en va t'en guerre*,[55] which Da Ponte replaced with an Italian canzonetta on the theme of 'cos' è l'amore?', a theme still popular even today in Italian street songs. The way in which the women are apostrophized in the poem and the guitar accompaniment with pizzicato strings[56] happily maintain the tone of a canzonetta. But the author of the poem – Cherubino – naturally treats the subject in his own way, adopting a standpoint familiar to us from his earlier aria. On that occasion we had been treated to a purely subjective outpouring of emotion, but this now becomes a poetic image, and the painfully sweet love that had then sung itself out in music now becomes the object that the boy's excitable poetic imagination attempts to master. Thus the situation demands, and Da Ponte duly obliged with, tried-and-tested images and rationalistic flashes of inspiration from *galant* poetry such as 'gelare', 'avvampare' and 'ricerco un bene fuori di me'. Mozart follows him in this, albeit at a discreet distance, lightly etching in all the images associated with 'diletto', 'martir', 'gemere', 'palpitar' and so on. But the real kernel of the piece goes deeper than this, for behind this canzonetta lies a sense of agitation repressed only with great difficulty, a state of affairs suggested not only by the regular metre, the uninterrupted bass line and the richer and more animated harmonies, but above all by the writing for the winds, which would have been superfluous in a song accompanied only by a guitar. 'Voi che sapete' is in fact the only solo number in the entire opera that brings together all the woodwinds as solo instruments, while adding two horns for good measure. They contribute sporadically to the vocal melody by seizing on individual outlines, before letting them drop again, but in general they are content with brief and expressive phrases and often with mere timbral effects: this is a language

---

54. There is something extraordinarily true to life about the musical symbolism of the ascending and descending melodic line at the final 'o mi rendi il mio tesoro o mi lascia almen morir!'
55. These *timbres*, too, are already familiar to us from *opéra comique*; see above.
56. The violas double the bass, thereby preserving the primitive character of the guitar accompaniment.

that seeks expression on a barely conscious level. In short, the winds tell the listener what is going on in the heart of the young poet and singer. For those listeners who have ears for such things, the tone colour alone is sufficient to round out the picture of this infatuated boy's soul: the naïve sound of the flute, the elegiac strains of the oboe, the sensually swelling tones of the clarinet, the darkly languishing sonorities of the bassoon and the prescient Romanticism of the horns – all follow each other in turn, overlapping, blending and combining with one another to form a psychological portrait of incomparable succinctness. In general terms, the aria expresses a sense of insistent, languishing desire, with stronger emotions occasionally adding highlights. Listen, for example, to the enchantingly childlike outburst for the flute and oboe on the words 'vedete' and 'nel cor'. At the words 'sospiro e gemo' the expressive language acquires a darker and more anguished colour through the chromaticisms in the basses and upper voices, and as if the winds have now given too much away, they fall silent at the *da capo*: Cherubino has regained his composure. Note also the subtle difference between his two arias in terms of their effect on his female audience: the first is more genuine, but also more unbridled and more childlike, hence, perhaps, the fact that it amuses Susanna rather than charms her, whereas the second is all the more dangerous for the fact that it is superficially more cultivated for all its essential intensity of emotion.

Its impact on Susanna becomes immediately clear from her own aria ('Venite, inginocchiatevi'), which has less to do with character than with the situation on stage, specifically Cherubino's disguise – ultimately a French device, hence the leading role of the orchestra in depicting the individual events, while the vocal writing is largely declamatory in style: at the beginning Susanna beckons to the page to come closer, after which she describes his ungainly movements in clothes that he is not used to wearing ('pian piano or via giratevi' and 'la faccia ora volgetemi'), his lovesick glances at the Countess and his tiny steps ('vedremo poscia il passo'). Even the main theme is clearly gestural in character:

re - sta - te   fer - mo   lì,   re - sta - te   fer - mo   lì

Here Susanna raises her finger, then lowers it (at the descending interval of a ninth) in order to point to the place where Cherubino should stand. Particularly charming is her reappraisal at the end when, seeing the attractive young lad, she comes to the conclusion that 'se l'amano le femmine, han certo il lor perchè' ('If women fall in love with him, they have good reason to'). And how subtly this is prepared for by Susanna's delightful whispering to the Countess! This theme is the recurrent refrain of the aria, which thus proves to be another example of Mozart's free approach to rondo form. Yet here, too, a little affair of the heart is played out behind the superficial tone painting. Susanna would not be the spirited hedonistic creature that she is if her senses were not in turmoil during this *travestimento*, as she starts to find the young lad increasingly attractive: her triplet melody at the end and, above all, the charming interjections from the winds are highly revealing in this regard. But the whole scene is authentically Mozartian, with all the natural grace of young people who feel drawn to other people of their own age without any trace of the lascivious eroticism in which certain moderns appear to recognize 'love's true nature'.[57] Figaro has no reason to doubt Susanna's fidelity.

57. ◆ This quotation is from Wagner's *Tannhäuser*.

The following trio ('Susanna or via sortite') differs from its predecessor ('Cosa sento!') by dint of its more lyrical character, which also affects its form: ternary form with a varied *da capo*. The situation remains the same from start to finish, with all three characters in a state of permanent and feverish excitement and with the tension maintained to the very end in a whole series of different ways. The only difference is the way in which the characters attempt to master their feelings and come to terms with the pressures upon them. The Count prepares to attack with a defiant motif borrowed from Paisiello, soon producing the first of the oppressive pedal points that are characteristic of the overall mood of the trio. The second of these pedal points is further intensified by the chromatic middle voices and occurs at the Countess's words 'un abito da sposa provando ella si sta' ('She's in there, trying on her wedding dress'), very quickly leading to a real feeling of oppressiveness and apprehension at the modulation to G minor. This second pedal point is all the more effective in that the Count and Countess are keen to preserve appearances at all costs: after all, the trio as a whole is based on a minuet rhythm symbolic of social etiquette. But trouble is already brewing, as is clear from the curiously agitated passage in E minor with its sequentially descending bass line and sforzato accents in the violins.[58] At this point, Susanna, revealing all her seriousness of purpose and depth of character, succeeds for a time in easing the tension at the painfully rising chromatic coloratura passage, following which the breathtaking momentum suddenly falters in order to make way for a tenderly dreamy passage under Susanna's leadership. The words tell of Susanna's resolve to ensure that all works out for the best, but the music already holds out the promise of fulfilment, and there is something profoundly poetic to the way in which this beautiful melody is immediately taken up by the anxious Countess.[59] But it is only a brief ray of light that pierces the gloom, and when it is repeated in the third section of the trio, this passage, too, acquires a darker coloration: the sense of confidence has become decidedly more subdued. But the piece as a whole could hardly be further removed from the *buffa*-like spirit of the Italian composers of the period. For them, the imbroglio, with its piquant situation, would have been the main point of interest, and it is more than likely that the Countess, forced into a corner, would have had to foot the bill, while Susanna, looking down on events from her position of contemptuous coquetry, would have escaped with impunity. But here, as elsewhere, Mozart flies in the face of convention. With him, the awkward situation in which they find themselves reduces neither the Count nor the Countess to the level of low comedy, and Susanna is concerned not to judge her mistress but to help her. As a result, she is immediately aware of the seriousness of the conflict that develops here and forgoes any desire to be smugly dismissive. Here, too, the ossified responses of masklike characters have been replaced by individual, entirely human concerns.

In its original form,[60] the duettino ('Aprite, presto') was ten bars longer than it appears in the complete edition. The extra bars comprise two groups of four bars each and one group of two. Their omission was noted in the autograph score by means of brackets and red pencil, but it is not clear whether the hand is Mozart's, while the justification for the cut – especially the second four-

58. This passage is related to a section of the quartet in scene eleven of Grétry's *La fausse magie*.
59. The Countess originally had the upper part, but Mozart later changed this in favour of Susanna, thereby necessitating various alterations to the text. This was presumably undertaken out of consideration for the singers. In the two finales this question was already resolved while Mozart was still working on them.
60. Reproduced in the appendix to the full score in AMA, 403ff.; see also p.80 of the critical commentary. Mozart appears to have planned yet another version of this duet, no more than a few bars of which have survived. They are headed 'Atto 2do Scene 3 in vece del Duetto di Susanna e Cherubino'; see NMA II/5/16/2, 613. ◆ Concerning a possible recitative replacement for this duet, see Anheißer, 'Die unbekannte Urfassung von Mozarts Figaro', and Tyson, 'Some Problems in the Text of *Le nozze di Figaro*: Did Mozart Have a Hand in Them?' Other important textual issues, including changes to the Countess and Susanna's parts, are discussed in Tyson, '*Le nozze di Figaro*: Lessons from the Autograph Score'.

bar period – remains disputed as it includes some words of Cherubino's that are later to prove important, 'un vaso o due di fiori, più mal non avverrà' ('a vase or two of flowers, nothing worse'). At the same time, it brings with it a violent release of tension in the orchestra's upper register following the mounting tension of the previous six bars, a release that the listener is unwilling to forgo from a dramatic point of view. The two earlier cuts, by contrast, may be sanctioned in the light of the tense situation that admits of no delay. The duet once again springs from the situation and, as such, takes its place in the French tradition. But on this occasion the motivic material includes only a single theme with its two subdivisions (bar 1[61] and bars 3–4) that are developed in the most varied ways. The accompaniment is continuous and consists only of strings, with a performance marking that remains *pianissimo* until the very end, when the quavers turn to semi-quavers and, to a sudden crescendo, Cherubino jumps out of the window. But the brief phrases for the singers are declamatory rather than sung. Only once, at Cherubino's words 'pria di nuocerle nel foco volerei' ('rather than harm her, I'd leap into the fire') towards the end, is there a hint of stronger emotion that suddenly grants a brief insight into Cherubino's soul. (Note the G minor tonality here.) For all its brevity, this is one of the most original numbers in the entire score, full of breathtaking, tingling excitement and animated by all manner of tensions on a larger and smaller scale, including the one mentioned above. Note also the way in which the middle voice accompanying the minim in the main theme alternates between a simple and a chromatic form:

This number places particularly great demands on its performers in terms of their acting and singing: every unevenness and sense of heaviness will seriously affect the overall impression.

The first finale ('Esci ormai, garzon malnato') begins with the return of the Count and Countess. Even today it continues to be regarded – quite rightly – as one of the finest examples of its kind. We do not know to what extent Mozart himself was involved in its poetic design, but there is no doubt that it was Da Ponte who laid the foundations on which this musico-dramatic edifice could be raised. The result is an ideal balance between drama and music. The drama moves inexorably towards its climax, without a single point of stasis, while not only allowing the music to unfold in the freest possible manner but even inviting it to do so. On a purely superficial level, this stems from the constant increase in the number of characters on stage, with two in the first section and seven in the last. Yet, however effective it may be from a purely musical standpoint, this increase in sonority invariably serves the aims of the drama, which develops in eight independent sections, each of which adds a further twist to the plot and even, to a certain extent, helps to resolve its complexities, but in such a way that the resolution is immediately retracted in the following section and replaced by a new complication, which inevitably leads in turn to a regrouping of the different characters. But each of these sections is also based on a particular mood that invites musical expression, lasting just long enough for the music to exhaust that mood with the formal resources at its disposal. The problem of achieving unity within diversity is solved here in the most perfect way imaginable, with the individual characters in a state of constant movement, forever developing at each other's expense, with coup followed by counter-coup and with the most

61. The same theme forms the basis of the finale of the D major symphony K504 ('Prague') of 1786. Further, see Tyson, *Le nozze di Figaro: eight variant versions = acht abweichende Fassungen.*

detailed individual characterization appearing alongside the general characterization of each particular section. The change that Da Ponte has made to the ending of Beaumarchais's act is a minor masterpiece of libretto writing, inasmuch as he brings down the curtain at the moment when the excitement has reached its height following the intervention of Marcellina and her cronies. This meant cutting the following discussion between Susanna and the Countess over the assignation in the garden. In consequence, the finale as a whole leads to a veritable tangle of comedy-like complications which, in spite of the discomfiture of Figaro's faction, still lacks a definitive solution and, as such, leaves the listener in a state of extreme excitement.

The first section is the duet for the Count and Countess and increases the tension in such a way that a catastrophe seems inevitable. So great is his rage and jealousy, the Count is barely able to control himself any longer, while the Countess is torn between feelings of wounded pride and a vague fear at her husband's fury. Whereas her own vocal line is generally limited to anxiously fluttering phrases,[62] the Count responds with harsh and defiant rhythms, notably with the following motif that he seems almost literally to tear from her lips:

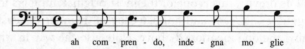

ah com - pren - do, inde - gna mo - glie

This is also the only motif to be repeated by all the parties involved, as the Count, in his unbridled passion, gets through a whole series of motifs that take him increasingly in the direction of tragic, high-flown emotion. There are even times when he comes close to the world of Othello with outbursts such as:

va lon - tan dagl' oc - chi mie - i, un' in - fi - da, un em - pia

se - i e mi cer - chi d'in - fa - mar

Or take the seething outburst, with its wind scales like tongues of darting flame:

mo - ra, mo - ra!

There are times when the music brings the opposing forces into the sharpest possible contrast, notably at the Count's brusque 'Qua la chiave' ('Give me the key!'), with full orchestra, and at the Countess's reply, 'Egli è innocente' ('He's innocent'), with its touching wind sonorities. This section is cast in binary form, but reveals total freedom, with only the endings of the two sections corresponding to each other. The end of this sombre and impassioned portrait comes as the key turns grindingly in the lock. As in the first trio ('Cosa sento'), the sense of surprise at Susanna's appearance is initially marked by a feeling of perplexity as the final motif is allowed to run itself out, followed by total silence, the only difference being that on this occasion there is a decisive modulation. The next two sections are related to each other inasmuch as the second brings with it a realization of all that has been prepared for in the first. Both are in total contrast to the preceding

---

62. Here, at the words 'Mi fa torto quel trasporto', we find the Piccinnian motif that Mozart had already used in *La finta giardiniera*; see above.

section. The wild-eyed emotion suddenly turns to irony, as the Count, with his unbridled passion, is now seen to have been in the wrong, but the Countess, too, clearly harbours feelings of guilt. Initially, however, in the opening section – a molto andante in B flat major in 3/8-time[63] – it is the situation itself that creates its impact through its sheer gravity. The motif in the orchestra recalls nothing so much as a heartbeat giving out.[64] A past mistress in the art of dissimulation, Susanna emerges 'tutta grave' from the dressing room and adapts to the new situation by pretending to have no idea what is going on, a pretence conducted to the strains of a lieder-like melody. And once again a lengthy pedal point expresses the oppressive astonishment felt by the other two characters, while above it in the soprano line the mischievous servant delights in the success of her stratagem in chuckling triplets. Not until we come to the third section – a common-time Allegro in B flat major – are any conclusions drawn from the changed situation, although the crisis remains unresolved and the Count and Countess accept the new situation only reluctantly: the Count has little choice but to forgive his wife, without, however, being convinced of her innocence, while in her case the pleasure of being forgiven is marred by her oppressive sense of guilt. Meanwhile Susanna continues to act as go-between, a role she assumes partly out of amusement, partly out of genuine concern. In short, feelings and ideas are in a constant state of flux, giving the music a perfect opportunity to deploy its ability to allow the listener to read between the lines. That Mozart saw this scene through the eyes of a humorist is clear from this section's two main motifs:

Both are Piccinnian in origin. The former sounds like secret giggling, in spite of its two keen suspensions, while the latter – first heard at Susanna's words 'più lieta, più franca' – increasingly expresses the idea of reconciliation, its element of roguery notwithstanding. This is the only motif that is properly developed in keeping with all the rules of music. It accompanies not only Susanna's attempts to persuade the others to make up but also the little war of words between the Count and Countess with its defiance and sulking, as well as its furtively lovestruck glances and desire for reconciliation, finally descending at the end like a dove of peace at the words 'Da questo momento'. But this victory is achieved not without setbacks. Between these main motifs we hear all manner of episodes in which the whole iridescent humour of the situation finds expression. Note, for example, the wild slide motif in the ninth bar: once again the Count flares up, not in remorse, but in his fury at the fact that he has fallen into the trap. Yet his initial plea for forgiveness tells of self-torment, only for all his old defiance to reassert itself at the end. How priceless is the torrent of words with which the two women tell him off ('Le vostre follie non mertan pietà!': 'Your foolish behaviour deserves no forgiveness'). Soon the Count becomes much more subdued ('quell' ira, Susanna, m'aita a calmar': 'Help me, Susanna, to calm her anger'), and at this juncture the situation develops into a dialogue between the Count and Susanna, who seizes the opportunity to give him a piece of her mind.[65] Finally she gets him to the point where he simply echoes her entreaty:

---

63. Not an andante con moto, as it appeared in earlier scores.
64. On the parallelism between this passage and Grétry's *L'amant jaloux*, see p.472 above.
65. On the way in which this motif is used to express vituperative abuse, see the parallel passage in Guglielmi quoted on p.315 above.

'Signora! – Rosina!' By the time that all three characters blend their voices together in A flat major to the motif marked (b) above ('Confuso, pentito'), we are already close to a state of reconciliation. But the Count then recalls Cherubino and his anger flares up again, with the earlier contrasts repeated in intensified form. Note the subtle way in which Susanna now lectures the Countess on the fate of women in a man's world, a lecture delivered to the same motif as the one she had earlier used to heap calumny on the Count. Next comes the passage already mentioned ('Da questo momento'), with its authentically Mozartian shift of direction and with the voices suddenly coming together in the simplest homophony to mysterious wind harmonies and the motif (b), which calls down its blessing upon the proceedings, adding a note of something approaching transfiguration. It is as though a gentle veil has descended on all these troubled hearts and as though their eyes have suddenly been opened to a paradise of peace in which the past now lies behind them like some terrible dream. It is hard to conceive of anything less Italian than this.

Once again the formal structure is highly idiosyncratic. Essentially, this section is cast in the form of a completely free rondo, the individual episodes of which are freely varied in keeping with the action, while the main themes – especially (b) – are developed over longer stretches, albeit on dramatic, rather than musical, lines. No less remarkable is the harmonic design of this section. The dominant (F major) is touched on only at the beginning, and in general subdominant harmonies (E flat and A flat major) prevail: rarely found in Mozart's works of this period, this dominance stems from the sombre, vacillating overall mood. It is this mood, after all, that forms the basis of this section, with its constant flood of movement for ever jolting itself into action and yet never leading to a goal. Not even the ending strikes us as providing a complete and real solution but suggests, rather, an escape into a dreamlike, unreal world, an escape which, however powerfully motivated from a psychological point of view by the previous build-up of tension, holds out no promise of permanence.

The unsuspecting Figaro now bursts in with his bright G major and completely changes the situation, ushering in an allegro con spirito in 3/8-time. Here, too, the new situation is initially depicted in wholly objective terms, with the music resembling a boisterous sequel to the earlier peasants' chorus ('Giovani liete') and with the jubilant blasts of the 'suonatori' interrupting his announcement. But it is not long before the others are struck by the implications of his remarks, so that the Count suddenly casts a pall over the mood of celebration, ignoring Figaro's agitated interjection 'La turba m'aspetta' ('The crowd is waiting for me') and bringing everything to an end with a sinister trill. With this the atmosphere becomes markedly more oppressive. Figaro notices at once that something is amiss and instinctively aligns himself with the womenfolk to form a self-contained group whose inner insecurity explodes at the sudden *forte* on 'com'ha da finir?' ('How will it end?'), while the Count, supported by the bassoon, assumes control of the situation. But it is the fifth section – a C major Andante in 2/4-time – that draws the actual consequences from Figaro's appearance. As such, this fifth section is related to the fourth in the same way that the third is related to the second. Although the Count is still in a conciliatory mood, he cannot let slip the opportunity to take Figaro to task over the letter that is responsible for the whole of their present predicament and in that way to delay his wedding still further. Gleefully and, of course, with a note of profound irony, he asks after the letter in the tone of a man of the people. Figaro's circumspect reply – 'Nol conosco' ('I don't know') – is accompanied by a knowing smirk in the orchestra. At this point the two women begin their anxious attempts to bring home to Figaro the fact that the time for joking is over. Here the orchestra secretly signals its unmistakable message. Especially remarkable in the following bars is the full orchestra's brusque entry on the consequent phrase of the main theme at the Count's words 'Tu c'intendi. Già capisci' ('You're deceiving me. You know

now'). Figaro behaves like a perfect diplomat. Indeed, the whole way in which the individual characters listen carefully to what the others are saying here is a model of its kind, tapping a comic vein of the subtlest nature. The three partners in crime come to an understanding in a passage that involves some remarkably strict part-writing over a pedal point. A minor skirmish between the Count and Figaro, followed by the women's mischievous tittering, leads back to the beginning, with Figaro – insolently taking up his master's melody – raising the matter of his wedding in order, as he says, to bring the whole issue to an end. The polyphonic writing is now extended to all four characters. Once again a mood of mystery descends on the ensemble, with not even the Count succeeding in escaping from its sway. The tender entreaties of the two women allay his suspicions, and only deep down in his heart does he continue to hope that Marcellina will arrive and resolve the whole situation.

But instead of Marcellina, it is the drunken gardener Antonio who now enters with his broken pot of carnations. This sixth section is a common-time allegro molto in F major, and the subtlety of the previous section now gives way to a coarseness bordering on the burlesque. It is hardly surprising, therefore, that the music now comes very close to the world of an Italian *opera buffa*, as is clear not only from the slides at the very beginning but also from the rolling triplets that predominate in the orchestra throughout virtually the whole of this section, both evident signs of the inebriated state of the new hero, who also needs plenty of time before he can begin his account which he delivers with foolish haste over an extended pedal point. The melodic writing, too, bears an extremely turbulent and realistic stamp throughout this section. For whole stretches it is only the dynamics that indicate the inner course of events, notably when the Count's passions typically flare up at 'Cosa sento?' ('What do I hear?'), then immediately afterwards, as Figaro's faction begins to feel afraid and makes a desperate attempt to shout the drunkard down and in that way prevent the Count from questioning Antonio, an interrogation that threatens to expose them. It is at this juncture that Figaro drops his bombshell and, to a tremendous crescendo, announces 'Sono io stesso saltato di lì' ('It was I who jumped down from there'). The rattling triplets now give way to the twitching slide motif, and then, for the first time in this section, the orchestra comes to a complete standstill at the gardener's half-astonished, half-insolent question 'Come mai diventasti sì grosso' ('How have you grown so tall, then?'). But Antonio quickly pulls himself together again, and the earlier breakneck pace returns. Indeed, the more urgent the situation becomes, the more Figaro seems to sprout wings. Drawing on a unison motif familiar from *Don Giovanni*, he passes ironical comment on his obdurate enemy, encouraging the latter, in his doltish simple-mindedness, to parry by simply continuing the motif. But there follows the far more dangerous confrontation between Figaro and the Count himself, with the tension suddenly shifting in the course of two weighty pedal points, as Figaro in his feverish excitement continues to weave his tissue of lies and, in his typically roguish manner, graphically describes his leap from the window and his oh! so painful injury to his foot. This section is the most loosely structured of the eight that make up the finale. Although individual passages are repeated, it is the dramatist who decides which ones they shall be. The seventh section – an andante ma non troppo in B flat major and 6/8-time almost one hundred bars in length – is totally different in this respect, dominated, as it is, by a single pounding motif in the orchestra:

In other words, the orchestra is limited here to depicting the underlying mood, without exploring individual aspects of the action. The sense of inner tension mounts to the point where it is ready to burst, but no release comes and, indeed, it is more oppressive in its restraint than it was in the previous section, with its physically far cruder outbursts. The psychological pressure on the Count is now considerably greater, his suspicions concerning the Countess not only revived but emphatically increased as a result of the thought that she and his servants are conspiring against him. Meanwhile, Figaro, who had barely escaped from one predicament, now finds himself suddenly implicated in another from which the two women can free him only at the cost of the greatest inner turmoil. By the end of this section the Count is at his wits' end and no longer knows what to make of the whole situation. When examining numbers such as this, we do well to recall that in any opera – and especially a comic opera – the performer, too, demands his due alongside the poet and musician. There are good reasons why Mozart repeatedly returns to the importance of the 'action': he does not always express the full extent of the underlying emotion in his music but occasionally merely hints at it, leaving it to the singer to complete the picture through his gifts as an actor, gifts that he will deploy with the greatest possible freedom. Of course, Mozart continues to hold the performer on a tight rein, invisibly preventing the latter from muddying his basic outline, while counting on his independent input to the extent that the picture remains incomplete without him. This is all too easily forgotten by those people who judge Mozart's operas only by the score, rather than by a living performance. Later composers often entrusted the whole of the work's emotional impact to the music alone, maintaining a constant state of tension from start to finish, preventing their singers from introducing any nuances in terms of expression and gesture, but turning them into mere puppets in their hands. In this way musicians have been fully avenged for the slights suffered at the hands of their former oppressors, but the musical drama is certainly the poorer in consequence. In this regard Mozart achieved a perfect balance, thereby demonstrating that he was not only a great musical genius, but a towering dramatic genius, too: after all, he knew that when the drama demanded it, he should allow the musician to take second place to the performer. But as someone who knew all about real life, he was also aware that people do not express their emotions at the same relentless pitch all the time. Assuming that they are not personified passions, even the most impassioned people have moments when we see them in everyday guise and in ordinary contact with others, when they behave like anyone else. It is sufficient to recall Shakespeare's tragedies in this respect. It is only natural that comic operas should count far more on this factor. Indeed, they have often suffered from the fact that, more especially in recent times, composers of comic operas have been misled by Wagner's music dramas to present their characters in a state of permanently heightened emotion, increasing the tension with every word and every speech and filling out the unemotional passages with thickly instrumented bombast.[66]

We have already encountered several scenes in *Le nozze di Figaro* in which, the subtlety of the writing notwithstanding, the musician makes way for the performer. (Examples include 'Via resti servita' and 'Aprite, presto'.) In the case of the present section, the music merely maintains the note of oppressive tension, defining the performers' tasks in only their most general outlines, while allowing them total freedom in their execution. Above all, it does not claim the listener's attention to such an extent that he or she is prevented from concentrating on the plot and, specifically, on

---

66.   There may soon come a time, therefore, when composers again take a serious interest in the problem of the unaccompanied recitative, which the Italians have never really given up (cf. Verdi).

the way in which the two women secretly work on Figaro and he cunningly falls in with their scheme.

A different relationship exists in the case of the final section of the finale, a common-time passage in E flat major[67] that begins as an allegro assai, changing first to a più moto and finally to a prestissimo. It is also the longest section in the finale, being divided into two sections in keeping with the plot. Of these, the first depicts the new situation, with the arrival of the enemy faction and their indictment of Figaro, while the second describes the effect of this change on the minds of all the characters. Both sections are motivically linked, inasmuch as we are again dealing with one of Mozart's relatively loosely structured dramatic rondos. Even on a superficial level, they feature a whole arsenal of resources, with the seven-part ensemble joined for the first time by the full orchestra, including trumpets and timpani. From the outset the mood is openly hostile and the listener is left in no doubt that everything is now to play for. Marcellina's faction arrives, resolute and sure of victory, initially reducing the opposition to total confusion. Only the Count strikes a note of self-satisfaction as he feels that he is now on firm ground once again and has a chance to gain revenge:

son ve - nu - ti___ a ven - di - car - mi___

In the following passage his motif – ultimately Italian in origin – repeatedly cuts through the musical textures like a sharp-edged sword, interrupting all attempts to prevent the new arrivals from getting a word in edgeways:

o - là, si - len - zio, si - len - zio, si - len - zio!

On the first occasion, flute and clarinet clearly indicate the Count's secret delight at his office as judge. Marcellina, Bartolo and Basilio explain the matter in a way that reflects their own characters, in other words, bawling out their concerns in a vulgarly triumphalistic manner that quickly turns into rapid patter. Again the events on stage unfold with perfect musical symmetry. The più moto describes the way in which this latest turn of events affects all the parties concerned. They now align themselves in two opposing groups, with Figaro's faction subdivided into Figaro himself, who remains relatively calm, and the two far more agitated womenfolk, while Marcellina's more compact group soon has the satisfaction of welcoming the Count into their midst. The latter, urged on by his darker emotions, forgets all social considerations and throws in his lot with these commoners. What is particularly original about this whole passage is that Marcellina's group does not burst into a shriek of triumphant delight, as would undoubtedly have been the case with an Italian composer, but expresses its joy at the success of its coup by striking a self-confident, hypocritical note of calm that is all the more appalling in consequence. They can sit back and allow their enemies to get worked up, and, indeed, the latter are generally accompanied by the full

67. Note the key sequence in the finale as a whole: E flat major, B flat major, B flat major, G major, C major, F major, B flat major and, again, E flat major. Compare this with the course of the action on stage.

orchestra, while their own four contented faces are lit by wind harmonies alone. On one occasion the winds even reward them with a regular fanfare. But then the contrast becomes especially acute. While Figaro's faction regards the intervention of the others as the work of the devil, the latter see in it the agency of a 'nume propizio', prompting them to launch into an *a cappella* melody of almost religious solemnity,[68] which naturally discountenances the others completely ('son confusa, son stordita'). From now on, moreover, Susanna grows increasingly spirited, as is clear from her second 'son confusa' with its doggedly ascending chromatic line as her enemies come within a bar of her. Of course, her anger remains ineffectual, and at its repeat this passage is accompanied by her enemies' drumming rhythm that plainly reveals their unbridled inner delight. The clash between the two factions is repeated for a third time, with ascending scalar figures for Susanna and the Countess. Soon after this, Susanna's anger finally boils over, her *sotto voce* singing notwithstanding, finding expression in a melody that writhes wildly and confusedly to and fro, with its desperate coloratura outburst, while the Countess and Figaro submit to their fate in a spirit of resignation. By the end all three of them are like caged birds, fluttering to and fro in their impotent rage. The prestissimo brings a final sudden unison outcry of indignation, whereupon the finale ends with both factions in a state of total agitation.[70] Figaro and his allies have been defeated. It is no wonder that, in spite of the fact that the two factions are otherwise evenly balanced, Figaro's is more individually treated. It is their fate that is ultimately at stake here, it is they who in essence have brought the plot to this point, they who must now foot the bill. All their efforts and ruses have been in vain. The relationship between the Count and Countess has again been placed under strain, Susanna's happiness is under serious threat and Figaro's wedding has been placed in question at the very last moment. For his part, the Count has regained the advantage, yet he has still not succeeded in wresting the prize – Susanna – from the dangerous and rebellious Figaro. The mood of his later aria ('Vedrò, mentr'io') is already adumbrated in this finale. His position of superiority is also undermined by the fact that in order to achieve his goal he has had to consort with the plebeian faction and thus become partly dependent on them, instead of getting his way through his own strength alone, even though he is not, of course, aware of this. As far as the onlooker is concerned, the Count simply looks foolish throughout the whole of this finale, as his attempt to preserve his dignity and maintain his seriousness of purpose is constantly thwarted both by the changing situation and by the dark forces within him. Moreover, he is increasingly distracted from his original and real aim, which was to enjoy his *ius primae noctis* with Susanna before her marriage, with the first such distraction resulting from his quarrel with his wife and subsequent reconciliation, after which he has to deal with the crafty Figaro. Only when he has inflicted a serious defeat on Figaro and his fellow conspirators, which he succeeds in doing, of course, only with considerable help from the plebeian faction, is there any prospect of his returning to his former plan. Adverse conditions have kept the two of them apart throughout the finale, but now his burning desire for Susanna is once again rekindled.

With the duet ('Crudel! perchè finora') that opens act three, fortune seems to smile on the Count and to offer him an opportunity to achieve his aims straightaway. Da Ponte has skilfully transferred the ending of Beaumarchais's second act – the Countess's decision to attend the tryst in the garden dressed in Susanna's clothes – to a brief scene of *secco* recitative at the start of the third act, with the result that Susanna's role in the duet is now clearly defined. She plays with the

---

68. An echo of it may be heard in the slow introduction to the overture to Weber's *Der Freischütz.*

Count and with his emotions not merely for the Countess's benefit but also because the situation itself invites her to do so. She would not be Susanna if she did not feel a certain thrill at the Count's impassioned wooing. And she knows only too well where it is all leading, and, as always, her resolve in fending him off grows with the force of his onslaught. However flattered she may be by his attentions, she is motivated far more powerfully by the desire not simply to assert herself in the face of her principal adversary, who threatens her entire future, but to use him for her own ends. The Count's boundlessly insensible passion is brought into conflict with her own no less powerful temperament, which is so self-assured that it can meet his onslaught with total freedom and even with a superior sense of wit. In consequence she is able to defeat him while preserving her outward status as his servant, while, for his part, naked human instinct now breaks through, triumphing over his consciousness of his aristocratic standing.[69]

Here we get to know the Count from a completely different aspect. All his overbearing insistence on his rank seems to have been forgotten. What we hear at the very beginning in his masterfully declaimed question[70] is the unadulterated voice of nature, an ardent sensual desire and the undisguised admission of the torment bound up with it. Here is one of those moments when we find ourselves very close to the world of tragedy: an Italian *contino* would hardly rise to this level of genuinely human suffering. But Susanna's evasive answer – 'Signor, la donna ognora tempo ha di dir di sì' ('My lord, a woman always needs time before she says yes') – creates a most curious impression with its chromatic shift towards C major:[71] it sounds as though she has to force herself to reach a decision. But the more compliant Susanna proves, the more insistent the Count becomes. The same agitated violin figure already winds its way around question and answer, and immediately afterwards, at his chromatic, wind-accompanied 'Verrai? Non mancherai?' ('You'll come? You won't fail me?'), his desire acquires unmistakable expression. Susanna calms him down only with difficulty, insistently repeating the same brief phrase. And now that all barriers between them have been lowered, the Count's surging passion bursts forth in all its force in A major. There are few melodies in the opera as luxuriantly sensuous as 'mi sento di contento',[72] and yet even here there is a *galant* streak. Susanna is momentarily at a loss, and her 'scusatemi se mento' ('Forgive my deception') sounds somewhat anxious and apprehensive, so that only at the Count's whispered 'Dunque in giardin verrai?' ('So I'll see you in the garden')[73] does she finally strike the same note. Yet only a moment later, of course, she is so confused by his increasingly urgent questions that she answers 'yes' instead of 'no' and vice versa, a reaction that is undoubtedly more than a simple *opera buffa* joke. Note the mischievous expression of delight that she feels at this game. By the end it

69. According to Holmes, *Life of Mozart*, 269, Mozart wrote this second-act finale in the space of two nights and a day, without interruption: 'In the course of the second night he was seized with an illness which compelled him to stop; but there remained a few pages only of the last piece to instrument.' Presumably this was again the definitive fair copy.

70. Mozart is fond of using the key of A minor in these tense situations; see above.

71. The initial descending line in flutes and second violins sounds like the answer to the chromatically ascending line of the second violins in the fifth bar.

72. Cf. the Paisiello theme quoted on pp.311–12 above. Related to the same type of theme is the melody of one of Piccinni's arias that Mozart took over into *Mitridate*; see above.

73. In act two, scene one of Piccinni's *L'Origille* of 1760, we find:

sounds like a somewhat impatient 'Yes, of course!' By the third section of the duet she is already capable of echoing the Count's love motif,[74] and from now on the two of them are apparently of one mind.

But the Count's ecstasy is short-lived, when he discovers that Susanna has been trifling with him, and in the following aria ('Cosa sento!') Mozart conveys his change of attitude with the same intensity of expression as he had earlier lavished on his lovesick frenzy. The two psychological portraits provided by the duet and by the aria are closely connected on an internal level, inasmuch as both finally unmask the Count, allowing us to see behind the social being the true face of a hot-blooded human being. Common to both is the way in which a basic human instinct – passion – is unleashed, except that, as a result of the intervening events, it is now forced in a different direction. The psychological process has been accurately grasped by Mozart: disappointment in love automatically revives the Count's feelings of virile self-confidence, which now erupt with the same unbridled force. What matters in this atmospheric portrait is not his rekindled sense of honour as a gentleman but the wounded pride of a man whose most basic feelings have been violated. As a result, his consciousness of his own status surfaces here, and the thought that it is his social inferior to whom he owes this defeat merely serves to twist the knife in his heart, but ultimately it is a far deeper and far truer emotion, because it is an aspect of our universal fate as human beings, before which all references to a particular period pale into insignificance. It is at this point that the character of the Count finally loses all last remaining vestiges of his *buffa* prototype and – as already suggested in the duet – enters the world of tragedy. Here in the world of comic opera Mozart achieved something that he had failed to achieve in his serious operas, where he was unable to break free from convention: here he found a new and genuine note suitable for high emotion. It is no accident that the aria is preceded by the first accompanied recitative of the whole opera. It expresses the bewilderment of a man brought down to earth with a bang. The constant sudden changes of tempo and tonality might recall the turbulent manner of the composer's early operas, were it not that on this occasion these changes reflect the character's inner life, rather than being the product of a teeming and purely musical imagination, as they had been before. In this context it is significant that we are immediately drawn into the sharp tonalities of E major and F sharp minor, two keys associated with burning emotions. There follows a brief moment of contemplation, a mocking sidelong glance at old Antonio, after which comes the volcanic outburst of the aria with a powerfully descending scale in the full orchestra, answered by a curiously austere passage in the winds involving tied and dotted notes and a defiant trill in the strings. The image is that of a husband determinedly drawing himself up to his full height at the expense of his rival. In both cases the *galant* undertone is impossible to overhear. There now follows one of the most inspired passages in the aria. At the words 'Vedrò per man d'amore' it is clear from the mocking trills that the Count attempts to see this affair from its contemptible side, but this idea in turn reminds him of his anguish at his lost happiness. (Listen in particular to the winds at the words 'chi in me destò un affetto'.[75]) Immediately afterwards he breaks down in utter anguish to the same words that had found such heroic expression at the beginning:

74. There is something especially piquant about the wind accompaniment here: the Count's entry is accompanied by flutes, Susanna's by bassoons.
75. The melodic writing for the voice bears an unconscious resemblance to the beginning of the duet, a resemblance that extends even to the key of A minor.

This outpouring of pain proves beyond doubt that the Count's love of Susanna is no mere trifle but genuine passion, and no less genuine is the anxious echo with its oppressive wind chords. But this painful rêverie comes to an abrupt end with a passage that significantly looks forward to a similar one in the 'Jupiter' symphony, with its impressive timpani roll. At this point there is a change of tempo and, with the second section of the aria, the Count's wounded pride is transformed into a burning desire for vengeance. It is clear from the sudden change in dynamics that the savagery of his outburst acquires a literally demonic expression – nothing that this character says and does is ever less than wholehearted. What sinister contempt lies in the urgency of 'per dare a me tormento' ('to cause me torment'), at the end of which a flame appears to dart upwards! Yet even here the Count's aristocratic defiance repeatedly comes to the surface ('Ah, no! Lasciarti in pace'). This section consists of two repeated subsections, at the end of the second of which the Count's wild fury erupts in a dazzling coloratura flourish on the word 'giubilar' (this passage was a later addition),[76] summing up the whole demonic nature of the character and the situation in which he finds himself.

In Beaumarchais's original there follows an elaborate trial scene, but this has been reduced to a single-sentence verdict pronounced by the stuttering judge Don Curzio, 'E decisa la lite: o pagarla o sposarla' ('The case is decided: pay up or marry her').[77] Figaro now turns out to be the stolen child of Bartolo and Marcellina – a revelation that was one of the hoarier elements of spoken and sung comedy at this time. But this means that the Count can no longer prevent Figaro from marrying Susanna. Equally, neither Susanna nor the Countess has any reason any longer to go through with their scheme to invite the Count to the garden. That they none the less do so is inadequately motivated. Although Da Ponte attempts to use Cherubino to deflect the Count's anger on to the Countess and thereby to motivate the new intrigue, we have virtually lost sight of the page as a result of all the other and more important new developments, quite apart from the fact that the Countess has already cleared herself of any suspicion that she has been conducting an affair with Cherubino and will be just as capable of reaffirming her innocence on any subsequent occasion, not least because nothing has happened in the meantime to justify the Count's suspicions. And Barbarina's new attempt to disguise Cherubino creates a rather feeble impression. Until now the whole plot had revolved around Figaro's wedding and the Count's attempts to thwart it by enforcing his rights as lord of the manor. Now the main focus of the action shifts to the reconciliation of the Count and Countess. But this shift of emphasis is far too weakly motivated and there

---

76. See above; Bulthaupt, *Dramaturgie der Oper*, 142, has completely misunderstood this coloratura outburst.
77. As a solution, Gerhäuser, *Stuttgarter Bühnenkunst*, 314, suggests that during the trial scene, Susanna should arrive with the 1000 thalers and announce that the Countess has given her the money in order to redeem Figaro's promise, thus rekindling the Count's feelings of anger against his wife and in that way remotivating her plot to catch him out. On a superficial level, this certainly offers a better solution to the problem, even though it still leaves many questions unanswered.

is no doubt that in the course of this third act the listener's interest in the action begins to flag, even though the tension is maintained on a superficial level by the brilliant wedding procession. The fourth act seems no more than an intermezzo tacked on to the end of the work, and it is no accident that it is precisely here that we find most of the stopgap arias.

For the present, Mozart allows the recognition scene between Figaro and his parents to climax in the sextet ('Riconosci in questo amplesso'), a number which, according to Michael Kelly,[78] was the most popular piece in the entire opera. As an ensemble,[79] it is very similar to the quartet from *Die Entführung aus dem Serail* ('Ach! Belmonte! Ach, mein Leben!'), containing, as it does, a brief and simple self-contained action: harmony, discord and reconciliation. As such, it contrasts well with the almost tragic tone of what comes before and afterwards: the world in which we find ourselves here is the everyday world of decent middle-class folk, people who until now have appeared as self-important, insolent and even malicious philistines but who, now that there is no longer any reason for them to flex their muscles, reveal a far more sympathetic side of their characters. The mood initially is one of a homely but good-natured sincerity for which the Count, with his dogged anger, is no match, and, however comical the situation, it is impossible not to be moved by the happiness felt by Figaro's parents:

Fi - glio a - ma - to!

At this point Susanna arrives with the money that is needed to pay off Marcellina but its origins, of course, remain obscure. We hear a contented chuckle in the orchestra. Figaro's parents refuse to allow their happiness to be disturbed, but the Count and his stooge Don Curzio draw Susanne's attention to the situation, causing her feelings to flare up as of old: note the sudden tremolando and minor-key harmonies. But the orchestra is in too good a mood to sustain this over-emotional tone for long and it ignores the box on the ears that Figaro gives Susanna. Once again the musician retires behind the singers and performers, and it is significant that the two characters who are the most highly strung, Susanna and the Count, involuntarily find themselves singing the same sharply dotted melodic line in spite of the fact that they are worked up for totally different reasons. There is considerable tension in the vocal lines, whereas the orchestra continues to strike a note of carefree charm, chuckling contentedly as it leads us back to the beginning and takes up the melody with which Marcellina had first greeted her son. Now she explains that she is his mother. There is something both amusing and true to life about the way in whic Susanna, surprised, asks each of the others in turn whether the news is true. Figaro's answer – 'e quello è mio padro che a te lo dirà' ('And this is my father, who'll tell you it's true') – is entirely in the spirit of an *opera buffa*. After dealing with this final obstacle to their happiness, the more unassuming characters celebrate their good fortune, and Susanna, who had earlier been leading the Count by the nose, takes control with a melody that expresses the general feeling of happiness in a way that is both spirited and charming.[80] The 'sotto voce' here is entirely typical of Mozart, who at moments of such sudden

78. Kelly, *Reminiscences*, i.260.
79. The roles of Basilio and Curzio, on the one hand, and Bartolo and Antonio, on the other, were doubled by the same singer, with the result that Curzio is not mentioned in the autograph score at this point. But, as we know from Kelly's reminiscences (i.260–1), Curzio took part in the sextet, so that Otto Jahn's suggestion that he be deleted as a 'musical pleonasm' or replaced by Basilio is completely unjustified; see Jahn, *W. A. Mozart*, ii.326.
80. Susanna's melody ('Al dolce contento') was originally accompanied by flute and bassoon, but these were later struck out; see p.81 of the critical commentary.

emotion invariably prefers tranquil introspective joy to raucous effusions. *Forte* outbursts are reserved for the two characters who are excluded from this happiness, the Count, who has difficulty controlling his anger at the failure of his plans, and his minion Don Curzio, who, after recovering from his initial embarrassment, adds his voice to that of his lord and master. Here, too, the contrasts are brought into sharp and immediate focus. While the others, to the accompaniment of the winds, express their delight in the following contented and quintessentially Mozartian motif

the other two keep interrupting them with a brusque string unison,[81] finally joining forces for a countermelody in octaves. Curzio simply parrots his master's outburst of anger in a higher register, without having any real idea of what it is all about. As a result, the Count once again has an unvoluntary joker beside him, but fails to notice him. He has no luck with his partners in crime as all of them are far too prone to make him look a fool. But nothing can destroy the family idyll and so the sextet ends with the liveliest contrast between the most disparate characters. In spite of Mozart's instructions to the contrary, Kelly even managed to stutter while singing, convincing the composer to allow him to keep the stutter by the way in which he achieved this.[82] This may be possible in the case of a particularly gifted performer who remains sufficiently discreet, but modern performers are right not to emulate him. There is a delightful echo of the sextet in the following recitative, when the four characters are left alone together and are accompanied by only the harpsichord: 'E schiatti il signor conte al gusto mio' ('And may the Count explode with anger at my happiness').

With the Countess's recitative and aria ('E Susanna non vien!-Dove sono I bei momenti') the music turns its back on this bourgeois still life, and although the situation is totally different from that in which the Count found himself in his aria ('Cosa sento!'), the two scenes do none the less have a number of points in common.[83] Both present their characters at important turning points in their lives and avail themselves of the old Italian form in such a way that the recitative depicts the impulse that arises out of the situation, while the aria takes the individual emotions aroused in this way and turns them into a complete psychological portrait of a profoundly lyrical kind. The Countess is overcome by fear and anxiety at the thought of the hazardous step that she is planning to take in order to win back her husband's love, hence the recitative's constant vacillation between hesitation and the wish to press on, a wish expressed by an agitated motif found elsewhere in Mozart's works and ultimately Italian in origin:[84]

---

81. Susanna answers with a passage behind whose melismatic writing her old Paisiello motif can be glimpsed; see above.
82. Kelly, *Reminiscences*, i.260.
83. There is even a textual parallel: just as the Count complains at having to yield to a social inferior, so the Countess laments the fact that she is reduced to seeking help from her chambermaid: 'Fammi or cercar da una mia serva aita'. In both cases, therefore, aristocratic feelings are roused.
84. It also appears at the end of the Count's recitative.

The recitative ends with an anxious question that is the helpless expression of a heart weighed down with unhappiness. There is great psychological subtlety, therefore, to the way in which the aria begins by recalling a happier past. The main melody of the andantino[85] steals through the Countess's soul like the sweetest of dreams, a dream delicately sustained by the wind instruments during breaks in the vocal line and moving to a full close in C major without modulating to any other key. At this point a sweet-toned figure appears in the winds, its purpose being to awaken the Countess's anguish at her loss, and with the modulation to G minor we find the voice entering into a veritable dialogue with the winds, before inveighing against fate in tones that are all the more moving for being so subdued. But memory retains the upper hand, ushering in a return to the opening section. The voice is then cut short at the thought of the Count's 'deceiving lips', at which point a sudden breath of air passes through the Countess's soul and, with the following allegro, her hopes are rekindled. The second section of the aria is clear proof of the psychological resolve that lies dormant in the Countess's heart, in spite of her emotional tenderness. On a formal level, too, this section is exceptional in that it modulates only briefly at the words 'nel languire amando ognor' ('always yearning lovingly for him'). But the modulation – from C major to C minor – is all the more effective as a result, with the melodic line freely following the text and with only the actual thought of hope

mi por - tas - se u - na   spe - ran - za

repeatedly rising up from the waves of the Countess's agitation, its final motif ascending higher and higher in this inspired dialogue between voice and winds, only for it to be followed at once by the breath of barely perceptible anguish that repeatedly casts its shadows over this section, too. In general, however, the mood remains bright-toned, most obviously following the full orchestra's *forte* entry, with its brief and mischievous consequent phrase in the winds. Here we find something of the spirit of the earlier Rosine, coquettishly playing with her fan and delighting in a risqué intrigue. In turn this forges a link with the following 'letter duet' ('Sull'aria').

The 'letter duet' deals with an idea very popular in Italian and French comic operas.[86] It is clear from the sketches[87] that Mozart only gradually discovered its definitive form. Indeed, it appears that there were originally two duets at this point, the first of which was later abandoned. This suggestion is supported by the older and more impassioned ending of the recitative, where the Countess asks 'sei per tradirmi tu d'accordo ancora?', words that were later deleted, as was the note 'dopo il Duettino' before an alternative version of the ending of the recitative.[88] Ultimately, Beaumarchais's version carried the day. The custom alluded to here by Beaumarchais is authentically French: we are dealing with a new text (in this case a 'canzonetta') to be sung to an existing melody. Here, of course, the existing melody has been invented by Mozart himself. The libretto gives only the beginning: the Count will know the rest. The opening is in fact markedly

85. This melody is already prefigured in the 'Agnus Dei' of the C major mass K317 of 1779.
86. See act three, scene three of Antonio Palomba's *Il finto turco*, which was set by Gioacchino Cocchi and first heard at the Teatro dei Fiorentini in Naples in 1753. ◆ In fact, this was a revised version of the work first performed at the same theatre in 1749.
87. ◆ See NMA II/15/16/2, 638–41 and X/30/3.
88. On all these versions, see the critical report to NMA II/15/16.

Rococo-like in tone, and the music soon takes up the image of the 'soavi zeffiretti' in the violins.[89] But the grove of pine trees swayed by the breeze is more than a mere background: in the increasingly closely intertwined voices of these two daughters of Eve dwell all the secret spirits of seduction that inhabit this evening scene. There is something inexpressibly delightful about the way in which the senses of these two women are stirred at the idea of this seductive setting. One might almost imagine a host of Cupids watching over this dictation with their winsome smiles. The melodic writing is entirely characteristic, proceeding, as it does, not stepwise but for the most part in broken chords (even more so in the second section than the first), increasingly avoiding popular sighlike suspensions in favour of the notes of the natural scale.[90] Here Mozart revels in this kind of melodic writing, with its constant rocking to and fro on broken chord harmonies, thereby determining the whole character of the piece, which suggests not sentimentality but naïve and even mischievous charm. The harmonic writing, too, is completely unproblematic: the first section modulates on one occasion to the dominant, the second section not at all. There is something extremely ingenious in the way in which the simple binary form with its brief coda is placed in the service of the situation on stage, with the opening section including actual dictation, so that there are long gaps between the entries of the two voices. Mozart was right to avoid giving the same melody to both singers, delaying this device – to wholly delightful effect – until the words 'Certo, certo il capirà', after which the two voices combine in charming high spirits. In the second section, as they read through the letter, the entries are closer together, with the melodic phrases of the first section now freely developed. The women's delight in what they have written becomes increasingly clear, finally finding release in a brief coloratura passage, after which they give each other an understanding nod of agreement in the coda, with which the duet comes to an end. The winds are used with particular intelligence here: they enter as soon as Susanna starts writing[91] and break off when the Countess resumes her dictation. Even so, they always complete the Countess's melodies, turning them into a full period,[92] while Susanna breaks in with brief phrases of a generally cadential nature. The inner process continues, entirely logically, as anyone dictating a letter generally tends to think most about its contents at the very moments when he or she has stopped dictating. The winds are less prominent when the letter is reread.[93]

The chorus of peasant girls ('Ricevete, o padroncina') closely resembles the other rustic numbers ('Giovani lieti' and 'Signori di fuori') in terms of its pastoral charm, the chief difference being that

89. The violins are almost always in unison. In much the same way the violas double the basses, so that the string writing is in two parts, thereby reflecting the character of a canzonetta; see also the discussion of Cherubino's canzona above.
90. The only exception is the Countess's words 'sotto i pini del boschetto' ('beneath the pines in the grove').
91. Note the attractive way in which Susanna first asks 'sotto i pini?' ('beneath the pines?'), then, reassured, repeats it.
92. Only right at the beginning do they have the same melody as the voice, but here we are dealing with the heading to the whole piece, which is underscored in this way.
93. The final fermata demands a brief melisma in the voices, perhaps as follows:

molto rit.
il ca - pi - ra

the tone is now somewhat more courteous and feminine. The folklike thirds and sixths in the voices that are found from start to finish create a particularly felicitous impression. The finale ('Ecco la marcia, andiamo!') now begins with a distant march, its distance suggested not only by the *pianissimo* marking but also by the fact that the other instruments enter gradually, rising to a *forte* climax. Above all, however, the initial sense of distance is established by dint of the fact that the march enters *in medias res*, with its second section, even omitting its upbeat.[94] In spite of the celebratory mood, there is something boorish and surly about this march. Its rhythms are strictly maintained, and at the end of every colon it moves inexorably towards the same rhythmic cadence ♩♩│♩.

In the first subject there is a certain obstinacy to the fact that the minim is generally *g″*. The rhythmic structure, too, departs from the norm inasmuch as the main section (beginning with bar 14) starts with two regular four-bar periods, only to be followed – at the modulation to A minor – by two three-bar periods. The same is true of the second section. These three-bar minor-key periods have something doggedly determined about them, not least as a result of the fact that we find in the winds the same astringent mordents that we already encountered accompanying Osmin. The voices declaim their parts with total freedom until the procession is properly formed.

Equally French in inspiration is the following ternary duet with chorus which, simple and song-like in character, is in marked contrast to the march. Particularly attractive here is the sense of jubilation in the orchestra when the two young women sing of the Count's decision to abandon his *droit de seigneur*. Note the oboe trills. In terms of its overall character, this brief chorus already anticipates similar numbers from *Die Zauberflöte*. The following dance is the only example of Spanish local colour in the entire opera. It derives from what was originally an Andalusian fandango melody[95] that must have been familiar in Vienna as early as 1760 as Gluck uses it in his ballet *Don Juan* of 1761 (no. 19: it, too, is in A minor). Mozart's use of it shows total freedom, with the bass and middle voices in particular freed from their stereotypical role of supporting and accompanying the main melody. The whole orchestra is caught up in the sense of movement, and, as before, the writing for the winds is particularly inspired. In turn, we find them joining in with the others, picking up only individual cues and adding their own independent sighs that time and again cast a melancholy sheen over this section as a whole. Take the following passage, for example:[96]

Everything is more subtly and individually nuanced. During this section, too, the characters continue to declaim the text as though in passing, the Count with fractious nonchalance, Figaro with some agitation. After a brief accompanied recitative for the Count, in which he reassumes his role as lord of the manor, the earlier duet is repeated, now with the full chorus, bringing the act to a brilliant conclusion.[97]

94. On the second march from *Idomeneo*, which is related to the present example, see above.
95. See Dohrn, *Neue Zeitschrift für Musik*, xi (1844), 168.
96. On the second occasion, the sigh motif appears in the bassoon as the Count pricks his finger with the pin.
97. ◆ Although it was not a concern for Abert, later writers – in particular Robert Moberly and Christopher Raeburn ('Mozart's "Figaro": The Plan of Act III') – have questioned the ordering of the action in the third act, noting in particular the brevity of the trial, Antonio's speedy discovery (by scene nine) of the plot, Susanna's delay in telling the Countess about Figaro's parents

Barbarina's cavatina ('L'ho perduta')[98] at the beginning of act four is a veritable masterpiece culled from real life. Who has not seen a terrified child, sobbing quietly to itself and searching for some object or other that it has lost in the street? In much the same way, Barbarina wanders around at dead of night with her lantern, inducing in us that frame of mind which, with its mixture of cheerfulness and emotion, grown-ups tend to feel when children are confronted by just such catastrophes as this. With its sombre F minor and sighing melodic line, the orchestra takes the case entirely seriously, while avoiding any more violent emotions, and the vocal line, too, is limited to a heart-rending sobbing and whimpering, with a fewer deeper sighs, but no violent outbursts. The piece suddenly breaks off completely unexpectedly on the dominant. Numbers such as this reveal how much Mozart had learnt from Piccinni, whose particular strength was very much this type of scene, with its depiction of childlike anguish.[99]

Beginning with Marcellina's aria ('Il capro e la capretta'), we find a whole series of stopgap arias intended to disguise the fact that the plot has ground to a halt. Here Da Ponte has drawn with particular enthusiasm on the stock-in-trade of some of the oldest types of *opera buffa*, attacking now men, now women, and interpolating between these two a narrative aria based on French models. And we can see at once that, as the dramatic momentum flags, so too does Mozart's interest. The music that he contributes here is pleasant and even witty, but it is most emphatically not dramatic. Of what concern to him here were Marcellina and Basilio and their Enlightenment sermons padded out with popular similes? As a result he approached these numbers as professional obligations, writing the inevitable arias for the singers, but not arias suitable for his musical comedy. Marcellina's aria is completely unrelated to her characterization elsewhere in the opera. How is it, after all, that she has suddenly acquired a penchant for coloratura? There is, however, one element of mischievous humour in her aria, namely, in the minuet-like strains to which the animals enter in its opening section: it is they who are the real gentlemen, they who know how to behave towards women. Humans have no such sensitivities. Here is a regular *opera buffa* aria in the usual two sections. Musically, too, it includes a number of authentically Mozartian features such as the allegro's syncopated main theme. But there is no trace whatsoever of any dramatic depth. The same is true of Basilio's aria ('In quegl' anni, in cui val poco'), in spite of its far more ambitious musical trimmings. Although Basilio remains in character here (in the opening act he had already appeared as a common hypocrite), it was certainly untypical of Mozart to lavish an elaborate character sketch on him at this point in the opera: after all, Mozart normally introduced his arias at points of high dramatic tension. As a result, the present aria appears in something of a vacuum. Nor is it any accident that Mozart pays a greater tribute here to *italianità* and tone-painting than anywhere else in the opera. The opening section could easily have been written by Paisiello, its only Mozartian elements being, at best, the tension-laden introduction of the adventurer with his ass's skin and the insistent emphasis on the 'somaro'. Melodically speaking, the slow tempo di menuetto and the following brief *tempesta* likewise stick to the beaten track. Conversely, the description of the adventurer donning his ass's skin (in G minor) and the approach of the wild animal with its terrifying chromatic roar is delightfully vivid.[100] Although the third section – an

---

(although she resolves to do so at the end of scene six, she does so only in scene ten) and of her meeting with the Count in scene two (by scene eight Susanna had not yet been to see the Countess), and the back-to-back arias for the Countess, 'Dove sono i bei momenti' and 'Che soave zeffiretto'. Yet while it is possible to reorder the action and remove many of these difficulties, the structure of the autograph score precludes the possibility that there was a late change due to problems of casting; see Tyson, '*Le nozze di Figaro*: Lessons from the Autograph Score'.

98. In Beaumarchais, the character in question is Fanchette.

99. Even the main theme and its tonality are Piccinnian in character; see above.

100. There is something particularly amusing about the way in which the beast clears off again in its contempt.

allegro – begins by striking a typically Italianate note, it is also the only section to include any trace of Mozart's characteristic sense of humour. At the words 'onte, pericoli, vergogna e morte' ('insults, dangers, shame and death'), the whole orchestra suddenly launches a terrible onslaught from which there seems to be no escape. But at the words 'col cuoio d'asino fuggir si può' ('can escape under an ass's skin'), Basilio – who looks at honour from a Falstaffian standpoint – succeeds in getting out of danger with a cheekily mischievous tune, with the orchestra then mockingly calling after him and repeating the whole of the heroic melody. There is no denying the fact that the aria constitutes an apt character sketch of Basilio, but it is dramatically superfluous at this point in the opera and, as a result, it holds up the action.

Only with Figaro's *scena* ('Tutto è disposto') do we pick up the threads of the plot once again. He, too, is honoured with an accompanied recitative, as also is Susanna in the following scene. This was not an easy challenge for poet and composer to meet. In Beaumarchais's original, we find the hero's famous monologue at this point, a monologue which, drawing on its author's own experience, holds up a mirror to the political world of the times and which had ultimately persuaded Louis XVI to ban the entire play. Da Ponte was in his element, of course, with *opera buffa* and, with the world of politics closed to him, he fell back on a tried and tested type of aria about women and their ways, but in the process he placed his composer in an undeniably difficult situation, as the *buffa* style on which such an aria would inevitably be based brought with it the danger that Figaro would be dragged down to the level of an *opera buffa* character at the very moment when the outward situation induces doubts in the one thing that he prizes above all else, Susanna's love. Mozart adopted an entirely serious approach to the recitative, in which Figaro expresses his anguish and indignation: note, in particular, the affecting little motifs at the end, when he praises his precious Susanna. And the aria, too, goes its own way, in spite of its *buffa* character. This is something that can be appreciated only by those listeners who are familiar with the brilliant pyrotechnics unleashed by the Italian composers of the period as soon as this subject is raised. Here Mozart recalls the Figaro of the first two scenes of the opera, the phlegmatic lad who, his good humour notwithstanding, retains a goodly measure of pessimism. Until now he has successfully and unhesitatingly played all the parts required of him by fate, but now he has the hardest and most ungrateful role: 'il scimunito mestiere di marito' ('the foolish art of being a husband'). For all the anguish that he feels, he is well aware of the ridiculousness of the situation in which he finds himself, hence the remarkable mixture of seriousness and humour – a sullen gallows humour – unknown to the Italians. Of course, the fact that he directs his inflammatory remarks about faithless women to the audience[101] strikes us nowadays as cold and old-fashioned, but Enlightenment poets were fond of expressing their feelings in the form of such wise saws, which were designed to be instructive or entertaining or both. It was not their intention to stir the audience to the very roots of their being. If there is any sense of individuality to this number, it stems entirely from Mozart's music. Even the performance marking, 'moderato', is strikingly un-Italian and already gives notice of the fact that we are not dealing here with one of the usual Italian *scherzi*. And the opening underscores this fact: with its sforzatos and heavy chords in the winds, it suggests palpable psychological pressure. Anyone who begins by striking such a note of resignation must already have gained a thorough understanding of women. Yet there is something almost frightening about the unexpected sense of revolt at the end of the main theme:[102]

---

101. This was an old *buffa* practice; see above.
102. Cf. the opening of the string quartet in E flat major K428.

The second subject in B flat major begins with a genuinely Mozartian dynamic contrast between *forte* and *piano,* and it, too, conceals within it a certain dogged anger, as is clear from the wide-ranging intervals in the vocal line over a pedal point in the orchestra, which depicts the ways in which men's senses are gradually fired. Note the havoc caused by these wicked sirens in the second violins and, hence, on the wits of poor men. Figaro describes all this, not as a joke, but with the grim humour of the most closely involved of all the participants, and his sarcasm grows in intensity, the more worked up he becomes. This explains why he moves closer and closer to the language of *opera buffa,* without, however, abandoning his underlying surliness. Certain phrases are typically repeated:

In a different form this phrase plays an important part in the second section of the aria. Following the passage 'che allettano per trarci le piume', with its keen and sullen thirds, we find the quotation from Paisiello, to whom Figaro now appeals for help in formulating his vow. And finally, via a series of rapid triplets and a large-scale crescendo, we approach the main sentiment of the aria: 'non senton pietà' ('they feel no pity'). Almost at once the underlying emotion changes ('il resto non dico'), and with the *d* flat on the diminished chord, Figaro appears overwhelmed by his whole sense of grief, followed by a suspicious stirring in the horns. This second section reuses the motivic material from the first, but adapts and combines it in remarkable ways. At 'son streghe che incantano' the dotted thirds appear to be on the point of beginning all over again, when suddenly he is seized by the thought of something too terrible to express ('il resto non dico'), and these words now attach themselves to his invective against women, where they are sung to the rhythm of the above-cited motif, so much so, indeed, that Figaro can no longer break free from them. There is something particularly vivid about the change of register in the vocal line and the concertante dialogue between strings and winds in the orchestra. It requires the Paisiello motif to tear Figaro away from this obsessive preoccupation with the same idea and allow the musical argument to develop along regular lines. In the coda the horns suddenly blare out, disastrously reminding us of the 'resto' that Figaro has consistently refused to spell out, a particularly vivid use of instrumental symbolism that Mozart himself appears to have devised. As a result of this muted *buffa* style, Figaro remains true to character even in this critical situation. Unlike his French prototype and in spite of his cunning, he remains a human being who is not always capable of dealing with life's problems, which occasionally involve him in a great deal of suffering. Mozart handles all this with his customary irony, sympathizing with his hero's anguish, while also finding it amusing. In this, the audience is particularly happy to agree with him, as we know from Susanna's plans that Figaro is unnecessarily worked up.[103]

There is a clear link between this scene and the following one and Susanna's aria 'Deh vieni'. Taken together, they develop the relationship between the two lovers that was already made clear in the first two scenes of the opera and that is now taken a logical stage further. From the outset, Figaro has been

103.   ◆ Further, see Rabin, 'Figaro as misogynist: on aria types and aria rhetoric'.

portrayed as the weaker of the two, not least where his jealousy is concerned, and this has now forced him into a position that induces a feeling of self-contempt and from which he can find no escape. As Figaro sinks deeper into self-loathing, so Susanna continues to rise above the situation, a superiority already found in the opening duets. Her love of Figaro is genuine, but precisely because of this she feels obliged to bring home to him her superiority whenever he feels these unjustified outbursts of jealousy. In keeping with her character, she does so not by expressing any over-emotional moral indignation but with a candid humour that allows her true thoughts to be heard behind the mask that she has assumed – if only Figaro would listen. The same is true in the present case. It is no accident that the Paisiello motif that we encountered in the opening scene of the opera and that we repeatedly hear on her lips – and on her lips alone – in the course of the opera now becomes the aria's main musical symbol, dominating the scene as a whole and adorned with all the delights of Mozart's musicianship. Nor can it be mere chance that Susanna reveals her own feelings here, rather than playing the part of the Countess, for all that she is dressed as the latter.[104] Her aria is an indirect reply to Figaro's earlier outpouring. In the darkness he will presumably not be able to see her disguise, but he must be able to recognize the voice with which she tells the night of her longing for her lover. Initially, of course, he will think that she is addressing the hated Count, as Susanna knows very well, hence her decision to test him and see whether, in his jealousy, he can still understand the true language of her heart.[105] As always, she feels fully equal to the situation and can therefore be uninhibited in revealing her whole nature. But Figaro is so blinded by his jealousy that he fails to understand her singing, even though it is directed at him, and all he hears is the seductive call to the Count.[106] As a result, a miniature tragedy is played out in Figaro's place of hiding during the aria. Its consequences will become clear in the fourth-act finale.

Susanna's aria marks the *ne plus ultra* of her characterization, revealing not only her powerful, sensual – sensual not merely in the erotic sense – temperament which, as a result of her unusual mental resolve, prevents her from simply being dominated by her physical urges, but also an inner freedom that is capable of combining seriousness of purpose and playfulness with an outstanding sense of humour. And there is something particularly beautiful and true to life about the way in which the *genius loci* succeeds in coaxing from her this innermost kernel of her being. As such, the aria is clear proof of Mozart's ability at high points in his works to transcend the barriers imposed on his age's feeling for nature. Once again the text is an example of Rococo poetry pure and simple, with its meticulously detailed tone-painting of all the individual features that make up the landscape – the stream, the caressing breeze, the smiling flowers and so on. It is clear, therefore, that the librettists of the time still felt close to nature, even if we can hear little more than a formulaic echo of the lofty poetry of the earlier period. There is now a rather greater concentration than before on concepts and individual observations, in other words, on conceptualized expressions of emotion, rather than on emotion itself. But this emotion may be heard in Mozart's music. An Italian composer would have highlighted all these features – the stream, the breeze and so on – with coloratura flourishes or at least with brief painterly descriptions in the winds, but Mozart merely

104. In his *Geschichte der Oper*, 242, Kretzschmar interprets the beginning and the whole of the opening section as a parody that is intentionally threadbare and banal in terms of its expression. Only in the second section, argues Kretzschmar, does Mozart step out of character and take the situation seriously. Kretzschmar is guilty not only of imputing more to the aria than it actually contains but of misinterpreting the significance of the opening theme. Schurig, too, goes too far in claiming that in assuming the Countess's clothes, Susanna has also assumed her mistress's mood of infatuation; see Schurig, *Mozart*, ii.88.
105. This emerges from her words in her recitative: 'Il birbo è in sentinella. Divertiamci anche noi, diamogli la mercè de dubbi suoi' ('The rascal's watching. So we, too, shall have some fun. We'll reward him for his doubts').
106. Cf. Figaro's words at the start of the following scene: 'Perfida! e in quella forma meco mentia' (The traitress! This is how she was deceiving me!).

hints at them: for him, neither night nor the countryside is a fixed and conventional backdrop any longer, but both have assumed a particular function, having been drawn into Susanna's world of yearning and thereby become part of her emotional agitation. It is sufficient to compare this aria with one of the popular simile arias based on idyllic natural themes to appreciate that we are not dealing here with a showpiece of painterly illusion but with a genre painting in which emotion and landscape are in perfect accord. The only element that Mozart has borrowed from the stock-in-trade of his age is the idea of a serenade, with its siciliana rhythm and pizzicato accompaniment in the strings. This is bound up with the whole way in which music was cultivated at this time, with its countless serenades, divertimentos and so on that were sung and played in the evening. Behind the aria lies the idea – familiar to every member of Mozart's audience – that by singing the serenade the singer hopes that her lover will grant her secret wishes. This is the only concession that Susanna makes to the fact that she is disguised as the Countess. Otherwise, the spell cast by the garden at night lifts her out of herself, allowing her longing to pour out in music of such emotional truth that the listener has the impression that the music no longer depicts her longing but has become that longing, a desire that seeks sensual fulfilment, not in the Beethovenian sense of a yearning impulse to soar aloft to inaccessible heights, but in a genuinely Mozartian spirit.

That Mozart laid particular emphasis on this aria is clear from the sketches and, more especially, from the numerous attempts that he made to draft its ending.[107] Nor is its structure as straightforward as it may seem at first sight. It is in three sections (bars 1–20, 21–32 and 33–50), each of which is linked to the others only by individual phrases and reminiscences. The harmonic language is simple in the extreme, its momentum being almost imperceptible. The emphasis lies on the melodic writing, which in the first two sections advances in three-bar periods, thereby giving the impression of a restrained urgency. Only with the third section do we find four-bar periods, but almost at once these are extended and expanded. In its predilection for intervals involving broken chords the aria recalls the 'letter duet', except that on this occasion these intervals are repeatedly replaced by stepwise progressions and especially by chromatic figures. At a number of points we find a subtle use of musical symbolism, notably at the descending line on 'notturna face' ('night's torch') and 'incoronar' ('to deck'). In the first two sections, the winds, too, are content to bridge the gaps in the vocal line with brief expressive phrases. Only in the third section, where the orchestra in general assumes a heightened form of expression, do they, too, become more eloquent, preparing the way for the following 'incoronar' in the vocal line with their semiquaver figure. For its part, the voice floats down on the expanded main idea, which is now invested with its full emotional force. In general these final bars, with their constant interplay between tonic and subdominant and their fermatas, achieve a note of wonderful raptness and in that way sum up the emotional content of the aria as a whole as it dies away like a gentle breeze in the night. As usual, the previous recitative establishes the aria's mood on the basis of the situation on stage. It is motivically unified, its basic idea being an intensified version of the agitated motif that we have already encountered on frequent occasions, except that this time it ends in a mischievously scurrying passage with reversed dotting. This sideways glance is directed at Figaro, as he lies in hiding. But there is something particularly appealing about the way in which, towards the end of the recitative, Susanna gradually slips into the mood of the aria. The mocking motif disappears and, with the modulation to F major, the aria's more expressive melodic writing, with its chordal intervals, slowly asserts itself. No less significant are the burgeoning syncopations in the strings.

---

107. See NMA II/5/16/2, 638–41 and X/30/3.

Le nozze di Figaro was revived in August 1789, and Mozart took the opportunity to replace the present aria with an alternative number, 'Al desio di chi t'adora' K577, which he wrote for Adriana Ferrarese del Bene,[108] a singer whom he did not hold in particularly high regard.[109] The existing recitative was retained.[110] Here Susanna appears to assume the Countess's musical persona, as least in the first part of the aria. It is a crude masquerade and, needless to say, it destroys the subtlety of her relationship with Figaro. Moreover, the illusion is not maintained, as neither the elaborate coloratura writing nor the emotionally charged tone of the allegro reflects the Countess's character, with the result that the aria remains a foreign body, a concession to a singer to whom Mozart was not particularly close on an artistic level. One can only marvel at the fact that, superficially at least, it has turned out to be so effective. With its two large-scale sections, it recalls the arias from *Così fan tutte*, with which it also shares its brilliant wind sonorities in the form of basset-horns, bassoons and horns. The various pre-echoes of the melodic writing of *Die Zauberflöte* – a work with which *Le nozze di Figaro* otherwise has little in common – likewise reflect the fact that the present aria postdates the rest of the opera.

That Mozart had already toyed with the idea of presenting Susanna in the Countess's musical mask is clear from the sketch of an aria headed 'Scena con Rondo' that has unfortunately survived in only incomplete form.[111] The opening of the recitative is identical to that of the version familiar to us, but it later becomes somewhat more discursive and ends in B flat major. The rondo is notated on a separate sheet and breaks off after only eight bars. Only the vocal line and bass survive:

Once again it is the voice of the Countess that we can hear in this sketch.

108.   She made her Viennese début on 11 October 1788 as Diana in Martín y Soler's *L'arbore di Diana*; see *Wiener Zeitung*, lxxxviii (1788), appendix. Soon afterwards Mozart wrote the role of Fiordiligi in *Così fan tutte* for her. ◆ See Gidwitz, 'Mozart's Fiordiligi: Adriana Ferrarese del Bene'.
109.   *Briefe*, iv.83 (letter of 16 April 1789).
110.   The aria was previously ascribed to the Countess, with Leopold von Sonnleithner suggesting it as a replacement for 'Dove sono'; see 'Mozartiana III', 721–2. But a copy from Mozart's estate and a copy of the vocal score containing Mozart's own cadenza both bear the name Susanna. The autograph manuscript is no longer extant. Jahn has shown that the aria was intended for Susanna, an argument which, as we have seen, is supported by internal evidence; see Jahn, *W. A. Mozart*, ii.308. In 1789 the Countess was sung by Cavalieri, not Villeneuve: see Zinzendorf's diary for 31 August 1789, reproduced in Pohl, *Joseph Haydn*, ii.124 [*Dokumente*, 308, *Documentary Biography*, 351]: 'charmant duo entre la Cavalieri e Ferraresi.' This can refer only to the 'letter duet'. Note also the later entry of 7 May 1790, reporting on the success of the aria: 'le duo des deux femmes, le rondeau de la Ferrarese plaît toujours' [*Dokumente*, 321, *Documentary Biography*, 366]. ◆ The vocal score referred to by Abert is a professional Viennese copy of the aria that includes Mozart's autograph cadenza; it is extant in the British Library, London.
111.   The original score of the opera contains the following note at the end of the unaccompanied recitative: 'Segue Recit. istrumentato con Rondo di Susanna.' This cannot refer to 'Deh vieni' but suggests that a different aria was originally intended here. ◆ The 'Recit. istrumentato con Rondo' is 'Non tardar, amato bene'; it is published in NMA II/5/16/2, 638–41.

Another number written for Adriana Ferrarese del Bene is the arietta 'Un moto di gioia' K579,[112] although it is unclear from its vapid text precisely where it would have been inserted in the opera. Its pleasant but insignificant music likewise gives no pointers in this direction.[113] Probably it was intended to replace Susanna's aria in act two, when she helps Cherubino into his disguise.[114] If so, it would prove yet again that Mozart had little faith in La Ferrarese.[115]

The fourth-act finale ('Pian, pianin le andrò più presso') differs from its second-act predecessor by virtue of the fact that, initially at least, it deals with outer, rather than inner, events. This, after all, was the ideal to which the Italian composers of the period aspired: confusion was to reign on stage, with the development of the characters secondary in importance. Mozart, too, must have been aware that in the present case the situation and, with it, the action on stage were the decisive factor. If he wrote too much music, he would obscure the fact that this was a comedy of intrigue. But, unlike composers of so many similar pieces, he was not content to use the orchestra merely to depict the general atmosphere. Instead – and this is perhaps the most remarkable aspect of this finale – he followed the situation step by step and, with inspired succinctness, depicted its repercussions on the individual characters, without ever unduly impeding the lively pace. Here, too, the outward situation was ultimately no more than a means to an end, that end being to bring out the contrasts and interplay between the characters. The first part of the finale is a particularly fine example of this. On a formal level, it is a ternary structure, as clear as it is free, and, as such, alive to every twist and turn of the plot. Its main motif

recalls Grétry with its comic depiction of the various characters cautiously stealing in and then running for cover. But immediately afterwards there ensues a characteristic exchange between Cherubino, who again deploys all his youthful charms as a *damerino*, and the Countess, who responds with considerable acerbity: both characters emerge in all their graphic clarity, and the way in which they draw closer together is hugely effective. By the second section, however, they are no longer alone, as the other characters arrive 'da lontano' as a self-contained group. Their agitation at the events that have been taking place initially welds them together as a body, while Cherubino, brazen as usual, continues to pursue his own independent interests. But the group is forced apart by his kiss and the ensuing blow, both of which miss their mark, and there is something particularly amusing about the way in which the page is ridiculed to the same melody (the section's second subject) as the one with which he had earlier made such tender overtures to the woman he thought was Susanna. The elaborate ensemble that follows very quickly assumes the note of tension that generally distinguishes these passages in Mozart's operas from the insane tittering of the Italians. In this regard it is enough to note the modulation to the minor and the great fermata. Only Susanna soon regains her old cheerfulness.

112.   NMA II/5/16/2, 602–17; also published as a song with piano accompaniment in NMA II/5/16/2, 624–7.
113.   The words 'Le nozze di Figaro n.13 Atto 2do' have been added above it in a different hand in the full score, together with the cue 'e pur n' ho paura', which was evidently inserted later. ◆ See the critical report to NMA II/5/16.
114.   This emerges if the numbering is continuous. But if the opera were given in two acts, 'Deh vieni' would be no. 13 in the second act.
115.   *Briefe*, iv.97 (letter of 19 August 1789): 'The little aria that I've written for La Ferraresi [*sic*] ought to be a success, provided she can sing it in a naïve way, which I very much doubt.' ◆ Mozart, at least, thought enough of the aria to arrange it for keyboard; see NMA II/5/16/2, 624–7. Also see Roger Parker, 'Ersatz Ditties: Adriana Ferrarese's Susanna'.

The second section – a common-time più moto in G major – strikes the same serenely cheerful note that we have already encountered in numbers such as the first-act duet ('Se a caso madama'), as the Count now condescends to his servant both socially and musically. On this occasion, however, his declaration of love is not as ardent as before ('Crudel! Perchè finora'): Mozart shows great tact in avoiding the earlier excess and in investing this section, in which the Count's involuntary humour achieves its high point, with an essentially comic tone, quite apart from the fact that the humour is increased by the presence of both Figaro and the real Susanna. Even so, the Count's impetuosity finds clear expression here, too, notably at 'Che dita tenerelle!' Here he is overwhelmed by passion, just as he had been in the duet, and there is something almost frightening about the unison passage at 'tu sai che là per leggere io non desio d'entrar' ('you know I don't want to go in there to read'). But there is also something subtle about the Countess's reserve here, with her eloquent 'giacchè così vi piace, eccomi qui, signor' ('as you wish, here I am, my lord') sufficing to indicate the musical mask. Moreover, it does not occur to the Countess to mimic Susanna's musical style, a point that emerges with particular clarity when Susanna herself joins in. Figaro's role, meanwhile, is a source of great amusement. His motif has much in common with the grim determination of his last aria:[116]

Che com-pia-cen-te fem-mi-na! che spo-sa di buon cor!

It is he who now introduces the note of devilry into the finale, a note that recurs with the regularity of a refrain, not only lending expression to his own indignation at women's malicious ways but affecting the mood in general and unexpectedly bringing Susanna together with her furious lover. The motif's appearance in the orchestral unison towards the end, where it accompanies Figaro's intervention, is irresistibly comical: here it drives the lovers apart, modulating to G minor and preparing the way for the brief triple-time larghetto in E flat major, in which Figaro alludes to the well-known dealings between Venus, Mars and Vulcan and sings with bitter sarcasm of the couple's happiness in love. As such, this passage is a delightful parody of Johann Christian Bach's larghettos in E flat major, with their tender, magical strains. It is no accident that this is the first time that the clarinets have been used in the finale. This brief idyll thus puts an effective stop to the earlier agitation, which is then released with all the greater force in the fourth section, an Allegro molto that is motivically related to the second section and in the same key as the third: it, too, is in E flat major and 3/4-time. And, like the second section, it is cast in the form of a free rondo with recurring refrain-like episodes. It is decision time for Susanna and Figaro. As long as he still thinks that she is the Countess, the orchestra remains wedded to its urgently insistent main motif, just as Figaro remains wedded to his. The new picture confuses him completely. He remains agitated, and, indeed, his agitation is now all the greater, but it is directed elsewhere. With razorlike rhythms he ends his speech:

toc-car io vi fa-rò, toc-car io vi fa-rò.

116.　It is related to the motif quoted above, but is also clearly connected to the main orchestral motif of the following section; cf. Figaro's words 'La perfida lo seguita' towards the end of this section.

Disguised as the Countess, Susanna adopts a similar tone but forgets to disguise her voice, precipitating a delightful game between them. Figaro has recognized Susanna and now attempts to lead her by the nose in exactly the same way that she was intending to lead him. This thought brings them back together again on a musical level, too. He then begins to declare his love in an exaggeratedly rhetorical manner – he has studied his master's ways to good effect, as emerges from the passage in E flat major ('eccomi a vostri piedi'), with its seductive wind sonorities and broadly flowing, overemotional melodic writing. Susanna's suspicions are already aroused, and she itches to hit him, and Figaro's mind, too, is partly elsewhere. Both take a hold on themselves. Figaro finally gets into his stride with an eloquent coloratura flourish, causing Susanna finally to lash out and suddenly bringing us back to the beginning and its agitated tone. This in turn is followed by the melody associated with their love – a particularly subtle stroke from a psychological point of view. Even during the earlier disguise, there had already been a hint of genuine emotion. Now it breaks out all the more sincerely at the words 'O schiaffi graziosissimi' ('How sweet these blows!'), especially when Susanna herself takes up the wide-ranging triadic melody. By the end of this section, and in spite of their anger, the two of them have been reconciled, their feelings of happiness finding expression in the sincere and folklike strains of the fifth section – a B flat major andante in 6/8-time.[117] Note in particular the tenderness of Susanna's smile in the winds at 'La mia voce?' When the Count enters a moment later, he, too, is drawn into this mood of tender-hearted forgiveness, but it is not long before his domineering nature reasserts itself, encouraging the other two to continue acting out their parts in their elation. Their comedy now verges on the burlesque, notably at the words 'Madama, voi siete il ben mio' ('My lady, you are my love'), which audibly recall the Count's earlier effusions (note the parodistically skipping bassoons), and at the grotesque 'un ristoro al mio cor concedete' ('Grant some solace to my heart'). All of this, and especially their harmonious duetting at the end, is bound to drive the Count to distraction and his anger duly explodes in all its force in the Italianate triadic motifs of the finale's sixth section, a common-time allegro assai in G major. Here, too, there is no trace of caricature: the Count's passion is as genuine and true to life as ever, his anger increased by the fact that he believes himself to have been cuckolded by his own servant. The whole orchestra is now in a state of constant agitation, and at the great unison at 'il scellerato m'ha tradito' ('the villain has deceived me') it acquires an almost demonic intensity. All the greater is its impact on Basilio and his cronies. Their motif, abruptly curtailed, recalls the 'in mal punto son qui giunto' of the first-act trio and is immediately parodied by Figaro. Even the episode with Cherubino, with its delightful and authentically Mozartian little trills over sustained notes in the winds, affords little respite. The Count is more defiant than ever in resisting the united appeals of the others, finally silencing them with his sixfold 'No!' to a tremendous unison outburst. Yet this very outburst is transformed to tenderness and deep emotion by the entrance of the Countess to the sound of tender wind sonorities. Not only is the abrupt contrast typical of Mozart, so too is its concision, with not a word or a note too many. All the greater, then, is its impact on the others – significantly the dynamic marking remains *pianissimo*. The sudden entry of G minor, the unstable staccato figure in the violins, the imitative writing for voices and winds – all this not only gives dramatic support to the Countess's earlier intervention, it also prepares the way for what is to follow. The G minor section between the two sections in G major creates the

117. Of deep significance is the off-beat emphasis given to the word 'pace' when the two characters sing together (bars 289 and 291).

impression that the characters are initially incapable of feeling the ray of warming light which, exuded by the Countess, now enters their hearts. The first to open his eyes is the Count in the famous passage 'Contessa, perdono' – significantly, it was the Count who only moments earlier had defiantly rejected all pleas for mercy. Like everything else he says, this plea, too, is impulsive, genuine and heartfelt. That he has just been duped by all that has taken place is no longer of any importance. His passion has exposed him to all the depths of human emotion, at times turning him into a comic figure and at other times drawing him into the world of tragedy. It now raises him to the full height of noble humanity. What we find here is no longer a gallant plea for forgiveness on the part of a grand seigneur[118] such as would have been expressed with a smile by a *contino burlato* at the end of an *opera buffa* but an impassioned outburst of genuine human emotion. To take *Die Zauberflöte* as an analogy, Almaviva is not a count but more than that – he is a human being, and it is no accident that in the later work Mozart twice recalls the present melody at points relating to the couple's ultimate purification.[119] In the case of *Le nozze di Figaro*, it clearly harks back to the tone of the Countess's arias, with the Count submitting to the Countess not only morally but musically, too. She has now achieved her highest goal and so the continuation of the melodic line flows from her soul as though of its own accord. And there is something particularly beautiful and affecting about the way in which this melody is taken up in a typically Mozartian *sotto voce* by the entire ensemble, creating another of those passages that tell of a tranquil and, therefore, all the deeper happiness that an Italian composer would simply have failed to grasp. What a din such a composer would have produced at the words 'ah contenti saremo così' ('then let us be happy'). Only at the brief *forte* on 'ah tutti' does the feeling of joy burst forth in all its splendour,[120] yet the full orchestra is permanently employed throughout the whole of this ensemble. A new motif is used to provide a muted transition to the final section, which begins with a *piano* drum roll: brief and laden with tension, this transition is a prototype of many such passages in later works, most notably in *Die Zauberflöte*. Once again Mozart's music speaks of all the 'tormenti' and 'capricci' and 'follia' that constitute the darker aspects of our human tragicomedy, before recalling the earlier chorus ('Ricevete, o padroncina') and issuing the sort of invitation that is typically found in Italian comic operas at this point, 'al ballo, al gioco!' Beginning quietly, it erupts in an explosive *forte* at the words 'solo amor può terminar' ('love can end only [in joy and contentment]'), words that touch on the opera's main theme. And once again Mozart suddenly stems the torrent of sound: a march tune seems to approach from the distance, with trumpets and timpani, a march clearly related to the serenade marches that were customary at this time.[121] Immediately afterwards the voices enter on 'ed al suon di lieta marcia', stating the theme in augmentation. Here, too, the *forte* suddenly erupts towards the end. A real Mannheim crescendo is found only in the following stretta, which is in fact nothing more than a sung fanfare accompanied by a brilliant unison figure for all the strings.[122] As a result, the earlier contrast prepares the way for this final chorus of jubilation in a manner found in none of the Italian

---

118. Thus Schurig, *Mozart,* ii.89.
119. At the beginning of the scene with the Men in Armour, 'Der, welcher wandert diese Straße voll Beschwerden', and in the final chorus, 'Heil sei euch Geweihten'.
120. The brief crescendos in the accompanying violin figure are also remarkable here.
121. The rhythm in the basses recalls the beginning of the overture, except that the first beat is missing.
122. Cf. Beethoven's overture to *Die Geschöpfe des Prometheus.*

works of the period, where the final chorus is often tacked on to the opera in a thoroughly schematized way. It, too, affords proof of Jahn's splendid assessment of Mozart:

> The noblest and highest form of comedy rests on this curious mixture of sincere interest in human emotions and the joviality that liberates the mind. There is no mistaking the fact that this view of comedy explores the depths in which tragedy and comedy are jointly rooted. Körner declared that Mozart was unique in being equally great in comedy and tragedy,[123] in a way that Plato demanded of the dramatic poet – and this is something achieved only by the supreme genius.[124]

A few words on the unaccompanied recitatives: here Mozart sticks more closely than many of his contemporaries[125] to the authentic Italian *buffa* style: for them these sections constituted the simplest musical stylization of everyday speech, unencumbered by any deeper emotions. It is these speech patterns alone that determine the melodic and rhythmic form of the recitatives. This is not to say that the *secco* recitatives are incoherent or that they lack variety. Cohesion is ensured by the syntactic structure of the dialogue, variety by the temperament of the individual speaker and by the emotion provoked by the situation in question. In Mozart's day, too, it was essentially different from musically fixed singing. In *Le nozze di Figaro*, Mozart is fond of employing an essentially Italian phrase, its striking frequency allowing us to regard it as typically Mozartian. In act three, scene twelve, for example, Barbarina sings:

Here the freely introduced seventh, *d″*, is one of those notes typical of unaccompanied recitative that reflect the intonational patterns of everyday speech and which, in the words of Joseph Riepel, are 'digressive passing notes'.[126] Under this same heading comes the highly effective imitation of brief motifs, including the following example from the opening scene:[127]

123. Körner's letter to Schiller of 28 March 1794; see *Schiller's Briefwechsel mit Körner*, iii.127.
124. Jahn, *W. A. Mozart*, ii.338.
125. Such as Fischietti; see Engländer, 'Domenico Fischietti als Buffokomponist in Dresden', 414–15.
126. Riepel, *Harmonisches Sylbenmaß*, i.20.
127. Conversely, the Count's repetition of Susanna's words 'hai già vinta la causa' ('you've already won your case') is meant to be taken seriously.

A similar motif passes among three characters following the decision in the court case in act three, scene five:[128]

The tendency to vacillate between brief, emotionally charged motifs is particularly delightful, as in act three, scene three:

Sometimes individual words are singled out for special emphasis. Here the speaker is generally Susanna. Listen, for example, to her 'io' at the end of act two, scene eight, 'bocca' at the end of act three, scene two, and, in act three, scene six, the words 'chi al par di me contenta', where we even find a fermata and a harmonized sigh. And, for all the animation, the declamation is always very vivid, with even old Antonio having the following to sing in act three, scene nine:

In the harmonic writing, we still find traces of the older view that in recitative there is no strict sequence of harmonies but only individual chords that underline the meaning of the words.[129] This produces the dissonances that are common in Mozart's case, too, especially in the form of non-harmonic relations, such as we find towards the end of act one, scene six:

It is clear that the second chord is produced simply by the word 'infelice' without reference to its non-harmonic relation to the first chord. This view also informs the interrupted cadences that are so popular in unaccompanied recitatives in general, even though by Mozart's day dissonances no longer exceeded the norm in harmonic writing in general. This was a device that different composers used in very different ways. For many of them, including Mozart in his early operas, the interrupted cadence was used especially in *opere serie* to indicate a change of character or at

128. The judge's stutter finds clear expression here.
129. Fux, *Gradus ad Parnassum*, 276.

some other critical juncture. In *Le nozze di Figaro*, this is very rarely so,[130] and in the case of changes of character Mozart prefers far smoother transitions. Conversely, he very often uses interrupted cadences for questions, notably at Susanna's question in the very first scene of the opera:

This form of question is very typical of Mozart, its unexpected harmonic shift giving his questions particular weight. In the above example there is an element of reproachful, ironical mockery. Another harmony that Mozart is fond of using for questions is the chord of a second, which is generally resolved by the answer (as at 'dov'è la canzonetta?' in act two, scene three). On the other hand, the well-known 'Phrygian question' is found only in accompanied recitatives in *Le nozze di Figaro*, never in unaccompanied ones. Mozart evidently felt it was too solemn for this. But individual actions on stage and especially individual words are also underscored by unusual harmonic progressions, mostly to comic effect. Here one thinks of the ringing of the Countess's bell in act one, scene one, of 'atterrir' in act one, scene three, and of 'drucciolando' in act two, scene three.

In general, however, the harmonic writing is light-footed and flexible. Even in *Idomeneo*, Mozart had had little time for Gluck's large-scale approach to harmony, where it is used not only to express passing emotions but to impose a logical structure on the dialogue. Inevitably he had even less time for this approach in his *buffa* recitatives.[131] His aim was a type of declamation that was not emotionally overcharged but which, in the true spirit of *opera buffa*, flowed smoothly and was quick to respond to every situation, and there is no doubt that he achieved this aim here. But a precondition is that speech follows speech in quick succession, without dragging, and that gesture and facial expression are not neglected. In addition, Mozart sometimes adopts a practice already found in Galuppi and Gassmann and interrupts the fixed progress of the long bass notes by means of more animated motifs at moments of intensified emotion such as the beginning of act one, scene six. On one occasion we even find him adopting this device over a longer period in act one, scene two, where he comes close to an accompanied recitative with his change of tempo, recurrent motif and more clear-cut declamation.

But the main point to note is that in the *secco* recitatives in *Le nozze di Figaro* all the characters receive their due. This aim lies behind all the individual features that we have mentioned, with Susanna's character clearly distinguished from Figaro's right from the outset: her speeches are rhythmically resolute, while his vacillate between ponderousness and gabbled agitation.[132] The brief recitative at the end of act one, scene seven is also particularly vivid, thanks to its contrast between the Count's peremptory but excitable tone and Susanna's sharp and ready tongue. Finally

130. But see act three, scene thirteen.
131. Gluck's chromatic basses with a sequential idea above them are found only once in the opera, in act one, scene seven, from 'ed allora di dietro io mi celai'.
132. As an example, take the passage already mentioned: Susanna: 'E tu credevi che fosse la mia dote merto del tuo bel muso.' Figaro: 'Me n'era lusingato.' (Susanna: 'Do you imagine he gave me the dowry for the sake of your beautiful face ' Figaro: 'So I'd flattered myself.')

they are joined by Cherubino's replies, half afraid, half naïvely insolent, with their innocent third-based endings. The calmest character is the Countess, yet even she becomes agitated in a way typical of all women, as soon as her situation becomes critical in act two, scene four. In much the same way, the Count's vacillation between aristocratic self-assurance and inner turmoil reflects his general characterization.

If the accompaniment is provided by a harpsichord and the bass line is static, simple chords, arpeggiated or otherwise, will suffice here,[133] mirroring the singer's delivery as closely as possible. The bass notes will also be played by a cello, although this may be dispensed with if the harpsichord is replaced by a modern piano.[134]

Mozart was fortunate with his singers for this opera. As always, they left at least part of their imprint on the music, most notably in the case of Francesco Benucci, on whom Mozart could place the highest demands as he was not only the possessor of a 'beautiful, round and full bass voice' but was also a fine actor and, thanks to his avoidance of all exaggeration, was particularly well suited to Mozart's aims.[135] Likewise Stefano Mandini, who played the part of the Count, was praised by Michael Kelly as one of the leading *buffo* singers of his day.[136] Choron, too, described him as the ideal singer.[137] Kelly himself sang Basilio. A versatile singer, he was equally at home in serious and comic roles, as well as being an outstanding actor.[138] Francesco Bussani, who played both Bartolo and Antonio, had been a member of the Italian opera in Vienna since 1772/3 and was praised for his 'expansive bass voice'.[139]

Preeminent among the women was the Susanna, Nancy Storace (1765–1817). It is to her that we owe much of the appeal of this part, for, according to one contemporary, she 'combined all the gifts of nature, education and skill that could ever be desired in Italian comic opera, combining them in a way such as no other singer in her own day, and few since, have demonstrated'.[140] Zinzendorf, too, noted that her forte was playing naïve and mischievous characters.[141] Conversely, Luisa Laschi,

133. Max Schneider, 'Die Begleitung des Secco-Rezitativs um 1750.'
134. ◆ Generally concerning *Figaro*, see Allanbrook, *Rhythmic Gesture in Mozart: Le nozze di Figaro and Don Giovanni*; Dent, *Mozart's Operas: A Critical Study*; Gallarati, 'Music and Masks in Lorenzo Da Ponte's Mozartian Librettos'; Levarie, *Mozart's 'Le Nozze di Figaro': A Critical Analysis*; Noske, *The Signifier and the Signified: Studies in the Operas of Mozart and Verdi*; Platoff, 'Tonal Organization in "Buffo" Finales and the Act II Finales of "Le nozze di Figaro"'; Steptoe, *The Mozart–Da Ponte Operas: The Cultural and Musical Background to Le nozze di Figaro, Don Giovanni, and Così fan tutte*; Charles Rosen, *The Classical Style*, 288–325; and Waldoff and Webster, 'Operatic Plotting in *Le nozze di Figaro*'.
135. See *Berlinische musikalische Zeitung historischen und kritischen Inhalts*, i (1793), 138–9. ◆ Further concerning Benucci, see Rushton, 'Buffo Roles in Mozart's Vienna: Tessitura and Tonality as Signs of Characterization', and Link, *Arias for Francesco Benucci, Mozart's First Figaro and Guglielmo*. For the Viennese careers and other details concerning the singers in Mozart's operas generally, see Link, *The National Court Theatre in Mozart's Vienna*.
136. Kelly, *Reminiscences*, i.121 and 196.
137. Scudo, *L'art ancien et l'art moderne*, 22–3. ◆ Also see Paissa, '"Questo è il conte, alla voce il conosco": Stefano Mandini prima di Mozart (1774–1783)'.
138. He himself recounts how he so impressed Casti and Paisiello with his acting that, in spite of his youth, they entrusted him with the difficult role of Gafforino in *Il re Teodoro*, a role that he performed to great acclaim; see Kelly, *Reminiscences*, i.241–2. ◆ Further, see Jenkins, *Mozart and the English Connection* and Ellis, *The Life of Michael Kelly, Musician, Actor and Bon Viveur*.
139. Johann Müller, *Genaue Nachrichten von beyden Kaiserlich-Königlichen Schaubühnen und anderen öffentlichen Ergötzlichkeiten in Wien*, 73. ◆ Also see Angermüller, 'Francesco Bussani – Mozarts erster Bartolo, Antonio und Alfonso und Dorothea Bussani – Mozarts erster Cherubino und erste Despina'.
140. *AmZ*, xxiv (1822), 284.
141. Pohl, *Joseph Haydn*, ii.123: 'jolie figure, voluptueuse, belle gorge, beaux yeux, cou blanc, bouche fraîche, belle peau, la naïveté et la petulance [sic] de l'enfance, chante comme un ange.' ◆ Concerning Storace, see Jenkins, *Mozart and the English Connection*; Brace, *Anna . . . Susanna: Anna Storace, Mozart's first Susanna: Her life, times and family*; Chancellor, 'Nancy Storace: Mozart's Susanna'; Gidwitz, 'Vocal Profiles of Four Mozart Sopranos'; Hodges, 'Lorenzo Da Ponte's first Susanna', and '"One of the most accomplished women of her age": Anna Storace, Mozart's first Susanna'; Link, *Arias for Nancy Storace, Mozart's First Susanna*; Matthews, 'The Childhood of Nancy Storace'; and Price, 'Mozart, the Storaces and Opera in London 1787–1790'.

the Countess, was far less popular in Vienna than in Italy.[142] None the less, she must have had considerable gifts as a singer and actress, otherwise Mozart would hardly have written the role in the way he did. Cherubino was played by Dorothea Bussani, who made her stage début in this role and who owed her success less to her singing than to her figure and unaffected acting.[143]

142.   Cramer, *Magazin der Musik*, ii (1788), 48. She first sang in Vienna, to great acclaim, on 24 September 1784; see *Wiener Zeitung*, lxxix (1784), Appendix, but did not appear again until *Le nozze di Figaro*. As Signora Mombelli, she sang Zerlina in *Don Giovanni* in 1788.
143.   *Berlinische musikalische Zeitung historischen und kritischen Inhalts*, i (1793), 134. Da Ponte even speaks of the 'smorfie' and 'pagliacciate' that made her very popular with the public at large; see Da Ponte, *Memorie*, i/2.111 and 135–6. ◆ Also see Angermüller, 'Francesco Bussani – Mozarts erster Bartolo, Antonio und Alfonso und Dorothea Bussani – Mozarts erster Cherubino und erste Despina'.

43

Between Figaro *and* Don Giovanni

For the time being, Mozart continued to eke out the same pitiful existence in Vienna as before, as though *Le nozze di Figaro* had never been written. No doubt his acquaintances – most of whom, especially those in the Jacquin household, admired him rather than understood him – felt much more respect for him now, but, in spite of its occasional patronage, the court still failed to take him entirely seriously as an opera composer, and the same was true of the public at large: in Vienna, as elsewhere, they were attracted only by big names. And Mozart was a big name only as a keyboard player, whereas his reputation as a music dramatist remained confined to Vienna,[1] with the result that he continued to have to rely on teaching and concerts to make ends meet.[2] There was thus a sense of profound resignation in the letter of farewell that he wrote to Adalbert Gyrowetz when the latter left for Italy: 'You lucky man! If only I could come to Italy with you, how happy I'd be! – Look, I now have to give another lesson, so that I can earn some money!'[3] This was the period

---

1. Even Count Zinzendorf had been bored by the opera; indeed he also commented on *Die Entführung aus dem Serail*: 'The opera, the music of which is pilfered from various others' [*Dokumente*, 180, *Documentary Biography*, 203]. ◆ Here Abert over-states the case, perhaps, for Mozart's lack of reputation as a dramatist. Not only was *Die Entführung* an immediate success throughout German-speaking Europe, but *Figaro*, especially in Vienna, became a rallying point for German composers. See, for example, the anonymous pamphlet, *Uiber das deutsche Singspiel den Apotheker des Hrn. v. Dittersdorf*, published at Vienna in 1786: 'It is almost unbelievable, and truly vexing, how the German singspiel, and those who are interested in it, are treated in the German capital. Until now there remained but a glimmer of hope, in spite of a conspiracy by the aristocracy and some influen-tial musical scholars, of some time seeing fulfilled the wishes of our monarch, himself the founder of it . . . it came to the point that – the poor German muse, hunted from the stage in order to tyrannize our taste with foreign nations . . . – it was unlikely ever again to find a German opera at the National Theatre . . . [or] to hear good music for an Italian singspiel by a German master. [But] they have completely lost their bet, for Mozart's *Nozze di Figaro*, and the subsequent reintroduction of German opera, have put to shame the ridiculous pride of this fashionable sect.' See Eisen, *New Mozart Documents*, 45.
2. 'Beethoven, who as a youth of great promise came to Vienna in the spring of 1787, but was obliged to return to Bonn after a brief sojourn, was taken to Mozart and at that musician's request played something for him which he, taking it for granted that it was a show-piece prepared for the occasion, praised in a rather cool manner. Beethoven, observing this, begged Mozart to give him a theme for improvisation. He always played admirably when excited and now he was inspired, too, by the presence of the master whom he reverenced greatly; he played in such a style that Mozart, whose attention and interest grew more and more, finally went silently to some friends who were sitting in an adjoining room, and said, vivaciously, "Keep your eyes on him; some day he will give the world something to talk about".' This report by Otto Jahn is evidently a true account of this memorable occa-sion, even down to the wording of Mozart's remark; it draws a striking portrait of the contrastive characters of the two composers, the critical Mozart and the equally sensitive and temperamental Beethoven, who was finally able to coerce Mozart's attention and interest; see Jahn, *W.A. Mozart*, fourth edition, ii.40–1; see also Thayer, *Ludwig van Beethovens Leben*, i.197–8. Conversely, the extraordinary knowledge of counterpoint that Beethoven is said to have shown is almost certainly apocryphal, given the state of his musical education at this time; see Seyfried, *Ludwig van Beethoven's Studien im Generalbaß, Contrapunkt und in der Compositions-Lehre*, Appendix p. 4. It seems certain that Beethoven had a number of lessons with Mozart, almost certainly in composition, but that Mozart never played for him, a circumstance that Beethoven himself later regretted; see Wegeler and Ries, *Biographische Notizen über Ludwig van Beethoven*, 86. This does not, of course, preclude the possibility that Beethoven heard Mozart play in public, a possibility confirmed by Czerny's report; see Thayer, *Ludwig van Beethovens Leben*. According to Beethoven, Mozart's playing was 'subtle, but choppy, with no legato'. Beethoven's lessons with Mozart cannot have lasted long, as the younger composer soon had to return to Bonn on receiving news that his mother was seriously ill. She died in her son's presence on 17 July 1787. ◆ There is no unequivocal evidence that Mozart and Beethoven met; modern opinion discounts the possibility.
3. Einstein, *Lebensläufe deutscher Musiker von ihnen selbst erzählt*, iii.16–17. ◆ This story may also be apocryphal.

shortly after the birth of Mozart's third son, Leopold, on 18 October 1786, when he seriously considered moving to England, a plan that foundered only on his father's opposition. And with the exception of Prague, *Le nozze di Figaro* had failed to make any real impression outside Vienna.[4]

As a result, the works that date from this period reveal the same old picture of official commissions and works written to order. Yet an important change can be detected here in terms of their style and content. The time when Mozart had drawn his artistic experiences from the civilized world around him and imbued the older spirit of music as a social art form with the refining fires of his own personality was now past. *Le nozze di Figaro* stands on the cusp between these two periods. On the one hand, it is still lit by the whole *galant* and hedonistic brilliance of this social art form, while on the other the archetypal aesthetic experience asserts itself so forcefully that the social element threatens to disappear completely. Brief though the interval was between these two great works, the radical change in Mozart's creative output could hardly have been more far-reaching.[5] Although these, too, were commissioned works, they increasingly reflect Goethe's well-known belief that the artist's archetypal experience grows more and more powerfully compelling, encouraging him to express things that are no longer of any concern to society but to himself alone. Mozart had assimilated all that aristocratic art had to offer him, and when this source of inspiration began to run dry, his inner voice grew increasingly audible. His own view of the world gradually became more remote from that of the people around him, and his art became more and more subjective, with the passionate, 'demonic' aspect of his character emerging with ever greater

4. One of the earliest performances after Prague was the one given at Frankfurt in 1788 by Gustav Friedrich Wilhelm Großmann's company; see Carl Valentin, *Geschichte der Musik in Frankfurt am Main*, 257. Bonn followed in 1789, when the piece was said to have 'found great favour'; see Thayer, *Ludwig van Beethovens Leben*, i.233. Next came Stuttgart on 16 July 1790; see Krauß, *Das Stuttgarter Hoftheater von den ältesten Zeiten bis zur Gegenwart*, 94. And Berlin first heard the work on 14 September 1790; see Louis Schneider, *Geschichte der Oper und des königlichen Opernhauses in Berlin*, 59. Critics praised the work as a masterpiece, but audiences preferred Martín y Soler and Dittersdorf; see *Chronik von Berlin*, viii (1790), 1229–30 and 1244 [*Dokumente*, 372–3, *Documentary Biography*, 328]; also *Musikalische Monathsschrift*, i (1792), 137. *Le nozze di Figaro* conquered other German theatres only in the wake of *Die Zauberflöte* in the course of the 1790s. Even today, it remains largely unsuccessful in Italy. The first attempt to stage the work in Italy was made in Florence in 1788; see *AmZ*, iii (1800/1), 182. After this, the Italians appear not to have troubled themselves with the work until March 1814, when it was performed at the Teatro del Fondo in Naples; see Florimo, *La scuola musicale di Napoli e i suoi conservatorii*, iv.366. Here the librettist is described as 'Anonimo'. It was performed at La Scala, Milan, on 27 March 1815, when it was repeated 23 times; see Cambiasi, *La Scala*, 306. This was the first attempt to stage any of Mozart's work at La Scala: *Don Giovanni* followed on 17 October 1814, with 40 subsequent performances; *Il flauto magico* was first staged there on 15 April 1816 and was given 38 times. Of course, these works failed to maintain a place for themselves in the repertory, and cities such as Venice and Bologna continue to turn their backs on *Figaro*. The first attempt to stage *Le nozze di Figaro* in Paris in 1793 was abandoned after five performances and the work was not heard again there until the end of 1802, when a German company, including Aloysia Weber, revived it. It was next heard at the Théâtre Italien in 1807 and remained in the repertory here for many years. A French adaptation was performed at the Théâtre Lyrique in 1858 and proved a great and lasting success; see Scudo, *Critique et littérature musicales*, ii.458–9. It was first performed at the Opéra-Comique on 24 February 1872; see *AmZ*, viii (1872), 213; and Wilder, *Mozart: L'homme et l'artiste*, 226. In London, *Le nozze di Figaro* was first performed at the King's Theatre on 18 June 1812, with Catalani as Susanna; see Pohl, *Mozart und Haydn in London*, i.147; Parke, *Musical Memoirs*, ii.82–3; and Thomae, 'Vier Mozart-Handschriften in der Bibliothek des British Museum London', 499. From then on it was one of the most popular of all operas in London. ◆ Abert's dates for the performance of Mozart's operas in Italy are slightly confused. *Figaro* was not the first attempt to stage any of Mozart's works at La Scala: *Don Giovanni* was first given there on 17 October 1814. For a general account of early performances of Mozart's operas, see Eisen, 'Reception'. Further, see Manfred Schuler, 'Die Aufführung von Mozarts *Le Nozze di Figaro* in Donaueschingen 1787: Ein Beitrag zur Rezeptionsgeschichte'; Würtz, 'Die Erstaufführungen von Mozarts Bühnenwerken in Mannheim'; Nägele, 'Die Rezeption der Mozart-Opern am Stuttgarter Hof 1790 bis 1810'; Beard, 'Figaro in England: Productions of Mozart's Opera, and the Early Adaptations of it in England Before 1850'; and Angermüller, 'Die Erstaufführung von Mozarts *Le Nozze di Figaro* an der Mailänder Scala, 27. März 1815'. An early and important Donaueschingen performance (1787) may have reflected the version of the opera performed in Prague in 1787: see Manfred Schuler, 'Das Donaueschinger Aufführungsmaterial von Mozarts *Le nozze di Figaro*'; for other textual questions, see Tyson, 'Some Problems in the Text of *Le nozze di Figaro*: Did Mozart Have a Hand in Them?'. Concerning the reception of the opera generally, see Ruf, 'Die Rezeption von Mozarts *Le Nozze di Figaro* bei den Zeitgenossen'; Carter, *W. A. Mozart: Le nozze di Figaro*, 122–47; and Gruber, *Mozart and Posterity*.

5. Wyzewa and Saint-Foix, *Wolfgang Amédée Mozart*, ii.416, quite rightly acknowledge this change but again speak of a 'Romantic' period, a term which strikes me as inappropriate on account of its ambiguity.

prominence, an aspect which – to stress only one characteristic – found particular expression in the increased importance of harmony and free counterpoint.

This new spirit already informs the keyboard music of this period. It is sufficient to compare the D major rondo K485 of 10 January 1786 with the A minor rondo K511 of 11 March 1787 to appreciate this difference. The former is an amiable enough example of the *galant* style, the latter a confession of a deeply personal kind, exploring emotional depths unsuspected by the earlier piece.[6] K511 is one of the most important keyboard rondos ever composed. With its exotically tinged theme, it is a typically Mozartian piece in A minor, its first four bars, with their characteristic chromaticisms and dynamics, revealing an impassioned tension that is maintained throughout the whole movement, without ever achieving any resolution in an optimistic sense. Symptomatic of this whole approach are the unusually broad proportions of the individual sections: the first and second subject-groups are all fully developed ternary structures. Unlike those of the rondos from the keyboard concertos, these themes are interrelated by more than merely a sense of contrast. The F major episode is linked to the first subject by the mordent that recurs with thematic regularity, while the A major episode emerges organically from the first subject's final bar and in the subsequent course of the movement likewise recalls the mordent motif. This is a further important feature of this new keyboard style that we shall rediscover in an even more developed state when we examine the sonatas for four hands. Mozart is no longer at pains to exploit the dazzling interplay of ideas but strives rather for unity, a unity based in the present case, of course, less on the logical development of those ideas than on their underlying mood. As a result, Mozart does not simply juxtapose the individual sections but attempts to create transitions, and it is here in particular that he has produced passages of unprecedented austerity and boldness at the point where the two episodes return to the main theme, the eerie intensity of which is now raised to the highest pitch using its own chromatic devices, thereby reintroducing the main theme with compelling psychological logic. Chromaticisms are crucial to the work as a whole. Even in the A major section[7] there is barely an idea into which they do not slip in one form or another, permeating the thematic material as well as the figurations and affecting the inner voices in addition to the main melody. In the D major rondo Mozart had drawn closer to Carl Philipp Emanuel Bach, and although he now moves away again by invariably sticking to the tonic for the main theme, he none the less varies the theme at each of its appearances, investing it with extremes of expressivity and exploring the full potential of its anguished chromatic line. The subsidiary themes, too, always appear in their traditional keys. There is no question here of the constant modulations typical of Carl Philipp Emanuel Bach, making the harmonic character of the links and transitions all the more surprising. The subdominant character of the first episode (in F major) is remarkably intensified in its middle section, while the sudden incursion of D flat major already anticipates the whole of Schubert. This tendency to explore the region of the subdominant (frequently by sidestepping the nearest degrees) is entirely typical of this period in Mozart's development.[8] The keyboard writing, too, has changed. Although the influence of the concerto is rarely far away, especially in the *majeur*, in general the writing is far more reminiscent of a string quartet, with Mozart avoiding the usual stereotypical accompanying figures and

6. See Marx, *Die Lehre von der musikalischen Komposition*, iii.150–1.
7. Its main theme recalls Cupid's aria in act one of Gluck's *Orfeo ed Euridice*.
8. Hans Gál is wrong, therefore, to claim that this characteristic is limited almost exclusively to Beethoven; see 'Die Stileigentümlichkeiten des jungen Beethoven', 65.

attempting to ensure that the middle voices are independent. Four-part writing is preferred and quartet-like passages such as the following point far into the future:

Only in the substantial coda is the polyphonic writing embedded in a figuration that recalls the first episode. Here the repressed passion of the theme acquires a note of sinister defiance, with the chromatic line being fully harmonized for the first time. And this is followed in turn by the first real *forte* outburst of the movement. The sense of a tenacious struggle is intensified by virtue of the fact that the theme is immediately repeated in the bass and the two hands reverse their roles. In turn this is followed by a gently rocking figure from the *majeur* that had previously appeared in a bright A major but which is now drawn into the sombre minor mood. The ending takes the form of a passage that already looks forward to Schumann: chromatic syncopations in the middle voice circle around the tonic, while above them the first motif from the main idea places its seal on the whole. A shadowy echo of this motif continues to be heard even in the two final *pianissimo* chords. The new style is still in a state of flux in the brief rondo in F major K 494 of 10 June 1786. A loosely structured example of the *galant* style, it none the less already reveals an attempt to allow the main idea to infiltrate the episodes, too, and to vary and intensify it at each subsequent appearance, before it finally and good-humouredly takes its leave in the coda, deep down in the bass.[9] The *minore* is already notable for its stricter procedures.

The least innovative of these works, at least when compared with its predecessors, is the set of twelve variations in B flat major on an allegretto K500 of 12 September 1786, even though the new spirit is already palpable in the fifth and seventh variations, as well as in the transition between the tenth and eleventh. Conversely, the work includes a handful of novel pianistic effects that are foreign to Mozart's earlier style and that clearly reflect the influence of Clementi, to whom Mozart had not long before adopted a superior tone.[10] Typical of Clementi are the triplet figuration in the first two variations, the bass figure in the fourth and the chordal textures in the eighth.[11]

The two sonatas in F major K497 and C major K 521 date from 1 August 1786 and 29 May 1787 and, as such, are probably coeval with the unfinished sonata in G major K357.[12] All are written for

9.   The 27-bar cadenza-like interpolation is missing from the autograph but was almost certainly added by Mozart for the first edition of the work. ◆ This revised version of the F major rondo became the third movement of the keyboard sonata K533.

10.   See Wyzewa and Saint-Foix, *Wolfgang Amédée Mozart*, ii.416. See also above, pp.624–6 and 885.

11.   The allegro KAnh. C25.04 in B flat major must likewise date from the autumn of 1786. It was later combined with the last two movements of the B flat major concerto K450 and a menuetto – likewise rearranged and clearly by Mozart himself – to form a sonata. Marx, *Die Lehre von der musikalischen Komposition*, iii.150–1. ◆ There is no evidence that KAnh. C25.04 is by Mozart and its posthumous publication together with arrangements from Mozart's concertos is a strike against its authenticity; the minuetto included in the putative sonata, KAnh. C25.05, is similarly uncertain.

12.   Köchel believes that it is coeval with the sonata in B flat major K358 and that it therefore dates from 1780, but this is inconceivable on stylistic grounds alone. At the very least, the distinctively French menuetto must date from a later period. But the opening movement, too, is stylistically so close to the above-named works that the dating suggested by Wyzewa and Saint-Foix – between August and November 1786 – has much in its favour; see Wyzewa and Saint-Foix, *Wolfgang Amédée Mozart*, ii.417. Mozart appears to have played a lot of duets with one of his pupils at around this time. ◆ Abert's suggestion that K357 is a coherent sonata is also problematic. First published by André in 1796, the work includes the incomplete sonata movement K497a

piano four hands and all are outstanding examples of the new style. Consider, for example, the unison opening of the F major sonata, with its striking use of dynamics:

This is one of the most substantial of Mozart's slow introductions. Its opening seems to be weighed down by fate. From it there rises up an imploring cantilena, but this then becomes caught up in its initial motif in a series of stabbing sforzatos, allowing itself to be drawn down deeper and deeper into subdominant harmonies, as though by some secret power.[13] The questioning end of this adagio is no less sinister and tension-laden than its opening. An answer is provided by the allegro, but it is by no means purely optimistic in tone. This theme, too, has something contemplative, even something tormented about it as a result of its syncopations, and if the rest of this movement attempts to strike a more positive note, it is invariably against the background of these sombre and defiant stirrings. Even the self-confident second subject, which enters fully prepared in keeping with the whole nature of this style, soon modulates not only to C minor but, highly significantly, to E flat major, forcing a return to the tonic via a canonic passage based on this section's dominant rhythm: ♪ ♫♫ | ♩ The main theme suddenly reappears and, retaining is anguished expression, conducts the musical argument quietly through to the end, an ending which, equally unexpectedly, finds tempestuous confirmation in a passage of double counterpoint based on the very same rhythm; the initial theme limps after it, *piano*, like some miserable sinner. As with so many other works from this period, the development section wastes no time in modulating to the remote key of A flat major and to a passage of strangely Romantic half-lights. The main theme has now lost all its melodic contours and makes what impact it can only through its harmonization and rhythm. But a mysterious murmuring rises up in the bass before passing to the upper voice, again by means of a passage of double counterpoint. The goal of this night-time journey is revealed in all its horror by the passage in D flat major in which the main theme is suddenly exposed to a life-and-death struggle. In the savagery of its passion as in the strict procedures used to express this emotion, this passage already anticipates the development sections of the G minor symphony. Mozart's ability to invest the delicate anguish of this theme with a very real grimace of pain is little less than astonishing. Even its capricious third bar is transformed into a roaring demon at the positively Beethovenian *fortissimo* passage. But there is something particularly beautiful about the way in which these Romantic veils waft down again over the battlefield at the end, making the whole encounter seem almost a bewildering dream. When they lift, the main theme emerges in its original form for the recapitulation. This proceeds along largely regular lines, after which a coda brings the whole work to an end, just as the main theme, still limping gamely along, brings the subject-group to an end on a note of roguish humour reminiscent of Till Eulenspiegel. The movement thus pursues its course through a remarkable interplay of light and

and the fragmentary variations K500a. Whether they belong together is questionable: in the absence of an autograph, K497a cannot be dated. And K500a, contrary to Abert's belief, now appears to have been written down in 1791. At the very least, then, the variations are considerably later than K497 and K521. It may be that K500a is related to a different work altogether, the variations K501; Constanze mooted as much in a letter of 31 May 1800 (*Briefe*, iv.357).
13. There is a similar passage in the first section of the C minor fantasia K475.

shade, joviality and earnestness that almost reminds us of Jean Paul. Problems such as these were clearly alien to Mozart during the period of the great keyboard concertos. In terms of its mood and structure, the middle movement follows on logically from the opening adagio, with a feeling of heavy-heartedness alternating with good-natured contentedness and, in the third subject, with whimsical good humour. Here, too, we may note a fondness for canonic procedures, especially in the case of the second and third subjects, and there is still the same tendency to impose a sense of unity on the movement as a whole by means of thematic repetition. The theme of the rondo suggests a belated addition to the series of rondos from the keyboard concertos, even to the extent that a tutti appears to enter in the tenth bar. The whole subject-group as far as the concerto-like ending in C major recalls the old spirit of hedonism, and only the double counterpoint in bars 24ff. and the dreamy theme in F major, with its intricate textures, goes beyond this mood. But from the D minor episode onwards, a different atmosphere prevails. It is in fact no more than a transitional link designed to lead back to the earlier dreamy subject, yet it refuses to be displaced by the latter and repeatedly interrupts it with its tempestuous scales, so that this subject, too, assumes an increasingly anguished expression. It is the old ghosts from the opening movement that burst in here in a highly dramatic dialogue. But in the process they throw the main theme off course. Even its modulation to the minor is disturbing, but then the scales shoot up in all their naked aggression, causing the theme to break down helplessly into its component parts. Only then can the old and carefree continuation begin. This final section includes a powerful canonic passage in which the soprano and bass play with the main theme. The earlier Mozart would have ended at this point, but now he suddenly comes to a standstill on a diminished chord, once again allowing the more contemplative elements to have their say, before bringing the whole movement to an end with a brief crescendo. Here, too, it is ultimately the subjective character of the whole work that finds expression in this interplay of opposing forces. In consequence, the keyboard writing is completely different from that found in the earlier sonatas, with the very nature of the themes meaning that when the two players engage in a concertante dialogue on the same idea, the result is no longer purely playful but positively dramatic. In ensemble passages, it is very rare for one or other of them to be accorded a merely accompanying role. Mozart's fondness for double counterpoint is in itself sufficient to ensure that this does not happen, quite apart from the fact that the individual voices are in general treated independently, whether canonically or in free imitation. Finally, we also find other tonal effects, such as the treatment of a melody in tenths (by the lower player) rather than in thirds or even octaves, just as in his orchestral writing Mozart often has the violas or even the bassoons doubling the first violins. In short, the usual concertante procedures and reciprocal accompaniment on the part of two players at the same instrument are replaced by a compact, genuine four-handed keyboard style.

Although far less important as a work, the C major sonata reveals the new stylistic characteristics particularly clearly, especially its opening movement: with the exception of a handful of virtuoso transitional groups, everything is derived from the main theme, even appearing in the final subject-group in the concentrated form of a three-bar period:

As in Mozart's earlier works, the notional second subject does not appear until the beginning of the development section, but here it is even better motivated by the whole character of the movement.

The beautiful andante is cast in the form of a French rondeau with a middle section in the minor, while the finale, with its amiably ambling theme (a favourite of the Viennese), takes the form of an Italian rondo. The unfinished sonata in G major, finally, likewise begins with a unison passage,[14] but here the whole of the musical argument is derived with even greater insistency from the main idea. Even the brief development section is entirely thematic. Both movements are in G major, a form that points to France. French, too, is the andante, the first section of which is a constant dialogue between the two players, while the second creates a remarkably pittoresque impression that makes one wonder whether there may be some hidden programme. The variations K 501 for piano four hands add nothing of any note to the picture that we have already drawn.

Among the chamber works with keyboard, the trio in E flat major K498 of 5 August 1786 stands out not least on account of the forces for which it is scored: keyboard, clarinet and viola. In itself, it was an inspired idea to harness together two instruments with such individual sonorities as the sensuously swelling clarinet and the melancholy resignation of the viola, and there is no doubt that this contrast left a decisive mark on the overall mood of the piece, which was written as a favour for the Jacquin household: Franziska played the keyboard, while Mozart himself took the viola part, hence the privileged role played by this instrument throughout the whole of the work. The order of its movements – andante, menuetto and rondo – suggests a suite rather than a sonata, but the manner in which they are elaborated is entirely typical of this period. Among the features that fall under this heading is the astonishing motivic unity of the opening movement, which is cast in ternary form, albeit without a development section. The opening motif is ever-present, even in the second subject, and its gradual development is particularly attractive, especially in terms of its sonorities. It is brusquely introduced at the beginning by the viola, and even the keyboard's reply sounds less than wholly confident. Only with the entry of the clarinet does it acquire the raptness and momentum that return each time this instrument assumes control of the musical argument. The more the piece develops, the greater the tendency towards imitative procedures,[15] which reach their high point in the beautiful coda. There are none of the antiphonal textures of the kind found in Mozart's earlier chamber works, an absence explained by the forces for which the work is scored. The writing reveals a uniquely calm and tender poetry that not even a number of darker emotions can exorcise. All the more majestically does the menuetto then swagger along, although it, too, has its sombre, even sullen moments, notably in its second section, when the left hand of the keyboard suddenly takes up the theme, but even more so in the trio, in which the anguished cry in the clarinet

inspires an extremely bad-tempered outburst of triplets on the part of the viola. And, as before, these two ideas refuse to give ground, but wander from instrument to instrument and from one register to another,[16] sometimes in free double counterpoint, finally reappearing in the

14. The theme belongs to the world of the opening movement of the C minor concerto. The first movement was completed by Mozart as far as the ninth bar of the development section, while the second movement survives almost complete. The work was completed by Julius André. ◆ Concerning this sonata, see n. 12 above.

15. Note the attractive way in which, at the recapitulation, the rests from the beginning of the movement are now bridged by the imitative entries.

16. The high point is reached in bar 15ff. of the second section with the imitative entry of all four voices within the narrowest confines. Here the dominant emotion is genuine, affecting sadness, but a sadness that acquires a humorous tinge with the viola's surly interruption.

coda.[17] The main theme of the rondo and the related first episode are both magnificent melodies for the clarinet, filled with a burgeoning love of life. Only the viola introduces a further surly, half-irritated note in the episode in C minor, agreeing to take up the main theme only after a relatively lengthy passage of triplets. But it is in the episode in A flat major that the note of elegiac raptness finds its fullest expression, and from now on the mood brightens, ultimately achieving a typically Mozartian degree of carefreeness and charm. New ideas now shoot up like flowers in spring and yet, on closer inspection, they all prove to be derived from a single source. Viola and clarinet now coexist in perfect harmony, their differences of opinion a thing of the past, as they make their way, generally in thirds, towards their common goal. The whole trio is a jewel of chamber-like intimacy.

Far more ambitious is the trio in B flat major K502 for keyboard, violin and cello that Mozart completed on 18 November 1786. Here, too, the whole of the subject-group is developed from the single main idea,[18] so that particularly towards the end it almost recalls a development section. But none of the theme's countermelodies is lost either: think only of the role that is later played by the brief and unprepossessing motif in the second bar of the violin part. Conversely, we again find a completely new theme at the start of the development section, reflecting the approach that we have already observed, even if it disappears again without trace almost immediately afterwards. The middle movement sounds like an echo of the magically beautiful Larghettos of the concertos, while the final movement recalls the gavotte themes of the earlier chamber works with keyboard. This movement is also a remarkable hybrid between sonata form and rondo form: the sequence of modulations, limited number of themes and recapitulation-like repeat of a great complex of ideas towards the end are all reminiscent of sonata form, while rondo form is suggested by the absence of a regular development section and by the freedom with which the individual ideas are treated. It is not that there are none of the procedures associated with a development section. Quite the opposite: the first and second subjects are often examined at points where one least expects it, and here the writing is not only thematic, it also, and more especially, involves contrapuntal proce-dures. Here, too, the aim is that absolute unity of ideas that is in such strange contrast to the loosely structured, multiform character of the young Mozart. The coda also extracts the last ounce of canonic potential from both themes. The piano writing is far more virtuosic than in the viola trio and sometimes recalls the concertos. The strict antiphonal style is far more often abandoned in favour of a free obbligato style. The writing is occasionally in four parts, two of which are entrusted to the keyboard. For the same reason the cello breaks free from the bass far more often than before and goes its own way. For the present it is not yet used as a solo instrument in the later sense. In other words, its unique sonorities are not yet exploited for their own sake. Rather, the instrument is used as an independent voice within the polyphonic textures.

The sonata in A major K526 for violin and keyboard is dated 24 August 1787. Mozart's last large-scale contribution to the medium, it reveals the vast distance that he had travelled since his first 'violin sonatas', in which the violin was merely an optional extra. Even the 'Romantic' sonatas of his youth still bear clear traces of the genre's origins, resembling trios in which one of the violin lines is taken by the keyboard's upper part,[19] while the left hand elaborates the continuo part. And

---

17. With an optimism entirely characteristic of this trio, the clarinet steers this motif towards the major, provoking a demon-strative reply in the minor from the keyboard's left hand, but it is not long before this instrument, too, is forced to submit, with only the viola continuing to gabble on till the end.

18. It is clearly related to the theme of the keyboard concerto K450 in B flat major. Mozart was remarkably fond of these third-based melodies, especially in the key of B flat major.

19. See Mersmann, 'Beiträge zur Aufführungspraxis der vorklassischen Kammermusik in Deutschland', 101–2. ◆ Concerning the 'Romantic' sonatas, see above.

the term 'keyboard duets' that was used to describe the Mannheim violin sonatas recalls this earlier practice, even though these traces are already beginning to disappear, allowing both instruments to engage in a concertante dialogue of a more modern kind, while the old continuo practice in the bass yields to the freedom of the 'classical' chamber style. The concertante features of the genre reveal an increasing tendency towards virtuosity, with the present sonata representing the culmination of this development. The two outer movements have an effervescent brilliance to them found in no other violin sonata by Mozart, whereas the features that are otherwise typical of this period are rather less conspicuous. Everything runs along the most orderly lines, and the opening molto allegro[20] is one of Mozart's most regular sonata movements. Only in its development section, with the Romantic to-ing and fro-ing of its final subject-group, and in its brief canonic passages do we find something of the spirit of the new age. All the more implacably does the middle movement avoid all virtuosity, plumbing emotional depths of a kind unexplored by any of the earlier sonatas. It is as though Mozart had suddenly laid aside the brilliant garb of the virtuoso that he now had to force himself to wear and, lost to the world, was starting to compose for himself alone with the deep sense of resignation that was to beset him increasingly frequently from now on. Even the main idea is different from anything we have previously encountered: a resolute unison striding motion in the keyboard, the regularity of which suggests something implacable and portentous, while above it we twice hear a sorrowful entreaty in the violin. It immediately becomes clear where all this is leading, with a sudden shift to the minor followed by a breathtaking crescendo with a cry on *b* flat, before the melody sinks back hopelessly into the key of D minor. The whole process is then repeated, but with the roles reversed, after which a new theme is introduced. The leaden-footed motion in the bass disappears, although the unison remains. A game of question and answer now begins on the basis of a simple triadic motif that is inverted in the keyboard's answer and that appears embedded in an ingratiating semiquaver figure. But it is not long, of course, before the main motif reasserts itself in the bass and at the *forte* section even ushers in a proudly triumphant passage. Yet it, too, is of only brief duration and, with the sudden shift from major to minor that is typical of the movement as a whole, the real second subject enters in A minor, a figure notable for its veiled and ineffably profound anguish and, at the same time, the only theme unrelated to the main theme's ponderous motion. Within the movement it appears to stand apart, for at the end the second theme simply continues in A major as though nothing untoward has happened. All that is new is a constant quaver motion derived from the main theme. Here also Mozart succeeds in generating an uncanny sense of tension with a syncopated passage coupled with a crescendo, but far from bringing any release from the pressure, it merely increases that tension to the point where it becomes almost intolerable. The quaver motion continues throughout the brief development section, suggesting nothing so much as an effortful search and wandering that fails to achieve any rest. Whenever a particular goal seems at hand, a powerful emotional pressure exerts itself, and when that pressure abates after a brief space of time we suddenly find ourselves in a completely unexpected environment, as though we have entered some unknown country through a dark and narrow gateway. These two modulatory miracles, in which enharmonic change plays a not inconsiderable part, are typical of Mozart's new style and stand far apart from the clear and transparent harmonies of the earlier period. The recapitulation runs along regular lines with the exception of the off-beat syncopations in the main theme in the right hand: it is as though the main character were constantly dogged by his shadow. In terms of its expressive subjectivity and the uniformity with which its ideas are structured, this movement is a

---

20. The main theme of the opening movement recalls Michael Haydn.

true product of this period in Mozart's career, almost seeming to be a throwback to the free ostinato movements of the older period. The finale, conversely, takes up and intensifies the mood of the opening movement. This is one of the most virtuosic rondos that Mozart ever wrote, its unity consisting for the most part in its incessantly rolling motion, which is interrupted only briefly by individual subsidiary themes. Virtually no trace remains of the anguish of the middle movement, and only rarely does a darker shadow steal over the bright scene, notably in the F sharp minor episode in the violin and in its modulation to A minor in the second subsidiary theme, together with the latter's continuation.

Chamber music for strings is also represented by the string quartet in D major K499 of 19 August 1786 and, more especially, by the two string quintets in C major K515 and G minor K516 of 19 April and 16 May 1787 respectively. All three works are not only the most perfect examples of the new style, they also mark a high point in Mozart's entire output. The rapt theme of the string quartet is launched by all four instruments in unison, an opening found in many other works of this period. There is no second subject as such. Instead, the main idea keeps on recurring in different guises, especially in canon. Finally, we find a genuinely 'Romantic' development of a kind that Schubert was especially fond of exploiting: an interrupted cadence on the relative minor, a contented rocking to and fro in this minor tonality with an apparently new theme, and a return via the main idea to the six-four chord of the major. This process is made even more intense by dint of the fact that at the repeat the key of F sharp minor is replaced by the major of the diminished submediant (F major). In the development section the main theme is joined by a subsidiary motif that had slipped in only with the very last bar of the subject-group. As in the F major sonata, the musical argument leads us deep into the region of the subdominant, from which it returns via enharmonic change. There is something particularly appealing about the way in which the subsidiary motif returns in the coda and brings the whole movement to an ethereal, elfinlike ending. The menuetto strikes a note of contemplative charm, with the trio already looking forward to the main theme of the finale. Both movements afford ample scope for contrapuntal procedures. The adagio shares with the other slow movements of this period the broad design of its themes. In general, it breathes the same spirit of hearty joviality that typifies the work's other movements. Only in the brief development section is there any greater feeling of passion, yet even here – as in the movement as a whole – thematic unity is maintained and, with it, a uniformity of mood. The quartet culminates in a finale of effervescent good humour. It begins with a figurative theme that seems to have been dashed off as though by way of a joke before gradually getting into its stride and sharing control with a tomboyish second subject. In the exceptionally ingenious development section, these two subjects struggle for supremacy, with the first subject finally emerging as the victor in the recapitulation. Only the second violin finds it impossible to break away from the canonic procedures, and the second subject, which now crops up, much to our surprise, in F major, fails to develop properly. Instead, the first subject is reworked – a further feature of the new, more subjective style, which involves the sudden appearance of brief development-like passages at points where they do not as a rule belong, either in the subject-group or, as here, in the recapitulation. In this way, conflicts are fomented and resolved for which the listener is initially not at all prepared but which explore the emotional world of the main themes in far greater depth than before. The coda, too, is designed along similar lines, except that here the conflicts are less acute and make no attempt to prevent the tension from falling, even making that relaxation seem all the more psychologically plausible.

The string quintet in C major begins with a typically Mozartian 'broken' theme over a curiously pounding quaver accompaniment in the middle voices. The bass presses forward in the familiar way[21] with an abruptly curtailed motif built up on a chord of C major and is answered by the first violin with a cantabile melody familiar from *Le nozze di Figaro*.[22] Here it sounds like an affecting sigh caused by a heavy burden of care. All this happens within the space of only five bars and is repeated three times before ending with a helpless question and a whole bar's rest. It is an authentically Mozartian picture made up of disparate moods and failing to find any clarification, but increasing the tension accordingly. At least initially, the following passage, too, brings with it no resolution, but merely adds to the tension by repeating the whole section in C minor, now with the roles reversed. Treated canonically, the sigh motif increases the sense of profound agitation when suddenly a ray of light enters the proceedings and sets the listener thinking of other thoughts, although even these are 'Romantic' in origin. There follows a subsidiary motif[23]

from which there evolves one of those dreamy Schubertiads *avant la lettre* that suddenly plunge deep down into the world of subdominant tonalities, where they perform a brief dance before abruptly leading straight back to the tonic by means of an enharmonic shift. A new theme enters, once again bringing with it a feeling of secret defiance and resulting in the musical argument slipping back into the principal theme. And once again it is the sigh motif which, powerfully intensified (it clambers up from the bass, step-wise and canonically, to the first violin), resists this move and introduces a new and unexpected turn of events. With the help of a transitional motif

the movement's actual second subject leads us back to a gently rocking rêverie for the first violin over a pedal point, a rêverie from which more clearly contoured melodic shapes emerge only when it is repeated by the violas. But the transitional motif is now developed along broader lines and, albeit not without a certain degree of resistance, leads us away from this world and to the open spaces of the G major ending. The mood then changes yet again. A new pedal point theme[24] appears, characterized by the whispered interplay between one note and its lower semitone, in other words, another dreamy, 'Romantic' idea that leads via a crescendo back to the beginning. The development section, too, begins with the main theme but immediately intensifies its sense of contrast not only harmonically but also by virtue of the fact that the bass, with its triadic motif, no longer allows the motif of entreaty to have its say. In this way the expressive force of the latter is likewise increased, the interval between its last two notes now widened to that of an octave, and in this form it carries the day at a particularly important point in the musical argument, defeating its enemy at one of the most tense and emotionally charged passages in the whole of this opening movement. This urgent entreaty calls forth a newcomer in the form of the final theme,[25] which,

21. Cf. the keyboard sonata in C minor K457, the main theme of which contains a similarly sudden shift of mood.
22. If the individual phrases are joined together, the result is the familiar Italian type of melody.
23. Even the previous variant on the chordal motif recalls Schumann and Brahms.
24. The affinity between this theme and that of the main theme of the overture to *Le nozze di Figaro* is immediately apparent.
25. Its first semibreve still has the character of a 'curtain', thereby adding even further to the similarity with the theme from *Le nozze di Figaro*.

beginning in the bass, steals through all the voices in turn. It then reveals the other facet of its character, its sinister, gnawing aspect, giving rise to an inevitable reaction as the sigh motif resists the intruder both in its original semitone form[26] and in its octave variant – in other words, with both entreaties and threats. In both cases its efforts are in vain. With this we enter one of those development sections that are so typical of the later Mozart and that are emphatically dramatic in character: two starkly contrasting thematic ideas are developed in double counterpoint with a constant increase in tension. It is also significant that the octave motif now disappears, while the quaver motif is treated canonically, thus drawing together the strands of the sinister fabric even more tightly. This passage culminates in a heavy dominant pedal point, above which a fragment of the second subject writhes to and fro in an agonized C minor. This feeling of agitation continues into the recapitulation, which from the outset includes darker colours. Structurally speaking, this passage runs along regular lines, except that the final theme is introduced very abruptly after a whole bar's rest and, moreover, is now treated canonically. This allows the writing to expand organically in the form of a coda that calms the mood to such an extent that the final theme can now end the piece in its original form – a remarkable form for the coda, which in fact consists of a development-like interpolation before the final link in the chain. Like all the menuettos in the works of this period with the exception of *Eine kleine Nachtmusik*, the present menuetto, too, is in second position and clearly picks up the mood of the opening movement.[27] Its thematically exceptionally unified first subject-group,[28] the main idea of which is Beethovenian in character, is dominated by a remarkably grim and sullen humour that refuses to abandon this one idea. All the greater is the range of moods contained within the trio. It takes half the opening section before we emerge from the vacillating dominant harmonies and find ourselves standing on firm ground. The most varied ideas are presented here, the most remarkable of them being at bar 9ff., where the writing for both the two violins and the two violas is in octaves. Here the music finally breaks free to what sounds like an anxious groan, as the opening motif soars upwards to C major, this time with a turn instead of the initial crotchet. Here, too, there follows an extremely tense development section, with the whole of the first half of the opening section repeated in the bass in expanded form. With the entry of the viola in the fifth bar of the andante, the devoutly religious chant of the opening acquires the subjective element that is typical of the quintet as a whole. Initially it recalls a recitative, sounding like nothing so much as a gentle sob, before developing into a broadly flowing chromatic melody. It is as though the mood of the opening had suddenly coaxed from a single member of this little group all his private griefs, and there is something particularly moving about the way in which the first violin appears to accept this in the second idea in F major and the viola takes the proferred hand, initially shyly, then with total commitment, allowing it to assume complete control at the end. This dialogue continues in the second theme, too, except that when repeated by the viola, everything sounds a degree more personal and anguished. As a result, this movement, too, contains a powerful dramatic streak, with the emotional world of the opening returning in the coda to particularly beautiful effect.

The final movement is a large-scale example of the sort of sonata-rondo form that we have already encountered on many previous occasions. It begins with a very broadly developed

26. These extended suspension motifs are now found more frequently in canon. Among notable examples is the opening movement of the great C major symphony (K551).

27. ◆ In Mozart's autograph, the minuetto is in third place; in the first edition, published by Artaria in 1789, the minuetto comes second. Concerning the disputed placement of this movement, see NMA VII/19/1, ix and Emerson, 'A Question of Order'.

28. It is typical of Mozart that even in such brief movements he is fond of returning to the main theme at the end. Here its effectiveness is increased by dint of the fact that he reintroduces it without the lengthening of its second half.

subject-group with resolute closure on the dominant, but this is followed not by a development section but by the main idea, first in C major, then in F major, in which key we then have a brief development section in the familiar contrapuntal style, with even an inversion of the main idea, after which the movement continues in the manner of a recapitulation with a subsidiary subject and final theme, followed by a thematic coda. Yet almost every theme, and especially the second of them, is followed by brief development-like pendants that explore the movement's basic emotions – strength and humour – from the most varied angles. But even this world of emotion is expressed in entirely personal ways. There is also a notional link between the two main ideas of the outer movements and their accompaniments, except that in the final movement there is no contrast in mood. As the movement pursues its course, so we find that the mood briefly clouds over, especially when the part-writing becomes chromatic. No less present are 'Romantic' subdominant harmonies, especially in the course of the second subject. But we also find new and intimate features such as the way in which the second subject gradually summons our attention. In the coda, which only hesitantly gets under way, all the spirits of spring gather to perform a festive dance that does not, however, prevent the thoughtful, dreamy aspect of the piece from once again finding expression in the passages marked *piano*.

Whereas the C major quintet rests on the conflict between opposing forces and the resolution of that conflict, the G minor quintet – the most profound of all Mozart's works in this key and, as such, a worthy counterpart of the G minor symphony – is an expression of one and the selfsame mood, the most anguished resignation, which it embraces with a resolution of literally harrowing impact. It is the complete opposite of the keyboard concertos, being the creation of a lonely individual who confronts the dark powers of fate, but who fails to master them in the Beethovenian sense of that term. Like the torments that they inspire, he accepts them as something irrevocable, and if, in the finale, he allows his earlier love of life to reassert itself, this must not be interpreted as a Beethovenian victory following an earlier struggle, but in the sense in which Mozart himself understands that term, that of a realist who again juxtaposes the opposing aspects of reality. (In the G minor symphony he dispenses with this contrast.)

The opening movement expresses this pessimism most consistently, being more succinct and laconic than its predecessor's opening movement.[29] Its main theme

already expresses every aspect of this underlying mood: a somewhat tense rise and fall, first into searing pain, then into wistful sobbing, while its second half reveals a greater intensity that borders on despair, before plunging back into fatalism. The disjointed phrases and constantly hammering

29. In terms of their length, even the subject-groups are in the proportion of 1:1½.

quavers in the accompaniment add an element of restlessness and persecution to this section, much as the fact that initially the harmonies are in only three parts adds to the intensity of the emotion. This theme is immediately repeated by the three lower instruments, but with a remarkable increase in tension in its second section. But, entirely typically, this sense of savage threat is followed by the unspeakable self-torment of a return to G minor with an agitated final phrase that is also found in the G minor symphony. A brief attempt to use the opening motif from the main theme to modulate to E flat major leads all the more hopelessly back to G minor, and it is in this key – from which there seems virtually no escape in the movement as a whole – that the second subject, flouting all tradition, now appears. It begins as follows:

This is one of Mozart's most striking ideas, ineffably wistful and yet filled with manly strength in spite of its anguish, an anguish which, even here, includes a sudden wild outburst of defiance in the form of its tremendous upward leap of a ninth. This theme, too, fails to break free from the spell that hangs over the work as a whole, with the highest point of its melodic line (*d'''*) followed by a painfully and helplessly descending dialogue between first violin and bass. It takes a canonic dialogue between first violin and viola to bring about the movement's first decisive modulation to the major, and there is a real feeling of emotional truth to the way in which the first motif of the main theme – the only expression of strength – takes control at this very point, as the music enters a brighter sphere. Of course, there are still sounds of anguish even here, but the mood brightens sufficiently for the subject-group to come to a calmly contemplative ending. Yet immediately afterwards the old goad becomes clearly visible again in the *g''♭* (*f''♯*). After the usual laconic transition, the development section plunges back down again into the world of the dark subdominant. The mood now becomes uncertain, filled, as it is, with a sense of anxious tension, as the second subject emerges in E flat minor, dominating all five parts with its imitative interplay, first with its opening half, then reduced to the phrase with the interval of a ninth. The strident dissonances of this ninth-based motif now leap up on all sides, while the quaver rhythm continues to beat implacably, after which violins and violas assail each other with the foreshortened motif from the main theme over a pedal point on D:

The melodic line keeps descending, *piano*, evoking a sense of suppressed embitterment, until we suddenly find ourselves back at the hopeless tragedy of the outset. This development section, too, differs from that of the C major quintet by dint of its far greater brevity and succinctness: the more the mature Mozart abandons himself to a single mood, the briefer and more concentrated the outer structure. The recapitulation runs along regular lines with the exception of a significant addition at the beginning, where the third motif from the main theme, together with its sighs, is itself briefly developed. Needless to add, the key of G minor is maintained from start to finish. But it is the coda that creates a particularly moving impression, with the first two motifs of the main theme heard in counterpoint. The rest is a state of total prostration. The melodic line threatens to fall apart, and the appearance of the second subject acquires a positively tragic dimension: the feeling of melancholy remains, but the keen-edged passion has gone. This idea, too, yields to the inevitable.

As with the C major quintet, so here, too, the menuetto builds on and intensifies the mood of the opening movement.[30] In conjunction with its bizarre dynamics, its fragmented melodic line suggests a spontaneous outburst of defiance that inevitably has to contend with weary resignation. This is especially clear from the brief final period:

Yet it is this very motif that the trio now picks up in a bright G major:

What is new here is not so much the motivic link between menuetto and trio as the psychological skill with which that link is forged. The wild defiance of the menuetto calls forth the keenest reaction and does so, moreover, with the selfsame idea that had earlier ended on so pessimistic a note, as though Mozart had suddenly glimpsed it in a completely new light that now filled him with hope. It is no accident that the whole movement clings to this idea with remarkable tenacity. Although the lighting is different, the motif's melodic core remains the same, as do its wistfulness and the inner agitation bound up with its three-bar structure, a sense of agitation that finds particularly clear expression in its middle section. Not even here is the feeling of happiness unalloyed, in spite of the mysterious morendo of the ending's peaceful strains.

The adagio is one of the most heartfelt pieces that Mozart ever wrote,[31] with even its main theme proving to be an extraordinarily complex structure. It begins on a note of profound, manly seriousness, but by the third bar the sense of anguish has already acquired a highly subjective expression,[32] only to sink into brooding two bars later, with some remarkable concertante writing for the instruments. But by the end of this passage there is a feeling of powerful uplift, making this theme as a whole entirely typical of Mozart in its multifarious variety. Yet even here there is a fly in the ointment in the form of the B flat minor idea that clearly conjures up the spirit of the opening movement with its pounding accompaniment, descending melodic line and the motif in the second viola. And just as the menuetto produced the trio, so the present theme unexpectedly draws after it a yearning prospect of happiness. This new theme in B flat major rests on a curiously insistent accompaniment that causes the whole soul to resonate in sympathy.[33] Yet not even here

---

30. An analysis of the two middle movements is given by Riemann, *Präludien und Studien: Gesammelte Aufsätze zur Ästhetik, Theorie und Geschichte der Musik*, iii.69ff. ◆ Further concerning Mozart's quintets, see Bockholdt, 'Der Schlußsatz von Mozarts Streichquintett in C-Dur, KV 515. Bau im Großen und Geschehen im Kleinen'; Schick, 'Ein Quintett im Diskurs mit dem Streichquartett. Mozarts Streichquintett C-Dur, KV 515'; Christoph Wolff, 'à 1, 2, 3, 4, et 5 parties'; Flothuis, *Wolfgang Amadeus Mozart: Streichquintett g-moll, KV516*; and Charles Rosen, *The Classical Style*, 264–87. For the broader context within which the works were written and performed, see Eisen, 'Mozart and the Viennese String Quintet'.

31. The performance marking is 'con sordino' throughout.

32. Note the cadence on the six-five chord, a cadence extremely unusual in Mozart's day.

33. Cf. the second section of Tamino's 'portrait aria' in *Die Zauberflöte* ('Dies Bildnis ist bezaubernd schön').

is there any real sense of liberation, as the musical journey leads back to the beginning, striking a serious note as it does so. This adagio is another binary movement that is notable for its concision. In the brief coda we seem to hear a note of urgent entreaty struggling to find expression, but instead of fulfilment we find ourselves plunged back into a mood of tragedy in the adagio introduction to the rondo, an introduction rarely found in this position in Mozart's works. His intention was to make the contrasts as harsh and stark as possible. As we have already observed, there is absolutely no sense of any struggle to achieve the cheerful high spirits of the rondo. Although this adagio is the most dramatic of the work's movements, it contains a conflict within itself, without reference to what follows, and a resolution in the Beethovenian sense is simply not attempted. Its mood is sustained by the ostinato bass motif that clearly recalls the 'Schreckenspforten, die Not und Tod mir dräun' – 'the gates of terror that threaten hardship and death' – in the second-act finale of *Die Zauberflöte*, while above it we hear the violin melody vehemently resisting its fate. Its first motif – the only motif which, significantly, briefly interrupts the bass line – manifestly harks back to the ponderous B flat minor motif of the previous movement. Many of Mozart's contemporaries would have cast this idea in the form of an instrumental recitative, and Mozart's melodic line, too, has elements of this, but in general it takes the form of a relatively free cantabile line. Yet the quavers in the three middle voices reflect the shifting moods that make up the background of this wholly remarkable movement. At the end the bass suddenly disappears as though avoiding some alien apparition, while in the upper voices there arises a curious whispering, after which they, too, begin to grow hesitant. It is at this point that the life-affirming theme of the rondo soars aloft in a radiant G major. Cast along the broadest lines, this final movement is a perpetual dance filled with a real love of life, now powerful, now charming and mischievous, without any darker aspects. Here Mozart's optimism forges ahead in its boundless enthusiasm. There may be a profound inner significance to this, coming, as it does, at the end of this tragic psychological portrait. The feeling of loneliness that must often have overcome the composer during these critical days finally yields to a proud feeling of strength inspired by the host of new artistic visions, allowing him to spread his wings and soar higher and higher aloft. The tragedy of the first three movements and the jubilation of the last stem from the very same source: the wealth of emotions that assailed Mozart as an artist also lent him an enhanced awareness of being alive.

Generally speaking, the quintets are no different stylistically from the quartets. Both are rigorous examples of chamber music. Only in terms of their execution and sonority do we find differences between them, although these differences then have clear repercussions for the overall structure and design of the individual movements and themes. The addition of the fifth instrument – for Mozart, unlike Schubert and Boccherini, it was always a viola rather than a cello[34] – made possible an impressive range of additional groupings. First and foremost one thinks of the division into two concertante groups of three voices each, with the first viola functioning first as a bass instrument and, secondly, as a melody instrument, as at the beginning of the G minor quintet. In this way it acquires a special role as the second chorus leader alongside the first violin. Indeed, there are even times, as in the andante of K515, where it appears as an independent character. At the same time, we find concertante pairings of the most disparate kind. Often – as at the beginning of K515 – the first violin and cello engage in a dialogue over the dense three-part

---

34. With Schubert, it was the sonorities that were decisive. Although this consideration was also of importance for Mozart, it was subordinated to the development of the musical ideas – significantly even more so in K516 than in K515.

textures of the three middle voices. It is the second viola that helps to make this possible by relieving the cello of part of its role as a bass instrument and thereby giving it more freedom of movement from a melodic point of view. To this may be added the octave doubling of individual voices, a practice taken over from the Viennese symphony and first applied to the quartet by Haydn. As we saw above, the trio of K515 is a good example of this. But the quintet was particularly well suited to Mozart's new approach to thematic and contrapuntal writing, and it is quite literally astonishing to discover the ease with which sections of the individual themes migrate from desk to desk. The art of double counterpoint and other forms of strict counterpoint are exploited with a technical mastery and, at the same time, a wealth of imagination that were unprecedented at this time. As listeners, we never have the impression that Mozart set out with the intention of impressing us with his contrapuntal skills. Rather, the contrapuntal passages emerge with the obviousness of a natural process, sometimes unexpectedly producing passages of highly dramatic tension, before unravelling once again in an equally casual manner. In this, they differ markedly from Mozart's earlier experiments in counterpoint, which were conducted under the influence of the north German school of composers. Here counterpoint had been an end in itself, whereas now it is a particularly effective means of developing the musical argument. It is not, of course, the only such means, as Mozart's thematic writing also becomes much more concentrated at this time, but it is far more common than with Haydn, who, although familiar with contrapuntal development sections, uses them far less frequently and far less consistently. The extent to which Mozart was attracted to the quintet as a medium (a medium cultivated by Boccherini especially) is also clear from various sketches.[35]

Eine kleine Nachtmusik K525 – 'consisting of an allegro, romance, menuetto and trio, and finale' [according to Mozart's thematic catalogue] – was completed on 10 August 1787 and, as is clear from the description 'Violoncello e Basso', was scored for multiple forces. It is a true occasional serenade with all the festive pomp but also all the delicate charm of such a piece. Deeper emotions are not explored, although we do find all the stylistic characteristics of this period, albeit in their most lightweight guise: in the opening movement, for example, there is a free return to reminiscences of the main themes of the subject-group, while in the romance we find an ingenious return to the main theme and in the 'Romantic' middle movement in C minor there is a canonic dialogue between first violin and bass. Mozart himself described the finale as a rondo, but it is clear, not least from the repeat signs following the cadence in D major, that it also includes features of sonata form. Even so, it is rondo form that predominates, with the movement's principal effect resting on the frequent return of its main idea in its entirety, this time in different keys, with the result that the movement is closer to the rondos of Carl Philipp Emanuel Bach than are Mozart's other rondos of this period. Moreover, this movement, too, reflects the period at which it was written, especially in the sudden entry of E flat major following the D major cadence and also in the contrapuntal writing in the coda. As an occasional piece, it is a sparklingly brilliant masterpiece.

---

35. K514a is reproduced in NMA VIII/19/1. On stylistic grounds it can probably be dated to the present period. ◆ Recent studies of Mozart's string quintet fragments – described by Abert as sketches but in fact works started by Mozart and left unfinished – suggest a wide range of dates for the manuscripts. K514a, 613b, 592b, 587a and 516a were probably written down between 1786 and 1788; K515c and 515a seem to date from 1791; and K613a is apparently early, 1784–5. The lost K626b/30, a fragment in E minor described in recent editions of Köchel as identical with K515c, probably never existed; according to Ulrich Konrad, 'Fragmente aus der Gegenwart', 180, the original reference in Nissen's biography of Mozart is a typographical error. For editions and facsimiles of all the quintet fragments, see NMA VIII/19/1 and X/30/4. Concerning a possible relationship between K613a and an early quintet by Pleyel, see Eisen, 'Mozart and the Viennese String Quintet'.

Completely different aims were served by *Ein musikalischer Spaß* K522 of 14 June 1787.[36] Scored for string quartet and two horns, this piece can look back on a venerable tradition, as the custom of caricaturing worthless and incompetent 'colleagues' was extremely popular at periods when art was still very much a craft or trade. In Mozart's day the divertimento was the place for such caricatures, and we know that Leopold Mozart was especially fond of the medium, a fondness hardly surprising, given what we know of his love of sarcasm. With the present composition, his great son created a work of timeless appeal. The two alternative titles that the work acquired after Mozart's death – 'The Village Musicians' and 'The Peasants' Symphony' – should be accepted only with great circumspection, as the piece, in spite of its conscious gaffes, is not a parody of village musicians of the kind that we find, for example, in the scherzo of Beethoven's 'Pastoral' symphony. The famous false notes in the winds and violins are not the main point, but merely an additional element that contributes to the humour of the piece. The real parody is directed at the work's imaginary composer. That he finds interpreters worthy of him no doubt serves to complete the delightful picture, but the real hero remains the composer. Rarely has so much wit been expended on creating an impression of such witlessness. This 'maestro' has no wish to write a mere divertimento, but is ambitious enough to want to compose a real four-movement symphony. And he has a vague idea of how to set about it, familiar, as he is, with the structure of the work in general and of the individual movements in particular. It is just regrettable that he has absolutely no idea of the spirit that created this form and even more regrettable that, no matter how hard he tries, he fails to come up with any ideas. That he produces such horrors as the infernal fifths in bars 12 and 13 may be mentioned merely in passing. In short, the man is decidedly more dogged than gifted, and during his years in Vienna Mozart will have got to know plenty of examples of such caricatures of true artistry, in whom sheer mindlessness and the dreariest craftsmanship replaced imagination and the powers of logical thought – perhaps he even had certain individuals in mind. Needless to say, this imaginary composer believes himself to be especially talented. He operates largely by the book, adding a goodly dose of pathos to the opening movement and a similar amount of sentimentality to the third, but the result, in the former instance, is hopelessly wooden, in the second, an insistently saccharine drone. Even the opening movement reveals a touching cluelessness about everything to do with symphonic form, notably the order and development of the ideas. The composer is just about able to present his main themes, but combining them together causes him terrible difficulties, as he has a very strained relationship with the concept of modulation and with harmony in general. So tenuous is his grasp of its logic that he often ends up in areas remote from those that he originally intended. By the end of the first seven bars[37] he has already run out of ideas and signally lacks the ability to develop the theme any further, with the result that he now introduces a new idea, a dreary display of triplets, but this, too, ends after only four bars. He is now dimly aware that the second subject should be in C major, and so he boldly adds his b' to the key of F major. But within a bar he has already modulated back to F major and to the three ominous crotchet beats on which he has invariably and irredeemably fallen back at the end of every period. Now he prefers to dispense with any transition and leaps feet first into C major. This subsidiary theme, too, is made up of two completely heterogeneous sections. In the second, the first violin suddenly falls silent and we hear only accompanying figures and a

36. ◆ Concerning the complicated origins of this work, see Tyson, 'Notes on the Genesis of Mozart's "Ein musikalischer Spass", K.522'.

37. Even the number seven is in itself suspicious, as the fourth bar ought really to have been repeated. The melodic line of this theme is one of Mozart's favourites. The peasants' music in act one of Anfossi's *Il geloso in cimento* begins with the same three crotchet beats over tonic and dominant harmonies.

contented purr from the viola player. But things pick up again with a heroic unison and by the end the composer can applaud his own achievement with a solemn flourish of a kind found in every one of the work's fast movements. He knows that the development section should be thematic, but what emerges is the most basic example of such a section: although it retains the given themes, it neither develops them melodically nor dissects them, but merely juxtaposes them in an entirely mechanical way.[38] The result is two primitive sequences, of which the second, moreover, is wide of the mark inasmuch as it ought to lead to A flat major. Instead, the composer arrives, somewhat against his will, in A minor, yet this proves to be his salvation, as it is far easier for him to find his way back to the recapitulation from here. This recapitulation rushes along in all its glory, with its first section foreshortened. For the coda the main theme is treated in a manner typical not only of Haydn but also of Mozart himself at this period, using the running basses that were then popular in Vienna. The menuetto adopts the approach found in Mozart's other works of this period and builds on and intensifies the heroic mood of the opening movement.[39] The 'style' is the same, except that the old delight in concertante procedures continues to find an echo here in the particularly florid horn parts with their well-known solo (*dolce*!!), including their painfully wrong notes. But the depths of grotesqueness are plumbed by the distended trio,[40] which is intended to display the skills of the first violinist. Here, too, the mood is one of the most pitiful lack of concentration that occasionally borders on the most total mindlessness. In the thematic middle section we even find something approaching timid double counterpoint, upon which the first violin staggers back to the beginning. The third movement is devoted to the first violinist's art of cantabile playing, which makes it all the more regrettable that he starts on $f'\sharp$, rather than f''. The whole art of emotionally charged ornaments is unleashed here. What is missing is any appreciation of the deeper meaning of this art. Everything is stuck on and added from the outside. The modulatory birthpangs at the return to the main theme in the second section are classics of their kind, and one can sympathize with the composer for introducing his theme in the minor in the wake of all this effort. At the end comes the inevitable cadenza, which is introduced in a crude and trivial manner. It, too, is made up of nothing but banal motifs and ends with a frightful mess at the top of the instrument's register, followed by an unexpected pizzicato *g*. But the best is reserved for the final rondo. Right from the outset, its vaguely folklike theme[41] acquires a worrying instability in terms of its tonality, with the result that it has to be wrenched back to F major at the end with a good deal of noise and effort. The first episode introduces a novel feature in the form of an actual fugato: our composer is evidently a contrapuntist. But the results are all too predictable: a dreary, vacuous, workaday theme, even more pitiful counterpoint and, above all, a development that inevitably breaks off in the fourth bar. After a single exposition of the subject, he has clearly had enough, and there now begins one of those passages that leaves none of us any the wiser. It drifts along, without any inner logic or any real sense of contrast, with disjointed themes and motifs (all of them strictly four bars in length) scurrying past and even double counterpoint briefly appearing in its most primitive conceivable form and with each phrase ending with the evil-sounding dissonance of *g* sharp – *a* – *b*. But just as, throughout the piece, Mozart says only what he needs to say and never allows his jokes to get out of hand, so he now introduces a new device and once again strikes lucky. This comes at the remarkable passage in C major, which is in fact nothing more nor

38. Not even here do the three crotchet beats give ground.
39. They are also related in terms of main theme's melodic line and the triplet motifs.
40. This basic type, with its semiquaver figure, is also found in the first menuetto of Mozart's divertimento K334 and in the menuetto of Beethoven's piano trio in C minor op. 1 no. 3.
41. A theme of a similar character, albeit one that inevitably has far more substance to it, may be found in the final movement of the F major concerto K459.

less than a large-scale ritardando written out in full. Our composer is evidently familiar with the tension-laden returns in 'classical' rondos and would clearly like to write one of his own. But he completely ruins it by interpolating all manner of extraneous features into this return to F major, chief of which is the main theme in C major with its *Bettelkadenz*. Yet there are two passages here that find our composer briefly entering Mozart's own world: the ritardando already mentioned and the final section that prepares the entry of F major and that includes a mysterious concertante dialogue among the strings over sustained notes in the horns in a manner reminiscent of Beethoven's eighth symphony. The coda is initially dominated by the following motif:

Throughout the movement this motif plays a role analogous to that of a crazed philistine wilfully and boorishly resisting the implacably rising lines in the two lowest instruments, after which the main theme comes merrily tripping along in the horns. The actual ending recalls that of a noisy serenade, and here Mozart once again comes up trumps with the fanfare in the horns joined by another in the strings in a different key. Is this a further dig at the composer, or are they simply too stupid to remain in control until the end of the piece? This whole musical joke is a masterpiece of its kind, a priceless satire behind whose jokes the sure hand of a master musician is time and again discernible.

Among the orchestral works of this period, pride of place goes to the symphony in D major K504, which was completed in Vienna on 6 December 1786. It has a large-scale slow introduction that runs along lines similar to those found in most of Mozart's other works of this kind, with an exceptionally tension-laden opening[42] followed by a soulful melody and then a long passage of a much more agitated character in which one and the selfsame motif is forced down into the remote regions of the subdominant by a series of stark dynamic contrasts, finally reaching the dominant, where the agitation dies away on a note of gentle nostalgia. The theme of the following allegro

---

42. The first three bars still have an Italianate ring to them. The emotional charge as a whole continues to find an echo even as late as Beethoven's first symphony.

is a genuine product of this period inasmuch as it includes all the different moods of the movement and, with a single exception, its whole motivic material, too: pensiveness (a), elation (b) and a feeling of strength (c), all in the remarkably inward tone of the works of this period. There is no longer any trace of Italian rhetoric in the opening, which with its syncopated motif presses forward so expressively towards G major.[43] At its repeat, the sense of resolve is further underlined by a fourth motif (d):

After a dogged struggle, it proudly achieves closure on the dominant. But it is not yet time for the second subject and instead we find a repeat of the main idea, but now expressive of greater yearning:

Together with the syncopations, this eloquent *e* sharp already looks forward to the world of the overture to *Don Giovanni*. It summons into existence a development-like, pugnacious passage based on motif (b). Only now, following a sudden change of mood, can the second subject appear, subtly prepared, as it is, by a transitional motif (e):

Yet, although it is twice repeated (the first time in the minor), it is only episodic in character as it appears only one more time in the course of the recapitulation. Motif (d) immediately takes up the reins again and brings the subject-group to an end with a full show of strength on the part on motif (a). Motif (c) briefly finds that its time has come in the development section, but it is soon joined by (b) and (d), thus investing this section with an exceptionally urgent character inasmuch as all these ideas keep attacking each other in double counterpoint. The awareness of strength already appears to gain the upper hand when motif (a) briefly raises its shadowy head in D minor just before the recapitulation, causing this turbulent world to begin to totter on its foundations. With weary resignation the musical argument now leads back to the recapitulation over a pedal point. It still bears traces of the foregoing struggle both in its variants – especially of motif (a) – and also in its evasive shift to B flat major,[44] but after this it runs along regular lines. Instead of a coda, motif (a) is briefly developed, leading to an increase in tension. The andante palpably picks up this earlier mood. Indeed, even the themes have a certain affinity, albeit one that is unconscious, of course,[45] and the plentiful chromaticisms show clearly not merely that this movement

43. At the repeat this is further reinforced by the countermelody in the oboe.
44. It is significant that this movement's development section avoids the region of the subdominant that is explored in the other works of this period.
45. Note the similarity between the main theme and motif (d) cited above.

breathes a spirit of unadulterated charm but that it also has to contend with extremely dark emotions.[46] Likewise, the pounding motif

has something remarkably agitated and tense about it. But it is the second subject in C minor that demonstrates most clearly that Mozart's allegedly untroubled godlike serenity is as apocryphal here as it is elsewhere. A cloudless sky looks down only on the second subsidiary subject in D major, a calmer predecessor of the duet for Don Giovanni and Zerlina.[47] But the development section immediately introduces a note of dramatic tension that propels the main theme through D and C minor, while the motif just cited pursues it with grim determination, almost literally snapping at its heels. Only towards the end of the movement does the mood begin to brighten, and it ends with the same motif, calm and intimate and not without a touch of humour.

We do not know why K504 has no minuet. As with all the other works of this period, it would most probably have appeared in second position. That its omission might be due to the symphony's greater interiority and its refusal to countenance a dance movement[48] is not a convincing argument, as Mozart was perfectly capable of writing minuets of great interiority at this time.[49]

Here, too, the affinity between the theme of the finale and one of the ideas from *Le nozze di Figaro* suggests a powerful sense of agitation that is further increased by the syncopations. It is a highly capricious joviality that unfolds here.[50] Structurally speaking, the movement is very similar to the first. Both repeat the main theme after a clear break on the dominant in the minor and only later proceed to the real second subject. And both treat this second subject as merely an episode, returning to the main idea at the end of the subject-group. The development sections, too, run along analogous lines, raising the note of agitation to a significant new high before meekly withdrawing into the recapitulation, the beginning of which is overcast by sombre shadows on both occasions. And both movements dispense with a large-scale coda, resulting in a symmetry shared by no other symphony by Mozart. The main difference here is that by the time we reach the finale the emotional conflict has lost much of its keenness, so that everything is now more intimate and homely, with even a trace of good humour occasionally making itself felt. On a more superficial level, too, the work is clothed in lighter, more piquant apparel, with strings and winds engaging in concertante dialogue and creating some particularly beautiful effects.

46. Jahn's assessment of this movement is symptomatic of attitudes to Mozart in his own day: 'The springlike, translucent andante is an expression of the utmost charm. For all its tenderness, the emotion expressed here never degenerates into effeminacy and only rarely and fleetingly strikes a note of yearning. It acquires its particular character from the brief, interrupted motif that permeates the movement as a whole, now in unison, now involving imitative procedures between upper voice and bass, and appearing in various harmonic guises, now teasingly provocative, now thoughtfully reserved'; Jahn, *W. A. Mozart*, ii.238. With its refusal to admit to the merest trace of passion, this is very much a Romantic view of Mozart.
47. At the words 'Andiam, andiam, mio bene' in the duet 'La ci darem la mano'. Even the sustained notes in the bass are the same.
48. Kretzschmar, *Führer durch den Konzertsaal*, i.181, which also includes an excellent analysis of this whole work. ◆ Also see Sisman, 'Genre, Gesture, and Meaning in Mozart's "Prague" Symphony', and Somfai, 'Sketches during the process of composition: Studies of K.504 and K.414'.
49. Mozart did, however, offer the people of Prague some genuine dance music in the form of his six German dances K509 of 6 February 1787. Each dance includes an 'alternativo' and the individual numbers are linked by transitional passages, ending with a coda which, in the manner of our waltzes, is based on earlier dance tunes. All six dances are scored for two violins and bass, flutes (with piccolos), oboes, clarinets, bassoons, horns, clarini and timpani.
50. Note also the brief wind chords on the brief sigh motif.

The vocal music that dates from the period between *Le nozze di Figaro* and *Don Giovanni* is made up in the main of what, for Mozart, is a strikingly large number of German lieder that summarize trends in the Viennese lied of the period and, to a certain extent, represent the culmination of all previous endeavours in this field.[51] It is entirely typical of Mozart that the two through-composed songs – *Als Luise die Briefe ihres ungetreuen Liebhabers verbrannte* K520 and *Abendempfindung* K523 – are the most important in the whole series. The former takes us straight to the heart of a dramatic situation that the keyboard writing reflects from its first eloquent gesture onwards. Songs such as this are a preliminary stage on the way to the later 'lyric monody' of Franz Schubert, inasmuch as we are dealing here with the expression of a particular character in a particular situation.[52] But in Mozart's case the dramatic treatment is predominant, allowing us to sense the proximity of the great operatic solo scenes, even if recitative is replaced by arioso. With its keenly emphasized minor-key character and its essentially chromatic nature, this whole song is a genuine product of this period,[53] subjective and impassioned from start to finish, and as unified in mood as it is succinct in expression.[54] *Abendempfindung*, by contrast, is more formally fixed inasmuch as the first two sections of the final strophe are a variant of the opening. Otherwise the setting is completely free. The unity of the whole is further underlined by a motif that is repeated like a refrain by the keyboard:

It derives from the final vocal phrase of the second line ('der Mondes Silberglanz').[55] A second feature that contributes to the feeling of unity is the gently rocking quaver accompaniment in broken triads, an accompaniment that ceases only at particularly important moments in the text. There is something especially inspired about the way in which Mozart treats the different strophes, in some cases linking them together, in others dividing them up, while using each of them in turn to shed new light on the underlying mood.[56] The song creates such a powerful impression because it touches on Mozart's views on death, views that he had only recently espoused following his

---

51. See Pollak-Schlaffenberg, *Die Wiener Liedmusik 1778–1789*, 138–9.
52. See Spitta, *Musikgeschichtliche Aufsätze*, 431–2.
53. Among the features characteristic of this period is the evasive modulation to A flat major in the fourth bar from the end.
54. Particularly striking are the various melodic pre-echoes of *Die Zauberflöte*.
55. It is found at the end of the first, third, fourth and sixth strophes, in addition to dividing the first two into two half-strophes.
56. The first two strophes are motivically linked in keeping with the text. The opening of the third is related to that of the first. There then follows a beautiful, hesitant, tone-painterly passage that launches the second half-strophe on its upward trajectory, just as, throughout the song as a whole, the second half of each strophe represents a powerfully intensified version of the first. This is particularly true of the fourth strophe with its mood of sombre mourning in E flat major. At the words 'dann, o Freunde, will ich Euch erscheinen' we suddenly find a heavily stressed variant of the dotted rhythms of the priests from *Die Zauberflöte*. The fifth strophe draws a contrast between tears (note the modulation to G minor) and an urgent sense of yearning expressed by means of syncopations, while the second half of the sixth strophe, finally, brings with it a magnificent outpouring of emotion that cannot repeat itself too often. It finally ends with a rapt phrase from the very first strophe and from the keyboard refrain

that permeates the whole song as a leading motif, occurring no fewer than three times in the course of its final section. It is here, too, that melismas are most frequently found.

contacts with his fellow Freemasons. The mysterious reminiscence of the world of Sarastro is no accident. The influence of the aria is still palpable, of course, yet the element of drama takes second place to a more lyrical aspect. Indeed, it could be said that in none of his lieder does Mozart come as close to Schubert's atmospheric lyricism as he does here. For here we find that sense of vibrant emotion that cannot be more accurately explained but which we tend to describe as 'atmosphere'. Mozart is no longer concerned to reexplore in his music the 'evening feeling' of the poem's title, as most earlier lieder composers would have done. After all, this theme has already been fully treated by the poet. Instead, the evening atmosphere as a theme or object of artistic treatment now takes second place to the artist's elemental experience of it, a psychological emotion that finds immediate expression in music. What we are dealing with here is no longer the depiction of a particular emotional state but a sense in which the emotion in question, in all its countless stirrings and immediacy, has taken on a vibrant, resonant existence. Herein lies the immense progress made by the Schubertian song, a form of progress that in turn made possible all its ground-breaking innovations in terms of structure, melody, rhythm, harmony and piano accompaniment. This spirit can already be discerned in the case of the present song: it is the same spirit as the one already revealed in the arias of Cherubino and Susanna. Mozart's other songs from this period still represent the older tradition, however much they may tower above their surroundings by dint of the greatness of Mozart's own personality. This is especially true of the anguished and impassioned *Lied der Trennung* K519 of 23 May 1787, a setting of a poem by Klamer Schmidt that is notable for the tenacity with which Mozart maintains the key and character of F minor, abandoning it only in the two penultimate new strophes. Conversely, the setting of Friedrich von Hagedorn's *Die Alte* K517 that Mozart completed five days earlier contains a delightful caricature, achieving its effect not only through its performance marking 'to be sung a little through the nose' but above all through its lachrymose tone due to its use of E minor, its nasal drone twice giving way to darting outbursts of malice at the lines 'doch alles mit Bescheidenheit' ('but everything in moderation') and 'sie reizten nicht der Mütter Neid' ('they did not provoke their mothers' envy'). This poem was popular with other composers of the period, and Mozart's own setting has clear affinities with the one by Joseph Anton Steffan. Two other songs are purely strophic in design: the arietta-like *Lied der Freiheit* K506 by Aloys Blumauer and the bitter-sweet pastoral *Die Verschweigung* K518 by Christian Felix Weiße.[57] The canzonetta-like *An Chloe* K524 is a setting of a poem by Johann Georg Jacobi and is cast in a free rondo form, making it a companion piece to *Abendempfindung*. An example of what was then the fashionable Italianate style, it owes its popularity to its delicate charm, a charm that is none the less not lacking in secret anguish. But it has no higher artistic ambitions.[58]

The recitative and aria *Non temer, amato bene* K505[59] was written for Nancy Storace on 26 December 1786 and has the same words as the additional aria composed for Idamante for the Viennese performance of *Idomeneo*. Exceptionally, the solo instrument is a piano. Aside from its ending, the piece is structurally and harmonically closely modelled on its predecessor,[60] with even

57. ◆ Mozart's autograph of *Die Verschweigung*, which is incomplete, includes additions possibly in the hand of Johann Anton André; see Ulrich Konrad, 'Zu Mozarts Lied "Die Verschweigung" KV518'.

58. ◆ Concerning Mozart's songs generally, see Ballin, *Das Wort-Ton-Verhältnis in den klavierbegleiteten Liedern Mozarts* and Rushton, 'Mozart's Lieder: A Survey'.

59. The autograph score bears the note 'composto per la Sgra Storace dal suo servo ed amico W. A. Mozart Vienna li 26 di decbr 1786'. According to his *Verzeichnüß*, Mozart wrote it 'for Mlle Storace and me'.

60. See Spiro, 'Die Entstehung einer Mozartschen Konzertarie (KV. 505)'.

the dialogue between voice and concertante instrument pursuing the same goals as before. At the same time, we find a number of clearly conscious reminiscences of *Le nozze di Figaro*.[61] And yet the characteristic style of this period has left its mark on this work, too, to an extent that precludes all thought of a mere revision. The new aria is not only far more subjective in tone than the old one, it is also far more unified in structure, with andante and allegretto linked by a number of highly poetical melodic allusions. Here, too, the rondo character is preserved, except that in the allegretto the third repeat of the main theme is suppressed in favour of an episode in A flat major.[62] Two bass arias date from this period: the aforementioned aria *Non sò d'onde viene* for Ludwig Fischer and *Mentre ti lascio, o figlia* K513 for Gottfried von Jacquin. This latter piece is a setting of words from Paisiello's *La disfatta di Dario*,[63] its addressee's identity evident from its absence of any more lofty dramatic passion and of what would have been its concomitant vocal demands. Even so, it remains entirely worthy of Mozart, with the father's farewell to his daughter finding noble and heartfelt expression. Its intimate tone and veiled anguish[64] reveal the period at which it was written no less than the motivic link between larghetto and allegro. Both sections are examples of binary form. And both are relatively brief.

61. The main idea of the andante starts with Cherubino and ends with Susanna.
62. ◆ Mozart and Storace performed K505 at her farewell concert on 23 February 1787; see Eisen, *New Mozart Documents*, 39–40.
63. For a note on the poet Morbilli, see Goldschmidt, *Tommaso Traetta: Ausgewählte Werke*, XVII.
64. In AMA, the figured bass indicated in the autograph by Mozart (bars 143–148) has been omitted. ◆ It is included, however, in NMA II/7/4.

44

Mozart in Prague

Constanze was delivered of her third child, Leopold, on 18 October 1786. He died in the spring of the following year.[1] Soon after his birth, Mozart was persuaded by his English friends to consider the possibility of moving to England, a plan that foundered only on his father's opposition. Shortly after this, a new and attractive prospect presented itself in the guise of an invitation to write a new opera for Prague, the one city where *Le nozze di Figaro* had already been taken into the repertory with a speed matched only by the success of the ensuing production.

Prague's offer came about as the result of a combination of particularly fortunate circumstances. The high reputation enjoyed by Bohemia since the days of the Bohemian Brethren has always rested not only on an intelligent approach to music that takes in the broadest cross-section of the people but also on a natural artistic gift.[2] In the wake of the Thirty Years War Prague admittedly lost some of the prestige that it had enjoyed under Rudolf II, but by the eighteenth century its fortunes had begun to revive thanks to the Church and its various institutions, including the monasteries and Jesuit seminaries. But schools and the aristocracy, with their private orchestras, also played a part in this development, with village schools in particular laying special emphasis on music. According to a valuable report from this period,[3] schoolteachers were required to write at least one new Mass a year and perform it with their pupils, thus presupposing that singing was actively taught. But we also know that the instruments that were especially popular in Bohemia were similarly in great demand, and there were occasions when 'Anton had to practise his horn in one corner, Andreas his oboe in another corner, Michel his violin in the third corner and Matthes his discant in the fourth, all for between four and five hours'.[4] Gifted musicians continued their studies at ecclesiastical foundations, but it was the village schools that were the real breeding grounds for the private orchestras of the aristocracy, including those of the Morzins, Pachtas, Czernins, Mansfelds and others. As elsewhere, the musicians wore special livery and were classed as servants.[5] They were required to provide *Tafelmusik* and concert music of every description.[6] It

1. ◆ In fact, Leopold died less than a month later, on 15 November.
2. See Batka, *Studien zur Geschichte der Musik in Böhmen* and *Geschichte der Musik in Böhmen*; Ambros, *Das Conservatorium zu Prag*; and Branberger, *Das Konservatorium für Musik in Prag*. ◆ The Bohemian Brethren, or Unitas Fratrum, founded in 1457, was a movement based on profound personal faith but at the same time allowing speculation along Scriptural lines concerning religious tenets. Concerning musical life in Bohemia generally, and Prague in particular, see Hogwood and Smaczny, 'The Bohemian lands'; Smaczny, 'Prague'; Všetecka and Berkovec, *Praga musicopolis Europae*; Berkovec, *Musicalia v pražském periodickém tisku 18. století* [Music references in 18th-century Prague periodicals]; and Schiwietz, 'Prag im "klassischen" Zeitalter der Musik'.
3. Schönfeld, *Jahrbuch der Tonkunst von Wien und Prag*, i.103–4; see also *AmZ*, ii (1799/1800), 488–9; and Reichardt, *Briefe eines aufmerksamen Reisenden die Musik betreffend*, ii.123–4.
4. This rural cultivation of instrumental music was maintained until well into the nineteenth century; see Abert, *Johann Joseph Abert*, 4–5. ◆ Abert's quotation derives from Schönfeld, *Jahrbuch der Tonkunst von Wien und Prag*, 103–4.
5. According to Schönfeld, *Jahrbuch der Tonkunst von Wien und Prag*, 'Their gun-chargers were not allowed to don their livery until they were fully proficient on the hand horn. Many employers in Prague demanded that their liveried servants should understand music before they were regarded as fit for service.'
6. See Einstein, *Lebensläufe deutscher Musiker von ihnen selbst erzählt*, iii: *Adalbert Gyrowetz*, 1ff.

is no wonder that – as is clear from the example of Johann Stamitz and the Bendas – Bohemian musicians were highly respected abroad. At the same time, a strong local tradition began to develop. A member of the minorite order, Bohuslav Černohorský (1684–1742), became head of a school whose leading members were two local musicians, František Tuma and Jan Zach, but that also included Tartini and Gluck.[7] Jan Dismas Zelenka is generally regarded as the first representative of a national Bohemian trend in instrumental music.[8] Both, moreover, had more or less close contacts with Italian music. A permanent Italian opera company, especially for *opera buffa*, was established in Prague in 1764 by Giuseppe Bustelli, whose company also appeared in Dresden in 1765, successfully presenting operas in both cities until around 1778. Alongside him, Johann Josef Brunian promoted German singspiels in Prague.[9] Bustelli's successor was Pasquale Bondini,[10] who later gave opera performances during the summer months in Leipzig, too. In Prague he championed Italian operas, initially at Count Thun's private theatre[11] and, from 1783, at the new National Theatre. In Johann Baptist Kucharz (Jan Křtitel Kuchař) and Johann Joseph Strobach he had two outstanding conductors. Indeed, the city as a whole could boast a whole number of distinguished musicians, including the conductor at St Vitus's Metropolitan Cathedral, Johann Antonin Kozeluch (a relative of Mozart's adversary), Václav Praupner and Vincenc Mašek. For Mozart, the most important contact was with the Duscheks, whom we have already met.[12]

Franz Duschek was born of peasant stock at Chotěborky on 8 December 1731. His musical abilities came to the attention of his lord of the manor, Count Johann Karl Spork,[13] who was persuaded to send the boy to the Jesuit Seminary at Königgrätz and, following an unfortunate accident in which Duschek was disfigured, to Vienna, where he devoted himself exclusively to music and, as a result of Wagenseil's teaching, developed into an outstanding keyboard player.[14] He long maintained this reputation in Prague and at the same time exerted a decisive influence on the city's musical life in general. He kept an open house that was much frequented by local musicians, not least because of his wife Josepha née Hambacher, who was born in Prague and baptized on 6 March 1754. She too became an excellent keyboard player under her future husband's tutelage and also turned her hand to composition, but her main strength was singing, and she was praised for her beautiful, full and well-rounded voice and also for her interpretative powers, which were said to be especially impressive in recitative. She triumphed easily over the difficulties of bravura singing, boasted an attractive use of portamento and was fully capable of combining power and ardour with emotion and charm with the result that by 1782 she was already being

7. Otto Schmid, 'Die musikgeschichtliche Bedeutung der altböhmischen Schule Czernohorsky's'.
8. ✦ For Zelenka, see Kohlhase, 'Der Dresdener Hofkirchenkomponist Jan Dismas Zelenka: ein Forschungsbericht'; Hausswald, 'Johann Dismas Zelenka als Instrumentalkomponist'; and Stockigt, *Jan Dismas Zelenka: A Bohemian Musician at the Court of Dresden.*
9. See Teuber, *Geschichte des Prager Theaters.* ✦ For Bustelli, see Haas, 'Beiträge zur Geschichte der Oper in Prag und Dresden' and Pokorny, 'Jossef Bustelli a jeho hudební pozustalost' [Bustelli and his musical legacy]; for the history of Italian opera in Prague, see Volek, 'Italienische Oper in Prag im 18. Jahrhundert'.
10. ✦ See Campana, 'La campagnia di Pasquale Bondini: Praga 1787'.
11. ✦ Concerning Thun, see Angermüller, 'Die Familie des "alten" Graf Thun'.
12. Cramer, *Magazin der Musik,* i (1783), 997–8; Schönfeld, *Jahrbuch der Tonkunst von Wien und Prag,* i.113–14; *AmZ,* i (1798/9), 444–5; and Procházka, *Mozart in Prag,* 1ff.
13. ✦ Johann Karl Spork (1722–90) was the nephew of Franz Anton Spork (1662–1738), an important early patron of Italian opera in Prague; see Freeman, *The Opera Theater of Count Franz Anton von Sporck in Prague* and 'The Foundation of Italian Operatic Traditions in Prague'.
14. Reichardt, *Briefe eines aufmerksamen Reisenden,* i.116, reckoned him among the finest pianists of the day (1773), adding that 'the fact that he performs Bach's music extremely well also means that he has a particularly delicate and brilliant way of playing'. ✦ Further, see Sýkora, *František Xaver Dušek: život a dílo* [Dušek: Life and Works].

described as 'Bohemia's Gabrieli'.[15] In 1785 and again in 1786 she sang to great acclaim in Dresden, so beguiling the Elector Friedrich August that he commissioned a portrait of her from Anton Graff, making her a present of the painting, which unfortunately disappeared after 1855. She had previously appeared in Vienna between 23 March and 6 April 1786, performing at private concerts organized by Count Johann Buquoy and Wenzel Johann Joseph, Prince Paar.[16] Leopold Mozart was less enthusiastic about her, and on 18 April 1786 we find him writing to his daughter on the occasion of the Duscheks' visit to Salzburg:

> Mme Duschek sang, how? – I can't help it, she screamed an aria by Naumann in a quite astonishing way, with exaggerated powers of expression, just as she did before, only worse. Who's to blame? Her husband, who knows no better, it's he who taught her and who continues to teach her, convincing her that she alone has true taste.[17]

Leopold even took exception to her physical appearance, writing on 13 April that 'it seems to me that you can already tell her age, she has a fairly broad face and was very negligently dressed'. Schiller said much the same when she visited Weimar in 1788, finding her very bold, 'not to say forward', and ridiculous in her appearance.[18] The ruling duchess even remarked that she looked like a discarded mistress. But thanks to the patronage of the Duchess Anna Amalie, she was able to give three concerts and prove that first impressions are not always to be trusted. Christian Gottfried Körner continued to criticize her, of course, finding her powers of expression 'too much of a caricature' and missing any sense of grace or charm.[19] But even as late as 1808 Reichardt, who had got to know the Duscheks in 1773,[20] could still praise her 'old warm-heartedness and her ardent enthusiasm for all things beautiful', even commending her voice and her 'grand and expressive style of delivery'.[21]

Duchess Luise of Weimar was quite right in her assessment, of course, for we know from Leopold Mozart[22] that Josepha had been the mistress of Count Christian Clam, one of the principal benefactors of the musical life of Prague,[23] reaping financial rewards of which Mozart, too, was later to take advantage.

We have already mentioned Mozart's first meeting with Josepha Duschek in Salzburg in 1777, including the artistic fruits of this encounter. As Leopold reports, the Duscheks 'sympathized deeply' with their worries in Salzburg, adding that Mozart, whom they described as 'now more of a scamp than ever', should go 'directly or indirectly to Prague, where he will always be given a very warm welcome'.[24] In 1783 *Die Entführung aus dem Serail* was successfully staged in Prague by the company managed by the impresario Karl Wahr, thereby paving the way for Mozart's other works in the city. According to Niemetschek,

15. Teuber, *Geschichte des Prager Theaters*, ii.203. ◆ Caterina Gabrielli (1730–96) was among the most celebrated sopranos of the time; see Casavola, 'La più grande interprete di Traetta: Caterina Gabrielli'.
16. Zinzendorf reacted very favourably to her singing; see Pohl, *Joseph Haydn*, ii.163.
17. Jahn, *W. A. Mozart*, fourth edition, ii.345 (these passages are missing from Schiedermair's edition). ◆ They are included in *Briefe*, iii.532 (letter of 18–22 April 1786).
18. *Schiller's Briefwechsel mit Körner*, i.217.
19. *Schiller's Briefwechsel mit Körner*, i.220. She had performed in Leipzig on 22 April. See also Busby, *A General History of Music, from the Earliest Times to the Present*.
20. Schletterer, *Johann Friedrich Reichardt*, i.134.
21. Reichardt, *Vertraute Briefe geschrieben auf einer Reise nach Wien und den österreichischen Staaten zu Ende 1808 und zu Anfang 1809*, i.132.
22. Jahn, *W. A. Mozart*, ii.345 [*Briefe*, iii.425, letter of 14 October 1785].
23. Branberger, *Das Konservatorium für Musik in Prag*, 13ff.
24. *Briefe*, ii.77 (letter of 28 September 1777).

Now the Bohemians began to search out his compositions; and in that same year all the better concerts contained pianoforte works and symphonies by Mozart. From this time forth Bohemia's preference for his works was decided! The greatest cognoscenti and artists of our city were also the greatest admirers of Mozart and the most ardent prophets of his fame.[25]

The prospects for *Le nozze di Figaro* were especially favourable, therefore, not least because the Duscheks had got to know the recently completed work in the spring of 1786 and, at the same time, had been witness to the intrigues that Mozart had had to face prior to the production in Vienna. As early as 1786 Bondoni decided to stage the work in Prague and duly presented it in December of that year. Niemetschek reports on its success:

It was performed in Prague in 1786 by Bondini's company and received with an enthusiasm at its first performance such as only *Die Zauberflöte* later knew. It is the strictest truth if I say that this opera was played almost uninterruptedly that whole winter, and that it completely allevi-ated the wretched circumstances of the entrepreneur. The enthusiasm it excited from the public had no previous parallel; people could not hear enough of it. It soon came out in a good piano reduction by one of our best masters, Herr Kucharz; it appeared in wind parts, as a chamber quintet, as German dances: in short, Figaro's songs rang out in the streets, in gardens – even the harper inside the tavern had to play 'Non più andrai' if he wanted a hearing.[26]

Around Christmas Mozart received an invitation to attend a performance of Bondini's produc-tion in person, and on 12 January 1787 we find Leopold writing to his daughter to say that her brother would already be in Prague from where 'the orchestra and a company of *great* connois-seurs and lovers of music sent him letters inviting him to Prague and also a poem that was written in his honour'.[27] Wolfgang and Constanze had arrived in Prague on 11 January and, at the sugges-tion of the Duscheks, stayed with one of the most musically influential members of Prague's aris-tocracy, Count Johann Joseph Thun, whom Mozart already knew from Vienna. In his letter to Gottfried von Jacquin of 14 January, Mozart himself reports on the warm reception that he received in Prague and on his initial impressions of the city:

Dearest friend,
    At last I've found a moment to write to you; – as soon as I arrived I resolved to write four letters to Vienna, but in vain! – I could manage only one (to my mother-in-law), and then only half of it. – My wife and Hofer[28] had to finish it. We'd no sooner arrived (at midday on Thursday the 11th) than we had the most dreadful rush to get ready for lunch at 1 o'clock. After the meal old Count Thun entertained us with some music, performed by his own people, which lasted

25. Niemetschek, *Leben des k. k. Kapellmeisters Wolfgang Gottlieb Mozart*, 23 [*Dokumente*, 434, *Documentary Biography*, 505].
26. Niemetschek, *Leben des k. k. Kapellmeisters Wolfgang Gottlieb Mozart*, 26 [*Dokumente*, 435, *Documentary Biography*, 506]; see also the report in the *Prager Oberpostamtszeitung* in Procházka, *Mozart in Prag*, 22–3 [*Dokumente*, 435, *Documentary Biography*, 280–81]. ◆ Concerning Kucharz's piano reduction, see Nettl, 'Der erste Klavierauszug des Don Giovanni', and Kyas, 'Otazníky nad Kuchařovým originálem: Brněnský klavírní výtah Mozartova Dona Giovanniho v úpravě J.K. Kuchaře' [Concerning Kucharz's source: the piano arrangement of Mozart's Don Giovanni by J. K. Kucharz]; and for his quartet arrangement, Krones, '"Il Dissoluto Punito o sia Il D: Giovanni. Quartetti Del Signore Gio: Kucharz". Bearbeitung oder Mitschrift des Mozartschen "Don Giovanni"'.
27. *Briefe*, iv.7 (letter of 12 January 1787).
28. The husband of Josepha Weber and brother-in-law of Mozart; see Blümml, 'Der Violinist Franz de Paula Hofer: Freund und Schwager Mozarts'.

about an hour and a half. This kind of *real entertainment* I can enjoy every day. At 6 o'clock I drove with Count Canal to the so-called Breitfeld ball,[29] where the cream of Prague's beauties tends to foregather. – That would have been something for you, my friend! I can just imagine you running – or rather limping – after all those pretty young girls and women! – I didn't dance or spoon with any of them, the former because I was too tired, the latter because of my natural bashfulness; – but it gave me a lot of pleasure to watch these people leaping around in sheer delight to the music of my Figaro, arranged as contredanses and German dances; – here people talk about nothing but Figaro, nothing is played, sung or whistled but Figaro, no opera is as well attended as Figaro – nothing but Figaro; certainly a great honour for me. But to return to my day's activities. As I got back very late from the ball and was in any case tired and sleepy from my journey, it was entirely natural that I should sleep for a long time; and that's just what I did. – As a result the whole of the next morning was again 'sine linea'. After lunch the Count's music cannot be ignored, and as a very good pianoforte had just been installed in my room, you'll readily imagine that I didn't leave it unused and unplayed that evening and that as a matter of course we played among ourselves a little 'Quatuor in caritatis camera' (and the 'schöne Bandel Hammera'), and in this way the whole evening was again lost 'sine linea'; and that's how it was. Now they're cross with Morpheus because of me, but this god is very propitious to us both in Prague; – I don't know the reason for this; but at all events we really overslept – even so, we still managed to be at Pater Ungar's at 11 for a tour of the Imperial and Royal Library and the General Theological Seminary; – by then our eyes had almost fallen out of their sockets from so much sightseeing and deep down inside us we thought we could hear a little stomach aria, and so we thought it a good idea to drive to Count Canal's for lunch; – before we knew where we were, it was evening and time for the opera. We heard [Paisiello's] *Le gare generose* – as far as the performance of this opera is concerned I can't give you a proper opinion as I talked a lot, the reason why, contrary to my usual custom, I talked so much may be because – enough! this evening, too, was wasted 'al solito'; – today is the first opportunity I've had to ask after the health of your dear parents and the whole Jacquin family. . . . Well, adieu. My concert will take place at the theatre next Friday the 19th, I'll probably give a second one, which will *unfortunately* prolong my stay here. . . . On Wednesday I'm to see and hear Figaro here, assuming I've not gone blind and deaf by then. – Perhaps I'll do so only after the opera.[30]

Mozart attended a performance of *Le nozze di Figaro* on 17 January. During the overture, the report that he was present spread like wildfire through the theatre and, according to Niemetschek, 'when the symphony was over, the whole public applauded and welcomed him with their clapping'.[31] On the 20th he conducted the opera himself and was again accorded a jubilant reception. So pleased was he by the performance that he wrote a letter of thanks to the conductor, Johann Joseph Strobach.[32] The Prague orchestra was small in size and included no famous virtuosos,[33] but its ensemble playing was outstandingly good and it followed its conductor's every instruction.

---

29. 'The Breitfeld balls were particularly brilliant during the winter of 1787. All who were distinguished by status, beauty, wealth and talent were invited'; see Meißner, *Rococo-Bilder*.
30. Schiedermair, *Briefe*, ii.272 (wrongly dated 15 January, but it is clear from the contents of the letter that it was written on the 14th) [*Briefe*, iv.9–12, where the letter is also dated 15 January 1787]; see Procházka, *Mozart in Prag*, 33.
31. Niemetschek, *Leben des k. k. Kapellmeisters Wolfgang Gottlieb Mozart*, 26. ◆ Niemetschek incorrectly states that this was the day of Mozart's arrival, 11 January.
32. ◆ Only a summary of the contents of this letter is known; see *Briefe*, iv. 22.
33. The strings were made up of three first and four second violins, together with two violas and two basses; see Procházka, *Mozart in Prag*, 23 and 165.

Strobach himself often insisted that he and his players were so fired by the music that, in spite of the hard work involved, they would happily have begun all over again.[34]

On 19 January,[35] between the two performances of the opera, Mozart gave a concert at which the enthusiasm of the local inhabitants reached new heights. The programme included the D major Symphony of 1786 (K504, 'Prague') and ended with a free fantasia that so impressed the audience that Mozart was obliged to perform two more extemporizations as encores, the second of which – in response to the audience's tempestuous demands – consisted of an elaborate set of variations on Figaro's 'Non più andrai'.[36] The concert also proved a great financial success, with the profits, according to Nancy Storace, amounting to 1000 florins. Niemetschek left the following account of the concert:

> Never had the theatre been so full of people as it was on this occasion; never had there been greater or more unanimous delight than his heavenly playing aroused. Indeed, we do not know what to admire the more – the extraordinary composition, or the extraordinary playing; both together made a total impression on our souls that could be compared only to a sweet enchantment.[37]

Because of all the distractions to which he was exposed, Mozart wrote relatively little during this first visit to Prague: the only works that date from this period are the contredanses for Count Pachta and the six German dances K509 of 6 February 1787. According to the latest research, the theme that Mozart gave to the harpist Joseph Häusler as the basis of a set of variations also dates from this period.[38] Yet, however meagre this harvest of works may have been, Mozart also achieved his ambition to write an opera for an audience that understood and respected him: Bondini signed a contract with him for an opera for the coming season.[39] The fee was the usual one at this time: 100 ducats. By February Mozart was back in Vienna.

Following his triumphs in Prague, Mozart must have found his straitened circumstances in Vienna all the more unbearable. When, in February, the Storaces set off back to London in the company of Kelly and Attwood,[40] he again cast a wistful glance in the direction of England, delaying his own departure only until such time as his friends might have found him a secure position. His anger was all the more justified in that he was now at an even greater disadvantage than

34. Niemetschek, *Leben des k. k. Kapellmeisters Wolfgang Gottlieb Mozart*, 26. Holmes heard something similar from the first bassoonist; see Holmes, *The Life of Mozart*, 278.

35. A second concert mentioned by Nissen and held out as a possibility by Mozart in his letter to Gottfried von Jacquin is not mentioned in any of Mozart's other letters or by any other sources; see Nissen, *Biographie W. A. Mozarts*, 517 and Procházka, *Mozart in Prag*, 39–40.

36. According to a report by Johann Nepomuk Stiepanek, who later ran the theatre in Prague; see Procházka, *Mozart in Prag*, 39.

37. Niemetschek, *Leben des k. k. Kapellmeisters Wolfgang Gottlieb Mozart*, 27 [*Dokumente*, 436, *Documentary Biography*, 507, translation emended].

38. See Procházka, *Mozart in Prag*, 44ff. The theme is reproduced by Freisauff, *Mozarts Don Juan 1787 bis 1887*, 17. Mozart got to know Häusler at the 'New Tavern' (now the Golden Angel), where Häusler used to entertain guests by improvising on his harp. Mozart invited Häusler to his rooms and asked him to extemporize on a given theme, which Häusler did to his satisfaction. Later this theme formed the basis of the virtuoso's *pièce de résistance*, which he performed only when specially asked. He clung tenaciously to his belief that Mozart was Bohemian by birth. Jahn and Deiters argue that these events took place in 1791, at the time of the performances of *La clemenza di Tito*; see Jahn, *W. A. Mozart*, ii.574–6. It is impossible to be entirely certain on this point, but the earlier date is suggested by both Dionys Weber and Friedrich Wilhelm Pixis, both of whom, however, confuse Häusler with another harpist by the name of Hofmann; see Procházka, *Mozart in Prag*, 44ff. ◆ See KAnh. C26.11.The theme reproduced by Freisauff differs slightly from the published version of Häusler's variations (Prague, 1848).

39. Niemetschek, *Leben des k. k. Kapellmeisters Wolfgang Gottlieb Mozart*, 28.

40. ◆ On 23 February, Nancy Storace gave a farewell concert at the Kärntnertor-Theater; according to a later reminiscence by Attwood, she and Mozart performed the scena *Ch'io mi scordi di te – Non temer, amato bene* K505; see Eisen, *New Mozart Documents*, 39–40. By 26 February, the Storaces, Kelly and Attwood were in Salzburg, where they visited Leopold Mozart.

before in the field of both German and Italian opera. Throughout the early months of 1787 the favourite Italian opera of the Viennese was Martín y Soler's *Una cosa rara*,[41] which, following Nancy Storace's departure, was also performed at the Marinelli Theatre in a German adaptation that enjoyed the same acclaim as the Italian original. In German opera, Dittersdorf was now the hero of the moment. He had come to Vienna during Lent 1786 in order to perform his oratorio *Giobbe* at the concerts of the Tonkünstler-Sozietät, but he also performed his twelve 'characteristic' (i.e., programme) symphonies 'after Ovid's *Metamorphoses*' in the course of two concerts at the Augarten and the Kärntnertor-Theater.[42] And he also received a commission to write an opera for the Nationaltheater: his setting of a libretto by Stephanie the younger, *Doktor und Apotheker*, was first performed on 11 July 1786 and proved such a success that he was acclaimed as the most famous representative of the genre as a whole. Commissions came pouring in, in marked contrast to Mozart: *Betrug durch Aberglauben* was unveiled on 3 October 1786, while *Die Liebe im Narrenhause* proved immensely successful when premièred on 12 April 1787. Only with his Italian opera *Democrito corretto*, which received its first performance on 24 January 1787, was he less fortunate. But his singspiels were deservedly successful. Textually speaking, they were a mixture of types and motifs from *opera buffa* and the local singspiel skilfully adapted to suit the taste of Viennese audiences of the time. Dittersdorf made no attempt to tamper with the stylistic structure of the music. He was decidedly more talented than all his rivals with the single exception of Mozart, with whom he stood in the relationship of the satirist to the ironist. Dittersdorf tended to be pitiless in poking fun at the petit bourgeois world, hence the fact that he was particularly successful when it came to burlesque and the low comedy associated with the world of *opera buffa*.[43] Bound up with this was his determined championship of the *buffa* finale in the Viennese singspiel, ensuring that after a lengthy period of indecision it now acquired a fixed place here. At the same time, of course, he revealed a pronounced gift for the popular German song and sound technical skills. With the exception of *Doktor und Apotheker*, however, none of his singspiels managed to maintain the same high level throughout but all too often was disfigured by hackwork, carelessness and outright dramatic shortcomings. Of some significance are the numerous and striking reminiscences of Mozart in the works written from 1786 onwards, reminiscences affecting not only the melodic writing,[44] but above all the dramatic treatment of the orchestra.[45]

41. Cramer, *Magazin der Musik*, (1788), 47–8 [*Dokumente*, 436, *Documentary Biography*, 507]. ◆ *Una cosa rara* was first given on 17 November 1786 and another nine times by 20 February 1787; see Link, *The National Court Theatre in Mozart's Vienna*, 94–9.
42. See his oft-cited *Lebensbeschreibung*; also Krebs, *Dittersdorfiana*, and Riedinger, 'Karl von Dittersdorf als Opernkomponist'.
43. 'The ridiculous never failed him', wrote Christian Friedrich Daniel Schubart in his *Ideen zu einer Ästhetik der Tonkunst*, 234; see also Dittersdorf's own comments on opera in *AmZ*, i (1798/9), 138–9.
44. Cf. the sextet (no. 9) in *Die Liebe im Narrenhause*:

This is the counterpart to Cimarosa's overture to *Gli Orazi ed i Curiazi*; see Kretzschmar, 'Mozart in der Geschichte der Oper', ii.276.
45. Riedinger, 'Dittersdorf als Opernkomponist', 301. ◆ Further, see Rafael Köhler, 'Dittersdorf und Mozart in der Geschichte des Singspiels'; Horsley, 'Dittersdorfs Singspiele' and 'Dittersdorf and the Finale in Late-Eighteenth-Century German Comic Opera'; Kantner, 'Dittersdorfs italienische Opern'; and Bauman, *North German Opera in the Age of Goethe*.

Unlike Mozart, therefore, Dittersdorf was a composer entirely after the emperor's heart, and Joseph duly and handsomely rewarded him when he left Vienna in 1787. The majority of audiences, too, were won over to his cause, with *Doktor und Apotheker* doing more for the international reputation of the Viennese singspiel, both at home and abroad, than *Die Entführung aus dem Serail* was ever able to do.

In the light of all this, Mozart inevitably remained dependent on the occasional commissions mentioned earlier, writing chamber works and other pieces for domestic consumption. Yet even here he often encountered a lack of understanding. We have already quoted from the following review:

The works of this composer [Kozeluch] maintain themselves and find access everywhere, whereas Mozart's works do not in general please quite so much. It is true, too, and his six quartets for violins, viola and bass dedicated to Haydn confirm it once again, that he has a decided leaning towards the difficult and the unusual. But then, what great and elevated ideas he has too, testifying to a bold spirit![46]

Following his return from Prague, Mozart spent most of his time working on his new opera. The success of *Le nozze di Figaro* made Da Ponte the natural choice as librettist, and according to the latter's self-regarding memoirs, it was he who suggested the subject of *Don Giovanni* to Mozart, a suggestion that the composer found exceptionally attractive. Da Ponte had agreed to provide three librettos simultaneously: an adaptation of Beaumarchais's *Tarare* for Salieri, *L'arbore di Diana* for Martín y Soler and *Don Giovanni* for Mozart. Although Joseph II had questioned the advisibility of his taking on such a workload, Da Ponte had boldly replied that he was determined to prove that it was possible: 'I shall write evenings for Mozart, imagining I am reading the *Inferno*; mornings I shall work for Martini [Martín y Soler] and pretend I am studying Petrarch; my afternoons will be for Salieri. He is my Tasso!'[47] He set to work, a bottle of Tokay to his right, a box of Spanish snuff to his left and his landlady's beautiful daughter as his muse. By the end of the first day he had completed the first two scenes of *Don Giovanni*, two scenes of *L'arbore di Diana* and more than half the opening act of *Tarare*. Within sixty-three days he had finished the whole of the first two operas and around two thirds of the last.

Unfortunately, we know no more about the contribution that Mozart must have made to the final form of the libretto than we do about his progress on the work in general. The question as to how much of the opera was written in Vienna and how much in Prague is even harder to answer as we do not know exactly when Mozart returned to Prague. He was still in Vienna on 24 August 1787, the day on which he completed his violin sonata in A major (K526), whereas his first letter from Prague, which is dated 15 October,[48] makes it clear that he had already been in the city for some time by that date. Stiepanek claimed that he had arrived during the month of September,[49] whereas Dlabač[50] reports that he spent the whole summer in the city, a claim contradicted by the

46. Cramer, *Magazin der Musik*, (1789), 53 [*Dokumente*, 306, *Documentary Biography*, 349].
47. Da Ponte, *Memorie*, i/2.98–9.
48. *Briefe*, iv.54–6 (letter of 15 October 1787).
49. See the preface to his Czech translation of *Don Giovanni* (Prague 1825). A German translation of this text appears in Nissen, *Biographie W. A. Mozarts*, 515.
50. Dlabač, *Allgemeines historisches Künstler-Lexikon für Böhmen und zum Theil auch für Mähren und Schlesien*; see also Procházka, *Mozart in Prag*, 69–70; Freisauff, *Mozarts Don Juan 1787 bis 1887*; and Teuber, *Geschichte des Prager Theaters*, ii.216–17.

evidence cited above. Since the entry of 24 August is the last in Mozart's thematic catalogue before *Don Giovanni*, we may assume that he left Vienna towards the end of August.[51]

If we may trust Da Ponte's account, the libretto must have been finished by June at the latest. And from all that we know about Mozart, it is inconceivable that he had not already begun to plan the music by this date. But we also know that it was not only Mozart's own practice but that of all other composers at this time to allow the singers to exert a significant influence on the definitive form of an opera, especially in the case of the arias and recitatives. Only in the case of the ensembles – as we know from *Idomeneo* – did Mozart refuse to be browbeaten by his singers. In short, the overall musical picture will already have been clear in his mind when he left Vienna, even if much of it was not yet written down. In Prague he will have limited himself to making changes and additions that seemed to him desirable in the light of what he discovered about the individual singers. Also in Prague he will finally have written out the full score. We shall never be in a position to describe this process in greater detail.[52] All that we can deduce from his letter to Gottfried von Jacquin of 15 October is that the opera was completed by an earlier date than is generally assumed.[53]

On his arrival in Prague,[54] Mozart was provided by Bondini with rooms at 'The Three Golden Lions' at no. 420 Kohlmarkt,[55] although Mozart preferred to spend his time with the Duscheks at their house in the country, the Villa Bertramka, near the village of Koschirsch, which they had bought in April 1784.[56] Visitors to the house can still see the room in which he stayed and the

51. ◆ A letter from Mozart to his brother-in-law Johann Baptist Berchtold zu Sonnenburg of 29 September 1787 (*Briefe*, iv.54) shows that he returned to Prague on 1 October, not late August as Abert claims.

52. ◆ The paper types in Mozart's autograph of the opera suggest that the following numbers were composed there: the second version of Masetto's 'Ho capito', Don Giovanni's 'Deh vieni alla finestra' and 'Metà di voi quà vadano', the recitative 'Dunque quello sei tu', the duet 'O statua gentilissima' and the second-act finale; see NMA II/5/17, critical report, 30–1. In Mozart's thematic catalogue, the overture is dated 28 October; see below.

53. See Teuber, *Geschichte des Prager Theaters*, ii.216. ◆ Mozart's letter to Jacquin is reproduced below.

54. This second journey to Prague is treated by Eduard Mörike in his famous and masterly novella, *Mozart auf der Reise nach Prag*, a work planned in 1847 as 'a fragment of poetry from his life' but not published until 1855. Its 'unhistorical' character has always had Mozart's biographers up in arms, with even Jahn taking Mörike to task for it; see Jahn, *W. A. Mozart*, ii.355. Although virtually all the details are invented and the characterization of Mozart himself is idealized in the Romantic tradition, Mörike none the less gained a far deeper insight into the composer's psyche than those of his biographers who are so busy collecting and analysing the historical evidence that they lose sight of him completely. To lump Mörike together with literary Leporellos like Heribert Rau, *Mozart. Ein Künstlerleben. Culturhistorischer Roman*, is little short of blasphemous. A laudable exception is Schurig, *Wolfgang Amade Mozart*, ii.98. ◆ More recently, see Vom Hofe, 'Göttlich-menschlicher Amadeus. Literarischer Mozart. Bilder im Horizont des romantischen Kunst- und Geniebegriffs'; Brandstetter and Neumann, 'Biedermeier und Postmoderne. Zur Melancholie des schöpferischen Augenblicks: Mörikes Novelle "Mozart auf der Reise nach Prag" und Shaffers "Amadeus"'; and Mahlendorf, 'Eduard Mörike's "Mozart on the way to Prague": stages and outcomes of the creative experience'.

55. Procházka, *Mozart in Prag*, 70–1.

56. On 4 March 1856, Carl Mozart wrote to the then owner, a certain Herr Popelka: 'Even blindfolded, I could still find my way there today – after 59 years! Leaving the city by the Ougezd City Gate, with what was then Count Buquoy's garden to the left and Wirtshaus no. 1 to the right, then along the highroad for about a quarter of a mile, after which you turn off into a narrower but still practicable road on the right, you come – or used to come – to an avenue lined with chestnut trees that led right up to the gates to the manor. I still remember every room in the house and every corner of the garden. In the garden – on the left – there was, first, a little flowerbed and, beyond it, a path leading uphill and overgrown by fruit trees, with a large pond on the right, then the greenhouse that I saw being built and, finally, the hillside that was used for farming and at the very top of which there was a pavilion from which you could look down on the cemetery. I also remember – and, as you can imagine, with special affection – the lower part of your estate, where the orchard was situated and where I tried to slip away whenever I could. It was like an Eden to me'; see Procházka, *Mozart in Prag*, 70–1. Since 1876 there has been a bust of Mozart by Thomas Seidan in one of the squares. Procházka also reproduces illustrations of the Villa Bertramka, including Mozart's workroom and Seidan's bust; see also Freisauff, *Mozarts Don Juan 1787 bis 1887*, 22, and Engl, 'Die Villa Bertramka', 63. ◆ Also see Deutsch, *Mozart und seine Welt*, 213.

stone table in the garden at which he worked on the score of *Don Giovanni* to the sound of lively conversation and skittles.

A tangled skein of legends has arisen around the genesis of *Don Giovanni*, foremost among which are the inevitable tales of Mozart's affairs with his female singers. We do not know whether there is any truth in these reports, but the form in which they have come down to us suggests no more than philistine gossip.[57] More important are other accounts that reveal quite clearly that at the rehearsals Mozart not only kept an eye on musical matters but also directed the staging. Although he found that 'the theatre staff here aren't as skilled as they are in Vienna and not able to rehearse such an opera in such a short space of time',[58] he achieved his goal with a characteristic mixture of energy, amiability and diplomacy. Da Ponte arrived from Vienna in early October and took rooms to the rear of the inn 'Zum Glatteis', so that poet and composer could talk to each other through their open windows.[59]

The accounts of these rehearsals are informative not only for what they tell us about Mozart's approach to them but also for the whole way in which operas were rehearsed at this time. First he had to console Luigi Bassi for the fact that Don Giovanni has no major aria to sing. Then he is said to have rewritten the duet 'Là ci darem la mano' five times before Bassi was satisfied with it.[60] The Zerlina, Caterina Bondini, then proved reluctant to utter the well-known scream in the first-act finale. After several unsuccessful attempts, Mozart himself finally went up on stage, asked for the whole passage to be repeated and then, at the critical moment, seized the singer so unexpectedly and so roughly that she screamed out in surprise. 'That's what it should sound like!' he said to her with a laugh. The Commendatore's words in the graveyard scene, it is also reported, were originally accompanied only by trombones, but the players could not perform the passage as Mozart wanted it, and so he collected up the parts and added the woodwinds there and then.[61] But the most important point to emerge from all this is that, according to one unassailable source, the *Tafelmusik* in the second-act finale was improvised at the rehearsals – a living example of one of the oldest *buffa* traditions.[62]

The first performance was set to take place on 14 October and was to have been a gala performance in honour of Prince Anton of Saxony and Archduchess Maria Theresia, a niece of Joseph II,

57. His first favourite, Teresa Saporiti, is said to have expressed astonishment at his unprepossessing appearance, whereupon Mozart – depending on which version of the anecdote one prefers – turned his attention either to Caterina Micelli or Caterina Bondini. ◆ In his life of Rossini, Stendhal recalled meeting Luigi Bassi in Dresden in 1813: 'If I were to tell of the respectful curiosity with which I tried to induce this kindly old man [Bassi] to talk, no one would take me seriously. "Mr Mozart", he would answer (how entrancing to hear someone who still said Mr Mozart!). "Mr Mozart was an extremely eccentric and absent-minded young man, but not without a certain spirit of pride. He was very popular with the ladies, in spite of his small size; but he had a most unusual face, and he could cast a spell on any woman with his eyes. . . ." On this subject, Bassi told me three or four little anecdotes . . .'. See Eisen, *New Mozart Documents*, 52.
58. *Briefe*, iv.54–5 (letter of 15 October 1787).
59. Da Ponte, *Memorie*, i/2.203.
60. According to Victor Wilder, the duet is written on the same paper and with the same ink as the rest of the score (Jahn claims that the paper is of a smaller size and the handwriting more cursory), but that Masetto's previous aria is on a different type of paper; see Wilder, *Mozart: L'homme et l'artiste*, 246. ◆ Neither Wilder nor Abert is correct: both the duet and Masetto's 'Ho capito' are on the same type of paper, which is found throughout the first act, as far as Zerlina's 'Batti, batti'.
61. The recitative that includes these two passages is missing from the original score, thereby appearing to confirm the accuracy of this anecdote, even though its authenticity has been questioned by Gugler, 'Zur Oper Don Giovanni: Controversfragen bezüglich der Darstellung auf der Bühne', 777. In *Idomeneo* the Oracle is accompanied only by trombones and horns.
62. Procházka, *Mozart in Prag*, 86. Missing from the Prague wordbook are all the speeches with which Leporello comments on the excerpts that are performed here; see Wolzogen, *Über die szenische Darstellung von Mozarts Don Juan mit Berücksichtigung des ursprünglichen Textbuches von Lorenzo da Ponte*, 57. Leporello's words 'They're musicians from Prague' in Mozart's fragmentary translation of his opera likewise come under this heading.

who passed through Prague on their honeymoon.[63] But the work was still under-rehearsed, and so *Le nozze di Figaro* was revived under Mozart's direction, eliciting the usual applause.[64]

Mozart reported on these events in his letter to Gottfried von Jacquin:

You'll probably think my opera is over by now – but you'd be wrong. In the first place, the theatre staff here aren't as skilled as they are in Vienna and not able to rehearse such an opera in such a short space of time. In the second place, I found on my arrival that so few preparations and other arrangements had been made that it would have been utterly impossible to have given it yesterday, the 14th. – So yesterday my Figaro was given in the fully illuminated theatre and I myself conducted. In this connection I must tell you a joke. A number of the leading ladies here (and one in particular who is very high and mighty) deigned to find it extremely ridiculous, inappropriate and goodness knows what else that the princess should be offered Figaro, the Mad Day (as they are pleased to call it); – it never occurred to them that no opera in the world, unless it is written specially for the occasion, can really be suitable and that it was therefore a matter of extreme indifference whether this or that opera was given, provided only that it was a good one and that the princess didn't know it; and Figaro at least met this last requirement – in short, the ringleader was so eloquent in her arguments that she managed to persuade the government to ban the impresario from performing the piece that day. – And so she was triumphant! – 'Hò vinta', she cried out one evening from her box, – presumably she never suspected that the 'hò' could be turned into a 'sono'! – The following day Le Noble appeared, bearing a command from His Majesty that if the new opera couldn't be given, Figaro was to be given instead! – My friend, if only you could have seen this lady's beautiful, magnificent nose! – Oh, it would have amused you as much as it did me! Don Giovanni is now fixed for the 24th.

– The 21st. – it *was* fixed for the 24th, but a further delay has been caused by the fact that one of the sopranos has been ill; as the company is small, the impresario is in a constant state of anxiety and has to spare his people as much as possible lest some unexpected indisposition place him in the most awkward of all situations, that of not being able to give a performance at all!

As a result, everything has been postponed indefinitely as the singers (out of sheer idleness) refuse to rehearse on opera days and the manager (out of fear and anxiety) refuses to force them. . . .

---

63. Their wedding opera was Martín y Soler's *L'arbore di Diana*, which was performed in Vienna on 1 October; see *Wiener Zeitung*, lxxix (1787), appendix. Martín y Soler's opera received nine further performances in 1787. The wordbook of the Prague production of *Don Giovanni* had already been printed in Vienna with the note 'Da rappresentarsi nel teatro di Praga per l'arrivo di S.A.R. Maria Teresa, Archiduchessa d'Austria, sposa del Ser. Principe Antonio di Sassonia l'anno 1787'. The first act ends with the quartet ('Non ti fidar, o misera'), the whole of the rest of the act being missing. The second act is complete. The royal party left on 15 October.

64. Bondini had sought permission to stage Beaumarchais's *Le mariage de Figaro*, but on 13 October was informed by the court that the play could be performed 'only as an Italian opera, as presented at the Vienna court theatre', not as a spoken drama; see Teuber, *Geschichte des Prager Theaters*, ii.190–1 [*Dokumente*, 264, *Documentary Biography*, 300]. The *Prager Oberpostamtszeitung* reported as follows on the performance on 14 October: 'The National Theatre was decorated and illuminated in a very special way for the occasion. The scene was so transfigured by the presence of so many distinguished guests that one has to admit to never having beheld such a magnificent sight. When they entered, Their Highnesses were greeted with the most evident marks of pleasure on the part of the whole audience. At their request the well-known opera *Le nozze di Figaro*, generally admitted to be so well performed here, was given. The enthusiasm of the musicians and the presence of the composer were a source of general acclaim and satisfaction for Their Highnesses. After the first act, a sonnet, organized by a number of Bohemian patriots for the occasion, was publicly distributed. Because of their early departure, Their Highnesses returned to the royal castle before the end of the opera' [*Dokumente*, 264–5, *Documentary Biography*, 300; translation emended]. See also the *Wiener Zeitung*, lxxxiv (20 October 1787) [*Dokumente*, 265, *Documentary Biography*, 301]; and Freisauff, *Mozarts Don Juan 1787 bis 1887*, 28–9.

The 25th. – Today is the eleventh day on which I've been scribbling away at this letter; – you'll gather from this that I'm not lacking in good intentions – if I find the time, I'll add a little more to this picture, – but I can't spend too long on it – as too many people have a claim on my time, over which I myself have too little claim; – that this is not the kind of life I prefer, I really don't need to tell you.

The opera is to be performed for the first time next Monday, the 29th – you'll receive a report on it the very next day – as for the aria, it's simply impossible for me to send it to you (for reasons I'll tell you in person). – –[65]

It is hardly surprising that Mozart contemplated this performance with some trepidation, not least because he was aware of the vast difference between his new opera and *Le nozze di Figaro*. Only when he received assurance on this point from the conductor Johann Baptist Kucharz[66] did he take heart, assuring the latter that he had made a very special effort for Prague.[67]

We have already discussed the genesis of the overture. The only point of disagreement is the actual date on which it is said to have been written. A number of commentators, anxious to stress the 'miraculous' nature of the occasion, have assumed that it was the night before the first performance, so that the orchestra had to sight-read the piece, for which the players were warmly praised by Mozart, in spite of the many wrong notes.[68] Others, including Constanze, state that it was two nights before the first performance, a date confirmed by Mozart's thematic catalogue, in which the entire opera, including the overture, is entered under 28 October. This suggests the night of 27/28 October, in other words, before the dress rehearsal. Neither composer nor conductor would surely have been so foolhardy as to expect the orchestra to play such a difficult piece from uncorrected parts on so important an occasion as this.

The first night was a brilliant success:

On Monday the 29th the Italian opera company gave the ardently awaited opera by Maestro Mozard, *Don Giovani* [*sic*], or *das steinerne Gastmahl.* Connoisseurs and musicians say that Prague had never yet heard the like. Herr Mozard conducted in person; when he entered the orchestra he was received with threefold cheers, which again happened when he left it. The opera is, moreover, extremely difficult to perform, and every one admired the good performance given in spite of this after such a short period of study. Everybody, on the stage and in the orchestra, strained every nerve to thank Mozart by rewarding him with a good performance. There are also heavy additional costs, caused by several choruses and changes of scenery, all of which Herr Guardasoni had brilliantly attended to. The unusually large attendance testifies to a unanimous approbation.[69]

65. *Briefe*, iv.54–6 (letter of 15–25 October 1787).
66. Johann Baptist Kucharz [Jan Křtitel Kuchař] (1751–1829) was born at Chotec and studied with Josef Seger. His first appointment was as organist at St Henry's Church in Prague. In 1790 he became organist at the Premonstratensian Abbey Church at Strahov and from 1791 to 1797 was conductor at the Prague Opera. He was a much-respected organ virtuoso and wrote numerous works for the instrument, in addition to music for the stage; see Procházka, *Mozart in Prag*, 76–8. Kucharz was also responsible for the first vocal scores of *Le nozze di Figaro, Don Giovanni, Così fan tutte, La clemenza di Tito* and *Die Zauberflöte*, for which he also wrote recitatives for a production in Prague in 1794. ◆ Further, see Jonášová, '"Ihre Versicherung beruhigt mich, sie kommt von einem Kenner": K biografii Jana Křtitele Kuchaře'.
67. See Niemetschek, *Leben des k. k. Kapellmeisters Wolfgang Gottlieb Mozart*, 85.
68. The various versions are reproduced by Teuber, *Geschichte des Prager Theaters*, ii.231–2, and Procházka, *Mozart in Prag*, 92ff.
69. *Prager Oberpostamtszeitung* (3 November 1787) [*Dokumente*, 267, *Documentary Biography*, 303–4]; see Teuber, *Geschichte des Prager Theaters*, ii.236–7; and Procházka, *Mozart in Prag*, 112; Procházka also includes Meißner's report, 110–11.

The cast was as follows:[70]

Don Giovanni giovane cavaliere estremamente licenzioso	Sign. Luigi Bassi
Donna Anna dama promessa sposa di	Sgra. Teresa Saporiti
Don Ottavio	Sign. Antonio Baglioni
Commendatore	Sign. Giuseppe Lolli
Donna Elvira dama di Burgos abbandonata da D. Giovanni	Sgra. Caterina Micelli
Leporello servo di D.G.	Sign. Felice Ponziani
Masetto amante di	Sign. Giuseppe Lolli
Zerlina contadina	Sgra. Teresina Bondini.

Guardasoni[71] wrote enthusiastically to Da Ponte, who had had to return to Vienna for the rehearsals of Salieri's *Axur* before *Don Giovanni* opened: 'Evviva da Ponte, evviva Mozart! Tutti gli impresarij, tutti i virtuosi devono benedirli! Finchè essi vivranno, non si saprà mai, cosa sia miseria teatrale.'[72] Mozart, too, wrote to inform Da Ponte of the opera's success and on 4 November wrote to Gottfried von Jacquin:

Dearest, best of friends,

I hope you received my letter. My opera Don Giovanni was staged on 29 October and received with the greatest applause. Yesterday it was performed for the 4th time (for my benefit). I'm thinking of leaving here on the 12th or 13th, you'll have the aria as soon as I get back. NB. *between ourselves* – How I wish my good friends (especially you and Bridi) could have been here for just one evening in order to have shared in my pleasure! – Perhaps it'll be performed in Vienna after all? I hope so. – People here are doing everything possible to talk me into staying a few more months and writing another opera; but, however flattering this offer, I can't accept it.[73]

The first Don Giovanni was the then twenty-two-year-old[74] Luigi Bassi. He was born in Pesaro in 1766[75] and studied with Norandini in Senigallia and with the Laschis in Florence. Even as late as 1823/4 Beethoven could still describe him in his conversation books as a 'fiery Italian'. Meißner, conversely, found him an 'extraordinarily handsome but deeply stupid fellow'. He joined Bondini's company in 1784 and in 1792 was described in the company's listings as follows: 'His voice is as melodious as his acting is masterly. As a result he is equally acclaimed in comic and tragic roles and wherever he has appeared he has been universally admired.' He was active in Prague until 1806. By the late 1790s, of course, he had already lost his voice, which was described as follows by an eyewitness in Prague:

70. The playbill from this performance has not survived, and so the present list is based on the Prague wordbook (see above) and the details given by Stiepanek. The Zerlina was Caterina, not Teresa, Bondini; see Procházka, *Mozart in Prag*, 24ff.
71. Guardasoni was currently co-director with Bondini. He later became sole director. An unflattering account of his greed and unscrupulousness may be found in *AmZ*, ii (1799/1800), 537. ◆ Further, see Teuber, *Geschichte des Prager Theaters*.
72. Da Ponte, *Memorie*, i/2.103. His fee was 50 ducats.
73. *Briefe*, iv.58 (letter of 4 November 1787).
74. As emerges from the illustrations by Kininger and Ramberg, he performed the role without a beard; see Deutsch, *Mozart und seine Welt*, 217.
75. See Procházka, *Mozart in Prag*, 73ff.; and Mantovani, 'Luigi Bassi e il "Don Giovanni" di Mozart'.

It lies between tenor and bass, and although it sounds somewhat bright, it is still very flexible, full and pleasant. Herr Bassi is furthermore a very skilled actor in tragedy with no trace of burlesque, and with no vulgarity or tastelessness in comedy. In his truly artful and droll way he can parody the faults of the other singers so subtly than only the audience notices and they themselves are unaware of it. His best roles are Axur, Don Giovanni, Teodoro [in Paisiello's *Il re Teodoro*], the Notary in [Paisiello's] *La molinara*, the Count in *Figaro*, and others. He never spoils a role and is the only actor in the present Italian company.[76]

Leporello was played by the *buffo* bass Felice Ponziani, who had already sung Figaro in Prague. He, too, was praised as a singer and actor, especially in character roles.[77] Contemporary reports stress the evenness of his voice throughout its whole range, as well as his excellent enunciation.[78] Before moving to Prague, he was active in Parma in 1784/5.[79] By 1792 he was working in Venice.[80]

Giuseppe Lolli, who played both Masetto and the Commendatore, was similarly praised as a singer.[81] He, too, was active in Parma and Venice in 1780/81.[82]

Mozart's first Don Ottavio was the excellent tenor Antonio Baglioni, who was particularly praised for his artistry and taste.[83] The list of company members referred to above reports that his voice was attractive, pure and expressive, so that few other companies could boast such a tenor.[84] He appeared in Venice in 1786 and again in 1793/4.[85]

Among the female singers, it was the then twenty-four-year-old Teresa Saporiti as Donna Anna who enjoyed the highest reputation at this time, a reputation that she owed not only to her vocal skills but also to her beauty. A portrait of her has survived in the form of a medallion now in the possession of Dr Schebek.[86] After triumphant appearances in Prague, she too appeared in Italy, including performances in Venice, Parma and Bologna.[87]

Of the first Donna Elvira, Caterina Micelli, we know only that she was a leading member of the Prague ensemble. The first Zerlina, by contrast, was Caterina Bondini, the wife of the director of the theatre. The declared favourite of local audiences on account of her gifts both as a singer and as an actress, she was almost literally overwhelmed by enthusiastic poems on the occasion of her benefit performance of *Le nozze di Figaro* on 14 December 1786.[88]

---

76. Teuber, *Geschichte des Prager Theaters*, ii.345. In 1806 Bassi entered the service of Prince Lobkowitz, returning to Prague in 1814, where he sang Don Giovanni under Carl Maria von Weber; see Max Maria von Weber, *Carl Maria von Weber*, i.434–5. From 1815 until his death he worked as stage director for the Italian opera in Dresden; see Weber, *Carl Maria von Weber*, ii.45. ◆ Also see Waidelich, '"Don Juan von Mozart, (für mich componirt.)" Luigi Bassi – eine Legende zu Lebzeiten, sein Nekrolog und zeitgenössische "Don Giovanni"-Interpretationen'.

77. See Teuber, *Geschichte des Prager Theaters*, ii.209 and 224. ◆ Also see Campana, 'Giuseppe Lolli da *L'italiana in Londra* a *Don Giovanni*'.

78. See Teuber, *Geschichte des Prager Theaters*, ii.130.

79. Ferrari, *Spettacoli drammatico-musicali e coreografici in Parma dal 1628 al 1883*, 42.

80. Wiel, *I teatri musicali veneziani nel Settecento*, 430ff.

81. Ferrari, *Spettacoli drammatico-musicali e coreografici in Parma*, 40; and Wiel, *I teatri musicali veneziani*, 349ff.

82. Dlabač, *Allgemeines historisches Künstler-Lexikon*. According to Stiepanek, he was still living in Vienna in 1823; see Nissen, *Biographie W. A. Mozarts*, 519.

83. Da Ponte, *Memorie*, i.80; see also *AmZ*, xxiv (1822), 301.

84. Procházka, *Mozart in Prag*, 75–6. He later sang the title role in *La clemenza di Tito*.

85. Wiel, *I teatri musicale veneziani*, 398–9 and 452.

86. Reproduced by Kruse, 'Die erste Donna Anna', 70–1; see also *Zeitschrift der Internationalen Musikgesellschaft*, ii (1900), 409. She died in Milan on 17 March 1869 at the age of 106. ◆ Also see Deutsch, *Mozart und seine Welt*, 218.

87. Wiel, *I teatri musicali veneziani*, 413–14; Ricci, *I teatri di Bologna nei secoli XVII e XVIII: Storia aneddotica*, 515; and Ferrari, *Spettacoli drammatico-musicali e coreografici in Parma*, 44. ◆ Further, see Clement Gruber and Reitterer, 'Biographien aus dem Umfeld von W. A. Mozart: Saporti Teresa'.

88. Examples are reproduced by Procházka, *Mozart in Prag*, 25–6.

Although these reports no doubt reflect a good deal of local patriotism, they also show that Mozart could generally be well satisfied with the first performers of these roles.

Following the first performance of his work, he remained in Prague for several weeks, fêted and acclaimed by all. His acquaintances in the city retained the fondest and liveliest memories of this period.[89] A number of compositions date from this period, chief of which is the *scena Bella mia fiamma* K528 for Josepha Duschek, which Mozart completed on 3 November. Here, too, he delayed putting pen to paper, with the result that the singer finally locked him in a garden room at the Villa Bertramka and declared that she would let him out only when he had finished it. Mozart set to work but for his part vowed in turn that he would give her the aria only if she could sight-read it, note-perfect.[90] And he proceeded to make the vocal line extremely demanding: at the words 'quest' affanno, questo passo è terribile per me' in the andante he introduced such unusual intervals over such striking harmonies that only a singer who was technically very secure would be capable of rising to the challenge and singing the piece *prima vista*. In general terms, this is one of the most important arias of its kind. Even its recitative is remarkably unified, largely as a result of the fact that each section ends with the same idea in the manner of a refrain. The tonalities, too, are entirely characteristic, with the underlying emotion ('bella mia fiamma, addio! Non piacque al cielo di renderci felici') breaking through in all its intensity in E minor, while the orchestral accompaniment is at its most expressive here. All that follows – the description of the hero's adverse fate and his plea to be remembered – takes place in the flattened keys of the subdominant of C major, with which the aria begins. For all its sense of melancholy, this two-part andante initally allows love to have the last word at the moment of farewell. But as the feeling of agitation continues to grow in the orchestra, so the mood becomes ever more anguished, until a real sense of pain is unleashed in all its Mozartian bitterness at the chromatic passage already mentioned – here, again, the voice takes the lead. In this section, too, the formal unity is remarkable, with the same basic motifs constantly recurring in both voice and orchestra. This also links this section to the recitative, which is further recalled by individual orchestral motifs.[91] The allegro section[92] strikes a positively heroic note as the character resolves to die, yet there is nothing Metastasian about this resolve. After all, the hero who is going to his death here makes no attempt to conceal his inner agitation, which breaks forth in all its fury at the words 'vieni, affretta la vendetta'. Later, when he repeats the words from the Andante 'oh cara, addio per sempre' – a passage that is over-whelming in its expressivity, expanding the section's formal parameters in the most inspired way – he is overcome by love in all its tenderness, just as the ending, with its repeat of 'questo affanno' and so on, clearly harks back to the feeling of anguish expressed in the andante. The result is not a bravura aria in the usual sense, as there is virtually no coloratura writing here, but one that demands a large voice in the true soprano range and a free, expressive grandiose style of delivery.

89. See Niemetschek, *Leben des k. k. Kapellmeisters Wolfgang Gottlieb Mozart*, 60. Freisauff, *Mozarts Don Juan 1787 bis 1887*, 41, contributes to our knowledge of Mozart's stay in the city with an account based on information given to him by Schebek. On his way home from the old city to the Villa Bertramka in the evening, Mozart used to call in at Steinitz's coffee house to drink 'another black coffee. If the place was closed, it was not unknown for Mozart to knock on the window and for the landlord to prepare the coffee for him personally. – – But the coffee had to be very strong. Mozart generally wore a blue dress-coat with gilt buttons, nankeen knee breeches, stockings and buckled shoes'; see Procházka, *Mozart in Prag*, 82ff.
90. Thus the version of events attested to by Mozart's son and reproduced in the *Berliner Musik-Zeitung Echo*, xxv (1856), 198–9; see also Procházka, *Mozart in Prag*, 115.
91. The interval of a diminished seventh is a typically recurrent feature of the vocal line in all three parts (at 'o pene!' and 'il mio furor' in the recitative, at the word 'terribile' in the andante and at 'amara' in the allegro).
92. The accompaniment of the opening bars recalls a passage from the recitative, 'Vivi! Cedi al destin' etc.

Two songs were written in Prague: *Des kleinen Friedrichs Geburtstag* K529, from Campe's *Kinderbibliothek*, and a setting of Hölty's *Das Traumbild* K530.[93] Both are dated 6 November 1787. The former is a simple strophic singspiel number with an opening familiar from the Viennese singspiel.[94] *Das Traumbild*, too, is strophic, but is more like an Italian arietta in character. The tender, ethereal element of the poem finds particularly fine expression here.[95]

It was presumably the great acclaim that Mozart enjoyed in Prague that prompted the authorities to arrange a performance of one of his masses to celebrate the Feast of St Nicholas on 6 December. The performance took place at St Nicholas's Church in the small side in Prague: 'Everyone', wrote a contemporary, 'admitted that in this kind of composition too he is a complete master.'[96]

Mozart himself had already returned to Vienna in mid-November. Gluck died there on the 15th, and Mozart's triumphs in Prague seem to have persuaded the emperor to appoint him chamber musician on 7 December 1787 in order to keep him in Vienna.[97]

But there was still some way to go before *Don Giovanni* was to be performed in the city. On 8 June 1787 Salieri's opera *Tarare* had opened in Paris, a setting of a libretto by Beaumarchais, who had once again used the stage as a vehicle for a discussion of political and philosophical ideas.[98] At the emperor's bidding, Salieri now prevailed on Da Ponte to revise the libretto of *Tarare* and turn it into a Italian opera, *Axur, re d'Ormus*, an adaptation that also involved extensive musical revisions. *Axur* received its first performance on 8 January 1788 to celebrate the wedding of Archduke Franz and Princess Elisabeth[99] and in the course of the year was performed, with mounting acclaim, a further twenty-nine times,[100] soon entering the repertory of foreign opera houses, even though it is on a far lower artistic level than the same composer's *Les Danaïdes*.

As a result, there was no room for *Don Giovanni* for the present. Mozart spent the first four months of 1788 essentially composing trifles in the form of two contredanses K534 and 535 and six German dances K536 for orchestra. He also wrote the song *Ich möchte wohl der Kaiser sein* K539 that the actor Friedrich Baumann performed at Vienna's Leopoldstädter Theater on 7 March 1788,[101] and the aria *Ah se in ciel* K538 that he composed on 4 March for Aloysia Lange. Only the keyboard works of this period reveal pieces of any greater substance: the D major concerto K537

---

93. ◆ Only the concluding strophe of K529 is by Campe; the others are by the poet and writer Johann Eberhard Friedrich Schall (1742–90).

94. On the strength of this song, Johann Evangelist Engl has posited the existence of a son by the name of Friedrich, who, he claims, was born at the Villa Bertramka on 6 November 1787; but this is impossible as Mozart's daughter Theresia was born on 27 December 1787; see Engl, 'Die den Vater überlebenden Söhne', 51; see also Blümml, 'Mozarts Kinder: Eine Matrikelstudie'. Whether this Fritz is Prince Friedrich von Anhalt-Dessau, as Köchel claims, is still not certain.

95. I have unfortunately not been able to examine the rondo for soprano and orchestra, *Donne vaghe*, that was discovered in Prague in 1912; see Wyzewa and Saint-Foix, *Wolfgang Amédée Mozart*, ii.418. ◆ *Donne vaghe* (KAnh. C7.05) is not by Mozart but composed by Paisiello for his *La serva padrona*, first given at St Petersburg in the late summer of 1781; according to K6, the manuscript was discovered by Guido Adler in 1891.

96. *Prager Oberpostamtszeitung* ([8?] December 1787), quoted by Teuber, *Mozart in Prag*, ii.240 [*Dokumente*, 270, *Documentary Biography*, 307].

97. ◆ See Link, 'Mozart's appointment to the Viennese court'.

98. Loménie, *Beaumarchais et son temps*, ii.399–400.

99. *Wiener Zeitung*, iii (1788); Müller, *Abschied von der National-Schaubühne*, 277–8.

100. Da Ponte, *Memorie*, i/2.208; *AmZ*, xxiv (1822), 284; *Musikalische Korrespondenz* (1790), 30; and *Musikalisches Wochenblatt* (1791), 5–6. ◆ For an account of performances of *Axur* in 1788, see Link, *The National Court Theatre in Mozart's Vienna*, 118–34 and Rice, *Antonio Salieri and Viennese Opera*, 403–20.

101. This had been preceded by *Die kleine Spinnerin* K531 on 11 December 1787. It is not known when the trio *Grazie agl'inganni tuoi* K532 was written. ◆ Concerning K539, see Beales, 'Court, Government and Society in Mozart's Vienna', 13–17. *Grazie agl'inganni tuoi* may have been composed as early as 1784 or 1785; concerning its disputed authorship, see Zaslaw, '"Grazie agl' inganni tuoi": Mozart or Kelly?'.

of 24 February (the 'Coronation' concerto); the allegro and andante K533 of 3 January;[102] and the adagio K540 in B minor of 19 March 1788.

It was not until 7 May 1788 that the performance of *Don Giovanni* went ahead on Joseph II's orders. Staged at the Burgtheater, it netted Da Ponte 100 florins and Mozart 225.[103] In the event, it proved a failure and reviewers merely noted that the performance had taken place.[104] Da Ponte reports that everyone with the exception of Mozart believed that something had been overlooked,[105] with the result that various additions were made and some of the arias altered, but success continued to elude the piece. Only when, at Da Ponte's instigation, further performances were arranged in rapid succession did Viennese audiences gradually come to terms with what they clearly regarded as an unusual work.[106] The cast was as follows:[107]

Don Giovanni	Sign. Francesco Albertarelli
Donna Anna	Sgra. Aloysia Lange
Donna Elvira	Sgra. Catarina Cavalieri
Don Ottavio	Sign. Francesco Morella
Leporello	Sign. Francesco Benucci
Don Pedro	
Masetto	Sign. Francesco Bussani
Zerlina	Signa. Luisa Mombelli.

According to his thematic catalogue (see entries of 24, 28 and 30 April), Mozart had in fact already undertaken the main additions to the score before the production opened, and these are duly shown in the printed wordbook. Dramatically speaking they are, without exception, unwelcome. The first is Donna Elvira's aria 'Mi tradì quell' alma ingrata' (K540c), which was merely a concession to Caterina Cavalieri;[108] the second was the aria in G major 'Dalla sua pace' (K540a) for the tenor Francesco Morella;[109] and the third was a *buffa* duet for Zerlina and Leporello, 'Per queste

---

102.   It was not Mozart who added the rondo K494 to these two movements to create a complete sonata. ◆ *Pace* Abert, there is every reason to believe it was Mozart who appended K494 to the sonata movements K533 and had the whole produced by one of his regular Vienna publishers, Hoffmeister, in 1788.

103.   According to the theatre accounts; see Jahn, *W. A. Mozart*, ii.365.

104.   *Wiener Zeitung* (10 May 1788) [*Dokumente*, 276, *Documentary Biography*, 314].

105.   Da Ponte, *Memorie*, i/2.104.

106.   *Don Giovanni* was performed 15 times in 1788, on 7, 9, 12, 16, 23, 30 May, 16, 23 June, 5, 11, 21 July, 2 August, 24, 31 October and 15 December; see Freisauff, *Mozarts Don Juan 1787 bis 1887*, 49. Lange's claim that the work was taken off after three performances rests, therefore, on an error; see Lange, *Biographie des Joseph Lange*, 171. Only after 1788 did it fall from the repertory and was not revived until 5 November 1792, when it was staged at the Theater auf der Wieden in a wretched German adaptation by Christian Heinrich Spieß. On 11 December 1798 the Court Theatre performed it in German; see Wlassak, *Chronik des k. k. Hof-Burgtheaters*, 99. According to Da Ponte, the emperor commented after hearing a performance of the work: 'The opera is divine, I should even venture that it is more beautiful than *Figaro*. But such music is not meat for the teeth of my Viennese!' Da Ponte reported this remark to Mozart, who allegedly replied 'Give them time to chew on it!' Joseph left for the field on 28 February 1788 and did not return to Vienna until 5 December, so he can have seen the opera only on 15 December. ◆ Abert's account of performances of *Don Giovanni* is essentially correct with one exception: the penultimate performance was on 3 November, not 31 October; see Link, *The National Court Theatre in Mozart's Vienna*, 125–31.

107.   Don Giovanni was sung by Francesco Albertarelli, not by Stefano Mandini, as claimed by Freisauff and others; see Freisauff, *Mozarts Don Juan 1787 bis 1887*, 48. Albertarelli had made his Viennese début in Salieri's *Axur* on 4 April 1788 (private communication from Eusebius Mandyczewski in Vienna to Hermann Deiters; see Jahn, *W. A. Mozart*, ii.366). ◆ Concerning Albertarelli, see Rice, 'Benedetto Frizzi on Singers, Composers and Opera in Late Eighteenth-Century Italy'.

108.   She also wanted to sing it in D instead of E flat major, once again requring Mozart's intervention. On Cavalieri's reputation at this time, see Cramer, *Magazin der Musik* (July 1789), 47. ◆ Further, see Gidwitz, '"Ich bin die erste Sängerin": Vocal Profiles of Two Mozart Sopranos'.

109.   He had made his début at Easter 1788 in Paisiello's *Il barbiere di Siviglia*.

tue manine' (K540b), an earthy little number that has little to do with the main action and that rides roughshod over the characterization of the two singers, serving only to amuse the general public.[110]

Mozart himself was half-hearted about these alterations, none of which helped his opera. We already know the objections raised against the work by Vienna's musicians and connoisseurs and that the only person to come out unequivocally in Mozart's favour was Joseph Haydn.

Like *Le nozze di Figaro*, *Don Giovanni* only slowly gained a foothold in the repertory of other German theatres, at least when compared with the popular and fashionable operas of the time.[111] The first production outside Vienna opened in Leipzig on 15 June 1788 under Guardasoni's management and with several of the singers from the Prague performances.[112] The opera was subsequently heard at the Electoral National Theatre in Mainz on 13 March 1789 in a translation by Heinrich Gottlieb Schmieder;[113] at Mannheim, to great acclaim, on 27 September;[114] at Bonn on 13 October (both here and in Mannheim Christian Gottlob Neefe's translation was used);[115] at Frankfurt am Main [on 3 May 1789];[116] and at Hamburg under Friedrich Ludwig Schröder on 27 October. Johann Friedrich Schink was critical of the libretto but all the more enthusiastic about the music:

> Is such magnificent, majestic and powerful song really stuff for ordinary opera-lovers, who only bring their *ears* to the singspiel and leave their *hearts* at home? . . . The beauty, greatness and nobility of the music for *Don Juan* will never appeal anywhere to more than a handful of the elect. It is not music to everyone's taste, merely tickling the ear and letting the heart starve. . . . *Mozart* is no ordinary composer. He is not content with light, pleasing melodies written down at random. His music is carefully planned, profoundly felt work, suited to the personalities, situations and sentiments of his characters. It shows study of the language, which he treats musically, and just knowledge of prosody. . . . He never ornaments his song with needless and soulless flourishes. For that is to banish expression from music, and expression never lies in single words but in the wise, natural combination of notes, through which speaks true feeling. This kind of expression *Mozart* has entirely in his power. With him every note proceeds from feeling and generates feeling. His expression is glowing, vivid and picturesque, yet without becoming fulsome and excessive. He has the richest and yet the most restrained imagination. He

110. The autograph score has not survived. The *secco* recitatives, too, have come down to us in an incomplete form. Bernhard Gugler has cast doubt on the authenticity of the surviving material; see his 'Die nachkomponierten Szenen zu "Don Juan"' and his preface to his 1868 edition of the full score (XIV). This number is relegated to appendix II of AMA V; see also the critical commentary 18. For an opposing view, see Wolzogen, *Über die szenische Darstellung*, 107. In the other editions of the full score, Masetto's aria 'Ho capito' was erroneously described as a late addition, but it appears in the original full score ◆ Mozart's score of 540b survives, with the rest of the opera autograph, in the Bibliothèque nationale, Paris.

111. On the following statistics, see Freisauff, *Mozarts Don Juan 1787 bis 1887*, 105–6; see also Schatz, 'Ergänzungen zur Bühnenstatistik des Don Juan in Freisauff's Buch'.

112. The playbill is reproduced in Freisauff, *Mozarts Don Juan 1787 bis 1887*, 148; see also Procházka, *Mozart in Prag*, 117–18.

113. Schatz, 'Ergänzungen zur Bühnenstatistik', 278; Peth, *Geschichte des Theaters und der Musik zu Mainz*, 87 (on Schmieder, 95). In December 1798 Zulehner in Mainz advertised a vocal score with German and Italian words.

114. *Journal des Luxus und der Moden* (1790), 50.

115. Thayer, *Ludwig van Beethovens Leben*, i.232. The reviewer in Reichard's *Theater-Kalender* – probably Neefe himself – writes: 'The music greatly pleased the connoisseurs. The action was not liked' [*Dokumente*, 338, *Documentary Biography*, 384].

116. It was given by Großmann's company; see Carl Valentin, *Geschichte der Musik in Frankfurt am Main vom Anfange des XIV. bis zum Anfange des XVIII. Jahrhunderts*, 257. In a letter written from Frankfurt on 3 October 1790, Mozart speaks of a performance in his honour by the elector's company, but this performance evidently failed to take place; *Briefe*, iv.116.

is the true virtuoso who never lets his imagination run away with intelligence. Reason guides his enthusiasm and calm judgment his presentation.[117]

An Austrian production took place in Brünn in December 1789 (the Graz performance of 1789 seems doubtful), but it failed to displace Dittersdorf's *Figaro* in the public's affections.[118] The following year there were productions in Budapest by Count Erdödy's company in a German translation by Franz Xaver Giržik (the date cannot be established with any certainty);[119] in Soest by the Toscani-Müller company on 26 June;[120] and, above all, in Berlin on 20 December, when the work was performed in the presence of the king in a verson by Friedrich Ludwig Schröder based on Neefe's translation.[121] The performance proved exceptionally successful,[122] yet the reviews were in part extraordinarily hostile:

If ever an opera was awaited with eagerness, if ever a Mozartian composition was trumpeted to the clouds even before it was performed, – it was this same *Don Juan*. . . . That Mozart is an *excellent*, a *great* composer, all the world will admit; but whether nothing *greater* had ever been written before him, or would ever be written after him, than this opera under review, we beg leave to doubt. . . . Theatrical music knows no other rule, no other judge, than our hearts, and *whether* and *how* it works upon them is what determines its whole value. Not the art of over-loading the instruments, but the heart, the feelings and the passions must be allowed to speak by the composer, for then he writes great music, then his name goes down to posterity, and an evergreen laurel blooms for him in the Temple of Immortality. Grétry, Monsigny and Philidor serve and will continue to serve as proof. *Mozart* in his *Don Juan* wanted to write something extraordinary, something *inimitably great*, that much is certain, and the extraordinary quality is there, but not the *inimitable greatness*! Whim, caprice, pride, but not the heart created *Don Juan*, and we would rather admire his great musical potentialities in an *oratorio* or some other solemn piece of church music, than in his *Don Juan*.[123]

Another reviewer praised the music but was all the more critical of the text – a common approach to the piece in these early years of its performance history. He found that the eye was sated and the ear enchanted, but that reason was offended and morality insulted, as virtue and feeling were trampled underfoot by vice:

If ever a nation were entitled to take pride in a compatriot, it would be Germany in regard to *Mozart*, the composer of this singspiel. Never, certainly never, has the greatness of a human spirit been more palpable, and never has the art of music reached to a higher degree! Melodies which seem to have been invented by an angel are here accompanied by heavenly harmonies, and anyone whose soul is even a little receptive to true beauty will surely forgive me for saying that *the ear is enchanted*.

---

117. *Dramaturgische Monate*, ii (1790), 320–1 [*Dokumente*, 310–13, *Documentary Biography*, 354–5].
118. Schatz, 'Ergänzungen zur Bühnenstatistik', 280. ◆ Dittersdorf's *Figaro* was first given at Brno in January 1789.
119. Schatz, 'Ergänzungen zur Bühnenstatistik', 280.
120. Schatz, 'Ergänzungen zur Bühnenstatistik', 283.
121. Louis Schneider, *Geschichte der Oper und des Königlichen Opernhauses in Berlin*, 59. According to the Berlin correspondent of the *Journal des Luxus und der Moden*, 'The music of this singspiel is beautiful, but here and there very artificial, difficult and over-loaded with instrumental detail'; *Journal des Luxus und der Moden* (1791), 76 [*Dokumente*, 524, *Documentary Biography*, 386].
122. The opera was given five times in ten days.
123. *Chronik von Berlin*, ix (5 February 1791), 132–3 [*Dokumente*, 334, *Documentary Biography*, 380–1].

Yet the same anonymous reviewer could not prevent himself from expressing the pious wish:

Oh, hadst thou not thus squandered the power of thy spirit! had thy sentiments been more in harmony with thine imagination and not led thee to take such unclean steps to greatness! . . . What could it avail thee if thy name were to be inscribed in letters of diamond upon a golden tablet – and this tablet were to hang on a pillory of shame?[124]

Karl Spazier acknowledged Mozart's 'genuine, original, natural wealth of ideas'[125] and claimed that individual arias in *Don Giovanni* had more true merit than whole operas by Paisiello,[126] but insisted elsewhere:

It is a great pleasure to see an artistic genius of this kind make light of a curious passage which, one suspects, would cost others the most enormous effort. This pleasure, however, turns into strenuous labour, which then has again to be turned to enjoyment by the circuitous route of study, if such an artist for once strives with all his might, which is especially true of Mozart's *Don Juan*, where he throws the whole store of his art at the hearer at once, whereby the excellent whole almost becomes lost to sight.[127]

The detailed review promised by Spazier did not materialize.

Genuine admiration for *Don Giovanni* was also expressed by Bernhard Anselm Weber, who had only recently come to Berlin:[128]

Let us unite profound knowledge of the art with the happiest talent for inventing lovely melodies, and then link both with the greatest possible originality, in order to obtain the most faithful picture of Mozart's musical genius. Nowhere in his work does one ever find an idea one had heard before: even his accompaniments are always novel. One is, as it were, incessantly pulled along from one notion to another, without rest or repose, so that admiration of the latest constantly swallows up admiration for what has gone before, and even by straining all one's forces one is scarcely able to absorb all the beauties that present themselves to the soul. If any fault had to be found with Mozart, it could surely be only this: that such abundance of beauty almost tires the soul and the effect of the whole is sometimes obscured thereby. But happy the artist whose only fault lies in an *all too great* perfection.[129]

It was almost impossible, Weber went on, to discuss a Mozart opera in detail as there was no obvious beginning or end to it. Even so, he singled out for special mention the overture, quartet, first-act finale, sextet and final scene of the opera, in which the horror of the situation was so accu-

124. ◆ *Chronik von Berlin*, ix (14 May 1791), 454; *Dokumente*, 342–4, *Documentary Biography*, 390–2.
125. *Musikalisches Wochenblatt*, xx (?25 February 1792), 158 [*Dokumente*, 387, *Documentary Biography*, 441].
126. *Musikalische Monatsschrift*, v (November 1792), 122 [*Dokumente*, 408–9, *Documentary Biography*, 466].
127. *Musikalisches Wochenblatt*, iii (?22 October 1791), 19 [*Dokumente*, 358, *Documentary Biography*, 410–11].
128. A similar view of Mozart was expressed by Dittersdorf in conversation with Joseph II: 'He is undoubtedly one of the greatest and most original geniuses that I know, and I have never met a composer with such an extraordinary wealth of ideas. I just wish he weren't so profligate with them. He doesn't allow the listener to breathe; you have scarcely begun to ponder on one beautiful idea before another, equally glorious, drives the earlier one from your mind, and so it goes on, so that by the end you can't recall a single one of these beautiful ideas'; Dittersdorf, *Lebensbeschreibung*, 176.
129. *Musikalisches Wochenblatt*, iv (?29 October 1791), 30–31 [*Dokumente*, 359–60, *Documentary Biography*, 411–12].

rately depicted that listeners' hair literally stood on end. And as proof that Mozart was also capable of striking a more cheerful note he also quoted the 'Peasants' chorus' and the delightful duet 'Là ci darem la mano', with its enchanting melody. This view was forcefully refuted by another reader, whose 'candid thoughts' were published in November 1792:

> His judgment on Mozart's *Don Juan* is extremely exaggerated and one-sided. No one will fail to recognize in Mozart the man of great talents and the experienced, prolific and genial composer. But I have yet to see him considered a correct, much less a perfect artist, by any thoroughgoing scholar of the art of music, and by so much the less will the critic endowed with taste hold him to be a correct and sensitive composer in his attitude towards poetry.[130]

The home of the German intelligentsia was fond of adopting this sort of tone in discussing Mozart:

> Mozart was a great genius; but he really had little higher culture and little or, rather, no learning or taste. For all their originality, the works that he wrote for the theatre failed to make any effect, which is all that matters in the theatre; and as for a true treatment of the text, let the man stand up who can justify the claim that Mozart really knew how to set this text and that his music always consorted with the poetry in such a way that poetry cannot rise up against him and arraign him at the tribunal of criticism.[131]

The various views that were expressed elsewhere do not need to detain us here. Both praise and censure show clearly enough that contemporaries everywhere felt that they were dealing with a new phenomenon of great significance.[132]

In 1791 there were productions of *Don Giovanni* in Hanover (on 4 March),[133] Kassel (on 16 April by Großmann's company)[134] and Munich, where the production, originally banned by the censor, opened at the elector's behest on 7 August.[135] In 1792 Wäser's company performed the work in Breslau on 20 January[136] and in Glogau on 26 July.[137] Prior to that – on 30 January – it had been heard in Weimar, where it was to prove no more successful than *Le nozze di Figaro* in 1793. Here, too, it was not until 1794 that the success of *Die Zauberflöte* paved the way for the earlier operas.[138] On 30 December 1797 we find Goethe writing to Schiller:

> The hope which you entertained for the opera you would have seen fulfilled to a high degree in *Don Juan* recently; however, this piece too stands quite alone, and all prospect of something similar has been frustrated by Mozart's death.[139]

130. *Musikalische Monatsschrift*, v (November 1792), 139 [*Dokumente*, 409, *Documentary Biography*, 467].
131. *Berlinische musikalische Zeitung historischen und kritischen Inhalts*, i (1793/4), 127.
132. In July 1792, admittedly, we find Jacobi writing to Herder: 'We found yesterday's opera tedious in the extreme; it really is intolerable, this Don Juan! Thank goodness it's over!'; Jacobi, *Auserlesener Briefwechsel*, ii.91.
133. Freisauff, *Mozarts Don Juan 1787 bis 1887*, 148.
134. Schatz, 'Ergänzungen zur Bühnenstatistik', 282.
135. Grandaur, *Chronik des Königlichen Hof- und Nationaltheaters in München*, 37.
136. Schlesinger, *Geschichte des Breslauer Theaters*, i.75.
137. Schatz, 'Ergänzungen zur Bühnenstatistik', 283.
138. Bode, *Die Tonkunst in Goethes Leben*, ii.201.
139. Vollmer, *Briefwechsel zwischen Schiller und Goethe*, i.352; Schiller's letter may be found on 351.

Bremen followed on 24 October 1792, the court theatres of Braunschweig, Passau and Münster in 1793. Also in 1793 Johann Böhm's company performed the work in Düsseldorf, Cologne and Aachen,[140] while Karl Steinberg Schuch took it to Königsberg in 1793 and to Danzig in 1794. The opera was also heard at Oels and Schleswig in 1794, and at Kiel, Magdeburg and Nuremberg in 1795.[141] The last of the major court theatres to stage the work was Stuttgart, where a burlesque form of the piece was unveiled on 28 March 1796.[142]

The work quickly found a place for itself in public esteem, and there were soon no German theatres where *Don Giovanni* was not a permanent part of the repertory. In Vienna, Sonnleithner calculated that there were no fewer than 531 performances up to the end of 1863.[143] According to figures compiled by Stiepanek, there were 116 performances in Prague within the first ten years of the opera's première. By 1855 that figure had risen to 360.[144] In Berlin, the fiftieth anniversary of the work's première was marked in 1837, by which date there had been more than two hundred performances of the opera in the city.[145] Similar celebrations were held in Prague[146] and Magdeburg.[147] The centenary of the first performance on 29 October 1887 sparked a whole series of gala performances in Germany in celebration of Mozart's memory. The Berlin performance was the 497th in the city's history, while the two performances in Prague, in Italian and German, were the 534th and 535th. Vienna marked the occasion with a new translation by Max Kalbeck.[148]

Paris first heard *Don Giovanni* in 1805 in a truly frightful adaptation by Kalkbrenner that completely distorted and garbled the piece. Suffice it to say that the masked trio was sung by three gendarmes to the words 'Courage, vigilance, / Adresse, défiance, / Que l'active prudence / Préside à nos desseins'. Kalkbrenner also added some new music of his own. In this guise the work proved popular with audiences for quite some time.[149] Not until 1811 was *Don Giovanni* heard in its original form with singers from the Italian opera, and since that date it has never been out of the repertory.[150] A French adaptation by Castil-Blaze[151] was first heard in Lyons in 1822 and at the Odéon in Paris in 1827. The work reached the Académie de Musique in 1834 with an outstanding cast and lavish sets in a version that was even closer to the original.[152] A further version was staged at the Théâtre Lyrique under Carvalho's direction in 1866.[153]

140.   ◆ According to Loewenberg, *Annals of Opera*, 449, the Cologne performance took place on 7 October 1791.
141.   Schatz, 'Ergänzungen zur Bühnenstatistik', 281ff.
142.   Krauß, *Das Stuttgarter Hoftheater*, 102.
143.   By 23 January 1869, there had been 356 performances at the old Kärntnertor-Theater. In the new Court Opera, which opened on 25 May 1869, there were a further 117 performances by 9 March 1890, making a grand total of 473.
144.   Kulhanek, *Bohemia*, cclxxviii (1887), appendix. By May 1890 there had been 556 performances in Prague, 560 by March 1892.
145.   *AmZ*, xxxix (1837), 800.
146.   *AmZ*, xxxix (1837), 810–1. By May 1890 there had been 523 performances at the Royal Theatre in Berlin. The 600th performance on 12 June 1902 was a special gala performance; see *Mitteilungen für die Mozart-Gemeinde in Berlin*, vii (1902), 137; Schatz, 'Ergänzungen zur Bühnenstatistik', 281.
147.   *AmZ*, xl (1838), 140.
148.   ◆ For general studies concerning the reception of *Don Giovanni*, see Werner-Jensen, *Studien zur Don Giovanni-Rezeption im 19. Jahrhundert (1800–1850)* and Bitter, *Wandlungen in den Inszenierungsformen des 'Don Giovanni' von 1787 bis 1928.*
149.   Castil-Blaze, *Théâtres lyriques de Paris: L'Académie impériale de musique de 1645 à 1855*, ii.98–9
150.   Castil-Blaze, *Molière musicien*, i.321–2; Sievers, 'Mozarts Beifall in Paris', 208–9; Schebest, *Aus dem Leben einer Künstlerin*, 202–3.
151.   Castil-Blaze, *Molière musicien*, i.268–9 and 323; and *Théâtres lyriques de Paris*, ii.241–2.
152.   *Leipziger Allgemeine musikalische Zeitung*, i (1866), 192–3; in general, see Schatz, 'Ergänzungen zur Bühnenstatistik', 284–5; and Freisauff, *Mozarts Don Juan 1787 bis 1887*, 161–2; also *AmZ*, new series, v (1870), 147–8 and 289–90. ◆ Further, see Henze-Döhring, 'E. T. A. Hoffmann-"Kult" und Don Giovanni-Rezeption im Paris des 19. Jahrhunderts: Castil-Blazes Don Juan im Théâtre de l'Académie Royale de Musique am 10. März 1834'.
153.   *Don Juan, opéra en 2 actes et 13 tableaux. Édition du Théâtre Lyrique.* ◆ See Delporte, 'Le Don Juan de Mozart à Paris en 1866: Extraits de la Revue Dramatique de Théophile Gautier' and, more generally, Angermüller, 'Pariser Don Juan-Rezensionen 1805 bis 1866'.

In London the hugely successful production of *Le nozze di Figaro* paved the way for *Don Giovanni*, which was first heard at the King's Theatre on 12 April 1817, thereafter remaining one of the most popular works in the Italian repertory. Indeed, the acclaim that this first Italian production enjoyed was so great that Covent Garden was persuaded to commission an English version of the work, which proved no less successful when it received its outstandingly fine first performance on 20 May 1817.[154]

Meanwhile, *Don Giovanni* continued to make a home for itself in northern Europe, with productions in Amsterdam (1794), Reval and St Petersburg (1797), Copenhagen (1807) and Stockholm (1813).[155] But in Italy, in spite of repeated attempts to establish a performing tradition, it failed to draw audiences, even though a number of connoisseurs acknowledged its merits. The first attempt to stage the work in Italy was made in Florence in 1792.[156] We do not know whether it was a success or not. In 1817 and again in 1818, when the work was performed in mutilated travesties, it proved a failure. Not until 1834, when it was given in its original form, did *Don Giovanni* enjoy any great acclaim in Florence.[157] Meanwhile, the original version had been staged in Rome in 1811 in a carefully rehearsed production, in which form it enjoyed a certain *succès d'estime*. The music was said to be 'bellissima, superba, sublime, un musicone', but not 'del gusto del paese', while the many 'stranezze' may well have been attractive but beyond the audience's grasp.[158] A similar impression was left by the Naples production of 1812.[159] In neither case did the work find lasting acclaim. In Milan in 1814 the work was whistled as much as it was applauded, although later performances proved more successful.[160] In Turin in 1815 it was said to have found favour in spite of a poor performance.[161] Bologna followed in 1817,[162] Parma in 1821, in the latter case to only modest acclaim.[163] In Genoa, in May 1824, the work was applauded by the cognoscenti but not by the public at large.[164] And in Venice, where it was first staged in 1833, it was slow to gain an even modest reputation.[165] Of some significance in this context is the comment by a later soprano: 'Non capisco niente a questa musica maledetta!'[166] To be set against this, of course, is Rossini's response when asked to name his favourite opera among his own compositions: 'Vous voulez connaître

154. The work was entitled *The Libertine*. The translator was Isaac Pocock and the music was arranged by Sir Henry Bishop; see Schatz, 'Ergänzungen zur Bühnenstatistik', 284, and *The Musical Times* (1887), 593–4. ◆ Also see Fend, 'Zur Rezeption von Mozarts Opern in London im fruhen 19. Jahrhundert', and Cowgill, '"Wise Men from the East": Mozart's Operas and their Advocates in Early Nineteenth-Century London'.

155. ◆ Concerning performances in Poland, see Tomaszewski, 'Mozarts Don Juan in Polen'.

156. ◆ This alleged performance is undocumented. Possibly the first Italian performance was in the summer of 1817; see Loewenberg, *Annals of Opera*, 454.

157. *AmZ*, xx (1818), 489; Freisauff, *Mozarts Don Juan 1787 bis 1887*, 166–7; Schatz, 'Ergänzungen zur Bühnenstatistik', 285. In 1857 a performance in Florence was so roundly booed on account of its 'old-fashioned hyperborean music' that all further performances were abandoned; see Jahn, *W. A. Mozart*, ii.375.

158. *AmZ*, xiii (1811), 524–5; Stendhal, *Vie de Rossini*, 6–7.

159. Florimo, *La scuola musicale di Napoli*, iv.364; *AmZ*, xiv (1812), 786–7, and xv (1813), 531.

160. *AmZ*, xvi (1814), 859–60; Cambiasi, *La Scala*, 304, notes an 'esito buonissimo' in 1814.

161. *AmZ*, xviii (1816), 232.

162. Schatz, 'Ergänzungen zur Bühnenstatistik', 285.

163. Ferrari, *Spettacoli drammatico-musicali e coreografici in Parma*, 62.

164. *AmZ*, xxvi (1824), 570.

165. *AmZ*, xxv (1823), 639. ◆ In general, see Petrobelli, 'Don Giovanni in Italia: La fortuna dell'opera ed il suo influsso'.

166. Scudo, *Critique et littérature musicales*, i.191; a similar view is expressed by the *AmZ*, xxv (1823), 869–70.

celui de mes ouvrages que j'aime le mieux: eh bien c'est Don Giovanni.'[167] The first Spanish performance of *Don Giovanni* took place in Madrid in 1834.[168]

Eight years earlier, in 1826, Da Ponte persuaded Manuel García, who was then organizing performances of Italian operas in New York, to stage the *Don Giovanni* there.[169] Although the performance left much to be desired,[170] it none the less met with a warm response, and Da Ponte, who had staked the proceeds of the sale of his librettos on the local lottery, made a handsome profit.[171]

---

167.   Viardot, 'Manuscrit autographe du Don Giovanni', 10. Rossini's reply dates from the period after his arrival in Paris in 1823, when his own music was frequently played off against Mozart's. ◆ Also see Everist, 'Enshrining Mozart: "Don Giovanni" and the Viardot Circle'.

168.   Schatz, 'Ergänzungen zur Bühnenstatistik', 286.

169.   Da Ponte, *Memorie*, iii/1.43–4.; and Scudo, *Critique et littérature musicales*, i.178.

170.   In the first-act finale, things went so awry that García, who was playing the part of Don Giovanni to admirable effect, finally waved his sword in the air in order to restore calm, shouting out that such a masterpiece should not be ruined in this way. The performers started again and this time brought the finale to a successful conclusion; see Castil-Blaze, *Molière musicien*, i.329–30. A friend of Da Ponte's who regularly fell asleep at the opera assured him that a work like *Don Giovanni* prevented him from sleeping the following night as well; Da Ponte, *Memorie*, iii/1.54.

171.   Da Ponte, *Memorie*, iii/1.58. ◆ Further, see Radomski, 'The life and works of Manuel del Pópulo Vicente García (1775–1832): Italian, French, and Spanish opera in early nineteenth-century Romanticism' and Müller and Panagl, *Don Giovanni in New York: Lorenzo Da Pontes italienisch-englisches Libretto für die US-Erstaufführung von Mozarts Oper (1826)*.

45

Don Giovanni

It says much for Da Ponte's deep and instinctive understanding of Mozart's personality that it was Don Giovanni that he suggested as a suitable subject for an opera. The character of Don Juan has exercised the imaginations of poets of all countries for at least the last three centuries, clear proof of the fact that the problems raised by the figure – like those associated with Faust – go to the very heart of human existence. Whereas the Faust legend is based on the struggle to find a higher meaning to life and on the desire for redemption, the world of Don Juan is simply that of the senses, an extreme affirmation of the life force that recognizes no other values than its own. Don Juan knows nothing of Faust's striving, but only the 'to be or not to be' of Renaissance man, and so it is no accident that the subject was first treated dramatically in the Catholic countries of southern Europe, where the medieval doctrine of the sinfulness of all flesh has always provoked the most extreme reaction on the part of the natural life force.

No historical foundation for the story has yet been identified.[1] Myth and legend have clearly provided most of the material in the form not only of the image of an unbridled sensualist (an image familiar from the Middle Ages and later surrounded by a particular aura in the Renaissance) but also of the ancient legend of the dead man who returns as a statue to avenge a crime. These two motifs were first combined in *El burlador de Sevilla, y combidado de pietra*, first printed in 1630, by Tirso de Molina, a monk and prior who wrote under the name of Gabriel Téllez but whose authorship has recently been called into question.[2] For all its poetic qualities, this is an oddly hybrid work. Even here, Don Juan has already far outgrown the role of a dastardly villain, revealing true greatness in committing his crimes and proving as chivalrous as he is fearless. Nor does he lack genuinely human features such as his inner vacillation before the decisive supper in the graveyard chapel. Only when he is certain of his end does his strength fail him and he asks for a priest in a vain show of remorse. Here the moralizing tendency of the piece emerges in all its clarity, as it does in the character of the Commendatore (here called Don Gonzalo de Ulloa), who no longer functions as a figure of retribution avenging a personal wrong but who is already the agent of a moral world order.

---

1. The poetic aspect of the legend is examined by Farinelli, *Don Giovanni: Note critiche*; see also Karl Engel, *Die Don Juan-Sage auf der Bühne*; Bévotte, *La légende de Don Juan: Son évolution dans la littérature, des origines au romantisme*; on the origins of the legend, see the articles by Zeidler and Bolte in Koch's *Zeitschrift für vergleichende Literaturgeschichte*, new series, vols ix and xiii; see also Schröder, *Die dramatischen Bearbeitungen der Don-Juan-Sage*; on the more recent period, see Heckel, *Das Don-Juan-Problem in der neueren Dichtung*.
2. Especially by Farinelli, *Don Giovanni*; for an opposing view, see Bévotte, *La légende de Don Juan*. Basing his arguments on the second surviving version of the piece entitled *Tan largo me lo fiáis?*, Schröder has even attempted to ascribe the play to Calderón.
◆ More recently, see Parr, 'Selected Evidence for Tirso's Authorship of *El burlador de Sevilla y convidado de piedra*' and Stratil and Oakley, 'A Disputed Authorship Study of Two Plays Attributed to Tirso de Molina'.

Don Juan's servant Catalinon is the *gracioso* – the buffoon – of the piece, devoted to his master but far from happy with the latter's goings-on. He is far less of a comic character than Leporello. In particular, his cowardice is not yet stressed with the relish that was later to be the case.

As for the female characters, it has to be said at once that Don Juan's only concern is to gratify his male egoism. There is as yet no trace of the demonic aspect of the character as an out-and-out sensualist. He sets about his business in a wholly unscrupulous manner, acting out of sheer delight at his ability to seduce women. Nor is it possible to speak of love or passion in the case of the women he seduces: he wins them over partly by deceit, partly by the promise of marriage. Donna Anna remains a two-dimensional figure, and although the impassioned Tisbea already reveals a number of the characteristics of the later Donna Elvira, it is really only in the case of the peasant couple Aminta and Patricio that we can already recognize the characters of Zerlina and Masetto. Of course, these subsidiary characters are only loosely connected with the main plot, and much the same is true of the Duchess Isabella, who is a further prototype of Donna Elvira. Donna Anna's fiancé, the Marquis de la Mota, was later combined with Duke Oktavio and turned into a single character. It is Duke Oktavio who at the end of Téllez's play receives the hand of Isabella, who was originally intended for Don Juan.

The play already contains the main features of the later libretto: the murder of the Commendatore, the country wedding followed by the seduction of the bride, the inscription on the tombstone and, finally, the invitation and appearance of the statue at Don Juan's house, except that after the meal the Commendatore invites his host to a further meal in the chapel where he is buried and where he is served scorpions, snakes and gall. Instead of *Tafelmusik*, we hear a penitential hymn. This is followed by Don Juan's punishment, after which the work ends with Catalinon's account of all that has happened and the wedding of the two couples.

From Spain the story travelled to Italy and, in particular, to Naples, where Onofrio Giliberti's *Il convitato di pietra, rappresentazione in prosa* was printed in 1652. No copies have survived, so that it is impossible to say how this version relates to *El burlador* or to any of the later works. We do not even know whether it predates a piece of the same name by Andrea Cicognini that was printed in 1671, some twenty years after its author's death. Both were evidently genuine *commedie dell'arte*, investing the material with an element of burlesque comedy. The plot was taken over in rough outline, but all its sublime elements and especially anything that smacked of religion were removed, with the emphasis now placed on the hero's servant – here called Arlecchino – and his pranks. A further version was made by Andrea Perucci in 1678. It, too, is lost.[3]

Whether two French verse dramas by Nicolas Drouin dit Dorimond (1658) and Claude Deschamps de Villiers (1659) are related to Giliberti's *Il convitato di pietra* is doubtful, although de Villiers mentions a translation from the Italian. Both were called *Le festin de pierre, ou Le fils criminel*[4] and both reflect the knockabout spirit of the Italian *commedia dell'arte*. As before, the rakish pranks of the master and especially the madcap jokes of the servant are really all that matter here.[5]

---

3. It remains unclear exactly what this 'opera tragica in prosa' looked like, although the term itself makes it highly unlikely that we are dealing with an opera here. ◆ Perrucci's text has since been recovered; for a modern edition, see Perrucci, *Il convitato di pietra*.

4. For more on this title, see Schröder, 'Die dramatischen Bearbeitungen', 131. ◆ For editions of de Villiers and Dorimon(d), see Bévotte, *Le Festin de pierre avant Molière: Dorimon–de Villiers–Scénario des Italiens–Cicognini*.

5. A novel feature is the character of the Pilgrim (Hermit) who is also found in Molière and the German folkplays. This scene was often interpolated into Mozart's opera, notably by Schikaneder when he performed the work in Vienna in 1792; see Heckel, *Das Don-Juan-Problem*, 12. Another novel feature is the repulsive relationship between the hero and his father Don Alvaro.

Molière's first prose comedy, *Dom Juan, ou Le festin de pierre*, was first performed at the Théâtre du Palais-Royal on 15 February 1665 and first published in his *Œuvres* in 1682. Molière probably knew *El burlador* and was almost certainly familiar with the improvised Italian farce, together with its two French derivatives, but all these models are completely overshadowed by the new spirit that he breathed into the subject. Molière was a true product of the age of Louis XIV inasmuch as his hero is motivated not by instinct and sensuality but by rationalism at its most logical. He is a typical cavalier of the time: fearless and in total command of courtly convention, but also a cold and, above all, egoistical creature of reason lacking in sensuality, passion and feeling. It is significant not only that he blasphemes like his predecessors, but that he even denies the existence of God. For him, piety is mere hypocrisy and a way of achieving his ends. As a result, his invitation to the statue inevitably loses much of its dramatic force: on his lips, it has the effect of a cynical game, rather than of a challenge to supernatural powers by a man whose demoniacal impulse knows no bounds. On a more general level, one wonders what purpose is served by all these fantastical, Romantic and, in short, irrational features in such a rationalistic and tendentious drama. Typically French is the confrontation with the supernatural in the guise of a veiled woman who at the end pronounces judgement on the hero before suddenly turning into an allegory of Time with its scythe. In this way Molière added psychological depth to the subject for the first time since *El burlador* and removed the coarseness and immorality of his most recent predecessors, but by turning it into a character drama he also found himself at odds with essential aspects of the story.

Dom Juan's servant Sganarelle bears a striking resemblance to the Italian Arlecchino, but he, too, has gained in depth as a result of Molière's decision to portray him as a foil to his hero. For Sganarelle's arguments are as moralistic as his master's are immoral. He is just as egoistical, but cowardly into the bargain.[6] Of the female characters, Donna Anna is virtually lost from sight, with both her seduction and the murder of the Commendatore being relegated to the wings. By contrast, the character of Donna Elvira is essentially Molière's creation, beside which all previous attempts to portray her pale into insignificance. Dom Juan abducts her from a convent and marries her, only to abandon her soon afterwards. She pursues him and in doing so discovers his true nature, whereupon she decides to return to her convent. First, however, she seeks him out, not to reproach him for his infidelity but to try to persuade him to repent and in that way to save him from perdition. This aspect of sublimity and renunciatory love bears the hallmark of a great dramatist, without, however, removing the work's basic defects. Elvira's two brothers, Dom Carlos and Dom Alonse, seek to avenge their sister's honour but fail to achieve their aim within the course of the play.

That the play's bitter satire was instantly felt is clear from the fact that it received only fifteen performances and remained unpublished in Molière's lifetime. Only when rewritten in alexandrines by Thomas Corneille in 1677 did it find a place for itself in the repertory, the most offensive passages, including the ending, all having been removed.[7] The most recent French adaptation of the legend, Rosimond's *Le nouveau festin de pierre, ou L'Athée foudroyé*, has no independent merit.[8]

---

6. His pathetic cry of 'Mes gages! mes gages' on Dom Juan's death caused considerable offence even at the first performance; see Max Wolff, *Molière*, 346ff.

7. It was not until 1841 that the original version was revived at the Odéon, with a further production at the Théâtre Français in 1847.

8. To be on the safe side, the action was transferred to pagan times in order to allow the 'atheist' to swagger with impunity.

◆ Further, see Ronzeaud, *Moliére/Dom Juan*.

Other versions of the legend began to appear throughout Europe but were initially dependent on the aforementioned French authors, most notably Molière. Thomas Shadwell's *The Libertine*, which was first performed in London in 1676, is based on Molière and Rosimond. It proved hugely successful, yet the overall impression was so unsettling 'as to render it little less than impiety to represent it on the stage'.[9] Among Dutch plays more or less clearly influenced by these French models are versions by Adrian Reys (1699) and van Maaler (1719). Meanwhile, in 1690, Johannes Velten had staged a German version in Torgau under the title *Don Juan oder Don Pedro Totengastmahl* (Don Juan, or Don Pedro's Banquet for the Dead),[10] after which the subject quickly found a home for itself in Germany, becoming popular with theatre companies that still specialized in improvisation. In 1716, for example, the actor Gottfried Prehauser, who was famous as the stock character of Hanswurst, made his Viennese début as Don Philippo in *Das steinerne Gastmahl*.[11] Another play, *Don Juan oder Das steinerne Gastmahl*, is also known to have been performed in Vienna during the first week of November until as late as 1772.[12] Unfortunately we do not know the contents of either piece, although in Prehauser's case we shall not go far wrong in assuming it to have been an improvised burlesque of a kind that was then popular in Vienna. Another play that almost certainly tapped a similar vein was *Der Schrecken im Spiegel ruchloser Jugend, oder Das lehrreiche Gastmahl des Don Pedro* (The Terror in the Mirror of Infamous Youth, or Don Pedro's Edifying Banquet) that was included in the repertory of Carolina Neuber's company in 1735, when it was advertised as 'sufficiently well known to most people'. Ackermann's company, too, performed an after-piece by the name of *Don Juan* in 1742. In 1752 the court actors to the King of Poland and Elector of Saxony in Dresden staged a piece based on Molière with the typically rationalistic title of *Das steinerne Totengastmahl, oder Die im Grabe noch lebende Rache, oder Die aufs höchste gestiegene, endlich übel angekommene Kühn- und Frechheit* (The Stone Banquet of the Dead, or Vengeance still living in the Grave, or Extreme Boldness and Impudence finally come to Grief). In 1766 Friedrich Ludwig Schröder triumphed as Sganarelle in Hamburg,[13] suggesting that it was a version of Molière's play that was performed here. Only one of these popular plays has survived from the eighteenth century, *Der Laufner Don Juan*, which treats the legend in a particularly knockabout manner.[14] In the same vein are the numerous contemporary puppet plays from Augsburg, Ulm, Strasbourg and elsewhere.[15] Titles such as *Don Juan, oder Der vierfache Mörder, oder Das Gastmahl um Mitternacht auf dem Kirchhof* (Don Juan, or The Fourfold Murderer, or The Banquet at Midnight in the Graveyard) speak for themselves.[16] Here Hanswurst

9. Baker, *Biographia dramatica*, ii.188. ◆ See Shadwell, *The Libertine: A Tragedy*; further, Kaufman, 'The Shadow of the Burlador: Don Juan on the Continent and in England'. For Purcell's music to *The Libertine*, see Spink, 'Purcell's music for *The Libertine*'.

10. Heine, *Johannes Velten*, 37.

11. Don Philippo also appears in the versions of Dorimond and de Villiers, but as a serious character corresponding to the later Don Ottavio. This has led writers to draw certain conclusions regarding the sources of the lost Viennese piece, but it is worth asking whether Prehauser would have contemplated such a serious role. Is it not more likely that behind the high-sounding name there lurks the Viennese comic character of Lipperl? See Johann Müller, *Abschied von der National-Schaubühne*, 63; Farinelli, *Don Giovanni*, 63; and Werner, 'Der Laufner Don Juan'.

12. Sonnenfels, *Gesammelte Schriften*, iii.139. According to Carl Ferdinand Pohl, quoted by Jahn, the full title was *Das steinerne Gastmahl oder die redende Statue samt Arie, welche Hanswurst singet, nebst denen Versen des Eremiten und den Verzweiflungsreden des Don Juan bei dessen unglückseeligem Lebens-Ende* (The Stone Banquet, or The Talking Statue, together with the Aria sung by Hanswurst, together with the Verses of the Hermit and Don Juan's Desperate Speeches at the End of his Unhappy Life); see Otto Jahn, *W. A. Mozart*, fourth edition, ii.389.

13. Friedrich Meyer, *Friedrich Ludwig Schröder: Beitrag zur Kunde des Menschen und des Künstlers*, i.153; ii.2, 55 and 144.

14. *Don Joann, ein Schauspill in 4 Aufzigen. Verfaßt von Herrn appen Beter Metastasia. K. K. Hofpoeten*; see Werner, 'Der Laufner Don Juan'. Needless to add, the name of Metastasio was used merely as a means of attracting audiences.

15. Scheible, *Das Kloster*, iii.699ff.; Engel, *Deutsche Puppenkomödien*.

16. One of these plays is reproduced by Engel, *Deutsche Puppenkomödien*.

is invariably the main character, but there is still a clear link with the older French tradition, as emerges, not least, from the Hermit scene, which is a regular feature of all these versions. None the less, it remains doubtful whether their authors drew directly on Dorimond or de Villiers. The final offshoot of these popular plays on the legend of Don Juan is the comedy *Don Juan, oder Der steinerne Gast nach Molière und dem Spanischen des Tirso de Molina bearbeitet mit Kaspars Lustbarkeit* (Don Juan, or The Stone Guest adapted from Molière and the Spanish of Tirso de Molina, with Kaspar's Merrymaking), which the director of the Leopoldstädter Theater in Vienna, Karl Marinelli, staged eighty-one times between 1783 and 1821.[17]

A new version turned up in Spain in 1725 under the title *No hay plazo que no se cumpla ni deuda que no se pague, y convidado de piedra* (There is Neither Time Unaccomplished nor Debt Unpaid, or The Stone Guest). Its author was Antonio de Zamora. A loosely structured piece, it turns the hero into a common-or-garden theatrical villain and would have been of no interest to Da Ponte.[18]

In Italy, too, the subject enjoyed lasting popularity in comic guise, with no less a dramatist than Carlo Goldoni resolving to replace what he regarded as the inferior Italian and French versions with something better.[19] Like Molière, but less successfully, he adopted a fundamentally rationalistic approach to the material, creating a comedy that was staged in Venice in 1736 under the title *Don Giovanni Tenorio ossia il Dissoluto* and that deals with commonsensical practicalities, with no room for passion or miracles: at the end the hero is simply struck dead by lightning and the statue's invitation has been cut completely. Although the burlesque aspect has been eradicated, so, too, has all profundity. Even more problematical is the fact that in the character of the coquettish Elisa (a failed attempt at a Zerlina figure), Goldoni was hoping to take personal revenge on the actress Anna Baccherini ('La Passalacqua'), who had been unfaithful to him,[20] with the result that it is one of the playwright's feeblest pieces. Thanks to Goldoni's reputation, however, it still provided a number of features of the later librettos. Just before he is challenged to his first duel, for example, Don Giovanni declares Isabella/Elvira to be mad. And Donna Anna is engaged to Don Ottavio, even though she feels no special affection for him but, at least for a time, is clearly more drawn to Don Giovanni. Don Ottavio is already the vacillating, passive character familiar from the libretto,[21] even the subtitle of which – 'il dissoluto' – derives from Goldoni.[22]

Meanwhile the subject had conquered the operatic stage.[23] In 1713 *Le festin de pierre* was performed at the Théâtre de la Foire in Paris. Described as being 'en vaudevilles sans prose', this three-act piece was evidently one of the vaudeville comedies with music of the kind that Alain-René Lesage was fond of staging. The composer was Le Tellier. Although it caught the public imagination, the piece was originally banned because of its depiction of hell at the end.[24] The subject was treated entirely in the style of these typical precursors of *opéra comique*. Not until 1734 did the figure of Don Juan set foot on the operatic stage in Italy in Eustacchio Bambini's *La pravità castigata* in a production by Angelo Mingotti's company.[25] Here the libretto was extremely loosely

---

17. Zeidler, 'Die Ahnen Don Juans'. ◆ Marinelli himself died in 1803.
18. Its contents are summarized by Bulthaupt, *Dramaturgie der Oper*, i.164–5.
19. Goldoni, *Mémoires*, i/29.163. ◆ Further, see Balmas, 'Carlo Goldoni: Il dissoluto' and Malachy, 'Don Giovanni Tenorio o sia Il Dissoluto: Une Tragi-comédie oubliée de Carlo Goldoni'.
20. Goldoni, *Mémoires*, i/29.163.
21. Farinelli, *Don Giovanni*, 77; and Bulthaupt, *Dramaturgie der Oper*, 162–3.
22. ◆ Concerning eighteenth-century Don Juan literary traditions generally, see Hall, 'Dom Juan, personnage européen du XVIIe siècle' and Lazzaro-Weis, 'Parody and Farce in the Don Juan Myth in the Eighteenth Century'.
23. Perrucci's *opera tragica* (see above) may be ignored on the grounds that we cannot be sure that it was an opera at all.
24. Parfaict, *Mémoires pour servir à l'histoire des spectacles de la foire*, i.153–4.
25. Müller von Asow, *Angelo und Pietro Mingotti*, 8 and CXXXIV–V. There is no proof that Angelo Mingotti was the librettist. ◆ Concerning the Mingotti company, see Müller von Asow, *Die Mingottischen Opernunternehmungen, 1732 bis 1756*.

structured in keeping with the popular improvised farces of the period[26] and also used stage machinery to create a lot of crude effects. In 1746 Colin Restier performed a ballet *Le grand festin de pierre* at the Théâtre de la Foire Laurent, but nothing is known about this work apart from its title. Conversely the ballet *Don Juan* that was performed at the Kärntnertor-Theater in Vienna in 1761 has survived in its entirety. Its scenario was by the then balletmaster at the theatre, Gasparo Angiolini, and its music was by Gluck. Earlier writers tended to dismiss the idea of treating the subject as a ballet, but this view has had to be revised in the wake of our greater understanding of the importance of Noverre and his circle. Angiolini, too, described his *Don Juan* as a 'ballet-pantomime dans le goût des anciens' and demanded simplicity and grandeur in terms of both characters and action.[27] And the action is certainly reduced to its barest essentials. Of the female characters, only Donna Anna survives as Don Juan's lover and the niece of the Commendatore. The first part includes a serenade for Don Juan outside Donna Anna's house, followed by the death of her uncle; the second depicts a party at Don Juan's attended by the statue, which invites Don Juan to visit it in turn; the third is given over to the Commendatore's attempts to persuade Don Juan to mend his ways, followed by Don Juan's descent into hell; and the fourth depicts his torment by the Furies and ultimate destruction in the fires of hell. This version certainly simplifies the action, but it also omits the most salient aspects of the hero's character and reduces Donna Anna to the point where she is simply a slave to his will. Thanks to Gluck's music, the work soon gained an international reputation, enjoying performances in Paris and, more especially, in Italy, where it was staged in Parma, Turin, Naples and Milan.[28] Another ballet on the same subject, probably based on a scenario by Friedrich Ludwig Schröder, was performed by Ackermann's company in 1769.[29]

From the 1770s onwards Italian theatres were almost literally overwhelmed by 'stone guests', thereby affording clear proof of the popularity enjoyed by the subject in this country. The first was a *dramma tragicomico* by Vincenzo Righini to a libretto by Nunzio Porta that was performed in Prague in 1776 and in Vienna in 1777. As in the older versions, it begins with a fisherman and his wife rescuing Don Giovanni and his servant Arlecchino from drowning. This is followed by Don Giovanni's assault on the virtue of Donna Anna, who in this version has been married against her will to the Duca Ottavio. In turn this leads to the murder of the Commendatore and to Donna Anna's vow to be avenged of his murderer. Don Giovanni decides to flee but is pursued by Isabella, whom he has seduced and who urges Don Alfonso to punish him. After a failed attempt to make Donna Anna change her mind, Arlecchino, acting on Don Giovanni's instructions, invites the statue to supper, which begins with the hero's toast to the audience and Arlecchino's toast to all beautiful young women, after which the statue appears and invites Don Giovanni to dine with him in turn. His fate is sealed at the meeting in the mausoleum. Anna and Alfonso are informed, and Don Giovanni is tormented by the Furies in hell.[30]

---

26. Rille, *Geschichte des Brünner Stadttheaters, 1734–1884*, 28ff.
27. Engländer, 'Glucks "Cinesi" und "Orfano della China"', 71–2; and Arend, 'Das Szenarium zu Glucks Ballett Don Juan', 293ff.
28. Farinelli, *Don Giovanni*, 260. ◆ Further, see Unfried, 'Von der geschmackvollen Armkunst zur spektakulären Beinkunst: Materialien zu einer eigenständigen Wiener Tanzkultur im 18. Jahrhundert an Hand von Glucks Ballettpantomime Don Juan' and Bruce Alan Brown, *Gluck and the French Theatre in Vienna*. Some time before 1772, Leopold Mozart arranged four dances from the ballet; for an edition, see Eisen, *Christoph W. Gluck: Four Dances from Don Juan, arranged by Leopold Mozart*. No doubt these were well known to Mozart.
29. Friedrich Meyer, *Friedrich Ludwig Schröder*, ii.2, 55 and 144.
30. ◆ Further, see Buch, 'The Don Juan Tradition, Eighteenth-Century Supernatural Musical Theatre and Vincenzo Righini's "Il convitato di pietra"'; Kunze, *Don Giovanni vor Mozart: Die Tradition der Don Giovanni-Opern im italienischen Buffo-Theater des 18. Jahrhunderts*; and Russell, *The Don Juan Legend before Mozart, with a Collection of Eighteenth-Century Opera Librettos*.

Righini's libretto is a lively mixture of serious and *buffa* elements. A further opera, *Il convitato di pietra*, with music by Giovanni Bertati was performed in Venice in 1777, but only the title survives,[31] and the same is true of a piece by Gioachino Albertini first seen in Venice in 1784.[32] Conversely, the poet Giambattista Lorenzi went back to the earlier version by Cicognini when preparing his libretto for Giacomo Tritto in Naples in 1783, giving the character of Pulcinella an important role to play.[33]

But it was in 1787 that the Italians' enthusiasm for the Don Juan legend reached its high point. Even as late as 1815, Goethe told his friend Zelter he could still remember the time when, in Rome, 'a Don Juan opera (not Mozart's) was played every evening for four weeks, throwing the city into such a state of excitement that the lowliest grocers' families were to be found in the stalls and boxes and there could not be a living soul who had not seen Don Juan roasted in hell and the Commendatore ascend to heaven as a blessed spirit'.[34] It is unclear which work Goethe is referring to here. In the autumn of 1787[35] a one-act farce with words by Lorenzi and music by Vincenzo Fabrizi, *Il convitato di pietra*, was performed at the Teatro della Valle,[36] but a *Nuovo convitato di pietra* is also known to have been given in Venice during the 1787 carnival.[37] The name of the librettist is not known, but the composer was Francesco Gardi.[38] The text is again a fairly crude farce. The adjective 'nuovo' suggests an earlier and particularly successful piece, which was presumably Giuseppe Gazzaniga's *Il convitato di pietra*, a setting of a libretto by Giuseppe Bertati first staged at the Teatro San Moisè in Venice on 5 February 1787.[39] Of all the versions under review, this was the most successful. It was prefaced by *Il capriccio drammatico*, itself adapted from a prologue by Bertati, *La novità*, of 1775. The plot of this last-named piece is as follows. The opera director Policastro informs his company that he intends to offer German audiences something new in the form of a one-act comedy *The Stone Guest*. An aristocratic patron attempts to dissuade the players from carrying out this plan, and they are all on the point of fleeing the rehearsal when the director threatens not to pay their fees, with the result that the rehearsal goes ahead after all, albeit accompanied by all manner of practical jokes. This prologue formed the first half of the evening's entertainment, with *Il convitato di pietra* as the second half. Although the librettist is not named, it was again almost certainly Bertati. The prologue is one of those parodies of theatrical life that were particularly popular in *opere buffe*. With the exception of a handful of interpolations, the music of the prologue was by Giovanni Valentini, while that of *Il convitato di pietra* was by

31. Wiel, *I teatri musicali veneziani nel Settecento*, 331. ◆ Since Abert's time, a score of Calegari's *Il convitato di pietra* has been found in the Bibliothèque nationale, Paris.

32. ◆ Albertini's opera appears to have been first given in Warsaw as *Don Juan albo Ukarany libertyn* (*Don Juan, or The Libertine Punished*); a Polish libretto, dated 1783, survives in the Biblioteka Jagiellońska, Kraków. A score of the Italian version survives in the library of the Conservatorio di Musica Luigi Cherubini, Florence.

33. Florimo, *La scuola musicale di Napoli e i suoi conservatorii*, iv.74. ◆ In fact, scores survive in the Bibliothèque nationale, Paris, and the library of the Conservatorio di Musica S. Pietro a Majella, Naples. Further, see Rousset, 'Don Juan dans l'opéra avant Mozart', and Brandenburg, 'Giacomo Tritto: *Il convitato di pietra*'. For Cocognini's text, see Bévotte, *Le festin de pierre avant Molière: Dorimon–de Villiers–Scénario des Italiens–Cicognini.*

34. Riemer, *Briefwechsel zwischen Goethe und Zelter*, i.406–7. Somewhat surprisingly, there is no mention of this performance in the *Italienische Reise*.

35. ◆ But possibly this was as early as carnival 1787.

36. Schatz, 'Giovanni Bertati', 261. ◆ Excerpts from Fabrizi's *Il convitato di pietra* survive in manuscripts at the British Library, London, and the Statens musiksamlingar–Musikbiblioteket, Stockholm.

37. Wiel, *I teatri musicali veneziani*, 403.

38. ◆ Gardi's *Don Giovanni, o Il nuovo convitato di pietra*, with a text after Bertati, was first given at the S. Samuele, Venice, on 5 February 1787; a score survives in the library of the Conservatorio di Musica S. Pietro a Majella, Naples (shelfmark Rari Cornicione 222).

39. Schatz, 'Giovanni Bertati', 260.

Gazzaniga.[40] The work was soon being staged all over Italy, with a veritable rash of productions in Varese, Bologna, Ferrara, Bergamo, Milan and Lucca. It was performed in Paris in 1791, when Cherubini contributed an additional quartet.[41] By 1792 it had reached Lisbon,[42] and two years later, in spite of opposition from Da Ponte, who was then in London, it was performed in the English capital in a version that included several numbers drawn from other works, not least of which was Leporello's 'catalogue aria' from Mozart's opera.[43]

The score of the opera survives only in the form of copies, none of which is complete, although in most cases they supplement each other. The libretto, by contrast, survives in its entirety.[44]

The list of characters contained in the original wordbook is as follows:

> *Don Giovanni.*
> *Donna Anna* figlia del Comendatore [*sic*] d'Oljola.
> *Donna Elvira* Sposa promessa di Don Giovanni.
> *Donna Ximena* Dama di Villena.
> *Il Comendatore* Padre di Donna Anna.
> *Duca Ottavio* Sposo promesso della medesima.
> *Maturina* Sposa promessa di Biagio.
> *Pasquariello* Servo confidente di Don Giovanni.
> *Biagio* Contadino Sposo di Maturina.
> *Lanterna* altro Servo di Don Giovanni.
> Servitori diversi, ch non parlono.
> La Scena è in Villena nell' Aragona.

The roles of Donna Anna and Maturina were doubled, as were those of the Commendatore and Biagio. The plot may be summarized as follows:

Pasquariello is ill-humouredly keeping watch outside the Commendatore's house when Don Giovanni rushes out, trying to break free from Donna Anna, who attempts to tear off his mask while calling on her father to help her. The latter appears and falls in the ensuing duel. The first scene ends with a trio for the three men. (There is no overture.) After a brief conversation Don Giovanni escapes with Pasquariello. Donna Anna hurries in with her fiancé, the Duca Ottavio, and to her horror discovers her father's body (accompanied recitative); regaining her composure, she explains in detail how she was attacked by Don Giovanni and declares her intention of retiring to a convent until such time as Ottavio discovers the murderer and punishes him (aria). Dismayed, Ottavio agrees to this (aria). (Donna Anna does not reappear after this.) Don Giovanni is waiting

---

40. See especially Chrysander, 'Die Oper Don Giovanni von Gazzaniga und von Mozart', 351–453, which includes part of the prologue and the whole of the libretto of the opera. A handful of bars of Gazzaniga's score are reproduced in Chrysander, 'Francesco Antonio Urio', 577, and by Bulthaupt, *Dramaturgie der Oper*, appendix 52ff. On individual points, see Chrysander and Gugler, '[Review of *Don Giovanni*]', 69, 110, 126 and 132. ◆ Cherubini's quartet, 'Non ti fidar, o misera', was performed in 1792 (see n. 45), not 1791; the autograph survives in the Biblioteka Jagiellońska, Kraków.
41. Chrysander, 'Die Oper Don Giovanni', 409.
42. Karl Engel, *Die Don-Juan-Sage*, 126 and 242.
43. Da Ponte, *Memorie*, ii/1.28; and Chrysander, 'Die Oper Don Giovanni', 410–11.
44. The London score was owned by Chrysander. Additional manuscripts may be found in Bologna (library of the Liceo musicale), Milan (Ricordi) and Vienna (library of the Gesellschaft der Musikfreunde). The following synopsis is taken from Jahn. ◆ Incomplete manuscript copies of Gazzaniga's *Il convitato di pietra* survive in the British Library, London (shelfmarks R.M.23.f.19.(3.) and R.M.23.f.19.(4.)) and the library of the Conservatorio di Santa Cecilia, Rome (shelfmark G.Mss.208). For an edition of the work, see Gazzaniga, *Don Giovanni: o sia, Il convitato di pietra*.

for Donna Ximena at a country house and is talking to Pasquariello when Donna Elvira enters in travelling clothes. Abandoned by Don Giovanni in Burgos, she has come in search of him (aria). They recognize each other. Don Giovanni tells her that Pasquariello will explain the reasons for his departure and then makes good his escape. Pasquariello shows her a list of his master's lovers (aria). She resolves either to insist on her rights or to exact vengeance. Don Giovanni arrives in amorous conversation with Ximena and, in reply to her jealous questions, assures her of his good faith (aria). A couple from the surrounding countryside, Biagio and Maturina, are celebrating their wedding (chorus and tarantella). Pasquariello joins them and pays court to Maturina but is forced to withdraw when Don Giovanni arrives. Don Giovanni is so rude to Biagio that the latter leaves in high dudgeon (aria). By flattering and promising to marry her, Don Giovanni seduces Maturina, who assures him that she loves him in return (aria). Ximena asks Pasquariello about his master and is overjoyed to be told that he is still faithful to her. Don Giovanni now enters and is questioned by Ximena, Elvira and Maturina in turn, reassuring each of them by declaring that the other two are out of their minds with love of him[45] (duet in which Elvira and Maturina quarrel after the others have left). The scene changes to the mausoleum that the Commendatore had had built while he was still alive. The Duca Ottavio places an inscription beneath the statue. Don Giovanni arrives with Pasquariello in order to inspect the tombstone and forces his servant to invite the statue to supper (duet). Back at Don Giovanni's house his cook Lanterna is preparing the meal and awaiting his master's return. Elvira arrives, and when Don Giovanni enters with Pasquariello, she begs him to show remorse, but he scornfully dismisses her entreaties. She leaves, announcing her intention of entering a convent (aria). Don Giovanni sits down cheerfully to dinner to the strains of *Tafelmusik* (concertino). Pasquariello has to sit with him while Lanterna serves the food and wine; they toast the city of Venice and its beautiful women (aria for Pasquariello).[46] There is a knock at the door, and to the horror of the two servants, the Commendatore enters. Don Giovanni bids him welcome and tells Pasquariello to entertain him. When the Commendatore invites him to sup with him in return, Don Giovanni accepts with a handshake, but rejects his summons to repent, whereupon the spirits of hell rise up to torment him. The vision of hell disappears and Ottavio enters with Ximena, Elvira and Maturina. The servants tell them what has happened, whereupon all join in the usual comic finale.

Gazzaniga's *Don Giovanni* must have reached Vienna very soon after its Venetian première. This was the period when Mozart had to write a new opera for Prague, and it is quite likely that familiarity with Bertati's libretto prompted Da Ponte and Mozart to choose this subject. Be that as it may, it was Bertati's text that formed the basis of the new piece, with Da Ponte taking over not only the main characters and scenes but even individual words and phrases. Whenever he made changes, his aim is clear. As with *Le nozze di Figaro*, he preferred to rework an older libretto, leaving its main features intact, rather than create a new one of his own. And in both cases he revealed undeniable dramatic skill. In the case of *Don Giovanni*, it is entirely typical of him that he not only concealed his dependency but later treated Bertati with open contempt and hostility when the latter replaced him at the Viennese court.

There is no doubt that Bertati raised the story to a higher and, above all, a more musical level. Following the subject's rationalistic treatment at the hands of Molière and Goldoni, the world of

---

45. It must have been at this point that Cherubini's quartet, 'Non ti fidar, o misera', written for the Paris production of 1792, was interpolated; see Scudo, *Critique et littérature musicales*, i.181.

46. This was changed, of course, depending on where the work was performed. The custom of a toast continued to be popular in Mozart's opera, too: in Stuttgart, even as late as the 1880s, Don Giovanni regularly toasted Mozart, 'the dear composer'.

sensuality, irrationality and instinctual desire that had already played an important role in *El burlador de Sevilla* comes into its own again here, with the result that the intervention of supernatural forces is now far better motivated than it was in the older versions, in which their authors' Enlightenment standpoint made it impossible for the mystical and fantastical element to be incorporated in any organic way. At the same time, Bertati must take the credit for having raised the subject above the level of mere farce to which it had sunk, especially in Germany and Italy, and for having invested it with a higher dramatic and psychological truth. Admittedly, he too envisaged no more than an ordinary *opera buffa*, and his libretto is certainly not lacking in elements of crude, knockabout humour, foremost among which are the scene in hell, which is genuinely *buffa* in character, and the traditional finale, the contents of which are already familiar to us:

Donne:	A a a, io vò cantare:
	Igo vò mettermi a saltar.
Don Ottavio:	La chitarra io vò suonare.
Lanterna:	Io suonar vò il contrabasso.
Pasquariello:	Ancor io per far del chiasso
	Il fagotto vò suonar.
Don Ottavio:	Tren, tren, trinchete, trinchete trè.
Lanterna:	Flon, flon, flon, flon, flon, flon.
Pasquariello:	Pu, pu, pu, pu, pu, pu, pu.
Tutti:	Che bellissima pazzia!
	Che stranissima armonia!
	Così allegro si va a star.

But these are no more than individual concessions to the popular *buffa* spirit. In general, Bertati aspired to the sort of more refined *buffa* style that was cultivated by Lorenzi and Casti, thereby creating a new *Don Giovanni* which, if not yet a perfect work of art, none the less pointed in that direction. This was no accident, of course, as this period was fond of heroes whose very greatness lay in their rejection of laws and morality – take Schiller's *Die Räuber*, for example. Contemporaries admired their unbridled love of life and their willingess to challenge even divine authority, regarding as a sign of their own superiority a mode of behaviour that would earlier have been dismissed as sinful. In short, there were good reasons why the subject of Don Juan was so popular at this time: with his demonic sensuality, the hero seemed to be the living embodiment of their protest against all that was unnatural about the old, rationalistic view of life. Of course, none of these poets, not even Bertati, considered the possibility of consciously elaborating this idea: all that they wanted to create was an effective *opera buffa*. On an unconscious level, however, Bertati clearly bowed to the new spirit. Even his substitution of the old subtitle of the 'dissoluto punito' by the more neutral 'convitato di pietra' is significant: the 'quod erat demonstrandum' – the old magic formula of rationalism – no longer had any appeal for him. His aim was not to teach or convert or to choose between good and evil, but only to stick to tangible reality. The events on stage should be effective in themselves and, in spite of all its *buffa* elements, there is clearly an awareness of tragedy in the way he shapes the final scene, a tragedy based not on guilt and atonement but simply on the impact of the drama as it unfolds. The importance of Bertati for Mozart lay precisely in ideas of this kind, however much his libretto may in other ways still be bound by tradition.

In part, it was practical considerations that prompted Da Ponte to change certain details of Bertati's libretto. Among these considerations was the relatively small number of singers available in Prague. The cook Lanterna was the first to be sacrificed to these cuts, with the result that Don Giovanni now had only one servant. Next to go was Donna Ximena, albeit not without leaving traces of her character on both Elvira and, more especially, Zerlina. This marked a decisive advance inasmuch as it meant that the three remaining women characters were now much more sharply delineated, thereby becoming more effective foils to the hero. Bound up with this is the most radical change undertaken by Da Ponte, the expansion of the role of Donna Anna, who in Bertati's version had disappeared from the opera after the opening scene, waiting for Ottavio to avenge her dishonour within the walls of a convent. In Da Ponte's version she is permanently involved in the action as Don Giovanni's most resolute adversary. As a result, not only is her own characterization significantly deepened, so, too, is that of Don Giovanni. Not without good reason, Mozart's hand has been suspected here.[47] In writing to his librettists, the composer had already expressed very specific views and wishes about his female characters, and it is scarcely conceivable that, as a fully mature artist, he should suddenly have refrained from doing so. In the case of the Countess in *Le nozze di Figaro*, moreover, he had already created a character who stands out clearly from her comic surroundings by dint of her darker and deeper emotions. With its starker contrasts, *Don Giovanni* emphatically demanded a corresponding figure. And when we consider the result, we shall have no hesitation in concluding that Donna Anna owes her undeniable dramatic life not to the librettist but to the composer. Da Ponte was content merely to elaborate hints already provided by Bertati, but he did not alter the figure's basic character and, above all, added not a single new motif. As a result, Donna Anna comes into her own only episodically in the libretto, whereas in his musical characterization Mozart has achieved something that only the greatest music dramatists have managed to do: through his music he has transformed a figure that Da Ponte had left in only vague and half-finished outline, turning her not only into a living, unified character but, more than that, into one of the main characters in the drama as a whole. In view of this, it is hard to see how at least one recent commentator has sought to deny Mozart's involvement in the libretto at all.[48]

Both Bertati and Da Ponte portrayed the figure of Donna Elvira along largely the same lines as she had been characterized by Molière. Both librettists force her to undergo a process of deep humiliation, in Bertati's case through her altercation with Maturina, in Da Ponte's in the scene with the disguised Leporello. But in both versions this passionate woman frustrates all the hero's nefarious plans and in her final warning to him rises to true greatness of character. In this way Molière's inspired creation has also benefited the opera.

By being combined with Ximena, Zerlina is far superior as a character to Maturina, who is little more than an earthy *buffa* figure. From Da Ponte she acquired not only her naïve charm but also the natural impulsiveness of a simple young woman from the people. Particularly successful from a psychological point of view is Da Ponte's idea of her reconciliation with Masetto, which rounds off her characterization in a pleasingly logical manner. But Masetto, too, has benefited from this new motif. Bertati's Biagio appears only once, in order to witness Maturina's infidelity and be driven away by Don Giovanni. Masetto's martyrdom is longer and more painful, but as a result,

---

47. See Chrysander, 'Die Oper Don Giovanni', 420.
48. Schurig, *Wolfgang Amade Mozart*, ii.170–1. Schurig goes on to show, quite rightly, that Da Ponte moved Donna Anna's account of Don Giovanni's assault on her and transferred it to after the recognition scene, making it incomparably more effective from a dramatic point of view. Yet he criticizes Mozart for treating this high point in the action as a *secco* recitative, describing it as 'the only musical weakness' of the piece. This shows a grave misunderstanding on Schurig's part, as this recitative is in fact an accompagnato on the grandest scale and, as such, an example of the type of recitative invariably used by composers at this time for particular high points in the action. Schurig's conclusion – that the passage proves 'that Mozart was indecisive as a dramatist' – actually proves the opposite.

Zerlina's return to him seems all the more convincing. Each supports the other, and instead of two *buffa* figures who are treated by the librettist with the usual implacable contempt, we have an innocently trusting everyday couple who, in spite of all their sins and the dangers to which they are exposed, are finally reconciled. Above all, however, the links between these characters and the others, especially the protagonist, are now much closer and filled with a greater sense of life.

Don Ottavio remains a passive character, more complex on a superficial level, but of no greater psychological depth. As for the Commendatore and his antithesis Leporello, they are modelled on Bertati with almost slavish exactitude, the only difference being that in Da Ponte's version Leporello is the only comic character, whereas in Bertati's case virtually all the characters are comic in one way or another.

We have already discussed Don Giovanni's character in general. Da Ponte has added little of substance to the picture presented by Bertati, whose comparatively sketchy portrayal was no doubt due to the fact that his opera was in a single act, whereas Da Ponte could work on a larger canvas and provide more detailed motivation. Yet in spite of the fact that Da Ponte worked with a finer brush, Don Giovanni remains essentially the same character as before.

In short, much of the credit for the libretto should go not to Da Ponte, as earlier writers claimed, but to Bertati. Indeed, there is one point on which Da Ponte proves to be much less progressive than his predecessor in his handling of the material, namely, in his greater emphasis on rationalistic morality, an emphasis already clear from his reintroduction of the Goldonian subtitle, 'Il dissoluto punito'. Da Ponte was incapable of conceiving of tragic seriousness without this additional feature. Fortunately the sheer wealth of action prevented him from laying undue emphasis upon it, and the dramatic poet in him happily proved more powerful than the moralist. Only in the final scene could he not resist the temptation to draw a moral and replace Bertati's burlesque ending with a series of scenes in which he first imposes a sense of order on the lives of Donna Anna and Donna Elvira but then attempts to do justice to both the spirit of *opera buffa* and to the 'tragic moral' that he had in mind, with all the characters joining 'allegramente' in the 'antichissima canzon': 'Questo è il fin di chi fa mal, / E de' perfidi la morte alla vita è sempre ugual' ('This is the end of the man who does wrong, and the death of wrongdoers is always a reflection of their life'). This is the favourite moral less of an *opera buffa* than of an *opéra comique*,[49] and it is surprising only that the individual characters do not give further examples of this precept in the manner of a vaudeville.

Even so, Da Ponte's contribution should not be underestimated. After all, he was demonstrably concerned to adapt Bertati's *buffa* text in such a way that it conformed with Mozart's unique qualities as a music dramatist, qualities for which the music of *Le nozze di Figaro* had considerably sharpened his perceptions. When he set about adapting Beaumarchais's comedy, his aim – as we have seen – was essentially still to create an *opera buffa*. The finished opera had showed him that Mozart saw his subjects with very different eyes, and although he can have had no clear idea about this new artistic ideal, he none the less felt instinctively how a libretto should be structured in order to meet those demands. One can almost literally see him developing Bertati's figures with Mozart's dramatic characterization in mind, intensifying and deepening the contrasts between them and, above all, taking account of Mozart's individuality in building on their basic musical character – a character already present in Bertati. Neither before nor afterwards was Mozart

---

49. See above. This final moral acquires a note of unintentional humour in Rochlitz's translation: 'Lasterglück flieht schnell wie Rauch; / wie man lebt, so stirbt man auch' ('The joys of sin pass swiftly by: / just as you live, so you shall die'). Not even Wilhelm Busch could have improved on this.

offered characters that cried out for music as much as they do in *Don Giovanni*. This is as true of Leporello as it is of the three female characters, but it applies most of all to the utterly original way in which the real hero of the drama is characterized. Throughout the opera nothing happens that is not in some way related to him and that expresses some aspect of his character: everything gravitates towards him and revolves around his actions and his destiny. This is very different from the multifaceted nature of *Le nozze di Figaro*. And yet Don Giovanni does not have a single aria of the older type to sing.[50] Not even his famous 'champagne aria' ('Finch' han dal vino') falls under this heading. As a man of action, he has no time for lyrical effusions but evolves by interacting with others. This was entirely new and exceptional in an age when operatic heroes habitually introduced themselves to their audiences through their arias. The result is a form of indirect characterization in which the apparently unintentional replaces the intentional. Here, too, the composer had to confront a new and difficult challenge. If the hero was to appear not only as an individual, unified character but also as the focus of the action and if he was to be not merely an impulsive adventurer but an exceptional human being bursting with energy and sensuality, then a musician of outstanding creative abilities was needed who was capable of finding new means to solve this novel problem. For Mozart, this was a far greater challenge than *Le nozze di Figaro*, yet it was also bound to be a particular stimulus to his universal genius.

On a purely technical level, all credit is due to Da Ponte, especially in the opening act, for developing Bertati's plot by introducing a series of highly effective contrasts and constantly building to a climax. The second act would have benefited, of course, from a new dramatic motif as the continuing pursuit of Don Giovanni is not in itself sufficient to maintain the tension at the same high level. But creative ideas on such a scale were not Da Ponte's strong point. And so, in order to pad out the second act, he fell back on the tried and tested expedients of *opera buffa* such as beatings and changing clothes, getting second wind only when reverting to Bertati towards the end, from the graveyard scene onwards. Even so, the individual situations that make up this act are in themselves effective on stage and extremely grateful from a musical point of view. Here, indeed, lies one of Da Ponte's greatest merits, inasmuch as he showed immense skill in constructing each scene in such a way that it lent itself to musical treatment. And this is particularly true of his ensembles, which were, of course, Mozart's great strength. In his depiction of passion, he was no match, of course, for a librettist such as Casti, and his libretto contains few traces of the courtly character of the Spanish original. Rather, it reflects the Rococo spirit, with its effortless ability to combine a boundless love of life with humanism and all manner of mystical ideas. It is this that gives the text its individual truthfulness. Equally Rococoesque is the skilful, precious and graceful mode of expression that distinguishes Da Ponte from the more robust Bertati.[51]

Da Ponte's libretto thus combines the most disparate preconditions that allowed Mozart's creative genius to soar aloft to particularly impressive heights. Indeed, he scaled peaks just as high as in *Le nozze di Figaro* but they were peaks of a totally different order, taking him into a world whose sublimities and profundities were barely glimpsed in the earlier work. There are good reasons why, in the context of *Don Giovanni*, Goethe thought that Mozart was the man to set his *Faust* to music.[52] His verdict was not reached simply on the basis of the affinities between individual situations in both works but on the strength of his instinctive feeling that here was an artist

---

50. As we have already seen, a number of singers of Mozart's own day found this hard to swallow. Bertati gives his hero an aria in his scene with Ximena (no. 9), an aria that Da Ponte has expanded and turned into a duet ('Là ci darem la mano').

51. ◆ Further concerning Bertati, Gazzaniga and Mozart's *Don Giovanni*, see Noiray, 'La construction de Don Giovanni' and Raffaelli, 'Il primo invito di Don Giovanni: Maschere e travestimenti in Mozart–Da Ponte'.

52. Eckermann, *Gespräche mit Goethe*, ii.87 (12 February 1829).

who was related to him not only in terms of his universality but in the whole way in which he shaped his vision of the world. Two years later we find him returning to this same point: 'How can one say that Mozart *composed* Don Juan! Composition – as if it were a cake or a biscuit stirred together from eggs, flour and sugar! It is a creation of the mind in which the individual details and the whole are pervaded by a single spirit and by the breath of a single life. The artist did not experiment or patch things together or operate in an arbitrary manner. No, the demonic spirit of his genius had him in its power, so that he was obliged to do exactly as he was told.'[53]

Let us begin by examining the plot in detail.[54] Leporello is on guard, impatiently awaiting his master, who has stolen away to an assignation. Don Giovanni appears, pursued by Donna Anna, from whom he tries in vain to break free. Her father, the Commendatore, arrives in response to her cries for help and forces the brazen intruder to fight with him. He falls to the ground, cut down by Don Giovanni's sword, a turn of events that leaves Don Giovanni himself as stunned as Leporello.[55] There is no time to lose, and Don Giovanni makes good his escape. No sooner has he left than Donna Anna returns with her fiancé, Don Ottavio. At the sight of her father's body she is distraught with grief and faints, but recovers her senses enough to make Don Ottavio swear an oath of vengeance.

Refusing to listen to Leporello's reproaches, Don Giovanni is in the process of informing his servant that he is already embarked on a new adventure when Donna Elvira arrives. She was once seduced by Don Giovanni in Burgos, but then abandoned by him.[56] Now she has come in pursuit of him to remind him of his obligation. He approaches her and is not a little taken aback to recognize her. She overwhelms him with reproaches, whereupon he refers her to Leporello, explaining that his servant will apologize on his behalf. He himself seizes the opportunity to escape. By way of consoling her, Leporello shows her the lengthy list of his master's lovers. Incensed at this latest insult, she resolves to renounce her love for the faithless Don Giovanni and devote her life to vengeance.

Together with some of their friends from the surrounding countryside, Masetto and Zerlina are celebrating their wedding near Don Giovanni's *casinetto*, where the latter has come for another assignation. The young Zerlina attracts him, and he introduces himself to the bridal couple, inviting the whole company to his house and, with a show of force, sending the jealous Masetto packing. He is on the point of winning over Zerlina by flattering her and declaring his love for her when Elvira intervenes, warning Zerlina and, when Don Giovanni whispers into her ear that Elvira is maddened by jealousy as a result of her own unrequited feelings for him, leading her away. Don Giovanni is now joined by Donna Anna and Don Ottavio, who welcome him as a family friend and ask his help in finding the murderer of the Commendatore and bringing him to justice. He is still talking to Donna Anna when Donna Elvira enters and warns them of his hypocrisy. Don Giovanni can find no way out of this new predicament except to declare that she is mad[57] and that the only means of calming her is to leave with her. Donna Anna's suspicions are aroused and, observing him closely, she realizes that he is her father's murderer. She tells Don Ottavio the whole story and demands that

53. Eckermann, *Gespräche mit Goethe*, ii.329–30 (20 June 1831).
54. Largely based on Jahn, *W. A. Mozart*, ii.399ff.
55. This is clear from the words 'Ah! già cadde il sciagurato' ('Ah! the wretch is down') and, above all, from the music. And it continues to make itself felt in Don Giovanni's words in scene two. On the psychological justification for this, see below.
56. Da Ponte gives no indication that Donna Elvira is married or engaged to Don Giovanni but simply describes her as 'abbandonata da Don Giovanni'. For Bertati she had been the 'sposa promessa di Don Giovanni'.
57. Elvira's alleged madness is taken over from Goldoni and Bertati and is a feature familiar to composers of *opera buffa* from time immemorial, but Da Ponte has shown considerable skill in using it to bring together characters who, in part, do not know each other and in that way to expose Don Giovanni.

he avenge her dishonour. Don Ottavio is unwilling to lend credence to so grave a suspicion, but resolves to make enquiries and find out all that he can about Don Giovanni. In the meantime, Don Giovanni has shaken off Donna Elvira and now gives instructions for a lavish banquet to be prepared in honour of the newly-wed couple. With honeyed words Zerlina has largely succeeded in allaying Masetto's fears. He hides when Don Giovanni enters; she is standoffish towards him, and when Masetto unexpectedly reappears, he quickly pulls himself together and manages to talk them both into attending the banquet at his country house. Donna Anna and Don Ottavio arrive with Donna Elvira. She has told them everything. At her suggestion, they wear masks, in order to observe Don Giovanni without being recognized in turn. Leporello notices them and, just as they had hoped, invites them to attend the celebrations, an invitation that they accept. This was a popular custom at this time, especially in Venice, where people would wear masks and, whenever a party was in progress, passing strangers would be invited in, with the masks breaking down all inhibitions. The newcomers enter the hall during a break in the dancing. The others are taking refreshments, Don Giovanni is talking to Zerlina, and Masetto, his jealousy rekindled, attempts to warn her to be careful. The arrival of the three masked figures attracts the attention of the others. They receive a friendly welcome, and the dancing starts up afresh. Mozart states explicitly that Donna Anna and Don Ottavio join in a minuet, the dance of the aristocracy.[58] Only with difficulty does Donna Anna succeed in suppressing her feelings of revulsion, which find expression in a series of individual outbursts, while Don Ottavio advises her to dissemble. Donna Elvira observes Don Giovanni's every move. The latter invites Zerlina to dance a contredanse, while Leporello attempts to distract Masetto's attention by forcing him to dance a *Deutscher*, the quick and boisterous dance of the people. Don Giovanni seizes the opportunity to abduct Zerlina. Leporello hurries after him to warn him. Her cry for help is heard, and everyone rushes to her assistance, but Don Giovanni comes out to meet them, dragging Leporello after him, accusing him of assaulting Zerlina and threatening him with death. But his enemies assail him from every quarter, the masks fall, and Don Giovanni sees himself surrounded by people whom he knows and who are bent on vengeance. For a brief moment master and servant hesitate, before the former, with bold resolve, forces his way through the ranks of his enemies. Thunder can be heard in the distance.[59]

The second act opens with Don Giovanni pacifying the outraged Leporello by means of money and placatory words. He admits that he is pursuing Elvira's pretty chambermaid and, in order to gain access to her house, changes clothes with his servant. Scarcely have they done so when Elvira herself appears at the window. In order to get rid of her, Don Giovanni amuses himself by repeating his earlier protestations of love with feigned passion. Elvira is weak enough to believe him. The disguised Leporello now has to respond to her expressions of love, until Don Giovanni enters noisily and drives them away. He then tries to attract the chambermaid with a tender song. Masetto now enters, armed and accompanied by a number of friends, in order to call Don Giovanni to account. Still in his disguise as Leporello, Don Giovanni promises to put them on the right track, skilfully contriving to disperse the group and talking Masetto into handing over his weapons, after which he beats him soundly and makes good his escape. Hearing Masetto's cries, Zerlina hurries in and attempts to comfort him with her caresses.

---

58. In Hamburg members of the aristocracy demanded that at masked balls minuets should be danced alternately with English dances 'because they did not wish to join the common herd'; Friedrich Meyer, *Friedrich Ludwig Schröder*, i.150–1. Mozart's note, 'Don Ottavio balla minuetto con Donna Anna', is not in the Prague wordbook. For this and other, internal reasons Alfred von Wolzogen felt justified in arguing that the aristocratic guests should not dance at all; see Wolzogen, *Don Juan*, 96. Gugler, too, omits Mozart's note, whereas there is in fact no justification for doing so [Deiters's note].
59. Thürlings, 'Der Donner im ersten Finale des Don Juan'.

Meanwhile, Leporello and Elvira have sought refuge in an anteroom of Donna Anna's house.[60] Leporello tries to slip away, while Elvira begs him not to leave her alone in the dark. He is about to escape when Donna Anna enters with Don Ottavio, who is still trying to assuage her grief. Elvira and Leporello both now try to steal away without the other noticing, but they find their path blocked by Zerlina and Masetto. Believing Leporello to be Don Giovanni, they resolve to put him on trial. To everyone's surprise, Donna Elvira intercedes on his behalf, but in vain. At this point Leporello reveals his true identity and attempts to justify his actions in spite of all their reproaches, before finally managing to escape. Don Ottavio is now convinced that it was Don Giovanni who murdered the Commendatore and declares his intention of pursuing him through the courts in order to bring him to justice. He asks his friends to comfort Donna Anna until he has avenged her father's death.[61]

Don Giovanni is waiting for Leporello near the memorial to the Commendatore. They are laughing at his latest adventure when an invisible voice rings out twice, uttering words of warning. Only now does Don Giovanni notice the Commendatore's statue and order Leporello to read the inscription: 'Retribution here awaits the evildoer who sent me to my grave.' High-spiritedly contemptuous of Leporello's dismay, he orders his servant to invite the statue to supper. The statue nods its head and when Don Giovanni notices this, he challenges it to reply. When it answers with an audible 'Yes', he flees in consternation.

Don Ottavio tells Donna Anna about Don Giovanni's imminent punishment before attempting once again to console her. He asks for her hand in marriage, but she declares that however much she may desire marriage in her heart, her grief for her father obliges her to postpone the fulfilment of that desire until some indeterminate date in the future. This scene looks suspiciously as though it was inserted in Prague, after the opera was already finished in essence, in order to give the soprano a final aria. The same situation arises at the end of the finale, where it contradicts Don Ottavio's appearance in the previous scene.

Don Giovanni is enjoying himself at his richly appointed table and sharing a few jokes with the sweet-toothed Leporello.[62] This is a scene in which master and servant traditionally indulged in the most uninhibited tomfoolery, and Mozart has taken the opportunity to add a number of musical jokes. The meal is accompanied by music featuring popular numbers from the latest operas. During the opening bars, Leporello exclaims: 'Bravi! Cosa rara!' The music in question is taken from the final section of the first-act finale of Martín y Soler's *Una cosa rara*, 'O quanto un si bel giubilo', which was then on everyone's lips and which Mozart parodies in the most delightful manner. In Martín y Soler's opera the unhappy lovers see their partners snatched away by their rivals before their very eyes, whereas in Mozart's opera the hungry Leporello watches his master feasting, so that the music seems tailor-made for the scene. Leporello acknowledges the second number with a delighted exclamation: 'Evvivano i "Litiganti"!' This is Mingone's popular aria from act one, scene eight of Sarti's *Fra i due litiganti il terzo gode*, on which Mozart had already written a set of variations (K460). Its words

---

60. Da Ponte's libretto refers explicitly to an 'atrio terreno oscuro in casa di Donna Anna'. Edward J. Dent argues that Da Ponte originally intended the whole opera to be in three acts, with the sextet ('Sola, sola in buio loco') as the second-act finale. Mozart, too, envisaged this number as a finale, but pressure of time prevented librettist and composer from carrying through this plan; see Dent, *Mozart's Operas*, 168.

61. This scene was altered, or rather extended, for the first Viennese production. Leporello has been caught and Zerlina drags him in by the hair and fastens him to a chair; left alone, he frees himself and escapes. Zerlina, Masetto and Elvira return and Masetto reports on another of Don Giovanni's atrocities. Zerlina and Masetto leave to tell Don Ottavio. Elvira remains behind and, torn between pity and her desire for revenge, pours out her feelings in a great lament; see below.

62. ◆ Concerning the insider jokes in the second act finale, see Volek, 'Prague Operatic Traditions and Mozart's Don Giovanni'.

Come un agnello,
Che va al macello,
Andrai belando
Per la città!

were particularly well known at this time and comically suited to Leporello's behaviour.[63] These musical interpolations replace Bertati's *brindisi* in honour of the beautiful women of Venice and, in keeping with contemporary custom, not only involve parody but also constitute a tribute to the composers in question. The scoring for winds creates a comic effect and is likewise typical of contemporary Tafelmusik. Finally, to please the Prague audiences that were so dear to his heart, Mozart quotes his own 'Non più andrai' from *Le nozze di Figaro*, prompting Leporello's comment, 'Questa poi la conosco pur troppo' ('I've heard this once too often'), and expressing Mozart's gratitude for the enthusiastic reception accorded to his opera in Prague.

The merry-making comes to an abrupt end with the arrival of Donna Elvira. She has abjured her love of Don Giovanni and intends to retire to a convent, but before she does so, she makes one last attempt to persuade him to repent. He counters all her objections with light-hearted scorn, and so she reluctantly leaves. From outside we hear her utter a terrible cry. Leporello hurries after her and returns trembling with fear: the statue of the Commendatore is outside. It knocks, and Don Giovanni has to go in person to admit it. He returns with his stone guest. The latter declines all offers of hospitality but asks Don Giovanni whether he is prepared to accept his own invitation in return; when Don Giovanni answers in the affirmative, the statue seizes him by the hand and demands that he atone for his sins. Defiantly, Don Giovanni repeatedly refuses to do so, whereupon the Commendatore leaves. Darkness descends, flames shoot up from the ground, which begins to shake, and invisible spirits raise their terrifying voices, surrounding Don Giovanni and drawing him down into the abyss. Just as he is snatched away from mortal vengeance, Don Ottavio enters with Donna Anna, Elvira, Zerlina and Masetto to punish the malefactor. Leporello, who in feverish fear has witnessed the terrifying scene, tells of his master's gruesome end. Their troubles over and their rightful relationships restored, the other characters unite in intoning the work's final moral, which we quoted above.

The idea that Don Giovanni has his way with none of the women he pursues is one that Da Ponte took over from Bertati and merely elaborated in greater detail. But it is difficult to accept Jahn's view that this is the source of the 'humour that permeates the whole opera'.[64] Rather, it may be seen as an extremely effective and dramatic means of characterizing the hero. A character like Don Giovanni is bound to be confirmed in his ways by the constant resistance that he faces. The force that drives him is maintained in a state of permanent tension, thereby precipitating his downfall. Moreover, Don Giovanni's essential character does not revolve around his ability to seduce whichever woman comes his way, however many of them there may be, but around the elemental sensual urge to live and love that rages with the force of nature unbound. The more he reveals himself, the more dangerous, but also the greater, he becomes. The fact that he confronts the Commendatore both at the beginning and end of the opera not only reflects skilful planning from the standpoint of dramatic technique, it is also compelling from a symbolic point of view.

---

63. The aria is reprinted in the *Niederrheinische Musikzeitung*, ii.413–14. Mozart has transposed it from A to B flat major and slightly shortened it. Both pieces are reproduced in the appendix to Bernhard Gugler's edition of the full score; see Genée, 'Aus Sartis "Due Litiganti" in Mozarts Don Giovanni'; on the aria from *Una cosa rara*, see Genée, '"Una cosa rara" in Mozarts Don Juan', 63–5.
64. Jahn, *W. A. Mozart*, ii.405–6.

The very opening scene ushers in a world of tragedy: we are shaken by the terrifying nature of the elemental force that dwells within Don Giovanni and that reveals him from the outset as a man who has total control over life and death. And yet this incident is far from taxing him to the limits of his powers. The old man easily falls prey to him, and he takes the Commendatore's life by exercising what seems to him the self-evident right of the stronger man. By the time that he confronts the statue, the situation has changed completely. Now he is faced by a power which, remote from his own material world, represents a more powerful reality than his own. Yet we would be wrong to see in this scene the intervention of a moral world order in the Schillerian sense. The battle that is fought out in the second-act finale is not between good and evil, but between two sublime realities, the weaker of which is finally overcome. The concept of radical evil is unknown to the wholly unphilosophical Mozart, and so he does not judge his hero and the latter's actions by some moral ideal but feels very clearly that a power as real as Don Giovanni's life force can be defeated only by a more powerful reality: one demon can be conquered only by another. In short, the work is not about guilt and retribution but simply about being and non-being, and the overwhelming tragedy of the conclusion rests on the grandeur and terror of the action as such, not on the triumph of moral laws over the world of appearances. It is the most authentic Renaissance spirit that finds expression here, a spirit that emerges completely logically from Mozart's view of the world, a view that measures reality by its own terms alone, not by any philosophical laws that lie outside it.

This explains why in *Don Giovanni* Mozart far transcended his librettist and the latter's world of ideas, rising further above them than in any of his other operas, in spite of the fact that Da Ponte did everything in his power to adapt to Mozart's own ways. Here the text really only resembles the frame around which the sculptor creates his sculpture, so much is Mozart himself responsible for the opera on every level, be it in terms of detail or overall conception.[65] From this point of view, the full score[66] is an unprecedented triumph of his musical and dramatic imagination.

With its combination of a slow section and a quick one, the overture is French in form, a form that Mozart was to use in all his operas from now on – not that this implies any change of attitude towards the overture in general. It remains, as before, an independent piece whose aim is to introduce the listener to the emotional world of the following drama, not to the course of the action itself. As a result, it admits of no individual poeticizing interpretations of the kind repeatedly attempted by nineteenth-century writers, with their intellectualizing tendencies.[67] Indeed, it is

---

65. Jahn, *W. A. Mozart*, ii.407.

66. On the original score, see Gottfried Weber, 'Über Mozarts Originalmanuskripte der Partitur der Oper: Il Dissoluto punito ossia il Don Giovanni'. Weber was the first to clarify the position with regard to the additional numbers. The autograph score was acquired by Pauline Viardot and on her death bequeathed to the library of the Paris Conservatoire. On a second full score that is claimed to be an original but which is probably a copy prepared under Mozart's supervision in Prague, see Procházka, *Mozart in Prag*, 132ff. For a critique of the score, see Gugler, *AmZ*, new series, i (1866), nos 8–10, 12 and 38; ii (1867), nos 1–3 and 7; iii (1868), no. 38 (on the *secco* recitatives); iv (1869), no. 4; and xi (1876), nos 2, 49 and 50. The first full score to be published on the basis of the autograph was Gugler's edition, published by Leuckart in Breslau in 1870; see Chrysander, 'Zur Partitur des "Don Giovanni"', and Baumgart, *AmZ*, new series, v (1870), no. 9 and vi (1871), nos 2–4. Gugler's edition was followed by Julius Rietz's, published by Breitkopf & Härtel in 1872. A revised version of this edition was used as the basis of the complete edition: see the critical commentary and Chrysander, 'Zur Partitur des "Don Giovanni"'. More generally, see Gounod, *Le Don Juan de Mozart*; Gustav Engel, 'Eine mathematisch-harmonische Analyse des Don Giovanni von Mozart'; Tiersot, 'Étude sur Don Giovanni'; and Heinemann, 'Ist Mozarts "Don Juan" eine tragische oder eine komische Oper?' ◆ Concerning Viardot and her ownership of the score – now in the Bibliothèque nationale, Paris – see Everist, 'Enshrining Mozart: "Don Giovanni" and the Viardot Circle'. Concerning various copies deriving from Prague and possibly representing aspects of early performances there, see below.

67. See, for example, E. T. A. Hoffmann, *Fantasiestücke in Callots Manier*, i.v; Oulibicheff, *Mozart*, iii.105–6; Merian, *Mozarts Meisteropern*, 169; Gounod, *Le Don Juan de Mozart*, 7; and Jahn, *W. A. Mozart*, ii.408ff. For a highly perceptive account, see Wagner, 'Über die Ouvertüre'. For a detailed musical analysis, see Lobe, 'Das Gehaltvolle in der Musik: Die Ouverture zu Don Juan von Mozart'.

these very interpretations that have introduced a note of vagueness and confusion to an overture that is wholly unambiguous from a musical and emotional standpoint. The overture to *Don Giovanni* differs from that to *Le nozze di Figaro* only to the extent that in the earlier work the world of emotion was unified, whereas in the later piece it is dominated by two fundamental opposites. As a result, binary form suggested itself as a matter of course to Mozart. Yet he is content for the present to state these contrasts and to leave the clash between them to the opera itself. Of course, there is an inner connection between the andante and the allegro, but we must be wary of adopting the popular model and interpreting the former as a 'slow introduction' to the latter. There is absolutely nothing to introduce. Rather, one of the two fundamental forces of the opera bursts forth here with elemental power and with a harsh clarity which, typical of the opera as a whole, borders on sheer terror. Doubly terrifying in its laconic brevity of expression, it is even here not merely the equal of the other force that informs the opera, but its palpable superior. This other force, too, has a keen, breathtaking demonicism to it. It also has something elemental and volcanic about it, taking it far from the world of the *Figaro* overture, the impression that it creates intensified yet further by the fact that the Andante constantly hangs over it like a heavy cloud. The nature of the two contrasting ideas that Mozart wants the listener to feel is expressed so clearly in the music that only intellectual hairsplitting could obscure it. We are not dealing with two portraits, as faithful and as detailed as possible, of the stone guest and Don Giovanni, but with the representation of, on the one hand, an awesomely sublime power imbued with all the terrors of the other world and, on the other, a demonic passion spurred on to ever greater heights by every act of resistance that it encounters. This is all that the impartial listener will feel, and this alone was Mozart's intention. But the implacable resolve with which this contrast is worked out instils in the listener a state of extreme agitation: we sense that these two superhuman forces can never be reconciled, yet we learn nothing about the struggle itself or its outcome. This tension is so important for Mozart that he does not break the artistic illusion by means of a perfect cadence, but allows the emotion to ebb away, as though a fine veil were descending, after which the overture leads without a break into the opening scene.

As a result, this is no programme overture in the sense understood either by the older Venetian composers or by the later Romantics, and if Mozart reverted to the supper scene for the music of the andante, he did so not in order to introduce the *convitato di pietra* in person, but because it struck him as entirely natural to use the same music to symbolize the same otherworldly power that is represented by the stone guest within the opera itself. Its tragic key of D minor[68] is also the same in both cases, except that it dominates the overture – with its lack of dramatic detail – far more implacably than is the case with the opera itself: however remote the keys that the modulatory line may appear to explore, it is always drawn back to it as though by a magic force. As in the opera, so in the overture the otherworldly power makes its appearance in the form of a four-bar introduction. There are only two chords in the full orchestra, one in the tonic, the other in the dominant, but what shattering resolve lies not only in the momentous rests that follow each of them but also in the incomparable effect of the syncopations, their impact significantly intensified by the minims in the basses that die away in so eerie a fashion. It is as though the head of some Medusa, contorted with pain, were staring at us. Only then does the actual development begin, compressing the music of the later scene to its furthest extreme. No motif is developed at any

68. Even Mozart's first 'tragic' overture, the one to *La Betulia liberata*, had been in D minor; see above.

length.[69] Rather, disembodied images of terror and grief pass before us in the briefest outline, as though glimpsed through a veil: they lack the tangible, three-dimensional reality of the later scene. Moreover, there is something elemental in the whole structure of the melodic lines that consist largely of motifs that create the impression of natural sounds and interjections; it is rhythm, dynamics and orchestral colour, together with the harmonic writing, that essentially determine the character of this section.[70] Yet, however starkly these ideas may contrast with each other on a superficial level, there is a clearly perceptible inner connection between them, with each stroke invariably producing a counterstroke. Following the two introductory chords, the other world begins to make itself heard, its *piano* marking merely the first of the dynamic contrasts in which the overture abounds. With firm resolve the harmony descends over the primeval chromatic interval of a fourth to a heavily dotted rhythm, while above it the octave motif unfolds in ever new combinations of winds, from flutes to horns and trumpets. But in bar 11 we return to the syncopated melody in the first violins, a melody which, seemingly paralysed, is soon joined by a dully murmuring semiquaver figure in the second violins, as though a sudden gust of wind were whipping up fallen leaves.[71] And so it goes on: in a brief, strident sforzato motif consisting of only two notes[72] the voice of the other world seems to speak in ever more terrifying tones, and on each occasion it is followed by a timid echo from the soul of the frightened creature that finally, in bars 21–22, submits, completely broken, to its fate. But then, in the second section, stroke and counterstroke come together. The dotted rhythm of the opening returns in the bass, but this time it moves up, rather than down, a fourth, drawing the harmonic writing into a sequence of chromatically rising chords of a sixth. These are now joined by the familiar scales in the first violins and flutes over a tremolando in the second violins and violas, allowing the listener to feel an almost physical dread of eternity,[73] rising in a crescendo, then seeping away again *piano* – an effect that should not be weakened by introducing a diminuendo. Similarly there should be no transitional crescendo in bars 23–7. Here the tension lies in the harmony alone, not in the dynamics. All the more terrifying, then, is the impact of the *forte* in bars 27–8, the high point of the whole, where the scalar figures break off. Yet the otherworldly force has scarcely asserted itself in all its terror when it, too, disappears in an equally sudden *piano* that derives its effectiveness from a dynamic shift of the motif in the winds:

69. This also explains why this 'introduction' is markedly different from the introductions to Mozart's instrumental works; see above.

70. Here we may well be right to hear an echo of Gluck's spirit.

71. Mozart's whole approach here is vaguely reminiscent of the scenes inside or at the gates of the underworld such as we find in the Italian composers of the period as well as in Gluck's *Alceste*: all contain pittoresque descriptions of sinister, paralysed nature and the 'orribili' or 'flebili accenti' of the spirit world in the winds. The only difference is that in Mozart's case the tone-painting originally used to evoke a particular situation is now used for psychological, purely emotional ends.

72. On its first appearance it assumes the simple form: At its second occurrence it appears in augmentation: Its intermediary form brings this section to an end:

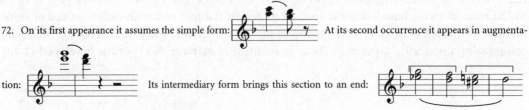

73. See Monsigny's version of this idea, p.467 above.

The dynamics of this whole section are pure Mozart. He gives the listener only three bars[74] in which to allow this terrible experience to die away, before the allegro enters, virtually unprepared, bringing with it the most abrupt of conceivable changes of mood. There is something utterly inspired about the way in which Mozart follows D minor with D major, with the purely musical change of tonality on the same degree serving not only to link the two sections but also to point up the starkest contrast between them. The present allegro differs from that in *Le nozze di Figaro* in that it is a fully developed sonata movement, rather than a motley assembly of disparate elements that prevents us from lingering over any of the individual ideas. Rather, Mozart explores and harnesses the forces that are dormant within the main ideas, not merely juxtaposing them, but examining their contrasts and interrelationships.

Much has been written on the nature of the theme of this allegro, with Romantic writers in particular attempting to see in every motif a different aspect of Don Giovanni's character: his demonic sensuality in the chromatic interval, his impetuous resolve in the syncopated section, his frivolousness in the quaver motif and, finally, his chivalry in the concluding wind passage.[75] But in the light of what we have already said, this is to read far too much into it. After all, we are not dealing with a musical portrait of Don Giovanni, to which every bar adds a new brushstroke, quite apart from the fact that such a mosaic-like approach runs counter to the laws of musical creativity. No, this theme – one of the most inspired of all Mozart's ideas – is a unified whole and demands to be perceived as such. Its first half:

shows clearly and without any need for rational explanation what we are dealing with here: on a purely musical level it is evident that what is at stake here is the build-up and release of the most tremendous vital energy. This is the underlying emotion that holds this whole multisectional structure together, its multisectionality controlled by a clear guiding will. This emerges from the rhythm and metre that are bound to strike every listener as particularly unusual and original. All the motifs[76] start on an upbeat,[77] always consisting of two notes followed by the main accent. This is the basic character of an anapaestic metre, which has always been felt to express a sense of vital energy. Only on the present occasion does this character remain to a certain extent latent, at least until the fourth bar, first having to assert itself in the face of the pressure inherent in the heavy upbeats and to overcome the division of its accentuated beat into two quavers in motifs (b²) and

74. With its open fifth, even the third bar (the first of the allegro) leaves the actual tonality in the balance, drawing our attention to what is to follow only by means of the gently pounding *d'* in the violas and cellos.

75. All these interpretations derive from E. T. A. Hoffmann. ◆ Further concerning Hoffmann, see Wittkowski, 'E. T. A. Hoffmanns musikalische Musikdichtungen Ritter Gluck, Don Juan, Rat Krespel'; Massalongo, 'Il Don Giovanni di Mozart in due "studi letterari" del romanticismo: Don Juan di E. T. A. Hoffmann e il Don Giovanni di Søren Kierkegaard'; Margotton, 'Don Juan ou Mozart vu par Hoffmann'; Kaiser, 'Mozarts Don Giovanni und E. T. A. Hoffmanns Don Juan: Ein Beitrag zum Verständnis des Fantasiestücks'.

76. Note the structural division indicated by letters and brackets above.

77. Even motif (a) is a 'general upbeat' as defined by Hugo Riemann.

(c), before entering in its pure form – a demonic fanfare – with explosive force in the winds. As a result of the constant foreshortening of the upbeats, the rhythmic change to this theme results in a unified, steadily mounting psychological development, in which a force that is subjected to the strongest pressure gradually breaks free, allowing it to unfold in all its unbridled intensity. This psychological process is now underlined in the most impressive manner imaginable by the melodic and harmonic writing. The melody emerges initially as the main vehicle of the secret forms of resistance that this force has to overcome. Among these features are the famous d'' sharp in the second bar, with its piercing dissonance, right from the outset forcing the harmony down to the minor of the subdominant and greatly intensifying the sense of pressure inherent in motif (a). In group (b) the rhythmic intensification seems initially to affect the melody, too, but the initial show of strength is invariably followed by a bending back of the melodic line, and the more the rhythm is intensified (group (c)), the more insistently the line is drawn back towards the tonic. The brief suspensions are the final show of resistance that it is capable of affording. Only in group (d) is the spell abruptly broken, effortlessly allowing it to reach the fifth (a'') after a brief run-up, thereby underlining the explosive nature of this passage. The harmonic writing is dominated in the first five bars by the tonic pedal. That this is no ordinary Neapolitan *Trommelbaß* pedal point is clear, not least from the fact that it is entrusted to cellos and violas alone (without basses). After the earlier heavy bass steps, this pounding on the high d' in the bass has something curiously unstable and unsettling about it, creating the sensation of a sudden change from icy cold to burning heat. But the pedal point itself proves to be the principal source of the energy that is stored up in the first half of the theme. In group (b) it initially leaves the harmony unclear, as Mozart was more concerned at this point to reinforce the melodic line by means of the lower sixth and third. Only in the second half of the theme does the latent dominant harmony on which the two minims are based really emerge. In the third bar from the end even this pressure is relaxed in the resolute cadential steps, and now the harmony, too, plays its part in the elemental outburst of the two last bars, an outburst in which dynamics and instrumentation are no less effective than rhythm and melody, forcing the musical argument towards the dominant harmony with lapidary simplicity. The impression left by this passage is very much that of the long-suppressed fires of passion suddenly shooting heavenwards.

As long as its metrical structure is properly recognized, this theme speaks for itself and needs no poetically redundant interpretation. Its second half initially resembles the first, except that the pedal point is reinforced by the horns and the harmonies are filled out by the winds, in both cases leading to an appreciable intensification of the underlying emotion.[78] But the final bars achieve their sense of uplift not through the earlier wind fanfare, but in a passage for the full orchestra which, more broadly developed, is much more emotionally intense, based, as it is, on the same anapaestic rhythm and rising by means of a powerful unison to d'', before breaking off on an almost brutal half-cadence. This is how Johann Christian Bach and his school used to introduce their second subjects. And a new idea in A major is indeed introduced at this point. Yet it brings no real sense of contrast, but only defiant strokes in the full orchestra, from which violin scales

---

78. Early printed scores include a flat sign before the b'' in the fourth bar. In the original there is a flat sign only in the third bar, giving rise to much controversy. Gugler, for example, includes the flat sign on both occasions, whereas Rietz has the note b in both cases, a reading in which he is followed by the complete edition; see *AmZ*, new series, vi (1871), 50 and xi (1876), 537 and 769–70. Both of these readings are arbitrary. In the third bar we are dealing with an accompanying voice that could be altered chromatically, not least because its b flat is well prepared by the c of the second bar, whereas in the fourth bar we have the main theme, which retains its original shape. Mozart's notation is certainly striking, but it is psychologically well motivated, and we have no reason to change it on the grounds of mere correctness; see Jahn, *W. A. Mozart*, ii.409–10. ◆ The NMA gives an editorial natural before the b'' (bar 43).

detach themselves three times. Here, too, there is no lack of contrast, which lies in the brief melody in the winds, once again over a pedal point in the violins, violas and cellos. But it serves to stem the floodtide only briefly, before it then breaks free with all the greater force.[79] This, too, occurs with the suddenness to which we have now grown accustomed – there are no transitional crescendos at any point in the overture – in the diminished chord that leads to A minor instead of A major. This A minor, which also plays a leading role in the actual second subject, gives a particularly wild coloration to the basic urge for pleasure, returning at later points in the work, notably in Don Giovanni's aria ('Finch' han dal vino'), where we once again feel its goad. Here, too, the passage ends with a defiant half-cadence, this time on the dominant of A minor. Only now does the actual second subject enter, sharply divided, with its two parts dominated in typically Mozartian fashion by the starkest possible contrast in terms of melody and instrumentation:[80]

This theme, too, has been interpreted along poetical lines, with commentators hearing the stone guest's words of warning in its first half and Don Giovanni's flippant reply in its second section. This desire to draw direct parallels between the overture and the characters and events of the opera itself may well be justified in the case of Weber and his contemporaries, but it is not so with Mozart. How could it enter his head to step so far out of character as to introduce a dialogue between two figures from the opera itself? And even if he had done so, his innate love of contrast would surely have persuaded him to distinguish musically between this reappearance of the other-worldly element and all that has gone before it. Instead, he simply continues in the dominant, without any change of harmony. No, this second subject brings with it no change of scene, still less any contrast with what has gone before. Rather, it brings a sense of completion to the earlier unfinished business. It is the old demonic life force that now finds expression with redoubled strength following the critical tension of the preceding passage. Mozart characteristically presents this theme in the form of two contrasting ideas, of which the one immediately calls forth the other. The wild defiance of the unison sforzato motif provides an answer to what has gone before, creating the impression of a heavy burden being forcibly shaken off. With its dominant seventh harmony, however, the motif also points the way ahead, and the answer comes in the form of the quaver motif. Here the anapaestic rhythm of motif (c) of the main theme again emerges with striking clarity, affording further proof of the inner links between the two thematic groups. Instead of 'frivolous dalliance' we again find an expression of the most intense and unsettling vital energy that is an entirely logical response to the defiant challenge. And the basses that had been absent from the main theme now have a role to play. In this way the second subject emphasizes the two extreme aspects of this life force: belligerent defiance and a self-satisfied delight in its own

79. Merian hears Don Giovanni's adventure with Zerlina in this passage; see Merian, *Mozarts Meisteropern*, 169.
80. The alleged origins of this motif, including its imitative writing, in the Kyrie of Gottfried Heinrich Stölzel's *Missa canonica*, which the north Germans Friedrich Wilhelm Marpurg and Johann Philipp Kirnberger thought they had discovered, have long been recognized as no more than a chance reminiscence; see Marpurg, *Abhandlung von der Fuge nach den Grundsätzen der besten deutschen und ausländischen Meister*, ii.77, Pl. 35–6; and Kirnberger, *Die Kunst des reinen Satzes in der Musik*, ii/2.18–19.

deployment. It is the mood of aggressivity that initially demands a say, its insistency intensified by means of a three-part canon. But at the surprising modulation to C major, which suddenly sheds a completely different light on everything, the motif loses its sforzato, and the imitative writing becomes freer – the sense of energy begins to flag, and the mood that now develops is one of weariness and, at the same time, typically Mozartian eeriness,[81] reflecting a psychologically well-observed relaxation of tension following its earlier concentration. But this is only the calm before the storm: the A major of the final subject-group erupts in a sudden *forte*, going back beyond the second subject to the strident outbursts of the main subject-group, which it also recalls motivically, finally culminating with a tremendous climax in the main group's cadential section, with the final word given to an irresistible display of unbridled energy.

The development section begins with the second subject, again without the change of key-signature that is so common in Mozart's works at this point. It, too, is made up of two contrasting ideas, but it succeeds in building a bridge between them by dint of the fact that the underlying harmony remains the same. The 'answer' comes only with the repeat of the whole theme in the fifth bar.[82] There follows a further series of stretta entries, but this time over a wide harmonic arc that takes us through all the sharp tonalities to G major. Meanwhile the theme's second motif keeps flaring up in the strings, creating harsh dissonances with its suspension.[83] This is the most inspired moment in the entire allegro, not least because it makes palpably clear that the two contrasting ideas are basically no more than different expressions of one and the selfsame force. The whole passage, moreover, is marked *piano*: this picture of teeming life floats past with weight-less ease. The situation changes with the arrival on the subdominant G major, as the main theme now reasserts itself, with its latent conflicts and strident fanfare, but it is not developed any further; its second half modulates to G minor, leading us down from there into the depths of the subdominant, a world that Mozart was particularly fond of exploring at this point in the works of this period. At the same time, however, it gradually loses its inherent energy and dies away, somewhat helplessly, on the dominant of B flat major – another of those deeply disturbing passages in which paralysis takes over. As in the overture as a whole, there is no sense of any gradual reassertion of courage here, but only an impulsive breaking free from a terrifying force. The listener feels very strongly that the forces at play here go far beyond everyday human experience. What the main theme had earlier failed to express is now made good by the second subject. It enters six times in all its force[84] over constantly changing degrees of the scale, without recourse of imitative procedures, naked, merely juxtaposing the contrasting ideas and accompanying the first three notes with strident chords in all the winds, together with a timpani roll. Harmonically, too, the six entries are wholly different: the first stands completely alone, while the next four are treated as pairs in the relationship of dominant to tonic.[85] The final entry attempts to continue this relationship, but lacks the second element, just as the first entry had essentially lacked the first element. This is the climax of the development section, with the musical idea acquiring its most intense expression. And again there is no gradual transition. Following another of the curiously whispered sections without double basses, the musical argument is forced back to the recapitula-

---

81. Note also the dull murmuring in the violins and especially the interval of an augmented fourth in the flutes.
82. ◆ Bar 125.
83. Only the final motif is altered, with the two upward-sliding crotchets creating a certain similarity with the corresponding passages in the opening movement of the G minor symphony K550.
84. The earlier sforzato is now replaced by a genuine *forte*.
85. The sequence of harmonies in this section is as follows: B flat – g^V – g^I (= d^{IV}) – d^V – d^I (= a^{IV}) – a^V – A^I. Note the minor keys.

tion through a series of sforzatos and a *forte* outburst in the full orchestra, with a typically Mozartian scale trickling quietly down in the violins between the recapitulation and the *forte* passages. Unlike the majority of Mozart's other sonata movements from this period, the present recapitulation itself is an almost note-perfect repeat of the exposition until the completely surprising ending, where it veers away to the subdominant and the wild defiance of the second subject rears its head in the full orchestra,[86] before vanishing as though in a mist, much as its adversary had done in the andante.

This powerful prologue contrasts the two opposing forces of fate with unrelenting harshness,[87] and is followed immediately – without any break in the aesthetic illusion – by the no less powerful Introduzione ('Notte e giorno faticar'), which, dramatically speaking, extends as far as the opening of scene four. Here the loosely structured *buffa* introduction of the older type of opera, with its madcap humour, has been totally transformed in the hands of the librettist and, more especially, of the composer. Instead of an introduction, we are immediately faced by a climax of the first order. Already at this early stage, the 'dramma giocoso' of the playbill is effectively given the lie, even though the first of the four sections that make up the Introduzione introduces us to the work's one comic character. Of course, Leporello is no longer the *servo ridicolo* of the older tradition, tending to accompany the action with his jokes, rather than being bound up with it. Instead, he is an entirely autonomous, independent figure of a wholly Mozartian kind, developing his inherent potential through his interaction with the other characters.

In discussing the earlier operas, we have already noted how Mozart saw the different characters in relation to one another, with each individual and group emerging in clear-cut outline from the light and shade cast by the others, so that each of them is not only an individual creation but also a yardstick by which the others may be judged. Leporello is one of the most inspired examples of this, inasmuch as he owes his entire dramatic existence to his lord and master Don Giovanni. In the first place, he unburdens him of all the comic characteristics that we still find in Bertati. For Mozart, this was simply impossible. Count Almaviva could still combine tragedy and comedy within his person, but with Don Giovanni the sheer size of the dramatic problem no longer made this feasible and he had no choice but to hand over to Leporello all those aspects of his character that might mar it by suggesting the finite and all-too-human. It is this that determines his character and his whole position within the opera: he is clearly related to his master, differing from him only in representing a different degree of reality. Don Giovanni's world is that of a primeval and, therefore, timeless existence, while Leporello is satisfied with the most superficial aspect of life, tedious everyday reality. As a result he remains contingent upon his environment, forever the plaything of chance and his own lack of freedom. Everything that is essential to Don Giovanni is merely apparent in him. The terrible destiny that overwhelms Don Giovanni passes him by, his whole existence is largely untouched by fate but is ruled merely by chance adventures. He is essentially an ordinary person, a man possessed of low cunning but none the less good-natured, like all such people who tend to moralize and who are capable of sentimentality. And so he repeatedly tries to break free from his dangerous and unsettling position and in that way to achieve the peace and quiet that he secretly longs to find. But the drop of Don Giovanni's blood that flows through

---

86. The fact that this motif always appears in a different instrumentation is significant.
87. Nägeli, *Vorlesungen über Musik*, 157 and 160, criticizes this 'exaggerated, dissipated use of contrast', a use which, for good reason, extends to individual themes in the present piece. He goes on (p. 168) to argue that bars 36 and 197 disrupt the eurhythmy of the piece. His views were quickly countered by Kahlert, 'Rechtfertigung Mozarts gegen H. G. Nägeli', 97–8. A complete ending to the overture, thirteen bars long instead of the present eleven and evidently dashed off at speed by Mozart, is included in the autograph score and reproduced in NMA II/5/17, 27. It is evidently a version intended for the concert hall.

his veins and that ultimately brought him to his master's side keeps stirring within him, lending him a degree of cunning which, right from the outset, encourages him to toy with the idea of playing the master himself one day. It is this trait that thwarts and frustrates all his philistine tendencies and forces him to keep on following his master, as a shadow follows the light. There are occasions when he lectures his master on the subject of morality, only to violate those very same morals through his own actions. However much he may fear or resent the tricks that Don Giovanni forces him to play, he none the less enjoys them in his heart of hearts. As a result, he yields little to his master in terms not only of his unscrupulousness but also of his slipperiness and cunning. But it would be wrong to place undue emphasis on his cowardice, as many earlier writers have done.[88] Nothing was further from Mozart's thoughts than to portray him as a typical coward. Even in the face of danger, Mozart's Leporello behaves in a way commensurate with his character as a whole: he has not enough courage to seek out danger or risk his own life, but enough to extricate himself with cunning – after all, Don Giovanni is unlikely to have chosen an out-and-out coward as his servant. Only in the face of the stone guest does Leporello go weak at the knees, with the supernatural affecting him in a way appropriate to his character, just as it affects Don Giovanni in a way appropriate to *his*. And his impact on the other figures is likewise in keeping with his character. As an exceptional figure, Don Giovanni inspires fear and terror, the greater and more dangerous he becomes, whereas Leporello, as someone who lives in the past, emerges from the same situations as a poor wretch, an equivocal, contemptible braggart. His dealings with Don Giovanni mean that he comes into lightning contact with all the other characters in the drama in turn, bringing him into conflict with passions and events whose depths he is incapable of fathoming – by the end he is exactly the same rogue as he was at the beginning. It is on this inner relationship with Don Giovanni that the comedy of his character rests, a comedy that goes far beyond the traditional jokes associated with *Hanswurst*: he is a brilliantly inspired foil to his hero. Everything that becomes part of Don Giovanni's destiny remains in the realm of chance and of common reality for him. Everything that assumes a tragic dimension for Don Giovanni ends up as merely comic for Leporello, with Mozart once again demonstrating the truth of the old saw, namely, that the true tragedian is also a genuine comic.

In his famous 'Notte e giorno faticar' (its melody immortalizes a traditional Italian tune), Leporello trudges angrily to and fro, bewailing his servant's lot, even his surly phrase endings revealing a good deal about his temperamental character. Yet this outburst of anger is merely an introduction to his ternary-form 'Voglio far il gentiluomo' in which we hear the first stirrings of the Giovannian aspect of his character. His aristocratic swagger finds delightful expression in the accompanying triplets and writing for the horns, with clear echoes of his master's titillating world in the brief wind passages after the word 'gentiluomo' and in the short interlude before 'oh che caro galantuomo'. Initially even the phrase 'e non voglio più servir' ('I no longer want to serve him') is affected by this mood, but by the time that we reach the consequent phrase Leporello's sense of pride has been overshadowed by his more immediate concerns in the form of the workaday hardship that once again draws him into its sway, finding dogged expression in a style of writing reminiscent of Piccinni.[89] It is significant that from now on this brief consequent phrase ends every section in the manner of a refrain, like some sullen 'ceterum censeo', even when noises from within the house force him to hide. The scene changes in a brief, explosive and typically Mozartian

---

88. This view is still held by Jahn, *W. A. Mozart*, ii.411–12, but rightly refuted by Schurig, *Wolfgang Amade Mozart*, ii.110.
89. See above. Note also the way in which the triplets and horn accompaniment ends.

crescendo that takes us to B flat major. The music here was clearly suggested by Gazzaniga,[90] but that is as far as the influence goes. Only the opening motif evoking a sense of tumult and the dotted rhythm of the initial vocal phrases are the same, but in every other respect Mozart has expanded and deepened this section in terms of both form and, more especially, dramatic expression. It is cast in abbreviated binary form with an introduction that is motivically linked to what follows. Even the fact that it is Donna Anna, rather than Don Giovanni as in Bertati, who enters first is significant, inasmuch as it reveals an important aspect of his character, namely, his remarkable ability to adapt musically to the character of the woman with whom he is dealing. It is this that makes his demonic nature all the more dangerous: he attracts his victims not only physically but musically, too, attacking their innermost being. He counters Donna Anna with the same vehement anger, following her every move, most notably at the wildly agitated motif on the words 'Come furia disperata'. Here the imitative writing adds incomparably to the sense of a breathless struggle, with both characters finally appearing to run out of breath. The situation is completely different in Gazzaniga, where it is Don Giovanni who sets the tone before joining forces musically with Leporello. Mozart, conversely, is entirely logical in drawing a clear distinction between Leporello on the one hand and Donna Anna and Don Giovanni on the other, placing him as it were in a completely different perspective within the overall picture. Leporello also sings in a far more naturalistic manner: after having recovered from his initial shock, he has – in contrast to the other two – only broken triads to sing, first in crotchets, then in rapid patter-like quavers. And he always enters *piano* each time that the other two pause for breath. It is impossible to conceive of a starker contrast between the world of the hero and that of this commonplace rogue – the man of action and the man of empty words, with Leporello chattering twice as much in order to vent his petty feelings, with the result that Mozart here falls back on the old parlando style of *opera buffa*.

There follows another of the sudden and violent transitions in which this opera abounds, as Donna Anna tears herself free with three wild outbursts and rushes away. She is replaced by the Commendatore for the third section of the Introduction. The choice of keys is significant. For Mozart, the G minor that appears first is certainly not the key of tragic emotion but, rather, of impassioned anguish and is initially also the basic motif associated with the spirited old man. Only when he has forced his adversary to fight with him does the tragic D minor gradually cast its shadow over the two combatants. Even so, the Commendatore's entry is dignified and determined.[91] Don Giovanni initially declines to engage in such an unequal contest, which runs counter to his code of honour. But at the sinister *piano* unison passages in the orchestra, which with Mozart invariably signify a state of heightened tension and which in this particular case finally lead the musical argument to D minor, the Commendatore's fate is sealed, and there is a cruel irony to the fact that it is at precisely this point that Leporello enters to express his profound dislike of all life-and-death decisions. Once again Don Giovanni hesitates with his 'Misero!', first *sotto voce*,[92] then *più voce*, a performance marking that should not be interpreted as a sign of weakness,[93] but merely as an expression of regret that his adversary is not his equal. The tension culminates in the whole bar's rest, when our hearts really seem to stop beating. For a third time Don Giovanni exclaims 'Misero!', this time *forte*. These eight bars, including the whole bar's rest, are the climax of this entire Introduction, with the hero's fateful nature emerging on the same grand scale as the

90. See Chrysander, 'Francesco Antonio Urio', 577.
91. He evidently draws his sword only at the whirring demisemiquavers in the violins following his opening speech.
92. ◆ Here (bar 256), the NMA has the marking 'mezza voce' for Don Giovanni.
93. The translation in the AMA – 'Mitleid fühl' ich' ('I feel pity') – strikes a false note here.

tragic horror that it provokes. The duel itself proceeds along entirely realistic lines,[94] with disaster overwhelming the participants in the fourth section with the same degree of shattering intensity as before. The cold hand of death descends on all of them, reducing them to a state of paralysed inactivity. Nowhere else in the whole history of opera has this mood found such succinct and, at the same time, such moving expression. Everything conspires to produce this effect: the key of F minor with its subdominant, the ensemble writing for the three low male voices, the weighty chords in the horns and bassoons, and the low register of the strings with their convulsive triplet motif.[95] While the Commendatore's life slowly ebbs away in his disjointed musical line, Don Giovanni – unlike many of his predecessors – is initially torn between the horror that he feels at the power of death (a horror that should not be seen as pity or remorse) and his innate and ruthless will to life.[96] Meanwhile Leporello is overcome by a feeling of general dismay and, after uttering two primitive cries of fear, manages only to stammer his lack of resolve. Finally flutes and oboes intone the mournful and, in its chromaticisms, typically Mozartian melody that brings to an end this whole complex scene, imprinting itself unforgettably on the listener and seeming to suggest a vigil by the Commendatore's dead body. All the more surprising, then, is the way in which this ending veers off into the following recitative, which, after all that has happened, creates a particularly *secco* impression. But unlike any ordinary *secco* recitative, the present passage pursues a particular dramatic aim, with Don Giovanni finally breaking free from the spell that has been cast upon him. Throughout this strange second scene, he maintains a permanent *sotto voce*, his resurgent thirst for action initially directed against Leporello, whom he reprimands and even threatens to beat but who cannot resist the temptation to offer his master an ironical lesson in morality. Finally the two men fade into the darkness.

This Introduction has often, and rightly, been hailed as a model of dramatic exposition,[97] and there is no doubt that in terms of its design and execution it is a masterpiece of its kind. But its significance goes far beyond this. Although Don Giovanni utters not a single word about himself, it presents a picture of his character and of the forces contained within it that knows no equal inasmuch as it reveals him as a sensual man of action locked from the outset in an impassioned struggle with the supreme powers of life on earth and, indeed, as a demonic individual playing with life and death, with the listener sensing right away that this single incident is typical of the whole of his previous life.

Romantic writers had much to say about this scene and the premisses on which it is based. The best known of these writers remains E. T. A. Hoffmann, whose theory that Donna Anna was violated by Don Giovanni continues to be repeated right down to the present day.[98] But there is not a word in Da Ponte or his source Bertati to sustain such a view, quite apart from the fact that

94. Compare the powerful octave intervals in the violins with the much smaller intervals in the bass. A similar device is found in Gluck's ballet. In both cases the model is probably French.

95. This, too, goes no higher than *c"* at the very end.

96. The similarity between his opening phrase and Donna Anna's previous 'Come furia disperata' is probably only fortuitous. In Gazzaniga, this section is elaborated at much greater length.

97. See Gounod, *Le Don Juan de Mozart*, 16.

98. See *Neue Berliner Musikzeitung*, i (1847), 319–20; and Rellstab, *Gesammelte Schriften*, vi.251–2. Individual singers such as Friederike Bethmann and Wilhelmine Schröder-Devrient have also adopted this view. See Genast, *Aus dem Tagebuch eines alten Schauspielers*, iii.171–2, and Wolzogen, *Wilhelmine Schröder-Devrient*, 163–4. Among more recent writers, see Søren Kierkegaard, *Gesammmelte Werke*; Schurig, *Wolfgang Amade Mozart*, ii.110–11; and Cohen, *Die dramatische Idee in Mozarts Operntexten*, 85–6. For an opposing view, see Bulthaupt, *Dramaturgie der Oper*, 180ff.; and Jahn, *W. A. Mozart*, ii.442. ◆ For Schröder-Devrient, also see Hagemann, *Wilhelmine Schroeder-Devrient* and Bab, *Die Devrients*.

it runs counter to the whole style of *opera buffa*, in which events of such importance are invariably spelt out for the spectator. *Opera buffa* prefers clarity on such points, and the more graphic the better, especially in the case of such an act of violation, which would have been presented with total frankness, albeit not in the style of a writer like Hoffmann. *Opera buffa* has absolutely no time for the complex psychological problems bound up with our sex lives but sticks instead to naked instincts, indifferent to the moral consequences of satisfying those drives. In the present case Don Giovanni would be admired as the victorious male, while his victim would have been a duped *poverina* for whom neither the librettist nor his Italian audience would have felt the least spark of sympathy. Readers familiar with the genre will have no difficulty imagining the sort of comments with which the comic servant would have accompanied these proceedings.

If we accept this premiss, then all E. T. A. Hoffmann's other conclusions are likewise rendered untenable, namely, Donna Anna's continuing hypocrisy towards her unloved fiancé Don Ottavio (this, too, is refuted by Da Ponte's text) and her secret love of Don Giovanni (here Hoffmann speaks of the 'sublime tragic solemnity' of the character), to say nothing of Don Giovanni himself, a character who, in Hoffmann's eyes, seeks to satisfy his desire for transcendency through love until, thoroughly satiated, he comes to despise the world and, in his contempt for God and nature, no longer wants to enjoy women but only to corrupt them. It is entirely typical of the nineteenth century and its interest in the problems of erotic love that it sought at all costs to read such an interpretation into Donna Anna's relationship with Don Giovanni. Whether or not we care to appeal to earlier versions of the legend, neither Bertati nor Da Ponte knows of any secret love on Donna Anna's part. Had they attached any importance to it, they would certainly not have missed the opportunity to write an aria or at least a cavatina describing her 'nascosa fiamma'. Above all, however, Mozart's music knows nothing of such a love. For Mozart, Donna Anna is the daughter of her father, a distinguished nobleman, an aristocratic figure who, unlike Donna Elvira – a woman completely obsessed by her passions – has all her feelings and desires under control. It is no wonder that, quite apart from her natural filial affection, so aristocratic a woman should be so deeply affected by her father's death. She feels his wounds as though they were her own. The blood-stained image of her murdered father impresses itself on her mind like the vision of a madwoman, so unthinkable is the very idea to her. But once this initial storm has blown itself out, her feelings become more clear-cut. The assault on her honour pales into insignificance beside her memory of the murderous deed. No doubt she, too, is in thrall to Don Giovanni, but she sees in him not a demonic seducer but an untamed tyrant who in his unbridled impulsiveness has set himself up as the ultimate authority over life and death. Her loathing of a man who, in murdering her father, dealt her, too, a mortal blow consumes all her other feelings. This hatred is not, there-fore, a concealed form of love, as it is with Donna Elvira. It is not a secret and self-tormenting desire to recapture love's bygone pleasures but a desire for the blood of the criminal and, as such, a wish to continue the game of life and death than he himself began. This is the only way in which Donna Anna reacts to Don Giovanni's sudden incursion on her life. Still less does she react in the manner of a vengeful Armida, so that it is wrong to cast a *hochdramatisch* soprano in the part,[99] as Mozart intended her as a young woman whose strength of purpose is tempered by maidenly tenderness and shyness. Unlike Donna Elvira, who invariably acts independently, she never takes the initiative but always leaves Don Ottavio to do so. That he is emotionally unequal to the task is

99. It was Schröder-Devrient who initiated this practice by singing Anna instead of Elvira.

part of her destiny, even if she herself is unaware of this fact. Neither Da Ponte nor Mozart questions her love of Don Ottavio, even if that love differs from that of Donna Elvira and Zerlina: it is not in any way sensual but is based on ethical considerations and, as such, typical of her character in general. In this way, Mozart has introduced a moral component into the drama, acknowledging moral law as one of the realities of human existence, albeit a reality that is neither transcendent nor immanent but merely one among many others. Thus this austere and noble figure – Mozart's very own creation – takes her place within the opera, standing in stark contrast to the other characters, while moving towards the same goal as all the other forces that motivate the drama as a whole. And we must be wary of adopting too circumscribed a view of these forces: Don Giovanni's demonic nature, for example, is not limited to the sexual sphere but affects every aspect of our material existence, unleashing not only love but all the forces of human life, drawing those forces along with it or provoking them into resistance. From this point of view, Donna Anna, too, has her place in the drama, without thereby having to succumb to the general fever of passion unleashed by Don Giovanni. All later interpretations merely serve to demonstrate the almost limitless possibilities inherent in the material, and it ill behoves us to pass moral judgement on their proponents. But it must be stressed that these later readings have nothing to do with Mozart's opera.

Donna Anna returns with Don Ottavio and discovers her father's body. The events that follow have been so fashioned by Mozart as to produce a great musical *scena* that combines accompanied recitative and free melodic sections with a dramatic flexibility that would not, of course, have been possible without the example of Gluck. Horror is the first emotion to find expression in the orchestral introduction, which flares up briefly and precipitately. Note in particular the declamatory style here: horrified, Donna Anna initially sees only a dead body, and it is only after a further and more intense outburst in the orchestra – now in F minor – that she recognizes her father, her voice rising breathlessly through a C major triad.[100] But then, in an affecting passage for winds, she relapses into her earlier grief and bewilderment. Four times we hear the same affecting lament in the winds, and each time it is followed by a whispered echo in the vocal line, a fifth lower and in diminution, with the full orchestra taking up the phrase on its last appearance and investing it with a tremendous increase in tension.[101] Grief-stricken she seeks in vain for a sign of life to the strains of a beautiful wind passage over tremolando strings, but then her mood becomes tormented and disjointed, with heavy shadows descending in the violins as she faints away. With Don Ottavio's entry comes a total change of tone, with brief and disjointed phrases in the vocal line and orchestra, while the tension again builds to a feverish climax at the point when Donna Anna recovers her senses.[102] Already Don Ottavio stands revealed as the antithesis of Don Giovanni, impulsive but weak-willed and sanguine, always full of the best intentions but lacking the strength to carry them through and, therefore, always someone who looks on and comments but never acts. There is something touching about his love of Donna Anna, which breaks through in this final passage. The duetto that follows ('Fuggi, crudele, fuggi') is a classic example of Mozart's inspired freedom in his approach to questions of form. It consists of two large-scale sections divided by a recitative, to which the second section freely refers. The first section, too, is remarkably free. It begins with Donna Anna imagining that she can see not Don Ottavio but her

---

100. It is significant that each time she repeats the words 'mio padre' in this scene, it is always the first word that she stresses.
101. Note Mozart's use of sharp keys here, rising in intensity to the particularly ardent F sharp major.
102. At the words 'Cercatemi, recatemi qualche odor' ('Find and bring me some smelling salts'), Mozart uses the highly effective Gluckian device of a chromatically rising bass line with sequential writing above it; see above.

father's murderer. She starts by striking a harsh and wildly impetuous note (in D minor!), with a steely rhythm reminiscent of Gluck,[103] but within six bars her vocal line has already dissolved into individual disjointed phrases, as her grief at her father's death gains the upper hand for some time to come. The orchestra now takes control, but only in order to paint a picture of utter despair in the restless figures in the second violins and off-beat crotchets in the first violins and violas. Don Ottavio's words of comfort strike a particularly truthful and beautiful note, at first haltingly emotional, but then gradually settling into a warm cantilena,[104] and there is something no less truthful about Donna Anna's reply as she recovers from her delusion to music that even here refutes the notion of the unloved fiancé. At his words of comfort, her convulsive despair turns to very feminine grief, even if the orchestra continues with the same motif as before and even adds to the note of suffering. And now Don Ottavio himself conjures up the old and unpleasant memory, his words 'Lascia, o cara, la rimembranza amara' ('Do not dwell, beloved, on this painful memory') creating a profoundly poetic impression by recalling the implacable rhythm of the opening, but only in order to dispel for good the earlier vision of horror, and even before he can utter the words 'Hai sposo e padre in me' ('You have both husband and father in me'), we hear the following motif in the oboes and bassoons, bringing with it a touching sense of consolation:

The writing for the winds here is authentically Mozartian and, as such, wholly unlike anything written by any Italian composer of this or any other period.[105] It is impossible to conceive of a more succinct or convincing contrast than that found in Don Ottavio's words: suffice it to note the harmonic writing and the melodic line, which, initially sharply declamatory, later assumes the form of a rapt cantabile. In order to intensify the starkness of the contrast and deepen the overall impression, Mozart now repeats this passage. Donna Anna then takes heart in one of the familiar scalar motifs with string tremolando that audibly anticipates the following 'Che giuramento, oh Dei!', briefly and forcefully exacting an oath from Don Ottavio in a passage of recitative. But it is highly significant that the music that accompanies his oath places greater emphasis on the words 'occhi tuoi' and 'nostro amor' than on the vow to avenge her father's death – if Don Ottavio had had a will of his own, Mozart would surely have made him swear in somewhat more forceful terms. The second section of the duet is itself in two sections with a large-scale coda. In terms of its emotional content, it is more than a furious demand for vengeance, as it is usually believed to be. The words make no mention of vengeance, but in fairly conventional terms reminiscent of Metastasio[106] describe the wild horror that the characters feel at being forced by this terrible deed to swear this oath and their dismay at the demonic tragedy into which they are suddenly drawn. But this demonic stirring of archetypal human instincts also dominates the music. The whole elemental savagery of this grandiose operatic opening breaks forth once again in boundless fury, drawing the two of them into its insane turmoil. At the very outset we hear a sinister motif

103. Note also the powerful upbeats on 'fuggi' and 'lascia'.
104. The gradual transition to F major is also beautifully effective here.
105. See Kretzschmar, 'Mozart in der Geschichte der Oper', 278.
106. Cf. the aria 'Fra cento affanni e cento' in act one, scene two of *Artaserse*.

that is treated imitatively in the winds, appearing like an echo from some dark abyss,[107] while a recurrent pedal point on A serves to intensify the impression, allowing the outburst on 'cento' to emerge with all the greater stridency. It is entirely natural that when feelings are as stirred as this the characters are no longer individualized. They are drawn into the vortex together, and even Don Ottavio's oath in the middle section now sounds not so much more heroic as more tormented and anxious as a result of the accompanying chromatic thirds. In the coda Mozart finally picks up the image of 'ondeggiar', depicting the raging floodtide of emotions now in wild quaver melismas,[108] now in tugging syncopations at which the very ground beneath our feet appears to shake; only with difficulty can the voices hold their own, with imitative writing occasionally used here in the coda to intensify the effect. The sense of agitation continues as far as the defiant semiquaver motif of the last two bars.[109]

The scene changes, and Donna Elvira enters ('Ah! chi mi dice mai'). We know her from Molière, but the figure of the 'sposa abbandonata' was also familiar to *opera buffa*, except that *opera buffa* always sided with the man and was implacable in its treatment of the woman as a dupe, as is clear from Bertati's opening aria for Elvira, 'Povere femmine', and from the way that Gazzaniga has set it. Nineteenth-century writers attempted to rewrite her previous life, on this occasion in a desire to invest her with bourgeois respectability,[110] but in vain. As Da Ponte's libretto makes clear, she is simply 'abbandonata da Don Giovanni' and, as such, no different from many others like her. At the same time, of course, she is a woman who is passionate by nature and for whom her love for Don Giovanni is no mere passing episode but the most decisive experience of her whole life. Of all the women in the opera, she is the one who is temperamentally closest to Don Giovanni. His kiss has kindled in her the same consuming passion that burns in him. But whereas sensual desire forces him, as a man, to keep on seeking out new women, she, as a woman, can find fulfilment of her desires only in him. As a result, her aim is not to be revenged but to win back his love, a love that is always in the background even during her most furious outbursts of loathing. And when she is forced to realize the impossibility of achieving this aim, she is concerned solely to save the man she loves from the consequences of his actions. When she returns at the end, it is neither as a sister of mercy anxious to save his soul[111] nor as a Gretchen-like figure wanting to 'redeem' him, an idea that could hardly have been further from Mozart's mind.[112] It is purely and simply to save the man

107. The phrase that comes later

involves only an extension of the initial upbeat crotchet.
108. It is enough to compare these 'coloratura' passages with the endless *fioriture* of the Neapolitan composers of the period to be conscious of the enormous difference between them. Even the sharp clash of the semitone interval is characteristic.
109. ◆ Further, see Kerman, 'On *Don Giovanni*, No. 2'.
110. Gugler and Wolzogen both assume that she was tricked into a sham marriage by Don Giovanni and, as a result, is his 'legal wife'. Bulthaupt rightly objects to this preposterous idea; see *Dramaturgie der Oper*, 189–90. But even Jahn's idea of a promise of marriage, assuming that he means a bourgeois engagement, is misconceived. The term 'sposa' covers a very wide range of meanings in *opera buffa* and does not always need to refer to an actual bride; see Adelmann, *Donna Elvira als Kunst-Ideal und in ihrer Verkörperung auf der Münchener Hof-Bühne*.
111. See Schurig, *Wolfgang Amade Mozart*, ii.163.
112. See Cohen, *Die dramatische Idee in Mozarts Opentexten*, 89ff.

she still loves and to prevent him from being destroyed. A clear expression of this character, her opening aria ('Ah! Chi mi dice mai') is a simple binary number interrupted in the true *buffa* manner by brief comments from Don Giovanni and Leporello that do not, however, affect its course in any way. Even the solemn pathos of its key of E flat major is significant, as is its extended ritornello, the abrupt dynamic contrasts of which are already indicative of Elvira's profound sense of inner agitation. This is followed by a strikingly large number of motifs[113] which, although very different from one another, all spring from the same psychological source, highlighting now one wave of emotion, now another. None of them takes precedence over any of the others, her inner turmoil finding expression now in injured pride, now in a defiant railing at her fate, before finally striking a revealingly tender note that the vocal line takes up with the well-known motif of a fourth expressive of great sensibility and associated with the Neapolitan school: all her anger and hatred are ultimately no more than unrequited love.[114] On this occasion, then, it is the vocal line that adds the final decisive touch to this animated portrait. But the orchestra again whips up her raging passion, with its razor-sharp slide motif and the syncopations of its second theme. Here, too, the vocal writing initially strikes a note of resignation, and it is only at the words 'vo' farne orrendo scempio' ('I'll torture him most horribly') that her hatred flares up,[115] finally finding explosive expression in an outburst of vehement defiance that is almost in the style of an *opera seria*. And this is the passage that Mozart uses to introduce the interjections on the part of the other two characters. The effect is strikingly realistic, initially mocking in its suggestion that Don Giovanni still languishes for her, but then all his old seductive wiles are rekindled, notably in the whispered monotone in the following orchestral motif[116]

that already contains a dangerous sensual lure, so that it is hardly surprising that Leporello, half smirking, half regretfully, adds his own particular comment to his master's words. At the repeat, Donna Elvira's feelings find explosive expression in an elaborate coloratura outburst based on the

---

113. Note the reminiscence between her opening phrase and Grétry: see p.475 above.
114. This is the first time that Mozart uses clarinets in the opera.
115. Italian composers had already taken over such wide-ranging intervals from *opera seria* into *opera buffa*. Thus Arsinda sings the following in act one, scene nine of Traetta's *Il cavaliere errante*:

traf - fig - ge - rò quel se - no se giun - gi a qual - che ecces - so

In act two, scene ten of Piccinni's *Il sposalizio di Don Pomponio* [presumably Abert means *Le gelosie* of 1755], Corrado has the following to sing:

e qua - le sa - ra ma - i se que - sto n'e do - lor?

116. Cf. Piccinni's *La Corsara* quoted on p.303 above.

triad of E flat major, which in turn provokes a wildly exultant outburst in the full orchestra. And once again we hear the gently soporific motif in the violins, now in a higher register and crescendo, to which Don Giovanni adds his beguiling 'Signorina!' – a supremely emotional moment. Then, once again, the action continues unexpectedly in a passage of *secco* recitative, with Donna Elivra's reproaches entrusted to the cut and thrust of this traditional *buffa* device.

It is entirely typical of the Italian operas of the period that, following this violent exchange, the poor abandoned Donna Elvira should be exposed to the whims of the work's one comic character. From de Villiers's version onwards, the list of Don Giovanni's loves that is kept by his servant plays a significant role and seems to have been so popular that it was taken over into other versions.[117] In Bertati's case the scene culminates in a duet for Pasquariello and Donna Elvira that highlights the contrasts between them in the true *buffa* style. But although Da Ponte sticks close to his source here, no less than elsewhere, he allows only Leporello to speak, a decision in which he was almost certainly encouraged by Mozart, given the fact that in writing this aria ('Madamina! Il catalogo è questo') the composer was following very different aims from those pursued by Gazzaniga in *his* duet. Although it has been regarded as a shortcoming that Elvira does not respond to her humil-iation with an aria[118] (Rochlitz even suggested inserting her second-act aria, 'Mi tradì quell' alma ingrata', at this point, but this is not a good idea, as the emotions expressed here would completely distort Elvira's character from the outset), is the humiliation that she suffers at Leporello's hands really so serious? She could hardly have been more hurt than she was by Don Giovanni in the previous scene, so that she is unlikely to feel particularly insulted by the outpourings of this rogue, to whose words she in any case only half listens in the recitative. However much he may go on, his mockery still falls short of the wrong done to her by his master. If his words leave any impression on her, it is not his smart-alecky derision but the image of Don Giovanni that is still clearly discernible even in this caricatured guise. This brings us to the true dramatic significance of this famous number, which contains a character sketch of Don Giovanni seen through the eyes of his servant, a figure both closely related to him and, at the same time, firmly rooted in everyday life. It is just enough to give us a convincing impression of the captivating elemental force that dwells within Don Giovanni, while repeatedly forcing us to smile at the effect that it has on a smaller mind. In this way, Don Giovanni is also present in this aria, but seen from a different perspective. As a result, all three numbers combine to present a magnificent exposition of the hero's character.

This dramatic aim not only explains the musical character of the piece, it also accounts for its unusual form, in which a fast movement is followed by a slow one, rather than the other way round.[119] The quick section paints a matchless portrait of the elemental and sensual life force, a force that seems to crepitate and flash at every point, increasingly drawing Leporello into its breathless turmoil, whereas the second section offers an account of his master's physical appear-ance, on which he invariably dwells with envious admiration. For Leporello, this aspect is more important as it is more tangible and, therefore, of greater significance to him. Here he describes his gentlemanly ways in the tone of an aristocratic minuet and his magic power over the most varied types of women, from the amiable to the demonic – and everything is seen in the remark-ably enigmatic humour of a man who is a rogue by nature and, as such, capable only of under-standing those aspects of a superior mind that correspond to his own nature. The allegro is in free

---

117. In act one, scene four of Piccinni's *L'incostante*, the lover disowns his mistress, whereupon his servant Pierotto informs the abandoned woman: 'Nel suo catalogo dove tien registrate tutte l'inammorate, questa Giulia non v'è.'
118. See Schurig, *Wolfgang Amade Mozart*, ii.122–3.
119. Paisiello had set a precedent here; see p.309 above.

binary form and characterized by the unsettling quaver motion that stops only once, at the now proverbial words 'Ma in Ispagna son già mille e tre' – this is also the only passage in which the vaguely declamatory tone gives way to actual singing. The winds have a markedly tone-painterly role to play in this display of teeming life, first with the slide motif in the flutes, at which Leporello seems to keep turning over a new page, and then in the chuckling motif in the oboes and horns indicative of Leporello's sheer delight in his own account. A similar purpose is served by the orchestra's heroic flourish following the words 'mille e tre'. There are no modulations at all in this opening section, with the result that the increase in tension at the sudden shift to A major at the start of the second section is all the more palpable, leaving its mark on all the other expressive devices in turn: the whole melodic line rises irresistibly upwards, accompanied by a titillating concertante passage for flutes and horns with oboes and bassoons, culminating in the almost brutal outburst at 'd'ogni forma, d'ogni età'. At this point even the cellos and double basses are drawn into this grotesque scalar writing, which is accompanied by more and more new wind sonorities. Finally, the vocal writing is affected by it, too: it is clear that the spirit of Don Giovanni increasingly draws his servant into its wild frenzy until the latter finally strikes a note of veritable triumph, as though he himself were the hero of all these adventures. But the ending on the dominant leads us to expect something new, and we are not disappointed: through the curiously shimmering haze, the source of this magic power emerges in the figure of Don Giovanni as he presents himself to the world. The floating, primitive, restless motifs of the earlier section are now replaced by more measured and graphic melodic writing. Again Mozart uses a free variant of binary form, with his description of the perfect gentleman initially cast in the form of a minuet, as though as a matter of course. The opening is far from original, but reflects a well-known type of Italianate melody, yet it achieves its originality through Mozart's subsequent treatment of it. Leporello understands his master perfectly and knows that his ability to adapt to the ways of the women he is pursuing is his most dangerous weapon. And so, adopting the note of gentle caricature typical of his nature, he describes the 'costanza' of the brunettes and the 'dolcezza' of the blondes, whereas the 'stout' and 'slender', whom the text invests with no particular qualities, are accompanied by the same motif in the music, a motif that later returns in a similar context, when it is reinforced by a trill, its fivefold repeat providing a graphic image of Don Giovanni and of the way in which he draws no distinction between these various types of women. Conversely, the image of 'large' and 'small' women – the simplest of all antitheses – rekindles Leporello's imagination, and here we see very clearly that in describing his master he uses only his own standards of comparison: he would lay it on just as thick in his own case. The contrast is worked out in delightfully graphic detail, with the music ascending stepwise at the description of the 'large' woman and with Leporello himself working his way up in long note-values to his sustained top d', with its horn fanfares and powerful chords in the full orchestra, until at the words 'la piccinna' he sets off back down the scale in the most rapid parlando,[120] the effect of which can barely be captured in German. Like all that has gone before it, it is inconceivable without lively Italian gesticulations. Once again, it settles on a pedal point. The second section includes a highly significant variant at the interrupted cadence on B flat major in its eighth bar, as Leporello suddenly assumes a mysterious air, his whispered remarks conjuring up the whole demonism of his master, albeit not without a hint of the ordinariness that we must always expect with Leporello. This time it resides in the unexpected appearance of a

---

120. This device, too, is Italian in origin.

staccato motif in the first bassoon, a sound that has an unmistakable symbolism to it.[121] Given Leporello's character, it is entirely natural that in describing sensual impulses, common lasciviousness is sooner or later bound to find expression. Here we can almost imagine him nudging Elvira in the ribs in order to make his point. And the bassoon motif likewise returns at the end of this section. The coda is addressed to Elvira, half in pity, half in scorn, with Leporello's coarse importunacy again taken up and underlined by the winds. It culminates in the syncopated coloratura flourish:

quel che fa

If correctly performed,[122] its veiled insolence is bound to create a particularly outrageous impression. Leporello leaves in triumph, but not without first paying Donna Elvira a grotesquely ironic compliment, although the latter, of course, takes no more notice than before. She listens because the portrait that Leporello has been painting is that of the man she loves, but the colouring that he gives to it and his importunate manner pass her completely by. There is no need for her to reply, and at this juncture an aria expressive of her general anger or indignation would merely weaken the impact left by her earlier aria. And so, after a brief *secco* recitative, Donna Elvira leaves the stage.[123]

Da Ponte was clearly at pains to ensure that all his hero's antagonists should be introduced at the very outset in a series of effective scenes. And so we now have a rustic wedding procession for Masetto and Zerlina ('Giovinette che fate all'amore'). The music follows French models in its division into several solo strophes and a choral refrain,[124] but in expression it is Italian. Its folklike character derives from its almost permanent use of passages in thirds and sixths, as well as from the sound of drones and the vigorous and earthy unison writing at the end of the refrain. Yet this is no ordinary folksong, as is clear from the three-bar structure of the opening period, which produces a remarkably agitated and unsettling effect when combined with the fourfold repeat of the motif $b'-c''-d''$. No less remarkable are the variants in Masetto's strophe, especially those of an harmonic nature.[125]

To his immense and secret anger, Masetto is now parted from Zerlina, with his aria ('Ho capito, signor, sì') admirably capturing this mood. Its main theme is *buffa*-like in character, its horn fanfare suggesting an imperious gesture on the part of Don Giovanni, a gesture to which the foolish lad must instinctively yield, whether he wants to or not – it is no accident that the musical argument invariably returns to this theme. Although he would like to show Don Giovanni that he has seen through him and wants him to feel his contempt, he fails to do so when faced with a man of his adversary's breeding. His contempt turns to agitated doggedness, and especially in the

121. There is a clear reminiscence here of the duet for Rosina and Bartolo in act one, scene five of Paisiello's *Il barbiere di Siviglia*, where we find a similar chordal motif with staccato bassoon accompaniment, although there the aim is purely comic.
122. According to Jahn, *W. A. Mozart*, ii.420, Luigi Lablache sang it somewhat nasally, with a sideways glance at Elvira. This is undoubtedly correct. In general, the role of Leporello requires a consummate actor and singer. ◆ Concerning Lablache, see Widén, *Luigi Lablache*.
123. ◆ For a discussion of Leporello's aria in the context of other 'catalogue arias', see Platoff, 'Catalogue Arias and the "Catalogue Aria"'.
124. Like Masetto's aria ('Ho capito, signor, sì'), it is written on a separate folio. This does not mean that it was a later interpolation, but merely that it was revised during the rehearsals in Prague.
125. This strophe is also a bar longer.

second subject ('cavalier voi siete già'), with its strident *relatio non harmonica*, his anguish can no longer be concealed. Note, too, his furious asides to Zerlina. But the expressive language becomes positively grotesque at the unison motif that suddenly dances in at the words 'faccia il nostro cavaliere cavaliera ancora te', an idea that becomes such an obsession that he cannot put it from his mind in the coda, with its recalcitrant syncopations. The orchestra then contemptuously repeats the 'cavaliera' idea,[126] thus investing this secondary character with a fully-rounded portrait.

It is no accident that the duettino 'Là ci darem la mano' has become so immensely popular, as it fulfils its dramatic purpose with such inspired ease and naturalness as to make us forget the implausible, *risqué* nature of the outward situation. But we must be clear from the outset about Zerlina's character. She is neither a coquette already gone to seed (as so many performers seem to think) nor one of those village beauties that delighted our novel-reading, romantic grandmothers. But we should also be wary about referring to her 'charming innocence'.[127] Zerlina has nothing in common with the rustic beauties of Rousseau's day, characters who in the folk operas of the period were held out as the antithesis of corrupt townswomen. Still less is she a *buffa* figure in the vein of Bertati's Maturina, but simply an untutored peasant girl with a lively temperament, natural charm and, above all, strong, healthy instincts. It is these that determine her actions and feelings, making it impossible for us to judge her by the higher moral standards of guilt and innocence. With the same naïvely sensual impulse that allows her to fall into Don Giovanni's trap she returns to Masetto afterwards. Mozart's music divests this natural, entirely unreflective sensuality of all its earthly trammels, thereby granting it artistic legitimacy. By ridding the scene of the all-too-human aspect that is normally a source of pleasure to lesser minds, Mozart approaches it from the standpoint of a higher reality and creates a slice of the most immediate and natural life that silences all reservations of a moral and, at the same time, dramaturgical kind.

It is clear from the outset that, given his personality, Don Giovanni will have no difficulty seducing Zerlina. But the way in which the two characters draw closer together is none the less a masterpiece of dramatic psychology. He knows that he will achieve his ends soonest by acting the part of the gentleman, and so he begins by adopting a gentlemanly tone as though he were dealing with a social equal, rather than with a peasant girl. But far more important is the peculiar warmth and suppressed urgency behind his wooing: note in this context the eloquent interval of a fourth in the second bar – its emotional impact can best be judged by imagining it being replaced by some more traditional formula such as a sigh motif. No less significant is the fact that Don Giovanni creates an initial impression simply through the power of his singing, without any other expedient. Only at the end of each phrase do we seem to hear a deep intake of breath in the winds. It is no wonder that Zerlina, suddenly awakened to womanhood, simply repeats these siren sounds as if

126. Note, too, the following two passages from Biagio's aria in Gazzaniga's setting:

127. Cohen, *Die dramatische Idee in Mozarts Operntexten*, 88.

under a spell – an inspired poetic use of the old Scarlatti duet principle – and even develops them at the end, so strangely affected does she feel. The duet as a whole is lit by the whole seductive ardour of Mozart's movements in A major.[128] And now, in the more intense E major and this time with support from the winds, Don Giovanni intensifies his attack with a broadly expansive, ardent melodic line. A touching, if brief, sideways glance at poor Masetto is Zerlina's reply.[129] But immediately afterwards her restless melody suggests nothing so much as a bird fluttering helplessly in a net. With uncanny assurance and without undue haste, Don Giovanni closes the trap by simply beginning all over again. Now he has got Zerlina to the point where she takes up each of his phrases even before it has died on his lips. Particularly significant here is the fact that he is joined by a flute,[130] she by a bassoon, until he draws all three woodwind instruments to his side, an octave apart, at the words 'Partiam, ben mio, da qui'. Zerlina's vocal line grows more and more agitated, while Don Giovanni's brief phrases seem to exude a curiously potent power, and his languishing final call of 'Andiam!' assures him of victory. For the second part of the duettino,[131] Don Giovanni – now sure of his victim – descends to her rustic world, bending her to his will by means of the deadliest of his weapons (see above). This is the meaning of this pastoral section, from its opening pedal point, with its gently rocking feeling of happiness, to its delightfully skipping conclusion.[132] The whole of this section is imagined from Zerlina's standpoint, just as the Andante was seen entirely from Don Giovanni's. Some writers have demanded more fire and passion here, but this is to misunderstand Don Giovanni's position. For him, this new conquest is nothing special, but merely an amusing game that involves no effort on his part. Zerlina's reaction, too, is decidedly undramatic: she has merely followed her instincts and, now that fulfilment beckons, she delights in the outcome with all the simple and warm impulsiveness of her nature. And so this happy idyll comes to pass, its rustic tone offering even the seducer himself a certain thrill. But how much more effective is this whole scene in the form of a duet, rather than having Don Giovanni open the proceedings by declaring his love for Zerlina in an aria, followed by a second aria for Zerlina, with a duet to conclude the scene.

At this point Donna Elvira enters to bar the deluded Zerlina's way. Her aria ('Ah, fuggi il traditor') is written in a most remarkable, pseudo-archaic style.[133] Among its archaic features are its concentrated ternary form (albeit with the third section much varied and expanded), the sequence of modulations, including E and B minor, in its middle section, its strict orchestral writing over an old-fashioned bass line reminiscent of the old ostinatos, the weighty cadences that recall earlier composers such as Handel and, above all, the taut dotted rhythm found throughout the piece. All these features help to set this aria apart from Mozart's normal method of conjuring up the most disparate feelings with the merest handful of brushstrokes. Here the overall character is remarkably unified, allowing for only a single independent orchestral interlude, near the beginning. The whole aria resembles a single violent outburst of emotion that continues to mount in tension, before finding release at the wild coloratura on 'fallace'. It is hardly a moral sermon aimed

128. Cf. the trio ('Ah taci! ingiusto core'), the only other piece in the opera that is in the key of A major.
129. The slide figure in the violins is another half-comic reminder of Masetto.
130. The flute plays a characteristic role in all Don Giovanni's arias; see below.
131. There is no tempo marking in the original score, and, indeed, it needs none, as the change in tempo and overall character is enough to add to the mounting tension.
132. It recalls the previous number: even the scoring for winds is the same. Clarinets are absent, as they are in the rustic choruses in *Le nozze di Figaro*.
133. Mozart's alleged heading, 'Nello stile di Haendel', is, however, pure invention; see Rochlitz, 'Verbürgte Anekdoten aus Wolfgang Gottlieb Mozarts Leben', 116; and Seyfried, 'Mozart der Opernkomponist: Don Giovanni'.

at Zerlina[134] – such an idea would be wholly untypical of Mozart. Clearly, the composer was anxious to express the starkest possible contrast with the tender, sensuous atmosphere of the preceding scene, hence the harshness and austerity that he piles as high as he can and that was in fact the main reason for his recourse to the earlier style. But didacticism could not be further from Elvira's mind: although her words may suggest otherwise, this element soon evaporates, such is the white-hot indignation that she feels on seeing the amorous couple.[135] Leporello's mockery had passed her by, but now, as she catches her former lover in the act, her passion knows no bounds. Furious passion is this aria's basic emotion and is directed less at Zerlina than at Don Giovanni. Elvira is forced to destroy this idyll, not out of hatred or even pity for her rival, who is of no interest to her as a person, but simply in order to oppose Don Giovanni's altogether boundless lust.

For the present she succeeds in depriving him of his prey. At this point Donna Anna and Don Ottavio enter in search of the murderer of the Commendatore, and Don Giovanni, immediately mastering the situation in spite of all his setbacks, offers them his help as a perfect gentleman, even soliciting Donna Anna with a tempting display of his sympathy. At this very moment Donna Elvira again intervenes, preparing the ground for the quartet ('Non ti fidar, o misera') which, in true Mozartian fashion, enters at a point in the plot when all the participants find themselves confronted by an entirely new situation. Anna and Ottavio do not know what to make of Elvira's intervention, while Elvira tries to unmask Don Giovanni, who for his part does everything in his power to get her out of the way. Cast in ternary form, the quartet is cyclical in structure, with a middle section which, unlike that of the previous aria, is by far the longest of the three, being divided in turn into several independent sections linked only by the fact that they all revolve around the dominant of B flat major and that they all avoid the tonic, which reasserts itself only at the end. There is something particularly attractive about the way in which the main theme, which dominates the quartet as a whole, is introduced. Elvira begins, not as explosively as she previously did with Zerlina, but it is none the less clear that her feelings are suppressed only with difficulty,[136] and this note is sustained until her melancholy final phrase:

This now becomes the shibboleth of the whole quartet, passing from voice to voice, before affecting the orchestra, too, and finally betraying Don Giovanni himself. The pity that Donna Elvira was unable to feel for Zerlina now overwhelms her in the presence of Donna Anna. Even more, this touching melody later begins to sound like the grieving voice of all the women trampled underfoot by Don Giovanni, inasmuch as it invariably recalls the words to which it was originally sung. It rises up in the orchestra, first in the violins, then in the clarinets and finally in the flutes, before being taken up by Donna Anna and Don Ottavio, who remain musically inseparable throughout this whole number and whose grief inspires their pity for the aristocratic Donna Elvira. Even Don Giovanni himself succumbs to this refrain, although his aim here is to render the

134. See Jahn, *W. A. Mozart*, ii.433–4; and Ambros, *Die Grenzen der Musik und Poesie*, 61–2.
135. Gounod, *Le Don Juan de Mozart*, 42.
136. The whole of the opening bar is a single powerful upbeat, with the dotted minim on 'Non' having the same forceful accent as the word 'fuggi' in the opera's opening duet.

whole situation ridiculous by claiming that Donna Elvira is mad. As a result, the motif acquires a note of irony and aristocratic condescension on his lips, while the orchestra stubbornly clings to its original version. But Elvira's passion flares up all the more powerfully and she now takes control of the musical argument, her agitation finding expression in a series of ever-changing motifs that oblige Don Giovanni to keep on following her. The more the contrast between them intensifies, the more powerful the tension between the other two, descending on all four characters like a dark stormcloud, from which Elvira's wild phrases dart forth like so many flames. It is easy to see why Don Giovanni, increasingly driven into a corner, finally prefers to deal directly with Donna Elvira, so that in terse semiquavers, accompanied by a unison passage in the full orchestra that clearly reveals his agitation, he whispers to her the words 'Siate un poco più prudente' ('Be a little more prudent'). This is no *opera buffa* patter, but barely suppressed anger at her obstinacy. All that it achieves, however, is to encourage Elvira to reply in the same furious tone, but this time *coram publico*. And their agitated conversation now serves to increase the others' suspicions: we return to the opening phrase, with the refrainlike motif associated with the words 'te vuol tradir ancor' now turning Donna Anna's forebodings into certainty.

Dull murmurings in the cellos and double basses in the recitative ('Don Ottavio, son morta!') that launches the following scene are followed by a strident outburst in the orchestra, including even trumpets, its piercing, heavily accentuated dissonances and cross-rhythms recalling the horrors of the previous night, to which Donna Anna's imagination keeps returning throughout the whole of the scene that follows.[137] This entire passage is a *locus classicus* of the most varied types of recitative, beginning with an expression of the most intense emotion in a passage in C minor, in which voice and instruments are particularly closely related, with notably wide-ranging writing for the cellos and double basses and the keenest declamatory line spanning wide intervals. There follow seven bars of pure *secco*, hastily whispered, over the same harmony, in a tone of the utmost secrecy, as though Donna Anna can only hesitantly bring herself to utter these thoughts. Then comes the actual narration, beginning in a dark E flat minor and exploring its basic harmonies to the full – there is a compelling atmospheric spell over this opening section, and it is entirely logical that at the mention of the stranger, the music modulates to B minor. But then, as Donna Anna recalls the actual attack, the orchestra returns in a violent stringendo[138] to the music of the opening,[139] before lapsing into a sinister silence interrupted only by a few isolated and brutal *forte* outbursts. What resources later composers would have used to depict this struggle! Mozart gives only slight, but unmistakable hints, such as the tugging syncopated motif at the words 'svincolarmi, torcermi' and the interrupted cadence on F major, with its sense of liberation, at Ottavio's 'Ohimè! respiro!' As always, Mozart achieves his effects through his contrastive use of dynamics. The ending is again dominated by the wild initial theme that returns in a much intensified form, with greatly extended cadences and, especially towards the end, a remarkable tension in the harmonic writing so that right up to the final bar it is impossible to know in what key this section

137. The C minor motif in the winds

is familiar from the opening movement of the C minor sonata K457, where it expresses wild emotion; see above.
138. Note also the breathless, disjointed declamation.
139. The wind instruments join in only for this main theme.

will end. Even the repetition of the words 'compie il misfatto suo' creates an uncommonly intense impression. It is from this powerful build-up of emotional tension that the aria now breaks free, a fine example of Mozart's ability to reduce old forms to their most succinct and to invest them with a psychological expressivity that is all the more powerful in consequence. Here, too, the old ternary form is still vaguely discernible, no longer, however, as a formal template, but as a natural vehicle for the emotions being expressed here. The relaxed loquacity of earlier composers gives way to a laconic concision that confines itself to only the most essential points. In terms of its emotional content, the aria paints a clear portrait of Donna Anna's character as outlined above. The spirit of *opera seria* lives on in the melodic writing, notably in the wide intervals used at the beginning to express her desire for revenge, but also in the sighlike character of the section that follows straight on from this ('che il padre mi tolse'). But at no point is there any sense of empty theatricality, thanks mainly to the highly original and independent writing for the orchestra that gives an air of austerity to the whole as a result of the absence of the more soft-toned woodwind, namely, the flutes and clarinets.[140] Instead of the usual *Trommelbässe*, the aria ('Or sai chi l'onore') begins with a restless seething in the upper strings, and only then do the cellos and double basses enter with a sombrely energetic motif that is immediately answered by the winds in a strikingly distant register. As with most of the numbers in the opera, the orchestral writing here is compellingly reminiscent of a force of nature, rather like the rumbling of a distant thunderstorm. But how truthful, then, is the impression created by the same orchestra when Donna Anna's feelings of anguish break through and it suddenly joins forces with the vocal line in the most intimate manner, only to break forth with renewed force in the defiant imitations and regain control of the situation. The middle section brings with it a distant echo of the sombre, visionary tone that we already heard on Donna Anna's lips in the first duet. Once again the blood-stained image passes before her mind's eye, accompanied by dull sounds of nature in the violas and bassoons, but the emotion that it now evokes is no longer horror but tear-choked anguish, and the section ends with the affecting sigh motif that Donna Anna uses to express her whole grief at her father's death, now that she has put aside all thoughts of vengeance and hatred. It is also heard in the third and final section, even though her desire for vengeance, fuelled by her memory of the terrible deed, now burns more brightly than ever. This memory, too, is drawn into the floodtide of emotion in the course of a few agitated bars, a floodtide that issues in the coda, where it rages with even greater force. The orchestral postlude is typically Mozartian, finally sinking back, *piano*, as if exhausted after so much effort.

A master of contrast, Mozart follows this up with Don Giovanni's famous aria ('Finch' han dal vino'), which could hardly be more different in tone. Don Giovanni is completely carried away by the thought of the imminent celebrations and the triumphs that he will enjoy. The whole sensual atmosphere intoxicates him in advance, with even the dances that will be performed – 'minuetto, follia, alemanna' – already leaving his head reeling. Above all, he looks forward to adding new names to his catalogue. This much is clear from the text. An Italian *opera buffa* composer would certainly not have missed the opportunity for a display of devilish high spirits, and even the rhythm adopted by Mozart was familiar to the Italians and used in similar contexts. But, for them, the aim of the music was merely to clarify the state of excitement depicted in the words. In Mozart's case, by contrast, we find the same process at work that we noted in several numbers from *Le nozze di Figaro*, in which the music not merely describes or clarifies the excitement with greater or lesser immediacy, it actually *is* that excitement. We are directly assailed by the whole pressure of

140.   I fail to understand how Marx could find it trivial and even ascribe it to Süßmayr, an attribution refuted, of course, by the autograph score; see Marx, *Die Lehre von der musikalischen Komposition*, iv.259.

the life force in full spate, a force which, freed from all constraints, races past us like an unbound force of nature, bearing absolutely no resemblance to an aria, however impassioned. Hence the impact of this frenzied musical outpouring, an impact as intense today as it ever was in the past. Its lifeblood is its rhythm, which continues to generate new melodic structures on the strength of its almost incessant quaver motion, relenting only for the long note-values on the triumphant cadences before each return of the main theme. The basic rhythm 2/4 ♩ ♫ | ♩♪ ♩ is not, however, made up of two identical bars: rather, the first must be seen as a notional upbeat, so that the main stress falls on the first crotchet of the second bar. It is this that brings a sense of unsettling power to the piece and gives it its distinctive stamp. Particularly characteristic are those passages in which this upbeat is extended by a further crotchet, notably at the second entry of 'chi'l minuetto'. A sudden shift brings an abrupt increase in resolve that is clearly bound up with the chromatically descending line that follows. Much the same is true of the later passage, 'd'una decina devi aumentar' ('By tomorrow, my list should have grown by a dozen or more'). These are all secret forms of psychological resistance that continue to add to the sense of excitement. They also occur in the melodic writing, especially in the brief chromatic sections that intensify the expressive language in highly original ways. Otherwise the writing is solidly diatonic, with the main idea, for example, based entirely on triadic intervals. But there is something deeply fascinating about the way in which the minor key enters at 'ed io frattanto', thereby capturing the whole demonicism of Don Giovanni's domineering character. It is no wonder, then, that in spite of its captivating unity, the aria is formally extremely free, being closest to a rondo, with Don Giovanni always returning to his main theme from the most varied angles. Such is Mozart's skill that each return of the theme strikes us as a new climax. It is also worth noting that the voice moves higher and higher, culminating in the coda, in which the composer – in keeping with Italian practice, but to striking psychological effect – keeps postponing the cadence. Moreover, there are only two bars in the whole aria during which the voice is silent and the beginning of the main theme rings out in the orchestra, striking a particularly ecstatic note. The aria is scored for all the winds except the trumpets and, apart from a handful of brief episodes,[141] they always appear as a self-contained body, the only exception being the flute which, together with the first violins, doubles the vocal line almost continuously, two octaves higher, significantly adding to the sensual colouring of the piece.[142] No less characteristic is the extremely full sound of the orchestra: right at the beginning, for example, the second violins and violas provide full four-part harmonies. Nor, finally, should we forget the dynamics: here, too, there are no transitions, but only the starkest contrasts. It is the orchestra, moreover, that acts as a vehicle for the wildly ecstatic *forte* and sforzato outbursts that erupt at odd moments in the aria. But it never drowns the singer, who must be careful not to try to characterize the role by unnecessary vocal swagger. The melody and especially the rhythm must emanate not just from his throat but from his whole appearance, from every glance and gesture. There are few arias, even today, in which the performer has such difficulty meeting the composer's demands as here.

---

141. These include the whiplike *forte* chord in the winds with an appoggiatura at the first mention of the dances. Both here and at each subsequent mention the cellos and double basses are invariably set in motion.
142. See also the duet ('Là ci darem la mano'). In *Die Entführung aus dem Serail* (the duet 'Vivat Bacchus, Bacchus lebe') and *Die Zauberflöte* (Monostatos's aria 'Alles fühlt der Liebe Freuden'), it is the piccolo that is used to depict sensuality, although the characters in these two cases are Osmin and Monastatos. It is striking that in the present aria, the clarinets are used only for the purposes of timbral nuance, never as solo instruments.

Whereas Don Giovanni's aria draws its strength from its rhythm, Zerlina's aria ('Batti, batti, o bel Masetto') relies largely on melodic devices. Her concern is to make up with Masetto, who has understandably been hurt by her scene with Don Giovanni. It is a theme, in short, that was as familiar to the Italians as the view that in all such cases the daughters of Eve were necessarily superior to a mere dull-witted man.[143] This was also the case with Blonde and Pedrillo, and it is even truer of Zerlina and Masetto, as Zerlina already has her experience of Don Giovanni behind her. Here, too, she remains true to her own character, and there is no more thought of remorse or rekindled passion than there is of any kind of sentimentality. Her affair with Don Giovanni seems as natural to her as her conviction that her relations with Masetto, to whom she remains devoted in her way, cannot be affected in the longer term. She is fully aware that the good-natured lad will not be able to resist her, not least because nothing serious took place during her scene with Don Giovanni. That she herself can claim no credit for this is of no further concern to her. But it is enough to allow her to play the wronged woman, and having unsettled Masetto in this way, she can intensify her attack and use all her feminine wiles to work on his senses. It is, of course, in her nature to do this, but the way in which she goes about it shows clearly that on this point she has learnt a good deal from Don Giovanni. She attempts to ensnare him with a tenderness of bewitching charm, an inspired mixture of genuine affection and the most cunning calculation. It is as though Masetto were now subjected to the same seductive spell to which she herself had succumbed in her encounter with Don Giovanni. After all, both numbers are completely identical in terms of their form and time-signature. And in both cases Andante and Allegro are in the same relationship of courtship and fulfilment. The only difference is that in Zerlina's case everything reflects a greater sense of devotion and femininity, although it is clear that since she came into contact with Don Giovanni she is fully conscious of her weapons as a woman. She obviously loves Masetto, but she also enjoys letting him feel her power.

In itself this is a simple situation, and one, moreover, that the petit-bourgeois composers of German singspiels much enjoyed depicting. But Mozart adorned and transfigured it with all the bewitching sweetness of his cantilena, without ever lapsing into inappropriate emotionalism or false sentimentality. Here, too, Zerlina sticks closely to the basic character of a child of nature, with rhythm and harmony taking second place to melody, and even this is virtually devoid of all chromaticisms, being limited to diatonic and chordal intervals. Even the main melody of the two-part Andante is typical of this approach, with its descending phrases and tendency to use folklike third-based formulas.[144] How authentic, for example, is the impression created by the consequent phrase, with its f'' not only marking the highest point in the melodic line but also exploiting the harmonic interplay I–V–I, with the simplest of all chordal intervals. Each phrase has the impact of a physical gesture, as though a gentle hand were stroking Masetto's cheek with ever-greater tenderness. The harmonic writing, too, is as simple as possible in both of Zerlina's arias, with tonic and dominant and nothing else. Conversely, the instruments clearly speak the language of flattery and endearment. Even the main theme is accompanied by the strings in octaves, before being taken up in the second section by all the winds three octaves apart. Above all, however, the solo cello plays the role of a suitor throughout the whole aria, entwining each idea in the vocal line with its ingratiating figuration, which generally – at the beginning, for example – implies two-part harmonies,

143. See Abert, 'Piccinni als Buffokomponist', 32 (on Piccinni's *La locandiera di spirito*).
144. The two phrases of the antecedent are metrically identical but melodically different. The second bends the line upwards,

reaching the third from the fifth with a delightful, typically Mozartian suspension: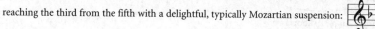

namely, a quiet melodic lower voice in parallel with the vocal line and an upper voice that remains on the fifth, *c′*. On one occasion – at the words 'e le care tue manine' – there is even an eloquent imitative dialogue between voice and cello. At the repeat the first upbeat in the winds is expanded in a highly individual manner, while its expressivity is further intensified by the syncopations in the oboes (in this way the descending melodic line is specifically stressed). Here, too, we find the melody slightly varied, before a trilled figure enters in the violins, endlessly repeated and suggesting a veritable hail of lovesick glances beating down on poor Masetto. Zerlina has him firmly under her spell thanks to her brief, triumphant motif

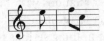

and its manifold variants, scoring an easy victory over Masetto while the cello cavorts merrily in demisemiquavers. A new section in 6/8-time is now launched by means of an extended form of this motif, continuing the mood of jubilation, with the cello now beside itself with happiness, dancing round the defeated Masetto, while suing for his love with an entirely natural, roguish sense of triumph, as the vocal line moves up and down in broken triads, with the occasional exultant coloratura. Zerlina can hardly stop herself, and at the end she continues to rock gracefully to and fro on the fifth,[145] before the orchestra brings the aria to an end while the cello purrs contentedly. Both of Zerlina's arias are like rays of warming sunshine in the dark and impassioned world of this drama.

On a poetic level, the first-act finale ('Presto, presto!') cannot compare with its predecessor in *Le nozze di Figaro*. Unlike this last-named piece, it does not grow from within, nor does it advance the plot in any consistent way but merely juxtaposes various scenes in an entirely mechanical manner, albeit with a skilful increase in tension. As such, it is a through-composed complex of scenes designed to end the first act, rather than an organically structured finale. This was an inevitable result of the sheer number of events that it contains. But where the librettist failed, the composer triumphantly succeeded, structuring the whole finale round its climax in the form of the ball, the festive strains of which are already heard at the outset and continue to be heard increasingly clearly between the individual episodes. These, too, are notionally related to it, adding to the sense of expectation, each according to its very different atmosphere, so that by the time we enter the ballroom, in spite of the festive merriment, there is already the overwrought atmosphere that tends to precede a catastrophe.

The opening section follows on immediately from the previous scene. Zerlina hears Don Giovanni's voice within and at once falls under his spell again. Needless to say, this reawakens Masetto's suspicions, while Zerlina attempts with some agitation to avert any outburst. The malicious snarl in the orchestra at the beginning and the muffled motifs in the vocal line, including the following which steals time and again through all the voices, sum up the tense situation to perfection. Now it is Zerlina's turn to struggle to regain her composure, her voice fluttering agitatedly round Masetto's grimly determined vocal line. In the brief middle section in G major, he spells out his feelings more clearly – note the crescendo and the following motif in the trumpets:

---

145. See the passage from Anfossi quoted on p.319 above.

By now she clings to his vocal phrases in the utmost anxiety. The repeat increases the tension by drawing on all the available resources, with Masetto's trumpet motif now striking a bashful note in the flutes:

Finally it becomes positively desperate in the violins:

At this point the ball is announced in the festive anapaestic rhythm with which we are all too familiar from all that has gone before. Don Giovanni invites the rustic company to his home and hastily gives his servants some last-minute orders. They repeat the invitation in a no less chivalrous tone – they, too, have picked up his gentlemanly manners. The chorus[146] slowly dies away and, as it does so, provides a transition to the following scene, which is the first of the finale's more important episodes. As such, it brings with it a change of tempo, time- and key-signature, and restores the earlier seductive mood of sensual desire that we recognize from the duettino ('Là ci darem la mano'). The upper strings strike up a mysterious, sweet-toned dialogue with the flutes, the somewhat uncertain tone adopted by Zerlina failing to conceal the fact that she is already beginning to succumb to the sorcerer's spell, and when the latter seizes her hand to the accompaniment of a brief intervention from the full orchestra, the old game starts to repeat itself. Don Giovanni begins by echoing each of her phrases, but he no longer needs to play the part of the rustic lover, as Zerlina is already trembling with secret desire, so that all he has to do is interpret her own bashfully stammered remarks. The situation is now much more tense than it was in the Duettino, almost brimming over with desire[147] when their voices come together to the accompaniment of a semiquaver motif in the winds that trickles continually downwards. Zerlina's semiquavers continue to flutter anxiously, suggesting that her resistance has finally been broken down, but at this point Masetto suddenly emerges from his hiding place, with the music that accompanies this unexpected event having a counterpart in the scene in *Le nozze di Figaro* in which the Count suddenly discovers Cherubino in the chair. There is no outburst in the orchestra, no change of time-signature or tempo, not even a *forte*, but the same tendency for the music to settle, as though paralysed, on a single motif that simultaneously produces an unexpected modulation to D minor:

146. Note the subtle way in which the dotted rhythm in the violins is transformed into a quaver figure six bars before the end, seeming to disappear as the chorus gradually dies away.
147. Don Giovanni's motif, 'Vieni un poco', corresponds to Almaviva's 'Son venuti a vendicarmi' in the second-act finale of *Le nozze di Figaro*. On both occasions, the motif expresses the triumph felt by the aristocrat as he achieves his desires.

At the same time we hear a further motif in the horns on the note *a*, its rhythm

suspiciously like Masetto's trumpet motif cited earlier. The musical argument simply comes to a rest on this combination of motifs, as if there were nothing more to expect, with the sense of surprise finding expression not in any overwrought effusion but in a general paralysis. But at least in Don Giovanni's case it does not last long. Pretending that nothing has happened, he leads Zerlina over to Masetto to the sound of mocking laughter in the orchestra, with the dull-witted Masetto even echoing his final phrase, 'Non può più star senza di te'. Once again our attention is drawn to the celebrations within (it is the contredanse that Don Giovanni will later dance with Zerlina[148]), and the tension that ensues ensures that the previous altercation is forgotten. All three characters are brought together by the same sense of exhilaration, as though the dance music that they have just heard has suddenly transported them into a completely different world.

At this point the lively motion stops with a sudden jolt and a dark veil seems to descend in the winds, while the key of F major yields to the tragic D minor that always has a special significance in this opera. This second episode brings together Donna Elvira, Donna Anna and Don Ottavio, who have come to unmask Don Giovanni at his own banquet. They, in turn, are masked, and the orchestra, picking up the semiquaver motion of the previous scene and even repeating individual phrases, reveals that they, too, await the coming celebrations in a state of extreme suspense, even if the reasons in their case are completely different. Behind their masks lurks the feverish restlessness that precedes any decisive action. This whole section remains rooted in the minor keys of D and G minor, so that the F major of the Menuetto later strikes the listener as an act of liberation, while the sense of apprehension is increased by the following recurrent rhythm:

The melodic writing, too, follows a model often found in Mozart's works in D minor, dominating the voices as well as the accompaniment:[149]

Note the subtle way in which Donna Elvira takes control of this passage, drawing Don Ottavio after her, while Donna Anna goes her own way. She does so not in the spirit of the opening section of her 'vengeance aria', even though she is now significantly closer to her real aim in life, but because, with true feminine hesitation, she sees herself faced with a decision and, above all, is afraid for Don Ottavio. This is clear from the chromatic sixths in the bassoons that introduce her first entry, and especially from the G minor section, with its sighs and vacillations. In this way, the feelings aroused

148. As with the march in *Le nozze di Figaro*, the two opening bars are suppressed.
149. See also the opening duet ('Fuggi, crudele') and the beginning of the D minor keyboard concerto K466. It also appears in the final movement of Beethoven's sonata op. 31 no. 2.

by this critical moment in all the players in the drama find strikingly succinct expression here. At this point the Menuetto is heard from the ballroom, still in F major, and the celebrations once again take centre-stage. The dialogue between Don Giovanni and Leporello – partly parlando – takes place over this dance melody, striking an extremely lively note, while the others comment on their appearance, before Leporello invites them to join them. We encountered something similar with the 'Wedding March' in *Le nozze di Figaro*, and it has been imitated in countless scenes since then. Here, too, individual features emerge with characteristic clarity, notably Don Giovanni's ebullient 'di' che ci fanno onor' and Leporello's splendidly naturalistic and courteous invitation, to which Don Ottavio responds in an equally courteous manner. But scarcely has Leporello disappeared when the tone changes completely, with a brief and tension-laden orchestral motif similar to the one heard before the section in D minor. After all, this famous trio is its notional continuation, the surprising opening and profound impact of which are prepared for in masterly fashion by the interpolated dance movement. For all its brevity, this section has been set apart from the rest of the finale in so many different ways that it virtually becomes the nub of the entire finale, certainly the heart of its inner action. Within the complex as a whole, it occupies the same position as the A major section in the quartet from *Die Entführung aus dem Serail*, which is introduced in an equally solemn manner. It is as though Mozart were drawing aside the last veil from his characters' inner lives and revealing them to us in an utterly transfigured light. Essentially, they remain the same as before, of course, but not even here can Mozart deny his tremendous ability to depict his individual characters in their interaction with one another. Yet it is as though they have suddenly been stripped of all that is random, contingent and constrained by material circumstances. In the episode in D minor the whole burden of the outward situation had continued to weigh heavily upon them, but now that their opponents have forced them to take a decision, the spell is lifted and they go to meet their destiny clear-sightedly and with their emotions purified. This is how Mozart interprets this prayer, to which he gives a distinctly religious tone. The voices reveal their full expressive power for the first time in the finale, with the wind accompaniment (the strings are silent) adding significantly to the effect. Even the voices enter *a cappella*, without any instrumental support. Donna Anna has regained her former confidence, but, once again, it is no wild cry for vengeance that she raises to heaven: all of that lies behind her, and the more the drama develops, the more mellow, one might almost say, the more ethereal the expression of her feelings becomes, and the looser become the bonds that tie her to this world of elemental passions and instincts. Even here, in this trio, we already find signs of a remarkably high-flown fervour and interiority, as her vocal line soars up and down in a broadly expansive melody, with even the scalar passages and brief ornaments merely serving to increase the impression of a confidence that springs from the very depths of her heart. Here, as elsewhere, Don Ottavio is her loyal companion, but on this occasion the angular melodic line of the far more impassioned Elvira rises up between them. It is she, not Donna Anna, who here gives candid expression to the desire for vengeance, even introducing a phrase towards the end ('vendichi, vendichi il giusto cielo') that recalls the equivalent passage in Donna Anna's 'vengeance aria'. Throughout this whole section her vocal line goes its own way, always entering only when the other two have completed their phrases, with her entry generally intensifying the underlying emotion, notably when she enters on a top *a″* flat. With their discreetly etched-in chords, the winds cast a radiant sheen over the trio as a whole. Only in the seventh bar (at Elvira's 'Protegga il giusto ciel') does a chordal figure enter in semiquavers in the lower register of the second clarinet over a sharply dotted motif in the first bassoon, a motif that later acquires a greater intensity in the form of semiquaver triplets, producing a highly individual effect, the dark coloration of which emphasizes the repetition of the words of the prayer to particularly striking effect. At the end the instruments take up Donna Anna's final phrase.

The following section takes us right to the heart of the ball with all its lively animation, a situation familiar from the Italian *opere buffe* of the period.[150] And, indeed, the scene is structured along essentially Italianate lines, with a swirling brio intercut by festive bustle, whispering and chuckling, describing the chaos that comes with a break in the dancing. Coffee, chocolate and sorbets are passed round – in a word, we find ourselves after the sublimities of the trio in the most insane bustle of everyday life and, at the same time, in the voluptuous and sensually exciting aura that surrounds Don Giovanni. Again it is the orchestra that independently sustains the mood, with the voices sometimes joining in with brief phrases, sometimes interrupting it, generally in a light parlando. In short, a lively picture unfolds in an entirely realistic manner. Only the jealous Masetto stands to one side, watching. There is something touching about his repeated cry of 'Ah Zerlina, giudizio!', but trouble starts to stir in the orchestra at his brief exchange with her, whereupon the cellos and double basses suddenly settle on a B flat, which they proceed to sustain for fourteen bars, as Don Giovanni again offers his hand to Zerlina, and Leporello, who is fond of playing the gentleman on such occasions, follows his example and sets off in pursuit of the other young women. Again it is the flutes that are Don Giovanni's loyal companions here, this time supported by the clarinets. And once again it is Masetto who represents the main obstacle, even though in his dimwittedness he merely stammers a few disjointed phrases. Zerlina is furious at this, while the other two draw their own conclusions in the following inimitable passage:[151]

Masetto must be kept busy. Their negotiations come to an end with an agitated repeat of the final passage from the opening section.

Until now the music has had a primitive, rustic character in honour of the countryfolk who are present, but now, at the entry of the three masked figures, it suddenly strikes a profoundly aristocratic note. Not only is there a sudden change of key, but the orchestra is joined by trumpets and timpani. Here is an official, ceremonial reception of high-born visitors, for which many a distinguished household in Vienna could have provided Mozart with a model. Even Leporello, who functions here as a majordomo, begins his speech as a grand seigneur, with the newcomers' answer, precious to a fault, preserving the same aristocratic tone. With the amiability of a man of the world, Don Giovanni keeps repeating the words 'È aperto a tutti quanti, viva la libertà' ('It's open house today! Here's to freedom'), a remark which, curiously enough, has prompted performers to raise a completely unmotivated toast to political freedom in which the chorus and

---

150. See, for example, act one, scene nine of Piccinni's *Le donne vendicate*, in which the newcomers likewise express their thanks.
151. This passage clearly recalls Figaro's 'Non più andrai'.

even the audience have occasionally taken part. But it would never occur to an aristocrat like Don Giovanni to champion political freedom: all that he is referring to is the freedom conferred by the wearing of masks, and if his distinguished visitors concur with this, it is merely out of courtesy towards their host: they are unwilling to give ground to him in matters of social refinement. The herd of peasants, meanwhile, is expected to remain silent during this ceremonial on the part of their social superiors, and the fact that Mozart depicts this ceremonial in such a realistic way invests the scene with bitter irony, especially for audiences of his own day.

Don Giovanni now gives a sign for the dancing to begin again, and when it does, the dramatic tension that has been slowly building up finally breaks. However many ball scenes opera can boast before[152] or since, Mozart's has never been surpassed either musically or dramatically. Its actual motif – the dancing – is purely musical in character, but Mozart immediately adds a dramatic dimension by coupling together no fewer than three different dances. This gives Don Giovanni an opportunity to divide up the characters and to avoid those he finds most tiresome. His aristocratic visitors begin a minuet, while he himself dances a contredanse with Zerlina, and Leporello forces an unwilling Masetto to perform a swirling allemande. As a result, three orchestras are involved, with the aristocrats accompanied by the well-appointed house orchestra that Don Giovanni maintains like any respected nobleman in Vienna, while the villagers have to make do with two two-part peasant orchestras consisting of two violins and bass.[153] This tripartite arrangement, which is also clearly reflected on a purely spatial level, is a precondition for the ensuing action, with the three dances forming the chief focus of interest, while the individual characters have to adapt to them, come what may. Detailed atmospheric descriptions are ruled out, therefore, from the outset. The combination of three dances that are completely different from each other in terms of both character and rhythm constitutes a contrapuntal masterpiece. Although the equation of two bars of 3/4-time = three bars of 2/4-time is straightforward, as is one bar of 3/8-time = one crotchet divided into triplets, it still requires immense skill to combine all three dances so that each retains its independent stamp and their combination, while sounding melodious, appears to be accidental. The successive entries of the three dances are presented very realistically, with both subsidiary bands preparing themselves by tuning up, the open strings sounding in fifths, a pizzicato effect is attempted, as is a brief little trill, while another player tries out all the strings and the bass tunes up in similar fashion – all this fits in quite naturally with all that has been going on.[154] The minuet itself is a true, festive dance movement and, as such, very different from Mozart's symphonic minuets, for example. The spendidly festive rhythm ³/₄ [musical notation] is repeated throughout the whole section,[155] and even the stiffly solemn cadence [musical notation] that ends every eight-bar period (there are no interpolations in this minuet) underlines its strictly

152.   Of Mozart's Italian contemporaries, suffice it to mention only Galuppi and the second finale of his opera *La partenza e il ritorno de' marinari* (1764), where the dance scene is likewise introduced by a minuet, and the first finale of Piccinni's *I viaggiatori*, in which a 'Tempo di Minuè' provides the outer framework of the action.

153.   The use of different orchestras was familiar not only to Gluck but also to Italian composers of the period, including Paisiello and Galuppi (see above). Wolzogen rightly rejects the idea of having three separate dance floors; see Wolzogen, *Don Juan*, 93–4, and 'Anmerkungen zu dem Artikel: "Don Juan im neuen Opernhause zu Paris"'. (For his attack on de la Génévais [production at the Paris Opéra], see Wolzogen, *Don Juan*, 147–8.) On this occasion, Mozart made no attempt to introduce any national colour into his dances, as he had with the fandango in *Le nozze di Figaro*. In terms of its music, this scene is more suited to the town house of an Austrian magnate than to the country house of a Spanish grandee.

154.   The tuning up of open strings was a popular joke with Italian composers. Later composers include Weber in the peasants' music in the opening scene of *Der Freischütz*.

155.   Cf. the A major violin sonata discussed on pp.843–4 above. Exactly the same rhythm is found in the passage from Guglielmi quoted on p.315 above.

dancelike character. The other dances, by contrast, are not strictly symmetrical – in the case of the contredanse, a four-bar antecedent is followed by a six-bar consequent phrase. Yet none of this disrupts the natural flow of this section.[156] It is against this brilliant background that the actual plot unfolds, generally in brief, half-suppressed exclamations that are only rarely extended into longer phrases. Yet even here the characterization is strenuously maintained. Right at the beginning, for example, Donna Elvira effortlessly stifles her feelings, hissing the words 'Quella è la contadina' to Donna Anna, with their keen-edged augmented fourth, and the latter, deeply disturbed by what she sees and scarcely able to control her emotions, answers with an anguished cry of 'Io moro!' Don Ottavio enjoins them both to remain calm. Don Giovanni then dances with Zerlina, while Leporello does what he can with the ill-tempered, ungainly Masetto. Only towards the end, when Don Giovanni drags away Zerlina, who is by now as alarmed as the other two women, do the three adversaries join ranks in anticipation of the approaching catastrophe. And this duly follows with Zerlina's scream. The whole situation now changes with the sudden entry of E flat major: the dance music breaks off abruptly, and the whole orchestra (minus horns, trumpets and timpani) depicts the general confusion in a wild and realistic unison interspersed with violent sforzatos. This allegro section is completely free in design, with even the harmonies constantly changing and leading from B flat minor via C minor to a tension-laden half-cadence on the dominant of D minor. Entirely typical are the brief crescendos that precede the polyphonic passages, while Zerlina's cries of terror, rising higher and higher, are accompanied by syncopations, marked *piano*, in the violins. Here, too, the voices remain in unison,[157] the long note-values in the two preceding bars for orchestra creating the effect of a powerful upbeat of tremendous tension. Only at the end, when Masetto enters, do the voices go their separate ways again. But instead of the expected D minor, with its suggestion of impending disaster, it is the key of F major that now appears with the return of Don Giovanni and Leporello. Supported by the orchestra to the best of its abilities, master and servant now act out an emotionally charged scene for the benefit of the others, with Don Giovanni leading the way with a theatrical slide motif familiar from *opera seria*, together with vigorous dotted rhythms and a unison trill in the strings reminiscent of an earlier period.[158] The comedy then continues with peremptory chords in the strings to which the poor victim Leporello responds to the sound of anxious calls in the winds. But their enemies refuse to be taken in by this and remove their masks, one after the other, to the same motif (a striking use of imitation), a brief tremolando in the strings suggesting that Don Giovanni has completely lost his composure. He can barely stammer odd words, and there is something particularly delightful about the way in which the music here recalls Leporello's fear in the previous passage.[159] The characters now regroup, with Zerlina and Masetto on the one hand and Ottavio, Donna Anna and Donna Elvira on the other, their interventions growing increasingly forceful and culminating in the fourfold threat of 'Tutto!' There follows an outburst of indignation, introduced by the familiar tragic unison motif in the full orchestra and cast in the form of a clearly structured, two-part movement with coda that is motivically closely related to what we have just heard. Note especially

---

156.   In Prague there seems to have been a shortage of players. The usual peasant orchestra is in three, not two, parts, so Mozart uses the winds from the main orchestra to fill out the harmonies. In the case of the allemande, for example, the rhythm is spelt out by the horns. (Note the naturalistic way in which this dance is introduced with the *g″* repeated three times, each time with an appoggiatura.) There is no doubt that if Mozart's hands had not been tied by his limited resources in Prague, he would either have added the winds to the individual orchestras or provided three-part textures for the two peasant bands. ◆ Further, see Heartz, 'An Iconography of the Dances in the Ballroom Scene of *Don Giovanni*'.

157.   The same rolling unison figure, this time in C major, is found in the second-act finale of Grétry's *Les événements imprévus*.

158.   A similar device is found in Count Almaviva's aria ('Hai già vinta la causa!').

159.   Even the wind accompaniment is the same.

the elemental tension of the first five bars with their solid F minor sonorities over a pedal point that is itself underscored by a timpani roll suggestive of thunder. But this crescendo, too, is suddenly interrupted at Don Giovanni's words and those of Leporello, who is now closely associated with him on a musical level, too. Don Giovanni feels far from crushed, even though his head is beginning to reel at all his misfortunes, and there is a subtle touch to the way in which his thoughts turn not to high-flown rhetoric but to the banquet that had started so well.[160] Once again his enemies close ranks and advance on him, and the rolling unison of the opening Allegro returns, but this time in C major, as does the barbed octave interval, but everything is now much more intense from an orchestral point of view, gradually assuming the character of a storm breaking out, not least because of the triplets that infiltrate the violins and that later spread to all the strings in the form of unison figures. Now even Don Giovanni starts to vacillate. There is a palpable increase in tension at Donna Anna's sustained *g″* on 'trema', beneath which the middle voices strain chromatically upwards in thirds. In turn this produces a more agitated response on the part of Don Giovanni and Leporello, and their two voices ascend the scale of C major in feverish haste, only to encounter irresistible opposition in the form of a harsh dissonance[161] – there is nothing in the least *buffa*-like about this passage, rather should it be seen as an example of a violent, desperate assault. It is entirely logical, therefore, that their opponents' indignation now reaches its high point, as their voices strain sequentially upwards in a powerful unison, while the cellos and double basses in the orchestra are now stirred into action. The voices end on the following characteristic phrase, with its searing interval of a diminished third, that had ended the opening section:

il suo ful - mi - ne ca - drà !

This whole section is now repeated, culminating in the coda as Don Giovanni's courage returns and he manages to fight his way through the serried ranks of his enemies. Once again we sense his spirit in the powerful theme in the first violins and the glitteringly descending scale in the winds:[162]

The others renew their attack to the slide motif heard earlier, as Don Giovanni challenges his opponents with his Horatian 'se cadesse ancor il mondo, nulla mai temer mi fà' ('let the world fall around my ears, nothing will make me afraid') in a Più stretto whose provocative fanfare motif is immediately taken up by the three women in imitation (undoubtedly an intentional feature), while the two other men, Don Ottavio and Masetto, form a group by themselves. Leporello naturally

160. The music is the same as that heard at his words 'Sù svegliatevi da bravi' at the beginning of the finale (bars 52–4). Even the little trills in the violins are the same.
161. Note also the way in which the melodic line moves in the opposite direction here.
162. It is entirely typical that, on a musical level, Don Giovanni and Leporello go their separate ways here, with the latter relapsing into his usual *opera buffa* tone.

sides with his master. The chorus is not involved in this section of the finale, an omission that is entirely understandable as the peasants are wary of interfering in the goings-on of the aristocracy. As soon as things become critical, musicians and dancers leave the ballroom, letting the others fight it out among themselves. Like *Die Zauberflöte*, *Don Giovanni* should not be reduced to the level of a Meyerbeerian grand opera.

In spite of all the dangers with which his fellow humans threaten him, Don Giovanni has again emerged triumphant. He knows that none of the women will lay a hand on him. Don Ottavio is as always content with good intentions and idle threats and is unequal, therefore, to a man of action like Don Giovanni. And Masetto, finally, is too much of a dull-witted booby to take the initiative, quite apart from the fact that he lives in fear of his lord of the manor. The only person to have to foot the bill is Leporello who, in the light of this new and unfortunate experience, once again decides to find a less dangerous post. In the distant rumble of thunder, however, we hear the voice of a higher power – a feature that points forward to Romantic opera and begs the question whether the elemental force embodied by Don Giovanni will master it, too.

The second act brings with it the aforementioned waning of the librettist's poetical powers. Incapable of maintaining the great dramatic sweep of the narrative by introducing new motifs, he is content to expand the old ones and attempts to fill the resultant vacuum with all manner of episodes of a largely *buffa*-like character, none of which is original, even if they are skilfully executed and, above all, very grateful from a musical point of view. Only in the graveyard scene does he again return to Bertati and, at the same time, rediscover his earlier level of inspiration. It is to Mozart's credit that he continues to enlist the listener's sympathies even during these loosely structured interpolations, a feat that he achieves by revealing greater skill than Da Ponte in linking them to the main narrative.

Even in the brief duet ('Eh via buffone') that opens act two Mozart manages to throw vivid light on the inner relationship between master and servant. Deeply dismayed at the role that he has been required to play in recent events, Leporello is determined to hand in his notice, but Don Giovanni is as adept at handling men as he knows how to deal with women and in both cases he uses essentially the same expedient, consciously descending to Leporello's emotional world and in that way winning him over. In short, he plays with his most dangerous weapon here and does so, moreover, in an utterly delightful way. The only difference is that on this occasion it is Don Giovanni himself who strikes a *buffa*-like note from the outset,[163] leading Leporello by the nose from one phrase to the next. The humour of the duet lies in the fact that for Don Giovanni it is all a joke, whereas for Leporello it is a matter of deadly earnest. Note, for example, the witty chuckle in the winds at Don Giovanni's words 'che sei matto' ('You're mad'), to which Leporello responds with his first independent idea, an angry 'No', accompanied by unison strings. This same idea returns in the orchestra at the end, to no avail of course, as Leporello has already eaten humble pie. Even if he had still had reservations, they would have been silenced by the fulfilment of his wish to play his master's part. This he is now required to do by Don Giovanni in order to deal with Donna Elvira, who has just come out on to her balcony. Don Giovanni lends him his voice in an attempt to keep her occupied while he gets to grips with her chambermaid. This is the starting point for the trio ('Ah taci! ingiusto core'), a piece that has always been held out as a pearl of Mozart's ensemble writing. Clearly laid out in ternary form (with a varied *da capo* of the opening section), it is also remarkably unified from a motivic point of view: with the exception of its some-what freer middle section, it is based on a very small number of recurrent motifs. In spite of this,

---

163. On the reminiscence of Domenico Fischietti's *Il mercato di Malmantile*, see above.

drama and music once again interact in the most wonderful way. Not only do the characters' thoughts and feelings speak to us from this music, so does the natural setting in which they find themselves. Within the first eight bars we have already discovered what it was that brought Elvira out on to her balcony: the harmony between her feelings and the tender, alluring and southern summer night. Here, once again, we find ourselves in the presence of one of those entirely modern images of nature which, innocent of any Rococo-like tone-painting, reveal nature's mysterious workings in musical terms.[164] The intangible aura that surrounds this piece is Don Giovanni's best possible ally. Everything conspires to create this effect: the key of A major, the gentle-toned instrumentation (the oboes are missing for the first time in the opera), and the raptly floating, slightly tremulous tone of the principal melody. Believing herself to be alone and with her heart no longer tossed by the storms of the world, Elvira gives voice to her innermost feelings, her love of Don Giovanni, an emotion which, having been confronted by his infidelity, she has been able to express hitherto only in the language of hatred. Longingly, she listens to the night, communing with her heart which, in spite of all Don Giovanni's infidelities, still beats for him with all its old passion. But here, too, she remains Elvira: at the thought of the 'empio traditore', impassioned scales suddenly shoot up in the violins, similar to those that we encountered in her very first aria, and her inner turmoil finds moving expression at the words 'è colpa aver pietà' ('it is wrong to pity him'). We then hear the second main motif on Leporello's lips:[165]

zit - to   di Donn' El - vi - ra

Mysterious and insinuating in character, it admirably sums up the dark machinations that have been set in train under cover of night. Don Giovanni intervenes on behalf of his puppet, Leporello, as always beginning with the same melody as Elvira, only in the more intense key of E major and with a greater degree of sensual ardour. Now this sinister motif takes hold of Elvira, too ('Numi! che strano affetto'). Note the masterful way in which Mozart tightens the threads of the deception on the strength of these two antithetical moods. A brief but typically Mozartian transition, with a surprising modulation and a chromatic melody over a short crescendo that fades softly away, brings us suddenly to C major. Don Giovanni no longer adopts Donna Elvira's tone but reverts to his own, singing what is perhaps the most seductive tune that we ever hear on his lips. It is no accident that its opening is similar to that of the following canzonetta.[166] But we should not conclude from this that Don Giovanni is already thinking of Donna Elvira's chambermaid.[167] Rather, it is Don Giovanni's sensuality as such that finds expression here, under the spell of the outward situation, a sensuality that has no specific object to it, his bewitching melody being directed not to any one particular woman but to womankind in general, and if he shortly returns to this mood when serenading the chambermaid to the sound of a mandolin and the rhythms of a dance, there is clearly a sense in which he is now toning down that feeling in a self-ironical way. And as so often with Mozart, this ardent outburst is followed by an equally violent reaction in the form of Elvira's

164. Cf. Susanna's aria in act four of *Le nozze di Figaro* ('Giunse alfin il momento').

165. The interval of a fourth at the end is missing in the instruments. Later, when they take it up, it emerges that its second note is actually conceived as the upbeat of the following repeat.

166. Even the suspension on the fourth, with its appoggiatura-like accented fifth, is repeated in the second phrase.

167. See *Fliegende Blätter für Musik*, iii (1857), 11–12. Schurig, too, tends to this same view; see Schurig, *Wolfgang Amade Mozart*, ii.147. But we must be careful when interpreting these motifs of reminiscence in an eighteenth-century context.

last remaining resistance with its passionately agitated, sharply accented melody over a string tremolando. With the syncopations in the violins at her final 'non ti credo' (again a crescendo followed by a *piano!*), her struggle reaches its climax. At the same time, the cynic in Don Giovanni breaks out in his emotionally charged, 'almost tearful' 'o m'uccido!' ('Believe me, or I'll kill myself!'), prompting Leporello to comment in his delightful and typically Italian way, 'Io rido' ('I'm laughing'). While the rogue has been laughing contentedly to himself, Elvira's discomfiture is complete. Again the purely musical development, modulating back from C major to A major, is closely bound up with the development of the drama – Elvira's change of mind –, and with the return of the original key, all three unite for the principal theme. Especially attractive is the way in which Elvira duets with Leporello, suggesting that in this extremity he feels something like pity for its victim, while Don Giovanni contemptuously rejoices in his victory. But the sinister motif returns, of course, its rolling thirds gradually assuming control of the voices and orchestra. At the same time a large-scale crescendo develops, as things seem to move increasingly towards a climactic outburst of agitation, only to end *piano*, as before. A staccato chord in the full orchestra consisting of only two notes captures to perfection the whole unsettling nature of the nocturnal events that have just unfolded. The whole trio is authentically Mozartian. As always he prefers to avoid crude dramatic explosions and with an unerring instinct feels very clearly that the Romantic lack of resolution, with its curious mixture of feminine devotion and the most ruthless male egoism in its most seductive guise, would not sustain such treatment. But at the same time he glosses over the crudity of the situation and draws a veil over the element of buffoonery that the librettist has introduced here, not in order to pretend that it is not there but because he sees more to it than Da Ponte, who, like all ordinary mortals, thought that what he saw first was more real and that what promised to be most effective was also the most vital. For an Italian, the masquerade would have been the main concern; for Mozart, it was the interplay of inner, psychological forces and the way in which those forces attract and repel one another, surrounded by the mysterious workings of nature. Where would there have been room in this picture for dull-wittedness, coarseness and crowd-pulling effects?

We have already mentioned the link between the rio and the canzonetta ('Deh, vieni alla finestra'). Once again we are dealing with a piece of music drawn from the everyday life of the time: serenades like this were an entirely common occurrence on warm summer nights on the streets of Vienna. And the practice of accompanying them with a mandolin was undoubtedly familiar to Mozart. Indeed, he himself wrote songs with mandolin accompaniment [K349 and 351, both possibly composed in Munich at the end of 1780 or in early 1781]. And in opera he knew of the practice from Paisiello and Grétry. But the popular nature of the piece emerges not only from its instrumentation, but also from its simple strophic form[168] and the strictly symmetrical

168. In the introduzione of Anfossi's *Il geloso in cimento*, the serenade begins as follows:

structure of its periods,[169] all of which is calculated to appeal to the chambermaid. Even so, we are not dealing with any old street song. Whether we are to imagine Don Giovanni singing a well-known song or improvising a serenade of his own, it is clearly his own world of emotion that finds expression here: only he could sing a song of such intoxicating sensuality. The echo of the trio indicates only that Don Giovanni still inhabits the same world of emotion, its folklike garb adding an ironical aspect that is further underlined by the exaggerated use of expressions such as 'pianto' and 'morire' ('tears' and 'death'). Although the singer undoubtedly empathizes with what he is singing, he also consciously delights in his superiority, which assures him of an easy victory in the present case. This high-spirited playfulness is merely another aspect of Don Giovanni's character.

But his plans are once again thwarted. Masetto arrives with his peasant friends in order to wreak vengeance, in his own inimitable way, on the man who has destroyed his own happiness. Here the text becomes indistinguishable from that of any ordinary *opera buffa*: Don Giovanni disguised as Leporello and the peasants spoiling for a fight are tried-and-tested set pieces with a long and venerable history. Needless to say, Don Giovanni has no difficulty in mastering the situation when confronted by adversaries of this order and simply takes charge in his guise as Leporello. The aria ('Metà di voi quà vadano') that he sings in the role of his servant is one of the most inspired of the whole opera. The text is content to describe the situation on stage: sentries are posted and the enemy is described in detail – musically speaking, it is a relatively thin idea. Mozart, too, naturally uses the language of *opera buffa* and describes the outward situation with graphic clarity. But he fills this framework with an inner life of unprecedented range and animation. For although Don Giovanni feels extremely comfortable wearing Leporello's mask, he is also keen to play his own superior game with it and to keep removing it, but in such a way that the dim-witted peasants are unaware of what he is doing. Indeed, he positively revels in his ironical self-characterization, repeatedly provoking the peasants' dull-witted responses. Above all, however, it is his violent demonic nature that keeps on breaking through here, the unbridled delight in giving these upstart simpletons a piece of his mind. As a result, this aria is a typically Mozartian creation, unified and yet filled with an almost inexhaustible wealth of emotions, a variety reflected in its external form. It is basically a ternary aria, but it also includes features of a rondo to the extent that new themes appear in the *da capo*, while the postlude reverts to the principal idea. This theme begins quietly, but full of tension, to the accompaniment of long notes in the horns and syncopations in the violins, striking a note which, vigorously peremptory, is supported by imperious gestures in the orchestra. But by the eleventh bar the picture has changed: in the delightful thirds of the bassoons and the little trills in the oboes and violins, Don Giovanni, still adopting the manner of Leporello, describes the usual course of his amorous escapades. Yet his own face already seems to appear from behind the mask in the sinister syncopations at 'ferite pur'.[170] But then, in C major, Don Giovanni begins his ironical self-portrayal in which it is the instruments that have the principal role to play – just as they do throughout the aria as a whole. Here we seem to see him standing before us, with the flowing plumes in his hat. And here, too, he delights in playing the devil. The following passage, with its diabolical trill, goes far beyond anything that Leporello might say:

---

169. Only the interludes are two bars long, although this also accords with popular practice. The simple songlike tone is also reflected in its modulatory structure, with the first section modulating to the dominant, the second returning to the tonic via the minor of the subdominant and the subdominant itself, as in countless Italian serenades.

170. Syncopations are also found in the orchestra at Blaisine's words 'Il me bat, le scélérat' in scene five of Philidor's *Blaise le savetier*.

e spa - da al fian - co e - gli ha, e___ spa - da al fian - co e - gli ha

And this double game continues in the following section. With the *da capo*, he peremptorily sends the peasants packing, so that, in a characteristic shift to the subdominant, he can deal with Masetto on his own. And now he is even more casual. He begins by detaining him, evidently to make a fool of him in the following passage, with double octaves in the strings but in only two-part harmony, and with a cheeky echo in the winds:

noi___ far dob - bia - mo il re - sto e già ve - drai cos' è.

His tone grows increasingly contemptuous, and the third-based motif *c'–a* that is endlessly repeated adds to the sense of infamy, especially when taken up by the orchestra in a whole series of different guises. The aria ends with a lengthy postlude based on the motif with which Don Giovanni had earlier sent the peasants on their way, suggesting a brief patrol of the neighbouring streets, while the music of the aria slowly dies away, striking a half mocking note as it does so. And so this curious aria, which is all about masks and disguises and which again demands considerable acting skills on the part of all concerned, fades away like a ghost in the dark.

But the storm that has been brewing now breaks over Masetto's unsuspecting head, and he is soundly beaten in a way entirely appropriate to such a character in an *opera buffa*. Zerlina now arrives to console him in her aria ('Vedrai, carino'). She is neither appalled by what has just happened nor particularly overcome by emotion, but is fully conscious of the absurdity of her fiancé's plight and is no doubt happy to give him a piece of her mind in order to punish him for his jealousy. But with Zerlina, too, old love never dies, and the remedy that she hopes will cure him is entirely in keeping with her character. The text expresses all this with the lack of ambiguity that is typical of *opera buffa*, but Mozart is no more interested in such graphic detail than he is in the case of the duet for Papageno and Papagena. There is, it is true, an underlying sensuality, to which the soft-toned winds – flutes, clarinets, bassoons and horns, but no oboes – contribute in no small way; and the melody, too, with its tender feminine suspensions,[171] sounds very much like a promise of imminent happiness. But he draws a veil of the most delightful kind over the aria as a whole, preventing the all-too-human from finding expression and, with the hand of genius, transforming nature into art. All glaring colours are avoided; and the tonic is abandoned only fleetingly. The aria is in two parts, the first of which is entirely folklike in terms of its expression and the structure of its themes:[172] it introduces us to the aria's basic emotion and contains a whole number of caressing phrases such as that in the cello in the third and fourth bars, the numerous little trills and, above all, the ravishing language of the winds, the handling of which affords particular pleasure throughout this aria in general. The second section follows the fermata in which Zerlina gives Masetto a long and loving look and harks back, textually and musically, to the image of the

171. Even the seventh and eighth bars exude a particular warmth with the unexpected entry of the winds.

172. The heartfelt tone is German, but the melodic type is entirely Italian with its rhythm: ³/₈ ♩♩ | ♩.♩♩ The same melodic type is found in many similar pieces by Majo and Piccinni.

beating heart, an image found in countless variants since Pergolesi's day. But here, too, tone-painting is not Mozart's main concern. As is clear, not least, from the unison figure in the three winds over the trembling pedal point, he adds decisively to Zerlina's sensual urgency, as, indeed, the aria's second section is intended as an intensification of the first. The instruments take control: particularly inspired is the passage in which the violins flutter down gently in octaves over the pounding staccato in the winds. But the underlying emotion is also emphasized in the vocal line as it strives towards the seventh with a motif which, at the final 'sentilo battere, toccami quà', is combined with the orchestral accompaniment mentioned above and seems no longer capable of controlling its longing. At the repeated 'qua' we again hear the caressing trills from the opening section. But Mozart goes no further with this sensuous element: there is one more mischievous staccato rocking figure in the winds, then gracefulness wins the day. The aria ends with a remarkably warm outburst in the full orchestra that combines the themes from both sections and then, as so often with Mozart, dies away *pianissimo*.

The sextet ('Sola, sola in buio loco') brings to an end this *buffa* episode in act two. With its nocturnal confusions, its bringing together of the various strands in the plot through the arrival of more and more characters at critical moments and its threats to the fearful Leporello, the text is a true product of the spirit of *opera buffa*. And Da Ponte treated it as such, even to the extent that in the second part of the sextet he falls back on entirely generalized, hackneyed phrases to describe the effect of the imbroglio on all concerned. An Italian composer would have responded with a scintillating and musically grateful piece that brought to an end all the multiple confusions on stage.

Mozart's setting of this scene has always been much admired, and there is no doubt that the scene is a brilliant and, indeed, triumphant example of his unique ability to combine tragedy and comedy. The sublime and the ridiculous and the most profound and most trivial emotions are found here side by side. Dramatically, too, this is far more than just another number from an *opera buffa*. For Da Ponte the sextet was merely a way of padding out the second act, but for Mozart it is an organic link in a large-scale dramatic development: for, although unseen, the hero of the sextet is not Leporello but Don Giovanni. This is not only because he is represented by his servant – even if, given the pitiful failure of his attempt to play the part of his master, we can see just how superficial is his character compared with that of Don Giovanni – but also because the other characters are palpably under Don Giovanni's spell. For the last time before the final catastrophe, all his enemies, suspecting his hand in this latest comedy of errors, unite in their common hatred of him, even though they are conscious of their own powerlessness in the face of his demonism. Although he himself is unaware of the fact, this is his final victory over his enemies before his insatiable desires drive him into the arms of a power superior even to his. But the music that expresses their grief in the second section of the sextet touches on the deepest human emotions, affecting us profoundly and rising to heights of transfigured mysticism which, far beyond even the highest theatricalism, are among the purest summits of art. Certainly, the second-act finale could have no finer foil than the present ensemble, which raises Don Giovanni's enemies to the heights of true humanity. Bound up with this development is Leporello's own fate, as the final veil falls away from his innermost character under the pressure of his extreme predicament: he stands there, naked and exposed, a pitiful everyday figure willing to sacrifice everything to save his own life, including even the outer and inner mask of his master, of which he was otherwise so proud. It is difficult to conceive of a more inspired way of incorporating into the drama the old theatrical role of the jester, whose principal function was to mediate between stage and audience. Note also the subtle way in which Leporello, following his discovery, becomes a matter of increasing indifference to the others: they no longer have anything in common with the poor beggar.[173]

Musically speaking, the sextet is laid out along extremely unified lines and comprises two large-scale sections – an andante and an allegro – that are both in E flat major. But the internal structure is remarkably free, especially in the andante, its unity being achieved in part through the repetition of individual passages but, more especially, through the recurrence of certain orchestral motifs, producing something like a free variant of rondo form. Following a two-bar introduction of a kind that Mozart liked to use in order to add to the feeling of suspense on the listener's part, Elvira begins by expressing her anxiety at the darkness of the place to which her supposed lover has brought her. Her hot-blooded temperament is made clear from the interval of a seventh with its sforzato marking in the fourth bar, from the impassioned counterfigure familiar from her earlier numbers in the seventh and, above all, the ending with its sinister chromatic orchestral unison in the eleventh bar. Yet there is also something affecting about this opening that immediately moves us to pity.[174] All the greater, then, is the contrast with the following passage for Leporello, as he gropes his way uncertainly around the stage, his only thought being how to escape from this dire situation. At first he is genuinely afraid, but when he finally finds the 'damned door', we hear a contented trill and chuckle in the orchestra, and with one of Mozart's eloquent unisons, he decides to make good his escape: we can almost literally see him tiptoeing towards the exit in a state of extreme agitation. Unfortunately, it is the wrong door, and with a modulation as abrupt as it is unexpected (the key of B flat major is respelt enharmonically as the triad of the flattened sixth degree of D major), Donna Anna and Don Ottavio enter with their torchbearers and bar his way. With its bright trumpet sonorities, this D major has an almost physical impact: a ray of bright light suddenly falls over the scene, not only making it impossible for Leporello to escape, but banishing the dark forces of deception and cunning.[175] Drawing on the whole sincerity of his emotions that is his peculiar strength, Don Ottavio consoles his lover: it is the same noble and warm-toned type of cantilena that he had already used to comfort her at the beginning of act one. The first violins cling to the same motif in the manner of an *opera buffa* (it is a motif that is often found in Mozart's works), while the semiquaver figures in the second violins reflect the profound emotions that stir within him. But Donna Anna's anguish will end only when she is dead. Note the extremely subtle way in which she initially attempts to strike the same note as her lover, while the orchestral accompaniment remains unchanged. Yet her lover's tone becomes very different on her lips. Not only the key of D minor is indicative of all this, so, too, is the melodic line of her opening phrase:

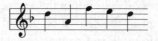

We have already heard this phrase in her opening duet and the first-act finale, both times in D minor and on each occasion symbolizing the wound that she bears in her heart,[176] thereby

173. Schaul, *Briefe über den Geschmack in der Musik*, 51, quotes the sextet as an example of Mozart's repeated infringement of the rules of common sense, arguing that it is tragic in tone, whereas it ought to be demi-caractère.
174. The opening recalls Leonore's great aria in act one of Beethoven's *Fidelio* ('Komm, Hoffnung').
175. Cf. the final movement of the C minor serenade K388. On the similar passage in *La finta giardiniera*, see p.337 above.
176. 'Sola, sola in buio loco', from bar 41.

affording further proof of the consistent way in which Mozart portrays his characters. But the radiance of D major is almost at once extinguished, as Donna Anna's cantilena, in keeping with her whole character, drifts more and more into high-flown passion (note the eloquent repeated melisma on 'sola'), ending in the most anguished chromatic lament in C minor. With this there begins the most idiosyncratic passage in the whole of this opening section, a passage almost frightening in its realism, as the comedy here is also tragic, and the tragic element borders on the grotesque. Elvira and Leporello return downstage, to the following orchestral motif that from now on becomes a recurrent feature of the andante:

With its sinuously descending chromatic line and convulsive rhythms,[177] it is remarkably ambiguous, oscillating, as it does, between tragedy and comedy. One after the other, it accompanies not only Elvira, whose fate now acquires a tragic aspect as she fears that she is about to lose the lover whom she thinks she has only just won back, but also Leporello who, more agitated than ever, again attempts to escape, before finally taking up his earlier unison motif, but now in a decidedly more timid version in the minor. The listener feels very clearly that things are building to a climax. On an outward level, this comes with the arrival of Zerlina and Masetto, which is followed in turn by the unmasking of Leporello. The music, too, now becomes more emotionally charged,[178] as everyone, apart from Elvira, demands vengeance on the traitor. To their amazement, Elvira intercedes on behalf of her lover: 'È mio marito! Pietà' ('He's my husband! Have mercy!'). It is with extreme fear that she utters these words, accompanied by the chromatic motif whose tragic tone is now underscored by the writing for the violas. With this outburst Donna Elvira attains to true grandeur as a tragic figure, with her whole passion for Don Giovanni – the very essence of her being – finding expression in these few brief phrases. The others are as surprised as they are affected by this, and the homophonic textures of the previous passage now give way to freer part-writing, initially involving imitative procedures, with the individual characters sharply differentiated, while the orchestra sticks unceasingly to the same motif as before. Only at the sudden *forte* that accompanies the entry of the full orchestra do the voices regroup as a solid mass, announcing their 'Morrà!' ('He shall die') with a blood-chilling unison leap of a seventh. More desperate than ever, Elvira repeats her appeal for mercy, but in vain. Only when Leporello himself raises his voice does the key of G minor – long prepared, but repeatedly delayed by a series of interrupted cadences – appear. And, like Elvira, he, too, reveals his innermost nature under the pressure of circumstances. The skills that Leporello has learnt from Don Giovanni are no longer equal to this onslaught and he throws aside his master's mask on both an outer and an inner level, standing before his persecutors as a pitiful wretch whining for his life to be spared. And he does so in a thoroughly grotesque manner, with his vocal line ('quasi piangendo' – 'as though weeping') sounding more like howling than singing. He becomes obsessed with certain phrases, each of which he repeats and ends with a sustained note. Yet everything is expressed with scrupulous detail: first the timid and whimpering plea for mercy set to the tonic and its chromatic auxiliaries, then the urgent admission 'quello io non sono' ('I'm

177.   It appears only in the strings in double octaves.
178.   The violin motif in the second bar is related to Elvira's motifs: see bar 7 of the sextet 'Sola, sola in buio loco'.

not who you think I am'), with its modulation to the dominant, and, finally and most importantly, 'viver lasciatemi per carità' ('Let me live for pity's sake'), rising convulsively to the subdominant (note the crescendo!) and reaching the sharply dissonant ninth, marked *piano*, before suddenly turning back on itself with an interval of a seventh and ending in a pitiful whine based on this same motif of a seventh. The cellos and double basses initially remain fixed, as though paralysed, on a series of long notes, while the violins double the voice in octaves,[179] and the same lachrymose chromatic motif trickles downwards five times in succession in double octaves in the winds, making our flesh creep.[180] Only at his final 'per carità' is Leporello robbed of his existing orchestral support, leaving the oboes alone – hitherto silent – to accompany his final plea. Above everything hovers the key of G minor, a key associated with anguish in Mozart's mind and here invested with a hint of irony. As with Elvira, so Leporello's outburst provokes a reaction in the other characters, except that on this occasion they appear as a self-contained group from the outset. Typically Mozartian is the *sotto voce* with which they express their general surprise: only the unexpected modulatory shift and the changed picture in the orchestra reveal the way in which the situation has altered. This *sotto voce* creates a more truthful and natural impression than any *forte* outcry of theatrical indignation. Not until two bars later does their anger at the way in which they have been deceived erupt in a sharply dotted rhythm. The effect is then repeated a whole tone higher, with the greater intensity on the second 'Leporello' being especially noteworthy. At the end of this section the chromatic motif returns, once again summing up the vacillating, tense situation in a highly poetical way. After all, everyone is afraid of some new and evil trick on Don Giovanni's part. The andante ends with an apprehensive question on the dominant of C minor.

The answer comes in the form of the monumental molto allegro, although it fails to lift the sense of emotional pressure. The source of the whole disturbance, Leporello, becomes less and less important in the eyes of the others, allowing their feelings of disenchantment and impotence in the face of this new and sinister trick on Don Giovanni's part to break through with all the greater intensity. In typically Mozartian manner, it finds expression in impulsive astonishment, followed, in turn, by impassioned anguish and silent grief, with the composer laying particular emphasis on the last of these, as is clear from the sustained passages in the vocal writing, notably the wonderful polyphonic section in the coda. Here the anguish acquires a transfigured tone, turning to profound grief at the tragedy of human destiny. Here Mozart avoids the noisy bustle suggested by the text and prefers to strike a note of the most profound interiority (*sotto voce* and *piano*!). In consequence, this section is no longer the uproarious ending that Italian practice would have demanded but is the climax of the whole sextet.

Yet even here the great realist in Mozart does not lose sight of the comic side of things. Indeed, he even underlines it by giving the lead to Leporello, who begins to sense that the wind is turning in his favour and, in spite of the fact that he still fears for his life, he now takes heart. The accompaniment shows clearly that he is slowly regaining his senses – as so often with his master, the flute doubles his vocal line. Indeed, he even manages to draw the others after him, as they echo his own motif in diminution,[181] for they, too, are initially overcome by feelings of boundless

179. The little ornament on the second phrase creates a particularly vivid impression.
180. The brief crescendo must not be overlooked here at bars 102, 104, 106, 108 and 110.
181. The diminution extends to the metric structure, with Leporello's five-bar period corresponding to the three-bar period of the others.

stupefaction. But their outburst disconcerts him, provoking a chattered ascent – marked crescendo – to *b* flat, again to a unison accompaniment. Now the vocal writing for the others acquires a darker colour, and at the words 'Che giornata' they are overwhelmed by the full force of their despair at once again being exposed to a sinister power. And once again we see its impact on Leporello, who, needless to say, has no idea what the others are feeling but simply hears in it a continuing threat to his own person. He, too, begins to feel uneasy, but in his own grotesque fashion, as is clear from his parlando on the two notes *a* and *b* flat to the accompaniment of concertante strings and winds, which seem to weigh so heavily on him. There follows the first of the *sotto voce* passages with descending scales in the violins, a curious mixture of grief and apprehension. From now on, Leporello withdraws increasingly into the background, while naturally retaining his independence and following the new developments, albeit in his own particular way. The others remain rooted to the chord of E flat major, as though transfixed, until it is followed completely unexpectedly by a chord of D flat major, marked *forte*, a sudden outburst of horror of shattering impact that musically and dramatically reflects the 'impensata novità' of the text. Even Leporello feels its impact and, as though shaken to the very roots of his being, he enters with his top *d'* flat a full beat after the others. At this point the ensemble breaks up into separate groups, within which the individual characters make their presence felt. In the case of Donna Anna, for example, her numbness melts into an extended coloratura outburst that sinks away, *piano*, in an expression of supreme anguish, before the other characters' feelings flare up again at the repeated 'mille torbidi pensieri'. This time it is Donna Elvira whose fiery temperament goes its own confused way. At this juncture the whole passage from Leporello's first parlando is repeated, followed by a large-scale coda, which is introduced by an interrupted cadence that increases the feeling of tension. Here Leporello is entirely swallowed up by the ensemble. By repeatedly introducing interpolations and thereby delaying the ending, the music raises the sense of anguish to a transfigured, mystical level, first at the passage where the cellos and double basses encircle the note *B* flat beneath a sustained *f''* in the upper voices. Here, in the extended cadence, with its strict and churchlike polyphony, there is even a religious feeling. With its disjointed crotchets and sharp accentuation of the word 'novità', the following section adds to the feeling of mystery, and it is immediately after this that the Sextet as a whole reaches its inner climax at the inspired *a cappella* passage in which the world of *opera buffa* lies far below us. Significantly, Leporello takes no part in this, reappearing only in the final section and thereby bringing this inspired sextet back to the point from which it set out.

In writing this sextet, Mozart turned an ordinary *opera buffa* joke into a psychological portrait that far transcends anything found in any of the comic or tragic operas of his time, touching, as it does, on the ultimate questions of human existence. And, once again, the manner of its execution is both musically and dramatically perfect. The allegro is a two-part section with a kind of introduction and a coda. Its atmospheric range is so wide that the repeated passages not only do not weaken the overall impression but are felt to be dramatically necessary. The grouping of the characters – Leporello against the others – is carried through with admirable symmetry, finding expression not only in the instrumentation but also in the harmonic writing. The ensemble never leaves the home key of E flat major,[182] whereas Leporello is always straining towards the dominant, without, however, being able to settle there for any length of time. In general, the sextet is clear proof of Mozart's ability to manage with a minimum of harmonic resources. Melody, rhythm,

---

182. The modulation to D flat major at bars 178 and 223 is only fleeting.

part-writing, orchestration and, last but not least, dynamics play a far greater role. That such an economical use of harmony is by no means a hard and fast rule with him is evident from the andante, with its far greater tendency to modulate to other keys. But here he is concerned to advance the plot, whereas the basic character of the allegro is lyrical, maintaining one and the self-same mood in countless different nuances. Occasional deviations on words such as 'novità' (see above) make the home key more, rather than less, effective.[183]

Leporello's aria ('Ah, pietà, signori miei') takes a stage further the situation depicted in the sextet, at least to the extent that the situation affects him personally. There is no longer any pressure on him, and so it is the mischievous, slippery trickster whom we see before us once again. Only at the beginning does his head still appear to throb, as the opening bars clearly hark back to his motif in the sextet. It is a genuine *opera buffa* aria in which he addresses each of the characters in turn and which requires a good deal of action on stage. It is binary in form, with the motifs appearing in no particular order, but with the mischievous theme in bars 8–13 playing the main part and finally helping Leporello to make good his escape. In general it contains some delightful individual episodes such as 'il padron con prepotenza l'innocenza mi rubò' ('My master bullied me into doing wrong'), with its defiant beginning and sanctimonious continuation. And the music always suits the character whom he is addressing. Only towards the end, when he comes to Don Ottavio, does it assume a mysterious aspect, from the grotesque canon between strings and winds onwards. We can almost literally see him slowly groping his way towards the door that will be his salvation and finally slipping through it.

By now even Don Ottavio has realized that his social equal, Don Giovanni, murdered the Commendatore, and so he decides on vengeance, an act for which he is uniquely suited both as a man and as a gentleman. That he intends to hand him over to the courts strikes us as cold-hearted, if not as downright comical. Don Giovanni has assailed the honour of his fiancée, while in the case of the Commendatore, he killed him in an open duel, rather than stabbing him insidiously in the back. According to his gentlemanly code of conduct, it is not the civil courts that should assume responsibility for his punishment, but the sword of the offended party. Of course, Don Ottavio is well aware – as the words of his aria make clear – that it is no less dangerous to hale Don Giovanni before a judge, so that we cannot accuse him of any lack of courage in taking this decision. Even so, it would have been far more natural if Da Ponte had abandoned the idea of the courts.

Don Ottavio has given exegetes a great deal of trouble.[184] That Da Ponte's characterization goes no further than that of a pallid adolescent is all too apparent. Even so, the shortcomings in his characterization are not so striking in act one. Although he is a very passive figure, he invariably behaves in an entirely noble and distinguished manner, eliciting our sympathy through the sincerity of his love of Donna Anna. That he does not attack Don Giovanni in the first-act finale is not so ridiculous, as at this stage he is still not convinced that Don Giovanni is guilty and so he has no reason to challenge him to a duel for his assault on a peasant girl.[185] In the second act, of

183. ◆ For a different reading of the sextet, see Platoff, 'Operatic Finales and the Problem of the *Don Giovanni* Sextet'.
184. Chrysander argues that Mozart's influence was as crucial here as it was with Donna Anna; see Chrysander, 'Die Oper Don Giovanni von Gazzaniga und von Mozart', 426. This is certainly plausible. But when he claims that Da Ponte turned Bertati's character into a weakling, he is certainly going too far. In Bertati, Ottavio is just as passive, albeit far more sketchy as a character. Among more recent writers, Max Kalbeck has sought to turn him into a more active figure, while Schurig sees him as a tragi-comic character; see Schurig, *Wolfgang Amade Mozart*, ii.134 and 144. Among earlier writers, see Oulibicheff, *Mozarts Opern*, iii.113–14; Lobe, *Fliegende Blätter für Musik*, i (1855), 221–2; and Jahn, *W. A. Mozart*, ii.445ff.
185. The idea of having him confront the hero with a pistol but of then failing to use it is not a happy one. Although it makes Don Ottavio more 'active' as a character, it places his courage in an unnecessarily poor light.

course, it is Don Ottavio, more than anyone else, who has to pay the price for the fact that, as we have already observed, the action grinds to a standstill. He becomes an increasingly pallid figure, a weak-willed lover whose function is to comfort Donna Anna and who forfeits our sympathies by deciding to act only when it is already far too late.

That Mozart failed to notice these shortcomings is out of the question. He, too, treats him as an adolescent, albeit after his own fashion. For Mozart, the basic motive for Don Ottavio's actions is love, as it is with Don Giovanni, but whereas in the case of the latter, love unleashes all his energies at their most intense, it reduces Don Ottavio to a state of utter paralysis. Apart from his love of Donna Anna, there is scarcely another thought in his mind, and the blows of fate that echo all around him barely reach his ear. Hence his characteristic lack of initiative. Whenever he is obliged to act, it is reason, not willpower, that motivates him. Nothing is more than a passing fancy that fails to engage his innermost being, and as always with such individuals, words – honestly and sincerely meant – have to take the place of actions. As such, Don Ottavio stands between Don Giovanni and Donna Anna, embodying a conscious irony on his creator's part that would have tempted many another composer to caricature him, however slightly. But here, as elsewhere, Mozart does not sit in judgement on his own creatures. Rather, he allows Don Ottavio to create an impression on the strength of his character and his relationship to his environment. He even gives him the noblest and warmest cantilenas of the whole opera, cantilenas that we need only compare with those of Don Giovanni to appreciate the differences between them as suitors. Yet Don Ottavio never grows sentimental in an effeminate way. What he feels is true, sincere, manly affection, and his weakness consists only in the fact that from his initial vow onwards he is so absorbed by this emotion that his strength of purpose and resolve simply atrophy. The only other quality that Da Ponte stresses is the importance that Ottavio attaches to the superficial aspects of gentlemanly behaviour. As such, he is nicely observed as a character, appearing in a particular light by dint of the fact that he stands alone in a world of wild passions. He is certainly not the embarrassing figure that so many inept performers make of him, but an organic part of the action, indissolubly linked with Donna Anna's fate as well as with that of Don Giovanni.

His aria ('Il mio tesoro intanto') is once again an accurate reflection of his character. As a result of the changed situation, it is now even more important that he should act, and he is fully conscious of the bitter struggle that lies ahead. But love is again uppermost in his mind,[186] and it is this that he expresses in the first section of his binary aria with very special inwardness and sweetness, but without any pathos (the performance marking is 'Andante grazioso'). The noble lyricism typical of his entire part reaches its high point here. Individual virtuoso features such as the sustained f'[187] and the various coloratura passages were clearly intended for the tenor Antonio Baglioni, but they are by no means unduly prominent, and the florid writing at the return from the heroic mood of the second section to the main theme is particularly finely expressed. Yet even this show of strength is typical of his character. The orchestra generates a great deal of energy, but the vocal writing itself remains remarkably irresolute and does not express the new feeling with anything like the same conviction as before. Earlier writers regarded this as a shortcoming,[188] but it is in fact admirably suited to our picture of Don Ottavio's character. And the same is true of the

---

186. The idea of having the hero entrust his lover to the care of his friends when obliged to leave her is a favourite of Metastasio.
187. Instead of sustaining the f', Rubini used to take his lead from the violins and produce a trill on a''. Whether this display of virtuosity is really what Mozart intended is an open question; see Jahn, *W. A. Mozart*, ii.451; and Schebest, *Aus dem Leben einer Künstlerin*, 203. ◆ Concerning the singer Rubini, see Gara, *Giovanni Battista Rubini nel centenario della morte*; Traini, *Il cigno di Romano: Giovanni Battista Rubini*; and Brewer, 'Rubini, the King of Tenors'.
188. See Jahn, *W. A. Mozart*, ii.451.

repeat of this passage, when a number individual details are changed in the interests of greater expressivity. Here the wide-ranging intervals in the vocal writing come close to the desperate, theatrical style of the Neapolitans. It is with all the greater truthfulness, then, that the postlude returns to the earlier and more tender mood.

In the graveyard scene ('O statua gentilissima'), Da Ponte returns to Bertati, even taking over individual turns of phrase. Don Giovanni's destiny has now reached its critical turning point, although not, as before, through an encounter with the temporal world, to which the demonic hero has always proved superior. Amatory escapades are now replaced by a new motif in the form of a crime committed against the dead.[189] But this will be seen as an inconsistency only by those who think of Don Giovanni solely in terms of his love affairs. In fact, his world is much more extensive than this: wherever the forces of sensuality stir, he feels that he is master. For this reason, the dead simply do not exist for him, as they are no longer a part of the world of the senses. He neither fears nor stands in awe of them, and even the graveyard is a place like any other, somewhere to engage in light-hearted, scintillating banter. It was an excellent idea on Da Ponte's part to introduce a new escapade here in the form of Don Giovanni's assault on the honour of Leporello's lover. It is at this point that the statue of the Commendatore suddenly starts to speak. Here the music immediately recalls the Oracle in Gluck's *Alceste* and thence Rameau – Gluckian features include the declamation on one note, the unusual orchestration and the singular note of pathos that it strikes. Yet here, too, Mozart retains his independence, which consists not only in the different time- and key-signature but, above all, in the inspired touch of melancholy that colours the words of the statue, their intransigence notwithstanding: note, for example, the chromatic line of the first bassoon in the second adagio. The harmonic writing, too, reflects this same underlying feeling, with the ghost beginning in the tragic key of D minor and ending in G minor.[190]

With this, a power enters Don Giovanni's life that is remote from his own world of the senses, a demon like Don Giovanni himself, but one not bound by human limitations and therefore superior to him from the outset. Many writers have commented that the ghost does not intervene as a messenger of any moral world order in the usual sense of that term, and it would be wrong to weaken the dramatic impact of the piece at its powerful final climax by introducing a moralizing element. Admittedly, there is a moral aspect to Don Giovanni's downfall, but only in the wider sense of an appraisal of reality. No final moral is proclaimed. Rather, the opera depicts a decisive struggle between two tremendous forces. We sense the ultimate link between the most passionate and turbulent human existence and the world as a whole, the identity of man and destiny.

The ghost's words instil a sense of superstitious fear in Leporello, whereas Don Giovanni, refusing to acknowledge the afterlife, thinks it is merely a joke on the part of some outsider and so he good-humouredly responds by inviting the statue to supper. In this way the ultimate catastrophe is introduced in an entirely *buffa* manner, and the irony is underlined by the fact that it is the terrified Leporello who has to issue the invitation. This is the starting point for their remarkable duet, a number striking not least for its key of E major and its searing intensity. For a Romantic composer, the sombre *genius loci* and the terrifying nature of the situation would no doubt have played an important role here. But it is precisely here that Mozart shows his greatest restraint, relegating these features to the extreme periphery. The stone statue has already revealed

189. Schnerich believes, quite rightly, that the sets for this scene were inspired by the Scaliger Tombs in Verona; see Schnerich, 'Wie sahen die ersten Vorstellungen von Mozarts Don Juan aus?', 107.
190. Eduard Mörike's wonderfully poetic account of this passage in *Mozart auf der Reise nach Prag* reads as follows: 'The sounds of silver trombones fall as if from distant stars, ice cold, cutting through the blue night and freezing the blood and marrow.'

his otherworldly nature sufficiently clearly, and in the finale he dominates the whole stage – here in the duet it is Leporello and Don Giovanni alone who are to hold the listener's attention. The opening suggests that Don Giovanni is right, after all, and that the statue is nothing more than an entertaining illusion. Leporello forces himself to adopt the tone of a majordomo, as he did with the three masked figures in the first-act finale. Yet there is something disturbing about the way in which he crumples up in terror in the fourth bar, going completely to pieces in the interval of a seventh in the consequent phrase:[191]

Don Giovanni barks at him impatiently, his servant's fears visibly adding to his sense of delight. Leporello begins again, this time in the more tension-laden key of B major, but his approach is far more timid than before, his terror all the greater. He then sees his master's flashing sword and, in mortal terror, summons up his last remaining strength to address the statue a third time, again to a unison passage in the strings. On this occasion his invitation creates a particularly tense and grotesque impression.[192] The cellos and basses fall silent, and a brief whispering motif rises up in

191. This interval also plays a major role in the sextet; see also the passage from Galuppi quoted on p.323 above.
192. Compare this with Pasquariello's authentically Italian invitation in Gazzaniga:

the violins over a pounding pedal point in the violas on the dominant of B major, then – with an eloquent syncopated shift – in the woodwind, too. Later the violins and winds are divided, with suspensions of quite unusual keenness. By now Leporello himself has lost all sense of dignity and he stammers out his invitation on two notes. When he thinks that he sees the statue nod, he feels an icy terror. With this interrupted cadence on G, the music suddenly leaves behind it the world of *opera buffa* and adopts a far more serious tone that clearly anticipates the second-act finale. At Don Giovanni's impetuous insistence, Leporello tells him what he has seen ('colla marmorea testa' and so on) and, unnerved by his terror, imitates the statue nodding. Don Giovanni then parodies him with the most cutting irony, after which his old resolve reasserts itself: whether he is dealing with a joke or with something more serious, he has to get to the bottom of it. Introduced by a sinister interrupted cadence on C major, his own invitation to the statue again leaves far behind it the world of *opera buffa*,[193] inspiring a note of strength that already looks forward to his later heroic encounter with the statue. This unexpected modulation creates a completely different mood. The titillating spirit of *opera buffa* appears to have fled,[194] and the statue, supported only by the two horns, answers the question, which culminates clearly on the dominant, with a 'Sì' on the tonic. This is all that Mozart considers necessary here to depict such an unprecedented moment: the statue is intended to create an impression first and foremost through its *voice*. But the horn call continues to reverberate like the voice of destiny, inviting the other winds to join in. The unexpected entry of the submediant, C, creates a totally different impression from eleven bars earlier by leaving the harmony completely vague but significantly adds to the sense of eeriness – even Don Giovanni finds it impossible to break away from his phrase as it writhes uncertainly to and fro. But the *buffa* element now slips back again, casting an oddly ambiguous light on all that follows. While Don Giovanni's thoughts are already directed towards the pleasures of the table and Leporello wants nothing more than to escape from this scene of horror, a remarkably agitated tingling and flickering rises up in the orchestra, its nervous intensity adding to the mood, which veers erratically between horror and madcap merriment, finally fading away in the dark as the two men disappear.[195] It is sufficient to compare Mozart's conception of this scene with that of Gazzaniga to appreciate its inspired nature. For Gazzaniga, the horror of the graveyard is merely a

193. At this point in Gazzaniga's opera we find a slow siciliana in D minor, to which the solo writing for the winds lends a highly picturesque character.
194. The dotted chords at Don Giovanni's question are also found in Gazzaniga, but the earlier composer weakens the impact of the Phrygian mode by adding a second question on the dominant and tonic.
195. A tone-painterly feature is the augmentation of the final motif in the violas, beginning in the third bar from the end. The semiquaver motion is also found in Gazzaniga's score at this point, but as a simple tremolando. The eerie passage at 'mover mi posso appena' is missing from Gazzaniga.

piquant device involving theatrical illusion, while for the later Romantics, these scenes reflected their attitude to nature, which was thus the focus of attention. For Mozart, the psychological element was foremost in importance, with the spirit world entering into it only to the extent that it is necessary to create this curious tingling sensation in the characters and kindle the audience's interest in the subsequent course of the action, without anticipating the display of superhuman power that it embodies. Formally, too, this duet is extremely remarkable, inasmuch as it follows the course of the action with total freedom, the only link being Leporello's motif of a falling seventh, which recurs on frequent occasions, always in a new guise. The harmonic writing, too, reflects this basic approach, with the bright glare of E, B and F sharp major only occasionally obscured by heavy, eerie shadows at the climaxes that look forward to the final conflict.

Dramaturgically speaking, the following scene for Donna Anna ('Crudele! Ah nò, mio bene – Non mi dir, bell'idol mio') is undoubtedly a weak point of the opera and was presumably inserted here in order to allow more time to change the sets for the final scene, which take up the whole depth of the stage. But Mozart made a virtue of this necessity by using this stopgap aria, immediately before Don Giovanni's downfall, to add the final touches to his portrayal of Donna Anna's character. In the process he also created a musically effective contrast not only with the previous scene but also with the one that follows. Don Ottavio, of course, remains more problematical than ever. Although his opening remarks show that he has indeed reported Don Giovanni to the authorities, his feelings and thoughts remain obsessed with his love of Donna Anna.[196]

The aria is introduced by an accompanied recitative that adopts the Italian practice[197] of anticipating the main motifs of the opening section of the aria. In terms of its form and treatment, too, especially its almost soloistic writing for the winds and its elaborate coloratura, it is much closer to the traditional Italian aria than all the opera's other arias, while still serving to characterize Donna Anna musically.[198] Ottavio's renewed courtship stirs a mood of affecting tenderness in her soul, providing a perfect solution to the difficult task of declaring her love for him and, at the same time, refusing him his ultimate desire. Even now she remains conscious of her duty towards her murdered father, but, as we have already seen, this feeling has gradually turned to sorrowful resignation, without losing any of its intensity. Here it comes into conflict with her affection for Don Ottavio and produces a division of loyalties in her soul that she gently suppresses. A woman like Donna Anna cannot divide her loyalties: she cannot give herself to her fiancé until her father's shadow has been avenged. This she announces to Don Ottavio with wonderful, authentically Mozartian tact that reveals both her fondness for him and the whole of her secret anguish. Even her main theme, with its leading note descending to the fifth and its octave motion in the second violins and violas, is touching in its interiority, without any trace of sentimentality. And it is altogether typical of Mozart's whole approach that the consequent phrase introduces entirely new material. Here, as she candidly confesses her love for him, the tone becomes markedly more intense with the insistent orchestral motif à la Paisiello[199] and the adoption of her melisma by the winds. The tender second subject in the clarinets also introduces her impassioned plea to Ottavio, its subsequent course revealing her inner distress in entirely modern terms:

---

196.   An earlier expedient was to cut Don Ottavio and have Donna Anna read out a letter from him instead, but this merely made the situation more obscure, without solving the basic problem; see Gugler, 'Zur Oper Don Juan: Controversfragen bezüglich der Darstellung auf der Bühne', 780–1. In his performing version of the work, Max Kalbeck has Don Ottavio report that he has challenged Don Giovanni to a duel. Kalbeck also provides a better motivation for Donna Anna's refusal to marry Don Ottavio without any further delay.

197.   See Abert, Nicolò Jommelli: Fetonte, 71ff.

198.   It is described as a rondo in the sense in which this term was used for many earlier arias; see above.

199.   A typically Mozartian feature, by contrast, is the fact that it begins on the fifth, rather than the third.

se di duol non vuoi ch'io mo - ra, non vuoi ch'io mo - ra

The repeat omits the second subject and also offers a much more compact version of the second section of the main theme, while adding considerably to its expressivity by means of modulatory procedures. There now begins the allegretto moderato, which should not be taken too quickly and which introduces a new emotion, albeit one well prepared for by the earlier section: the hope that heaven will take pity on her in her distress. Silently and secretly, her soul appears to begin to seethe with emotion: the way in which the string theme is taken up and developed by the winds is particularly expressive. Then the voice has a florid passage probably inspired by the soprano for whom the role was written but which should not be condemned simply because the present age is hostile to coloratura, as it undoubtedly serves to express the sense of hope that soars aloft on glittering wings, before gradually sinking back again. In much the same way, the constantly shifting harmonies, with their interrupted cadences and six-five chords, create a feeling of ethereal otherworldliness before finally reaching the six-four chord of F major and savouring it to the full. It is merely a question of how this passage is sung. Immediately afterwards, in the syncopated passage, Donna Anna's old resolve resurfaces, bringing the aria to an end after a brief moment of sorrowful trepidation. The aria has been much misunderstood, but it is a necessary part of Donna Anna's characterization.

The design of the second-act finale ('Già la mensa è preparata') reveals particular dramatic and poetic skill.[200] Once again we see Don Giovanni and his shadow Leporello surrounded by all the pleasures of earthly existence.[201] Right from the outset we are caught up in the whole festive atmosphere of an aristocratic banquet of the time, an atmosphere summed up here by the brilliant key of D major. Then the resident orchestra strikes up, as it always did on these occasions in

200. In Gazzaniga, this scene is much more loosely structured. It begins with a *secco* recitative, the first musical number being a concertino for the onstage band that opens in the style of a Viennese serenade:

The brief middle section features French-style oboe solos, with the bass line entrusted to the violins. In turn this is followed by an accompanied recitative, with the actual finale – a C major allegro non tanto in 3/4-time – not beginning until Don Giovanni's words 'Far devi un brindisi alla città'. There follows Pasquariello's toast to Venice (a common-time andante *sotto voce* in C major, with a solemn flourish in the horns), then his toast to the beautiful women of the city (an andantino in F major and in 6/8-time). At this point the stone guest is heard knocking, its arrival announced by the terrified Lanterna (a common-time andante in D major, followed by a common-time allegro in A). The entry of the statue is preceded by an accompanied recitative (a D minor largo, as in Mozart), its speech beginning in a solemn E flat major. Here, above all, we see the vast difference between the two composers. Although there is an increase in tempo, the statue's words lack any sense of weight or unity, being set, rather, to brief and commonplace passages of accompanied recitative. Don Giovanni descends into hell to a passage in E flat major headed 'Furia', after which the whole ensemble brings the opera to an end in the manner described above. This final section is a common-time allegro in G major.

201. In his fragmentary translation, Mozart speaks of beautiful young women accompanying the individual dances on stage, but there is nothing to substantiate this in the libretto or full score. At all events, they would be merely decorative and take no part in the meal itself. Significantly, Don Giovanni makes no mention of them, with the result that they have been omitted from recent productions. Only Emil Gerhäuser's Stuttgart production used the opportunity to introduce modern dances; see also Schnerich, 'Wie sahen die ersten Vorstellungen von Mozarts Don Juan aus?', 107.

Vienna. In this case it is a wind band, the sonorities of which are in themselves sufficient to create a comic impression. Here, too, we are dealing with a 'musical joke', albeit one of a far subtler kind, and it is easy to imagine that the idea for this Tafelmusik came to Mozart only during the rehearsals. The first two pieces that he introduces are relatively monotonous numbers from the two named operas, works which, for precisely that reason, were then enormously popular – Mozart knew his audience. Particularly amusing is the satire on their words, which are reinterpreted to refer to the present situation in all its materiality. When the voices occasionally double the melody, they sound to be making fun of the old parodies familiar to Mozart from his early sketchbook. But then the players regale us with the theme from *Le nozze di Figaro*. Here, too, the description of the young aristocrat Cherubino is delightfully transferred to Leporello as he gobbles his food and especially to praise of the excellent cook.

In this way the intervention of a supernatural power is preceded by a picture of an entirely ordinary day in the life of a member of the nobility, the main attractions of which – eating, drinking and music – are so compelling that Don Giovanni and his servant have long since forgotten the statue. The tone abruptly changes with Donna Elvira's entry. She has come, as she says, to give him 'one last proof' of her love, a task that he makes even more difficult for her than before as a result of his frivolous attitude. She intends to warn him against the consequences of his actions, consequences that she herself, being closest to him emotionally, foresees very clearly.[202] It is the old idea that we found in Molière: so much does she go in fear of her lover's life that she desires only one thing, to save him from damnation. The idea is as simple as it is beautiful, and we should be wary of seeing in her a Gretchen figure, a role that could hardly be further removed from Mozart's way of thinking.[203] With true psychological insight, therefore, he chose not to reduce her passion to lofty resignation but, conversely, to intensify it to the point where it acquires a hitherto unsuspected ardour – what a contrast to the way in which Donna Anna develops as a character. Her melodic line pours out in breathless haste, mostly in disjointed phrases that often sound like mere screams, her passion intensified by Don Giovanni's resistance. Nowhere else in the opera does her inner affinity with his elemental nature emerge as clearly as it does here. It is as though a part of his own being had risen up against him. But with him, too, the unexpected opposition causes him to summon up all his energies, with his superiority finding expression in icy contempt and only his equally disjointed phrases revealing that he, too, is in a state of great agitation. His contempt seems all the more appalling in that it never becomes offensive: even here he remains the true gentleman. His scorn culminates in the following theme, which, repeated several times, stands out from the full-toned harmonies of this section by dint of its bare two-part writing:

202. There is absolutely nothing in the text to support Schurig's suggestion that she would like to 'see him die in a state of grace'; see Schurig, *Wolfgang Amade Mozart*, ii.163.
203. See Cohen, *Die dramatische Idee in Mozarts Operntexten*, 89ff.

This comes close to the world of a popular street song.[204] It is also worth noting here that Don Giovanni makes no reference to anything that Donna Elvira has said. Instead, he begins by inviting her to dine with him, then drinks the health of women in general – this is all that remains of the usual toast. Musically speaking, this section is a brilliant example of Mozart's inspired freedom in his handling of formal questions. It develops directly out of the dramatic situation, while never doing less than full justice to the formal laws of musical structure. He achieves this through the meaningful, free repetition of individual motifs that he continues to develop in new ways. The orchestra, too, contributes to the sense of musical unity by developing a motif based on the following rhythm ♩ that assumes the greatest possible variety of melodic forms and complements the basic rhythm that generally strides along in the vocal lines in weighty equal crotchets. Throughout this whole section the declamation is syllabic, the only exceptions being Elvira's two melismas on the words 'pietate' and 'cangi', in which all her feelings are focused to tremendous effect, and Leporello's dull mutterings ('Se non si muore') – as before, he feels genuine pity for Donna Elvira. A final unifying element is the harmonic structure, which never ventures beyond the two dominants in the whole of this wildly agitated passage. Only at Elvira's final scream are the harmonic foundations of this section suddenly undermined. Within these narrow confines, certain individual features create a correspondingly powerful impression, notably the tremendous upward surge in the basses right at the beginning, followed by a pedal point and the decisive shift to the dominant at Elvira's melisma. Her first breathless speech has a psychological subtlety and intensity to it that are uniquely well observed. Even the entry of the full orchestra (but without the trumpets and timpani heard in the finale's festive opening bars) is strikingly effective following the music for the onstage wind band. The dynamics, too, are remarkable, with the whole section abounding in sudden changes from *forte* to *piano*, as well as sforzatos and brief crescendos ending in a *piano*. This is genuine Mozart, speaking the language of passion based on the Mannheim school. Only once is there a crescendo that adds significantly to the sense of tension, at the terrifying moment when Elvira hurls out her eleven-bar accusation of Don Giovanni on the notes f'' and f', while he high-spiritedly continues his praise of women. Here the conflict builds to a terrible climax, with the whole orchestra in a state of wild agitation, so that the cynical contempt of the following passage (see above) is all the more searing in its impact. Even Leporello finds this attitude too much to take. His sympathy for Elvira increases, and the quaver writing for him

204. Consciously or unconsciously Mozart falls back on an old folktune here. Dreyßer's *Dantzbüchlein* of 1720 includes the following dance on p.14:

The opening phrase was popular from an even earlier period, occurring, for example, in the sixteenth century in the following example from Johann Hermann Schein:

following the return of the opening section shows clearly the impression that this tremendous figure of fate has made on him.

At Elvira's scream the picture changes, and the orchestra, in a state of extreme agitation, ascends chromatically to a diminished chord on B which, both in itself and through the syncopations bound up with it, clearly looks forward to the ghostly music that is to follow. The entire passage is repeated a whole tone higher, leading us to the very gates of D minor, with its associations with fate. But the time has not yet come for this and, as a master of contrast, Mozart interpolates a comic scene for Leporello between these two decisive sections.[205] With its pounding pedal point, trembling violins and chromatic sixths in the accompanying winds, this F major section strikes a different note from its predecessor, while adding to the sense of agitation by presenting tragedy in a comic form. And how differently Leporello now expresses his fear when compared with the sextet, for example. Terror has totally paralysed his otherwise glib tongue, allowing Don Giovanni's forceful interjections to emerge all the more keenly against the background of his terrified stammering. We hear the stone guest pounding on the door, each beat interrupted by a shudder on Leporello's part, after which Don Giovanni seizes the initiative to a darker unison in which he seems for the first time to recall his invitation, while Leporello crawls under the table to the selfsame melody.

This masterly introduction takes the listener from the noisy bustle of everyday life through the highs and lows of human passion and, finally, to the very gates of eternity. At this point the stone guest enters to strains of shattering impact.[206] The power that he symbolizes is far removed from the world inhabited by Don Giovanni: it knows no earthly passions, neither anger, nor pity, nor love. The elemental life force that has allowed Don Giovanni to triumph in the past is powerless in the face of his present adversary, so that the outcome of the battle between these two demonic figures is obvious from the outset. In spite of this, Don Giovanni rises to his full tragic stature as a result of the way in which he invests every last ounce of his personality with an energy that takes him to the very limits of his resources. Even at the moment of his downfall he acquires a superhuman dimension, and we are shaken by the power and awesome nature of the event as such, without needing to see in it a pointer to divine justice.

We mentioned the general character of this music when discussing the overture. The emotional weight of the Commendatore's music, with its powerful rhythms and a melodic line that alternates between a single reiterated note and wide-ranging intervals, is entirely Gluckian in spirit, a spirit that Mozart had already evoked in his music to *König Thamos*. It is permanently supported not only by a weighty rhythm ♩ ♪♩. ♪│♩. , that is heard now in the orchestra, now in the bass line alone, but also by the accompaniment for the full orchestra that falls silent for only brief stretches, before reentering with redoubled force, notably at the words 'Non si pasce di cibo mortale' ('Those

205. It had also introduced the Commendatore's death scene at the beginning of act one.
206. The entry of the trombones remains a problem. They do not appear in the autograph score, although this in itself is no argument against their authenticity, as the brass were often notated on separate sheets of paper in early scores. In the present case no such sheet has survived, either for the trombones or for trumpets and timpani. Julius Rietz reports that he saw such a sheet in Mozart's hand in 1834 and 1836 in André's possession; by 1865, by which date the score had passed into the ownership of Pauline Viardot, the sheet was missing; see *AmZ*, new series, ii (1867). The Prague copy formerly owned by Luigi Bassi included trombones. Bernhard Gugler has tried to show that they may have been added for the Viennese production, not by Mozart but by Süßmayr, whose handwriting, as we know, was so very similar to Mozart's; see his 'Sind im 2. Finale des Don Juan die Posaunen von Mozart?', 59. This suggestion was refuted by Jahn, 'Mozarts Handschrift', 155. It is scarcely conceivable that Süßmayr's addition would later have been entered into the original score. Among more recent writers, Hans Merian supports Gugler's hypothesis, but without giving any reasons for doing so; see Merian, *Mozarts Meisteropern*, 212. Jahn argues that the trombones are authentic; see *W. A. Mozart*, ii.418, while Schurig avoids the question, as does Egon Komorzynski, who simply assumes that they are authentic; see Komorzynski, *Mozarts Kunst der Instrumentation*, 38.

who have tasted the food of heaven do not eat the food of mortals'), with its strange and austere unison, and, later, at 'Dammi la mano in pegno' ('Give me your hand on it!'), the mysterious G minor chord which suddenly flares up in the wildest *fortissimo*. At the same time, the orchestral writing is full of the subtlest nuances: the scales that trickle up and down are already familiar to us from the Overture, but only now, at the words 'Altre cure più gravi' ('Other, weightier concerns'), do they reveal their full expressive force and, supported by unusual, urgent harmonies, allow listeners to sense all the horrors of eternity.

Don Giovanni's part is in the starkest possible contrast with this. His stunned surprise at his eerie visitor, whom he had earlier dismissed as an illusion and then completely forgotten, is clearly reflected in the syncopations and whispered figure in the second violins, soon affecting the trembling Leporello, whose sense of terror is even greater. But by his second rejoinder, their paths have begun to diverge: while Don Giovanni, with somewhat desperate resolve, asks the statue what he wants, Leporello's teeth start to chatter in the triplets of his vocal line. The role played by this whining everyman in this life-and-death struggle is arguably the *ne plus ultra* of Mozart's art of combining tragedy and comedy, with its profoundly terrifying way of presenting tragedy in comic form. Leporello prattles away, interrupting not only his master, but also the ghost. Meanwhile the Commendatore grows more and more insistent, and in a powerful vocal line that ascends chromatically over the boldest sequence of harmonies, he seems to grow in size, assuming gigantic dimensions, while Don Giovanni shudders once more,[207] before immediately regaining his composure and rising to his full stature. The Commendatore intones the words 'Risolvi! Verrai?' ('Decide! Will you come?') to a series of terrifying intervals,[208] Leporello interjects with his indescribable

Di - te di nò, di - te di nò!

and Don Giovanni announces his decision to the accompaniment of a remarkably strict and dotted orchestral passage. Here, in all its force, we see a side of Don Giovanni that is generally overlooked by commentators who see in him only the seducer of young women: here, rather, is the heroic embodiment of the most unbridled life force, a man who prefers self-annihilation to the voluntary abandonment of even the tiniest part of that power. This decision is followed by the Più stretto, for which Mozart holds in reserve his strongest trumps. Here his treatment differs perceptibly, with question and answer following each other in brief phrases and finally in only wild outbursts. The dotted rhythm continues to echo in the vocal writing not only of the Commendatore but also of Don Giovanni who, after suppressing another brief shudder, summons up every ounce of his strength and comes close to the world of expression inhabited by his superhuman adversary. As a result the contest between these two forces acquires a transcendental dimension. What happens here is far more than the punishment of a crime, it is the acting out of an elemental destiny that overwhelms us with the violence of a thunderstorm. The accompaniment here is provided by timpani rolls and terrifying crashes in the winds over a string

207. At this point, the Italian text contains a remnant of earlier versions of the legend in which the stone guest invited Don Giovanni back to his mausoleum, where his fate finally caught up with him. But this is contradicted by Da Ponte's account, according to which Don Giovanni is dragged down to hell in his own house, immediately after the Commendatore has left.
208. In all seriousness, a number of writers have supported Meyerbeer's suggestion, first put forward in 1822, that the Commendatore should be played by an actor, while the part is sung through an offstage megaphone; see *AmZ*, xxiv (1822), 230–1.

tremolando, while powerful scales surge incessantly upwards in the cellos and double basses. Although these scales initially recall the analogous passage in the duel in the opening act,[209] they differ from it quite radically not only as a result of the absence of any imitative procedures but also

by dint of the presence of the following characteristic interval of a seventh

so that it would be wrong to think of an intentional reminiscence. Here, too, we find the starkest dynamic contrasts, without a single crescendo. Only the interplay between *forte* and *piano* becomes more frequent in the course of this section. Shortly before the moment of decision, a terrified Leporello once again interjects his 'Sì! sì!', immediately followed by the two powerful crashes of Don Giovanni's last 'No!', which gives way in turn to the statue's eerie *pianissimo* unison passage before it disappears. Here the conflict reaches its ultimate, supreme climax. In the allegro we can already hear the voice of hell itself, embodied by a unison male-voice chorus in the manner of Gluck. In the cellos and double basses the statue's dotted rhythm continues for a time to reverberate, but then the orchestra devotes itself entirely to describing the upheaval taking place in nature with its fiery figures and tugging syncopations. The fact that nature raises its voice here signifies far more than a mere increase in tension but adds something approaching a mythic element to the finale, so that it is with a real sense of horror that we become aware of the oneness of fate, nature and man. Following Don Giovanni's disappearance, the storm abates in a wonderful plagal cadence, its fury continuing to echo in the chromatic writing for the inner voices. A powerful crescendo then leads to the chord of D major that creates an incomparable impression here, not – of course – in the sense of a happy ending, but implying cold, implacable majesty.[210]

Even today this section of the finale continues to be regarded as one of the unsurpassed high points of music drama in general. Jahn's description of it is both apt and beautiful: 'The mood of the sublime and of the supernatural to which we submit unconditionally here is maintained so unshakeably throughout this relatively lengthy scene that the listener is carried along in Mozart's powerful grip, soaring above the abyss in breathless suspense but with no sense of dizziness.'[211] It is necessary only to ensure that the shattering impact of the music is not weakened by all manner of spectacular stage effects such as fireworks, hellish masks, conflagrations and collapsing buildings. In Prague such effects were ruled out by the theatre's modest technical resources,[212] but it was not long before directors seized upon this 'grateful' scene and brought in their big guns in the form of every conceivable kind of crude effect borrowed from the popular plays of the period.[213] Later, the stage machinery associated with Romantic operas was brought into play, allowing Don Giovanni's house to collapse in ruins, reintroducing an equestrian statue into the graveyard scene and so on.

The way in which this scene is staged is bound up, in part, with our attitude to the finale's final sections, which were soon felt to be an anticlimax after the scene with the Commendatore. The original score includes an attempt to solve this problem by cutting the larghetto, in which the

209. See Bulthaupt, *Dramaturgie der Oper*, 178.
210. This point is well made by Heuß, 'Das dämonische Element in Mozarts Werken', 180. This majestic character is produced by the almost exclusive use of minor tonalities.
211. Jahn, *W. A. Mozart*, ii.461.
212. See Schnerich, 'Wie sahen die ersten Vorstellungen von Mozarts Don Juan aus?', 101–8, esp. 107.
213. Panic broke out at a performance in Berne in 1810, when the six devils engaged for the occasion were joined by a self-appointed seventh and two of them came to grief; see Kretzschmar, 'Mozart in der Geschichte der Oper', ii.272.

relationships between the individual characters are resolved.[214] In other words, Mozart clearly toyed with the idea of at least shortening this scene while still in Prague. In Vienna he wanted Don Giovanni's pursuers to appear on stage at the last moment and cry out in horror on the D major chord. But this, too, he abandoned, and we do not know if the idea was ever carried out.[215] But both in Vienna and, for the most part, elsewhere, the opera now ended with Don Giovanni's descent into hell, the chief exception being Dresden, where the complete ending was still being performed as late as 1836.[216] The Romantic period also witnessed a number of highly unfortunate attempts to change the ending. At the Paris performances Don Giovanni's descent into hell was followed by the spectacle of Donna Anna's coffin surrounded by a group of mourners to the strains of the 'Dies irae' from the composer's *Requiem*.[217] Then Bernhard Gugler suggested that the scene should change to the Commendatore's chapel and that the 'Lux perpetua' from the same work be sung at his obsequies. (In this case, the words 'Lux perpetua luceat eis' would have to be changed to 'ei', 'as only one person is involved'.) The 'Hosanna' would then make a 'suitable' ending.[218] Most recently, Arthur Schurig[219] has suggested that, following the disappearance of the Commendatore, Don Giovanni and Leporello should rush to the graveyard to see whether the statue is still standing on its pedestal. They find it fantastically illuminated. From the vault comes the sound of sacred singing. Tormented by an inner fire, Don Giovanni finally dies, 'unrepentant', praising his paradise – love – while Leporello 'sinks to his knees in prayer', day breaks and the chanting is heard anew. It is impossible to demand more than this by way of modern 'atmosphere'. But it remains unclear what music Schurig has in mind here.

This catalogue of the sins committed against the ending of the opera may suffice to demonstrate that we moderns have no reason to be particularly proud of our sense of style. We have no right to distort Mozart's masterpiece by grafting a colourful ending on to it, whether that ending be Meyerbeerian or in keeping with the most modern tastes. There can really only be two alternatives: either the original ending in its entirety or bringing down the curtain with Don Giovanni's descent into hell. Dramatically speaking, it is difficult to object to this second alternative, as we already know all that we need to know about the fate of the remaining characters, and the opera now ends at its high point. But in this way it is tragedy, in its most extreme form, that has the last word. The most recent adaptations, by contrast, reflect our age's historicist and stylistic concerns and revert to the complete ending, thereby emphasizing the *opera buffa* aspect of the work. This is prompted by the undoubtedly correct feeling that, following the horrors of the previous night-piece, the opera should end on a note of reassurance. But such an ending can be justified only if it brings the whole opera to an organic conclusion. In this we are helped neither by 'historical accuracy', which in the present instance would ultimately lead only to the world of the circus, nor by the style of an Italian *opera buffa*, which would reduce Mozart's whole conception to the level of the Italian composers he had already left behind him. In fact we need none of these outside expedients to

---

214. Reproduced on p.368 of the complete edition; Gugler thinks that it was Süßmayr who was responsible for this cut; see Gugler, 'Zweifelhafte Stellen im Manuscripte der Don Juan-Partitur', 93–4. Jahn rightly refutes this view in 'Mozarts Handschrift', 155. See also Freisauff, *Mozarts Don Juan 1787 bis 1887*, 67.

215. In his critical commentary, Rietz wonders whether the final scene was omitted in Prague, as the Commendatore and Masetto were played by the same singer and there was no time for him to change costume, unless – that is – another singer stood in for him.

216. Karl Engel, *Die Don Juan-Sage auf der Bühne*, 114.

217. Castil-Blaze, *Molière musicien*, i.338.

218. *Argo* (1854), i.365–6; Oulibicheff, *Mozart* (revised Ludwig Gantter), iii.361; Viol, too, is in favour of this same scene of mourning, but with Mozart's original ending; see his *Don Juan*, 25–6.

219. Schurig, *Wolfgang Amade Mozart*, ii.167.

justify this ending as long as we do not lose sight of Mozart's own conception of his material. What happens in these three sections? Following Don Giovanni's descent into hell, all his victims reappear and describe the impression that his death has had on them. Each of them then draws practical conclusions for his or her own future. The only feeling that remains is their moral satisfaction at the ultimate victory of good over evil. Da Ponte certainly took very seriously this scene in which, as we have seen, the everyday world sits in judgement on the exceptional. But if Mozart allows the familiar everyday sun to shine again following the night-time battle between two demonic figures, he does so with the irony typical of his whole approach to drama. This is most obvious from the two most antithetical male characters, Leporello and Don Ottavio. Leporello, whom these tremendous events have passed by without their taking the slightest notice of him, is allowed to report on them in his own way – and not without pride: he, the arch-philistine, tells the world about his wholly exceptional master. Ottavio then follows up this report with more of his love-sick melodies, as though nothing untoward has happened, then has to agree to a further year's delay before he can marry Donna Anna. But this does not mean that all the characters are suddenly reduced to the same level, for it is clear, not least from Donna Anna, that they continue to occupy different dramatic planes. None the less, the basic feeling remains the same, merely expressing itself in different ways. In the religious tone of the Presto section at the end we even find something approaching a celebration of everyday life, causing hearts to beat faster at the thought of divine retribution. Here, too, Mozart looks down on his own creatures with an ironic smile. He feels their prejudices, which he depicts from a higher, more exalted standpoint.

If interpreted in this way, these three final sections soon lose the character of mere appendages but bring the opera to an organic ending that is entirely Mozartian in spirit. Even the oft-heard reproach that they represent a falling off in musical quality when compared with what has gone before now becomes untenable. The world in which we find ourselves here could never sustain the sort of imaginative outpouring that we found in the previous scene, with its otherworldly dimension. Mozart certainly did not miss the opportunity to write an effective ending, but the present one differs from the usual high-spirited Italian finales by emerging in a wholly idiosyncratic way from within the opera's overall framework.

These three sections are clearly interrelated, with the first and third devoted mainly to the whole ensemble, while the second concentrates on them as soloists. Essentially, this reflects the principle of the French vaudeville, except that the three sections are completely independent. The first is in G major, thereby picking up the preceding plagal cadence, and is fresh-toned and lively in character, its somewhat conventional beginning gradually striking a more individual note, first with Leporello's narration, in which we can still hear an echo of the preceding catastrophe and all its terrors, and, above all, in the impression that this account leaves on the other characters: they are all evidently overcome by horror in the last eleven bars. The following Larghetto is bewitching in its loveliness. It begins by bringing Donna Anna and Don Ottavio to the fore, but the ironical way in which the latter's happiness is once again postponed for a year is further underlined by the fact that immediately afterwards, with Donna Elvira's entry, the tone becomes increasingly reminiscent of an *opera buffa*. By the time that we reach the words 'Resti dunque quel birbon con Proserpina e Pluton' ('Then let the scoundrel stay with Proserpine and Pluto') it has even acquired a note of parody. Note, finally, the delightful way in which the three representatives of the lower orders strike a contentedly folklike tone in announcing the 'antichissima canzon'.[220]

---

220. ◆ Further concerning 'ending' conventions in eighteenth-century opera, and in Mozart in particular, see Allanbrook, 'Mozart's happy endings: A new look at the "convention" of the "lieto fine"'.

When it comes to performing this, of course, the two female members of the aristocracy take the words out of their inferiors' mouths. Mozart did not want to end his work on the *buffa*-like note associated with Italian opera, with the performers stepping down to the footlights and removing their masks with a smile. Instead, he gives Don Giovanni's adversaries their dramatic due in an entirely typical section of impetuous, fiery resolve that grips the listener at once. Even the aforementioned echo of the more austere style associated with sacred music is taken no further than was demanded by his basic approach to the scene as a whole.[221]

Of the numbers that were subsequently written for Vienna,[222] Don Ottavio's aria ('Dalla sua pace') is dramatically weak.[223] Not only does it contradict the preceding recitative, in which Don Ottavio speaks of his duty to avenge the Commendatore's murder, it is also out of place in the wake of the profound emotional shock suffered by Donna Anna. Although this tender outpouring of affection is entirely typical of Don Ottavio, it was not at all like Mozart to insert such features into the drama in such a primitive manner, without reference to the situation. Evidently there were certain constraints on him when he adapted the work for Vienna, although it remains unclear how much he was influenced by consideration for the singer or for Viennese audiences' predilection for languishing lovers. But if we ignore this basic shortcoming, the aria is one of Mozart's most beautiful love songs, transfiguring the sentimental Italian type of aria, while avoiding any false sentimentality. Binary form is handled with typical Mozartian freedom. The first section uses the whole text, treating the authentically Italian G minor passage, with the 'sospiri' in the winds, as the second and more intense section, before leading back to the beginning by means of an inspired modulation via B minor. The second section no longer refers back to the 'sospiri', but develops the main idea by expanding it along highly poetical lines. Particularly beautiful, finally, is the little coda, in which the voice suddenly doubles the bass line.

The situation is no better when we turn to the second of the changes made for Vienna, the duet for Leporello and Zerlina ('Per queste tue manine') and Elvira's well-known aria ('Mi tradì quell'alma ingrata'), which together replaced Don Ottavio's aria ('Il mio tesoro intanto'). The duet is not only out of place dramatically, but is also deeply insignificant from a purely musical point of view, with not a single element in it that might make one think of Mozart. Elvira's aria, by contrast, is admittedly a stopgap that makes sense only in the context of the interpolation as a whole,[224] but at least it has a certain musical charm to it, even if it is difficult to square with Elvira's character in general. Of course, her change from her earlier impassioned desire to win back her lover to pity for the man she has lost can be justified psychologically, but the result does not correspond to the

---

221. The final section of the quartet from *Die Entführung aus dem Serail* is elaborated along similar lines, the similarities extending even to the accompanying figures and scales in the violins. The sustained chord on the word 'morte' and the pedal point on 'sempre ugual' are likewise reminiscent of the whole style of church music.

222. ◆ *Don Giovanni* was first given in Vienna at the Burgtheater on 7 May 1788.

223. Vincent's suggestion that the aria (minus its recitative) be interpolated before the quartet in act one has been accepted by Wolzogen, Grandaur and Kalbeck, without, however, solving the basic problem. The only solution is to relegate the aria to the concert hall. The AMA adopts an inconsistent approach here, including both this and Donna Elvira's aria in the main body of the text, rather than relegating them to the appendix, together with the duet 'Per queste tue manine'. ◆ K[6] similarly conflates the two versions of the opera – a curious state of affairs considering that it makes a distinction between the 'original' version of *Le nozze di Figaro* and its later version (cf. K577 and 579). Possibly this reflects *Don Giovanni*'s prestige, as if every number of the work were 'sacred'. Or it may be that both the AMA and K[6] privilege Vienna over all other performing venues. Regardless, the different treatment of the operas reflects an inconsistency with respect to the concept of a 'definitive' version while at the same time promoting the idea that Mozart's works are, somehow, unitary – a dubious suggestion at best. The NMA correctly gives the additional Viennese numbers for *Don Giovanni* in an appendix.

224. Elvira has now learnt of Don Giovanni's latest outrage. If the whole scene is omitted, as it should be, the aria is left hanging in mid-air. It makes no sense as a response to Ottavio's aria, while Rochlitz's suggestion that it be sung after Leporello's 'catalogue aria' in act one is particularly unfortunate. Equally impossible is Schurig's suggestion that it follow Donna Anna's final aria; see Schurig, *Wolfgang Amade Mozart*, ii.155. There is no alternative, then, but to relegate it, too, to the concert hall.

real Elvira who, in typically Mozartian fashion, would have expressed this struggle in all its antitheses, reliving every moment of it with the ardour that is uniquely hers, rather than remaining content with this remarkably calm admission of her mental anguish. Only the recitative refers to this inner conflict. Indeed, the gradual change from violent passion to silent grief[225] that the main motif undergoes in the course of the recitative is a particularly fine example of Mozart's skill at accompagnato writing. The aria itself is a fully developed rondo, but the opportunity for contrast that it would have offered is not exploited at all. Quite the opposite: the aria acquires its remarkable unity by dint of the fact that the main motif is constantly repeated, while the perpetual quaver motion lends it its peculiar stamp, producing a constant flood of emotion, without any real goal and with no sense of any contrast. The chief feature of all these interpolated pieces – their indebtedness to existing types – applies to this aria, too, with even the principal motif being familiar to the Italians. The solo nature of the accompaniment is unique in *Don Giovanni* and already looks forward to *Così fan tutte*.

Like those of *Le nozze di Figaro*, the *secco* recitatives are entirely *buffa* in character and as a result have the same principal features. Some of these features are, in fact, more developed than in the earlier work, notably the use of a final rising third in the melodic line in order to indicate a question (the simplest case) or the use of the chord of the second or, finally, an interrupted cadence with a freely entering bass.[226] A new feature – and a highly effective one, too, in terms of its ability to generate tension – is found at the end of some of the recitatives, which reach the tonic not through the typical interval of a fifth in the bass, but stepwise, from the supertonic (the tenor clausula of the older theorists). It is in this way that Zerlina introduces her first aria and Donna Elvira the sextet. In general, the harmonic writing in the *secco* recitatives, in keeping with the nature of the drama, is more characterful and austere in *Don Giovanni* than it was in *Le nozze di Figaro*. The Gluckian style of declamation involving a sequentially rising melodic line over chromatically ascending basses in passages of growing excitement is found more frequently here and is also used in an almost comic way, notably at the beginning of act two, scene nine, where, one after the other, the characters all turn on poor Leporello. But in cases such as these Mozart is also fond of using chords of the second together with their resolution, often writing several of them in a row. A typical example of his harmonic writing in passages of heightened emotion is Elvira's impassioned speech following her opening aria, 'Cosa puoi dire dopo azion sì nera?' ('What can you say after such vile actions?'), as far as the Phrygian close.[227] A similar device is found in the brief recitative before Ottavio's interpolated aria, where the thought of the 'nero delitto' ('black crime') produces the chord of the diminished seventh that is otherwise only rarely encountered. Ottavio's B flat minor aria is similarly preceded by a recitative in which the harmonic writing is remarkably emotionally charged. A final example occurs before the quartet ('Non ti fidar, o misera'), when Don Giovanni, pulling himself together, approaches Donna Anna to assure her of his friendship and moves further and further down into flat tonalities, until Donna Elvira peremptorily cuts him off:[228] this, too, is highly effective and undoubtedly intentional.

The calm of the cellos and double basses is often disturbed by brief animated motifs, although these are not found over such long stretches as they are in *Le nozze di Figaro*. A few of them serve

---

225. The nucleus of this already lies in the motif itself, with its heroic opening and remarkably questioning ending.
226. The 'Phrygian question' is found only once in *Don Giovanni*, significantly on Donna Elvira's lips in act one, scene five (at 'che t'amai cotanto', bar 24), where it accompanies not a question but a reproach.
227. Recitative following 'Ah chi mi dice mai', bars 10–18.
228. Act one, scene twelve (bars 1–2).

to intensity the *Affekt,* but most of them signify a musical gesture[229] or prepare the way for a particular procedure.[230]

All these examples prove that, even within the limits imposed by the *secco* style, Mozart was at pains to distinguish between the individual characters. Typical of this endeavour is the dialogue between master and servant in the graveyard. It bubbles along (semiquavers predominate), with one speech following another like balls tossed to and fro, calling for lively gestures. Only occasionally do we find more intense emotions, and here they are tinged with irony, as at Don Giovanni's 'Leporello, mio caro'. Don Giovanni has his own particular way of declaiming his music and it marks him off from the others even in the *secco* recitatives. Here, too, he is always superior, whether revealing his domineering nature or displaying his boisterous capriciousness. The tendency in *secco* recitative to set syntactically important words to the notes of the underlying chord is particularly marked in his case, as is clear from the opening of the scene under discussion:

This simple, almost fanfare-like melody is typical of Don Giovanni and on one occasion – in act one, scene fifteen [the recitative preceding 'Finch' han dal vino'] – it is even parodied by Leporello to particularly delightful effect:

229. 'Madamina, il catalogo è questo', bars 51–61 (the unrolling of the catalogue); and act two, scene 3, recitative bars 29–30 (preparing for the serenade).
230. Act two, scene eleven, bar 71 (before Leporello reads the inscription on the plinth).

Rhythmically, too, Don Giovanni's speeches are especially forceful and resolute, with dactyls and anapaests predominating. By repeating his line a whole tone higher while beating Masetto [in the recitative succeeding 'Metà di voi qua vadano' in act two], Mozart creates a particularly graphic effect:

In contrast, Leporello's melodic line is far less wide-ranging, except when he feels that he is master of the situation and attempts to mimic Don Giovanni.[231] Rhythmically, too, his part has a restless, prattling quality to it, with a tendency to move in semiquavers. Only once, when he has to read the inscription, does his vocal writing become emotionally charged. Of the female characters, Donna Elvira is the most clearly characterized in the *secco* recitatives. The harmonic writing corresponds to the melodic writing, which is in complete contrast to Don Giovanni's lapidary style, bearing, as it does, a far more complex and tortuous stamp. Take the beginning of act one, scene twelve [preceding the quartet 'Non ti fidar, o misera'] with its interval and fermata:

In act two, scene three [preceding Don Giovanni's serenade, 'Deh vieni alla finestra'], Elvira even has a brief sighlike suspension on the words 'mio tesoro'.[232] Her impassioned temperament also finds expression in her agitated rhythms, which assume the most varied forms. Donna Anna's contribution to the *secco* recitatives is much smaller as she prefers *recitativo accompagnato* and fuller musical forms, whereas Don Ottavio's loving nature emerges very clearly from the *secco* recitatives. In much the same way, Zerlina's *naïveté* palpably sets her apart from the treatment accorded to Don Giovanni as well as to Masetto.

These sections thus contribute to the opera's overall unity, although, as always, this presupposes that the performers have not only assimilated their roles but are consummate actors. Obviously, *secco* recitative, as a true product of Italy, can never be as successful when sung in German, but, given the right training, significantly more can be achieved than is offered by the average modern German theatre. The once popular substitution of the *secco* sections by spoken dialogue is an unsubtle cure and has rightly been almost universally abandoned in recent times.

That Mozart could, within a year, create two masterpieces which, although sprung from the same historical foundations, are as radically different in terms of their content and aims as *Le nozze di Figaro* and *Don Giovanni* is one of the most brilliant proofs of the universality of his genius. In spite of its passing shadows, *Le nozze di Figaro* presents an essentially bright and hedonistic picture of a world still lit by the gleam of a moribund aristocracy. At the same time, it brings to an end a very particular phase in Mozart's inner and outer development that had found its purest expression in his keyboard concertos. *Don Giovanni*, by contrast, was preceded by works such as the great string quartets, in which the focus of Mozart's interest shifted from the

---

231. This is especially true when he addresses Donna Elvira before his 'catalogue aria'.
232. Bar 17.

audience to himself as a creative artist, and his artistic bond with the outside world grew more and more tenuous. Although he continued to work to commission, he tended increasingly to listen to his own inner voice when carrying out those commissions. This was also the period when his health began to fail him and he withdrew into himself and brooded on all manner of problems. Recent writers have quite rightly drawn attention to the links between his final letter to his father, with its observations on death, and his contemporary work on *Don Giovanni*,[233] but in this respect the opera needs to be interpreted, rather, as an antithetical complement to the letter. In writing to his father, Mozart held out death as man's friend, whereas the music of *Don Giovanni* unleashes all its terrors. It is clear that, in spite of all the teachings of Freemasonry, there were times when the sensual side of Mozart's nature – the side related to Goethe – continued to stir within him.

This change of heart explains why he was no longer concerned, as he had been in *Le nozze di Figaro*, to adopt an ironical tone in depicting the interplay of psychological forces within the tragicomedy of human existence. What now fascinates him is the fatal nature of this play of forces. In this way he succeeds in raising everything to the level of an exceptional event, intensifying every passion to breaking point and even conjuring up those supernatural powers with which he may have communed in many a quiet moment. Whereas, in the music of *Le nozze di Figaro*, we feel its creator's heart-warming joy, the music of *Don Giovanni* springs from a tremendous resolve that admits of only one goal: to exploit its material to the full. It is easy to understand why it alienated and even repelled the composer's contemporaries. *Don Giovanni* was no longer 'amusing', even in the better sense of that term, but kept the listener in a state of feverish suspense with its well-calculated, searing contrasts. The instrumention reveals a clarity of expression that is terrifying in its harshness and that is markedly different from that of *Le nozze di Figaro*. Even more extreme are the dynamic markings which, in *Don Giovanni* as in no other opera by Mozart, toss the listener to and fro between the most glaring contrasts, with scarcely any transitions. With terrible savagery this music storms across the highs and lows of human destiny, leading us into a world whose sombre sublimity makes our hearts miss a beat, only to bring us a moment later to the closely circumscribed, gloomy world of everyday existence, a world portrayed with such accuracy that even its representatives in the audience would be forced to smile at it. Nowhere was Mozart more successful at relating his characters to one another and measuring against each other the realities that they represent. It is this skill that is revealed most clearly as the principal source of his inspired ability to fuse tragedy with comedy.

For all his attempts at realism, Mozart never violates the language of musical expression or uses it for merely superficial effect. Although considerable demands were placed on contemporary listeners, those demands were never anti-musical. And although formal questions were frequently answered with a freedom that perplexed his more conservative audiences, it is impossible to describe the work as formless. Mozart merely made use of the genius's natural right to find new forms for his whole new world of experience. That he himself was fully conscious of what was necessary and appropriate to his art goes without saying. Even the most unbridled outbursts of passion are subjected to a firm and self-assured desire to fashion his material and to turn nature into culture and, thence, into the highest art. In this way he created a work that is in the same relation to its predecessors as Goethe's *Faust* is to earlier versions of the Faust legend. However much later exegetes may have cudgelled their brains on the subject, he himself never addressed the ques-

---

233. Lert, *Mozart auf dem Theater*, 386; and Schurig, *Wolfgang Amade Mozart*, ii.108.

tion as to whether it is a tragic or a comic opera.[234] Indeed, the question is futile because, however many points of contact it may have with *opera buffa* on a purely stylistic level, it became something far more than that. The materials may be the same, but the building that Mozart erected remains his, a work of genius and, hence, unique. As such, attempts to force it into an existing straitjacket serve no useful purpose whatsoever.[235]

Few other operas have been as frequently 'adapted' as *Don Giovanni*, a state of affairs attributable, in part, to differing views as to its basic meaning and, in part, to the technical difficulties of staging it.[236] We have already mentioned some of the attempts to deal with the ending. Other versions involved all manner of 'effective' interpolations designed to endear the work to audiences and include Schikaneder's adaptation of 1792, which featured the popular figure of the pilgrim. Such aberrations are now a thing of the past and need be mentioned only in passing. As with *Le nozze di Figaro*, however, there is still no satisfactory answer to the problem of an adequate German translation.[237] Virtually all the attempts to provide such a translation are bound up with more or less far-reaching revisions. We have already mentioned the earliest translations by Schmieder, Spieß, Giržik, Neefe and Schröder.[238] The most successful of these early translations was the one by Friedrich Rochlitz, published in Leipzig in 1801. Based on Neefe and Schröder, it is a model of tastelessness and, as such, a classic example of the irresponsible attitudes to translating at this time.[239] Among later versions, suffice it to mention those by W. Viol (Breslau, 1858), Alfred von Wolzogen (Schwerin, 1860), Bernhard Gugler (Breslau) and Franz Grandaur (Munich, 1871).[240] The last two are the first not only to raise the linguistic level but to attempt to restore a sense of order and logic to the drama. Carl Niese's 1872 translation for the *AMA* was followed in 1886 by the most successful translation to date, that by Max Kalbeck,[241] which was especially noteworthy for its sympathetic view of Don Ottavio. Kalbeck's translation was prompted by a meeting of German theatre managers under the presidency of Karl von Perfall, their aim being to produce an authentic text of the opera that all German opera houses could use. Grandaur's version was to be used as the basis of this version. In fact, the attempt proved even less successful than a similar one undertaken in 1913, so that it now seems inevitable that every major opera house should have its own version of the work. The 1890s witnessed a whole series of often brilliant productions of the opera drawing on all the resources of modern technology, not in the sense of superficial effects

234. ◆ Although Abert's point is that *Don Giovanni* transcends both genre and generic labels, the question of the work's generic designation as a *dramma giocoso* nevertheless remains; see Henze-Döhring, *Opera seria, opera buffa und Mozarts Don Giovanni: Zur Gattungskonvergenz in der italienischen Oper des 18. Jahrhunderts* and Heartz, 'Goldoni, Don Giovanni and the dramma giocoso'.

235. ◆ In general, see Kerman, 'Reading *Don Giovanni*'; Rushton, *W. A. Mozart: Don Giovanni*; Bauman, 'The Three Trials of Don Giovanni'; Pirrotta, *Don Giovanni's Progress: A Rake Goes to the Opera*; Zeiss, 'Permeable Boundaries in Mozart's *Don Giovanni*'; Charles Rosen, *The Classical Style*, 288–325; and Gay, 'The Father's Revenge'.

236. On the original staging of the work, see especially Schnerich, 'Wie sahen die ersten Vorstellungen von Mozarts Don Juan aus?', 101–8.

237. According to Lyser, *Mozart-Album*, 86, Mozart himself began a translation of the opera, but his attempt remained incomplete. Lyser claimed to have seen the lost fragment in 1834 and later explicitly rejected the charge of mystification. He copied out the translation and reproduced the finished numbers in the *Neue Zeitschrift für Musik*, xxi (1855), 174ff. and xxii (1856), 133ff. They were reprinted by Jahn, *W. A. Mozart*, iv.757ff., and by Batka, *W. A. Mozarts gesammelte Poesien*, 42ff. ◆ This fragment is now considered not to be by Mozart and is not included in *Briefe*.

238. ◆ Concerning Schmieder and Neefe, see Dieckmann, '"Don Giovanni" deutsch: Mozarts "Don Giovanni" in der deutschen Fassung von Schmieder und Neefe Frankfurt 1789'. Singspiel versions, with spoken dialogue or with dialogue in part, were also important in the early reception of the opera; see Oehl, 'Die eingeschobenen Dialogszenen in Mozarts Don Juan im 18.-19. Jahrhundert'.

239. From 1845 onwards, the recitatives were generally sung in the equally wooden translation of Johann Philipp Samuel Schmidt.

240. See Bulthaupt, *Dramaturgie der Oper*, i.211ff.

241. Kalbeck, *Mozarts Don Juan*.

and empty spectacle but with the aim of overcoming the technical shortcomings bound up with earlier performing practices. The most definitive of these productions was the one staged by Ernst von Possart[242] in Munich in 1896, when the conductor was Hermann Levi. Its starting point was the Prague version and took the work away from the world of large opera houses into the intimate confines of Munich's Residenztheater. The orchestra was reduced in size to the sort of forces found in Mozart's day, whereas, conversely, only the finest singers were used. The work benefited above all from the use of Karl Lautenschläger's revolve, which obviated the need for disruptive breaks between the scenes and thereby significantly added to the overall impact of the drama. Grandaur's translation was radically overhauled by Levi. This Munich version had the great merit of removing the work from the rut of operatic routine[243] and of awakening and reinforcing a sense of the classical operatic style among the widest cross-section of the public. In this way Wagner's ideas on the reform of opera were applied to the performance of a classical opera.[244] A completely new translation by E. Heinemann appeared in 1904 and remained in use, alongside Levi's version, until 1913, when the Deutscher Bühnenverein organized a competition with the aim of establishing a version that all German opera houses could use. The prize was awarded to Karl Scheidemantel of Dresden,[245] but the decision encountered a good deal of opposition on the part of critics and individual intendants, and rightly so, as Scheidemantel's version was by no means ideal, with the result that we continue to be thrown back on compromise. Among recent productions, those by Emil Gerhäuser in Stuttgart and Ernst Lert in Leipzig have caused the greatest stir.[246]

242. Possart, *Über die Neueinstudierung und Neuinszenierung des Mozartschen Don Giovanni*. ◆ Possart was director of the Munich Hoftheater from 1893 to 1905.
243. This production had a predecessor in Eduard Devrient's Mozart performances in Karlsruhe: he, too, removed all later accretions and went back to the original form of the opera, replacing the dialogue with Mozart's *secco* recitatives.
244. In 'The Public in Time and Space', Wagner asked: 'How could it ever occur to us to wish to alter anything in *Don Giovanni*, for instance? . . . Almost every opera director has at some time attempted to adapt the work and bring it into line with his own day, whereas every sensible person should tell himself that it is not the work that needs to be adapted to fit our times, but we ourselves who should adapt ourselves to the age of *Don Giovanni* in order to find ourselves in accord with Mozart's creation'; Wagner, *Gesammelte Schriften und Dichtungen*, x.97.
245. The same year also witnessed the appearance of Schurig's attempt at a translation in his monograph on Mozart; see Schurig, *Wolfgang Amade Mozart*, ii.108ff.
246. Both productions are described in their authors' oft-cited studies. ◆ Curiously, Abert does not mention here Gustav Mahler's production, which used Kalbeck's text; see Blaukopf, 'Musiktheater als Gesamtkunstwerk: Am Beispiel von Gustav Mahlers "Don Giovanni"-Produktion in Budapest und Wien' and 'Max Kalbecks Don Giovanni-Text von 1905: Ein Beitrag zum 200-Jahrjubiläum der Oper aller Opern'. The reception of *Don Giovanni* has, of course, been significant not only for the history of opera but culturally as well. See, among others, Petrobelli, 'Don Giovanni in Italia: La fortuna dell'opera ed il suo influsso'; Kummel, 'Aus der Frühzeit der Mozart-Pflege in Italien'; Noiray, 'Le répertoire d'opéra italien au Théâtre de Monsieur et au Théâtre Feydeau: Janvier 1789–août 1792'; Mongrédien, 'Les mystères d'Isis (1801) and reflections on Mozart from the Parisian press at the beginning of the nineteenth century'; Angermüller, 'Les mystères d'Isis (1801) und Don Juan (1805, 1834) auf der Bühne der Pariser Oper'; Delporte, 'Le Don Juan de Mozart à Paris en 1866: Extraits de la Revue Dramatique de Théophile Gautier'; Cowgill, 'Regendering the libertine, or, The taming of the rake: Lucy Vestris as Don Giovanni on the early 19th-century London stage'; Fend, 'Zur Rezeption von Mozarts Opern in London im frühen 19. Jahrhundert'; Müller and Panagl, *Don Giovanni in New York: Lorenzo Da Pontes italienisch-englisches Libretto für die US-Erstaufführung von Mozarts Oper (1826). Mit dem Libretto der Oper Mozart in New York*; Franze, 'Die Erstaufführung des Don Giovanni, 1827 in Buenos Aires'; Werner-Jensen, *Studien zur Don Giovanni-Rezeption im 19. Jahrhundert (1800–1850)*; Parakilas, 'The afterlife of "Don Giovanni": Turning production history into criticism'; Wates, '"Die Oper aller Opern": Don Giovanni as text for the Romantics'; Zelechow, 'Kierkegaard, the Aesthetic and Mozart's "Don Giovanni"'; Eisen, 'Don Giovanni'; and Gruber, *Mozart and Posterity*. For a guide to the extensive literature on the opera, see Du Mont, *The Mozart–Da Ponte operas: An annotated bibliography*.

46

The period of the three great symphonies

Don Giovanni brought no more of an improvement to Mozart's financial situation than *Le nozze di Figaro* had done. Quite the opposite: the letters that he wrote to Puchberg in June and July 1788 reveal only too clearly that he was sinking deeper and deeper into debt.[1] And, however significant some of them may be, his compositions from this period likewise tell the same old story, being written almost entirely for teaching purposes or for some other specific occasion. Even the three great symphonies that were composed over a three-month period in the summer of 1788 were intended for subscription concerts that were originally scheduled to take place in June but which were then repeatedly postponed before apparently being abandoned altogether.[2] In addition to the works already mentioned, the following pieces date from the period between the first performance of *Don Giovanni* and Mozart's departure for northern Germany: the three symphonies K543 in E flat major, K550 in G minor and K551 in C major, completed on 26 June, 25 July and 10 August respectively; the divertimento K563 in E flat major for violin, viola and cello of 27 September; three trios or 'terzette' for keyboard, violin and cello, K542 in E major, K548 in C major and K564 in G major, completed on 22 June, 14 July and 27 October; the adagio and transcription for string quartet of the C minor fugue for two keyboards K546, completed on 26 June; a keyboard sonata in C major K545 that dates from around the same time and a violin sonata K547 in F major that was completed on 10 July, both of which are described as being 'for beginners'; a keyboard sonata K570 in B flat major dating from February 1789; the canzonetta for 2 sopranos and bass, *Più non si trovano* K549, with an accompaniment for three basset-horns that Mozart completed on 16 July; the aria 'Un bacio di mano' K541 that Mozart wrote in May 1788 for Francesco Albertarelli for a performance of Anfossi's *Le gelosie fortunate*; a lost German aria, *Ohne Zwang aus eignem Triebe* K569; and, finally, a song, also lost, *Beim Auszug ins Feld* K552, that Mozart entered in his catalogue on 11 August 1788.[3]

For those who see in the works of great composers only a reflection of their outer existence, the symphony in E flat major, with its healthy, even boisterous zest for life, is bound to be a puzzle, as

---

1. On the chronology of these letters, see Spitta, 'Zur Herausgabe der Briefe Mozarts', 401–5 and 417–21.
2. See Spitta, 'Zur Herausgabe der Briefe Mozarts', 417. ◆ The idea that Mozart's last three symphonies were written for upcoming concerts derives from an undated letter to Michael Puchberg: 'I . . . implore you to help me out with 100 gulden until next week, when my concerts in the Casino begin' (*Briefe*, iv.69). There is no unequivocal evidence, however, that the letter is from June 1788, as traditionally assumed, nor is there a record of the concerts Mozart planned to give. For various theories concerning the original intent of the symphonies, see Zaslaw, *Mozart's Symphonies: Context, Performance Practice, Reception*, 421–31; Steptoe, 'Mozart and his last three symphonies – a myth laid to rest?'; Jones, 'Why did Mozart compose his last three Symphonies? Some new Hypotheses'; and Grattan-Guinness, 'Why did Mozart write three symphonies in the summer of 1788?'.
3. The *Wiener Zeitung*, lxi (1789), appendix [*Dokumente*, 306–7, *Documentary Biography*, 349], announced a *Freiheitslied* and *Kriegslied* by Mozart. The march in D major K544 for violin, flute, viola, horn and cello that dates from this period is likewise lost. ◆ Although the autograph of K552 remains lost, the work survives in an edition published in Vienna in 1788 by the Taubstummen-Institut (Institute for the Deaf and Dumb).

it was written between the two most desperate letters to Puchberg.[4] It is clear from this just how little the world of the imagination – Mozart's real world – had to do with the everyday world and its cares. Never for a moment did it occur to Mozart to 'set to music' his present predicament or, to quote the popular cliché, get it off his chest. Not even the G minor symphony has anything in common with this: the dark forces that are at work here derive from a completely different, higher reality than that of everyday life and had a far more shattering impact on his inner life than the world around him.

It has often been remarked that, of these three symphonies, the one in E flat major is the most Haydnesque in terms of its formal structure and – especially in the case of its finale – its spirit. Yet in drawing this comparison we should not forget the even more important fact that for all their affinities, K543 expresses Mozart's essential nature at its most distinctive. Indeed, the process of drawing closer to Haydn that had begun in 1782 had by this point led to Mozart's total intellectual and spiritual independence, as least as far as the symphony as a genre is concerned. It is the Mozart of *Don Giovanni* who speaks to us here, just as it had been the Mozart of *Le nozze di Figaro* who spoke to us from the earlier D major symphony (K504). Reinforced by the sharply dotted rhythm that is characteristic of Mozart's other pieces in this key, the tonality of E flat major immediately reveals the whole dark-toned splendour which, following on from the Italian tradition, is so typical of him. This high-flown emotion[5] is maintained throughout the whole of the adagio, gaining in intensity throughout this section until it acquires a note of sombreness and eeriness interspersed, in typically Mozartian fashion, by the brief moments of apprehension and faint-heartedness that this unusual phenomenon evokes in our hearts. At the same time, these are the only passages in which the melodic writing acquires a more cantabile aspect (Mozart here dispenses with a fully developed cantilena in the sense in which this is found in his earlier introductions). Both clearly recall the world of *Don Giovanni* (bars 7–9 and 22 to the end). The unifying melodic link, moreover, is provided by the great scalar motifs that already anticipate Beethoven and that finally acquire a note of wild defiance in the contrary motion in the basses. But it is the harmonic writing and the rhythm that invest this section with its sense of highly charged emotion. The former strives towards the dominant pedal point by means of the vigorous stepwise bass line, while fully exploiting the rhythm with true Mozartian suspensions that glide in and out of each other, turning back to the subdominant via the tonic through a series of piercingly dissonant suspensions, before finally reaching the home key once again in a final section that tells of ineffable weariness and resignation. It bears the unmistakable imprint of the creator of *Don Giovanni*, not least in the way in which it, too, reveals an abrupt change of rhythm, with the festively dotted rhythm of the earlier section assuming a more resolute form ♪ 𝅘𝅥𝅮 𝄾 𝅘𝅥𝅮 ♪ with the entry of the pedal point, in the process affecting the whole of the movement's inner life – one of the most powerful rhythmic effects in Mozart's entire instrumental output. After raising the pitch of agitation to the point at which it erupts in bar 21, he suddenly breaks off and in this way adds to the deep sense of pessimism that brings this proud section to an end.

The following allegro is every bit as exceptional as this introduction, with the essentially strictly instrumental adagio giving way to a section whose theme is strikingly vocal in quality, as though

---

4. *Briefe*, iv.65–70 (letters of 17 and 27 June 1788). Even Hermann Kretzschmar writes that 'If we are to see it as an expression of Mozart's own private mood, the period at which he wrote this symphony must have been a very happy one for him'; see Kretzschmar, *Führer durch den Konzertsaal*, fourth edition, i.182.
5. The keyboard concerto K482 also belongs under this heading.

the only means of escaping from the oppressive mood of the foregoing section is by approaching a vocal style. In this way Mozart found a particularly poetic use for the 'singing allegro' with which he had been familiar from his youth. Nor is it entirely unprepared, as its opening is already clearly adumbrated in the flute motif in bars 9–14 and, more especially, in the shadowy motif in bar 22:

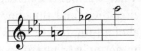

What is new, however, is the keenness with which the vocal character of the theme is stressed and the poetic way in which it is introduced. The melody is initially everything, with the harmonies no more than lightly etched in.[6] It was a particularly inspired and, at the same time, a genuinely Romantic idea not only to follow up the opening motif with its echo in the horns and then in the bassoons but to allow this mood to continue to reverberate in the continuation of the theme – not even Haydn had begun an allegro in this way. Not only does this Romantic opening provide a link between the allegro and the adagio, but the whole character of the theme avoids the naïve joviality of Haydn, preferring a note of Schillerian sentimentality that takes the form of an overwhelming sense of yearning. No less perfect is the way in which this opening is structured: the fifth, *b* flat, that is held by the winds with such emphatic resolve lies right in the middle of the melodic line, the first section rising raptly to a high *g″*, before sinking back with a feminine ending to the third of the dominant chord, while the second section reaches the fifth from above, rather than from below, answering with the feminine third-based ending of the tonal triad, introduced from below, a corresponsion often found in Mozart's works. The second section of the period picks up the rhythm of the final element ♩ ♩ | ♩ ♩ and uses it to increase its expressiveness melodically, harmonically and instrumentally. At the same time, the second element becomes a bar shorter. This varied repeat of the theme is likewise exceptional: the basses suddenly launch into the earlier yearning melody, with the echo now heard in the clarinets and flutes. But in the new, chromatic countermelody in the violins the elegiac mood that characterizes the main theme now finds uninhibited expression: here, too, the ending has something resigned and questioning about it. At this point the Haydnesque tutti enters, picking up the heroic strains of the introduction, with even the violin scales putting in a reappearance. Above all, however, the characteristic features of the key of E flat major, as described above, are once again sharply emphasized.[7] This section races along with a certain gruffness and not without an echo of the noisily festive tone of the time, a tone to which the *Trommelbässe* and expansive motifs in the violins make a by no means inconsiderable contribution. It ends, emphatically, in E flat major. The following transitional group is dominated by the scalar motif accompanied by chords in the winds based on a rhythm related to the one that was quoted above: ♩ ♩ | ♩. ♩ The F major harmonies are then emphatically stressed by means of the triadic melodic writing that typifies the whole of this movement's *forte* passages. Following the unison final bars

---

6. They always enter belatedly on the weak beat of the bar, thereby stressing the ethereal nature of the melody and avoiding the fashionably flirtatious tone of the period. Note also the fact that, with the exception of the first, the suspensions are all fully harmonized.

7. The triadic motif with a chromatically filled-in third at the end is already found in the coda of the opening movement of the violin sonata K481 in E flat major of 1785.

the earlier Mozart would no doubt have introduced his second subject. But here these final bars are so important to him that he uses them and the above-mentioned rhythm in the winds to descend through the entire interval of a fifth, from *f″* to *b′* flat, ending with a vigorous sforzato on the *b′* flat. And the dotted minim not only brings to an end the previous section, it also forms a kind of 'curtain' on what is to come. This second subject picks up the mood of the main theme, as though by a process of natural reaction, except that the underlying note of elegy has now become more tender and more intimate. The earlier sense of agitation continues to be felt in the pedal point, while above it there unfolds the concertante interplay between the violins and winds, creating a feeling of tender, half-suppressed sadness. Here, too, the metre is especially fascinating, with the four bars of pure wind writing that follow the second reply in the winds linked in a curious manner not only with what has gone before but also with what is to follow,[8] the latter bringing with it an old favourite of Mozart's. But the whole of the second subject appears within the movement as though inside a special frame, inasmuch as its final note reintroduces the old, belligerent tone that even uses earlier motifs and ends the subject-group with the transitional passage quoted above.[9]

The development section of the E flat major symphony is far shorter than that of either of its two companion pieces. Although strictly thematic, it merely juxtaposes the existing contrasts within a relatively narrow area, rather than exploring their emotional range in any greater depth. Even the beginning is typical, inasmuch as it allows the transitional theme to reverberate timidly in G minor before rising up, completely unexpectedly, on the chord of the second of A flat major, thus creating a sense of terrifying defiance. Equally unexpectedly, the second subject's rapt consequent phrase comes floating in, as though nothing has happened. Apart from the fact that it is now in A flat major, it otherwise appears in its original form, with only its final phrase revelling in its emotions as it is spun out at greater length, finally propelling the musical argument towards the key of C minor, but scarcely has this key been reached when the surly transitional theme suddenly intervenes in the form of the concertante interplay between two orchestras over a string tremolando, with cellos and double basses, brass and timpani pitted against first violins and woodwinds. As in the first subject-group, its melodic line attempts to move downwards by degrees, its line pointing in the process to the conclusion of the previous second subject (cf. the *a*-flat‴ – *a*-flat′ – *g*‴ – *g*‴ – *f*‴ – *f*‴ – *f*-sharp‴ – *g*‴ in the flutes). Yet this motif, too, retains its original form, rather than being broken down into smaller elements. But the most important point to note is its unexpected entry and the definitive modulation to C minor that it brings with it. The pugnacious defiance invariably associated with this key in Mozart's mind emerges clearly here, even acquiring a demonic aspect in the following section, which is likewise derived from the subject-group, an intensification due to the fact that it suddenly interrupts the interplay between tonic and domi-

8. In terms of their outward structure, they are the antecedent of what follows. The consequent phrase is now five bars long as a result of the lengthening of its initial motif, and thanks to its changed modulation it produces an increase in tension when repeated. Mozart often develops the first element of a consequent phrase from the final element of its antecedent, while the completely new treatment of the second element of the consequent phrase is entirely in keeping with all that we have learnt to expect of him.

9. Only the bass motif in the second bar harks back to the penultimate bar of the second subject in terms of its phrasing.

nant harmonies by introducing subdominant harmonies (with even the second degree flattened) – the earlier Mozart would no doubt have been satisfied with a noisy half-cadence on the dominant of C minor, which would then have been followed by the recapitulation. But the mature Mozart has placed his personal seal on the end of the development section, just as he did on its beginning, suddenly interrupting the weighty emotions of the C minor section with a whole bar's rest and revealing in the process an abruptness which, typical of the movement as a whole, takes the form of three bars of woodwind writing over chords of the seventh with austere ninth-based suspensions.[10] And with this we find ourselves at the recapitulation. In this way, the main theme reemerges, just as it emerged from the adagio at the beginning, by means of a powerful increase in tension that at the very last moment suddenly turns into its opposite. On both occasions the eloquent brevity of these transitional sections is entirely typical of Mozart. With few exceptions, the recapitulation runs along far more regular lines than in the next two symphonies, and even the brief coda, which once again falls back on the earlier scalar figures, serves merely to reinforce the movement's heroic aspect, an aspect that now acquires a particularly festive stamp as a result of the prominence given to the brass and timpani.

The E flat major symphony has been described as Mozart's 'Eroica' on the strength of this movement.[11] Yet, quite apart from the fact that this title presupposes a sense of conflict, the heroic aspect is held in check here by contemplative and elegiac elements. Above all, the movement is characterized by its brusque interplay of contrasts. The underlying emotions are not explored in any regular way. Rather, the mood keeps changing abruptly, so that we would be far more justified in describing the work as Mozart's 'Romantic' symphony.

This description is confirmed by the andante, which consists of two large-scale sections based on the same three thematic complexes. It ends with a coda based on the main theme. This theme maintains its privileged position not least by dint of the fact that its main motifs also infiltrate the other themes, thereby lending the movement as a whole its tauter sense of unity. A further Romantic feature is its pronounced insistence on A flat major, with all the dreamily wistful associations of that key. Its march rhythm harks back to Haydn, and to Austrian models in general, but from the outset it is far more tender and intimate than these. In general, the movement inclines strongly in the direction of chamber music, with the woodwinds in particular being treated with Classical subtlety and translucency. Typical of the main theme is the absence of all *empfindsam* suspensions in the melodic line, with even the feminine endings of the fourth and eighth bars avoiding the heavy suspension harmonies that are normally found here and cadencing within the root chords. The second characteristic is the prominence of the cantilena and the fact that the supporting harmonies are limited to their barest essentials, as we already found to be the case with the main theme of the allegro. Taken together, these two features invest this movement with something naïvely affecting and yet spiritualized. As a result, the ascending line in the first violins that follows the innocent plagal opening and that ends over plagally coloured harmonies supported only by the high cellos, rather than by the double basses, has something ethereal and transfigured about it. The middle section of the main theme is an inspired combination of the two main motifs from the opening sections of the movement over a pedal point on *e* flat gently hammered out in

---

10. Motivically speaking, these three bars are connected with the final bar in C minor, with the sighs in the flutes continuing its last two beats, while the three minims in the other winds represent an augmented version of this bar.
11. See Kretzschmar, *Führer durch den Konzertsaal*, i.182.

the violas. The rising bass line contains within it a vague sense of tension, whose resolution in the beautiful dotted cantilena in the first violins produces a feeling of tender happiness. There follows a repeat of the opening, but its second section is suddenly interrupted by the sombre A flat minor that sounds like a final echo of the old and popular interplay between major and minor, while also suggesting a pre-echo of Schubert. Yet almost at once this mood is exorcized by a wonderful increase in rapt interiority.

Once again a transitional motif of laconic brevity appears in the winds. It seems initially to be no more than a connecting link, only for it later to turn out to be the third main idea of the movement. First, however, the second theme in F minor brings with it an outburst of the same passionate character that we have already encountered in the opening movement, but made even more intense as a result of typically Mozartian devices such as slide motifs and syncopations in the accompaniment. The key of B flat major is finally reached with great resolve, whereupon the beginning of the second part of the main section suddenly reappears, but with the roles completely changed: the pedal point has migrated to the violins, the main motif to the clarinets and bassoons, and the answer, finally, to the cellos and double basses. And this time the sense of secret tension leads not to a feeling of release but to a new outburst of emotion, with the main troublemaker proving to be the dissonances in the second thematic motif, which is now held fast in the bass. In contrast to the main theme, the harmonies are now sharply underlined by the staccato semiquavers in the winds.[12] Only when entrusted to the violins does this motif reacquire its ethereal character, which it does in a passage that is strikingly reminiscent of bars 7–8 of the introductory adagio. Even now, the mood still seems too agitated for the main theme to be reintroduced, and so Mozart falls back on the transitional theme in the winds that had introduced the second subject. Firmly planted on the pedal point on E flat, it is introduced in a highly effective manner by means of a dissonance and rises up, imitatively, from the bassoons to the flutes. As such, it is admirably well suited to lowering the emotional temperature and to restoring the dreamy atmosphere of the opening. Particularly subtle from a psychological point of view is the sense of powerful confidence that enters after four bars in the strings, a feeling that strikes us as the first sign of the new dispensation. We then slip back to the main theme by means of the same theme over typically Mozartian pedal point harmonies. This repeat reveals exactly the same contrapuntal variant that we found in the overture to *Le nozze di Figaro*, with the new countermelodies derived from the theme appearing in the strings whenever the winds have the theme, and vice versa. The result is a sense of greatly enhanced vitality that extends the Romantic mood of the theme in the direction both of yearning raptness and of the pittoresque. In turn, this leads to an extremely significant expansion of the ending. The A flat minor of the theme no longer remains a mere episode, as it was before, but leads to B major (C flat major) in the winds and thence to the second subject, which now enters, unprepared, in B minor (C flat minor).[13] This theme, too, is harmonically intensified, whereas the rest of the musical argument, with the exception of a few individual variants and a different sequence of modulations, follows the same lines as before. The third theme, too, is extended only at the end by means of a beautiful thematic dialogue between strings and winds. The main theme then brings the movement to an end in the form of a coda. There are no further modulations, although this third variation acquires a note of tired resignation through its typically Mozartian, chromatically descending melodic line:

---

12. In this way they pick up and continue the previous pedal point. The sequence of chords is one that is found very often in Mozart's music $\left(\begin{smallmatrix} 6 & 5 & 6 & 5 \\ 5 & 3 & 5 & 3 \end{smallmatrix}\right)$, with a bass line that descends by steps.

13. C flat minor is the key of the diminished upper third of A flat, just as F minor was that of the diminished lower third.

The sense of resignation is in no way attenuated by the somewhat forced elation of the final bars. It palpably recalls the end of the first adagio.

The opening of the menuetto – in contrast to the string quartets, the menuetto is in third position in all three symphonies – recalls the heroically festive tone of the opening movement,[14] while its consequent phrase picks up that movement's gentle grace. It is structured along the strictly symmetrical lines of a dance movement. Just as the main section adopts the old Viennese practice of exploiting violin sonorities to great effect, so the trio is a wind idyll inspired by Haydn – 'one of the loveliest ever created in music', according to one writer.[15] Here the clarinet expounds a theme that Mozart was later to use as the basis of the andante of the C major symphony. Particularly enchanting are the little echoes with which the flute takes the words from the clarinet's lips at the end of each phrase.

The menuetto opens up the way for the boisterous high spirits of the finale. Of all Mozart's great symphonic movements, this one comes closest to Haydn not only in terms of its exuberance but also in respect of its unified structure, with the whole movement developed from a single theme and with the composer eschewing all subsidiary ideas. Equally Haydnesque is the beginning, scored for first and second violins alone, followed by the tutti. (This, it may be added, was an effect that Mozart had successfully exploited in Paris in order to seize his audience's attention.[16]) This opening is followed in turn by the whirring violin figures over broken triads that are typical of the symphony as a whole but that now acquire a particularly whimsical aspect as a result of the merrily skipping basses:

As in the opening movement, the ending on the dominant is sharply accentuated, with the following fanfare rhythm even appearing at the end and adding to the sense of closure: (this rhythm has a further role to play in the subsequent course of the movement).

At this point the main theme reappears in place of a second subject, but even its second motif is snatched from the strings by the winds, so that, in their surprise, the former fail to pick up the theme and, following a belated and futile attempt to do so, bring the theme to a different conclusion, so that, as a result of this unexpected intervention, it is extended from four to six bars in length. Nor does the situation improve with the repeat. Quite the opposite: thanks to the ill humour of the strings, with their minor tonality and *c* flat enharmonically rewritten as *b*, the F sharp minor passage acquires a perceptible tension between both groups: to the accompaniment of heavy syncopations in the strings, bassoon and flute cavort delightedly on the basis of the first of the theme's motifs. But with the return to B flat major, concord returns (the fanfare rhythm now plays an important role) and the musical argument moves purposefully towards its

---

14. Even the chordal passages are common to both movements.
15. Kretzschmar, *Führer durch den Konzertsaal*, i.183.
16. See *Briefe*, ii.388 (letter of 3 July 1778).

conclusion in this key to the strains of festive splendour, a third-based trill and a timpani roll. Yet the ending is delayed once again by an extremely witty intermezzo for the three woodwind soloists based on the beginning of the theme – it is as though three good-natured friends were amusing themselves with a few special somersaults. Only now does a further variant of the main theme appear as the final subject-group, now clearly recalling a Haydnesque funfair, with bagpipe-like drones and a humming in all the strings.[17] It is clear that at these exuberant celebrations all kinds of humour come into their own. The development section again begins with one of those surprising shifts involving a whole bar's rest in which the composer suddenly seems to turn over a whole new page. The main theme then enters in its original guise, except that now it is in A flat major. But even by the fourth bar the momentum starts to flag and, thanks to a new enharmonic respelling, we find ourselves in E major. The actual development section now begins. As always in these symphonies, it avails itself of contrapuntal procedures and begins with an imitative dialogue between first violin and bass over a new, off-beat rhythm in the winds: ♪♩ . This, in turn, is followed by a series of keen stretta entries in the strings, above which the winds launch a new idea related to the opening of the G minor quintet (K516). The result is a weighty imperfect cadence on C minor, similar to the one found at the start of the development section and in the opening movement of the work.[18] But on this occasion the return to the recapitulation has none of the urgent brevity of the opening movement, preferring, instead, to introduce one of the most poetical passages in the entire symphony, with the work's yearning, Romantic spirit breaking through once again in the dreamily songlike writing for the three winds, while the main motif keeps swirling round this tender bloom like a goblin.[19] In this way we slip imperceptibly back to the secret whisperings of the opening, to which a handful of solo wind instruments now add their voices. With the exception of a few minor variants, the recapitulation runs along regular lines, and the coda, too, merely has the function of allowing the mood of carefree celebration to find expansive expression before dying away, as in the opening movement. Only the very ending brings with it a surprise, with the usual final chords replaced by the main motif that twice sweeps over the scene like a whirlwind, creating an effect that would undoubtedly have delighted Haydn.[20]

It has often been remarked that the emotional world of this symphony is largely conditioned by the forces for which it is scored and by the appeal exerted by their sonorities. Of the three, it is the only one that demands clarinets instead of oboes, a demand that in itself lends the piece its soft-edged colours and rounded tone. Above all, however, it is a particularly fine example of the art of orchestration of the Classical Viennese period, which treats the woodwind department in a more subtle and individual manner than the Mannheimers, who handled the strings and winds as equals and tended to merge them together. We have already seen how entire sections of this symphony, including the whole of the andante, are far closer to chamber music than to orchestral music, on

---

17. This humming is related to the earlier third-based trill, whereas the wind phrase above it can trace back its roots to the third and fourth bars of the theme.

18. This parallel between the sequence of modulations in the two outer movements is clear from the decisive shift to A flat major at the beginning.

19. Equally characteristic is the fact that the bass line is taken by the cellos.

20. Hans Georg Nägeli, in his *Vorlesungen über Musik* (1826), 158, found this ending 'so stylelessly inconclusive, so disjointedly abrupt, that the unprejudiced listener does not know what is happening'. The symphony later became known as Mozart's 'Schwanengesang'. It is not known who was responsible for this wholly inappropriate title. For a Romantically poeticizing account of it, see Hoffmann, *Fantasiestücke in Callots Manier*, i.4; Apel's poem on the piece is reproduced in the *AmZ*, viii (1805/6), 453–4; see also Ludwig Bauer, *Schriften* (1847), 471. ◆ For a discussion of Apel's poem, see Helbing, 'Mozarts "Eros-Sinfonie": Die Es-dur-Sinfonie KV 543, nachgebildet und aufbereitet für Leser der AMZ von August Apel'. Further, see Gülke, *Im Zyklus eine Welt: Mozarts letzte Sinfonien*, and Subotnik, 'Evidence of a Critical World View in Mozart's Last Three Symphonies'. For performance suggestions nearly contemporary with Abert, see Weingartner, *Ratschläge für Aufführungen klassischer Sinfonien. Band III: Mozart*.

which point Mozart almost goes further than Haydn. However much he may earlier have felt indebted to the Mannheim school (a debt more evident in his keyboard music than in his orchestral works), his handling of the orchestra finds him moving increasingly in the direction of the Viennese. This is unequivocally clear from a comparison with the symphonies then being written by the composers of the Mannheim school.

In the G minor symphony, too, the choice of instruments is closely bound up with the work's general world of emotion. Here Mozart replaces the clarinets with oboes and dispenses with trumpets and timpani. Only for a later performance did he rewrite the original oboe parts on a separate sheet, dividing their lines between clarinets and oboes or both, evidently in an attempt to achieve a great fulness of sound; the original scoring was retained only in the menuetto. It must be admitted that much of the characteristically austere oboe sound associated with the symphony was lost in this way.

At no other point in his life was Mozart to write two symphonies that are in starker contrast than these. The black pessimism of the opening movement of the piano quartet in G minor (K478) and and, even more, of the string quintet (K516)[21] is now taken to its bitter conclusion. Mozart's contemporaries immediately recognized this, even if they had distinctly mixed feelings about it, whereas it is symptomatic of changing views of Mozart during the Romantic period that the symphony was generally regarded as cheerful and charming, and even as an insignificant work.[22] Only more recently has this view – which has, of course, been reinforced by the way in which the work has been performed – been revised and due account been taken of the way in which Mozart and his contemporaries regarded the piece.[23]

The work has no introduction, merely a bar of anticipatory accompaniment. The theme follows a melodic prototype that was very common at this period and that was later to leave its mark on *Die Zauberflöte* in particular:

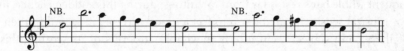

But it differs in two important respects from this prototype. First, it expands the anacrusis (NB) to three times its original length, while none the less retaining its essential character as an upbeat (the main stress still lies on the third and seventh bars of the theme); and, secondly (and related), the second note of the rising sixth coincides with the weak beat of the bar, thereby robbing the prototype of much of its original vitality, a process intensified by the fact that the extended upbeat is rhythmically and melodically varied:

---

21. ◆ For a technical account of this relationship, see William S. Newman, 'Mozart's G minor Quintet (K. 516) and its Relationship to the G minor Symphony (K. 550)'.

22. Writing in the *Neue Zeitschrift für Musik*, viii (1838), 190, Hirschbach described 'this so-called symphony' as 'distinguished neither by its level of invention nor by the treatment of its themes, a commonplace, inoffensive piece of music that cannot have been very difficult to write (leaving aside all the more profound demands of our age) and that Beethoven would presumably not have regarded as a great masterpiece'. Robert Schumann, too, brought out the difference between then and now when criticizing Christian Friedrich Daniel Schubart's *Ideen zu einer Ästhetik der Tonkunst*: 'In G minor he [Schubart] finds dissatisfaction, uneasiness, wrestling with an unworkable plan, gritting of the teeth in anger, etc. Now just listen to Mozart's Symphony in G minor, with its buoyant Hellenic charm'; *Gesammelte Schriften über Musik und Musiker*, i.105. Even the Swabian theologian Christian Palmer found nothing but 'love and life' in the symphony; *Evangelische Hymnologie*, 246. This is the same Romantic view of music that defined Beethoven as a 'titan', even though his music is about far more than 'titanism'. ◆ For an overview of K550's reception, see Broder, *Wolfgang Amadeus Mozart, Symphony in G minor, K. 550: The Score of the New Mozart Edition, Historical Note, Analysis, Views, and Comments*.

23. See Kretzschmar, *Führer durch den Konzertsaal*, i.184–5.

It is melodically varied by means of the heavy sigh motif (NB) and rhythmically varied by the sigh's anapaestic character, its forward momentum having nothing positive or life-affirming about it in its present surroundings: rather, it introduces a note of disquiet and tension from the very outset. Even the recurrent feminine cadences are typical. The theme reveals the same broad sweep as the corresponding theme from the E flat major symphony,[24] except that the second section of its antecedent phrase brings with it a considerable increase in tension in its underlying emotion, an increase due to its metrical extension and to the sharp emphasis given to the half-cadence on the dominant: at this point the passion that has been effortfully suppressed breaks forth in naked savagery. The consequent phrase of the theme is interrupted after its first group by the tutti's extremely pugnacious transitional group. We are already in B flat major, the key of the second subject. But this is reached only after a hard-won struggle. In this way the B flat major is reinterpreted as the subdominant of F major, with the underlying harmonies following the usual sequence IV–V–I, except that the final F major itself soon acquires the force of a dominant. Notionally, then, this whole section reveals the following sequence of harmonies:

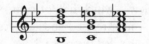

This then takes on physical form in the second subject. In this way, this second subject struggles to break free within this group (a group which is anything but a purely mechanical connecting link), assuming the status of a demand that lies within the nature of the movement as a whole. Even the eloquent whole bar's rest is far from fortuitous: during this sudden silence, listeners with any degree of musical sensitivity are bound to feel a mood reverberating within them that makes the entry of the second subject seem utterly inevitable. In terms of its scoring, this theme is a particularly fine example of the Classical relationship between strings and winds already mentioned. Indeed, their concertante interplay leads here to an example of the *durchbrochene Arbeit* associated with more modern composers, in other words, the same theme is divided up among different groups of instruments. But in keeping with its character, it reduces the agitation of the main theme to the point where it acquires a note of touching lament, although this contemplative mood is short-lived, as the development section refuses to subscribe to it, and when the idea reappears in the recapitulation, it assumes an air of the deepest resignation within the sombre mood of G minor, thereby affording affecting proof of the profound human emotions that lie concealed within this movement. No less inspired is the way in which the theme is expanded at the end, sinking dreamily down to A flat major, a move that inevitably produces a natural reaction with the return to B flat major.[25] The end of the subject-group again belongs to the main theme,

24. See Wilhelm Fischer, 'Zur Entwicklungsgeschichte des Wiener klassischen Stils', 54–5.
25. Only the unison

is related to the chromaticisms of the second subject.

with imitative writing in the winds based on the sigh motif, while a heavy, groanlike sigh, also involving imitative procedures, struggles to break free in the strings. This relatively intimate section and, with it, the subject-group is brought to an end on a note of sullen defiance. When these themes are repeated, the orchestral groups are invariably interchanged, with double counterpoint in the last of them, a procedure that also plays an important role in the development section. This section differs from all the others by virtue of the fact that it never breaks free from the main theme but explores every aspect of it to the full, rather than examining the interplay between the individual moods, as was the case with the symphony in E flat major. Typically for Mozart, it begins with a transitional passage that is as surprising as it is laconic and that takes us suddenly – and yet in a way that is internally justified by all that has gone before – to the remote, 'hot' key of F sharp minor. From now on only the first eight bars of the main theme have a say in the musical argument. This structure descends stepwise, creating a sense of curious oppressiveness as it does so, with the lower melodic line moving chromatically from *c*-sharp″ via *b*′ sharp, *b*′, *a*′ sharp and *a*′ to *g*′, supported by corresponding steps in the bassoons and basses. There follows a veritable explosion with the *forte* entry of the theme in the basses in E minor – again without a transition. At the same time a new voice enters in counterpoint in staccato quavers

in the opening bar of which we hear an echo of the chordal motif from the transitional group. In the first half, the suspension harmonies in the winds are no less powerfully effective than the way in which, in the second half, theme and counterpoint strive to go their separate melodic ways. And now the sense of unleashed passion rages in double counterpoint over the regular harmonic sequence E minor, A minor, D minor, G minor, C major, F major and B flat major, not stopping until it reaches the dominant of D minor, while the first element of the theme, which has been hurled through every tonality but which is now compressed to the semitone step of its sigh motif, brings this whole section to an end like some shrill outburst. As such, it constitutes the climax of this highly charged development section. From a purely technical point of view, this section is further proof of Mozart's increasing interest in counterpoint at this time, and on this point, more than any other, it stands well apart from Haydn, for whom counterpoint was merely a passing phase on his way to a new kind of thematic development. Here, by contrast, the sudden eruption of contrapuntal procedures in the wake of the gentle melodic flow of the earlier passage creates an extraordinarily weighty and dramatic impression. The mood then disappears as unexpectedly as it arrived, with no dynamic preparation, giving way to thematic development in the Haydnesque sense of that term, with the result that this development section includes examples of every kind of thematic reworking: melodic *Fortspinnung*, counterpoint and modern thematic writing. All that remains is the section of the theme that was stated last and that now utters its final sighs, softly and alone in the first violins, creating an impression of helplessness. But this moving lament is now intensified by the winds until it acquires a note of self-torment. The original sigh motif, hitherto heard in a purely melodic form, is from now on fully harmonized, acquiring ever-greater keenness between now and the end of the development section. Note also the masterly way in which the instrumentation is placed in the service of expressivity: the first violins force their way desperately upwards over the dark-toned sonorities of the sustained notes in the bassoons and oboes, with each phrase ending intensified in expression as a result of the entry of the two upper winds. Even when the melodic line is recast in the other strings[26] and the first violins rediscover their natural support, the winds remain the real proponents of the mood of anguished agitation thanks to such searing echo-like dissonances as the following:

The harmonic writing, too, is in a state of constant unrest throughout this section. Only in the tutti section, which again enters with startling suddenness, is terra firma reached with the dominant harmony of G minor. By now all that remains of the main theme is its ur-motif, which the strings take over from the final call in the winds, while the winds in turn return to the old transitional idea. The result is a new build-up of tension that compresses the work's emotional content to its simplest and most basic idea – we can see from this just how logical this development section is. In terms of its sequence of modulations, there would be nothing at this point to prevent the recapitulation from entering, but Mozart follows up this final outburst of agitation with a gentle echo that at the same time brings the music back to the beginning. Only the sforzato accents in the bassoons hark back to the earlier section, while above them the ur-motif descends chromatically in the winds, its final note extended to three times its original length: this is the weariest and most resigned passage in the entire movement, with the result that the return of the main theme – effected by a keen dissonance and heavily underscored by the dominant character of its opening – strikes us as an act of liberation. In this way the development section intensifies the emotional content of the subject-group in every way possible, with a powerful peak of agitation at its heart, flanked by two sections which, although related to it, are more restrained in expression, all three being distinguished by the manner in which the material is treated,[27] while clearly offshoots of the same stem and expressions of the same organic emotional development – few other development sections by Mozart are sustained by the same degree of emotional energy.

This also affects the recapitulation, which, as a result of its variants and additions, is far more intense expressively than that of the E flat major symphony. Even the main theme is now scored for additional winds, but above all it is the transitional group that has been extended in a highly significant manner. The ultimate goal of this whole process is the second subject, now in G minor, a key that Mozart now has as firmly in mind as he had in the case of the string quintet. Yet even this important change has to be properly prepared and motivated. Herein lies the significance of the varied transitional group which, in keeping with the subject-group, begins in E flat major, before modulating to F minor, finally reaching G minor to the accompaniment of wild stretta entries of the crotchet motif.[28] The earlier version of this whole section is now repeated in this key.

---

26. The use of cellos instead of basses suggests an echo of the old concertino groups.
27. The differences extend to tonality and instrumentation.
28. It may be possible to detect an echo of the main theme's melodic line in the new contrapuntal motif:

We have already mentioned the second subject itself, which only now acquires its full expressive force. Its ending, too, is now expanded in the direction of greater expressive resolve. The final group begins by running along regular lines, but in its final section, which is likewise expanded, the movement's two basic antitheses – wild onslaught[29] and a weary ebbing away of the underlying emotion – are once again forced together within the narrowest possible confines. There follows the actual coda, which on this occasion does not merely have the effect of reinforcing the ending but brings the whole of the movement's emotional world to a psychologically fitting conclusion. The main theme returns, but its second element is already obscured by a syncopated passage that seems to grow increasingly static, with the imitative entries designed merely to increase the feeling of resignation. Only now does the final section break through, powerfully conjuring up the old warring factions one last time. Here the anapaestic rhythm affects even the final chords:

The andante is closely related to this opening movement in terms of both form and expression. A sonata-form movement, it is characterized by the same degree of thematic unity and by the same importance of contrapuntal procedures. That it belongs to the same world of emotion is clear from its main theme,[30] with its oppressive repeated notes intensified by the use of imitation, by its heavy suspensions and by its chromatic bass line wending its gloomy way beneath them. The answer comes in the form of the consequent phrase, a Paisiello-like motif in which the underlying emotion almost spills over, but by the second element the motif has disappeared again. Even the horns that had accompanied this upsurge of emotion now fall silent again, and the antecedent phrase of the whole theme dies away in a series of anguished chromaticisms. But the demisemi-

quaver motif 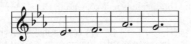 that is now introduced in so striking a manner continues to grow in

importance, in which respect it recalls the sigh motif of the opening movement. To it falls the task of conveying a sense of agitation that is offset by the contemplative, meditative aspects of the theme. The consequent phrase immediately brings with it a significant increase in tension, not least through its use of double counterpoint. It begins with a weighty pedal point, above which the earlier bass motif, now heard in the violins, is transformed into a moving threnody. It leads to one of those 'singing basses' (with the theme) that are characteristic of all three of these symphonies. Only the ending achieves a note of greater confidence thanks to the motif that was quoted above. The second theme enters suddenly on the dominant, releasing the pressure that was latent in the first theme – or, rather, it attempts to find release, for here, too, the energy is dissipated in the second bar as a result of the aforementioned demisemiquaver motif. Yet this motif has the ability

---

29. This section, too, is thematic.
30. Note that all this symphony's main themes begin on the upbeat. The basic melodic line of the first element of the theme produces Mozart's old favourite:

This idea is later found in the finale of the C major symphony. The repeated note with the following suspension is related to the third theme of the andante of the symphony in E flat major.

not only to interrupt the musical argument, but also to built it up: it now takes control, initially by pouring oil on troubled waters, but then, following the cadence on F major, unexpectedly providing a transition to the passage in D flat major, performing an ethereal dance around the opening motif of the main theme, which now makes its dreamy entrance. Even here the sounds of nature already begin to resonate very softly, soon rising to a powerful murmur in the full orchestra, from which arabesques proudly arise at the wonderful enharmonic change to B flat major. Once again the musical argument is suddenly interrupted, then all at once we hear, as the final theme, the unmistakable call of a nightingale, first in the strings,[31] then in the winds, as though enticing us from various quarters, accompanied by the same motif as before. How beautiful and truthful, then, is the overwhelming expression of sadness that now breaks free in the full orchestra at the renewed descent into G flat major. But it does not last long. This section ends on a note of indescribable tenderness and interiority, with precedence given to the aforementioned motif.

At the beginning of the development section the sombre spirit of the main theme reasserts itself, first in a dull pounding, then in a more forceful hammering, drawing even the brief demisemi-quaver motif into its thrall: each time it flutters down through the chords prescribed by the chro-matic line that rises up resolutely in the basses. The regularly pounding rhythm of the main theme is the chief source of this sense of tension, which finally erupts on the dominant of C minor. Once again the earlier motif attempts to unravel the situation, but too great a dampener has been placed on the earlier mood for it to achieve any sense of liberation. The main theme is then reannounced in the bassoons to an open, harsh-sounding fourth, producing a passage of almost spine-chilling eeriness, but almost at once it is supplanted by its tender, elegiac counterpoint:

This brings the present section to an end with its expressive opening dissonance, which, accompa-nied by the demisemiquaver motif, already looks forward to the world of the Romantics. Borne aloft on these pinions of wistful sadness, the musical argument slips mysteriously into the recapit-ulation. In this way, the entire development section forms a single large-scale emotional diminu-endo, even though no such performance marking appears at this point in the score. As such, it is an instructive example of Mozart's ability to deal with these problems in his own idiosyncratic way. The recapitulation brings with it an utterly inspired extension of the consequent phrase of the theme, which is now combined with the second theme, while the counterpoint quoted above comes close to a recitative in its expressivity, playing a decisive role here. Only when the theme is taken up by the basses (note, in particular, the effectiveness of the low notes in the horns) does the musical argument again proceed along regular lines, from now on closely adopting the same line of development as the subject-group.[32]

31. Here, too, the old contrast between tutti and concertino is revived, with the latter even assuming the form of a trio for the two violins and viola.
32. ◆ The andante of K550 was for many years performed in a corrupt edition including eight extra bars that were later inter-preted as alternative versions of the same passage. The discovery of a copy used by Mozart to perform the symphony shows not only that he revised the scoring in anticipation of an upcoming performance, but also that he rewrote and replaced the passage in the andante; see Eisen, 'Another Look at the "Corrupt Passage" in Mozart's G minor Symphony K550: Its Sources, "Solution" and Implications for the Composition of the Final Trilogy'.

The menuetto takes up the bellicose mood of the opening movement and raises it to a new pitch of intensity.[33] This movement, too, finds it impossible to break away from the same basic idea; and it, too, makes extensive use of counterpoint in the course of its development. Metrically it is exceptional, with its main theme beginning with two three-bar periods, followed by a consequent phrase in which the earlier material is developed for a further two bars, before ending with another three-bar period. This ratio is then continued in its second section, in which the three-bar units are intermeshed by means of imitative procedures, and by the time that the brief epilogue enters seven bars from the end, we feel clearly that the rhythmic emphasis of the main idea lies not on its first bar, but on its second. All this gives the movement a sense of grim and wild defiance, with the second section adding immeasurably to this feeling of surliness by the harshness and severity of its two-part textures, from which its opposite then emerges in the form of richly polyphonic stretta entries. The voices do not allow each other to complete what they are saying, while the theme itself is significantly transformed as a result of its modulation to the dominant. It is this, in turn, that produces the epilogue, which repeats the theme in its original form. In terms of its expression, this epilogue picks up the mood of the work as a whole, with the sense of immense agitation ending once again in resignation. Again it is the winds that convey this sense of radical upheaval, and again it takes the form of that elegiac, chromatic part-writing that typifies these sections in the symphony as a whole.

At the same time, however, the epilogue clears the way for the enchanting sadness of the trio, the theme of which – related to that of the main movement[34] – recalls a folksong. In particular, its refrainlike consequent phrase is well known in Austrian folk music:

The movement as a whole is yet another fine example of Mozart's ability to write a concertante dialogue for strings and winds of a kind that Viennese composers traditionally introduced at this point. Here the winds are invariably more adventurous than the strings in exploring the whole range of their compass, allowing the sense of yearning to burgeon perceptibly. But it is the horns – held in reserve until the third section of the movement – that are given the trump card to play, suddenly clothing the beautiful song tune in their Romantic sonorities.[35]

As its main theme, the allegro assai has a regularly structured, two-part period, thirty-two bars in length, that recalls the older tradition with its dynamic interplay of soli and tutti within very narrow confines. The ascending triad of its opening bars likewise belongs to an older prototype,

---

33. Kretzschmar quite rightly describes it as 'one of the most argumentative movements ever constructed on the basis of this old and precious dance form'; see *Führer durch den Konzartsaal*, i.186.

34. Compare its opening with the melodic line of the main theme:

The beginning of the finale likewise picks up its first three notes.

35. ◆ For detailed analysis of the menuetto, including discussion of its metric complexity, see Leonard B. Meyer, 'Grammatical Simplicity and Relational Richness: The Trio of Mozart's G minor Symphony'; and Cohn, 'Metric and hypermetric dissonance in the menuetto of Mozart's symphony in G minor, K. 550'.

but Mozart introduces an individual note with the suspension with which this ascending line culminates and which from the very outset lends the theme an element of agitation and even of despair: even here the arrow hits home and inflicts a keen wound. The wild echo in the tutti with its authentically Mozartian warlike rhythm ♩♩ | ♩ ♩ ♩ ♩ | ♩ 𝄾 𝄾 [36] continues here, while the constant interplay between *piano* and *forte* likewise continues to express a curious feeling of agitation that even dulls the senses. The listener has the clear feeling that the basic mood of the work is intensified here one last time, acquiring an element of savagery and demonism. The motif that is entrusted to the tutti audibly recalls the ending of the first movement. At the same time, the tutti continues the transitional group, which is dominated by the same rhythmic motif (but without its upbeat) and is filled with all manner of pugnacious quaver motifs. Unlike so many of their predecessors, however, these are no mere random and noisy links, for, quite apart from the principal motif, which finally migrates to the basses, the motifs that appear here are both thematic in origin:

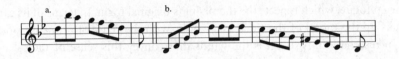

(b) derives from the main theme, whereas (a) is identical to an important motif from the analogous section of the first movement. The second subject is introduced as a proper trio (both violins and viola) in the manner of a traditional concertino. It initially avoids the element of anguish found in its counterpart in the opening movement. Rather, its emotionally charged and uplifting modulation to the subdominant suggests rapt yearning. Indeed, its initial section – as in the andante – recalls nothing so much as the siren call of nature. By the time that we reach the consequent phrase, however, the melodic line has already been infiltrated by the anguished chromaticisms that we know only too well from the earlier movements. This passage is even strikingly similar to the analogous section in the opening movement. When repeated by the winds, the theme acquires two upbeats that add to the element of tension, but in its consequent phrase its melodic outlines are drawn into an oppressive chromatic motion that seizes hold of all the voices, and immediately afterwards the tutti motif enters, bringing with it all the old sense of unrest. As a result, the second subjects of both outer movements are extraordinarily closely related on their innermost level. As in the opening movement, the second subject is ignored in the development section, but, as if in compensation, it acquires a far greater depth of expression in the recapitulation when it is heard in the tonic, G minor.

The opening of the development section brings with it even more of the surprises that Mozart regularly holds in store at this point in his works, appearing to reject a regular development following the initial assault of the main theme (with the added intensity of its major seventh). Here the demonic quality of the movement as a whole finds expression in horrors of disturbing savagery. Lurking behind these unison chords and grotesque intervals is the theme and its various subdivisions:

---

36. It also clearly recalls the anapaestic form of the opening movement: ♫♩ | ♩ ♫ | ♩ ♫ | ♩.

But in the white-hot glow of passion, this melody evaporates, leaving only its barest outlines, in some cases metrically realigned under the weight of the experience to which it has been subjected (see, in particular, bars 3, 5 and 8). Elsewhere, as in the searing triplet in bar 4, the metre is intensified. Twice – in bars 6–7 and 9–10 – a ritardando is written into the music, the second time in the winds, whose transitional motif also recalls the analogous passage for the winds in the opening movement. A further link between the two outer movements is found in the contrapuntal treatment of the following passage and in the fact that the musical material is limited to the main theme. In terms of their mood, however, they are markedly different. In the finale the sense of agitation is not allowed to flag once it has reached its climax: although briefly interrupted at the passage in C minor, it is then whipped up with all the greater ferocity, before being abruptly curtailed at the shrill dissonance of the chord of the diminished seventh just before the recapitulation. Virtually the whole of the development section maintains a constant *forte*, with a quieter passage appearing only at the beginning, when the first violins and winds toss the theme to and fro. At the same time the underlying harmonies descend through the circle of fifths from A minor to F minor over the sharply accented crotchet rhythm. It is at this point that the *forte* enters on a keen-edged horn call. At the same time, the theme is subjected to a further development, initially in two-part harmonies, and expanded by means of a scalar motif

behind which we can recognize an inverted form of the theme. Later it is joined by the quaver motif familiar from the transitional group. Characteristic of this section are the abruptly curtailed horn calls that accompany it. Yet this section is no more than a preparation for the first climax of the development section, which now enters in C minor. And once again Mozart falls back on the strictest form of counterpoint, with stretta entries of the theme in all four voices repeated no fewer than three times – on the first two occasions, the entries are in the same order, whereas on the third occasion the order is different. The counterpoint is provided by an abbreviated version of the above-cited theme. But the harmonic framework, with its constant succession of $IV–V–\frac{I}{IV}–V–\frac{I}{IV}$ and so on, acquires a keen melodic edge as a result of the motif that is developed *alternatim* in the winds:

In this way, the musical argument finally migrates to C sharp minor, the dominant of which – flickering in quavers in the violins – raises the agitation to boiling point. There is something authentically Mozartian about the weary *piano* continuation with the timid theme in the winds following the surly interrupted cadence. But immediately afterwards the orchestra is assailed by a further outburst of fury, once again descending through the circle of fifths, this time to D major, the dominant of G minor. Although this leads to a loosening of the contrapuntal textures, the harmonies now keep changing on the fourth beat of the theme, thereby intensifying its underlying emotion, while at the same time two orchestral groups attack each other, with violins and bassoons aligned against cellos and basses and the rest of the winds. In this way the powerful floodtide of passion in the recapitulation is channelled back into its former course. But in contrast to the opening movement there is no sense of resolution, still less of resignation. There is something profoundly right, therefore, about the fact that at the start of the recapitulation the main theme is reduced to half its original length and the transitional group to almost half *its* original length. And there is something no less right about the fact that the whole movement is increasingly taken over by G minor. The second subject is the best possible demonstration of this, inasmuch as it explores the anguished world of this tonality to the point of self-torment in the form of the new chromatic variations to which its consequent phrase is now subjected. The final section, too, retains the mood of sombreness and savagery, thereby placing its seal on the symphony as a whole.[37]

The G minor symphony thus constitutes the most extreme expression of the deep and fatalistic pessimism that was always a part of Mozart's character and that strove particularly forcefully for artistic expression in the final years of his life. Of course, he was now sufficiently mature not to limit himself to this sombre world, and he never returned to it with such ruthless consistency. Rather, works such as *Die Zauberflöte* and the *Requiem*, by reducing this pessimism to calm, yet all the more profound, sadness, reveal that the G minor symphony is merely one stage in his intellectual and spiritual growth. Perhaps this change stemmed from the fact that in the present piece Mozart explored every aspect of this feeling with an almost literally pitiless resolve, evincing a ruthless objectivity that the work shares with *Don Giovanni*. Related to this is the absence of an ethical element in the Beethovenian sense of liberation and reconciliation. For a composer as strong-willed as Beethoven, experiences of this kind inevitably bore within them the seeds of a struggle that demanded a resolution within the work itself. This is not true of Mozart even in those movements where the clouds part at the end. For him, too, there was a sense of liberation, but it

37. The rhythm of the main theme ♩ | ♩ ♩ ♩ ♩ | ♩. emerges here in the winds, just as it did before. The last two chords repeat the theme's last two notes in augmentation.

occurred outside the piece in question: the nature of the work that he felt impelled to write found such implacable expression that it no longer exercised him on an internal level.[38]

Was it this feeling of liberation that inspired Mozart to write a third symphony in C major?[39] On a purely superficial level, it is the most brilliant of his symphonies. Constructed on the largest scale, it also breathes a spirit of proud strength found nowhere else in his output. Even the themes of its opening movement are laid out along incomparably broader lines than in either of the symphony's two predecessors. Indeed, the first subject essentially extends as far as the entry of the second subject, with no transitional group, taking the form of two large-scale complexes divided by a fermata, with the second of these complexes extending and varying the ideas of the first in the same order as that in which they first appeared. There is none of the passage-work and none of the scalar figures found in the earlier transitional groups. The opening of the theme

creates a genuinely Mozartian mood involving *durchbrochene Arbeit*, with the heroic overture-like opening of the Neapolitans answered by a meditative motif of noble *cantabilità* in the string concertino.[40] In this way, the basic tone of the movement and, indeed, of the symphony as a whole is established from its very first bars. Unlike that of the G minor symphony, this tone is emphatically life-affirming, embracing, as it does, both masculine strength and feminine caution, two aspects that acquire their ultimate truthfulness as a result of their constant and typically Mozartian intermingling and cross-fertilization, merging together even in the first subject's extended consequent phrase. At this point the heroic opening returns softly in the strings, accompanied by one of those wide-ranging contrapuntal lines with a descending scale in the winds of which Mozart was especially fond. But the songlike continuation, further developed, now reveals the nostalgic side of its nature[41] – and all this on the basis of the witty, intimate interplay between strings and winds that characterizes this group of symphonies in general. Soon, however, the darker colours are forced to yield to a further entry of the first subject in the tutti, which now drives motif (b) powerfully upwards[42] and brings the whole complex to an end with the heroic step of the antecedent phrase. As the second subject, one of Mozart's most heart-warming and charming ideas floats into view, an imitative game of question and answer between first violin and bass accompanied by a

---

38. ◆ Further concerning K550, see Leonard B. Meyer, 'Grammatical Simplicity and Relational Richness: The Trio of Mozart's G minor Symphony'; Hortschansky, 'Die g-Moll-Sinfonie zur Zeit der Wiener Klassik'; and Gjerdingen, 'Revisiting Meyer's "Grammatical Simplicity and Relational Richness"'.

39. Not until after Mozart's death did it become known as his 'Jupiter' symphony. It is not known who invented this title. ◆ According to Vincent Novello, the nickname was first mooted by the London violinist and impresario Johann Peter Salomon; during a visit to Salzburg in 1829, Novello wrote in his diary that 'Mozart's son said he considered the Finale to his father's sinfonia in C – which Salomon christened the Jupiter – to be the highest triumph of Instrumental Composition . . .'; see Medici di Marignano and Hughes, *A Mozart Pilgrimage: Being the Travel Diaries of Vincent & Mary Novello in the Year 1829*, 99. Certainly it was in use by the late 1810s and early 1820s: it appears in programmes for the Edinburgh Music Festival on 20 October 1819 and a concert by the Philharmonic Society on 26 March 1821. The earliest known appearance of the nickname on an edition of the work is Clementi's arrangement for piano, flute, violin and violoncello, published in 1822 or shortly afterwards; see King, *Mozart in Retrospect*, third edition, 264, with a facsimile of Clementi's title page as the frontispiece.

40. Motif (b) is related to bars 2–3 of the andante of the E flat major symphony.

41. In bar 27 we find a rare instance of a suspension producing a consonance, while its resolution gives rise to a dissonance.

42. Note especially the keenly cutting *relationes non harmonicae* in bars 44–6 of both first and second violins.

contrapuntal line that is both graceful and warm-hearted at once[43] – no wonder, then, that Mozart finds it so hard to break away from this passage, even allowing the basses to join in with motif (b). But this graceful episode then breaks off on a whole bar's rest, and the full orchestra now enters unexpectedly in a sombre C minor. Yet this typically Mozartian warning shot is not meant to be entirely tragic, being no more than a surly 'quos ego' that counters the note of contentment and recalls the heroic side of the work's underlying mood.[44] Once again motif (b) is forced upwards, this time in diminution, adding to its emotional intensity. With this, we might assume that we had reached the end of the subject-group, but instead Mozart breaks off once again and, in keeping with the work's expansive design, interpolates a further dancelike passage of delightful folklike appeal,[45] in which the movement's whole godlike delight in existence seems once again to be focused. In the passage that follows, Haydn, too, appears to give his friendly blessing, before the pugnacious motif from the first subject brings this section to an end.

How important to Mozart this dancelike passage was becomes clear from the development section, a full two-thirds of which it now dominates. Following the usual brief modulatory shift of the wind unison, behind whose outlines its theme already emerges, it immediately appears with the fifth in the winds in E flat major that casts its radiance over it like sunshine. On the basis of this material there now unfolds a passage filled with an astonishing variety of life involving the most elaborate use of contrapuntal procedures and thematic development. The result is an outpouring of the most immediate musical creativity that appears to revel in its own power and energy. This is true above all of the final section of the dance theme, which is developed in a series of inexhaustible combinations. The winds initially accompany it with the festive rhythm of the main theme 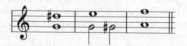, but then add a wide-ranging motif consisting of only two notes, before finally helping to develop the dancelike theme. The harmonies move sequentially to the dominant of A minor, where the dance slowly dies away. At this point the first subject is reintroduced in F major, after having been prepared for by the violins by means of a series of modulations that add significantly to the tension. We might almost be reminded of one of the false recapitulations so popular with Haydn, were it not for the fact that the subject enters in such a quiet and hesitant manner. In fact, no answer follows on even the second occasion, with motif (a) continuing alone with its wind counterpoint, always a degree higher. At this point the whole sense of defiance that is latent within it suddenly erupts. This is the passage in which the slide motif, with its emphatically off-beat winds and basses, finally forces its way back to G major, the dominant of C major, over a chromatically descending bass line underpinned by changing harmonies involving syncopated entries. Yet not even here does the sense of heightened emotion have the last word. Instead, the violins enter with the same final phrase from the third theme with which they had ended before the entry of the first. In turn, this is followed by an echo in the winds. Bassoons and oboes

---

43. Here we find another of Mozart's favourite phrases, again borrowed from Paisiello.

44. The E flat soon turns out to be a far more harmless D sharp, its chromatic development even recalling the beginning of the second subject. We even find a chromatic answer in the lower voice:

45. The theme is taken from the aria 'Un bacio di mano' K541 that Mozart wrote for Francesco Albertarelli in May 1788. There the melody is set to the words 'Voi siete un po tondo, mio caro Pompeo, l'usanze del mondo andate a studiar'. For the present purposes, Mozart subjected it to a slight but expressive alteration.

reveal a distinct desire to repeat the contrapuntal round dance from earlier (one of the most amusing passages in all Mozart's symphonies), but the power of the pedal point soon draws them into the recapitulation. In this way the present development section expresses the same free interplay of emotions as the operas, combining contrastive moods with sovereign freedom, while always revealing their common source.

Even before the antecedent phrase has reached an end, the recapitulation modulates to E flat major, clearly under the influence of the development section, with brief stretta entries of every kind serving to add a note of intensity to the subsequent course of this section, while the second subject, too, becomes more expressively charged as a result of the greater contribution of the winds. The warning shot, too, reverberates more powerfully and at greater length, with the minor tonality now being explored in greater depth, and only the dance theme reappears in its old form, its enhanced sonorities notwithstanding. The movement concludes with one of the festive fanfares that Mozart was fond of using to end his more light-hearted movements.

Structured along similar lines to its predecessor, the andante cantabile takes as its main theme one of the favourite ideas of the Classical period,[46] its broadly expansive dignity and strength entirely in keeping with the basic character of the symphony as a whole. Here, too, the consequent phrase plays a complementary role. While emphasizing the 'cantabile' element of the movement, it affords a brilliant demonstration of Mozart's inspired ability to expand traditional metrical patterns, with the sudden cantabile outpouring in the seventh bar extending the second element from two to three bars. But, not content with this, Mozart then uses an interrupted cadence to add a further two bars under the pressure of the underlying emotion, so that the consequent phrase is now seven bars long. This powerful outburst of emotion then brings with it a much-varied repeat of the theme in the bass, accompanied over wind chords by a figural countermotif in the violins derived from bars 7–8 of the cantabile consequent phrase. Its own consequent phrase now descends to a half-cadence on the dominant, creating a profoundly elegiac mood and in this way preparing the ground for the profound emotional pressure of the second subject, which it does with great psychological subtlety. With this second subject comes a clouding over of the dominant harmonies from C major to C minor, a sign that, in spite of its sense of contrast, this theme none the less emerges from all that has gone before, its oppressive pedal point, syncopations and sudden interruption in its second bar (a point that recalls the analogous passage in the G minor symphony) revealing it to be the vehicle of an impassioned emotion which, struggling desperately to find expression, culminates in the latent introduction of the two-part bar in bar 5ff. Yet not even here do these moments of sombreness last, and a sense of calm returns in the deeply felt third theme in C major.[47] Only in the semiquaver triplets of its consequent phrase

---

46. It is already found in Orpheus's solo, 'Che puro ciel', in Gluck's opera; on Mozart's use of it, see above. For examples in Haydn, see the middle movements of sonatas nos 35, 38 and 39 in the complete edition of his works. The *Don Giovanni* motifs in D minor are likewise related to it. The same idea is also found in the finale of Beethoven's C minor symphony. The end of the movement was originally shorter, with Mozart writing out the longer version on a separate sheet of paper; see also Mendelssohn, *Briefe aus den Jahren 1833 bis 1847*, 44.

47. It recalls Susanna's words in the second-act finale of *Le nozze di Figaro*, 'il brando prendete, il paggio uccidete'.

do we still hear a distant echo of the mood of wistful nostalgia. Here, too, the motif is raptly developed, leading to an expansion of the whole period; and here, too, the two-part bar, combined with a crescendo, steals in towards the end. The subject-group comes to an end with a dialogue between strings and winds, the sheer sound of which is peerless in its beauty.

Development section and recapitulation are handled on this occasion with inspired freedom, while at the same time affording matchless examples of structures as brief as they are filled with ideas. How expressive and almost recitative-like is the brief transitional passage for the first violins! In the short development section wave upon wave of passion builds up on the basis of the second theme, while the harmonies continue to change, slipping from D minor to E flat minor in the seventh bar and from now on giving particularly keen emphasis to the recalcitrant two-part bar. Yet not even this outburst of wild agitation is of any real duration, and once again the triplet motif from the final group takes it upon itself to pour oil on troubled waters and lead us back to the main theme by means of a dialogue between the winds involving a gentle chromatic line. The changes that this theme has undergone allow us to feel with particular keenness the transformation that took place in the previous section. There is no longer any sign of its cantabile consequent phrase. Instead Mozart prefers to stick to the countermotif with its impulsive demisemiquavers, a motif which first appears – by no means fortuitously – in the basses, after which it is taken up and expanded by the violins, before leading the whole of the musical argument to the subdominant. Once again the theme reasserts itself in the basses, only to be literally overwhelmed by the demisemiquaver motion, which now raises the music to a higher level, bringing to it a powerful, heroic element that culminates in the resolute entry of C major and in a passage of overwhelming power.[48] The original theme backs this up in the winds, assuming a guise that involves diminution and that compresses the melodic outlines of its first two bars to their ultimate extreme:

Its dotted rhythm complements this proud image in the most effective way imaginable. The second theme is merely hinted at and can therefore conjure up only a fleeting and shadowy picture of all that has gone before. What follows, by contrast, bespeaks a sense of calm and peaceful hope, with the different sonorities in the winds creating a particularly beautiful impression. But then the main theme appears once again in the wonderful coda – a passage added in the very last stages of composition – and again the demisemiquaver motif, now in the winds, attempts to intervene, but it is silenced by a radical curtailment of the antecedent from four to two bars, and in its place we hear the original form of the consequent phrase's noble melody, a melody suppressed in the recapitulation. The movement comes to an end with a very brief final group that has only one point in common with the earlier group: its magical horn sonorities. No other coda by the composer bears so unmistakable an imprint of his genius.

As with the earlier symphonies, the menuetto picks up the mood of the opening movement, except that on this occasion the more thoughtful elements initially take precedence. Its first subject-group is characterized by the same strict motivic unity that had typified the G minor symphony, with the whole of the movement evolving from a single initial motif:

48. Here, too, the two-part bar is incorporated into the three-part bar.

Also common to both movements is the extent to which the opening is varied in the third section, which is followed once again by the main theme in the winds, albeit in a new contrapuntal and highly chromatic variant, so that the final element of the theme ultimately has to put an end to these timorous goings-on. The highly original trio seems initially intent on reinforcing the previous cadential harmonies with its wind sonorities, but it is answered in a much higher register by a comical quaver motif of Haydnesque stamp, and with this the structure of this tiny main section is complete. The middle section is entirely dominated by the opening motif.[49] It begins with an obstinate but good-humoured struggle between the brass and strings over the following rhythmic figure: ♪♪ ♩ 𝄾 . This same motif then leads us back unexpectedly to a repeat of the beginning, which is now varied instrumentally (note the low-lying writing for the horn).

In spite of its traditional description as 'the C major symphony with final fugue', the final movement is not a fugue but is an example of sonata form in which fugue technique plays an important but far from predominant role. Although Mozart's current interest in counterpoint finds its supreme expression here, he was by no means concerned with questions of purely technical mastery. Rather, his mastery serves to give the richest and most varied expression to the animated free play of forces that informs the symphony as a whole and to do so, moreover, one last time. Although other composers of the period, including Michael Haydn and Dittersdorf,[50] attempted something similar, Mozart surpasses them all not only in terms of the playful lightness with which he sets and solves contrapuntal problems (after all, he has been described with some justification as the last great contrapuntalist of the old school) but also in respect of the consummate harmonic writing that dominates this movement between its purely homophonic and contrapuntal sections, allowing the latter to emerge completely naturally from the former. The first complex of themes is laid out along lines very similar to those of its predecessor from the opening movement, except that it is more broadly structured than in the earlier movement, extending, as it does, as far as bar 73.[51] Like its predecessor, it is divided into two almost equal halves by a clear half-cadence. The familiar theme enters quietly and secretively. Like the final theme of the E flat major symphony, it is in two-part harmony. But unlike the theme of the opening movement, *cantabilità* now takes precedence, with a cantabile line emerging even from the more animated consequent phrase:[52]

---

49. In its opening we may already hear a pre-echo of the theme of the finale:

50. See Kretzschmar, *Führer durch den Konzertsaal*, i.260–61. ◆ No doubt the example best known to Mozart was Michael Haydn's MH287, composed about 1780; in 1783 Mozart made a partial copy of the symphony's fugato finale (KAnh. A52).
51. The reader may gain an idea of the dimensions of this movement from the fact that the subject-group is 157 bars long, the development section 68, the recapitulation 131 and the coda 66.
52. The rhythmic accents lie on the second and fourth beats. A similar cantabile hexachord theme also forms the basis of the 'Cum Sancto Spiritu' fugue in the C minor mass K427.

This consequent phrase is the only idea in the whole movement that is not contrapuntally developed but appended to the contrapuntal sections in the manner of a refrain. Scarcely has it been repeated by the tutti when contrapuntal procedures enter with the simple ligature counterpoint familiar from an earlier generation of composers:

Meanwhile, the semiquaver motif from (b) appears in the bass, it, too, an idea familiar from the opening allegro's subject-group. This section is followed by a new idea that is heroic in stamp:

This idea soon rises majestically upwards through the notes of the ascending triad over rolling basses, leading to a noisy half-cadence on the dominant, exactly as in the opening movement. The whole section is now repeated, with the contrapuntal procedures serving to add to the energy inherent in the themes, as they do whenever the themes of this movement are repeated or developed. The result is not a fugue, but only the first, five-part exposition of one. The theme is now a bar longer:

The new idea that is introduced immediately afterwards and that is likewise treated imitatively is derived from the contrapuntal continuation (e):

while its own continuation (see above) already contains within it the seeds of the second theme (in inversion). Once again it is the heroic motif (d) – this time in stretta – that brings the passage to an end. The second, cantabile theme[53]

---

53. Its melodic line belongs to a well-known older type:

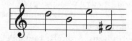

On the first three notes, see also the Eleison motif from the Kyrie of the C minor mass K427.

likewise comprises a single vast complex of ideas, with increased contrapuntal activity in its second half. This time, however, it is joined in its first section – as though by chance – by motif (f^2), which now appears in its original form, as a second subject in diminution, with (f^1) and (d) in counterpoint. But it is only after the vast pedal point on D that the theme reaches its true climax: and again there develops a contrapuntal passage, again with stretta entries, initially based on the first three notes of the theme, later with the theme in its entirety, its entries following each other within the narrow confines of a minim. In this way the music generates a power that seems almost impossible to surpass. The main theme's homophonic consequent phrase then returns to highly impressive effect,[54] again with a varied repeat, the expression of a self-conscious and contented feeling of strength. And again motif (d) places its seal on all this, initially in a more intense contrapuntal guise (with contrary motion), before dying away softly in the winds.

The actual development section has difficulty in asserting itself in the face of this vast block of a subject-group, which contains within it the material for two development sections. It limits itself in essence to the single theme (d), using (a) only by way of an introduction and in brief episodes. The introduction picks up the previous mood to the sound of two mysterious, tension-laden pedal points on *a* and *d*, after which the brass suddenly and noisily enters with the beginning of motif (d), thus signalling the start of the contrapuntal treatment of this theme, too. As before, the stretta entries seem to spur on each other with their battle cry. This is the most militant passage in the movement, not least because of the violent clash between the dotted motifs, with their constantly shifting accents. As so often with passages of this kind in Mozart's works, the harmonies simply move upwards through the circle of fifths, with only the mode occasionally changing. At this point, motif (a) suddenly asserts itself in the winds, resulting in an almost dramatic confrontation between the two and, hence, between the heroic and thoughtful and intimate aspects of the whole. There is something extraordinarily subtle about the way in which the emotional world of (a) continues to expand, forcing motif (d) to abandon its contrapuntal ambitions and to moderate its volume to a *piano* from which it rises once again for a final show of strength over a typically Mozartian pedal point, before quietly leading back to the recapitulation via a transitional passage as brief as it is inspired over chromatically descending cellos and double basses.

In keeping with the whole character of this movement, the recapitulation is notable for its particularly far-reaching changes, all of which are designed to increase the emotional charge. To this end the two sections that make up the main thematic block are reduced to a single section[55] that is harmonically and contrapuntally far deeper in consequence.[56] Less far-reaching are the changes to the second thematic block, which is repeated in its entirety. Following a powerful shift of theme (d) to the subdominant, Mozart adds the impressive coda to this second thematic block, a coda which, in the present case, resembles a second and more potent development section inasmuch as it takes all the ideas that have already been treated contrapuntally and plays them off, the one against the other, in a tremendous fugato. As though in a dream, theme (d) is initially answered by theme (a) in inversion, but from the *forte* marking onwards, fugal procedures take over, procedures based here on theme (a) and, in counterpoint to it, theme (g). As soon as a new voice enters, one of the other main themes appears in counterpoint to it, with the result that we hear in succession (f^1) and its continuation (f^2) and (d). In short, there is not a single bar in this whole section that is not thematic in origin. Using this material, Mozart now opens all the

---

54. The only contrapuntal feature here is the imitation of the following rhythm in the winds: ♩ ♩ ♩| ○ |♩
55. In the light of the development section, the first entry of (d) is initially omitted.
56. The first signs of an inversion of (a) are found here in the cellos and double basses.

floodgates of multiple counterpoint, with all the old familiar ideas striking the listener's ear in ever-new combinations, leaving us astonished at the wonderful ease with which this vital energy, now increased to a hitherto unknown pitch of intensity, impresses itself upon us here.[57] Not even this section is a fully worked-out fugue, of course. Rather, it contents itself with a twofold exposition involving regular entries on the tonic, dominant and tonic (dominant). Only on the second occasion is the last entry of the dominant displaced by the tonic, with the whole entry, moreover, being a bar shorter. This increase in tension also prepares for the entry of theme (b), a theme which, followed by (d), now brings the movement to an end on a note of festive brilliance and celebration – this is also the section that was previously suppressed in the recapitulation. A powerful fanfare concludes the movement and, with it, the symphony.[58]

Apart from these three symphonies, the most significant work from this period is the divertimento in E flat major K563 for violin, viola and cello that Mozart wrote for Puchberg.[59] It is in six movements, a number that Mozart had already preferred in the past: allegro, adagio, menuetto, andante with variations, menuetto and rondo. As always, the problem of the actual sound of the piece – only three string instruments, without a second violin – has had a decisive impact on its musical structure, and one can only admire the mastery with which Mozart handles these limitations. The expedient of double-stopping is relatively rarely used. Rather more frequent, by contrast, are broken chords, but in general the writing is in three parts and, thanks to the often virtuosic exploitation of the expressive potential of each of the three instruments for which the work is scored, the result is a sound of almost inexhaustible fullness and variety. Even the opening allegro's beautiful second subject demonstrates this quality in a surprising way: the melody – a close relative of that of the romance from the D minor keyboard concerto – is expounded in two-part harmonies by the first violin and cello, while the viola takes the bass line. In its choice and treatment of its themes, too, the work is a genuine example of chamber music. All three players are treated as equals: even when one of them takes control, the others explore independent ideas in a spirit of contradiction or affirmation, so that we always have the impression of the most animated life. The expressive world is that of the symphonies, extending from the lightest homophony to strict counterpoint. Only the tone is far more intimate and delicate in keeping with the character of a divertimento, with any suggestion of pessimism or heroism replaced by a healthy, youthful feeling of strength that is as capable of rapt infatuation as it is of good-humoured ribaldry. Take the opening movement's development section, in which the main theme pursues its dreamy course to distant keys in a typically Mozartian manner. Yet by the third bar this theme has already been

---

57. With the exception of the flutes, the winds are divided and double the violins either in unison or at the octave, while the brass and timpani accompany them with heavy fanfare-like motifs.

58. ◆ Further concerning the 'Jupiter' in particular, see Sechter, 'Analysis of the Finale of Mozart's Symphony no. 41 in C (K.551, "Jupiter") (1843)' (for a significant nineteenth-century analysis); Sisman, *Mozart: The 'Jupiter' Symphony, No. 41 in C major, K. 551* (concerning rhetoric, learned style and the sublime); Chua, 'Haydn as Romantic: A Chemical Experiment with Instrumental Music' (for a provocative discussion of how the symphony may have been read by the early Romantics); Keefe, 'The "Jupiter" Symphony in C, K. 551: New Perspectives on the Dramatic Finale and its Stylistic Significance in Mozart's Orchestral Œuvre' (concerning dialogue procedures); and A. Peter Brown, 'Eighteenth-century traditions and Mozart's "Jupiter" symphony K.551' (for an account of other late eighteenth-century, C major trumpet and drums symphonies). Further concerning the final trilogy generally, see Subotnik, 'Evidence of a Critical World View in Mozart's Last Three Symphonies'; Gülke, *Im Zyklus eine Welt: Mozarts letzte Sinfonien*; and for an instructive performance analysis virtually contemporaneous with Abert, Weingartner, *Ratschläge für Aufführungen klassischer Sinfonien. Band III: Mozart.*

59. See Nottebohm, *Mozartiana*, 54. ◆ The idea that K563 was composed for Puchberg assumes the identity of that work with the trio mentioned in Mozart's letter to Constanze, written at Dresden on 16 April 1789 – 'We arranged a quartet among ourselves. . . . At this little concert I introduced the trio that I wrote for Herr von Puchberg' – and his letter to Puchberg of about 8 April 1790: 'Tomorrow . . . Count Hadik has invited me to perform for him Stadler's quintet [K581] and the trio I composed for you' (*Briefe*, iv.82–3 and 105).

joined by a further motif derived by a process of foreshortening from an earlier subsidiary idea. Melodically speaking, it strikes out in completely the opposite direction, with its original form finally giving rise to increasingly agitated canonic clashes between all three. An admonitory voice good-humouredly asserts itself here:

And, as in the symphonies, so here, too, Mozart finds his way back to the recapitulation by means of a surprising series of modulations.[60] The marvellous rêverie of the adagio is built up on a simple triadic motif:[61]

This is then taken up by the violin in its own inimitable language to produce the following lively and expansive flourish that immediately awakens a competitive spirit in the other two instruments:

It also forms the actual nub of the movement, as even the brief motif that is found in the development section is derived from it:

The ending in particular revels insatiably in this idea, which soars aloft in each of the three instruments in turn. Of the two menuettos, the first is notable not least for the inspired way in which its repeats, both in its main movement and in its Trio, are varied and expanded, just as was the case with the symphonies. Whereas the second menuetto is melodic in character, the first is notable for its animated figurations. Between them comes the andante, a set of variations on a folklike theme. Each section is immediately varied at its repeat, resulting in a double variation of a kind that we have already occasionally encountered in the past, with the two variations alternating within the complex as a whole in such a way that each of the initial sections and repeats forms a

60. Of significance here is the little crescendo that soon makes way for a *piano* marking. ◆ Abert's concern for detail – including both dynamics (as here) and articulation – distinguishes his writings from those of his Mozartian contemporaries. In the case of K563, however, dynamics and articulation are especially problematic; no autograph survives and the earliest known source for the work is Artaria's posthumous first edition of 1792. For an account of the trio's textual complexities, see Seiffert, 'Mozarts Streichtrio KV 563: Eine quellen- und textkritische Erörterung'.
61. The rising triadic line mirrors the descending line of the themes in both the opening movement and the first menuetto.

self-contained variation. In the first variation, for example, the theme is heard in its original form on the viola, with independent contrapuntal lines in the violin and cello. At the repeat, by contrast, we find free figurations in the violin supported by the other two instruments, whose accompaniment is light-textured but, harmonically speaking, often considerably altered. In the second variation, a fiery dialogue between viola and violin is followed by a free canon between violin and cello. In the particularly thoughtful *minore*, the contrapuntal lines in the three voices are interchanged, so that the violin now has the viola's melody, the viola that of the cello, and the cello that of the violin. In the *maggiore* that follows this sombre picture the viola pursues its own course, seriously and sedately, with the theme now reduced to its simplest melodic outlines, while accompanied by an extremely lively figure in the violin and an old-fashioned running bass in the cello. It is as though the old and cheerful tune has been transformed into a penitent pilgrim's chant, with one phrase above all emerging with particular dignity:

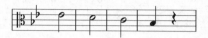

Significantly, this image is not offset by any counterimage but brings the scene to an end with a plagal coda, although not before the theme has briefly taken its leave of us one last time in its original form. The following menuetto takes us back to the world of hedonistic pleasure with its imitation of horn textures in its opening bars. This is not only one of Mozart's most charming minuets, it is also one of his most ingenious compositions in this field, as is clear not least from the superior and almost whimsical way in which the various elements are interchanged and recombined within the narrowest confines of the second section of the main movement, while maintaining the lightest of touches. It is on this basis that the viola's delightful melody blossoms in the first trio, a pre-echo of Schubert's German dances that are also recalled in the brief development section that revels in the tenderest sadness. The second trio, too, reveals a secret anguish in spite of its charmingly flirtatious main theme, an anguish that emerges more especially from its development section, with its strains of G minor and fully written-out ritardando. Mozart evidently had great difficulty taking his leave of this menuetto, and in a remarkably lengthy coda he returns to the main section, once again playing whimsically with its principal motifs. The final movement, too, reveals him at the very peak of his creative powers: here he handles rondo form with a freedom found in virtually none of his earlier rondos. Not only does he vary the themes each time that he repeats them, he also develops them. In this way, the main theme suddenly appears in the viola in A flat major, after which it is broken down into its individual motivic components and, by a series of bold modulations, brought to the dominant of C minor. The following idea

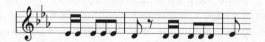

is then treated in a similar fashion, its manifold rhythmic shifts revealing it as the joker of the pack. The same is true of the remaining themes. As a whole, the movement is unadulterated Mozart in terms of its winning charm[62] and its tendency to revel in its own wealth of ideas. The work itself

---

62. The first theme's consequent phrase points clearly to the well-known song *Sehnsucht nach dem Frühling* K596 and especially to the line 'Wie möcht' ich doch so gerne ein Veilchen wieder sehn' ('How much I'd like to see a violet again').

is not only one of Mozart's most mature chamber pieces, it also represents an unsurpassed high point within the genre in general.

The three keyboard trios that date from this period, K542, 548 and 564, are not quite on the same high level, even though they are all entirely worthy of their creator and represent a considerable stylistic advance on their predecessors. Above all, the interplay between the keyboard on the one hand and the string instruments on the other is now more fully developed and the cello's older role as a continuo instrument almost completely abandoned. Concerto form is recalled by the three-movement design of all three trios, by the choice of rondo form for the finale and by the often virtuosic treatment not only of the keyboard but of the violin, too. Although the G major trio was originally intended as a keyboard sonata,[63] an origin still clearly discernible in the finished piece, the concertante interplay between the two parties is skilfully worked out. The work was presumably revised in response to external pressure, and it was no doubt for a similar occasion that the other two pieces were composed.[64] All three works, and especially the first two, reveal the characteristic features of Mozart's instrumental style at this period, chief among which are his contrapuntal leanings and his reworking of what were originally subsidiary ideas in the development sections. The most substantial of the three works is the trio in E major (K542), which is also the most broadly developed. In its treatment of its second subject it reveals a surprising contrapuntal depth, while the very beginning of the recapitulation adds immeasurably to the expressive intensity of this passage. In the analogous movement in the C major trio, the main emphasis lies on the development section thanks to Mozart's elaborate and sophisticated treatment of a motif made up of only two notes. The middle movements depart from the noble Italianate tone of the earlier chamber works with keyboard, opting instead for the more popular tone of autochthonous songs. Here, too, the E major trio towers above its companion pieces, its andante grazioso – cast in the form of a French rondeau with *mineur* – proving a veritable pearl of the whole trio repertory, not least as a result of its *mineur*, whose exotically tinged melody, derived from its main theme, and surprisingly bold harmonies attest to exceptional musical inspiration. While the andante of the C major trio is distinguished above all by its soaring cantilenas and intricate figural writing, that of the G major trio is a set of variations on a simple song tune, the affecting sadness of which goes straight to our hearts. Although neither as elaborate nor as profound as the variations in the string trio, the present variations develop the theme's basic mood in such a natural, truthful and, above all, melodious way that the movement fully justifies its place in popular affections. Of the rondo finales, that of the E major trio sounds like an echo of the final movements of the great concertos, with its broadly developed themes and transitions interspersed by passages of pronounced virtuosity, highly effective contrasts and, at the same time, a desire for unity that is peculiar to all the works of this period. This final quality emerges even more clearly from the delightful Rococo finale of the C major trio, a French rondeau whose *mineur* is motivically linked to its main section. The most loosely structured of these final movements is that of the G major trio, an innocently light-hearted siciliana.

---

63. ◆ This hypothesis is based on the survival of two autograph leaves (now in the Biblioteka Jagiellońska, Kraków) with fragments of what is apparently a piano part for bars 41–105 of the andante of K564; see Weismann, 'Zur Urfassung von Mozarts Klaviertrio KV 564'.

64. On the E major trio, see Mozart's letter to Puchberg; *Briefe*, iv.67 (letter of 17 June 1788). ◆ In his postscript to this letter, asking Puchberg for a loan, Mozart writes, 'When will we have a small musical party at your house again? I have composed a new trio!', which presumably refers to K542. Contrary to Abert's implication – that the works were composed for private performance – it may be that the trios were intended in the first instance for publication, though not all at the same time. K542 and K548 were published together with the earlier trio, K502, by Artaria in 1788. K564, the G major trio, was first published in London, by Mozart's English friend Stephen Storace, and may have been composed for him; the edition published by Artaria in 1790, presumably with Mozart's authority, transmits a text different in some details.

On a formal level, Mozart's final violin sonata K547 harks back to the 'Romantic' sonatas of his youth inasmuch as it is more of a suite than a sonata. A slow prelude in simple ternary form is followed by a loosely structured sonata movement whose thematic writing, too, is reminiscent of that of a suite. The final movement is a set of variations. By far the most profound of these movements, all three of which are in the same key, is the set of variations, which resembles that of the string trio in terms of its design and execution, with the fifth and sixth variations in particular pointing clearly to this model, the former by dint of its thoughtful contrapuntal writing, the latter by virtue of the simplified version of the melody of the theme in the violin.

Of the keyboard works of this period, pride of place must go to the D major concerto K 537, the so-called 'Coronation' concerto.[65] Although it resembles its predecessors in general terms, there are many points of detail in which it reveals the distinctive features of Mozart's later style.[66] Among these features are the splendid way in which the second subject is introduced in the tutti (already we seem to hear in it a pre-echo of the later, second subsidiary theme in the keyboard) and the interpolation of Mozart's old favourite idea in a new guise before the end of the tutti. On this occasion the soloist enters with the main idea without any preliminaries, but then insists on his own second subject, only later returning to that of the orchestra, the final section of which is subjected to a lengthy contrapuntal development. The development section picks up the final motif in what is now a familiar manner, reworking it along highly elaborate lines in order to produce another new motif as though at random:

In its more compact and cantabile form

this motif then dominates the section that follows. Here, too, the recapitulation is much altered, with the independent treatment of Mozart's favourite theme proving particularly attractive. The larghetto picks up the tone of a naïve romance familiar from earlier concertos, its second theme developed by the soloist from a preparatory tutti idea:

65. On its performance in the modern concert hall, see Reinecke, *Zur Wiederbelebung der Mozartschen Clavier-Concerte*, 25ff.
◆ Further, see the performance practice discussion in chapter 39 above.
66. ◆ Concerning the style of K537 and its possible relationship to Mozart's other 'late' piano concerto, K595, see Keefe, 'A Complementary Pair: Stylistic Experimentation in Mozart's Final Piano Concertos, K. 537 in D and K. 595 in B♭'. Paper studies show that K537 was probably started up to a year before Mozart entered it in his thematic catalogue on 24 February 1788. And in the event, a text for the piano part was never fully written down in the autograph; a left-hand part is lacking for much of the first and third movements, and for the middle movement in its entirety.

In its most general terms, this movement is one of the most delicate and fragrant blooms among Mozart's concertos. The final movement is a familiar combination of rondo and sonata form and is distinguished not only by its remarkable wealth of themes and the brilliant virtuosity of its bridge passages but above all by its harmonic liberties. The soloist's second subject, for example, makes its second appearance following a sudden enharmonic shift to B flat major, only gradually working its way back to G major. In this way, the D major Concerto inhabits the expressive world of its predecessors, while at the same time clearly reflecting the period at which it was written.

The two finished keyboard sonatas from this period, K545 in C major[67] and K570 in B flat major,[68] prefer particularly free types of rondo form for their middle and final movements. The first of these pieces is a stylish example of teaching material for beginners, its opening movement illustrating what was by now the antiquated practice of introducing the recapitulation in the subdominant. Of the two, the B flat major sonata is the more substantial piece. Its opening movement has in fact two subsidiary themes, one in the subdominant, the other in the dominant. Of these, the latter is closely related to the main theme, attracting attention in the development section by its use of double counterpoint. The adagio is notable for its particularly noble cantilena and, in its second subject-groups, for the highly subjective nature of the emotions depicted here. In the very loosely structured final rondo, it is the second episode in E flat major that stands out most of all, again on account of the role accorded to double counterpoint here. No less ingenious is the way in which the themes of both episodes are recalled at the end in an abbreviated and varied form.

But the stylistic features of this period are most pronounced in the two sonata movements K533 in F and B flat major. (For reasons that remain unclear, the sonata was never completed.[69]) The first movement, in particular, provides a parallel with the finale of the C major symphony to the extent that in both cases sonata form is filled with teeming contrapuntal life. Both subject-groups – first and second – have scarcely stated their themes before these latter are contrapuntally developed in the most varied ways. No less typical of this whole approach is the introduction of a third main idea, which enters provocatively in the bass:

---

67. Its last movement was later combined by an unknown hand with the first movement of the violin sonata in F major K547 to produce a further keyboard sonata K547a. ◆ K547a is almost certainly not an arrangement by Mozart.
68. The published version of this sonata arbitrarily includes a violin part. ◆ There is no convincing evidence that the violin part is by Mozart.
69. In later editions they were combined with the rondo K494 in F major to produce a complete sonata. ◆ The idea of a sonata including K533 and the rondo K494, published in Vienna by Hoffmeister in 1788, was unquestionably Mozart's and the two movements of K533 may have been intended from the start to accompany the expanded version of K494 published as part of the sonata.

Only towards the end of the subject-group does the writing become homophonic, and here it acquires a decidedly virtuosic aspect. All these themes exude a keen, belligerent resolve, which in the development section assumes a note of sombreness and defiance. Most of this section is in the minor and accompanied by rolling triplets between which the beginning of the main theme appears only intermittently. The recapitulation is again much altered. Note especially the way in which the first subject moves playfully towards D flat major, before returning to the tonic through a broad series of sequences, a feature entirely typical of Mozart's style at this time. But when the third idea enters, the main theme is treated contrapuntally. Here, too, its continuation is characteristic of the Mozart at this period:

The last four bars are utterly inspired as an interpolation. Two features that the B flat major andante shares with this movement are sonata form and strict counterpoint. This andante is also one of the most broodingly introspective movements that Mozart ever wrote for the keyboard. Even the main theme is unusual from a melodic[70] and, more especially, an harmonic point of view. Both themes, moreover, are broadly developed, so that their continuation creates the impression of independent ideas – this is especially true of the expressive second subject in F major, in which the tension is brilliantly increased through the use of modulation.[71] The development section begins with the combined elaboration of both themes on the basis of a motif derived from the main theme:

This in turn is followed by one of the most austere passages in the whole of Mozart's output. Certainly none of his contemporaries ever wrote anything to match the present passage in terms of its searing *relationes non harmonicae*. Together with its contrapuntal accompaniment, which is

---

70. Note the way in which Mozart expands the consequent phrase by developing its highly expressive first element.
71. Particularly unusual here is the apparent minor tonality of the sixth bar before the double barline, with only the following bar making it clear that the *a* flat in the middle voice is in fact a *g* sharp.

reinforced by thirds, the motif just quoted strives upwards with its sforzato accents, creating a feeling of the bitterest self-torment, until it reaches the dominant harmony of B flat major, thereby producing a sense of emotional tension unique in Mozart's sonatas. The recapitulation begins by restating the first subject in the bass, as in the symphonies. Meanwhile, in the soprano register, we hear a motif from the development section. Later, too, the parts are interchanged. In this way the mood associated at this time with *Don Giovanni* finds consummate expression in these two masterly movements for the keyboard. And it continues to reverberate in the profoundly thoughtful adagio K540 in B minor. Although this last-named piece is cast in sonata form and is based on strict thematic procedures, it resembles nothing so much as a fantasia, a resemblance due to its emphatically subjective expression as manifest in its disjointed, recitative-like melodic writing, its often extremely bold and constantly shifting harmonies and its keen dynamic accents. But the work is also of particular interest in terms of its keyboard technique: note the crossing of hands, the singing basses, the expressive middle voices and the use of figuration.

Mozart's official activities as Imperial chamber composer were initially[72] limited to writing all manner of dances for the masked balls in the Imperial and Royal Redoutensäle. These halls were situated in a wing of the Hofburg on the right-hand side of the Josefsplatz and originally included a theatre where operas and ballets were performed for the court on festive occasions. In 1752, following the building of the Burgtheater, this theatre at the Hofburg was turned into the two Redoutensäle, one of which was larger in size than the other. They were used not only for court festivities but also for public concerts and masked balls. These balls were held every Sunday during the carnival season, as well as on the last Thursday before Lent and on the last three days of the carnival. Joseph II was very keen on these balls as a way of drawing closer to his subjects and frequently attended them, together with his court, encouraging the lively participation of members of every social class. The wearing of masks allowed certain liberties. The chief dances were minuets and German dances (waltzes), later also contredanses and ländlers. Only the lower orders took part in waltzes and ländlers as they involved a good deal of jostling – just as in *Don Giovanni*. The Redoutensäle were normally run by the same lessee as the opera house. In 1778 the court assumed control of the opera house, adding the Kärntnertor-Theater to its responsibilities in 1785, a state of affairs that remained in force until August 1794. As a result, it was the management of the Imperial court theatres that commissioned the dance music for these balls, attempting to attract respected composers in spite of the pitiful fee of only a handful of ducats. In this way, not only Mozart himself wrote sets of dances for the Redoutensäle, so too did Haydn, Eybler, Gyrowetz, Hummel and Beethoven.[73]

Between his appointment at the end of 1787 and his death in 1791 Mozart wrote a whole series of dances for these masked balls:[74]

72. The large-scale pasticcio *L'ape musicale* compiled by Da Ponte includes a number of arias by Mozart; see *Wiener Zeitung*, xxiii (1789), appendix [*Dokumente*, 294–6, *Documentary Biography*, 335–7]. ◆ It is not clear why Abert cites this work here; it is unrelated to Mozart's court appointment and performances of the pasticcio probably had nothing to do with Mozart. First given in February 1789, the extant libretto suggests it may have included a parody of the duet 'Là ci darem la mano' from *Don Giovanni*. Copies of the work offered for sale by the music dealer Lausch in the *Wiener Zeitung* for 21 March 1789, however, do not list this number; instead they list 'Voi che sapete' and 'Non più andrai', both from *Le nozze di Figaro*.
73. Pohl, *Joseph Haydn*, i.102–3 and ii.152–3; Nottebohm, *Ein Skizzenbuch von Beethoven*, 39. ◆ Concerning the size of the orchestras that might have played Mozart's dance music, see Edge, 'Mozart's Viennese Orchestras'.
74. Published in AMA/IX, with additional material in XXIV; see Chrysander, 'Mozarts Tänze für Orchester', 756–7. ◆ A more recent and comprehensive edition is NMA IV/13/1/1–2.

1788	14 January	Contredanse K534 ('Das Donnerwetter')
	23 January	Contredanse K535 ('Die Bataille')
	27 January	6 German dances K536
	30 October	2 contredanses K 565 (lost)
	6 December	6 German dances K567
	24 December	12 minuets K568
1789	21 February	6 German dances K571[75]
	December	12 minuets K585[76]
		12 German dances K586
		Contredanse K587 ('Der Sieg vom Helden Coburg')
1791	23 January	6 minuets for the Redoutensaal K599
	29 January	6 German dances K600
	5 February	4 minuets K601
		4 German dances K602[77]
		2 contredanses K603
	12 February	2 minuets K604
		3 German dances K605[78]
	28 February	Contredanse K607 ('Il trionfo delle donne')
		6 German dances K606
	6 March	Contredanse K610 ('Die Leyerer'; called 'Les filles malicieuses' in the autograph)[79]
	6 March	5 contredanses K609[80]

No dances are recorded for 1790, when the illness and death of Joseph II on 20 February meant that most of the celebrations were abandoned. The most striking aspect of these dances is their almost literally inexhaustible fund of invention. Although their form offers only limited scope for experimentation, each dance differs from the others. With the exception of the very simple

75. The Malherbe collection in Paris [now at the Bibliothèque nationale] includes an autograph score of the wind and percussion parts not known to AMA. The string parts are indicated here by rests, suggesting that Mozart added the winds at a later date. ◆ For an edition including both the wind and timpani parts, see NMA IV/13/1/1. The autograph of the string parts is in the Österreichische Nationalbibliothek, Vienna.

76. ◆ The exact number of minuets composed by Mozart, and now identified as K585, is uncertain. The autograph (Staatsbibliothek zu Berlin) includes only four minuets although Mozart explicitly gives '6 Menuette' on the first page. At the same time, his thematic catalogue reads '12 Menuette'.

77. The dance reproduced in AMA XI, no. 12/3 is identical with the German dance catalogued by Mozart himself as no. 132 (2) (K611 of 6 March 1791). ◆ That is, K611 is identical with K602 no. 3.

78. The older copies and editions (see critical commentary to AMA XI, no. 11, and, hence, Köchel (605) and the complete edition add a third German dance (with the 'Sleighride trio') to the two listed in Mozart's own catalogue. ◆ As Abert notes, Mozart's thematic catalogue lists only two dances for K605. The third, 'Die Schlittenfahrt', is known from a contemporaneous copy in the library of the Gesellschaft der Musikfreunde, Vienna; there is no unequivocal evidence it is by Mozart. NMA IV/13/1/1 includes 'Die Schlittenfahrt' as part of K605.

79. André's catalogue also includes five minuets headed 'di Wolfgango Amadeo Mozart Vienna 1784' (K461). Several other dances, presumably dating from an earlier period, are also listed alongside the German dances written in Prague (K509). To these may be added the contredanses K535a, all of which were published in keyboard arrangements by Artaria with K462/3, 534 and 535. Printed and manuscript collections of dances in the most varied transcriptions circulated under Mozart's name, but their authenticity is highly doubtful. ◆ The dating of K610 is the most vexing among the late dances. Although Mozart listed it in his thematic catalogue under the date 6 March 1791, the paper on which it is written apparently dates from 1782–4. It may be that in 1791 Mozart wrote the dance on a scrap of old paper; or possibly that he pressed into service a short composition nearly ten years old. For a comprehensive account of the confusing source situation for Mozart's late dances, see the critical report to NMA IV/13/1/2.

80. Only no. 5 is dated, although no. 1 – based on the theme of 'Non più andrai' – may be from around 1786. No. 6 is merely another version of K610.

ländlers, all are in either two parts (with a trio in the same key or, at most, in the minor) or in several parts. Into the first group fall the minuets and German dances, while the contredanses belong to the second group.[81] The German dances generally include a coda, which in most cases relates back to the final dance and frequently includes all manner of orchestral jokes such as the great Mannheim crescendo and ending of K571. The character of the individual dances is strictly maintained, as is clear from a comparison between the minuets and the German dances. The minuets are more elaborate in style and reveal all the delights of Mozart's handling of the orchestra at this time, with their instrumental garb frequently changing at the repeat. In the German dances, conversely, he was at pains to preserve the popular tone and ensure that sentimentality had as much of a say (especially in the minor-key trios) as rustic earthiness. In particular we find the appoggiatura slides familiar from *Don Giovanni* in the trio of K571, no. 6:

Indeed, the trios not infrequently contain unadulterated echoes of folk music, notably in K602, no. 3, which appears to be played by a hurdy-gurdy. Others include particular surprises such as the sullen chromaticisms of K571, no. 6:

Hungarian and Spanish features may be found in K568, no. 11 and K586, no. 5. Occasionally – as in K567, no. 3 – there are even motivic links between the main movement and the trio.

A popular feature of the contredanses are allusions to songs and operatic arias that were well known in their day. Just as K609 quotes from *Le nozze di Figaro*, so K607 cites Anfossi's *Il trionfo delle donne* and K587 a marching song in praise of General Friedrich Josias von Coburg-Saalfeld, whose victory over the Turks on 22 September 1789 is indicated by a minor-key theme in the style of Mozart's other Turkish music. Closely related to this is the naïve tone-painting of a number of these pieces, notably in 'Die Bataille' K535, which includes not only trumpet signals but also a march with fife and drum and, at the end, a further 'alla turca'. 'Les filles malicieuses' K610 is another programmatic piece, while the trio of K600, no. 5 features a canary (represented by the piccolo) and that of K605, no. 3 a sleighride with three tuned bells and a posthorn that ultimately have the last word. In general, the instrumentation of these pieces includes many subtle features, especially of a concertante kind, quite apart from the passages that are meant to be comical. In every case the basis is a three-part string orchestra comprising two violins and bass, with no viola. To these are added various combinations of winds,[82] with trumpets (clarini) and timpani playing a prominent role here. Also represented are unusual instruments such as the tambourine in the

---

81. K603 no. 2 even has a change of time-signature familiar to us from earlier.
82. The Haydnesque doubling of first violin and bassoon missing from the mature symphonies is frequently found here.

trio of K586, no. 5. In general, these works are much undervalued, for in every respect they attest to the hand of the mature composer even within the limited artistic world that they inhabit.[83]

Totally different demands were made of Mozart at this time by Gottfried van Swieten, who had conceived a fondness for Handel's oratorios in Berlin and who was now anxious to introduce them to Vienna. In addition to the concerts that he held in his own home ('Zu den drei Hacken' in the Renngasse next to the 'Hotel zum Römischen Kaiser'), he also mounted these oratorios in the Grand Hall of the court library and in the private mansions of his aristocratic subscribers including the Princes Schwarzenberg, Lobkowitz and Dietrichstein, and Counts Apponyi, Batthyány and Franz Esterházy. The concerts took place in the afternoon before invited guests, generally during the spring months, before their lordships left for their country estates. In the main the performers were drawn from the Hofkapelle and the opera orchestra, with rehearsals being held at van Swieten's own home. He himself adapted *Athalia* and, most probably, *The Choice of Hercules*, although in both cases the works in question were almost certainly performed only after Mozart's death. The conductor was initially Joseph Starzer, who also adapted *Judas Maccabaeus*.[84] Following Starzer's death on 22 April 1787, Mozart took over, with the young Joseph Weigl as his keyboard accompanist.[85]

According to Mozart's own *Verzeichnüß* of November 1788, the first Handel oratorio that he adapted was *Acis and Galatea*.[86] This was followed in March 1789 by *Messiah*,[87] which was probably taken in hand under the impression left by the sensational performances mounted by Johann Adam Hiller at the Domkirche in Berlin on 19 May 1786 (to an Italian text),[88] at the Universitätskirche in Leipzig on 3 November 1786 and 11 May 1788[89] and in Breslau on 30 May 1788.[90] (In turn, these

83. Hummel also published a further work under Mozart's name, an *Anleitung Walzer oder Schleifer mit zwei Würfeln zu komponieren, soviel man will, ohne musikalisch zu seyn, noch etwas von der Composition zu verstehen* (Instructions on how to Write a Waltz or Slide with Two Dice, as Much as One Wants, without Being Musical or Understanding Anything about Composition). The piece appeared in Amsterdam and Berlin in four languages, but the title alone is sufficient to call Mozart's authorship into question. ◆ Hummel's *Anleitung*, published in 1793 and subsequently reprinted in Bonn, Hamburg and Paris, is almost certainly not by Mozart; it is listed in the most recent edition of Köchel as Anh. C30.01. Mozart's authentic attempt at a musical dice game – not uncommon in the later eighteenth century – is K516f of 1787; see Noguchi, 'Mozart: Musical Game in C major K. 516f' and Zaslaw, 'Mozart's Modular Minuet Machine'.
84. See Sonnleithner, 'Über Mozarts angebliche Bearbeitung und Instrumentierung des Händel'schen Oratorium "Judas Maccabäus"', 242–3, and *AmZ*, xxii (1820), 30–1. The work had already been performed in 1779 as a benefit for the Tonkünstler-Sozietät. ◆ Concerning a recently-discovered manuscript that is claimed possibly to transmit Mozart's otherwise lost version of *Judas Maccabaeus*, see Cowgill, 'The Halifax *Judas*: an unknown Handel arrangement by Mozart?'
85. This information was communicated by Sonnleithner to Jahn; see Jahn, *W. A. Mozart*, fourth edition, ii.472. On 26 February and 4 March 1788 Carl Philipp Emanuel Bach's *Die Auferstehung und Himmelfahrt Jesu* of 1774 was performed at Count Esterházy's at van Swieten's instigation. Mozart conducted, with Ignaz Umlauf at the keyboard. The singers included Adamberger and Aloysia Lange; see *Musikalischer Almanach für Deutschland auf das Jahr 1789*, 121 [*Dokumente*, 273, *Documentary Biography*, 310–11]. ◆ For this performance, Mozart arranged flute, oboe and trumpet parts for the aria 'Ich folge dir, verklärter Held', K537d.
86. Pichler, *Denkwürdigkeiten aus meinem Leben*, iv.21–2; on a benefit performance for Mozart in November 1788 with Adamberger, Tobias Gsur and Catarina Cavalieri, see Pohl, *Joseph Haydn*, ii.136. ◆ According to Zinzendorf's diary, *Acis and Galatea* was also performed on 30 December 1788 at Prince Johann Esterházy's (*Dokumente*, 290, *Documentary Biography*, 331).
87. Carpani, *Le Haydine*, first edition, 64, mentions a performance at the Schwarzenberg Palais, but this may date from a later period. ◆ *Messiah* was first performed on 6 March 1789, with a repeat performance, at Johann Esterházy's, on 7 April (*Dokumente*, 294 and 297, *Documentary Biography*, 333 and 338).
88. Hiller, *Nachricht von der Aufführung des Händelschen Messias in Berlin den 19. May 1786*; see also *Ephemeriden der Litteratur und des Theaters*, iii.335–6 and iv.333–4. Around 300 performers took part.
89. Here, too, Hiller wrote a number of essays on the performance: *Fragmente aus Händels Messias, nebst Betrachtungen über die Aufführung Händelscher Singcompositionen*; *Über Alt und Neu in der Musik*; and *Der Messias von Händel nebst angehängten Betrachtungen darüber*; on the performance, see Reichardt's *Berlinische musikalische Zeitung*, i (1805), 126–7; and *AmZ*, xxx (1828), 491.
90. Hiller added his own explanations to the wordbook; his report was published in the *Schlesische Provinzialblätter* (1788), 549–8; see Baumgart, 'Die erste Aufführung des Händel'schen Messias in Breslau in Jahre 1788'.

performances were inspired by the Handel celebrations in London in 1784 and 1785.[91]) In July 1790 Mozart went on to adapt *Alexander's Feast* and the *Ode for St Cecilia's Day*.[92]

This cult of Handel is one of the more gratifying aspects of van Swieten's musical activities and is a particular credit to those of his colleagues in Vienna who thought as he did. Although Handel never fell into such total neglect as Bach, whom van Swieten knew only as a composer of keyboard music, his works still represented a challenge for conductors of the time, taking them far beyond the world of their usual obligations.

Whereas the music of Mozart's contemporaries prescribed what the performer should play right down to the very last detail, the music of the older generation allowed performers a far greater degree of creative involvement. In the works of these earlier composers, performers had to distinguish between the obbligato voices prescribed by the composer himself and what were originally the improvised additions of the conductor, singer and, from the seventeenth century onwards, the continuo player or players. Long and bitter battles were fought before this relationship was properly recognized and the foundations laid for a type of performing practice that did justice to the essential nature of early music. Initially, it was rationalism that caused the greatest confusion: when the continuo style began to die out, contemporaries, lacking in all sense of historical perspective, came to regard it as outdated and, failing to understand its meaning, either ignored it or, at best, entrusted it not to the instruments for which it was originally intended but to those of the 'modern' orchestra. This, of course, was something that early music had itself done as a point of principle,[93] but it had always meticulously maintained the original obbligato textures. Not for a moment did it set out to 'complete' the orchestration by adding choirs of instruments or to invest the music with a particular 'colour', which was the aim of such early arrangers as Hiller and Mozart and such zealous successors as Robert Franz and his school.

Hiller himself made no secret of the fact that the allegedly primitive nature of Handel's instrumentation left him feeling dissatisfied. Even though he had grown up in the older tradition, he now aligned himself with the newer school of orchestration, which was influenced by the tone colour and articulation of the individual instruments, regarding the original merely as a sketch that he had to complete and colour in. 'Many an improvement could be made to Handel's compositions by using the wind instruments in a way commensurate with today's compositional practices. At no point in *Messiah* does Handel appear to have thought of oboes, flutes or horns, instruments that have such a characteristic contribution to make to our modern orchestras, thereby increasing and reinforcing the effectiveness of the whole. That this requires much thought and discretion I cannot deny.'[94] Yet Hiller went further than this, making changes and cuts to the works themselves, especially in arias and recitatives, in order to produce 'an entirely new score,

91. Burney's report [*An Account of the Musical Performances in Westminster Abbey and the Pantheon, May 26th, 27th, 29th; and June the 3rd and 5th, 1784*] was translated by Johann Joachim Eschenburg and published in Berlin in 1785. At the first performance more than 500 performers were involved, at the second more than 600. For a report on the performance in Copenhagen in March 1786, see Cramer, *Magazin der Musik*, ii (1786), 960–1.

92. ◆ See Zelter, 'Händel's Messias und Mozart's Bearbeitung desselben'; Winkler, 'Mozarts Bearbeitung des Messias: Händels Oratorium in neuer geographischer und geistesgeschichtlicher Umwelt'; Baselt, 'Georg Friedrich Händels "Ode for St. Cecilia's Day" und ihre Bearbeitung durch Wolfgang Amadè Mozart (KV 592)'; Holschneider, 'Mozarts Bearbeitung von Händels Messias'; and Schildkret, 'On Mozart Contemplating a Work of Handel: Mozart's Arrangement of "Messiah"'.

93. These are the 'Capellae fidiciniae' of Michael Praetorius in the third part of his *Syntagma musicum* of 1619 (see Bernoulli, *Syntagma Musicum*, 91ff.); see also Max Schneider, 'Die Besetzung der vielstimmigen Musik des 16. und 17. Jahrhunderts', 205–34. ◆ Further concerning continuo, see Howard Mayer Brown and Sadie, *Performance Practice: Music after 1600*; Borgir, *The Performance of the Basso Continuo in Italian Baroque Music*; Dreyfus, *Bach's Continuo Group*; Reidemeister, '"Was der Generalbass sey?" Beiträge zu Theorie und Praxis'; and Ledbetter, *Continuo Playing According to Handel*, in addition to the bibliography cited in chapter 39 above.

94. Hiller, *Nachricht von der Aufführung des Händelschen Messias*, 14.

more or less as Handel himself would have written it if he had been alive today'.[95] This was an approach, he believed, that would be criticized 'only by a pedantic admirer of ancient fashions or a pedantic castigator of all the good that more recent composers have achieved'.[96]

With all the unconscious self-righteousness of the rationalist, Hiller was proposing a disastrous programme of reform that ran completely counter to the style of early music and prevented audiences from achieving a proper understanding of it for decades to come. That the original continuo instruments – organs, harpsichords, lutes and harps – were replaced by the modern orchestra was bad enough. Even worse was the fact that the fundamental relationship between fully composed and improvised sections and, hence, the preponderance of line over colour was virtually abandoned.

In essence, Mozart adopted this same approach, but the fact that he had no time for Hiller's musings meant that he was spared the latter's most arbitrary excesses. Yet there was still a long way to go before stylistic considerations were based on any sense of historical awareness, with the result that he set to work with his usual uninhibitedness, regarding his own feelings as his ultimate authority. Only in one respect did he follow Hiller's lead in that his attention was directed, in the main, at the winds. The vocal lines and string parts, conversely, were taken over into his score unchanged. Only in those cases where Handel had written a single violin part did he add a second violin and viola in order to fill out the harmonies. But the wind instruments had to be omitted by the copyist. In those passages where Handel had used them to characteristic effect, namely, in numbers involving obbligato winds, Mozart left them unchanged, but whenever the oboes appeared merely to represent the winds, he either replaced them with other winds (rarely with flutes, more frequently with clarinets) or used the full choir of wind instruments. But this is also used on occasions when Handel did not even demand oboes, thereby producing a much fuller and more powerful sound. In this way the orchestral garb of the original was transformed into something completely different, as the parts that were not changed now sounded very different in their new environment. The characteristic sound of Handel's orchestra, with its obbligato voices on the one hand and, on the other, the accompanying organ and harpsichords, together with the lutes and harps that reinforce and replace these latter, has vanished.

In short, Mozart, too, adopted the principle of having the continuo part played by a choir of orchestral instruments, a principle that he adopted unwittingly, albeit with aims which, quite different from those of Hiller, cannot be justified from a stylistic point of view. The result is a treatment of the continuo part that is open to serious stylistic question, as he, too, set out from the view that his source was no more than a sketch that he had to complete. He, too, failed to recognize that the link between figures and notes in early scores is not arbitrary but that it was designed to bring out the fundamental difference between those parts that were actually composed and those that were intended to accompany them and fill out the textures. In consequence, he often committed the mistake of making these accompanying voices 'obbligato' by developing Handel's motifs along thematic and contrapuntal lines, occasionally even adding new contrapuntal voices. In this, his genius prevented him from committing the errors made by many later arrangers, who often rendered the original lines unrecognizable by incorporating them into a fabric of independent contrapuntal lines that completely undermined what had once been their dominant position. In the lightness and transparency of its textures, his adaptation consistently reveals the hand of a master, and yet it confuses the role of the adapter with that of the composer and, no matter how

---

95. Hiller, *Fragmente aus Händels Messias*, 16.
96. Hiller, *Fragmente aus Händels Messias*, 18–19.

well-intentioned Mozart undoubtedly was, it finds the latter unconsciously imposing his own personality on the work.

This is certainly the picture that emerges from Mozart's original scores of *Acis and Galatea* K566, the *Ode for St Cecilia's Day* K592 and *Alexander's Feast* K591 that are now in the Royal Library in Berlin.[97] It is one, moreover, that is complemented by his adaptation of *Messiah* K572.[98] Here the great length of the work meant that Mozart was also obliged to make cuts. Indeed, he seems to have planned even more far-reaching changes, as emerges from van Swieten's letter to him of 21 March 1789:

> Your idea of setting the text of the cold aria ['If God be for us'] as a recitative is admirable, and, uncertain as to whether you have retained the words, I am sending you a copy herewith. Anyone who can clothe Handel in such festive and tasteful guise that he pleases the modish fop on the one hand and, on the other, reveals him in his sublimity has felt Handel's worth, has understood him, has reached the source of his expression and is both able and certain to draw from this source. This is how I view all that you have achieved, and I need say no more about my confidence in you but only about my wish to receive the recitative soon.[99]

To judge by the full score, this idea was not carried out, although it shows very clearly that Mozart felt able to adopt a far freer approach to the present work than was the case with the other three oratorios. A different reason – the lack of a solo trumpeter capable of playing in the old clarino register – obliged him to rework the air 'The trumpet shall sound'. But even when there were no reasons for introducing any such changes, he altered not only the instrumentation but also the harmonization of individual passages. In short, the urge to impose his own character on the work increased decisively and, with it, the stylistic gulf between the original and his adaptation. The most extreme example of this process is the air 'The people that walked in darkness', which has been turned into something completely different from anything that Handel envisaged, with the original providing little more than the basis for a new piece.

The files on Mozart's adaptations are now closed. Now that we are aware of the sort of performance practice that obtained in Handel's day, we are far more sensitive towards such revisions and prefer to educate audiences so that they learn to appreciate the original work, rather than attempting to make it palatable by modernizing it and thereby trying to serve two masters at once. At the same time, however, it would be historically unjustified to demand that Mozart should have shared this standpoint.[100] In his own day it was invariably the living composer who was right; that

---

97. *Acis and Galatea* was composed at Cannons in 1718, *Alexander's Feast* in 1736 and the *Ode for St Cecilia's Day* in 1739; see Chrysander, *Georg Friedrich Händel*, i.479–80, ii.415–16 and 430–31. ◆ Only the autograph of K591 remains in Berlin (Staatsbibliothek zu Berlin); K566 is now at the Biblioteka Jagiellońska, Kraków, while an autograph for K592 is unknown. Original performing parts, including Mozart's autograph corrections, survive for all three works at the Národná Muzeum, Hudebná Oddelěná, Prague.

98. Not all the numbers in the published score are by Mozart. The air 'If God is for us', for example, with its bassoon accompaniment, was taken over from Hiller's adaptation; see Baumgart, *Niederrheinische Musik-Zeitung*, v (1862), 35–6. Mozart's autograph score, on which this edition was said to be based, is lost; see Reichardt's *Berlinische musikalische Zeitung*, i (1805), 127. On Mozart's first encounter with *Messiah* in Mannheim, see above. ◆ A partial autograph and the original performing parts are now housed at the Národná Muzeum, Hudebná Oddelěná, Prague (shelfmark X.B.b.4). In the event, Mozart set 'If God is for us' as a recitative.

99. Niemetschek, *Leben des k. k. Kapellmeisters Wolfgang Gottlieb Mozart*, 31 [*Dokumente*, 296, *Documentary Biography*, 337]. ◆ The authenticity of this letter is now thought to be uncertain.

100. ◆ Here Abert betrays an early to mid-twentieth-century perspective on performance and performance practice; while exempting Mozart from any sort of historical awareness, his formulation at the same time begs the question how a modern, strictly 'authenticist' view – apparently the opposite of Mozart's – is itself justifiable.

the living composer was right in his own day and had to be helped to enjoy this right would never have entered his mind. Such considerations are found only rarely and fleetingly,[101] and so it was no wonder that Mozart's adaptations, especially that of *Messiah*, soon found general acceptance. Although criticisms were eventually made, notably by Zelter[102] and Rochlitz,[103] it was only much later that this whole question was properly discussed. After all, even Zelter used Mozart's version of *Messiah* for his own performances, albeit with a number of alterations and cuts.[104] As a mere curiosity, it is finally worth mentioning Ernst Ludwig Gerber's suggestion that the choruses from *Messiah* should be performed in Mozart's arrangement but that the arias should all be newly written by tried and tested composers.[105]

A further adaptation ascribed to Mozart – a concert arrangement of the end of the overture to Gluck's *Iphigénie en Aulide* (KAnh. C5.01) – is in fact the work of the Berlin privy counsellor Johann Philipp Samuel Schmidt.[106]

101.   'No, David [a reference to Jacques-Louis David (1748–1825)] must not wish to paint over Michel Angelo's painting', we read in a report from Hamburg published in Reichardt's *AmZ*, i (1798/9), 197. Jahn, it is true, attempted to exculpate Mozart by citing the countless self-borrowings on the part of earlier composers and the frequent changes that they made for the purposes of particular performances, but this merely shows that he, too, never really got to the heart of the matter; see Jahn, *W. A. Mozart*, ii.478.
102.   Reichardt's *Musikalische Zeitung*, i (1805), 41–2, reprinted in the *AmZ*, new series, xii (1877), 357.
103.   *Jenaer Allgemeine Zeitung*, i (1804), 601–2; reprinted in the *AmZ*, new series, xii (1877), 357; see also Rochlitz, *Für Freunde der Tonkunst*, i.158ff.
104.   *Berliner allgemeine musikalische Zeitung*, i (1824), 427–8.
105.   *AmZ*, xx (1818), 832–3.
106.   Marx, *Gluck und die Oper*, ii.71. ◆ The authenticity of the concert ending to *Iphigénie en Aulide* remains unresolved: because it is first mentioned in Heinse's 1795 novel *Hildegard von Hohenthal*, it is unlikely to have been composed by Schmidt, who was born only in 1779.

47

Visit to north Germany

Mozart's last journey of any duration dates from the spring of 1789. In terms of its aims and execution, it differed substantially from all his earlier journeys, which had been concert tours well planned in advance, each with a programme worked out to the very last detail. The present journey, by contrast, was undertaken more or less on the spur of the moment and was suggested by Prince Karl Lichnowsky, the son-in-law of Countess Thun and a great music lover in his own right. He had studied with Mozart and was evidently very fond of him. His estates in Silesia and his position in the Prussian army obliged him to spend part of the year in Berlin, and when he set off there in the spring of 1789 he invited Mozart to accompany him, an invitation that Mozart was very happy to accept. The fact that King Friedrich Wilhelm II was interested in music and that Prince Lichnowsky was a patron of the arts encouraged him to hope that here was an opportunity to escape from his increasingly straitened circumstances in Vienna. The request for a loan that he addressed to Franz Hofdemel on 2 April 1789 was clearly bound up with this journey.[1] Constanze remained at home and, as usual, was regaled with examples of Mozart's earthy humour. She received the comic quartet *Caro mio Schluck und Druck* (K571a) and also the following lines 'on the planned journey', for which she herself presumably provided the rhymes:

Wenn ich werde nach Berlin ver-	Reisen
Hoff' ich mir fürwahr viel Ehr und	Ruhm
Doch acht' ich geringe alles –	Preisen
bist du, Weib, bey meinem Lobe –	stumm;
Wenn wir uns dann wieder sehen,	küssen,
drücken, o der wonnevollen –	lust!
aber Thränen – Trauerthränen –	fließen
noch ehvor – und spalten Herz und	Brust.

[When I leave for Berlin, I hope for much honour and fame, but I hold all praise in low regard if you, my wife, remain silent. When we see each other again, kiss and hug, O joy! – but tears – tears of grief – must first flow, and heart and breast must be riven.][2]

Mozart left Vienna on 8 April 1789, writing from Budwitz later that same day to report that Lichnowsky was 'busy haggling over horses'. But, in general, the letter reveals only tender concern for his wife.[3] They arrived in Prague at midday on Good Friday, 10 April, and put up at the

---

1. ◆ Mozart's bill of exchange in favour of Hofdemel is reproduced in *Dokumente*, 296, *Documentary Biography*, 338.
2. ◆ It is not certain that K571a dates from 1789 or even that it is by Mozart. No autograph is known and the versions published in AMA XXIV/50 and NMA X/30/4 are based on a copy, owned by Breitkopf & Härtel, that was lost during World War II.
3. *Briefe*, iv.79 (letter of 8 April 1789).

'Unicorn'. None of Mozart's old patrons was at home. Of the Duscheks, he saw only Franz, as Josepha had left for Dresden the previous day. On the other hand, he was 'virtually able'[4] to sign a contract with Guardasoni for a new opera for Prague. The fee was 200 ducats, plus 50 ducats as travelling expenses. In the event, the contract was not carried out.[5] Meanwhile, he discovered from his old friend Friedrich Ramm that King Friedrich Wilhelm had been asking when he would be arriving in Berlin.

They reached Dresden on 12 April, and Mozart immediately went to see Josepha Duschek, who was staying with Johann Leopold Neumann. Neumann, who was secretary to the Saxon War Council, played a significant role in the literary and musical life of Dresden at this time, not least as a result of his friendly relations with Johann Gottlieb Naumann (1741–1801), the Oberkapellmeister to the elector in Dresden, for whom Neumann translated the opera and *opéra-ballet Cora* and *Amphion*, respectively. Neumann founded an academy of music in 1777,[6] while his wife was described by Goethe[7] as a particularly fine keyboard player. Mozart was delighted by the Neumanns, who introduced him to musical circles in the city. Foremost among the people he met was Schiller's friend, the Consistorial Councillor Christian Gottfried Körner, whom he saw on several occasions. According to a much later account, Mozart on one occasion became so absorbed in improvising at Körner's house that he forgot all about the meal that was waiting for him.[8] This was also the occasion on which Körner's sister-in-law Doris Stock produced a particularly successful silverpoint drawing of Mozart. The first musical event was a mass by Naumann, conducted by the composer himself that Mozart found 'very mediocre'. Also present was the 'Directeur des plaisirs' to the elector, Friedrich August von König, to whom Mozart was introduced by Neumann and who was 'extremely nice', asking him whether he would like to perform at court.[9] The resulting concert took place on the evening of 14 April, when Mozart played his new concerto in D major K 537 and the following day received one hundred ducats in a handsome snuffbox.[10] He also performed in private circles, notably on 13 April, when he played quartets at the Hôtel de Pologne, where he was staying, with the Dresden organist Anton Teyber (1756–1822) and the cellist Anton Kraft (1749–1820).[11] They also played the composer's string trio in E flat major, and Josepha Duschek sang arias from *Le nozze di Figaro* and *Don Giovanni*. The following day, after lunch with the Russian ambassador, he engaged in a trial of strength in the court church

---

4. *Briefe*, iv.80 (letter of 10 April 1789).

5. Guardasoni had been running the Nationaltheater since 1788. In 1789 he left for Warsaw, where the Polish parliament was meeting, and did not return to Prague until 1791; see Teuber, *Geschichte des Prager Theaters*, ii.260 and 264.

6. Meißner, *Bruchstücke zur Biographie J. G. Naumann's*, ii.267–8. ◆ Further, see Engländer, *Johann Gottlieb Naumann als Opernkomponist* and *Die Dresdner Instrumentalmusik in der Zeit der Wiener Klassik*.

7. Wahle, *Goethes Briefe an Frau von Stein*, i.465.

8. Gustav Parthey in his memoirs of his youth, published by Genée in 'Mozart in Dresden und Doris Stock', 222–3. Doris Stock's memory was at fault when she claimed that Mozart dined with Körner almost every day; see Schurig, *Wolfgang Amade Mozart*, ii.189. ◆ Parthey's *Jugenderinnerungen* of 1871 are reproduced in *Dokumente*, 481, *Documentary Biography*, 568–9.

9. *Briefe*, iv.82 (letter of 16 April 1789).

10. See the *Musikalische Real-Zeitung* (17 June 1789), 191: 'On 14 April the famous composer Herr *W. A. Mozart* of *Vienna* was heard at the fortepiano by *His Elect. Highness* – furthermore he also played here at *Dresden* in many noble and private houses with boundless success; his agility on the clavier and on the fortepiano is inexpressible – and to this is added an extraordinary ability to read at sight, which truly borders on the incredible: – for he himself is hardly able to play a thing better after practice than he does for the very first time. On the organ too he showed his great skill in the strict style. – He goes to *Berlin* from here' [*Dokumente*, 304, *Documentary Biography*, 347].

11. ◆ Mozart probably knew the Viennese-born Teyber from his first years in the imperial capital where he was active until his appointment at Dresden in 1787. Teyber returned to Vienna in late 1791; in 1793 he succeeded Mozart as court composer. Kraft was Joseph Haydn's principal cellist at Eszterháza from 1778 to 1790. Further, see Pfannhauser, 'Wer war Mozarts Amtsnachfolger?' and Biba, 'Nachrichten zu Mozart in Briefen seiner Zeitgenossen'.

with the Erfurt organist Johann Wilhelm Häßler (1747–1822). Häßler was a pupil of Johann Christian Kittel, who in turn had studied with Johann Sebastian Bach.[12] He was much admired as a harpsichordist and organist, not only on account of his virtuoso technique but also because of his stylish and expressive playing.[13] In Dresden, too, he was praised for his 'inexpressibly emotional playing' as early as 1788 and there were claims in the press that he wanted to travel to Vienna 'in order to show the Viennese musical public in a competition on the clavier with the great Mozart that the latter, powerful as he is on the fortepiano, cannot play the clavier'.[14] Mozart reported on the encounter in a letter of 16 April:

> After lunch it was agreed to seek out an organ; we drove there at 4 o'clock; Naumann was there as well. – At this point I should add that a certain Häßler (organist in Erfurt) was there, too; – he's a pupil of a pupil of Bach; – his forte is the organ and the clavier (clavichord). Now people here think that because I come from Vienna I'm unfamiliar with this style and way of playing. – So I sat down at the organ and played. – Prince Lichnowsky knows Häßler well but had some difficulty persuading him to play, – this Häßler's forte is his foot-work on the organ, which is not such a great skill, as the pedals here are arranged stepwise; also, he has simply memorized the harmony and modulations of old Sebastian Bach and is incapable of playing a proper fugue, and his playing lacks solidity – he's far from being another Albrechtsberger.[15] Afterwards it was decided to return to the Russian ambassador's so that Häßler could hear me on the fortepiano. – Häßler played too. – On the fortepiano I find Fräulein Aurnhammer just as good, so you can imagine that he has sunk considerably in my estimation.[16]

Mozart found the opera in Dresden 'truly wretched', although it remains unclear whether he was referring to performance standards in general or to the works of Naumann in particular. Be that as it may, he was pleased to renew contact with Rosa Manservisi, whom he knew from Munich.[17]

The two visitors left Dresden on 18 April and arrived in Leipzig on the 20th. Here Mozart called on another of Bach's pupils, the present Thomaskantor Johann Friedrich Doles (1715–97).[18] A former pupil at the Thomasschule, Friedrich Rochlitz, was a frequent visitor to Doles's house and has left us an account of Mozart from which we have already quoted, albeit one that he embroidered in his usual manner.[19] During the short time that he was in Dresden, Mozart regaled audiences with his skills as a keyboard player and chamber musician, and, even as an old man, a local violinist by the name of Berger would still whisper to friends whenever such a piece was

---

12. His autobiography was published in the second volume of his *Sechs leichte Sonaten* (Erfurt, 1786–7); see also *AmZ*, ii (1799/1800), 635; *Cäcilia*, ii (1825), 229; and Meinardus, 'Johann Wilhelm Hässler', 505–6. ◆ Further, see Hogwood, '"The Inconstant and Original Johann Wilhelm Hässler: His 1786 Autobiography and a Thematic Catalogue of his Keyboard Works to 1790'.

13. Cramer, *Magazin der Musik*, ii (1784/6), 404. On 18 August 1787 Schiller wrote to Körner: 'His playing is masterly. He is also a very fine composer. As a man, he is highly original, with a fiery temperament'; see *Schiller's Briefwechsel mit Körner*, i.122; see also Friedrich Meyer, *Friedrich Ludwig Schröder*, ii/1.360.

14. *Musikalische Real-Zeitung* (13 August 1788), 56 [*Dokumente*, 283, *Documentary Biography*, 323].

15. Johann Georg Albrechtsberger (1736–1809) was then court organist in Vienna. He later taught Beethoven.

16. *Briefe*, iv.83 (letter of 16 April 1789). ◆ Further, see Hamann, 'W. A. Mozart – J. W. Hässler: Der Dresdener Orgelwettstreit im Jahre 1789'.

17. She had created the role of Sandrina in *La finta giardiniera*.

18. ◆ See Banning, *Johann Friedrich Doles: Leben und Werk*, and Schering, *J. S. Bach und das Musikleben Leipzigs im 18. Jahrhundert*.

19. Rochlitz, *Für Freunde der Tonkunst*, third edition, iii.136. Rochlitz was exaggerating when he claimed that chamber music was performed 'every evening' in Leipzig in honour of Mozart's visit, as there can have been no more than three such evenings in all.

played: 'I myself once had the honour of accompanying the great Mozart in this work.'[20] Far more important is another eyewitness account:

> On 22 April he played on the Thomaskirche organ without any preliminary announcement and with no remuneration. He played there for an hour to the delight of a large audience, his playing marked by great beauty and artistry. The then organist Karl Friedrich Görner and the late Kantor Johann Friedrich Doles drew the stops for him. I saw him myself, a young, fashionably dressed man of average height. Doles was enchanted by his playing and thought that his teacher, old Sebastian Bach, had been reborn. Mozart displayed all the arts of harmony with immense grace and the greatest ease, gloriously improvising on the various themes, including the chorale *Jesu meine Zuversicht*.[21]

Doles revered Mozart. In 1790 he dedicated his cantata *Ich komme vor Dein Angesicht* to Mozart and Naumann and in order to show his gratitude for Mozart's organ playing arranged for his pupils to perform Bach's motet *Singet dem Herrn ein neues Lied*. According to Rochlitz,[22] Mozart listened with extreme attention, before exclaiming in delight at the end: 'Here's something that we can all learn from!' He also asked to see the parts of Bach's other motets, which he then laid out all round him and worked through them all, before asking for copies of them. In this way he again came much closer to Bach, just as he had come much closer to Handel only a short time earlier, and we shall soon see traces of this interest in his own works.

Shortly afterwards, on 22 or 23 April,[23] the travellers left for Potsdam, where the court was currently in residence.

Friedrich Wilhelm II shared his great uncle's aptitude for, and interest in, music, but was far more catholic in his tastes. He had studied with Jean-Pierre Duport (1741–1818) and was a fine cellist, appearing as a soloist and chamber musician and even taking part in orchestral rehearsals.[24] As crown prince, he had maintained a full orchestra under Duport's direction, inviting foreign virtuosos to play at its concerts.[25] As king he opened up Berlin to all the different trends in contemporary music, especially those excluded by his predecessor.[26] It was at his instigation that Reichardt founded the Concert Spirituel in imitation of the Paris institution of that name. Here it was in general the older Italian composers whose works were performed. He also thought highly of Handel and Gluck – the latter a composer for whom Frederick the Great had never had much time. And he encouraged performances of Italian, French and German works in both the theatre and the concert hall. Above all, Haydn found in him a sympathetic patron, while Boccherini,

20. Rochlitz, *Für Freunde der Tonkunst*, iii.136.

21. Reichardt, *Berlinische musikalische Zeitung*, i (1805), 132.

22. Rochlitz, 'Verbürgte Anekdoten aus Wolfgang Gottlieb Mozarts Leben', 117. ◆ In this instance, Rochlitz's anecdote appears to be confirmed by a contemporaneous copy of Bach's motet (now in the Gesellschaft der Musikfreunde, Vienna, shelfmark III/31685) with a note by Mozart, 'NB. Needs to be set for full orchestra'. Given the survival of this manuscript, it is likely that in Leipzig he also acquired *Jauchzet dem Herrn, alle Welt*, BWV Anh. III, 160 Chor I; a manuscript of this work (also in the Gesellschaft der Musikfreunde, Vienna, shelfmark A169b) is by the same copyist, and on the same type of paper, as *Singet dem Herrn*. Further, see Ernst Fritz Schmid, 'Zu Mozarts Leipziger Bach-Erlebnis'.

23. According to *Briefe*, iv.86 (letter of 16 May 1789), Mozart spent 17 days in Potsdam. He returned to Leipzig on 8 May (see *Briefe*, iv.89; letter of 23 May 1789), with the result that – assuming that his memory was not at fault – he must have left Leipzig on 22 April.

24. Meißner, *Bruchstücke zur Biographie J. G. Naumanns*, ii.199.

25. Ernst Wilhelm Wolf, *Auch eine Reise*, 10–11.

26. Reichardt, *Musikalische Monatsschrift*, 70–1; *Berlinische musikalische Zeitung*, i (1805), 2–3.

currently living in Madrid, was appointed court composer on an annual salary, an arrangement that lasted from 1787 to 1797. Following his accession in 1786, his private orchestra was merged with the royal orchestra and both placed under Reichardt's direction. During the carnival season, Italian grand operas continued to be staged but were now commissioned from Reichardt and his assistant conductor Felice Alessandri, and also occasionally from outsiders such as Naumann. The Deutsches Schauspiel became the Nationaltheater and received a regular subsidy, a state of affairs that also benefited the German singspiel. But French and Italian comic operas were also encouraged, with the result that one of the court's festivities during the summer of 1789 was accompanied by performances of Cimarosa's *Il falegname*, Dalayrac's *Nina* and Reichardt's *Claudine von Villabella* all on the same evening. Meanwhile, the king's concerts continued under Duport's direction. Friedrich Wilhelm treated leading artists – both foreign and local – with extreme friendliness and paid them generously, with the result that they respected him and placed the greatest hopes in the Berlin court.[27]

Of Mozart's operas, neither *Le nozze di Figaro* nor *Don Giovanni* had yet been staged in Berlin. On the other hand, Friedrich Wilhelm was familiar with *Die Entführung aus dem Serail*, which had been performed there to great acclaim, and he also thought highly of Mozart's instrumental music, especially his quartets. In short, Mozart had high hopes of Berlin and wrote to tell Constanze that he was 'held in favour' by the king.[28] This is in fact his only reference to his standing in royal circles. All the more numerous, by contrast, are the more or less anecdotal stories that later became associated with his visit to Berlin. One point that appears to emerge from them, however, is that Mozart encountered all manner of resistance from the other musicians at court. Above all, he seems to have aroused the distrust of the notoriously domineering and scheming Duport.[29] According to a much later report, he is said to have responded to Duport's suggestion that they should speak French at their first meeting by retorting that 'A foreign rogue who has lived for years in Germany and who eats German bread should also be able to speak German or, rather, murder it, however well or badly his French mouth is suited to it'.[30] Given Mozart's outspoken manner and nationalist outlook, this is by no means out of the question. At all events, relations between the two men remained extremely cool, in spite of the variations on a minuet by Duport K573 that Mozart wrote on 29 April. His letters fail to mention the cellist. Even so, he was invited to perform at the king's concerts. When asked what he thought of the orchestra, he is said to have told Friedrich Wilhelm that it included the greatest virtuosos in the world, but if the gentlemen were to play together, they could do even better.[31] Reichardt, who set the tone in musical circles in Berlin at this time, was not in fact present during Mozart's visit,[32] so that the evident ill humour that finds expression in his assessment of Mozart and in the reactions of his hangers-on can have had no personal basis to it. Rather, it was grounded in Reichardt's own nature as man and artist, a nature familiar to us from remarks by Goethe and Schiller and typified by its curious combination of a highly significant talent with an odd intellectual restlessness and a particularly liberal conscience.

---

27. See Meißner, *Bruchstücke zur Biographie J. G. Naumanns*, ii.189–90, 267; and Dittersdorf, *Lebensbeschreibung*, 186–9.
28. *Briefe*, iv.90 (letter of 23 May 1789).
29. Reichardt, *Musikalische Monatsschrift*, 20; Schletterer, *Johann Friedrich Reichardt*, i.457–8; and Louis Schneider, *Geschichte der Oper und des Königlichen Opernhauses in Berlin*, supplement XXXVI.15 and 16.
30. See *Neue Berliner Musikzeitung*, x/5 (30 January 1856), 35. ◆ Further concerning Mozart and Duport, see Milliot, 'Mozart et les violoncellistes français de la cour de Prusse' and Rummenhöller, 'Mozart auf der Reise nach Berlin'.
31. Rochlitz, 'Verbürgte Anekdoten', 22.
32. Pauli, *J. F. Reichardt: Sein Leben und seine Stellung in der Geschichte des deutschen Liedes*, 86.

We have already noted that Friedrich Wilhelm's offer to appoint Mozart his Kapellmeister and the latter's rejection of the offer have no basis in historical fact.[33]

While in Potsdam, Mozart stayed with the outstanding horn player Carl Türrschmidt,[34] whom he knew from Paris. He also saw a lot of a certain Herr Sartory, who made architectural ornaments and who had spent some time in Italy, where he had acquired his great love of music. Here Mozart met other music lovers, winning them over with his playing and good humour.[35] He was also a frequent visitor to the home of the singer Sophie Niclas, the sister of the chamber musician Franz Xaver Semler. She had been acclaimed as Konstanze in *Die Entführung aus dem Serail* as long before as 1784.[36]

He was once invited to extemporize there. He was always willing to do so and made no exception now. He sat down at the keyboard; two themes had been given him by the musical experts who were present. The singer placed herself near his chair in order to watch him play. Mozart enjoyed joking with her and looked up at her, saying: 'Well? Have you, too, got a little theme on your mind?' She sang one to him. He now began to play most delightfully, now with this theme, now with that, and finally he combined all three, to the greatest pleasure and astonishment of those present.[37]

Lichnowsky returned to Vienna at the beginning of May, and Mozart gladly allowed himself to be talked into accompanying him to Leipzig to renew acquaintance with their mutual friends there. They arrived on 8 May and on the 12th gave a concert in response to their friends' entreaties.[38] Rochlitz reports that he took the opening allegro from one of his symphonies[39] exceptionally quickly at the rehearsal, and as the orchestra was unable to keep up with him, he twice repeated the beginning. In doing so he beat time so violently with his foot that his steel buckle broke off.[40] Only when the players, with immense reluctance, had performed it at the required speed was he satisfied. Later he told a number of connoisseurs that he was a sworn enemy of excessively fast speeds, but that he had been afraid that, in view of the advanced age of most of the players, they would start to drag and so he had 'put a bomb under them, with the result that they had then given of their best out of sheer anger'. He took everything else at a more measured tempo, and when they had finished rehearsing an aria with Josepha Duschek,[41] he praised the orchestral accompaniment and announced that it was no longer necessary to rehearse his two concertos,

---

33. All the documentary evidence relating to Mozart's visit to Berlin may be found in Friedländer, 'Mozarts Beziehungen zu Berlin'. According to Friedländer, the king was informed of Mozart's arrival on 26 April. ◆ The date 26 April is confirmed by a memo to Friedrich Wilhelm: 'One Motzart (who on his arrival declared himself to be a Capellmeister from Vienna) reports that he was brought here in the company of Prince Lichnowsky, that he desired to lay his talents before Your Sovereign Majesty's feet, and awaited the command whether he may hope that Your Sovereign Majesty will receive him' (*Dokumente*, 298, *Documentary Biography*, 340).
34. Türrschmidt gave a concert in Vienna in 1782 with Johann Palsa; see Pohl, *Joseph Haydn*, ii.143.
35. *Neue Berliner Musikzeitung*, x/5 (30 January 1856), 35. The tradition whereby Mozart wrote his *Ave verum* in Potsdam is called into question by his own dating of 18 June 1791.
36. *Litteratur- und Theater-Zeitung*, ii (1784), 160; Dittersdorf, *Lebensbeschreibung*, 204.
37. Semler's account was published in the *Vossische Zeitung* (11 March 1857), supplement, 7 [*Dokumente*, 533, *Documentary Biography*, 567–8].
38. The concert was advertised in the *Leipziger Zeitungen* on 12 May 1789; tickets cost one florin each [*Dokumente*, 300, *Documentary Biography*, 342].
39. According to Rochlitz, there were two symphonies, but no further details are known. ◆ See n. 44 below.
40. One of the viola players made an exact note of the passage in his part; an orchestral assistant by the name of Griel kept the buckle as a souvenir.
41. *Non temer, amato bene* K505.

[presumably] K503 in C major and K456 in B flat major: 'The parts are correctly written out, you'll play them correctly and so shall I.' The success of the concert lived up to his expectations.[42]

In the event, the concert was poorly attended, with the result that the journey was largely a waste of time.[43] Half the audience had been given free tickets, and when the choir members who were not involved in the concert asked if it was possible for them to attend, Mozart admitted them free of charge, too: 'Who's going to worry unduly one way or the other?' he asked. This concert, too, ended with a free fantasia that began in C minor, later passing into the variations in E flat major that were published afterwards.[44] Following the concert Mozart returned to the rooms of the violinist Berger and played duets with him until late into the night. On 17 May another Leipzig musician, Carl Immanuel Engel, who was organist at the Schloßkapelle, received a present from him in the form of the little gigue in G major K574.[45]

In view of the large number of travellers trying to leave Leipzig at this time, Mozart was forced to delay his own departure until 17 May,[46] with the result that it was not until the 19th that he was back in Berlin. On this occasion he stayed with a certain Herr Möser on the Gendarmenmarkt,[47] later giving his host a neat copy of his six op. 10 string quartets [the 'Haydn' quartets]. That same evening *Die Entführung aus dem Serail* was performed 'by request' at the Nationaltheater.[48] Mozart himself attended, thereby giving rise to a further anecdote that is almost certainly grounded in truth. Mozart went and stood near the orchestra, where he attracted attention with his running commentary on the performance. When the second violins played a *d*-sharp' instead of a *d* (in Pedrillo's aria ('Frisch zum Kampfe! Frisch zum Streite!'), he exclaimed: 'Damn it, why can't you play your *d*!'[49] At this point, he was recognized and at the end of the act was called on to the stage. The soprano Henriette Baranius, who was singing the part of Blonde, used the occasion to extort from him the promise that he would work through her role with her.[50] A gifted singer, she was also a celebrated beauty and no doubt aware of her charms.[51] According to Rochlitz, Mozart, too, fell into her clutches and it was only with some difficulty that his friends succeeded in rescuing him.[52]

42. Rochlitz, 'Verbürgte Anekdoten', 85–6 and 179.
43. *Briefe*, iv.86 (letter of 16 May 1789).
44. Variations on 'Je suis Lindor' K354. *Pace* Schurig, the C minor beginning does not need to be K475; see Schurig, *Wolfgang Amade Mozart*, ii.192. ◆ *Pace* Abert, the concert did not end with a free fantasia, but with a symphony or a movement of a symphony. And it is by no means certain that the variations were those on 'Je suis Lindor' (which in any case were not published shortly afterwards but more than ten years earlier, in Paris in 1778). According to a bill announcing the concert, the programme consisted of a symphony, a *scena* sung by Josepha Duschek, a piano concerto, and a symphony in the first part; and a concerto, another *scena* sung by Duschek, a fantasy and a symphony in the second part. Furthermore, 'All these musical pieces are of Herr Kapellmeister Mozart's composition' (*Dokumente*, 300, *Documentary Biography*, 342). Whether one or two symphonies were performed is unclear. Almost certainly it was not three, given the custom of splitting movements of a symphony between the beginning and ending of concerts or parts of concerts. The same was true of Mozart's performance of the 'Haffner' symphony K385 (see above).
45. ◆ The exact date of K574 is uncertain: it is given as 16 May in Mozart's thematic catalogue, 17 May on the autograph, and 18 May on a copy owned by Johann Anton André, who had purchased Mozart's estate from the composer's widow. The date 18 May is almost certainly wrong, since Mozart left Leipzig on 17 May.
46. *Briefe*, iv.86 (letter of 16 May 1789).
47. It is the same building as the one that later housed the Stehelysche Konditorei; see Rellstab, *Ludwig Berger*, 97.
48. Friedländer, 'Mozarts Beziehungen zu Berlin', 117. The performance was repeated 'by command' on the 28th.
49. The scene was later immortalized in a copperplate engraving evidently based on Rochlitz's account in 'Verbürgte Anekdoten', 20–1. The engraving was reproduced in *Mitteilungen für die Mozartgemeinde in Berlin*, i (1897), 105.
50. Rochlitz, 'Verbürgte Anekdoten', 20–1.
51. Friedrich Meyer, *Friedrich Ludwig Schröder*, ii/1.93.
52. *Neue Berliner Musikzeitung*, x/5 (30 January 1856). ◆ There is no evidence to suggest this story is true. What is more, the entire episode smacks of mythologizing. Wilhelm Backhaus, who sang the role of Antonio at the Mannheim premiere of *Le nozze di Figaro* on 24 October 1790, described Mozart's visit there: 'Kapellmeister Motzard was here on the 23rd and gave numerous tempos at the rehearsal of Figaro. I embarrassed myself with Motzard. I took him for a journeyman tailor. I was standing at the door during the rehearsal. He came and asked me if one could listen to the rehearsal. I sent him away: "But surely you would let

More harmless was another encounter at the theatre, this time with the then sixteen-year-old Ludwig Tieck.[53] According to an anecdotal report of the meeting, Tieck arrived for one of the Berlin performances of *Die Entführung* some time before it was due to begin and spotted a stranger in the orchestra pit, a smallish man, rapid of movement, wearing a grey overcoat and busily inspecting the parts on the music stands. Tieck struck up a conversation with him, and the two men chatted about the theatre and opera, with Tieck finally expressing his admiration for Mozart's operas. 'So you often hear Mozart's operas and are fond of them?' asked the stranger. 'That's very good of you, young man.' They continued to talk as the theatre started to fill, and finally the stranger was called up on to the stage. It was only later that Tieck, who had been strangely moved by the stranger's remarks, discovered that it was none other than Mozart himself.

Meanwhile, Hummel had given a concert in Dresden on 10 March, when he had advertised himself as Mozart's pupil.[54] He gave a further concert in Berlin on 23 May,[55] without being aware of Mozart's presence in the city. When he noticed him among the audience, he could scarcely restrain himself but, as soon as he had finished playing, he plunged into the auditorium and rushed over to him, hugging him and overwhelming him with the tenderest expressions of his affection.[56]

On 26 May Mozart played for the queen. 'I shan't make much money', he told his wife in advance of the event. 'I announced my arrival only because it's the custom here and because she would otherwise have taken it amiss.'[57] He gave no public concerts in Berlin, as Friedrich Wilhelm was not keen on the idea, and Mozart's own experiences in Leipzig in any case advised caution. Even so, he received a gift of one hundred friedrichs d'or (about nine hundred florins) from the king, together with a commission to write six quartets for Friedrich Wilhelm himself and a similar number of easy keyboard sonatas for his eldest daughter, Princess Friederike.[58] Apart from the one hundred ducats that he earned in Dresden, this was all that Mozart brought home with him. Of this sum, he gave one hundred florins to an unidentified friend, whose request for a loan he was typically unable to turn down. There were good reasons, therefore, why he wrote to Constanze on 23 May: 'My darling little wife, when I return you must look forward to *me* more than to the money.'[59]

Mozart left Berlin on 28 May, travelling by way of Dresden and Prague, where he stayed between 31 May and 2 June, and arriving back in Vienna on 4 June.

Kapellmeister Mozart listen?" he said. Then I was more embarrassed than ever' (Eisen, *New Mozart Documents*, 65). This story, like the Berlin *Entführung* episode, is reminiscent of myths describing Zeus's disguised or unrecognized appearance among 'common people'.

53. Köpke, *Ludwig Tieck: Erinnerungen aus dem Leben des Dichters nach dessen mündlichen und schriftlichen Mitteilungen*, i.86–7.

54. *Musikalische Real-Zeitung* (20 May 1789), col. 156 [*Dokumente*, 303, *Documentary Biography*, 346].

55. Friedländer, 'Mozarts Beziehungen zu Berlin', 116.

56. Personal communication from Hummel's widow communicated to Jahn in 1855; see Otto Jahn, *W. A. Mozart*, fourth edition, ii.492. ◆ No contemporaneous document confirms this anecdote. Hummel's concert was advertised in the *Spenersche Zeitung* for 21 May 1789: 'On Saturday, 23 May, a virtuoso aged ten, Mons. Hummel from Vienna, will be heard on the fortepiano in a finely wrought concerto in the Corsika Hall. He is a pupil of the famous Herr Mozart and exceeds all expectation in agility, sureness and delicacy' (*Dokumente*, 303–4, *Documentary Biography*, 346).

57. *Briefe*, iv.89 (letter of 23 May 1789).

58. ◆ It is unclear whether Mozart received a commission from the king or whether he took it upon himself to compose six quartets and six sonatas for the Berlin court; the earliest reference to the works is his letter to Puchberg of 12 July 1789 in which he states only, 'I am composing six easy keyboard sonatas for Princess Friederike and six quartets for the King' and for which he had to bear the printing costs (*Briefe*, iv.93).

59. ◆ It may be that Mozart made at least a little money on the trip. On 9 May 1789 the publisher Johann Friedrich Carl Rellstab advertised 'the complete works of Mozart' in the *Berlinische Nachrichten von Staats- und gelehrten Sachen* (Eisen, *Dokumente: Addenda*, 63, *New Mozart Documents*, 59). Since few of Mozart's works had been advertised in Berlin to this time, it is possible that Rellstab acquired copies from Mozart. For a sinister view of Mozart's trip to Berlin, and in particular his deception of Constanze and relationship with Josepha Duschek, see Solomon, *Mozart: A Life*, 437–54.

The journey had proved unrewarding both financially and artistically. Although the Duport variations K573 are soundly structured and grateful from a pianistic point of view, clearly revealing the hand of their creator, their musical ideas fail to live up to the standards set by their great predecessors and, formally speaking, contain nothing that is not found there.[60] The gigue K574, conversely, is a miniature masterpiece. Clearly written under the influence of the impressions of Bach to which Mozart was exposed in Leipzig, it begins by striking a strictly contrapuntal note, while its second section resembles Bach's own contributions to the medium by exploring the theme and its inversion. Generally, however, the counterpoint is relatively free and notable for all manner of whimsical ideas. Even the subject sets out as if its chromatic line intends to contribute to the old fugue subjects over chromatically descending intervals of a fourth, but the line then breaks off on the *e″*, and the subject hurries to its conclusion. Only in the second section is the chromatic interval fully explored and even expanded at the end. Elsewhere, too, Mozart plays fast and loose with the subject, alternately shortening and lengthening it and also using it as the basis of the contrapuntal lines, only one of which maintains its independence by insisting obstinately on the fifth in the upper voice. It then appears in the bass, too, at the end. In the subjectivity of its expressive language, including all its contrapuntal, rhythmic and harmonic surprises, this little piece already looks forward to many similar fantasias by Schumann.

60. The opening of the minuet repeats the idea which, familiar from Paisiello, had played such an important role in *Le nozze di Figaro*.

48

Così fan tutte

On his return to Vienna, Mozart set to work at once on the first of the six quartets that Friedrich Wilhelm II had commissioned from him: K575 in D major was completed in June and sent off to Berlin, eliciting in return a gold snuffbox containing one hundred friedrichs d'or and a flatteringly worded accompanying letter.[1] None the less, Mozart's situation was by now extremely desperate, with Constanze so ill that he was 'constantly torn between fear and hope' and had to send her to the health resort of Baden, incurring an expense that weighed increasingly heavily on him, not least because his attempts to organize subscription concerts at his own home proved unsuccessful. The hopelessness of his situation is clear from his letters to his friend Michael Puchberg, to whom we find him writing on 12 July:

> God! I wouldn't wish my present situation on my worst enemy; and if you, most beloved friend and brother, abandon me, I shall *unfortunately – and through no fault of my own* – be lost, together with my poor sick wife and child. – Only recently, when I was with you, I wanted to pour out my heart to you – only I didn't have the heart to do so! – indeed, I still wouldn't have the heart . . . were I not certain that you know me and are aware of my circumstances and are fully convinced of my *innocence* as far as my unfortunate and utterly deplorable situation is concerned. O God! instead of thanks, I come to you with fresh entreaties! . . . If you really know me, you will share my anguish at having to do so.[2]

A few days later, Constanze seemed to be getting better:

> I am now feeling more inclined to work – but on the other hand I see myself faced by misfortunes of another kind, even if only for the present! – Dearest, most beloved friend and brother – you know my *present circumstances*, but you *also* know *my prospects*; let things remain as we agreed; *thus* or *thus*, you understand me; – meanwhile I'm writing 6 easy keyboard sonatas for Princess Friederika and 6 quartets for the king, all of which Kozeluch is engraving at my expense; at the same time, the 2 dedications will bring me in something; within a couple of months my fate must have been decided *in every detail*, and so, my dearest of friends, you won't

---

1. *Neue Berliner Musikzeitung*, x/5 (30 January 1856), 35. ◆ This claim is incorrect: although Mozart entered K575 in his thematic catalogue in June 1789, there is no evidence that a copy was sent to Berlin or that he received payment for it. When he sold the three quartets K575, 589 and 590 to Artaria in 1790, Mozart wrote to Puchberg, 'I have now been obliged to give away my quartets (those very difficult works) for a mere song, simply in order to have cash in hand to meet my present difficulties' (letter of 12 June 1790, *Briefe*, iv.110). He is unlikely to have done so if the work had been commissioned – and paid for – by Friedrich Wilhelm II. In any event, Mozart – as Abert notes – had written to Puchberg as early as 12 July 1789 that he expected an honorarium from the king only after the quartets' publication.
2. *Briefe*, iv.92 (letter of 12 July 1789).

be taking a risk with me; now, my only friend, it depends simply on whether you're willing and able to lend me another 500 florins.[3]

Although Mozart promised to repay this sum at a rate of ten florins a month until his affairs were settled – he seems to have pinned his hopes either on Berlin or on an imperial commission in Vienna – Puchberg was evidently not in a position to advance such a large sum of money. As a result he delayed replying for a few days, plunging Mozart into a further state of consternation:

You must be angry with me as you haven't replied to my letter! – When I compare the proofs of your friendship with my present demands, I think that you're perfectly right. But when I compare my misfortunes (for which I'm not to blame) with your friendly attitude towards me, I think that I deserve to be forgiven. My dear friend, in my last letter I told you quite openly all that was burdening my heart, so there would be nothing left for me now but to repeat all that I said then; but I must add, 1st, that I'd not require such a large sum if I didn't have to pay the horrendous expenses of my wife's treatment, especially if she has to go to Baden; 2nd, I'm sure that my circumstances will soon change for the better, and so the sum that I have to repay is a matter of great indifference, but for the present I'd prefer it to be a large sum, which would make me feel more secure; 3rd, I must ask you – if it really is completely impossible to help me with this sum on this occasion – to show your friendship and brotherly love for me by supporting me now with *as much as you can spare*, for I really am in great need; you certainly can't doubt my integrity, you know me too well for that; – nor can you distrust what I say or question my behaviour and way of life, as you know my lifestyle and conduct; – forgive me, then, for confiding in you.[4]

'I really am very unhappy!' he added in a postscript. And this mood refused to leave him:

Since the time you did me such a great favour as a friend, I have been living in such *misery* that for very grief I have not only been unable to go out, I have also been unable to write. – She [Constanze] is now calmer . . . she is extraordinarily resigned to her fate and awaits recovery or death with true philosophical composure, I'm writing this with tears in my eyes. – Come and visit us, my dear friend, if you can; and if you *can*, help us in word and deed in the matter *of which you know.*[5]

Constanze had indeed gone to take the waters at Baden, where she quickly recovered, as emerges from a letter that Mozart wrote to her during the first half of August,[6] a letter that is also eloquent proof of the fact that whenever the typical Weber temperament was spurred into action by some external occurrence she immediately lost sight of all sense of moral duty. Her frivolous behaviour in Baden merely added to Mozart's burden of care. 'I'm delighted when you're happy, of course I am,' he wrote to her, 'I only wish you didn't carry on in such a vulgar way.' And he went on to complain that an acquaintance of his who normally had the greatest respect of women had written

3. ◆ *Briefe*, iv.92 (letter of 12 July 1789).
4. *Briefe*, iv.94 (letter of 17 July 1789). At the foot of the letter, Puchberg added the note: 'Replied to same on 17 July and sent 150 florins.'
5. ◆ *Briefe*, iv.95 (letter of second half of July 1789).
6. *Briefe*, iv.96–7 (letter written before mid-August 1789). On the chronology of this and the following letters, see Spitta, 'Zur Herausgabe der Briefe Mozarts', 401–5 and 417–21.

'the most disgusting and crudest sottises' about her. In a moving appeal, he asked her to forgive him for being so honest,

> but my peace of mind demands it as much as our mutual happiness. . . . Remember, too, the promise that you gave me – O God! – just try, my love! – be happy and contented and do what you can to please me – don't torment us both with unnecessary jealousy – trust in my love, you've enough proof of it – and you'll see how happy we'll be, believe me, only by her prudent actions can a wife bind her husband to her.[7]

Mozart went to visit Constanze at Baden, evidently in order to discuss his feelings in person, but no sooner had he returned to Vienna than he was already writing again to express his fears: 'My love! – *Never* go out walking alone – the very thought of it appals me.'[8]

This period of financial misery and personal unhappiness coincided with the revival of *Le nozze di Figaro* in Vienna on 29 August, for which Mozart wrote an additional aria for Adriana Ferrarese del Bene.[9] In the course of the next three months he also wrote three insertion arias for Louise Villeneuve: 'Alma grande e nobil core' K578 for Cimarosa's *I due baroni*, 'Chi sà qual sia' K582 for Martín y Soler's *Il burbero di buon cuore* and 'Vado, ma dove?' K583 for the same work. For his sister-in-law Josepha Hofer he wrote the aria 'Schon lacht der holde Frühling' K580 for insertion in Paisiello's *Il barbiere di Siviglia*; and for Francesco Benucci he wrote the aria 'Rivolgete a lui lo squardo' K584, which he originally intended for *Così fan tutte*. Otherwise, this bleak period produced only a meagre crop of works that consisted of the keyboard sonata in D major K576 of July 1789 (the only one of the six that he completed for Princess Friederike of Prussia); the clarinet quintet in A major K581 that he completed on 29 September 1789; and twelve minuets and twelve German dances dating from the December of that year (K585 and 586).

The success of *Le nozze di Figaro*[10] served to remind the emperor of Mozart's existence, with the result that he was invited to write a new opera. The result was a setting of Da Ponte's *Così fan tutte ossia La scuola degli amanti*.[11] 'It was not in his power to turn down the commission, and the libretto was expressly forced upon him', Niemetschek wrote, half apologetically.[12] By December we find Mozart hard at work on the score. The two hundred ducats that he was promised for it and that he later received were enough for him to approach his friend Michael Puchberg with the request for a further loan, which he claimed to need urgently in view of the 'apothecaries and

---

7. ◆ *Briefe*, iv.96–7.

8. *Briefe*, iv.97 (letter of ?19 August 1789).

9. ◆ 'Al desio di chi t'adora', K577.

10. It was performed 11 times in 1789 (on 29 and 31 August, 2, 11 and 19 September, 3, 9 and 24 October, 5, 13 and 27 November). In 1790 it was seen 14 times, and in 1791 3 times. ◆ In 1790, *Figaro* was performed on 8 January, 1, 7, 9 and 30 May, 22 and 26 June, 24 and 26 July, 22 August, 3 and 25 September, and 11 October; in 1791 it was given on 4 and 20 January and 9 February. See Link, *The National Court Theatre in Mozart's Vienna*.

11. Da Ponte mentions it only briefly in his *Memorie*, ii.109.

12. Niemetschek, *Leben des k. k. Kapellmeisters Wolfgang Gottlieb Mozart*, 29. According to Heinse, *Reise- und Lebens-Skizzen nebst dramaturgischen Blättern*, i.184–5, the libretto was based on a real-life incident that the emperor explicitly wanted to have dramatized. ◆ The idea that *Così* was inspired by a real-life incident is now generally discredited. By the same token it is likely that Mozart, who was apparently not the first choice to set Da Ponte's libretto, welcomed the commission: probably it was originally intended for Salieri, who wrote one trio and the vocal line of another before giving up the composition; see Bruce Alan Brown and Rice, 'Salieri's "Così fan tutte"'. According to a later reminiscence of Constanze's, 'Salieri first tried to set this opera but failed, and the great success of Mozart in accomplishing what he could make nothing of is supposed to have excited his envy and hatred, and have been the first origin of his enmity and malice towards Mozart'; see Medici and Hughes, *A Mozart Pilgrimage*, 127.

doctors' who would have to be paid in the New Year.[13] In the same letter he also invited Puchberg and Haydn to attend 'a little opera rehearsal' in his rooms on 31 December, ending by mentioning 'Salieri's plots which have, however, already come to nothing'. The first orchestral rehearsal took place in the Burgtheater on 21 January 1790, followed on the 26th[14] by the first performance, with the following cast:

Fiordiligi	}	Dame Ferraresi e sorelle abitanti in Napoli	Sgra. Ferraresi del Bene.
Dorabella			Sgra. L. Villeneuve.
Guillelmo	}	amanti delle medesime	Sign. Benucci.
Ferrando			Sign. Calvesi.
Despina cameriera			Sigra. Bussani.
Don Alfonso vecchio filosofo			Sign. Bussani.

The opera appears to have been a success,[15] even though it did not remain in the repertory for long.[16] Zinzendorf noted in his diary: 'La musique de Mozart charmante et le sujet assez amusant.'[17] Otherwise we know nothing about the opera's genesis and staging. The plot is as follows:

Two young officers from Naples,[18] Ferrando (tenor) and Guglielmo (bass), are engaged to be married to the sisters Fiordiligi and Dorabella. At the local coffee-house the officers become embroiled in an argument with their friend Don Alfonso, who doubts whether their fiancées, if put to the test, will prove faithful. Women's fidelty, he maintains, is a phoenix that no one has yet seen.[19] Finally they decide on a wager, with the two officers promising to do all that Don Alfonso tells them to do in the next twenty-four hours in order to test the two women, but without giving anything away. A day is long enough for Don Alfonso to prove his point and tempt the women into being unfaithful. The two officers are confident of success and already look forward to the celebrations that they plan to hold with their winnings of one hundred zecchini.

We now meet the two young women, who are lost in rapt contemplation of portraits of their lovers. Don Alfonso enters to report that the latter have to go off to the front with their regiment, resulting in a touching farewell accompanied by the most impassioned assurances that they will

---

13. *Briefe*, iv.100 (letter of December 1789). ◆ Although Mozart claimed to have been offered 200 ducats, records show that he received only 100, the standard fee for an opera at the time; see Edge, 'Mozart's fee for "Così fan tutte"'.

14. The date of 16 January in the *Wiener Zeitung*, ix (30 January 1790), appendix [*Dokumente*, 318, *Documentary Biography*, 362], is a printing error; see Wlassak, *Chronik des k. k. Hof-Burgtheaters*, 67.

15. See *Journal des Luxus und der Moden* (March 1790), 148–9: 'I can again announce an excellent work to you, which has been taken up by our theatre. Yesterday, that is, it was given for the first time at the I. & R. National Theatre. It is entitled *Cosi* [*sic*] *fan tutte, o sia, la Scuola degli Amanti* . . . . That the music is by Mozart says, I believe, everything' [*Dokumente*, 318–9, *Documentary Biography*, 363].

16. It was performed on 26, 28, 30 January, 7, 11 February, then – following the period of national mourning following the death of Joseph II – 6, 12 June, 6, 16 July and 7 August, after which date it disappeared from the stage. ◆ This was not, however, a reflection on the success of the opera, as is sometimes claimed; rather it it was a result of the court theatres' reorganization under the new emperor, Leopold II; see Rice, 'Emperor and impresario: Leopold II and the transformation of Viennese musical theater, 1790–1792' and 'Leopold II, Mozart, and the return to a Golden Age'. Records show that the first performance of *Così* was more heavily attended than any other première in the 1789/90 operatic year; see Edge, 'Mozart's reception in Vienna, 1787–1791'.

17. Pohl, *Joseph Haydn*, ii.125.

18. 'Trieste', mentioned in act one, scene nine, was later changed to 'Napoli'.

19. Alfonso's words 'È la fede delle femmine / Come l'araba fenice: / Che vi sia, ciascun lo dice, / Dove sia, nessun lo sa' ('Woman's constancy is like the Arabian Phoenix: everyone swears it exists, but no one knows where') are taken from act two, scene three of Metastasio's *Demetrio*, where 'delle femmine' appears as 'degli amanti'. The lines were set as a canon by Metastasio himself.

remain faithful. A military march with chorus[20] frames the officers' departure. The sobbing of the lovers is accompanied by Alfonso's gloating laughter.

Despina, the sisters' maid, advises them not to take their separation too seriously but to find ways of amusing themselves: men's inconstancy deserves no better.[21] Alfonso bribes Despina into helping two strangers, who are in love with the sisters, to gain entry to the house. Ferrando and Guglielmo now appear, disguised as Albanian noblemen with long beards, and proceed to declare their love for the horrified young women. In spite of all attempts to mediate on the part of Don Alfonso, who pretends to be a good friend of the two strangers, the women remain steadfast and finally refuse to have anything more to do with their suitors. To the delight of the two officers, the first assault on their virtue has successfully been fought off, leaving Alfonso to hatch a new plot with Despina.

While the two sisters are strolling around their garden, lost in thoughts of their lovers, the two Albanians come rushing in and, to the women's horror, pretend to take poison. Alfonso and Despina hurry off in search of a doctor, while pity for the two men, who appear to be in the throes of death, begins to stir in the sisters' hearts. Alfonso returns with Despina, now disguised as a doctor, and the two sisters have to hold the patients' heads while Despina attempts to cure them by magnetizing out the poison à la Mesmer. The two men return to life, twitching convulsively, and finally ask for a kiss. The first-act finale ends with the women's indignation at this request and a scene of general confusion.

The second act begins with Despina attempting to persuade her employers to abandon their restraint and indulge in a little flirtation. Immediately afterwards Dorabella tells Guglielmo that she is not averse to the idea, a declaration echoed by Fiordiligi in conversation with Ferrando. In a garden by the sea, the Albanians greet the sisters with a serenade, after which Alfonso and Despina bring about a reconciliation. Guglielmo has no difficulty in winning Dorabella's love. He gives her a golden heart and in return receives Ferrando's portrait. Ferrando has more difficulty winning over Fiordiligi: although she is inwardly torn, she finally spurns his advances and vows to resist temptation.

The two friends exchange experiences, which causes great distress to Ferrando, who is still devoted to Dorabella. Don Alfonso demands a new assault on Fiordiligi, who bitterly reproaches her sister for her infidelity and decides to disguise herself as a man and follow her lover into battle. But while she is preparing to leave, Ferrando rushes in, begging her to kill him before she abandons him. This is too much for Fiordiligi, who is overcome by compassion, with the result that, vanquished, she sinks upon his breast. Now it is Guglielmo's turn to be beside himself with anger. Both men decide to break off their engagements, and it is only with difficulty that Don Alfonso persuades them to accept his philosophical credo: 'Così fan tutte' ('All women are like that'). They agree to marry their fiancées but first plan to punish them for their infidelity. At that point Despina announces that the women have decided to marry their new lovers that very evening and that she has been sent to find a notary.

It is in fact Despina herself who now arrives disguised as a notary in order to read out the terms of the marriage contract at the ensuing banquet. Scarcely has it been signed when we hear the march and chorus from the opening act and Alfonso announces the return of the sisters' old

---

20. In the autograph score the march is initially played by the orchestra alone, entering *piano*, with a crescendo in its second section; only at the repeat does the chorus enter *forte*.
21. This scene was originally intended to begin with a cavatina for Despina, or so it would appear from a note appended to the recitative, 'Dopo la cavatina di Despina'. But Mozart then deleted these words, evidently because a better place had been found for Despina's aria.

lovers. The Albanians and the notary are quickly concealed, and the women, mortified and embarrassed, welcome back their fiancés. Don Alfonso then pretends to discover the notary in the next room, and Despina reveals her true identity, claiming that she is on her way home from a masked ball. But when Guglielmo comes across the marriage contract, the sisters are forced to confess. Their lovers then reveal themselves as the Albanians, with Guglielmo returning Ferrando's portrait to the melody of his earlier love duet with Dorabella, and with both men acknowledging Despina as the ostensible doctor. Alfonso reconciles the lovers and brings the opera to an end on a note of Enlightenment morality:

> Fortunato l'uom che prende
> Ogni cosa pel buon verso,
> E tra i casi e le vicende
> Da ragion guidar si fa.
> Quel che suole altrui far piangere
> Fia per lui cagion di riso,
> E del mondo in mezzo i turbini
> Bella calma troverà.

[Happy is the man who looks at everything on the right side and through trials and tribulations makes reason his guide. All that makes another man weep will for him be a cause of mirth and amid the tempests of this world he will find sweet peace.]

During Mozart's lifetime, the opera was staged in both Prague, by Guardasoni,[22] and in Dresden, where it was the first of his operas to be performed.[23] On both occasions it was given in the original Italian. Shortly afterwards Guardasoni took the Prague production to Leipzig. The Berlin production opened on 3 August 1792 under the title *Eine macht's wie die andere* (literally, 'One woman is just like the rest')[24] and was merely the first in a long series of German translations and adaptations. In 1805, for example, the work was published in Berlin in Bretzner's translation as *Weibertreue, oder Die Mädchen sind von Flandern* ('Women's Fidelity, or The Girls are from Flanders') – this version was first heard in Leipzig in 1794.[25] In 1820 Carl Alexander Herklots's adaptation appeared under the title *Die verfängliche Wette* ('The Insidious Wager'). In 1825 the older version was used for a production at the Königstädtisches Theater,[26] but in 1831, 1832 and 1835 this was replaced by a new one by Carl August Ludwig von Lichtenstein.[27] This in turn was followed by Louis Schneider's version, *So machen es alle* ('That's how they all do it'), of 1846.[28] Much the same story was found in Vienna, where Gieseke's translation – staged at the Theater auf der Wieden in 1794 as *Die Schule der Liebe* ('The School of Love') – gave way to *Mädchentreue* ('Girls' Fidelity') at the Hoftheater on 19 September 1804. By 1814 the Theater an der Wien was staging Treitschke's adaptation *Die Zauberprobe* ('The Magic Trial'). In 1819 and 1840 the earlier translation was again used, with Schneider's version being preferred in 1863 and again on 18

22. Teuber, *Geschichte des Prager Theaters*, ii.268.
23. *AmZ*, xiv (1812), 189, and xvi (1814), 154.
24. Louis Schneider, *Geschichte der Oper und des Königlichen Opernhauses in Berlin*, 61.
25. Schneider, *Geschichte der Oper*, 76.
26. *AmZ*, xxviii (1826), 26; *Berliner allgemeine musikalische Zeitung*, iii (1826), 12–13.
27. Wolzogen, 'Mozarts "Così fan tutte" auf der deutschen Bühne', 137–8.
28. *AmZ*, xlviii (1846), 870.

October 1872 – the first performance in the new house. In Prague the opera was staged in 1808 as *Mädchentreue*[29] and in 1823 as *Die Zauberprobe*,[30] on both occasions in evident emulation of Vienna. In 1831 it was heard in Czech[31] and in 1839 in Italian, this time in a performance by pupils from the local conservatory.[32] In Leipzig, too, it was staged as *Weibertreue* in 1805,[33] reaching Dresden in Italian in 1830.[34] Of other German towns and cities, suffice it to mention: Breslau on 16 January 1795 (in Bretzner's version);[35] Frankfurt in 1796 (Stegmann's adaptation, *Liebe und Versuchung* ['Love and Temptation'], had already been staged in the city as early as 1791);[36] Stuttgart on 16 May 1796 as *Die Wette oder Mädchenlist und Liebe* ('The Wager or Girls' Cunning and Love') (in 1816 it was revived in a version by Krebel as *Mädchen sind Mädchen* ['Girls are Girls']);[37] and Weimar, where the opera was adapted by Christian August Vulpius as *So sind sie alle, alle* ('That's how they all are, all of them') and first staged on 10 January 1797.[38] In Paris it was performed by the Italian Opera at the Odéon in 1811, 1817 and 1820, each time to great acclaim.[39] In 1863 Barbier and Carré attempted to adapt the music to a new text based on Shakespeare's *Love's Labour's Lost*. Needless to say, the result, *Les peines d'amour perdues*, was a failure.[40] In England *Così fan tutte* was first heard in Italian in 1811, followed in 1828 by an English version [probably] by Samuel James Arnold.[41] The Italian Opera staged it in 1842[?]. Italy itself proved typically resistant to the work. La Scala performed it on 19 September 1807, when it was a success, and again on 31 May 1814, when it was a failure.[42] It was seen at the Teatro del Fondo in Naples during the 1815 carnival[43] and in Turin in 1816.[44] The Teatro del Fondo made a further attempt to revive the work during the summer of 1870.[45]

Although the music was much admired, the text soon came in for criticism. It found a number of eulogists among the Romantics,[46] it is true, foremost among whom was E. T. A. Hoffmann, who considered it genuinely operatic.[47] But the anonymous judgement passed on the piece in 1792 continues to affect perceptions of it even today: 'The present singspiel is the silliest thing in the world, and audiences attend performances of it only out of respect for the admirable composi-

29. *AmZ*, x (1808), 409.
30. *AmZ*, xxv (1823), 428. ◆ Probably the second Prague staging (as *Die Zauberprobe*) was on 7 March 1815, not in 1823; see Loewenberg, *Annals of Opera*, 477.
31. *AmZ*, xxxiii (1831), 222.
32. *AmZ*, xl (1838), 440; Branberger, *Das Konservatorium für Musik in Prag*, 60.
33. *AmZ*, viii (1806), 240.
34. *AmZ*, xxxii (1830), 375; Heinse, *Reise- und Lebens-Skizzen*, i.183–4.
35. Schlesinger, *Geschichte des Breslauer Theaters*, 75.
36. Carl Valentin, *Geschichte der Musik in Frankfurt am Main vom Anfange des XIV. bis zum Anfange des XVIII. Jahrhunderts*, 25–6.
37. Krauß, *Das Stuttgarter Hoftheater von den ältesten Zeiten bis zur Gegenwart*, 102. ◆ According to Loewenberg, *Annals of Opera*, 477, the translation was by Johann Baptist Krebs and the opera opened on 7 January 1817.
38. On 15 May 1797 Goethe's mother wrote: 'The opera Cosa van Tutti [*sic*] – or that's how they all are – is said to have gained so much in Weimar through the improved text – the one we have here is frightful – and so it's this improved text that Herr Bernhardt asks you to send him'; see Burckhardt, *Das Repertoire des Weimarer Theaters unter Goethes Leitung*, 144; and *Schriften der Goethe-Gesellschaft*, iv (1889), 126.
39. *AmZ*, xiii (1811), 526 and 720; xix (1817), 550; xxii (1820), 813.
40. Wilder, *Mozart: L'homme et l'artiste*, 270.
41. Under the title *Tit for Tat*; see Pohl, *Mozart und Haydn in London*, 146–7; Parke, *Musical Memoirs*, ii.259. ◆ Further, see Angermüller, 'Von Salieris und Mozarts "Così fan tutte" über "Die zwey Tanten aus Meyland" – "Tit for tat; or The Tables Turned" – "Die Guerillas" – "Winzer und Sänger" zu "Dame Kobold". Metamorphosen eines Librettos'. Concerning an early American adaptation, see Clark, 'The enlightened transposition: "Così fan tutte" in colonial America, Philadelphia, 1785'.
42. Cambiasi, *La Scala 1778–1906*, 300 and 304.
43. Florimo, *La scuola musicale di Napoli e i suoi conservatorii*, iv.368.
44. *AmZ*, xviii (1816), 895. ◆ According to Loewenberg, *Annals of Opera*, 454, *Così* was first given at Turin in the autumn of 1815.
45. Florimo, *La scuola musicale di Napoli*, iv.398.
46. Notably in the 'Musical Correspondence' published in the *Berlinische musikalische Zeitung*, i (1805), 293–4, where the opera is hailed as the epitome of genuine irony.
47. Hoffmann, *Die Serapionsbrüder*, i/2.1.

tion.'[48] Improbability and frivolousness were the chief reproaches traditionally levelled against the text, and the various adaptations have all attempted to counter what they perceived as this twofold 'evil'. In his *Zauberprobe*, Treitschke turned Alfonso into a sorcerer and Despina into a spirit of the air, while Krebs had the two men make their bet only after their return from a long journey and before they had seen their fiancées again. In this version, Despina undertakes to cure them herself, without assuming any disguise, and at the end a real notary appears, whom she later introduces as her lover. The plot was completely changed in this way, and virtually all the musical numbers were traduced and wrenched from their context. In Herklots's version[49] the sisters are not even tested by their lovers but – with their agreement – by two friends. A servant Pedrillo appears as doctor and notary. In Lichtenstein's version, the maid reveals the whole of Alfonso's plan to her employers right at the very outset, so that it is the men who are now led by the nose. Much the same is true of Arnold's version.[50] In the adaptation by Louis Schneider, this betrayal takes place only in the second act, with the sisters now feigning weakness in order to punish their lovers.[51] These are all desperate remedies that effectively destroyed the piece. Among other suggestions that deserve to be taken more seriously is the one by Oulibicheff,[52] who proposed that the sisters' second choice be regarded as definitive, thereby making good a twofold injustice and allowing the work to end on a traditional note, with the tenor ultimately marrying the prima donna and the baritone being paired off with the seconda donna (an arrangement which is, in fact, not true in the case of *opera buffa*). In the version that he published in Stuttgart in 1858, Bernhard Gugler had each of the officers test his own lover, a change that likewise required a number of alterations to the musical numbers.[53] The most radical adaptations are those by librettists who set the existing music to completely different texts: here one thinks above all of the Shakespearean setting by Barbier and Carré (see above) and, more recently, the version of Karl Scheidemantel, whose *Die Dame Kobold*, first staged in Dresden in 1909, borrowed its subject matter from Calderón.[54]

All these attempts to adapt the piece commit the same basic mistake of trying to salvage Mozart's music by more or less depriving it of its actual basis, namely, its text. In the case of a dramatist like Mozart, this can only be a bad thing. Whatever we may think of the libretto, this is the text that fired his imagination and inspired this particular music, with all its specific qualities, so that we shall not salvage the music by robbing it of this basis but will merely render it meaningless and, by preferring some cheap and superficial solution, deprive ourselves of the pleasure afforded by an organic, unified work of art.

Every reader familiar with *opera buffa* will have no difficulty in rejecting the two main charges of frivolity and implausibility. We need to stop demanding that such operas should be moralistic in tone. Women's fickleness was one of its oldest and most popular themes, and one to which it repeatedly brought new variants with its typical lack of moral scruples. Martín y Soler's successful

48. *Journal des Luxus und der Moden* (1792), 404; see also Hanslick, *Die moderne Oper*, 45.
49. In this form the opera was staged in Berlin in 1820; in Braunschweig in 1822 (*AmZ*, xxiv (1822), 378); in Kassel and Stuttgart in 1823 (*AmZ*, xxv (1823), 450 and 766); and in Munich in 1824 (*AmZ*, xxvi (1824), 588).
50. Hogarth, *Memoirs of the Opera*, ii.188–9. The Danish version by Adam Gottlob Oehlenschläger turned the subject matter on its head; see Oehlenschläger's *Meine Lebens-Erinnerungen*, i.121 and iv.43–4.
51. This version continues to enjoy the greatest success even today and is the one published by Breitkopf & Härtel in its series of opera librettos (no. 230).
52. Oulibicheff, *Mozarts Opern*, 254ff.
53. Gugler's translation remains the most successful. Among more recent versions, two that deserve to be mentioned here are those by Carl Friedrich Niese for the complete edition and by Schletterer for Breitkopf & Härtel's *Textbibliothek* edition (no. 19).
54. ◆ Further concerning early adaptations of the text, see Gruber, *Mozart and Posterity* and Goehring, *Three Modes of Perception in Mozart: The Philosophical, Pastoral and Comic in Così fan tutte*, especially 1–28. For French adaptations specifically, see Angermüller, 'Bemerkungen zu französischen Bearbeitungen des 19. Jahrhunderts'.

Una cosa rara falls effortlessly into this category. But even the most implausible twists of the plot were not only accepted as part of the deal, audiences even took a positive delight in them, always assuming, of course, that they were theatrically effective and powerful in their impact. And it is here that the most egregious weaknesses of the present text are to be found, with the plot being advanced in a way that is awkward, lame and wearisome in its repetitions. These shortcomings are particularly keenly felt in the second act, with its two similar seduction scenes[55] and its superficial treatment of the structurally important quartet ('La mano a me date'). Italian *opera buffa* is far less able to cope with these shortcomings than it can with even the worst violations of sound common sense, and from this point of view the criticisms of the libretto are fully justified. As such, it provides clear proof that Da Ponte was not a creative writer and that his strength lay in reworking and adapting other writers' ideas. Here we spend an entire evening in the company of the librettist responsible for the additions to Bertati's *Don Giovanni*, a poet familiar with the tried and tested stereotypes and motifs from *opera buffa* and able on that basis to develop a new plot requiring only modest skill and scant powers of invention. Apart from the basic idea, virtually everything is modelled on well-known prototypes, including the characters of the notary and doctor,[56] who acquires a contemporary gloss only through his association with Mesmer's magnetism. The other stock characters are the cunning chambermaid and the 'vecchio filosofo', whose insipid rationalism was still effective at this time. Other old friends are Guglielmo's diatribe against women ('Donne mie, la fate a tanti'), Despina's philippic against men ('In uomini! In soldati'), Dorabella's outburst against the rogue Cupid ('È amore un ladroncello') and Despina's thoughts on the right way to love ('Una donna a quindici anni'). Equally typical of *opera buffa* is the role played by eating and drinking, by *Tafelmusik*, serenades and individual examples of tone-painting such as beating hearts ('Il core vi dono' and 'È amore un ladroncello'), but above all we find one of the favourite themes of *opera buffa*, namely, the parody of *opera seria*, a theme that is barely represented in *Le nozze di Figaro* and *Don Giovanni*. Among the features that appear under this heading are the quotation from Metastasio,[57] Dorabella's aria about the Eumenides ('Smanie implacabili che m'agitate'), Fiordiligi's simile aria ('Come scoglio immoto resta') and most of the scenes in which the two officers, in disguise, feign love and which were traditionally set as accompanied recitatives. Related to these scenes is the one is which the two men take poison, a popular idea that conceals a dig at death scenes in *opera seria*. A final feature that deserves to be mentioned here is the delight in learned mythological references, as in act two, scene thirteen.[58]

In short, Viennese audiences must have been struck by the libretto's distinct lack of novelty. And there was another reason why many listeners will have found it reactionary, as Da Ponte avoided

55. Here improvements can be made by means of cuts, as was the case under Leopold Sachse at the Stadttheater in Halle an der Saale in 1917, but this is the only way of making the work 'more accessible' to modern audiences without destroying its basic character.

56. Cf. the Dottore in act one, scene eleven of Piccinni's *Il curioso di se stesso* [presumably Abert means *Il curioso del suo proprio danno* of 1755/6]; in the first-act finale of Piccinni's *Lo sposo burlato*; and Luigi's aria in act two, scene three of Piccinni's *La bella verità*; and the notary in act two, scene ten of Piccinni's *La notte critica* and in act two, scene eight of Pietro Alessandro Guglielmi's *I cacciatori*.

57. Now a symbol of rejuvenation, the phoenix was then predominantly an emblem of something that had never existed or that was otherwise inconceivable; cf. Carl Philipp Emanuel Bach's setting of Johann Adolf Schlegel's *Der Phönix* (1782 or earlier) and the second-act finale of Guglielmi's *L'azzardo*. ◆ Abert's reference to *Der Phönix* is a mystery: no such work by C. P. E. Bach is known. Possibly, however, he means *Phillis und Thirsis*, published in 1766 and based on a text by Johann Elias Schlegel, brother of Johann Adolf. No other Schegel settings by Bach – by either brother – are known. I am indebted to Mark Knoll for this information.

58. ◆ Further, see Hunter, *The Culture of Opera Buffa in Mozart's Vienna* and Farnsworth, '*Così fan tutte* as Parody and Burlesque'.

the element of sentimentality that had been traditional since Piccinni's day, preferring instead to restrict himself to the older, purer type of *opera buffa*. From this point of view, *La finta giardiniera* was a far more 'modern' piece.

How, one wonders, did the composer of *Le nozze di Figaro* and *Don Giovanni* come to set such a text, especially since its lack of originality and dramatic skill could hardly have been lost on him? And did this opera represent no more than a return to a style that he had long since abandoned, just as was to be the case with *La clemenza di Tito* in the field of *opera seria*? Or does it reflect a new aspect of his artistry?

The unease that many people have felt both in the past and more recently is no doubt understandable, as it reflects the widespread tendency to see a great artist's development as a clearly visible straight line that always runs in the same direction. As a result, there have been the most varied attempts to excuse this apparent lapse from the straight and narrow. Foremost among such excuses, inevitably, is Mozart's allegedly uncritical attitude towards his texts, while others writers, taking their cue from Niemetschek, have drawn attention to the predicament in which the composer is said to have found himself at this time. But it is hard to accept that, if the libretto had not had some appeal for him, he would have accepted it unseen and not asked for some alternative. Nor does his score reveal the least sign of embittered forced labour. Rather, he took on the commission whole-heartedly, otherwise it would undoubtedly have suffered the same fate as *L'oca del Cairo* and *Lo sposo deluso*.

It is always dangerous to judge the work of a creative genius by the norms of lesser mortals. After all, there are plenty of examples in the history of art in which artists suddenly depart from the course that they have been following, appearing to play games with their life's work and leaving posterity to detect any sense of intellectual unity. That we cannot judge an *opera buffa* by its moral, we already know. Still less can we do so in the case of a composer like Mozart, given all that we know about his intellectual outlook. No more can his new opera be judged by non-artistic criteria: it no more preaches immorality than *Don Giovanni* preaches morality, so that it is impossible in this regard to claim that Mozart was 'untrue to himself'. All that we can say with any certainty is that, after the inspired flight of fancy of *Don Giovanni*, *Così fan tutte* constitutes a superior, playful game with the shadowy side of everyday human existence. Mozart does not take this world seriously, in which respect he differs radically from the composers of *opera buffa*, a genre which, no matter how much they may caricature it, is invariably rooted in the world around them. Rather, Mozart is always aware of the masklike, random, contingent aspect of characters and events, yet at the same time he takes immense pleasure in playing with this world of human inadequacy, a world familiar to him as an inspired observer of humankind. In this, he is not in the least concerned to follow Italian practice and paint it in its worst possible colours, hence the much reduced role of caricature in his music. Rather, he is himself acutely conscious of the confines and limitations of this world, which he measures by the yardstick of his own, far more Olympian view of the world, resulting in the typically Mozartian irony that we encountered in the case of the comic characters in his earlier operas, except that these earlier characters also included tragic features, whereas now it is irony that is uniquely dominant.[59] Mozart reveals a wonderful instinct in maintaining this basic tone, a tone which certainly brought him closer to *opera buffa* than before but which essentially belongs to a completely different world. In this way he created a work which, for all its

---

59. ◆ Also see Burnham, 'Mozart's *felix culpa: Così fan tutte* and the Irony of Beauty'.

novelty, is none the less quintessentially Mozartian. A genius does not repeat himself; and so we may accept this work, too, in a spirit of gratitude and seek to understand it as a reflection of Mozart's own spirit, instead of attempting to excuse it in a way that Mozart emphatically does not require.

The opera's basic theme provided a link with his earlier works: that theme is love and, more specifically, the relationship between men and women, which he had already treated from the most disparate angles, from the delightful fairytale innocence of *Die Entführung aus dem Serail* to the demonic terrors of *Don Giovanni*. In *Così fan tutte*, too, love is the driving force, but on this occasion it does not turn its characters into either gods or demons. For that, they are far too much like everyday creatures, lacking in any real sense of destiny, with mere impulsiveness instead of willpower and capriciousness instead of any deeper feelings. The couples all have something instinctively primitive about them: they express their feelings with all the impulsiveness and inconstancy of people ruled solely by their five senses. In some ways, they are still children for whom laughter and tears, playfulness and earnestness are closely related. Even the two men repeatedly require outside help to prevent them from vacillating in the comedy that they themselves have sanctioned. The rational characters, by contrast, Don Alfonso and Despina, are unimaginative types with a concern for utilitarian principles that never extends beyond their most immediate interests. The result is a comedy of all-too-human concerns and superficialities in which the unconsciously superficial couples are led in circles by Alfonso and Despina, who turn superficiality into a principle and attempt to make capital out of it.

In consequence, the opera is essentially ironical in character, rather than being merely satirical in the manner of the Italians: the ironist is not only aware of the conditional nature of the world's phenomena, he also keeps a constant eye on life in its entirety. The fact that irony dominates an entire work – a work, be it added, that is so musically full-blooded – merely proves how powerfully developed was this aspect of Mozart's personality. There is more of it in this work than later writers, including Wagner,[60] were willing to concede. The result is an authentically Mozartian view of the world, rather than a more or less successful work of art wrung from his genius against his will. Given his basic belief that the opera librettist had to take account of musical considerations above all others, Mozart may have been fascinated by another outstanding quality of the text, the parallelism between the different groups of characters. On the one hand we have the two sisters, on the other the two men. Between them are the two like-minded, manipulative figures of Don Alfonso and Despina – such symmetry recalls the three groups of characters in *Die Zauberflöte* and promised to provide Mozart with ample opportunities for effective sonorities, not only in duets, but also in large-scale ensembles with their sharply contrasted groupings. As a result, *Così fan tutte* has more ensembles than any other opera by Mozart. In the opening act, Da Ponte divided up these numbers with undoubted skill, whereas in the second act he fell far short of this ideal with a monotonous sequence of five arias unique in Mozart's mature operas, all of them, moreover, based on the same idea.

But even this preponderance of ensembles over arias reflects Mozart's basic attitude towards his material. After all, the action as a whole takes place not between individual characters but between

---

60. 'O how doubly dear and above all honour is Mozart to me that it was not possible for him to invent music for *La clemenza di Tito* like that of *Don Giovanni*, or for *Così fan tutte* like that of *Le nozze di Figaro*! . . . A frivolously artful librettist handed him arias, duets and ensembles for him to set to music, and he duly set them in a way that depended on the warmth that they were able to awaken in him, so that they always acquired the most appropriate expression of which they were capable in terms of their content'; Wagner, 'Oper und Drama', iii.247.

the three groups of individuals and, more especially, between the pairs of lovers. And Mozart treats these groups as self-contained entities at least until act one, scene nine, and then from scene fifteen of act two onwards, with only insignificant nuances between the various characters. But even in the middle section of the opera, where the characters are more sharply distinguished from each other, Mozart is concerned more with differences in temperament than with differences of character. Significantly, these differences emerge more clearly in the case of the two women than with the men.

As a result, Mozart's usual approach to the drama, with its depiction of the living interplay between the characters, is ruled out in the case of *Così fan tutte*. Although his basic theme is still present in the guise of the love interest, it is acted out by puppets, unable to strike sparks from their souls or to become part of their living destiny. The result, therefore, is no more than a light-footed, *galant* contredanse in which the couple changes places, before returning to their former positions with the same ease as they left them. However superior their behaviour may be, the two individuals who arrange all this are little better than poor devils, for, although they may think that they know all about love, they know it only as a type of parlour game. Yet even here Mozart reveals his characteristic sense of irony by occasionally removing the masks and allowing us to see the human souls within these puppets and, at the same time, allowing the characters to feel love's *coup de foudre*, with all its joys and torments. This love is not to be interpreted tragically, however, as the characters themselves do not know what is happening to them. They merely have a vague awareness of a power which, with their limited horizons, they are unable grasp in its entirety. This emerges most clearly from the reconciliation at the end, a scene which musically speaking goes far beyond the trivial rationalism of the poem. Here the feeling of release from a game that had begun so light-heartedly and threatened to end so disastrously allows all hearts to beat more freely and with greater ease.

All these features take us far beyond the world of *opera buffa*. The Italians had no experience of this wistful humour that consists in the fact that grand feelings lead to utter humiliation in the hearts and souls of small-minded everyday types. But as a genuine humourist, Mozart had the gift of being able both to empathize and to observe and so he was unable to dispense with these aspects in the present piece, however much he may appear to step back from the seriousness of purpose that marks out his artistry in general and to produce not his usual type of drama but a light-hearted shadow-show that results in a temporary sense of liberation on his own part and helps to entertain others. Does this reflect a natural reaction on Mozart's part following the tremendous emotional upheaval of *Don Giovanni*? Or was it perhaps experiences in his own house at this time, with its lifeless quotidian round and dependency on base instincts, that prompted him to write this insane comedy of love and excess? Whatever the answer, we do not have the right to argue with Mozart over this. If Da Ponte's text paid tribute to its age, the new and original expression of Mozart's view of the world that it contains has not been lost to posterity. But we must now turn to the music itself.

The overture corresponds in every way to the basic view of the work outlined above. The andante begins with a genuinely Mozartian melody in the oboes, expressive of love, their burgeoning longing recalling the world of Belmonte. But the tutti chords that interrupt it seem like interlopers, and after eight bars the enchanting figure disappears without trace. It is replaced in the consequent phrase by a shadowy shape in the basses with the 'Così fan tutte' motto from Don Alfonso's aria ('Tutti accusan le donne'). In its third bar – on the word 'tutte' – it is continued, half smiling and half wistful, with a suspension and interrupted cadence, before being repeated in a convulsive *forte* by the full orchestra:

It is as if the composer were slowly donning his mask in these first fourteen bars. Only with the presto does he introduce us to his real world of comedy. And here he is not entirely serious even on the level of musical form. Although it is possible to see in this section an example of sonata form in its general outlines, Mozart plays more freely with its structure than in any other of his overtures. It consists, in fact, of the lively interplay of three different themes:[61]

These are then joined by a fourth theme that is introduced in the manner of a trio, with a lower line reminiscent of the overture to *Le nozze di Figaro*:

61. In the earliest copies of the score and in the first engraved edition, motif (c) is eight bars shorter. On each occasion the passages in question are repeats, albeit differently instrumented. To judge from the autograph score, these cuts can hardly be by Mozart. In other passages, it is more difficult to reach a decision.

But this is the only point in common between these two overtures. Otherwise their relationship is that of a masquerade to a portrayal of the most elemental life. Even the themes of the later overture have something rigid and conventional about them, with the result that they lack the incomparable terseness of those of *Le nozze di Figaro*. Here, too, we find more temperament than character. But within this limited sphere Mozart reveals himself at his most high-spirited, and in this he is abetted above all by the instrumentation. Motif (a) remains the preserve of the strings, motif (c) that of the winds, with one of the overture's main attractions residing in this motif's unexpected visits to the most disparate desks. But motif (b) repeatedly interrupts the mysterious bustle with its booming laughter, assuming the most varied forms as it does so. Finally the whole masquerade is interrupted by the same motto that had called it into existence: 'Così fan tutte!' And the overture ends with a brilliant Mannheim crescendo rising up through a C major triad.

The introductory sequence of three trios for the same three men's voices ('La mia Dorabella capace non è', 'È la fede delle femmine' and 'Una bella serenata') was in itself a risk, but one that evidently fired Mozart's imagination. He construes them as a single whole – not, it is true, on a motivic level, but at least in terms of their underlying dramatic idea, showing in three relatively brief numbers the sort of people that these three men are. The most striking aspect of all this is that, although the discussion is about love and fidelity, we never hear a note of true passion on the lips of either of the two officers. Sanguine by nature, they get tremendously worked up, but this is as far as it goes. All the more, conversely, do they become preoccupied with trivia and superficialities. In the opening trio, for example, we are introduced to them as gallant gentlemen who regard their fiancées' fidelity as a question of honour and who are therefore immediately ready to engage in a duel in a particularly felicitous passage ('O fuori la spada'). As a result, this opening trio is predominantly belligerent and agitated in tone. In the second trio, Don Alfonso, with his light but patronizing irony, is highly effectively contrasted with these two spirited beaux as he delivers himself of his Metastasian dictum rather in the manner of an adult telling fairy stories to a child. Particularly delightful is the contrast between the 'ciascun lo dice', to which the garrulous winds keep returning, and the shadowy 'nessun lo sa', with its string accompaniment. Once again the two officers break free with their impulsive praise of their lovers, and there is something especially attractive about the way in which, at the end, they interject the names of their lovers *sotto voce* into Don Alfonso's speech, while the orchestra points out that it is the latter who has already been proved right. By the third duet the officers are convinced that they have won their wager and are completely obsessed by the idea of the pleasures that await them: serenade, *Tafelmusik* and cheers already resound in their ears, and with a courteousness befitting their rank they invite Alfonso to the celebrations. With a fine sense of irony he joins in their jubilation and the trio ends with the strains of festive music.

The duet for the two women ('Ah guarda, sorella')[62] deals with similar emotions but in far more tender tones and with far more of the sensuality that is typical of so many of the opera's more leisurely numbers that deal with the subject of love. After all, this is the first time since the overture that clarinets have appeared in the orchestra. This feature emerges with particular prominence in the andante, in which the two women praise their lovers' physical attractions. Yet even here there is a lack of depth and, above all, of the element of yearning that normally distinguishes love in Mozart's works. For all its charm, it tends rather in the direction of a sensually coloured

---

62. Between now and the first-act finale the upper voice in the ensembles is always Dorabella's, with Fiordiligi's appearing beneath it. Only later did Mozart reverse them. The original order was undoubtedly an error, as it is clear from the melodic line that the upper line was intended from the outset for Adriana Ferrarese, whose wide-ranging compass was uniquely suited to the part.

frivolousness that finds expression in the coloratura flourishes in the Andante and in the vocal writing for Dorabella, who even here is already the more impulsive of the pair. In the Allegro, this frivolousness then becomes the dominant mood thanks to the teasing syncopations and coquettish coloratura on the word 'amore'. Note the high-spirited way in which one note is sustained in each voice while the other slips gracefully past like a dancer in her lover's arms. This duet, too, reveals that for the sisters, as for the officers, love – however truthful within its own terms – is not so much a matter of the heart as a matter of temperament and, indeed, almost a gallant party game that never delves beneath the surface. In this, the sisters are entirely worthy of their lovers.

A character like Don Alfonso is bound to be largely impenetrable in terms of his musical persona. As a result he generally pretends to be a different person from the one that he actually is, changing his role in keeping with the situation in which he happens to find himself. His F minor aria ('Vorrei dir, e cor non ho') sets the basic tone for the farewell scene that follows, with all its contrasting moods. Here he plays the part of a man shocked beyond all measure, and so the music, clearly aiming to create a sense of exaggeration, comes particularly close in style to an *opera buffa*, while remaining limited to the briefest ternary form. Pretending to be the bringer of bad tidings, he rushes in like a hunted animal and gasps out his news in a stumbling, irregular metre, supported by a breathless orchestra. Only towards the end does he allow himself to repeat individual phrases. The real comedy begins with the quintet ('Sento oddio, che questo piede') in which the lovers say goodbye to each other. A free example of binary form, it is an atmospheric number that acquires an ironic overtone from its solemn opening in E flat major. There is something typically Mozartian about the extremely symmetrical and clear opposition between the different groups, of which each has its own independent musical ideas. With a well-acted display of *galant* emotion, the two officers launch into their farewells, keenly urged on by Don Alfonso's wise dictum. With the entry of the women's voices we again hear no genuine sounds of anguish, but nor do we hear any parodistic lament in the style of an *opera seria* that an Italian composer would almost certainly have introduced at this point. Instead we hear a restless, helpless lament that finally turns into heartbreaking sobbing of almost childlike intensity. For the present this is all that these everyday characters can bring themselves to express, and there is a certain irony to the fact that the text mentions daggers and death at this point. Of course, they are entirely serious when they speak of the pain of parting, but these thoughts of violent death are not much more than bombastic phrases on their lips: not for a moment would it occur to them to put these thoughts into practice. Here the humour lies in the fact that the two men are limited enough in outlook to believe in them and already begin to exult. In this opera, the characters not only deceive each other, they also delude themselves, and Mozart typically refuses to fall back each time on the Italian devices of caricature and parody, preferring instead to allow the nature of these people to create its due effect simply on its own terms. There is something particularly beautiful and truthful about the following climax on the words 'Il destin così defrauda le speranze de' mortali' ('Thus destiny confounds our mortal hopes'). At this coldly commonplace remark on the part of his librettist, Mozart responds with an outburst of intense agitation in the hearts of the two sisters, again without any sense of pretentious pathos: note the typically Mozartian *sotto voce* and the especially subtle way in which Ferrando, as the more sentimental of the two officers, breaks free from the group of menfolk and moves over to the women, no longer able to suppress his pity. Alfonso's ironic interjections ensure that things do not become too serious. Throughout the number Mozart – as masterful as ever – takes the listener to the very edge of emotional involvement, without ever stepping over that boundary, but surrounding the whole situation in an ironical chiaroscuro, while allowing us to glimpse the two officers' inner uncertainty as they waver between fear and hope, very much in need of Alfonso's encouraging 'finem lauda'. The number is also perfect in its design and magical in its sheer beauty of sound. It is sufficient to recall the bitter dissonances of *Don Giovanni* to be aware of just how different the two works are in terms of their conception and style.

In the following duettino ('Al fato dàn legge') the two officers pull themselves together and offer their fiancées a few well-chosen words of comfort. They keep their remarks very short, while making a decent stab at wearing their heroic masks. Hence the entirely conventional character of this number, with even the sudden coloratura outburst on 'tornar' that Guglielmo takes over from Ferrando as if on command proving part of the picture. Immediately afterwards we hear the march with chorus ('Bella vita militar!'), a delightful number completely different from any of Mozart's other operatic marches and one, moreover, that acquires a hint of humour through its martial unison writing and the tone-painterly evocation of 'trombe e pifferi, schioppi e bombe' ('trumpets and fifes, guns and shells'). It is repeated after the actual farewell in the quintet ('Di scrivermi ogni giorno'), its original description in the autograph score of a 'Recitativo con stromenti' helping to explain its completely free form. In the fundamental change of mood following the previous march we again see the born dramatist in Mozart, and yet we feel that both numbers belong together. The pomp and circumstance of this warlike picture leaves the two women completely devastated. Like children, they begin to sob incoherently[63] – a realistic effect that was very popular in *opera buffa* – and it is not long before the men join in, half amused, half genuinely affected. But although this *buffa* atmosphere is heightened by Alfonso's 'io crepo se non rido' ('I'll burst if I don't laugh'), Mozart does not linger over it for long. A lament of such overwhelming inwardness breaks free from the sisters' hearts that even the men are moved by it and Alfonso's mockery is silenced. This is one of those moments when these everyday creatures are touched by rays of a higher reality and briefly rise above themselves, as Mozart reminds us that these characters of his are not just social beings but human beings, too. Admittedly, the veil descends again very quickly with Alfonso's renewed intervention, and the repeat of the march brings us unequivocally back to earth again with a bump. Yet the same note of radiance continues to affect the following terzettino ('Soave sia il vento'), which picks up the tradition of Italian numbers on the subject of wind and waves, differing from them only in its note of German Romanticism, which finds an unmistakable echo here in the evocation of nature and one of its moods. Here the actual pain of parting is overshadowed by the sisters' ardent desires that accompany their menfolk as they sail away, allowing the impassioned note of the quintet to mellow into tender yearning. Like all the sisters' outpourings, it has a powerful sensual element to it, as they abandon themselves to the new feeling with all the impulsiveness of their nature. A whole world of languorous sensuality lies in the surprising interrupted cadence on 'desir', with its keen-edged dissonance, that twice delays the actual closure. And how beautifully this interrupted cadence is prepared by the brief episode ('ed ogni elemento') with the wind trio and its insistent imitations. In much the same way, the murmured accompaniment in tender thirds in the muted strings that is initially conjured up by the image of a journey by sea comes imperceptibly to symbolize inner emotions. The wind instruments, too, are used in a typically Mozartian manner, entering only when the strings have filled in the outer picture and expressed the sisters' heartfelt desires. From then on they provide an almost constant accompaniment, bringing the whole trio to an end with a series of sustained chords.

---

63. Particularly attractive here is the 'write soon' topos of the text, which is in delightful contrast to the heroic tirades of only a few moments earlier.

That Don Alfonso joins in the trio and even reveals a certain importunity in doing so is entirely logical, given his theory that the most passionate people are the first to fall. As a result, it suits him to confirm the sisters in their feelings and to strike a similar note. The following accompanied recitative, in which he expresses his true thoughts, even picks up and parodies the terzettino's tone-painterly portrayal of waves.

The whole of this second part of the exposition, with its extended farewell, is masterly in its design. It begins by striking the ironical note of a piece of harmless roguery that acquires a rousing brilliance with the entry of the chorus. But in the midst of this festive clangour, the fires of true emotion are kindled at the most farcical point, in the quintet ('Di scrivermi ogni giorno'), casting their radiance over all that follows, before gradually fading away. The early ensembles all include a climax of one sort or another. Only in the case of the last of them does the emotion gradually die away. Every aspect of the pain of parting is fully explored here, from the conventional and primitively childlike to an elemental outburst of grief and heartfelt yearning – and all these ensembles are Andantes. As so often, the librettist's old-fashioned text shadows the music as the latter accompanies the characters' actions with its sense of Olympian irony, seeming to laugh and weep with them in turn, while never allowing us listeners to forget that in essence we are dealing with no more than a light-hearted game. But the music also reveals a further characteristic of the whole opera, namely, its delight in the sensuous beauty of its melodic writing and instrumentation. Mozart revels in 'beautiful music' here, in a melodiousness of iridescently changing colours that is itself a further aspect of his masquerade.

With Dorabella's aria ('Smanie implacabili che m'agitate) the individual characters begin to emerge from their various groups and take on a life of their own. In terms of their words, both recitative and aria are a genuine parody of the great solo scenes from *opera seria*. This in itself has given rise to considerable misgivings,[64] and it is certainly true that Mozart himself hesitated over his setting of this number.[65] None the less, it accords with the whole of Dorabella's later behaviour. She is the more impulsive and carefree of the sisters, abandoning herself to her feelings with greater passion, while at the same time forgetting them all the more promptly. By now the pain of parting, which had still been real when she had said goodbye to Ferrando, has been more or less forgotten. But as a society lady who knows how to behave, especially in the presence of servants, she plays the part of the abandoned Ariadne in all her disconsolate grief, a grief all the more spurious in that she can no longer express any genuine emotions. This is how Mozart has attempted to provide a psychological motive for a scene that composers of *opera buffa* tradition-ally – and with huge acclaim – treated as a parody. But unlike the Italian composers of the period, Mozart did not take the parody to the point of caricature. As a result, there are none of the wide-ranging intervals and coloratura outbursts that are otherwise inevitable here. Only the broad *seria* design, the insistently extended cadences, the Eumenides' retinue of winds and the tone-painting at the words 'suono orribile de' miei sospiri' ('the dreadful sound of my sighs') recall the tried and tested devices of the older type of parody. But nor is there any sign of the broad and emotional sweep of the melodic line found in such cases in Italian operas. Dorabella is psychologically inca-

---

64. See Jahn, *W. A. Mozart*, fourth edition, ii.515.
65. According to Köchel, a second version of this aria has survived with German words. Two folios from the autograph manu-script are currently in the possession of G. A. Petter in Vienna. ◆ The manuscript cited by Abert (now in the Staatsbibliothek zu Berlin) is not by Mozart but a copy said to have been made from the composer's score. In the absence of any unequivocal evidence for his authorship, and considering that an autograph has never been known, the version is unlikely to be by Mozart; possibly the anonymous arrangement was made in connection with a later performance. See K⁶ Anh. C7.06.

pable of this full-throated emotion and contents herself instead with short-breathed, almost convulsively agitated phrases, with only the orchestra giving full expression to her fury with its uninterrupted sextuplets[66] and violent dynamic contrasts. The particular qualities of the singer Louise Villeneuve – the sister of Adriana Ferrarese del Bene[67] – may also have played a part here. To judge by the music that Mozart wrote for her, she had a soprano voice of modest range that was particularly well suited to simple expressive singing.

Despina's first aria ('In uomini! In soldati') is a direct response to Dorabella's outburst and reveals her as a worthy descendant of Pergolesi's Serpina, one of a long line of Italian maids who with their immense cunning embody the crassest egoism. Nor was Mozart the first composer to take it upon himself 'to ensure that this character never for a moment degenerates into vulgarity'.[68] His Italian models had already achieved this aim by combining her basic instincts with mischievous charm and sincere, folklike freshness. As a result these characters were always the real favourites of *opera buffa* audiences, regaling them with most of the folklike songs. Mozart largely took over the character as he found it and wisely avoided investing her with the psychological depth found in the case of Susanna or even Zerlina. Textually and musically she behaves likes a true child of *opera buffa*, expressing her contempt of men in the form of a siciliana, in which men's falseness is underlined by drones involving a pedal point and appoggiaturas that tell the same old story. More individual is the introductory allegretto, which is also a delightful example of the language of musical gesture. It begins by striking a note of comic indignation, which is followed by a typically Mozartian phrase expressive of boundless contempt:

Finally, Despina makes fun of the sisters' credulous trust with a scherzando triplet motif – the second time round the triplet is intensified by wind accents on the weak beat of the bar. Particularly delightful is the emphatic repeat of 'fedeltà'. A typically Italian passage of quasi-recitative then leads into the Allegretto, which is chuckled rather than sung, but which none the less feels to be related to the siciliana theme, making it seem the natural sequel of the opening Allegretto.

With the sextet ('Alla bella Despinetta') the real comedy begins. The 'Albanians' enter on a note of delightful, solemn dignity, and with impassioned gallantry, supported by clarinets and bassoons, they attempt to win over Despina to their cause. She expresses her comic delight at the bearded strangers, a delight in no way lessened when the two men attempt, *sotto voce*, to boost their own failing spirits. The two sisters call out from offstage, thereby introducing the action proper. They come rushing in at the start of the allegro to a rapid unison passage, and proceed to

---

66. The same figure is found in the finale of Paisiello's *Il re Teodoro*.

67. Hence the reference to 'quelle dame ferraresi' in the second-act finale (bars 269–272), an echo of the old custom of improvised comedy. Louise Villeneuve had made her début as Amor in Martín y Soler's *L'arbore di Diana* on 1 October 1789 and had been 'rightfully acclaimed for her delightful appearance, subtle and expressive acting and beautiful and artistic singing'; see *Wiener Zeitung*, lii (1789), appendix.

68. Jahn, *W. A. Mozart*, ii.526.

scold poor Despina in a way that is highly strung and precious and, above all, true to life,[69] with the orchestration even extending to trumpets. But the Albanians, whom Despina now introduces, refuses to be blown off course and, supported by only clarinets, bassoons and, later, cellos, act out the part of sentimental admirers. There is something irresistibly comical about their melodic line, with its languorous sighs and tearful chromaticisms. Only with the entry of the Neapolitan sixth on the *b'* flat and of the cellos does it appear to acquire a regular metrical structure. Above all, however, it is the key of A minor[70] – invariably associated with exoticism in Mozart's works – that creates the sense of comedy. That the two sisters initially regard this as a painful insult is nicely observed, while the way in which the two groups retain their own particular orchestration is also highly effective. Their indignation then finds uninhibited expression in the great two-part molto allegro. Here the thirds that characterize the sisters throughout the whole of the opera and that are now supported by strings and winds acquire a particularly threatening, flickering hue. The men likewise form a group in opposition to them, to the accompaniment of a motif that Mozart had often used in the past to express male triumphalism. The third group is made up of Alfonso and Despina, and it is this group which, in keeping with the situation on stage, initially dominates the proceedings, with Despina even picking up the final motif from the previous episode. This group becomes even more prominent at the following passage:

Here it can hardly be an accident that Don Alfonso repeats the phrase 'che vi sia ciascun lo dice' ('everyone swears it exists') from the earlier trio ('Fuor la spada'). The two sisters remain self-contained as a group, while the other two groups occasionally join forces, before all combine together at the end in a great unison emblematic of the general confusion. The section that follows is striking for its interplay of *secco* and accompagnato, something found in no other opera by Mozart. Particularly amusing here is the comic scene in which Don Alfonso pretends to recognize the strangers, a brief episode over a chromatically descending bass line, first staccato, then legato. In declaring their love, the two men again appear as a self-contained group, each taking up where the other leaves off, finally coming together in two-part harmonies in a particularly exaggerated outpouring of emotion. Only with Fiordiligi's intervention does the tone switch from the lyrical to the dramatic, with its highly charged intensity preparing the way for her aria ('Come scoglio immoto resta'), the slow introduction of which is motivically and atmospherically a heightened continuation of the recitative. As a character, Fiordiligi is no deeper than her sister, merely prouder

69. It is based on a rhythm regularly used by Mozart to create a feeling of agitation: ♪ ♪| ♩. ♫ | ♩ See also Osmin's aria 'Solche hergelauf'ne Laffen' in *Die Entführung aus dem Serail*.
70. In the course of the whole opera, the minor tonality is used only in Alfonso's caricature-like aria ('Vorrei dir, e cor non ho'), during the scene in the first-act finale when the two men pretend to take poison and in certain episodes in Ferrando's aria ('Tradito, schernito').

and more domineering. Whereas Dorabella opts to strike a note of tragic pathos in order to fake an emotion that is already fading in intensity, Fiordiligi is able to allow her emotions to well up from inside her: even in her recitative she seems already fully armed like some Amazon warrior about to do battle. As a result, she is far more successful than her sister at capturing the style of *opera seria*. The words recall the popular simile arias of the period, and within the first fourteen bars the music already conjures up the familiar scene-stealing style of the Neapolitans, except that the rising melodic line is audibly reminiscent of the first version of Donna Anna's 'vengeance aria' ('Or sai chi l'onore'). On that occasion Mozart had rejected the version as too high-flown, but for Fiordiligi it struck him as just right. The shortened two-part allegro develops this tone a stage further. Here, too, at the words 'e potrà la morte sola', we find certain elements in the thematic writing and the accompaniment that are related to Donna Anna's aria, except that here, too, the relationship is that of a mask to the person's actual face. The elaborate cadence at 'far che cangi affetto il cor', with its trifling coloratura, reveals all too clearly what Fiordiligi understands by 'affetto', and there is something entirely logical about the way in which the orchestra now breaks in with its noisy and vacuous scales. This vocal virtuosity climaxes in the Più allegro and, above all, in the dazzling coloratura on 'speranza' and the subsequent doubling of voice and violas, which here take the bass line. Both these aspects serve to point up the sense of irony. Of course, the aria was written to accommodate Ferrarese's particular vocal skills. As Da Ponte's lover at this time,[71] she was well provided for in the opera. Elsewhere he praised the beauty of her singing and her moving delivery. Mozart was far more critical.[72] Above all, he was keen to stress the drama of the role. In this aria, too, the parody is clearly felt, as Fiordiligi is incapable of any deeper emotion, but only of a defiant independence of mind and a powerful sense of her own worth, a feeling that dresses itself in the gaudy robes of tragedy. This basic feeling is, however, genuine and, as such, well calculated to cause her suitor serious difficulties in the future.

Clearly this heroic aria initially persuaded Mozart to follow it up with an equally large-scale *buffa* aria for Guglielmo, 'Rivolgete a lui lo sguardo' K584,[73] which was intended for Benucci. This is undoubtedly one of Mozart's greatest achievements in the field of *opera buffa*, but it would be going too far to compare it with Leporello's 'catalogue aria', which grows organically out of the action. Guglielmo's aria, by contrast, is only loosely connected to the plot and actually contradicts the character of the two fiancées. In the best *opera buffa* manner, Da Ponte is largely unconcerned about this but offloads on to his hero a whole array of mythological and other allusions that are difficult to ascribe to him in the light of all that we know of his character.[74] Mozart, too, brings a larger-than-life aspect to the comedy. In itself the aria is a worthy monument to Mozart's humour with its witty underlining of the individual ideas, its colourful tone-painting and other allusions, especially in the winds, to say nothing of a typically Mozartian joviality that borders on the demonic. Certainly, the way in which the tension builds up towards the end, culminating in an outburst reminiscent of Count Almaviva, creates an incomparable impression

71. *Memorie di Lorenzo da Ponte*, ii.108–9 and 117.

72. See above and *Briefe*, iv.83 (letter of 16 April 1789). In London, too, observers admired her skills but were reluctant to hail her as a real prima donna; see Parke, *Musical Memoirs*, i.48–9. She was not particularly pretty, nor were her skills as an actress at all impressive, but she had an attractive mouth and beautiful eyes, and audiences warmed to her.

73. According to Mozart's *Verzeichnüß* it was written in December 1789 and is here described as an 'aria that was intended for the opera Così fan tutte. For Benucci'. In other words it had already been replaced by 'Non siate ritrosi' by the date of the first performance. It is reproduced in NMA II/5/18/2, 603–23. It originally demanded not only oboes, bassoons and trumpets but also horns, but these were later deleted for reasons that remain unclear.

74. There is even a mention of the solo dancer Charles Le Picq, who was famous at this time; see above.

e - ro - i - ne di___ co - stan - za   spec - chi son   di fe - del - tà.

before Guglielmo breaks off as though shocked and whispers his delight to Don Alfonso.

Rightly realizing that such a large-scale character aria was unsuited to the opera, Mozart replaced it with a second aria ('Non siate ritrosi'), cast in rondo form, from which Guglielmo emerges as an urbane gentleman well versed in the ways of the world, who, in spite of the snub that he has received, once again attempts to win over the women, half in earnest, half in jest. Yet at the same time his remarks reveal a smile of contentment at his rejection: confident that he retains Fiordiligi's love, he can good-humouredly play the gallant philanderer. Finally, even the orchestra takes a real delight in depicting masculine attractions, thereby leading directly into the following trio ('E voi ridete?') for the three men, an example of a popular type of number found in *opera buffa* that takes laughter as its subject.[75] In the present case the two officers reduce Alfonso to a state of virtual despair with their laughter, and there is something particularly amusing about the way in which the crescendos evaporate into a sudden *piano*, with Ferrando and Guglielmo laughing so hard that they run out of breath. The buzzing triplets in the generally unison strings complete this picture of exuberant high spirits.[76]

There follows an aria ('Un'aura amorosa') for Ferrando,[77] whose rapt infatuation had already found expression in the farewell scene. The saccharine words clearly pick up and parody the previous conversation about food, but Mozart's setting finds him – once again – going over his librettist's head. Rarely did he write a melody of such beguiling sensual beauty or such tender emotion. Ferrando is a deeply emotional, even sentimental, individual and, as such, was a figure of fun for the Italians, a factor that should not be forgotten in the present case. What we also find here is a burgeoning sensuality that finds particularly powerful expression in the wind accompaniment in the second section of the aria, at the end of which we again have a glimpse of the work's underlying irony: not once in the course of the aria have we heard a note of powerful masculine resolve on the part of this sanguine visionary, and so the orchestra now tries to make good that omission in a postlude based on a much altered version of the earlier motifs, only for it to sink back, of course, into the old mood of languorous passion.

The first-act finale ('Ah che tutta in un momento') begins with a broadly developed duet for the two sisters that is introduced by a lengthy ritornello and that is again intended to express their feeling of abandonment. The underlying mood is again one of tender yearning, with the same element of powerful sensuality as before. At the same time, however, the fluttering figures in the flutes immediately introduce a note of coquetry: in spite of their grief-stricken words, it is clear

---

75. Cf. the ensemble in act three, scene one of Piccinni's *La Corsara*. In both versions Guglielmo's aria passes into the trio without full closure. This trio itself is marked 'ride smoderatamente' (not *fortissimo*).

76. ◆ Further, see Heartz, 'When Mozart Revises: Guglielmo in *Così*'. More generally on his writing for particular singers, see Woodfield, 'Mozart's Compositional Methods: Writing for his Singers'.

77. The tenor Vincenzo Calvesi had made his Viennese début with his wife in April 1785; see *Wiener Zeitung*, xxxiii (1785), appendix. It was for Calvesi that Mozart wrote the insertion arias for *La villanella rapita* in 1785. In 1786 he sang Eufemio of Syracuse in Storace's *Gli equivoci*, with Michael Kelly as Eufemio of Ephesus; see Kelly, *Reminiscences*, i.237. In 1781 he sang in Venice; see Wiel, *I teatri musicali veneziani nel Settecento*; and in 1787 he appeared in Naples; see Florimo, *La scuola musicale di Napoli*, iv.353. ◆ Concerning Calvesi, see Link, *The National Court Theatre in Mozart's Vienna*.

that the sisters have not lost their appetite for life. Listen, for example, to the setting of the words 'Ah, che un mar pien di tormento' ('Ah, what a sea of torment [is life henceforth for me]'), with its accompanying winds, at which point the two officers, fully resolved to die, burst in with their strident diminished seventh, their phrases, breathlessly expelled, standing out sharply from the sisters' lengthy scream.[78] With the heroic shift to B flat major ('L'arsenico mi liberi': 'May arsenic set me free') they swallow the poison, the effect of their action on the two sisters rapidly finding expression in a motif that keeps on recurring, helplessly, in the orchestra:

The harmonies change to a tragic G minor, where they remain for some time, supported by a rolling motif in the orchestra:

No stone has been left unturned in painting this tragic portrait, from the sisters' bewildered horror to Alfonso's ironic regret and the men's heroic yet wistful farewell. Finally, their hearts begin to beat more slowly, at which point the sisters join their group, allowing them to sense both their fever[79] and their failing strength with all the greater immediacy. As a result, they already seem to be half won over. The men sink into unconsciousness. With Alfonso's solemn E flat major, the mood changes to one that comes close to recalling an *ombra* scene: note, in particular, the solemn wind sonorities. All the more vivid are the sisters' calls for help and Despina's Zerlina-like feigned regret: 'Morti i meschini io credo' ('I think the poor things are dead').[80] This section develops along entirely natural lines, with the orchestra repeatedly falling back on old motifs and thereby ensuring a sense of unity and clarity. Despina proves to be a consummate actress, inviting the sisters to

She then insists that Alfonso accompany her in search of a doctor, leaving the two couples alone. The sisters are still extremely concerned, while the two men, now in the best of spirits, delight in their comic role, with Ferrando – as always the more volatile of the two – proving particularly ebullient. At this point a new and important double motif enters:

---

78. Note the way in which their screams typically break off nervously to the rhythm: ♪ ♪♩ .
79. There is a clear reminiscence here of the beginning of Donna Anna's recitative ('Ma qual mai s'offre, oh Dei') in *Don Giovanni*.
80. Cf. Zerlina's 'Ah lasciatemi andar via' in the first-act finale in *Don Giovanni*.

The two men seem to writhe on the ground with racing pulses. The instruments of the orchestra now take control, and over their two mischievous motifs the women engage in a delightful game, drawing closer to the handsome men in their sensual inquisitiveness and examining them as their lives slip away. Their pity is genuinely stirred, but this merely serves to make the men feel apprehensive: might Don Alfonso have been right after all? These two motifs then disappear, giving way to a remarkable sense of anxiety and tension that finds expression in terse imitative polyphony and chromatic motifs. The women are close to tears, while the men are deeply worried at this unwelcome turn of events: what had begun as a light-hearted game now threatens to become much more serious. There is genuine comedy here, with the true and honest feelings of both parties resting on completely different assumptions and taking a very different course from the one that appears to be the case. In terms of its concept and execution, this section of the finale – from the entry of the double motif to the reappearance of Despina in disguise – is a veritable masterpiece, with its gradual increase in tension from a witty situation comedy to an expression of the subtlest irony. With the doctor's entrance the weighty C minor is abruptly replaced by G major,[81] thereby recalling the earlier situation, and with this we return to the world of *opera buffa*. Typical of this section is the regular rhythm ♩ ♩ ♩ | ♩. ♪ ♩ with its alternative form in diminution 𝄽 𝄾 ♪ ♪ ♪ | ♪. ♪ ♪ ♪. These provide the basis for the questions and answers, the chuckles and pompous preenings – in short, all the impish sparks of the *buffa* composer's art – that typify this section. The self-styled medic conducts his examination to mounting agitation on the part of Fiordiligi, Dorabella and Alfonso, before reassuring them in the most delightful manner, finally and gravely playing his trump card with the modulation to the subdominant C major: Dr Mesmer's magnetic therapy is now duly applied to the accompaniment of an incomparably comical passage in the winds notable for its affected pomposity.[82] Again the sisters have to place their hands on the men in an agitated passage involving syncopations and a tremolando. Adopting a suitably dignified tone, the doctor confirms the success of his cure, earning the praise of the two sisters, who are much relieved, and of Alfonso, whose reaction is one of mockery: 'Ah, questo medico vale un Perù' ('Ah, this doctor is worth all the gold in Peru'). The whole section bubbles along with all the high spirits associated with comedy, with no sense of exaggeration, while revealing the most wonderful unity. The number of new ideas that Mozart is able to coax from his basic rhythm is almost literally inexhaustible, making this scene an utter delight even if only from a musical standpoint. Again the music abruptly modulates, this time from G to B flat major. The men think that they have woken up in Elysium – an extremely popular feature in opera librettos of this period – and the orchestra responds by replacing the flutes, oboes and horns by clarinets, bassoons and trumpets, producing strange-sounding sonorities, half solemn, half ornate in a typi-

81.   The changes of tonality are more volatile here than in the second-act finale of *Le nozze di Figaro* or the first-act finale of *Don Giovanni*. Here the sequence is D major–G minor–E flat major–C minor–G major–B flat major–D major.

82.   The repeat of the passage 'Che poi sì celebre là in Francia fu' in the winds is missing from the autograph score and has been notated for flutes and bassoons alone on a separate folio in an unknown hand. That the passage is authentic is virtually certain. Presumably the comic idea that it expresses occurred to Mozart only during the rehearsals. ◆ The NMA version of this passage is based on the original conducting score of the opera (Österreichische Nationalbibliothek, Vienna, shelfmark O.A. 146).

cally Rococo manner, that continue throughout the whole of this section. The lovers seize the opportunity provided by the elevated mood to declare their love, a rapt declaration accompanied by the winds. At this latest turn of events, the sisters lose all self-control and reply with the same delightfully love-struck melody which, even if more timidly expressed, reminds their lovers of the comic nature of the situation. Alfonso and Despina between them form the third group, attempting to encourage the women with their hypocritical comments. The sisters pull themselves together one last time, with Fiordiligi underlining her proud resolve with a dazzling coloratura outburst, thereby bringing this section to an end on a note of extreme tension. This is the nub of the finale: while the orchestra continues to sing of the joys of Elysium, a decisive change in this game of love takes place in the voices. 'Più resister non poss'io', sing the sisters: 'I can resist no longer.' Melodically, too, they are now completely under the control of their new lovers. They can take no credit for the fact that in the following passage the men's awkward importunity recalls them to the path of duty. With its change of instrumentation – flutes and violins in unison and trembling quaver motion in the middle voices – the final allegro makes it clear that the officers are resolved to play their highest trump in the art of sensual seduction and, waking as though from an otherworldly vision, they demand a remarkably worldly kiss. This is too much for the sisters who, to the sound of powerful horn calls, interrupt the torrent of words and erupt in sheer anger. But it is unclear whether this anger is directed at their lovers' courtship as such or merely at the awkward, importunate form that it assumes. The latter seems the more likely, given the sisters' extreme reaction: they are furious at the fact that the men suddenly make so little effort, when they would have expected a different, more well-mannered approach. Because it springs from disappointment, their anger inevitably acquires a note of exaggeration that ultimately makes even the two officers afraid. As a whole, the scene again reveals Mozart's shrewd understanding of the female psyche. This lengthy section is in two parts, with a concluding stretta.[83] The three groups are maintained as before, but only the two sisters remain a self-contained entity throughout the whole of this section, while the other two groups soon merge to the sound of secret chuckling.[84] Meanwhile, the women's fury continues to mount, acquiring a note of high tragedy at the chromatic ascent to B flat major, which is immediately followed by a typically Mozartian combination of ideas: while the others, *sotto voce*, express their mischievous glee, Fiordiligi vents her anger in an agitated quaver-based melody with a final coloratura flourish on 'furor' and Dorabella's voice strives upwards in a series of recalcitrant suspensions. In the second section all the foregoing material is repeated in a more intense form, with the various groups now coming together to create a full ensemble. In the coda Fiordiligi manages for a time to assert herself in the face of the others by dint of her sustained and penetrating *a''*, thereby causing Ferrando to lose control of his own melodic line, a device that Mozart introduces to highly amusing effect: clearly Ferrando is terrified at Fiordiligi's behaviour. On this, Mozart now builds the presto, making the confusion complete. It begins with one of the descending scalar motifs with syncopated upbeat that are so often found in his works and that all convey a sense of breathlessness.[85] The men's group is now broken down, with Ferrando moving over to the side of the women, Guglielmo to that of Alfonso and Despina. The tumult reaches its climax in the tremendous chromatic crescendo in all six voices, with flames

83. At the repeat the main theme is reduced from four bars to three.
84. On the clipped melody at 'un quadretto più giocondo', see the trio ('Cosa sento!') in *Le nozze di Figaro*, where it again has an ironical significance.
85. Examples in *Don Giovanni* include the passage at 'mille torbidi pensieri' in the sextet ('Sola, sola in buio loco') and Leporello's aria ('Ah, pietà, signori miei!').

appearing to issue from the broken octaves in the strings that remain on *d*. The act ends on a typically Mozartian note, with all the characters reduced to a state of indecision that produces an insane whirl of the most contradictory emotions. The sisters are no longer entirely serious about their anger, the two officers grow unsure of themselves and of the comedy that they are playing and become suspicious, and Alfonso and Despina, too, appear to be mildly agitated, now that there is all to play for. Yet none of the characters is able to master the situation on his or her own initiative, resulting in a sense of general confusion, an aimless tension, a lively whirl of emotions that is all the more amusing in that the characters all attempt to lie to each other, while failing to find the courage needed to launch a proper attack. In this way love leads these characters a merry dance, making all their actions seem basically specious, pitiful and lacking in freedom, while at the time they take themselves incredibly seriously. This tangle of emotions was tailor-made for Mozart. He, too, makes no attempt to view it tragically but, delighting in his own gifts as a creative artist, leads his foolish creatures around in a circle. In all his earlier finales, there had always been an undertow of more or less dark-hued emotions, whereas here he created a masterpiece in the form of a purely *buffa* finale of a quintessentially Mozartian kind, with no crude effects and little sense of caricature but, rather, simply allowing the light-hearted masquerade to pursue its natural course and transfiguring it with the whole of his mature musical mastery. Significantly the Italians, with their instinctive sensitivity in such matters, rejected the work as essentially alien to their nature: after all, it is not an Italian *opera buffa*, but one, rather, that is typically Mozartian.

The second act opens with Despina regaling her listeners with her 'ars amandi' in an aria ('Una donna a quindici anni') that begins as a siciliana and ends as a quick waltz full of bubbling, pert high spirits, as if she were singing some old familiar ditty. Only a few passages are genuinely comical: note, for example, the high-flown 'e qual regina dall'alto soglio' ('and like a queen on her lofty throne') and the line 'viva Despina che sà servir' ('long live Despina, for she knows how to do it'), which rocks complacently back and forth on the chord of the ninth. In the fast section she grows even more impassioned, vociferating her domineering demands with almost tragic emotion. In the coda – a surprising and delightfully inspired appendage – the orchestra then coaxes her into picking up the earlier tone, until the very end, when her ingratiating triadic melody places an authentically Mozartian garland on her cunning little head.

In the following duet ('Prenderò quel brunettino') the sisters agree with Despina that there is no harm in a little flirtation. Their anger has been completely forgotten, and sensuality and curiosity rear their heads once more. Initially they regard the affair as no more than a game that does not affect their loyalty towards their fiancés. As the far more impulsive of the two, Dorabella takes control, with Fiordiligi following, initially at a considerable distance but later, once her senses have been fired, much more closely. In keeping with the *galant* lyric poetry of the period, the text revels in charming ideas and images, with the music exploring these images in greater detail than is normally the case with Mozart: note, in particular, the mischievous double coloratura and the repeatedly delayed ending.[86] But the music also reveals the sisters' powerful sensual desire and in that way lays the foundations for the decisive events that are to follow. Their lovers appear and launch into an emotionally charged wind-accompanied serenade with chorus ('Secondate, aurette amiche') of a kind drawn from real life at this time. But they still lack the courage for the final assault, and so Despina and Alfonso have to stand in for them in the following quartet ('La mano

---

86. The same sequence of chords (IV–V–V–I) is repeated six times in succession.

a me date').[87] At this important point in the action, the men are revealed – to utterly delightful effect – as mere puppets of Don Alfonso, incapable of doing anything more than simply echoing his phrases. And, for all the humour of the situation, Mozart has been particularly successful in capturing the note of great urgency with which he spurs them into action. Despina begins by striking a similar note when addressing the sisters, but in evident deference to Fiordiligi she introduces a passage of emotionally charged recitative. Unlike the men, the women do not echo her phrases, and it is left to the winds to provide a response, a state of affairs that undoubtedly reflects the underlying situation. But the fact that the sisters are left out here, allowing no large-scale sextet to develop and bring the couples closer together, is clearly a weakness on the part of the libretto. What a plan might Mozart himself have offered! The whole of the double seduction would have unfolded along far more striking and succinct lines than in the present case, where Da Ponte was reduced to a monotonous series of arias and duets. Instead, the ensemble dissolves into a mocking *buffa* duet for the two opportunists: not even the clever variation of the initial theme[88] can alter the fact that a particularly favourable dramatic opportunity was missed here.

The game of seduction brings with it a reversal of roles, with the tender-hearted and volatile Ferrando now brought together with the proud Fiordiligi, while the *galant* bon vivant Guglielmo is paired off with the easy-going Dorabella. In the following duet ('Il core vi dono') it transpires that Dorabella is particularly receptive to gallantry, with the result that she soon succumbs to the perfect gentleman in Guglielmo, whose courtship has something extraordinarily eloquent about it. This emerges not only from the numerous fermatas but also from the rising fourth with change of harmony at the end of the phrase, a device that recalls Don Giovanni's 'Là ci darem la mano'. Dorabella loses no time in adopting this tone in turn. Even the inevitable description of her beating heart is found here. Only once – at the words 'Nel petto un Vesuvio' ('I feel I have a volcano in my bosom') – do her feelings well up inside her, allowing her to take the initiative, and here Guglielmo accompanies her with his sense of superior gallantry, yet every section of this number ends with a motif which, in one form or another, suggests a seductive and lovesick glance:

It finally comes to dominate the end of the duet, with the winds once again revelling insatiably in the joys of *galant* love.

Ferrando's situation is more difficult. True to her character, Fiordiligi gives him his marching orders in an accompanied recitative which, emotionally overblown, involves a lively dialogue. Only at the end does she cast a seductive and snakelike glance at him with the full support of the orchestra. It is this glance that Ferrando picks up in his aria ('Ah lo veggio, quell'anima bella'),

---

87. Something different was originally intended here, with the recitative achieving full closure:

Alongside this is a note 'segue l'aria di Don Alfonso'. The *d* was then struck out and the word 'attacca' written next to it. In other words, a solo aria was originally planned at this point, perhaps with a following ensemble. The passage shows that Mozart was aware of the weakness of his text at this juncture.

88. This is a feature often found in Piccinni; see above.

which Mozart specifically described as 'lietissimo' ('very happy'). From a psychological point of view, the absence of all caricature is nicely observed, as is the fact that in this moment of outward dissimulation the aria develops solely out of Ferrando's own character. Sanguine by nature, he makes straight for his goal and plunges into a real turmoil of emotions, including hope for the future, that is undoubtedly intended on its deepest level to be an expression of feigned emotion but which immediately draws him into its sway to such an extent that he is no longer conscious of its inauthenticity. Here we see the man of temperament who, acting according to the dictates of reason, sets himself a particular goal, only to find himself swept along by his temperament in a totally different direction. Ferrando simply does not realize that his youthful heart is surreptitiously and at least for the present taking entirely seriously what had originally been intended as a game, and an additional irony lies in the fact that in this way he becomes far more of a threat to Fiordiligi than if he were consciously playing a part. As a result, the floodtide of this aria flows impetuously along, a single, powerful expression of emotion, in a constant state of unrest, never allowing the orchestra to have an independent say. In its most general terms, it recalls the aria that Mozart wrote for Donna Elvira for the Vienna production of *Don Giovanni*, except that it is far more agitated and lacks its motivic unity. It is in binary form, with the allegro taking its cue from the quartet ('La mano a me date') and, in its emotional exuberance, freely developing the main theme and transferring it to the orchestra. We also hear a clear reminiscence of a phrase from Zerlina's first aria ('Pace, pace, o mia vita').

This outpouring of emotion leaves a profound impression on Fiordiligi, whose emotional life is likewise well developed, but the impression is not the one intended by Don Alfonso and Despina. She feels remorse at her frivolous behaviour and yearns once more to recapture her earlier happiness in love. Both of these feelings assail her in her recitative in keeping with her volatile temperament, but then, in the radiant E major of her aria ('Per pietà, ben mio, perdona'), she sees the image of her absent lover in her mind's eye and seems to sink remorsefully to the ground in the adagio's half-sobbing portamento opening.[89] This and Ferrando's aria ('Un aura amorosa') contain the most beguiling melodies in the whole opera, with the present aria surpassing its predecessor only in that it has none of the former's irony. Its emotions are entirely authentic, even if – like all the sisters' outpourings – it is markedly sensuous in tone. A considerable part in this colouring is played by the concertante winds, alternately echoing the calls of yearning and supporting them with independent motifs – especially beautiful at the words 'perderà la rimembranza'. The fact that, however much she may revel in her own emotions, we are still dealing with the old Fiordiligi is clear from the wide-ranging and emotionally charged intervals that are scattered throughout the adagio and, even more, from the dazzling bravura of the allegro, which in terms of both its structure and themes recalls one of Sarti's rondòs,[90] a type that is certainly appropriate here inasmuch as it prevents the underlying mood from becoming too serious and picks up the note of the comedy as a whole.

Guglielmo tells Ferrando about Dorabella's infidelity, precipitating an outburst of appalled despair that finds expression in a wild accompanied recitative.[91] Guglielmo, too, comments on this

---

89. In terms of its key-signature, form and mood, there is a clear affinity between the present aria and Leonore's 'Komm, Hoffnung' from *Fidelio*. Jahn rightly draws attention to the parallel with the aria that Mozart wrote for Ferrarese for the 1789 revival of *Le nozze di Figaro* (see above); see Jahn, *W. A. Mozart*, ii.520.

90. Even the upbeat with the four quavers and the translucent melodic line demonstrate this affinity.

91. The recitative originally ended in C minor with the words 'Dammi consiglio!', followed by the note 'Segue l'aria di Guillelmo'. Later, the last two bars were deleted and the present version of the recitative continued on a separate folio, ending with the same note as before.

turn of events in his aria ('Donne mie, la fate a tanti'), but his own tone is ironical and that of a man of the world. He now believes himself peculiarly entitled to adopt this superior tone in that he has not only replaced his friend in Dorabella's affections but, according to Ferrando, can still count on Fiordiligi's love. It does not occur to him, of course, that this state of affairs may change, and herein lies the comedy of the situation. Wittily discursive, his aria is directed at the women whom he earlier valued so highly but whom he now regards as fickle and, as such, is half reproachful, half couched in the form of a tribute. It is a rondo, with a middle section that is bellicose and sentimental by turns. The way in which Guglielmo repeatedly returns to his reproachful 'ma quel farla a tanti a tanti' ('but such treatment of so many') creates a wonderful comic effect. But there are other ways, too, in which the aria stands out from its surroundings, not only as a result of its considerable length but also because of the leisurely, almost nonchalant manner of its expression, a quality already apparent in the metre of its main idea. The theme, which is stated right at the outset by the flutes, violins and bassoons two octaves apart, babbles along at a comfortable pace. Time and again this volatile and roguish figure slips out, reminding Guglielmo of the matter in hand and, following the second episode, reducing the whole orchestra to a state of total unease with its chuckling.

This has no effect on Ferrando, of course, and in the following accompanied recitative, which is particularly unified from a motivic point of view, he wallows in his anguish, but in his beautiful cavatina ('Tradito, schernito') his anger flares up again after only seven bars, followed in the winds by a radiant picture of the woman whom he still loves. It is the sort of melody which, filled with yearning, already anticipates Beethoven in its expressivity. Like Fiordiligi before him, Ferrando is deadly serious about his fidelity. Again his anger flares up briefly, before the earlier melody reappears, but now heard in the oboes, rather than the clarinets, and in the key of C major, where it creates a particularly beautiful impression, casting its transfiguring radiance over the whole of the rest of the aria. Here, too, Ferrando remains true to himself, a man of deep emotions but little taste for action – Alfonso still has a struggle on his hands with him. Dorabella, too, pours out the whole of her superficial, sensual nature in her following aria ('È amore un ladroncello'): the love that she praises is a titillating affair of the moment, a gallant game that stirs the senses but never goes beyond the surface. In this it corresponds to a commonplace of *opera buffa* as found in the text. Mozart responds in kind, setting it as an Italianate, siciliana-like rondo with a varied main theme,[92] mischievous and graceful, but without depth. The prominent winds, especially the clarinets, ensure that the sensual aspect of Dorabella's character finds full expression here.

Meanwhile, Fiordiligi has taken the romantic decision of dressing as a man and following her fiancé into battle. She is busy preparing to leave, when Ferrando interrupts her in a state of tense expectancy. He, too, is deeply agitated as a result of recent events, thereby providing the starting point for the most remarkable number in the entire opera apart from the two finales, a duet ('Fra gli amplessi in pochi istanti') that is noteworthy not least for its free form. In the opening adagio Fiordiligi begins by picking up the raptly infatuated mood of her recent aria. Her thoughts are still consumed with tender longing, and her heart is already beginning to beat a little faster in the E major section (con moto) when suddenly, in E minor, she hears a lovesick lament that is akin to her own yearning but which comes from another world: it is Ferrando who, on entering this world of emotion, once again forgets the role that he is playing. The radiance of A major suddenly fades and Fiordiligi withdraws into C major for the allegretto, a fragrant bloom that closes its petals

92. The opening recalls Paisiello's 'E vero sò fegliuola' from the second finale of *Gli amanti comici*, a number that is also in B flat major.

when touched against its will. Only one more phrase struggles to cross her lips, the same phrase that had accompanied the sisters' first rejection in the earlier quintet ('Sento oddio, che questo piede'), except that now it is harsher. But even the flickering accompaniment in the violins is the same. Ferrando now begins to emerge more clearly from the curious half-light, the phrase in question becoming for him a symbol of death at Fiordiligi's hands. How eloquent is his admonishment at the words 'E se forza, oh Dio, non hai, io la man ti reggerò' ('And if you lack the strength, by God, I'll guide your hand myself')! Even at this point Fiordiligi has already begun to vacillate, as is clear from her helpless, vaguely recitative-like melodic line at 'taci ahimè'. From now on he has her in tow melodically: he begins with bassoons, she follows with oboes, and at the words 'incomincia a vacillar', the vocal lines of both of them already exude a suspicious warmth of emotion. Once more she tries to break free from this delightful spell with her disjointed entreaty, but by the words 'ah non son, non son più forte' ('Ah, I no longer have any strength') she is fluttering around like a caged bird. At the same time the seductive A major reappears with increasing insistence in the distance, emerging from Ferrando's vocal line in the following larghetto to exert its magic power. It is a melody of a sensuous beauty unique to this opera and, at the same time, very closely related to Fiordiligi's world of emotion. But the enchantment of the moment draws Ferrando, too, out of himself, so that he no longer thinks of acting a part and instead enjoys its beauty to the full. Fiordiligi's change of heart is typical of Mozart: in spite of the previous crescendo, it is accompanied not by an agitated outburst of emotion but by an oboe melody of tranquil bliss. Which of us, when listening to this whole love scene, thinks of it as no more than a hypocritical game? Fiordiligi has forgotten her fiancé, Ferrando has forgotten the role that he was playing and the listener has forgotten the whole dramatic context as a result of the music, which is the true victor in this battle of love, so that even these characterless creatures are permitted a fleeting glimpse of Mozart's paradise of love. And is it not an ancient right of *opera buffa* occasionally to turn dramatic logic on its head for the sake of the music, a privilege of which Mozart now makes the noblest use? Which of us, in the presence of such rapt bliss, thinks of logic or of Da Ponte?[93] In the following andante – there are no fast sections in this duet – the couple's happiness pours forth in all its inwardness, first in folklike thirds and sixths, as though we are dealing with some fairytale princess who has just been released from her captivity, then in a passage involving brief canonic entries, mounting in intensity all the time, as though there is no end to the feeling of bliss. Only in the following scene does the beautiful illusion evaporate and the plot reasserts its claims. In a scene that is calculated to create the greatest possible contrast, the arch-rationalist Don Alfonso – a man who can never take time off to explore the irrational – draws his own conclusion, culminating in the moral 'così fan tutte': 'all women are the same'. Melodically, too, this aria is the diametrical opposite of the duet, with the burgeoning lines of the earlier piece replaced by self-righteous, stilted and arid declamation. Particularly delightful here are the trenchant dynamics and orchestral writing: note especially the contrasting use of legato and staccato and the complacent tone that Alfonso adopts at the words 'ed a me par necessità del core' ('but I think that it's an inborn need'). His diatribe grows increasingly embittered, climaxing in the final moral familiar from the overture that is now repeated by the lovers, who have finally been persuaded to believe in it, too. That this uninspired dictum follows immediately after the love scene between Fiordiligi and Ferrando is a further example of the opera's subtle irony, reminding us that the work is not a series of random numbers

---

93. Not even Jahn is free of such reservations; see Jahn, *W. A. Mozart*, ii.521.

but one that demands to be seen as a whole, the individual parts of which are internally linked with one another.[94]

Like the first-act finale of *Don Giovanni*, the second-act finale of *Così fan tutte* ('Fate presto, o cari amici') begins with hectic preparations for the coming celebrations. The bubbling high spirits of the music are also related, except that here the tone is more leisurely, more good-natured and more bourgeois. With wit and dignity Don Alfonso takes control of the situation, slipping away at the end with Despina, with a half-suppressed chuckle at the success of his prank. With the sudden entry of a festive E flat major comes a description – clearly modelled on contemporary life[95] – of the wedding celebrations of the two couples. The chorus begins the proceedings with a lively number, with the men greeting the two bridegrooms, the women greeting the brides. But they have also brought some music with them and end with a festive fanfare. The chorus is then repeated following an ensemble for the two couples that lends burgeoning expression to their feelings of happiness to the accompaniment of tender wind sonorities. Once again Fiordiligi and Ferrando step outside their respective groups with their fiery *fioriture*. And once again the pressure to dissemble has been completely forgotten, as the two men abandon themselves to the happiness of the moment with the same ardour as the two women. To the strains of Tafelmusik, they then sit down to eat and to drink each other's health while casting lovesick glances at one another, while their glasses chink merrily in the orchestra. In keeping with contemporary custom, the meal culminates in a canon initiated by Fiordiligi. In this way Mozart succeeds in allowing the lovers to luxuriate in their feelings of bliss to a degree that one would hardly have thought possible. In a far nobler sense than is suggested by the text, all thoughts of the past are overtaken by this flood of beauty and harmony, with only the coolly superior Guglielmo refusing to be drawn into the flood-tide of emotion.[96] Seething with quiet fury, he curses the whole comedy and thus maintains a link with the outer action. But he remains completely apart from the others, as the winds add their voices to the canon.

With a surprising enharmonic shift from A flat to a strident E major, the notary's *buffa* scene begins.[97] Here Mozart adopts the Italian practice of emphasizing his formal dignity, just as he

94.   ◆ Concerning the duet, also see Stiefel, 'Mozart's Seductions', and de Médicis, 'Chanter pour se faire entendre: Le duo d'influence dans les opéras de Mozart'.

95.   We have already found similar allusions to everyday customs and practices in *Le nozze di Figaro* and, even more, in *Don Giovanni*. They reveal the links between Mozart's operas and the older tradition which, as is clear from Bach's passions, for example, laid special emphasis on such connections.

96.   It was originally planned that Guglielmo should join in the canon, but this idea was then abandoned; in the critical commentary to AMA V/19, Rietz suggests that the canon would have been too high for Guglielmo's voice, but, had he wanted to, Mozart could undoubtedly have overcome this technical difficulty. ◆ Concerning the context of Mozart's canon, and in particular its relation to Martín y Soler's *Una cosa rara* and *L'arbore di Diana*, see Link, 'The Viennese operatic canon and Mozart's *Così fan tutte*'.

97.   In this scene Bernhard Gugler assumes an error on Mozart's part and alters the bass line in the autograph score from

to

stressed the medic's vulgar charlatanism. Even his greeting is accompanied by a delightful little old-fashioned flourish in the orchestra. When he then reads out the contract, he assumes his self-important official expression in a vivid motif that he is instructed to sing 'pel naso' ('through the nose'):

The orchestra keeps inventing new and more roguish accompanying figures that finally drive the two bridal couples to vent their exasperation, at which point a drumroll and the shrill sound of flutes, coupled by a sudden shift from A to D major, usher in a repeat of the chorus from the opening act ('Bella vita militar'), which now enters *pianissimo* in the distance. This is the first of a series of very brief sections. After all, the listener knows in advance how the affair will end and demands its swift resolution, with the result that the composer, too, is content to emphasize individual features and to characterize each of them only briefly. In consequence, there is no grand, free rondo-like ending to the work. Alfonso's feigned alarm is suitably underscored by the sudden entry of E flat major. This section is related, above all rhythmically, to the scene with the doctor in the first-act finale. It opens with one of those motifs which, descending triadically before suddenly breaking off, invariably signifies an outpouring of extreme emotion in Mozart's music.[98] The two women then repeat it in a more succinct form. For all its brevity, this section is extremely unified in structure and filled with a real sense of tension. Its second half rests on two equally structured harmonic arches, first on F, then, by means of an interrupted cadence, on E flat. The fluttering of the voices in minor thirds over the diminished chords creates a particularly pitiable impression, sinking to the ground in a highly realistic manner at the change of time-signature. All the more effective, then, is the half *galant*, half trusting tone of the two officers on their apparent return, with their delightful fermatas at the ends of their lines.[99] They know very well how to play the part of innocents. Meanwhile, the two puppeteers continue to pull the strings of the comedy. Particularly priceless is Despina's lie about the masked ball, with the innocent tone of the opening suddenly turning into mischievous giggling. The discovery of the marriage contract provokes in the men an outburst of tragic emotion that clearly contains an element of parody. All the more powerful is the response on the part of the totally annihilated sisters. Here, too, the text strikes a tragic pose, but the composer takes pity on his creatures and simply lets them sing and reveal the genuine emotions that they feel in their anxious young hearts. At the words 'Il mio fallo tardi vedo' ('Too late I see my error') they suddenly and movingly take refuge in the melody with which the men had greeted them, as though this might offer them some means of escape. After a few moments of fear and bewilderment, the two Albanians are wittily unmasked in a series of very brief episodes, with Guglielmo quoting the melody of his love duet ('Il core vi dono') and then, together with Ferrando, repeating the doctor's melody from the first-act finale, while the

As a result the bass now doubles the voice. See Gugler, 'Zwei eingewurzelte Druckfehler', 30. Chrysander ('Zur Partitur des *Don Giovanni*', 534–5) and Köchel (written communication) agree, whereas Rietz, in the collected edition, disagrees. The new edition gives the original version, but changes the viola line, a change that the critical commentary ought to have stressed, whereas it does not discuss the passage at all. I share Deiters's reservations about this change; see Jahn, *W. A. Mozart*, ii.539. It undermines the notary's self-importance, which finds highly effective expression in the chord of the seventh on F sharp, and above all it destroys the wonderful effect of the ninth that enters on 'stipulato'. There is no compelling reason to change Mozart's autograph score at this point.

98. Cf. the Count's 'Quà la chiave' in *Le nozze di Figaro* and, below, the passage 'Giusto ciel! Voi qui scriveste!'
99. Note also the way in which the violas double the violins at the lower octave.

orchestra, too, insists repeatedly on its motif from the same scene. Alfonso then adopts his typical tone of discreetly smiling irony (note also the gentle murmuring in the middle voices) and removes his own mask. Note the delightful way in which the sisters completely ignore him and, drawing on all the feminine wiles at their disposal, beg their lovers' forgiveness. Again their characteristic shimmering sequences of thirds have to do all that they can on their behalf. How fervent are their fermatas, how irresistible the following phrase, which is so typical of the opera as a whole:

a - do - rar - ti o - gnor sa - prò

The men forgive them, even if their forgiveness is initially somewhat grudging. Meanwhile, Despina's voice flutters uneasily through the ensemble, suggesting that she may even feel the pricks of conscience here. Total reconciliation comes only with the final Allegro, but whereas the Italian composers of the period would have struck a note of wild exuberance, here we find a quiet cantabile for the winds, which the voices likewise take up *sotto voce*, with the feeling of happiness finding expression with no sense of stridency or exaggeration. In the course of the following pages Mozart explores in detail individual ideas in his wooden text, from 'ogni cosa', 'casi', 'piangere' and 'riso' to 'turbini' and 'bella calma', but he takes these pearls of wisdom no more seriously than his characters, who are the last people to allow their happiness to be spoilt by Da Ponte's moral. Instead, they enjoy the moment with all the impulsiveness of their nature, with sheer bliss radiating in their eyes at the beautiful writing for the winds before 'bella calma troverà'. It is as though love, having led them such a merry dance, were smiling and offering them its forgiveness here. And with a silent and wistful smile the composer brings down the curtain.

The recitatives are markedly *buffa*-like in character, in other words, they are far more concerned with quick-wittedness than with expressivity. The *secco* recitative between the second and third trios includes a dialogue consisting of very brief phrases that are generally tossed to and fro like balls. Mostly, it is the same chord on which the battle of words is fought out. As a result, the recitatives are essentially more flowing and flexible than in the earlier operas. Not only do they often pass without full closure into the following number but are occasionally and effortlessly combined with brief accompanied recitatives, as in act one, scene twelve. This also explains the more frequent appearance of animated basses. Just before the decisive scene with Despina in act one, scene ten, for example, Don Alfonso has a motif in the bass which, carefully harmonized, is repeated seven times, providing an admirable reflection of his concerns. Otherwise, the emotionally charged passages are far fewer than in the other operas. The brief recitative at the start of act one, scene three is a good example of this, as is the recitative in act one, scene nine, in which Alfonso tells Despina of his plan for the officers to take poison. In act two, scene eight, when Ferrando learns that Dorabella has been unfaithful to him, there is even a chromatically rising line in the bass that recalls Gluck. And in much the same way, the temperament of the two sisters occasionally breaks through, as with Fiordiligi in act one, scene four and with Dorabella in act one, scene nine. And since the couples often appear in self-contained groups, we encounter a surprising number of recitatives involving more than one voice at a time, notably in act one, scene four, where the two officers sing together for no fewer than five bars in a row. On one occasion, the entrance of Don Alfonso means that we even have three-part writing.

Like each of its great predecessors, *Così fan tutte* has its own particular style, a style that emerged entirely naturally from Mozart's basic conception of his subject.[100] In this case the difference is much greater than that between *Le nozze di Figaro* and *Don Giovanni*, for *Così fan tutte* represents far more of a triumph for Mozart as a musician than as a delineator of character. The austere objectivity of *Don Giovanni* is replaced by a veritable indulgence in the purely musical, with all its sensual delights.[101] This indulgence manifests itself in the predilection for tone-painting as well as in the colourful instrumentation, with its fondness for beautiful sonorities, especially the characteristically tender sound of the clarinets, and in the melodic writing, which bears all the hallmarks of the composer's grace and sweetness. Nowhere else did he write more sensuously beguiling love songs. Of course, there is no underlying sense of the portentous primeval urges of the human psyche, as in *Le nozze di Figaro* and *Don Giovanni*. What we find instead is *galant* lyricism: these feelings, after all, are always bound up with society. Yet within this sphere they have all the delightful mellifluousness of this Rococo art form, without any sense of self-complacent insistency. It is this that distinguishes *Così fan tutte* from Italian *opera buffa*, a genre with which it otherwise shares the preponderance of the musical over the psychological. The insane jokes and caricatures of Italian *opera buffa* are only lightly touched on, and instead the prevailing tone is a superior, far more aristocratic humour that prefers to leave everything in this masquerade to create its effect through itself alone, learning to recognize and love the human element even in the inadequate and superficial. In consequence, the work reveals an aspect of Mozart's view of the world that we should not like to forgo. We have every reason to take off our hats to the genius who conjured up this fragrant rosebush between the towering achievements of *Don Giovanni* and *Die Zauberflöte*.

Among the arias that date from this period, the least important is 'Schon lacht der holde Frühling' K580, which Mozart wrote for Josepha Hofer and which survives only in the form of a draft score. It was presumably in order to accommodate his sister-in-law's modest musical abilities that he fell back on the form of the old *da capo* aria here, a form he had long ago abandoned, varying only the end of the *da capo*. On a higher level are the three insertion arias written for Louise Villeneuve, K578, 582 and 583.[102] The first of these, 'Alma grande', is a binary aria, powerful in expression, that makes only limited demands on the singer's range and vocal flexibility. Its accompaniment includes a number of effective pointers in the direction of an imitative treatment of the main theme. The second aria, 'Chi sà qual sia', is a single andante movement that stands out more for the beauty of its wind writing than for its depth of expression. And the third, 'Vado, ma dove?', comprises a fast section followed, exceptionally, by a slow one. The andante that finally develops out of the tempestuous allegro floats along on a Mozartian minuet rhythm

♪ with a cantilena whose tender melodiousness recalls *Così fan tutte*. Its instrumentation, too, reveals the same masterly qualities.

100. ◆ Further concerning *Così fan tutte*, see Bruce Alan Brown, *W. A. Mozart: Così fan tutte*; Dent, *Mozart's Operas: A Critical Study*; Kunze, *Mozarts Opern*; Steptoe, *The Mozart–Da Ponte operas: The Cultural and Musical Background to Le nozze di Figaro, Don Giovanni, and Così fan tutte*; Till, *Mozart and the Enlightenment: Truth, virtue and beauty in Mozart's operas*; and Vill, *Così fan tutte: Beiträge zur Wirkungsgeschichte von Mozarts Oper*.
101. Mozart's consideration for the individual qualities of his performers also falls under this heading.
102. K578 was discovered by Jahn in Carl August André's possession in 1856 in a copy that was almost certainly among Mozart's papers at the time of his death. An entry on the title-page is in Nissen's hand. ◆ Mozart's autograph for K578 is lost; the best surviving source for the work is a Viennese copy from 1789 now in the library of the Gesellschaft der Musikfreunde, Vienna (shelfmark K. T. 56). Further concerning K578, see Lazarevich, 'Mozart's Insertion Aria "Alma grande e nobil core", K. 578: Criticism of Cimarosa or a Compliment to the Composer?' Concerning K582 and 583, see Wiesend, 'Opernhandwerk und Originalität: Mozarts Arien KV 582 und 583 als Einlagen in Martín y Solers "Il burbero di buon cuore"'.

49

Increasing hardship and work[1]

The accession of the Emperor Leopold II on 13 March 1790 seemed to bode little good for opera and music in general. After all, Leopold was not regarded as a great lover or connoisseur of music. At all events, he no longer took a personal interest in the musical life of Vienna in the way that his predecessor had done. Consciously or unconsciously he ushered in a period of marked political and artistic reaction. The old favourites of the princely courts of Europe – ballet and *opera seria* – were revived. Rumour had it that a new opera house was to be built with boxes that could also be used for card games.[2] It was also reported that Salieri was so disgruntled by this new development that he was thinking of quitting his post and would be replaced by Cimarosa.[3] Initially Leopold showed absolutely no interest in opera and music: by July 1790 he had still not been to the theatre or organized any private concerts. Only his wife, the Empress Louise, was seen at the opera, to which she seemed to bring a genuine understanding, even though she appeared unimpressed by musical standards in Vienna. The princes, too, received music lessons.[4] But gradually the emperor became less withdrawn, and it was Joseph II's favourites who were the first to be affected by this change of heart. On 25 January 1791 Count Rosenberg was dismissed from his post and replaced by Count Ugarte,[5] and the same fate overtook Adriana Ferrarese and Da Ponte, who had marked the emperor's accession with a typically bombastic tribute.[6] Salieri, to whom Leopold was particularly ill disposed,[7] preferred not to wait for further developments but stepped down as director of the opera and was replaced by Joseph Weigl, in order – it was said – 'to honour the master in the pupil'.[8]

Mozart himself had certainly not been one of the favourites of the old regime and was allowed to remain in office. But that was all. In general, even less notice was taken of him than before and he was treated with open contempt, a point that emerges with particular clarity from his attempt – undertaken with the help of Gottfried van Swieten – to obtain the post of second Kapellmeister

---

1. ◆ In some respects this is the most surprising chapter in Abert. To be sure, research since his time has clarified aspects of the genesis and chronology of *La clemenza di Tito*, *Die Zauberflöte* and the *Requiem* that could not have been known to him. Nevertheless, his uncritical faith in unsupported anecdotal evidence concerning these works is atypical of the book as a whole. At the same time, however, it clearly serves his teleological purpose, as the chapter's concluding sentence makes clear.

2. This, too, was a long-established custom in Italy, as is clear from the lively account of de Brosses, *Lettres familières écrites en Italie en 1739 et 1740*, ii.236: 'Les échecs sont inventés à merveille pour remplir le vide de ces longs récitatifs, et la musique pour interrompre la trop grande assuidité aux échecs.'

3. *Musikalisches Wochenblatt*, i (1791), 15; and Lange, *Biographie des Joseph Lange*, 167.

4. *Musikalische Korrespondenz der Teutschen Filarmonischen Gesellschaft*, i (1790), 30.

5. Wlassak, *Chronik des k. k. Hof-Burgtheaters*, 67.

6. Da Ponte, *Memorie*, i/2.114–15.

7. According to Da Ponte, Leopold described him as an 'egoista insupportabile che non vorrebbe che piacessero nel mio teatro che le sue opere e la sua bella; egli non è solo nemico vostro, ma lo è di tutti i maestri di cappella, di tutte le cantanti'; Da Ponte, *Memorie*, ii.135. ◆ For detailed discussions of Leopold's musical taste and changes in Vienna's musical life at this time, see Rice, 'Emperor and impresario: Leopold II and the transformation of Viennese musical theater, 1790–1792', 'Vienna under Joseph II and Leopold II', 'Leopold II, Mozart, and the return to a Golden Age' and *Antonio Salieri and Viennese Opera*; further, see Link, *The National Court Theatre in Mozart's Vienna: Sources and documents, 1783–1792*.

8. Mosel, *Ueber das Leben und die Werke des Anton Salieri*, 138; and *Musikalisches Wochenblatt*, i (1791), 62.

and to teach the keyboard to the young princes. In early April 1790 he was still buoyed up with hopes for the future, as is clear from his letter to Puchberg:

When I arrived home from visiting you the other day I found the enclosed note from B. Swieten. You'll see from this, as I did, that my prospects are now better than ever. I now stand on the very brink of good fortune – yet the opportunity will be lost for ever if I cannot make use of it this time. But my present circumstances are such that in spite of my excellent prospects I must abandon all hope of furthering my fortunes unless I can count on the help of a staunch friend. You will have noticed that I have been very sad recently – and only the very many kindnesses that you have already shown me have prevented me from speaking out: but now – once more and for the last time, in my hour of greatest need, which will determine the whole of my future happiness – I call on you, fully trusting in your tried and tested friendship and brotherly love, to ask you to stand by me as best you can. You know that if my present circumstances were to become known, they would harm my application to the court and so it is necessary that they remain a secret, as they do not judge by circumstances at court, but, unfortunately, merely by appearances.[9]

In May Mozart went a stage further and appealed to Archduke Franz to use his 'most gracious influence' on his behalf. Significantly he stressed his work as a church composer,[10] hoping in that way to commend himself to the court, as this was a field that Salieri had entirely neglected. Even as late as 17 May he was still telling himself that the emperor had not sent back his petition and that this was a good sign.[11] But we then hear no more of the matter, and the resulting disappointment merely added to his burden of care. He was also passed over when King Ferdinand and Queen Caroline of Naples arrived in Vienna on 14 September to celebrate the double wedding of their daughters Maria Theresia and Luisa with the Archdukes Franz and Ferdinand on the 19th. Apart from hunting,[12] King Ferdinand listed only music and playing the lyre among his interests. On 15 September he was regaled with a performance of Weigl's new opera *La caffettiera bizzarra*;[13] and on the 21st the emperor appeared with him for the first time at the opera for Salieri's *Axur*. The wedding celebrations themselves took place at the Redoutensaal, with the musicians – including Cavalieri, Calvesi and the Stadler brothers – placed in the gallery under Salieri's direction. The programme included a symphony by Haydn that the king knew by heart, encouraging him to sing along with it. Haydn was introduced to him and was not only invited to Naples but also honoured with a number of new commissions,[14] whereas Mozart's name was not mentioned: he was not even asked to play for the king, a snub that left him feeling deeply offended.[15]

Mozart's situation thus became increasingly deplorable. Constanze's health showed no sign of any improvement, with the result that in the summer of 1790 she had to take the waters at Baden near Vienna. Nor did Mozart have much success with his teaching: in May 1790 he had only two pupils and had to ask his friends to help him increase this number to eight. The loyal Puchberg helped out as best he could but was unable to prevent Mozart from falling into the hands of

9. *Briefe*, iv.108 (letter of early April 1790); see also Spitta, 'Zur Herausgabe der Briefe Mozarts'.
10. *Briefe*, iv.107 (letter of early May 1790).
11. *Briefe*, iv.108 (letter written on or before 17 May 1790).
12. *Wiener Zeitung*, xxix (1791).
13. *Wiener Zeitung*, lxxv (1790), appendix.
14. Pohl, *Joseph Haydn*, ii.245. ◆ It is not clear that Haydn received 'a number of new commissions' at this time. He had composed six lira organizzata concertos for Naples as early as 1786–7 (including Hob. VIIh:1–5) and between 1788 and 1790 he wrote at least nine notturnos (including Hob. II:25–7 and 30–2).
15. *Briefe*, iv.121 (letter written before 4 November 1790).

usurers in May, so that his situation now became desperate. Even the two new string quartets K589 and 590 in B flat major and F major that he wrote for Friedrich Wilhelm II in May and June had to be handed over 'for a risible sum simply in order to have cash in hand'.[16] Apart from his adaptations of Handel's *Ode for St Cecilia's Day* and *Alexander's Feast*, these were the only works entered in his *Verzeichnüß* in 1790 between *Così fan tutte* and the December of that year. To make matters worse he now fell ill himself, complaining in April and May of severe headaches and toothache. By June he had recovered sufficiently to conduct a performance of *Così fan tutte*. But by 14 August we find him writing again to Puchberg:

> I felt tolerably well yesterday, but feel wretched today; I couldn't sleep all night for pain: I must have got too hot yesterday from so much walking, then caught a chill without realizing it; just imagine the state I'm in, ill and filled with cares and worries – such a state prevents me from getting appreciably better. In a week or two I'll be all right, no doubt about it, but at present I'm running short of money. Could you not help me out with a trifle? – *anything* would help me right now.[17]

Scarcely had Mozart recovered when he was already planning another concert tour to help him out of his predicament. Leopold II was to be crowned emperor in Frankfurt on 9 October 1790. Salieri as Hofkapellmeister was sent on in advance, together with Ignaz Umlauf as his deputy and fifteen chamber musicians, all of whom were part of the emperor's retinue. On this occasion, too, Mozart was passed over, and so he decided to go to Frankfurt on his own, hoping that he would at least be able to recover his expenses by taking part in the celebrations. In order to raise money for the journey, he first had to pawn his silverware. He set off on 23 September together with his brother-in-law, the violinist Franz Hofer,[18] who, he hoped, would take a share of the profits. They travelled in their own carriage and arrived in Frankfurt on 28 September. Because of the large numbers of visitors, they had some difficulty finding accommodation.[19] Mozart wrote to Constanze to report on the journey:

> In Regensburg we had a splendid lunch to the accompaniment of some divine Tafelmusik, angelic cooking and a wonderful Moselle wine. We breakfasted at Nuremberg – a hideous town. In Würzburg we fortified our precious stomachs with coffee, a beautiful, splendid town – the food was everywhere tolerable – but at Aschaffenburg, only 2 and a 1/2 stages from here, our host was kind enough to fleece us in the most pitiful way. – I am longing to hear your news and to know whether you're well and how our affairs are progressing etc. – I'm now firmly resolved to make as much money as I can here and am then looking forward to seeing you again. What a splendid life we'll lead, I'll work – work so hard that no unforeseen circumstances will ever reduce us to such desperate straits again.

16. *Briefe*, iv.110 (letter written on or before 12 June 1790). ◆ See p.1162, n.58 above.
17. *Briefe*, iv.111–12 (letter of 14 August 1790).
18. See Blümml, 'Der Violinist Franz de Paula Hofer: Freund und Schwager Mozarts'.
19. Their first lodgings were a hostelry at Sachsenhausen, after which they moved into a room in the Eagle, an apothecary's on the corner of Töngesgasse and Hasengasse. The building no longer exists. A fellow lodger was Johann Böhm, whose company had been performing in Frankfurt since 1780. On 12 October 1790, two days before Mozart's concert, Böhm staged *Die Entführung aus dem Serail*, following it up on the 22nd by *La finta giardiniera*, which was given in German; see *Frankfurter Generalanzeiger* (15 and 16 October 1890). Another old friend from the 'Auge Gottes' in Vienna whom Mozart met in Frankfurt was Frau Porsch, the wife of an actor at the Nationaltheater in the town [and an actress in her own right]. ◆ In fact, Mozart and Hofer did not remain at the Eagle but moved on 30 September to Böhm's house (Kalbächer-Gasse no. 167), where they paid 30 florins per month rent.

'My love,' he continued on 30 September,

there is no doubt whatever that I'll make something here, but it certainly won't be as much as you and various friends imagine. That I'm well known and respected here is certain. Well, we'll see. . . . I'm as happy as a sandboy at the thought of seeing you again – if people could see into my heart, I'd be almost ashamed – to me everything is cold – cold as ice. If you were with me, I might take more pleasure in the kindness of those I meet here – but, as it is, everything seems so empty. Adieu, my love.[20]

Initially Mozart led a 'very retiring' existence in Frankfurt and got on with his work. In the evening he went to the theatre, where he met various acquaintances, including the horn player Franz Lang and 'old Wendling and his Dorothé' from Mannheim. Reluctantly, he spent part of this period working on an 'adagio for the clockmaker', hoping to be able to force himself to finish it, but in vain. 'If it were for a large instrument and the work sounded like an organ piece, I'd be happy, but the mechanism consists of nothing but little pipes that sound too high-pitched and are too childish for me.'[21] The piece – K594 – was not completed until December.[22]

But if Mozart was hoping for a quiet life, he was soon to be disabused. On 5 October the theatre company maintained by the elector of Mainz planned a performance of *Don Giovanni*, although in the event nothing came of the idea.[23] Nor was it long before the composer was being 'invited everywhere', and, however reluctant he was to be placed on public display in this way, he had no choice in the matter, given the fact that his concert was about to take place. His general impression was one of disappointment: 'All this talk of imperial towns is no more than idle chatter. . . . The people here are even more stingy than in Vienna.'[24] If his concert were to prove a success, he would have only the Countess Hatzfeld and the Schweitzer family to thank: they alone were working hard on his behalf.[25] He was also invited to the home of Dr Johann Friedrich Wilhelm Dietz, who lived on the Zeil opposite the 'Römischer Kaiser' and who was on friendly terms with the director of the Stadttheater, Johann August Tabor, proving a generous host to visiting artists. Mozart spent a good deal of time at Dietz's house, where he also gave concerts.[26]

Mozart's concert was held at the Stadttheater on 15 October, six days after the coronation. His own report runs as follows:

20. *Briefe*, iv.113–14 (letters of 28 and 30 September 1790). ◆ The same day, 30 September, Constanze and their son, Karl, moved to Rauhensteingasse 970 (today no. 8) in the inner city. On 1 October, Mozart took a loan of 1000 gulden from Heinrich Lackenbacher. (The promissory note reproduced in *Dokumente*, 327, *Documentary Biography*, 371–2, was presumably signed before Mozart left for Frankfurt. The debt may have been discharged before Mozart's death; Lackenbacher does not appear among his creditors.)
21. *Briefe*, iv.116 (letter of 3 October 1790).
22. ◆ See also Haspels, 'Mozart and Automatic Music'.
23. See Mentzel's article in the Frankfurt weekly *Die kleine Chronik* (1887), nos 22ff. ◆ Dittersdorf's *Die Liebe im Narrenhause* was performed instead.
24. *Briefe*, iv.117 (letter of 8 October 1790).
25. Countess Hatzfeld lived at Heddernheim near Frankfurt. The Schweitzers were presumably the family of the banker and privy counsellor Franz Maria Schweitzer, who was married to Paula Maria Allesina and who had moved to Frankfurt in 1766. There were close links between the Schweitzers and the Dietzes. Hermann Deiters also mentions the senator and justice of the peace, Friedrich Karl Schweizer, who was an early friend of Goethe's; see Jahn, *W. A. Mozart*, fourth edition, ii.548; see also Gustav von Löper's critical commentary on *Dichtung und Wahrheit* iii.382 in the *Sophien-Ausgabe* of Goethe's works.
26. See Dietz, *Der Superintendent und erste Hofprediger M. Joh. Hektor Dietz, seine Vorfahren und Nachkommen: Ein Familienbuch*, 110 [Deiters's note]. Mozart's letters and autograph scores that were once in the family's possession are unfortunately no longer extant.

My concert took place at 11 o'clock this morning and was a splendid success from the stand-point of honour but a failure as far as money is concerned. Unfortunately some prince or other was giving a big dejeuné and the Hessian troops were on manoeuvres – there has been some obstacle or other every day I've been here. You can't imagine how – – –, – but in spite of this I was on such good form and people were so delighted with me that they begged me to give another concert next Sunday.[27] – And so I'll now be leaving on Monday.[28]

The programme was made up entirely of works by Mozart, foremost among which were almost certainly the two keyboard concertos in F and D major K459 and 537. The soprano soloist was Margarethe Schick née Hamel, whose performance is said to have inspired Mozart to comment afterwards that he no longer desired to hear any other singer.[29] He is also reported to have met old Ignaz von Beecke in Frankfurt and to have performed a double keyboard concerto[30] with him, in addition to playing a 'duo concertante' for keyboard and violin with his brother-in-law. One of the double-bass players at the concert, a certain Herr Ludwig, later recalled that at the rehearsal the composer, small of stature and extremely lively and restless, kept getting up from the keyboard and jumping down into the orchestra pit over the prompt box, then, after a lively exchange with the players, clambering back up on to the stage. Mozart is also said to have struck up a friendship with the leader of the orchestra, Heinrich Anton Hoffmann, with whom he and others would go to Kran's wine bar on the Bleidenstraße opposite the Kleine Sandgasse in the evening. Finally, Adolf Hesse reported meeting a former organist from the Katharinenkirche, who in 1790 had been a young pupil of his predecessor in the post. The latter told him that

One Sunday, when the service had finished, Mozart came up into the organ loft at St Catharine's and asked the old organist if he could play something on the organ. He sat down on the bench and was following the bold flight of his imagination when the old organist suddenly pushed him aside in the most discourteous manner imaginable, saying to his pupil: 'Did you hear that last modulation that Herr Mozart made? He claims to be a famous man but commits such serious violations of strict counterpoint.'[31]

27. This concert did not take place: by the Sunday in question Mozart was already in Mainz; see *Briefe*, iv.119 (letter of 17 October 1790).
28. *Briefe*, iv.118 (letter of 15 October 1790). See also the *Rats- und Schöffenprotokoll der Reichsstadt Frankfurt zur Wahl und Krönung des Kaisers Leopold*, 400: 'Wednesday, 13 October 1790. It being requested that the Imperial Concert-Meister Mozart be given permission to hold a concert to-morrow morning at the Municipal Playhouse: this is to be granted without establishing a precedent for other such cases' [*Dokumente*, 329, *Documentary Biography*, 373]. According to the playbill and *Briefe*, iv.118 (letter of 15 October 1790), the concert was given not on the 14th, but on the 15th.
29. Lewezow, *Leben und Kunst der Frau Margarete Luise Schick, gebornen Hamel, Königl. Preuss. Kammersängerin und Mitgliedes des Nationaltheaters zu Berlin*, 14–15. She was the wife of the Hofkapellmeister in Mainz and sang Blonde, Susanna and Zerlina.
◆ According to a surviving concert bill, the programme for Mozart's Frankfurt concert, which began at 11 am, included 'a grand new symphony', arias sung by Schick and Ceccarelli, a duet (Schick and Ceccarelli), an improvisation, and two concertos. Neither the symphony nor the concertos can be identified with certainty. The claim that K537 and 459 were performed on this occasion derives from the title-pages of the first editions; that to K459, published by André in 1794, reads: 'Ce Concerto a été exécuté par l'Auteur à Francfort sur le Mein à l'occasion du Couronnement de l'Empéreur Léopold II'. According to the travel diary of Count Ludwig von Bentheim-Steinfurt, 'the last symphony [which was supposed to follow the improvisation] was not given for it was almost two o'clock and everybody was sighing for dinner. The music thus lasted three hours which was due to the fact that between all the pieces there were very long pauses. The orchestra was no more than rather weak with five or six violins but apart from that very accurate'; see *Dokumente*, 329–30, *Documentary Biography*, 374–5.
30. Lipowsky, *Baierisches Musik-Lexikon*, 16.
31. *Breslauer Zeitung*, ccxl (1855), 1366. According to Mentzel, Mozart also visited the Karmeliterkirche and Dreikönigskirche, where he heard concertos by Georg Joseph Vogler.

The pupil had made a note of the modulation, which Hesse found beautiful and not even unusual.

From Frankfurt Mozart visited Offenbach, where he made contact with the André family. We may assume that he was a frequent visitor there.

But on one occasion, as chance would have it, Mozart found himself at a light-hearted, carefree party at which dancing played a prominent role, and since there was a shortage of female dancers, he quickly made up his mind to plight himself to the prettiest paper-folder from André's music press and to dance with her. – – For the whole of the rest of her life this 'prettiest paper-folder' boasted that the great Mozart had once invited her to dance. This story came to light again through her daughter, who later married the tax collector Herr Becker at the Kanalthor in Hanau.[32]

By 16 October at the latest Mozart had set off back via Mainz, where [on 20 October] he performed for the elector, Friedrich Karl Joseph Baron von Erthal, but received only 'a meagre 15 carolins'.[33] It is here that Tischbein is said to have painted the well-known portrait of Mozart for the elector,[34] but there are so many compelling arguments against this attribution that the matter can safely be laid to rest,[35] as can the claim that the aria 'Io ti lascio' is by Mozart, whereas it is in fact by Gottfried von Jacquin.[36]

Mozart then appears to have hesitated over whether to continue his journey via Regensburg or to return to Vienna via Mannheim and Munich. He also seems to have been tormented once more by Constanze's feelings of jealousy when the four letters that he sent her from Frankfurt were slow to reach her:

You seem to doubt my punctuality or rather my eagerness to write to you, which pains me very much. You should know me better than this – O God! love me only half as much as I love you, and I'll be content.[37]

PS: While I was writing the last page, tear after tear fell on to the paper, but now I must cheer up – catch! – an incredible number of kisses are flying about – what the devil! – I can see a whole host of them! – ha ha! – I've caught three of them – they're very precious to me! –[38]

In the end, Mozart decided to return to Vienna via Mannheim, where he spent several days renewing contact with those of his former friends who were still there. On 24 October he visited

32. Pirazzi, *Bilder und Geschichten aus Offenbachs Vergangenheit*, 188.
33. *Briefe*, iv.119 (letter of 23 October 1790). Arentz's claim that Mozart played for the elector 'on frequent occasions' is an exaggeration; see Engl, *W. A. Mozart in den Schilderungen seiner Biographen, in seiner körperlichen Erscheinung im Leben und im Bilde*, 45 and 48, based on information supplied by André [Deiters's note].
34. André, quoting a musician by the name of Haunz, states that in 1792 the elector gave the portrait to a court musician called Stutzl; see Engl, *W. A. Mozart*, 46.
35. Schurig, *Leopold Mozarts Reise-Aufzeichnungen 1763–1771*, 97; and *Wolfgang Amade Mozart*, ii.364. ◆ The Tischbein portrait is reproduced in Deutsch, *Mozart und seine Welt*, 289.
36. ◆ K621a, the aria 'Io ti lascio, oh cara, addio', is a problematic work. Although a single leaf (the second) survives in Mozart's autograph, and the work is probably to be dated some time between 1788 and 1791, Constanze later disowned it, writing to Breitkopf on 25 May 1799, 'I *and many experts* do not think it is his [Mozart's] work. My copy seems to me to be in the hand of the late Gottfried von Jacquin' (*Briefe*, iv.239).
37. *Briefe*, iv.118 (letter of 15 October 1790).
38. In spite of Jahn's and Nohl's assumptions to the contrary, this postscript does not belong with the letter of 30 September (see Deiters's note in Jahn, *W. A. Mozart*, ii.551) but probably with the lost letter that Mozart wrote in Mainz on 17 October 1790 [*Briefe*, iv.119].

Schwetzingen, 'in order to see the park', but above all he was detained by a performance of *Le nozze di Figaro* that same evening in Mannheim. The company had already begged him to attend the dress rehearsal on the 23rd.[39] The actor Wilhelm Backhaus noted in his diary of the Mannheim theatre: 'I had a very embarrassing encounter with Mozart. When I saw him, I thought he was some tailor's apprentice. I was standing by the door while we were rehearsing. He came over to me and asked about the rehearsal and whether it was possible to listen in. I sent him packing. But surely you'll allow Kapellmeister Mozart to attend? By now I was really embarrassed.'[40] At the age of eighty, the former court organist at the Trinitatiskirche could still remember Mozart visiting his father and playing the organ with him. At the rehearsal for *Le nozze di Figaro*, he had criticized the slow tempi of the conductor Ignaz Fränzl and suggested quicker ones.[41] One of the rank-and-file violinists was Johann Anton André, who reports that at the rehearsal Mozart looked small and slight of stature. André particularly recalled his pale complexion, prominent eyes and large nose.[42]

Mozart arrived in Munich on 29 October and stayed with his old friend, Franz Albert, the landlord of the Black Eagle in the Kaufingerstraße.[43] He intended to remain in the city for only a day but was detained by the elector, who wanted him to perform at a concert in honour of King Ferdinand of Naples, who was spending two days in Munich on his way home from Frankfurt.[44] 'A great honour for the Viennese court,' Mozart wrote, 'that the king has to hear me in a foreign country.' But the delay enabled him to see as much as he liked of his old friends in Munich:

As you can imagine, I've been having a good time with the Cannabichs, la bonne Ramm, Marchand and Brochard and we've talked a lot about you, my love. – I'm looking forward to seeing you, as I've lots to tell you; I'm thinking of making this very same journey with you, my love, at the end of next summer, so that you can take the waters in some other place, at the same time the company, exercise and change of air will do you good, just as they have done me good. . . . Forgive me for not writing as much as I'd like, but you can't imagine what a fuss they're making of me. – I must now be off to Cannabich's, where they're rehearsing a concerto.[45]

It was not long after Mozart got back to Vienna that Salomon arrived from London and invited Haydn to go to England and write a series of works for his concerts in the capital.[46] Negotiations were also started with Mozart, and it was provisionally agreed that following Haydn's return he, too, would go to London under similarly advantageous conditions. Shortly before this Mozart had been approached by Robert Bray O'Reilly, the director of the Italian Opera in London, inviting him to go to England and remain there until June 1791. While in England he would write at least two operas, for which he would be paid three hundred pounds.[47] It is easy to understand why he did

39. *Briefe*, iv.119 (letter of 23 October 1790).
40. Nohl, *Musikalisches Skizzenbuch*, 190.
41. Koffka, *Iffland und Dalberg: Geschichte der classischen Theaterzeit Mannheims*, 185. Mozart declared himself satisfied with the cast and production.
42. Henkel, *Der Klavierlehrer*, xiii (1890), 1.
43. *Kurfürstl. gnädigst privilegiertes Münchner Wochen- oder Anzeigsblatt*, xliv (3 November 1790) [*Dokumente*, 333, *Documentary Biography*, 378].
44. According to the *Kurfürstl. gnädigst privilegiertes Münchner Wochen- oder Anzeigsblatt*, clxxiii–clxxv (1790), the king's arrival on 4 November was attended by a court gala and concert, followed the next day by a hunt, with a play in the evening, followed by a formal supper.
45. *Briefe*, iv.121 (letter written before 4 November 1790).
46. Pohl, *Mozart und Haydn in London*, ii.101ff.
47. O'Reilly's letter of 26 October 1790 reads as follows: 'Through a person attached to H.R.H. the Prince of Wales I have learnt of your plan to visit England, and as I wish to make the personal acquaintance of men of talent and am at present in a position to contribute to their advantage, I am offering you, Sir, the position of composer in England. If you are able to come to London

not take up this invitation straightaway and why, in 1791, his work in Prague and Vienna prevented him from doing so. We have already had occasion to mention how difficult it was for him to say goodbye to Haydn, whom he regarded as his only true friend.

Mozart's aim of devoting himself to his work without having to worry about how to survive was one that he was unable to achieve either through his visit to Frankfurt or by his other financial dealings.[48] But his creativity could not in the long run be curbed. Quite the opposite: following the period in 1790 when he wrote very little, the final twelve months of his life witnessed an unexpected increase in productivity, as if it were a question of gathering in as much of the harvest as possible before the onset of darkness.

He began in December 1790 with his string quintet in D major K593, which he followed up with a similar piece in E flat major K614 completed on 12 April 1791. According to his publisher, both were written in response to 'the very active encouragement of a music lover',[49] who evidently hoped that by commissioning these pieces he might be able to assist Mozart in his straitened circumstances. It is unclear whether Mozart also wrote any chamber works for winds at this time: it seems likely that he did, even though there are no such entries in his own thematic catalogue. The anthologies of works for wind ensemble published by Simrock, Breitkopf and others contain such an assortment of original compositions and transcriptions that it is difficult to establish which pieces are authentic. Two works that are now believed to date from this period[50] are the canonic adagio in F major K410 for two basset-horns and bassoon and the adagio in B flat major K411 for two clarinets and three basset-horns. This dating would appear to be confirmed by the mature mastery of the former piece and by the whole expressive language of the latter. Equally unresolved is the dating of the five divertimentos for two clarinets and bassoon, an uncertainty due to the lack of any documentary evidence concerning their authenticity.[51] That they are by Mozart seems beyond question. Only their dating remains problematic. The suggestion that they were written as early as 1783–5 seems unlikely, given their approach in general and the advanced style of the menuettos in particular, a style that recalls the period of *Don Giovanni* and the three great symphonies. On the other hand, it is not impossible that the collection includes pieces from different periods.[52] Conversely, there is no doubt that the period under discussion witnessed the

towards the end of December next, 1790, and to remain there until the end of June 1791 and within that space of time to write at least two operas, serious or comic, according to the choice of the management, I can offer you three hundred pounds sterling, with the additional opportunity of writing for the professional concerts or any other concert hall with the sole exception of the other theatres. If this proposal is acceptable to you and you are in a position to accept it, kindly let me have your reply by return, and this letter will serve as a contract'; see Nottebohm, *Mozartiana*, 67 [*Dokumente*, 332, *Documentary Biography*, 377–8].

48. Mozart's letters of 28 and 30 September and 8 and 23 October 1790 (*Briefe*, iv.113, 114, 117 and 119) all contain allusions to these financial dealings, the full extent of which remains unclear. What seems to have been involved was an arrangement with Hoffmeister, who had lent him a relatively large sum of money, in return for which Mozart had agreed to write something for him. These plans were evidently concealed from Puchberg.

49. *Wiener Zeitung* (18 May 1793), 1492. The Artaria edition described K614 as 'composto per un Amatore Ongarese'.

50. See Wyzewa and Saint-Foix, *Wolfgang Amédée Mozart*, ii.421, although the second piece is here described, erroneously, as being in B flat major.

51. Their editor, Ernst Lewicki [AMA XXIV, supplement 62], deserves our gratitude for removing the extremely inept writing for the horns. Lewicki believes that these works were written by Gottfried von Jacquin and his circle in the years between 1783 and 1785. ◆ The twenty-six pieces for three basset-horns K439b are now considered doubtful as works by Mozart; the earliest surviving source is an incomplete eighteenth-century manuscript of uncertain provenance and the works were not published until the early years of the nineteenth century, by Breitkopf & Härtel, in a version for two basset-horns and bassoon (nos 7–9 and 11), and – the source used by Lewicki – by Simrock, in a version for two clarinets, two horns and bassoon (nos 1–10 and 12–26). None of the works can be accurately dated. Further, see Federici, 'Kennzeichen und Eigenart der Triobesetzung in der Musik für Bassetthorn in Wien zur Zeit Mozarts'.

52. ◆ A study of the autographs shows that K410 is likely to date from 1784–5, K411 from 1782–3.

composition of the adagio and rondo in C minor K617 for musical glasses,[53] flute, oboe, viola and cello entered in Mozart's catalogue under 23 May 1791 and probably also the little adagio in C major K356 for musical glasses. Both were probably written for the blind virtuoso Marianne Kirchgäßner (1769–1808), who was a pupil of Joseph Aloys Schmittbaur[54] and who elicited Mozart's sympathy when she visited Vienna in 1791. Her performances of these works were much applauded.[55]

Other curiosities that date from this period are the works that Mozart wrote for 'an organ in a clock', the adagio and allegro K594 in F minor, which Mozart completed in December 1790, the fantasia in F minor K608 of 3 March 1791 and the andante in F major K616 of 4 May 1791. All these pieces were commissioned by Count Joseph Deym, who pseudonymously ran the Müller Gallery on the Stock am Eisen Platz in Vienna.[56] Mozart himself had no hand in any of the later transcriptions of these pieces.

This period begins and ends with a concerto. It was for himself – evidently for a performance that he was planning to give[57] – that Mozart wrote his keyboard concerto K595 in B flat major, his final contribution to the medium, which he completed on 5 January 1791. The A major clarinet concerto K622 was written 'for Herr Stadler the Elder' between 28 September and 7 October 1791. At the same time, as we noted above, Mozart was busy writing dances for the court's festivities.[58]

The keyboard music of this period is represented by only a handful of trifles such as the little *Albumblatt* in E flat major K236 for Johann Baptist Cramer;[59] the menuetto in D major K355;[60] and the eight variations on *Ein Weib ist das herrlichste Ding* K613. Vocal music, by contrast, plays a rather greater role – and not only because this period witnessed the composition of Mozart's last two operas and the *Requiem*. This series of works was launched by the three German songs K596–598 that were intended for a collection of children's songs and entered in Mozart's catalogue

53. The glass harmonica is a musical instrument made of tuned glass bowls that are rubbed with the tip of a moistened finger. In 1761 Benjamin Franklin fitted the bowls to a horizontal rod actuated by a crank attached to a pedal. Schmittbaur extended the compass to *c–f′* and then to *c–c‴*; see Pohl, *Zur Geschichte der Glasharmonika*; and Sachs, *Real-Lexikon der Musikinstrumente*, 159–60. ◆ For two contemporaneous sources on playing the glass harmonica, see Ford, *Instructions for the Playing of the Musical Glasses*; and Bartl, *Nachrichten von der Harmonika*. Further, see O'Donoghue, *An Irish Musical Genius: Richard Pockrich, the Inventor of the Musical Glasses*; and Sonneck, 'Benjamin Franklin's Musical Side'.
54. *Musikalische Korrespondenz der Teutschen Filarmonischen Gesellschaft*, i (1790), 170–71 and ii (1791), 69. On 13 August 1791 the *Wiener Zeitung*, lxv (1791), appendix, announced that on the 19th Marianne Kirchgäßner would perform 'an entirely new and surpassingly beautiful concert quintet accompanied by wind instruments by Herr Kapellmeister Mozart' [*Dokumente*, 350–1, *Documentary Biography*, 399–400]; see also *Musikalische Korrespondenz*, iii (1792), 146; and *AmZ*, iii (1800), 127–8. The fragment of a further quintet K616a is now in the Mozarteum in Salzburg. ◆ Further concerning Kirchgäßner, see Ullrich, *Die blinde Glasharmonikavirtuosin Marianne Kirchgessner und Wien: Eine Künstlerin der empfindsamen Zeit*.
55. In Berlin and Leipzig she was criticized for her unduly virtuosic manner; see Reichardt, *Musikalische Monatsschrift*, 25; *Berlinische musikalische Zeitung historischen und kritischen Inhalts*, i (1793/4), 150; and *AmZ*, ii (1799/1800), 254.
56. On 17 August 1791, Müller announced that visitors to his gallery would be able to see 'the magnificent mausoleum erected to the great Field Marshal Baron von Loudon. Here listeners will be amazed by the choice funeral music composed by the famous Herr Capellmeister Mozart, music wholly appropriate to the purpose for which it has been written'; *Wiener Zeitung*, lxvi (1791), appendix. ◆ Earlier, on 26 March 1791, Müller had advertised the 'mausoleum erected by him, which he has at great expense built in memory of the unforgettable and world-famous Field Marshal Baron von Loudon . . . upon the stroke of each hour a funeral musique will be heard, and will be different every week. This week the composition is by Herr Kapellmeister Mozart.' Presumably the work is K594. See *Dokumente*, 400–1, *Documentary Biography*, 388–9.
57. Perhaps for that of the clarinettist Joseph Beer on 4 March 1791. ◆ It is possible that the concerto was performed earlier, in January 1791; see Edge, 'Mozart's reception in Vienna, 1787–1791'.
58. The contredanses with introductory overture K106 probably also date from 1790; see Wyzewa and Saint-Foix, *Wolfgang Amédée Mozart*, ii.422. ◆ There is no unequivocal evidence that K106 is by Mozart; the earliest documentary reference to the work is an advertisement for manuscript copies offered by Johann Traeg in the *Wiener Zeitung* for 14 January 1792.
59. Czerny dated it to 1790. ◆ Recent research suggests that the date is more likely to be 1782 or 1783. For a facsimile, see King, *Mozart in Retrospect*, 112.
60. Harmonically speaking, this piece cannot possibly have been written in 1780: stylistically, it bears all the hallmarks of Mozart's final period. ◆ Although it was apparently composed in the 1780s, the fragmentary K355 cannot be dated with certainty. The trio was composed by Maximilian Stadler.

on 14 January 1791. (They include the famous *Komm, lieber Mai* K596.) These were followed on 8 March by a bass aria, *Per questa bella mano* K612, with obbligato double bass, an occasional aria for the first Sarastro, Franz Gerl, and the double-bass virtuoso Friedrich Pischlberger. On 20 April he completed a final chorus, 'Viviamo felici' K615, for Sarti's *Le gelosie villane*. Written 'for amateurs', it is now lost. In July he wrote the cantata *Die ihr des unermeßlichen Weltalls Schöpfer ehrt* K619, a setting of a text by Franz Heinrich Ziegenhagen; and on 15 November he completed his *Kleine Freimaurerkantate* K623. Even more important are the sacred compositions to which he now returned after a long break and that culminated in the *Requiem*.

Foremost among this last group of works is the *Ave verum corpus* K618 of 17 June 1791, a motet-like work scored for chorus, four-part strings and organ. As we know, Constanze had spent the summer and autumn of 1790 taking the waters at Baden, whither she returned with her son Carl the following summer. She was in an advanced state of pregnancy and in poor health. Here Mozart had found an ardent admirer in the local schoolmaster and choirmaster Anton Stoll, who helped him in all manner of ways, including finding a small apartment for Constanze for the summer: 'She needs only 2 rooms or one room and a dressing room, but the main thing is that they are on the ground floor.'[61] Like so many others, Stoll had to put up with the occasional outburst of Mozart's high spirits. His first surviving letter to him, for example, ends with the words, 'This is the stupidest letter I've written in my entire life, but it's just the thing for you.'[62] And his letter of 12 July begins with some lines of doggerel verse:

> Liebster Stoll!
> Bester Knoll!
> Größter Schroll!
> Bist Sternvoll!
> Gelt das Moll!
> Tut Dir wohl![63]

In return Mozart helped Stoll out with church music, lending him the parts for various pieces, including his Masses in B flat and C major K275 and 317. When it turned out that the soprano soloist was unwilling to comply with his instructions, he immediately replaced her with Stoll's ten- or eleven-year-old sister-in-law Antonie Huber, the daughter of a civil servant in the employment of Karl von Doblhoff-Dier in Baden. After a week's intensive rehearsals, Mozart was so pleased with her that after the performance he is said to have exclaimed, 'Good, Tonerl [a diminutive of Antonia], very good', and gave her a kiss and a ducat. On another occasion he told her: 'Tonerl, hurry up and become a big girl, and then I'll take you with me to Vienna.'[64] It was no doubt during one of his visits to Baden that he wrote the *Ave verum corpus* at Stoll's suggestion. To judge by its words, it may have been intended for the Feast of Corpus Christi.[65]

61. *Briefe*, iv.133 (letter of late May 1791). Here Mozart announces that his wife will arrive 'on Saturday or Monday at the latest'. His first letter to Constanze is dated 5 June, a Sunday, suggesting that she arrived on the 4th.
62. *Briefe*, iv.133 (letter of late May 1791).
63. *Briefe*, iv.152 (letter of 12 July 1791).
64. Antonie Huber later married a Herr Haradauer and settled in Graz. Her reminiscences were published in the *Wiener Fremdenblatt* (22 January 1856); see also Rudolf Lewicki, 'Antonia Haradauer'.
65. In spite of claims to the contrary (see Wyzewa and Saint-Foix, *Wolfgang Amédée Mozart*, ii.424), the hymn *Adoramus te* K327 for four voices, bass and organ is by Quirino Gasparini; see above.

Constanze probably remained in Baden until 11 July.[66] For Mozart, her absence meant a period of restlessness and disorganization, as vividly emerges from his letters of the time. Here we learn of his domestic and financial concerns, of work and performances and of new and old acquaintances. Above all, however, we see the tenderest concern for Constanze's well-being. Among the individuals and families whom Mozart saw at this time are not only old acquaintances, but also new ones, including Montecuculi,[67] and the Schwingenschuh, Rechberg and Wildburg families, although in none of these cases did the friendship extend beyond superficialities. The Wildburgs are mentioned in the context of one of Constanze's dresses,[68] while Mozart appears to have had a relatively low opinion of the Rechbergs,[69] who lived near his old friend Joseph Leutgeb. For the Schwingenschuhs he once obtained a box at the theatre,[70] on another occasion warning Constanze against going to the casino with them if he himself was not present.[71] He generally ate out, either with friends or at one of the local inns. As he often gave their servant 'Lorl' permission to take the evening off, he occasionally spent the night with friends, including Leutgeb.[72] All this was passed on to Constanze with his usual high spirits and tenderness. Sometimes he wrote in French. On 7 June, for example, we find him writing to her as follows:

It was with indescribable pleasure that I received your letter of the 6th and saw from it that you are well and in good health and – very sensibly – not taking baths. God! How happy I'd have been if you'd come with the Wildburgs! – I was annoyed with myself for not asking you to drive into town – but I was afraid of the expense. But it would have been charmant if you'd come. We're setting off at 5 in the morning, 3 carriagefuls of us – and so I hope that between 9 and 10 I'll find in your arms all the pleasure that a man can feel who loves his wife as I love you.[73]

Yesterday I lunched with Süßmaier at the 'Ungarische Krone', as I still had business in the town at 1, S- has to eat early and Frau S-, who had been wanting to invite me for lunch these last few days, had an engagement at Schönbrunn.[74] As you know, I'm having lunch with Schicaneder today, as you, too, were invited. – Still haven't received a letter from Frau Duschek – I'll enquire again today.[75]

This letter is important as it contains the first mention of the names of Süßmayr and Schikaneder. Süßmayr, it seems, was as much the butt of Mozart's high spirits as Leutgeb, for example.

Mozart visited his family in Baden on several occasions, including 8 June and, finally, on 10 July, when he arrived to take them back to Vienna. He was planning to go on 12 June, but, to his annoyance, had to abandon the visit, as a concert by Marianne Kirchgäßner had unexpectedly been brought forward to the 10th. On the 11th he wrote to Constanze:

---

66. See Spitta, 'Zur Herausgabe der Briefe Mozarts', 403. The Mozarts' fourth son, Franz Xaver Wolfgang, was born in Vienna on 26 July.

67. Probably the Margrave Franz Ludwig Marchese di Montecuculi, who later became Commander of the Maltese Order at Maidelberg in Austrian Silesia; see Deiters's note in Jahn, *W. A. Mozart*, ii.557. He may have been Mozart's pupil.

68. *Briefe*, iv.136 (letter of 7 June 1791).

69. *Briefe*, iv.138 (letter of 12 June 1791).

70. *Briefe*, iv.134 (letter of 6 June 1791).

71. *Briefe*, iv.138 (letter of 12 June 1791).

72. *Briefe*, iv.134 (letter of 5 June 1791).

73. Mozart drove out to Baden with the Schwingenschuhs; see *Briefe*, iv.134 (letter of 5 June 1791); on Mozart's frequent visits to Baden, see Rollett, 'Mozart in Baden'.

74. For some reason, Nissen struck out all the names here. S- may be the composer Benedikt Schack, whose wife, a contralto, sang the Third Lady in *Die Zauberflöte*.

75. *Briefe*, iv.135–6 (letter of 7 June 1791). The Ungarische Krone was a tavern in the Himmelpfortgasse in Vienna.

Criés avec moi contre mon mauvais sort! – Mad^selle Kirchgessner ne donne pas son Academie Lundi! – par consequent j'aurais pu vous posseder, ma chère, tout ce jour de Dimanche – mercredi je viendrai sûrement. – [Rail with me against my ill fortune! Mad^selle Kirchgessner is not giving her concert on Monday! As a result I could have had you, my dear, all Sunday – I'll definitely come on Wednesday.]

I must hurry as it's already a 1/4 to 7 – and the coach leaves at 7 – – mind you don't slip when bathing, and never stay in on your own – if I were you, I'd have the occasional day off in order not to force things. I hope that someone kept you company during the night. – I can't tell you what I'd give to be with you at Baaden instead of being stuck here. – From sheer boredom I wrote an aria for the opera[76] today – I've been up since 1/2 past 4. . . . Adieu, my love! – Today I'm having lunch with Puchberg – I kiss you 1000 times and in my thoughts say with you: 'Death and despair were his reward!'[77]

Mozart's annoyance increased as the day wore on:

Why didn't I receive a letter from you yesterday evening? So that you can continue to keep me in a state of anxiety over your baths? – this and something else spoilt the whole of yesterday for me; – I spent the morning with N.N. and he promised me on his word of honour to call on me between 12 and 1 to sort everything out. As a result I couldn't have lunch with Puchberg but had to wait, – I waited – 1/2 past 2 came and went, – he still hadn't come, so I wrote a note and got our servant to take it to his father, – meanwhile I went off to the Ungarische Krone, as it was too late for anywhere else – even *there* I had to eat on my own, as the other guests had already left – by now I was not only anxious about you but annoyed with N.N., so you can imagine the sort of lunch I had, – if only I'd had someone to console me a little. – It's not good for me to be on my own when I've got things on my mind, – and by 1/2 past 3 I was back home – the servant still hadn't returned – I waited and waited – she finally turned up with a note at 1/2 past 6. – Waiting is never agreeable – but it's even more disagreeable when the result isn't what you expect – it was only excuses for his inability to obtain any definite information and assurances that he'd certainly not forget me and would certainly keep his word, – to cheer myself up I went to see Kasperle in the new opera *Der Fagottist*,[78] which is causing quite a stir, but which is nothing to write home about. – As I was passing the coffee-house, I looked in to see if Löbel[79] was there – but he wasn't. – In the evening I again ate at the 'Krone' (simply in order not to be alone), – at least I had an opportunity to talk to people there – then went straight to bed – I was up again at 5 – got dressed at once – went to see Montecuculi – I found him in – then to N.N., but he'd already fled – I'm only sorry that, *having achieved nothing*, I wasn't able to write to you this morning – I'd so much wanted to write!

I'm now going to the Rechbergs for a great *banquet that they're giving for their friends* – if I'd not given them my solemn promise and if it weren't so impolite to stay away, I'd not go – but what good would it do me? – well, I'm leaving here tomorrow and driving out to see you! – if only my affairs were in order! – who'll now keep prodding N.N. on my behalf? – if he's not

76. *Die Zauberflöte*, a line from which is quoted at the end of the present excerpt.
77. *Briefe*, iv.136 (letter of 11 June 1791).
78. *Kaspar der Fagottist* by Wenzel Müller had received its first performance on 8 June 1791.
79. Perhaps Johann Martin Loib(e)l; see above.

prodded, he loses interest – I've been to see him every single morning, otherwise he wouldn't even have done as much as he has done.[80]

The matter that was causing Mozart such disquiet was evidently another loan, as he had promised Puchberg that he would repay the sum of 2000 florins by 25 June.[81] Following another visit to Baden, he seems to have been hopeful that the money would be provided, with the result that his former spirits returned. 'Today', he wrote on 25 June,

I gave N.N. a surprise – I first went to the Rechbergs – and Frau Rechberg sent one of her daughters upstairs to tell him that a dear old friend of his had arrived from Rome and had searched every house without being able to find him! – he sent back a message asking me to wait a moment, meanwhile the poor fellow put on his Sunday best. His finest clothes, his hair splendidly done – you can imagine how we made fun of him, I can never resist making a fool of people – if it's not N.N., it's N.N. or Snai.[82] . . . I'll reply to Süßmayr in person – it's a waste of paper to write. . . . Tomorrow I'll join the procession in the Josephstadt with a candle in my hand! Snai! – Don't forget my warnings about the morning and evening air – or about bathing too long – give my best wishes to Count and Countess Wagensperg. – –[83]

By the end of June Mozart was back in Baden. Throughout the first part of July, however, he was in particularly lively contact by letter, with barely a day going by without his writing to Constanze. His chief concern was that, in her present condition, she could undermine her health by bathing too frequently or for too long. But we also learn something about his work on *Die Zauberflöte*. On 2 July, for example, he asks 'that idiotic fellow' Süßmayr to send him his score of act one, from the Introduction to the finale, so that he can orchestrate it.[84] On 3 July we find him writing to say that he still believes that his situation is about to improve and announcing that he has dined at Puchberg's and Schikaneder's, in the latter case 'with the Lieutenant-Colonel, who is also taking the Antony baths'.[85] On the 4th he sent Constanze three florins to pay for her treatment, enclosing a further twenty-five the next day.[86] Later that day he followed this up with a longer letter that expresses his longing for rest and for his wife's company:

I hope to be able to hug you on Saturday [9 July], perhaps before then, as soon as my business is over, I'll be with you – for I fully intend to rest in your arms; – and I'll certainly need it as this mental worry and anxiety and all the running around connected with it is really rather tiring. Many thanks for your latest parcel, which has arrived safely. – I can't tell you how happy I am that you're not taking any more baths – in a word, all I need now is your company – I don't think I can wait so long; once my business is dealt with, I could of course have you back for

80. *Briefe*, iv.137–8 (letter of 12 June 1791).
81. *Briefe*, iv.139–40 (letter of 25 June 1791).
82. Probably Süßmayr.
83. *Briefe*, iv.141–2 (letter of 25 June 1791); see also the previous, undated note. In this case N.N. is probably Joseph Leutgeb, whom Mozart had met in Italy in 1773; see *Briefe*, i.477 (letter of 23 January 1773). ◆ Almost certainly they had met earlier, during the later 1760s when Leutgeb was attached to the Salzburg court music. The identity of 'N.N.' remains unclear; for an attempt to unravel the mystery, see Arthur, '"N.N." revisited: New light on Mozart's late correspondence'.
84. *Briefe*, iv.144 (letter of 2 July 1791).
85. *Briefe*, iv.143 (letter of 3 July 1791).
86. *Briefe*, iv.146 (letters of 4 and 5 July 1791).

good – but I'd like to spend a few more days with you in Baden. – N.N. is with me now and tells me that I ought to do so – he's taken a liking to you and thinks you must have noticed it.

What's my second fool doing? – it's hard for me to choose between the 2 fools! – when I went to the Krone yesterday evening, I found the English lord lying there completely exhausted, as he was still waiting for Snai. – Today, when I was going to Wetzlar's, I saw a couple of oxen yoked to a waggon and when they began to pull, they moved their heads just like our foolish N.N. – Snai! . . . Tell Carl to behave himself, then I might answer his letter.[87]

By 6 July the mysterious business was still not resolved:

Even as I write these lines Blanchard will either ascend into the air or fool the Viennese for a 3rd time. This whole episode with Blanchard is most unwelcome to me, today of all days – it's preventing me from completing my business – N.N. promised that he'd come and see me before he left, – but he hasn't come, – perhaps he'll come when the fun is over, – I'll wait till 2, then I'll shove some food inside me – and hunt him down. – Things aren't easy for us at present. – Be patient! they'll improve, and then I'll rest in your arms! I'm grateful to you for your advice not to rely entirely on N.N., but in such cases you have to deal with only one person at a time – if you turn to two or three and the affair becomes common property, other people with whom you can't deal regard you as a fool or as unreliable. –

But you can now do me no greater favour than to be happy and contented – for if I *know for certain* that you've *everything* you need, I don't mind how much trouble I have to put up with – the most difficult and complicated situation in which I could possibly find myself becomes a mere trifle as long as I know that you're *well* and *happy* – and now look after yourself – make good use of your table-fool – think and speak of me often – love me for ever as I love you, and always be my Stanzi Marini, just as I shall always be

Your

Stu! Knaller paller

Schnip – schnap – schnur –

Schnepeperl –

snai! –

Give N.N. a box on the ears and tell him that you had to kill a fly that *I* saw sitting there! adieu – look out – bi – bi – bi 3 kisses, as sweet as sugar are flying your way![88]

On 7 July he reported on all the trouble he was having in 'not allowing N.N. to escape'. He had been to see him at seven every morning. He then returned to the subject of Blanchard, whom he had not seen, then teased 'Sauermayer' a little, before going on:

There's nothing I'd like more than that my affairs had already been settled, so that I can be with you again, you can't imagine what I've been feeling for you all this time! – I can't describe what I've been feeling, it's a kind of emptiness that really hurts, – a kind of longing that's never satisfied and that therefore never stops but continues to grow worse by the day; – when I think how happy and childlike we were in Baaden – and what sad, tedious hours I'm spending here – not

---

87. *Briefe*, iv.147 (letter of 5 July 1791).
88. *Briefe*, iv.148–9 (letter of 6 July 1791). On 6 July the hot-air balloonist Jean-Pierre Blanchard set off from the Prater in his Montgolfier balloon, landing later at Groß-Enzersdorf; see *Wiener Zeitung*, lv (1791).

even my work gives me any pleasure because I've always been used to stopping every so often and exchanging a few words with you, whereas this pleasure is unfortunately now out of the question – if I go over to the piano and sing something from the opera,[89] I have to stop at once – it makes me too emotional – basta! – the moment I finish my business here, I'll be off. . . .[90]

The final letter is dated 8 July and lends comic expression to the pleasure that Mozart felt at the prospect of seeing Constanze again, even if he was also clearly concerned that he had still not sorted out his affairs:

I've received your letter of the 7th together with the receipt for the correct payment; I only wish for your sake that you'd had it signed by a witness, – for if N.N. chooses to be dishonest, he could one day make things difficult for you in terms of the *genuineness* and *weight*, – as it says simply a 'box on the ear', he can send you a legal summons out of the blue, demanding a violent or a sound or even a gentle box on the ear – what will you do then? You'll have to pay him at once, which is not always possible. My advice would be that you come to some arrangement with your adversary and give him a couple of violent boxes on the ear, followed by 3 sound ones and 1 gentle one, and even more if he's still not satisfied, for I think that kindness solves all problems, magnanimous and meek behaviour has often reconciled the bitterest enemies. . . .

My dearest wife, I hope you received yesterday's letter; now the time, the happy time of our reunion is drawing ever closer, be patient, and just be as cheerful as possible. Your letter yesterday left me so depressed that I was on the point of leaving the present matter unresolved and driving out to see you at once, but what good would it have done? – I'd only have had to drive back into town again or, instead of being happy, I'd have been worried; matters will have resolved themselves within a few days – Z.[91] has given me his solemn promise – then I'll be with you at once. But if you want, I can send you the money you need and you can pay for everything and then come back to town! – I don't mind; – but I think that Baaden will be good for you as long as the weather remains fine and that it will benefit your health, as far as the glorious walks are concerned. – You yourself must feel this better than anyone; – if you find that the air and exercise are good for you, stay there – and I'll then come and fetch you or, if you like, spend a few days there – or, as I say, you can return to town tomorrow if you like; tell me frankly which you prefer. – Now farewell, dearest Stanzi Marini! – I kiss you millions of times and am ever Your

Mozart.[92]

In the end Mozart drove out to Baden on 9 July, in keeping with his original plan, performing his B flat major Mass (K275) there on the 10th and returning to Vienna with his family on the 11th.[93]

Mozart's letters from this period refer frequently to Schikaneder and *Die Zauberflöte*. And there is also a connection between them and the above-mentioned aria with obbligato double bass, inasmuch as the double-bass player Friedrich Pischlberger and Franz Gerl, together with Gerl's wife

---

89. *Die Zauberflöte*.
90. *Briefe*, iv.150 (letter of 7 July 1790).
91. The letter is unclear: the copy owned by Breitkopf & Härtel has B. = Bridi or Bauernfeind/Pauernfeind? ◆ According to *Briefe*, vi.420, the reference may be to the banker Raimund Wetzlar.
92. *Briefe*, iv.151–2 (letter of 9 July 1791).
93. Spitta, 'Zur Herausgabe der Briefe Mozarts', 403, proves this virtually beyond doubt.

Barbara née Reisinger, were all members of Schikaneder's company. According to contemporary reports Mozart was completely ensnared by Barbara Gerl's charms. Be that as it may, there was regular contact between the composer and Schikaneder's company, a contact that was also to have repercussions for his music.

Johann Emanuel Schikaneder[94] was born in Straubing in 1751. He came from a humble background and as a youth earned his living as an itinerant musician, before joining a company of touring actors – probably Schopf's – in 1773, having previously attended their performances in Augsburg. He not only appeared as an actor with the company, he also sang and soon started to direct. He married his fellow actress Eleonore Arth on 9 February 1777 and, together with her, joined Moser's company, becoming its director in 1778 and embarking on an itinerant existence that was as turbulent as it was glorious and that took him in the course of the next ten years to Swabia, Bavaria, Styria, Carinthia, Carniola and, twice, to Vienna. By then his troupe was regarded as one of the finest in Germany, performing Shakespeare (Schikaneder was a famous Hamlet), Lessing and Goethe, as well as Schiller's early plays. In the field of opera, his company performed works by Gluck, Mozart and Haydn, in addition to numerous German singspiels. Meanwhile Schikaneder was also active as a poet and arranger, revealing an incredible inventiveness, albeit one that was sometimes somewhat indiscriminating in the devices that he used whenever he wanted to appeal to the public at large. When the company appeared in Salzburg between 17 September 1780 and Lent 1781, it was not the innocent heroine but the evil Vizedom who was drowned at the end of a performance of Josef August Törring's *Agnes Bernauerin*, a reversal of roles that met with general acclaim. In Graz he performed Heinrich Ferdinand Möller's *Der Graf von Walltron* in the open air in a camp comprising two hundred tents, with officers on horseback and a real coach for the Countess. All these successes filled his coffers. Only when he reached Preßburg did his fortunes begin to turn. His productions lost their power to pull in audiences, and a comedy starring a cast of hens, with a goose as its hero, proved a failure. He was obliged to disband his company and in the autumn of 1784 he set out for Vienna with a handful of loyal supporters. Here he managed to enlist the support of Joseph II for his performances of German singspiels at the Kärntnertor-Theater.[95] Yet this period of glory proved equally short-lived and the company dispersed following a series of amorous intrigues, leaving Schikaneder to take work as an actor at the Nationaltheater between 1 March 1785 and 28 February 1786. Here his lack of success in serious roles obliged him to limit himself almost exclusively to comic parts. But Schikaneder was too restless by nature to remain in so subordinate a position for long, and after further peregrinations he took over the running of the court theatre in his native Regensburg, far surpassing all his previous achievements through the magnificence of the productions that he mounted here.[96] But ultimately audiences and critics tired of such extravagance and by 1788 his position in Regensburg had become untenable and early in 1789 he moved back to Vienna with the whole of his company and renewed contact with his ex-wife, from whom he had separated in 1786 following her affair with the actor Johann Friedel. Together with her lover, she had taken over the running of the recently opened Freihaus-Theater auf der Wieden in 1788. Friedel died at the end of March 1789

94. See Komorzynski, *Emanuel Schikaneder: Ein Betrag zur Geschichte des deutschen Theaters*; and Blümml, *Aus Mozarts Freundes- und Familienkreis*, 90ff. and 140ff. ◆ Further, see Sonnek, *Emanuel Schikaneder: Theaterprinzipal, Schauspieler und Stückeschreiber*, and Honolka, *Papageno: Emanuel Schikaneder. Man of the theater in Mozart's time.*
95. ◆ Schikaneder had performed Mozart's *Die Entführung aus dem Serail* at the Kärntnertor-Theater as early as 5 November 1784; see Eisen, *New Mozart Documents*, 33.
96. Here he performed Schiller's *Die Räuber* in the open air as a vast spectacle, with the Moors' castle literally going up in flames; see Komorzynski, *Emanuel Schikaneder*, 18.

and Schikaneder nimbly stepped into the breach, making his peace with his wife and becoming co-director of the Theater auf der Wieden, with its imperial and royal privilege, on 1 April 1789. As such, he became the main rival of Marinelli and his Theater in der Leopoldstadt. Here he revealed his usual chameleon-like qualities and had soon assimilated the Viennese mentality to such an extent that he was able to leave his mark on the subsequent development of the popular Viennese theatre, capturing to perfection the element of *naïveté*, sentimentality and irony that typified the local tone and learning to take advantage of local patriotism with an acquisitiveness unique in the annals of the Viennese theatre. In the end he was even able to set up a successful rival to Marinelli's Kasperl in the guise of his 'Foolish Anton', a figure of fun who was the hero of seven of his farces. At the same time he was an excellent employer, describing his company as his 'children' and taking a particular interest in newcomers, although, given his roving eye, female employees always had to be on their guard against non-artistic approaches. In short, this remarkable man was a true product of his time, when charlatans and men of genius lived in such close proximity. His education barely encompassed the skills of writing and arithmetic and his character was that of the born vagabond, with its blend of good-natured amiability, quick-wittedness, showmanship and an extraordinary lack of moral scruples that he was invariably able to conceal behind his charm and good humour. He combined an undeniable business acumen with extreme extravagance and a fondness for cutting an impressive figure so that money flowed through his fingers like water. Even so, his fast living and lavish parties impressed the Viennese just as much as his numerous love affairs.[97] Moreover, and in spite of all his lapses, Schikaneder was far more than a run-of-the-mill director of some provincial flea-pit. In Mozartian terms, he had a unique understanding of the theatre, an understanding that he owed not only to an unusual routine but also to his innate and inspired ability to see what was theatrically effective, in which regard he was far superior to many much better-educated poets. This emerges with particular clarity from his opera librettos, with *Die Zauberflöte* as the best possible proof of his superiority.

The Freihaus-Theater that owed its reputation to him was a wooden building, rectangular in shape, and no bigger than the Josefstädter Theater.[98]

In Vienna Schikaneder renewed contact with Mozart, whose sister-in-law, Josepha Hofer, joined his company soon after her marriage in 1788.[99] She had already performed Mozart's insertion aria for Paisiello's *Il barbiere di Siviglia* (see above). On the other hand, the duet 'Nun, liebes Weibchen, ziehst mit mir' K625 that Mozart is said to have written for Schikaneder's *Der Stein der Weisen* on 11 September 1790 is dubious, to say the least: it is an extremely modest piece in the style of contemporary comedies and, as such, not one that one would wish to be associated with Mozart.[100] The links between Schikaneder and Mozart became closer when Schikaneder became a member of Mozart's Masonic Lodge 'Zur gekrönten Hoffnung im Orient in Wien' ('Crowned

---

97. For a character sketch, see Seyfried, *Neue Zeitschrift für Musik*, xii (1845), 180. He died insane in Vienna on 21 September 1812.

98. In addition to the literature listed by Komorzynski, *Emanuel Schikaneder*, 26, see Cloeter, *Häuser und Menschen von Wien*, 39, where the exact location of the theatre – between the first and sixth courts of the Freihaus – is established.

99. See Blümml, 'Josefa Weber-Hofer: Die erste "Königin der Nacht"', 14.

100. ◆ Abert's certainty notwithstanding, at least part of the work appears to be by Mozart, as a study of his partial autograph shows; see Buch 'On Mozart's Partial Autograph of the Duet "Nun, liebes Weibchen", K. 625/592a'. Concerning the disputed possibility that other numbers from *Der Stein der Weisen* are also by Mozart, see Buch, 'Mozart and the Theater auf der Wieden: New attributions and perspectives', '"Der Stein der Weisen", Mozart, and Collaborative Singspiels at Emanuel Schikaneder's Theater auf der Wieden', 'Die Hauskomponisten am Theater auf der Wieden zur Zeit Mozarts (1789–1791)' and 'Texts and contexts: Eighteenth-century performing materials from the archive of the Theater an der Wien and Mozart's *Die Zauberflöte*'.

Hope in the Orient in Vienna'). This was an influential Order that evidently struck Schikaneder as particularly useful in furthering his own ends.

It was at a time of pressing financial embarrassment that Schikaneder turned to Mozart in the early months of 1791 – later reports state that it was on 7 March – and explained that without some new crowd-puller he could not hold out much longer.[101] He told Mozart that he had discovered an excellent subject for a *Zauberoper* and one, moreover, that was tailor-made for him. The latter's natural willingness to help, especially where a fellow Mason was concerned, together with his irrepressible urge to write an opera and – it is said – the intercession of Barbara Gerl, persuaded him to agree, albeit on one condition: 'If it turns out a disaster, there's nothing I can do about it as I've never written a magic opera.' Schikaneder sent him a draft of the new work and, knowing the composer's dilatoriness and wanting to keep an eye on him, offered him the use of the little summer-house in the grounds of the Freihaus, right next to the theatre.[102] It was here and at Josephsdorf on the Kahlenberg (where Mozart's room was still being shown to visitors many years later[103]) that most of the work was written. We have already seen traces of its genesis in his letters of 11 June and 7 July. On 2 July Mozart announced his intention of starting to orchestrate the first act, which was already finished in draft score.[104] And by July work on it was already so far advanced that he was able to enter it in his thematic catalogue as virtually finished. The rehearsals had already begun at a time when the score contained only the vocal parts and bass line: as usual, the instrumentation was added only later. Work was then interrupted by two other commissions, the *Requiem* and *La clemenza di Tito*, an interruption that appears to have lasted until September. The chorus 'O Isis und Osiris', Papageno's arias and the second-act finale were apparently not started until after 12 September.[105] The overture and Priests' March were completed on 28 September, two days before the first performance. Much has been written – most of it of a speculative nature – on the working relationship between librettist and composer. Mozart is said to have made various attempts to set the song 'Ein Mädchen oder Weibchen', for example, before Schikaneder finally hummed a tune of his own invention that provided the basis of Mozart's final version. In much the same way Schikaneder is said to have left his mark on the music of the duets 'Bei Männern, welche Liebe fühlen' and 'Papageno! Papagena!' But the melody of 'Ein Mädchen oder Weibchen' is that of an old German folksong,[106] and the two duets are so quintessentially Mozartian in character that any part that Schikaneder may have played in their genesis pales into insignificance. Also worth quoting in this context is the following note in Schikaneder's hand:

---

101.   On the genesis of *Die Zauberflöte*, see Treitschke, 'Die Zauberflöte, Der Dorfbarbier, Fidelio: Beiträge zur musikalischen Kunstgeschichte'; *Illustriertes Familienbuch des österreichischen Lloyd* (1852), ii.119–20; and *Monatsschrift für Theater und Musik* (1857), 444–5. All too often, of course, even reliable accounts include demonstrably inaccurate information. ◆ Some aspects of Treitschke's account have been discredited; see Branscombe, *W. A. Mozart: Die Zauberflöte*, 70–1. It now seems clear that except for the overture and Priests' March and three vocal numbers (or parts of them: the terzetto 'Seid uns zum zweiten Mal willkommen', Pamina's 'Ach, ich fühl's' and the terzetto 'Soll ich dich Teurer nicht mehr sehn?'), the opera was largely completed before Mozart's departure for Prague at the end of August. For a thorough account of the opera's origin and composition, see Branscombe, *W. A. Mozart: Die Zauberflöte*, 4–34 and 67–86.

102.   This summer-house was later rebuilt on the Kapuzinerberg in Salzburg; see Engl, 'Das Zauberflöten-Häuschen', 69–70.

103.   *Allgemeine Wiener Musik-Zeitung*, i (1841), 128.

104.   *Briefe*, iv.144 (letter of 2 July 1791).

105.   Treitschke, 'Die Zauberflöte', 246; and *Monatsschrift für Theater und Musik*, 445.

106.   See, for example, the opening bars of the folksong *Es freit ein wilder Wassermann* in Erk and Böhme, *Deutscher Liederhort*, i.1; see also Friedrich Ludwig Aemilius Kunzen's romance *Au bord d'une fontaine* in Friedlaender, *Das deutsche Lied im 18. Jahrhundert*, i.300. At a later date – but no earlier than 1793 – Mozart's melody was also used for Hölty's song *Üb' immer Treu und Redlichkeit*.

Dear Wolfgang, I'm returning your Pa-Pa-Pa herewith. It's now more or less acceptable to me. It'll do. I'll see you this evening at the usual place.

Yours, E. Schikaneder.[107]

This does not sound as if Mozart had given in to his librettist on every point. Of course, Schikaneder was keen that Mozart should provide him with a good and grateful role. His bass voice was neither particularly powerful nor well trained, but he was more than capable of making up for these shortcomings through his talents as a musician and as an actor. None the less, Mozart's willingness to compromise had its limits, and we should not assume that Schikaneder surprised Mozart by presenting him with the finished libretto. Rather, we may imagine the work's genesis as follows: Schikaneder will have begun by informing Mozart of the subject matter, after which they will have drafted an outline, presumably together, as this was something on which Mozart always laid special emphasis. Schikaneder will then have set about working it up into a finished libretto, again in close contact with Mozart. On none of his earlier operas had Mozart worked in such close collaboration with his librettist, and it certainly benefited the work as a whole. But such an approach was also entirely in keeping with Mozart's whole outlook: here he had finally found the librettist whom he had failed for so long to trace and who, more than any other, 'understood the theatre and was himself capable of making suggestions'. The subsequent fate of the libretto up to and including its completion will occupy us in due course.

Meanwhile Schikaneder continued to do everything in his power to keep Mozart's spirits up. The composer was feeling lonely and so he often invited him to eat with him. Their meals were invariably lively occasions. Schikaneder also introduced him to his rakish friends, including the clarinettist Anton Stadler of inglorious memory.[108] Mozart was certainly no killjoy and, given his character, he will have been more than welcome as a member of this circle, but there is absolutely no justification for the later rumours that sprang up concerning his gluttony and moral depravity. If nothing else, this is clear from his letters to Constanze quoted above, with their expressions of longing for his wife and family and their feelings of emptiness and abandonment, feelings that none of Schikaneder's orgies could have banished, quite apart from the fact that his illness and worries made him increasingly sombre and serious at this time.

While he was working on his new opera, his former librettist Lorenzo da Ponte renewed contact with the suggestion that he should accompany him to London and work for the Italian opera. Mozart was not ill disposed to the idea but demanded a six-month delay in order to complete and perform *Die Zauberflöte*, a request to which Da Ponte was unable to accede.[109]

In July Mozart received a second and rather more remarkable visitor in the person of a mysterious messenger, a tall, thin man dressed in grey who cut a striking figure and who brought with him an anonymous letter. After complimenting Mozart on his previous achievements, the letter went on to ask him whether he would be prepared to write a Mass for the Dead, what his fee would be and how long he would need to complete it. Mozart consulted his wife and told her that he was willing to accept the commission. After all, he had been wanting for some time to return to the field of sacred music and had already reminded both Leopold II and the municipal authorities in

107. Formerly in the private collection of Aloys Fuchs. ◆ This letter is now considered spurious.
108. ◆ Mozart and Stadler had met long before 1791: the clarinettist had been a fellow Mason (performing some of Mozart's works at Lodge meetings) at least since 1785 and in 1786 Wolfgang composed the clarinet part in the trio K498 for him. They may have become acquainted as early as 1781.
109. Da Ponte, *Memorie*, i/2.124.

Vienna of his standing as a church composer.[110] Moreover, the reforms of Joseph II had been abandoned and the older form of the liturgy had been reintroduced. Constanze persuaded him to accept and so Mozart agreed to the offer, demanding fifty ducats (one hundred according to some sources), but refusing to be tied down to a particular deadline. The messenger returned, bringing with him the sum demanded and the promise of more when the work was finished. The manner in which the commission was completed was to be left to Mozart's discretion, but he was advised against trying to find out who had commissioned the work, as he would not succeed in doing so.

Only after Mozart's death was the mystery solved. Count Franz von Walsegg zu Stuppach wanted a Requiem in memory of his wife, Baroness Anna von Flammberg, who had died on 14 February 1791. It was his steward Leitgeb who dealt with the negotiations. Walsegg himself was a great music lover, a decent flautist and mediocre cellist, who performed quartets every Tuesday and Thursday, and on Sundays even performed plays, in which his family and servants all played an active part.[111] But he also wanted to be thought of as a composer and so he commissioned quartets from various other composers, always anonymously and always well-paid,[112] which he would then copy out, before having the parts prepared from his own copy. When the piece in question was performed, he would ask all those who were present to guess the identity of the composer and his fellow performers would invariably flatter him by naming him as the composer, even though they knew that this was not the case. This charade was always rewarded with a smile of agreement on the count's part.[113] This was by no means an exceptional case with the higher aristocracy.[114] This, then, is the background to the *Requiem* and its mysterious commission. It, too, was copied out by the count in a tall folio and headed 'Requiem composto del conte Walsegg', on which basis the parts were then prepared. He himself conducted its first performance on 14 December 1793.

In mid-August, before Mozart was able to make much progress on the *Requiem*, he received another commission that brooked no delay and that required him to write a festival opera for the coronation of Leopold II as king of Bohemia in Prague. Once again the reputation that Mozart enjoyed in the eyes of the people of Prague bore fruit. At Guardasoni's recommendation, the Bohemian Estates invited him to set a text of their own choosing, Metastasio's *La clemenza di Tito*, a text that had already graced many a festivity in honour of one princely house or another. Time was of the essence, as the commission – for unknown reasons[115] – was very late in reaching Mozart: the coronation was due to take place on 6 September, leaving him only a few weeks in

110. On the genesis of the *Requiem*, see Niemetschek, *Leben des k. k. Kapellmeisters Wolfgang Gottlieb Mozart*, 32–3; Nissen, *Biographie W. A. Mozarts*, 551–2; for an embellished account, see Rochlitz, 'Verbürgte Anekdoten aus Wolfgang Gottlieb Mozarts Leben', 149–50 and 177–8, and Zawrzel and Krüchten, 'Anzeige', 12–13 and 217–18; see also Anton Herzog's account in Köchel, 'Mozarts Requiem: Nachlese zu den Forschungen über dessen Entstehen'; and Jahn, *W. A. Mozart*, ii.570–71. ◆ The genesis of the *Requiem* remains shrouded in mystery and Abert's account, like all others, relies chiefly on posthumous hearsay evidence or unsupported claims by members of Mozart's immediate circle. As far as is known, Mozart was approached in July 1791 by a clerk employed by Walsegg's Viennese lawyer, Johann Nepomuk Sortschan. The traditional 'grey messenger', identified by Abert below as Franz Anton Leitgeb, was in fact well known to both Mozart and Constanze. The work was probably started about the time the commission was received but interrupted by the composition of *La clemenza di Tito* and the final preparations for *Die Zauberflöte*. There is no compelling evidence that Mozart continued to work on the *Requiem* after the onset of his final illness at the end of November 1791 or on his deathbed. For a full account, see Christoph Wolff, *Mozart's Requiem: Historical and Analytical Studies, Documents, Score*.

111. In 1787, for example, he performed Haydn's *Seven Last Words*; see Cramer, *Magazin der Musik*, i (1789), 51.

112. According to Niemetschek, Walsegg's emissary also invited Mozart to write a number of quartets; see Niemetschek, *Leben des k. k. Kapellmeisters Wolfgang Gottlieb Mozart*, 36.

113. ◆ Further, see Brauneis, 'Franz Graf Wallsegg – Mozarts Auftraggeber für das Requiem: Neue Forschungsergebnisse zur Musikpflege auf Schloß Stuppach' and Biba, 'Par Monsieur François Comte de Walsegg'.

114. That same year, on 6 March, Beethoven's music was used for a ballet and performed in Bonn under the name of Count Waldstein; see Thayer, *Ludwig van Beethovens Leben*, second edition, i.285–6.

115. Schurig assumes that the reason for the delay was resistance on the part of the Lord Chamberlain's office in Vienna; see Schurig, *Wolfgang Amade Mozart*, ii.247.

which to write the opera. After making only the most urgent preparations, Mozart set off for Prague, this time in the company of Constanze. They were just on the point of getting into their coach when the unknown messenger reappeared, tugged at Constanze's coat and asked how the *Requiem* was progressing. Mozart apologized by explaining his predicament and pointing out that it had been impossible to inform his client of this latest turn of events, but promised to take the *Requiem* in hand the moment that he returned, assuming that he was allowed to defer its completion until then. The messenger agreed to the delay.[116]

Mozart worked on the new opera during the journey to Prague, sketching it in the coach and orchestrating the sketches in his hotel room in the evening. It appears from the two sketches[117] that he must have assumed that Sesto would be a tenor and that it was not until he reached Prague that he learnt the definitive casting. Here he continued to work on the score with the same degree of enthusiasm, with the result that the opera as a whole was written and rehearsed within the space of eighteen days.[118] In order to help him, he took with him on the journey his young friend and pupil Franz Süßmayr, who is believed to have written the *secco* recitatives, a custom often found in Italy at this time. Certainly, these passages are missing from the original score. Conversely, there is no truth to the claim that Süßmayr also composed the arias of Servilia, Annio and Publio and that he orchestrated various other numbers:[119] almost all these numbers have survived in their entirety in Mozart's hand.[120] On 2 September, *Don Giovanni* was performed at the emperor's behest and in the presence of their imperial majesties and the court. Mozart himself may have conducted the performance.[121] On the day of the coronation itself, 6 September, the new opera was performed after supper. Staged with the greatest magnificence,[122] it was given at the National Theatre with the following cast:[123]

116. ◆ There is no evidence to confirm this story.

117. ◆ At least seven sketches survive for *La clemenza di Tito*, including draft material for the duet of Vitellia and Sesto; the terzetto for Vitellia, Annio and Publio; two for the chorus no. 15; and the terzetto for Vitellia, Sesto and Publio. See Ulrich Konrad, *Mozarts Schaffensweise*, 197–200. Further, see Durante, 'The Chronology of Mozart's "La clemenza di Tito" Reconsidered'.

118.   The entry in Mozart's catalogue reads: '5 September – performed in Prague on 6 September. La Clemenza di Tito. Opera seria in due atti, per l'incoronazione di sua Maestà l'imperatore Leopoldo II. – ridotta a vera opera dal Sgre. Mazzolà, poeta di sua A. S. l'Elettore di Sassonia . . . – 24 pezzi.' The score is lodged in the Berlin Library. Excluding the overture, it contains 26 numbers, with the accompanied recitatives counted separately. ◆ Neither the traditional claim, that *La clemenza di Tito* was composed in eighteen days, nor Abert's account of the order in which Mozart composed the numbers of the opera, is tenable. Research into the history of the coronation festivities shows that Guardasoni concluded his agreement to provide a coronation opera with the Estates of Bohemia on 8 July 1791; the crucial clause in the contract, at least insofar as Mozart was to become involved, reads: 'I [Guardasoni] promise to have the poetry of the libretto composed on [one of] the two subjects given to me by [Governor Rottenhan] and to have it set by a distinguished composer; but in the case it should not be at all possible to accomplish this in the short time remaining, I promise to procure an opera newly composed on the subject of Metastasio's *Tito*.' Guardasoni first approached Salieri, who declined the commission; he then turned to Mozart, probably in the middle of July, some seven weeks before the opera's première. Mozart began to set the opera almost immediately but without knowing exactly who the singers were to be; accordingly he began with the ensembles and turned to the arias only later. One aria, however, has been the subject of considerable chronological speculation, Vitellia's 'Non più di fiori'. Volek, 'Über den Ursprung von Mozarts Oper "La clemenza di Tito"', was the first to suggest it may have been composed for Josepha Duschek's Prague concert of 26 April 1791, which included a 'rondò with obbligato basset-horn' by Mozart; the paper on which the autograph is written does not rule out this early date (Tyson, '"La clemenza di Tito" and its chronology'). Nevertheless, the matter remains unresolved. In general, see Rice, *W. A. Mozart. La clemenza di Tito*, 45–51. The partial autograph now in the Staatsbibliothek zu Berlin lacks nos 2, 3, 11, 12 and 25; these are at the Biblioteka Jagiellońska, Kraków. A score copy and autograph parts for the opera, including the earliest source for no. 25, can be found in the Archiv Lobkowitz at the Národní Muzeum, Prague.

119.   See Gottfried Weber, 'Weitere Nachrichten', 295.

120.   The only numbers missing are the duettino (no. 3), which survives in a copy revised by the Abbé Stadler, and the accompanied recitative no. 25. ◆ See note 118.

121.   See Freisauff, *Mozarts Don Juan 1787 bis 1887: Ein Beitrag zur Geschichte der Oper*, 122.

122.   The sets for the first three scenes were by Pietro Travaglia, that for the fourth by a Herr Preising from Koblenz. The costumes were designed by Cherubino Babbini of Mantua. ◆ See also Durante, 'Le Scenographie di Pietro Travaglia per "La clemenza di Tito" (Praga, 1791): Problemi di identificazione ed implicazioni'.

123.   The origin of this cast-list remains obscure; Debrois, *Urkunde über die vollzogene Krönung S. M. des Königs von Böhmen Leopold des Zweiten*, 110, does not include it, although he mentions the famous Portuguese mezzo-soprano Luisa Todi as one of

Tito Vespasiano, imperator di Roma	Sgre. Baglioni.
Vitellia, figlia del imperator Vitellio	Sgra. Marchetti-Fantozzi.
Servilia, sorella di Sesto	Sgra. Antonini.
Sesto, amico di Tito	Sgra. Car. Perini.
Annio, amico di Sesto	Sgre. Bedini.
Publio, prefetto del pretorio	Sgre. Campi.

The performance was only moderately successful, with the empress apparently dismissing the music as 'porcheria tedesca' and the audience taking little pleasure in the piece, a state of affairs that the loyal Niemetschek ascribed to the festive atmosphere that prevented people from enjoying the work's many beauties.[124] It was Mozart's first failure in Prague, and not even the fee of two hundred ducats could console him for this.[125] Moreover, he was already ill when he arrived in the city. It is unclear where he stayed, but it was presumably with the Duscheks at the Villa Bertramka. With the rest of Prague packed to the rafters, this was the obvious place for him to go.[126] None the less, we hear nothing of a repeat of the carefree stay of 1787. The rushed preparations and the failure of the production added to Mozart's ill health. Niemetschek reports that he was 'ill all the time and for ever taking medicines. His colour was pale and his expression sad, even though in the company of his friends his lively humour often found expression in light-hearted banter'.[127] When he took his leave of his friends in Prague in mid-September, he was so overcome with grief that he burst into tears: he suspected that this was the last time that he would see them.

---

the performers, a singer not mentioned by Jahn, *W. A. Mozart*, ii.470; see also Freisauff, *Mozarts Don Juan*, 122. In fact, the official report on the coronation does not mention *Don Giovanni* on 2 September, which merely confirms our belief that it is unreliable. It looks as though Jahn confused his sources, for all that his cast-list appears to be authentic; see also Procházka, *Mozart in Prag*, 161–2. The *Tagebuch der böhmischen Königskrönung* noted: 'In the evening there was given a free opera, to attend which His Majesty, the Imperial Family and the Court shortly after 8 o'clock entered the boxes prepared for Their Highnesses. They were accompanied thither through all the streets by unanimous and joyous huzzahs, and Their Highnesses were also received in the theatre with similar manifestations'; see Freisauff, *Mozarts Don Juan*, 122 [*Dokumente*, 524–5, *Documentary Biography*, 405].
◆ Concerning the cast list, see Raeburn, 'Mozarts Opern in Prag', and Westrup, 'Two First Performances: Monteverdi's "Orfeo" and Mozart's "La Clemenza di Tito"'.
124. Niemetschek, *Leben des k. k. Kapellmeisters Wolfgang Gottlieb Mozart*, 74.
125. Teuber, *Geschichte des Prager Theaters*, ii.267.
126. Procházka, *Mozart in Prag*, 150–1. On Mozart's meeting with Häusler, which Jahn dates to this period, see above; also see Jahn, *W. A. Mozart*, ii.574–5.
127. Niemetschek, *Leben des k. k. Kapellmeisters Wolfgang Gottlieb Mozart*, 34.

50

Instrumental and vocal works of the
final two years

This final period opens with the three string quartets K575, 589 and 590 that Mozart wrote for Friedrich Wilhelm II[1] and with the clarinet quintet K581 that takes its natural place alongside them. In all four cases the chronological proximity of *Così fan tutte* is clear from the importance that Mozart attaches to the sensuous beauty of their melodic invention and, indeed, to the question of their sonorities in general. In the case of the clarinet quintet, the involvement of the clarinet inevitably contributed to this end, whereas in the quartets Mozart took due heed of their dedicatee's instrument, the cello, which is given special prominence. Not only is it used independently, it is often treated as a soloist, frequently electing to expound the melody in its highest register. All this helps to explain the vast difference between these quartets and the earlier ones, especially those dedicated to Haydn. In the case of the earlier works, Mozart had been entirely himself, whereas here, in spite of the authenticity of the emotions explored, he had in mind a completely different world of feeling and culture, a difference due to the purpose for which they were written. There can, of course, be no question here of a return to an impersonal, conventional style. Quite the opposite: there is something particularly appealing about the manner in which the old ideal of music written to entertain society now finds expression in ways that differ from those found in the keyboard concertos, for example. The brilliance and *galant* tone of the concertos is replaced by a far calmer, more inward spirit. The hedonistic tendency to revel in beauty pure remains, but it now includes a hint of sadness, reminding us of Schiller's belief – in his poem *Nänie* of 1799 – that 'Even the beautiful, which vanquishes men and gods, must die'. There is something genuinely touching about these works, not least because this sense of sadness never degenerates into conscious pessimism. As a result, Mozart continues to develop stylistically, too. Rather, these quartets already clearly reflect the fundamental change that was ultimately to give his music its totally different stamp.

   The very first theme of the D major quartet (K575) is typical of this period:

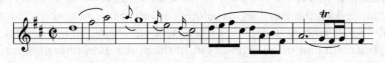

Mozart had already written 'singing' allegro themes at an earlier date, but few melodies of such

---

1. ◆ It is unclear whether these quartets were commissioned by Friedrich Wilhelm II or whether Mozart wrote them on speculation, intending to dedicate the works to the king; see p.1162, n.58 above.

burgeoning beauty. Above all, the emotions of a teeming heart lead to a remarkable expansion and extension of the movement's metrical relationships,[2] while the brief section that follows is entirely typical of the mature composer. Built upon a triplet motif, it unexpectedly introduces a note of resolve at the end of the theme, a feature which, as emerges very shortly, was particularly important to Mozart. This section is prepared for by the accompaniment of the main theme which, with its pounding crotchets and murmuring quavers, adds an active, allegro-like feature to the contemplative cantilena. It is from this material that the whole of the movement evolves: launched by the cello, the second subject, too, is internally related to the main subject, as is clear from its triadically rising opening and from its third and fifth bars (cf. bars 5–6 of the main theme). This is not, of course, a sign of rational calculation but of the power and permanence of the artistic experience. And here, too, the triplet motif rounds off the section, before the main theme produces another offshoot towards the end of the subject-group. A curious feature of all these late works is the transitional passage that follows the actual ending of the subject-group. The development section is relatively short, but it reveals an important characteristic of the new style, namely, the tendency to treat the various themes contrapuntally. The andante, too, is brief, its A major tonality intensifying the first movement's thirst for beauty. Above all, however, it takes up and builds on the tendency already found there for the instruments to duet with each other, as the individual players seem to keep on throwing to one another the melody's blossoming arabesques. The main theme's consequent phrase

is an old favourite of Mozart's that we shall soon encounter again. In the menuetto, it is the trio that sustains the cantabile tone with its delightful cello cantilena.[3] As guarantor of the work's overriding unity is the fact that the main theme of the final movement

picks up earlier material, referring back not only to the opening movement, but also to the second (see the music example quoted above). But the music no longer revels in its own beauty with the same degree of unthinking contentedness as before. The new theme and, with it, the movement as a whole, literally bursts with an energy that finds expression above all through the free contrapuntal writing that from now on emerges as one of the principal features of Mozart's late style.

2. This becomes clear when we compare it with its 'regular' form, to which Mozart later alludes in the final subject-group:

3. It is preceded by a two-bar 'upbeat' similar to the one found in the trio of the menuetto of Beethoven's piano trio in C minor op 1. no. 3.

Like Haydn, Mozart passed through an intermediary stage typified by the use of strict counterpoint – the finale of the C major symphony (K551) represents the *ne plus ultra* in this regard – before establishing a new style that combines thematic development and contrapuntal procedures, the only difference being that Mozart places far greater emphasis on counterpoint as such than Haydn did. In the present case, for example, we find him using a device that is to be increasingly frequent from now on: the symmetrical inversion of his themes. Here the main theme now appears as follows:

Few other themes succeed in asserting themselves in the face of this one theme. The finale is cast in the form of an exceptionally solidly structured rondo, except that, unlike Mozart's earlier rondos, it is concerned not with variety but with unity, with the main theme producing more and more new offshoots that reveal an inexhaustible wealth of inventiveness. In turn, these offshoots generate new countermelodies, suggesting the spirit of Carl Philipp Emanuel Bach permeated by the whole energy and wealth of Mozart's powers of invention.

A related work, albeit one that is less unified in structure, is the B flat major quartet [K589], in which the new style is immediately apparent from the opening movement's development section. Perhaps Mozart was also trying to show off his abilities to his audience in Berlin and place those abilities in a particularly favourable light. In this work, too, there is a marked increase in energy towards the end, with even the trio of the menuetto – almost twice the length of the main section – acquiring a highly original life of its own that finally builds in tension in a previously unsuspected way thanks to an impressive pedal point. Following this exploration of more rhetorical emotions, Mozart then good-humouredly returns at the end to the tone of the menuetto. The strictest procedures are again reserved for the final rondo, with the viola revealing contrapuntal proclivities even within the opening bar. Here, too, contrapuntal procedures permeate the entire style, offsetting individual ideas one against the other, inverting them and repeatedly interpolating them between thematic and homophonic sections, as in the main theme, which, following the example of Carl Philipp Emanuel Bach, suddenly enters in the remote key of D flat major.

The opening movement of the F major string quartet (K590) reveals the same degree of thematic unity as the one in B flat major: here, too, the second subject is derived from the main idea. This is also the most capricious of the three quartets, striking a note that it retains tenaciously until the very end. Particularly remarkable is the similar handling of the development section in all three works: each begins by playing light-heartedly with the previous phrase (in the present case this involves a witty dialogue between a surly two-crotchet motif and a sentimental chromatic quaver motif), followed by a strictly contrapuntal development of individual ideas ending on the dominant. This ends with a brief and simple return to the recapitulation lacking the modulatory subtleties so frequently found in the previous series of works.[4] The present quartet, by contrast, introduces two new features that were to be important from now on: a profoundly modified recapitulation and a coda that harks back to the beginning of the development section. No less unified in its structure is the andante, which continues the note of whimsy in a more contemplative, one might even say respectable, form. Its theme has something French about it. Here, too, imitative procedures play a major role, with all manner of bizarre arabesques shooting up between these

---

4. The modulatory shift that normally occurs at the start of the development section is found only in K575.

passages. In the menuetto the spirit of capriciousness avails itself of particularly realistic means, setting out from one of the motifs suggestive of enticement, with appogiaturas, familiar from the German dances,[5] a motif which in the middle section is combined with an inner part that ascends and descends through the whole of the chromatic scale, before finally reappearing in the third section in the guise of a grotesque growling in the bass. And here, too, the final movement – this time cast in sonata form – sums up and intensifies the emotional mood of the work as a whole. With its cheerfully ebullient wit, the first subject recalls the world of Haydn, and even the way in which it is developed in the subject-group immediately after being introduced is Haydnesque in spirit. But the character of the movement becomes unmistakably Mozartian with the D minor episode – as before, there is no real second subject in this movement. Note the delightful entry of C minor with its emotionally charged chromatic counterpoint and mordent. The polyphonic textures become increasingly dense here, there is the same symmetrical inversion as before, and only in the final section, with its earthy drones in the bass, is Haydn again invoked. It also dominates the development section, while the recapitulation undergoes the usual changes.

The clarinet quintet K581 that Mozart wrote for Stadler is completely different in character. Earlier writers have criticized this fact by comparing it with the string quintets,[6] but such criticisms are wide of the mark. Mozart himself was fully aware that the present resources demanded a wholly different style. After all, we are not dealing here with five similar instruments and, as a result, with what we earlier described as a 'conversation between five intelligent persons, each of them enjoying equal status'. Rather, the clarinet is an outsider that inhabits its own emotional world and as a result has its own way of expressing that world. Above all, however, we now find a new element on which the pure string quartet had laid less and less weight, the more intellectualized it had become: consideration for the actual sound of the piece. All this demanded an entirely new approach not only to the nature of the themes themselves but also to the way in which those themes are developed. The clarinet always leads the way, and although the other instruments are never condemned to a rigid accompaniment, they invariably acknowledge the clarinet's leadership. The latter leads them into a world of mature and sweet sensuality,[7] with the result that the piece as a whole is a triumph of *cantabilità* and, as such, the radiant centrepiece of this entire series of works, all of which luxuriate in sheer beauty. Even before the clarinet has made itself heard in the opening movement, we already find ourselves immersed in the atmosphere of a cloudless spring morning, a mood inspired by the glorious and authentic theme in A major. Even with this burgeoning cantabile line the strings come closer to their colleague in terms of their character, so that the latter, now supremely happy, soars up and down above them in a triadic figure that is twice repeated. The transitional group breathes the same sense of effusive contentment that imbues all these themes. The second subject,[8] which is likewise introduced by the strings, is again written with the clarinet in mind. On this occasion, the clarinet takes it up in the minor of the dominant, investing it with a note of yearning and thereby adding to its intensity. Following the usual surprising harmonic transition based on the first subject, the development section is built up

---

5. The actual nub of this remarkable phrase appears only in the third bar, with all that precedes it – the motif of enticement and the previous musical gesture – falling under the heading of an upbeat. There is genuine humour to the way in which the primitive slide in the actual main idea suddenly acquires melodic significance. The main theme of the trio likewise turns out to be five bars long as the result of its extended upbeat.

6. See Jahn, *W. A. Mozart*, fourth edition, ii.35.

7. Ambros, *Die Grenzen der Musik und Poesie*, 57.

8. Metrically speaking, it reveals the same typically Mozartian structure, with a four-bar antecedent answered by a three-bar consequent phrase. It is also found at the words 'Der Götter Wille mag geschehen' in the trio 'Soll ich dich Teurer nicht mehr sehn?'

entirely on the first figure in the clarinet, a figure that descends progressively through each of the strings in turns. This is not, of course, thematic writing in the sense of the string quintets, rather is it an example of a stealthy modulatory procedure which, in the present case, is complemented by the sonorities of the ascending and descending clarinet line. Indeed, there is never any question in this piece of thematic development, and the themes are not designed with this aim in mind. The famous larghetto is a veritable jewel of beauty and mellifluence. In its second section the low notes of the noble-toned clarinet are used to particularly impressive effect to produce a dialogue between it and the first violin, while the other instruments accompany them with gently undulating chordal figures. The main section of the menuetto features all five players, whereas the first of the two trios is limited to the strings alone. Here a darker note is struck for the first time in the work. At the repeat the theme is heard in canon between first violin and viola. The second trio, conversely, belongs initially to the clarinet, which gives itself the airs of a folk instrument. The folk-like tone is then brilliantly stylized with the gently rocking expansion of the first subject's consequent phrase, a stylization that is also clear from the mysterious return to the repeat and from the way in which this repeat is varied. Finally comes a set of Haydnesque variations on a simple theme reminiscent of a children's song, and here, once again, the clarinet displays all its luxuriant sonorities. In this way it summons the first violin into action, with the viola grumpily reporting for duty in the minor-key variation. There is even an adagio variation. The movement ends with a carefree allegro that plays fast and loose with the theme.

Of the two string quintets, the first in D major K593 is again a genuine example of chamber music for strings. It is the only such piece that prefaces its opening allegro with a slow introduction and – exceptionally – repeats it at the very end: a brief coda based on the theme of the allegro then brings the movement to a close. This dreamy and wistful larghetto bears all the hallmarks of the late Mozart, with the melodic line, weary and resigned, finally sinking chromatically to the dominant. The allegro, too, reflects the stylistic differences between the present work and the earlier quintets. By the second bar the pugnacious first subject has already moved purposefully to the minor of the subdominant, a shift by no means exceptional in the works of this period. There follows – unexpectedly – a passage of triplets that creates a powerful sense of tension, after which the musical argument moves through a series of violent chords back to the tonic, a journey that takes it via the dominant. The following four bars, all of which introduce new melodic material, serve to reinforce this dominant ending. It is sufficient to recall the discursive themes of the two earlier quintets to appreciate the difference. But the way in which the movement continues is equally new: here the final idea is developed in such a way that it unexpectedly acquires a note of greater intensity through its use of contrapuntal procedures. As so often in the works of this period, the second subject is derived from the first, again through the use of canonic procedures. The development section ushers in a witty interlude based on a rhythmic motif derived from the theme that vacillates constantly between *piano* and *forte* – the sort of passage that we often find in Beethoven. Predictably, the musical argument then picks up the triplet motif and follows the circle of fifths, but it no longer modulates to a remote key, which would have required Mozart to modulate back to the home key in a succinct and daring manner. Instead, he heads straight for the dominant, thereby allowing him to return entirely naturally to the recapitulation. This is considerably varied, above all as a result of the disappearance of the triplet passage, but also by virtue of the unexpected entry of the first subject in the minor and the way in which the voices are frequently interchanged. The minor-key colouring continues to leave its mark on the whole of the rest of this section and prepares the way for the return of the larghetto, which now acquires a more anguished note as a result of its constant vacillation between major and minor. The allegro then struggles to break free from this spell, convulsively clinging to the triplet passage that returns at this point. Like the andante of the C major symphony (K551), the adagio derives its effectiveness from the contrast between its main theme and its sombrely impassioned second subject in D minor.[9] No less remarkable is its extremely substantial development section, which introduces the main theme in B flat major. The concertante writing for the five instruments in the third and fourth bars of the theme, first in groups, then with all the voices entering in succession, allows a gradual return to the beginning. In essence, this movement is homophonic in style and designed to create its impact through its use of sonorities. It is followed by a powerful and characterful menuetto that reasserts the role of strict counterpoint through its canonic writing, thereby laying the foundations for the final movement, in which contrapuntal procedures reach their climax. Heralded by a capricious upbeat, its main theme reflects the masculine, almost stubborn character of all the piece's fleet-footed themes. The chief result of this – and this is another of the hallmarks of Mozart's new style – is the gradual disappearance of the feminine suspensions in the melodic line that had earlier been found here. At the same time Mozart no longer tends to divide the strong beats of the bar in the Lombardic manner. These features are still found, of course, but by no means as frequently, and in the case of the suspension formulas, there is now a clear tendency to write out their harmonies in full. The allegro themes in the present quintet are particularly instructive examples of this change of style: in every case Mozart makes straight for his goal without any digressions of a melodic, harmonic or rhythmic kind, with the result that his whole style acquires an emphatically masculine note that not infrequently reminds us of Beethoven. It is immediately clear that the second subject of the present movement has been devised in terms of its usefulness from a contrapuntal point of view,[10] and it is not long before it is, indeed, developed along regular lines. The development section begins with the usual abrupt transitional passage based on an inversion of the upbeat motif, a feature that Mozart probably first got to know through the gigues of Johann Sebastian Bach. Here, too, a concertante section gives way to a strict fugato that finally leads back to the recapitulation with a great dominant pedal point, but not without a genuinely Mozartian solo for the first violin by way of a conclusion. Mozart uses the recapitulation to allow the second subject to appear in counterpoint at its entry with the first subject. The following section, too, is considerably varied, above all as a result of the fact that the sequence of harmonies B flat A A D is explored to the full. This is something that we find on frequent occasions during the last five years of Mozart's life. New, however, are the far more complex textures.

The E flat major quintet K614 is essentially a far more light-hearted and lovable piece. For all its solid craftsmanship, therefore, it lays greater emphasis on its outward sonorities, notably in the form of the free concertante dialogue between the individual groups. Once again the whole of the opening movement derives from the simple main idea:

This chirruping motif, which also steals into the second subject, assumes the most ingenious combinations as it flutters cheerfully through the whole movement up to and including the coda,

9. At the end we hear an expressive cantabile phrase from the first andante of the 'Haffner' serenade K250.
10. The opening recalls the second subject of the finale of the C major symphony (K551).

where it even calls on the motif associated with allurement that features a short appoggiatura and that is heard first in the first violin, then in the bass. The andante is based on a familiar prototype that goes back ultimately to French models.[11] It is cast in rondo form, with a contentedly sauntering theme that Mozart subjects to ever new variations each time that it returns, each variation suggesting birdcalls and other natural sounds. The menuetto is made up of a thoughtful, finely wrought main section contrasted with a trio in the same key, whose unadulterated folklike melody attracts first the first viola, then the second violin as though with magic force, until it finally appears in threefold concentration. The final movement is a cross between sonata form and rondo form. Thematically speaking, it is exceptionally unified and once again provides a Mozartian gloss on Haydn's sense of humour. Here, too, contrapuntal procedures steal into the musical argument unawares, initially in the form of a filigree canon, but, following the second return of the theme, the consequent phrase suddenly emerges in counterpoint with its antecedent, resulting in a regular fugato. No less appealing is the way in which Mozart extricates himself from this tangle, with the second violin suddenly stating the theme in the minor and thereby providing a chance for the music to wander some distance away from the tonic before the actual recapitulation. The movement ends on a good-humoured note, with the main theme appearing four times, on each occasion with a different counterpoint. On the last occasion, it even appears in inversion.[12]

Of the pieces written – in Mozart's words – 'for an organ in a clock', the andante in F major K616 follows a well-trodden path from a thematic point of view, while revealing aspects of the composer's new style in terms of the way in which the material is treated. Of greater significance are the two pieces in F minor, of which the first – K594 – survives only in a transcription for keyboard duet. Its opening adagio is notable for its harmonic austerities that clearly reflect the composer's late style and is followed by an allegro in F major, a brief and highly unified sonata-form movement involving strict contrapuntal procedures, after which the adagio returns, only now acquiring its full expressive potential as a result of the masterful changes to which it has been subjected. It brings the work as a whole to a reassuring conclusion. The second piece is notated on four staves and begins with an allegro comprising a lively introduction followed by a masterly fugue that even involves stretto entries of its subject in inversion, after which an extremely bold and agitated modulation leads back to the introduction in F sharp minor. Only when the mood has grown calmer does the middle movement begin, an andante in A flat major filled with the wistful sadness of Mozart's late style and distinguished above all by its expressive figurations. The allegro then returns, with a further level of intensity added to the fugue through a new counter-subject, resulting in a sense of lively agitation that continues to reverberate in the turbulent final bars. Such is its profundity, this piece deserves a far wider circulation than it currently enjoys.[13]

The adagio and rondo K617 for musical glasses, flute, oboe, viola and cello, by contrast, is concerned entirely with questions of sonority, although its effectiveness is, of course, fully achieved only if the musical glasses are not replaced by a piano. The harmonica has no bass notes and is a true *empfindsam* instrument that demands an emotionally charged and legato singing style, a style happily reflected in the veiled moonlit raptness of the adagio that gives way to the sustained and delightful joviality of the rondo which, for all its structural translucency, cannot deny its date of

---

11. Typical of this model are its keen rhythms and the broad sweep of its opening, with its two crotchets; cf. the corresponding movement from *Eine kleine Nachtmusik* K525.

12. ◆ Concerning Mozart's late chamber music, including the quartets and quintets, see Eisen, 'Mozart's Chamber Music', 113–17; and Finscher, 'Über einen Finaletypus bei Mozart' and 'Bemerkungen zu den späten Streichquintetten'.

13. ◆ Further, see Haspels, 'Mozart and Automatic Music' and Richards, 'Automatic Genius: Mozart and the Mechanical Sublime'.

composition in terms of its striving for unity and the range of tonalities that it explores.[14] The volatile nature of the dialogue between the chordal instrument and the other instruments recalls the piano quartets and trios.

The keyboard, too, is the beneficiary of Mozart's late style in the keyboard sonata K576. The composer's final contribution to the medium, it shares with its predecessors the same tendency to engage in contrapuntal procedures, while surpassing them in terms of its thematic unity.[15] A surviving trace of the older approach is the opening movement's beautiful final theme, which assumes the role of a second subject in the markedly altered recapitulation. Only the middle movement, for all its intensity of expression, continues to rely for its effectiveness on *cantabilità* and tasteful ornamentation, whereas the final movement – a free rondo – harks back to the contrapuntal tendencies of the opening movement. Although its theme was not primarily designed for contrapuntal treatment, it is remarkable to discover the number of combinations that Mozart has been able to coax from it.

The eight variations on 'Ein Weib ist das herrlichste Ding' K613 are likewise among Mozart's finest contributions to the genre, even though they are like most such works in being purely melodic in character. Particularly remarkable is his initial refusal to vary the first section of his theme, which he even includes independently, in a slightly ornamented version, before the minor-key variation. Even more striking, however, is the final variation, with its change of time-signature: note especially the typically Mozartian sudden shift to D flat major that prepares the way for the following cadence, which ushers in a passage that plays freely with the theme, the individual phrases of which are heard in counterpoint with one another, before a witty game with the cadential formula brings the movement to an end.[16]

This series of works for the keyboard culminates in the keyboard concerto in B flat major K595, the last of its kind. In terms of its form and structure it is largely modelled on its predecessors, while departing markedly from them in respect of its general tenor. Here the listener has the impression that Mozart was writing for himself, rather than for the public at large, for the old life-affirming brilliance has now given way to a far more personal and, at the same time, remarkably resigned tone that sets it clearly apart from the impassioned language of the two earlier concertos in minor keys. In all these works, Mozart is more reluctant to reveal his contrapuntal abilities, even though the development section of the opening movement of the present piece cannot, from this point of view, deny the period at which it was written. All the more clearly does the desire for unity and inwardness emerge here. Although this concerto, too, demands a brilliant technique, this is now placed in the service of the developing musical ideas in a way that was not found at an earlier date. By the same token, the concept of a concertante dialogue is now more rigorously defined, with the result that the development section is no longer content to allow the soloist to display all his or her skills while accompanied by simple chords in the orchestra that merely hint at the theme. Rather, both parties engage in a dialogue that already anticipates Beethoven.

Even the opening takes us far from the world of works written only to entertain society at large: as though lost in thought, the first subject rocks back and forth on the notes of the B flat major

---

14. Its theme is related to that of the rondo from the keyboard trio in E major.
15. Another modern feature is the whole harmonic disposition, from the repeat of the main theme on the second degree of the scale in the consequent phrase. ◆ Further, see Irving, *Mozart's Piano Sonatas: Contexts, Sources, Style*.
16. ◆ Also see Buch, 'On the Context of Mozart's Variations to the Aria, "Ein Weib ist das herrlichste Ding auf der Welt", KV 613' and Cavett-Dunsby, *Mozart's Variations Reconsidered: Four Case Studies (K.613, K.501, and the Finales of K.421 (417b) and K.491)*.

triad but is unexpectedly answered by a keen battle-cry in the winds. This tendency for the musical argument to summon up all its reserves, only to sink back again in exhaustion almost immediately afterwards,[17] is typical of the whole of the opening movement, although the scales tip increasingly in the direction of resignation. Characteristic of this tendency are various weary minor-key passages that enter completely unexpectedly, notably towards the end of the tutti and in the brief section in the minor that the soloist interpolates following the first subject. This conflict builds to a pitch of extreme intensity in the development section, a section which, harmonically too, is highly expressive. Here the battle-cry gradually dies away and a series of increasingly stretta-like imitative entries of the main idea leads back to the recapitulation by means of a surprising modulation familiar from the symphonies. Particularly beautiful is the way in which the soloist catches up with the tutti's minor-key idea only towards the very end.[18] The larghetto picks up the dreamily wistful romance-like tone of earlier concertos, but also strikes a darker and sadder note. Note the curiously impressive way in which the melody of the theme returns in the solo and is finally taken up by the flutes and first violins. The rondo finale likewise departs from existing practice inasmuch as its theme does not always return in the same key but occasionally modulates to the minor, even in the middle of the refrain – a witty variant on the earlier minor-key episodes. Above all, its individual components are thematically developed in the transitional groups. The theme is clearly related to that of the song *Sehnsucht nach dem Frühling* (K596), which was written only eight days later, allowing the concerto as a whole to come to a harmonious end within this same atmospheric world.

Mozart's final concerto was the clarinet concerto K622 that he wrote for Anton Stadler.[19] Its opening movement survives in the form of a twelve-page draft score for basset-horn (K621b). The solo line in this version, which dates from an earlier period[20] and is in G major, is largely identical to that of the later clarinet version, the only difference being some of the low notes. It seems highly unlikely that the concerto was completed at this time. The present version is geared to the character of the clarinet in every detail, with the contrasting tone colours of the instrument's different registers being used in the most effective ways imaginable. This is especially true of the low notes, the characteristic effects of which, whether in the cantilena or the accompanying figures, were first explored by Mozart. There is no expressive area of the clarinet that he did not exploit in the most consummate way, from tender, burgeoning cantilenas to the supplest agility, and there is an almost palpable sense of the inner warmth with which he explored the instrument's magical sonorities. The instrument dominates the concerto in a way found in no other concerto by the composer and is ultimately responsible for the broad structure and whole nature of the work's conception – the affinity with the clarinet quintet not only lies in the fact that both are in the same key, it also extends to points of detail, especially in the middle movement. Yet Mozart remains true to his late style even here, especially in the harmonies and in individual imitative passages, even if the concerto as a whole belongs in essence to its soloist and the orchestra is limited, rather, to the role of an accompanist.

---

17. Typical of this are various reminiscences of the G minor symphony (K550).

18. ◆ For an account of Mozart's structural thinking in the first movement of K595, see David Rosen, 'The composer's "standard operating procedure" as evidence of intention: The case of a formal quirk in Mozart's K. 595'; also see Keefe, 'A Complementary Pair: Stylistic Experimentation in Mozart's Final Piano Concertos, K. 537 in D and K. 595 in B♭'.

19. According to *Briefe*, iv.157, it must have been completed after 7 October 1791. The whereabouts of the autograph manuscript are unknown.

20. ◆ It could be as early as 1787.

The three German songs K596–598 are all strophic settings intended for children and, as such, are undemanding. Of the three, the first, *Komm, lieber Mai*, is by far the most successful and remains popular with children even today. Old memories seem to have stirred in Mozart while he was writing it, as the first period contains an audible reminiscence of a folksong, *Ich bin ein Schwabenmädchen*, that he has changed very slightly, but in a way that adds a certain stylization and creates an even more beautiful impression.[21] The second section, with its unmistakably Mozartian opening, is entirely his own invention. In general, Mozart strikes a note of heartfelt sincerity that rises far above the *fausse naïveté* of Overbeck's text. Conversely, his setting of Sturm's *Im Frühlingsanfange* is a failure as a result of his attempt to adopt a childlike tone in setting the poet's high-flown religious verse.

However attractive as a work, the bass aria with obbligato double bass K612 must be seen as something of a curiosity and one, moreover, that the resourceful Schikaneder no doubt forced on the composer. In spite of the seriousness of the words, the incongruously virtuosic treatment of the double bass, combined with the relatively stately writing for the bass soloist, creates an impression that can be described only as mildly comical.

The famous *Ave, verum corpus* K618 could hardly be more different from Mozart's previous sacred works. Its simple songlike character is no doubt attributable to the fact that it was probably written for the church choir at Baden and for the Feast of Corpus Christi.[22] But the whole of its noble and wistful manner recalls the series of Italianate motets that ultimately go back to the old and authentic ecclesiastical tradition that existed alongside the operatic tradition: Jommelli, for example, left a number of similar pieces.[23] But Mozart's setting stands apart from these others by dint of the way in which it perfectly captures the overall mood, as well as by virtue of its individual ideas. It is also eloquent proof of the composer's profound religious feelings. With the single exception of its extended ending, the work never steps outside the folklike symmetry of its four-bar structure, while perfectly mirroring the text's train of thought, just as it effortlessly dispenses with end-rhyme in favour of a meaningful declamation of the words. It begins by apostrophizing the body of our Lord in an affecting mixture of emotion and silent sadness – 'sotto voce' is the only performance marking in the movement – after which the sense of agitation grows perceptibly greater with the mounting intensity implied by the words 'passum', 'immolatum'[24] and 'in cruce': listen in particular to the melodic line and to the evolving harmonies here. This mood dies away quickly and expressively in the movement's only interlude. The second section follows on without a break and adds to the feeling of intensity. The image of the crucified Saviour transfixed by the spear elicits from the chorus an outburst of muted anguish that finds moving expression in the modulation to F major. The melodic line then sinks down again in a profoundly resigned D minor, sequentially picking up what went before. But the entry of D major then brings with it a new sense of release that finds expression above all in the imitative entry of the two halves of the choir, an entry all the more striking in that the writing hitherto has been wholly homophonic. The plea to be purged of sin through the blood of Christ at the moment of death struggles to find expression, first calmly but then, at the renewed thought of death, as a fervent outpouring of emotion prepared for by the interrupted cadence on the chord of the sixth of the subdominant.[25] With the

---

21. See Friedlaender, *Das deutsche Lied im 18. Jahrhundert*, ii.380–1.
22. See Kretzschmar, *Führer durch den Konzertsaal*, fourth edition, ii.512.
23. Leichtentritt, *Geschichte der Motette*, 205.
24. The melodic line here recalls the Countess's cavatina from *Le nozze di Figaro*.
25. It recurs in a similar context in the 'Priests' March' from *Die Zauberflöte*.

soprano's resolute leap of a fifth we soon reach the highest point of the melodic line. The extraordinarily eloquent melisma here, together with the chromatic bass line and the bold harmonies built up over it, completes the picture of fear that then fades away with the word 'mortis'. In this way the prayer, with its sense of tender wistfulness, seems to emerge naturally from the words as the ultimate expression of the principles that the young Mozart had once set forth in his letter to Padre Martini.[26] The writing is entirely homophonic and whereas the opening is dominated by the soprano, the other voices become more animated as the movement unfolds. Particularly striking here is the way in which the feminine suspension formulas are all fully harmonized in the manner of the later Mozart. The choir is accompanied by organ and orchestra, while the prelude, interludes and postlude are entrusted to the orchestra and organ bass alone. At the beginning the way in which the instruments gradually rise to the a' on which the voices enter is particularly beautiful, but no less inspired is the gently rocking motion with which they accompany the vocal line, now drawing closer to it, now moving further away from it. Often they emphasize individual ideas, such as the words 'de Maria virgine' with its upper octave and cessation of all movement, but they are also exploited at the phrase 'in cruce' with its intensifying syncopation and, finally, at the parallel passage 'mortis in', with its expressive unison writing for second violins and violas.[27]

26. It is related to the gradual *Sancta Maria* (K273) discussed above.
27. ◆ Further, see Wolfgang Hoffmann, 'Satztechnische Bemerkungen zu Mozarts "Ave verum corpus" KV 618'; Faravelli, 'Mozart e il mottetto: Un'ipotesi critica e note su "Ave verum corpus"'; and Edelmann, 'Dichtung und Komposition in Mozarts "Ave verum corpus" KV 618'.

51

La clemenza di Tito

By a curious quirk of destiny Mozart ended his career as a music dramatist with a work that belongs to the same genre as the one with which he had first triumphed as a boy: *opera seria*. For *La clemenza di Tito* is even more of an *opera seria* than *Idomeneo* had been. After all, the words are by the great Metastasio himself and date back to 1734. They were set that same year by Antonio Caldara, and the resultant work was heard for the first time on Charles VI's name-day.[1] As an act of homage for crowned heads of state, the poem was tailor-made and, as a result, it was set to music on frequent occasions.[2] For Prague, Caterino Mazzolà, who had been the Saxon court poet since 1780, made a number of changes, reducing the three acts of the original to two and removing the scene in which Sesto changes cloaks with Annio, thereby making the latter seem the guilty party. Various vocal numbers were added, not always to the work's advantage, but in general the opera's overall character remained untouched.[3] The characters are all of the older type, largely allegorical and geared to specific qualities. The eternally vacillating, passive and youthful Sesto and especially the all-forgiving and resigned Tito are additionally typical of an age for which sentiment was far more important than heroism.[4] Mozart must have felt that there was a certain affinity with *Die Zauberflöte* in this glorification of goodness and the eschewal of revenge. This is all clothed in Metastasio's familiar, elegant style with his precious *sententiae*, similes, flowers of rhetoric and other outpourings of emotion that spring merely from rational reflection.[5] The plot, in outline, is as follows:

1. ◆ Caldara's *Tito* was first given on 4 November 1734 at the Hoftheater in Vienna.
2. The most important settings were those by Leonardo Leo (Venice, 1735), Hasse (Pesaro, 1735), Wagenseil (Vienna, 1746), Carlo Pietro Grua (Mannheim, 1748), Gluck (Naples, 1752), Jommelli (Stuttgart, 1753), Holzbauer (Mannheim, 1757), Giuseppe Scarlatti (Venice, 1757), Naumann (Dresden, 1769) and Pietro Alessandro Guglielmi (Turin, 1785). ◆ The attribution of a *Tito* setting to Guglielmi is now believed to be doubtful or even spurious. Other early settings of the text include those by Francesco Peli (Munich, 1736), Giovanni Francesco Marchi (Milan, 1737), Francesco Maria Veracini (with text revisions by Angelo Maria Cori, London, 1737), Giuseppe Arena (Turin, 1738), Joseph Camerloher (Munich, ?1741), David Perez (Naples, 1749), Andrea Adolfati (Vienna, 1753), Michelangelo Valentini (Bologna, 1753), Antonio Mazzoni (Lisbon, 1755), Vincenzo Ciampi (Venice, 1757), Gioacchino Cocchi (London, 1760), Baldassare Galuppi (Vienna, 1760), Niccolò Jommelli (Stuttgart, 1753; second version, Ludwigsburg, 1765), Andrea Bernasconi (Munich, 1768), Pasquale Anfossi (Rome, 1769), Giuseppe Sarti (Padua, 1771), Josef Mysliveček (Venice, 1774), Anton Bachschmidt (Eichstätt, 1776), Luigi Beltrami (Verona, 1779) and David August von Apell (Kassel, 1787). Concerning Camerloher's setting, see Haberkamp, 'Die Oper La clemenza di Tito von Joseph Anton Camerloher (4.7.1710–17.6.1743)'; for musical accounts of some of these works, see Lühning, *Titus-Vertonungen im 18. Jahrhundert – Untersuchungen zur Tradition der Opera seria von Hasse bis Mozart.*
3. ◆ Concerning Mazzolà's revisions to Metastasio's text, see Durante, 'Mozart and the Idea of "Vera Opera": A Study of "La Clemenza di Tito"' and '"La clemenza di Tito" and Other Two-Act Reductions of the Late 18th Century'; and Kreutzer, 'Von der Opera seria zur "vera opera": Die neue musikdramatische Form von Mozarts "La clemenza di Tito"'.
4. In 1819 Zelter wrote to Goethe, 'The Titus has yet to be born who falls in love with all young women, all of whom want to kill him'; see Riemer, *Briefwechsel zwischen Goethe und Zelter*, ii.20.
5. 'Deh se piacer mi vuoi', 'Serbate, oh Dei custodi', 'Del più sublime soglio', 'Ah, se fosse intorno al trono', 'Parto, ma tu ben mio', 'Tardi s'avvede', 'Se all'impero, amici Dei', 'S'altro che lacrime', 'Che del ciel, che degli Dei' and the accompanied recitatives 'Oh Dei, che smania è questa', 'Ecco il punto, oh Vitellia' and 'Ma che giorno è mai questo?' are all by Metastasio, while the rest

Vitellia, the volatile daughter of the deposed Emperor Vitellius, prevails on her lover Sesto to conspire against his friend the Emperor Tito, in return for which she promises him her hand. Annio then reports that Tito has banished his wife Berenice. He asks Sesto to intercede with Tito and obtain the latter's permission for him to marry Sesto's sister Servilia, a request that Tito readily grants. But in the presence of the Roman people, Tito then demands Servilia's hand in marriage. When Sesto remains silent in his dismay, the noble Annio confirms the emperor in his decision. But Servilia remains true to Annio and tells Tito that she and Annio are in love, whereupon Tito magnanimously withdraws in favour of Annio. Meanwhile Vitellia is furious to discover that Servilia has been elevated to the throne and orders Sesto to join his fellow conspirators and set to work at once. He obeys her. But scarcely has Sesto left when the prefect of the Praetorian guard, Publio, enters to announce that Tito is on his way to visit her in order to ask for her hand in marriage. She hurries away to meet him in a state of utter confusion. All the characters foregather in front of the Capitol, which the conspirators have set on fire. Sesto reports that Tito has been murdered, a report that gives rise to feelings of anguish and horror.

The second act opens with Sesto, plagued by pangs of conscience, confessing his guilt to Annio. Both Annio and Vitellia, who is now concerned for her own safety, advise him to flee, but he is prevented from doing so by Publio, who, acting on information received from those of the conspirators who have been captured, has come to arrest him. Tito has in fact survived the attempt on his life and appears before the jubilant populace at a meeting of the senate. He thanks his audience for the love that they have shown him.[6] Sesto has confessed and been condemned to death by the senate. Tito summons him into his presence, ready to forgive him if he confides in him. But Sesto maintains an obstinate silence out of consideration for Vitellia, with the result that Tito confirms the death sentence, only to tear up the document and decide to exercise clemency. Meanwhile Servilia begs Vitellia to plead with the emperor for Sesto's life, and so Vitellia decides to renounce all her hopes of becoming empress and to admit to her guilt. She duly does so at the very moment that sentence is due to be exacted on Sesto in the Roman amphitheatre. Tito finally forgives her, just as he forgives Sesto and the other conspirators. All join in praising his clemency.

It is clear at a glance that we are dealing here with a type of drama that Mozart had long since outgrown. This is in no way changed by Mazzolà's adaptation, an adaptation wrongly attributed to Mozart himself,[7] even though the addition of the sort of ensemble movements that reflected contemporary developments in opera at least met him halfway as a musician. Yet not even Mozart was able to breathe life into these shadowy figures that had long since vanished from sight and that could never be revived in the spirit of *Le nozze di Figaro* or *Don Giovanni*. Nor was this required of him. Quite the opposite: audiences wanted to hear a regular *opera seria* of a kind which, like the usual pomp and official ideas, invariably accompanied these official celebrations.[8] No one cared about the mental anguish that he was bound to suffer: after all, he had the honour of the commission and his fee. The fact that he had so little time to complete the commission and that he was ill also played a part, with observers genuinely interested to see whether he would rise to the challenge. He was helped in his predicament by one of his principal characteristics as a composer, his

are by Mazzolà, although the latter also used Metastasian motifs, including even individual lines and turns of phrase. A copy of the wordbook from the first performances is lodged in the Dresden Landesbibliothek. ◆ The libretto at the Dresden Landesbibliothek was lost during World War II; further copies survive at the Staatsbibliothek zu Berlin (shelfmark Mus. Tm 1125), the Library of Congress, Washington (shelfmark ML50.2.C58M75), and the Gesellschaft der Musikfreunde, Vienna.
6. This scene is the work of Mazzolà but has not been used to create a large-scale ensemble.
7. See Rochlitz, 'Verbürgte Anekdoten aus Wolfgang Gottlieb Mozarts Leben', 151–2; Seyfried, 'Mozart der Opernkomponist: Ein skizzirter Versuch', 191.
8. ◆ See Beránek, 'Zum musikalischen Rahmenprogramm während der böhmischen Krönungsfeierlichkeiten für Leopold II. im Jahr 1791: Bemerkungen zu einem Problem der Mozart-Historiographie'.

remarkable adaptability. At home in every style, he could trust himself to conjure up the spirit of *opera seria* and create, if not an archetypal image, at least a stylistically correct afterimage of a type of work that already existed.[9] In this he was not deluded. Although his new opera was not based on authentic experience in the way that his other operas, including even *Così fan tutte*, were, but on an experience derived from a cultural world that its creator had long since left behind him, it none the less attests to an exceptionally assured and subtle sense of style, and herein lies its main strength. We should not expect more of the piece than the genre itself permitted.[10]

The first eight bars of the overture strike the same festive and pathos-laden note familiar from *Idomeneo*. In the earlier work, however, the festively rising triad had been followed by an image of the most subjective imaginable passion, showing how seriously Mozart took *opera seria* at that time, whereas here it culminates in a far more impersonal idea whose chief characteristic is the highly effective interplay between *forte* and *piano*:

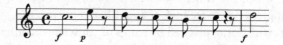

When the opening is repeated, it is varied in the form of a Mannheim crescendo, which Mozart planned to be especially effective here. The cantabile second subject is not particularly original[11] and is introduced in the manner of a French trio, but in general it plays no more than an episodic role and is almost immediately supplanted by the above-cited subject. The development section modulates almost at once to E flat major, thus echoing the opening movement of the C major symphony (K551), but, by interpolating a new unison figure, it lacks the inspired brevity of the earlier work.[12] The main theme is then reworked with a contrapuntal seasoning in the style of the late Mozart, except that the emotion that is kindled here leaves a very much cooler impression. Only towards the end do the accents become keener. Here, too, dynamics are typically strident. In the recapitulation, first and second subject are reversed, thereby adding to the sense of festive splendour, with the full orchestra playing its part here. The opening Neapolitan motif acquires a degree of power that suggests that the festive magnificence of *opera seria* cannot be sufficiently emphasized.[13]

9.   ◆ It may be, too, that Mozart's *Tito* is in part representative of the operatic style encouraged by Leopold II during his time at Florence; see McClymonds, 'Mozart's La clemenza di Tito and opera seria in Florence as a reflection of Leopold II's musical taste'; Heartz, 'Mozart and his Italian contemporaries: La clemenza di Tito'; and Rice, 'Emperor and impresario: Leopold II and the transformation of Viennese musical theater, 1790–1792'. Concerning the original scenography for the opera, see Durante, 'Le Scenographie di Pietro Travaglia per "La clemenza di Tito" (Praga, 1791): Problemi di identificazione ed implicazioni'.

10.   ◆ For a contrary view, that *La clemenza di Tito* represents a different slice of Enlightenment philosophy rather than an obsolete one, see Herklotz, 'Metastasios La clemenza di Tito und die Philosophie der Aufklärung'.

11.   It is introduced in a typically Mozartian manner, with a modulation to the subdominant F major, but the F is then peremptorily raised to F sharp, thereby reaching the dominant.

12.   In order to stress the E flat major tonality, Mozart prefaces the contrapuntal treatment of the subject with a statement of the subject itself, but without any counterpoint.

13.   This overture, too, is said to have been written at the last minute, a claim that is not implausible in the light of the circumstances surrounding the commission; see Procházka, *Mozart in Prag*, 163–4. ◆ The late composition of the overture is apparently confirmed by the distribution of paper types in the autograph score; see Tyson, '"La clemenza di Tito" and its chronology' and Rice, *W. A. Mozart: La clemenza di Tito*, 47–9. Further, see Heartz, 'Mozart's overture to Titus as dramatic argument' and Küster, 'An Early Form in Mozart's Late Style: The Overture to "La clemenza di Tito"'.

One significant chronological problem not considered by Abert – it first surfaced in the 1950s – is the dating of the aria 'Non più di fiori'. Tomislav Volek was the first to suggest that Mozart composed the aria, and may have started work on *Tito*, as early as the spring of 1791; the chief evidence for this assertion is an announcement for a concert on 26 April at which Mozart's friend the soprano Josepha Duschek sang a rondò by Mozart 'with obbligato basset-horn'; according to Rice, *W. A. Mozart: La clemenza di Tito*, 50, the text of 'Non più di fiori' supports Volek's hypothesis: its imagery matches the recitative that precedes it in the opera. At the same time, however, the evidence of the autograph is equivocal: the aria is on a type of paper otherwise not found

It was no doubt as a favour to the two leading sopranos that Mazzolà added a duet for Sesto and Vitellia at the very beginning of the opera ('Come ti piace imponi').[14] Like Sesto, Annio is sung by a soprano, except that a woman's voice was preferred to that of a castrato here, a preference that no doubt represents progress in humanitarian terms, even if the drama suffers in consequence. In the present case, however, the drama was not the decisive factor. The duet is cast in the form of a slow movement followed by a fast one, a form that had been taken over by *opera seria* from *opera buffa* at this time. Yet even here we can already see clearly that Mozart knew very well where he was heading in this opera. There are no complex psychological problems, no individual characters: Sesto is simply the passive and sentimental young lover, Vitellia the proud heroine, ambitious and vengeful by turns. Both characters are almost like allegories and, as such, indistinguishable from similar characters who had already appeared under countless different names in earlier *opere serie*. Musically, too, they take turns, each taking over from the other in keeping with the rationalistic spirit of this art form. When their voices come together in the allegro, they do not interact on a psychological level but simply join forces to express a common feeling which, however agitated, is none the less impersonal. That the music as such plays a decisive role here is only natural, as it alone was capable of breathing any warmth and life into these antiquated plaster-of-Paris figures. Sesto in particular is the beneficiary of Mozart's sweet-toned melodies, whereas Vitellia is closer to the rhetorical style of the Neapolitans with her leaping intervals and wide-ranging compass. The allegro begins with a familiar Mozartian melody expressive of agitation. Here, above all, the imitative entries that had always been traditional at this juncture produce a tone which, although more universally appealing, is none the less somewhat neutral in expression.

The part of Vitellia was taken by Maria Marchetti, who was born about 1760 and who married the tenor Angelo Fantozzi around 1783. She had acquired a considerable reputation in Naples and Milan before being invited to Prague. Wherever she appeared, she impressed her audiences with her beautiful, full-toned voice and with her excellent enunciation and skills as an actress, the latter being enhanced by her pleasing appearance and nobility of manner.[15] How little store was set by consistent characterization in the real Mozartian sense is clear from her very first aria ('Deh se piacer mi vuoi'), in which a completely different, lyrically sentimental Vitellia suddenly confronts us. Its slow section expresses a wholly uncomplicated feeling of tenderness, while the fast section is an example of the sort of music that Metastasio's frosty words of wisdom invariably inspired his composers to produce.[16] Not knowing where to start with his text, Mozart begins by allowing

in *La clemenza di Tito*, and while this may lend weight to Volek's hypothesis concerning the dating of 'Non più di fiori', it may also discount his suggestion that the opera itself was started earlier than the summer of 1791 since it is the only number from the work on this type of paper. See Volek, 'Über den Ursprung von Mozarts Oper "La clemenza di Tito"'; Tyson, '"La clemenza di Tito" and its chronology'; and Rice, *W. A. Mozart: La clemenza di Tito*, 48–51. More recently, see Durante, 'The Chronology of Mozart's "La clemenza di Tito" Reconsidered'.

14. See Genée, 'Über einige Musikhandschriften von Mozart', 121–2.

15. Gerber, *Neues historisch-biographisches Lexikon der Tonkünstler*, ii.75; *AmZ*, iv (1801/2), 318–19; Reichardt, *Berlinische musikalische Zeitung*, i (1805), 112; Florimo, *La scuola musicale di Napoli e i suoi conservatorii*, iv.351; and Cambiasi, *La Scala 1778–1906*, 289ff. From Prague she went to Venice in 1791; see Wiel, *I teatri musicali veneziani nel Settecento*, 424 and 428. After that she moved to Berlin; see Louis Schneider, *Geschichte der Oper und des Königlichen Opernhauses zu Berlin*, 248. A Berlin report of 1799, by contrast, describes her merely as a caricature; see *AmZ*, i (1798/9), 348–9. ◆ Concerning Marchetti, see Rice, 'Mozart and his singers: The case of Maria Marchetti Fantozzi, the first Vitellia'. According to the *Berlinische musikalische Zeitung historischen und kritischen Inhalts* for 9 February 1793, 'The compass of [Marchetti's] voice is not big; the low register is rough and dull and the upper reaches are such that she can reach high C only in passing. Yet her otherwise full voice is completely at her command; her tone is quite pure, and she has the Italian expressivity with its good aspects and without too much exaggeration; she sings with great feeling and, when it is necessary, with considerable virtuosity, although it requires much effort of her. . . . But her acting, her delivery are masterful; they are such as only she, the best actress on the operatic stage, can have'; see Rice, *W. A. Mozart: La clemenza di Tito*, 52.

16. The settings of Hasse and Gluck are likewise fairly conventional at this point.

Vitellia's temperament to flare up in a way remotely reminiscent of Donna Anna's 'vengeance aria' ['Fuggi, crudele, fuggi!' from *Don Giovanni*], but then he alights on the words 'inganni' and, later, 'alletta' – here the typically Mozartian painterly motif obliges him to extend the underlying metre. The result is that instead of describing an inner emotion, Mozart has set mere concepts that he singles out as musically useable just as an Italian composer would have done in similar circumstances.

The following duettino for Sesto and Annio ('Deh prendi un dolce amplesso') is equally problematic from a dramatic point of view. Indeed, it even falls short of Metastasio, who had at least ended the scene with an aria for the anxious Annio. Mozart steps outside his role for the one and only time in the opera by investing Mazzolà's pretentious expression of friendship with the homely sounds of a German singspiel. No doubt this was much appreciated by his audience, but it reflects neither the drama in particular nor the style of *opera seria* in general, whose aims are far better served by the following march[17] and chorus ('Serbate, oh Dei custodi'),[18] with their festive, albeit somewhat impersonal character.

Tito now sings his first aria ('Del più sublime soglio'). Antonio Baglioni, who had earlier created the role of Don Ottavio, is said to have complained that Mozart had been given the commission in preference to an Italian composer, with the result that Mozart saddled him with such an ungrateful role.[19] This is clearly no more than theatre gossip. Quite apart from its slight on Mozart's character, it ignores the fact that too much was at stake for the composer and that a coronation opera was hardly the opportunity to engage in acts of personal revenge. In fact, Mozart seems to have had the creator of Don Ottavio specifically in mind when writing this role, even though he was unable to achieve more than a pale imitation of the tender melodies of the earlier figure. In total contrast to Gluck, for example, he was not trying to conjure up a picture of a Roman emperor but attempting to capture his clemency in music, with the result that the only Mozartian element that the composer has added to this pale and idealized figure is a vague sense of sadness and resignation. In the present aria we can hear a distant echo of Sarastro's 'In diesen heil'gen Hallen'.[20] In general, the mood is one of tender, lyrical half-lights. Above all, however, the listener is aware of the absence of Mozart's individual treatment of the winds. It is an example of the brief ternary form that was then fashionable and that also provides the basis of the following duet for Servilia and Annio ('Ah, perdona al primo affetto'). Whereas the older Neapolitan composers would have struck a more emotional note here, the younger generation, including Mozart, preferred a more intimate and heartfelt note for their secondary characters, something that they owed to the spirit of *opera buffa*. The emotion that finds expression here in such tender and delightful tones is a sincere and innocent feeling of love. In the best Neapolitan tradition, it is Annio who begins, accompanied by a single bassoon as the only expression of his manliness and followed by Servilia, who adopts the same melody, this time to a flute accompaniment. Both voices combine in the middle section in simple homophony, which is maintained in the da capo and the intimate coda.[21] Tito's second aria ('Ah, se fosse intorno al trono') adopts a freer approach to ternary form by developing the da capo along independent lines after the first six bars. In terms

---

17. Like the aria 'Ah, se fosse intorno al trono' and the accompanied recitatives and overture, this march was originally unnumbered, but was written on the same special type of paper that was used for all these other numbers, thereby indicating that they were completed at a later date.

18. Hasse's setting of this chorus includes clear reminiscences of the 'Hallelujah' chorus from *Messiah*.

19. Seyfried, 'Mozart der Opernkomponist: Ein skizzirter Versuch', 193–4. ◆ Concerning Baglioni, see Rice, *W. A. Mozart: La clemenza di Tito*, 54–9.

20. Apart from the main theme, note also the passage at the words 'tormento e servitù' with its imitative motif in the strings.

21. It is introduced by the interrupted cadence on the chord of the sixth of the subdominant.

of its expression, it is more manly than its predecessor, but also more impersonal. We look in vain here for any sign of Mozart's true greatness.

Only when we turn to Sesto's aria ('Parto, ma tu ben mio') do we find a genuine example of an *opera seria* aria. Here the debt extends even to the use of an obbligato clarinet, which was especially popular with the younger generation of Neapolitan composers and which in the present case is handled with great virtuosity. Formally, too, the influence of *opera seria* is palpable, with an opening adagio followed by an allegro and a final allegro assai that adds to the sense of tension. In terms of its text, the aria reveals nothing that we do not already know about Sesto's steadfast love for Vitellia and his willingness to turn his words into actions. Mozart made no attempt to explore any new aspects of a theme long familiar to *opera seria*. Instead, he invested in the aria his most noble melodies and his whole sense of sonority. With its typically Mozartian metre and heartfelt interweaving of voice and solo instrument, the adagio in particular is notable for the way in which the expression of love gains in intensity and ultimately achieves a note of rapt enchantment. But in the allegro, where heroism is supposed to be given its due, the tone again becomes relatively conventional.[22] By the time that we reach the allegro assai, with its elaborate coloratura flourishes divided between voice and clarinet, the Neapolitanisms have become even more extreme, although it must be conceded that, unlike his early operas, with their indiscriminate use of coloratura on random words, Mozart now limits the *fioriture* to those words that justify its use from a psychological or tone-painterly point of view. Only in the middle section, with its evocation of more tender emotions, do we hear the true Mozart. Yet there is something utterly Rococoesque about the love-struck glance that is cast by the clarinet before the words 'A questo sguardo solo'. The characterization is no more distinctive here than it is in the rest of the opera. Rather, Mozart takes from the individual character and the situation on stage only enough to create a general atmospheric portrait, just as in his concert arias.

The trio for Vitellia, Annio and Publio ('Vengo . . . aspettate') occurs at one of those critical points where Mozart normally included an ensemble. Vitellia has just urged Sesto to overthrow the emperor and now discovers that she is to be Tito's wife. Profoundly agitated, she hopes to call him back. Meanwhile, Annio offers the future empress a heartfelt tribute, while Publio maintains his official attitude. The number begins with one of those brief and agitated orchestral motifs from which Mozart generally develops his *buffa* ensembles. But it soon emerges that we are not dealing here with three independent participants in the drama, as Annio and Publio are treated as a self-contained group pitted against Vitellia. The latter begins by expressing her agitation in a disjointed vocal line which, in keeping with the text, had been standard practice in such situations with the older generation of Neapolitan composers.[23] The language becomes Mozartian only with the sudden entry of E flat major, when Vitellia appears almost literally to shake with fever. The two men then enter, unaware of the true situation and misinterpreting her confusion as an expression of boundless happiness. This contrast is fully worked out, thereby avoiding a solo aria with two accompanying voices.[24] The modern listener may be disturbed, of course, by the homely note struck by Annio and Publio, but we must not forget that we are dealing here with a prima donna and two subsidiary figures. In other words, Mozart remained stylistically consistent by maintaining this distance and allowing the two subsidiary characters to be recognized as such through his music. They express their feelings in a subdued manner befitting their rank, without jeopardizing the

---

22. The phrase ending with the fully harmonized dominant and tonal triad on the strong beat of the bar creates a sense of stilted pathos that is often found in this opera.
23. Only the suspensions in the winds attest to any greater individuality.
24. See Oulibicheff, *Mozart's Leben*, 340.

dominant position of the leading singer. Her strength of feeling loses none of its vehemence,[25] as is clear from her lengthy outburst on 'Che angustia, che tormento' and especially from the sudden changes from *sotto voce* to *forte* and back, during which she seems to grow hot and cold by turns. In general, this and the other ensembles in the opera afford adequate proof of the fact that, however widespread it may have been at this time, ensemble singing in *opera seria* did not enjoy the same degree of freedom as it did in *opera buffa*. Musical values were still deemed far more important than dramatic ones.

Numbered separately, Sesto's solo *scena* ('Oh Dei, che smania è questa') launches the first-act finale ('Deh conservate, oh Dei'), which constitutes the climax of the whole opera. The difference between it and an *opera buffa* finale is immediately apparent: here we are no longer dealing with a constant unfolding of the plot, including all its vicissitudes, but with a single situation, a variously nuanced atmospheric picture. But the situation itself is of genuine grandeur, and Mozart rose to the challenge with a resolve reminiscent of Gluck. Structurally, too, this section is as masterly as it is original, with an impassioned *accompagnato* to start, followed by a climactic allegro and, finally, an andante that would have been simply impossible in a *buffa* finale, but which here allows the tension to subside into grief and anguish. Even Sesto's solo *scena* has few precedents in Mozart's works. A brief andante is embedded in a wildly impassioned and motivically exceptionally unified section: within it the figure of the magnanimous emperor is conjured up in Sesto's thoughts in a recitative that is strikingly reminiscent of Gluck. The harmonic writing, too, avoids the tendency to modulate to remote keys that is normally found in such scenes. In the first section it revolves around the C minor that is struck so resolutely at the outset, descending to the region of its subdominant at each renewed outburst of passion. Only when Sesto comes to rest on the words 'Io non credea che fosse sì difficile impresa esser malvagio' ('I had not realized it would be so difficult to be evil') does the key of E flat major enter. At the end of this section ('Sesto infelice, tu traditor! Che orribil nome': 'Unhappy Sesto! A traitor, you! What a terrible name!') the cadence following the word 'nome' forces the musical argument back towards C minor. Here Mozart follows his usual practice of rewriting the F sharp in the bass as the leading note of G minor and ending in this key, manifestly using its sombre associations to lay the foundations for what follows. None the less, the andante begins with a D flat that is literally terrifying in its ambiguity. The third section initially plunges still deeper into flattened tonalities. And not even here does the main motif, with its realistically convulsive expression, yield any ground. Only when the Capitol goes up in flames – a development that Mozart ignores in his music just as his predecessors had done – does the tension rise and build to a tremendous climax accompanying Sesto's desperate resolve, for all that this comes too late. With the beginning of the allegro an ardent prayer for Tito – in E flat major! – struggles to break free from Sesto's breast, a genuinely great moment that reveals the hand of the master dramatist. The confused Annio hears first a sudden flaring up of emotion, then a series of hesitant, mysterious remarks that acquire an almost eerie expression as a result of the sudden modulation to G flat major. Following Sesto's departure, he stands helplessly rooted to the spot. With Servilia's arrival we again become aware of the general situation with its sense of widespread confusion. From now on each of the new arrivals – Servilia, Publio and Vitellia – expresses the sense of common horror by means of the same musical phrase, while the orchestral accompaniment remains the same, with its tremolando, wild bass motif and heavy *forte* wind chords above it, as does the soloists' Phrygian cadence and the agitated outcry of the distant chorus that throws the harmonies into wild disarray at the end of every section. The harmonies in fact mirror those

---

25. See Jahn, *W. A. Mozart*, fourth edition, ii.585.

found in the previous recitative: C minor dominates with its two dominants of F and G minor. Only with the return of Sesto, who initially follows in his predecessors' musical footsteps, is there a decisive shift to A flat major. The following section is again highly significant for Mozart's concept of dramatic effectiveness, not only on account of its impressive treatment of the horrifying news of Tito's death (such moments are also found in operas by Italian composers) but because of his whole approach to the situation. Sesto's recitative slowly subsides and comes to rest on a dissonance, followed by a grand pause. Now, instead of a tempestuous outpouring of horror, the ensemble answers quietly, *andante*, as though transfixed, then stammering its response. Such suppressed tragedy is typical of Mozart. For all its simplicity, the following build-up of tension is indescribably effective. The foundations are laid for Sesto's terrible confession of his guilt with eloquent sequencing suggestive of tremendous psychological pressure, but before he can say anything he is interrupted by an appalled Vitellia in a hurried recitative. There follows another anxious and tension-laden grand pause that signifies a violent change of mood: in the following andante all personal feelings are silenced,[26] and even Sesto and Vitellia are submerged within the unified ensemble, which now launches into a moving dirge for the murdered emperor, their voices alternating with those of the equally subdued chorus. This final section is dominated by the spirit of Gluck and, in part, by the same composer's expressive resources. One might even say that it is the spirit of classical tragedy that finds expression here. The two groups of singers are particularly finely shaded in terms of their language of expression, with the solemnly measured tread and symmetrical structures of the chorus offset against the more animated and freer ensemble. Only in the case of a handful of individual outbursts, especially on the word 'tradimento', does the feeling of agitation suddenly flare up. Particularly significant in this context is the ending, where the chorus twice groans loudly, while the voices of the soloists – utterly broken by all that they have witnessed – die away *piano*. The orchestra, too, is divided, with the chorus accompanied by horns, trumpets and timpani and, at its initial entry, unison writing in the upper strings that creates an impressive effect, while the ensemble relies on the remaining winds and on the string choir, which is here treated more individually. At the end there is a muffled timpani roll with horns (but without trumpets). But there is never any question here of Mozart renouncing his independence in favour of Gluck. What he had in mind was merely a general Gluckian model, the scene of lamentation, but the way in which he works up his model is entirely his own, from the touching sadness of the opening line, with its rising fourth, to the final phrase of the ensemble, which recalls *Die Zauberflöte*. Nor should we see in this scene a fundamental shift in the direction of Gluck, a shift precluded by the whole of the rest of the opera's character. After all, the other representatives of *opera seria* at this time were not averse to borrowing certain features from Gluck for individual scenes. If Mozart picked up these experiments here in so independent and successful a way, we clearly owe this to *Die Zauberflöte*, on which he was working at more or less the same time and whose pure and sublime spirit can still be heard in the present piece. Mozart's distinguished audience in Prague, by contrast, may have heard this scene with mixed feelings, and it is impossible not to be reminded here of the spiteful comment about 'porcheria tedesca'. Unfortunately, this is the only such scene in the opera.

The second act opens with an aria for Annio ('Torna di Tito a lato')[27] that immediately brings us back to the world of convention: it is a simple number for a subsidiary character, with no individual features. Not even the following trio ('Se al volto mai ti senti') is an ensemble in the Mozartian sense of the term. Rather, it is typical of an *opera seria*, being more musical than

---

26. This mood is subtly prepared in the andante section of the recitative, which, melodically too, anticipates what follows.
27. The words are by Mazzolà. It was inserted at a later date and numbered 13½.

dramatic, even though Sesto's tender farewell to Vitellia, who is now torn between fear and shame, would have provided a grateful starting point. Although this contrast is hinted at, especially in the andante, there is no question here of any dramatic synthesis filled with any real sense of life, while Publio never emerges from behind his neutral stance. The result is a number that deals with a valedictory mood and that is tender-hearted in a typically Neapolitan manner, including even the usual tone-painterly underlining of the words 'lieve aura' and 'estremi miei sospiri' in the winds. In spite of the freer handling of the voices, the purely musical character of the number emerges more clearly in the allegretto, the basic tone of which is again determined by Sesto. It is he who launches the phrase that is repeated by the others in the manner of a refrain:

Only towards the end does the agitation begin to grow palpably more intense with the dotted motif in the strings that is heard here in conjunction with a crescendo. The brief postlude clearly depicts Sesto being led away by Publio's guards. The words of the trio are modelled on those of Metastasio's aria 'Se mai senti spirarti sul volto' from act two, scene fifteen of his original libretto, an aria that an older generation of composers had been particularly fond of setting.[28]

The following chorus ('Ah grazie si rendano') frames a solo for Tito and is likewise typical of the Neapolitan school, simultaneously contemplative and charming, but with no deeper emotions involved and with Tito himself fully subscribing to this tone. There is no trace here of inner turmoil or even imperial dignity. With different words, this solo could equally well be sung by a member of the chorus, a practice frequently found in French operas of the period. Mozart's authorship is recalled by no more than a handful of purely musical features[29] such as the two introductory bars that later recur in diminution and the characteristic change of harmony on the weak beat of the bar, a feature often found in *La clemenza di Tito*. There follow two arias for two of the subsidiary characters, Publio ('Tardi s'avvede') and Annio ('Tu fosti tradito'). Of these, the first, with its ice-cold morality, is no more than a product of Mozart's embarrassment, while the second at least expresses a certain warmth in the form of Annio's feeling of pity for his bride's brother. As in the older tradition of *opera seria*, the two contrasting ideas – those of betrayal and of the hapless Sesto's fate – are strictly segregated in the music, but the tender-hearted entreaty emerges as movingly authentic: it is easy to imagine such a plea having an effect on Tito.

Tito himself begins scene seven on a surprisingly impassioned note in his *accompagnato*. The orchestra makes only a modest contribution to this scene, which achieves its impact through its use of succinct declamation and especially through its expressive harmonic language. The music modulates through a wide range of keys, but always in close association with the ideas contained in the text. The more that Tito's anger towards Sesto grows, the more the harmonies descend into

28. Hasse had set this as a beautiful slow aria in C minor with flutes, while Gluck later reworked his setting as the heroine's aria at the end of act two of *Iphigénie en Tauride*, 'O malheureuse Iphigénie', proof of how highly he regarded it; see Wotquenne, *Thematisches Verzeichnis der Werke von Chr. W. v. Gluck*, 217. In the list of songs that Constanze Mozart sent to Breitkopf on 25 February 1799, Metastasio's incipit appears as no. 13; see Nottebohm, *Mozartiana*, 123 [*Briefe*, iv.229]. Nottebohm draws the no doubt correct conclusion that this lost work was originally intended for *La clemenza di Tito* but that it was later replaced by the present trio.

29. By contrast, the tendency to delay the cadence that is so frequently found in this opera is Italian in origin.

flattened tonalities, reaching D flat major with the death sentence. But as soon as Tito's fury abates and he begins to reflect on a monarch's lot,[30] the modulation retraces its steps until the image of the poor and enviable peasant brings us back to A minor. By now the orchestral writing, too, has grown calmer with its series of familiar sustained chords in the strings. Only gradually do the flat keys return, but now as an expression of wistful sadness.

Sesto is then led in, giving rise to a trio ('Quello di Tito è il volto!') whose introductory larghetto brings with it a decisive change of tone. Again, it is not a true Mozartian ensemble, as the characters – initially at least – are merely juxtaposed, rather than played off against each other. But in the case of Sesto and Tito the result is grippingly effective from a dramatic point of view, resulting in a moment of genuine grandeur. Each of the two men is appalled at the other's changed appearance. Sesto is accompanied by a convulsive tremolando motif in the orchestra, a realistic device that points far into the future, and by dark-toned, strange-sounding harmonies, while Tito's astonishment is expressed by means of a simpler, two-note motif that is constantly repeated. Finally Publio, as impersonal as ever, expresses the feelings of a third party, a reaction that later composers and even Mozart in his other operas would have entrusted to the orchestra alone. The two main characters are now brought into direct confrontation, with Sesto rising to truly tragic greatness. Unfortunately the following allegro fails to maintain this same high level but allows the keen sense of personal antithesis to evaporate into generalities. Tito and Publio form a self-contained group in which Publio begins by simply repeating his imperial master's thoughts – this is a particularly appealing idea. Here the use of imitation produces a musically effective picture but in terms of its expression the image is somewhat blurred. Sesto stands out more clearly by dint of his disjointed melodic line, which is twice interrupted by expressive, cadenza-like passages on the words 'a piacere'.[31] Entirely typical of Mozart is the ending, which dies away softly on a plagal cadence.

After a bitter mental struggle, Sesto rejects the emperor's friendly overtures and in doing so forfeits his life. His feelings overwhelm him in his following aria ('Deh per questo istante solo'). Here Metastasio expressed only the character's desperate resolve to die, but Mazzolà begins by conjuring up the painful memory of his earlier friendship, and Mozart lends visionary expression to this mood even in the opening adagio,[32] with even the key of A major pointing in this direction. This whole section is made up of one of those tender pictures of lost happiness that were among the favourite themes of *opera seria*. Only the word 'orror' causes a darker cloud to pass momentarily overhead. All the starker are the contrasts in the following allegro, where they produce a freer form that sets it apart from the simple ternary structure of the adagio. This allegro is a kind of rondo, except that the theme ('tanto affanno soffre un core') enters not at the beginning but only in the course of the section. Each time it is in the home key of A major. The allegro is related to the gavotte-like movements that are French in origin and that we have already encountered in the case of Sarti. In terms of its overall expression it is indebted to the rapt tone of the adagio but it needs to be well performed if it is to avoid the sense of monotony that affects this type of piece in general.[33] But the way in which the theme is invariably prepared for by passages evocative of contrasting moods creates a subtle psychological impression. Twice the mood of A major is

---

30. Hasse treated this aria as a pastoral idyll, while Gluck, who from the outset saw Tito as a far more manly figure, simply cut this entire outpouring.

31. He begins with one of Mozart's favourite ideas, an idea already familiar from *Le nozze di Figaro*.

32. The ritornello at the beginning and end has been written out by a copyist. Presumably the aria originally passed straight into an accompanied recitative for Tito that has not survived; on the change to the aria's metre, see above.

33. Schaul, *Briefe über den Geschmack in der Musik*, 5. Schaul points out that Sesto expresses his pangs of conscience in the form of a rondo and quotes this as an example of the way in which Mozart frequently offends against common sense. Carl Maria von Weber immediately leapt to Mozart's defence; see Max Maria von Weber, *Carl Maria von Weber*, iii.4.

interrupted by a brief and typically Mozartian harmonic shift, first to C major, then to F major.[34] As a result, the expression of high emotion turns out to be more convincing here than that of sentimentality, a situation rarely found among the younger generation of Neapolitan composers. It is also worth noting that Mozart refrains from introducing any coloratura writing here.[35]

For a time Mozart himself seems to have hesitated over this allegro, evidently because he was not entirely sure that the main theme would create an effect. The opening was originally more resolute and defiant in character:

At this point the sketch breaks off at the foot of the page, and the later allegro begins on a new side. It seems highly unlikely that the earlier version was elaborated any further.

Structurally speaking, Tito's aria ('Se all'impero, amici Dei') harks back to an earlier form, in which a slow middle section is interpolated between a main section and its repeat. Its expressive language is extremely conventional, including even coloratura passages, which seem added almost as an afterthought. With its gently undulating dance-like character (it is headed 'Tempo di Minuetto'), Servilia's aria ('S'altro che lacrime') is a fashionable number of a kind often heard on the lips of the subsidiary characters in *opera seria*, a sentimental number that falls pleasingly on the ear but offers little in the way of characterization.[36] As in Annio's arias, Mozart strikes the heartfelt note that we also find in his *empfindsam* songs. Vitellia's *scena* ('Ecco il punto, oh Vitellia' – 'Non più di fiori vaghe catene') then lifts us out of these shallows. Even the accompanied recitative is remarkable for its declamatory and harmonic writing,[37] with the tension building over a

34. The opening also avails itself of an orchestral motif reminiscent of the beginning of the overture to *Le nozze di Figaro*.
35. Gluck is much more succinct in his own setting of this aria in act three, scene six, stressing only the character's resolve to die and pangs of conscience. The equivalent aria in Hasse's setting is one of the most substantial in the whole opera.
36. Gluck's setting is in C minor, a pugnacious and, harmonically speaking, highly impressive number in which Servilia's reproaches are expressed in far more characterful terms.
37. The initial motif in the orchestra is one of a type that is often found in Mozart's accompanied recitatives, with a sforzato opening followed by a brief, sharply rhythmical motif with a trill by way of an upbeat: for other examples, see Donna Elvira's insertion aria in *Don Giovanni*, the recitative preceding Susanna's 'Deh vieni' in *Le nozze di Figaro*, the scene with the Speaker in *Die Zauberflöte* and Sesto's accompanied recitative ('Oh Dei, che smania è questo') that launches the first-act finale.

single powerful line and culminating in the wild outburst at the words 'Ah! mi vedrei sempre Sesto d'intorno' ('Ah, I should always see Sesto near me'), at which point Vitellia's despair rises to the highest pitch of intensity, before gradually growing calmer as she heroically renounces all her proud dreams. Textually speaking, the aria is based on the typically Metastasian contrast between the dream of marital happiness and the very real threat of death, with all its terrors. Once again it comprises a slow and a fast section but is in fact a self-contained whole as the slow section is repeated in the course of the fast one. Instrumentally, too, the aria is particularly lavishly scored, not least as a result of the participation of an obbligato basset-horn which, regardless of its virtuosity, underlines the drama in the most felicitous manner imaginable.[38] The opening is a tender idyll inspired by Italian models, except that the ornate Rococo melodies found there are replaced by a typically Mozartian, warm-hearted, songlike tone. In the middle section of its simple ternary larghetto, the first shadows descend over the bright scene at the unison passages accompanying the words 'veggo la morte ver me avanzar' ('I see death drawing near'), but for the present they are unable to cast a permanent pall over it. The allegro recalls the corresponding section from Sesto's aria ('Deh per questo istante solo') inasmuch as here, too, the melody first heard belatedly at the words 'Chi vedesse il mio dolore, pur avria di me pietà' ('Could they see my suffering, all would pity me') is later repeated in the manner of a rondo. Structurally, it also recalls the earlier type, except that its language of expression is far more characterful, not least as a result of its searing chromaticisms which express a sense of the pitiful helplessness that motivates Vitellia more than any other character in the work. This theme is again prepared for by a section in the minor, but here it does not have a merely transitional significance, plunging us instead right into the heart of Vitellia's despair.[39] The melody of the larghetto is used for the first episode, but as a result of the common-time signature it is now significantly intensified (note the syncopation at the beginning), while also being robbed of its idyllic character. Above all, the menacing picture of death, previously merely hinted at, is now depicted in broad detail, with the vocal line doubling the unison strings, which now take the bass line. The harmonies are indicated by flutes and bassoons, as well as by the basset-horn with its fluttering figuration. The opening of the allegro is now repeated in a much abbreviated form, and this in turn is followed by the main theme in A flat major, which serves as a sort of second episode. These twenty-one bars are flanked by two rests in the full orchestra, creating an interpolation that is, however, fully justified by the tremendous build-up in tension that has preceded it. Only afterwards does the main theme enter in F major, except that on this occasion the voice takes precedence over the instruments. Also of importance from this point onwards is Mozart's entirely free approach to individual ideas in the text, all of which reappear within the narrowest possible confines, with Vitellia even harking back to her lost happiness, albeit without repeating the wistful melody heard on the earlier occasion. This section culminates in another of the rests in the full orchestra that are so characteristic of this aria, which prepares the way for the ultimate climax, a climax built up on a very free variant of the main theme of which the winds initially state only the bass. The roles of the voice and orchestra are then reversed, with the aria ending on a note of extreme agitation involving the usual emotionally charged extensions of the old cadential harmonies, but avoiding the *Bettelkadenz* that is not infrequently found in Mozart's works, especially in his concert arias. Admittedly, the grand emotions expressed in this most substantial of arias are only loosely connected to the characterization of Vitellia found

---

38. Stadler's involvement in the production explains the solo use of the clarinet and basset-horn in the opera; see Mozart's letter of 7 October 1791 (*Briefe*, iv.157). See also Procházka, *Mozart in Prag*, 173ff.
39. The first bar of the three-bar structure should be interpreted as an upbeat.

elsewhere in the opera,[40] but it should be remembered that the figures of intrigue in *opera seria* cannot be judged by the standards of strict psychological development, being generally depicted at the outset as impassioned, black-hued villains. Once they have performed their duty within the course of the piece and at the end – as is only fitting – succumbed to the principle of good, they retire from the scene of action as figures of despair fired by the same impassioned rhetoric as before. We must be grateful to Mazzolà for rejecting Metastasio's simile aria at this point, 'Getta il nocchier talora', in favour of a direct emotional confession on Vitellia's part. Here Mozart seized his opportunity with both hands and created an atmospheric portrait in which we see a purely human face, with all its individual features, behind the conventional mask.

The aria passes without a break into a solemn and transitional andante maestoso that gives way in turn to a chorus ('Che del ciel, che degli Dei') whose strict, archaizing, almost churchlike tone evokes the sense of horror at the attempt on Tito's life that still haunts the minds of all involved in the drama, conjuring up a mood that finds expression in the solemnly measured, independent accompaniment, with its rhythmic ostinato in the bass, and in the numerous dissonant suspensions in the part-writing. The listener will be reminded of similar pieces by Handel. Shortly before the end Mozart uses these devices to achieve an effective increase in tension. Only when Vitellia accepts responsibility for all that has happened and Tito expresses his resolve to pardon all concerned in another expressive *accompagnato* ('Ma che giorno è mai questo?') do the heavens brighten for the finale ('Tu, è ver, m'assolvi Augusto'). By now Hasse's brief and vacuous closing choruses had already given way to longer French-inspired complexes for soloists and chorus, and this is the model that Mozart adopts in order to bring the now complete action to a musically effective conclusion. Needless to say, the emotions described here can only be of a very generalized kind, with happiness and gratitude uppermost in the characters' minds. Yet Mozart shows great skill in working them up into an effective climax, with the exchange between Sesto and Tito followed by a more animated ensemble for the soloists. Only then does the chorus enter, an entry ushered in by a mighty unison in the full orchestra, which now includes trumpets and timpani, and by Vitellia's dramatically effective triadic ascent to a top g'', which soars above the others like a radiant star over the chorus's hymnlike 'Eterni dei'. Following this first general tutti, the dialogue between Tito, who continues to be accompanied by strings alone, and the other characters becomes livelier. On some occasions Tito himself spins out the melodic thread, on others he completes the line begun by the tutti, ending it in the manner of a refrain. Even when this dialogue takes place within very narrow confines, as at the exchange 'Vegliate' – 'Troncate', he maintains his melodic independence. Here, too, the way in which the soloists and chorus are subtly differentiated creates a very fine impression. The opera thus ends entirely in the spirit of an *opera seria*, not in a dramatic way, but with a section which, musically speaking, is finely structured and extremely felicitously nuanced in terms of its sonorities.

Any comparison between *Idomeneo* and *La clemenza di Tito* is bound to be to the latter's disadvantage, as the later work lacks the sense of profound personal experience that we find in the earlier piece. In *Idomeneo* Mozart still believed in his artistic mission even in the field of *opera seria*. By the time that he wrote *La clemenza di Tito*, this world lay far behind him, and his only concern was to carry out his professional duty and complete a task that only sporadically engaged his interest. Although there is undoubtedly progress on a formal level (the distended and noisy ritornellos have gone and musical forms are generally handled in a more concise and flexible

---

40. See Jahn, *W. A. Mozart*, ii.583.

manner), the work falls surprisingly short of *Idomeneo* even on a purely instrumental level. In the case of *Idomeneo* Mozart had successfully exploited all the impressions gleaned in Mannheim and Paris, whereas, with the exception of a handful of numbers that are festive in character, *La clemenza di Tito* tends rather towards the more intimate and translucent instrumentation of the later works, yet without coming anywhere near them in terms of its subtlety. In general one looks in vain for the inspired use of the orchestra that was one of Mozart's supreme dramatic achievements. One reason for this may be the limited time that he had at his disposal to work on the piece, but in general it reflects current practices in the world of *opera seria*, in which the voices were regarded as more important than the orchestra, sensuous beauty and theatrical effectiveness more important than characterization. In short, Mozart found himself in the position of a composer who, at the instigation of a third party, completes a task that has little appeal for him but which he none the less carries out with the assured taste and sense of style of the mature artist. Herein lies the work's strength, but also its weakness.

Understandably responses to the piece varied depending on the individual critic's standpoint. According to Niemetschek, many observers regarded *La clemenza di Tito* as Mozart's most consummate work, as everything about it, including the 'modest' instrumentation, expressed 'the simplicity and calm sublimity of Tito's character and of the action as a whole'.[41] Niemetschek himself saw the work as a shining example of pure taste and apt characterization.[42] Another reviewer criticized Metastasio's text but was all the warmer in his praise of the musical characterization not only of the mild-mannered Tito, but also of the sublime Vitellia and of the ideal tenderness of the friendship between Sesto and Annio. On the whole, he concluded, the work was worthy of standing alongside Goethe's *Tasso*.[43] Johann Baptist Schaul, by contrast, thought that, with the exception of a handful of numbers, everything was so dry and tedious that one would assume it was the work of a novice rather than of a mature composer.[44] According to a highly respected Italian writer living in Naples, it was only in the serious arias that one occasionally glimpsed Mozart's genius, revealing what the composer could have achieved if he had been better guided. The keenest, but also the most justified, criticisms came from Berlin in 1796.[45] Rochlitz struck a more tolerant note:

> He was no god, and so he saw himself obliged either to deliver an entirely mediocre piece or to rework only the main numbers as best he could and to dash off the less interesting ones in keeping with the fashionable tastes of the public at large; he rightly chose the latter course.[46]

In Prague *La clemenza di Tito* was initially repeated several times with mounting success, its final performance on 30 September 1791 coinciding with the first night of *Die Zauberflöte*.[47] It then disappeared from the repertory until given at the Burgtheater in Vienna on 31 March 1795 as a benefit performance for Mozart's widow.[48] Its fortunes were also helped, albeit only modestly, by

---

41. Niemetschek, *Leben des k .k. Kapellmeisters Wolfgang Gottlieb Mozart*, 73.
42. Niemetschek, *Leben des k .k. Kapellmeisters Wolfgang Gottlieb Mozart*, 47.
43. *AmZ*, iv (1801/2), 822–3.
44. Schaul, *Briefe über den Geschmack*, 59.
45. *Deutschland*, i (1796), 269–70 and ii (1797), 363–4. Reichardt emphatically denied authorship of these articles in his *Berlinische musikalische Zeitung*, i (1805), 6.
46. Rochlitz, 'Verbürgte Anekdoten', 151.
47. *Briefe*, iv.157 (letter of 7/8 October 1791).
48. Wlassak, *Chronik des k. k. Hof-Burgtheaters*, 98. The part of Sesto was sung by Aloysia Lange; see Hanslick, *Geschichte des Concertwesens in Wien*, 192.

the success of *Die Zauberflöte*. From the end of the century it crops up both in the theatre and in the concert hall in individual towns and cities, including concert performances in Vienna and Breslau[49] and a fully staged production in Frankfurt am Main, all in 1799.[50] In London it was given as a benefit performance for Elizabeth Billington in 1806, the first of Mozart's operas to be heard in the capital.[51] Later performances include productions at the San Carlo in Naples in 1809,[52] in Paris in 1816[53] and at La Scala, Milan, in 1818.[54]

49. Schlesinger, *Geschichte des Breslauer Theaters*, 95.

50. Carl Valentin, *Geschichte der Musik in Frankfurt am Main vom Anfange des XIV. bis zum Anfange des XVIII. Jahrhunderts*, 257. In 1800 Goethe's mother heard the work and was moved to tears at the appearance of the Capitol and at Tito's entry; see *Schriften der Goethe-Gesellschaft*, iv (1889), 198.

51. Reichardt, *Berlinische musikalische Zeitung*, ii (1806), 123; Parke, *Musical Memoirs*, ii.3–4; and Pohl, *Mozart und Haydn in London*, 145–6.

52. Florimo, *La scuola musicale di Napoli*, iv.266.

53. *AmZ*, xviii (1816), 463.

54. Cambiasi, *La Scala*, 308. ◆ The pan-European and nineteenth-century reception of *La clemenza di Tito* has been widely studied since Abert's time. For specific case studies, see Hiltner, '"La clemenza di Tito" von W. A. Mozart im Berliner Musikleben der ersten Hälfte des 19. Jahrhunderts' and '*La clemenza di Tito*' von Wolfgang Amadé Mozart im Spiegel der musikalischen Fachpresse zwischen 1800 und 1850: Rezeptionsgeschichtliche Untersuchungen unter besonderen Berücksichtigungen der Wiener Quellen und Verhältnisse; Senici, '"Adapted to the modern stage": *La clemenza di Tito* in London'; and Cowgill, '"Wise men from the East": Mozart's operas and their advocates in early nineteenth-century London'. More generally, see Senici, *La Clemenza di Tito di Mozart: I Primi Trent'anni (1791–1821)*; Durante, 'Mozarts *La clemenza di Tito* und der deutsche Nationalgedanke: Ein Beitrag zur Titus-Rezeption im 19. Jahrhundert'; and Rice, *W. A. Mozart: La clemenza di Tito*, 104–59.

52

Die Zauberflöte

Disappointed and in failing health,[1] Mozart returned to Vienna in mid-September 1791 in order to resume work on *Die Zauberflöte* and the *Requiem*. The opera was finished on 28 September – the last pieces to be written were the overture and Priests' march – and after extensive rehearsals under the young conductor Johann Baptist Henneberg,[2] the first performance took place on the 30th at Schikaneder's Theater auf der Wieden. Mozart himself conducted it from the keyboard, while Süßmayr turned the pages.

The playbill ran as follows:[3]

Today, Friday 30 Sept. 1791, the Actors of the Imperial and Royal Privileged Theater auf der Wieden will have the honour to perform for the first time

Die Zauberflöte

A grand opera in two acts by Emanuel Schikaneder.

Characters:

Sarastro	Herr Gerl
Tamino	Herr Schack
Speaker	Herr Winter
First ⎫	Herr Schikaneder senior[4]
Second ⎬ Priests	Herr Kistler
Third ⎭	Herr Moll
Queen of Night	Mme Hofer
Pamina, her daughter	Mlle Gottlieb
First ⎫	Mlle Klöpfer
Second ⎬ Ladies	Mlle Hofmann
Third ⎭	Mme Schack
Papageno	Herr Schikaneder junior
An Old Woman	Mme Gerl
Monostatos, a Moor	Herr Nouseul

1. ◆ Although Mozart had been ill in Prague, there is no compelling evidence to link his health at the time, even implicitly, to his final illness. By the same token, there is no unequivocal evidence that he was disappointed and, as Abert notes later, his letters from September and October 1791 are 'high-spirited'. For his biographical agenda, however, it is almost necessary for Abert to see Mozart's high-spirited letters as masking a fatal disappointment, and his failing health as a sign not only of his approaching death, but of the dismal trajectory of his final year.
2. ◆ See Komorzynski, 'Johann Baptist Henneberg, Schikaneders Kapellmeister (1768–1822)'.
3. Copy in the Salzburg Mozarteum. ◆ A facsimile is published in Deutsch, *Mozart und seine Welt*, 257.
4. Schikaneder's elder brother Urban; see Cloeter, *Häuser und Menschen von Wien*, 64ff.

First		Herr Gieseke
Second	} Slaves	Herr Frasel
Third		Herr Starke
Priests, Slaves, Followers		

The music is by Herr *Wolfgang Amade Mozart*, Kapellmeister and actual I. & R. Chamber Composer. Out of his regard for a kind and much-respected audience and out of his friendship for the author of the piece, Herr Mozard will today direct the orchestra himself.

The book of the opera, which includes two copperplate engravings showing Herr Schikaneder wearing his actual costume as Papageno is on sale at the theatre box office for 30 kr.[5]

Herr Gayl, the theatre painter, and Herr Neßlthaler as designer flatter themselves that they have worked with the utmost zeal as artists according to the prescribed plan of the piece.

Prices of admission are as usual.

The performance begins at 7 o'clock.[6]

The work was slow to catch fire, and after the first act Mozart, pale and dismayed, is said to have gone up on stage to see Schikaneder, who did what he could to console him. But the situation improved during the second act, and at the end Mozart was called out on stage. He had hidden, and it was only with difficulty that he could be persuaded to appear. The difference between his own artistic aims and the way in which Viennese audiences responded to his work must have been particularly upsetting at a time when he was so hypersensitive.[7] He also conducted the second performance,[8] and by now the reception was much warmer. Before long *Die Zauberflöte* was proving to be the most successful opera in living memory. Mozart's delight at this development was the one ray of light in the final weeks of his life, as emerges from the high-spirited letters that he dashed off to his wife, who, together with her sister Sophie, had returned to Baden on 7 October. That same day he wrote to her:

> I've just got back from the opera; it was as full as ever. The duetto 'Mann und Weib' etc. and the glockenspiel in the first act was repeated as usual – also the Boys' trio in the 2nd act – but what I like best is the *silent approval*! – you can see the opera continuing to rise in people's estima-tion. As for my own activities: – immediately after you'd sailed away, I played 2 games of billiards

---

5. ◆ Both the engraving of Schikaneder as Papageno and an elaborate title-page are reproduced in Deutsch, *Mozart und seine Welt*, 252–3. For a Masonic interpretation of the title-page, see Brauneis, 'Das Frontispiz im Alberti-Libretto von 1791 als Schlüssel zu Mozarts "Zauberflöte"'.

6. The Three Boys were sung by Nanette Schikaneder, later Mme Eikof, Matthias Tuscher and Handlgruber. Tuscher was later replaced by Franz Maurer, who four years later went on to sing Sarastro. Treitschke, 'Die Zauberflöte, Der Dorfbarbier, Fidelio: Beiträge zur musikalischen Kunstgeschichte', in his transcription of the playbill, gives names in brackets as well. Presumably these parts were doubled: Speaker–Herr Winter (J. Schuster); Second Priest–Herr Kistler (Weiß); Second Lady–Mlle Hofmann (Mme Haselböck); Third Lady–Mme Schack (Mme Gerl); First Slave–Herr Gieseke (Helmböck); Second Slave–Herr Frasel (Strassier); Third Slave–Herr Starke (Trittenwein). ◆ Further concerning the singers at the first performance, see Heinz Schuler, 'Das Zauberflöten-Ensemble des Jahres 1791: Biographische Miszellen'.

7. Among the musicians, by contrast, there were several who recognized the significance of the work from the outset. In his auto-biography, Johann Baptist Schenk, who had a seat in the orchestra at the first performance, crept over to the conductor's chair at the end of the overture and, beside himself with delight, seized Mozart's hand and kissed it, while the latter gave him a friendly glance and stroked his cheek, while continuing to conduct with his right hand. Conversely, the claim that Haydn consoled Mozart with his applause is a myth, as Haydn was already in London by this date; see *Wiener allgemeine Musikzeitung* (1842), 58.

8. The later performances were conducted by Henneberg.

with Herr von Mozart (he's the one who wrote the opera for Schikaneder). – I then sold my nag for 14 ducats. Then I got Joseph to call Primus and fetch some black coffee, while I smoked a wonderful pipe of tobacco.[9]

The following day he returned to the opera and wrote to Constanze immediately afterwards:

Although Saturday is always a bad day as it's post-day, the opera was performed to a full house, with the usual applause and repeats. It'll be given again tomorrow, but there'll be no performance on Monday – and so Süßmayr[10] will have to bring Stoll in on Tuesday, when it will be given again for the *first time*; I say for the *first time* as I expect it'll again be given several times in a row. . . . Leitgeb asked me to take him back, and so I did. Tomorrow I'll take Mama; Hofer has already given her the libretto to read. With Mama, it's a case of *seeing* the opera, rather than *hearing* it. N.N.[11] had a box today, [she] applauded everything, but he, the know-all, proved so typical a *Bavarian* that I had to leave, otherwise I'd have called him an ass. Unfortunately, I was still there when the second act began and, as a result, was present during the most solemn scene, – he laughed at everything. Initially I was patient enought to draw his attention to a number of speeches, but he just laughed at everything; this was too much for me – I called him Papageno and left – but I don't think that the fool understood me.[12] So I went to another box where Flamm was sitting with his wife.[13] There everything was to my liking, and so I stayed to the end. During Papageno's aria with the glockenspiel I went on stage as I felt a great urge to play it myself today; – at the point where Schikaneder stops playing, I played an arpeggio as a joke – he was startled – looked into the wings and saw me – the next time round I did nothing – this time he stopped and refused to continue – I guessed what he was thinking and again played a chord – he then struck the glockenspiel and said 'Shut up'. Everyone then laughed – I think that it was only as a result of this joke that people realized that he doesn't play the instrument himself. By the way, you can't imagine how delightful the music sounds from a box close to the orchestra, much better than from the gallery; you must try it for yourself as soon as you get back.[14]

Even the Italians were fulsome in their praise, as Mozart reported on 14 October:

Yesterday, Thursday the 13th, Hofer drove out with me to see Carl – we lunched there, then drove back into town – at 6 o'clock I collected Salieri and Mme Cavalieri in the carriage and took them to my box – then I hurried back to fetch Mama and Carl, whom I'd left at Hofer's. You can't imagine how kind they both were – and how much they liked not only my music but also the libretto and everything else. They both said it was an opera worthy of being performed at the grandest festivals and before the greatest monarch and that they'd often go and see it – as

9. *Briefe*, iv.157 (letter of 7 October 1791).
10. Illegible. Jahn and Schiedermair read it as 'Sie', which might refer to the opera, but a more plausible reading is 'Snai', Süßmayr's nickname. That he was currently in Baden emerges from the end of this same letter: 'Pull Siessmayer's nose for him and give his hair a proper tug, and give Stoll a thousand greetings. Adieu. The hour is striking – – farewell – we'll meet again!' ◆ *Briefe*, iv.161, agrees that the reference is to Süßmayr. The last eight words are a quotation from *Die Zauberflöte*.
11. ◆ See Arthur, '"N.N." revisited: New light on Mozart's late correspondence'.
12. Perhaps *Schwingenschuh*; see above.
13. Franz Xaver Flamm was a clerk of chancery in Vienna. Well known for his love of music, he was the son-in-law of Haydn's friend, the tenor Johann Michael Spangler; his daughter Antonie began her career as a solo singer in 1794; see Pohl, *Joseph Haydn*, i.119.
14. *Briefe*, iv.159–60 (letter of 8 October 1791).

they'd never seen a more beautiful or delightful piece. – He [Salieri] listened and watched with total attentiveness, and from the overture to the final chorus there wasn't a number that didn't call forth from him a 'bravo' or a 'bello' – they could hardly thank me enough for my kindness. They had intended in any case to go to the opera yesterday, but they'd have had to be in their seats by 4 o'clock – instead they were able to see and hear everything in comfort. – After the performance I drove them home and had supper with Carl at Hofer's – I then drove home with him and we both slept soundly. I couldn't have made Carl happier than by taking him to the opera.[15]

Needless to say, the performances do not appear to have been uniformly excellent, a problem endemic to suburban theatres in general.[16] Even so, Schikaneder continued to mount the work: within the single month of October it was given no fewer than twenty-four times, and by 23 November 1792 he was able to announce the one hundredth performance. By 22 October 1795 it had been performed two hundred times.[17]

For years Schikaneder had been content to perform a mix of serious works, farces and singspiels calculated to appeal to middle-class audiences,[18] but on 11 September 1790 he entered the world of the *Zauberoper* with *Der Stein der Weisen, oder Die Zauberinsel*, a work written by a consortium of composers, including Benedikt Schack.[19] In a move clearly aimed at his rival Karl von Marinelli at the Leopoldstädter Theater, he now began to take an interest in this more highbrow offshoot of the older Viennese machine comedies from the days of Prehauser and Kurz. At that stage in its history the dialogue was still improvised as a concession to its real hero, Hanswurst, in all his manifold guises. Their plots were based on gruesome stories of the crudest kind set in remote or mythical lands and calculated to place extreme demands on the magic skills of the machinist and director. As such, these works were the most primitive representatives of the fairytale element that had been found in *opera buffa* since the time of Cerlone and in *opéra comique* since Duni, whence it had entered the world of the north German singspiel.[20] Under the influence of these various types of work, together with similar trends in literature, the machine play became more respectable in its outward form, coming closer to the singspiel but essentially leaving unchanged

15. *Briefe*, iv.161–2 (letter of 14 October 1791). Mozart's son Karl was currently a boarder at Wenzel Bernhard Heeger's school in Perchtoldsdorf, but Mozart was so unhappy with the arrangement that he was toying with the idea of having him transferred to the Piarists' School; see *Briefe*, iv.161 and 162 (letters of 9 and 14 October 1791). The present letter is a fine example of Mozart's concern for his children's education. He planned to drive out to Baden with Karl on 15 October.

16. On 9 October a report appeared in the *Musikalisches Wochenblatt* in Berlin, claiming that the opera had failed to achieve the hoped-for success 'because the content and language of the piece are simply too bad'; *Musikalisches Wochenblatt*, x (1791), 79 [*Dokumente*, 358, *Documentary Biography*, 409]. Two years later, another Berlin-based journal, the *Berlinische musikalische Zeitung*, reported that 'Mozart's wonderful music for *Die Zauberflöte* is so badly mauled at Schikaneder's theatre that one feels like turning tail and running from such a pitiful sight. And there is not a single singer, male or female, who rises above mediocrity in terms of singing or acting'; *Berlinische musikalische Zeitung historischen und kritischen Inhalts*, i (1793), 142.

17. Thayer, *Ludwig van Beethovens Leben*, i.346; Treitschke, 'Die Zauberflöte', 248, insists that the performance announced as the 200th was in fact the 135th.

18. In 1789 he mounted Schenk's *Das unvermutete Seefest*, in 1790 Part II of *Una cosa rara*, with music by Benedikt Schack [that is, *Der Fall ist noch weit seltner*], and also Schenk's *Das Singspiel ohne Titel*. These were followed in 1791 by *Die Wienerzeitung* by Schenk and others, and in 1792 by *Das Schlaraffenland* by Schack and Franz Gerl. ◆ Concerning Gerl, see Orel, 'Sarastro . . . Hr. Gerl/Ein altes Weib . . . Mad. Gerl' and 'Neue Gerliana'. In general, see Deutsch, 'Das Freihaus-Theater auf der Wieden' and Buch, 'Die Hauskomponisten am Theater auf der Wieden zur Zeit Mozarts (1789–1791)'.

19. ◆ Concerning the possibility that Mozart also contributed to *Der Stein der Weisen*, see Buch, 'Mozart and the Theater auf der Wieden: New attributions and perspectives' and '"Der Stein der Weisen", Mozart, and Collaborative Singspiels at Emanuel Schikaneder's Theater auf der Wieden'; for an edition of the text, see Buch and Jahrmärker, *Schikaneders heroisch-komische Oper "Der Stein der Weisen" – Modell für Mozarts "Zauberflöte". Kritische Ausgabe des Textbuches*.

20. ◆ Concerning fairytale opera in Vienna, see Buch, '"Die Zauberflöte", Masonic Opera, and Other Fairy Tales' and 'Fairy-tale literature and "Die Zauberflöte"'.

the desire for crudely material theatrical spectacle. There is barely a trace of the true spirit of the fairytale in any of these 'fairytale operas'. In Paris, the moribund culture of the French generally sought to combine it with the usual 'contemporary' allusions, while misusing its characters for allegorical ends, whereas in Vienna, by contrast, it often degenerated to the point where, instead of innocently playing with the wondrous, it was often enough concerned only with titillating the senses in the most superficial ways possible. Throughout Europe the Enlightenment did what it could to rob the fairytale of its final vestiges of innocence, with the result that not infrequently these pieces consciously or unconsciously are parodistic in character. The plots, too, are highly circumscribed, with the hero having to brave countless dangers to win back his lover from distant and exotic lands, as in Mozart's *Die Entführung aus dem Serail,* or else he has to call on the help of powerful spirits to rescue her from the hands of an evil sorcerer. In both cases, however, the hero is accompanied by Hanswurst or – as he became known in Vienna from the time of Johann Joseph Laroche – Kasperl.[21] And in the course of the action, this comic character likewise finds a lover for himself. A welcome sourcebook was opened up to these poets by Christoph Martin Wieland's *Oberon* of 1780 and, even more so, by his later collection of stories, *Dschinnistan,*[22] from which Schikaneder had probably already taken the plot of his *Stein der Weisen.*[23] Encouraged by the success of this last-named piece, Schikaneder took up Wieland's collection again and on this occasion his eye was caught by the story 'Lulu oder die Zauberflöte' that was included in the third volume.[24] This was the story that he suggested to Mozart as the basis of their new opera.[25]

The wicked sorcerer Dilsenghuin has stolen a gilt tinderbox from the 'radiant fairy' Perifirime. Its sparks make its owner the lord of the whole of the spirit world. Prince Lulu is the son of the king of Korassan and as yet is untouched by love. It is he, therefore, whom Perifirime chooses to win back the talisman. As a reward she offers him the hand of her daughter Sidi, who has likewise been abducted by the magician and who is now the object of the latter's unwelcome attentions. Perifirime gives Lulu a flute that has the power to win the hearts of all who hear it, together with a ring that allows him to assume whatever shape he wishes. If he throws it from him, it will summon help in the person of the fairy herself. Thus armed, Lulu sets out in the guise of an old man and enters the magician's castle, playing on his flute and in that way taming the beasts of the forest, ingratiating himself with his enemy and, at the same time, winning Sidi's love. At a banquet the magician is drugged and the tinderbox recaptured. With the help of the spirits and finally of the fairy herself his resistance is eventually broken down and he escapes in the shape of an owl. His castle is destroyed and the lovers' union is celebrated at the fairy palace.

This story resembles the opera both in its basic idea and in the role of the miraculous flute, but departs from it so radically in every other respect that it cannot be considered the only source of *Die Zauberflöte.* Like Bretzner before him, Schikaneder drew on a whole series of other works, to some of which he was introduced only while he was already working on his libretto.

---

21. ◆ In general, see Asper, *Hanswurst.*

22. The full title of the original three-volume collection, published in Winterthur between 1786 and 1789, was *Dschinnistan oder auserlesene Feen- und Geistermärchen, teils neu erfunden, teils neu übersetzt und umgearbeitet* (*Dschinnistan or Selected Fairytales and Ghost Stories, partly newly invented, partly newly translated and reworked*).

23. Here, too, there is a persecuted couple, together with a comic child of nature and matching companion, a good and a bad spirit and an ordeal by fire and water. The parallels with *Die Zauberflöte* are obvious; see *Der Freimütige,* ccix (1804); and *AmZ,* vii (1805), 41. Mozart contributed the duet 'Nun liebes Weibchen' K625; see above.

24. The author is August Jakob Liebeskind; the story was published separately in Vienna by Mathias Ludwig in 1791.

25. The Lulu story was later used by Carl Christian Frederik Güntelberg as the basis of a Danish opera set by Friedrich Kuhlau; see *AmZ,* xxx (1828), 540. New light has recently been shed on the genesis of *Die Zauberflöte* by Komorzynski, *Schikaneder,* 109ff. The following remarks are based in the main on Komorzynski's findings.

This is particularly true of Paul Wranitzky's magic opera *Oberon, König der Elfen*, a setting of a poem by one of Schikaneder's actors, Karl Ludwig Gieseke, first staged on 23 July 1791.[26] Here the hero, acting under Oberon's aegis and armed with the latter's magic horn, rescues his lover from the powerful sultan. He is accompanied by his squire Scherasmin, who is absent from the other story and who in *Oberon* wins a wife for himself in the comic character of Fatme. Both sources were merged and further features borrowed from *Dschinnistan*. In this way the 'radiant fairy' became the 'star-flaming queen of night'[27] who, heavily veiled and attended by her female torch-bearers, is discovered seated on her throne.[28] Meanwhile, the magician became the lascivious Moor with his cohort of slaves. The hero is given a portrait of the young woman[29] and also acquires three wise boys as his companions.[30]

On this basis, poet and composer set to work and completed the opera as far as the first-act finale.

The 'Japanese' Prince Tamino is rescued from a wild serpent by the Three Ladies of the 'star-flaming queen'. The birdcatcher Papageno pretends to be Tamino's saviour and as a punishment for his lie has a padlock placed over his mouth. For his part, Tamino receives the portrait of a beautiful young woman that immediately fires his heart with feelings of love. When he discovers that it is Pamina, the daughter of the star-flaming queen, and that she has been abducted by a powerful and wicked magician, he decides to free her. The Queen now arrives in person and promises him her daughter's hand if he succeeds. Papageno's padlock is removed and the Three Ladies order him to accompany Tamino to the wicked Sarastro's castle. To protect them, Tamino is given a flute, Papageno a glockenspiel and, in the words of the Three Ladies, they are to have three additional travelling companions in the persons of 'three little boys, young, comely, lovely and wise'.

The scene changes to Sarastro's castle, where Pamina has attempted to escape from the attentions of her guard, the lascivious Moor Monostatos, but has been recaptured by him. Papageno arrives and the two men flee in terror, but Papageno then recovers sufficiently to tell Pamina that she will shortly be rescued by Prince Tamino. Both hurry off in search of him.

The close parallels with the Lulu story and also with *Oberon* are clear: in both cases the Queen and her Three Ladies and Spirits represent Good, while Sarastro represents Evil – or probably it was not even Sarastro[31] but only the Moor Monostatos who was no doubt intended to be defeated by the power of the magic instruments and of the Queen herself in the course of the following act. But then something strange happened: the whole plan was abruptly turned on its head, with the Queen and her Three Ladies becoming representatives of Evil, while Sarastro became a sublime luminary inhabiting not an enchanted castle but the Temple of Wisdom itself. Sarastro orders the lovers' ordeals not in order to torment them, but in order to purify them. Monostatos remained on the side of Evil, while the Three Boys changed sides and joined the opposing forces, where they found themselves in the company of a whole host of servants of enlightenment. Finally, the lovers are not only united but initiated into the mysteries of enlightened brotherhood. Only Papageno is excluded from these ultimate solemnities. Here, too, *Dschinnistan* offered certain

---

26. His source was not Wieland's version but Friederike Sophie Seyler's 'Romantic Singspiel in 3 Acts after Wieland's *Oberon, or The King of the Elves*'. Gieseke showed little originality and great nerve in using Seyler's version, which first appeared in print in 1789.
27. Wieland, *Dschinnistan*, iii.105ff.
28. Wieland, *Dschinnistan*, i.85 and ii.162.
29. Wieland, *Dschinnistan*, i.118. This motif was already familiar to *opéra comique*; see above.
30. See Komorzynski, *Schikaneder*, 112.
31. Sarastro may have been added only when the plot was revised. Certainly, the fairytale tradition made the Moor a far better embodiment of villainous intrigue than Sarastro.

points of reference, especially for the trials of fire and water (see above) and the injunction to remain silent.[32] In rewriting the story, Schikaneder drew above all on Karl Friedrich Hensler's *Das Sonnenfest der Brahminen*, which Marinelli had staged on 9 September 1790, using it for the Priests' scenes, the appearance of the Temple of the Sun and the new idea of a universal brotherhood of men.[33] Here Mozart found himself back in a world that he had already explored with his incidental music for Gebler's *Thamos, König in Egypten*. This earlier work is set in the Temple of the Sun at Heliopolis and is closely related to the definitive version of *Die Zauberflöte*, except that the heroic note of the earlier piece is replaced by a fairytale element. Recent writers have quite rightly noted a direct link between Gebler's drama and the whole structure of Mozart's opera.[34] Both here and in individual sections of *Dschinnistan* the spirit of Freemasonry is clearly at work, and in both cases the source was the Abbé Jean Terrasson's novel *Sethos, histoire ou vie tirée des monumens anecdotes de l'ancienne Égypte, traduite d'un manuscrit grec*, first published in Paris in 1731. Matthias Claudius's German translation appeared in Breslau in 1777/8[35] and was undoubtedly available to Schikaneder and Mozart. Here the sacred mysteries of the Egyptians are equated with their purported historical descendant, Freemasonry, an equation entirely in keeping with the spirit of the age.[36] Sarastro now became the head of the 'Brotherhood', and Tamino and Papageno, followed by Tamino and Pamina, were required, as novices, to undertake the traditional 'journey through the elements' before they could be accepted into the realm of light and truth. In this way the opera ultimately became a glorification of Freemasonry. This may have been intended as a criticism of Leopold II, who had withdrawn the imperial privileges granted by Joseph II,[37] but, whether or nor this is true, the idea of a universal brotherhood of men, which is heavily stressed in the opera, clearly suggests an act of homage to the late emperor.

Earlier writers[38] attributed this change of plan to Wenzel Müller's opera *Kaspar der Fagottist, oder Die Zauberzither*, a setting of a libretto by Joachim Perinet that Marinelli staged on 8 June 1791 and that was closely based on the Lulu story.[39] Prince Armidoro receives a magic zither from Perifirime, while his companion, the inevitable Kasperl, is given a magic bassoon, which is the inspiration behind some extremely dubious jokes: this in itself is sufficient to give one an idea of the note of low farce that dominates the work as a whole. The music, too, follows the well-worn paths of the contemporary Viennese singspiel, a motley assembly of pieces that fails to come up to the same high level as the better works by Müller, who was in fact not ungifted as a singspiel composer.[40] In spite of all this, the work proved a huge success, a success repeated in 1792 with a sequel by the same team, *Pizichi oder Fortsetzung Kaspars des Fagottisten*. As recent writers have pointed out,[41] it was by no means unusual for different librettists and composers to rework the same material, and not even Mozart's dismissive remark about Müller's opera[42] suggests the least annoyance at the unwelcome competition. In consequence, the reason for the change of plan must be sought elsewhere. Although we have no firm evidence to support this claim, it seems not

32. Komorzynski, *Schikaneder*, 115–16.
33. Komorzynski, *Schikaneder*, 117–18.
34. Komorzynski, *Schikaneder*, 118–19.
35. Komorzynski, *Schikaneder*, 120.
36. Born, 'Ueber die Mysterien der Aegyptier'.
37. Thus Jahn, *W. A. Mozart*, fourth edition, ii.600–1; Jahn's view is refuted by Komorzynski, *Schikaneder*, 121–2.
38. See Jahn, *W. A. Mozart*, ii.598ff.
39. Castelli, *Memoiren meines Lebens*, i.111–12.
40. ◆ Concerning Müller, see Raab, *Wenzel Müller: Ein Tonkünstler Altwiens*; Krone, *Wenzel Müller: Ein Beitrag zur Geschichte der komischen Oper* and Branscombe, 'Music in the Viennese Popular Theatre of the Eighteenth and Early Nineteenth Centuries'.
41. Komorzynski, *Schikaneder*, 114.
42. *Briefe*, iv.137 (letter of 12 June 1791).

unreasonable to suppose that Mozart himself had a hand in it. We know the changes that had taken place within him during the final years of his life and that had long since alienated him from current trends in music. In the case of *La clemenza di Tito*, he had been forced by external factors to return to a world that he thought he had left behind him, while in the case of *Die Zauberflöte* he was initially threatened with an even more dangerous descent into the most primitive of artistic spheres, and we know how insecure he initially felt in this area. Was he to squander his gifts once again on a mere trifle? It was perhaps at this point that he was reminded of the humanitarian ideas that were associated with Freemasonry and that appear to have provided a solution to the problem that he was facing. Mozart no doubt realized that these ethical ideas would raise the work far above all similar pieces and, at the same time, offer him a chance to express freely and uninhibitedly all that he had on his mind. His comment on 'silent approval' shows clearly that he was not interested in writing a work that would merely entertain his suburban audience. Schikaneder, for his part, was happy with the new turn of events, less for ideological reasons than because he hoped to gratify both his audience and the influential Craft by introducing a Masonic element that was entirely new to his theatre. But the introduction of the symbolic notion of the struggle between light and darkness meant that the Queen of Night could no longer embody the principle of Good. Against this background, it seems likely that, as the embodiment of light, Sarastro was introduced into the opera only after the new plan had already been conceived.[43]

This new plot begins with the first-act finale and with the Three Boys leading Tamino to the grove. All that precedes this scene was left unaltered on the grounds that the Queen and her Three Ladies had simply tricked Tamino. Later interpreters have thought that they could justify this inconsistency in all manner of different ways,[44] in certain cases even by having to add new details.[45] In general, far too much is read into the opera. After all, we must never forget that we are dealing with a fairytale whose laws are not those of logical thought processes. Fairytales attach no weight to a pragmatic treatment of the events that they describe but are content to depict a very general mood based on the imagination or on atmosphere. Such a mood is undoubtedly present in *Die Zauberflöte*, which neatly avoids all the pitfalls of illogicality, while there is absolutely nothing in the music of the earlier part of the opera to suggest that the plot has been turned on its head. True, the music here does not introduce us to a world of light, but nor does it usher us into a world of darkness. Rather, it remains true to Mozart's earlier principles and takes us into a world of pure and naïve humanity that is self-sufficient and still innocent of all ethical standards. Least of all would the Queen of Night's aria suggest a good fairy: rather, she appears as an impassioned, sinister, magic figure whose sombre ardour sets her far apart from the world of the other characters. In general, *Die Zauberflöte* proceeds along much calmer lines than any of the composer's earlier operas: abruptness, chaos and uncontrolled emotions are either missing completely or, as in the case of the Queen of Night, are part of an infinitely remote realm. Moreover, we are on what might be termed hallowed ground where humans acquire a life of their own only through their attitude to morality. If Mozart simply retained his existing music for the opening scenes, he was

43. ◆ The alleged plot change can also be read as part of a common 'recognition' topos; see Waldoff, 'The music of recognition: Operatic enlightenment in *The Magic Flute*'.

44. Schurig, for example, draws attention to Nietzsche's ideas in *Jenseits von Gut und Böse* and argues that the way in which good contains an element of evil and vice versa is intentionally symbolic; see Schurig, *Wolfgang Amade Mozart*, ii.259.

45. In his own version of the work, Vulpius, for example, made the Queen of Night Sarastro's sister-in-law, Sarastro's aim being to make over to the God-fearing Tamino the Queen of Night's kingdom to which he himself is the rightful heir. All this is spelt out by Sarastro in his dialogue with the Priests at the beginning of act two. ◆ Further, see Branscombe, '*Die Zauberflöte*: A lofty sequel and some lowly parodies'.

guided by the aim of gradually introducing this sublime idea into the drama, then allowing it to unfold with increasing refulgence. Only with the solemn strains of the Three Boys does a higher order enter the naïve world that we have seen until now. Only now is the fundamental question raised about the opposing forces of good and evil, light and darkness. Only now does the sun of conscious morality rise on a world of unconsciousness. It does not yet shine in all its brilliance, however, but only gradually penetrates the mists of the fairytale. Within this finale the note of naïve innocence that has characterized the work hitherto is now mixed with a note of sublimity. Only with the second act do we enter the hallowed realm itself. In other words, Mozart did not thoughtlessly turn black into white but, with the instinct that comes with genius he developed his main idea, setting out from a broad basis and allowing it to unfold with a powerful increase in intensity. It is not, of course, a logical development that we are dealing with here, but an imaginative and emotional framework that leaves a far greater impression on the listener who responds impartially to Mozart's music than the much-discussed inconsistency, which tends to strike listeners only when they belatedly dissect Schikaneder's libretto from a rational point of view.

If there is now a more or less general consensus concerning the sources of the libretto of *Die Zauberflöte*,[46] the question of its authorship is still unresolved. Even during Schikaneder's own lifetime there were already rumours that he had claimed glory for others' achievements,[47] and following his death other writers began to assert that Johann Georg Karl Ludwig Gieseke, an actor in Schikaneder's company, was the real author of *Die Zauberflöte*.[48] Gieseke was born in Augsburg in 1761 and studied law and mineralogy at Göttingen between 1781 and 1783. After working as an actor with various companies, he was taken on by Schikaneder in 1789 and by 1796 had been appointed the theatre's official poet. But in 1801 he turned his back on the stage and resumed his interest in natural science, building up a reputation in this field, first in Denmark and then as professor of mineralogy in Dublin, where he died on 5 March 1833. As an actor, he was notable more for his skill and versatility than for any original talent, but he distinguished himself as a librettist, arranging pieces for the theatre and writing occasional verses, often of a patriotic stamp. We have already encountered him as the librettist of Wranitzky's *Oberon*.

The remarkable thing about this whole question is that it was only long after Schikaneder's death and only in the course of a single conversation that Gieseke is said to have claimed credit for a work that by then was extremely famous. His long silence was attributed to his fear of reprisals for his Masonic proclivities, a fear that seems implausible when we recall that both Mozart and Schikaneder were Masons. Gieseke was right to assert this claim to the extent that his *Oberon* inspired his employer to embark on his original version of *Die Zauberflöte*, and, as was often the case with such popular pieces, he may even have made a modest contribution to its continuation, but this would not justify us in ascribing to him authorship of the work as a whole. Moreover, the finished libretto reflects Schikaneder's hand far more than that of the far less skilful Gieseke. Until

---

46. ◆ For further, detailed discussion of the opera's literary sources, including the Arthurian romance *Yvain or Le Chevalier au Lion*, Terrasson's *Sethos*, Gebler's *Thamos, König in Egypten*, Born's essay on the mysteries of the Egyptians, Wieland's *Dschinnistan*, Wranitzky's *Oberon* and Perinet's *Der Fagottist, oder Die Zauberzither*, see Branscombe, *W. A. Mozart: Die Zauberflöte*, 4–34.

47. According to one rumour, a cleric at the Paulanerkirche on the Wieden, Pater Cantes, wrote the arias for Schikaneder's operas out of his sheer love of the medium; another name mentioned in this context is that of the curate at St Stephen's, one Herr Wüst; see Komorzynski, *Schikaneder*, 123.

48. See Dent, *Mozart's Opera: The Magic Flute*, 33ff.; and Blümml, 'Karl Ludwig Gieseke als Gelegenheitsdichter'. His real name was Metzler and in 1819 he is said to have told the opera manager Julius Cornet that he was the real author of *Die Zauberflöte*; see Cornet, *Die Oper in Deutschland*, 24–5; see also *Illustriertes Familienbuch zur Unterhaltung & Belehrung häuslicher Kreise,* ii (1852), 19. Jahn was told something similar by Neukomm; see Jahn, *W. A. Mozart*, ii.601. ◆ More recently, see Heinz Schuler, 'Schikaneder contra Gieseke: Eine Dokumentation zur Verfasserfrage des Zauberflöten-Librettos'.

there is convincing proof to the contrary, we shall do well to regard Schikaneder and Mozart as the true authors of *Die Zauberflöte* and to limit Gieseke's contribution to the input outlined above.[49]

Quite apart from its alleged inconsistency, the libretto of *Die Zauberflöte* has been condemned and criticized more than all other Mozart's opera librettos put together. From a purely literary point of view, it is not difficult, of course, to find fault with its crudely fashioned structure, its primitive characters and situations and a text that is banal and tasteless by turns.[50] Yet none of these shortcomings has prevented the work from making an impression, with not only the public at large but its spiritual leaders, too, invariably speaking out in its defence. Goethe conceded that the text was 'full of implausibilities and jokes that not everyone can understand and appreciate, but one must at all events grant that the author was well versed in the art of making effective use of contrasts and of producing grand theatrical effects'.[51] Although it was never completed, he began his own sequel to *Die Zauberflöte* as early as 1795, 'in order not only to meet the public on the path of its own pleasure but also to make it easier for actors and theatre managements to perform a new and complex piece'.[52] As the main reason for the opera's success, Herder singled out its basic idea of the struggle between light and darkness.[53] And Beethoven, too, preferred it to all Mozart's other operas. Or at least he did not dismiss its libretto, as he did in the case of both *Le nozze di Figaro* and *Don Giovanni*.[54] Of the impressive list of later writers who leapt to the text's defence, suffice it to mention only Hegel,[55] Otto Ludwig[56] and David Friedrich Strauß.[57] More recently, it has even been described as the finest opera libretto ever written.[58]

These assessments certainly come far closer to the truth than those of the opposing faction that set out from a literary and technical standpoint. Quite apart from the fact that the text has many of the features of a fairytale which, as we pointed out above, never feels indebted to the laws of common logic, it can boast a whole series of other qualities that raise it far above so many later librettos, for all that these may be superior in linguistic and logical terms, and that explain its lasting success. These qualities reside not only in the naïve depiction of the elemental conflict that lies at the root of all popular drama and that cries out to be set to music, namely, the conflict between light and darkness and good and evil, but also in the detailed way in which this conflict is portrayed. As we have seen, the action unfolds so that the tension gradually increases, using theatrically effective contrasts that reveal the man of the theatre and culminating in the ordeal by fire and water, after which the tension is released without any sense of discursiveness. There are never any points at which the action grinds to a halt, as it occasionally does in the earlier operas,

49. Of Mozart's various biographers, Jahn declared his cautious support for Gieseke's claim in the first three editions of his life of the composer, but in revising Jahn for its fourth edition, Deiters aligned himself instead with Komorzynski's opposing view, which had been published in the meantime. Schurig follows him in this; see Schurig, *Wolfgang Amade Mozart*, ii.253. Dent, by contrast, continues to insist that the librettist was Gieseke, without, however, adducing any convincing reasons for doing so; Dent, *Mozart's Opera: The Magic Flute*, 45–6. Blümml leaves the question open; Blümml, 'Karl Ludwig Gieseke', 113.
50. ◆ Further, see Manfred Schuler, 'Zeitgenössische Kritik an Schikaneders Textbuch "Die Zauberflöte"', and Meinhold, *Zauberflöte und Zauberflötenrezeption: Studien zu Emanuel Schikaneders Libretto "Die Zauberflöte" und seiner literarischen Rezeption*.
51. Eckermann, *Gespräche mit Goethe*, ii.358 (entry of 13 April 1823).
52. Letter to Wranitzky of 24 January 1796. Wranitzky also offered to set the libretto, in which Zelter had already shown an interest; see *Briefwechsel zwischen Goethe und Zelter*, i.368. On Goethe's work on the libretto, see his correspondence with Schiller; *Briefwechsel zwischen Goethe und Schiller*, ii.459–61, and *Briefwechsel zwischen Goethe und Zelter*, i.42 and 376. On the poem itself, see Junk, *Goethes Fortzetzung der Mozartschen Zauberflöte*; and Morris, *Goethe-Studien*, i.310ff. The fragment is a kind of preliminary study for *Faust*. Goethe also had a hand in Vulpius's reworking of the text; see Wustmann, 'Zum Text der Zauberflöte'.
53. Herder, *Adrastea*, ii.284.
54. Thayer, *Ludwig van Beethovens Leben*, iv.211 and v.199.
55. Hegel, *Vorlesungen über die Ästhetik*, 203.
56. Bartels, *Otto Ludwigs Werke*, vi.307.
57. Strauß, *Der alte und der neue Glaube*, 351; see also the two poems in Strauß's *Poetisches Gedenkbuch*.
58. See the eminently readable study by Waltershausen, *Die Zauberflöte: Eine operndramatische Studie*.

especially in *Le nozze di Figaro*, either as a result of a lack of dramatic skill on the part of the librettist or out of consideration for individual singers. Here the uncomplicated characterization allows the composer the greatest possible scope for further development, with the librettist making his task easier for him chiefly by dint of the fact that all the characters are borne along by the drama from the moment of their first vital appearance. None of them stops to brood on the situation but is immediately overwhelmed by it, thereby playing his or her part in advancing the action.

This is true not only of the individual characters but also of the groups of Three Ladies and Three Boys that are so typical of the work. Inspired by the Masonic symbolism of the number three, which plays such a major role elsewhere in the work, they lend the piece its perfect symmetry.[59] Each of the two main factions has its own group, with the Three Ladies aligned with the Queen of Night, the Three Boys with Sarastro. Sarastro is additionally accompanied by the Speaker, the Queen of Night by Monostatos. Between them, equally symmetrically, stands the serious couple and, behind the latter, the comic couple. For Mozart, the Masonic symbolism proved particularly fruitful, not least because he had already experimented with this kind of symmetrical arrangement in *Così fan tutte*, with its three groups of couples.

But the greatest advantage that the text could offer was that it ideally complemented Mozart's idiosyncratic working method. Here he had everything that he demanded: a 'plan' that was well developed and theatrically effective and verse that could be used for dramatic ends while at the same time proving itself 'the obedient daughter of the music', for, although unpretentious, it cried out to be set to music, being succinct and unambiguous and, as such, not the sort that 'ruin the composer's whole idea'. There is no doubt that Mozart recognized Schikaneder's often intolerable trivialities for what they are, but he knew that the scenes are all well motivated and filled with life. And he could trust himself to write music that would allow listeners to overlook Schikaneder's wooden verse just as it had enabled them to overlook Da Ponte's stilted poetry. Indeed, Schikaneder's verse was less dangerous in that Da Ponte could never resist the temptation to play the part of the self-regarding man of letters and thereby get in his way.

Mozart exploited these advantages in a highly particular way. Of the many surprises that characterize his development, *Die Zauberflöte* is arguably the greatest as it is based on a completely new approach to drama and, indeed, on a completely new view of the world. With the exception of *La clemenza di Tito*, his last three operas had allowed the action on stage to make its impact on its own terms, without applying any moral standards, whereas *Die Zauberflöte* relates everything, be it plot or characters, to a single basic moral idea. Its figures are no longer the products of a naïve delight in artistic creativity that is content to depict the emotional and psychological forces contained within each and every one of them. Instead, the characters draw their lifeblood from this single basic idea. This is the goal to which they all aspire, and, depending on their relationship to it, they are divided into good and evil. Even in *Die Entführung aus dem Serail* – the work that is closest to this new approach to drama – Mozart ascribes far less importance to the unfolding ethical belief.

The idea of giving symbolic expression to this idea is entirely typical of the final decades of the eighteenth century. Love and friendship are the forces that show Tamino the way to goodness. But this goodness consists in acting for the general happiness of future humanity, a happiness that contemporaries hoped would be achieved if all men became brothers and aspired to the noblest humanity. The old world, with its divisive class differences, has vanished. When the Speaker questions Tamino's steadfastness in act two on the grounds that he is a prince, Sarastro retorts: 'More than that – he is a man!' Here the king's son becomes a willing student of the cosmopolitan

59. The number of Priests at the beginning of act two, for example, is $18 = 2 \times 3 \times 3$.

representative of supreme wisdom – a favourite dream of the age and one that was bound up with its whole longing for a better world. Sarastro was merely echoing the mood of the time when he described this meeting of initiates as 'one of the most important of our age'. And Mozart's music subscribes to this ideal with a sense of mystically sublime awe, thus placing it in the tradition of other 'classical' works that adopt a similar outlook and that range from Lessing's *Nathan der Weise* to Schiller's *Don Carlos*, Goethe's *Iphigenie auf Tauris* and Beethoven's ninth symphony. There is something profoundly symbolic to the fact that *Die Zauberflöte* was unveiled to the world not in one of the great theatres of the court and aristocracy but in the popular Theater auf der Wieden: from the outset it was aimed not merely at 'connoisseurs and music lovers' but at a far wider community that had no monopoly of artistic understanding. At the end of his life its creator revealed that he had after all been affected by the powerful intellectual movement that had found its most potent expression in the French Revolution of two years earlier. From the very beginning he had been predisposed to develop in this direction, as his whole moral outlook was rooted in humanism and on a desire, based on freedom of conscience and of the individual, to live only for himself and, hence, for the community as a whole. In *Die Zauberflöte* this aspect of his character assumed the form of an artistic creed.

Love had been the basic theme of all Mozart's earlier operas, but in this final work it was subordinated to the ethical idea discussed above. It is no longer a basic human instinct that expresses itself with the violence of a force of nature but a quality that acquires its value only when combined with virtue and wisdom. It is 'the possession of love and virtue' that Tamino seeks at a particularly significant point in his scene with the Speaker in the Temple of Wisdom. And the way in which Mozart brings out this basic idea through the use of contrast is entirely worthy of him, with the pair of idealized lovers contrasted with Papageno and Papagena. Traditionally, this was the place for the inevitable buffoonery, but the approach that Mozart adopted to this last-named couple is similar to the one that he adopted to Leporello, incorporating them organically into the action and using them to throw the main pair of lovers into sharper dramatic focus. The higher world of Tamino is constantly measured by the standards of Papageno's lower world, and in that way the exceptional nature of his quest is emphasized. Yet Papageno should certainly not be seen as a caricature of the hero. Although virtue and wisdom are denied him and, indeed, beyond his comprehension, he, too, regards love as the source of supreme happiness in his life. He can therefore echo Pamina's comment: 'Wir leben durch die Lieb' allein' ('We live by love alone'), and when he is threatened with the loss of this supreme happiness, he immediately resolves to end his worthless existence, only to be prevented from doing so by the same Three Boys. Like Tamino, he has a magic instrument which, in spite of all the dangers to which he is exposed, finally helps him to achieve his heart's desire. Although he is prevented from achieving the highest sanctity in love, that love still rests on the basis of a naïve and heartfelt emotion and, hence, of natural morality. Here it is enough to compare his final duet with the deeply offensive numbers that treat this theme in other Viennese singspiels in order to appreciate how morally noble is Mozart's whole approach to this character. Above all, he avoids any suspicion of lubricity and lewdness. That this was intentional is clear from the figure of the Moor. Here sensual love becomes a caricature of itself and, as in the case of Osmin, assumes the character of lasciviousness. Like *Don Giovanni*, albeit from a completely different standpoint, *Die Zauberflöte* shows us love in its most manifold guises, each of which supports and explains the other.

This new approach to drama naturally resulted in a completely different style. Not without good reason commentators have often expressed their astonishment at Mozart's ability to create two such different works as *Don Giovanni* and *Die Zauberflöte* within such a relatively short space of time. The fact that they are examples of different genres is not in itself sufficient to explain this difference, as *Die Zauberflöte* occupies a special place even within its own genre, the German singspiel. What is new about *Die Zauberflöte* is not its range of styles, extending from the simple popular song to the figural chorale and to choral scenes of Gluckian grandeur – the older Viennese singspiel composers had had all these styles at their disposal – but the inspired way in which Mozart places this variety in the service of the drama, an approach that attests to the highest understanding of art. Whereas composers of the older generation often drew on this range of styles in a thoroughly indiscriminate way and were thereby prevented from achieving the effects that they might otherwise have done, each of the styles that Mozart uses acquires a special dramatic significance as a result of the care with which he chooses to use it in each individual instance. It is not only on this, however, that the greatness of his work lies, but on the wonderful musical unity that it displays and that sets it apart from its predecessors. Only a creative genius of Mozart's stature could risk melting down and recasting all these different elements to create a new artistic whole. As proof of this we may cite not only the extraordinarily unified musical design as such but also the return of certain melodic, harmonic and rhythmic types with quite specific dramatic aims, individual examples of which we shall see in a moment.[60]

As with *Don Giovanni*, so with *Die Zauberflöte*, the listener seems to be transported into a totally alien world from the very first bars of the overture. The three solemn dotted chords – in E flat major, which represents the most awesome sublimity in this opera – recall Masonic number symbolism, while the dotted rhythm will later be found within the opera itself as a musical symbol of the world of the Priests.[61] It, too, clearly reflects the influence of Masonic ideas. But even on a purely musical level, this rising triadic melody functions as a powerful motto for the work as a whole, with the notes of the triad and their various melodic and harmonic possibilities proving particularly important for the music of the opera in general.[62] This solemn call initially produces a curiously tense, yet mystically thoughtful mood repeatedly interrupted by the mysteriously shuddering sforzatos in the full orchestra (including trombones). The rhythmic motif from the first three bars continues in the cellos and double basses, before being taken up by the first violins.[63] But the tension stems, in the main, from the way in which the music encircles the dominant B flat in the bass, initially leading down to the subdominant, then, following a particularly expressive shift to the minor by means of a typically Mozartian sharpening of the A flat to A, growing increasingly purposeful, with the intervals becoming narrower, until the dominant is reached three bars from the end of the Adagio and at the same time keenly reinforced. The tremendous tension generated by this harmonic process is further emphasized by the syncopated accompaniment, which at the point where the note-values are halved is joined by a twofold crescendo and by *piano* chords in the trombones, the mysterious impact of which had already been tried out in *Don Giovanni*. Never has the sense of reverential awe evoked in the human soul by a mysteriously

60. For a select bibliography, see Wurzbach, *Mozart-Buch*, 156, and Curzon, *Essai de bibliographie Mozartine: Revue critique des ouvrages relatifs à W. A. Mozart et ses œuvres*, 29–30; for more recent writings, see Dent, *Mozart's Opera: The Magic Flute*, and Waltershausen, *Die Zauberflöte*. The autograph manuscript of the full score (K620) is in the Staatsbibliothek zu Berlin; see Schnyder von Wartensee, 'Notizen über die Zauberflöte von Mozart', 41–3. ◆ For more recent literature, see in particular the bibliography in Branscombe, *W. A. Mozart: Die Zauberflöte*.
61. See Waltershausen, *Die Zauberflöte*, 62–3.
62. I am grateful to the as yet unpublished investigations of my pupil, Fritz Jöde, for a number of ideas in this regard. ◆ See Jöde, 'Durchgeführte harmonische Organisierung bei Mozart'.
63. Here, too, the number three plays an important role. The call rings out three times; and the whole three-bar structure (bars 1–3) is repeated three times in triadic steps in the bass, before being repeated three times in a different form in the first violins, violas and cellos.

sublime phenomenon been expressed in so inspired a way as in these first sixteen bars, in which the tension builds from the third bar onwards with no appreciable interruption.

The tension is then released in the allegro. It is not a fugue but a sonata movement that occasionally comes close to a fugue in style, notably at the very beginning, but in general reveals the sort of free amalgamation of contrapuntal and thematic procedures that we already know as a characteristic feature of Mozart's late style. But this strict style reappears only once more in the course of the opera, in the scene with the two Men in Armour, suggesting a particular aim here, as a symbol of the work's supreme idea, the triumph of full and noble humanity over all hostile forces. As a result, the allegro follows on logically from the adagio: awe of the divine gives way to the free deployment of all the forces that strive towards this ultimate goal. But the overture tells us nothing about the dramatic conflict that is to follow. Like its predecessors, it was the last number to be written and in consequence is a kind of general lyrical admission of Mozart's feelings about the work as a whole. Once more he relives the artistic experience that produced the opera, but instead of the work in its concrete form, it is the mood that inspired *Die Zauberflöte* that he now intends to instil in the listener before the following drama can make its impression – but it is, of course, the mood of the work as he, its creator, felt it. The most remarkable aspect of this allegro is the fact that the most profound earnestness is clothed in the most ethereal, weightless form. Mozart's starting point had been the fairytale, which struck him as the best possible basis for the symbolism of his plot, yet it was the fairytale not as a storehouse of frosty allegories or crudely titillating assaults on the listener's nerves but as a world far removed from common reality and, as such, reminiscent of Schiller's 'What has never happened anywhere, that alone never grows old'.[64] Like the overture to *Die Entführung aus dem Serail*, the present allegro ushers us into a world of genuine fairytale poetry, except that on this occasion it is far more spiritualized and profound. Only once, in the three wind chords, does Mozart allude directly to the sublime idea that underpins the work as a whole and remind the listener of the spiritual goal to which these ethereal measures aspire, while at the same time looking back to the solemn mood of the adagio.

The opening bar of the allegro overlaps with the final bar of the adagio. Its first subject is as follows:

It consists of two parts. The highest notes in the melodic line in the first part again produce the sharply accented degrees of the E flat major triad, except that there is now a new element in the form of a dominant-based tension that is further intensified by the energetic leap of a fifth with its sforzato slide. But its chief characteristic continues to be its return to the third.[65] Its melodic resolve is weaker than that of the interval of the fifth, which explains why, in the second section, this reduction in energy is made good by the music's twice encircling the third-based ending by

64. ◆ From his 'An die Freunde' of 1802.
65. Herein lies the fundamental difference between Mozart's theme and Clementi's, quoted above, which is no more than an ordinary Italian 'rocket' theme. In short, Clementi's pride in his priority was singularly ill founded.

means of the latent sequence of cadences familiar from the older period: VI–IV–V–I.[66] The upper melodic line

contains within itself the nucleus of a later, important contrapuntal line. As a result, the subject is far from trifling in tone, but energetic and purposeful, however much the recurrent staccato quavers lend it an air of lightness and fantastical immateriality. Its musical qualities are not, of course, Mozart's own invention: melodically speaking, it is based on a model that can be traced back to Hasse's time. But classical period composers were not concerned with the originality of their thematic ideas, preferring to base their movements on material generally derived from musical archetypes that serves merely as the starting point for further creative development.[67] In keeping with his normal practice at this time, Mozart develops all two hundred and eleven bars of the present section from the theme quoted above, first treating it fugally, then in free counterpoint. None of the countermelodies that it generates is overlooked in the course of what follows. The most important of these countermelodies is as follows, its two main elements (a) and (b) even being independently developed:[68]

The first statement of the subject is followed not by the old tutti entry but by the theme itself in an intensified form, with its first two elements extended. In the case of the second, the intervals are reversed, so that the interval of a fifth now comes at the end:

With the firm harmonic steps that characterize this overture, the music now proceeds to F major, the dominant of the expected second subject. But instead of an abrupt conclusion, there follows an intimate, thematic transitional passage in which the earlier pedal point continues to reverberate on a purely notional level and the flute descends stepwise from *g″* to *d″*, filling out the triadic harmonies with chromatic scales.[69] What had originally been a mere detail becomes the main element in the actual second subject, providing the starting point for a ravishing dialogue between flute and oboe[70] over the thematic exchange between bassoons and clarinets that likewise harks back to the earlier section. This delightful idyll for the winds is the most intimate passage in this

---

66. This encircling motion recalls older fugue subjects, including the first from Bach's *Well-Tempered Clavier*.

67. In the works of Romantic composers, conversely, this creative energy is often already spent within the initial 'original' themes, with the result that it then has to be maintained by all manner of other initiatives imposed from without and designed to create a sense of atmosphere.

68. This descending scalar counterpoint is frequently found in Mozart.

69. This is the last remaining trace of the brief chromatic scalar passages that Mozart had previously been fond of using in order to reach his second subjects.

70. Here, too, we are dealing with the simple tonic–dominant relationship. Note also the fondness for the degrees of the triad, a fondness that becomes clearer at the recapitulation.

whole section,[71] with even the powerful first element of the theme acquiring a note of innocent and light-hearted playfulness. And the second element now joins in, not *in propria persona*, however, but in the guise of a variant of its syncopated counterpoint – this is a particularly inspired touch that serves at the same time to heighten the atmosphere. Ultimately, then, this second subject is an utterly inspired variant of the first. The final idea

is likewise developed from the second element of the theme, with the intervals now in a different direction. Once again a tremendous amount of tension is generated through the encircling of the tonic of B flat major, the constant interplay between tonic and dominant and the sixfold repeat of the motif over a crescendo which on this occasion does not adopt the Mannheim model but uses register to create its effect.[72] As a result, the end of this section acquires a particularly solid foundation that looks forward to the following mystical appearance of the three wind chords. Although remarkable in its own right, this final group may also contain an element of Masonic symbolism. The famous three wind chords, thrice repeated and again ascending triadically, later return in the assembly of the Brotherhood as a sign that Tamino should be accepted into their midst and admitted to the trials. The same rhythm is used in Masonic Lodges, in the form of knocking or some other means, to welcome a member who has come to be tested.[73] An echo of this solemn ritual is found in the Allegro's development section, with its use of minor keys (previously hardly touched on) and increased use of counterpoint. Even the d'' flat of the second violins has an elemental force to it. Above all, however, the second element of the theme now contracts and acquires a note of timidity and weariness:

It then disappears completely, allowing greater prominence to the scalar counterpoint, which by moving in the opposite direction to the theme's interval of a fifth serves to increase the impression of a conflict. In the development section the crisis indicated by these wind chords casts its dark shadows over this carefree scene, symbolizing the struggle over the high ideal that they represent. The first element of the theme rises higher and higher, powerfully exploiting the tension between tonic and dominant, with the conflict reaching its climax in the section in G minor. The modulations cease. The upper voice follows the bass with the first element of the theme in canon, its rhythm strangely distorted and twisted. The theme now throws up a sixth instead of its earlier

71. Waltershausen's attempt to relate this to Papageno and Papagena strikes me as somewhat forced; see Waltershausen, *Die Zauberflöte*, 64.
72. The reinforcement always occurs after two bars, thereby producing three elements. Perhaps there is another allusion to the mystic trinity here.
73. This settles the doubts expressed by earlier writers, who had wondered whether the second and third chords should be tied; see André's preface to his edition of the overture. Peter Winter gives even greater emphasis to this rhythm in *Das Labyrinth*, the official sequel to *Die Zauberflöte*.

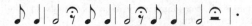

fifth, but in vain, as the bass draws the musical argument irrevocably downwards, step by step, to the subdominant of G minor, emphatically preparing the way for this section to end in this key. But then, instead of this ending, there is a full bar's rest, as though the composer had suddenly shied away from drawing this ultimate conclusion and indicating a stagnation of the rhythmic life of this section. The main beat is avoided by means of the rest or, rather, it is steered in a different direction that offers a way out of the crisis. This is the point at which Mozart generally returns to the recapitulation along lines as brief as they are harmonically bold, but here he prefers a broader canvas that recalls the second subject in terms of its treatment and sonorities. Interrupted by a figure in the flutes and bassoons two octaves apart, the opening motif from the main theme flutters mysteriously through the circle of fourths from C minor to E flat minor, unable to gain a firm foothold, when suddenly the sun breaks through the mist with the unexpected entry of E flat major, and the recapitulation begins. Initially it is treated very freely. The fugal textures are missing, as is the second element of the theme. And at the outset the tone is still fairly hesitant, its old freedom returning only with the basses' ascent through a fifth, in canon with the violas.[74] Once again the scalar counterpoint that trickles incessantly downwards in countermotion to it creates an effective contrast. From now on the development section pursues its anticipated course, except that the main idea now emerges more clearly in the second subject. The tension-laden crescendo of the final subject that had previously prepared the way for the wind chords now summons into existence an apparently new idea:[75]

But it, too, turns out to be rooted in the second element of the theme and to be palpably related to the final theme heard earlier. What is striking about this idea is not only the diminished interval based around the third of the subdominant,[76] but also the two-part harmonies and the *fortissimo* marking, the first such marking since the beginning of the adagio. These thunderous three chords again suggest a symbolic significance, while at the same time bringing the overture to an end on a note of the greatest splendour and the most sublime earnestness. The idea of a deeper symbolism is further increased by the unexpected *piano* that enters eight bars later. Here, for the first time in this allegro, the main theme descends through the whole of the E flat major triad, before the brilliant ending begins. If we accept the popular image of a bright light constantly increasing in intensity throughout the whole of this final section,[77] we may well imagine a single radiant star disappearing in a universal sea of light at this point.

The Introduction ('Zu Hilfe! zu Hilfe! sonst bin ich verloren') launches straight into the liveliest dramatic action, with Tamino, in desperate straits, rescued from the serpent by the Three Ladies. Mozart deals with this idea in a series of independent sections linked together by vague motivic reminiscences, their basic tonalities those of the triad C–E flat–G–C. And it is with this triad that the Introduction begins:

74. It is again the interval of the E flat major triad that is traversed here.
75. The bar in parentheses is an upbeat of elemental tension.
76. This close encircling of the degrees of the triad is a characteristic feature not only of the overture but of the opera as a whole.
77. See Oulibicheff, *Mozart's Leben*, iii.400–1; and Jahn, *W. A. Mozart*, ii.610.

The prelude is extremely long by Mozart's standards and clearly depicts Tamino's desperation, his violent onslaught followed by his retreat and, finally, his mortal fear as he gasps for breath. This is not the sort of introduction that we associate with a hero,[78] but we are not dealing here, of course, with an *opera seria*, but with a fairytale, quite apart from the fact that the attack by the serpent – the Masonic symbol of evil[79] – has a special significance: here we encounter Tamino at the most critical phase in his earthly existence, almost succumbing to the powers of darkness. In view of the situation in which he finds himself, his vocal interjections are extremely brief, yet strikingly expressive. He begins with two breathless three-bar phrases, with a palpable sense of relief coming on the word 'Götter', the whole of this section being manly in tone, with no trace of effeminate fear.[80] The wicked serpent then slithers in to the sound of heavy triadic intervals, one of the few examples in the opera of tone-painting. Tamino's desperate calls become increasingly realistic, while the dark character of C minor asserts itself with ever greater intensity and implacability,[81] at which point the Three Ladies rescue him with a simple interrupted cadence on A flat, again with the help of a unison triadic motif.[82] The deployment of timpani and trumpets here allows a trace of irony to enter the music, and this becomes more pronounced in the following sections, ultimately becoming one of the number's principal attractions. After all, these women are not the brave Amazons that the powerful orchestration and resplendent sonorities would have us think. At least, they themselves attach no particular importance to this, but turn their attentions to quite different matters. Their magic nature is revealed by the combination of three women's voices with two soft-toned winds (generally flutes and clarinets), with the violins or, at most, cellos taking the bass line, producing a remarkably ethereal, weightless sound that might well indicate their original nature as good fairies, especially at the translucent textures at 'Durch unsres Armes Tapferkeit'. But it soon emerges that behind their fay exterior lurk three extremely earthly daughters of Eve. It is with masterly subtlety that the stirring of their senses is depicted by the brief and swelling entry of a tender A flat major after the solemn strains of E flat major. For the first time the three voices now go their separate ways, but the underlying emotion remains the same, as is clear from the good-humoured fourfold repeat of the same sequence of harmonies I–IV–V–I. The Third Lady reveals herself as a humorist with the interval of a seventh in the phrase 'Ja, ja, gewiß, zum Malen schön' ('Yes, yes, of course, as pretty as a picture'). And in all subsequent ensemble passages she has

---

78. This impression is increased, but with no justification, if he enters without his bow, which is specifically mentioned in the stage directions and which indicates that he has already begun fighting with the serpent, albeit in vain.
79. The beast was originally a 'fierce lion', but Mozart evidently replaced this by the 'cunning serpent' when the plot was reworked in the spirit of Freemasonry.
80. Compare this with an Italianate setting of the same text:

sonst bin ich ver - lo - ren

81. With the expansion of the ending, *Affekt* and musical logic are again in perfect congruity: in the wake of the earlier section ('Ach, rettet mich'), musical logic demands a broader conclusion.
82. Note the striking brevity with which the serpent is 'cut into three pieces' with the vigorous thrust of the sudden chord of the seventh.

a tendency to strike out on her own, notably at 'Würd' ich mein Herz',[83] where the characteristic sonorities of all the trios for the Three Ladies find particularly attractive expression. But as they gaze at the handsome youth, we feel divisions arising among them, and with the entry of the staccato motif and its triplet upbeat, the ethereal glow that attends these characters fades, and during their description of their Queen and her peace of mind,[84] they begin to eye each other like cats defending their territory. Minor keys enter for the first time, their remarks become more cutting and sharp-tongued, and the triadic motif at the word 'Ich bleib' indessen hier' ('But I'll stay here') already starts to sound like a fanfare. In short, we are faced by the threat of a distinctly unfairylike quarrel between women of a kind familiar from *opera buffa*.[85] But Mozart shows his usual tact in avoiding the coarseness so often associated with such scenes, using the section in G major to introduce a German folklike tone, with a type of melody that is often found in *Die Zauberflöte*.[86] In this way the threatening quarrel is defused and transformed into an expression of charming roguery in keeping with the whole tone of the fairytale, with all seriousness removed from the situation at this most critical juncture in the text. Unlike their squabbling colleagues in *opera buffa*, the Three Ladies can still appreciate the humour of their situation. How mischievous are the little wind figures that we hear between their own contributions! Meanwhile, the music follows each twist and turn of the text, beginning with the amused 'Ei, ei, wie fein' ('How smart'), followed by the delightful but highly revealing 'Sie wären gern bei ihm allein' ('They'd like to be alone with him') and its contrasting consequent phrase, which charmingly gives the lie to the idea contained in the antecedent as though it were the most natural thing in the world.[87] As none of the Ladies is prepared to give ground to the others, they are left with no choice but to leave together, but this decision causes their feelings to flare up anew, and once again a genuine *buffa* scene seems to be inevitable in the allegro: even the motif in the orchestra is familiar from Mozart's Italian operas,[88] while the scalar motifs that shoot up and down are equally *buffa*-like. Note the finely observed way in which, at this moment of disappointment, the Three Ladies' feelings get the better of them and how, whenever they deny their higher natures, their tone ceases to be German and becomes Italian. But, as before, their agitation is short-lived, and the ending ('Du Jüngling schön und liebevoll') brings us back once again to the folklike tone, while at the same time clothing them in its gossamer-like instrumental raiment. With its third-based sonorities the melodic line suggests the somewhat wistful air of a German folksong,[89] yet it acquires a subtle humour as a result of the brief languishing motif in the first oboe at the end of the phrase. The women look forward to seeing Tamino again with a delight that is both appealing and typically Mozartian, their pleasure finding

83. Her entry is splendidly prepared by the previous triadic motif in the violas and bassoons.
84. Strangely enough, their previous love tune returns at the words 'Vielleicht, daß dieser schöne Mann'. Note the subtle contribution of the bassoons here.
85. Cf. the trio 'Ich bin die erste Sängerin' from *Der Schauspieldirektor*; see above.
86. It is the simple sequence

The opening third, *b'*, is generally reached by an upbeat from the fifth; for other examples, see Papageno's 'Schön Mädchen jung und rein' in the trio 'Du feines Täubchen' and 'Das klinget so herrlich' in the first-act finale.
87. At this point the cellos and double basses again fall silent.
88. Cf. the trio ('Susanna or via sortite') in *Le nozze di Figaro*.
89. It is a type of melody that returns in the first-act finale at 'Könnte jeder brave Mann'.

expression in a descending G major triad and a syncopated melody to the rhythm ♪ | ♪ ♪ 𝄽 .[90] The coda, too, emphasizes the third, and the sense of humour that is intrinsic to this number again comes into its own in the Third Lady's melancholic line.[91]

Papageno now enters and introduces himself as the 'well-known birdcatcher'. Certainly, the Viennese had been familiar with this particular manifestation of Hanswurst since Marinelli's *Kaspar, der Guckguckfänger* of 1783 and its sequel *Kasperl, der glückliche Vogelkrämer* of 1791. Schikaneder's own comedy about birds may also have played a part here.[92] Meanwhile Gieseke had treated Scherasmin as a child of nature in his *Oberon*. Such characters represented the ultimate debasement of Rousseauesque ideas, with Schikaneder himself having led the way by creating a similar character in his *Herzog Ludwig von Steyermark*. Even in this particular guise, of course, Kasperl retained not only his earthy humour but also his cowardly, garrulous and gluttonous nature, all qualities that find clear expression in the case of Papageno, too. Schikaneder wrote this role with himself in mind and later had himself depicted as Papageno on the front of the new Schauspielhaus auf der Wieden that he built with the proceeds of *Die Zauberflöte*.

Mozart introduces him with the singspiel equivalent of an entrance aria ('Der Vogelfänger bin ich ja'), from which he emerges not as a crafty jack of all trades in the Italian tradition but as a young lad who is good-humoured and stolid by nature,[93] an aspect that finds particularly clear expression in the abrupt phrase ending that is always comically underscored by the horns: [**Music example no. 604; p.643**] This song, too, is a fine example of Mozart's inspired ability to handle local folktunes of the kind introduced into the Viennese singspiel by Ignaz Umlauf. Melody and harmony are as simple as possible. Tonic and dominant harmonies suffice. Halfway through the strophe (at the words 'Bei alt und jung im ganzen Land') the dominant itself becomes the tonic with its own dominant. This is also the point at which the vocal line ranges further afield and the orchestra intervenes with comic resolve in order to underline what it has just heard. Then, with a corresponding rewriting of the harmonies, we return to G major, briefly flirting with the subdominant in the form of the top *e'* shortly before the end. Each of the eight-bar periods has its own two-bar postlude – a masterly feature that allows the tension to increase both melodically and harmonically each time that the singing stops, with this build-up of tension requiring a relatively extended resolution from a musical point of view. The interludes for the panpipes – a descendant of the ancient syrinx – are merely piquant interpolations, by contrast.[94] Schikaneder may well have been familiar with the instrument from the numerous accounts of eighteenth-century travel that describe it as an instrument used by primitive peoples. Everything comes together here to produce a picture of perfect, warm-hearted naturalness as free from banality as it is from lasciviousness.

90. Cf. the D major symphony K504; see above.
91. The Introduction originally ended with a cadenza for all Three Ladies, but this was later – and quite rightly – cut.
92. See above; see also Komorzynski, *Schikaneder*, 126–7. As early as 1704, the joker had appeared dressed in eagle's feathers, with talons, in the Hamburg première of Reinhard Keiser's *Nebucadnezar*.
93. That he also has Viennese blood in his veins is clear from the recurrent march rhythm:

94. The wind chords associated with them have no melodic significance but merely serve to reinforce the triad that is concealed

in the flute figure, too:

Although the lad's desire for love is innocent of any higher ethical goals, it is equally free of hothouse sensuality. As such he is entirely worthy of being Tamino's companion.

The role of Tamino was created by Benedikt Schack (1758–1826). A native of Bohemia, he had studied both music and science, was an excellent flautist and also wrote several operas for Schikaneder's company, of which he was a member from 1786. He became friendly with Mozart during the final years of the latter's life and had also known Leopold Mozart. Mozart seems to have treated him in the same good-humoured way as his other musical friends: whenever he went to collect Schack so that the two of them could go walking together, he would often sit at Schack's desk while the latter was dressing and make changes to his operas. He was praised for his beautiful, metallic, flexible and genuine tenor voice and his thoughtful delivery, whereas his acting skills left much to be desired. He left Vienna for Graz in 1793 and three years later moved to Munich, where he turned his attentions to church music.[95]

It is doubtless largely thanks to Schack that the role of Tamino is of such high quality. His 'portrait aria' ('Dies Bildnis ist bezaubernd schön') deals with a theme familiar not only from fairytales but also from French and German[96] comic operas, namely, the love of a mere portrait, a true fairytale miracle that music alone can turn into a real-life experience for the listener. Few, if any, experiences lend themselves to musical treatment as much as the mysterious burgeoning of love in a young heart. It was an experience that had already preoccupied Mozart's attentions in the case of Cherubino. Now, of course, we are no longer dealing with an adolescent but with an already mature young man. Moreover, Tamino does not experience love as a state of turmoil in which all his senses are assaulted, as is the case with Count Almaviva, for example, but nor is it a magic force that paralyses all his energies, as it does with Don Ottavio. Rather, it is with reverent awe that he feels the unknown yet divine miracle burgeoning within him. From the outset, this lends his emotions a high degree of moral purity and prevents him from becoming sentimental. Love immediately becomes a moral ideal that determines his life and actions for now on. Of course, his emotions, like Cherubino's, are in a state of constant upheaval, allowing him to experience the joys and sweet torments of love in all their intensity, but ultimately his love repeatedly aspires to a particular goal that is revealed by the rapt and dreamy final section of each of its two halves: 'mein Herz mit neuer Regung füllt' ('fills my heart with new emotion') and 'und ewig wäre sie dann mein' ('she'd then be mine for ever'). In this way Mozart explores yet another new facet of his old familiar theme, singing of love with unique perspicacity.

In keeping with its psychological content, the form of the aria is completely free in spite of a ternary structure imposed by its key scheme.[97] And yet the aria reveals a wonderful sense of unity of a kind that none of the usual cyclical forms could have achieved. Once again a very simple triadic effect is used to create the necessary mood. The orchestra sighs twice as it leads directly up to the g' on which the voice enters with Mozart's favourite theme, a descending scale setting out from the third, preceded by a sixth from below, the whole phrase repeated to the sequence of harmonies I–V–V–I,[98] which is here expressive of transfigured ecstasy increased by the gentle sighing in the winds (clarinets!). Throughout the aria, declamatory and melodic lines are interwoven in the closest possible ways. In the first section, for example, the essentially declamatory

95. See Lipowsky, *Baierisches Musik-Lexicon*, 297ff.; *AmZ*, xxix (1827), 519–21 [Schack's obituary]; Friedrich Meyer, *Friedrich Ludwig Schröder*, ii/1.85. On his relations with Mozart, see Constanze's letter to him of 16 February 1826 (*Briefe*, iv.475–9).
96. Cf. Schiebeler and Hiller's *Lisuart und Dariolette* (noted above); see also Calmus, *Die ersten deutschen Singspiele von Standfuß und Hiller*, 28.
97. The first section ends, exceptionally, on the tonic, rather than the dominant.
98. Cf. also the beginning of the violin sonata in F major K377. It recurs in the opera on frequent occasions.

opening exclamation[99] is immediately followed by the melodic 'ich fühl' es', with its bitter-sweet chromaticisms so typical of all the lovers' music.[100] In turn, this gives way to the overwhelming outburst on 'Götterbild' and, finally, to the rapt cantilena of the *Abgesang*. In the second section we hear an independent and typically Mozartian love theme in the orchestra that is later to return on frequent occasions in the course of the opera:[101]

It is related to what has gone before not only through its first two notes but also through its chromaticisms. The clarinets express what the singer is unable to articulate. Note, too, the extremely subtle psychological way in which he twice recalls the lovely vision. Here the instruments build meaningful bridges between his individual phrases, just as voice and instruments interact throughout the whole of the aria to produce a perfect example of dramatic psychology. It is left to the winds, for example, to usher in a reply to the wonderful Phrygian question 'Soll die Empfindung Liebe sein?' ('Could this feeling be love?'), a reply that fills Tamino with feelings of happiness and that is followed in turn by his dreamy confession with its typically Mozartian *piano* marking, 'Die Liebe ist's allein' ('It is love alone'). Note the beautiful, truthful way in which this emotion wells forth in the final part of this section, a section that alludes motivically to the earlier 'ich fühl' es'.[102] The realization that he is in love now rouses in Tamino a desire to possess his beloved and causes his emotions to flare up even higher. Here Mozart avails himself of a great pedal point on B flat that raises to its highest pitch the tension inherent in the dominant harmony. The orchestra is in a state of constant motion, its motif[103] repeatedly flaring up, only to sink back down once again, with the vocal line following its contours with an ascending scalar figure that overflows with emotion and that is related to the aria's opening idea, finally struggling to find linguistic and melodic expression in a series of disjointed phrases. The tension culminates in a realistic whole bar's rest, as though Tamino were waiting for an answer from elsewhere. The answer, when it eventually comes, is wholly un-Italianate and takes the form of an intimate dialogue between first violin and voice, again over a pedal point. Only in the marked emphasis on the *d'* flat of 'drücken' does the suppressed agitation suddenly break through.[104] Once again – at the words 'und ewig wäre sie dann mein' – Mozart alludes to the underlying scalar motif, and the beautiful *Abgesang* returns, with its ending expanded as it literally overflows with emotion and revels in its triadic melody.[105] The brief orchestral postlude[106] leaves us with an echo of one of the

---

99. Waltershausen draws attention to the predilection for 'uncomfortable' vowels i and ü on high notes, a feature that is found throughout the opera as a whole and that he attributes to Schack's particular qualities as a singer; see Waltershausen, *Die Zauberflöte*, 74.

100. The same idea is also found in the G minor symphony (see above), where it is intensified by the use of imitative procedures in the strings (with the *d'* flat).

101. Waltershausen, *Die Zauberflöte*, 75.

102. Particularly effective is the sudden and typically Mozartian shift to the subdominant on the weak beat. Bars 32–35 contain a distant echo of bars 9–12, thereby affording further proof of the unity of the number as a whole.

103. Note also the off-beat winds and the dynamics.

104. This passage, too, has its counterpart in bar 29.

105. Note in particular the emotionally charged emphasis of the third, *g'*.

106. Its melodic line recalls that of the postlude to the duet for Susanna and the Count ('Crudel, perchè finora') in *Le nozze di Figaro*.

aria's principal characteristics, with the underlying emotion welling up in all its intensity, only to withdraw into itself immediately afterwards.

Just as Papageno's aria strikes a folklike tone, so the present aria is an example of an *empfindsam* arietta combining German and Italian elements, a kind of aria, moreover, that was then being developed in Vienna and that involved a far more intricate style as a result of its use of chromaticisms. In this way the contrasting and, at the same time, complementary nature of the two characters – Papageno's thoughts, too, are directed at love – is reflected on a purely superficial level in the choice of styles adopted here.

A new and significant change of style comes with the *scena* for the Queen of Night ('O zittre nicht, mein lieber Sohn'), inasmuch as we now enter the world of *opera seria*. Even now these coloratura arias are still regarded as a blot of the opera's escutcheon[107] and a mere concession to the soprano Josepha Hofer.[108] But this is a one-sided view that reflects only modern sensibilities. Of course, the singer's abilities influenced the music that Mozart wrote for her, but it is inherently implausible that Mozart, who was normally fully conscious of his ability to exploit the different styles for his own dramatic ends, should have fallen back on the principle of his early operas for as important a part as this and written arias merely to please his singers. We also know of his whole attitude to *opera seria* at this time. Is it likely that, simply to please a particular soprano, he would have donned the mask of *opera seria* in a work whose every note is otherwise an expression of his innermost being? This is a conclusion that even the most zealous advocate of Mozart's *naïveté* is bound to shrink away from drawing. In fact, the reason for his recourse to the formal repertory of *opera seria* is not hard to find. Of all the characters in *Die Zauberflöte*, the Queen of Night is furthest removed from the visible world: her realm is the cold, shimmering splendour of the starry heavens. Whereas her adversary Sarastro, for all his majesty, represents the noblest humanity, the Queen of Night strikes Mozart as a larger-than-life figure, a character who, in everything she says and does, including her high-flown emotions, has something superhuman about her. For an eerily majestic figure who sits enthroned above the stars, the style of *opera seria* seemed best suited precisely because Mozart now saw it as something fossilized and remote from reality. But, far from taking it over as a dead letter, he filled it with new life – an utterly original, flickering, ghostly life – with the help of a curiously ardent emotion that allowed him to depict this demonic woman in the starkest possible contrast with the calmly radiant world of light of the Priests. In order to appreciate Mozart's aim, it is enough to listen to her second aria ('Der Hölle Rache kocht in meinem Herzen') and the following aria for Sarastro. In the case of her opening recitative, even the orchestral prelude heralds an otherworldly figure. The oft-cited similarity with the music that depicts the rising sun in Benda's *Ariadne* undoubtedly exists[109] but is in itself insufficient to prove that the Queen of Night was originally on the side of good. The rising triadic harmonies with their syncopations and crescendo[110] could just as well portray the mountains parting asunder or, as we often find in French works of the period, the approach of a divine figure *tout court*. Among the many masterly features of this brief recitative[111] are not only the keenly declamatory style but also

107. Kretzschmar, 'Mozart in der Geschichte der Oper', ii.265.
108. Blümml, 'Josefa Weber-Hofer: Die erste "Königin der Nacht"'. The affinities with the aria *Schon lacht der holde Frühling* (see above) are obvious. Schröder was very dismissive of her performance in Wranitzky's *Oberon* in 1791: 'A very unpleasant singer, who does not have the high notes for the role and squeaks them. At the same time she opens up her mouth like Stephanie the Elder'; Friedrich Meyer, *Friedrich Ludwig Schröder*, ii/1.85.
109. See Jahn, *W. A. Mozart*, ii.629–30.
110. Again, it is not a Mannheim crescendo but is based on register; cf. the aria 'Divinités du Styx' from Gluck's *Alceste*.
111. Note also the triadic opening, which later returns in the allegro.

the way in which the melodic line steadily rises to the dissonance on *e″* flat ('Mutterherz'), while the tension continues to rise both melodically and harmonically. The larghetto[112] is a further example of the free binary form that is content to repeat certain succinct motifs. It is also one of the most dissonant G minor movements that Mozart ever wrote. Although the Queen's anguish as a mother is its underlying emotion, her grief is far from passive and tender-hearted. Violent outbursts such as those in the third bar (instead of the sighlike clausula that one would otherwise expect here) and in bars 11–14 ('ein Bösewicht'), as well as the sinister melody in the violas and bassoons in the second half of this section, reveal very clearly that behind her lament lies an ardour that is suppressed only with difficulty and that finds explosive expression in the following allegro. The whole section could hardly be more intense in its expression: it is enough in this context to note the varied ways in which Mozart treats the simple iambic metre of his text. Even the passage at the words 'Ach helft' is a model of dramatic declamation. In the allegro the sombre passion flares up in all its intensity, revealing another facet of the Queen: her eerie, ghostlike nature. It is a facet that finds expression in the fanfare-like melodies of the opening section, whereas in the second section ('und werd' ich dich als Sieger sehen') her music assumes an ecstatic quality.[113] The following coloratura passage, extending to a high *f‴*, is not intended as mere decoration or even as light relief but affords a final, powerful increase in the intensity of the underlying emotion. This is clear even from the upward thrust of the octave line in the first six bars:

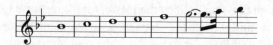

Immediately afterwards this same ascending scale is repeated in shorter note-values, giving rise to the broken staccato chord that suggests nothing so much as glittering stars. Everything evolves with compelling musical logic, including the descent over an aggressive anapaestic rhythm[114] to the cadence that typically ends Italian arias. With its hostility to coloratura, our own age may regard this passage as vapid and tawdry, if not as an actual parody,[115] but Mozart's age, with its Medeas and Armidas and its conception of night as 'nobody's friend', saw things differently. Within their present setting, these arias struck them as the expression of a dark and otherworldly magic power. What may appear to us to be a brilliant display of pyrotechnics seemed to Mozart's contemporaries to express a ghostly flickering passion.

The quintet ('Hm! hm! hm!') is also in B flat major[116] and, formally speaking, is one of the freest numbers in the whole opera, its individual sections generally linked together by transitional

112. It is indicated as such in the complete edition; the autograph score includes no such indication. ◆ The earliest surviving non-autograph sources give the tempo as andante. This is the reading taken over in the NMA edition of the work. For a facsimile of the autograph score, see Köhler, *Wolfgang Amadeus Mozart: Die Zauberflöte. Faksimile der autographen Partitur.*

113. The melodic writing is similar to that found at the equally ecstatic passage in Tamino's 'portrait aria', 'Ich würde sie voll Entzücken'.

114. Here, too, the degrees of the triad are sharply accented: *d‴–b″* flat–*g″*; *b″* flat–*g″–e″* flat; *g″–e″* flat–*c″*.

115. Thus Waltershausen, *Die Zauberflöte*, 78, who sees in this figure a precursor of the 'soulless mythical creatures of Romanticism' and, as such, the prototype of Undine and Melusine; a more apt assessment is given by Schurig, *Wolfgang Amade Mozart*, ii.257.

116. Note the keys of this whole complex of scenes leading up to the finale: they are limited to E flat major (with C minor), G major and B flat major, in other words, the degrees of the E flat major triad. Only with the finale do we find a change with the entry of C major. The introductory triadic motif is the same as the one that we have already encountered in *Idomeneo* and that we shall meet again in the scene with the Priests.

passages of typically Mozartian, laconic brevity, yet each section emerges from its predecessor as though it could not be otherwise, thanks to a strict sense of logic that never gives the impression of a patchwork of disparate ideas. The first section is in ternary form and is self-contained. It deals with the encounter between Tamino and the silent and pitifully whimpering Papageno[117] and is notable for the recurrent three-crotchet upbeat on the same three notes that gives lively expression to the poor rogue's despair. Note the subtle humour to the way in which Tamino initially takes up the melody, only to feel increasing sympathy with Papageno's plight. This is followed by the first shift to F major and the appearance of the Three Ladies, with which the music strikes a naïvely popular note. By now the Three Ladies have cast aside their otherworldly ways and adopt a manner close to Papageno's. Note the curious impression made as the melodic line rocks luxuriantly to and fro on the fifth, *c*, throughout this section, a note which Papageno seizes as soon as the spell has been removed from him – a priceless passage in which Schikaneder was undoubtedly in his element, as he must have been throughout the quintet in general. Indeed, the whole of this *echt*-Viennese conversation between Papageno and the Three Ladies is unusually charming.[118] Note in particular the good-humoured way in which Mozart expresses Schikaneder's trite wisdom ('Bekämen doch die Lügner alle': 'Oh, would that all liars had their mouths padlocked') and especially the contrast between, on the one hand, hatred and slander, the mere thought of which seems to make all five characters shudder with loathing, and, on the other, the words 'Lieb und Bruderbund' ('Love and brotherhood'). This contrast is conveyed by means of a brief oboe motif

that derives from the earlier triadic motif and that is later to prove particularly fertile. The handing over of the flute to Tamino is preceded by another striking harmonic shift, which on this occasion takes the musical argument back to B flat major. The music now slips into a higher gear with a melody that represents one of the main melodic types in *Die Zauberflöte*:[119]

O Prinz, nimm dies Ge-schenk von mir! Dies sen-det un-sre Für-stin dir.

Together with the dotted motif quoted above, the last two bars prepare the ground for the musical idea that accompanies the handing over of the flute. Like the later passage with the glockenspiel, it is treated with playful grace – it is clear what little respect these magic operas had for the miraculous powers of their own instruments. Often they serve only to add an extra degree of poetic or musical piquancy, and not even Schikaneder was interested in attaching any particular importance

117. For another example of this stammering, see Philidor (p.461 above). In Mozart's case, Papageno has a comic companion in the guise of a bassoon.

118. Particularly witty is the sudden sound of the winds at Papageno's 'Ich lüge nimmermehr, nein, nein!' ('I'll never lie again, no, never!')

119. Cf. '[Zauberflöten] sind zu eurem Schutz vonnöten' ('[Magic flutes] are needed to protect you') and especially the trio 'Soll ich dich Teurer nicht mehr sehn?'

to the symbolic character of the flute, especially after the change of plan outlined above. Looked at closely, its eponymous heroine plays an extremely dubious and contradictory role in the opera.

A more solemn note returns with the words 'Hiermit kannst du allmächtig handeln', a passage that owes its colourful ethereality to its absence of cellos and double basses, yet one that still contains an element of humour.[120] Only with the beautiful *sotto voce* at 'O, so eine Flöte' and its idea of human happiness and contentment does a loftier feeling find expression. As so often on such occasions, it produces vaguely imitative procedures in the voices.[121] Immediately afterwards the folklike tone comes into its own again with the entry of G minor, its motifs in some ways reminiscent of the second section, and the roguish spirit that is abroad in the orchestra now assumes the following aspect:

It becomes attached to Papageno, functioning as a kind of cunning smile that periodically flits across his face.[122] Here, too, the Three Ladies retain their airy orchestral garb, while the fearful Papageno acquires all manner of eerily insidious accompanying figures. One of the most remarkable features of this section, however, is the simplicity of its melodic and harmonic resources: essentially it revolves around the leading note with its simple relationship of dominant and tonic, most vividly at Papageno's words 'Sicher ließ' ohn' alle Gnaden'.[123] In other respects, too, this section reveals a natural musical logic,[124] with a particularly sophisticated use of sonority, notably at the delightfully tone-painterly 'Silberglöckchen, Zauberflöten' sung by the whole ensemble,[125] which in this section adopts a heartfelt fairytale-like tone in contrast to the comic episodes. In the andante this fairytale-like note becomes positively transfigured. Accompanied by pizzicato strings, these triads in the winds conjure up a picture of radiant brightness, and the Three Ladies continue to strike this same note with their staccato quaver chords, creating an impression that is half mischievous, half mysterious. The whole movement breathes a spirit of the most noble and folklike innocence, not least as a result of the way in which the two men alternate with the Three Ladies, each group being accompanied by its own orchestra as they continue to spin out the delightful fairytale melody,[126] before all five of them briefly come together to bid each other farewell, after which they set off slowly in opposite directions to the strains of genuinely folklike fifths reminiscent of the sound of horns.[127] The quintet thus ends on an utterly transfigured note of German folk music without any attempt to build to a climax. As such, it could hardly be more different from an Italian ensemble.

120. Cf. the horn calls that herald the bachelor.
121. For another example, see the sextet 'Sola, sola in buio loco' in *Don Giovanni*, although here, of course, we find a more intense form.
122. In the first-act finale it introduces his glockenspiel ('Komm, du schönes Glockenspiel').
123. Cf. the downward-pointing leading note in the bass. The upward-pointing leading note also appears in the bass at 'Mein Leben ist mir lieb'.
124. Cf. the continuation of the chromatic line ('setzte mich den Hunden für') in the women's voices. Melodically speaking, the words 'ei, ei, was mag darinnen sein' mirror the earlier 'O, so eine Flöte'.
125. Here, in the violins, we already find a winged motif that later dominates the orchestral writing in the trio ('Seid uns zum zweitenmal willkommen').
126. At the words 'sie werden eure Führer sein' we again find a turn of phrase typical of *Die Zauberflöte* in general.
127. Remarkably, they are not played by the horns themselves.

With the trio ('Du feines Täubchen') we again enter a completely different world, with even the violin trill having something sensuously exciting about it. The situation now develops with typically Mozartian power, with Monostatos drawing Pamina after her not only physically but melodically, too,[128] after which the two go their separate ways, Monostatos with brief and brutal phrases, Pamina with a broadly flowing, impassioned vocal line. Note the masterly way in which the D minor suddenly enters at the words 'sie stirbt vor Gram'. Here, in a *relatio non harmonica*, the dying mother appears before the mortally terrified daughter like some pallid vision. Also worth noting is the way in which Pamina's two speeches are clearly related to each other on a musical level. The terrified Papageno now peers in through the window, creating an incomparably lively impression as the sight of Pamina reawakens the thought of attractive young women and a genuinely roguish tune comes tripping along, partly recalling his entrance song, partly anticipating the Slaves' dance,[129] at which point he and Monostatos spot each other. The ensuing scene reveals each of them as a direct descendant of the devil of the folk imagination and clearly recalls the Kasperl theatre. As such, it was particularly close to Schikaneder's heart, and there is no doubt that Mozart, too, took great pleasure in a scene that describes the very capers to which he was so receptive, for all that he dealt with them briefly and with a sense of superiority. There is real humour to the way in which the line 'Das ist der Teufel sicherlich' ('It's the devil, no doubt about it') turns out to be a comically horrified variant of the roguish tune heard only a moment earlier.[130] In much the same way the orchestral motif that is later so graphically inverted in 'Hab' Mitleid' has already been prepared for in the earlier part of the scene. The ending is as resolute as it is comical, with the musical lines forced higher and higher and culminating in the merest hint of a chuckle in the winds.

In the following duet for Pamina and Papageno ('Bei Männern') it appears that Schikaneder initially wanted to retain the same folklike tone. Mozart is said to have set the piece three times – five times, according to other accounts – before winning his librettist's approval.[131] The daughter of the Queen of Night and the child of nature join forces here to praise love in the spirit of rationalism,[132] a spirit that creates a distinctly odd impression on their lips and that becomes positively intolerable as a result of Schikaneder's banal verse. Mozart's used this doggerel as no more than a linguistic prop for his music, preferring instead to concentrate on the emotional content of the situation. For him, too, the union of man and woman is a divine mystery, but one that he approaches from the standpoint of these two childlike beings, the innocent and virginal Pamina and the naïve Papageno, 'half in a childish game, half with a heart for God'.[133] As a result the duet is notable for its solemnly elevated tone, a tone such as is felt by innocent minds, without any sense of high-flown emotion, but also without any sentimentality. Nor should we forget that it is Pamina who sets the tone, still filled, as she is, by the spell cast upon her by the word love.[134] How

---

128. Again bars 2–6 are based on the notes of the triad, although on this occasion the intervals are filled in.

129. Note the reminiscence of Grétry here; see p.472 above.

130. Note, too, their respective bass lines. The only difference is the subdominant instead of the dominant in the second bar, but this is clearly inspired by the word 'Teufel'.

131. See *AmZ*, i (1798/9), 448. ◆ It is questionable whether this anecdote, which derives from the notoriously unreliable Rochlitz, is credible.

132. The idea of the divine nature of the union between man and woman was widespread at this time; see also Schiller's poem 'Der Triumph der Liebe'.

133. ◆ Goethe, *Faust I*, ll.3781–2.

134. This needs to be stressed in order to refute Jahn's claim that it is Papageno who leads the way here; Jahn, *W. A. Mozart*, ii.640ff.

beautiful and warm-hearted are her two brief coloratura passages that add to the sense of climax in the second strophe! The brief prelude is divided between the strings and winds in a thoroughly modern way and is again closely connected with what follows: the tonic–dominant harmonies on which the first element of the vocal line rocks gently to and fro are already indicated in outline here.[135] The melody, which is again in the basic key of *Die Zauberflöte*, E flat major, develops exponentially:

Bei Männern,   wel-che Lie - be fühlen, fehlt auch ein gu-tes Her- ze nicht.

In its second section ('Wir leben durch die Lieb' allein'), it acquires a mystic character (note the *pianissimo* marking!) that recalls Sarastro's aria ('O Isis und Osiris') and especially its prelude and postlude. Not until the end are the instruments allowed a say. This dialogue between voices and winds is one of the most beautiful ideas in the opera as a whole, admirably summing up the mood of the duet, with its combination of naïve charm and genuine emotion. The situation that it describes is certainly unusual: here, after all, are two young people who, yearning for love, sing of the power of this emotion, while feeling nothing for each other beyond innocent friendship. The times are long since past when composers were still able to strike such a note, but Mozart evidently struck a chord with his own age, as is clear from the fact that this number received the greatest applause at its first performance.[136] According to the Prague conductor Josef Triebensee, who played the oboe in Schikaneder's orchestra, a discarded version of the duet in a grand operatic style later alternated with the familiar version, with the playbills announcing 'with the old duet' or 'with the new duet', depending on which was to be performed.[137] At the first performance in the new Theater an der Wien in 1802, Schikaneder included a note on the playbill:

> As I was fortunate enough to enjoy Mozart's friendship and as he set my original work to his masterly music out of true brotherly love for me, I may perhaps afford today's much-respected audience a pleasant surprise by offering them two numbers of Mozart's own composition, which he bequeathed to me alone.[138]

One of these duets was undoubtedly the one that Mozart later discarded, but the identity of the other remains a mystery.[139]

135. Much the same is true of the first interlude, which initially creates an impression by harmonic means alone, before acquiring its melodic contours through the violins alone.

136. In 1793 a critic for whom all things Mozartian were clearly a thorn in the flesh noted with annoyance that 'at concerts the heads of the ladies sway to and fro like light-stemmed poppies whenever this poetic nonsense is sung: Man and Wife and Wife and Man (making a total of four) attain to Divinity'; *Berlinische musikalische Zeitung historischen und kritischen Inhalts*, i (1793/4), 148.

137. Schnyder von Wartensee, 'Notizen über die Zauberflöte', 43. ◆ This claim is almost certainly wrong: no surviving playbill includes this announcement; see Branscombe, *W. A. Mozart: Die Zauberflöte*, 209.

138. *Allgemeine Wiener Musik-Zeitung* (1842), 58.

139. A duet for Tamino and Papageno in which they express their longing for their respective lovers ('Pamina, wo bist du') was discovered by Georg Kruse in an old hand-written score of the opera in the holdings of the old Theater an der Wien, a copy that reflects the published score in every other respect. The volume bears the inscription 'The music is by the late Herr Amade Mozart' and includes the duet as no. 13. The quintet with the Three Ladies ('Wie? wie? wie?') is here renumbered as no. 13½; see Genée, 'Ein bisher unbekannt gebliebenes Duett zu Mozarts "Zauberflöte"', 206–7. As far as the plot of the opera is concerned, this number is eminently dispensable, while the music, too, contains a number of suspect features, such as the coloratura writing and *Bettelkadenz* for Tamino and the dramatic characterization. Even so, I consider the piece authentic, not least because a number of its phrases are so typical of the music of *Die Zauberflöte* in general:

The first-act finale ('Zum Ziele führt dich diese Bahn') shares with its second-act counterpart the distinction of having absolutely nothing in common with a typical Italian *opera buffa* finale. What we are dealing with here is not an action that sets out from a single point and progresses purposefully towards its goal through all manner of complications, but a lively array of scenes which, loosely held together by the thread of the plot, engage our attention more by their changing situations than by any sense of progressive development. This was bound to have a decisive effect on their musical structure. Only once, when Monostatos leads in Tamino, do we find any motivic writing in the Italian sense. The other sections all eschew such writing and are either very brief or else they are examples of the same formal freedom that we have already found in the ensembles. The scene with the Speaker, with its large-scale recitative, is a separate matter. In spite of this formal variety, the finale is none the less dominated by a clearly palpable unity of artistic mood that is based in particular upon a degree of harmonc unity not found in Italian finales. The basic key is C major, with its two dominants and its relative, A minor. More remote tonalities are touched on only in passing in the recitative. Even the instrumentation – flutes, clarinets, bassoons, muted trumpets, timpani and trombones, as well as strings, but without double basses – tells us that a more elevated spirit is now entering the naïve fairytale world that we have inhabited hitherto. And these instruments are now joined by three bright-toned voices which – a point generally overlooked – are intended to be boys' voices, not women's.[140] The sustained g'' in the highest woodwind gazes down on their singing like some gentle star.[141] Yet, in spite of all its sublimity, this section, too, is based on a folktune, thereby creating a link with what has gone before.[142] That these Three Boys are from Sarastro's realm is clear from the dotted rhythm that dominates this section, but especially from their threefold exhortation 'Sei standhaft, duldsam und verschwiegen' ('Be steadfast, patient and tight-lipped'), with its wind colouring and three trombone chords. Note also the beautiful way in which the dotted crotchets become quavers as the vocal line unfolds, an indication of the fact that, for all their dignity, these are young boys who are bright and cheerful by nature. Tamino's interjection is as brief as it is filled with expressive tension[143] and adds incomparably to the effectiveness of this whole section. So masterly is the way in which they are prepared that the words 'Dies kundzutun' leave an incomparable impression. Quite apart from its intrinsic

In the allegro it is initially Tamino who takes the lead, followed by a passage beginning 'Stille, stille' that recalls similar passages ('zitto, zitto') in *opere buffe*. But Mozart was right to discard this stopgap number: not only is it undramatic but, precisely because of that, it fails to come up to the same high level as the other numbers in the score. ◆ There is no unequivocal evidence to support the claim that 'Pamina, wo bist du' is by Mozart: the words are not included in the original libretto or the earliest musical sources; the duet appears in vocal scores of the opera published by Peters Edition. See Branscombe, *W. A. Mozart: Die Zauberflöte*, 208.
140. This explains why the Three Boys were not included on the original playbill.
141. This effect is enhanced by the Second Boy's sustained g'.
142. On this melody, which Mozart had already used in his divertimento K252, see above.
143. The tension lies in the wide-ranging intervals in the vocal lines, in the resolute shift to G major and in the triplet accompaniment, while the bass line continues the Boys' dotted rhythm.

qualities, this whole introductory section admirably fulfils the function of providing an internally valid reason for Tamino's change of heart in his meeting with the Speaker.

Most commentators describe this recitative as the birthplace of the later dramatic recitative, and there is no doubt that its traces can still be found in much later Romantic operas. Moreover, the stylistic advance on Mozart's own accompanied recitatives, including those in *La clemenza di Tito*, is immediately apparent. The Italian accompagnato had never been able to rid itself entirely of its originally lyric nature, while at the same time sticking in essence to the principle that the orchestra should either precede or follow the voice when elucidating the situation on stage. The melodrama had taken up this principle and developed it. As we have already seen in the case of Mozart, this in turn affected the accompanied recitative.

The scene with the Speaker, by contrast, makes up a large part of the dramatic action itself and only exceptionally includes the traditional juxtaposition of singing and orchestral tone-painting.[144] The individual emotions are no longer decribed in loving detail. Rather, the whole passage deals with a single large-scale emotion, with the result that vocal line and orchestra are now far more closely integrated. This does not mean, however, that the orchestra now has a larger part to play. An Italian composer, for example, would not have missed the chance to turn the words 'Sitz der Götter hier' ('home of the gods here') into a brief orchestral idyll, whereas Mozart deals with it relatively peremptorily in a series of resolute rising string chords that stick to the point and allow the listener to share Tamino's feeling of expectancy. But immediately afterwards, recitative gives way to a fully developed cantilena: what is new about this recitative style is that declamatory and melodic lines constantly permeate and interact with one another, as is abundantly clear even from the first three bars, including the fermata on 'mir'.[145] This scene is undoubtedly modelled on Gluck, and especially on his French operas,[146] the main difference being that in Mozart's case everything is more flexible and free-flowing. Tamino's mixture of reverential awe and astonishment, his mounting agitation as he tries to pluck up courage and, finally, his liberating decision are all expressed in ways that seem uniquely truthful: note the broadly arching melodic lines and especially the harmonic writing which, however much it may waver, moves increasingly purposefully towards D major.[147] Equally resolute is the way in which it leads us down into the mystic world of the Priests' A flat major by means of the familiar Gluckian motif at the thrice repeated 'Zurück!'[148] Here a new spirit envelops us, as the Priest asks his question,[149] striking a note of incomparable dignity that he maintains even in the face of Tamino's outbursts of anger. The latter answers the question in a purely melodic way, an answer that acquires peculiar emphasis through the key of E flat major,[150] the unexpected wind accompaniment[151] and the whole melodic and harmonic writing of this andante section. After all, it is an answer that contains Tamino's whole

144. Particularly instructive in this respect is a comparison with the recitative in 'O zittre nicht, mein lieber Sohn', which still follows the older tradition.
145. Here, too, Waltershausen draws attention to the curious word setting, with the high notes set to the vowel i; Waltershausen, *Die Zauberflöte*, 85.
146. Cf. Agamemnon's opening scene in act one, scene one of *Iphigénie en Aulide*.
147. The only examples of the old *secco* cadence with its interval of a fourth are found at the words 'ist mir Pflicht', at the very end of the recitative and at the F minor cadence at the words 'das ist mir schon genug'. Otherwise, Mozart goes out of his way to avoid it, preferring a third-based formula such as we find at the words 'und Künste hier weilen'. The fourth-based ending is used with the same peculiarly resolute tone as is occasionally found in Gluck's works, notably at Amor's opening words in *Orfeo ed Euridice*.
148. The motif soon changes direction here.
149. Note the interval of a seventh, which Mozart uses to great effect elsewhere in *Die Zauberflöte*: the present passage recalls Sarastro's phrase 'die ihr der Wandrer Schritte lenket' in his aria 'O Isis und Osiris'. Tamino's reply is also related to the question.
150. This key returns when the Temple of Wisdom is mentioned.
151. Mozart originally asked for flutes, not clarinets.

ethos in life, with the Priest's adagio and its sombre C minor unison following it as night follows day. All the more searing, then, is Tamino's rapid G major fanfare that follows and that ends in G minor, giving rise to a remarkable passage of dialogue in which Tamino's response ('Sarastro herrscht in diesen Gründen': 'Sarastro rules in these parts') distorts the Priest's dignified exclamation ('Den wirst du wohl bei uns nicht finden': 'I do not think you'll find him here'). Immediately afterwards the Priest responds in a similar, melodically related way: 'doch in der Weisheit Tempel nicht' ('but not in the Temple of Wisdom'). This results in Tamino's wild outburst 'So ist denn alles Heuchelei' ('So it is all hypocrisy') in the most remote key of the whole recitative, B flat minor. In turn this is followed by a gesture of leave-taking in the orchestra.[152] From now on the Priest's speeches, too, become more agitated, while Tamino's anger rises. There is something particularly affecting about his grief when he first mentions Pamina's abduction. The music then modulates back to A minor, which it reaches at the Priest's solemnly dotted line 'Sobald dich führt der Freundschaft Hand' ('As soon as you are led by the hand of friendship'), which resembles a mysterious greeting from the world of the Priests, reminding us that for Mozart the key of A minor invariably signifies something alien. Immediately afterwards the orchestra repeats the motif associated with leave-taking, but now in the form of an extended cry of yearning.[153] Twice more we hear the mystical melody, now entrusted to invisible men's voices and trombone chords, on each occasion introduced by the same Phrygian question from Tamino. In this way the need for a musical climax reflects the dramatic situation and the unmistakable mystical symbolism. And now the weight is lifted from Tamino's mind, as the recitative ends with a declamatory passage which, masterly in its animation, is entirely worthy of Gluck. For Tamino, however, the news that Pamina is still alive is for the present all that matters, and he remains untouched by the wise teachings of the Brotherhood. With its concertante writing for solo flute, the following andante depicts him completely obsessed with his love, thereby providing a link with the carefree high spirits of the following section. The fact that his magic flute is involved in this scene and attracts wild animals is a survival of the old fairytale about Prince Lulu and is unrelated to the present situation on stage or to the work's symbolism. Mozart uses the flute as a delightful ornament that accompanies the tender love melody, without placing any great virtuosic demands on it.[154] It falls silent at the passage in C minor during which Tamino recalls his absent lover, only to reassert the earlier carefree mood immediately afterwards. With its tender, yearning chromaticisms, the tune itself is entirely typical of a sentimental Viennese arietta. Note the delightful manner in which Mozart gradually prepares for the game of question and answer with Papageno's flute,[155] leading the listener to expect the music to return to the beginning, but instead the tremendous build-up of emotion results in a presto[156] that begins by striking a note that is half recitative-like, half melodic,[157] only to end like the fast section of an aria that has been hitherto suppressed. In the

---

152. It is worth emphasizing that this orchestral motif appears three times in two variants, as do the tremolando and, later, the A minor section.

153. The words 'O ew'ge Nacht' ('O eternal night') are clearly reminiscent of the Queen of Night's recitative 'O zittre nicht, mein lieber Sohn' ('Oh, do not tremble, my dear son'). ◆ Further, see Christoph Wolff, '"O ew'ge Nacht! wann wirst zu [*sic*] schwinden?" Zum Verständnis der Sprecherszene im ersten Finale von Mozarts "Zauberflöte"'.

154. The tenor Benedikt Schack was himself a flautist.

155. The piping motif is first heard at the beginning of the second section at the words 'Pamina, höre mich', after which the flute scale from *g′* to *d‴* evolves completely logically out of the previous 'Wo, ach wo find' ich dich'. Papageno's reply initially sounds like an echo.

156. The adagio is only a powerful ritardando.

157. The fifth at the beginning ('Vielleicht sah er Paminen schon') is an echo of the flute motif; note the dominant-based tension that continues to mount melodically here.

last two bars we even hear the usual triumphant rhythm with Mozart's typical cadential harmonies G $^6_4$ $^5_3$ C.[158]

There follows a complex of scenes in G major, a tonality introduced with typically Mozartian succinctness and wholly appropriate to the carefree action that now unfolds, with Mozart refusing to take seriously either the fears felt by the childlike couple of Pamina and Papageno or the fearful bluster of the wicked Moor. In the brief duet 'Schnelle Füße' he even comes close to the tone of an Italian *opera buffa*, without, however, degenerating into the coarseness so often associated with it. Among the elements that mark it out in this way are the whirring orchestral motif in the very first bar (a motif incidentally reminiscent of the similar motif in the quintet ('Hm! hm! hm!') and especially the melodic line, which includes a number of turns of phrase familiar to us from Anfossi. Note the subtle humour of the ending, with its insistent repeats that result in the couple wasting their time gossiping and thus falling into their enemy's hands. The lieder-like structure typical of this section is even clearer in the following allegro. Here the actual folktune good-humouredly emerges from the terrible tumult stirred up by the triumphant Moor, whose vocal line, when looked at closely, turns out to be made up of well-worn, vacuous phrases of a kind found nowhere else in the whole of *Die Zauberflöte*, his bluster quickly destroyed by Papageno's lively folktune, like some evil spirit that fades with the dawn. The whole passage acquires its particular appeal through the use of the glockenspiel. According to the libretto, it is a 'machine like wooden laughter',[159] while in the score Mozart describes it as an 'istromento d'acciajo', making it clear that the instrument in question comprises a frame with metal bars.[160] The double-bass player Friedrich Pischlberger – or, according to Treitschke, the conductor Johann Baptist Henneberg – 'belaboured' the instrument in the wings. As we have already noted, Mozart himself played it on one occasion. Supported by pizzicato writing in the strings, it accompanies the melody that is later sung by Monostatos and the chorus,[161] with the whole passage creating an utterly delightful impression as a result of its innocence and simplicity.[162] Papageno's enemies leave, and the carefree and, at the same time, heartfelt aspect of the folksong now comes into its own in the sentimental little section 'Könnte jeder brave Mann', with its fifths in the horns and folklike canon. Once again Pamina and Papageno are united in their innocent folk tone. And once again their good-humoured gossip proves their undoing, as they are suddenly interrupted by a trumpet fanfare, and a distant chorus announces Sarastro. At the same time, the music returns to the C major of the beginning before modulating to the subdominant, F major, with the entrance of

---

158. Cf. the entrance of the Three Ladies (in the Introduction) and the end of the Queen of Night's first aria ('O zittre nicht, mein lieber Sohn').

159. A popular name for the xylophone; see Sachs, *Real-Lexikon der Musikinstrumente*, 188.

160. Sachs, *Real-Lexikon der Musikinstrumente*, 356 ('Stahlspiel'). Mozart also calls it 'steel laughter'. A striking feature is the polyphonic bass line found in the full score and presupposing several players. At a performance in Bad Godesberg in 1793, Christian Gottlob Neefe used a *Stahlklavier*, an instrument that had been invented only the previous year; see *Berlinische musikalische Zeitung historischen und kritischen Inhalts*, i (1793/4), 151.

161. On the particular type of folktune, see p.1263 above; the folksong offers many examples of this.

162. In the travesty of the opera seen in Paris, the noble shepherd Bochoris sings this song in order to persuade the guards to release Pamina. According to one eyewitness, he 'gradually sets the twelve Moors and guard in motion, their movements proving so wittily comical and sensual that they perform an extremely characterful pantomimic dance, capering around him in their inquisitiveness and delight while he sings his song of entreaty. The chorus of guards then joins in, while Lais continues to sing in his beautiful voice and the chorus of Moorish guards, drugged and overcome by delight, lies at his feet in picturesque groups. It is impossible to imagine anything more piquant or perfect in composition and execution'; Reichardt, *Vertraute Briefe aus Paris*, i.438–9. The dance made such an impression that it had to be repeated, an event unique in the annals of the Paris Opéra: see *AmZ*, iv (1802), 72. The changes that had to be made to the music were reproduced in a supplement to the same issue of the journal. ◆ This Parisian production is described in more detail below.

Sarastro, a modulation that proves uncommonly effective. This climax is in fact prepared for in a whole series of masterly ways, not only through the gradual approach of the procession, but also by the differing impressions that it makes on Papageno and Pamina, who now go their separate ways, with Papageno starting to quake and literally writhing on the ground at the delightful unison passage, while Pamina shows that she not only has a sense of humour but also that she is fully prepared to take responsibility for her actions. The moment of danger brings out emotional strengths that reveal her to be entirely worthy of Tamino but also to be the equal of Sarastro, even before the latter has set foot on stage. She has little to say to the garrulous Papageno, but passages such as 'Dies kündigt den Sarastro an' ('This heralds Sarastro') and especially the glorious outburst at 'Die Wahrheit! sei sie auch Verbrechen' ('The truth, even though it were a crime') leave no room for argument. The way in which the march, with its accompanying chorus, enters immediately after these words, is finely calculated, the march itself being the simplest of all Mozart's operatic marches from an harmonic point of view, but precisely because of that it is also the most powerful and dignified.[163] Sarastro appears here not yet as the leader of the Brotherhood, but as a ruler over his subjects, a true fairytale prince,[164] thereby providing a link between the old and 'new' plots. Only the larghetto, with its three triadic chords and basset-horns, brings us closer to the world of the Brotherhood. The very free dialogue between Pamina and Sarastro is another dramatic masterpiece: it is impossible to imagine a more eloquent melody than the one with which Pamina, sinking to her knees, begins her confession. No less inspired is the mixture of virginal modesty and profound agitation with which she seeks to justify herself.[165] Sarastro's musical language breathes a spirit of incomparable majesty and clemency at the words 'Steh auf, erheitre dich, o Liebe' ('Arise, be of good cheer, my love'), followed by a cantilena of such peculiarly affecting sadness that we sense his profound understanding of Pamina's heartfelt anguish. Only with his wide-ranging melodic line at the end ('Zur Liebe will ich dich nicht zwingen'[166]) does his towering majesty return with his ultimate resolution.[167] The speeches now become more animated, with Pamina resorting to a well-known type of melody[168] and with the contrasts coming to a head at Sarastro's C minor, with its energetic dotted rhythms, and at Pamina's imploring answer.[169] The sense of agitation continues to reverberate even in the acute dissonance in Sarastro's vocal line at the word 'Wirkungskreis', after which the mood abruptly changes with the arrival of Monostatos and Tamino. The Moor initially sets the tone with the recurrent, agitated orchestral motif:

---

163. The rising triad again plays a significant role in the melodic line.

164. According to the libretto, he arrives on a 'triumphal car drawn by six lions'.

165. Even the entry of D minor creates an unusual impression here. Note also the sense of agitation in the orchestra and the keen-edged declamation with its ride-ranging intervals, including the seventh already heard in Tamino's reply to the Three Boys.

166. *Pace* Hermann Cohen, there is nothing to suggest that Sarastro loves Pamina, an imputation totally alien to the spirit of the opera; see Cohen, *Die dramatische Idee in Mozarts Operntexten*, 112.

167. Its climax comes with the famous low F on 'doch', a note that was long used to test new bass singers in Vienna; see Kretzschmar, 'Mozart in der Geschichte der Oper', ii.274. This is no mere vocal effect but serves to characterize Sarastro.

168. In the following exchange, Pamina prefers descending triads in her melodic lines: 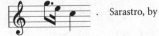 . Sarastro, by contrast, favours broken triads:

169. At this point Sarastro's vocal line recalls the Speaker's phrase 'weil Tod und Rache dich entzünden' ('because you are stirred by thoughts of death and vengeance').

Meanwhile the lovers see each other for the first time, an impassioned encounter evoked with typically Mozartian, striking brevity. The orchestral floodtide briefly ceases at its two climaxes, only to resume with the above-quoted motif, its strength unimpaired. Monostatos again takes control of the situation – in G minor! – first with his usual brutal and disjointed phrases, then pouring out his accusation in a gabbled and chaotic manner. The humour of the situation, which amuses even Sarastro, culminates in the pitiful F minor after the Moor has been condemned to be lashed. Introduced by the same three chords as before, the recitative that follows reveals Sarastro rising to his full stature as High Priest, after which the closing chorus enters with the whole radiant force of a secular choir.[170] In the main it owes its infectious, almost ecstatic force to its exploitation of the tension inherent in the leading note with the two dominant harmonies (first F major, then G major): with the most simple devices a great effect is achieved. Its impact continues in the postlude, where the motif suddenly flickers up on the third of the scale.

The Priests' March introduces not only the following scene but the whole of the second act, in which the work's humanitarian ideas find their fullest expression. At the same time, the world of the Brotherhood now casts its mystical and sublime glow over the whole of the opera. The March is part of a tradition that can trace back its roots to French *tragédie lyrique* and that Gluck had already taken over and developed in act one, scene three of *Alceste*,[171] while Mozart himself had adopted it in *Idomeneo*.[172] But whereas Gluck's priests had been the servants of an inaccessible deity remote from all human passions, the priests in *Idomeneo*, especially at the beginning, strike a more tender, more subjective note, and in the case of *Die Zauberflöte* this sense of greater humanity has produced a march which, in keeping with the tenor of the whole work, inhabits an emotional world all of its own. We are aware from the outset that these Priests serve not only the gods but also humankind, whom they hope to reform through their work. For all its majesty, this march contains an affecting element of sadness, as do all the Priests' other numbers up to and including the finale. This combination of dignity and humanity is clear from the first four bars, with their interrupted cadence, a device so typical of the music of *Die Zauberflöte* in general.[173] Note, too, the equally typical way in which the melody glides gently along over sixth-chord harmonies. The opening section consists of two motivically unrelated parts, the second of which adds palpably to the tension of the first, a relationship repeated on a larger scale following the repeat signs. Whereas Gluck's march describes a mood that is fixed from the outset, Mozart's is all about emotional development. As a result, the middle section adds appreciably to the elegiac note,[174] and this in turn affects the way in which we hear the opening section when it returns. Its consequent phrase includes an *f"* sharp that adds to the note of intensity, while the winds evoke an image of the music dying mystically away. Only then does the build-up of emotion already

170. The choral sopranos rise through the notes of the C major triad at the start of this final section, in which triadic melodies proliferate.

171. When an acquaintance accused him of theft, Mozart refuted the charge with a laugh, pointing out that this was impossible, as the march was still in *Alceste*. ◆ The source of this anecdote is unknown.

172. See above. Its first section is harmonically very close to the march from *Die Zauberflöte*; see also the Chorus of Priestesses, 'Chaste fille de Latone', from Gluck's *Iphigénie en Tauride* and Mozart's own exercise example quoted on p.829 above.

173. See 'Bei Männern' (bars 13ff.) and the beginning of 'O Isis und Osiris'.

174. Cf. the *d* flat in the 6th bar and the inspired inversion of the motif from bars 2–3 of the opening section.

adumbrated at the end of the opening section find its fullest expression. As in the trio for the Three Boys in act one, the dotted rhythm associated with the Priests is reduced from crotchets to quavers, thereby producing a tremendous increase in power, which in turn delays the actual ending through two interrupted cadences.[175] This produces three elements with a powerfully ascending melodic line, c'''–d'''–f''', emphasized by sforzato accents. As before, the number symbolism is surely not without significance. It is as though the Priests were now raising themselves to their full, majestic height.[176] The instrumentation, too, reflects this picture of wistful sublimity, with the dark, muted sound of the basset-horns[177] and bassoons lightened and rendered less austere through the use of a single flute, while the horns and trombones lend it power and fullness. The strings bind everything together to produce a unified whole. The march's key-signature and instrumentation provide a link with the following aria for Sarastro ('O Isis und Osiris'),[178] except that the flute and horns are now silent and the strings are limited to violas and cellos, resulting in a mysteriously dark colour from which the bass voice emerges all the more vividly. Nor should we overlook the B flat major of the three preceding wind chords, its plagal sonorities creating an impression of solemn sublimity between the two numbers in F major. The aria's religious overtones are clear on even the most superficial level from the combination of a prayer leader in the person of Sarastro and a chorus that picks up the final words of his prayer in the manner of a refrain.[179] It is cast in binary form, except that at the end the second section returns imperceptibly to the tune of the first. Writers have often, and with some justification, seen in this prayer a statement of Mozart's own religious beliefs. Certainly, the element of mysticism that Mozart discovered in Freemasonry and that sees death as the key to true happiness finds moving expression here. The melodic line[180] moves solemnly yet consolingly, without any sense of pretentious pathos, with the old tendency for bass arias to indulge in wide-ranging intervals[181] now placed in the service of a sublime and priestlike tone. As before, the second section brings with it a perceptible increase in tension, here of a modulatory kind: it occurs at the point where Sarastro mentions the ordeals that the lovers must undergo and, hence, the mortal danger to which they will be exposed. Following this passage in a sombre F minor, Sarastro's final plea in F major ('nehmt sie in euren Wohnsitz auf') sounds all the more heartfelt. Note, finally, the uniquely inspired way in which Sarastro's closing phrases are taken up by the middle voices of the chorus, thereby investing these words with their full mystic expression.[182] These brief refrains contain more depth than many a fully developed chorale. Here the instruments double the choral lines, whereas they otherwise accompany the soloist either with calmly reassuring chords or with a vague indication of the outlines of his melodic line. There are no interludes whatsoever.[183]

The words of the Priests' duet ('Bewahret euch vor Weibertücken') were clearly written with the following quintet ('Wie? wie? wie?') in mind, whereas the music, with its broadly flowing

---

175. On D (see bar 2 of the whole piece). On the first occasion the simple chord of D minor rises up above it, while on the second occasion we find the typically Mozartian chord of the sixth of the subdominant.

176. The ending, too, acquires a particular weight as a result of the brief semiquaver figure and the fully harmonized suspension. In this, it contrasts with the end of the first section.

177. They are the male counterpart of the clarinets in the first trio for the Three Boys.

178. The first three chords are also harmonically related to each other.

179. ◆ This gesture is typical of Masonic songs generally; see Autexier, *La Lyre maçonne: Mozart–Haydn–Spohr–Liszt*.

180. On the reminiscences of Holzbauer's *Günther von Schwarzburg*, see above; individual phrases also recur in the eleventh number of Monsigny's *Rose et Colas* and the eighteenth number of Gluck's *La rencontre imprévue*.

181. Here, too, a particular role is played by the typically Mozartian interval of a seventh.

182. Its impact rests above all on the appearance of the previously missing bass note B flat (F), which only now adds its true expressive force to the suspension on c' sharp (g sharp).

183. Note also the different harmonization of the prelude and postlude.

melodies, bears all the hallmarks of a solemn and urgent entreaty. Here, too, we find the weighty tones of the music associated with the Priests, notably at the words 'er fehlte'.[184] Mozart's ability to create an impression within the narrowest confines is clear, not least, from the duet's second section, in which a remarkable degree of tension is built up over the broken octaves in the strings, reaching its unexpected climax at the sudden chord of E major, before abruptly breaking off on a minim rest and ending with a vigorous final section ('Tod und Verzweiflung'), the dotted rhythms of which recall the music of the Priests. It is hard to imagine the implacability of fate being under-scored more clearly than by this ending, which owes its effectiveness not only to its deployment of trumpets and trombones but, more especially, to the characteristically sardonic effect of its use of staccato.[185]

The Priests' warning about garrulousness is followed at once by the temptation to be garrulous, a temptation to which the Three Ladies succumb in the ensuing quintet ('Wie? wie? wie?'). Their characterization is the same as before, especially in terms of the purely musical means used to depict them: there is still no trace whatsoever of their demonic nature. The only difference is that they are now much more agitated, which is only natural: after all, they hope to talk Tamino and Papageno into becoming garrulous and believe that they are most likely to achieve this by being garrulous themselves. As a result, Mozart quite rightly emphasizes the comic nature of the situation, with the whole number unfolding in the bright and amiable key of G major, whose immediate circle of tonalities is never once abandoned. Only at the end, with the entry of the invisible Priests' chorus, do darker storm-clouds gather over the heads of the five characters in the form of C minor and of the two powerful chords of the diminished seventh,[186] plunging the Three Ladies down through one of the traps. But the sense of comedy returns with Papageno's pitiful G minor cadence. Formally speaking, the number is again structured along extremely loose lines, its unity being ensured not only by its overall mood but also by recurrent phrases in the vocal lines and orchestra, foremost among which is the Italianate *buffa* motif:

Note the particularly amusing way in which the Three Ladies deploy all their arts in turn, attempting first to terrify Tamino and Papageno with a surprise attack, a ploy that naturally works better with Papageno, who at the words 'Immer stille' lapses into the tone of an Italian *opera buffa*. Note, also, the finely observed way in which Tamino tries to reassure him by initially taking up each of his phrases in turn. As in *Così fan tutte*, the Three Ladies' scales finally shoot up in thirds at the words 'Ganz nah ist euch die Königin'. In the section in C major ('Man zischelt viel sich in die Ohren') they attempt to get their way with vicious slander, producing a veritable hail of *buffa*-like patter,[187] while Tamino shares in the humour of the situation: 'A wise man examines and does not heed what the common rabble says.' This sounds so arid and almost self-righteous that one

184. The first three harmonies (I–V–VI) are the same as in the two previous numbers.
185. In Stuttgart even as late as the 1880s Papageno used to respond to the disappearance of the Priests by improvising the following comment during the last two bars of the orchestral postlude: 'They're now going off again with their light!' See also Mozart's letter of 11 June 1791 (*Briefe*, iv.136). ◆ Abert's reference to Mozart's letter of 11 June 1791 is unclear: except for the comment 'Out of sheer boredom I've written an aria for my opera today', it does not refer to *Die Zauberflöte*.
186. The listener is reminded of the entrance of the statue in *Don Giovanni*; even the syncopations are the same.
187. In this, Mozart was much helped by the repeated i's in Schikaneder's text.

wonders whether Mozart was himself making fun of his librettist's dreary commonplace remark. Papageno is again infected by the Three Ladies' *buffa* spirit and only with difficulty is reassured by Tamino and his holier-than-thou melody. But soon afterwards, at the words 'Denk' deiner Pflicht', we already find him adopting the tone associated with the Priests. At this point the Three Ladies draw on the most powerful of their arts, launching into a melody as sweet as any Siren's: 'Warum bist du mit uns so spröde?' ('Why are you so shy of us?'). Their words echo in the men's hearts in the form of the phrase's harmonies and accompaniment, with only the melody missing. Yet even this final assault is in vain, and the concluding section of the quintet maintains the homely tone of a popular singspiel. The Three Ladies adopt a far from tragic approach to their failure, with the result that both groups can join good-humouredly in the final moral,[188] in which man's 'firm resolve' and his praiseworthy readiness 'to think before he speaks'[189] finds mischievous, picturesque expression. And since the idle chatter continues unabated in this place devoted to silence, the storm, when it finally breaks out, proves all the more intense.

Here Mozart plays ironically with the forces of evil by good-humouredly showing only their most harmless aspect, namely, their superficial garrulousness, but in the next two numbers he reveals them in all their sinister menace, first as sultry lasciviousness and then as wild hatred that seeks to 'break all ties of nature', an outburst followed in turn by Sarastro's lofty statement of his ethical beliefs. Schikaneder may have been a pitiful poetaster, but few librettists were as adept as he at creating effective climaxes and contrasts. Previously depicted in only the broadest outlines, Monostatos had originally been Tamino's main enemy but, following the revisions to the plot, his role became that of a kind of turncoat. In his aria ('Alles fühlt der Liebe Freuden') he becomes a character of the first order. In contrast to Papageno he represents love in its basest and most distorted form as common lust, which here finds particularly overpowering expression. The moonlight setting is no mere ornament but is closely bound up with the whole mood and, above all, is necessary for our understanding of the music, with Mozart using it to create one of his most original dramatic character-pieces. It includes no wild outbursts in the manner of Osmin, but maintains an almost constant *pianissimo*,[190] with only two *mfp* accents in its middle section. Against this background the aria unfolds with a sensual flickering and tingling that causes the listener's blood to race through his veins and makes his nerves tingle. Only once does the semiquaver motion in the orchestra falter, before finding release at the end in a veritable orgy of febrile activity. Here the orchestral colour is determined above all by the keen sonorities of the piccolo, which is used only in this aria, its line doubling that of the flute and violin.[191] Note also the tremolando in the strings[192] and marcato accents in the clarinets and bassoons.[193] The voice emerges in an extremely unusual way from this sensuously intoxicating activity in the orchestra, with even its metre strenuously avoiding all sense of symmetry. Particularly significant in this context is the brutally ejaculated dotted crotchet at the beginning of the phrase 'Alles fühlt der

---

188. Nor are the two groups as strictly segregated as before: initially the vocal lines of the two men correspond with those of the Second and Third Ladies, whereas later the Third Lady and two men join forces against the First and Second Ladies.

189. The clipped and half-suppressed melody at these words alludes to this.

190. Schikaneder notes in his stage direction: 'Everything is sung and played *piano*, as though the music were in the far distance.'

191. Note the analogous use of the instrument in the Bacchus duet from *Die Entführung aus dem Serail* discussed above. In both cases the model is probably Grétry's *L'amitié à l'épreuve*, in which the Black Amilcar is also accompanied by piccolos in act one, scene eight.

192. Waltershausen pertinently draws attention to the subtly calculated distinction between legato and staccato here; Waltershausen, *Die Zauberflöte*, 98.

193. At the end they spell out the rattling rhythm that Mozart always uses to provide exotic colour:

Liebe Freuden'. In the most general terms, the whole of the melodic structure has something disorganized, even chaotic about it, notably at the very beginning:

It writhes around the note *c'* with dogged savagery,[194] touching on the other degrees of the scale in a fairly primitive order. In this way, the most extreme figure in the opera is raised from the depths of an ordinary comic singspiel and, thanks to Mozart's inspired touch, elevated to the heights of the true art of characterization, yet without abandoning the field of the simple singspiel song. Like Osmin's opening aria, the present number is arguably the finest proof of Mozart's ability to develop the most striking character portraits on the basis of these simple songs.

The onslaught of the forces of darkness reaches its high point in the Queen's second aria ('Der Hölle Rache kocht in meinem Herzen'). Here Mozart's tragic key of G minor comes into its own, its opening phrase familiar from Donna Anna's impassioned call for vengeance. Again, therefore, there is no reason to interpret this aria as a parody of the style of *opera seria*.[195] Quite the opposite: it deserves to be taken entirely seriously as the most impassioned outburst in the whole opera and as one of Mozart's most significant achievements in the field of high emotion. Even its opening is arresting in its power, with a dark-hued chord of D minor in the full orchestra abruptly conjured up out of a seething tremolando before furiously driving up the harmonies to the chord of the sixth of the subdominant. The descending vocal line with its Neapolitan sixth returns twice in the second part of the aria as a particularly important motif:

Another typically Mozartian feature is the *piano* ending to the crescendo. A full *forte* appears only at the following orchestral transition, the tremendous energy of which forces a shift to F major, and here the Queen of Night, borrowing increasingly from the Italian style, announces her decision to use Pamina to kill Sarastro. Like its predecessor, this section, too, is driven down to the subdominant by the sheer pressure of the feelings expressed here, breaking away only on the *a″* flat at 'meine Tochter'. But this *a″* flat feels to be clearly related to the repeated *a″* of the following outburst on 'so bist du mein', meine Tochter nimmermehr', which in turn finds release in the coloratura passage that follows. It, too, then, is no mere superficial flourish but the climactic expression of the underlying emotion, demanding an appropriately intense delivery. Even though this kind of expression may no longer appeal to our modern sensitivities, this wilful staccato outburst,[196] with its vigorous fifths and wildly flickering passion, reflects a demonically flashing hatred that is entirely in keeping with this sinister woman's nature. In the concertante writing for the orchestra, too, flames seem to leap up on every side. The second section of the aria acquires a note of dark resolve as a result of its ostinato motif's constant vacillation between *forte* and *piano*

194. This feature reappears in an even more intensified form in the final section of the aria.
195. See Waltershausen, *Die Zauberflöte*, 99ff.
196. Oulibicheff suggests turning the staccato quavers into 'polished semiquavers', but this would destroy the whole expressive force of this passage; see Oulibicheff, *Mozart's Leben*, 311.

and its obsessional insistence first on the note f', then on g''. In essence, this whole section is built up on the upwardly thrusting bass line F–F sharp–G–G sharp–A,[197] the final note of which again produces a full-scale coloratura flourish. On this occasion the pent-up emotion is released in triplets that only gradually revert to the earlier flickering staccato. But it is the ending that proves most inspired, with Mozart using the form of a recitative as his trump card. The Neapolitan sixth in the motif quoted above forces the musical argument to modulate to E flat major at the point where the vocal line achieves its greatest intensity, before the Queen of Night sinks back below ground to the strains of a chromatic tremolando postlude that shoots up like a blazing fire.

Sarastro's aria ('In diesen heil'gen Hallen') is in the radiant key of E major and, as such, in conscious contrast to the dark D minor of its predecessor, a German song alongside an Italian aria. The power of evil fades like some nocturnal vision before Sarastro's noble humanity. Its form is as simple and clear as possible. The fact that Sarastro now avoids the tone adopted by the Priests and instead adopts that of the German folksong, albeit ennobled to its highest degree,[198] is entirely natural as he is speaking, of course, to Pamina. And yet, for all its gentleness and warmth, this song is remarkable for the air of mysticism that lies over it, an air that becomes more pronounced as it pursues its course. The brief prelude again indicates the harmonic sequence that is particularly characteristic of the aria as a whole (I–IV–V–I), in this way providing a masterly anticipation of the mood to come. Here the *forte* bar creates the impression of an impulsive gesture, as though Sarastro were finally and decisively driving away all evil spirits. When he begins to sing, it is as a father figure offering comfort and consolation.[199] That he is susceptible to human emotions in spite of his purity was clear from the first-act finale, and we now hear an echo of this, especially in the b sharp of the consequent phrase ('und ist ein Mensch gefallen': 'and if a man falls'), in which his sadness finds uninhibited expression. Even within this opening section, the use of bright, gentle-toned flutes combined with the deep bass voice produces an extremely unusual tonal effect. At the start of the second section a sense of mysterious life suddenly starts to stir in the orchestra, with a scalar motif rising up staccato in the violins and immediately answered by an ascending, then a descending motif in the cellos and double basses. The flutes give way to bassoons and horns, while the voice keeps company for a time with the violins, in a musical evocation of the Masonic image of two friends who, hand in helping hand, set off on the road to a 'better land'. In a different guise this symbolism is continued in the following section, with Sarastro's heartfelt melody soon migrating to the orchestra, while he himself provides support for the bass line. The tone colour afforded by the low register recalls the corresponding passages in the first-act finale; only at the end ('ins bessre, bessre Land') does Sarastro pick up the melodic thread again and bring it to an end on a note of supreme transfiguration. The brief postlude belongs to the world of the Brotherhood: with changed harmonies it also ends the Chorus of the Priests ('O Isis und Osiris, welche Wonne!'). The aria as a whole constitutes an artistic echo of the gospel of universal human love in Mozart's heart, and it is arguably the most perfect musical expression of what was a favourite theme at this time. A comparison between the present aria and its predecessor makes

197. The transitional motif in minims supported by the winds in double octaves is found elsewhere in Mozart's works to express the demonic, most characteristically at the words 'Non si pasce di cibo mortale' in the second-act finale of *Don Giovanni*.

198. This helps to explain why the aria soon became very popular, initially in Masonic circles; later other words were set to the same melody; see Friedlaender, *Das deutsche Lied im 18. Jahrhundert*, ii.471.

199. Friedlaender draws attention to the similarity between this opening and that of a song by Johann Abraham Peter Schulz dating from 1786; see Friedlaender, *Das deutsche Lied*, i.261. But in Schulz's case we are dealing with a cadential phrase. It is a phrase, moreover, that is found in various forms at this time.

it abundantly clear which world represented reality for Mozart and which was no more than a cheerless world of appearances.

Once again, comedy follows tragedy as night follows day but on this occasion it is limited to a brief dialogue,[200] which is followed in turn by the trio for the Three Boys ('Seid uns zum zweiten Mal willkommen'), the very tonality of which – A major – recalls its inner affinity with Sarastro's aria. In both the finales the Three Boys are clearly related to the Priests in terms of their character, but here they appear as spirits of the air. Indeed, writers have repeatedly concluded on the basis of the trio's ethereal lightness of touch and its utterly delightful and inspired violin figure that they should appear in one of the flying machines so popular at this period.[201] This is open to question, although the music certainly suggests the idea of winged spirits similar to the Cupids so often found in contemporary iconography.[202] But, initially at least, the tone-painterly motif is merely a delightful extra, adding to the charming and innocent folktune and its utterly enchanting sonorities. The bright, radiant tone of all Mozart's movements in A major is enhanced here in a completely unexpected way through his exploitation of the very nature of a trio for boys' voices, a use that he explores with a wonderful sense of sonority. It is sufficient in this context to note the combination of the two upper voices, which generally move in thirds and sixths, with the lower voice which, wide-ranging in its compass, tends by preference to revel in broken triads. Only towards the end ('Tamino, Mut!') is there a kind of question and answer between the tone-painterly motif in the orchestra and the voices, as though the Three Boys were circling ever more closely round their protégés. The prelude and postlude provide the framework in which the vocal writing etches in this delightful image.

Pamina's G minor aria ('Ach, ich fühl's') brings with it a new and arresting change of mood. Poetically speaking, we are dealing here with a motif that can be traced back to Gluck's *Orfeo*: the divine decree that prevents the lovers from being reunited in the way they so passionately desire. Structurally, the aria bears a striking similarity to Tamino's 'portrait aria': the same *Abgesang* ends both sections and in doing so provides a concentrated summation of the emotional content of the section as a whole. On this occasion, however, the tone is one of the bitterest anguish, yet behind it there is neither any unnatural passion, as in the Queen of Night's G minor aria ('O zittre nicht'), nor the kind of wild despair that is associated with this key in *opera seria*. Rather, it expresses what Jahn called 'the unalloyed feeling of pain that a young person's mind is still capable of experiencing in all its purity'.[203] As such, the aria represents the culmination of a line of development beginning with Konstanze in *Die Entführung aus dem Serail* (where it is clouded, however, by all manner of Italian influences[204]) and passing through the female characters in *Le nozze di Figaro* and *Don Giovanni*: feminine feelings no longer avail themselves of a conventional mask, nor do these women force themselves to sing of their anguish in carefree and charming Rococo strains, but reflect a very real emotional truth. The aria is dominated by a uniformly pulsating rhythm in the orchestra that suggests nothing so much as an inescapable pressure filled with the fear of death, while above it there unfolds the vocal line, every note of which is imbued with emotion. Like Tamino's vocal line, it wavers between recitative and actual song and, more than in any other

200. The joke of the lover disguised as an old woman is already found in Hiller's *Lisuart und Dariolette*; see Calmus, *Die ersten deutschen Singspiele von Standfuß und Hiller*, 29.
201. See Merian, *Mozarts Meisteropern*, 277; and Waltershausen, *Die Zauberflöte*, 102. They both mention the 'flying machine' in the stage directions to the second-act finale.
202. Amor, for example, appears as a winged Rococo god in his opening aria in Gluck's *Orfeo ed Euridice*.
203. Jahn, *W. A. Mozart*, ii.625.
204. See in particular her G minor aria ('Traurigkeit ward mir zum Lose') discussed above.

number in the opera, tends to break down its clear outlines with chromatic alterations, suspensions and so on, thereby exploring the individual tensions in the minutest possible detail.[205] Of some significance here is the fact that the double basses repeatedly fall silent in favour of the cellos, thus investing these outpourings with a note of affecting helplessness. It is clear from bars 5–7, in which the sense of anguish is already raised to its highest pitch of intensity, that the inner tension, with its inherent contrasts, is uniquely powerful.[206] This is followed at once by an insistent modulation from D major to B flat major,[207] with its beautiful and eloquent echo of *Le nozze di Figaro* at the words 'Nimmer kommt ihr Wonnestunden', its dreamy triadic melody followed all too soon by a passage of searing chromatic intensity at 'meinem Herzen mehr zurück'. The *Abgesang*, finally, is an emotionally intensified variant of part of Orpheus's opening aria from Gluck's opera of the same name:[208]

In the second section of the aria the instruments acquire greater independence. Particularly moving is the passage at which the voice ('diese Tränen fließen Trauter dir allein': 'these tears are flowing for you alone, my love'), again without double basses, appears rooted to the dominant harmony of G minor as though by some magic spell, encircling it with an increasing sense of entreaty before culminating in the anguished resignation of the words 'so wird Ruh' im Tode sein' ('then I shall find peace in death'). The melody here is a further minor-key variant of the Gluckian idea just cited. The following bars (27–33) are an extremely compressed and, as a result, exceptionally intensified repeat of the second section,[209] constituting an *Abgesang* which, like so many of the second subjects in Mozart's instrumental movements in G minor, acquires its full expressive potential only in this key.[210] The coda is introduced by one of the interrupted cadences on the sixth that is so frequently found in *Die Zauberflöte*, increasing the sense of anguish to the point where it becomes total paralysed hopelessness, where even the tears seem to dry up: there follows a wild outburst during which the violins remain fixed on the seventh *a–g'*, while the violas, cellos and double basses encircle the dominant *d*,[211] at which point the vocal line abruptly plunges down, as though into an open grave. Finally there comes the last desperate cry of lamentation on the ninth, *e''* flat, with its fermata. The tension is maintained undiminished in the postlude, its brief motif derived from the cry of 'Tamino'

in bar 17:   It seems to echo unendingly in Pamina's heart like some mute plaint

---

205. Right at the beginning all the phrases are feminine.

206. Note the clash between the ascending leading note *c* sharp and the descending E flat at the second 'ewig hin der Liebe Glück', a clash that almost tears the chord apart.

207. This is a typically Mozartian device; see also bars 10–11 of the Queen of Night's second aria ('Der Hölle Rache kocht in meinem Herzen').

208. Only the six-four chord in bar 4 is extended by Mozart's coloratura. This, too, is intended to add to the expression, as is clear from the way in which the demisemiquaver figure is slowed down to semiquavers in the second bar.

209. All that is missing is the earlier tendency to hover around the dominant. Instead, bars 28–30 hark back to bars 6–7.

210. Note the small intervals and the Neapolitan sixth *a* flat.

211. Mozart is fond of using this device to evoke related moods, as in the wind adagios in the graveyard scene in *Don Giovanni* and at the words 'movermi posso appena' in the following duet. It is also worth drawing attention in this context to the adagio from the overture to *Die Zauberflöte* (see above). In the present case the power of the ascending and descending leading note (for it is on this that the whole phenomenon rests) creates a particularly chilling impression.

levelled against Tamino and his apparent infidelity. As so often in this aria, the listener has the impression that he is hearing entirely modern sounds here.[212] It is worth noting, finally, that the expressivity of the aria will be impaired if the tempo is dragged.[213]

Following this moving picture of human suffering, the Chorus of the Priests ('O Isis und Osiris, welche Wonne!') takes us straight back to the battle between light and darkness. Tamino has survived the first ordeal and is solemnly welcomed by the Priests, but the storm clouds have not yet vanished, hence the serious and solemn note that is struck by this chorus and, more especially, its frequent changes of dynamics juxtaposing night and day. Its basic character is *piano*: following the solemn invocation of the opening, a mist seems to descend over the orchestra in bars 7–9, with the harmony modulating to the dark subdominant key of G minor – the shades of darkness appear to descend in a particularly vivid way. But almost immediately afterwards the ascent towards the light is as brief as it is clear, thanks to the *forte* that suddenly flares up and the resolute modulation to A major, evoking the image of the whole assembly all at once lit by a celestial light.[214] Everything breathes a spirit of utter transfiguration, not least as a result of the word setting, initially in equal crotchets, then with the single Gluckian anapaest at 'bald ist er', a device that creates an indescribable effect, as does the barely audible, organ-like echo in the orchestra. Once more the chorus rises to a climax of magnificent splendour ('Sein Geist ist kühn'), but within four bars the *piano* marking has returned. The tone remains confident, but muted,[215] suggesting mystic presentiment rather than a genuine vision of future majesty.[216] The voices die away at the end on a note of silent and solemn devotion, again with a double interrupted cadence and clearly alluding to the postludial motif from Sarastro's aria ('In diesen heil'gen Hallen'). The striking brevity of this chorus, which sets it apart from the related choruses in *Thamos*, is a genuine hallmark of the mature Mozart. Yet its instrumental substructure is impressive in the extreme, with trombones accompanying the voices and with trumpets (without timpani) doubling the horns and repeatedly casting a radiant glow over the number as a whole at the main accents, while the woodwind trio of flutes, oboes and bassoons accompanies the voices at the upper octave. In turn the voices are doubled by the strings, chiefly in their lower register.

The trio ('Soll ich dich Teurer nicht mehr sehn?') is entirely worthy of standing alongside Mozart's finest dramatic ensembles, the psychological situation that it describes being tailor-made to suit his abilities. It describes the lovers' farewell before the decisive ordeal, but they are prevented from giving free expression to their feelings of love, as Tamino is required as part of the test to resist Pamina's impassioned and urgent appeal, thereby exposing him once again to the suspicion that he does not love her. Behind both of them, however, stands Sarastro, consoling them and, at the same time, encouraging them to face up to their obligations. The mood is one of extreme intensity, which Mozart has succeeded in capturing, initially at least, through the recurrent and insistent figure in the unison violas, cellos and bassoons, which achieves its full impact, of course, only if the tempo is not too slow.[217] But the voices are dominated by a curious sense of

212. This rests above all on the introduction of the various applied dominants. Note the six leading note steps in the bass, whereas the corresponding steps in the upper voice are always delayed by suspensions. All these phenomena were familiar to the later Romantics. ◆ Further concerning 'Ach, ich fühl's', see Bauman, 'At the North Gate: Instrumental Music in *Die Zauberflöte*'.
213. See Weber in the *AmZ*, xvii (1815), 247–8 ('Ein Zweifel'), and the evidence of Mozart's contemporaries reproduced on page 571 of the same issue.
214. Note especially the insistent syncopations in the strings in the tenth bar and the trill in the eleventh.
215. Note the characteristic role that is now played in the orchestra by the anapaestic rhythm.
216. It is the suppressed outburst on the thrice-repeated word 'bald' that creates the greatest impact here.
217. Mozart himself gave slight emphasis to the first quaver and took the piece almost twice as fast as was later to become usual; see *AmZ*, xvii (1815), 571. Waltershausen suggests M.M. minim = 72, with a tempo marking of 'Passionately animated, but not too fast'. Even the *alla breve* time-signature should warn against dragging.

unease. What an extravagant outpouring of emotion we would have found in an *opera seria* for this 'ultimo amplesso'! Mozart, by contrast, begins on a note of eloquent taciturnity with very brief phrases, the sense of the imminent decision sealing the characters' lips. In the contrast between the three characters, dramatic and musical considerations again coincide. The greatest distance is between Pamina and Sarastro, with Tamino naturally mediating between them. But it is the harmonic language that is especially inspired here, with Pamina invariably creating the tension, initially in the direction of the dominant and subdominant,[218] while the men contrive to release that tension with equal regularity. As the trio develops, so the speeches become longer, while the characters' despair drives the musical argument to G minor ('O liebtest du'), yet here, too, at the words 'Glaub mir, ich fühle gleiche Triebe', the menfolk succeed in resolving the tension in a moving modulation to E flat major – the solemn key associated with the Priests in the opera. No less significant is Sarastro's sombre modulation to the minor at 'Die Stunde schlägt', when the accompanying figure suddenly ceases, allowing the anguish of the two lovers to find its fullest expression. This is also the first time in the trio that we hear the oboes.[219] From now on the textures grow increasingly dense, introducing a polyphonic element in a typically Mozartian manner. The floodtide of sound rolls along in a series of separate waves, their crests invariably represented by Pamina's impassioned outbursts. In her time of greatest need, Tamino moves increasingly over to Pamina, as their farewell grows more and more tender and filled with yearning.[220] At the same time, however, Sarastro becomes more determined, and with his renewed 'Die Stunde schlägt' ('The hour has struck'), the drama reaches its high point, a climax which, to quote Gluck, 'draws blood'. With a dull pounding in the strings, the bass line moves chromatically upwards, forcing the lovers' vocal lines to move in the same direction in an increasingly impassioned outburst.[221] But immediately afterwards, at the modulation to E flat major, the emotion typically switches to mute sadness that creates an all the more moving impression through the anguished coloratura.[222] The lovers' genuinely German farewell dies away on a note of extreme tenderness,[223] as though they were already receding into the distance.[224]

Between this trio and its consequences for Pamina comes a scene for Papageno that textually recalls the figure of Kasperl. Like Tamino and Pamina, he longs more than anything for love, but in his case ethical considerations could not be further from his mind. What he understands by love is simply the gratification of a natural and innate urge, which explains why the Speaker's announcement that he is excluded from the 'heavenly joys of the Brotherhood' leaves him completely cold. A good glass of wine is far more welcome than all the solemnities of the Temple of Wisdom. Needless to say, he himself has no inkling of this moral flaw in his personality, and herein lies the comedy associated with his character. The wine loosens his tongue, and in his little song ('Ein Mädchen oder Weibchen') he tells us all about his longings, a song as simple, heartfelt and stolid as his entrance number. Here the music is even closer in tone to that of a folksong, a similarity that it owes, not least, to its traditional combination of a slow section in duple metre and a quick section in triple time. The preludes to both sections are particularly delightful in terms of

---

218. Of great significance in this context is her increasing emotion at 'Dein warten tödliche Gefahren' ('Mortal dangers await you'). In bars 5–7 we glimpse the melody of Tamino's 'portrait aria'.

219. Their love motif is related to that of the clarinets in the 'portrait aria'.

220. It is significant that it is at this moment ('Nun eile fort') that Sarastro takes over the accompanying figure from the basses.

221. Note the way in which the brief sighlike phrase increases in intensity, culminating in its final syncopated form.

222. Particularly beautiful in its impact is the dissonance on 'wieder', which is resolved only by Sarastro.

223. In an entirely Romantic spirit, Mozart avoids the root chords on F–G–E flat–F, preferring more tender-sounding altered chords with F sharp–G–E–F.

224. The same device is found in the quintet ('Hm! hm! hm!'): here, too, the voices fade away in the distance as they bid each other farewell.

their sonorities. In the first two strophes they are entrusted to the glockenspiel alone, with only its main accents supported by the strings, but in the third strophe it is joined by woodwinds and horns. The glockenspiel part itself is varied, becoming more brilliant with each successive strophe, while the vocal melody itself retains the same contented semiquaver accompaniment as Papageno's entrance number. It comprises a simple eight-bar period followed by an additional four-bar phrase in which the listener feels that the tension built up in bars 6–7 is now able to find release. Here, too, the horns put in a good-humoured appearance. The allegro is more complex, the playful ease with which the consequent phrase modulates from C major to the subdominant F major concealing from us the fact that such a modulation is extremely rare in a German folksong. And the F major feels to be consolidated only by the entry of its own subdominant, B flat major, followed by a return to F major. The folklike note culminates in the postlude to the whole number, where Papageno's delight appears to be utterly unbounded.[225]

The second-act finale ('Bald prangt, den Morgen zu verkünden') brings us back to the world of the Brotherhood with its solemn strains of E flat major. The Three Boys now enter for the third time, their singing revealing palpable affinities with the beginning of the first-act finale, the only difference being that there is now a matitudinal mood of glorious freshness: the following decision could hardly be introduced in a more poetical manner. The instrumentation is less brilliant than in the first-act finale, although clarinets now return for the first time since the scene with the Speaker,[226] a reappearance that is undoubtedly intentional. The dialogue between strings (without cellos and double basses) and winds is also especially meaningful, as is clear from such a heartfelt passage as 'O holde Ruhe, steig hernieder' and from the significant expansion of the ending at 'und Sterbliche den Göttern gleich'.[227]

Immediately afterwards the celestial radiance fades, and the Three Boys descend into the world of human feelings inhabited by Pamina. Hitherto self-contained, the trio is now divided up and the metre becomes freer. Words and music mirror each other in the closest ways imaginable. Above all, the harmonies modulate to C minor as the melodic lines are increasingly infiltrated by chromaticisms.[228] Finally, the impression left on the Three Boys by Pamina's approach is given particular emphasis.[229] She introduces herself with the words:

Du al - so bist mein Bräu-ti-gam? Durch Dich voll - end' ich mei-nen Gram!

There is no trace here of the fantastical and emotionally charged madness found in *opera seria*, and yet these bars contain a masterly account of the 'half-distraught' state in which Pamina enters. The music has a remarkably intransigent feel to it, but one that creates an even more moving impression inasmuch as Pamina's decision to kill herself is not the result of any great mental turmoil and anguish. As Jahn points out, she is 'a young woman determined not to come to terms with her

225. Cf. the authentically folklike *c′ a–c′ b* flat–*c′ a*, the noisy accompaniment in the second violins and violas, and the delighted bray of the horns.
226. Cf. Tamino's words 'Der Lieb' und Tugend Eigentum' ('The sanctuary of love and virtue', bars 88–9).
227. The words 'Dann ist die Erd' ein Himmelreich, und Sterbliche den Göttern gleich' ('Then the earth will be a heavenly kingdom and mortals will be like gods') are the same as those heard at the end of the first-act finale. It was an idea particularly close to Schikaneder's heart.
228. The chromatically descending line at 'Fürwahr, ihr Schicksal geht uns nah' ('Indeed, her fate affects us deeply') strikes an almost modern note with its ending on the Neapolitan sixth chord.
229. The threefold 'Sie kommt', followed by the quaver motion in the orchestra, creates a particularly vivid impression: we can almost see the Three Boys stepping hastily aside.

anguish, but to be vanquished by it'.[230] As in love, so in anguish she will stop at nothing, and it goes without saying that, young and desperately unhappy as she is, the loss of her lover leaves her with no choice but to die,[231] reminding us involuntarily of Goethe's lines: 'Wo so ein Köpfchen keinen Ausgang sieht, stellt er sich gleich das Ende vor' ('Where such a little mind sees no way out, he thinks at once that it must be the end').[232] This state of mind emerges even more clearly in the following episode in F minor with its strangely determined melodic line ('bald werden wir vermählet sein': 'soon we shall be married'), and whereas the Three Boys had previously been merely shaken by what they have seen, they are now seized by a very real sense of horror. But immediately afterwards, at the beautiful passage in A flat major ('holdes Mädchen'), their bright, otherworldly glow returns.[233] From now on, whether offering words of comfort or exhortation, they are again messengers from the realm of light. In the case of Pamina, the listener will note the subtle way in which the weight begins to lift from her mind[234] and feelings that have slumbered in the depths of her young soul now flood to the surface in wild confusion: despair, helplessness,[235] her love for Tamino,[236] and even anger at her mother. Meanwhile, the Three Boys can interject only brief phrases that are keenly declamatory in style. Particularly significant is this section's decisive shift towards Pamina's traditionally anguished key of G minor, in which, motivated by the deepest grief,[237] she takes the ultimate decision to kill herself. With the intervention of the Three Boys,[238] the key of E flat major returns for good, a few passing modulations in Pamina's part notwithstanding. The trio of Boys' voices remains self-contained, its delightfully comforting melody preparing the way for the later folk tone and holding the whole section together. Even the very first orchestral motif sounds like a charmingly flattering gesture:

Note, especially, its gently descending, soft-toned sequence of chords of the sixth, a sequence which time and again introduces the Boys' vocal line, their heart-warming words of encouragement finally persuading Pamina to change her mind. Now all her despair is banished by the single thought of seeing her lover again, and her fourfold 'Ich möcht' ihn sehen' ('I long to see him') expresses an almost literally indescribable yearning,[239] thereby opening up the way for the folklike ending of the scene ('zwei Herzen, die von Liebe brennen') that unites all four characters. Thus

---

230. Jahn, *W. A. Mozart*, ii.627.

231. On this point, too, she reveals her affinities with Papageno, who later harbours identical thoughts.

232. ◆ *Faust I*, ll.3368–9.

233. The descending melodic line, *e'* flat–*d'* flat–*c'*–*b* flat–*a* flat–*g*–*a* flat, is related to the earlier passage.

234. The convulsive motif is the same as the one heard in the larghetto from the first-act finale.

235. Her half-discreet, half-hesitant reference to the dagger ('Dies gab meine Mutter mir': 'My mother gave me this') is particularly well observed from a psychological point of view. Note especially the Three Boys' extraordinarily effective enharmonic respelling of the *c'* flat as *b*.

236. Mozart's ability to explore every last detail of his text is clear from the phrase 'Sterben will ich' ('I long to die'), with its masterly word-setting combining resolve with the most touching anguish in love. Note especially the entry of the winds here.

237. The descending chromatic line in the voice part at 'Ja, des Jammers Maß ist voll!' ('Ah, my cup of suffering runneth over!') corresponds to the rising line in the winds a moment later.

238. This follows identical musical lines to that of the Three Ladies in the Introduction ('Stirb, Ungeheur'), with its interrupted cadence and following dominant harmony.

239. The sense of yearning lies not only in the repeated phrase with its suspension but more especially in the *c* flat in the bass, which lends the harmony an element of anguish.

Pamina's tragic turmoil ends in pure, heartfelt, fairytale happiness. One has the impression that she has already reached the same stage of transfiguration as the Three Boys and can now go forward, pure in heart, to face the final ordeal. Harmonically speaking, this is one of the simplest sections of the whole opera, with only tonic and dominant appearing here. But what bliss is expressed by the way in which, towards the end, the music rocks luxuriantly to and fro on these two harmonies![240] In more general terms, the enchanting and ethereal sonorities of the four high voices produce a literally paradisal radiance throughout the whole of this section, a radiance, moreover, that is unique in this work. No less remarkable in this context is the postlude with its curious upsurge of activity,[241] as though the light has suddenly flared up once again.

With the sombrely sublime strains of C minor in the strings and trombones – note the special role played by this tonality in the opera – we find ourselves standing at the drama's decisive turning point. These strains hover like dark storm clouds over this whole tremendous scene,[242] which Mozart saw as central to the whole conceptual development of the work and for which he therefore chose the strictest counterpoint. The words sung by the two Men in Armour standing outside the Gates of Terror are inspired by the type of song sung in Masonic Lodges at this period, while the melody is that of the old chorale *Ach Gott vom Himmel, sieh darein*.[243] With the exception of the replacement of the minims by crotchets (a move necessitated by the text) and Mozart's addition of the final line, it has been taken over unaltered and is sung by the two Men in Armour in octaves, supported by flutes, oboes and bassoons in minims, while the trombones play the notes of the melody, each note reduced to a crotchet and followed by a crotchet rest.[244] Mozart undoubtedly discovered the melody in Kirnberger, who often uses it as an example and twice treats it as a cantus firmus.[245] This assumption is based on the fact that both Mozart and Kirnberger raised the first note of the second line by a third and is confirmed by the fact that as a countermotif Mozart uses a motif that Kirnberger had himself used in his adaptation of the chorale *Es woll' uns Gott genädig sein*:[246]

A sketch in the Austrian National Library shows that Mozart also transcribed this melody in four parts, basing himself even more closely on Kirnberger.[247] The handwriting of the version taken

---

240. Note also the wind sonorities, especially the use of clarinets.

241. The basses descend with great power over a line comprising a sequence of thirds, E flat–C–A flat–F–D.

242. The melody returns in E flat major in the final chorus at the words 'Heil sei euch Geweihten'. On the melodic prototype, see p.978 above.

243. First recorded in 1524 in the two Erfurt enchiridions; see Winterfeld, *Der evangelische Kirchengesang und sein Verhältniß zur Kunst des Tonsatzes*, i, Appendix 14/II, p.VII; and Tucher, *Schatz des evangelischen Kirchengesangs im ersten Jahrhundert der Reformation*, melody no. 236.

244. The melody was often confused with other chorales; see *Caecilia*, viii (1828), 134; and *AmZ*, xlviii (1846), 481.

245. Kirnberger, *Die Kunst des reinen Satzes in der Musik*, i.237–8.

246. Kirnberger, *Die Kunst des reinen Satzes*, i.243; see also Stadler, *Nachtrag zur Rechtfertigung*, 12–13. The motif bears all the hallmarks of the school of Johann Sebastian Bach.

247. Two other melodies, *O Gottes Lamm* and *Als aus Ägypten*, exist with partly figured bass: K343.

over into the opera shows clearly that it was copied from an existing sketch.[248] Alongside the Protestant chorale, however, we also find a Catholic melody in the form of its counterpoint:

The Kyrie from Heinrich Biber's *Missa S Henrici* of 1701[249] includes the following phrase:

Biber, too, had been active in Salzburg, and so old memories may have played a part in Mozart's decision to use this theme. Be that as it may, it was clearly his intention to give this section of the work a strictly ecclesiastical colouring, and although he evidently wanted to depict all the horrors of this moment, there is also a more subjective element here that emerges from the original words to which both melodies were set: awareness of our sinful nature and a plea for divine mercy.[250] The whole movement is imbued with a sense of deep anguish, as is clear from the sighlike motif of lamentation[251] and the chromatic part-writing that enters in the third bar. As a result, this figural chorale,[252] whose ultimate origins can be traced back to Johann Sebastian Bach, paints a shattering atmospheric portrait of our journey down the dark street of life, at the end of which death lies in wait for us, together with the feeling of powerlessness that increasingly oppresses the traveller. There is a sense of demonic restlessness in the incessant and regular ticking of the Kyrie theme and in the sighs that invariably answer it, while the chorale melody moves through the intricate weft of the voices like the voice of implacable fate itself. This whole section attests to the greatest contrapuntal rigour, limiting the interludes to their absolute minimum, so that the course of the chorale is never interrupted. The key remains C minor,[253] even at the ends of the lines and even where, in keeping with the text, E flat major appears at the beginning of the lines. In the final line, where the downward motion affects the whole orchestra, the mood of deathly anxiety seems to envelop the whole of the piece. In this way the tendency to indulge in contrapuntal procedures that had typified Viennese opera since the days of old Johann Joseph Fux finds its supreme dramatic and spiritualized expression in this section of the opera.[254]

With dark resolve Tamino answers the chorale in F minor,[255] at which point Pamina's voice is heard off-stage and the music modulates abruptly to D flat major. This allegretto is remarkably

248. According to Aloys Fuchs, this was the first number to be composed. If true, this would suggest that it was based on an existing piece; see Fuchs, 'Beitrag zur Geschichte der Oper "Die Zauberflöte"'.

249. Adler, *Heinrich Ignaz Franz Biber: Missa Sti. Henrici*. ◆ The Bohemian violinist and composer Heinrich Iganz Franz von Biber (1644–1704) was active at Salzburg from 1670 (Kapellmeister from 1684). See Walterskirchen, *Heinrich Franz Biber: Kirchen- und Instrumentalmusik*; Hintermaier, 'Heinrich Ignaz Franz Biber (1644–1704) und das Musikleben Salzburgs'; and Chafe, *The Church Music of Heinrich Biber*.

250. The melody of the Kyrie speaks for itself, but the original words of the chorale likewise ask God to have mercy on a world of 'false appearances'.

251. Even the first contrapuntal line belongs under this heading. It may be regarded as the later quaver motif in augmentation.

It is also found in the overture: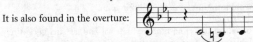

252. A figural cantus firmus is also found in the Masonic Funeral Music: see above.

253. With the exception of the third line.

254. ◆ For another view of the significance of counterpoint and the chorale of the Men in Armour in *Die Zauberflöte*, see Chapin, 'Strict and Free Reversed: The Law of Counterpoint in Koch's *Musikalisches Lexikon* and Mozart's *Zauberflöte*'.

255. We have already heard a major-key version of the phrase 'Ich wage froh den kühnen Lauf' in the first-act finale. On that occasion, too, the singer was Tamino.

agitated in character, thereby raising the tension to its highest pitch and suggesting that Tamino has suddenly lost all his fears and inhibitions. Already we hear phrases from the later ordeal with the fire and water,[256] and there is something particularly wonderful about the way in which the music takes wing at the words 'Welch Glück, wenn wir uns wiedersehn' ('What joy to meet again') and jubilantly recalls the melody of Tamino's 'portrait aria'. Even the two Men in Armour are moved; and clarinets reappear in the orchestra.[257] The end of the section ('ist würdig und wird eingeweiht') picks up the festive and emotionally charged rhythm of the world of the Brotherhood. A brief, tone-painterly orchestral transition is followed by Pamina's F major at the words 'Tamino mein', releasing the pent-up tension and bringing with it almost a feeling of redemption in the wake of so many flattened tonalities. Inwardly, the two lovers are already victorious as a result of their decision to remain true to each other in spite of all the dangers, and for the first time in the opera the bright sun of happiness shines on their union, and the terrors that threaten from the depths of the orchestra serve merely to make this light seem even more radiant.[258] Yet, such are the dangers that threaten them, their feelings are free from all earthly passion, and the whole section has something transfigured and, at the same time, irresistibly heartfelt about it, a quality that finds particularly clear expression in the case of Pamina.[259] Sounds of such naïve sincerity have not been heard in the opera before. Again there is an echo of the motif from Tamino's 'portrait aria' at the words 'Sie mag den Weg mit Rosen streun' ('Love will strew the way with roses'), followed immediately by the phrase ('Spiel du die Zauberflöte an': 'Now play your magic flute'), a phrase entirely typical of the opera as a whole, with its triadic melody, interrupted cadence and ascent to the fifth.[260] There is something almost Romantic about the sombre episode in G minor that describes the flute's origins,[261] but the picture soon brightens and ushers in the quartet, one of those profound ensembles that Mozart had tended to use from the time of the A major section of the quartet from *Die Entführung* in order to bring his dramatic crises to an end. Here the sense of transfiguration assumes a mystical character. Pamina's voice rocks gently to and fro on the fifth, c'',[262] evidently a musical symbol inspired by the words 'des Tones Macht' ('the power of music'), while Tamino encircles the tonic, f', with an agitated figure very popular with Mozart,[263] and the two Men in Armour contribute third-based sonorities in the form of a wonderfully reassuring motif. The lovers then exchange roles, as do the two Men in Armour. Right at the end the words 'des Todes düstre Nacht' ('death's dark night') cast a further shadow over this section with their two heavily stressed diminished chords.

The difference between classical and Romantic opera could hardly be more clearly underlined than by the fact that in the following ordeals by fire and water the natural elements are nowhere described in the music but remain a mere extra. There is no suggestion that they are filled with an animate force, and the lovers appear to be wholly without fear. The unconscious, the eerily sinister and the sense of primeval chaos are powerless in the face of the conscious. Mozart depicts the couple advancing to a slow march tune of solemnly mystical sonorities, with the flute stating the

256. Cf. the phrase 'Wohl mir, nun kann sie mit mir gehn' and the later passage at 'Wir wandelten durch Feuergluten'.
257. Note also the octave reinforcement by the divided violas at 'Wohl mir, nun kann sie mit mir gehn'.
258. Cf. the dull pizzicato writing in the cellos and double basses in bars 9ff.
259. The first duet comprises a self-contained eight-bar period based on the same motivic material and, as such, is entirely typical of Mozart and classical-period opera in general. Pamina establishes the tension with the dominant and Tamino resolves it by returning to the tonic – the simplest possible expression of the psychological process that lies behind their actions.
260. The semiquaver figure already alludes to the magic flute.
261. Note the free word-setting at 'mein Vater'.
262. This device is found in Mozart's works from an early date.
263. It returns in semiquavers in the following march.

melody, which acquires a curiously tense quality as a result of the fact that the elements that make it up are so clearly differentiated.[264] It is accompanied by muted chords in the horns, trumpets and trombones, followed by mysterious off-beat strokes on the timpani.[265] But as soon as the voices enter, the tension is released in a folktune that is a supremely transfigured expression of the opera's German fairytale tone. We hear no echo of the dangers that have been overcome, nor any sounds of impassioned jubilation, but only the calm and dreamy happiness that comes from finally possessing what the lovers have long sought to possess. The vocal line blossoms on the strength of a very simple phrase and is borne aloft on a gently rocking figure in the strings, with the section as a whole resting firmly and securely on a pedal point on C. 'I am yours, you are mine', to quote the words of an old German folksong. The second strophe is interrupted by the blaring trumpets of the following chorus of celebration, an example of genuine festive music that sounds like a ceremonial fanfare. This is the first spontaneous expression of delight in the lovers' triumph following the dangers of the ordeal. A more profound expression of joy is reserved for the final chorus.[266] The C major brings with it a radiant resolution of the dull pressure that had begun with the C minor of the figural chorale, thereby underlining the importance of the key structure of this whole section. But the time has not yet come for E flat major, the basic key of the finale and of the opera as a whole. First, the comic action demands its due with its characteristic bright G major, before the hostile C minor sinks away with the quintet and is replaced by the E flat major of the ending.

Papageno's tragicomedy is the comic counterpart to the scene in which Pamina contemplates suicide and, indeed, mirrors it closely. Papageno's destiny, too, has to be fully worked out, and worked out, moreover, for the good, even if only in the way in which Papageno understands that term. He, too, is wholly without guile, albeit ignorant of conscious morality, which explains why he is given a companion who suits him. The 'dear little children' that they will bring into the world will ensure that the lofty ideals of Tamino and Pamina remain no more than ideals for him and never become reality. Musically speaking, this section is cast in the form of a free rondo in which the following idea, symbolizing Papageno's repeated decision to kill himself, keeps on returning:

264. The phrase

is related to the opening of both the previous quartet and Tamino's 'portrait aria'. Note also the appearance of the ascending triad in this march.

265.   The combination of flutes, trumpets and timpani is already found in Mozart's Salzburg divertimentos; see above.

266.   But the threefold 'kommt' recalls the 'bald' of the Chorus of the Priests ('O Isis und Osiris, welche Wonne!'). The festive brilliance of the postlude, by contrast, is related to the end of the opening act.

This also explains the relatively strict style of the subject.[267] Papageno, too, finds himself standing outside 'the dark gates of destiny', just as Tamino had done in the figural chorale. The phrase contains within it the effect of a double dominant, which lends it its peculiar resolve and invests it with a fatalism that is irresistibly comical. It is always prepared by the sequence D[7]–G, so that its opening seems like its natural continuation.[268] At the start of the section as a whole there is another very primitive triadic effect. The vocal line is now declamatory, now melodic, with the instruments following it closely. They achieve their greatest independence in the minor-key episodes, first of all in the tragicomic passage in E minor, where thoughts of the magic wine that Papageno has enjoyed inspire chromaticisms in the violins. The pain that he feels in his heart is wittily captured in the orchestra. He is entirely serious, of course, and yet his motifs have something playful about them,[269] thereby maintaining a sense of constant irony. The same is true of the section in G minor, in which the bassoon plays a considerable role in striking the note of lament. Here the motifs are particularly good at conjuring up images, notably at 'Diesen Baum da will ich zieren' ('I plan to decorate this tree') and the signalling gesture at 'Will sich eine um mich Armen' ('Won't one take pity on me, poor wretch that I am'). Particularly powerful in its impact is the dominant-seventh chord following the final 'Ja oder nein', in which the cellos and double basses suddenly fall silent.[270] On the second occasion Mozart adds to this effect by having the sound of Papageno's flute followed by total silence. Papageno has now lost his sense of composure and he bids farewell to the false world in a genuinely pitiful G minor andante with a descending melodic line[271] and Neapolitan sixth. At this point the Three Boys take pity on him[272] in a brief allegretto that is likewise highly unified in form, with the phrase 'man lebt nur einmal, das sei dir genug' ('We've only one life, let that be enough') forming the refrainlike ending to each section.[273] The Boys set the tone with their usual determination,[274] and on this occasion Papageno responds in kind,[275] while the sound of what seem to be little bells rises up from the orchestra. There follows a brief, dancelike song with glockenspiel accompaniment, after which the duet for Papageno and Papagena reestablishes the key of G major after the previous C major. The birdman and bird-woman recognize each other, drawing closer and encircling each other before finally falling into each other's arms. The opening is delightfully reminiscent of a love scene in a farmyard, with the cockerel and hen strutting around in their stiff-legged way, puffing themselves up and only then beginning to gurgle and finally to cackle.[276] This rapid parlando on a single note repeatedly returns in the course of the following duet, where the text adopts another favourite device from the world of Harlequin and Columbine, namely, praise of a prospective brood of children.[277] Schikaneder

---

267. Especially effective are the two trills in the violas and second violins.

268. Melodically, too, this preparation emerges with increasing clarity: note its final appearance at 'also ist es euer Wille'.

269. This becomes particularly clear when the E minor idea later appears in G major.

270. As a result the main tune that follows creates a correspondingly powerful effect.

271. Under this heading comes the melancholy triadic descent in the unison winds, followed immediately afterwards, of course, by an ascending line, suggesting that the orchestra is giving the lie to the poor lad's remarks.

272. The open fifth with which the previous passage ends is entirely typical.

273. On the final occasion ('Ich muß mein liebes Mädchen sehn': 'I must see my dear little girl'), there is a reminiscence of the duet 'Bei Männern, welche Liebe fühlen' ('Wir leben durch die Lieb' allein': 'We live by love alone').

274. Initially they operate only within the harmonies of C–G.

275. The triplet accompaniment with off-beat crotchets recalls Tamino's scene with the Three Boys in the first-act finale.

276. According to the bass Friedrich Sebastian Mayer, it was Schikaneder – the author of the earlier comedy about birds – who inspired this idea; see Castelli, *Illustriertes Familienbuch zur Unterhaltung & Belehrung häuslicher Kreise*, ii.119.

277. In the intermezzo *Pimpinella e Marcantonio* from Hasse's *Numa Pompilio* of 1741, the Sabine lovers recall their origins as follows:

The clucking of hens was equally popular with older composers. An example may be found in the second intermezzo from Hasse's *Attalo* of 1728.

associates this with the parental happiness that stems from marriage and that he describes as 'the greatest of feelings'.[278] This two-part section is again completely free in its design, its unity consisting simply in its ascent to the dominant and return to the tonic and in the repetition of individual motifs. As soon as what we might call the 'language of the birds' ends and gives way to human speech at the words 'Bist du mir nun ganz ergeben' ('Are you really mine now?'), the winds enter, bassoons for Papageno, flutes for Papagena, and from now on she obediently follows her husband phrase by phrase.[279] The D major adds greatly to the sense of climax at 'Welche Freude wird das sein' ('What a joy that will be'): here, at the words 'unsrer Liebe Kinder schenken' ('if the gods bestow children on our love'), we even find an unexpected reminiscence of an old love theme from *Die Zauberflöte*.[280] Particularly affecting is the half naïve, half coy sincerity with which the two sing of the 'dear little children' at the ritardando, as if they, too, are momentarily overwhelmed by this mystery. But now the little ones themselves come crawling out of the eggs, one after another, so that their parents no longer know whether they are coming or going. Again we hear a more inward tone,[281] after which Papageno seems to dance in his lover's outstretched arms on the sustained *d″*, as though taking part in a folkdance, after which the roles are reversed. By the end the sense of delight has given way to the greatest high spirits, a mood taken up by the orchestra in the postlude, thus marking the apotheosis of the 'comic' couple, an apotheosis unsanctified by any ethical concerns but, at the same time, lacking in any of the sensual desire on which other composers placed such great value in an attempt to curry favour with their middle-class audiences. Here the tone is all innocence and sincerity and, moreover, ennobled by the charm of genius.

Once again the shadows of darkness are cast over the beauty of the world in the following quintet, in which all its representatives are united under the Queen's sceptre, with the result that the characterization of the realm of night culminates here. One sign of this is the recurrent, dull unison motif in the strings which strive towards the dark world of the subdominant:

Now the Three Ladies reveal themselves unequivocally as servants of the night. The exchange between the Moor and the Queen is accompanied by a tremolando, an effect only rarely used by Mozart, and creates a sense of dark and eerie passion. A melody that he often employs to suggest a state of agitation[282] suddenly acquires a demonic aspect, as the Queen gives her blessing to the Moor's demand, a consent that becomes even more insistent when repeated by the ensemble. Here, too, the choice of keys is highly significant: the negotiations concerning Pamina take place in the key of G minor, while the decision to attack the Priests is taken in A flat major and F minor, at

278. The duet originally ended with the following words: 'Wenn dann die Kleinen um sie spielen, / Die Eltern gleiche Freude fühlen, / Sich ihres Ebenbildes freun, / O, welch ein Glück kann größer sein?' ('When the little ones then play around them and the parents feel the same pleasure and delight in their own image, what joy can be greater?'). The Three Boys originally introduced Pamina with the words: 'Komm her, du holdes, liebes Weibchen! / Dem Mann sollst du dein Herzchen weihn. / Er wird dich lieben, süßes Weibchen, / Dein Vater, Freund und Bruder sein; / Sei dieses Mannes Eigentum!' ('Come here, you sweet and lovely wife! You must give your heart to your husband. He'll love you, sweet little wife, and be your father, friend and brother. Be your husband's property!'). On both occasions Mozart was right not to set these words. His music needed no moralizing long-windedness.
279. The first of these phrases is again related to the beautiful clarinet phrase from Tamino's 'portrait aria'.
280. It is Tamino's love theme from 'Dies Bildnis ist bezaubernd schön'. All these echoes of the world of the ideal lovers prove that Mozart believed that the purely earthly love of the comic couple could also be transfigured in its own way.
281. The bassoons now accompany Papagena, while Papageno is accompanied by the flutes.
282. It accompanies Tamino's words 'Ihr holden Kleinen sagt mir an' in the first-act finale and 'Ich wage froh den kühnen Lauf' in the second-act finale.

which point the voices are seized by a flurry of wild agitation. Meanwhile the whole modulatory thrust of this passage moves with sinister certainty back to C minor, culminating in the sombrely majestic tribute to the 'great Queen of Night'. Set to the keenest-edged rhythms, it is held as though spellbound to the note *c'* and supported only by chords in the clarinets and bassoons followed by the string motif quoted above. It explores the subdominant harmonies of A flat and F, before a heavy cadence brings us back to C minor. As in 'Wie? wie? wie?', a chord of a diminished seventh accompanies the disappearance of the enemy forces to the sound of thunder and lightning. But on this occasion this powerful unison is followed by a second unison passage that plunges down through the notes of the chord of F minor (with the *c* altered to *d* flat[283]), before disappearing on the dominant harmony on *b* as though in some yawning void. The following transformation music has only to be compared with corresponding numbers in later operas for us to appreciate the whole change in perceptions that took place over this period: it is not the transition, but the opposition between night and day, that fascinates the classical composer. And yet the mere existence of this brief transformation music already anticipates the Romantic period, otherwise Mozart would have ended this scene with a ritornello of a kind familiar from older operas, before beginning anew. There is also an element of tone-painting here, with the first four bars sounding like the thunderclaps of a storm as it recedes into the distance.[284] But the real action between now and the entry of the chorus takes place on the level of harmony. First, Mozart shows his usual resolve in modulating to the dominant of B flat major by means of a tension-laden chromatic bass line B–C–B–B flat–A, while at the same time the melodic line, which has previously flickered unsteadily, now acquires a greater sense of purpose,[285] so that the abyss gradually seems to close. But the B flat major in which the three dotted chords of the Brotherhood ring out in all their resolve continues to modulate via dominant harmonies to E flat major in the course of Sarastro's powerfully wide-ranging recitative, finally culminating over the latter's subdominant, A flat, in the first bar of the following andante by means of a cadence that is associated in Mozart's mind with the idea of triumph and that brings this transformation to an end in a supremely dignified manner. The chorus enters in a solemn E flat major, repeating the melody that we earlier heard in the orchestra in a sombre C minor before the figural chorale, with the echo in the winds now creating a powerful impression. The imprecatory tone assumes a mystical quality at the brief and quasi-polyphonic passage 'Ihr dranget durch Nacht', the melodic line of which is continued in the threefold cry of 'Dank'. At the same time, a flickering figure enters in the violins, a figure which, ultimately rooted in Handel and Gluck, was to leave numerous traces on Romantic operas.[286] The following allegro suggests nothing so much as a festive dance and in doing so picks up older traditions in terms of its choral textures, orchestral writing and accompanying figure,[287] with the music acquiring a more personal note only from the great crescendo at 'und krönet zum Lohn', with Mozart's smiling eyes gazing down at us once again at the following *piano* passage at 'Die Schönheit und Weisheit mit ewiger Lohn'.[288]

283. This passage is a good example of Kurth's theory in his *Romantische Harmonik und ihre Krise in Wagners 'Tristan'*, 133–4.
284. The melodic writing based on the chord of the sixth recalls the threatening passage at the words 'Hier sind die Schreckenspforten' in the andante in F major.
285. But note the sense of hesitancy on points of detail, notably at the angular ascent from *a* to *e'''* flat and the cautiously syncopated descent from *e'''* flat to *d''*.
286. The best-known are in Wagner's *Tannhäuser*.
287. A further characteristic feature is the old bass line in bars 5–8: E flat–D–C–G–A flat–B flat–E flat. A concealed version of this line also underpins the Priests' March.
288. We have already encountered this melody elsewhere in *Die Zauberflöte*: see p.1292; a minor-key variant is mentioned on p.1281 above.

The German character of *Die Zauberflöte* has always been singled out for special praise. Of course, this aspect was also present in *Le nozze di Figaro* and *Don Giovanni*, to say nothing of *Die Entführung aus dem Serail*. In the case of the two Italian operas, the German element consisted principally in the fact that the characters were not fixed from the outset, as they were in the operas of French and Italian composers, but were Mozart's own creations. The failure of these operas to make any impression in Italy shows clearly that this basic difference was felt more keenly than the affinities due to subject matter, language and formal repertory. And although *Die Entführung aus dem Serail* openly proclaimed itself a German singspiel, it also unwittingly included a number of French characteristics. In *Die Zauberflöte*, by contrast, Mozart's long-standing wish to write a German opera was finally realized. It, too, of course, was only a singspiel, rather than a through-composed opera, but, as we have seen, this form was enough to allow him to express his unique approach to dramatic art.

The German language was naturally of decisive influence on the music. Schikaneder had no time for the mannered verse of the Italians, with their precious imagery and florid phraseology that time and again forced composers to produce tone-paintings in miniature. Of all Mozart's operas, *Die Zauberflöte* is the most economical in this regard: whenever the music singles out an individual idea in the text, its aim is not superficial tone-painting but a deeper symbolism. All the more, then, does it seek to explore the emotional resonances of the text, with the arias of the lovers and Sarastro classic examples of this approach.[289] Schikaneder gave his composer only the most primitive of popular metres,[290] making the variety of rhythmic shapes that Mozart was able to coax from this uniform material all the more astonishing. His word-setting follows the stresses of individual words and sentences in the closest possible manner, yet he does not turn this into a hard-and-fast rule in the way that Gluck does. Here, too, logical order goes hand in hand with musical creativity. The earthbound nature of the libretto shows very clearly that Mozart was ultimately not interested in slavishly following his librettist but in recreating his work from the spirit of music. There is a great difference between Mozart setting the text in a not entirely 'correct' way and a composer such as Weber committing a similar violation. In Weber's case such passages are invariably an indication of the fact that his own response as the composer was not entirely the same as his librettist's and that the emotional content of the situation had not been fully grasped. In Mozart's case, conversely, the musician was always more perceptive than the poet, so that one has the clear impression that it was so much the worse for Schikaneder.

With the exception of the consciously Italianate role of the Queen, the whole style, moreover, is German. Of the various elements from which this work's outer raiment is so brilliantly woven together, the two most diverse – folksong and figural chorale – both sprang from German soil, while the predilection for contrapuntal procedures was also based on an old Viennese tradition. The numbers that go beyond the lower forms of folk poetry – above all those sung by the lovers and by Sarastro – are related to the sentimental Viennese arietta, with its mixture of German and Italian ideas, but as a result of their amalgamation with a more refined German folk tone they have acquired so powerful an infusion of German blood that their national character is established once

---

289. See Bulthaupt, *Dramaturgie der Oper*, i.252–3.
290. Two thirds of all the numbers (that is, fourteen) are purely iambic and only two ('Alles fühlt der Liebe Freuden' and 'Ach, ich fühl's') are purely trochaic. In the two finales both metres alternate. Dactylic and anapaestic metres occur much less frequently and only episodically, but are found, for example, in the Introduction.

and for all. Here the Italian element is no more than a secondary influence that merely added a little warmth.[291]

German, finally and above all, is the work's mixture of a sincere love of life and profound yearning. The music transfigures the simplest and most innocent of ideas with its sunlike rays, only to rise at the very next moment to the supreme heights of mystic wisdom. Schikaneder no doubt hoped to cash in on the topicality of the opera's Masonic garb, and even Mozart, as a convinced Freemason, was happy to accept this, occasionally referring to Masonic rites and symbols in his music.[292] But the most important aspect of this secret society, with its devotion to goodness, truth and beauty, was its eternal and timeless teachings. In this regard we should not impute to him any desire to proselytize or preach. All that he seeks to give us is his own personal experience, which in this particular case means the genius's innate quest for the numinous in his own life. But, whereas for the later Romantics, this authentically German longing for direct contemplation of the metaphysical led to the intermediary realms of twilight and night, for the classical composer in Mozart the numinous lay in the bright world of day. He conjures up the spirits of night only in order to turn to the light with all the greater fervour. The numinous is merely a symbol which, in the case of the ordeal by fire and water, for example, he depicts on a purely external level, while his music explores what for him was far more important, namely, the mystery behind the symbol. At no point in *Die Zauberflöte* do we find a scene of terror similar to the apparition of the Commendatore in *Don Giovanni*, however many opportunities there may have been for such descriptions. The stone guest is no mere symbol, but a miraculous apparition of blood-curdling reality that intervenes in the drama as an independent force.

We have already noted how the development of the work's underlying concept and the symbolism bound up with it affected the characterization of the individual figures. All of them move as though behind a light veil that causes the sharp outlines of their characters to become somewhat blurred, with Mozart treating them more as stereotypes than as fully rounded, living people in the spirit of Italian opera. But this merely demonstrates the unity and strength of Mozart's artistic vision, a unity that permeates every aspect of the work with equal force.[293]

This unity is equally clear from the whole of the musical design. We have already seen how certain musical symbols recur in the course of the opera, above all the rising and falling triad and the descending line of the 'Portrait aria'. But it would be completely wrong to see in these symbols precursors of the later leitmotif.[294] Here, after all, we are dealing with forms of the most basic kind,

---

291. It was this masterly ability to merge together the most disparate styles that Beethoven admired above all in *Die Zauberflöte*; see Schindler, *Biographie von Ludwig van Beethoven*, ii.164–5 and 322. As a result of this, Beethoven declared it the greatest of German operas; see also Seyfried, *Ludwig van Beethoven's Studien im Generalbasse, Contrapuncte und in der Compositions-Lehre*, Appendix p.21.

292. ◆ Unlike many writers since his time, Abert does not dwell on the purported Masonic symbolism of *Die Zauberflöte*. See, among others, Brauneis, 'Die Wiener Freimaurer unter Kaiser Leopold II: Mozarts "Zauberflöte" als emblematische Standortbestimmung'; Manfred Wagner, 'Zur Freimaurerei in Mozarts "Zauberflöte"'; Strebel, 'Ein Hohelied der Maurerei: Bemerkungen zur Zauberflöte Mozarts und . . . Schikaneders'; Irmen, *Mozart's Masonry and The Magic Flute*; Chailley, *The Magic Flute unveiled: Esoteric symbolism in Mozart's Masonic opera. An interpretation of the libretto and the music*; and Eckelmeyer, *The cultural context of Mozart's Magic Flute: Social, aesthetic, philosophical*.

293. Cf. David Friedrich Strauß: 'In Lessing's *Nathan* we no more miss the more powerfully arresting impressions of what are in fact more graphic pieces than we miss the multifarious characterization and effervescent passion of the melodies of *Don Giovanni* when hearing the profoundly peaceful strains of *Die Zauberflöte*. For all their differences, both these final works – that of the poet as well as that of the composer – reveal a spirit of perfection that has found clarity and peace only after a struggle and which, precisely because it has overcome all sense of inner turmoil, can no longer be seriously troubled by any external disruption'; see Strauß, *Lessing's Nathan der Weise*, 77–8.

294. The closest that Mozart comes to this is his conscious repeat of the earlier theme in C minor in the final chorus of the opera, 'Heil sei euch Geweihten'.

all of which are ultimately derived from the music, scarcely crossing the threshold of consciousness, hence their primitive and ductile character: they are symbols of universal moods that have only just broken free from the depths of consciousness. Some are still relatively close to their undifferentiated origins, while others have already acquired a more individual emotional content.[295] Yet none of them moves out of the world of the purely musical into that of the modern leitmotif. As a result, they are used in a completely different way. We noted this in the case of *Le nozze di Figaro* and *Don Giovanni*, but *Die Zauberflöte* goes far beyond its predecessors in this respect and is striking evidence not only of the unified artistic impulse to which it owes its genesis but also of the fact that the overall tone was more important to Mozart than any particular emphasis on individual features.

Under this same heading comes the frequent and recurrent use of certain harmonic and rhythmic elements and the choice of specific keys, the symbolism of which was so much admired by Beethoven.[296] This choice was certainly no accident even in earlier operas, but in the case of *Die Zauberflöte* it is again placed in the service of the work's basic idea, so that the return of the same key invariably has a particular significance to it.[297] Finally, we must mention the instrumentation, which reveals neither the dissonant austerity of *Don Giovanni* nor the sensual mellifluousness of *Così fan tutte*, but is mellower and more adaptable, and in a certain sense also more progressive, at least as far as the close links between voice and orchestra are concerned. Light and translucent where purely human emotions are involved, it immediately produces entirely new and strange-sounding sonorities as soon as the work's mystical dimension comes into its own. In the two groups of three high voices, moreover, the opera has opportunities such as few other operas can boast, resources that Mozart was able to exploit in a way that no later composer has succeeded in doing. But quite apart from this, the mystical scenes reveal combinations of tone colours that were not only unique in their own day but have remained so ever since. They range from solemn sadness to radiant splendour, with all the myriad gradations in between, while always maintaining the basic tone of solemnity and sublimity and holding the listener spellbound in a world removed from everyday life. Above all, however, the instrumentation forges symbolic links with remote scenes by means of similar or related colours.

All these features ensure that, for all its stylistic variety, *Die Zauberflöte* has a unity and purity found in very few other music dramas.[298]

The acclaim that the work enjoyed produced countless imitations at the Theater auf der Wieden and the Theater in der Leopoldstadt:

Everything is under a magic spell at these theatres; they have, for example, *The Magic Flute*, *The Magic Ring*, *The Magic Arrow*, *The Magic Mirror*, *The Magic Crown* and other pitiful tricks that

---

295. One example of this is the clarinet theme from Tamino's 'portrait aria'.
296. Schindler, *Biographie von Ludwig van Beethoven*, ii.165.
297. The key of the work's fundamental idea is the mystical E flat major, that of the world of the Priests F major, and that of the hostile powers of darkness C minor, while G major is the preserve of the carefree world of the comic characters. G minor is the tonality associated with anguish. At climactic points the representatives of the two opposing forces emerge from their usual world and avail themselves of keener tonalities, with the Queen of Night adopting D minor, Sarastro E major.
298. Wagner's comments on the opera are especially beautiful: 'The German can never overestimate this work. Until then German opera had virtually not existed; with this work it was created. . . . What godlike magic suffuses this work, from the most popular song to the sublimest of hymns! What variety and diversity! . . . What unforced and, at the same time, what noble popularity in every melody, from the simplest to the most powerful! In fact, genius took almost too gigantic a stride here, for in creating German opera, it also created the most perfect masterpiece, a work that could never be surpassed, nay, whose very genre could not be expanded or taken up and continued'; 'Über deutsches Musikwesen', 162–3.

it would make one sick to see and hear. Words and music dance their pathetic measures along-side each other – *The Magic Flute* excepted – so that it is impossible to know whether the poet wanted to outdo the composer or vice versa in terms of their hackwork, added to which these wretched products are wretchedly performed.[299]

Schikaneder was particularly adept at taking advantage of the work's success, with the result that all his later librettos were influenced by *Die Zauberflöte*. The first was *Der wohltätige Derwisch* of 1793, with music by Schack, Gerl and others.[300] Even more important were *Der Spiegel von Arkadien*, set by Süßmayr in 1794, *Babylons Pyramiden*, which was set by Johann Mederitsch-Gallus and Peter von Winter in 1797, and *Das Labyrinth, oder Der Kampf mit den Elementen, der zweyte Teil der Zauberflöte*, which Winter set to music in 1798.[301]

Even so, the success of *Die Zauberflöte* was initially limited to Vienna, allowing Schikaneder to continue for some time to reap the rewards of his crowd-puller undisturbed. Not until 24 February 1801 was it staged at the Kärntnertor-Theater with new sets by Sacchetti.[302] Schikaneder was not even named as the librettist, an omission that gave rise to an unmannerly literary quarrel.[303] He responded with a brilliantly staged production of the work at his new Theater an der Wien,[304] parodying his rival's defective machinery[305] and making all manner of far-reaching changes.[306] In November 1810 the Theater in der Leopoldstadt tried its hand at a production,[307] and two years later the Kärntnertor-Theater and the Theater an der Wien engaged in a regular contest to mount the most brilliant staging of the piece.[308]

The first production outside Vienna was at Prague, where it was seen on 25 October 1792 and where it soon found a regular niche in the repertory.[309] Frankfurt followed on 16 August 1793,[310]

299. *Berlinische musikalische Zeitung historischen und kritischen Inhalts*, i (1793), 142.

300. See Komorzynski, *Schikaneder*, 140ff., where the others, too, are listed.

301. This last-named work was staged with great magnificence in Berlin in 1806; see *AmZ*, v (1803), 778 and 794; see also *Briefwechsel zwischen Goethe und Zelter*, i.78. ◆ For an edition of the text, see Jahrmärker and Waidelich, *Der Zauberflöte zweyter Theil unter dem Titel: Das Labyrinth oder Der Kampf mit den Elementen. Eine große heroisch-komische Oper in zwey Aufzügen von Emanuel Schikaneder. In Musik gesetzt von Herrn Peter Winter Kapellmeister in Churpfalz-bayerischen Diensten. Vollständiges Textbuch. Erstveröffentlichung nach den zeitgenössischen Quellen*. Further, see Henderson, 'The "Magic Flute" of Peter Winter'.

302. *AmZ*, iii (1800/1801), 484; and *Zeitung für die elegante Welt*, i (1801), 315.

303. Anonymous, *Mozart und Schikaneder: Ein theatralisches Gespräch über die Aufführung der Zauberflöte im Stadttheater, in Knittelversen von **; see *Zeitung für die elegante Welt*, i (1801), 326–7. Also Anonymous, *Mozarts Traum nach Anhörung seiner Oper 'Die Zauberflöte' im Stadttheater: Jupitern und Schikanedern erzählt im Olymp in Knittelversen von F. H. v. TZ*.

304. He recommended it as Papageno with the following words: 'Der Papageno ist zwar da, / Doch singt er noch nicht hopsasa; / Nach eurem Urtheil bloß allein / Wird er sich seines Sieges freun. / Versprochen hab ich zwar schon lang / Der Zauberflöte Sang und Klang, / doch Maler, Schneider, Maschinist / Erheischten diese lange Frist' ('Though Papageno's here again, he's not yet singing "oops-a-daisy". Only when he hears your verdict will he rejoice in his victory. Although I long ago promised to give you The Magic Flute, painters, tailors and machinist required this lengthy delay').

305. Treitschke, 'Die Zauberflöte', 248; and *AmZ*, iii (1800/1801), 484.

306. Anonymous, *Jupiter, Mozart und Schikaneder nach der ersten Vorstellung der Zauberflöte im neuen Theater an der Wien*.

307. *AmZ*, xii (1810), 1057.

308. *AmZ*, xiv (1812), 558–9; and Treitschke, 'Die Zauberflöte', 249–50.

309. Procházka, *Mozart in Prag*, 193–4. ◆ In Prague, *Die Zauberflöte* was first given in Czech the next year; see Volek, 'Die erste Aufführung der "Zauberflöte" in tschechischer Sprache in Prag 1794'.

310. Goethe's mother wrote about the production in a letter to her son dated 9 November 1793: 'There's nothing to report except that the Magic Flute has been given here 18 times and the house was always packed – no one will have it said of them that they haven't seen the work – all the craftsmen – gardeners – even the inhabitants of Sachsenhausen whose children play the apes and lions have been to see it, nothing like it has ever been seen here before – the house has to be opened before 4 o'clock each time – and even so several hundred are turned away as they can't get a seat – it has certainly brought in the money. The last time the king was here he paid 100 carolins for the 3 times he went – and he had only Willmer's single small box'; *Schriften der Goethe-Gesellschaft*, iv (1889), 28–9. On 6 February 1794 she wrote again: 'Last week The Magic Flute was given for the 24th time before a full house and has already brought in 22,000 florins! How was your own performance? Are your monkeys as good as our inhabitants of Sachsenhausen?'; *Schriften der Goethe-Gesellschaft*, 45.

followed by Weimar on 16 January 1794 (in the oft-mentioned version by Vulpius)[311] and above all Berlin in a particularly brilliant production that opened on 12 May 1794.[312] Its success in Berlin proved a turning point in the work's performance history, while in Berlin itself it helped German opera to triumph over its Italian counterpart.[313] From now on, *Die Zauberflöte* not only conquered permanent theatres such as Hamburg (15 November 1793)[314] and Stuttgart (18 December 1795),[315] it also became the favourite opera of all the various singspiel companies, one of which was responsible for the Breslau performance on 25 February 1795,[316] and it led in turn to productions of Mozart's Italian operas in German translations. As a result it helped to determine Mozart's historical position and ensured that, in Hermann Kretzschmar's words, he 'triumphed as a German'.[317] It speaks volumes for the conditions that obtained in German opera houses at this time that it was performed in Braunschweig in a French translation[318] and that it reached Dresden in 1794 in an Italian adaptation.[319] Not until 1818 was Carl Maria von Weber able to present it in Dresden in its original German.[320]

The literary impact of the work was no less great than its musical repercussions, a development clear not only from the career of Schikaneder himself but also from that of his Viennese rivals such as Karl Friedrich Hensler.[321] Mozart's ability to capture the spirit of his times with the opera emerges from Hermann's words in Goethe's *Hermann und Dorothea*:

> Mina was at the piano, her father was there, he was listening
> To his dear daughters singing, and seemed in a very good temper.
> I couldn't make out much of the songs they performed, but I kept on
> Hearing them mention 'Pamina', and somebody else called 'Tamino';
> And I felt I must say something too, so when they had finished
> I at once asked what the text had been, and about the two characters.
> They were all silent at that, and smiled; but their father's reply was:
> 'Why, young fellow, are Adam and Eve the last couple you've heard of?'

We have already mentioned Goethe's continuation, which appeared in 1802.[322] Two years later Rochlitz published his *Liebhabereyen, oder Die neue Zauberflöte*, followed in 1814 by Costenoble's *Die Zauberflöte*. Grillparzer, too, having got to know the work as a child, produced a satirical sequel in 1826.[323] Clear allusions to the piece may be found in August Wilhelm Schlegel's *Ehrenpforte* and Tieck's *Der gestiefelte Kater*. Tieck also describes a third-rate performance of *Die Zauberflöte* in

311. Bode, *Die Tonkunst in Goethes Leben*, i.201.
312. Reichardt, *Vertraute Briefe aus Paris*, i.163.
313. Louis Schneider, *Geschichte der Oper und des Königlichen Opernhauses in Berlin*, 63–4.
314. Friedrich Meyer, *Friedrich Ludwig Schröder*, ii/1.115. ◆ Further, see Freyhan, 'Rediscovery of the 18th Century Score and Parts of "Die Zauberflöte": Showing the Text Used at the Hamburg Première in 1793'.
315. Krauß, *Das Stuttgarter Hoftheater von den ältesten Zeiten bis zur Gegenwart*, 102.
316. Schlesinger, *Geschichte des Breslauer Theaters*, 76.
317. Kretzschmar, 'Mozart in der Geschichte der Oper', ii.274.
318. *AmZ*, vii (1805), 208.
319. *AmZ*, i (1798/9), 341; and Treitschke, 'Die Zauberflöte', 250–1.
320. *AmZ*, xx (1818), 839–40; and *Caecilia*, viii (1828), 170.
321. See Komorzynski, *Schikaneder*, 136ff., where the reader will find a more detailed discussion of these literary responses to the opera. Suffice it to mention the travesty by the Viennese playwright Karl Meisl.
322. See Junk, 'Goethes Fortsetzung der Mozartschen Zauberflöte'; and Morris, *Goethe-Studien*, i.310ff.
323. The brief fragment 'L'hermite en prison' of 1826 also alludes to *Die Zauberflöte*.

Phantasus, while E. T. A. Hoffmann treats another such performance as a *comédie larmoyante* in *Die Lieden eines Theaterdirektors*. But the influence of *Die Zauberflöte* also extends to poetry, from Goethe's 'Löwenstuhl', 'Das Märchen von der schönen Lilie' and part two of *Faust*[324] to Grillparzer's *Der Traum ein Leben* and Raimund's magic plays.

The opera also triumphed in many other parts of the world, with translations into Dutch,[325] Swedish,[326] Danish[327] and Polish.[328] The fact that Italy remained less receptive to this 'musica scellerata without any tunes' is understandable. Milan experimented with the work in 1816 and managed a total of thirty-eight performances,[329] but a production in Florence in 1818 proved a failure.[330]

In London, *Die Zauberflöte* was first staged in Italian in 1811,[331] followed by an English version on 10 March 1838.[332] A German company performed it in German in 1840.[333] It found little favour in the theatre, although individual numbers proved enormously popular.[334]

The most insane chapter in the work's history is the one bound up with the Paris production of 1801, a version cobbled together by 'le Citoyen Lachnith' and performed under the title *Les mystères d'Isis*.[335] A native of Bohemia, Ludwig Wenzel Lachnith had the tasteless temerity to remove all the numinous and comical elements from the work and to turn Papageno, for example, into a wiseacre shepherd by the name of Bochoris. Rarely, if ever, can a work of art have been treated with such contempt. Entire numbers ('Ihr an diesem Schreckensort?', 'Ach, ich fühl's', 'O Isis und Osiris, welche Wonne!', 'Soll ich dich Teurer nicht mehr sehn?') were omitted and replaced by pieces from other operas by Mozart, including the 'champagne aria' from *Don Giovanni* and an aria from *La clemenza di Tito*, both of them adapted as duets. The existing numbers, too, were reordered and altered, so that the opera began with the final chorus and Sarastro's recitative, followed by the trio (no. 16), here sung by six Priestesses, then a chorus from *La clemenza di Tito* ('Ah grazie si rendano') and finally the original Introduction. Monostatos's aria was allotted to Papagena (now called Mona), the Queen's first aria to Pamina, and the duet ('Bei Männern') was turned into a trio. Even the Parisians found this too much to take and renamed the opera 'Les misères d'ici',[336] dubbing Lachnith a 'dérangeur' rather than an 'arrangeur'.[337] Yet in spite of these objections, Lachnith's 'opération' was to the liking of French audiences in other ways, who

324. There may also be an allusion to Schikaneder in the Theatre Manager's final words in the 'Vorspiel auf dem Theater'.

325. *AmZ*, xiv (1812), 239.

326. *AmZ*, xiv (1812), 593–4, 804 and 864.

327. *AmZ*, xxxi (1829), 820.

328. *AmZ*, xiv (1812), 327.

329. Cambiasi, *La Scala 1778–1906*, 306–7. The production opened on 15 April 1816.

330. *AmZ*, xxi (1819), 42. In 1809 a ballet by Tinti and Cocchi was staged in Parma under the title *Il flauto magico*, but it is impossible to know whether it had anything to do with Mozart's opera; see Ferrari, *Spettacoli drammatico-musicali e coreografici in Parma dal 1628 al 1883*, 55.

331. Pohl, *Mozart und Haydn in London*, 147.

332. Hogarth, *Memoirs of the Opera*, ii.193. ◆ In fact, the opera had already been staged in German at Covent Garden on 27 May 1833. The earliest English-language production may have been mounted at Norwich on 1 June 1829; see Fawcett, 'The first undoubted "Magic Flute"?'

333. *AmZ*, xlii (1840), 736, and xliv (1842), 610.

334. *AmZ*, iii (1800/1), 135.

335. See *AmZ*, iv (1801/2), 69–70; and Wilder, *Mozart: L'homme et l'artiste*, 298.

336. *AmZ*, iv (1801/2), 47; German protests may be found in Reichardt, *Vertraute Briefe aus Paris*, i.162–3 and 457–8; Solger, *Nachgelassene Schriften*, i.69–70; Johann Jakob Engel, *Journal de Paris*, cccxlvi (1801); Friedrich Schlegel, *Europa*, ii/1 (1804), 178. Cramer, conversely, defended the adaptation, *Anecdotes sur Mozart*, 18–19; see also *Zeitung für die elegante Welt*, i (1801).

337. Castil-Blaze, *Théâtres lyriques de Paris: L'Académie impériale de musique de 1645 à 1855*, ii.86. Further, see Angermüller, '"Les Mystères d'Isis" (1801) und "Don Juan" (1805, 1834) auf der Bühne der Pariser Oper'.

particularly admired the brilliant ballets and sets. Indeed, the whole production and especially the admirable performances of the orchestra and chorus left such an impression that this caricature of the original had none the less chalked up no fewer than 134 performances by 1827.[338] Not until 23 February 1865 was the work performed in its original form at the Théâtre Lyrique and proved a brilliant success. The translation on this occasion was by Nuitter and Beaumont.[339]

338.   *AmZ*, xx (1818), 858, and xxxiii (1831), 82–3 and 142–3. But in 1829 a German production of *Die Zauberflöte* met with great acclaim; see *AmZ*, xxxi (1829), 466; see also Karl Julius Weber's report in his letter from Paris dated 27 April 1806 reproduced in Anonymous, 'Eine Verballhornung der Zauberflöte'.

339.   *Revue des deux mondes*, lvi (1865), 412–13; for the numerous, often extremely bizarre interpretations of *Die Zauberflöte*, see Blümml, 'Ausdeutungen der "Zauberflöte"'. ◆ In addition to productions and editions of the work, *Die Zauberflöte* was frequently arranged for small instrumental ensembles for domestic performance; see Funk, 'Die "Zauberflöte" in der bürgerlichen Wohnstube des 19. Jahrhunderts: Reduktionen für kleinere Besetzungen'. For general accounts of the opera's reception, see Branscombe, *W. A. Mozart: Die Zauberflöte*, 142–77, and Gruber, *Mozart and Posterity*, in particular.

53

Illness and death

Following the first performance of *Die Zauberflöte*, Mozart was keen to resume work on his *Requiem*.[1] Constanze had returned to Baden for a short break with her sister Sophie on 7 October 1791, and on the 8th we find Mozart writing to her: 'If I weren't so busy, I'd have gone off at once to spend a week with you; but it's not *easy* for me to work out *there*, and as far as possible I'd prefer to avoid all *inconvenience*; there's nothing I'd like more than to be able to live in peace, but to achieve this you have to work hard, which is what I'm doing.'[2] This is the only time that Mozart mentions his work on the *Requiem* in his final letters to Constanze,[3] all of which reveal his usual half-joking, half-anxious tone when writing to her. Yet the piece was evidently preoccupying him, persuading him to accept no more pupils until it was completed.[4] This feverish haste was already clearly bound up with his illness, which in turn merely reflected the way in which his health had over the years been undermined by a poor diet, overwork and endless worries. Even in his youth he had suffered a whole series of serious illnesses, most of which were the result of the stresses of travel, and we also know from Sigmund Barisani of two further cases during his early years in Vienna. Mozart was already very ill when he arrived in Prague to work on *La clemenza di Tito*, and from now on his health continued to deteriorate.[5] While putting the finishing touches to *Die Zauberflöte* he began to suffer from fainting fits, while his mood became noticeably more sombre. This is clear from a letter that he wrote in Italian to an unknown correspondent – perhaps Da Ponte, who was then in London – on 7 September 1791:

---

1. The following is based on Constanze's accounts in Niemetschek, *Leben des k. k. Kapellmeisters Wolfgang Gottlieb Mozart*, 34ff., and Nissen, *Biographie W. A. Mozarts*, 563–4. These accounts are confirmed by the report that Constanze gave to an English visitor to Salzburg in 1829; see Novello, 'A Visit to Mozart's Widow and Sister'; see also Hogarth, *Memoirs of the Opera*, ii.196–7. An additional authentic source is Sophie Haibel's letter of 7 April 1825, excerpts of which were reproduced by Nissen, *Biographie W. A. Mozarts*, 573–4. The complete text is reproduced in Nohl, *Musikalisches Skizzenbuch* and *Mozart nach den Schilderungen seiner Zeitgenossen*, 390 [*Briefe* iv.462–5]. ◆ It should be noted, in this context, that the evidence cited by Abert is selective and suits the intended trajectory of his biography. With the exception of citations from Mozart's letters, all of the testimony is posthumous and prompted by complicated personal motives both personal and financial. Although it is 'authentic' in the sense that it derives from those who witnessed Mozart's death, or were close to him, it is not necessarily accurate. Vincent and Mary Novello's accounts of their conversations with Constanze are given complete in Medici and Hughes, ed., *A Mozart Pilgrimage Being the Travel Diaries of Vincent & Mary Novello in the Year 1829*.
2. *Briefe*, iv.158 (letter of 7/8 October 1791).
3. ◆ Much as Abert wants to read Mozart's letter as referring to the *Requiem*, it does not necessarily do so: at the time he was also working on the clarinet concerto K622 and possibly the Masonic cantata *Laut verkünde unsre Freude* K623, which he entered in his thematic catalogue on 15 November.
4. He turned down a keyboard player recommended by Joseph von Jacquin, for example; see Mosel, *Über die Originalpartitur des Requiem von W. A. Mozart*, 5; and Stadler, *Nachtrag zur Vertheidigung der Echtheit des Mozart'schen Requiem*, 17.
5. ◆ To be sure, Mozart was under the weather in Prague. But there is no evidence that he was 'very' ill and it is not true that his health 'continued to deteriorate'. As Abert himself notes later in this chapter, Mozart's health improved in October and early November.

Affmo Signore. Vorrei seguire il vostro consiglio, ma come riuscirvi? ho il capo frastornato, conto a forza, e non poßo levarmi dagli occhi l'immagine di questo incognito. Lo vedo di continuo, esso mi prega, mi sollecita, ed impaziente mi chiede il lavoro. Continuo, perchè il comporre mi stanca meno del riposo. Altronde no ho più da tremere. Lo sento a quel chel provo, che l'ora suona; sono in procinto di spirare; ho finito prima di avar goduto del mio talento. La vita era pur si bella, la carriera s'appriva sotto auspici tanto fortunati, ma non si può cangiare il proprio destino. Nessuno misura i propri giorni, bisogna rassegnarsi, sarà quel che piacerà alla providenza, termino ecco il mio canto funebre non devo lasciarlo imperfetto.[6]

[My very dear Sir, I'd like to follow your advice, but how? my head is in a whirl, I cannot get out of my thoughts the image of that stranger. I see him constantly, begging me, urging me on, and impatiently demanding the work from me. I'm continuing with it, because composing tires me less than rest. On the other hand, I've no reason to be afraid. I feel it from what I know, namely, that the hour has struck; I am about to die; I have reached the end of my life without having enjoyed my talent. Life was so beautiful, my career had begun under such favourable auspices, but we cannot change our own destinies. No one can reckon the length of his days, we have to submit, howsoever it shall please Providence. And so I am completing my own funeral anthem, I cannot leave it unfinished.]

Following her return from Baden, Constanze did everything in her power to stop her husband from working and to cheer him up, but he remained listless and depressed. During a visit to the Prater he began to talk to her about death and, with tears in his eyes, told her that he was writing the *Requiem* for himself. 'I feel very strongly', he went on, 'that things can't go on like this for much longer; I'm sure I've been poisoned – I can't get this thought out of my head.'[7] This remark, which later gave rise to the completely unfounded suspicion that Salieri had poisoned Mozart,[8] is eloquent proof of his morbidly over-sensitive state of mind. Deeply disturbed, Constanze did all

6. Formerly in the possession of Mr Gouny in London, the letter's present whereabouts are unknown; reproduced in *Briefe*, iv.156. ◆ This letter is almost certainly a posthumous fabrication. The existence of the original has never been verified and the only known copy, formerly owned by the (then) Royal Library in Berlin, is also lost. This is not the only instance of a spurious letter by or to Mozart; in addition to the examples from van Swieten and Schikaneder cited above, see Eisen, 'Mozart Apocrypha'.
7. Even Niemetschek wondered whether Mozart's early death was 'artificially induced'; see Niemetschek, *Leben des k. k. Kapellmeisters Wolfgang Gottlieb Mozart*, 44. Destouches mentioned the poisoning story to Sulpiz Boisserée; see Boisserée, *Selbstbiographie, Tagebücher und Briefe*, i.292 [*Dokumente*, 442–3, *Documentary Biography*, 515–16]. And Marianne Sessi [Sesto in the 1804 Vienna production of *La clemenza di Tito*] believed in it, too; see *Neue Berliner Musikzeitung*, xiv (1860), 340. In a letter that she wrote to Carl Anton Ziegler in Munich on 25 August 1837, even Constanze said that her son knew that, unlike his father, he had no need to fear people who were envious of him and who had designs on his life [*Briefe*, iv.515]. ◆ This anecdote, too, cannot be confirmed. The composer Franz Seraph Destouches (1772–1844) is said to have studied with Joseph Haydn in 1787.
8. On his deathbed Salieri is said to have confessed to poisoning Mozart; see *AmZ*, xxvii (1825), 413. This was emphatically rejected by Carpani in 'Lettera del sig. G. Carpani in difesa del Mo. Salieri calumniato dell'avvelenamento del M. Mozart', who drew explicit attention to statements by Salieri's orderlies Rosenberg and Porsche and to a medical report according to which Mozart had died of a brain fever [*Dokumente*, 449, *Documentary Biography*, 522–3]. According to Moscheles, the dying Salieri described the rumour as untrue; Moscheles, *Aus Moscheles' Leben*; Neukomm, too, leapt to Salieri's defence, *Berliner allgemeine musikalische Zeitung*, i (1824), 172. According to Beethoven's conversation books, Schindler told Beethoven at the beginning of 1824: 'Salieri is in a poor way again. His health is completely undermined. He imagines that he was responsible for Mozart's death and that he poisoned him. It's true, he means to confess to it. – Once again we see the truth of the saying that everything receives its reward' [not in *Dokumente*; *Documentary Biography*, 524]. Needless to say, the ramblings of a dying man have no value as evidence when offset against other, more reliable reports. Salieri's friend in Braunschweig, the conductor Johann Gottfried Schwanenberger, is even said to have responded to the rumour that Mozart was a victim of Italian envy by exclaiming: 'Pazzi! non ha fatto niente per meritar un tal onore'; see *AmZ*, xxi (1819), 120, and Sievers, *Mozart und Süßmayer*, 3–4. Georg Friedrich Daumer, *Aus der Mansarde*, iv (1861), 75–6, even claimed that Mozart had been poisoned by his Masonic order. The legend that Salieri poisoned Mozart was even made the subject of a sad little tale by Gustav Nicolai, *Der Musikfeind*.

that she could to reassure him, finally taking away the score of the *Requiem* and turning for advice to Dr Closset.

Mozart's health did in fact improve at this point, allowing him to complete his masonic cantata on 15 November and to conduct its first performance three days later.[9] Indeed, he felt so much better that he ascribed the idea of his having been poisoned to the fact that he had simply been unwell. He persuaded Constanze to return the score of the *Requiem* and continued to work on it.

But the improvement to his health was only short-lived, and within days his earlier mood of depression had returned, bringing with it the renewed belief that he had been poisoned. He began to lose strength, his hands and feet became swollen, and he suffered from almost total immobility, followed by sudden vomiting. According to Joseph Deiner's version of events, Mozart went to the Silver Snake in November 1791. He looked terrible and, complaining about his state of health, asked Deiner to call on him the next morning as he wanted to buy some wood for the winter. When Deiner turned up the next morning, the Mozarts' serving girl reported that her master was feeling so ill that she had had to call a doctor. Deiner found Mozart in bed. 'There's nothing doing today, Joseph,' Mozart told him, barely audibly, 'today we're busy with doctors and apothecaries.'[10] By 28 November Mozart's health was giving rise to such serious concern that Closset sought the advice of Dr Mathias von Sallaba, who was head physician at the Vienna General Hospital. Mozart remained lucid throughout the two weeks that he was in bed: he thought of death constantly, facing it with equanimity, while taking his leave of life with feelings of regret, not least because only a few days before his death he received two offers that would have solved all his financial worries: not only had a number of members of the Hungarian aristocracy guaranteed him an income of 1000 florins a year, but an even more favourable offer had reached him from Amsterdam.[11] Instead, he was obliged to abandon his family and leave them to an uncertain future. Yet not even now did his goodness of heart abandon him, and he never revealed the least impatience. It was with great reluctance that he agreed to having his pet canary removed, first to the adjacent room, and then even further away, because he could no longer bear the sound of its singing.

Sophie Haibel recalled:

When Mozart fell ill, we both made him a nightshirt that he could put on from the front, as he could not turn over because of the swelling; and as we did not know how ill he was, we also made him a quilted dressing gown – – so that he would be well protected when he got up, and so we visited him regularly; he made it plain that he was genuinely pleased with the dressing gown. I visited him in town every day, and once when I went in on a Saturday, M. said to me, 'Now, dear Sophie, tell Mama that I am getting on very well and that I'll come out to see her during the week beginning with her name-day [22 November] to give her my very best wishes.'

9. ◆ The Masonic cantata *Laut verkünde unsre Freude* K623 was performed on 17 November, not 18 November as claimed here; see Eisen, *New Mozart Documents*, 71.

10. *Morgen-Post* (28 January 1856), 2; see also Nohl, *Mozart in den Schilderungen seiner Zeitgenossen*, 384–5, and Procházka, *Mozart in Prag*, 180–1 [*Dokumente*, 477–80, *Documentary Biography*, 563–6].

11. See Constanze's later petition. ◆ '. . . besides the reversion which he recently obtained of the position of Kapellmeister at St Stephen's Cathedral, he was assured shortly before his death of an annual subscription of 1000 florins from a number of the Hungarian nobility; while from Amsterdam he was advised of a still larger annual sum, for which he would have had to compose only a few works for the exclusive use of the subscribers' [*Dokumente*, 372, *Documentary Biography*, 421–2].

Mozart also took the liveliest interest in the increasing success of *Die Zauberflöte* and, watch in hand, followed every performance in his thoughts: 'The first act has just ended – now it's the passage "Dir, große Königin der Nacht".'[12] On the eve of his death, he told Constanze that he would like to hear *Die Zauberflöte* one more time and hummed 'Der Vogelfänger bin ich ja' quietly to himself. The conductor Johann Georg Roser happened to be present and went over to the keyboard and played the song, to Mozart's evident delight.[13] The *Requiem*, too, occupied him continuously. On completing each movement, he would immediately have it sung, while he himself accompanied it on the keyboard, at least as long as he had the strength to do so. At two o'clock in the afternoon of the day before he died, he asked for the score to be brought to his bed and sang the alto line himself,[14] while Schack took the soprano part, his brother-in-law Franz Hofer the tenor part and Gerl the bass part. They had reached the opening bars of the 'Lacrimosa' when Mozart, realizing that he would never complete the work, broke down and, crying uncontrollably, pushed the score to one side.[15]

When Sophie Haibel arrived that evening, Constanze greeted her despairingly: 'Thank God you've come, he was so bad last night that I thought he'd never get through today; if he's as bad again today, he'll die during the night.' When she went over to the bed, Mozart said to her, 'Ah, dear Sophie, it's good of you to come, you must stay here tonight, you must see me die.' Sophie tried to regain her composure and persuade Mozart to put such thoughts from his mind, but he only replied: 'I already have the taste of death on my tongue, who'll look after my dearest Constanze if you don't stay?' She asked to be allowed to return home briefly in order to tell her mother what was happening, and at Constanze's bidding she called in at St Peter's to ask if one of the priests would look in on Mozart, as if on a chance visit. She had 'great difficulty in persuading one of those inhuman priests' to come. Perhaps they were deterred by Mozart's Freemasonry, or perhaps there was some other reason, but it seems that a priest did finally come.[16] On her return Sophie found her brother-in-law in lively conversation with Süßmayr on the subject of the *Requiem*. 'Didn't I tell you that I was writing this *Requiem* for myself?' she heard him ask with tears in his eyes. He was so convinced that he was about to die that he told his wife to keep his death a secret until she had informed Albrechtsberger, as his post at St Stephen's belonged to the latter 'in the eyes of God and the world'.

Late that evening they sent for the doctor and eventually found him at the theatre. He offered to come when the performance was over. When he finally arrived, he took Süßmayr to one side and told him that the situation was hopeless, then prescribed cold compresses on Mozart's head, inducing such a state of shock that Mozart lost consciousness and from then on fantasized deliriously, apparently still preoccupied with his *Requiem*. He puffed up his cheeks and tried to imitate the sound of the timpani. Towards midnight he sat up and stared into space, then leant his head

12. Rochlitz, 'Verbürgte Anekdoten aus Wolfgang Gottlieb Mozarts Leben', 149.
13. *Monatsschrift für Theater und Musik*, iii (1857), 446. ◆ Manuscript biographies of Johann Georg Roser (1740–97) and his son Franz de Paula (1779–1830), now in the library of the Gesellschaft der Musikfreunde, Vienna, include at least two references to Mozart, neither of them, however, concerning the *Requiem*. Furthermore, the anecdotes that are transmitted cannot be reconciled with known facts; see *Dokumente*, 453, *Documentary Biography*, 528–9. Roser's deathbed visit to Mozart cannot be confirmed.
14. Mozart had a gentle tenor voice. Only when he was conducting and became excitable did he raise his voice; see Hogarth, *Memoirs of the Opera*, ii.198.
15. See the obituary of Benedikt Schack, *AmZ*, xxix (1827), 520–1, and Nissen, *Biographie W. A. Mozarts*, Anhang 169. ◆ Sophie Haibel's reminiscences derive from a letter that she wrote to Georg Nikolaus Nissen on 7 April 1825 (*Dokumente*, 449–52, *Documentary Biography*, 524–7).
16. See Kreitmaier, *W. A. Mozart: Eine Charakterzeichnung des großen Meisters nach den literarischen Quellen*, 111. Kreitmaier attributes this gross infringement of their professional duties to the priests' training in the Vienna of Joseph II.

against the wall and seemed to fall asleep. He died at five minutes to one[17] in the early hours of 5 December.[18]

Moments later Count Deym appeared and took Mozart's death mask.[19] Deiner was summoned in the morning 'in order to dress the master'. The body was laid out on a bier and covered with black drapery from a funeral society, then taken into the study and placed near the keyboard, where a crowd of mourners came to pay their last respects. The *Wiener Zeitung* reported:

> The I. & R. court chamber composer Wolfgang *Mozart* died here during the night of the 4th and 5th of this month. Known from childhood as the possessor of the rarest musical talent in all *Europe*, he ranked alongside the greatest composers thanks to the happiest development of his outstanding natural gifts and the most persistent application of those gifts; his works, loved and admired by all, bear witness to this and are the measure of the irreplaceable loss that the noble art of music has suffered through his death.[20]

A letter from Prague dated 12 December 1791 reports:

> Mozart is – dead. He returned home from Prague a sick man, and from then on continued to ail; he was thought to be suffering from dropsy and died in Vienna at the end of last week. His body swelled up after death, leading people to believe that he had been poisoned. One of his last works is said to be a Mass for the Dead that was performed at his obsequies. Only now that he is dead will the Viennese finally realize what they have lost in him.[21] During his lifetime he was always the object of cabals, which he may occasionally have provoked himself as a result of his sans souci manner. Neither his Figaro nor his Don Juan was successful in Vienna, but was all the more successful in Prague. May he rest in peace![22]

Constanze had been so ill herself on the previous day that she, too, required medical help. She now collapsed completely and lay in Mozart's bed in the hope of contracting the same fatal illness

---

17. ◆ A bronze death mask said to be Mozart's was discovered in 1947; it is reproduced in Deutsch, *Mozart und seine Welt*, 284. Further, see Krieg, 'Um Mozarts Totenmaske: Ein Beitrag zur Mozartikonographie'; Schwarz, 'Das Geheimnis um Mozarts Totenmaske'; Günther Duda, 'Die Totenmaske W. A. Mozarts'; and Heinrich Schuler, 'W. A. Mozarts Totenmaske: Bemerkungen zu ihrer Geschichte'.

18. The death certificate describes Mozart's illness as 'heated miliary fever'. His doctors could not agree on its true nature; see Niemetschek, *Leben des k. k. Kapellmeisters Wolfgang Gottlieb Mozart*, 37. The suggestion that he was suffering from hypertensive encephalopathy has little in its favour as Mozart remained lucid until shortly before his death. In 1824 Eduard Guldener von Lobes argued that Mozart was suffering from the rheumatic inflammatory fever that had then reached epidemic proportions in Vienna (see Carpani, 'Lettera del sig. G. Carpani in difesa del Mo. Salieri'), while others diagnosed dropsy (see above) and consumption; see Nissen, *Biographie W. A. Mozarts*, 571. Barraud, finally, suggested Bright's Disease, that is, nephritis; see Schurig, *Wolfgang Amade Mozart*, ii.277. ◆ It is now generally accepted that Mozart died of natural causes, probably rheumatic fever complicated by excessive blood-letting; see Bär, *Mozart: Krankheit, Tod, Begräbnis*. For further accounts, including different diagnoses, see Ludewig, 'Zum derzeitigen Stand der Forschung über die Ursachen des Todes von Mozart'; Davies, 'Mozart's health, illness, and death' and 'The death of Mozart'; Neumayr, 'Wolfgang Amadeus Mozart – Krankheit, Tod und Begräbnis'; and Anderson, 'Mozart's Death – The Case of Complications of Rheumatic Heart Disease'.

19. Nissen, *Biographie W. A. Mozarts*, 574 and Anhang 181; for Constanze's letter, see Nottebohm, *Mozartiana*, 133. The death mask later disappeared. Constanze is said to have destroyed a copy of it; see Nohl, *Mozart nach den Schilderungen seiner Zeitgenossen*, 392; and Engl, *Mozart in den Schilderungen seiner Biographen*, 50.

20. *Wiener Zeitung* (7 December 1791) [*Dokumente*, 369, *Documentary Biography*, 418].

21. Niemetschek quotes an unnamed composer in Vienna (one suspects that it was Salieri) as saying: 'It's a shame that such a great genius has died, but a blessing for the rest of us; had he lived any longer, in truth the world would not have given us any more scraps of bread for our own compositions'; see Niemetschek, *Leben des k. k. Kapellmeisters Wolfgang Gottlieb Mozart*, 84.

22. *Musikalisches Wochenblatt*, xii (?31 December 1791), 94 [*Dokumente*, 380, *Documentary Biography*, 431–2].

and accompanying him on his final journey. Here, too, she remained true to her own nature, as did Gottfried van Swieten. He arrived very quickly and, attempting to comfort her, persuaded her to spend the next few days with a family of her acquaintance. At the same time, however, he advised her – in view of her limited means – to keep the burial as simple as possible. Accordingly, Mozart was given a third-class burial costing 8 florins 36 kreutzers, plus 3 florins for the hearse. Thus the immensely wealthy and influential van Swieten rewarded Mozart for all the services that he had rendered him over a period of nearly ten years.

The body was consecrated in the Crucifix Chapel on the northern side of St Stephen's, near the Capistrano Pulpit, at three o'clock on the afternoon of 6 December. Heavy rain and snow meant that the few mourners who were present – they included van Swieten, Salieri, Süßmayr, Deiner, Roser and the cellist Joseph Orsler[23] – stood around the bier holding umbrellas, before making their way along the Schulerstraße to St Marx's Cemetery. As the weather continued to deteriorate, the mourners decided to turn back at the Stubentor,[24] with the result that none of Mozart's friends was at his graveside when the coffin was lowered into the ground. Swieten had advised a pauper's grave, which normally took between fifteen and twenty coffins and was cleared every ten years. And so Mozart found his final resting place among the poorest of Vienna's poor, with no mark attesting to the place where he was buried. Deiner asked Constanze whether she wanted a simple cross placed over the grave. She replied that she assumed that Mozart would be given one as a matter of course as the parish where the burial had taken place would see to this.[25] By the time that she had recovered and returned to the cemetery with a group of friends, there was a new gravedigger who was unable to show her where her husband had been buried. All their enquiries were in vain. Later, too, it has proved equally impossible to establish Mozart's final resting place with any degree of certainty.[26] Constanze's attitude in all this is inexcusable. It was entirely typical

23. *Monatsschrift für Theater und Musik*, iii (1857), 446; and Nottebohm, *Mozartiana*, 55. It seems likely that the mourners also included Mozart's two brothers-in-law, Joseph Lange and Franz Hofer, as well as Benedikt Schack. According to Nissen, Schikaneder was not present; he is said to have been deeply shaken by Mozart's death and to have exclaimed: 'His ghost follows me everywhere, I see him wherever I look'; see Nissen, *Biographie W. A. Mozarts*, 572. ◆ It is not true that the weather was inclement on the day of Mozart's funeral; Zinzendorf's diary for 6 December records 'mild weather and frequent mist'; similarly, a weather report in the court-sanctioned *Wiener Zeitung* notes only a light north wind and temperatures hovering slightly over freezing. See *Dokumente*, 397, *Documentary Biography*, 418. The traditional account, of course, is more atmospheric. It seems likely, too, that the funeral procession from Mozart's apartment to St Stephen's included a crossbearer, four pallbearers, choirboys, Constanze, her sister and other members of the Weber family, van Swieten, Mozart's students Franz Jakob Freystädtler, Süßmayr and Otto Hatwig, and his friends and colleagues Johann Georg Albrechtsberger, Anselm Hüttenbrenner and Salieri; see Christoph Wolff, *Mozart's Requiem: Historical and Analytical Studies, Documents, Score*. Further, the traditional tale of few (and apparently not very distraught) mourners reinforced the idea that Vienna did not really care about Mozart. Recently discovered documents, however, show that a Requiem Mass was held for Mozart at St Michael's, the parish church of the Hofburg. Organized by Schikaneder and his colleague Joseph von Bauernfeld on behalf of Vienna's court and theatre musicians, parts of the *Requiem* may have been performed on this occasion. See Brauneis, 'Exequien für Mozart' and 'Unveröffentlichte Nachrichten zum Dezember 1791 aus einer Wiener Lokalzeitung'.

24. *Morgen-Post* (28 January 1856), 2. ◆ This assertion derives from Deiner's memoirs; see note 10 above.

25. ◆ The origin of the legends surrounding Mozart's burial – and their meaning – remains obscure. But it is certainly not the case that Mozart was buried in a pauper's grave: individual graves were the exception, not the rule, in Josephine Vienna and while the nobility and some wealthy merchants may have erected family vaults, gravestones were otherwise permitted only along cemetery walls; Joseph's 'court decree on religious and police matters' of 23 August 1784 makes it clear that bodies were to be sewn into linen sacks and that if several bodies arrived at the cemetery at the same time, they could be placed in a single grave. Nor was it common practice, once cemeteries were relocated beyond the city limits, to accompany bodies to the gravesite. All in all, then, Mozart had a 'normal' burial for the time. For a level-headed account of Viennese burial practice, including a translation of Joseph's decree, see Braunbehrens, *Mozart in Vienna*, 413–24. Abert's characterization of Constanze's behaviour in what follows – or van Swieten's, mentioned above – must accordingly be taken with a grain of salt.

26. See the *Journal des Luxus und der Moden* (1808), ii.801–2. All the older works on this contentious issue are discussed by Wurzbach, *Mozart-Buch*, 148ff. Particularly worth mentioning in this context are the researches of Aloys Fuchs in Gräffer, 'Das Mozarthaus. Mozarts Grab', 227–8 (with negative results). A deceptive lead that came to light in 1845 was reported in the Österreichischer Lloyd *Illustriertes Familienbuch zur Unterhaltung & Belehrung häuslicher Kreise* ii (1852), 117. New material was

of her to allow things to take whatever course they liked. Even her characteristic outbursts of emotion do nothing to alter this assessment. On the back of Sigmund von Barisani's entry in Mozart's album, for example, she wrote the following:

What you once wrote to your friend on this page, I now write, bent low over you, dearly beloved husband! Mozart, never to be forgotten by me or by the whole of Europe – you too are now at rest, eternal rest!

At 1 o'clock on the morning of 5 December this year he left this good but ungrateful world in his 36th year – alas, all too soon! – O God! – For eight years we were joined together by the most tender bond, never to be broken here below! Oh, if only I could be joined with you for ever,

Your grievously afflicted wife
Constance Mozart née Weber.

Vienna, 5 December 1791.[27]

Mozart's death left his family in a precarious financial position.[28] They had sixty florins in cash, in addition to which they were owed 133 florins and 20 kreutzers in arrears on Mozart's annual salary, but all other claims had to be abandoned.[29] The whole of Mozart's household effects, including his clothes and library,[30] were valued at less than 500 florins. Conversely, there were substantial debts that had to be paid, not only to Puchberg, who forbore to raise the matter but simply got on with helping Constanze to sort out the estate, but also to various artisans and shop-keepers of every description, all of whom demanded payment.[31] In total, these debts amounted to 3000 florins.[32] In the circumstances, Constanze decided to appeal to the emperor's generosity, but first she had to counter the slanderous rumour that Mozart had been guilty of extravagance and run up debts of 30,000 florins. In particular, she had to deal with a domestic tragedy that had taken

presented by Johann von Lucam in 1856; see his *Die Grabesfrage Mozarts: Nach brieflichen Originalurkunden der Witwe Mozarts selbst.* Lucam questioned two musicians who had known Mozart, Franz Jakob Freystädtler and (Carl?) Scholl, and was told that the grave was in the third or fourth row to the right of the main cross. This is confirmed by details given by Nissen, *Biographie W. A. Mozarts*, 576. Official enquiries undertaken in 1856 have made it likely that Mozart was buried in the fourth row to the right of the cross, close to a willow bush; see *Wiener Blätter für Musik, Theater und Kunst* (1859), 97–8. According to a report from Dresden published in the *Neue Zeitschrift für Musik*, lii (1890), 589, the gravedigger had been an admirer of Mozart's from his boyhood and had made a note of the location of the grave. In 1801, when the mass grave was cleared, he had taken Mozart's skull, which was acquired in turn by his successor. In 1842 this skull passed into the possession of the engraver Jakob Hyrtl, whence to the latter's brother Joseph, who was a well-known anatomist in Vienna. On Joseph's death it came into the possession of the Mozarteum in Salzburg, where it is still to be found; Johann Evangelist Engl believes the skull to be genuine; see his, 'W. A. Mozarts Schädel'. In fact, its authenticity is far from clear; see Schafhäutl, 'Wolfgang Amadäus Mozart: Wie hat er eigentlich ausgesehen?'; and Anonymous, 'Noch einmal der Schädel Mozarts', 466. ◆ The authenticity of the skull continues to be a matter of controversy. See Ullrich, 'Wolfgang Amadeus Mozart – Ein falscher Schädel ruht im Mozarteum in Salzburg'; Karhausen, 'The Mozarteum's skull: a historical saga'; and Murray, 'The Skull of Mozart'.

27. See above [*Dokumente*, 367, *Documentary Biography*, 416], with Mozart's postscript; for a facsimile of Constanze's entry, see Schurig, *Wolfgang Amade Mozart*, ii.333.

28. The papers relating to Mozart's estate were reproduced in the *Deutsche Musik-Zeitung* (9 September 1861), 284–5. ◆ For a fuller account, see *Dokumente*, 493–511, *Documentary Biography*, 583–604.

29. They were owed 300 florins by Franz Gilowsky, who in July 1787 was reported to have fled the city in debt – see the *Posttägliche Anzeigen aus dem k. k. Frag- und Kundschaftsamt in Wien*, xxxv (1787); and another 500 florins by Anton Stadler.

30. Mozart's books and scores were valued at 23 florins 41 kreutzers.

31. The apothecary's bills alone amounted to more than 200 florins.

32. ◆ Not included in this total is the sum of just over 1435 gulden that a Viennese court awarded Prince Karl Lichnowsky as a result of a lawsuit against Mozart barely a month before the composer's death. The cause of Lichnowsky's action, the legal proceedings surrounding it, and details of any settlement are unknown. See Brauneis, '". . . wegen schuldigen 1435 f 32 xr": Neuer Archivfund zur Finanzmisere Mozarts im November 1791', *Mitteilungen der Internationalen Stiftung Mozarteum*, xxxix (1991), 159–63.

place at the home of Franz Hofdemel, a clerk of the Supreme Judiciary, who was said to have killed himself out of jealousy on 10 December 1791 on discovering that his wife's name had been linked with Mozart's.[33] Constanze discovered this from one of Mozart's pupils, who at the same time urged her to obtain an audience with the incensed emperor and prove that the rumour was groundless. As a result she handed her petition to the emperor in person on 11 December, pointing out that her husband had attracted these calumnies simply because he was talented. His enemies and those who envied him had increased his debts tenfold: 3000 florins would be enough to meet all outstanding liabilities. Not even these debts had been frivolously incurred but were the result of the family's depressed finances, including frequent illnesses and confinements. Leopold II agreed to help and encouraged Constanze to organize a concert, to which he generously contributed, allowing her to pay off all her debts.[34] Following Leopold's death on 1 March 1792, her request for a pension was authorized by his successor, Franz II, on the recommendation of Prince Starhemberg. She received 266 florins 40 kreutzers a year.[35]

33. See Jahn, *Gesammelte Aufsätze über Musik*, 230–1; and Bischoff, 'Zur Geschichte der Frau Magdalena Hofdemel'. For a long time, Beethoven, too, refused to play in Maria Magdalena Hofdemel's presence 'because of her affair with Mozart'; see Thayer, *Ludwig van Beethovens Leben*, ii/2.150–51. ◆ Further, see Gärtner, *Adieu, Mozart: Die Hofdemel-Tragödie und die Selbstzerstörung eines Genies*.
34. The concert took place on 29 December 1794. ◆ The programme included an unstaged version of *La clemenza di Tito* and, between the acts of the opera, a performance by Anton Eberl, who may have been a pupil of Mozart's, of an unidentified concerto by Mozart. Eberl, whose C minor sonata op. 1 was originally, and incorrectly, published under Mozart's name, toured Germany with Constanze and Aloysia Lange in 1795 and 1796; Haas, 'Anton Eberl'.
35. ◆ For the documents relating to Constanze's petition and its resolution, see *Dokumente*, 388–92, *Documentary Biography*, 442–7.

54

The Requiem

Constanze's immediate concern was her husband's unfinished *Requiem* K626.[1] She was worried that the stranger who had commissioned it might refuse to accept the unfinished work and demand the return of the fee that had already been paid, and so she and her advisers hit on the idea of completing the work and in that way satisfying the stranger's demands. The first composer to be invited to complete it was Joseph Eybler,[2] who began by instrumenting the existing score as far as the 'Confutatis' and adding two more bars to the 'Lacrimosa',[3] before abandoning the exercise as too problematical. A number of other musicians are said to have turned down Constanze's request before her choice finally fell on Süßmayr. Süßmayr had studied composition with Mozart during the final months of his life, had helped with *La clemenza di Tito* and had worked through each of the completed sections of the *Requiem* with him. Mozart had initiated him into the exact

---

1. Among recent studies, see Pressel, 'Die aufgefundene Original-Handschrift der Nummern VIII und IX des Mozart'schen Requiems' and Johann Evangelist Engl, 'Das Requiem und Requiem-Frage'. Both writers discuss a manuscript score of the 'Domine Jesus' and 'Hostias' in André's possession. Fully instrumented, this manuscript is said to be by Mozart himself. Both writers then go on to argue in favour of the existence of a second, complete original draft that was used by Süßmayr. But this flies in the face of Mozart's whole working method and cannot be reconciled with the accounts of Constanze and Stadler and may therefore be safely ignored. See also André, *Beiträge zur Geschichte des Requiems von W. A. Mozart*; Mosel, *Über die Originalpartitur des Requiem von W. A. Mozart*; and Köchel, 'Mozarts Requiem: Nachlese zu den Forschungen über dessen Entstehen'. Analyses have been published by Hahn, *Mozarts Requiem: Zum besseren Verständnis mit einer neuen Übersetzung nebst einem Nachtrag und den Resultaten eines Vergleiches der Breitkopf & Härtelschen Partitur mit den Original-Manuskripten der k. k. Hofbibliothek zu Wien*, and Kretzschmar, *Führer durch den Konzertsaal*, fourth edition, ii/1.274ff. The whole question of the work's authenticity has recently been reexamined from a stylistic point of view by Handke, whose approach has proved particularly fruitful; see his 'Zur Lösung der Benedictus-Frage in Mozarts Requiem'. Of importance, finally, is Alfred Schnerich's facsimile edition of the autograph score, published in 1914. ✦ The literature concerning Mozart's *Requiem* is vast. For summaries of the history of the manuscripts and the controversies surrounding its completion, see in particular Moseley, 'Mozart's Requiem: A Revaluation of the Evidence'; Christoph Wolff, *Mozart's Requiem: Historical and Analytical Studies, Documents, Score*; and Gmeiner, 'Der sogenannte "Echtheitsstreit"'. For analyses of the work in the context of other similar works, see especially Manfred Schuler, 'Mozarts Requiem in der Tradition gattungsgeschichtlicher Topoi' and Reutter, 'Trauersymbolik im Introitus des Requiem: Jommelli und die Gattungstradition'. And for analyses centred almost exclusively on the work itself, see Manfred Hermann Schmid, 'Introitus und Communio im Requiem: Zum Formkonzept von Mozart und Süßmayr' and 'Das "Lacrimosa" in Mozarts Requiem'; Wolff, *Mozart's Requiem: Historical and Analytical Studies, Documents, Score*; and Wolf-Dieter Seiffert, 'Wolfgang Amadeus Mozart: Requiem'. A high-quality facsimile of the autograph was produced by the Österreichische Nationalbibliothek in 1991.
2. See Eybler's statement: 'The undersigned hereby acknowledges that the composer's widow, Frau Konstanzie [*sic*] Mozart, has entrusted him with the completion of the Requiem Mass begun by her late husband; the same undertakes to complete it by the middle of the coming Lent and at the same time guarantees that it shall neither be copied nor entrusted to hands other than those of the aforementioned widow. Vienna, 21 Dec. 1791' [*Dokumente*, 375, *Documentary Biography*, 426–7]. Mozart had written a reference for Eybler on 30 May 1790: 'I, the undersigned, attest herewith that I have found the bearer of this testimonial, Herr Joseph Eybler, to be a worthy pupil of his famous master Albrechtsberger. He is a deeply knowledgeable composer, equally skilled in chamber music and the church style, fully versed in the art of composition, and also an accomplished organist and keyboard player, in short a young musician of a kind that regrettably has few equals'; see *Neue Berliner Musikzeitung* (1858), 244 [*Dokumente*, 322, *Documentary Biography*, 366–7]. In a letter to Constanze that Spitta dates to the autumn of 1789, Deiters to the year 1790, Mozart notes: 'We're invited to a service and to lunch at Schwechat.' Eybler's father was a schoolteacher and choirmaster at Schwechat; see Jahn, *W. A. Mozart*, fourth edition, ii.660 [*Briefe*, iv.110, letter of ?2 June 1790].
3. See Köchel, 'Mozarts Requiem', 753.

nature of his work on the score, including the instrumentation,[4] so that, familiar as he was with Mozart's working method, he would no doubt have been able to form an impression of the composer's aims and intentions, at least as far as this was at all possible.

The position was as follows. The first two movements – the Introit and the Kyrie – were both complete in Mozart's score.[5] Of the 'Dies irae', only the vocal parts and meticulously figured basso continuo were written out in full, in keeping with Mozart's usual practice. As for the instrumentation, only a handful of motifs were indicated in the preludes and interludes and at other characteristic points. All were intended to show how these passages should later be developed. The 'Lacrimosa' breaks off at the words 'qua resurget ex favilla judicandus homo reus'. Of the Offertory, the 'Domine Jesu' and the 'Hostias' were completed in draft score, while the Sanctus, Benedictus and Agnus Dei are missing in their entirety.

In dealing with the question of the work's authenticity, earlier writers almost always took this original score as their starting point, while failing to ask themselves whether Süßmayr had other sources at his disposal, either in the form of excerpts that Mozart played to him or that he had communicated in some other way but which he had failed to write down, or in the form of loose sketches. We know, for example, that Constanze told Stadler[6] that at the time of Mozart's death she had found 'a number of scraps of paper with music on them' and passed them on to Süßmayr, without knowing what they contained. Likewise, Schack's report of the deathbed performance of the *Requiem* by Mozart and his friends presupposes the existence of written parts, including vocal parts and figured bass for the complete 'Lacrimosa'.[7] Although the absence of evidence will never allow us to be absolutely clear on this point, we may still hope to be able to establish certain findings on the strength of a stylistic examination, even if it is only to realize that the earlier method of relying entirely on the evidence of the original score and on the information provided by Süßmayr is incapable of providing a satisfactory answer to the question.[8]

4. Constanze later told Stadler: 'When Mozart felt weak, Süßmayr often had to sing through what he had written with him and me, and in this way he received formal instruction from him. And I can still hear Mozart telling Süßmayr: "Well, you're still standing there like a cow at a five-barred gate, you still don't understand."' Stadler, *Nachtrag zur Vertheidigung der Echtheit des Mozart'schen Requiem*, 40. Constanze's sister Sophie also remembered this remark.
5. The two movements are written on five sheets of the twelve-line oblong-format Italian manuscript paper that Mozart normally used. Each folio is numbered from one to ten, but there is no separate pagination; the last three sides are blank. The work is headed 'Di me W. A. Mozart 1792'. Evidently Mozart anticipated completing the work in 1792. ◆ Abert's account is not quite correct. Although Mozart completed the Introit, in the Kyrie, only the vocal parts and orchestral bass part are by him; the two violins, viola, basset-horns and bassoons were written by Franz Jakob Freystädtler, and the trumpets and timpani by Süßmayr. Similarly, the inscription 'Di me W. A. Mozart 792' is not by Mozart but by Süßmayr: why he would have fabricated the inscription, however, remains unclear.
6. Stadler, *Vertheidigung der Echtheit des Mozart'schen Requiem*, 46.
7. Deiters rightly draws attention to this point in Jahn, *W. A. Mozart*, ii.691. ◆ This assumes, of course, that Schack's memory was reliable. It seems more likely, however, to be an affecting tale than an eyewitness account of the composer's final hours. By the time Schack's report was published, it was widely believed that the fragmentarily transmitted 'Lacrimosa' represented Mozart's last work on the composition – as such it was a fitting moment for Mozart to 'break down'. As the autograph shows, however, Mozart also wrote down the vocal and orchestral bass part for the 'Domine Jesu' and 'Quam olim Abrahae' (with a few bars for the first violin in the fugue); there is no compelling reason to think that the 'Lacrimosa' was composed later. The passage in Schack's report reads: '. . . they were at the first bars of the "Lacrimosa" when Mozart began to weep bitterly' (*Dokumente*, 460, *Documentary Biography*, 537). More generally, paper studies suggest that none of the *Requiem* was committed to paper before Mozart's return from Prague about 13 or 14 September 1791; see Tyson, *Mozart: Studies of the Autograph Scores*, 35. Similarly, it is unlikely that any of the work was written down after the onset of Mozart's terminal illness, about 20 November.
8. ◆ Since Abert's time, a single sketchleaf relating to the *Requiem* has been discovered, for an 'Amen' apparently intended to conclude the 'Lacrimosa'; see Plath, 'Über Skizzen zu Mozarts Requiem'. For transcriptions of the sketch, see Christoph Wolff, *Mozart's Requiem: Historical and Analytical Studies, Documents, Score*, 30, and NMA X/30/4; for a facsimile, see Wolff, *Mozart's Requiem: Historical and Analytical Studies, Documents, Score*, 54.

Süßmayr began by copying out Mozart's own copy of the work 'so that the two scripts would not overlap with each other'.[9] He then added the missing instrumentation to his own copy, adopting an approach that he believed most closely reflected Mozart's own intentions.[10] He added a new ending to the 'Lacrimosa' (from 'judicandus homo reus' onwards) and, in his own words, 'prepared' the Sanctus, Benedictus and Agnus Dei that are not found in Mozart's autograph. In order to 'give the work greater unity', he repeated the fugue from the Kyrie for the 'Cum sanctis'.

The whole work was now handed over to Walsegg's emissary, the first two movements in Mozart's original, the rest in Süßmayr's hand.[11] Süßmayr's handwriting was in fact so similar to Mozart's that not only Walsegg himself but many later commentators thought that it was Mozart's original score that they had before them.[12] Not until 10 February 1839 did Constanze clarify the situation by answering a question on the subject. Minor discrepancies between the two manuscripts had already been noted. But now there could be no doubt any longer that Süßmayr had written out the score from the 'Dies irae' onwards. This section is also separately paginated, beginning with the Sanctus.[13]

Constanze was initially keen for the world to believe that Mozart himself had completed the *Requiem*. In 1796, for example, Friedrich Rochlitz consulted her in Leipzig on the genesis of the work and was told that Mozart had finished it before he died.[14] But the deception could not be sustained for long. When Gottfried van Swieten performed it in the Jahnscher Saal in Vienna in 1792[15] on the basis of a copy retained by Constanze, the performers already knew which parts were by Mozart and which by Süßmayr.[16] The same was true in Munich[17] and Prague, where a performance was given soon after Mozart's death using a copy from Vienna and the sections from the Sanctus onwards were recognized as the work of Süßmayr.[18] Constanze gave individual copies to various members of the aristocracy[19] and allowed others to make copies of their

9. Constanze's letter to André quoted in *Caecilia*, vi (1827), 202 [*Briefe*, iv.387; letter of 26 November 1800].

10. Of Mozart's original drafts, Maximilian Stadler was given folios 11–32 (from the 'Dies irae' to the end of the 'Confutatis'). In turn, he left them to the Vienna Court Library [now the Österreichische Nationalbibliothek]. Folios 33–45, covering the 'Lacrimosa', 'Domine' and 'Hostias', were acquired by Eybler, who likewise gave them to the Vienna Court Library. André published an exact copy of all these folios in 1829 under the title *Partitur des 'Dies irae' etc.* Curiously, he also reconstructed a similar draft score for the 'Requiem' and Kyrie. For more on the attempts to elaborate Mozart's draft (the hand responsible for these attempts is almost certainly Eybler's), see Brahms's critical commentary to his edition, AMA XXIV/1. Eybler and Stadler received their sections of the score from Constanze after Süßmayr had returned them to her; see Constanze's letter of 2 June 1802 [*Briefe*, iv.421–2]. ◆ Further concerning Constanze, André and André's editions, see Plath, 'Requiem-Briefe: Aus der Korrespondenz Johann Anton Andrés 1825–1831'.

11. Stadler, *Vertheidigung der Echtheit des Mozart'schen Requiem*, 17. Count Walsegg's sister, Countess Sternberg, sold his music library to his steward Franz Anton Leitgeb, from whom the score passed into the possession of the count's secretary Karl Haag, thence to the wife of the Stuppach court usher Johann Adelpoller, Katharina Adelpoller. Another of Count Walsegg's former stewards, a legal commissioner by the name of Novak of Schottwien, drew the attention of the Imperial and Royal Court Librarian, Count Moritz von Dietrichstein, to the existence of the score, and Dietrichstein duly bought it for his Library for 50 ducats.

12. *AmZ*, xli (1839), 81; and Gottfried Weber, 'Die vollständige eigenhändige Partitur', 279.

13. Jahn was unsure of the provenance of the last six bars of the 'Tuba mirum'; see Jahn, *W. A. Mozart*, ii.695–6. Their instrumentation is not in fact by Mozart but is the work of a third party (Eybler or Stadler?), whose treatment of the viola line at another point in the score is preferable to Süßmayr's; see Brahms's critical commentary and Deiters's commentary on Jahn, *W. A. Mozart*, ii.670. ◆ The last six bars of the 'Tuba mirum' were orchestrated by Süßmayr.

14. Rochlitz, 'Verbürgte Anekdoten aus Wolfgang Gottlieb Mozarts Leben', 178; and Gottfried Weber, 'Weitere Nachrichten', 288.

15. ◆ In fact, this was on 2 January 1793.

16. Stadler, *Nachtrag zur Vertheidigung der Echtheit des Mozart'schen Requiem*, 6; see also Constanze's letter of 17 November 1799 reproduced in Nohl, *Mozart nach den Schilderungen seiner Zeitgenossen*, 331 [*Briefe*, iv.290–6].

17. *AmZ*, xxix (1827), 520.

18. Weber, 'Weitere Nachrichten', 308. The Dresden singer Antonio Mariottini copied out the Introit, Kyrie and 'Dies irae', presumably on the basis of a copy from Prague or Vienna, adding: 'L'offertorio, il Sanctus e l'Agnus Dei non gl'ho trascritti perché non mi anno parso essere del valore del precedente, ne credo ingannarmi nel crederli opera di un' altra penna'; quoted by Weber, 'Weitere Nachrichten', 301–2 and 310–11.

19. From Friedrich Wilhelm II she received 100 ducats for the copy that she sent him; see Zawrzel and Krüchten, 'Anzeige', 211.

own.[20] Johann Adam Hiller, for example, copied out the full score, adding to it the title 'Opus summum viri summi' ('The greatest work by the greatest man') and performed it without any indication of the fact that it was not all by Mozart.[21] The work soon became the most sought after of all settings of the Mass for the Dead, with the result that Constanze began to consider ways of publishing it and turning it to her material advantage. Believing that Walsegg – whose identity remained concealed from her – had expressly forbidden this, she even thought of advertising in the press and asking him for his permission, an idea that she very soon abandoned.[22] Meanwhile she had been informed by Breitkopf & Härtel in Leipzig that they were planning to publish the work on the basis of several copies in their possession and, in order to establish a reliable edition, asked if they could consult her own copy. Unable to prevent publication, she agreed to Härtel's request. Rumour had it that there was more than one *Requiem*, and so we find her writing to the firm on 27 March 1799:

> As far as the *Requiem* is concerned, I have, of course, the famous one that he wrote shortly before his death. [...] I am not aware of any other setting, all the rest must be inauthentic.[23] How far it is by Mozart himself – it is so virtually to the end – I shall tell you when I send it to you. The facts are as follows. When he saw that his end was approaching, he spoke with Herr Süßmayr, now I. & R. Kapellmeister, and asked that, in the event of his dying without completing it, the opening fugue should be repeated in the final movement, as is in any case customary, and also told him how to deal with the end of the work, of which the main substance was already finished in the form of parts. And this is what Herr Süßmayr in fact did.[24]

Later Constanze referred Härtel to Süßmayr himself, and the latter replied on 8 February 1800, supplying the information already mentioned but avoiding all reference to any instructions on Mozart's part: clearly Constanze was concerned above all to ensure that the work was seen as a unified whole.

Breitkopf & Härtel duly announced publication of the *Requiem*, which they advertised as 'based on the manuscript communicated by Mozart's widow',[25] prompting a reaction from the hitherto silent Count Walsegg who, as we have seen, had been happy to pass himself off as its composer. He sent the copy of the score that he had received from Mozart to his lawyer Johann Nepomuk Sortschan in Vienna and demanded an explanation and compensation from Constanze. The negotiations were conducted in her name by Stadler and Nissen. Stadler reported on the way in which the work had been completed and the relative contributions of Mozart and Süßmayr, and Sortschan undertook to convey this information to the count.[26] According to Constanze's letter to

20. Häser recalls that an excellent copyist at the Thomasschule by the name of Jost prepared two copies of the score for Constanze during her visits to Leipzig; see Gottfried Weber, 'Weitere Nachrichten', 297.
21. Rochlitz, *Für Freunde der Tonkunst*, third edition, i.17
22. In a letter to Härtel of 18 October 1799, she encloses a draft of her demand: 'As the noble and anonymous gentleman who gave the late Mozart the commission to compose a *Requiem* a few months before his death has still not published the work after more than 7 years, his widow gratefully regards this as proof that he may be willing to grant her some advantage from its publication. In the meantime she considers it an increased safeguard for herself and her duty, in view of the sentiments which he has occasioned in her, to invite this noble gentleman, through the columns of the Vienna, Hamburg and Frankfurt newspapers, to be kind enough to acquaint her of his intentions within a period of three months, after which time she will take the liberty of publishing the *Requiem* in her late husband's collected works' [*Briefe*, iv.278].
23. Thus we need have no hesitation in dismissing as inauthentic the *Missa brevis* in D minor KAnh. C 1.90 that Simrock published in Bonn without any attempt to authenticate it on internal or external grounds.
24. ◆ *Briefe*, iv.233–4.
25. *AmZ*, i (1798/9), Intelligenzblatt 97–8.
26. Stadler, *Verteidigung der Echtheit des Mozart'schen Requiem*, 14–15.

Härtel of 30 January 1800, Walsegg demanded the return of his fifty ducats, although she thought that he might settle for a number of copies of the score. After a number of 'serious complaints and threats', Nissen finally persuaded the count to accept copies of several unpublished works by Mozart[27] and to allow Constanze to compare the printed score with his own copy.[28]

When discussing the *Ave verum corpus*, we noted the distance that Mozart had travelled since 1780 and how far he had progressed from the style associated with his earlier sacred works.[29] The *Requiem* reveals the full extent of this gulf: in its whole character and spiritual aims it is a completely different piece from even the C minor Mass of 1783. Mozart's attitude to religion had changed beyond recognition – not that the ideas associated with Catholicism had lost their power over him, for even as a Freemason he remained a convinced Catholic. But dogma, as such, was no longer enough for him, and he now sought to internalize his Church's soteriological truths. Even as a boy he had felt powerfully drawn to mysticism, and this tendency now emerged with increasing clarity during the last five years of his life, with the idea of death and the afterlife preoccupying his thoughts to a much greater extent than before, as the once hedonistic composer became increasingly conscious of the existence of a metaphysical world whose terrors he had first felt in *Don Giovanni*, before revealing its purifying and elevating force to him in *Die Zauberflöte*, a work that proclaims this force as the highest goal of human aspirations, while the *Requiem* addresses it from its metaphysical aspect, as a power which, remote from all temporal concerns, arouses man's feelings of guilt and need for redemption. In this, Mozart found himself on common ground with the Church's teachings on the Last Judgement and divine mercy. The threads thus lead directly from *Die Zauberflöte* to the *Requiem*, a relationship clear even on the most superficial level, with the combination of basset-horns, bassoons and trombones, occasionally complemented by trumpets and timpani in addition to strings, that had already been used in *Die Zauberflöte* to express a sense of mystic sublimity returning in the *Requiem* and with only the absence of the remaining woodwinds and horns making the colours much darker. Its orchestral character rests solely on the way in which these various instruments are combined. Another feature that the two works have in common is the greater use of a strict ecclesiastical style that is found in the opera in the chorale for the two Men in Armour and that is developed and intensified in the *Requiem*. It is this feature which, reflecting the influence of Bach and Handel, determines the character of the *Requiem* and sets it apart from Mozart's earlier sacred works. There is no longer any trace of the former mixture of contrapuntai and homophonic sections and of liturgical, aria-like and instrumental forms. Nor is there any trace of the discursiveness and volubility that meant that the spiritual element was sometimes overwhelmed by the purely musical. The strictly sacred character of the present setting, coupled with Mozart's immense skill in investing the briefest forms with the most significant ideas, lends this piece its characteristic stamp and at the same time affords an insight into the sort of sacred works that Mozart, had he lived, would

27. Nissen, *Anhang zu Wolfgang Amadeus Mozart's Biographie*, 169–70.
28. This new comparison produced only a few corrections to Härtel's 1800 score. Constanze passed them on to Härtel in her letters of 6 and 13 August 1800 [*Briefe*, iv.363–5]; see also *AmZ*, iv (1801/2), 30–1. This revised copy was used as the basis for André's edition of both the vocal score and the full score of 1827, in which the respective contributions of Mozart and Süßmayr are distinguished by means of the letters M and S. The preface was reprinted in Zawrzel and Krüchten, 'Anzeige'.
29. On Mozart's very earliest works, see the recent study by Kurthen, 'Studien zu W. A. Mozarts kirchenmusikalischen Jugendwerken (bis zur 1. italienischen Reise)'. Kurthen examines them in detail, paying particular attention to the influence of Hasse, Eberlin and Leopold Mozart, thereby earning our gratitude for increasing our understanding of these historical sources. Only his assumption that Mozart was also influenced by Gluck, Handel and the *tombeau* of French operas of the period seems to me problematical. ◆ Further, see Rosenthal, 'The Salzburg Church Music of Mozart and his Predecessors' and 'Zur Stilistik der Salzburger Kirchenmusik von 1600 bis 1730'; and Manfred Hermann Schmid, *Mozart und die Salzburger Tradition*.

have bequeathed to the world in his appointment at St Stephen's. He would have breathed new life into Viennese church music in the spirit of the older north German school, a development already clearly adumbrated by his *Requiem*.[30]

The Kyrie is preceded by an Introit – a prayer that the dead may rest in peace – that establishes this austere tone in a wholly unambiguous manner.

The work opens in a portentous D minor,[31] around which the whole *Requiem* continues to circle for the whole of its duration. The theme – one of the most important in the entire work – rings out in the basset-horns and bassoons to a simple string accompaniment involving off-beat chords:

It is characterized by the tonic with its lower leading note and stepwise ascent to the third, and also by its entry on the weak beat of the bar, so that the first minim immediately produces a stridently dissonant suspension.[32] In itself, it is no more original than most of the rest of the ideas contained within this movement,[33] but Mozart is concerned less with a subjective outpouring of emotion than with an expression of the work's strictly liturgical character. To quote Hermann Kretzschmar, 'the pain of grief is eased by the language of the Church, a language tested and hallowed from time immemorial'.[34] Initially, Mozart is content to borrow elements from the sacred style in general and to wait until the 'Te decet hymnus' before allowing the Church to speak in person. The whole way in which imitative procedures are used to introduce the Requiem theme in the winds is clearly influenced by Johann Sebastian Bach.[35] It is a genuine prelude in the spirit of the later Mozart, rather than a mere ritornello of the older type. The basic mood, initially at least, is one of calmly composed grief, but this grows perceptibly in intensity from the third bar onwards (note the irregular entries of the voices and the way in which the melodic line thrusts upwards), only to die away again on a note of resignation and sink back to the dominant, A minor. But Mozart is not interested in a symmetrical return to the tonic in the sense of the older ritornellos, preferring instead to force his way back to it as quickly as possible by means of four shattering chords on the trombones, which sound like the voice of the Last Judgement and which are not used again until the

30. ◆ Further, see Schlager, *Kirchenmusik in romantischer Sicht: Zeugnisse des Musikjournalisten und des Komponisten E. T. A. Hoffmann* and Bauman, 'Requiem but No Piece'.

31. It is also found in the mass K65, in the unfinished Kyrie K90, the 'Munich' Kyrie K341, and the *Misericordias* K222, the opening bars of which prefigure the first theme of the present movement.

32. The same dissonance is often found in counterpoint in other works of this period; see above.

33. Hermann Kretzschmar recalls the opening of Handel's 'Funeral Anthem for Queen Caroline'; see his *Führer durch den Konzertsaal*, ii/1.277. Cf. also the opening bars of the chorale *Herr Jesu Christ, du höchstes Gut* and, in the Huguenot psalter, *Mon Dieu, preste moy l'oreille par ta bonté non pareille* in Douen, *Clément Marot et le Psautier Huguenot*, i.650. ◆ Mozart's modelling of the Introit on Handel's funeral anthem was noted as early as 1826, in Maximilian Stadler's *Vertheidigung der Echtheit des Mozart'schen Requiem*; the chorale setting in the second half of the Handel quotes two well-known Lutheran funeral hymns, 'Wenn mein Stündlein vorhanden ist' and 'Herr Jesu Christ, du höchstes Gut'. See Christoph Wolff, *Mozart's Requiem: Historical and Analytical Studies, Documents, Score*, 74.

34. Kretzschmar, *Führer durch den Konzertsaal*, ii/1.277.

35. The *Requiem* also contains a number of typical old-fashioned cadential phrases that recall an even older period. Here one thinks, for example, of the following:

moment when the Last Judgement actually arrives. With the *forte* entrance of the chorus the congregation's mood of sorrow bursts forth in all its anguish, with the trombone chords continuing to reverberate above all in the trenchant syncopated figure in the violins that seems like the musical equivalent of the wringing of hands. Stretto entries of the Requiem theme are heard in all four voices, which enter in ascending order, beginning with the bass. The theme is then repeated in the soprano, acquiring a particular intensity through the accelerated rhythm of the three lower voices. Before the final emphatic half-cadence on A[36] the voices come together for a sharply declaimed homophonic passage. The same eloquent brevity typifies the first interlude, 'Et lux perpetua luceat eis'. Its F major tonality is introduced with typically Mozartian resolve and recalls the transfigured mellowness of those of the Priests' choruses in *Die Zauberflöte* that are in the same key. The notes of the triad are now strongly accented in the melodic line and again point to the changed picture. The unison motif in the strings

represents a melodic type that recurs on other occasions in the *Requiem*, notably in the 'Tuba mirum'. This brief, self-contained choral passage, the main motif of which is treated imitatively by the winds, likewise builds to a fervent climax, before finally sinking back again into a state of tranquil wistfulness.[37] There follows the more extended second interlude, which is superbly prepared for by its predecessor and which is based on Psalm 65: 'Praise is due to you in Sion, and prayer will be offered to you'. In order to indicate that these words derive from Scripture, Mozart has set them to an old chorale melody, the two-part trope of the ninth church mode traditionally associated with the Psalm *In exitu Israel de Aegypto* – the very same mode as the one that Mozart has already used in *Betulia liberata*.[38] It is first stated by the soprano soloist and introduced by a brief transitional passage that initially recalls the Requiem theme before introducing a new motif that is later set to the words 'Dona eis requiem':

It is the shortened and inverted version of the Requiem theme that twines around the consolatory chorale melody both *rectus* and *inversus*. The choral sopranos take it up at the words 'Exaudi orationem meam, ad te omnis caro veniet' ('Hear my prayer, to you will all flesh come'), while the other voices are treated contrapuntally in the manner of Bach's chorale choruses.[39] But even before the chorale melody enters, the mood intensifies markedly, not least as a result of the appearance of a dotted ostinato motif in the orchestra that creates an impression of old-fashioned rigour.[40]

---

36. It is striking that this dominant ending is studiously avoided in the previous section and that, in spite of all deviations, the D minor character of the work is steadfastly maintained.

37. There is something profoundly moving about the *d″*flat at the second 'luceat' that emerges from the previous semitone step, *a″*–*b″flat*, and transfers the sadness of the orchestral interlude to the vocal writing, too.

38. See above. The way in which composers have treated this passage depends on the ritual in question: in his own *Requiem*, Jommelli includes both verses of the psalm, Hasse and Zelenka the first and Asola only the words 'Te decet hymnus in Sion', while Pitoni offers a free setting of both verses. ◆ Asola's and Pitoni's *Requiems* are published in Proske, *Musica Divina*, i.

39. The expansive motif on 'exaudi' is already found on the word 'eleison' in the Kyrie of the C minor mass K427.

40. Something similar is already found in the 'Gratias' of the C minor mass. Here, too, the listener will note the keen *relatio non harmonica*, *f″*–*f* sharp in bar 27.

This liturgical section ends in the same way as it started: its opening section returns, but the above-quoted theme from the middle section is now heard in constant counterpoint with its main idea, acquiring its full expressive potential only at the words 'dona eis, Domine', with the listener clearly aware that it, too, is derived from the main theme by inversion. In this way the mood of grief is powerfully enhanced. Moreover, the entries of the subject are no longer regular, as they were before, but enter freely on *d, a, g'* and *f''*. The semiquaver theme gradually draws more and more voices into its sway, thereby allowing the underlying emotion to build to a climax at the F major entry of the main theme in the soprano, after which the tension begins to relax with the magnificent descent of both themes, pausing briefly on B flat major before 'et lux perpetua' in order to allow the idea of 'perpetual light' to illumine our souls once again. Now, however, the chorus is divided instead of being a unified mass, and the motif

et lux per - pe - tu - a

to which the sopranos cling with remarkable tenacity once again recalls the beginning of the chorale. But this B flat major does not indicate full closure as F major had previously done. Instead it functions as a leading note, urging the musical argument towards A and thence back to the world of D minor. To the dominant harmonies of this last-named key, the desire for perpetual light dies away on a note of the most profound earnestness. There follows the great double fugue based on the following two subjects:

Both subjects are inspired by Handel and Bach and even older models,[41] with Mozart consciously availing himself of them in his desire to set out from the typical and universally familiar and to raise it to a more individual plane by dint of his treatment of it. All that he needed at this point in his work had already found perfect expression in these older themes, and so he used them with the same justification as Bach, Handel and Gluck had done in countless similar cases – only ignorance and pedantry could speak in such circumstances of plagiarism and lack of inventiveness.[42] The two subjects belong together, being closely related and yet antithetical in character, as are the words to which they are set. The first appears to emerge from the text as though of its own accord, with its powerful appeal to God the Father followed at once by the shattering plea of 'eleison'. But even

41.   There is no doubt that the first subject was inspired by the chorus 'And with his stripes we are healed' from *Messiah*, while the idea of combining the first and the second subjects clearly came from the chorus 'Alleluia! We will rejoice in thy salvation' from Handel's *Joseph*. On the old prototype, with its interval of a diminished seventh, see above. ◆ It is now generally accepted that the Kyrie fugue is based on Handel's Dettingen Anthem HWV265; see Christoph Wolff, *Mozart's Requiem: Historical and Analytical Studies, Documents, Score*, 78.
42.   This note was struck with regard to Mozart's masses from an early date; see Sievers, *Mozart und Süßmayer: Ein neues Plagiat, ersterm zur Last gelegt und eine neue Vermuthung, die Entstehung des Requiems betreffend*, 15–16; Schiffner, *AmZ*, xlv (1843), 581; Fuchs, 'Aufforderung an Herrn Albert Schiffner', 95–6.

before it ends, this tremendous figure calls forth the second theme with its invocation of Christ as mediator, an invocation normally reserved for a separate middle section. Here the sense of subjectivity streams out in a vast wave of emotion. Initially both subjects move in the same direction, but at the end the first of them reaches the fifth, *a*, as the climax of its melodic line, while the second turns back on itself, moving stepwise through the same diminished interval, *b'* flat–*c'* sharp, as is found at the start of the first. Here the emotions stirred up by the Introit reach a climax whose overriding unity borders on real drama.

The double fugue has been criticized as often as it has been admired.[43] With the exception of its first four entries, which proceed along regular lines,[44] it does in fact depart from textbook rules on a number of important points, not least in the way in which it races along in such an unstoppable, agitated floodtide of sound that it hardly finds a point of structural repose and has none of the lengthier interludes that normally prepare for the reentry of the subject and thereby add to the tension. All are replaced by very short transitions, most of which are derived from the second subject. In particular, the listener never feels safe from the entry of the main theme, its thunderous message repeatedly ringing out from the most disparate quarters. This is clearly intentional, for both the main idea and its tugging accompaniment are no longer designed to express calm and God-fearing humility, as they were in the Introit, but reflect the state of guilt-laden humanity at the imminence of Divine Judgement, thus providing a transition to the following 'Dies irae'. Indeed, the movement as a whole is truly demonic in its emotional expression, occasionally verging on very real despair, a state reflected in its modulatory progress, for, however purposefully it may move towards its goal, it remains fluid in its structure, with every point of repose either preempted by an interrupted cadence or quickly abandoned. It is significant that, as in the Introit and all the later passages in D minor, dominant tonalities are overshadowed by the darker world of the subdominant.[45] The brightest tonality, which is touched on only briefly, is the F major at the soprano entry in bar 16, which does indeed lead to a lightening of the pressure. All the more oppressive, then, is the way in which the musical argument darkens with the following G and C minor. The sopranos, now at the top of their register, later succeed in turning it back to a more friendly B flat major and in parting the clouds one more time,[46] but once again the earlier mood reasserts itself and the last decisive climax starts to build with the entry of F minor. For the first time stretto entries appear in the second subject, and at the same time its ascending diatonic line is compressed to the point where it becomes chromatic: these are the 'wild gurglings' and 'chromatic meanderings' that caused contemporaries such difficulties – as if such devices were not familiar from Bach. To the sound of the keenest dissonances, this almost literally terrifying section finally forces its way back to the home key of D minor,[47] a key which, with the exception of a handful of applied dominants, it maintains until the very end.[48] The second subject retains its

43. According to Nägeli, it offends against key relationships, especially the relationship between major and minor, and becomes no more than a barbaric confusion of sounds; see Nägeli, *Vorlesungen über Musik*, 99–100. Gottfried Weber criticized the 'wild gurglings' in the choral parts and the 'confusedly trimmed meanderings' of the 'Christe', a response that Beethoven vehemently rejected in his own copy of the score; see Weber, 'Über die Echtheit des Mozart'schen Requiem', 216–17. Schwencke, too, found the subject of the 'Christe' inadequate when it came to depicting the solemn plea and humble entreaty; see *AmZ*, iv (1801/2), 8.
44. The dominant A minor is twice touched upon here, only to disappear from the rest of the fugue.
45. See Handke, 'Zur Lösung der Benedictus-Frage', 120.
46. The bass, too, answers in B flat major, while the second subject makes two attempts to start before getting under way, retaining its upward thrust as it does so.
47. Here, for the first time, the first subject adopts the final motif from the second subject, thereby increasing the impact of the diminished interval.
48. Note the sequence of tonalities of the section as a whole: D minor – A minor – D minor – A minor – F major – G minor – C minor – B flat major – F minor – D minor. The first subject appears twelve times, the second subject eighteen times.

chromatic form and, with its stretto entries, finally ascends to *a″*, before hurrying on to the end. But, all at once, the singers pause on an interrupted cadence on the diminished chord,[49] as though the face of some appalling Medusa has risen up before their eyes. When coupled with the following portentous rest, the chord creates an utterly terrifying impression. The chorus then brings this section to an end with the firm tread of a Handelian adagio, a classic example of the way in which a composer of genius can use very general, stereotypical material to create something utterly personal. Its critics notwithstanding, this passage is filled with the most immediate and gripping life and is seen through the eyes of a dramatist, but without ever becoming theatrical and violating the *Requiem*'s sacred character. As always, the ideas inherent in the text generate the movement's free form.

The Last Judgement had already cast its shadows over the fugue and now breaks in with all its terrors. This large-scale section extends as far as the Offertory ('Domine Jesu Christe') and to a certain extent replaces the Gloria and Credo. It forms the sequence of the Mass for the Dead.[50] The sequence – a type of religious verse dating back to the ninth century – is derived from the alleluia, its first important representative being Notker Balbulus of St Gall (830–912).[51] Thanks to their popular nature, these sequences eventually got so out of hand that in 1568 Pope Pius V banned them, with the exception of the five that are still in use today. These are the sequences for Easter (*Victimae Paschali laudes*), Pentecost (*Veni, Sancte Spiritus*) and Corpus Christi (*Lauda Sion*) and two non-specific sequences, the *De septem doloribus Mariae Virginis* (the famous *Stabat mater*, the words of which were written by Jacopone da Todi, who died in 1306) and the present *Dies irae*, which was written by Thomas of Celano at the time of the Black Death in the mid-thirteenth century. These last two cannot really be termed sequences as they are unconnected with the alleluia. Here the term simply indicates a hymn-related chant that serves a particular purpose.

The words of the Dies irae are extremely beautiful, albeit far more subjective than those of the Gloria and Credo. As a result, they have always been very popular with composers, a popularity increased by the vivid and graphic depiction of the Last Judgement. With it, of course, came a serious danger that composers would be misled into investing this section with a thrilling sense of drama and making it central to the Mass as a whole, whereas the latter is essentially concerned with the tranquil memory of the dead and prayers for their eternal rest. The leading composers of requiems, including Mozart, have always recognized this danger and sought to use the images of terror merely as a background for this entreaty, whose fervour is increased as a result.

The opening section deals with the end of the world and looks forward to the Second Coming. This section is entrusted to the chorus, which, with a single exception, remains a unified mass. The orchestra assumes the task of depicting the superficial horrors of the Last Judgement, with tremolando passages in the strings – a device normally used only rarely by Mozart – repeatedly interrupted by typically Mozartian syncopations. This movement, it may be added, is scored for the same forces as its predecessor, with only the trombones missing, an absence compensated for by the increased prominence of the trumpets and timpani, resulting in completely different sonorities. They are joined by the voices in a high, strident register – Mozart consciously reserves the starkest realism for this opening section. Yet it, too, is clearly related to its predecessor – and not only in terms of its tonality. Bars 4–6 of the choral soprano line

49.   Cf. the end of the quartet 'Wir wandeln durch des Tones Macht' from *Die Zauberflöte*.
50.   Peter Wagner, *Geschichte der Messe I: Bis 1600*, 20ff.
51.   Peter Wagner, *Einführung in die gregorianischen Melodien: Ein Handbuch der Choralwissenschaft*, i: *Ursprung und Entwicklung der liturgischen Gesangsformen bis zum Ausgange des Mittelalters*, second edition, i.253ff.; Riemann, *Handbuch der Musikgeschichte*, i/2, 116ff.; and Bartsch, *Die lateinischen Sequenzen des Mittelalters in musikalicher und rhythmischer Beziehung*.

sol - vet   sae-clum   in   fa - vil - la

take up the Requiem theme,[52] as, too, does the start of the bass line. The expressive language is of the boldest plasticity, the chorus's disjointed phrases suggesting that they are wracked by fever. The first of the orchestral interludes appears following the half-cadence on the dominant A: in all of them we seem to hear the whistling of the tempest. The powerful modulation to F major is familiar from other similar movements by Mozart, and, as we shall see in a moment, is a particular characteristic of the *Requiem*. The second section ('Quantus tremor') acquires its expressive force chiefly through its bass line, which thrusts impetuously upwards from F to e, first chromatically, then diatonically, creating a sense of demonic unrest, while the fear of death finds additional expression in the soprano line, which, with its strident top notes, races up and down through the notes of the triad in the manner of a fanfare, before the tenors suddenly join in with their imitative entries. It is not impossible that Mozart was influenced here by the image of the earthquake traditionally associated with the end of the world.[53] The musical argument comes to rest in a solid A minor, after which the first section is repeated in a more intensified form. Here the sudden descent from the chord of E major to the dark world of C minor is daring in the extreme, with the most glaring of antitheses brought into direct conflict. But the storm quickly passes, and the musical development immediately presses on sequentially[54] to D minor, on the dominant of which it comes to rest, as before. Mozart now proceeds to exploit the effect of this dominant on the most colossal scale in order to make the terrors of the Last Judgement seem even more vivid, with the whole of the next ten bars reflecting this development and sucking everything into its wake, as though there were no longer any escape from this paralysing horror. For the first time the chorus is now divided,[55] with the basses launching into their terrifying, trill-like motif as though from subterranean vaults,[56] encircling the *a* with its two leading notes, g sharp and b flat, while the 'Dies irae' reverberates timidly[57] in the other voices. That this is meant to be sung *piano*, in contrast to the bass motif, emerges from the cello line, which here assumes the function of the bass line. At the end of this awesome dialogue, the trill motif affects the whole chorus, and only with the return of D minor is the spell broken. The movement ends with a compressed repeat of the very first section, although the chorus does not, of course, regain its former self-contained unity.

Following the wild emotion of the 'Dies irae', in which minds and the elements are all thrown into turmoil, the 'Tuba mirum' brings with it a feeling of tranquillity. The chorus now makes way for the quartet of soloists. A tenor trombone announces the approach of the Lord with a solemn, descending triadic motif.[58] The bass soloist takes up the melody, while the tenor trombone provides a concertante accompaniment in the form of motifs reminiscent of Sarastro.[59] The plagal phrase over the sustained note in the vocal line is particularly dignified in its impact. It is clear,

52. Handke, 'Zur Lösung der Benedictus-Frage', 122.

53. Chromatically ascending basses also play a major role in the depiction of the earthquake in Bach's *St Matthew Passion*, a work which Mozart did not of course know.

54. On this occasion the chromatically ascending line is in the soprano: c'' – c''sharp – d'' – e''flat – f''sharp – g''.

55. Kretzschmar recommends having the tenors double the basses here; Kretzschmar, *Führer durch den Konzertsaal*, ii/1.277.

56. Here Mozart may have been inspired by František Tuma's *Missa della morte*.

57. Note Mozart's predilection for the semitone step in this section as a whole.

58. Here, too, there is a parallel with the Introit; see above. The first 'Quantus tremor' comes under this same heading.

59. Hiller's soloist was unequal to the part and so he transcribed it for the bassoon from bar 5 onwards, a version that subsequently found its way into the first printed edition of the score; see Gottfried Weber, 'Beitrag zur Verunstaltungsgeschichte des Mozartischen Requiem', 54–5; and *AmZ*, iv (1801/2), 10. Tuma, too, includes a part for solo trombone.

moreover, from the later trombone melody that Mozart pictures the Lord not as a strict and implacable judge but as a lenient, albeit just and serious, God. This is entirely consonant with his other known views on the subject and explains the confident, even intimate, tone on which this section ends but which Mozart's admirers, including even Jahn, have found to be too lightweight.[60] The entries of the four voices reflect the impression evoked by the majestic vision. Here our journey takes us upwards from the bass to the soprano, and the expressive register that Mozart ascribes to each of the voices is easy to follow. With his usual wide-ranging intervals the bass stresses the sublimity of the Lord as he wakes the dead, the vacillation between major and minor at the end adding to the sense of mystery. The tenor soloist, by contrast, restates the opening motif in the minor and in diminution. Here there is already a note of impassioned astonishment at all that is happening, a feeling that culminates in anxious fear at the line beginning 'Liber scriptus' (note the repetition of the word 'mundus'). This explains why the tenor explores a wider range of tonalities[61] that finally takes him to the home key, D minor, to the accompaniment of a powerful string unison, and here the alto enters with the most intense expression of impassioned emotion. All that remains of the opening motif is its general sense of direction, while its final phrase appears in diminution under the pressure of the emotion that is expressed here. As the alto enters, so the trombone falls silent. But now the soprano enters with her bright B flat major, like some manifestation from another world. Breaking completely free from the movement's main idea,[62] she sings her 'Quid sum miser tunc dicturus?' with such naïve and heartfelt confidence and, at the same time, with such conviction that she is quickly joined by the other voices as well as by the hitherto unused basset-horns and bassoons. The soprano is thus the only one of the four soloists to have noticed the undertow of grace in the voice of the Lord, allowing the movement to end on a note of consolation no longer clouded by any hint of anxiety.

This is in no way contradicted by the following 'Rex tremendae majestatis', in which the Lord is revealed in all his sombre majesty and a mood of supreme emotion is once again explored. A powerful dotted ostinato motif[63] appears in the orchestra, where it is freely treated in the style of Bach. From the third bar onwards the choral voices, completely overwhelmed, interject their threefold call of 'Rex' on the weak beat of the bar, followed by the exclamation 'Rex tremendae majestatis!', a model of detailed word-setting that is supported by the winds alone. After this tremendous invocation the voices are divided, with the alto and soprano repeating the words canonically in a melody filled with fervent reverence, while the two lower voices recall the Lord's mercy, timidly at first and in disjointed phrases. Here, too, canonic procedures are used. Meanwhile, a third canon, based on the ostinato motif, unfolds in the orchestra. After a brief interjection from the full chorus, this opening section is repeated, but with the choral groups interchanged. At the same time a change takes place in the harmonies, with the musical argument modulating emphatically from the G minor with which this section had begun to D minor,[64] on the dominant of which the whole chorus finally comes together again for its cry of 'qui salvandos salvas gratis' in a passage reminiscent of the 'Dies irae'. Suddenly the tone becomes quiet and muted, and, with his usual brevity, Mozart follows up the earlier grandiose image with a simple entreaty, 'Salva me!', intoned by the

60. At the end of the first section, the main motif appears as a link in the unison orchestra.

61. There is the same encircling of the note *a* as we found in the earlier 'Quantus tremor est futurus'.

62. The only point that it has in common with the other voices is its Mozartian third-based endings opening towards the fifth, a feature found with great frequency in the *Requiem* as a whole.

63. At the beginning, the cadential sequence I–IV–V–I is used to great effect to establish the key of G minor.

64. Schwencke was wrong to criticize the D minor ending as it is fully justified by both the character of the work as a whole and the F major of the following section; see *AmZ*, iv (1801/2), 11.

two choral groupings, while the ostinato motif is heard very softly in the first violins. On closer examination, this deeply affecting final section proves to correspond harmonically with the opening of the movement, now transposed to D minor,[65] but with the chord of the sixth, *g–b* flat–*e* flat, replacing the expected G minor three bars from the end and creating an indescribable impression by allowing the earlier emotion to resonate once more in this final entreaty.[66]

Mozart himself told his wife that, even if he failed to complete the *Requiem*, it was immensely important to him that he had written out the 'Recordare',[67] which is indeed one of the high points of the work. It picks up the mood of the final request from the previous movement, but the sense of devotion is now far less intense, comfort and trust having entered the supplicants' hearts. As a result it is more discursive than its predecessor, being cast in rondo form, with the main idea returning after the 'Recordare', at 'Juste judex' and 'Preces meae':

The result is a wonderful combination of Mozartian interiority and sacred rigour that is achieved by the imitative entry of the second voice and the dissonant suspensions bound up with it. These are accompanied by a recurrent motif in the orchestra from which virtually the whole of the orchestral part is derived:

Note the particularly appealing way in which it is treated in canon in the violins over a pedal point in the bass in the second part of the prelude, where, in comparison with the first part, it acquires the character of a musical gesture expressive of moving entreaty. The four vocal soloists to whom this movement belongs are grouped along lines that reveal Mozart's usual symmetrical thinking, with the alto and bass entering in the typically mellow home key of F major followed by the soprano and tenor in the dominant. The main theme is then followed by a consequent phrase that allows terror to enter this movement, too, in the form of motifs familiar from earlier movements.[68] The first episode ('Quaerens me') adds considerably to the intensity of this mood. In a series of very short phrases, the soloists take the words from each other's mouths, while the harmonies shift abruptly from C minor to D minor,[69] at which point the sense of emotion reaches its high point at the words 'tantus labor non sit cassus', the setting of which is impassioned in the extreme. The main theme then returns in a shortened form in B flat major – a darker key than before – and in this way conveys a moving picture of man's consciousness of his guilt in the second episode ('Ingemisco, tamquam reus'), in which the gentle accompanying figure significantly falls completely silent for the first time, while the voices remain together in the simplest homophony. With its upwardly thrusting basses, keen *sforzato* accents and sudden changes of register, especially in the soprano and bass, this passage speaks for itself: the hand of the dramatist can be

65. Cf. the bass line, which was previously G – E flat – C – D, but which is now D – B flat – G – A.
66. It is the chord of the sixth of the actual harmonies of the interrupted cadence on E flat major.
67. Hogarth, *Memoirs of the Opera*, ii.199.
68. It is the bass line F – G – A flat – G, later F sharp – G – A flat – G, which, with its increasingly narrow intervals, encircles the dominant G in typically Mozartian fashion.
69. The sudden juxtaposition of these two minor keys is also found in the 'Dies irae' and the alto solo from the 'Tuba mirum'.

clearly felt here. The way in which the movement continues at the words 'Qui Mariam absolvisti' creates a highly unusual effect, not least as a result of its constantly changing tonality. The menacing D minor is quickly overcome and, after lengthy hesitation, the musical argument finally seems to decide in favour of a calming F major, at which point Mozart surprises us by playing his trump card, suddenly ushering in C major at the final 'spem dedisti' and, with it, a ray of hope of inconceivable radiance. Here the soloists finally find a solid support after their lengthy fervent entreaties, and the main idea now returns in a spirit of utter confidence. At the thought of hellfire, the singers are again seized by a sense of wild terror,[70] leading to a slightly extended version of the consequent phrase, but the voices then come together again in a wonderfully reassuring coda that brings this beautiful movement to an end.

The depiction of the torment of the damned in the 'Confutatis' creates an impression that is all the more searing in consequence. As before, Mozart has produced a dramatic portrait by contrasting the two male voices, representing the damned, with the two female voices begging to be numbered among the elect. The key is A minor, a key undoubtedly chosen with reference to the strangely unsettling character that it always has with Mozart. To the accompaniment of an Italianate slide figure in the unison strings that writhes back and forth in torment – as so often, Mozart uses the ascent of the bass to the fifth to add to the intensity of expression – we hear the cries of anguish of the damned in sharply dotted phrases that are treated imitatively and that are followed, with the usual abrupt modulation to C major, by the entreaty in the women's voices accompanied only by the unison violins,[71] a passage whose brevity and simplicity[72] recalls the prayers of supplication of the early church. Once again we hear the voices of the damned, but now to the accompaniment of curiously heightened harmonies,[73] so that the women's plea sounds more agitated in consequence. And now the whole gathering comes together for the shattering entreaty of the 'Oro supplex et acclinis', a passage which, harmonically speaking, is one of the most overwhelming that Mozart ever wrote. It rests on a sequence made up of four elements that draw not only the melody but the whole of the musical argument, with its attendant sonorities, relentlessly down into the depths. The starting point here is the enharmonic respelling of the diminished-seventh chord of the opening, the bass note of which – initially D sharp – is held as E flat instead of progressing to E. In this way it finally leads to A flat minor, a modulation repeated in the following section, too. The third element that makes up the sequence ('gere curam') is shortened, with the full closure on G flat minor omitted and a simple chromatic interval of a second appearing in the bass following the suppression of the diminished fifth. The fourth element is again complete, albeit slightly modified. This section already anticipates the harmonic writing of the Romantics[74] and reveals the whole of Mozart's deep mysticism and, at the same time, a degree of psychological insight that is little short of inspired. All that we have heard so far has been confined to the world of warm-blooded, human emotion, including the emotions of terror, horror

70. Again it is supported by the bass line B – C – D flat – C.
71. The figure is related to the one from the 'Recordare'.
72. The semitone interval is again characteristic.
73. Underpinning this passage is a latent chromatic polyphony that is closely related to the sequencing of the ending:

74. See Kurth, *Romantische Harmonik und ihre Krise in Wagners 'Tristan'*, 302ff.

and impassioned, childlike entreaty. But here we begin to breathe the spirit of eternity and to enter a world free from desires and anxieties but instinctively, with an unconscious awareness of the divine mystery. As a result, the movement ends not in a sombre F minor, but in F major, the mystic key of the Brotherhood in *Die Zauberflöte*.

The final section of this sequence is the 'Lacrimosa', which picks up the sequence's basic key of D minor and takes us back to the world of a funeral service in church, allowing the section to end on a note of moving lamentation, while at the same time containing a hint of the terrors of the Last Judgement within its opening section. A very brief prelude, built up on a sigh motif and entrusted to the strings (without cellos and double basses), introduces a choral passage that begins with a motif of striking pictoriality in a typically Mozartian D minor:[75]

But the terrifying ghosts rise up again at the words 'qua resurget ex favilla', a vast ascending scale from *d'* to *a"* suggesting the image of sinful humanity rising up from the grave. It begins diatonically with punched-out quavers, then proceeds chromatically with dotted crotchets, over a powerful crescendo, while the harmonies continue to change all the time. At this point Mozart's score breaks off and for the first time confronts us with the difficult problem of completing the piece, a problem which, in the light of Benedikt Schack's above-cited account, cannot be satisfactorily resolved: we simply cannot say for certain that the rest of this movement is the work of Süßmayr alone. Here and in the following disputed movements there are stylistic considerations that have to be taken into account and that remind us once again that the final word has not yet been spoken in this matter.

Franz Xaver Süßmayr was born in 1766 at Schwanenstadt in Upper Austria and was not only one of Mozart's pupils,[76] he was also a member of the group of young musicians with whom Mozart was in close personal contact. That Mozart called him his 'fool' suggests that he had a somewhat low opinion of him; and the fact that Eybler and, probably, others were preferred to him when the question of completing the *Requiem* was raised tends to confirm this assessment. In spite of this, he was one of the best musicians to emerge from Mozart's school. This influence emerges at every turn, not only from his operas, of which *Der Spiegel von Arkadien* (1794) and *Soliman der Zweite* (1799) long maintained a place for themselves in the repertory, but also from his sacred works. Here we find signs of a notable talent, especially in terms of charm and interiority, while the borrowings were markedly Mozartian whenever he was called upon to depict serious or tragic situations. At the same time, his music clearly shows that there is a great step from talent to genius and that, in spite of all their merits, his works fail to match up to Mozart's in terms of their aesthetic value: none of them approaches the level of *Die Zauberflöte* or those sections of the *Requiem* that we know to be by Mozart.

In considering the work's completion, we should concern ourselves less, therefore, with the question of Süßmayr's ability to create a work worthy of Mozart than with the question of his ability to imitate Mozart's style and enter Mozart's own aesthetic world of experience when

75. Cf. the rising sixth, *a'–f"*.
76. He later studied with Salieri. In its edition of 8 July 1793, the *Wiener Zeitung* reported on a production of his opera *L'incanto superato* and described him as 'a pupil of Herr Salieri'. It is unlikely that Süßmayr would have studied simultaneously with Mozart and Salieri during the former's lifetime.

working on the completion.[77] That this was not always the case is clear from the instrumentation of the movements ascribed to him. Even in the 'Lacrimosa' the listener will surely be struck by the elaborate use of the trombones, a use that is bound to puzzle anyone familiar with *Die Zauberflöte* and the authentic movements of the *Requiem*, quite apart from the fact that in a movement devoted to the subject of lamentation Mozart would undoubtedly have been satisfied with basset horns and bassoons. Admittedly, trombones were commonly used to support the voices in the church music of this period and are found in this capacity in the sacred works from Mozart's own youth. But in the *Requiem*, this mechanical use is replaced by something far subtler and more individualized: they are no longer merely traditional but are employed for expressive ends. All the more astonishing is the Mozartian grandeur and unity of the 'Lacrimosa', including even the section after Mozart's manuscript breaks off.[78] Following the break, the 'qua resurget' is again underscored by a tension-laden chromatically ascending line, this time in the bass, followed by a typically Mozartian change of mood at the words 'Huic ergo parce Deus', which are set, moreover, to a motif that encircles the dominant C and its immediate neighbours in a way that we have already encountered on frequent occasions in the course of the work.[79] No less worthy of Mozart is the heartfelt 'Pie Jesu Domine'. But this movement – like all its precedessors it is extremely brief – reaches its high point following the repeat of its opening section, with the sequence as a whole coming to a conciliatory ending in a genuinely religious spirit at the second 'dona eis requiem', the descending diatonic line of which is clearly related to the earlier chromatic ascent. At the end the word 'requiem' is set to the old Requiem theme. Such a stroke of genius is found nowhere in any of Süßmayr's own sacred works. In short, we must decide whether, in completing the *Requiem*, Süßmayr suddenly transcended the gulf between talent and genius or whether he used Mozart's sketches, a suggestion that is far more in keeping not only with the whole nature of the exercise but also with Benedikt Schack's account of Mozart's final days.

All that survives of the traditional Offertory from the Mass for the Dead is the discursiveness of the liturgical chants associated with it.[80] Its text deals with the request that the souls of the dead should not go to hell but that the Archangel Michael may guide them to the light that God once promised to Abraham and his seed. In this movement, too, the images of hell, which are given particular emphasis here, add a dark and even sombre colour to this pious entreaty. Mozart divided the movement into three sections, the third of which ('Quam olim Abrahae') is a broadly developed choral fugue in keeping with tradition. The other two are distinguished from each other in terms of their general character and the contrastive sonorities that stem from the use

77. ◆ Further, see Duda, *Das musikalische Werk Franz Xaver Süßmayrs: Thematisches Werkverzeichnis (SmWV) mit ausführlichen Quellenangaben und Skizzen der Wasserzeichen*; Winterberger, *Franz Xaver Süßmayr: Leben, Umwelt und Gestalt*; Fuhrmann, 'War Franz Xaver Süßmayr Mozarts Schüler und Assistent?'; and Wlcek, *Franz Xaver Süssmayr als Kirchenkomponist*. For the contentious issue of his work on the *Requiem*, see Maunder, 'Süßmayr's Work in Mozart's Requiem: A Study of the Autograph Score'; Leeson, 'Franz Xaver Süssmayr and the Mozart Requiem: A Computer Analysis of Authorship Based on Melodic Affinity'; Levin, 'Zu den von Süßmayr komponierten Sätzen des Requiems KV 626'; and Gloede, 'Süssmayrs Requiem-Ergänzungen und das Wort-Ton-Problem'.
78. It must be admitted, of course, that according to Eduard Sievers's analysis of the score, the break occurs not in the 9th but in the 12th bar. I should like to take this opportunity to thank my Leipzig colleague Eduard Sievers for the support that he has given me in helping to identify the respective contributions of Mozart and Süßmayr. I shall have frequent occasion to return to his findings in the course of the following pages. ◆ In fact, Mozart completed only eight bars of the Lacrimosa. And this is the one documentable instance where Süßmayr chose *not* to follow sketches left by Mozart (see again n. 7 above). The implications of this for the question of other possible sketches (or verbal instructions) and the extent to which Süßmayr may or may not have relied on them have yet to be addressed.
79. See especially the steps in the bass, D – C – B – C.
80. Peter Wagner, *Geschichte der Messe*, i.5.

of both chorus and soloists. Motivically, by contrast, they are linked with the triadic motif from the beginning

Do - mi - ne Je - su Chri - ste

returning at the words 'sed signifer sanctus Michael', just as it had previously done at the words 'libera eas', producing something formally akin to a free rondo, the only difference being that everything is marked by the same extreme succinctness as before. Particularly admirable is the sense of symmetry that is achieved within such formal freedom. The opening sections of the first part ('Domine' and the second 'Libera') both begin with the main idea, which is succeeded by an expressive, rising sequential structure, with the third, fugal section following on as an *Abgesang*, again building to a great climax at the end. Common to all three sections is the harsh and powerful semiquaver figure in the strings. But the dramatist is clearly revealed in the striking brevity with which individual passages – especially those of a demonic nature – are singled out in a typically Mozartian manner by means of the starkest dynamic contrasts. The subdued and churchlike opening is immediately followed, for example, by the impassioned and repeated 'Rex gloriae!' and thereafter[81] by the keenly cutting 'de poenis inferni',[82] a passage that instils terror not least through its sudden dynamic reversal and that acquires a mystical element at the words 'et de profundo lacu' as a result of one of the modulations – from a dark A flat major to C minor – that are so typical of the work in general. Much the same is true of the later passage at the word 'libera', where the figure of the lion rears up in terror. Only the colours are darker here. In the wake of all these tormenting images, the fugato, with its intervals of a seventh[83] and wild orchestral unison, provides a psychologically subtle portrait of the universal sense of agitation caused by the uncertain fate of the dead. The harmonies, too, have something curiously unstable to them, whereas the underlying rhythm ♩ ♩ ♩ | ♩ constantly urges the music forwards. The order in which the voices enter is completely free and unrelated to any textbook rules.[84] Like its predecessors, the movement ends with two sharply juxtaposed antitheses, with the words 'ne cadant' flung forth five times in wild succession, then followed at once by the eerie 'in obscurum'.[85] The quartet of soloists now enters, initially picking up the fugal procedures of the preceding passage.[86] It is significant that, at the mention of the Archangel Michael, the minor key modulates to the major and a bright light illumines the dark image for the first time in this movement, which continues with the melody from the first 'Libera eas', thereby rounding off this section and producing a self-contained whole. At this point the fugue begins. It occurs at this juncture not only because

81. The modulation to B flat major is one that is typical of the *Requiem* as a whole.
82. Cf. the way in which the triadic motif moves in the opposite direction to that of the main idea.
83. Behind it lies a hidden polyphony:

84. The notes *gc–ad* reveal a harmonic sequence. Both pairs of voices produce a descending scale, tenor and alto from *g* to *f*, soprano and bass from *a* to *b* flat, with each voice invariably starting with the final note of the other.
85. Note the characteristic semitone step that we also found at the words 'de ore leonis'.
86. The entries again represent a sequence: *g–c, f–b* flat.

tradition demands that it should do so, but because it also allows the whole mood of the foregoing section, with its stark contrast between trust in God and oppressive fear of hell's chastisements, to find expression in a single powerful floodtide of sound. In spite of its relative clause, the text involves no subsidiary ideas[87] but justifies the trust at the heart of the entreaty, thereby providing the section as a whole with its poetical foundation. The theme is again typical of the older church tradition:

quam o - lim A - brahae   pro - mi - si - sti   et se - mi - ni e - ius

Its first two bars are based on the fixed harmonic sequence that is found in this tradition (tonic–dominant–dominant–tonic) and that is retained throughout the whole fugue, with all its changing tonalities, even if it is occasionally obscured by interrupted cadences. But the word-setting is typically Mozartian, with its characteristic rests and a third element ('et semini eius') that is invested with a particular weight of expression. It is the poetic idea behind this element that finally calms the mood of agitation. But the most typically Mozartian feature is the free form of the fugue:[88] although the voices initially enter along regular lines, there are in general fewer transitional elements than in the fugue in the Kyrie. The whole of the musical material is derived from the main theme, which always appears in stretto. Conversely, no new ideas are introduced here with the exception of the Bachian accompanying motif in the orchestra that is treated strictly imitatively. The underlying emotion grows in intensity until the point where the choral sopranos enter, only for them to sink back again timidly with the altos to B flat major. They fail to reach the third element but continue to cling to their imploratory 'promisisti'. Only when they return to this element in the bright key of D major does the whole picture change and the voices abandon their strict polyphony and form more unified groups and at the same time establish a more melodic style. The feeling of agitation ebbs gently away over the great pedal point on D, with the first element of the theme in inversion coming to a tranquil, *piano* ending on the words 'et semini eius', where the accompaniment falls silent for the first time. The new-found feeling of peace spreads to the whole of the chorus in the following passage, which is especially affecting in consequence. The 'quam olim Abrahae' returns once more over the old chromatically descending fourth in the bass line, but it has lost its earlier sense of muted entreaty and now breathes a spirit of confidence and strength, achieving a feeling of calm composure and culminating in a beautiful plagal cadence.

As a result it is with total inner composure that the community can offer up its sacrifices to the Lord in the following 'Hostias'. The key of E flat major and the movement's stately dancelike step suggest a religious act of the most solemn kind, with only the syncopations in the violins still implying an element of agitation. The brief movement is divided into two parts, each of which is a setting of the same text. The first treats it in a subdued and objective way appropriate to the Church, while the second introduces a greater degree of subjectivity. In both, however, the choral writing is almost exclusively homophonic and declamatory. Likewise, the musical language becomes more expressive in both sections at the words 'Tu suscipe', not least as a result of the harmonic resources that are used here. At the second 'Hostias' the dark B flat minor and the stark contrast in terms of dynamics and register that recalls the 'Ingemisco, tamquam reus' from the

87. This was criticized by Gottfried Weber, 'Über die Echtheit des Mozart'schen Requiem', 222–3, but defended by Ignaz von Seyfried; see Gottfried Weber, 'Weitere Nachrichten', 296.
88. Hermann Kretzschmar argues on the basis of the blank pages in the autograph score that Mozart intended the fugue to be longer, but this seems unlikely in view of its unified nature; see Kretzschmar, *Führer durch den Konzertsaal*, 281.

'Recordare' both come as a surprise. From the 'tu suscipe' onwards, the harmonic writing assumes the profound and mystical character that we know from the earlier movements, while the dynamics, too, express a sense of reverential awe. The brief coda ('Fac eas, Domine') allows this mood to die away on a note of tranquil emotion. There follows a note-for-note repeat of the Offertory fugue.

Up to this point it has been possible to consult the full score to establish the extent of Süßmayr's contribution to the instrumentation. Although any competent composer would generally have known from Mozart's instructions which direction he was to follow, he was still left with considerable latitude on points of detail, and even if we ignore individual aberrations such as the trombones in the 'Lacrimosa', there is no doubt that many of Mozart's subtleties in the accompaniment have been lost to us. He left virtually no indications for the wind instruments, for example, and here in particular there are a number of doubts, in spite of any verbal instructions that Mozart may have given. On the other hand, we have to admit that Süßmayr never attempted to smuggle any ideas of his own into the work and that his accompaniment does not create a disruptive impression.

The last three movements are all missing from the original score and, as such, they throw into particularly sharp focus the problem of the work's completion. From the moment that Süßmayr claimed them as his own in the letter referred to above, it was argued that 'the artistic products of Herr Süßmayer with which we are familiar call into serious question the claim that he made an essential contribution to this great work'.[89] Rochlitz later expressed his reservations in even more emphatic terms.[90] Gottfried Weber was another writer who believed that the final movements betrayed Mozart's hand in a way that he felt the earlier movements often did not.[91] Adolf Bernhard Marx argued in favour of the authenticity of the entire work, although his argument was inevitably based solely on aesthetic criteria and on the belief that the movements in question were too good to be attributed to Süßmayr,[92] while according to Seyfried it was widely rumoured in Vienna that Süßmayr had completed the last three movements on the basis of an existing draft and that Mozart had wanted to elaborate the 'Hosanna' fugue after the Benedictus and had already had in his head a new subject for the final fugue at 'Cum Sanctis'.[93] No evidence has come to light to substantiate this view, with the result that there was an increasing tendency to credit Süßmayr with these movements. Yet, as Jahn noted in this context,[94] it is striking that these three movements – if they really had been missing – had not been lifted from other masses by Mozart that were then unpublished and, as such, unknown in Vienna, rather than being newly composed by Süßmayr. More recently, stylistic considerations have persuaded writers such as Robert Handke to conclude that in the main these movements are by Mozart.[95]

In terms of its whole character and the treatment of its text, the Sanctus is based on a model already exemplified by Mozart's earlier masses,[96] although this, of course, proves nothing for or against Süßmayr's authorship. More striking, by contrast, is the similarity between its opening and

---

89. *AmZ*, iv (1801/2), 4.
90. Gottfried Weber, 'Weitere Nachrichten', 289; *AmZ*, xxv (1823), 687.
91. Gottfried Weber, 'Über die Echtheit des Mozart'schen Requiem', 226, and 'Weitere Nachrichten', 279.
92. *Berliner allgemeine musikalische Zeitung*, ii (1825), 378–9.
93. Gottfried Weber, 'Weitere Nachrichten', 307.
94. Jahn, *W. A. Mozart*, ii.695.
95. Handke, 'Zur Lösung der Benedictus-Frage'. ◆ See again n. 76 above.
96. See, for examples, K66 and 139. The harmonic writing is also similar, the one exception being the later tendency to modulate to the subdominant.

the first strophe of the 'Dies irae'.[97] The melody proceeds along similar lines, albeit in D major rather than D minor. The only real difference is that in the 'Dies irae' the Requiem theme was interpolated as the second element ('solvet saeclum in favilla'). Given the significant motivic unity of the work as a whole, there is a strong likelihood that this section, too, is based on authentic material. The firm and purposeful harmonic progressions (I–IV–V–I–V) are likewise entirely Mozartian, with only the coarse and impersonal instrumentation pointing to Süßmayr. The situation is more problematical with the 'Pleni sunt', for in the vast majority of Mozart's earlier Masses the 'Hosanna' is preceded by either a perfect or an imperfect cadence on the dominant. In the present case, however, we find full closure in D major, which is the result, moreover, of a somewhat uncertain modulatory process that also reflects the far feebler nature of the word-setting. This ending finally collides with the first D of the theme of the 'Hosanna', thereby weakening the impact of this section and undermining the build-up of tension that Mozart aimed to achieve at this point in all his earlier Masses. The listener has the clear impression that this is a makeshift solution and that the arranger was unclear what Mozart himself intended here.[98] By contrast, the subject of the 'Hosanna'

O - san - na in___ ex - cel - - - - sis !

fits meaningfully into the thematic structure of the work as a whole: its first two motifs are related to the 'quam olim Abrahae', while its final section rests on the interval of a seventh as in the first subject from the Kyrie, the only difference being that on this occasion the interval is traversed stepwise. It remains highly questionable, of course, whether Mozart himself is responsible for the exposition, not least because from bar 15 onwards, following the first entry of all four voices, the fugue lacks the characteristic harmonic vitality found in the *Requiem*'s other fugues.[99] It is then elaborated along increasingly feeble and superficial lines before coming to a particularly trivial conclusion.

The situation is even more complicated when we come to the Benedictus. That its opening idea is Mozart's is clear from the exercise book mentioned earlier. And the form that it assumes within the *Requiem* bears the unmistakable imprint of his genius: we can see it emerging from the seeds of his earlier settings of the Benedictus and acquiring its ultimate and most mature expression not only in its two opening phrases, each of which is closely related to the other, but also in the beautiful and typically Mozartian *Abgesang* at the words 'in nomine Domini'.[100] No less harmonious is the way in which the same idea is taken up and varied by the soprano soloist, who extends the original interval of a third (on the word 'benedictus'), first disjunctly, then conjunctly, to a seventh ('in nomine Domini'), resulting in a metrical extension and the addition of a further element. It is impossible to imagine the delight in the approach of the God-sent Saviour finding a nobler or more intense expression than it does here. That the overall mood of the movement – tender and

97. See Handke, 'Zur Lösung der Benedictus-Frage', 122.

98. Handke recommends simply omitting this final chord and ending with a fermata on the previous beat; see Handke, 'Zur Lösung der Benedictus-Frage', 129. But this would be felt merely as a breaking off of the musical argument, rather than a genuine preparatory half-cadence, in spite of the final semitone interval in the soprano line that looks forward to the 'Hosanna'. This has no special motivic significance but is a much older cadential formula.

99. According to Sievers, Süßmayr's contribution begins with bar 15.

100. All this is aptly and sensitively demonstrated by Handke, 'Zur Lösung der Benedictus-Frage', 109ff.

sweet-toned – is entirely typical of the Mozart we know from the Masses that he wrote in his youth.[101]

The twofold invocation on the part of the soprano and alto soloists gives way to an imitative passage for all four soloists, the motivic material being developed in such a natural way that – with the continuing exception of the instrumentation – it is hard to believe in any foreign involvement here, especially in view of the assured harmonic writing. The dominant key of F major is seized and consolidated with a firm hand. All the more puzzling, by contrast, is the following passage, which introduces a new idea corresponding to the earlier 'et lux perpetua' and does so, moreover, in what strikes one as a somewhat importunate manner. This flies in the face of Mozart's whole approach. Nor does the idea come to a proper conclusion but, after vacillating uncertainly, ends with an embarrassed-sounding solo for the basset-horns on the half-cadence on C major, while the middle section of the vocal part is equally lacking in harmonic assurance. Normally Mozart's middle sections are far more purposeful, with far greater tension, whereas the present one flutters around F major in a relatively inconstant manner and, by anticipating the B flat major itself, is robbed of the impact that this key should have at its reentry in the third section. Under this same heading come this section's vapid and inexpressive motifs in both the orchestra and the vocal writing, none of which is related to anything that has gone before. The living forms that we heard earlier have now been replaced by something bloodless and shadowy. But what was it that persuaded Süßmayr, whose hand is clearly in evidence here, to interpolate this section? The most obvious answer is an orchestral motif that Mozart may have sketched in bar 18, namely:

This would not have been intended, however, to introduce a new section, but to lead back to the beginning along lines similar to those found in bar 27.[102] If this is so, then the Benedictus that Mozart was planning would have been in two sections. This second section allows the two lower voices to have their say with the main idea and begins by reducing the tenor's vocal line by a bar and compensating for this by extending the contribution of the ensemble as a whole. The motivation for this may be found in the passage beginning in bar 31, with its descent into the world of the subdominant that then leads to a tremendous climax in bar 38. From here until bar 46, the harmonies move along lines identical to those found in the opening section. But, although the individual motifs and harmonic writing are related to those of the earlier section, their emotional expression is far more intense: here we find the same ability to coax fuller and more noble shoots from a single stem as we encountered in the case of the very first two entries. No less typically Mozartian is the coda that begins in bar 46, its ecstatic opening culminating in the *dolce* tranquillity of the final 'in nomine Domini'. The postlude picks up Süßmayr's unfortunate idea from the middle section. In the light of all this, there is much to be said for Handke's assumption that the vocal parts of the first and third sections, together with the figured bass, are by Mozart, whereas the middle section and postlude are by Süßmayr.[103] The instrumentation of the whole movement likewise raises doubts, not only because of the two trombones, which are used here in total

101. See above. Sievers, too, considers the first 18 bars to be genuine.
102. This assumption on Handke's part is very plausible; see Handke, 'Zur Lösung der Benedictus-Frage', 117. Sievers, too, believes that the middle section is the work of another composer.
103. Handke, 'Zur Lösung der Benedictus-Frage', 119.

contravention of Mozart's normal practice, but above all because of its impersonal, mechanical deployment, with inexpressive figures, tremolandos and so on replacing Mozart's subtle approach.[104] The result reflects the style of Süßmayr's sacred works, not that of Mozart's *Requiem*.

The inept ending of the 'Benedictus' robs the following 'Hosanna' of its impact, making it seem like some inorganic appendage, whereas it should in fact allow the mood of the previous solo ensemble to end with a powerful tutti effect. The part-writing is unlike that of the 'Hosanna' from the Sanctus. It is also shortened by five bars following the first exposition, although its overall impression remains the same.

Mozart's image rises up more radiantly in the Agnus Dei than in either of the two movements just discussed: not only is the language of expression more authentically Mozartian, so, too, are the links between its motifs and the work as a whole.[105] The threefold call of 'Agnus Dei' divides the movement into three sections, all of which begin in the upper voice with a semitone motif typical of the *Requiem* in its entirety:

All, moreover, are accompanied by the same bass motif

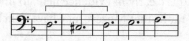

On its first appearance, this motif is expanded to produce the old Requiem theme, as was already the case at the beginning of the 'Dies irae', as a result of which the first nine bars seem like an intensified and more fervent variant of the Requiem idea.[106] Accompaniment is provided throughout by the following figure:

This figure can be traced back to the 'Qui tollis' from the Mass K66, and, with its encircling motion around the fifth, is already found in bar 27 of the Benedictus.[107] With its two semitone steps it fits organically into the work as a whole. Each of the Agnus Dei's three sections, moreover, has a wonderful structural symmetry to it. Each begins with an entreaty that seems to come from the very depths of the heart and evokes the image of a wringing of hands, building to a tremendous harmonic climax and driving the musical argument to an emphatic half-cadence. On each occasion this is followed by an interrupted cadence[108] that gives way in turn to a moving and genuinely Mozartian shift to the irenic mood of the 'Dona eis requiem', whose musical idea, entirely Mozartian in spirit, brings each section to an end in the manner of a refrain. The second

104.   Handke argues that the instrumentation of the first section is also by Mozart; see Handke, 'Zur Lösung der Benedictus-Frage', 118–19.

105.   Jahn, too, attributes the main idea to Mozart and only its elaboration to Süßmayr; see Jahn, *W. A. Mozart*, ii.698. According to Sievers, the whole movement is by Mozart.

106.   See Handke, 'Zur Lösung der Benedictus-Frage', 121ff.

107.   Handke, 'Zur Lösung der Benedictus-Frage', 126.

108.   Even in the first section we already find the music modulating from the dominant of the minor to the relative major, but without any preparation. This type of modulation is typical of the *Requiem* as a whole; see above.

section creates an impression of greater intensity not only as a result of its more agitated harmonies but also thanks to its descending melodic line, the individual phrases of which sound like nothing so much as sobs. In consequence, its antithetical section is laid out along broader lines. Its melody

do - na, do - na e - is re - - - - - qui - em

constitutes one of the most overwhelming sections of the whole work and is a masterly variant of the original refrain

that soon reverberates in the orchestra, too. The third section explores a greater range of tonalities, not least as a result of the respelling of the B in the bass as C flat, a beautiful effect that recalls the 'Confutatis' and leads ultimately to the half-cadence on B flat. On this occasion, the change of mood at the word 'dona' is not as abrupt, culminating instead in the half-cadence on the diminished chord that holds the note *b′* flat on 'sempiternam' in a mysterious state of suspension before passing through the wonderful intermediate harmonies of G flat major and emerging as a suspension of the final chord of F major.

The whole of the Agnus Dei is sustained by such a high level of inspiration and so closely bound up with the rest of the work that Süßmayr's authorship is virtually ruled out, no matter how much respect we may have for his abilities. The only alternative is to believe in miracles and argue that one genius – Süßmayr – has here succeeded in entering the world of another to the total denial of his own personality.

From the 'Lux aeterna' onwards, the whole of the Introit from the 'Te decet hymnus' and the fugue from the Kyrie are repeated with suitably altered words. According to Constanze, this was Mozart's intention. But we should not overlook her remark 'if he were to die without completing it', as this indicates that Mozart's suggestion was no more than a makeshift solution intended to preempt any attempt on Süßmayr's part to give the work an original ending. This kind of repeat of the opening section at the end of a work was not uncommon at this period and is in fact found in two of Mozart's masses in G major K220 and K317. In the *Requiem*, too, we may be prepared to sanction the repeat of the old liturgical melody and the 'Dona', even though the organic link which, in the opening movement, binds them together with the work as a whole is loosened here and the connection is now much more superficial. Far more serious doubts are raised by the repeat of the fugue from the Kyrie to completely different words, namely, 'Cum sanctis tuis in aeternum'. For what possible connection is there between the impassioned anguish of the Kyrie subject and the saints in heaven? At the same time the countersubject loses much of its expressivity by forfeiting its original words. Indeed, the whole character of this fugue makes it seem inappropriate for the work's confident and acquiescent conclusion, for although it ends the opening movement, its inherent agitation already looks forward to the 'Dies irae'. When other composers repeated themselves, it was mostly musical ideas of a very general nature, where the change of words was not so strongly felt and where such a change was offset by the general religious tone and the impression of a formal rounding off. But, although it retains a religious stamp, Mozart's *Requiem* is a far more personal work that seeks to explore the detailed meaning of its words, most notably and most outstandingly in the Agnus Dei. Indeed, this tremendous opening section of the final movement points to a different continuation in which, had he been able to complete the work himself, Mozart would have achieved a sense of unity not by rounding it off in a formal way but by structuring the music on the basis of the text and in the spirit of the work as a whole. This ending, which would have been the work's crowning glory, has of course been lost, but at least in the other disputed movements the composer's artistic intentions can still be more or less clearly established.

Mozart's *Requiem* is a sacred work in the best sense of the word and at the same time is a thoroughly modern piece. Among its sacred aspects are not only its use of liturgical melodies and strict counterpoint but above all its desire to set out from the familiar and typical and, by dint of the treatment to which that material is subjected, to raise it to a level of greater individuality. Finally, there is the concisely objective way in which the music always serves the text without ever indulging in purely musical pleasures. Those critics who, evidently influenced by their knowledge of the work's genesis, complain of its lack of unity are completely wrong.[109] Such criticisms can be refuted not only by reference to the melodic and harmonic formulae that recur throughout the work but also by its uniformity of mood. In turn, this links the *Requiem* with *Die Zauberflöte*, a work with which it also shares its dramatically motivated contrasts. Here we find a modern feature that is no longer content to stir specific emotions in the most general terms but that seeks to reflect the detailed psychological development of the work. Time and again it is Mozart the dramatist who emerges from the score, not in the sense of an opera composer or man of the theatre,[110] but in the way in which Bach in his vocal works and Schubert in his lieder occasionally plays the part of the dramatist. Mozart was right when he said that he was writing his *Requiem* for himself, but his remark goes far deeper than he himself intended: it is his most individual and personal confession of his thoughts about life and death, with Count Walsegg's commission merely providing him with an excuse to give voice to his innermost thoughts.

That he struck a chord with contemporaries is clear from the *Requiem*'s tremendous and constantly growing acclaim, with Haydn, for example, prophesying that Mozart would achieve immortality with this one work alone. In north Germany especially, where Bach's works were actively promoted by his pupils at the end of the eighteenth century, there was an immediate and instinctive recognition that the *Requiem* was Bachian in spirit. The Thomaskantor's last pupil, the Erfurt organist Johann Christian Kittel, felt powerfully attracted to the work, even though he was initially unaware who its composer was, and was astonished to discover that it was by Mozart, a composer of popular operas, with which he was likewise unfamiliar. He asked to see copies of these operas and was sufficiently unbiased to recognize in them the composer of the *Requiem* and to value them as such.[111]

In Leipzig, Johann Adam Hiller admired the work sufficiently to arrange a performance of it, establishing a place for it in the local repertory.[112] In Berlin the Singakademie performed it on 8

---

109. His admiration notwithstanding, Zelter described it as 'fissured, uneven, consisting of individual interpolated pieces'; Riemer, *Briefwechsel zwischen Goethe und Zelter*, ii.506–7. Jean Paul expressed similar reservations in a letter to Herder; see Herder, *Aus dem Nachlaß*, i.313.

110. Zelter thought that many movements represented 'the last remaining vestiges of a great school' and, at the same time, reflected 'the passionate understanding of a theatre composer'; Riemer, *Briefwechsel zwischen Goethe und Zelter*, ii.506–7. In Tieck's *Phantasus*, Ernst praises Mozart's genius – 'only you must not expect me to listen to his *Requiem*'; see Tieck, *Schriften*, iv.426. A similar sentiment is expressed by Krüger, *Beiträge für Leben und Wissenschaft der Tonkunst*, 199–200.

111. Jahn, *W. A. Mozart*, ii.700–1.

112. Rochlitz, *Für Freunde der Tonkunst*, i.16–17; Häser in Gottfried Weber, 'Weitere Nachrichten', 297; see also Körner's letter to Goethe of 29 May 1796 in *Goethe-Jahrbuch*, vii (1886), 54.

October 1800 in memory of its founder, Carl Friedrich Christian Fasch, who had died only two months earlier. It was the Singakademie's first public performance.[113] It was not long before Mozart's setting of the Mass for the Dead had overtaken all others as the version that was most often performed in memory of great men, especially musicians. In Berlin,[114] as elsewhere,[115] Zelter thought that it could never be killed off, either by bad reviews or by bad performances.[116] In many cities – and even in some of the smaller towns – it remained the most frequently performed work at memorial services throughout the whole of the nineteenth century.[117] In Paris, Cherubini mounted a spectacular performance in 1804,[118] and in 1840 it was even preferred to the works of French composers and performed at the ceremony accompanying the reburial of Napoleon's mortal remains.[119] And the work even succeeded where the composer's operas had failed, conquering the Italian cities of Venice,[120] Turin, Florence and Naples, and even reaching Lisbon, Lemberg, Warsaw, St Petersburg and Stockholm.[121] A performance in Rio de Janeiro was its first in the New World.[122] Its reputation was so high that in the first three decades of the nineteenth century it completely overshadowed more significant Masses for the Dead by other composers.[123]

113. Blumner, *Geschichte der Sing-Akademie zu Berlin*, 30–1.
114. Among the individuals so commemorated were the Dowager Queen (1805), the director of the Berlin Akademie der Künste, Johann Christian Frisch (1815), Andreas Romberg (1821), Bernhard Klein (1832), Prince Radziwill (1833), Count Brühl (1837), Ludwig Berger (1839), King Friedrich Wilhelm III (1840) and King Friedrich Wilhelm IV (1861).
115. The *Requiem* was performed in Prague on 16 February 1803 in memory of the horn player Giovanni Punto; see Procházka, *Mozart in Prag*, 196; and on 12 May 1805 it was performed in Weimar in memory of Schiller; see Vulpius's correspondence in *Goethe-Jahrbuch*, ii (1881), 421. There were also performances in Leipzig in 1823 in memory of Johann Gottfried Schicht (*AmZ*, xxv (1823), 405); and in Vienna in memory of Carl Maria von Weber (*AmZ*, xxviii (1826), 734), Beethoven (*AmZ*, xxix (1827), 367) and Franz Grillparzer (*AmZ*, new series, vii (1872), 166). In Munich it was performed in 1867 in memory of Peter Cornelius. In Mozart's home town of Salzburg the *Requiem* was performed at St Peter's on 17 February 1816 in memory of Elisabeth Neukomm; see Hammerle, *Mozart und einige Zeitgenossen*, 53.
116. Riemer, *Briefwechsel zwischen Goethe und Zelter*, iii.441–2.
117. One such performance took place in Halle, for example; see Abert, *Geschichte der Robert-Franz-Singakademie*, 99 and 101.
118. *Berlinische musikalische Zeitung*, i (1805), 28.
119. Kretzschmar, *Führer durch den Konzertsaal*, ii.283.
120. In this case it was a music lover who used his legacy to ensure that three *Requiems*, including Mozart's, were performed annually; see *AmZ*, xlii (1840), 54. In Senftenberg in Bohemia a society was founded in 1857 with the express aim of performing the *Requiem* every year; see *Neue Wiener Zeitung* (1857), 167–8.
121. See Kretzschmar, *Führer durch den Konzertsaal*, ii.283.
122. *AmZ*, xxii (1820), 501–2. ◆ The performance took place in 1819; it included a newly-composed concluding 'Libera me, Domine' written by the Salzburg composer and pupil of Michael Haydn, Sigismund Neukomm (1778–1858), who also conducted. See Ulrich Konrad, 'Sigismund von Neukomm: "Libera me, Domine" d-Moll NV 186: Ein Beitrag zur liturgischen Komplettierung von Wolfgang Amadé Mozarts "Requiem" d-Moll KV 626'.
123. ◆ Among many attempts in recent years to 'complete' Mozart's *Requiem*, or to correct Süßmayr's perceived faults, the most important are by Franz Beyer (1983), Richard Maunder (1987), H. C. Robbins Landon (1991), Duncan Druce (1993) and Robert Levin (1994). Further, see Maunder, *Mozart's Requiem: On preparing a new edition*; Beyer, 'Zur Neuinstrumentation des Mozart-Requiems – Eine Werkstattbetrachtung'; Levin, 'Zu den Ergänzungen von Mozarts Requiem in der 2. Hälfte des 20. Jahrhunderts'; and Bauman, 'Requiem, but No Piece' and 'On Completing the Requiem'. Concerning some important aspects of the work's reception, see Ebisawa, 'The Requiem: Mirror of Mozart performance history' and 'The Requiem of Mozart and the Attitude toward Death in Late Eighteenth-Century Europe'; and Eisen, 'Mozart's leap in the dark'.

55

Beyond the grave

Mozart's unexpected and untimely death at a period when, thanks to *Die Zauberflöte*, he had renewed contact with a broad cross-section of the population soon brought home to the world the full magnitude of its loss.[1] The first sign of this was the lively and sympathetic response encountered by Constanze and by the various concerts that she organized. A benefit performance of *La clemenza di Tito* was held at the Burgtheater in Vienna on 31 March 1795, with Aloysia Lange as Sesto. Beethoven played one of Mozart's keyboard concertos at the end of the first act.[2] In Prague, Constanze gave a concert early in 1796 at which the six-year-old Wolfgang sang Papageno's 'Der Vogelfänger bin ich ja'.[3] From Prague they travelled to Berlin, where Friedrich Wilhelm II allowed her to use the opera house and royal orchestra for a benefit concert on 28 February in the course of which she herself appeared as a singer.[4] According to a minute in Friedrich Wilhelm's hand, 'His Majesty the King of Prussia is pleased to demonstrate, by acceding to the wish of Mozart's widow, how deeply He esteemed her late husband's talent and how much He regrets the unfortunate circumstances that prevented him from reaping the fruits of his works'.[5] In Leipzig, Constanze was granted use of the Gewandhaus for a concert on 20 April at which the *Requiem* was performed. The programme also included a keyboard concerto played by the local organist August Eberhard Müller. Constanze again appeared as a soloist.[6] In Dresden she appeared at the Hôtel de Pologne on 25 May and performed 'some of her husband's compositions that have not yet been heard in Dresden'.[7]

Mozart's unpublished manuscripts could not, of course, be turned to any great material advantage as his works could easily be disseminated in print and in manuscript copies without

1. ◆ Mozart's death attracted international notice: brief obituaries of the composer were published not only in Vienna, but in Hamburg, Frankfurt and London as well; a lengthy obituary was published in the 4 January issue of *Musikalische Korrespondenz der Teutschen Filarmonischen Gesellschaft*, published at Speyer; see Eisen, *New Mozart Documents*, 72–6 and 154.

2. See Wlassak, *Chronik des k. k. Hof-Burgtheaters*, 98. It was probably the D minor concerto K466 that Beethoven played. This was a work of which he was especially fond and for which he wrote a set of cadenzas [*Dokumente*, 414, *Documentary Biography*, 473].

3. Procházka, *Mozart in Prag*, 206; Josef Fischer, *Wolfgang Amadeus Mozart (Sohn): Eine biographische Skizze sowie zwei bisher unbekannte Briefe Mozarts (Vater)*, 6. At the end of 1796 Constanze announced a concert in Graz with *Idomeneo* and excerpts from *La clemenza di Tito* [*Dokumente*, 420–1 and 484–5, *Documentary Biography*, 476 and 483].

4. Genée, 'Constanze Mozart in Berlin', 277. The second part of the concert included 'a selection of the most substantial excerpts' from *La clemenza di Tito*, in which Constanze again took part.

5. Niemetschek, *Leben des k. k. Kapellmeisters Wolfgang Gottlieb Mozart*, 42.

6. Dörffel, *Geschichte der Gewandhauskonzerte zu Leipzig*, 195. The programme also included two numbers from *Idomeneo* and a symphony by Mozart.

7. Nottebohm, *Mozartiana*, 15–16. ◆ Abert's chronology of Constanze Mozart's travels and concerts is slightly skewed: she performed at Graz on 4 September 1795 and at Leipzig on 11 November 1795; in 1796 she gave concerts at Berlin on 11 February (Friedrich Wilhelm II's minute is dated 14 February), at Leipzig on 16 and 25 April, and at Dresden probably on 21 May; she then played at Linz on 19 November and at Graz on 30 December. Her Prague concert took place on 15 November 1797. For the documents relating to her concert tours, see *Dokumente*, 415–21, *Documentary Biography*, 476–85.

Constanze being even so much as asked.[8] Indeed, she herself regarded it as a favour when this happened and she received a fee.[9] Certainly she was more than satisfied when André bought all Mozart's unpublished works for 1000 carolins in 1799.[10] A few of his manuscript scores had been missing at the time of his death, and others were given away by André, but the rest were itemized in the 'Thematic Catalogue of Mozart's Original Manuscripts owned by Court Councillor André in Offenbach' that was published in Offenbach in 1841. The manuscripts that remained in the possession of André and his brothers were bought for 20,000 thalers by the Berlin Royal Library in 1873.[11]

In 1797 Constanze met Georg Nikolaus Nissen, who was then chargé d'affaires at the Danish Embassy in Vienna and who, as is clear from the numerous letters that he wrote in her name, helped her to sort out her affairs. He was an honest and decent individual, albeit melancholy by nature and inclined to fuss. As we have already seen, he managed to turn Constanze into a thoroughly respectable housewife following their marriage in 1809. Between 1810 and 1820 they lived in Copenhagen, where Nissen was responsible for censoring political newspapers. The holder of the Order of the Danebrog and a Danish Councillor of State, he retired in 1820 and settled in Salzburg, where Mozart's sister was still living. Outwardly, relations between the two sisters-in-law seem to have improved, although Marianne inevitably continued to regard Constanze as a typical Weber. Nissen died on 24 March 1826[12] and Constanze now moved in with her widowed sister Sophie Haibel, devoting her energies to administering her fortune and sorting out the various papers relating to Nissen's estate and his life of Mozart, while at the same time keeping up a lively

8. Of some significance in this context is Marianne's letter to Breitkopf & Härtel of 4 August 1799; see Nottebohm, *Mozartiana*, 135. ◆ See *Briefe*, iv.259–60: 'All of my brother's scores that were still in our father's possession I immediately sent to my brother in Vienna on our father's death in 1787, but I regret that I did not keep back some of his earlier compositions myself, they'd have been well looked after with me, whereas I have it on good authority, and from an eyewitness, that his scores were always left lying around under the piano and that copyists were able to help themselves to whatever they wanted, and I'm all the more willing to believe this in that I knew that the more my brother developed as a composer, the more intolerant he became towards his older works, and so I don't doubt that many of his earlier works will have been lost.'
9. Constanze was heavily involved in the edition of Mozart's 'Oeuvres' instigated by Breitkopf & Härtel; for excerpts from her correspondence with the firm, see Nottebohm, *Mozartiana*, 121–2. ◆ Constanze's correspondence with Breitkopf & Härtel between 1795 and 1802 is reproduced in *Briefe*, iv.206–432. For an overview of the edition, published between 1798 and 1806, see K⁶, 915–17. Concerning Constanze's promotion of Mozart in the years following his death, her business dealings and her participation in the creation of a Mozart 'myth', see Weikl, 'Die Vermarktung des Mythos "Mozart"'; Erich Valentin, 'Das Testament der Constanze Nissen: Mit biographischen Notizen über Constanze und Georg Nikolaus Nissen'; Gärtner, *Mozarts Requiem und die Geschäfte der Constanze Mozart*; and Stafford, *Mozart's Death: A Corrective Survey of the Legends*.
10. Henkel, 'Über Mozartsche Manuskripte', 157. ◆ Concerning André, see August André, *Zur Geschichte der Familie André*; Hortschansky, *Die Andrés. Familie und Verlag: Ihr Beitrag zur Musik-Druck-Stadtgeschichte. Ausstellung Stadtmuseum Offenbach a.M.*; Uta-Margrit and Hans-Jörg André, *Festschrift André zum 225. Firmenjubiläum*; Matthäus, *Johann André Musikverlag zu Offenbach am Main: Verlagsgeschichte und Bibliographie 1782–1800*; Constapel, *Der Musikverlag Johann André in Offenbach am Main: Studien zur Verlagstätigkeit von Johann Anton André und Verzeichnis der Musikalien von 1800 bis 1840*; and Rehm, 'Mozarts Nachlaß, die Andrés und kein Ende'. For Constanze's contract and correspondence with André between 1799 and 1803, see *Briefe*, iv.281–431. Further concerning the cataloguing of Mozart's musical estate, see Eichenauer, *Johann Anton André (1775–1842) und der Mozart-Nachlass: Ein Notenschatz in Offenbach am Main (Ausstellung: 29.1.–28.5.2006)*; Rehm, *Mozarts Nachlaß und die Andrés: Dokumente zur Verteilung und Verlosung von 1854*; Finscher, 'Maximilian Stadler und Mozarts Nachlaß'; and Deutsch, 'Mozarts Nachlaß: Aus den Briefen Konstanzens an den Verlag André'.
11. See *AmZ*, new series, viii (1873), 762; a list of the Mozart manuscripts lodged in Berlin may be found in Genée, 'Verzeichniß der Musikhandschriften W. A. Mozarts im Besitze der Königlichen Bibliothek in Berlin'. ◆ The majority of these manuscripts are now housed at the Biblioteka Jagiellońska, Kraków. During World War II, the Berlin library's rich manuscript collection was housed throughout parts of German-conquered Europe; the Mozart autographs, stored at the Grüßau monastery in Poland, were not rediscovered until 1979. Given the mobility of these treasures, together with the fact that some autographs remain in private hands, there is, even today, no single, up-to-date source for locating all of Mozart's manuscripts; the most reliable information can be found in the critical reports to the NMA.
12. He was buried in Leopold Mozart's grave at St Sebastian's. The tombstone was removed on Constanze's instructions, and it was only very recently that his name reappeared on the new tombstone.

correspondence with her two sons Carl and Wolfgang.[13] She died on 6 March 1842, only hours after receiving a model of the Mozart statue intended for Salzburg.[14] Of Mozart's six children,[15] only the second and sixth survived their father.

Carl Thomas Mozart was born at no. 591 Graben on 21 September 1784 and was educated first at Perchtoldsdorf and then, between 1792 and 1797, by Franz Xaver Niemetschek in Prague. It was intended that he should go into business and in 1798 he began his apprenticeship in Livorno, but for a long time he hesitated over whether to become a musician, before finally embarking on a career as a civil servant. He studied the piano with Duschek in Prague and conducted private performances both at the home of a certain Colonel Casella and subsequently at his own home, too.[16] His activities were concentrated in the main on Milan, where shortly before his death he bought a country house for 10,000 francs – the royalties that he received for three performances of *Le nozze di Figaro* in Paris.[17] He died on 31 October 1858, having retired from his post as an official of the state accountancy in Austrian Lombardy.[18]

Mozart's youngest son, Franz Xaver Wolfgang Mozart (later renamed Wolfgang Amadeus by his mother), was born at no. 970 Rauhensteingasse on 26 July 1791. Like his brother, he spent part of his childhood with Niemetschek in Prague, before moving to Vienna, where his teachers included Johann Nepomuk Hummel, Salieri, the Abbé Vogler and possibly also Albrechtsberger. He organized his first public concert in 1804. Between 1808 and 1814 he was music teacher to two aristocratic families in Lemberg. In 1819 he undertook an extended tour of Poland, Germany, Denmark and Italy, ending up in Prague, before returning to Lemberg in 1822. With the exception of a brief visit to Salzburg, he remained in Lemberg until 1838, teaching music and running the local choral society. In 1838 he moved to Vienna and four years later took part in the official celebrations marking the unveiling of his father's statue in Salzburg, performing the D minor concerto K466. He was made honorary Kapellmeister of the Dom-Musik-Verein and the Mozarteum in Salzburg. He died of a stomach disorder at Karlsbad on 29 July 1844. This is not the place to examine his artistic importance. Suffice it to say that neither his talent nor his character predestined him to greatness. There is a widespread view that the sons of great men are martyrs to their name, but the opposite is often the case and their fathers' reputations may help them to achieve a level of success that would otherwise have been denied them on the strength of their own artistic achievements

13. Cf. her oft-mentioned diary, recently published in Abert, 'Konstanze Nissens Tagebuch aus den Jahren 1824–1837'. ◆ For modern editions, see *Briefe*, 497–510 and Angermüller, *TageBuch meines Brief Wechsels*. Constanze's correspondence with her children is published in *Briefe*, iv.444–53.

14. *Wiener Musik-Zeitung* (1842), 150; on Vincent Novello's visit in 1829, see *AmZ*, new series, vii (1872), 80; on Julius André's visit in 1841, see Heinrich Henkel, *Der Klavierlehrer*, xiii/1. She told André that the two most compelling likenesses of Mozart were Posch's medallion and Mansfeld's engraving. In general, André had the impression that she had never really understood what a genius Mozart had been. ◆ The Posch medallion and Mansfeld engraving are reproduced in Deutsch, *Mozart und seine Welt*, 19–20. Vincent and Mary Novello, who visited Constanze in 1829, kept a diary of their visit with her; see Medici di Marignano and Hughes, *A Mozart Pilgrimage: Being the Travel Diaries of Vincent & Mary Novello in the Year 1829*.

15. For a long time considerable confusion surrounded Mozart's children, a confusion only recently cleared up by Emil Karl Blümml, who has examined the relevant registers; see Blümml, 'Mozarts Kinder: Eine Matrikelstudie'. The six children were Raimund Leopold (*b* 17 June 1783; *d* 19 August 1783); Carl; Johann Thomas Leopold (*b* 18 October 1786; *d* 15 November 1786); Theresia (*b* 27 December 1787; *d* 29 June 1788); Anna (*b* and *d* 16 November 1789); and Franz Xaver Wolfgang.

16. Reichardt, *Vertraute Briefe geschrieben auf einer Reise nach Wien und den österreichischen Staaten zu Ende 1808 und zu Anfang 1809*, i.244; and *AmZ*, xx (1818), 512; for a letter to Popelka, see Teuber, *Geschichte des Prager Theaters*, ii.221.

17. See Engl, 'Die den Vater überlebenden Söhne Carl und Wolfgang und die übrigen Kinder W. A. Mozarts'; *Katalog des Mozarteums im Geburts- und Wohnzimmer Mozarts zu Salzburg*, 10; and Schurig, *Wolfgang Amade Mozart*, ii.341–2.

18. ◆ For recently-discovered letters by Carl, not included in *Briefe*, see Angermüller, 'Carl Mozart an Alois Taux, Mailand, 4. April 1856' and 'Ein ungedruckter Brief Carl Mozarts (Mailand, 14. Oktober 1820)'; and [Mozart, Carl], 'Ein Brief von Karl Mozart'.

alone. This seems to have been the case with Franz Xaver Wolfgang. An exhaustive study of his work as a musician has yet to be written, of course.[19]

The fame and honours that had eluded Mozart during his final years were heaped upon him in death. In many places his memory was marked by performances of his works or by funeral cantatas specially written for the occasion,[20] and in many private houses[21] it soon became standard practice to commemorate his birth and death with concerts. Large-scale celebrations were held in 1856, 1891 and 1906 to mark the centenary of his birth and death and the sesquicentenary of his birth. The anniversaries of individual works were likewise celebrated, notably that of *Don Giovanni* in 1887.

To examine the traces left by Mozart's music on the nineteenth century, especially on the Romantics, would require a volume to itself. Such traces may be found not only in Germany itself, but in the whole of European music, even in Italy, a country otherwise so remote from Mozart. No attempt has yet been made to examine Mozart's influence on the whole of our intellectual development – but the same is true, of course, of Bach and Beethoven.[22]

The earliest memorial to Mozart was erected in Graz in 1792 by a local art dealer by the name of Franz Deyerkauf. It is no longer extant.[23] Likewise, Mozart's friend Giuseppe Antonio Bridi set up a monument to him in his garden at Rovereto with an inscription in Latin and German.[24] It,

19. See Wurzbach, *Mozart-Buch*, 277ff.; Engl, 'Die den Vater überlebenden Söhne', 41ff.; Josef Fischer, *Wolfgang Amadeus Mozart (Sohn)*; Kaufmann, 'Wolfgang Amadeus Mozart der Sohn: Sein Aufenthalt in Karlsbad, seine Begräbnisstätte und Biographisches'; and Schurig, *Wolfgang Amade Mozart*, ii.342ff. (with portrait). On Werner Wolffheim's research on his travel diary of 1819–21, see *Wolffheim, 'W. A. Mozart Sohn'*. ◆ Also see Fuchs, 'Biographische Skizze von Wolfgang Amadeus Mozart (dem Sohne)'; Hummel, *W. A. Mozarts Söhne*; Tournier, 'Le Dernier des Mozart'; and Hans Hoffmann, 'Mozart – Genialer Vater, vergessene Söhne'. For letters by F. X. Mozart not in *Briefe*, see Senigl, 'Ein unveröffentlichter Brief Franz Xaver Mozarts an Franz Edlen von Hilleprandt'; and Angermüller, 'Ein ungedruckter Brief Franz Xaver Wolfgang Mozarts an Caroline Ungher-Sabatier, Wien, 26. Dezember 1842', 'Neuerwerbungen der Bibliotheca Mozartiana' and 'Verschollene Briefe von und an Franz Xaver Wolfgang Mozart'. F. X. Mozart's works include a lost cantata written for Joseph Haydn (1805); *Der erste Frühlingstag*, a cantata for four solo voices, chorus and orchestra op. 28; a cantata for the 1842 unveiling of the Mozart memorial in Salzburg op. 30; the songs 'In der Väter Hallen ruht' op. 12 (1808), 'In questa tomba oscura' (1808), *6 Lieder* op. 21 (1820), 'An Emma' op.24 (1820) and *3 deutsche Lieder* op.27 (1820); two piano concertos opp. 14 and 25 (published in 1809 and 1818, respectively); the piano quartet op. 1 (1805); two violin sonatas opp. 7 and 15 (published in 1808 and 1813); a sonata for violoncello or violin and piano op. 19 (1820); and twelve polonaises for piano op. 17 (c1815), among other works.
20. By Carl Bernhard Wessely in Berlin [*Mozard's Urne*, 1792] and Cannabich in Munich [*Mozarts Gedächtnis Feyer seinen Manen gewidmet*, published 1797], for example; see *Musikalisches Wochenblatt*, xxiv (?24 March 1792), 191, and Niemetschek, *Leben des k. k. Kapellmeisters Wolfgang Gottlieb Mozart*, 66; on the memorial service in Prague in 1791, see Teuber, *Geschichte des Prager Theaters*, ii.273 and Procházka, *Mozart in Prag*, 184–5. ◆ A description of the Prague memorial service was published in the *Musikalische Korrespondenz der Teutschen Filarmonischen Gesellschaft* for 4 January 1792: 'on the day itself, all the bells of the parish church were rung uninterruptedly for a full half-hour. Almost the entire city turned out, so that the Italian Square could not accommodate the carriages, nor the church, with room for nearly 4000 people, those who came to honour the deceased. The Requiem was by the famous Kapellmeister Rosetti . . . and it was so admirably performed by 120 of the best musicians, first among whom was the famous singer Duschek, that Mozart's great spirit in Elysium must have rejoiced. In the middle of the church stood a finely illuminated catafalque; three choirs of timpani and trumpets played in muffled tones. The Mass was celebrated by his Excellency, the parish priest Herr Rudolph Fischer; he was assisted by twelve students from the small side gymnasium, who carried torches, wore mourning-crepes draped diagonally across one shoulder, and carried white cloths in their hands. A solemn silence reigned on all sides and, what is more, a thousand tears flowed for the worthy Mozart, who with his heavenly harmonies had so often filled all hearts with the most tender feelings.' See Eisen, *New Mozart Documents*, 73–6.
21. *AmZ*, ii (1799/1800), 239.
22. Important pointers in this direction may be found in Kretzschmar, 'Mozart in der Geschichte der Oper', ii.275–9. ◆ Mozart reception studies, both historical and historiographical, have blossomed in the nearly ninety years since Abert wrote his text. Among numerous significant studies, see, in particular, Gruber, *Mozart and Posterity*; Daverio, 'Mozart in the nineteenth century'; Ulrich Konrad, 'Mozart an den Zeitwenden 1800 – 1900 – 2000'; Jung, *Mozart – Aspekte des 19. Jahrhunderts*; Botstein, 'Nineteenth-century Mozart: The fin de siècle Mozart revival'; and Smaczny, 'Mozart and the twentieth century'.
23. Anonymous, 'Grazer Mozartiana', which also mentions a second monument to Mozart at Mariagrün near Graz. This second monument, a bust, is no longer extant. ◆ Concerning Deyerkauf, see Rüdiger Wolf, 'Wiener Wirtschaftsadel um Mozart, 1781–1791'; his memorial has subsequently been recovered and restored.
24. Bridi, *Breve notizie intorno ad alcuni più celebri compositori di musica e cenni sullo stato presente del canto italiano*, 63–4; and *AmZ*, xxvi (1824), 92 and xxx (1828), 680–81. ◆ See Bisesti and Muzi, 'Giuseppe Antonio Bridi: Un amico Roveretano di W. A. Mozart', and *Un'architettura iniziatica: Il Giardino Bridi a Rovereto dall'abbandono al recupero. Relazione storica*.

too, has disappeared, as has Gottlieb Klauer's terracotta monument, which the Duchess Anna Amalie of Weimar commissioned for the park at Tiefurt in 1799.[25]

The idea of commemorating Mozart with a large-scale monument in Salzburg was first mooted by Julius Schilling in 1835[26] and an appeal launched in September 1836.[27] The statue was cast on 22 May 1841 and officially unveiled in the Michaelsplatz in Salzburg on 4 September 1842 and on the days that followed.[28] Unfortunately Schwanthaler failed to do justice either to Mozart as an individual or to his artistry. The composer is depicted wearing his usual coat, his head turned slightly upwards and to one side, his position evidently suggested by the inscription 'Tuba mirum' on the sheet of paper that he holds in his hand. On the base of the statue, Mozart's church music, concertos and operas are allegorically represented in reliefs, as is an eagle depicted flying heavenwards with a lyre. The inscription reads simply: 'Mozart'. Soon after this, Mozart's bust was set up in Walhalla near Regensburg at the behest of Ludwig I.

In 1856 the city of Vienna decided to erect a monument to Mozart in St Marx's Cemetery. The work of Hanns Gasser, it was officially unveiled on 5 December 1859 and moved to the Währinger Central Cemetery in 1891. The bronze statue of a grieving Muse sits on a granite plinth, with the score of the *Requiem* in her right hand, while her left hand, resting on a pile of Mozart's works, holds a laurel wreath. The plinth itself includes a relievo portrait of Mozart and the Vienna coat of arms, together with a number of brief inscriptions.

In Prague a bust of Mozart by Thomas Seidan was unveiled in the garden at the Villa Bertramka on 3 June 1876.[29] And on 8 April 1881 a huge bronze bust by the Viennese sculptor Edmund Hellmer was erected in front of the Mozart House on the Kapuzinerberg.[30] Vienna can boast three additional monuments to the composer: the bronze bust by Johann Baptist Feßler in Mozart's house at Rauhensteingasse no. 8; the marble statue by Victor Tilgner that rests on a plinth surrounded by Cupids and tutelary spirits and that was unveiled in the Albrechtsplatz on 24 April 1896; and the Mozart Fountain on the Marktplatz, a memorial designed jointly by the sculptor Carl Wollek and the architect Otto Schönthal and unveiled on 18 October 1905. It represents Tamino with his flute and Pamina preparing to face the ordeal by fire and water. Dresden, too, has a Mozart Fountain on the Bürgerwiese. Unveiled in 1907, it is the work of Hermann Hosaeus and comprises a column inscribed with the word 'Mozart' and surrounded by the three allegorical figures of Grace, Serenity and Wistfulness.[31]

Mozart's name has also been honoured by means of foundations. The Salzburg Mozarteum was founded in 1841 and from the outset set itself the task of collecting all Mozart's family documents and other memorabilia, initially from the family estate, later from elsewhere, too. In particular, it has done much to promote church music in Salzburg. In 1871 a society was formed in the town

---

25. *Journal des Luxus und der Moden* (November 1799); *AmZ*, ii (1799/1800), 239 and 420; illustration in Schurig, *Wolfgang Amade Mozart*, ii.377. ◆ Although Duchess Anna Amalie's monument does not survive, it is pictured in the *Journal des Luxus und der Moden* (November 1799), plate 33. Bridi's temple, on the other hand, does survive, although only in part: both the frescoes inside and the busts of Haydn and Mozart are lost. Located at Viale Trento 42, the garden also contains a stone monument in remembrance of W. A. Mozart erected in 1831.
26. See *Salzburger Zeitung* (12 August 1835).
27. Hammerle, *Mozart und einige Zeitgenossen*, 85–6.
28. Mielichhofer, *Das Mozart-Denkmal zu Salzburg und dessen Enthüllungs-Feier im September 1842*; *AmZ*, xliv (1842), 722–3, 780–1 and 806–7. The total contributions amounted to more than 30,000 florins. ◆ More recently, see Angermüller, *Das Salzburger Mozart-Denkmal: Eine Dokumentation (bis 1845) zur 150–Jahre-Enthüllungsfeier*.
29. Procházka, *Mozart in Prag*, 211.
30. Engl, *W. A. Mozart in den Schilderungen seiner Biographen*, 50; a plaster cast is in the room in which Mozart was born.
31. On the various monuments to Mozart, see Wurzbach, *Mozart-Buch*, 193–4, and Schurig, *Wolfgang Amade Mozart*, ii.367–8.

with the aim of establishing an international Mozart foundation that would set up a school of music, dispense bursaries, perform classical works, build a 'Mozart House' and so on. The foundation soon found widespread support,[32] with the result that by 1880 it had replaced the old Mozarteum and was able to set about achieving its aims in the guise of the Internationale Stiftung Mozarteum.[33] It runs not only the music school that reopened in the new 'Mozart House' in September 1914 but also the museum in the house in which Mozart was born.[34] In addition it administers the Mozart House on the Kapuzinerberg and organizes concerts and festivals.[35] It was this organization that in 1888 helped to found the Internationale Mozartgemeinde that seeks to bring together all admirers of Mozart's music.[36] In comparison with the work of societies devoted to other composers such as Bach and Wagner, it has so far enjoyed only modest successes, of course.

Salzburg was in fact preempted by Frankfurt am Main, which established its own Mozart Foundation in 1838 with the aim of awarding grants to talented young musicians in order for them to train as composers. In 1895 the newly founded Berlin Mozart-Gemeinde published the first issue of its new journal.[37] It, too, organizes regular performances.[38] Various other towns and cities have Mozart Societies, the most active of them being the Dresden Mozart Society, which was founded in 1897.[39]

In spite of all the good will and often significant successes chalked up by these organizations, it is unfortunately still not possible to say that Mozart and his music have been promoted in a wholly satisfactory, coherent and purposeful way. This is all the more regrettable in that during the last twenty years our attitude to Mozart has changed considerably, a change reflected in the writings quoted above. It is a gratifying sign of its vitality that his music is not merely uncritically admired but discussed in a serious way and that this new spirit is discernible not only in the world of scholarship but also in practical terms, a sure sign that Mozart is more alive today than he was only thirty years ago. It is all the more important, therefore, that these resources are not dissipated in

---

32. Engl, *General-Bericht des Provisorischen Ausschusses der Internationalen Mozart-Stiftung*, 16 and 20. In 1877 it arranged for the 'Zauberflötenhäuschen' to be moved from Vienna to Salzburg.

33. The new Mozarteum, too, publishes annual reports by its secretary Johann Evangelist Engl. ◆ The *Jahresbericht der Internationalen Stiftung Mozarteum* was superseded by the *Mitteilungen der Internationalen Stiftung Mozarteum*. The Internationale Mozart-Stiftung, whose broad initial programme included supporting and encouraging musicians and music students, promoting concerts, building a library and archive and organizing periodic conventions of musicians, was founded in 1870 by Karl Freiherr von Sterneck (1813–93); in 1875 it started the first complete edition of Mozart's works. In 1880 Sterneck succeeded in freeing the Mozarteum from its administrative association with the Dommusikverein and it united with the Internationale Mozart-Stiftung to form the Internationale Stiftung Mozarteum. The first director of the public music school was Joseph Friedrich Hummel; it later became a conservatory (1914, state controlled from 1922), a Reichshochschule für Musik (1939–45), a Musikakademie (1953) and the Hochschule für Musik und Darstellende Kunst (1971). Among its outstanding directors were Bernhard Paumgartner (1917–38 and 1945–9), Clemens Krauss (1938–45) and Eberhard Preussner (1959–64). In 1956, the bicentenary of Mozart's birth, the Internationale Stiftung Mozarteum initiated an annual series of concerts held at the end of January, the Salzburg Mozartwoche. Since 1950 it has also published the more substantial *Mozart-Jahrbuch*, a sequel to the *Mozart-Jahrbuch* (1923–9) and the *Neues Mozart-Jahrbuch* (1941–3). Further, see Karl Wagner, *Das Mozarteum: Geschichte und Entwicklung einer kulturellen Institution*, and Rehm, *Internationale Stiftung Mozarteum Salzburg: Geschichte – Gegenwart – Aufgaben der Zukunft*.

34. ◆ Getreidegasse 9. The other significant Mozart site in Salzburg is the newly-reconstructed 'Tanzmeisterhaus' on the Makartplatz, where the Mozarts lived from 1773.

35. A further point is the organization of Mozart conferences to discuss important musical questions, but in spite of its importance for Mozart himself, this point has yet to be effectively implemented.

36. See Horner, ['Nachricht'].

37. Genée, 'Zum zehnjährigen Bestehen der Mozart-Gemeinde in Berlin', 297–8.

38. *AmZ*, xlii (1841), 735. ◆ The *Mitteilungen für die Mozart-Gemeinde in Berlin* was published between 1895 and 1925.

39. ◆ See *Festschrift zum hundertjährigen Bestehen des Mozarts-Vereins zu Dresden, 1886–1996* and, more generally, Brusniak, 'Organisierte und institutionalisierte Mozart-Pflege in Deutschland im 19. und 20. Jahrhundert'. Of particular importance now is the Deutsche Mozart-Gesellschaft, which since 1954 has published *Acta Mozartiana*.

an aimless and incoherent manner but that they acquire a firm focus, allowing for an exchange of common ideas and ensuring that scholarly findings can always be implemented.[40] The fact that the last word has not been spoken on Mozart and that it will never be spoken is clearer to us today than ever before and one of the main aims of this study has been to make contemporaries aware of this. A whole host of questions of a stylistic and dramaturgical nature, to say nothing of those bound up with the psychology of art, still await an answer, quite apart from old, unsettled debts of honour such as the preparation of acceptable translations of Mozart's Italian operas. Even the complete edition of Mozart's works that was published by Breitkopf & Härtel in Leipzig between 1876 and 1886 and that resulted from the collaboration of leading artists and researchers, although a monumental work of which we Germans can be proud, is very uneven in quality and in urgent need of an overhaul.[41] In short, there is still a lot of work to be done. Is it not possible for a German Mozart Society to be established in order to achieve what has long been the case with Bach and what is now the case with Brahms, Reger and Schumann, in other words, a society that will place itself in the service of the composer and his art in a way that is divorced from local concerns?[42]

The present writer has devoted many years of his life to Mozart and derived immense enjoyment from his work. He hopes that the reader will not hold it against him if he now takes his leave with a certain feeling of sadness. Above all, he hopes that he will be spared the need to search for the sort of brief and convenient formula that many biographers feel called upon to provide in order to sum up their hero's essential character: such a formula simply cannot be found. Earlier writers have fallen back on analogies and compared Mozart with Raphael, Shakespeare, Watteau and Goethe. But, although such comparisons have produced many a word of wisdom, they have failed to explain the essence of Mozart as a phenomenon. After all, comparisons of this kind tend to become meaningful – if at all – only when they stress not merely the affinities between the artists in question but also their fundamental differences.

There is only one further point that needs to be made here: in spite of all the Italian influences and models to which Mozart was exposed, it is the German spirit that he embodies. What matters here is not so much his epistolary professions of his Germanness nor even individual details of his work such as the inspired way in which he was able to transform *opera buffa* and lend it greater depth but, rather, the fact that, following the hegemony of French rationalism, his works reflected the new German desire to see the world not as a well-ordered system of forces that could be comprehended and predicted by rational means but as the source of endlessly new ideas that no longer lent themselves to rational explanation. Mozart's creative urge invariably set out from a visible world that could be grasped by means of the senses, without any preconceived theoretical speculations, thereby allowing all his works to appear veritable miracles of creation. As such, this was the direct opposite of the demands advanced by French aesthetics. This creativity, it must be stressed, is not the same as formlessness, and the claim that Mozart is one of the greatest masters of form remains as valid as ever. But for him form was not a fixed pattern or dead letter: rather, it was something that was created anew with each new work, a living force inextricably bound up

---

40. ◆ Abert's reasonable and disinterested wish has been fulfilled, but only in part, by the Internationale Stiftung Mozarteum and the NMA.

41. ◆ The AMA has now been superceded by the NMA, the first volumes of which appeared in 1955. See Rehm, '1956–1991–2006: Milestones in the "Neue Mozart-Ausgabe"'.

42. This notion is actively advocated by Schurig, *Wolfgang Amade Mozart*, ii.347. ◆ Even today, however, Schurig and Abert's call for a Mozart society divorced from local concerns has not been realized.

with him and his inner life. In the circumstances it is hardly surprising that Goethe felt drawn to Mozart. His comment to Eckermann may bring this study to a close:

> What is genius if not the creative force by which acts arise that can reveal themselves before God and Nature and which, precisely for that reason, produce results and are permanent? All Mozart's works are of this kind; they contain a generative force that continues to leave its mark on generation upon generation and as a result may not so soon be exhausted or consumed.[43]

43.   Goethe, *Gespräche mit Eckermann*, ii.5–6 (entry of 11 March 1828).

APPENDIX I

Marianne Mozart[1]
by Otto Jahn

Known to her family and friends as 'Nannerl', Wolfgang Mozart's sister, Maria Anna Walburga Ignatia, was born on 30 July 1751 and was therefore five years older than her brother. From an early age she revealed such a decisive gift for music that she made the most extraordinary progress under her father's instruction, appearing as a keyboard player during the family's first concert tours in 1762, 1763–6 and 1767, and standing comparison with the leading performers of her day. Only her younger brother's unprecedented achievements surpassed her own. Her father was not alone in praising her accomplishments when he wrote from London on 8 June 1764: 'It is enough that my little girl is one of the most skilful players in Europe, even though she is only 12.'[2] Other assessments amply confirm this view. During their visit to The Hague in October 1765 she was struck down by a serious illness that brought her close to death, but she recovered, to the great relief of her parents, both of whom had despaired of her recovery. In November 1767 both she and Wolfgang were affected by smallpox in Olmütz. Once again she survived.

She did not accompany her father and brother on their later visits to Italy but remained at home with her mother, continuing to develop as a keyboard player, with the result that even at a later date she could claim to be regarded as a virtuoso, and as such she is described by Burney in 1772.[3] As she herself willingly admitted, it was to the example and instruction of her brother, with whom she made music whenever he was in Salzburg, that she owed her finest achievements. In his letter of 25 January 1778, Leopold informed his son that two members of Prince Kraft Ernst von Oettingen-Wallerstein's orchestra, the violinist Anton Janitsch and the cellist Josef Reicha, had given a concert in Salzburg and had 'absolutely insisted on hearing Nannerl play, admitting that their sole reason for doing so was so that they could tell from her own style of playing what yours

---

1. See also Genée, 'Mozarts Schwester Nannerl'. ◆ For more recent biographical accounts, see Hummel, *Nannerl: Wolfgang Amadeus Mozarts Schwester;* Geffray, 'Mozart, Maria Anna' and Rieger, *Nannerl Mozart: Leben einer Künstlerin im 18. Jahrhundert.* A psychological interpretation of the relationship between Mozart and his sister is Solomon, 'Marianne Mozart: "Carissima sorella mia"', but see also Halliwell, *The Mozart Family: Four Lives in a Social Context.* For a carnivalesque reading of the letters, see Schroeder, *Mozart in Revolt: Strategies of Resistance, Mischief and Deception,* 126–40 ('Scatology and the "Bäsle" Letters').

2. ◆ *Briefe,* i.154 (letter of 8 June 1764).

3. Burney, *The Present State of Music in Germany, the Netherlands, and United Provinces,* ii.323. ◆ In fact, the description of Nannerl is not original to Burney but a reworking of a comment by one of his correspondents, Louis De Visme. And it is hardly complimentary either to Nannerl or to Mozart. The passage reads, in full: 'I passed lately some days at Salsburg and had a great deal of Musick at the Archbishop's, as he is a Dilettante & plays well on the Fiddle. He takes pains to reform his Band, which, like others, is too harsh. He has put Fischietti at the head of it, Composer of il Mercato di Malmantile & il Dottore &c. There is among them an excellent Composer for the Bassoon & other wind Musick. Secchi & Raineri (for so Reiner is to be called for the future by my direction) are to go there on purpose to play before him, that he may learn their stile & write for them. Young Mozhart is too of the band, you remember this prodigy in England. He composed an Opera at Milan for the marriage of the Archduke & he is now to do the same this Carnaval tho' but sixteen years of age. He is [a] great master of his Instrument; for I went to his Father's house to hear him. He and his Sister can play together on the same Harpsicord, but she is at her summit which is not marvellous, and if I may judge by the Musick I heard of his composition in the Orchestra, he is one further instance of early Fruit, which is more extraordinary than excellent.' De Visme's letter to Burney is dated Munich, 30 November 1772; see Eisen, *New Mozart Documents,* 23.

must be like, and so they were especially keen to hear one of your works. She gave a wonderful performance of your Mannheim sonata, with all the necessary expression. They were amazed at her playing and at the work. – They also accompanied Nannerl in your trio in B flat [K254], and did so most admirably.'[4] Leopold went on to report that his two visitors now felt the greatest respect for Mozart's achievements on the basis of these works and Nannerl's style of playing. 'I am only my brother's pupil', she had kept repeating. Whenever he was away from home, Mozart would always send his sister his keyboard compositions and set store by her opinions. As a result he also sent her reports and reviews, especially of other keyboard players such as Clementi.[5]

She also tried her hand at composition: a song that she sent to her brother in Rome elicited his admiration, and he found her exercises in thoroughbass faultless and to his complete satisfaction (see letters of 19 May and 7 July 1770).[6] On 25 February 1778 Leopold reported that she had learnt to play a figured bass and to extemporize as she had realized that, when her father died, she would have to look after herself and her mother.[7] On 20 July 1778, as a belated present for her name-day, Mozart sent her a prelude from Paris, describing it as 'a kind of capriccio with which to test a keyboard'.[8] As a joke, she used it to test her father. She received it at four o'clock in the afternoon and immediately committed it to memory, so that, when her father returned home at five, she told him that she had thought up a new piece and that if he liked it, she would write it down. With that she began the prelude. 'I stared at her in wide-eyed amazement,' reported Leopold, 'and said: "Where the devil have you got those ideas from?" She laughed and pulled the letters out of the bag.'[9]

She began giving keyboard lessons at an early age, so that on 12 December 1772, for example, we find her father writing from Milan: 'Tell Nannerl to be patient and to work hard when teaching little Zezi; I know that she herself will benefit from showing someone to do something thoroughly and patiently, I have not written this in vain.'[10] Later her lessons became a welcome source of income for the family, whose means were very limited, allowing her to see to her personal needs and, at least as long as she was still living with her father, to lighten his burden of care.[11] Even within her own family she was regarded as selfish, so that Leopold was agreeably surprised when

4. ◆ *Briefe*, ii.241–2. In fact, Leopold's letter was written on 25 January but dated 26 January.

5. ◆ For Mozart and Clementi, see above.

6. ◆ *Briefe*, ii.349–50 and 369 (letters of 19 May and 7 July 1770).

7. ◆ *Briefe*, ii.300 (letter of 25 February 1778). Further, see Plath, 'Leopold Mozart und Nannerl: Lehrer und Schülerin. Fragmentarische Bemerkungen zu zwei Fragmenten'.

8. ◆ *Briefe*, ii.409–11 (letter of 20 July 1778). ◆ According to Wyzewa and Saint-Foix (*W. A. Mozart*, ii.405) and *Briefe*, v.540, this may be the four praeambula K395. However, Mozart's description does not match that work (*Briefe*, ii.49, letter of 10 October 1777); further, see Christoph Wolff, 'Mozarts Präludien für Nannerl: Zwei Rätsel und ihre Lösung'. Confusingly, *Briefe* (vi.612) also claims that K395 is the composition mentioned by Constanze in her letter to André of 28 October 1825 (*Briefe*, iv.472), but as Constanze herself notes, that work was composed by Mozart 'for his sister later, if not in his last years' and includes an allegretto in C, a capriccio, andantino, cantabile and concluding capriccio allegro; this corresponds to neither the date of K395 nor Mozart's description. Another possibility is K394, identified by *Briefe* (vi.516) as the work sent by Nannerl to Breitkopf & Härtel on 8 February 1800, 'a fugue and praeludium that my brother composed for me'. However, K394 also cannot be identical with the work mentioned in Mozart's letter of 20 July 1778; it is written on a kind of paper that suggests it was composed in Vienna about 1782. Possibly, then, Mozart's 'kind of capriccio' is lost. Further, see Levin, 'Mozart's non-metrical keyboard preludes'.

9. ◆ *Briefe*, ii.446 (letter of 13 August 1778).

10. ◆ *Briefe*, i.467 (letter of 12 December 1772).

11. ◆ Nannerl's pupils in Salzburg during the 1770s and 1780s included Barbara Zezi, a daughter of the local merchant Johann Bernhard Zezi; Elisabeth Maria Magdalena Katharina Antretter, daughter of the court councillor Johann Ernst von Antretter; the countesses Antonia Maria and Maria Anna Aloisia of the prominent Lodron family; Maria Margarethe ('Gretl') Marchand, daughter of Theobald Marchand, director of the German court theatre at Munich; and Maria Johanna Josepha ('Hanchen') Brochard, also of Munich. Marchand was a resident pupil of Leopold and Nannerl in Salzburg from 1782 to 1784, Brochard a resident pupil in 1783–4.

she heard that during his visit to Paris her brother had encountered unexpected difficulties: 'Thank God it was nothing more serious!' she exclaimed, even though she knew that, in order to help Mozart, she herself would have to run up debts. In other respects, too, she proved tender-hearted, if slightly excitable, and was not only deeply affected by the loss of her mother but was also genuinely concerned about her brother's fate, sometimes taking a livelier interest in it than he himself would have wished. His annoyance finds expression in the letter that he wrote from Mannheim on 19 February 1778: 'I embrace my sister with all my heart, but she shouldn't cry about every little shit, otherwise I'll never come home again.'[12] Leopold's remonstration followed as surely as night follows day.

In general, however, the relationship between brother and sister was extremely close and affectionate from childhood onwards. The other children had all died in infancy, with the result that Mozart and his sister were thrown back on each other alone. The strict discipline to which they were subjected at home, their joint travels and, above all, their interest in music – an interest fostered by both disposition and education – inevitably increased their natural affection, not least because of the total absence of any trace of jealousy or envy. Mozart's propensity for jokes and teasing was often directed at his 'rascally sister', and the letters that he wrote to her while touring Italy afford ample evidence of the delight with which he joked with her and of the innocent way in which he made fun of her cleverness and wit. Even at a much later date, he continued to maintain this tone of boisterous, even childish high spirits. On 20 December 1777, for example, he sent her the following doggerel verse from Mannheim. The lines are addressed not only to Nannerl but also to an otherwise unknown family friend by the name of Rosalie:

> Dearest Sallerl, sweetheart mine,
> Dearest Nannerl, sister mine.
> Thank you, my angel, for all your good wishes.
> Here's one from Mozart, that oddest of fishes.
> I wish you good luck and great joy for you, too,
> And hope that you'll love me as Woferl loves you;
> I tell you in truth that it's you I admire:
> For you, if you wished it, I'd go through the fire.
> I have to write just as I speak. With what zeal
> I see it all clearly, the love that I feel
> For you, pretty Sallerl, and you, sister Nan!
> So off with you, darlings, as fast as you can!
> Long life to you all, to Papa and Mama,
> To sister and brother, heysa, hopsasa!
> And his mistress and Woferl as well, just as long,
> Just as long, just as long as he still f-ts about,
> Just as long as he can p-s and s-t and pong,
> So long will he and Nan and Sallerl, too, be out
> In front, a splendid crew! But now I'll creep
> To bed, it's twelve o'clock and we should be asleep.[13]

12.   ◆ *Briefe*, ii.287 (letter 19 February 1778).
13.   ◆ *Briefe*, ii.199–200 (letter of 20 December 1777).

On another occasion, when he and his wife were on a visit to Salzburg, he sent his good wishes to Nannerl on her birthday:

> Today I went out shopping, you couldn't know the reason why,
> But all I'll say is this: it was so that I could buy
> A trifling gift that would give you a little pleasure,
> No matter what it cost in terms of time and leisure.
> I'm not quite sure if punch is what you drink,
> But don't you say it isn't, or else there'll be a stink.
> But then I thought, you're all for English places,
> For if you favoured Paris, I'd give you lots of laces,
> A bunch of posies and some eau de toilette,
> But you, my dearest sister, you are no coquette,
> So take this punch – it's good and very strong.
> Enjoy it while you can: for that alone I long.

Salzburg, 31 July 1783.

W. A. Mozart
Poet Laureate of the Marksmen[14]

On 10 December 1783, following his return to Vienna, he wrote to his sister again, sending her a couple of boxes on the ear, a couple of slaps on the face, a couple of raps on the cheek, a couple of whacks on the jaw, a couple of smacks on the jowl and a couple of cuffs on the mug.

The affectionate relationship between brother and sister found expression not only in these jokes, however, but also in their ability to share life's more serious aspects. When Mozart reached maturity and life in Salzburg was often made unbearable for him, his sister's situation, too, was far from happy. When mother and son left for Paris, she took over the running of the household, and Leopold had nothing but praise for her extraordinary hard work and attentiveness to detail. With the maidservant, who was dirty and deceitful, she was punctilious and resolute. Following her mother's death, she continued to look after the house for her father, including taking in lodgers from time to time. Keyboard practice – generally for several hours with her father in the evening – and the lessons that she gave for young ladies took up the rest of her time. She was popular as a teacher, and her pupils were distinguished by the precision and neatness of their playing. Whenever her brother was at home, the whole house came alive, their father was in a good mood, and she had someone with whom she could share her pleasures and unhappiness. When he left, Leopold was generally depressed and beset by care: he found it difficult to live without Mozart, and there was nothing that Nannerl could do to make life less irksome for him. Still less could she replace Mozart in his affections. By the same token, the distractions afforded by the social life of Salzburg were a poor substitute for the loneliness of her life at home, even though she took a lively interest in the individual members who made up her circle of friends and in the minor incidents that befell them, an interest maintained by her brother even after he had left Salzburg. 'Write to me often,' he begged her from Vienna on 4 July 1781, 'when you have nothing better to do, for I'd dearly like to hear some news occasionally, and you're Salzburg's living chronicle – you already write down every single thing that happens, so write it down twice, just to please me.'[15] Leopold

14. ◆ *Briefe*, iii.319–20 (letter of 31 July 1783). Mozart's wishes were for Nannerl's nameday (26 July), not her birthday.
15. ◆ *Briefe*, iii.138–9 (letter of 4 July 1781).

had insisted that the two of them should keep a regular diary, which Mozart did in his youth, while Nannerl continued the practice even in later life. Fragments from her diaries have survived,[16] while her letters to her brother include two very detailed accounts of the performances given by Schikaneder's company in Salzburg (November and December 1780).[17]

Towards the end of 1780, while Mozart was working on *Idomeneo* in Munich, Marianne was struck down by an illness that threatened for a time to turn to consumption; it was a long time before she was fully recovered. It seems that a tendency that had to contend with unfavourable circumstances was partly to blame for her ill health. Even as a child she had been physically attractive and it is clear from the family portrait in the Mozarteum in Salzburg that she developed into a young woman of imposing beauty who cannot have lacked for suitors. Mozart's jokes at the expense of a certain Herr von Mölk, one of Marianne's unrequited lovers (letter of 26 January 1770[18]), and other mysterious hints in his letters from Italy and later show that brother and sister also confided in each other where matters of the heart were concerned.

Once Mozart had settled in Vienna, he attempted to ingratiate himself with his sister by running all manner of errands for her. 'Ma très chère soeur,' he wrote to her on 4 July 1781,

> I'm delighted that the ribbons were to your liking, as for the price of the painted and unpainted ones I'll make enquiries, as I don't know at present, as Fräulein von Auerhammer, who was kind enough to obtain them for me, refused to accept any payment but begged me to send you all manner of good wishes, even though she does not know you, and to assure you that she will be pleased to run errands for you at any time; I've already passed on your very best wishes to her. My dearest sister, I recently wrote to our dear father to say that if there is anything that you would like me to send you from Vienna, no matter what it is, it would give me genuine pleasure to do so for you; I repeat this offer now, adding only that it would upset me very much if I were to hear that you were commissioning someone else in Vienna to run around for you.[19]

Later Constanze, too, went out of her way to run errands for her sister-in-law. But it was Mozart who continued to take a serious interest in Marianne's affairs of the heart. 'I'd very much like to know how things are going between you and a certain good friend', he wrote to her on 4 July 1781. 'Write and tell me, or have I lost your confidence in this matter?' The friend in question was Franz d'Ippold, a captain in the Imperial and Royal Army, tutor to the Salzburg Court pages from 1774,[20] and a member of the war council from 1777.[21] His feelings for Marianne were reciprocated, but his circumstances did not allow him to marry her. Mozart realized that his sister's health and peace of mind were at stake and, since things would never work out in Salzburg, he suggested that d'Ippold should move to Vienna and try his luck there. He himself would do everything in his power to help d'Ippold by introducing him to his acquaintances. Marianne would earn far more through teaching in Vienna than she would in Salzburg, and she would soon be able to marry

---

16. ◆ See Geffray, *"meine tag Ordnungen": Nannerl Mozarts Tagebuchblätter 1775–1783 mit Eintragungen ihres Bruders Wolfgang und ihres Vaters Leopold*. Further, see Halliwell, *The Mozart Family: Four Lives in a Social Context*, 215–17.

17. ◆ See *Briefe*, iii.35–8 (letter of 30 November 1780) and iii.61–3 (letter of 18 December 1780); further, see Friedrich Johann Fischer, 'Emanuel Schikaneder und Salzburg'.

18. ◆ *Briefe*, i.309–11 (letter of 26 January 1770).

19. ◆ *Briefe*, iii.138–9 (letter of 4 July 1781).

20. Sterneck has cast doubt on this claim; see his 'Der Freundeskreis Mozarts in Salzburg', 102 [Deiters's note]. ◆ In fact, d'Ippold held both these positions; see Heinz Schuler, *Mozarts Salzburger Freunde und Bekannte: Biographien und Kommentare*, 131.

21. ◆ Further, see Breitinger, 'Mozart Nannerls unglücklicher Verehrer'.

d'Ippold there. Then their father, too, would quit his post in Salzburg and move to Vienna to be with his children. Unfortunately this splendid plan seems to have been impracticable, and as there was no prospect of their marrying, the two lovers drifted apart again, even though d'Ippold remained on friendly terms with both Leopold and Marianne, towards whom he continued to show both sympathy and devotion. His greatest pleasure was Leopold's grandson, who was staying with his grandfather and with whom he talked, laughed and played, visiting the child every day during one of Leopold's absences from Salzburg.[22]

Just as Mozart stood by his sister during her affair with d'Ippold, so Marianne took a lively interest in her brother's love for his future wife. He could open his heart to her and complain of the difficulties placed in the way of himself and Constanze, encouraging the latter to instigate a correspondence of her own with Marianne at a time when Leopold was still opposed to their union.[23] Once Mozart had moved to Vienna, they inevitably wrote to each other less frequently as his turbulent existence and numerous other preoccupations left him with little time for lengthy or regular correspondence. When she reproached him for this, he sought to justify himself in his reply of 13 February 1782:

You must not conclude from my lack of a reply that you and your letters are a nuisance to me. – I shall always be delighted, dear sister, to have the honour of receiving a letter from you; – if the necessary business of earning my living allowed me, God knows I'd answer your letters at once! – When have I ever failed to reply to you? –Well, then! – It can't be forgetfulness, – nor can it be negligence, therefore it's entirely due to immediate hindrances – genuine impossibility! Do I not write to my father little enough? – That's bad enough, you'll say! But for heaven's sake, you both know Vienna! – In a place like this, has not a man (who has not a kreutzer of assured income) enough to think about and to work at day and night? – When our father has finished his duties in church and you have got rid of your few pupils, you can both do as you like for the rest of the day and write letters containing whole litanies; but I can't do that. – – – My dearest sister, if you think that I could ever forget my dearest, most beloved father and you, well – – but hush! God know the truth of the matter and that's consolation enough for me, – may He punish me if ever I forget you.[24]

On 23 August 1784 Marianne married Baron Johann Baptist von Berchthold zu Sonnenburg, a privy counsellor in Salzburg and magistrate at St Gilgen.[25] Mozart wrote to her on 18 August:

Ma très chère soeur,

Good Gracious! It's high time that I wrote to you if I want my letter to reach you while you're still a vestal virgin! – A few more days, and it'll be too late! – My wife and I wish you all joy and happiness in your change of state and are sorry only that we cannot have the pleasure of

---

22. ◆ Abert's explanation for Nannerl and d'Ippold's failure to marry and move to Vienna notwithstanding, the reason remains entirely unknown. For Mozart's suggestion, see *Briefe*, iii.158–9.

23. Essentially her views were no different from those of her father. [Abert's footnote] ◆ The notion that Nannerl, like Leopold, was antithetical to Constanze derives in the first instance from comments appended by Albert von Mölk to Nannerl's 1792 reminiscences, which were then passed on to Mozart's early biographer, Friedrich Schlichtegroll. It appears, however, that Nannerl was unaware of Mölk's interpolations and that the opinions expressed by him did not originate with her. See Clarke, 'Albert von Mölk: Mozart Myth-Maker?' and Halliwell, *The Mozart Family*, 581–5.

24. ◆ *Briefe*, iii.197–8 (letter of 13 February 1782).

25. See Engl, 'Studien über W. A. Mozart. Fünfte Folge', 34.

attending your wedding in person; but we hope to embrace you as Frau von Sonnenburg, together with your husband, both in Salzburg and St Gilgen next spring. Our only regrets are for our dear father, who will now be on his own! – Of course, you will not be far away and he can often drive out and visit you – but he's tied to that damned Kapellhaus again! – If I were in my father's place, I'd do as follows: – having served the archbishop for so long, I'd ask him if I could retire – and on receiving my pension I'd go and live with my daughter in St Gilgen and lead a life of peace and quiet there. – If the archbishop refused my request, I'd apply for my discharge and join my son in Vienna, – and it's this that I chiefly ask, namely, that you do your utmost to persuade him to do this; – I've said the same in my letter to him today. And now I send you 1000 good wishes from Vienna to Salzburg and hope in particular that the two of you will live together as harmoniously as we two. – So take this small piece of advice from my poetical brainbox. Listen:

> In wedlock you'll learn things, by God,
> That once seemed really very odd;
> You'll soon discover – yes, you too –
> What Eve herself was forced to do
> Before she could give birth to Cain.
> But wedlock's duties are so light
> That you'll perform them with delight
> And easily ignore the pain.
> But wedlock's joys are also mixed.
> So if your husband's scowl is fixed
> And if he look at you in ways that you,
> Dear sister, feel you don't deserve
> And if he proves bad-tempered too,
> Remember he's a man and say
> 'Thy will be done, O Lord, by day,
> But then by night my own I'll do!'
> > Your honest brother
> > W. A. Mozart.[26]

A whole series of letters from Leopold to his daughter attest to the loving care that he lavished on her throughout her life. He was tireless in running errands for her, seeing to her domestic needs and providing her with reading matter, occasionally receiving game or fish in return and faithfully retailing the local gossip. And he was equally ready to dispense advice not only to Marianne but also to her brother, who occasionally struck him as 'too deeply immersed in the spirit of dispensation'. Sarcasm is found, too, although Leopold is more reticent towards Marianne than he is towards Mozart. His healthy outlook and sound mind never wavered. When Marianne and her husband showed undue haste in applying for a stewardship at Neumarkt, Leopold repeatedly raised objections, advising them to think the matter over carefully, but once they had agreed on a course of action, they should stick to it. 'I am writing all this', he added on 20 November 1786, 'as

---

26. ◆ *Briefe*, iii.320–1 (letter of 18 August 1784).

I can easily imagine that from time to time unnecessary and tiresome things may be said and thought on this subject: but if it is bound to happen, no one can oppose what God ordains.'[27] If Marianne's husband seems to have made life difficult for her, her five stepchildren merely exacerbated the situation. Leopold describes them as malicious, ill-bred and ignorant. One of them, Wolfgang, even boasted of having 'bullied his second mother, and whenever he was naughty, his father invariably blamed the womenfolk and his mother, whom he then proceeded to berate'.[28]

She returned to Salzburg in June 1785 in order to be delivered of her first child at her father's house. She remained ill for some time afterwards, and so Leopold kept his grandson in Salzburg, lavishing the tenderest care on him and beginning each of his subsequent letters with an account of his state of health. 'I cannot look at the child's right hand without feeling moved', he wrote on 11 November 1785:

> The most skilled keyboard player cannot place his hand as beautifully on the keys as he constantly holds his own hand; as soon as he stops moving his fingers, they come to rest in the position used for playing, with his little hand straightened out, and when he is asleep he has his little hand lying like this, as though the fingers are actually on the keys, with the most well-balanced tension and bending of the fingers: in short, you couldn't imagine a prettier picture! It often makes me sad to see it and I wish he were already 3 years old, I mean so that he would be able to play straightaway.

He found it hard to part with the child, and while criticizing its father for never coming to see his son, declared: 'I tell you, I'll keep little Leopold for as long as I live.'[29]

On Leopold's death, Mozart wrote to his sister as follows on 16 June 1787:

> Dearest, most beloved sister,
>
> I was not at all surprised, as I could easily guess the reason why you yourself did not inform me of the sad news of our dear father's completely unexpected death. – God rest his soul! – Rest assured, my dear, that if you want a kind brother to love and protect you, you will always find one in me. – My dearest, most beloved sister! If you were still unprovided for, all this would be unnecessary. As I have already thought and said a thousand times, it would give me the greatest pleasure to leave everything to you; but as it is now of no use to you, as it were, whereas it would be of considerable help to me, I think it my duty to consider my wife and child.[30]

It is unclear from this letter what Mozart claimed under the terms of his father's will, still less do we know how the estate was divided up.[31]

27. ◆ *Briefe*, iii.608–10 (letter of 20 November 1786). For Leopold Mozart's correspondence with Nannerl – his earliest letter is dated 30 August 1784, his last 10 May 1787 – see *Briefe*, iii.322–629 and iv.1–45.
28. ◆ Nannerl and Berchtold zu Sonnenburg had three children of their own: Leopold Alois Pantaleon (1785–1840), Johanna (known as 'Jeanette', 1789–1805) and Marie Babette (1790–1).
29. ◆ *Briefe*, iii.443–8, especially 446–7 (letter of 11 November 1785).
30. ◆ *Briefe*, iv.51 (letter of 16 June 1787).
31. In his letter of 1 August 1787 [*Briefe*, iv.52], Mozart agreed to accept his brother-in-law's offer 'on the understanding that the 1000 fl.' were paid to him 'in Viennese currency and, moreover, as a bill of exchange'. He also asked to be sent his scores [Abert's footnote]. ◆ For an account of the disposition of Leopold's estate, see Halliwell, *The Mozart Family*, 545–64; further, see Hamerníková, '"Licitations-Protokoll über die Leopold Mozartische Verlassenschaft" im Familienarchiv Berchtold'.

It is undoubtedly no accident that a letter that Mozart wrote shortly after this in August 1788 deals with his financial situation:

In reply to your question about my appointment, the emperor has taken me into his household and as a result has formally *decreed* it, but *for the present* on only 800 florins: but there is no one else in the household who has as much. On the playbill that appeared when my Prague opera *Don Giovanni* was performed (it's being given again today) and on which there's certainly not *too much* information as it's published by the management of the I. & R. Theatres, it said: 'The music is by Herr Mozart, *Kapellmeister in the Actual Service of His I. & R. Majesty*.'[32]

I am not aware of any subsequent letters. There was no real affinity between Marianne and her brother's wife; Marianne's opinion of Constanze, in part influenced by her father, continued to remain unfavourable. In her comments to Breitkopf & Härtel, for example, we read: 'He could not handle money and married a completely unsuitable young woman against his father's will, hence the great domestic disorder at and following his death.' Whether it was because of this antipathy or because of the events surrounding the administration of Leopold's estate, there seems – at least on an outer level – to have been a breach in Mozart's relations with his sister during the final years of his life, a breach that emerges from the fact that she took no note of the events of this period or at least refused to answer any questions on the subject. Yet on a deeper level she clearly remained fond of him, with the result that on 8 February 1800, for example, we find her writing to Breitkopf & Härtel: 'Herr Professor Niemetscheck's biography rekindled my sisterly feelings for my so dearly beloved brother, so that I often burst into tears as it was only now that I became aware of the sad situation in which my brother found himself.'[33] It would appear, therefore, that following Mozart's death there was initially no contact between Marianne and the composer's widow. It emerges from a letter that Marianne wrote to Joseph Sonnleithner on 2 July 1819 that she had not received any letters from her sister-in-law since 1801: she knew nothing about the latter's children and it was only through strangers that she had learnt of Constanze's remarriage.[34]

Baron von Sonnenburg had in fact died in 1801 and his widow had moved back to Salzburg with her children, where she lived in conditions which, if not opulent, were at least comfortable. She returned to piano teaching – not out of need, but merely for the extra income, her simple and economical lifestyle allowing her to spend more, rather than less. Her fellow Salzburgers were very fond of her: she was well respected and universally liked. In 1820 she had the misfortune of going blind, a fate that she bore with fortitude and composure and even with cheerfulness, as emerges from an incident that took place on the occasion of a visit from a woman whom she found deeply unpleasant – as she herself was very popular, people sought to entertain her by visiting her often. 'What a torment to make conversation with this person', she exclaimed when the woman had finally left. 'How fortunate that I can't see her!'[35] As we may expect, closer relations seem to have

---

32. ◆ *Briefe*, iv.52 (letter of August 1787). Apparently this was Mozart's last letter to his sister; it is presumed to date 2 August.
33. ◆ *Briefe*, iv. 311–13 (letter of 8 February 1800).
34. ◆ *Briefe*, iv.455–6 (letter of 2 July 1819).
35. This information comes from a letter from Nissen to Privy Counsellor André who, having been told, erroneously, that she was living in poverty offered to arrange a performance of the *Requiem* for her benefit. When she heard of this plan, she sent word via Nissen that, grateful though she was, she had no need of his assistance. ◆ See *Briefe*, iv.481–5 (letter of 16 March 1826).

developed in Salzburg between Marianne, her sister-in-law and Nissen. In Constanze's letter to Schack,[36] the former reports that 'a few years ago' Marianne made her and her husband a present of Mozart's correspondence with his father. Shortly before her death she was visited by Vincent Novello and his wife. In the diary incorporated into his biography he gives a moving account of the impressions gleaned on that occasion.[37]

She died in Salzburg at an advanced age on 29 October 1829.[38]

36. ◆ *Briefe*, iv.475–9 (letter of 16 February 1826).

37. See Thomae, *Allgemeine musikalische Zeitung* (1872), 77–8. He had brought her a gift of money from some English admirers, a gift that she accepted. [footnote added by Deiters to Jahn and taken over by Abert] ◆ The Novellos' conversations with Nannerl are published in Medici and Hughes, *A Mozart Pilgrimage: Being the Travel Diaries of Vincent and Mary Novello in the Year 1829*.

38. ◆ For Nannerl's will, see Angermüller, 'Testament, Kodizill, Nachtrag und Sperrelation der Freifrau Maria Anna von Berchtold zu Sonnenburg, geb. Mozart (1751–1829)'; further concerning Nannerl, particularly in the broader context of eighteenth-century Salzburg women and artists, see Mittendorfer, 'Unterdrückte Kreativität: Cornelia Goethe und Nannerl Mozart', and Morath and Andessner, *Salzburger Museum Carolino Augusteum: Frauen zu Salzburg. Caroline Auguste, Constanze Mozart, Nannerl Mozart, Barbara Krafft, Emilia Viktoria Kraus ('Hundsgräfin')*.

Transcriptions of Mozart's church music
by Otto Jahn[1]

Seven cantatas published under Mozart's name have achieved a popularity almost as widespread as that of his operas and in doing so have largely affected our views of Mozart as a church composer. Yet only one of these cantatas, the second, was written as such by Mozart, and even here the words have been rewritten. The remainder were all compiled after his death from individual sections of various sacred works that bear little relation to one another in terms of their date, style and essential purpose. All, moreover, were subjected to arbitrary changes and additions. Only their new words provide them with any sense of cohesion and these words, being generally extraordinarily trivial and feeble, not infrequently contradict the original texts.

As an example, take the following parody of a Goethe song, which appears in cantata 4 in place of the original *Alma Dei creatoris*.[2]

> Der du Leid und Sehnsucht stillest
> und das Herz mit Trost erfüllest,
> das sich reuvoll seiner Schuld bewußt,
> ach, ich bin des Wogens müde,
> banger Schmerzen, unruhvoller Lust;
> Geist vom Himmel, Gottes Friede,
> komm und wohn' in meiner Brust!

[You who ease suffering and longing and fill with solace the heart that, overcome with remorse, is conscious of its guilt, ah, I am weary of upheaval, fearful anguish and restless desire! Spirit from Heaven, God's peace, come and dwell within my breast.]

Here Mozart has been traduced twice over, a state of affairs attributable to the tendency of an age that sought to anaesthetize music and reduce it to the level of harmless enjoyment, having little understanding for the work as a whole, in other words, little respect for the artist's right to the integrity of his works. Least of all did this age have any historical understanding.

The following table provides an overview of these cantatas and their component parts:

Cantata 1 is made up of the Kyrie, 'Panis omnipotentiae', 'Viaticum' and 'Pignus futurae gloriae' from the litany K125.
Cantata 2 is the litany K109.

---

1. ◆ Although this appendix deals with only a few examples of the reuse and rearrangement of Mozart's music during the late-eighteenth and nineteenth centuries, it nevertheless serves as an important reminder – not otherwise mentioned by Abert – that a very large number of his compositions were adapted to differing local, national, religious, social and purely musical circumstances. More importantly, it shows that many of Mozart's works, and as a result changing views of the composer, often depended on a body of 'non-authentic' performances rather than a corpus of 'authentic' works. For extensive, but still only partial, lists of late-eighteenth and nineteenth-century arrangements of Mozart's compositions, see K⁶, 771–803 (Anh. B) and *Wolfgang Amadeus Mozart: Verzeichnis von Erst- und Frühdrucken bis etwa 1800.*
2. Anton Thibaut quite rightly inveighs against these insipid translations in *Über Reinheit der Tonkunst*, 102–3.

Cantata 3 is compiled from the Sanctus from the mass K259, the Benedictus from mass K220, the Gloria from the mass K259, the Offertory K72, and the Credo from the mass K 259.

Cantata 4 consists of the Kyrie and Gloria from the mass K220, the offertory K277, the 'Gratias' and 'Domine' from the mass in C minor K427 (also used in *Davidde penitente* K469 as the chorus 'Sii pur sempre' and the duet 'Sorgi o Signore') and the Magnificat from the vespers K193.

Cantata 5 is formed from the Kyrie, 'Et incarnatus' to the end of the Credo, Benedictus, Agnus Dei and Gloria from the mass K258.

Cantata 6 contains the 'Dixit' from the Vespers K193, and the 'Laudate Dominum' and Magnificat from the vespers K321.

Cantata 7 is made up of the Kyrie and Benedictus from the mass K259, the aria 'Lungi le cure ingrate' from *Davidde penitente* K469, the Agnus Dei and 'Dona' from the mass K259 and the 'Dixit' from the vespers K321.

In the light of all this, it comes as no surprise to discover that the choruses from *König Thamos* were reused with different words as sacred works[3] or that the Masonic cantata K471 was likewise recycled.[4] Nor should it surprise us that the words of other sacred works were replaced by alternative sacred texts.[5]

But secular music, too, was reused in church.[6] The beautiful adagio from the great serenade for wind instruments K361 reappeared as an offertory *Quis te comprehendat*. The aria for Nancy Storace, *Ch'io mi scordi di te* K505, acquired the words *In te domine speravi*, with the obbligato keyboard part transcribed for the organ. An aria from *La clemenza di Tito*, 'Deh per questo istante', was reused as an offertory with the words 'O Deus ego te amo', while a similar fate befell Adamberger's aria *Per pietà non ricercate* K420, which was retexted as 'Omni die dic Mariae'. Vincent Novello published the wonderful ensemble from act four of *Le nozze di Figaro*, 'Più docile io sono e dico di sì', as a motet with organ accompaniment, *O Iesu mi, miserere nobis!*, adding the note: 'This motett may be used at Benediction.' One hopes that it was merely as a joke that Leporello's 'Notte e giorno faticar' was travestied as a *Docti sacris* and Don Giovanni's 'champagne aria' as a *Lauda Sion*.[7]

---

3. ◆ The chorus 'Schon weichet dir, Sonne' was performed as a hymn, 'Preis dir! Gottheit', at Leipzig as early as 1796 and published as such by Breitkopf & Härtel in 1804, while the chorus 'Gottheit, Gottheit über alle' was published as a hymn, also by Breitkopf, in 1797. Further, an early manuscript copy survives with the offertory text 'Jesu, Jesu, Rex tremendae majestatis' (Prague, National Museum).

4. ◆ As 'Sehen wie der heiß gewünschte Friede' (manuscript at the monastic library of St Florian, Austria) and as a church cantata, 'Sehen, jenes Irrtums Macht verschwinden' (manuscript in the library of the Gesellschaft der Musikfreunde, Vienna, formerly owned by Köchel).

5. ◆ The numbers used by Abert to identify these arrangements, KAnh. 114–119, were subsumed in K[6] under the works from which the compositions were redacted: the 'Laudate pueri' of K339 as the offertory *Sancti et justi in Domino* and the 'Laudate dominum' of the same work as a gradual; the 'Viaticum' and 'Pignus' of K125 as the offertory *Adoratio tibi*; the 'Tremendum' and 'Pignus' of K243 as *Tremendum ac vivificum*; the Kyrie fragment K323 as a *Regina Coeli*; and the 'Laudate pueri' of K321 as the offertory *Amavit eum Dominus*. The vespers K321 were particularly well-known as psalms in an arrangement published in Vienna by Artaria in 1828, where the six movements of the original were retexted as 'Gott, der Schöpfung Herr', 'Dich will ich bekennen', 'Heil sei dem Mann', 'Lobpreiset des Herren', 'Lobpreiset Gott den Herrn' and 'Den ewigen Gott'.

6. This was not a new procedure, of course. According to an eyewitness report dating from 1788, the numbers that made up a piece of sacred music from 1755 that was still being performed in a Franconian principality 33 years later consisted simply of a collection of Italian arias underlaid with sacred German texts; see *Musikalische Realzeitung*, i (1788), 177. ◆ It was, in any case, a long-standing tradition in Catholic countries to perform instrumental music during the Mass, the so-called epistle sonatas (of which Mozart composed 17 for Salzburg: K67–69, 144–145, 212, 224–225, 241, 244–245, 263, 274, 278, 328–329 and 336). And in many localities, the epistle sonata was replaced by a symphony or a concerto; see Zaslaw, 'Mozart, Haydn, and the *Sinfonia da chiesa*'. Mozart himself composed not only a mass and offertory for the dedication of the Waisenhauskirche in Vienna in 1768, but also a trumpet concerto (K47c), now lost.

7. *Deutsche Musik-Zeitung*, i (1860), 112. ◆ The arrangement of K361 was published by Artaria at Vienna in 1824; Nancy Storace's 'sacred' aria survives in manuscript copies at the Bayerische Staatsbibliothek, Munich, and in the library of the Gesellschaft der Musikfreunde, Vienna; and both K420 and the aria from *Tito* were published at Augsburg, by Lotter, in 1789 as part of *XXVII Ariae Selectissimae Praeclarorum virorum*.

But whole masses have been cobbled together on the basis of Mozart's operas, and at the beginning of the century neither a *Missa di Figaro* nor a *Don Giovanni* with church choruses was in any way exceptional. One particular example deserves to be examined in greater detail as typical of this approach.

Carl Zulehner's collection in Mainz formerly included under Mozart's name a 'Coronation' mass in C major, a copy of which I have been sent by Schott in Mainz.

With the exception of the Credo, all the movements are identical with whole numbers or shorter sections from *Così fan tutte*, with only the keys and instrumentation changed and the occasional voice being added or omitted.[8]

The Kyrie is the trio, 'Soave sia il vento', transposed to C major, but with two flutes and with the addition of a tenor voice to fill out the harmonies and produce a four-part chorus.

The Christe eleison is the first section of the duet, 'Ah guarda sorella', transposed to G major and rescored for soprano and tenor, with two oboes and two horns. Individual passages have been shortened and the ritornello moved to the end.

In essence, the opening of the Gloria is made up of motifs from the opening chorus from the second-act finale, the compiler adding a mere handful of highly insignificant bars of his own composition before helping himself to the first seventy bars of the aria 'Smanie implacabili', now a soprano solo in F major, for the 'Gratias agimus'. The 'Qui tollis' comprises seven original bars, while the 'Miserere' includes four bars from the first-act finale (at 'Ed in polso'). The original 'Qui tollis' is then repeated, after which comes the 'Suscipe', which is based on the passage beginning with 'Ah se tarda' in the first-act finale and continuing to the end of this section. From the 'Quoniam tu solus' to the end of the Gloria the source is the trio 'Una bella serenata', a number taken over unchanged except for the addition of a fourth voice in the tuttis and the omission of the final ritornello. Wind instruments – flutes, oboes, horns and trumpets and timpani – are used throughout the Gloria, alternating in the usual manner.

The Sanctus and 'Hosanna' are based on the andante from the first-act finale, 'Dove son', with the passage transposed to C major and shortened by six bars and with the part-writing slightly adapted to fit the new words.

The Benedictus is the duet and chorus, 'Secondate', transposed to F major and accompanied by strings, flutes and oboes. The chorus enters for the 'Hosanna'.

The Agnus Dei begins with eleven bars of the arranger's own invention, followed by 'Idol mio' from the second-act finale, with Despina's part omitted.

The 'Dona nobis' is the opera's final ensemble.

It appears from a letter to Gottfried Weber that Zulehner was convinced that Mozart wrote this mass before the opera. That the Mass was in fact cobbled together from the opera by some second-rate church musician or other requires no further demonstration.[9]

---

8. ◆ Carl Zulehner (1770–1841) was a music publisher in Mainz. The mass derived from *Così fan tutte* is listed in K[6] under Anh. B zu 588.

9. ◆ The example of *Così fan tutte* is in many ways typical of most of Mozart's works. In addition to the mass arrangement described by Jahn (which also survives in a manuscript copy in the library of the Conservatorio 'Luigi Cherubini', Florence), the aria 'Come scoglio' was arranged as 'Omni die dic Mariae', the aria 'Un' aura amorosa' as an *Aria soloemnis pro communi unius Martyris* ('Quando per mare ignotum'), the duet 'Secondate, aurette amiche' as 'Ave Jesu, summe bonus', and the duet 'Il core vi dono' as both 'Quo progrederis, Pater' and 'Non ego te linquo' – all survive in manuscripts at the National Museum, Prague. Additionally, manuscript arrangements of the opera are known for piano quintet (by Maximilian Stadler), for string quintet, and for an ensemble of two oboes, two english horns and two bassoons (by Johann Wendt). Published editions include arrangements for flute quartet (Bonn: Simrock, 1795), for string quartet (Vienna: Artaria, 1805), for two violins or two flutes (Vienna: Artaria, 1806), for piano four hands (Vienna: Mollo, 1798) and for two pianos eight hands (Prague: Marco Berra, n.d.), among others. Further, see K[6], 797, and *Wolfgang Amadeus Mozart: Verzeichnis von Erst- und Frühdrucken bis etwa 1800*, 53–8.

APPENDIX III

Mozart's cousin[1]
by Otto Jahn

Maria Anna Mozart was the daughter of one of Leopold Mozart's brothers in Augsburg, Franz Alois. She was born on 14 January 1758[2] and was therefore two years younger than her cousin. They first met in Augsburg in the autumn of 1777, when their acquaintance rapidly became as intimate as it was lively, as is clear from Mozart's surviving letters, letters that reveal a side of his character that we should not ignore if we want to understand his nature in its entirety.

There is a sense of fun, a tendency to make jokes and indulge in pranks intended purely and simply to make people laugh that we find as a matter of course among children, where mental effort is proportionate to this ability to relax and recover from such exertions. This tendency to indulge in foolish and childish jokes – as we are bound to describe it in the case of adults – remained one of Mozart's abiding characteristics, even in his later years. His brother-in-law Joseph Lange had the following to say on the subject:

> Never was Mozart less recognizably a great man in his conversation and actions than when he was preoccupied with some important piece. At such times he not only spoke confusedly and disjointedly but made jokes of a kind that one was simply not used to from him; indeed, he was deliberately negligent in his behaviour. Yet he did not appear to be brooding or thinking about anything. Either he intentionally concealed his inner effort behind superficial frivolity, for reasons that cannot be explained; or he enjoyed drawing a sharp distinction between the divine ideas contained in his music and whatever occurred to him on the humdrum level of everyday existence, delighting in a kind of self-irony.[3]

It is difficult to speak of conscious self-irony here, but rather of unconscious self-help on the part of the mind anxious to offset inner agitation and work with an activity that would distract from the latter, without itself affording any new and significant stimulus. Related to this is the fact that certain physical movements and exercises that occupy the body without tiring it and that require only a certain degree of attention such as the billiards of which Mozart was inordinately fond were well calculated to allow him to maintain his sense of balance so that he could devote himself inwardly to his musical ideas and their elaboration, without being worn down by them.[4] This tendency to indulge in farcical behaviour and thereby to free his mind to deal with ideas (a tendency that has been described as the spirit of the Salzburg Hanswurst) is not without importance, of course, in the case of a composer who scaled such heights in comic opera, yet it must be

---

1. See also Genée, 'Aus Mozarts Liebesleben nach seinen Briefen geschildert'.
2. ◆ In fact she was born on 25 September 1758.
3. ◆ Lange, *Selbstbiographie*, 46 (*Dokumente*, 433, *Documentary Biography*, 503).
4. ◆ Concerning Mozart and billiards, see Günther G. Bauer, '"Das Billardspiel liebte er leidenschaftlich": W. A. Mozart der Billard- und Kegelspieler'.

stressed all the more emphatically that this farcical element never appears in his work as an artist and that he tends, rather, to raise all comic elements into the higher world of art, with the result that a number of critics have even denied altogether that he had any real sense of comedy. The expressions of man's intellectual nature, which to a certain extent emerge only from the needs of its real-life existence, differ substantially from its artistic achievements; but they spring from a common source, which is why they are not unworthy of our consideration.

It was thought advisable to include only excerpts from these letters, a decision prompted not only by the desire not to weary the reader but also because a number of the jokes offend our age's sense of seemliness and good taste, if not its sense of morality. These excerpts are enough to demonstrate Mozart's boisterous high spirits and the deftness with which he was able to dash off his improvised jokes in rapid succession. It is a skill that finds expression in doggerel verse, in the way in which he twists and dissects words and in the refrainlike repeats which, for all their lack of genuine wit and meaning, reveal a certain sense of form and a lively appreciation of sound and rhythm that survives in the sayings and songs still found in the mouths of children and the common people, often at the expense of meaning and in some cases dispensing with any meaning at all.[5]

Shortly after arriving in Mannheim Mozart wrote to his cousin:[6]

My dearest little cousin cozen,

I've duly received retrieved your kind letter and see free from it that my uncle furuncle, aunt can't and you stew are very well tell; we too, thank God, are in good health stealth. Today I got spot the letter better from my papa haha. I hope you'll have received aggrieved the letter wetter I sent you from Mannheim. All the better, better the all. But now for something sensible. I'm very sorry to hear that the prelate pellet has had another stroke bloke, but I hope that with God's sod's help the consequences won't be serious deleterious. You tell me knee that you'll keep the promise[7] that you gave me before I left Augsburg and do so soon moon; well, I certainly look forward to that.[8]. You also write, nay, disclose, reveal, announce, let me know, declare, make it abundantly plain, demand, desire, wish, want, would like, order, hint, inform me, tell me that I should also send my portrait to you screw. Eh bien, I'll certainly send spend it to you. Oui par ma la fois – – – – [I'll shit on your nose so it runs down your chin. By the way, have you got the spuni cuni fait too? – – – What? [9]] Do you still love me – I think you do. All the better, better the all. Well, that's the way of the world, so I'm told; Tom has the purse, and Dick has the gold; whom do you prefer? – it's me, isn't it? I think it is. – – – [But now it gets worse. By the way, don't you want to go and see Herr Goldschmid again soon? But what'll you do there? – – what? – – nothing! – – just ask him about the spuni cuni fait, nothing else. nothing else? – – Very well;

---

5. When sending some music and letters to Breitkopf & Härtel on 28 August 1799, Constanze noted: 'Although in dubious taste, the letters to his cousin are full of wit and deserve mentioning, although they cannot, of course, be published in their entirety'; see Nottebohm, *Mozartiana*, 128 (*Briefe*, iv.269). ◆ Mozart's correspondence with his cousin from 5 November 1777 to 23 October 1781 is given in *Briefe* between ii.104 and iii.169.
6. According to Nohl, the original was in the possession of Wilhelm Speyer of Frankfurt am Main [footnote added by Deiters to Jahn and taken over by Abert]. ◆ The original of this letter is now in the British Library, London. It is reproduced in *Briefe*, ii.104–6 (letter of 5 November 1777).
7. ◆ Jahn has 'versprechen' ('promise'), which is reproduced in Abert; the original, however, has 'verbrechen'('crime').
8. Here Jahn and Abert have 'freuen'; the original has 'reuen' ('I certainly regret that').
9. ◆ These two sentences are omitted by Jahn and Abert; in what follows, sentences omitted from the originals are given in square brackets.

all right. Long live all those who – who – – who – – – how does it go on?] Now I wish you good night, [may your bed burst with shite; sleep sound as a log and shove your arse in your gob; now I'm off to fool about, then I'll sleep a bit, no doubt]. Tomorrow we'll talk more sensibly defensibly; I've things of lots to tell you, you simply believe it can't, but tomorrow you hear it will. Till then, goodbye! – – – – – [Ow, my *arse* is burning like fire. what can that mean? – – perhaps some *shit* wants to get out? – yes, yes, *shit, I* know you, see you, taste you – – and – – what's that? – – is it possible? – – ye gods! – – Can I believe my *ears*? – – Yes, indeed, it's – – what a long, sad sound! – –]

Today written I've letter fifth the is this. Yesterday I spoke with the strict electress and tomorrow, the 6th, I'm playing at the great gala concert, and then I'll play again for her in private, or so the tresselec tells me. Now for something sensible! (1) a letter or letters addressed to me will fall into your hands and I must ask you – what? – well, a fox is no hare – yes, where was I? yes, indeed, I was just coming, – – [yes, yes, they'll come – – yes, who? – who'll come – –] yes, now I have it, letters, letters will arrive – but what sort of letters? well, letters to me, of course; please be sure to forward them, I'll let you know where I'll be going after Mannheim. Now for no. (2)! I must ask you – why not? I must ask you, my dearest loon – why not? if you write to Mme Tavernier in Munich, please remember me to the two Mlles Freysinger – why not? Strange, why not? and please ask the younger of them, Fräulein Josepha, to forgive me – why not? why shouldn't I ask for her forgiveness? strange, I don't know why I shouldn't. I ask her to forgive me for not yet having sent her the sonata I promised, but I'll forward it as soon as possible – why not? what do you mean, why not? why shouldn't I send it? – why shouldn't I forward it? why not? strange, I don't know why I shouldn't. Well, will you do this favour for me? – why not? [– – why shouldn't you? – – why not, strange! I'd do it for you if you wanted, why not? – – why shouldn't I do it for you? – –] Strange! why not? I don't know why not. Don't forget to convey my best wishes to the Papa and Mama of the two young ladies, as it's a gross failing to forget bet let wet your father and mother. Once the sonata's finished, I'll send it to you with an accompanying letter and hope you'll be good enough to forward it to Munich. But now I must stop, I'm so mad I could hop. Good sir,[10] let's go at once to the Holy Cross and see if anyone's still up. We'll not stay long, just ring the bell, nothing more. – [But now I must tell you a sad little story that has just this minute happened. just as I was doing my best to write this letter, I heard something in the street outside. I stopped writing – – got up, went over to the window – – and – couldn't hear anything any more – – I sat down again, resumed writing – – I'd hardly written 10 words when I heard another sound, this time quite faint – – but I could smell something burning – – wherever I went, it stank. when I looked out of the window the smell disappeared, but when I looked back into the room, the smell got worse – – finally Mama said to me: I bet you've let one off. – – I don't think so, Mama. Yes, I'm certain. I made a test, put my first finger up my arse and then to my nose, and – – Ecce Provatum est; Mama was right.] Goodbye now, I kiss you 10,000 times and remain as always your little old Piggy Wolfgang Amadè Rosenkranz – to all my good friends blends my best wishes fishes! addio loony moony – [333][11] unto the grave as long as I live.

10. ◆ 'Herr Ritter' although *Briefe*, ii.106, has 'herr vetter', that is, 'dear cousin'.
11. ◆ Possibly meaning 'treu, treu, treu' in Salzburg dialect, that is, 'thrice faithful unto death'; see Spaethling, *Mozart's Life, Mozart's Letters*, 89.

A thousand good wishes from us 2 travellers to my uncle and aunt.
Miehnnam eht ht5 rebotco[12] 7771.

There was soon a lively exchange of letters, as is clear from the following letter dated 13 November 1777:[13]

Ma très chère Nièce! Cousine! Fille! Mère, Sœur et Epouse!

Bless my soul, a thousand curses, Croatians, sore distress, devils, witches, hags, hell's battalions and no end to them, by all the elements, air, water, earth and fire, Europe, Asia, Africa and America, Jesuits, Augustinians, Benedictines, Capuchins, Minorites, Franciscans, Dominicans, Carthusians and Brothers of the Holy Cross, canons regular and irregular, and idlers, knaves, cowards, scoundrels and hangers-on all higgledy-piggledy, asses, buffaloes, oxen, fools, idiots and loons! What sort of conduct is that, my dears? a quartet of soldiers and 3 bandoliers! – a packet, but no portrait? – I was all eagerness – I was sure – you yourself wrote recently that I'd receive it soon, very soon. Perhaps you doubt that I'll keep my word? I hope not. Well, I beg you, send it to me, the sooner the better, I hope it will be done as I asked, namely in French costume.

How do I like Mannheim? – as well as I could like anywhere without my little cousin. [Sorry my writing's so bad, but the nib's worn to a shred, it's said that I've been shitting through the same hole for nearly 22 years, but it's not frayed one whit, though I've often used it to shit, then bitten the shit with my teeth where I sit.] On the contrary, I hope that, however that may be, you've received the letters I sent you; namely, one from Hohenaltheim and 2 from Mannheim, and this one; however that may be, this is the third from Mannheim, but the fourth in all, however that may be. I must stop now, however that may be, as I'm not yet dressed and we're about to eat [so we can have another good shit afterwards], however that may be. Go on loving me as I love you, and we'll never stop loving each other. – Though the lion hovers round the walls and doubt's hard-won victory may not be well thought-through and the tyranny of brutes has crept away, yet Codrus, the wise philosopher, often eats soot instead of porridge, and the Romans, the props of my a[rse] have always been and will always be – free of charge.[14]

Adieu. j'espère que vous aurés deja pris quelque lection dans la langue française, et je ne doute point, que – – Ecoutés: que vous saurés bientôt mieux le françois que moi; car il y a certainement deux ans, que je n'ai pas écrit un môt dans cette langue. Adieu cependant. Je vous baise vos mains, votre visage, vos genoux et votre – – afin, tout ce que vous me permettés de baiser. Je suis de tout mon cœur

votre

très affectioné Neveu et Cousin

Wolfg. Amadé Mozart.

[Farewell. I hope you've already had a French lesson, I don't doubt that – listen – that you'll soon be better at French than I am, as it's a good two years since I wrote a word in this language.

---

12. A mistake for November.
13. The original is owned by Heinrich Seligmann of Cologne; see Nottebohm, *Mozartiana*, 51 [*Briefe*, ii.121–3]. ◆ The original is now in the Pierpont Morgan Library, New York.
14. This final section appears to contain jocular allusions to Mozart's reading matter at this time.

Goodbye for now. I kiss your hands, your face, your knees and your – –, in a word, everything you allow me to kiss. I am, with all my heart, your very affectionate Nephew and Cousin, Wolfg. Amadé Mozart.]

No less high-spirited and, in part, unreproducible is a letter dated 3 December 1777:[15]

Ma très chère Cousine!

[Before I write to you, I must go to the closet – – – well, that's over! ah! – – that's a weight off my mind! – I feel much better for that – now I can stuff my face again! – it's true, when you've emptied yourself, life's worth living again.] I'd have received your letter of 25 Nov. if you hadn't written that you had pains in your head, throat and arms, but as you say that now, at present, for the moment, for the nonce, you're no longer in pain, I've received your letter of the 26th. Yes, indeed, my dearest Mistress Cousin, thus it was ever so; Tom has the purse, and Dick has the gold, which do you prefer? – – with your ☞ I'll wager. Huzza, coppersmith, [hold the wench for me, don't squeeze her, hold the wench for me, don't squeeze her, lick my arse, coppersmith], yes, and it's true that whoever believes it will be happy, and whoever doesn't will go to heaven, but straight, not the way I'm writing. You can see now that I can write just as I like, both neatly and untidily, both straight and crooked. The other day I was in a bad mood and so my writing was neat, straight and serious; today I'm in a good mood, and so my writing is untidy, crooked and comical; it just depends on what you prefer, – – you must choose, as I've no golden mean to offer you, neat or untidy, straight or crooked, serious or comical; the first 3 words, or the last 3; I await your decision in your next letter. [My decision is taken; when nature calls, I go; but it all depends on the circumstances, if I've diarrhoea, I run, and if I can't wait, I shit my trousers. God preserve you, foot, your leg lies on the windowsill.] I am much obliged to you, my dear Mistress Cousin, for passing on Fräulein Freysinger's good wishes, which your dear Fräulein Juliana was kind enough to send me. – You tell me that although I know a lot more, too much is too much; – in a letter, I admit that it may be too much, but in the longer term one could write a lot; do you see what I mean, as for the sonata, the world must possess itself in patience a little longer. Had it been for my little cousin, it would have been finished long ago – – who knows whether Mlle Freysinger still remembers it – – all the same, I'll finish it as soon as possible and write a letter to go with it and ask my dear little cousin to deliver them to her. By the way [I've not taken off my trousers once since leaving Augsburg – except at night, before going to bed.] What will you think when I tell you that I'm still at Mannheim, up to my neck in it? That's because I've not yet left and gone somewhere else. But now I think that Mannheim will soon be off. But Augsburg can continue to write to me through you and address letters to Mannheim until further notice. My uncle, aunt and cousin ask to be remembered to my Mama and me. They were afraid that we were ill as they'd received no letter from us for so long. But they were delighted to receive our letter of the 26th two days ago, and today, the 3rd of Dec., they have had the pleasure of replying to me. So shall I keep my promise to you? – You'd like that. Don't forget to compose Munich for the sonata, for once you've kept something you must promise it, you must always be a word of one's man. – Now let's be serious.

I must tell you something very briefly: I didn't lunch at home today but with a certain Monsieur Wendling; but I should add that he always lunches at half past one, he's married and

---

15. See Nottebohm, *Mozartiana*, 48–9 [*Briefe*, ii.163–5].

has a daughter who's always ill. His wife will be singing in the new opera and he himself will play the flute. Well, just imagine, at half past one all of us except the daughter, who remained in bed, sat down to table and began to eat.

[Please give a whole arseful of good wishes from us both to all our good friends, male and female. Our good wishes to your parents will be found on p. 3 line 12. I've nothing else to report except that an old cow has shit a new turd] and so now adieu, Anna Maria Schlosser née Schlüsselmacher. Take care of yourself and continue to love me; write to me without delay, as it's turned very cold today; and keep your word or I'll drop a turd. addieu, mon Dieu, a thousand times I kiss you and miss you.

Mannheim	Ma très chère Cousine?
without slime	were you never in Berlin?
the 3rd of Decembr.	Your cousin of virtues rare
Today's not Quatembr.	in weather foul or fair
1777 in darkest night	W. A. Mozart
from now until the end of time	[sh: shitting] is very hard.
Amen.	

The portrait arrived in Salzburg in February 1778 and is now in the archives of the Mozarteum.[16] A pencil drawing, it is not the work of a major artist. It shows Maria Anna's good-natured, smiling but somewhat coarse features: her face is pleasant enough, without being beautiful. She is wearing an embroidered ornamental cap of a kind worn by Bavarian women. It suits her. Around her neck is a small black shawl.

Life in Mannheim, with all its new impressions and the new acquaintances that kept Mozart fully occupied, but above all his feelings for Aloysia Weber – all this brought a temporary halt to Mozart's correspondence with his cousin. None the less, the following letter was sent to her shortly before his departure from the town, and when we recall his situation and frame of mind at this time – 28 February 1778 – we shall be not a little surprised at the tone that he was able to adopt and at the way in which he was able to develop a joke as though it was a piece of music. Yet such apparent psychological contradictions are deeply rooted in our nature and every observer will note them in the most varied situations both in himself and in others. In the case of so exceptionally sensitive and volatile a nature as Mozart's, these reflexes of caprice must have been particularly lively. It is typical of his whole character that, no matter how strenuously and earnestly Leopold reminded him of his duty, the bitter struggle that he fought with his own inclinations never left him feeling embittered towards his father, never made him refractory or grimly determined. Rather, he abandoned himself uninhibitedly to the natural stirrings of his essentially jovial nature, a facility that contributed in no small way to his ability to maintain a sense of equilibrium. As is clear from all his letters and other remarks, the fact that he invariably acted in such a simple and truthful manner in every situation and mood shows that the harmony that typified his nature as an artist was true of the whole of his mental make-up.

---

16. ◆ It is reproduced in Deutsch, *Mozart und seine Welt*, 139.

The letter in question reads as follows:

Mademoiselle, ma très chère Cousine!

I expect you think I'm dead! – that I've pegged out? – or kicked the bucket? – but no, don't believe it, I beg you – [for thinking and shitting are not at all the same!] how could I write such a beautiful hand if I were dead? how could that be possible? – I shan't apologize for my long silence, as you'd never believe me, but what is true remains true, I've had so much to do that, although I had time to think of my little cousin, I had no time to write to her, you see, and so I simply had to let things be. Let me ask you how you are feeling: are you well or is your head reeling? Would you say that your movements are regular? or do you think that you might have got scrofula? can you still bear to think of me at all? do you still write in chalk upon the wall? does your love for me cause you the slightest pang or – be honest – would you rather go hang? were you cross at little old me? (What a fool I shall always be!) If you won't make it up in your heart, I swear I'll let rip a great fart. But you're laughing – I've won! [our arses'll signal our newly-found peace.] I knew you'd not be able to resist me for much longer, yes, I'm certain of my success, [even though I may make a mess] as I'm off to Paris in 2 weeks or less. So if you want to reply from Augsburg, do try and write me a letter, the sooner the better, for once I've left this place, I'll get not a letter but shit on my face. [shit! – – shit! O shit! – sweet word! – shit! Scheiße! – what could be nicer! shite, Mahlzeit! – shit! – lick – O charmante – shit, lick! – I like it! – shit, lick, bon appétit! – eat shit and lick it! – –] And now for something completely different, did you enjoy yourself during the carnival? you can enjoy yourself far more in Augsburg at this time than here, I wish I was with you, so we could run around together. My Mama and I send our best wishes to your father and mother and to my little cousin and hope that all 3 of you are well. [Praise and thanks be to God, we are in good health. don't you believe it.] All the better, better the all. By the way, how are you getting on with the French language? shall I soon be able to send you a whole letter in French? from Paris, eh? – [tell me whether you still have the spunicunifait? – I imagine so.]

Well I must tell you something before I close, for I really must stop soon, as I'm in a hurry because at present I've nothing to do, and also because I've no more room, as you can see, the paper will soon be full, and besides I'm tired, and my fingers are hurting from so much writing, and even if I had any room, I wouldn't know what to write, apart from this story that I plan to tell you. Listen, then, it happened quite recently, it took place hereabouts and caused quite a stir, as it seems so incredible; and, between ourselves, no one knows how it will turn out. Well, to cut a long story short, about four hours from here, I forget the name of the place, but it was some village or other – well, it doesn't matter whether it was tribsterill [where shit runs into the sea] or burmesquick [where they make the crooked arseholes] – in short it was a hole. There was a herdsman or shepherd there who was already fairly old but who still looked hale and hearty; he was unmarried and well off and he enjoyed life – yes, there's something else I should tell you before I go on with my story, the sound of his voice was quite terrifying, people were always afraid when he spoke. Well, to make a long story short, you must know that he also had a dog that he called Bellot, a large and very beautiful dog, white with black spots. Well, one day he was walking along with his sheep, of which he had eleven thousand, and carrying a stick with a beautiful rose-coloured ribbon, for he never went anywhere without a stick – that was his custom. Now let me get back to the story. He'd been walking for a good hour when he began to feel tired and sat down by a river. Finally he fell asleep; he then dreamt that he'd lost his sheep – and in his terror he woke up, but to his immense delight saw all his sheep beside him. Finally he got up and continued his journey, but not for long, as he'd hardly been walking for half an hour when he came to a bridge that was very long but well protected on both sides so that you couldn't fall off. Well, he looked at his flock, and as he had to cross over, he began to drive his eleven thousand sheep across. Now kindly wait for the eleven thousand sheep to cross the river and then I'll finish my story. I've already told you that no one knows how it will turn out, but I hope that before I write again the sheep will be safely over the river – if not, I don't care, for as far as I'm concerned, they could have stayed where they were. So you'll have to be satisfied with this for now; I've told you all I know and it's better to stop now rather than make up the rest, for then you wouldn't have believed any of the story, but as it is, you're bound to believe me – or at least half of it.

Well, now I've got to stop, although it makes me hop; whoever starts must stop or people start to drop; my compliments to each and every friend, and whoever doesn't believe me can lick me, world without end, yea, from now unto eternity or until I regain my sanity; but he'll have to lick and lick, and I worry myself sick [that my shit will soon dry up and he won't have enough on which to sup]. Adieu, bääsle! I am, I was, I would be, I have been, I had been, I would have been, O if only I had been, O that I might have been, would to God that I had been; I would be, I shall be, if I were to be, O that I might be, I might have been, I would have been, O if only I had been, O that I might have been, would to God that I had been – what? – a blockhead! Adieu, ma chère Cousine! where now? – I'm your same faithful cousin

Wolfgang Amade Mozart.[17]

We do not know whether Mozart continued to write to his cousin after he arrived in Paris: at all events, no letters have survived from this period. But on his way home, Mozart wrote to her again from Kaisersheim on 23 December 1778. He was unsure whether his journey would take him via Augsburg, and so he invited her to meet him in Munich:

Ma très chère Cousine!

In the greatest haste and with extreme regret and sorrow and fixed resolve I am writing to inform you that I am leaving for Munich tomorrow. Cousin dearie, don't be dreary! I'd very much like to have come to Augsburg, I assure you, but the Imperial Prelate wouldn't let me, and I can't hold it against him, as that would be against the laws of both God and Nature, and, what's more, whoever doubts this is a wh-re; well, that's how it is at present. Perhaps I could nip over to Augsburg from Munich, but I'm not sure whether I'll be able to; if it would really give you as much pleasure to see me as it would give me to see you, come to Munich, that worthy city. Make sure you get here by the New Year, and I'll take a good look at you from the front and the rear and take you everywhere, [and if necessary clyster you], I'm only sorry that I shan't be able to put you up, as I'll not be staying at an inn but shall be staying – where? I wish I knew.[18] Well, joooking apart, that's exactly why I need you to come and stay – you may have an important role to play – so come for a bit [or I'll be in the shit]; there I can thank you [and certainly spank you, I'll kiss you, my dear, shoot a gun up your rear], embrace you, [wash your front and behind], repay you in kind and let off a f[art – my word – and perhaps drop a turd]. Now, farewell, my angel and sweetheart, I am aching to see you,

Your sincere cousin
W. A.

---

17. ◆ *Briefe*, ii.307–10 (letter of 28 February 1778).
18. Mozart stayed with the Webers.

Write to me, poste restante, in Munich, a little 24-page letter, but don't say where you'll be staying, so that we won't be able to find each other.
[P.S.: Shit-Dibitari, the priest at Rodampl
licked his cook's arse, so to set an example;
vivat – vivat –][19]

Maria Anna Thekla duly came to Munich, and Mozart in turn invited her to visit him in Salzburg, writing to inform his father of his plans in his letter of 8 January 1779:[20]

My little cousin is here? – why? to please her cousin? – that's the ostensible reason! but – well, we'll talk about it in Salzburg, which is why I'd like her to come to Salzburg with me. . . . She'd like to come, so, if you'd really like to have her in your house, perhaps you'd be good enough to write to your brother at once, saying that it's all right – when you see her and get to know her, you'll be bound to like her, everyone does.

On the back of the letter Maria Anna added her own appeal, and as she was writing in Mozart's presence, the latter could not resist the temptation to interject his own commentary, producing the following comic duet:

Monsieur, mon très cher Oncle,
    I trust that you and Mademoiselle my cousin are well. I have had the honour of finding your son in excellent health in Munich; he wants me to come to Salzburg with him, but I don't yet know whether I'll have the honour of seeing you.

There follows a large ink blot, to which Mozart has added a note:

A portrait of my cousin, she's writing in shirtsleeves.

Maria Anna then continues:

but my cousin is a complete fool, as you can see. I wish you a long life, mon cher oncle, and a thousand good wishes to Mademoiselle my cousin. Je suis de tout mon coeur
Fräulein Mozart

Added by Mozart at the end:

Monsieur, [where the latter has not yet shit], votre invariable cochon.

Maria Anna's parents raised no objection to her visit, and she duly stayed in Salzburg for several weeks early in 1779. On her return to Augsburg, Mozart wrote to her as follows:

Dearest, kindest, most beautiful,   Salzburg, 10 May one
most amiable, most enchanting   thousand 7 hundred and nine

19. ◆ *Briefe*, ii.524–5 (letter of 23 December 1778).
20. ◆ *Briefe*, ii.536–8 (letter of 8 January 1779).

little bass[21] or little cello
placed in harness
by an unworthy cousin!

blow into my behind
it's good,
your health!

Whether I, Johannes Chrysostomus Sigismundus Amadeus Wolfgangus Mozartus, shall ever be in a position to quell, mitigate or soften the anger that doubtless raises your enchanting beauty (visibilia et invisibilia) by the height of a full slipper heel is a question that I fully intend to answer. To soften means, 1st, to carry someone softly in a soft chair – I am by nature very soft and I also like to eat mustard,[22] especially with roast beef – so it is quite all right about Leipzig, even though Monsieur Feigelrapée asserts or, rather, arserts that it's all pie in the sky, a vol in the vent, something I simply refuse to believe; it's not even worth bending over for; if it were a purse full of convention kreutzers, one might after all pick it up or reach out for it – as I say, I shan't let it go for less. That's my lowest price, I refuse to haggle, I'm not a woman, so that's that! Yes, my dear little cello, that's the way of the world, I'm told; Tom has the purse, and Dick has the gold, and whoever has neither has nothing, and nothing is very little and little is not much, and so nothing is still less than little, and little is still more than not much, and – thus it is, was and ever shall be. Put an end to the letter, seal it and send it off – Feigele:

please turn over, V. S. [= volti subito]
Your most humble and obedient servant
[my arse, if you please, isn't Viennese].

P. S. Has Böhm's troupe left town – tell me, my dear, in heaven's name – ah, they'll now be rehearsing [in Ulm?], won't they? Do set my mind at rest on this point, I entreat you by all that's sacred – the gods know that I mean it. How's the Thüremichele? blow into my hole? How's Vogt getting on with his wife? is she still a source of strife? so many questions, upon my life.

A tender ode[23]
Your likeness sweet, O cousin,
is forever before my eyes;
and yet I weep and languish
that you yourself aren't here.
I see your image when evening
falls; and when the moon appears
I see it, too, and weep
that you yourself aren't here.
By all the valley's flowers
that I would pick for her,
by all the myrtle branches
that I would twine for her,

---

21. ◆ Here Mozart writes an untranslatable play on words: *Bäschen* = little cousin, while *Bäßchen* = little bass.
22. ◆ Another series of untranslatable puns: *besänftigen* = to soften or lessen; *sanft* = soft; *Sänfte* = a sedan chair; and *Senf* = mustard.
23. Klopstock's ode *Du süßes Bild, Edone*, virtually unchanged.

I conjure up your image:
arise, transform yourself,
transform yourself, fair image,
and be my little cousin!
                    Finis coronat opus
        S.V. [*salva verecundia* = with modesty preserved]
        P.T. [*pleno titulo* = with full title]
                    Baron von Pigstail.

Every good wish from all of us to the father and mother who produced you [I mean, to him who made the effort and to her who submitted to it]. Adieu angel! My father gives him his avuncular blessing and my sister a thousand cousinly kisses; [and your cousin gives you what he's not allowed to give you]. Adieu – adieu – angel!

I'll write more by the next ordinary post – something very sensible and important. And we must be satisfied with that until further notice. Adieu – Adieu – angel![24]

From now on, Mozart's letters to his cousin – only two more have survived – strike a more sombre note, with the following letter of 24 April 1780 clearly avoiding the high-spirited jokes of the earlier ones:

                                        Salzburg, 24 April 1780.
    Ma très chère Cousine!
You answered my last letter so beautifully that I really don't know where to find words to express my thanks and at the same time to assure you yet again that I am
            Your most obedient servant and sincere
                        cousin
                Wolfgang Amadi Mozart.
    I wanted to write more, but, as you see, the space
            is
            too   adieu! adieu!
            small.

[On the following page:]
    Well, jest to be serious for a moment: you must forgive me on this occasion for not replying to your most delightful letter in the way that it deserves, i.e., word for word, and let me say only what is most necessary – next time I'll do all in my power to make up for my shortcoming –
    It's now a fortnight since I replied to Monsieur Böhm – I hope my letter hasn't gone missing, I'd be very sorry if it has – I know only too well that Monsieur Böhm is extremely busy every day – be that as it may, I would ask you, my little chou, to give him a thousand good wishes and say that as soon as I receive a sign of life from him his aria will be finished. –
    I hear that Munschhauser is ill, too, is that true? – That wouldn't be good for Monsieur Böhm. – Well, my dear, I expect you'll be going to the theatre every day, come hell or high water, as you

---

24. These final sentences are written around Mozart's caricature of his cousin, reproduced in Nottebohm, *Mozartiana*, 70 [*Briefe*, ii.facing 545]; see Anonymous, 'Eine Zeichnung Mozarts vom Bäsle"' and Genée, 'Aus Mozarts Liebesleben', 270. ◆ This letter is reproduced in *Briefe*, ii.547–9 (letter of 10 May 1779).

have free entry. – I've no news to tell you, except that Joseph Hagenauer (in whose bow window you drank chocolate with me and my sister) has unfortunately died, a great loss for his father – his brother Johannes (the one who is married) had previously been able to rely entirely on his late brother and got more or less used to leading the life of an idler, but must now buckle to, something he finds rather distasteful. –

Now, my dearest, best, most beautiful, most charming and most lovable cousin – write to me soon! Please! Tell me all the news both at home and abroad – and to all the people who have sent me their best wishes, send twice as many in return – Adieu – Next time I'll write a whole page – but first, my love, you must send me a whole book – Adieu

All manner of messages from my dear Papa and my sister Zizibe – to your parents from all three of us, 2 boys and a girl, 12345678987654321 good wishes, and to all our good friends from myself 624, from my father 100 and from my sister 150, together 1774 and summa summarum 12345678987656095 good wishes.[25]

The final letter is dated 23 October 1781[26] and differs completely in tone from the earlier letters with their jokes and witticisms. It deals on the whole with business matters.

Maria Anna Thekla seems to have taken her cousin's courtship more seriously than Mozart himself. Certainly, the people close to her later thought that they detected a sense of disappointed hopes in the way she spoke about him. She rarely talked about this period and when she did, it was with some reluctance. She was unmusical and cannot, therefore, have formed any clear impression of Mozart's artistic significance. Indeed, she regarded as simply comical his tendency to become so lively and animated during performances of music. We know little about her subsequent fate. She later married and went to live in Bayreuth with the director of posts Franz Joseph Streitel, dying there on 25 January 1841 at the advanced age of eighty-three. One of her daughters married a certain Pümpel, and their descendants now live at Feldkirch.[27]

---

25. ◆ *Briefe*, iii.4–5 (letter of 24 April 1780).
26. See Jahn, 'Briefe Mozart's', 203. ◆ *Briefe*, iii.170–1 (letter of 23 October 1781).
27. Wurzbach, *Mozart-Buch*, 238. ◆ Maria Anna Thekla had married on 31 May 1802. Further concerning her, see Schad and Klotz-Reill, *Mozarts erste Liebe: Das Bäsle Marianne Thekla Mozart*; Breitinger, 'Das Augsburger Bäsle'; and Schwerin, 'W. A. Mozart (1756–91) and Maria Anna Thekla Mozart (1758–1841) the Bäsle'.

APPENDIX IV

Mozart as a comic poet
by Otto Jahn

The ease with which Mozart was able to take in and depict comic situations and ideas prompted him to produce a number of shorter works. There were the usual occasional verses with fairly rough-and-ready rhymes, of which we have already encountered a handful of examples.[1] For fancy-dress balls he drafted a series of brief pantomimes, for which he then wrote the music. And he even embarked on various comedies or, rather, farces, none of which – understandably – ever proceeded beyond its initial stages. Indeed, it would have been a pity if Mozart had wasted any more time on them. But a number of vestiges of these works have survived, and so they may find their rightful place here.

One of these farces bears the eloquent title of *Der salzburger Lump in Wien* (The Rogue from Salzburg in Vienna) and may have been intended as a satire. Only the opening of the draft has survived.[2]

Act One.
Scene One.

Herr Stachelschwein [= Porcupine] is just reading a letter that he has received from his mother in Salzburg, informing him of the death of his father. – He grieves at the loss but at the same time is pleased at the thought of his inheritance. – He is joined by

Scene 2.

Herr Intriguant. The two men are pleased to see each other. – Herr Intriguant tells him about everything that has happened to him since the time that they shared the same police cell. – Herr Stachelschwein tells his friend that following his father's death he expects his circumstances to improve; – he will tell him more on another occasion, but for the present he has to hurry away –. Herr Intriguant asks whether he is going to see Fiala or Scultettj. – Herr Stachelschwein says that he is going to see neither, but to see Kitscha – and so they go their separate ways.

---

1. Batka, *W. A. Mozarts gesammelte Poesien*. Wurzbach, relying on a correspondent in Nuremberg, reproduces a poem about the noses of both Mozart and his son; see Wurzbach, *Mozart-Buch*, 176. But the poem is of doubtful authenticity.
2. The original was formerly in the possession of Aloys Fuchs, who kindly allowed me to make a copy of it. ◆ K^6 509b. The original remains lost; the full text is known only from Jahn and is reproduced in *Briefe*, iv.167–8. The dating of this fragment is uncertain. Its placement in K^6 implies a date of 1787. *Briefe*, vi.428, however, suggests it may date from early 1786, based on the appearance of the name Fiala in scene 2: Joseph Fiala, a Salzburg oboist well known to Mozart, quit Salzburg in September, making his way to Vienna, where he briefly lodged with Wolfgang. Branscombe, 'Mozart as author', 334, suggests it may date from carnival 1783, about the time of the masquerade K446.

Scene 3.
Frau von Scultetti and her daughter.

Frau von Scult. complains that although it is already 10 o'clock, Herr Stachelschwein has not yet arrived. – Her daughter says that she is pleased, as she is spared having to smoke. – They discuss various matters; finally there is a knock at the door.

Scene 4.
Herr Stachelschwein and the same. –

Herr Stachelschwein says: 'Your most obedient servant.' – They discuss various matters, including the new opera. – Herr von Stachelschwein asks her if she has seen it and whether she liked it. – Frau von Sculteti says she didn't like it at all. – When asked why not, she replies that it was too hot for her.

The draft ends at this point, at the start of the second page. It is clear that this is how it was left. Mozart made more progress on a second piece, a comedy in three acts, *Die Liebesprobe* (The Trial of Love), of which a single folio survives.[3] On this occasion, the page has been filled and the dialogue breaks off in mid-sentence, suggesting that Mozart continued to work on the piece, although it is unlikely that he ever completed it. The opening runs as follows:[4]

The Trial of Love.
A Comedy in Three Acts.
Dramatis personae:
Herr von Dumkopf.
Rosaura. His daughter.
Trautel. His chambermaid.
Leander. Rosaura's lover.
Wurstl. His servant.
Herr von Knödl. Rosaura's lover.
Kasperl. Herr von Dumkopf's hostler.
The Witch Slinzkicotinzki.
A female dwarf.
A female giant.

Act One.
Scene One.

The stage represents a pleasance. – To the left and right are identical houses.

There is the sound of fingers being snapped and of a posthorn being blown. Wurstl enters, pushing Leander in a wheelbarrow, sounding the horn and snapping his fingers.

---

3. ✦ K⁶ 509c. Like *Der Salzburger Lump in Wien, Die Liebesprobe* is undated. *Briefe*, vi.428, suggests early 1787; Branscombe, 334, thinks it was written about the same time as K⁶ 509b, about carnival 1783. The complete text is given in *Briefe*, iv.168–73.
4. The original is owned by Dr Hermann Härtel and was published as 'Bruchstück eines Lustspiels von Wolfgang Amadeus Mozart', *AmZ*, xliii (1841), 17–21. ✦ Mozart's autograph is now in the Staatsbibliothek zu Berlin. The complete text is given in *Briefe*, iv.168–73.

Wurstl (empting the wheelbarrow).

We're here.

Leander (getting up from the ground).

You clumsy oaf, look what you've done!

Wurstl.

Allons! Relax!

Leander.

You damned fool! – That's no way to treat your master! – It's a miracle that I haven't broken every bone in my body. There's nothing I'd like more than to give you a sound thrashing. – But – you're lucky that my desire to see my beloved Rosaura again and to embrace her as quickly as possible is too great for me to waste time on the likes of you, my fine fellow.

Wurstl.

Dear Sir Poltroon . . .

Leander.

What did you say, you churl? – Poltroon? – You mean 'patron'.

Wurstl.

Well, yes, patron. It was a slip of the tongue. – Well, then, my dearest, kindest Herr Pol . . . , I mean Patron; don't take it amiss, I didn't do it out of clumsiness, it was on purpose; in my enthusiasm to get you here as soon and as quickly as possible I was so enthusiastic and hasty that out of sheer enthusiasm and haste I didn't know whether to throw you or toss you here.

Leander.

You and your enthusiasm and haste! You're the biggest fool I've ever set eyes on in my life; – oh well, I'll forgive you just this once, but next time . . .

Wurstl.

Next time I'll make a better job of it.

Leander.

What? – You'll make a better job of it?

Wurstl.

Of course! – If I've made a bad job of it today, I'll have to make a better job of it next time.

Leander.

Yes, all right. – Now be off with you and see to it that I soon have the good fortune to speak to my dearest and most adorable Rosaura. – Allons: get a move on; knock. – What in the devil's name – which house is it? – This one on the right, or that one on the left? –I've been away for three whole years and I can't tell any longer which of these two houses is the right one.

Wurstl.

Odds fish! I can't either. – Quod est faciendi? What's to be done?

Leander.

I don't know. – I don't want to knock up the wrong people. – Do you know something, Wurstl? – Listen at both houses and let me know whether you can hear a woman's voice that sounds anything like my beautiful Rosaura's enchanting voice. –

Wurstl.

That's a good idea. – When my Trautel talks, I can recognize her at once – she has a voice like a cowbell. – Well, let's get cracking! (He goes over to both houses and sniffs.)

Leander.

O Rosaura! How I yearn for the happy moment when I'll see you again – and embrace you. – Well, Wurstl – can you hear anything? – What the devil are you doing? – Why are you sniffing around like that? –

Wurstl.

Quiet! – If my Trautel is in one of these houses, I'm bound to get a whiff of her; – I still remember what she smelt like; but be quiet as a mouse, I say, otherwise I'll lose the scent, and then . . .

Leander.

Well, just get a move on.

Wurstl (sniffing at the house on the right).

Fie! For shame! . . . What a pong! – It's not there. (Sniffing at the house on the left.) Haha! – What a heavenly, sweet perfume! – Yes, yes, it's coming from my dear Trautel; – now – I've sniffed you out, I'd like to see you, too. (He knocks.) Darling, come on out; – darling dear!

Scene Two.

A Giantess and the same.

Giantess.

Here I am, what does the gentleman want?

Wurstl (leaping back).

Upon my soul! How she's grown! – (To the Giantess.) Well – is it you – or isn't it?

Giantess.

Yes, my dear little Wurstl, it's me; – I'm your dear, true little Trautel; – come here and let me hug you. (Hugging him.)

Wurstl.

Ow! – Don't get carried away: you'll crush me to death. – And you used to be such a sweet little thing, so small, too, and now you're such a strapping great hulk of a woman; tell me, what happened to make you suddenly shoot up like this? –

Giantess.

Well, I'll tell you, my dear little Wurstl. – Listen.

Leander.

Trautel dear – although it's rather difficult for me to call you by that name as it seems to me almost impossible that you're Trautel the chambermaid of my adored Rosaura, but I'll make every effort to believe it and call you Trautel; – and so I would ask you, dear Trautel, to save your explanation for a more convenient time and instead prevail on my beautiful Rosaura to come out: I simply must see her, talk to her, hug her – and goodness knows what else.

Giantess.

All right, you'll see her instantly; oh, what a joy it will be! – But – here she comes of her own accord.

Scene Three.

A Female Dwarf and the same.

Giantess (to Leander).

Well, go and say hello to her.

Leander.

Where? – I can't see anything.

Wurstl.

I can't either.

Giantess.

Well, there; – be careful – Oh dear, you've trodden on her.
(The Dwarf cries and screams like a small child.)

Leander.

I'm sorry – but – in God's name, this can't be my Rosaura –

Wurstl.

It's just a babe in arms.

Dwarf.

But it really is me, my love; yes, I'm your faithful Rosaura, though I don't know if I'm still your beloved Rosaura!

Leander.

Ah, now I recognize you! – Though you don't look at all like the woman you once were; – but your ideas are still the same.

Wurstl (to Leander).

Patron, yours has got smaller, mine's got bigger, and so it follows that mine is more distinguished.

Leander (to Wurstl).

Yes, but yours has got *too* big.

Wurstl (to Leander).

And yours has got too small.

Dwarf.

My dear Leander, I can't blame you for being surprised at seeing me so small. But I hope that you'll soon get over your surprise and once again be my beloved and tender Leander.

Leander.

Angelic Rosaura; you do me a great wrong; – permit me to kiss your pretty hand or, rather, your pretty little hand in token of my utterly unshakeable fidelity and love. (He kneels and kisses her hand.) – – – –

According to Nissen,[5] Mozart's estate included 'an unfinished German operetta similar in manner to *Die Entführung aus dem Serail*'. The names of its characters are identical to those of *Die Liebesprobe*. It is scarcely credible that Mozart could have worked up this same material twice, once as a comedy and once as an operetta. If the scenes just quoted were to be used for an operetta, it is conceivable that Mozart copied out the text, just as he copied out the words of the opening scene of *Die Entführung*, a fair copy that I myself have seen at the home of my friend Franz Hauser.[6] But they are of no use in such a context and I fear that Nissen was labouring under a misapprehension. No musical sketches have survived.[7]

---

5. ◆ Nissen, *Biographie W. A. Mozart*, appendix p. 20.
6. ◆ The baritone Franz Hauser (1794–1870) was a leading figure in the nineteenth-century Bach revival; see Jorgenson, *The Life and Legacy of Franz Xaver Hauser: A Forgotten Leader in the Nineteenth-Century Bach Movement*.
7. The work under discussion is *Zaide* K344; see above [Abert's footnote]. ◆ Mozart's handwritten copy of the opening of the text of *Die Entführung* is now privately owned. Neither Jahn nor Abert mentions one other poem by Mozart, the undated 'Der kunstreiche Hund' ('The artistically gifted dog'). The original of the poem is lost and the text known only from Nottebohm, *Mozartiana*, 6–8 (reproduced in *Briefe*, iv.164–7).

APPENDIX V

On the genesis of Idomeneo
by Hermann Abert

1. *The relationship between words and music.*

Thanks to the correspondence between father and son, we know more about Mozart's attitude to his text in the case of *Idomeneo* than with any of his other operas.[1] Leopold acted as intermediary between the librettist Giovanni Battista Varesco in Salzburg and the composer in Munich, informing the former of his son's wishes and typically making no secret of his own thoughts on the matter. When taken together with the surviving variants and cuts to various passages, these letters grant an extremely instructive insight into Mozart's practice of proceeding along dramatic lines at this time. As a result, a detailed examination of the question seems appropriate. After all, it sheds light not only on Mozart's whole attitude towards his text and to *opera seria* in general, it also touches on one of the most important and specific problems for any opera composer at this time, namely, his attitude to the demands of his singers.

'As for the libretto,' Mozart wrote on 8 November 1780, immediately after his arrival in Munich,

the count says that Abbate Varesco doesn't need to copy it out again before sending it, as it's to be printed here. But I thought that he should finish it and not forget the *little notes*,[2] and only then send it here, together with the *argomento*.[3] As for the names of the singers, this is my least concern as it is simplest to add these here. Some slight alterations will have to be made here and there. And the recitatives will have to be shortened a bit – but *everything will be printed*. I've a request for Herr Abbate: Ilia's aria in the second scene of act two I'd like to change a little in order to produce what I need. – *Se il padre perdei, in te lo ritrovo*: this strophe couldn't be better. But now comes what has always seemed unnatural to me – I mean, in an aria – and that is an aside. In a *dialogue* these things are entirely natural, a character can hurriedly say a few words in an aside, but in an aria, where the words have to be repeated, it creates a bad impression, and even if this were not the case, I'd still prefer an aria that flows along naturally (the beginning can stay as it is, if it suits him, as it's charming), I'd prefer not to be so tied to the words but to be able to feel that the aria was virtually writing itself: we've agreed that there should be an *aria andantino* here, with four concertante wind instruments, namely, flute, oboe, horn and bassoon, and so I'd like to have it as soon as possible.[4]

---

1. ◆ Mozart's letters concerning the genesis of *Idomeneo* are widely discussed in the literature, and frequently cited in biographical studies, in studies of the opera and in works describing Mozart's compositional methods. Abert thinks they are important, too, and presumably his relegation of them to an appendix is a sign of his reluctance to disrupt the flow of his narrative in chapter 26. Nevertheless, they are an important adjunct to the book. Needless to say, they relate chiefly to work on the opera prior to its first performance at Munich on 29 January 1781 and do not reflect changes to the opera made after the premiere. For further discussion, see in particular Rushton, *W. A. Mozart: Idomeneo*, 25–47.
2. That is, the stage directions.
3. The *argomento* is the brief introduction to the subject matter of the drama. It was regularly prefaced to the libretto.
4. *Briefe*, iii.13 (letter of 8 November 1780).

Leopold sent Mozart a new aria by return of post: 'Here is the aria,' he wrote on 11 November. 'I think it will be suitable, if not – let me know at once.' Wolfgang acknowledged receipt of it on the 15th, describing it as 'excellent'.[5]

Here we are struck not only by the wish to shorten the *secco* recitatives, a move already adopted by Hasse and his school, including Gluck in his mature Italian operas, but also by Mozart's basic dislike of asides in arias. In spite of the repetitions that are typical of these arias, Italian composers of the period had had no difficulty in accepting the unnaturalness of this device.

But the most important point to emerge from this letter is Mozart's refusal to be 'tied to the words' from the outset and his plan to write for four concertante winds. This is the first time that, in contrast to Gluck, he demands that the musician be given precedence over the poet. Yet even here it is clear that he was by no means willing to forgo his rights as a dramatist. This scene depicts what is essentially an inner event, namely, Ilia's act of self-betrayal in the face of Idomeneo and, as Mozart rightly felt, this could be far more vividly described by a musician than by a librettist – even by a better librettist than the coldly unfeeling Varesco. Later, too, he continued to insist on the musician's right to ignore a mediocre text and go straight to the emotional heart of a situation on stage. In the present case it encouraged him to invest the passage with a depth of expression of which Varesco can never have dreamt.

A further difficulty arose over the scene in which Idomeneo is shipwrecked (act one, scene eight). Mozart wrote to his father on this point on 13 November:

To act one, *scene VIII* Herr Quaglio has raised the same objection that we ourselves made at the very beginning, namely, that it isn't right that the king should be all on his own on board ship. If the Herr Abbé thinks that he can be reasonably represented in a terrible storm, abandoned by everyone, *without a ship*, completely alone and exposed to the greatest danger, then so be it, but please cut the ship, as he can't be alone on board a ship – otherwise a few generals who are in his confidence (extras) must disembark with him, but then the king must say a few words to his men, namely, that they should leave him on his own, a desire that is entirely natural in the sad situation in which he finds himself. – *The 2nd duetto* is to be omitted altogether and, indeed, with more profit than loss to the opera: if you read through the scene as a whole, you'll see that it becomes weak and cold through the addition of an aria or a duet and very tedious for the other actors who have to stand around doing nothing, and, besides, the *combat de générosité* between Ilia and Idamante would be too long and lose its entire force.[6]

Leopold responded to this point in his letter of 18 November:

Idomeneo must disembark with his retinue. There follow the words that he addresses to his retinue, who then withdraw. You know that I told Munich of this objection but that they wrote back to say that thunderstorms and seas pay no heed to the laws of *etiquette*. Yes, indeed, if a shipwreck had actually occurred! But the vow spares them. Besides, this landing will produce a splendid impression.

For a long time Herr Varesco was unwilling to make a start on the duet *Deh soffri in pace o cara etc.*, but I've persuaded him to do so. Ilia and Idamante still have a very short argument

---

5. ◆ *Briefe*, iii.15 and 19 (letter of 15 November 1780).
6. *Briefe*, iii.17–18 (letter of 13 November 1780). This duet was originally planned for act three, scene ten. Authentically Italian in spirit, it would have been placed immediately before the oracle.

conducted in a few words of recitative interrupted, *as it were,* by a subterranean noise, after which the oracle is proclaimed by a subterranean voice, which voice and *its accompaniment* must be moving, terrifying and exceptional, it can be a masterpiece of harmony. You'll find enclosed the alteration that has been made.[7]

The problems surrounding the scene with the shipwreck had still not been resolved, however, and on 22 December we find Leopold writing again:

In *act one, scene VIII,* for example, where it says *Nettuno esce etc.* and then *Nel fondo della Prospettiva si vede Idomeneo che si sforza arrampicarsi sopra quei dirupi etc.* [At the back of the stage we see Idomeneo trying to clamber over the rocks], here, as I say, you'll have to draw up the stage direction and an explanation of this scene in the way you want it staged, in other words, depending on whether *Idomeneo remains on board* or whether, while not being shipwrecked, he becomes aware of the apparent danger and abandons ship with his men and seeks refuge on the rocks. In short, it depends on how it's staged. This can be left to Herr *Quaglio,* who is skilled and experienced in these matters. But there must be shipwrecked vessels, for in his *recitative* in *Scene 10* Idamante says *Vedo fra quegl' avanzi di fracassate navi su quel lido sconosciuto guerrier* [I see among the remnants of wrecked ships an unknown warrior on the beach].[8]

This refers to a pantomime which in Varesco's libretto follows the chorus for the sailors. Here Neptune appeared, calmed the sea and, with an angry glance at Idomeneo, disappeared beneath the waves once again. Mozart showed true dramatic instinct in dispensing with this superficial effect. Idomeneo comes ashore as the sea grows calmer and dismisses his followers in a few words.

In his letter of 18 November, Leopold raised a number of minor objections to the libretto, noting, for example, that 'Argivo' should be replaced by 'Achivo', as Ilia is referring not to the inhabitants of Argos but to the whole of Greece. He also had the following to say about the recitative for Ilia and Idamante immediately before the oracle:

The end of this recitative must be extremely animated, with Ilia running to the altar, while Idamante holds her back, whereupon she turns to the Priest himself with great resolve, throws herself on her knees and before she has finished her speech and during the words *a te sacro Ministro – –* the subterranean noise prevents her from speaking and fills everyone with amazement and fear. If this is done properly, with one peal of thunder following another, it will make a great impression on the audience, especially as it is followed by the subterranean voice. All this will strike the audience as unexpected and highly unusual and surprising.[9]

Although Mozart agreed with this, he none the less had reservations about the way in which the oracle was phrased, reservations no doubt inspired by Gluck's *Alceste.* Thus we find him writing to Leopold on 29 November:

7. *Briefe,* iii.22–3 (letter of 18 November 1780).
8. *Briefe,* iii.67 (letter of 22 December 1780).
9. *Briefe,* iii.23 (letter of 18 November 1780).

Tell me, don't you think that the speech of the subterranean voice is too long? Consider it carefully. – Imagine the theatre, the voice must be terrifying, it must be penetrating, people must believe that it really exists – how can it achieve this if the speech is too long and the audience is increasingly convinced that it means nothing? If the Ghost's speech in Hamlet weren't so long, it would be even more effective. – This speech here can easily be shortened and will gain more than it loses in the process.[10]

Leopold failed to reply by return, and so Mozart reminded him of the problem in his letter of 5 December 1780: 'I mentioned too that I (and others, too) thought the subterranean speech too long to be effective – think about it.'[11] But Leopold was in full agreement and had already written to his son to this effect on the 4th: 'You know that I too thought the subterranean speech too long. I've told him [Varesco] my honest opinion, and it will now be as short as possible.'[12] But this was still not short enough for Mozart: 'The oracle', he wrote on 18 January 1781, 'is still far too long – I've shortened it; Varesco doesn't need to know all this, as it will all be printed just as he wrote it.'[13]

Mozart's mention of *Hamlet* is not without significance here. He may have seen the play in Salzburg shortly beforehand in a performance by Schikaneder's company. The passage in *Idomeneo* continued to preoccupy him: he was convinced that it was too long and so he strove increasingly to approach his Gluckian model, without, of course, equalling it. Leopold wrote to Mozart on 29 December, offering him the following advice on how to deal with the oracle:

I assume that you'll use deep wind instruments to *accomp.* the subterranean voice. How would it be if after the *vague* subterranean noise the instruments were to *sustain* their notes or, *rather, begin to sustain them piano,* followed by a *crescendo that adds to the element of terror,* with the voice entering at the decrescendo and with another terrifying *crescendo each time the voice falls silent?* The noise, which must be brief and like the shock of an earthquake, causing the statue of Neptune to move, captures everyone's attention, and this attention is increased by the entry of a quiet and sustained passage for winds that grows louder and louder and instils a sense of extreme terror, building to a climax, at which point *a single voice* is heard – I can already hear and see it in my imagination.[14]

It is clear from the way in which Mozart dealt with this passage that he followed his father's advice in at least the first two versions that he produced.

In another scene – act two, scene six – he was more successful in shortening a problematical passage. In the printed wordbook, the chorus 'Placido è il mar' has four strophes, of which Mozart set only one choral strophe and one of Elettra's solo strophes. But, according to his letter of 24 November, the number still struck him as 'far too long'.[15]

He had more difficulties reconciling his own aims as composer with the demands of his singers. Even Panzacchi, who was singing one of the smaller roles, wanted Arbace's recitative in act three,

10.   *Briefe*, iii.34–5 (letter of 29 November 1780).
11.   *Briefe*, iii.48 (letter of 5 December 1780).
12.   *Briefe*, iii.44 (letter of 4 December 1780).
13.   *Briefe*, iii.90 (letter of 18 January 1780).
14.   *Briefe*, iii.74–5 (letter of 29 December 1780).
15.   *Briefe*, iii.32 (letter of 24 November 1780). For Leopold's reply of 30 November, see *Briefe*, iii.39.

scene five to be lengthened. It is clear from his letter of 5 December that Mozart felt that this wish was justified:

> As a result of the *chiaro e oscuro* and the fact that he is a good actor, this will create an excellent impression. For example, after the line *sei la città del pianto, e questa reggia quella del duol*, there is a mere glimmer of hope, and then: how foolish I am! how my grief confounds me! *A Creta tutta io vedo etc.*[16]

Mozart's interpretation of this scene was accepted by Varesco, who duly added the lines from 'Dunque per noi dal cielo' to 'Ah sordo è il cielo'. It is an interpretation, moreover, that is highly characteristic of the composer. Varesco began by depicting a state of total despair, whereas Mozart demanded what he termed 'chiaro e oscuro', in other words, contrasting moods, allowing him to invest this solo scene with far greater depth. He also set great store by his performer's abilities and had evidently watched Panzacchi closely, evincing an awareness of the man's acting skills that had been evident from his early youth.

But it was his dealings with Anton Raaff that were to prove most revealing. For all his goodwill, Raaff was particularly demanding, as Mozart had already discovered by 15 November:

> There's a further alteration, for which Raaff is to blame; but he's right, and even if he weren't, one should still respect his grey hairs. He came to see me yesterday, I ran through his 1st aria with him, and he was very pleased with it. But the man is old: in an aria like the one in the second act *Fuor del mar ho un mare in seno etc.* he can't show off any longer; – and so, as he has no aria in the third act and as his aria in the first act can't be as cantabile as he'd like because of the sentiments expressed by the words, he'd like to sing a pretty aria instead of the quartet following the words: *O Creta fortunata! O me felice!*, and in this way we'll get rid of a superfluous number, and the third act will be far more effective.[17]

Here, then, an ensemble had to be sacrificed to a singer, even though such a number would have been dramatically appropriate at such a juncture, where the listener expects the characters who have been affected by this latest turn of events to express their reactions to it. But Italian composers of the period were still baulking at larger ensemble passages and for them an aria was perfectly adequate. Mozart's final remark in his letter to his father – 'in this way we'll get rid of a superfluous number' – throws significant light on his attitude to such an aria. The later, fully mature composer would almost certainly not have found this ensemble 'superfluous'. He then goes on:

> In the final scene in the 2nd act Idomeneo has an aria or, rather, a sort of cavatina between the two choruses; here it will be better to have just a recitative in which the instruments can be put through their paces; for in this scene – which, to judge by the action and groupings that we recently discussed with Le Grand, will be the finest in the whole opera – there'll be so much noise and confusion on stage that an aria at this point would cut a sorry figure, quite apart from the thunderstorm, which is hardly likely to subside just for Herr Raaff's aria – and the effect of a recitative between the choruses will be infinitely better.[18]

16. *Briefe*, iii.48 (letter of 5 December 1780); see also above.
17. *Briefe*, iii.19–20 (letter of 15 November 1780).
18. *Briefe*, iii.20 (letter of 15 November 1780).

Mozart, who was evidently recalling similar scenes in French operas of the period, was guided here by a far sounder instinct than his librettist. The cavatina did not even find its way into the printed wordbook. Leopold expressed a similar point of view in his letter of 18 November: 'The aria between the choruses will be turned into a spirited recitative that can be accompanied, if you like, by thunder and lightning.'[19] Conversely, Raaff's final aria caused almost insuperable difficulties, with Leopold reporting on its initial version in his letter of 25 November:

I'm not happy about the fact that in the first line of Herr Raaff's aria the words *ed era* belong to the second line. True, this is often found with Metastasio, but this depends on the skill of the composer. Many Italian idiots have set the melody *il cuor languiva, ed era* and only then devised some other disconnected melody for *gelida messa in petto*.[20]

Raaff and Mozart were even less happy with the aria, as the latter wrote to inform his father on 29 November:

The aria for Raaff that you've sent me pleases neither of us. I shan't even begin to comment on the *era*, which is always a mistake in an aria of this kind. You sometimes find it in Metastasio, but it's extremely rare and these arias are not among his best; and is there any need for this? But in any case the aria isn't at all what we wanted, it's supposed to express only peace and content-ment, and this emerges only in its second section: we've already had ample opportunity to see, hear and feel the misfortune that he's had to endure throughout the opera, whereas he can now speak, rather, of his present situation. In fact we don't even need a second section – all the better. – Metastasio's opera *Achille in Sciro* includes an aria of this kind and of the kind that Raaff would like:

> Or che mio figlio sei,
> O fido il destin nemico,
> Sento degl' anni miei
> Il Peso a leggierir.[21]

This reference to Metastasio shows clearly how a singer such as Raaff, who had grown up in the Metastasian tradition, could not get these stereotyped scenes out of his head, with the result that he judged every new libretto by their standards. Simply to fall back on an older version for a new situation was all too easy an option. Raaff, too, was ultimately resolved to take what he needed from Metastasio, especially when the new words that he received from Varesco and that were printed in the wordbook failed to satisfy him. These new words ran as follows:

> Sazio è il destino al fine,
> Mostrami lieto aspetto,
> Spirto novello il petto
> Vien mi a rinvigorir.

19. *Briefe*, iii.24 (letter of 18 November 1780).
20. *Briefe*, iii.33 (letter of 25 November 1780).
21. *Briefe*, iii.34 and 40 (letters of 29 November and 1 December1780). The aria is from act three, scene seven of *Achille in Sciro*.

> Tal serpe in frà le spine
> Lascia le antiche spoglie,
> E vinte l'aspre doglie
> Torna a ringiovenir.

As Mozart wrote to inform his father on 27 December, Raaff raised technical objections to this: 'The other day he got very annoyed about the words of his final aria, *rinvigorir* and *ringiovenir*, especially *vien mi a rinvigorir*, five *i*'s, it's true, at the end of an aria this is very disagreeable.'[22]

Leopold responded to these objections on 29 December:

> As for the *vieni a rinvigorir*, it's true that there are 5 *i*'s, but it's also true that I can pronounce it 20 times without difficulty, and with the greatest ease and speed. In the aria from Metastasio's *Achille in Sciro* that you sent me as a model, the closing lines, *il peso alleggerir* and *lo vede rinfiorir*, especially the final *rinfiorir* on account of its initial *r*, are far more difficult. basta! To please everyone, the devil himself may go on tinkering till the end of time. Signor Raaff is being far too pernickety.[23]

But Raaff refused to be placated and in all seriousness demanded the interpolation of a text by Metastasio, as Mozart reported on 30 December:

> I am now in some difficulty over Raaff's final aria, and you'll have to help me out of it. He can't stomach the *rinvigorir* and *ringiovenir*, and because of these 2 words he hates the whole aria. It's true that the *mostrami* and *vien mi* aren't good either, but the two words at the end are the worst of all – to avoid the trill on the *i* in the first *rinvigorir*, I should really move it to the *o*. Raaff has now found an aria well suited to his situation in *Natal di Giove* (a work which, I admit, is very little known), I think it's the *aria di licenza*:

> > Bell' alme al ciel dilette
> > Si Ah! respirate
> > Già palpitaste assai,
> > È tempo di goder.
> > Creta non oda intorno,
> > Non vegga in sì bel giorno
> > Che accenti di contenti,
> > Che oggetti di piacer.[24]

> – and I'm now expected to write this aria for him – no one knows it, he says, and we won't say anything. He knows that we can't expect the Herr Abbate to alter this aria a third time – yet he won't sing it as it stands.[25]

22. *Briefe*, iii.73 (letter of 27 December 1780).
23. *Briefe*, iii.74 (letter of 29 December 1780).
24. Metastasio, *Il natale di Giove*, scene 8.
25. *Briefe*, iii.77–8 (letter of 30 December 1780).

This is a significant example of the way in which singers sometimes played around with the words. In the meantime, Varesco had after all agreed to provide a third version of the aria, distasteful though he found this haggling. It was with some relief that Mozart was able to write to his father on 3 January:

I'm delighted to have the aria for Raaff as he was determined that I should set the aria he'd turned up – with a man like Raaff I'd have had no choice but to have Varesco's aria printed and to have left Raaff to sing his own.[26]

Varesco's revised version finally found favour in Raaff's eyes and was printed and set by Mozart, only to be omitted from the production, as Mozart explained in his letter of 18 January 1781:

But the text [of act three] is too long and so, too, is the music (something I've said all along); as a result, Idamante's aria *Nò, la morte io non pavento* is to be omitted – it was in any case out of place here, although those who have heard it with the music regret its omission; – and Raaff's final aria, too, an even more regrettable omission; but we must make a virtue of necessity.[27]

This whole business is extremely revealing for the light that it sheds on the decisive role played by the singers in the genesis of operas at this period, a role that Gluck refused steadfastly to accept. But Raaff was one of Mozart's closest friends, as well as being a thoughtful and well-educated singer. Moreover, Mozart still tended to vacillate at this time: while his dramatic awareness was now much keener than it had been in his earlier operas, the ease with which he dispensed with the second quartet shows that he was still held back by old ideas and, above all, that, at least in the case of the arias, he did not yet have the courage and necessary resolve to oppose his friend Raaff, however much he was aware of the latter's weaknesses. In the two final arias for Dal Prato and Raaff he was even prepared, albeit reluctantly, to sacrifice his own convictions and was heartily relieved when the situation was resolved to his own satisfaction. Given such constant haggling over the arias, it is no wonder, therefore, that he failed to scale the heights of consistent dramatic characterization in this work. Indeed, Mozart himself was no doubt fully conscious of the fact that Varesco's libretto was not without its flaws, so that on 18 January we find him writing to his father to announce that there was 'still a great deal to alter' and that Varesco 'would not have come off so well with any other composer'.[28]

He also disagreed with his father over certain *secco* passages, even though Leopold generally lent him powerful support. It is a disagreement that throws instructive light on Mozart's attitude to these scenes in general. This is the first time that he admits to feeling the old *tedio del recitativo*, as there was nothing that he feared so much as the excessive length of the *secco* recitatives, a length that could be mitigated only by great skill on the part of the performers. Thus we find him writing on 19 December:

By the way! – The scene between father and son in the first act and the first scene in the second act between Idomeneo and Arbace are both too long; they are bound to be boring, especially because in the first scene both men are poor actors and in the 2nd scene one of them is; besides,

---

26. *Briefe*, iii.80 (letter of 3 January 1781).
27. *Briefe*, iii.90 (letter of 18 January 1781).
28. *Briefe*, iii.90 (letter of 18 January 1781).

they contain only a recital of all that the audience has already seen with its own eyes. These scenes are to be printed as they stand, but I hope that Herr Abbate will indicate how I can shorten them and make them as short as possible, otherwise I'll have to do so myself, as these 2 scenes can't remain as they are – when set to music, I mean.[29]

Leopold answered on the 22nd:

So you're absolutely set on having two of the recitatives shortened. I sent for Varesco at once, as I received your letter at 5 o'clock this evening and the mail coach leaves tomorrow morning. We read it over several times and neither of us finds any occasion to shorten it. It has been translated from the French, as the plan demanded. Indeed, if you look at the plan, you'll see that it was demanded that this recitative should be a little longer, so that the two don't recognize each other so quickly, and now you want to make it ridiculous by having them recognize each other after only a few words. – Let me explain. Idamante must surely say why he's there, he sees the stranger and offers to help him. Idomeneo now goes so far as to speak of his sufferings and at the same time must return his greetings, Idamante will then tell him that he sympathizes with all who have suffered misfortune, as he himself has experienced it. Idomeneus's reply is a necessary question. Idamantes now tells him of the king's misfortunes, and Idomeneus's mysterious comment *non più di questo!* gives Idamantes a ray of hope, so that he asks in his eagerness *dimmi amico, dimmi dov'è?* This eagerness makes Idomeneus ask: *ma d'onde etc.* Surely Idamantes must now explain himself and describe himself as a son worthy of his father, awakening in Idomeneus amazement, respect and a desire to know who this youth is, thereby making the whole story more interesting when he does finally realize that it is his son? – But if something has *par force* to be omitted, I wondered if it should be after Idamantes's recitative *Che favelli? vive egli ancor? etc.*, which ends with *dove quel dolce aspetto vita mi rendera? Idomeneo. Ma d'onde nasce questa che per lui nutri tenerezza d'amor?* then straight to *Perchè qual tuo parlar si mi conturba? Idamante. E qual mi sento anch' io* and so on. In this way you'll lose 1½ pages from the copy of the libretto that Varesco is sending you at present (p. 32), including the beautiful description of his heroic deed, where *Idamante* begins: *Potessi almeno etc.* This may shorten it by 1 *minute*, yes, *exactly* a minute. A great gain! Or do you want father and son to run in and recognize each other like the disguised Harlequin and Brigella, two servants in a foreign land who suddenly discover each other and embrace? Don't forget that this is one of *the most beautiful scenes in the opera, indeed, the main scene,* on which the whole of the rest of the story depends. Such a scene can hardly weary the audience *as it is in the first act.* – Nothing can be omitted from the second act except part of Idomeneo's second speech: *Un sol consiglio or mi fa d'uopo. Ascolta. Tu sai quanto a' Troiani fu il mio brando fatal. Arbace. Tutto m'è noto.* Then we continue and from now on not a single word can reasonably be omitted. This whole recitative can't last long as it contains many things that must be declaimed quickly and eagerly, and here you'd gain *half a minute!* A great gain! This recitative, too, won't weary a soul as it's the *first* in the second act. One passage that you could omit is after Arbace's recitative *Male s'usurpa un re etc.* and Idomeneo says at once: *Il voto è ingiusto.* You could then omit *Idom. Intendo Arbace etc.* and *Arb. Medica man etc.* But I really don't know whether it's worth all this for such a trifle, which amounts to no more than 2½ minutes at most, especially as these recitatives occur at places where they can't weary anyone.

---

29. *Briefe,* iii.66 (letter of 19 December 1780).

In the first act everyone is patient, and the first recitative in the second act will weary no one. It strikes me as absurd: at a rehearsal, where there's nothing to see, it's very boring, of course, but in the theatre, where there are so many distractions between the stage and the audience, a recitative like this is over before you've even noticed. You may tell everyone this from me. If, in spite of all this, something has to be omitted, I would ask that everything be printed. Herr Varesco knows nothing of what I have written here.[30]

Again it was out of consideration for the performers that Mozart demanded cuts, even though he agreed with his father on this point. And so we find him writing to Leopold on 27 December:

With regard to the 2 scenes that have to be shortened, it wasn't my idea, merely one to which I gave my consent; and the reason I agreed to it was because Raaff and dal Prato sing the recitative without any spirit and fire and in such a monotonous manner – and they're the most pitiful actors ever to have set foot on a stage. I had a desperate row the other day with Seeau about the awkwardness, unnaturalness and virtual impossibility of omitting anything. It's enough that everything is to be printed, something he absolutely refused to agree to at first, but he finally said yes after I'd given him a good talking to.[31]

Mozart finally got his way with his cuts, even if they were not the ones that Leopold had suggested. Two passages were cut in act two, scene one: not only the one proposed by Leopold, but also a considerably longer one. In other cases, Mozart was able to solve the problem himself, and so we find him writing to his father on 3 January 1781:

No doubt we shall have a good many observations to make in Act III once it gets into the theatre; – in s*cene VI*, for example, after Arbace's aria, it says: *Idomeneo. Arbace etc*. But how can the latter reappear so soon?[32] Fortunately he can be cut completely – but to be on the safe side I've written a somewhat longer *Introduzion* to the High Priest's recitative. – Following the chorus of mourners, the king, populace and everyone else leaves – and in the following scene, it says: *Idomeneo in ginocchione nel tempio*. But this is impossible; he has to enter with his whole retinue; and so we need a *Marche* here – I've written a very simple march for 2 violins, viola, bass and 2 oboes, to be played *a mezza voce*, during which the king enters and the priests prepare the equipment for the sacrifice; the king then kneels and begins to pray.

In the recitative for Elettra after the subterranean voice, it should say *Partono*, I forgot to look at the copy that's been prepared for the printer to see whether it's there and, if so, where it comes – it strikes me as rather silly that they hurry away so quickly simply in order to leave Madame Elettra alone.[33]

Only on one point did Mozart remain obdurate in the face of Raaff's objections, and that was the quartet 'Andrò ramingo e solo'. He wrote to his father on this point on 27 December:

30. *Briefe*, iii.67–9 (letter of 22 December 1780).
31. *Briefe*, iii.71 (letter of 27 December 1780).
32. There has been a change of scene in the meantime.
33. *Briefe*, iii.80 (letter of 3 January 1781).

I've now had problems with him over the quartet. The more I think about this quartet, as it will be performed on stage, the more effective I think it will be, and certainly everyone who has heard it on the harpsichord has liked it. Only Raaff thinks it will have no effect. When we were on our own together, he said: *non c'è da spianar la voce* [There's nothing in it to iron out the voice] – *it's too restricting* – as if the words in a *quartetto* should not be spoken rather than sung! He simply doesn't understand such things. I just said: My very dear friend, if I knew of a single note that needed to be altered in this *quartetto*, I'd alter it at once, but there's nothing in this opera with which I'm as satisfied as I am with this quartet, and when you've heard it all together, you'll certainly change your mind. I've made every effort to serve you well with your 2 arias, and I'll do the same with the third one, and I hope I'll succeed, but as far as trios and quartets are concerned, the composer must have a free hand. He said he was happy with this.[34]

This is one of Mozart's most important admissions of his attitude to dramatic ensembles, which from now on he was to invest with an ever greater potential for development. This is the point on which he first gives unconditional precedence to the composer over the singer and to the dramatist over the musician, with the work itself clearly showing what he meant by his comment that 'the words should be spoken rather than sung', in other words, the individual characters should be carefully worked out in association with the dramatic situation (see above). This naturally excluded any suggestion that the composer should 'serve' the singer. A comparison between these comments and his decision to cut the 'superfluous' quartet (see above) shows clearly that Mozart still had mixed feelings about the drama, for on that occasion he was still in thrall to Italian thinking, with its hostility to ensembles, whereas these other remarks already reveal the great dramatist that he was later to become.

Varesco continued to cause difficulties with his libretto right up to the end. Even though the text was printed as he had written it, he still demanded an extra fee for the many changes that he had to make, prompting Leopold to comment that, although 'only half-Italian', he was '*peggio dell' Italiano vero* [worse than a real Italian], who, even with his income, is riddled with debts'.[35] But Mozart wrote to inform him that he would receive only the sum already agreed as the changes had been made merely for the composer and to his own advantage; he would not have 'come off so well with another composer' (see above). Varesco had to be satisfied with this, although even then this 'greedy, money-grubbing fool' could not wait for the money to reach him from Munich but pestered Leopold to such an extent that the latter was finally moved to comment, uncharacteristically colourfully, that 'Varesco mi a seccato i cuglioni' [Varasco has bored the balls off me].[36]

34. *Briefe*, iii.72–3 (letter of 27 December 1780).
35. ◆ These characterizations derive from Leopold's letters of 4 January 1781 (*Briefe*, iii.8) and 27 January 1781 (*Briefe*, iii.91).
36. *Briefe*, iii.92 (letter of 22 January 1781). ◆ Many of the passages cut or changed by Mozart during December 1780 and January 1781 (and discussed here by Abert) are reproduced in NMA II/5/11, 535–626; further see the critical report to the edition. It is worth noting, too, that two printed librettos survive for the opera. One, now at the Bayerische Staatsbibliothek, Munich, gives both Varesco's Italian text and Schachtner's German translation; it is thought to date from approximately one month before the opera's first performance. The second libretto, also in the Bayerische Staatsbibliothek, gives the Italian text only (including changes) and probably dates from mid- to late January, closer in time to the work's premiere; accordingly it better approximates to the text used by Mozart (although neither text exactly reproduces what was in fact performed). Abert, in his study of the opera, relied on the edition published as part of the AMA, which in turn relied on the first libretto (the second was not known at the time). The changes in the second libretto do not, however, substantially affect his reading of the work.

2. *Changes for the later performance*

In spite of the acclaim that it received in Munich, *Idomeneo* shared the fate of all Mozart's early operas and not only failed to be taken up elsewhere but soon disappeared from the Munich repertory as well. Mozart, too, looked on the work with more critical eyes after the first few performances, and when Grand Duke Paul passed through Vienna in the autumn of 1781 and Mozart thought of staging the work as part of the celebrations, he could envisage it only in German and in a substantially different form. As translator he hoped to enlist the services of the 'excellent poet' Johann von Alxinger, who had more than justified Mozart's favourable opinion of him with his translation of Gluck's *Iphigénie en Tauride*, a translation prepared under Gluck's supervision.[37] As for the musical revisions, Mozart wrote to his father on 12 September 1781: 'I'd have completely altered Idomeneo's part and rewritten it as a bass role for Fischer and would also have made several other changes and arranged it more in the French style. Bernasconi, Adamberger and Fischer would have been only too pleased to have sung in it.'[38] This passage makes it clear that Mozart was fully conscious of the undoubted disjunction between the Italian and French elements in *Idomeneo*, a discrepancy that he sought to overcome by laying greater emphasis on the French element. Unfortunately nothing came of this plan as the two gala operas were Gluck's *Iphigénie* and *Alceste*. A third work was not considered.

But in March 1786 *Idomeneo* was performed in Vienna by a group of aristocratic amateurs. According to his own thematic catalogue, Mozart wrote two new numbers for it, a duet for Ilia and Idamante in act three, scene two (with new words) and a new scena and rondo for Idamante in act two, scene one (K489, 'Spiegarti non poss'io', and K490, 'Non più, tutto ascoltai – Non temer, amato bene').[39] Ilia was sung by Anna von Pufendorf, Idamante by Baron Pulini, and Idomeneo probably by Antonio Giacomo Bridi.[40]

In the circumstances, there could be no question of any far-reaching dramatic changes: on the whole, the performance represented a concession to the taste and abilities of the performers. The *secco* recitatives were heavily cut, suggesting that Mozart had very little trust in his singers' dramatic abilities.

The main change was that Idamante was rewritten for tenor voice. Although the rondo is notated in the soprano clef, it bears the name of Baron Pulini, for whom the role of Idamante was written in the duet, where a tenor clef is used, so that there can be no doubt on the point. Mozart opted for a soprano clef here as it is used constantly throughout the score. Changes also had to be made to the trio ('Pria di partir, o Dio!') and quartet ('Andrò ramingo e solo'), with Idamante's part being transposed up an octave wherever it would otherwise have gone below Idomeneo's. In the trio Mozart entered the changes himself in the full score, whereas for the quartet the new version of the vocal lines was written out again on a separate folio,[41] with Idamante's part again being notated in the soprano clef for simplicity's sake.

No suitable singer seems to have been found for the role of Elettra as her last two arias ('Idol mio, se ritroso' and 'D'Oreste, d'Ajace') were simply cut, while in most of the ensembles her vocal line was exchanged with that of Ilia. The part of Arbace was likewise cut with the exception of a mere handful of *secco* passages indispensable to the action. Even the main characters lost arias,

37. See Arend, 'Die unter Gluck's Mitwirkung hergestellte, verschollene älteste deutsche Übersetzung der "Iphigenia auf Tauris"'.
38. *Briefe*, iii.157 (letter of 12 September 1781).
39. Both are dated 10 March 1786.
40. See Jahn, *W. A. Mozart*, fourth edition, ii.828ff.
41. The last twenty bars are missing; see the critical commentary in AMA, p.71.

with Idamante losing two ('Il padre adorato' and 'No, la morte, la morte io non pavento') and Idomeneo one ('Torna la pace al core'). The latter's prayer ('Accogli, o rè del mar') was shortened and his aria ('Fuor del mar') deprived of its coloratura passages and final cadenza. But it was in the *secco* recitatives that the most far-reaching cuts were made, generally reducing them to the point where they are only just intelligible.

In two respects, at least by Mozartian standards, the revisions represent a genuine improvement: the replacement of a castrato part by a tenor and the removal of the coloratura writing from the aria 'Fuor del mar'. The new duet is also decidedly superior to its predecessor in terms of its fully rounded form and interiority of expression. Conversely, the new rondo aria with solo violin at the beginning of act two, while melodious, elegant and grateful, reveals the same preponderance of purely musical elements that was later to characterize many of the numbers in *La clemenza di Tito*. On the whole, however, we should not forget that these revisions were undertaken not for dramaturgical reasons but to accommodate the resources of amateur performers, with the result that the work lost so much in the process that it is difficult to share Jahn's view that it could serve as a model for modern performances.[42] If, by contrast, Mozart had revised the work for Grand Duke Paul, as he had thought of doing, its fortunes would no doubt be far greater than is now the case. In the absence of such a revision we can only fall back on the existing score, while retaining the right to undertake minor changes to it.

---

42. Jahn, *W. A. Mozart*, ii.831.

Bibliography

Abbate, Carolyn and Roger Parker. 'Dismembering Mozart', *Cambridge Opera Journal*, ii (1990), 187–95

Abert, Anna Amalie. *Christoph Willibald Gluck* (Munich, 1959)

Abert, Hermann. 'Eine Nationalhymnen-Sammlung', *Zeitschrift der Internationalen Musikgesellschaft*, ii (1900/1), 69–79

Abert, Hermann. *Herzog Karl Eugen von Württemberg und seine Zeit* (Eßlingen, 1905)

Abert, Hermann. 'Die dramatische Musik', *Herzog Karl Eugen von Württemberg und seine Zeit* (Eßlingen, 1905), 555–611

Abert, Hermann. *Nicolò Jommelli: Fetonte* (Leipzig, 1907 = Denkmäler deutscher Tonkunst xxxii/xxxiii)

Abert, Hermann. 'J. G. Noverre und sein Einfluß auf die dramatische Ballettkomposition', *Jahrbuch der Musikbibliothek Peters 1908*, 29–45

Abert, Hermann. *Niccolò Jommelli als Opernkomponist* (Halle, 1908)

Abert, Hermann. *Geschichte der Robert-Franz-Singakademie* (Halle, 1908)

Abert, Hermann. *Die Magd als Herrin: Giovanni Battista Pergolesi* (Munich, 1910)

Abert, Hermann. *Ausgewählte Ballette Stuttgarter Meister aus der 2. Hälfte des 18. Jahrhunderts* (Leipzig, 1913 = Denkmäler der Tonkunst in Bayern xliii/xliv)

Abert, Hermann. 'Piccinni als Buffokomponist', *Jahrbuch der Musikbibliothek Peters 1913*, 29–42

Abert, Hermann. *Christoph Willibald Gluck: Orfeo ed Euridice* (Leipzig, 1914 = Denkmäler der Tonkunst in Österreich xliva)

Abert, Hermann. *Christoph Willibald Gluck: Le nozze d'Ercole e d'Ebe* (Leipzig, 1914 = Denkmäler der Tonkunst in Bayern xiv/2)

Abert, Hermann. 'Glucks italienische Opern bis zum "Orfeo"', *Gluck-Jahrbuch*, ii (1915), 1–25

Abert, Hermann. 'Zum Kapitel Entstellungen und Parodien Gluckscher Opern', *Gluck-Jahrbuch*, ii (1915), 108–9

Abert, Hermann. *Carlo Pallavicino: La Gierusalemme liberata* (Leipzig, 1916 = Denkmäler deutscher Tonkunst lv)

Abert, Hermann. *Johann Joseph Abert* (Leipzig, 1916)

Abert, Hermann. 'Leopold Mozarts Notenbuch von 1762', *Gluck-Jahrbuch*, iii (1917), 51–87

Abert, Hermann. 'Paisiellos Buffokunst und ihre Beziehung zu Mozart', *Archiv für Musikwissenschaft*, i (1918/19), 402–21

Abert, Hermann. 'Über Aufgaben und Ziele der musikalischen Biographie', *Archiv für Musikwissenschaft* ii (1919/20), 417–33

Abert, Hermann. 'Joh. Christian Bachs italienische Opern und ihr Einfluß auf Mozart', *Zeitschrift für Musikwissenschaft*, i (1919/20), 313–28

Abert, Hermann. 'Schwäbisches bei Mozart', *Der Schwäbische Bund*, i (1919/20), 433–43

Abert, Hermann. 'Konstanze Nissens Tagebuch aus den Jahren 1824–1837', *Mozarteums-Mitteilungen*, ii/2–3 (1920), 38–62 and 65–75

Abraham, Otto. 'Das absolute Tonbewußtsein: Psychologisch-musikalische Studie', *Sammelbände der Internationalen Musikgesellschaft*, iii (1901/2), 1–86

Adam, Adolphe. *Souvenirs d'un musicien* (Paris, 1857)

Adelmann, Karl. *Donna Elvira als Kunst-Ideal und in ihrer Verkörperung auf der Münchener Hof-Bühne* (Munich, 1888)

Ademollo, Alessandro. 'Le cantanti italiane celebri del secolo decimottavo: Vittoria Tesi', *Nuova antologia*, ser.3, xxii (1889), 308–27

Adler, Guido. 'Die Kaiser Ferdinand III., Leopold I., Joseph I., und Karl VI. als Tonsetzer und Förderer der Musik', *Vierteljahrsschrift für Musikwissenschaft*, viii (1892), 252–68

Adler, Guido. *Johann Froberger: Orgel- und Clavierwerke* (Leipzig, 1897–1903 = Denkmäler der Tonkunst in Österreich viii, xiii and xxi)

Adler, Guido. *Orazio Benevoli: Festmesse und Hymnus zur Einweihung des Domes in Salzburg 1628* (Leipzig, 1903 = Denkmäler der Tonkunst in Österreich xx)

Adler, Guido. *Wiener Instrumentalmusik vor und um 1750* (Leipzig, 1908–12)

Adler, Guido. *Der Stil in der Musik* (Leipzig, 1911)

Adler, Guido. *Heinrich Ignaz Franz Biber: Missa Sti. Henrici* (Vienna, 1918 = Denkmäler der Tonkunst in Österreich xxv/1)

Adler, Guido, ed. *Handbuch der Musikgeschichte* (Frankfurt, 1924)

Adlung, Philipp. *Mozarts Opera seria 'Mitridate, re di Ponto'* (Eisenach, 1996)

Adrian, Irene. 'Rolle und Bedeutung der Kastraten in Leben und Werk Wolfgang Amadeus Mozarts', *Mozart: Gli orientamenti della critica moderna. Atti del convegno internazionale Cremona, 24–26 novembre 1991*, ed. Giacomo Fornari (Lucca, 1994), 27–45

Agricola, Johann Friedrich. *Anleitung zur Singkunst* (Berlin, 1757)

Agricola, Johann Friedrich. 'Alceste: Tragedia messa in musica dal Signore Cavaliere Christoforo Gluck', *Allgemeine deutsche Bibliothek*, xiv (1779), 3–27

Aigner, Theodor. 'Der Eggenfeldener Lehrersohn Franz Ignaz Lipp (1718–1798)', *Heimat an Rott und Inn: Heimatbuch für die Landkreise des Rottals*, vi (1969), 1–5

Alaleona, Domenico. *Studi su la storia dell'oratorio musicale in Italia* (Turin, 1908)

Alberti-Radanowicz, Editha. 'Das Wiener Lied von 1789–1815', *Studien zur Musikwissenschaft*, x (1923), 37–78

Allanbrook, Wye Jamison. *Rhythmic Gesture in Mozart: Le Nozze di Figaro and Don Giovanni* (Chicago, 1983)

Allanbrook, Wye Jamison. 'Mozart's happy endings: A new look at the "convention" of the "lieto fine"', *Mozart-Jahrbuch 1984/85*, 1–5

Allanbrook, Wye Jamison. 'Ear-tickling Nonsense': A New Context for Musical Expression in Mozart's "Haydn-Quartets"', *The St. John's Review*, xxxviii (1988), 1–24

Allanbrook, Wye Jamison. 'Mozart's tunes and the comedy of closure', *On Mozart*, ed. James M. Morris (Cambridge, 1994), 169–86

Allanbrook, Wye Jamison. '"To Serve the Private Pleasure": Expression and Form in the String Quartets', *Wolfgang Amadè Mozart: Essays on his Life and his Music*, ed. Stanley Sadie (Oxford, 1996), 132–60

Allihn, Ingeborg. 'Die Darstellung der Konstanze Mozart in der neueren Mozart-Literatur', *Kongreßbericht zum VII. Internationalen Gewandhaus-Symposium. Wolfgang Amadeus Mozart: Forschung und Praxis im Dienst von Leben, Werk, Interpretation und Rezeption anläßlich der Gewandhaus-Festtage in Leipzig vom 3. bis 6. Oktober 1991* (Leipzig, 1993), 66–71

Allroggen, Gerhard. 'Zur Frage der Echtheit der Sinfonie KV Anh. 216 = 74g', *Colloquium 'Mozart und Italien' (Rom 1974)*, ed. Friedrich Lippmann (Cologne, 1978 = Analecta musicologica xviii), 237–45

Allroggen, Gerhard. 'Mozarts Lambacher Sinfonie: Gedanken zur musikalischen Stilkritik', *Leopold Mozart: Auf dem Weg zu einem Verständnis*, ed. Josef Mančal and Wolfgang Plath (Augsburg, 1994), 119–30

Altenburg, Johann Ernst. *Versuch einer Anleitung zur heroisch-musikalischen Trompeter- und Pauker-Kunst* (Halle, 1795)

Ambros, August Wilhelm. *Die Grenzen der Musik und Poesie* (Prague, 1856)

Ambros, August Wilhelm. *Das Conservatorium zu Prag* (Prague, 1858)

Ambros, August Wilhelm. *Geschichte der Musik*, third edition, ed. Hugo Leichtentritt (Leipzig, 1909)

Anderson, Emily. *The Letters of Mozart and his Family* (London, 1935; second edition, ed. A. Hyatt King and Monica Carolan, London, 1966; third edition, ed. Stanley Sadie and Fiona Smart, London, 1985)

Anderson, R. N. 'Mozart's Death: The Case of Complications of Rheumatic Heart Disease', *Dalhousie Review*, lxxiii/2 (1993), 234–40

André, Anton. *Beiträge zur Geschichte des Requiems von W. A. Mozart* (Offenbach, 1829)

André, August Hermann. *Zur Geschichte der Familie André* (Garmisch, 1963)

André, Johann Anton. *Thematisches Verzeichnis W. A. Mozartscher Manuskripte, chronologisch geordnet von 1764 bis 1784* (Offenbach, 1833)

André, Uta-Margrit and Hans-Jörg André. *Festschrift André zum 225. Firmenjubiläum* (Offenbach, 1999)

Angelucci, Eugenia. 'La forma della comunicazione nel sistema didattico della "Violinschule" di Leopold Mozart', *Beiträge des Internationalen Leopold-Mozart-Kolloquiums Augsburg 1994*, ed. Josef Mančal and Wolfgang Plath (Augsburg, 1997 = Beiträge zur Leopold-Mozart-Forschung ii), 107–45

Angermüller, Rudolph. 'Nissens Kollektaneen für seine Mozartbiographie', *Mozart-Jahrbuch 1971/72*, 217–26

Angermüller, Rudolph. *W. A. Mozart: Lucio Silla. Faksimiledruck des Librettos von G. de Gamerra. Mailand 1772* (Munich, 1975)

Angermüller, Rudolph. 'Wer war der Librettist von *La finta giardiniera*?', *Mozart-Jahrbuch 1976/77*, 1–8

Angermüller, Rudoph. 'Bemerkungen zu französischen Bearbeitungen des 19. Jahrhunderts', *Così fan tutte: Beiträge zur Wirkungsgeschichte von Mozarts Oper*, ed. Susanne Vill (Bayreuth, 1978), 67–90

Angermüller, Rudolph. 'Ein neuentdecktes Salzburger Libretto (1769) zu Mozarts "La Finta semplice"', *Die Musikforschung*, xxxi/3 (1978), 318–22

Angermüller, Rudolph. 'Wer spielte die Uraufführung von Mozarts "Pariser Symphonie" KV 297?', *Mitteilungen der Internationalen Stiftung Mozarteum*, xxvi/3–4 (1978), 12–20

Angermüller, Rudolph. 'Les mystères d'Isis (1801) und Don Juan (1805, 1834) auf der Bühne der Pariser Oper', *Mozart-Jahrbuch 1980/83*, 32–97

Angermüller, Rudolph. *Antonio Salieri: Fatti e documenti* (Vicenza and Belluno, 1985)

Angermüller, Rudolph. 'Testament, Kodizill, Nachtrag und Sperrelation der Freifrau Maria Anna von Berchtold zu Sonnenburg, geb. Mozart (1751–1829)', *Mozart-Jahrbuch 1986*, 97–132

Angermüller, Rudolph. *Das Salzburger Mozart-Denkmal: Eine Dokumentation (bis 1845) zur 150–Jahre-Enthüllungsfeier* (Salzburg, 1992)

Angermüller, Rudolph. 'Verschollene Briefe von und an Franz Xaver Wolfgang Mozart', *Mitteilungen der Internationalen Stiftung Mozarteum*, xl/1–4 (1992), 145–62

Angermüller, Rudolph. 'Neuerwerbungen der Bibliotheca Mozartiana', *Mitteilungen der Internationalen Stiftung Mozarteum*, xli/1–2 (1993), 69–76

Angermüller, Rudolph. 'Ein ungedruckter Brief Franz Xaver Wolfgang Mozarts an Caroline Ungher-Sabatier, Wien, 26. Dezember 1842', *Mitteilungen der Internationalen Stiftung Mozarteum*, xliii/3–4 (1995), 86–92

Angermüller, Rudolph. '"Des Vaters Name war es eben, was deiner Tatkraft Keim zerstört." Franz Xaver Wolfgang Mozart – Wie lebte er mit dem Erbe seines Vaters?', *Mitteilungen der Internationalen Stiftung Mozarteum*, xlvi/3–4 (1998), 29–48

Angermüller, Rudolph. 'Die Familie des "alten" Graf Thun', *Mitteilungen der Internationalen Stiftung Mozarteum*, xliv/1–2 (1998), 26–35

Angermüller, Rudolph. 'Pariser "Don Juan"-Rezensionen 1805 bis 1866' *Mozart-Studien*, viii (1998), 153–224

Angermüller, Rudolph. 'Carl Mozart an Alois Taux, Mailand, 4. April 1856', *Mitteilungen der Internationalen Stiftung Mozarteum*, xlvii/3–4 (1999), 94–6

Angermüller, Rudolph. 'Die Sänger der Erstaufführung von Mozarts Dramma per musica "Lucio Silla" KV 135, Mailand, 26. Dezember 1772. Morgnoni – de Amicis – Rauzzini, Suardi – Mienci – Onofrio', *Mitteilungen der Internationalen Stiftung Mozarteum*, xlvii/3–4 (1999), 3–18

Angermüller, Rudolph. 'Die Sänger der Erstaufführung von Mozarts Festa teatrale "Ascanio in Alba" KV 111, Mailand, 17. Oktober 1771. Falchini – Manzuoli – Girelli – Tibaldi – Solzi', *Mitteilungen der Internationalen Stiftung Mozarteum*, xlvii/1–2 (1999), 1–27

Angermüller, Rudolph. *TageBuch meines Brief Wechsels in Betref der Mozartischen Biographie (1828–1837)* (Bad Honnef, 1999)

Angermüller, Rudolph. 'Ein Mozart-Tenor aus Niederbayern: Johann Valentin Adamberger zu seinem 260. Geburtstag', *Musik in Bayern*, lix (2000), 93–110

Angermüller, Rudolph. 'Francesco Bussani – Mozarts erster Bartolo, Antonio und Alfonso und Dorothea Bussani – Mozarts erster Cherubino und erste Despina', *Mozart-Studien*, x (2000), 213–29

Angermüller, Rudolph. 'Die Sänger der Erstaufführung von Mozarts "Mitridate, Re di Ponto" KV 87 (Mailand, 26. Dezember 1770). d'Ettore – Bernasconi – Benedetti – Aldobrandini – (Cicognani) – Varese – Bassano – Muschietti', *Mitteilungen der Internationalen Stiftung Mozarteum*, xlix/1–2 (2001), 10–29

Angermüller, Rudolph. '"ein Gottförchtiger, erlicher Mann": Anton Raaff, Mozarts erster Idomeneo', *Mitteilungen der Arbeitsgemeinschaft für rheinische Musikgeschichte e. V., Köln* (December 2001), 10–29

Angermüller, Rudolph. 'Das Wunderkind in Paris: Ein unbekanntes Mozart-Autograph und seine Geschichte', *Mozart-Studien*, xi (2002), 189–99

Angermüller, Rudolph. 'Die Erstaufführung von Mozarts *Le Nozze di Figaro* an der Mailänder Scala, 27. März 1815', *Hudební věda*, xl/2–3 (2003), 155–68

Angermüller, Rudolph. 'Von Salieris und Mozarts "Così fan tutte" über "Die zwey Tanten aus Meyland" – "Tit for tat; or The Tables Turned" – "Die Guerillas" – "Winzer und Sänger" zu "Dame Kobold": Metamorphosen eines Librettos', *Almanach der Mozartwoche 2003 vom 24. Jänner bis 2. Februar* (Salzburg, 2003), 23–31

Angermüller, Rudolph. 'Die Sänger der Erstaufführung des "Idomeneo" KV 366', *In signo Wolfgang Amadé Mozart: Mitteilungen der Mozart-Gesellschaft Zürich*, xiv (2004), 1–24

Angermüller, Rudolph. 'Theateraufführungen während Mozarts Paris-Aufenthalt 1778 (23. März–26. September 1778)', *Hudební věda*, xli/3–4 (2004), 267–94

Angermüller, Rudolph und Elena Biggi Parodi, ed. *Da Beaumarchais a Da Ponte: Convegno su Antonio Salieri. Verona, 9 aprile 1994* (Turin, 1996)

Angermüller, Rudolph and Gabriele Ramsauer, '"du wirst, wenn uns Gott gesund zurückkommen läst, schöne Sachen sehen": Veduten aus dem Nachlaß Leopold Mozarts in der Graphiksammlung des Salzburger Museums Carolino Augusteum', *Mitteilungen der Internationalen Stiftung Mozarteum*, xlii/1–2 (1994), 1–48

Anheißer, Siegfried. 'Die unbekannte Urfassung von Mozarts Figaro', *Zeitschrift für Musikwissenschaft*, xv (1933), 301–17

Anonymous. 'Die Hochzeit des Figaro, Oper', *Rheinische Musen*, i/3 (1794), 273–4

Anonymous. 'Aus einem Briefe des Herrn Geheimen Raths, Freyherrn van Swieten', *Allgemeine musikalische Zeitung*, i (1798/9), 252–5

Anonymous. *Mozart und Schikaneder: Ein theatralisches Gespräch über die Aufführung der Zauberflöte im Stadttheater, in Knittelversen von* ** (Vienna, 1801)

Anonymous. *Mozarts Traum nach Anhörung seiner Oper 'Die Zauberflöte' im Stadttheater: Jupitern und Schikanedern erzählt im Olymp in Knittelversen von F. H. v. TZ* (Vienna, 1801)

Anonymous. *Jupiter, Mozart und Schikaneder nach der ersten Vorstellung der Zauberflöte im neuen Theater an der Wien* (Vienna, 1802)

Anonymous. 'Auszug aus dem Sarti'schen Manuscripte, worin Mozart bitter getadelt wird', *Allgemeine musikalische Zeitung*, xxxiv (1832), 373–4 and xxxvi (1834), 540

Anonymous. 'Autograph von Michael Haydn', *Caecilia*, xvi (1834), 212

Anonymous. 'Das Mozarteum zu Salzburg', *Allgemeine Wiener Musik-Zeitung*, iii/25–6 (1843), 101–2

Anonymous. *Biographien Salzburgischer Tonkünstler* (Salzburg, 1845)

Anonymous. 'Zur Säcularfeier Mozart's in Berlin', *Neue Berliner Musikzeitung*, x/5 (1856), 34–5

Anonymous. 'Oulibischeff's und Jahn's "Mozart": Eine Parallele', *Recensionen und Mittheilungen über Theater und Musik*, v (1859), 80–2

Anonymous. 'Eine Zeichnung Mozarts vom Bäsle', *Mitteilungen für die Mozart-Gemeinde in Berlin*, ii (1908), 66

Anonymous. 'Eine Verballhornung der Zauberflöte', *Mozarteums-Mitteilungen*, i (1918), 20–1

Anonymous. 'Grazer Mozartiana', *Mozarteums-Mitteilungen*, ii (1919), 94ff.

Anonymous. 'Noch einmal der Schädel Mozarts', *Mitteilungen für die Mozart-Gemeinde in Berlin*, xxii (n.d.), 466

Anwand, Oskar. *Die Primadonna Friedrichs des Großen* (Berlin, 1930)

Apfel, Ernst. *Zur Vor- und Frühgeschichte der Symphonie* (Baden-Baden, 1972)

Arbogast, Jochen. *Stilkritische Untersuchungen zum Klavierwerk des Thomaskantors Johann Kuhnau* (Regensburg,1983)

Arend, Max. 'Das Szenarium zu Glucks Ballett *Don Juan*', *Zur Kunst Glucks* (Regensburg, 1914), 31–7

Arend, Max. 'Die unter Gluck's Mitwirkung hergestellte, verschollene älteste deutsche Übersetzung der "Iphigenia auf Tauris"', *Zeitschrift der Internationalen Musikgesellschaft*, vii (1905/6), 261–7

Arienzo, Nicola. *Die Entstehung der komischen Oper* (Berlin, 1899)

Aringer-Grau, Ulrike. *Marianische Antiphonen von Wolfgang Amadeus Mozart, Johann Michael Haydn und ihren Salzburger Zeitgenossen* (Tutzing, 2002)

Armbruster, Richard. 'Mozart und der "Stein der Weisen": Bedeutender Fund in einer Hamburger Bibliothek', *Neue Zürcher Zeitung*, xxiii/xxiv (August 1997), n.p.

Arneth, Alfred. *Briefe der Kaiserin Maria Theresia an ihre Kinder und Freunde* (Vienna, 1881)

Arnheim, Amalie. 'Le devin du village von J. J. Rousseau und die Parodie "Les amours de Bastien et Bastienne"', *Sammelbände der Internationalen Musik-Gesellschaft*, iv (1902/3), 686–727

Arnold, Denis. 'Orphans and Ladies: The Venetian Conservatoires (1680–1790)', *Proceedings of the Royal Musical Association*, lxxxix (1962/3), 31–47

Arnold, Ignaz. *Mozarts Geist* (Erfurt, 1803)

Arnoldson, Louise Parkinson. *Sedaine et les musiciens de son temps* (Paris, 1934)

Arteaga, Esteban de. *Le rivoluzioni del teatro musicale italiano dalla sua origine fino al presente* (Bologna, 1783)

Arthur, John. '"N.N." revisited: New light on Mozart's late correspondence', *Haydn, Mozart and Beethoven: Studies in the Music of the Classical Period. Essays in honour of Alan Tyson*, ed. Sieghard Brandenburg (Oxford, 1998), 127–45

Artuso, Pacifica. *Monsieur Egidio Romualdo Duni tra scuola napoletana e opéra-comique* (Rome, 1996)

Asper, Helmut G. *Hanswurst* (Emsdetten, 1980)

Auld, Louis E. *The lyric art of Pierre Perrin, founder of French opera* (Henryville, PA, 1986)

Autexier, Philippe. 'Wann wurde die Maurerische Trauermusik uraufgeführt?', *Mozart-Jahrbuch 1984*, 56–8

Autexier, Philippe. 'Cinq lieder inconnus de W. A. Mozart', *International Journal of Musicology*, i (1992), 67–79

Autexier, Philippe. *La Lyre maçonne: Mozart – Haydn – Spohr – Liszt* (Paris, 1997)

Bab, Julius. *Die Devrients* (Berlin, 1932)

Bach, Carl Philipp Emanuel. *Versuch über die wahre Art das Clavier zu spielen*, ed. Walter Neumann (Leipzig, 1906); trans. William J. Mitchell as *Essay on the True Art of Playing Keyboard Instruments* (New York, 1949)

Bachaumont, Louis Petit de. *Mémoires secrets* (Paris, 1777–89)

Badura-Skoda, Eva. 'Zur Frühgeschichte des Hammerklaviers', *Florilegium musicologicum: Helmut Federhofer zum 75. Geburtstag*, ed. Christoph-Hellmut Mahling (Tutzing, 1988), 37–44

Badura-Skoda, Eva. 'On Improvised Embellishments and Cadenzas in Mozart's Piano Concertos', *Mozart's Piano Concertos: Text, Context, Interpretation*, ed. Neal Zaslaw (Ann Arbor, MI, 1996), 365–71

Baggesen, Jens Immanuel. *Briefwechsel*, ed. Hans Schulz (Leipzig, 1910)

Baini, Giuseppe. *Memorie storico-critiche della vita e delle opere di Giovanni Pierluigi da Palestrina* (Rome, 1828)

Baiocco, Monica. 'Su Baldassarre Ferri, cantante evirato del Seicento' (dissertation, University of Perugia, 1992/3)

Baker, D. Erskine. *Biographia dramatica* (London, 1782)

Ballin, Ernst A. *Das Wort-Ton-Verhältnis in den klavierbegleiteten Liedern Mozarts* (Kassel, 1984)

Balmas, Enea. 'Carlo Goldoni: Il dissoluto', *Don Giovanni a più voci*, ed. Anna Maria Finoli and Enea Balmas (Bologna, 1996), 39–57

Banning, Helmut. *Johann Friedrich Doles: Leben und Werk* (Leipzig, 1939)

Bär, Carl. 'Die Lodronischen Nachtmusiken', *Mitteilungen der Internationalen Stiftung Mozarteum*, x (1961), 19–22

Bär, Carl. *Mozart: Krankheit, Tod, Begräbnis* (Salzburg, 1972)

Barak, Helmut. 'Valentin Adamberger – Mozarts Belmonte und Freund', *Internationaler Musikwissenschaftlicher Kongreß zum Mozartjahr 1991 Baden-Wien*, ed. Ingrid Fuchs (Tutzing, 1993), 463–74

Barak, Helmut. 'Buff, Herz und Vogelsang – Die Theaterfamilien Stephanie, Lange und Adamberger im Wien Mozarts', *Wege zu Mozart: W. A. Mozart in Wien und Prag. Die großen Opern*, ed. Herbert Zeman (Vienna, 1993), 92–113

Barbier, Patrick. *Farinelli: Le castrat des Lumières* (Paris, 1994)

Bardon, Yves. 'L'esthétique des passions: Marmontel et l'opéra', *Dix-huitième siècle*, xxi (1989), 329–40

Barilier, Étienne. 'Le philosophe et le mythe: Kierkegaard et Don Juan', *Mythen in der Musik: Essays zu den Internationalen Festwochen Luzern 1999*, ed. Erich Singer, Rudolf Bossard and Karina Wisniewska (Wabern-Bern, 1999), 112–17

Barlow, Jeremy. *The Music of John Gay's The Beggar's Opera* (Oxford, 1990)

Barnes, Clifford. 'Vocal Music at the "Théâtres de la Foire" 1697–1762, i: Vaudeville', *Recherches sur la musique française classique*, viii (1968), 141–60

Barr, Raymond Arthur. 'Carl Friedrich Zelter: A Study of the Lied in Berlin during the Late Eighteenth and Early Nineteenth Centuries' (dissertation, University of Wisconsin, 1968)

Barrington, Daines. *Miscellanies* (London, 1781)

Bartels, Adolf. *Otto Ludwigs Werke* (Leipzig, 1900)

Barthold, Friedrich Wilhelm. *Die geschichtlichen Persönlichkeiten in Jacob Casanova's Memoiren* (Berlin, 1846)

Bartl, Franz Conrad. *Nachrichten von der Harmonika* (Prague, 1796)

Bartsch, Karl. *Die lateinischen Sequenzen des Mittelalters in musikalicher und rhythmischer Beziehung* (Rostock, 1868)

Barzun, Jacques and R. H. Bowen, trans. and ed., *Rameau's Nephew* (Indianapolis, 1964)

Baselt, Bernd, 'Georg Friedrich Händels "Ode for St. Cecilia's Day" und ihre Bearbeitung durch Wolfgang Amadè Mozart (KV 592)', *Händel-Jahrbuch*, xxxviii (1992), 94–8

Batka, Richard. *Studien zur Geschichte der Musik in Böhmen* (Prague, 1902)

Batka, Richard. *Geschichte der Musik in Böhmen* (Prague, 1906)

Batka, Richard, ed. *W. A. Mozarts gesammelte Poesien* (Prague, 1906)

Bauer, Günther G. 'Spielen in Salzburg im 18. Jahrhundert', *Homo ludens: Der spielende Mensch. Internationale Beiträge des Institutes für Spielforschung und Spielpädagogik an der Hochschule "Mozarteum" Salzburg*, i (1991), 115–47

Bauer, Günther G. '"Das Billardspiel liebte er leidenschaftlich." W.A. Mozart der Billard- und Kegelspieler', *Homo ludens: Der spielende Mensch. Internationale Beiträge des Institutes für Spielforschung und Spielpädagogik an der Hochschule Mozarteum*, v (1995), 167–228

Bauer, Günther G. 'Bölzelschießen – das "Dartfieber" der Mozartzeit: Salzburg 1770–1795', *Automatenspiele: Homo ludens: Der spielende Mensch. Internationale Beiträge des Institutes für Spielforschung und Spielpädagogik, Universität Mozarteum, Salzburg 9 (1999)* (Munich and Salzburg, 1999), 159–201

Bauer, Günther G. '"Wer nicht spielen kann, dem traut man heutigen Tags kaum gute Sitten zu." Die Spiele der Nannerl Mozart', *Maria Anna Mozart: Die Künstlerin und ihre Zeit*, ed. Siegrid Düll und Otto Neumaier (Möhnesee, 2001), 49–71

Bauer, Günther G. *Mozart: Glück Spiel und Leidenschaft*, second edition (Bad Honnef, 2005)

Bauer, Ludwig Amandus. *Schriften* (Stuttgart, 1847)

Bauer, Wilhelm, Otto Erich Deutsch, Joseph Heinz Eibl and Ulrich Konrad, *Mozart: Briefe und Aufzeichnungen* (Kassel, 1962–2006)

Bauman, Thomas. *North German Opera in the Age of Goethe* (Cambridge, 1985)

Bauman, Thomas. *W. A. Mozart: Die Entführung aus dem Serail* (Cambridge, 1987)

Bauman, Thomas. 'At the North Gate: Instrumental Music in *Die Zauberflöte*', *Mozart's Operas*, ed. Daniel Heartz (Berkeley, 1990), 277–98

Bauman, Thomas. 'Mozart's Belmonte', *Early Music*, xix/4 (1991), 557–62

Bauman, Thomas. 'On Completing the Requiem', *Mozart-Jahrbuch 1991: Bericht über den Internationalen Mozart-Kongreß Salzburg 1991*, 494–8

Bauman, Thomas. 'Requiem, but No Piece', *19th-Century Music*, xv (1991), 151–61

Bauman, Thomas. 'The Three Trials of Don Giovanni', *The Pleasures and Perils of Genius: Mostly Mozart*, ed. Peter Ostwald and Leonard S. Zegans (Madison, WI, 1993), 133–44

Baumgart, Friedrich. 'Die erste Aufführung des Händel'schen Messias in Breslau im Jahre 1788', *Abhandlungen der Schlesischen Gesellschaft für vaterländische Cultur* (Breslau, 1862)

Beales, Derek. 'Court, Government and Society in Mozart's Vienna', *Wolfgang Amadè Mozart: Essays on his Life and his Music*, ed. Stanley Sadie (Oxford, 1996), 3–20

Beard, Harry R. 'Figaro in England: Productions of Mozart's Opera, and the Early Adaptations of it in England Before 1850', *Maske und Kothurn*, x (1964), 498–513

Beaussant, Philippe. 'Le récitatif lulliste', *Goûts réunis*, iii (1978), 1–13

Becher, A. J. 'Die Mozartfeier zu Salzburg als Musikfest', *Sonntags-Blätter für heimathliche Interessen*, ed. Ludwig August Frankl (Vienna, [2 October 1842]), 713–17

Beck, Rudolf. 'Geschichte und Genealogie der Hofmusikerfamilie Cannabich, 1707–1806', *Archiv für Musikwissenschaft*, xxxiv (1977), 298–309

Becker, Carl Ferdinand. 'Die Klaviersonate in Deutschland', *Neue Zeitschrift für Musik*, vii (1837), 25–6, 29–30 and 33–4

Becq, Annie. *Genèse de l'esthétique française moderne: De la raison classique à l'imagination créatrice, 1680–1815* (Pisa, 1984)

Beechey, Gwilym. 'Thomas Linley, Junior: His Life, Work and Times' (dissertation, University of Cambridge, 1965)

Beitrag zur pfälzischen Schaubühne (Mannheim, 1780)

Bekker, Paul. *Beethoven* (Berlin, 1911)

Belli-Gontard, Maria. *Leben in Frankfurt am Main* (Frankfurt, 1850)

Bellina, Anna Laura, ed. *Ranieri Calzabigi: Scritti teatrali e letterari* (Rome, 1994)

Bellucci la Salandra, L. 'Opere teatrali serie e buffe di Nicolò Piccinni dal 1754 al 1794', *Note d'archivio per la storia musicale*, xii (1935), 43–54, 114–25 and 235–48

Beránek, Jirí. 'Zum musikalischen Rahmenprogramm während der böhmischen Krönungsfeierlichkeiten für Leopold II. im Jahr 1791: Bemerkungen zu einem Problem der Mozart-Historiographie', *Mitteilungen der Internationalen Stiftung Mozarteum*, xliii/3–4 (1995), 48–69

Berchtold zu Sonnenburg, Johann Baptist Franz. 'Noch einige Anekdoten aus Mozarts Kinderjahren. Mitgetheilt von dessen Schwester, der Reichsfreyin Frau von Berchtold zu Sonnenburg', *Allgemeine musikalische Zeitung*, ii (1799/1800), 300–1

Berger, Karl. *Schiller* (Munich, 1914)

Berger, Karol. 'The First-Movement Punctuation Form in Mozart's Piano Concertos', *Mozart's Piano Concertos: Text, Context, Interpretation*, ed. Neal Zaslaw (Ann Arbor, MI, 1996), 239–59

Berger, Ludwig. 'Erläuterungen eines Mozartschen Urtheils über Muzio Clementi', *Caecilia*, x (1829), 238–40

Bergeron, Katharine. 'The Castrato as History', *Cambridge Opera Journal*, viii (1996), 167–84

Bergh, Herman van den. *Giambattista Casti (1724–1803): L'homme et l'œuvre* (Amsterdam and Brussels, 1951)

Berkovec, Jirí. *Musicalia v pražském periodickém tisku 18. století* [Music references in 18th-century Prague periodicals] (Prague, 1989)

Berlioz, Hector. *A travers chants* (Paris, 1862)

Bernardin, Napoléon Maurice. *La Comédie italienne en France et les Théâtres de la foire et du boulevard (1570–1791)* (Paris, 1902)

Bernoulli, Edward. *Syntagma Musicum* (Leipzig, 1916)

Berwaldt, Jacek. 'Życie Feliksa Janiewicza' [Life], *Muzyka* , xi/3–4 (1966), 98–105

Berwaldt, Jacek. 'Twórczość Feliksa Janiewicza' [Work], *Muzyka*, xii/1 (1967), 44–58

Bettelheim, Anton. *Beaumarchais: Eine Biographie*, second edition (Frankfurt, 1911)

Betzwieser, Thomas. 'Singspiel in Mannheim: *Der Kaufmann von Smyrna* von Abbé Vogler', *Mozart und Mannheim* (Mannheim, 1991), 119–44

Betzwieser, Thomas. 'Auf der Suche nach der verlorenen "Zaide": Die Probleme mit Mozarts Opernfragment', *Österreichische Musikzeitschrift*, lxi/5 (2006), 16–24

Bevan, Clifford. 'The low brass', *The Cambridge Companion to Brass Instruments*, ed. Trevor Herbert and John Wallace (Cambridge, 1997), 143–56

Bévotte, Georges Gendarme de. *Le festin de pierre avant Molière: Dorimon – de Villiers – Scénario des Italiens – Cicognini* (Paris, 1907)

Bévotte, Georges Gendarme de. *La légende de Don Juan: Son évolution dans la littérature, des origines au romantisme* (Paris, 1911)

Beyer, Franz. 'Zur Neuinstrumentation des Mozart-Requiems: Eine Werkstattbetrachtung', *Musikalische Aufführungspraxis und Edition: Johann Sebastian Bach, Wolfgang Amadeus Mozart, Ludwig van Beethoven* (Regensburg, 1990), 81–121

Beyschlag, Adolf. *Die Ornamentik der Musik* (Leipzig, 1908)

Biba, Otto. 'Ludwig Ritter von Köchel (1800–1877): Zur Erinnerung an seinen vor 100 Jahren erfolgten Tod', *Österreichische Musikzeitschrift*, xxii (1977), 310–17

Biba, Otto. 'Ludwig Ritter von Köchels Verdienste um die Mozart-Gesamtausgabe', *Bürgerliche Musikkultur im 19. Jahrhundert*, ed. Rudolph Angermüller (Salzburg, 1980), 93–104

Biba, Otto. '"Par Monsieur François Comte de Walsegg"', *Mitteilungen der Internationalen Stiftung Mozarteum*, xxix/3–4 (1981), 34–40

Biba, Otto. 'Nachrichten zu Mozart in Briefen seiner Zeitgenossen: Unbeachtete Dokumente aus dem Archiv der Gesellschaft der Musikfreunde in Wien', *Mozartiana: The Festschrift for the Seventieth Birthday of Professor Ebisawa Bin*, ed. Yoshihiko Tokumaru (Tokyo, 2001), 607–24

Biba, Otto. 'Wiener Freimaurer-Musiken – nicht von Mozart: Nachweise und Rezeption', *Mozart. Le arie di concerto. Mozart e la musica massonica dei suoi tempi / Die Konzertarien. Mozart und die Freimaurermusik seiner Zeit. Atti del Convegno internationale di studi Rovereto 26–27 Settembre 1998 / Bericht des internationalen Kongresses Rovereto 26.–27. September 1998*, ed. Rudolph Angermüller and Giacomo Fornari (Bad Honnef, 2001), 233–41

Biedenfeld, Ferdinand Leopold Carl von. *Die komische Oper der Italiener, der Franzosen und der Deutschen* (Leipzig, 1848)

Bieler, Maria. *Binärer Satz – Sonate – Konzert: Johann Christian Bachs Klaviersonaten op. V im Spiegel barocker Formprinzipien und ihrer Bearbeitung durch Mozart* (Kassel, 2002)

Biener, Roland. 'Zu Leopold Mozarts Liedern', *Acta Mozartiana*, i/3–4 (2003), 105–17

Birsak, Kurt and Manfred König. *Das große Salzburger Blasmusikbuch* (Salzburg, 1983)

Bischoff, Ferdinand. 'Zur Geschichte der Frau Magdalena Hofdemel', *Mitteilungen der Mozart-Gemeinde in Berlin*, i (1900), 304–6

Bisesti, Luana und Emanuela Muzi. *Un'architettura iniziatica: Il Giardino Bridi a Rovereto dall'abbandono al recupero. Relazione storica* (Milan, 1990)

Bisesti, Luana and Emanuela Muzi. 'Giuseppe Antonio Bridi: Un amico Roveretano di W. A. Mozart', *W. A. Mozart: Associazione Mozart Italia*, ii/1 (1993), 7–9

Bitter, Christof. *Wandlungen in den Inszenierungsformen des 'Don Giovanni' von 1787 bis 1928* (Regensburg, 1961)

Björnstahl, Jacob Jonas. *Jacob Jonas Björnstahl's Briefe auf seinen ausländischen Reisen*, second edition (Leipzig and Rostock, 1780–83)

Blanchetti, Francesco. 'Tipologia musicale dei concertati nell'opera buffa di Giovanni Paisiello', *Rivista italiana di musicologia*, xix (1984), 234–60

Blank, Hugo. 'Jean-Jacques Rousseaus Devin du village und sein Weg über Favart zu Mozarts Bastien und Bastienne', *Schweizer Jahrbuch für Musikwissenschaft*, xviii (1998), 11–122

Blankenburg, Walter. *Die Messe* (Kassel, 1985)

Blaukopf, Herta. 'Max Kalbecks Don Giovanni-Text von 1905: Ein Beitrag zum 200–Jahrjubiläum der Oper aller Opern', *Nachrichten zur Mahler-Forschung*, xviii (October 1987), 12–15

Blaukopf, Herta. 'Musiktheater als Gesamtkunstwerk: Am Beispiel von Gustav Mahlers 'Don Giovanni'-Produktion in Budapest und Wien', *Das Musiktheater um die Jahrhundertwende: Wien – Budapest um 1900*, ed. Reinhard Farkas (Vienna, 1990), 11–16

Blazin, Dwight, 'The Two Versions of Mozart's Divertimento K. 113', *Music & Letters*, lxxiii (1992), 32–47

Bloch, Henry. 'Tommaso Traetta's Reform of Italian Opera', *Collectanea historiae musicae*, iii (1962–3), 5–13

Blomhert, Bastiaan. *The Harmoniemusik of Die Entführung aus dem Serail by Wolfgang Amadeus Mozart: A Study of its Authority and a Critical Edition* (The Hague, 1987)

Blomhert, Bastiaan. 'Mozart's own 1782 Harmoniemusik based on "Die Entführung aus dem Serail" and its place in the repertory for wind ensembles', *Mozart-Studien*, xii (2003), 77–113

Blume, Friedrich. 'Die formgeschichtliche Stellung der Klavierkonzerte Mozarts', *Mozart-Jahrbuch*, ii (1924), 83–107

Blümml, Emil Karl. 'Der Violinist Franz de Paula Hofer: Freund und Schwager Mozarts', *Mozarteums-Mitteilungen*, ii (1919), 17–24

Blümml, Emil Karl. 'Josefa Weber-Hofer: Die erste "Königin der Nacht"', *Mozarteums-Mitteilungen*, i (1919), 7–8

Blümml, Emil Karl. 'Mozarts Kinder: Eine Matrikelstudie', *Mozarteums-Mitteilungen*, i (1919), 1–6

Blümml, Emil Karl. 'Johann von Thorwart', *Mozarteums-Mitteilungen*, ii (1920), 81–91

Blümml, Emil Karl. 'Karl Ludwig Gieseke als Gelegenheitsdichter', *Mozarteums-Mitteilungen*, ii (1920), 112–21 and iii (1920), 25–8

Blümml, Emil Karl. *Aus Mozarts Freundes- und Familienkreis* (Vienna, 1923)

Blümml, Emil Karl. 'Ausdeutungen der "Zauberflöte"', *Mozart-Jahrbuch*, i (1923), 109–46

Blümner, Heinrich. *Geschichte des Theaters in Leipzig* (Leipzig, 1818)

Blumner, Martin. *Geschichte der Sing-Akademie zu Berlin* (Berlin, 1891)

Boas, Hans. 'Lorenzo da Ponte als Wiener Theaterdichter', *Sammelbände der Internationalen Musikgesellschft*, xv (1913/14), 325–38

Boberski, Heiner. *Das Theater der Benediktiner an der alten Universität Salzburg (1617–1778)* (Vienna, 1978)

Bockholdt, Rudolf. 'Der Schlußsatz von Mozarts Streichquintett in C-Dur, KV 515: Bau im Großen und Geschehen im Kleinen', *Mozarts Streichquintette: Beiträge zum musikalischen Satz, zum Gattungskontext und zu Quellenfragen*, ed. Cliff Eisen and Wolf-Dieter Seiffert (Stuttgart, 1994), 103–26

Bockholdt, Rudolf. 'Liebe zu einer unterschätzten Komposition Joseph Haydns: Die Finalsätze von Haydns "Russischem" Quartett in G-Dur und Mozarts "Haydn"-Quartett in d-Moll', *Studien zur Musik der Wiener Klassiker: Eine Aufsatzsammlung zum 70. Geburtstag des Autors*, ed. Christian Speck (Bonn, 2001), 61–70

Bode, Wilhelm F. *Die Tonkunst in Goethes Leben* (Berlin, 1912)

Boecklin, Franz Friedrich Siegmund August, Baron von. *Beyträge zur Geschichte der Musik, besonders in Deutschland* (Freiburg im Breisgau, 1790)

Böhmer, Karl. *Wolfgang Amadeus Mozarts Idomeneo und die Tradition der Karnevalsopern in München* (Tutzing, 1998)

Bohn, Emil. *Die Nationalhymnen der europäischen Völker* (Breslau, 1908)

Boisserée, Sulpiz. *Selbstbiographie, Tagebücher und Briefe*, ed. Mathilde Boisserée (Stuttgart, 1862)

Bolt, Rodney. *Lorenzo Da Ponte: The Adventures of Mozart's Librettist in the Old and New Worlds* (London, 2006)

Bonds, Mark Evan. 'The sincerest form of flattery? Mozart's "Haydn" quartets and the question of influence', *Studi musicali*, xxii/2 (1993), 365–410

Bonds, Mark Evan. 'Ästhetische Prämissen der musikalischen Analyse im ersten Viertel des 19. Jahrhunderts, anhand von Friedrich August Kannes "Versuch einer Analyse der Mozartschen Clavierwerke" (1821)', *Mozartanalyse im 19. und frühen 20. Jahrhundert: Bericht über die Tagung Salzburg 1996*, ed. Gernot Gruber and Siegfried Mauser (Laaber, 1999), 63–80

Bonnet, George-Edgar. *Philidor et l'évolution de la musique française au XVIIIe siècle* (Paris, 1921)

Borgir, Tharald. *The Performance of the Basso Continuo in Italian Baroque Music* (Ann Arbor, 1987)

Born, Ignaz von. 'Ueber die Mysterien der Aegyptier', *Journal für Freymaurer*, i (1784), 15–132

Borowitz, Albert. 'Lully and the Death of Cambert', *Music Review*, xxxv (1974), 231–9

Borrel, Eugène. *Jean-Baptiste Lully: Le cadre, la vie, l'œuvre, la personnalité, le rayonnement, les œuvres, bibliographie* (Paris, 1949)

Bossler, Heinrich Philipp. *Musikalische Korrespondenz der Teutschen Filarmonischen Gesellschaft* (Speier, 1790–2)

Botstein, Leon. 'Nineteenth-century Mozart: The fin de siècle Mozart revival', *On Mozart*, ed. James M. Morris (Cambridge, 1994), 204–26

Botstiber, Hugo. *Geschichte der Ouvertüre und der freien Orchesterformen* (Leipzig, 1913)

Bouissou, Sylvie. 'Ariette', *Dictionnaire de la musique en France aux XVIIe et XVIIIe siècles*, ed. Marcelle Benoit (Paris, 1992)

Bourdelot, Pierre. *Histoire de la musique et de ses effets depuis son origine jusqu'à présent*, ed. Jacques Bonnet (Amsterdam 1722, 1725 and 1726; The Hague and Frankfurt, 1743)

Boyer, Noël. *La Guerre des Bouffons et la musique française* (Paris, 1945)

Brace, Geoffrey. *Anna . . . Susanna: Anna Storace, Mozart's first Susanna: Her life, times and family* (London, 1991)

Branberger, Jan. *Das Konservatorium für Musik in Prag* (Prague, 1911)

Brandenburg, Daniel. 'Giacomo Tritto: *Il convitato di pietra*', *Napoli e il teatro musicale in Europa tra Sette e Ottocento: Studi in onore di Friedrich Lippmann*, ed. Friedrich Lippmann and Bianca Maria Antolini (Florence, 1993), 145–74

Brandes, Johann Christian. *Meine Lebensgeschichte* (Berlin, 1799–1800)

Brandstetter, Gabriele und Gerhard Neumann. 'Biedermeier und Postmoderne: Zur Melancholie des schöpferischen Augenblicks: Mörikes Novelle "Mozart auf der Reise nach Prag" und Shaffers "Amadeus"', *Studien zur Literatur des Frührealismus*, ed. Günter Blamberger (Frankfurt am Main, 1991), 306–37

Branscombe, Peter. 'Music in the Viennese Popular Theatre of the Eighteenth and Early Nineteenth Centuries', *Proceedings of the Royal Musical Association*, xcviii (1971/2), 101–12

Branscombe, Peter. '*Die Zauberflöte*: A lofty sequel and some lowly parodies', *The Publications of the English Goethe Society*, xlviii (1978), 22–36

Branscombe, Peter. *W. A. Mozart: Die Zauberflöte* (Cambridge, 1991)

Branscombe, Peter. 'Mozart as Author', *The Cambridge Mozart Encyclopedia*, ed. Cliff Eisen and Simon P. Keefe (Cambridge, 2005), 333–5

Braunbehrens, Volkmar. *Mozart in Vienna* (New York, 1989)

Brauneis, Walther. 'Exequien für Mozart', *Singende Kirche*, xxxvii (1991), 8–11

Brauneis, Walther. 'Unveröffentlichte Nachrichten zum Dezember 1791 aus einer Wiener Lokalzeitung', *Mitteilungen der Internationalen Stiftung Mozarteum*, xxxix (1991), 165–8

Brauneis, Walther. '". . . wegen schuldigen 1435 f 32 xr": Neuer Archivfund zur Finanzmisere Mozarts im November 1791', *Mitteilungen der Internationalen Stiftung Mozarteum*, xxxix (1991), 159–63

Brauneis, Walther. 'Das Frontispiz im Alberti-Libretto von 1791 als Schlüssel zu Mozarts "Zauberflöte"', *Mitteilungen der Internationalen Stiftung Mozarteum*, xli/3–4 (1993), 49–59

Brauneis, Walther. 'Franz Graf Wallsegg – Mozarts Auftraggeber für das Requiem: Neue Forschungsergebnisse zur Musikpflege auf Schloß Stuppach', *Musik Mitteleuropas in der 2. Hälfte des 18. Jahrhunderts: Bericht über die Internationale musikwissenschaftliche Konferenz Bratislava, 23. bis 25. März 1992*, ed. Pavol Polák (Bratislava, 1993), 207–21

Brauneis, Walther. '"Wir weihen diesen Ort zum Heiligtum . . .": Marginalien zur Uraufführung von Mozarts "Kleiner Freimaurer-Kantate" und des ihm zugeschriebenen Kettenliedes "Zum Schluß der Loge" (ident mit der späteren österreichischen Bundeshymne)', *Österreichische Musikzeitschrift*, xlviii/1 (1993), 12–16

Brauneis, Walther. 'Die Wiener Freimaurer unter Kaiser Leopold II.: Mozarts "Zauberflöte" als emblematische Standortbestimmung', *Studies in Music History presented to H. C. Robbins Landon on his Seventieth Birthday*, ed. Otto Biba and David Wyn Jones (London, 1996), 115–64

Breitinger, Friedrich. 'Ältester väterlicher Abstammungsnachweis aus Augsburg', *Mozartiana: 'Gaulimauli Malefisohu'. Erhebungen von Friedrich Breitinger*, ed. Friederike Prodinger (Salzburg, 1992), 12–13

Breitinger, Friedrich. 'Das Augsburger Bäsle', *Mozartiana: 'Gaulimauli Malefisohu'. Erhebungen von Friedrich Breitinger*, ed. Friederike Prodinger (Salzburg, 1992), 66–74

Breitinger, Friedrich. 'Mozart Nannerls unglücklicher Verehrer', *Mozartiana: 'Gaulimauli Malefisohu'. Erhebungen von Friedrich Breitinger*, ed. Friederike Prodinger (Salzburg, 1992), 75–80

Breitinger, Friedrich. 'Aloisia Lange, die erste große Liebe Mozarts', *Mozartiana: 'Gaulimauli Malefisohu'. Erhebungen von Friedrich Breitinger*, ed. Friederike Prodinger (Salzburg, 1992), 135–41

Bremner, Robert. *The Compleat Tutor for the Violin* (Edinburgh, c1750)

Brenet, Michel. *Grétry: Sa vie et ses œuvres* (Paris, 1884)

Brenet, Michel. 'La librairie musicale en France de 1653 à 1780', *Sammelbände der Internationalen Musikgesellschaft*, viii (1906/7), 401–66

Brenner, Clarence Dietz. *The Théâtre Italien: Its Repertory 1716–1793* (Berkeley, 1961)

Brèque, Jean-Michel. 'Mithridate de Racine à Mozart', *L'avant-scène opéra*, liv (July 1983), 8–13

Brewer, Bruce. 'Rubini, the King of Tenors', *Opera*, xxx (1979), 326–9

Bridi, Giuseppe. *Breve notizie intorno ad alcuni più celebri compositori di musica e cenni sullo stato presente del canto italiano* (Rovereto, 1827)

'Briefe an Salzmann von Gottlieb Hufeland, aus Danzig', *Alsatia*, iii (1853), 91–101

Briefe eines Biedermanns über die Freimaurer in Wien (Munich, 1786)

Briefwechsel des Großherzogs Carl August von Sachsen-Weimar-Eisenach mit Goethe in den Jahren 1775 bis 1828 (Weimar, 1863)

Brink, Guido. *Die Finalsätze in Mozarts Konzerten: Aspekte ihrer formalen Gestaltung und ihrer Funktion als Abschluß des Konzerts* (Kassel, 2000)

Broder, Nathan, ed. *Wolfgang Amadeus Mozart, Symphony in G minor, K. 550: The Score of the New Mozart Edition, Historical Note, Analysis, Views, and Comments* (New York, 1967)

Brook, Barry S. 'The Symphonie Concertante: Its Musical and Sociological Bases', *International Review of the Aesthetics and Sociology of Music*, vi (1975), 9–28

Brooks, William. *Bibliographie critique du théâtre de Quinault* (Paris, 1988)

Brosses, Charles de. *Lettres familières écrites en Italie en 1739 et 1740*, second edition (Paris, 1858)

Broughton, Mrs. Vernon Delves, ed. *Court and Private Life in the Time of Queen Charlotte: Being the Journals of Mrs. Papendiek* (London, 1887)

Brown, A. Peter. 'The Trumpet Overture and Sinfonia in Vienna (1715–1882): Rise, Decline and Reformulation', *Music in Eighteenth-Century Austria*, ed. David Wyn Jones (Cardiff, 1991), 2–69

Brown, A. Peter, 'Haydn and Mozart's 1773 Stay in Vienna: Weeding a Musical Garden', *Journal of Musicology*, x (1992), 192–230

Brown, A. Peter. 'Song', *Oxford Composer Companions: Haydn*, ed. David Wyn Jones (Oxford, 2002), 366–71

Brown, A. Peter. 'Eighteenth-century traditions and Mozart's "Jupiter" symphony K.551', *Journal of Musicology*, xx/2 (2003), 13–69

Brown, Bruce Alan. *Gluck and the French Theatre in Vienna* (Oxford, 1991)

Brown, Bruce Alan. *W. A. Mozart: Così fan tutte* (Cambridge, 1995)

Brown, Bruce Alan. 'Beaumarchais, Paisiello, and the Genesis of *Così fan tutte*', *Wolfgang Amadè Mozart: Essays on his Life and his Music*, ed. Stanley Sadie (Oxford, 1996), 312–38

Brown, Bruce Alan. 'Elementi di classicismo nei balli viennesi di Gasparo Angiolini', *Creature di Prometeo: Il ballo teatrale dal divertimento al dramma – Studi offerti a Aurel M. Milloss*, ed. Giovanni Morelli (Florence, 1996), 121–38

Brown, Bruce Alan. 'Lo specchio francese: Viennese opera buffa and the legacy of French theatre', *Opera buffa in Mozart's Vienna*, ed. Mary Hunter and James Webster (Cambridge, 1997), 50–81

Brown, Bruce Alan. 'Metastasio und das Ballett', *Händel-Jahrbuch*, xlv (1999), 37–63

Brown, Bruce Alan und John A. Rice. 'Salieri's "Così fan tutte"', *Cambridge Opera Journal*, viii/1 (1996), 17–43

Brown, Clive. *Classical and Romantic Performing Practice 1750–1900* (Oxford, 1999)

Brown, Edward. *A Brief Account of Some Travels in divers Parts of Europe, viz. Hungaria, Servia, Bulgaria, Macedonia, Thessaly, Austria, Styria, Carinthia, Carniola, and Friuli. Through a great part of Germany, and The Low-Countries*, second edition (London, 1687)

Brown, Howard Mayer. *Music in the French Secular Theatre 1400–1550* (Cambridge, MA, 1963)

Brown, Howard Mayer. 'Ut musica poesis: Music and Poetry in France in the Late Sixteenth Century', *Early Music History*, xiii (1994), 1–64

Brown, Howard Mayer and Stanley Sadie. *Performance Practice: Music after 1600* (London, 1989)

Brown, Leslie E. 'The *récit* in the Eighteenth-Century *Tragédie en musique*', *Music Review*, xlv (1984), 96–111

Brück, Marion. *Die langsamen Sätze in Mozarts Klavierkonzerten: Untersuchungen zur Form und zum musikalischen Satz* (Munich, 1994)

Brückner, Fritz. 'Georg Benda und das deutsche Singspiel', *Sammelbände der Internationalen Musikgesellschaft*, v (1903/4), 571–621

Brulart de Genlis, Stéphanie Félicité. *Mémoires inédits pour servir à l'histoire des dix-huitième et dix-neuvième siècles* (Paris, 1825–6)

Brusniak, Friedhelm. '". . . um dem europäischen Meister der Töne – Mozart – zu huldigen": Zu einigen weniger bekannten Mozart-Unternehmungen der ersten Hälfte des 19. Jahrhunderts', *Acta Mozartiana*, xlii/1 (1995), 21–31

Brusniak, Friedhelm. 'Organisierte und institutionalisierte Mozart-Pflege in Deutschland im 19. und 20. Jahrhundert', *Musikgeschichte in Mittel- und Osteuropa*, ed. Helmut Loos and Eberhard Möller (Chemnitz, 1997), 69–84

Buch, David J. 'Fairy-tale literature and "Die Zauberflöte"', *Acta musicologica*, lxiv/1 (1992), 30–49

Buch, David J. 'Mozart and the Theater auf der Wieden: New attributions and perspectives', *Cambridge Opera Journal*, ix/3 (1997), 195–232

Buch, David J. 'On Mozart's Partial Autograph of the Duet "Nun, liebes Weibchen", K. 625/592a', *Journal of the Royal Musical Association*, cxxiv (1999), 53–85

Buch, David J. 'On the Context of Mozart's Variations to the Aria, "Ein Weib ist das herrlichste Ding auf der Welt", KV 613', *Mozart-Jahrbuch 1999*, 72–80

Buch, David J. '"Der Stein der Weisen", Mozart, and Collaborative Singspiels at Emanuel Schikaneder's Theater auf der Wieden', *Mozart-Jahrbuch 2000*, 91–126

Buch, David J. 'Texts and contexts: Eighteenth-century performing materials from the archive of the Theater an der Wien and Mozart's *Die Zauberflöte*', *Musical Quarterly*, lxxxiv/2 (2000), 287–322

Buch, David J. 'Die Hauskomponisten am Theater auf der Wieden zur Zeit Mozarts (1789–1791)', *Acta Mozartiana*, xlviii/1–4 (2001), 75–81

Buch, David J. '"Die Zauberflöte", Masonic Opera, and Other Fairy Tales', *Acta musicologica*, lxxvi/2 (2004), 193–219

Buch, David J. 'The Don Juan Tradition, Eighteenth-Century Supernatural Musical Theatre and Vincenzo Righini's "Il convitato di pietra"', *Hudební věda*, xli/3–4 (2004), 295–307

Buch, David J. and Manuela Jahrmärker. *Schikaneders heroisch-komische Oper "Der Stein der Weisen" – Modell für Mozarts Zauberflöte". Kritische Ausgabe des Textbuches* (Göttingen, 2002)

Bücken, Ernst. 'Tagebuch der Gattin Mozarts', *Beiträge zur Forschung: Studien und Mitteilungen aus dem Antiquariat Jacques Rosenthal* (Munich, 1915)

Buelow, George J. 'A Lesson in Operatic Performance Practice by Madame Faustina Bordoni', *A Musical Offering: Essays in Honor of Martin Bernstein*, ed. Edward H. Clinkscale and Claire Brook (New York, 1977), 79–96

Buff, Adolf. 'Mozarts Augsburger Vorfahren', *Zeitschrift des Historischen Vereins für Schwaben*, xviii (1891), 1–36

Buhle, Edward. *Singende Muse an der Pleiße* [*von*] *Sperontes* (Leipzig, 1909 = Denkmäler deutscher Tonkunst xxxv–xxxvi)

Bulthaupt, Heinrich. *Dramaturgie der Oper* (Leipzig, 1887)

Burckhardt, Carl August Hugo. *Das Repertoire des Weimarer Theaters unter Goethes Leitung* (Hamburg and Leipzig, 1891)

Burdach, Konrad. 'Schillers Chordrama und die Geburt des tragischen Stils aus der Musik', *Deutsche Rundschau*, cxlii (1910), 232–62, 400–33 and cxliii (1910), 91–112

Burney, Charles. *The Present State of Music in France and Italy, or the Journal of a Tour through those Countries, undertaken to collect Materials for a General History of Music* (London, 1771)

Burney, Charles. *The Present State of Music in Germany, the Netherlands, and the United Provinces, or the Journal of a Tour through those Countries, undertaken to collect Materials for a General History of Music* (London, 1773)

Burney, Charles. *Carl Burney's Tagebuch seiner Musikalischen Reisen* (Hamburg, 1773)

Burney, Charles. *A General History of Music from the Earliest Ages to the Present Period* (London, 1776–89)

Burney, Charles. *An Account of the Musical Performances in Westminster Abbey and the Pantheon, May 26th, 27th, 29th; and June the 3rd and 5th, 1784, in Commemoration of Handel* (London, 1785)

Burney, Charles. *Memoirs of the Life and Writings of the Abate Metastasio* (London, 1796)

Burnham, Scott. 'Mozart's *felix culpa: Così fan tutte* and the Irony of Beauty', *Musical Quarterly*, lxxviii (1994), 77–98

Burrows, Donald. 'London: Commercial Wealth and Cultural Expansion', *The Late Baroque Era from the 1680s to 1740*, ed. George J. Buelow (Englewood Cliffs, NJ, 1994), 355–92

Burton, Humphrey. 'Les académies de musique en France au XVIIIe siècle', *Revue de musicologie*, xxxvii (1955), 122–47

Busby, Thomas. *A General History of Music, from the Earliest Times to the Present* (London, 1819)

Busi, Leonida. *Il Padre G. B. Martini* (Bologna, 1891)

Bustico, Guido. *Pier Alessandro Guglielmi: Appunti biografici* (Massa, 1898)

Cadieux, Daniel. 'Linzer Schmerzensmann: De la *Grande Messe en Ut Mineur* K.427 au fantasme "Ein Kind Wird Geschlagen"', *Mozart-Jahrbuch 2002*, 37–86

Callegari Hill, Laura. *L'Accademia filarmonica di Bologna 1666–1800: Statuti, indici degli aggregati e catalogo degli esperimenti d'esame nell'archivio, con un'introduzione storica* (Bologna, 1991)

Callegari Hill, Laura. 'Padre Martini and the Accademia filarmonica of Bologna', *Musicologia humana: Studies in Honor of Warren and Ursula Kirkendale*, ed. S. Gmeinwieser, D. Hiley and J. Riedlbauer (Florence, 1994), 457–71

Calmus, Georgy. 'Die Beggar's Opera von Gay und Pepusch: Ihre musikalisch-parodistische Seite und ihre Nachahmungen in England', *Sammelbände der Internationalen Musikgesellschaft*, viii (1906/7), 286–335

Calmus, Georgy. *Die ersten deutschen Singspiele von Standfuß und Hiller* (Leipzig, 1908)

Calmus, Georgy. *Zwei Opernburlesken aus der Rokokozeit* (Berlin, 1912)

Calzabigi, Ranieri de'. 'Dissertazione su le poesie drammatiche del signor abate Pietro Metastasio', *Poesie del signor abate Pietro Metastasio* (Paris, 1755)

Cambiasi, Pompeo. *La Scala 1778–1906* (Milan, 1906)

Camesi, David. 'Eighteenth-Century Conducting Practices', *Journal of Research in Music Education*, xviii (1970), 365–76

Campan, Mme de. *Mémoires sur la vie privée de Marie Antoinette* (Paris, 1827)

Campana, Alessandra. 'La campagnia di Pasquale Bondini: Praga 1787' (dissertation, University of Rome, 1987/8)

Campana, Alessandra. 'Giuseppe Lolli da *L'italiana in Londra* a *Don Giovanni*', *Mozart, Padova e la Betulia liberata: Committenza, interpretazione e fortuna delle azioni sacre metastasiane nel '700* (Florence, 1991), 417–22

Campana, Alessandra. 'Il libretto de *Lo sposo deluso*', *Mozart-Jahrbuch 1989/90*, 73–87

Campardon, Émile. *Les spectacles des foires* (Paris, 1880)

Candiani, Rosy. *Libretti e librettisti italiani per Mozart* (Rome, 1994)

Candiani, Rosy. 'Giovanni De Gamerra e il libretto del "Lucio Silla"', *Libretti e librettisti italiani per Mozart* (Rome, 1994), 13–45

Canevazzi, Giovanni. *Papa Clemente IX poeta* (Modena, 1900)

Canova-Green, Marie-Claude. 'Le ballet de cour en France', *Spectaculum Europaeum: Theater and spectacle in Europe/Histoire du spectacle en Europe (1580–1750)* (Wiesbaden, 1999)

Cantone, Gaetana and Franco Carmelo Greco, ed. *Il Teatro del Re: Il San Carlo da Napoli all' Europa* (Naples, 1987)

Capone, Stefano. *Piccinni e l'opera buffa: Modelli e varianti di un genere alla moda* (Foggia, 2002)

Cappelletto, Sandro. *La voce perduta: Vita di Farinelli evirato cantore* (Turin, 1995)

Cardamone, Donna G. *The Canzone villanesca alla napolitana and Related Forms, 1537–1570* (Ann Arbor, 1981)

Cardy, Michael. *The Literary Doctrines of Marmontel* (Oxford, 1982)

Carli Ballola, Giovanni. 'Mozart e l'opera seria di Jommelli, De Majo e Traetta', *Analecta musicologica*, xviii (1978), 138–47

Carlson, David M. 'The Vocal Music of Leopold Mozart (1719–1787): Authenticity, Chronology and Thematic Catalogue' (dissertation, University of Michigan, 1976)

Carmody, Francis J. *Le répertoire de l'Opéra-Comique en vaudevilles de 1708 à 1764* (Berkeley and Los Angeles, 1933)

Carpani, Giuseppe. *Le Haydine*, second edition (Padua, 1823)

Carpani, Giuseppe. 'Lettera del sig. G. Carpani in difesa del Mo. Salieri calumniato dell'avvelenamento del M. Mozart', *Biblioteca Italiana*, xxxv (1824), 262–73

Carter, Tim. *W. A. Mozart: Le nozze di Figaro* (Cambridge, 1987)

Casavola, Franco. *Tommaso Traetta di Bitonto (1727–1779): La vita e le opere* (Bari, 1957)

Casavola, Franco. 'La più grande interprete di Traetta: Caterina Gabrielli', *Tommaso Traetta di Bitonto (1727–1779): La vita e le opere* (Bari, 1957), 103–114

Castelli, Ignaz Franz. *Memoiren meines Lebens* (Vienna, 1861)

Castelli, Ignaz Franz. *Illustriertes Familienbuch zur Unterhaltung & Belehrung häuslicher Kreise*, ed. Österreichischer Lloyd (Vienna, 1852)

Castil-Blaze. *Molière musicien* (Paris, 1852)

Castil-Blaze. *Théâtres lyriques de Paris: L'Académie impériale de musique de 1645 à 1855* (Paris, 1855)

Catanzaro, Christine de and Werner Rainer. *Anton Cajetan Adlgasser (1729–1777): A Thematic Catalogue of His Works* (Hillsdale, NY, 2000)

Cattoretti, Anna. '1771–1773: Gli ultimi quintetti per archi di Giovanni Battista Sammartini, i primi di Luigi Boccherini', *Chigiana*, xliii (1993), 193–229

Cattoretti, Anna, ed. *Giovanni Battista Sammartini and his Musical Environment* (Turnhout, 2004)

Cavett-Dunsby, Esther. *Mozart's Variations Reconsidered: Four Case Studies (K.613, K.501, and the Finales of K.421 (417b) and K.491)* (New York, 1989)

Cerami, Antonella. 'Il Saggio sopra l'opera in musica di Francesco Algarotti: Analisi e critica nel contesto culturale del XVIII secolo' (dissertation, Università degli Studi di Roma La Sapienza, 1988)

Chafe, Eric. *The Church Music of Heinrich Biber* (Ann Arbor, 1987)

Chailley, Jacques. 'Joseph Haydn and the Freemasons', *Studies in Eighteenth-Century Music: A Tribute to Karl Geiringer*, ed. H. C. Robbins Landon and R. E. Chapman (New York and London, 1970), 117–24

Chailley, Jacques. *The Magic Flute Unveiled: Esoteric Symbolism in Mozart's Masonic Opera. An Interpretation of the Libretto and the Music* (Rochester, VT, 1992)

Chambers, David. 'The Earlier "Academies" in Italy', *Italian Academies of the Sixteenth Century*, ed. David Chambers and François Quiviger (London, 1995), 1–14

Chancellor, Valerie E. 'Nancy Storace: Mozart's Susanna', *Opera Quarterly*, vii/2 (1990), 104–24

Chapin, Keith. 'Strict and Free Reversed: The Law of Counterpoint in Koch's *Musikalisches Lexikon* and Mozart's *Zauberflöte*', *Eighteenth-Century Music*, iii/1 (2006), 91–107

Charlton, David. *Grétry and the Growth of Opéra-Comique* (Cambridge, 1986)

Charlton, David. *French Opera 1730–1830: Meaning and Media* (Aldershot, 1999)

Charlton, David and Mark Ledbury, eds. *Michel Sedaine, 1719–1797: Theatre, Opera and Art* (Aldershot, 2000)

Charters, Murray R. 'Abel in London', *Musical Times*, cxiv (1973), 1224–6

Christensen, Jesper B. *Die Grundlagen des Generalbassspiels* (Kassel, 1992)

Christout, Marie-Françoise. *Le ballet de cour au XVIIe siècle* (Geneva, 1987)

Chrysander, Friedrich. 'Zur Partitur des "Don Giovanni"', *Allgemeine musikalische Zeitung*, new series, xi (1876), 529–34

Chrysander, Friedrich. 'Mozarts Lieder', *Allgemeine musikalische Zeitung*, new series, xii (1877), 17–20, 33–7, 54–5, 145–8, 161–4

Chrysander, Friedrich. 'Francesco Antonio Urio', *Allgemeine musikalische Zeitung*, new series, xiii (1878), 513–19, 529–35, 545–50, 561–4, 577–81, 625–9, 641–3, 657–64, 785–9, 801–6, 817–23; xiv (1879), 6–10, 21–6, 36–40, 71–4, 86–9, 101–4, 118–23

Chrysander, Friedrich. 'Mozarts Werke: Litaneien und Vespern', *Allgemeine musikalische Zeitung*, new series, xv (1880), 545–7, 561–3, 577–80, 593–4, 609–13, 625–7, 641–3, 665–6

Chrysander, Friedrich. 'Mozarts Ballettmusik zur Oper "Idomeneo"', *Allgemeine musikalische Zeitung*, new series, xvi (1881), 512–16, 529–34

Chrysander, Friedrich. 'Mozarts Werke: Zaide' *Allgemeine musikalische Zeitung*, new series, xvi (1881), 625–7, 641–4, 657–9, 673–5, 689–94, 705–12, 721–6, 739–44

Chrysander, Friedrich. 'Mozarts Tänze für Orchester', *Allgemeine musikalische Zeitung*, new series, xvi (1881), 756–60, 773–7

Chrysander, Friedrich. 'Mitridate, italienische Oper von Mozart', *Allgemeine musikalische Zeitung*, new series, xvi (1881), 785–8, 801–2, 817–21; xvii (1882), 8–12, 25–7, 36–42, 54–9, 70–4, 85–9, 103–7, 122–4, 893

Chrysander, Friedrich. 'Die Oper Don Giovanni von Gazzaniga und von Mozart', *Vierteljahrsschrift für Musikwissenschaft*, iv (1888), 351–453

Chrysander, Friedrich. 'Ludovico Zacconi als Lehrer des Kunstgesangs', *Vierteljahrsschrift für Musikwissenschaft*, vii (1891), 337–96; ix (1893), 249–310; x (1894), 531–67

Chrysander, Friedrich. *Georg Friedrich Händel*, second edition (Leipzig, 1919)

Chua, Daniel. 'Haydn as Romantic: A Chemical Experiment with Instrumental Music', *Haydn Studies*, ed. W. Dean Sutcliffe (Cambridge, 1999), 120–51

Churgin, Bathia. 'The Italian Symphonic Background to Haydn's Early Symphonies and Opera Overtures', *Haydn Studies: Washington DC 1975*, ed. Jens Peter Larsen, Howard Serwer and James Webster, 329–36

Churgin, Bathia. 'Did Sammartini Influence Mozart's Earliest String Quartets?', *Mozart-Jahrbuch 1991*, 529–39

Churgin, Bathia. 'Sammartini and Boccherini: Continuity and Change in the Italian Instrumental Tradition of the Classic Period', *Chigiana: Luigi Boccherini e la musica strumentale dei maestri italiani. Siena 1993*, new series, xxiii (1993), 171–91

Clark, Caryl. 'Reading and Listening: Viennese *Frauenzimmer* Journals and the Sociocultural Context of Mozartean Opera Buffa', *Musical Quarterly*, lxxxviii/1 (2004), 140–75

Clark, Jonathan Charles Douglas. *English Society 1688–1832* (Cambridge, 1985)

Clark, Kenneth. *The Romantic Rebellion* (London, 1973)

Clark, Mark Ross. 'The enlightened transposition: "Così fan tutte" in Colonial America, Philadelphia, 1785' (D.M.A. dissertation, University of Washington, DC, 1996)

Clarke, Bruce Cooper. 'Albert von Mölk: Mozart Myth-Maker? Study of an 18th-Century Correspondence', *Mozart-Jahrbuch 1995*, 155–91

Clercx, Suzanne. *Grétry, 1741–1813* (Brussels, 1944)

Clive, Peter. *Mozart and His Circle: A Biographical Dictionary* (New Haven and London, 1993)

Cloeter, Hermine. *Häuser und Menschen von Wien* (Vienna, 1915–20)

Cloeter, Hermine. *Johann Thomas Trattner: Ein Großunternehmer im Theresianischen Wien* (Graz, 1952)

Closson, Ernest. 'Pascal Taskin', *Sammelbände der Internationalen Musikgesellschaft*, xii (1910/11), 234–67

Cohen, Hermann. *Die dramatische Idee in Mozarts Operntexten* (Berlin, 1915)

Cohn, Richard L. 'Metric and hypermetric dissonance in the menuetto of Mozart's symphony in G minor, K. 550', *Intégral*, vi (1992), 1–33

Colt, C. F. and Antony Miall. *The Early Piano* (London, 1981)

Conesa, Gabriel. *Trilogie de Beaumarchais: Écriture et dramaturgie* (Paris, 1985)

Conestabile, Giovanni Carlo. *Notizie biografiche di Baldassarre Ferri, musico celebratissimo* (Perugia, 1846)

Constable, M. V. 'The Venetian "Figlie del Coro": Their Environment and Achievement', *Music & Letters*, lxiii (1982), 181–212

Constapel, Britta. *Der Musikverlag Johann André in Offenbach am Main: Studien zur Verlagstätigkeit von Johann Anton André und Verzeichnis der Musikalien von 1800 bis 1840* (Tutzing, 1998)

Contant d'Orville, André-Guillaume. *Histoire de l'opéra bouffon* (Amsterdam and Paris, 1768)

Coquéau, Claude-Philibert. *Entretiens sur l'état de l'Opéra de Paris* (Paris, 1776)

Corneilson, Paul. 'Opera at Mannheim, 1770–1778' (dissertation, University of North Carolina, 1992)

Corneilson, Paul. 'Reconstructing the Mannheim court theatre', *Early Music*, xxv/1 (1997), 63–81

Corneilson, Paul. 'Vogler's Method of Singing', *Journal of Musicology*, xvi (1998), 91–109

Corneilson, Paul. 'An Intimate Vocal Portrait of Dorothea Wendling: Mozart's "Basta, vincesti" – "Ah non lasciarmi, no" K. 295a', *Mozart-Jahrbuch 2000*, 29–45

Corneilson, Paul and Eugene K. Wolf. 'Newly identified manuscripts of operas and related works from Mannheim', *Journal of the American Musicological Society*, xlvii/2 (1994), 244–74

Cornet, Julius. *Die Oper in Deutschland* (Hamburg, 1849)

Corrette, Michel. *L'école d'Orphée, méthode pour apprendre facilement à jouer du violon dans le goût françois et italien avec des principes de musique et beaucoup de leçons* (Paris, 1738)

Coulet, Henri, ed. *Diderot: Les beaux-arts et la musique* (Aix-en-Provence, 1986)

Couvreur, Manuel. *Jean-Baptiste Lully: Musique et dramaturgie au service du prince* (Brussels, 1992)

Couvreur, Manuel. 'Le récitatif lullyste et le modèle de la Comédie-Française', *Entre théâtre et musique: Récitatifs en Europe aux XVIIe et XVIIIe siècles*, ed. Raphaëlle Legrand and Laurine Quétin (Tours, 2000), 33–45

Couvreur, Manuel and Philippe Vendrix. 'Les enjeux théoriques de l'opéra-comique', *L'opéra-comique en France au XVIIIe siècle*, ed. Philippe Vendrix (Liège, 1992), 213–81

Cowart, Georgina. *The Origins of Modern Musical Criticism: French and Italian Music 1600–1750* (Ann Arbor, 1981)

Cowgill, Rachel. 'Re-gendering the libertine, or, The taming of the rake: Lucy Vestris as Don Giovanni on the early 19th-century London stage', *Cambridge Opera Journal*, x/1 (1998), 45–66

Cowgill, Rachel. '"Wise Men from the East": Mozart's Operas and their Advocates in Early Nineteenth-Century London', *Music and British culture, 1785–1914: Essays in honour of Cyril Ehrlich*, ed. Christina Bashford and Leanne Langley (Oxford, 2000), 39–64

Cowgill, Rachel. 'The Halifax *Judas*: An unknown Handel arrangement by Mozart?', *Musical Times*, cxliii (2002), 19–36

Cramer, Carl Friedrich. *Magazin der Musik* (Hamburg, 1783–6)

Cramer, Carl Friedrich. *Anecdotes sur Mozart* (Paris, 1801)

Cristini, C. 'Vita dell'abate Pietro Metastasio', *Opere del signor abate Pietro Metastasio* (Nice, 1785)

Croce, Benedetto. *I teatri di Napoli* (Naples, 1891)

Croll, Gerhard. 'Im tonus peregrinus: Bemerkungen zur "Betulia liberata" von Mozart', *Mozart-Studien*, ii (1993), 73–89

Croll, Gerhard and Kurt Vössing. *Johann Michael Haydn, sein Leben, sein Schaffen, seine Zeit: Eine Bildbiographie* (Vienna, 1987)

Croll, Gerhard and Hans Wagner, ed. *Vita di Giuseppe Afflisio: Lebensgeschichte des Giuseppe Afflisio. Aus dem Nachlaß von Bernhard Paumgartner* (Kassel, 1977)

Csampai, Attila and Dietmar Holland. *Wolfgang Amadeus Mozart: Die Entführung aus dem Serail* (Reinbek bei Hamburg, 1983)

Cucuel, Georges. 'La question des clarinettes dans l'instrumentation du XVIIIe siècle', *Zeitschrift der Internationalen Musikgesellschaft*, xii (1910/11), 280–4

Cucuel, Georges. 'Notes sur Jean-Jacques Rousseau musicien', *Zeitschrift der Internationalen Musikgesellschaft*, xiii (1911/12), 287–92

Cucuel, Georges. 'Quelques documents sur la librairie musicale du XVIIIe siècle', *Sammelbände der Internationalen Musikgesellschaft*, xiii (1911/12), 385–92

Cucuel, Georges. *Les créateurs de l'opéra-comique français* (Paris,1914)

Cudworth, Charles. 'The English Symphonists of the Eighteenth Century', *Proceedings of the Royal Musical Association*, lxxviii (1951/2), 31–51

Curzon, Henri de. *Essai de bibliographie Mozartine: Revue critique des ouvrages relatifs à W. A. Mozart et ses œuvres* (Paris, 1906)

Curzon, Henri de. *Grétry: Biographie critique* (Paris, 1907)

Cuvay, Maria. 'Beiträge zur Lebensgeschichte des Salzburger Hofkapellmeisters Johann Ernst Eberlin', *Mitteilungen der Gesellschaft für Salzburger Landeskunde*, xcv (1955), 179–88

Czucha, Eckehard. 'Mozarts "Die Gans von Kairo": Zum Verhältnis von Satire und Lustspiel am Beispiel eines Opernfragments', *Kairoer Germanistische Studien*, vi (1991), 267–79

Daffner, Hugo. *Die Entwicklung des Klavierkonzertes bis Mozart* (Leipzig, 1906)

Dahms, Sibylle. 'Das musikalische Repertoire des Salzburger Fürsterzbischöflichen Hoftheaters (1775–1803)', *Österreichische Musikzeitschrift*, xxxi (1976), 340–54

Dahms, Sibylle. 'Mozarts Festa teatrale "Ascanio in Alba"', *Österreichische Musikzeitschrift*, xxxi (1976), 15–24

Dahms, Sibylle. 'Étienne Lauchery, der Zeitgenosse Noverres', *Mozart und Mannheim: Mannheim 1991*, 145–55

Dahms, Sibylle. 'Mozart und Noverres "Ballet en action"', *Mozart-Jahrbuch 1991: Bericht über den Internationalen Mozart-Kongreß Salzburg 1991*, 431–7

Dahms, Sibylle. 'Das Repertoire des "Ballet en action": Noverre–Angiolini–Lauchery', *De editione musices: Festschrift Gerhard Croll*, ed. Wofgang Gratzer and Andrea Lindmayer (Laaber, 1992), 125–42

Dahms, Sibylle. 'Entlehnungspraktiken in der zweiten Hälfte des 18. Jahrhunderts und zur Ballettmusik aus Mozarts "Ascanio in Alba"', *Mozart-Jahrbuch 1993*, 133–42

Dahms, Sibylle. 'Tanz und Ballett in Wien zur Zeit Mozarts', *Europa im Zeitalter Mozarts*, ed. Moritz Csáky and Walter Pass (Vienna, 1995), 365–71

Dahms, Sibylle. 'Anmerkungen zu den "Tanzdramen" Angiolinis und Noverres und zu deren Gattungsspezifik', *Tanzdramen – Opéra-comique: Kolloquiumsbericht der Gluck-Gesamtausgabe*, ed. Gabriele Buschmeier and Klaus Hortschansky (Kassel, 2000), 67–73

Dahms, Sibylle. 'Wiener Ballett zur Zeit Metastasios', *Pietro Metastasio: Uomo universale (1698–1782) – Festgabe der Österreichischen Akademie der Wissenschaften zum 300. Geburtstag von Pietro Metastasio*, ed. Andrea Sommer-Mathis (Vienna, 2000), 157–68

Dale, William. *Tschudi, the harpsichord maker* (Boston, 1974)

Danzel, Theodor Wilhelm. *Gottsched und seine Zeit* (Leipzig, 1848)

Da Ponte, Lorenzo. *Memorie di Lorenzo da Ponte, da Ceneda*, second edition (New York, 1829–30)

Darlow, Mark. 'Les parodies du Devin du village de Rousseau et la sensibilité dans l'opéra-comique français', *Revue de la Société Liégeoise de Musicologie*, xiii/xiv (1999), 123–41

Das deutsche Singspiel im 18. Jahrhundert: Colloquium der Arbeitsstelle 18. Jahrhundert, Gesamthochschule Wuppertal, Universität Münster, Amorbach vom 2. bis 4. Oktober 1979 (Heidelberg, 1981)

Daumer, Georg Friedrich. *Aus der Mansarde* (Mainz, 1860–2)

Dauphin, Claude. *Rousseau musicien des Lumières* (Montreal, 1992)

Dauphin, Claude. *La musique au temps des Encyclopédistes* (Ferny, 2001)

Daverio, John. 'Mozart in the nineteenth century', *The Cambridge Companion to Mozart*, ed. Simon P. Keefe (Cambridge, 2003), 171–84

David, Hans T. *Johann Schobert als Sonatenkomponist* (Borna, 1928)

Davies, Peter J. 'The death of Mozart', *Journal of the Royal Society of Medicine*, lxxxiv (1991), 246

Davies, Peter J. 'Mozart's health, illness, and death', *The Pleasures and Perils of Genius: Mostly Mozart*, ed. Peter Ostwald and Leonard S. Zegans (Madison, WI, 1993), 97–115

Davis, Shelley. 'H. C. Koch, the Classic Concerto, and the Sonata-Form Retransition', *Journal of Musicology*, ii (1983), 45–61

Dean, Winton and John Merrill Knapp. *Handel's Operas 1704–1726*, revised edition (Oxford, 1995)

Debrois, Johann. *Urkunde über die vollzogene Krönung S. M. des Königs von Böhmen Leopold des Zweiten* (Prague, 1818)

de Catanzaro, Christine and Werner Rainer, *Anton Cajetan Adlgasser: A Thematic Catalogue of his Works* (Stuyvesant, NY, 2000)

Deffand, Marie de Vichy, marquise du. *Lettres de la Marquise du Deffand à Horace Walpole* (Paris, 1824)

DeFord, Ruth. 'Musical Relationships between the Italian Madrigal and Light Genres in the Sixteenth Century', *Musica disciplina*, xxxix (1985), 107–68

Degrada, Francesco. 'Le sonate per cembalo e per organo di Giovanni Battista Pescetti', *Chigiana*, new series, iii (1966), 89–108

Degrada, Franceso. 'L'opera napoletana', *Storia dell'opera*, ed. Guglielmo Barblan and Alberto Basso (Turin, 1977), i.237–332

Degrada, Francesco. '"Lo frate 'nnamorato" e l'estetica della commedia musicale napoletana', *Napoli e il teatro musicale in Europa tra Sette e Ottocento: Studi in onore di Friedrich Lippmann*, ed. Bianca Maria Antolini and Wolfgang Witzenmann (Florence, 1993), 21–35

Degrada, Francesco. 'Lo Sposo deluso da Cimarosa a Mozart', *Convegno italo-tedesco "Mozart, Paisiello, Rossini e l'opera buffa" (Rom 1993). Bericht*, ed. Markus Engelhardt and Wolfgang Witzenmann (Laaber, 1998), 1–31

Deininger, Heinz Friedrich. 'Die Deutsche Schauspielergesellschaft unter der Direktion von Johann Heinrich Böhm, einem Freunde der Familie Mozart, in Augsburg in den Jahren 1779 und 1780', *Augsburger Mozartbuch* (Augsburg, 1942–3), 299–397

DeJean, Joan, ed. *Le Festin de pierre (Dom Juan)* (Geneva, 1999)

DelDonna, Anthony Robert. 'The Operas of Pietro Alessandro Guglielmi (1728–1804): The Relationship of His Dialect Operas to His *Opere Serie*' (dissertation, Catholic University of America)

Della Corte, Andrea. *L'opera comica italiana nel '700: Studi ed appunti* (Bari, 1923)

Della Corte, Andrea. *Baldassare Galuppi: Profilo critico* (Siena, 1948)

dell'Antonio, Andrew. '"Il compositore deluso": The fragments of *Lo sposo deluso*', *Wolfgang Amadè Mozart: Essays on his Life and his Music*, ed. Stanley Sadie (Oxford, 1996), 403–12

Del Monte, Claudio and Vincenzo Raffaele Segreto, ed. *Christoph Willibald Gluck nel 200o anniversario della morte* (Parma, 1987)

Delporte, Michel. 'Le Don Juan de Mozart à Paris en 1866: Extraits de la Revue Dramatique de Théophile Gautier', *Bulletin de la Société Théophile Gautier*, viii (1986), 85–96

de Médicis, François. 'Chanter pour se faire entendre: Le duo d'influence dans les opéras de Mozart', *Acta musicologica*, lxxiv/1 (2002), 35–54

Demuth, Norman. *French Opera: Its Development to the Revolution* (Horsham, 1963)

DeNora, Tia. *Beethoven and the Construction of Genius: Musical Politics in Vienna, 1792–1803* (Berkeley, CA, 1996)

Dent, Edward J. *Alessandro Scarlatti* (London, 1905)

Dent, Edward J. 'Leonardo Leo', *Sammelbände der Internationalen Musikgesellschaft*, viii (1906/7), 550–66

Dent, Edward J. 'Ensembles and Finales in Eighteenth-Century Italian Opera', *Sammelbände der Internationalen Musikgesellschaft*, xi (1909/10), 543–69 and xii (1910/11), 112–38

Dent, Edward J. *Mozart's Opera: The Magic Flute* (Cambridge, 1911)

Dent, Edward J. 'Giuseppe Maria Buini', *Sammelbände der Internationalen* Musikgesellschaft, xiii (1911/12), 329–54

Dent, Edward J. *Mozart's Operas: A Critical Study*, second edition (Oxford, 1970)

De Nys. Carl. *La musique religieuse de Mozart*, second edition (Paris, 1991)

Derr, Ellwood. 'Composition with Modules: Intersections of Musical Parlance in Works of Mozart and J. C. Bach', *Mozart-Jahrbuch 1997*, 249–91

Desarbres, Nérée. *Deux siècles de l'opéra (1669–1868)* (Paris, 1868)

Désastre, Jean. *Carlo Brioschi: Kuriose Abenteuer eines Sopranisten*, trans. René Rabelais (Zurich, 1903)

Desboulmiers [Jean-Auguste Jullien]. *Histoire du Théâtre de l'Opéra Comique* (Paris, 1770)

Desnoiresterres, Gustave Le Brisoys de. *Gluck et Piccinni* (Paris, 1875)

Detenbeck, L. 'Dramatized Madrigals', *The Science of Buffoonery: Theory and History of the Commedia dell'Arte*, ed. Domenico Pietropaolo (Toronto, 1989), 59–68

Deutsch, Otto Erich. 'Das Freihaus-Theater auf der Wieden', *Mitteilungen des Vereines für Geschichte der Stadt Wien*, xvi (1937), 30–73

Deutsch, Otto Erich. 'Kozeluch ritrovato', *Music & Letters*, xxvi (1945), 47–50

Deutsch, Otto Erich. 'The First Lady Hamilton', *Notes and Queries*, cxcvii (1952), 540–43 and 560–65

Deutsch, Otto Erich. 'Mozarts Nachlaß: Aus den Briefen Konstanzens an den Verlag André', *Mozart-Jahrbuch 1953*, 32–7

Deutsch, Otto Erich. 'Die Mesmers und die Mozarts', *Mozart-Jahrbuch 1954*, 54–64

Deutsch, Otto Erich. 'Innenansicht einer Wiener Freimaurer-Loge', *Wiener Schriften*, v (1957), 96–102

Deutsch, Otto Erich. 'Das Fräulein von Auernhammer', *Mozart-Jahrbuch 1958*, 17–19

Deutsch, Otto Erich. *Mozart und seine Welt in zeitgenössischen Bildern* (Kassel, 1961 = NMA X/32)

Deutsch, Otto Erich. *Mozart: Die Dokumente seines Lebens* (Kassel, 1961; in English as *Mozart: A Documentary Biography*, second edition [London, 1966])

Deutsch, Otto Erich. 'Aus Köchels Jugendtagen', *Festschrift Hans Engel zum siebzigsten Geburtstag*, ed. Horst Heussner (Kassel, 1964), 70–5

Devrient, Eduard. *Geschichte der deutschen Schauspielkunst* (Leipzig, 1848–74)

DiChiera, David. 'The Life and Operas of Gian Francesco de Majo' (dissertation, University of California, Los Angeles, 1962)

Didier, Béatrice. *La musique des Lumières* (Paris, 1985)

Dieckmann, Friedrich. '"Don Giovanni" deutsch: Mozarts "Don Giovanni" in der deutschen Fassung von Schmieder und Neefe, Frankfurt 1789', *Beiträge zur Musikwissenschaft*, xxxiv (1992), 1–78

Dieckmann, Friedrich. 'Mozart im Bilde: Die Porträts der Wiener Jahre', *Gespaltene Welt und ein liebendes Paar. Oper als Gleichnis*, ed. Friedrich Dieckmann (Frankfurt am Main, 1999), 96–104

Dies, Albert. *Biographische Nachrichten von Joseph Haydn* (Vienna, 1810)

Dietrich, Margret, ed., *Das Burgtheater und sein Publikum* (Vienna, 1989)

Dietz, Alexander. *Der Superintendent und erste Hofprediger M. Joh. Hektor Dietz, seine Vorfahren und Nachkommen: Ein Familienbuch* (Frankfurt, 1889)

Diezmann, August, ed. *Aus Weimars Glanzzeit: Ungedruckte Briefe von und über Göthe und Schiller* (Leipzig, 1855)

Diezmann, August. *Goethe-Schiller-Museum* (Leipzig, 1858)

Dill, Charles William. 'The reception of Rameau's *Castor et Pollux* in 1737 and 1754' (dissertation, Princeton University, 1989)

Dill, Charles William. *Monstrous Opera: Rameau and the Tragic Tradition* (Princeton, NJ, 1998)

Di Mauro, Graziella. 'A Stylistic Analysis of Selected Keyboard Sonatas by Baldassare Galuppi (1706–1785)' (dissertation, University of Miami, 1989)

Di Profio, Alessandro and Mariagrazia Melucci, ed. *Niccolò Piccinni, musicista europeo* (Bari, 2002)

Dittersdorf, Karl Ditters von. *Karl von Dittersdorfs Lebensbeschreibung, seinem Sohne in die Feder diktiert* ed. Edgar Istel (Leipzig, 1908)

Dittrich, Marie-Agnes. 'Dichterleid und Damenzank: Zu Salieris "Prima la musica e poi le parole" und Mozarts "Schauspieldirektor"', *Zeit in der Musik in der Zeit: 3. Kongreß für Musiktheorie, 10.–12. Mai 1996, Hochschule für Musik und darstellende Kunst Wien*, ed. Diether de la Motte (Frankfurt am Main, 1997), 90–104

Dixon, Susan M. 'Women in Arcadia', *Eighteenth-Century Studies*, xxxii/xxxiii (1999), 371–5

Dlabač, Jan Bohumír. *Allgemeines historisches Künstler-Lexikon für Böhmen und zum Theil auch für Mähren und Schlesien* (Prague, 1815)

Doering, Johann Michael Heinrich. *Leben A. L. v. Schlözer's* (Zeitz, 1836)

Dohrn, Carl August. *Neue Zeitschrift für Musik*, xi (1844), 168

Dominicus, Alexander. *Coblenz unter dem letzten Kurfürsten von Trier* (Koblenz, 1869)

Dömling, Wolfgang. 'Musikgeschichte als Stilgeschichte: Bemerkungen zum musikhistorischen Konzept Guido Adlers', *International Review of the Aesthetics and Sociology of Music*, iv (1973), 35–49

Donath, Gustav. 'Florian Leopold Gaßmann als Opernkomponist', *Studien zur Musikwissenschaft*, ii (1914), 34–211

Doolittle, James. *Rameau's Nephew: A Study of Diderot's 'Second Satire'* (Paris, 1960)

Dopsch, Heinz. *Geschichte Salzburgs: Stadt und Land* (Salzburg, 1981–3)

Dörffel, Alfred. *Geschichte der Gewandhauskonzerte zu Leipzig* (Leipzig, 1884)

Dotoli, Giovanni. *Le jeu de Dom Juan* (Fasano, 2004)

Douen, Emmanuel-Orentin. *Clément Marot et le Psautier Huguenot* (Paris, 1878–9)

Doussot, Joëlle-Elmyre. *Grimm et la musique d'après 'La correspondance'* (Paris, 1994)

Downes, Edward O. 'The Operas of Johann Christian Bach as a Reflection of the Dominant Trends in Opera Seria 1750–1780' (dissertation, Harvard University, 1958)

Dresden Mozartverein. *Festschrift zum hundertjährigen Bestehen des Mozarts-Vereins zu Dresden 1886–1996* (Dresden, 1996)

Dreßler, Ernst Christoph. *Gedanken, die Vorstellung der Alceste, ein deutsches ernsthaftes Singspiel betreffend* (Frankfurt and Leipzig, 1774)

Dreßler, Ernst Christoph. *Theater-Schule für die Deutschen, das ernsthafte Singe-Schauspiel betreffend* (Hanover, 1777)

Dreyfus, Laurence. *Bach's Continuo Group* (Cambridge, MA, 1987)

Druilhe, Paule. *Monsigny* (Paris, 1955)

DuBois, Ted Alan. 'Christian Friedrich Daniel Schubart's Ideen zu einer Ästhetik der Tonkunst: An Annotated Translation' (dissertation, University of Southern California, 1983)

Dubowy, Norbert. *Arie und Konzert: Zur Entwicklung der Ritornellanlage im 17. und frühen 18. Jahrhundert* (Munich, 1991)

Duda, Erich. *Das musikalische Werk Franz Xaver Süßmayrs: Thematisches Werkverzeichnis (SmWV) mit ausführlichen Quellenangaben und Skizzen der Wasserzeichen* (Kassel, 2000)

Duda, Gunther, 'Die Totenmaske W. A. Mozarts', *Der Quell*, xii (1960), 79–85

Dudley, Sherwood. 'Les premières versions françaises du *Mariage de Figaro* de Mozart', *Revue de musicologie*, lxix (1983), 55–83

Dufourcq, Norbert. 'Concerts parisiens et associations de "Symphonistes"', *Revue belge de musicologie*, viii (1954), 46–55

Dufourcq, Norbert, ed. *La musique à la cour de Louis XIV et de Louis XV, d'après les 'Mémoires' de Sourches et Luynes, 1681–1758* (Paris, 1970)

Düll, Siegrid und Otto Neumaier, ed. *Maria Anna Mozart: Die Künstlerin und ihre Zeit* (Möhnesee, 2001)

Du Mont, Mary. *The Mozart–Da Ponte operas: An annotated bibliography* (Westport, CT, 2000)

Dunning, Albert, ed. *Intorno a Locatelli: Studi in occasione del tricentenario della nascita di Pietro Antonio Locatelli* (Lucca, 1995)

Düntzer, Johann Heinrich Joseph. *Frauenbilder aus Goethes Jugendzeit* (Stuttgart, 1852)

Durand-Sendrail, Béatrice, ed. *Denis Diderot: Écrits sur la musique* (Paris, 1987)

Durante, Sergio. '"La clemenza di Tito" and Other Two-Act Reductions of the Late 18th Century', *Mozart-Jahrbuch 1991: Bericht über den Internationalen Mozart-Kongreß Salzburg 1991*, 733–41

Durante, Sergio. 'Mozart and the Idea of "Vera Opera": A Study of "La Clemenza di Tito"' (dissertation, Harvard University, 1993)

Durante, Sergio. 'Le Scenographie di Pietro Travaglia per "La clemenza di Tito" (Praga, 1791): Problemi di identificazione ed implicazioni', *Mozart-Jahrbuch 1994*, 157–69

Durante, Sergio. 'The Chronology of Mozart's "La clemenza di Tito" Reconsidered', *Music & Letters*, lxxx (1999), 560–93

Durante, Sergio. 'Mozarts *La clemenza di Tito* und der deutsche Nationalgedanke: Ein Beitrag zur Titus-Rezeption im 19. Jahrhundert', *Die Musikforschung*, liii/4 (2000), 389–400

Dutens, Louis. *Mémoires un voyageur qui se repose* (Paris, 1786)

Eberhard, Johann August. 'Abhandlung über das Melodrama', *Neue vermischte Schriften* (Halle, 1788), 1–22

Ebisawa, Bin. 'The Requiem: Mirror of Mozart performance history', *Early Music*, xx/2 (1992), 279–94

Ebisawa, Bin. 'The Requiem of Mozart and the Attitude toward Death in Late Eighteenth-Century Europe', *Mozart and Japan: Selected Papers*, ed. Bin Ebisawa and Chieko Watanabe (Tokyo, 2001), 109–22

Eckelmeyer, Judith A. *The cultural context of Mozart's Magic Flute: Social, aesthetic, philosophical* (Lewiston, NY, 1991)

Eckermann, Johann Peter. *Gespräche mit Goethe* (Leizpig, 1908)

Edelmann, Bernd. 'Dichtung und Komposition in Mozarts "Ave verum corpus" KV 618', *Mozart-Studien*, ii (1993), 11–55

Eder, Petrus, OSB. *Salzburger Klaviermusik des 18. Jahrhunderts* (Salzburg, 2005 = Denkmäler der Musik in Salzburg xvi)

Edge, Dexter. 'Mozart's Fee for "Così fan tutte"', *Journal of the Royal Musical Association*, cxvi/2 (1991), 211–35

Edge, Dexter. 'Mozart's Viennese Orchestras', *Early Music*, xx/1 (1992), 64–88

Edge, Dexter. 'A Newly Discovered Autograph Source for Mozart's Aria, K. 365a (Anh. 11a)', *Mozart-Jahrbuch 1996*, 177–96

Edge, Dexter. 'Mozart's Reception in Vienna, 1787–1791', *Wolfgang Amadè Mozart: Essays on his Life and his Music*, ed. Stanley Sadie (Oxford, 1996), 66–117

Edge, Dexter. 'Mozart's Viennese Copyists' (dissertation, University of California at Los Angeles, 2001)

Ehrard, Jean, ed. *De l'Encyclopédie à la contre-révolution: Jean-François Marmontel (1723–1799): Études réunies* (Clermont-Ferrand, 1970)

Ehrlich, Cyril. 'Economic History and Music', *Proceedings of the Royal Musical Association*, ciii (1976/7), 188–99

Eibl, Joseph Heinz. 'Die Mozarts und der Erzbischof', *Österreichische Musikzeitschrift*, xxx (1975), 329–41

Eibl, Joseph Heinz. *Wolfgang Amadeus Mozart: Chronik eines Lebens* (Kassel, 1977)

Eibl, Joseph Heinz. *Mozart: Die Dokumente seines Lebens. Addenda und Corrigenda* (Kassel, 1978)

Eibl, Joseph Heinz. 'Zur Überlieferungsgeschichte der Bäsle-Briefe', *Mitteilungen der Internationalen Stiftung Mozarteum*, xxvii (1979), 9–17

Eichborn, Hermann. *Die Trompete in alter und neuer Zeit* (Leipzig, 1881)

Eichborn, Hermann. *Das alte Clarinblasen auf Trompeten* (Leipzig, 1894)

Eichenauer, Jürgen, ed. *Johann Anton André (1775–1842) und der Mozart-Nachlass: Ein Notenschatz in Offenbach am Main. (Ausstellung: 29.1.–28.5.2006)* (Weimar, 2006)

Eigeldinger, Jean-Jacques, ed. *Jean-Jacques Rousseau et la musique* (Neuchâtel, 1988)

Einstein, Alfred. 'Calzabigis "Erwiderung" von 1790', *Gluck-Jahrbuch*, ii (1915), 56–102 and iii (1917), 25–50

Einstein, Alfred. *Lebensläufe deutscher Musiker von ihnen selbst erzählt, iii: Adalbert Gyrowetz* (Leipzig, 1915)

Einstein, Alfred. *Gluck* (London, 1936)

Eisen, Cliff. 'Contributions to a New Mozart Documentary Biography', *Journal of the American Musicological Society*, xxxix/3 (1984), 615–32

Eisen, Cliff. 'Mozart Apocrypha', *Musical Times*, cxxvii (1986), 683–5

Eisen, Cliff. 'Leopold Mozart Discoveries', *Mitteilungen der Internationalen Stiftung Mozarteum*, xxxv (1987), 1–10

Eisen, Cliff. 'New Light on Mozart's "Linz" Symphony, K425', *Journal of the Royal Musical Association*, cxiii (1988), 81–96

Eisen, Cliff. 'Problems of Authenticity among Mozart's Early Symphonies: The Examples of K. Anh. 220 (16a) and 76 (42a)', *Music & Letters*, lxx (1989), 505–16

Eisen, Cliff. 'Salzburg under Church Rule', *The Classical Era: From the 1740s to the End of the 18th Century*, ed. Neal Zaslaw (London, 1989), 166–87

Eisen, Cliff. 'Dissemination of Mozart's music', *The Mozart Compendium: A Guide to Mozart's Life and Music*, ed. H. C. Robbins Landon (London and New York, 1990), 185–204

Eisen, Cliff. *Leopold Mozart: Ausgewählte Werke*, i: *Sinfonien* (Bad Reichenhall, 1990)

Eisen, Cliff. 'The Mozarts' Salzburg Copyists: Aspects of Attribution, Chronology, Text, Style and Performance Practice', *Mozart Studies*, ed. Cliff Eisen (Oxford, 1991), 253–307

Eisen, Cliff. *New Mozart Documents* (London, 1991; in German as *Mozart: Die Dokumente seines Lebens. Addenda. Neue Folge* (Kassel, 1997 = NMA X/31/2)

Eisen, Cliff. 'Mozart's Salzburg Orchestras', *Early Music*, xx (1992), 65–79

Eisen, Cliff. 'Mozart and the Viennese String Quintet', *Mozarts Streichquintette: Beiträge zum musikalischen Satz, zum Gattungskontext und zu Quellenfragen*, ed. Cliff Eisen and Wolf-Dieter Seiffert (Stuttgart, 1994), 127–52

Eisen, Cliff. *Orchestral Music in Salzburg 1740–1780* (Madison, WI, 1994 = Recent Researches in the Music of the Classic Period xl)

Eisen, Cliff. 'Mozart e l'Italia: Il Ruolo di Salisburgo', *Rivista italiana di musicologia*, xxx (1995), 51–84

Eisen, Cliff. 'The Orchestral Bass Part in Mozart's Salzburg Keyboard Concertos: The Evidence of the Authentic Copies', *Mozart's Piano Concertos: Text, Context, Interpretation*, ed. Neal Zaslaw (Ann Arbor, MI, 1996), 411–25

Eisen, Cliff. 'The Salzburg Symphonies: A Biographical Interpretation', *Wolfgang Amadè Mozart: Essays on His Life and his Music*, ed. Stanley Sadie (Oxford, 1996), 178–212

Eisen, Cliff. 'Another Look at the "Corrupt Passage" in Mozart's G minor Symphony K550: Its Sources, "Solution" and Implications for the Composition of the Final Trilogy', *Early Music*, xxv (1997), 373–81

Eisen, Cliff. *Christoph W. Gluck: Four Dances from Don Juan, arranged by Leopold Mozart* (Wellington, New Zealand, 1997)

Eisen, Cliff. 'The Mozarts' Salzburg Music Library', *Mozart Studies 2*, ed. Cliff Eisen (Oxford, 1997), 85–138

Eisen, Cliff. 'The Present State of Research on Leopold Mozart's Symphonies', *Beiträge des Internationalen Leopold-Mozart-Kolloquiums Augsburg 1994*, ed. Joseph Mančal and Wolfgang Plath (Augsburg, 1997), 57–68

Eisen, Cliff. 'Mozart and the Four-Hand Sonata K. 19d', *Haydn, Mozart, & Beethoven: Studies in the Music of the Classical Period. Essays in Honour of Alan Tyson*, ed. Sieghard Brandenburg (Oxford, 1998), 91–9

Eisen, Cliff. 'Concerto, §3: The Classical Period', *The New Grove Dictionary of Music and Musicians*, second edition ed. Stanley Sadie and John Tyrrell (London, 2001), vi.246–51

Eisen, Cliff. 'Notation and Interpretation', *A Performer's Guide to Music of the Classical Period*, ed. Anthony Burton (London, 2002), 15–38

Eisen, Cliff. 'Mozart's Chamber Music', *The Cambridge Companion to Mozart*, ed. Simon P. Keefe (Cambridge, 2003), 105–17

Eisen, Cliff. 'Don Giovanni', *Encyclopedia of the Romantic Era*, ed. Christopher John Murray (London, 2004), 281–2

Eisen, Cliff. 'Mozart, Johann Georg Leopold', *Die Musik in Geschichte und Gegenwart: Allgemeine Enzyklopädie der Musik begründet von Friedrich Blume. Zweite, neubearbeitete Ausgabe*, ed. Ludwig Finscher (Kassel, 2004), Personenteil xii.579–90

Eisen, Cliff. 'The primacy of performance: Text, act and continuo in Mozart's keyboard concertos', *Essays on Mozart in Honour of Stanley Sadie*, ed. Dorothea Link and Judith Nagley (Woodbridge, 2005), 107–20

Eisen, Cliff. 'Reception', *The Cambridge Mozart Encyclopedia*, ed. Cliff Eisen and Simon P. Keefe (Cambridge, 2005), 408–11

Eisen, Cliff. 'Sources', *The Cambridge Mozart Encyclopedia*, ed. Cliff Eisen and Simon P. Keefe (Cambridge, 2005), 477–89

Eisen, Cliff. *Mozart: A Life in Letters* (London, 2006)

Eisen, Cliff. 'Mozart's leap in the dark', *Mozart Studies*, ed. Simon P. Keefe (Cambridge, 2006), 1–19

Eisen, Cliff and Christopher Wintle. 'Mozart's C minor Fantasy, K475: An Editorial "Problem" and its Analytical and Critical Consequences', *Journal of the Royal Musical Association*, cxxiv (1999), 26–52

Eitner, Robert. 'Die Sonate: Vorstudien zur Entstehung der Form', *Monatshefte für Musikgeschichte*, xx (1888), 163–70 and 179–85

Elias, Norbert. *Mozart: Portrait of a Genius*, trans. Edmund Jephcott (Cambridge, 1993)

Ellis, Stewart Marsh. *The Life of Michael Kelly, Musician, Actor and Bon Viveur* (London, 1930)

Emerson, Isabelle. 'A Question of Order: Andante, Minuet, Or Minuet, Andante – Mozart's String Quintet in C major, K. 515', *Mozart-Jahrbuch 1989/90*, 89–98

Emery, Ted. *Goldoni as Librettist: Theatrical Reform and the drammi giocosi per musica* (New York, 1991)

Engel, Carl. *Deutsche Puppenkomödien* (Oldenburg, 1875)

Engel, Gustav. 'Eine mathematisch-harmonische Analyse des Don Giovanni von Mozart', *Vierteljahresschrift für Musikwissenschaft*, iii (1887), 491–560

Engel, Hans. *Die Entwicklung des deutschen Klavierkonzertes von Mozart bis Liszt* (Leipzig, 1927)

Engel, Hans. *Das Concerto Grosso* (Cologne, 1962 = *Das Musikwerk*)

Engel, Karl. *Die Don Juan-Sage auf der Bühne* (Dresden and Leipzig, 1887)

Engel, Leopold. *Geschichte des Illuminatenordens* (Berlin, 1906)

Engelbrecht, Helmut. 'Ludwig Alois Friedrich Köchel (1842 Ritter von) (1800–1877)', *Wiener Figaro: Mitteilungsblatt der Mozartgemeinde Wien*, lviii/1 (2001), 5–11

Engl, Johann Evangelist. *General-Bericht des Provisorischen Ausschusses der Internationalen Mozart-Stiftung* (Salzburg, 1880)

Engl, Johann Evangelist. *W. A. Mozart in den Schilderungen seiner Biographen* (Salzburg, 1887)

Engl, Johann Evangelist. *Festschrift zur Mozart-Centenarfeier in Salzburg am 15., 16. und 17. Juli 1891* (Salzburg, 1891)

Engl, Johann Evangelist. 'Das Requiem und Requiem-Frage', *Festschrift zur Mozart-Centenarfeier* (Salzburg, 1891), 73–123

Engl. Johann Evangelist. 'Die Villa Bertramka', *Mozart-Jahrbuch 1891*, 63

Engl, Johann Evangelist. 'Das Zauberflöten-Häuschen', *Mozart-Jahrbuch 1891*, 69–70

Engl, Johann Evangelist. 'Die den Vater überlebenden Söhne Carl und Wolfgang und die übrigen Kinder W. A. Mozarts', *Jahresbericht der Internationalen Stiftung Mozarteum*, xiii (1893), 38–40

Engl, Johann Evangelist. 'W. A. Mozarts Schädel', *Studien über Mozart* (Salzburg, 1893), 3ff., 21ff.

Engl, Johann Evangelist. 'Über die Lieder W. A. Mozarts und die Echtheit des Wiegenliedes: Schlafe mein Prinzchen, schlaf ein', *Studien über W. A. Mozart* (Salzburg, 1893), 11ff.

Engl, Johann Evangelist. 'Studien über W. A. Mozart: Fünfte Folge', *17. Jahresbericht der Internationalen Stiftung Mozarteum* (Salzburg, 1898), 24–43

Engl, Johann Evangelist. *Katalog des Mozarteums im Geburts- und Wohnzimmer Mozarts zu Salzburg*, fourth edition (Salzburg, 1906)

Engl, Johann Evangelist. *Zum Gedächtnis Johann Michael Haydns* (Salzburg, 1906)

Engl, Johann Evangelist. 'Mozarts Krönungsmesse', *Salzburger Volksblatt*, xxxvii (30 March 1907), 8

Engl, Johann Evangelist. 'W. A. Mozarts Wiegenlied und Konstanzes Tagebuch', *25. [sic] Jahresbericht des Konservatoriums Mozarteum für 1915* (Salzburg, 1915)

Engländer, Richard. 'Glucks "Cinesi" und "Orfano della China"', *Gluck-Jahrbuch*, i (1913), 54–81

Engländer, Richard. 'Zu den Münchener Orfeo-Aufführungen 1773 und 1775', *Gluck-Jahrbuch*, ii (1915), 26–55

Engländer, Richard. 'Domenico Fischietti als Buffokomponist in Dresden', *Zeitschrift für Musikwissenschaft*, ii (1919/20), 321–52 and 399–422

Engländer, Richard. *Johann Gottlieb Naumann als Opernkomponist (1741–1801)* (Leipzig, 1922)

Engländer, Richard. 'Les sonates de violon de Mozart et les "Duetti" di Joseph Schuster', *Revue de musicologie*, xx (1939), 6–19

Engländer, Richard. 'Problem kring Mozarts violinsonat i e-moll K. 304', *Svensk Tidskrift för Musikforskning*, xxxiii (1951), 127–35

Engländer, Richard. 'Die Echtheitsfrage in Mozarts Violinsonaten KV 55–60', *Die Musikforschung*, viii (1955), 292–8

Engländer, Richard. *Die Dresdner Instrumentalmusik in der Zeit der Wiener Klassik* (Uppsala, 1956)

Engländer, Richard. 'Nochmals Mozart und der Dresdner Joseph Schuster', *Svensk Tidskrift för Musikforskning*, xxxix (1957), 141–3

Erk, Ludwig and Franz Magnus Böhme. *Deutscher Liederhort* (Leipzig, 1893–4)

Escal, Françoise. 'Les concertos-pastiches de Mozart, ou la citation comme procès d'appropriation du discours', *International Review of the Aesthetics and Sociology of Music*, xii/2 (1981), 117–39

Esch, Christian. *'Lucio Silla': Vier Opera-Seria-Vertonungen aus der Zeit zwischen 1770 und 1780* (Baden-Baden, 1994)

Everist, Mark. '"Madame Dorothea Wending is arcicontentissima": The performers of *Idomeneo*', *W. A. Mozart: Idomeneo*, ed. Julian Rushton (Cambridge, 1993), 48–61

Everist, Mark. 'Enshrining Mozart: "Don Giovanni" and the Viardot Circle', *19th-Century Music*, xxv/2–3 (2001/2), 165–89

Everson, Jane E. 'Of Beaks and Geese: Mozart, Varesco and Francesco Cieco', *Music & Letters*, lxxvi/3 (1995), 369–83

Eybl, Martin. 'Franz Bernhard Ritter von Keeß: Sammler, Mäzen und Organisator. Materialien zu Wiens Musikleben im Geist der Aufklärung', *Österreichische Musik – Musik in Österreich: Beiträge zur Musikgeschichte Mitteleuropas. Theophil Antonicek zum 60. Geburtstag*, ed. Elisabeth Theresia Hilscher (Tutzing, 1998), 239–50

Eybl, Martin. 'Mozarts erster Konzertsatz: Die Pasticcio-Konzerte KV 37, 39, 40, 41 im zeitgenössischen Wiener Kontext', *Musikgeschichte als Verstehensgeschichte: Festschrift für Gernot Gruber zum 65. Geburtstag*, ed. Joachim Brügge (Tutzing, 2004), 199–214

Eynard, Marcello. *Il musicista Pietro Antonio Locatelli: Un itinerario artistico da Bergamo a Amsterdam* (Bergamo, 1995)

Faißt, Immanuel. 'Beiträge zur Geschichte der Claviersonate von ihrem ersten Auftreten an bis auf C. P. Emanuel Bach', *Caecilia*, xxv (1846), 129–58, 201–31; xxvi (1847), 1–28 and 73–83

Falck, Martin. *Wilhelm Friedemann Bach: Sein Leben und seine Werke, mit thematischem Verzeichnis und zwei Bildern* (Leipzig, 1913)

Faravelli, Danilo. 'Mozart e il mottetto: Un'ipotesi critica e note su "Ave verum corpus"', *Rivista internazionale di musica sacra*, xv/3–4 (1994), 230–53

Faravelli, Danilo. *Mozart e Paisiello* (Milan, 2000)

Farinelli, Arturo. *Don Giovanni: Note critiche* (Turin and Rome, 1896)

Farmer, Henry G. 'Diderot and Rameau', *Music Review*, xxii (1961), 181–8

Farnsworth, Rodney. '*Così fan tutte* as Parody and Burlesque', *Opera Quarterly*, vi/2 (1988/9), 50–68

Fauquet, Joël-Marie. 'Regards sur "Lucio Silla" de Jean-Chrétien Bach', *L'avant-scène opéra*, cxxxix (May–June 1991), 108–19

Faustini-Fasini, Eugenio. 'Gli astri maggiori del bel canto napoletano: Gaetano Majorano detto "Caffarelli"', *Note d'archivio per la storia musicale*, xv (1938), 121–8, 157–70 and 258–70

Favart, Antoine-Pierre-Charles. *Mémoires et correspondances littéraires, dramatiques et anecdotiques de C. S. Favart* (Paris, 1808)

Fawcett, Trevor. 'The first undoubted "Magic Flute"?', *Royal Musical Association Research Chronicle*, xii (1974), 106–14

Federici, Piera. 'Kennzeichen und Eigenart der Triobesetzung in der Musik für Bassetthorn in Wien zur Zeit Mozarts', *Internationaler Musikwissenschaftlicher Kongreß zum Mozartjahr 1991 Baden-Wien*, ed. Ingrid Fuchs (Tutzing, 1993), ii.579–86

Fehr, Max. *A. Zeno und seine Reform des Operntextes* (Zurich, 1912)

Fehr, Max. 'Die Familie Mozart in Zürich', *130. Neujahrsblatt der allgemeinen Musikgesellschaft auf das Jahr 1942* (Zurich, 1942)

Feldman, Martha. 'Staging the Virtuoso: Ritornello Procedure in Mozart, from Aria to Concerto', *Mozart's Piano Concertos: Text, Context, Interpretation*, ed. Neal Zaslaw (Ann Arbor, MI, 1996), 149–86

Fellerer, Karl. *Die Kirchenmusik W. A. Mozarts* (Berlin, 1985)

Fellmann, Hans Georg. *Die Böhmsche Theatertruppe und ihre Zeit* (Leipzig, 1928)

Fellner, A. 'Mozart als Freimaurer in der Wiener Loge "Zur gekrönten Hoffnung"', *Mitteilungen für die Mozart-Gemeinde in Berlin*, ii (1902), 115–18

Fend, Michael. 'Zur Rezeption von Mozarts Opern in London im frühen 19. Jahrhundert', *Internationaler Musikwissenschaftlicher Kongress zum Mozartjahr 1991, Baden-Wien*, ed. Ingrid Fuchs (Tutzing, 1993), ii.601–14

Ferguson, Faye. 'The Classical keyboard concerto: Some thoughts on authentic performance', *Early Music*, xii (1984), 437–45

Ferguson, Faye. 'Mozart's Keyboard Concertos: Tutti Notations and Performance Models', *Mozart-Jahrbuch 1984/85*, 32–9

Ferrari, Paolo Emilio. *Spettacoli drammatico-musicali e coreografici in Parma dal 1628 al 1883* (Parma, 1884)

Fétis, François-Joseph. *Curiosités historiques de la musique* (Paris, 1830)

Finscher, Ludwig. 'Maximilian Stadler und Mozarts Nachlaß', *Mozart-Jahrbuch 1960/61*, 168–72

Finscher, Ludwig. *Studien zur Geschichte des Streichquartetts, i: Die Entstehung des klassischen Streichquartetts: Von den Vorformen zur Grundlegung durch Joseph Haydn* (Kassel, 1974)

Finscher, Ludwig, ed. *Die Mannheimer Hofkapelle im Zeitalter Carl Theodors* (Mannheim, 1992)

Finscher, Ludwig. 'Über einen Finaletypus bei Mozart', *Begegnungen: Festschrift für Peter Anselm Riedl zum 60. Geburtstag*, ed. Klaus Güthlein and Franz Matsche (Worms, 1993), 356–63

Finscher, Ludwig. 'Bemerkungen zu den späten Streichquintetten', *Mozarts Streichquintette: Beiträge zum musikalischen Satz, zum Gattungskontext und zu Quellenfragen*, ed. Cliff Eisen and Wolf-Dieter Seiffert (Stuttgart, 1994), 154–62

Finscher, Ludwig, Bärbel Pelker and Jochen Reutter, ed. *Mozart und Mannheim* (Frankfurt am Main, 1994)

Fischer, Friedrich Johann. 'Emanuel Schikaneder und Salzburg', *Jahrbuch der Gesellschaft für Wiener Theaterforschung*, xv–xvi (1966), 179–216

Fischer, Georg-Helmut. 'Abbé Georg Joseph Vogler: A "Baroque" Musical Genius', *Gustav III and the Swedish stage: Opera, theatre, and other foibles. Essays in honor of Hans Åstrand*, ed. Bertil Van Boer (Lewiston, NY, 1993), 75–102

Fischer, Josef. *Wolfgang Amadeus Mozart (Sohn): Eine biographische Skizze sowie zwei bisher unbekannte Briefe Mozarts (Vater)* (Karlsbad, 1888)

Fischer, Kurt von. 'C. Ph. E. Bachs Variationenwerke', *Revue Belge de Musicologie*, vi (1952), 190–218

Fischer, Kurt von. 'Zur Theorie der Variation im 18. und beginnenden 19. Jahrhundert', *Festschrift Joseph Schmidt-Görg*, ed. Dagmar Weise (Bonn, 1957), 117–30

Fischer, Wilhelm. *Wiener Instrumentalmusik vor und um 1750. Heft II* (Leipzig, 1912 = Denkmäler der Tonkunst in Österreich xxxix)

Fischer, Wilhelm. 'Zur Entwicklungsgeschichte des Wiener klassichen Stils', *Studien zur Musikwissenschaft*, iii (1915), 24–84

Fischer-Dieskau, Dietrich. *'Weil nicht alle Blütenträume reiften': Johann Friedrich Reichardt, Hofkapellmeister dreier Preußenkönige: Porträt und Selbstporträt* (Stuttgart, 1992)

Fischer-Dieskau, Dietrich. *Carl Friedrich Zelter und das Berliner Musikleben seiner Zeit: Eine Biographie* (Berlin, 1997)

Flaherty, Gloria. *Opera in the Development of German Critical Thought* (Princeton, NJ, 1978)

Flamm, Christa. 'Leopold Koželuch: Biographie und stilkritische Untersuchung der Sonaten für Klavier, Violine und Violoncello' (dissertation, University of Vienna, 1968)

Fleischer, Oskar. *Mozart* (Berlin, 1900)

Flögel, Karl Friedrich. *Geschichte des Grotesk-Komischen: Ein Beitrag zur Geschichte der Menschheit*, ed. Max Bauer (Munich, 1914)

Florimo, Francesco. *La scuola musicale di Napoli e i suoi conservatorii* (Naples, 1880–3)

Flothuis, Marius. 'Ridente la calma – Mozart oder Mysliveček', *Mozart-Jahrbuch 1973*, 241–3

Flothuis, Marius. *Wolfgang Amadeus Mozart: Streichquintett g-moll, KV516* (Munich, 1987)

Flothuis, Marius. *Mozart's Piano Concertos* (Amsterdam, 2001)

Flueler, Max. 'Die norddeutsche Sinfonie zur Zeit Friedrichs des Großen und besonders die Werke Ph. Em. Bachs' (dissertation, University of Berlin, 1908)

Font, Auguste. *Favart, l'opéra-comique et la comédie-vaudeville aux XVIIe et XVIIIe siècles* (Paris, 1894)

Ford, Anne. *Instructions for the Playing of the Musical Glasses* (London, 1761)

Forkel, Johann Nikolaus. *Musikalisch-kritische Bibliothek* (Gotha, 1778–9)

Forkel, Johann Nikolaus. *Musikalischer Almanach für Deutschland* (Leipzig, 1782–9)

Forkel, Johann Nikolaus. *Ueber Johann Sebastian Bachs Leben, Kunst und Kunstwerke* (Leipzig, 1802)

Forman, Dennis. *Mozart's Concerto Form: The First Movements of the Piano Concertos* (London, 1971)

Fornari, Giacomo. 'Das anerkannte Genie: Mozart in biographischen Quellen der Lombardei während der ersten zwei Jahrzehnte des 19. Jahrhunderts', *Salieri sulle tracce di Mozart (Katalogbuch zur Ausstellung anläßlich der Wiedereröffnung der Mailänder Scala am 7. Dezember 2004. 3. Dezember 2004–30. Jänner 2005)*, ed. Herbert Lachmayer, Theresa Haigermoser and Reinhard Eisendle (Kassel, 2004), 81–85

Forster, Johann Georg Adam. *Sämtliche Schriften* (Leipzig, 1843)

Forster, Robert. *Die Kopfsätze der Klavierkonzerte Mozarts und Beethovens: Gesamtaufbau, Solokadenz und Schlußbildung* (Munich, 1992)

Fournier, Édouard. 'Mozart à Paris 1778', *Revue française*, ii/7 (1856), 28–39

Francine, Jean-Nicolas. *Recueil général des opéra* (Paris 1703–45)

Frank, Joseph. 'Aus den ungedruckten Denkwürdigkeiten der Aerzte Peter und Joseph Frank', ed. Robert Prutz and Wilhelm Wolfsohn, *Deutsches Museum*, ii/1 (January 1852), 24–8

Franze, Juan Pedro. 'Die Erstaufführung des Don Giovanni, 1827 in Buenos Aires', *Mitteilungen der Internationalen Stiftung Mozarteum*, xvii/1–2 (1969), 5–15

Frati, Lodovico. 'Antonio Bernacchi e la sua scuola di canto', *Rivista musicale italiana*, xxix (1922), 473–91

Freeman, Daniel E. *The Opera Theater of Count Franz Anton von Sporck in Prague* (Stuyvesant, NY, 1992)

Freeman, Daniel E. 'Johann Christian Bach and the Early Classical Italian Masters', *Eighteenth-Century Keyboard Music*, ed. Robert Marshall (New York, 1994), 230–69

Freeman, Daniel E. 'The Foundation of Italian Operatic Traditions in Prague', *Il melodramma italiano in Italia e in Germania nell'età Barocca: Como 1993*, ed. Alberto Colzani, Andrea Luppi, Maurizio Padoan and Norbert Dubowy (Loveno di Menaggio, 1995), 115–25

Freeman, Robert S. 'Apostolo Zeno's Reform of the Libretto', *Journal of the American Musicological Society*, xxi (1968), 321–41

Freeman, Robert S. *Opera without Drama: Currents of Change in Italian Opera, 1675–1725* (Ann Arbor, MI, 1981)

Freiberger, Heinz. *Anton Raaff (1714–1797): Sein Leben und Wirken als Beitrag zur Musikgeschichte des 18. Jahrhunderts* (Cologne, 1929)

Freisauff, Rudolf von. *Mozarts Don Juan 1787 bis 1887: Ein Beitrag zur Geschichte dieser Oper* (Salzburg, 1887)

Freyhan, Michael. 'Rediscovery of the 18th Century Score and Parts of "Die Zauberflöte": Showing the Text Used at the Hamburg Première in 1793', *Mozart-Jahrbuch 1997*, 109–47

Friedel, Johann. *Briefe aus Wien verschiedenen Inhalts an einen Freund in Berlin* (Vienna, 1784)

Friedlaender, Max. 'Briefe aus Goethes Autographensammlung: Zwei Schreiben W. A. Mozarts', *Goethe-Jahrbuch*, xii (1891), 100–10, 129–32

Friedlaender, Max. 'Mozarts Wiegenlied', *Vierteljahrsschrift für Musikwissenschaft*, viii (1892), 275–85

Friedlaender, Max. *Das deutsche Lied im 18. Jahrhundert* (Stuttgart and Berlin, 1902)

Friedlaender, Max. 'Leopold Mozarts Klaviersonaten', *Die Musik*, iv (1904/5), 38–40

Friedländer, Ernst. 'Mozarts Beziehungen zu Berlin', *Mitteilungen für die Mozartgemeinde in Berlin*, i (1897), 115–21

Fröhlich, Joseph. [Review article], *Allgemeine musikalische Zeitung*, xix (1817), 96

Fröhlich, Joseph. *Biographie des großen Tonkünstlers Abt G. J. Vogler* (Würzburg, 1845)

Froidcourt, Georges de, ed. *La correspondance générale de Grétry* (Brussels, 1962)

Fubini, Enrico. *Les philosophes et la musique* (Paris, 1983)

Fubini, Enrico. *Music and culture in eighteenth-century Europe: A source book*, ed. and trans. Bonnie Blackburn (Chicago, 1994), 233–40

Fuchs, Aloys. 'Beitrag zur Geschichte der Oper "Die Zauberflöte"', *Wiener Allgemeine Theater-Zeitung*, xxxi (1842), 142–3

Fuchs, Aloys. 'Aufforderung an Herrn Albert Schiffner in Dresden', *Caecilia*, xxiii (1844), 95–6

Fuchs, Aloys. 'Biographische Skizze von Wolfgang Amadeus Mozart (dem Sohne)', *Allgemeine Wiener Musik-Zeitung*, iv/9 (1844), 441–4

Fuhrmann, Roderich. *Mannheimer Klavier-Kammermusik* (Marburg, 1963)

Fuhrmann, Roderich. 'War Franz Xaver Süßmayr Mozarts Schüler und Assistent?', *Kongreßbericht zum VII. Internationalen Gewandhaus-Symposium: Wolfgang Amadeus Mozart. Forschung und Praxis im Dienst von Leben, Werk, Interpretation und Rezeption anläßlich der Gewandhaus-Festtage in Leipzig vom 3. bis 6. Oktober 1991* (Leipzig, 1993), 78–81

Funk, Vera. 'Die "Zauberflöte" in der bürgerlichen Wohnstube des 19. Jahrhunderts: Reduktionen für kleinere Besetzungen', *Musikalische Metamorphosen: Formen und Geschichte der Bearbeitung*, ed. Silke Leopold (Kassel, 1992), 123–36

Fürstenau, Moritz. *Beiträge zur Geschichte der königlich sächsischen musikalischen Kapelle* (Dresden, 1849)

Fürstenau, Moritz. *Zur Geschichte der Musik und des Theaters am Hofe zu Dresden* (Dresden, 1861)

Fürstenau, Moritz. 'Maria Antonia Walpurgis, Kurfürstin von Sachsen: Eine biographische Skizze', *Monatshefte für Musikgeschichte*, xi (1879), 167–81

Fux, Johann Joseph. *Gradus ad Parnassum* (Vienna, 1725)

Gál, Hans. 'Die Stileigentümlichkeiten des jungen Beethoven', *Studien zur Musikwissenschaft*, iv (1916), 58–115

Galiani, Ferdinando. *Correspondance inédite de l'abbé Ferdinand Galiani, conseiller du roi, pendant les années 1765 à 1783* (Paris, 1818)

Galkin, Elliott W. *A History of Orchestral Conducting in Theory and Practice* (New York, 1988)

Gallarani, Marina Vaccarini. 'La festa teatrale tra Vienna e Milano', *Intorno all'Ascanio in Alba di Mozart: Una festa teatrale a Milano*, ed. Guido Salvetti (Lucca, 1995), 101–35

Gallarati, Paolo. 'La poetica di Giacomo Durazzo e la *Lettre sur le méchanisme de l'opéra italien*', *Musica/Realtà*, xxvi (1988), 53–73

Gallarati, Paolo. 'Music and Masks in Lorenzo Da Ponte's Mozartian Librettos', *Cambridge Opera Journal*, i/3 (1989), 225–47

Gallois, Jean. *Jean-Baptiste Lully, ou La naissance de la tragédie lyrique* (Geneva, 2001)

Gambassi, Osvaldo. *L'Accademia Filarmonica di Bologna: Fondazione, statuti e aggregazione* (Florence, 1992)

Gamerra, Giovanni de. 'Osservazioni sullo spettacolo in generale . . . per servire allo stabilmento del novo Teatro nazionale', *Novo teatro di Giovanni de Gamerra* (Venice, 1790)

Gandolfi, Bruno and Marino Mora. 'La forma dell'aria nelle opere milanesi di Mozart', *Intorno all'Ascanio in Alba di Mozart: Una festa teatrale a Milano*, ed. Guido Salvetti (Lucca, 1995), 23–38

Gandolfi, Riccardo. *Elogio di Giovanni Battista Martini* (Bologna, 1813)

Gara, Eugenio. *Giovanni Battista Rubini nel centenario della morte* (Bergamo, 1954)

Garat, Dominique-Joseph. *Mémoires sur la vie de M. Suard, sur ses écrits, et sur le XVIIIe siècle* (Paris, 1820)

Gardien, Jacques. *Jean-Philippe Rameau* (Paris, 1949)

Gärtner, Heinz. *Mozarts Requiem und die Geschäfte der Constanze Mozart* (Munich, 1986; trans. as *Constanze Mozart: After the Requiem* [Portland, OR, 1991])

Gärtner, Heinz. *Johann Christian Bach, Mozarts Freund und Lehrmeister* (Munich, 1989; trans. as *Johann Christian Bach: Mozart's Friend and Mentor* [Portland, OR, 1994])

Gärtner, Heinz. *Adieu, Mozart: Die Hofdemel-Tragödie und die Selbstzerstörung eines Genies* (Frankfurt, 2004)

Gaspari, Gaetano. *La musica in Bologna* (Milan, 1858)

Gathy, Auguste. 'Un manscrit inédit de Mozart', *Revue et gazette musicale de Paris*, xii (23 March 1856), 90–1

Gay, Peter. 'The Father's Revenge', *The Don Giovanni Book: Myths of Seduction and Betrayal*, ed. Jonathan Miller (London, 1990), 70–80

Gazzaniga: Don Giovanni, o sia Il convitato di pietra, ed. Stefan Kunze (Kassel, 1974)

Geffray, Geneviève and Rudolph Angermüller, ed. *'meine tag Ordnungen': Nannerl Mozarts Tagebuchblätter 1775–1783 mit Eintragungen ihres Bruders Wolfgang und ihres Vaters Leopold* (Bad Honnef, 1998)

Geffray, Geneviève. 'Mozart, Maria Anna', *Die Musik in Geschichte und Gegenwart: Allgemeine Enzyklopädie der Musik begründet von Friedrich Blume. Zweite, neubearbeitete Ausgabe*, ed. Ludwig Finscher (Kassel, 2004), Personenteil xii.590–1

Gehmacher, Monica. 'Luigi Gatti: Sein Leben und seine Oratorien' (dissertation, University of Vienna, 1959)

Geiringer, Karl. 'The Rise of Chamber Music', *The New Oxford History of Music* (Oxford, 1973), vii.515–73

Geminiani, Francesco. *The Art of Playing on the Violin* (London, 1751)

Genast, Eduard. *Aus dem Tagebuch eines alten Schauspielers* (Leipzig, 1862)

Genée, Rudolph. 'Verzeichniß der Musikhandschriften W. A. Mozarts im Besitze der Königlichen Bibliothek in Berlin', *Mitteilungen für die Mozart-Gemeinde in Berlin*, i (1895), 5–17

Genée, Rudolph. 'Zur Geschichte des Mozartschen Schauspieldirektor und der verschiedenen Bearbeitungen', *Mitteilungen für die Mozart-Gemeinde in Berlin*, ii (1896), 60–2

Genée, Rudolph. '"Una cosa rara" in Mozarts Don Juan', *Mitteilungen für die Mozart-Gemeinde in Berlin*, ii (1896), 63–5

Genée, Rudolph. 'Mozarts Schwester Nannerl', *Mitteilungen für die Mozart-Gemeinde in Berlin*, iii (1896), 98–103

Genée, Rudolph. 'Ein bisher unbekannt gebliebenes Duett zu Mozarts "Zauberflöte"', *Mitteilungen für die Mozart-Gemeinde in Berlin*, iv (1899), 205–9

Genée, Rudolph. 'Aus Sartis "Due Litiganti" in Mozarts Don Giovanni', *Mitteilungen für die Mozart-Gemeinde in Berlin*, iv (1899), 210–13

Genée, Rudolph. 'Abbé Stadler', *Mitteilungen für die Mozart-Gemeinde in Berlin*, v (1900), 265–70

Genée, Rudolph. 'Mozarts Partitur-Entwurf seiner Oper "L'Oca del Cairo"', *Mitteilungen für die Mozart-Gemeinde in Berlin*, v (1900), 271–7

Genée, Rudolph. 'Caron de Beaumarchais und seine Lustspiele als Opernstoffe', *Mitteilungen für die Mozart-Gemeinde in Berlin*, vi (1901), 3–22

Genée, Rudolph. 'Mozarts Partitur der "Hochzeit des Figaro"', *Mitteilungen für die Mozart-Gemeinde in Berlin*, vi (1901), 66–9

Genée, Rudolph. 'Die ersten Entwürfe Mozarts zu "Figaros Hochzeit"', *Mitteilungen für die Mozart-Gemeinde in Berlin*, vii (1902), 83–91

Genée, Rudolph. 'Über einige Musikhandschriften von Mozart', *Mitteilungen für die Mozart-Gemeinde in Berlin*, vii (1902), 119–23

Genée, Rudolph, 'Mozart in Dresden und Doris Stock', *Mitteilungen für die Mozart-Gemeinde in Berlin*, viii (1903), 222–4

Genée, Rudolph. 'Aus Mozarts Liebesleben nach seinen Briefen geschildert', *Mitteilungen für die Mozart-Gemeinde in Berlin*, ix (1904), 245–76

Genée, Rudolph. 'Constanze Mozart in Berlin', *Mitteilungen für die Mozart-Gemeinde in Berlin*, ix (1904), 277–9

Genée, Rudolph. 'Zum zehnjährigen Bestehen der Mozart-Gemeinde in Berlin', *Mitteilungen für die Mozart-Gemeinde in Berlin*, ix (1904), 297–8

Genée, Rudolph. 'Mozarts musikalische Erziehung und ein bisher unbekannt gebliebenes Notenbuch von Leopold Mozart', *Mitteilungen für die Mozart-Gemeinde in Berlin*, xiii (1908), 71–80

Gerber, Ernst Ludwig. *Historisch-biographisches Lexicon der Tonkünstler* (Leipzig, 1790–2)

Gerber, Ernst Ludwig. *Neues historisch-biographisches Lexikon der Tonkünstler* (Leipzig, 1812–14)

Gerhäuser, Emil. *Stuttgarter Bühnenkunst* (Stuttgart, 1917)

Gerlach, Sonja. 'Joseph Haydns Sinfonien bis 1774: Studien zur Chronologie', *Haydn-Studien*, vii/1–2 (1996), 1–287

Gersthofer, Wolfgang. 'Mozarts frühe Sinfonien und ihre Londoner Vorbilder: Überlegungen zum Verhältnis Mozart – Abel – J. C. Bach', *Der junge Mozart: Le jeune Mozart*, ed. Joseph Willimann (Berne, 1992 = Schweizer Jahrbuch für Musikwissenschaft, new series, xii)

Gersthofer, Wolfgang. *Mozarts frühe Sinfonien (bis 1772): Aspekte frühklassischer Sinfonik* (Kassel, 1993)

Gersthofer, Wolfgang. 'Zur Melodramtechnik in "Zaide"', *Mozart-Jahrbuch 2001: Bericht über das Mozart-Symposion zum Gedenken an Wolfgang Plath (1930–1995). Augsburg, 13. bis 16. Juni 2000*, 205–19

Gervinus, Georg Gottfried. *Geschichte der poetischen National-Literatur der Deutschen* (Leipzig, 1835–42)

Gherardi, Evaristo. *Le théâtre italien* (Amsterdam, 1700)

Gianturco, Carolyn. *Mozart's Early Operas* (London, 1981)

Giazotto, Remo. *La musica a Genova nella vita pubblica e privata del XIII al XVIII secolo* (Genoa, 1952)

Gibson, Elisabeth. 'Italian Opera in London, 1750–1775: Management and Finances', *Early Music*, xviii (1990), 47–59

Gidel, Henry. *Le vaudeville* (Paris, 1986)

Gidwitz, Patricia Lewy. '"Ich bin die erste Sängerin": Vocal Profiles of Two Mozart Sopranos', *Early Music*, xix (1991), 565–74

Gidwitz, Patricia Lewy. 'Vocal Profiles of Four Mozart Sopranos' (dissertation, University of California, Berkeley, 1991)

Gidwitz, Patricia Lewy, 'Mozart's Fiordiligi: Adriana Ferrarese del Bene', *Cambridge Opera Journal*, viii/3 (1996), 199–214

Gilman, Todd S. 'The beggar's opera and British opera', *University of Toronto Quarterly*, lxvi/3 (1997), 539–61

Ginguené, Pierre Louis. *Notice sur la vie et les ouvrages de Nicolas Piccinni* (Paris, 1800–1)

Girdlestone, Cuthbert M. *Mozart et ses concertos pour piano* (Paris, 1939; trans. as *Mozart and his Piano Concertos*, London, 1948)

Gisi, Martin. *Sedaine: Sein Leben und sein Werk* (Berlin, 1883)

Giuntini, Francesco. *I drammi per musica di Antonio Salvi: Aspetti della 'riforma' del libretto nel primo Settecento* (Bologna, 1994)

Gjerdingen, Robert. 'Revisiting Meyer's "Grammatical simplicity and relational richness"', *Cognitive bases of musical communication*, ed. Mari Reiss Jones and Susan Holleran (Washington, DC, 1991), 225–43

Glasow, E. Thomas. 'Jungfrau Martha – Martha Hagenauer: Lamentable passing as the inspiration for Mozart's 1st operatic Ode to death – Mitridate's "Pallid Shade"', *Opera Quarterly*, x/1 (1993), 13–22

Glixon, Beth. 'Recitative in Seventeenth-Century Venetian Opera: Its Dramatic Function and Musical Language' (dissertation, Rutgers University, 1985)

Gloede, Wilhelm. 'Süßmayrs Requiem-Ergänzungen und das Wort-Ton-Problem', *Mozart-Jahrbuch 1999*, 81–103

Gmeiner, Josef. 'Der sogenannte "Echtheitsstreit"', *Requiem, Wolfgang Amadeus Mozart 1791–1991: Ausstellung der Musiksammlung der Österreichischen Nationalbibliothek, Prunksaal, Wien 1, Josefsplatz 1, 17. Mai bis 5. Dezember 1991. Katalog* (Graz, 1991), 271–82

Godt, Irving. 'Marianna in Italy: The International Reputation of Marianna Martines (1744–1812)', *Journal of Musicology*, xiii (1995), 538–61

Godt, Irving. 'Marianna in Vienna: A Martines Chronology', *Journal of Musicology*, xvi (1998), 136–58

Goeckingk, Leopold Friedrich Günther von. *Friedrich Nicolai's Leben und literarischer Nachlaß* (Berlin, 1820)

Goedeke, Karl. *Grundriß zur Geschichte der deutschen Literatur* (Dresden, 1859–1910)

Goehring, Edmund. *Three Modes of Perception in Mozart: The Philosophical, Pastoral, and Comic in Così fan tutte* (Cambridge, 2004)

Goethe, Johann Wolfgang von. *Aus meinem Leben: Dichtung und Wahrheit* (Tübingen, 1811–22)

Goethe, Johann Wolfgang von. *Werke* (Weimar, 1887–1920)

Goethe, Johann Wolfgang von. *Goethes Briefe an Frau von Stein*, ed. Adolf Schöll; third edition ed. Julius Wahle (Frankfurt, 1900)

Goethe. Johann Wolfgang von. *Sämtliche Werke: Jubiläums-Ausgabe* (Stuttgart and Berlin, 1902–12)

Goldoni, Carlo. *Mémoires* (Paris, 1787)

Goldschmidt, Hugo. *Studien zur Geschichte der italienischen Oper im 17. Jahrhundert* (Leipzig, 1901–4)

Goldschmidt, Hugo. 'Claudio Monteverdis Oper: Il ritorno d'Ulisse in patria', *Sammelbände der Internationalen Musikgesellschaft*, iv (1902–3), 671–6 and ix (1907–8), 570–92

Goldschmidt, Hugo. *Die Lehre von der vokalen Ornamentik* (Charlottenburg, 1907)

Goldschmidt, Hugo. *Tommaso Traetta: Ausgewählte Werke* (Leipzig, 1914 = Denkmäler deutscher Tonkunst xiv/1)

Goldschmidt, Hugo. *Die Musikästhetik des 18. Jahrhunderts* (Zurich, 1915)

Gollmick, Carl. 'Eine nachgelassene Oper Mozarts', *Recensionen und Mittheilungen über Theater und Musik*, xvi (1860), 25–253

Goncourt, Edmond and Jules de. *La femme au XVIIIième siècle* (Paris, 1862)

Goschler, Abbé. *Mozart, d'après de nouveaux documents* (Paris, 1866)

Gottron, Adam. 'Kleine Beiträge zur Mainzer Musikgeschichte, i: Die Selbstbiographie des Bassisten Ludwig Fischer aus Mainz', *Mainzer Almanach* (1959), 113–25

Gottron, Adam. *Mainzer Musikgeschichte von 1500 bis 1800* (Mainz, 1959)

Gottsched, Johann Christoph. *Das Neueste aus der anmuthigen Gelehrsamkeit* (Leipzig, 1751–62)

Gounod, Charles. *Le Don Juan de Mozart* (Paris, 1890)

Gourret, Jean. *Histoire de l'Opéra-Comique* (Paris, 1983)

Gräffer, Franz. 'Das Mozarthaus. Mozarts Grab', *Kleine Wiener Memoiren* (Vienna, 1845), 227–8

Gräffer, Rudolf. *Neue Sammlung von Vergnügen und Unterricht* (Vienna, 1768–9)

Grandaur, Franz. *Chronik des Königlichen Hof- und Nationaltheaters in München* (Munich, 1878)

Grattan-Guinness, Ivor. 'Why did Mozart write three symphonies in the summer of 1788?', *The Music Review*, liii (1994), 1–6

Grave, Floyd and Margaret Grave. *In Praise of Harmony: The Teachings of Abbé Georg Joseph Vogler* (Lincoln, NE, 1987)

Grétry. André-Ernest-Modeste. *Memoiren: oder, Essays über die Musik*, ed. Peter Gülke (Wilhelmshaven, 1978)

Grétry, André-Ernest-Modeste. *Mémoires, ou Essais sur la musique* (Paris, 1797)

Grey, Thomas S. 'Metaphorical modes in nineteenth-century music criticism: Image, narrative, and idea', *Music and text: Critical inquiries* (New York, 1992), 93–117

Griesinger, Georg August. *Biographische Notizen über Joseph Haydn* (Leipzig, 1810)

Grimm, Friedrich Melchior. *Correspondance littéraire, philosophique et critique*, ed. Maurice Tourneux (Paris, 1877–82)

Griswold, Harold E. 'Mozart's "Good Wood-Biter": Georg Wenzel Ritter (1748–1808)', *Galpin Society Journal*, xlix (1996), 103–12

Grochotow, Sergei. 'Mozart und Hummel', *Acta Mozartiana*, xl/3–4 (1993), 94–103

Groman, Mary Alyce. 'The Mannheim Orchestra under the Leadership of Christian Cannabich' (dissertation, University of California, Berkeley, 1979)

Gros, Étienne. *Philippe Quinault: Sa vie et son œuvre* (Paris, 1926)

Grout, Donald J. *Alessandro Scarlatti: An Introduction to his Operas* (Berkeley, 1979)

Grove, George. 'Mozart's Sonata', *Athenaeum* (27 July 1872), 119

Gruber, Clemens M. und Hubert Reitterer. 'Biographien aus dem Umfeld von W. A. Mozart: Saporti Teresa', *Wiener Figaro: Mitteilungsblatt der Mozartgemeinde Wien*, lii/4 (1996), 11–12

Gruber, Gernot. 'Glucks Tanzdramen und ihre musikalische Dramatik', *Österreichische Musikzeitschrift*, xxix (1974), 17–24

Gruber, Gernot. *Mozart and Posterity* (London, 1991)

Gruber, Gernot. 'Otto Jahns Bedeutung für die Mozart-Forschung', *Otto Jahn (1813–1868): Ein Geisteswissenschaftler zwischen Klassizismus und Historismus*, ed. William M. Calder, Hubert Cancik and Bernhard Kytzler (Stuttgart, 1991), 144–50

Gubernatis, Angelo de. *Pietro Metastasio: Corso di lezioni fatte nell'Università di Roma nell'anno scolastico 1909–1910* (Florence, 1910)

Gugler, Bernhard. 'Zur Oper Don Giovanni: Controversfragen bezüglich der Darstellung auf der Bühne', *Morgenblatt für Gebildete Leser*, xxxii (1865), 745–51; xxxiii (1865), 772–81; xxxiv (1865), 799–802

Gugler, Bernhard. 'Zwei eingewurzelte Druckfehler', *Allgemeine musikalische Zeitung*, new series, i (1866), 29–31

Gugler, Bernhard. 'Zweifelhafte Stellen im Manuscripte der Don Juan-Partitur', *Allgemeine musikalische Zeitung*, new series, i (1866), 61–2, 77–9, 93–6

Gugler, Bernhard. 'Sind im 2. Finale des Don Juan die Posaunen von Mozart?', *Allgemeine musikalische Zeitung*, new series, ii (1867), 2–4, 13–15 and 21–4

Gugler, Bernhard. 'Die nachkomponierten Szenen zu "Don Juan"', *Allgemeine musikalische Zeitung*, new series, iv (1869), 25–7

Gülke, Peter. *Rousseau und die Musik* (Wilhelmshaven, 1984)

Gülke, Peter. *Im Zyklus eine Welt: Mozarts letzte Sinfonien* (Munich, 1997)

Günther, Ladislas. *L'œuvre dramatique de Sedaine* (Paris, 1908)

Haas, Robert. *Ignaz Umlauff: Die Bergknappen* (Leipzig, 1911 = Denkmäler der Tonkunst in Österreich xxxvi)

Haas, Robert. *Florian Gassmann: La contessina* (Leipzig, 1914 = Denkmäler der Tonkunst in Österreich xlii/xliv)

Haas, Robert. 'Beiträge zur Geschichte der Oper in Prag und Dresden', *Neues Archiv für sächsische Geschichte und Altertumskunde*, xxxvii (1916), 68–96

Haas, Robert. 'Eberlins Schuldramen und Oratorien', *Studien zur Musikwissenschaft*, viii (1921), 9–44

Haas, Robert. 'Anton Eberl', *Mozart-Jahrbuch 1951*, 123–30

Haberkamp, Gertraut. 'Eine bisher unbekannte Widmung Mozarts an die Kurfürstin Maria Elisabeth von Bayern zur Erstausgabe der Sonaten für Klavier und Violine KV 301–306', *Musik in Bayern*, xviii/xix (1979), 5–13

Haberkamp, Gertraut. *Die Erstdrucke der Werke von Wolfgang Amadeus Mozart: Bibliographie* (Tutzing, 1986)

Haberkamp, Gertraut. 'Die Oper La clemenza di Tito von Joseph Anton Camerloher (4.7.1710 – 17.6.1743)', *Collectanea Mozartiana*, ed. Cordelia Ruloff (Tutzing, 1988), 59–71

Hadamowsky, Franz. 'Leitung, Verwaltung und ausübende Künstler . . . am Burgtheater (französisches Theater) und am Kärntnertortheater (deutsches Theater) in Wien 1754–1764', *Jahrbuch der Gesellschaft für Wiener Theaterforschung 1958–9*, 113–33

Hadatsch, Franz J. *Die Launen des Schicksals* (Vienna, 1834)

Haering, Kurt. 'Christian Ludwig Dieter: Hofmusiker und Singspielkomponist, 1757 bis 1822', *Schwäbische Lebensbilder*, i (1940), 98–104

Hagedorn, Friedrich. *Sämmtliche poetische Werke* (Hamburg, 1757)

Hagemann, Carl. *Wilhelmine Schroeder-Devrient* (Berlin, 1904)

Hahn, Albert. *Mozarts Requiem: Zum besseren Verständnis mit einer neuen Übersetzung nebst einem Nachtrag und den Resultaten eines Vergleiches der Breitkopf & Härtelschen Partitur mit den Original-Manuskripten der k. k. Hofbibliothek zu Wien* (Bielefeld, 1867)

Hajdecki, Alexander. 'Mozarts Taufnamen', *Beethoven-Forschung: Lose Blätter*, vi/vii (August 1916), 103–6

Hall, H. Gaston. 'Dom Juan, personnage européen du XVIIe siècle', *Horizons européens de la littérature française au XVIIe siècle: L'Europe: Lieu d'échanges culturels? La Circulation des œuvres et des jugements au XVIIe siècle*, ed. Wolfgang Leiner (Tübingen, 1988), 139–47

Hallays, André. *Beaumarchais* (Paris, 1897)

Halliwell, Ruth. *The Mozart Family: Four Lives in a Social Context* (Oxford, 1998)

Hamann, Heinz-Wolfgang. 'W.A. Mozart – J. W. Hässler: Der Dresdener Orgelwettstreit im Jahre 1789', *Musik und Kirche*, xxxiii (1963), 126–8

Hamerníková, Anna: '"Licitations-Protokoll über die Leopold Mozartische Verlassenschaft" im Familienarchiv Berchtold', *Mozart-Jahrbuch 1991: Bericht über den Internationalen Mozart-Kongreß Salzburg 1991*, 122–5

Hammer, Karl. *W. A. Mozart: Eine theologische Deutung*, second edition (Weil am Rhein, 2006)

Hammerle, Alois Joseph. *Chronik des Gesanges und der Musik in Salzburg* (Salzburg, 1874–6)

Hammerle, Alois Joseph. *Mozart und einige Zeigenossen: Neue Beiträge für Salzburgische Geschichte, Literatur und Musik* (Salzburg, 1877)

Handke, Robert. 'Zur Lösung der Benedictus-Frage in Mozarts Requiem', *Zeitschrift für Musikwissenschaft*, i (1918), 108–30

Hanning, Barbara Russano. 'The Iconography of a Salon Concert: A Reappraisal', *French Musical Thought, 1600–1800*, ed. Georgia Cowart (Ann Arbor, MI, 1989), 129–48

Hansell, Kathleen Kuzmick. *Opera and Ballet at the Regio Ducal Teatro of Milan, 1771–1776: A Musical and Social History* (Berkeley, CA, 1980)

Hansell, Sven H. 'Sacred Music at the Incurabili in Venice at the Time of J. A. Hasse', *Journal of the American Musicological Society*, xxiii (1970), 282–301, 505–21; xv (1972), 118–20

Hanslick, Eduard. *Geschichte des Concertwesens in Wien* (Vienna, 1869)

Hanslick, Eduard. *Die moderne Oper* (Vienna, 1885)

Hanslick, Eduard. 'Mozart', *Die moderne Oper* (Vienna, 1885), 29–60

Hanslick, Eduard. *Suite: Aufsätze über Musik und Musiker* (Vienna, 1885)

Hanslick, Eduard. *Sämtliche Schriften*, ed. Dietmar Strauss (Vienna, 1993—)

Hardie, Graham. 'Gennaro Antonio Federico's *Amor vuol sofferenza* (1739) and the Neapolitan Comic Opera', *Studies in Music* [Australia], x (1976), 62–6

Harley, Brian. 'Music and Chess', *Music & Letters*, xii (1931), 276–83

Harley, John. 'Music at the English Court in the Eighteenth and Nineteenth Centuries', *Music & Letters*, l (1969), 332–51

Harmon, Thomas. 'The performance of Mozart's Church Sonatas', *Music & Letters*, li/1 (1970), 51–60

Harpe, Jean-François de La. *Correspondance littéraire* (Paris, 1801–7)

Haspels, Jan Jaap. 'Mozart and Automatic Music', *Mozart and the Netherlands: A Bicentenarian Retrospect*, ed. Arie Peddemors and Leo Samama (Zutphen, 2003), 113–25

Hasquin, Hervé and Roland Mortier, ed. *Fêtes et musiques révolutionnaires: Grétry et Gossec* (Brussels, 1990)

Haug, Fr. 'Raff', *Cäcilia*, v (1826), 44

Häusser, Ludwig. *Die Geschichte der rheinischen Pfalz* (Heidelberg, 1845)

Haußwald, Günter. 'Johann Dismas Zelenka als Instrumentalkomponist', *Archiv für Musikwissenschaft*, xiii (1956), 243–62

Head, Matthew. 'Myths of a Sinful Father: Maynard Solomon's "Mozart"', *Musical Times*, lxxx/1 (1999), 74–85

Head, Matthew. *Orientalism, Masquerade and Mozart's Turkish Music* (London, 2000)

Heartz, Daniel. 'From Garrick to Gluck: The Reform of Theatre and Opera in the Mid-Eighteenth Century', *Proceedings of the Royal Musical Association*, xciv (1967/8), 111–27

Heartz, Daniel. '*Voix de ville*', *Words and Music: The Scholar's View . . . in Honor of A. Tillman Merritt*, ed. L. Berman (Cambridge, MA, 1972), 115–35

Heartz, Daniel. 'Raaff's last aria: A Mozartian idyll in the spirit of Hasse', *Musical Quarterly*, lx/4 (1974), 517–43

Heartz, Daniel. 'The Creation of the Buffo Finale in Italian Opera', *Proceedings of the Royal Musical Association*, civ (1977/8), 67–78

Heartz, Daniel. 'Diderot et le Théâtre lyrique', *Revue de musicologie*, lxiv (1978), 229–51

Heartz, Daniel. 'Mozart's Overture to *Titus* as Dramatic Argument', *Musical Quarterly*, lxiv (1978), 29–49

Heartz, Daniel. 'Goldoni, *Don Giovanni* and the dramma giocoso', *The Musical Times*, cxx (1979) 993–8

Heartz, Daniel. 'Mozart and his Italian contemporaries: *La clemenza di Tito*', *Mozart und seine Umwelt* (Kassel, 1979), 275–93

Heartz, Daniel. 'The great quartet in Mozart's *Idomeneo*', *The Music Forum*, v (1980), 233–56

Heartz, Daniel. 'The Beginnings of Operatic Romance: Rousseau, Sedaine, and Monsigny', *Eighteenth-Century Studies*, xv (1981/2), 149–78

Heartz, Daniel. 'An Iconography of the Dances in the Ballroom Scene of *Don Giovanni*', *Mozart's Operas*, ed. Thomas Bauman (Berkeley, 1990), 178–93

Heartz, Daniel. 'Mozart's sense for nature', *19th-Century Music*, xv/2 (1991), 107–15

Heartz, Daniel. *Haydn, Mozart and the Viennese School 1740–1780* (New York, 1995)

Heartz, Daniel, 'When Mozart Revises: Guglielmo in *Così*', *Wolfgang Amadè Mozart: Essays on his Life and his Music*, ed. Stanley Sadie (Oxford, 1996), 355–61

Heartz, Daniel. 'Goldoni, opera buffa, and Mozart's advent in Vienna', *Opera buffa in Mozart's Vienna*, ed. Mary Hunter and James Webster (Cambridge, 1997), 25–49

Heartz, Daniel. 'Vis comica: Goldoni, Galuppi, and *L'Arcadia in Brenta*', *From Garrick to Gluck: Essays on Opera in the Age of Enlightenment*, ed. John A. Rice (Hillsdale, NY, 2004), 11–39

Heckel, Hans. *Das Don-Juan-Problem in der neueren Dichtung* (Stuttgart, 1915)

Hegel, Georg Wilhelm Friedrich. *Vorlesungen über die Ästhetik* (Berlin, 1835)

Heine, Carl. *Johannes Velten* (Halle, 1887)

Heinemann, Ernst. 'Ist Mozarts "Don Juan" eine tragische oder eine komische Oper?', *Die Musik*, iv (1904/5), 17–24

Heinse, Friedrich. *Reise- und Lebens-Skizzen nebst dramaturgischen Blättern* (Leipzig, 1837)

Heinse, Johann Jakob Wilhelm. *Sämtliche Schriften* (Leipzig, 1838)

Heinse, Johann Jakob Wilhelm. *Hildegard von Hohenthal* (Berlin, 1795)

Heinz, Rudolf. 'Guido Adlers Musikhistorik als historisches Dokument', *Die Ausbreitung des Historismus über die Musik*, ed. Walter Wiora (Regensburg, 1969), 209–19

Helbing, Volker. 'Mozarts "Eros-Sinfonie": Die Es-dur-Sinfonie KV 543, nachgebildet und aufbereitet für Leser der AMZ von August Apel', *Musica*, i (1996), 84–92

Helfert, Joseph Alexander von. *Die österreichische Volksschule: Geschichte, System, Statistik* (Prague and Vienna, 1860)

Hell, Helmut. *Die neapolitanische Opernsinfonie in der ersten Hälfte des 18. Jahrhunderts* (Tutzing, 1971)

Helm, Eugene E. *Thematic Catalogue of the Works of Carl Philipp Emanuel Bach* (New Haven, CT, 1989)

Helm, Eugene E. 'C. P. E. Bach and the Great Chain of Variation', *Carl Philipp Emanuel Bach und die europäische Musikkultur: Hamburg 1988*, ed. Hans Joachim Marx (Göttingen, 1990), 223–8

Henderson, Donald G. 'The "Magic Flute" of Peter Winter', *Music & Letters*, lxiv/3–4, 193–205

Henkel, Heinrich. 'Über Mozartsche Manuskripte', *Mitteilungen für die Mozart-Gemeinde in Berlin*, i (1898), 156–63

Henri, Jacques. *Mozart Frère Maçon: La Symbolique Maçonnique dans l'Œuvre de Mozart* (Paris, 1997)

H[ensler], Karl Friedrich. *Masonic Oration on Mozart's Death. Delivered on the Occasion of the Admission of a Master to the Most Worthy Lodge of St John called the Crowned Hope of the Orient in Vienna, by Br. H . . . R.* (Vienna, 1792)

Henze-Döhring, Sabine. 'E. T. A. Hoffmann-"Kult" und Don Giovanni-Rezeption im Paris des 19. Jahrhunderts: Castil-Blazes Don Juan im Théâtre de l'Académie Royale de Musique am 10. Marz 1834', *Mozart-Jahrbuch 1984/85*, 193–229

Henze-Döhring, Sabine. *Opera seria, opera buffa und Mozarts Don Giovanni: Zur Gattungskonvergenz in der italienischen Oper des 18. Jahrhunderts* (Laaber, 1986)

Henze-Döhring, Sabine. 'Orchester und Orchestersatz in Christian Cannabichs Mannheimer Sinfonien', *Mozart und Mannheim*, ed. Ludwig Finscher, Bärbel Pelker and Jochen Reutter (Frankfurt am Main, 1994), 257–71

Herbert, Trevor and John Wallace, ed. *The Cambridge Companion to Brass Instruments* (Cambridge, 1997)

Herder, Johann Gottfried. *Aus dem Nachlaß* (Frankfurt, 1856–7)

Herder, Johann Gottfried. *Adrastea* (Berlin, 1879)

Heriot, Angus. *The Castrati in Opera* (London, 1956)

Herklotz, Renate. 'Metastasios *La clemenza di Tito* und die Philosophie der Aufklärung', *Kongreßbericht zum VII. Internationalen Gewandhaus-Symposium: Wolfgang Amadeus Mozart – Forschung und Praxis im Dienst von Leben, Werk, Interpretation und Rezeption anläßlich der Gewandhaus-Festtage in Leipzig vom 3. bis 6. Oktober 1991* (Leipzig, 1993), 35–40

Hermann, Albert Ritter von. *Antonio Salieri: Eine Studie zur Geschichte seines künstlerischen Wirkens* (Vienna, 1897)

Heuß, Alfred. 'Die Instrumental-Stücke des "Orfeo"', *Sammelbände der Internationalen Musikgesellschaft*, iv (1902/3), 175–224

Heuß, Alfred. 'Mozart als Kritiker', *Die Musik*, iv (1904/5), 25–37

Heuß, Alfred. 'Das dämonische Element in Mozarts Werken', *Zeitschrift der Internationalen Musikgesellschaft*, vii (1906), 175–86

Heuß, Alfred. 'Mozarts siebentes Violinkonzert', *Zeitschrift der Internationalen Musikgesellschaft*, ix (1907/8), 124–9

Heuß, Alfred. 'Zum Thema: Mannheimer Vorhalt', *Zeitschrift der Internationalen Musikgesellschaft*, ix (1907/8), 277–80

Heuss, Alfred. '[Review of Georg Schünemann, *Mozart als achtjähriger Komponist*]', *Zeitschrift der Internationalen Musikgesellschaft*, x (1908/9), 181–2

Heuß, Alfred. 'Über die Dynamik der Mannheimer Schule', *Riemann-Festschrift* (Leipzig, 1909), 433–55

Heuß, Alfred. 'Zu Umlauf's Singspiel "Die Bergknappen"', *Zeitschrift der Internationalen Musikgesellschaft*, xiii (1911/12), 164–71

Heuß, Alfred. 'Gluck als Musikdramatiker', *Zeitschrift der Internationalen Musikgesellschaft*, xv (1913/14), 274–91

Hickman, Roger. 'The Nascent Viennese String Quartet', *Musical Quarterly*, lxvii (1981), 193–212

Hickman, Roger. 'The Flowering of the Viennese String Quartet in the Late Eighteenth Century', *Music Review*, i (1989), 157–80

Hiller, Johann Adam. *Wöchentliche Nachrichten und Anmerkungen die Musik betreffend* (Leipzig, 1766–70)

Hiller, Johann Adam. *Lebensbeschreibung berühmter Musikgelehrten und Tonkünstler neuerer Zeit* (Leipzig, 1784)

Hiller, Johann Adam. *Der Messias von Händel nebst angehängten Betrachtungen darüber* (Berlin, 1786)

Hiller, Johann Adam. *Nachricht von der Aufführung des Händelschen Messias in Berlin den 19. May 1786* (Berlin, 1786)

Hiller, Johann Adam. *Fragmente aus Händels Messias, nebst Betrachtungen über die Aufführung Händelscher Singcompositionen* (Leipzig, 1787)

Hiller, Johann Adam. *Über Alt und Neu in der Musik* (Leipzig, 1787)

Hilmar, Rosemary. *Der Musikverlag Artaria & Comp.: Geschichte und Probleme der Druckproduktion* (Tutzing, 1977)

Hilscher, Elisabeth and Andrea Sommer-Mathis, ed. *Pietro Metastasio, uomo universale (1698–1782)* (Vienna, 2000)

Hiltner, Beate. *'La clemenza di Tito' von Wolfgang Amadé Mozart im Spiegel der musikalischen Fachpresse zwischen 1800 und 1850: Rezeptionsgeschichtliche Untersuchungen unter besonderen Berücksichtigungen der Wiener Quellen und Verhältnisse* (Frankfurt, 1994)

Hiltner, Beate. '"La clemenza di Tito" von W. A. Mozart im Berliner Musikleben der ersten Hälfte des 19. Jahrhunderts', *Neue Berlinische Musikzeitung*, ix/2 (1994), 33–9

Hintermaier, Ernst. 'Die Salzburger Hofkapelle von 1700 bis 1806: Organisation und Personal' (dissertation, University of Salzburg, 1972)

Hintermaier, Ernst. 'Das Fürsterzbischöfliche Hoftheater zu Salzburg (1775–1803)', *Österreichische Musikzeitschrift*, xxx/7 (1975), 351–63

Hintermaier, Ernst. '"Missa salisburgensis": Neue Erkenntnisse über Entstehung, Autor und Zweckbestimmung', *Musicologica austriaca*, i (1977), 154–96

Hintermaier, Ernst. 'Mozart und das Theater am Salzburger fürsterzbischöflichen Hof', *Mozart und seine Umwelt* (Kassel, 1979), 144–8

Hintermaier, Ernst. 'Zur Urheberschaft des Introitus Cibavit eos KV 44/73u: Mozarts mißglückter Transkriptionsversuch einer mensural notierten Musik', *Mozart-Jahrbuch 1991*, 509–17

Hintermaier, Ernst. 'Eine vermutlich authentische Sinfonie-Fassung der Ouvertüre zu Mozarts Lucio Silla KV 135', *Mozart-Studien*, i (1992), 125–34

Hintermaier, Ernst. 'Heinrich Ignaz Franz Biber (1644–1704) und das Musikleben Salzburgs', *Barockberichte*, xviii/ix (1994), 265–73

Hirasawa, Hiroko. 'Josepha Barbara von Auernhammer: Schülerin Mozarts, Pianistin, Komponistin' (dissertation, University of Vienna, 1993)

Hirsch, Paul. 'A Mozart Problem', *Music & Letters*, xxv/4 (1944), 209–12

Hirsch, Rudolf. *Mozarts Schauspieldirektor: Musikalische Reminiscenzen* (Leipzig, 1856)

Hirschberg, Eugen. *Die Enzyklopädisten und die französische Oper im 18. Jahrhundert* (Leipzig, 1903)

Hirschfeld, Robert. 'Mozarts "Zaide" in der Wiener Hofoper', *Zeitschrift der Internationalen Musikgesellschaft*, iv (1902/3), 66–71

Hochradner, Thomas. 'Matthias Siegmund Biechteler: Leben und Werk eines Salzburger Hofkapellmeisters' (dissertation, University of Salzburg, 1991)

Hochradner, Thomas. '"Meistens nur um eine Uebung in der Radierkunst zu machen": Leopold Mozarts kompositorisches Erstlingswerk: Die Sonate Sei (1740)', *Beiträge des Internationalen Leopold-Mozart-Kolloquiums Augsburg 1994*, ed. Josef Mančal and Wolfgang Plath (Augsburg, 1997 = Beiträge zur Leopold-Mozart-Forschung ii), 29–46

Hochstein, Wolfgang. 'Die Gestaltung des Gloria in konzertierenden Messvertonungen "neapolitanischer" Komponisten', *JbMw*, viii (1985), 45–64

Hocquard, Jean-Victor. *La pensée de Mozart* (Paris, 1958)

Hocquard, Jean-Victor. *L'Enlèvement au Sérail (Die Entführung aus dem Serail) précédé de Zaïde* (Paris, 1980)

Hocquard, Jean-Victor. *Mozart dans ses airs de concert* (Paris, 1989)

Hocquard, Jean-Victor. *Mozart ou la voix du comique* (Paris, 1999)

Hodges, Sheila. '"One of the most accomplished women of her age": Anna Storace, Mozart's first Susanna,' *Music Review* l/2 (1989), 93–102

Hodges, Sheila. 'Venanzio Rauzzini: "The First Master for Teaching in the Universe"', *Music Review*, lii (1991), 12–30

Hodges, Sheila. 'Lorenzo Da Ponte's first Susanna', *Omaggio a Lorenzo Da Ponte: Atti del Convegno "Lorenzo Da Ponte: Librettista di Mozart"* (Rome, 1992), 357–64

Hodges, Sheila. *Lorenzo Da Ponte: The Life and Times of Mozart's Librettist* (Madison, WI, 2002)

Hoesli, Irma. *Wolfgang Amadeus Mozart: Briefstil eines Musikgenies* (Zurich, 1948)

Hoffmann, Ernst Theodor Amadeus. *Fantasiestücke in Callots Manier* (Bamberg, 1814)

Hoffmann, Ernst Theodor Amadeus. *Die Serapionsbrüder* (Berlin, 1819)

Hoffmann, Hans. *Mozart: Genialer Vater, vergessene Söhne* (Schwarzach, 1999)

Hoffmann, Samuel Friedrich Wilhelm. *Lebensbilder berühmter Humanisten. 1. Reihe: Friedrich Jacobs, August Böckh, Karl Zell, Angelo Poliziano* (Leipzig, 1837)

Hoffmann, Wolfgang. 'Satztechnische Bemerkungen zu Mozarts "Ave verum corpus" KV 618', *Mozart-Studien*, viii (1998), 113–24

Hoffmann-Erbrecht, Lothar. *Deutsche und italienische Klaviermusik zur Bachzeit* (Leipzig and Wiesbaden, 1954)

Höft, Brigitte. 'Komponisten, Komponistinnen und Virtuosen', *Die Mannheimer Hofkapelle im Zeitalter Carl Theodors*, ed. Ludwig Finscher (Mannheim, 1972), 59–70

Hogarth, George. *Memoirs of the Opera* (London, 1851)

Hogwood, Christopher. '"The Inconstant and Original Johann Wilhelm Hässler", his 1786 Autobiography and a Thematic Catalogue of his Keyboard Works to 1790', *De Clavicordio III: Magnano 1997* (Magnano, 1997), 151–220

Hogwood, Christopher and Jan Smaczny. 'The Bohemian lands', *The Classical Era: From the 1740s to the end of the 18th Century*, ed. Neal Zaslaw (London, 1989), 188–212

Hohenemser, Richard. *Cherubini: Sein Leben und seine Werke* (Leipzig, 1913)

Holden, Raymond. 'Richard Strauss' performing version of *Idomeneo*', *Richard Strauss-Blätter*, xxxvi (1996), 83–131

Holl, Moritz. 'Mozarts Ohr: Eine anatomische Studie', *Mitteilungen der Anthropologischen Gesellschaft in Wien*, xxxi (1901), 1–12

Holman, Peter. '"A solo on the viola da gamba": Carl Friedrich Abel as a performer', *Ad Parnassum*, ii/4 (2004), 45–71

Holmes, Edward. *The Life of Mozart* (London, 1845)

Holschneider, Andreas. 'Die musikalische Bibliothek Gottfried van Swietens', *Gesellschaft für Musikforschung: Kongreß-Bericht Kassel 1962*, 174–8

Holschneider, Andreas. 'Mozarts Bearbeitung von Händels Messias', *Zwischen Bach und Mozart: Vorträge des Europäischen Musikfestes Stuttgart 1988*, ed. Ulrich Prinz (Kassel, 1994), 166–79

Honolka, Kurt. *Schubart, Dichter und Musiker, Journalist und Rebell: Sein Leben, sein Werk* (Stuttgart, 1985)

Honolka, Kurt. *Papageno: Emanuel Schikaneder. Man of the theater in Mozart's time* (Portland, OR, 1990)

Högg, Margarete. *Die Gesangskunst der Faustina Hasse und das Sängerinnenwesen ihrer Zeit in Deutschland* (Berlin, 1931)

Hormayr, Joseph von. *Wien: Seine Geschichte und Denkwürdigkeiten* (Vienna, 1823–5)

Horsley, Paul J. 'Dittersdorf and the Finale in Late-Eighteenth-Century German Comic Opera' (dissertation, Cornell University, 1988)

Horsley, Paul J. 'Dittersdorfs Singspiele', *Carl Ditters von Dittersdorf: Leben, Umwelt, Werk*, ed. Hubert Unverricht (Tutzing, 1997), 123–35

Hortschansky, Klaus, ed. *Die Andrés: Familie und Verlag. Ihr Beitrag zur Musik-Druck-Stadtgeschichte. Ausstellung Stadtmuseum Offenbach a. M.* (Offenbach am Main, 1974)

Hortschansky, Klaus. 'Mozarts Ascanio in Alba und der Typus der Serenata', *Analecta musicologica* xviii (1978), 148–58

Hortschansky, Klaus. 'Autographe Stimmen zu Mozarts Klavierkonzert KV 175 im Archiv André zu Offenbach', *Mozart-Jahrbuch 1989/90*, 37–54

Hortschansky, Klaus. 'Musiktheater in Mannheim als gestelltes Bild', *Mozart und Mannheim*, ed. Ludwig Finscher, Bärbel Pelker and Jochen Reutter (Frankfurt am Main, 1994), 65–80

Hortschansky, Klaus. 'Die g-Moll-Sinfonie zur Zeit der Wiener Klassik' *Traditionen – Neuansätze: Für Anna Amalie Abert (1906–1996)*, ed. Klaus Hortschansky (Tutzing, 1997), 329–48

Hörwarthner, Maria. 'Joseph Haydns Bibliothek: Versuch einer literaturhistorischen Rekonstruktion', *Haydn und die Literatur seiner Zeit*, ed. Z. Heman (Eisenstadt, 1976), 157–207; Eng. trans. in *Joseph Haydn and his World*, ed. Elaine Sisman (Princeton, NJ, 1997), 395–462

Horwitz, Karl and Karl Riedel, *Wiener Instrumentalmusik vor und um 1750. Heft I* (Leipzig, 1908 = Denkmäler der Tonkunst in Österreich xxxi)

Hosler, Bellamy. *Changing Aesthetic Views of Instrumental Music in 18th-Century Germany* (Ann Arbor, MI, 1981)

Howard, Patricia. *Gluck: An Eighteenth-Century Portrait in Letters and Documents* (Oxford, 1995)

Hucke, Helmut. 'Alessandro Scarlatti und die Musikkomödie', *Colloquium Alessandro Scarlatti Würzburg 1975*, ed. Wolfgang Osthoff and Jutta Ruile-Dronke (Tutzing, 1979), 177–90

Hudson, Richard. *Stolen Time: The History of Tempo Rubato*, second edition (Oxford, 1997)

Hummel, Walter. *Nannerl: Wolfgang Amadeus Mozarts Schwester* (Vienna, 1952)

Hummel, Walter. *W. A. Mozarts Söhne* (Kassel, 1956)

Hunkemöller, Jürgen. *W. A. Mozarts frühe Sonaten für Violine und Klavier: Untersuchungen zur Gattungsgeschichte im 18. Jahrhundert* (Berne, 1970)

Hunt, Jno Leland. *Giovanni Paisiello: His Life as an Opera Composer* (New York, 1975)

Hunter, Alfred Collinson. *J.-B.-A. Suard, un introducteur de la littérature anglaise en France* (Paris, 1925)

Hunter, Mary. '"Pamela": The Offspring of Richardson's Heroine in Eighteenth-Century Opera', *Mosaic: A Journal for the Interdisciplinary Study of Literature*, viii (1985), 61–76

Hunter, Mary. 'The Fusion and Juxtaposition of Genres in Opera Buffa 1770–1800: Anelli and Piccinni's "Griselda"', *Music & Letters*, lxviii (1986), 363–80

Hunter, Mary. 'Some representations of *opera seria* in *opera buffa*', *Cambridge Opera Journal*, iii (1992), 89–108

Hunter, Mary. 'Landscapes, Gardens and Gothic Settings in the *Opere Buffe* of Mozart and his Contemporaries', *Current Musicology*, li (1993), 94–105

Hunter, Mary. *The Culture of Opera Buffa in Mozart's Vienna: A Poetics of Entertainment* (Princeton, 1999)

Hurwitz, Joachim. 'Haydn and the Freemasons', *Haydn Yearbook 1985*, 5–98

Hutchings, Arthur. *A Companion to Mozart's Piano Concertos* (London, 1948)

Hüttenbrenner, Anselm. 'Kleiner Beytrag zu Salieri's Biographie', *Allgemeine musikalische Zeitung*, xxvii (1825), 797

Iacuzzi, Alfred. *The European Vogue of Favart: The Diffusion of the Opéra-Comique* (New York, 1932)

Inzaghi, Luigi and Danilo Prefumo. *Giambattista Sammartini, primo maestro della sinfonia (1700–1775)* (Turin, 1996)

Irmen, Hans-Josef. *Mozart: Mitglied geheimer Gesellschaften* (Mechernich, 1988)

Irmen, Hans-Josef, Ruth Ohm and Chantal Spenke. *Mozart's Masonry and The Magic Flute* (Zülpich, 1996)

Irmen, Hans-Josef und Heinz Schuler, ed. *Die Wiener Freimaurerlogen 1786–1793: Die Protokolle der Loge "Zur Wahrheit" (1785–1787) und die Mitgliederverzeichnisse der übrigen Wiener Logen (1786–1793)* (Zülpich, 1998)

Irving, John. 'Johann Schobert and Mozart's Early Sonatas', *Irish Musical Studies*, v (1996), 82–95

Irving, John. *Mozart: The 'Haydn' Quartets* (Cambridge, 1998)

Irving, John. *Mozart's Piano Concertos: Contents, Sources, Style* (Aldershot, 2003)

Isherwood, Robert M. *Music in the Service of the King: France in the Seventeenth Century* (Ithaca, 1973)

Isherwood, Robert M. *Farce and Fantasy: Popular Entertainment in Eighteenth-Century Paris* (New York, 1986)

Isherwood, Robert M. 'Nationalism and the Querelle des Bouffons', *D'un opéra l'autre: Hommage à Jean Mongrédien*, ed. Jean Gribenski, Marie-Claire Mussat and Herbert Schneider (Paris, 1994), 323–30

Istel, Edgar. *Jean-Jacques Rousseau als Komponist seiner lyrischen Scene 'Pygmalion'* (Leipzig, 1901)

Istel, Edgar. 'Die Entstehung des deutschen Melodramas', *Die Musik*, v (1905/6), 143–67, 231–56, 308–30, 367–90

Istel, Edgar. *Das Libretto* (Berlin, 1915)

Jacobi, Friedrich Heinrich. *F. H. Jacobi's Auserlesener Briefwechsel* (Leipzig, 1825–7)

Jacobi, Friedrich Heinrich. *Aus F. H. Jacobi's Nachlaß: Ungedruckte Briefe von und an Jacobi und Andere* (Leipzig, 1869)

Jakubcova, Alena. '"Ihr, Furien, kommt . . . !" Theatrales Vergnügen am Schrecklichen um 1790', *Hudební věda*, xxxviii/3–4 (2001), 343–75

Jahn, Otto. *W. A. Mozart* (Leipzig, 1856; fourth edition, ed. Hermann Deiters: Leipzig, 1905–7)

Jahn, Otto. 'Mozart-Paralipomenon', *Allgemeine musikalische Zeitung*, new series, i (1863), 171–4

Jahn, Otto. *Gesammelte Aufsätze über Musik* (Leipzig, 1866)

Jahn, Otto. 'Mozarts Handschrift', *Allgemeine musikalische Zeitung*, new series, ii (1867), 155, 163

Jahn, Otto. 'Briefe Mozart's', *Allgemeine musikalische Zeitung*, new series, ii (1867), 202–3, 211, 266–7, 243, 250

Jahrmärker, Manuela and Till Gerrit Waidelich, ed. *Der Zauberflöte zweyter Theil unter dem Titel: Das Labyrinth oder Der Kampf mit den Elementen. Eine große heroisch-komische Oper in zwey Aufzügen von Emanuel Schikaneder. In Musik gesetzt von Herrn Peter Winter Kapellmeister in Churpfalz-bayerischen Diensten. Vollständiges Textbuch* (Tutzing, 1992)

Jalowetz, Heinrich. 'Beethovens Jugendwerke in ihren melodischen Beziehungen zu Mozart, Haydn und Ph. E. Bach', *Sammelbände der Internationalen Musikgesellschaft*, xii (1910), 417–74

Jansen, Albert. *Jean-Jacques Rousseau als Musiker* (Berlin, 1884)

Jeffery, Brian. 'The Idea of Music in Ronsard's Poetry', *Ronsard the Poet*, ed. Terence Cave (London, 1973), 209–39

Jenkins, John. *Mozart and the English Connection* (London, 1998)

Jöde, Fritz. 'Durchgeführte harmonische Organisierung bei Mozart', *Die Musikantengilde*, vii (1929/30), 56–61

Johnson, Douglas, Alan Tyson and Robert Winter. *The Beethoven Sketchbooks: History, Reconstruction, Inventory* (Oxford, 1985)

Johnstone, H. Diack and Roger Fiske, ed. *Music in Britain: The Eighteenth Century* (Oxford, 1990)

Jonášová, Milada. '"Ihre Versicherung beruhigt mich, sie kommt von einem Kenner": K biografii Jana Křtitele Kuchaře', *Hudební věda*, lx (2003), 329–60

Jones, David Wyn. 'Why did Mozart compose his last three symphonies? Some new hypotheses', *Music Review*, li/4 (1990), 280–9

Jones, David Wyn. 'The origins of the quartet', *The Cambridge Companion to the String Quartet*, ed. Robin Stowell (Cambridge, 2003), 177–84

Jorgenson, Dale A. *The Life and Legacy of Franz Xaver Hauser: A Forgotten Leader in the Nineteenth-Century Bach Movement* (Carbondale, IL, 1996)

Jullien, Adolphe. *La musique et les philosophes au dix-huitième siècle* (Paris, 1873)

Jung, Hermann, ed. *Mozart-Aspekte des 19. Jahrhunderts* (Mannheim, 1995)

Junk, Viktor. *Goethes Fortsetzung der Mozartschen Zauberflöte* (Munich, 1899)

Junker, Carl Ludwig. *Zwanzig Komponisten* (Berne, 1776)

Kabelková, Markéta. 'Hudební archív a kapela hrabete Jana Josefa Filipa Pachty', *Hudební věda*, xxviii/4 28 (1991), 329–33

Kahlert, August. 'Rechtfertigung Mozarts gegen H. G. Nägeli', *Neue Zeitschrift für Musik*, xix (1843), 97–8

Kaiser, Hartmut. 'Mozarts Don Giovanni und E. T. A. Hoffmanns Don Juan: Ein Beitrag zum Verständnis des Fantasiestücks', *Mitteilungen der E. T. A. Hoffmann-Gesellschaft*, xxi (1975), 6–26

Kalbeck, Max. *Mozarts Don Juan* (Vienna, 1886)

Kamienski, Lucian. 'Zum "Tempo rubato"', *Archiv für Musikwissenschaft*, i (1918/9), 108–26

Kammermayer, Max. *Emanuel Schikaneder und seine Zeit: Ein Spiegelbild zu Mozarts Zauberflöte* (Grafenau, 1992)

Kandler, Franz Sales. *Cenni storico-critici intorno alla vita ed alle opere del celebre compositore di musica Giovanni Adolfo Hasse detto il Sassone* (Venice, 1820)

Kandler, Franz Sales. *Über das Leben und die Werke des G. Pierluigi da Palestrina* (Leipzig, 1834)

Kanduth, Erika. 'The Literary and Dramaturgical Aspects of the Viennese *Sepolcro* Oratorio, with Particular Reference to Fux', *Johann Joseph Fux and the Music of the Austro-Italian Baroque*, ed. Harry White (Aldershot, 1992) 153–63

Kantner, Leopold M. 'Dittersdorfs italienische Opern', *Carl Ditters von Dittersdorf: Leben, Umwelt, Werk* (Tutzing, 1997), 111–21

Kaplan, James M. *Marmontel et 'Polymnie'* (Oxford, 1984)

Karhausen, Lucien Richard. 'The Mozarteum's skull: A historical saga', *Journal of Medical Biography*, ix (2001), 109–17

Karro-Pélisson, Françoise. 'Livrets et librettistes parisiens à la cour de Vienne au temps de Marie-Thérèse: Modèles français pour *Die Entführung aus dem Serail*', *Mozart: Les chemins de l'Europe* (Strasbourg, 1997), 137–48

Kaufman, Anthony. 'The Shadow of the Burlador: Don Juan on the Continent and in England', *Comedy from Shakespeare to Sheridan: Change and Continuity in the English and European Dramatic Tradition*, ed. Eugene Waith and James C. Bulman (Newark, NJ, 1986)

Kaufmann, M. 'Wolfgang Amadeus Mozart der Sohn: Sein Aufenthalt in Karlsbad, seine Begräbnisstätte und Biographisches', *Neue Zeitschrift für Musik*, lxxxii (1915), 145–8

Kaul, Oskar. *Anton Rosetti: Ausgewählte Sinfonien des Fürstl. Oettinger-Wallersteinischen Kapellmeisters* (Leipzig, 1912 = Denkmäler der Tonkunst in Bayern xii/1)

Kaulitz-Niedeck, Rosa. *Die Mara: Das Leben einer berühmten Sängerin* (Heilbronn, 1929)

Kawada, Kyoko. *Studien zu den Singspielen von Johann Adam Hiller (1728–1804)* (Marburg an der Lahn, 1969)

Kearns, Andrew. 'The Orchestral Serenade in Eighteenth-Century Salzburg', *Journal of Musicological Research*, xvi/3 (1997), 163–97

Kearns, Andrew. *Six Orchestral Serenades from South Germany and Austria. Part 2* (Middleton, WI, 2003 = Recent Researches in the Music of the Classical Era lxx)

Keefe, Simon P. 'A Complementary Pair: Stylistic Experimentation in Mozart's Final Piano Concertos, K. 537 in D and K. 595 in B flat', *Journal of Musicology*, xviii (2001), 658–84

Keefe, Simon P. '"An Entirely Special Manner": Mozart's Piano Concerto No. 14 in E Flat, K. 449, and the Stylistic Implications of Confrontation', *Music & Letters*, lxxxii (2001), 559–81

Keefe, Simon P. *Mozart's Piano Concertos: Dramatic Dialogue in the Age of Enlightenment* (Woodbridge, 2001)

Keefe, Simon P. 'An Integrated "Dissonance": Mozart's "Haydn" Quartets and the Slow Introduction of K. 465', *Mozart-Jahrbuch 2002*, 87–103

Keefe, Simon P. 'The "Jupiter" Symphony in C, K. 551: New Perspectives on the Dramatic Finale and its Stylistic Significance in Mozart's Orchestral Œuvre', *Acta musicologica*, lv/1 (2003), 17–43

Keefe, Simon P. 'Mozart's late piano sonatas (K457, 533, 545, 570, 576): Aesthetic and stylistic parallels with his piano concertos', *Words About Mozart: Essays in Honour of Stanley Sadie*, ed. Dorothea Link and Judith Nagley (Woodbridge, 2005), 59–75

Keller, Sigismund. 'Wolfgang Amadeus Mozart in Salzburg im Jahre 1769', *Monatshefte für Musik-Geschichte*, v (1873), 122–3

Kelly, Michael. *Reminiscences of Michael Kelly, of the King's Theatre* (London, 1826)

Kende, Götz Klaus. 'Gustav Mahlers Wiener Figaro', *Acta Mozartiana*, xviii/3–4 (1971), 60–7

Kennedy, Philip. 'The First French Opera', *Recherches sur la musique française classique*, viii (1968), 77–88

Kerman, Joseph. 'Reading *Don Giovanni*', *The Don Giovanni Book: Myths of Seduction and Betrayal*, ed. Jonathan Miller (London, 1990), 108–25

Kerman, Joseph. 'On *Don Giovanni*, No. 2', *Opera and the Enlightenment*, ed. Thomas Bauman and Marita Petzoldt McClymonds (Cambridge, 1995), 260–70

Kessler, Daniel. 'Der Ur-Urgroßvater W. A. Mozarts als Erbauer des Achteckaufsatzes auf dem Dillinger Stadtpfarrkirchenturm', *Jahrbuch des Historischen Vereins Dillingen*, liii (1951), 80–3

Kessler von Sprengseysen, Christian Friedrich. *Anti-Saint-Nicaise: Ein Turnier im XVIII. Jahrhundert gehalten von zwey T**** H**** als etwas für Freymaurer und die es nicht sind* (Leipzig, 1786–7)

Keyssler, Johann Georg. *Neueste Reisen durch Teutschland, Böhmen, Ungarn, die Schweitz, Italien und Lothringen*, third edition, ed. G. Schütze (Hanover, 1776)

Kierkegaard, Søren. *Gesammmelte Werke* (Jena, 1911)

Kiernan, Colm. 'Rousseau and Music in the French Enlightenment', *French Studies*, xxvi (1972), 156–65

King, Alec Hyatt. *Mozart in Retrospect* (London, 1955)

King, Alec Hyatt. 'The Mozarts at the British Museum', *Festschrift Albi Rosenthal*, ed. Rudolf Elvers (Tutzing, 1984), 157–80

Kink, Rudolf. *Geschichte der kaiserlichen Universität zu Wien* (Vienna, 1854)

Kintzler, Catherine. *Jean-Philippe Rameau: Splendeur et naufrage de l'esthétique du plaisir à l'âge classique* (Paris, 1983)

Kintzler, Catherine. *Poétique de l'opéra français de Corneille à Rousseau* (Paris, 1991)

Kipper, Christian. *Musikalische Aktion in der Opera buffa: Il mercato di Malmantile von Carlo Goldoni* (Frankfurt, 1999)

Kirkendale, Warren. 'KV 405: Ein unveröffentlichtes Mozart-Autograph', *Mozart-Jahrbuch 1962/63*, 224–39

Kirkendale, Warren. 'More Slow Introductions by Mozart to Fugues of J. S. Bach?', *Journal of the American Musicological Society*, xvii (1964), 43–65

Kirkendale, Warren. *Fugue and Fugato in Rococo and Classical Chamber Music*, second edition (Durham, NC, 1979)

Kirnberger, Johann Philipp. *Die Kunst des reinen Satzes in der Musik* (Berlin and Königsberg, 1771–9)

Kirnberger, Johann Philipp. *Grundsätze des Generalbasses als erste Linien zur Composition* (Berlin, 1781)

Klafsky, Anton Maria. 'Michael Haydn als Kirchenkomponist', *Studien zur Musikwissenschaft*, iii (1915), 5–23

Klafsky, Anton Maria. *Michael Haydn: Kirchenwerke* (Leipzig, 1915 = Denkmäler der Tonkunst in Österreich xlv)

Klaver, Richard. *The Litany of Loreto* (London, 1954)

Klein, Anton von. *Über Wielands Rosamund, Schweizers Musik und die Vorstellung dieses Singspiels in Mannheim* (Frankfurt, 1781)

Kleiner, Hans and Erhard Nowak. *'Nur wer die Musik liebt . . .': Valentin Rathgeber (1682–1750)* (Bad Neustadt an der Saale, 1981)

Kleinertz, Rainer. 'Musik als Parodie: Bemerkungen zu Florian Leopold Gaßmanns Dramma giocoso La contessina', *Die Oper in Böhmen, Mähren und Sudetenschlesien*, ed. Widmar Hader (Regensburg, 1996), 40–50

Kloiber, Rudolf. *Die dramatischen Ballette von Christian Cannabich* (Munich, 1928)

Kluger, Martin. *Die Mozarts: Die deutsche Mozartstadt Augsburg und die Mozartstätten in der Region* (Augsburg, 2004)

Knape, Walther. *Karl Friedrich Abel: Leben und Werk eines frühklassischen Komponisten* (Bremen, 1973)

Knepler, Georg. *Wolfgang Amadé Mozart: Annäherungen* (Frankfurt am Main, 1993)

Kneschke, Julius Emil. *Das deutsche Lustspiel in Vergangenheit und Gegenwart* (Leipzig, 1861)

Knigge, Adolf von. *Aus einer alten Kiste: Originalbriefe, Handschriften und Dokumente aus dem Nachlasse eines bekannten Mannes*, ed. Philipp Friedrich Hermann Klencke (Leipzig, 1853)

Knighton, Tess and Michael Burden, ed. 'Metastasio, 1698–1782', *Early Music*, xxvi/4 (1998)

Koch, Charles E. 'The Dramatic Ensemble Finale in the Opéra Comique of the Eighteenth Century', *Acta musicologica*, xxxix (1967), 72–83

Koch, Klaus-Peter. *Reinhard Keiser (1674–1739): Leben und Werk* (Teuchern, 1989)

Koch, Michael. *Die Oratorien Johann Adolf Hasses: Überlieferung und Struktur* (Pfaffenweiler, 1989)

Koch, Richard. *Mozart: Freimaurer und Illuminaten* (Bad Reichenhall, 1911)

Koch-Sternfeld, Josef Ernst Ritter von. *Die letzten dreißig Jahre des Hochstifts und Erzbisthums Salzburg* (n.p., 1816)

Köchel, Ludwig Ritter von. *Chronologisch-thematisches Verzeichniss sämmtlicher Tonwerke Wolfgang Amade Mozart's* (Leipzig, 1862; second edition, ed. Paul Graf von Waldersee: Leipzig, 1905; third edition, ed. Alfred Einstein: Leipzig, 1937; sixth edition, ed. Franz Giegling, Alexander Weinmann and Gerd Sievers: Wiesbaden, 1964)

Köchel, Ludwig Ritter von. 'Nachträge und Berichtigungen zu von Köchels Verzeichnis der Werke Mozarts', *Allgemeine musikalische Zeitung*, ii, new series (1864), 493–6

Köchel, Ludwig Ritter von. 'Mozarts Requiem: Nachlese zu den Forschungen über dessen Entstehen', *Rezensionen über Theater und Musik*, x (1864), 753–6

Köchel, Ludwig Ritter von. *Die Pflege der Musik am österreichischen Hofe vom Schlusse des XV. bis zur Mitte des XVIII. Jahrhunderts* (Vienna, 1866)

Köchel, Ludwig Ritter von. *Johann Josef Fux* (Vienna, 1872)

Koerte, Friedrich Heinrich Wilhelm, ed. *Briefe deutscher Gelehrten: Aus Gleims litterarischem Nachlasse*, ii and iii: *Briefe zwischen Gleim, W. Heinse, und J. von Müller* (Zurich, 1804–6)

Koffka, Wilhelm. *Iffland und Dalberg: Geschichte der classischen Theaterzeit Mannheims* (Berlin, 1865)

Köhler, Karl-Heinz, ed. *Wolfgang Amadeus Mozart: Die Zauberflöte. Faksimile der autographen Partitur* (Leipzig, 1979)

Köhler, Rafael. 'Dittersdorf und Mozart in der Geschichte des Singspiels', *Musik in Bayern*, xl (1990), 35–45

Kohlhase, Thomas. 'Der Dresdener Hofkirchenkomponist Jan Dismas Zelenka: Ein Forschungsbericht', *Musik des Ostens*, xii (1992), 115–212

Komlós, Katalin. 'The Viennese Keyboard Trio in the 1780s: Sociological Background and Contemporary Reception', *Music & Letters*, lxviii (1987), 222–34

Komlós, Katalin. 'Mozart and Clementi: a Piano Competition and its Interpretation', *Historical Performance*, ii (1989), 3–9

Komlós, Katalin. 'Fantasia and Sonata K. 475/457 in Contemporary Context', *Mozart-Jahrbuch 1991: Bericht über den Internationalen Mozart-Kongreß Salzburg 1991*, 816–19

Komlós, Katalin. '"Ich praeludirte und spielte Variazionen": Mozart the Fortepianist', *Perspectives on Mozart Performance*, ed. R. Larry Todd and Peter Williams (Cambridge, 1991), 27–54

Komlós, Katalin. *Fortepianos and their Music: Germany, Austria, and England, 1760–1800* (Oxford, 1995)

Komorzynski, Egon. *Emanuel Schikaneder: Ein Beitrag zur Geschichte des deutschen Theaters* (Berlin, 1901)

Komorzynski, Egon. *Mozarts Kunst der Instrumentation* (Stuttgart, 1906)

Komorzynski, Egon. 'Johann Baptist Henneberg, Schikaneders Kapellmeister (1768–1822)', *Mozart-Jahrbuch 1955*, 243–5

Konrad, Thomas. *Ludwig Ritter von Köchel* (Vienna, 1998)

Konrad, Ulrich. 'Zu Mozarts Lied "Die Verschweigung" KV518', *Mozart-Jahrbuch 1989/90*, 99–113

Konrad, Ulrich. '"In seinem Kopfe lag das Werk immer schon vollendet . . . ": Bemerkungen zu Mozarts Schaffensweise am Beispiel des Klaviertrios B-Dur KV 502', *Mozart-Jahrbuch 1991: Bericht über den Internationalen Mozart-Kongreß Salzburg 1991*, 540–51

Konrad, Ulrich. 'Fragment bei Mozart', *Acta Mozartiana*, xxxix/2 (1992), 36–51

Konrad, Ulrich. *Mozarts Schaffensweise: Studien zu den Werkautographen, Skizzen und Entwürfen* (Göttingen, 1992)

Konrad, Ulrich. 'Fragmente aus der Gegenwart: Mozarts unvollendete Kompositionen für Streichquintett', *Mozarts Streichquintette: Beiträge zum musikalischen Satz, zum Gattungskontext und zu Quellenfragen*, ed. Cliff Eisen and Wolf-Dieter Seiffert (Stuttgart, 1994), 163–93

Konrad, Ulrich. 'Neuentdecktes und wiedergefundenes Werkstattmaterial Wolfgang Amadeus Mozarts: Erster Nachtrag zum Katalog der Skizzen und Entwürfe', *Mozart-Jahrbuch 1995*, 1–28

Konrad, Ulrich. '". . . mithin liess ich meinen gedanken freyen lauf": Erste Überlegungen und Thesen zu den "Fassungen" von W. A. Mozarts Die Entführung aus dem Serail KV 384', *Opernkomposition als Prozeß*, ed. Werner Breig (Kassel, 1996), 47–64

Konrad, Ulrich. 'Vier Briefe über die Mode in der Musik: Eine wenig beachtete Quelle zur Einschätzung zeitgenössischer Musik im letzten Drittel des 18. Jahrhunderts', *Acta Mozartiana*, xliv/1–2 (1997), 1–16

Konrad, Ulrich. 'Mozarts Skizzen', *Acta Mozartiana*, xlv/3–4 (1998), 45–58

Konrad, Ulrich. 'Mozart an den Zeitwenden 1800 – 1900 – 2000', *Acta Mozartiana*, xlvi/3–4 (1999), 69–75

Konrad, Ulrich. 'Sigismund von Neukomm: "Libera me, Domine" d-Moll NV 186. Ein Beitrag zur liturgischen Komplettierung von Wolfgang Amadé Mozarts "Requiem" d-Moll KV 626', *Im Dienst der Quellen zur Musik: Festschrift Gertraut Haberkamp zum 65. Geburtstag*, ed. Paul Mai (Tutzing, 2002), 425–34

Konrad, Ulrich. 'Compositional Method', *The Cambridge Mozart Encyclopedia*, ed. Cliff Eisen and Simon P. Keefe (Cambridge, 2005), 100–8

Konrad, Ulrich and Martin Staehelin. *allzeit ein buch: Die Bibliothek Wolfgang Amadeus Mozarts* (Weinheim, 1991)

Köpke, Rudolf. *Ludwig Tieck: Erinnerungen aus dem Leben des Dichters nach dessen mündlichen und schriftlichen Mitteilungen* (Leipzig, 1855)

Koury, Daniel J. *Orchestral Performance Practices in the Nineteenth Century: Size, Proportions, and Seating* (Ann Arbor, 1986)

Krämer, Jörg. *Deutschsprachiges Musiktheater im späten 18. Jahrhundert: Typologie, Dramaturgie und Anthropologie einer populären Gattung* (Tübingen, 1988)

Kramer, Kurt. 'Antike und christliches Mittelalter in Varescos "Idomeneo", dem Libretto zu Mozarts gleichnamiger Oper', *Mitteilungen der Internationalen Stiftung Mozarteum*, xxviii/1–2 (1980), 6–20

Kraus, Hedwig. 'W. A. Mozart und die Familie Jacquin', *Zeitschrift für Musikwissenschaft*, xv (1932/3), 155–68

Krause, Christian Gottfried. *Von der musikalischen Poesie* (Berlin, 1752)

Krauß, Rudolf. *Das Stuttgarter Hoftheater von den ältesten Zeiten bis zur Gegenwart* (Stuttgart, 1908)

Krautwurst, Franz. 'Valentin Rathgeber OSB (1682–1750)', *Fränkische Lebensbilder*, xiv (1991), 141–61

Krautwurst, Franz and Werner Zorn. *Bibliographie des Schrifttums zur Musikgeschichte der Stadt Augsburg* (Tutzing, 1989)

Krebs, Carl. *Dittersdorfiana* (Berlin, 1900)

Kreitmaier, Josef S J. *W. A. Mozart: Eine Charakterzeichnung des großen Meisters nach literarischen Quellen* (Düsseldorf, 1919)

Kreitz, Helmut. 'Abbé Georg Joseph Vogler als Musiktheoretiker' (dissertation, University of the Saarland, 1957)

Kretschmer, Helmut. 'Mozarts "geläufige Gurgel": Die Sängerin Catarina Cavalieri', *Wiener Figaro*, lvi/3–4 (1999), 9–16

Kretzschmar, Hermann. 'Die venetianische Oper und die Werke Cavallis und Cestis', *Vierteljahrsschrift für Musikwissenschaft*, viii (1892), 1–76

Kretzschmar, Hermann. 'Monteverdi's "Incoronazione di Poppea"', *Vierteljahrsschrift für Musikwissenschaft*, x (1894), 483–530

Kretzschmar, Hermann. 'Das erste Jahrhundert der deutschen Oper', *Sammelbände der Internationalen Musikgesellschaft*, iii (1901/2), 270–93

Kretzschmar, Hermann. 'Hasse über Mozart', *Zeitschrift der Internationalen Musikgesellschaft*, iii (1902), 263–5

Kretzschmar, Hermann. *Ignaz Holzbauer: Günther von Schwarzburg* (Leipzig, 1902 = Denkmäler deutscher Tonkunst in Bayern viii–ix)

Kretzschmar, Hermann. 'Aus Deutschlands italienischer Zeit', *Gesammelte Aufsätze über Musik* (Leipzig, 1911), ii.137–50d

Kretzschmar, Hermann. 'Die Correspondance littéraire als musikgeschichtliche Quelle', *Gesammelte Aufsätze über Musik* (Leipzig, 1911), ii.210–25

Kretzschmar, Hermann. 'Einige Bemerkungen über den Vortrag alter Musik', *Gesammelte Aufsätze über Musik* (Leipzig, 1911), ii.100–19

Kretzschmar, Hermann. *Geschichte des neuen deutschen Liedes* (Leipzig, 1911)

Kretzschmar, Hermann. 'Die Jugendsymphonien Joseph Haydns', *Gesammelte Aufsätze über Musik* (Leipzig, 1911), ii.401–27

Kretzschmar, Hermann. 'Mozart in der Geschichte der Oper', *Gesammelte Aufsätze über Musik* (Leipzig, 1911), ii.257–79

Kretzschmar, Hermann. 'Über die Bedeutung von Cherubinis Ouvertüren und Hauptopern für die Gegenwart', *Gesammelte Aufsätze über Musik* (Leipzig, 1911), ii.325–42

Kretzschmar, Hermann. 'Zum Verständnis Glucks', *Gesammelte Aufsätze über Musik* (Leipzig, 1911), ii.193–209

Kretzschmar, Hermann. 'Zwei Opern Nicolo Logroscinos', *Gesammelte Aufsätze über Musik* (Leipzig, 1911), ii.374–400

Kretzschmar, Hermann. *Führer durch den Konzertsaal*, fourth edition (Leipzig, 1913)

Kretzschmar, Hermann. *Geschichte der Oper* (Leipzig, 1919)

Kreutzer, Hans Joachim. 'Von der Opera seria zur "vera opera": Die neue musikdramatische Form von Mozarts "La clemenza di Tito"', *Acta Mozartiana*, xlvii/3–4 (2000), 65–71

Krieg, Walter. 'Um Mozarts Totenmaske: Ein Beitrag zur Mozartikonographie', *Neues Mozart-Jahrbuch*, iii (1943), 118–43

Krone, Walter. *Wenzel Müller: Ein Beitrag zur Geschichte der komischen Oper* (Berlin, 1906)

Krones, Hartmut. '"Il Dissoluto Punito o sia Il D: Giovanni: Quartetti Del Signore Gio: Kucharz". Bearbeitung oder Mitschrift des Mozartschen "Don Giovanni"', *Festschrift Christoph-Hellmut Mahling zum 65. Geburtstag*, ed. Axel Beer, Kristina Pfarr and Wolfgang Ruf (Tutzing, 1997), i.721–35

Kroyer, Theodor. *Gregor Aichinger: Ausgewählte Werke* (Leipzig, 1909 = Denkmäler der Tonkunst in Bayern x/1)

Krüger, Eduard. *Beiträge für Leben und Wissenschaft der Tonkunst* (Leipzig, 1847)

Krüger, Walther. *Das Concerto grosso in Deutschland* (Wolfenbüttel and Berlin, 1932)

Kruse, Georg Richard. 'Die erste Donna Anna', *Mitteilungen für die Mozart-Gemeinde in Berlin*, ii (1901), 70–71

Krutmann, Johannes. 'Mozarts Litaneien', *Mozarts Kirchenmusik*, ed. Harald Schützeichel (Freiburg, 1992), 52–72

Kucaba, John. 'The Symphonies of G. C. Wagenseil' (dissertation, Boston University, 1967)

Kucaba, John. *Georg Christoph Wagenseil: Fifteen Symphonies* (New York, 1981 = The Symphony 1720–1840, Series B Volume iii)

Kühn, Arnold. 'Komik, Humor und Musikalität in Mozarts Bäslebriefen', *Neues Augsburger Mozartbuch* (Augsburg, 1962), 107–89

Kumbier, William A. 'Rousseau's *Lettre sur la musique française*', *Stanford French Review*, vi (1982), 221–37

Kummel, Werner Friedrich. 'Aus der Frühzeit der Mozart-Pflege in Italien', *Analecta musicologica*, vii (1969), 145–63

Kunze, Stefan. 'Die Vertonungen der Aria "Non sò d'onde viene" von J. C. Bach und Mozart', *Analecta musicologica*, ii (1965), 85–110

Kunze, Stefan. *Don Giovanni vor Mozart: Die Tradition der Don-Giovanni-Opern im italienischen Buffa-Theater des 18. Jahrhunderts* (Munich, 1972)

Kunze, Stefan. *Mozarts Opern* (Stuttgart, 1984)

Kunze, Stefan. *Die Sinfonie im 18. Jahrhundert: Von der Opernsinfonie zur Konzertsinfonie* (Laaber, 1993)

Kurth, Ernst. 'Die Jugendopern Glucks bis Orfeo', *Studien zur Musikwissenschaft*, i (1913), 193–277

Kurth, Ernst. *Romantische Harmonik und ihre Krise in Wagners 'Tristan'* (Berne, 1920)

Kurthen, Wilhelm. 'Studien zu W. A. Mozarts kirchenmusikalischen Jugendwerken (bis zur 1. italienischen Reise)', *Zeitschrift für Musikwissenschaft*, iii (1921), 194–222 and 337–81

Küster, Konrad. *Formale Aspekte des ersten Allegros in Mozarts Konzerten* (Kassel, 1991)

Küster, Konrad. *Das Konzert: Form und Forum der Virtuosität* (Kassel, 1993)

Küster, Konrad. 'Mozarts "Thamos" und der Kontext', *Acta Mozartiana*, xlii/4 (1995), 124–43

Küster, Konrad. 'An Early Form in Mozart's Late Style: The Overture to "La clemenza di Tito"', *Wolfgang Amadè Mozart: Essays on his Life and his Music*, ed. Stanley Sadie (Oxford, 1996), 477–82

Küster, Konrad. *Mozart: A Musical Biography* (Oxford, 1996)

Kutscher, Artur. *Vom Salzburger Barocktheater zu den Salzburger Festspielen* (Düsseldorf, 1939)

Kyas, Vojtech. 'Otazníky nad Kucharovým originálem: Brnenský klavírní výtah Mozartova Dona Giovanniho v úprave J.K. Kuchare', *Opus musicum*, xxiv (1992), 104–10

Lach, Robert. *Studien zur Entwicklungsgeschichte der ornamentalen Melopöie* (Leipzig, 1913)

Lach, Robert. 'Sebastian Sailers "Schöpfung" in der Musik', *Denkschrift der Kaiserlichen Akademie der Wissenschaften in Wien: philosophisch-historische Klasse*, lx/1 (1916)

Lach, Robert. *W. A. Mozart als Theoretiker* (Vienna, 1918)

La Gorce, Jérôme de. *L'opéra à Paris au temps de Louis XIV: Histoire d'un théâtre* (Paris, 1992)

Lagrave, Henri. *Le théâtre et le public à Paris de 1715 à 1750* (Paris, 1972)

Lajarte, Théodore de. *Bibliothèque musicale du Théâtre de l'opéra: Catalogue historique, chronologique, anecdotique* (Paris, 1878)

Laloy, Louis. *Jean-Philippe Rameau* (Paris, 1908)

Landon, H. C. Robbins. *The Symphonies of Joseph Haydn* (London, 1955)

Landon, H. C. Robbins. 'The Concertos: (2) Their Musical Origin and Development', *The Mozart Companion*, ed. H. C. Robbins Landon and Donald Mitchell (London, 1956), 234–82

Landon, H. C. Robbins. 'Crisis Years: *Sturm und Drang* and the Austrian Musical Crisis', *Haydn: Chronicle and Works*, ii: *Haydn at Eszterháza, 1766–1790* (Bloomington, IN, and London, 1978), 266–393

Landon, H. C. Robbins. *Mozart and the Masons: New Light on the Lodge 'Crowned Hope'* (London, 1982)

Landon, H. C. Robbins. 'Controversial Köchels: On the authenticity of Mozart's sixth and seventh violin concertos', *The Strad*, ic (1988), 571–2

Landon, H. C. Robbins. *Mozart and Vienna* (New York, 1992)

Landon, H. C. Robbins. 'Mozart's incidental music to Thamos, König in Ägypten (K.345)', *The Mozart Essays* (New York, 1995), 38–55

Lang, Karl Heinrich von. *Memoiren* (Braunschweig, 1842)

Lang, Paul Henry. 'Diderot as Musician', *Diderot Studies*, x (1968), 95–107

Lange, Joseph. *Biographie des Joseph Lange* (Vienna, 1808)

La Roche, Sophie. *Briefe über Mannheim* (Zurich, 1791)

Larsen, Jens Peter. 'Zur Entstehung der österreichischen Symphonietradition (ca. 1750–1775)', *Haydn-Jahrbuch* 1978, 72–80

Larsen, Jens Peter. 'Zur Vorgeschichte der Symphonik der Wiener Klassik', *Studien zur Musikwissenschaft*, xliii (1994), 67–143

Latcham, Michael. 'Mozart and the pianos of Gabriel Anton Walter', *Early Music*, xxv/3 (1997), 382–99

Latcham, Michael. 'Historische Belege zum Mozart-Flügel', *Mitteilungen der Internationalen Stiftung Mozarteum*, xlviii/1–4 (2000), 10–12

Latcham, Michael. 'Zur Frage der Authentizität und Datierung der Klaviere von Anton Walter zwischen 1780 und 1800', *Mitteilungen der Internationalen Stiftung Mozarteum*, xlviii/1 (2000), 114–45

Latcham, Michael und Alfons Huber. 'Instrumentenkundliche Daten des Mozart-Flügels', *Der Hammerflügel von Anton Walter aus dem Besitz von Wolfgang Amadeus Mozart: Befund – Dokumentation – Analyse*, ed. Rudolph Angermüller and Alfons Huber (Salzburg, 2000), 226–31

Lauer, Enrik. *Mozart und die Frauen* (Bergisch Gladbach, 2005)

Launay, Denise, ed. *La Querelle des Bouffons* (Geneva, 1973)

Laurencie, Lionel de La. *Rameau* (Paris, 1908)

Laurencie, Lionel de La. *Lully* (Paris, 1911)

Layer, Adolf. 'Johann Ernst Eberlin', *Lebensbilder aus dem bayerischen Schwaben*, ed. G. F. von Pölnitz (Munich, 1958), vi.388–405

Layer, Adolf, 'Zur Tätigkeit des Augsburger Barockbaumeisters David Mozart und seiner Söhne im Donautal: Ein Beitrag zur Geschichte der Architektur Dillingens im 17. Jahrhundert', *Jahrbuch des Historischen Vereins Dillingen*, lxxii (1970), 140–3

Layer, Adolf. *Eine Jugend in Augsburg: Leopold Mozart 1719–1737* (Augsburg, 1975)

Lazarevich, Gordana. 'Mozart's Insertion Aria "Alma grande e nobil core", K. 578: Criticism of Cimarosa or a Compliment to the Composer?' *Mozart-Jahrbuch 1991: Bericht über den Internationalen Mozart-Kongreß Salzburg 1991*, 262–7

Lazzaro-Weis, Carol. 'Parody and Farce in the Don Juan Myth in the Eighteenth Century', *Eighteenth-Century Life*, viii/3 (1983), 35–48

Lazzeri, Ghino. *La vita e l'opera letteraria di Ranieri Calzabigi* (Città di Castello, 1907)

Lebègue, Raymond. 'Ronsard et la musique', *Musique et poésie au XVIe siècle* (Paris, 1953), 105–19

Lebermann, Walter. 'Biographische Notizen über Johann Anton Fils, Johann Anton Stamitz, Carl Joseph und Johann Baptist Toeschi', *Die Musikforschung*, xix (1966), 40–41

Lebermann, Walter. 'Zu Franz Xaver Richters Sinfonien', *Die Musikforschung*, xxv (1972), 471–80

Lebermann, Walter. 'Zur Genealogie der Toeschi', *Die Musikforschung*, xxii (1969), 200–2 and xxvii (1974), 464–5

Lebermann, Walter. 'Mozart–Eck–André: Ein Beitrag zu KV 268', *Die Musikforschung*, xxxi (1978), 452–65

Le Blond, Gaspard Michel. *Mémoires pour servir à l'histoire de la révolution opérée dans la musique par M. le Chevalier Gluck* (Paris, 1781); German trans. by J. G. Siegmeyer, *Über den Ritter Gluck und seine Werke* (Berlin, 1823; second edition: Berlin, 1837)

Le Cerf de la Viéville, Jean Laurent. *Comparaison de la musique italienne et de la musique françoise* (Brussels, 1704–6)

Ledbetter, David. *Continuo Playing According to Handel*, fourth edition (Oxford, 1995)

Leeson, Daniel N. 'Franz Xaver Süssmayr and the Mozart Requiem: A Computer Analysis of Authorship Based on Melodic Affinity', *Mozart-Jahrbuch 1995*, 111–53

Leeson, Daniel N. and Robert D. Levin, 'On the Authenticity of K. Anh. C 14.01 (297b), a Symphonia Concertant for Four Winds and Orchestra', *Mozart-Jahrbuch 1975/76*, 70–96

Leeson, Daniel N. and David Whitwell, 'Mozart's Thematic Catalogue', *Musical Times*, cxiv (1973), 781–3

Legband, Paul. 'Münchener Bühne und Literatur im 18. Jahrhundert', *Oberbayerisches Archiv*, li (1904), 422–3

Lehmann-Gugolz, Ursula. *Deutsches und italienisches Wesen in der Vorgeschichte des klassischen Streichquartetts* (Würzburg, 1939)

Leichtentritt, Hugo. *Geschichte der Motette* (Leipzig, 1908)

Leichtentritt, Hugo. *Mozarts Briefe* (Berlin, 1912)

Leitzmann, Albert. *Mozarts Briefe* (Leipzig, 1910)

Leitzmann, Albert. *Mozarts Persönlichkeit: Urteile der Zeitgenossen* (Leipzig, 1914)

Lenneberg, Hans. 'Hermann Abert's Biography of Mozart', *Notes*, xxxv/4 (1979), 847–53

Lennhoff, Eugen and Oskar Posner, *Internationales Freimaurerlexikon* (Vienna and Munich, 1932)

Lenoir, Yves, ed. *Documents Grétry dans les collections de la Bibliothèque Royale Albert 1er* (Brussels, 1989)

Lenoir, Yves, ed. *A.-E.-M. Grétry: Lettres autographes conservées à la Bibliothèque Royale Albert 1er* (Brussels, 1991)

Leo, Giacomo. *Leonardo Leo, musicista del secolo XVIII e le sue opere musicali* (Naples, 1905)

Lequin, Frank. 'Mozarts ". . . rarer Mann"', *Mitteilungen der Internationalen Stiftung Mozarteum*, xxix/1–2 (1981), 3–19

Leris, Antoine de. *Dictionnaire portatif historique et littéraire des théâtres*, second edition (Paris, 1763)

Lert, Ernst. *Mozart auf dem Theater* (Berlin, 1918)

Lesage, Alain-René. *Théâtre de la Foire* (Amsterdam, 1723–34)

Lessing, Gotthold Ephraim. *Hamburgische Dramaturgie* (Hamburg, 1767–8)

Lessing, Gotthold Ephraim. *Werke* (Berlin, 1883–90)

Lesure, François. 'Éléments populaires dans la chanson française au début du XVIe siècle', *Musique et poésie au XVIe siècle* (Paris, 1953), 169–84

Lesure, François. *Querelle des Gluckistes et des Piccinnistes* (Geneva, 1984)

Leupold, Carl Friedrich Benjamin. *Allgemeines Adels-Archiv der österreichischen Monarchie* (Vienna, 1789–92)

Levarie, Siegmund. *Mozart's 'Le Nozze di Figaro': A Critical Analysis* (Chicago, 1952)

Levin, Robert. *Who Wrote the Mozart Four-Wind Concertante?* (New York, 1988)

Levin, Robert. 'Zu den von Süßmayr komponierten Sätzen des Requiems KV 626', *Mozart-Jahrbuch 1991: Bericht über den Internationalen Mozart-Kongreß Salzburg 1991*, 475–93

Levin, Robert. 'Zu den Ergänzungen von Mozarts Requiem in der 2. Hälfte des 20. Jahrhunderts', *Musik Mitteleuropas in der 2. Hälfte des 18. Jahrhunderts: Bericht über die internationale musikwissenschaftliche Konferenz Bratislava, 23. bis 25. März 1992*, ed. Pavol Polák (Bratislava, 1993), 179–205

Levin, Robert. 'Performance practice in the music of Mozart', *The Cambridge Companion to Mozart*, ed. Simon P. Keefe (Cambridge, 2002), 227–45

Levin, Robert. 'Mozart's non-metrical keyboard preludes', *The Keyboard in Baroque Europe*, ed. Christopher Hogwood (Cambridge, 2003), 198–216

Levy, Kenneth Jay. 'Vaudeville, vers mesurés et airs de cour', *Musique et poésie au XVIe siècle*, ed. Jean Jacquot (Paris, 1953), 185–201

Lewezow, Konrad. *Leben und Kunst der Frau Margarete Luise Schick, gebornen Hamel, Königl. Preuss. Kammersängerin und Mitgliedes des Nationaltheaters zu Berlin* (Berlin, 1809)

Lewicki, Ernst. 'Mozarts Verhältnis zu Sebastian Bach', *Mitteilungen für die Mozart-Gemeinde in Berlin*, ii (1903), 163–79

Lewicki, Ernst. 'Zur Wiederbelebung des Mozartschen Musikdramas "Idomeneus": Ein Wort der Anregung und praktische Vorschläge', *Die Musik*, iv/11 (1904/5), 317–25

Lewicki, Ernst. 'Auf Mozartschen Vorlagen fußende Bühnen-Neubearbeitung der ernsten Oper "Idomeneus"', *Mitteilungen für die Mozart-Gemeinde in Berlin*, iv/3 (1905), 86ff.

Lewicki, Ernst. 'Die Vervollständigung von Mozarts Großer c-Moll-Messe durch Alois Schmitt in ihrem Werdegang nach authentischen Quellen dargestellt', *Die Musik*, v (1905/6), 3–12 and 168–75

Lewicki, Ernst. 'Musikalien', *Die Musik*, vii/4 (1907/8), 233–5

Lewicki, Ernst. 'Mozarts Deutschtum nach seinen Briefen', *Mozarteums-Mitteilungen*, i (1918), 14–18

Lewicki, Ernst. 'Über Mozarts Naturliebe', *Mozarteums-Mitteilungen*, i (1919), 1–4

Lewicki, Rudolf. 'Mozarts Jugendtagebuch', *Mozarteums-Mitteilungen*, i/1 (1918), 4–6

Lewicki, Rudolf. 'Antonia Haradauer', *Mozarteums-Mitteilungen*, ii (1920), 106–8

Lewis, Ludwig. *Geschichte der Freimaurerei in Österreich im allgemeinen und der Wiener Loge zu St. Joseph insbesondere* (Vienna, 1861)

Lewy, Heinrich. 'Christian Gottlob Neefe' (dissertation, University of Rostock, 1901)

Libin, Kathryn L. Shanks. 'The Emergence of an Idiomatic Fortepiano Style in the Keyboard Concertos of Mozart' (dissertation, New York University, 1998)

Liebeskind, Josef. 'Mozarts Konzert mit dem Straßburger', *Musikhandel und Musikpflege*, ix (1908), 8

Liebeskind, Josef. 'Leopold Mozart: Ausgewählte Werke', *Zeitschrift der Internationalen Musikgesellschaft*, xi (1910), 361–2

Lindemann, Friedrich. 'Die Operntexte Ph. Quinaults vom literarischen Standpunkte aus betrachtet' (dissertation, University of Leipzig, 1904)

Lindgren, Lowell. 'Il dramma musicale a Roma durante la carriera di Alessandro Scarlatti (1660–1725)', *Le muse galanti: La musica a Roma nel Settecento*, ed. Bruno Cagli (Rome, 1985), 35–57

Lindner, Dolf. *Ignaz von Born: Meister der Wahren Eintracht. Wiener Freimaurerei im 18. Jahrhundert* (Vienna, 1986)

Lindner, Otto. *Geschichte des deutschen Liedes im XVIII. Jahrhundert* (Leipzig, 1871)

Link, Dorothea. 'The Viennese operatic canon and Mozart's *Così fan tutte*', *Mitteilungen der Internationalen Stiftung Mozarteum*, xxxviii (1990), 111–21

Link, Dorothea. *The National Court Theatre in Mozart's Vienna* (Oxford, 1998)

Link, Dorothea. *Arias for Nancy Storace, Mozart's First Susanna* (Madison, WI, 2002 = Recent Researches in Music of the Classic Period xxx)

Link, Dorothea. *Arias for Francesco Benucci, Mozart's First Figaro and Guglielmo* (Madison, WI, 2004 = Recent Researches in Music of the Classic Period xxx)

Link, Dorothea. 'Mozart's appointment to the Viennese court', *Words About Mozart: Essays in Honour of Stanley Sadie*, ed. Dorothea Link and Judith Nagley (Woodbridge, 2005), 153–78

Lintilhac, Eugène. *Beaumarchais et ses œuvres* (Paris, 1887)

Lipowsky, Felix Joseph. *Baierisches Musik-Lexicon* (Munich, 1811)

Lippmann, Friedrich. '"Il mio ben quando verrà": Paisiello creatore di una nuova semplicità', *Studi musicali*, xix (1990), 385–405

Lippmann, Friedrich. 'Mozart und Paisiello: Zur stilistischen Position des "Lucio Silla"', *Mozart-Jahrbuch 1991: Bericht über den Internationalen Mozart-Kongreß Salzburg 1991*, 580–93

Lippmann, Friedrich. 'Tendenzen der italienischen Opera seria am Ende des 18. Jahrhunderts – und Mozart', *Studi musicali*, xxi (1992), 307–58

Lippmann, Friedrich. 'Paisiello und Mozart in der Opera Buffa', *Convegno italo-tedesco 'Mozart, Paisiello, Rossini e l'opera buffa' (Rom 1993): Bericht*, ed. Markus Engelhardt and Wolfgang Witzenmann (Laaber, 1998), 117–202

Lipton, Kay. 'The opere buffe of Pietro Alessandro Guglielmi in Vienna and Eszterháza: Contributions to the Development of opera buffa between 1768 and 1793' (dissertation, UCLA, 1995)

Literarische Anekdoten auf einer Reise durch Deutschland (Frankfurt am Main, 1790)

Littger, Klaus Walter, ed. *Johann Anton Fils (1733–1760): Ein Eichstätter Komponist der Mannheimer Klassik* (Tutzing, 1983)

Lobe, Johann Christian. 'Das Gehaltvolle in der Musik: Die Ouverture zu Don Juan von Mozart', *Allgemeine musikalische Zeitung*, xlviii (1846), 681–4; il (1847), 369–74, 385–9, 417–20, 441–5

Loewenberg, Alfred. *Annals of Opera* (St. Claire Shores, MI, 1971)

Loewenthal, Erich, ed. *Sturm und Drang: Kritische Schriften* (Heidelberg, 1972)

Loménie, Louis Léonard de. *Beaumarchais et son temps* (Paris, 1856)

Loos, Helmut and Eberhard Möller, ed. *Mozart-Rezeption in Mittel- und Osteuropa* (Chemnitz, 1997)

Lorenz, Franz. *Haydns, Mozarts und Beethovens Kirchenmusik und ihre katholischen und protestantischen Gegner* (Breslau, 1866)

Lorenz, Franz. *W. A. Mozart als Klavierkomponist* (Breslau, 1866)

Lorenz, Michael. 'Gottfried Ignaz von Ployers Haus in Döbling – eine vergessene Mozartstätte: Nebst biographischen Bemerkungen zu Babette Ployer', *Acta Mozartiana*, xlvii/1–2 (2000), 11–24

Lorenz, Michael. 'Konzert für Klavier und Orchester Es-Dur, KV 271 (1777) "Jenamy" (bisher "Jeunehomme")', *Programmheft der Jeunesse, Saison 2003/2004, Orchestergastspiel am 18. März 2004 im Großen Konzerthaussaal* (Vienna, 2004)

Lucam, Johann von. *Die Grabesfrage Mozarts: Nach brieflichen Originalurkunden der Witwe Mozarts selbst* (Vienna, 1856)

Lucarelli, Nicola. 'Girolamo Crescentini: la vita, la tecnica vocale analizzata attraverso alcune sue arie tipiche' (dissertation, University of Perugia, 1984)

Ludewig, R. 'Zum derzeitigen Stand der Forschung über die Ursachen des Todes von Mozart', *Mozart-Jahrbuch 1991: Bericht über den Internationalen Mozart-Kongreß Salzburg 1991*, 132–44

Lühning, Helga. *Titus-Vertonungen im 18. Jahrhundert – Untersuchungen zur Tradition der Opera seria von Hasse bis Mozart* (Laaber, 1983 = Analecta musicologica, xx)

Lühning, Helga. 'Das Theater Carl Theodors und die Idee der Nationaloper', *Mozart und Mannheim*, ed. Ludwig Finscher, Bärbel Pelker, and Jochen Reutter (Frankfurt am Main, 1994), 89–99

Lütolf, Max, ed. *Alessandro Scarlatti und seine Zeit* (Berne, 1995)

Lütteken, Laurenz. '"Es musste nur blos der Musick wegen aufgefuhrt werden": Text und Kontext in Mozarts Thamos, König in Ägypten Melodrama', *Mozart und Mannheim*, ed. Ludwig Finscher, Bärbel Pelker and Jochen Reutter (Frankfurt am Main, 1994), 167–86

Lynham, Deryck. *The Chevalier Noverre: Father of Modern Ballet* (London and New York, 1950)

Lynker, Wilhelm. *Geschichte des Theaters und der Musik in Kassel* (Kassel, 1865)

Lyser, Johann Peter. 'Mozartiana: Mozart's Leben', *Mozart-Album*, ed. Johann F. Kayser (Vienna, 1856)

McClymonds, Marita P. 'The Evolution of Jommelli's Operatic Style', *Journal of the American Musicological Society*, xxxiii (1980), 326–55

McClymonds, Marita P. *Niccolò Jommelli: The Last Years, 1769–1774* (Ann Arbor, 1980)

McClymonds, Marita P. 'Mozart's *La clemenza di Tito* and *opera seria* in Florence as a reflection of Leopold II's musical taste', *Mozart-Jahrbuch 1984/85*, 61–70

McCredie, Andrew. 'Symphonie Concertante and Multiple Concerto in Germany, 1780–1850: Some Problems and Perspectives for a Source-Repertory Study', *Miscellanea musicologica* [Australia], viii (1975), 115–47

McGowan, Margaret M. *L'art du ballet de cour en France, 1581–1643* (Paris, 1963)

McGowan, Margaret M. 'The Origins of French Opera', *New Oxford History of Music*, v (1975), 169–205

MacIntyre, Bruce C. *The Viennese Concerted Mass of the Early Classic Period* (Ann Arbor, MI, 1986)

McKendrick, Neil, John Brewer and J. H. Plumb, *The Birth of a Consumer Society: The Commercialization of Eighteenth-Century England* (London, 1982)

McVeigh, Simon. *The Violinist in London's Concert Life, 1750–1784: Felice Giardini and his Contemporaries* (New York, 1989)

McVeigh, Simon. *Concert Life in London from Mozart to Haydn* (Cambridge, 1993)

Mahillon, Victor-Charles. *La trompette, son histoire, sa théorie, sa construction* (Brussels, 1907)

Mahlendorf, Ursula. 'Eduard Mörike's "Mozart on the way to Prague": Stages and outcomes of the creative experience', *Mörike's muses: Critical essays on Eduard Mörike*, ed. Jeffrey Adams (Columbia, 1990), 95–111

Mahling, Christoph-Hellmut. 'Die Gestalt des Osmin in Mozarts Entführung: Von Typus zur Individualität', *Archiv für Musikwissenschaft*, xxx/2 (1973), 96–108

Mahling, Christoph-Hellmut. 'Bemerkungen zum Violinkonzert D-dur KV 271^i', *Mozart-Jahrbuch 1978/79*, 252–68

Mahling, Christoph-Hellmut. '". . . new and altogether special and astonishingly difficult": Some Comments on Junia's Aria in "Lucio Silla"', *Wolfgang Amadè Mozart: Essays on his Life and his Music*, ed. Stanley Sadie (Oxford, 1996), 377–94

Malachy, Thérèse. 'Don Giovanni Tenorio o sia Il Dissoluto: Une Tragi-comédie oubliée de Carlo Goldoni', *Revue de littérature comparée*, lxvii/3 (1993), 361–9

Malherbe, Charles. 'Autographiana', *Revue internationale de musique*, i (1898), 15–31

Mamy, Sylvie. 'Tradizione pedagogica del canto a Napoli: Giuseppe Aprile', *Musicisti nati in Puglia ed emigrazione musicale tra Seicento e Settecento* (Lecce, 1985), 281–311

Mamy, Sylvie. *Les grands castrats napolitains à Venise au XVIIIe siècle* (Liège, 1994)

Mančal, Josef. 'Briefe – nur "Briefe"? Vorüberlegungen zur Informationsbewertung einer Quellengattung der Mozart-Forschung', *Acta Mozartiana*, xl/2 (1993), 50–73

Mančal, Josef. *Mozart-Schätze in Augsburg* (Augsburg, 1995 = Beiträge zur Leopold-Mozart-Forschung iii)

Mančal, Josef. 'Der Mensch als Schöpfer seiner Wirklichkeit', *Beiträge des Internationalen Leopold-Mozart-Kolloquiums Augsburg 1994*, ed. Josef Mančal and Wolfgang Plath (Augsburg, 1997), 149–73

Mančal, Josef. 'Augsburg "Meine Vaterstadt" (L. Mozart 1756), "die vatterstadt meines Papa" (W. A. Mozart 1777), "meine eigentliche Stammstadt" (Fr. X. W. A. Mozart 1821)', *Acta Mozartiana*, xlvi/1–2 (1999), 3–31

Mančal Josef. 'Die "Zengersammlung": Zu einem der wichtigsten Bestände des Augsburger Mozarthauses', *50. Deutsches Mozartfest 2001 der Deutschen Mozart-Gesellschaft e. V. Augsburg vom 5. bis 20. Mai. Festschrift und Programm* (Augsburg, 2001), 20–7

Mančal, Josef und Wolfgang Plath, ed. *Leopold Mozart: Auf dem Weg zu einem Verständnis* (Augsburg, 1994 = Beiträge zur Leopold-Mozart-Forschung i)

Mancini, Franco, Maria Teresa Muraro and Elena Povoledo, ed. *I teatri del Veneto* (Venice, 1995–6)

Mancini, Giambattista. *Pensieri, e riflessioni pratiche sul canto figurato*, third edition (Vienna, 1774)

Mandyczewski, Eusebius. *Joseph Haydns Werke* (Leipzig, 1907–33)

Mann, Alfred. 'Haydn and Mozart', *Theory and Practice: The Great Composer as Student and Teacher* (New York, 1987), 41–62

Mann, Michael. *Sturm-und-Drang Drama: Studien und Vorstudien zu Schillers 'Räubern'* (Berne, 1974)

Mann, William. *The Operas of Mozart* (London, 1977)

Mannlich, Johann Christian von. *Histoire de ma vie: Mémoires*, ed. Karl-Heinz Bendes and Hermann Kleber (Trier, 1989–93)

Mantovani, T. 'Luigi Bassi e il "Don Giovanni" di Mozart', *La cronaca musicale*, iii/3 (1898), 89–98

Marcello, Benedetto. *Il teatro alla moda* (Venice, 1733)

Marchesan, Angelo. *Della vita e delle opere di Lorenzo da Ponte* (Treviso, 1900)

Margotton, Jean-Charles. 'Don Juan ou Mozart vu par Hoffmann', *Mozart: Origines et transformations d'un mythe*, ed. Jean-Louis Jam (Paris, 1994), 171–84

Marks, Paul Frederick. 'The Rhetorical Element in Musical *Sturm und Drang*: Christian Gottfried Krause's *Von der musikalischen Poesie*', *Music Review*, xxxiii (1972), 93–107

Markstrom, Kurt Sven. 'The Operas of Leonardo Vinci' (dissertation, University of Toronto, 1993)

Marmontel, Jean François. *Oeuvres complètes* (Paris, 1787)

Marpurg, Friedrich Wilhelm. *Die Kunst das Clavier zu spielen, durch den Verfasser des critischen Musicus an der Spree* (Berlin, 1750)

Marpurg, Friedrich Wilhelm. *Abhandlung von der Fuge nach den Grundsätzen der besten deutschen und ausländischen Meister* (Berlin, 1753–4)

Marpurg, Friedrich Wilhelm. *Historisch-kritische Beyträge zur Aufnahme der Musik* (Berlin 1754–78)

Marpurg, Friedrich Wilhelm. *Anleitung zum Clavierspielen der schönen Ausübung der heutigen Zeit gemäß* (Berlin, 1755)

Marpurg, Friedrich Wilhelm. *Handbuch bey dem Generalbasse und der Composition mit zwey- drey- vier- fünf- sechs- sieben- acht und mehreren Stimmen* (Berlin, 1755–8)

Marpurg, Friedrich Wilhelm. *Anleitung zur Singcomposition* (Berlin, 1758)

Marpurg, Friedrich Wilhelm. *Kritische Briefe über die Tonkunst* (Berlin, 1760–4)

Marshall, Robert L., ed. *Mozart Speaks: Views on Music, Musicians, and the World* (New York, 1991)

Marshall, Robert L., ed. *Eighteenth-Century Keyboard Music* (New York, 1994)

Martini, Giovanni Battista. *Storia della musica* (Bologna, 1761–81)

Martini, Giovanni Battista. *Esemplare, o sia Saggio fondamentale pratico di contrappunto sopra il canto fermo* (Bologna, 1774–6)

Martinotti, Sergio. 'Italiani e italianisti a Vienna da Bonno a Salieri', *Il teatro musicale italiano nel Sacro Romano Impero nei secoli XVII e XVIII*, ed. Alberto Colzani, Andrea Luppi, Maurizio Padoan and Norbert Dubowy (Como, 1999), 461–81

Martorana, Pietro. 'Trinchera, Pietro', *Notizie biografiche e bibliografiche degli scrittori del dialetto napoletano* (Naples, 1874)

Marx, Adolf Bernhard. *Die Lehre von der musikalischen Komposition* (Leipzig, 1837–8)

Marx, Adolf Bernhard. *Gluck und die Oper* (Berlin, 1863)

Mas, Christian. 'Influence française sur l'évolution de la suite instrumentale en Allemagne', *Aspects de la baroque et classique à Lyon et en France*, ed. Daniel Paquette (Lyons, 1989), 118–24

Masi, Ernesto. 'Gio. De Gamerra o il segreto d'un cuor sensibile', *Studi e ritratti* (Bologna, 1881), 267–97

Masi, Ernesto. 'Giovanni de Gamerra e i drammi lagrimosi', *Sulla storia del teatro nel secolo XVIII* (Florence, 1891)

Massalongo, Mileana. 'Il Don Giovanni di Mozart in due "studi letterari" del romanticismo: Don Juan di E. T. A. Hoffmann e il Don Giovanni di Søren Kierkegaard', *Hortus musicus*, v/20 (2004), 68–78

Mattern, Volker. *Das Dramma giocoso: 'La finta giardiniera': Ein Vergleich der Vertonungen von Pasquale Anfossi und W. A. Mozart* (Laaber, 1989)

Matthäus, Wolfgang. *Johann André Musikverlag zu Offenbach am Main: Verlagsgeschichte und Bibliographie 1782–1800* (Tutzing, 1973)

Mattheson, Johann. *Das neu-eröffnete Orchestre* (Hamburg, 1713)

Mattheson, Johann. *Critica musica* (Hamburg, 1722–5)

Mattheson, Johann. *Matthesons Mithridat wider den Gift einer welschen Satyre* (Hamburg, 1749)

Matthews, Betty. 'The Childhood of Nancy Storace', *Musical Times*, cx (1969), 733–5

Matthews, Betty. 'The Davies Sisters, J. C. Bach and the Glass Harmonica', *Music & Letters*, lvi (1975), 150–69

Maunder, Richard. *Mozart's Requiem: On Preparing a New Edition* (Oxford, 1988)

Maunder, Richard. 'Süßmayr's Work in Mozart's Requiem: A Study of the Autograph Score', *Mozart-Studien*, vii (1997), 57–80

Maunder, Richard and David Rowland. 'Mozart's pedal piano', *Early Music*, xxiii/2 (1995), 287–96

Maurer, Julius. *Anton Schweitzer als dramatischer Komponist* (Leipzig, 1912)

Maylender, Michele. *Storia delle Accademie d'Italia* (Bologna, 1926–30)

Mayr, Josef. *Die ehemalige Universität Salzburg* (Salzburg, 1859)

Mazzeo, Antonio. *I tre 'Senesini': Musici ed altri cantanti evirati senesi* (Siena,1979)

Medici di Marignano, Nerina and Rosemary Hughes, ed. *A Mozart Pilgrimage: Being the Travel Diaries of Vincent & Mary Novello in the Year 1829* (London, 1955)

Meinardus, Ludwig Siegfried. 'Johann Wilhelm Häßler', *Allgemeine musikalische Zeitung*, iii, new series (1865), 505–6

Meinhold, Günter. *Zauberflöte und Zauberflötenrezeption: Studien zu Emanuel Schikaneders Libretto 'Die Zauberflöte' und seiner literarischen Rezeption* (Frankfurt, 2001)

Meißner, Alfred. *Bruchstücke zur Biographie J. G. Naumanns* (Prague, 1803–4)

Meißner, Alfred. *Rococo-Bilder: Aufzeichnungen meines Großvaters* (Gumbinnen, 1871)

Melamed, Daniel. 'Evidence on the Genesis of *Die Entführung aus dem Serail* from Mozart's Autograph Score', *Mozart-Jahrbuch 2003/4*, 25–42

Mellace, Raffaele. *Johann Adolf Hasse* (Palermo, 2004)

Meloncelli, Raoul. 'Un operista italiano alla corte di Vienna: Giuseppe Bonno (1710–1788)', *Chigiana*, xxix/xxx (1975), 331–42

Mendelssohn, Felix. *Reisebriefe aus den Jahren 1830 bis 1832* (Leipzig, 1861)

Mendelssohn, Felix. *Briefe aus den Jahren 1833 bis 1847* (Leipzig, 1863)

Mennicke, Carl. *Hasse und die Brüder Graun als Symphoniker* (Leipzig, 1906)

Merck, Johann Heinrich. *Briefe an und von Johann Heinrich Merck* (Darmstadt, 1838)

Merian, Hans. *Mozarts Meisteropern* (Leipzig, 1900)

Mersmann, Hans. 'Beiträge zur Aufführungspraxis der vorklassichen Kammermusik in Deutschland', *Archiv für Musikwissenschaft*, ii (1919/20), 99–143

Messina, Nuccio, ed. *Carlo Goldoni: Vita, opere, attualità* (Rome, 1993)

Metastasio, Pietro. *Lettere* (Venice, 1794)

Metastasio, Pietro. *Opere postume* (Vienna, 1795)

Meyer, Daniel. 'Deux vedettes chez le Prince de Conti', *Connaissance des arts*, no.479 (1992), 52–7

Meyer, Friedrich Ludwig Wilhelm. *Friedrich Ludwig Schröder: Beitrag zur Kunde des Menschen und des Künstlers* (Hamburg, 1819)

Meyer, John A. 'The keyboard concertos of Johann Christian Bach and their influence on Mozart', *Miscellanea musicologica* [Australia], x (1979), 59–73

Meyer, Leonard B. 'Grammatical Simplicity and Relational Richness: The Trio of Mozart's G minor Symphony', *Critical Inquiry*, ii (1975/6), 693–761

Meyer, Ralph. 'Die Behandlung des Rezitativs in Glucks italienischen Reformopern', *Gluck-Jahrbuch*, iv (1918), 1–90

Michaelis, Rainer und Wolfgang Seiller. 'Ein unbekanntes Bildnis Wolfgang Amadeus Mozarts in der Berliner Gemäldegalerie', *Mozart-Jahrbuch 1999*, 1–12

Michel, Hertha. 'Ranieri Calzabigi als Dichter von Musikdramen und als Kritiker', *Gluck-Jahrbuch*, iv (1918), 99–171

Michelitsch, Helga. *Das Klavierwerk von Georg Christoph Wagenseil: Thematischer Katalog* (Vienna, 1966)

Michot, Pierre. 'Le créateur de Cecilio: Venanzio Rauzzini', *L'avant-scène opéra*, no.139 (1991), 92–5

Michot, Pierre. 'Les créateurs de la Flûte', *L'avant-scène opéra* (May/June 2000), 122–5

Michtner, Otto. *Das alte Burgtheater als Opernbühne: Von der Einführung des deutschen Singspiels (1778) bis zum Tod Kaiser Leopolds II. (1792)* (Vienna, 1970)

Mieder, Wolfgang. '"Nun sitz ich wie der Haass im Pfeffer": Sprichwörtliches in Mozarts Briefen', *Mozart-Jahrbuch 2003/4*, 165–98

Mielichhofer, Ludwig. *Das Mozart-Denkmal zu Salzburg und dessen Enthüllungs-Feier im September 1842* (Salzburg, 1843)

Miller, Norbert. 'Die Schule der Intrige oder der Bürger als Parvenu: Zur Figaro-Trilogie von Pierre Augustin Caron de Beaumarchais', *Beaumarchais: Die Figaro-Trilogie*, ed. Gerda Scheffel (Frankfurt, 1976), 347–94

Miller, Norbert. 'Die Komödie "Le mariage de Figaro" von Beaumarchais', *Wolfgang Amadeus Mozart: Die Hochzeit des Figaro. Texte, Materialien, Kommentare*, ed. Attila Csampai and Dietmar Holland (Reinbek bei Hamburg, 1982)

Milliot, Sylvette. 'Mozart et les violoncellistes français de la cour de Prusse', *Itinéraires mozartiens en Bourgogne: Colloque de Dijon des 11 et 12 avril 1991*, ed. Francis Claudon (Paris, 1992), 221–5

Millner, Frederick. *The Operas of Johann Adolf Hasse* (Ann Arbor, 1979)

Minor, Jakob. *Christian Felix Weiße und seine Beziehungen zur deutschen Literatur des achtzehnten Jahrhunderts* (Innsbruck, 1880)

Mishkin, Henry G. 'Incomplete notation in Mozart's piano concertos', *Musical Quarterly*, lxi/3 (1975), 345–59

Mittendorfer, Monika. 'Unterdrückte Kreativität: Cornelia Goethe und Nannerl Mozart', *Maria Anna Mozart: Die Künstlerin und ihre Zeit*, ed. Siegrid Düll and Otto Neumaier (Möhnesee, 2001), 134–53

Moberly, Robert and Christopher Raeburn, 'Mozart's "Figaro": The Plan of Act III', *Music & Letters*, xlvi (1965), 134–6

Modica, Massimo. *Il sistema delle arti: Batteux e Diderot* (Palermo, 1987)

Mongrédien, Jean. 'Les mystères d'Isis (1801) and reflections on Mozart from the Parisian press at the beginning of the nineteenth century', *Music in the Classic period: Essays in honor of Barry S. Brook*, ed. Allan Atlas (New York, 1985), 195–211

Mongrédien, Jean. *La musique en France, des Lumières au Romantisme: de 1789 à 1830* (Paris, 1986)

Mongrédien, Jean. 'Paris: The End of the Ancien Régime', *The Classical Era from the 1740s to the end of the 18th Century*, ed. Neal Zaslaw (London, 1989), 61–98

Mongrédien, Jean. 'La France à la découverte de Mozart ou le véritable enjeu d'une mythification (1791–1815)', *Mozart: Origines et transformations d'un mythe. Actes du colloque international organisé dans le cadre du bicentenaire de la mort de Mozart. Clermont-Ferrand, décembre 1991*, ed. Jean-Louis Jam (Berne, 1994), 71–8

Montéclair, Michel Pignolet de. *Méthode facile pour apprendre à jouer du violin* (Paris, 1711–12)

Monterosso, Raffaello. 'L'oratorio musicale in Bologna nel secolo XVIII', *Risultati e prospettive della ricerca sul movimento dei Disciplinati: Convegno internazionale di studio, Perugia, 5–7 dicembre 1969* (Perugia, 1972), 99–120

Moolenijzer, J. H. and Sas Bunge, *Mozart en de Hollanders: een winter in Mannheim* (Haarlem, 1969)

Moore, Julia. 'Mozart in the Market Place', *Journal of the Royal Musical Association*, cxiv (1989), 18–42

Morath, Wolfram and Irene Andessner, ed. *Salzburger Museum Carolino Augusteum: Frauen zu Salzburg. Caroline Auguste, Constanze Mozart, Nannerl Mozart, Barbara Krafft, Emilia Viktoria Kraus ('Hundsgräfin'). Ausstellung vom 23. Juli bis 12. September 1999* (Salzburg, 1999)

Morea, Nicola. *Tommaso Traetta: Riformatore del melodramma* (Bitonto, 1982)

Mörike, Eduard. *Mozart auf der Reise nach Prag* (Stuttgart, 1856)

Morris, Max. *Goethe-Studien*, second edition (Berlin, 1902)

Morris, Max. 'Goethe als Bearbeiter von italienischen Operntexten', *Goethe-Jahrbuch*, xxvi (1905), 3–51

Morrow, Mary Sue. *Concert Life in Haydn's Vienna: Aspects of a Developing Musical and Social Institution* (New York, 1989)

Morrow, Mary Sue. *German Music Criticism in the Late Eighteenth Century: Aesthetic Issues in Instrumental Music* (New York, 1997)

Moscheles, Charlotte, ed. *Aus Moscheles' Leben* (Leipzig, 1872–3)

Mosel, Ignaz von. *Ueber das Leben und die Werke des Anton Salieri* (Vienna, 1827)

Mosel, Ignaz von. *Über die Originalpartitur des Requiem von W. A. Mozart* (Vienna, 1839)

Moseley, Paul. 'Mozart's Requiem: A Revaluation of the Evidence', *Journal of the Royal Musical Association*, cxiv (1989), 203–37

Moss, Harold Gene. 'Popular music and the ballad opera', *Journal of the American Musicological Society*, xxvi/3 (1973), 365–82

Mozart: Bilder und Klänge (Salzburg, 1991)

Mozart, Carl Thomas. 'Brief Karl Thomas Mozarts an Adolf Popelka vom 4. März 1856', *Briefe vom Bertramhof* (Prague, 1944), 1–4

Mozart, Carl Thomas. 'Ein Brief von Karl Mozart', *Arbeits- und Kulturbericht der Mozartgemeinde Wien (Wiener Figaro)*, ii/3–4 (1944), 8–10

Mozart, Constanze. 'Einige Anekdoten aus Mozarts Leben, von seiner hinterlassenen Gattin uns mitgetheilt', *Allgemeine musikalische Zeitung*, i (1798/9), 289–91

Mozart, Constanze. 'Noch einige Kleinigkeiten aus Mozarts Leben', *Allgemeine musikalische Zeitung*, i (1798/9), 854–6

Mozart, Leopold. *Versuch einer gründlichen Violinschule* (Augsburg, 1756); Dutch trans. *Grondig Onderwys in het behandelen der Violin* (Haarlem, 1766)

Mozart, Wolfgang Amadeus. 'Bruckstück eines Lustspiels', *Allgemeine musikalische Zeitung*, xliii (1843), 17–21

Mozart, Wolfgang Amadeus. *Eigenhändiges Werkverzeichnis: Faksimile. British Library Stefan Zweig MS 63*, ed. Albi Rosenthal and Alan Tyson (London and Kassel, 1991 = NMA X/33/1)

Mozarts Idomeneo und die Musik in München zur Zeit Karl Theodors: Bericht über das Symposion der Gesellschaft für Bayerische Musikgeschichte (Munich, 2001)

Mueller von Asow, Erich H. and H., ed. *The Collected Correspondence and Papers of Christoph Willibald Gluck* (London, 1962)

Müller, Johann Heinrich Friedrich. *Genaue Nachrichten von beyden Kaiserlich-Königlichen Schaubühnen und anderen öffentlichen Ergötzlichkeiten in Wien* (Preßburg, 1772)

Müller, Johann Heinrich Friedrich. *Abschied von der k. k. Hof- und National-Schaubühne: Mit einer kurzen Biographie seines Lebens und einer gedrängten Geschichte des hiesigen Hoftheaters* (Vienna, 1802)

Müller, Ulrich and Oswald Panagl. *Don Giovanni in New York: Lorenzo Da Pontes italienisch-englisches Libretto für die US-Erstaufführung von Mozarts Oper (1826). Mit dem Libretto der Oper Mozart in New York von Herbert Rosendorfer/Helmut Eder (1991)* (Anif, 1991)

Müller, Walther. *Johann Adolf Hasse als Kirchenkomponist* (Leipzig, 1911)

Müller von Asow, Erich H. *Die Mingottischen Opernunternehmungen, 1732 bis 1756* (Leipzig, 1915)

Müller von Asow, Erich H. *Angelo und Pietro Mingotti* (Leipzig, 1917)

Müller von Asow, Erich H. 'Gluck und die Brüder Mingotti', *Gluck-Jahrbuch*, iii (1917), 1–14

Müller von Asow, Erich H. 'Regina Mingotti: Eine italienische Primadonna aus österreichischer Familie', *Musikblätter*, iv (1950), 79–82

Münster, Robert. 'Nissens "Biographie W.A. Mozarts": Zu ihrer Entstehungsgeschichte', *Acta Mozartiana*, ix (1962), 2–14

Münster, Robert. 'Neues zu Leopold Mozarts Augsburger Gymnasialjahren', *Acta Mozartiana*, xii (1965), 57–60

Münster, Robert. 'Mozart "... beym Herzoge Clemens ...": Ein Beitrag zum Thema Mozart in München', *Mozart-Jahrbuch 1965/66*, 133–41

Münster, Robert. 'Mozarts Münchener Aufenthalt von 1777, der "H: von Hamm" und "die Finalmusik mit dem Rondeau auf die letzt"', *Acta Mozartiana*, xxii/2 (1975), 21–37

Münster, Robert. 'Mozart's Kirchenmusik in München im 18. und beginnenden 19. Jahrhundert: Stiftskirche zu Unserer Lieben Frau – Augustinerkloster – Kurfürstliche und Königliche Hofkapelle', *Festschrift Erich Valentin zum 70. Geburtstag*, ed. Günther Weiß (Regensburg, 1976), 143–53

Münster, Robert. 'Die beiden Fassungen der Motette *Exsultate, jubilate* KV 165', *Mozart-Studien*, ii (1993), 119–33

Münster, Robert. *'Ich bin hier sehr beliebt': Mozart und das kurfürstliche Bayern* (Tutzing, 1993)

Münster, Robert. 'Neues zum Münchener "Idomeneo" 1781', *'Ich bin hier sehr beliebt': Mozart und das kurfürstliche Bayern* (Tutzing, 1993), 125–35

Munter, Friedrich. 'Ignaz von Beecke (1733–1803) und seine Instrumentalkompositionen', *Zeitschrift für Musikwissenschaft*, iv (1921/2), 586–603

Muresu, Gabriele. *La parola cantata: Studi sul melodramma italiano del Settecento* (Rome, 1982)

Murray, Sterling. 'Bohemian Musicians in South German Hofkapellen during the Late Eighteenth Century', *Hudební věda*, xv (1978), 153–73

Murray, Sterling. *Seven Symphonies from the Court of Oettingen-Wallerstein, 1773–1795* (New York, 1981 = The Symphony 1720–1840, series C, volume vi)

Murray, T. J. 'The Skull of Mozart', *Dalhousie Review*, lxxiii/2 (1993), 246–51

Mussafia, Adolfo. *Pietro Metastasio* (Vienna, 1882)

Nägele, Reiner. 'Die Rezeption der Mozart-Opern am Stuttgarter Hof 1790 bis 1810', *Mozart-Studien*, v (1995), 119–37

Nägele, Reiner. 'Die wiederentdeckte "Stuttgarter Kopie (Prager Provenienz)" von Mozarts "Don Giovanni"', *Musik in Baden-Württemberg*, ii (1995), 159–66

Nägele, Reiner. 'Belmont und Constanze in den Vertonungen von Dieter und Mozart: Ein Vergleich', *Die Musikforschung*, l/3 (1997), 277–94

Nägeli, Hans Georg. *Vorlesungen über Musik: Mit Berücksichtigung der Dilettanten* (Stuttgart, 1826)

Nagler, Alois Maria. *Theatre Festivals of the Medici 1539–1637* (New Haven, CT, and London, 1964)

Nalbach, Daniel. *The King's Theatre, 1704–1867: London's first Italian opera house* (London, 1972)

Nascimbene, Anelide. 'Mysliveček e i Mozart a Bologna: Documenti, cronaca e critica', *Mozart: Gli orientamenti della critica moderna. Atti del convegno internazionale Cremona, 24–26 novembre 1991*, ed. Giacomo Fornari (Lucca, 1994), 3–25

Nettl, Paul. 'Der erste Klavierauszug des Don Giovanni', *Mitteilungen der Internationalen Stiftung Mozarteum*, xvi (1956), 36–8

Neumann, A. R. 'The Changing Concept of the *Singspiel* in the Eighteenth Century', *Studies in German Literature*, ed. Carl Hammer (Baton Rouge, LA, 1963), 63–71

Neumann, Frederick. *Ornamentation in Baroque and Post-Baroque Music: With special emphasis on J. S. Bach* (Princeton, NJ, 1978)

Neumann, Frederick. *Performance Practices of the Seventeenth and Eighteenth Centuries* (New York, 1993)

Neumayr, Anton. 'Wolfgang Amadeus Mozart: Krankheit, Tod und Begräbnis', *Genie und Alltag: Bürgerliche Stadtkultur zur Mozartzeit*, ed. Gunda Barth-Scalmani, Brigitte Mazohl-Wallnig and Ernst Wangermann (Salzburg, 1994), 119–34

Newman, Ernest. *Gluck and the Opera* (London, 1895)

Newman, William S. 'Mozart's G minor Quintet (K. 516) and its Relationship to the G minor Symphony (K. 550)', *Music Review*, xvii (1956), 287–303

Newman, William S. *The Sonata in the Classic Era* (Chapel Hill, 1963)

Newman, William S. *The Sonata in the Baroque Era* (Chapel Hill, 1966)

Nichelmann, Christoph. *Die Melodie, nach ihrem Wesen sowohl, als nach ihren Eigenschaften* (Danzig, 1755)

Nicolai, Friedrich. *Beschreibung einer Reise durch Deutschland und die Schweiz im Jahre 1781* (Berlin, 1783–96)

Nicolai, Gustav. 'Der Musikfeind: Ein Nachtstück', *Arabesken für Musikfreunde*, second edition (Leipzig, 1838)

Niderst, Alain. 'Marmontel et la musique', *Papers on French Seventeenth-Century Literature*, xv/29 (1988), 577–91

Niecks, Friedrich. 'Pianoforte four-hand compositions', *Zeitschrift der Internationalen Musikgesellschaft*, v (1903/4), 275–7

Niedecken, Hans. *Jean Georges Noverre 1727–1810: Sein Leben und seine Beziehungen zur Musik* (Halle, 1914)

Niemetschek, Franz Xaver. *Leben des k. k. Kapellmeisters Wolfgang Gottlieb Mozart nach Originalquellen beschrieben*, ed. Ernst Rychnowsky (Prague, 1905)

Niemöller, Klaus Wolfgang. 'Joseph Aloys Schmittbaurs Werke und ihre Würdigung im 18. Jahrhundert', *Festschrift Karl Gustav Fellerer zum sechzigsten Geburtstag*, ed. Heinrich Hüschen (Regensburg, 1962), 377–90

Niggli, Arnold. 'Gertrud Elisabeth Mara', *Sammlung musikalischer Vorträge*, ed. Paul von Waldersee (Leipzig, 1881), iii.163–208

Nissen, Georg Nikolaus von. *Biographie W. A. Mozarts* (Leipzig, 1828)

Noel, Édouard and Edmond Stoullig. *Les annales du théâtre et de la musique* (Paris, 1876–1918)

Noguchi, Hideo. 'Mozart: Musical Game in C major K. 516f', *Mitteilungen der Internationalen Stiftung Mozarteum*, xxxviii (1990), 89–101

Nohl, Hermann. *Typische Kunststile in Dichtung und Musik* (Jena, 1915)

Nohl, Ludwig. *Musikalisches Skizzenbuch* (Leipzig, 1866)

Nohl, Ludwig. *Musiker-Briefe* (Leipzig, 1873)

Nohl, Ludwig. *Mozart nach den Schilderungen seiner Zeitgenossen* (Leipzig, 1880)

Noinville, Jacques-Bernard Durey de. *Histoire du Théâtre de l'Opéra en France depuis l'établissement de l'Académie royale de musique, jusqu'à présent*, second edition (Paris, 1757)

Noiray, Michel. 'La répertoire d'opéra italien au Théâtre de Monsieur et au Théâtre Feydeau: Janvier 1789–août 1792', *Revue de musicologie*, lxxxi/2 (1995), 259–75

Noiray, Michel. 'La construction de Don Giovanni', *L'avant-scène opéra*, clvii (July-August 1996), 126–133

Norman, Buford. 'The *tragédie-lyrique* of Lully and Quinault: Representation and Recognition of Emotion', *Literature and the Other Arts: Continuum*, v (1993), 111–42

Norman, Buford. *Touched by the Graces: The Libretti of Philippe Quinault in the Context of French Classicism* (Birmingham, AL, 2001)

Noske, Frits. *The Signifier and the Signified: Studies in the Operas of Mozart and Verdi* (The Hague, 1977)

Nottebohm, Gustav. *Ein Skizzenbuch von Beethoven* (Leipzig, 1865)

Nottebohm, Gustav. *Beethoveniana* (Leipzig, 1872)

Nottebohm, Gustav. *Ein Skizzenbuch von Beethoven aus dem Jahre 1803* (Leipzig, 1880)

Nottebohm, Gustav. *Mozartiana* (Leipzig, 1880)

Nottebohm, Gustav. *Zweite Beethoveniana*, ed. Eusebius Mandyczewski (Leipzig, 1887)

Novello, Mary Sabilla. 'A Visit to Mozart's Widow and Sister', *The Musical World* (18 August – 22 September 1837)

Noverre, Jean-Georges. *Lettres sur la danse et sur les ballets* (Lyons and Stuttgart, 1760)

Nuitter, Charles and Ernest Thoinan, *Les origines de l'opéra français* (Paris, 1886)

Oboussier, Philippe. 'The French String Quartet, 1770–1800', *Music and the French Revolution*, ed. Malcolm Boyd (Cambridge, 1992), 74–92

Ochs, Michael. '"L.m.i.a": Mozart's suppressed canon texts', *Mozart-Jahrbuch 1991: Bericht über den Internationalen Mozart-Kongreß Salzburg 1991*, 254–61

O'Donoghue, David James. *An Irish Musical Genius: Richard Pockrich, the Inventor of the Musical Glasses* (Dublin, 1899)

Oehl. Kurt Helmut. 'Die eingeschobenen Dialogszenen in Mozarts Don Juan im 18.–19. Jahrhundert', *Florilegium musicologicum: Hellmut Federhofer zum 75. Geburtstag*, ed. Christoph-Hellmut Mahling (Tutzing, 1988), 247–66

Oehl, Kurt Helmut. 'Mozarts "Figaro" mit Singspieldialog von Knigge', *Festschrift Christoph-Hellmut Mahling zum 65. Geburtstag*, ed. Axel Beer, Kristina Pfarr and Wolfgang Ruf (Tutzing, 1997), 1043–56

Oehlenschläger, Adam Gottlob. *Meine Lebens-Erinnerungen* (n.p., 1850)

Oliver, Alfred Richard. *The Encyclopedists as Critics of Music* (New York, 1947)

Olleson, Edward. 'Gottfried van Swieten, Patron of Haydn and Mozart', *Proceedings of the Royal Musical Association*, lxxxix (1962–3), 63–74

Oncken, Wilhelm. *Das Zeitalter Friedrichs des Großen* (Berlin, 1881–2)

Orel, Alfred. 'Die Legende um Mozarts "Bastien und Bastienne"', *Schweizerische Musikzeitung*, xci (1951), 137–43

Orel, Alfred. 'Sarastro . . . Hr. Gerl/Ein altes Weib . . . Mad. Gerl', *Mozart-Jahrbuch 1955*, 66–89

Orel, Alfred. 'Neue Gerliana', *Mozart-Jahrbuch 1957*, 212–22

Ortolani, Giuseppe. *La riforma del teatro nel Settecento e altri scritti* (Venice, 1962)

Osborne, Charles. *The Complete Operas of Mozart: A Critical Guide* (New York, 1978)

Ott, Alfons. 'Von der frühdeutschen Oper zum deutschen Singspiel', *Musik in Bayern* (1974), 165–77

Oulibicheff, Alexander D. *Mozarts Opern: Kritische Erläuterungen aus dem französischen Originale übersetzt von C. Kossmaly* (Leipzig, 1848)

Oulibicheff, Alexander D. *Mozart's Leben, nebst einer Uebersicht der allgemeinen Geschichte der Musik und einer Analyse der Hauptwerke Mozart's* (Stuttgart, 1847; second edition, ed. Ludwig Gantter: Stuttgart, 1864)

Paczkowski, Szymon and Alina Zorawska-Witkowska, ed. *Johann Adolf Hasse in seiner Epoche und in der Gegenwart: Studien zur Stil- und Quellenproblematik* (Warsaw, 1999)

Padoan, Giorgio, ed. *Problemi di critica goldoniana*. *II* (Ravenna: Longon, 1995 = Atti ed inchieste di Quaderni Veneti iv)

Pagano, Roberto. 'L'inserimento di Nicolò Logroscino nella realtà musicale palermitana', *Musicisti nati in Puglia ed emigrazione musicale tra Seicento e Settecento* (Rome, 1988), 49–55

Paissa, Robert. '"Questo è il conte, alla voce il conosco": Stefano Mandini prima di Mozart (1774–1783)', *Rivista italiana di musicologia*, xxii (1987), 145–82

Palisca, Claude V. 'The "Camerata Fiorentina": A Reappraisal', *Studi musicali*, i (1972), 203–36

Palisca, Claude V. 'The Recitative of Lully's Alceste: French Declamation or Italian Melody?', *Actes de Baton Rouge: Papers on 17th-Century Literature*, xxx (1986), 19–34

Palisca, Claude V. *The Florentine Camerata: Documentary Studies and Translations* (New Haven, CT, 1989)

Palmer, Christian. *Evangelische Hymnologie* (Stuttgart, 1865)

Pandolfi, Vito. *La commedia dell'arte: Storia e testo* (Florence, 1988)

Paquette, Daniel. *Jean-Philippe Rameau: Musicien bourguignon* (Saint-Seine-l'Abbaye, 1984)

Parakilas, James. 'The afterlife of "Don Giovanni": Turning production history into criticism', *Journal of Musicology*, viii/2 (1990), 251–65

Parfaict, Claude and François. *Mémoires pour servir à l'histoire des spectacles de la foire* (Paris, 1743)

Parisini, Federico. *Della vita e delle opere del Padre G. B. Martini* (Bologna, 1887)

Parke, William Thomas. *Musical Memoirs* (London, 1830)

Parker, Mildred. 'Some Speculations on the French Keyboard Suites of the Seventeenth and Early Eighteenth Centuries', *International Review of the Aesthetics and Sociology of Music*, vii (1976), 203–18

Parker, Roger, ed. *The Oxford Illustrated History of Opera* (Oxford, 1994)

Parker, Roger. 'Ersatz Ditties: Adriana Ferrarese's Susanna', *Remaking the Song: Operatic visions and revisions from Handel to Berio* (Berkeley, CA, 2006), 42–66

Les parodies du nouveau théâtre italien, second edition (Paris, 1738)

Parr, James A. 'Selected Evidence for Tirso's Authorship of *El burlador de Sevilla y convidado de piedra*', *Hispanic Essays in Honor of Frank P. Casa*, ed. A. Robert Lauer and Henry Sullivan (New York, 1997), 156–64

Pastore, Giuseppe A. *Leonardo Leo* (Galatina, 1957)

Pastore, Giuseppe A. 'Le "arielle co'wioline" di Antonicco Arefece', *Studi salentini*, xx (1965), 249–62

Pastore, Giuseppe A. *Don Lionardo: Vita e opere di Leonardo Leo* (Cuneo, 1994)

Patier, Dominique. 'Vers une meilleure compréhension de l'expression de Léopold Mozart: Le "vermanierierte Mannheimer Goût"', *Off-Mozart: Musical Culture and the 'Kleinmeister' of Central Europe 1750–1820*, ed. Vjera Katalinič (Zagreb, 1995), 153–66

Pauer, Ernst. *Alte Meister: Sammlung wertvoller Klavierstücke des 17. und 18. Jahrhunderts* (Leipzig, 1868–91)

Pauli, Walther. *J. F. Reichardt: Sein Leben und seine Stellung in der Geschichte des deutschen Liedes* (Berlin, 1903)

Paulin, Du Route de. *La vie et les œuvres d'Antoine d'Auvergne* (Paris, 1911)

Pauly, Reinhard G. 'Johann Ernst Eberlin's Concerted Liturgical Music', *Musik und Geschichte/Music and History: Leo Schrade zum sechzigsten Geburtstag* (Cologne, 1963), 146–77

Pauly, Reinhard and Ernst Hintermaier, 'Eberlin, Johann Ernst', *The New Grove Dictionary of Music and Musicians*, second edition ed. Stanley Sadie and John Tyrrell (London, 2001), vii.849–50

Payer von Thurn, Rudolph, ed. *Joseph II. als Theaterdirektor: Ungedruckte Briefe und Aktenstücke aus den Kinderjahren des Burgtheaters* (Vienna, 1920)

Pečman, Rudolf. *Franz Xaver Richter und seine 'Harmonische Belehrungen'*, ed. E. Thom (Blankenburg, Harz, 1990)

Peiretti, Rita. '"Vado incontro al fato estremo": Eine bisher fälschlich Mozart zugeschriebene Arie der Oper "Mitridate, Re di Ponto"', *Mitteilungen der Internationalen Stiftung Mozarteum*, xliv/3–4 (1996), 40–1

Pelker, Bärbel, ed. *Günther von Schwarzburg: Singspiel in drei Aufzügen* (Munich, 2000)

Pendle, Karin. 'The Opéras Comiques of Grétry and Marmontel', *Musical Quarterly*, lxii (1976), 409–34

Pendle, Karin. 'L'opéra-comique à Paris de 1762 à 1789', *L'opéra-comique en France au XVIIIe siècle*, ed. Philippe Vendrix (Liège, 1992), 79–178

Penninger, Julia. 'Der historische Opernwettstreit von 1786: Untersuchungen zur Problematik der Gattungsbegriffe "Deutsches Singspiel" und "Opera buffa" in der Auseinandersetzung um Mozarts "Der Schauspieldirektor" und Salieris "Prima la musica, poi le parole" und Darstellung der vermeintlich konkurrierenden Position beider Komponisten anhand historischer Dokumente' (dissertation, University of Vienna, 1992)

Perey, Lucien [Luce Herpin] and Gaston Maugras, *Une femme du monde au XVIIIe siècle: La jeunesse de Madame d'Épinay, d'après des lettres et des documents inédits* (Paris, 1882)

Perger, Lothar H. *Michael Haydn: Instrumentalwerke* (Leipzig, 1907 = Denkmäler der Tonkunst in Österreich xxix)

Perrucci, Andrea and Roberto De Simone, ed. *Il convitato di pietra* (Turin, 1998)

Pestelli, Giorgio. 'Mozart e Rutini', *Mozart und Italien*, ed. Friedrich Lippmann (Köln, 1978 = *Analecta musicologica* xviii), 290–307

Peth, Jakob. *Geschichte des Theaters und der Musik zu Mainz* (Mainz, 1879)

Petrobelli, Pierluigi. 'The Italian Years of Anton Raaff', *Mozart-Jahrbuch 1973/74*, 233–73

Petrobelli, Pierluigi. 'Un cantante fischiato e le appoggiature di mezza battuta: Cronaca teatrale e prassi esecutiva alla metà del '700', *Studies in Renaissance and Baroque Music in Honor of Arthur Mendel*, ed. Robert L. Marshall (Kassel, 1974), 363–76

Petrobelli, Pierluigi. 'Don Giovanni in Italia: La fortuna dell'opera ed il suo influsso', *Colloquium 'Mozart und Italien' (Rom 1974)*, ed. Friedrich Lippmann (Cologne, 1978 = *Analecta musicologica* xviii), 30–51

Petrobelli, Pierluigi. 'Leopold Mozart e la "Ausbildung" di Wolfgang', *Beiträge des Internationalen Leopold-Mozart-Kolloquiums Augsburg 1994*, ed. Josef Mančal and Wolfgang Plath (Augsburg, 1997), 105–6

Petty, Fred C. 'Italian Opera in London, 1760–1800' (dissertation, Yale University, 1971)

Petzholdt, Julius. 'Biographisch-litterarische Mittheilungen über Maria Antonia Walpurgis von Sachsen', *Neuer Anzeiger für Bibliographie und Bibliothekwissenschaft*, xi (1856), 336–45, 367–90

Pezzl, Johann. *Skizze von Wien* (Vienna, 1786–90)

Pfannhauser, Karl. 'Wer war Mozarts Amtsnachfolger?', *Acta Mozartiana*, iii/3 (1956), 6–16

Pichler, Karoline. *Denkwürdigkeiten aus meinem Leben* (Vienna, 1844)

Pieri, Marzia, ed. *Il teatro di Goldoni* (Bologna, 1993)

Pierre, Constant. *Histoire du Concert Spirituel 1725–1790* (Paris, 1975)

Pies, Eike. *Prinzipale: Zur Genealogie des deutschsprachigen Berufstheaters vom 17. bis 19. Jahrhundert* (Ratingen, Kastellaun and Düsseldorf, 1973)

Pietropaolo, Domenico, ed. *Goldoni and the Musical Theatre* (New York, 1995)

Pillwein, Benedikt. *Biographische Schilderungen oder Lexikon Salzburgischer, teils verstorbener, teils lebender Künstler* (Salzburg, 1821)

Piovano, Francesco. 'Elenco cronologico delle opere (1757–1802) di Pietro Guglielmi (1727–1804)', *Rivista italiana di musicologia*, xii (1905), 407–47

Piovano, Francesco. 'Baldassare Galuppi: Note bio-bibliografiche', *Rivista italiana di musicologia*, xiii (1906), 676–726; xiv (1907), 333–65; xv (1908), 233–74

Piovano, Francesco. 'A propos d'une récente biographie de Léonard Leo', *Sammelbände der Internationalen Musikgesellschaft*, viii (1906/7), 70–95

Piovano, Francesco. 'Notizie storico-bibliografiche sulle opere di Pietro Carlo Guglielmi (Guglielmini) con appendice su Pietro Guglielmi', *Rivista musicale italiana*, xvi (1909), 243–70, 475–505 and 785–820; xvii (1910), 59–90, 376–414, 554–89 and 827–77

Pirazzi, Emil. *Bilder und Geschichten aus Offenbachs Vergangenheit* (n.p., 1879)

Pirckmayer, Friedrich, 'Zur Lebensgeschichte Mozarts', *Mitteilungen der Gesellschaft für Salzburger Landeskunde*, xvi (1876), 130–51

Pirckmayer, Friedrich. *Über Musik und Theater am f. e. Salzburger Hofe 1762–1775* (Salzburg, 1886)

Pirrotta, Nino. 'Commedia dell'arte and Opera', *Musical Quarterly*, xli (1955), 305–24; reprinted in *Music and Culture in Italy from the Middle Ages to the Baroque* (Cambridge, MA, 1984), 343–60

Pirrotta, Nino. *Don Giovanni's Progress: A Rake Goes to the Opera* (New York, 1994)

Pisarowitz, Karl M. 'Allerhand Neues vom vergessenen Mozart-Schüler Danner', *Mitteilungen der Internationalen Stiftung Mozarteum*, xvi/1–2 (1968), 7–10

Pisarowitz, Karl M. 'Mozarts Schnorrer Leutgeb', *Mitteilungen der Internationalen Stiftung Mozarteum*, xviii/3–4 (1970), 21–7

Piscitelli, Maurizio. 'I libretti napoletani di Ranieri de' Calzabigi', *Critica letteraria*, xix (1991), 328–40

Pitou, Spire. *The Paris Opera: An Encyclopedia of Operas, Ballets, Composers and Performers* (Westport, CT, and London, 1983)

Plantinga, Leon. 'Clementi, Virtuosity, and the "German Manner"', *Journal of the American Musicological Society*, xxv (1972), 303–30

Plantinga, Leon. *Clementi: His Life and Music* (London, 1977)

Plath, Wolfgang. 'Beiträge zur Mozart-Autographie I: Die Handschrift Leopold Mozarts', *Mozart-Jahrbuch 1960/61*, 82–117

Plath, Wolfgang. 'Miscellanea Mozartiana I', *Festschrift Otto Erich Deutsch zum 80. Geburtstag*, ed. Walter Gerstenberg, Jan LaRue and Wolfgang Rehm (Kassel, 1963), 135–40

Plath, Wolfgang. 'Über Skizzen zu Mozarts Requiem', *Bericht über den Internationalen Musikwissenschaftlichen Kongreß Kassel 1962*, ed. Georg Reichert and Martin Just (Kassel, 1963), 184–7

Plath, Wolfgang. 'Der Ballo des "Ascanio" und die Klavierstücke KV Anh. 207', *Mozart-Jahrbuch 1964*, 111–29

Plath, Wolfgang. 'Überliefert die dubiose Klavierromanze in As KV Anh.205 das verschollene Quintett-Fragment KV Anh.54 (452a)?', *Mozart-Jahrbuch 1965/66*, 71–86

Plath, Wolfgang. 'Leopold Mozarts Notenbuch für Wolfgang (1762) – eine Fälschung?', *Mozart-Jahrbuch 1971/72*, 337–41

Plath, Wolfgang. 'Zur Datierung der Klaviersonaten KV 279–284', *Acta Mozartiana*, xxi (1974), 26–30

Plath, Wolfgang. 'Mozart und Galuppi: Bemerkungen zur Szene "Ah non lasciarmi, no" K295a', *Festschrift Walter Senn zum 70. Geburtstag*, ed. Erich Egg and Ewald Fäßler (Munich, 1975), 174–8

Plath, Wolfgang. 'Beiträge zur Mozart-Autographie II: Schriftchronologie 1770–1780', *Mozart-Jahrbuch 1976/77*, 131–73

Plath, Wolfgang. 'Requiem-Briefe: Aus der Korrespondenz Johann Anton Andrés 1825–1831', *Mozart-Jahrbuch 1978*, 174–203

Plath, Wolfgang. 'Leopold Mozart und Nannerl: Lehrer und Schülerin. Fragmentarische Bemerkungen zu zwei Fragmenten', *Maria Anna Mozart: Die Künstlerin und ihre Zeit*, ed. Siegrid Düll and Otto Neumaier (Möhnesee, 2001), 85–92

Plath, Wolfgang and Wolfgang Rehm. *Wolfgang Amadeus Mozart: Fantasie und Sonate c-Moll für Klavier KV 475 + 457. Faksimile nach dem Autograph in der Bibliotheca Mozartiana Salzburg* (Salzburg, 1991)

Platoff, John. 'Writing about influences: Idomeneo, a case study', *Explorations in music, the arts, and ideas: Essays in honor of Leonard B. Meyer*, ed. Ruth Solie and Eugene Narmour (Stuyvesant, 1988), 43–65

Platoff, John. 'Tonal Organization in the "Buffo" Finales and the Act II Finale of "Le nozze di Figaro"', *Music & Letters*, lxxii/3 (1991), 387–403

Platoff, John. 'Catalogue Arias and the "Catalogue Aria"', *Wolfgang Amadè Mozart: Essays on his Life and his Music*, ed. Stanley Sadie (Oxford, 1996), 296–311

Platoff, John. 'Operatic Finales and the Problem of the *Don Giovanni* Sextet', *Opera Buffa in Mozart's Vienna*, ed. Mary Hunter and James Webster (Cambridge, 1997), 378–405

Plümicke, Carl Martin. *Entwurf einer Theatergeschichte von Berlin* (Berlin and Stettin, 1781)

Pohl, Carl Ferdinand. *Zur Geschichte der Glas-Harmonika* (Vienna, 1862)

Pohl, Carl Ferdinand. 'Über Originalhandschriften von Mozart, Haydn etc.', *Allgemeine musikalische Zeitung*, new series, i (1863), 853–6

Pohl, Carl Ferdinand. 'Mozarts erstes dramatisches Werk', *Allgemeine musikalische Zeitung*, new series, iii (1865), 225–44

Pohl, Carl Ferdinand, *Mozart und Haydn in London* (Vienna, 1867)

Pohl, Carl Ferdinand. *Denkschrift aus Anlaß des hundertjährigen Bestehens der Tonkünstler-Societät in Wien* (Vienna, 1871)

Pohl, Carl Ferdinand. *Joseph Haydn* (Leipzig, 1875–82)

Poisot, Charles. *Lecture sur Mozart à propos du 116e anniversaire de la naissance de ce maître* (Dijon and Paris, 1872)

Pokorny, Josef. 'Jossef Bustelli a jeho hudební pozustalost', *Miscellanea musicologica*, xxxiii (1992), 85–111

Pollak-Schlaffenberg, Irene. *Die Wiener Liedmusik 1778–1789* (Vienna, 1918)

Pollens, Stewart. 'The Pianos of Bartolomeo Cristofori', *Journal of the American Musical Instrument Society*, x (1984), 32–68

Pollens, Stewart. *The Early Pianoforte* (Cambridge, 1995)

Popovici, Josefine Dagmar. *La buona figliuola von Nicola Piccinni* (Vienna, 1920)

Possart, Ernst von. *Über die Neueinstudierung und Neuinszenierung des Mozartschen Don Giovanni* (Munich, 1896)

Pougin, Arthur. 'La querelle des bouffons', Supplément Anonyme to Fétis's *Biographie universelle des musiciens* (Paris, 1863)

Pougin, Arthur. *Rameau: Essai sur sa vie et ses œuvres* (Paris, 1876)

Pougin, Arthur. *Madame Favart: Étude théâtrale* (Paris, 1912)

Preibisch, Walter. 'Quellenstudien zu Mozarts "Entführung aus dem Serail"', *Sammelbände der Internationalen Musikgesellschaft*, x (1908/9), 430–76

Pressel, Gustav Adolf. 'Die aufgefundene Original-Handschrift der Nummern VIII und IX des Mozart'schen Requiems', *Der Klavier-Lehrer*, iv (1881), nos. 18–27

Pretzsch, O. 'Johann André und seine Stellung in der Berliner Liederschule' (dissertation, University of Leipzig, 1924)

Price, Curtis. *Music in the Restoration Theatre* (Ann Arbor, 1979)

Price, Curtis. 'Mozart, the Storaces and Opera in London 1787–1790', *Europa im Zeitalter Mozarts,* ed. Moritz Csáky and Walter Pass (Vienna, 1995), 209–13

Procházka, Rudolph von. *Mozart in Prag* (Prague, 1892)

Prod'homme, Jacques-Gabriel. *Gluck* (Paris, 1948; second edition 1985)

Prod'homme, Jacques-Gabriel. *François-Joseph Gossec* (Paris, 1949)

Proske, Carl. *Musica divina* (Regensburg, 1849–64)

Prossnitz, Gisela. 'Vom fürsterzbischöflichen Hoftheater zum Stadttheater (1775–1893): Theaterleben im 19. Jahrhundert in Salzburg', *Bürgerliche Musikkultur im 19. Jahrhundert in Salzburg,* ed. Rudolph Angermüller (Salzburg, 1981), 130–43

Prota-Giurleo, Ulisse. *Nicola Logroscino, 'il dio dell'opera buffa' (la vita e le opere)* (Naples, 1927)

Prota-Giurleo, Ulisse. *Sacchini a Napoli* (Naples, 1956)

Prunières, Henry. *Lully: Biographie critique* (Paris, 1909)

Prunières, Henry. 'Notes sur les origines de l'ouverture française', *Sammelbände der Internationalen Musikgesellschaft,* xii (1910/11), 565–85

Prunières, Henry. *Le ballet de cour en France avant Benserade et Lully* (Paris, 1914)

Prunières, Henry. 'Lully and the Académie de musique et de danse', *Musical Quarterly,* xi (1925), 528–46

Prunières, Henry. 'La première tragédie en musique de Lully: Cadmus et Hermione', *Revue musicale,* c–cv (1930), 385–94

Pryer, Anthony. 'Mozart's operatic audition: The Milan concert, 12 March 1770: A reappraisal and revision', *Eighteenth-Century Music,* i (2004), 265–88

Pullman, David E. 'A Catalog of the Keyboard Sonatas of Baldassare Galuppi (1706–1785)' (dissertation, American University, Washington DC, 1972)

Puncuh, Dino. 'Giacomo Durazzo: Famiglia, ambiente, personalità', *Gluck in Wien,* ed. Gerhard Croll and Monika Woitas (Kassel, 1989), 69–77

Quantz, Johann Joachim. *Versuch einer Anweisung die Flöte traversiere zu spielen* (Berlin, 1752); trans. Edward R. Reilly as *On Playing the Flute* (New York, 1966)

Quittard, Henri. 'Les origines de la suite de clavecin', *Courrier musical,* xiv (1911), 675–9 and 740–46

Raab, Leopold. *Wenzel Müller: Ein Tonkünstler Altwiens* (Baden, 1928)

Raabe, Felix. *Galuppi als Instrumentalkomponist* (Frankfurt an der Oder, 1929)

Rabin, Ronald. 'Figaro as misogynist: On aria types and aria rhetoric', *Opera Buffa in Mozart's Vienna,* ed. Mary Hunter and James Webster (Cambridge, 1997), 232–60

Radet, Edmond. *Lully, homme d'affaires, propriétaire et musicien* (Paris, 1891)

Radiciotti, Giuseppe. *G. B. Pergolesi* (Rome, 1910)

Radomski, James. 'The life and works of Manuel del Pópulo Vicente García (1775–1832): Italian, French, and Spanish opera in early nineteenth-century Romanticism' (dissertation, University of California, Los Angeles, 1992)

Raeburn, Christopher. 'Mozarts Opern in Prag', *Musica,* xiii/3 (1959), 158–63

Raffaelli, Renato. 'Il primo invito di Don Giovanni: Maschere e travestimenti in Mozart–Da Ponte', *Il saggiatore musicale: Rivista semestrale di musicologia,* iii/1 (1996), 71–103

Raguenet, François. *Paralèle des italiens et des françois, en ce qui regarde la musique et les opéra [sic]* (Paris, 1702)

Raguenet, François. *Défense du Parallèle des italiens et des françois* (Paris, 1705)

Ratschy, Josef Franz. *Gedichte,* second edition (Vienna, 1791)

Rattay, Kurt. *Die Ostracher Liederhandschrift und ihre Stellung in der Geschichte des deutschen Liedes* (Halle, 1911)

Rau, Heribert. *Mozart: Ein Künstlerleben. Culturhistorischer Roman* (Frankfurt, 1858)

Rech, Geza. 'Böhm und Schikaneder: Zwei Salzburger Theaterimpresarios der Mozart-Zeit', *Festschrift Walter Senn zum 70. Geburtstag,* ed. Erich Egg and Ewald Fäßler (Munich, 1975), 188–95

Recherches sur la musique française classique, xxviii (1993–5) [Philidor issue]

Reese, William Heartt. *Grundsätze und Entwicklung der Instrumentation in der vorklassischen und klassischen Sinfonie* (Gräfenhainichen, 1939)

Reeser, Eduard. *Ein Augsburger Musiker in Paris: Johann Gottfried Eckard (1735–1809)* (Augsburg, 1984)

Reeser, Eduard and Johan Ligtelijn, *Johann Gottfried Eckard: Oeuvres complètes pour le clavecin ou le piano forte* (Amsterdam, 1956)

Rehm, Wolfgang. 'Nochmals: Ritter von Köchels Verdienste um die "Alte Mozart-Ausgabe"', *Neue Musik und Tradition: Festschrift Rudolf Stephan zum 65. Geburtstag,* ed. J. Kuckertz (Laaber, 1990), 171–8

Rehm, Wolfgang, ed. *Internationale Stiftung Mozarteum Salzburg. Geschichte – Gegenwart – Aufgaben der Zukunft* (Salzburg, 1992)

Rehm, Wolfgang. 'Zur Prager Fassung 1787', *Wolfgang Amadeus Mozart – Don Giovanni in der Prager Fassung von 1787: Programmbuch der Salzburger Festspiele 1995* (Klagenfurt, 1995), 9–16

Rehm, Wolfgang. *Mozarts Nachlaß und die Andrés: Dokumente zur Verteilung und Verlosung von 1854* (Offenbach am Main, 1999)

Rehm, Wolfgang. 'Mozarts Nachlaß, die Andrés und kein Ende', *Resonanzen: Festschrift für Hans Joachim Kreutzer zum 65. Geburtstag*, ed. Sabine Doering, Waltraud Maierhofer and Peter Philipp Riedl (Würzburg, 2000), 109–17

Rehm, Wolfgang. '1956 – 1991 – 2006: Milestones in the "Neue Mozart-Ausgabe"', *Mozart Society of America Newsletter*, v/2 (2001), 1–2 and 4–5

Reichardt, Johann Friedrich. *Ueber die deutsche comische Oper* (Hamburg, 1774)

Reichardt, Johann Friedrich. *Briefe eines aufmerksamen Reisenden die Musik betreffend* (Frankfurt, 1774–6)

Reichardt, Johann Friedrich. *Musikalisches Kunstmagazin* (Berlin, 1782)

Reichardt, Johann Friedrich. *Geist des musikalischen Magazins* (Berlin, 1791)

Reichardt, Johann Friedrich. *Musikalische Monatsschrift* (Berlin, 1792)

Reichardt, Johann Friedrich. *Musikalischer Almanach* (Berlin, 1796)

Reichardt, Johann Friedrich. *Lieder geselliger Freude* (Leipzig, 1796–7)

Reichardt, Johann Friedrich. *Vertraute Briefe aus Paris* (Hamburg, 1804)

Reichardt, Johann Friedrich. *Vertraute Briefe geschrieben auf einer Reise nach Wien und den österreichischen Staaten zu Ende 1808 und zu Anfang 1809* (Amsterdam, 1810)

Reichardt, Johann Friedrich. 'Bruchstücke aus Reichardt's Autobiographie', *Allgemeine musikalische Zeitung*, xv (1813), 601–16, 633–42, 665–74; xvi (1814), 21–34

Reidemeister, Peter. ed. '"Was der Generalbass sey?" Beiträge zu Theorie und Praxis', *Basler Jahrbuch für historische Musikpraxis*, xviii (1994); xix (1995)

Reijen, Paul van. *Vergleichende Studien zur Klaviervariationstechnik von Mozart und seinen Zeitgenossen* (Buren, 1988)

Reimann, Margarete. *Untersuchungen zur Formgeschichte der französischen Klaviersuite mit besonderer Berücksichtigung von Couperins Ordres* (Regensburg, 1940)

Reimer, Erich. 'National consciousness and music historiography in Germany 1800–1850', *History of European Ideas*, xvi/4–6 (1993), 721–8

Reinecke, Carl. *Zur Wiederbelebung der Mozartschen Clavier-Conzerte* (Leipzig, 1891)

Reinhold, Ernst. *Karl Leonhard Reinhold's Leben und litterarisches Wirken* (Jena, 1825)

Reissinger, Marianne. *Die Sinfonien Ernst Eichners (1740–1777)* (Wiesbaden, 1970)

Reißmann, August. *Allgemeine Geschichte der Musik* (Munich and Leipzig, 1863–4)

Rellstab, Ludwig. *Gesammelte Schriften* (Leipzig, 1843–4)

Rellstab, Ludwig. *Ludwig Berger* (Berlin, 1846)

Rengger, Albrecht, ed. *Joh. Gg. Zimmermann's Briefe an einige seiner Freunde in der Schweiz* (Aarau, 1830)

Renz, Willi. 'Leopold Mozart als Komponist', *Die Musik*, iv (1904/5), 351–61

Reuter, R. and Eberhard Wächtler. 'Die künstlerische und historische Bedeutung des Singspiels "Die Bergknappen" von Ignaz Umlauf am Beginn der Geschichte der deutschen Nationaloper', *Freiberger Forschungshefte*, xlviii (1965), 9–35

Reutter, Jochen. 'Franz Xaver Richters Bemerkungen über das Komponieren einer Sinfonie in Kompositionstheorie und Kompositionspraxis', *Mozart und Mannheim*, ed. Ludwig Finscher, Bärbel Pelker and Jochen Reutter (Frankfurt am Main, 1994), 257–71

Reutter, Jochen. 'Trauersymbolik im Introitus des Requiem. Jommelli und die Gattungstradition', *Mozart-Studien*, vii (1997), 81–103

Rex, Walter E. The "storm" music of Beaumarchais' "Barbier de Séville"', *Opera and the Enlightenment*, ed. Thomas Bauman and Marita Petzoldt McClymonds (Cambridge, 1995), 243–59

Ricci, Corrado. 'Mozart e Bologna (con documenti inediti)', *Gazzetta musicale di Milano*, xlvi/31 (2 August 1891), 495–8 and xlvi/32 (9 August 1891), 511–13

Ricci, Corrado. *I teatri di Bologna nei secoli XVII e XVIII* (Bologna, 1888)

Rice, John A. 'Emperor and impresario: Leopold II and the transformation of Viennese musical theater, 1790–1792' (dissertation, University of California, Berkeley, 1987)

Rice, John A. 'Vienna under Joseph II and Leopold II', *The Classical Era: From the 1740s to the End of the 18th Century*, ed. Neal Zaslaw (London, 1989), 126–65

Rice, John A. *W. A. Mozart: La clemenza di Tito* (Cambridge, 1991)

Rice, John A. 'Benedetto Frizzi on Singers, Composers and Opera in Late Eighteenth-Century Italy', *Studi musicali*, xxiii (1994), 367–93

Rice, John A. 'Leopold II, Mozart, and the return to a Golden Age', *Opera and the Enlightenment*, ed. Thomas Bauman and Marita Petzoldt McClymonds (Cambridge, 1995), 271–96

Rice, John A. 'Mozart and his singers: The case of Maria Marchetti Fantozzi, the first Vitellia', *Opera Quarterly*, xi/4 (1995), 31–52

Rice, John A. *Antonio Salieri and Viennese Opera* (Chicago, 1998)

Rice, Paul F. *The Performing Arts at Fontainebleau from Louis XIV to Louis XVI* (Ann Arbor, 1989)

Richards, Annette. 'Automatic Genius: Mozart and the Mechanical Sublime', *Music & Letters*, lxxx/3 (1999), 366–89

Richardson, John. 'John Gay, The beggar's opera, and forms of resistance', *Eighteenth-Century Life*, xxiv/3 (2000), 19–30

Ridgewell, Rupert. 'Mozart's Publishing Plans with Artaria in 1787: New Archival Evidence', *Music & Letters*, lxxxiii/1 (2002), 30–74

Riedel, Friedrich Justus, ed. *Ueber die Musik des Ritters Christoph von Gluck* (Vienna, 1775)

Riedel, Friedrich Wilhelm. *Kirchenmusik am Hofe Karl VI. (1711–1740): Untersuchungen zum Verhältnis von Zeremoniell und musikalischem Stil im Barockzeitalter* (Munich and Salzburg, 1977)

Riedlbauer, Jörg. 'Tommaso Trajetta – Ein Wegbereiter Mozarts', *Internationaler Musikwissenschaftlicher Kongreß zum Mozartjahr 1991 Baden-Wien*, ed. Ingrid Fuchs (Tutzing, 1993), 859–64

Riedlbauer, Jörg. *Die Opern von Tommaso Trajetta* (Hildesheim, 1994)

Riedlbauer, Jörg. 'Zur stilistischen Wechselwirkung zwischen Niccolò Jommelli und Tommaso Trajetta', *Musik in Baden-Württemberg*, iii (1996), 205–12

Riedinger, Lothar. 'Karl von Dittersdorf als Opernkomponist', *Studien zur Musikwissenschaft*, ii (1914), 212–349

Rieger, Eva. *Nannerl Mozart: Leben einer Künstlerin im 18. Jahrhundert* (Frankfurt, 1992)

Riemann, Hugo. *Präludien und Studien: Gesammelte Aufsätze zur Ästhetik, Theorie und Geschichte der Musik* (Frankfurt, 1895–1901)

Riemann. Hugo. *J. C. Bach: Trio in D-Dur* (Leipzig, 1903 = Collegium musicum xix)

Riemann, Hugo. *Handbuch der Musikgeschichte* (Leipzig, 1904–13)

Riemann, Hugo. 'Zur Geschichte der deutschen Suite', *Sammelbände der Internationalen Musikgesellschaft*, vi (1904/5), 501–20

Riemann, Hugo. *Sinfonien der Pfalzbayerischen Schule I–III* (Leipzig, 1902–7 = Denkmäler der Tonkunst in Bayern iii, iv, vii, viii, xiii)

Riemann, Hugo. *Johann Schobert: Ausgewählte Werke* (Leipzig, 1909 = Denkmäler deutscher Tonkunst xxxix)

Riemann, Hugo. 'Spontane Phantasietätigkeit und verstandesmäßige Arbeit in der tonkünstlerischen Produktion', *Jahrbuch der Musikbibliothek Peters*, xvi (1909), 33–46

Riemann, Hugo. *Agostino Steffani: Ausgewählte Werke* (Leipzig, 1912 = Denkmäler der Tonkunst in Bayern xxiii)

Riemann, Hugo. *Mannheimer Kammermusik des 18. Jahrhunderts* (Leipzig, 1914 = Denkmäler der Tonkunst in Bayern xv/xvi)

Riemer, Friedrich Wilhelm. *Briefwechsel zwischen Goethe und Zelter* (Berlin, 1833–4)

Riepel, Joseph. *Harmonisches Sylbenmaß* (Regensburg, 1776)

Riesbeck, Johann Caspar. *Briefe eines reisenden Franzosen über Deutschland an seinen Bruder zu Paris* (Zurich, 1784)

Riesemann, Otto von, ed. 'Eine Selbstbiographie der Sängerin Gertrud Elisabeth Mara', *Allgemeine musikalische Zeitung*, new series, x (1875), 497–501, 513–17, 529–35, 545–50, 561–5, 577–82, 593–7, 609–13

Rietsch, Heinrich. 'Ein Sonatenthema bei Mozart', *Zeitschrift der Internationalen Musikgesellschaft*, xiv (1912/13), 278–80

Riggs, Robert. 'Mozart's Sonata for Piano and Violin, K. 379: Perspectives on the "One-hour" Sonata', *Mozart-Jahrbuch 1991: Bericht über den Internationalen Mozart-Kongreß Salzburg 1991*, 708–15

Rille, Albert. *Geschichte des Brünner Stadttheaters 1734–1884* (Brünn, 1885)

Rivara, Annie. 'Don Juan et la mort ou la difficulté d'être libertin: Dorimon, Villiers, Molière, Th. Corneille, Rosimond et les Don Juan de la Foire', *Études & recherches sur le XVIIIe siècle* (Aix-en-Provence, 1980), 1–55

Robinson, Michael. *Naples and Neapolitan Opera* (Oxford, 1972)

Robinson, Michael. 'The alternative endings of Mozart's *Don Giovanni*', *Opera Buffa in Mozart's Vienna*, ed. Mary Hunter and James Webster (Cambridge, 1997), 261–85

Robinson, Philip. 'Vaudevilles et genre comique à Paris au milieu du XVIIIe siècle', *Timbre und Vaudeville: Zur Geschichte und Problematik einer populären Gattung im 17. und 18. Jahrhundert*, ed. Herbert Schneider (Hildesheim, 1998), 292–305

Robinson, Philip. 'Beaumarchais et la tradition comique', *Beaumarchais: Homme de lettres, homme de société*, ed. Philip Robinson and René Pomeau (Oxford, 2000), 133–46

Rochlitz, Friedrich. 'Verbürgte Anekdoten aus Wolfgang Gottlieb Mozarts Leben', *Allgemeine Musikzeitung*, i (1798/9), 17–24, 49–55, 81–6, 113–17, 145–52, 177–83, 289–91, 480, 854–6; iii (1800/1), 450–2, 493–7, 590–6

Rochlitz, Friedrich. *Für Freunde der Tonkunst* (Leipzig, 1824; third edition: Leipzig, 1868)

Roe, Stephen. 'J. C. Bach (1735–1782): Towards a New Biography', *Musical Times*, cxxiii (1982), 23–6

Roeder, Michael. *A History of the Concerto* (Portland, OR, 1994)

Roeder, Michael Thomas. 'Das Klassische Konzert. Kapitel: Wolfgang Amadeus Mozart', *Das Konzert*, ed. Michael Roeder and Siegfried Mauser (Laaber, 2000), 119–58

Rogers, Daniel, ed. *Tirso de Molina: El burlador de Sevilla* (London, 1977)

Rolland, Romain. *Musiciens d'autrefois* (Paris, 1908)

Rollett, Hermann. 'Mozart in Baden', *Mozarteums-Mitteilungen*, ii (1920), 109–12

Rollin, Corrado. *Philidor: Il musicista che giocava a scacchi* (Brescia, 1994)

Ronzeaud, Pierre, ed. *Molière/Dom Juan* (Paris, 1993)

Rosand, Ellen. *Opera in Seventeenth-Century Venice: The Creation of a Genre* (Berkeley, 1991)

Roscoe, Christopher. 'Two 18th-century non-events', *Musical Times*, cxii (1971), 18–19

Rosen, Charles. *The Classical Style* (New York, 1971)

Rosen, Charles. *Sonata Forms* (New York, 1980)

Rosen, David. 'The composer's "standard operating procedure" as evidence of intention: The case of a formal quirk in Mozart's K. 595', *Journal of Musicology*, v/1 (1987), 79–90

Rosenblum, Sandra P. *Performance Practices in Classic Piano Music* (Bloomington, Indiana, 1988)

Rosenblum, Sandra P. 'The Uses of *Rubato* in Music, Eighteenth to Twentieth Centuries', *Performance Practice Review*, vii (1994), 33–53

Rosenstrauch-Königsberg, Edith. 'Zur Philosophie der österreichischen Freimaurer und Illuminaten mit Blick auf Mozart', *Genie und Alltag: Bürgerliche Stadtkultur zur Mozartzeit*, ed. Gunda Barth-Scalmani, Brigitte Mazohl-Wallnig and Ernst Wangermann (Salzburg, 1994), 317–50

Rosenthal, Karl A. 'Zur Stilistik der Salzburger Kirchenmusik von 1600 bis 1730', *Studien zur Musikwissenschaft*, xvii (1930), 77–94 and xix (1932), 3–32

Rosenthal, Karl A. 'The Salzburg Church Music of Mozart and his Predecessors', *Musical Quarterly*, xviii (1932), 559–77

Rosselli, John. 'The Castrati as a Professional Group and a Social Phenomenon, 1550–1850', *Acta musicologica*, lx (1988), 143–79

Rössig, Carl Gottlob. *Versuche im musikalischen Drama* (Bayreuth, 1779)

Rousseau, Jean-Jacques. *Dictionnaire de musique* (Paris, 1768)

Rousseau, Jean-Jacques. *Le devin du village*, ed. Cynthia Verba (Madison, WI, 1998 = Recent Researches in the Music of the Classical era xxx)

Rousset, Jean. 'Don Juan dans l'opéra avant Mozart', *L'opéra aux XVIIIe siècle* (Aix-en-Provence, 1982), 97–110

Rudhart, Franz Michael. *Geschichte der Oper am Hofe zu München. Erster Theil: Die italiänische Oper von 1654–1787* (Freising, 1865)

Rudolf, Kenneth E. 'The Symphonies of Georg Mathias Monn (1715–1750)' (dissertation, University of Washington, DC, 1982)

Rudolf, Kenneth E., *Georg Mathias Monn: Five Symphonies* (New York, 1985 = The Symphony, 1720–1840, Series B/1)

Ruf, Wolfgang. *Die Rezeption von Mozarts Le Nozze di Figaro bei den Zeitgenossen* (Freiburg, 1974)

Ruf, Wolfgang. 'Mozart in der Musiktheorie des frühen 19. Jahrhunderts', *Mozart – Aspekte des 19. Jahrhunderts*, ed. Hermann Jung (Mannheim, 1995), 44–58

Rummenhöller, Peter. 'Mozart auf der Reise nach Berlin', *Zwischen Aufklärung & Kulturindustrie: Festschrift für Georg Knepler zum 85. Geburtstag*, ed. Hanns-Werner Heister, Karin Heister-Grech and Gerhard Scheit (Hamburg, 1993), 73–82

Rushton, Julian. 'Music and Drama at the Académie Royale de Musique (Paris), 1774–1789' (dissertation, University of Oxford, 1969)

Rushton, Julian. 'The Theory and Practice of Piccinnisme', *Proceedings of the Royal Musical Association*, xcviii (1971/2), 31–46

Rushton, Julian. 'Iphigénie en Tauride: The operas of Gluck and Piccinni', *Music & Letters*, liii/4 (1972), 411–30

Rushton , Julian. 'Philidor and the Tragédie Lyrique', *Musical Tiimes*, cxvii (1976), 734–7

Rushton, Julian. *W. A. Mozart: Don Giovanni* (Cambridge, 1981)

Rushton, Julian. *W. A. Mozart: Idomeneo* (Cambridge, 1993)

Rushton, Julian. '". . . hier wird es besser seyn – ein blosses Recitativ zu machen . . .": Observations on recitative organization in *Idomeneo*', *Wolfgang Amadè Mozart: Essays on his Life and his Music*, ed. Stanley Sadie (Oxford, 1996), 436–48

Rushton, Julian. 'Buffo Roles in Mozart's Vienna: Tessitura and Tonality as Signs of Characterization', *Opera buffa in Mozart's Vienna*, ed. Mary Hunter and James Webster (Cambridge, 1997), 406–25

Rushton, Julian. 'Mozart and opera seria', *The Cambridge Companion to Mozart*, ed. Simon P. Keefe (Cambridge, 2003), 147–55

Rushton, Virginia. 'Mozart's Lieder: A Survey', *Mozart in History, Theory, and Practice: Selected Papers from the International Symposium, Faculty of Music, The University of Western Ontario 1990–91*, ed. Don Neville (London, 1996), 105–30

Russell, Charles C. *The Don Juan legend before Mozart, with a collection of eighteenth-century opera librettos* (Ann Arbor, MI, 1993)

Rutz, Ottmar. *Musik, Wort und Körper als Gemütsausdruck* (Leipzig, 1911)

Sacaluga, Servando. 'Diderot, Rousseau et la querelle musicale de 1752: nouvelle mise au point', *Diderot Studies*, x (1968), 133–73

Saccenti, Mario, ed. 'Metastasio e altro settecento', *Italianistica*, xiii/1–2 (1984)

Sachs, Curt. *Musik und Oper am kurbrandenburgischen Hof* (Berlin, 1910)

Sachs, Curt. *Die Briefe Mozarts* (Berlin, 1911)

Sachs, Curt. *Real-Lexikon der Musikinstrumente* (Berlin, 1913)

Sadie, Stanley, ed. *History of Opera* (Basingstoke, 1989)

Sadie, Stanley. 'Genesis of an operone', Julian Rushton, *W. A. Mozart: Idomeneo* (Cambridge, 1993), 25–47

Sainte-Beuve, Charles-Augustin. *Causeries du lundi* (Paris, 1851–2)

Saint-Foix, Georges de. 'Zwei Berichtigungen zum Köchelschen Verzeichnis der Werke Mozarts', *Neue Musikzeitung*, xxix (1908), 323–4

Saint-Foix, Georges de. 'Les débuts milanais de Gluck', *Gluck-Jahrbuch*, i (1913), 28–46

Saint-Foix, Georges de. 'La chronologie de l'œuvre instrumentale de Jean Baptiste Sammartini', *Sammelbände der Internationalen Musikgesellschaft*, xv (1913/14), 308–24

Saint-Foix, Georges de. 'Les premiers pianistes parisiens, i: Jean Schobert, vers 1740–1767', *Revue musicale*, iii/9–10 (1921/2), 121–36

Saint-Foix, Georges de. 'Le Théâtre à Salzbourg en 1779–1780', *Revue de musicologie*, xvi (1935), 193–204

Salinger, Nicole, ed. *Mozart à Paris* (Paris, 1991)

Salvioli, Giovanni. *I teatri musicali di Venezia nel secolo XVII* (Milan, 1879)

Sandberger, Adolf. 'Zur Geschichte des Haydnschen Streichquartetts', *Altbayerische Monatshefte*, ii (1900), 41–64

Sandberger, Adolf. 'Mozartiana', *Jahrbuch der Musikbibliothek Peters*, viii (1901), 63–76

Sandberger, Adolf. 'Roland Lassus' Beziehung zur italienischen Literatur', *Sammelbände der Internationalen Musikgesellschaft*, v (1903/4), 402–41

Sandberger, Adolf. '[Review of Edgar Istel, *Die Entstehung des deutschen Melodrams*]', *Zeitschrift der Internationalen Musikgesellschaft*, vii (1905/6), 66–71

Sandberger, Adolf. [Article on Cannabich], *Festschrift Hermann Kretzschmar zum siebzigsten Geburtstage* (Leipzig, 1918)

Sanders, Donald C. 'The Keyboard Sonatas of Giustini, Paradisi, and Rutini: Formal and Stylistic Innovation in Mid-Eighteenth-Century Italian Keyboard Music' (dissertation, University of Kansas, 1983)

Sanders, Donald C. 'Early Italian prototypes of the classic sonata-rondo form', *The Music Review*, liii/3 (1992), 179–190

Sands, Mollie. 'Venanzio Rauzzini: Singer, Composer, Traveller', *Musical Times*, xciv (1953), 15–19, 108–11

Sannipoli, Sabrina. 'Dalle "Donne rivali" di Cimarosa allo "Sposo deluso" di Mozart: Alcune ipotesi sull'autore del libretto', *Musica e poesia: Celebrazioni in onore di Carlo Goldoni (1707–1793). Atti dell'incontro di studio. Narni, 11–12 dicembre 1993*, ed. Galliano Ciliberti and Biancamaria Brumana (Perugia, 1994), 83–7

Sartori, Egida. 'Le sonate per cembalo di Baldassarre Galuppi', *Galuppiana 1985: Studi e ricerche. Atti del convegno internazionale* (Florence, 1986)

Sattler, Magnus. *Ein Mönchsleben aus der 2. Hälfte des 18. Jahrhunderts: Nach dem Tagebuche des P. Placidus Scharl O. S. B. von Andechs* (Regensburg, 1868)

Schachter, Carl. 'The violet: An analysis of the music', *Ostinato: Revue internationale d'études musicales* (1993), 163–73

Schad, Martha and Eva Klotz-Reill, ed. *Mozarts erste Liebe: Das Bäsle Marianne Thekla Mozart* (Augsburg, 2004)

Schafhäutl, Karl Emil von. 'Moll und Dur in der Natur, und in der Geschichte der neuern und neuesten Harmonielehre: Mit besonderer Berücksichtigung der Systeme von Vallotti und Abt Vogler', *Allgemeine musikalische Zeitung*, xiii, new series (1878), 1–6, 22–7, 38–42, 53–7, 69–73, 87–92, 101–5, 115–20, 132–7

Schafhäutl, Karl Emil von. *Abt Georg Joseph Vogler* (Augsburg, 1888)

Schafhäutl, Karl Emil von. 'Wolfgang Amadäus Mozart: Wie hat er eigentlich ausgesehen?' *Neue Musikzeitung*, ix (1888), 241–3

Scharnagl, Augustin. *Johann Franz Xaver Sterkel* (Würzburg, 1943)

Schatz, Albert. 'Ergänzungen zur Bühnenstatistik des Don Juan in Freisauff's Buch', *Vierteljahrsschrift für Musikwissenschaft*, iv (1888), 278–86

Schatz, Albert. 'Giovanni Bertati', *Vierteljahrsschrift für Musikwissenschaft*, v (1889), 231–71

Schaul, Johann Baptist. *Briefe über den Geschmack in der Musik* (Karlsruhe, 1809)

Schebest, Agnese. *Aus dem Leben einer Künstlerin* (Stuttgart, 1857)

Scheible, Johann. *Das Kloster* (Stuttgart, 1845–9)

Scheible, Johann Adolph. *Der critische Musikus* (Hamburg, 1738–40)

Scheibler, Ludwig. 'Mozarts Mannheimer Klaviersonate', *Die Rheinlande*, xii (1906), 145–52

Schenk, Erich. *Giuseppe Antonio Paganelli* (Salzburg, 1928)

Scherillo, Michele. *L'opera buffa napoletana durante il Settecento: Storia letteraria* (Naples, 1883)

Schering, Arnold. 'Zur Bachforschung', *Sammelbände der Internationalen Musikgesellschaft*, v (1903/4), 565–70

Schering, Arnold. *Geschichte des Instrumentalkonzerts* (Leipzig, 1905)

Schering, Arnold. *Johann Adolph Hasse: La conversione di Sant'Agostino* (Leipzig, 1905 = Denkmäler deutscher Tonkunst xx)

Schering, Arnold. 'Die Musikästhetik der deutschen Aufklärung', *Zeitschrift der Internationalen Musikgesellschaft*, viii (1906/7), 263–71

Schering, Arnold. *Geschichte des Oratoriums* (Leipzig, 1911)

Schering, Arnold. *J. S. Bach und das Musikleben Leipzigs im 18. Jahrhundert* (Leipzig, 1941)

Scheurleer, Daniel François. *Mozart's verblijf in Nederland* (The Hague, 1883)

Schick, Hartmut. 'Ein Quintett im Diskurs mit dem Streichquartett: Mozarts Streichquintett C-Dur, KV 515', *Mozarts Streichquintette: Beiträge zum musikalischen Satz, zum Gattungskontext und zu Quellenfragen*, ed. Cliff Eisen and Wolf-Dieter Seiffert (Stuttgart, 1994), 69–101

Schiebeler, Daniel. 'Anmerkung zu Lisuart und Dariolette', *Wöchentliche Nachrichten*, ii (2 November 1767), 135–9

Schiedermair, Ludwig. 'Die Blütezeit der Öttingen-Wallerstein'schen Hofkapelle', *Sammelbände der Internationalen Musikgesellschaft*, ix (1907/8), 83–130

Schiedermair, Ludwig. *Die Briefe W. A. Mozarts und seiner Familie* (Munich and Leipzig, 1914)

Schildkret, David. 'On Mozart Contemplating a Work of Handel: Mozart's Arrangement of "Messiah"', *Festa Musicologica: Essays in Honor of George J. Buelow*, ed. Thomas J. Mathiesen and Benito V. Rivera (Stuyvesant, NY, 1995), 129–46

Schiller, Friedrich von. *Die Rheinische Thalia* (Leipzig, 1785–93)

Schiller, Friedrich von. *Schiller's Briefwechsel mit Körner* (Berlin, 1847)

Schimek, Martin. *Musikpolitik in der Salzburger Aufklärung: Musik, Musikpolitik und deren Rezeption am Hof des Salzburger Fürsterzbischofs Hieronymus Graf Colloredo* (Frankfurt, 1995)

Schindler, Anton. *Biographie von Ludwig van Beethoven* (Münster, 1840)

Schindler, Otto. 'Das Publikum des Burgtheaters in der Josephinischen Ära: Versuch einer Strukturbestimmung', *Das Burgtheater und sein Publikum*, ed. Margret Dietrich (Vienna, 1976), i.11–95

Schink, Johann Friedrich. *Litterarische Fragmente* (Graz, 1784–5)

Schink, Johann Friedrich. *Dramaturgische Fragmente* (Graz, 1782)

Schink, Johann Friedrich. *Dramaturgische Monate* (Schwerin, 1790)

Schinn, Georg Johann and Franz Joseph Otter. *Biographische Skizze von Michael Haydn* (Salzburg, 1808)

Schiwietz, Lucian. 'Prag im "klassischen" Zeitalter der Musik', *Deutsche Musik in Ost- und Südosteuropa*, ed. Gabriel Adriányi (Cologne, 1997), 37–54

Schizzi, Florimo. *Elogio storico di W. A. Mozart* (Cremona, 1817)

Schlager, Karlheinz. *Kirchenmusik in romantischer Sicht: Zeugnisse des Musikjournalisten und des Komponisten E. T. A. Hoffmann* (Regensburg, 1993)

Schlegel, Friedrich von. *Deutsches Museum* (Vienna, 1812–13)

Schlesinger, Maximilian. *Geschichte des Breslauer Theaters* (Breslau, 1898)

Schletterer, Hans Michel. *Das deutsche Singspiel von seinen Anfängen bis auf die neueste Zeit* (Augsburg, 1863)

Schletterer, Hans Michel. *Johann Friedrich Reichardt* (Augsburg, 1865)

Schleuning, Peter. *Die Freie Fantasie: Ein Beitrag zur Erforschung der klassischen Klaviermusik* (Göppingen, 1973)

Schlichtegroll, Friedrich. 'Joannes Chrysostomus Wolfgang Gottlieb Mozart', *Nekrolog auf das Jahr 1791* (Gotha, 1793)

Schlosser, Johann Aloys. *W. A. Mozarts Biographie*, third edition (Augsburg, 1844)

Schlösser, Rainer. *Vom Hamburger Nationaltheater zur Gothaer Hofbühne* (Hamburg and Leipzig, 1895)

Schmid, Anton. 'Zwei musikalische Berühmtheiten Wien's aus dem Schönen Geschlecht in der zweiten Hälfte des verflossenen Jahrhunderts', *Wiener allgemeine Musikzeitung*, vi (1846), 513 and 517

Schmid, Anton. *Christoph Willibald Ritter von Gluck* (Leipzig, 1854)

Schmid, Christian Heinrich. *Das Parterr* (Erfurt, 1771)

Schmid, Christian Heinrich. *Chronologie des deutschen Theaters* (Leipzig, 1775)

Schmid, Hans. 'Zur Biographie des bayerischen Hofsängers Giovanni Valesi (Walleshauser)', *Musik in Bayern*, x (1975), 28–30

Schmid, Ernst Fritz. *Ein schwäbisches Mozartbuch* (Lorch/Stuttgart, 1948)

Schmid, Ernst Fritz. 'Zu Mozarts Leipziger Bach-Erlebnis', *Neue Zeitschrift für Musik*, cxi/6 (1950), 297–303

Schmid, Ernst Fritz. 'Ignaz von Beecke', *Lebensbilder aus dem bayerischen Schwaben*, ed. G. F. von Pölnitz (Munich, 1952–4), i.343–64

Schmid, Ernst Fritz. 'Leopold Mozart', *Lebensbilder aus dem bayerischen Schwaben*, ed. G. F. von Pölnitz (Munich, 1952–4), iii.346–68

Schmid, Ernst Fritz. 'Neues zu Leopold Mozarts Bildungsgang', *Acta Mozartiana*, iii/1 (1956), 21–4

Schmid, Ernst Fritz. 'Mozart und Monsigny', *Mozart-Jahrbuch 1957*, 57–62

Schmid, Manfred Hermann. *Mozart und die Salzburger Tradition* (Tutzing, 1976)

Schmid, Manfred Hermann. 'Die Romanze des Pedrillo aus Mozarts *Entführung*', *De editione musices: Festschrift Gerhard Croll zum 65. Geburtstag*, ed. Wofgang Gratzer and Andrea Lindmayer (Laaber, 1992), 305–14

Schmid, Manfred Hermann. 'Musikalische Syntax in Menuetten Mozarts: Anmerkungen zur Bläserserenade KV 361 und zum Streichquintett KV 614', *Gesellschaftsgebundene instrumentale Unterhaltungsmusik des 18. Jahrhunderts*, ed. Hubert Unverricht (Tutzing, 1992), 119–30

Schmid, Manfred Hermann. 'Typen des Orchestercrescendo im 18. Jahrhundert', *Untersuchungen zu Musikbeziehungen zwischen Mannheim, Böhmen und Mähren im späten 18. und frühen 19. Jahrhundert*, ed. Christine Heyter-Rauland and Christoph-Hellmut Mahling (Mainz, 1993), 96–132

Schmid, Manfred Hermann. *Italienischer Vers und musikalische Syntax in Mozarts Opern* (Tutzing, 1994)

Schmid, Manfred Hermann. 'Das "Lacrimosa" in Mozarts Requiem', *Mozart-Studien*, vii (1997), 115–41

Schmid, Manfred Hermann. 'Introitus und Communio im Requiem: Zum Formkonzept von Mozart und Süßmayr', *Mozart-Studien*, vii (1997), 11–55

Schmid, Manfred Hermann. 'Zu den Klaviersonaten von Leopold Mozart', *Beiträge des Internationalen Leopold-Mozart-Kolloquiums Augsburg 1994*, ed. Josef Mančal and Wolfgang Plath (Augsburg, 1997), 47–55

Schmid, Manfred Hermann. 'Zur Mitwirkung des Solisten am Orchester-Tutti bei Mozarts Konzerten', *Basler Jahrbuch für historische Musikpraxis*, xvii (1993), 89–112

Schmid, Manfred Hermann. 'Das Orakel in Mozarts *Idomeneo*', *Mozart-Studien*, x (2001), 103–38

Schmid, Otto. 'Die musikgeschichtliche Bedeutung der altböhmischen Schule Czernohorsky's', *Sammelbände der Internationalen Musikgesellschaft*, ii (1900/1), 133–41

Schmid, Otto. *Johann Michael Haydn* (Langensalza, 1906)

Schmidt, Ernst. 'Goethes Proserpina', *Vierteljahrschrift für Literaturgeschichte*, i (1888), 27ff.

Schmidt, Ernst. *Lessing: Geschichte seines Lebens und seiner Schriften*, third edition (1910)

Schmidt, Leopold. *W. A. Mozart* (Berlin, 1912)

Schmidt, Matthias. 'Das Andere der Aufklärung: Zur Kompositionsästhetik von Mozarts Glasharmonika-Quintett KV 617', *Archiv für Musikwissenschaft*, lx/4 (2003), 279–302

Schmidt, Matthias. 'Mozarts "Don Giovanni" und die italienische Buffa-Tradition: Methodologische und analytische Studien zum Motiv der lebenden Statue', *Mozart-Jahrbuch 2003/04*, 94–127

Schmidt-Görg, Joseph. *Geschichte der Messe* (Cologne, 1967 = *Das Musikwerk*)

Schmierer, Elisabeth. 'Die deutsche Rezeption der Querelle des Gluckistes et Piccinnistes', *Studien zu den deutsch-französischen Musikbeziehungen im 18. und 19. Jahrhundert: Bericht über die erste gemeinsame Jahrestagung der Gesellschaft für Musikforschung und der Société Française de Musicologie* (Saarbrücken, 1999), 196–217

Schmitt, Alois. 'W. A. Mozarts große Messe in c-Moll, ihre Entstehung und ihr Schicksal', *Allgemeine Musikzeitung*, xxviii (1901), 175–6

Schmitt, Eduard. *Kirchenmusik der Mannheimer Schule* (Wiesbaden, 1980–1982 = Denkmäler der Tonkunst in Bayern, new series, ii–iii)

Schneider, Constantin. 'Zur Lebensgeschichte des Salzburger Komponisten A. C. Adlgasser', *Salzburger Museumsblätter*, iv (1925)

Schneider, Constantin. *Geschichte der Musik in Salzburg* (Salzburg, 1935)

Schneider, Herbert. 'Zur Gattungsgeschichte der frühen Opéra-Comique', *Gesellschaft für Musikforschung: Bericht über den Internationalen Wissenschaftlichen Kongreß Bayreuth 1981*, ed. Christoph-Hellmut Mahling and Sigrid Wiesmann (Bayreuth, 1981), 107–16

Schneider, Herbert, ed. *Das Vaudeville: Funktionen eines multimedialen Phänomens* (Hildesheim, 1996)

Schneider, Herbert. 'Gluck and Lully', *Lully Studies*, ed. John Hajdu Heyer (Cambridge, 2000), 243–71

Schneider, Herbert and Reinhard Wiesend, ed. *Die Oper im 18. Jahrhundert* (Laaber, 2001)

Schneider, Louis. *Geschichte der Oper und des Königlichen Opernhauses in Berlin* (Berlin, 1852)

Schneider, Max. 'Die Begleitung des Secco-Rezitativs um 1750', *Gluck-Jahrbuch*, iii (1917), 88–107

Schneider, Max. 'Die Besetzung der vielstimmigen Musik des 16. und 17. Jahrhunderts', *Archiv für Musikwissenschaft*, i (1918/19), 205–34

Schneider-Cuvay, Michaela. 'Die Instrumentalwerke Johann Ernst Eberlins' (dissertation, University of Salzburg, 1975)

Schnerich, Alfred. *Der Messentypus von Haydn bis Schubert* (Vienna, 1892)

Schnerich, Alfred. *Messe und Requiem seit Haydn und Mozart* (Vienna, 1909)

Schnerich, Alfred. 'Wie sahen die ersten Vorstellungen von Mozarts Don Juan aus?', *Zeitschrift der Internationalen Musikgesellschaft*, xii (1911), 101–8

Schnerich, Alfred. *Mozarts Requiem: Nachbildung der Originalhandschrift (Cod. 17561) der Nationalbibliothek Wien in Lichtdruck* (Vienna, 1913)

Schnoebelen, Anne. 'The Growth of Padre Martini's Library as Revealed in his Correspondence', *Music & Letters*, lvii (1976), 379–97

Schnyder von Wartensee, Franz Xaver. 'Notizen über die Zauberflöte von Mozart', *Neue Zeitschrift für Musik*, xlv (1856), 41–3

Scholes, Percy. 'George III as Music Lover', *Musical Quarterly*, xxviii (1942), 78–92

Scholz-Michelitsch, Helga. 'Georg Christoph Wagenseil als Klavierkomponist: Eine Studie zu seinen zyklischen Soloklavierwerken' (dissertation, University of Vienna, 1967)

Scholz-Michelitsch, Helga. *Das Orchester- und Kammermusikwerk von Georg Christoph Wagenseil: Thematischer Katalog* (Vienna, 1972)

Scholz-Michelitsch, Helga. *Georg Christoph Wagenseil* (Vienna, 1980)

Schönfeld, Johann Ferdinand. *Jahrbuch der Tonkunst von Wien und Prag* (Vienna, 1796)

Schöttl, Julius. 'Mozarts Ur-Urgroßvater', *Der Heimatfreund*, ix/1 (1958), 1

Schröder, Theodor August Emil. *Die dramatischen Bearbeitungen der Don-Juan-Sage in Spanien, Italien und Frankreich* (Halle, 1912)

Schroeder, David. *Mozart in Revolt: Strategies of Resistance, Mischief and Deception* (London, 1999)

Schubart, Christian Friedrich Daniel. *Deutsche Chronik* (Heidelberg, 1774–7)

Schubart, Christian Friedrich Daniel. *Leben und Gesinnungen* (Stuttgart, 1791–3)

Schubart, Christian Friedrich Daniel. *Ideen zu einer Ästhetik der Tonkunst* (Vienna, 1806)

Schubert, Gustav. *Mozart und die Freimaurerei* (Berlin, 1891)

Schulenberg, David. 'Carl Philipp Emanuel Bach', *Eighteenth-Century Keyboard Music*, ed. Robert L. Marshall (New York, 1994), 191–229

Schuler, Heinz. 'Johann Michael Haydn und sein Salzburger Familienkreis', *Genealogie*, vii (1981), 603–18

Schuler, Heinz. 'W. A. Mozarts Totenmaske: Bemerkungen zu ihrer Geschichte', *Vom Winkel zum Zirkel*, i (1988), Beilage, 1–8

Schuler, Heinz. 'Mozarts Akademien im Trattnersaal 1784: Ein Kommentar zum Mozart-Brief – Wien, 20. März 1784', *Mitteilungen der Internationalen Stiftung Mozarteum*, xxxviii/1–4 (1990), 1–47

Schuler, Heinz. 'Das Zauberflöten-Ensemble des Jahres 1791: Biographische Miszellen', *Mitteilungen der Internationalen Stiftung Mozarteum*, xxxix (1991), 92–124

Schuler, Heinz. 'Die St. Johannis-Freimaurerloge "Zur wahren Eintracht": Die Mitglieder der Wiener Elite-Loge 1781 bis 1785', *Genealogisches Jahrbuch*, xxxi (1992), 5–41

Schuler, Heinz. 'Mozarts "Maurerische Trauermusik" KV 477/ 479a: Eine Dokumentation', *Mitteilungen der Internationalen Stiftung Mozarteum*, xl/1–4 (1992), 46–70

Schuler, Heinz. *Mozart und die Freimaurerei: Daten, Fakten, Biographien* (Wilhelmshaven, 1992)

Schuler, Heinz. 'Die Mozart-Loge "Zur Wohltätigkeit" im Orient von Wien 1783 bis 1785: Entwicklung und Mitgliederbestand', *Genealogisches Jahrbuch*, xxxii (1993), 5–52

Schuler, Heinz. *Mozarts Salzburger Freunde und Bekannte: Biographien und Kommentare* (Wilhelmshaven, 1995)

Schuler, Heinz. 'Schikaneder contra Gieseke: Eine Dokumentation zur Verfasserfrage des Zauberflöten-Librettos', *Quatuor Coronati*, xxxiii (1996), 199–215

Schuler, Manfred. 'Mozarts Don Giovanni in Donaueschingen', *Mitteilungen der Internationalen Stiftung Mozarteum*, xxxv/1–4 (1987), 63–72

Schuler, Manfred. 'Das Donaueschinger Aufführungsmaterial von Mozarts *Le nozze di Figaro*', *Florilegium musicologicum: Hellmut Federhofer zum 75. Geburtstag*, ed. Cordelia Ruloff (Tutzing, 1988), 375–88

Schuler, Manfred. 'Die Aufführung von Mozarts *Le Nozze di Figaro* in Donaueschingen 1787: Ein Beitrag zur Rezeptionsgeschichte', *Archiv für Musikwissenschaft*, xlv/2 (1988), 111–31

Schuler, Manfred. 'L'esecuzione delle "Nozze di Figaro" di Mozart a Donaueschingen nel 1787', *Danubio–- Una civiltà musicale, i: Germania*, ed. Carlo de Incontrera and Birgit Schneider (Monfalcone, 1991), 117–38

Schuler, Manfred. 'Zeitgenössische Prager Abschriften von Werken Mozarts', *Hudební věda*, xxviii/4 (1991), 291–8

Schuler, Manfred. 'Mozarts Requiem in der Tradition gattungsgeschichtlicher Topoi', *Studien zur Musikgeschichte: Eine Festschrift für Ludwig Finscher*, ed. Annegrit Laubenthal (Kassel, 1995), 317–27

Schuler, Manfred. 'Zeitgenössische Kritik an Schikaneders Textbuch "Die Zauberflöte"', *Mitteilungen der Internationalen Stiftung Mozarteum*, xlv/3–4 (1997), 53–8

Schuler, Manfred. 'Zum Stile antico in Leopold Mozarts kirchenmusikalischem Schaffen', *Beiträge des Internationalen Leopold-Mozart-Kolloquiums Augsburg 1994*, ed. Josef Mančal and Wolfgang Plath (Augsburg, 1997), 213–18

Schultz, Detlef. *Mozarts Jugendsinfonien* (Leipzig, 1909)

Schumann, Robert. *Gesammelte Schriften über Musik und Musiker*, ed. Martin Kreisig (Leipzig, 1914)

Schünemann, Georg. *Mozart als achtjähriger Komponist: Ein Notenbuch Wolfgangs* (Leipzig, 1909)

Schünemann, Georg. *Geschichte des Dirigierens* (Leipzig, 1913)

Schurig, Arthur. 'Die Briefe Mozarts und seiner Familie', *Mozarteums-Mitteilungen*, ii (1919), 7–9

Schurig, Arthur. *Leopold Mozarts Reise-Aufzeichnungen 1763–1777* (Dresden, 1920)

Schurig, Arthur. *Wolfgang Amade Mozart: Sein Leben, seine Persönlichkeit und sein Werk*, second edition (Leipzig, 1923)

Schwab, Heinrich W. *Sangbarkeit, Popularität und Kunstlied: Studien zu Lied und Liedästhetik der mittleren Goethezeit* (Regensburg, 1965)

Schwarte, Michael. "'in des Fedi Parnass . . .": Bildnisse des Sängers Anton Raaff (1714–1797)', *Traditionen – Neuansätze: Für Anna Amalie Abert (1906–1996)*, ed. Klaus Hortschansky (Tutzing, 1997), 587–618

Schwarz, Max. 'Johann Christian Bach', *Sammelbände der Internationalen Musikgesellschaft*, ii (1900/1), 401–54

Schwarz, Richard. 'Das Geheimnis um Mozarts Totenmaske', *Neue Musik-Zeitschrift*, ii (1948), 367–70

Schweitzer, Albert. *J. S. Bach*, second edition (Leipzig, 1915)

Schwerin, Erna. 'W. A. Mozart (1756–91) and Maria Anna Thekla Mozart (1758–1841) the Bäsle, Mozart's Transitional', *Friends of Mozart Inc. Newsletter* (New York, spring 2005), 1–6

Schwindt-Gross, Nicole. 'Zwei bisher unbekannte Salzburger "L'isola disabitata"-Vertonungen', *Mitteilungen der Internationalen Stiftung Mozarteum*, xxxvii/1–4 (1989), 161–76

Scott, Ralph Henry. *Jean-Baptiste Lully* (London, 1973)

Scudo, Paul. *Critique et littérature musicales* (Paris, 1850–59)

Scudo, Paul. *L'art ancien et l'art moderne* (Paris, 1854)

Sechter, Simon. 'Analysis of the Finale of Mozart's Symphony no.41 in C (K.551, "Jupiter") (1843)', *Music Analysis in the Nineteenth Century, i: Fugue, Form and Style*, ed. Ian Bent (Cambridge, 1993), 79–96

Sedelmayr, Romanus. *Historia almae et archi-episcopalis Universitatis Salisburgensis sub cura PP. Benedictorum* (Bonndorf, 1728)

Seiffert, Max. *Geschichte der Klaviermusik* (Leipzig, 1899)

Seiffert, Max. *Leopold Mozart: Ausgewählte Werke* (Leipzig, 1908 = Denkmäler der Tonkunst in Bayern ix/2)

Seiffert, Max. 'Die Mannheimer "Messias"-Aufführung 1777', *Jahrbuch der Musikbibliothek Peters für 1916*, 61–71

Seiffert, Wolf-Dieter. 'Mozarts "Salzburger" Streichquintett', *Mozarts Streichquintette: Beiträge zum musikalischen Satz, zum Gattungskontext und zu Quellenfragen*, ed. Cliff Eisen and Wolf-Dieter Seiffert (Stuttgart, 1994), 29–68

Seiffert, Wolf-Dieter. 'Wolfgang Amadeus Mozart: Requiem', *Werkanalyse in Beispielen: Große Chorwerke*, ed. Siegmund Helms and Reinhard Schneider (Regensburg, 1994)

Seiffert, Wolf-Dieter. 'Mozart's "Haydn" Quartets: An Evaluation of the Autographs and First Edition, with Particular Attention to mm. 125–42 of the Finale of K. 387', *Mozart Studies 2*, ed. Cliff Eisen (Oxford, 1997), 175–200

Seiffert, Wolf-Dieter. 'Mozarts Streichtrio KV 563: Eine quellen- und textkritische Erörterung', *Mozart-Jahrbuch 1998*, 53–83

Senici, Emanuele. "'Adapted to the modern stage": La clemenza di Tito in London', *Cambridge Opera Journal*, vii/1 (1995), 1–22

Senici, Emanuele. *La clemenza di Tito di Mozart: I primi trent'anni (1791–1821)* (Brebols, 1997)

Senigl, Johanna. 'Ein unveröffentlichter Brief Franz Xaver Mozarts an Franz Edlen von Hilleprandt', *Musica conservata: Günter Brosche zum 60. Geburtstag*, ed. Josef Gmeiner, Zsigmond Kokits, Thomas Leibnitz and Inge Pechotsch-Feichtinger (Tutzing, 1999), 347–53

Serwe, Johannes. 'Komposition und Disposition: Über rhetorische Strukturen in Mozarts Briefen', *Mitteilungen der Internationalen Stiftung Mozarteum*, xlvi/1–2 (1998), 4–25

Seuffert, Bernhard. *Anzeiger für deutsches Altertum und deutsche Litteratur* (Berlin, 1876—)

Seuffert, Bernhard. *Prolegomena zu einer Wieland-Ausgabe* (Berlin, 1904—)

Seyfried, Ignaz Ritter von. *Ludwig van Beethoven's Studien im Generalbasse, Contrapuncte und in der Compositions-Lehre* (Vienna, 1832)

Seyfried, Ignaz Ritter von. 'Mozart der Opernkomponist: Don Giovanni', *Caecilia*, xviii (1836), 65–70

Seyfried, Ignaz Ritter von. 'Mozart der Opernkomponist: Ein skizzirter Versuch, als Beitrag zur Charakteristik dieses Meisters', *Caecilia*, xx (1839), 178–94

Sherman, Charles T. and T. Donley Thomas, *Johann Michael Haydn (1737–1806): A Chronological Thematic Catalogue of His Works* (Stuyvesant, NY, 1993)

Siepmann, Jeremy. 'The history of direction and conducting', *The Cambridge Companion to the Orchestra*, ed. Colin Lawson (Cambridge, 2003), 112–25

Sievers, Georg Ludwig Peter. 'Das Miserere von Allegri in der Sixtinischen Capelle in Rom, und Nachtrag zu der Notiz über den Sopransänger Mariano', *Cäcilia*, ii (1825), 66–82

Sievers, Georg Ludwig Peter. 'Mozarts Beifall in Paris', *Caecilia*, ix (1828), 208–16

Sievers, Georg Ludwig Peter. *Mozart und Süßmayer, ein neues Plagiat, ersterm zur Last gelegt, und eine neue Vermuthung, die Entstehung des Requiems betreffend* (Mainz, 1829)

Silin, Charles Intervale. *Benserade and his Ballets de cour* (Baltimore, 1940)

Simon, Edwin J. 'The Double Exposition in the Classic Concerto', *Journal of the American Musicological Society*, x (1957), 111–18

Simon, Edwin J. 'Sonata into Concerto: A Study of Mozart's First Seven Concertos', *Acta musicologica*, xxxi (1959), 170–85

Simon, James. *Abt Voglers kompositorisches Wirken* (Berlin, 1904)

Simon, Julia. 'Rousseau and aesthetic modernity: Music's power of redemption', *Eighteenth-Century Music*, ii/1 (2005), 41–56

Sisman, Elaine R. *The 'Jupiter' Symphony, No. 41 in C major, K. 551* (Cambridge, 1993)

Sisman, Elaine R. 'Form, Character, and Genre in Mozart's Piano Concerto Variations', *Mozart's Piano Concertos: Text, Context, Interpretation*, ed. Neal Zaslaw (Ann Arbor, MI, 1996), 335–61

Sisman, Elaine R. 'Learned Style and the Rhetoric of the Sublime in the "Jupiter" Symphony', *Wolfgang Amadè Mozart: Essays on his Life and his Music*, ed. Stanley Sadie (Oxford, 1996), 213–38

Sisman, Elaine R. 'Genre, Gesture, and Meaning in Mozart's "Prague" Symphony', *Mozart Studies 2*, ed. Cliff Eisen (Oxford, 1997), 27–84

Smaczny, Jan. 'Mozart and the twentieth century', *The Cambridge Companion to Mozart*, ed. Simon P. Keefe (Cambridge, 2003), 185–99

Smaczny, Jan. 'Prague', *The Cambridge Mozart Encyclopedia*, ed. Cliff Eisen and Simon P. Keefe (Cambridge, 2005), 397–402

Smith, Bill. *The Vaudevillians* (New York, 1976)

Smith, Kent Maynard. 'Egidio Duni and the Development of the Opéra-Comique from 1753 to 1770' (dissertation, Cornell University, 1980)

Smither, Howard E. *A History of the Oratorio* (Chapel Hill, NC, 1977–2000)

Solerti, Angelo. *Gli albori del melodramma* (Milan, 1904–5)

Solger, Karl Wilhelm Ferdinand. *Nachgelassene Schriften* (Leipzig, 1826)

Solomon, Maynard. 'The Rochlitz Anecdotes: Issues of Authenticity in Early Mozart Biography', *Mozart Studies*, ed. Cliff Eisen (Oxford, 1991), 1–59

Solomon, Maynard. 'Marianne Mozart: "Carissima sorella mia"', *On Mozart*, ed. James M. Morris (Cambridge, 1994), 130–50

Solomon, Maynard. *Mozart: A Life* (New York, 1995)

Somfai, László. 'Sketches during the process of composition: Studies of K.504 and K.414', *Wolfgang Amadè Mozart: Essays on his Life and his Music*, ed. Stanley Sadie (Oxford, 1996), 53–65

Sondheimer, Robert. 'Die Sinfonien Franz Becks', *Zeitschrift für Musikwissenschaft*, iv (1921/2), 323–51 and 449–84

Sondheimer, Robert. 'Die formale Entwicklung der vorklassischen Sinfonie', *Archiv für Musikwissenschaft*, iv (1922), 85–99 and 123–39

Sondheimer, Robert. *Die Theorie der Sinfonie und die Beurteilung einzelner Sinfoniekomponisten bei den Musikschriftstellern des 18. Jahrhunderts* (Leipzig, 1925)

Sonneck, Oscar. 'Benjamin Franklin's Musical Side', *Suum cuique: Essays in Music* (New York, 1916)

Sonnek, Anke. *Emanuel Schikaneder: Theaterprinzipal, Schauspieler und Stückeschreiber* (Kassel, 1999)

Sonnenfels, Joseph von. *Gesammelte Schriften* (Vienna, 1783–7)

Sonnenfels, Joseph von. *Briefe über die wienerische Schaubühne* (Vienna, 1768)

Sonnleithner, Leopold von. 'Über Mozarts angebliche Bearbeitung und Instrumentierung des Händel'schen Oratorium "Judas Maccabäus"', *Caecilia*, xviii (1836), 242–50

Sonnleithner, Leopold von. 'Über Mozarts Opern aus seiner frühen Jugend', *Caecilia*, xxiii (1844), 233–56

Sonnleithner, Leopold von. [Review article], *Recensionen und Mittheilungen über Theater und Musik* viii/2 (1862), 18ff.

Sonnleithner, Leopold von. 'Mozartiana III', *Recensionen und Mittheilungen über Theater und Musik*, xi (1865), 721–3

Sørensen, Inger. 'Ein Mozart-Porträt in Dänemark', *Mozart-Jahrbuch 1994*, 79–88

Soubies, Albert and Charles Malherbe, *Précis de l'histoire de l'Opéra-Comique* (Paris, 1887)

Spaethling, Robert. *Mozart's Letters, Mozart's Life* (London, 2001)

Spazier, Karl. *Grétrys Versuche über die Musik* (Leipzig, 1800)

Speck, Christian. *Boccherinis Streichquartette: Studien zur Kompositionsweise und zur gattungsgeschichtlichen Stellung* (Munich, 1987)

Speck, Christian. 'Mozart und Boccherini: Zur Frage der Italianità in Mozarts frühen Streichquartetten', *Gesellschaft für Musikforschung: Kongreß-Bericht Baden 1991*, 921–32

Spieß, Hermann. 'Ist die Motette "Adoramus te" (KV. 327, Krit. Ges. Ausg. Ser. III, Nr. 30) von W. A. Mozart?', *Gregorius-Blatt*, xlvii/4–5 (1922), 25–9

Spindler, Carl. *Belletrisisches Ausland* (Stuttgart, 1847)

Spink, Ian. 'Purcell's music for The Libertine', *Music & letters*, lxxxi/4 (2000), 520–31

Spiro, Friedrich. 'Die Entstehung einer Mozartschen Konzertarie (KV. 505)', *Vierteljahrsschrift für Musikwissenschaft*, iv (1888), 255–69

Spitta, Philipp. *Johann Sebastian Bach* (Leipzig, 1873–80)

Spitta, Philipp. 'Zur Herausgabe der Briefe Mozarts', *Allgemeine musikalische Zeitung*, new series, xv (1880), 401–5, 417–21

Spitta, Philipp. 'Rinaldo di Capua', *Vierteljahrsschrift für Musikwissenschaft*, iii (1887), 92–121

Spitta, Philipp. *Musikgeschichtliche Aufsätze* (Berlin, 1894)

Spitzer, John and Neal Zaslaw, *The Birth of the Orchestra: History of an Institution* (Oxford, 2004)

Spohr, Louis. *Selbstbiographie* (Kassel and Göttingen, 1860–61)

Stadler, Maximilian. *Verteidigung der Echtheit des Mozart'schen Requiem* (Vienna, 1826)

Stadler, Maximilian. *Nachtrag zur Rechtfertigung* (Vienna, 1827)

Stafford, William. *Mozart's Death: A Corrective Survey of the Legends* (London, 1991)

Staral, Susanne. 'Zwei Klavierschulen des späteren 18. Jahrhunderts von Francesco Pasquale Ricci', *Muzyka fortepianowa* (Gdańsk, 1995), 253–67

Stauder, Wilhelm. 'Johann André: Ein Beitrag zur Geschichte des deutschen Singspiels', *Archiv für Musikwissenschaft*, i (1936), 318–60

Steglich, Rudolf. 'Karl Philipp Emanuel Bach und der Dresdner Kreuzkantor Gottfried August Homilius im Musikleben ihrer Zeit', *Bach-Jahrbuch*, xii (1915), 39–145

Steinbeck, Wolfram. 'Zur Entstehung der Konzertform in den Pasticcio-Konzerten Mozarts', *Beiträge zur Geschichte des Konzerts: Festschrift Siegfried Kross zum 60. Geburtstag*, ed. Reinmar Emans and Matthias Wendt (Bonn, 1990), 125–39

Stendhal. *Vie de Rossini* (Paris, 1824)

Stendhal. *Vies de Haydn, de Mozart et de Métastase* (Paris, 1887)

Steptoe, Andrew. 'Mozart and Poverty', *Musical Times*, cxxv (1984), 196–201

Steptoe, Andrew. *The Mozart–Da Ponte Operas: The Cultural and Musical Background to Le Nozze di Figaro, Don Giovanni, and Così fan tutte* (Oxford, 1988)

Steptoe, Andrew. 'Mozart and his last three symphonies – a myth laid to rest?', *Musical Times*, cxxxii (1991), 550–1

Steptoe, Andrew. 'Mozart's personality and creativity', *Wolfgang Amadè Mozart: Essays on his Life and his Music*, ed. Stanley Sadie (Oxford, 1996), 21–34

Sterneck, Carl Freiherr von. 'Der Freundeskreis Mozarts in Salzburg', *Studien über Mozart*, ed. Johann Evangelist Engl (Salzburg, 1896)

Sternfeld, Frederick W. 'The Concerto', *The Age of Enlightenment 1745–1790*, ed. Egon Wellesz and Frederick Sternfeld (London, 1974 = The Oxford History of Music), 434–502

Sternfeld, Frederick W. *The Birth of Opera* (Oxford, 1993)

Stetten, Paul von. *Kunst-, Gewerb- und Handwerks-Geschichte der Reichs-Stadt Augsburg* (Augsburg, 1779)

Stevens, Jane. 'An 18th-Century Description of Concerto First-Movement Form', *Journal of the American Musicological Society*, xxiv (1971), 85–95

Stevens, Jane. 'Theme, Harmony, and Texture in Classic-Romantic Descriptions of Concerto First-Movement Form', *Journal of the American Musicological Society*, xxvii (1974), 25–60

Stevenson, Robert. 'Marianna Martines = Martínez (1744–1812): Pupil of Haydn and Friend of Mozart', *Inter-American Music Review*, xi (1990–91), 25–44

Stiefel, Richard. 'Mozart's Seductions', *Current Musicology*, xxxvi (1983), 151–66

Stockigt, Janice B. *Jan Dismas Zelenka: A Bohemian Musician at the Court of Dresden* (New York, 2000)

Stone, G[eorge] W[inchester], ed., *The London Stage 1660–1800: Part 4 (1747–76)* (Carbondale, 1962)

Storck, Karl. *Mozarts Briefe in Auswahl* (Stuttgart, 1906)

Storck, Karl. *Mozart: Sein Leben und Schaffen* (Stuttgart, 1908)

Storer, Mary Elizabeth. 'Abbé François Raguenet: Deist, Historian, Music and Art Critic', *Romantic Review*, xxxvi (1945), 283–96

Stratil, Marie and Robert J. Oakley. 'A Disputed Authorship Study of Two Plays Attributed to Tirso de Molina', *Literary and Linguistic Computing: Journal of the Association for Literary and Linguistic Computing*, ii/3 (1987), 154–60

Stratton, S. 'Coincidence or Design', *Zeitschrift der Internationalen Musikgesellschaft*, v (1903–4), 450–1

Strauß, David Friedrich. *Lessing's Nathan der Weise* (Berlin, 1864)

Strauß, David Friedrich. *Der alte und der neue Glaube* (Leipzig, 1872)

Strebel, Harald. 'Ein Hohelied der Maurerei: Bemerkungen zur Zauberflöte Mozarts und … Schikaneders', *Alpina: Revue maçonnique suisse – Schweizer Freimaurer-Rundschau – Rivista massonica svizzera*, cxxxvi/5 (2000), 120–7

Strebel, Harald. 'Freimaurerische Musik und Loge', *Handbuch des Freimaurers*, second edition (Lausanne, 2002), 363–75

Strebel, Harald. 'La musique maçonnique dans la vie de la Loge', *Masonica: Revue du Groupe de Recherche Alpina / Zeitschrift der Forschungsgruppe Alpina 2002*, xii (2002), 5–21

Strebel, Harald. '"Nun ist der Paesiello Hier (…)": Mozart's Beziehungen zu Giovanni Paisiello', *Mitteilungen der Mozart-Gesellschaft Zürich*, xii/20 (2002), 7–18

Strohm, Reinhard. *Die italienische Oper im 18. Jahrhundert* (Wilhelmshaven, 1979)

Strohm, Reinhard. 'Alessandro Scarlatti and the Settecento', *Essays on Handel and Italian Opera* (Cambridge, 1985), 15–34

Strohm, Reinhard. 'The crisis of Baroque opera in Germany', *Dramma per musica: Italian opera seria of the eighteenth century* (New Haven, CT, 1997), 81–96

Strohm, Reinhard. 'Tradition und Fortschritt in der opera seria: Tommaso Traetta: *Ifigenia in Tauride* (Wien, 1763); Christoph Willibald Gluck: *Il Telemaco, o sia l'isola di Circe* (Wien, 1765)', *Christoph Willibald Gluck und die Opernreform*, ed. Klaus Hortschansky (Darmstadt, 1989), 325–52

Suard, Jean-Baptiste-Antoine. *Mélange de littérature* (Paris, 1804)

Subotnik, Rose Rosengard. 'Evidence of a Critical World View in Mozart's Last Three Symphonies', *Music and Civilization: Essays in Honor of Paul Henry Lang*, ed. E. Strainchamps, Maria Rika Maniates and Christopher Hatch (New York, 1984), 29–43; reprinted in Rose Rosengard Subotnik, *Developing Variations: Style and Ideology in Western Music* (Minneapolis, 1991), 98–111

Sühring, Peter. 'Eine vierhändige Sonata – "bis dahin noch nirgends gemacht"?', *Mozart-Studien*, xiii (2004), 209–30

Sulzer, Johann Georg. *Allgemeine Theorie der schönen Künste* (Leipzig, 1771)

Sulzer, Wolfgang. 'Christoph Friedrich Bretzner: Sein Anteil an Mozarts Entführung aus dem Serail', *Mitteilungen der Internationalen Stiftung Mozarteum*, xxxviii/1–4 (1990), 49–87

Sutcliffe, W. Dean. 'Change and Constancy in Mozart's Keyboard Variations K. 180, K. 345 and K. 455', *Mozart-Jahrbuch 2003/4*, 73–94

Sutcliffe, W. Dean. *The Keyboard Sonatas of Domenico Scarlatti and Eighteenth-Century Musical Style* (Cambridge, 2004)

Swain, Joseph P. 'Musical Disguises in Mozart's Late Comedies', *Opera Quarterly*, xiii/4 (1997), 47–58

Sýkora, Václav Jan. *František Xaver Dušek: zivot a dílo* [Dušek: Life and Works] (Prague, 1958)

Szabo, Franz A. *Kaunitz and Enlightened Absolutism, 1753–1780* (Cambridge, 1994)

Tagebuch der böhmischen Königskrönung (Prague, 1791)

Tajetti, Oscar. 'Francesco Zappa: violoncellista e compositore milanese', *Antiquae musicae italicae studiosi*, iii/6 (1987), 9–12

Tanejew, Sergius Iwanow. 'Der Inhalt des Arbeitsheftes von W. A. Mozarts eigenhändig geschriebenen Übungen, mit den Unterweisungen durch seinen Vater im strengen Kontrapunkt und reinen Satz', *Jahresbericht der Internationalen Stiftung Mozarteum*, xxxiii (1913), 29–39

Tangeman, Robert S. 'Mozart's Seventeen Epistle Sonatas', *Musical Quarterly*, xxxii (1946), 588–601

Tenschert, Roland. *Christoph Willibald Gluck, der große Reformator der Oper* (Olten, 1951)

Terry, Charles Stanford. *John Christian Bach* (London, 1929)

Teuber, Oskar. *Geschichte des Prager Theaters* (Prague, 1883–7)

Teuber, Oskar. *Die Theater Wiens* (Vienna, 1903)

Thalker, C. 'Rousseaus *Devin du village*', *Das deutsche Singspiel im 18. Jahrhundert* (Amorbach, 1979), 119–24

Thayer, Alexander Wheelock. 'Mozart und Salieri', *Allgemeine musikalische Zeitung*, new series, iii (1865), 241–61

Thayer, Alexander Wheelock. *Ludwig van Beethovens Leben*, ed. Hermann Deiters and Hugo Riemann (Berlin and Leipzig, 1907–17; revised English edition as *Thayer's Life of Beethoven*, ed. Elliot Forbes [Princeton, 1967])

Théâtre de M. et Mme Favart, ou Recueil des comédies, parodies et opéra-comiques (Paris, 1763–72)

Thibaut, Anton. *Über Reinheit der Tonkunst* (Heidelberg, 1826)

Thoinan, Ernest. *Notes bibliographiques sur la guerre musicale des Gluckistes et Piccinnistes* (Paris, 1878)

Thoma, Clemens. '"Betulia liberata": Bemerkungen zum literatur- und geistesgeschichtlichen Hintergrund des Mozart-Oratoriums KV 118', *Mozart 1991: Die Kirchenmusik von W. A. Mozart in Luzern*, ed. Alois Koch (Lucerne, 1992), 113–18

Thomae, Friedrich. 'Vier Mozart-Handschriften in der Bibliothek des British Museum in London', *Allgemeine musikalische Zeitung*, new series, vi (1871), 481–6, 497–501

Thomas, Downing A. *Aesthetics of Opera in the Ancien Régime, 1647–1785* (Cambridge, 2002)

Thomas, Downing A. *Music and the Origins of Language: Theories from the French Enlightenment* (Cambridge, 1995)

Thomson, Katharine. *The Masonic Thread in Mozart* (London, 1977)

Thouret, Georg. 'Das Mozartfest der Königlichen Oper in Berlin', *Zeitschrift der Internationalen Musikgesellschaft*, iii (1901/2), 138–46

Thürlings, Adolf. 'Der Donner im ersten Finale des Don Juan', *Berner Bund*, lxxx (1903)

Tieck, Ludwig. *Dramaturgische Blätter* (Breslau, 1826)

Tieck, Ludwig. *Schriften* (Berlin, 1828–54)

Tiersot, Julien. 'Étude sur Don Giovanni', *Le ménestrel*, lxii (1896), 393–4, 401–2, 409–11; and lxiii (1897), 9–10, 73–4 and 89–90

Tiersot, Julien. 'Ronsard et la musique de son temps', *Sammelbänder der Internationalen Musikgesellschaft*, iv (1902/3), 70–142

Tiersot, Julien. *Gluck* (Paris, 1910)

Tiersot, Julien. *Jean-Jacques Rousseau* (Paris, 1912)

Till, Nicholas. *Mozart and the Enlightenment: Truth, Virtue and Beauty in Mozart's Operas* (London, 1991)

Tintori, Giampiero. *L'opera napoletana* (Milan, 1958)

Toguetti, Francesco. *Discorso su i progressi della musica in Bologna* (Bologna, 1818)

Toldo, Pietro. *Figaro et ses origines* (Milan, 1893)

Tomaszewski, Mieczyslaw. 'Mozarts Don Juan in Polen', *Musikgeschichte in Mittel- und Osteuropa*, ed. Helmut Loos and Eberhard Möller (Chemnitz, 1997), 21–32

Tomita, Yo. 'Bach reception in pre-Classical Vienna: Baron von Swieten's circle edits the Well-tempered Clavier II', *Music & Letters*, lxxxi/3 (2000), 364–91

Tomlinson, Gary. *Monteverdi and the End of the Renaissance* (Berkeley, 1987)

Torrefranca, Fausto. 'Le origini della sinfonia: Le sinfonie dell'imbrattacarte (G. B. Sammartini)', *Rivista musicale italiana*, xx (1913), 291–346; xxi (1914), 97, 278–312; xxii (1915), 431–46

Torrefranca, Fausto. 'Il primo maestro di W. A. Mozart (Giovanni Maria Rutini)', *Rivista musicale italiana*, xl (1936), 239–53

Toscani, Bernard. 'Introduction', *Antonio Caldara: Six Introduzioni and one Sinfonia* (New York, 1983 = The Symphony 1720–1840, Series B/ii), xxxvii–xlviii

Tosi, Pier Francesco. *Opinioni de' cantori antichi e moderni* (Bologna, 1723)

Toth, Karl. *Französisches Salonleben um Charles Pinot Duclos 1704–1772* (Vienna, 1918)

Tournier, Jacques. *Le Dernier des Mozart* (Paris, 2000)

Tovey, Donald F. 'The Classical Concerto', *Essays in Musical Analysis*, iii: *Concertos* (London, 1936), 3–27

Tozzi, Lorenzo. *Il balletto pantomimo del Settecento: Gaspare Angiolini* (L'Aquila, 1972)

Traini, Carlo. *Il cigno di Romano: Giovanni Battista Rubini* (Bergamo, 1954)

Treitschke, Friedrich. 'Die Zauberflöte, Der Dorfbarbier, Fidelio: Beiträge zur musikalischen Kunstgeschichte', *Orpheus: Musikalisches Tagebuch für das Jahr 1841*, 242–3

Troy, Charles E. *The Comic Intermezzo: A Study in the History of Eighteenth-Century Opera* (Ann Arbor, 1979)

Tucher, Gottlieb von. *Schatz des evangelischen Kirchengesangs im ersten Jahrhundert der Reformation* (Leipzig, 1848–67)

Tugal, Pierre. *Jean-Georges Noverre, der große Reformator des Balletts* (Berlin, 1959)

Turrentine, Herbert C. 'Johann Schobert and French Clavier Music from 1700 to the Revolution' (dissertation, University of Iowa, 1962)

Turrentine, Herbert C. 'The Prince de Conti, a Royal Patron of Music', *Musical Quarterly*, liv (1968), 309–15

Tutenberg, Fritz. *Die Sinfonik Johann Christian Bachs* (Wolfenbüttel, 1928)

Tyler, Linda L. 'Aria as drama: A sketch from Mozart's *Der Schauspieldirektor*', *Cambridge Opera Journal*, ii/3 (1990), 251–67

Tyler, Linda L. '"Zaide" in the development of Mozart's operatic language', *Music & Letters*, lxxii/2 (1991), 214–35

Tyler, Linda L. 'Bastien und Bastienne and the Viennese Volkskomödie', *Bericht über den Internationalen Mozart-Kongreß Salzburg 1991* (Kassel, 1992), 576–9

Tyson, Alan. '*La clemenza di Tito* and its chronology', *Musical Times*, cxvi (1975), 221–7

Tyson, 'Mozart's Truthfulness', *Musical Times*, cxvii (1978), 938

Tyson, Alan. 'A Reconstruction of Nannerl Mozart's Music Book (Notenbuch)', *Music & Letters*, lx (1979), 389–400

Tyson, Alan. 'The Mozart Fragments in the Mozarteum, Salzburg: A Preliminary Study of Their Chronology and Their Significance', *Journal of the American Musicological Society*, xxxiv (1981), 471–510

Tyson, Alan. '*Le nozze di Figaro*: Lessons from the Autograph Score', *Musical Times*, cxxii (1981), 456–61

Tyson, Alan. 'The Two Slow Movements of Mozart's Paris Symphony K. 297', *Musical Times*, cxxii (1981), 17–21

Tyson, Alan. 'The Dates of Mozart's *Missa brevis* K. 258 and *Missa longa* K. 262 (246a)', *Bachiana et alia musicologica: Festschrift Alfred Dürr zum 65. Geburtstag*, ed. Wolfgang Rehm (Kassel, 1983), 328–39

Tyson, Alan. *Mozart: Studies of the Autograph Scores* (Cambridge, MA, 1987)

Tyson, Alan. 'Notes on the Genesis of Mozart's "Ein musikalischer Spass", K.522', Alan Tyson, *Mozart: Studies of the Autograph Scores* (Cambridge, MA, 1987), 234–45

Tyson, Alan. 'Some Problems in the Text of *Le nozze di Figaro*: Did Mozart Have a Hand in Them?', *Journal of the Royal Musical Association*, cxii/1 (1987), 99–131

Tyson, Alan. *Le nozze di Figaro: eight variant versions = acht abweichende Fassungen* (Oxford, 1989)

Tyson, Alan. 'Die Prager Version von Mozarts "Figaro" 1786: Zur Donaueschinger Partitur', *Musik in Baden-Württemberg*, ii (1995), 143–58

Tyson, Alan. 'Mozart's Piano Concerto Fragments', *Mozart's Piano Concertos: Text, Context, Interpretation*, ed. Neal Zaslaw (Ann Arbor, MI, 1996), 67–72

Ullrich, Herbert. 'Maria Theresia Paradis' große Kunstreise', *Österreichische Musikzeitschrift*, xv (1960), 470–80; xvii (1962), 11–26; xviii (1963), 475–83; xix (1964), 430–35; xx (1965), 589–97

Ullrich, Herbert. 'Das Stammbuch der Maria Theresia Paradis', *Jahrbuch des Bonner Heimat- und Geschichtsvereins*, xv (1961), 340–84

Ullrich, Herbert. 'Maria Theresia Paradis in London', *Music & Letters*, xliii (1962), 16–24

Ullrich, Herbert. *Die blinde Glasharmonikavirtuosin Mariane Kirchgessner und Wien: Eine Künstlerin der empfindsamen Zeit* (Tutzing, 1971)

Ullrich, Herbert. 'Wolfgang Amadeus Mozart – Ein falscher Schädel ruht im Mozarteum in Salzburg', *Schädel-Schicksale historischer Persönlichkeiten*, ed. Herbert Ullrich (Munich, 2004), 33–49

Unfried, Hannelore. 'Von der geschmackvollen Armkunst zur spektakulären Beinkunst: Materialien zu einer eigenständigen Wiener Tanzkultur im 18. Jahrhundert an Hand von Glucks Ballettpantomime Don Juan', *Tanzdramen – Opéra-comique: Kolloquiumsbericht der Gluck-Gesamtausgabe*, ed. Gabriele Buschmeier and Klaus Hortschansky (Kassel, 2000), 75–87

Unger, Max. 'Muzio Clementis Leben' (dissertation, University of Leipzig, 1914)

Universität Salzburg 1662 – 1962 – 1972: Festschrift (Salzburg, 1972)

Unverricht, Hubert. *Gesellschaftsgebundene instrumentale Unterhaltungsmusik des 18. Jahrhunderts* (Tutzing, 1992)

Ursprung, Otto. *Jacobus de Kerle (1531/2–1591): Sein Leben und seine Werke* (Munich, 1913)

Ursprung, Otto. *Die katholische Kirchenmusik* (Potsdam, 1931)

Valentin, Carl. *Geschichte der Musik in Frankfurt am Main vom Anfange des XIV. bis zum Anfange des XVIII. Jahrhunderts* (Frankfurt, 1906)

Valentin, Erich. 'Das Testament der Constanze Nissen: mit biographischen Notizen über Constanze und Georg Nikolaus Nissen', *Neues Mozart-Jahrbuch 1942*, 128–75

Valle, Guillemus della. *Memorie storiche del p. m. Giambattista Martini* (Naples, 1785)

van Boer, Bertil. 'Coffey's *The Devil to Pay*, the Comic War, and the Emergence of the German *Singspiel*', *Journal of Musicological Research*, viii (1988), 119–39

Vaupél, Emil. 'Mozarts Freimaurer-Gesellenlied', *Zeitschrift der Internationalen Musikgesellschaft*, i (1900), 135

Vecchi, Giuseppe, ed. *L'Accademia Filarmonica di Bologna (1666–1966): Notizie storiche, manifestazioni* (Bologna, 1966)

Vecchi, Giuseppe, ed. *La musica come arte e come scienza, ricordando Padre Martini: Bologna 1984* [*Quadrivium*, xxvi/1 (1985)]

Vecchi, Giuseppe. 'L'Accademia Filarmonica e le sue fonti storiche: Padre G. B. Martini . . . ridimensionato', *Studi e materiali, per la storia dell'Accademia Filarmonica*, iii (1991), 3–15

Vehse, Karl Eduard. *Geschichte des östreichischen Hofes und Adels und der östreichischen Diplomatie* (Hamburg, 1851–3)

Vendrix, Philippe, ed. *Grétry et l'Europe de l'opéra-comique* (Liège, 1992)

Vendrix, Philippe, ed. *L'opéra-comique en France au XVIIIe siècle* (Liège, 1992)

Vendrix, Philippe. *Aux origines d'une discipline historique: La musique et son histoire en France aux XVIIe et XVIIIe siècles* (Liège, 1993)

Verba, Cynthia. 'Jean-Jacques Rousseau: Radical and Traditional Views in his *Dictionnaire de musique*', *Journal of Musicology*, vii (1989), 303–26

Verba, Cynthia. *Music and the French Enlightenment* (Oxford, 1993)

Vertrees, Julie Anne. 'Mozart's String Quartet K. 465: The History of a Controversy', *Current Musicology*, xvii (1974), 96–114

Viardot, Louis. 'Manuscrit autographe du Don Giovanni de Mozart', *L'illustration*, xxvii (1856), 10–11

Vignal, Marc. *Haydn et Mozart* (Paris, 2001)

Vill, Susanne, ed. *Così fan tutte: Beiträge zur Wirkungsgeschichte von Mozarts Oper* (Bayreuth, 1978)

Viol, W. *Don Juan, komisch-tragische Oper in zwei Akten, von W. A. Mozart* (Breslau, 1858)

Vít, Peter. 'Kompositionsprinzipien der Sinfonien des Anton Fils', *Sborník prací filosofické fakulty Brnenské University. H: Rada hudebnevedná, Czech Republic*, vii (1972) 43–52

Vitali, Carlo and Francesca Boris, ed. *Carlo Broschi Farinelli: Senza sentimento oscuro* (Palermo, 2000)

Vogel, Emil. 'Claudio Monteverdi', *Vierteljahrsschrift für Musikwissenschaft*, iii (1887), 315–450

Vogler, Georg Joseph. *Betrachtungen der Mannheimer Tonschule* (Mannheim, 1778–81)

Vogler, Georg Joseph. 'Ueber die Musik der Oper *Rosamunde*', *Rheinische Beiträge zur Gelehrsamkeit*, vi (Mannheim, 1780), 497–514

Voisine, Jacques. 'Le *Devin du village* de Rousseau et son adaptation anglaise par le musicologue Charles Burney', *Le théâtre dans l'Europe des Lumières: Programmes, pratiques, échanges: Wrocław 1983*, ed. Mieczysław Klimowicz and Aleksander Wit Labuda (Wrocław, 1985), 133–46

Völckers, Jürgen W. *Johann Rudolph Zumsteeg als Opernkomponist: Ein Beitrag zur Geschichte des deutschen Singspiels und der Musik am Württembergischen Hofe um die Wende des 18. Jahrhunderts* (Erfurt, 1944)

Volek, Tomislav. 'Über den Ursprung von Mozarts Oper "La clemenza di Tito"', *Mozart-Jahrbuch 1959*, 274–86

Volek, Tomislav. 'Die erste Aufführung der "Zauberflöte" in tschechischer Sprache in Prag 1794', *Mozart-Jahrbuch 1967*, 387–91

Volek, Tomislav. 'Prague Operatic Traditions and Mozart's Don Giovanni', *Mozart's Don Giovanni in Prague*, ed. Jan Kristek (Prague, 1987), 21–91

Volek, Tomislav. 'Italienische Oper in Prag im 18. Jahrhundert', *Europa im Zeitalter Mozarts*, ed. Moritz Csáky and Walter Pass (Vienna, 1995), 222–5

Vollmer, Wilhelm. *Briefwechsel zwischen Schiller und Goethe*, fourth edition (Stuttgart, 1881)

Vom Hofe, Gerhard. 'Göttlich-menschlicher Amadeus: Literarischer Mozart. Bilder im Horizont des romantischen Kunst- und Geniebegriffs', *Athenäum: Jahrbuch für Romantik*, iv (1994), 189–218

Vom Hofe, Gerhard. 'Die Konstellation des Genies: Raffael und Shakespeare in Mozart. Mozarts Kunstgeist in parallelisierter Deutung des frühen 19. Jahrhunderts', *Mozart: Aspekte des 19. Jahrhunderts*, ed. Hermann Jung (Mannheim, 1995), 23–43

Voß, Johann Heinrich. *Briefe* (Berlin, 1829–33)

Všetecka, Jiří and Jiří Berkovec. *Praga musicopolis Europae* (Prague, 1983)

Wade, Rachel W. 'Carl Friedrich Christian Fasch, Geburtshelfer des Musiklebens in Berlin', *Carl Friedrich Christian Fasch (1736–1800) und das Berliner Musikleben seiner Zeit*, ed. Konstanze Musketa and Susanne Oschmann (Dessau, 1999), 182–93

Waeber, Jacqueline. 'Le Devin du village de Jean-Jacques Rousseau: Histoire, orientations esthétiques, réception, 1752–1829' (dissertation, University of Geneva, 2002)

Wagner, Günther. *Die Sinfonien Carl Philipp Emanuel Bachs: Werdende Gattung und Originalgenie* (Stuttgart, 1994)

Wagner, Guy. *Bruder Mozart: Freimaurer im Wien des 18. Jahrhunderts* (Vienna, 1996)

Wagner, Karl. *Das Mozarteum: Geschichte und Entwicklung einer kulturellen Institution* (Innsbruck, 1993)

Wagner, Manfred. 'Zur Freimaurerei in Mozarts "Zauberflöte"', *Musikgeschichte als Verstehensgeschichte: Festschrift für Gernot Gruber zum 65. Geburtstag*, ed. Joachim Brügge (Tutzing, 2004), 371–81

Wagner, Peter. *Einführung in die gregorianischen Melodien: Ein Handbuch der Choralwissenschaft*, i: *Ursprung und Entwicklung der liturgischen Gesangsformen bis zum Ausgange des Mittelalters*, second edition (Fribourg, 1901)

Wagner, Peter. *Geschichte der Messe*, i: *Bis 1600* (Leipzig, 1913)

Wagner, Richard. 'Oper und Drama', *Gesammelte Schriften und Dichtungen* (Leipzig, 1907), iii.222–iv.229

Wagner, Richard. 'Über deutsches Musikwesen', *Gesammelte Schriften und Dichtungen* (Leipzig, 1907), i.149–66

Waidelich, Till Gerrit. '"Don Juan von Mozart, (für mich componirt.)" Luigi Bassi – eine Legende zu Lebzeiten, sein Nekrolog und zeitgenössische "Don Giovanni"-Interpretationen', *Mozart-Studien*, x (2001), 118–211

Waldersee, Paul von. 'Neue Publikationen der Mozart-Ausgabe', *Allgemeine musikalische Zeitung*, new series, xii (1877), 737–40

Waldersee, Paul von. 'Varesco's L'Oca del Cairo, nach der Originalhandschrift herausgegeben', *Allgemeine musikalische Zeitung*, new series, xvii (1882), 693–8, 710–15, 728–34, 745–50

Waldkirch, Franz. *Die konzertanten Sinfonien der Mannheimer im 18. Jahrhundert* (Ludwigshafen, 1931)

Waldoff, Jessica. 'The music of recognition: Operatic enlightenment in The Magic Flute', *Music & Letters*, lxxv/2 (1994), 214–35

Waldoff, Jessica and James Webster, 'Operatic Plotting in Le nozze di Figaro', *Wolfgang Amadè Mozart: Essays on his Life and his Music*, ed. Stanley Sadie (Oxford, 1996), 250–95

Walter, Friedrich. *Geschichte des Theaters und der Musik am kurpfälzischen Hofe* (Leipzig, 1898)

Walter, Friedrich. *Archiv und Bibliothek des Großherzoglichen Hof- und Nationaltheaters zu Mannheim* (Leipzig, 1899)

Waltershausen, Hermann Wolfgang von. *Die Zauberflöte: Eine operndramatische Studie* (Munich, 1920)

Walterskirchen, Gerhard, ed. *Heinrich Franz Biber: Kirchen- und Instrumentalmusik* (Salzburg, 1997)

Walton, Chris. 'The performing version by Richard Strauss and Lothar Wallerstein', *W. A. Mozart: Idomeneo*, ed. Julian Rushton (Cambridge, 1993), 89–94

Warburton, Ernest. 'A Study of Johann Christian Bach's Operas' (dissertation, University of Oxford, 1969)

Warburton, Ernest, ed. *The Collected Works of Johann Christian Bach 1735–1782* (New York, 1984–99)

Warburton. Ernest. 'Lucio Silla – by Mozart and J. C. Bach', *Musical Times*, cxxvi (1985), 726–30

Warburton, Ernest, ed. *The Librettos of Mozart's Operas*, ii: *The Works for Munich and Vienna* (New York, 1992)

Warburton, Ernest. *The Collected Works of Johann Christian Bach 1735–1782: Thematic Catalogue* (New York, 1995)

Wasielewski, Wilhelm Joseph von. 'Die Collection Philidor', *Vierteljahrsschrift für Musikwissenschaft*, i (1885), 531ff.

Wates, Roye E. '"Die Oper aller Opern": Don Giovanni as text for the Romantics', *Musik als Text*, ii (1998), 209–14

Weber, Gottfried. 'Ein Zweifel', *Allgemeine musikalische Zeitung*, xvii (1815), 247–9

Weber, Gottfried. 'Über die Echtheit des Mozart'schen Requiem', *Cäcilia*, iii (1825), 205–29

Weber, Gottfried. 'Erläuterungen zum Nachtrag zur Verteidigung der Echtheit des Mozart'schen Requiem', *Caecilia*, vi (1827), 133–53

Weber, Gottfried. 'Weitere Nachrichten über die Echtheit des Mozartschen Requiem', *Cäcilia*, iv (1826), 257–352

Weber, Gottfried. 'Beitrag zur Verunstaltungsgeschichte des Mozartischen Requiem von G. B. Bierney', *Caecilia*, viii (1828), 53–9

Weber, Gottfried. 'Geschichte der Mozart'schen Hymne: "Die Ihr des unermeßlichen"', *Caecilia*, xviii (1836), 210–13

Weber, Gottfried. 'Über Mozarts Originalmanuskripte der Partitur der Oper: Il Dissoluto punito ossia il Don Giovanni', *Caecilia*, xviii (1836), 91–120

Weber, Gottfried. 'Die vollständige eigenhändige Partitur des Mozartischen Requiem, aufgefunden und herausgegeben von Hofrath von Mosel', *Caecilia*, xx (1839), 279–99

Weber, Karl von. *Maria Antonia Walpurgis, Churfürstin zu Sachsen* (Dresden, 1857)

Weber, Max Maria von. *Carl Maria von Weber* (Leipzig, 1864–6)

Weber, William. 'London: A City of Unrivalled Riches', *The Classical Era*, ed. Neal Zaslaw (Basingstoke, 1989), 293–326

Webster, James. 'Towards a History of Viennese Chamber Music in the Early Classical Period', *Journal of the American Musicological Society*, xxvii (1974), 212–47

Webster, James. 'The Bass Part in Haydn's Early String Quartets', *Musical Quarterly*, lxiii (1977), 390–424

Webster, James. 'On the Absence of Keyboard Continuo in Haydn's Symphonies', *Early Music*, xviii (1990), 599–608

Webster, James. *Haydn's 'Farewell' Symphony and the Idea of Classical Style: Through-Composition and Cyclic Integration in his Instrumental Music* (Cambridge, 1991)

Webster, James. 'Are Mozart's Concertos "Dramatic"? Concerto Ritornellos versus Aria Introductions in the 1780s', *Mozart's Piano Concertos: Text, Context, Interpretation*, ed. Neal Zaslaw (Ann Arbor, 1996), 107–37

Webster, James and Georg Feder. *The New Grove Haydn* (London and New York, 2002)

Wegeler, Franz Gerhard and Ferdinand Ries. *Biographische Notizen über Ludwig van Beethoven* (Berlin, 1906)

Weigel, Max. *Mozarts Briefe* (Berlin, 1910)

Weikl, Rudolf. 'Die Vermarktung des Mythos "Mozart"', *Kongreßbericht zum VII. Internationalen Gewandhaus-Symposium: Wolfgang Amadeus Mozart. Forschung und Praxis im Dienst von Leben, Werk, Interpretation und Rezeption anläßlich der Gewandhaus-Festtage in Leipzig vom 3. bis 6. Oktober 1991* (Leipzig, 1993), 182–5

Weilen, Alexander von. *Geschichte des Wiener Theaterwesens* (Vienna, 1899)

Weilen, Alexander von. *Geschichte des Burgtheaters* (Vienna, 1902)

Weingartner, Felix. *Ratschläge für Aufführungen klassischer Sinfonien. Band III: Mozart* (Leipzig, 1923)

Weismann, Wilhelm. 'Zur Urfassung von Mozarts Klaviertrio KV 564', *Deutsches Jahrbuch der Musikwissenschaft für 1958*, 35–40

Weiss, Piero. 'Venetian Commedia dell'Arte "Operas" in the Age of Vivaldi', *Musical Quarterly*, lxx (1984), 195–217

Weiss, Piero. 'La diffusione del repertorio operistico nell'Italia del Settecento: Il caso dell'opera buffa', *Civiltà teatrale e Settecento emiliano*, ed. Susi Davoli (Bologna, 1986), 241–56

Weiße, Christian Felix. *Selbstbiographie*, ed. Christian Ernst Weiße and Samuel Gottlob Frisch (Leipzig, 1806)

Weißensteiner, Friedrich. *Die Frauen der Genies* (Wien, 2001)

Welck, Karin von and Lieselotte Homering, ed. *176 Tage W. A. Mozart in Mannheim* (Mannheim, 1991)

Wellesz, Egon. 'Giuseppe Bonno (1710–1788): Sein Leben und seine dramatischen Werke', *Sammelbände der Internationalen Musikgesellschaft*, xi (1909/10), 395–442

Wellesz, Egon. 'Cavalli und der Stil der venetianischen Oper von 1640–1660', *Studien zur Musikwissenschaft*, i (1913), 1–103

Wellesz, Egon and Frederick W. Sternfeld. 'The Early Symphony', *New Oxford History of Music*, vii (1973), 366–433

Welti, Heinrich. 'Gluck und Calsabigi', *Vierteljahrsschrift für Musikwissenschaft*, vii (1891), 26–42

Werner, Richard Maria. *Aus dem Josephinischen Wien* (Berlin, 1888)

Werner, Richard Maria. 'Der Laufner Don Juan', *Theatergeschichtliche Forschungen*, iii (1891), 72ff.

Werner-Jensen, Karin. *Studien zur Don Giovanni-Rezeption im 19. Jahrhundert (1800–1850)* (Tutzing, 1980)

Wertheim, Ursula and Hans Böhm, *C. F. D. Schubart: Briefe* (Munich, 1984)

Westrup, Jack. 'Two First Performances: Monteverdi's "Orfeo" and Mozart's "La Clemenza di Tito"', *Music & Letters*, xxxix (1958), 327–35

Westrup, Jack and Mary Hunter, 'Aria, § 2: 17th-Century Vocal Music' and '4: 18th Century', *The New Grove Dictionary of Music and Musicians*, second edition ed. Stanley Sadie and John Tyrrell (London, 2001), i.888–9 and 890–4

Wheelock, Gretchen. *Haydn's Ingenious Jesting with Art* (New York, 1992)

White, Harry M. 'The *Sepolcro* Oratorios of Fux: An Assessment', *Johann Joseph Fux and the Music of the Austro-Italian Baroque*, ed. Harry M. White (Aldershot, 1992), 164–230

White, Harry M. 'The Oratorios of Johann Joseph Fux and the Imperial Court in Vienna', *Studies in Music from the University of Western Ontario*, xv (1995), 1–16

Whittaker, Alfred. 'Karl Ludwig Giesecke: His life, performance and achievements', *Mitteilungen der Österreichischen Mineralogischen Gesellschaft*, cxlvi (2001), 451–79

Whitwell, Daniel. 'The Incredible Vienna Octet School', *The Instrumentalist*, xxiv (1969/70), no. 3, 31–5; no. 4, 40–43; no. 5, 42–6; no.6, 38–40; no. 7, 31; and no.8, 31–3

Widén, Gust. *Luigi Lablache* (Göteborg, 1897)

Wiel, Taddeo. *I teatri musicali veneziani nel Settecento* (Venice, 1897)

Wieland, Christoph Martin. 'Briefe an einen Freund [F. H. Jacobi] über das deutsche Singspiel, *Alceste*', *Der Teutsche Merkur*, i (1773), i.34–72 and iii.223–43

Wieland, Christoph Martin. *Geschichte der Abderiten* (Leipzig, 1782)

Wieland, Christoph Martin. *Dschinnistan oder Auserlesene Feen- und Geister-Mährchen* (Winterthur, 1786–9)

Wieland, Christoph Martin. *Auswahl denkwürdiger Briefe*, ed. Ludwig Wieland (Vienna, 1815)

Wieland, Christoph Martin. *Briefe an Sophie von La Roche* (Berlin, 1820)

Wieland, Christoph Martin. *Briefe an und von Johann Heinrich Merck* (Darmstadt, 1838)

Wieland, Christoph Martin. *Werke* (Berlin, 1882–7)

Wiese, Berthold and Erasmo Percopo. *Geschichte der italienischen Litteratur von den ältesten Zeiten bis zur Gegenwart* (Leipzig, 1899)

Wiese, Henrik. 'Zur Entstehungsgeschichte der Flötenkonzerte', *Mozart-Jahrbuch 1997*, 149–56

Wiesend, Reinhard. *Studien zur opera seria von Baldassare Galuppi: Werksituation und Überlieferung – Form und Satztechnik. Inhaltsdarstellung, mit einer Biographie und einem Quellenverzeichnis der Opern* (Tutzing, 1984)

Wiesend, Reinhard. 'Opernhandwerk und Originalität: Mozarts Arien KV 582 und 583 als Einlagen in Martín y Solers "Il burbero di buon cuore"', *Mozart e la Drammaturgia Veneta / Mozart und die Dramatik des Veneto: Bericht über das Colloquium Venedig 1991*, ed. Wolfgang Osthoff and Reinhard Wiesend (Tutzing, 1996), 129–77

Wiesmann, Sigrid. 'Giuseppe Sartis *Giulio Sabino* als representative Opera seria der Haydn-Zeit', *Joseph Haydn und die Oper seiner Zeit*, ed. Gerhard Winkler (Eisenstadt, 1988), 127–30

Wignall, Harrison James. 'Mozart and the "Duetto Notturno" tradition', *Mozart-Jahrbuch 1993*, 145–61

Wignall, Harrison James. 'Guglielmo Dettore – Mozart's 1st Mitridate', *Opera Quarterly*, x/3 (1994), 93–112

Wignall, Harrison James. 'The Genesis of "Se di lauri": Mozart's Drafts and Final Version of Guglielmo D'Ettore's Entrance Aria from "Mitridate"', *Mozart-Studien*, v (1995), 45–99

Wild, Nicole. *Dictionnaire des théâtres parisiens au XIXe siècle* (Paris, 1989)

Wilder, Victor. 'Mozart à Paris en 1778: Une partition inédite ("Les petits riens")', *Le ménestrel*, xxxviii (1872), 418–19

Wilder, Victor. *Mozart: L'homme et l'artiste* (Paris, 1880)

Williams, Hermine. *Francesco Bartolomeo Conti: His Life and Music* (Aldershot, 1999)

Winckelmann, Johann Joachim. *Briefe* (Berlin, 1824–5)

Winkler, Klaus. 'Mozarts Bearbeitung des Messias: Händels Oratorium in neuer geographischer und geistesgeschichtlicher Umwelt', *Wissenschaften und Musik unter dem Einfluß einer sich ändernden Geisteshaltung* (Bochum, 1992), 87–102

Winterberger, Johann. *Franz Xaver Süßmayr: Leben, Umwelt und Gestalt* (Frankfurt, 1999)

Winterfeld, Carl Georg Vivigens von. *Der evangelische Kirchengesang und sein Verhältniß zur Kunst des Tonsatzes* (Leipzig, 1843–7)

Winternitz, Emanuel. 'Gnagflow Trazom: An Essay on Mozart's Script, Pastimes, and Nonsense Letters', *Journal of the American Musicological Society*, xi (1958), 200–16

Wittkowski, Wolfgang. 'E. T. A. Hoffmanns musikalische Musikdichtungen Ritter Gluck, Don Juan, Rat Krespel', *Aurora*, xxxviii (1978), 54–74

Witzenmann, Wolfgang. 'Stilphasen in Hasses Kirchenmusik', *Johann Adolf Hasse und die Musik seiner Zeit: Siena 1983* [= *Analecta musicologica*, xxv (1987)], 329–71

Witzmann, Reingard. '"Amici, al ballo, al gioco . . .": Wiener Ballkultur zur Mozartzeit', *Wiener Figaro*, liii/1 (1996), 3–6

Wlassak, Eduard. *Chronik des k. k. Hof-Burgtheaters* (Vienna, 1876)

Wlcek, Walter. *Franz Xaver Süßmayr als Kirchenkomponist* (Tutzing, 1978)

Woelcke, Karl. 'Mozart in Frankfurt', *Alt Frankfurt*, ed. Bernhard Müller (Frankfurt, 1917), 103–21

Wokler, Robert. 'La Querelle des Bouffons and the Italian Liberation of France: A Study of Revolutionary Foreplay', *Eighteenth-Century Life*, xi (1987), 94–116

Wolf, Ernst Wilhelm. *Auch eine Regie* (Weimar, 1784)

Wolf, Eugene K. 'On the Origins of the Mannheim Symphonic Style', *Studies in Musicology in Honor of Otto E. Albrecht*, ed. John W. Hill (Kassel, 1980), 197–239

Wolf, Eugene K. *The Symphonies of Johann Stamitz: A Study in the Formation of the Classic Style with a Thematic Catalogue of the Symphonies and Orchestral Trios* (Utrecht, 1981)

Wolf, Eugene K. 'The Mannheim Court', *The Classical Era: From the 1740s to the End of the 18th Century*, ed. Neal Zaslaw (London, 1989), 213–39

Wolf, Eugene K. 'The Rediscovered Autograph of Mozart's Fantasy and Sonata in C minor, K. 475/457', *Journal of Musicology*, x (1992), 3–47

Wolf, Eugene K. 'Mannheimer Symphonik um 1777/1778 und ihr Einfluß auf Mozarts symphonischen Stil', *Mozart und Mannheim*, ed. Ludwig Finscher, Bärbel Pelker and Jochen Reutter (Frankfurt am Main, 1994), 309–30

Wolf, Eugene K. and Jean K. Wolf. *The Symphony at Mannheim: Johann Stamitz, Christian Cannabich* (New York, 1984 = The Symphony 1720–1840, series C/iii)

Wolf, Rüdiger. 'Wiener Wirtschaftsadel um Mozart, 1781–1791', *Mitteilungen der Internationalen Stiftung Mozarteum*, l/1–2 (2002), 16–48

Wölfel, Kurt, ed. *Christian Garve: Gesammelte Werke* (Hildesheim, 1985–7)

Wolff, Christoph. '"O ew'ge Nacht! wann wirst zu [*sic*] schwinden?" Zum Verständnis der Sprecherszene im ersten Finale von Mozarts "Zauberflöte"', *Analysen: Beiträge zu einer Problemgeschichte des Komponierens. Festschrift für Hans Heinrich Eggebrecht zum 65. Geburtstag*, ed. Werner Breig, Reinhold Brinkmann and Elmar Budde (Stuttgart, 1984), 234–47

Wolff, Christoph. 'Mozarts Präludien für Nannerl: Zwei Rätsel und ihre Lösung', *Festschrift Wolfgang Rehm zum 60. Geburtstag*, ed. Dietrich Berke and Harald Heckmann (Kassel, 1989), 114–17

Wolff, Christoph. 'Cadenzas and Styles of Improvisation in Mozart's Piano Concertos', *Perspectives on Mozart Performance*, ed. R. Larry Todd and Peter Williams (Cambridge, 1991), 228–38

Wolff, Christoph. 'à 1, 2, 3, 4, et 5 parties', *Mozarts Streichquintette: Beiträge zum musikalischen Satz, zum Gattungskontext und zu Quellenfragen*, ed. Cliff Eisen and Wolf-Dieter Seiffert (Stuttgart, 1994), 13–27

Wolff, Christoph. *Mozart's Requiem: Historical and Analytical Studies, Documents, Score* (Oxford, 1994)

Wolff, Helmut Christoph. *Die venezianische Oper in der zweiten Hälfte des 17. Jahrhunderts* (Berlin, 1937)

Wolff, Max J. *Molière* (Munich, 1910)

Wolffheim, Werner. 'W. A. Mozart Sohn', *Zeitschrift der Internationalen Musikgesellschaft*, x (1908/9), 20–7

Wölfflin, Heinrich. *Kunstgeschichtliche Grundbegriffe* (Munich, 1915)

Wolfgang Amadeus Mozart: Verzeichnis von Erst- und Frühdrucken bis etwa 1800 (Kassel, 1978 = Répertoire International des Sources Musicales A/I/6)

Wollenberg, Susan. 'Vienna under Joseph I and Charles VI', *Man & Music: The Late Baroque Era*, ed. George J. Buelow (London, 1993), 324–54

Wolzogen, Alfred von. *Über die szenische Darstellung von Mozarts Don Juan mit Berücksichtigung des ursprünglichen Textbuches von Lorenzo da Ponte* (Breslau, 1860)

Wolzogen, Alfred von. 'Mozarts "Così fan tutte" auf der deutschen Bühne', *Deutsche Musik-Zeitung*, ii (1861), 137–40, 145–8

Wolzogen, Alfred von. *Wilhelmine Schröder-Devrient* (Leipzig, 1863)

Wolzogen, Alfred von. 'Zur Mozart-Biographie', *Recensionen und Mittheilungen über Theater und Musik*, xi/6 (11 Feb. 1865), 81–3

Wolzogen, Alfred von. 'Anmerkungen zu dem Artikel: "Don Juan im neuen Opernhause zu Paris"', *Allgemeine musikalische Zeitung*, new series, xi (1876), 289–92

Wood, C. *Music and Drama in the Tragédie en musique, 1673–1715: Jean-Baptiste Lully and his Successors* (New York, 1996)

Woodfield, Ian. 'New light on the Mozarts' London visit: A private concert with Manzuoli', *Music & Letters*, lxxvi/2 (1995), 187–208

Woodfield, Ian. 'Mozart's Compositional Methods: Writing for his Singers', *The Cambridge Companion to Mozart*, ed. Simon P. Keefe (Cambridge, 2003), 35–47

Wortsmann, Stephan. 'Die deutsche Gluck-Literatur' (dissertation, University of Leipzig, 1914)

Wotquenne, Alfred. *Baldassare Galuppi, 1706–1785: Étude bibliographique sur ses œuvres dramatiques* (Brussels, 1902)

Wotquenne, Alfred. *Thematisches Verzeichnis der Werke von Chr. W. v. Gluck* (Leipzig, 1904)

Wotquenne, Alfred. *Alphabetisches Verzeichnis der Stücke in Versen aus den dramatischen Werken von Zeno, Metastasio und Goldoni* (Leipzig, 1905)

Wotquenne, Alfred. *Thematisches Verzeichnis der Werke von Carl Philipp Emanuel Bach* (Leipzig, 1905)

Würtz, Roland. *Ignaz Fränzl: Ein Beitrag zur Musikgeschichte der Stadt Mannheim* (Mainz, 1970)

Würtz, Roland. 'Die Erstaufführungen von Mozarts Bühnenwerken in Mannheim', *Mozart und seine Umwelt* (Kassel, 1979), 163–71

Würtz, Roland. 'Das Turkische im Singspiel des 18. Jahrhunderts bis zu Mozarts *Entführung aus dem Serail*', *Wiener Figaro*, xlvii (1980), 8–14

Würtz, Roland. 'Anton Schweitzer and Christoph Martin Wieland: The Theory of the Eighteenth-Century Singspiel', *Crosscurrents and the Mainstream of Italian Serious Opera* (London, ON, 1982 = *Studies in Music from the University of Western Ontario* vii), 148–54

Wurzbach, Constantin von. *Mozart-Buch* (Vienna, 1869)

Wustmann, Rudolf. 'Zum Text der Zauberflöte', *Sammelbände der Internationalen Musikgesellschaft*, xi (1909/10), 468

Wyzewa, Théodore. 'Un maître inconnu de Mozart', *Zeitschrift der Internationalen Musikgesellschaft*, x/5 (1908/9), 35–41

Wyzewa, Théodore de and Georges de Saint-Foix, *Wolfgang Amédée Mozart* (Paris, 1912–46)

Young, Percy M. *The Bachs 1500–1850* (London, 1970)

Yudkin, Jeremy. 'Beethoven's "Mozart" Quartet', *Journal of the American Musicological Society*, xliv/1 (1992), 30–74

Zaccaria, Vittore. *Padre Giambattista Martini: Compositore musicologo e maestro* (Padua, 1969)

Zanetti, Roberto. 'Il teatro: Alessandro Scarlatti', *La musica italiana nel Settecento* (Busto Arsizio,1978), 65–129

Zaslaw, Neal. 'Mozart's Modular Minuet Machine', *Essays in Honour of László Somfai on his 70th Birthday*, ed. László Vikárius and Vera Lampert (Lanham, 2005), 219–35

Zaslaw, Neal. 'Mozart, Haydn, and the *Sinfonia da chiesa*', *Journal of Musicology*, i (1982), 95–124

Zaslaw, Neal. '"Grazie agl' inganni tuoi": Mozart or Kelly?', *Im Dienst der Quellen zur Musik: Festschrift Gertraut Haberkamp zum 65. Geburtstag*, ed. Paul Mai (Tutzing, 2002), 409–24

Zaslaw, Neal. 'Leopold Mozart's List of His Son's Works', *Music in the Classical Period: Essays in Honor of Barry S. Brook*, ed. Allan Atlas (New York, 1985), 323–58

Zaslaw, *Mozart's Symphonies: Context, Performance Practice, Reception* (Oxford, 1989)

Zaslaw, 'Waiting for *Figaro*', *Wolfgang Amadè Mozart: Essays on his Life and his Music*, ed. Stanley Sadie (Oxford, 1996) 413–35

Zaslaw, Neal. 'Wolfgang Amade Mozart's allegro and andante ("Fantasy") in F minor for mechanical organ, K. 608', *The Rosaleen Moldenhauer Memorial: Music History from Primary Sources – A Guide to the Moldenhauer Archives* (Washington, DC, 2000), 327–40

Zawrzel, Joseph and Joseph Krüchten, 'Anzeige der von A. André veranstalteten neuen, nach Mozarts und Süßmayers Handschriften berichtigten und mit einem historischen Vorberichte versehenen Ausgabe der Requiems-Partitur', *Caecilia*, vi (1827), 193–230

Zeidler, Jakob. 'Die Ahnen Don Juans', *Wiener Zeitung*, cxxxv (1886)

Zeiss, Laurel. 'Permeable Boundaries in Mozart's *Don Giovanni*', *Cambridge Opera Journal*, xiii/2 (2001), 115–39

Zelechow, Bernard. 'Kierkegaard, the Aesthetic and Mozart's "Don Giovanni"', *Kierkegaard on Art and Communication*, ed. George Pattison (New York, 1992), 64–77

Zelter, Carl Friedrich. *Eine Lebensbeschreibung nach autobiographischen Manuscripten*, ed. Wilhelm Rintel (Berlin, 1861)

Zelter, Carl Friedrich. 'Händel's Messias und Mozart's Bearbeitung desselben', *Allgemeine musikalische Zeitung*, new series, xii/22–23 (1877), 340–5 and 357–8

Ziegenhagen, Franz Heinrich. *Lehre vom richtigen Verhältnisse zu den Schöpfungswerken und die durch öffentliche Einführung derselben allein zu bewürkende allgemeine Menschenbeglückung* (Hamburg, 1792)

Zito, Maria. *Studio su Pietro Metastasio* (Naples, 1904)

Zimmermann, Johann Georg. *Briefe an einige seiner Freunde in der Schweiz* (Aarau, 1830)

Zörrer, Ferdinand. 'La franc-maçonnerie à Vienne et à Prague', *Mozart: Les chemins de l'Europe. Actes du Congrès de Strasbourg 14–16 octobre 1991*, ed. Brigitte Massin (Strasbourg, 1997), 253–61

Index of Mozart's Works by Köchel Numbers

Index of Mozart's Works by Genre

Index of Names and Subjects

Music examples are shown in bold type